W9-CZD-421

Financial Markets and Institutions

SIXTH EDITION

The Prentice Hall Series in Finance

Alexander/Sharpe/Bailey
Fundamentals of Investments

Andersen
Global Derivatives: A Strategic Risk Management Perspective

Bear/Moldonado-Bear
Free Markets, Finance, Ethics, and Law

Berk/DeMarzo
*Corporate Finance**
*Corporate Finance: The Core**

Bierman/Smidt
The Capital Budgeting Decision: Economic Analysis of Investment Projects

Bodie/Merton/Cleeton
Financial Economics

Click/Coval
The Theory and Practice of International Financial Management

Copeland/Weston/Shastri
Financial Theory and Corporate Policy

Cornwall/Vang/Hartman
Entrepreneurial Financial Management

Cox/Rubinstein
Options Markets

Dorfman
Introduction to Risk Management and Insurance

Dietrich
Financial Services and Financial Institutions: Value Creation in Theory and Practice

Dufey/Giddy
Cases in International Finance

Eakins
Finance in .learn

Eiteman/Stonehill/Moffett
Multinational Business Finance

Emery/Finnerty/Stowe
Corporate Financial Management

Fabozzi
Bond Markets, Analysis and Strategies

Fabozzi/Modigliani
Capital Markets: Institutions and Instruments

Fabozzi/Modigliani/Jones/Ferri
Foundations of Financial Markets and Institutions

Finkler
Financial Management for Public, Health, and Not-for-Profit Organizations

Francis/Ibbotson
Investments: A Global Perspective

Fraser/Ormiston
Understanding Financial Statements

Geisst
Investment Banking in the Financial System

Gitman
*Principles of Managerial Finance**
*Principles of Managerial Finance—Brief Edition**

Gitman/Joehnk
*Fundamentals of Investing**

Gitman/Madura
Introduction to Finance

Guthrie/Lemon
Mathematics of Interest Rates and Finance

Haugen
The Inefficient Stock Market: What Pays Off and Why
Modern Investment Theory
The New Finance: Overreaction, Complexity, and Uniqueness

Holden
Excel Modeling and Estimation in the Fundamentals of Corporate Finance
Excel Modeling and Estimation in the Fundamentals of Investments
Excel Modeling and Estimation in Investments
Excel Modeling and Estimation in Corporate Finance

Hughes/MacDonald
International Banking: Text and Cases

Hull
Fundamentals of Futures and Options Markets
Options, Futures, and Other Derivatives
Risk Management and Financial Institutions

Keown
Personal Finance: Turning Money into Wealth

Keown/Martin/Petty/Scott
Financial Management: Principles and Applications
Foundations of Finance: The Logic and Practice of Financial Management

Kim/Nofsinger
Corporate Governance

Levy/Post
Investments

May/May/Andrew
Effective Writing: A Handbook for Finance People

Madura
Personal Finance

Marthinsen
Risk Takers: Uses and Abuses of Financial Derivatives

McDonald
Derivatives Markets
Fundamentals of Derivatives Markets

Megginson
Corporate Finance Theory

Melvin
International Money and Finance

Mishkin/Eakins
Financial Markets and Institutions

Moffett
Cases in International Finance

Moffett/Stonehill/Eiteman
Fundamentals of Multinational Finance

Nofsinger
Psychology of Investing

Ogden/Jen/O'Connor
Advanced Corporate Finance

Pennacchi
Theory of Asset Pricing

Rejda
Principles of Risk Management and Insurance

Schoenebeck
Interpreting and Analyzing Financial Statements

Scott/ Martin/ Petty/Keown/Thatcher
Cases in Finance

Seiler
Performing Financial Studies: A Methodological Cookbook

Shapiro
Capital Budgeting and Investment Analysis

Sharpe/Alexander/Bailey
Investments

Solnik/McLeavey
Global Investments

Stretcher/Michael
Cases in Financial Management

Titman/Martin
Valuation: The Art and Science of Corporate Investment Decisions

Trivoli
Personal Portfolio Management: Fundamentals and Strategies

Van Horne
Financial Management and Policy
Financial Market Rates and Flows

Van Horne/Wachowicz
Fundamentals of Financial Management

Vaughn
Financial Planning for the Entrepreneur

Weston/Mitchel/Mulherin
Takeovers, Restructuring, and Corporate Governance

Winger/Frasca
Personal Finance

* denotes 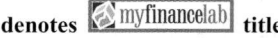 titles   Log onto www.myfinancelab.com to learn more

Financial Markets and Institutions

SIXTH EDITION

FREDERIC S. MISHKIN
Graduate School of Business, Columbia University

STANLEY G. EAKINS
East Carolina University

PEARSON
Prentice Hall

Boston San Francisco New York
London Toronto Sydney Tokyo Singapore Madrid
Mexico City Munich Paris Cape Town Hong Kong Montreal

Editor in Chief: Denise Clinton
Executive Editor: Donna Battista
Assistant Editor: Kerri McQueen
Managing Editor: Nancy Fenton
Senior Production Supervisor: Meredith Gertz
Cover Designer: Beth Paquin
Design Manager: Joyce Wells
Text Designer: Gillian Hall, The Aardvark Group
Supplements Editor: Heather McNally
Senior Media Producer: Bethany Tidd
Senior Marketing Manager: Andrew Watts
Permissions Editor: Dana Weightman
Senior Prepress Supervisor: Caroline Fell
Senior Manufacturing Buyer: Carol Melville
Production Coordination, Composition, and Illustrations:
   Thompson Steele, Inc.
Cover/part opener/chapter opener images: New York and Toronto
   Stock Exchanges: © 2009 Flickr; Tokyo Stock Exchange: © 2009 PhotoVault;
   London Stock Exchange: © 2009 Rueters

Library of Congress Cataloging-in-Publication Data

CIP data is on file with Library of Congress.

ISBN-13: 978-0-321-37421-9
ISBN-10: 0-321-37421-5

Financial Markets and Institutions

1 2 3 4 5 6 7 8 9 10—QWT—12 11 10 09 08

To My Dad

—F. S. M.

To My Wife, Laurie

—S. G. E.

Contents in Brief

Contents in Detail

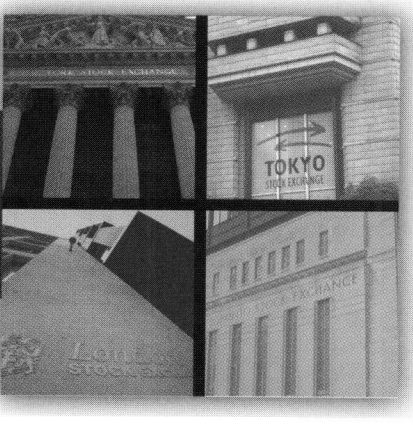

ix

Contents on the Web

The following updated chapter and appendices are available
on our Companion Web site at www.prenhall.com/mishkin_eakins.

Preface

A Note from Frederic Mishkin

Despite my accepting a position in September 2006 (see About the Authors) that restricts my activities, I remain as committed as ever to educating financial markets and institutions students. I am honored that each year thousands of students throughout the world learn about the financial markets and institutions by reading this book. With this honor comes a personal responsibility that I take very seriously. In every new edition, and this one is no exception, I, with my coauthor Stan Eakins, take great care to craft a better book, page by page. While not typical of many textbook authors, I also write most of the Instructor's Manual so that I have the opportunity to share my teaching experiences with other professors teaching this course. In order to make sure that this revision is the best possible, I delayed my start date for my new position in order to complete my work on this new edition before I began working there. The result is that with Stan Eakins's help, the sixth edition of *Financial Markets and Institutions* is another major revision that features substantial changes throughout the book, including substantial reorganization of old chapters, and much new material to keep the book current. I believe that this sixth edition of *Financial Markets and Institutions* will be as exciting as previous editions, if not more so, for students new to the subject.

August 2007

Hallmarks

Although this text has undergone a major revision, it retains the basic hallmarks that make it the best-selling textbook on financial markets and institutions. The sixth edition of *Financial Markets and Institutions* is a practical introduction to the workings of today's financial markets and institutions. Moving beyond the descriptions and definitions provided by other textbooks in the field, *Financial Markets and Institutions* encourages students to understand the connection between the theoretical concepts and their real-world applications. By enhancing students' analytical abilities and concrete problem-solving skills, this textbook prepares students for successful careers in the financial services industry or successful interactions with financial institutions, whatever their jobs.

To prepare students for their future careers, *Financial Markets and Institutions* provides the following features:

- A unifying analytic framework that uses a few basic principles to organize students' thinking. These principles include:

    Asymmetric information (agency) problems
    Conflicts of interest
    Transaction costs
    Supply and demand
    Asset market equilibrium
    Efficient markets
    Measurement and management of risk

- "The Practicing Manager," nearly twenty hands-on applications that emphasize the financial practitioner's approach to financial markets and institutions.
- A careful step-by-step development of models that enables students to master the material more easily.
- A high degree of flexibility that allows professors to teach the course in the manner they prefer.
- Complete integration of international perspectives throughout the text.
- "Following the Financial News" and "Case: The *Wall Street Journal,*" features that encourage the reading of a financial newspaper.
- Numerous cases that increase students' interest by applying theory to real-world data and examples.
- A focus on the impact of electronic (computer and telecommunications) technology on the financial system. The text makes extensive use of the Internet with Web exercises, Web sources for charts and tables, and Web references in the margins. It also features special E-Finance boxes that explain how changes in technology have affected financial markets and institutions.

What's New in the Sixth Edition

In addition to the expected updating of all data through the end of 2007 whenever possible, there is major new material in every part of the text.

New Material on Financial Markets and Institutions

In light of ongoing research and changes in financial markets and institutions, we have added the following new material to keep the text current:

- Discussion of the yield curve as a forecasting tool for inflation and the business cycle (Chapter 5)
- A new box on the problems of the Pension Benefit Guarantee Corporation ("Penny Benny") (Chapter 22)
- A new section on the rapidly growing markets in credit derivatives, including a discussion of credit options, credit swaps, and credit-linked notes (Chapter 25)

Enhanced Coverage of the European Central Bank

Until recently, the U.S. Federal Reserve had no rivals in terms of importance in the central banking world. However, this situation changed in January 1999 with the start-up of the European Central Bank (ECB). The ECB now conducts monetary policy for countries that are members of the European Monetary Union, which collectively have a population that exceeds that in the United States and a GDP comparable to that of the United States. In recognition of students' growing interest in the workings of the ECB, we have added the following new material:

- A new section, "The Structure and Independence of the European Central Bank" (Chapter 7)
- A new section, "Monetary Policy Tools of the European Central Bank" (Chapter 8)
- Discussion of the European Central Bank's monetary policy strategy (Chapter 8)

New Material on Monetary Policy

Drawing on my continuing involvement with central banks around the world, we have added new material to keep the discussion of monetary theory and policy current:

- A new section on whether price stability should be the primary goal of monetary policy (Chapter 8)
- An examination of whether hierarchical versus dual mandates are better for central banks (Chapter 8)
- A new box on the new Federal Reserve Chairman, Ben Bernanke, and his views on inflation targeting (Chapter 8)

Increased International Perspective and Coverage of China

Given the continuing and growing importance of the global economy and China's role in it, we have incorporated new material with an international focus. A special "global icon" designates these text sections and cases, and Global boxes report on specific international developments.

New to this edition:

- A box on why the large U.S. current account deficit worries economists (Chapter 14)
- An exploration of how China has accumulated over $1 trillion of international reserves and has become one of the largest holders of U.S. Treasury securities (Chapter 14)
- A discussion of whether China is a counter-example to the importance of financial development for economic growth (Chapter 15)
- An examination of problems in the Chinese banking system (Chapter 20)

Simpler Supply and Demand Analysis for the Foreign Exchange Market

Using the interest parity condition to explain the determination of exchange rates has always been challenging for some students. We have used this approach in past editions, however, because it is based on the modern asset market approach to exchange rate determination—a standard in the literature. It emphasizes that what drives exchange rate fluctuations are changes in relative expected returns and, as a result, can explain large day-to-day fluctuations in foreign exchange rates, which are not well explained by older supply and demand frameworks often used in other texts.

Although the asset market approach is the way economists currently think about exchange rate determination, it has one major drawback: It is difficult for many students to understand. Through our teaching we discovered that there is a way to explain an asset market approach to exchange rate determination that is embedded in a more conventional supply and demand framework, which many students find far easier to comprehend. Chapters 13 and 14 now provide a supply and demand analysis for assets denominated in a currency, and emphasize that the demand for these assets depends on their expected return relative to assets denominated in foreign currencies. Not only is this framework easier for students to work with, but it also allows the instructor to discuss cases in which domestic and foreign assets are not perfect substitutes for each other and, therefore, has the additional advantage of being more general. Nonetheless, this new framework produces all of the same results that the interest-parity model of previous editions produces (as is pointed out in the text). In our experience, this new approach has enjoyed great success in the classroom.

Improved Exposition and Organization

Helpful comments from reviewers prompted us to simplify the exposition in Chapters 4 and 5 by eliminating the right-hand axis on the graphs, which had interest rates going in the wrong direction. The analysis now focuses on what happens to bond prices and emphasizes that when bond prices rise, interest rates fall, and vice versa.

We have also thoroughly reorganized Chapter 8, "Conduct of Monetary Policy: Tools, Goals, Strategy, and Tactics," to make it logically more coherent and of greater relevance to students. This chapter begins by discussing the tools of monetary policy. It then goes on to explain modern theories of central banking: It first discusses the price stability goal and the role of a nominal anchor in solving the time-inconsistency problem; it then reviews the other goals of monetary policy and explains why price stability is now viewed as the primary goal of monetary policy. From this theoretical perspective, the chapter is better able to explore the strategies and tactics employed by central banks. Material on monetary policy strategy is covered next, with a discussion of monetary targeting and a much more extensive treatment of inflation targeting. Inflation targeting as a monetary policy strategy for the United States is now being actively debated due to a new chairman of the Fed, Ben Bernanke, coming on board. The remainder of the chapter deals with the tactics of monetary policy.

Appendices on the Web

The Web site for this book, **www.prenhall.com/mishkin_eakins**, has allowed us to retain and add new material for the book by posting content online. The appendices include:

Chapter 4: Models of Asset Pricing

Chapter 4: Applying the Asset Market Approach to a Commodity Market: The Case of Gold

Chapter 4: Loanable Funds Framework

Chapter 4: Supply and Demand in the Market for Money: The Liquidity Preference Framework

Chapter 8: The Fed's Balance Sheet and the Monetary Base

Chapter 14: Balance of Payments

Chapter 20: Evaluating FDICIA and Other Proposed Reforms of the Bank Regulatory System

Chapter 25: More on Hedging with Financial Derivatives

Instructors can either use these appendices in class to supplement the material in the textbook, or recommend them to students who want to expand their knowledge of the financial markets and institutions field.

Flexibility

There are as many ways to teach financial markets and institutions as there are instructors. Thus, there is a great need to make a textbook flexible in order to satisfy the diverse needs of instructors, and that has been a primary objective in writing this book. This textbook achieves this flexibility in the following ways:

- Core chapters provide the basic analysis used throughout the book, and other chapters or sections of chapters can be assigned or omitted according to instructor preferences. For example, Chapter 2 introduces the financial system and basic concepts such as transaction costs, adverse selection, and moral hazard. After covering Chapter 2, an instructor can decide to teach a more detailed treatment of financial structure or conflicts of interest in Chapters 15 and 16, or can skip these chapters and take any of a number of different paths.

- The approach to internationalizing the text using separate, marked international sections within chapters and separate chapters on the foreign exchange market and the international monetary system is comprehensive yet flexible. Although many instructors will teach all the international material, others will choose not to. Instructors who want less emphasis on international topics can easily skip Chapter 13 (on the foreign exchange market) and Chapter 14 (on the international financial system).

- "The Practicing Manager" applications, as well as Part 7 on the management of financial institutions, are self-contained and so can be skipped without loss of continuity. Thus, an instructor wishing to teach a less managerially oriented course, who might want to focus more on public policy issues, will have no trouble doing so. Alternatively, Part 7 can be taught earlier in the course, immediately after Chapter 17 on bank management.

The course outlines listed next for a semester teaching schedule illustrate how this book can be used for courses with a different emphasis. More detailed information about how the text can offer flexibility in your course is available in the *Instructor's Resource Manual.*

Financial markets and institutions emphasis: Chapters 1–5, 9–11, 15, 17, 18, 20, and six other text chapters

Financial markets and institutions with international emphasis: Chapters 1–5, 9–11, 13–15, 17, 18, 20, and four other text chapters

Managerial emphasis: Chapters 1–5, 17, 18, 20, 24, 25, and eight other text chapters

Public policy emphasis: Chapters 1–5, 7, 8, 15, 16, 17, 20, and seven other text chapters

Making It Easier to Teach Financial Markets and Institutions

The demands for good teaching at business schools have increased dramatically in recent years. To meet these demands, we have provided the instructor with supplementary materials, unavailable with any competing text, that should make teaching the course substantially easier.

Along with the usual items in the *Instructor's Resource Manual*—sample course outlines, chapter outlines, overviews, teaching tips, and answers to the end-of-chapter questions and quantitative problems—this manual includes over 850 pages of lecture notes. The lecture notes are comprehensive and outline all the major points covered in the text. They have been class-tested successfully by the authors and should make it much easier for other instructors to prepare their lecture notes as well. The lecture notes are perforated so that they can be easily detached for class use or to make transparency masters.

This edition of the book comes with a powerful teaching tool: an *Instructor's Resource CD-ROM.* Fully compatible with Windows and Macintosh computers, the CD-ROM contains Word™ files for the entire contents of the *Instructor's Resource Manual* (including the lecture notes), PowerPoint™ presentations, Computerized Test Bank files, and animated graphs. Using this handy supplement, instructors can prepare student handouts such as solutions to problem sets made up of end-of-chapter problems or the outline of the lecture of the day. We have used handouts of this type in our classes and have found them to be very effective. To facilitate classroom presentation even further, the PowerPoint presentations include all the book's figures and tables in full color, as well as all the lecture notes; all are fully customizable. The Computerized Test Bank software (TestGen-EQ with QuizMaster-EQ for Windows and Macintosh) is a valuable test preparation tool that allows professors to view, edit, and add questions. Instructors have our permission and are encouraged to reproduce all of the materials on the CD-ROM and use them as they see fit in class.

Pedagogical Aids

A textbook must be a solid motivational tool. To this end, we have incorporated a wide variety of pedagogical features.

1. **Chapter Previews** at the beginning of each chapter tell students where the chapter is heading, why specific topics are important, and how they relate to other topics in the book.
2. **Cases** demonstrate how the analysis in the book can be used to explain many important real-world situations. A special set of cases called "Case: The *Wall Street Journal*" shows students how to read daily columns in this leading financial newspaper.

3. **"The Practicing Manager"** is a set of special cases that introduce students to real-world problems that managers of financial institutions have to solve.
4. **Numerical Examples** guide students through solutions to financial problems using formulas, time lines, and calculator key strokes.
5. **"Following the Financial News" boxes** introduce students to relevant news articles and data that are reported daily in the *Wall Street Journal* and other financial news sources and explain how to read them.
6. **"Inside the Fed" boxes** give students a feel for what is important in the operation and structure of the Federal Reserve System.
7. **"Global" boxes** include interesting material with an international focus.
8. **"E-Finance" boxes** relate how changes in technology have affected financial markets and institutions.
9. **"Conflicts of Interest" boxes** outline conflicts of interest in different financial service industries.
10. **"Mini-Case" boxes** highlight dramatic historical episodes or apply the theory to the data.
11. **Study Guides** are highlighted statements scattered throughout the text that provide hints on how to think about or approach a topic as students work their way through it.
12. **Summary Tables** are useful study aids for reviewing material.
13. **Key Statements** are important points that are set in boldface type so that students can easily find them for later reference.
14. **Graphs** with captions, numbering over 60, help students understand the interrelationship of the variables plotted and the principles of analysis.
15. **Summaries** at the end of each chapter list the chapter's main points.
16. **Key Terms** are important words or phrases that appear in boldface type when they are defined for the first time and are listed at the end of each chapter.
17. **End-of-Chapter Questions** help students learn the subject matter by applying economic concepts, and feature a special class of questions that students find particularly relevant, titled "Predicting the Future."
18. **End-of-Chapter Quantitative Problems,** numbering over 250, help students to develop their quantitative skills.
19. **Web Exercises** encourage students to collect information from online sources or use online resources to enhance their learning experience.
20. **Web Sources** report the URL source of the data used to create the many tables and charts.
21. **Marginal Web References** point the student to Web sites that provide information or data that supplement the text material.
22. **Glossary** at the back of the book defines all the key terms.
23. **Full Solutions to the Questions and Quantitative Problems** appear in the *Instructor's Resource Manual* and on the *Instructor's Resource CD-ROM*. Professors have the flexibility to share the solutions with their students as they see fit.

Supplementary Materials

The sixth edition of *Financial Markets and Institutions* includes the most comprehensive program of supplementary materials of any textbook in its field. These items are available to qualified domestic adopters but in some cases may not be available to international adopters. These include the following items:

For the Professor

1. **Instructor's Manual:** This manual, prepared by the authors, includes sample course outlines, chapter outlines, overviews, teaching tips, and complete solutions to questions and problems in the text.
2. **PowerPoint:** Prepared by John Banko (University of Central Florida). The presentation, which contains lecture notes and the complete set of figures and tables from the textbook, contains more than 850 slides that comprehensively outline the major points covered in the text.
3. **Instructor's Resource CD-ROM:** Contains Word and PDF files for the Instructor's Manual and Test Bank, PowerPoint presentations, the Computerized Test Bank, and animated graphs from the text.
4. **Test Bank:** Updated and revised by Stanley G. Eakins, Emanual Hill, and Kyle Reeves (East Carolina University). Available in both print and electronic form, the Test Bank comprises over 2500 multiple-choice, true-false, and essay test items. The Test Bank is computerized so that the instructor can easily produce exams automatically.
5. **Mishkin-Eakins Companion Web Site** (located at **http://www.prenhall.com/ mishkin_eakins**), which features a Web chapter on finance companies, Web appendices, mini-cases, animated graphs, and links to relevant data sources and Federal Reserve Web sites. The site also offers multiple-choice quizzes for each chapter.
6. The student materials on the Companion Web site and the instructor's test bank are also available in Blackboard™. This powerful course management system enable professors to tailor content and functionality to meet their individual course needs. Please contact your local sales representative or visit our Instructor Resource Center at **http://www.prenhall.com/irc**), for more information.

For the Student

1. **Study Guide:** Updated and revised by Frederick P. Schadler (East Carolina University). Includes chapter synopses and completions, exercises, self-tests, and answers to the exercises and self-tests.
2. **Readings in Financial Markets and Institutions,** edited by James W. Eaton of Bridgewater College and Frederic S. Mishkin. Updated annually, with numerous new articles each year, this valuable resource is available online at the book's Web site (**www.prenhall.com/mishkin_eakins**).
3. **Mishkin-Eakins Companion Web site** (located at **www.prenhall.com/ mishkin_eakins**) includes a Web chapter on finance companies, Web appendices, animated graphs, glossary flashcards, numerical and integrative mini-cases, self-assessment quizzes, Web exercises, and links from the textbook.

Acknowledgments

As always in so large a project, there are many people to thank. Our special gratitude goes to Bruce Kaplan, former economics editor at HarperCollins; Donna Battista, finance editor at Prentice Hall; Jane Tufts, development editor; and Kerri McQueen, editorial assistant. We would also like to give a special thanks to Jim Eaton, who diligently reviewed each chapter for accuracy and currency, and was a vital part of the team. We also have been assisted by comments from my colleagues at Columbia and from my students.

In addition, we have been guided in this edition and its predecessors by the thoughtful comments of outside reviewers and correspondents. Their feedback has made this a better book. In particular, we thank:

Ibrahim J. Affanen, Indiana University of Pennsylvania

Senay Agca, George Washington University

Ronald Anderson, University of Nevada–Las Vegas

Bala G. Arshanapalli, Indiana University Northwest

Christopher Bain, Ohio State University

James C. Baker, Kent State University

John Banko, University Central Florida

Mounther H. Barakat, University of Houston Clear Lake

Joel Barber, Florida International University

Thomas M. Barnes, Alfred University

Marco Bassetto, Northwestern University

Dallas R. Blevins, University of Montevallo

Matej Blusko, University of Georgia

Paul J. Bolster, Northeastern University

Lowell Boudreaux, Texas A&M University Galveston

Deanne Butchey, Florida International University

Mitch Charklewicz, Central Connecticut State University

Yea-Mow Chen, San Francisco State University

N.K. Chidambaran, Tulane University

Wan-Jiun Paul Chiou, Shippensburg University

Jeffrey A. Clark, Florida State University

Robert Bruce Cochran, San Jose State University

William Colclough, University of Wisconsin–La Crosse

Elizabeth Cooperman, University of Baltimore

Carl Davison, Mississippi State University

Erik Devos, Ohio University at SUNY Binghamton

Alan Durell, Dartmouth College

Franklin R. Edwards, Columbia University

Marty Eichenbaum, Northwestern University

Elyas Elyasiani, Temple University

Edward C. Erickson, California State University, Stanislaus

E. Bruce Fredrikson, Syracuse University

James Gatti, University of Vermont

Paul Girma, SUNY–New Paltz

Susan Glanz, St. John's University

Gary Gray, Pennsylvania State University

Charles Guez, University of Houston

Beverly L. Hadaway, University of Texas

John A. Halloran, University of Notre Dame

Billie J. Hamilton, East Carolina University

John H. Hand, Auburn University

Don P. Holdren, Marshall University

Adora Holstein, Robert Morris College

Sylvia C. Hudgins, Old Dominion University

Jerry G. Hunt, East Carolina University

Boulis Ibrahim, Heroit-Watt University

William E. Jackson, University of North Carolina–Chapel Hill

Joe James, Sam Houston State University

Melvin H. Jameson, University of Nevada–Las Vegas

Kurt Jessewein, Texas A&M International University

Jack Jordan, Seton Hall University

Tejendra Kalia, Worcester State College

Taeho Kim, Thunderbird: The American Graduate School of International Management

Taewon Kim, California State University, Los Angeles

Elinda Kiss, University of Maryland

Glen A. Larsen, Jr., University of Tulsa

James E. Larsen, Wright State University

Rick LeCompte, Wichita State University

Baeyong Lee, Fayetteville State University

Boyden E. Lee, New Mexico State University

Kartono Liano, Mississippi State University

John Litvan, Southwest Missouri State

Richard A. Lord, Georgia College

Robert L. Losey, American University

Anthony Loviscek, Seton Hall University

James Lynch, Robert Morris College

Judy E. Maese, New Mexico State University

Inayat Mangla, Western Michigan University

William Marcum, Wake Forest University

David A. Martin, Albright College

Lanny Martindale, Texas A&M University

Joseph S. Mascia, Adelphi University

Khalid Metabdin, College of St. Rose

David Milton, Bentley College

A. H. Moini, University of Wisconsin–Whitewater

Russell Morris, John Hopkins University

Chee Ng, Fairleigh Dickinson University

Srinivas Nippani, Texas A&M Commerce

Terry Nixon, Indiana University
William E. O'Connell, Jr., The College of William and Mary
Masao Ogaki, Ohio State University
Evren Ors, Southern Illinois University
Coleen C. Pantalone, Northeastern University
Scott Pardee, University of Chicago
James Peters, Fairleigh Dickinson University
Fred Puritz, SUNY–Oneonta
Mahmud Rahman, Eastern Michigan University
Anoop Rai, Hofstra University
Mitchell Ratner, Rider University
David Reps, Pace University–Westchester
Terry Richardson, Bowling Green University
Jack Rubens, Bryant College
Charles B. Ruscher, James Madison University
William Sackley, University of Southern Mississippi
Kevin Salyer, University of California–Davis

Siamack Shojai, Manhattan College
Donald Smith, Boston University
Sonya Williams Stanton, Ohio State University
Michael Sullivan, Florida International University
Rick Swasey, Northeastern University
Anjan Thackor, University of Michigan
Janet M. Todd, University of Delaware
James Tripp, Western Illinois University
Carlos Ulibarri, Washington State University
John Wagster, Wayne State University
Bruce Watson, Wellesley College
David A. Whidbee, California State University–Sacramento
Arthur J. Wilson, George Washington University
Shee Q. Wong, University of Minnesota–Duluth
Criss G. Woodruff, Radford University
Tong Yu, University of Rhode Island

Finally, I want to thank my wife, Sally, my son, Matthew, and my daughter, Laura, who provide me with a warm and happy environment that enables me to do my work, and my father, Sydney, now deceased, who a long time ago put me on the path that led to this book.

Frederic S. Mishkin

I would like to thank Rick Mishkin for his excellent comments on my contributions. By working with Rick on this text, not only have I gained greater skill as a writer, but I have also gained a friend. I would also like to thank my wife, Laurie, for patiently reading each draft of this manuscript and for helping make this my best work. Through the years, her help and support have made this aspect of my career possible.

Stanley G. Eakins

About the Authors

© Peter Murphy

Frederic S. Mishkin is the Alfred Lerner Professor of Banking and Financial Institutions at the Graduate School of Business, Columbia University. Starting in September 2006 he became a member of the Board of Governors of the Federal Reserve System.

He is also a research associate at the National Bureau of Economic Research and past president of the Eastern Economics Association. Since receiving his Ph.D. from the Massachusetts Institute of Technology in 1976, he has taught at the University of Chicago, Northwestern University, Princeton University, and Columbia University. He has also received an honorary professorship from the People's (Renmin) University of China. From 1994 to 1997, he was executive vice president and director of research at the Federal Reserve Bank of New York and an associate economist of the Federal Open Market Committee of the Federal Reserve System.

Professor Mishkin's research focuses on monetary policy and its impact on financial markets and the aggregate economy. He is the author of more than fifteen books, including *The Economics of Money, Banking and Financial Markets,* Eighth Edition (Addison Wesley, 2007); *Monetary Policy Strategy* (MIT Press, 2007); *The Next Great Globalization: How Disadvantaged Nations Can Harness Their Financial Systems to Get Rich* (Princeton University Press, 2006); *Inflation Targeting: Lessons from the International Experience* (Princeton University Press, 1999); *Money, Interest Rates, and Inflation* (Edward Elgar, 1993); and *A Rational Expectations Approach to Macroeconometrics: Testing Policy Ineffectiveness and Efficient Markets Models* (University of Chicago Press, 1983). In addition, he has published more than 150 articles in such journals as *American Economic Review, Journal of Political Economy, Econometrica, Quarterly Journal of Economics, Journal of Finance,* and *Journal of Monetary Economics.*

Professor Mishkin has served on the editorial board of the *American Economic Review* and has been an associate editor at the *Journal of Business and Economic Statistics* and *Journal of Applied Econometrics;* he also served as the editor of the Federal Reserve Bank of New York's *Economic Policy Review.* He is currently an associate editor (member of the editorial board) at six academic journals, including *Journal of Money, Credit and Banking; Macroeconomics and Monetary Economics Abstracts; Journal of International Money and Finance; International Finance; Finance India;* and *Economic Policy Review.* He has been a consultant to the Board of Governors of the Federal Reserve System, the World Bank and the International Monetary Fund, as well as to many central banks throughout the world. He was also a member of the International Advisory Board to the Financial Supervisory Service of South Korea and an adviser to the Institute for Monetary and Economic Research at the Bank of Korea. Professor Mishkin has also served as a senior fellow at the Federal Deposit Insurance Corporation's Center for Banking Research, and as an academic consultant to and member of the Economic Advisory Panel of the Federal Reserve Bank of New York.

Stanley G. Eakins has notable experience as a financial practitioner, serving as vice president and comptroller at the First National Bank of Fairbanks and as a commercial and real estate loan officer. A founder of the Denali Title and Escrow Agency, a title insurance company in Fairbanks, Alaska, he also ran the operations side of a bank and was the chief finance officer for a multimillion-dollar construction and development company.

Professor Eakins received his Ph.D. from Arizona State University. He is the Associate Dean for the College of Business at East Carolina University. His research is focused primarily on the role of institutions in corporate control and how they influence investment practices. He is also interested in integrating multimedia tools into the learning environment and has received grants from East Carolina University in support of this work.

A contributor to journals such as the *Quarterly Journal of Business and Economics,* the *Journal of Financial Research,* and the *International Review of Financial Analysis,* Professor Eakins is also the author of *Finance,* 3rd edition (Addison-Wesley, 2008).

PART 1

Introduction

Why Study Financial Markets and Institutions?

Preview

On the evening news you have just heard that the bond market has been booming. Does this mean that interest rates will fall so that it is easier for you to finance the purchase of a new computer system for your small retail business? Will the economy improve in the future so that it is a good time to build a new building or add to the one you are in? Should you try to raise funds by issuing stocks or bonds, or instead go to the bank for a loan? If you import goods from abroad, should you be concerned that they will become more expensive?

This book provides answers to these questions by examining how financial markets (such as those for bonds, stocks, and foreign exchange) and financial institutions (banks, insurance companies, mutual funds, and other institutions) work. Financial markets and institutions not only affect your everyday life but also involve huge flows of funds—trillions of dollars—throughout our economy, which in turn affect business profits, the production of goods and services, and even the economic well-being of countries other than the United States. What happens to financial markets and institutions is of great concern to politicians and can even have a major impact on elections. The study of financial markets and institutions will reward you with an understanding of many exciting issues. In this chapter we provide a road map of the book by outlining these exciting issues and exploring why they are worth studying.

Why Study Financial Markets?

Parts 2 and 3 of this book focus on **financial markets,** markets in which funds are transferred from people who have an excess of available funds to people who have a shortage. Financial markets, such as bond and stock markets, are crucial to promoting greater economic efficiency by channeling funds from people who do not have a productive use for them to those who do. Indeed, well-functioning financial markets are a key factor in producing high economic growth, and poorly performing financial markets are one reason that many countries in the world remain desperately poor. Activities in financial markets also have direct effects on personal wealth, the behavior of businesses and consumers, and the cyclical performance of the economy.

Debt Markets and Interest Rates

A **security** (also called a *financial instrument*) is a claim on the issuer's future income or **assets** (any financial claim or piece of property that is subject to ownership). A **bond** is a debt security that promises to make payments periodically for a specified period of time.[1] Debt markets, also often referred to generically as the *bond* market, are especially important to economic activity because they enable corporations and governments to borrow to finance their activities and because they are where interest rates are determined. An **interest rate** is the cost of borrowing or the price paid for the rental of funds (usually expressed as a percentage of the rental of $100 per year). There are many interest rates in the economy—mortgage interest rates, car loan rates, and interest rates on many different types of bonds.

Interest rates are important on a number of levels. On a personal level, high interest rates could deter you from buying a house or a car because the cost of financing it would be high. Conversely, high interest rates could encourage you to save because you can earn more interest income by putting aside some of your earnings as savings. On a more general level, interest rates have an impact on the overall health of the economy because they affect not only consumers' willingness to spend or save but also businesses' investment decisions. High interest rates, for example, might cause a corporation to postpone building a new plant that would provide more jobs.

Because changes in interest rates have important effects on individuals, financial institutions, businesses, and the overall economy, it is important to explain fluctuations in interest rates that have been substantial over the past 20 years. For example, the interest rate on three-month Treasury bills peaked at over 16% in 1981. This interest rate fell to 3% in late 1992 and 1993, rose to above 5% in the mid- to late 1990s, and fell to below 1% in 2004, only to begin rising again.

Because different interest rates have a tendency to move in unison, economists frequently lump interest rates together and refer to "the" interest rate. As Figure 1.1 shows, however, interest rates on several types of bonds can differ substantially. The interest rate on three-month Treasury bills, for example, fluctuates more than the other interest rates and is lower, on average. The interest rate on Baa (medium-quality) corporate bonds is higher, on average, than the other interest rates, and the spread between it and the other rates became larger in the 1970s, narrowed in the 1990s, and rose briefly in the early 2000s, before narrowing again.

[1]The definition of *bond* used throughout this book is the broad one in common use by academics, which covers both short- and long-term debt instruments. However, some practitioners in financial markets use the word *bond* to describe only specific long-term debt instruments such as corporate bonds or U.S. Treasury bonds.

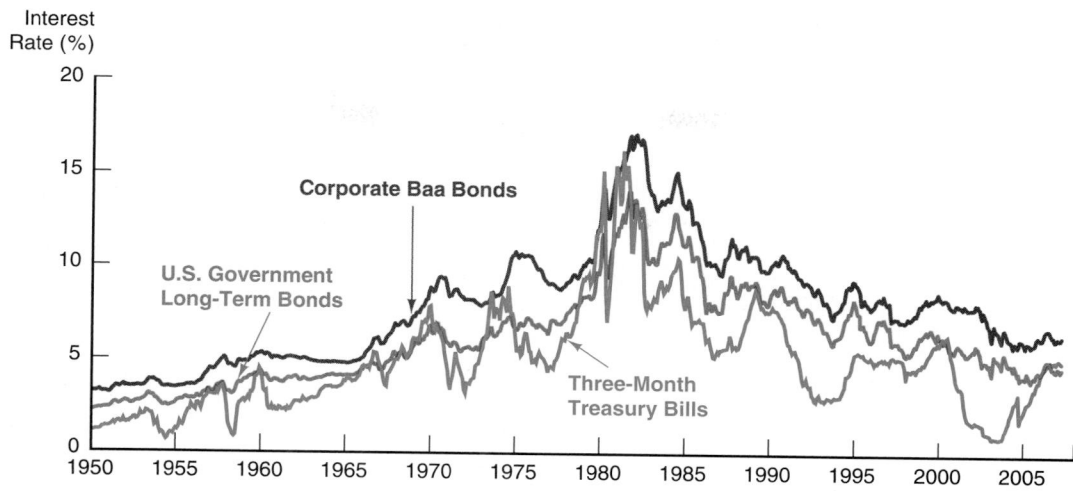

Figure 1.1 Interest Rates on Selected Bonds, 1950–2007

Sources: Federal Reserve *Bulletin;* www.federalreserve.gov/releases/H15/data.htm.

In Chapters 2, 9, 10 and 12 we study the role of debt markets in the economy, and in Chapters 3 through 5 we examine what an interest rate is, how the common movements in interest rates come about, and why the interest rates on different bonds vary.

The Stock Market

go online
http://stockcharts.com/
charts/historical/
Historical charts of various
stock indexes over differing
time periods.

A **common stock** (typically just called a **stock**) represents a share of ownership in a corporation. It is a security that is a claim on the earnings and assets of the corporation. Issuing stock and selling it to the public is a way for corporations to raise funds to finance their activities. The stock market, in which claims on the earnings of corporations (shares of stock) are traded, is the most widely followed financial market in almost every country that has one; that's why it is often called simply "the market." A big swing in the prices of shares in the stock market is always a major story on the evening news. People often speculate on where the market is heading and get very excited when they can brag about their latest "big killing," but they become depressed when they suffer a big loss. The attention the market receives can probably be best explained by one simple fact: It is a place where people can get rich—or poor—quickly.

As Figure 1.2 indicates, stock prices are extremely volatile. After the market rose in the 1980s, on "Black Monday," October 19, 1987, it experienced the worst one-day drop in its entire history, with the Dow Jones Industrial Average (DJIA) falling by 22%. From then until 2000, the stock market experienced one of the great bull markets in its history, with the Dow climbing to a peak of over 11,000. With the collapse of the high-tech bubble in 2000, the stock market fell sharply, dropping by over 30% by late 2002. It then recovered again, reaching the 14,000 level in 2007. These considerable fluctuations in stock prices affect the size of people's wealth and as a result may affect their willingness to spend.

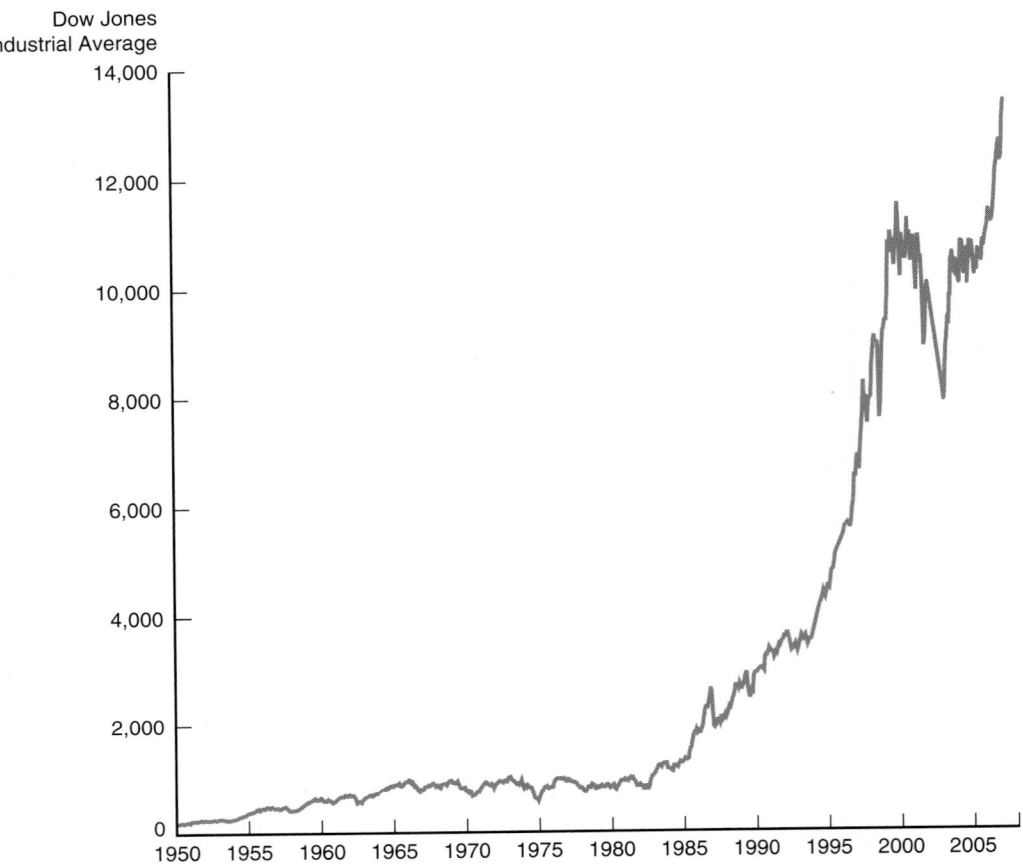

Figure 1.2   Stock Prices as Measured by the Dow Jones Industrial Average, 1950–2007

Source: Dow Jones Indexes: http://finance.yahoo.com/?u.

The stock market is also an important factor in business investment decisions, because the price of shares affects the amount of funds that can be raised by selling newly issued stock to finance investment spending. A higher price for a firm's shares means that it can raise a larger amount of funds, which can be used to buy production facilities and equipment.

In Chapter 2 we examine the role that the stock market plays in the financial system, and we return to the issue of how stock prices behave and respond to information in the marketplace in Chapters 6 and 11.

The Foreign Exchange Market

For funds to be transferred from one country to another, they have to be converted from the currency in the country of origin (say, dollars) into the currency of the country they are going to (say, euros). The **foreign exchange market** is where this conversion takes place, so it is instrumental in moving funds between countries. It is also

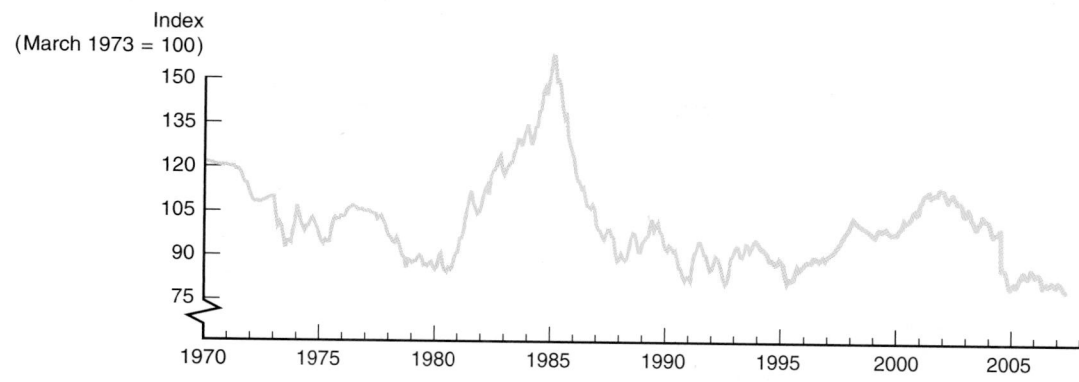

Figure 1.3 Exchange Rate of the U.S. Dollar, 1970–2007

Source: Federal Reserve: www.federalreserve.gov/releases/H10/summary/indexbc_m.txt/.

important because it is where the **foreign exchange rate,** the price of one country's currency in terms of another's, is determined.

Figure 1.3 shows the exchange rate for the U.S. dollar from 1970 to 2007 (measured as the value of the U.S. dollar in terms of a basket of major foreign currencies). The fluctuations in prices in this market have also been substantial: The dollar's value weakened considerably from 1971 to 1973, rose slightly until 1976, and then reached a low point in the 1978–1980 period. From 1980 to early 1985, the dollar's value appreciated dramatically, and then declined again, reaching another low in 1995. The dollar appreciated from 1995 to 2000, only to depreciate thereafter.

What have these fluctuations in the exchange rate meant to the American public and businesses? A change in the exchange rate has a direct effect on American consumers because it affects the cost of imports. In 2001, when the euro was worth around 85 cents, 100 euros of European goods (say, French wine) cost $85. When the dollar subsequently weakened, raising the cost of a euro to around $1.40, the same 100 euros of wine now cost $140. Thus, a weaker dollar leads to more expensive foreign goods, makes vacationing abroad more expensive, and raises the cost of indulging your desire for imported delicacies. When the value of the dollar drops, Americans decrease their purchases of foreign goods and increase their consumption of domestic goods (such as travel in the United States or American-made wine).

Conversely, a strong dollar means that U.S. goods exported abroad will cost more in foreign countries, and hence foreigners will buy fewer of them. Exports of steel, for example, declined sharply when the dollar strengthened in the 1980–1985 and 1995–2001 periods. A strong dollar benefited American consumers by making foreign goods cheaper but hurt American businesses and eliminated some jobs by cutting both domestic and foreign sales of their products. The decline in the value of the dollar from 1985 to 1995 and 2001 to 2007 had the opposite effect: It made foreign goods more expensive, but made American businesses more competitive. Fluctuations in the foreign exchange markets thus have major consequences for the American economy.

In Chapter 13 we study how exchange rates are determined in the foreign exchange market, in which dollars are bought and sold for foreign currencies.

Why Study Financial Institutions?

The second major focus of this book is financial institutions. Financial institutions are what make financial markets work. Without them, financial markets would not be able to move funds from people who save to people who have productive investment opportunities. They thus play a crucial role in improving the efficiency of the economy.

Central Banks and the Conduct of Monetary Policy

go online
www.federalreserve.gov
General information,
monetary policy, banking
system, research, and
economic data of the Federal
Reserve.

The most important financial institution in the financial system is the **central bank,** the government agency responsible for the conduct of monetary policy, which in the United States is the **Federal Reserve System** (also called simply **the Fed**). **Monetary policy** involves the management of interest rates and the quantity of **money,** also referred to as the **money supply** (defined as anything that is generally accepted in payment for goods and services or in the repayment of debt). Because monetary policy affects interest rates, inflation, and business cycles, all of which have a major impact on financial markets and institutions, we study how monetary policy is conducted by central banks in both the United States and abroad in Chapters 7 and 8.

Structure of the Financial System

The financial system is complex, comprising many different types of private sector financial institutions, including banks, insurance companies, mutual funds, finance companies, and investment banks, all of which are heavily regulated by the government. If you wanted to make a loan to IBM or General Motors, for example, you would not go directly to the president of the company and offer a loan. Instead, you would lend to such companies indirectly through **financial intermediaries,** institutions such as commercial banks, savings and loan associations, mutual savings banks, credit unions, insurance companies, mutual funds, pension funds, and finance companies that borrow funds from people who have saved and in turn make loans to others.

Why are financial intermediaries so crucial to well-functioning financial markets? Why do they give credit to one party but not to another? Why do they usually write complicated legal documents when they extend loans? Why are they the most heavily regulated businesses in the economy?

We answer these questions by developing a coherent framework for analyzing financial structure both in the United States and in the rest of the world in Chapters 15 and 16.

Banks and Other Financial Institutions

Banks are financial institutions that accept deposits and make loans. Included under the term *banks* are firms such as commercial banks, savings and loan associations, mutual savings banks, and credit unions. Banks are the financial intermediaries that the average person interacts with most frequently. A person who needs a loan to buy a house or a car usually obtains it from a local bank. Most Americans keep a large proportion of their financial wealth in banks in the form of checking accounts, savings accounts, or other types of bank deposits. Because banks are the largest financial intermediaries in our economy, they deserve careful study. However, banks are not the only important financial institutions. Indeed, in recent years, other financial institutions such as insurance companies, finance companies, pension funds, mutual funds, and investment banks have been growing at the expense of banks, and so we need to study them as well. We study banks and all these other institutions in Parts 5 and 6.

Financial Innovation

In the good old days, when you took cash out of the bank or wanted to check your account balance, you got to say hello to a friendly human. Nowadays, you are more likely to interact with an automatic teller machine (ATM) when withdrawing cash, and can get your account balance from your home computer. To see why these options have developed, we study why and how financial innovation takes place in Chapters 18 and 20, with particular emphasis on how the dramatic improvements in information technology have led to new means of delivering financial services electronically, in what has become known as **e-finance.** We also study financial innovation because it shows us how creative thinking on the part of financial institutions can lead to higher profits. By seeing how and why financial institutions have been creative in the past, we obtain a better grasp of how they may be creative in the future. This knowledge provides us with useful clues about how the financial system may change over time and will help keep our knowledge about banks and other financial institutions from becoming obsolete.

Managing Risk in Financial Institutions

In recent years, the economic environment has become an increasingly risky place. Interest rates have fluctuated wildly, stock markets have crashed both here and abroad, speculative crises have occurred in the foreign exchange markets, and failures of financial institutions have reached levels unprecedented since the Great Depression. To avoid wild swings in profitability (and even possibly failure) resulting from this environment, financial institutions must be concerned with how to cope with increased risk. We look at techniques that these institutions use when they engage in risk management in Chapter 24. Then in Chapter 25, we look at how these institutions make use of new financial instruments, such as financial futures, options, and swaps, to manage risk.

Applied Managerial Perspective

Another reason for studying financial institutions is that they are among the largest employers in the country and frequently pay very high salaries. Hence, some of you have a very practical reason for studying financial institutions: It may help you get a good job in the financial sector. Even if your interests lie elsewhere, you should still care about how financial institutions are run because there will be many times in your life, as an individual, an employee, or the owner of a business, when you will interact with these institutions. Knowing how financial institutions are managed may help you get a better deal when you need to borrow from them or if you decide to supply them with funds.

This book emphasizes an applied managerial perspective in teaching you about financial markets and institutions by including special case applications headed "The

Practicing Manager." These cases introduce you to the real-world problems that managers of financial institutions commonly face and need to solve in their day-to-day jobs. For example, how does the manager of a financial institution come up with a new financial product that will be profitable? How does a financial institution manager manage the risk that the institution faces from fluctuations in interest rates, stock prices, or foreign exchange rates? Should a manager hire an expert on Federal Reserve policymaking, referred to as a "Fed watcher," to help the institution discern where monetary policy might be going in the future?

Not only do "The Practicing Manager" cases, which answer these questions and others like them, provide you with some special analytic tools that you will need if you make your career at a financial institution, but they also give you a feel for what a job as the manager of a financial institution is all about.

How We Will Study Financial Markets and Institutions

Instead of focusing on a mass of dull facts that will soon become obsolete, this textbook stresses a unifying, analytic framework to study financial markets and institutions. This framework uses a few basic concepts to help organize your thinking about the determination of asset prices, the structure of financial markets, bank management, and the role of monetary policy in the economy. The basic concepts are equilibrium, basic supply and demand analysis to explain behavior in financial markets, the search for profits, and an approach to financial structure based on transaction costs and asymmetric information.

The unifying framework used in this book will keep your knowledge from becoming obsolete and make the material more interesting. It will enable you to learn what *really* matters without having to memorize a mass of dull facts that you will forget soon after the final exam. This framework will also provide you with the tools needed to understand trends in the financial marketplace and in variables such as interest rates and exchange rates.

To help you understand and apply the unifying analytic framework, simple models are constructed in which the variables held constant are carefully delineated, each step in the derivation of the model is clearly and carefully laid out, and the models are then used to explain various phenomena by focusing on changes in one variable at a time, holding all other variables constant.

To reinforce the models' usefulness, this text also emphasizes the interaction of theoretical analysis and empirical data in order to expose you to real-life events and data. To make the study of financial markets and institutions even more relevant and to help you learn the material, the book contains, besides "The Practicing Manager" cases, numerous additional cases and mini-cases that demonstrate how you can use the analysis in the book to explain many real-world situations.

To function better in the real world outside the classroom, you must have the tools to follow the financial news that appears in leading financial publications. To help and encourage you to read the financial section of the newspaper, this book contains two special features. The first is a set of special boxed inserts titled "Following the Financial News" that contain actual columns and data from *The Wall Street Journal* (subscription required on the Web at **http://online.wsj.com/home/us**) or other financial publications that typically appear daily or periodically. These boxes give you the detailed information and definitions you need to evaluate the data being presented. The second feature is a set of special case applications titled "Reading *The Wall Street Journal*" that expand on the Following the Financial News boxes. These cases show you how you can use the analytic framework in the book directly to make sense of the daily columns in the United States' leading financial newspaper. In addition to these cases, this book also contains nearly 400 end-of-chapter problems that ask you to apply the analytic concepts you have learned to other real-world issues. Particularly relevant is a special class of problems headed "Predicting the Future." These questions give you an opportunity to review and apply many of the important financial concepts and tools presented throughout the book.

Exploring the Web

The World Wide Web has become an extremely valuable and convenient resource for financial research. We emphasize the importance of this tool in several ways. First, wherever we utilize the Web to find information to build the charts and tables that appear throughout the text, we include the source site's URL. These sites often contain additional information and are updated frequently. Second, we have added Web exercises to the end of each chapter. These exercises prompt you to visit sites related to the chapter and to work with real-time data and information. We have also added Web references to the end of each chapter that list the URLs of sites related to the material being discussed. Visit these sites to further explore a topic you find of particular interest. Web site URLs are subject to frequent change. We have tried to select stable sites, but we realize that even government URLs change. The publisher's Web site (**www.prenhall.com/mishkin_eakins**) will maintain an updated list of current URLs for your reference.

Collecting and Graphing Data

The following Web exercise is especially important because it demonstrates how to export data from a Web site into Microsoft® Excel™ for further analysis. We suggest you work through this problem on your own so that you will be able to perform this activity when prompted in subsequent Web exercises.

Web Exercise

You have been hired by Risky Ventures, Inc., as a consultant to help the company analyze interest-rate trends. Your employers are initially interested in determining the historical relationship between long- and short-term interest rates. The biggest task you must immediately undertake is collecting market interest-rate data. You know the best source of this information is the Web.

1. You decide that your best indicator of long-term interest rates is the 10-year U.S. Treasury note. Your first task is to gather historical data. Go to **www.federalreserve.gov/releases/H15**. The site should look like Figure 1.4. At the top, click on Historical Data. Now scroll down to "Treasury Constant Maturities" and click on the annual tag to the right of the 10 Year category.
2. Now that you have located an accurate source of historical interest-rate data, the next step is getting it onto a spreadsheet. You recall that Excel will let you convert text data into columns. Begin by highlighting the two columns of data (the year and rate). Right-click the mouse and choose COPY. Now open Excel

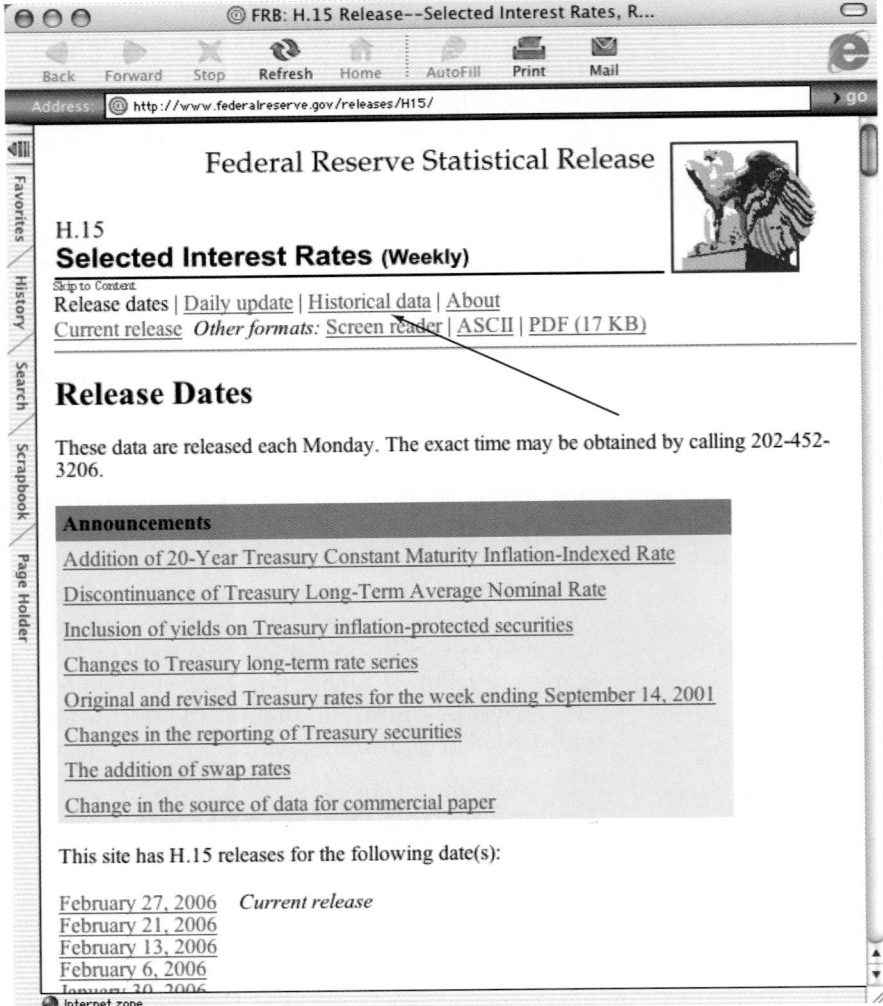

Figure 1.4 Federal Reserve Board Web Site

and put the cursor in a cell. Click PASTE. Now choose data from the menu bar and click on TEXT TO COLUMNS. Follow the wizard (Figure 1.5), checking the fixed-width option. The list of interest rates should now have the year in one column and the interest rate in the next column. Label your columns.

Repeat the preceding steps to collect the one-year interest rate series. Put it in the column next to the 10-year series. Be sure to line up the years correctly and delete any years that are not included in both series.

3. You now want to analyze the interest rates by graphing them. Highlight the two columns of interest-rate data you just created in Excel. Click on the Chart Wizard icon on the toolbar (or INSERT/CHART). Select the Scatter chart type and choose any type of scatter chart sub-type that connects the dots. Let the Excel wizard take you through the steps of completing the graph. (See Figure 1.6.)

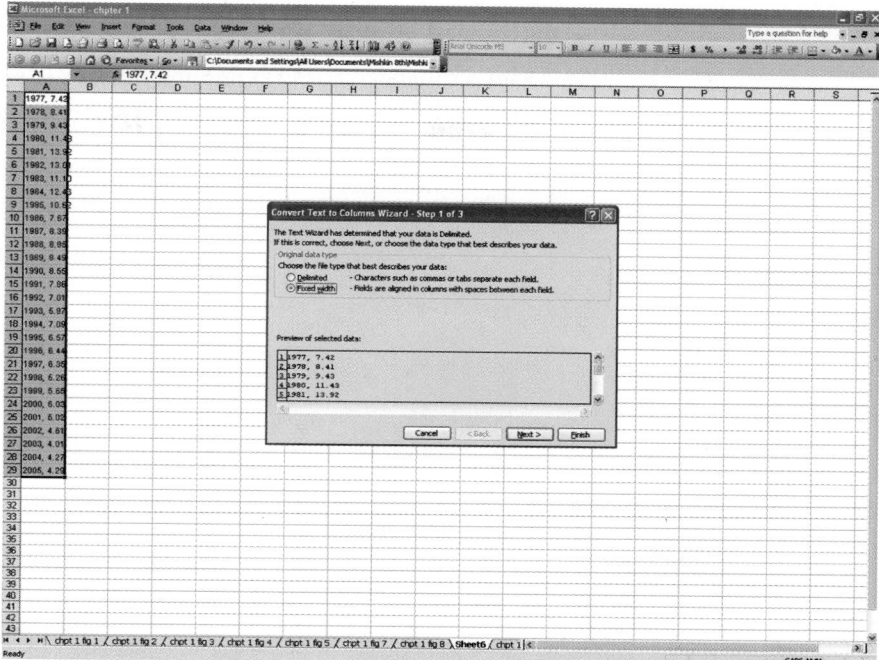

Figure 1.5 Excel Spreadsheet with Interest-Rate Data

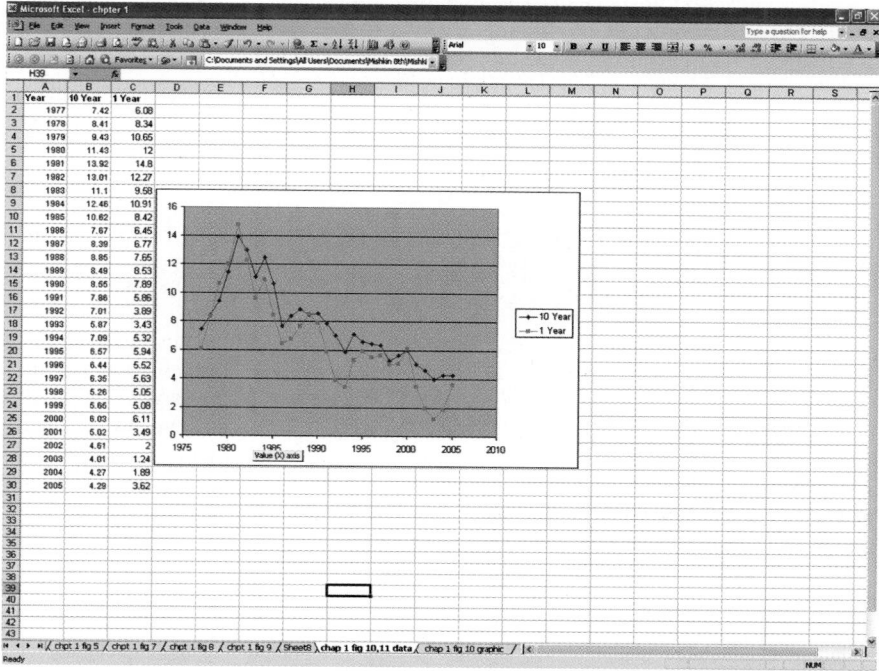

Figure 1.6 Excel Graph of Interest-Rate Data

Concluding Remarks

The field of financial markets and institutions is an exciting one. Not only will you learn material that directly affects your life—for example gaining skills that would be valuable in your career—but you will also gain a clearer understanding of events in financial markets and institutions you frequently hear about in the news media. Your study of financial markets and institutions will introduce you to many of the controversies that are hotly debated in the current political arena.

SUMMARY

1. Activities in financial markets have direct effects on individuals' wealth, the behavior of businesses, and the efficiency of our economy. Three financial markets deserve particular attention: the bond market (where interest rates are determined), the stock market (which has a major effect on people's wealth and on firms' investment decisions), and the foreign exchange market (because fluctuations in the foreign exchange rate have major consequences for the U.S. economy).

2. Because monetary policy affects interest rates, inflation, and business cycles, all of which have an important impact on financial markets and institutions, we need to understand how monetary policy is conducted by central banks in the United States and abroad.

3. Banks and other financial institutions channel funds from people who might not put them to productive use to people who can do so and thus play a crucial role in improving the efficiency of the economy.

4. Understanding how financial institutions are managed is important because there will be many times in your life, as an individual, an employee, or the owner of a business, when you will interact with them. "The Practicing Manager" cases provide special analytic tools that are useful if you make your career at a financial instituition and also give you a feel for what a job as the manager of a financial instition is all about.

5. This textbook stresses an analytic way of thinking by developing a unifying framework for the study of financial markets and instituitions using a few basic principles. This textbook also emphasizes the interaction of theoretical analysis and empirical data.

KEY TERMS

asset, *p. 4*
banks, *p. 8*
bond, *p. 4*
central bank, *p. 8*
common stock, *p. 5*
e-finance, *p. 9*
Federal Reserve System (the Fed), *p. 8*
financial intermediaries, *p. 8*

financial markets, *p. 4*
foreign exchange market, *p. 6*
foreign exchange rate, *p. 7*
interest rate, *p. 4*
monetary policy, *p. 8*
money (money supply), *p. 8*
security, *p. 4*

QUESTIONS

1. Why are financial markets important to the health of the economy?

2. When interest rates rise, how might businesses and consumers change their economic behavior?

3. How can a change in interest rates affect the profitability of financial institutions?

4. Is everybody worse off when interest rates rise?

5. What effect might a fall in stock prices have on business investment?

6. What effect might a rise in stock prices have on consumers' decisions to spend?

7. How does a decline in the value of the pound sterling affect British consumers?

8. How does an increase in the value of the pound sterling affect American businesses?

9. How can changes in foreign exchange rates affect the profitability of financial institutions?

10. Looking at Figure 1.3, in what years would you have chosen to visit the Grand Canyon in Arizona rather than the Tower of London?

11. What is the basic activity of banks?

12. What are the other important financial intermediaries in the economy besides banks?

13. Can you think of any financial innovation in the past ten years that has affected you personally? Has it made you better or worse off? In what way?

14. What types of risks do financial institutions face?

15. Why do managers of financial institutions care so much about the activities of the Federal Reserve System?

QUANTITATIVE PROBLEMS

1. The following table lists foreign exchange rates between U.S. dollars and British pounds (GBP) during April.

Which day would have been the best day to convert $200 into British pounds? Which day would have been the worst day? What would be the difference in pounds?

Date	U.S. Dollars per GBP
4/1	1.9564
4/4	1.9293
4/5	1.914
4/6	1.9374
4/7	1.961
4/8	1.8925
4/11	1.8822
4/12	1.8558
4/13	1.796
4/14	1.7902
4/15	1.7785
4/18	1.7504
4/19	1.7255
4/20	1.6914
4/21	1.672
4/22	1.6684
4/25	1.6674
4/26	1.6857
4/27	1.6925
4/28	1.7201
4/29	1.7512

WEB EXERCISES

Working with Financial Market Data

1. In this exercise we will practice collecting data from the Web and graphing it using Excel. Use the example on page 13 as a guide. Go to **www.forecasts.org/data/index.htm**, click on "Data" at the top of the page, then click on "Stock Index Data," then choose the "U.S. Stock Indices—Monthly" option. Finally, choose the "Dow Jones Industrial Average" option.

   a. Using the method presented in this chapter, move the data into an Excel spreadsheet.

   b. Using the data from part a, prepare a chart. Use the Chart Wizard to properly label your axes.

2. In Web Exercise 1 you collected and graphed the Dow Jones Industrial Average. This same site reports forecast values of the DJIA. Go to **www.forecasts.org/data/index.htm**. Click on the Dow Jones Industrials link under "6 Month Forecasts" in the far left column.

   a. What is the Dow forecast to be in three months?

   b. What percentage increase is forecast for the next three months?

CHAPTER 2

Overview of the Financial System

Preview

Suppose that you want to start a business that manufactures a recently invented low-cost robot that cleans the house (even does windows), mows the lawn, and washes the car, but you have no funds to put this wonderful invention into production. Walter has plenty of savings that he has inherited. If you and Walter could get together so that he could provide you with the funds, your company's robot would see the light of day, and you, Walter, and the economy would all be better off: Walter could earn a high return on his investment, you would get rich from producing the robot, and we would have cleaner houses, shinier cars, and more beautiful lawns.

Financial markets (bond and stock markets) and financial intermediaries (banks, insurance companies, pension funds) have the basic function of getting people such as you and Walter together by moving funds from those who have a surplus of funds (Walter) to those who have a shortage of funds (you). More realistically, when Apple invents a better iPod, it may need funds to bring it to market. Similarly, when a local government needs to build a road or a school, it may need more funds than local property taxes provide. Well-functioning financial markets and financial intermediaries are crucial to our economic health.

To study the effects of financial markets and financial intermediaries on the economy, we need to acquire an understanding of their general structure and operation. In this chapter we learn about the major financial intermediaries and the instruments that are traded in financial markets.

This chapter offers a preliminary overview of the fascinating study of financial markets and institutions. We will return to a more detailed treatment of the regulation, structure, and evolution of financial markets and institutions in Parts 3 through 7.

Function of Financial Markets ▮

Financial markets perform the essential economic function of channeling funds from households, firms, and governments that have saved surplus funds by spending less than their income to those that have a shortage of funds because they wish to spend more than their income. This function is shown schematically in Figure 2.1. Those who have saved and are lending funds, the lender-savers, are at the left, and those who must borrow funds to finance their spending, the borrower-spenders, are at the right. The principal lender-savers are households, but business enterprises and the government (particularly state and local government), as well as foreigners and their governments, sometimes also find themselves with excess funds and so lend them out. The most important borrower-spenders are businesses and the government (particularly the federal government), but households and foreigners also borrow to finance their purchases of cars, furniture, and houses. The arrows show that funds flow from lender-savers to borrower-spenders via two routes.

In *direct finance* (the route at the bottom of Figure 2.1), borrowers borrow funds directly from lenders in financial markets by selling them *securities* (also called *financial instruments*), which are claims on the borrower's future income or assets. Securities are assets for the person who buys them but they are **liabilities** (IOUs or debts) for the individual or firm that sells (issues) them. For example, if General Motors needs to borrow funds to pay for a new factory to manufacture electric

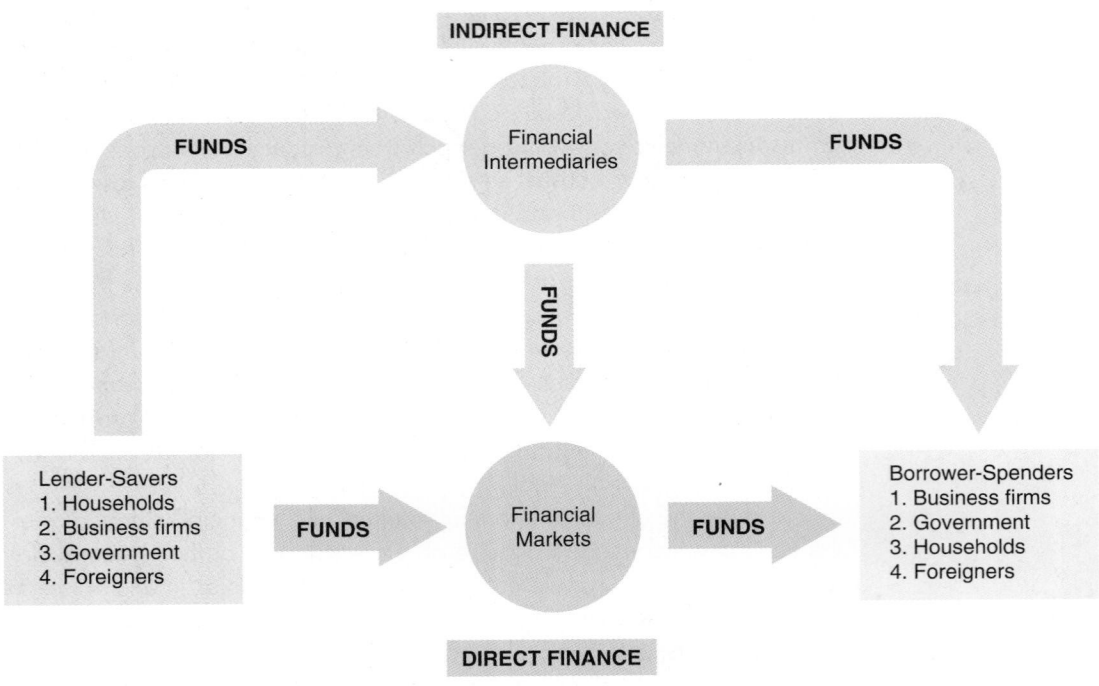

Figure 2.1　Flows of Funds Through the Financial System

cars, it might borrow the funds from savers by selling them a *bond*, a debt security that promises to make payments periodically for a specified period of time, or a *stock*, a security that entitles the owner to a share of the company's profits and assets.

Why is this channeling of funds from savers to spenders so important to the economy? The answer is that the people who save are frequently not the same people who have profitable investment opportunities available to them, the entrepreneurs. Let's first think about this on a personal level. Suppose that you have saved $1,000 this year, but no borrowing or lending is possible because there are no financial markets. If you do not have an investment opportunity that will permit you to earn income with your savings, you will just hold on to the $1,000 and will earn no interest. However, Carl the Carpenter has a productive use for your $1,000: He can use it to purchase a new tool that will shorten the time it takes him to build a house, thereby earning an extra $200 per year. If you could get in touch with Carl, you could lend him the $1,000 at a rental fee (interest) of $100 per year, and both of you would be better off. You would earn $100 per year on your $1,000, instead of the zero amount that you would earn otherwise, while Carl would earn $100 more income per year (the $200 extra earnings per year minus the $100 rental fee for the use of the funds).

In the absence of financial markets, you and Carl the Carpenter might never get together. You would both be stuck with the status quo, and both of you would be worse off. Without financial markets, it is hard to transfer funds from a person who has no investment opportunities to one who has them. Financial markets are thus essential to promoting economic efficiency.

The existence of financial markets is beneficial even if someone borrows for a purpose other than increasing production in a business. Say that you are recently married, have a good job, and want to buy a house. You earn a good salary, but because you have just started to work, you have not saved much. Over time, you would have no problem saving enough to buy the house of your dreams, but by then you would be too old to get full enjoyment from it. Without financial markets, you are stuck; you cannot buy the house and must continue to live in your tiny apartment.

If a financial market were set up so that people who had built up savings could lend you the funds to buy the house, you would be more than happy to pay them some interest so that you could own a home while you are still young enough to enjoy it. Then, over time, you would pay back your loan. If this loan could occur, you would be better off, as would the persons who made you the loan. They would now earn some interest, whereas they would not if the financial market did not exist.

Now we can see why financial markets have such an important function in the economy. They allow funds to move from people who lack productive investment opportunities to people who have such opportunities. Financial markets are critical for producing an efficient allocation of **capital** (wealth, either financial or physical, that is employed to produce more wealth), which contributes to higher production and efficiency for the overall economy. Indeed, as we will explore in Chapter 15, when financial markets break down during financial crises, as they have in Mexico, East Asia, and Argentina in recent years, severe economic hardship results, which can even lead to dangerous political instability.

Well-functioning financial markets also directly improve the well-being of consumers by allowing them to time their purchases better. They provide funds to young people to buy what they need and can eventually afford without forcing them to wait until they have saved up the entire purchase price. Financial markets that are operating efficiently improve the economic welfare of everyone in the society.

Structure of Financial Markets

Now that we understand the basic function of financial markets, let's look at their structure. The following descriptions of several categorizations of financial markets illustrate essential features of these markets.

Debt and Equity Markets

A firm or an individual can obtain funds in a financial market in two ways. The most common method is to issue a debt instrument, such as a bond or a mortgage, which is a contractual agreement by the borrower to pay the holder of the instrument fixed dollar amounts at regular intervals (interest and principal payments) until a specified date (the maturity date), when a final payment is made. The **maturity** of a debt instrument is the number of years (term) until that instrument's expiration date. A debt instrument is **short-term** if its maturity is less than a year and **long-term** if its maturity is ten years or longer. Debt instruments with a maturity between one and ten years are said to be **intermediate-term.**

The second method of raising funds is by issuing **equities,** such as common stock, which are claims to share in the net income (income after expenses and taxes) and the assets of a business. If you own one share of common stock in a company that has issued one million shares, you are entitled to 1 one-millionth of the firm's net income and 1 one-millionth of the firm's assets. Equities often make periodic payments (**dividends**) to their holders and are considered long-term securities because they have no maturity date. In addition, owning stock means that you own a portion of the firm and thus have the right to vote on issues important to the firm and to elect its directors.

The main disadvantage of owning a corporation's equities rather than its debt is that an equity holder is a *residual claimant*; that is, the corporation must pay all its debt holders before it pays its equity holders. The advantage of holding equities is that equity holders benefit directly from any increases in the corporation's profitability or asset value because equities confer ownership rights on the equity holders. Debt holders do not share in this benefit, because their dollar payments are fixed. We examine the pros and cons of debt versus equity instruments in more detail in Chapter 15, which provides an economic analysis of financial structure.

The total value of equities in the United States has typically fluctuated between $4 trillion and $20 trillion since the early 1990s, depending on the prices of shares. Although the average person is more aware of the stock market than any other financial market, the size of the debt market is often substantially larger than the size of the equities market: The value of debt instruments was $43.4 trillion at the end of 2006, while the value of equities was $19.3 trillion at the end of 2006.

Primary and Secondary Markets

go online
www.nyse.com
New York Stock Exchange. Find listed companies, quotes, company historical data, real-time market indices, and more.

A **primary market** is a financial market in which new issues of a security, such as a bond or a stock, are sold to initial buyers by the corporation or government agency borrowing the funds. A **secondary market** is a financial market in which securities that have been previously issued can be resold.

The primary markets for securities are not well known to the public because the selling of securities to initial buyers often takes place behind closed doors. An important financial institution that assists in the initial sale of securities in the primary market is the **investment bank.** It does this by **underwriting** securities: It guarantees a price for a corporation's securities and then sells them to the public.

The New York Stock Exchange and NASDAQ (National Association of Securities Dealers Automated Quotation System), in which previously issued stocks are traded, are the best-known examples of secondary markets, although the bond markets, in which previously issued bonds of major corporations and the U.S. government are bought and sold, actually have a larger trading volume. Other examples of secondary markets are foreign exchange markets, futures markets, and options markets. Securities brokers and dealers are crucial to a well-functioning secondary market. **Brokers** are agents of investors who match buyers with sellers of securities; **dealers** link buyers and sellers by buying and selling securities at stated prices.

When an individual buys a security in the secondary market, the person who has sold the security receives money in exchange for the security, but the corporation that issued the security acquires no new funds. A corporation acquires new funds only when its securities are first sold in the primary market. Nonetheless, secondary markets serve two important functions. First, they make it easier and quicker to sell these financial instruments to raise cash; that is, they make the financial instruments more **liquid.** The increased liquidity of these instruments then makes them more desirable and thus easier for the issuing firm to sell in the primary market. Second, they determine the price of the security that the issuing firm sells in the primary market. The investors who buy securities in the primary market will pay the issuing corporation no more than the price they think the secondary market will set for this security. The higher the security's price in the secondary market, the higher the price that the issuing firm will receive for a new security in the primary market, and hence the greater the amount of financial capital it can raise. Conditions in the secondary market are therefore the most relevant to corporations issuing securities. It is for this reason that books like this one, which deal with financial markets, focus on the behavior of secondary markets rather than primary markets.

Exchanges and Over-the-Counter Markets

go online

www.nasdaq.com
Detailed market and security information for the Nasdaq OTC stock exchange.

Secondary markets can be organized in two ways. One method is to organize **exchanges,** where buyers and sellers of securities (or their agents or brokers) meet in one central location to conduct trades. The New York and American Stock Exchanges for stocks and the Chicago Board of Trade for commodities (wheat, corn, silver, and other raw materials) are examples of organized exchanges.

The other method of organizing a secondary market is to have an **over-the-counter (OTC) market,** in which dealers at different locations who have an inventory of securities stand ready to buy and sell securities "over the counter" to anyone who comes to them and is willing to accept their prices. Because over-the-counter dealers are in computer contact and know the prices set by one another, the OTC market is very competitive and not very different from a market with an organized exchange.

Many common stocks are traded over-the-counter, although a majority of the largest corporations have their shares traded at organized stock exchanges. The U.S. government bond market, with a larger trading volume than the New York Stock Exchange, by contrast, is set up as an over-the-counter market. Forty or so dealers establish a "market" in these securities by standing ready to buy and sell U.S.

government bonds. Other over-the-counter markets include those that trade other types of financial instruments such as negotiable certificates of deposit, federal funds, banker's acceptances, and foreign exchange.

Money and Capital Markets

Another way of distinguishing between markets is on the basis of the maturity of the securities traded in each market. The **money market** is a financial market in which only short-term debt instruments (generally those with original maturity of less than one year) are traded; the **capital market** is the market in which longer-term debt (generally with original maturity of one year or greater) and equity instruments are traded. Money market securities are usually more widely traded than longer-term securities and so tend to be more liquid. In addition, as we will see in Chapter 3, short-term securities have smaller fluctuations in prices than long-term securities, making them safer investments. As a result, corporations and banks actively use the money market to earn interest on surplus funds that they expect to have only temporarily. Capital market securities, such as stocks and long-term bonds, are often held by financial intermediaries such as insurance companies and pension funds, which have little uncertainty about the amount of funds they will have available in the future.

Internationalization of Financial Markets

The growing internationalization of financial markets has become an important trend. Before the 1980s, U.S. financial markets were much larger than financial markets outside the United States, but in recent years the dominance of U.S. markets has been disappearing. (See the Global box, "Are U.S. Capital Markets Losing Their Edge?") The extraordinary growth of foreign financial markets has been the result of both large increases in the pool of savings in foreign countries such as Japan and the deregulation of foreign financial markets, which has enabled foreign markets to expand their activities. American corporations and banks are now more likely to tap international capital markets to raise needed funds, and American investors often seek investment opportunities abroad. Similarly, foreign corporations and banks raise funds from Americans, and foreigners have become important investors in the United States. A look at international bond markets and world stock markets will give us a picture of how this globalization of financial markets is taking place.

International Bond Market, Eurobonds, and Eurocurrencies

The traditional instruments in the international bond market are known as **foreign bonds.** Foreign bonds are sold in a foreign country and are denominated in that country's currency. For example, if the German automaker Porsche sells a bond in the United States denominated in U.S. dollars, it is classified as a foreign bond. Foreign bonds have been an important instrument in the international capital market for centuries. In fact, a large percentage of U.S. railroads built in the nineteenth century were financed by sales of foreign bonds in Britain.

A more recent innovation in the international bond market is the **Eurobond,** a bond denominated in a currency other than that of the country in which it is

global

Are U.S. Capital Markets Losing Their Edge?

Over the past few decades the United States lost its international dominance in a number of manufacturing industries, including automobiles and consumer electronics, as other countries became more competitive in global markets. Recent evidence suggests that financial markets now are undergoing a similar trend: Just as Ford and General Motors have lost global market share to Toyota and Honda, U.S. stock and bond markets recently have seen their share of sales of newly issued corporate securities slip. In 2006 the London and Hong Kong stock exchanges each handled a larger share of initial public offerings (IPO) of stock than did the New York Stock Exchange, which had been by far the dominant exchange in terms of IPO value just three years before. Likewise, the portion of new corporate bonds issued worldwide that are initially sold in U.S. capital markets has fallen below the share sold in European debt markets in each of the past two years.*

Why do corporations that issue new securities to raise capital now conduct more of this business in financial markets in Europe and Asia? Among the factors contributing to this trend are quicker adoption of technological innovation by foreign financial markets, tighter immigration controls in the United States following the terrorist attacks in 2001, and perceptions that listing on American exchanges will expose foreign securities issuers to greater risks of lawsuits.

Many people see burdensome financial regulation as the main cause, however, and point specifically to the Sarbanes-Oxley Act of 2002. Congress passed this act after a number of accounting scandals involving U.S. corporations and the accounting firms that audited them came to light. Sarbanes-Oxley aims to strengthen the integrity of the auditing process and the quality of information provided in corporate financial statements. The costs to corporations of complying with the new rules and procedures are high, especially for smaller firms, but largely avoidable if firms choose to issue their securities in financial markets outside the United States. For this reason, there is much support for revising Sarbanes-Oxley to lessen its alleged harmful effects and induce more securities issuers back to United States financial markets. However, there is not conclusive evidence to support the view that Sarbanes-Oxley is the main cause of the relative decline of U.S. financial markets and therefore in need of reform.

Discussion of the relative decline of U.S. financial markets and debate about the factors that are contributing to it likely will continue. Chapter 16 provides more detail on the Sarbanes-Oxley Act and its effects on the U.S. financial system.

*Down on the Street," *The Economist*, November 25, 2006, pp. 69–71.

sold—for example, a bond denominated in U.S. dollars sold in London. Currently, over 80% of the new issues in the international bond market are Eurobonds, and the market for these securities has grown very rapidly. As a result, the Eurobond market is now larger than the U.S. corporate bond market.

A variant of the Eurobond is **Eurocurrencies,** which are foreign currencies deposited in banks outside the home country. The most important of the Eurocurrencies are **Eurodollars,** which are U.S. dollars deposited in foreign banks outside the United States or in foreign branches of U.S. banks. Because these short-term deposits earn interest, they are similar to short-term Eurobonds. American banks borrow Eurodollar deposits from other banks or from their own foreign branches, and Eurodollars are now an important source of funds for American banks (over $190 billion outstanding).

Note that the euro, the currency used by countries in the European Monetary System, can create some confusion about the terms Eurobond, Eurocurrencies, and

Eurodollars. A bond denominated in euros is called a Eurobond only *if it is sold outside the countries that have adopted the euro.* In fact, most Eurobonds are not denominated in euros but are instead denominated in U.S. dollars. Similarly, Eurodollars have nothing to do with euros, but are instead U.S. dollars deposited in banks outside the United States.

World Stock Markets

go online

http://stockcharts.com/
def/servlet/Favorites
.CServlet?obj=msummary
&cmd=show&disp=SXA

This site contains historical stock market index charts for many countries around the world.

Until recently, the U.S. stock market was by far the largest in the world, but foreign stock markets have been growing in importance, with the United States not always being number one. The increased interest in foreign stocks has prompted the development in the United States of mutual funds that specialize in trading in foreign stock markets. American investors now pay attention not only to the Dow Jones Industrial Average but also to stock price indexes for foreign stock markets such as the Nikkei 300 Average (Tokyo) and the Financial Times Stock Exchange (FTSE) 100-Share Index (London).

go online

http://quote.yahoo
.com/m2?u

Major world stock indexes, with charts, news, and components.

The internationalization of financial markets is having profound effects on the United States. Foreigners, particularly Japanese investors, are not only providing funds to corporations in the United States, but are also helping finance the federal government. Without these foreign funds, the U.S. economy would have grown far less rapidly in the last 20 years. The internationalization of financial markets is also leading the way to a more integrated world economy in which flows of goods and technology between countries are more commonplace. In later chapters, we will encounter many examples of the important roles that international factors play in our economy (see the Following the Financial News box).

Function of Financial Intermediaries: Indirect Finance

As shown in Figure 2.1 (p. 18), funds also can move from lenders to borrowers by a second route called *indirect finance* because it involves a financial intermediary that stands between the lender-savers and the borrower-spenders and helps transfer funds from one to the other. A financial intermediary does this by borrowing funds from the lender-savers and then using these funds to make loans to borrower-spenders. For example, a bank might acquire funds by issuing a liability to the public (an asset for the public) in the form of savings deposits. It might then use the funds to acquire an asset by making a loan to General Motors or by buying a U.S. Treasury bond in the financial market. The ultimate result is that funds have been transferred from the public (the lender-savers) to GM or the U.S. Treasury (the borrower-spender) with the help of the financial intermediary (the bank).

The process of indirect finance using financial intermediaries, called **financial intermediation,** is the primary route for moving funds from lenders to borrowers. Indeed, although the media focus much of their attention on securities markets, particularly the stock market, financial intermediaries are a far more important source of financing for corporations than securities markets are. This is true not only for the United States but for other industrialized countries as well (see the Global box on p. 26). Why are financial intermediaries and indirect finance so important in financial markets? To answer this question, we need to understand the role of transaction costs, risk sharing, and information costs in financial markets.

Foreign Stock Market Indexes

International Stock Indexes

Region/Country	Index	Close	LATEST Net chg	LATEST % chg	YTD % chg
World	**DJ World Index**	**299.53**	−0.15	−0.05	7.9
	DJ World ex U.S.	**265.12**	0.27	0.10	9.1
	MSCI EAFE*	**2242.88**	2.80	0.12	8.1
Americas	**DJ Americas**	**377.60**	−0.97	−0.26	7.4
Brazil	Sao Paulo Bovespa	**50510.76**	−391.62	−0.77	13.6
Canada	S&P/TSX Comp	**13903.28**	−100.54	−0.72	7.7
Mexico	IPC All-Share	**29766.33**	−292.42	−0.97	12.5
Venezuela	Caracas General	**42471.63**	−508.40	−1.18	−18.7
Europe	**DJ Stoxx 600**	**388.96**	−0.82	−0.21	6.5
Euro zone	DJ Euro Stoxx	**428.00**	−0.69	−0.16	8.2
Belgium	Bel-20	**4658.76**	−8.36	−0.18	6.2
France	CAC 40	**6026.42**	−24.21	−0.40	8.7
Germany	DAX	**7459.61**	−19.73	−0.26	13.1
Israel	Tel Aviv	**1114.25**	−2.24	−0.20	20.3
Italy	S&P/MIB	**43629**	39	0.09	5.3
Netherlands	AEX	**529.89**	−1.31	−0.25	7.0
Spain	IBEX 35	**14686.0**	−50.3	−0.34	3.8
Sweden	SX All Share	**408.53**	2.77	0.68	9.1
Switzerland	Swiss Market	**9387.29**	−20.96	−0.22	6.8
U.K.	FTSE 100	**6555.5**	−10.2	−0.16	5.4
Asia-Pacific	**DJ Asia-Pacific**	**155.97**	0.81	0.52	6.7
Australia	S&P/ASX 200	**6345.1**	47.7	0.76	11.9
China	DJ CBN China 600	**29951.59**	209.38	0.70	92.1
Hong Kong	Hang Seng	**20979.24**	511.03	2.50	5.1
India	Bombay Sensex	**13965.86**	169.70	1.23	1.3
Japan	Nikkei Stock Avg	**17677.94**	124.22	0.71	2.6
Russia	DJ Russia Titans 10	**6525.12**	31.13	0.48	−2.1
Singapore	Straits Times	**3501.10**	54.18	1.57	17.3
South Korea	Kospi	**1605.77**	2.21	0.14	11.9
Taiwan	Weighted	**8030.56**	−0.98	−0.01	2.6

*Europe, Australia, Far East, U.S.-dollar terms   Sources: Reuters; WSJ Market Data Group

Foreign stock market indexes are published daily in the *Wall Street Journal* next to the "World Markets" column, which reports developments in foreign stock markets.

The first two columns identify the foreign stock exchange and the market index; for example, the colored entry is for the DAX for the German Stock Exchange. The third column, "CLOSE," gives the closing value of the index, which was 7460 for the DAX on May 15, 2007. The "NET CHG" column indicates the change in the index from the previous trading day, −19.73, and the "% CHG" column indicates the percentage change in the index, −0.26. The next column indicates the year-to-date percentage change of the index (+13.1%).

Source: Wall Street Journal, May 15, 2007, p. C16. Republished by permission of Dow Jones, Inc. via Copyright Clearance Center, Inc. ©2004 Dow Jones and Company, Inc. All Rights Reserved Worldwide.

Transaction Costs

Transaction costs, the time and money spent in carrying out financial transactions, are a major problem for people who have excess funds to lend. As we have seen, Carl the Carpenter needs $1,000 for his new tool, and you know that it is an excellent investment opportunity. You have the cash and would like to lend him the money, but to protect your investment, you have to hire a lawyer to write up the loan contract that specifies how much interest Carl will pay you, when he will make these interest payments, and when he will repay you the $1,000. Obtaining the contract will

global

The Importance of Financial Intermediaries Relative to Securities Markets: An International Comparison

Patterns of financing corporations differ across countries, but one key fact emerges: Studies of the major developed countries, including the United States, Canada, the United Kingdom, Japan, Italy, Germany, and France, show that when businesses go looking for funds to finance their activities, they usually obtain them indirectly through financial intermediaries and not directly from securities markets.* Even in the United States and Canada, which have the most developed securities markets in the world, loans from financial intermediaries are far more important for corporate finance than securities markets are. The countries that have made the least use of securities markets are Germany and Japan; in these two countries, financing from financial intermediaries has been almost 10 times greater than that from securities markets. However, after the deregulation of Japanese

securities markets in recent years, the share of corporate financing by financial intermediaries has been declining relative to the use of securities markets.

Although the dominance of financial intermediaries over securities markets is clear in all countries, the relative importance of bond versus stock markets differs widely across countries. In the United States, the bond market is far more important as a source of corporate finance: On average, the amount of new financing raised using bonds is 10 times the amount raised using stocks. By contrast, countries such as France and Italy make more use of equities markets than of the bond market to raise capital.

*See, for example, Colin Mayer, "Financial Systems, Corporate Finance, and Economic Development," in *Asymmetric Information, Corporate Finance, and Investment,* ed. R. Glenn Hubbard (Chicago: University of Chicago Press, 1990), pp. 307–332.

cost you $500. When you figure in this transaction cost for making the loan, you realize that you can't earn enough from the deal (you spend $500 to make perhaps $100) and reluctantly tell Carl that he will have to look elsewhere.

This example illustrates that small savers like you or potential borrowers like Carl might be frozen out of financial markets and thus be unable to benefit from them. Can anyone come to the rescue? Financial intermediaries can.

Financial intermediaries can substantially reduce transaction costs because they have developed expertise in lowering them, and because their large size allows them to take advantage of **economies of scale,** the reduction in transaction costs per dollar of transactions as the size (scale) of transactions increases. For example, a bank knows how to find a good lawyer to produce an airtight loan contract, and this contract can be used over and over again in its loan transactions, thus lowering the legal cost per transaction. Instead of a loan contract (which may not be all that well written) costing $500, a bank can hire a topflight lawyer for $5,000 to draw up an airtight loan contract that can be used for 2,000 loans at a cost of $2.50 per loan. At a cost of $2.50 per loan, it now becomes profitable for the financial intermediary to lend Carl the $1,000.

Because financial intermediaries are able to reduce transaction costs substantially, they make it possible for you to provide funds indirectly to people like Carl with productive investment opportunities. In addition, a financial intermediary's low transaction costs mean that it can provide its customers with **liquidity services,** services that make it easier for customers to conduct transactions. For example, banks provide depositors with checking accounts that enable them to pay their bills easily. In addition, depositors can earn interest on checking and savings accounts and yet still convert them into goods and services whenever necessary.

Risk Sharing

Another benefit made possible by the low transaction costs of financial institutions is that they can help reduce the exposure of investors to **risk**—that is, uncertainty about the returns investors will earn on assets. Financial intermediaries do this through the process known as **risk sharing:** They create and sell assets with risk characteristics that people are comfortable with, and the intermediaries then use the funds they acquire by selling these assets to purchase other assets that may have far more risk. Low transaction costs allow financial intermediaries to share risk at low cost, enabling them to earn a profit on the spread between the returns they earn on risky assets and the payments they make on the assets they have sold. This process of risk sharing is also sometimes referred to as **asset transformation,** because in a sense, risky assets are turned into safer assets for investors.

Financial intermediaries also promote risk sharing by helping individuals to diversify and thereby lower the amount of risk to which they are exposed. **Diversification** entails investing in a collection (**portfolio**) of assets whose returns do not always move together, with the result that overall risk is lower than for individual assets. (Diversification is just another name for the old adage, "You shouldn't put all your eggs in one basket.") Low transaction costs allow financial intermediaries to do this by pooling a collection of assets into a new asset and then selling it to individuals.

Asymmetric Information: Adverse Selection and Moral Hazard

The presence of transaction costs in financial markets explains, in part, why financial intermediaries and indirect finance play such an important role in financial markets. An additional reason is that in financial markets, one party often does not know enough about the other party to make accurate decisions. This inequality is called **asymmetric information.** For example, a borrower who takes out a loan usually has better information about the potential returns and risks associated with the investment projects for which the funds are earmarked than the lender does. Lack of information creates problems in the financial system on two fronts: before the transaction is entered into and after.[1]

Adverse selection is the problem created by asymmetric information *before* the transaction occurs. Adverse selection in financial markets occurs when the potential borrowers who are the most likely to produce an undesirable (*adverse*) outcome—the bad credit risks—are the ones who most actively seek out a loan and are thus most likely to be selected. Because adverse selection makes it more likely that loans might be made to bad credit risks, lenders may decide not to make any loans even though there are good credit risks in the marketplace.

To understand why adverse selection occurs, suppose that you have two aunts to whom you might make a loan—Aunt Louise and Aunt Sheila. Aunt Louise is a conservative type who borrows only when she has an investment she is quite sure will pay off. Aunt Sheila, by contrast, is an inveterate gambler who has just come across a get-rich-quick scheme that will make her a millionaire if she can just borrow $1,000 to invest in it. Unfortunately, as with most get-rich-quick schemes, there is a high probability that the investment won't pay off and that Aunt Sheila will lose the $1,000.

---

[1]Asymmetric information and the adverse selection and moral hazard concepts are also crucial problems for the insurance industry.

Which of your aunts is more likely to call you to ask for a loan? Aunt Sheila, of course, because she has so much to gain if the investment pays off. You, however, would not want to make a loan to her because there is a high probability that her investment will turn sour and she will be unable to pay you back.

If you knew both your aunts very well—that is, if your information were not asymmetric—you wouldn't have a problem, because you would know that Aunt Sheila is a bad risk and so you would not lend to her. Suppose, though, that you don't know your aunts well. You are more likely to lend to Aunt Sheila than to Aunt Louise because Aunt Sheila would be hounding you for the loan. Because of the possibility of adverse selection, you might decide not to lend to either of your aunts, even though there are times when Aunt Louise, who is an excellent credit risk, might need a loan for a worthwhile investment.

Moral hazard is the problem created by asymmetric information *after* the transaction occurs. Moral hazard in financial markets is the risk (*hazard*) that the borrower might engage in activities that are undesirable (*immoral*) from the lender's point of view, because they make it less likely that the loan will be paid back. Because moral hazard lowers the probability that the loan will be repaid, lenders may decide that they would rather not make a loan.

As an example of moral hazard, suppose that you made a $1,000 loan to another relative, Uncle Melvin, who needs the money to purchase a computer so he can set up a business typing students' term papers. Once you have made the loan, however, Uncle Melvin is more likely to slip off to the track and play the horses. If he bets on a 20-to-1 long shot and wins with your money, he is able to pay you back your $1,000 and live high off the hog with the remaining $19,000. But if he loses, as is likely, you don't get paid back, and all he has lost is his reputation as a reliable, upstanding uncle. Uncle Melvin therefore has an incentive to go to the track because his gains ($19,000) if he bets correctly are much greater than the cost to him (his reputation) if he bets incorrectly. If you knew what Uncle Melvin was up to, you would prevent him from going to the track, and he would not be able to increase the moral hazard. However, because it is hard for you to keep informed about his whereabouts—that is, because information is asymmetric—there is a good chance that Uncle Melvin will go to the track and you will not get paid back. The risk of moral hazard might therefore discourage you from making the $1,000 loan to Uncle Melvin, even if you were sure that you would be paid back if he used it to set up his business.

Another way of describing the moral hazard problem is that it leads to **conflicts of interest,** in which one party in a financial contract has incentives to act in its own interest rather than in the interests of the other party. Indeed, this is exactly what happens if your Uncle Melvin is tempted to go to the track and gamble at your expense.

study guide

Because the concepts of adverse selection and moral hazard are extremely useful in understanding the behavior we examine in this and many of the later chapters (and in life in general), you must understand them fully. One way to distinguish between them is to remember that adverse selection is a problem of asymmetric information *before* entering into a transaction, whereas moral hazard is a problem of asymmetric information *after* the transaction has occurred. A helpful way to nail down these concepts is to think of other examples, for financial or other types of transactions, in which adverse selection or moral hazard plays a role. Several problems at the end of the chapter provide additional examples of situations involving adverse selection and moral hazard.

The problems created by adverse selection and moral hazard are an important impediment to well-functioning financial markets. Again, financial intermediaries can alleviate these problems.

With financial intermediaries in the economy, small savers can provide their funds to the financial markets by lending these funds to a trustworthy intermediary—say, the Honest John Bank—which in turn lends the funds out either by making loans or by buying securities such as stocks or bonds. Successful financial intermediaries have higher earnings on their investments than small savers, because they are better equipped than individuals to screen out bad credit risks from good ones, thereby reducing losses due to adverse selection. In addition, financial intermediaries have high earnings because they develop expertise in monitoring the parties they lend to, thus reducing losses due to moral hazard. The result is that financial intermediaries can afford to pay lender-savers interest or provide substantial services and still earn a profit.

As we have seen, financial intermediaries play an important role in the economy because they provide liquidity services, promote risk sharing, and solve information problems, thereby allowing small savers and borrowers to benefit from the existence of financial markets. The success of financial intermediaries in performing this role is evidenced by the fact that most Americans invest their savings with them and obtain loans from them. Financial intermediaries play a key role in improving economic efficiency because they help financial markets channel funds from lender-savers to people with productive investment opportunities. Without a well-functioning set of financial intermediaries, it is very hard for an economy to reach its full potential. We will explore further the role of financial intermediaries in the economy in Parts 5 and 6.

Types of Financial Intermediaries

We have seen why financial intermediaries play such an important role in the economy. Now we look at the principal financial intermediaries themselves and how they perform the intermediation function. They fall into three categories: depository institutions (banks), contractual savings institutions, and investment intermediaries. Table 2.1 provides a guide to the discussion of the financial intermediaries that fit into these three categories by describing their primary liabilities (sources of funds) and assets (uses of funds). The relative size of these intermediaries in the United States is indicated in Table 2.2, which lists the amount of their assets at the end of 1980, 1990, 2000, and 2007.

Depository Institutions

Depository institutions (for simplicity, we refer to these as *banks* throughout this text) are financial intermediaries that accept deposits from individuals and institutions and make loans. These institutions include commercial banks and the so-called **thrift institutions (thrifts):** savings and loan associations, mutual savings banks, and credit unions.

Commercial Banks These financial intermediaries raise funds primarily by issuing checkable deposits (deposits on which checks can be written), savings deposits (deposits that are payable on demand but do not allow their owner to write checks), and time deposits (deposits with fixed terms to maturity). They then use these funds

TABLE 2.1 Primary Assets and Liabilities of Financial Intermediaries

Type of Intermediary	Primary Liabilities (Sources of Funds)	Primary Assets (Uses of Funds)
Depository institutions (banks)		
Commercial banks	Deposits	Business and consumer loans, mortgages, U.S. government securities and municipal bonds
Savings and loan associations	Deposits	Mortgages
Mutual savings banks	Deposits	Mortgages
Credit unions	Deposits	Consumer loans
Contractual savings institutions		
Life insurance companies	Premiums from policies	Corporate bonds and mortgages
Fire and casualty insurance companies	Premiums from policies	Municipal bonds, corporate bonds and stock, U.S. government securities
Pension funds, government retirement funds	Employer and employee contributions	Corporate bonds and stock
Investment intermediaries		
Finance companies	Commercial paper, stocks, bonds	Consumer and business loans
Mutual funds	Shares	Stocks, bonds
Money market mutual funds	Shares	Money market instruments

Source: Federal Reserve Flow of Funds Accounts: www.federalreserve.gov/releases/Z1/.

to make commercial, consumer, and mortgage loans and to buy U.S. government securities and municipal bonds. There are slightly fewer than 7,500 commercial banks in the United States, and as a group, they are the largest financial intermediary and have the most diversified portfolios (collections) of assets.

Savings and Loan Associations (S&Ls) and Mutual Savings Banks These depository institutions, of which there are approximately 1,300, obtain funds primarily through savings deposits (often called *shares*) and time and checkable deposits. In the past, these institutions were constrained in their activities and mostly made mortgage loans for residential housing. Over time, these restrictions have been loosened so that the distinction between these depository institutions and commercial banks has blurred. These intermediaries have become more alike and are now more competitive with each other.

Credit Unions These financial institutions, numbering about 9,500, are typically very small cooperative lending institutions organized around a particular group: union members, employees of a particular firm, and so forth. They acquire funds from deposits called *shares* and primarily make consumer loans.

Contractual Savings Institutions

Contractual savings institutions, such as insurance companies and pension funds, are financial intermediaries that acquire funds at periodic intervals on a contractual basis. Because they can predict with reasonable accuracy how much they will have to pay

TABLE 2.2 Principal Financial Intermediaries and Value of Their Assets

Type of Intermediary	Value of Assets ($ billions, end of year)			
	1980	1990	2000	2006
Depository institutions (banks)				
Commercial banks	1,481	3,334	6,469	7,613
Savings and loan associations and mutual savings banks	792	1,365	1,218	1,715
Credit unions	67	215	441	719
Contractual savings institutions				
Life insurance companies	464	1,367	3,136	4,709
Fire and casualty insurance companies	182	533	862	1,365
Pension funds (private)	504	1,629	4,355	5,558
State and local government retirement funds	197	737	2,293	2,979
Investment intermediaries				
Finance companies	205	610	1,140	1,889
Mutual funds	70	654	4,435	7,093
Money market mutual funds	76	498	1,812	2,313

Source: Federal Reserve Flow of Funds Accounts: www.federalreserve.gov/releases/Z1/.

out in benefits in the coming years, they do not have to worry as much as depository institutions about losing funds quickly. As a result, the liquidity of assets is not as important a consideration for them as it is for depository institutions, and they tend to invest their funds primarily in long-term securities such as corporate bonds, stocks, and mortgages.

Life Insurance Companies Life insurance companies insure people against financial hazards following a death and sell annuities (annual income payments upon retirement). They acquire funds from the premiums that people pay to keep their policies in force and use them mainly to buy corporate bonds and mortgages. They also purchase stocks, but are restricted in the amount that they can hold. Currently, with $4.7 trillion in assets, they are among the largest of the contractual savings institutions.

Fire and Casualty Insurance Companies These companies insure their policyholders against loss from theft, fire, and accidents. They are very much like life insurance companies, receiving funds through premiums for their policies, but they have a greater possibility of loss of funds if major disasters occur. For this reason, they use their funds to buy more liquid assets than life insurance companies do. Their largest holding of assets is municipal bonds; they also hold corporate bonds and stocks and U.S. government securities.

Pension Funds and Government Retirement Funds Private pension funds and state and local retirement funds provide retirement income in the form of annuities to employees who are covered by a pension plan. Funds are acquired by contributions from employers and from employees, who either have a contribution automatically deducted from their paychecks or contribute voluntarily. The largest asset holdings of pension funds are corporate bonds and stocks. The establishment of pension funds has been actively encouraged by the federal government, both through legislation requiring pension plans and through tax incentives to encourage contributions.

Investment Intermediaries

This category of financial intermediaries includes finance companies, mutual funds, and money market mutual funds.

Finance Companies Finance companies raise funds by selling commercial paper (a short-term debt instrument) and by issuing stocks and bonds. They lend these funds to consumers, who make purchases of such items as furniture, automobiles, and home improvements, and to small businesses. Some finance companies are organized by a parent corporation to help sell its product. For example, Ford Motor Credit Company makes loans to consumers who purchase Ford automobiles.

Mutual Funds These financial intermediaries acquire funds by selling shares to many individuals and use the proceeds to purchase diversified portfolios of stocks and bonds. Mutual funds allow shareholders to pool their resources so that they can take advantage of lower transaction costs when buying large blocks of stocks or bonds. In addition, mutual funds allow shareholders to hold more diversified portfolios than they otherwise would. Shareholders can sell (redeem) shares at any time, but the value of these shares will be determined by the value of the mutual fund's holdings of securities. Because these fluctuate greatly, the value of mutual fund shares will, too; therefore, investments in mutual funds can be risky.

Money Market Mutual Funds These financial institutions have the characteristics of a mutual fund but also function to some extent as a depository institution because they offer deposit-type accounts. Like most mutual funds, they sell shares to acquire funds that are then used to buy money market instruments that are both safe and very liquid. The interest on these assets is paid out to the shareholders.

A key feature of these funds is that shareholders can write checks against the value of their shareholdings. In effect, shares in a money market mutual fund function like checking account deposits that pay interest. Money market mutual funds have experienced extraordinary growth since 1971, when they first appeared. By 2006, their assets had climbed to nearly $2.3 trillion.

Investment Banks Despite its name, an investment bank is not a bank or a financial intermediary in the ordinary sense; that is, it does not take in deposits and then lend them out. Instead, an investment bank is a different type of intermediary that helps a corporation issue securities. First it advises the corporation on which type of securities to issue (stocks or bonds); then it helps sell (underwrite) the securities by purchasing them from the corporation at a predetermined price and reselling them in the market. Investment banks also act as deal makers and earn enormous fees by helping corporations acquire other companies through mergers or acquisitions.

Regulation of the Financial System

go online

www.sec.gov
The United States Securities and Exchange Commission home page. It contains vast SEC resources, laws and regulations, investor information, and litigation.

The financial system is among the most heavily regulated sectors of the American economy. The government regulates financial markets for two main reasons: to increase the information available to investors and to ensure the soundness of the financial system. We will examine how these two reasons have led to the present regulatory environment. As a study aid, the principal regulatory agencies of the U.S. financial system are listed in Table 2.3.

Increasing Information Available to Investors

Asymmetric information in financial markets means that investors may be subject to adverse selection and moral hazard problems that may hinder the efficient operation of financial markets. Risky firms or outright crooks may be the most eager to sell securities to unwary investors, and the resulting adverse selection problem may keep investors out of financial markets. Furthermore, once an investor has bought a security, thereby lending money to a firm, the borrower may have incentives to engage in risky activities or to commit outright fraud. The presence of this moral hazard problem may also keep investors away from financial markets. Government regulation can reduce adverse selection and moral hazard problems in financial

TABLE 2.3 Principal Regulatory Agencies of the U.S. Financial System

Regulatory Agency	Subject of Regulation	Nature of Regulations
Securities and Exchange Commission (SEC)	Organized exchanges and financial markets	Requires disclosure of information, restricts insider trading
Commodities Futures Trading Commission (CFTC)	Futures market exchanges	Regulates procedures for trading in futures markets
Office of the Comptroller of the Currency	Federally chartered commercial banks	Charters and examines the books of federally chartered commercial banks and imposes restrictions on assets they can hold
National Credit Union Administration (NCUA)	Federally chartered credit unions	Charters and examines the books of federally chartered credit unions and imposes restrictions on assets they can hold
State banking and insurance commissions	State-chartered depository institutions	Charter and examine the books of state-chartered banks and insurance companies, impose restrictions on assets they can hold, and impose restrictions on branching
Federal Deposit Insurance Corporation (FDIC)	Commercial banks, mutual savings banks, savings and loan associations	Provides insurance of up to $100,000 for each depositor at a bank, examines the books of insured banks, and imposes restrictions on assets they can hold
Federal Reserve System	All depository institutions	Examines the books of commercial banks that are members of the system, sets reserve requirements for all banks
Office of Thrift Supervision	Savings and loan associations	Examines the books of savings and loan associations, imposes restrictions on assets they can hold

markets and increase their efficiency by increasing the amount of information available to investors.

As a result of the stock market crash in 1929 and revelations of widespread fraud in the aftermath, political demands for regulation culminated in the Securities Act of 1933 and the establishment of the Securities and Exchange Commission (SEC). The SEC requires corporations issuing securities to disclose certain information about their sales, assets, and earnings to the public and restricts trading by the largest stockholders (known as *insiders*) in the corporation. By requiring disclosure of this information and by discouraging insider trading, which could be used to manipulate security prices, the SEC hopes that investors will be better informed and protected from some of the abuses in financial markets that occurred before 1933. Indeed, in recent years, the SEC has been particularly active in prosecuting people involved in insider trading.

Ensuring the Soundness of Financial Intermediaries

Asymmetric information can lead to the widespread collapse of financial intermediaries, referred to as a **financial panic.** Because providers of funds to financial intermediaries may not be able to assess whether the institutions holding their funds are sound, if they have doubts about the overall health of financial intermediaries, they may want to pull their funds out of both sound and unsound institutions. The possible outcome is a financial panic that produces large losses for the public and causes serious damage to the economy. To protect the public and the economy from financial panics, the government has implemented six types of regulations.

Restrictions on Entry   State banking and insurance commissions, as well as the Office of the Comptroller of the Currency (an agency of the federal government), have created tight regulations governing who is allowed to set up a financial intermediary. Individuals or groups that want to establish a financial intermediary, such as a bank or an insurance company, must obtain a charter from the state or the federal government. Only if they are upstanding citizens with impeccable credentials and a large amount of initial funds will they be given a charter.

Disclosure   There are stringent reporting requirements for financial intermediaries. Their bookkeeping must follow certain strict principles, their books are subject to periodic inspection, and they must make certain information available to the public.

Restrictions on Assets and Activities   There are restrictions on what financial intermediaries are allowed to do and what assets they can hold. Before you put your funds into a bank or some other such institution, you would want to know that your funds are safe and that the bank or other financial intermediary will be able to meet its obligations to you. One way of doing this is to restrict the financial intermediary from engaging in certain risky activities. Legislation passed in 1933 (repealed in 1999) separated commercial banking from the securities industry so that banks could not engage in risky ventures associated with this industry. Another way to limit a financial intermediary's risky behavior is to restrict it from holding certain risky assets, or at least from holding a greater quantity of these risky assets than is prudent. For example, commercial banks and other depository institutions are not allowed to hold common stock because stock prices experience substantial fluctuations. Insurance companies are allowed to hold common stock, but their holdings cannot exceed a certain fraction of their total assets.

Deposit Insurance The government can insure people's deposits so that they do not suffer great financial loss if the financial intermediary that holds these deposits should fail. The most important government agency that provides this type of insurance is the Federal Deposit Insurance Corporation (FDIC), which insures each depositor at a commercial bank, savings and loan association, or mutual savings bank up to a loss of $100,000 per account ($250,000 for individual retirement accounts). Premiums paid by these financial intermediaries go into the FDIC's Deposit Insurance Fund, which is used to pay off depositors if an institution fails. The FDIC was created in 1934 after the massive bank failures of 1930–33, in which the savings of many depositors at commercial banks were wiped out. The National Credit Union Share Insurance Fund (NCUSIF) provides similar insurance protection for deposits (shares) at credit unions.

Limits on Competition Politicians have often declared that unbridled competition among financial intermediaries promotes failures that will harm the public. Although the evidence that competition has this effect is extremely weak, state and federal governments at times have imposed restrictions on the opening of additional locations (branches). In the past, banks were not allowed to open up branches in other states, and in some states, banks were restricted from opening branches in additional locations.

Restrictions on Interest Rates Competition has also been inhibited by regulations that impose restrictions on interest rates that can be paid on deposits. For decades after 1933, banks were prohibited from paying interest on checking accounts. In addition, until 1986, the Federal Reserve System had the power under *Regulation Q* to set maximum interest rates that banks could pay on savings deposits. These regulations were instituted because of the widespread belief that unrestricted interest-rate competition helped encourage bank failures during the Great Depression. Later evidence does not seem to support this view, and Regulation Q has been abolished (although there are still restrictions on paying interest on checking accounts held by businesses).

In later chapters we will look more closely at government regulation of financial markets and will see whether it has improved their functioning.

Financial Regulation Abroad

Not surprisingly, given the similarity of the economic system here and in Japan, Canada, and the nations of western Europe, financial regulation in these countries is similar to financial regulation in the United States. The provision of information is improved by requiring corporations issuing securities to report details about assets and liabilities, earnings, and sales of stock, and by prohibiting insider trading. The soundness of intermediaries is ensured by licensing, periodic inspection of financial intermediaries' books, and the provision of deposit insurance (although its coverage is smaller than in the United States and its existence is often intentionally not advertised).

The major differences between financial regulation in the United States and abroad relate to bank regulation. In the past, the United States was the only industrialized country to subject banks to restrictions on branching, which limited banks' size and restricted them to certain geographic regions. (These restrictions were abolished by legislation in 1994.) U.S. banks are also the most restricted in the range of assets they may hold. Banks abroad frequently hold shares in commercial firms; in Japan and Germany, those stakes can be sizable.

SUMMARY

1. The basic function of financial markets is to channel funds from savers who have an excess of funds to spenders who have a shortage of funds. Financial markets can do this either through direct finance, in which borrowers borrow funds directly from lenders by selling them securities, or through indirect finance, which involves a financial intermediary that stands between the lender-savers and the borrower-spenders and helps transfer funds from one to the other. This channeling of funds improves the economic welfare of everyone in the society. Because they allow funds to move from people who have no productive investment opportunities to those who have such opportunities, financial markets contribute to economic efficiency. In addition, channeling of funds directly benefits consumers by allowing them to make purchases when they need them most.

2. Financial markets can be classified as debt and equity markets, primary and secondary markets, exchanges and over-the-counter markets, and money and capital markets.

3. An important trend in recent years is the growing internationalization of financial markets. Eurobonds, which are denominated in a currency other than that of the country in which they are sold, are now the dominant security in the international bond market and have surpassed U.S. corporate bonds as a source of new funds. Eurodollars, which are U.S. dollars deposited in foreign banks, are an important source of funds for American banks.

4. Financial intermediaries are financial institutions that acquire funds by issuing liabilities and, in turn, use those funds to acquire assets by purchasing securities or making loans. Financial intermediaries play an important role in the financial system because they reduce transaction costs, allow risk sharing, and solve problems created by adverse selection and moral hazard. As a result, financial intermediaries allow small savers and borrowers to benefit from the existence of financial markets, thereby increasing the efficiency of the economy.

5. The principal financial intermediaries fall into three categories: (a) banks—commercial banks, savings and loan associations, mutual savings banks, and credit unions; (b) contractual savings institutions—life insurance companies, fire and casualty insurance companies, and pension funds; and (c) investment intermediaries—finance companies, mutual funds, and money market mutual funds.

6. The government regulates financial markets and financial intermediaries for two main reasons: to increase the information available to investors and to ensure the soundness of the financial system. Regulations include requiring disclosure of information to the public, restrictions on who can set up a financial intermediary, restrictions on the assets financial intermediaries can hold, the provision of deposit insurance, limits on competition, and restrictions on interest rates.

KEY TERMS

adverse selection, *p. 27*
asset transformation, *p. 27*
asymmetric information, *p. 27*
brokers, *p. 21*
capital, *p. 19*
capital market, *p. 22*
conflicts of interest, *p. 28*
dealers, *p. 21*
diversification, *p. 27*
dividends, *p. 20*
economies of scale, *p. 26*
equities, *p. 20*
Eurobond, *p. 22*
Eurocurrencies, *p. 23*
Eurodollars, *p. 23*
exchanges, *p. 21*

financial intermediation, *p. 24*
financial panic, *p. 34*
foreign bonds, *p. 22*
intermediate-term, *p. 20*
investment bank, *p. 21*
liabilities, *p. 18*
liquid, *p. 21*
liquidity services, *p. 26*
long-term, *p. 20*
maturity, *p. 20*
money market, *p. 22*
moral hazard, *p. 28*
over-the-counter (OTC) market, *p. 21*
portfolio, *p. 27*
primary market, *p. 20*
risk, *p. 27*

risk sharing, *p. 27*
secondary market, *p. 20*
short-term, *p. 20*

thrift institutions (thrifts), *p. 29*
transaction costs, *p. 25*
underwriting, *p. 21*

QUESTIONS

1. Why is a share of Microsoft common stock an asset for its owner and a liability for Microsoft?

2. If I can buy a car today for $5,000 and it is worth $10,000 in extra income next year to me because it enables me to get a job as a traveling anvil seller, should I take out a loan from Larry the Loan Shark at a 90% interest rate if no one else will give me a loan? Will I be better or worse off as a result of taking out this loan? Can you make a case for legalizing loan-sharking?

3. Some economists suspect that one of the reasons that economies in developing countries grow so slowly is that they do not have well-developed financial markets. Does this argument make sense?

4. The U.S. economy borrowed heavily from the British in the nineteenth century to build a railroad system. What was the principal debt instrument used? Why did this make both countries better off?

5. "Because corporations do not actually raise any funds in secondary markets, they are less important to the economy than primary markets." Comment.

6. If you suspect that a company will go bankrupt next year, which would you rather hold, bonds issued by the company or equities issued by the company? Why?

7. How can the adverse selection problem explain why you are more likely to make a loan to a family member than to a stranger?

8. Think of one example in which you have had to deal with the adverse selection problem.

9. Why do loan sharks worry less about moral hazard in connection with their borrowers than some other lenders do?

10. If you are an employer, what kinds of moral hazard problems might you worry about with your employees?

11. If there were no asymmetry in the information that a borrower and a lender had, could there still be a moral hazard problem?

12. "In a world without information and transaction costs, financial intermediaries would not exist." Is this statement true, false, or uncertain? Explain your answer.

13. Why might you be willing to make a loan to your neighbor by putting funds in a savings account earning a 5% interest rate at the bank and having the bank lend her the funds at a 10% interest rate rather than lend her the funds yourself?

14. How does risk sharing benefit both financial intermediaries and private investors?

15. Discuss some of the manifestations of the globalization of world capital markets.

WEB EXERCISES

The Financial System

1. One of the single best sources of information about financial institutions is the U.S. Flow of Funds report produced by the Federal Reserve. This document contains data on most financial intermediaries. Go to **www.federalreserve.gov/releases/Z1/**. Go to the most current release. You may have to load Acrobat Reader if your computer does not already have it; the site has a link for a free patch. Go to the Level Tables and answer the following questions.

  a. What percentage of assets do commercial banks hold in loans? What percentage of assets are held in mortgage loans?

  b. What percentage of assets do savings and loans hold in mortgage loans?

  c. What percentage of assets do credit unions hold in mortgage loans and in consumer loans?

2. The most famous financial market in the world is the New York Stock Exchange. Go to **www.nyse.com**.

  a. What is the mission of the NYSE?

  b. Firms must pay a fee to list their shares for sale on the NYSE. What would be the fee for a firm with five million common shares outstanding?

PART 2

Fundamentals of
Financial Markets

CHAPTER 3

What Do Interest Rates Mean and What Is Their Role in Valuation?

Preview

go online
www.bloomberg.com/
markets/
Under "Rates & Bonds,"
you can access information
on key interest rates, U.S.
Treasuries, government
bonds, and municipal bonds.

Interest rates are among the most closely watched variables in the economy. Their movements are reported almost daily by the news media because they directly affect our everyday lives and have important consequences for the health of the economy. They affect personal decisions such as whether to consume or save, whether to buy a house, and whether to purchase bonds or put funds into a savings account. Interest rates also affect the economic decisions of businesses and households, such as whether to use their funds to invest in new equipment for factories or to save their money in a bank.

Before we can go on with the study of financial markets, we must understand exactly what the phrase *interest rates* means. In this chapter, we see that a concept known as the *yield to maturity* is the most accurate measure of interest rates; the yield to maturity is what financial economists mean when they use the term *interest rate*. We discuss how the yield to maturity is measured on credit market instruments and how it is used to value these instruments. We also see that a bond's interest rate does not necessarily indicate how good an investment the bond is because what it earns (its rate of return) does not necessarily equal its interest rate. Finally, we explore the distinction between real interest rates, which are adjusted for changes in the price level, and nominal interest rates, which are not.

Although learning definitions is not always the most exciting of pursuits, it is important to read carefully and understand the concepts presented in this chapter. Not only are they continually used throughout the remainder of this text, but a firm grasp of these terms will give you a clearer understanding of the role that interest rates play in your life as well as in the general economy.

Measuring Interest Rates

Different debt instruments have very different streams of cash payments to the holder (known as **cash flows**), with very different timing. Thus, we first need to understand how we can compare the value of one kind of debt instrument with another before we see how interest rates are measured. To do this, we make use of the concept of *present value*.

Present Value

The concept of **present value** (or **present discounted value**) is based on the commonsense notion that a dollar of cash flow paid to you one year from now is less valuable to you than a dollar paid to you today: This notion is true because you can deposit a dollar in a savings account that earns interest and have more than a dollar in one year. Economists use a more formal definition, as explained in this section.

Let's look at the simplest kind of debt instrument, which we will call a **simple loan.** In this loan, the lender provides the borrower with an amount of funds (called the *principal*) that must be repaid to the lender at the *maturity date*, along with an additional payment for the interest. For example, if you made your friend Jane a simple loan of $100 for one year, you would require her to repay the principal of $100 in one year's time along with an additional payment for interest; say, $10. In the case of a simple loan like this one, the interest payment divided by the amount of the loan is a natural and sensible way to measure the interest rate. This measure of the so-called *simple interest rate*, i, is:

$$i = \frac{\$10}{\$100} = 0.10 = 10\%$$

If you make this $100 loan, at the end of the year you would have $110, which can be rewritten as:

$$\$100 \times (1 + 0.10) = \$110$$

If you then lent out the $110, at the end of the second year you would have:

$$\$110 \times (1 + 0.10) = \$121$$

or, equivalently,

$$\$100 \times (1 + 0.10) \times (1 + 0.10) = \$100 \times (1 + 0.10)^2 = \$121$$

Continuing with the loan again, you would have at the end of the third year:

$$\$121 \times (1 + 0.10) = \$100 \times (1 + 0.10)^3 = \$133$$

Generalizing, we can see that at the end of n years, your $100 would turn into:

$$\$100 \times (1 + i)^n$$

The amounts you would have at the end of each year by making the $100 loan today can be seen in the following timeline:

This timeline immediately tells you that you are just as happy having $100 today as having $110 a year from now (of course, as long as you are sure that Jane will pay you back). Or that you are just as happy having $100 today as having $121 two years from now, or $133 three years from now, or $100 × (1 + 0.10)^n in n years from now. The timeline tells us that we can also work backward from future amounts to the present. For example, $133 = $100 × (1 + 0.10)^3 three years from now is worth $100 today, so that:

$$\$100 = \frac{\$133}{(1 + 0.10)^3}$$

The process of calculating today's value of dollars received in the future, as we have done above, is called *discounting the future*. We can generalize this process by writing today's (present) value of $100 as *PV*, the future cash flow of $133 as *CF*, and replacing 0.10 (the 10% interest rate) by i. This leads to the following formula:

$$PV = \frac{CF}{(1 + i)^n} \tag{1}$$

Intuitively, what Equation 1 tells us is that if you are promised $1 of cash flow for certain ten years from now, this dollar would not be as valuable to you as $1 is today because if you had the $1 today, you could invest it and end up with more than $1 in 10 years.

example 3.1 Simple Present Value

What is the present value of $250 to be paid in two years if the interest rate is 15%?

Solution
The present value would be $189.04. Using Equation 1:

$$PV = \frac{CF}{(1 + i)^n}$$

where

CF = cash flow in two years = $250
i = annual interest rate = 0.15
n = number of years = 2

Thus,

$$PV = \frac{\$250}{(1 + 0.15)^2} = \frac{\$250}{1.3225} = \$189.04$$

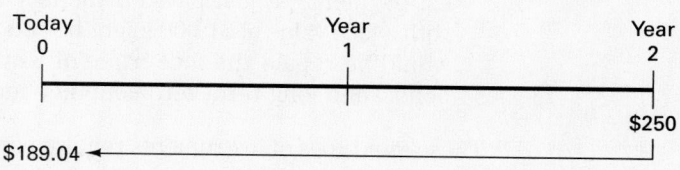

The concept of present value is extremely useful because it allows us to figure out today's value of a credit market instrument at a given simple interest rate i by just adding up the present value of all the future cash flows received. The present value concept allows us to compare the value of two instruments with very different timing of their cash flows.

Four Types of Credit Market Instruments

In terms of the timing of their cash flows, there are four basic types of credit market instruments.

1. A simple loan, which we have already discussed, in which the lender provides the borrower with an amount of funds, which must be repaid to the lender at the maturity date along with an additional payment for the interest. Many money market instruments are of this type: for example, commercial loans to businesses.

2. A **fixed-payment loan** (which is also called a **fully amortized loan**) in which the lender provides the borrower with an amount of funds, which must be repaid by making the same payment every period (such as a month), consisting of part of the principal and interest for a set number of years. For example, if you borrowed $1,000, a fixed-payment loan might require you to pay $126 every year for 25 years. Installment loans (such as auto loans) and mortgages are frequently of the fixed-payment type.

3. A **coupon bond** pays the owner of the bond a fixed interest payment (coupon payment) every year until the maturity date, when a specified final amount (**face value** or **par value**) is repaid. The coupon payment is so named because the bondholder used to obtain payment by clipping a coupon off the bond and sending it to the bond issuer, who then sent the payment to the holder. Nowadays, it is no longer necessary to send in coupons to receive these payments. A coupon bond with $1,000 face value, for example, might pay you a coupon payment of $100 per year for 10 years, and at the maturity date repay you the face value amount of $1,000. (The face value of a bond is usually in $1,000 increments.)

   A coupon bond is identified by three pieces of information. First is the corporation or government agency that issues the bond. Second is the maturity date of the bond. Third is the bond's **coupon rate,** the dollar amount of the yearly coupon payment expressed as a percentage of the face value of the bond. In our example, the coupon bond has a yearly coupon payment of $100 and a face value of $1,000. The coupon rate is then $100/$1,000 = 0.10, or 10%. Capital market instruments such as U.S. Treasury bonds and notes and corporate bonds are examples of coupon bonds.

4. A **discount bond** (also called a **zero-coupon bond**) is bought at a price below its face value (at a discount), and the face value is repaid at the maturity date. Unlike a coupon bond, a discount bond does not make any interest payments; it just pays off the face value. For example, a discount bond with a face value of $1,000 might be bought for $900; in a year's time the owner would be repaid the face value of $1,000. U.S. Treasury bills, U.S. savings bonds, and long-term zero-coupon bonds are examples of discount bonds.

These four types of instruments require payments at different times: Simple loans and discount bonds make payment only at their maturity dates, whereas fixed-payment loans and coupon bonds have payments periodically until maturity. How would you decide which of these instruments provides you with more income? They all seem so different because they make payments at different times. To solve this problem, we use the concept of present value, explained earlier, to provide us with a procedure for measuring interest rates on these different types of instruments.

Yield to Maturity

Of the several common ways of calculating interest rates, the most important is the **yield to maturity,** the interest rate that equates the present value of cash flows received from a debt instrument with its value today. Because the concept behind the calculation of the yield to maturity makes good economic sense, financial economists consider it the most accurate measure of interest rates.

To understand the yield to maturity better, we now look at how it is calculated for the four types of credit market instruments.

Simple Loan Using the concept of present value, the yield to maturity on a simple loan is easy to calculate. For the one-year loan we discussed, today's value is $100, and the cash flow in one year's time would be $110 (the repayment of $100 plus the interest payment of $10). We can use this information to solve for the yield to maturity i by recognizing that the present value of the future payments must equal today's value of a loan.

example 3.2 **Simple Loan**

If Pete borrows $100 from his sister and next year she wants $110 back from him, what is the yield to maturity on this loan?

Solution
The yield to maturity on the loan is 10%.

$$PV = \frac{CF}{(1+i)^n}$$

where

PV = amount borrowed   = $100
CF = cash flow in one year = $110
n = number of years   = 1

Thus,

$$\$100 = \frac{\$110}{(1+i)}$$

$$(1+i)\$100 = \$110$$

$$(1+i) = \frac{\$110}{\$100}$$

$$i = 1.10 - 1 = 0.10 = 10\%$$

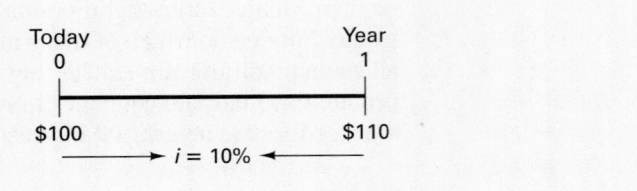

This calculation of the yield to maturity should look familiar because it equals the interest payment of $10 divided by the loan amount of $100; that is, it equals the simple interest rate on the loan. An important point to recognize is that **_for simple loans, the simple interest rate equals the yield to maturity._** Hence the same term i is used to denote both the yield to maturity and the simple interest rate.

study guide

The key to understanding the calculation of the yield to maturity is equating today's value of the debt instrument with the present value of all of its future cash flows. The best way to learn this principle is to apply it to other specific examples of the four types of credit market instruments in addition to those we discuss here. See if you can develop the equations that would allow you to solve for the yield to maturity in each case.

Fixed-Payment Loan Recall that this type of loan has the same cash flow payment every year throughout the life of the loan. On a fixed-rate mortgage, for example, the borrower makes the same payment to the bank every month until the maturity date, when the loan will be completely paid off. To calculate the yield to maturity for a fixed-payment loan, we follow the same strategy we used for the simple loan—we equate today's value of the loan with its present value. Because the fixed-payment loan involves more than one cash flow payment, the present value of the fixed-payment loan is calculated as the sum of the present values of all cash flows (using Equation 1).

Suppose the loan is $1,000, and the yearly cash flow payment is $85.81 for the next 25 years. The present value is calculated as follows: At the end of one year, there is a $85.81 cash flow payment with a PV of $85.81/(1 + i)$; at the end of two years, there is another $85.81 cash flow payment with a PV of $85.81/(1 + i)^2$; and so on until at the end of the twenty-fifth year, the last cash flow payment of $85.81 with a PV of $85.81/(1 + i)^{25}$ is made. Making today's value of the loan ($1,000) equal to the sum of the present values of all the yearly cash flows gives us

$$\$1,000 = \frac{\$85.81}{1 + i} + \frac{\$85.81}{(1 + i)^2} + \frac{\$85.81}{(1 + i)^3} + \cdots + \frac{\$85.81}{(1 + i)^{25}}$$

More generally, for any fixed-payment loan,

$$LV = \frac{FP}{1 + i} + \frac{FP}{(1 + i)^2} + \frac{FP}{(1 + i)^3} + \cdots + \frac{FP}{(1 + i)^n} \tag{2}$$

where LV = loan value
FP = fixed yearly cash flow payment
n = number of years until maturity

For a fixed-payment loan amount, the fixed yearly payment and the number of years until maturity are known quantities, and only the yield to maturity is not. So we can solve this equation for the yield to maturity i. Because this calculation is not easy, many pocket calculators have programs that allow you to find i given the loan's numbers for LV, FP, and n. For example, in the case of the 25-year loan with yearly payments of $85.81, the yield to maturity that solves Equation 2 is 7%. Real estate brokers always have a pocket calculator that can solve such equations so that they can immediately tell the prospective house buyer exactly what the yearly (or monthly) payments will be if the house purchase is financed by taking out a mortgage.

example 3.3 **Fixed-Payment Loan**

You decide to purchase a new home and need a $100,000 mortgage. You take out a loan from the bank that has an interest rate of 7%. What is the yearly payment to the bank to pay off the loan in 20 years?

Solution

The yearly payment to the bank is $9,439.29.

$$LV = \frac{FP}{1 + i} + \frac{FP}{(1 + i)^2} + \frac{FP}{(1 + i)^3} + \cdots + \frac{FP}{(1 + i)^n}$$

where

LV = loan value amount = $100,000

i = annual interest rate = 0.07

n = number of years   = 20

Thus,

$$\$100,000 = \frac{FP}{1 + 0.07} + \frac{FP}{(1 + 0.07)^2} + \frac{FP}{(1 + 0.07)^3} + \cdots + \frac{FP}{(1 + 0.07)^{20}}$$

To find the monthly payment for the loan using a financial calculator:

n = number of years   = 20

PV = amount of the loan (LV) = −100,000

FV = amount of the loan after 20 years = 0

i = annual interest rate   = .07

Then push the *PMT* button = fixed yearly payment (*FP*) = $9,439.29.

Coupon Bond To calculate the yield to maturity for a coupon bond, follow the same strategy used for the fixed-payment loan: Equate today's value of the bond with its present value. Because coupon bonds also have more than one cash flow payment, the present value of the bond is calculated as the sum of the present values of all the coupon payments plus the present value of the final payment of the face value of the bond.

The present value of a $1,000 face value bond with 10 years to maturity and yearly coupon payments of $100 (a 10% coupon rate) can be calculated as follows: At the end of one year, there is a $100 coupon payment with a *PV* of $100/(1 + *i*); at the end of two years, there is another $100 coupon payment with a *PV* of $100/(1 + *i*)^2; and so on until at maturity, there is a $100 coupon payment with a *PV* of $100/(1 + *i*)^{10} plus the repayment of the $1,000 face value with a *PV* of $1,000/(1 + *i*)^{10}. Setting today's value of the bond (its current price, denoted by *P*) equal to the sum of the present values of all the cash flows for this bond gives

$$P = \frac{\$100}{1 + i} + \frac{\$100}{(1 + i)^2} + \frac{\$100}{(1 + i)^3} + \cdots + \frac{\$100}{(1 + i)^{10}} + \frac{\$1,000}{(1 + i)^{10}}$$

More generally, for any coupon bond,[1]

$$P = \frac{C}{1 + i} + \frac{C}{(1 + i)^2} + \frac{C}{(1 + i)^3} + \cdots + \frac{C}{(1 + i)^n} + \frac{F}{(1 + i)^n} \tag{3}$$

where
P = price of coupon bond
C = yearly coupon payment
F = face value of the bond
n = years to maturity date

In Equation 3, the coupon payment, the face value, the years to maturity, and the price of the bond are known quantities, and only the yield to maturity is not. Hence we can solve this equation for the yield to maturity i.[2] Just as in the case of the fixed-payment loan, this calculation is not easy, so business-oriented software and calculators have built-in programs that solve this equation for you.

[handwritten in margin: COMPUTE THE PRESENT VALUE OF AN ANNUITY]

example 3.4 **Coupon Bond**

Find the price of a 10% coupon bond with a face value of $1,000, a 12.25% yield to maturity, and eight years to maturity.

Solution
The price of the bond is $889.20. To solve using a financial calculator:

n	= years to maturity	= 8
FV	= face value of the bond	= 1,000
i	= annual interest rate	= 12.25%
PMT	= yearly coupon payments	= 100

Then push the *PV* button = price of the bond = $889.20.

---

[1]Most coupon bonds actually make coupon payments on a semiannual basis rather than once a year as assumed here. The effect on the calculations is only very slight and will be ignored here.

[2]In other contexts, it is also called the *internal rate of return*.

TABLE 3.1 Yields to Maturity on a 10% Coupon Rate Bond Maturing in 10 Years (Face Value = $1,000)

Price of Bond ($)	Yield to Maturity (%)
1,200	7.13
1,100	8.48
1,000	10.00
900	11.75
800	13.81

Table 3.1 shows the yields to maturity calculated for several bond prices. Three interesting facts emerge:

1. When the coupon bond is priced at its face value, the yield to maturity equals the coupon rate.
2. The price of a coupon bond and the yield to maturity are negatively related; that is, as the yield to maturity rises, the price of the bond falls. If the yield to maturity falls, the price of the bond rises.
3. The yield to maturity is greater than the coupon rate when the bond price is below its face value.

These three facts are true for any coupon bond and are really not surprising if you think about the reasoning behind the calculation of the yield to maturity. When you put $1,000 in a bank account with an interest rate of 10%, you can take out $100 every year and you will be left with the $1,000 at the end of 10 years. This is similar to buying the $1,000 bond with a 10% coupon rate analyzed in Table 3.1, which pays a $100 coupon payment every year and then repays $1,000 at the end of 10 years. If the bond is purchased at the par value of $1,000, its yield to maturity must equal the interest rate of 10%, which is also equal to the coupon rate of 10%. The same reasoning applied to any coupon bond demonstrates that if the coupon bond is purchased at its par value, the yield to maturity and the coupon rate must be equal.

It is straightforward to show that the valuation of a bond and the yield to maturity are negatively related. As i, the yield to maturity, rises, all denominators in the bond price formula must necessarily rise. Hence a rise in the interest rate as measured by the yield to maturity means that the value and hence the price of the bond must fall. Another way to explain why the bond price falls when the interest rises is that a higher interest rate implies that the future coupon payments and final payment are worth less when discounted back to the present; hence the price of the bond must be lower.

The third fact, that the yield to maturity is greater than the coupon rate when the bond price is below its par value, follows directly from facts 1 and 2. When the yield to maturity equals the coupon rate, then the bond price is at the face value; when the yield to maturity rises above the coupon rate, the bond price necessarily falls and so must be below the face value of the bond.

There is one special case of a coupon bond that is worth discussing because its yield to maturity is particularly easy to calculate. This bond is called a **perpetuity** or a **consol;** it is a perpetual bond with no maturity date and no repayment of

go online
www.teachmefinance.com
A review of the key financial concepts: time value of money, annuities, perpetuities and so on.

principal that makes fixed coupon payments of $C forever. The formula in Equation 3 for the price of a perpetuity, P_c, simplifies to the following:[3]

$$P_c = \frac{C}{i_c} \qquad (4)$$

where
P_c = price of the perpetuity (consol)
C = yearly payment
i_c = yield to maturity of the perpetuity (consol)

One nice feature of perpetuities is that you can immediately see that as i_c goes up, the price of the bond falls. For example, if a perpetuity pays $100 per year forever and the interest rate is 10%, its price will be $1000 = $100/0.10. If the interest rate rises to 20%, its price will fall to $500 = $100/0.20. We can also rewrite this formula as

$$i_c = \frac{C}{P_c} \qquad (5)$$

example 3.5 **Perpetuity**

What is the yield to maturity on a bond that has a price of $2,000 and pays $100 annually forever?

Solution
The yield to maturity would be 5%.

$$i_c = \frac{C}{P_c}$$

where

C = yearly payment $= \$100$
P_c = price of perpetuity (consol) $= \$2,000$

---

[3]The bond price formula for a perpetuity is

$$P_c = \frac{C}{1 + i_c} + \frac{C}{(1 + i_c)^2} + \frac{C}{(1 + i_c)^3} + \cdots$$

which can be written as

$$P_c = C(x + x^2 + x^3 + \dots)$$

in which $x = 1/(1 + i)$. From your high school algebra you might remember the formula for an infinite sum:

$$1 + x + x^2 + x^3 + \cdots = \frac{1}{1 - x} \quad \text{for } x < 1$$

and so

$$P_c = C\left(\frac{1}{1 - x} - 1\right) = C\left[\frac{1}{1 - 1/(1 + i_c)} - 1\right]$$

which by suitable algebraic manipulation becomes

$$P_c = C\left(\frac{1 + i_c}{i_c} - \frac{i_c}{i_c}\right) = \frac{C}{i_c}$$

Thus,

$$i_c = \frac{\$100}{\$2,000}$$

$$i_c = 0.05 = 5\%$$

The formula in Equation 5, which describes the calculation of the yield to maturity for a perpetuity, also provides a useful approximation for the yield to maturity on coupon bonds. When a coupon bond has a long term to maturity (say, 20 years or more), it is very much like a perpetuity, which pays coupon payments forever. This is because the cash flows more than 20 years in the future have such small present discounted values that the value of a long-term coupon bond is very close to the value of a perpetuity with the same coupon rate. Thus, i_c in Equation 5 will be very close to the yield to maturity for any long-term bond. For this reason, i_c, the yearly coupon payment divided by the price of the security, has been given the name **current yield** and is frequently used as an approximation to describe interest rates on long-term bonds.

Discount Bond The yield-to-maturity calculation for a discount bond is similar to that for the simple loan. Let us consider a discount bond such as a one-year U.S. Treasury bill, which pays a face value of $1,000 in one year's time. If the current purchase price of this bill is $900, then equating this price to the present value of the $1,000 received in one year, using Equation 1, gives

$$\$900 = \frac{\$1,000}{1 + i}$$

and solving for i,

$$(1 + i) \times \$900 = \$1,000$$

$$\$900 + \$900i = \$1,000$$

$$\$900i = \$1,000 - \$900$$

$$i = \frac{\$1,000 - \$900}{\$900} = 0.111 = 11.1\%$$

More generally, for any one-year discount bond, the yield to maturity can be written as

$$i = \frac{F - P}{P} \tag{6}$$

where
$$F = \text{face value of the discount bond}$$
$$P = \text{current price of the discount bond}$$

In other words, the yield to maturity equals the increase in price over the year $F - P$ divided by the initial price P. In normal circumstances, investors earn positive returns from holding these securities and so they sell at a discount, meaning that the current price of the bond is below the face value. Therefore, $F - P$ should be positive, and the yield to maturity should be positive as well. However, this is not always the case, as extraordinary events in Japan indicated (see the Global box on p. 52).

Negative T-Bill Rates? Japan Shows the Way

We normally assume that interest rates must always be positive. Negative interest rates would imply that you are willing to pay more for a bond today than you will receive for it in the future (as our formula for yield to maturity on a discount bond demonstrates). Negative interest rates therefore seem like an impossibility because you would do better by holding cash that has the same value in the future as it does today.

The Japanese have demonstrated that this reasoning is not quite correct. In November 1998, interest rates on Japanese six-month Treasury bills became negative, yielding an interest rate of −0.004%, with investors paying more for the bills than their face value. This was an extremely unusual event because no other country in the world has seen negative interest rates during the past 50 years. How could this happen?

As we will see in Chapter 4, the weakness of the Japanese economy and a negative inflation rate have driven Japanese interest rates to low levels, but they can't explain the negative rates. The answer is that large investors find it more convenient to hold these six-month bills as a store of value rather than holding cash because the bills are denominated in larger amounts and can be stored electronically. These advantages of the Japanese T-bills result in some investors being willing to hold them, given their negative rates, even though in monetary terms the investors would be better off holding cash. Clearly, the convenience of T-bills only goes so far, and thus their interest rates can go only a little bit below zero.

An important feature of this equation is that it indicates that for a discount bond, the yield to maturity is negatively related to the current bond price. This is the same conclusion that we reached for a coupon bond. For example, Equation 6 shows that a rise in the bond price from $900 to $950 means that the bond will have a smaller increase in its price over its lifetime, and the yield to maturity falls from 11.1% to 5.3%. Similarly, a fall in the yield to maturity means that the price of the discount bond has risen.

Summary The concept of present value tells you that a dollar in the future is not as valuable to you as a dollar today because you can earn interest on this dollar. Specifically, a dollar received n years from now is worth only $\$1/(1 + i)^n$ today. The present value of a set of future cash flows on a debt instrument equals the sum of the present values of each of the future cash flows. The yield to maturity for an instrument is the interest rate that equates the present value of the future cash flows on that instrument to its value today. Because the procedure for calculating the yield to maturity is based on sound economic principles, this is the measure that financial economists think most accurately describes the interest rate.

Our calculations of the yield to maturity for a variety of bonds reveal the important fact that *current bond prices and interest rates are negatively related: When the interest rate rises, the price of the bond falls, and vice versa.*

The Distinction Between Real and Nominal Interest Rates

So far in our discussion of interest rates, we have ignored the effects of inflation on the cost of borrowing. What we have up to now been calling the interest rate makes no allowance for inflation, and it is more precisely referred to as the **nominal interest**

rate. We distinguish it from the **real interest rate,** the interest rate that is adjusted by subtracting expected changes in the price level (inflation) so that it more accurately reflects the true cost of borrowing. This interest rate is more precisely referred to as the *ex ante real interest rate* because it is adjusted for *expected* changes in the price level. The *ex ante* real interest rate is most important to economic decisions, and typically it is what financial economists mean when they make reference to the "real" interest rate. The interest rate that is adjusted for *actual* changes in the price level is called the *ex post real interest rate*. It describes how well a lender has done in real terms *after the fact*.

go online

www.martincapital.com/
main/charts.htm
Go to charts of real versus
nominal rates to view
30 years of nominal interest
rates compared to real rates
for the 30-year T-bond and
90-day T-bill.

The real interest rate is more accurately defined by the *Fisher equation*, named for Irving Fisher, one of the great monetary economists of the twentieth century. The Fisher equation states that the nominal interest rate i equals the real interest rate i_r plus the expected rate of inflation π^e.[4]

$$i = i_r + \pi^e \tag{7}$$

Rearranging terms, we find that the real interest rate equals the nominal interest rate minus the expected inflation rate:

$$i_r = i - \pi^e \tag{8}$$

To see why this definition makes sense, let us first consider a situation in which you have made a one-year simple loan with a 5% interest rate ($i = 5\%$) and you expect the price level to rise by 3% over the course of the year ($\pi^e = 3\%$). As a result of making the loan, at the end of the year you expect to have 2% more in **real terms,** that is, in terms of real goods and services you can buy.

In this case, the interest rate you expect to earn in terms of real goods and services is 2%; that is,

$$i_r = 5\% - 3\% = 2\%$$

as indicated by the Fisher definition.

---

example 3.6 **Real and Nominal Interest Rates**

What is the real interest rate if the nominal interest rate is 8% and the expected inflation rate is 10% over the course of a year?

Solution

The real interest rate is −2%. Although you will be receiving 8% more dollars at the end of the year, you will be paying 10% more for goods. The result is that you will be able to buy 2% fewer goods at the end of the year, and you will be 2% worse off in real terms.

$$i_r = i - \pi^e$$

---

[4]A more precise formulation of the Fisher equation is

$$i = i_r + \pi^e + (i_r \times \pi^e)$$

because

$$1 + i = (1 + i_r)(1 + \pi^e) = 1 + i_r + \pi^e + (i_r \times \pi^e)$$

and subtracting 1 from both sides gives us the first equation. For small values of i_r and π^e, the term $i_r \times \pi^e$ is so small that we ignore it, as in the text.

where

i = nominal interest rate = 0.08

π^e = expected inflation rate = 0.10

Thus,

$$i_r = 0.08 - 0.10 = -0.02 = -2\%$$

As a lender, you are clearly less eager to make a loan in Example 6 because in terms of real goods and services you have actually earned a negative interest rate of 2%. By contrast, as the borrower, you fare quite well because at the end of the year, the amounts you will have to pay back will be worth 2% less in terms of goods and services—you as the borrower will be ahead by 2% in real terms. ***When the real interest rate is low, there are greater incentives to borrow and fewer incentives to lend.***

The distinction between real and nominal interest rates is important because the real interest rate, which reflects the real cost of borrowing, is likely to be a better indicator of the incentives to borrow and lend. It appears to be a better guide to how people will be affected by what is happening in credit markets. Figure 3.1, which presents estimates from 1953 to 2007 of the real and nominal interest rates on three-month

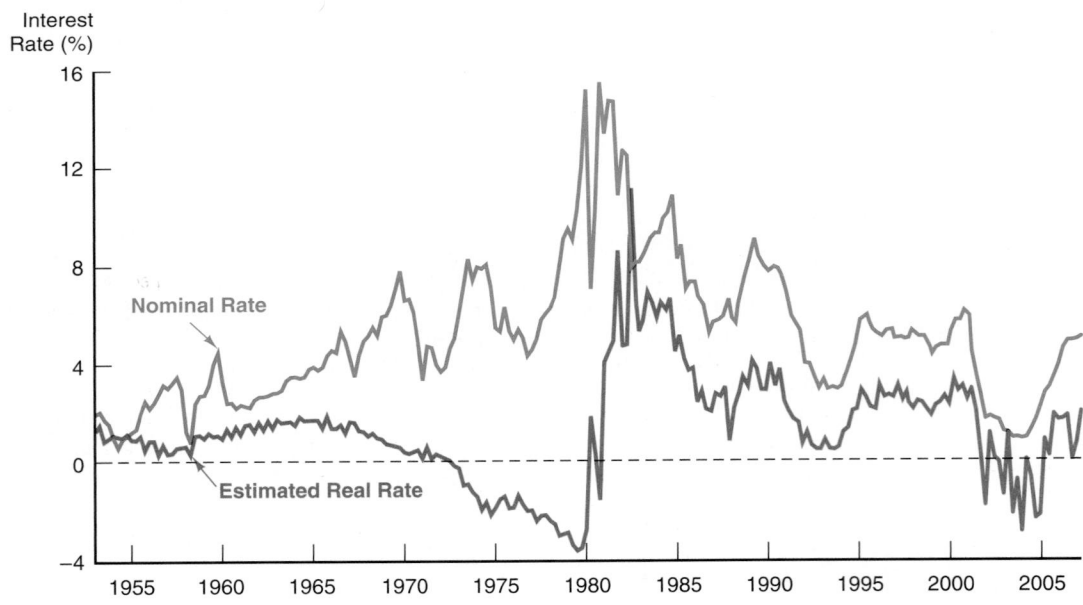

Figure 3.1 Real and Nominal Interest Rates (Three-Month Treasury Bill), 1953–2007

Sources: Nominal rates from the Citibase databank. The real rate is constructed using the procedure outlined in Frederic S. Mishkin, "The Real Interest Rate: An Empirical Investigation," *Carnegie–Rochester Conference Series on Public Policy* 15 (1981): 151–200. This involves estimating expected inflation as a function of past interest rates, inflation, and time trends and then subtracting the expected inflation measure from the nominal interest rate.

U.S. Treasury bills, shows us that nominal and real rates often do not move together. (This is also true for nominal and real interest rates in the rest of the world.) In particular, when nominal rates in the United States were high in the 1970s, real rates were actually extremely low, often negative. By the standard of nominal interest rates, you would have thought that credit market conditions were tight in this period because it was expensive to borrow. However, the estimates of the real rates indicate that you would have been mistaken. In real terms, the cost of borrowing was actually quite low.[5]

Until recently, real interest rates in the United States were not observable, because only nominal rates were reported. This all changed in January 1997, when the U.S. Treasury began to issue **indexed bonds,** bonds whose interest and principal payments are adjusted for changes in the price level (see the Mini-Case box on p. 56) .

The Distinction Between Interest Rates and Returns

Many people think that the interest rate on a bond tells them all they need to know about how well off they are as a result of owning it. If Irving the Investor thinks he is better off when he owns a long-term bond yielding a 10% interest rate and the interest rate rises to 20%, he will have a rude awakening: As we will shortly see, Irving has lost his shirt! How well a person does by holding a bond or any other security over a particular time period is accurately measured by the **return,** or, in more precise terminology, the **rate of return.** For any security, the rate of return is defined as the payments to the owner plus the change in its value, expressed as a fraction of its purchase price. To make this definition clearer, let us see what the return would look like for a $1,000-face-value coupon bond with a coupon rate of 10% that is bought for $1,000, held for one year, and then sold for $1,200. The payments to the

---

[5]Because most interest income in the United States is subject to federal income taxes, the true earnings in real terms from holding a debt instrument are not reflected by the real interest rate defined by the Fisher equation but rather by the *after-tax real interest rate*, which equals the nominal interest rate *after income tax payments have been subtracted*, minus the expected inflation rate. For a person facing a 30% tax rate, the after-tax interest rate earned on a bond yielding 10% is only 7% because 30% of the interest income must be paid to the Internal Revenue Service. Thus, the after-tax real interest rate on this bond when expected inflation is 20% equals −13% (= 7% − 20%). More generally, the after-tax real interest rate can be expressed as

$$i(1 - \tau) - \pi^e$$

where τ = the income tax rate.

This formula for the after-tax real interest rate also provides a better measure of the effective cost of borrowing for many corporations and individuals in the United States because in calculating income taxes, they can deduct interest payments on loans from their income. Thus, if you face a 30% tax rate and take out a mortgage loan with a 10% interest rate, you are able to deduct the 10% interest payment and thus lower your taxes by 30% of this amount. Your after-tax nominal cost of borrowing is then 7% (10% minus 30% of the 10% interest payment), and when the expected inflation rate is 20%, the effective cost of borrowing in real terms is again −13% (= 7% − 20%).

As the example (and the formula) indicates, after-tax real interest rates are always below the real interest rate defined by the Fisher equation. For a further discussion of measures of after-tax real interest rates, see Frederic S. Mishkin, "The Real Interest Rate: An Empirical Investigation," *Carnegie-Rochester Conference Series on Public Policy* 15 (1981): 151–200.

With TIPS, Real Interest Rates Have Become Observable in the United States

When the U.S. Treasury decided to issue TIPS (Treasury Inflation Protection Securities), a version of indexed coupon bonds, it was somewhat late in the game. Other countries such as the United Kingdom, Canada, Australia, and Sweden had already beaten the United States to the punch. (In September 1998, the U.S. Treasury also began issuing the Series I savings bond, which provides inflation protection for small investors.)

These indexed securities have successfully acquired a niche in the bond market, enabling governments to raise more funds. In addition, because their interest and principal payments are adjusted for changes in the price level, the interest rate on these bonds provides a direct measure of a real interest rate. These indexed bonds are very useful to policymakers, especially monetary policymakers, because by subtracting their interest rate from a nominal interest rate, they generate more insight into expected inflation, a valuable piece of information. For example, on September 6, 2007, the interest rate on the 10-year Treasury bond was 4.51%, while that on the 10-year TIPS was 2.32%. Thus, the implied expected inflation rate for the next 10 years, derived from the difference between these two rates, was 2.19%. The private sector finds the information provided by TIPS very useful: Many commercial and investment banks routinely publish the expected U.S. inflation rates derived from these bonds.

owner are the yearly coupon payments of $100, and the change in its value is $1,200 − $1,000 = $200. Adding these together and expressing them as a fraction of the purchase price of $1,000 gives us the one-year holding-period return for this bond:

$$\frac{\$100 + \$200}{\$1,000} = \frac{\$300}{\$1,000} = 0.30 = 30\%$$

You may have noticed something quite surprising about the return that we have just calculated: It equals 30%, yet as Table 3.1 indicates, initially the yield to maturity was only 10%. This demonstrates that ***the return on a bond will not necessarily equal the interest rate on that bond.*** We now see that the distinction between interest rate and return can be important, although for many securities the two may be closely related.

The concept of return discussed here is extremely important because it is used continually throughout the book. Make sure that you understand how a return is calculated and why it can differ from the interest rate. This understanding will make the material presented later in the book easier to follow.

More generally, the return on a bond held from time t to time $t + 1$ can be written as

$$R = \frac{C + P_{t+1} - P_t}{P_t} \tag{9}$$

where R = return from holding the bond from time t to time $t + 1$
                                       P_t = price of the bond at time t
                                       P_{t+1} = price of the bond at time $t + 1$
                                       C = coupon payment

example 3.7 **Rate of Return**

What would the rate of return be on a bond bought for $1,000 and sold one year later for $800? The bond has a face value of $1,000 and a coupon rate of 8%.

Solution
The rate of return on the bond for holding it one year is −12%.

$$R = \frac{C + P_{t+1} - P_t}{P_t}$$

where

C = coupon payment = $1,000 × 0.08 = $80

P_{t+1} = price of the bond one year later = $800

P_t = price of the bond today = $1,000

Thus,

$$R = \frac{\$80 + (\$800 - \$1,000)}{\$1,000} = \frac{-120}{1,000} = -0.12 = -12\%$$

A convenient way to rewrite the return formula in Equation 9 is to recognize that it can be split into two separate terms:

$$R = \frac{C}{P_t} + \frac{P_{t+1} - P_t}{P_t}$$

The first term is the current yield i_c (the coupon payment over the purchase price):

$$\frac{C}{P_t} = i_c$$

The second term is the **rate of capital gain,** or the change in the bond's price relative to the initial purchase price:

$$\frac{P_{t+1} - P_t}{P_t} = g$$

where g = rate of capital gain. Equation 9 can then be rewritten as

$$R = i_c + g \tag{10}$$

which shows that the return on a bond is the current yield i_c plus the rate of capital gain g. This rewritten formula illustrates the point we just discovered. Even for a bond for which the current yield i_c is an accurate measure of the yield to maturity, the return can differ substantially from the interest rate. Returns will differ from

TABLE 3.2 One-Year Returns on Different-Maturity 10% Coupon Rate Bonds When Interest Rates Rise from 10% to 20%

(1) Years to Maturity When Bond Is Purchased	(2) Initial Current Yield (%)	(3) Initial Price ($)	(4) Price Next Year ($)	(5) Rate of Capital Gain (%)	(6) Rate of Return (2 + 5) (%)
30	10	1,000	503	−49.7	−39.7
20	10	1,000	516	−48.4	−38.4
10	10	1,000	597	−40.3	−30.3
5	10	1,000	741	−25.9	−15.9
2	10	1,000	917	− 8.3	+ 1.7
1	10	1,000	1,000	0.0	+10.0

the interest rate especially if there are sizable fluctuations in the price of the bond that produce substantial capital gains or losses.

To explore this point even further, let's look at what happens to the returns on bonds of different maturities when interest rates rise. Table 3.2 calculates the one-year return on several 10% coupon rate bonds all purchased at par when interest rates on all these bonds rise from 10% to 20%. Several key findings in this table are generally true of all bonds:

- The only bond whose return equals the initial yield to maturity is one whose time to maturity is the same as the holding period (see the last bond in Table 3.2).
- A rise in interest rates is associated with a fall in bond prices, resulting in capital losses on bonds whose terms to maturity are longer than the holding period.
- The more distant a bond's maturity, the greater the size of the price change associated with an interest-rate change.
- The more distant a bond's maturity, the lower the rate of return that occurs as a result of the increase in the interest rate.
- Even though a bond has a substantial initial interest rate, its return can turn out to be negative if interest rates rise.

At first, it frequently puzzles students that a rise in interest rates can mean that a bond has been a poor investment (as it puzzles poor Irving the Investor). The trick to understanding this is to recognize that a rise in the interest rate means that the price of a bond has fallen. A rise in interest rates therefore means that a capital loss has occurred, and if this loss is large enough, the bond can be a poor investment indeed. For example, we see in Table 3.2 that the bond that has 30 years to maturity when purchased has a capital loss of 49.7% when the interest rate rises from 10% to 20%. This loss is so large that it exceeds the current yield of 10%, resulting in a negative return (loss) of −39.7%. If Irving does not sell the bond, the capital loss is often referred to as a "paper loss." This is a loss nonetheless because if he had not bought this bond and had instead put his money in the bank, he would now be able to buy more bonds at their lower price than he presently owns.

Maturity and the Volatility of Bond Returns: Interest-Rate Risk

The finding that the prices of longer-maturity bonds respond more dramatically to changes in interest rates helps explain an important fact about the behavior of bond markets: ***Prices and returns for long-term bonds are more volatile than those for shorter-term bonds.*** Price changes of +20% and −20% within a year, with corresponding variations in returns, are common for bonds more than 20 years away from maturity.

We now see that changes in interest rates make investments in long-term bonds quite risky. Indeed, the riskiness of an asset's return that results from interest-rate changes is so important that it has been given a special name, **interest-rate risk.** Dealing with interest-rate risk is a major concern of managers of financial institutions and investors, as we will see in later chapters (see also the Mini-Case box below).

Although long-term debt instruments have substantial interest-rate risk, short-term debt instruments do not. Indeed, bonds with a maturity that is as short as the holding period have no interest-rate risk.[6] We see this for the coupon bond at

mini-case

Helping Investors Select Desired Interest-Rate Risk

Because many investors want to know how much interest-rate risk they are exposed to, some mutual fund companies try to educate investors about the perils of interest-rate risk, as well as to offer investment alternatives that match their investors' preferences.

Vanguard Group, for example, offers eight separate high-grade bond mutual funds. In its prospectus, Vanguard separates the funds by the average maturity of the bonds they hold and demonstrates the effect of interest-rate changes by computing the percentage change in bond value resulting from a 1% increase and decrease in interest rates. Three of the

funds invest in bonds with average maturities of one to three years, which Vanguard rates as having the lowest interest-rate risk. Three other funds hold bonds with average maturities of five to ten years, which Vanguard rates as having medium interest-rate risk. Two funds hold long-term bonds with maturities of 15 to 30 years, which Vanguard rates as having high interest-rate risk.

By providing this information, Vanguard hopes to increase its market share in the sales of bond funds. Not surprisingly, Vanguard is one of the most successful mutual fund companies in the business.

---

[6]The statement that there is no interest-rate risk for any bond whose time to maturity matches the holding period is literally true only for discount bonds and zero-coupon bonds that make no intermediate cash payments before the holding period is over. A coupon bond that makes an intermediate cash payment before the holding period is over requires that this payment be reinvested at some future date. Because the interest rate at which this payment can be reinvested is uncertain, there is some uncertainty about the return on this coupon bond even when the time to maturity equals the holding period. However, the riskiness of the return on a coupon bond from reinvesting the coupon payments is typically quite small, and so the basic point that a coupon bond with a time to maturity equaling the holding period has very little risk still holds true.

the bottom of Table 3.2, which has no uncertainty about the rate of return because it equals the yield to maturity, which is known at the time the bond is purchased. The key to understanding why there is no interest-rate risk for *any* bond whose time to maturity matches the holding period is to recognize that (in this case) the price at the end of the holding period is already fixed at the face value. The change in interest rates can then have no effect on the price at the end of the holding period for these bonds, and the return will therefore be equal to the yield to maturity known at the time the bond is purchased.

Reinvestment Risk

Up to now, we have been assuming that all holding periods are short and equal to the maturity on short-term bonds and are thus not subject to interest-rate risk. However, if an investor's holding period is longer than the term to maturity of the bond, the investor is exposed to a type of interest-rate risk called **reinvestment risk.** Reinvestment risk occurs because the proceeds from the short-term bond need to be reinvested at a future interest rate that is uncertain.

To understand reinvestment risk, suppose that Irving the Investor has a holding period of two years and decides to purchase a $1,000 one-year bond at face value and then purchase another one at the end of the first year. If the initial interest rate is 10%, Irving will have $1,100 at the end of the year. If the interest rate on one-year bonds rises to 20% at the end of the year, as in Table 3.2, Irving will find that buying $1,100 worth of another one-year bond will leave him at the end of the second year with $1,100 $\times$ (1 + 0.20) = $1,320. Thus, Irving's two-year return will be ($1,320 − $1,000)/$1,000 = 0.32 = 32%, which equals 14.9% at an annual rate. In this case, Irving has earned more by buying the one-year bonds than if he had initially purchased the two-year bond with an interest rate of 10%. Thus, when Irving has a holding period that is longer than the term to maturity of the bonds he purchases, he benefits from a rise in interest rates. Conversely, if interest rates on one-year bonds fall to 5% at the end of the year, Irving will have only $1,155 at the end of two years: $1,100 $\times$ (1 + 0.05). Thus, his two-year return will be ($1,155 − $1,000)/$1,000 = 0.155 = 15.5%, which is 7.2% at an annual rate. With a holding period greater than the term to maturity of the bond, Irving now loses from a fall in interest rates.

We have thus seen that when the holding period is longer than the term to maturity of a bond, the return is uncertain because the future interest rate when reinvestment occurs is also uncertain—in short, there is reinvestment risk. We also see that if the holding period is longer than the term to maturity of the bond, the investor benefits from a rise in interest rates and is hurt by a fall in interest rates.

Summary

The return on a bond, which tells you how good an investment it has been over the holding period, is equal to the yield to maturity in only one special case: when the holding period and the maturity of the bond are identical. Bonds whose term to maturity is longer than the holding period are subject to interest-rate risk: Changes in interest rates lead to capital gains and losses that produce substantial differences between the return and the yield to maturity known at the time the bond is purchased. Interest-rate risk is especially important for long-term bonds, where the capital gains and losses can be substantial. This is why long-term bonds are not considered to be safe assets with a sure return over short holding periods. Bonds whose term to maturity is shorter than the holding period are also subject to reinvestment risk. Reinvestment risk occurs because the proceeds from the short-term bond need to be reinvested at a future interest rate that is uncertain.

THE PRACTICING MANAGER

Calculating Duration to Measure Interest-Rate Risk

Earlier in our discussion of interest-rate risk, we saw that when interest rates change, a bond with a longer term to maturity has a larger change in its price and hence more interest-rate risk than a bond with a shorter term to maturity. Although this is a useful general fact, in order to measure interest-rate risk, the manager of a financial institution needs more precise information on the actual capital gain or loss that occurs when the interest rate changes by a certain amount. To do this, the manager needs to make use of the concept of **duration,** the average lifetime of a debt security's stream of payments.

The fact that two bonds have the same term to maturity does not mean that they have the same interest-rate risk. A long-term discount bond with 10 years to maturity, a so-called zero-coupon bond, makes all of its payments at the end of the 10 years, whereas a 10% coupon bond with 10 years to maturity makes substantial cash payments before the maturity date. Since the coupon bond makes payments earlier than the zero-coupon bond, we might intuitively guess that the coupon bond's *effective maturity*, the term to maturity that accurately measures interest-rate risk, is shorter than it is for the zero-coupon discount bond.

Indeed, this is exactly what we find in Example 3.8.

example 3.8 **Rate of Capital Gain**

Calculate the rate of capital gain or loss on a 10-year zero-coupon bond for which the interest rate has increased from 10% to 20%. The bond has a face value of $1,000.

Solution
The rate of capital gain or loss is −49.7%.

$$g = \frac{P_{t+1} - P_t}{P_t}$$

where

P_{t+1} = price of the bond one year from now $= \dfrac{\$1,000}{(1 + 0.20)^9} = \$193.81$

P_t = price of the bond today $= \dfrac{\$1,000}{(1 + 0.10)^{10}} = \$385.54$

Thus,

$$g = \frac{\$193.81 - \$385.54}{\$385.54}$$

$$g = -0.497 = -49.7\%$$

But as we have already calculated in Table 3.2, the capital gain on the 10% 10-year coupon bond is −40.3%. We see that interest-rate risk for the 10-year coupon bond is less than for the 10-year zero-coupon bond, so the effective maturity on the coupon bond (which measures interest-rate risk) is, as expected, shorter than the effective maturity on the zero-coupon bond.

Calculating Duration

To calculate the duration or effective maturity on any debt security, Frederick Macaulay, a researcher at the National Bureau of Economic Research, invented the concept of duration more than half a century ago. Because a zero-coupon bond makes no cash payments before the bond matures, it makes sense to define its effective maturity as equal to its actual term to maturity. Macaulay then realized that he could measure the effective maturity of a coupon bond by recognizing that a coupon bond is equivalent to a set of zero-coupon discount bonds. A 10-year 10% coupon bond with $1,000 face value has cash payments identical to the following set of zero-coupon bonds: a $100 one-year zero-coupon bond (which pays the equivalent of the $100 coupon payment made by the $1,000 10-year 10% coupon bond at the end of one year), a $100 two-year zero-coupon bond (which pays the equivalent of the $100 coupon payment at the end of two years), . . . , a $100 10-year zero-coupon bond (which pays the equivalent of the $100 coupon payment at the end of 10 years), and a $1,000 10-year zero-coupon bond (which pays back the equivalent of the coupon bond's $1,000 face value). This set of coupon bonds is shown in the following timeline:

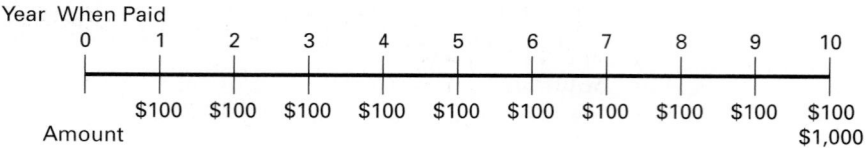

This same set of coupon bonds is listed in column (2) of Table 3.3, which calculates the duration on the 10-year coupon bond when its interest rate is 10%.

To get the effective maturity of this set of zero-coupon bonds, we would want to sum up the effective maturity of each zero-coupon bond, weighting it by the percentage of the total value of all the bonds that it represents. In other words, the duration of this set of zero-coupon bonds is the weighted average of the effective maturities of the individual zero-coupon bonds, with the weights equaling the proportion of the total value represented by each zero-coupon bond. We do this in several steps in Table 3.3. First we calculate the present value of each of the zero-coupon bonds when the interest rate is 10% in column (3). Then in column (4) we divide each of these present values by $1000, the total present value of the set of zero-

TABLE 3.3 Calculating Duration on a $1,000 Ten-Year 10% Coupon Bond When Its Interest Rate Is 10%

(1) Year	(2) Cash Payments (Zero-Coupon Bonds) ($)	(3) Present Value (PV) of Cash Payments (i = 10%) ($)	(4) Weights (% of total PV = PV/$1,000) (%)	(5) Weighted Maturity (1 × 4)/100 (years)
1	100	90.91	9.091	0.09091
2	100	82.64	8.264	0.16528
3	100	75.13	7.513	0.22539
4	100	68.30	6.830	0.27320
5	100	62.09	6.209	0.31045
6	100	56.44	5.644	0.33864
7	100	51.32	5.132	0.35924
8	100	46.65	4.665	0.37320
9	100	42.41	4.241	0.38169
10	100	38.55	3.855	0.38550
10	1,000	385.54	38.554	3.85500
Total		1,000.00	100.000	6.75850

coupon bonds, to get the percentage of the total value of all the bonds that each bond represents. Note that the sum of the weights in column (4) must total 100%, as shown at the bottom of the column.

To get the effective maturity of the set of zero-coupon bonds, we add up the weighted maturities in column (5) and obtain the figure of 6.76 years. This figure for the effective maturity of the set of zero-coupon bonds is the duration of the 10% 10-year coupon bond because the bond is equivalent to this set of zero-coupon bonds. In short, we see that ***duration is a weighted average of the maturities of the cash payments.***

The duration calculation done in Table 3.3 can be written as follows:

$$DUR = \sum_{t=1}^{n} t\frac{CP_t}{(1+i)^t} \bigg/ \sum_{t=1}^{n} \frac{CP_t}{(1+i)^t} \tag{11}$$

where
DUR = duration
t = years until cash payment is made
CP_t = cash payment (interest plus principal) at time t
i = interest rate
n = years to maturity of the security

This formula is not as intuitive as the calculation done in Table 3.3, but it does have the advantage that it can easily be programmed into a calculator or computer, making duration calculations very easy.

TABLE 3.4   Calculating Duration on a $1,000 Ten-Year 10% Coupon Bond
When Its Interest Rate Is 20%

(1)	(2)	(3)	(4)	(5)
Year	Cash Payments (Zero-Coupon Bonds) ($)	Present Value (PV) of Cash Payments (i = 20%) ($)	Weights (% of total PV = PV/$580.76) (%)	Weighted Maturity (1 × 4)/100 (years)
1	100	83.33	14.348	0.14348
2	100	69.44	11.957	0.23914
3	100	57.87	9.965	0.29895
4	100	48.23	8.305	0.33220
5	100	40.19	6.920	0.34600
6	100	33.49	5.767	0.34602
7	100	27.91	4.806	0.33642
8	100	23.26	4.005	0.32040
9	100	19.38	3.337	0.30033
10	100	16.15	2.781	0.27810
10	$1,000	161.51	27.808	2.78100
Total		580.76	100.000	5.72204

If we calculate the duration for an 11-year 10% coupon bond when the interest rate is again 10%, we find that it equals 7.14 years, which is greater than the 6.76 years for the 10-year bond. Thus, we have reached the expected conclusion: ***All else being equal, the longer the term to maturity of a bond, the longer its duration.***

You might think that knowing the maturity of a coupon bond is enough to tell you what its duration is. However, that is not the case. To see this and to give you more practice in calculating duration, in Table 3.4 we again calculate the duration for the 10-year 10% coupon bond, but when the current interest rate is 20% rather than 10% as in Table 3.3. The calculation in Table 3.4 reveals that the duration of the coupon bond at this higher interest rate has fallen from 6.76 years to 5.72 years. The explanation is fairly straightforward. When the interest rate is higher, the cash payments in the future are discounted more heavily and become less important in present-value terms relative to the total present value of all the payments. The relative weight for these cash payments drops as we see in Table 3.4, and so the effective maturity of the bond falls. We have come to an important conclusion: ***All else being equal, when interest rates rise, the duration of a coupon bond falls.***

The duration of a coupon bond is also affected by its coupon rate. For example, consider a 10-year 20% coupon bond when the interest rate is 10%. Using the same procedure, we find that its duration at the higher 20% coupon rate is 5.98 years versus 6.76 years when the coupon rate is 10%. The explanation is that a higher coupon rate means that a relatively greater amount of the cash payments is made earlier in the life of the bond, and so the effective maturity of the bond must fall. We have thus established a third fact about duration: ***All else being equal, the higher the coupon rate on the bond, the shorter the bond's duration.***

---

study guide

To make certain that you understand how to calculate duration, practice doing the calculations in Tables 3.3 and 3.4. Try to produce the tables for calculating duration in the case of an 11-year 10% coupon bond and also for the 10-year 20% coupon bond mentioned in the text when the current interest rate is 10%. Make sure your calculations produce the same results found in the text. You can get more practice by doing some of the problems involving duration calculations at the end of the chapter.

One additional fact about duration makes this concept useful when applied to a portfolio of securities. Our examples have shown that duration is equal to the weighted average of the durations of the cash payments (the effective maturities of the corresponding zero-coupon bonds). So if we calculate the duration for two different securities, it should be easy to see that the duration of a portfolio of the two securities is just the weighted average of the durations of the two securities, with the weights reflecting the proportion of the portfolio invested in each.

---

example 3.9 **Duration**

A manager of a financial institution is holding 25% of a portfolio in a bond with a five-year duration and 75% in a bond with a 10-year duration. What is the duration of the portfolio?

Solution
The duration of the portfolio is 8.75 years.

$$(0.25 \times 5) + (0.75 \times 10) = 1.25 + 7.5 = 8.75 \text{ years}$$

We now see that *the duration of a portfolio of securities is the weighted average of the durations of the individual securities, with the weights reflecting the proportion of the portfolio invested in each.* This fact about duration is often referred to as the *additive property of duration*, and it is extremely useful because it means that the duration of a portfolio of securities is easy to calculate from the durations of the individual securities.

To summarize, our calculations of duration for coupon bonds have revealed four facts:

1. The longer the term to maturity of a bond, everything else being equal, the greater its duration.
2. When interest rates rise, everything else being equal, the duration of a coupon bond falls.
3. The higher the coupon rate on the bond, everything else being equal, the shorter the bond's duration.
4. Duration is additive: The duration of a portfolio of securities is the weighted average of the durations of the individual securities, with the weights reflecting the proportion of the portfolio invested in each.

Duration and Interest-Rate Risk

Now that we understand how duration is calculated, we want to see how it can be used by the practicing financial institution manager to measure interest-rate risk. Duration is a particularly useful concept because it provides a good approximation, particularly when interest-rate changes are small, for how much the security price changes for a given change in interest rates, as the following formula indicates:

$$\%\Delta P \approx -DUR \times \frac{\Delta i}{1 + i} \qquad (12)$$

where $\%\Delta P = (P_{t+1} - P_t)/P_t$ = percentage change in the price of the security from t to $t + 1$ = rate of capital gain

DUR = duration

i = interest rate

example 3.10 **Duration and Interest-Rate Risk**

A pension fund manager is holding a 10-year 10% coupon bond in the fund's portfolio and the interest rate is currently 10%. What loss would the fund be exposed to if the interest rate rises to 11% tomorrow?

Solution

The approximate percentage change in the price of the bond is −6.15%.

As the calulation in Table 3.3 shows, the duration of a 10-year 10% coupon bond is 6.76 years.

$$\%\Delta P \approx -DUR \times \frac{\Delta i}{1 + i}$$

where

DUR = duration   = 6.76

Δi = change in interest rate = 0.11 − 0.10 = 0.01

i = current interest rate   = 0.10

Thus,

$$\%\Delta P \approx -6.76 \times \frac{0.01}{1 + 0.10}$$

$$\%\Delta P \approx -0.0615 = -6.15\%$$

example 3.11 **Duration and Interest-Rate Risk**

Now the pension manager has the option to hold a 10-year coupon bond with a coupon rate of 20% instead of 10%. As mentioned earlier, the duration for this 20% coupon bond is 5.98 years when the interest rate is 10%. Find the approximate change in the bond price when the interest rate increases from 10% to 11%.

Solution

This time the approximate change in bond price is −5.4%. This change in bond price is much smaller than for the higher-duration coupon bond.

$$\%\Delta P \approx -DUR \times \frac{\Delta i}{1+i}$$

where

DUR = duration $\qquad\qquad$ = 5.98

Δi = change in interest rate = 0.11 − 0.10 = 0.01

i = current interest rate $\qquad$ = 0.10

Thus,

$$\%\Delta P \approx -5.98 \times \frac{0.01}{1+0.10}$$

$$\%\Delta P \approx -0.054 = -5.4\%$$

The pension fund manager realizes that the interest-rate risk on the 20% coupon bond is less than on the 10% coupon, so he switches the fund out of the 10% coupon bond and into the 20% coupon bond.

Examples 3.10 and 3.11 have led the pension fund manager to an important conclusion about the relationship of duration and interest-rate risk: ***The greater the duration of a security, the greater the percentage change in the market value of the security for a given change in interest rates. Therefore, the greater the duration of a security, the greater its interest-rate risk.***

This reasoning applies equally to a portfolio of securities. So by calculating the duration of the fund's portfolio of securities using the methods outlined here, a pension fund manager can easily ascertain the amount of interest-rate risk the entire fund is exposed to. As we will see in Chapter 24, duration is a highly useful concept for the management of interest-rate risk that is widely used by managers of banks and other financial institutions.

SUMMARY

1. The yield to maturity, which is the measure that most accurately reflects the interest rate, is the interest rate that equates the present value of future cash flows of a debt instrument with its value today. Application of this principle reveals that bond prices and interest rates are negatively related: When the interest rate rises, the price of the bond must fall, and vice versa.

2. The real interest rate is defined as the nominal interest rate minus the expected rate of inflation. It is a better measure of the incentives to borrow and lend than the nominal interest rate, and it is a more accurate indicator of the tightness of credit market conditions than the nominal interest rate.

3. The return on a security, which tells you how well you have done by holding this security over a stated period of time, can differ substantially from the interest rate as measured by the yield to maturity. Long-term bond prices have substantial fluctuations when interest rates change and thus bear interest-rate risk. The resulting capital gains and losses can be large, which is why long-term bonds are not considered to be safe assets with a sure return. Bonds whose maturity is shorter than the holding period are also subject to reinvestment risk, which occurs because the proceeds from the short-term bond need to be reinvested at a future interest rate that is uncertain.

4. Duration, the average lifetime of a debt security's stream of payments, is a measure of effective maturity, the term to maturity that accurately measures interest-rate risk. Everything else being equal, the duration of a bond is greater the longer the maturity of a bond, when interest rates fall, or when the coupon rate of a coupon bond falls. Duration is additive: The duration of a portfolio of securities is the weighted average of the durations of the individual securities, with the weights reflecting the proportion of the portfolio invested in each. The greater the duration of a security, the greater the percentage change in the market value of the security for a given change in interest rates. Therefore, the greater the duration of a security, the greater its interest-rate risk.

KEY TERMS

cash flows, *p. 42*
coupon bond, *p. 44*
coupon rate, *p. 44*
current yield, *p. 51*
discount bond (zero-coupon bond), *p. 44*
duration, *p. 61*
face value (par value), *p. 44*
fixed-payment loan (fully amortized loan), *p. 44*
indexed bond, *p. 55*
interest-rate risk, *p. 59*

nominal interest rate, *p. 52*
perpetuity (consol), *p. 49*
present value (present discounted value), *p. 42*
rate of capital gain, *p. 57*
real interest rate, *p. 53*
real terms, *p. 53*
reinvestment risk, *p. 60*
return (rate of return), *p. 55*
simple loan, *p. 42*
yield to maturity, *p. 45*

QUESTIONS

1. Write down the formula that is used to calculate the yield to maturity on a 20-year 10% coupon bond with $1,000 face value that sells for $2,000.

2. If there is a decline in interest rates, which would you rather be holding, long-term bonds or short-term bonds? Why? Which type of bond has the greater interest-rate risk?

3. A financial adviser has just given you the following advice: "Long-term bonds are a great investment because their interest rate is over 20%." Is the financial adviser necessarily right?

4. If mortgage rates rise from 5% to 10%, but the expected rate of increase in housing prices rises from 2% to 9%, are people more or less likely to buy houses?

QUANTITATIVE PROBLEMS

1. Calculate the present value of a $1,000 zero-coupon bond with five years to maturity if the yield to maturity is 6%.

2. A lottery claims its grand prize is $10 million, payable over 20 years at $500,000 per year. If the first payment is made immediately, what is this grand prize really worth? Use a discount rate of 6%.

3. Consider a bond with a 7% annual coupon and a face value of $1,000. Complete the following table.

Years to Maturity	Yield to Maturity	Current Price
3	5	
3	7	
6	7	
9	7	
9	9	

What relationships do you observe between maturity and discount rate and the current price?

4. Consider a coupon bond that has a $1,000 par value and a coupon rate of 10%. The bond is currently selling for $1,150 and has eight years to maturity. What is the bond's yield to maturity?

5. You are willing to pay $15,625 now to purchase a perpetuity that will pay you and your heirs $1,250 each year, forever, starting at the end of this year. If your required rate of return does not change, how much would you be willing to pay if this were a 20-year, annual payment, ordinary annuity instead of a perpetuity?

6. What is the price of a perpetuity that has a coupon of $50 per year and a yield to maturity of 2.5%? If the yield to maturity doubles, what will happen to its price?

7. Property taxes in DeKalb County are roughly 2.66% of the purchase price every year. If you just bought a $100,000 home, what is the PV of *all* the future property tax payments? Assume that the house remains worth $100,000 forever, property tax rates never change, and that a 9% discount rate is used for discounting.

8. Assume you just deposited $1,000 into a bank account. The current real interest rate is 2%, and inflation is expected to be 6% over the next year. What nominal rate would you require from the bank over the next year? How much money will you have at the end of one year? If you are saving to buy a stereo that currently sells for $1,050, will you have enough to buy it?

9. A 10-year, 7% coupon bond with a face value of $1,000 is currently selling for $871.65. Compute your rate of return if you sell the bond next year for $880.10.

10. You have paid $980.30 for an 8% coupon bond with a face value of $1,000 that matures in five years. You plan on holding the bond for one year. If you want to earn a 9% rate of return on this investment, what price must you sell the bond for? Is this realistic?

11. Calculate the duration of a $1,000, 6% coupon bond with three years to maturity. Assume that all market interest rates are 7%.

12. Consider the bond in the previous question. Calculate the expected price change if interest rates drop to 6.75% using the duration approximation. Calculate the actual price change using discounted cash flow.

13. The duration of a $100 million portfolio is 10 years. $40 million in new securities are added to the portfolio, increasing the duration of the portfolio to 12.5 years. What is the duration of the $40 million in new securities?

14. A bank has two 3-year commercial loans with a present value of $70 million. The first is a $30 million loan that requires a single payment of $37.8 million in three years, with no other payments till then. The second loan is for $40 million. It requires an annual interest payment of $3.6 million. The principal of $40 million is due in three years.

    a. What is the duration of the bank's commercial loan portfolio?

    b. What will happen to the value of its portfolio if the general level of interest rates increases from 8% to 8.5%?

15. Consider a bond that promises the following cash flows. The required discount rate is 12%.

Year	0	1	2	3	4
Promised Payments	160	160	170	180	230

You plan to buy this bond, hold it for 2.5 years, and then sell the bond.

    a. What total cash will you receive from the bond after the 2.5 years? Assume that periodic cash flows are reinvested at 12%.

    b. If immediately after buying this bond, all market interest rates drop to 11% (including your reinvestment rate), what will be the impact on your total cash flow after 2.5 years? How does this compare to part (a)?

    c. Assuming all market interest rates are 12%, what is the duration of this bond?

Understanding Interest Rates

1. Investigate the data available from the Federal Reserve at **http://www.federalreserve.gov/releases/**. Then answer the following questions.

   a. What is the difference in the interest rates on commercial paper for financial firms versus nonfinancial firms?

   b. What was the interest rate on the one-month Eurodollar at the end of 1971?

   c. What is the most recent interest rate reported for the 10-year Treasury note?

2. Figure 3.1 in the chapter shows the estimated real and nominal rates for three-month Treasury bills. Go to **http://www.martincapital.com/main/charts.htm**. Click on "Interest Rates and Yields" then on "Nominal vs. Real Market Rates."

   a. Compare the three-month real rate to the long-term real rate. Which is greater?

   b. Compare the short-term nominal rate to the long-term nominal rate. Which appears most volatile?

CHAPTER 4

Why Do Interest Rates Change?

Preview

In the early 1950s, nominal interest rates on three-month Treasury bills were about 1% at an annual rate; by 1981, they had reached over 15%, then fell to 3% in 1993, rose above 5% by the mid-1990s, dropped to near 1% in 2003, then began rising again to over 5% by 2007. What explains these substantial fluctuations in interest rates? One reason we study financial markets and institutions is to provide some answers to this question.

In this chapter we examine why the overall level of *nominal* interest rates (which we refer to simply as "interest rates") changes and the factors that influence their behavior. We learned in Chapter 3 that interest rates are negatively related to the price of bonds, so if we can explain why bond prices change, we can also explain why interest rates fluctuate. Here we will apply supply and demand analysis to examine how bond prices and interest rates change.

Determinants of Asset Demand

An **asset** is a piece of property that is a store of value. Items such as money, bonds, stocks, art, land, houses, farm equipment, and manufacturing machinery are all assets. Facing the question of whether to buy and hold an asset or whether to buy one asset rather than another, an individual must consider the following factors:

1. **Wealth,** the total resources owned by the individual, including all assets
2. **Expected return** (the return expected over the next period) on one asset relative to alternative assets

71

3. **Risk** (the degree of uncertainty associated with the return) on one asset relative to alternative assets

4. **Liquidity** (the ease and speed with which an asset can be turned into cash) relative to alternative assets

Wealth

When we find that our wealth has increased, we have more resources available with which to purchase assets and so, not surprisingly, the quantity of assets we demand increases.[1] Therefore, the effect of changes in wealth on the quantity demanded of an asset can be summarized as follows: ***Holding everything else constant, an increase in wealth raises the quantity demanded of an asset.***

Expected Returns

In Chapter 3 we saw that the return on an asset (such as a bond) measures how much we gain from holding that asset. When we make a decision to buy an asset, we are influenced by what we expect the return on that asset to be. If an Exxon- Mobil Corporation bond, for example, has a return of 15% half of the time and 5% the other half of the time, its expected return (which you can think of as the average return) is 10%. More formally, the expected return on an asset is the weighted average of all possible returns, where the weights are the probabilities of occurrence of that return:

$$R^e = p_1 R_1 + p_2 R_2 + \cdots + p_n R_n \tag{1}$$

where R^e = expected return
         n = number of possible outcomes (states of nature)
         R_i = return in the ith state of nature
         p_i = probability of occurrence of the return R_i

example 4.1 Expected Return

What is the expected return on the Exxon-Mobil bond if the return is 12% two-thirds of the time and 8% one-third of the time?

---

[1] Although it is possible that some assets (called *inferior assets*) might have the property that the quantity demanded does not increase as wealth increases, such assets are rare. Hence we will always assume that demand for an asset increases as wealth increases.

Solution

The expected return is 10.68%.

$$R^{\text{e}} = p_1 R_1 + p_2 R_2$$

where

p_1 = probability of occurrence of return 1 = $\frac{2}{3}$ = 0.67

R_1 = return in state 1   = 12% = 0.12

p_2 = probability of occurrence return 2   = $\frac{1}{3}$ = 0.33

R_2 = return in state 2   = 8% = 0.08

Thus,

$$R^{\text{e}} = (.67)(0.12) + (.33)(0.08) = 0.1068 = 10.68\%$$

If the expected return on the Exxon-Mobil bond rises relative to expected returns on alternative assets, holding everything else constant, then it becomes more desirable to purchase it, and the quantity demanded increases. This can occur in either of two ways: (1) when the expected return on the Mobil Oil bond rises while the return on an alternative asset—say, stock in IBM—remains unchanged or (2) when the return on the alternative asset, the IBM stock, falls while the return on the Mobil Oil bond remains unchanged. To summarize, *an increase in an asset's expected return relative to that of an alternative asset, holding everything else unchanged, raises the quantity demanded of the asset.*

Risk

The degree of risk or uncertainty of an asset's returns also affects the demand for the asset. Consider two assets, stock in Fly-by-Night Airlines and stock in Feet-on-the-Ground Bus Company. Suppose that Fly-by-Night stock has a return of 15% half of the time and 5% the other half of the time, making its expected return 10%, while stock in Feet-on-the-Ground has a fixed return of 10%. Fly-by-Night stock has uncertainty associated with its returns and so has greater risk than stock in Feet-on-the-Ground, whose return is a sure thing.

To see this more formally, we can use a measure of risk called the **standard deviation.** The standard deviation of returns on an asset is calculated as follows. First you need to calculate the expected return, R^{e}; then you subtract the expected return from each return to get a deviation; then you square each deviation and multiply it by the probability of occurrence of that outcome; finally, you add up all these weighted squared deviations and take the square root. The formula for the standard deviation, σ, is thus:

$$\sigma = \sqrt{p_1(R_1 - R^{\text{e}})^2 + p_2(R_2 - R^{\text{e}})^2 + \cdots + p_n(R_n - R^{\text{e}})^2} \qquad (2)$$

The higher the standard deviation, σ, the greater the risk of an asset.

example 4.2 **Standard Deviation**

What is the standard deviation of the returns on the Fly-by-Night Airlines stock and Feet-on-the Ground Bus Company, with the same return outcomes and probabilities described above? Of these two stocks, which is riskier?

Solution
Fly-by-Night Airlines has a standard deviation of returns of 5%.

$$\sigma = \sqrt{p_1(R_1 - R^e)^2 + p_2(R_2 - R^e)^2}$$

$$R^e = p_1R_1 + p_2R_2$$

where

p_1 = probability of occurrence of return 1 = $\frac{1}{2}$ = 0.50

R_1 = return in state 1   = 15%   = 0.15

p_2 = probability of occurrence of return 2 = $\frac{1}{2}$ = 0.50

R_2 = return in state 2   = 5%   = 0.05

R^e = expected return   = (.50)(0.15) + (.50)(0.05)   = 0.10

Thus,

$$\sigma = \sqrt{(.50)(0.15 - 0.10)^2 + (.50)(0.05 - 0.10)^2}$$

$$\sigma = \sqrt{(.50)(0.0025) + (.50)(0.0025)} = \sqrt{0.0025} = 0.05 = 5\%$$

Feet-on-the-Ground Bus Company has a standard deviation of returns of 0%.

$$\sigma = \sqrt{p_1(R_1 - R^e)^2}$$

$$R^e = p_1R_1$$

where

p_1 = probability of occurrence of return 1 = 1.0

R_1 = return in state 1 = 10%   = 0.10

R^e = expected return = (1.0)(0.10)   = 0.10

Thus,

$$\sigma = \sqrt{(1.0)(0.10 - 0.10)^2}$$

$$= \sqrt{0} = 0 = 0\%$$

Clearly, Fly-by-Night Airlines is a riskier stock because its standard deviation of returns of 5% is higher than the zero standard deviation of returns for Feet-on-the-Ground Bus Company, which has a certain return.

A *risk-averse* person prefers stock in the Feet-on-the-Ground (the sure thing) to Fly-by-Night stock (the riskier asset), even though the stocks have the same expected return, 10%. By contrast, a person who prefers risk is a *risk preferrer* or *risk lover*. Most people are risk-averse, especially in their financial decisions: Everything else being equal, they prefer to hold the less risky asset. Hence, ***holding everything else constant, if an asset's risk rises relative to that of alternative assets, its quantity demanded will fall.***[2]

Liquidity

Another factor that affects the demand for an asset is how quickly it can be converted into cash at low cost—its liquidity. An asset is liquid if the market in which it is traded has depth and breadth, that is, if the market has many buyers and sellers. A house is not a very liquid asset because it may be hard to find a buyer quickly; if a house must be sold to pay off bills, it might have to be sold for a much lower price. And the transaction costs in selling a house (broker's commissions, lawyer's fees, and so on) are substantial. A U.S. Treasury bill, by contrast, is a highly liquid asset. It can be sold in a well-organized market where there are many buyers, so it can be sold quickly at low cost. ***The more liquid an asset is relative to alternative assets, holding everything else unchanged, the more desirable it is, and the greater will be the quantity demanded.***

Summary

All the determining factors we have just discussed can be summarized by stating that, holding all of the other factors constant:

1. The quantity demanded of an asset is usually positively related to wealth, with the response being greater if the asset is a luxury than if it is a necessity.
2. The quantity demanded of an asset is positively related to its expected return relative to alternative assets.
3. The quantity demanded of an asset is negatively related to the risk of its returns relative to alternative assets.
4. The quantity demanded of an asset is positively related to its liquidity relative to alternative assets.

These results are summarized in Table 4.1.

Supply and Demand in the Bond Market

We approach the analysis of interest-rate determination by studying the supply of and demand for bonds. Because interest rates on different securities tend to move together, in this chapter we will act as if there is only one type of security and a single interest rate in the entire economy. In Chapter 5, we will expand our analysis to look at why interest rates on different securities differ.

The first step is to use the analysis of the determinants of asset demand to obtain a **demand curve,** which shows the relationship between the quantity demanded and

---

[2]Diversification, the holding of many risky assets in a portfolio, reduces the overall risk an investor faces. If you are interested in how diversification lowers risk and what impact this has on the price of an asset, you can look at an appendix to this chapter describing models of asset pricing that is on the book's Web site at www.prenhall.com/mishkin_eakins.

Table 4.1 Summary Response of the Quantity of an Asset Demanded to Changes in Wealth, Expected Returns, Risk, and Liquidity

Variable	Change in Variable	Change in Quantity Demanded
Wealth	↑	↑
Expected return relative to other assets	↑	↑
Risk relative to other assets	↑	↓
Liquidity relative to other assets	↑	↑

Note: Only increases in the variables are shown. The effect of decreases in the variables on the change in quantity demanded would be the opposite of those indicated in the rightmost column.

the price when all other economic variables are held constant (that is, values of other variables are taken as given). You may recall from previous finance and economics courses that the assumption that all other economic variables are held constant is called *ceteris paribus*, which means "other things being equal" in Latin.

Demand Curve

To clarify our analysis, let us consider the demand for one-year discount bonds, which make no coupon payments but pay the owner the $1,000 face value in a year. If the holding period is one year, then as we have seen in Chapter 3, the return on the bonds is known absolutely and is equal to the interest rate as measured by the yield to maturity. This means that the expected return on this bond is equal to the interest rate i, which, using Equation 6 in Chapter 3, is

$$i = R^e = \frac{F - P}{P}$$

where

i = interest rate = yield to maturity
R^e = expected return
F = face value of the discount bond
P = initial purchase price of the discount bond

This formula shows that a particular value of the interest rate corresponds to each bond price. If the bond sells for $950, the interest rate and expected return are

$$\frac{\$1,000 - \$950}{\$950} = 0.53 = 5.3\%$$

At this 5.3% interest rate and expected return corresponding to a bond price of $950, let us assume that the quantity of bonds demanded is $100 billion, which is plotted as point A in Figure 4.1.

At a price of $900, the interest rate and expected return are

$$\frac{\$1,000 - \$900}{\$900} = 0.111 = 11.1\%$$

Because the expected return on these bonds is higher, with all other economic variables (such as income, expected returns on other assets, risk, and liquidity)

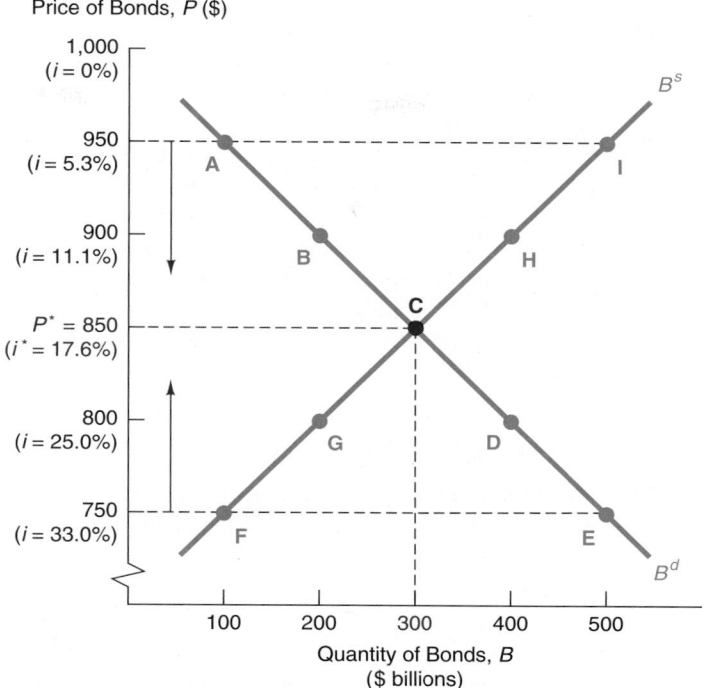

Price of Bonds, P ($)

Figure 4.1 Supply and Demand for Bonds

Equilibrium in the bond market occurs at point C, the intersection of the demand curve B^d and the bond supply curve B^s. The equilibrium price is $P^* = \$850$, and the equilibrium interest rate is $i^* = 17.6\%$.

held constant, the quantity demanded of bonds will be higher as predicted by the theory of asset demand. Point B in Figure 4.1 shows that the quantity of bonds demanded at the price of $900 has risen to $200 billion. Continuing with this reasoning, if the bond price is $850 (interest rate and expected return = 17.6%), the quantity of bonds demanded (point C) will be greater than at point B. Similarly, at the lower prices of $800 (interest rate = 25%) and $750 (interest rate = 33.3%), the quantity of bonds demanded will be even higher (points D and E). The curve B^d, which connects these points, is the demand curve for bonds. It has the usual downward slope, indicating that at lower prices of the bond (everything else being equal), the quantity demanded is higher.[3]

Supply Curve

An important assumption behind the demand curve for bonds in Figure 4.1 is that all other economic variables besides the bond's price and interest rate are held constant. We use the same assumption in deriving a **supply curve,** which shows the

---

[3]Although our analysis indicates that the demand curve is downward-sloping, it does not imply that the curve is a straight line. For ease of exposition, however, we will draw demand curves and supply curves as straight lines.

relationship between the quantity supplied and the price when all other economic variables are held constant.

When the price of the bonds is $750 (interest rate = 33.3%), point F shows that the quantity of bonds supplied is $100 billion for the example we are considering. If the price is $800, the interest rate is the lower rate of 25%. Because at this interest rate it is now less costly to borrow by issuing bonds, firms will be willing to borrow more through bond issues, and the quantity of bonds supplied is at the higher level of $200 billion (point G). An even higher price of $850, corresponding to a lower interest rate of 17.6%, results in a larger quantity of bonds supplied of $300 billion (point C). Higher prices of $900 and $950 result in even greater quantities of bonds supplied (points H and I). The B^s curve, which connects these points, is the supply curve for bonds. It has the usual upward slope found in supply curves, indicating that as the price increases (everything else being equal), the quantity supplied increases.

Market Equilibrium

In economics, **market equilibrium** occurs when the amount that people are willing to buy (*demand*) equals the amount that people are willing to sell (*supply*) at a given price. In the bond market, this is achieved when the quantity of bonds demanded equals the quantity of bonds supplied:

$$B^d = B^s \tag{3}$$

In Figure 4.1, equilibrium occurs at point C, where the demand and supply curves intersect at a bond price of $850 (interest rate of 17.6%) and a quantity of bonds of $300 billion. The price of $P^* = \$850$, where the quantity demanded equals the quantity supplied, is called the *equilibrium* or *market-clearing* price. Similarly, the interest rate of $i^* = 17.6\%$ that corresponds to this price is called the equilibrium or market-clearing interest rate.

The concepts of market equilibrium and equilibrium price or interest rate are useful, because there is a tendency for the market to head toward them. We can see that it does in Figure 4.1 by first looking at what happens when we have a bond price that is above the equilibrium price. When the price of bonds is set too high, at, say, $950, the quantity of bonds supplied at point I is greater than the quantity of bonds demanded at point A. A situation like this, in which the quantity of bonds supplied exceeds the quantity of bonds demanded, is called a condition of **excess supply.** Because people want to sell more bonds than others want to buy, the price of the bonds will fall, which is why the downward arrow is drawn in the figure at the bond price of $950. As long as the bond price remains above the equilibrium price, there will continue to be an excess supply of bonds, and the price will continue to fall. This decline will stop only when the price has reached the equilibrium price of $850, where the excess supply of bonds has been eliminated.

Now let's look at what happens when the price of bonds is below the equilibrium price. If the price of the bonds is set too low, at, say, $750, the quantity demanded at point E is greater than the quantity supplied at point F. This is called a condition of **excess demand.** People now want to buy more bonds than others are willing to sell, so the price of bonds will be driven up. This is illustrated by the upward arrow drawn in the figure at the bond price of $750. Only when the excess demand for bonds is eliminated by the price rising to the equilibrium level of $850 is there no further tendency for the price to rise.

We can see that the concept of equilibrium price is a useful one because it indicates where the market will settle. Because each price on the vertical axis of Figure 4.1 corresponds to a particular value of the interest rate, the same diagram also shows that the interest rate will head toward the equilibrium interest rate of 17.6%. When the interest rate is below the equilibrium interest rate, as it is when it is at 5.3%, the price of the bond is above the equilibrium price, and there will be an excess supply of bonds. The price of the bond then falls, leading to a rise in the interest rate toward the equilibrium level. Similarly, when the interest rate is above the equilibrium level, as it is when it is at 33.3%, there is excess demand for bonds, and the bond price will rise, driving the interest rate back down to the equilibrium level of 17.6%.

Supply and Demand Analysis

Our Figure 4.1 is a conventional supply and demand diagram with price on the vertical axis and quantity on the horizontal axis. Because the interest rate that corresponds to each bond price is also marked on the vertical axis, this diagram allows us to read the equilibrium interest rate, giving us a model that describes the determination of interest rates. It is important to recognize that a supply and demand diagram like Figure 4.1 can be drawn for *any type* of bond because the interest rate and price of a bond are *always* negatively related for any type of bond, whether a discount bond or a coupon bond.

An important feature of the analysis here is that supply and demand are always in terms of *stocks* (amounts at a given point in time) of assets, not in terms of *flows*. The **asset market approach** for understanding behavior in financial markets—which emphasizes stocks of assets rather than flows in determining asset prices—is the dominant methodology used by economists, because correctly conducting analyses in terms of flows is very tricky, especially when we encounter inflation.[4]

Changes in Equilibrium Interest Rates

We will now use the supply and demand framework for bonds to analyze why interest rates change. To avoid confusion, it is important to make the distinction between *movements along* a demand (or supply) curve and *shifts in* a demand (or supply) curve. When quantity demanded (or supplied) changes as a result of a change in the price of the bond (or, equivalently, a change in the interest rate), we have a *movement along* the demand (or supply) curve. The change in the quantity demanded when we move from point A to B to C in Figure 4.1, for example, is a movement along a demand curve. A *shift in* the demand (or supply) curve, by contrast,

---

[4]The asset market approach developed in the text is useful in understanding not only how interest rates behave but also how any asset price is determined. A second appendix to this chapter, which is on this book's Web site at www.prenhall.com/mishkin_eakins, shows how the asset market approach can be applied to understanding the behavior of commodity markets; in particular, the gold market. The analysis of the bond market that we have developed here has another interpretation using a different terminology and framework involving the supply and demand for loanable funds. This loanable funds framework is discussed in a third appendix to this chapter, which is also on the book's Web site.

occurs when the quantity demanded (or supplied) changes *at each given price (or interest rate)* of the bond in response to a change in some other factor besides the bond's price or interest rate. When one of these factors changes, causing a shift in the demand or supply curve, there will be a new equilibrium value for the interest rate.

In the following pages, we will look at how the supply and demand curves shift in response to changes in variables, such as expected inflation and wealth, and what effects these changes have on the equilibrium value of interest rates.

Shifts in the Demand for Bonds

The theory of asset demand demonstrated at the beginning of the chapter provides a framework for deciding which factors cause the demand curve for bonds to shift. These factors include changes in four parameters:

1. Wealth
2. Expected returns on bonds relative to alternative assets
3. Risk of bonds relative to alternative assets
4. Liquidity of bonds relative to alternative assets

To see how a change in each of these factors (holding all other factors constant) can shift the demand curve, let us look at some examples. (As a study aid, Table 4.2 summarizes the effects of changes in these factors on the bond demand curve.)

Wealth When the economy is growing rapidly in a business cycle expansion and wealth is increasing, the quantity of bonds demanded at each bond price (or interest rate) increases as shown in Figure 4.2. To see how this works, consider point B on the initial demand curve for bonds B_1^d, With higher wealth, the quantity of bonds demanded at the same price must rise, to point B′. Similarly, for point D the higher wealth causes the quantity demanded at the same bond price to rise to point D′. Continuing with this reasoning for every point on the initial demand curve B_1^d, we can see that the demand curve shifts to the right from B_1^d, to B_2^d as is indicated by the arrows.

The conclusion we have reached is that ***in a business cycle expansion with growing wealth, the demand for bonds rises and the demand curve for bonds shifts to the right.*** Using the same reasoning, ***in a recession, when income and wealth are falling, the demand for bonds falls, and the demand curve shifts to the left.***

Another factor that affects wealth is the public's propensity to save. If households save more, wealth increases and, as we have seen, the demand for bonds rises and the demand curve for bonds shifts to the right. Conversely, if people save less, wealth and the demand for bonds will fall and the demand curve shifts to the left.

Expected Returns For a one-year discount bond and a one-year holding period, the expected return and the interest rate are identical, so nothing besides today's interest rate affects the expected return.

For bonds with maturities of greater than one year, the expected return may differ from the interest rate. For example, we saw in Chapter 3, Table 2, that a rise in the interest rate on a long-term bond from 10% to 20% would lead to a sharp decline in price and a very large negative return. Hence, if people began to think

Table 4.2 Summary Factors That Shift the Demand Curve for Bonds

Variable	Change in Variable	Change in Quantity Demanded at Each Bond Price	Shift in Demand Curve
Wealth	↑	↑	P → B_1^d B_2^d B
Expected interest rate	↑	↓	P ← B_2^d B_1^d B
Expected inflation	↑	↓	P ← B_2^d B_1^d B
Riskiness of bonds relative to other assets	↑	↓	P ← B_2^d B_1^d B
Liquidity of bonds relative to other assets	↑	↑	P → B_1^d B_2^d B

Note: Only increases in the variables are shown. The effect of decreases in the variables on the change in demand would be the opposite of those indicated in the remaining columns.

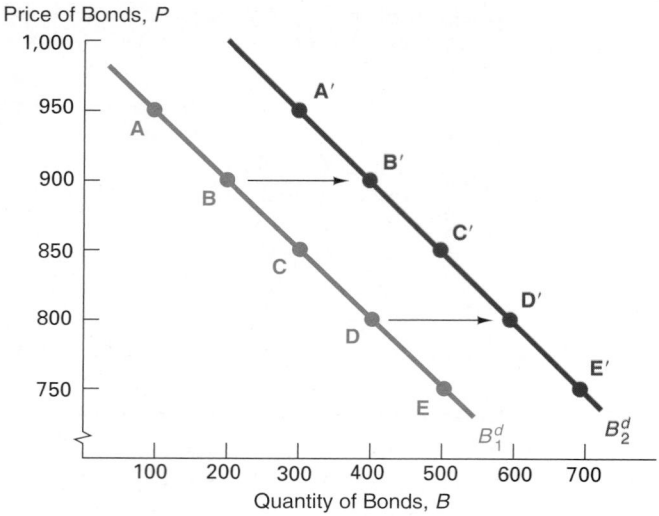

Figure 4.2   Shift in the Demand Curve for Bonds

When the demand for bonds increases, the demand curve shifts to the right as shown.

that interest rates would be higher next year than they had originally anticipated, the expected return today on long-term bonds would fall, and the quantity demanded would fall at each interest rate. ***Higher expected interest rates in the future lower the expected return for long-term bonds, decrease the demand, and shift the demand curve to the left.***

By contrast, a revision downward of expectations of future interest rates would mean that long-term bond prices would be expected to rise more than originally anticipated, and the resulting higher expected return today would raise the quantity demanded at each bond price and interest rate. ***Lower expected interest rates in the future increase the demand for long-term bonds and shift the demand curve to the right*** (as in Figure 4.2).

Changes in expected returns on other assets can also shift the demand curve for bonds. If people suddenly became more optimistic about the stock market and began to expect higher stock prices in the future, both expected capital gains and expected returns on stocks would rise. With the expected return on bonds held constant, the expected return on bonds today relative to stocks would fall, lowering the demand for bonds and shifting the demand curve to the left.

A change in expected inflation is likely to alter expected returns on physical assets (also called *real assets*) such as automobiles and houses, which affect the demand for bonds. An increase in expected inflation, say, from 5% to 10%, will lead to higher prices on cars and houses in the future and hence higher nominal capital gains. The resulting rise in the expected returns today on these real assets will lead to a fall in the expected return on bonds relative to the expected return on real assets today and thus cause the demand for bonds to fall. Alternatively, we can think of the rise in expected inflation as lowering the real interest rate on bonds, and the resulting decline in the relative expected return on bonds will cause the demand for bonds to fall.

An increase in the expected rate of inflation lowers the expected return for bonds, causing their demand to decline and the demand curve to shift to the left.

Risk If prices in the bond market become more volatile, the risk associated with bonds increases, and bonds become a less attractive asset. *An increase in the riskiness of bonds causes the demand for bonds to fall and the demand curve to shift to the left.*

Conversely, an increase in the volatility of prices in another asset market, such as the stock market, would make bonds more attractive. *An increase in the riskiness of alternative assets causes the demand for bonds to rise and the demand curve to shift to the right* (as in Figure 4.1).

Liquidity If more people started trading in the bond market, and as a result it became easier to sell bonds quickly, the increase in their liquidity would cause the quantity of bonds demanded at each interest rate to rise. *Increased liquidity of bonds results in an increased demand for bonds, and the demand curve shifts to the right* (see Figure 4.2). *Similarly, increased liquidity of alternative assets lowers the demand for bonds and shifts the demand curve to the left.* The reduction of brokerage commissions for trading common stocks that occurred when the fixed-rate commission structure was abolished in 1975, for example, increased the liquidity of stocks relative to bonds, and the resulting lower demand for bonds shifted the demand curve to the left.

Shifts in the Supply of Bonds

Certain factors can cause the supply curve for bonds to shift, among them these:

1. Expected profitability of investment opportunities
2. Expected inflation
3. Government budget

We will look at how the supply curve shifts when each of these factors changes (all others remaining constant). (As a study aid, Table 4.3 summarizes the effects of changes in these factors on the bond supply curve.)

Expected Profitability of Investment Opportunities The more profitable plant and equipment investments that a firm expects it can make, the more willing it will be to borrow to finance these investments. When the economy is growing rapidly, as in a business cycle expansion, investment opportunities that are expected to be profitable abound, and the quantity of bonds supplied at any given bond price will increase (see Figure 4.3). *Therefore, in a business cycle expansion, the supply of bonds increases, and the supply curve shifts to the right. Likewise, in a recession, when there are far fewer expected profitable investment opportunities, the supply of bonds falls, and the supply curve shifts to the left.*

Expected Inflation As we saw in Chapter 3, the real cost of borrowing is more accurately measured by the real interest rate, which equals the (nominal) interest rate minus the expected inflation rate. For a given interest rate (and bond price), when

Table 4.3 Summary Factors That Shift the Supply of Bonds

Variable	Change in Variable	Change in Quantity Supplied at Each Bond Price	Shift in Supply Curve
Profitability of investments	↑	↑	
Expected inflation	↑	↑	
Government deficit	↑	↑	

Note: Only increases in the variables are shown. The effect of decreases in the variables on the change in supply would be the opposite of those indicated in the remaining columns.

expected inflation increases, the real cost of borrowing falls; hence the quantity of bonds supplied increases at any given bond price. ***An increase in expected inflation causes the supply of bonds to increase and the supply curve to shift to the right*** (see Figure 4.3).

Government Budget The activities of the government can influence the supply of bonds in several ways. The U.S. Treasury issues bonds to finance government deficits, the gap between the government's expenditures and its revenues. When these deficits are large, the Treasury sells more bonds, and the quantity of bonds supplied at each bond price increases. ***Higher government deficits increase the supply of bonds and shift the supply curve to the right*** (see Figure 4.3). ***On the other hand, government surpluses, as occurred in the late 1990s, decrease the supply of bonds and shift the supply curve to the left.***

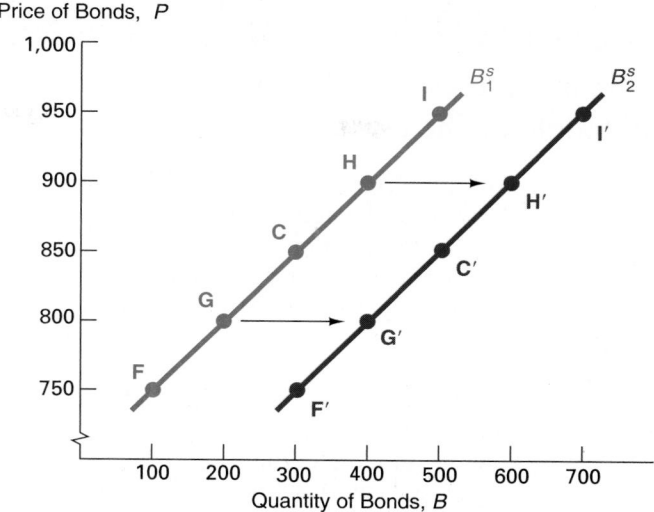

Figure 4.3   Shift in the Supply Curve for Bonds

When the supply of bonds increases, the supply curve shifts to the right.

State and local governments and other government agencies also issue bonds to finance their expenditures, and this can also affect the supply of bonds. We will see in later chapters that the conduct of monetary policy involves the purchase and sale of bonds, which in turn influences the supply of bonds.

We now can use our knowledge of how supply and demand curves shift to analyze how the equilibrium interest rate can change. The best way to do this is to pursue several case applications that are particularly relevant to our understanding of how monetary policy affects interest rates.

study guide

Supply and demand analysis for the bond market is best learned by practicing case applications. When there is a case in the text and we look at how the interest rate changes because some economic variable increases, see if you can draw the appropriate shifts in the supply and demand curves when this same economic variable decreases. While you are practicing case applications, keep two things in mind:

1. *When you examine the effect of a variable change, remember that we are assuming that all other variables are unchanged; that is, we are making use of the ceteris paribus assumption.*

2. *Remember that the interest rate is negatively related to the bond price, so when the equilibrium bond price rises, the equilibrium interest rate falls. Conversely, if the equilibrium bond price moves downward, the equilibrium interest rate rises.*

CASE

Changes in the Interest Rate Due to Expected Inflation: The Fisher Effect

We have already done most of the work to evaluate how a change in expected inflation affects the nominal interest rate, in that we have already analyzed how a change in expected inflation shifts the supply and demand curves. Figure 4.4 shows the effect on the equilibrium interest rate of an increase in expected inflation.

Suppose that expected inflation is initially 5% and the initial supply and demand curves B_1^s and B_1^d intersect at point 1, where the equilibrium bond price is P_1. If expected inflation rises to 10%, the expected return on bonds relative to real assets falls for any given bond price and interest rate. As a result, the demand for bonds falls, and the demand curve shifts to the left from B_1^d to B_2^d. The rise in expected inflation also shifts the supply curve. At any given bond price and interest rate, the real cost of borrowing has declined, causing the quantity of bonds supplied to increase, and the supply curve shifts to the right, from B_1^s to B_2^s.

go online
ftp://ftp.bls.gov/pub/
special.requests/cpi/
cpiai.txt
Contains historical
information about inflation.

When the demand and supply curves shift in response to the change in expected inflation, the equilibrium moves from point 1 to point 2, the intersection of B_2^d and B_2^s. The equilibrium bond price has fallen from P_1 to P_2, and because the bond price is negatively related to the interest rate, this means that the interest rate has risen. Note that Figure 4.4 has been drawn so that the equilibrium quantity of bonds remains the same for both point 1 and point 2. However, depending on the size of the shifts in the supply and demand curves, the equilibrium quantity of bonds could either rise or fall when expected inflation rises.

Our supply and demand analysis has led us to an important observation: **When expected inflation rises, interest rates will rise.** This result has been named

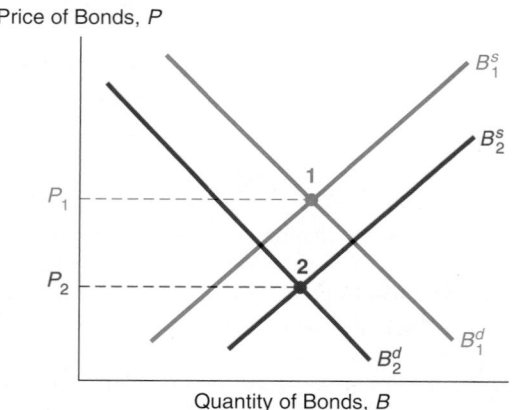

Figure 4.4 Response to a Change in Expected Inflation

When expected inflation rises, the supply curve shifts from B_1^s to B_2^s, and the demand curve shifts from B_1^d to B_2^d The equilibrium moves from point 1 to point 2, with the result that the equilibrium bond price falls from P_1 to P_2 and the equilibrium interest rate rises.

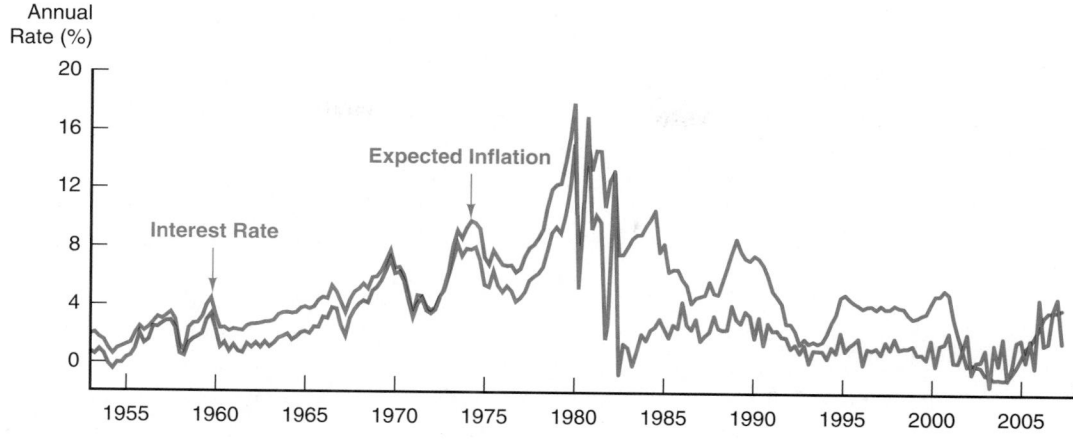

Figure 4.5 Expected Inflation and Interest Rates (Three-Month Treasury Bills), 1953–2007

Source: Expected inflation calculated using procedures outlined in Frederic S. Mishkin, "The Real Interest Rate: An Empirical Investigation," *Carnegie-Rochester Conference Series on Public Policy* 15 (1981): 151–200. These procedures involve estimating expected inflation as a function of past interest rates, inflation, and time trends.

the **Fisher effect,** after Irving Fisher, the economist who first pointed out the relationship of expected inflation to interest rates. The accuracy of this prediction is shown in Figure 4.5. The interest rate on three-month Treasury bills has usually moved along with the expected inflation rate. Consequently, it is understandable that many economists recommend that inflation must be kept low if we want to keep nominal interest rates low.

CASE

Changes in the Interest Rate Due to a Business Cycle Expansion

Figure 4.6 analyzes the effects of a business cycle expansion on interest rates. In a business cycle expansion, the amounts of goods and services being produced in the economy increase, so national income increases. When this occurs, businesses will be more willing to borrow, because they are likely to have many profitable investment opportunities for which they need financing. Hence at a given bond price, the quantity of bonds that firms want to sell (that is, the supply of bonds) will increase. This means that in a business cycle expansion, the supply curve for bonds shifts to the right (see Figure 4.6) from B_1^s to B_2^s.

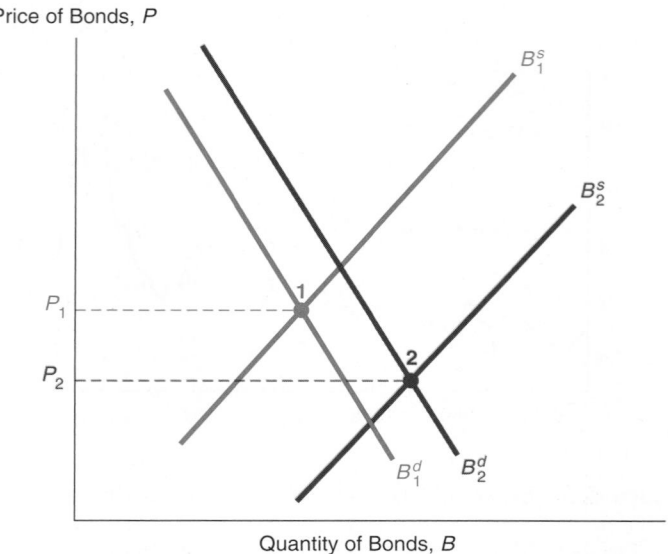

Price of Bonds, *P*

Quantity of Bonds, *B*

Figure 4.6 Response to a Business Cycle Expansion

In a business cycle expansion, when income and wealth are rising, the demand curve shifts rightward from B_1^d to B_2^d and the supply curve shifts rightward from B_1^s to B_2^s. If the supply curve shifts to the right more than the demand curve, as in this figure, the equilibrium bond price moves down from P_1 to P_2, and the equilibrium interest rate rises.

Expansion in the economy will also affect the demand for bonds. As the business cycle expands, wealth is likely to increase, and the theory of asset demand tells us that the demand for bonds will rise as well. We see this in Figure 4.6, where the demand curve has shifted to the right, from B_1^d to B_2^d.

Given that both the supply and demand curves have shifted to the right, we know that the new equilibrium reached at the intersection of B_2^d and B_2^s must also move to the right. However, depending on whether the supply curve shifts more than the demand curve, or vice versa, the new equilibrium interest rate can either rise or fall.

The supply and demand analysis used here gives us an ambiguous answer to the question of what will happen to interest rates in a business cycle expansion. Figure 4.6 has been drawn so that the shift in the supply curve is greater than the shift in the demand curve, causing the equilibrium bond price to fall to P_2, leading to a rise in the equilibrium interest rate. The reason the figure has been drawn so that a business cycle expansion and a rise in income lead to a higher interest rate is that this is the outcome we actually see in the data. Figure 4.7 plots the movement of the interest rate on three-month U.S. Treasury bills from 1951 to 2007 and indicates when the business cycle is undergoing recessions (shaded areas). As you can see, the interest rate tends to rise during business cycle expansions and falls during recessions, which is what the supply and demand diagram indicates.

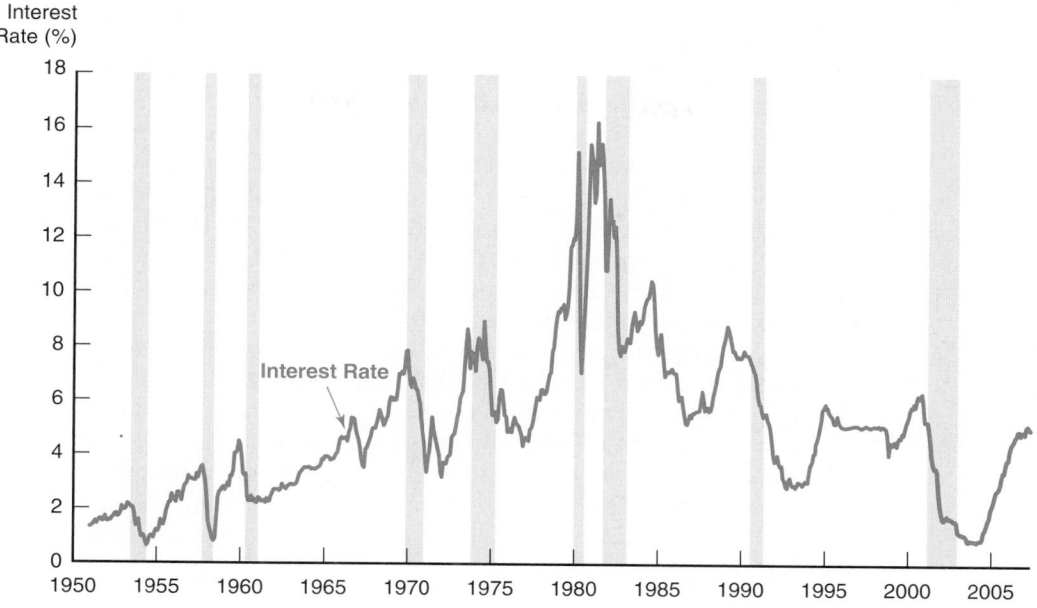

Figure 4.7 Business Cycle and Interest Rates (Three-Month Treasury Bills), 1951–2007

Shaded areas indicate periods of recession. The figure shows that interest rates rise during business cycle expansions and fall during contractions, which is what Figure 4.6 suggests would happen.

Source: Federal Reserve: www.federalreserve.gov/releases/H15/data.htm.

CASE

Explaining Low Japanese Interest Rates

In the 1990s and early 2000s, Japanese interest rates became the lowest in the world. Indeed, in November 1998, an extraordinary event occurred: Interest rates on Japanese six-month Treasury bills turned slightly negative (see Chapter 3). Why did Japanese rates drop to such low levels?

In the late 1990s and early 2000s, Japan experienced a prolonged recession, which was accompanied by deflation, a negative inflation rate. Using these facts, analysis similar to that used in the preceding application explains the low Japanese interest rates.

Negative inflation caused the demand for bonds to rise because the expected return on real assets fell, thereby raising the relative expected return on bonds and in turn causing the demand curve to shift to the right. The negative inflation also raised the real interest rate and therefore the real cost of borrowing for any given nominal rate, thereby causing the supply of bonds to contract and the supply curve to shift to the left. The outcome was then exactly the opposite of that graphed Figure 4.4: The rightward shift of the demand curve and leftward shift of the supply curve led to a rise in the bond price and a fall in interest rates.

The business cycle contraction and the resulting lack of profitable investment opportunities in Japan also led to lower interest rates, by decreasing the supply of bonds and shifting the supply curve to the left. Although the demand curve also would shift to the left because wealth decreased during the business cycle contraction, we have seen in the preceding application that the demand curve would shift less than the supply curve. Thus, the bond price rose and interest rates fell (the opposite outcome to that in Figure 4.6).

Usually, we think that low interest rates are a good thing, because they make it cheap to borrow. But the Japanese example shows that just as there is a fallacy in the adage, "You can never be too rich or too thin" (maybe you can't be too rich, but you can certainly be too thin and do damage to your health), there is a fallacy in always thinking that lower interest rates are better. In Japan, the low and even negative interest rates were a sign that the Japanese economy was in real trouble, with falling prices and a contracting economy. Only when the Japanese economy returns to health will interest rates rise back to more normal levels.

CASE

Reading the *Wall Street Journal* "Credit Markets" Column

Now that we have an understanding of how supply and demand determine prices and interest rates in the bond market, we can use our analysis to understand discussions about bond prices and interest rates appearing in the financial press. Every day, the *Wall Street Journal* reports on developments in the bond market on the previous business day in its "Credit Markets" column, an example of which is found in the *Wall Street Journal*: Following the Financial News box on the next page. Let's see how statements in the "Credit Markets" column can be explained using our supply and demand framework.

The column featured in the Following the News box begins by stating that a report of strength in the nonmanufacturing sector of the economy helped to lower the prices of Treasury bonds and raise their yields. This is exactly what our demand and supply analysis says should happen.

A stronger economy raises the demand for bonds because of increased wealth and income and thus shifts the demand curve for bonds to the right, while it also creates more profitable investment opportunities for firms, shifting the supply curve for bonds to the right as well. (Note that the column mentions a "blitz" of new corporate bond issues coming to market.) As Figure 4.6 illustrates, however, because the supply curve generally shifts by more than the demand curve when the economy gets stronger, the price of bonds is likely to fall rather than rise.

The column also points to rising yields on government bonds in Germany and Japan. With yields rising on these assets, the relative return on Treasury bonds has

following the financial news

The "Credit Markets" Column

The "Credit Markets" column appears daily in the *Wall Street Journal*; an example is presented here. It is found in the third section, "Money and Investing."

Treasurys Fall on Robust Data

Nonmanufacturing Report's Strength Damps Fed-Cut Bets

By DEBORAH LYNN BLUMBERG

A robust report on the services and construction sectors pushed Treasury-bond prices lower and yields higher, with the two-year yield touching a nine-month high of 5% during the session.

The 10-year note wasn't far behind, as the surprisingly strong May report from the Institute for Supply Management on the nonmanufacturing sector added to signs the economy is picking up, forcing investors to reverse bets the Federal Reserve will cut interest rates to help a soft economy.

After the report, the 10-year yield pushed as high as 4.99%, though triple-digit declines in the Dow Jones Industrial Average later in the session helped keep the yield from reaching 5%, an important psychological level.

The benchmark 10-year note was down 12/32 point, or $3.75 per $1,000 face value, at 96 10/32. Its yield rose to 4.976% from 4.927% Monday, as yields move inversely to prices. The two-year note fell 2/32 to 99 25/32 to yield 4.992%.

"Data really drive home the point of how robust the U.S. and global economies are," said T.J. Marta, fixed-income strategist at RBC capital Markets in New York. "The general feeling is that people think [government bond] yields are going up."

Losses in U.S. Treasury also came amid weakness in government bonds abroad, with yields on 10-year German government bonds at their highest levels since December 2003 and 10-year yields on Japanese government bonds at a seven-month high.

Amid the run of firm data, rate-cut expectations have been scaled back, with Goldman Sachs yesterday the latest Wall Street dealer to reverse its call for a Federal Reserve rate cut this year, given the resilience of labor markets in the face of slower growth.

The Fed has kept the Fed fund rate at 5.25% for seven meetings in a row, and the number of banks expecting a

rate cut this year is dwindling. Monday, Merrill Lynch also abandoned its forecast that the Fed would cut rates this year.

Short-term interest-rate futures markets have already come to the conclusion that the Fed will remain on hold for the rest of the year. The December 2007 Eurodollar contract is reflecting 80% odds of a Fed funds rate at 5.25%

The 5% yield mark on the 10-year Treasury note has been flagged by strategists as a clear invitation for buyers among the institutional investors, including pension funds.

Jason Evans, head of government trading at Deutsche Bank, said buying by such investors may already be afoot. "We've seen real money [long-term

Treasury Yields

2-year note: **4.992%**
10-year note: **4.976%**

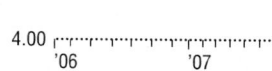

Source: WSJ Market Data Group

investors] buying as market valuations get back to comparatively rational levels."

However, any such interest could be outweighed by selling from mortgage-bond holders adjusting their hedges to account for higher yields.

Appetites Are Healthy For Corporate Bonds

With a blitz of more than $11 billion of investment-grade corporate-bond deals hitting the market, it is hard to

miss the point that investor appetite for corporate bonds is healthy-and growing.

"If the market absorbs this, you'll see more before the summer slowdown," said Scott MacDonald, research director at Aladdin Capital Holdings in Stamford, Conn. "The tone is good, and people are confident."

Strong demand for corporate bonds has helped push risk premium to historical lows, providing companies with cheap financing for share-buy-back programs and leveraged buyouts.

Yesterday's wave of new supply is on top of the note than $4 billion of bonds sold Monday. June 2006 saw $95 billion, and market participants ay this month could match it.

Sid Bakst at Robeco Weiss Peck & Greer in New York, which has $9 billion in assets under management, said deals that include change-of-control provisions for bondholders are proving most popular with investors who have grown more cautious amid the current leveraged-buyout frenzy. Change-of-control covenants protect bondholders from losses that could result from leveraged buyouts.

Monday, **Countrywide Financial** Corp.'s $2.5 billion offer had a change-of-control clause that would be triggered by a downgrade by three ratings agencies. **Valero Energy** Corp.'s $2.25 billion two-part note and **WellPoint** Inc.'s $1.5 billion two-point had similar language.

—*Anusha Shrivastava*

Auction Results

Here are the results of the Treasury auction of four-week bills. All bids are awarded at a single price at the market-clearing yield. Rates are determined by the difference between that price and the face value.

Applications	$34,142,474,000
Accepted bids	$10,000,144,000
Accepted noncompetitively	$428,474,000
Foreign noncompetitively	$0
Auction price (rate)	99.638333 (4.650)
Coupon equivilent	4.745%
Bids at market-clearing yld accepted	87.29%
Cusip number	912795ZP9

The bills are dated June 7 and mature July 5.

fallen. This lowers the demand for Treasury bonds and shifts the demand curve to the left. This provides another reason why the price of Treasury bonds fell.

Finally, strong growth in the economy gives investors less reason to expect the Federal Reserve to cut interest rates anytime soon, as there is less need for a rate cut to boost the economy. Since bond prices and yields move inversely, the lower likelihood of a rate cut implies lower likelihood of a boost in bond prices. This reduces the expected return on Treasury bonds relative to other assets and is another factor that shifts the demand curve for Treasury bonds to the left and lowers their price.

THE PRACTICING MANAGER

Profiting from Interest-Rate Forecasts

Given the importance of interest rates, the media frequently report interest-rate forecasts, as the Following the Financial News box on page 93 indicates. Because changes in interest rates have a major impact on the profitability of financial institutions, financial managers care a great deal about the path of future interest rates. Managers of financial institutions obtain interest-rate forecasts either by hiring their own staff economists to generate forecasts or by purchasing forecasts from other financial institutions or economic forecasting firms.

Several methods are used to produce interest-rate forecasts. One of the most popular is based on the supply and demand for bonds framework described in this chapter, and it is used by financial institutions such as Salomon Smith Barney, Morgan Guaranty Trust Company, and the Prudential Insurance Company.[5] Using this framework, analysts predict what will happen to the factors that affect the supply of and demand for bonds—factors such as the strength of the economy, the profitability of investment opportunities, the expected inflation rate, and the size of government deficits and borrowing. They then use the supply and demand analysis outlined in the chapter to come up with their interest-rate forecasts. A variation of this approach makes use of the *Flow of Funds Accounts* produced by the Federal Reserve. These data show the sources and uses of funds by different sectors of the American economy. By looking at how well the supply of credit and the demand for credit by different sectors match up, forecasters attempt to predict future changes in interest rates.

Forecasting done with the supply and demand for bonds framework often does not make use of formal economic models but rather depends on the judgment or "feel" of the forecaster. An alternative method of forecasting interest rates makes use of **econometric models,** models whose equations are estimated with statistical procedures using past data. These models involve interlocking equations that, once input variables such as the behavior of government spending and monetary policy are plugged in, produce simultaneous forecasts of many variables including interest rates.

---

[5]Another framework used to produce forecasts of interest rates, developed by John Maynard Keynes, analyzes the supply and demand for money and is called the *liquidity preference framework.* This frameword is discussed in a fourth appendix to this chapter which can be found on the book's Web site at www.prenhall.com/mishkin_eakins.

following the financial news

Forecasting Interest Rates

Forecasting interest rates is a time-honored profession. Financial economists are hired (sometimes at very high salaries) to forecast interest rates because businesses need to know what the rates will be in order to plan their future spending, and banks and investors require interest-rate forecasts in order to decide which assets to buy. Interest-rate forecasters predict what will happen to the factors that affect the supply and demand for bonds and for money—factors such as the strength of the economy, the profitability of investment opportunities, the expected inflation rate, and the size of government budget deficits and borrowing. They then use the supply and demand analysis we have outlined in this chapter to come up with their interest-rate forecasts.

The *Wall Street Journal* reports interest-rate forecasts by leading prognosticators twice a year (early January and July) on its Web site. Forecasting interest rates is a perilous business. To their embarrassment, even the top experts are frequently far off in their forecasts.

Economist	RATES						DOLLAR			
	3-MONTH BILLS		10-YR NOTES		FED TARGET FUNDS		vs. YEN		vs. EURO	
	Dec '07	June '08	Dec '07	June '08	Dec '07	June '08	Dec '07	June '08	Dec '07	June '08
Bruce Kasman, JP Morgan Chase & Co	5.55	5.8	5.5	5.55	5.25	6	125	126	1.36	1.33
Dean Maki, Barclays Capital	5.45	5.65	5.4	5.4	5.75	6	122	123	1.36	1.36
Tracy Herrick, The Private Bank	5.4	4.4	5.6	4.7	5.5	4.5	120	115	1.22	1.26
John Ryding, Bear Stearns & Co., Inc.	5.4	5.6	5.4	5.7	5.5	5.75	118	117	1.31	1.29
Brain S. Wesbury, First Trust Advisors, L. P.	5.35	5.7	5.75	6.2	5.5	6	128	132	1.28	1.26
Stephen Stanley, RBS Greenwich Capital	5.3	5.65	5.55	5.7	5.5	5.75	125	126	1.32	1.3
Diane Swonk, Mesirow Financial	5.2	5.4	5.3	5.6	5.25	5.5	120	119	1.32	1.28
Jan Hatzius, Goldman Sachs & Co.	5.15	5.15	5	5.1	5.25	5.25	118	112	1.35	1.35
Richard Berner/David Greenlaw, Morgan Stanley	5.1	4.9	5.25	5.25	5.25	5	118	115	1.28	1.24
Stephen Gallagher, Societe Generale	5.1	5.5	5.25	5.5	5.25	5.75	124	123	1.34	1.3
Gene Huang, FedEx Corp.	5.1	5.3	5.5	5.9	5.5	5.5	120	115	1.3	1.25
Daniel Laufenberg, Ameriprise Financial	5.1	5.4	5.25	5.8	5.25	5.5	118	112	1.34	1.34
Edward Leamer, UCLA Anderson Firecast	5.1	4.8	4.9	4.8	5	4.5	0	0	0	0
Mickey D. Levy, Bank of America	5.1	5.1	5.2	5.2	5.25	5.25	121	121	1.32	1.32
David Rosenberg, Merrill Lynch	5.1	4.5	5.1	4.45	5.25	4.5	0	0	0	0
Dana Johnson, Comerica Bank	5.05	5.25	5.3	5.5	5.25	5.25	120	120	1.32	1.32
Allen Sinai, Decision Economics, Inc.	5.05	5.38	5.45	5.62	5.5	5.75	118	114	1.42	1.46
Jim Meil/Tianlun Jian, Eaton Corp.	5.01	4.76	5.2	5.3	4.98	5.05	120	118	1.34	1.32
Joseph Carson, AllianceBernstein	5	5.25	4.95	5.3	5.25	5.25	121	118	1.37	1.38
Robert DiClemente, Citigroup	5	4.75	5.15	5.2	5.25	5	123	121	1.32	1.32
Steve East, Friedman Billings Ramsey	5	5	5.25	5.25	5.25	5.25	122	0	1.36	0
Ian Shepherdson, High Frequency Economics	5	4	4.5	4	5	4	135	140	1.35	1.4
Douglas Duncan, Mortgage Bankers Association	4.95	5	5.2	5.25	5.25	5.25	125	128	1.45	1.35
Stuart Hoffman, PNC Financial Services Group	4.95	4.65	5.15	4.85	5.25	4.75	120	118	1.35	1.37
David Resler, Nomura Securities International Inc.	4.95	4.5	5.25	5.1	5.25	5	124	118	1.3	1.25
David W. Berson, Fannie Mae	4.94	4.71	4.7	5.04	5.25	5	123	125	1.22	1.24
Saul Hymans/Joan Crary/Janet Wolfe, RSQE, University of Michigan	4.94	4.95	4.99	5.17	5.25	5.25	116	114	1.38	1.4
Scott Anderson, Wells Fargo & Co.	4.9	4.9	5	5	5.25	5.25	122	120	1.35	1.36
Nariman Behravesh, Global Insight	4.9	5	5.1	5.2	5.25	5.25	111	107	1.42	1.45
Lou Crandall, Wrightson ICAP	4.9	5.15	5.1	5.1	5.25	5.5	118	110	1.38	1.42
J. Dewey Daane, Vanderbuilt University	4.9	5.1	5.5	5.75	5.5	5.5	118	115	1.4	1.45
Maria Fiorini Ramirez, Maria Fiorini Ramirez Inc.	4.9	4.9	4.75	5	5.25	5.25	122	124	1.34	1.32
Ethan S. Harris, Lehman Brothers	4.9	5	5.1	5.1	5.25	5.25	115	110	1.31	1.28
Michael P. Niemira, International Council of Shopping Centers	4.9	4.9	5.5	5.75	5.25	5.25	124	126	1.3	1.28
Joel Prakken/Chris Varvares, Macroeconomic Advisers	4.9	4.9	5.1	5.2	5.25	5.25	118	118	1.36	1.36
John Silvia, Wachovia Corp.	4.9	5.25	5.4	5.7	5.25	5.5	116	112	1.4	1.42
Gary Thayer, A. G. Edwards	4.9	4.7	4.9	5.2	5	4.75	126	130	1.29	1.24
David Wyss, Standard and Poor's	4.9	4.5	5.3	5.5	5.25	4.75	115	110	1.4	1.43
Richard DeKaser, National City Corporation	4.87	4.89	5.4	5.46	5.25	5.25	121	116	1.34	1.35
John Lonski, Moody's Investors Service	4.85	5.25	5.25	5.35	5.25	5.25	118	117	1.33	1.29
Mike Cosgrove, Econoclast	4.8	4.8	5.25	5.25	5.25	5.25	120	112	1.31	1.2
Peter Hooper/Joseph A. LaVorgna, Deutsche Bank Securities Inc.	4.8	4.9	5.25	5.5	5.25	5.25	105	96	1.35	1.37
David Lereah, National Association of Realtors	4.8	4.6	5.1	5	5.25	4.75	118	118	1.35	1.35
Sung Won Sohn, Hanmi Bank	4.8	4.5	5	4.8	5	4.75	123	118	0.74	0.73
Paul Ashworth, Capital Economics	4.75	5	5	5.25	4.75	4.75	110	100	1.35	1.35
Lawrence Kudlow, Kudlow & Co. LLC	4.75	4.75	4.95	5.1	5.25	5.25	125	125	1.31	1.29
William B. Hummer, Wayne Hummer Investments LLC	4.7	4.4	4.9	4.7	5.25	4.75	128	121	1.24	1.19
Kurt Karl/Arun Raha, Swiss Re	4.7	4.6	5.2	5	5	5	116	111	1.34	1.35
Ram Bhagavatula Combinatorics Capital	4.6	4.4	4.75	5	4.5	4.25	118	110	1.25	1.2
Maury Harris, UBS	4.6	4.6	4.75	4.8	4.75	4.75	108	105	1.4	1.35
Susan M. Sterne, Economic Analysis	4.6	4	4.8	4.5	4.75	4.25	120	126	1.3	1.2
Kathleen M. Camilli, Camilli Economics, LLC	4.5	4.3	5.35	5.25	5.25	5	118	117	1.35	1.3
Robert T. McGee, U. S. Trust	4.5	4.35	5.15	5.15	5	4.5	120	118	1.35	1.35
Nicolas S. Perna, Perna Associates	4.37	4.42	5.38	5.58	4.75	4.75	120	117	1.37	1.44
Paul Kasriel, The Northern Trust	4.3	3.8	4.5	4.25	4.75	4.25	119	119	1.35	1.37
Charles Dumas, Lombard Street Research	4	3	4.5	4	4.5	3.5	125	125	1.37	1.39
James F. Smith, Western Carolina University and Parsec Financial Management	2.48	3.68	4.14	4.42	2.5	3.75	129	133	1.14	0.99
Neal Soss, Credit Suisse			5.35	4.75	5.25	5.25	118	116	1.37	1.35
AVERAGE FORECASTS	4.9	4.88	5.16	5.2	5.6	5.09	120	118	1.32	1.31

Wall Street Journal, July 2, 2007, p. C7. http://online.wsj.com/public/resources/documents/info-fore-070frameset.htm.

The basic assumption of these forecasting models is that the estimated relationships between variables will continue to hold up in the future. Given this assumption, the forecaster makes predictions of the expected path of the input variables and then lets the model generate forecasts of variables such as interest rates.

Many of these econometric models are quite large, involving hundreds and sometimes over a thousand equations, and consequently require computers to produce their forecasts. Prominent examples of these large-scale econometric models used by the private sector include those developed by Wharton Econometric Forecasting Associates, Chase Econometric Associates, and Data Resources, Inc. To generate its interest-rate forecasts, the Board of Governors of the Federal Reserve System makes use of its own large-scale econometric model, although it makes use of judgmental forecasts as well.

Managers of financial institutions rely on these forecasts to make decisions about which assets they should hold. A manager who believes that the forecast that long-term interest rates will fall in the future is reliable would seek to purchase long-term bonds for the asset account because, as we have seen in Chapter 3, the drop in interest rates will produce large capital gains. Conversely, if forecasts say that interest rates are likely to rise in the future, the manager will prefer to hold short-term bonds or loans in the portfolio in order to avoid potential capital losses on long-term securities.

Forecasts of interest rates also help managers decide whether to borrow long-term or short-term. If interest rates are forecast to rise in the future, the financial institution manager will want to lock in the low interest rates by borrowing long-term; if the forecasts say that interest rates will fall, the manager will seek to borrow short-term in order to take advantage of low interest-rate costs in the future.

Clearly, good forecasts of future interest rates are extremely valuable to the financial institution manager, who, not surprisingly, would be willing to pay a lot for accurate forecasts. Unfortunately, interest-rate forecasting is a perilous business, and even the top forecasters, to their embarrassment, are frequently far off in their forecasts.

SUMMARY

1. The quantity demanded of an asset is (a) positively related to wealth, (b) positively related to the expected return on the asset relative to alternative assets, (c) negatively related to the riskiness of the asset relative to alternative assets, and (d) positively related to the liquidity of the asset relative to alternative assets.

2. Diversification (the holding of more than one asset) benefits investors because it reduces the risk they face, and the benefits are greater the less returns on securities move together.

3. The supply and demand analysis for bonds provides a theory of how interest rates are determined. It predicts that interest rates will change when there is a change in demand because of changes in income (or wealth), expected returns, risk, or liquidity, or when there is a change in supply because of changes in the attractiveness of investment opportunities, the real cost of borrowing, or government activities.

KEY TERMS

asset, *p. 71*
asset market approach, *p. 79*
demand curve, *p. 75*
econometric models, *p. 92*
excess demand, *p. 78*
excess supply, *p. 78*
expected return, *p. 71*

Fisher effect, *p. 87*
liquidity, *p. 72*
market equilibrium, *p. 78*
risk, *p. 72*
standard deviation, *p. 73*
supply curve, *p. 77*
wealth, *p. 71*

QUESTIONS

1. Explain why you would be more or less willing to buy a share of Polaroid stock in the following situations:
   a. Your wealth falls.
   b. You expect it to appreciate in value.
   c. The bond market becomes more liquid.
   d. You expect gold to appreciate in value.
   e. Prices in the bond market become more volatile.

2. Explain why you would be more or less willing to buy a house under the following circumstances:
   a. You just inherited $100,000.
   b. Real estate commissions fall from 6% of the sales price to 4% of the sales price.
   c. You expect Polaroid stock to double in value next year.
   d. Prices in the stock market become more volatile.
   e. You expect housing prices to fall.

3. "The more risk-averse people are, the more likely they are to diversify." Is this statement true, false, or uncertain? Explain your answer.

4. I own a professional football team, and I plan to diversify by purchasing shares in either a company that owns a pro basketball team or a pharmaceutical company. Which of these two investments is more likely to reduce the overall risk I face? Why?

5. "No one who is risk-averse will ever buy a security that has a lower expected return, more risk, and less liquidity than another security." Is this statement true, false, or uncertain? Explain your answer.

For items 6–13, answer each question by drawing the appropriate supply and demand diagrams.

6. An important way in which the Federal Reserve decreases the money supply is by selling bonds to the public. Using a supply and demand analysis for bonds, show what effect this action has on interest rates.

7. Using the supply and demand for bonds framework, show why interest rates are procyclical (rising when the economy is expanding and falling during recessions).

8. Find the "Credit Markets" column in the *Wall Street Journal*. Underline the statements in the column that explain bond price movements, and draw the appropriate supply and demand diagrams that support these statements.

9. What effect will a sudden increase in the volatility of gold prices have on interest rates?

10. How might a sudden increase in people's expectations of future real estate prices affect interest rates?

11. Explain what effect a large federal deficit might have on interest rates.

12. Using a supply and demand analysis for bonds, show what the effect is on interest rates when the riskiness of bonds rises.

13. Will there be an effect on interest rates if brokerage commissions on stocks fall? Explain your answer.

Predicting the Future

14. The president of the United States announces in a press conference that he will fight the higher inflation rate with a new anti-inflation program. Predict what will happen to interest rates if the public believes him.

15. The chairman of the Fed announces that interest rates will rise sharply next year, and the market believes him. What will happen to today's interest rate on AT&T bonds, such as the $8\frac{1}{8}$ s of 2022?

16. Predict what will happen to interest rates if the public suddenly expects a large increase in stock prices.

17. Predict what will happen to interest rates if prices in the bond market become more volatile.

QUANTITATIVE PROBLEMS

1. You own a $1,000-par zero-coupon bond that has five years of remaining maturity. You plan on selling the bond in one year, and believe that the required yield next year will have the following probability distribution:

Probability	Required Yield %
0.1	6.60%
0.2	6.75%
0.4	7.00%
0.2	7.20%
0.1	7.45%

   a. What is your expected price when you sell the bond?

   b. What is the standard deviation of the bond price?

2. Consider a $1,000-par junk bond paying a 12% annual coupon with two years to maturity. The issuing company has a 20% chance of defaulting this year; in which case, the bond would not pay anything. If the company survives the first year, paying the annual coupon payment, it then has a 25% chance of defaulting in the second year. If the company defaults in the second year, neither the final coupon payment nor par value of the bond will be paid.

   a. What price must investors pay for this bond to expect a 10% yield to maturity?

   b. At that price, what is the expected holding period return and standard deviation of returns? Assume that periodic cash flows are reinvested at 10%.

3. Last month, corporations supplied $250 billion in one-year discount bonds to investors at an average market rate of 11.8%. This month, an additional $25 billion in one-year discount bonds became available, and market rates increased to 12.2%. Assuming that the demand curve remained constant, derive a linear equation for the demand for bonds, using prices instead of interest rates.

4. An economist has concluded that, near the point of equilibrium, the demand curve and supply curve for one-year discount bonds can be estimated using the following equations:

$$B^d: \text{Price} = \frac{-2}{5}\text{Quantity} + 940$$

$$B^s: \text{Price} = \text{Quantity} + 500$$

   a. What is the expected equilibrium price and quantity of bonds in this market?

   b. Given your answer to part (a), which is the expected interest rate in this market?

5. The demand curve and supply curve for one-year discount bonds were estimated using the following equations:

$$B^d: \text{Price} = \frac{-2}{5}\text{Quantity} + 940$$

$$B^s: \text{Price} = \text{Quantity} + 500$$

Following a dramatic increase in the value of the stock market, many retirees started moving money out of the stock market and into bonds. This resulted in a parallel shift in the demand for bonds, such that the price of bonds at all quantities increased $50. Assuming no change in the supply equation for bonds, what is the new equilibrium price and quantity? What is the new market interest rate?

6. The demand curve and supply curve for one-year discount bonds were estimated using the following equations:

$$B^d: \text{Price} = \frac{-2}{5}\text{Quantity} + 990$$

$$B^s: \text{Price} = \text{Quantity} + 500$$

As the stock market continued to rise, the Federal Reserve felt the need to increase the interest rates. As a result, the new market interest rate increased to 19.65%, but the equilibrium quantity remained unchanged. What are the new demand and supply equations? Assume parallel shifts in the equations.

WEB EXERCISES

Interest Rates and Inflation

1. One of the largest single influences on the level of interest rates is inflation. There are a number of sites that report inflation over time. Go to **ftp://ftp.bls .gov/pub/special.requests/cpi/cpiai.txt** and review the data available. Note that the last columns report various averages. Move these data into a spreadsheet using the method discussed in the Web exploration at the end of Chapter 1. What has the average rate of inflation been since 1950, 1960, 1970, 1980, and 1990? Which year had the lowest level of inflation? Which year had the highest level of inflation?

2. Increasing prices erode the purchasing power of the dollar. It is interesting to compute what goods would have cost at some point in the past after adjusting for inflation. Go to **http://minneapolisfed.org/ Research/data/us/calc/**. What would a car that cost $22,000 today have cost the year that you were born?

3. One of the points made in this chapter is that inflation erodes investment returns. Go to **www.moneychimp .com/articles/econ/inflation_calculator.htm** and review how changes in inflation alter your real return. What happens to the difference between the adjusted value of an investment compared to its inflation-adjusted value as

    a. Inflation increases?

    b. The investment horizon lengthens?

    c. Expected returns increase?

WEB APPENDICES

Please visit our Web site at **www.prenhall.com/mishkin_ eakins** to read the Web appendices to Chapter 4:

- **Appendix 1:** Models of Asset Pricing
- **Appendix 2:** Applying the Asset Market Approach to a Commodity Market: The Case of Gold
- **Appendix 3:** Loanable Funds Framework
- **Appendix 4:** Supply and Demand in the Market for Money: The Liquidity Preference Framework

CHAPTER 5

How Do Risk and Term Structure Affect Interest Rates?

Preview

In our supply and demand analysis of interest-rate behavior in Chapter 4, we examined the determination of just one interest rate. Yet we saw earlier that there are enormous numbers of bonds on which the interest rates can and do differ. In this chapter we complete the interest-rate picture by examining the relationship of the various interest rates to one another. Understanding why they differ from bond to bond can help businesses, banks, insurance companies, and private investors decide which bonds to purchase as investments and which ones to sell.

We first look at why bonds with the same term to maturity have different interest rates. The relationship among these interest rates is called the **risk structure of interest rates,** although risk, liquidity, and income tax rules all play a role in determining the risk structure. A bond's term to maturity also affects its interest rate, and the relationship among interest rates on bonds with different terms to maturity is called the **term structure of interest rates.** In this chapter we examine the sources and causes of fluctuations in interest rates relative to one another and look at a number of theories that explain these fluctuations.

Risk Structure of Interest Rates

Figure 5.1 shows the yields to maturity for several categories of long-term bonds from 1919 to 2007. It shows us two important features of interest-rate behavior for bonds of the same maturity: Interest rates on different categories of bonds differ from one another in any given year, and the spread (or difference)

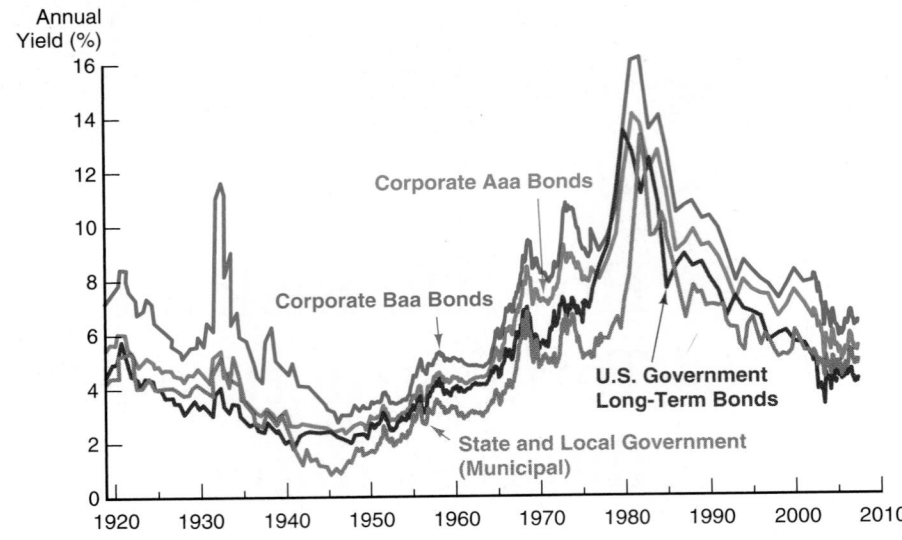

Figure 5.1 Long-Term Bond Yields, 1919–2007

Sources: Board of Governors of the Federal Reserve System, *Banking and Monetary Statistics, 1941–1970*; Federal Reserve: www.federalreserve.gov/releases/h15/data.htm.

between the interest rates varies over time. The interest rates on municipal bonds, for example, are higher than those on U.S. government (Treasury) bonds in the late 1930s but lower thereafter. In addition, the spread between the interest rates on Baa corporate bonds (riskier than Aaa corporate bonds) and U.S. government bonds is very large during the Great Depression years 1930–1933, is smaller during the 1940s–1960s, and then widens again afterward. Which factors are responsible for these phenomena?

Default Risk

One attribute of a bond that influences its interest rate is its risk of **default,** which occurs when the issuer of the bond is unable or unwilling to make interest payments when promised or pay off the face value when the bond matures. A corporation suffering big losses, such as the major airline companies like United, Delta, US Airways, and Northwest in the mid-2000s, might be more likely to suspend interest payments on its bonds. The default risk on its bonds would therefore be quite high. By contrast, U.S. Treasury bonds have usually been considered to have no default risk because the federal government can always increase taxes to pay off its obligations. Bonds like these with no default risk are called **default-free bonds.** The spread between the interest rates on bonds with default risk and default-free bonds, both of the same maturity, called the **risk premium,** indicates how much additional interest people must earn to be willing to hold that risky bond. Our supply and demand analysis of the bond market in Chapter 4 can be used to explain why a bond with default risk always has a positive risk premium and why the higher the default risk is, the larger the risk premium will be.

To examine the effect of default risk on interest rates, let us look at the supply and demand diagrams for the default-free (U.S. Treasury) and corporate long-term bond markets in Figure 5.2. To make the diagrams somewhat easier to read, let's assume that initially corporate bonds have the same default risk as U.S. Treasury bonds. In this case, these two bonds have the same attributes (identical risk and maturity); their equilibrium prices and interest rates will initially be equal ($P_1^c = P_1^T$ and $i_1^c = i_1^T$), and the risk premium on corporate bonds ($i_1^c - i_1^T$) will be zero.

If the possibility of a default increases because a corporation begins to suffer large losses, the default risk on corporate bonds will increase, and the expected return on these bonds will decrease. In addition, the corporate bond's return will be more uncertain. The theory of asset demand predicts that because the expected return on the corporate bond falls relative to the expected return on the default-free Treasury bond

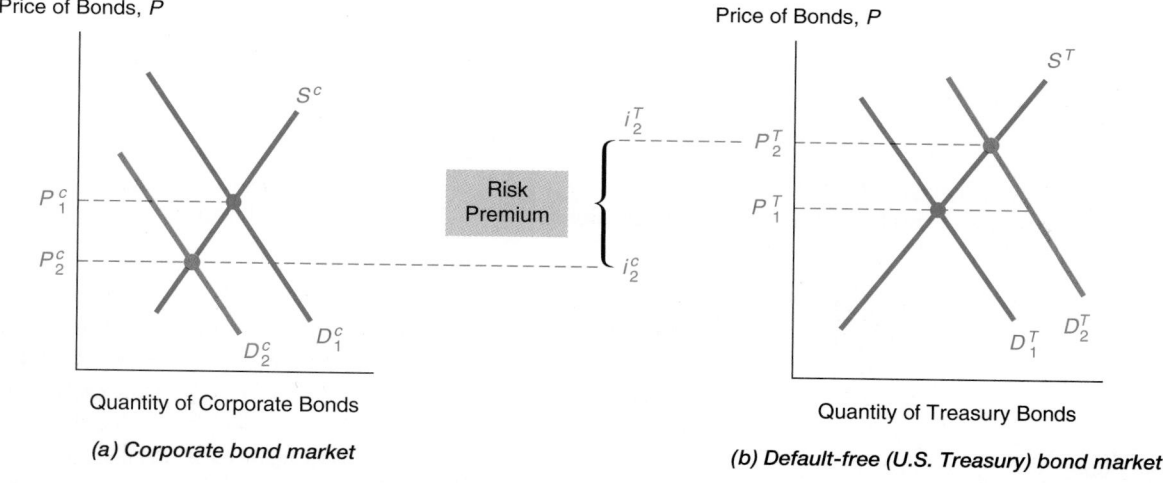

Quantity of Corporate Bonds

(a) Corporate bond market

Quantity of Treasury Bonds

(b) Default-free (U.S. Treasury) bond market

Figure 5.2   Response to an Increase in Default Risk on Corporate Bonds

Initially $P_1^c = P_1^T$ and the risk premium is zero. An increase in default risk on corporate bonds shifts the demand curve from D_1^c to D_2^c. Simultaneously, it shifts the demand curve for Treasury bonds from D_1^T to D_2^T. The equilibrium price for corporate bonds falls from P_1^c to P_2^c and the equilibrium interest rate on corporate bonds rises to i_2^c. In the Treasury market, the equilibrium bond price rises from P_1^T to P_2^T and the equilibrium interest rate falls to i_2^T. The brace indicates the difference between i_2^c and i_2^T, the risk premium on corporate bonds. (Note that because P_2^c is lower than P_2^T, i_2^c is greater than i_2^T.)

while its relative riskiness rises, the corporate bond is less desirable (holding everything else equal), and demand for it will fall. The demand curve for corporate bonds in panel (a) of Figure 5.2 then shifts to the left, from D_1^c to D_2^c.

At the same time, the expected return on default-free Treasury bonds increases relative to the expected return on corporate bonds, while their relative riskiness declines. The Treasury bonds thus become more desirable, and demand rises, as shown in panel (b) by the rightward shift in the demand curve for these bonds from D_1^T to D_2^T.

As we can see in Figure 5.2, the equilibrium price for corporate bonds falls from P_1^c to P_2^c, and since the bond price is negatively related to the interest rate, the equilibrium interest rate on corporate bonds rises to i_2^c. At the same time, however, the equilibrium price for the Treasury bonds rises from P_1^T to P_2^T, and the equilibrium interest rate falls to i_2^T. The spread between the interest rates on corporate and default-free bonds—that is, the risk premium on corporate bonds—has risen from zero to $i_2^c - i_2^T$. We can now conclude that *a bond with default risk will always have a positive risk premium, and an increase in its default risk will raise the risk premium.*

Because default risk is so important to the size of the risk premium, purchasers of bonds need to know whether a corporation is likely to default on its bonds. This information is provided by **credit-rating agencies,** investment advisory firms that rate the quality of corporate and municipal bonds in terms of the probability of default. Table 5.1 provides the ratings and their description for the two largest credit-rating agencies, Moody's Investor Service and Standard and Poor's Corporation. Bonds with relatively low risk of default are called *investment-grade* securities and have a rating of Baa (or BBB) and above. Bonds with ratings below Baa (or BBB) have higher default risk and have been aptly dubbed speculative-grade or **junk**

go online
www.federalreserve.gov/
Releases/h15/update/
The Federal Reserve reports the yields on different quality bonds. Look at the bottom of the listing of interest rates for AAA- and BBB-rated bonds.

TABLE 5.1 Bond Ratings by Moody's and Standard and Poor's

Moody's	Standard and Poor's	Descriptions	Examples of Corporations with Bonds Outstanding in 2007
Aaa	AAA	Highest quality (lowest default risk)	General Electric, Johnson & Johnson, Exxon-Mobil
Aa	AA	High quality	Shell Canada Ltd., Abbott Laboratories, Amoco Argentina Oil
A	A	Upper medium grade	Harley-Davidson, Hewlett-Packard, McDonald's, Inc.
Baa	BBB	Medium grade	Best Buy, FexEx, DaimlerChrysler
Ba	BB	Lower medium grade	Advanced Auto Parts, Hilton Hotels, US Steel
B	B	Speculative	Ford Motor, General Motors, Logan's Roadhouse
Caa	CCC, CC	Poor (high default risk)	Charter Communications, Atlantis Plastics, Bally Total Fitness
C	D	Highly speculative	Calpine Corp., Citation Corp., Delta Airlines

bonds. Because these bonds always have higher interest rates than investment-grade securities, they are also referred to as high-yield bonds.

Next let's look at Figure 5.1 at the beginning of the chapter and see if we can explain the relationship between interest rates on corporate and U.S. Treasury bonds. Corporate bonds always have higher interest rates than U.S. Treasury bonds because they always have some risk of default, whereas U.S. Treasury bonds do not. Because Baa-rated corporate bonds have a greater default risk than the higher-rated Aaa bonds, their risk premium is greater, and the Baa rate therefore always exceeds the Aaa rate. We can use the same analysis to explain the huge jump in the risk premium on Baa corporate bond rates during the Great Depression years 1930–1933 and the rise in the risk premium after 1970 (see Figure 5.1). The depression period saw a very high rate of business failures and defaults. As we would expect, these factors led to a substantial increase in the default risk for bonds issued by vulnerable corporations, and the risk premium for Baa bonds reached unprecedentedly high levels. Since 1970, we have again seen higher levels of business failures and defaults, although they were still well below Great Depression levels. Again, as expected, both default risks and risk premiums for corporate bonds rose, widening the spread between interest rates on corporate bonds and Treasury bonds.

CASE

The Enron Bankruptcy and the Baa–Aaa Spread

In December 2001, Enron Corporation, a firm specializing in trading in the energy market and once the seventh-largest corporation in the United States, was forced to declare bankruptcy after it became clear that it had used shady accounting to hide its financial problems. (The Enron bankruptcy, the largest ever in the United States, will be discussed further in Chapter 15.) Because of the scale of the bankruptcy and the questions it raised about the quality of the information in accounting statements, the Enron collapse had a major impact on the corporate bond market. Let's see how our supply and demand analysis explains the behavior of the spread between interest rates on lower quality (Baa-rated) and highest quality (Aaa-rated) corporate bonds in the aftermath of the Enron failure.

As a consequence of the Enron bankruptcy, many investors began to doubt the financial health of corporations with lower credit ratings such as Baa. The increase in default risk for Baa bonds made them less desirable at any given interest rate, decreased the quantity demanded, and shifted the demand curve for Baa bonds to the left. As shown in panel (a) of Figure 5.2, the interest rate on Baa bonds should have risen, which is indeed what happened. Interest rates on Baa bonds rose by 24 basis points (0.24 percentage point) from 7.81% in November 2001 to 8.05% in December 2001. But the increase in the perceived default risk for Baa bonds after the Enron bankruptcy made the highest-quality (Aaa) bonds relatively more attractive and shifted the demand curve for these securities to the right—an outcome described by some analysts as a "flight to quality." Just as our analysis predicts in Figure 5.2, interest rates on Aaa bonds fell by 20 basis points, from 6.97% in November to 6.77% in December. The overall outcome was that the spread between interest rates on Baa and Aaa bonds rose by 44 basis points from 0.84% before the bankruptcy to 1.28% afterward.

Liquidity

Another attribute of a bond that influences its interest rate is its liquidity. As we learned in Chapter 4, a liquid asset is one that can be quickly and cheaply converted into cash if the need arises. The more liquid an asset is, the more desirable it is (holding everything else constant). U.S. Treasury bonds are the most liquid of all long-term bonds, because they are so widely traded that they are the easiest to sell quickly and the cost of selling them is low. Corporate bonds are not as liquid, because fewer bonds for any one corporation are traded; thus, it can be costly to sell these bonds in an emergency, because it might be hard to find buyers quickly.

How does the reduced liquidity of the corporate bonds affect their interest rates relative to the interest rate on Treasury bonds? We can use supply and demand analysis with the same figure that was used to analyze the effect of default risk, Figure 5.2, to show that the lower liquidity of corporate bonds relative to Treasury bonds increases the spread between the interest rates on these two bonds. Let us start the analysis by assuming that initially corporate and Treasury bonds are equally liquid and all their other attributes are the same. As shown in Figure 5.2, their equilibrium prices and interest rates will initially be equal: $P_1^c = P_1^T$ and $i_1^c = i_1^T$. If the corporate bond becomes less liquid than the Treasury bond because it is less widely traded, then (as the theory of asset demand indicates) demand for it will fall, shifting its demand curve from D_1^c to D_2^c as in panel (a). The Treasury bond now becomes relatively more liquid in comparison with the corporate bond, so its demand curve shifts rightward from D_1^T to D_2^T as in panel (b). The shifts in the curves in Figure 5.2 show that the price of the less liquid corporate bond falls and its interest rate rises, while the price of the more liquid Treasury bond rises and its interest rate falls.

The result is that the spread between the interest rates on the two bond types has risen. Therefore, the differences between interest rates on corporate bonds and Treasury bonds (that is, the risk premiums) reflect not only the corporate bond's default risk but also its liquidity. This is why a risk premium is more accurately a "risk and liquidity premium," but convention dictates that it is called a *risk premium*.

Income Tax Considerations

Returning to Figure 5.1, we are still left with one puzzle—the behavior of municipal bond rates. Municipal bonds are certainly not default-free: State and local governments have defaulted on the municipal bonds they have issued in the past, particularly during the Great Depression and even more recently in the case of Orange County, California, in 1994 (more on this in Chapter 25). Also, municipal bonds are not as liquid as U.S. Treasury bonds.

Why is it, then, that these bonds have had lower interest rates than U.S. Treasury bonds for at least 40 years, as indicated in Figure 5.1? The explanation lies in the fact that interest payments on municipal bonds are exempt from federal income taxes, a factor that has the same effect on the demand for municipal bonds as an increase in their expected return.

Let us imagine that you have a high enough income to put you in the 35% income tax bracket, where for every extra dollar of income you have to pay 35 cents to the government. If you own a $1,000-face-value U.S. Treasury bond that sells for $1,000 and has a coupon payment of $100, you get to keep only $65 of the payment after taxes. Although the bond has a 10% interest rate, you actually earn only 6.5% after taxes.

Suppose, however, that you put your savings into a $1,000-face-value munici-pal bond that sells for $1,000 and pays only $80 in coupon payments. Its interest rate is only 8%, but because it is a tax-exempt security, you pay no taxes on the $80 coupon payment, so you earn 8% after taxes. Clearly, you earn more on the municipal bond after taxes, so you are willing to hold the riskier and less liquid munic-ipal bond even though it has a lower interest rate than the U.S. Treasury bond. (This was not true before World War II, when the tax-exempt status of municipal bonds did not convey much of an advantage because income tax rates were extremely low.)

example 5.1 **Income Tax Considerations**

Suppose you had the opportunity to buy either a municipal bond or a corporate bond, both of which have a face value and purchase price of $1,000. The municipal bond has coupon payments of $60 and a coupon rate of 6%. The corporate bond has coupon payments of $80 and an interest rate of 8%. Which bond would you choose to purchase, assum-ing a 40% tax rate?

Solution

You would choose to purchase the municipal bond because it will earn you $60 in coupon payments and an interest rate after taxes of 6%. Since municipal bonds are tax-exempt, you pay no taxes on the $60 coupon payments and earn 6% after taxes. However, you have to pay taxes on corporate bonds. You will keep only 60% of the $80 coupon pay-ment because the other 40% goes to taxes. Therefore, you receive $48 of the coupon payment and have an interest rate of 4.8% after taxes. Buying the municipal bond would yield you higher earnings.

Another way of understanding why municipal bonds have lower interest rates than Treasury bonds is to use the supply and demand analysis depicted in Figure 5.3. We assume that municipal and Treasury bonds have identical attributes and so have the same bond prices as drawn in the figure: $P_1^m = P_1^T$, and the same interest rates. Once the municipal bonds are given a tax advantage that raises their after-tax expected return relative to Treasury bonds and makes them more desirable, demand for them rises, and their demand curve shifts to the right, from D_1^m to D_2^m. The result is that their equilibrium bond price rises from P_1^m to P_2^m, and their equilibrium inter-est rate falls. By contrast, Treasury bonds have now become less desirable relative to municipal bonds; demand for Treasury bonds decreases, and D_1^T shifts to D_2^T. The Treasury bond price falls from P_1^T to P_2^T, and the interest rate rises. The resulting lower interest rates for municipal bonds and higher interest rates for Treasury bonds explain why municipal bonds can have interest rates below those of Treasury bonds.[1]

Summary

The risk structure of interest rates (the relationship among interest rates on bonds with the same maturity) is explained by three factors: default risk, liquidity, and the income tax treatment of a bond's interest payments. As a bond's default risk

[1]In contrast to corporate bonds, Treasury bonds are exempt from state and local income taxes. Using the analysis in the text, you should be able to show that this feature of Treasury bonds provides an additional reason why interest rates on corporate bonds are higher than those on Treasury bonds.

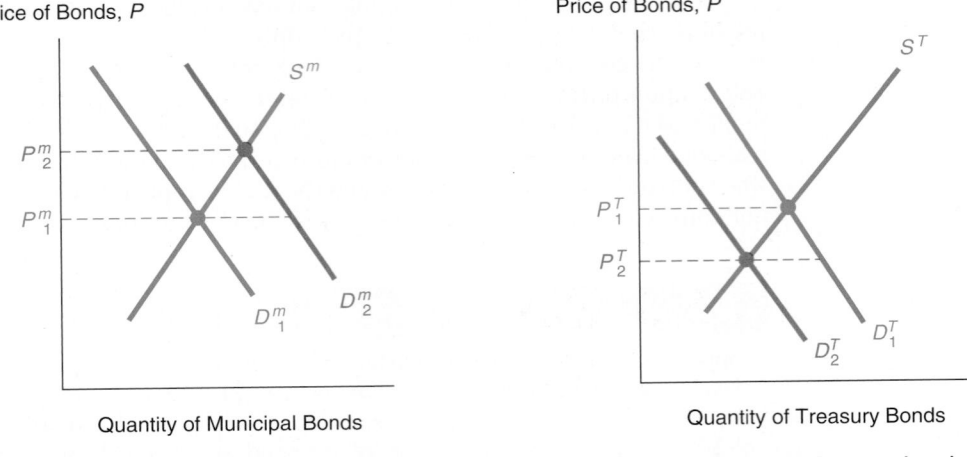

Price of Bonds, *P*

P^m_2
P^m_1
S^m
D^m_1
D^m_2

Quantity of Municipal Bonds

(a) Market for municipal bonds

Price of Bonds, *P*

S^T
P^T_1
P^T_2
D^T_2
D^T_1

Quantity of Treasury Bonds

(b) Market for Treasury bonds

Figure 5.3 Interest Rates on Municipal and Treasury Bonds

When the municipal bond is given tax-free status, demand for the municipal bond shifts rightward from D^m_1 to D^m_2 and demand for the Treasury bond shifts leftward from D^T_1 to D^T_2. The equilibrium price of the municipal bond rises from P^m_1 to P^m_2, so its interest rate falls, while the equilibrium price of the Treasury bond falls from P^T_1 to P^T_2 and its interest rate rises. The result is that municipal bonds end up with lower interest rates than those on Treasury bonds.

increases, the risk premium on that bond (the spread between its interest rate and the interest rate on a default-free Treasury bond) rises. The greater liquidity of Treasury bonds also explains why their interest rates are lower than interest rates on less liquid bonds. If a bond has a favorable tax treatment, as do municipal bonds, whose interest payments are exempt from federal income taxes, its interest rate will be lower.

CASE

Effects of the Bush Tax Cut on Bond Interest Rates

The Bush tax cut passed in 2001 scheduled a reduction of the top income tax bracket from 39% to 35% over a 10-year period. What is the effect of this income tax decrease on interest rates in the municipal bond market relative to those in the Treasury bond market?

Our supply and demand analysis provides the answer. A decreased income tax rate for wealthy people means that the after-tax expected return on tax-free municipal bonds relative to that on Treasury bonds is lower, because the interest on Treasury bonds is now taxed at a lower rate. Because municipal bonds now become less desirable, their demand decreases, shifting the demand curve to the left, which lowers their price and raises their interest rate. Conversely, the lower income tax rate makes Treasury bonds more desirable; this change shifts their demand curve to the right, raises their price, and lowers their interest rates.

Our analysis thus shows that the Bush tax cut raised the interest rates on municipal bonds relative to interest rates on Treasury bonds.

Term Structure of Interest Rates

We have seen how risk, liquidity, and tax considerations (collectively embedded in the risk structure) can influence interest rates. Another factor that influences the interest rate on a bond is its term to maturity: Bonds with identical risk, liquidity, and tax characteristics may have different interest rates because the time remaining to maturity is different. A plot of the yields on bonds with differing terms to maturity but the same risk, liquidity, and tax considerations is called a **yield curve,** and it describes the term structure of interest rates for particular types of bonds, such as government bonds. The Following the Financial News box shows several yield curves for Treasury securities that were published in the *Wall Street Journal*. Yield curves can be classified as upward-sloping, flat, and downward-sloping (the last sort is often referred to as an **inverted yield curve**). When yield curves slope upward, the most usual case, the long-term interest rates are above the short-term interest rates; when yield curves are flat, as in the Following the Financial News box, short- and long-term interest rates are the same; and when yield curves are inverted, long-term interest rates are below short-term interest rates. Yield curves can also have

following the financial news

Yield Curves

The *Wall Street Journal* publishes a daily plot of the yield curves for Treasury securities, an example of which is presented here. It is typically found on page 2 of the "Money and Investing" section.

The numbers on the vertical axis indicate the interest rate for the Treasury security, with the maturity given by the numbers on the horizontal axis. For example, the yield curve marked "Friday" indicates that the interest rate on the three-month Treasury bill was 4.85%, while the two-year bond had an interest rate of 4.73% and the 10-year bond had an interest rate of 4.69%. The yield curve shown here is relatively flat, indicating there is little financial reward for investing in longer-term bonds.

Source: Wall Street Journal, May 14, 2007, p. C2. Republished by permission of Dow Jones, Inc. via Copyright Clearance Center, Inc. 2004 Dow Jones and Company, Inc. All Rights Reserved Worldwide.

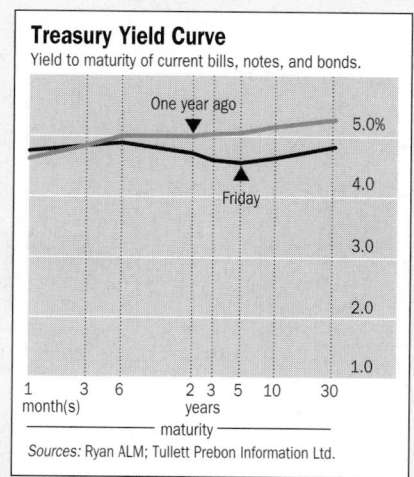

Treasury Yield Curve
Yield to maturity of current bills, notes, and bonds.

Sources: Ryan ALM; Tullett Prebon Information Ltd.

more complicated shapes in which they first slope up and then down, or vice versa. Why do we usually see upward slopes of the yield curve but sometimes other shapes?

Besides explaining why yield curves take on different shapes at different times, a good theory of the term structure of interest rates must explain the following three important empirical facts:

1. As we see in Figure 5.4, interest rates on bonds of different maturities move together over time.
2. When short-term interest rates are low, yield curves are more likely to have an upward slope; when short-term interest rates are high, yield curves are more likely to slope downward and be inverted.
3. Yield curves almost always slope upward, as in the Following the Financial News box.

Three theories have been put forward to explain the term structure of interest rates—that is, the relationship among interest rates on bonds of different maturities reflected in yield curve patterns: (1) the expectations theory, (2) the market segmentation theory, and (3) the liquidity premium theory, each of which is described in the following sections. The expectations theory does a good job of explaining the first two facts on our list, but not the third. The market segmentation theory can explain fact 3 but not the other two facts, which are well explained by the expectations theory. Because each theory explains facts that the other cannot, a natural way to seek a better understanding of the term structure is to combine features of both theories, which leads us to the liquidity premium theory, which can explain all three facts.

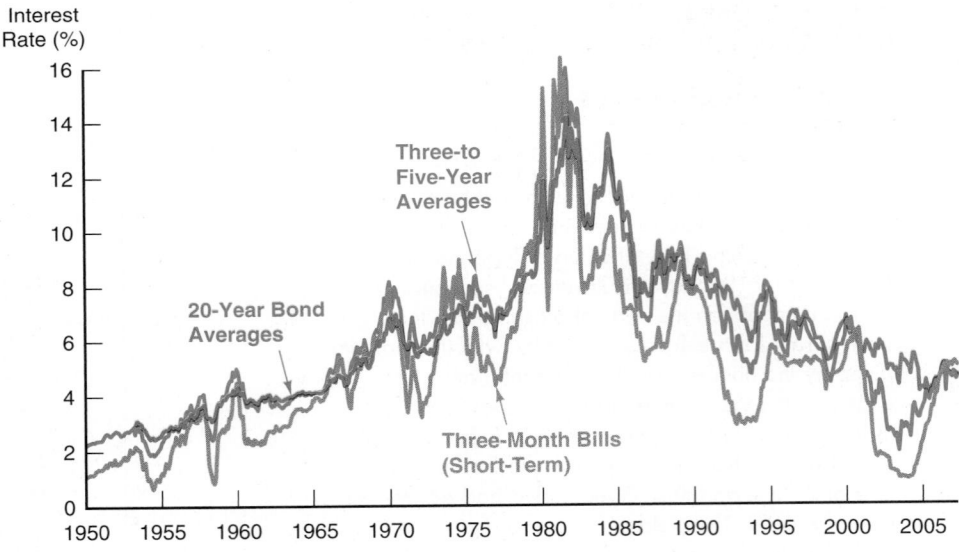

Figure 5.4 Movements over Time of Interest Rates on U.S. Government Bonds with Different Maturities

Source: Federal Reserve: www.federalreserve.gov/releases/h15/data.htm.

If the liquidity premium theory does a better job of explaining the facts and is hence the most widely accepted theory, why do we spend time discussing the other two theories? There are two reasons. First, the ideas in these two theories lay the groundwork for the liquidity premium theory. Second, it is important to see how economists modify theories to improve them when they find that the predicted results are inconsistent with the empirical evidence.

Expectations Theory

The **expectations theory** of the term structure states the following commonsense proposition: The interest rate on a long-term bond will equal an average of the short-term interest rates that people expect to occur over the life of the long-term bond. For example, if people expect that short-term interest rates will be 10% on average over the coming five years, the expectations theory predicts that the interest rate on bonds with five years to maturity will be 10%, too. If short-term interest rates were expected to rise even higher after this five-year period, so that the average short-term interest rate over the coming 20 years is 11%, then the interest rate on 20-year bonds would equal 11% and would be higher than the interest rate on five-year bonds. We can see that the explanation provided by the expectations theory for why interest rates on bonds of different maturities differ is that short-term interest rates are expected to have different values at future dates.

The key assumption behind this theory is that buyers of bonds do not prefer bonds of one maturity over another, so they will not hold any quantity of a bond if its expected return is less than that of another bond with a different maturity. Bonds that have this characteristic are said to be *perfect substitutes*. What this means in practice is that if bonds with different maturities are perfect substitutes, the expected return on these bonds must be equal.

To see how the assumption that bonds with different maturities are perfect substitutes leads to the expectations theory, let us consider the following two investment strategies:

1. Purchase a one-year bond, and when it matures in one year, purchase another one-year bond.
2. Purchase a two-year bond and hold it until maturity.

Because both strategies must have the same expected return if people are holding both one- and two-year bonds, the interest rate on the two-year bond must equal the average of the two one-year interest rates.

---

example 5.2 **Expectations Theory**

The current interest rate on a one-year bond is 9%, and you expect the interest rate on the one-year bond next year to be 11%. What is the expected return over the two years? What interest rate must a two-year bond have to equal the two one-year bonds?

Solution

The expected return over the two years will average 10% per year ([9% + 11%]/2 = 10%). The bondholder will be willing to hold both the one- and two-year bonds only if the expected return per year of the two-year bond equals 10%. Therefore, the interest rate on the two-year bond must equal 10%, the average interest rate on the two one-year bonds. Graphically, we have:

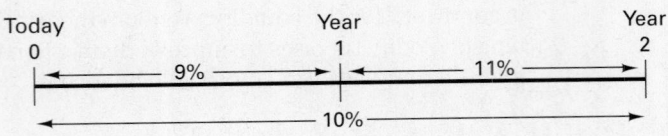

We can make this argument more general. For an investment of $1, consider the choice of holding, for two periods, a two-period bond or two one-period bonds. Using the definitions

i_t = today's (time t) interest rate on a one-period bond

i^e_{t+1} = interest rate on a one-period bond expected for next period (time $t + 1$)

i_{2t} = today's (time t) interest rate on the two-period bond

the expected return over the two periods from investing $1 in the two-period bond and holding it for the two periods can be calculated as

$$(1 + i_{2t})(1 + i_{2t}) - 1 = 1 + 2i_{2t} + (i_{2t})^2 - 1 = 2i_{2t} + (i_{2t})^2$$

After the second period, the $1 investment is worth $(1 + i_{2t})(1 + i_{2t})$. Subtracting the $1 initial investment from this amount and dividing by the initial $1 investment gives the rate of return calculated in the previous equation. Because $(i_{2t})^2$ is extremely small—if $i_{2t} = 10\% = 0.10$, then $(i_{2t})^2 = 0.01$—we can simplify the expected return for holding the two-period bond for the two periods to

$$2i_{2t}$$

With the other strategy, in which one-period bonds are bought, the expected return on the $1 investment over the two periods is

$$(1 + i_t)(1 + i^e_{t+1}) - 1$$
$$= 1 + i_t + i^e_{t+1} + i_t(i^e_{t+1}) - 1 = i_t + i^e_{t+1} + i_t(i^e_{t+1})$$

This calculation is derived by recognizing that after the first period, the $1 investment becomes $1 + i_t$, and this is reinvested in the one-period bond for the next period, yielding an amount $(1 + i_t)(1 + i^e_{t+1})$. Then subtracting the $1 initial investment from this amount and dividing by the initial investment of $1 gives the expected return for the strategy of holding one-period bonds for the two periods. Because $i_t(i^e_{t+1})$ is also extremely small—if $i_t = i^e_{t+1} = 0.10$, then $i_t(i^e_{t+1}) = 0.01$—we can simplify this to

$$i_t + i^e_{t+1}$$

Both bonds will be held only if these expected returns are equal—that is, when

$$2i_{2t} = i_t + i^e_{t+1}$$

Solving for i_{2t} in terms of the one-period rates, we have

$$i_{2t} = \frac{i_t + i^e_{t+1}}{2} \tag{1}$$

which tells us that the two-period rate must equal the average of the two one-period rates. Graphically, this can be shown as

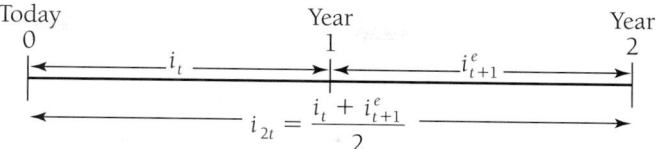

We can conduct the same steps for bonds with a longer maturity so that we can examine the whole term structure of interest rates. Doing so, we will find that the interest rate of i_{nt} on an n-period bond must be

$$i_{nt} = \frac{i_t + i_{t+1}^e + i_{t+2}^e + \cdots + i_{t+(n-1)}^e}{n} \tag{2}$$

Equation 2 states that the n-period interest rate equals the average of the one-period interest rates expected to occur over the n-period life of the bond. This is a restatement of the expectations theory in more precise terms.[2]

example 5.3 **Expectations Theory**

The one-year interest rates over the next five years are expected to be 5%, 6%, 7%, 8%, and 9%. Given this information, what are the interest rates on a two-year bond and a five-year bond? Explain what is happening to the yield curve.

Solution

The interest rate on the two-year bond would be 5.5%.

$$i_{nt} = \frac{i_t + i_{t+1}^e + i_{t+2}^e + \cdots + i_{t+(n-1)}^e}{n}$$

where

$$i_t = \text{year 1 interest rate} = 5\%$$
$$i_{t+1}^e = \text{year 2 interest rate} = 6\%$$
$$n = \text{number of years} \quad = 2$$

Thus,

$$i_{2t} = \frac{5\% + 6\%}{2} = 5.5\%$$

The interest rate on the five-year bond would be 7%.

$$i_{nt} = \frac{i_t + i_{t+1}^e + i_{t+2}^e + \cdots + i_{t+(n-1)}^e}{n}$$

---

[2]The analysis here has been conducted for discount bonds. Formulas for interest rates on coupon bonds would differ slightly from those used here, but would convey the same principle.

where

$$i_t = \text{year 1 interest rate} = 5\%$$
$$i^e_{t+1} = \text{year 2 interest rate} = 6\%$$
$$i^e_{t+2} = \text{year 3 interest rate} = 7\%$$
$$i^e_{t+3} = \text{year 4 interest rate} = 8\%$$
$$i^e_{t+4} = \text{year 5 interest rate} = 9\%$$
$$n = \text{number of years} \quad = 5$$

Thus,

$$i_{5t} = \frac{5\% + 6\% + 7\% + 8\% + 9\%}{5} = 7.0\%$$

Using the same equation for the one-, three-, and four-year interest rates, you will be able to verify the one-year to five-year rates as 5.0%, 5.5%, 6.0%, 6.5%, and 7.0% respectively. The rising trend in short-term interest rates produces an upward-sloping yield curve along which interest rates rise as maturity lengthens.

The expectations theory is an elegant theory that explains why the term structure of interest rates (as represented by yield curves) changes at different times. When the yield curve is upward-sloping, the expectations theory suggests that short-term interest rates are expected to rise in the future, as we have seen in our numerical example. In this situation, in which the long-term rate is currently higher than the short-term rate, the average of future short-term rates is expected to be higher than the current short-term rate, which can occur only if short-term interest rates are expected to rise. This is what we see in our numerical example. When the yield curve is inverted (slopes downward), the average of future short-term interest rates is expected to be lower than the current short-term rate, implying that short-term interest rates are expected to fall, on average, in the future. Only when the yield curve is flat does the expectations theory suggest that short-term interest rates are not expected to change, on average, in the future.

The expectations theory also explains fact 1, which states that interest rates on bonds with different maturities move together over time. Historically, short-term interest rates have had the characteristic that if they increase today, they will tend to be higher in the future. Hence a rise in short-term rates will raise people's expectations of future short-term rates. Because long-term rates are the average of expected future short-term rates, a rise in short-term rates will also raise long-term rates, causing short- and long-term rates to move together.

The expectations theory also explains fact 2, which states that yield curves tend to have an upward slope when short-term interest rates are low and are inverted when short-term rates are high. When short-term rates are low, people generally expect them to rise to some normal level in the future, and the average of future expected short-term rates is high relative to the current short-term rate. Therefore, long-term interest rates will be substantially higher than current short-term rates, and the yield curve would then have an upward slope. Conversely, if short-term rates are high, people usually expect them to come back down. Long-term rates would then drop below short-term rates because the average of expected future short-term rates would be lower than current short-term rates and the yield curve would slope downward and become inverted.[3]

The expectations theory is an attractive theory because it provides a simple explanation of the behavior of the term structure, but unfortunately it has a major shortcoming: It cannot explain fact 3, which says that yield curves usually slope upward. The typical upward slope of yield curves implies that short-term interest rates are usually expected to rise in the future. In practice, short-term interest rates are just as likely to fall as they are to rise, and so the expectations theory suggests that the typical yield curve should be flat rather than upward-sloping.

Market Segmentation Theory

As the name suggests, the **market segmentation theory** of the term structure sees markets for different-maturity bonds as completely separate and segmented. The interest rate for each bond with a different maturity is then determined by the supply of and demand for that bond, with no effects from expected returns on other bonds with other maturities.

The key assumption in market segmentation theory is that bonds of different maturities are not substitutes at all, so the expected return from holding a bond of one maturity has no effect on the demand for a bond of another maturity. This theory of the term structure is at the opposite extreme to the expectations theory, which assumes that bonds of different maturities are perfect substitutes.

The argument for why bonds of different maturities are not substitutes is that investors have strong preferences for bonds of one maturity but not for another, so they will be concerned with the expected returns only for bonds of the maturity they prefer. This might occur because they have a particular holding period in mind, and if they match the maturity of the bond to the desired holding period, they can obtain a certain return with no risk at all.[4] (We have seen in Chapter 3 that if the term to maturity equals the holding period, the return is known for certain because it equals the yield exactly, and there is no interest-rate risk.) For example, people who have a short holding period would prefer to hold short-term bonds. Conversely, if you were putting funds away for your young child to go to college, your desired holding period might be much longer, and you would want to hold longer-term bonds.

In market segmentation theory, differing yield curve patterns are accounted for by supply and demand differences associated with bonds of different maturities. If, as

---

[3]The expectations theory explains another important fact about the relationship between short-term and long-term interest rates. As you can see in Figure 5.4, short-term interest rates are more volatile than long-term rates. If interest rates are *mean-reverting*—that is, if they tend to head back down after they are at unusually high levels or go back up when they are at unusually low levels—then an average of these short-term rates must necessarily have less volatility than the short-term rates themselves. Because the expectations theory suggests that the long-term rate will be an average of future short-term rates, it implies that the long-term rate will have less volatility than short-term rates.

[4]The statement that there is no uncertainty about the return if the term to maturity equals the holding period is literally true only for a discount bond. For a coupon bond with a long holding period, there is some risk because coupon payments must be reinvested before the bond matures. Our analysis here is thus being conducted for discount bonds. However, the gist of the analysis remains the same for coupon bonds because the amount of this risk from reinvestment is small when coupon bonds have the same term to maturity as the holding period.

seems sensible, investors have short desired holding periods and generally prefer bonds with shorter maturities that have less interest-rate risk, market segmentation theory can explain fact 3, which states that yield curves typically slope upward. Because in the typical situation the demand for long-term bonds is relatively lower than that for short-term bonds, long-term bonds will have lower prices and higher interest rates, and hence the yield curve will typically slope upward.

Although market segmentation theory can explain why yield curves usually tend to slope upward, it has a major flaw in that it cannot explain facts 1 and 2. First, because it views the market for bonds of different maturities as completely segmented, there is no reason for a rise in interest rates on a bond of one maturity to affect the interest rate on a bond of another maturity. Therefore, it cannot explain why interest rates on bonds of different maturities tend to move together (fact 1). Second, because it is not clear how demand and supply for short- versus long-term bonds change with the level of short-term interest rates, the theory cannot explain why yield curves tend to slope upward when short-term interest rates are low and to be inverted when short-term interest rates are high (fact 2).

Because each of our two theories explains empirical facts that the other cannot, a logical step is to combine the theories, which leads us to the liquidity premium theory.

Liquidity Premium Theory

The **liquidity premium theory** of the term structure states that the interest rate on a long-term bond will equal an average of short-term interest rates expected to occur over the life of the long-term bond plus a liquidity premium (also referred to as a term premium) that responds to supply and demand conditions for that bond.

The liquidity premium theory's key assumption is that bonds of different maturities are substitutes, which means that the expected return on one bond *does* influence the expected return on a bond of a different maturity, but it allows investors to prefer one bond maturity over another. In other words, bonds of different maturities are assumed to be substitutes but not perfect substitutes. Investors tend to prefer shorter-term bonds because these bonds bear less interest-rate risk. For these reasons, investors must be offered a positive liquidity premium to induce them to hold longer-term bonds. Such an outcome would modify the expectations theory by adding a positive liquidity premium to the equation that describes the relationship between long- and short-term interest rates. The liquidity premium theory is thus written as

$$i_{nt} = \frac{i_t + i^e_{t+1} + i^e_{t+2} + \cdots + i^e_{t+(n-1)}}{n} + l_{nt} \qquad (3)$$

where l_{nt} is the liquidity (term) premium for the n-period bond at time t, which is always positive and rises with the term to maturity of the bond, n.

The relationship between the expectations theory and the liquidity premium theory is shown in Figure 5.5. There we see that because the liquidity premium is always positive and typically grows as the term to maturity increases, the yield curve implied by the liquidity premium theory is always above the yield curve implied by the expectations theory and generally has a steeper slope. (Note that for simplicity we are assuming that the expectations theory yield curve is flat.)

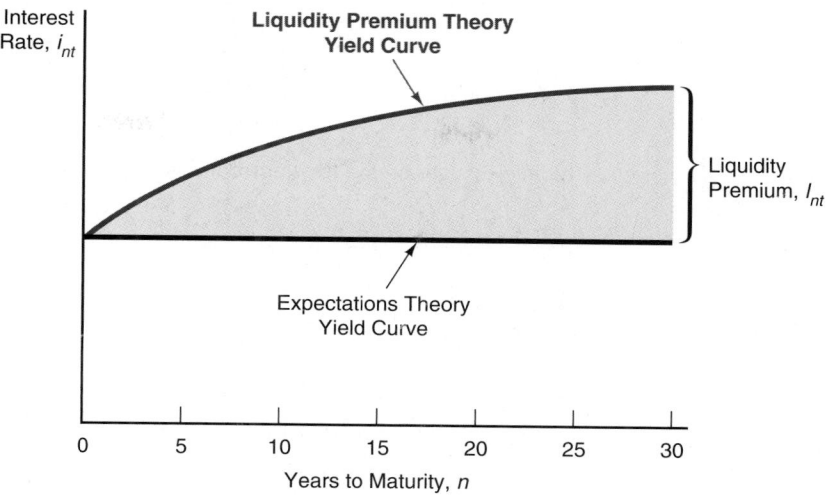

Interest Rate, i_{nt}

Liquidity Premium Theory Yield Curve

Liquidity Premium, l_{nt}

Expectations Theory Yield Curve

Years to Maturity, n

0   5   10   15   20   25   30

Figure 5.5 The Relationship Between the Liquidity Premium and Expectations Theory

Because the liquidity premium is always positive and grows as the term to maturity increases, the yield curve implied by the liquidity premium theory is always above the yield curve implied by the expectations theory and has a steeper slope. For simplicity, the yield curve implied by the expectations theory is drawn under the scenario of unchanging future one-year interest rates.

example 5.4 **Liquidity Premium Theory**

As in Example 3, let's suppose that the one-year interest rates over the next five years are expected to be 5%, 6%, 7%, 8%, and 9%. Investors' preferences for holding short-term bonds have the liquidity premiums for one-year to five-year bonds as 0%, 0.25%, 0.5%, 0.75%, and 1.0%, respectively. What is the interest rate on a two-year bond and a five-year bond? Compare these findings with the answer from Example 3 dealing with the pure expectations theory.

Solution

The interest rate on the two-year bond would be 5.75%.

$$i_{nt} = \frac{i_t + i_{t+1}^e + i_{t+2}^e + \cdots + i_{t+(n-1)}^e}{n} + l_{nt}$$

where

i_t = year 1 interest rate = 5%

i_{t+1}^e = year 2 interest rate = 6%

l_{nt} = liquidity premium = 0.25%

n = number of years = 2

Thus,

$$i_{2t} = \frac{5\% + 6\%}{2} + 0.25\% = 5.75\%$$

The interest rate on the five-year bond would be 8%.

$$i_{nt} = \frac{i_t + i_{t+1}^e + i_{t+2}^e + \cdots + i_{t+(n-1)}^e}{n} + l_{nt}$$

where

$$i_t = \text{year 1 interest rate} = 5\%$$
$$i_{t+1}^e = \text{year 2 interest rate} = 6\%$$
$$i_{t+2}^e = \text{year 3 interest rate} = 7\%$$
$$i_{t+3}^e = \text{year 4 interest rate} = 8\%$$
$$i_{t+4}^e = \text{year 5 interest rate} = 9\%$$
$$l_{2t} = \text{liquidity premium} = 1\%$$
$$n = \text{number of years} = 5$$

Thus,

$$i_{5t} = \frac{5\% + 6\% + 7\% + 8\% + 9\%}{5} + 1\% = 8.0\%$$

If you did similar calculations for the one-, three-, and four-year interest rates, the one-year to five-year interest rates would be as follows: 5.0%, 5.75%, 6.5%, 7.25%, and 8.0%, respectively. Comparing these findings with those for the pure expectations theory, we can see that the liquidity preference theory produces yield curves that slope more steeply upward because of investors' preferences for short-term bonds.

Let's see if the liquidity premium theory is consistent with all three empirical facts we have discussed. They explain fact 1, which states that interest rates on different-maturity bonds move together over time: A rise in short-term interest rates indicates that short-term interest rates will, on average, be higher in the future, and the first term in Equation 3 then implies that long-term interest rates will rise along with them.

They also explain why yield curves tend to have an especially steep upward slope when short-term interest rates are low and to be inverted when short-term rates are high (fact 2). Because investors generally expect short-term interest rates to rise to some normal level when they are low, the average of future expected short-term rates will be high relative to the current short-term rate. With the additional boost of a positive liquidity premium, long-term interest rates will be substantially higher than current short-term rates, and the yield curve will then have a steep upward slope. Conversely, if short-term rates are high, people usually expect them to come back down. Long-term rates will then drop below short-term rates because the average of expected future short-term rates will be so far below current short-term rates that despite positive liquidity premiums, the yield curve will slope downward.

The liquidity premium theory explains fact 3, which states that yield curves typically slope upward, by recognizing that the liquidity premium rises with a bond's maturity because of investors' preferences for short-term bonds. Even if short-term interest rates are expected to stay the same on average in the future, long-term interest rates will be above short-term interest rates, and yield curves will typically slope upward.

How can the liquidity premium theory explain the occasional appearance of inverted yield curves if the liquidity premium is positive? It must be that at times short-term interest rates are expected to fall so much in the future that the average of the expected short-term rates is well below the current short-term rate. Even when the positive liquidity premium is added to this average, the resulting long-term rate will still be lower than the current short-term interest rate.

As our discussion indicates, a particularly attractive feature of the liquidity premium theory is that it tells you what the market is predicting about future short-term interest rates just from the slope of the yield curve. A steeply rising yield curve, as in panel (a) of Figure 5.6, indicates that short-term interest rates are expected to rise in the future. A moderately steep yield curve, as in panel (b), indicates that short-term interest rates are not expected to rise or fall much in the future. A flat yield curve, as in panel (c), indicates that short-term rates are expected to fall moderately in the future. Finally, an inverted yield curve, as in panel (d), indicates that short-term interest rates are expected to fall sharply in the future.

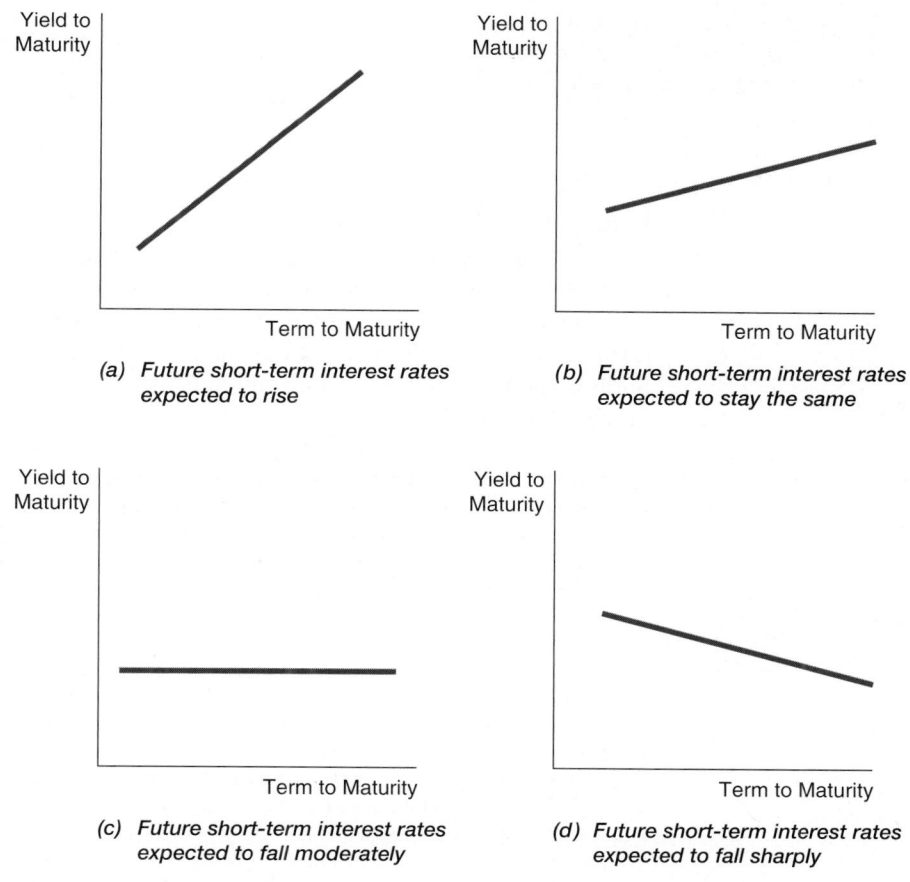

Figure 5.6 Yield Curves and the Market's Expectations of Future Short-Term Interest Rates According to the Liquidity Premium Theory

mini-case

The Yield Curve as a Forecasting Tool for Inflation and the Business Cycle

Because the yield curve contains information about future expected interest rates, it should also have the capacity to help forecast inflation and real output fluctuations. To see why, recall from Chapter 4 that rising interest rates are associated with economic booms and falling interest rates with recessions. When the yield curve is either flat or downward-sloping, it suggests that future short-term interest rates are expected to fall and, therefore, that the economy is more likely to enter a recession. Indeed, the yield curve is found to be an accurate predictor of the business cycle.[a]

In Chapter 3, we also learned that a nominal interest rate is composed of a real interest rate and expected inflation, implying that the yield curve contains information about both the future path of nominal interest rates and future inflation. A steep yield curve predicts a future increase in inflation, while a flat or downward-sloping yield curve forecasts a future decline in inflation.[b]

The ability of the yield curve to forecast business cycles and inflation is one reason why the slope of the yield curve is part of the toolkit of many economic forecasters and is often viewed as a useful indicator of the stance of monetary policy, with a steep yield curve indicating loose policy and a flat or downward-sloping yield curve indicating tight policy.

------

[a]For example, see Arturo Estrella and Frederic S. Mishkin, "Predicting U.S. Recessions: Financial Variables as Leading Indicators," *Review of Economics and Statistics*, 80 (February 1998): 45–61.

[b]Frederic S. Mishkin, "What Does the Term Structure Tell Us About Future Inflation?" *Journal of Monetary Economics* 25 (January 1990): 77–95; and Frederic S. Mishkin, "The Information in the Longer-Maturity Term Structure About Future Inflation," *Quarterly Journal of Economics* 55 (August 1990): 815–828.

Evidence on the Term Structure

In the 1980s, researchers examining the term structure of interest rates questioned whether the slope of the yield curve provides information about movements of future short-term interest rates.[5] They found that the spread between long- and short-term interest rates does not always help predict future short-term interest rates, a finding that may stem from substantial fluctuations in the liquidity (term) premium for long-term bonds. More recent research using more discriminating tests now favors a different view. It shows that the term structure contains quite a bit of information for the very short run (over the next several months) and the long run (over several years) but is unreliable at predicting movements in interest rates over the intermediate term (the time in between).[6] Research also finds that the yield curve helps forecast future inflation and business cycles (see the Mini-Case box).

------

[5]Robert J. Shiller, John Y. Campbell, and Kermit L. Schoenholtz, "Forward Rates and Future Policy: Interpreting the Term Structure of Interest Rates," *Brookings Papers on Economic Activity* 1 (1983): 173–217; N. Gregory Mankiw and Lawrence H. Summers, "Do Long-Term Interest Rates Overreact to Short-Term Interest Rates?" *Brookings Papers on Economic Activity* 1 (1984): 223–242.

[6]Eugene Fama, "The Information in the Term Structure," *Journal of Financial Economics* 13 (1984): 509–528; Eugene Fama and Robert Bliss, "The Information in Long-Maturity Forward Rates," *American Economic Review* 77 (1987): 680–692; John Y. Campbell and Robert J. Shiller, "Cointegration and Tests of the Present Value Models," *Journal of Political Economy* 95 (1987): 1062–1088; John Y. Campbell and Robert J. Shiller, "Yield Spreads and Interest Rate Movements: A Bird's Eye View," *Review of Economic Studies* 58 (1991): 495–514.

Summary

The liquidity premium theory is the most widely accepted theory of the term structure of interest rates because it explains the major empirical facts about the term structure so well. It combines the features of both the expectations theory and market segmentation theory by asserting that a long-term interest rate will be the sum of a liquidity (term) premium and the average of the short-term interest rates that are expected to occur over the life of the bond.

The liquidity premium theory explains the following facts: (1) Interest rates on bonds of different maturities tend to move together over time, (2) yield curves usually slope upward, and (3) when short-term interest rates are low, yield curves are more likely to have a steep upward slope, whereas when short-term interest rates are high, yield curves are more likely to be inverted.

The theory also helps us predict the movement of short-term interest rates in the future. A steep upward slope of the yield curve means that short-term rates are expected to rise, a mild upward slope means that short-term rates are expected to remain the same, a flat slope means that short-term rates are expected to fall moderately, and an inverted yield curve means that short-term rates are expected to fall sharply.

CASE

Interpreting Yield Curves, 1980–2008

Figure 5.7 illustrates several yield curves that have appeared for U.S. government bonds in recent years. What do these yield curves tell us about the public's expectations of future movements of short-term interest rates?

study guide

Try to answer the preceding question before reading further in the text. If you have trouble answering it with the liquidity premium theory, first try answering it with the expectations theory (which is simpler because you don't have to worry about the liquidity premium). When you understand what the expectations of future interest rates are in this case, modify your analysis by taking the liquidity premium into account.

The steep inverted yield curve that occurred on January 15, 1981, indicated that short-term interest rates were expected to decline sharply in the future. For longer-term interest rates with their positive liquidity premium to be well below the short-term interest rate, short-term interest rates must be expected to decline so sharply that their average is far below the current short-term rate. Indeed, the public's expectations of sharply lower short-term interest rates evident in the yield curve were realized soon after January 15; by March, three-month Treasury bill rates had declined from the 16% level to 13%.

The steep upward-sloping yield curve on March 28, 1985 indicated that short-term interest rates would climb in the future. The long-term interest rate is higher than the short-term interest rate when short-term interest rates are expected to

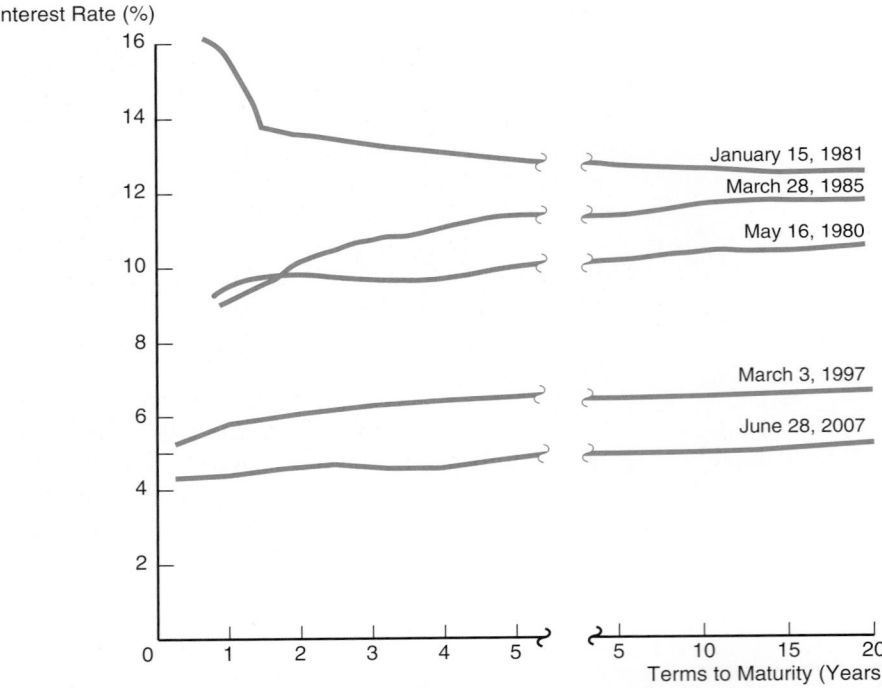

Figure 5.7 Yield Curves for U.S. Government Bonds

Sources: Federal Reserve Bank of St. Louis; *U.S. Financial Data,* various issues; *Wall Street Journal,* various dates.

rise because their average plus the liquidity premium will be higher than the current short-term rate. The moderately upward-sloping yield curves on May 16, 1980, March 3, 1997, and June 28, 2007 indicated that short-term interest rates were expected neither to rise nor to fall in the near future. In this case, their average remains the same as the current short-term rate, and the positive liquidity premium for longer-term bonds explains the moderate upward slope of the yield curve.

THE PRACTICING MANAGER

Using the Term Structure to Forecast Interest Rates

As was discussed in Chapter 4, interest-rate forecasts are extremely important to managers of financial institutions because future changes in interest rates have a significant impact on the profitability of their institutions. Furthermore, interest-rate forecasts are needed when managers of financial institutions have to set interest rates on loans that are promised to customers in the future. Our discussion of the term structure of interest rates has indicated that the slope of the yield curve provides general information about the market's prediction of the future path of interest rates. For example, a steeply upward-sloping yield curve indicates that short-term interest rates are predicted to rise in the future, and a downward-sloping yield curve indicates that short-term interest rates are predicted to fall. However, a financial institution manager needs much more specific information on interest-rate forecasts than this. Here we show how the manager of a financial institution can generate specific forecasts of interest rates using the term structure.

To see how this is done, let's start the analysis using the approach we took in developing the pure expectations theory. Recall that because bonds of different maturities are perfect substitutes, we assumed that the expected return over two periods from investing \$1 in a two-period bond, which is $(1 + i_{2t})(1 + i_{2t}) - 1$, must equal the expected return from investing \$1 in one-period bonds, which is $(1 + i_t)(1 + i_{t+1}^e) - 1$. This is shown graphically as follows:

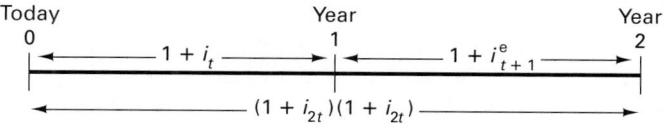

In other words,

$$(1 + i_t)(1 + i_{t+1}^e) - 1 = (1 + i_{2t})(1 + i_{2t}) - 1$$

Through some tedious algebra we can solve for i_{t+1}^e:

$$i_{t+1}^e = \frac{(1 + i_{2t})^2}{1 + i_t} - 1 \tag{4}$$

This measure of i_{t+1}^e is called the **forward rate** because it is the one-period interest rate that the pure expectations theory of the term structure indicates is expected to prevail one period in the future. To differentiate forward rates derived from the term structure from actual interest rates that are observed at time t, we call these observed interest rates **spot rates.**

Going back to Example 3, which we used to discuss the pure expectations theory earlier in this chapter, at time t the one-year interest rate is 5% and the two-year rate is 5.5%. Plugging these numbers into Equation 4 yields the following estimate of the forward rate one period in the future:

$$i_{t+1}^e = \frac{(1 + 0.055)^2}{1 + 0.05} - 1 = 0.06 = 6\%$$

Not surprisingly, this 6% forward rate is identical to the expected one-year interest rate one year in the future that we used in Example 3. This is exactly what we should find, as our calculation here is just another way of looking at the pure expectations theory.

We can also compare holding the three-year bond against holding a sequence of one-year bonds, which reveals the following relationship:

$$(1 + i_t)(1 + i_{t+1}^e)(1 + i_{t+2}^e) - 1 = (1 + i_{3t})(1 + i_{3t})(1 + i_{3t}) - 1$$

and plugging in the estimate for i^{e}_{t+1} derived in Equation 4, we can solve for i^{e}_{t+2}:

$$i^{\text{e}}_{t+2} = \frac{(1 + i_{3t})^3}{(1 + i_{2t})^2} - 1$$

Continuing with these calculations, we obtain the general solution for the forward rate n periods into the future:

$$i^{\text{e}}_{t+n} = \frac{(1 + i_{n+1t})^{n+1}}{(1 + i_{nt})^n} - 1 \tag{5}$$

Our discussion indicated that the pure expectations theory is not entirely satisfactory because investors must be compensated with liquidity premiums to induce them to hold longer-term bonds. Hence we need to modify our analysis, as we did when discussing the liquidity premium theory, by allowing for these liquidity premiums in estimating predictions of future interest rates.

Recall from the discussion of those theories that because investors prefer to hold short-term rather than long-term bonds, the n-period interest rate differs from that indicated by the pure expectations theory by a liquidity premium of l_{nt}. So to allow for liquidity premiums, we need merely subtract l_{nt} from i_{nt} in our formula to derive i^{e}_{t+n}:

$$i^{\text{e}}_{t+n} = \frac{(1 + i_{n+1t} - l_{n+1t})^{n+1}}{(1 + i_{nt} - l_{nt})^n} - 1 \tag{6}$$

This measure of i^{e}_{t+n} is referred to, naturally enough, as the *adjusted forward-rate forecast*.

In the case of i^{e}_{t+1}, Equation 6 produces the following estimate

$$i^{\text{e}}_{t+1} = \frac{(1 + i_{2t} - l_{2t})^2}{1 + i_t} - 1$$

Using Example 4 in our discussion of the liquidity premium theory, at time t the l_{2t} liquidity premium is 0.25%, $l_{1t} = 0$, the one-year interest rate is 5%, and the two-year interest rate is 5.75%. Plugging these numbers into our equation yields the following adjusted forward-rate forecast for one period in the future:

$$i^{\text{e}}_{t+1} = \frac{(1 + 0.0575 - 0.0025)^2}{1 + 0.05} - 1 = 0.06 = 6\%$$

which is the same as the expected interest rate used in Example 3, as it should be.

Our analysis of the term structure thus provides managers of financial institutions with a fairly straightforward procedure for producing interest-rate forecasts. First they need to estimate l_{nt}, the values of the liquidity premiums for various n. Then they need merely apply the formula in Equation 6 to derive the market's forecasts of future interest rates.

example 5.5 **Forward Rate**

A customer asks a bank if it would be willing to commit to making the customer a one-year loan at an interest rate of 8% one year from now. To compensate for the costs of making the loan, the bank needs to charge one percentage point more than the expected interest rate on a Treasury bond with the same maturity if it is to make a profit. If the bank manager estimates the liquidity premium to be 0.4%, and the one-year Treasury bond rate is 6% and the two-year bond rate is 7%, should the manager be willing to make the commitment?

Solution

The bank manager is unwilling to make the loan because at an interest rate of 8%, the loan is likely to be unprofitable to the bank.

$$i_{t+n}^e = \frac{(1 + i_{n+1t} - l_{n+1t})^{n+1}}{(1 + i_{nt} - l_{nt})^n} - 1$$

where

$$i_{n+1t} = \text{two-year bond rate} = 0.07$$
$$l_{n+1t} = \text{liquidity premium} = 0.004$$
$$i_{nt} = \text{one-year bond rate} = 0.06$$
$$l_{1t} = \text{liquidity premium} = 0$$
$$n = \text{number of years} = 1$$

Thus,

$$i_{t+1}^e = \frac{(1 + 0.07 - 0.004)^2}{1 + 0.06} - 1 = 0.072 = 7.2\%$$

The market's forecast of the one-year Treasury bond rate one year in the future is therefore 7.2%. Adding the 1% necessary to make a profit on the one-year loan means that the loan is expected to be profitable only if it has an interest rate of 8.2% or higher.

As we will see in Chapter 6, the bond market's forecasts of interest rates may be the most accurate ones possible. If this is the case, the estimates of the market's forecasts of future interest rates using the simple procedure outlined here may be the best interest-rate forecasts that a financial institution manager can obtain.

study guide

To make sure you understand how to generate interest-rate forecasts from the term structure, calculate the forecasts of the one-year interest rates using Equation 6 for two, three, and four years in the future using the liquidity premiums and one-year through five-year interest rates in Example 4. The resulting forecasts should equal the expected future interest rates found in the example. Problems at the end of the chapter will give you more practice in generating interest-rate forecasts from the term structure.

SUMMARY

1. Bonds with the same maturity will have different interest rates because of three factors: default risk, liquidity, and tax considerations. The greater a bond's default risk, the higher its interest rate relative to other bonds; the greater a bond's liquidity, the lower its interest rate; and bonds with tax-exempt status will have lower interest rates than they otherwise would. The relationship among interest rates on bonds with the same maturity that arise because of these three factors is known as the *risk structure of interest rates*.

2. Several theories of the term structure provide explanations of how interest rates on bonds with different terms to maturity are related. The expectations theory views long-term interest rates as equaling the average of future short-term interest rates expected to occur over the life of the bond. By contrast, the market segmentation theory treats the determination of interest rates for each bond's maturity as the outcome of supply and demand in that market only.

Neither of these theories by itself can explain the fact that interest rates on bonds of different maturities move together over time and that yield curves usually slope upward.

3. The liquidity premium theory combines the features of the other two theories, and by so doing is able to explain the facts just mentioned. It views long-term interest rates as equaling the average of future short-term interest rates expected to occur over the life of the bond plus a liquidity premium. This theory allows us to infer the market's expectations about the movement of future short-term interest rates from the yield curve. A steeply upward-sloping curve indicates that future short-term rates are expected to rise, a mildly upward-sloping curve indicates that short-term rates are expected to stay the same, a flat curve indicates that short-term rates are expected to decline slightly, and an inverted yield curve indicates that a substantial decline in short-term rates is expected in the future.

KEY TERMS

credit-rating agencies, *p. 102*
default, *p. 100*
default-free bonds, *p. 100*
expectations theory, *p. 109*
forward rate, *p. 121*
inverted yield curve, *p. 107*
junk bonds, *p. 102*

liquidity premium theory, *p. 114*
market segmentation theory, *p. 113*
risk premium, *p. 100*
risk structure of interest rates, *p. 99*
spot rate, *p. 121*
term structure of interest rates, *p. 99*
yield curve, *p. 107*

QUESTIONS

1. Which should have the higher risk premium on its interest rates, a corporate bond with a Moody's Baa rating or a corporate bond with a C rating? Why?

2. Why do U.S. Treasury bills have lower interest rates than large-denomination negotiable bank CDs?

3. Risk premiums on corporate bonds are usually anti-cyclical; that is, they decrease during business cycle expansions and increase during recessions. Why is this so?

4. "If bonds of different maturities are close substitutes, their interest rates are more likely to move together."

Is this statement true, false, or uncertain? Explain your answer.

5. If yield curves, on average, were flat, what would this say about the liquidity premiums in the term structure? Would you be more or less willing to accept the pure expectations theory?

6. If a yield curve looks like the one shown on the next page, what is the market predicting about the movement of future short-term interest rates? What might the yield curve indicate about the market's predictions about the inflation rate in the future?

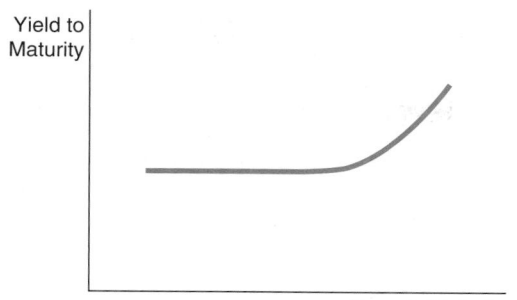

Yield to Maturity — Term to Maturity

7. If a yield curve looks like the one below, what is the market predicting about the movement of future short-term interest rates? What might the yield curve indicate about the market's predictions about the inflation rate in the future?

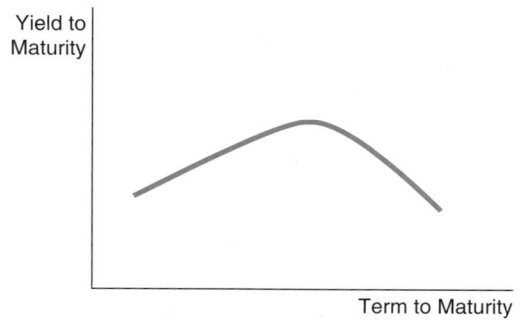

Yield to Maturity — Term to Maturity

8. What effect would reducing income tax rates have on the interest rates of municipal bonds? Would interest rates of Treasury securities be affected and, if so, how?

Predicting the Future

9. Predict what will happen to interest rates on a corporation's bonds if the federal government guarantees today that it will pay creditors if the corporation goes bankrupt in the future. What will happen to the interest rates on Treasury securities?

10. Predict what would happen to the risk premiums on corporate bonds if brokerage commissions were lowered in the corporate bond market.

11. If the income tax exemption on municipal bonds were abolished, what would happen to the interest rates on these bonds? What effect would it have on interest rates on U.S. Treasury securities?

QUANTITATIVE PROBLEMS

1. Assuming that the expectations theory is the correct theory of the term structure, calculate the interest rates in the term structure for maturities of one to five years, and plot the resulting yield curves for the following series of one-year interest rates over the next five years:

a. 5%, 7%, 7%, 7%, 7%

b. 5%, 4%, 4%, 4%, 4%

How would your yield curves change if people preferred shorter-term bonds over longer-term bonds?

2. Government economists have forecasted one-year T-bill rates for the following five years, as follows:

Year	1-year rate (%)
1	4.25
2	5.15
3	5.50
4	6.25
5	7.10

You have a liquidity premium of 0.25% for the next two years and 0.50% thereafter. Would you be willing to purchase a four-year T-bond at a 5.75% interest rate?

3. How does the after-tax yield on a $1,000,000 municipal bond with a coupon rate of 8% paying interest annually, compare with that of a $1,000,000 corporate bond with a coupon rate of 10% paying interest annually? Assume that you are in the 25% tax bracket.

4. Consider the decision to purchase either a five-year corporate bond or a five-year municipal bond. The corporate bond is a 12% annual coupon bond with a par value of $1,000. It is currently yielding 11.5%. The municipal bond has an 8.5% annual coupon and a par value of $1,000. It is currently yielding 7%. Which of the two bonds would be more beneficial to you? Assume that your marginal tax rate is 35%.

5. Debt issued by Southeastern Corporation currently yields 12%. A municipal bond of equal risk currently yields 8%. At what marginal tax rate would an investor be indifferent between these two bonds?

6. One-year T-bill rates are expected to steadily increase by 150 basis points per year over the next six years. Determine the required interest rate on a three-year T-bond and a six-year T-bond if the current one-year interest rate is 7.5%. Assume that the expectations hypothesis for interest rates holds.

7. The one-year interest rate over the next ten years will be 3%, 4.5%, 6%, 7.5%, 9%, 10.5%, 13%, 14.5%, 16%, and 17.5%. Using the expectations theory, what will be the interest rates on a three-year bond, six-year bond, and nine-year bond?

8. Using the information from the previous question, now assume that investors prefer holding short-term bonds. A liquidity premium of 10 basis points is required for each year of a bond's maturity. What will be the interest rates on a three-year bond, six-year bond, and nine-year bond?

9. Which bond would produce a greater return if the expectations theory were to hold true, a two-year bond with an interest rate of 15% or two one-year bonds with sequential interest payments of 13% and 17%?

10. Little Monsters, Inc., borrowed $1,000,000 for two years from NorthernBank, Inc., at an 11.5% interest rate. The current risk-free rate is 2%, and Little Monsters' financial condition warrants a default risk premium of 3% and a liquidity risk premium of 2%. The maturity risk premium for a two-year loan is 1%, and inflation is expected to be 3% next year. What does this information imply about the rate of inflation in the second year?

11. One-year T-bill rates are 2% currently. If interest rates are expected to go up after three years by 2% every year, what should be the required interest rate on a 10-year bond issued today? Assume that the expectations theory holds.

12. One-year T-bill rates over the next four years are expected to be 3%, 4%, 5%, and 5.5%. If four-year T-bonds are yielding 4.5%, what is the liquidity premium on this bond?

13. At your favorite bond store, Bonds-R-Us, you see the following prices:

    One-year $100 zero selling for $90.19

    Three-year 10% coupon $1,000 par bond selling for $1,000

    Two-year 10% coupon $1,000 par bond selling for $1,000

    Assume that the expectations theory for the term structure of interest rates holds, no liquidity premium exists, and the bonds are equally risky. What is the implied one-year rate two years from now?

14. You observe the following market interest rates, for both borrowing and lending:

    One-year rate = 5%

    Two-year rate = 6%

    One-year rate one year from now = 7.25%

    How can you take advantage of these rates to earn a riskless profit? Assume that the expectations theory for interest rates holds.

15. If the interest rates on one- to five-year bonds are currently 4%, 5%, 6%, 7%, and 8%, and the term premiums for one- to five-year bonds are 0%, 0.25%, 0.35%, 0.40%, and 0.50%, predict what the one-year interest rate will be two years from now.

WEB EXERCISES

The Risk and Term Structures of Interest Rates

1. The amount of additional interest investors receive due to the various risk premiums changes over time. Sometimes the risk premiums are much larger than at other times. For example, the default risk premium was very small in the late 1990s when the economy was so healthy that business failures were rare. This risk premium increases during recessions.

   Go to **www.federalreserve.gov/releases/h15** (historical data) and find the interest rate listings for AAA- and Baa-rated bonds at three points in time: the most recent; June 1, 1995; and June 1, 1992. Prepare a graph that shows these three time periods (see Figure 5.1 for an example). Are the risk premiums stable or do they change over time?

2. Figure 5.7 shows a number of yield curves at various points in time. Go to **www.bloomberg.com**, and click on "Markets" at the top of the page. Find the Treasury yield curve. Does the current yield curve fall above or below the most recent one listed in Figure 5.7? Is the current yield curve flatter or steeper than the most recent one reported in Figure 5.7?

3. Investment companies attempt to explain to investors the nature of the risk the investor incurs when buying shares in their mutual funds. For example, go to **http://flagship5.vanguard.com/VGApp/hnw/FundsStocksOverview**.

   a. Select the bond fund you would recommend to an investor who has a very low tolerance for risk and a short investment horizon. Justify your answer.

   b. Select the bond fund you would recommend to an investor who has a very high tolerance for risk and a long investment horizon. Justify your answer.

CHAPTER 6

Are Financial Markets Efficient?

Preview

Throughout our discussion so far of how financial markets work, you may have noticed that the subject of expectations keeps cropping up again and again. Expectations of returns, risk, and liquidity are central elements in the demand for assets; expectations of inflation have a major impact on bond prices and interest rates; expectations about the likelihood of default are the most important factor that determines the risk structure of interest rates; and expectations of future short-term interest rates play a central role in determining the term structure of interest rates. Not only are expectations critical in understanding behavior in financial markets, but as we will see later in this book, they are also central to our understanding of how financial institutions operate.

To understand how expectations are formed so that we can understand how securities prices move over time, we look at the *efficient market hypothesis.* In this chapter we examine the basic reasoning behind the efficient market hypothesis in order to explain some puzzling features of the operation and behavior of financial markets. You will see, for example, why changes in stock prices are unpredictable and why listening to a stock broker's hot tips may not be a good idea.

Theoretically, the efficient market hypothesis should be a powerful tool for analyzing behavior in financial markets. But to establish that it is *in reality* a useful tool, we must compare the theory with the data. Does the emperical evidence support the theory? Though mixed, the available evidence indicates that for many purposes, this theory is a good starting point for analyzing expectations.

The Efficient Market Hypothesis

go online

www.investorhome.com/
emh.htm

Learn more about the
efficient market hypothesis.

To more fully understand how expectations affect securities prices, we need to look at how information in the market affects these prices. To do this we examine the **efficient market hypothesis** (also referred to as the **theory of efficient capital markets**), which states that prices of securities in financial markets fully reflect all available information. But what does this mean?

You may recall from Chapter 3 that the rate of return from holding a security equals the sum of the capital gain on the security (the change in the price) plus any cash payments, divided by the initial purchase price of the security:

$$R = \frac{P_{t+1} - P_t + C}{P_t} \tag{1}$$

where
R = rate of return on the security held from time t to time $t + 1$ (say, the end of 2008 to the end of 2009)

P_{t+1} = price of the security at time $t + 1$, the end of the holding period

P_t = the price of the security at time t, the beginning of the holding period

C = cash payment (coupon or dividend payments) made in the period t to $t + 1$

Let's look at the expectation of this return at time t, the beginning of the holding period. Because the current price and the cash payment C are known at the beginning, the only variable in the definition of the return that is uncertain is the price next period, P_{t+1}.[1] Denoting the expectation of the security's price at the end of the holding period as P_{t+1}^e, the expected return R^e is

$$R^e = \frac{P_{t+1}^e - P_t + C}{P_t}$$

The efficient market hypothesis views expectations as equal to optimal forecasts using all available information. What exactly does this mean? An optimal forecast is the best guess of the future using all available information. This does not mean that the forecast is perfectly accurate, but only that it is the *best possible* given the available information. This can be written more formally as

$$P_{t+1}^e = P_{t+1}^{of}$$

which in turn implies that the expected return on the security will equal the optimal forecast of the return:

$$R^e = R^{of} \tag{2}$$

Unfortunately, we cannot observe either R^e or P_{t+1}^e, so the equations above by themselves do not tell us much about how the financial market behaves. However, if we

---

[1]There are cases where C might not be known at the beginning of the period, but that does not make a substantial difference to the analysis. We would in that case assume that not only price expectations but also the expectations of C are optimal forecasts using all available information.

can devise some way to measure the value of R^e, these equations will have important implications for how prices of securities change in financial markets.

The supply and demand analysis of the bond market developed in Chapter 4 shows us that the expected return on a security (the interest rate in the case of the bond examined) will have a tendency to head toward the equilibrium return that equates the quantity demanded to the quantity supplied. Supply and demand analysis enables us to determine the expected return on a security with the following equilibrium condition: The expected return on a security R^e equals the equilibrium return R^*, which equates the quantity of the security demanded to the quantity supplied; that is,

$$R^e = R^* \tag{3}$$

The academic field of finance explores the factors (risk and liquidity, for example) that influence the equilibrium returns on securities. For our purposes, it is sufficient to know that we can determine the equilibrium return and thus determine the expected return with the equilibrium condition.

We can derive an equation to describe pricing behavior in an efficient market by using the equilibrium condition to replace R^e with R^* in Equation 2. In this way we obtain

$$R^{of} = R^* \tag{4}$$

This equation tells us that *current prices in a financial market will be set so that the optimal forecast of a security's return using all available information equals the security's equilibrium return.* Financial economists state it more simply: A security's price fully reflects all available information in an efficient market.

example 6.1 **The Efficient Market Hypothesis**

Suppose that a share of Microsoft had a closing price yesterday of $90, but new information was announced after the market closed that caused a revision in the forecast of the price for next year to go to $120. If the annual equilibrium return on Microsoft is 15%, what does the efficient market hypothesis indicate the price will go to today when the market opens? (Assume that Microsoft pays no dividends.)

Solution
The price would rise to $104.35 after the opening.

$$R^{of} = \frac{P^{of}_{t+1} - P_t + C}{P_t} = R^*$$

where

R^{of} = optimal forecast of the return = 15% = 0.15

R^* = equilibrium return = 15% = 0.15

P^{of}_{t+1} = optimal forecast of price next year = $120

P_t = price today after opening

C = cash (dividend) payment = 0

Thus,

$$0.15 = \frac{\$120 - P_t}{P_t}$$

$$P_t \times 0.15 = \$120 - P_t$$

$$P_t(1.15) = \$120$$

$$P_t = \$104.35$$

Rationale Behind the Hypothesis

To see why the efficient market hypothesis makes sense, we make use of the concept of **arbitrage,** in which market participants (*arbitrageurs*) eliminate **unexploited profit opportunities,** i.e., returns on a security that are larger than what is justified by the characteristics of that security. There are two types of arbitrage, *pure arbitrage*, in which the elimination of unexploited profit opportunities involves no risk, and the type of arbitrage we discuss here, in which the arbitrageur takes on some risk when eliminating the unexploited profit opportunities. To see how arbitrage leads to the efficient market hypothesis, suppose that, given its risk characteristics, the normal return on a security, say, Exxon-Mobil common stock, is 10% at an annual rate, and its current price P_t is lower than the optimal forecast of tomorrow's price P_{t+1}^{of} so that the optimal forecast of the return at an annual rate is 50%, which is greater than the equilibrium return of 10%. We are now able to predict that, on average, Exxon-Mobil's return would be abnormally high, so there is an unexpected profit opportunity. Knowing that, on average, you can earn such an abnormally high rate of return on Exxon-Mobil because $R^{of} > R^*$, you would buy more, which would in turn drive up its current price relative to the expected future price P_{t+1}^{of}, thereby lowering R^{of}. When the current price had risen sufficiently so that R^{of} equals R^* and the efficient market condition (Equation 4) is satisfied, the buying of Exxon-Mobil will stop, and the unexploited profit opportunity will have disappeared.

Similarly, a security for which the optimal forecast of the return is −5% while the equilibrium return is 10% ($R^{of} < R^*$) would be a poor investment because, on average, it earns less than the equilibrium return. In such a case, you would sell the security and drive down its current price relative to the expected future price until R^{of} rose to the level of R^* and the efficient market condition is again satisfied. What we have shown can be summarized as follows:

$$\left.\begin{array}{l} R^{of} > R^* \rightarrow P_t\uparrow \rightarrow R^{of}\downarrow \\ R^{of} < R^* \rightarrow P_t\downarrow \rightarrow R^{of}\uparrow \end{array}\right\} \text{ until } R^{of} = R^*$$

Another way to state the efficient market condition is this: ***In an efficient market, all unexploited profit opportunities will be eliminated.***

An extremely important factor in this reasoning is that ***not everyone in a financial market must be well informed about a security or have rational expectations for its price to be driven to the point at which the efficient market condition holds.*** Financial markets are structured so that many participants can play. As long as a few (who are often referred to as "smart money") keep their eyes open for unexploited profit opportunities, they will eliminate the profit opportunities that appear because in so doing, they make a profit. The efficient market hypothesis makes sense because it does not require everyone in a market to be cognizant of what is happening to every security.

Stronger Version of the Efficient Market Hypothesis

Many financial economists take the efficient market hypothesis one step further in their analysis of financial markets. Not only do they define an efficient market as one in which expectations are optimal forecasts using all available information, but they also add the condition that an efficient market is one in which prices reflect the true fundamental (intrinsic) value of the securities. Thus, in an efficient market, all prices are always correct and reflect **market fundamentals** (items that have a direct impact on future income streams of the securities). This stronger view of market efficiency has several important implications in the academic field of finance. First, it implies that in an efficient capital market, one investment is as good as any other because the securities' prices are correct. Second, it implies that a security's price reflects all available information about the intrinsic value of the security. Third, it implies that security prices can be used by managers of both financial and nonfinancial firms to assess their cost of capital (cost of financing their investments) accurately and hence that security prices can be used to help them make the correct decisions about whether a specific investment is worth making or not. The stronger version of market efficiency is a basic tenet of much analysis in the finance field.

Evidence on the Efficient Market Hypothesis

Early evidence on the efficient market hypothesis was quite favorable to it, but in recent years, deeper analysis of the evidence suggests that the hypothesis may not always be entirely correct. Let's first look at the earlier evidence in favor of the hypothesis and then examine some of the more recent evidence that casts some doubt on it.

Evidence in Favor of Market Efficiency

Evidence in favor of market efficiency has examined the performance of investment analysts and mutual funds, whether stock prices reflect publicly available information, the random-walk behavior of stock prices, and the success of so-called technical analysis.

Performance of Investment Analysts and Mutual Funds We have seen that one implication of the efficient market hypothesis is that when purchasing a security, you cannot expect to earn an abnormally high return, a return greater than the equilibrium return. This implies that it is impossible to beat the market. Many studies shed light on whether investment advisers and mutual funds (some of which charge steep sales commissions to people who purchase them) beat the market. One common test that has been performed is to take buy and sell recommendations from a group of advisers or mutual funds and compare the performance of the resulting selection of stocks with the market as a whole. Sometimes the advisers' choices have even been compared to a group of stocks chosen by putting a copy of the financial page of the newspaper on a dartboard and throwing darts. The *Wall Street Journal,* for example, used to have a regular feature called "Investment Dartboard" that compared how well stocks picked by investment advisers did relative to stocks picked by throwing darts. Did the advisers win? To their embarrassment, the dartboard beat them as often as they beat the dartboard. Furthermore, even when the comparison included only advisers who had been successful in the past in predicting the stock market, the advisers still didn't regularly beat the dartboard.

Consistent with the efficient market hypothesis, mutual funds are also not found to beat the market. Mutual funds not only do not outperform the market on average, but when they are separated into groups according to whether they had the highest or lowest profits in a chosen period, the mutual funds that did well in the first period did not beat the market in the second period.[2]

The conclusion from the study of investment advisers and mutual fund performance is this: ***Having performed well in the past does not indicate that an investment adviser or a mutual fund will perform well in the future.*** This is not pleasing news to investment advisers, but it is exactly what the efficient market hypothesis predicts. It says that some advisers will be lucky and some will be unlucky. Being lucky does not mean that a forecaster actually has the ability to beat the market. (An exception that proves the rule is discussed in the Mini-Case box.)

go online

http://stocks.
tradingcharts.com
Access detailed stock quotes, charts, and historical stock data.

Do Stock Prices Reflect Publicly Available Information? The efficient market hypothesis predicts that stock prices will reflect all publicly available information. Thus, if information is already publicly available, a positive announcement about a company will not, on average, raise the price of its stock because this information is already reflected in the stock price. Early empirical evidence also confirmed this conjecture from the efficient market hypothesis: Favorable earnings announcements or announcements of stock splits (a division of a share of stock into multiple shares, which is usually followed by higher earnings) do not, on average, cause stock prices to rise.[3]

Random-Walk Behavior of Stock Prices The term **random walk** describes the movements of a variable whose future changes cannot be predicted (are random) because, given today's value, the variable is just as likely to fall as to rise. An important implication of the efficient market hypothesis is that stock prices should approximately follow a random walk; that is, ***future changes in stock prices should, for all practical purposes, be unpredictable.*** The random-walk implication of the efficient market hypothesis is the one most commonly mentioned in the press because it is the most readily comprehensible to the public. In fact, when people mention

---

[2]An early study that found that mutual funds do not outperform the market is Michael C. Jensen, "The Performance of Mutual Funds in the Period 1945–64," *Journal of Finance* 23 (1968): 389–416. More recent studies on mutual fund performance are Mark Grimblatt and Sheridan Titman, "Mutual Fund Performance: An Analysis of Quarterly Portfolio Holdings," *Journal of Business* 62 (1989): 393–416; R. A. Ippolito, "Efficiency with Costly Information: A Study of Mutual Fund Performance, 1965–84," *Quarterly Journal of Economics* 104 (1989): 1–23; J. Lakonishok, A. Shleifer, and R. Vishny, "The Structure and Performance of the Money Management Industry," *Brookings Papers on Economic Activity, Microeconomics* (1992); and B. Malkiel, "Returns from Investing in Equity Mutual Funds, 1971–1991," *Journal of Finance* 50 (1995): 549–72.

[3]Ray Ball and Philip Brown, "An Empirical Evaluation of Accounting Income Numbers," *Journal of Accounting Research* 6 (1968): 159–178; Eugene F. Fama, Lawrence Fisher, Michael C. Jensen, and Richard Roll, "The Adjustment of Stock Prices to New Information," *International Economic Review* 10 (1969): 1–21.

mini-case

An Exception That Proves the Rule: Ivan Boesky

The efficient market hypothesis indicates that investment advisers should not have the ability to beat the market. Yet that is exactly what Ivan Boesky was able to do until 1986, when he was charged by the Securities and Exchange Commission with making unfair profits (rumored to be in the hundreds of millions of dollars) by trading on inside information. In an out-of-court settlement, Boesky was banned from the securities business, fined $100 million, and sentenced to three years in jail. (After serving his sentence, Boesky was released from jail in 1990.) If the stock market is efficient, can the SEC legitimately claim that Boesky was able to beat the market? The answer is yes.

Ivan Boesky was the most successful of the so-called *arbs* (short for *arbitrageurs*) who made hundreds of millions in profits for himself and his clients by investing in the stocks of firms that were about to be taken over by other firms at an above-market

price. Boesky's continuing success was assured by an arrangement whereby he paid cash (sometimes in a suitcase) to Dennis Levine, an investment banker who had inside information about when a takeover was to take place because his firm was arranging the financing of the deal. When Levine found out that a firm was planning a takeover, he would inform Boesky, who would then buy the stock of the company being taken over and sell it after the stock had risen.

Boesky's ability to make millions year after year in the 1980s is an exception that proves the rule that financial analysts cannot continually outperform the market; yet it supports the efficient markets claim that only information *unavailable to the market* enables an investor to do so. Boesky profited from knowing about takeovers before the rest of the market; this information was known to him but unavailable to the market.

the "random-walk theory of stock prices," they are in reality referring to the efficient market hypothesis.

The case for random-walk stock prices can be demonstrated. Suppose that people could predict that the price of Happy Feet Corporation (HFC) stock would rise 1% in the coming week. The predicted rate of capital gains and rate of return on HFC stock would then be over 50% at an annual rate. Since this is very likely to be far higher than the equilibrium rate of return on HFC stock ($R^{of} > R^*$), the efficient market hypothesis indicates that people would immediately buy this stock and bid up its current price. The action would stop only when the predictable change in the price dropped to near zero so that $R^{of} = R^*$.

Similarly, if people could predict that the price of HFC stock would fall by 1%, the predicted rate of return would be negative ($R^{of} < R^*$), and people would immediately sell. The current price would fall until the predictable change in the price rose back to near zero, where the efficient market condition again holds. The efficient market hypothesis suggests that the predictable change in stock prices will be near zero, leading to the conclusion that stock prices will generally follow a random walk.[4]

Financial economists have used two types of tests to explore the hypothesis that stock prices follow a random walk. In the first, they examine stock market records

[4]Note that the random-walk behavior of stock prices is only an *approximation* derived from the efficient market hypothesis. It would hold exactly only for a stock for which an unchanged price leads to its having the equilibrium return. Then, when the predictable change in the stock price is exactly zero, $R^{of} = R^*$.

to see if changes in stock prices are systematically related to past changes and hence could have been predicted on that basis. The second type of test examines the data to see if publicly available information other than past stock prices could have been used to predict changes. These tests are somewhat more stringent because additional information (money supply growth, government spending, interest rates, corporate profits) might be used to help forecast stock returns. Early results from both types of tests generally confirmed the efficient market view that stock prices are not predictable and follow a random walk.[5]

Technical Analysis A popular technique used to predict stock prices, called *technical analysis,* is to study past stock price data and search for patterns such as trends and regular cycles. Rules for when to buy and sell stocks are then established on the basis of the patterns that emerge. The efficient market hypothesis suggests that technical analysis is a waste of time. The simplest way to understand why is to use the random-walk result derived from the efficient market hypothesis that holds that past stock price data cannot help predict changes. Therefore, technical analysis, which relies on such data to produce its forecasts, cannot successfully predict changes in stock prices.

Two types of tests bear directly on the value of technical analysis. The first performs the empirical analysis described earlier to evaluate the performance of any financial analyst, technical or otherwise. The results are exactly what the efficient market hypothesis predicts: Technical analysts fare no better than other financial analysts; on average, they do not outperform the market, and successful past forecasting does not imply that their forecasts will outperform the market in the future. The second type of test takes the rules developed in technical analysis for when to buy and sell stocks and applies them to new data.[6] The performance of these rules is then evaluated by the profits that would have been made using them. These tests also discredit technical analysis: It does not outperform the overall market.

---

[5]The first type of test, using only stock market data, is referred to as a test of *weak-form efficiency* because the information that can be used to predict stock prices is restricted solely to past price data. The second type of test is referred to as a test of *semistrong-form efficiency* because the information set is expanded to include all publicly available information, not just past stock prices. A third type of test is called a test of *strong-form efficiency* because the information set includes insider information, known only to the owners of the corporation, as when they plan to declare a high dividend. Strong-form tests do sometimes indicate that insider information can be used to predict changes in stock prices. This finding does not contradict efficient markets theory because the information is not available to the market and hence cannot be reflected in market prices. In fact, there are strict laws against using insider information to trade in financial markets. For an early survey on the three forms of tests, see Eugene F. Fama, "Efficient Capital Markets: A Review of Theory and Empirical Work," *Journal of Finance* 25 (1970): 383–416.

[6]Sidney Alexander, "Price Movements in Speculative Markets: Trends or Random Walks?" *Industrial Management Review,* May 1961, pp. 7–26; and Sidney Alexander, "Price Movements in Speculative Markets: Trends or Random Walks? No. 2" in The *Random Character of Stock Prices,* ed. Paul Cootner (Cambridge, MA: MIT Press, 1964), pp. 338–372. More recent evidence also seems to discredit technical analysis, for example, F. Allen and R. Karjalainen, "Using Genetic Algorithms to Find Technical Trading Rules," *Journal of Financial Economics* (1999) 51: 245–71. However, some other research is more favorable to technical analysis, e.g., P. Sullivan, A. Timmerman, and H. White, "Data-Snooping, Technical Trading Rule Performance and the Bootstrap," Centre for Economic Policy Research Discussion Paper No. 1976, 1998.

CASE

Should Foreign Exchange Rates Follow a Random Walk?

Although the efficient market hypothesis is usually applied to the stock market, it can also be used to show that foreign exchange rates, like stock prices, should generally follow a random walk. To see why this is the case, consider what would happen if people could predict that a currency would appreciate by 1% in the coming week. By buying this currency, they could earn a greater than 50% return at an annual rate, which is likely to be far above the equilibrium return for holding a currency. As a result, people would immediately buy the currency and bid up its current price, thereby reducing the expected return. The process would stop only when the predictable change in the exchange rate dropped to near zero so that the optimal forecast of the return no longer differed from the equilibrium return. Likewise, if people could predict that the currency would depreciate by 1% in the coming week, they would sell it until the predictable change in the exchange rate was again near zero. The efficient market hypothesis therefore implies that future changes in exchange rates should, for all practical purposes, be unpredictable; in other words, exchange rates should follow random walks. This is exactly what empirical evidence finds.[7]

Evidence Against Market Efficiency

All the early evidence supporting the efficient market hypothesis appeared to be overwhelming, causing Eugene Fama, a prominent financial economist, to state in his famous 1970 survey of the empirical evidence on the efficient market hypothesis, "The evidence in support of the efficient markets model is extensive, and (somewhat uniquely in economics) contradictory evidence is sparse."[8] However, in recent years, the theory has begun to show a few cracks, referred to as *anomalies,* and empirical evidence indicates that the efficient market hypothesis may not always be generally applicable.

Small-Firm Effect One of the earliest reported anomalies in which the stock market did not appear to be efficient is called the *small-firm effect.* Many empirical studies have shown that small firms have earned abnormally high returns over long periods of time, even when the greater risk for these firms has been taken into account.[9]

---

[7]See Richard A. Meese and Kenneth Rogoff, "Empirical Exchange Rate Models of the Seventies: Do They Fit out of Sample?" *Journal of International Economics* 14 (1983): 3–24.

[8]Eugene F. Fama, "Efficient Capital Markets: A Review of Theory and Empirical Work," *Journal of Finance* 25 (1970): 383–416.

[9]For example, see Marc R. Reinganum, "The Anomalous Stock Market Behavior of Small Firms in January: Empirical Tests of Tax Loss Selling Effects," *Journal of Financial Economics* 12 (1983): 89–104; Jay R. Ritter, "The Buying and Selling Behavior of Individual Investors at the Turn of the Year," *Journal of Finance* 43 (1988): 701–717; and Richard Roll, "Vas Ist Das? The Turn-of-the-Year Effect: Anomaly or Risk Mismeasurement?" *Journal of Portfolio Management* 9 (1988): 18–28.

The small-firm effect seems to have diminished in recent years but is still a challenge to the theory of efficient markets. Various theories have been developed to explain the small-firm effect, suggesting that it may be due to rebalancing of portfolios by institutional investors, tax issues, low liquidity of small-firm stocks, large information costs in evaluating small firms, or an inappropriate measurement of risk for small-firm stocks.

January Effect Over long periods of time, stock prices have tended to experience an abnormal price rise from December to January that is predictable and hence inconsistent with random-walk behavior. This so-called **January effect** seems to have diminished in recent years for shares of large companies but still occurs for shares of small companies.[10] Some financial economists argue that the January effect is due to tax issues. Investors have an incentive to sell stocks before the end of the year in December because they can then take capital losses on their tax return and reduce their tax liability. Then when the new year starts in January, they can repurchase the stocks, driving up their prices and producing abnormally high returns. Although this explanation seems sensible, it does not explain why institutional investors such as private pension funds, which are not subject to income taxes, do not take advantage of the abnormal returns in January and buy stocks in December, thus bidding up their price and eliminating the abnormal returns.[11]

Market Overreaction Recent research suggests that stock prices may overreact to news announcements and that the pricing errors are corrected only slowly.[12] When corporations announce a major change in earnings, say, a large decline, the stock price may overshoot, and after an initial large decline, it may rise back to more normal levels over a period of several weeks. This violates the efficient market hypothesis because an investor could earn abnormally high returns, on average, by buying a stock immediately after a poor earnings announcement and then selling it after a couple of weeks when it has risen back to normal levels.

Excessive Volatility A closely related phenomenon to market overreaction is that the stock market appears to display excessive volatility; that is, fluctuations in stock prices may be much greater than is warranted by fluctuations in their fundamental value. In an important paper, Robert Shiller of Yale University found that fluctuations in the S&P 500 stock index could not be justified by the subsequent fluctuations in the dividends of the stocks making up this index. There has been much subsequent technical work criticizing these results, but Shiller's work, along with research that finds that there are smaller fluctuations in stock prices when stock markets are

---

[10]For example, see Donald B. Keim, "The CAPM and Equity Return Regularities," *Financial Analysts Journal* 42 (May–June 1986): 19–34.

[11]Another anomaly that makes the stock market seem less than efficient is the fact that the *Value Line Survey*, one of the most prominent investment advice newsletters, has produced stock recommendations that have yielded abnormally high returns on average. See Fischer Black, "Yes, Virginia, There Is Hope: Tests of the Value Line Ranking System," *Financial Analysts Journal* 29 (September–October 1973): 10–14, and Gur Huberman and Shmuel Kandel, "Market Efficiency and Value Line's Record," *Journal of Business* 63 (1990): 187–216. Whether the excellent performance of the *Value Line Survey* will continue in the future is, of course, a question mark.

[12]Werner F. M. De Bondt and Richard Thaler, "Further Evidence on Investor Overreaction and Stock Market Seasonality," *Journal of Finance* 62 (1987): 557–580.

closed, has produced a consensus that stock market prices appear to be driven by factors other than fundamentals.[13]

Mean Reversion Some researchers have also found that stock returns display **mean reversion:** Stocks with low returns today tend to have high returns in the future, and vice versa. Hence stocks that have done poorly in the past are more likely to do well in the future because mean reversion indicates that there will be a predictable positive change in the future price, suggesting that stock prices are not a random walk. Other researchers have found that mean reversion is not nearly as strong in data after World War II and so have raised doubts about whether it is currently an important phenomenon. The evidence on mean reversion remains controversial.[14]

New Information Is Not Always Immediately Incorporated into Stock Prices Although it is generally found that stock prices adjust rapidly to new information, as is suggested by the efficient market hypothesis, recent evidence suggests that, inconsistent with the efficient market hypothesis, stock prices do not instantaneously adjust to profit announcements. Instead, on average stock prices continue to rise for some time after the announcement of unexpectedly high profits, and they continue to fall after surprisingly low profit announcements.[15]

Overview of the Evidence on the Efficient Market Hypothesis

As you can see, the debate on the efficient market hypothesis is far from over. The evidence seems to suggest that the efficient market hypothesis may be a reasonable starting point for evaluating behavior in financial markets. However, there do seem to be important violations of market efficiency that suggest that the efficient market hypothesis may not be the whole story and so may not be generalizable to all behavior in financial markets.

---

[13]Robert Shiller, "Do Stock Prices Move Too Much to Be Justified by Subsequent Changes in Dividends?" *American Economic Review* 71 (1981): 421–436, and Kenneth R. French and Richard Roll, "Stock Return Variances: The Arrival of Information and the Reaction of Traders," *Journal of Financial Economics* 17 (1986): 5–26.

[14]Evidence for mean reversion has been reported by James M. Poterba and Lawrence H. Summers, "Mean Reversion in Stock Prices: Evidence and Implications," *Journal of Financial Economics* 22 (1988): 27–59; Eugene F. Fama and Kenneth R. French, "Permanent and Temporary Components of Stock Prices," *Journal of Political Economy* 96 (1988): 246–273; and Andrew W. Lo and A. Craig MacKinlay, "Stock Market Prices Do Not Follow Random Walks: Evidence from a Simple Specification Test," *Review of Financial Studies* 1 (1988): 41–66. However, Myung Jig Kim, Charles R. Nelson, and Richard Startz, "Mean Reversion in Stock Prices? A Reappraisal of the Evidence," *Review of Economic Studies* 58 (1991): 515–528, question whether some of these findings are valid. For an excellent summary of this evidence, see Charles Engel and Charles S. Morris, "Challenges to Stock Market Efficiency: Evidence from Mean Reversion Studies," Federal Reserve Bank of Kansas City *Economic Review,* September–October 1991, pp. 21–35. See also N. Jegadeesh and Sheridan Titman, "Returns to Buying Winners and Selling Losers: Implications for Stock Market Efficiency," *Journal of Finance* 48 (1993): 65–92, which shows that mean reversion also occurs for individual stocks.

[15]For example, see R. Ball and P. Brown, "An Empirical Evaluation of Accounting Income Numbers," *Journal of Accounting Research* (1968) 6: 159–78; L. Chan, N. Jegadeesh, and J. Lakonishok, "Momentum Strategies," *Journal of Finance* (1996) 51: 1681–171; and Eugene Fama, "Market Efficiency, Long-Term Returns and Behavioral Finance," *Journal of Financial Economics* (1998) 49: 283–306.

THE PRACTICING MANAGER

Practical Guide to Investing in the Stock Market

The efficient market hypothesis has numerous applications to the real world. It is especially valuable because it can be applied directly to an issue that concerns managers of financial institutions (and the general public as well): how to make profits in the stock market. A practical guide to investing in the stock market, which we develop here, provides a better understanding of the use and implications of the efficient market hypothesis.

How Valuable Are Published Reports by Investment Advisers?

Suppose that you have just read in the "Heard on the Street" column of the *Wall Street Journal* that investment advisers are predicting a boom in oil stocks because an oil shortage is developing. Should you proceed to withdraw all your hard-earned savings from the bank and invest it in oil stocks?

The efficient market hypothesis tells us that when purchasing a security, we cannot expect to earn an abnormally high return, a return greater than the equilibrium return. Information in newspapers and in the published reports of investment advisers is readily available to many market participants and is already reflected in market prices. So acting on this information will not yield abnormally high returns, on average. As we have seen, the empirical evidence for the most part confirms that recommendations from investment advisers cannot help us outperform the general market. Indeed, as the Mini-Case box below suggests, human investment advisers in San Francisco do not on average even outperform an orangutan!

Probably no other conclusion is met with more skepticism by students than this one when they first hear it. We all know or have heard of somebody who has been successful in the stock market for a period of many years. We wonder, how could someone be so consistently successful if he or she did not really know how to predict when returns would be abnormally high? The following story, reported in the press, illustrates why such anecdotal evidence is not reliable.

mini-case

Should You Hire an Ape as Your Investment Adviser?

The *San Francisco Chronicle* came up with an amusing way of evaluating how successful investment advisers are at picking stocks. They asked eight analysts to pick five stocks at the beginning of the year and then compared the performance of their stock picks to those chosen by Jolyn, an orangutan living at Marine World/Africa USA in Vallejo, California.

Consistent with the results found in the "Investment Dartboard" feature of the *Wall Street Journal,* Jolyn beat the investment advisers as often as they beat her. Given this result, you might be just as well off hiring an orangutan as your investment adviser as you would hiring a human being!

A get-rich-quick artist invented a clever scam. Every week, he wrote two letters. In letter A, he would pick team A to win a particular football game, and in letter B, he would pick the opponent, team B. A mailing list would then be separated into two groups, and he would send letter A to the people in one group and letter B to the people in the other. The following week he would do the same thing but would send these letters only to the group who had received the first letter with the correct prediction. After doing this for ten games, he had a small cluster of people who had received letters predicting the correct winning team for every game. He then mailed a final letter to them, declaring that since he was obviously an expert predictor of the outcome of football games (he had picked winners ten weeks in a row) and since his predictions were profitable for the recipients who bet on the games, he would continue to send his predictions only if he were paid a substantial amount of money. When one of his clients figured out what he was up to, the con man was prosecuted and thrown in jail!

What is the lesson of the story? Even if no forecaster is an accurate predictor of the market, there will always be a group of consistent winners. A person who has done well regularly in the past cannot guarantee that he or she will do well in the future. Note that there will also be a group of persistent losers, but you rarely hear about them because no one brags about a poor forecasting record.

Should You Be Skeptical of Hot Tips?

Suppose that your broker phones you with a hot tip to buy stock in the Happy Feet Corporation (HFC) because it has just developed a product that is completely effective in curing athlete's foot. The stock price is sure to go up. Should you follow this advice and buy HFC stock?

The efficient market hypothesis indicates that you should be skeptical of such news. If the stock market is efficient, it has already priced HFC stock so that its expected return will equal the equilibrium return. The hot tip is not particularly valuable and will not enable you to earn an abnormally high return.

You might wonder, though, if the hot tip is based on new information and would give you an edge on the rest of the market. If other market participants have gotten this information before you, the answer is no. As soon as the information hits the street, the unexploited profit opportunity it creates will be quickly eliminated. The stock's price will already reflect the information, and you should expect to realize only the equilibrium return. But if you are one of the first to know the new information (as Ivan Boesky was—see the Mini-Case box), it can do you some good. Only then can you be one of the lucky ones who, on average, will earn an abnormally high return by helping eliminate the profit opportunity by buying HFC stock.

Do Stock Prices Always Rise When There Is Good News?

If you follow the stock market, you might have noticed a puzzling phenomenon: When good news about a stock, such as a particularly favorable earnings report, is announced, the price of the stock frequently does not rise. The efficient market hypothesis and the random-walk behavior of stock prices explain this phenomenon.

Because changes in stock prices are unpredictable, when information is announced that has already been expected by the market, the stock price will remain unchanged. The announcement does not contain any new information that should lead to a change in stock prices. If this were not the case and the announcement led to a change in stock prices, it would mean that the change was predictable. Because that is ruled out in an efficient market, **_stock prices will respond to announcements only when the information being announced is new and unexpected._** If the news is expected, there will be no stock price response. This is exactly what the evidence that we described earlier suggests will occur—that stock prices reflect publicly available information.

Sometimes a stock price declines when good news is announced. Although this seems somewhat peculiar, it is completely consistent with the workings of an efficient market. Suppose that although the announced news is good, it is not as good as expected. HFC's earnings may have risen 15%, but if the market expected earnings to rise by 20%, the new information is actually unfavorable, and the stock price declines.

Efficient Markets Prescription for the Investor

What does the efficient market hypothesis recommend for investing in the stock market? It tells us that hot tips, investment advisers' published recommendations, and technical analysis—all of which make use of publicly available information—cannot help an investor outperform the market. Indeed, it indicates that anyone without better information than other market participants cannot expect to beat the market. So what is an investor to do?

The efficient market hypothesis leads to the conclusion that such an investor (and almost all of us fit into this category) should not try to outguess the market by constantly buying and selling securities. This process does nothing but boost the income of brokers, who earn commissions on each trade.[16] Instead, the investor should pursue a "buy and hold" strategy—purchase stocks and hold them for long periods of time. This will lead to the same returns, on average, but the investor's net profits will be higher because fewer brokerage commissions will have to be paid.[17]

It is frequently a sensible strategy for a small investor, whose costs of managing a portfolio may be high relative to its size, to buy into a mutual fund rather than individual stocks. Because the efficient market hypothesis indicates that no mutual fund can consistently outperform the market, an investor should not buy into one that has high management fees or that pays sales commissions to brokers but rather should purchase a no-load (commission-free) mutual fund that has low management fees.

As we have seen, the evidence indicates that it will not be easy to beat the prescription suggested here, although some of the anomalies to the efficient market hypothesis suggest that an extremely clever investor (which rules out most of us) may be able to outperform a buy-and-hold strategy.

---

[16]The investor may also have to pay Uncle Sam capital gains taxes on any profits that are realized when a security is sold—an additional reason why continual buying and selling does not make sense.

[17]The investor can also minimize risk by holding a diversified portfolio. The investor will be better off by pursuing a buy-and-hold strategy with a diversified portfolio or with a mutual fund that has a diversified portfolio.

CASE

What Do the Black Monday Crash of 1987 and the Tech Crash of 2000 Tell Us About the Efficient Market Hypothesis?

On October 19, 1987, dubbed "Black Monday," the Dow Jones Industrial Average declined more than 20%, the largest one-day decline in U.S. history. The collapse of the high-tech companies' share prices from their peaks in March 2000 caused the heavily tech-laden NASDAQ index to fall from around 5000 in March 2000 to around 1500 in 2001 and 2002, for a decline of well over 60%. These two crashes have caused many economists to question the validity of the efficient market hypothesis. They do not believe that an efficient market could have produced such massive swings in share prices. To what degree should these stock market crashes make us doubt the validity of the efficient market hypothesis?

Nothing in the efficient market hypothesis rules out large changes in stock prices. A large change in stock prices can result from new information that produces a dramatic decline in optimal forecasts of the future valuation of firms. However, economists are hard pressed to come up with fundamental changes in the economy that can explain the Black Monday and tech crashes. One lesson from these crashes is that factors other than market fundamentals probably have an effect on stock prices. Hence these crashes have convinced many economists that the stronger version of the efficient market hypothesis, which states that asset prices reflect the true fundamental (intrinsic) value of securities, is incorrect. They attribute a large role in determination of stock prices to market psychology and to the institutional structure of the marketplace. However, nothing in this view contradicts the basic reasoning behind the weaker version of the efficient market hypothesis—that market participants eliminate unexploited profit opportunities. Even though stock market prices may not always solely reflect market fundamentals, this does not mean that rational expectations do not hold. As long as stock market crashes are unpredictable, the basic lessons of the theory of rational expectations hold.

Some economists have come up with theories of what they call *rational bubbles* to explain stock market crashes. A **bubble** is a situation in which the price of an asset differs from its fundamental market value. In a rational bubble, investors can have rational expectations that a bubble is occurring because the asset price is above its fundamental value but continue to hold the asset anyway. They might do this because they believe that someone else will buy the asset for a higher price in the future. In a rational bubble, asset prices can therefore deviate from their fundamental value for a long time because the bursting of the bubble cannot be predicted and so there are no unexploited profit opportunities.

However, other economists believe that the Black Monday crash of 1987 and the tech crash of 2000 suggest that there may be unexploited profit opportunities and that the theory of rational expectations and the efficient market hypothesis might be fundamentally flawed. The controversy over whether capital markets are efficient continues.

Behavioral Finance

Doubts about the efficient market hypothesis, particularly after the stock market crash of 1987, have led to a new field of study, **behavioral finance,** which applies concepts from other social sciences, such as anthropology, sociology, and particularly psychology, to understand the behavior of securities prices.[18]

As we have seen, the efficient market hypothesis assumes that unexploited profit opportunities are eliminated by "smart money." But can smart money dominate ordinary investors so that financial markets are efficient? Specifically, the efficient market hypothesis suggests that smart money sells when a stock price goes up irrationally, with the result that the stock falls back down to what is justified by fundamentals. However, for this to occur, smart money must be able to engage in **short sales,** in which they borrow stock from brokers and then sell it in the market, with the hope that they earn a profit by buying the stock back again ("covering the short") after it has fallen in price. However, work by psychologists suggests that people are subject to loss aversion: That is, they are more unhappy when they suffer losses than they are happy from making gains. Short sales can result in losses way in excess of an investor's initial investment if the stock price climbs sharply above the price at which the short sale is made (and these losses have the possibility of being unlimited if the stock price climbs to astronomical heights). Loss aversion can thus explain an important phenomenon: Very little short selling actually takes place. Short selling may also be constrained by rules restricting it because it seems unsavory that someone would make money from another person's misfortune. The fact that there is so little short selling can explain why stock prices sometimes get overvalued. Not enough short selling can take place by smart money to drive stock prices back down to their fundamental value.

Psychologists have also found that people tend to be overconfident in their own judgments (just as in "Lake Woebegon," everyone believes they are above average). As a result, it is no surprise that investors tend to believe that they are smarter than other investors and so are willing to assume that the market typically doesn't get it right and therefore to trade on their beliefs. This can explain why securities markets have so much trading volume, something that the efficient market hypothesis does not predict.

Overconfidence and social contagion provide an explanation for stock market bubbles. When stock prices go up, investors attribute their profits to their intelligence and talk up the stock market. This word-of-mouth enthusiasm and the media then can produce an environment in which even more investors think stock prices will rise in the future. The result is then a so-called positive feedback loop in which prices continue to rise, producing a speculative bubble, which finally crashes when prices get too far out of line with fundamentals.[19]

The field of behavioral finance is a young one, but it holds out hope that we might be able to explain some features of securities markets' behavior that are not well explained by the efficient market hypothesis.

[18]Surveys of this field can be found in Hersh Shefrin, *Beyond Greed and Fear: Understanding of Behavioral Finance and the Psychology of Investing* (Boston: Harvard Business School Press, 2000); Andrei Shleifer, *Inefficient Markets* (Oxford: Oxford University Press, 2000); and Robert J. Shiller, "From Efficient Market Theory to Behavioral Finance," Cowles Foundation Discussion Paper No. 1385 (October 2002).

[19]See Robert J. Shiller, *Irrational Exuberance* (New York: Broadway Books, 2001).

SUMMARY

1. The efficient market hypothesis states that current security prices will fully reflect all available information because in an efficient market, all unexploited profit opportunities are eliminated. The elimination of unexploited profit opportunities necessary for a financial market to be efficient does not require that all market participants be well informed.

2. The evidence on the efficient market hypothesis is quite mixed. Early evidence on the performance of investment analysts and mutual funds, whether stock prices reflect publicly available information, the random-walk behavior of stock prices, or the success of so-called technical analysis, was quite favorable to the efficient market hypothesis. However, in recent years, evidence on the small-firm effect, the January effect, market overreaction, excessive volatility, mean reversion, and that new information is not always incorporated into stock prices suggests that the hypothesis may not always be entirely correct. The evidence seems to suggest that the efficient market hypothesis may be a reasonable starting point for evaluating behavior in financial markets but may not be generalizable to all behavior in financial markets.

3. The efficient market hypothesis indicates that hot tips, investment advisers' published recommenda-

tions, and technical analysis cannot help an investor outperform the market. The prescription for investors is to pursue a buy-and-hold strategy—purchase stocks and hold them for long periods of time. Empirical evidence generally supports these implications of the efficient market hypothesis in the stock market.

4. The stock market crashes of 1987 and 2000 have convinced many financial economists that the stronger version of the efficient market hypothesis, which states that asset prices reflect the true fundamental (intrinsic) value of securities, is not correct. It is less clear that the stock market crashes show that the weaker version of the efficient market hypothesis is wrong. Even if the stock market was driven by factors other than fundamentals, the crashes do not clearly demonstrate that many of the basic lessons of the efficient market hypothesis are no longer valid as long as the crashes could not have been predicted.

5. The new field of behavioral finance applies concepts from other social sciences, such as anthropology, sociology, and particularly psychology, to understand the behavior of securities prices. Loss aversion, overconfidence, and social contagion can explain why trading volume is so high, stock prices get overvalued, and speculative bubbles occur.

KEY TERMS

arbitrage, *p. 130*
behavioral finance, *p. 142*
bubble, *p. 141*
efficient market hypothesis, *p. 128*
January effect, *p. 136*
market fundamentals, *p. 131*

mean reversion, *p. 137*
random walk, *p. 132*
short sales, *p. 142*
theory of efficient capital markets, *p. 128*
unexploited profit opportunity, *p. 130*

QUESTIONS

1. "Forecasters' predictions of inflation are notoriously inaccurate, so their expectations of inflation cannot be optimal." Is this statement true, false, or uncertain? Explain your answer.

2. "Whenever it is snowing when Joe Commuter gets up in the morning, he misjudges how long it will take him to drive to work. Otherwise, his expectations of the driving time are perfectly accurate. Considering that it snows only once every 10 years where Joe

lives, Joe's expectations are almost always perfectly accurate." Are Joe's expectations optimal? Why or why not?

3. If a forecaster spends hours every day studying data to forecast interest rates, but his expectations are not as accurate as predicting that tomorrow's interest rates will be identical to today's interest rates, are his expectations optimal?

4. "If stock prices did not follow a random walk, there would be unexploited profit opportunities in the market." Is this statement true, false, or uncertain? Explain your answer.

5. Suppose that increases in the money supply lead to a rise in stock prices. Does this mean that when you see that the money supply has had a sharp rise in the past week, you should go out and buy stocks? Why or why not?

6. If I read in the *Wall Street Journal* that the "smart money" on Wall Street expects stock prices to fall, should I follow that lead and sell all my stocks?

7. If my broker has been right in her five previous buy and sell recommendations, should I continue listening to her advice?

8. Can a person with optimal expectations expect the price of Google to rise by 10% in the next month?

9. "If most participants in the stock market do not follow what is happening to the monetary aggregates, prices of common stocks will not fully reflect information about them." Is this statement true, false, or uncertain? Explain your answer.

10. "An efficient market is one in which no one ever profits from having better information than the rest." Is this statement true, false, or uncertain? Explain your answer.

11. If higher money growth is associated with higher future inflation and if announced money growth turns out to be extremely high but is still less than the market expected, what do you think would happen to long-term bond prices?

12. "Foreign exchange rates, like stock prices, should follow a random walk." Is this statement true, false, or uncertain? Explain your answer.

13. Can we expect the value of the dollar to rise by 2% next week if our expectations are optimal?

14. "Human fear is the source of stock market crashes, so these crashes indicate that expectations in the stock market cannot be optimal." Is this statement true, false, or uncertain? Explain your answer.

QUANTITATIVE PROBLEMS

1. A company has just announced a 3-for-1 stock split, effective immediately. Prior to the split, the company had a market value of $5 billion with 100 million shares outstanding. Assuming that the split conveys no new information about the company, what is the value of the company, the number of shares outstanding, and price per share after the split? If the actual market price immediately following the split is $17.00 per share, what does this tell us about market efficiency?

2. If the public expects a corporation to lose $5 a share this quarter and it actually loses $4, which is still the largest loss in the history of the company, what does the efficient market hypothesis say will happen to the price of the stock when the $4 loss is announced?

WEB EXERCISES

The Efficient Market Hypothesis

1. Visit **http://www.forecasts.org/data/index.htm**. Click on "Stock Index Data" at the very top of the page. Now choose "U.S. Stock Indices-Monthly." Review the indices for the DJIA, the S&P 500, and the NASDAQ composite. Which index appears most volatile? In which index would you have rather invested in 1985 if the investment had been allowed to compound until now?

2. The Internet is a great source of information on stock prices and stock price movements. Go to **http://finance.yahoo.com** and click on the DOW ticker in the Market Summary section to view current data on the Dow Jones Industrial Average. Click on the chart to manipulate the different variables. Change the time range and observe the stock trend over various intervals. Have stock prices been going down over the last day, week, three months, and year?

PART 3

Central Banking and the Conduct of Monetary Policy

CHAPTER **7**

Structure of Central Banks and the Federal Reserve System

Preview

Among the most important players in financial markets throughout the world are central banks, the government authorities in charge of monetary policy. Central banks' actions affect interest rates, the amount of credit, and the money supply, all of which have direct impacts not only on financial markets, but also on aggregate output and inflation. To understand the role that central banks play in financial markets and the overall economy, we need to understand how these organizations work. Who controls central banks and determines their actions? What motivates their behavior? Who holds the reins of power?

In this chapter we look at the institutional structure of major central banks and focus particularly on the Federal Reserve System, the most important central bank in the world. We start by focusing on the formal institutional structure of the Fed and then examine the more relevant informal structure that determines where the true power within the Federal Reserve System lies. By understanding who makes the decisions, we will have a better idea of how they are made. We then look at several other major central banks, particularly the European Central Bank, and see how they are organized. With this information, we will be better able to comprehend the actual conduct of monetary policy described in the following chapter.

Origins of the Federal Reserve System

Of all the central banks in the world, the Federal Reserve System probably has the most unusual structure. To understand why this structure arose, we must go back to before 1913, when the Federal Reserve System was created.

147

Before the twentieth century, a major characteristic of American politics was the fear of centralized power, as seen in the checks and balances of the Constitution and the preservation of states' rights. This fear of centralized power was one source of the American resistance to the establishment of a central bank (see Chapter 18). Another source was the traditional American distrust of moneyed interests, the most prominent symbol of which was a central bank. The open hostility of the American public to the existence of a central bank resulted in the demise of the first two experiments in central banking, whose function was to police the banking system: The First Bank of the United States was disbanded in 1811, and the national charter of the Second Bank of the United States expired in 1836 after its renewal was vetoed in 1832 by President Andrew Jackson.

The termination of the Second Bank's national charter in 1836 created a severe problem for American financial markets, because there was no lender of last resort that could provide reserves to the banking system to avert a bank panic. Hence, in the nineteenth and early twentieth centuries, nationwide bank panics became a regular event, occurring every 20 years or so, culminating in the panic of 1907. The 1907 panic resulted in such widespread bank failures and such substantial losses to depositors that the public was finally convinced that a central bank was needed to prevent future panics.

The hostility of the American public to banks and centralized authority created great opposition to the establishment of a single central bank like the Bank of England. Fear was rampant that the moneyed interests on Wall Street (including the largest corporations and banks) would be able to manipulate such an institution to gain control over the economy and that federal operation of the central bank might result in too much government intervention in the affairs of private banks. Serious disagreements existed over whether the central bank should be a private bank or a government institution. Because of the heated debates on these issues, a compromise was struck. In the great American tradition, Congress wrote an elaborate system of

inside the fed

The Political Genius of the Founders of the Federal Reserve System

The history of the United States has been one of public hostility to banks and especially to a central bank. How were the politicians who founded the Federal Reserve able to design a system that has become one of the most prestigious institutions in the United States?

The answer is that the founders recognized that if power was too concentrated in either Washington, DC, or New York, cities that Americans often love to hate, an American central bank might not have enough public support to operate effectively. They thus decided to set up a decentralized system with 12 Federal Reserve banks spread throughout the country to make sure that all regions of the country were represented in monetary policy deliberations. In addition, they made the Federal Reserve banks quasi-private institutions overseen by directors from the private sector living in each district who represent views from their region and are in close contact with the president of their district's Federal Reserve bank. The unusual structure of the Federal Reserve System has promoted a concern in the Fed with regional issues as is evident in Federal Reserve bank publications. Without this unusual structure, the Federal Reserve System might have been far less popular with the public, making the institution far less effective.

checks and balances into the Federal Reserve Act of 1913, which created the Federal Reserve System with its 12 regional Federal Reserve banks (see the Inside the Fed box, "The Political Genius of the Founders of the Federal Reserve System").

Structure of the Federal Reserve System

go online

www.federalreserve.gov/
pubs/frseries/frseri.htm

Information on the structure of the Federal Reserve System.

The writers of the Federal Reserve Act wanted to diffuse power along regional lines, between the private sector and the government, and among bankers, business people, and the public. This initial diffusion of power has resulted in the evolution of the Federal Reserve System to include the following entities: the **Federal Reserve banks,** the **Board of Governors of the Federal Reserve System,** the **Federal Open Market Committee (FOMC),** the Federal Advisory Council, and around 2,800 member commercial banks. Figure 7.1 outlines the relationships of these

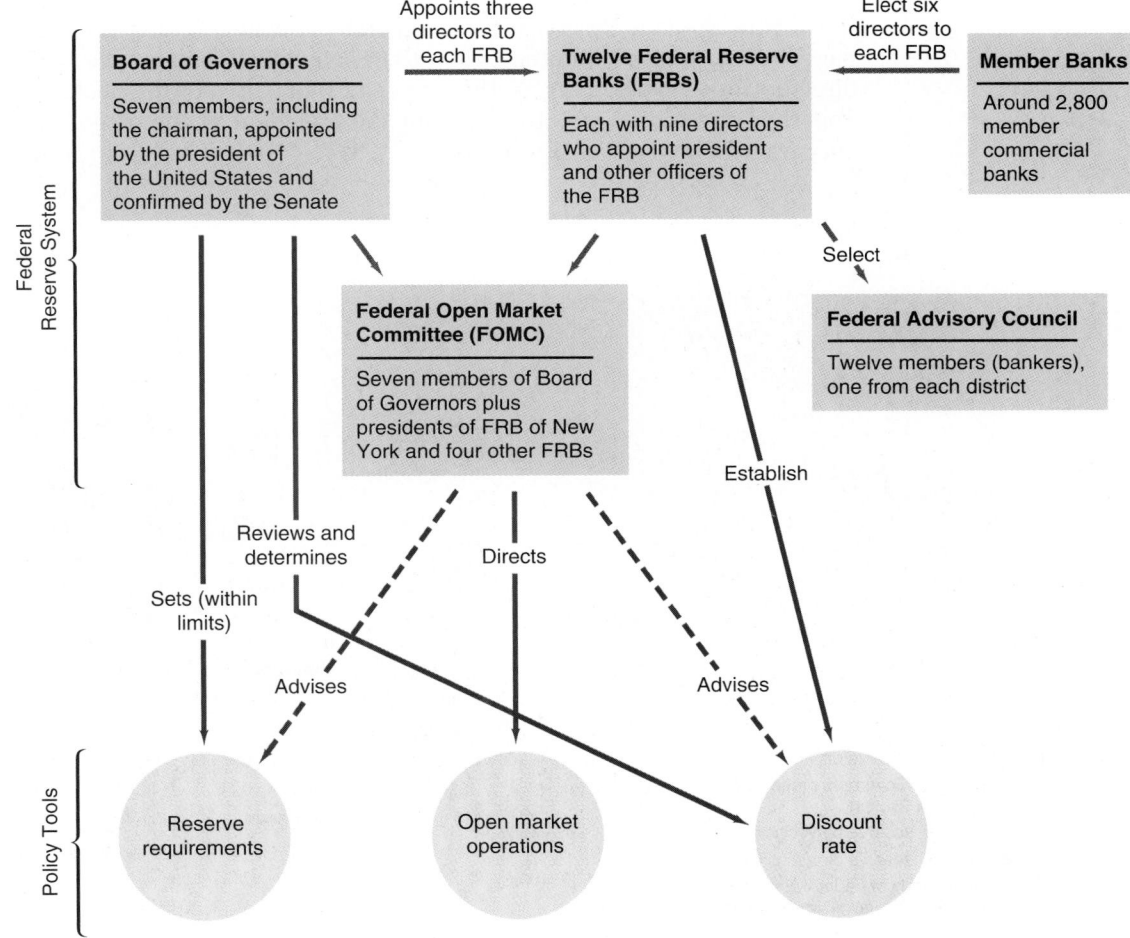

Figure 7.1 Structure and Responsibility for Policy Tools in the Federal Reserve System

Dashed lines indicate that the FOMC "advises" on the setting of reserve requirements and the discount rate.

entities to one another and to the three policy tools of the Fed (open market operations, the discount rate, and reserve requirements) discussed in Chapter 8.

Federal Reserve Banks

go online

www.federalreserve.gov/
otherfrb.htm

Addresses and phone
numbers of Federal Reserve
Banks, branches, and RCPCs
and links to the main pages
of the 12 reserve banks and
Board of Governors.

Each of the 12 Federal Reserve districts has one main Federal Reserve bank, which may have branches in other cities in the district. The locations of these districts, the Federal Reserve banks, and their branches are shown in Figure 7.2. The three largest Federal Reserve banks in terms of assets are those of New York, Chicago, and San Francisco—combined they hold more than 50% of the assets (discount loans, securities, and other holdings) of the Federal Reserve System. The New York bank, with around one-quarter of the assets, is the most important of the Federal Reserve banks (see Inside the Fed box, "The Special Role of the Federal Reserve Bank of New York").

Each of the Federal Reserve banks is a quasi-public (part private, part government) institution owned by the private commercial banks in the district that are members of the Federal Reserve System. These member banks have purchased stock in their district Federal Reserve bank (a requirement of membership), and the dividends paid by that stock are limited by law to 6% annually. The member banks elect six directors for each district bank; three more are appointed by the Board of Governors. Together, these nine directors appoint the president of the bank (subject to the approval of the Board of Governors).

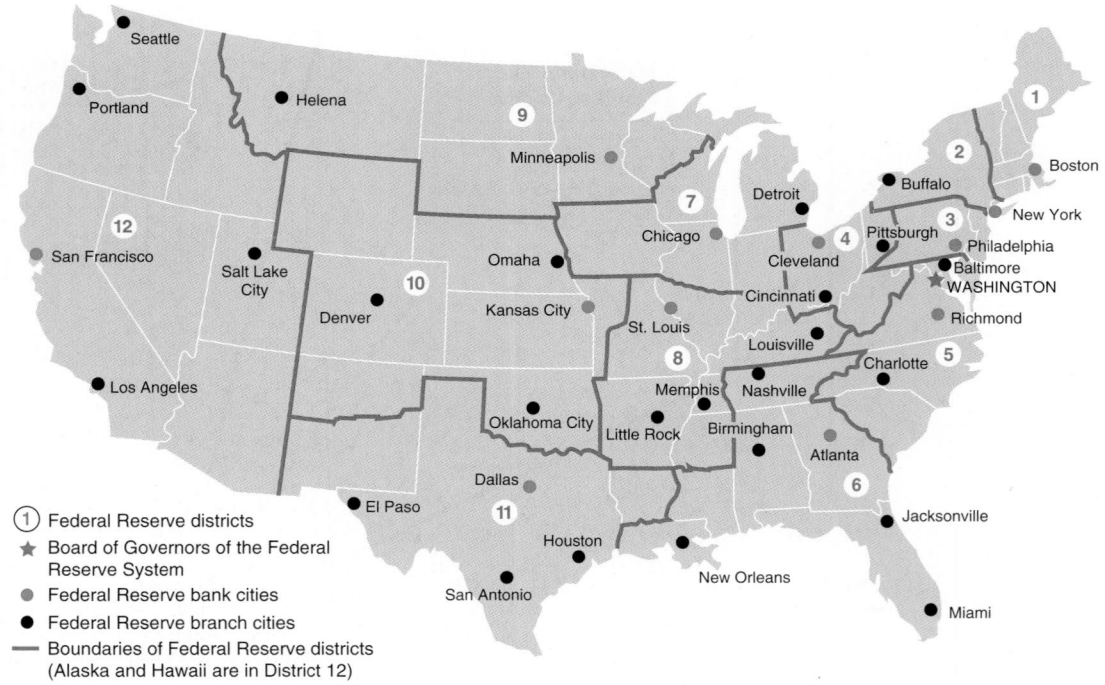

① Federal Reserve districts
★ Board of Governors of the Federal
   Reserve System
● Federal Reserve bank cities
● Federal Reserve branch cities
— Boundaries of Federal Reserve districts
   (Alaska and Hawaii are in District 12)

Figure 7.2 Federal Reserve System

Source: Federal Reserve *Bulletin.*

The Special Role of the Federal Reserve Bank of New York

The Federal Reserve Bank of New York plays a special role in the Federal Reserve System for several reasons. First, its district contains many of the largest commercial banks in the United States, the safety and soundness of which are paramount to the health of the U.S. financial system. The Federal Reserve Bank of New York conducts examinations of bank holding companies and state-chartered member banks in its district, making it the supervisor of some of the most important financial institutions in our financial system. Not surprisingly, given this responsibility, the bank supervision group is one of the largest units of the New York Fed and is by far the largest bank supervision group in the Federal Reserve System.

The second reason for the New York Fed's special role is its active involvement in the bond and foreign exchange markets. The New York Fed houses the open market desk, which conducts open market operations—the purchase and sale of bonds—that determine the amount of reserves in the banking system. Because of this involvement in the Treasury securities market, as well as its walking-distance location near the New York and American Stock Exchanges, the officials at the Federal Reserve Bank of New York are in constant contact with the major domestic financial markets in the United States. In addition, the Federal Reserve Bank of New York houses the foreign exchange desk, which conducts foreign exchange interventions on behalf of the Federal Reserve System and the U.S. Treasury. Its involvement in these financial markets means that the New York Fed is an important source of information on what is happening in domestic and foreign financial markets, particularly during crisis periods, as well as a liaison between officials in the Federal Reserve System and private participants in the markets.

The third reason for the Federal Reserve Bank of New York's prominence is that it is the only Federal Reserve bank to be a member of the Bank for International Settlements (BIS). Thus, the president of the New York Fed, along with the chairman of the Board of Governors, represents the Federal Reserve System in its regular monthly meetings with other major central bankers at the BIS. This close contact with foreign central bankers and interaction with foreign exchange markets means that the New York Fed has a special role in international relations, both with other central bankers and with private market participants. Adding to its prominence in international circles, the New York Fed is the repository for more than $100 billion of the world's gold, an amount greater than the gold at Fort Knox.

Finally, the president of the Federal Reserve Bank of New York is the only permanent member of the FOMC among the Federal Reserve bank presidents, serving as the vice-chairman of the committee. Thus, he and the chairman and vice-chairman of the Board of Governors are the three most important officials in the Federal Reserve System.

The directors of a district bank are classified into three categories: A, B, and C. The three A directors (elected by the member banks) are professional bankers, and the three B directors (also elected by the member banks) are prominent leaders from industry, labor, agriculture, or the consumer sector. The three C directors, who are appointed by the Board of Governors to represent the public interest, are not allowed to be officers, employees, or stockholders of banks. This design for choosing directors was intended by the framers of the Federal Reserve Act to ensure that the directors of each Federal Reserve bank would reflect all constituencies of the American public.

The 12 Federal Reserve banks perform the following functions:

- Clear checks
- Issue new currency

- Withdraw damaged currency from circulation
- Administer and make discount loans to banks in their districts
- Evaluate proposed mergers and applications for banks to expand their activities
- Act as liaisons between the business community and the Federal Reserve System
- Examine bank holding companies and state-chartered member banks
- Collect data on local business conditions
- Use their staffs of professional economists to research topics related to the conduct of monetary policy

The 12 Federal Reserve banks are involved in monetary policy in several ways:

1. Their directors "establish" the discount rate (although the discount rate in each district is reviewed and determined by the Board of Governors).
2. They decide which banks, member and nonmember alike, can obtain discount loans from the Federal Reserve bank.
3. Their directors select one commercial banker from each bank's district to serve on the Federal Advisory Council, which consults with the Board of Governors and provides information that helps in the conduct of monetary policy.
4. Five of the twelve bank presidents each have a vote on the Federal Open Market Committee, which directs **open market operations** (the purchase and sale of government securities that affect both interest rates and the amount of reserves in the banking system). As explained in the Inside the Fed box, "The Special Role of the Federal Reserve Bank of New York," the president of the New York Fed always has a vote on the FOMC, making it the most important of the banks; the other four votes allocated to the district banks rotate annually among the remaining 11 presidents.

Member Banks

All *national banks* (commercial banks chartered by the Office of the Comptroller of the Currency) are required to be members of the Federal Reserve System. Commercial banks chartered by the states are not required to be members, but they can choose to join. Currently, 37% of the commercial banks in the United States are members of the Federal Reserve System, having declined from a peak figure of 49% in 1947.

Before 1980, only member banks were required to keep reserves as deposits at the Federal Reserve banks. Nonmember banks were subject to reserve requirements determined by their states, which typically allowed them to hold much of their reserves in interest-bearing securities. Because no interest is paid on reserves deposited at the Federal Reserve banks, it was costly to be a member of the system, and as interest rates rose, the relative cost of membership rose, and more and more banks left the system.

This decline in Fed membership was a major concern of the Board of Governors: one reason was that it lessened the Fed's control over the money supply, making it more difficult for the Fed to conduct monetary policy. The chairman of the Board of Governors repeatedly called for new legislation requiring all commercial banks to be members of the Federal Reserve System. One result of the Fed's pressure on Congress was a provision in the Depository Institutions Deregulation and Monetary Control Act of 1980: All depository institutions became subject (by 1987) to the same requirements to keep deposits at the Fed, so member and nonmember banks would be on an equal footing in terms of reserve requirements. In addition, all depository institutions were given access to the Federal Reserve facilities, such as the discount window (discussed in Chapter 8) and Fed check clearing, on an equal basis. These provisions ended the decline in Fed membership and reduced the distinction between member and nonmember banks.

Board of Governors of the Federal Reserve System

go online

www.federalreserve.gov/
bios/boardmembership.htm
Lists all the members of the
Board of Governors of the
Federal Reserve since its
inception.

At the head of the Federal Reserve System is the seven-member Board of Governors, headquartered in Washington, DC. Each governor is appointed by the president of the United States and confirmed by the Senate. To limit the president's control over the Fed and insulate the Fed from other political pressures, the governors can serve one full nonrenewable 14-year term plus part of another term, with one governor's term expiring every other January.[1] The governors (many are professional economists) are required to come from different Federal Reserve districts to prevent the interests of one region of the country from being overrepresented. The chairman of the Board of Governors is chosen from among the seven governors and serves a four-year, renewable term. It is expected that once a new chairman is chosen, the old chairman resigns from the Board of Governors, even if there are many years left to his or her term as a governor.

The Board of Governors is actively involved in decisions concerning the conduct of monetary policy. All seven governors are members of the FOMC and vote on the conduct of open market operations. Because there are only twelve voting members on this committee (seven governors and five presidents of the district banks), the Board has the majority of the votes. The Board also sets reserve requirements (within limits imposed by legislation) and effectively controls the discount rate by the "review and determination" process, whereby it approves or disapproves the discount rate "established" by the Federal Reserve banks. The chairman of the Board advises the president of the United States on economic policy, testifies in Congress, and speaks for the Federal Reserve System to the media. The chairman and other governors may also represent the United States in negotiations with foreign governments on economic matters. The Board has a staff of professional economists (larger than those of individual Federal Reserve banks), which provides economic analysis that the board uses in making its decisions. (See the Inside the Fed box, "The Role of the Research Staff.")

Through legislation, the Board of Governors has often been given duties not directly related to the conduct of monetary policy. In the past, for example, the Board set the maximum interest rates payable on certain types of deposits under Regulation Q. (After 1986, ceilings on time deposits were eliminated, but there is still a restriction on paying any interest on business demand deposits.) Under the Credit Control Act of 1969 (which expired in 1982), the Board had the ability to regulate and control credit once the president of the United States approved. The Board of

---

[1]Although technically the governor's term is nonrenewable, a governor can resign just before the term expires and then be reappointed by the president. This explains how one governor, William McChesney Martin, Jr., served for 28 years. Since Martin, the chairman from 1951 to 1970, retired from the Board in 1970, the practice of allowing a governor to, in effect, serve a second full term has not been continued and this is why Alan Greenspan had to retire from the Board after his 14-year term expired in 2006.

The Role of the Research Staff

The Federal Reserve System is the largest employer of economists not just in the United States, but in the world. The system's research staff has around 1,000 people, about half of whom are economists. Of these 500 economists, approximately 250 are at the Board of Governors, 100 are at the Federal Reserve Bank of New York, and the remainder are at the other Federal Reserve banks. What do all these economists do?

The most important task of the Fed's economists is to follow the incoming data on the economy from government agencies and private sector organizations and provide guidance to the policymakers on where the economy may be heading and what the impact of monetary policy actions on the economy might be. Before each FOMC meeting, the research staff at each Federal Reserve bank briefs its president and the senior management of the bank on its forecast for the U.S. economy and the issues that are likely to be discussed at the meeting. The research staff also provides briefing materials or a formal briefing on the economic outlook for the bank's region, something that each president discusses at the FOMC meeting. Meanwhile, at the Board of Governors, economists maintain a large econometric model (a model whose equations are estimated with statistical procedures) that helps them produce their forecasts of the national economy, and they, too, brief the governors on the national economic outlook.

The research staffers at the banks and the board also provide support for the bank supervisory staff, tracking developments in the banking sector and other financial markets and institutions and providing bank examiners with technical advice that they might need in the course of their examinations. Because the Board of Governors has to decide on whether to approve bank mergers, the research staff at both

the board and the bank in whose district the merger is to take place prepare information on what effect the proposed merger might have on the competitive environment. To assure compliance with the Community Reinvestment Act, economists also analyze a bank's performance in its lending activities in different communities.

Because of the increased influence of developments in foreign countries on the U.S. economy, the members of the research staff, particularly at the New York Fed and the Board, produce reports on the major foreign economies. They also conduct research on developments in the foreign exchange market because of its growing importance in the monetary policy process, and to support the activities of the foreign exchange desk. Economists help support the operation of the open market desk by projecting reserve growth and the growth of the monetary aggregates.

Staff economists also engage in basic research on the effects of monetary policy on output and inflation, developments in the labor markets, international trade, international capital markets, banking and other financial institutions, financial markets, and the regional economy, among other topics. This research is published widely in academic journals and in Reserve bank publications. (Federal Reserve bank reviews are a good source of supplemental material for finance students.)

Another important activity of the research staff primarily at the Reserve banks is in the public education area. Staff economists are called on frequently to make presentations to the board of directors at their banks or to make speeches to the public in their district.

Governors also sets margin requirements, the fraction of the purchase price of securities that has to be paid for with cash rather than borrowed funds. It also sets the salary of the president and all officers of each Federal Reserve bank and reviews each bank's budget. Finally, the Board has substantial bank regulatory functions: It approves bank mergers and applications for new activities, specifies the permissible activities of bank holding companies, and supervises the activities of foreign banks in the United States.

Federal Open Market Committee (FOMC)

The FOMC usually meets eight times a year (about every six weeks) and makes decisions regarding the conduct of open market operations, which influence the money supply and interest rates. Indeed, the FOMC is often referred to as the "Fed" in the press: For example, when the media say that the Fed is meeting, they actually mean that the FOMC is meeting. The committee consists of the seven members of the Board of Governors, the president of the Federal Reserve Bank of New York, and the presidents of four other Federal Reserve banks. The chairman of the Board of Governors also presides as the chairman of the FOMC. Even though only the presidents of five of the Federal Reserve banks are voting members of the FOMC, the other seven presidents of the district banks attend FOMC meetings and participate in discussions. Hence they have some input into the committee's decisions.

go online

www.federalreserve.gov/
fomc

Find general information
on the FOMC; its schedule
of meetings, statements,
minutes, and transcripts;
information on its members;
and the "beige book."

Because open market operations are the most important policy tool that the Fed has for controlling the money supply, the FOMC is necessarily the focal point for policymaking in the Federal Reserve System. Although reserve requirements and the discount rate are not actually set by the FOMC, decisions in regard to these policy tools are effectively made there, and this is why Figure 7.1 has dashed lines indicating that the FOMC "advises" on the setting of reserve requirements and the discount rate. The FOMC does not actually carry out securities purchases or sales. Instead, it issues directives to the trading desk at the Federal Reserve Bank of New York, where the manager for domestic open market operations supervises a roomful of people who execute the purchases and sales of the government or agency securities. The manager communicates daily with the FOMC members and their staffs concerning the activities of the trading desk.

The FOMC Meeting

The FOMC meeting takes place in the boardroom on the second floor of the main building of the Board of Governors in Washington, DC. The seven governors and the twelve Reserve Bank presidents, along with the secretary of the FOMC, the Board's director of the Research and Statistics Division and his deputy, and the directors of the Monetary Affairs and International Finance Divisions, sit around a massive conference table. Although only five of the Reserve Bank presidents have voting rights on the FOMC at any given time, all actively participate in the deliberations. Seated around the sides of the room are the directors of research at each of the Reserve banks and other senior board and Reserve Bank officials, who, by tradition, do not speak at the meeting.

The meeting starts with a quick approval of the minutes of the previous meeting of the FOMC. The first substantive agenda item is the report by the manager of system open market operations on foreign currency and domestic open market operations and other issues related to these topics. After the governors and Reserve Bank presidents finish asking questions and discussing these reports, a vote is taken to ratify them.

The next stage in the meeting is a presentation of the Board staff's national economic forecast, referred to as the "green book" forecast (see the Inside the Fed box, "Green, Blue, and Beige"), by the director of the Research and Statistics Division at the board. After the governors and Reserve Bank presidents have queried the division director about the forecast, the *go-round* occurs: Each bank president presents an overview of economic conditions in his or her district and the bank's assessment of the national outlook, and each governor, including the chairman, gives

Green, Blue, and Beige: What Do These Colors Mean at the Fed?

Three research documents play an important role in the monetary policy process and at Federal Open Market Committee meetings. The national forecast for the next two years, generated by the Federal Reserve Board of Governors' Research and Statistics Division, is placed between green covers and is thus known as the "green book." It is provided to all who attend the FOMC meeting. The "blue book," in blue covers, also provided to all participants at the FOMC meeting, contains the projections for the monetary aggregates prepared by the Monetary Affairs Division at the Board of Governors and typically presents three alternative scenarios for the stance of monetary policy (labeled A, B, and C). The "beige book," with beige covers, is produced by the Reserve banks and details evidence gleaned either from surveys or from talks with key businesses and financial institutions on the state of the economy in each of the Federal Reserve districts. This is the only one of the three books that is distributed publicly, and it often receives a lot of attention in the press.

a view of the national outlook. By tradition, remarks avoid the topic of monetary policy at this time.

The agenda then turns to current monetary policy and the domestic policy directive. The Board's director of the Monetary Affairs Division leads off the discussion by outlining the different scenarios for monetary policy actions outlined in the "blue book" (see the aforementioned Inside the Fed box) and may describe an issue relating to how monetary policy should be conducted. After a question-and-answer period, each of the FOMC members, as well as the nonvoting bank presidents, expresses his or her views on monetary policy and on the monetary policy statement. The chairman then summarizes the discussion and proposes specific wording for the directive on the federal funds rate target transmitted to the open market desk and the monetary policy statement. The secretary of the FOMC formally reads the proposed statement and the members of the FOMC vote.[2] A public announcement about the monetary policy statement is made around 2:15 PM.

Why the Chairman of the Board of Governors Really Runs the Show

At first glance, the chairman of the Board of Governors is just one of 12 voting members of the FOMC and has no legal authority to exercise control over this body. So why does the media pay so much attention to every word the chairman speaks? Does the chairman really call the shots at the Fed? And if so, why does the chairman have so much power?

The chairman does indeed run the show. He is the spokesperson for the Fed and negotiates with Congress and the president of the United States. He also exercises control by setting the agenda of Board and FOMC meetings. The chairman also influences the Board through the force of stature and personality. Chairmen of the Board of Governors (including Marriner S. Eccles, William McChesney Martin, Jr.,

---

[2]The decisions expressed in the directive may not be unanimous, and the dissenting views are made public. However, except in rare cases, the chairman's vote is always on the winning side.

Arthur Burns, Paul A. Volcker, Alan Greenspan, and Ben Bernanke) have typically had strong personalities and have wielded great power.

The chairman also exercises power by supervising the Board's staff of professional economists and advisers. Because the staff gathers information for the Board and conducts the analyses that the Board uses in its decisions, it has some influence over monetary policy. In addition, in the past, several appointments to the Board itself have come from within the ranks of its professional staff, making the chairman's influence even farther-reaching and longer-lasting than a four-year term.

How Independent Is the Fed?

When we look, in the next chapter, at how the Federal Reserve conducts monetary policy, we will want to know why it decides to take certain policy actions but not others. To understand its actions, we must understand the incentives that motivate the Fed's behavior. How free is the Fed from presidential and congressional pressures? Do economic, bureaucratic, or political considerations guide it? Is the Fed truly independent of outside pressures?

Stanley Fischer, who was a professor at MIT and is now Governor of the Bank of Israel, has defined two different types of independence of central banks: **instrument independence,** the ability of the central bank to set monetary policy instruments, and **goal independence,** the ability of the central bank to set the goals of monetary policy. The Federal Reserve has both types of independence and is remarkably free of the political pressures that influence other government agencies. Not only are the members of the Board of Governors appointed for a 14-year term (and so cannot be ousted from office), but also the term is technically not renewable, eliminating some of the incentive for the governors to curry favor with the president and Congress.

Probably even more important to its independence from the whims of Congress is the Fed's independent and substantial source of revenue from its holdings of securities and, to a lesser extent, from its loans to banks. In recent years, for example, the Fed has had net earnings after expenses of around $18 billion per year—not a bad living if you can find it! Because it returns the bulk of these earnings to the Treasury, it does not get rich from its activities, but this income gives the Fed an important advantage over other government agencies: It is not subject to the appropriations process usually controlled by Congress. Indeed, the General Accounting Office, the auditing agency of the federal government, cannot audit the monetary policy or foreign exchange market functions of the Federal Reserve. Because the power to control the purse strings is usually synonymous with the power of overall control, this feature of the Federal Reserve System contributes to its independence more than any other factor.

Yet the Federal Reserve is still subject to the influence of Congress, because the legislation that structures it is written by Congress and is subject to change at any time. When legislators are upset with the Fed's conduct of monetary policy, they frequently threaten to take control of the Fed's finances and force it to submit a budget request like other government agencies. A recent example was the call by Senators Dorgan and Reid in 1996 for Congress to have budgetary authority over the nonmonetary activities of the Federal Reserve. This is a powerful club to wield, and it certainly has some effect in keeping the Fed from straying too far from congressional wishes.

Congress has also passed legislation to make the Federal Reserve more accountable for its actions. Under the Federal Reserve Act, the Federal Reserve is required to issue a *Monetary Policy Report to the Congress* semiannually, with accompanying testimony by the chairman of the Board of Governors, to explain how the conduct of monetary policy is consistent with the objectives given by the Federal Reserve Act.

The president can also influence the Federal Reserve. First, because congressional legislation can affect the Fed directly or affect its ability to conduct monetary policy, the president can be a powerful ally through his influence on Congress. Second, although ostensibly a president might be able to appoint only one or two members to the Board of Governors during each presidential term, in actual practice the president appoints members far more often. One reason is that most governors do not serve out a full 14-year term. (Governors' salaries are substantially below what they can earn in the private sector, thus providing an incentive for them to take private sector jobs before their term expires.) In addition, the president is able to appoint a new chairman of the Board of Governors every four years, and a chairman who is not reappointed is expected to resign from the board so that a new member can be appointed.

The power that the president enjoys through his appointments to the Board of Governors is limited, however. Because the term of the chairman is not necessarily concurrent with that of the president, a president may have to deal with a chairman of the Board of Governors appointed by a previous administration. Alan Greenspan, for example, was appointed chairman in 1987 by President Ronald Reagan and was reappointed to another term by a Republican president, George H. W. Bush, in 1992. When Bill Clinton, a Democrat, became president in 1993, Greenspan had several years left to his term. Clinton was put under tremendous pressure to reappoint Greenspan when his term expired and did so in 1996 and again in 2000, even though Greenspan is a Republican.[3] George W. Bush, a Republican, then reappointed Greenspan in 2004.

You can see that the Federal Reserve has extraordinary independence for a government agency and is one of the most independent central banks in the world. Nonetheless, the Fed is not free from political pressures. Indeed, to understand the Fed's behavior, we must recognize that public support for the actions of the Federal Reserve plays a very important role.[4]

Structure and Independence of the European Central Bank

Until recently, the Federal Reserve had no rivals in terms of its importance in the central banking world. However, this situation changed in January 1999 with the start-up of the European Central Bank (ECB) and European System of Central Banks (ESCB), which now conducts monetary policy for countries that are members of

---

[3]Similarly, William McChesney Martin, Jr., the chairman from 1951 to 1970, was appointed by President Truman (Dem.) but was reappointed by Presidents Eisenhower (Rep.), Kennedy (Dem.), Johnson (Dem.), and Nixon (Rep.). Also Paul Volcker, the chairman from 1979 to 1987, was appointed by President Carter (Dem.) but was reappointed by President Reagan (Rep.).

[4]An inside view of how the Fed interacts with the public and the politicians can be found in Bob Woodward, *Maestro: Greenspan's Fed and the American Boom* (New York: Simon and Schuster, 2000).

go online

www.ecb.int
The Web site for the
European Central Bank.

the European Monetary Union. These countries, taken together, have a population that exceeds that in the United States and a GDP comparable to that of the United States. The Maastricht Treaty, which established the ECB and ESCB, patterned these institutions after the Federal Reserve, in that central banks for each country (referred to as *National Central Banks*, or *NCBs*) have a similar role to that of the Federal Reserve banks. The European Central Bank, which is housed in Frankfurt, Germany, has an Executive Board that is similar in structure to the Board of Governors of the Federal Reserve; it is made up of the president, the vice president, and four other members, who are appointed to eight-year, nonrenewable terms. The Governing Council, which comprises the Executive Board and the presidents of the National Central Banks, is similar to the FOMC and makes the decisions on monetary policy. While the presidents of the National Central Banks are appointed by their countries' governments, the members of the Executive Board are appointed by a committee consisting of the heads of state of all the countries that are part of the European Monetary Union.

Differences Between the European System of Central Banks and the Federal Reserve System

In the popular press, the European System of Central Banks is usually referred to as the European Central Bank (ECB), even though it would be more accurate to refer to it as the *Eurosystem*, just as it would be more accurate to refer to the Federal Reserve System rather than the Fed. Although the structure of the Eurosystem is similar to that of the Federal Reserve System, some important differences distinguish the two. First, the budgets of the Federal Reserve Banks are controlled by the Board of Governors, while the National Central Banks control their own budgets *and* the budget of the ECB in Frankfurt. The ECB in the Eurosystem therefore has less power than does the Board of Governors in the Federal Reserve System. Second, the monetary operations of the Eurosystem are conducted by the National Central Banks in each country, so monetary operations are not centralized as they are in the Federal Reserve System. Third, in contrast to the Federal Reserve, the ECB is not involved in supervision and regulation of financial institutions; these tasks are left to the individual countries in the European Monetary Union.

Governing Council

Just as there is a focus on meetings of the FOMC in the United States, there is a similar focus in Europe on meetings of the Governing Council, which meets monthly at the ECB in Frankfurt to make decisions on monetary policy. Currently, 12 countries are members of the European Monetary Union, and the head of each of the 12 National Central Banks has one vote in the Governing Council; each of the six Executive Board members also has one vote. In contrast to FOMC meetings, which staff from both the Board of Governors and individual Federal Reserve banks attend, only the 18 members of the Governing Council attend the meetings, with no staff present.

The Governing Council has decided that although its members have the legal right to vote, no formal vote will actually be taken; instead, the Council operates by consensus. One reason the Governing Council has decided not to take votes is because of worries that the casting of individual votes might lead the heads of National Central Banks to support a monetary policy that would be appropriate for their individual countries, but not necessarily for the countries in the European Monetary Union as a whole. This problem is less severe for the Federal Reserve: Although Federal Reserve bank presidents do live in different regions of the country, all have the same nationality and are more likely to take a national view in monetary policy decisions rather than a regional view.

Just as the Federal Reserve releases the FOMC's decision on the setting of the policy interest rate (the federal funds rate) immediately after the meeting is over, the ECB does the same after the Governing Council meeting concludes (announcing the target for a similar short-term interest rate for interbank loans). However, whereas the Fed simply releases a statement about the setting of the monetary policy instruments, the ECB goes further by having a press conference in which the president and vice president of the ECB take questions from the news media. Holding such a press conference so soon after the meeting is tricky because it requires the president and vice president to be quick on their feet in dealing with the press. The first president of the ECB, Willem F. Duisenberg, put his foot in his mouth at some of these press conferences, and the ECB came under some sharp criticism. His successor, Jean-Claude Trichet, a more successful communicator, has encountered fewer problems in this regard.

Although currently only 12 countries in the European Monetary Union have representation on the Governing Council, this situation is likely to change in the future. Three countries in the European Community already qualify for entering the European Monetary Union: the United Kingdom, Sweden, and Denmark. Ten other countries entered the European Community in 2004 (Cyprus, the Czech Republic, Estonia, Hungary, Latvia, Lithuania, Malta, Poland, Slovakia, and Slovenia), and many of them plan to enter the European Monetary Union once they qualify, which will not be too far in the distant future. The possibly expansion of membership in the Eurosystem presents a particular dilemma. The current size of the Governing Council (18 voting members) is substantially larger than the FOMC (12 voting members). Many commentators have wondered whether the Governing Council is already too unwieldy—a situation that would get considerably worse as more countries join the European Monetary Union. To deal with this potential problem, the Governing Council has decided on a complex system of rotation, somewhat like that for the FOMC, in which National Central Banks from the larger countries will vote more often than National Central Banks from the smaller countries.

How Independent Is the ECB?

Although the Federal Reserve is a highly independent central bank, the Maastricht Treaty, which established the Eurosystem, has made the latter the most independent central bank in the world. Like the Board of Governors, the members of the Executive Board have long terms (8 years), while heads of National Central Banks are required to have terms at least five years long. Like the Fed, the Eurosystem determines its own budget, and the governments of the member countries are not allowed to issue instructions to the ECB. These elements of the Maatricht Treaty make the ECB highly independent.

The Maastricht Treaty specifies that the overriding, long-term goal of the ECB is price stability, which means that the goal for the Eurosystem is more clearly specified than it is for the Federal Reserve System. However, the Maastricht Treaty did not specify exactly what "price stability" means. The Eurosystem has defined the quantitative goal for monetary policy to be an inflation rate slightly less than 2%, so from this perspective, the ECB is slightly less goal-independent than the Fed. The Eurosystem is, however, much more goal-independent than the Federal Reserve System in another way: The Eurosystem's charter cannot be changed by legislation; it can be changed only by revision of the Maastricht Treaty—a difficult process because *all* signatories to the treaty must agree to accept any proposed change.

Structure and Independence of Other Foreign Central Banks

Here we examine the structure and degree of independence of three other important foreign central banks: the Bank of Canada, the Bank of England, and the Bank of Japan.

Bank of Canada

go online
www.bank-banque-canada.ca/
The Web site for the Bank of Canada.

Canada was late in establishing a central bank: The Bank of Canada was founded in 1934. Its directors are appointed by the government to three-year terms, and they appoint the governor, who has a seven-year term. A governing council, consisting of the four deputy governors and the governor, is the policymaking body comparable to the FOMC that makes decisions about monetary policy.

The Bank Act was amended in 1967 to give the ultimate responsibility for monetary policy to the government. So on paper, the Bank of Canada is not as instrument-independent as the Federal Reserve. In practice, however, the Bank of Canada does essentially control monetary policy. In the event of a disagreement between the bank and the government, the minister of finance can issue a directive that the bank must follow. However, because the directive must be in writing and specific and applicable for a specified period, it is unlikely that such a directive would be issued, and none has been to date. The goal for monetary policy, a target for inflation, is set jointly by the Bank of Canada and the government, so the Bank of Canada has less goal independence than the Fed.

Bank of England

go online
www.bankofengland.co.uk/index.htm
The Web site for the Bank of England.

Founded in 1694, the Bank of England is one of the oldest central banks. The Bank Act of 1946 gave the government statutory authority over the Bank of England. The Court (equivalent to a board of directors) of the Bank of England is made up of the governor and two deputy governors, who are appointed for five-year terms, and sixteen non-executive directors, who are appointed for three-year terms.

Until 1997, the Bank of England was the least independent of the central banks examined in this chapter because the decision to raise or lower interest rates resided not within the Bank of England but with the Chancellor of the Exchequer (the equivalent of the U.S. Secretary of the Treasury). All of this changed when the current Labour government came to power in May 1997. At this time, the Chancellor of the Exchequer, Gordon Brown, made a surprise announcement that the Bank of England would henceforth have the power to set interest rates. However, the Bank was not granted total instrument independence: The government can overrule the Bank and set rates "in extreme economic circumstances" and "for a limited period."

Nonetheless, as in Canada, because overruling the Bank would be so public and is supposed to occur only in highly unusual circumstances and for a limited time, it is likely to be a rare occurrence.

Because the United Kingdom is not a member of the European Monetary Union, the Bank of England makes its monetary policy decisions independently from the European Central Bank. The decision to set interest rates resides in the Monetary Policy Committee, made up of the governor, two deputy governors, two members appointed by the governor after consultation with the chancellor (normally central bank officials), plus four outside economic experts appointed by the chancellor. (Surprisingly, two of the four outside experts initially appointed to this committee were not British citizens—one was Dutch and the other American, although both were residents of the United Kingdom.) The inflation target for the Bank of England is set by the Chancellor of the Exchequer, so the Bank of England is also less goal-independent than the Fed.

Bank of Japan

go online
www.boj.or.jp/en/
index.htm
The Web site for the Bank of Japan.

The Bank of Japan (Nippon Ginko) was founded in 1882 during the Meiji Restoration. Monetary policy is determined by the Policy Board, which is composed of the governor; two vice-governors; and six outside members appointed by the cabinet and approved by the parliament, all of whom serve for five-year terms.

Until recently, the Bank of Japan was not formally independent of the government, with the ultimate power residing with the Ministry of Finance. However, the Bank of Japan Law, which took effect in April 1998 and was the first major change in the powers of the Bank of Japan in 55 years, changed this situation. In addition to stipulating that the objective of monetary policy is to attain price stability, the law granted greater instrument and goal independence to the Bank of Japan. Before this, the government had two voting members on the Policy Board, one from the Ministry of Finance and the other from the Economic Planning Agency. Now the government may send two representatives from these agencies to board meetings, but they no longer have voting rights, although they do have the ability to request delays in monetary policy decisions. In addition, the Ministry of Finance lost its authority to oversee many of the operations of the Bank of Japan, particularly the right to dismiss senior officials. However, the Ministry of Finance continues to have control over the part of the Bank's budget that is unrelated to monetary policy, which might limit its independence to some extent.

The Trend Toward Greater Independence

As our survey of the structure and independence of the major central banks indicates, in recent years we have been seeing a remarkable trend toward increasing independence. It used to be that the Federal Reserve was substantially more independent than almost all other central banks, with the exception of those in Germany and Switzerland. Now the newly established European Central Bank is far more independent than the Fed, and greater independence has been granted to central banks like the Bank of England and the Bank of Japan, putting them more on a par with the Fed, as well as to central banks in such diverse countries as New Zealand, Sweden, and the euro nations. Both theory and experience suggest that more independent central banks produce better monetary policy, thus providing an impetus for this trend.

Explaining Central Bank Behavior

One view of government bureaucratic behavior is that bureaucracies serve the public interest (this is the *public interest view*). Yet some economists have developed a theory of bureaucratic behavior that suggests other factors that influence how bureaucracies operate. The *theory of bureaucratic behavior* suggests that the objective of a bureaucracy is to maximize its own welfare, just as a consumer's behavior is motivated by the maximization of personal welfare and a firm's behavior is motivated by the maximization of profits. The welfare of a bureaucracy is related to its power and prestige. Thus, this theory suggests that an important factor affecting a central bank's behavior is its attempt to increase its power and prestige.

What predictions does this view of a central bank like the Fed suggest? One is that the Federal Reserve will fight vigorously to preserve its autonomy, a prediction verified time and time again as the Fed has continually counterattacked congressional attempts to control its budget. In fact, it is extraordinary how effectively the Fed has been able to mobilize a lobby of bankers and business people to preserve its independence when threatened.

Another prediction is that the Federal Reserve will try to avoid conflict with powerful groups that might threaten to curtail its power and reduce its autonomy. The Fed's behavior may take several forms. One possible factor explaining why the Fed is sometimes slow to increase interest rates and so smooths out their fluctuations is that it wishes to avoid a conflict with the president and Congress over increases in interest rates. The desire to avoid conflict with Congress and the president may also explain why in the past the Fed was not at all transparent about its actions and is still not fully transparent (see the Inside the Fed box, "Federal Reserve Transparency").

inside the fed

Federal Reserve Transparency

As the theory of bureaucratic behavior predicts, the Fed has incentives to hide its actions from the public and from politicians to avoid conflicts with them. In the past, this motivation led to a penchant for secrecy in the Fed, about which one former Fed official remarked that "a lot of staffers would concede that [secrecy] is designed to shield the Fed from political oversight."* For example, the Fed pursued an active defense of delaying its release of FOMC directives to Congress and the public. However, as we have seen, in 1994 it began to reveal the FOMC directive immediately after each FOMC meeting. In 1999, it also began to immediately announce the "bias" toward which direction monetary policy was likely to go, later expressed as the balance of risks in the economy. In 2002, the Fed started to report the roll call vote on the federal funds rate target taken at the

FOMC meeting. In December 2004, it moved up the release date of the minutes of FOMC meetings to three weeks after the meeting from six weeks, its previous policy. Obviously, the Fed has increased its transparency in recent years.

In contrast to the Fed, the European Central Bank has decided it will not make the minutes of the Governing Council meetings public for 20 years. In this regard, the European Central Bank is much less transparent than the Fed. Yet even today, the Fed is not fully transparent: It does not publish its forecasts of the economy or its target for the inflation rate, as some other central banks do.

---

*Quoted in "Monetary Zeal: How the Federal Reserve Under Volcker Finally Slowed Down Inflation," *Wall Street Journal*, December 7, 1984, p. 23.

The desire of the Fed to hold as much power as possible also explains why it vigorously pursued a campaign to gain control over more banks. The campaign culminated in legislation that expanded jurisdiction of the Fed's reserve requirements to *all* banks (not just the member commercial banks) by 1987.

The theory of bureaucratic behavior seems applicable to the Federal Reserve's actions, but we must recognize that this view of the Fed as being solely concerned with its own self-interest is too extreme. Maximizing one's welfare does not rule out altruism. (You might give generously to a charity because it makes you feel good about yourself, but in the process you are helping a worthy cause.) The Fed is surely concerned that it conduct monetary policy in the public interest. However, much uncertainty and disagreement exist over what monetary policy should be.[5] When it is unclear what is in the public interest, other motives may influence the Fed's behavior. In these situations, the theory of bureaucratic behavior may be a useful guide to predicting what motivates the Fed and other central banks.

Should the Fed Be Independent?

As we have seen, the Federal Reserve is probably the most independent government agency in the United States. Every few years, the question arises in Congress whether the independence of the Fed should be curtailed. Politicians who strongly oppose a given Fed policy often want to bring it under their supervision so as to impose a policy more to their liking. Should the Fed be independent, or would we be better off with a central bank under the control of the president or Congress?

The Case for Independence

The strongest argument for an independent Federal Reserve rests on the view that subjecting the Fed to more political pressures would impart an inflationary bias to monetary policy. In the view of many observers, politicians in a democratic society are shortsighted because they are driven by the need to win their next election. With this as the primary goal, they are unlikely to focus on long-run objectives, such as promoting a stable price level. Instead, they will seek short-run solutions to problems, such as high unemployment and high interest rates, even if the short-run solutions have undesirable long-run consequences. For example, high money growth might lead initially to a drop in interest rates but might cause an increase later as inflation heats up. Would a Federal Reserve under the control of Congress or the president be more likely to pursue a policy of excessive money growth when interest rates are high, even though it would eventually lead to inflation and even higher interest rates in the future? The advocates of an independent Federal Reserve say yes. They believe that a politically insulated Fed is more likely to be concerned with long-run objectives and thus be a defender of a sound dollar and a stable price level.

A variation on the preceding argument is that the political process in America could lead to a **political business cycle,** in which just before an election, expansionary policies are pursued to lower unemployment and interest rates. After the election, the bad effects of these policies—high inflation and high interest rates—come

---

[5]Economists are not sure how best to measure money. So even if economists agreed that controlling the quantity of money is the appropriate way to conduct monetary policy (a controversial position, as we will see in Chapter 8), the Fed cannot be sure which monetary aggregate it should control.

home to roost, requiring contractionary policies that politicians hope the public will forget before the next election. There is some evidence that such a political business cycle exists in the United States, and a Federal Reserve under the control of Congress or the president might make the cycle even more pronounced.

Putting the Fed under the control of the Treasury (thus making it more subject to influence by the president) is also considered dangerous because the Fed can be used to facilitate Treasury financing of large budget deficits by its purchases of Treasury bonds.[6] Treasury pressure on the Fed to "help out" might lead to more inflation in the economy. An independent Fed is better able to resist this pressure from the Treasury.

Another argument for Fed independence is that control of monetary policy is too important to leave to politicians, a group that has repeatedly demonstrated a lack of expertise at making hard decisions on issues of great economic importance, such as reducing the budget deficit or reforming the banking system. Another way to state this argument is in terms of the principal-agent problem discussed in Chapters 15 and 16. Both the Federal Reserve and politicians are agents of the public (the principals), and as we have seen, both politicians and the Fed have incentives to act in their own interest rather than in the interest of the public. The argument supporting Federal Reserve independence is that the principal-agent problem is worse for politicians than for the Fed because politicians have fewer incentives to act in the public interest.

Indeed, some politicians may prefer to have an independent Fed, which can be used as a public "whipping boy" to take some of the heat off their backs. It is possible that a politician who in private opposes an inflationary monetary policy will be forced to support such a policy in public for fear of not being reelected. An independent Fed can pursue policies that are politically unpopular yet in the public interest.

The Case Against Independence

Proponents of a Fed under the control of the president or Congress argue that it is undemocratic to have monetary policy (which affects almost everyone in the economy) controlled by an elite group that is responsible to no one. The current lack of accountability of the Federal Reserve has serious consequences: If the Fed performs badly, there is no provision for replacing members (as there is with politicians). True, the Fed needs to pursue long-run objectives, but elected officials of Congress also vote on long-run issues (foreign policy, for example). If we push the argument further that policy is always performed better by elite groups like the Fed, we end up with such conclusions as the Joint Chiefs of Staff should determine military budgets or the IRS should set tax policies with no oversight from the president or Congress. Would you advocate this degree of independence for the Joint Chiefs or the IRS?

The public holds the president and Congress responsible for the economic well-being of the country, yet they lack control over the government agency that may well be the most important factor in determining the health of the economy. In addition, to achieve a cohesive program that will promote economic stability, monetary policy must be coordinated with fiscal policy (management of government spending and

---

[6]The Federal Reserve Act prohibited the Fed from buying Treasury bonds directly from the Treasury (except to roll over maturing securities); instead, the Fed buys Treasury bonds on the open market. One possible reason for this prohibition is consistent with the foregoing argument: The Fed would find it harder to facilitate Treasury financing of large budget deficits.

taxation). Only by placing monetary policy under the control of the politicians who also control fiscal policy can these two policies be prevented from working at cross-purposes.

Another argument against Federal Reserve independence is that an independent Fed has not always used its freedom successfully. The Fed failed miserably in its stated role as lender of last resort during the Great Depression, and its independence certainly didn't prevent it from pursuing an overly expansionary monetary policy in the 1960s and 1970s that contributed to rapid inflation in this period.

Our earlier discussion also suggests that the Federal Reserve is not immune from political pressures.[7] Its independence may encourage it to pursue a course of narrow self-interest rather than the public interest.

There is yet no consensus on whether Federal Reserve independence is a good thing, although public support for independence of the central bank seems to have been growing in both the United States and abroad. As you might expect, people who like the Fed's policies are more likely to support its independence, while those who dislike its policies advocate a less independent Fed.

Central Bank Independence and Macroeconomic Performance Throughout the World

We have seen that advocates of an independent central bank believe that macroeconomic performance will be improved by making the central bank more independent. Recent research seems to support this conjecture: When central banks are ranked from least independent to most independent, inflation performance is found to be the best for countries with the most independent central banks.[8] Although a more independent central bank appears to lead to a lower inflation rate, this is not achieved at the expense of poorer real economic performance. Countries with independent central banks are no more likely to have high unemployment or greater output fluctuations than countries with less independent central banks.

SUMMARY

1. The Federal Reserve System was created in 1913 to lessen the frequency of bank panics. Because of public hostility to central banks and the centralization of power, the Federal Reserve System was created with many checks and balances to diffuse power.

2. The formal structure of the Federal Reserve System consists of 12 regional Federal Reserve banks, around 2,800 member commercial banks, the Board of Governors of the Federal Reserve System, the Federal Open Market Committee (FOMC), and the Federal Advisory Council.

---

[7]For evidence on this issue, see Robert E. Weintraub, "Congressional Supervision of Monetary Policy," *Journal of Monetary Economics* 4 (1978): 341–362. Some economists suggest that lessening the independence of the Fed might even reduce the incentive for politically motivated monetary policy; see Milton Friedman, "Monetary Policy: Theory and Practice," *Journal of Money, Credit and Banking* 14 (1982): 98–118.

[8]Alberto Alesina and Lawrence H. Summers, "Central Bank Independence and Macroeconomic Performance: Some Comparative Evidence," *Journal of Money, Credit and Banking* 25 (1993): 151–162. However, Adam Posen, "Central Bank Independence and Disinflationary Credibility: A Missing Link," Federal Reserve Bank of New York Staff Report No. 1, May 1995, has cast some doubt on whether the causality runs from central bank independence to improved inflation performance.

3. Although on paper the Federal Reserve System appears to be decentralized, in practice it has come to function as a unified central bank controlled by the Board of Governors, especially the board's chairman.

4. The Federal Reserve is more independent than most agencies of the U.S. government, but it is still subject to political pressures because the legislation that structures the Fed is written by Congress and can be changed at any time.

5. The European System of Central Banks has a similar structure to the Federal Reserve System, with each member country having a National Central Bank, and an Executive Board of the European Central Bank being located in Frankfurt, Germany. The Governing Council, which is made up of the six members of the Executive Board (which includes the president of the European Central Bank) and the presidents of the National Central Banks, makes the decisions on monetary policy. The Eurosystem, which was established under the terms of the Maastricht Treaty, is even more independent than the Federal Reserve System because its charter cannot be changed by legislation. Indeed, it is the most independent central bank in the world.

6. There has been a remarkable trend toward increasing independence of central banks throughout the world. Greater independence has been granted to central banks such as the Bank of England and the Bank of Japan in recent years, as well as to other central banks in such diverse countries as New Zealand and Sweden. Both theory and experience suggest that more independent central banks produce better monetary policy.

7. The theory of bureaucratic behavior suggests that one factor driving central banks' behavior might be an attempt to increase their power and prestige. This view explains many central bank actions, although central banks may also act in the public interest.

8. The case for an independent Federal Reserve rests on the view that curtailing the Fed's independence and subjecting it to more political pressures would impart an inflationary bias to monetary policy. An independent Fed can afford to take the long view and not respond to short-run problems that will result in expansionary monetary policy and a political business cycle. The case against an independent Fed holds that it is undemocratic to have monetary policy (so important to the public) controlled by an elite that is not accountable to the public. An independent Fed also makes the coordination of monetary and fiscal policy difficult.

KEY TERMS

Board of Governors of the Federal Reserve System, *p. 149*
Federal Open Market Committee (FOMC), *p. 149*
Federal Reserve banks, *p. 149*

goal independence, *p. 157*
instrument independence, *p. 157*
open market operations, *p. 152*
political business cycle, *p. 164*

QUESTIONS AND PROBLEMS

1. Why was the Federal Reserve System set up with twelve regional Federal Reserve banks rather than one central bank, as in other countries?

2. What political realities might explain why the Federal Reserve Act of 1913 placed two Federal Reserve banks in Missouri?

3. "The Federal Reserve System resembles the U.S. Constitution in that it was designed with many checks and balances." Discuss.

4. In what ways can the regional Federal Reserve banks influence the conduct of monetary policy?

5. Which entities in the Federal Reserve System control the discount rate? Reserve requirements? Open market operations?

6. Do you think that the 14-year nonrenewable terms for governors effectively insulate the Board of Governors from political pressure?

7. Compare the structure and independence of the Federal Reserve System and the European System of Central Banks.

8. The Fed is the most independent of all U.S. government agencies. What is the main difference between it and other government agencies that explains the Fed's greater independence?

9. What is the primary tool that Congress uses to exercise some control over the Fed?

10. In the 1960s and 1970s, the Federal Reserve System lost member banks at a rapid rate. How can the theory of bureaucratic behavior explain the Fed's campaign for legislation to require all commercial banks to become members? Was the Fed successful in this campaign?

11. "The theory of bureaucratic behavior indicates that the Fed never operates in the public interest." Is this statement true, false, or uncertain? Explain your answer.

12. Why might eliminating the Fed's independence lead to a more pronounced political business cycle?

13. "The independence of the Fed leaves it completely unaccountable for its actions." Is this statement true, false, or uncertain? Explain your answer.

14. "The independence of the Fed has meant that it takes the long view and not the short view." Is this statement true, false, or uncertain? Explain your answer.

15. The Fed promotes secrecy by not releasing the minutes of the FOMC meetings to Congress or the public immediately. Discuss the pros and cons of this policy.

WEB EXERCISES

The Structure of the Federal Reserve System

1. Go to **www.federalreserve.gov/general.htm** and click on the link to general information. Choose "Structure of the Federal Reserve." According to the Federal Reserve, what is the most important responsibility of the Board of Governors?

2. Go to the above site and click on "Monetary Policy" to find the beige book. According to the summary of the most recently published book, is the economy weakening or strengthening?

CHAPTER 8

Conduct of Monetary Policy: Tools, Goals, Strategy, and Tactics

Preview

Understanding the conduct of monetary policy is important because it affects not only the money supply and interest rates but also the level of economic activity and hence our well-being. To explore this subject, we look first at the Federal Reserve's balance sheet and how the tools of monetary policy affect the money supply and interest rates. Then we examine in more detail how the Fed uses these tools and what goals the Fed and other countries' central banks establish for monetary policy. After examining strategies for conducting monetary policy, we can evaluate central banks' conduct of monetary policy in the past, with the hope that it will give us some clues to where monetary policy may head in the future.

The Federal Reserve's Balance Sheet

The conduct of monetary policy by the Federal Reserve involves actions that affect its balance sheet (holdings of assets and liabilities). Here we discuss the following simplified balance sheet:[1]

Federal Reserve System	
Assets	Liabilities
Government securities	Currency in circulation
Discount loans	Reserves

---

[1]A detailed discussion of the Fed's balance sheet and the factors that affect reserves and the monetary base can be found in the appendix to this chapter, which you can find on this book's Web site at **www.prenhall.com/mishkin_eakins**.

Liabilities

The two liabilities on the balance sheet, currency in circulation and reserves, are often referred to as the *monetary liabilities* of the Fed. They are an important part of the money supply story because increases in either or both will lead to an increase in the money supply (everything else being constant). The sum of the Fed's monetary liabilities (currency in circulation and reserves) and the U.S. Treasury's monetary liabilities (Treasury currency in circulation, primarily coins) is called the **monetary base.** When discussing the monetary base, we will focus only on the monetary liabilities of the Fed because the monetary liabilities of the Treasury account for less than 10% of the base.[2]

go online

www.federalreserve.gov/releases/H3

Historic and current data on the aggregate reserves of depository institutions and the monetary base.

1. *Currency in circulation.* The Fed issues currency (those green-and-gray pieces of paper in your wallet that say "Federal Reserve Note" at the top). Currency in circulation is the amount of currency in the hands of the public (outside of banks)—an important component of the money supply. (Currency held by depository institutions is also a liability of the Fed but is counted as part of reserves.)

   Federal Reserve notes are IOUs from the Fed to the bearer and are also liabilities, but unlike most, they promise to pay back the bearer solely with Federal Reserve notes; that is, they pay off IOUs with other IOUs. Accordingly, if you bring a $100 bill to the Federal Reserve and demand payment, you will receive two $50s, five $20s, ten $10s, or one hundred $1 bills.

   People are more willing to accept IOUs from the Fed than from you or me because Federal Reserve notes are a recognized medium of exchange; that is, they are accepted as a means of payment and so function as money. Unfortunately, neither you nor I can convince people that our own IOUs are worth anything more than the paper on which they are written.[3]

2. *Reserves.* All banks have an account at the Fed in which they hold deposits. **Reserves** consist of deposits at the Fed plus currency that is physically held by banks (called vault cash because it is stored in bank vaults). Reserves are assets for the banks but liabilities for the Fed because the banks can demand payment on them at any time and the Fed is obliged to satisfy its obligation by paying Federal Reserve notes. As you will see, an increase in reserves leads to an increase in the level of deposits and hence in the money supply.

---

[2]It is also safe to ignore the Treasury's monetary liabilities when discussing the monetary base because the Treasury cannot actively supply its monetary liabilities to the economy due to legal restrictions.

[3]The currency item on the Fed's balance sheet refers only to currency in circulation, that is, the amount in the hands of the public. Currency that has been printed by the U.S. Bureau of Engraving and Printing is not automatically a liability of the Fed. For example, consider the importance of having $1 million of your own IOUs printed up. You give out $100 worth to other people and keep the other $999,900 in your pocket. The $999,900 of IOUs does not make you richer or poorer and does not affect your indebtedness. You care only about the $100 of liabilities from the $100 of circulated IOUs. The same reasoning applies for the Fed in regard to its Federal Reserve notes.

For similar reasons, the currency component of the money supply, no matter how it is defined, includes only currency in circulation. It does not include any additional currency that is not yet in the hands of the public. The fact that currency has been printed but is not circulating means that it is not anyone's asset or liability and thus cannot affect anyone's behavior. Therefore, it makes sense not to include it in the money supply.

Total reserves can be divided into two categories: reserves that the Fed requires banks to hold (**required reserves**) and any additional reserves the banks choose to hold (**excess reserves**). For example, the Fed might require that for every dollar of deposits at a depository institution, a certain fraction (say, 10 cents) must be held as reserves. This fraction (10%) is called the **required reserve ratio.** Currently, the Fed pays no interest on reserves. (However, this may change at some point in the future because of legislation passed in 2006 that authorizes the Fed to pay interest on reserve deposits of depository institutions beginning in 2011.)

Assets

The two assets on the Fed's balance sheet are important for two reasons. First, changes in the asset items lead to changes in reserves and consequently to changes in the money supply. Second, because these assets (government securities and discount loans) earn interest while the liabilities (currency in circulation and reserves) do not, the Fed makes billions of dollars every year—its assets earn income, and its liabilities cost nothing. Although it returns most of its earnings to the federal government, the Fed does spend some of it on "worthy causes," such as supporting economic research.

1. *Government securities.* This category of assets covers the Fed's holdings of securities issued by the U.S. Treasury. As you will see, the Fed provides reserves to the banking system by purchasing securities, thereby increasing its holdings of these assets. An increase in government securities held by the Fed leads to an increase in the money supply.
2. *Discount loans.* The Fed can provide reserves to the banking system by making discount loans to banks. An increase in discount loans can also be the source of an increase in the money supply. The interest rate charged banks for these loans is called the **discount rate.**

Open Market Operations

Open market operations, the central bank's purchase or sale of bonds in the open market, are the most important monetary policy tool because they are the primary determinant of changes in reserves in the banking system and interest rates. To see how they work, let's use T-accounts to examine what happens when the Fed conducts an open market purchase in which $100 of bonds are bought from the public.

When the person or corporation that sells the $100 of bonds to the Fed deposits the Fed's check in the local bank, the nonbank public's T-account after this transaction is

Nonbank Public		
Assets		Liabilities
Securities	−$100	
Checkable deposits	+$100	

When the bank receives the check, it credits the depositor's account with the $100 and then deposits the check in its account with the Fed, thereby adding to its reserves. The banking system's T-account becomes

Banking System			
Assets		Liabilities	
Reserves	+$100	Checkable deposits	+$100

The effect on the Fed's balance sheet is that it has gained $100 of securities in its assets column, while reserves have increased by $100, as shown in its liabilities column:

Federal Reserve System			
Assets		Liabilities	
Securities	+$100	Reserves	+$100

As you can see, the result of the Fed's open market purchase is an expansion of reserves and deposits in the banking system. Another way of seeing this is to recognize that open market purchases of bonds expand reserves because the central bank pays for the bonds with reserves. Because the monetary base equals currency plus reserves, we have shown that an open market purchase increases the monetary base by an equal amount. Also, because deposits are an important component of the money supply, another result of the open market purchase is an increase in the money supply. This leads to the following important conclusion: ***An open market purchase leads to an expansion of reserves and deposits in the banking system and hence to an expansion of the monetary base and the money supply.***

Similar reasoning indicates that when a central bank conducts an open market sale, the public pays for the bonds by writing a check that causes deposits and reserves in the banking system to fall. Thus, ***an open market sale leads to a contraction of reserves and deposits in the banking system and hence to a decline in the monetary base and the money supply.***

Discount Lending

Open market operations are not the only way the Federal Reserve can affect the amount of reserves. Reserves are also changed when the Fed makes a discount loan to a bank. For example, suppose that the Fed makes a $100 discount loan to the First National Bank. The Fed then credits $100 to the bank's reserve account. The effects on the balance sheets of the banking system and the Fed are illustrated by the following T-accounts:

Banking System				Federal Reserve System			
Assets		Liabilities		Assets		Liabilities	
Reserves	+$100	Discount loans	+$100	Discount loans	+$100	Reserves	+$100

We thus see that ***a discount loan leads to an expansion of reserves, which can be lent out as deposits, thereby leading to an expansion of the monetary base and the money supply.*** Similar reasoning indicates that ***when a bank repays its discount loan and so reduces the total amount of discount lending, the amount of reserves decreases along with the monetary base and the money supply.***

The Market for Reserves and the Federal Funds Rate

We have just seen how open market operations and discount lending affect the balance sheet of the Fed and the amount of reserves. Now we will analyze the market for reserves to see how the resulting changes in reserves affect the **federal funds rate,** the interest rate on overnight loans of reserves from one bank to another. The federal funds rate is particularly important in the conduct of monetary policy because it is the interest rate that the Fed tries to influence directly. Thus, it is indicative of the Fed's stance on monetary policy.

Open market operations and discount policy are the principal tools that the Fed uses to influence the federal funds rate. In addition, there is a third tool, **reserve requirements,** the regulations making it obligatory for depository institutions to keep a certain fraction of their deposits as reserves with the Fed. We will also analyze how reserve requirements affect the market for reserves and thereby affect the federal funds rate.

Demand and Supply in the Market for Reserves

The analysis of the market for reserves proceeds in a similar fashion to the analysis of the bond market we conducted in Chapter 4. We derive a demand and supply curve for reserves. Then the market equilibrium in which the quantity of reserves demanded equals the quantity of reserves supplied determines the federal funds rate, the interest rate charged on the loans of these reserves.

Demand Curve To derive the demand curve for reserves, we need to ask what happens to the quantity of reserves demanded, holding everything else constant, as the federal funds rate changes. Recall from the previous section that the amount of reserves can be split up into two components: (1) required reserves, which equal the required reserve ratio times the amount of deposits on which reserves are required, and (2) excess reserves, the additional reserves banks choose to hold. Therefore, the quantity of reserves demanded equals required reserves plus the quantity of excess reserves demanded. Excess reserves are insurance against deposit outflows, and the cost of holding these excess reserves is their opportunity cost, the interest rate that could have been earned on lending these reserves out, which is equivalent to the federal funds rate. Thus, as the federal funds rate decreases, the opportunity cost of holding excess reserves falls and, holding everything else constant, including the quantity of required reserves, the quantity of reserves demanded rises. Consequently, the demand curve for reserves, R^d, slopes downward in Figure 8.1.

Supply Curve The supply of reserves, R^s, can be broken up into two components: the amount of reserves that are supplied by the Fed's open market operations, called *nonborrowed reserves* (*NBR*), and the amount of reserves borrowed from the Fed, called *borrowed reserves* (*BR*). The primary cost of borrowing from the Fed is the interest rate the Fed charges on these loans, the discount rate (i_d). Because borrowing federal funds from other banks is a substitute for borrowing (taking out discount loans) from the Fed, if the federal funds rate i_{ff} is below the discount rate i_d, then banks will not borrow from the Fed and borrowed reserves will be zero because borrowing in the federal funds market is cheaper. Thus, as long as i_{ff} remains below

go online

www.economagic.com/
A comprehensive listing of sites that offer a wide variety of economic summary data and graphs.

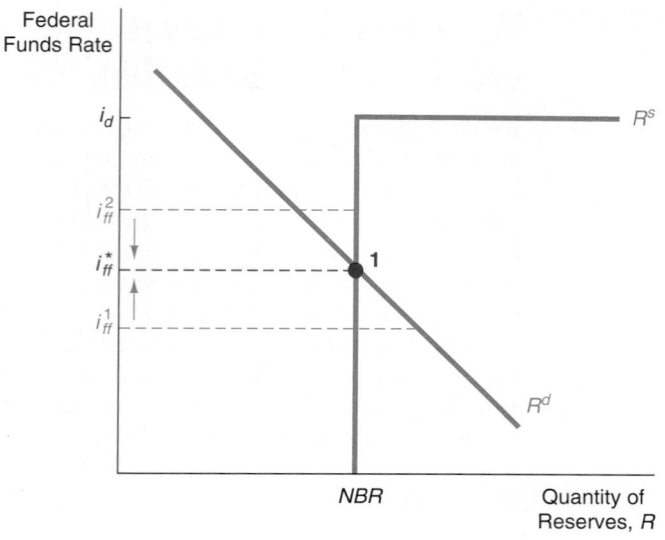

Figure 8.1 Equilibrium in the Market for Reserves

Equilibrium occurs at the intersection of the supply curve R^s and the demand curve R^d at point 1 and an interest rate of i_{ff}^*.

i_d, the supply of reserves will just equal the amount of nonborrowed reserves supplied by the Fed, *NBR*, and so the supply curve will be vertical, as shown in Figure 8.1. However, as the federal funds rate begins to rise above the discount rate, banks would want to keep borrowing more and more at i_d and then lending out the proceeds in the federal funds market at the higher rate, i_{ff}. The result is that the supply curve becomes flat (infinitely elastic) at i_d, as shown in Figure 8.1.

Market Equilibrium Market equilibrium occurs where the quantity of reserves demanded equals the quantity supplied, $R^s = R^d$. Equilibrium therefore occurs at the intersection of the demand curve R^d and the supply curve R^s at point 1, with an equilibrium federal funds rate of i_{ff}^*. When the federal funds rate is above the equilibrium rate at i_{ff}^2, there are more reserves supplied than demanded (excess supply) and so the federal funds rate falls to i_{ff}^* as shown by the downward arrow. When the federal funds rate is below the equilibrium rate at i_{ff}^1, there are more reserves demanded than supplied (excess demand) and so the federal funds rate rises, as shown by the upward arrow. (Note that Figure 8.1 is drawn so that i_d is above i_{ff}^* because the Federal Reserve now keeps the discount rate substantially above the target for the federal funds rate.)

go online
www.federalreserve.gov/fomc/fundsrate.htm
This site lists historical federal funds rates and discusses Federal Reserve targets.

How Changes in the Tools of Monetary Policy Affect the Federal Funds Rate

Now that we understand how the federal funds rate is determined, we can examine how changes in the three tools of monetary policy—open market operations, discount lending, and reserve requirements—affect the market for reserves and the equilibrium federal funds rate.

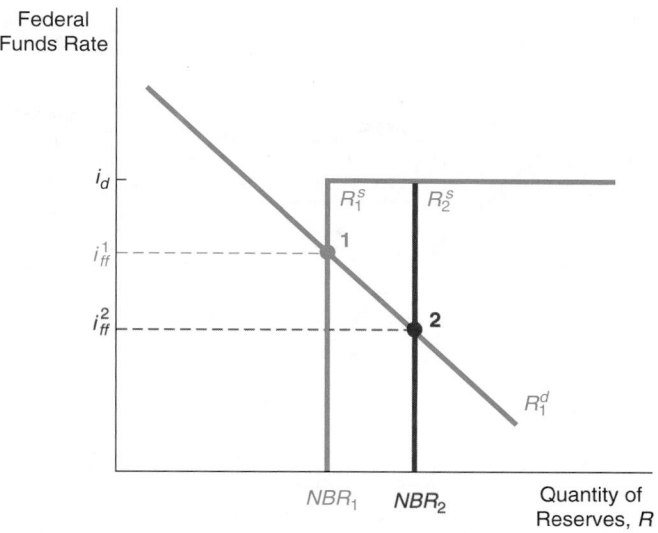

Figure 8.2   Response to an Open Market Operation

An open market purchase increases nonborrowed reserves and hence the reserves supplied, and shifts the supply curve from R_1^s to R_2^s. The equilibrium moves from point 1 to point 2, lowering the federal funds rate from i_{ff}^1 to i_{ff}^2

Open Market Operations We have already seen that an open market purchase leads to a greater quantity of reserves supplied; this is true at any given federal funds rate because of the higher amount of nonborrowed reserves, which rises from NBR_1 to NBR_2. An open market purchase therefore shifts the supply curve to the right from R_1^s to R_2^s and moves the equilibrium from point 1 to point 2, lowering the federal funds rate from i_{ff}^1 to i_{ff}^2 (see Figure 8.2). The same reasoning implies that an open market sale decreases the quantity of nonborrowed reserves supplied, shifts the supply curve to the left, and causes the federal funds rate to rise.

The result is that ***an open market purchase causes the federal funds rate to fall, whereas an open market sale causes the federal funds rate to rise.***

go online
www.frbdiscountwindow
.org/
Information on the operation
of the discount window and
data on current and historical
interest rates.

Discount Lending The effect of a discount rate change depends on whether the demand curve intersects the supply curve in its vertical section versus its flat section. Panel (a) of Figure 8.3 shows what happens if the intersection occurs in the vertical section of the supply curve so there is no discount lending and borrowed reserves, BR, are zero. In this case, when the discount rate is lowered by the Fed from i_d^1 to i_d^2, the horizontal section of the supply curve falls, as in R_2^s, but the intersection of the supply and demand curve remains at point 1. Thus, in this case, there is no change in the equilibrium federal funds rate, which remains at i_{ff}^1. Because this is the typical situation—since the Fed now usually keeps the discount rate above its target for the federal funds rate—the conclusion is that ***most changes in the discount rate have no effect on the federal funds rate.***

However, if the demand curve intersects the supply curve on its flat section, so there is some discount lending (*i.e.*, $BR > 0$), as in panel (b) of Figure 8.3, changes in the discount rate do affect the federal funds rate. In this case, initially discount

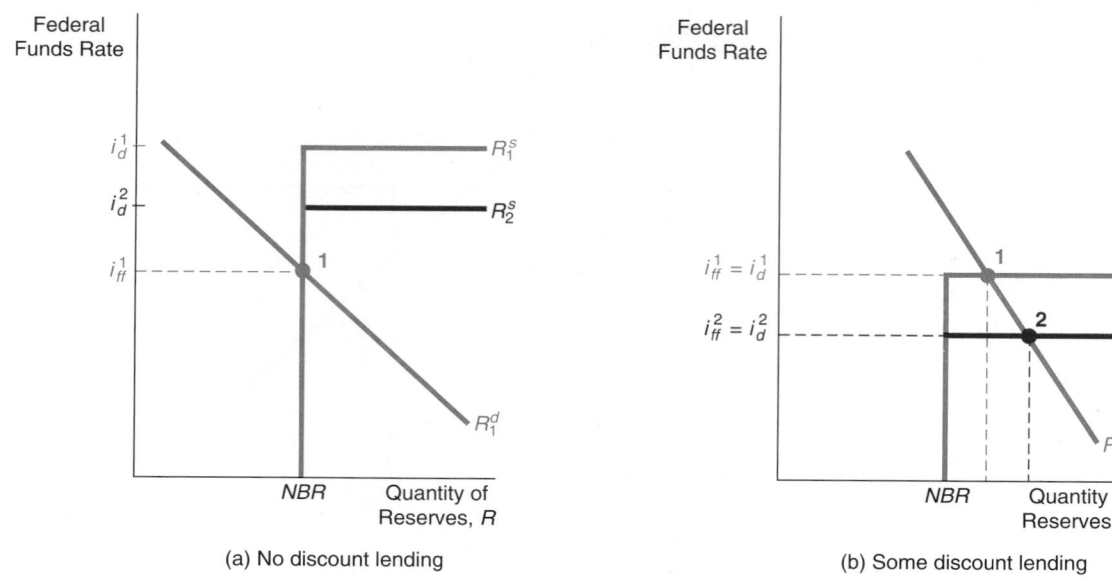

Figure 8.3 Response to a Change in the Discount Rate

In panel (a), when the discount rate is lowered by the Fed from i_1^d to i_2^d, although the horizontal section of the supply curve falls, as in R_2^s, the equilibrium federal funds rate remains unchanged at i_{ff}^1. In panel (b), when the discount rate is lowered by the Fed from i_1^d to i_2^d, the horizontal section of the supply curve R_2^s falls, and the equilibrium federal funds rate falls from i_{ff}^1 to i_{ff}^2.

lending is positive and the equilibrium federal funds rate equals the discount rate, $i_{ff}^1 = i_d^1$. When the discount rate is lowered by the Fed from i_d^1 to i_d^2, the horizontal section of the supply curve R_2^s falls, moving the equilibrium from point 1 to point 2, and the equilibrium federal funds rate falls from i_{ff}^1 to $i_{ff}^2(= i_d^2)$ in panel (b).

go online

www.federalreserve.gov/
monetarypolicy/
reservereq.htm
Historical data and discussion
about reserve requirements.

Reserve Requirements When the required reserve ratio increases, required reserves increase and hence the quantity of reserves demanded increases for any given interest rate. Thus, a rise in the required reserve ratio shifts the demand curve to the right from R_1^d to R_2^d in Figure 8.4, moves the equilibrium from point 1 to point 2, and in turn raises the federal funds rate from i_{ff}^1 to i_{ff}^2. The result is that **when the Fed raises reserve requirements, the federal funds rate rises.**

Conversely, a decline in the required reserve ratio lowers the quantity of reserves demanded, shifts the demand curve to the left, and causes the federal funds rate to fall. **When the Fed decreases reserve requirements, the federal funds rate falls.**

Tools of Monetary Policy

Now that we understand how the three tools of monetary policy—open market operations, discount lending, and reserve requirements—can be used by the Fed to manipulate the money supply and interest rates, we will look at each of them in turn to see how the Fed wields them in practice and how relatively useful each tool is.

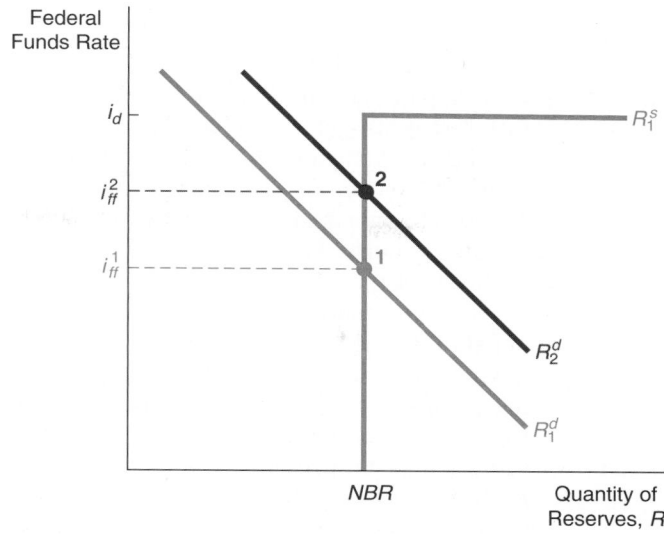

Figure 8.4 Response to a Change in Required Reserves

When the Fed raises reserve requirements, required reserves increase, which increases the demand for reserves. The demand curve shifts from R_1^d to R_2^d. the equilibrium moves from point 1 to point 2, and the federal funds rate rises from i_{ff}^1 to i_{ff}^2.

Open Market Operations

Open market operations are the primary tool used by the Fed to set interest rates. There are two types of open market operations: **Dynamic open market operations** are intended to change the level of reserves and the monetary base, and **defensive open market operations** are intended to offset movements in other factors that affect reserves and the monetary base. The Fed conducts open market operations in U.S. Treasury and government agency securities, especially U.S. Treasury bills.[4] The Fed conducts most of its open market operations in Treasury securities because the market for these securities is the most liquid and has the largest trading volume. It has the capacity to absorb the Fed's substantial volume of transactions without experiencing excessive price fluctuations that would disrupt the market.

As we saw in Chapter 7, the decision-making authority for open market operations is the Federal Open Market Committee (FOMC), which sets a target for the federal funds rate. The actual execution of these operations, however, is conducted by the trading desk at the Federal Reserve Bank of New York. The best way to see how these transactions are executed is to look at a typical day at the trading desk, located in a newly built trading room on the ninth floor of the Federal Reserve Bank of New York.

go online

www.federalreserve
.gov/fomc

A discussion about the Federal Open Market Committee, list of current members, meeting dates, and other current information.

---

[4]To avoid conflicts of interest, the Fed does not conduct open market operations in privately issued securities. (For example, think of the conflict if the Federal Reserve purchased bonds issued by a company owned by the chairman's brother-in-law.)

A Day at the Trading Desk

The manager of domestic open market operations supervises the analysts and traders who execute the purchases and sales of securities in the drive to hit the federal funds rate target. To get a grip on what might happen in the federal funds market that day, her workday and that of her staff begins with a review of developments in the federal funds market the previous day and with an update on the actual amount of reserves in the banking system the day before. Later in the morning, her staff issues updated reports that contain detailed forecasts of what will be happening to some of the short-term factors affecting the supply and demand of reserves.

This information will help the manager of domestic open market operations and her staff decide how large a change in nonborrowed reserves is needed to reach the federal funds rate target. If the amount of reserves in the banking system is too large, many banks will have excess reserves to lend that other banks may have little desire to hold, and the federal funds rate will fall. If the level of reserves is too low, banks seeking to borrow reserves from the few banks that have excess reserves to lend may push the funds rate higher than the desired level. Also during the morning, the staff will monitor the behavior of the federal funds rate and contact some of the major participants in the funds market, which may provide independent information about whether a change in reserves is needed to achieve the desired level of the federal funds rate.

Early in the morning, members of the manager's staff contact several representatives of the **primary dealers,** government securities dealers (who operate out of private firms or commercial banks) that the open market desk trades with. Her staff finds out how the dealers view market conditions to get a feel for what may happen to the prices of the securities they trade in over the course of the day. They also call the Treasury to get updated information on the expected level of Treasury balances at the Fed to refine their estimates of the supply of reserves.

Shortly after 9 AM, members of the Monetary Affairs Division at the Board of Governors are contacted, and the New York Fed's forecasts of reserve supply and demand are compared with the board's. On the basis of these projections and the observed behavior of the federal funds market, the desk will formulate and propose a course of action to be taken that day, which may involve plans to add reserves to or drain reserves from the banking system through open market operations. If an operation is contemplated, the type, size, and maturity will be discussed.

At 9:20 AM, a daily conference call is arranged linking the desk with the Office of the Director of Monetary Affairs at the Board of Governors and with one of the four voting Reserve Bank presidents outside of New York. During the call, a member of the open market operations unit will outline the desk's proposed reserve management strategy for the day. After the plan is approved, the desk is instructed to execute immediately any temporary open market operations that were planned for that day. (Outright operations, to be described shortly, may be conducted at other times of the day.)

The desk is linked electronically with its domestic open market trading counterparties by a computer system called TRAPS (Trading Room Automated Processing System), and all open market operations are now performed over this system. A message will be electronically transmitted simultaneously to all the primary dealers over TRAPS indicating the type and maturity of the operation being arranged. The dealers are given several minutes to respond via TRAPS with their propositions to buy or sell government securities. The propositions are then assembled and displayed on a computer screen for evaluation. The desk will select all propositions, beginning with the most attractively priced, up to the point where the desired amount is purchased or sold, and it will then notify each dealer via TRAPS which of its propositions have been chosen. The entire selection process is typically completed in a matter of minutes.

These temporary transactions are of two basic types. In a **repurchase agreement** (often called a **repo**), the Fed purchases securities with an agreement that the seller will repurchase them in a short period of time, anywhere from one to fifteen days from the original date of purchase. Because the effects on reserves of a repo are reversed on the day the agreement matures, a repo is actually a temporary open market purchase and is an especially desirable way of conducting a defensive open market purchase that will be reversed shortly. When the Fed wants to conduct a temporary open market sale, it engages in a **matched sale-purchase transaction** (sometimes called a **reverse repo**) in which the Fed sells securities and the buyer agrees to sell them back to the Fed in the near future.

At times, the desk may see the need to address a persistent reserve shortage or surplus and wish to arrange an operation that will have a more permanent impact on the supply of reserves. Outright transactions, which involve a purchase or sale of securities that is not self-reversing, are also conducted over TRAPS. These operations are traditionally executed at times of day when temporary operations are not being conducted.

Discount Policy

The facility at which banks can borrow reserves from the Federal Reserve is called the **discount window.** The easiest way to understand how the Fed affects the volume of borrowed reserves is by looking at how the discount window operates.

Operation of the Discount Window

The Fed's discount loans to banks are of three types: primary credit, secondary credit, and seasonal credit.[5] *Primary credit* is the discount lending that plays the most important role in monetary policy. Healthy banks are allowed to borrow all they want at very short maturities (usually overnight) from the primary credit facility, and it is therefore referred to as a **standing lending facility.** The interest rate on these loans is the discount rate, and as we mentioned before, it is set higher than the federal funds rate target, usually by 100 basis points (one percentage point), and thus in most circumstances the amount of discount lending under the primary credit facility is very small. If the amount is so small, why does the Fed have this facility?

The answer is that the facility is intended to be a backup source of liquidity for sound banks so that the federal funds rate never rises too far above the federal funds target set by the FOMC. To see how the primary credit facility works, let's

---

[5]The procedures for administering the discount window were changed in January 2003. The primary credit facility replaced an adjustment credit facility whose discount rate was typically set below market interest rates, so banks were restricted in their access to this credit. In contrast, now healthy banks can borrow all they want from the primary credit facility. The secondary credit facility replaced the extended credit facility, which focused somewhat more on longer-term credit extensions. The seasonal credit facility remains basically unchanged.

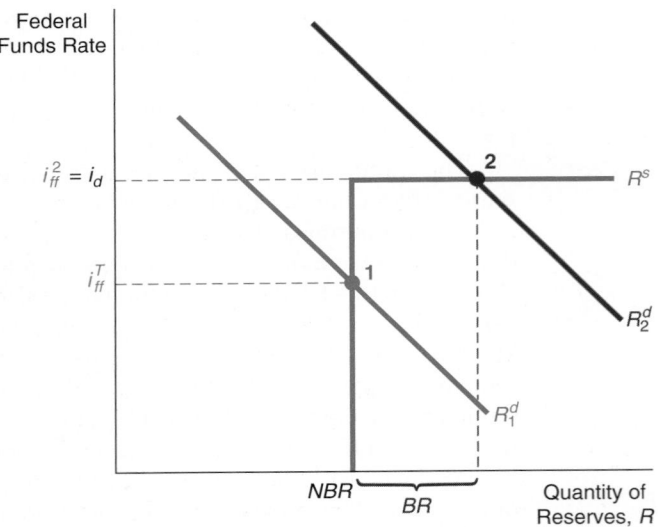

Figure 8.5   How the Primary Credit Facility Puts a Ceiling on the Federal Funds Rate

The rightward shift of the demand curve for reserves from R_1^d to R_2^d moves the equilibrium from point 1 to point 2 where $i_{ff}^2 = i_d$ and borrowed reserves increase from zero to BR.

see what happens if there is a large increase in the demand for reserves, say because deposits have surged unexpectedly and have led to an increase in required reserves. This situation is analyzed in Figure 8.5. Suppose that initially the demand and supply curves for reserves intersect at point 1 so that the federal funds rate is at its target level, i_{ff}^T. Now the increase in required reserves shifts the demand curve to R_2^d and the equilibrium moves to point 2. The result is that borrowed reserves increase from zero to BR and the federal funds rate rises to i_d and can rise no further. The primary credit facility has thus put a ceiling on the federal funds rate of i_d.

Secondary credit is given to banks that are in financial trouble and are experiencing severe liquidity problems. The interest rate on secondary credit is set at 50 basis points (0.5 percentage point) above the discount rate. The interest rate on these loans is set at a higher, penalty rate to reflect the less-sound condition of these borrowers. *Seasonal credit* is given to meet the needs of a limited number of small banks in vacation and agricultural areas that have a seasonal pattern of deposits. The interest rate charged on seasonal credit is tied to the average of the federal funds rate and certificate of deposit rates. The Federal Reserve has questioned the need for the seasonal credit facility because of improvements in credit markets and is thus contemplating eliminating it in the future.

Lender of Last Resort

In addition to its use as a tool to influence reserves, the monetary base, and the money supply, discounting is important in preventing financial panics. When the Federal Reserve System was created, its most important role was intended to be as the **lender of last resort;** to prevent bank failures from spinning out of control, it was to provide reserves to banks when no one else would, thereby preventing bank and financial panics. Discounting is a particularly effective way to provide reserves to the banking system during a banking crisis because reserves are immediately channeled to the banks that need them most.

Using the discount tool to avoid financial panics by performing the role of lender of last resort is an extremely important requirement of successful monetary policy-making. Financial panics can also severely damage the economy because they interfere with the ability of financial intermediaries and markets to move funds to people with productive investment opportunities (see Chapter 15).

Unfortunately, the discount tool has not always been used by the Fed to prevent financial panics, as the massive failures during the Great Depression attest. The Fed learned from its mistakes of that period and has performed admirably in its role of lender of last resort in the post–World War II period. The Fed has used its discount lending weapon several times to avoid bank panics by extending loans to troubled banking institutions, thereby preventing further bank failures. The largest of these occurred in 1984, when the Fed lent Continental Illinois, at that time one of the 10 largest banks in the United States, more than $5 billion.

At first glance, it might seem that the presence of the FDIC, which insures depositors up to a limit of $100,000 per account from losses due to a bank's failure, would make the lender-of-last-resort function of the Fed superfluous. There are two reasons why this is not the case. First, it is important to recognize that the FDIC's insurance fund amounts to around 1% of the amount of these deposits outstanding. If a large number of bank failures occurred, the FDIC would not be able to cover all the depositors' losses. Indeed, the large number of bank failures in the 1980s and early 1990s, described in Chapter 20, led to large losses and a shrinkage in the FDIC's insurance fund, which reduced the FDIC's ability to cover depositors' losses. This fact has not weakened the confidence of small depositors in the banking system because the Fed has been ready to stand behind the banks to provide whatever reserves are needed to prevent bank panics. Second, the nearly $1.8 trillion of large-denomination deposits in the banking system are not guaranteed by the FDIC because they exceed the $100,000 limit. A loss of confidence in the banking system could still lead to runs on banks from the large-denomination depositors, and bank panics could still occur despite the existence of the FDIC. The importance of the Federal Reserve's role as lender of last resort is, if anything, more important today because of the high number of bank failures experienced in the 1980s and early 1990s.

Not only can the Fed be a lender of last resort to banks, but it can also play the same role for the financial system as a whole. The existence of the Fed's discount window can help prevent financial panics that are not triggered by bank failures, as was the case during the Black Monday stock market crash of 1987 and the terrorist destruction of the World Trade Center in September 2001 (see the following Inside the Fed box).

Although the Fed's role as the lender of last resort has the benefit of preventing bank and financial panics, it does have a cost. If a bank expects that the Fed will provide it with discount loans when it gets into trouble, as occurred with Continental Illinois, it will be willing to take on more risk knowing that the Fed will come to the rescue. The Fed's lender-of-last-resort role has thus created a moral hazard problem similar to the one created by deposit insurance (discussed in Chapter 20): Banks take on more risk, thus exposing the deposit insurance agency, and hence taxpayers, to greater losses. The moral hazard problem is most severe for large banks, which may believe that the Fed and the FDIC view them as "too big to fail"; that is,

Using Discount Policy to Prevent a Financial Panic

The Black Monday Stock Market Crash of 1987 and the Terrorist Destruction of the World Trade Center in September 2001. Although October 19, 1987, dubbed "Black Monday," will go down in the history books as the largest one-day percentage decline in stock prices to date (the Dow Jones Industrial Average declined by more than 20%), it was on Tuesday, October 20, 1987, that financial markets almost stopped functioning. Felix Rohatyn, one of the most prominent men on Wall Street, stated flatly: "Tuesday was the most dangerous day we had in 50 years."* Much of the credit for prevention of a market meltdown after Black Monday must be given to the Federal Reserve System and then-chairman of the Board of Governors, Alan Greenspan.

The stress of keeping markets functioning during the sharp decline in stock prices on Monday, October 19, meant that many brokerage houses and specialists (dealer-brokers who maintain orderly trading on the stock exchanges) were severely in need of additional funds to finance their activities. However, understandably enough, New York banks, as well as foreign and regional U.S. banks, growing very nervous about the financial health of securities firms, began to cut back credit to the securities industry at the very time when it was most needed. Panic was in the air. One chairman of a large specialist firm commented that on Monday, "from 2 PM on, there was total despair. The entire investment community fled the market. We were left alone on the field." It was time for the Fed, like the cavalry, to come to the rescue.

Upon learning of the plight of the securities industry, Alan Greenspan and E. Gerald Corrigan, then president of the Federal Reserve Bank of New York and the Fed official most closely in touch with Wall Street, became fearful of a spreading collapse of securities firms. To prevent this from occurring, Greenspan announced before the market opened on Tuesday, October 20, the Federal Reserve System's "readiness to serve as a source of liquidity to support the economic and financial system." In addition to this extraordinary announcement, the Fed made it clear that it would provide discount loans to any bank that would make loans to the securities industry, although this did not prove to be necessary. As one New York banker said, the Fed's message was, "We're here. Whatever you need, we'll give you."

The outcome of the Fed's timely action was that a financial panic was averted. The markets kept functioning on Tuesday, and a market rally ensued that day, with the Dow Jones Industrial Average climbing over 100 points.

A similar lender-of-last-resort operation was carried out in the aftermath of the destruction of the World Trade Center in New York City on Tuesday, September 11, 2001—the worst terrorist incident in U.S. history. Because of the disruption to the most important financial center in the world, the liquidity needs of the financial system skyrocketed. To satisfy these needs and to keep the financial system from seizing up, within a few hours of the incident, the Fed made an announcement similar to that made after the crash of 1987: "The Federal Reserve System is open and operating. The discount window is available to meet liquidity needs."** The Fed then proceeded to provide $45 billion to banks through the discount window, a 200-fold increase over the previous week. As a result of this action, along with the injection of as much as $80 billion of reserves into the banking system through open market operations, the financial system kept functioning. When the stock market reopened on Monday, September 17, trading was orderly, although the Dow Jones average did decline 7%.

The terrorists were able to bring down the twin towers of the World Trade Center, with nearly 3,000 dead. However, they were unable to bring down the U.S. financial system because of the timely actions of the Federal Reserve.

---

*"Terrible Tuesday: How the Stock Market Almost Disintegrated a Day After the Crash," *Wall Street Journal*, November 20, 1987, p. 1. This article provides a fascinating and more detailed view of the events described here and is the source of all the quotations cited.

**"Economic Front: How Policy Makers Regrouped to Defend the Financial System," *Wall Street Journal*, September 18, 2001, p. A1, provides more detail on this episode.

they will always receive Fed loans when they are in trouble because their failure would be likely to precipitate a bank panic.

Similarly, Federal Reserve actions to prevent financial panic may encourage financial institutions other than banks to take on greater risk. They, too, expect the Fed to ensure that they could get loans if a financial panic seems imminent. When the Fed considers using the discount weapon to prevent panics, it therefore needs to consider the trade-off between the moral hazard cost of its role as lender of last resort and the benefit of preventing financial panics. This trade-off explains why the Fed must be careful not to perform its role as lender of last resort too frequently.

Reserve Requirements

Changes in reserve requirements affect the demand for reserves: A rise in reserve requirements means that banks must hold more reserves, and a reduction means that they are required to hold less. The Depository Institutions Deregulation and Monetary Control Act of 1980 provided a simpler scheme for setting reserve requirements. All depository institutions, including commercial banks, savings and loan associations, mutual savings banks, and credit unions, are subject to the same reserve requirements: Required reserves on all checkable deposits—including non-interest-bearing checking accounts, NOW accounts, super-NOW accounts, and ATS (automatic transfer savings) accounts—are equal to 0% of a bank's first $8.5 million of checkable deposits, 3% of a bank's checkable deposits from $8.5 million to $45.8 million, and 10% of checkable deposits over $45.8 million,[6] and the percentage set initially at 10% can be varied between 8% and 14%, at the Fed's discretion. In extraordinary circumstances, the percentage can be raised as high as 18%.

Reserve requirements have rarely been used as a monetary policy tool because raising them can cause immediate liquidity problems for banks with low excess reserves. When the Fed increased these requirements in the past, it usually softened the blow by conducting open market purchases or by making the discount loan window (borrowed reserves) more available, thereby providing reserves to banks that needed them. Continually fluctuating reserve requirements would also create more uncertainty for banks and make their liquidity management more difficult.

Monetary Policy Tools of the European Central Bank

go online
www.federalreserve.gov/general.htm
The Federal Reserve provides links to other central bank Web pages.

Like the Federal Reserve, the European System of Central Banks (which is usually referred to as the European Central Bank) signals the stance of its monetary policy by setting a **target financing rate,** which in turn sets a target for the **overnight cash rate.** Like the federal funds rate, the overnight cash rate is the interest rate for very short-term interbank loans. The monetary policy tools used by the European Central Bank are similar to those used by the Federal Reserve and involve open market operations, lending to banks, and reserve requirements.

[6]The $45.8 million figure is as of the beginning of 2007. Each year, the figure is adjusted upward (or downward) by 80% of the previous year's percentage increase (or decrease) in checkable deposits in the United States. **www.federalreserve.gov/pubs/supplement/2007/02/200702statsup.pdf**.

Open Market Operations

Like the Federal Reserve, the European Central Bank uses open market operations as its primary tool for conducting monetary policy and setting the overnight cash rate at the target financing rate. **Main refinancing operations** are the predominant form of open market operations and are similar to the Fed's repo transactions. They involve weekly **reverse transactions** (purchase or sale of eligible assets under repurchase or credit operations against eligible assets as collateral) that are reversed within two weeks. Credit institutions submit bids, and the European Central Bank decides which bids to accept. Like the Federal Reserve, the European Central Bank accepts the most attractively priced bids and makes purchases or sales to the point where the desired amount of reserves are supplied. In contrast to the Federal Reserve, which conducts open market operations in one location at the Federal Reserve Bank of New York, the European Central Bank decentralizes its open market operations by having them be conducted by the individual national central banks.

A second category of open market operations is the **longer-term refinancing operations,** which are a much smaller source of liquidity for the euro-area banking system and are similar to the Fed's outright purchases or sales of securities. These operations are carried out monthly and typically involve purchases or sales of securities with a maturity of three months. They are not used for signaling the monetary policy stance, but instead are aimed at providing euro-area banks with additional longer-term refinancing.

Lending to Banks

As for the Fed, the next most important tool of monetary policy for the European Central Bank involves lending to banking institutions, which is carried out by the national central banks, just as discount lending is performed by the individual Federal Reserve Banks. This lending takes place through a standing lending facility called the **marginal lending facility.** There, banks can borrow (against eligible collateral) overnight loans from the national central banks at the **marginal lending rate,** which is set at 100 basis points above the target financing rate. The marginal lending rate provides a ceiling for the overnight market interest rate in the European Monetary Union, just as the discount rate does in the United States. In contrast to the U.S. system, but similar to the systems in Canada, Australia, and New Zealand, the Eurosystem has another standing facility, the **deposit facility,** in which banks are paid a fixed interest rate that is 100 basis points below the target financing rate. The prespecified interest rate on the deposit facility provides a floor for the overnight market interest rate, while the marginal lending rate sets a ceiling.

Reserve Requirements

Like the Federal Reserve, the European Central Bank imposes reserve requirements such that all deposit-taking institutions are required to hold 2% of the total amount of checking deposits and other short-term deposits in reserve accounts with national central banks. All institutions that are subject to minimum reserve requirements have access to the European Central Bank's standing lending facilities and participate in open market operations. Unlike the Federal Reserve, the European Central Bank pays interest on reserves. Consequently, the banks' cost of complying with reserve requirements is low.

The Price Stability Goal and the Nominal Anchor

Over the past few decades, policymakers throughout the world have become increasingly aware of the social and economic costs of inflation and more concerned with maintaining a stable price level as a goal of economic policy. Indeed, **price stability,** which central bankers define as low and stable inflation, is increasingly viewed as the most important goal of monetary policy. Price stability is desirable because a rising price level (inflation) creates uncertainty in the economy, and that uncertainty might hamper economic growth. For example, when the overall level of prices is changing, the information conveyed by the prices of goods and services is harder to interpret, which complicates decision making for consumers, businesses, and government, thereby leading to a less efficient financial system.

Not only do public opinion surveys indicate that the public is hostile to inflation, but a growing body of evidence also suggests that inflation leads to lower economic growth.[7] The most extreme example of unstable prices is *hyperinflation*, such as Argentina, Brazil, and Russia have experienced in the recent past. Hyperinflation has proved to be very damaging to the workings of the economy.

Inflation also makes it difficult to plan for the future. For example, it is more difficult to decide how much to put aside to provide for a child's college education in an inflationary environment. Furthermore, inflation can strain a country's social fabric: Conflict might result, because each group in the society may compete with other groups to make sure that its income keeps up with the rising level of prices.

The Role of a Nominal Anchor

Because price stability is so crucial to the long-run health of an economy, a central element in successful monetary policy is the use of a **nominal anchor,** a nominal variable such as the inflation rate or the money supply, which ties down the price level to achieve price stability. Adherence to a nominal anchor that keeps the nominal variable within a narrow range promotes price stability by directly promoting low and stable inflation expectations. A more subtle reason for a nominal anchor's importance is that it can limit the **time-inconsistency problem,** in which monetary policy conducted on a discretionary, day-by-day basis leads to poor long-run outcomes.[8]

The Time-Inconsistency Problem

The time-inconsistency problem is something we deal with continually in everyday life. We often have a plan that we know will produce a good outcome in the long run, but when tomorrow comes, we just can't help ourselves and we renege on our

---

[7]For example, see Stanley Fischer, "The Role of Macroeconomic Factors in Growth," *Journal of Monetary Economics* 32 (1993): 485–512.

[8]The time-inconsistency problem was first outlined in papers by Nobel Prize winners Finn Kydland and Edward Prescott, "Rules Rather Than Discretion: The Inconsistency of Optimal Plans," *Journal of Political Economy* 85 (1977): 473–491; Guillermo Calvo, "On the Time Consistency of Optimal Policy in the Monetary Economy," *Econometrica* 46 (November 1978): 1411–1428; and Robert J. Barro and David Gordon, "A Positive Theory of Monetary Policy in a Natural Rate Model," *Journal of Political Economy* 91 (August 1983): 589–610.

plan because doing so has short-run gains. For example, we make a New Year's resolution to go on a diet, but soon thereafter we can't resist having one more bite of that rocky road ice cream—and then another bite, and then another bite—and the weight begins to pile back on. In other words, we find ourselves unable to *consistently* follow a good plan over *time;* the good plan is said to be *time-inconsistent* and will soon be abandoned.

Monetary policymakers also face the time-inconsistency problem. They are always tempted to pursue a discretionary monetary policy that is more expansionary than firms or people expect because such a policy would boost economic output (or lower unemployment) in the short run. The best policy, however, is *not* to pursue expansionary policy, because decisions about wages and prices reflect workers' and firms' expectations about policy; when they see a central bank pursuing expansionary policy, workers and firms will raise their expectations about inflation, driving wages and prices up. The rise in wages and prices will lead to higher inflation, but will not result in higher output on average.

A central bank will have better inflation performance in the long run if it does not try to surprise people with an unexpectedly expansionary policy, but instead keeps inflation under control. However, even if a central bank recognizes that discretionary policy will lead to a poor outcome (high inflation with no gains in output), it still may not be able to pursue the better policy of inflation control, because politicians are likely to apply pressure on the central bank to try to boost output with overly expansionary monetary policy.

A clue as to how we should deal with the time-inconsistency problem comes from how-to books on parenting. Parents know that giving in to a child to keep him from acting up will produce a very spoiled child. Nevertheless, when a child throws a tantrum, many parents give him what he wants just to shut him up. Because parents don't stick to their "do not give in" plan, the child expects that he will get what he wants if he behaves badly, so he will throw tantrums over and over again. Parenting books suggest a solution to the time-inconsistency problem (although they don't call it that): Parents should set behavior rules for their children and stick to them.

A nominal anchor is like a behavior rule. Just as rules help to prevent the time-inconsistency problem in parenting by helping the adults to resist pursuing the discretionary policy of giving in, a nominal anchor can help prevent the time-inconsistency problem in monetary policy by providing an expected constraint on discretionary policy.

Other Goals of Monetary Policy

While price stability is the primary goal of most central banks, five other goals are continually mentioned by central bank officials when they discuss the objectives of monetary policy: (1) high employment, (2) economic growth, (3) stability of financial markets, (4) interest-rate stability, and (5) stability in foreign exchange markets.

High Employment

High employment is a worthy goal for two main reasons: (1) the alternative situation—high unemployment—causes much human misery, and (2) when unemployment is high, the economy has both idle workers and idle resources (closed factories and unused equipment), resulting in a loss of output (lower GDP).

Although it is clear that high employment is desirable, how high should it be? At what point can we say that the economy is at full employment? At first, it might seem that full employment is the point at which no worker is out of a job—that is, when unemployment is zero. But this definition ignores the fact that some unemployment, called *frictional unemployment*, which involves searches by workers and firms to find suitable matchups, is beneficial to the economy. For example, a worker who decides to look for a better job might be unemployed for a while during the job search. Workers often decide to leave work temporarily to pursue other activities (raising a family, travel, returning to school), and when they decide to reenter the job market, it may take some time for them to find the right job.

Another reason that unemployment is not zero when the economy is at full employment is *structural unemployment*, a mismatch between job requirements and the skills or availability of local workers. Clearly, this kind of unemployment is undesirable. Nonetheless, it is something that monetary policy can do little about.

This goal for high employment is not an unemployment level of zero but a level above zero consistent with full employment at which the demand for labor equals the supply of labor. This level is called the **natural rate of unemployment.**

Although this definition sounds neat and authoritative, it leaves a troublesome question unanswered: What unemployment rate is consistent with full employment? In some cases, it is obvious that the unemployment rate is too high: The unemployment rate in excess of 20% during the Great Depression, for example, was clearly far too high. In the early 1960s, on the other hand, policymakers thought that a reasonable goal was 4%, a level that was probably too low, because it led to accelerating inflation. Current estimates of the natural rate of unemployment place it between 4.5% and 6%, but even this estimate is subject to much uncertainty and disagreement. It is possible, for example, that appropriate government policy, such as the provision of better information about job vacancies or job training programs, might decrease the natural rate of unemployment.

Economic Growth

The goal of steady economic growth is closely related to the high-employment goal because businesses are more likely to invest in capital equipment to increase productivity and economic growth when unemployment is low. Conversely, if unemployment is high and factories are idle, it does not pay for a firm to invest in additional plants and equipment. Although the two goals are closely related, policies can be specifically aimed at promoting economic growth by directly encouraging firms to invest or by encouraging people to save, which provides more funds for firms to invest. In fact, this is the stated purpose of *supply-side economics* policies, which are intended to spur economic growth by providing tax incentives for businesses to invest in facilities and equipment and for taxpayers to save more. There is also an active debate over what role monetary policy can play in boosting growth.

Stability of Financial Markets

Financial crises can interfere with the ability of financial markets to channel funds to people with productive investment opportunities and lead to a sharp contraction in economic activity. The promotion of a more stable financial system in which financial crises are avoided is thus an important goal for a central bank. Indeed, as discussed in Chapter 7, the Federal Reserve System was created in response to the bank panic of 1907 to promote financial stability.

Interest-Rate Stability

Interest-rate stability is desirable because fluctuations in interest rates can create uncertainty in the economy and make it harder to plan for the future. Fluctuations in interest rates that affect consumers' willingness to buy houses, for example, make it more difficult for consumers to decide when to purchase a house and for construction firms to plan how many houses to build. A central bank may also want to reduce upward movements in interest rates for the reasons we discussed in Chapter 7: Upward movements in interest rates generate hostility toward central banks and lead to demands that their power be curtailed.

The stability of financial markets is also fostered by interest-rate stability, because fluctuations in interest rates create great uncertainty for financial institutions. An increase in interest rates produces large capital losses on long-term bonds and mortgages, losses that can cause the failure of the financial institutions holding them. In recent years, more pronounced interest-rate fluctuations have been a particularly severe problem for savings and loan associations and mutual savings banks, many of which got into serious financial trouble in the 1980s and early 1990s (as we will see in Chapter 19).

Stability in Foreign Exchange Markets

With the increasing importance of international trade to the U.S. economy, the value of the dollar relative to other currencies has become a major consideration for the Fed. A rise in the value of the dollar makes American industries less competitive with those abroad, and declines in the value of the dollar stimulate inflation in the United States. In addition, preventing large changes in the value of the dollar makes it easier for firms and individuals purchasing or selling goods abroad to plan ahead. Stabilizing extreme movements in the value of the dollar in foreign exchange markets is thus an important goal of monetary policy. In other countries, which are even more dependent on foreign trade, stability in foreign exchange markets takes on even greater importance.

Should Price Stability Be the Primary Goal of Monetary Policy?

In the long run, there is no inconsistency between the price stability goal and the other goals mentioned earlier. The natural rate of unemployment is not lowered by high inflation, so higher inflation cannot produce lower unemployment or more employment in the long run. In other words, there is no long-run trade-off between inflation and employment. In the long run, price stability promotes economic growth as well as financial and interest-rate stability. Although price stability is consistent with the other goals in the long run, in the short run price stability often conflicts with the goals of high employment and interest-rate stability. For example, when the economy is expanding and unemployment is falling, the economy may become overheated, leading to a rise in inflation. To pursue the price stability goal, a central bank would prevent this overheating by raising interest rates, an action that would initially lower employment and increase interest-rate instability. How should a central bank resolve this conflict among goals?

Hierarchical Versus Dual Mandates

Because price stability is crucial to the long-run health of the economy, many countries have decided that price stability should be the primary, long-run goal for central banks. For example, the Maastricht Treaty, which created the European Central Bank, states, "The primary objective of the European System of Central Banks [ESCB] shall be to maintain price stability. Without prejudice to the objective of price stability, the ESCB shall support the general economic policies in the Community," which include objectives such as "a high level of employment" and "sustainable and non-inflationary growth." Mandates of this type, which put the goal of price stability first, and then say that as long as it is achieved other goals can be pursued, are known as **hierarchical mandates.** They are the directives governing the behavior of central banks such as the Bank of England, the Bank of Canada, and the Reserve Bank of New Zealand, as well as for the European Central Bank.

In contrast, the legislation defining the mission of the Federal Reserve states, "The Board of Governors of the Federal Reserve System and the Federal Open Market Committee shall maintain long-run growth of the monetary and credit aggregates commensurate with the economy's long-run potential to increase production, so as to promote effectively the goals of maximum employment, stable prices, and moderate long-term interest rates." Because, as we learned in Chapter 4, long-term interest rates will be high if there is high inflation, to achieve moderate long-term interest rates, inflation must be low. Thus, in practice, the Fed has a **dual mandate** to achieve two co-equal objectives: price stability and maximum employment.

Is it better for an economy to operate under a hierarchical mandate or a dual mandate?

Price Stability as the Primary, Long-Run Goal of Monetary Policy

Because there is no inconsistency between achieving price stability in the long run and the natural rate of unemployment, these two types of mandates are not very different *if* maximum employment is defined as the natural rate of unemployment. In practice, however, there could be a substantial difference between these two mandates, because the public and politicians may believe that a hierarchical mandate puts too much emphasis on inflation control and not enough on reducing business-cycle fluctuations.

Because low and stable inflation rates promote economic growth, central bankers have come to realize that price stability should be the primary, long-run goal of monetary policy. Nevertheless, because output fluctuations should also be a concern of monetary policy, the goal of price stability should be seen as the primary goal only in the long run. Attempts to keep inflation at the same level in the short run no matter what would likely lead to excessive output fluctuations.

As long as price stability is a long-run goal, but not a short-run goal, central banks can focus on reducing output fluctuations by allowing inflation to deviate from the long-run goal for short periods of time and, therefore, can operate under a dual mandate. However, if a dual mandate leads a central bank to pursue short-run expansionary policies that increase output and employment without worrying about the long-run consequences for inflation, the time-inconsistency problem may recur. Concerns that a dual mandate might lead to overly expansionary policy is a key reason why central bankers often favor hierarchical mandates in which the pursuit of price stability takes precedence. Hierarchical mandates can also be a problem if they lead to a central bank behaving as what the Governor of the Bank of England, Mervyn King, has referred to as an "inflation nutter"—that is, a central bank that focuses solely on inflation control, even in the short run, and so undertakes policies that lead to large output fluctuations. The choice of which type of mandate is better for a central bank ultimately depends on the subtleties of how it will work in practice. Either type of mandate is acceptable as long as it operates to make price stability the primary goal in the long run, but not the short run.

In the following sections, we examine two monetary policy strategies by which policymakers can achieve price stability: monetary targeting and inflation targeting. Both strategies feature a strong nominal anchor and have price stability as the primary, long-run goal of monetary policy.

Monetary Targeting

In pursuing a strategy of **monetary targeting,** the central bank announces that it will achieve a certain value (the target) of the annual growth rate of a monetary aggregate, such as a 5% growth rate of M1 or a 6% growth rate of M2. The central bank then is accountable for hitting the target.

Monetary Targeting in the United States, Japan, and Germany

In the 1970s, monetary targeting was adopted by several countries—most notably, Germany, Switzerland, Canada, the United Kingdom, Japan, and the United States. Monetary targeting as practiced during this decade was quite different from Milton Friedman's suggestion that the chosen monetary aggregate be targeted to grow at a constant rate. Indeed, in all of these countries, the central banks never adhered to strict, ironclad rules for monetary growth. In some of these countries, monetary targeting was not pursued very seriously.

United States In 1970, Arthur Burns was appointed chairman of the Board of Governors of the Federal Reserve, and soon thereafter the Fed stated that it was committing itself to the use of monetary targets to guide monetary policy. In 1975, in response to a congressional resolution, the Fed began to announce publicly its targets for money supply growth, though it often missed them. In October 1979, two months after Paul Volcker became chairman of the Board of Governors, the Fed switched to an operating procedure that focused more on nonborrowed reserves and control of the monetary aggregates and less on the federal funds rate. Despite the change in focus, the performance in hitting monetary targets was even worse: In all three years of the 1979–1982 period, the Fed missed its M1 growth target ranges. What went wrong?

There are several possible answers to this question. The first is that the U.S. economy was exposed to several shocks during this period that made monetary control more difficult: the acceleration of financial innovation and deregulation, which added new categories of deposits such as NOW accounts to the measures of monetary aggregates; the imposition by the Fed of credit controls from March to July 1980, which restricted the growth of consumer and business loans; and the back-to-back recessions of 1980 and 1981–1982.[9]

A more persuasive explanation for poor monetary control, however, is that controlling the money supply was never really the intent of Volcker's policy shift. Despite Volcker's statements about the need to target monetary aggregates, he was not committed to these targets. Rather, he was far more concerned with using interest-rate movements to wring inflation out of the economy. Volcker's primary reason for changing the Fed's operating procedure was to free his hand to manipulate interest rates and thereby fight inflation. It was necessary to abandon interest-rate targets if Volcker were to be able to raise interest rates sharply when a slowdown in the economy was required to dampen inflation. This view of Volcker's strategy suggests that the Fed's announced attachment to monetary aggregate targets may have been a smokescreen to keep the Fed from being blamed for the high interest rates that would result from the new interest-rate policy.

In 1982, with inflation in check, the Fed decreased its emphasis on monetary targets. In July 1993, Board of Governors Chairman Alan Greenspan testified in Congress that the Fed would no longer use any monetary aggregates as a guide for conducting monetary policy.

The Bank of Canada and the Bank of England also made commitments to monetary targets around the same time as the Federal Reserve and had similar experiences to that in the United States. By the 1980s, they found that monetary aggregates were not a reliable guide to monetary policy and, like the Federal Reserve, abandoned monetary targeting. Gerald Bouey, the governor of the Bank of Canada, described his bank's experience colorfully by saying, "We didn't abandon monetary aggregates; they abandoned us."

Japan The increase in oil prices in late 1973 was a major shock for Japan, which experienced a huge jump in the inflation rate, to greater than 20% in 1974—a surge facilitated by money growth in 1973 in excess of 20%. The Bank of Japan, like the other central banks discussed here, began to pay more attention to money supply growth rates. In 1978, the Bank of Japan began to announce "forecasts" at the beginning of each quarter for M2 + CDs. Although the Bank of Japan was not officially committed to monetary targeting, monetary policy appeared to be more money-focused after 1978. For example, after the second oil price shock in 1979, the Bank of Japan quickly reduced M2 + CDs growth, rather than allowing it to shoot up as occurred after the first oil shock. The Bank of Japan now conducts monetary policy with operating procedures that are similar in many ways to those of the Federal Reserve. It uses the interest rate in the Japanese inter-bank market (similar to the federal funds market) as its daily operating target, just as the Fed does.

The Bank of Japan's monetary policy performance during the 1978–1987 period was much better than the Fed's. Money growth in Japan slowed gradually, beginning in the mid-1970s, and was much less variable than in the United States. The outcome was a more rapid braking of inflation and a lower average inflation rate. In

---

[9]Another explanation focuses on the technical difficulties of monetary control when using a non-borrowed reserves operating target under a system of lagged reserve requirements, in which required reserves for a given week are calculated on the basis of the level of deposits two weeks earlier. See David Lindsey, "Nonborrowed Reserve Targeting and Monetary Control," in *Improving Money Stock Control*, ed. Laurence Meyer (Boston: Kluwer-Nijhoff, 1983), pp. 3–41.

addition, these excellent results on inflation were achieved with lower variability in real output than in the United States.

In parallel with the United States, financial innovation and deregulation in Japan began to reduce the usefulness of the M2 + CDs monetary aggregate as an indicator of monetary policy. Because of concerns about the appreciation of the yen, the Bank of Japan significantly increased the rate of money growth from 1987 to 1989. Many observers blame speculation in Japanese land and stock prices (the *bubble economy*) on the increase in money growth. To reduce this speculation, in 1989 the Bank of Japan switched to a tighter monetary policy aimed at slower money growth. The aftermath was a substantial decline in land and stock prices and the collapse of the bubble economy.

The collapse of land and stock prices helped provoke a severe banking crisis, discussed in Chapter 20, that was a severe drag on the economy. As a result, the Japanese economy was in a slump until quite recently. The resulting weakness of the economy even led to deflation, promoting further financial instability. The outcome has been an economy that has stagnated for over a decade. Many critics believe that the Bank of Japan has pursued overly tight monetary policy and needs to substantially increase money growth in order to lift the economy out of its stagnation.

Germany Starting in the mid-1970s and continuing through the next two decades, both Germany and Switzerland engaged in monetary targeting. The success of monetary targeting in controlling inflation in these two countries explains why monetary targeting still has strong advocates and is an element of the official policy regime for the European Central Bank (see the Global box). Because the success of the German monetary targeting regime in producing low inflation has received the most attention, we'll concentrate on Germany's experience.

Germany's central bank, the Bundesbank, chose to focus on a narrow monetary aggregate called *central bank money*, the sum of currency in circulation and bank deposits weighted by the 1974 required reserve ratios. In 1988, the Bundesbank switched targets from central bank money to M3.

The key fact about the monetary targeting regime in Germany is that it was not a Friedman-type monetary targeting rule in which a monetary aggregate is kept on a constant-growth-rate path and is the primary focus of monetary policy. The Bundesbank allowed growth outside of its target ranges for periods of two to three years, and overshoots of its targets were subsequently reversed. Monetary targeting in Germany was instead primarily a method of communicating the strategy of monetary policy focused on long-run considerations and the control of inflation.

The calculation of monetary target ranges put great stress on making policy transparent (clear, simple, and understandable) and on regular communication with the public. First and foremost, a numerical inflation goal was prominently featured in the setting of target ranges. Second, monetary targeting, far from being a rigid policy rule, was flexible in practice. The target ranges for money growth were missed about 50% of the time in Germany, often because of the Bundesbank's concern about other objectives, including output and exchange rates. Furthermore, the Bundesbank demonstrated its flexibility by allowing its inflation goal to vary over time and to converge gradually with the long-run inflation goal.

The monetary-targeting regime in Germany demonstrated a strong commitment to clear communication of the strategy to the general public. The money growth targets were continually used as a framework to explain the monetary policy strategy, and the Bundesbank expended tremendous effort in its publications and in frequent speeches by central bank officials to communicate to the public what the

The European Central Bank's Monetary Policy Strategy

The European Central Bank (ECB) pursues a hybrid monetary policy strategy that has elements in common with the monetary-targeting strategy previously used by the Bundesbank but also includes some elements of inflation targeting.* Like inflation targeting, the ECB has an announced goal for inflation over the medium term of "below, but close to, 2%." The ECB's strategy has two key "pillars." First, monetary and credit aggregates are assessed for "their implications for future inflation and economic growth." Second, many other economic variables are used to assess the future economic outlook. (Until 2003, the ECB employed something closer to a monetary target, setting a "reference value" for the growth rate of the M3 monetary aggregate.)

The ECB's strategy is somewhat unclear and has been subject to criticism for this reason. Although the "below, but close to, 2%" goal for inflation sounds like an inflation target, the ECB has repeatedly stated that it does not have an inflation target. This central bank seems to have decided to try to "have its cake and eat it, too" by not committing too strongly to either a monetary-targeting strategy or an inflation-targeting strategy. The resulting difficulty of assessing the ECB's strategy has the potential to reduce the accountability of the institution.

*For a description of the ECB's monetary policy strategy, go to the ECB's Web site at www.ecb.int.

central bank was trying to achieve. Given that the Bundesbank frequently missed its money growth targets by significant amounts, its monetary-targeting framework is best viewed as a mechanism for transparently communicating how monetary policy is being directed to achieve inflation goals and as a means for increasing the accountability of the central bank.

There are two key lessons to be learned from our discussion of German monetary targeting. First, a monetary targeting regime can restrain inflation in the longer run, even when the regime permits substantial target misses. Thus, adherence to a rigid policy rule is not necessary to obtain good inflation outcomes. Second, the key reason why monetary targeting was reasonably successful, despite frequent target misses, is that the objectives of monetary policy were clearly stated and the central bank actively engaged in communicating the strategy of monetary policy to the public, thereby enhancing the transparency of monetary policy and the accountability of the central bank.

As we will see in the next section, these key elements of a successful monetary-targeting regime—flexibility, transparency, and accountability—are also important elements in inflation-targeting regimes. German monetary policy was actually closer in practice to inflation targeting than it was to Friedman-like monetary targeting, and thus might best be thought of as "hybrid" inflation targeting.

Advantages of Monetary Targeting

One advantage of monetary targeting is that information on whether the central bank is achieving its target is known almost immediately—figures for monetary aggregates are typically reported within a couple of weeks. Thus, monetary targets can send almost immediate signals to the public and markets about the stance of monetary policy and the intentions of the policymakers to keep inflation in check. In turn, these signals help fix inflation expectations and produce less inflation. Monetary targets also allow almost immediate accountability for monetary policy to keep inflation low, thus helping to constrain the monetary policymaker from falling into the time-inconsistency trap.

Disadvantages of Monetary Targeting

All of the above advantages of monetary aggregate targeting depend on a big *if*: There must be a strong and reliable relationship between the goal variable (inflation or nominal income) and the targeted monetary aggregate. If the relationship between the monetary aggregate and the goal variable is weak, monetary aggregate targeting will not work; this seems to have been a serious problem in the United States and other countries that pursued monetary targets. The weak relationship implies that hitting the target will not produce the desired outcome on the goal variable and thus the monetary aggregate will no longer provide an adequate signal about the stance of monetary policy. As a result, monetary targeting will not help fix inflation expectations and will not be a good guide for assessing central bank accountability. In addition, an unreliable relationship between monetary aggregates and goal variables makes it difficult for monetary targeting to serve as a communications device that increases the transparency of monetary policy and makes the central bank accountable to the public.

Inflation Targeting

Given the breakdown of the relationship between monetary aggregates and goal variables such as inflation, many countries have recently adopted inflation targeting as their monetary policy strategy to achieve price stability. New Zealand was the first country to formally adopt inflation targeting in 1990, followed by Canada in 1991, the United Kingdom in 1992, Sweden and Finland in 1993, and Australia and Spain in 1994. Israel, Chile, and Brazil, among others, have also adopted a form of inflation targeting.

Inflation targeting involves several elements: (1) public announcement of medium-term numerical targets for inflation; (2) an institutional commitment to price stability as the primary, long-run goal of monetary policy and a commitment to achieve the inflation goal; (3) an information-inclusive approach in which many variables (not just monetary aggregates) are used in making decisions about monetary policy; (4) increased transparency of the monetary policy strategy through communication with the public and the markets about the plans and objectives of monetary policymakers; and (5) increased accountability of the central bank for attaining its inflation objectives.

Inflation Targeting in New Zealand, Canada, and the United Kingdom

We begin our look at inflation targeting with New Zealand, because it was the first country to adopt it. We then go on to look at the experiences in Canada and the United Kingdom, which were next to adopt this strategy.[10]

---

[10]For further discussion of experiences with inflation targeting, particularly in other countries, see Leonardo Leiderman and Lars E. O. Svensson, *Inflation Targeting* (London: Centre for Economic Policy Research, 1995); Frederic S. Mishkin and Adam Posen, "Inflation Targeting: Lessons from Four Countries," Federal Reserve Bank of New York, *Economic Policy Review* 3 (August 1997), pp. 9–110; and Ben S. Bernanke, Thomas Laubach, Frederic S. Mishkin, and Adam S. Posen, *Inflation Targeting: Lessons from the International Experience* (Princeton: Princeton University Press, 1999).

New Zealand As part of a general reform of the government's role in the economy, the New Zealand parliament passed a new Reserve Bank of New Zealand Act in 1989, which became effective on February 1, 1990. Besides increasing the independence of the central bank, moving it from being one of the least independent to one of the most independent among the developed countries, the act committed the Reserve Bank to a sole objective of price stability. The act stipulated that the minister of finance and the governor of the Reserve Bank should negotiate and make public a Policy Targets Agreement, a statement that sets out the targets by which monetary policy performance will be evaluated, specifying numerical target ranges for inflation and the dates by which they are to be reached. An unusual feature of the New Zealand legislation is that the governor of the Reserve Bank is held highly accountable for the success of monetary policy. If the goals set forth in the Policy Targets Agreement are not satisfied, the governor is subject to dismissal.

The first Policy Targets Agreement, signed by the minister of finance and the governor of the Reserve Bank on March 2, 1990, directed the Reserve Bank to achieve an annual inflation rate within a 3–5% range. Subsequent agreements lowered the range to 0–2% until the end of 1996, when the range was changed to 0–3% and later to 1–3% in 2002. As a result of tight monetary policy, the inflation rate was brought down from above 5% to below 2% by the end of 1992, but at the cost of a deep recession and a sharp rise in unemployment. Since then, inflation has typically remained within the targeted range, with the exception of brief periods in 1995 and 2000 when it exceeded the range by a few tenths of a percentage point. (Under the Reserve Bank Act, the governor, Donald Brash, could have been dismissed, but after parliamentary debates he was retained in his job.) Since 1992, New Zealand's growth rate has generally been high, with some years exceeding 5%, and unemployment has come down significantly.

Canada On February 26, 1991, a joint announcement by the minister of finance and the governor of the Bank of Canada established formal inflation targets. The target ranges were 2–4% by the end of 1992, 1.5–3.5% by June 1994, and 1–3% by December 1996. After the new government took office in late 1993, the target range was set at 1–3% from December 1995 until December 1998 and has been kept at this level. Canadian inflation has also fallen dramatically since the adoption of inflation targets, from above 5% in 1991, to a 0% rate in 1995, and to around 2% subsequently. As was the case in New Zealand, however, this decline was not without cost: Unemployment soared to above 10% from 1991 until 1994, but then declined substantially.

United Kingdom In October 1992, the United Kingdom adopted an inflation target as its nominal anchor, and the Bank of England began to produce an *Inflation Report*, a quarterly report on the progress being made in achieving that target. The inflation target range was initially set at 1–4% until the next election (spring 1997 at the latest), with the intent that the inflation rate should settle down to the lower half of the range (below 2.5%). In May 1997, the inflation target was set at 2.5% and the Bank of England was given the power to set interest rates henceforth, granting it a more independent role in monetary policy.

Before the adoption of inflation targets, inflation had already been falling in the United Kingdom, with a peak of 9% at the beginning of 1991 and a rate of 4% at the time of adoption. By the third quarter of 1994, it was at 2.2%, within the intended range. Subsequently inflation rose, climbing slightly above the 2.5% level by the end of 1995, but then fell and has remained close to the target since then. In December 2003, the target was changed to 2.0% for a slightly different measure of inflation. Meanwhile, growth of the UK economy has been strong, causing a substantial reduction in the unemployment rate.

Advantages of Inflation Targeting

Inflation targeting has several advantages over monetary targeting as a strategy for the conduct of monetary policy. With inflation targeting, stability in the relationship between money and inflation is not critical to its success, because it does not rely on this relationship. An inflation target allows the monetary authorities to use all available information, not just one variable, to determine the best settings for monetary policy.

Inflation targeting also has the key advantage that it is readily understood by the public and is thus highly transparent. Monetary targets, in contrast, are less likely to be easily understood by the public, and if the relationship between the growth rates of monetary aggregates and the inflation goal variable is subject to unpredictable shifts, as has occurred in many countries, monetary targets lose their transparency because they are no longer able to accurately signal the stance of monetary policy.

Because an explicit numerical inflation target increases the accountability of the central bank, inflation targeting has the potential to reduce the likelihood that the central bank will fall into the time-inconsistency trap of trying to expand output and employment in the short run by pursuing overly expansionary monetary policy. A key advantage of inflation targeting is that it can help focus the political debate on what a central bank can do in the long run—that is, control inflation, rather than what it cannot do, permanently increase economic growth and the number of jobs through expansionary monetary policy. Thus, inflation targeting has the potential to reduce political pressures on the central bank to pursue inflationary monetary policy and thereby to reduce the likelihood of the time-inconsistency problem.

Inflation-targeting regimes also put great stress on making policy transparent and on regular communication with the public. Inflation-targeting central banks have frequent communications with the government, some mandated by law and some in response to informal inquiries, and their officials take every opportunity to make public speeches on their monetary policy strategy. While these techniques are also commonly used in countries that have not adopted inflation targeting, inflation-targeting central banks have taken public outreach a step further: Not only do they engage in extended public information campaigns, including the distribution of glossy brochures, but they also publish documents like the Bank of England's *Inflation Report*. The publication of these documents is particularly noteworthy, because they depart from the usual dull-looking, formal reports of central banks and use fancy graphics, boxes, and other eye-catching design elements to engage the public's interest.

The above channels of communication are used by central banks in inflation-targeting countries to explain the following concepts to the general public, financial market participants, and politicians: (1) the goals and limitations of monetary policy, including the rationale for inflation targets; (2) the numerical values of the inflation targets and how they were determined; (3) how the inflation targets are to be achieved, given current economic conditions; and (4) reasons for any deviations from targets. These communications have improved private sector planning by reducing uncertainty about monetary policy, interest rates, and inflation; they have promoted public debate of monetary policy, in part by educating the public about what a central bank can and cannot achieve; and they have helped clarify the responsibilities of the central bank and of politicians in the conduct of monetary policy.

Another key feature of inflation-targeting regimes is the tendency toward increased accountability of the central bank. Indeed, transparency and communication go hand in hand with increased accountability. The strongest case of accountability of a central bank in an inflation-targeting regime is in New Zealand, where the government has the right to dismiss the Reserve Bank's governor if the inflation targets are breached, even for one quarter. In other inflation-targeting countries, the central bank's accountability is less formalized. Nevertheless, the transparency of policy associated with inflation targeting has tended to make the central bank highly accountable to the public and the government. Sustained success in the conduct of monetary policy as measured against a pre-announced and well-defined inflation target can be instrumental in building public support for a central bank's independence and for its policies. This building of public support and accountability occurs even in the absence of a rigidly defined and legalistic standard of performance evaluation and punishment.

The performance of inflation-targeting regimes has been quite good. Inflation-targeting countries seem to have significantly reduced both the rate of inflation and inflation expectations beyond what would likely have occurred in the absence of inflation targets. Furthermore, once down, inflation in these countries has stayed down; following disinflations, the inflation rate in targeting countries has not bounced back up during subsequent cyclical expansions of the economy.

Disadvantages of Inflation Targeting

Critics of inflation targeting cite four disadvantages of this monetary policy strategy: delayed signaling, too much rigidity, the potential for increased output fluctuations, and low economic growth. We look at each in turn and examine the validity of these criticisms.

Delayed Signaling In contrast to monetary aggregates, inflation is not easily controlled by the monetary authorities. Furthermore, because of the long lags in the effects of monetary policy, inflation outcomes are revealed only after a substantial lag. Thus, an inflation target is unable to send immediate signals to both the public and markets about the stance of monetary policy. However, we have seen that the signals provided by monetary aggregates may not be very strong. Hence, it is not at all clear that monetary targeting is superior to inflation targeting on these grounds.

Too Much Rigidity Some economists have criticized inflation targeting because they believe it imposes a rigid rule on monetary policymakers and limits their ability to respond to unforeseen circumstances. However, useful policy strategies exist that are "rule-like," in that they involve forward-looking behavior that limits policymakers from systematically engaging in policies with undesirable long-run consequences. Such policies avoid the time-inconsistency problem and would best be described as "constrained discretion."

Indeed, inflation targeting can be described exactly in this way. Inflation targeting, as actually practiced, is far from rigid and is better described as "flexible inflation targeting." First, inflation targeting does not prescribe simple and mechanical instructions on how the central bank should conduct monetary policy. Rather, it requires the central bank to use all available information to determine which policy actions are appropriate to achieve the inflation target. Unlike simple policy rules, inflation targeting never requires the central bank to focus solely on one key variable. Second, inflation targeting as practiced contains a substantial degree of policy discretion. Inflation targets have been modified depending on economic circumstances, as we have seen. Moreover, central banks under inflation-targeting regimes have left themselves considerable scope to respond to output growth and fluctuations through several devices.

Potential for Increased Output Fluctuations An important criticism of inflation targeting is that a sole focus on inflation may lead to monetary policy that is too tight when inflation is above target and thus may lead to larger output fluctuations. Inflation targeting does not, however, require a sole focus on inflation—in fact, experience has shown that inflation targeters display substantial concern about output fluctuations. All the inflation targeters have set their inflation targets above zero.[11] For example, currently New Zealand has the lowest midpoint for an inflation target, 1.5%, while Canada and Sweden set the midpoint of their inflation target at 2%; and the United Kingdom and Australia currently have their midpoints at 2.5%.

The decision by inflation targeters to choose inflation targets above zero reflects the concern of monetary policymakers that particularly low inflation can have substantial negative effects on real economic activity. Deflation (negative inflation in which the price level actually falls) is especially to be feared because of the possibility that it may promote financial instability and precipitate a severe economic contraction (Chapter 15). The deflation in Japan in recent years has been an important factor in the weakening of the Japanese financial system and economy. Targeting inflation rates of above zero makes periods of deflation less likely. This is one reason why some economists, both within and outside of Japan, have been calling on the Bank of Japan to adopt an inflation target at levels of 2% or higher.

Inflation targeting also does not ignore traditional stabilization goals. Central bankers in inflation-targeting countries continue to express their concern about fluctuations in output and employment, and the ability to accommodate short-run stabilization goals to some degree is built into all inflation-targeting regimes. All inflation-targeting countries have been willing to minimize output declines by gradually lowering medium-term inflation targets toward the long-run goal.

Low Economic Growth Another common concern about inflation targeting is that it will lead to low growth in output and employment. Although inflation reduction has been associated with below-normal output during disinflationary phases in inflation-targeting regimes, once low inflation levels were achieved, output and employment returned to levels at least as high as they were before. A conservative conclusion is that once low inflation is achieved, inflation targeting is not harmful to the real economy. Given the strong economic growth after disinflation in many countries (such as New Zealand) that have adopted inflation targets, a case can be made that inflation targeting promotes real economic growth, in addition to controlling inflation.

---

[11]Consumer price indexes have been found to have an upward bias in the measurement of true inflation, so it is not surprising that inflation targets would be chosen to exceed zero. However, the actual targets have been set to exceed the estimates of this measurement bias, indicating that inflation targeters have decided to have targets for inflation that exceed zero even after measurement bias is accounted for.

inside the fed

The New Fed Chairman and Inflation Targeting

Ben Bernanke, a former professor at Princeton University, became the new Federal Reserve Chairman in February 2006, after serving as a member of the Board of Governors from 2002–2005 and then as the chairman of the Council of Economic Advisers. Bernanke is a world-renowned expert on monetary policy and while an academic wrote extensively on inflation targeting, including articles and a book written with the author of this text.*

Bernanke's writings suggest that he is a strong proponent of inflation targeting and increased transparency in central banks. In an important speech given at a conference at the Federal Reserve Bank of St. Louis in 2004, he described how the Federal Reserve might approach a movement toward inflation targeting.** Bernanke suggested that the Fed should announce a numerical value for its long-run inflation goal, which he labeled the *optimal level of the inflation rate* (OLIR). Bernanke emphasized that announcing the OLIR would be completely consistent with the Fed's dual mandate of achieving price stability and maximum employment because it would be set above zero to avoid deflations, which have harmful effects

on employment, and would not be intended to be a short-run target that might lead to too tight control of inflation at the expense of overly high employment fluctuations.

Since becoming Fed chairman, Bernanke has made it clear that any movement toward inflation targeting must result from a consensus within the Federal Reserve. Under Chairman Bernanke, some movement toward greater transparency about the Fed's inflation goals is likely, but how far the Fed will move toward inflation targeting is still uncertain.

*Ben S. Bernanke and Frederic S. Mishkin, "Inflation Targeting: A New Framework for Monetary Policy," *Journal of Economic Perspectives*, vol. 11, no. 2 (1997); Ben S. Bernanke, Frederic S. Mishkin and Adam S. Posen, "Inflation Targeting: Fed Policy After Greenspan," *Milken Institute Review*, (Fourth Quarter, 1999): 48–56; Ben S. Bernanke, Frederic S. Mishkin and Adam S. Posen, "What Happens When Greenspan is Gone," *Wall Street Journal*, January 5, 2000: p. A22; and Ben S. Bernanke, Thomas Laubach, Frederic S. Mishkin and Adam S. Posen, *Inflation Targeting: Lessons from the International Experience* (Princeton, NJ: Princeton University Press 1999).

**Ben S. Bernanke, "Inflation Targeting," Federal Reserve Bank of St. Louis, *Review*, vol 86, no. 4 (July/August 2004), pp. 165–168.

The Fed's monetary policy strategy may move more toward inflation targeting in the future, particularly with the appointment of a new chairman of the Fed, Ben Bernanke, who has been an advocate of inflation targeting. (See the Inside the Fed box, "The New Fed Chairman and Inflation Targeting.") Inflation targeting is not too far from the Fed's current policymaking philosophy, which has stressed the importance of price stability as the overriding, long-run goal of monetary policy. Also, a move to inflation targeting is consistent with recent steps by the Fed to increase the transparency of monetary policy, such as shortening the time before the minutes of the FOMC meeting are released, the practice of announcing the FOMC's decision about whether to change the target for the federal funds rates immediately after the conclusion of the FOMC meeting, and the announcement of the "balance of risks" in the future, whether toward higher inflation or toward a weaker economy.

Tactics: Choosing the Policy Instrument

Now that we are familiar with the alternative strategies for monetary policy, let's look at how monetary policy is conducted on a day-to-day basis. Central banks directly control the tools of monetary policy—open market operations, reserve requirements, and the discount rate—but knowing the tools and the strategies for implementing a monetary policy does not tell us whether policy is easy or tight. The **policy instrument** (also called an **operating instrument**) is a variable that responds to the central bank's tools and indicates the stance (easy or tight) of monetary policy. A central bank like the Fed has at its disposal two basic types of policy instruments: reserve aggregates (total reserves, nonborrowed reserves, the monetary base, and the nonborrowed base) and interest rates (federal funds rate and other short-term interest rates). (Central banks in small countries can choose another policy instrument, the exchange rate. The policy instrument might be linked to an **intermediate target,** such as a monetary aggregate like M2 or a long-term interest rate. Intermediate targets stand between the policy instrument and the goals of monetary policy (e.g., price stability, output growth); they are not as directly affected by the tools of monetary policy, but might be more closely linked to the goals of monetary policy.

As an example, suppose the central bank's employment and inflation goals are consistent with a nominal GDP growth rate of 5%. The central bank might believe that the 5% nominal GDP growth rate will be achieved by a 4% growth rate for M2 (an intermediate target), which will in turn be achieved by a growth rate of 3% for nonborrowed reserves (the policy instrument). Alternatively, the central bank might believe that the best way to achieve its objectives would be to set the federal funds rate (a policy instrument) at, say, 4%. Can the central bank choose to target both the nonborrowed-reserves and the federal-funds-rate policy instruments at the same time? The answer is no. The application of supply and demand analysis to the market for reserves that we developed earlier in the chapter explains why a central bank must choose one or the other.

Let's first see why an aggregate target involves losing control of the interest rate. Figure 8.6 contains a supply and demand diagram for the market for reserves.

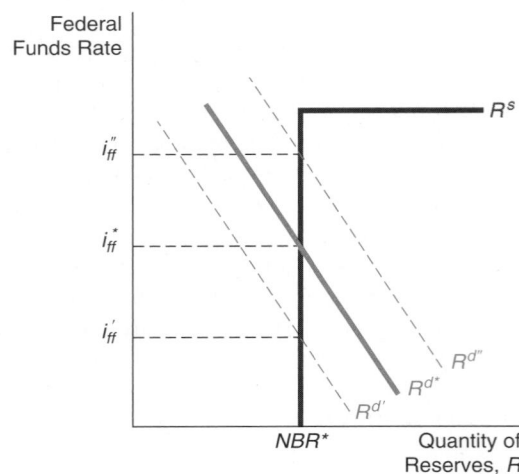

Figure 8.6 Result of Targeting on Nonborrowed Reserves

Targeting on nonborrowed reserves of NBR^* will lead to fluctuations in the federal funds rate between i_{ff}' and i_{ff}'' because of fluctuations in the demand for reserves between $R^{d'}$ and $R^{d''}$.

Although the central bank expects the demand curve for reserves to be at R^{d*}, it fluctuates between $R^{d'}$ and $R^{d''}$ because of unexpected fluctuations in deposits (and hence requires reserves) and changes in banks' desire to hold excess reserves. If the central bank has a nonborrowed reserves target of NBR^* (say, because it has a target growth rate of the money supply of 4%), it expects that the federal funds rate will be i_{ff}^*. However, as the figure indicates, the fluctuations in the reserves demand curve between $R^{d'}$ and $R^{d''}$ will result in a fluctuation in the federal funds rate between i_{ff}' and i_{ff}''. Pursuing an aggregate target implies that interest rates will fluctuate.

The supply and demand diagram in Figure 8.7 shows the consequences of an interest-rate target set at i_{ff}^*. Again, the central bank expects the reserves demand curve to be at R^{d*}, but it fluctuates between $R^{d'}$ and $R^{d''}$ due to unexpected changes in deposits or banks' desire to hold excess reserves. If the demand curve rises to $R^{d''}$, the federal funds rate will begin to rise above i_{ff}^* and the central bank will engage in open market purchases of bonds until it raises the supply of nonborrowed reserves to NBR'', at which point the equilibrium federal funds rate is again at i_{ff}^*. Conversely, if the demand curve falls to $R^{d'}$ and lowers the federal funds rate, the central bank would keep making open market sales until nonborrowed reserves fall to NBR' and the federal funds rate returns to i_{ff}^*. The central bank's adherence to the interest-rate target thus leads to a fluctuating quantity of nonborrowed reserves and the money supply.

The conclusion from the supply and demand analysis is that interest-rate and reserve (monetary) aggregate targets are incompatible. A central bank can hit one or the other, but not both. Because a choice between them has to be made, we need to examine what criteria should be used to select a policy instrument.

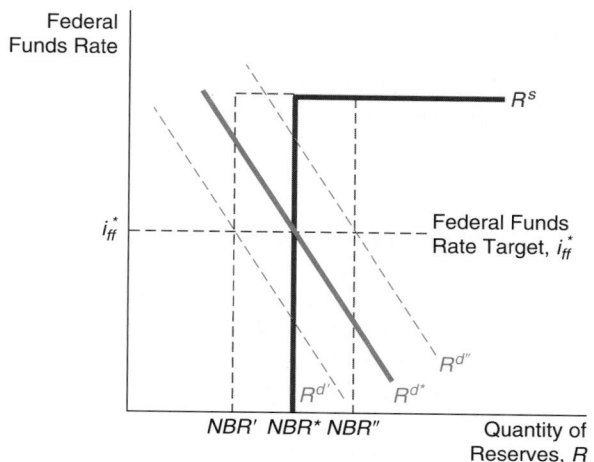

Figure 8.7   Result of Targeting on the Federal Funds Rate

Targeting on the interest rate i_{ff}^* will lead to fluctuation of nonborrowed reserves because of fluctuations in the demand for reserves between $R^{d'}$ and $R^{d''}$.

Criteria for Choosing the Policy Instrument

Three criteria apply when choosing a policy instrument: The instrument must be observable and measurable, it must be controllable by the central bank, and it must have a predictable effect on the goals.

Observability and Measurability Quick observability and accurate measurement of a policy instrument is necessary, because it will be useful only if it signals the policy stance rapidly. Reserve aggregates like nonborrowed reserves are straightforward to measure, but there is still some lag in reporting of reserve aggregates (a delay of two weeks). Short-term interest rates like the federal funds rate, by contrast, not only are easy to measure, but also are observable immediately. Thus, it seems that interest rates are more observable and measurable than are reserves and, therefore, are a better policy instrument.

However, as we learned in Chapter 3, the interest rate that is easiest to measure and observe is the nominal interest rate. It is typically a poor measure of the real cost of borrowing, which indicates with more certainty what will happen to the real GDP. This real cost of borrowing is more accurately measured by the real interest rate—that is, the nominal interest rate adjusted for expected inflation ($i_r = i - \pi^e$). Unfortunately, real interest rates are extremely difficult to measure, because we do not have a direct way to measure expected inflation. Given that both interest rates and aggregates have observability and measurability problems, it is not clear whether one should be preferred to the other as a policy instrument.

Controllability A central bank must be able to exercise effective control over a variable if it is to function as a useful policy instrument. If the central bank cannot control the policy instrument, knowing that it is off track does little good, because the central bank has no way of getting it back on track.

Because of shifts in and out of currency, even reserve aggregates such as nonborrowed reserves are not completely controllable. Conversely, the Fed can control short-term interest rates such as the federal funds rate very tightly. It might appear, therefore, that short-term interest rates would dominate reserve aggregates on the controllability criterion. However, a central bank cannot set short-term real interest rates because it does not have control over expectations of inflation. Once again, a clear-cut case cannot be made that short-term interest rates are preferable to reserve aggregates as a policy instrument, or vice versa.

Predictable Effect on Goals The most important characteristic of a policy instrument is that it must have a predictable effect on a goal. If a central bank can accurately and quickly measure the price of tea in China and can completely control its price, what good will that do? The central bank cannot use the price of tea in China to affect unemployment or the price level in its country. Because the ability to affect goals is so critical to the usefulness of any policy instrument, the tightness of the link from reserve or monetary aggregates to goals (output, employment, and inflation) or, alternatively, from interest rates to these goals, is a matter of much debate. In recent years, most central banks have concluded that the link between interest rates and goals such as inflation is tighter than the link between aggregates and inflation. For this reason, central banks throughout the world now generally use short-term interest rates as their policy instrument.

THE PRACTICING MANAGER

Using a Fed Watcher

go online

www.federalreserve.gov/
pf/pf.htm

Review what the Federal
Reserve reports as its
primary purposes and
functions.

As we have seen, the most important player in the determination of the U.S. money supply and interest rates is the Federal Reserve. When the Fed wants to inject reserves into the system, it conducts open market purchases of bonds, which cause their prices to increase and their interest rates to fall, at least in the short term. If the Fed withdraws reserves from the system, it sells bonds, thereby depressing their price and raising their interest rates. From a longer-run perspective, if the Fed pursues an expansionary monetary policy with high money growth, inflation will rise and interest rates will rise as well. Contractionary monetary policy is likely to lower inflation in the long run and lead to lower interest rates.

Knowing what actions the Fed might be taking can thus help financial institution managers predict the future course of interest rates with greater accuracy. Because, as we have seen, changes in interest rates have a major impact on a financial institution's profitability, the managers of these institutions are particularly interested in scrutinizing the Fed's behavior. To help in this task, managers hire so-called Fed watchers, experts on Federal Reserve behavior who may have worked in the Federal Reserve System and so have an insider's view of Federal Reserve operations.

Divining what the Fed is up to is by no means easy. The Fed does not disclose the content of the minutes of FOMC meetings at which it decides the course of monetary policy until three weeks after each meeting. In addition, the Fed does not provide information on the amount of certain transactions and frequently tries to obscure from the market whether it is injecting reserves into the banking system by making open market purchases and sales simultaneously.

Fed watchers, with their specialized knowledge of the ins and outs of the Fed, scrutinize the public pronouncements of Federal Reserve officials to get a feel for where monetary policy is heading. They also carefully study the data on past Federal Reserve actions and current events in the bond markets to determine what the Fed is up to.

If a Fed watcher tells a financial institution manager that Federal Reserve concerns about inflation are high and the Fed will pursue a tight monetary policy and raise short-term interest rates in the near future, the manager may decide immediately to acquire funds at the currently low interest rates in order to keep the cost of funds from rising. If the financial institution trades foreign exchange, the rise in interest rates and the attempt by the Fed to keep inflation down might lead the manager to instruct traders to purchase dollars in the foreign exchange market. As we will see in Chapter 13, these actions by the Fed would be likely to cause the value of the dollar to appreciate, so the purchase of dollars by the financial institution should lead to substantial profits.

If, conversely, the Fed watcher thinks that the Fed is worried about a weak economy and will thus pursue an expansionary policy and lower interest rates, the financial institution manager will take very different actions. Now the manager might instruct loan officers to make as many loans as possible so as to lock in the higher interest rates that the financial institution can earn currently. Or the manager might buy bonds, anticipating that interest rates will fall and their prices will rise, giving the institution a nice profit. The more expansionary policy is also likely to lower the value of the dollar in the foreign exchange market, so the financial institution manager might tell foreign exchange traders to buy foreign currencies and sell dollars in order to make a profit when the dollar falls in the future.

A Fed watcher who is right is a very valuable commodity to a financial institution. Successful Fed watchers are actively sought out by financial institutions and often earn high salaries, well into the six-figure range.

SUMMARY

1. The three basic tools of monetary policy are open market operations, discount policy, and reserve requirements. Open market operations are the primary tool used by the Fed to control interest rates.

2. The conduct of monetary policy involves actions that affect the Federal Reserve's balance sheet. Open market purchases lead to an expansion of reserves and deposits in the banking system and hence to an expansion of the monetary base and the money supply. An increase in discount loans leads to an expansion of reserves, thereby causing an expansion of the monetary base and the money supply.

3. A supply and demand analysis of the market for reserves yields the following results: When the Fed makes an open market purchase or lowers reserve requirements, the federal funds rate declines. When the Fed makes an open market sale or raises reserve requirements, the federal funds rate rises. Changes in the discount rate may also affect the federal funds rate.

4. The monetary policy tools used by the European Central Bank are similar to those used by the Federal Reserve System and involve open market operations, lending to banks, and reserve requirements. Main financing operations—open market operations in repos that are typically reversed within two weeks—are the primary tool to set the overnight cash rate at the target financing rate. The European Central Bank also operates standing lending facilities that ensure that the overnight cash rate remains within 100 basis points of the target financing rate.

5. The six basic goals of monetary policy are price stability (the primary goal), high employment, economic growth, interest-rate stability, stability of financial markets, and stability in foreign exchange markets.

6. A nominal anchor is a key element in monetary policy strategies. It helps promote price stability by tying down inflation expectations and limiting the time-

inconsistency problem, in which monetary policymakers conduct monetary policy in a discretionary way that produces poor long-run outcomes.

7. Monetary targeting has the advantage that information on whether the central bank is achieving its target is known almost immediately. Monetary targeting suffers from the disadvantage that it works well only if there is a reliable relationship between the monetary aggregate and the goal variable, inflation—a relationship that has often not held in many different countries.

8. Inflation targeting has several advantages: (1) It enables monetary policy to focus on domestic considerations; (2) stability in the relationship between money and inflation is not critical to its success; (3) it is readily understood by the public and is highly transparent; (4) it increases accountability of the central bank; and (5) it appears to ameliorate the effects of inflationary shocks. It does have some disadvantages, however: (1) Inflation is not easily controlled by the monetary authorities, so that an inflation target is unable to send immediate signals to both the public and markets; (2) it might impose a rigid rule on policymakers, although this has not been the case in practice; and (3) a sole focus on inflation may lead to larger output fluctuations, although this has also not been the case in practice.

9. Because interest-rate and aggregate policy instruments are incompatible, a central bank must choose between them on the basis of three criteria: measurability, controllability, and the ability to affect goal variables predictably. Central banks now typically use short-term interest rates as their policy instrument.

10. Because predicting the Federal Reserve's actions can help managers of financial institutions predict the course of future interest rates, which has a major impact on financial institutions' profitability, such managers value the services of Fed watchers, experts on Federal Reserve behavior.

KEY TERMS

defensive open market operations, *p. 177*
deposit facility, *p. 184*
discount rate, *p. 170*
discount window, *p. 179*
dual mandate, *p. 189*
dynamic open market operations, *p. 177*
excess reserves, *p. 171*
federal funds rate, *p. 173*
hierarchical mandate, *p. 189*
inflation targeting, *p. 194*
intermediate target, *p. 200*
lender of last resort, *p. 180*
longer-term financing operations, *p. 184*
main refinancing operations, *p. 184*
marginal lending facility, *p. 184*
marginal lending rate, *p. 184*
matched sale-purchase transaction
   (reverse repo), *p. 179*
monetary base, *p. 170*

monetary targeting, *p. 190*
natural rate of unemployment, *p. 187*
nominal anchor, *p. 185*
open market operations, *p. 171*
operating instrument, *p. 200*
overnight cash rate, *p. 183*
policy instrument, *p. 200*
price stability, *p. 185*
primary dealers, *p. 178*
repurchase agreement (repo), *p. 179*
required reserve ratio, *p. 171*
required reserves, *p. 171*
reserve requirements, *p. 173*
reserves, *p. 170*
reverse transactions, *p. 184*
standing lending facility, *p. 179*
target financing rate, *p. 183*
time-inconsistency problem, *p. 185*

QUESTIONS

1. "Unemployment is a bad thing, and the government should make every effort to eliminate it." Do you agree or disagree? Explain your answer.

2. Which goals of the Fed frequently conflict?

3. "If the demand for reserves did not fluctuate, the Fed could pursue both a nonborrowed reserves target and an interest-rate target at the same time." Is this statement true, false, or uncertain? Explain your answer.

4. Classify each of the following as either an operating target or an intermediate target, and explain why.

   a. The three-month Treasury bill rate

   b. The monetary base

   c. M2

5. What procedures can the Fed use to control the three-month Treasury bill rate? Why does control of this interest rate imply that the Fed will lose control of the money supply?

6. If the Fed has an interest-rate target, why will an increase in the demand for reserves lead to a rise in the money supply?

7. "Interest rates can be measured more accurately and more quickly than the money supply. Hence an interest rate is preferred over the money supply as an intermediate target." Do you agree or disagree? Explain your answer.

8. Compare the monetary base to M2 on the grounds of controllability and measurability. Which do you prefer as an intermediate target? Why?

9. "Discounting is no longer needed because the presence of the FDIC eliminates the possibility of bank panics." Is this statement true, false, or uncertain? Explain your answer.

10. The benefits of using Fed discount operations to prevent bank panics are straightforward. What are the costs?

11. What are the benefits of using a nominal anchor for the conduct of monetary policy?

12. Give an example of the time-inconsistency problem that you experience in your everyday life.

13. What incentives arise for a central bank to fall into the time-inconsistency trap of pursuing overly expansionary monetary policy?

14. What are the advantages of monetary targeting as a strategy for the conduct of monetary policy?

15. What is the big *if* necessary for the success of monetary targeting? Does the experience with monetary targeting suggest that the big *if* is a problem?

16. What methods have inflation-targeting central banks used to increase communication with the public and increase the transparency of monetary policymaking?

17. Why might inflation targeting increase support for the independence of the central bank to conduct monetary policy?

18. "Because the public can see whether a central bank hits its monetary targets almost immediately, whereas it takes time before the public can see whether an inflation target is achieved, monetary targeting makes central banks more accountable than inflation targeting does." Is this statement true, false, or uncertain? Explain your answer.

19. "Because inflation targeting focuses on achieving the inflation target, it will lead to excessive output fluctuations." Is this statement true, false, or uncertain? Explain your answer.

20. "A central bank with a dual mandate will achieve lower unemployment in the long run than a central bank with a hierarchical mandate in which price stability takes precedence." Is this statement true, false, or uncertain?

QUANTITATIVE PROBLEMS

1. Consider a bank policy to maintain 12% of deposits as reserves. The bank currently has $10 million in deposits and holds $400,000 in excess reserves. What is the required reserve on a new deposit of $50,000?

2. Estimates of unemployment for the upcoming year have been developed as follows:

Economy	Probability	Unemployment Rate (%)
Bust	0.15	20
Average	0.5	10
Good	0.2	5
Boom	0.15	1

What is the expected unemployment rate? The standard deviation?

3. The Federal Reserve wants to increase the supply of reserves, so it purchases $1 million dollars worth of bonds from the public. Show the effect of this open market operation using T-accounts.

4. Use T-accounts to show the effect of the Federal Reserve being paid back a $500,000 discount loan from a bank.

5. The short-term nominal interest rate is 5%, with an expected inflation of 2%. Economists forecast that next year's nominal rate will increase by 100 basis points, but inflation will fall to 1.5%. What is the expected change in real interest rates?

For Problems 6–8, recall from introductory macroeconomics that the money multiplier = 1/(required reserve ratio).

6. If the required reserve ratio is 10%, how much of a new $10,000 deposit can a bank lend? What is the potential impact on the money supply?

7. A bank currently holds $150,000 in excess reserves. If the current reserve requirement is 12.5%, how much could the money supply change? How could this happen?

8. The trading desk at the Federal Reserve sold $100,000,000 in T-bills to the public. If the current reserve requirement is 8.0%, how much could the money supply change?

Conduct of Monetary Policy: Tools, Goals, Strategy, and Tactics

1. Go to **www.federalreserve.gov/releases/h15/ update/**. What is the current federal funds rate (define this rate as well)? What is the current Federal Reserve discount rate (define this rate as well)? Have short-term rates increased or declined since the end of 2005?

2. The Federal Open Market Committee (FOMC) meets about every six weeks to assess the state of the economy and to decide what actions the central bank should take. The minutes of this meeting are released three weeks after the meeting; however, a brief press release is made available immediately. Find the schedule of minutes and press releases at **www .federalreserve.gov/fomc/**.

   a. When was the last scheduled meeting of the FOMC? When is the next meeting?

   b. Review the press release from the last meeting. What did the committee decide to do about short-term interest rates?

   c. Review the most recently published meeting minutes. What areas of the economy seemed to be of most concern to the committee members?

3. It is possible to access other central bank Web sites to learn about their structure. One example is the European Central bank. Go to **www.ecb.int/index.html**. On the ECB home page, find information about the ECB's strategy for monetary policy.

4. Many countries have central banks that are responsible for their nation's monetary policy. Go to **www .bis.org/cbanks.htm** and select one of the central banks (for example, Norway). Review that bank's Web site to determine its policies regarding application of monetary policy. How does this bank's policies compare to those of the U.S. central bank?

Please visit our Web site at **www.prenhall.com/mishkin_ eakins** to read the Web appendix to Chapter 8:

* **Appendix:** The Fed's Balance Sheet and the Monetary Base

PART 4

Financial Markets

CHAPTER 9

The Money Markets

Preview

If you were to review Microsoft's annual report for 2006, you would find that the company had over $6 billion in cash and equivalents. The firm also listed $27 billion in short-term securities. The firm chose to hold over $30 billion in highly liquid short-term assets in order to be ready to take advantage of investment opportunities and to avoid the risks associated with other types of investments. Microsoft will have much of these funds invested in the money markets. Recall that money market securities are short-term, low-risk, and very liquid. Because of the high degree of safety and liquidity these securities exhibit, they are close to being money, hence their name.

The money markets have been active since the early 1800s but have become much more important since 1970, when interest rates rose above historic levels. In fact, the rise in short-term rates, coupled with a regulated ceiling on the rate that banks could pay for deposits, resulted in a rapid outflow of funds from financial institutions in the late 1970s and early 1980s. This outflow in turn caused many banks and savings and loans to fail. The industry regained its health only after massive changes were made to bank regulations with regard to money market interest rates.

This chapter carefully reviews the money markets and the securities that are traded there. In addition, we discuss why the money markets are important to our financial system.

The Money Markets Defined

The term *money market* is actually a misnomer. Money—currency—is not traded in the money markets. Because the securities that do trade there are short-term and highly liquid, however, they are close to being money. Money market securities, which are discussed in detail later in this chapter, have three basic characteristics in common:

- They are usually sold in large denominations.
- They have low default risk.
- They mature in one year or less *from their original issue date*. Most money market instruments mature in less than 120 days.

Money market transactions do not take place in any one particular location or building. Instead, traders usually arrange purchases and sales between participants over the phone and complete them electronically. Because of this characteristic, money market securities usually have an active *secondary market*. This means that after the security has been sold initially, it is relatively easy to find buyers who will purchase it in the future. An active secondary market makes money market securities very flexible instruments to use to fill short-term financial needs. For example, Microsoft's annual report states that "we consider all highly liquid interest-earning investments with a maturity of 3 months or less at date of purchase to be cash equivalents."

Another characteristic of the money markets is that they are **wholesale markets**. This means that most transactions are very large, usually in excess of $1 million. The size of these transactions prevents most individual investors from participating directly in the money markets. Instead, dealers and brokers, operating in the trading rooms of large banks and brokerage houses, bring customers together. These traders will buy or sell $50 or $100 million in mere seconds—certainly not a job for the faint of heart!

As you may recall from Chapter 2, flexibility and innovation are two important characteristics of any financial market, and the money markets are no exception. Despite the wholesale nature of the money market, innovative securities and trading methods have been developed to give small investors access to money market securities. We will discuss these securities and their characteristics later in the chapter, and in greater detail in Chapter 21.

Why Do We Need the Money Markets?

In theory, the money markets should not be needed. The banking industry exists primarily to provide short-term loans and to accept short-term deposits. Banks should have an efficiency advantage in gathering information, an advantage that should eliminate the need for the money markets. Thanks to continuing relationships with customers, banks should be able to offer loans more cheaply than diversified markets, which must evaluate each borrower every time a new security is offered. Furthermore, short-term securities offered for sale in the money markets are neither as liquid nor as safe as deposits placed in banks and thrifts. Given the advantages that banks have, why do the money markets exist at all?

The banking industry exists primarily to mediate the asymmetric information problem between saver-lenders and borrower-spenders, and banks can earn profits by capturing economies of scale while providing this service. However, the banking industry is subject to more regulations and governmental costs than are the money markets. In situations where the asymmetric information problem is not severe, the money markets have a distinct cost advantage over banks in providing short-term funds.

Money Market Cost Advantages

Banks must put aside a portion of their deposits in the form of reserves that are held without interest at the Federal Reserve. Thus, a bank may not be able to invest 100% of every dollar it holds in deposits.[1] This means that it must pay a lower interest rate to the depositor than if the full deposit could be invested.

Interest-rate regulations were a second competitive obstacle for banks. One of the principal purposes of the banking regulations of the 1930s was to reduce competition among banks. With less competition, regulators felt, banks were less likely to fail. The cost to consumers of the greater profits banks earned because of the lack of free market competition was justified by the greater economic stability that a healthy banking system would provide.

One way that banking profits were assured was by regulations that set a ceiling on the rate of interest that banks could pay for funds. The Glass-Steagall Act of 1933 prohibited payment of interest on checking accounts and limited the interest that could be paid on time deposits. The limits on interest rates were not particularly relevant until the late 1950s. Figure 9.1 shows that the limits became especially troublesome to banks in the late 1970s and early 1980s when inflation pushed short-term interest rates above the level that banks could pay. Investors pulled their money out of banks and put it into money market security accounts offered by many brokerage firms. These new investors caused the money markets to grow rapidly.

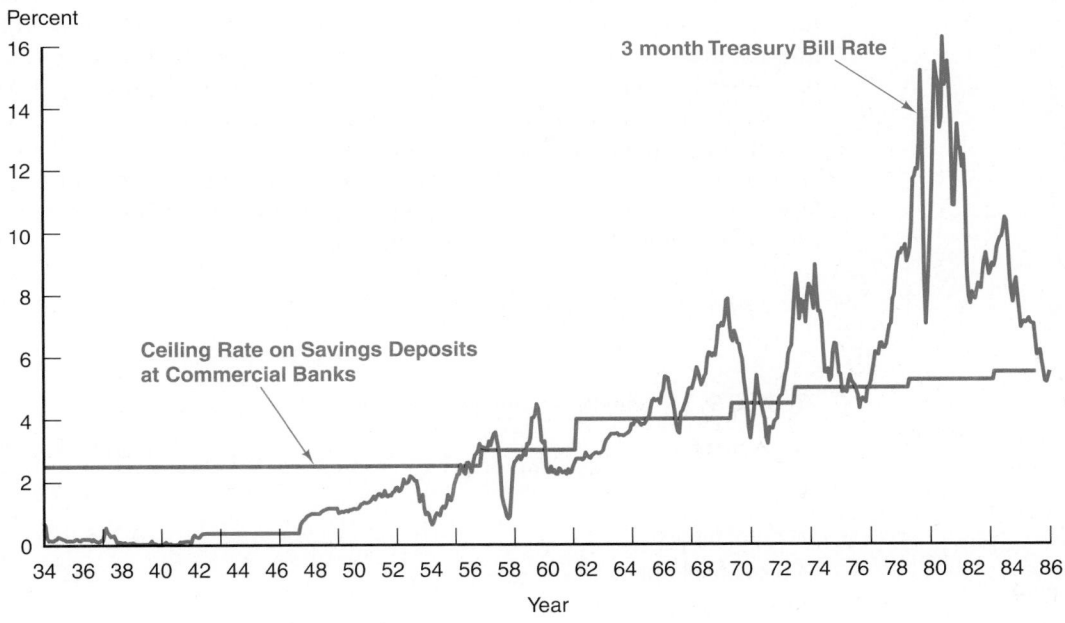

Figure 9.1 3-Month Treasury Bill Rate and Ceiling Rate on Savings Deposits at Commercial Banks

Source: http://www.stlouisfed.org/default.cfm.

---

[1]The reserve requirement on nonpersonal time deposits with an original maturity of less than $1\frac{1}{2}$ years was reduced from 3% to 0% in December 1990.

Commercial bank interest rate ceilings were removed in March of 1986, but by then the retail money markets were well established.

Banks continue to provide valuable intermediation, as we will see in several later chapters. In some situations, however, the cost structure of the banking industry makes it unable to compete effectively in the market for short-term funds against the less restricted money markets.

The Purpose of the Money Markets

The well-developed secondary market for money market instruments makes the money market an ideal place for a firm or financial institution to "warehouse" surplus funds until they are needed. Similarly, the money markets provide a low-cost source of funds to firms, the government, and intermediaries that need a short-term infusion of funds.

Most investors in the money market who are temporarily warehousing funds are ordinarily not trying to earn unusually high returns on their money market funds. Rather, they use the money market as an interim investment that provides a higher return than holding cash or money in banks. They may feel that market conditions are not right to warrant the purchase of additional stock, or they may expect interest rates to rise and hence not want to purchase bonds. It is important to keep in mind that holding idle surplus cash is expensive for an investor because cash balances earn no income for the owner. Idle cash represents an *opportunity cost* in terms of lost interest income. Recall from Chapter 4 that an asset's opportunity cost is the amount of interest sacrificed by not holding an alternative asset. The money markets provide a means to invest idle funds and to reduce this opportunity cost.

Investment advisers often hold some funds in the money market so that they will be able to act quickly to take advantage of investment opportunities they identify. Most investment funds and financial intermediaries also hold money market securities to meet investment or deposit outflows.

The sellers of money market securities find that the money market provides a low-cost source of temporary funds. Table 9.1 shows the interest rates available on

TABLE 9.1 Sample Money Market Rates, May 15, 2007

Instrument	Interest Rate (%)
Prime rate	8.25
Federal funds	5.28
Commercial paper	5.23
Banker's acceptance	5.29
London interbank offer rate	5.32
Foreign prime rates	
Canada	6.0
European Central Bank	3.75
Japan	1.875
Treasury bills (4 week)	4.665

Source: Wall Street Journal, May 16, 2007, p. C9.

a variety of money market instruments sold by a variety of firms and institutions. For example, banks may issue federal funds (we will define the money market securities later in this chapter) to obtain funds in the money market to meet short-term reserve requirement shortages. The government funds a large portion of the U.S. debt with Treasury bills. Finance companies like GMAC (General Motors Acceptance Company, the financing division of General Motors) may enter the money market to raise the funds that it uses to make car loans.

Why do corporations and the U.S. government sometimes need to get their hands on funds quickly? The primary reason is that cash inflows and outflows are rarely synchronized. Government tax revenues, for example, usually come only at certain times of the year, but expenses are incurred all year long. The government can borrow short-term funds that it will pay back when it receives tax revenues. Businesses also face problems caused by revenues and expenses occurring at different times. The money markets provide an efficient, low-cost way of solving these problems.

Who Participates in the Money Markets?

An obvious way to discuss the players in the money market would be to list those who borrow and those who lend. The problem with this approach is that most money market participants operate on both sides of the market. For example, any large bank will borrow aggressively in the money market by selling large commercial CDs. At the same time, it will lend short-term funds to businesses through its commercial lending departments. Nevertheless, we can identify the primary money market players—the U.S. Treasury, the Federal Reserve System, commercial banks, businesses, investments and securities firms, and individuals—and discuss their roles (summarized in Table 9.2).

U.S. Treasury Department

The U.S. Treasury Department is unique because it is always a demander of money market funds and never a supplier. The U.S. Treasury is the largest of all money market borrowers worldwide. It issues Treasury bills (often called T-bills) and other securities that are popular with other money market participants. Short-term issues enable the government to raise funds until tax revenues are received. The Treasury also issues T-bills to replace maturing issues.

Federal Reserve System

The Federal Reserve is the Treasury's agent for the distribution of all government securities. The Fed holds vast quantities of Treasury securities that it sells if it believes that the money supply should be reduced. Similarly, the Fed will purchase Treasury securities if it believes that the money supply should be expanded. The Fed's responsibility for the money supply makes it the single most influential participant in the U.S. money market. The Federal Reserve's role in controlling the economy through open market operations is discussed further in Chapters 7 and 8.

Commercial Banks

Commercial banks hold a larger percentage of U.S. government securities than any other group of financial institutions, approximately 12%. This is partly because of regulations that limit the investment opportunities available to banks. Specifically, banks

TABLE 9.2 Money Market Participants

Participant	Role
U.S. Treasury Department	Sells U.S. Treasury securities to fund the national debt
Federal Reserve System	Buys and sells U.S. Treasury securities as its primary method of controlling the money supply
Commercial banks	Buy U.S. Treasury securities; sell certificates of deposit and make short-term loans; offer individual investors accounts that invest in money market securities
Businesses	Buy and sell various short-term securities as a regular part of their cash management
Investment companies (brokerage firms)	Trade on behalf of commercial accounts
Finance companies (commercial leasing companies)	Lend funds to individuals
Insurance companies (property and casualty insurance companies)	Maintain liquidity needed to meet unexpected demands
Pension funds	Maintain funds in money market instruments in readiness for investment in stocks and bonds
Individuals	Buy money market mutual funds
Money market mutual funds	Allow small investors to participate in the money market by aggregating their funds to invest in large-denomination money market securities

are prohibited from owning risky securities, such as stocks or corporate bonds. There are no restrictions against holding Treasury securities because of their low risk and high liquidity.

Banks are also the major issuer of negotiable certificates of deposit (CDs), banker's acceptances, federal funds, and repurchase agreements (we will discuss these securities in the next section). In addition to using money market securities to help manage their own liquidity, many banks trade on behalf of their customers.

Not all commercial banks deal in the secondary money market for their customers. The ones that do are among the largest in the country and are often referred to as *money center banks*. The biggest money center banks include Citigroup, Bank of America, J.P. Morgan, and Wachovia.

Businesses

Many businesses buy and sell securities in the money markets. Such activity is usually limited to major corporations because of the large dollar amounts involved. As discussed earlier, the money markets are used extensively by businesses both to warehouse surplus funds and to raise short-term funds. We will discuss the specific money market securities that businesses issue later in this chapter.

Investment and Securities Firms

The other financial institutions that participate in the money markets are listed in Table 9.2.

Investment Companies Large diversified brokerage firms are active in the money markets. The largest of these include Bear Stearns, Salomon Smith Barney, Merrill Lynch, PaineWebber, and Morgan Stanley Dean Witter. The primary function of these dealers is to "make a market" for money market securities by maintaining an inventory from which to buy or sell. These firms are very important to the liquidity of the money market because they ensure that sellers can readily market their securities. We discuss investment companies in Chapter 23.

Finance Companies Finance companies raise funds in the money markets primarily by selling commercial paper. They then lend the funds to consumers for the purchase of durable goods such as cars, boats, or home improvements. Finance companies and related firms are discussed in Chapter 26 (on the Web at **www.prenhall.com/ mishkin_eakins**).

Insurance Companies Property and casualty insurance companies must maintain liquidity because of their unpredictable need for funds. When four hurricanes hit Florida in 2004, for example, insurance companies paid out billions of dollars in benefits to policyholders. To meet this demand for funds, the insurance companies sold some of their money market securities to raise cash. Insurance companies are discussed in Chapter 22.

Pension Funds Pension funds invest a portion of their cash in the money markets so that they can take advantage of investment opportunities that they may identify in the stock or bond markets. Like insurance companies, pension funds must have sufficient liquidity to meet their obligations. However, because their obligations are reasonably predictable, large money market security holdings are unnecessary. Pension funds are discussed in Chapter 22.

Individuals

When inflation rose in the late 1970s, the interest rates that banks were offering on deposits became unattractive to individual investors. At this same time, brokerage houses began promoting money market mutual funds, which paid much higher rates.

Banks could not stop large amounts of cash from moving out to mutual funds because regulations capped the rate they could pay on deposits. To combat this flight of money from banks, the authorities revised the regulations. Banks quickly raised rates in an attempt to recapture individual investors' dollars. This halted the rapid movement of funds, but money market mutual funds remain a popular individual investment option. The advantage of mutual funds is that they give investors with relatively small amounts of cash to invest access to large-denomination securities. We will discuss money market mutual funds in more depth in Chapter 21.

Money Market Instruments

A variety of money market instruments are available to meet the diverse needs of market participants. One security will be perfect for one investor; a different security may be best for another. In this section we gain a greater understanding of money market security characteristics and how money market participants use them to manage their cash.

Treasury Bills

To finance the national debt, the U.S. Treasury Department issues a variety of debt securities. The most widely held and most liquid security is the Treasury bill. Treasury bills are sold with 28, 91, and 182-day maturities. The Treasury bill had a minimum denomination of $10,000 until 1998, at which time new $1,000 T-bills became available. The Fed has set up a direct purchase option that individuals may use to purchase Treasury bills over the Internet. First available in September 1998, this method of buying securities represented an effort to make Treasury securities more widely available.

The government does not actually pay interest on Treasury bills. Instead, they are issued at a discount from par (their value at maturity). The investor's yield comes from the increase in the value of the security between the time it was purchased and the time it matures.

CASE

Discounting the Price of Treasury Securities to Pay the Interest

Most money market securities do not pay interest. Instead, the investor pays less for the security than it will be worth when it matures, and the increase in price provides a return. This is called **discounting** and is common to short-term securities because they often mature before the issuer can mail out interest checks. (We discussed discounting in Chapter 3.)

Table 9.3 shows the results of a typical Treasury bill auction as reported on the Treasurydirect Web site. If we look at the first listing we see that the 28-day Treasury bill sold for $99.637167 per $100. This means that a $1,000 bill was discounted to $996.37. The table also reports the Discount rate % and the Investment Rate % is computed as:

$$i_{discount} = \frac{F - P}{F} \times \frac{360}{n} \tag{1}$$

where $i_{discount}$ = annualized discount rate %
P = purchase price
F = face or maturity value
n = number of days until maturity

Notice a few features about this equation. First, the return is computed using the face amount in the denominator. You will actually pay less than the face amount, since this is sold as a discount instrument, so the return is underestimated. Second, a 360-day year (30 × 12) is used when annualizing the return. This also underestimates the return when compared to using a 365-day year.

The investment rate % is computed as

$$i_{investment} = \frac{F - P}{P} \times \frac{365}{n} \tag{2}$$

The investment rate % is a more accurate representation of what an investor will earn since it uses the actual number of days per year and the true initial investment in

TABLE 9.3   Recent Bill Auction Results

Security Term	Issue Date	Maturity Date	Discount Rate %	Investment Rate %	Price Per $100	CUSIP
28-day	05-17-2007	06-14-2007	4.665	4.760	99.637167	912795ZL8
91-day	05-17-2007	08-16-2007	4.730	4.867	98.804361	912795ZV6
182-day	05-17-2007	11-15-2007	4.735	4.932	97.606194	912795B26
28-day	05-10-2007	06-07-2007	4.640	4.734	99.639111	912795ZK0
91-day	05-10-2007	08-09-2007	4.760	4.898	98.796778	912795ZU8

Source: http://www.treasurydirect.gov/RI/OFBills.

its calculation. Note that when computing the investment rate % the Treasury uses the actual number of days in the following year. This means that there are 366 days in leap years.

example 9.1   **Discount and Investment Rate Percent Calculations**

You submit a noncompetitive bid in May 2007 to purchase a 28-day $1,000 Treasury bill and you find that you are buying the bond for $996.37. What are the discount rate % and the investment rate %?

Solution
Discount rate %

$$I_{discount} = \frac{F - P}{F} \times \frac{360}{n}$$

$$I_{discount} = \frac{\$1,000 - \$996.37}{\$1,000} \times \frac{360}{28}$$

$$I_{discount} = 4.665\%$$

Investment rate %

$$I_{investment} = \frac{F - P}{P} \times \frac{366}{n}$$

$$I_{investment} = \frac{\$1,000 - \$996.37}{\$996.37} \times \frac{366}{28}$$

$$I_{investment} = 4.760\%$$

Note that since 2008 is a leap year there are 366 days between 05-17-2007 and 05-17-2008. These solutions for the discount rate % and the investment rate % match those reported by Treasurydirect for the first Treasury bill in Table 9.3.

Risk Treasury bills have virtually zero default risk because even if the government ran out of money, it could simply print more to redeem them when they mature. The risk of unexpected changes in inflation is also low because of the short term to maturity. The market for Treasury bills is extremely deep and liquid. A **deep market** is one with many different buyers and sellers. A **liquid market** is one in which securities can be bought and sold quickly and with low transaction costs. Investors in markets that are deep and liquid have little risk that they will not be able to sell their securities when they want to.

go online
www.treasurydirect.gov
Visit this site to study how
Treasury securities are
auctioned.

The budget debates in early 1996 almost caused the government to default on its debt, despite the long-held belief that such a thing could not happen. Congress attempted to force President Clinton to sign a budget bill by refusing to approve a temporary spending package. If the stalemate had lasted much longer, we would have witnessed the first-ever U.S. government security default. We can only speculate what the long-term effect on interest rates might have been if the market decided to add a default risk premium to all government securities.

Treasury Bill Auctions Each week the Treasury announces how many and what kind of Treasury bills it will offer for sale. The Treasury accepts the bids offering the highest price. The Treasury accepts competitive bids in ascending order of yield until the accepted bids reach the offering amount. Each accepted bid is then awarded at the highest yield paid to any accepted bid.

As an alternative to the **competitive bidding** procedure just outlined, the Treasury also permits **noncompetitive bidding**. When competitive bids are offered, investors state both the amount of securities desired and the price they are willing to pay. By contrast, noncompetitive bids include only the amount of securities the investor wants. The Treasury accepts all noncompetitive bids. The price is set as the highest yield paid to any accepted competitive bid. Thus, noncompetitive bidders

mini-case

Treasury Bill Auctions Go Haywire

Every Thursday, the Treasury announces how many 28-day, 91-day, and 182-day Treasury bills it will offer for sale. Buyers must submit bids by the following Monday, and awards are made the next morning. The Treasury accepts the bids offering the highest price.

The Treasury auction of securities is supposed to be highly competitive and fair. To ensure proper levels of competition, no one dealer is allowed to purchase more than 35% of any one issue. About 40 primary dealers regularly participate in the auction.

In 1991, the disclosure that Salomon Smith Barney had broken the rules to corner the market cast the fairness of the auction in doubt. Salomon Smith Barney purchased 35% of the Treasury securities in

its own name by submitting a relatively high bid. It then bought additional securities in the names of its customers, often without their knowledge or consent. Salomon then bought the securities from the customers. As a result of these transactions, Salomon cornered the market and was able to charge a monopoly-like premium. The investigation of Salomon Smith Barney revealed that during one auction in May 1991, the brokerage managed to gain control of 94% of an $11 billion issue. During the scandal that followed this disclosure, John Gutfreund, the firm's chairman, and several other top executives with Salomon retired. The Treasury has instituted new rules since then to ensure that the market remains competitive.

pay the same price paid by competitive bidders. The significant difference between the two methods is that competitive bidders may or may not end up buying securities whereas the noncompetitive bidders are guaranteed to do so.

In 1976, the Treasury switched the entire marketable portion of the federal debt over to **book entry** securities, replacing engraved pieces of paper. In a book entry system, ownership of Treasury securities is documented only in the Fed's computer: Essentially, a ledger entry replaces the actual security. This procedure reduces the cost of issuing Treasury securities as well as the cost of transferring them as they are bought and sold in the secondary market.

The Treasury auction of securities is supposed to be highly competitive and fair. To ensure proper levels of competition, no one dealer is allowed to purchase more than 35% of any one issue. About 40 primary dealers regularly participate in the auction. Salomon Smith Barney was caught violating the limits on the percentage of one issue a dealer may purchase, with serious consequences. (See the Mini-Case box "Treasury Bill Auctions Go Haywire.")

Treasury Bill Interest Rates Treasury bills are very close to being risk-free. As expected for a risk-free security, the interest rate earned on Treasury bill securities is among the lowest in the economy. Investors in Treasury bills have found that in some years, their earnings did not even compensate them for changes in purchasing power due to inflation. Figure 9.2 shows the interest rate on Treasury bills and the inflation rate over the period 1973–2006. As discussed in Chapter 3, the *real rate* of interest has occasionally been less than zero. For example, in 1973–1977, 1990–1991, and 2002–2004, the inflation rate matched or exceeded the earnings on T-bills. Clearly, the T-bill is not an investment to be used for anything but temporary storage of excess funds, because it barely keeps up with inflation.

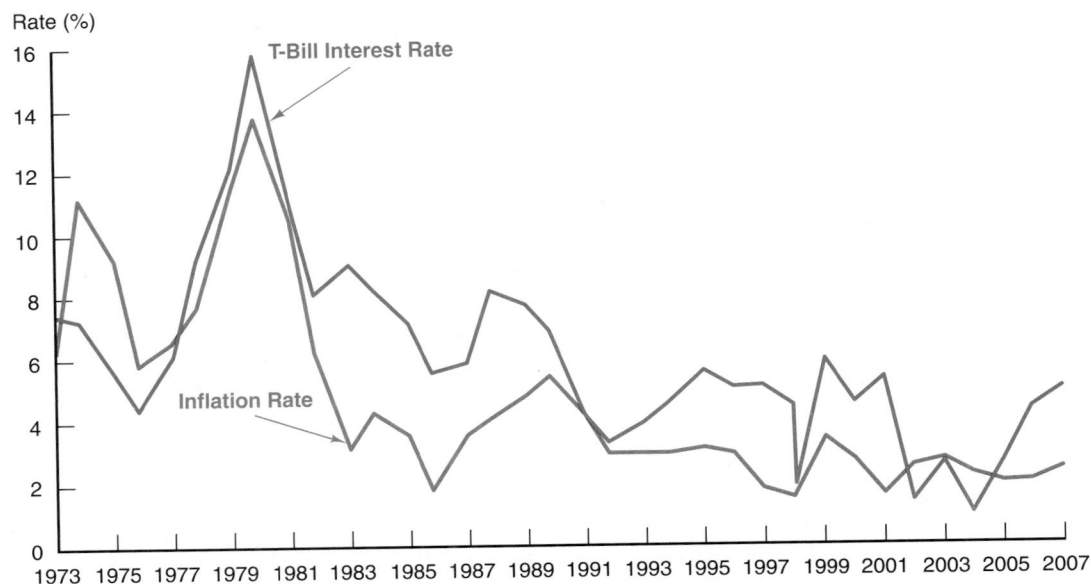

Figure 9.2   Treasury Bill Interest Rate and the Inflation Rate, January 1973–January 2007

Source: ftp://ftp.bls.gov/special.requests/cpi/cpiai.txt.

Federal Funds

Federal funds are short-term funds transferred (loaned or borrowed) between financial institutions, usually for a period of one day. The term *federal funds* (or *fed funds*) is misleading. Fed funds really have nothing to do with the federal government. The term comes from the fact that these funds are held at the Federal Reserve bank. The fed funds market began in the 1920s when banks with excess reserves loaned them to banks that needed them. The interest rate for borrowing these funds was close to the rate that the Federal Reserve charged on discount loans.

Purpose of Fed Funds The Federal Reserve has set minimum reserve requirements that all banks must maintain. To meet these reserve requirements, banks must keep a certain percentage of their total deposits with the Federal Reserve. The main purpose for fed funds is to provide banks with an immediate infusion of reserves should they be short. Banks can borrow directly from the Federal Reserve, but the Fed actively discourages banks from regularly borrowing from it. The reason that banks like to lend in the fed funds market is that money held at the Federal Reserve in excess of what is required does not earn any interest. So even though the interest rate on fed funds is low, it beats the alternative. One indication of the popularity of fed funds is that on a typical day a quarter of a trillion dollars in fed funds will change hands.

Terms for Fed Funds Fed funds are usually overnight investments. Banks analyze their reserve position on a daily basis and either borrow or invest in fed funds, depending on whether they have deficit or excess reserves. Suppose that a bank finds that it has $50 million in excess reserves. It will call its correspondent banks (banks that have reciprocal accounts) to see if they need reserves that day. The bank will sell its excess funds to the bank that offers the highest rate. Once an agreement has been reached, the bank with excess funds will communicate to the Federal Reserve bank instructions to take funds out of the seller's account at the Fed and deposit the funds in the borrower's account. The next day, the funds are transferred back, and the process begins again.

Most fed funds borrowings are unsecured. Typically, the entire agreement is established by direct communication between buyer and seller.

Federal Funds Interest Rates The forces of supply and demand set the fed funds interest rate. This is a competitive market that analysts watch closely for indications of what is happening to short-term rates. The fed funds rate reported by the press is known as the *effective rate,* which is defined in the *Federal Reserve Bulletin* as the weighted average of rates on trades through New York brokers.

The Federal Reserve cannot directly control fed funds rates. It can and does indirectly influence them by adjusting the level of reserves available to banks in the system. The Fed can increase the amount of money in the financial system by buying securities, as was demonstrated in Chapter 8. When investors sell securities to the Fed, the proceeds are deposited in their banks' accounts at the Federal Reserve. These deposits increase the supply of reserves in the financial system and lower interest rates. If the Fed removes reserves by selling securities, fed funds rates will increase. The Fed will often announce its intention to raise or lower the fed funds rate in advance. Though these rates directly affect few businesses or consumers, analysts consider them an important indicator of the direction in which the Federal Reserve wants the economy to move. Figure 9.3 compares the fed funds rate with the T-bill rate. Clearly, the two track together.

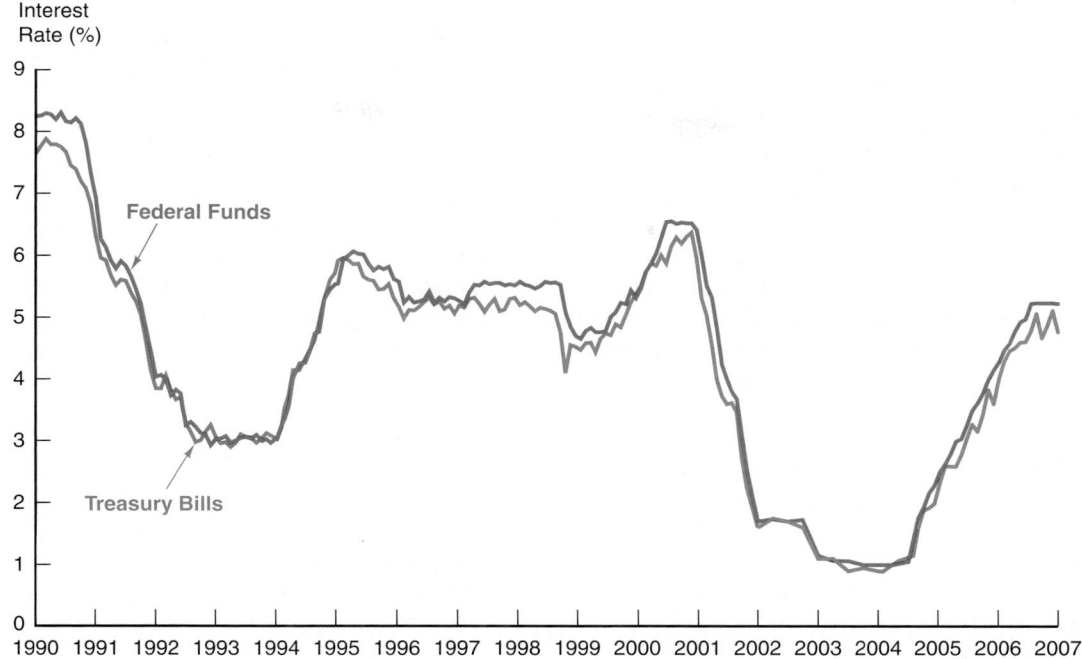

Figure 9.3 Federal Funds and Treasury Bill Interest Rates, January 1990–January 2007

Source: http://www.federalreserve.gov/releases/H15/data.htm/.

Repurchase Agreements

Repurchase agreements (repos) work much the same as fed funds except that non-banks can participate. A firm can sell Treasury securities in a repurchase agreement whereby the firm agrees to buy back the securities at a specified future date. Most repos have a very short term, the most common being for 3 to 14 days. There is a market, however, for one- to three-month repos.

The Use of Repurchase Agreements Government securities dealers frequently engage in repos. The dealer may sell the securities to a bank with the promise to buy the securities back the next day. This makes the repo essentially a short-term collateralized loan. Securities dealers use the repo to manage their liquidity and to take advantage of anticipated changes in interest rates.

The Federal Reserve also uses repos in conducting monetary policy. We presented the details of monetary policy in Chapter 8. Recall that the conduct of monetary policy typically requires that the Fed adjust bank reserves on a temporary basis. To accomplish this adjustment, the Fed will buy or sell Treasury securities in the repo market. The maturities of Federal Reserve repos never exceed 15 days.

Interest Rate on Repos Because repos are collateralized with Treasury securities, they are usually low-risk investments and therefore have low interest rates. Though rare, losses have occurred in these markets. For example, in 1985, ESM Government Securities and Bevill, Bresler & Schulman declared bankruptcy. These firms had used the same securities as collateral for more than one loan. The resulting losses to municipalities that had purchased the repos exceeded $500 million. Such losses also caused the failure of the state-insured thrift insurance system in Ohio.

Negotiable Certificates of Deposit

A negotiable certificate of deposit is a bank-issued security that documents a deposit and specifies the interest rate and the maturity date. Because a maturity date is specified, a CD is a **term security** as opposed to a **demand deposit**: Term securities have a specified maturity date; demand deposits can be withdrawn at any time. A negotiable CD is also called a **bearer instrument**. This means that whoever holds the instrument at maturity receives the principal and interest. The CD can be bought and sold until maturity.

Terms of Negotiable Certificates of Deposit The denominations of negotiable certificates of deposit range from $100,000 to $10 million. Few negotiable CDs are denominated less than $1 million. The reason that these instruments are so large is that dealers have established the round lot size to be $1 million. A round lot is the minimum quantity that can be traded without incurring higher than normal brokerage fees.

Negotiable CDs typically have a maturity of one to four months. Some have six-month maturities, but there is little demand for ones with longer maturities.

History of the CD Citibank issued the first large certificates of deposit in 1961. The bank offered the CD to counter the long-term trend of declining demand deposits at large banks. Corporate treasurers were minimizing their cash balances and investing their excess funds in safe, income-generating money market instruments such as T-bills. The attraction of the CD was that it paid a market interest rate. There was a problem, however. The rate of interest that banks could pay on CDs was restricted by Regulation Q. As long as interest rates on most securities were low, this regulation did not affect demand. But when interest rates rose above the level permitted by Regulation Q, the market for these certificates of deposit evaporated. In response, banks began offering the certificates overseas, where they were exempt from Regulation Q limits. In 1970, Congress amended Regulation Q to exempt certificates of deposit over $100,000. By 1972, the CD represented approximately 40% of all bank deposits. The certificate of deposit is now the second most popular money market instrument, behind only the T-bill.

Interest Rate on CDs Figure 9.4 plots the interest rate on negotiable CDs along with that on T-bills. The rates paid on negotiable CDs are negotiated between the bank and the customer. They are similar to the rate paid on other money market instruments because the level of risk is relatively low. Large money center banks can offer rates a little lower than other banks because many investors in the market believe that the government would never allow one of the nation's largest banks to fail. This belief makes these banks' obligations less risky.

Commercial Paper

Commercial paper securities are unsecured promissory notes, issued by corporations, that mature in no more than 270 days. Because these securities are unsecured, only the largest and most creditworthy corporations issue commercial paper. The interest rate the corporation is charged reflects the firm's level of risk.

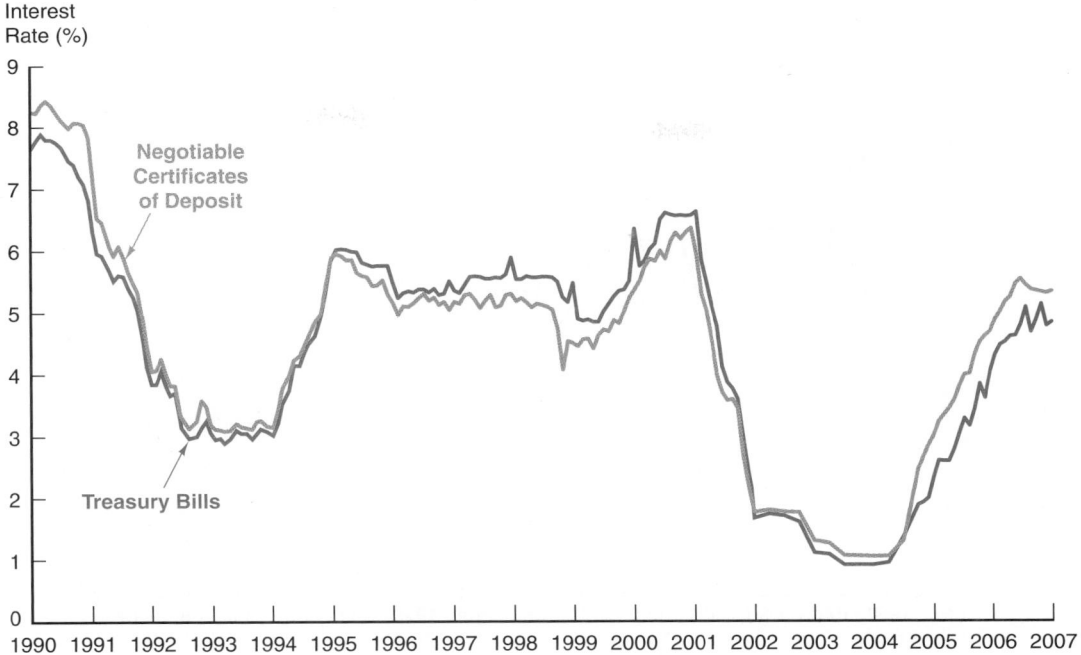

Figure 9.4   Interest Rates on Negotiable Certificates of Deposit and on Treasury Bills, 1990–2007

Source: http://www.federalreserve.gov/releases.

Terms and Issuance Commercial paper always has an original maturity of less than 270 days. This is to avoid the need to register the security issue with the Securities and Exchange Commission. (To be exempt from SEC registration, the issue must have an original maturity of less than 270 days and be intended for current transactions.) Most commercial paper actually matures in 20 to 45 days. Like T-bills, most commercial paper is issued on a discounted basis.

About 60% of commercial paper is sold directly by the issuer to the buyer. The balance is sold by dealers in the commercial paper market. A strong secondary market for commercial paper does not exist. A dealer will redeem commercial paper if a purchaser has a dire need for cash, though this is generally not necessary.

History of Commercial Paper Commercial paper has been used in various forms since the 1920s. In 1969, a tight-money environment caused bank holding companies to issue commercial paper to finance new loans. In response, to keep control over the money supply, the Federal Reserve imposed reserve requirements on bank-issued commercial paper in 1970. These reserve requirements removed the major advantage to banks of using commercial paper. Bank holding companies still use commercial paper to fund leasing and consumer finance.

The use of commercial paper increased substantially in the early 1980s because of the rising cost of bank loans. Figure 9.5 graphs the interest rate on commercial paper against the bank prime rate for the period January 1990–January 2007, Commercial paper has become an important alternative to bank loans primarily because of its lower cost.

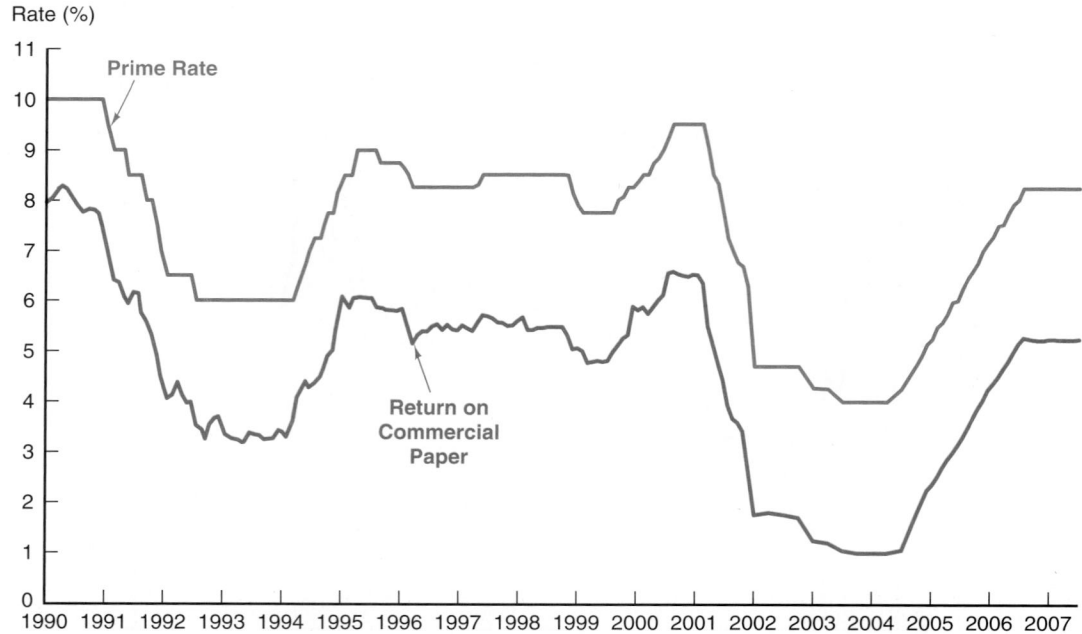

Figure 9.5 Return on Commercial Paper and the Prime Rate, 1990–2007

Source: http://www.federalreserve.gov/releases.

Market for Commercial Paper Nonbank corporations use commercial paper extensively to finance the loans that they extend to their customers. For example, General Motors Acceptance Corporation (GMAC) borrows money by issuing commercial paper and uses the money to make loans to consumers buying General Motors cars. Similarly, GE Capital and Chrysler Credit use commercial paper to fund loans made to consumers. The total number of firms issuing commercial paper varies between 600 to 800, depending on the level of interest rates. Most of these firms use one of about 30 commercial paper dealers who match up buyers and sellers. The large New York City money center banks are very active in this market. Some of the larger issuers of commercial paper choose to distribute their securities with **direct placements**. In a direct placement, the issuer bypasses the dealer and sells directly to the end investor. The advantage of this method is that the issuer saves the 0.125% commission that the dealer charges.

Most issuers of commercial paper back up their paper with a line of credit at a bank. This means that in the event the issuer cannot pay off or roll over the maturing paper, the bank will lend the firm funds for this purpose. The line of credit reduces the risk to the purchasers of the paper and so lowers the interest rate. The bank that provides the backup line of credit agrees in advance to make a loan to the issuer if needed to pay off the outstanding paper. The bank charges a fee of 0.5% to 1% for this commitment. Issuers pay this fee because they are able to save more than this in lowered interest costs by having the line.

Commercial banks were the original purchasers of commercial paper. Today the market has greatly expanded to include large insurance companies, nonfinancial busi-

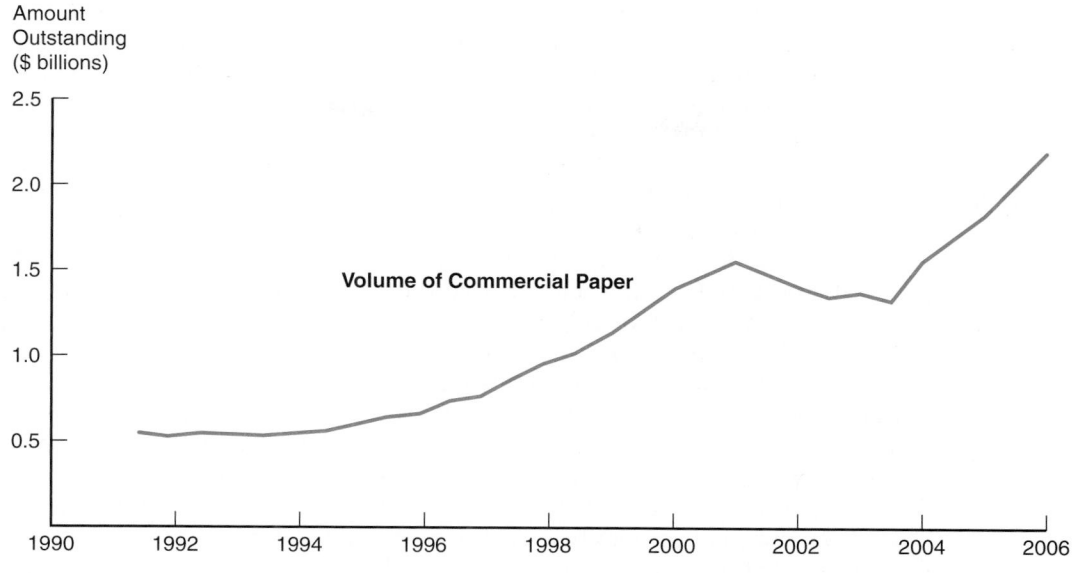

Figure 9.6 Volume of Commercial Paper Outstanding

Source: http://www.federalreserve.gov/releases/cp/histouts.txt.

nesses, bank trust departments, and government pension funds. These firms are attracted by the relatively low default risk, short maturity, and high yields these securities offer. Currently, about $2.0 trillion in commercial paper is outstanding (see Figure 9.6).

Banker's Acceptances

A banker's acceptance is an order to pay a specified amount of money to the bearer on a given date. Banker's acceptances have been in use since the twelfth century. However, they were not major money market securities until the volume of international trade ballooned in the 1960s. They are used to finance goods that have not yet been transferred from the seller to the buyer. For example, suppose that Builtwell Construction Company wants to buy a bulldozer from Komatsu in Japan. Komatsu does not want to ship the bulldozer without being paid because Komatsu has never heard of Builtwell and realizes that it would be difficult to collect if payment were not forthcoming. Similarly, Builtwell is reluctant to send money to Japan before receiving the equipment. A bank can intervene in this standoff by issuing a banker's acceptance.

Using a Banker's Acceptance The transaction would begin with Builtwell obtaining a letter of credit from its bank. A letter of credit simply says that if Builtwell has not paid its obligation by a certain time, the bank will make payment. This particular letter of credit will also authorize the exporter (Komatsu or its bank) to draw a time draft for the amount of the sale. A time draft is like a postdated check: It can be cashed only after a certain date. Builtwell sends the order for the bulldozer, along with the letter of credit, to Komatsu.

When Komatsu receives these documents, it is willing to ship the equipment because the bank's credit standing has been substituted for that of the actual buyer. Once the equipment has been shipped, Komatsu will present the letter of credit and the shipping documents to its own bank in Japan. This bank will create the time draft authorized by the letter of credit and send it to Builtwell's bank. When Builtwell's bank receives the time draft and the shipping documents, it will stamp the time draft "accepted" and return it to Komatsu's bank.

This accepted time draft is now a banker's acceptance. Because it is backed by the credit of a bank, it can be traded on the secondary market. Typically, the exporter's bank will sell it so that the exporter can receive funds before the maturity date. It will be sold at a discount so that the buyer can earn a fair return for holding it until its maturity date.

The transaction is completed when Builtwell deposits the funds in its bank to cover the amount of the time draft (now a banker's acceptance). When the banker's acceptance finally matures and is presented for payment, the issuing bank withdraws funds from Builtwell's account to make payment. Of course, if for some reason Builtwell was unable to make the required deposit, its bank would pay the acceptance anyway and attempt to collect from Builtwell later.

Let us summarize the steps for using banker's acceptances.

1. The importer requests its bank to send an irrevocable letter of credit to the exporter.
2. The exporter receives the letter, ships the goods, and is paid by presenting to its bank the letter along with proof that the merchandise was shipped.
3. The exporter's bank creates a time draft based on the letter of credit and sends it along with proof of shipment to the importer's bank.
4. The importer's bank stamps the time draft "accepted" and sends the banker's acceptance back to the exporter's bank so that the exporter's bank can sell it on the secondary market to collect payment.
5. The importer deposits funds at its bank sufficient to cover the banker's acceptance when it matures.

Advantages of Banker's Acceptances As the bulldozer example demonstrates, banker's acceptances are crucial to international trade. Without them, many transactions simply would not occur because the parties would not feel properly protected from losses. There are other advantages as well:

- The exporter is paid immediately. This is important when delivery times are long after shipment.
- The exporter is shielded from foreign exchange risk because the local bank pays in domestic funds.
- The exporter does not have to assess the creditworthiness of the importer because the importer's bank guarantees payment.

Secondary Market for Banker's Acceptances Because banker's acceptances are payable to the bearer, they can be bought and sold until they mature. They are sold on a discounted basis like commercial paper and T-bills. Dealers in this market match up firms that want to discount a banker's acceptance (sell it for immediate payment) with companies wishing to invest in banker's acceptances.

Interest rates on banker's acceptances are low because the risk of default is very low. For example, no investor in banker's acceptances in the United States has suffered a loss of principal in more than 60 years. The reason is that only large money center banks are involved in this market.

Eurodollars

Many contracts around the world call for payment in U.S. dollars due to the dollar's stability. For this reason, many companies and governments choose to hold dollars. Prior to World War II, most of these deposits were held in New York money center banks. However, as a result of the Cold War that followed, there was fear that deposits held on U.S. soil could be expropriated. Some large London banks responded to this opportunity by offering to hold dollar-denominated deposits in British banks. These deposits were dubbed Eurodollars (see the Global box).

The Eurodollar market has continued to grow rapidly. The primary reason is that depositors receive a higher rate of return on a dollar deposit in the Eurodollar market than in the domestic market. At the same time, the borrower is able to receive a more favorable rate in the Eurodollar market than in the domestic market. This is because multinational banks are not subject to the same regulations restricting U.S. banks and because they are willing and able to accept narrower spreads between the interest paid on deposits and the interest earned on loans.

London Interbank Market   Some large London banks act as brokers in the interbank Eurodollar market. Recall that fed funds are used by banks to make up temporary shortfalls in their reserves. Eurodollars are an alternative to fed funds. Banks from around the world buy and sell overnight funds in this market. The rate paid by banks buying funds is the **London interbank bid rate (LIBID)**. Funds are offered for sale in this market at the **London interbank offer rate (LIBOR)**. Because many banks participate in this market, it is extremely competitive. The spread between the bid and the offer rate seldom exceeds 0.125%. Eurodollar deposits are time deposits, which means that they cannot be withdrawn for a specified period of time. Although the most common time period is overnight, different maturities are available. Each maturity has a different rate.

The overnight LIBOR and the fed funds rate tend to be very close to each other. This is because they are near-perfect substitutes. Suppose that the fed funds rate exceeded the overnight LIBOR. Banks that need to borrow funds will borrow overnight Eurodollars, thus tending to raise rates, and banks with funds to lend will lend fed funds, thus tending to lower rates. The demand and supply pressure will cause a rapid adjustment that will drive the two rates together.

At one time, most short-term loans with adjustable interest rates were tied to the Treasury bill rate. However, the market for Eurodollars is so broad and deep that it has recently become the standard rate against which others are compared. For example, the U.S. commercial paper market now quotes rates as a spread over LIBOR, rather than over the T-bill rate.

The Eurodollar market is not limited to London banks anymore. The primary brokers in this market maintain offices in all of the major financial centers worldwide.

Eurodollar Certificates of Deposit Because Eurodollars are time deposits with fixed maturities, they are to a certain extent illiquid. As usual, the financial markets created new types of securities to combat this problem. These new securities were transferable negotiable certificates of deposit (negotiable CDs). Because most Eurodollar deposits have a relatively short term to begin with, the market for Eurodollar negotiable CDs is relatively limited, comprising less than 10% of the amount of regular Eurodollar deposits. The market for the negotiable CDs is still thin.

Other Eurocurrencies The Eurodollar market is by far the largest short-term security market in the world. This is due to the international popularity of the U.S. dollar for trade. However, the market is not limited to dollars. It is possible to have an account denominated in Japanese yen held in a London or New York bank. Such an account would be termed a Euroyen account. Similarly, you may also have Euromark or Europeso accounts denominated in marks and pesos, respectively, and held in various banks around the world. Keep in mind that if market participants have a need for a particular security and are willing to pay for it, the financial markets stand ready and willing to create it.

Comparing Money Market Securities

Although money market securities share many characteristics, such as liquidity, safety, and short maturities, they all differ in some aspects.

Interest Rates

Figure 9.7 compares the interest rates on many of the money market instruments we have discussed. The most notable feature of this graph is that all of the money market instruments appear to move very closely together over time. This is because all have very low risk and a short term. They all have deep markets and so are priced competitively. In addition, because these instruments have so many of the same risk and term characteristics, they are close substitutes. Consequently, if one rate should temporarily depart from the others, market supply and demand forces would

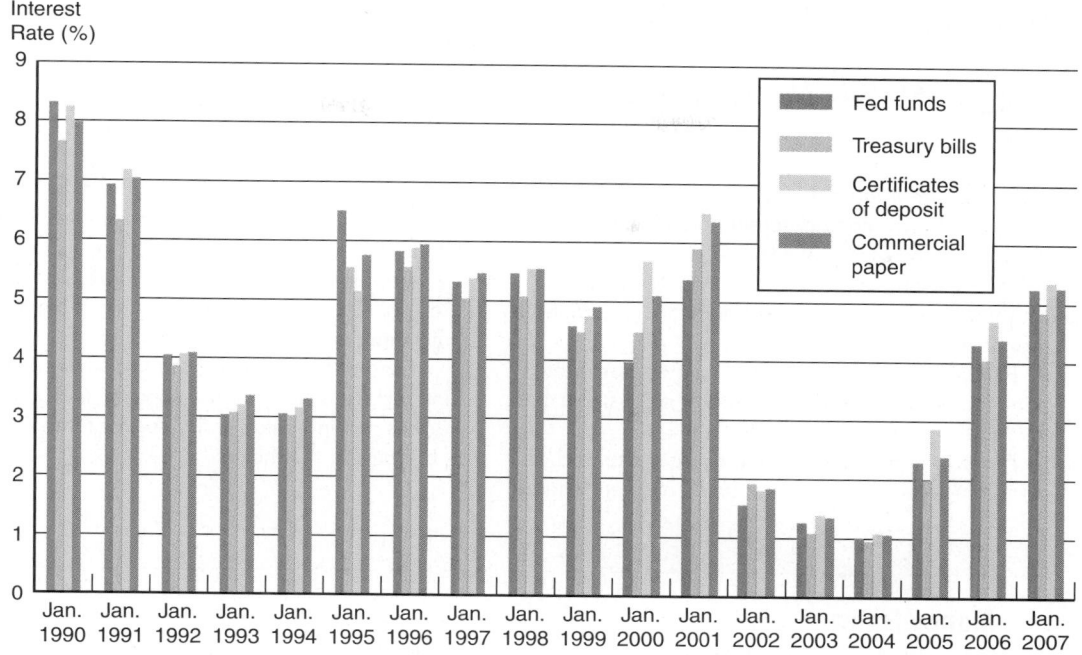

Figure 9.7   Interest Rates on Money Market Securities, 1990–2007

Source: http://www.federalreserve.gov/releases.

soon cause a correction. The *Wall Street Journal* reports money market rates in a table called "Money Rates," which appears daily in the third section (see the Following the Financial News box).

Liquidity

As we discussed in Chapter 4, the *liquidity* of a security refers to how quickly, easily, and cheaply it can be converted into cash. Typically, the depth of the secondary market where the security can be resold determines its liquidity. For example, the secondary market for Treasury bills is extensive and well developed. As a result, Treasury bills can be converted into cash quickly and with little cost. By contrast, there is no well-developed secondary market for commercial paper. Most holders of commercial paper hold the securities until maturity. In the event that a commercial paper investor needed to sell the securities to raise cash, it is likely that brokers would charge relatively high fees.

In some ways, the depth of the secondary market is not as critical for money market securities as it is for long-term securities such as stocks and bonds. This is because money market securities are short-term to start with. Nevertheless, many investors desire *liquidity intervention:* They seek an intermediary to provide liquidity where it did not previously exist. This is one function of money market mutual funds (discussed in Chapter 21).

following the financial news

Money Market Rates

The *Wall Street Journal* publishes daily a listing of interest rates on many different financial instruments in its "Money Rates" column.

The four interest rates in the "Money Rates" column that are discussed most frequently in the media are these:

Prime rate: The base interest rate on corporate bank loans, an indicator of the cost of business borrowing from banks

Federal funds rate: The interest rate charged on overnight loans in the federal funds market, a sensi-tive indicator of the cost to banks of borrowing funds from other banks and the stance of monetary policy

Treasury bill rate: The interest rate on U.S. Treasury bills, an indicator of general interest-rate movements

Federal Home Loan Mortgage Corporation rates: Interest rates on "Freddie Mac"—guaranteed mortgages, an indicator of the cost of financing residential housing purchases

Money Rates

July 5, 2007

Key annual interest rates paid to borrow or lend money in U.S. and international markets. Rates below are a guide to general levels but don't always represent actual transactions.

Inflation

	May index level	CHG FROM (%) April '07	May '06
U.S. consumer price index			
All items	207.9	0.6	2.7
Core	210.3	...	2.2

International rates

	Latest	Week ago	–52-WEEK– High	Low
Prime rates				
U.S.	**8.25**	8.25	8.25	8.25
Canada	**6.00**	6.00	6.00	6.00
Euro zone	**4.00**	4.00	4.00	2.75
Japan	**1.875**	1.875	1.875	1.375
Switzerland	**4.58**	4.47	4.60	2.74
Britain	**5.75**	5.50	5.75	4.50
Australia	**6.25**	6.25	6.25	5.75
Hong Kong	**8.00**	8.00	8.00	8.00
Overnight repurchases				
U.S.	**5.06**	4.98	5.28	4.48
U.K. (BBA)	**5.757**	5.675	6.583	4.342
Euro zone	**4.04**	4.14	4.14	2.73

U.S. government rates

Discount	**6.25**	6.25	6.25	6.25
Federal funds				
Effective rate	**5.25**	5.27	5.42	5.20
High	**5.3750**	5.3750	7.0000	5.2813
Low	**5.0000**	4.7500	5.2500	3.5000
Bid	**5.1250**	4.5000	6.7500	3.0000
Offer	**5.2500**	4.7500	7.0000	4.5000

	Latest	Week ago	–52-WEEK– High	Low
60 days	**5.31**	5.31	5.43	5.28
90 days	**5.32**	53.2	5.49	5.28
120 days	**5.33**	5.32	5.51	5.26
150 days	**5.33**	5.33	5.56	5.24
180 days	**5.35**	5.34	5.60	5.21

Other short-term rates

	Latest	Week ago	–52-WEEK– High	Low
Call money	**7.00**	7.00	7.00	7.00
Commercial paper				
30 to 75 days	**5.24**	...	...	...
76 to 90 days	**5.22**	...	...	...
91 to 120 days	**5.21**	...	...	...
121 to 151 days	**5.20**	...	...	...
152 to 181 days	**5.17**	...	...	...
182 to 210 days	**5.17**	...	...	...
211 to 242 days	**5.16**	...	...	...
243 to 270 days	**5.14**	...	...	...
Dealer commercial paper				
30 days	**5.28**	5.28	5.36	5.25
60 days	**5.30**	5.29	5.41	5.24
90 days	**5.30**	5.31	5.46	5.21
Euro commercial paper				
30 day	**4.05**	4.08	4.08	2.00
Two month	**4.08**	4.08	4.08	2.92
Three month	**4.14**	4.12	4.14	3.01
Four month	**4.19**	4.17	4.19	3.08
Five month	**4.22**	4.21	4.22	3.13
Six month	**4.29**	4.24	4.29	3.20

Euro Libor

	Latest	Week ago	–52-WEEK– High	Low
One month	**4.107**	4.114	4.120	2.884
Three month	**4.190**	4.174	4.190	3.059
Six month	**4.338**	4.312	4.338	3.255
One year	**4.564**	4.528	4.564	3.510

Euro interbank offered rate (Euribor)

One month	**4.103**	4.114	4.119	2.884
Three month	**4.190**	4.172	4.190	3.062
Six month	**4.337**	4.313	4.337	3.255
One year	**4.563**	4.525	4.563	3.511

Hibor

One month	**4.597**	4.458	4.660	3.662
Three month	**4.518**	4.470	4.707	3.904
Six month	**4.560**	4.525	4.852	3.950
One year	**4.712**	4.688	5.688	3.964

Asian dollars

One month	**5.336**	5.340	5.425	5.328
Three month	**5.368**	5.368	5.525	3.570
Six month	**5.389**	5.385	5.637	5.277
One year	**5.419**	5.408	5.752	5.119

Eurodollars (mid rates)

	Latest Offer	Bid	Week ago	52-WEEK High	Low
One month	**5.28**	5.31	5.30	5.35	5.27
Two month	**5.30**	5.32	5.31	5.44	5.27
Three month	**5.32**	5.33	5.33	5.51	5.27
Four month	**5.33**	5.34	5.33	5.54	5.25
Five month	**5.32**	5.34	5.33	5.57	5.24
Six month	**5.34**	5.35	5.34	5.61	5.22

Treasury bill auction

4 weeks	**4.660**	4.490	5.175	4.335
13 weeks	**4.790**	4.685	5.035	4.490
26 weeks	**4.810**	4.810	5.105	4.715

Secondary market
Freddie Mac
30-year mortgage yields

30 days	**6.58**	6.54	6.67	5.81
60 days	**6.60**	6.57	6.70	5.82
One-year RNY **3.375**	3.375	3.375	3.375

Constant maturity debt index

Three months	**5.295**	5.305	5.445	5.207
Six months	**5.297**	5.290	5.563	5.210
One year	**5.280**	5.270	5.603	4.953

Fannie Mae
30-year mortgage yields

30 days	**6.614**	6.603	6.775	5.913
60 days	**6.633**	6.623	6.795	5.924

Bankers acceptances

30 days	**5.30**	5.31	5.38	5.27

London interbank offered rate, or Libor

One month	**5.32000**	5.32000	5.42000	5.31913
Three month	**5.36000**	5.36000	5.52000	5.33000
Six month	**5.38625**	5.38000	5.63000	5.25913
One year	**5.41750**	5.40375	5.74938	5.11000

Weekly survey

Freddie Mac	Latest	Week ago	Year ago
30-year fixed	6.63	6.67	6.79
15-year fixed	6.30	6.34	6.44
Five-year ARM	6.29	6.30	6.39
One-year ARM	5.71	5.65	5.83

Notes on data:
U.S. prime rate and discount rate are effective June 29, 2006. **U.S. prime rate** is the base rate on corporate loans posted by at least 75% of the 30 largest U.S. banks; **Other prime rates** aren't directly comparable; lending practices vary widely by location; **Discount rate** is the charge on loans to depository institutions by the New York Federal Reserve Banks; **Federal-funds rate** is on reserves traded among commercial banks for overnight use in amounts of $1 million or more; **Call money rate** is the charge on loans to brokers on stock-exchange collateral; **Dealer commercial paper rates** are for high-grade unsecured notes fold through dealers by major corporations; **Freddie Mac RNY** is the required net yield for the one-year 2% rate-capped ARM. **Libor** is the British Banker's Association average of interbank offered rates for dollar deposits in the London market.

Sources: Merrill Lynch; Bureau of Labor Statistics; Reuters; General Electric Capital Corp.; Garban Intercapital; Tullett Prebon Information, Ltd.

Reuters Group PLC is the primary data provider for several statistical tables in The Wall Street Journal, including foreign stock quotations, futures and foreign exchange tables. Reuters real-time data feeds are used to calculated various Dow Jones indexes.

Table 9.4 summarizes the types of money market securities and the depth of the secondary market.

How Money Market Securities Are Valued

Suppose that you work for Merrill Lynch and that it is your job to submit the bid for Treasury bills this week. How would you know what price to submit? Your first step would be to determine the yield that you require. Let us assume that, based

TABLE 9.4 Money Market Securities and Their Markets

Money Market Security	Issuer	Buyer	Usual Maturity	Secondary Market
Treasury bills	U.S. government	Consumers and companies	4, 13 weeks, and 26 weeks	Excellent
Federal funds	Banks	Banks	1 to 7 days	None
Repurchase agreements	Businesses and banks	Businesses and banks	1 to 15 days	Good
Negotiable certificates of deposit	Large money center banks	Businesses	14 to 120 days	Good
Commercial paper	Finance companies and businesses	Businesses	1 to 270 days	Poor
Banker's acceptance	Banks	Businesses	30 to 180 days	Good
Eurodollar deposits	Non-U.S. banks	Businesses, governments, and banks	1 day to 1 year	Poor

on your understanding of interest rates learned in Chapters 3 and 4, you decide you need a 2% return. To simplify our calculations, let us also assume we are bidding on securities with a one-year maturity. We know that our Treasury bill will pay $1,000 when it matures, so to compute how much we will pay today we find the present value of $1,000. The process of computing a present value was discussed in Example 1 in Chapter 3. The formula is

$$PV = \frac{FV}{(1 + i)^n}$$

In this example FV = $1000, the interest rate = 0.02, and the period until maturity is 1, so

$$\text{Price} = \frac{\$1,000}{(1 + 0.02)} = \$980.39$$

Note what happens to the price of the security as interest rates rise. Since we are dividing by a larger number, the current price will decrease. For example, if interest rates rise to 3%, the value of the security would fall to $970.87 [$1,000/(1.03) = $970.87].

This method of discounting the future maturity value back to the present is the method used to price most money market securities.

SUMMARY

1. Money market securities are short-term instruments with an original maturity of less than one year. These securities include Treasury bills, commercial paper, federal funds, repurchase agreements, negotiable certificates of deposit, banker's acceptances, and Eurodollars.

2. Money market securities are used to "warehouse" funds until needed. The returns earned on these investments are low due to their low risk and high liquidity.

3. Many participants in the money markets both buy and sell money market securities. The U.S. Treasury, commercial banks, businesses, and individuals all benefit by having access to low-risk short-term investments.

4. Interest rates on all money market securities tend to follow one another closely over time. Treasury bill returns are the lowest because they are virtually devoid of default risk. Banker's acceptances and negotiable certificates of deposit are next lowest because they are backed by the creditworthiness of large money center banks.

KEY TERMS

bearer instrument, *p. 224*
book entry, *p. 221*
competitive bidding, *p. 220*
deep market, *p. 220*
demand deposit, *p. 224*
direct placements, *p. 226*
discounting, *p. 218*

liquid market, *p. 220*
London interbank bid rate, (LIBID), *p. 229*
London interbank offer rate, (LIBOR), *p. 229*
noncompetitive bidding, *p. 220*
term security, *p. 224*
wholesale markets, *p. 212*

QUESTIONS

1. What characteristics define the money markets?

2. Is a Treasury bond issued 29 years ago with six months remaining before it matures a money market instrument?

3. Why do banks not eliminate the need for money markets?

4. Distinguish between a term security and a demand security.

5. What was the purpose motivating regulators to impose interest ceilings on bank savings accounts? What impact did this eventually have on the money markets?

6. Why does the U.S. government use the money markets?

7. Why do businesses use the money markets?

8. What purpose initially motivated Merrill Lynch to offer money market mutual funds to its customers?

9. Why are more funds from property and casualty insurance companies than funds from life insurance companies invested in the money markets?

10. Which of the money market securities is the most liquid and considered the most risk-free? Why?

11. Distinguish between competitive bidding and non-competitive bidding for Treasury securities.

12. Who issues federal funds, and what is the usual purpose of these funds?

13. Does the Federal Reserve *directly* set the federal funds interest rate? How does the Fed influence this rate?

14. Who issues commercial paper and for what purpose?

15. Why are banker's acceptances so popular for international transactions?

QUANTITATIVE PROBLEMS

1. What would be your annualized discount rate % and your annualized investment rate % on the purchase of a 182-day Treasury bill for $4,925 that pays $5,000 at maturity?

2. What is the annualized discount rate % and your annualized investment rate % on a Treasury bill that you purchase for $9,940 that will mature in 91 days for $10,000?

3. If you want to earn an annualized discount rate of 3.5%, what is the most you can pay for a 91-day Treasury bill that pays $5,000 at maturity?

4. What is the annualized discount and investment rate % on a Treasury bill that you purchase for $9,900 that will mature in 91 days for $10,000?

5. The price of 182-day commercial paper is $7,840. If the annualized investment rate is 4.093%, what will the paper pay at maturity?

6. How much would you pay for a Treasury bill that matures in 182 days and pays $10,000 if you require a 1.8% discount rate?

7. The price of $8,000 face value commercial paper is $7,930. If the annualized discount rate is 4%, when will the paper mature? If the annualized investment rate % is 4%, when will the paper mature?

8. How much would you pay for a Treasury bill that matures in one year and pays $10,000 if you require a 3% discount rate?

9. The annualized discount rate on a particular money market instrument, is 3.75%. The face value is $200,000 and it matures in 51 days. What is its price? What would be the price if it had 71 days to maturity?

10. The annualized yield is 3% for 91-day commercial paper, and 3.5% for 182-day commercial paper. What is the expected 91-day commercial paper rate 91 days from now?

11. In a Treasury auction of $2.1 billion par value 91-day T-bills, the following bids were submitted:

Bidder	Bid Amount	Price
1	$500 million	$0.9940
2	$750 million	$0.9901
3	$1.5 billion	$0.9925
4	$1 billion	$0.9936
5	$600 million	$0.9939

If only these competitive bids are received, who will receive T-bills, in what quantity, and at what price?

12. If the Treasury also received $750 million in non-competitive bids, who will receive T-bills, in what quantity, and at what price? (Refer to the table under problem 11.)

WEB EXERCISES

The Money Markets

1. Up-to-date interest rates are available from the Federal Reserve at **http://www.federalreserve.gov/ releases**. Locate the current rate on the following securities:

   a. Prime rate

   b. Federal funds

   c. Commercial paper (financial)

   d. Certificates of deposit

   e. Discount rate

   f. One-month Eurodollar deposits

   Compare these rates on a–c to those reported in Table 9.1. Have short-term rates generally increased or decreased?

2. The Treasury conducts auctions of money market treasury securities at regular intervals. Go to **http:// www.treasurydirect.gov/RI/OFAnnce.htm** and locate the schedule of auctions. When is the next auction of 4-week bills? When is the next auction of 13- and 26-week bills? How often are these securities auctioned?

CHAPTER 10

The Bond Market

Preview

The last chapter discussed short-term securities that trade in a market we call the money market. This chapter talks about the first of several securities that trade in a market we call the capital market. Capital markets are for securities with an original maturity that is greater than one year. These securities include bonds, stocks, and mortgages. We will devote an entire chapter to each major type of capital market security due to their importance to investors, businesses, and the economy. This chapter begins with a brief introduction on how the capital markets operate before launching into the study of bonds. In the next chapter we will study stocks and the stock market. We will conclude our look at the capital markets in Chapter 12 with mortgages.

Purpose of the Capital Market

Firms that issue capital market securities and the investors who buy them have very different motivations than those who operate in the money markets. Firms and individuals use the money markets primarily to warehouse funds for short periods of time until a more important need or a more productive use for the funds arises. By contrast, firms and individuals use the capital markets for long-term investments.

Suppose that after a careful financial analysis, your firm determines that it needs a new plant to meet the increased demand for its products. This analysis will be made using interest rates that reflect the *current* long-term cost of funds to the firm. Now suppose that your firm chooses to finance this plant by issuing money market securities, such as commercial paper. As long as interest rates do not rise, all is well: When these short-term securities mature, they can be reissued at the same interest rate. However, if interest rates rise, as they did dramatically in 1980, the firm may find that it does not have the cash flows or income to support the plant because when the short-term securities mature, the firm will have to reissue them at a higher interest rate. If long-term securities, such as bonds or stock, had been used, the increased interest rates would not have been as critical. The primary reason that individuals and firms choose to borrow long-term is to reduce the risk that interest rates will rise before they pay off their debt. This reduction in risk comes at a cost, however. As you may recall from Chapter 5, most long-term interest rates are higher than short-term rates due to risk premiums. Despite the need to pay higher interest rates to borrow in the capital markets, these markets remain very active.

Capital Market Participants

The primary issuers of capital market securities are federal and local governments and corporations. The federal government issues long-term notes and bonds to fund the national debt. State and municipal governments also issue long-term notes and bonds to finance capital projects, such as school and prison construction. Governments never issue stock because they cannot sell ownership claims.

Corporations issue both bonds and stock. One of the most difficult decisions a firm faces can be whether it should finance its growth with debt or equity. The distribution of a firm's capital between debt and equity is its capital structure. (The factors that influence the capital structure decision are discussed in Chapter 15.) Corporations may enter the capital markets because they do not have sufficient capital to fund their investment opportunities. Alternatively, firms may choose to enter the capital markets because they want to preserve their capital to protect against unexpected needs. In either case, the availability of efficiently functioning capital markets is crucial to the continued health of the business sector.

The largest purchasers of capital market securities are households. Frequently, individuals and households deposit funds in financial institutions that use the funds to purchase capital market instruments such as bonds or stock.

Capital Market Trading

go online

Initial public offering news and information, including advanced search tools for IPO offerings, venture capital research reports, etc., is available at www.ipomonitor.com.

Capital market trading occurs in either the *primary market* or the *secondary market*. The primary market is where new issues of stocks and bonds are introduced. Investment funds, corporations, and individual investors can all purchase securities offered in the primary market. You can think of a primary market transaction as one where the issuer of the security actually receives the proceeds of the sale. When firms sell securities for the very first time, the issue is an **initial public offering (IPO).** Subsequent sales of a firm's new stocks or bonds to the public are simply primary market transactions (as opposed to an initial one).

The capital markets have well-developed secondary markets. A secondary market is where the sale of previously issued securities takes place, and it is important because most investors plan to sell long-term bonds before they reach maturity and

go online

Find listed companies, member information, real-time market indices, and current stock quotes at **www.nyse.com**.

eventually to sell their holdings of stock as well. There are two types of exchanges in the secondary market for capital securities: *organized exchanges* and *over-the-counter exchanges*. Whereas most money market transactions originate over the phone, most capital market transactions, measured by volume, occur in organized exchanges. An organized exchange has a building where securities (including stocks, bonds, options, and futures) trade. Exchange rules govern trading to ensure the efficient and legal operation of the exchange, and the exchange's board constantly reviews these rules to ensure that they result in competitive trading.

Types of Bonds

Bonds are securities that represent a debt owed by the issuer to the investor. Bonds obligate the issuer to pay a specified amount at a given date, generally with periodic interest payments. The par, face, or maturity value of the bond is the amount that the issuer must pay at maturity. The coupon rate is the rate of interest that the issuer must pay. This rate is usually fixed for the duration of the bond and does not fluctuate with market interest rates. If the repayment terms of a bond are not met, the holder of a bond has a claim on the assets of the issuer. Look at Figure 10.1. The face value of the bond is given in the top right corner. The interest rate of $8\frac{5}{8}\%$, along with the maturity date, is reported several times on the face of the bond.

Long-term bonds traded in the capital market include long-term government notes and bonds, municipal bonds, and corporate bonds.

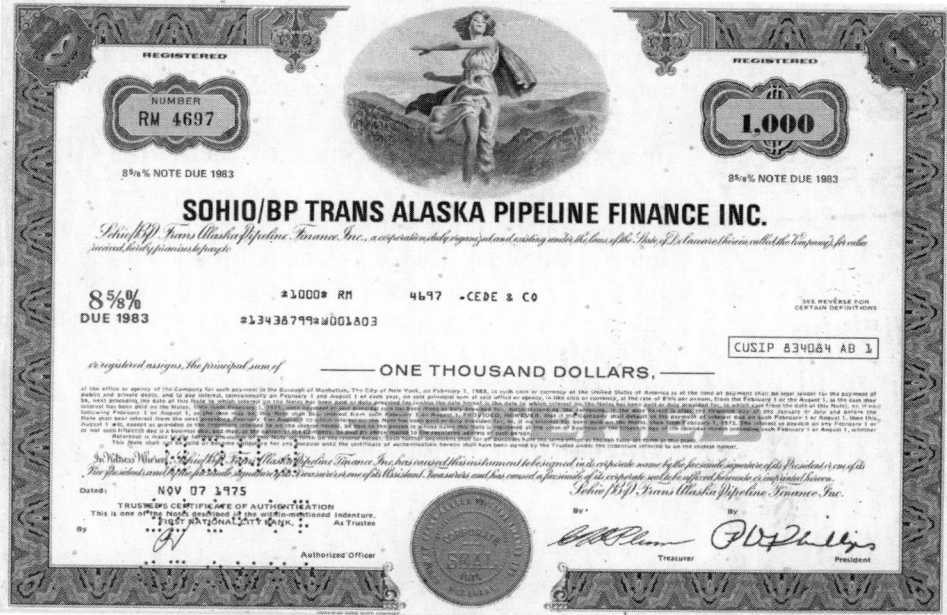

Figure 10.1 Sohio/BP Corporate Bond

Source: Eakins, *Finance: Investments, Institutions, & Management*, p. 39.

Treasury Notes and Bonds

The U.S. Treasury issues notes and bonds to finance the national debt. The difference between a note and a bond is that notes have an original maturity of 1 to 10 years while bonds have an original maturity of 10 to 30 years. (Recall from Chapter 9 that Treasury *bills* mature in less than one year.) The treasury currently issues notes with 2-, 5-, and 10-year maturities. The treasury resumed issuing 30-year bonds in February 2006. Table 10.1 summarizes the maturity differences among Treasury securities. The prices of Treasury notes, bonds, and bills are quoted as a percentage of $100 face value.

Federal government notes and bonds are free of default risk because the government can always print money to pay off the debt if necessary.[1] This does *not* mean that these securities are risk-free. We will discuss interest-rate risk applied to bonds later in this chapter.

Treasury Bond Interest Rates

Treasury bonds have very low interest rates because they have no default risk. Although investors in Treasury bonds have found themselves earning less than the rate of inflation in some years (see Figure 10.2), most of the time the interest rate on Treasury notes and bonds is above that on money market securities because of interest-rate risk.

Figure 10.3 plots the yield on 20-year Treasury bonds against the yield on 90-day Treasury bills. Two things are noteworthy in this graph. First, in most years, the rate of return on the short-term bill is below that on the 20-year bond. Second, short-term rates are more volatile than long-term rates. Short-term rates are more influenced by the current rate of inflation. Investors in long-term securities expect extremely high or low inflation rates to return to more normal levels, so long-term rates do not typically change as much as short-term rates.

Treasury Inflation Protected Securities (TIPS)

In 1997, the Treasury Department began offering an innovative bond designed to remove inflation risk from holding treasuries. The inflation-indexed bonds have an interest rate that does not change throughout the term of the security. However, the principal amount used to compute the interest payment does change based on the consumer price index. At maturity, the securities are redeemed at the greater of their inflation-adjusted principal or par amount at original issue.

TABLE 10.1 Treasury Securities

Type	Maturity
Treasury bill	Less than 1 year
Treasury note	1 to 10 years
Treasury bond	10 to 30 years

---

[1]We noted in Chapter 9 that Treasury bills were also considered default-risk-free except that a budget stalemate in 1996 almost caused default. The same small chance of default applies to Treasury bonds.

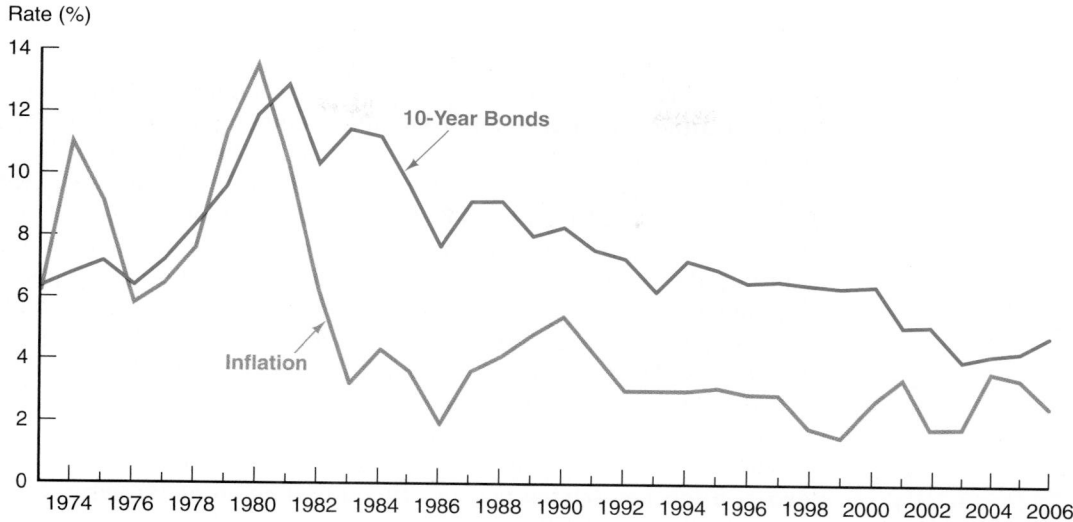

Figure 10.2   Interest Rate on Treasury Bonds and the Inflation Rate, 1973–2006

Sources: http://www.federalreserve.gov/releases and ftp://ftp.bls.gov/pub/special.requests/cpi/cpiai.txt.

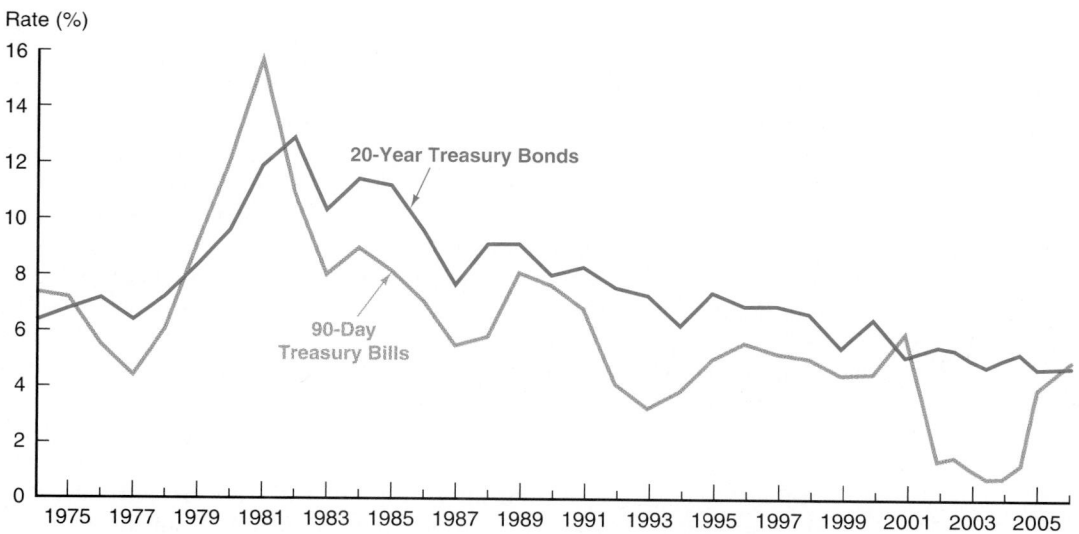

Figure 10.3   Interest Rate on Treasury Bills and Treasury Bonds, 1974–2006 (January of each year)

Source: http://www.federalreserve.gov/releases.

The advantage of inflation-indexed securities, also referred to as inflation pro-tected securities, is that they give both individual and institutional investors a chance to buy a security whose value won't be eroded by inflation. These securities can be used by retirees who want to hold a very low-risk portfolio.

Treasury STRIPS

In addition to bonds, notes, and bills, in 1985 the Treasury began issuing to depository institutions bonds in book entry form called **Separate Trading of Registered Interest and Principal Securities,** more commonly called **STRIPS.** Recall from Chapter 9 that to be sold in book entry form means that no physical document exists; instead, the security is issued and accounted for electronically. A STRIP separates the periodic interest payments from the final principal repayment. When a Treasury fixed-principal or inflation-indexed note or bond is stripped, each interest payment and the principal payment becomes a separate zero-coupon security. Each component has its own identifying number and can be held or traded separately. For example, a Treasury note with five years remaining to maturity consists of a single principal payment at maturity and ten interest payments, one every six months for five years. When this note is stripped, each of the ten interest payments and the principal payment becomes a separate security. Thus, the single Treasury note becomes 11 separate securities that can be traded individually. STRIPS are also called **zero-coupon securities** because the only time an investor receives a payment during the life of a STRIP is when it matures.

Before the government introduced these securities, the private sector had created them indirectly. In the early 1980s, Merrill Lynch created the Treasury Investment Growth Fund (TIGRs, pronounced "tigers"), in which it purchased Treasury securities and then stripped them to create principal-only securities and interest-only securities. Currently, more than $50 billion in stripped Treasury securities are outstanding.

Agency Bonds

Congress has authorized a number of U.S. agencies to issue bonds. The government does not explicitly guarantee agency bonds, though most investors feel that the government would not allow the agencies to default. Issuers of agency bonds include the Government National Mortgage Association, the Farmers Home Administration, the Federal Housing Administration, the Veterans Administrations, the Federal National Mortgage Association (Fannie Mae), the Federal Land Banks, and the Federal Home Loan Mortgage Corporation. These agencies issue bonds to raise funds that are used for purposes that Congress has deemed to be in the national interest. For example, the Government National Mortgage Association (Ginnie Mae) issues bonds to raise funds that are used to finance home loans.

The risk on agency bonds is actually very low. They are usually secured by the loans that are made with the funds raised by the bond sales. In addition, the federal agencies may use their lines of credit with the Treasury Department should they have trouble meeting their obligations. Finally, it is unlikely that the federal government would permit its agencies to default on their obligations.

Despite this low level of risk, these securities offer interest rates that are significantly higher than those available on Treasury securities. For example, on May 15, 2007, 30-year Fannie Mae bonds yielded 5.64%, while 30-year Treasury bonds yielded 4.79%. A portion of the higher yield available on agencies may be due to their lower liquidity: Though a secondary market in agency securities exists, it is not as well developed or as deep as the market for government securities. (Chapter 5 discusses the effect liquidity has on interest rates.) Many investors feel that agency bonds represent an attractive alternative to low-interest-rate Treasuries.

Municipal Bonds

go online
www.bloomberg.com/
markets/rates/index.html
supplies the latest municipal
bond events, experts'
insights and analyses,
and a municipal bond
yields table.

Municipal bonds are securities issued by local, county, and state governments. The proceeds from these bonds are used to finance public interest projects such as schools, utilities, and transportation systems. Municipal bonds that are issued to pay for essential public projects are exempt from federal taxation. As we saw in Chapter 5, this allows the municipality to borrow at a lower cost because investors will be satisfied with lower interest rates on tax-exempt bonds. You can use the following equation to determine what tax-free rate of interest is equivalent to a taxable rate:

$$\text{Equivalent tax-free rate} = \text{taxable interest rate} \times (1 - \text{marginal tax rate})$$

example 10.1 **Municipal Bonds**

Suppose that the interest rate on a taxable corporate bond is 9% and that the marginal tax is 28%. Suppose a tax-free municipal bond with a rate of 6.75% were available. Which security would you choose?

Solution
The tax-free equivalent municipal interest rate is 6.48%.

$$\text{Equivalent tax-free rate} = \text{taxable interest rate} \times (1 - \text{marginal tax rate})$$

where

Taxable interest rate = 0.09

Marginal tax rate = 0.28

Thus,

$$\text{Equivalent tax-free rate} = 0.09 \times (1 - 0.28) = 0.0648 = 6.48\%$$

Since the tax-free municipal bond rate (6.75%) is higher than the equivalent tax-free rate (6.48%), choose the municipal bond.

There are two types of municipal bonds: general obligation bonds and revenue bonds. **General obligation bonds** do not have specific assets pledged as security or a specific source of revenue allocated for their repayment. Instead, they are backed by the "full faith and credit" of the issuer. This phrase means that the issuer promises to use every resource available to repay the bond as promised. Most general obligation bond issues must be approved by the taxpayers because the taxing authority of the government is pledged for their repayment.

Revenue bonds, by contrast, are backed by the cash flow of a particular revenue-generating project. For example, revenue bonds may be issued to build a toll bridge, with the tolls being pledged as repayment. If the revenues are not sufficient to repay the bonds, they may go into default, and investors may suffer losses. This occurred on a large scale in 1983 when the Washington Public Power Supply System (since called "WHOOPS") used revenue bonds to finance the construction of two nuclear power plants. As a result of falling energy costs and tremendous cost overruns, the plants never became operational, and buyers of these bonds lost $225 billion. This

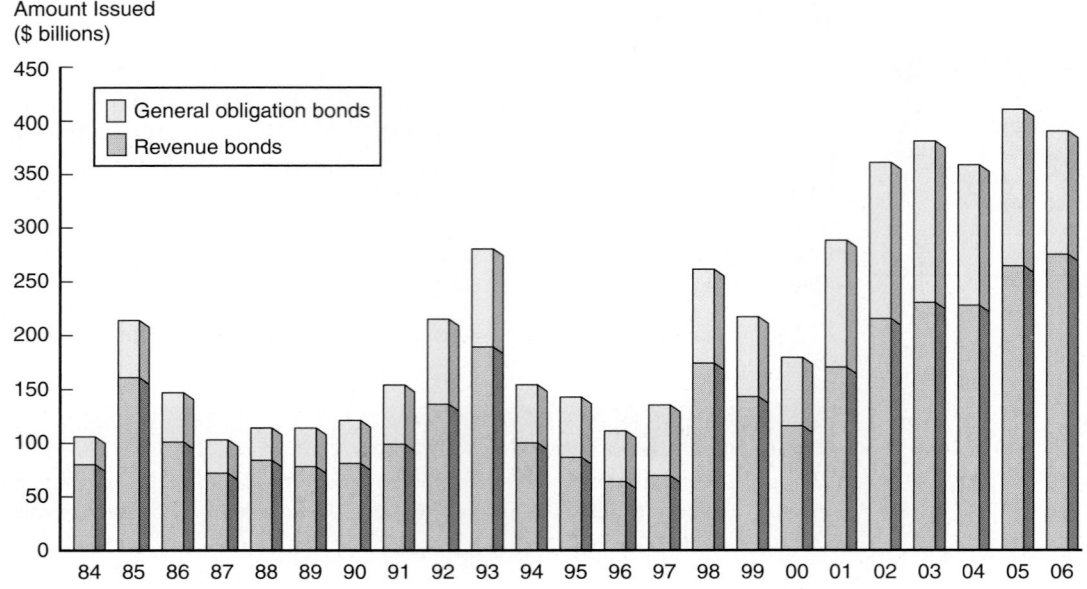

Amount Issued
($ billions)

Figure 10.4 Issuance of Revenue and General Obligation Bonds, 1984–2006 (End of year)

Source: Federal Reserve Bulletin, various issues, Table 1.45.

remains the largest public debt default on record. Revenue bonds tend to be issued more frequently than general obligation bonds (see Figure 10.4). Note that the low interest rates seen in recent years have prompted municipalities to issue record amounts of bonds.

Risk in the Municipal Bond Market

Municipal bonds are not default-free. For example, a study by Fitch Ratings reported a 0.63% default rate on municipal bonds. Default rates are higher during periods when the economy is weak. This points out that governments are not exempt from financial distress. Unlike the federal government, local governments cannot print money, and there are real limits on how high they can raise taxes without driving the population away.

Corporate Bonds

When large corporations need to borrow funds for long periods of time, they may issue bonds. Most corporate bonds have a face value of $1,000 and pay interest semiannually (twice per year). Most are also callable, meaning that the issuer may redeem the bonds after a specified date.

The **bond indenture** is a contract that states the lender's rights and privileges and the borrower's obligations. Any collateral offered as security to the bondholders will also be described in the indenture.

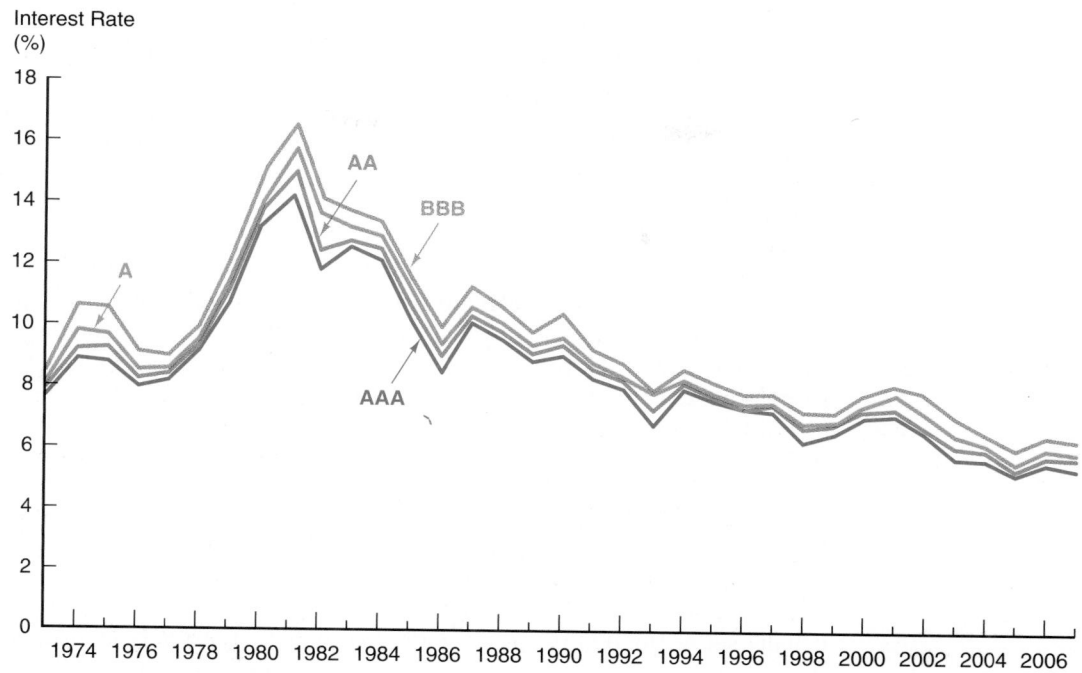

Interest Rate (%)

Figure 10.5 Corporate Bond Interest Rates, 1973–2006 (End of year)

Source: Federal Reserve Bulletin, Table 1.35, various issues.

The degree of risk varies widely among issues because the risk of default depends on the company's health, which can be affected by a number of variables. The interest rate on corporate bonds varies with the level of risk, as we discussed in Chapter 5. As Figure 10.5 shows, bonds with lower risk and a higher rating (AAA being the highest) have lower interest rates than more risky bonds (BBB). A bond's interest rate will depend on its features and characteristics, which are described in the following sections.

Characteristics of Corporate Bonds

At one time bonds were sold with attached coupons that the owner of the bond clipped and mailed to the firm to receive interest payments. These were called *bearer bonds* because payments were made to whoever had physical possession of the bonds. The Internal Revenue Service did not care for this method of payment, however, because it made tracking interest income difficult. Bearer bonds have now been largely replaced by **registered bonds,** which do not have coupons. Instead, the owner must register with the firm to receive interest payments. The firms are required to report to the IRS the name of the person who receives interest income. Despite the fact that bearer bonds with attached coupons have been phased out, the interest paid on bonds is still called the "coupon interest payment," and the interest rate on bonds is the coupon interest rate.

Restrictive Covenants A corporation's financial managers are hired, fired, and compensated at the direction of the board of directors, which represents the corporation's *stockholders*. This arrangement implies that the managers will be more interested in protecting stockholders than they are in protecting bondholders. You should recognize this as an example of the moral hazard problem introduced in Chapter 2 and discussed further in Chapter 15. Managers may not use the funds provided by the bonds as the bondholders might prefer. Since bondholders cannot look to managers for protection when the firm gets into trouble, they must include rules and restrictions on managers designed to protect the bondholders' interests. These are known as **restrictive covenants.** They usually limit the amount of dividends the firm can pay and the ability of the firm to issue additional debt. Other financial policies, such as the firm's involvement in mergers, may also be restricted. Restrictive covenants are included in the bond indenture. Typically, the interest rate will be lower the more restrictions are placed on management through restrictive covenants because the bonds will be considered safer by investors.

Call Provisions Most corporate indentures include a **call provision,** which states that the issuer has the right to force the holder to sell the bond back. The call provision usually requires a waiting period between the time the bond is initially issued and the time when it can be called. The price bondholders are paid for the bond is usually set at the bond's par price or slightly higher (usually by one year's interest cost). For example, a 10% coupon rate $1,000 bond may have a call price of $1,100.

If interest rates fall, the price of the bond will rise. If rates fall enough, the price will rise above the call price, and the firm will call the bond. Because call provisions put a limit on the amount that bondholders can earn from the appreciation of a bond's price, investors do not like call provisions.

A second reason that issuers of bonds include call provisions is to make it possible for them to buy back their bonds according to the terms of the **sinking fund.** A sinking fund is a requirement in the bond indenture that the firm pay off a portion of the bond issue each year. This provision is attractive to bondholders because it reduces the probability of default when the issue matures. Because a sinking fund provision makes the issue more attractive, the firm can reduce the bond's interest rate.

A third reason firms usually issue only callable bonds is that firms may have to retire a bond issue if the covenants of the issue restrict the firm from some activity that it feels is in the best interest of stockholders. Suppose that a firm needed to borrow additional funds to expand its storage facilities. If the firm's bonds carried a restriction against adding debt, the firm would have to retire its existing bonds before issuing new bonds or taking out a loan to build the new warehouse.

Finally, a firm may choose to call bonds if it wishes to alter its capital structure. A maturing firm with excess cash flow may wish to reduce its debt load if few attractive investment opportunities are available.

Because bondholders do not generally like call provisions, callable bonds must have a higher yield than comparable noncallable bonds. Despite the higher cost, firms still typically issue callable bonds because of the flexibility this feature provides the firm.

Conversion Some bonds can be converted into shares of common stock. This feature permits bondholders to share in the firm's good fortunes if the stock price rises. Most convertible bonds will state that the bond can be converted into a certain number of common shares at the discretion of the bondholder. The conversion ratio will be such that the price of the stock must rise substantially before conversion is likely to occur.

Issuing convertible bonds is one way firms avoid sending a negative signal to the market. If a firm chooses to issue stock, the market usually interprets this action as indicating that the stock price is relatively high or that it is going to fall in the future. The market makes this interpretation because it believes that managers are most concerned with looking out for the interests of existing stockholders and will not issue stock when it is undervalued. If managers believe that the firm will perform well in the future, they can, instead, issue convertible bonds. If the managers are correct and the stock price rises, the bondholders will convert to stock at a relatively high price that managers believe is fair. Alternatively, bondholders have the option not to convert if managers turn out to be wrong about the company's future.

Bondholders like a conversion feature. It is very similar to buying just a bond but receiving both a bond and a stock option (stock options are discussed fully in Chapter 25). The price of the bond will reflect the value of this option and so will be higher than the price of comparable nonconvertible bonds. The higher price received for the bond by the firm implies a lower interest rate.

Types of Corporate Bonds

A variety of corporate bonds are available. They are usually distinguished by the type of collateral that secures the bond and by the order in which the bond is paid off if the firm defaults.

Secured Bonds Secured bonds are ones with collateral attached. *Mortgage bonds* are used to finance a specific project. For example, a building may be the collateral for bonds issued for its construction. In the event that the firm fails to make payments as promised, mortgage bondholders have the right to liquidate the property in order to be paid. Because these bonds have specific property pledged as collateral, they are less risky than comparable unsecured bonds. As a result, they will have a lower interest rate.

Equipment trust certificates are bonds secured by tangible non-real-estate property, such as heavy equipment or airplanes. Typically, the collateral backing these bonds is more easily marketed than the real property backing mortgage bonds. As with mortgage bonds, the presence of collateral reduces the risk of the bonds and so lowers their interest rates.

Unsecured Bonds *Debentures* are long-term unsecured bonds that are backed only by the general creditworthiness of the issuer. No specific collateral is pledged to repay the debt. In the event of default, the bondholders must go to court to seize assets. Collateral that has been pledged to other debtors is not available to the holders of debentures. *Debentures* usually have an attached contract that spells out the terms of the bond and the responsibilities of management. The contract attached to the debenture is called an *indenture*. (Be careful not to confuse the terms *debenture* and *indenture*.) Debentures have lower priority than secured bonds if the firm defaults. As a result, they will have a higher interest rate than otherwise comparable secured bonds.

Subordinated debentures are similar to debentures except that they have a lower priority claim. This means that in the event of a default, subordinated debenture holders are paid only after nonsubordinated bondholders have been paid in full. As a result, subordinated debenture holders are at greater risk of loss.

Variable-rate bonds (which may be secured or unsecured) are a financial innovation spurred by increased interest-rate variability in the 1980s and 1990s. The interest rate on these securities is tied to another market interest rate, such as the rate on Treasury bonds, and is adjusted periodically. The interest rate on the bonds will change over time as market rates change.

Junk Bonds Recall from Chapter 5 that all bonds are rated by various companies according to their default risk. These companies study the issuer's financial characteristics and make a judgment about the issuer's possibility of default. A bond with a rating of AAA has the highest grade possible. Bonds *at or above* Moody's Baa or Standard and Poor's BBB rating are considered of investment grade. Those rated *below* this level are usually considered speculative (see Table 10.2). Speculative-grade bonds are often called **junk bonds.** Before the late 1970s, primary issues of speculative-grade securities were very rare; almost all new bond issues consisted of investment-grade bonds. However, when companies ran into financial difficulties, their bond ratings would fall. Holders of these downgraded bonds found that they were difficult to sell because no well-developed secondary market existed. It is easy to understand why investors would be leery of these securities, as they were usually unsecured.

In 1977, Michael Milken, at the investment banking firm of Drexel Burnham Lambert, recognized that there were many investors who would be willing to take on greater risk if they were compensated with greater returns. First, however, Milken had to address two problems that hindered the market for low-grade bonds. The first was that they suffered from poor liquidity. Whereas underwriters of investment-grade bonds continued to make a market after the bonds were issued, no such market maker existed for junk bonds. Drexel agreed to assume this role as market maker for junk bonds. That assured that a secondary market existed, an important consideration for investors, who seldom want to hold the bonds to maturity.

The second problem with the junk bond market was that there was a very real chance that the issuing firms would default on their bond payments. By comparison, the default risk on investment-grade securities was negligible. To reduce the probability of losses, Milken acted much as a commercial bank for junk bond issuers. He would renegotiate the firm's debt or advance additional funds if needed to prevent the firm from defaulting. Milken's efforts substantially reduced the default risk, and the demand for junk bonds soared.

During the early and mid-1980s, many firms took advantage of junk bonds to finance the takeover of other firms. When a firm greatly increases its debt level (by issuing junk bonds) to finance the purchase of another firm's stock, the increase in leverage makes the bonds high-risk. Frequently, part of the acquired firm is eventually sold to pay down the debt incurred by issuing the junk bonds. Some 1800 firms accessed the junk bond market during the 1980s.

Milken and his brokerage firm were very well compensated for their efforts. Milken earned a fee of 2% to 3% of each junk bond issue, which made Drexel the most profitable firm on Wall Street in 1987. Milken's personal income between 1983 and 1987 was in excess of $1 billion.

Unfortunately for holders of junk bonds, both Milken and Drexel were caught and convicted of insider trading. With Drexel unable to support the junk bond market, 250 companies defaulted between 1989 and 1991. Drexel itself filed bankruptcy in 1990 due to losses on its own holdings of junk bonds. Milken was sentenced to three

TABLE 10.2 Debt Ratings

Standard and Poor's	Moody's	Average Interest Rate* (%)	Definition
AAA	Aaa	5.47	Best quality and highest rating. Capacity to pay interest and repay principal is extremely strong. Smallest degree of investment risk.
AA	Aa	5.81	High quality. Very strong capacity to pay interest and repay principal and differs from AAA/Aaa in a small degree.
A	A	5.99	Strong capacity to pay interest and repay principal. Possess many favorable investment attributes and are considered upper-medium-grade obligations. Somewhat more susceptible to the adverse effects of changes in circumstances and economic conditions.
BBB	Baa	6.39	Medium-grade obligations. Neither highly protected nor poorly secured. Adequate capacity to pay interest and repay principal. May lack long-term reliability and protective elements to secure interest and principal payments.
BB	Ba		Moderate ability to pay interest and repay principal. Have speculative elements and future cannot be considered well assured. Adverse business, economic, and financial conditions could lead to inability to meet financial obligations.
B	B		Lack characteristics of desirable investment. Assurance of interest and principal payments over long period of time may be small. Adverse conditions likely to impair ability to meet financial obligations.
CCC	Caa		Poor standing. Identifiable vulnerability to default and dependent on favorable business, economic, and financial conditions to meet timely payment of interest and repayment of principal.
CC	Ca		Represent obligations that are speculative to a high degree. Issues often default and have other marked shortcomings.
C	C		Lowest-rated class of bonds. Have extremely poor prospects of attaining any real investment standard. May be used to cover a situation where bankruptcy petition has been filed, but debt service payments are continued.
CI			Reserved for income bonds on which no interest is being paid.
D			Payment default.
NR			No public rating has been requested.
(+) or (−)			Ratings from AA to CCC may be modified by the addition of a plus or minus sign to show relative standing within the major rating categories.

*Average interest rates are reported in the *Bulletin* only for the top four risk categories.
Source: *Federal Reserve Bulletin*, Table 1.35, Lines 27–30. March 2007.

years in prison for his part in the scandal. *Fortune* magazine reported that Milken's personal fortune still exceeded $400 million.[2]

The junk bond market has recovered since its low in 1990 and now continues to permit medium-size firms to obtain financing that might otherwise be unavailable to them because of the relatively high risk.

Financial Guarantees for Bonds

Financially weaker security issuers frequently purchase **financial guarantees** to lower the risk of their bonds. A financial guarantee ensures that the lender (bond purchaser) will be paid both principal and interest in the event the issuer defaults. Large, well-known insurance companies write what are actually insurance policies to back bond issues. With such a financial guarantee, bond buyers no longer have to be concerned with the financial health of the bond issuer. Instead, they are interested only in the strength of the insurer. Essentially, the credit rating of the insurer is substituted for the credit rating of the issuer. The resulting reduction in risk lowers the interest rate demanded by bond buyers. Of course, issuers must pay a fee to the insurance company for the guarantee. Financial guarantees make sense only when the cost of the insurance is less than the interest savings that result.

Financial guarantees were developed in the early 1970s to insure municipal bonds. More recently, their use has been expanded to cover a variety of corporate bonds as well. In recent years, 40% to 50% of all new U.S. municipal bonds have carried insurance.

Current Yield Calculation

Chapter 3 introduced interest rates and described the concept of yield to maturity. If you buy a bond and hold it until it matures, you will earn the yield to maturity. This represents the most accurate measure of the yield from holding a bond.

Current Yield

The **current yield** is an approximation of the yield to maturity on coupon bonds that is often reported because it is easily calculated. It is defined as the yearly coupon payment divided by the price of the security,

$$i_c = \frac{C}{P} \tag{1}$$

where
i_c = current yield
P = price of the coupon bond
C = yearly coupon payment

This formula is identical to the formula in Equation 5 of Chapter 3, which describes the calculation of the yield to maturity for a perpetuity. Hence for a perpetuity, the current yield is an exact measure of the yield to maturity. When a coupon bond has

---

[2]A complete history of Milken was reported in *Fortune,* September 30, 1996, pp. 80–105.

a long term to maturity (say, 20 years or more), it is very much like a perpetuity, which pays coupon payments forever. Thus, you would expect the current yield to be a rather close approximation of the yield to maturity for a long-term coupon bond, and you can safely use the current yield calculation instead of looking up the yield to maturity in a bond table. However, as the time to maturity of the coupon bond shortens (say, it becomes less than five years), it behaves less and less like a perpetuity and so the approximation afforded by the current yield becomes worse and worse.

We have also seen that when the bond price equals the par value of the bond, the yield to maturity is equal to the coupon rate (the coupon payment divided by the par value of the bond). Because the current yield equals the coupon payment divided by the bond price, the current yield is also equal to the coupon rate when the bond price is at par. This logic leads us to the conclusion that when the bond price is at par, the current yield equals the yield to maturity. This means that the nearer the bond price is to the bond's par value, the better the current yield will approximate the yield to maturity.

The current yield is negatively related to the price of the bond. In the case of our 10% coupon rate bond, when the price rises from $1,000 to $1,100, the current yield falls from 10% (=$100/$1,000) to 9.09% (=$100/$1,100). As Table 3.1 in Chapter 3 indicates, the yield to maturity is also negatively related to the price of the bond; when the price rises from $1,000 to $1,100, the yield to maturity falls from 10% to 8.48%. In this we see an important fact: The current yield and the yield to maturity always move together; a rise in the current yield always signals that the yield to maturity has also risen.

example 10.2 **Current Yield**

What is the current yield for a bond that has a par value of $1,000 and a coupon interest rate of 10.95%? The current market price for the bond is $921.01.

Solution
The current yield is 11.89%.

$$i_c = \frac{C}{P}$$

where

C = yearly payment $= 0.1095 \times \$1,000 = \$109.50$

P = price of the bond $= \$921.01$

Thus,

$$i_c = \frac{\$109.50}{\$921.01} = 0.1189 = 11.89\%$$

The general characteristics of the current yield (the yearly coupon payment divided by the bond price) can be summarized as follows: The current yield better approximates the yield to maturity when the bond's price is nearer to the bond's par value and the maturity of the bond is longer. It becomes a worse approximation when the bond's price is further from the bond's par value and the bond's maturity is shorter. Regardless of whether the current yield is a good approximation of the yield to maturity, a change in the current yield *always* signals a change in the same direction of the yield to maturity.

Finding the Value of Coupon Bonds

Before we look specifically at how to price bonds, let us first look at the general theory behind computing the price of any business asset. Luckily, the value of all financial assets is found the same way. The current price is the present value of all future cash flows. Recall the discussion of present value from Chapter 3. If you have the present value of a future cash flow, you can exactly reproduce that future cash flow by investing the present value amount at the discount rate. For example, the present value of $100 that will be received in one year is $90.90 if the discount rate is 10%. An investor is completely indifferent between having the $90.90 today or having the $100 in one year. This is because the $90.90 can be invested at 10% to provide $100.00 in the future ($90.90 × 1.10 = $100). This represents the essence of value. The current price must be such that the seller is indifferent between continuing to receive the cash flow stream provided by the asset or receiving the offer price.

One question we might ask is why prices fluctuate if everyone knows how value is established. It is because not everyone agrees about what the future cash flows are going to be. Let us summarize how to find the value of a security:

1. Identify the cash flows that result from owning the security.
2. Determine the discount rate required to compensate the investor for holding the security.
3. Find the present value of the cash flows estimated in step 1 using the discount rate determined in step 2.

The rest of this chapter focuses on how one important asset is valued: bonds. In the next chapter we discuss stock valuation.

Finding the Price of Semiannual Bonds

Recall that a bond usually pays interest semiannually in an amount equal to the coupon interest rate times the face amount (or par value) of the bond. When the bond matures, the holder will also receive a lump sum payment equal to the face amount. Most corporate bonds have a face amount of $1,000. Basic bond terminology is reviewed in Table 10.3.

The issuing corporation will usually set the coupon rate close to the rate available on other similar outstanding bonds at the time the bond is offered for sale. Unless the bond has an adjustable rate, the coupon interest payment remains unchanged throughout the life of the bond.

The first step in finding the value of the bond is to identify the cash flows the holder of the bond will receive. The value of the bond is the present value of these cash flows. The cash flows consist of the interest payments and the final lump sum repayment.

In the second step these cash flows are discounted back to the present using an interest rate that represents the yield available on other bonds of like risk and maturity.

TABLE 10.3 Bond Terminology

Coupon interest rate	The stated annual interest rate on the bond. It is usually fixed for the life of the bond.
Current yield	The coupon interest payment divided by the current market price of the bond.
Face amount	The maturity value of the bond. The holder of the bond will receive the face amount from the issuer when the bond matures. *Face amount* is synonymous with *par value*.
Indenture	The contract that accompanies a bond and specifies the terms of the loan agreement. It includes management restrictions, called covenants.
Market rate	The interest rate currently in effect in the market for securities of like risk and maturity. The market rate is used to value bonds.
Maturity	The number of years or periods until the bond matures and the holder is paid the face amount.
Par value	The same as *face amount*.
Yield to maturity	The yield an investor will earn if the bond is purchased at the current market price and held until maturity.

The technique for computing the price of a simple bond with annual cash flows was discussed in detail in Chapter 3. Let us now look at a more realistic example. Most bonds pay interest semiannually. To adjust the cash flows for semiannual payments, divide the coupon payment by 2 since only half of the annual payment is paid each six months. Similarly, to find the interest rate effective during one-half of the year, the market interest rate must be divided by 2. The final adjustment is to double the number of periods because there will be two periods per year. Equation 2 shows how to compute the price of a semiannual bond:[3]

$$P_{semi} = \frac{C/2}{1+i} + \frac{C/2}{(1+i)^2} + \frac{C/2}{(1+i)^3} + \cdots + \frac{C/2}{(1+i)^{2n}} + \frac{F}{(1+i)^{2n}} \quad (2)$$

where

P_{semi} = price of semiannual coupon bond
C = yearly coupon payment
F = face value of the bond
n = years to maturity date
$i = \frac{1}{2}$ annual market interest rate

___

[3]There is a theoretical argument for discounting the final cash flow using the full-year interest rate with the original number of periods. Derivative securities are sold, in which the principal and interest cash flows are separated and sold to different investors. The fact that one investor is receiving semiannual interest payments should not affect the value of the principal-only cash flow. However, virtually every text, calculator, and spreadsheet computes bond values by discounting the final cash flow using the same interest rate and number of periods as is used to compute the present value of the interest payments. To be consistent, we will use that method in this text.

> example 10.3 **Bond Valuation, Semiannual Payment Bond**
>
> Let us compute the price of a Chrysler bond recently listed in the *Wall Street Journal*. The bonds have a 10% coupon rate, a $1,000 par value (maturity value), and mature in two years. Assume semiannual compounding and that market rates of interest are 12%.
>
> **Solution**
>
> 1. Begin by identifying the cash flows. Compute the coupon interest payment by multiplying 0.10 times $1,000 to get $100. Since the coupon payment is made each six months, it will be one-half of $100, or $50. The final cash flow consists of repayment of the $1,000 face amount of the bond. This does not change because of semiannual payments.
> 2. We need to know what market rate of interest is appropriate to use for computing the present value of the bond. We are told that bonds being issued today with similar risk have coupon rates of 12%. Divide this amount by 2 to get the interest rate over six months. This provides an interest rate of 6%.
> 3. Find the present value of the cash flows. Note that with semiannual compounding the number of periods must be doubled. This means that we discount the bond payments for four periods.
>
> **Solution: Equation**
>
> $$P = \frac{\$100/2}{(1 + .06)} + \frac{\$100/2}{(1 + .06)^2} + \frac{\$100/2}{(1 + .06)^3} + \frac{\$100/2}{(1 + .06)^4} + \frac{\$1,000}{(1 + .06)^4}$$
>
> $$P = \$47.17 + \$44.50 + \$41.98 + \$39.60 + \$792.10 = \$965.35$$
>
> **Solution: Financial Calculator**
>
> $N = 4$
> $FV = \$1,000$
> $I = 6\%$
> $PMT = \$50$
> Compute PV = price of bond = $965.35.

Notice that the market price for the bond in Example 3 is below the $1,000 par value of the bond. When the bond sells for less than the par value, it is selling at a **discount.** When the market price exceeds the par value, the bond is selling at a **premium.**

What determines whether a bond will sell for a premium or a discount? Suppose that you are asked to invest in an old bond that has a coupon rate of 10% and $1,000 par. You would not be willing to pay $1,000 for this bond if new bonds with similar risk were available yielding 12%. The seller of the old bond would have to lower the price on the 10% bond to make it an attractive investment. In fact, the seller would have to lower the price until the yield earned by a buyer of the old bond exactly equaled the yield on similar new bonds. This means that as interest rates in the market rise, the value of bonds with fixed interest rates falls. Similarly, as interest rates available in the market on new bonds fall, the value of old fixed-interest-rate bonds rises.

Investing in Bonds

Bonds represent one of the most popular long-term alternatives to investing in stocks (see Figure 10.6). Bonds are lower risk than stocks because they have a higher priority of payment. This means that when the firm is having difficulty meeting its obligations, bondholders get paid before stockholders. Additionally, should the firm have to liquidate, bondholders must be paid before stockholders.

Even healthy firms with sufficient cash flow to pay both bondholders and stockholders frequently have very volatile stock prices. This volatility scares many investors out of the stock market. Bonds are the most popular alternative. They offer relative security and dependable cash payments, making them ideal for retired investors and those who want to live off their investments.

Many investors think that bonds represent a very low risk investment since the cash flows are relatively certain. It is true that high-grade bonds seldom default; however, bond investors face fluctuations in price due to market interest-rate movements in the economy. As interest rates rise and fall, the value of bonds changes in the opposite direction. As discussed in Chapter 3, the possibility of suffering a loss because of interest-rate changes is called **interest-rate risk.** The longer the time until the bond matures, the greater will be the change in price. This does not cause a loss to those investors who do not sell their bonds; however, many investors do not hold their bonds until maturity. If they attempt to sell their bonds after interest rates have risen, they will receive less than they paid. Interest-rate risk is an important consideration when deciding whether to invest in bonds.

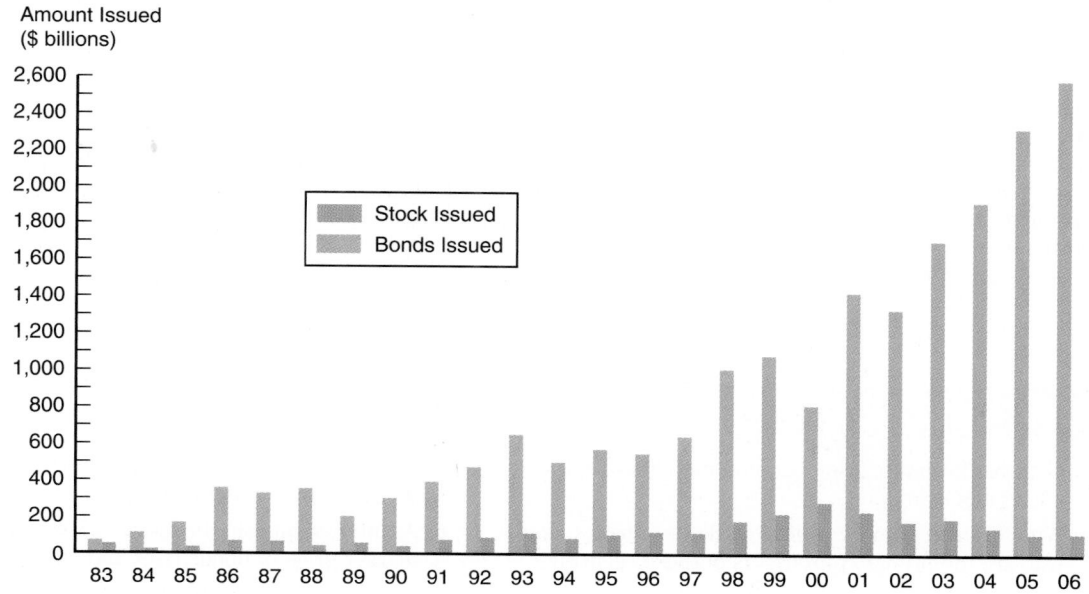

Figure 10.6 Bonds and Stocks Issued, 1983–2006

Source: Federal Reserve Bulletin, various issues. Table 1.46.

SUMMARY

1. The capital markets exist to provide financing for long-term capital assets. Households, often through investments in pension and mutual funds, are net investors in the capital markets. Corporations and the federal and state governments are net users of these funds.

2. The three main capital market instruments are bonds, stocks, and mortgages. Bonds represent borrowing by the issuing firm. Stock represents ownership in the issuing firm. Mortgages are long-term loans secured by real property. Only corporations can issue stock. Corporations and governments can issue bonds. In any given year, far more funds are raised with bonds than with stock.

3. Firm managers are hired by stockholders to protect and increase their wealth. Bondholders must rely on a contract called an indenture to protect their interests. Bond indentures contain covenants that restrict the firm from activities that increase risk and hence the chance of default on the bonds. Bond indentures

also contain many provisions that make them more or less attractive to investors, such as a call option, convertibility, or a sinking fund.

4. The value of any business asset is computed the same way, by computing the present value of the cash flows that will go to the holder of the asset. For example, a commercial building is valued by computing the present value of the net cash flows the owner will receive. We compute the value of bonds by finding the present value of the cash flows, which consist of periodic interest payments and a final principal payment.

5. The value of bonds fluctuates with current market prices. If a bond has an interest payment based on a 5% coupon rate, no investor will buy it at face value if new bonds are available for the same price with interest payments based on 8% coupon interest. To sell the bond, the holder will have to discount the price until the yield to the holder equals 8%. The amount of the discount is greater the longer the term to maturity.

KEY TERMS

bond indenture, *p. 244*
call provision, *p. 246*
current yield, *p. 250*
discount, *p. 254*
financial guarantees, *p. 250*
general obligation bonds, *p. 243*
initial public offering, *p. 238*
interest-rate risk, *p. 255*
junk bonds, *p. 248*

premium, *p. 254*
registered bonds, *p. 245*
restrictive covenants, *p. 246*
revenue bonds, *p. 243*
Separate Trading of Registered Interest and Principal Securities (STRIPS), *p. 242*
sinking fund, *p. 246*
zero-coupon securities, *p. 242*

QUESTIONS

1. Contrast investors' use of capital markets with their use of money markets.

2. What are the primary capital market securities, and who are the primary purchasers of these securities?

3. Distinguish between the primary market and the secondary market for securities.

4. A bond provides information about its par value, coupon interest rate, and maturity date. Define each of these.

5. The U.S. Treasury issues bills, notes, and bonds. How do these three securities differ?

6. As interest rates in the market change over time, the market price of bonds rises and falls. The change in the value of bonds due to changes in interest rates is a risk incurred by bond investors. What is this risk called?

7. In addition to Treasury securities, some agencies of the government issue bonds. List three such agencies, and state what the funds raised by the bond issues are used for.

8. A call provision on a bond allows the issuer to redeem the bond at will. Investors do not like call provisions and so require higher interest on callable bonds. Why do issuers continue to issue callable bonds anyway?

9. What is a sinking fund? Do investors like bonds that contain this feature? Why?

10. What is the document called that lists the terms of a bond?

11. Describe the two ways whereby capital market securities pass from the issuer to the public.

QUANTITATIVE PROBLEMS

1. A bond makes an annual $80 interest payment (8% coupon). The bond has five years before it matures, at which time it will pay $1,000. Assuming a discount rate of 10%, what should be the price of the bond? (Review Chapters 3 and 9.)

2. A zero-coupon bond has a par value of $1,000 and matures in 20 years. Investors require a 10% annual return on these bonds. For what price should the bond sell? (Note: Zero-coupon bonds do not pay any interest. Review Chapter 3.)

3. Consider the two bonds described below:

	Bond A	Bond B
Maturity (years)	15	20
Coupon rate (%)		
(paid semiannually)	10	6
Par value	$1,000	$1,000

a. If both bonds had a required return of 8%, what would the bonds' prices be?

b. Describe what it means if a bond sells at a discount, a premium, and at its face amount (par value). Are these two bonds selling at a discount, premium, or par?

c. If the required return on the two bonds rose to 10%, what would the bonds' prices be?

4. A two-year $1,000 par zero-coupon bond is currently priced at $819.00. A two-year $1,000 annuity is currently priced at $1,712.52. If you want to invest $50,000 in one of the two securities, which is a better buy? Hint: Compute the yield of each security.

5. Consider the following cash flows. All market interest rates are 12%.

Year	0	1	2	3	4
Cash Flow		160	170	180	230

a. What price would you pay for these cash flows? What total wealth do you expect after 2.5 years if you sell the rights to the remaining cash flows? Assume interest rates remain constant.

b. What is the duration of these cash flows?

c. Immediately after buying these cash flows, all market interest rates drop to 11%. What is the impact on your total wealth after 2.5 years?

6. The yield on a corporate bond is 10%, and it is currently selling at par. The marginal tax rate is 20%. A par value municipal bond with a coupon rate of 8.50% is available. Which security is a better buy?

7. If the municipal bond rate is 4.25% and the corporate bond rate is 6.25%, what is the marginal tax rate, assuming investors are indifferent between the two bonds?

8. M&E, Inc., has an outstanding convertible bond. The bond can be converted into 20 shares of common equity (currently trading at $52/share). The bond has five years of remaining maturity, a $1,000 par value, and a 6% annual coupon. M&E's straight debt is currently trading to yield 5%. What is the minimum price of the bond?

9. Assume the debt in the previous question is trading at $1,035. How can you earn a riskless profit from this situation (arbitrage)?

10. A ten-year, $1,000 par value bond with a 5% annual coupon is trading to yield 6%. What is the current yield?

11. A $1,000 par bond with an annual coupon has only one year until maturity. Its current yield is 6.713%, and its yield to maturity is 10%. What is the price of the bond?

12. A one-year discount bond with a face value of $1,000 was purchased for $900. What is the yield to maturity? What is the yield on a discount basis? (See Chapters 3 and 9.)

13. A seven-year, $1,000 par bond has an 8% annual coupon and is currently yielding 7.5%. The bond can be called in two years at a call price of $1,010. What is the bond yielding, assuming it will be called (known as the yield to call)?

14. A 20-year $1,000 par value bond has a 7% annual coupon. The bond is callable after the tenth year for a call premium of $1,025. If the bond is trading with a yield to call of 6.25%, what is the bond's yield to maturity?

15. A 10-year $1,000 par value bond has a 9% semiannual coupon and a nominal yield to maturity of 8.8%. What is the price of the bond?

16. Your company owns the following bonds:

Bond	Market Value	Duration
A	$13 million	2
B	$18 million	4
C	$20 million	3

If general interest rates rise from 8% to 8.5%, what is the approximate change in the value of the portfolio? (Review Chapter 3.)

WEB EXERCISES

The Bond Market

1. Stocks tend to get more publicity than bonds, but many investors, especially those nearing or in retirement, find that bonds are more consistent with their risk preferences. Go to **http://finance.yahoo.com/calculator/index**. Under Retirement find the calculator "How should I allocate my assets?" After answering the questionnaire, discuss whether you agree with the recommended asset destination.

CHAPTER 11

The Stock Market

Preview

In the last chapter we identified the capital markets as where long-term securities trade. We then examined the bond market and discussed how bond prices are established. In this chapter we continue our investigation of the capital markets by taking a close look at the stock market. The market for stocks is undoubtedly the financial market that receives the most attention and scrutiny. Great fortunes are made and lost as investors attempt to anticipate the market's ups and downs. We have witnessed an unprecedented period of volatility over the last decade. Stock indexes hit record highs in the late 1990s, largely led by technology companies, and then fell precipitously in 2000. By 2007 they had returned to record highs. In this chapter we look at how this important market works.

We begin by discussing the markets where stocks trade. We will then examine the fundamental theories that underlie the valuation of stocks. These theories are critical to an understanding of the forces that cause the value of stocks to rise and fall minute by minute and day by day. We will learn that determining a value for a common stock is very difficult and that it is this difficulty that leads to so much volatility in the stock markets.

Investing in Stocks

A share of stock in a firm represents ownership. A stockholder owns a percentage interest in a firm, consistent with the percentage of outstanding stock held.

Investors can earn a return from stock in one of two ways. Either the price of the stock rises over time, or the firm pays the stockholder dividends. Frequently, investors earn a return from both sources. Stock is riskier than bonds because stockholders have a lower priority than bondholders when the firm is in trouble, the returns to investors are less assured because dividends can be easily changed, and stock price increases are not guaranteed. Despite these risks, it is possible to make a great deal of money by investing in stock, whereas that is very unlikely by investing in bonds. Another distinction between stock and bonds is that stock does not mature.

Ownership of stock gives the stockholder certain rights regarding the firm. One is the right of a *residual claimant:* Stockholders have a claim on all assets and income left over after all other claimants have been satisfied. If nothing is left over, they get nothing. As noted, however, it is possible to get rich as a stockholder if the firm does well.

Most stockholders have the *right to vote* for directors and on certain issues, such as amendments to the corporate charter and whether new shares should be issued.

Notice that the stock certificate shown in Figure 11.1 does not list a maturity date, face value, or an interest rate, which were indicated on the bond shown in Chapter 10.

Common Stock Versus Preferred Stock

There are two types of stock, common and preferred. A share of **common stock** in a firm represents an ownership interest in that firm. Common stockholders vote, receive dividends, and hope that the price of their stock will rise. There are various classes of common stock, usually denoted as type A, type B, and so on. Unfortunately, the type does not have any meaning that is standard across all companies. The differences among the types usually involve either the distribution of dividends or voting rights. It is important for an investor in stocks to know exactly what rights go along with the shares of stock being contemplated.

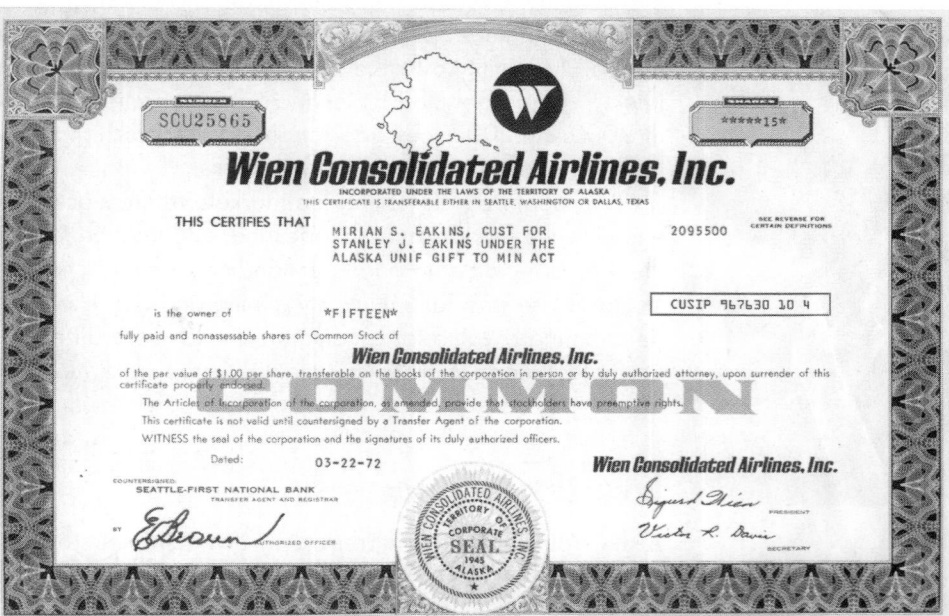

Figure 11.1 Wien Consolidated Airlines Stock

Source: Eakins, *Finance Investments, Institutions, & Management,* p. 43.

Preferred stock is a form of equity from a legal and tax standpoint. However, it differs from common stock in several important ways. First, because preferred stockholders receive a fixed dividend that never changes, a share of preferred stock is as much like a bond as it is like common stock. Second, because the dividend does not change, the price of preferred stock is relatively stable. Third, preferred stockholders do not usually vote unless the firm has failed to pay the promised dividend. Finally, preferred stockholders hold a claim on assets that has priority over the claims of common shareholders but after that of creditors such as bondholders.

Less than 25% of new equity issues are preferred stock, and only about 5% of all capital is raised using preferred stock. This may be because preferred dividends are not tax-deductible to the firm but bond interest payments are. Consequently, issuing preferred stock usually costs the firm more than issuing debt, even though it shares many of the characteristics of a bond.

How Stocks Are Sold

Literally billions of shares of stock are sold each business day in the United States. The orderly flow of information, stock ownership, and funds through the stock markets is a critical feature of well-developed and efficient markets. This efficiency encourages investors to buy stocks and to provide equity capital to businesses with valuable growth opportunities. We traditionally discuss stocks as trading on either an organized exchange or over the counter. Recently, this distinction is blurring as electronic trading grows in both volume and influence.

Organized Securities Exchanges Historically, the New York Stock Exchange (NYSE) has been the best known of the organized exchanges. The NYSE first began trading in 1792, when 24 brokers began trading a few stocks on Wall Street. The NYSE is still the world's largest and most liquid equities exchange. On an average trading day about 2 billion shares are traded. The traditional definition of an organized exchange is that there is a specified location where buyers and sellers meet on a regular basis to trade securities using an open-outcry auction model. As more sophisticated technology has been adapted to securities trading, this model is becoming less frequently used. The NYSE currently advertises itself as a hybrid market that combines aspects of electronic trading and traditional auction-market trading. In March of 2006, the NYSE merged with Archipelago, an electronic communication network (ECN) firm. At this time, the NYSE stopped selling seats representing membership and now operates as a traditional for profit, publicly traded company with shares trading on the NYSE under the symbol NYX.

go online

Find listed companies, member information, real-time market indices, and current stock quotes at **www.nyse.com**.

There are also major organized stock exchanges around the world. The most active exchange in the world is the Nikkei in Tokyo. Other major exchanges include the London Stock Exchange in England, the DAX in Germany, and the Toronto Stock Exchange in Canada.

To have a stock listed for trading on one of the organized exchanges, a firm must file an application and meet certain criteria set by the exchange designed to enhance trading. For example, the NYSE encourages only the largest firms to list so that transaction volume will be high. To list on the NYSE, a firm must meet the following minimum requirements:

- At least 2,200 shareholders with a monthly trading volume of 100,000 shares
- Earnings of at least $10 million for the last three years
- $100 million market value

About 2,800 companies around the world list their shares on the New York Stock Exchange. More than 70% of NYSE-listed companies have joined the exchange since 1986. The average firm on the exchange has a market value of $8.5 billion. On October 28, 1998, the NYSE volume topped 1 billion shares for the first time.[1] By 2007, daily volume was occasionally in excess of 4 billion shares.

The second-largest organized stock exchange in the United States is the American Stock Exchange. About 700 firms trade on it. The American Stock Exchange has less restrictive listing requirements. Regional exchanges, such as the Philadelphia and Pacific Stock Exchanges, are even easier to list on. Some firms choose to list on more than one exchange, believing that more exposure will increase the demand for their stock and hence its price. Many firms also believe that there is a certain amount of prestige in being listed on one of the major exchanges. They may even include this fact in their advertising. There is little conclusive research to support this belief, however. Microsoft, for example, is not listed on any organized exchange, yet its stock had a total market value of over $292 billion in late 2007.

Over-the-Counter Markets If Microsoft's stock is not traded on any of the organized stock exchanges, where does it sell its stock? Securities not listed on one of the exchanges trade in the over-the-counter (OTC) market. This market is not organized in the sense of having a building where trading takes place. Instead, trading occurs over sophisticated telecommunications networks. One such network is called the **National Association of Securities Dealers Automated Quotation System (NASDAQ).** This system, introduced in 1971, provides current bid and ask prices on about 3,200 actively traded securities. Dealers "make a market" in these stocks by buying for inventory when investors want to sell and selling from inventory when investors want to buy. These dealers provide small stocks with the liquidity that is essential to their acceptance in the market. Total volume on the NASDAQ is usually slightly lower than on the NYSE; however, NASDAQ volume has been growing and occasionally exceeds NYSE volume.

Not all publicly traded stocks list on one of the organized exchanges or on NASDAQ. Securities that trade very infrequently or trade primarily in one region of the country are usually handled by the regional offices of various brokerage houses. These offices often maintain small inventories of regionally popular securities. Dealers that make a market for stocks that trade in low volume are very important to the success of the over-the-counter market. Without these dealers standing ready to buy or sell shares, investors would be reluctant to buy shares of stock in regional or unknown firms, and it would be very difficult for start-up firms to raise needed capital. Recall from Chapter 4 that the more liquid an asset is, the greater the quantity demanded. By providing liquidity intervention, dealers increase demand for thinly traded securities.

Organized Versus Over-the-Counter Trading There is a significant difference between how organized and OTC exchanges operate. Organized exchanges are characterized as auction markets that use floor traders who specialize in particular stocks. These specialists oversee and facilitate trading in a group of stocks. Floor traders, representing various brokerage firms with buy and sell orders, meet at the trading post on the exchange and learn about current bid and ask prices. These quotes are called out loud. In about 90% of trades, the specialist matches buyers with sellers.

---

[1]*NYSE Fact Book*, www.nyse.com.

In the other 10%, the specialists may intervene by taking ownership of the stock themselves or by selling stock from inventory. It is the specialist's duty to maintain an orderly market in the stock even if that means buying stock in a declining market.

About one of four orders on the New York Stock Exchange is filled by floor traders personally approaching the specialist on the exchange. The other three-quarters of trades are executed by the SuperDOT system (Super Designated Order Turnaround system). The SuperDOT is an electronic order routing system that transmits orders directly to the specialist who trades in a stock. This allows for much faster communication of trades than is possible using floor traders. SuperDOT is for trades under 100,000 shares and gives priority to trades of under 2,100 shares. About 95% of orders to buy or sell on the NYSE are executed using this system.

Whereas organized exchanges have specialists who facilitate trading, over-the-counter markets have market makers. Rather than trading stocks in an auction format, they trade on an electronic network where bid and ask prices are set by the market makers. There are usually multiple market makers for any particular stock. They each enter their bid and ask quotes. Once this is done, they are obligated to buy or sell at least 1,000 securities at that price. Once a trade has been executed, they may enter a new bid and ask quote. Market makers are important to the economy in that they assure there is continuous liquidity for every stock, even those with little transaction volume. Market makers are compensated by the spread between the **bid price** (the price they pay for stocks) and **ask price** (the price they sell the stocks for). They also receive commissions on trades.

Although NASDAQ, the NYSE, and the other exchanges are heavily regulated, they are still public for-profit businesses. They have shareholders, directors, and officers who are interested in market share and generating profits. This means that the NYSE is vigorously competing with NASDAQ for the high-volume stocks that generate the big fees. For example, the NYSE has been trying to entice Microsoft to leave the NASDAQ and list with them for many years.

Electronic Communications Networks (ECNs) ECNs have been challenging both NASDAQ and the organized exchanges for business in recent years. An ECN is an electronic network that brings together major brokerages and traders so that they can trade between themselves and bypass the middleman. ECNs have a number of advantages that have led to their rapid growth.

- *Transparency:* All unfilled orders are available for review by ECN traders. This provides valuable information about supply and demand that traders can use to set their strategy. Although some exchanges make this information available, it is not always as current or complete as what the ECN provides.
- *Cost reduction:* Because the middleman and that commission is cut out of the deal, transaction costs can be lower for trades executed over an ECN. The spread is usually reduced and sometimes eliminated.
- *Faster execution:* Since ECNs are fully automated, trades are matched and confirmed faster than can be done when there is human involvement. For many traders this is not of great significance, but for those trying to trade on small price fluctuations, this is critical.
- *After-hours trading:* Prior to the advent of ECNs only institutional traders had access to trading securities after the exchanges had closed for the day. Many news reports and information become available after the major exchanges have closed, and small investors were locked out of trading on this data. Since ECNs never close, trading can continue around the clock.

Along with the advantages of ECNs there are disadvantages. The primary one is that they work well only for stocks with substantial volume. Since ECNs require there to be a seller to match against each buyer and vice versa, thinly traded stocks may go long intervals without trading. One of the largest ECNs is Instinet. It is mainly for institutional traders. Instinet also owns Island, which is for active individual trades.

The major exchanges are fighting the ECNs by expanding their own automatic trading systems. For example, the NYSE recently announced changes to its own Direct+ order routing system and merged with Archipelago to give it an established place in this market. Although the NYSE still dominates the American stock market in terms of share and dollar volume, its live auction format may not survive technological challenges for many more years.

Exchange Traded Funds (ETFs) Exchange traded funds (ETFs) have become the latest market innovation to capture investor interest. They were first introduced in 1990 and by 2007 over 400 separate ETFs were being traded. In their simplest form, ETFs are formed when a basket of securities is purchased and a stock is created based on this basket that is traded on an exchange. The makeup and structure are continuing to evolve, but ETFs share the following features:

1. They are listed and traded as individual stocks on a stock exchange. Currently, all available offerings are traded on the American Stock Exchange.
2. They are indexed rather than actively managed.
3. Their value is based on the underlying net asset value of the stocks held in the index basket. The exact content of the basket is public so that intraday arbitrage keeps the ETF price close to the implied value.

In many ways ETFs resemble stock index mutual funds in that they track the performance of some index, such as the S&P 500 or the Dow Jones industrial average. They differ in that ETFs trade like stocks, so they allow for limit orders, short sales, stop-loss orders, and the ability to buy on margin. ETFs tend to have lower management fees than do comparable index mutual funds. For example, the Vanguard extended market ETF reports an expense ratio of .08% compared to an expense ratio of .25% for its extended market index mutual fund. Another advantage of ETFs is that they usually have no minimum investment amount, whereas mutual funds often require $3,000–$5,000 minimums.

The primary disadvantage of ETFs is that since they trade like stocks, investors have to pay a broker commission each time they buy or sale shares. This provides a cost disadvantage compared to mutual funds for those who want to frequently invest small amounts, such as through a 401K.

ETFs feature some of the more exotic names found in finance, including Vipers, Diamonds, Spiders, and Qubes. These names are derived from the index that is tracked or the name of the issuing firm. For example, Diamonds are indexed to the Dow Jones Industrial Average, Spiders track the S&P 500, and Qubes follow the NASDAQ (ticker symbol QQQQ). Vipers are Vanguard's ETFs. The list of available indexes that can be tracked by purchasing EFTs is rapidly expanding to include virtually every sector, commodity, and investment style (value, growth, capitalization, etc). Their popularity is likely to increase as more investors learn about how they can be effectively used as a low cost way to help diversify a portfolio.

Computing the Price of Common Stock ▪

One basic principle of finance is that the value of any investment is found by computing the value today of all cash flows the investment will generate over its life. For example, a commercial building will sell for a price that reflects the net cash flows (rents – expenses) it is projected to have over its useful life. Similarly, we value common stock as the value in today's dollars of all future cash flows. The cash flows a stockholder may earn from stock are dividends, the sales price, or both.

To develop the theory of stock valuation, we begin with the simplest possible scenario. This assumes that you buy the stock, hold it for one period to get a dividend, then sell the stock. We call this the *one-period valuation model.*

The One-Period Valuation Model

Suppose that you have some extra money to invest for one year. After a year you will need to sell your investment to pay tuition. After watching *Wall Street Week* on TV you decide that you want to buy Intel Corp. stock. You call your broker and find that Intel is currently selling for $50 per share and pays $0.16 per year in dividends. The analyst on *Wall Street Week* predicts that the stock will be selling for $60 in one year. Should you buy this stock?

To answer this question you need to determine whether the current price accurately reflects the analyst's forecast. To value the stock today, you need to find the present discounted value of the expected cash flows (future payments) using the formula in Equation 1 of Chapter 3 in which the discount factor used to discount the cash flows is the required return on investments in equity. The cash flows consist of one dividend payment plus a final sales price, which, when discounted back to the present, leads to the following equation that computes the current price of the stock.

$$P_0 = \frac{Div_1}{(1 + k_e)} + \frac{P_1}{(1 + k_e)} \tag{1}$$

where
P_0 = the current price of the stock. The zero subscript refers to time period zero, or the present.
Div_1 = the dividend paid at the end of year 1.
k_e = the required return on investments in equity.
P_1 = the price at the end of the first period. This is the assumed sales price of the stock.

---

example 11.1 Stock Valuation: One-Period Model

Find the value of the Intel stock given the figures reported above. You will need to know the required return on equity to find the present value of the cash flows. Since a stock is more risky than a bond, you will require a higher return than that offered in the bond market. Assume that after careful consideration you decide that you would be satisfied to earn 12% on the investment.

Solution

Putting the numbers into Equation 1 yields the following:

$$P_0 = \frac{.16}{1 + 0.12} + \frac{\$60}{1 + 0.12} = \$.14 + \$53.57 = \$53.71$$

Based on your analysis, you find that the stock is worth $53.71. Since the stock is currently available for $50 per share, you would choose to buy it. Why is the stock selling for less than $53.71? It may be because other investors place a different risk on the cash flows or estimate the cash flows to be less than you do.

The Generalized Dividend Valuation Model

The one-period dividend valuation model can be extended to any number of periods. The concept remains the same. The value of stock is the present value of all future cash flows. The only cash flows that an investor will receive are dividends and a final sales price when the stock is ultimately sold. The generalized formula for stock can be written as in Equation 2.

$$P_0 = \frac{D_1}{(1 + k_e)^1} + \frac{D_2}{(1 + k_e)^2} + \cdots + \frac{D_n}{(1 + k_e)^n} + \frac{P_n}{(1 + k_e)^n} \qquad (2)$$

If you were to attempt to use Equation 2 to find the value of a share of stock, you would soon realize that you must first estimate the value the stock will have at some point in the future before you can estimate its value today. In other words, you must find P_n in order to find P_0. However, if P_n is far in the future, it will not affect P_0. For example, the present value of a share of stock that sells for $50 seventy-five years from now using a 12% discount rate is just one cent [$50/(1.12^{75}) = \$0.01$]. This means that the current value of a share of stock can be found as simply the present value of the future dividend stream. The **generalized dividend model** is rewritten in Equation 3 without the final sales price.

$$P_0 = \sum_{t=1}^{\infty} \frac{D_t}{(1 + k_e)^t} \qquad (3)$$

Consider the implications of Equation 3 for a moment. The generalized dividend model says that the price of stock is determined only by the present value of the dividends and that nothing else matters. Many stocks do not pay dividends, so how is it that these stocks have value? *Buyers of the stock expect that the firm will pay dividends someday.* Most of the time a firm institutes dividends as soon as it has completed the rapid growth phase of its life cycle. The stock price increases as the time approaches for the dividend stream to begin.

The generalized dividend valuation model requires that we compute the present value of an infinite stream of dividends, a process that could be difficult, to say the least. Therefore, simplified models have been developed to make the calculations easier. One such model is the **Gordon growth model** that assumes constant dividend growth.

The Gordon Growth Model

Many firms strive to increase their dividends at a constant rate each year. Equation 4 rewrites Equation 3 to reflect this constant growth in dividends.

$$P_0 = \frac{D_0 \times (1+g)^1}{(1+k_e)^1} + \frac{D_0 \times (1+g)^2}{(1+k_e)^2} + \cdots + \frac{D_0 \times (1+g)^\infty}{(1+k_e)^\infty} \qquad (4)$$

where

D_0 = the most recent dividend paid
g = the expected constant growth rate in dividends
k_e = the required return on an investment in equity

Equation 4 has been simplified using algebra to obtain Equation 5.[2]

$$P_0 = \frac{D_0 \times (1+g)}{(k_e - g)} = \frac{D_1}{(k_e - g)} \qquad (5)$$

This model is useful for finding the value of stock, given a few assumptions:

1. *Dividends are assumed to continue growing at a constant rate forever.* Actually, as long as they are expected to grow at a constant rate for an extended period of time, the model should yield reasonable results. This is because errors about distant cash flows become small when discounted to the present.
2. *The growth rate is assumed to be less than the required return on equity, k_e.* Myron Gordon, in his development of the model, demonstrated that this is a reasonable assumption. In theory, if the growth rate were faster than the rate demanded by holders of the firm's equity, in the long run the firm would grow impossibly large.

---

[2]To generate Equation 5 from Equation 4, first multiply both sides of Equation 4 by $(1 + k_e)/(1 + g)$ and subtract Equation 4 from the result. This yields

$$\frac{P_0 \times (1 + k_e)}{(1 + g)} - P_0 = D_0 - \frac{D_0 \times (1+g)^\infty}{(1 + k_e)^\infty}$$

Assuming that k_e is greater than g, the term on the far right will approach zero and can be dropped. Thus, after factoring P_0 out of the left-hand side,

$$P_0 \times \left[\frac{1 + k_e}{1 + g} - 1\right] = D_0$$

Next, simplify by combining terms to

$$P_0 \times \frac{(1 + k_e) - (1 + g)}{1 + g} = D_0$$

$$P_0 = \frac{D_0 \times (1 + g)}{k_e - g} = \frac{D_1}{k_e - g}$$

example 11.2 **Stock Valuation: Gordon Growth Model**

Find the current market price of Coca-Cola stock assuming dividends grow at a constant rate of 10.95%, $D_0 = \$1.00$, and the required return is 13%.

Solution

$$P_0 = \frac{D_0 \times (1 + g)}{k_e - g}$$

$$P_0 = \frac{\$1.00 \times (1.1095)}{.13 - .1095}$$

$$P_0 = \frac{\$1.1095}{0.0205} = \$54.12$$

Coca-Cola stock should sell for $54.12 if the assumptions regarding the constant growth rate and required return are correct.

Price Earnings Valuation Method

Theoretically, the best method of stock valuation is the dividend valuation approach. Sometimes, however, it is difficult to apply. If a firm is not paying dividends or has a very erratic growth rate, the results may not be satisfactory. Other approaches to stock valuation are sometimes applied. Among the more popular is the price/earnings multiple.

The **price earnings ratio (PE)** is a widely watched measure of how much the market is willing to pay for $1 of earnings from a firm. A high PE has two interpretations.

1. A higher than average PE may mean that the market expects earnings to rise in the future. This would return the PE to a more normal level.
2. A high PE may alternatively indicate that the market feels the firm's earnings are very low risk and is therefore willing to pay a premium for them.

The PE ratio can be used to estimate the value of a firm's stock. Note that algebraically the product of the PE ratio times expected earnings is the firm's stock price.

$$\frac{P}{E} \times E = P \tag{6}$$

Firms in the same industry are expected to have similar PE ratios in the long run. The value of a firm's stock can be found by multiplying the average industry PE times the expected earnings per share.

example 11.3 **Stock Valuation: PE Ratio Approach**

The average industry PE ratio for restaurants similar to Applebee's, a pub restaurant chain, is 23. What is the current price of Applebee's if earnings per share are projected to be $1.13?

Solution

Using Equation 6 and the data given we find:

$$P_0 = P/E \times E$$
$$P_0 = 23 \times \$1.13 = \$26$$

The PE ratio approach is especially useful for valuing privately held firms and firms that do not pay dividends. The weakness of the PE approach to valuation is that by using an industry average PE ratio, firm-specific factors that might contribute to a long-term PE ratio above or below the average are ignored in the analysis. A skilled analyst will adjust the PE ratio up or down to reflect unique characteristics of a firm when estimating its stock price.

How the Market Sets Security Prices

Suppose you go to an auto auction. The cars are available for inspection before the auction begins, and you find a little Mazda Miata that you like. You test-drive it in the parking lot and notice that it makes a few strange noises, but you decide that you would still like the car. You decide $5,000 would be a fair price that would allow you to pay some repair bills should the noises turn out to be serious. You see that the auction is ready to begin, so you go in and wait for the Miata to enter.

Suppose there is another buyer who also spots the Miata. He test-drives the car and recognizes that the noises are simply the result of worn brake pads that he can fix himself at a nominal cost. He decides that the car is worth $7,000. He also goes in and waits for the Miata to enter.

Who will buy the car and for how much? Suppose only the two of you are interested in the Miata. You begin the bidding at $4,000. He ups your bid to $4,500. You bid your top price of $5,000. He counters with $5,100. The price is now higher than you are willing to pay, so you stop bidding. The car is sold to the more informed buyer for $5,100.

This simple example raises a number of points. First, the price is set by the buyer willing to pay the highest price. The price is not necessarily the highest price the asset could fetch, but it is incrementally greater than what any other buyer is willing to pay.

Second, the market price will be set by the buyer who can take best advantage of the asset. The buyer who purchased the car knew that he could fix the noise easily and cheaply. Because of this he was willing to pay more for the car than you were. The same concept holds for other assets. For example, a piece of property or a building will sell to the buyer who can put the asset to the most productive use. Consider why one company often pays a substantial premium over current market prices to acquire ownership of another (target) company. The acquiring firm may believe that it can put the target firm's assets to work better than they are currently and that this justifies the premium price.

Finally, the example shows the role played by information in asset pricing. Superior information about an asset can increase its value by reducing its risk. When you consider buying a stock, there are many unknowns about the future cash flows. The buyer who has the best information about these cash flows will discount them at a lower interest rate than will a buyer who is very uncertain.

Now let us apply these ideas to stock valuation. Suppose that you are considering the purchase of stock expected to pay dividends of $2 next year. The firm is expected to grow at 3% indefinitely. You are quite *uncertain* about both the constancy of the dividend stream and the accuracy of the estimated growth rate. To compensate yourself for this risk, you require a return of 15%.

Now suppose Jennifer, another investor, has spoken with industry insiders and feels more confident about the projected cash flows. Jennifer only requires a 12% return because her perceived risk is lower than yours. Bud, on the other hand, is dating the CEO of the company. He knows with near certainty what the future of the firm actually is. He thinks that both the estimated growth rate and the estimated cash flows are lower than what they will *actually* be in the future. Because he sees almost no risk in this investment, he only requires a 7% return.

What are the values each investor will give to the stock? Applying the Gordon growth model yields the following stock prices.

Investor	Discount Rate	Stock Price
You	15%	$16.67
Jennifer	12%	$22.22
Bud	7%	$50.00

You are willing to pay $16.67 for the stock. Jennifer would pay up to $22.22, and Bud would pay $50. The investor with the lowest perceived risk is willing to pay the most for the stock. If there were no other traders, the market price would be just above $22.22. If you already held the stock, you would sell it to Bud.

The point of this section is that the players in the market, bidding against each other, establish the market price. When new information is released about a firm, expectations change, and with them, prices change. New information can cause changes in expectations about the level of future dividends or the risk of those dividends. Since market participants are constantly receiving new information and constantly revising their expectations, it is reasonable that stock prices are constantly changing as well.

Errors in Valuation

In this chapter we learned about several asset valuation models. An interesting exercise is to apply these models to real firms. Students who do this find that computed stock prices do not match market prices much of the time. Students often question whether the models are wrong or incomplete or whether they are simply being used incorrectly. There are many opportunities for errors in applying the models. These include problems estimating growth, estimating risk, and forecasting dividends.

Problems with Estimating Growth

The constant growth model requires the analyst to estimate the constant rate of growth the firm will experience. You may estimate future growth by computing the historical growth rate in dividends, sales, or net profits. This approach fails to consider any changes in the firm or economy that may affect the growth rate. Robert Haugen, a professor of finance at the University of California, writes in his book, *The New Finance,* that competition will prevent high-growth firms from being able to maintain their historical growth rate. He demonstrates that, despite this, the stock prices of historically high-growth firms tend to reflect a continuation of the high growth rate. The result is that investors in these firms receive lower returns than they

TABLE 11.1 Stock Prices for a Security with $D_0 = \$2.00$, $k_e = 15\%$, and Constant Growth Rates as Listed

Growth (%)	Price
1	$ 14.43
3	17.17
5	21.00
10	44.00
11	55.50
12	74.67
13	113.00
14	228.00

would by investing in mature firms. This just points out that even the experts have trouble estimating future growth rates. Table 11.1 shows the stock price for a firm with a 15% required return, a $2 dividend, and a range of different growth rates. The stock price varies from $14.43 at 1% growth to $228 at 14% growth rate. Estimating growth at 13% instead of 12% results in a $38.33 price difference.

Problems with Estimating Risk

The dividend valuation model requires the analyst to estimate the required return for the firm's equity. Table 11.2 shows how the price of a share of stock offering a $2 dividend and a 5% growth rate changes with different estimates of the required return. Clearly, stock price is highly dependent on the required return, despite our uncertainty regarding how it is found.

Problems with Forecasting Dividends

Even if we are able to accurately estimate a firm's growth rate and its required return, we are still faced with the problem of determining how much of the firm's earnings will be paid as dividends. Clearly, many factors can influence the dividend payout ratio. These will include the firm's future growth opportunities and management's concern over future cash flows.

TABLE 11.2 Stock Prices for a Security with $D_0 = \$2.00$, $g = 5\%$, and Required Returns as Listed

Required Return (%)	Price
10	$42.00
11	35.00
12	30.00
13	26.25
14	23.33
15	21.00

Putting all of these concerns together, we see that stock analysts are seldom very certain that their stock price projections are accurate. This is why stock prices fluctuate so widely on news reports. For example, information that the economy is slowing can cause analysts to revise their growth expectations. When this happens across a broad spectrum of stocks, major market indexes can change.

Does all this mean that you should not invest in the market? No, it only means that short-term fluctuations in stock prices are expected and natural. Over the long term, the stock price will adjust to reflect the true earnings of the firm. If high-quality firms are chosen for your portfolio, they should provide fair returns over time.

CASE

The September 11 Terrorist Attack, the Enron Scandal, and the Stock Market

In 2001, two big shocks hit the stock market: the September 11 terrorist attack and the Enron scandal. Our analysis of stock price evaluation, again using the Gordon growth model, can help us understand how these events affected stock prices.

The September 11 terrorist attack raised the possibility that terrorism against the United States would paralyze the country. These fears led to a downward revision of the growth prospects for U.S. companies, thus lowering the dividend growth rate g in the Gordon model. The resulting rise in the denominator in Equation 5 should lead to a decline in P_0 and hence a decline in stock prices.

Increased uncertainty for the U.S. economy would also raise the required return on investment in equity. A higher k_e also leads to a rise in the denominator in Equation 5, a decline in P_0, and a general fall in stock prices. As the Gordon model predicts, the stock market fell by over 10% immediately after September 11.

Subsequently, the U.S. successes against the Taliban in Afghanistan and the absence of further terrorist attacks reduced market fears and uncertainty, causing g to recover and k_e to fall. The denominator in Equation 5 then fell, leading to a recovery in P_0 and the stock market in October and November. However, by the beginning of 2002, the Enron scandal and disclosures that many companies had overstated their earnings caused many investors to doubt the formerly rosy forecast of earnings and dividend growth for corporations. The resulting revision of g downward, and the rise in k_e because of increased uncertainty about the quality of accounting information, should have led to a rise in the denominator in the Gordon Equation 5, thereby lowering P_0 for many companies and hence the overall stock market. As predicted by our analysis, this is exactly what happened. The stock market recovery was aborted and it entered a downward slide.

Stock Market Indexes

A stock market index is used to monitor the behavior of a group of stocks. By reviewing the average behavior of a group of stocks, investors are able to gain some insight as to how a broad group of stocks may have performed. Various stock market indexes are reported to give investors an indication of the performance of different groups

History of the Dow Jones Industrial Average

The Dow Jones Industrial Average (DJIA) is an index composed of 30 "blue chip" industrial firms. On May 26, 1896, Charles H. Dow added up the prices of 12 of the best-known stocks and created an average by dividing by the number of stocks. In 1916, eight more stocks were added, and in 1928, the 30-stock average made its debut.

Today the editors of the *Wall Street Journal* select the firms that make up the DJIA. They take a broad view of the type of firm that is considered "industrial": In essence, it is almost any company that is not in the transportation or utility business (because there are also Dow Jones averages for those kinds of stocks). In choosing a new company for DJIA, they look among substantial industrial companies with a

history of successful growth and wide interest among investors. The components of the DJIA are changed periodically. For example, in 2004, AT&T, Eastman Kodak, and International Paper were replaced with American International Group, Pfizer, and Verizon Communications.

Most market watchers agree that the DJIA is not the best indicator of the market's overall day-to-day performance. Indeed, it varies substantially from broader-based stock indexes in the short run. It continues to be followed so closely primarily because it is the oldest index and was the first to be quoted by other publications. But it tracks the performance of the market reasonably well over the long run.

go online
A wealth of information about the current DJIA and its history can be found at **www.djindexes.com**.

of stocks. The most commonly quoted index is the Dow Jones Industrial Average (DJIA), an index based on the performance of the stocks of 30 large companies. The Mini-Case box above provides more background on this famous index. Table 11.3 lists the 30 stocks that made up the index in November 2005.

Other indexes, such as Standard and Poor's 500 Index, the NASDAQ composite, and the NYSE composite, may be more useful for following the performance of different groups of stocks. The *Wall Street Journal* reports on 20 different indexes in its "Markets Lineup" column. Figure 11.2 shows the DJIA since 1980.

TABLE 11.3 The Thirty Companies That Make Up the Dow Jones Industrial Average

Alcoa Inc.	Exxon Mobil Corp.	McDonald's Corp.
Altria	General Electric Co.	Merck & Co. Inc.
American Express Co.	General Motors Corp.	Microsoft Corp.
American International Group	Hewlett-Packard Co.	Minnesota Mining & Manufacturing Co.
AT&T Inc.	Home Depot Inc.	Pfizer
Boeing Co.	Honeywell International Inc.	Procter & Gamble Co.
Caterpillar Inc.	Intel Corp.	United Technologies Corp.
Citigroup Inc.	International Business Machines Corp.	Verizon Communications
Coca-Cola Co.	J. P. Morgan Chase & Co.	Wal-Mart Stores Inc.
E.I. DuPont de Nemours & Co.	Johnson & Johnson	Walt Disney Co.

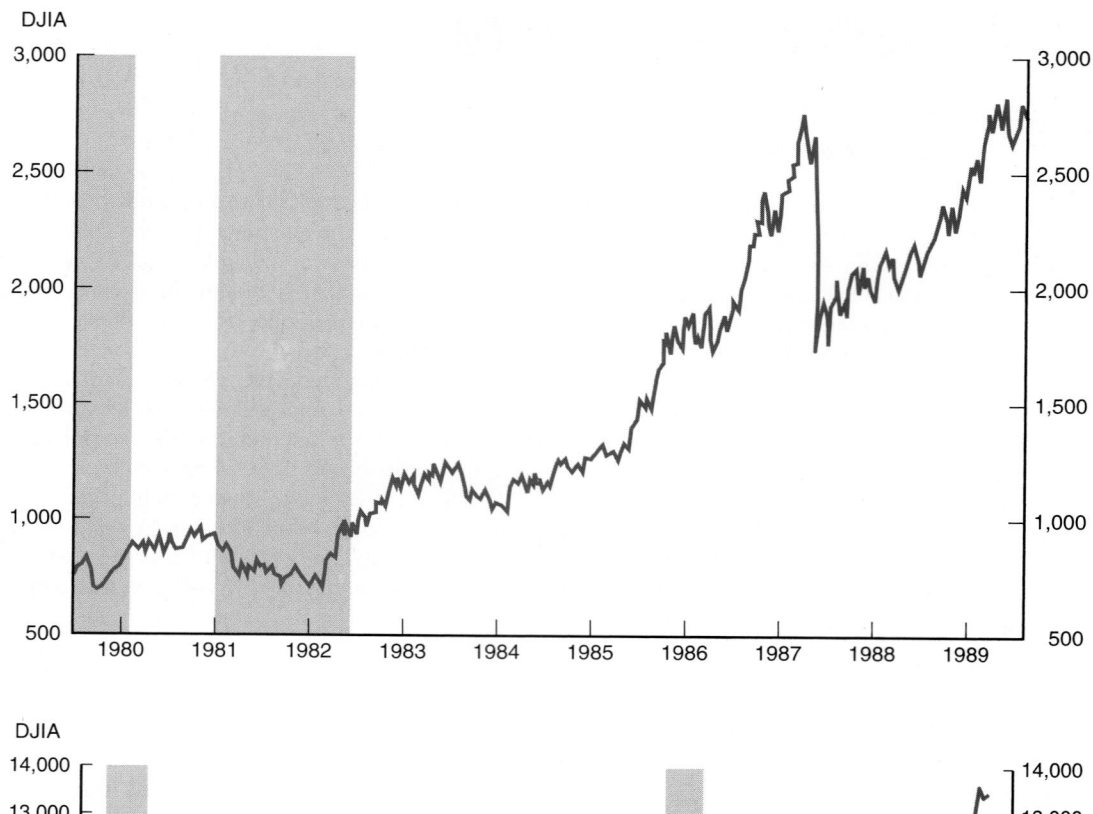

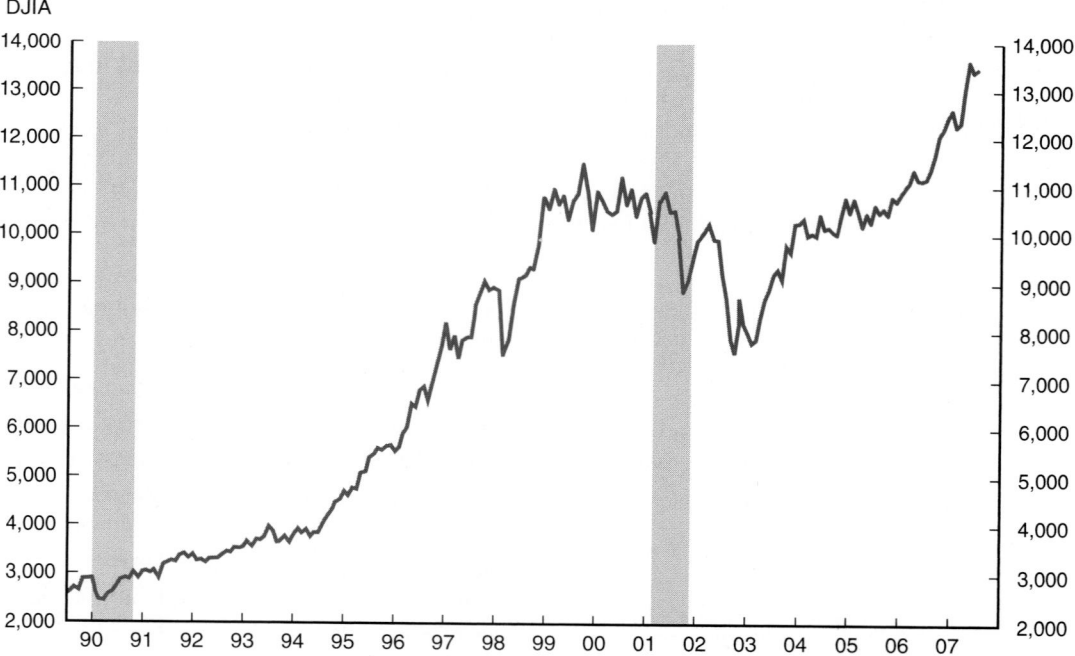

Figure 11.2 Dow Jones Indusrial Averages, 1980–2007

Shaded areas indicate periods of recession.

Source: http://finance.yahoo.com/?u.

Buying Foreign Stocks

In Chapter 4 we learned that diversification of a portfolio reduces risk. In recent years, investors have come to realize that some risk can also be eliminated by diversifying across different countries. When one country is suffering from a recession, others may be booming. If inflationary concerns in the United States cause stock prices to drop, falling inflation in Japan may cause Japanese stocks to rise.

The problem with buying foreign stocks is that most foreign companies are not listed on any of the U.S. stock exchanges, so the purchase of shares is difficult. Intermediaries have found a way to solve this problem by selling **American depository receipts (ADRs).** A U.S. bank buys the shares of a foreign company and places them in its vault. The bank then issues receipts against these shares, and these receipts can be traded domestically, usually on the NASDAQ. Trade in ADRs is conducted entirely in U.S. dollars, and the bank converts stock dividends into U.S. currency. One advantage of the ADR is that it allows foreign firms to trade in the United States without the firms having to meet the disclosure rules required by the SEC.

Foreign stock trading has been growing rapidly. Since 1979, cross-border trade in equities has grown at a rate of 28% a year and now exceeds $2 trillion annually. Interest is particularly keen in the stocks of firms in emerging economies such as Mexico, Brazil, and South Korea.

Regulation of the Stock Market

Properly functioning capital markets are a hallmark of an economically advanced economy. For an economy to flourish, firms must be able to raise funds to take advantage of growth opportunities as they become available. Firms raise funds in the capital markets, and for these to function properly investors must be able to trust the information that is released about the firms that are using them. Markets can collapse in the absence of this trust. The most notable example of this in the United States was the Great Depression. During the 1920s, about $50 billion in new securities were offered for sale. By 1932, half had become worthless. The public's confidence in the capital markets justifiably plummeted, and lawmakers agreed that for the economy to recover, public faith had to be restored. Following a series of investigative hearings, Congress passed the Securities Act of 1933, and shortly after the Securities Act of 1934. The main purpose of these laws was to (1) require firms to tell the public the truth about their businesses, and (2) require brokers, dealers, and exchanges to treat investors fairly. Congress established the Securities and Exchange Commission (SEC) to enforce these laws.

The Securities and Exchange Commission

The SEC Web site states the following:

> The primary mission of the U.S. Securities and Exchange Commission is to protect investors and maintain the integrity of the securities markets.[3]

It accomplishes this daunting task primarily by assuring a constant, timely, and accurate flow of information to investors, who can then judge for themselves if a company's

---

[3]www.sec.gov/about/whatwedo.shtml.

securities are a good investment. Thus, the SEC is primarily focused on promoting disclosure of information and reducing asymmetric information rather than determining the strength or well-being of any particular firm. The SEC brings 400 to 500 civil enforcement actions against individuals and companies each year in its effort to maintain the quality of the information provided to investors.

The SEC is organized around four divisions and 18 offices and employs about 3,100 people. One way to better understand how it accomplishes its goals is to review the duties assigned to each division.

- The Division of Corporate Finance is responsible for collecting the many documents that public companies are required to file. These include annual reports, registration statements, quarterly filings, and many others. The division reviews these filings to check for compliance with the regulations. It does not verify the truth or accuracy of filings. The division staff also provides companies with help interpreting the regulations and recommends new rules for adoption.
- The Division of Market Regulation establishes and maintains standards for an orderly and efficient market by regulating the major securities market participants. This is the division that reviews and approves new rules and changes to existing rules.
- The Division of Investment Management oversees and regulates the investment management industry. This includes oversight of the mutual fund industry. Just as the Division of Market Regulation establishes rules governing the markets, the Division of Investment Management establishes rules governing investment companies.
- The Division of Enforcement investigates violation of any of the rules and regulations established by the other divisions. The Division of Enforcement conducts its own investigations into various types of securities fraud and acts on tips provided by the SEC's other divisions. The SEC itself can only bring civil lawsuits; however, it works closely with various criminal authorities to bring criminal cases when appropriate.

Later, in Chapter 16 and again in Chapter 21, we discuss specific instances where the SEC has addressed fraud and violations of ethical standards.

SUMMARY

1. There are both organized and over-the-counter exchanges. Organized exchanges are distinguished by a physical building where trading takes place. The over-the-counter market operates primarily over phone lines and computer links. Typically, larger firms trade on organized exchanges and smaller firms trade in the over-the-counter market, though there are many exceptions to this rule. In recent years, ECNs have begun to capture a significant portion of business traditionally belonging to the stock exchanges. These electronic networks are likely to become increasingly significant players in the future.

2. Stocks are valued as the present value of the dividends. Unfortunately, we do not know very precisely what these dividends will be. This introduces a great deal of error to the valuation process. The Gordon growth model is a simplified method of computing stock value that depends on the assumption that the dividends are growing at a constant rate forever. Given our uncertainty regarding future dividends, this assumption is often the best we can do.

3. An alternative method for estimating stock price is to multiply the firm's earnings per share times

the industry price earnings ratio. This ratio can be adjusted up or down to reflect specific characteristics of the firm.

4. The interaction among traders in the market is what actually sets prices on a day-to-day basis. The trader that values the security the most, either because of less uncertainty about the cash flows or because of greater estimated cash flows, will be willing to pay the

most. As new information is released, investors will revise their estimates of the true value of the security and will either buy or sell it depending upon how the market price compares to their estimated valuation. Because small changes in estimated growth rates or required return result in large changes in price, it is not surprising that the markets are often volatile.

KEY TERMS

American depository receipts (ADRs), *p. 275*
ask price, *p. 263*
bid price, *p. 263*
common stock, *p. 260*
generalized dividend model, *p. 266*

Gordon growth model, *p. 266*
NASDAQ, *p. 262*
preferred stock, *p. 261*
price earnings ratio (PE), *p. 268*

QUESTIONS

1. What basic principle of finance can be applied to the valuation of any investment asset?

2. Identify the cash flows available to an investor in stock. How reliably can these cash flows be estimated? Compare the problem of estimating stock cash flows to estimating bond cash flows. Which security would you predict to be more volatile?

3. Discuss the features that differentiate organized exchanges from the over-the-counter market.

4. What is the National Association of Securities Dealers Automated Quotation System (NASDAQ)?

5. What distinguishes stocks from bonds?

6. Review the list of firms now included in the Dow Jones Industrial Average listed in Table 3. How many firms appear to be technology related? Discuss what this means in terms of the risk of the index.

QUANTITATIVE PROBLEMS

eBay, Inc., went public in September of 1998. The following information on shares outstanding was listed in the final prospectus filed with the SEC.[4]

In the IPO, eBay issued 3,500,000 new shares. The initial price to the public was $18.00 per share. The final first-day closing price was $44.88.

1. If the investment bankers retained $1.26 per share as fees, what were the net proceeds to eBay? What was the market capitalization of the new shares of eBay?

2. Two common statistics in IPOs are *underpricing* and *money left on the table*. Underpricing is defined as percentage change between the offering price and the first day closing price. Money left on the table is the difference between the first day closing price and the offering price, multiplied by the number of shares offered. Calculate the underpricing and money left on the table for eBay. What does this suggest about the efficiency of the IPO process?

---

[4]This information is summarized from http://www.sec.gov/Archives/edgar/data/1065088/0001012870-98-002475.txt.

3. The shares of Misheak, Inc., are expected to generate the following possible returns over the next 12 months:

Return (%)	Probability
−5	.10
5	.25
10	.30
15	.25
25	.10

If the stock is currently trading at $25 per share, what is the expected price in one year? Assume that the stock pays no dividends.

4. Suppose SoftPeople, Inc. is selling at $19.00 and currently pays an annual dividend of $0.65 per share. Analysts project that the stock will be priced around $23.00 in one year. What is the expected return?

5. Suppose Microsoft, Inc. is trading at $27.29 per share. It pays an annual dividend of $0.32 per share, and analysts have set a one-year target price around $33.30 per share. What is the expected return of this stock?

6. LaserAce is selling at $22.00 per share. The most recent annual dividend paid was $0.80. Using the Gordon growth model, if the market requires a return of 11%, what is the expected dividend growth rate for LaserAce?

7. Huskie Motors just paid an annual dividend of $1.00 per share. Management has promised shareholders to increase dividends at a constant rate of 5%. If the required return is 12%, what is the current price per share?

8. Suppose Microsoft, Inc. is trading at $27.29 per share. It pays an annual dividend of $0.32 per share, which is double last year's dividend of $0.16 per share. If this trend is expected to continue, what is the required return on Microsoft?

9. Gordon & Co.'s stock has just paid its annual dividend of $1.10 per share. Analysts believe that Gordon will maintain its historic dividend growth rate of 3%. If the required return is 8%, what is the expected price of the stock next year?

10. Macro Systems just paid an annual dividend of $0.32 per share. Its dividend is expected to double for the next four years (D_1 through D_4), after which it will grow at a more modest pace of 1% per year. If the required return is 13%, what is the current price?

11. Nat-T-Cat Industries just went public. As a growing firm, it is not expected to pay a dividend for the first five years. After that, investors expect Nat-T-Cat to pay an annual dividend of $1.00 per share (i.e., D_6 = 1.00), with no growth. If the required return is 10%, what is the current stock price?

12. Analysts are projecting that CB Railways will have earnings per share of $3.90. If the average industry PE ratio is about 25, what is the current price of CB Railways?

13. Suppose Microsoft, Inc. reports earnings per share of around $0.75. If Microsoft is in an industry with a PE ratio ranging from 30 to 40, what is a reasonable price range for Microsoft?

14. Consider the following security information for four securities making up an index:

Security	Price Time = 0	Price Time = 1	Shares Outstanding
1	8	13	20 million
2	22	25	50 million
3	35	30	120 million
4	50	55	75 million

What is the change in the value of the index from Time = 0 to Time = 1 if the index is calculated using a value-weighted arithmetic mean?

15. An index had an average (geometric) mean return over 20 years of 3.8861%. If the beginning index value was 100, what was the final index value after 20 years?

16. Compute the price of a share of stock that pays a $1 per year dividend and that you expect to be able to sell in one year for $20, assuming you require a 15% return.

17. The projected earnings per share for Risky Ventures, Inc., is $3.50. The average PE ratio for the industry composed of Risky Ventures' closest competitors is 21. After careful analysis, you decide that Risky Ventures is a little more risky than average, so you decide a PE ratio of 23 better reflects the market's perception of the firm. Estimate the current price of the firm's stock.

WEB EXERCISES

The Stock Market

1. Visit **http://www.forecasts.org/data/index.htm**. Click on "Stock Index Data" at the very top of the page and then click on "U.S. Stock Indices–monthly." Review the indexes for the DJIA, the S&P 500, and the NASDAQ composite. Which index appears most volatile? In which index would you have rather invested in 1985 if the investment had been allowed to compound until now?

2. There are a number of indexes that track the performance of the stock market. It is interesting to review how well they track along with each other. Go to **http://bloomberg.com**. Click on the "Charts" tab at the top of the screen. Alternatively, choose to display the DJIA, S&P 500, NASDAQ, and the Russell 2000. Set the time frame to five years. Click on "Get Chart."

   a. Which index has been most volatile over the last five years?

   b. Which index has posted the greatest gains over the last five years?

   c. Now adjust the time frame to intraday. Which index has performed the best today? Which has been most volatile?

CHAPTER 12

The Mortgage Markets

Preview

Part of the classic American dream is to own one's own home. With the price of the average house now over $140,000, few of us could hope to do this until late in life if we were not able to borrow the bulk of the purchase price. Similarly, businesses rely on borrowed capital far more than on equity investment to finance their growth. Many small firms do not have access to the bond market and must find alternative sources of funds. Consider the state of the mortgage loan markets 100 years ago. They were organized mostly to accommodate the needs of businesses and the very wealthy. Much has changed since then. The purpose of this chapter is to discuss these changes.

Chapter 9 discussed the *money markets,* the markets for short-term funds. Chapters 10 and 11 discussed the *bond and stock markets.* This chapter discusses the *mortgage markets,* where borrowers—individuals, businesses, and governments—can obtain long-term collateralized loans. From one perspective, the mortgage markets form a subcategory of the capital markets because mortgages involve long-term funds. But the mortgage markets differ from the stock and bond markets in important ways. First, the usual borrowers in the capital markets are government entities and businesses, whereas the usual borrowers in the mortgage markets are individuals. Second, mortgage loans are made for varying amounts and maturities, depending on the borrowers' needs, features that cause problems for developing a secondary market.

In this chapter we will identify the characteristics of typical residential mortgages, discuss the usual term and types of mortgages available, and review who provides and services these loans. We will also discuss the growth of the mortgage-backed security market.

What Are Mortgages?

A **mortgage** is a long-term loan secured by real estate. A developer may obtain a mortgage loan to finance the construction of an office building, or a family may obtain a mortgage loan to finance the purchase of a home. In either case, the loan is **amortized:** The borrower pays it off over time in some combination of principal and interest payments that result in full payment of the debt by maturity. Table 12.1 shows the distribution of mortgage loan borrowers. Because over 82% of mortgage loans finance residential home purchases, that will be the primary focus of this chapter.

One way to understand the modern mortgage is to review its history. Originally, many states had laws that prevented banks from funding mortgages so that banks would not tie up their funds in long-term loans. The National Banking Act of 1863 further restricted mortgage lending. As a result, most mortgage contracts in the past were arranged between individuals, usually with the help of a lawyer who brought the parties together and drew up the papers. Such loans were generally available only to the wealthy and socially connected. As the demand for long-term funds increased, however, more mortgage brokers surfaced. They often originated loans in the rapidly developing western part of the country and sold them to savings banks and insurance companies in the East.

By 1880, mortgage bankers had learned to streamline their operations by selling bonds to raise the long-term funds they lent. They would gather a portfolio of mortgage contracts and use them as security for an issue of bonds that were sold publicly. Many of these loans were used to finance agricultural expansion in the Midwest. Unfortunately, an agricultural recession in the 1890s resulted in many defaults. Land prices fell, and a large number of the mortgage bankers went bankrupt.

Thereafter, it was very difficult to obtain long-term loans until after World War I, when national banks were authorized to make mortgage loans. This regulatory change caused a tremendous real estate boom, and mortgage lending expanded rapidly.

The mortgage market was again devastated by the Great Depression in the 1930s. Millions of borrowers were without work and were unable to make their loan payments. This led to foreclosures and land sales that caused property values to collapse. Mortgage-lending institutions were again hit hard, and many failed.

One reason that so many borrowers defaulted on their loans was the type of mortgage loan they had. Most mortgages in this period were **balloon loans:** The borrower paid only interest for three to five years, at which time the entire loan amount became due. The lender was usually willing to renew the debt with some reduction in prin-

TABLE 12.1 Mortgage Loan Borrowing, 2006

Type of Property	Mortgage Loans Issued ($ millions)	Proportion of Total (%)
One- to four-family dwelling	10,199	76.6
Multifamily dwelling	731	5.49
Commercial building	2,221	16.68
Farm	163	1.22

Source: Federal Reserve Bulletin, 2006, Table 1.54.

cipal. However, if the borrower were unemployed, the lender would not renew, and the borrower would default.

As part of the recovery program from the depression, the federal government stepped in and restructured the mortgage market. The government took over delinquent balloon loans and allowed borrowers to repay them over long periods of time. It is no surprise that these new types of loans were very popular. The surviving savings and loans began offering home buyers similar loans, and the high demand contributed to restoring the health of the mortgage industry.

Characteristics of the Residential Mortgage

The modern mortgage lender has continued to refine the long-term loan to make it more desirable to borrowers. Even in the past 20 years, both the nature of the lenders and the instruments have undergone substantial changes. One of the biggest changes is the development of an active secondary market for mortgage contracts. We will examine the nature of mortgage loan contracts and then look at their secondary market.

The mortgage market has become very competitive in recent years. Twenty years ago, savings and loan institutions and the mortgage departments of large banks originated most mortgage loans. Currently, there are many loan production offices that compete in real estate financing. Some of these offices are subsidiaries of banks, and others are independently owned. As a result of the competition for mortgage loans, borrowers can choose from a variety of terms and options.

Mortgage Interest Rates

go online

Track mortgage rates and shop for mortgage rates in different geographic areas at **www.interest.com**.

The interest rate borrowers pay on their mortgages is probably the most important factor in their decision of how much and from whom to borrow. The interest rate on the loan is determined by three factors: current long-term market rates, the life (term) of the mortgage, and the number of discount points paid.

1. *Market rates.* Long-term market rates are determined by the supply of and demand for long-term funds, which are in turn influenced by a number of global, national, and regional factors. As Figure 12.1 shows, mortgage rates tend to stay above the less risky Treasury bonds most of the time but tend to track along with them.
2. *Term.* Longer-term mortgages have higher interest rates than shorter-term mortgages. The usual mortgage lifetime is either 15 or 30 years. Lenders also offer 20-year loans, though they are not as popular. Because interest-rate risk falls as the term to maturity decreases, the interest rate on the 15-year loan will be substantially less than on the 30-year loan. For example, in May, 2007, the average 30-year mortgage rate was 5.9%, and the 15-year rate was 5.6%.
3. *Discount points.* **Discount points** (or simply *points*) are interest payments made at the beginning of a loan. A loan with one discount point means that the borrower pays 1% of the loan amount at *closing,* the moment when the borrower signs the loan paper and receives the proceeds of the loan. In exchange for the points, the lender reduces the interest rate on the loan. In considering whether to pay points, borrowers must determine whether the reduced interest rate over the life of the loan fully compensates for the

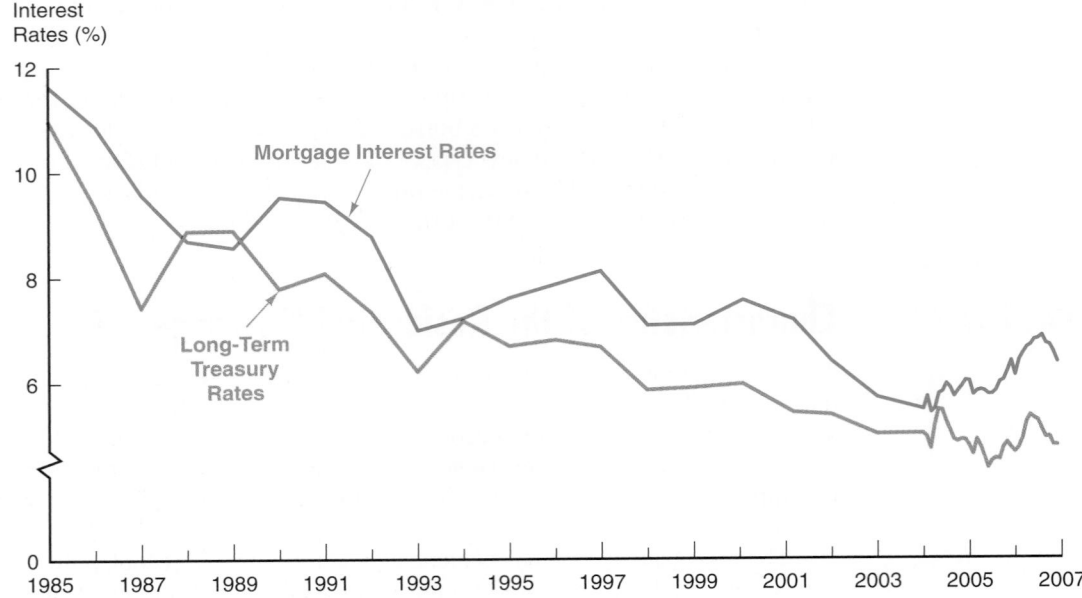

Figure 12.1   Mortgage Rates and Long-Term Treasury Interest Rates, 1985–2007

Source: Federal Reserve Bulletin, various issues, Table 1.53 Line 7 and Table 1.35 Line 23.

increased up-front expense. To make this determination, borrowers must take into account how long they will hold on to the loan. Typically, discount points should not be paid if the borrower will pay off the loan in five years or less. This breakeven point is not surprising since the average home sells every five years.

CASE

The Discount Point Decision

Suppose that you are offered two loan alternatives. In the first, you pay no discount points and the interest rate is 12%. In the second, you pay 2 discount points but receive a lower interest rate of 11.5%. Which alternative do you choose?

To answer this question you must first compute the effective annual rate without discount points. Since the loan is compounded monthly, you pay 1% per month. Because of the compounding, the effective annual rate is greater than the simple annual rate. To compute the effective rate, raise 1 plus the monthly rate to the twelfth power and subtract 1. The effective annual rate on the no-point loan is thus

$$\text{Effective annual rate} = (1.01)^{12} - 1 = 0.1268 = 12.68\%$$

Because of monthly compounding, a 12% annual percentage rate has an effective annual rate of 12.68%. On a 30-year, $100,000 mortgage loan, your payment will be $1,028.61 as found on a financial calculator.

TABLE 12.2 Effective Rate of Interest on a Loan at 12% with 2 Discount Points

Year of Prepayment	Effective Rate of Interest (%)	Year of Prepayment	Effective Rate of Interest (%)
1	14.54	6	12.65
2	13.40	7	12.60
3	13.02	10	12.52
4	12.84	15	12.45
5	12.73	30	12.42

Now compute the effective annual rate if you pay 2 discount points. Let's assume that the amount of the loan is still $100,000. If you pay 2 points, instead of receiving $100,000, you will receive only $98,000 ($100,000 − $2000). Your payment is computed on the $100,000, but at the lower interest rate. Using a financial calculator, we find that the monthly payment is $990.29 and your monthly rate is 0.9804%.[1] The effective annual rate after compounding is

$$\text{Effective annual rate} = (1.009804)^{12} - 1 = 0.1242 = 12.42\%$$

As a result of paying the 2 discount points, the effective annual rate has dropped from 12.68% to 12.42%. On the surface, it would seem like a good idea to pay the points. The problem is that these calculations were made assuming the loan would be held for 30 years. What happens if you sell the house before the loan matures?

If the loan is paid off early, the borrower will benefit from the lower interest rate for a shorter length of time, and the discount points are spread over a shorter period of time. The result of these two factors is that the effective interest rate rises the shorter the time the loan is held before being paid. This relationship is demonstrated in Table 12.2. If the 2-point loan is held for 15 years, the effective rate is 12.45%. At 10 years, the effective rate is up to 12.52%. Even at 6 years, when the effective rate is 12.65%, paying the discount points has saved the borrower money. However, if the loan is paid off at 5 years, the effective rate is 12.73%, which is higher than the 12.68% effective rate if no points were paid.[2]

Loan Terms

Mortgage loan contracts contain many legal and financial terms, most of which protect the lender from financial loss.

Collateral One characteristic common to mortgage loans is the requirement that collateral, usually the real estate being financed, be pledged as security. The lending institution will place a **lien** against the property, and this remains in effect until the

[1]The case on p. 288 discusses how mortgage loan payments are computed.

[2]For example, to compute the effective rate if the loan is prepaid after 2 years, find the FV if I = 11.5%, PV = 100,000, N = 360, and PMT = 990.29. Now set PV equal to 98,000 and compute I. Divide this I by 12, add 1, and raise the result to the twelfth power.

loan is paid off. A lien is a public record that attaches to the title of the property, advising that the property is security for a loan, and it gives the lender the right to sell the property if the underlying loan defaults.

No one can buy the property and obtain clear title to it without paying off this lien. For example, if you purchased a piece of property with a loan secured by a lien, the lender would file notice of this lien at the public recorder's office. The lien gives notice to the world that if there is a default on the loan, the lender has the right to seize the property. If you try to sell the property without paying off the loan, the lien would remain attached to the title or deed to the property. Since the lender can take the property away from whoever owns it, no one would buy it unless you paid off the loan. The existence of liens against real estate explains why a title search is an important part of any mortgage loan transaction. During the title search, a lawyer or title company searches the public record for any liens. Title insurance is then sold that guarantees the buyer that the property is free of *encumbrances*, any questions about the state of the title to the property, including the existence of liens.

Down Payments To obtain a mortgage loan, the lender also requires the borrower to make a **down payment** on the property, that is, to pay a portion of the purchase price. The balance of the purchase price is paid by the *loan proceeds*. Down payments (like liens) are intended to make the borrower less likely to default on the loan. A borrower who does not make a down payment could walk away from the house and the loan and lose nothing. Furthermore, if real estate prices drop even a small amount, the balance due on the loan will exceed the value of the collateral. As we discussed in Chapter 2, the down payment reduces *moral hazard* for the borrower. The amount of the down payment depends on the type of mortgage loan. Many lenders require that the borrower pay 5% of the purchase price; in other situations, up to 20% may be required.

Private Mortgage Insurance Another way that lenders protect themselves against default is by requiring the borrower to purchase **private mortgage insurance (PMI).** PMI is an insurance policy that guarantees to make up any discrepancy between the value of the property and the loan amount, should a default occur. For example, if the balance on your loan was $120,000 at the time of default and the property was worth only $100,000, PMI would pay the lending institution $20,000. The default still appears on the credit record of the borrower, but the lender avoids sustaining the loss. PMI is usually required on loans that have less than a 20% down payment. If the loan-to-value ratio falls because of payments being made or because the value of the property increases, the borrower can request that the PMI requirement be dropped. PMI usually costs between $20 and $30 per month for a $100,000 loan.

Borrower Qualification Before granting a mortgage loan, the lender will determine whether the borrower qualifies for it. Qualifying for a mortgage loan is different from qualifying for a bank loan because most lenders sell their mortgage loans to one of a few federal agencies in the secondary mortgage market. These agencies establish very precise guidelines that must be followed before they will accept the loan. If the lender gives a mortgage loan to a borrower who does not fit these guidelines, the lender may not be able to resell the loan. That ties up the lender's funds. Banks can be more flexible with loans that will be kept on the bank's own books.

The rules for qualifying a borrower are complex and constantly changing, but a rule of thumb is that the loan payment, including taxes and insurance, should not exceed 25% of gross monthly income. Furthermore, the sum of the monthly payments on all loans to the borrower, including car loans and credit cards, cannot exceed 33% of gross monthly income. A borrower who fails this income test can pay off some of the outstanding debt, increase the down payment, or find a less expensive house to buy.

Lenders will also order a credit report from one of the major credit reporting agencies. The credit score is based on a model that weights a number of variables found to be valid predictors of credit worthiness. The most common score is called the FICO, named after its creator, Fair Isaac Company. **FICO scores** may range from a low of 300 to a maximum of 850. Scores above 720 are considered good while scores below 660 are likely to cause problems obtaining a loan. The FICO score is determined by your past payment history, outstanding debt, length of credit history, number or recent credit applications and types of credit and loans you have. It is interesting to note that simply applying for and holding a number of credit cards can significantly affect your FICO score.

Mortgage Loan Amortization

Mortgage loan borrowers agree to pay a monthly amount of principal and interest that will fully amortize the loan by its maturity. "Fully amortize" means that the payments will pay off the outstanding indebtedness by the time the loan matures. During the early years of the loan, the lender applies most of the payment to the interest on the loan and a small amount to the outstanding principal balance. Many borrowers are surprised to find that after years of making payments, their loan balance has not dropped appreciably.

Table 12.3 shows the distribution of principal and interest for a 30-year, $130,000 loan at 8.5% interest. Only $78.75 of the first payment is applied to reduce the loan balance. At the end of two years, the balance due is $127,947, and at the end of five years, the balance due is $124,137. Put another way, of $59,975.40 in loan payments made during the first five years, only $5862.69 is applied to the principal. Over the life of the $130,000 loan, a total of $229,850 in interest will be paid.

If the loan in Table 12.3 had been financed for 15 years instead of for 30, the payment would have increased by about $280 per month to $1279.59, but the interest savings over the life of the loan would be nearly $130,000. It is no wonder why so many borrowers prefer the shorter-term loans.

TABLE 12.3 Amortization of a 30-Year, $130,000 Loan at 8.5%

Payment Number	Beginning Balance of Loan	Monthly Payment	Amount Applied to Interest	Amount Applied to Principal	Ending Balance of Loan
1	130,000.00	999.59	920.83	78.75	129,921.24
24	128,040.25	999.59	906.95	92.66	127,947.62
60	124,256.74	999.59	880.15	119.43	124,137.31
120	115,365.63	999.59	817.17	182.41	115,183.22
180	101,786.23	999.59	720.99	278.60	101,507.63
240	81,046.41	999.59	574.08	425.51	80,620.90
360	991.77	999.59	7.82	991.77	0

CASE

Computing the Payment on Mortgage Loans

We can apply the techniques for computing loan payments introduced in Chapter 3 to computing the payment on mortgage loans. Suppose that you have graduated and want to buy a condominium instead of renting an apartment. The condo costs $100,000, and a 5% down payment is required by your mortgage lender. How much will your monthly loan payment be?

To compute fixed-amount loan payments, we recognize that the lender must equate the present value of the stream of payments you will pay to the amount of the loan. In equation form,

$$\text{Loan amount} = \frac{P}{1+i} + \frac{P}{(1+i)^2} + \frac{P}{(1+i)^3} + \cdots + \frac{P}{(1+i)^n} \qquad (1)$$

where

P = fixed payment
i = interest rate on the loan
n = term of the loan

An alternative form for Equation 1, which takes advantage of present value tables included at the end of most introductory finance texts, is

$$\text{Loan amount} = P(PVIFA_{i,n}) \qquad (2)$$

where *PVIFA* is the present value interest factor with an interest rate of i for n periods. P can then be found by looking up the factor for the term and interest rate on the loan you are interested in and dividing this factor into the loan amount. Most factor tables include only 50 or 60 periods, so we cannot use this method to compute the payment on 30-year loans with monthly payments (30 × 12 = 360 periods). Instead, a close approximation of the monthly payment can be found by computing the annual payment and dividing by 12.

example 12.1 **Mortgage Loans**

You obtain a 30-year loan at 8% on the $95,000 you need to finance your new condo. The price of the condo is $100,000 minus a $5,000 down payment. Use Table 12.4 and Equation 2 to calculate the fixed payment on the loan.

TABLE 12.4 Present Value Interest Factor at Various Rates of Interest

Payment Periods	Interest Rate					
	5%	6%	7%	8%	9%	10%
15	10.3797	9.7122	9.1079	8.5595	8.0607	7.6061
20	12.4622	11.4699	10.5940	9.8181	9.1285	8.5136
25	14.0939	12.7834	11.6536	10.6748	9.8226	9.0770
30	15.3725	13.7648	12.4090	11.2578	9.8226	9.0770

Solution
The fixed payment on the loan would be $703 per month.

$$\text{Loan amount} = P(PVIFA_{i,n})$$

where

$$\text{Loan amount} = \text{amount loaned by the bank} = \$95,000$$
$$i = \text{interest rate on the loan} = 0.08$$
$$n = \text{term of the loan} = 30$$

Thus,

$$\$95,000 = P_{ann}(PVIFA_{8\%,30})$$
$$\$95,000 = P_{ann}(11.2578)$$

$$P_{ann} = \frac{\$95,000}{11.2578}$$

$$P_{ann} = \$8,439$$

$$P_{mo} = \frac{\$8,439}{12 \text{ months}} = \$703 \text{ per month}$$

To find the present value interest factor in Table 12.4, pick out the payment period in the left-hand column and then move across the row to the entry in the column for the interest rate on the loan. For a 30-year loan at 8%, the present value interest factor is 11.2578.
    To solve using a financial calculator:

$$N = \text{number of periods} = 30 \text{ years} \times 12 \text{ months} = 360$$
$$PV = \text{amount of the loan } (LV) = -95,000$$
$$FV = \text{amount of the loan after 30 years} = 0$$
$$I = \text{monthly interest rate} = 8/12 \text{ months} = 0.6667$$

Then push the PMT button = fixed monthly payment (P) = $697
    (Note: small differences between the table solution and the calculator solution are due to rounding.)

Types of Mortgage Loans

A number of types of mortgage loans are available in the market. Different borrowers may qualify for different ones. A skilled mortgage banker can help find the best type of mortgage loan for each particular situation.

Insured and Conventional Mortgages

Mortgages are classified as either *insured* or *conventional*. **Insured mortgages** are originated by banks or other mortgage lenders but are guaranteed by either the Federal Housing Administration (FHA) or the Veterans Administration (VA). Applicants for FHA and VA loans must meet certain qualifications, such as having served in the military or having income below a given level, and can borrow only up to a certain amount. The FHA or VA then guarantees the bank making the loans against any losses—that is, the agency guarantees that it will pay off the mortgage loan if the borrower defaults. One important advantage to a borrower who qualifies for an FHA or VA loan is that only a very low or zero down payment is required.

Conventional mortgages are originated by the same sources as insured loans but are not guaranteed. Private mortgage companies now insure many conventional loans against default. As we noted, most lenders require the borrower to obtain private mortgage insurance on all loans with a loan-to-value ratio exceeding 80%.

Fixed- and Adjustable-Rate Mortgages

In standard mortgage contracts, borrowers agree to make regular payments on the principal and interest they owe to lenders. As we saw earlier, the interest rate significantly affects the size of this monthly payment. In *fixed-rate mortgages,* the interest rate and the monthly payment do not vary over the life of the mortgage.

The interest rate on *adjustable-rate mortgages (ARMs)* is tied to some market interest rate and therefore changes over time. ARMs usually have limits, called *caps,* on how high (or low) the interest rate can move in one year and during the term of the loan. A typical ARM might tie the interest rate to the average Treasury bill rate plus 2%, with caps of 2% per year and 6% over the lifetime of the mortgage. Caps make ARMs more palatable to borrowers.

Borrowers tend to prefer fixed-rate loans to ARMs because ARMs may cause financial hardship if interest rates rise. However, fixed-rate borrowers do not benefit if rates fall unless they are willing to refinance their mortgage (pay it off by obtaining a new mortgage at a lower interest rate). The fact that individuals are risk-averse means that fear of hardship most often overwhelms anticipation of savings.

Lenders, by contrast, prefer ARMs because ARMs lessen interest-rate risk. Recall from Chapter 3 that interest-rate risk is the risk that rising interest rates will cause the value of debt instruments to fall. The effect on the value of the debt is greatest when the debt has a long term to maturity. Since mortgages are usually long-term, their value is very sensitive to interest-rate movements. Lending institutions can reduce the sensitivity of their portfolios by making ARMs instead of standard fixed-rate loans.

Seeing that lenders prefer ARMs and borrowers prefer fixed-rate mortgages, lenders must entice borrowers by offering lower initial interest rates on ARMs than on fixed-rate loans. For example, in April 2007, the reported interest rate for 30-year fixed-rate mortgage loans was 5.52%. The rate at that time for adjustable-rate mortgages was 5.9%. The rate on the ARM would have to rise .52% before the borrower of the ARM would be in a worse position than the fixed-rate borrower.

Other Types of Mortgages

As the market for mortgage loans becomes more competitive, lenders are offering more innovative mortgage contracts in an effort to attract borrowers. We discuss some of these mortgages here.

Graduated-Payment Mortgages (GPMs)   Graduated-payment mortgages are useful for home buyers who expect their incomes to rise. The GPM has lower payments in the first few years; then the payments rise. The early payments may not even be sufficient to cover the interest due, in which case the principal balance increases. As time passes, the borrower expects income to increase so that the higher payment will not be a burden.

The advantage of the GPM is that borrowers will qualify for a larger loan than if they requested a conventional mortgage. This may help buyers purchase adequate housing now and avoid the need to move to more expensive homes as their family size increases. The disadvantage is that the payments escalate whether the borrower's income does or not.

Growing-Equity Mortgages (GEMs) Lenders designed the growing-equity mortgage loan to help the borrower pay off the loan in a shorter period of time. With a GEM, the payments will initially be the same as on a conventional mortgage. However, over time the payment will increase. This increase will reduce the principal more quickly than the conventional payment stream would. For example, a typical contract may call for level payments for the first two years. The payments may increase by 5% per year for the next five years, then remain the same until maturity. The result is to reduce the life of the loan from 30 years to about 17.

GEMs are popular among borrowers who expect their incomes to rise in the future. It gives them the benefit of a small payment at the beginning while still retiring the debt early. Although the increase in payments is *required* in GEMs, most mortgage loans have no prepayment penalty. This means that a borrower with a 30-year loan could create a GEM by simply increasing the monthly payments beyond what is required and designating that the excess be applied entirely to the principal.

The GEM is similar to the graduated-payment mortgage; the difference is that the goal of the GPM is to help the borrower qualify by reducing the first few years' payments. The loan still pays off in 30 years. The goal of the GEM is to let the borrower pay off early.

Shared-Appreciation Mortgages (SAMs) When interest rates are high, the monthly payments on mortgage loans are also high. That prevents many borrowers from qualifying for loans. To help borrowers qualify and to keep loan volume high, lenders created the shared-appreciation mortgage. In a SAM, the lender lowers the interest rate on the mortgage in exchange for a share of any appreciation in the real estate (if the property sells for more than a stated amount, the lender is entitled to a portion of the gain). As interest rates and inflation fell in the late 1980s and into the 1990s, the popularity of these loans also diminished.

Equity Participation Mortgages In a shared-appreciation mortgage, the lender shares in the appreciation of the property. In an equity participation mortgage, an outside investor rather than the lender shares in the appreciation of the property. This investor will either provide a portion of the purchase price of the property or supplement the monthly payments. In return, the investor receives a portion of any appreciation in the property. As with the SAM, the borrower benefits by being able to qualify for a larger loan than without such help.

Second Mortgages Second mortgages are loans that are secured by the same real estate that is used to secure the first mortgage. The second mortgage is junior to the original loan. This means that should a default occur, the second mortgage holder will be paid only after the original loan has been paid off, if sufficient funds remain.

Second mortgages have two purposes. The first is to give borrowers a way to use the equity they have in their homes as security for another loan. An alternative to the second mortgage would be to refinance the home at a higher loan amount than is currently owed. The cost of obtaining a second mortgage is often much lower than refinancing.

Another purpose of the second mortgage is to take advantage of one of the few remaining tax deductions available to the middle class. The interest on loans secured by residential real estate is tax-deductible (the tax laws allow borrowers to deduct the interest on the primary residence and one vacation home). No other kind of consumer loan has this tax deduction. Many banks now offer lines of credit secured by second mortgages. In most cases, the value of the security is not of great interest to the bank. Consumers prefer that the line of credit be secured so that they can deduct the interest on the loan from their taxes.

Reverse Annuity Mortgages (RAMs) The reverse annuity mortgage is an innovative method for retired people to live on the equity they have in their homes. The contract for a RAM has the bank advancing funds on a monthly schedule. This increasing-balance loan is secured by the real estate. The borrower does not make any payments against the loan. When the borrower dies, the borrower's estate sells the property to retire the debt.

The advantage of the RAM is that it allows retired people to use the equity in their homes without the necessity of selling it. For retirees in need of supplemental funds to meet living expenses, the RAM can be a desirable option.

The various mortgage types are summarized in Table 12.5.

TABLE 12.5 Summary of Mortgage Types

Conventional mortgage	Loan is not guaranteed; usually requires private mortgage insurance; 5% to 20% down payment
Insured mortgage	Loan is guaranteed by FHA or VA; low or zero down payment
Adjustable-rate mortgage (ARM)	Interest rate is tied to some other security and is adjusted periodically; size of adjustment is subject to annual limits
Graduated-payment mortgage (GPM)	Initial low payment increases each year; loan amortizes in 30 years
Growing-equity mortgage (GEM)	Initial payment increases each year; loan amortizes in less than 30 years
Shared-appreciation mortgage (SAM)	In exchange for providing a low interest rate, the lender shares in any appreciation of the real estate
Equity participation mortgage	In exchange for paying a portion of the down payment or for supplementing the monthly payments, an outside investor shares in any appreciation of the real estate
Second mortgage	Loan is secured by a second lien against the real estate; often used for lines of credit or home improvement loans
Reverse annuity mortgage	Lender disburses a monthly payment to the borrower on an increasing-balance loan; loan comes due when the real estate is sold

Mortgage-Lending Institutions

Originally, the thrift industry was established with the mandate from Congress to provide mortgage loans to families. Congress gave these institutions the ability to attract depositors by allowing S&Ls to pay slightly higher interest rates on deposits. For many years, the thrift industry did its job well. Thrifts raised short-term funds by attracting deposits and used these funds to make long-term mortgage loans. The growth of the housing industry owes much of its success to these institutions. (The thrift industry is discussed further in Chapter 19.)

Until the 1970s, interest rates remained relatively stable, and when fluctuations did occur, they tended to be small and short-lived. But in the 1970s, interest rates rose rapidly, along with inflation, and thrifts became the victims of interest-rate risk. As market interest rates rose, the value of their fixed-rate mortgage loan portfolios fell. Because of the losses the thrifts suffered, they stopped being the primary source of mortgage loans.

Another serious problem with the early mortgage market was that thrift institutions were restricted from nationwide branching by federal and state laws and were forbidden to lend outside of their normal lending territory, about 100 miles from their offices. So even if an institution appeared very diversified, with thousands of different loans, all of the loans were from the same region. When that region had economic problems, many of the loans would default at the same time. For example, Texas and Oklahoma experienced a recession in the mid-1980s due to falling oil prices. Many mortgage loans defaulted because real estate values fell at the same time as the region's unemployment rate rose. That other areas of the country remained healthy was of no help to local lenders.

Figure 12.2 shows the share of the total mortgage market held by the major mortgage-lending institutions in the United States. (Mortgage pools and trusts are discussed later in this chapter.)

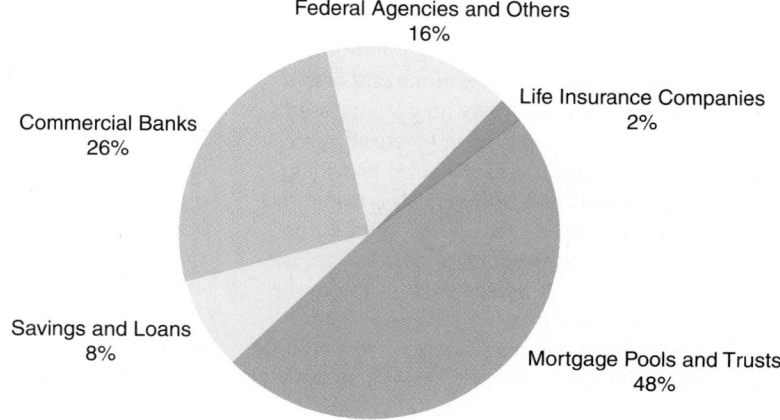

Figure 12.2   Share of the Mortgage Market Held by
Major Mortgage-Lending Institutions

Source: Federal Reserve Bulletin, April 2007, Table 1.54.

Loan Servicing

Many of the institutions making mortgage loans do not want to hold large port-folios of long-term securities. Commercial banks, for example, obtain their funds from short-term sources. Investing in long-term loans would subject them to unacceptably high interest-rate risk. Commercial banks, thrifts, and most other loan originators do, however, make money through the fees that they earn for packaging loans for other investors to hold. Loan origination fees are typically 1% of the loan amount, though this varies with the market.

Once a loan has been made, many lenders immediately sell the loan to another investor. The borrower may not even be aware that the original lender transferred the loan. By selling the loan, the originator frees up funds that can be lent to another borrower, thereby generating additional fee income.

Some of the originators also provide servicing of the loan. The loan-servicing agent collects payments from the borrower, passes the principal and interest on to the investor, keeps required records of the transaction, and maintains **reserve accounts.** Reserve accounts are established for most mortgage loans to permit the lender to make tax and insurance payments for the borrower. Lenders prefer to make these payments because they protect the security of the loan. Loan-servicing agents usually earn 0.5% per year of the total loan amount for their efforts.

Borrowers Shop the Web for Mortgages

One business area that has been significantly affected by the Web is mortgage banking. Historically, borrowers went to local banks, savings and loans, and mortgage banking companies to obtain mortgage loans. These offices packaged the loans and resold them. In recent years, hundreds of new Web-based mortgage banking companies have emerged.

The mortgage market is well suited to providing on-line service for several reasons. First, it is information-based and no products have to be shipped or inventoried. Second, the product (a loan) is homogeneous across providers. A borrower does not really care who provides the money as long as it is provided efficiently. Third, because home buyers tend not to obtain mortgage loans very often, they have little loyalty to any local lender. Finally, on-line lenders can often offer loans at lower cost because they can operate with lower overhead than firms that must greet the public.

The on-line mortgage market makes it much easier for borrowers to shop interest rates and terms. By fill-ing out one application, a borrower can obtain a number of alternative loan options from various Web service companies. Borrowers can then select the option that best suits their requirements.

On-line mortgage firms, such as Lending Tree, have made mortgage lending more competitive. This may lead to lower rates and better service. It has also led lenders to offer an often confusing array of loan alternatives that most borrowers have difficulty interpreting. This makes comparison shopping more difficult than simply comparing interest rates.

Borrowers using online services to shop for loans must be aware that scam artists have found this an easy way to obtain personal information. They set up a bogus loan site and offer extremely attractive interest rates to draw in customers. Once they have collected all the information needed to wipe out your checking, savings, and credit card accounts, they close their site and open another.

In summary, there are three distinct elements to most mortgage loans:

1. The originator packages the loan for an investor.
2. The investor holds the loan.
3. The servicing agent handles the paperwork.

One, two, or three different intermediaries may provide these functions.

Mortgage loans are increasingly obtained from the Web. The E-Finance box discusses this new source of mortgage loans.

Secondary Mortgage Market

The federal government founded the secondary market for mortgages. As we noted earlier, the mortgage market had all but collapsed during the Great Depression. To help spur the nation's economic activity, the government established several agencies to buy mortgages. The Federal National Mortgage Association (Fannie Mae) was set up to buy mortgages from thrifts so that these institutions could make more mortgage loans. This agency would fund these purchases by selling bonds to the public.

At about the same time, the Federal Housing Administration was established to insure certain mortgage contracts. This made it easier to sell the mortgages because the buyer did not have to be concerned with the borrower's credit history or the value of the collateral. A similar insurance program was set up through the Veterans Administration to insure loans to veterans after World War II.

One advantage of the insured loans was that they were required to be written on a standard loan contract. This standardization was an important factor in the growth of the secondary market for mortgages.

As the secondary market for mortgage contracts took shape, a new intermediary, the mortgage bank, emerged. Because this firm did not accept deposits, it was able to open offices across the country. The mortgage bank originated the loans, funding them initially with its own capital. After a group of similar loans were made, they would be bundled and sold, either to one of the federal agencies or to an insurance or pension fund. There were several advantages to the mortgage banks. Because of their size, they were able to capture economies of scale in loan origination and servicing. They were also able to bundle loans from different regions together, which helped reduce their risk. The increased competition for loans among these intermediaries led to lower rates for borrowers.

Securitization of Mortgages

Intermediaries still faced several problems when trying to sell mortgages. The first was that mortgages are usually too small to be wholesale instruments. The average mortgage loan is now about $200,000. This is far below the $5 million round lot established for commercial paper, for example. Many institutional investors do not want to deal in such small denominations.

The second problem with selling mortgages in the secondary market was that they were not standardized. They have different times to maturity, interest rates, and contract terms. That makes it difficult to bundle a large number of mortgages together.

Third, mortgage loans are relatively costly to service. Compare the servicing a mortgage loan requires to that of a corporate bond. The lender must collect monthly payments, often pay property taxes and insurance premiums, and service reserve accounts. None of this is required if a bond is purchased.

Finally, mortgages have unknown default risk. Investors in mortgages do not want to spend a lot of time evaluating the credit of borrowers. These problems inspired the creation of the **mortgage-backed security.**

What Is a Mortgage-Backed Security?

By the late 1960s, the secondary market for mortgages was declining, mostly because fewer veterans were obtaining guaranteed loans. The government reorganized Fannie Mae and also created two new agencies: the Government National Mortgage Association (GNMA, or Ginnie Mae) and the Federal Home Loan Mortgage Corporation (FHLMC, or Freddie Mac). These three agencies were now able to offer new securities backed by both insured and, for the first time, uninsured mortgages (see the Mini-Case box).

An alternative to selling mortgages directly to investors is to create a new security backed by (secured by) a large number of mortgages assembled into what is called a *mortgage pool.* A trustee, such as a bank or a government agency, holds the mortgage pool, which serves as collateral for the new security. This process is called *securitization.* The most common type of mortgage-backed security is the **mortgage pass-through,** a security that has the borrower's mortgage payments pass through the trustee before being disbursed to the investors in the mortgage pass-through. If borrowers prepay their loans, investors receive more principal than expected. For example, investors may buy mortgage-backed securities on which the average interest rate is 9%. If interest rates fall and borrowers refinance at lower

mini-case

Are Fannie Mae and Freddie Mac Getting Too Big for Their Britches?

With the growth of Fannie Mae and Freddie Mac to immense proportions, there are growing concerns that these federally sponsored agencies could pose a threat to the health of the financial system. Fannie Mae and Freddie Mac either own or insure the risk on nearly 75% of America's residential mortgages. In fact, their publicly issued debt is well over half that issued by the federal government. A failure of either of these institutions would therefore pose a grave shock to the financial system. Because the federal government would be unlikely to stand by and just let them fail, there would be substantial costs to the taxpayer, as occurred in the S&L crisis.

Concerns about the safety and soundness of these institutions arise because they have much smaller capital-to-asset ratios than banks. Critics also are concerned that Fannie Mae and Freddie Mac have become so large that they wield too much political influence. In addition, these federally sponsored agencies have conflicts of interest because they have to serve two masters: As publicly traded corporations they are supposed to maximize profits for the shareholders, but as government agencies they are supposed to work in the interests of the public. These concerns have led to calls for reform of these agencies, with many calling for full privatization as was done voluntarily by the Student Loan Market Association (Sallie Mae) in the mid-1990s.

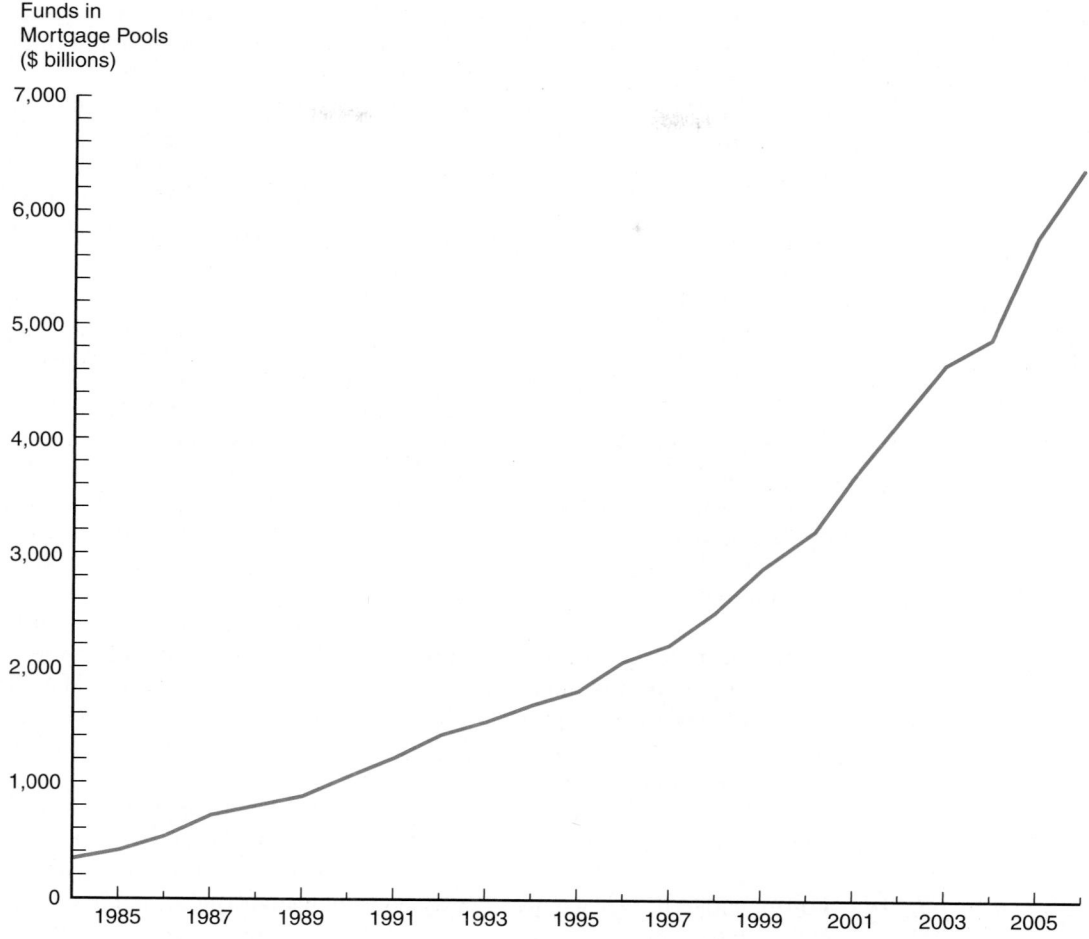

Funds in
Mortgage Pools
($ billions)

Figure 12.3 Value of Mortgage Principal Held in Mortgage Pools, 1984–2006

Source: Federal Reserve Bulletin, various issues, Table 1.54, Line 55.

rates, the securities will pay off early. The possibility that mortgages will prepay and force investors to seek alternative investments, usually with lower returns, is called *prepayment risk.*

As is evident in Figure 12.3, the dollar volume of outstanding mortgage pools has increased steadily since 1984. The reason that mortgage pools have become so popular is that they permit the creation of new securities (like mortgage pass-throughs) that make investing in mortgage loans much more efficient. For example, an institutional investor can invest in one large mortgage pass-through secured by a mortgage pool rather than investing in many small and dissimilar mortgage contracts.

Types of Pass-Through Securities

There are several types of mortgage pass-through securities: GNMA pass-throughs, FHLMC pass-throughs, and private pass-throughs.

Government National Mortgage Association (GNMA) Pass-Throughs Ginnie Mae began guaranteeing pass-through securities in 1968. Since then, the popularity of these instruments has increased dramatically.

A variety of financial intermediaries, including commercial banks and mortgage companies, originate Ginnie Mae mortgages. Ginnie Mae aggregates these mortgages into a pool and issues pass-through securities that are collateralized by the interest and principal payments from the mortgages. Ginnie Mae also guarantees the pass-through securities against default. The usual minimum denomination for pass-throughs is $25,000. The minimum pool size is $1 million. One pool may back up many pass-through securities.

Federal Home Loan Mortgage Corporation (FHLMC) Pass-Throughs Freddie Mac was created to assist savings and loan associations, which are not eligible to originate Ginnie Mae–guaranteed loans. Freddie Mac purchases mortgages for its own account and also issues pass-through securities similar to those issued by Ginnie Mae. Pass-through securities issued by Freddie Mac are called *participation certificates (PCs)*. Freddie Mac pools are distinct from Ginnie Mae pools in that they contain conventional (nonguaranteed) mortgages, are not federally insured, contain mortgages with different rates, are larger (ranging up to several hundred million dollars), and have a minimum denomination of $100,000.

A relatively recent innovation in the FHLMC pass-through market has been the **collateralized mortgage obligation (CMO).** CMOs are securities classified by when prepayment is likely to occur and are issued by Freddie Mac. These differ from traditional mortgage-backed securities in that they are offered in different maturity groups. These securities help reduce prepayment risk, which is a problem with other types of pass-through securities.

CMOs backed by a particular mortgage pool are divided into classes. When principal is repaid, the investors in the first class are paid first, then those in the second class, and so on. Investors choose a class that matches their maturity requirements. For example, if they will need cash from their investment in a few years, they purchase class 1 or 2 CMOs. If they want the investment to be long-term, they can purchase CMOs from the last class.

Even when an investor purchases a CMO, there are no guarantees about how long the investment will last. If interest rates fall significantly, many borrowers will pay off their mortages early by refinancing at lower rates.

Real estate mortgage investment conduits (REMICs) were authorized by the 1986 Tax Reform Act to allow originators to pass through all interest payments tax-free. Only their legal and tax consequences distinguish REMICs from CMOs.

Private Pass-Throughs (PIPs) In addition to the agency pass-throughs, intermediaries in the private sector have offered privately issued pass-through securities. The first of these PIPs was offered by BankAmerica in 1977.

One mortgage market opportunity available to private institutions is for mortgages larger than the maximum size set by the government. These so-called *jumbo mortgages* are often bundled into pools to back private pass-throughs.

Mortgage-Backed Securities Clearing Corporation

The Mortgage-Backed Securities Clearing Corporation (MBSCC) was formed by the Midwest Stock Exchange in 1979 to automate the trading of mortgage-backed securities. Both parties to an exchange of mortgage-backed securities submit information

go online

The homepage of the MBSCC, **www.ficc.com**, gives information on this provider of automated post-trade comparison, netting, risk management, and pool-notification services to the mortgage-backed securities market.

to the MBSCC. The computer system checks that the information is in agreement and then confirms the trade.

Mortgage-Backed Mutual Funds Mortgage-backed mutual funds offer individual investors an opportunity to invest in mortgage-backed securities despite their large denomination. Since mortgage-backed securities offer a higher return than Treasury bonds but are considered only slightly riskier, investors find them attractive. A typical mortgage-backed mutual fund will hold a combination of pass-throughs, CMOs, and Treasury bonds. Investors in these funds must be aware that when interest rates fall, many of the loans will pay off and be replaced with lower-interest mortgages. As a result, the fund's return will fall.

The Impact of Securitized Mortgages on the Mortgage Market

Mortgage-backed securities (also called **securitized mortgages**) have been a very important development in the financial markets in recent years. These new debt instruments compete for funds with government bonds, corporate bonds, and stocks. Securitized mortgages are low-risk securities that have higher yields than comparable government bonds and attract funds from around the world.

One benefit of the securitized mortgage is that it reduces the problems caused by regional lending institutions' sensitivity to local economic fluctuations. Because the loans are sold nationally and internationally, regional variations are no longer as great a source of risk to lenders.

A second benefit of the securitized mortgage is that borrowers now have access to a national capital market. In the early twentieth century, borrowers could choose among mortgages offered by only a few local lenders. The new securitized mortgages function much more like the rest of the capital markets. As a result, rates in the mortgage market follow other capital market rates much more closely.

Another benefit of securitized mortgages is that an investor can enjoy the low-risk and long-term nature of investing in mortgages without having to service the loan.

A side effect of the development of securitized mortgages has been that mortgage rates are now more open to national and international influences. As a result, mortgage rates are more volatile than they were in the past.

Subprime Mortgages

Subprime loans are those made to borrowers who do not qualify for loans at the usual market rate of interest because of a poor credit rating or because the loan is larger than justified by their income. There can be subprime car loans or credit cards, but subprime mortgages have been highly publicized recently due to the high default rates realized when real estate values began dropping in 2006.

Before the securitized market made it easy to bundle and sell mortgages, if you did not meet the qualifications for one of the major mortgage agencies, you were unlikely to be able to buy a house. These qualifications were strictly enforced and each element was verified to assure compliance. Once it became possible to sell bundles of loans to other investors, different lending rules emerged. These new rules gave rise to a new class of mortgage loans known as subprime mortgages.

According to the Mortgage Bankers Association, in 2000 about 70% of all loans were conventional prime, 20% were FHA, 8% were VA, and only 2% were subprime.

In 2006, 70% were still conventional prime, but now fully 17% were subprime, with the balance being FHA and VA. The FICO score is computed for virtually every borrower. This score is computed by the different credit rating agencies as an index of credit risk. Though each agency uses a slightly different algorithm, all include payment history, level of current debt, length of credit history, types of credit held, and the number of new credit inquiries made as criteria for rating credit worthiness. The average subprime FICO score was 624 versus 742 for prime mortgage loans.

Several innovative lending practices have led to this increase in lending to less credit worthy borrowers. First, 2/28 ARMs (sometimes called "teaser" loans) have become popular. These loans freeze the interest rate for 2 years, and then it increases, often substantially, after that. Piggyback loans are another example that consists of a combination of two loans made at the same time. The first and second mortgages eliminate the need for any down payment. These loans result in high payments for the borrower as well as little incentive not to walk away when debts begin piling up. Stretch loans allow the borrower to commit more than 50% of their gross income to make the monthly payment. Finally, "stated income" loans permit the borrower to state their income, without any verification, as the only prerequisite for the mortgage. Other variations on the graduated payment mortgage, as discussed in the last section, encourage borrowers to commit to larger loans than they can realistically handle.

When real estate values were rapidly increasing, borrowers could easily sell their property if they found themselves unable to make the payments. Once the real estate market cooled in 2006 and 2007, it became much more difficult to sell property and many borrowers were forced into default and bankruptcy. This brought the subprime market to the attention of regulators and congress.

Subprime lending has become controversial. On one side are those who point to predatory advertising and bait and switch tactics that coerce naïve home borrowers into obtaining loans they cannot possibly repay. On the other side are those who point to the increase in home ownership attributable to these loans as a positive outcome. It will take a number of years before the extent of the subprime problem is fully understood.

SUMMARY

1. Mortgages are long-term loans secured by real estate. Both individuals and businesses obtain mortgage loans to finance real estate purchases.

2. Mortgage interest rates are relatively low due to competition among various institutions that want to make mortgage loans. In addition to keeping interest rates low, the competition has resulted in a variety of terms and options for mortgage loans. For example, borrowers may choose to obtain a 30-year fixed-rate loan or an adjustable-rate loan that has its interest rate tied to the Treasury bill rate.

3. Several features of mortgage loans are designed to reduce the likelihood that the borrower will default. For example, a down payment is usually required so that the borrower will suffer a loss if the lender repossesses the property. Most lenders also require that the borrower purchase private mortgage insurance unless the loan-to-value ratio drops below 80%.

4. A variety of mortgages are available to meet the needs of most borrowers. The graduated-payment mortgage has low initial payments that increase over time. The growing-equity mortgage has increasing payments that cause the loan to be paid off in a shorter period than a level-payment loan. Shared-appreciation loans were used when interest rates and inflation were high. The lender shared in the increase in the real estate's value in exchange for lower interest rates.

5. Securitized mortgages have been growing in popularity in recent years as institutional investors look for attractive investment opportunities. Securitized mortgages are securities collateralized by a pool of mortgages. The payments on the pool are passed through to the investors. Ginnie Mae, Freddie Mac, and private banks issue pass-through securities.

KEY TERMS

amortized, *p. 282*
balloon loan, *p. 282*
collateralized mortgage obligation (CMO), *p. 298*
conventional mortgages, *p. 290*
discount points, *p. 283*
down payment, *p. 286*
FICO scores, *p. 287*
insured mortgages, *p. 289*

lien, *p. 285*
mortgage, *p. 282*
mortgage-backed security, *p. 296*
mortgage pass-through, *p. 296*
private mortgage insurance (PMI), *p. 286*
reserve accounts, *p. 294*
securitized mortgages, *p. 299*
subprime loans, *p. 299*

QUESTIONS

1. What distinguishes the mortgage markets from other capital markets?

2. Most mortgage loans once had balloon payments; now most current mortgage loans fully amortize. What is the difference between a balloon loan and an amortizing loan?

3. What features contribute to keeping long-term mortgage interest rates low?

4. What are discount points, and why do some mortgage borrowers choose to pay them?

5. What is a lien, and when is it used in mortgage lending?

6. What is the purpose of requiring that a borrower make a down payment before receiving a loan?

7. What kind of insurance do lenders usually require of borrowers who have less than an 80% loan-to-value ratio?

8. Lenders tend not to be as flexible about the qualifications required of mortgage customers as they can be for other types of bank loans. Why is this so?

9. Distinguish between conventional mortgage loans and insured mortgage loans.

10. Interpret what is meant when a lender quotes the terms on a loan as "floating with the T-bill plus 2 with caps of 2 and 6."

11. The monthly payments on both graduated-payment loans and growing-equity loans increase over time. Despite this similarity, the two types of loans have different purposes. What is the motivation behind each type of loan?

12. Many banks offer lines of credit that are secured by a second mortgage (or lien) on real property. These loans have been very popular among bank customers. Why are homeowners so willing to pledge their homes as security for these lines of credit?

13. The reverse annuity mortgage (RAM) allows retired people to live off the equity they have in their homes without having to sell the home. Explain how a RAM works.

14. What is a securitized mortgage?

15. Describe how a mortgage pass-through works.

QUANTITATIVE PROBLEMS

1. Compute the required monthly payment on an $80,000 30-year fixed-rate mortgage with a nominal interest rate of 5.80%. How much of the payment goes toward principal and interest during the first year?

2. Compute the face value of a 30-year fixed-rate mortgage with a monthly payment of $1,100, assuming a nominal interest rate of 9%. If the mortgage requires 5% down, what is the maximum house price?

3. Consider a 30-year fixed-rate mortgage for $100,000 at a nominal rate of 9%. If the borrower wants to pay off the remaining balance on the mortgage after making the 12th payment, what is the remaining balance on the mortgage?

4. Consider a 30-year fixed-rate mortgage for $100,000 at a nominal rate of 9%. If the borrower pays an additional $100 with each payment, how fast will the mortgage be paid off?

5. Consider a 30-year fixed-rate mortgage for $100,000 at a nominal rate of 9%. An S&L issues this mortgage on April 1 and retains the mortgage in its portfolio. However, by April 2 mortgage rates have increased to a 9.5% nominal rate. By how much has the value of the mortgage fallen?

6. Consider a 30-year fixed-rate mortgage of $100,000 at a nominal rate of 9%. What is the duration of the loan? If interest rates increase to 9.5% immediately after the mortgage is made, how much is the loan worth to the lender?

7. Consider a 5-year balloon loan for $100,000. The bank requires a monthly payment equal to that of a 30-year fixed-rate loan with a nominal annual rate of 5.5%. How much will the borrower owe when the balloon payment is due?

8. A 30-year variable-rate mortgage offers a first-year teaser rate of 2%. After that, the rate starts at 4.5%, adjusted based on actual interest rates. The maximum rate over the life of the loan is 10.5%, and the rate can increase by no more than 200 basis points a year. If the mortgage is for $250,000, what is the monthly payment during the first year? Second year? What is the maximum payment during the fourth year? What is the maximum payment ever?

9. Consider a 30-year fixed-rate mortgage for $500,000 at a nominal rate of 6%. What is the difference in required payments between a monthly payment and a bimonthly payment (payments made twice a month)?

10. Consider the following options available to a mortgage borrower:

	Loan Amount	Interest Rate (%)	Type of Mortgage	Discount Points
Option 1	$100,000	6.75	30-yr fixed	none
Option 2	$150,000	6.25	30-yr fixed	1
Option 3	$125,000	6.0	30-yr fixed	2

What is the effective annual rate for each option?

11. Two mortgage options are available: a 15-year fixed-rate loan at 6% with no discount points, and a 15-year fixed-rate loan at 5.75% with 1 discount point. Assuming you will not pay off the loan early, which alternative is best for you? Assume a $100,000 mortgage.

12. Two mortgage options are available: a 30-year fixed-rate loan at 6% with no discount points, and a 30-year fixed-rate loan at 5.75% with 1 discount point. How long do you have to stay in the house for the mortgage with points to be a better option? Assume a $100,000 mortgage.

13. Two mortgage options are available: a 30-year fixed-rate loan at 6% with no discount points, and a 30-year fixed-rate loan at 5.75% with points. If you are planning on living in the house for 12 years, what is the most you are willing to pay in points for the 5.75% mortgage? Assume a $100,000 mortgage.

14. A mortgage on a house worth $350,000 requires what down payment to avoid PMI insurance?

15. Consider a shared-appreciation mortgage (SAM) on a $250,000 mortgage with yearly payments. Current market mortgage rates are high, running at 13%, 10% of which is annual inflation. Under the terms of the SAM, a 15-year mortgage is offered at 5%. After 15 years, the house must be sold, and the bank retains $400,000 of the sale price. If inflation remains at 10%, what are the cash flows to the bank? To the owner?

16. Consider a 30-year graduated-payment mortgage on a $250,000 mortgage with yearly payments. The stated interest rate on the mortgage is 6%, but the first annual payment is calculated assuming a 3% rate for the life of the loan. Thereafter, the annual payment will grow by 3.151222%. Develop an amortization table for this loan, assuming the initial payment is based on 30 years and the loan pays off in 15.

17. Consider a growing equity mortgage on a $250,000 mortgage with yearly payments. The stated interest rate on the mortgage is 6%, but this only applies to the first annual payment. Thereafter, the annual payment will grow by 5.5797%. Develop an amortization table for this loan, assuming the initial payment is based on 30 years and the loan pays off in 15 years.

18. Rusty Nail owns his house free and clear, and it's worth $400,000. To finance his retirement, he acquires a reverse annuity mortgage (RAM) from his bank. The RAM provides a fixed monthly payment over 15 years on 70% of the value of his home at 5%. The payments are made at the beginning of the month. How much does Rusty get each month?

19. You are working with a pool of 1,000 mortgages. Each mortgage is for $100,000 and has a stated annual interest rate (nominal) of 6.00%. The mortgages are all 30-year fixed rate and fully amortizing. Mortgage servicing fees are currently 0.25% annually. Complete the following table.

Month	(1) Beginning Balance	(2) Required Payment	(3) Interest	(4) Principal	(5) Expected Prepayment	(6) Servicing Fees	(7) Ending Balance
1	100,000,000		500,000	99,551	16,665		
2					33,322		99,750,430

WEB EXERCISES

The Mortgage Markets

1. You may be looking into acquiring a home in the near future. One common question you may have is how large a mortgage loan you can afford. Go to **http://interest.com** and click on the "Mortgage" tab and then on "calculators." Choose the "mortgage required income calculator." Input your expected future salary data. How large a mortgage can you afford according to the calculator? Increase your debt to see the impact on the amount of mortgage loan you will qualify for.

2. One of the more difficult decisions faced by homeowners is whether it pays to refinance a mortgage loan when rates have dropped. Go to **http:// interest .com** and click on the calculator labeled "Refinance interest savings calculator." Compute how long it will take to recoup the interest of refinancing your mortgage loan. Assume you obtained a 30-year $130,000 loan four years ago at 7%. Now rates have dropped and your income is higher. Determine how much you will save if you get a new loan for 15 years at 6.25%.

CHAPTER 13

The Foreign Exchange Market

Preview

In the mid-1980s, American businesses became less competitive with their foreign counterparts; subsequently, in the 1990s and 2000s, their competitiveness increased. Did this swing in competitiveness occur primarily because American management fell down on the job in the 1980s and then got its act together afterwards? Not really. American business became less competitive in the 1980s because American dollars became worth more in terms of foreign currencies, making American goods more expensive relative to foreign goods. By the 1990s and 2000s, the value of the U.S. dollar had fallen appreciably from its highs in the mid-1980s, making American goods cheaper and American businesses more competitive.

The price of one currency in terms of another is called the **exchange rate.** As you can see in Figure 13.1, exchange rates are highly volatile. The exchange rate affects the economy and our daily lives, because when the U.S. dollar becomes more valuable relative to foreign currencies, foreign goods become cheaper for Americans and American goods become more expensive for foreigners. When the U.S. dollar falls in value, foreign goods become more expensive for Americans and American goods become cheaper for foreigners.

We begin our study of international finance by examining the **foreign exchange market,** the financial market where exchange rates are determined.

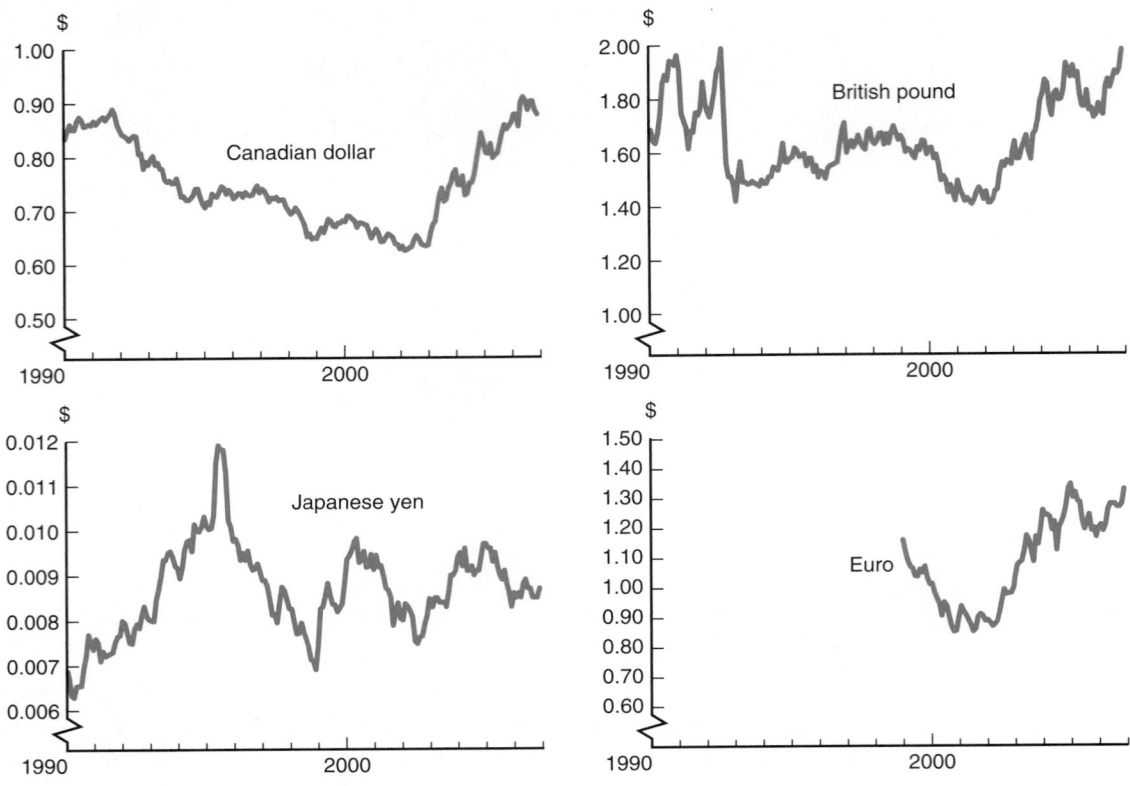

Figure 13.1 Exchange Rates, 1990–2007

Dollar prices of selected currencies. Note that a rise in these plots indicates a strengthening of the currency (weakening of the dollar).

Source: Federal Reserve: www.federalreserve.gov/releases/h10/hist.

Foreign Exchange Market

go online

www.newyorkfed.org/
markets/foreignex.html
Get detailed information
about the foreign exchange
market in the United States.

Most countries of the world have their own currencies: The United States has its dollar; the European Monetary Union, its euro; Brazil, its real; and China, its yuan. Trade between countries involves the mutual exchange of different currencies (or, more usually, bank deposits denominated in different currencies). When an American firm buys foreign goods, services, or financial assets, for example, U.S. dollars (typically, bank deposits denominated in U.S. dollars) must be exchanged for foreign currency (bank deposits denominated in the foreign currency).

The trading of currencies and bank deposits denominated in particular currencies takes place in the foreign exchange market. Transactions conducted in the foreign exchange market determine the rates at which currencies are exchanged, which in turn determine the cost of purchasing foreign goods and financial assets.

What Are Foreign Exchange Rates?

There are two kinds of exchange rate transactions. The predominant ones, called **spot transactions,** involve the immediate (two-day) exchange of bank deposits. **Forward transactions** involve the exchange of bank deposits at some specified future date. The **spot exchange rate** is the exchange rate for the spot transaction, and the **forward exchange rate** is the exchange rate for the forward transaction.

go online

http://quotes.ino.com/chart/

Go to this Web site and click on "Foreign Exchange" to get market rates and time charts for the exchange rate of the U.S. dollar to major world currencies.

When a currency increases in value, it experiences **appreciation;** when it falls in value and is worth fewer U.S. dollars, it undergoes **depreciation.** At the beginning of 1999, for example, the euro was valued at $1.18 and, as indicated in the Following the Financial News box, on May 22, 2007, it was valued at $1.35. The euro appreciated by 14%: $(1.35 - 1.18)/1.18 = 0.144 = 14\%$. Conversely, we could say that the U.S. dollar, which went from a value of 0.85 $(= 1/1.18)$ euros to a value of 0.74 $(= 1/1.35)$ euros by May 2007, depreciated by 13%: $(0.74 - 0.85)/0.85 = -0.129 = -13\%$.

Why Are Exchange Rates Important?

Exchange rates are important because they affect the relative price of domestic and foreign goods. The dollar price of French goods to an American is determined by the interaction of two factors: the price of French goods in euros and the euro/dollar exchange rate.

Suppose that Wanda the Winetaster, an American, decides to buy a bottle of 1961 (a very good year) Château Lafite Rothschild to complete her wine cellar. If the price of the wine in France is 1,000 euros and the exchange rate is $1.19 to the euro, the wine will cost Wanda $1,190 ($= 1,000$ euros $\times$ $1.19/euro). Now suppose that Wanda delays her purchase by two months, at which time the euro has appreciated to $1.40 per euro. If the domestic price of the bottle of Lafite Rothschild remains 1,000 euros, its dollar cost will have risen from $1,190 to $1,400.

The same currency appreciation, however, makes the price of foreign goods in that country less expensive. At an exchange rate of $1.19 per euro, a Dell computer priced at $2,000 costs Pierre the Programmer 1,681 euros; if the exchange rate increases to $1.40 per euro, the computer will cost only 1,429 euros.

A depreciation of the euro lowers the cost of French goods in America but raises the cost of American goods in France. If the euro drops in value to $1.00, Wanda's bottle of Lafite Rothschild will cost her only $1,000 instead of $1,190, and the Dell computer will cost Pierre 2,000 euros rather than 1,681.

Such reasoning leads to the following conclusion: ***When a country's currency appreciates (rises in value relative to other currencies), the country's goods abroad become more expensive and foreign goods in that country become cheaper (holding domestic prices constant in the two countries). Conversely, when a country's currency depreciates, its goods abroad become cheaper and foreign goods in that country become more expensive.***

Depreciation of a currency makes it easier for domestic manufacturers to sell their goods abroad and makes foreign goods less competitive in domestic markets. From 2002 to 2007, the depreciating dollar helped U.S. industries sell more goods, but it hurt American consumers because foreign goods were more expensive. The prices of French wine and cheese and the cost of vacationing abroad all rose as a result of the weak dollar.

following the financial news

Foreign Exchange Rates

Currencies

May 22, 2007

U.S.-dollar foreign-exchange rates in late New York trading

Country/currency	Tues in US$	Tues per US$	US$ vs, YTD chg (%)
Americas			
Argentina peso*	.3249	3.0779	0.6
Brazil real	.5133	1.9482	-8.8
Canada dollar	.9207	1.0861	-6.9
1-mos forward	.9216	1.0851	-6.9
3-mos forward	.9231	1.0833	-6.8
6-mos forward	.9250	1.0811	-6.8
Chile peso	.001902	525.76	-1.2
Colombia peso	.0005114	1955.42	-12.7
Ecuador US dollar	1	1	unch
Mexico peso*	.0927	10.7898	-0.1
Peru new sol	.3160	3.165	-1.0
Uruguay peso†	.04190	23.87	-2.1
Venezuela bolivar	.000466	2145.92	unch
Asia-Pacific			
Australian dollar	.8193	1.2206	-3.6
China yuan	.1306	7.6545	-2.0
Hong Kong dollar	.1278	7.8240	0.6
India rupee	.02485	40.241	-8.8
Indonesia rupiah	.0001152	8681	-3.5
Japan yen	.008225	121.58	2.2
1-mos forward	.008260	121.07	2.2
3-mos forward	.008324	120.13	2.2
6-mos forward	.008421	118.75	2.1
Malaysia ringgit§	.2952	3.3875	-4.0
New Zealand dollar	.7263	1.3768	-3.0
Pakistan rupee	.01647	60.717	-0.1
Philippines peso	.0217	46.062	-6.1
Singapore dollar	.6533	1.5307	-0.2
South Korea won	.0010749	930.32	unch
Taiwan dollar	.02994	33.400	2.5
Thailand baht	.03065	32.626	-8.0

Country/currency	Tues in US$	Tues per US$	US$ vs, YTD chg (%)
Europe			
Czech Rep. koruna**	.04767	20.978	0.7
Denmark krone	.1805	5.5402	-1.9
Euro area euro	1.3450	.7435	-1.8
Hungary forint	.005423	184.40	-3.2
Malta lira	3.1331	.3192	-1.8
Norway krone	.1654	6.0459	-3.0
Poland zloty	.3554	2.8137	-3.1
Russia ruble‡	.03863	25.887	-1.7
Slovak Rep koruna	.03985	25.094	-3.9
Sweden krona	.1463	6.8353	-0.1
Switzerland franc	.8132	1.2297	0.9
1-mos forward	.8154	1.2264	0.9
3-mos forward	.8192	1.2207	1.0
6-mos forward	.8248	1.2124	1.0
Turkey lira**	.7524	1.3290	-6.1
UK pound	1.9750	.5063	-0.9
1-mos forward	1.9746	.5064	-0.8
3-mos forward	1.9733	.5068	-0.7
6-mos forward	1.9706	.5075	-0.6
Middle East/Africa			
Bahrain dinar	2.6525	.3770	unch
Egypt pound*	.1757	5.6925	-0.3
Israel shekel	.2520	3.9683	-5.9
Jordan dinar	1.4112	.7086	-0.1
Kuwait dinar	3.4715	.2881	-0.3
Lebanon pound	.0006612	1512.40	unch
Saudi Arabia riyal	.2666	3.7509	unch
South Africa rand	.1419	7.0472	0.8
UAE dirham	.2723	3.6724	unch
SDR††	1.5129	.6610	-0.6

*Floating rate †Financial §Government rate ‡Russian Central Bank rate **Rebased as of Jan 1, 2005 ††Special Drawing Rights (SDR); from the International Monetary Fund; based on exchange rates for U.S., British and Japanese currencies.
Note: Based on trading among banks of $1 million and more, as quoted at 4 p.m. ET by Reuters.

Foreign exchange rates are published daily and appear in the "Currency Trading" column of the *Wall Street Journal*. The entries from one such column, shown here, are explained in the text.

The first entry for the euro lists the exchange rate for the spot transaction (the spot exchange rate) on May 22, 2007, and is quoted in two ways: $1.3450 per euro and 0.7435 euro per dollar. Americans generally regard the exchange rate with the euro as $1.3450 per euro, while Europeans think of it as 0.7435 euro per dollar. The three entries immediately below the spot exchange rates for some currencies give the rates for forward transactions (the forward exchange rates) that will take place one month, three months, and six months in the future.

Source: *Wall Street Journal*, May 22, 2007, p. C12.

How Is Foreign Exchange Traded?

You cannot go to a centralized location to watch exchange rates being determined; currencies are not traded on exchanges such as the New York Stock Exchange. Instead, the foreign exchange market is organized as an over-the-counter market in which several hundred dealers (mostly banks) stand ready to buy and sell deposits denominated in foreign currencies. Because these dealers are in constant telephone and computer contact, the market is very competitive; in effect, it functions no differently from a centralized market.

An important point to note is that while banks, companies, and governments talk about buying and selling currencies in foreign exchange markets, they do not take a fistful of dollar bills and sell them for British pound notes. Rather, most trades involve the buying and selling of bank deposits denominated in different currencies. So when we say that a bank is buying dollars in the foreign exchange market, what we actually mean is that the bank is buying *deposits denominated in dollars*. The volume in this market is colossal, exceeding $3 trillion per day.

Trades in the foreign exchange market consist of transactions in excess of $1 million. The market that determines the exchange rates in the Following the Financial News box is not where one would buy foreign currency for a trip abroad. Instead, we buy foreign currency in the retail market from dealers such as American Express or from banks. Because retail prices are higher than wholesale, when we buy foreign exchange, we obtain fewer units of foreign currency per dollar than exchange rates in the box indicate.

Exchange Rates in the Long Run

Like the price of any good or asset in a free market, exchange rates are determined by the interaction of supply and demand. To simplify our analysis of exchange rates in a free market, we divide it into two parts. First, we examine how exchange rates are determined in the long run; then we use our knowledge of the long-run determinants of the exchange rate to help us understand how they are determined in the short run.

Law of One Price

The starting point for understanding how exchange rates are determined is a simple idea called the **law of one price:** If two countries produce an identical good, and transportation costs and trade barriers are very low, the price of the good should be the same throughout the world no matter which country produces it. Suppose that American steel costs $100 per ton and identical Japanese steel costs 10,000 yen per ton. For the law of one price to hold, the exchange rate between the yen and the dollar must be 100 yen per dollar ($0.01 per yen) so that one ton of American steel sells for 10,000 yen in Japan (the price of Japanese steel) and one ton of Japanese steel sells for $100 in the United States (the price of U.S. steel). If the exchange rate were 200 yen to the dollar, Japanese steel would sell for $50 per ton in the United States or half the price of American steel, and American steel would sell for 20,000 yen per ton in Japan, twice the price of Japanese steel. Because American steel would be more expensive than Japanese steel in both countries and is identical to Japanese steel, the demand for American steel would go to zero. Given a fixed dollar price for American steel, the resulting excess supply of American steel will be eliminated only if the exchange rate falls to 100 yen per dollar, making the price of American steel and Japanese steel the same in both countries.

example 13.1 **Law of One Price**

Recently, the yen price of Japanese steel has increased by 10% (to 11,000 yen) relative to the dollar price of American steel (unchanged at $100). By what amount must the dollar increase or decrease in value for the law of one price to hold true?

Solution

For the law of one price to hold, the exchange rate must rise to 110 yen per dollar, which is a 10% appreciation of the dollar.

The exchange rate rises to 110 yen so that the price of Japanese steel in dollars remains unchanged at $100 (= 11,000 yen/110 yen per dollar). In other words, the 10% depreciation of the yen (10% appreciation of the dollar) just offsets the 10% increase in the yen price of the Japanese steel.

Theory of Purchasing Power Parity

go online

www.oecd.org/department/
0,2688,en_2649_34357
_1_1_1_1_1_1,00.html
The purchasing power parities home page includes the PPP program overview, statistics, research, publications, and OECD meetings on PPP.

One of the most prominent theories of how exchange rates are determined is the **theory of purchasing power parity (PPP).** It states that exchange rates between any two currencies will adjust to reflect changes in the price levels of the two countries. The theory of PPP is simply an application of the law of one price to national price levels.

As Example 1 illustrates, if the law of one price holds, a 10% rise in the yen price of Japanese steel results in a 10% appreciation of the dollar. Applying the law of one price to the price levels in the two countries produces the theory of purchasing power parity, which maintains that if the Japanese price level rises 10% relative to the U.S. price level, the dollar will appreciate by 10%. As our U.S./Japanese example illustrates, *the theory of PPP suggests that if one country's price level rises relative to another's, its currency should depreciate (the other country's currency should appreciate).*

As you can see in Figure 13.2, this prediction of the theory of PPP is borne out in the long run. From 1973 to 2007, the British price level rose 85% relative to the U.S. price level, and as the theory of PPP predicts, the dollar appreciated against sterling, though by 28%, an amount smaller than the 85% increase predicted by PPP.

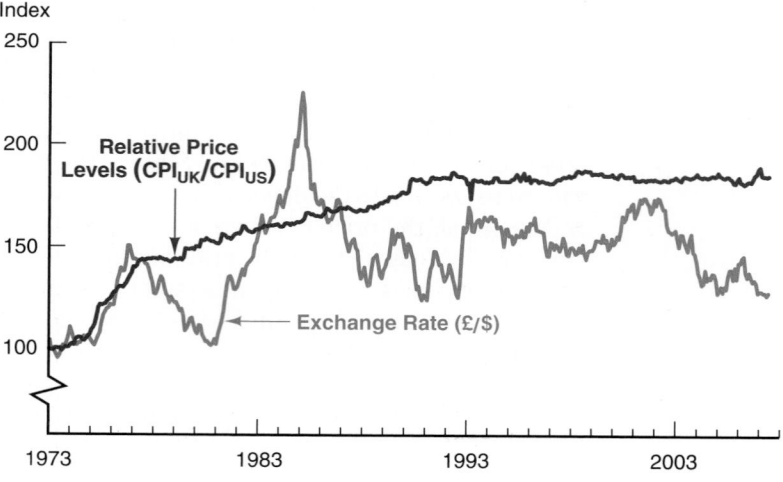

Figure 13.2 Purchasing Power Parity, United States/United Kingdom, 1973–2007 (Index: March 1973 = 100.)

Source: www.statistics.gov.uk/statbase/tsdataset2.asp.

Yet, as the same figure indicates, PPP theory often has little predictive power in the short run. From early 1985 to the end of 1987, for example, the British price level rose relative to that of the United States. Instead of appreciating, as PPP theory predicts, the U.S. dollar actually depreciated by 40% against the pound. So even though PPP theory provides some guidance to the long-run movement of exchange rates, it is not perfect and in the short run is a particularly poor predictor. What explains PPP theory's failure to predict well?

Why the Theory of Purchasing Power Parity Cannot Fully Explain Exchange Rates

The PPP conclusion that exchange rates are determined solely by changes in relative price levels rests on the assumption that all goods are identical in both countries and that transportation costs and trade barriers are very low. When this assumption is true, the law of one price states that the relative prices of all these goods (that is, the relative price level between the two countries) will determine the exchange rate. The assumption that goods are identical may not be too unreasonable for American and Japanese steel, but is it a reasonable assumption for American and Japanese cars? Is a Toyota the equivalent of a Chevrolet?

Because Toyotas and Chevys are obviously not identical, their prices do not have to be equal. Toyotas can be more expensive relative to Chevys and both Americans and Japanese will still purchase Toyotas. Because the law of one price does not hold for all goods, a rise in the price of Toyotas relative to Chevys will not necessarily mean that the yen must depreciate by the amount of the relative price increase of Toyotas over Chevys.

PPP theory furthermore does not take into account that many goods and services (whose prices are included in a measure of a country's price level) are not traded across borders. Housing, land, and services such as restaurant meals, haircuts, and golf lessons are not traded goods. So even though the prices of these items might rise and lead to a higher price level relative to another country's, there would be little direct effect on the exchange rate.

Factors That Affect Exchange Rates in the Long Run

In the long run, four major factors affect the exchange rate: relative price levels, tariffs and quotas, preferences for domestic versus foreign goods, and productivity. We examine how each of these factors affects the exchange rate while holding the others constant.

The basic reasoning proceeds along the following lines: Anything that increases the demand for domestically produced goods that are traded relative to foreign traded goods tends to appreciate the domestic currency because domestic goods will continue to sell well even when the value of the domestic currency is higher. Similarly, anything that increases the demand for foreign goods relative to domestic goods tends to depreciate the domestic currency because domestic goods will continue to sell well only if the value of the domestic currency is lower.

Relative Price Levels In line with PPP theory, when prices of American goods rise (holding prices of foreign goods constant), the demand for American goods falls and the dollar tends to depreciate so that American goods can still sell well. By contrast, if prices of Japanese goods rise so that the relative prices of American goods fall, the demand for American goods increases, and the dollar tends to appreciate because American goods will continue to sell well even with a higher value of the domestic currency. *In the long run, a rise in a country's price level (relative to the foreign price level) causes its currency to depreciate, and a fall in the country's relative price level causes its currency to appreciate.*

Trade Barriers Barriers to free trade such as **tariffs** (taxes on imported goods) and **quotas** (restrictions on the quantity of foreign goods that can be imported) can affect the exchange rate. Suppose that the United States increases its tariff or puts a lower quota on Japanese steel. These increases in trade barriers increase the demand for American steel, and the dollar tends to appreciate because American steel will still sell well even with a higher value of the dollar. *Increasing trade barriers cause a country's currency to appreciate in the long run.*

Preferences for Domestic Versus Foreign Goods If the Japanese develop an appetite for American goods—say, for Florida oranges and American movies—the increased demand for American goods (exports) tends to appreciate the dollar, because the American goods will continue to sell well even at a higher value for the dollar. Likewise, if Americans decide that they prefer Japanese cars to American cars, the increased demand for Japanese goods (imports) tends to depreciate the dollar. *Increased demand for a country's exports causes its currency to appreciate in the long run; conversely, increased demand for imports causes the domestic currency to depreciate.*

Productivity When productivity in a country rises, it tends to rise in domestic sectors that produce traded goods rather than nontraded goods. Higher productivity, therefore, is associated with a decline in the price of domestically produced traded goods relative to foreign traded goods. As a result, the demand for domestic goods rises, and the domestic currency tends to appreciate. If, however, a country's productivity lags behind that of other countries, its traded goods become relatively more expensive, and the currency tends to depreciate. *In the long run, as a country becomes more productive relative to other countries, its currency appreciates.*[1]

---

[1]A country might be so small that a change in productivity or the preferences for domestic or foreign goods would have no effect on prices of these goods relative to foreign goods. In this case, changes in productivity or changes in preferences for domestic or foreign goods affect the country's income but will not necessarily affect the value of the currency. In our analysis, we are assuming that these factors can affect relative prices and consequently the exchange rate.

Table 13.1 Summary Factors That Affect Exchange Rates in the Long Run

Factor	Change in Factor	Response of the Exchange Rate, E^*
Domestic price level†	↑	↓
Trade barriers†	↑	↑
Import demand	↑	↓
Export demand	↑	↑
Productivity†	↑	↑

*Units of foreign currency per dollar: ↑ indicates domestic currency appreciation; ↓, depreciation.
†Relative to other countries.
Note: Only increases (↑) in the factors are shown; the effects of decreases in the variables on the exchange rate are the opposite of those indicated in the "Response" column.

Our long-run theory of exchange rate behavior is summarized in Table 13.1. We use the convention that the exchange rate E is quoted so that an appreciation of the currency corresponds to a rise in the exchange rate. In the case of the United States, this means that we are quoting the exchange rate as units of foreign currency per dollar (say, yen per dollar).[2]

Exchange Rates in the Short Run

go online
www.federalreserve.gov/
releases/
The Federal Reserve reports current and historical exchange rates for many countries.

We have developed a theory of the long-run behavior of exchange rates. However, because factors driving long-run changes in exchange rates move slowly over time, if we are to understand why exchange rates exhibit such large changes (sometimes several percent) from day to day, we must develop a theory of how current exchange rates (spot exchange rates) are determined in the short run.

The key to understanding the short-run behavior of exchange rates is to recognize that an exchange rate is the price of domestic assets (bank deposits, bonds, equities, etc., denominated in the domestic currency) in terms of foreign assets (similar assets denominated in the foreign currency). Because the exchange rate is the price of one asset in terms of another, the natural way to investigate the short-run determination of exchange rates is to use an asset market approach that relies heavily on our analysis of the determinants of asset demand developed in Chapter 4. As

[2]Exchange rates can be quoted either as units of foreign currency per domestic currency or as units of domestic currency per foreign currency. In professional writing, many economists quote exchange rates as units of domestic currency per foreign currency so that an appreciation of the domestic currency is portrayed as a fall in the exchange rate. The opposite convention is used in the text here, because it is more intuitive to think of an appreciation of the domestic currency as a rise in the exchange rate.

you will see, however, the long-run determinants of the exchange rate we have just outlined also play an important role in the short-run asset market approach.[3]

In the past, approaches to exchange rate determination emphasized the role of import and export demand. The more modern asset market approach used here emphasizes stocks of assets rather than the flows of exports and imports over short periods, because export and import transactions are small relative to the amount of domestic and foreign assets at any given time. For example, foreign exchange transactions in the United States each year are well over 25 times greater than the amount of U.S. exports and imports. Thus, over short periods, decisions to hold domestic or foreign assets play a much greater role in exchange rate determination than the demand for exports and imports does.

Comparing Expected Returns on Domestic and Foreign Assets

In this analysis, we treat the United States as the home country, so domestic assets are denominated in dollars. For simplicity, we use euros to stand for any foreign country's currency, so foreign assets are denominated in euros. The theory of asset demand suggests that the most important factor affecting the demand for domestic (dollar) assets and foreign (euro) assets is the expected return on these assets relative to each other. When Americans or foreigners expect the return on dollar assets to be high relative to the return on foreign assets, there is a higher demand for dollar assets and a correspondingly lower demand for euro assets. To understand how the demands for dollar and foreign assets change, we need to compare the expected returns on dollar assets and foreign assets.

To illustrate further, suppose that dollar assets pay an interest rate of i^D and do not have any possible capital gains, so that they have an expected return payable in dollars of i^D. Similarly, foreign assets have an interest rate of i^F and an expected return payable in the foreign currency, euros, of i^F. To compare the expected returns on dollar assets and foreign assets, investors must convert the returns into the currency unit they use.

First let us examine how François the Foreigner compares the returns on dollar assets and foreign assets denominated in his currency, the euro. When he considers the expected return on dollar assets in terms of euros, he recognizes that it does not equal i^D; instead, the expected return must be adjusted for any expected appreciation or depreciation of the dollar. If François expects the dollar to appreciate by 3%, for example, the expected return on dollar assets in terms of euros would be 3% higher than i^D because the dollar is expected to become worth 3% more in terms of euros. Thus, if the interest rate on dollar assets is 4%, with an expected appreciation of the dollar of 3%, the expected return on dollar assets in terms of euros is 7%: the 4% interest rate plus the 3% expected appreciation of the dollar. Conversely, if the dollar were expected to depreciate by 3% over the year, the expected return on dollar assets in terms of euros would be only 1%: the 4% interest rate minus the 3% expected depreciation of the dollar.

Writing the current exchange rate (the spot exchange rate) as E_t and the expected exchange rate for the next period as E_{t+1}^e, we can write the expected rate

[3]For a further description of the modern asset market approach to exchange rate determination that we use here, see Paul Krugman and Maurice Obstfeld, *International Economics*, 7th ed. (Boston: Pearson Addison Wesley, 2006).

of appreciation of the dollar as $(E_{t+1}^e - E_t)/E_t$. Our reasoning indicates that the expected return on dollar assets R^D in terms of foreign currency can be written as the sum of the interest rate on dollar assets plus the expected appreciation of the dollar:[4]

$$R^D \text{ in terms of euros} = i^D + \frac{E_{t+1}^e - E_t}{E_t}$$

However, François's expected return on foreign assets R^F in terms of euros is just i^F. Thus, in terms of euros, the relative expected return on dollar assets (that is, the difference between the expected return on dollar assets and euro assets) is calculated by subtracting i^F from the expression above to yield

$$\text{Relative } R^D = i^D - i^F + \frac{E_{t+1}^e - E_t}{E_t} \tag{1}$$

As the relative expected return on dollar assets increases, foreigners will want to hold more dollar assets and fewer foreign assets.

Next, let us look at the decision to hold dollar assets versus euro assets from Al the American's point of view. Following the same reasoning we used to evaluate the decision for François, we know that the expected return on foreign assets R^F in terms of dollars is the interest rate on foreign assets i^F plus the expected appreciation of the foreign currency, equal to minus the expected appreciation of the dollar, $-(E_{t+1}^e - E_t)/E_t$:

$$R^F \text{ in terms of dollars} = i^F - \frac{E_{t+1}^e - E_t}{E_t}$$

If the interest rate on euro assets is 5%, for example, and the dollar is expected to appreciate by 3%, then the expected return on euro assets in terms of dollars is 2%. Al earns the 5% interest rate, but he expects to lose 3% because he expects the euro to be worth 3% less in terms of dollars as a result of the dollar's appreciation.

---

[4]This expression is actually an approximation of the expected return in terms of euros, which can be more precisely calculated by thinking how a foreigner invests in dollar assets. Suppose that François decides to put one euro into dollar assets. First he buys $1/E_t$ of U.S. dollar assets (recall that E_t, the exchange rate between dollar and euro assets, is quoted in euros per dollar), and at the end of the period he is paid $(1 + i^D)(1/E_t)$ in dollars. To convert this amount into the number of euros he expects to receive at the end of the period, he multiplies this quantity by E_{t+1}^e. François's expected return on his initial investment of one euro can thus be written as $(1 + i^D)(E_{t+1}^e/E_t)$ minus his initial investment of one euro:

$$(1 + i^D)\left(\frac{E_{t+1}^e}{E_t}\right) - 1$$

This expression can be rewritten as

$$i^D\left(\frac{E_{t+1}^e}{E_t}\right) + \frac{E_{t+1}^e - E_t}{E_t}$$

which is approximately equal to the expression in the text because E_{t+1}^e/E_t is typically close to 1. To see this, consider the example in the text in which $i^D = 0.04$; $(E_{t+1}^e - E_t)/E_t = 0.03$, so $E_{t+1}^e/E_t = 1.03$. Then François's expected return on dollar assets is $0.04 \times 1.03 + 0.03 = 0.0712 = 7.12\%$, rather than the 7% reported in the text.

Al's expected return on the dollar assets R^D in terms of dollars is just i^D. Hence, in terms of dollars, the relative expected return on dollar assets is calculated by subtracting the expression just given from i^D to obtain

$$\text{Relative } R^D = i^D - \left(i^F - \frac{E^e_{t+1} - E_t}{E_t} \right) = i^D - i^F + \frac{E^e_{t+1} - E_t}{E_t}$$

This equation is the same as Equation 1 describing François's relative expected return on dollar assets (calculated in terms of euros). The key point here is that the relative expected return on dollar assets is the same whether it is calculated by François in terms of euros or by Al in terms of dollars. Thus, as the relative expected return on dollar assets increases, both foreigners and domestic residents respond in exactly the same way—both will want to hold more dollar assets and fewer foreign assets.

Interest Parity Condition

We currently live in a world in which there is **capital mobility:** Foreigners can easily purchase American assets, and Americans can easily purchase foreign assets. If there are few impediments to capital mobility and we are looking at assets that have similar risk and liquidity—say, foreign and American bank deposits—then it is reasonable to assume that the assets are perfect substitutes (that is, equally desirable). When capital is mobile and when assets are perfect substitutes, if the expected return on dollar assets is above that on foreign assets, both foreigners and Americans will want to hold only dollar assets and will be unwilling to hold foreign assets. Conversely, if the expected return on foreign assets is higher than on dollar assets, both foreigners and Americans will not want to hold any dollar assets and will want to hold only foreign assets. For existing supplies of both dollar assets and foreign assets to be held, it must therefore be true that there is no difference in their expected returns; that is, the relative expected return in Equation 1 must equal zero. This condition can be rewritten as

$$i^D = i^F - \frac{E^e_{t+1} - E_t}{E_t} \tag{2}$$

This equation, which is called the **interest parity condition,** states that the domestic interest rate equals the foreign interest rate minus the expected appreciation of the domestic currency. Equivalently, this condition can be stated in a more intuitive way: The domestic interest rate equals the foreign interest rate plus the expected appreciation of the foreign currency. If the domestic interest rate is higher than the foreign interest rate, this means that there is a positive expected appreciation of the foreign currency, which compensates for the lower foreign interest rate.

example 13.2 **Interest Parity Condition**

If interest rates in the United States and Japan are 6% and 3%, respectively, what is the expected rate of appreciation of the foreign (Japanese) currency?

Solution
The expected appreciation of the foreign currency is 3%.

$$i^D = i^F - \frac{E_{t+1}^e - E_t}{E_t}$$

where

$\quad i^D$ = interest rate on dollars $\quad$ = 6%

$\quad i^F$ = interest rate on foreign currency = 3%

Thus,

$$6\% = 3\% - \frac{E_{t+1}^e - E_t}{E_t}$$

$$-\frac{E_{t+1}^e - E_t}{E_t} = \text{rate of appreciation of the foreign currency} = 6\% - 3\% = 3\%$$

There are several ways to look at the interest parity condition. First, we should recognize that interest parity means simply that the expected returns are the same on both dollar assets and foreign assets. To see this, note that the left side of the interest parity condition (Equation 2) is the expected return on dollar assets, while the right side is the expected return on foreign assets, both calculated in terms of a single currency, the U.S. dollar. Given our assumption that domestic and foreign assets are perfect substitutes (equally desirable), the interest parity condition is an equilibrium condition for the foreign exchange market. Only when the exchange rate is such that expected returns on domestic and foreign assets are equal—that is, when interest parity holds—will the domestic and foreign assets be willingly held.

The interest parity condition can be used to explain how the exchange rate is determined,[5] but in many circumstances it is not reasonable to assume that there is perfect capital mobility or that foreign and domestic assets are perfect substitutes. Here we develop a supply and demand analysis of the foreign exchange market that does not require us to make either of these assumptions.

Demand Curve for Domestic Assets

What determines the demand curve for domestic (dollar) assets is the relative expected return of domestic assets. This relative expected return equals the difference between the interest rate paid on dollar assets and the interest rate paid on foreign assets, plus the expected appreciation of the dollar: $i^D - i^F + (E_{t+1}^e - E_t)/E_t$. Suppose, for simplicity, that the domestic and foreign interest rates are both 5%

---

[5]By suitable algebraic manipulation, the interest parity condition in Equation 2 can be rewritten as

$$E_t = \frac{E_{t+1}^e}{i^F - i^D + 1}$$

This equation produces exactly the same results that we find in the supply and demand analysis to follow: If i^D rises, E_t rises; if i^F rises, E_t falls; and if E_{t+1}^e rises, E_t rises.

(so the expected interest differential is zero) and that the expected exchange rate next period E^e_{t+1} is 1.0 euro per dollar. When the current exchange rate is 1.05 euros per dollar, the expected appreciation of the dollar is $(1.00 - 1.05)/1.05 = -0.048 = -4.8\%$. The expected appreciation in this case is also the expected return on dollar assets relative to foreign assets because the interest differential is zero. In other words, holding dollar assets is not a very good deal because their relative expected return is negative; the quantity demanded of dollar assets will be low, as represented by point A in Figure 13.3. Note that not only is the expected return on dollar assets negative, it is also less than the expected return on foreign assets. Despite this, investors still will hold some dollar assets because we are no longer assuming that dollar and foreign assets are perfect substitutes. At a lower current exchange rate of $E_t = 1.0$ euro per dollar, the expected appreciation of the dollar is zero because E^e_{t+1} also equals 1.0 euro per dollar and the relative expected return is zero. Dollar assets are now a better deal, so the amount of dollar assets demanded is higher, as indicated by point B. At an even lower exchange rate of $E_t = 0.95$ euro per dollar, the expected appreciation and relative expected return of the dollar assets becomes $(1.00 - 0.95)/0.95 = 0.52 = 5.2\%$. With this higher expected return, the quantity of dollar assets demanded rises further, as indicated by point C. The resulting demand curve, D, which connects these points, is downward-sloping, indicating that at lower current values of the dollar (everything else equal), the quantity demanded of dollar assets is higher.

Another way of seeing that the demand curve is downward-sloping is to recognize that the lower the current exchange rate, E_t, the greater the expected appreciation of the dollar, $(E^e_{t+1} - E_t)/E_t$, and thus the higher the expected return on dollar assets relative to foreign assets. The lower the current exchange rate, the higher the quantity demanded of dollar assets (everything else held equal), so that the demand curve slopes down.

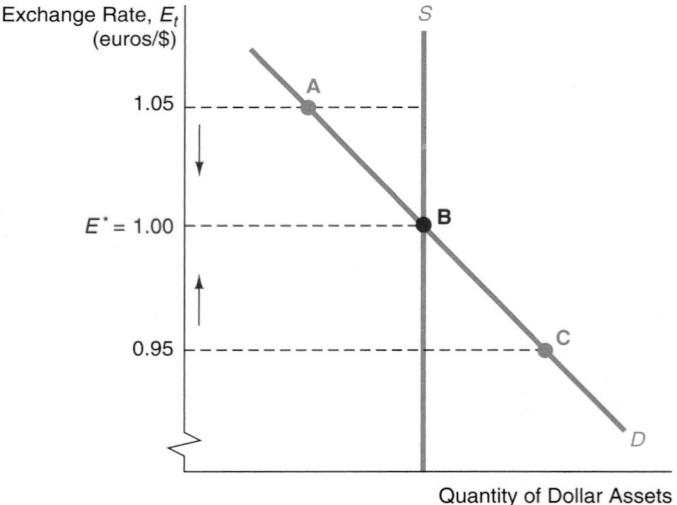

Figure 13.3 Equilibrium in the Foreign Exchange Market

Equilibrium in the foreign exchange market occurs at point B, the intersection of the demand curve D and the supply curve S. The equilibrium exchange rate is $E^* = 1$ euro per dollar.

Supply Curve for Domestic Assets

Because the quantity of dollar assets supplied is primarily the amount of bank deposits, bonds, and equities in the United States, we will take this amount as fixed with respect to the exchange rate. The quantity supplied at any exchange rate does not change, so the supply curve, S, is vertical, as shown in Figure 13.3.

Equilibrium in the Foreign Exchange Market

As in the usual supply and demand analysis, the market is in equilibrium when the quantity of dollar assets demanded equals the quantity supplied. In Figure 13.3, equilibrium occurs at point B, the intersection of the demand and supply curves. At point B, the exchange rate is 1 euro per dollar.

Suppose that the exchange rate is 1.05 euros per dollar, which is higher than the equilibrium exchange rate. As we can see in Figure 13.3, the quantity of dollar assets supplied is then greater than the quantity demanded, a condition of excess supply. Given that more people want to sell dollar assets than want to buy them, the value of the dollar will fall. As long as the exchange rate remains above the equilibrium exchange rate, there will continue to be an excess supply of dollar assets, and the dollar will fall in value until it reaches the equilibrium exchange rate of 1 euro per dollar.

Similarly, if the exchange rate is less than the equilibrium exchange rate at 0.95 euro per dollar, the quantity of dollar assets demanded will exceed the quantity supplied, a condition of excess demand. Given that more people want to buy dollar assets than want to sell them, the value of the dollar will rise until the excess demand disappears and the value of the dollar is again at the equilibrium exchange rate of 1 euro per dollar.

Explaining Changes in Exchange Rates

go online

http://fx.sauder.ubc.ca
The Pacific Exchange Rate Service at the University of British Columbia's Sauder School of Business provides information on how market conditions are affecting exchange rates and allows easy plotting of exchange rate data.

The supply and demand analysis of the foreign exchange market can explain how and why exchange rates change. This analysis is simplified by assuming the amount of dollar assets is fixed: The supply curve is vertical at a given quantity and does not shift. Under this assumption, we need look at only those factors that shift the demand curve for dollar assets to explain how exchange rates change over time.

Shifts in the Demand for Domestic Assets

As we have seen, the quantity of domestic (dollar) assets demanded depends on the relative expected return of dollar assets, $i^D - i^F + (E_{t+1}^e - E_t)/E_t$. To see how the demand curve shifts, we need to ask how the quantity demanded changes, holding the current exchange rate, E_t, constant, when i^D, i^F, and E_{t+1}^e change.

Domestic Interest Rate, i^D When the domestic interest rate on dollar assets i^D rises, holding the current exchange rate E_t and everything else constant, the return on dollar assets increases relative to foreign assets, so people will want to hold more dollar assets. The quantity of dollar assets demanded increases at every value of the exchange rate, as shown by the rightward shift of the demand curve in Figure 13.4 from D_1 to D_2. The new equilibrium is reached at point 2, the intersection of D_2 and S, and the equilibrium exchange rate rises from E_1 to E_2. ***An increase in the***

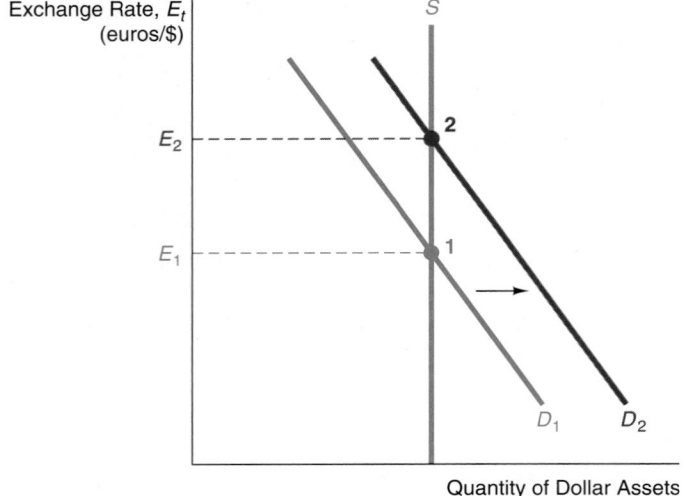

Figure 13.4 Response to an Increase in the Domestic Interest Rate, i^D

When the domestic interest rate i^D increases, the relative expected return on domestic (dollar) assets increases and the demand curve shifts to the right. The equilibrium exchange rate rises from E_1 to E_2.

domestic interest rate $\mathbf{i^D}$ *shifts the demand curve for domestic assets,* **D,** *to the right and causes the domestic currency to appreciate (* **E** ↑*).*

Conversely, if i^D falls, the relative expected return on dollar assets falls, the demand curve shifts to the left, and the exchange rate falls. *A decrease in the domestic interest rate* $\mathbf{i^D}$ *shifts the demand curve for domestic assets,* **D,** *to the left and causes the domestic currency to depreciate (* **E** ↓*).*

study guide

To grasp how the demand curve shifts, just think of yourself as an investor who is considering putting funds into domestic (dollar) assets. When a variable changes (i^D, for example), decide whether at a given level of the current exchange rate, holding all other variables constant, you would earn a higher or lower expected return on dollar assets versus foreign assets. This decision tells you whether you want to hold more or fewer dollar assets and thus whether the quantity demanded increases or decreases at each level of the exchange rate. Knowing the direction of the change in the quantity demanded at each exchange rate then tells you which way the demand curve shifts.

Foreign Interest Rate, i^F When the foreign interest rate i^F rises, holding the current exchange rate, E_t, and everything else constant, the return on foreign assets rises relative to dollar assets. Thus, the relative expected return on dollar assets falls. Now people want to hold fewer dollar assets, and the quantity demanded decreases at every value of the exchange rate. This is shown by the leftward shift of the demand curve in Figure 13.5 from D_1 to D_2. The new equilibrium is reached at point 2, when

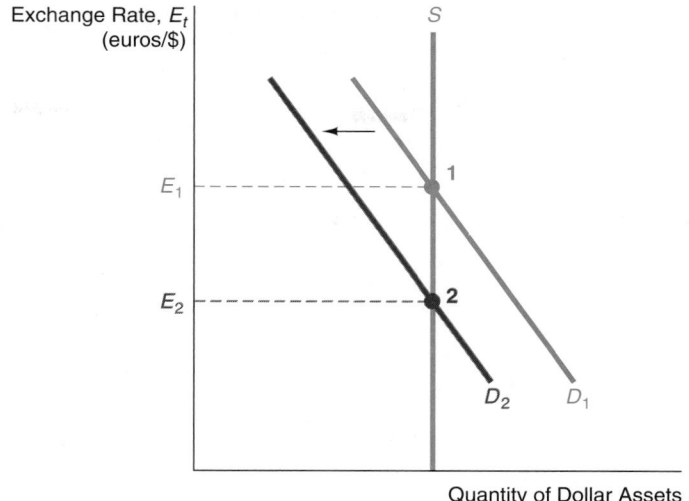

Figure 13.5   Response to an Increase in the Foreign Interest Rate, i^F

When the foreign interest rate i^F increases, the relative expected return on domestic (dollar) assets falls and the demand curve shifts to the left. The equilibrium exchange rate falls from E_1 to E_2.

the value of the dollar has fallen. Conversely, a decrease in i^F raises the relative expected return on dollar assets, shifts the demand curve to the right, and raises the exchange rate. To summarize, ***an increase in the foreign interest rate $\mathbf{i^F}$ shifts the demand curve D to the left and causes the domestic currency to depreciate; a fall in the foreign interest rate $\mathbf{i^F}$ shifts the demand curve D to the right and causes the domestic currency to appreciate.***

Changes in the Expected Future Exchange Rate, E_{t+1}^e Expectations about the future value of the exchange rate play an important role in shifting the current demand curve because the demand for domestic assets, like the demand for any durable good, depends on the future resale price. Any factor that causes the expected future exchange rate, E_{t+1}^e, to rise increases the expected appreciation of the dollar. The result is a higher relative expected return on dollar assets, which increases the demand for dollar assets at every exchange rate, thereby shifting the demand curve to the right in Figure 13.6 from D_1 to D_2. The equilibrium exchange rate rises to point 2 at the intersection of the D_2 and S curves. ***A rise in the expected future exchange rate, $\mathbf{E_{t+1}^e}$, shifts the demand curve to the right and causes an appreciation of the domestic currency.*** Using the same reasoning, ***a fall in the expected future exchange rate, $\mathbf{E_{t+1}^e}$, shifts the demand curve to the left and causes a depreciation of the currency.***

Earlier in the chapter we discussed the determinants of the exchange rate in the long run: the relative price level, relative tariffs and quotas, import and export demand, and relative productivity (refer to Table 13.1). These four factors influence the expected future exchange rate. The theory of purchasing power parity suggests that if a higher American price level relative to the foreign price level is expected to persist, the dollar will depreciate in the long run. A higher expected

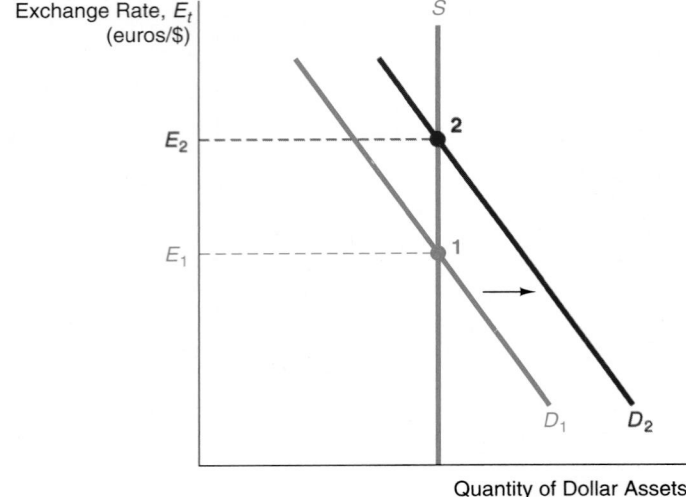

Figure 13.6   Response to an Increase in the Expected Future Exchange Rate, E^e_{t+1}

When the expected future exchange rate increases, the relative expected return on domestic (dollar) assets rises and the demand curve shifts to the right. The equilibrium exchange rate rises from E_1 to E_2.

relative American price level should thus have a tendency to lower E^e_{t+1}, lower the relative expected return on dollar assets, shift the demand curve to the left, and lower the current exchange rate.

Similarly, the other long-run determinants of the exchange rate can influence the relative expected return on dollar assets and the current exchange rate. Briefly, the following changes, all of which increase the demand for domestic goods relative to foreign goods, will raise E^e_{t+1}: (1) expectations of a fall in the American price level relative to the foreign price level; (2) expectations of higher American trade barriers relative to foreign trade barriers; (3) expectations of lower American import demand; (4) expectations of higher foreign demand for American exports, and (5) expectations of higher American productivity relative to foreign productivity. By increasing E^e_{t+1}, all of these changes increase the relative expected return on dollar assets, shift the demand curve to the right, and cause an appreciation of the domestic currency, the dollar.

study guide

As a study aid, the factors that shift the demand curve D and lead to changes in the current exchange rate E_t are listed in Table 13.2. The table shows what happens to the exchange rate when each of the variables increases, holding everything else constant. To give yourself practice, try to work out what happens to the demand curve and the exchange rate if each of these factors falls rather than rises. Check your answers by seeing if you get the opposite changes in the exchange rate compared to the changes indicated in Table 13.2.

Table 13.2 Summary	Factors That Shift the Demand Curve for Domestic Assets and Affect the Exchange Rate

Factor	Change in Factor	Change in Quantity Demanded of Domestic Assets at Each Exchange Rate	Response of Exchange Rate, E_t	
Domestic interest rate, i^D	↑	↑	↑	
Foreign interest rate, i^F	↑	↓	↓	
Expected domestic price level*	↑	↓	↓	
Expected trade barriers*	↑	↑	↑	
Expected import demand	↑	↓	↓	
Expected export demand	↑	↑	↑	
Expected productivity*	↑	↑	↑	

*Relative to other countries.

Note: Only increases (↑) in the factors are shown; the effects of decreases in the variables on the exchange rate are the opposite of those indicated in the "Response" column.

CASE

Changes in the Equilibrium Exchange Rate: Two Examples

Our analysis has revealed the factors that affect the value of the equilibrium exchange rate. Now we use this analysis to take a close look at the response of the exchange rate to changes in interest rates and money growth.

Changes in Interest Rates

Changes in domestic interest rates i^D are often cited as a major factor affecting exchange rates. For example, we see headlines in the financial press like this one: "Dollar Recovers as Interest Rates Edge Upward." But is the view presented in this headline always correct?

Not necessarily, because to analyze the effects of interest rate changes, we must carefully distinguish the sources of the changes. The Fisher equation (Chapter 3) states that a nominal interest rate such as i^D equals the *real* interest rate plus expected inflation: $i = i_r + \pi^e$. The Fisher equation thus indicates that the interest rate i^D can change for two reasons: Either the real interest rate i_r changes or the expected inflation rate π^e changes. The effect on the exchange rate is quite different, depending on which of these two factors is the source of the change in the nominal interest rate.

Suppose that the domestic real interest rate increases so that the nominal interest rate i^D rises while expected inflation remains unchanged. In this case, it is reasonable to assume that the expected appreciation of the dollar will be unchanged because expected inflation is unchanged. In this case, the increase in i^D increases the relative expected return on dollar assets, increases the quantity of dollar assets demanded at each level of the exchange rate, and shifts the demand curve to the right. We end up with the situation depicted in Figure 13.4, which analyzes an increase in i^D, holding everything else constant. Our model of the foreign exchange market produces the following result: ***When domestic real interest rates rise, the domestic currency appreciates.***

When the nominal interest rate rises because of an increase in expected inflation, we get a different result from the one shown in Figure 13.4. The rise in expected domestic inflation leads to a decline in the expected appreciation of the dollar, which is typically thought to be larger than the increase in the domestic interest rate i^D.[6] As a result, at any given exchange rate, the relative expected return on domestic (dollar) assets falls, the demand curve shifts to the left, and the exchange rate falls from E_1 to E_2 as shown in Figure 13.7. Our analysis leads to this conclusion: ***When***

---

[6]This conclusion is standard in asset market models of exchange rate determination; see Rudiger Dornbusch, "Expectations and Exchange Rate Dynamics," *Journal of Political Economy* 84 (1976): 1061–1076. It is also consistent with empirical evidence that suggests that nominal interest rates do not rise one-for-one with increases in expected inflation. See Frederic S. Mishkin, "The Real Interest Rate: An Empirical Investigation," *Carnegie-Rochester Conference Series on Public Policy* 15 (1981): 151–200; and Lawrence Summers, "The Nonadjustment of Nominal Interest Rates: A Study of the Fisher Effect," in *Macroeconomics, Prices and Quantities*, ed. James Tobin (Washington, DC: Brookings Institution, 1983), pp. 201–240.

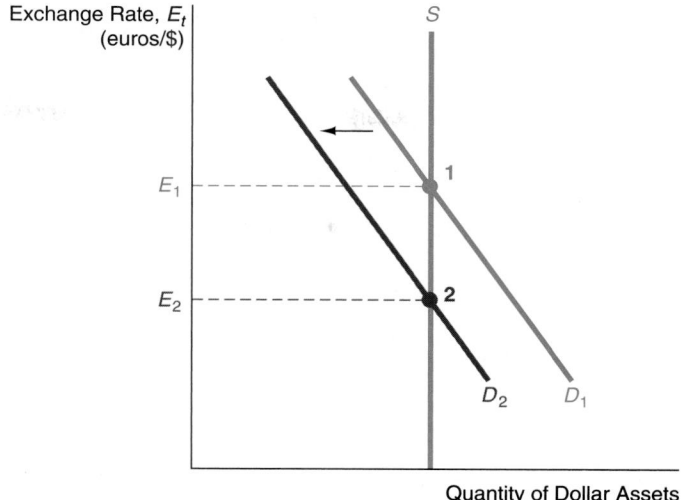

Figure 13.7 Effect of a Rise in the Domestic Interest Rate as a Result of an Increase in Expected Inflation

Because a rise in domestic expected inflation leads to a decline in expected dollar appreciation that is larger than the increase in the domestic interest rate, the relative expected return on domestic (dollar) assets falls. The demand curve shifts to the left, and the equilibrium exchange rate falls from E_1 to E_2.

domestic interest rates rise due to an expected increase in inflation, the domestic currency depreciates.

Because this conclusion is completely different from the one reached when the rise in the domestic interest rate is associated with a higher real interest rate, we must always distinguish between *real* and *nominal* measures when analyzing the effects of interest rates on exchange rates.

Changes in the Money Supply

Suppose that the Federal Reserve decides to increase the level of the money supply in an attempt to reduce unemployment, which it believes to be excessive. The higher money supply will lead to a higher American price level in the long run and hence to a lower expected future exchange rate. The resulting decline in the expected appreciation of the dollar lowers the quantity of dollar assets demanded at each level of the exchange rate and shifts the demand curve to the left. In addition, the higher money supply will lead to a higher real money supply M/P, because the price level does not immediately increase in the short run. The resulting rise in the real money supply causes the domestic interest rate to fall, which also lowers the relative expected return on dollar assets, providing a further reason why the demand curve shifts to the left. As we can see in Figure 13.8, the demand curve shifts to D_2, and the exchange rate declines from E_1 to E_2. The conclusion: *A higher domestic money supply causes the domestic currency to depreciate.*

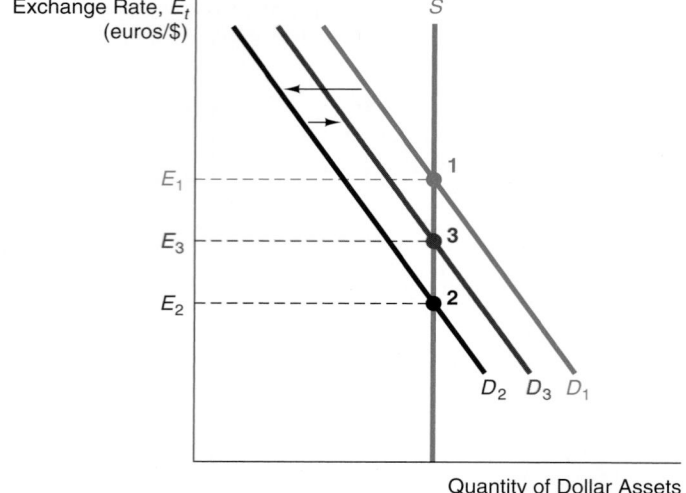

Figure 13.8   Effect of a Rise in the Money Supply

A rise in the money supply leads to a higher domestic price level, which in turn leads to a lower expected future exchange rate. In addition, the higher money supply leads to a decline in domestic interest rates. The decline in both the expected appreciation of the dollar and the domestic interest rate lowers the relative expected return on dollar assets, shifting the demand curve leftward from D_1 to D_2. In the short run, the equilibrium exchange rate falls from E_1 to E_2. In the long run, however, the interest rate rises back up again to its initial level and the demand curve shifts rightward to D_3. The exchange rate rises from E_2 to E_3 in the long run.

Exchange Rate Overshooting

Our analysis of the effect of an increase in the money supply on the exchange rate is not yet over—we still need to look at what happens to the exchange rate in the long run. A basic proposition in monetary theory, called **monetary neutrality,** states that in the long run, a one-time percentage rise in the money supply is matched by the same one-time percentage rise in the price level, leaving unchanged the real money supply and all other economic variables such as interest rates. An intuitive way to understand this proposition is to think of what would happen if our government announced overnight that an old dollar would now be worth 100 new dollars. The money supply in new dollars would be 100 times its old value and the price level would also be 100 times higher, but nothing in the economy would really have changed: Real and nominal interest rates and the real money supply would remain the same. Monetary neutrality tells us that in the long run, the rise in the money supply would not lead to a change in the domestic interest rate so it would rise back to its old level. The demand curve would shift to the right to D_3, but not all the way back to D_1, because the price level will still be higher in the long run. As we can see in Figure 13.8, this means that the exchange rate would rise from E_2 to E_3 in the long run.

The phenomenon we have described here in which the exchange rate falls by more in the short run than it does in the long run when the money supply increases is called **exchange rate overshooting.** It is important because, as we will see in the following application, it can help explain why exchange rates exhibit so much volatility.

Another way of thinking about why exchange rate overshooting occurs is to recognize that when the domestic interest rate falls in the short run, equilibrium in the foreign exchange market means that the expected return on foreign deposits must be lower. With the foreign interest rate given, this lower expected return on foreign deposits means that there must be an expected appreciation of the dollar (depreciation of the euro) for the expected return on foreign deposits to decline when the domestic interest rate falls. This can occur only if the current exchange rate falls below its long-run value.

CASE

Why Are Exchange Rates So Volatile?

The high volatility of foreign exchange rates surprises many people. Thirty or so years ago, economists generally believed that allowing exchange rates to be determined in the free market would not lead to large fluctuations in their values. Recent experience has proved them wrong. If we return to Figure 13.1, we see that exchange rates over the 1990–2007 period have been very volatile.

The asset market approach to exchange rate determination that we have outlined in this chapter gives a straightforward explanation of volatile exchange rates. Because expected appreciation of the domestic currency affects the expected return on foreign deposits, expectations about the price level, inflation, trade barriers, productivity, import demand, export demand, and the money supply play important roles in determining the exchange rate. When expectations about any of these variables change, as they do—and often at that—our model indicates that there will be an immediate effect on the expected return on foreign deposits and therefore on the exchange rate. Because expectations on all these variables change with just about every bit of news that appears, it is not surprising that the exchange rate is volatile. In addition, we have seen that our exchange rate analysis produces exchange rate overshooting when the money supply increases. Exchange rate overshooting is an additional reason for the high volatility of exchange rates.

Because earlier models of exchange rate behavior focused on goods markets rather than asset markets, they did not emphasize changing expectations as a source of exchange rate movements, and so these earlier models could not predict substantial fluctuations in exchange rates. The failure of earlier models to explain volatility is one reason why they are no longer so popular. The more modern approach developed here emphasizes that the foreign exchange market is like any other asset market in which expectations of the future matter. The foreign exchange market, like other asset markets such as the stock market, displays substantial price volatility, and foreign exchange rates are notoriously hard to forecast.

CASE

The Dollar and Interest Rates, 1973–2007

In the chapter preview, we mentioned that the dollar was weak in the late 1970s, rose substantially from 1980 to 1985, and declined thereafter. We can use our analysis of the foreign exchange market to understand exchange rate movements and help explain the dollar's rise and fall in the 1980s.

Some important information for tracing the dollar's changing value is presented in Figure 13.9, which plots measures of real and nominal interest rates and the value of the dollar in terms of a basket of foreign currencies (called an **effective exchange rate index**). We can see that the value of the dollar and the measure of real interest rates tend to rise and fall together. In the late 1970s, real interest rates were at low levels, and so was the value of the dollar. Beginning in 1980, however, real interest rates in the United States began to climb sharply, and at the same time so did the dollar. After 1984, the real interest rate declined substantially, as did the dollar.

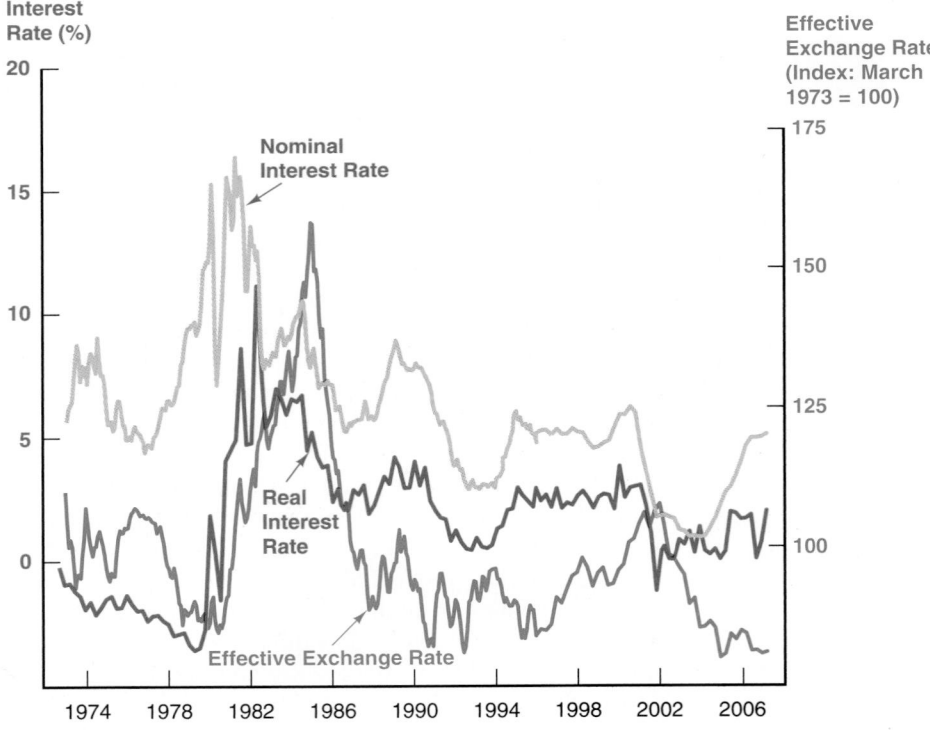

Figure 13.9 Value of the Dollar and Interest Rates, 1973–2007

Sources: Federal Reserve: www.federalreserve.gov/releases/h10/summary/indexn_m.txt; real interest rate from Figure 3.1 in Chapter 3.

Our model of exchange rate determination helps explain the rise and fall in the dollar in the 1980s. As Figure 13.4 indicates, a rise in the U.S. real interest rate raises the relative expected return on dollar assets, which leads to purchases of dollar assets that raise the exchange rate. This is exactly what happened in the 1980–1984 period. The subsequent fall in U.S. real interest rates then lowered the relative expected return on dollar assets, which lowered the demand for them and thus lowered the exchange rate.

The plot of *nominal* interest rates in Figure 13.9 also demonstrates that the correspondence between nominal interest rates and exchange rate movements is not nearly as close as that between *real* interest rates and exchange rate movements. This is also exactly what our analysis predicts. The rise in nominal interest rates in the late 1970s was not reflected in a corresponding rise in the value of the dollar; indeed, the dollar actually fell in the late 1970s. Figure 13.9 explains why the rise in nominal rates in the late 1970s did not produce a rise in the dollar. As a comparison of the real and nominal interest rates in the late 1970s indicates, the rise in nominal interest rates reflected an increase in expected inflation and not an increase in real interest rates. As our analysis in Figure 13.7 demonstrates, the rise in nominal interest rates stemming from a rise in expected inflation should lead to a decline in the dollar, and that is exactly what happened.

If there is a moral to the story, it is that a failure to distinguish between real and nominal interest rates can lead to poor predictions of exchange rate movements: The weakness of the dollar in the late 1970s and the strength of the dollar in the early 1980s can be explained by movements in *real* interest rates but not by movements in *nominal* interest rates.

CASE

The Euro's First Nine Years

With much fanfare, the euro debuted on January 1, 1999, at an exchange rate of 1.18 dollars per euro. Despite early hopes that the euro would be a strong currency, it initially proved to be weak. It declined 30% to a low of 83 cents per euro in October 2000, and then began a steady recovery to around the $1.45 level by late-2007. What explains the weakness of the euro in its first two years, and the subsequent recovery thereafter?

The previous case showed that changes in real interest rates are an important factor determining the exchange rate. When the domestic real interest rate falls relative to the foreign real interest rate, the domestic currency declines in value. While the euro was coming into existence, European economies were experiencing slow recoveries from recessions which had caused both real and nominal interest rates to fall. In contrast, the United States experienced very rapid growth in 1999 and 2000, substantially higher than the growth in its European counterparts. As in the analysis of the previous application, low real interest rates in Europe relative to those in the United States drove down the value of the euro.

With the slowing of the U.S. economy, after the recession started in the spring of 2001, both real and nominal U.S. interest rates began to fall to low levels, thereby weakening the dollar relative to the euro.

Reading the *Wall Street Journal*: The "Currency Trading" Column

Now that we have an understanding of how exchange rates are determined, we can use our analysis to understand discussions about developments in the foreign exchange market reported in the financial press.

Every day, the *Wall Street Journal* reports on developments in the foreign exchange market on the previous business day in its "Currency Trading" column, an example of which is presented in the Following the Financial News box, "The 'Currency Trading' Column." (Occasionally, as in the example presented here, the column is titled "Currency Markets" instead.)

The column states that the dollar fell to a record low against the euro on concerns about the U.S. housing sector and the risk of mortgage bonds and expectations that the Fed may cut interest rates even as central banks in other countries are raising theirs. Our analysis of the foreign exchange market explains why these developments led to a weaker dollar.

The warning by Home Depot that its earnings may be lower and the news that Standard & Poor's may downgrade some mortgage bonds signal weakness in housing, a major sector of the U.S. economy. These signs raise expectations that the Fed might cut interest rates later in the year to provide stimulus and avoid a slowdown in the economy. Expectations of a cut in U.S. interest rates lower the expected return on dollar assets in the future. If, in addition, other central banks move to raise their interest rates as the column suggests, then the expected return on foreign assets will rise in the future. Therefore, traders in the currency markets will expect that in the future the relative expected return for dollar assets will be lower and, as a result, there will be a smaller quantity of dollar assets demanded at each exchange rate. Thus, they expect that in the future the demand curve for dollar assets will shift to the left, as in Figure 13.5, and the dollar will depreciate. Because currency traders expect a lower future exchange rate for the dollar, the expected appreciation of the dollar falls today. This lowers the expected return for dollar assets relative to foreign assets now, which causes the demand for dollar assets to decline and causes the current exchange rate to fall, as in Figure 13.5.

following the financial news

The "Currency Trading" Column

The "Currency Trading" column appears daily in the *Wall Street Journal*; an example is presented here.

It is usually found in the third section, "Money and Investing."

Dollar Hits Record Low to Euro

BY DAN MOLINSKI

Concern about the U.S. housing sector, crystallized in an earnings warning from home-improvement retailer Home Depot and downgrade threats for some mortgage bonds by debt rater Standard & Poor's sent the dollar to record lows against the euro.

The euro reached a series of highs against the struggling dollar, busting through both its previous $1.3682 high and $1.3700 and reaching a new high of $1.3471 before retracing. The dollar also made a 26-year low against sterling, at $2.0273, and a four-week low of 121.88 yen.

CURRENCY MARKETS

In New York, the euro was at $1.3730 from $1.3622 late Monday, while the dollar was at 121.97 yen compared with 123.40 yen. The euro was at 167.46 yen fro 168.09 yen, while sterling was at $2.0273 from $2.0150. The dollar was at 1.2048 Swiss francs from 1.2165 Swiss francs late Monday.

The housing market's woes raised expectations that the Federal Reserve might be pushed to cut interest rates by late 2007, with short-term interest-rate futures pricing in a small possibility of a quarter percentage point cut by end-year to 5%.

"Expectations are starting to creep back in that the Fed will have to cut interest rates by the end of the year. . . . The dollar is on a new track," said Mark Meadows, a currency strategist at Tempus Consulting in Washington.

That comes just as central banks around the world are raising interest rates, shrinking the yield advantage that the dollar enjoys over many other currencies. The key interest rate in the euro zone, for example, is 4%, but plans are afoot for increases.

"The Fed is on hold, and with the other central banks on a bias to tighten, the outlook for the dollar is for weakness," said Divyang Shah, chief strategist at Commonwealth Bank in London.

The Bank of Canada announced a widely expected quarter percentage-point rate increase to 4.5%, the first in more than a year. However, its accompanying statement seemed more moderate than many had expected, and the greenback eked out small gains against its neighbor, which had reached a new 30-year high Monday.

Late yesterday, the U.S. dollar was at 1.0515 Canadian dollars from C$1.0495.

The greenback registered gains in Latin America as worries about the U.S. economy weigh heavily on local economies there. Late in the session, the dollar rose to 10.8354 Mexican pesos from 10.7583 late Monday. And the dollar increased to 1,963 Colombian pesos from 1,945.

Source: Wall Street Journal, July 11, 2007, p. C6.

THE PRACTICING MANAGER

Profiting from Foreign Exchange Forecasts

Managers of financial institutions care a great deal about what foreign exchange rates will be in the future because these rates affect the value of assets on their balance sheet that are denominated in foreign currencies. In addition, financial institutions often engage in trading foreign exchange, both for their own account and for their customers. Forecasts of future foreign exchange rates can thus have a big impact on the profits that financial institutions make on their foreign exchange trading operations.

Managers of financial institutions obtain foreign exchange forecasts either by hiring their own staff economists to generate them or by purchasing forecasts from other financial institutions or economic forecasting firms. In predicting exchange rate movements, forecasters look at the factors mentioned in this chapter. For example, if they expect domestic real interest rates to rise, they will predict, in line with our analysis, that the domestic currency will appreciate; conversely, if they expect domestic inflation to increase, they will predict that the domestic currency will depreciate.

Managers of financial institutions, particularly those engaged in international banking, rely on foreign exchange forecasts to make decisions about which assets denominated in foreign currencies they should hold. For example, if a financial institution manager has a reliable forecast that the euro will appreciate in the future but the yen will depreciate, the manager will want to sell off assets denominated in yen and instead purchase assets denominated in euros. Alternatively, the manager might instruct loan officers to make more loans denominated in euros and fewer loans denominated in yen. Likewise, if the yen is forecast to appreciate and the euro to depreciate, the manager would want to switch out of euro-denominated assets into yen-denominated assets and would want to make more loans in yen and fewer in euros.

If the financial institution has a foreign exchange trading operation, a forecast of an appreciation of the yen means that the financial institution manager should tell foreign exchange traders to buy yen. If the forecast turns out to be correct, the higher value of the yen means that the trader can sell the yen in the future and pocket a tidy profit. If the euro is forecast to depreciate, the trader can sell euros and buy them back in the future at a lower price if the forecast turns out to be correct, and again the financial institution will make a profit.

Accurate foreign exchange rate forecasts can thus help a financial institution manager generate substantial profits for the institution. Unfortunately, exchange rate forecasters are no more or less accurate than other economic forecasters, and they often make large errors. Reports on foreign exchange rate forecasts and how well forecasters are doing appear from time to time in the *Wall Street Journal* and in the trade magazine *Euromoney*.

SUMMARY

1. Foreign exchange rates (the price of one country's currency in terms of another's) are important because they affect the price of domestically produced goods sold abroad and the cost of foreign goods bought domestically.

2. The theory of purchasing power parity suggests that long-run changes in the exchange rate between two countries' currencies are determined by changes in the relative price levels in the two countries. Other factors that affect exchange rates in the long run are tariffs and quotas, import demand, export demand, and productivity.

3. In the short run, exchange rates are determined by changes in the relative expected return on domestic assets, which cause the demand curve to shift. Any factor that changes the relative expected return on domestic assets will lead to changes in the exchange

rate. Such factors include changes in the interest rates on domestic and foreign assets as well as changes in any of the factors that affect the long-run exchange rate and hence the expected future exchange rate. Changes in the money supply lead to exchange rate overshooting, causing the exchange rate to change by more in the short run than in the long run.

4. The asset market approach to exchange rate determination can explain both the volatility of exchange rates and the rise of the dollar in the 1980–1984 period and its subsequent fall.

5. Forecasts of foreign exchange rates are very valuable to managers of financial institutions because these rates influence decisions about which assets denominated in foreign currencies the institutions should hold and what kinds of trades should be made by their traders in the foreign exchange market.

KEY TERMS

appreciation, *p. 307*
capital mobility, *p. 316*
depreciation, *p. 307*
effective exchange rate index, *p. 328*
exchange rate, *p. 305*
exchange rate overshooting, *p. 327*
foreign exchange market, *p. 305*
forward exchange rate, *p. 307*
forward transactions, *p. 307*

interest parity condition, *p. 316*
law of one price, *p. 309*
monetary neutrality, *p. 326*
quotas, *p. 312*
spot exchange rate, *p. 307*
spot transactions, *p. 307*
tariffs, *p. 312*
theory of purchasing power
  parity (PPP), *p. 310*

QUESTIONS

1. When the euro appreciates, are you more likely to drink California or French wine?

2. "A country is always worse off when its currency is weak (falls in value)." Is this statement true, false, or uncertain? Explain your answer.

3. In a newspaper, check the exchange rates for the foreign currencies listed in the Following the Financial News box on page 308. Which of these currencies have appreciated and which have depreciated since May 22, 2007?

4. If the Japanese price level rises by 5% relative to the price level in the United States, what does the theory

of purchasing power parity predict will happen to the value of the Japanese yen in terms of dollars?

5. If the demand for a country's exports falls at the same time that tariffs on imports are raised, will the country's currency tend to appreciate or depreciate in the long run?

6. In the mid- to late 1970s, the yen appreciated relative to the dollar even though Japan's inflation rate was higher than America's. How can this be explained by an improvement in the productivity of Japanese industry relative to American industry?

Predicting the Future

Answer the remaining questions by drawing the appropriate exchange market diagrams.

7. The president of the United States announces that he will reduce inflation with a new anti-inflation program. If the public believes him, predict what will happen to the exchange rate for the U.S. dollar.

8. If the British central bank prints money to reduce unemployment, what will happen to the value of the pound in the short run and the long run?

9. If the Indian government unexpectedly announces that it will be imposing higher tariffs on foreign goods one year from now, what will happen to the value of the Indian rupee today?

10. If nominal interest rates in America rise but real interest rates fall, predict what will happen to the U.S. exchange rate.

11. If American auto companies make a breakthrough in automobile technology and are able to produce a car that gets 60 miles to the gallon, what will happen to the U.S. exchange rate?

12. If Mexicans go on a spending spree and buy twice as much French perfume, Japanese TVs, English sweaters, Swiss watches, and Italian wine, what will happen to the value of the Mexican peso?

13. If expected inflation drops in Europe so that interest rates fall there, predict what will happen to the exchange rate for the U.S. dollar.

14. If the European central bank decides to contract the money supply to fight inflation, what will happen to the value of the U.S. dollar?

15. If there is a strike in France, making it harder to buy French goods, what will happen to the value of the euro?

QUANTITATIVE PROBLEMS

1. A German sports car is selling for 70,000 euros. What is the dollar price in the United States for the German car if the exchange rate is 0.90 euros per dollar?

2. An investor in England purchased a 91-day T-bill for $987.65. At that time, the exchange rate was $1.75 per pound. At maturity, the exchange rate was $1.83 per pound. What was the investor's holding period return in pounds?

3. An investor in Canada purchased 100 shares of IBM on January 1 at $93.00 per share. IBM paid an annual dividend of $0.72 on December 31. The stock was sold that day as well for $100.25. The exchange rate was $0.68 per Canadian dollar on January 1 and $0.71 per Canadian dollar on December 31. What is the investor's total return in Canadian dollars?

4. The current exchange rate is 0.75 euro per dollar, but you believe the dollar will decline to 0.67 euro per dollar. If a euro-denominated bond is yielding 2%, what return do you expect in U.S. dollars?

5. The six-month forward rate between the British pound and the U.S. dollar is $1.75 per pound. If six-month interest rates are 3% in the United States and 150 basis points higher in England, what is the current exchange rate?

6. If the Canadian dollar to U.S. dollar exchange rate is 1.28 and the British pound to U.S. dollar exchange rate is 0.62, what must the Canadian dollar to British pound exchange rate be?

7. The New Zealand dollar to U.S. dollar exchange rate is 1.36, and the British pound to U.S. dollar exchange rate is 0.62. If you find that the British pound to New Zealand dollar were trading at 0.49, what would you do to earn a riskless profit?

8. In 1999, the euro was trading at $0.90 per euro. If the euro is now trading at $1.16 per euro, what is the percentage change in the euro's value? Is this an appreciation or depreciation?

9. The Brazilian real is trading at 0.375 real per U.S. dollar. What is the U.S. dollar per real exchange rate?

10. The Mexican peso is trading at 10 pesos per dollar. If the expected U.S. inflation rate is 2% while the expected Mexican inflation rate is 23% over the next year, what is the expected exchange rate in one year?

11. The current exchange rate between the United States and Britain is $1.825 per pound. The six-month forward rate between the British pound and the U.S. dollar is $1.79 per pound. What is the percentage difference between current six-month U.S. and British interest rates?

12. The current exchange rate between the Japanese yen and the U.S. dollar is 120 yen per dollar. If the dollar is expected to depreciate by 10% relative to the yen, what is the new expected exchange rate?

13. If the price level recently increased by 20% in England while falling by 5% in the United States, how much must the exchange rate change if PPP holds? Assume that the current exchange rate is 0.55 pound per dollar.

14. A one-year CD in Europe is currently paying 5%, and the exchange rate is currently 0.99 euros per dollar. If you believe the exchange rate will be 1.04 euros per dollar one year from now, what is the expected return in terms of dollars?

15. Short-term interest rates are 2% in Japan and 4% in the United States. The current exchange rate is 120 yen per dollar. What is the expected forward exchange rate?

16. Short-term interest rates are 2% in Japan and 4% in the United States. The current exchange rate is 120 yen per dollar. If you can enter into a forward exchange rate of 115 yen per dollar, how can you arbitrage the situation?

17. The interest rate in the United States is 4%, and the euro is trading at 1 euro per dollar. The euro is expected to depreciate to 1.1 euros per dollar. Calculate the interest rate in Germany.

WEB EXERCISES

The Foreign Exchange Market

1. The Federal Reserve maintains a Web site that lists the exchange rates between the U.S. dollar and many other currencies. Go to **www.newyorkfed.org/markets/foreignex.html**. Go to the historical data from 2000 and later and find the euro.

a. What has the percentage change in the euro–dollar exchange rate been between the euro's introduction and now?

b. What has been the annual percentage change in the euro–dollar exchange rate for each year since the euro's introduction?

2. International travelers and business people frequently need to accurately convert from one currency to another. It is often easy to find the rate needed to convert the U.S. dollar into another currency. It can be more difficult to find exchange rates between two non-U.S. currencies. Go to **www.oanda.com/convert/classic**. This site lets you convert from any currency into any other currency. How many Lithuanian litas can you currently buy with one Chilean peso?

14

The International Financial System

Preview

Thanks to the growing interdependence between the U.S. economy and the economies of the rest of the world, the international financial system now plays a more prominent role in economic events in the United States. In this chapter we see how fixed and managed exchange rate systems work and how they can provide substantial profit opportunities for financial institutions. We also look at the controversies over what role capital controls and the International Monetary Fund should play in the international financial system.

Intervention in the Foreign Exchange Market

In Chapter 13 we analyzed the foreign exchange market as if it were a completely free market that responds to all market pressures. Like many other markets, however, the foreign exchange market is not free of government intervention; central banks regularly engage in international financial transactions called **foreign exchange interventions** to influence exchange rates. In our current international environment, exchange rates fluctuate from day to day, but central banks attempt to influence their countries' exchange rates by buying and selling currencies. We can use the exchange rate analysis we developed in Chapter 13 to explain the impact of central bank intervention on the foreign exchange market.

Foreign Exchange Intervention and the Money Supply

The first step in understanding how central bank intervention in the foreign exchange market affects exchange rates is to see the impact on the monetary base from a central bank sale in the foreign exchange market of some of its holdings of assets denominated in a foreign currency (called **international reserves**). Suppose that the Fed decides to sell $1 billion of its foreign assets in exchange for $1 billion of U.S. currency. (This transaction is conducted at the foreign exchange desk at the Federal Reserve Bank of New York—see the Inside the Fed box.) The Fed's purchase of dollars has two effects. First, it reduces the Fed's holding of international reserves by $1 billion. Second, because the Fed's purchase of currency removes it from the hands of the public, currency in circulation falls by $1 billion. We can see this in the following T-account for the Federal Reserve:

Federal Reserve System			
Assets		Liabilities	
Foreign assets (international reserves)	−$1 billion	Currency in circulation	−$1 billion

Because the monetary base is made up of currency in circulation plus reserves, this decline in currency implies that the monetary base has fallen by $1 billion.

If instead of paying for the foreign assets sold by the Fed with currency, the persons buying the foreign assets pay for them with checks written on accounts at domestic banks, and then the Fed deducts the $1 billion from the reserve deposits it holds for these banks. The result is that deposits with the Fed (reserves) decline by $1 billion, as shown in the following T-account:

Federal Reserve System			
Assets		Liabilities	
Foreign assets (international reserves)	−$1 billion	Deposits with the Fed (reserves)	−$1 billion

In this case, the outcome of the Fed sale of foreign assets and the purchase of dollar deposits is a $1 billion decline in reserves and, as before, a $1 billion decline in the monetary base because reserves are also a component of the monetary base.

We now see that the outcome for the monetary base is exactly the same when a central bank sells foreign assets to purchase domestic bank deposits or domestic currency. This is why when we say that a central bank has purchased its domestic currency, we do not have to distinguish whether it actually purchased currency or bank deposits denominated in the domestic currency. We have thus reached an important conclusion: ***A central bank's purchase of domestic currency and corresponding sale of foreign assets in the foreign exchange market leads to an equal decline in its international reserves and the monetary base.***

We could have reached the same conclusion by a more direct route. A central bank sale of a foreign asset is no different from an open market sale of a government bond. We learned in our exploration of monetary policy that an open market sale leads to an equal decline in the monetary base; therefore, a sale of foreign assets

A Day at the Federal Reserve Bank of New York's Foreign Exchange Desk

Although the U.S. Treasury is primarily responsible for foreign exchange policy, decisions to intervene in the foreign exchange market are made jointly by the U.S. Treasury and the Federal Reserve's FOMC (Federal Open Market Committee). The actual conduct of foreign exchange intervention is the responsibility of the foreign exchange desk at the Federal Reserve Bank of New York, which is right next to the open market desk.

The manager of foreign exchange operations at the New York Fed supervises the traders and analysts who follow developments in the foreign exchange market. Every morning at 7:30, a trader on staff who has arrived at the New York Fed in the predawn hours speaks on the telephone with counterparts at the U.S. Treasury and provides an update on overnight activity in overseas financial and foreign exchange markets. Later in the morning, at 9:30, the manager and his or her staff hold a conference call with senior staff at the Board of Governors of the Federal Reserve in Washington. In the afternoon, at 2:30, they have a second conference call, which is a joint briefing of officials at the board and the Treasury. Although by statute the Treasury has the

lead role in setting foreign exchange policy, it strives to reach a consensus among all three parties—the Treasury, the Board of Governors, and the Federal Reserve Bank of New York. If they decide that a foreign exchange intervention is necessary that day—an unusual occurrence, as a year may go by without a U.S. foreign exchange intervention—the manager instructs his traders to carry out the agreed-on purchase or sale of foreign currencies. Because funds for exchange rate intervention are held separately by the Treasury (in its Exchange Stabilization Fund) and the Federal Reserve, the manager and his or her staff are not trading the funds of the Federal Reserve Bank of New York; rather, they act as an agent for the Treasury and the FOMC in conducting these transactions.

As part of their duties, before every FOMC meeting, the staff helps prepare a lengthy document full of data for the FOMC members, other Reserve bank presidents, and Treasury officials. It describes developments in the domestic and foreign markets over the previous five or six weeks, a task that keeps them especially busy right before the FOMC meeting.

also leads to an equal decline in the monetary base. By similar reasoning, a central bank purchase of foreign assets paid for by selling domestic currency, like an open market purchase, leads to an equal rise in the monetary base. Thus, we reach the following conclusion: *A central bank's sale of domestic currency to purchase foreign assets in the foreign exchange market results in an equal rise in its international reserves and the monetary base.*

The intervention we have just described, in which a central bank allows the purchase or sale of domestic currency to have an effect on the monetary base, is called an **unsterilized foreign exchange intervention.** But what if the central bank does not want the purchase or sale of domestic currency to affect the monetary base? All it has to do is to counter the effect of the foreign exchange intervention by conducting an offsetting open market operation in the government bond market. For example, in the case of a $1 billion purchase of dollars by the Fed and a corresponding $1 billion sale of foreign assets, which, as we have seen, would decrease the monetary base by $1 billion, the Fed can conduct an open market purchase of $1 billion of government bonds, which would increase the monetary base by $1 billion. The resulting T-account for the foreign exchange intervention and the offsetting open market operation leaves the monetary base unchanged:

Federal Reserve System			
Assets		Liabilities	
Foreign assets (international reserves)	−$1 billion	Monetary base (reserved)	0
Government bonds	+$1 billion		

A foreign exchange intervention with an offsetting open market operation that leaves the monetary base unchanged is called a **sterilized foreign exchange intervention.**

Now that we understand that there are two types of foreign exchange interventions—unsterilized and sterilized—let's look at how each affects the exchange rate.

Unsterilized Intervention

Your intuition might lead you to suspect that if a central bank wants to lower the value of the domestic currency, it should sell its currency in the foreign exchange market and purchase foreign assets. Indeed, this intuition is correct for the case of an unsterilized intervention.

Recall that in an unsterilized intervention, if the Federal Reserve decides to sell dollars so that it can buy foreign assets in the foreign exchange market, this works just like an open market purchase of bonds to increase the monetary base. Hence the sale of dollars leads to an increase in the money supply, and we find ourselves analyzing a similar situation to that described in Figure 8 of Chapter 13, which is reproduced here as Figure 14.1.[1] The higher money supply leads to a higher U.S. price level in the long run and so to a lower expected future exchange rate. The resulting decline in the expected appreciation of the dollar lowers the relative expected return on dollar assets and shifts the demand curve to the left. In addition, the increase in the money supply will lead to a higher real money supply in the short run, which causes the interest rate on dollar assets to fall, also lowering the relative expected return on dollar assets, and providing another reason for the demand curve to shift to the left. The demand curve shifts from D_1 to D_2, and the exchange rate falls to E_2. Because the domestic interest rate will rise back to its initial level in the long run, the relative expected return of dollar assets will increase somewhat, sending the demand curve to D_3, but not all the way back to D_1 because the price level will still be higher in the long run. The exchange rate thus rises from E_2 to E_3, which is still below the initial value of E_1. The result is the same one we found in the previous chapter, in which there is exchange rate overshooting—that is, the exchange rate falls by more in the short run than in the long run.

Our analysis leads us to the following conclusion about unsterilized interventions in the foreign exchange market: ***An unsterilized intervention in which domestic currency is sold to purchase foreign assets leads to a gain in inter-***

[1]An unsterilized intervention, in which the Fed sells dollars, increases the amount of dollar assets slightly because it leads to an increase in the monetary base while leaving the amount of government bonds in the hands of the public unchanged. The curve depicting the supply of dollar assets would thus shift to the right slightly, which also works toward lowering the exchange rate, yielding the same conclusion derived from Figure 14.1. Because the resulting increase in the monetary base would be only a minuscule fraction of the total amount of dollar assets outstanding, the supply curve would shift by an imperceptible amount. This is why Figure 14.1 is drawn with the supply curve unchanged.

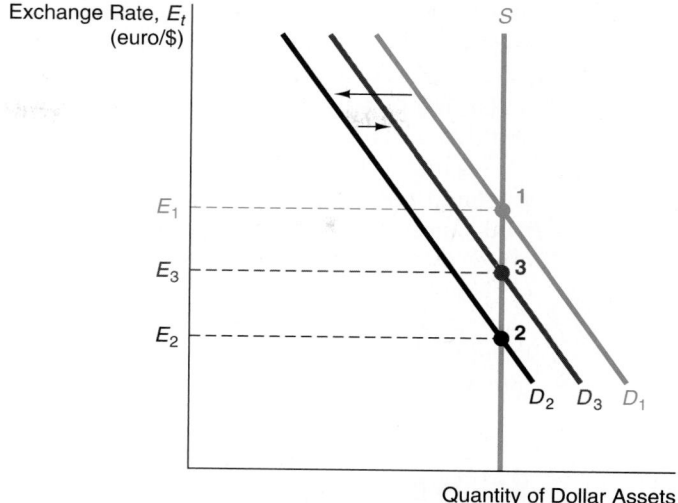

Figure 14.1   Effect of an Unsterilized Sale of Dollars and Purchase of Foreign Assets

A sale of dollars and the consequent open market purchase of foreign assets increase the monetary base. The resulting rise in the money supply leads to a decline in domestic interest rates and a higher domestic price level in the long run, which produces a lower expected future exchange rate. The decline in both the expected appreciation of the dollar and the domestic interest rate lowers the relative expected return on dollar assets, shifting the demand curve leftward from D_1 to D_2. In the short run, the equilibrium exchange rate falls from E_1 to E_2. In the long run, the interest rate rises back to its initial level and the demand curve shifts rightward to D_3. The exchange rate rises from E_2 to E_3 in the long run.

national reserves, an increase in the money supply, and a depreciation of the domestic currency.

The reverse result is found for an unsterilized intervention in which domestic currency is purchased by selling foreign assets. The purchase of domestic currency by selling foreign assets (reducing international reserves) works like an open market sale to reduce the monetary base and the money supply. The decrease in the money supply raises the interest rate on dollar assets and lowers the long-run price level, thereby increasing the future expected exchange rate. The resulting increase in the relative expected return on dollar assets means that people will buy more dollar assets, so the demand curve shifts to the right and the exchange rate rises. *An unsterilized intervention in which domestic currency is purchased by selling foreign assets leads to a drop in international reserves, a decrease in the money supply, and an appreciation of the domestic currency.*

Sterilized Intervention

The key point to remember about a sterilized intervention is that the central bank engages in offsetting open market operations, so that there is no impact on the monetary base and the money supply. In the context of the model of exchange rate determination we have developed here, it is straightforward to show that a sterilized intervention has almost *no effect* on the exchange rate. A sterilized intervention leaves the money supply unchanged and so has no direct way of affecting interest rates or the expected future exchange rate.[2] Because the relative expected return on dollar assets is unaffected, the demand curve would remain at D_1 in Figure 14.1, and the exchange rate would remain unchanged at E_1.

At first it might seem puzzling that a central bank purchase or sale of domestic currency that is sterilized does not lead to a change in the exchange rate. A central bank purchase of domestic currency cannot raise the exchange rate, because with no effect on the domestic money supply or interest rates, any resulting rise in the exchange rate would mean that there would be an excess supply of dollar assets. With more people willing to sell dollar assets than to buy them, the exchange rate would have to fall back to its initial equilibrium level, where the demand and supply curves intersect.

Balance of Payments

Because international financial transactions such as foreign exchange interventions have considerable effects on monetary policy, it is worth knowing how these transactions are measured. The **balance of payments** is a bookkeeping system for recording all receipts and payments that have a direct bearing on the movement of funds between a nation (private sector and government) and foreign countries. Here we examine the key items in the balance of payments that you often hear about in the media.

The **current account** shows international transactions that involve currently produced goods and services. The difference between merchandise exports and imports, the net receipts from trade, is called the **trade balance.** When merchandise imports are greater than exports (by $838 billion in 2006), we have a trade deficit; if exports are greater than imports, we have a trade surplus.

Additional items included in the current account are the net receipts (cash flows received from abroad minus cash flows sent abroad) from three categories: investment income, service transactions, and unilateral transfers (gifts, pensions, and foreign aid). In 2006, for example, net investment income was $37 billion for the United States because Americans received more investment income from abroad than they paid out. Americans bought less in services from foreigners than foreigners bought from Americans, so net services generated $80 billion in receipts. Because Americans made more unilateral transfers to foreign countries (especially foreign aid) than foreigners made to the United States, net unilateral transfers were negative $90 bil-

---

[2]A sterilized intervention changes the amount of foreign securities relative to domestic securities in the hands of the public, called a *portfolio balance effect.* Through this effect, the central bank might be able to affect the interest differential between domestic and foreign assets, which in turn affects the relative expected return of domestic assets. Empirical evidence has not revealed this portfolio balance effect to be significant. However, a sterilized intervention *could* indicate what central banks want to happen to the future exchange rate and so might provide a signal about the course of future monetary policy. In this way a sterilized intervention could lead to shifts in the demand curve for domestic assets and ultimately affect the exchange rate. However, the future change in monetary policy—not the sterilized intervention—is the source of the exchange rate effect. For a further discussion of the signaling and portfolio balance effects and the possible differential effects of sterilized versus unsterilized intervention, see Paul Krugman and Maurice Obstfeld, *International Economics*, 7th ed. (Boston: Addison-Wesley, 2006).

lion. The sum of the previous three items plus the trade balance is the current account balance, which in 2006 showed a deficit of −$811 billion (−$838 + $37 + $80 − $90 = −$811 billion).

Another important item in the balance of payments is the **capital account,** the net receipts from capital transactions (e.g., purchases of stocks and bonds, bank loans, etc.). In 2006 the capital account was −$4 billion, indicating that $4 billion more capital flowed out of the United States than came in. Another way of saying this is that the United States had a net capital outflow of $4 billion.[3] The sum of the current account and the capital account equals the **official reserve transactions balance** (net change in government international reserves), which was negative $815 billion in 2006 (−$811 − $4 = −$815 billion). When economists refer to a surplus or deficit in the balance of payments, they actually mean a surplus or deficit in the official reserve transactions balance.

Because the balance of payments must balance, the official reserve transactions balance, which equals the current account plus the capital account, tells us the net amount of international reserves that must move between governments (as represented by their central banks) to finance international transactions: i.e.,

$$\text{Current account} + \text{capital account} = \\ \text{net change in government international reserves}$$

This equation shows us why the current account receives so much attention from economists and the media. The current account balance tells us whether the United States (private sector and government combined) is increasing or decreasing its claims on foreign wealth. A surplus indicates that America is increasing its claims on foreign wealth and thus is increasing its holdings of foreign assets (both good things for Americans); a deficit (as in 2006) indicates that the United States is reducing its holdings of foreign assets and foreign countries are increasing their claims on the United States.[4] The rapid growth in the U.S. current account deficit in recent years, which is now near $1 trillion, has raised serious concerns that these large deficits may have negative consequences for the U.S. economy (see the Global box, "Why the Large U.S. Current Account Deficit Worries Economists").

Exchange Rate Regimes in the International Financial System

Exchange rate regimes in the international financial system are classified into two basic types: fixed and floating. In a **fixed exchange rate regime,** the value of a currency is pegged relative to the value of one other currency (called the **anchor**

---

[3]The capital account balance number reported here includes a statistical discrepancy item that represents errors due to unrecorded transactions involving smuggling and other capital flows (−$18 billion in 2006). Many experts believe that the statistical discrepancy item, which keeps the balance of payments in balance, is primarily the result of large hidden capital flows, and this is why it is included in the capital account balance.

[4]The current account balance can also be viewed as showing the amount by which total saving exceeds private sector and government investment in the United States. Total U.S. saving equals the increase in total wealth held by the U.S. private sector and government. Total investment equals the increase in the U.S. capital stock (wealth physically in the United States). The difference between them is the increase in U.S. claims on foreign wealth.

Why the Large U.S. Current Account Deficit Worries Economists

The massive U.S. current account deficit in recent years, which now exceeds 6% of GDP (the highest level reached over the past century), worries economists for several reasons. First, it indicates that at current exchange rate values, foreigners' demand for U.S. exports is far less than Americans' demand for imports. As we saw in the previous chapter, low demand for U.S. exports and high U.S. demand for imports may lead to a future decline in the value of the U.S. dollar. Some economists estimate that this decline could be very large, with the U.S. dollar depreciating by as much as 50%.

Second, the current account deficit means that foreigners' claims on U.S. assets are growing, and these claims will have to be paid back at some point. Americans are mortgaging their future to foreigners; when the bill comes due, Americans will be poorer. Furthermore, if Americans have a greater preference for dollar assets than foreigners do, the movement of American wealth to foreigners could decrease the demand for dollar assets over time, also causing the dollar to depreciate.

The hope is that the eventual decline in the dollar resulting from the large U.S. current account deficits will be a gradual one, occurring over a period of several years. If the decline is precipitous, however, it could potentially disrupt financial markets and hurt the U.S. economy.

currency) so that the exchange rate is fixed in terms of the anchor currency. In a **floating exchange rate regime,** the value of a currency is allowed to fluctuate against all other currencies. When countries intervene in foreign exchange markets in an attempt to influence their exchange rates by buying and selling foreign assets, the regime is referred to as a **managed float regime** (or a **dirty float**).

Fixed Exchange Rate Regimes

After World War II, the victors set up a fixed exchange rate system that became known as the **Bretton Woods system,** after the New Hampshire town in which the agreement was negotiated in 1944. The Bretton Woods system remained in effect until 1971.

The Bretton Woods agreement created the **International Monetary Fund (IMF),** headquartered in Washington, DC, which had 30 original member countries in 1945 and currently has over 180. The IMF was given the task of promoting the growth of world trade by setting rules for the maintenance of fixed exchange rates and by making loans to countries that were experiencing balance-of-payments difficulties. As part of its role of monitoring the compliance of member countries with its rules, the IMF also took on the job of collecting and standardizing international economic data.

The Bretton Woods agreement also set up the International Bank for Reconstruction and Development, commonly referred to as the **World Bank.** Headquartered in Washington, DC, it provides long-term loans to help developing countries build dams, roads, and other physical capital that would contribute to their economic development. The funds for these loans are obtained primarily by issuing World Bank bonds, which are sold in the capital markets of the developed countries. In addition, the General Agreement on Tariffs and Trade (GATT), headquartered in Geneva, Switzerland, was set up to monitor rules for the conduct of trade between countries (tariffs and quotas). The GATT has since evolved into the **World Trade Organization (WTO).**

Because the United States emerged from World War II as the world's largest economic power, with over half of the world's manufacturing capacity and the greater part of the world's gold, the Bretton Woods system of fixed exchange rates was based on the convertibility of U.S. dollars into gold (for foreign governments and central banks only) at $35 per ounce. The fixed exchange rates were to be maintained by intervention in the foreign exchange market by central banks in countries besides the United States that bought and sold dollar assets, which they held as international reserves. The U.S. dollar, which was used by other countries to denominate the assets that they held as international reserves, was called the **reserve currency.** Thus, an important feature of the Bretton Woods system was the establishment of the United States as the reserve currency country. Even after the breakup of the Bretton Woods system, the U.S. dollar has kept its position as the reserve currency in which most international financial transactions are conducted. However, with the creation of the euro in 1999, the supremacy of the U.S. dollar may be subject to a serious challenge (see the Global box, "The Euro's Challenge to the Dollar").

The fixed exchange rate, dictated by the Bretton Woods system was abandoned in 1971. From 1979 to 1990, however, the European Union instituted among its members its own fixed exchange rate system, the European Monetary System (EMS). In the *exchange rate mechanism (ERM)* in this system, the exchange rate between any pair of currencies of the participating countries was not supposed to fluctuate outside narrow limits, called the "snake." In practice, all of the countries in the EMS pegged their currencies to the German mark.

How a Fixed Exchange Rate Regime Works

Figure 14.2 shows how a fixed exchange rate regime works in practice by using the supply and demand analysis of the foreign exchange market we learned in the previous chapter. Panel (a) describes a situation in which the domestic currency is

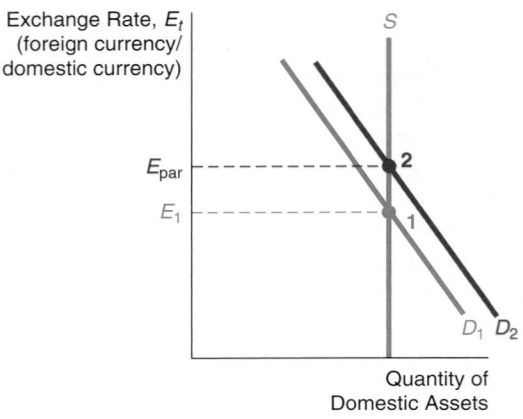
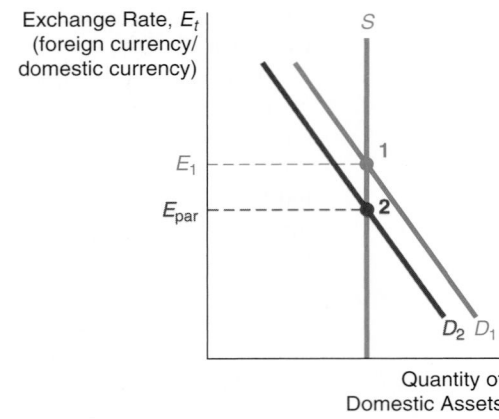

(a) Intervention in the case of an overvalued exchange rate

(b) Intervention in the case of an undervalued exchange rate

Figure 14.2 Intervention in the Foreign Exchange Market Under a Fixed Exchange Rate Regime

In panel (a), the exchange rate at E_{par} is overvalued. To keep the exchange rate at E_{par} (point 2), the central bank must purchase domestic currency to shift the demand curve to D_2. In panel (b), the exchange rate at E_{par} is undervalued, so the central bank must sell domestic currency to shift the demand curve to D_2 and keep the exchange rate at E_{par} (point 2).

fixed relative to an anchor currency at E_{par}, while the demand curve has shifted left to D_1, perhaps because foreign interest rates have risen, thereby lowering the relative expected return of domestic assets. At E_{par} the exchange rate is now *overvalued:* The demand curve D_1 intersects the supply curve at exchange rate E_1, which is lower than the fixed (par) value of the exchange rate E_{par}. To keep the exchange rate at E_{par}, the central bank must intervene in the foreign exchange market to purchase domestic currency by selling foreign assets. This action, like an open market sale, means that both the monetary base and the money supply decline, driving up the interest rate on domestic assets, i^D.[5] This increase in the domestic interest rate raises the relative expected return on domestic assets, shifting the demand curve to the right. The central bank will continue purchasing domestic currency until the demand curve reaches D_2 and the equilibrium exchange rate is at E_{par} at point 2 in panel (a).

We have thus come to the conclusion that *when the domestic currency is overvalued, the central bank must purchase domestic currency to keep the exchange rate fixed, but as a result it loses international reserves.*

Panel (b) in Figure 14.2 describes the situation in which the demand curve has shifted to the right to D_1 because the relative expected return on domestic assets has risen and hence the exchange rate is undervalued: The initial demand curve D_1 intersects the supply curve at exchange rate E_1, which is above E_{par}. In this situation, the central bank must sell domestic currency and purchase foreign assets. This action works like an open market purchase to increase the money supply and lower the interest rate on domestic assets i^D. The central bank keeps selling domestic currency and lowering i^D until the demand curve shifts all the way to D_2, where the equilib-

---

[5]Because the exchange rate will continue to be fixed at E_{par}, the expected future exchange rate remains unchanged and so does not need to be addressed in the analysis.

rium exchange rate is at E_{par}—point 2 in panel (b). Our analysis thus leads us to the following result: ***When the domestic currency is undervalued, the central bank must sell domestic currency to keep the exchange rate fixed, but as a result, it gains international reserves.***

As we have seen, if a country's currency is overvalued, its central bank's attempts to keep the currency from depreciating will result in a loss of international reserves. If the country's central bank eventually runs out of international reserves, it cannot keep its currency from depreciating, and a **devaluation** must occur, in which the par exchange rate is reset at a lower level.

If, by contrast, a country's currency is undervalued, its central bank's intervention to keep the currency from appreciating leads to a gain of international reserves. As we will see shortly, the central bank might not want to acquire these international reserves, and so it might want to reset the par value of its exchange rate at a higher level (a **revaluation**).

If there is perfect capital mobility—that is, if there are no barriers to domestic residents purchasing foreign assets or foreigners purchasing domestic assets—then a sterilized exchange rate intervention cannot keep the exchange rate at E_{par} because, as we saw earlier in the chapter, the relative expected return of domestic assets is unaffected. For example, if the exchange rate is overvalued, a sterilized purchase of domestic currency will leave the relative expected return and the demand curve unchanged—so pressure for a depreciation of the domestic currency is not removed. If the central bank keeps purchasing its domestic currency but continues to sterilize, it will just keep losing international reserves until it finally runs out of them and is forced to let the value of the currency seek a lower level.

One important implication of the foregoing analysis is that a country that ties its exchange rate to an anchor currency of a larger country loses control of its monetary policy. If the larger country pursues a more contractionary monetary policy and decreases its money supply, this would lead to lower expected inflation in the larger country, thus causing an appreciation of the larger country's currency and a depreciation of the smaller country's currency. The smaller country, having locked in its exchange rate to the anchor currency, will now find its currency overvalued and will therefore have to sell the anchor currency and buy its own to keep its currency from depreciating. The result of this foreign exchange intervention will then be a decline in the smaller country's international reserves, a contraction of its monetary base, and thus a decline in its money supply. Sterilization of this foreign exchange intervention is not an option because this would just lead to a continuing loss of international reserves until the smaller country was forced to devalue its currency. The smaller country no longer controls its monetary policy, because movements in its money supply are completely determined by movements in the larger country's money supply.

Another way to see that when a country fixes its exchange rate to a larger country's currency it loses control of its monetary policy is through the interest parity condition discussed in the previous chapter. There we saw that when there is capital mobility, the domestic interest rate equals the foreign interest rate minus the expected appreciation of the domestic currency. With a fixed exchange rate, expected appreciation of the domestic currency is zero, so that the domestic interest rate equals the foreign interest rate. Therefore, changes in the monetary policy in the large anchor country that affect its interest rate are directly transmitted to interest rates in the small country. Furthermore, because the monetary authorities in the small country cannot make their interest rate deviate from that of the larger country, they have no way to use monetary policy to affect their economy.

global

Argentina's Currency Board

Argentina has had a long history of monetary instability, with inflation rates fluctuating dramatically and sometimes surging to beyond 1,000% per year. To end this cycle of inflationary surges, Argentina decided to adopt a currency board in April 1991. The Argentine currency board worked as follows: Under Argentina's convertibility law, the peso/dollar exchange rate was fixed at one to one, and a member of the public could go to the Argentine central bank and exchange a peso for a dollar, or vice versa, at any time.

The early years of Argentina's currency board looked stunningly successful. Inflation, which had been running at an 800% annual rate in 1990, fell to less than 5% by the end of 1994, and economic growth was rapid, averaging almost 8% per year from 1991 to 1994. In the aftermath of the Mexican peso crisis, however, concern about the health of the Argentine economy resulted in the public pulling money out of the banks (deposits fell by 18%) and exchanging pesos for dollars, thus causing a contraction of the Argentine money supply. The result was a sharp drop in Argentine economic activity, with real GDP shrinking by more than 5% in 1995 and the unemployment rate jumping above 15%. Only in 1996 did the economy begin to recover.

Because the central bank of Argentina had no control over monetary policy under the currency board system, it was relatively helpless to counteract the contractionary monetary policy stemming from the public's behavior. Furthermore, because the cur-

rency board did not allow the central bank to create pesos and lend them to the banks, it had very little capability to act as a lender of last resort. With help from international agencies, such as the IMF, the World Bank, and the Interamerican Development Bank, which lent Argentina more than $5 billion in 1995 to help shore up its banking system, the currency board survived.

However, in 1998 Argentina entered another recession, which was both severe and very long lasting. By the end of 2001, unemployment reached nearly 20%, a level comparable to that experienced in the United States during the Great Depression of the 1930s. The result has been civil unrest and the fall of the elected government, as well as a major banking crisis and a default on nearly $150 billion of government debt. Because the Central Bank of Argentina had no control over monetary policy under the currency board system, it was unable to use monetary policy to expand the economy and get out of its recession. Furthermore, because the currency board did not allow the central bank to create pesos and lend them to banks, it had very little capability to act as a lender of last resort. In January 2002, the currency board finally collapsed and the peso depreciated by more than 70%. The result was the full-scale financial crisis (described in Chapter 15), with inflation shooting up and an extremely severe depression. Clearly, the Argentine public is not as enamored of its currency board as it once was.

go online

http://users.erols.com/
kurrency/intro.htm
A detailed discussion of
the history, purpose, and
function of currency boards.

Smaller countries are often willing to tie their exchange rate to that of a larger country in order to inherit the more disciplined monetary policy of their bigger neighbor, thus ensuring a low inflation rate. An extreme example of such a strategy is the **currency board,** in which the domestic currency is backed 100% by a foreign currency (say dollars) and in which the note-issuing authority, whether the central bank or the government, establishes a fixed exchange rate to this foreign currency and stands ready to exchange domestic currency for the foreign currency at this rate whenever the public requests it. Currency boards have been established in countries such as Hong Kong (1983), Argentina (1991), Estonia (1992), Lithuania (1994), Bulgaria (1997), and Bosnia (1998). Argentina's currency board, which operated from 1991 to 2002, is one of the most interesting and is described in the Global box, "Argentina's Currency Board.") An even more extreme strategy is **dollarization,**

global

Dollarization

Dollarization, which involves the adoption of another country's currency, usually the U.S. dollar (but other sound currencies like the euro or the yen are also possibilities), is a more extreme version of a fixed exchange rate than is a currency board. A currency board can be abandoned, allowing a change in the value of the currency, but a change of value is impossible with dollarization: A dollar bill is always worth one dollar whether it is held in the United States or outside of it. Panama has been dollarized since the inception of the country in the early twentieth century, while El Salvador and Ecuador have recently adopted dollarization.

Dollarization, like a currency board, prevents a central bank from creating inflation. Another key advantage is that it completely avoids the possibility of a speculative attack on the domestic currency (because there is none) that is still a danger even

under a currency board arrangement. However, like a currency board, dollarization does not allow a country to pursue its own monetary policy or have a lender of last resort. Dollarization has one additional disadvantage not characteristic of a currency board: Because a country adopting dollarization no longer has its own currency, it loses the revenue that a government receives by issuing money, which is called *seigniorage*. Because governments (or their central banks) do not have to pay interest on their currency, they earn revenue (seigniorage) by using this currency to purchase income-earning assets such as bonds. In the case of the Federal Reserve in the United States, this revenue is on the order of $20 billion dollars per year. If an emerging-market country dollarizes and give up its currency, it needs to make up this loss of revenue somewhere, which is not always easy for a poor country.

in which a country abandons its currency altogether and adopts that of another country, typically the U.S. dollar (see the Global box, "Dollarization").

A serious shortcoming of fixed exchange rate systems such as the Bretton Woods system or the European Monetary System is that they can lead to foreign exchange crises involving a "speculative attack" on a currency—massive sales of a weak currency or purchases of a strong currency that cause a sharp change in the exchange rate. In the following case, we use our model of exchange rate determination to understand how the September 1992 exchange rate crisis that rocked the European Monetary System came about.

CASE

The Foreign Exchange Crisis of September 1992

In the aftermath of German reunification in October 1990, the German central bank, the Bundesbank, faced rising inflationary pressures, with inflation having accelerated from below 3% in 1990 to near 5% by 1992. To get monetary growth under control and to dampen inflation, the Bundesbank raised German interest rates to near double-digit levels. Figure 14.3 shows the consequences of these actions by the Bundesbank in the foreign exchange market for British pounds. Note that in the diagram, the pound is the domestic currency and the German mark (deutsche mark, DM, Germany's currency before the advent of the euro in 1999) is the foreign currency.

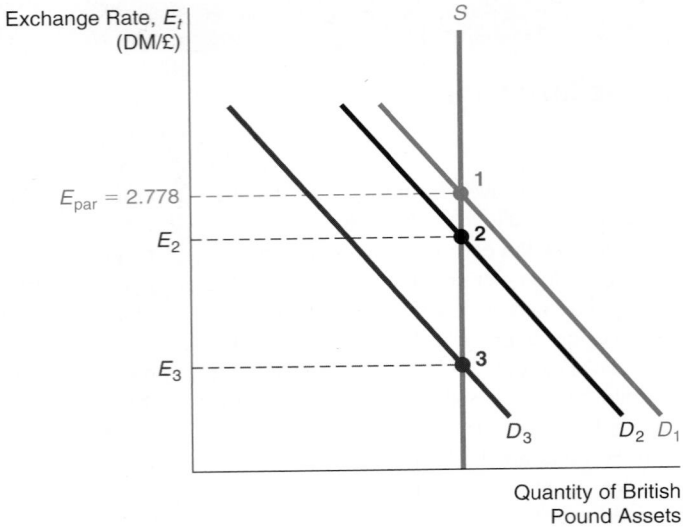

Exchange Rate, E_t
(DM/£)

$E_{par} = 2.778$

E_2

E_3

S

1

2

3

D_3 D_2 D_1

Quantity of British
Pound Assets

Figure 14.3 Foreign Exchange Market for British Pounds in 1992

The realization by speculators that the United Kingdom would soon devalue the pound decreased the relative expected return on British pound assets, resulting in a leftward shift of the demand curve from D_2 to D_3. The result was the need for a much greater purchase of pounds by the British central bank to raise the interest rate so that the demand curve would shift back to D_1 and keep the exchange rate E_{par} at 2.778 German marks per pound.

The increase in German interest rates i^F lowered the relative expected return of British pound assets and shifted the demand curve to D_2 in Figure 14.3. The intersection of the supply and demand curves at point 2 was now below the lower exchange rate limit at that time (2.778 marks per pound, denoted E_{par}). To increase the value of the pound relative to the mark and to restore the mark/pound exchange rate to within the exchange rate mechanism limits, one of two things had to happen. The Bank of England would have to pursue a contractionary monetary policy, thereby raising British interest rates sufficiently to shift the demand curve back to D_1 so that the equilibrium would remain at point 1, where the exchange rate would remain at E_{par}. Alternatively, the Bundesbank would have to pursue an expansionary monetary policy, thereby lowering German interest rates. Lower German interest rates would raise the relative expected return on British assets and shift the demand curve back to D_1 so the exchange rate would be at E_{par}.

The catch was that the Bundesbank, whose primary goal was fighting inflation, was unwilling to pursue an expansionary monetary policy, and the British, who were facing their worst recession in the postwar period, were unwilling to pursue a contractionary monetary policy to prop up the pound. This impasse became clear when in response to great pressure from other members of the EMS, the Bundesbank was willing to lower its lending rates by only a token amount on September 14 after a speculative attack was mounted on the currencies of the Scandinavian countries. So at some point in the near future, the value of the pound would have to decline to point 2. Speculators now knew that the depreciation of the pound was imminent.

As a result, the relative expected return of the pound fell sharply, shifting the demand curve left to D_3 in Figure 14.3.

As a result of the large leftward shift of the demand curve, there was now a huge excess supply of pound assets at the par exchange rate E_{par}, which caused a massive sell-off of pounds (and purchases of marks) by speculators. The need for the British central bank to intervene to raise the value of the pound now became much greater and required a huge rise in British interest rates. After a major intervention effort on the part of the Bank of England, which included a rise in its lending rate from 10% to 15%, which still wasn't enough, the British were finally forced to give up on September 16: They pulled out of the ERM indefinitely and allowed the pound to depreciate by 10% against the mark.

Speculative attacks on other currencies forced devaluation of the Spanish peseta by 5% and the Italian lira by 15%. To defend its currency, the Swedish central bank was forced to raise its daily lending rate to the astronomical level of 500%! By the time the crisis was over, the British, French, Italian, Spanish, and Swedish central banks had intervened to the tune of $100 billion; the Bundesbank alone had laid out $50 billion for foreign exchange intervention. Because foreign exchange crises lead to large changes in central banks' holdings of international reserves and thus significantly affect the official reserve asset items in the balance of payments, these crises are also referred to as **balance-of-payments crises.**

The attempt to prop up the European Monetary System was not cheap for these central banks. It is estimated that they lost $4 to $6 billion as a result of exchange rate intervention during the crisis.

THE PRACTICING MANAGER

Profiting from a Foreign Exchange Crisis

Large banks and other financial institutions often conduct foreign exchange trading operations that generate substantial profits for their parent institution. When a foreign exchange crisis like the one that occurred in September 1992 comes along, foreign exchange traders and speculators are presented with a golden opportunity. The foregoing analysis of this crisis helps explain why.

As we saw in Figure 14.3, the high German interest rates resulted in a situation in which the British pound was overvalued, in that the equilibrium exchange rate in the absence of intervention by the British and German central banks was below the lower exchange rate limit of 2.778 German marks per British pound. Once foreign exchange traders realized that the central banks would not be willing to intervene sufficiently or alter their policies to keep the value of the pound above the 2.778-mark-per-pound lower limit, the traders were presented with a "heads I win, tails you lose" bet. They knew that there was only one direction in which the exchange rate could go—down—and so they were almost sure to make money by buying marks and selling pounds. Our analysis of Figure 14.3 reflects this state of affairs; another way of looking at this one-sided bet is to recognize that it implies that the expected return on mark-denominated deposits increased sharply, shifting the R^F schedule to R_3^F in Figure 14.3.

Savvy foreign exchange traders, who read the writing on the wall early in September 1992, sold pounds and bought marks. When the pound depreciated 10% against the mark after September 16, they made huge profits because the marks they had bought could now be sold at a price 10% higher. Foreign exchange traders at Citibank are reported to have made $200 million in the week of the September 1992 exchange rate crisis—not bad for a week's work! But these profits pale in comparison to those made by George Soros, an investment fund manager whose funds are reported to have run up profits of $1 billion during the crisis. (However, Soros gave some of these profits back in 1994 when he acknowledged that he had suffered a $600 million loss from trades on the yen.) Clearly, foreign exchange trading can be a highly profitable enterprise for financial institutions, particularly during foreign exchange rate crises.

CASE

Recent Foreign Exchange Crises in Emerging Market Countries: Mexico 1994, East Asia 1997, Brazil 1999, and Argentina 2002

Major currency crises in emerging market countries have been a common occurrence in recent years. We can use Figure 14.3 to understand the sequence of events during the currency crises in Mexico in 1994, East Asia in 1997, Brazil in 1999, and Argentina in 2002. To do so, we just need to recognize that dollars are the foreign currency, while the domestic currency was either pesos, baht, or reals. (Note that the exchange rate label on the vertical axis would be in terms of dollars/domestic currency and that the label on the horizontal axis would be the quantity of domestic currency (say, pesos) assets.

In Mexico in March 1994, political instability (the assassination of the ruling party's presidential candidate) sparked investors' concerns that the peso might be devalued. The result was that the relative expected return on peso assets fell, thus moving the demand curve from D_1 to D_2 in Figure 14.3. In the case of Thailand in May 1997, the large current account deficit and the weakness of the Thai financial system raised similar concerns about the devaluation of the domestic currency, with the same effect on the demand curve. In Brazil in late 1998 and Argentina in 2001, concerns about fiscal situations that could lead to the printing of money to finance the deficit, and thereby raise inflation, also meant that a devaluation was more likely to occur. The concerns thus lowered the relative expected return on domestic assets and shifted the demand curve from D_1 to D_2. In all of these cases, the result was that the intersection of the supply and demand curves was below the pegged value of the domestic currency at E_{par}.

To keep their domestic currencies from falling below E_{par}, these countries' central banks needed to buy the domestic currency and sell dollars to raise interest rates and shift the demand curve to the right, in the process losing international reserves. At first, the central banks were successful in containing the speculative attacks. However, when more bad news broke, speculators became even more confident that these countries could not defend their currencies. (The bad news was everywhere: In Mexico, there was an uprising in Chiappas and revelations about problems in the banking system; in Thailand, there was a major failure of a financial institution; Brazil had a worsening fiscal situation, along with a threat by a governor to default on his state's debt; and in Argentina, a full-scale bank panic and an actual default on the government debt occurred.) As a result, the relative expected returns on domestic assets fell further, and the demand curve moved much farther to the left to D_3, and the central banks lost even more international reserves. Given the stress on the economy from rising interest rates and the loss of reserves, eventually the monetary authorities could no longer continue to defend the currency and were forced to give up and let their currencies depreciate. This scenario happened in Mexico in December 1994, in Thailand in July 1997, in Brazil in January 1999, and in Argentina in January 2002.

Concerns about similar problems in other countries then triggered speculative attacks against them as well. This contagion occurred in the aftermath of the Mexican crisis (jauntily referred to as the "Tequila effect") with speculative attacks on other Latin American currencies, but there were no further currency collapses. In the East Asian crisis, however, fears of devaluation spread throughout the region, leading to a scenario akin to that depicted in Figure 14.3. Consequently, one by one, Indonesia, Malaysia, South Korea, and the Philippines were forced to devalue sharply. Even Hong Kong, Singapore, and Taiwan were subjected to speculative attacks, but because these countries had healthy financial systems, the attacks were successfully averted.

As we will see in Chapter 15, the sharp depreciations in Mexico, East Asia, and Argentina led to full-scale financial crises that severely damaged these countries' economies. The foreign exchange crisis that shocked the European Monetary System in September 1992 cost central banks a lot of money, but the public in European countries were not seriously affected. By contrast, the public in Mexico, Argentina, and the crisis countries of East Asia were not so lucky: The collapse of these currencies triggered by speculative attacks led to financial crises, producing severe depressions that caused hardship and political unrest.

CASE

How Did China Accumulate Over $1 Trillion of International Reserves?

By the end of 2007, China had accumulated more than $1 trillion of international reserves, and its international reserves are expected to keep growing in the near future. How did the Chinese get their hands on this vast amount of foreign assets? After all, China is not yet a rich country.

The answer is that China pegged its exchange rate to the U.S. dollar at a fixed rate of 8.28 yuan (also called renminbi) to the dollar in 1994. Because of China's rapidly growing productivity and an inflation rate that is lower than in the United States, the long-run value of the yuan has increased, leading to a higher relative expected return for yuan assets and a rightward shift of the demand for yuan assets. As a result, the Chinese have found themselves in the situation depicted in panel (b) of Figure 14.2, in which the yuan is undervalued. To keep the yuan from appreciating above E_{par} to E_1 in the figure, the Chinese central bank has been engaging in massive purchases of U.S. dollar assets. Today the Chinese government is one of the largest holders of U.S. government bonds in the world.

The pegging of the yuan to the U.S. dollar has created several problems for Chinese authorities. First, the Chinese now own a lot of U.S. assets, particularly U.S. Treasury securities, which have very low returns. Second, the undervaluation of the yuan has meant that Chinese goods are so cheap abroad that many countries have threatened to erect trade barriers against these goods if the Chinese government does not allow an upward revaluation of the yuan. Third, the Chinese purchase of dollar assets has resulted in a substantial increase in the Chinese monetary base and money supply, which has the potential to produce high inflation in the future. Because the Chinese authorities have created substantial roadblocks to capital mobility, they have been able to sterilize most of their exchange rate interventions while maintaining the exchange rate peg. Nevertheless, they still worry about inflationary pressures. In July 2005, China finally made its peg somewhat more flexible by letting the value of the yuan rise 2.1%. The central bank also indicated that it would no longer fix the yuan to the U.S. dollar, but would instead maintain its value relative to a basket of currencies.

Why have the Chinese authorities maintained this exchange rate peg for so long despite the problems? One answer is that they want to keep their export sector humming by keeping the prices of their export goods low. A second answer might be that they want to accumulate a large amount of international reserves as a "war chest" that could be sold to buy yuan in the event of a speculative attack against the yuan at some future date. Given the pressure on the Chinese government to further revalue its currency from government officials in the United States and Europe, there are likely to be further adjustments in China's exchange rate policy in the future.

Managed Float

Although most exchange rates are currently allowed to change daily in response to market forces, many central banks have not been willing to give up their option of intervening in the foreign exchange market. Preventing large changes in exchange rates makes it easier for firms and individuals purchasing or selling goods abroad to plan into the future. Furthermore, countries with surpluses in their balance of payments frequently do not want to see their currencies appreciate, because it makes their goods more expensive abroad and foreign goods cheaper in their country. Because an appreciation might hurt sales for domestic businesses and increase unemployment, surplus countries have often sold their currency in the foreign exchange market and acquired international reserves.

Countries with balance-of-payments deficits do not want to see their currency lose value, because it makes foreign goods more expensive for domestic consumers and can stimulate inflation. To keep the value of the domestic currency high, deficit countries have often bought their own currency in the foreign exchange market and given up international reserves.

The current international financial system is a hybrid of a fixed and a flexible exchange rate system. Rates fluctuate in response to market forces but are not determined solely by them. Furthermore, many countries continue to keep the value of their currency fixed against other currencies.

Capital Controls

Because capital flows were an important element in the currency crises in Mexico and East Asia, politicians and some economists have advocated that emerging market countries avoid financial instability by restricting capital mobility. Are capital controls a good idea?

Controls on Capital Outflows

Capital outflows can promote financial instability in emerging market countries, because when domestic residents and foreigners pull their capital out of a country, the resulting capital outflow forces a country to devalue its currency. This is why some politicians in emerging market countries have recently found capital controls particularly attractive. For example, Prime Minister Mahathir of Malaysia instituted capital controls in 1998 to restrict outflows in the aftermath of the East Asian crisis.

Although these controls sound like a good idea, they suffer from several disadvantages. First, empirical evidence indicates that controls on capital outflows are seldom effective during a crisis because the private sector finds ingenious ways to evade them and has little difficulty moving funds out of the country.[6] Second, the evidence suggests that capital flight may even increase after controls are put into place, because confidence in the government is weakened. Third, controls on capital outflows often lead to corruption, as government officials get paid off to look the other way when domestic residents are trying to move funds abroad. Fourth, controls on capital outflows may lull governments into thinking they do not have to take the steps to reform their financial systems to deal with the crisis, with the result that opportunities to improve the functioning of the economy are lost.

Controls on Capital Inflows

Although most economists find the arguments against controls on capital outflows persuasive, controls on capital inflows receive more support. Supporters reason that if speculative capital cannot come in, then it cannot go out suddenly and create a crisis. Our analysis of the financial crises in East Asia in Chapter 15 provides support for this view by suggesting that capital inflows can lead to a lending boom and excessive risk taking on the part of banks, which then helps trigger a financial crisis.

However, controls on capital inflows have the undesirable feature that they may block from entering a country funds that would be used for productive investment opportunities. Although such controls may limit the fuel supplied to lending booms

---

[6]See Sebastian Edwards, "How Effective are Capital Controls?," *Journal of Economic Perspectives* 13, (Winter 2000): pp. 65–84.

through capital flows, over time they produce substantial distortions and misallocation of resources as households and businesses try to get around them. Indeed, just as with controls on capital outflows, controls on capital inflows can lead to corruption. There are serious doubts whether capital controls can be effective in today's environment, in which trade is open and where there are many financial instruments that make it easier to get around these controls.

On the other hand, there is a strong case for improving bank regulation and supervision so that capital inflows are less likely to produce a lending boom and encourage excessive risk taking by banking institutions. For example, restricting banks in how fast their borrowing can grow might substantially limit capital inflows. Supervisory controls that focus on the sources of financial fragility, rather than the symptoms, can enhance the efficiency of the financial system rather than hampering it.

The Role of the IMF

The International Monetary Fund was originally set up under the Bretton Woods system to help countries deal with balance-of-payments problems and stay with the fixed exchange rates by lending to deficit countries. When the Bretton Woods system of fixed exchange rates collapsed in 1971, the IMF took on new roles.

Although the IMF no longer attempts to encourage fixed exchange rates, its role as an international lender has become more important recently. This role first came to the fore in the 1980s during the Third World debt crisis, in which the IMF assisted developing countries in repaying their loans. The financial crises in Mexico in 1994–1995 and in East Asia in 1997–1998 led to huge loans by the IMF to these and other affected countries to help them recover from their financial crises and to prevent the spread of these crises to other countries. This role, in which the IMF acts like an international lender of last resort to cope with financial instability, is indeed highly controversial.

Should the IMF Be an International Lender of Last Resort?

As we will see in Chapter 15, in industrialized countries when a financial crisis occurs and the financial system threatens to seize up, domestic central banks can address matters with a lender-of-last-resort operation to limit the degree of instability in the banking system. In emerging market countries, however, where the credibility of the central bank as an inflation fighter may be in doubt and debt contracts are typically short-term and denominated in foreign currencies, a lender-of-last-resort operation becomes a double-edged sword—as likely to exacerbate the financial crisis as to alleviate it. For example, when the U.S. Federal Reserve engaged in a lender-of-last-resort operation during the 1987 stock market crash (Chapter 8), there was almost no sentiment in the markets that there would be substantially higher inflation. However, for a central bank with less inflation-fighting credibility than the Fed, central bank lending to the financial system in the wake of a financial crisis—even under the lender-of-last-resort rhetoric—may well arouse fears of inflation spiraling out of control, causing an even greater currency depreciation and still greater deterioration of balance sheets. The resulting increase in moral hazard and adverse selection problems in financial markets would only worsen the financial crisis.

Central banks in emerging market countries therefore have only a very limited ability to successfully engage in a lender-of-last-resort operation. However, liquidity provided by an international lender of last resort does not have these undesirable consequences, and in helping to stabilize the value of the domestic currency, it strengthens domestic balance sheets. Moreover, an international lender of last resort may be able to prevent contagion, the situation in which a successful speculative attack on one emerging market currency leads to attacks on other emerging market currencies, spreading financial and economic disruption as it goes. Because a lender of last resort for emerging market countries is needed at times, and because it cannot be provided domestically, there is a strong rationale for an international institution to fill this role. Indeed, since Mexico's financial crisis in 1994, the International Monetary Fund and other international agencies have stepped into the lender-of-last-resort role and provided emergency lending to countries threatened by financial instability.

However, support from an international lender of last resort brings risks of its own, especially the risk that the perception it is standing ready to bail out irresponsible financial institutions may lead to excessive risk taking of the sort that makes financial crises more likely. In the Mexican and East Asian crises, governments in the crisis countries used IMF support to protect depositors and other creditors of banking institutions from losses. This safety net creates a well-known moral hazard problem because the depositors and other creditors have less incentive to monitor these banking institutions and withdraw their deposits if the institutions are taking on too much risk. The result is that these institutions are encouraged to take on excessive risks. Indeed, critics of the IMF—most prominently, the Congressional Commission headed by Professor Alan Meltzer of Carnegie-Mellon University—contend that IMF lending in the Mexican crisis, which was used to bail out foreign lenders, set the stage for the East Asian crisis, because these lenders expected to be bailed out if things went wrong, and thus provided funds that were used to fuel excessive risk taking.[7]

An international lender of last resort must find ways to limit this moral hazard problem, or it can actually make the situation worse. The international lender of last resort can make it clear that it will extend liquidity only to governments that put the proper measures in place to prevent excessive risk taking. In addition, it can reduce the incentives for risk taking by restricting the ability of governments to bail out stockholders and large uninsured creditors of domestic financial institutions. Some critics of the IMF believe that the IMF has not put enough pressure on the governments to which it lends to contain the moral hazard problem.

One problem that arises for international organizations like the IMF engaged in lender-of-last-resort operations is that they know that if they don't come to the rescue, the emerging market country will suffer extreme hardship and possible political instability. Politicians in the crisis country may exploit these concerns and engage in a game of chicken with the international lender of last resort: They resist necessary reforms, hoping that the IMF will cave in. Elements of this game were present in the Mexican crisis of 1994 and were also a particularly important feature of the negotiations between the IMF and Indonesia during the Asian crisis.

---

[7]See International Financial Institution Advisory Commission, *Report* (IFIAC: Washington, DC, 2000).

How Should the IMF Operate?

The IMF would produce better outcomes if it made clear that it will not play this game. Just as giving in to ill-behaved children may be the easy way out in the short run, but supports a pattern of poor behavior in the long run, some critics worry that the IMF may not be tough enough when confronted by short-run humanitarian concerns. For example, these critics have been particularly critical of the IMF's lending to the Russian government, which resisted adopting appropriate reforms to stabilize its financial system.

The IMF has also been criticized for imposing on the East Asian countries so-called austerity programs that focus on tight macroeconomic policies rather than on microeconomic policies to fix the crisis-causing problems in the financial sector. Such programs are likely to increase resistance to IMF recommendations, particularly in emerging market countries. Austerity programs allow politicians in these countries to label institutions such as the IMF as being anti-growth, rhetoric that helps them mobilize the public against the IMF and avoid doing what they really need to do to reform the financial system in their country. IMF programs focused instead on reforms of the financial sector would increase the likelihood that the IMF will be seen as a helping hand in the creation of a more efficient financial system.

An important historical feature of successful lender-of-last-resort operations is that the faster the lending is done, the lower the amount that actually has to be lent. An excellent example involving the Federal Reserve occurred in the aftermath of the stock market crash on October 19, 1987 (Chapter 8). At the end of that day, to service their customers' accounts, securities firms needed to borrow several billion dollars to maintain orderly trading. However, given the unprecedented developments, banks were nervous about extending further loans to these firms. Upon learning this, the Federal Reserve engaged in an immediate lender-of-last-resort operation, making it clear that it would provide liquidity to banks making loans to the securities industry. What is striking about this episode is that the extremely quick intervention of the Fed not only resulted in a negligible impact of the stock market crash on the economy, but also meant that the amount of liquidity that the Fed needed to supply to the economy was not very large.

The ability of the Fed to engage in a lender-of-last-resort operation within a day of a substantial shock to the financial system stands in sharp contrast to the amount of time it has taken the IMF to supply liquidity during the recent crises in emerging market countries. Because IMF lending facilities were originally designed to provide funds after a country was experiencing a balance-of-payments crisis and because the conditions for the loan had to be negotiated, it took several months before the IMF made funds available. By this time, the crises had gotten much worse—and much larger sums of funds were needed to cope with the crisis, often stretching the resources of the IMF. One reason central banks can lend so much more quickly than the IMF is that they have set up procedures in advance to provide loans, with the terms and conditions for this lending agreed upon beforehand. The need for quick provision of liquidity, to keep the loan amount manageable, argues for similar credit facilities at the international lender of last resort, so that funds can be provided quickly as long as the borrower meets conditions such as properly supervising its banks or keeping budget deficits low. A step in this direction was made in 1999 when the IMF set up a new lending facility, the Contingent Credit Line, so that it can provide liquidity faster during a crisis.

The debate on whether the world will be better off with the IMF operating as an international lender of last resort is currently a hot one. Much attention is being focused on making the IMF more effective in performing this role, and redesign of the IMF is at the center of proposals for a new international financial architecture to help reduce international financial instability.

SUMMARY

1. An unsterilized central bank intervention in which the domestic currency is sold to purchase foreign assets leads to a gain in international reserves, an increase in the money supply, and a depreciation of the domestic currency. Available evidence suggests, however, that sterilized central bank interventions have little long-term effect on the exchange rate.

2. The balance of payments is a bookkeeping system for recording all payments between a country and foreign countries that have a direct bearing on the movement of funds between them. The official reserve transactions balance is the sum of the current account balance plus the items in the capital account. It indicates the amount of international reserves that must be moved between countries to finance international transactions.

3. After World War II, the Bretton Woods system and the IMF were established to promote a fixed exchange rate system in which the U.S. dollar, the reserve currency, was convertible into gold. The Bretton Woods system collapsed in 1971. We now have an international financial system that has elements of a managed float and a fixed exchange rate system. Some exchange rates fluctuate from day to day, although central banks intervene in the foreign exchange market, while other exchange rates are fixed.

4. Controls on capital outflows receive support because they may prevent domestic residents and foreigners from pulling capital out of a country during a crisis and make devaluation less likely. Controls on capital inflows make sense under the theory that if speculative capital cannot flow in, then it cannot go out suddenly and create a crisis. However, capital controls suffer from several disadvantages: They are seldom effective, they lead to corruption, and they may allow governments to avoid taking the steps needed to reform their financial systems to deal with the crisis.

5. The IMF has recently taken on the role of an international lender of last resort. Because central banks in emerging market countries are unlikely to be able to perform a lender-of-last-resort operation successfully, an international lender of last resort like the IMF is needed to prevent financial instability. However, the IMF's role as an international lender of last resort creates a serious moral hazard problem that can encourage excessive risk taking and make a financial crisis more likely, but refusing to lend may be politically hard to do. In addition, it needs to be able to provide liquidity quickly during a crisis to keep manageable the amount of funds lent.

KEY TERMS

anchor currency, *p. 343*
balance of payments, *p. 342*
balance-of-payments crises, *p. 351*
Bretton Woods system, *p. 344*
capital account, *p. 343*
currency board, *p. 348*
current account, *p. 342*
devaluation, *p. 347*
dollarization, *p. 348*
fixed exchange rate regime, *p. 343*
floating exchange rate regime, *p. 344*
foreign exchange interventions, *p. 337*

International Monetary Fund (IMF), *p. 344*
international reserves, *p. 338*
managed float regime (dirty float), *p. 344*
official reserves transactions balance, *p. 343*
reserve currency, *p. 345*
revaluation, *p. 347*
sterilized foreign exchange intervention, *p. 340*
trade balance, *p. 342*
unsterilized foreign exchange intervention, *p. 339*
World Bank, *p. 344*
World Trade Organization (WTO), *p. 345*

QUESTIONS

1. If the Federal Reserve buys dollars in the foreign exchange market but conducts an offsetting open market operation to sterilize the intervention, what will be the impact on international reserves, the money supply, and the exchange rate?

2. If the Federal Reserve buys dollars in the foreign exchange market but does not sterilize the intervention, what will be the impact on international reserves, the money supply, and the exchange rate?

3. For each of the following, identify in which part of the balance-of-payments account it appears (current account, capital account, or net change in international reserves) and whether it is a receipt or a payment.

   a. A British subject's purchase of a share of Johnson & Johnson stock

   b. An American's purchase of an airline ticket from Air France

   c. The Swiss government's purchase of U.S. Treasury bills

   d. A Japanese's purchase of California oranges

   e. $50 million of foreign aid to Honduras

   f. A loan by an American bank to Mexico

   g. An American bank's borrowing of Eurodollars

4. Why does a balance-of-payments deficit for the United States have a different effect on its international reserves than a balance-of-payments deficit for the Netherlands?

5. Under fixed exchange rates, if Britian becomes more productive relative to the United States, what foreign exchange intervention is necessary to maintain the fixed exchange rate between dollars and pounds? Which country undertakes this intervention?

6. What is the exchange rate between dollars and Swiss francs if one dollar is convertible into $\frac{1}{20}$ ounce of gold and one Swiss franc is convertible into $\frac{1}{40}$ ounce of gold?

7. If a country's par exchange rate was undervalued during the Bretton Woods fixed exchange rate regime, what kind of intervention would that country's central bank be forced to undertake, and what effect would it have on its international reserves and the money supply?

8. How can a large balance-of-payments surplus contribute to the country's inflation rate?

9. "If a country wants to keep its exchange rate from changing, it must give up some control over its money supply." Is this statement true, false, or uncertain? Explain your answer.

10. Why can balance-of-payments deficits force some countries to implement a contractionary monetary policy?

11. "Balance-of-payments deficits always cause a country to lose international reserves." Is this statement true, false, or uncertain? Explain your answer.

12. How can persistent U.S. balance-of-payments deficits stimulate world inflation?

13. Why did the exchange rate peg lead to difficulties for the countries in the ERM when German reunification occurred?

14. Why is it that in a pure flexible exchange rate system, the foreign exchange market has no direct effects on the monetary base and the money supply? Does this mean that the foreign exchange market has no effect on monetary policy?

15. "The abandonment of fixed exchange rates after 1973 has meant that countries have pursued more independent monetary policies." Is this statement true, false, or uncertain? Explain your answer.

16. Are controls on capital outflows a good idea? Why or why not?

17. Discuss the pros and cons of controls on capital inflows.

18. Why might central banks in emerging-market countries find that engaging in a lender-of-last-resort operation might be counterproductive? Does this provide a rationale for having an international lender of last resort like the IMF?

19. Has the IMF done a good job in performing the role of the international lender of last resort?

20. What steps should an international lender of last resort take to limit moral hazard?

QUANTITATIVE PROBLEMS

1. The Federal Reserve purchases $1,000,000 of foreign assets for $1,000,000. Show the effect of this open market operation using T-accounts.

2. Again, the Federal Reserve purchases $1,000,000 of foreign assets. However, to raise the funds, the trading desk sells $1,000,000 in T-bills. Show the effect of this open market operation using T-accounts.

3. If the interest rate is 4% on euro deposits and 2% on dollar deposits, while the euro is trading at $1.30 per euro, what does the market expect the exchange rate to be one year from now?

4. If the dollar begins trading at $1.30 per euro, with the same interest rates given in Problem 3, and the ECB raises interest rates so that the rate on euro deposits rises by 1 percentage point, what will happen to the exchange rate (assuming that the expected future exchange rate is unchanged)?

5. If the balance in the current account increases by $2 billion while the capital account is off $3.5 billion, what is the impact on governmental international reserves?

WEB EXERCISES

The International Financial System

1. The Federal Reserve publishes information online that explains the workings of the foreign exchange market. One such publication can be found at **www .ny.frb.org/pihome/addpub/usfxm/**. Review the table of contents and open Chapter 10, Evolution of the International Monetary System. Read this chapter and write a one-page summary that discusses why each monetary standard was dropped in favor of the succeeding one.

2. The International Monetary Fund stands ready to help nations facing monetary crises. Go to **www.imf .org**. Click on the tab labeled "About the IMF." What is the stated purpose of the IMF? How many nations participate and when was it established?

WEB APPENDICES

Please visit our Web site at **www.prenhall.com/mishkin_ eakins** to read the Web appendix to Chapter 14:

- **Appendix:** Balance of Payments

PART 5

Fundamentals of Financial Institutions

CHAPTER 15

Why Do Financial Institutions Exist?

Preview

A healthy and vibrant economy requires a financial system that moves funds from people who save to people who have productive investment opportunities. But how does the financial system make sure that your hard-earned savings get channeled to those with productive investment opportunities?

This chapter answers that question by providing a theory for understanding why financial institutions exist to promote economic efficiency. The theoretical analysis focuses on a few simple but powerful economic concepts that enable us to explain features of our financial markets, such as why financial contracts are written as they are, why financial intermediaries are more important than securities markets for getting funds to borrowers, and why financial crises occur and have such severe consequences for the health of the economy.

Basic Facts About Financial Structure Throughout the World

The financial system is complex in structure and function throughout the world. It includes many different types of institutions: banks, insurance companies, mutual funds, stock and bond markets, and so on—all of which are regulated by government. The financial system channels trillions of dollars per year from savers to people with productive investment opportunities. If we take a close look at financial structure all over the world, we find eight basic facts, some of which are quite surprising, that we need to explain to understand how the financial system works.

The bar chart in Figure 15.1 shows how American businesses financed their activities using external funds (those obtained from outside the business itself) in the period 1970–2000 and compares U.S. data to those of Germany, Japan, and Canada. The *Bank Loans* category is made up primarily of loans from depository institutions; *Nonbank Loans* is composed primarily of loans by other financial intermediaries; the *Bonds* category includes marketable debt securities such as corporate bonds and commercial paper; and *Stock* consists of new issues of new equity (stock market shares).

Now let us explore the eight facts.

1. ***Stocks are not the most important source of external financing for businesses.*** Because so much attention in the media is focused on the stock market, many people have the impression that stocks are the most important sources of financing for American corporations. However, as we can see from the bar chart in Figure 15.1, the stock market accounted for only a small fraction of the external financing of American businesses in the 1970–2000 period: 11%.[1] Similarly small figures apply in the other countries presented in Figure 15.1 as well. Why is the stock market less important than other sources of financing in the United States and other countries?

2. ***Issuing marketable debt and equity securities is not the primary way in which businesses finance their operations.*** Figure 15.1 shows that bonds are a far more important source of financing than stocks in the United States (32% versus 11%). However, stocks and bonds combined (43%), which make up the total share of marketable securities, still supply less than one-half of the external funds corporations need to finance their activities. The fact that issuing marketable securities is not the most important source of financing is true elsewhere in the world as well. Indeed, as we see in Figure 15.1, other countries have a much smaller share of external financing supplied by marketable securities than the United States. Why don't businesses use marketable securities more extensively to finance their activities?

3. ***Indirect finance, which involves the activities of financial intermediaries, is many times more important than direct finance, in which businesses raise funds directly from lenders in financial markets.*** Direct finance involves the sale to households of marketable securities such as stocks and bonds. The 43% share of stocks and bonds as a source of external financing for American businesses actually greatly overstates the impor-

---

[1]The 11% figure for the percentage of external financing provided by stocks is based on the flows of external funds to corporations. However, this flow figure is somewhat misleading, because when a share of stock is issued, it raises funds permanently; whereas when a bond is issued, it raises funds only temporarily until they are paid back at maturity. To see this, suppose that a firm raises $1,000 by selling a share of stock and another $1,000 by selling a $1,000 one-year bond. In the case of the stock issue, the firm can hold on to the $1,000 it raised this way, but to hold on to the $1,000 it raised through debt, it has to issue a new $1,000 bond every year. If we look at the flow of funds to corporations over a 30-year period, as in Figure 15.1, the firm will have raised $1,000 with a stock issue only once in the 30-year period, while it will have raised $1,000 with debt 30 times, once in each of the 30 years. Thus, it will look as though debt is 30 times more important than stocks in raising funds, even though our example indicates that they are actually equally important for the firm.

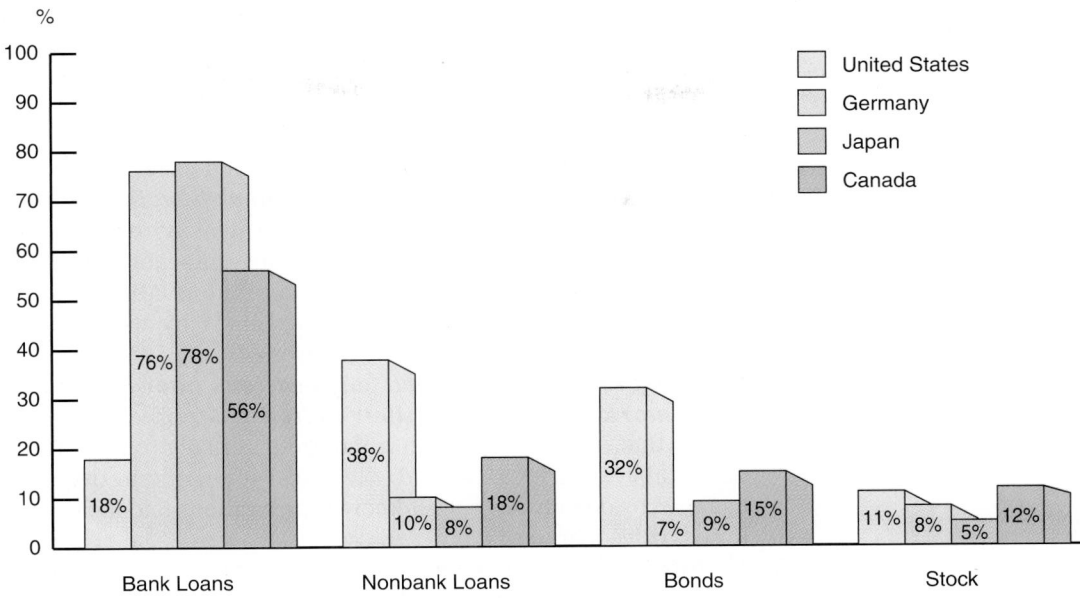

Figure 15.1   Sources of External Funds for Nonfinancial Businesses:
A Comparison of the United States with Germany, Japan, and Canada

Source: Andreas Hackethal and Reinhard H. Schmidt, "Financing Patterns: Measurement Concepts and Empirical Results," Johann Wolfgang Goethe-Universitat Working Paper No. 125, January 2004. The data are from 1970–2000 and are gross flows as percentages of the total, not including trade and other credit data, which are not available.

tance of direct finance in our financial system. Since 1970, less than 5% of newly issued corporate bonds and commercial paper and less than one-third of stocks have been sold directly to American households. The rest of these securities have been bought primarily by financial intermediaries such as insurance companies, pension funds, and mutual funds. These figures indicate that direct finance is used in less than 10% of the external funding of American business. Because in most countries marketable securities are an even less important source of finance than in the United States, direct finance is also far less important than indirect finance in the rest of the world. Why are financial intermediaries and indirect finance so important in financial markets? In recent years, however, indirect finance has been declining in importance. Why is this happening?

4. ***Financial intermediaries, particularly banks, are the most important source of external funds used to finance businesses.*** As we can see in Figure 15.1, the primary source of external funds for businesses throughout the world comprises loans made by banks and other nonbank financial intermediaries (56% in the United States, but more than 70% in Germany, Japan, and Canada). In other industrialized countries, bank loans are the largest category of sources of external finance (more than 70% in Germany and Japan and more than 50% in Canada). Thus, the data suggest that

banks in these countries have the most important role in financing business activities. In developing countries, banks play an even more important role in the financial system than they do in the industrialized countries. What makes banks so important to the workings of the financial system? Although banks remain important, their share of external funds for businesses has been declining in recent years. What is driving this decline?

5. ***The financial system is among the most heavily regulated sectors of the economy.*** The financial system is heavily regulated in the United States and all other developed countries. Governments regulate financial markets primarily to promote the provision of information, and to ensure the soundness (stability) of the financial system. Why are financial markets so extensively regulated throughout the world?

6. ***Only large, well-established corporations have easy access to securities markets to finance their activities.*** Individuals and smaller businesses that are not well established are less likely to raise funds by issuing marketable securities. Instead, they most often obtain their financing from banks. Why do only large, well-known corporations find it easier to raise funds in securities markets?

7. ***Collateral is a prevalent feature of debt contracts for both households and businesses.*** **Collateral** is property that is pledged to a lender to guarantee payment in the event that the borrower is unable to make debt payments. Collateralized debt (also known as **secured debt** to contrast it with **unsecured debt,** such as credit card debt, which is not collateralized) is the predominant form of household debt and is widely used in business borrowing as well. The majority of household debt in the United States consists of collateralized loans: Your automobile is collateral for your auto loan, and your house is collateral for your mortgage. Commercial and farm mortgages, for which property is pledged as collateral, make up one-quarter of borrowing by nonfinancial businesses; corporate bonds and other bank loans also often involve pledges of collateral. Why is collateral such an important feature of debt contracts?

8. ***Debt contracts typically are extremely complicated legal documents that place substantial restrictions on the behavior of the borrower.*** Many students think of a debt contract as a simple IOU that can be written on a single piece of paper. The reality of debt contracts is far different, however. In all countries, bond or loan contracts typically are long legal documents with provisions (called **restrictive covenants**) that restrict and specify certain activities that the borrower can engage in. Restrictive covenants are not just a feature of debt contracts for businesses; for example, personal automobile loan and home mortgage contracts have covenants that require the borrower to maintain sufficient insurance on the automobile or house purchased with the loan. Why are debt contracts so complex and restrictive?

As you may recall from Chapter 2, an important feature of financial markets is that they have substantial transaction and information costs. An economic analysis of how these costs affect financial markets provides us with explanations of the eight facts, which in turn provide us with a much deeper understanding of how our financial system works. In the next section, we examine the impact of transaction costs on the structure of our financial system. Then we turn to the effect of information costs on financial structure.

Transaction Costs

Transaction costs are a major problem in financial markets. An example will make this clear.

How Transaction Costs Influence Financial Structure

Say you have $5,000 you would like to invest, and you think about investing in the stock market. Because you have only $5,000, you can buy only a small number of shares. Even if you use online trading, your purchase is so small that the brokerage commission for buying the stock you picked will be a large percentage of the purchase price of the shares. If instead you decide to buy a bond, the problem is even worse because the smallest denomination for some bonds you might want to buy is as much as $10,000, and you do not have that much to invest. You are disappointed and realize that you will not be able to use financial markets to earn a return on your hard-earned savings. You can take some consolation, however, in the fact that you are not alone in being stymied by high transaction costs. This is a fact of life for many of us: Only around one-half of American households own any securities.

You also face another problem because of transaction costs. Because you have only a small amount of funds available, you can make only a restricted number of investments because a large number of small transactions would result in very high transaction costs. That is, you have to put all your eggs in one basket, and your inability to diversify will subject you to a lot of risk.

How Financial Intermediaries Reduce Transaction Costs

This example of the problems posed by transaction costs and the example outlined in Chapter 2 when legal costs kept you from making a loan to Carl the Carpenter illustrate that small savers like you are frozen out of financial markets and are unable to benefit from them. Fortunately, financial intermediaries, an important part of the financial structure, have evolved to reduce transaction costs and allow small savers and borrowers to benefit from the existence of financial markets.

Economies of Scale One solution to the problem of high transaction costs is to bundle the funds of many investors together so that they can take advantage of *economies of scale*, the reduction in transaction costs per dollar of investment as the size (scale) of transactions increases. Bundling investors' funds together reduces transaction costs for each individual investor. Economies of scale exist because the total cost of carrying out a transaction in financial markets increases only a little as the size of the transaction grows. For example, the cost of arranging a purchase of 10,000 shares of stock is not much greater than the cost of arranging a purchase of 50 shares of stock.

The presence of economies of scale in financial markets helps explain why financial intermediaries developed and have become such an important part of our financial structure. The clearest example of a financial intermediary that arose because of economies of scale is a mutual fund. A *mutual fund* is a financial intermediary that sells shares to individuals and then invests the proceeds in bonds or stocks. Because it buys large blocks of stocks or bonds, a mutual fund can take advantage of lower transaction costs. These cost savings are then passed on to individual investors after the mutual fund has taken its cut in the form of management fees for administering their accounts. An additional benefit for individual investors is that a mutual fund is large enough to purchase a widely diversified portfolio of securities. The increased diversification for individual investors reduces their risk, making them better off.

Economies of scale are also important in lowering the costs of things such as computer technology that financial institutions need to accomplish their tasks. Once a large mutual fund has invested a lot of money in setting up a telecommunications system, for example, the system can be used for a huge number of transactions at a low cost per transaction.

Expertise Financial intermediaries are also better able to develop expertise to lower transaction costs. Their expertise in computer technology enables them to offer customers convenient services like being able to call a toll-free number for information on how well their investments are doing and to write checks on their accounts.

An important outcome of a financial intermediary's low transaction costs is the ability to provide its customers with *liquidity services*, services that make it easier for customers to conduct transactions. Money market mutual funds, for example, not only pay shareholders high interest rates, but also allow them to write checks for convenient bill-paying.

Asymmetric Information: Adverse Selection and Moral Hazard

The presence of transaction costs in financial markets explains in part why financial intermediaries and indirect finance play such an important role in financial markets (fact 3). To understand financial structure more fully, however, we turn to the role of information in financial markets.[2]

Asymmetric information—a situation that arises when one party's insufficient knowledge about the other party involved in a transaction makes it impossible to make accurate decisions when conducting the transaction—is an important aspect of financial markets. For example, managers of a corporation know whether they are honest or have better information about how well their business is doing than the stockholders do. The presence of asymmetric information leads to adverse selection and moral hazard problems, which were introduced in Chapter 2.

Adverse selection is an asymmetric information problem that occurs *before* the transaction: Potential bad credit risks are the ones who most actively seek out loans. Thus, the parties who are the most likely to produce an undesirable outcome are the ones most likely to want to engage in the transaction. For example, big risk takers or outright crooks might be the most eager to take out a loan because they know that they are unlikely to pay it back. Because adverse selection increases the chances that a loan might be made to a bad credit risk, lenders might decide not to make any loans, even though there are good credit risks in the marketplace.

---

[2]An excellent survey of the literature on information and financial structure that expands on the topics discussed in the rest of this chapter is contained in Mark Gertler, "Financial Structure and Aggregate Economic Activity: An Overview," *Journal of Money, Credit and Banking* 20 (1988): 559–588.

Moral hazard arises *after* the transaction occurs: The lender runs the risk that the borrower will engage in activities that are undesirable from the lender's point of view because they make it less likely that the loan will be paid back. For example, once borrowers have obtained a loan, they may take on big risks (which have possible high returns but also run a greater risk of default) because they are playing with someone else's money. Because moral hazard lowers the probability that the loan will be repaid, lenders may decide that they would rather not make a loan.

The analysis of how asymmetric information problems affect economic behavior is called **agency theory.** We will apply this theory here to explain why financial structure takes the form it does, thereby explaining the facts outlined at the beginning of the chapter.

The Lemons Problem: How Adverse Selection Influences Financial Structure

go online

www.nobel.se/economics/
laureates/2001/public.html

A complete discussion of the lemons problem on a site dedicated to Nobel prize winners.

A particular aspect of the way the adverse selection problem interferes with the efficient functioning of a market was outlined in a famous article by Nobel prize winner George Akerlof. It is called the "lemons problem," because it resembles the problem created by lemons in the used-car market.[3] Potential buyers of used cars are frequently unable to assess the quality of the car; that is, they can't tell whether a particular used car is a car that will run well or a lemon that will continually give them grief. The price that a buyer pays must therefore reflect the *average* quality of the cars in the market, somewhere between the low value of a lemon and the high value of a good car.

The owner of a used car, by contrast, is more likely to know whether the car is a peach or a lemon. If the car is a lemon, the owner is more than happy to sell it at the price the buyer is willing to pay, which, being somewhere between the value of a lemon and a good car, is greater than the lemon's value. However, if the car is a peach, the owner knows that the car is undervalued at the price the buyer is willing to pay, and so the owner may not want to sell it. As a result of this adverse selection, few good used cars will come to the market. Because the average quality of a used car available in the market will be low and because few people want to buy a lemon, there will be few sales. The used-car market will function poorly, if at all.

Lemons in the Stock and Bond Markets

A similar lemons problem arises in securities markets—that is, the debt (bond) and equity (stock) markets. Suppose that our friend Irving the Investor, a potential buyer of securities such as common stock, can't distinguish between good firms with high expected profits and low risk and bad firms with low expected profits and high risk. In this situation, Irving will be willing to pay only a price that reflects the *average*

---

[3]George Akerlof, "The Market for 'Lemons': Quality, Uncertainty and the Market Mechanism," *Quarterly Journal of Economics* 84 (1970): 488–500. Two important papers that have applied the lemons problem analysis to financial markets are Stewart Myers and N. S. Majluf, "Corporate Financing and Investment Decisions When Firms Have Information That Investors Do Not Have," *Journal of Financial Economics* 13 (1984): 187–221; and Bruce Greenwald, Joseph E. Stiglitz, and Andrew Weiss, "Information Imperfections in the Capital Market and Macroeconomic Fluctuations," *American Economic Review* 74 (1984): 194–199.

quality of firms issuing securities—a price that lies between the value of securities from bad firms and the value of those from good firms. If the owners or managers of a good firm have better information than Irving and *know* that they are a good firm, they know that their securities are undervalued and will not want to sell them to Irving at the price he is willing to pay. The only firms willing to sell Irving securities will be bad firms (because his price is higher than the securities are worth). Our friend Irving is not stupid; he does not want to hold securities in bad firms, and hence he will decide not to purchase securities in the market. In an outcome similar to that in the used-car market, this securities market will not work very well because few firms will sell securities in it to raise capital.

The analysis is similar if Irving considers purchasing a corporate debt instrument in the bond market rather than an equity share. Irving will buy a bond only if its interest rate is high enough to compensate him for the average default risk of the good and bad firms trying to sell the debt. The knowledgeable owners of a good firm realize that they will be paying a higher interest rate than they should, so they are unlikely to want to borrow in this market. Only the bad firms will be willing to borrow, and because investors like Irving are not eager to buy bonds issued by bad firms, they will probably not buy any bonds at all. Few bonds are likely to sell in this market, so it will not be a good source of financing.

The analysis we have just conducted explains fact 2—why marketable securities are not the primary source of financing for businesses in any country in the world. It also partly explains fact 1—why stocks are not the most important source of financing for American businesses. The presence of the lemons problem keeps securities markets such as the stock and bond markets from being effective in channeling funds from savers to borrowers.

Tools to Help Solve Adverse Selection Problems

In the absence of asymmetric information, the lemons problem goes away. If buyers know as much about the quality of used cars as sellers, so that all involved can tell a good car from a bad one, buyers will be willing to pay full value for good used cars. Because the owners of good used cars can now get a fair price, they will be willing to sell them in the market. The market will have many transactions and will do its intended job of channeling good cars to people who want them.

Similarly, if purchasers of securities can distinguish good firms from bad, they will pay the full value of securities issued by good firms, and good firms will sell their securities in the market. The securities market will then be able to move funds to the good firms that have the most productive investment opportunities.

Private Production and Sale of Information The solution to the adverse selection problem in financial markets is to eliminate asymmetric information by furnishing the people supplying funds with full details about the individuals or firms seeking to finance their investment activities. One way to get this material to saver-lenders is to have private companies collect and produce information that distinguishes good from bad firms and then sell it. In the United States, companies such as Standard and Poor's, Moody's, and Value Line gather information on firms' balance sheet positions and investment activities, publish these data, and sell them to subscribers (individuals, libraries, and financial intermediaries involved in purchasing securities).

The system of private production and sale of information does not completely solve the adverse selection problem in securities markets, however, because of the **free-rider problem.** The free-rider problem occurs when people who do not pay for information take advantage of the information that other people have paid for. The free-rider problem suggests that the private sale of information will be only a partial solution to the lemons problem. To see why, suppose that you have just purchased information that tells you which firms are good and which are bad. You believe that this purchase is worthwhile because you can make up the cost of acquiring this information, and then some, by purchasing the securities of good firms that are undervalued. However, when our savvy (free-riding) investor Irving sees you buying certain securities, he buys right along with you, even though he has not paid for any information. If many other investors act as Irving does, the increased demand for the undervalued good securities will cause their low price to be bid up immediately to reflect the securities' true value. Because of all these free riders, you can no longer buy the securities for less than their true value. Now because you will not gain any profits from purchasing the information, you realize that you never should have paid for this information in the first place. If other investors come to the same realization, private firms and individuals may not be able to sell enough of this information to make it worth their while to gather and produce it. The weakened ability of private firms to profit from selling information will mean that less information is produced in the marketplace, so adverse selection (the lemons problem) will still interfere with the efficient functioning of securities markets.

Government Regulation to Increase Information The free-rider problem prevents the private market from producing enough information to eliminate all the asymmetric information that leads to adverse selection. Could financial markets benefit from government intervention? The government could, for instance, produce information to help investors distinguish good from bad firms and provide it to the public free of charge. This solution, however, would involve the government in releasing negative information about firms, a practice that might be politically difficult. A second possibility (and one followed by the United States and most governments throughout the world) is for the government to regulate securities markets in a way that encourages firms to reveal honest information about themselves so that investors can determine how good or bad the firms are. In the United States, the Securities and Exchange Commission (SEC) is the government agency that requires firms selling their securities to have independent **audits,** in which accounting firms certify that the firm is adhering to standard accounting principles and disclosing accurate information about sales, assets, and earnings. Similar regulations are found in other countries. However, disclosure requirements do not always work well, as the recent collapse of Enron and accounting scandals at other corporations, such as WorldCom and Parmalat (an Italian company) suggest (see the Conflicts of Interest box, "The Enron Implosion").

The asymmetric information problem of adverse selection in financial markets helps explain why financial markets are among the most heavily regulated sectors in the economy (fact 5). Government regulation to increase information for investors is needed to reduce the adverse selection problem, which interferes with the efficient functioning of securities (stock and bond) markets.

Although government regulation lessens the adverse selection problem, it does not eliminate it. Even when firms provide information to the public about their sales, assets, or earnings, they still have more information than investors: There is a lot more to knowing the quality of a firm than statistics can provide. Furthermore, bad firms have an incentive to make themselves look like good firms, because this would enable them to fetch a higher price for their securities. Bad firms will slant the information they are required to transmit to the public, thus making it harder for investors to sort out the good firms from the bad.

conflicts of interest

The Enron Implosion

Until 2001, Enron Corporation, a firm that specialized in trading in the energy market, appeared to be spectacularly successful. It had a quarter of the energy-trading market and was valued as high as $77 billion in August 2000 (just a little over a year before its collapse), making it the seventh-largest corporation in the United States at that time. However, toward the end of 2001, Enron came crashing down. In October 2001, Enron announced a third-quarter loss of $618 million and disclosed accounting "mistakes." The SEC then engaged in a formal investigation of Enron's financial dealings with partnerships led by its former finance chief. It became clear that Enron was engaged in a complex set of transactions by which it was keeping substantial amounts of debt and financial contracts off of its balance sheet. These transactions enabled Enron to hide its financial difficulties. Despite securing as

much as $1.5 billion of new financing from J. P. Morgan Chase and Citigroup, the company was forced to declare bankruptcy in December 2001, the largest bankruptcy in U.S. history.

The Enron collapse illustrates that government regulation can lessen asymmetric information problems, but cannot eliminate them. Managers have tremendous incentives to hide their companies' problems, making it hard for investors to know the true value of the firm.

The Enron bankruptcy not only increased concerns in financial markets about the quality of accounting information supplied by corporations, but also led to hardship for many of the firm's former employees, who found that their pensions had become worthless. Outrage against the duplicity of executives at Enron has been high, and several have been indicted, with some being already convicted and sent to jail.

Financial Intermediation So far we have seen that private production of information and government regulation to encourage provision of information lessen, but do not eliminate, the adverse selection problem in financial markets. How, then, can the financial structure help promote the flow of funds to people with productive investment opportunities when there is asymmetric information? A clue is provided by the structure of the used-car market.

An important feature of the used-car market is that most used cars are not sold directly by one individual to another. An individual considering buying a used car might pay for privately produced information by subscribing to a magazine like *Consumer Reports* to find out if a particular make of car has a good repair record. Nevertheless, reading *Consumer Reports* does not solve the adverse selection problem, because even if a particular make of car has a good reputation, the specific car someone is trying to sell could be a lemon. The prospective buyer might also bring the used car to a mechanic for a once-over. But what if the prospective buyer doesn't know a mechanic who can be trusted or if the mechanic would charge a high fee to evaluate the car?

Because these roadblocks make it hard for individuals to acquire enough information about used cars, most used cars are not sold directly by one individual to another. Instead, they are sold by an intermediary, a used-car dealer who purchases used cars from individuals and resells them to other individuals. Used-car dealers produce information in the market by becoming experts in determining whether a car is a peach or a lemon. Once they know that a car is good, they can sell it with some form of a guarantee: either a guarantee that is explicit, such as a warranty, or an implicit guarantee, in which they stand by their reputation for honesty. People are more likely to purchase a used car because of a dealer's guarantee, and the dealer is able to make a profit on the production of information about automobile quality by being able to sell the used car at a higher price than the dealer paid for it. If dealers purchase and then resell cars on which they have produced information, they avoid the problem of other people free-riding on the information they produced.

Just as used-car dealers help solve adverse selection problems in the automobile market, financial intermediaries play a similar role in financial markets. A financial intermediary, such as a bank, becomes an expert in producing information about firms, so that it can sort out good credit risks from bad ones. Then it can acquire funds from depositors and lend them to the good firms. Because the bank is able to lend mostly to good firms, it is able to earn a higher return on its loans than the interest it has to pay to its depositors. The resulting profit that the bank earns gives it the incentive to engage in this information production activity.

An important element in the bank's ability to profit from the information it produces is that it avoids the free-rider problem by primarily making private loans rather than by purchasing securities that are traded in the open market. Because a private loan is not traded, other investors cannot watch what the bank is doing and bid up the loan's price to the point that the bank receives no compensation for the information it has produced. The bank's role as an intermediary that holds mostly nontraded loans is the key to its success in reducing asymmetric information in financial markets.

Our analysis of adverse selection indicates that financial intermediaries in general—and banks in particular, because they hold a large fraction of nontraded loans—should play a greater role in moving funds to corporations than securities markets do. Our analysis thus explains facts 3 and 4: why indirect finance is so much more important than direct finance and why banks are the most important source of external funds for financing businesses.

Another important fact that is explained by the analysis here is the greater importance of banks in the financial systems of developing countries. As we have seen, when the quality of information about firms is better, asymmetric information problems will be less severe, and it will be easier for firms to issue securities. Information about private firms is harder to collect in developing countries than in industrialized countries; therefore, the smaller role played by securities markets leaves a greater role for financial intermediaries such as banks. A corollary of this analysis is that as information about firms becomes easier to acquire, the role of banks should decline. A major development in the past 20 years in the United States has been huge improvements in information technology. Thus, the analysis here suggests that the lending role of financial institutions, such as banks in the United States, should have declined, and this is exactly what has occurred (see Chapter 18).

Our analysis of adverse selection also explains fact 6, which questions why large firms are more likely to obtain funds from securities markets, a direct route, rather than from banks and financial intermediaries, an indirect route. The better known a corporation is, the more information about its activities is available in the marketplace. Thus, it is easier for investors to evaluate the quality of the corporation and determine whether it is a good firm or a bad one. Because investors have fewer worries about adverse selection with well-known corporations, they will be willing to invest directly in their securities. Our adverse selection analysis thus suggests that there should be a pecking order for firms that can issue securities. The larger and more established a corporation is, the more likely it will be to issue securities to raise funds, a view that is known as the **pecking order hypothesis.** This hypothesis is supported in the data and is what fact 6 describes.

Collateral and Net Worth Adverse selection interferes with the functioning of financial markets only if a lender suffers a loss when a borrower is unable to make loan payments and thereby defaults. *Collateral*, property promised to the lender if the borrower defaults, reduces the consequences of adverse selection because it reduces the lender's losses in the event of a default. If a borrower defaults on a loan, the lender can sell the collateral and use the proceeds to make up for the losses on the loan. For example, if you fail to make your mortgage payments, the lender can take title to your house, auction it off, and use the receipts to pay off the loan. Lenders are thus more willing to make loans secured by collateral, and borrowers are willing to supply collateral because the reduced risk for the lender makes it more likely they will get the loan in the first place and perhaps at a better loan rate. The presence of adverse selection in credit markets thus provides an explanation for why collateral is an important feature of debt contracts (fact 7).

Net worth (also called **equity capital**), the difference between a firm's assets (what it owns or is owed) and its liabilities (what it owes), can perform a similar role to collateral. If a firm has a high net worth, then even if it engages in investments that cause it to have negative profits and so defaults on its debt payments, the lender can take title to the firm's net worth, sell it off, and use the proceeds to recoup some of the losses from the loan. In addition, the more net worth a firm has in the first place, the less likely it is to default, because the firm has a cushion of assets that it can use to pay off its loans. Hence, when firms seeking credit have high net worth, the consequences of adverse selection are less important and lenders are more willing to make loans. This analysis lies behind the often-heard lament, "Only the people who don't need money can borrow it!"

Summary So far we have used the concept of adverse selection to explain seven of the eight facts about financial structure introduced earlier: The first four emphasize the importance of financial intermediaries and the relative unimportance of securities markets for the financing of corporations; the fifth, that financial markets are among the most heavily regulated sectors of the economy; the sixth, that only large, well-established corporations have access to securities markets; and the seventh, that collateral is an important feature of debt contracts. In the next section, we will see that the other asymmetric information concept of moral hazard provides additional reasons for the importance of financial intermediaries and the relative unimportance of securities markets for the financing of corporations, the prevalence of government regulation, and the importance of collateral in debt contracts. In addition, the concept of moral hazard can be used to explain our final fact (fact 8): why debt contracts are complicated legal documents that place substantial restrictions on the behavior of the borrower.

How Moral Hazard Affects the Choice Between Debt and Equity Contracts

Moral hazard is the asymmetric information problem that occurs after the financial transaction takes place, when the seller of a security may have incentives to hide information and engage in activities that are undesirable for the purchaser of the security. Moral hazard has important consequences for whether a firm finds it easier to raise funds with debt than with equity contracts.

Moral Hazard in Equity Contracts: The Principal–Agent Problem

Equity contracts, such as common stock, are claims to a share in the profits and assets of a business. Equity contracts are subject to a particular type of moral hazard called the **principal–agent problem.** When managers own only a small fraction of the firm they work for, the stockholders who own most of the firm's equity (called the *principals*) are not the same people as the managers of the firm, who are the *agents* of the owners. This separation of ownership and control involves moral hazard, in that the managers in control (the agents) may act in their own interest rather than in the interest of the stockholder-owners (the principals) because the managers have less incentive to maximize profits than the stockholder-owners do.

To understand the principal–agent problem more fully, suppose that your friend Steve asks you to become a silent partner in his ice cream store. The store requires an investment of $10,000 to set up and Steve has only $1,000. So you purchase an equity stake (stock shares) for $9,000, which entitles you to 90% of the ownership of the firm, while Steve owns only 10%. If Steve works hard to make tasty ice cream, keeps the store clean, smiles at all the customers, and hustles to wait on tables quickly, after all expenses (including Steve's salary), the store will have $50,000 in profits per year, of which Steve receives 10% ($5,000) and you receive 90% ($45,000).

But if Steve doesn't provide quick and friendly service to his customers, uses the $50,000 in income to buy artwork for his office, and even sneaks off to the beach while he should be at the store, the store will not earn any profit. Steve can earn the additional $5,000 (his 10% share of the profits) over his salary only if he works hard and forgoes unproductive investments (such as art for his office). Steve might decide that the extra $5,000 just isn't enough to make him expend the effort to be a good manager; he might decide that it would be worth his while only if he earned an extra $10,000. If Steve feels this way, he does not have enough incentive to be a good manager and will end up with a beautiful office, a good tan, and a store that doesn't show any profits. Because the store won't show any profits, Steve's decision not to act in your interest will cost you $45,000 (your 90% of the profits if he had chosen to be a good manager instead).

The moral hazard arising from the principal–agent problem might be even worse if Steve were not totally honest. Because his ice cream store is a cash business, Steve has the incentive to pocket $50,000 in cash and tell you that the profits were zero. He now gets a return of $50,000 and you get nothing.

Further indications that the principal–agent problem created by equity contracts can be severe are provided by recent scandals in corporations such as Enron and Tyco International, in which managers have been accused and convicted of diverting funds for their own personal use. Besides pursuing personal benefits, managers might also pursue corporate strategies (such as the acquisition of other firms) that enhance their personal power but do not increase the corporation's profitability.

The principal–agent problem would not arise if the owners of a firm had complete information about what the managers were up to and could prevent wasteful expenditures or fraud. The principal–agent problem, which is an example of moral hazard, arises only because a manager, such as Steve, has more information about his activities than the stockholder does—that is, there is asymmetric information. The principal–agent problem would also not arise if Steve alone owned the store and there were no separation of ownership and control. If this were the case, Steve's hard work and avoidance of unproductive investments would yield him a profit (and extra income) of $50,000, an amount that would make it worth his while to be a good manager.

Tools to Help Solve the Principal–Agent Problem

Production of Information: Monitoring You have seen that the principal–agent problem arises because managers have more information about their activities and actual profits than stockholders do. One way for stockholders to reduce this moral hazard problem is for them to engage in a particular type of information production, the monitoring of the firm's activities: auditing the firm frequently and checking on what the management is doing. The problem is that the monitoring process can be expensive in terms of time and money, as reflected in the name economists give it, **costly state verification.** Costly state verification makes the equity contract less desirable, and it explains, in part, why equity is not a more important element in our financial structure.

As with adverse selection, the free-rider problem decreases the amount of information production undertaken to reduce the moral hazard (principal–agent) problem. In this example, the free-rider problem decreases monitoring. If you know that other stockholders are paying to monitor the activities of the company you hold shares in, you can take a free ride on their activities. Then you can use the money you save by not engaging in monitoring to vacation on a Caribbean island. If you can do this, though, so can other stockholders. Perhaps all the stockholders will go to the islands, and no one will spend any resources on monitoring the firm. The moral hazard problem for shares of common stock will then be severe, making it hard for firms to issue them to raise capital (providing an additional explanation for fact 1).

Government Regulation to Increase Information As with adverse selection, the government has an incentive to try to reduce the moral hazard problem created by asymmetric information, which provides another reason why the financial system is so heavily regulated (fact 5). Governments everywhere have laws to force firms to adhere to standard accounting principles that make profit verification easier. They also pass laws to impose stiff criminal penalties on people who commit the fraud of hiding and stealing profits. However, these measures can be only partly effective. Catching this kind of fraud is not easy; fraudulent managers have the incentive to make it very hard for government agencies to find or prove fraud.

Financial Intermediation Financial intermediaries have the ability to avoid the free-rider problem in the face of moral hazard, and this is another reason why indirect finance is so important (fact 3). One financial intermediary that helps reduce the moral hazard arising from the principal–agent problem is the **venture capital firm.** Venture capital firms pool the resources of their partners and use the funds to help budding entrepreneurs start new businesses. In exchange for the use of the venture capital, the firm receives an equity share in the new business. Because verification of earnings and profits is so important in eliminating moral hazard, venture capital firms usually insist on having several of their own people participate as members of the managing body of the firm, the board of directors, so that they can keep a close watch on the firm's activities. When a venture capital firm supplies start-up funds, the equity in the firm is not marketable to anyone *except* the venture capital firm. Thus, other investors are unable to take a free ride on the venture capital firm's verification activities. As a result of this arrangement, the venture capital firm is able to garner the full benefits of its verification activities and is given the appropriate incentives to reduce the moral hazard problem. Venture capital firms have been important in the development of the high-tech sector in the United States, which has resulted in job creation, economic growth, and increased international competitiveness.

Debt Contracts Moral hazard arises with an equity contract, which is a claim on profits in all situations, whether the firm is making or losing money. If a contract could be structured so that moral hazard would exist only in certain situations, there would be a reduced need to monitor managers, and the contract would be more attractive than the equity contract. The debt contract has exactly these attributes because it is a contractual agreement by the borrower to pay the lender *fixed* dollar amounts at periodic intervals. When the firm has high profits, the lender receives the contractual payments and does not need to know the exact profits of the firm. If the managers are hiding profits or are pursuing activities that are personally beneficial but don't increase profitability, the lender doesn't care as long as these activities do not interfere with the ability of the firm to make its debt payments on time. Only when the firm cannot meet its debt payments, thereby being in a state of default, is there a need for the lender to verify the state of the firm's profits. Only in this situation do lenders involved in debt contracts need to act more like equity holders; now they need to know how much income the firm has to get their fair share.

The less frequent need to monitor the firm, and thus the lower cost of state verification, helps explain why debt contracts are used more frequently than equity contracts to raise capital. The concept of moral hazard thus helps explain fact 1, why stocks are not the most important source of financing for businesses.[4]

How Moral Hazard Influences Financial Structure in Debt Markets

Even with the advantages just described, debt contracts are still subject to moral hazard. Because a debt contract requires the borrowers to pay out a fixed amount and lets them keep any profits above this amount, the borrowers have an incentive to take on investment projects that are riskier than the lenders would like.

For example, suppose that because you are concerned about the problem of verifying the profits of Steve's ice cream store, you decide not to become an equity partner. Instead, you lend Steve the $9,000 he needs to set up his business and have

---

[4]Another factor that encourages the use of debt contracts rather than equity contracts in the United States is our tax code. Debt interest payments are a deductible expense for American firms, whereas dividend payments to equity shareholders are not.

a debt contract that pays you an interest rate of 10%. As far as you are concerned, this is a surefire investment because there is a strong and steady demand for ice cream in your neighborhood. However, once you give Steve the funds, he might use them for purposes other than you intended. Instead of opening up the ice cream store, Steve might use your $9,000 loan to invest in chemical research equipment because he thinks he has a 1-in-10 chance of inventing a diet ice cream that tastes every bit as good as the premium brands but has no fat or calories.

Obviously, this is a very risky investment, but if Steve is successful, he will become a multimillionaire. He has a strong incentive to undertake the riskier investment with your money, because the gains to him would be so large if he succeeded. You would clearly be very unhappy if Steve used your loan for the riskier investment, because if he were unsuccessful, which is highly likely, you would lose most, if not all, of the money you gave him. And if he were successful, you wouldn't share in his success—you would still get only a 10% return on the loan because the principal and interest payments are fixed. Because of the potential moral hazard (that Steve might use your money to finance a very risky venture), you would probably not make the loan to Steve, even though an ice cream store in the neighborhood is a good investment that would provide benefits for everyone.

Tools to Help Solve Moral Hazard in Debt Contracts

Net Worth and Collateral When borrowers have more at stake because their net worth (the difference between their assets and their liabilities) is high or the collateral they have pledged to the lender is valuable, the risk of moral hazard—the temptation to act in a manner that lenders find objectionable—will be greatly reduced because the borrowers themselves have a lot to lose. Let's return to Steve and his ice cream business. Suppose that the cost of setting up either the ice cream store or the research equipment is $100,000 instead of $10,000. So Steve needs to put $91,000 of his own money into the business (instead of $1,000) in addition to the $9,000 supplied by your loan. Now if Steve is unsuccessful in inventing the no-calorie nonfat ice cream, he has a lot to lose—the $91,000 of net worth ($100,000 in assets minus the $9,000 loan from you). He will think twice about undertaking the riskier investment and is more likely to invest in the ice cream store, which is more of a sure thing. Hence, when Steve has more of his own money (net worth) in the business, you are more likely to make him the loan. Similarly, if you have pledged your house as collateral, you are less likely to go to Las Vegas and gamble away your earnings that month because you might not be able to make your mortgage payments and might lose your house.

One way of describing the solution that high net worth and collateral provides to the moral hazard problem is to say that it makes the debt contract **incentive compatible;** that is, it aligns the incentives of the borrower with those of the lender. The greater the borrower's net worth and collateral pledged, the greater the borrower's incentive to behave in the way that the lender expects and desires, the smaller the moral hazard problem in the debt contract, and the easier it is for the firm or household to borrow. Conversely, when the borrower's net worth and collateral are lower, the moral hazard problem is greater, and it is harder to borrow.

Monitoring and Enforcement of Restrictive Covenants As the example of Steve and his ice cream store shows, if you could make sure that Steve doesn't invest in anything riskier than the ice cream store, it would be worth your while to make him the loan. You can ensure that Steve uses your money for the purpose *you* want it to be used for by writing provisions (restrictive covenants) into the debt contract that restrict his firm's activities. By monitoring Steve's activities to see whether he is complying with the restrictive covenants and enforcing the covenants if he is not, you can make sure that he will not take on risks at your expense. Restrictive covenants are directed at reducing moral hazard either by ruling out undesirable behavior or by encouraging desirable behavior. There are four types of restrictive covenants that achieve this objective:

1. *Covenants to discourage undesirable behavior.* Covenants can be designed to lower moral hazard by keeping the borrower from engaging in the undesirable behavior of undertaking risky investment projects. Some covenants mandate that a loan can be used only to finance specific activities, such as the purchase of particular equipment or inventories. Others restrict the borrowing firm from engaging in certain risky business activities, such as purchasing other businesses.

2. *Covenants to encourage desirable behavior.* Restrictive covenants can encourage the borrower to engage in desirable activities that make it more likely that the loan will be paid off. One restrictive covenant of this type requires the breadwinner in a household to carry life insurance that pays off the mortgage upon that person's death. Restrictive covenants of this type for businesses focus on encouraging the borrowing firm to keep its net worth high because higher borrower net worth reduces moral hazard and makes it less likely that the lender will suffer losses. These restrictive covenants typically specify that the firm must maintain minimum holdings of certain assets relative to the firm's size.

3. *Covenants to keep collateral valuable.* Because collateral is an important protection for the lender, restrictive covenants can encourage the borrower to keep the collateral in good condition and make sure that it stays in the possession of the borrower. This is the type of covenant ordinary people encounter most often. Automobile loan contracts, for example, require the car owner to maintain a minimum amount of collision and theft insurance and prevent the sale of the car unless the loan is paid off. Similarly, the recipient of a home mortgage must have adequate insurance on the home and must pay off the mortgage when the property is sold.

4. *Covenants to provide information.* Restrictive covenants also require a borrowing firm to provide information about its activities periodically in the form of quarterly accounting and income reports, thereby making it easier for the lender to monitor the firm and reduce moral hazard. This type of covenant may also stipulate that the lender has the right to audit and inspect the firm's books at any time.

We now see why debt contracts are often complicated legal documents with numerous restrictions on the borrower's behavior (fact 8): Debt contracts require complicated restrictive covenants to lower moral hazard.

Financial Intermediation Although restrictive covenants help reduce the moral hazard problem, they do not eliminate it completely. It is almost impossible to write covenants that rule out *every* risky activity. Furthermore, borrowers may be clever enough to find loopholes in restrictive covenants that make them ineffective.

Another problem with restrictive covenants is that they must be monitored and enforced. A restrictive covenant is meaningless if the borrower can violate it knowing that the lender won't check up or is unwilling to pay for legal recourse. Because monitoring and enforcement of restrictive covenants are costly, the free-rider problem arises in the debt securities (bond) market just as it does in the stock market. If you know that other bondholders are monitoring and enforcing the restrictive covenants, you can free-ride on their monitoring and enforcement. But other bondholders can do the same thing, so the likely outcome is that not enough resources are devoted to monitoring and enforcing the restrictive covenants. Moral hazard therefore continues to be a severe problem for marketable debt.

As we have seen before, financial intermediaries—particularly banks—have the ability to avoid the free-rider problem as long as they make primarily private loans. Private loans are not traded, so no one else can free-ride on the intermediary's monitoring and enforcement of the restrictive covenants. The intermediary making private loans thus receives the benefits of monitoring and enforcement and will work to shrink the moral hazard problem inherent in debt contracts. The concept of moral hazard has provided us with additional reasons why financial intermediaries play a more important role in channeling funds from savers to borrowers than marketable securities do, as described in facts 3 and 4.

Summary

The presence of asymmetric information in financial markets leads to adverse selection and moral hazard problems that interfere with the efficient functioning of those markets. Tools to help solve these problems involve the private production and sale of information, government regulation to increase information in financial markets, the importance of collateral and net worth to debt contracts, and the use of monitoring and restrictive covenants. A key finding from our analysis is that the existence of the free-rider problem for traded securities such as stocks and bonds indicates that financial intermediaries—particularly banks—should play a greater role than securities markets in financing the activities of businesses. Economic analysis of the consequences of adverse selection and moral hazard has helped explain the basic features of our financial system and has provided solutions to the eight facts about our financial structure outlined at the beginning of this chapter.

study guide

To help you keep track of all the tools that help solve asymmetric information problems, Table 15.1 summarizes the asymmetric information problems and tools that help solve them. In addition, it notes how these tools and asymmetric information problems explain the eight facts of financial structure described at the beginning of the chapter.

Table 15.1 Summary Asymmetric Information Problems and Tools to Solve Them

Asymmetric Information Problem	Tools to Solve It	Explains Fact Number
Adverse selection	Private production and sale of information	1, 2
	Government regulation to increase information	5
	Financial intermediation	3, 4, 6
	Collateral and net worth	7
Moral hazard in equity contracts (principal–agent problem)	Production of information: monitoring	1
	Government regulation to increase information	5
	Financial intermediation	3
	Debt contracts	1
Moral hazard in debt contracts	Collateral and net worth	6, 7
	Monitoring and enforcement of restrictive covenants	8
	Financial intermediation	3, 4

Note: List of facts:
1. Stocks are not the most important source of external financing.
2. Marketable securities are not the primary source of finance.
3. Indirect finance is more important than direct finance.
4. Banks are the most important source of external funds.
5. The financial system is heavily regulated.
6. Only large, well-established firms have access to securities markets.
7. Collateral is prevalent in debt contracts.
8. Debt contracts have numerous restrictive covenants.

CASE

Financial Development and Economic Growth

Recent research has found that an important reason why many developing countries or ex-communist countries like Russia (which are referred to as *transition countries*) experience very low rates of growth is that their financial systems are underdeveloped (a situation referred to as *financial repression*).[5] The economic analysis of financial structure helps explain how an underdeveloped financial system leads to a low state of economic development and economic growth.

The financial systems in developing and transition countries face several difficulties that keep them from operating efficiently. As we have seen, two important tools used to help solve adverse selection and moral hazard problems in credit markets are collateral and restrictive covenants. In many developing countries, the

---

[5]See World Bank, *Finance for Growth: Policy Choices in a Volatile World* (World Bank and Oxford University Press, 2001) for a survey of the literature linking economic growth with financial development and a list of additional references.

system of property rights (the rule of law, constraints on government expropriation, absence of corruption) functions poorly, making it hard to make effective use of these two tools. In these countries, bankruptcy procedures are often extremely slow and cumbersome. For example, in many countries, **creditors** (holders of debt) must first sue the defaulting debtor for payment, which can take several years; then, once a favorable judgment has been obtained, the creditor has to sue again to obtain title to the collateral. The process can take in excess of five years, and by the time the lender acquires the collateral, it well may have been neglected and thus have little value. In addition, governments often block lenders from foreclosing on borrowers in politically powerful sectors such as agriculture. Where the market is unable to use collateral effectively, the adverse selection problem will be worse, because the lender will need even more information about the quality of the borrower so that it can screen out a good loan from a bad one. The result is that it will be harder for lenders to channel funds to borrowers with the most productive investment opportunities. There will be less productive investment, and hence a slower-growing economy. Similarly, a poorly developed or corrupt legal system may make it extremely difficult for lenders to enforce restrictive covenants. Thus, they may have a much more limited ability to reduce moral hazard on the part of borrowers and so will be less willing to lend. Again the outcome will be less productive investment and a lower growth rate for the economy.

Governments in developing and transition countries often use their financial systems to direct credit to themselves or to favored sectors of the economy by setting interest rates at artificially low levels for certain types of loans, by creating development finance institutions to make specific types of loans, or by directing existing institutions to lend to certain entities. As we have seen, private institutions have an incentive to solve adverse selection and moral hazard problems and lend to borrowers with the most productive investment opportunities. Governments have less incentive to do so because they are not driven by the profit motive and thus their directed credit programs may not channel funds to sectors that will produce high growth for the economy. The outcome is again likely to result in less efficient investment and slower growth.

In addition, banks in many developing and transition countries are owned by their governments. Again, because of the absence of the profit motive, these **state-owned banks** have little incentive to allocate their capital to the most productive uses. Not surprisingly, the primary loan customer of these state-owned banks is often the government, which does not always use the funds wisely for productive investments to promote growth.

We have seen that government regulation can increase the amount of information in financial markets to make them work more efficiently. Many developing and transition countries have an underdeveloped regulatory apparatus that retards the provision of adequate information to the marketplace. For example, these countries often have weak accounting standards, making it very hard to ascertain the quality of a borrower's balance sheet. As a result, asymmetric information problems are more severe, and the financial system is severely hampered in channeling funds to the most productive uses.

The institutional environment of a poor legal system, weak accounting standards, inadequate government regulation, and government intervention through directed credit programs and state ownership of banks all help explain why many countries stay poor while others, unhindered by these impediments, grow richer.

CASE

Is China a Counter-Example to the Importance of Financial Development?

Although China appears to be on its way to becoming an economic powerhouse, its financial development remains in the early stages. The country's legal system is weak so that financial contracts are difficult to enforce, while accounting standards are lax, so that high-quality information about creditors is hard to find. Regulation of the banking system is still in its formative stages, and the banking sector is dominated by large state-owned banks. Yet the Chinese economy has enjoyed one of the highest growth rates in the world over the last 20 years. How has China been able to grow so rapidly given its low level of financial development?

As noted above, China is in an early state of development, with a per capita income that is still less than $5,000, one-eighth of the per capita income in the United States. With an extremely high savings rate, averaging around 40% over the last two decades, the country has been able to rapidly build up its capital stock and shift a massive pool of underutilized labor from the subsistence-agriculture sector into higher-productivity activities that use capital. Even though available savings have not been allocated to their most productive uses, the huge increase in capital combined with the gains in productivity from moving labor out of low-productivity, subsistence agriculture have been enough to produce high growth.

As China gets richer, however, this strategy is unlikely to continue to work. The Soviet Union provides a graphic example. In the 1950s and 1960s, the Soviet Union shared many characteristics with modern-day China: high growth fueled by a high savings rate, a massive buildup of capital, and shifts of a large pool of underutilized labor from subsistence agriculture to manufacturing. During this high-growth phase, however, the Soviet Union was unable to develop the institutions needed to allocate capital efficiently. As a result, once the pool of subsistence laborers was used up, the Soviet Union's growth slowed dramatically and it was unable to keep up with the Western economies. Today no one considers the Soviet Union to have been an economic success story, and its inability to develop the institutions necessary to sustain financial development and growth was an important reason for the demise of this superpower.

To move into the next stage of development, China will need to allocate its capital more efficiently, which requires that it must improve its financial system. The Chinese leadership is well aware of this challenge: The government has announced that state-owned banks are being put on the path to privatization. In addition, the government is engaged in legal reform to make financial contracts more enforceable. New bankruptcy law is being developed so that lenders have the ability to take over the assets of firms that default on their loan contracts. Whether the Chinese government will succeed in developing a first-rate financial system, thereby enabling China to join the ranks of developed countries, is a big question mark.

Financial Crises and Aggregate Economic Activity

Agency theory, the economic analysis of the effects of adverse selection and moral hazard, can help us understand **financial crises,** major disruptions in financial markets that are characterized by sharp declines in asset prices and the failures of many financial and nonfinancial firms. Financial crises have been common in most countries throughout modern history. The United States has experienced major financial crises in the past, but has not had a full-scale financial crisis in recent times.[6] Studying financial crises is worthwhile because they have led to severe economic downturns in the past and have the potential for doing so in the future.

Financial crises occur when a disruption in the financial system causes such a sharp increase in adverse selection and moral hazard problems in financial markets that the markets are unable to channel funds efficiently from savers to people with productive investment opportunities. As a result of this inability of financial markets to function efficiently, economic activity contracts sharply.

Factors Causing Financial Crises

To understand why banking and financial crises occur and, more specifically, how they lead to contractions in economic activity, we need to examine the factors that cause them. Five categories of factors can trigger financial crises: increases in interest rates, increases in uncertainty, asset market effects on balance sheets, problems in the banking sector, and government fiscal imbalances.

Increases in Interest Rates As we saw earlier, individuals and firms with the riskiest investment projects are those who are willing to pay the highest interest rates. If market interest rates are driven up sufficiently because of increased demand for credit or because of a decline in the money supply, good credit risks are less likely to want to borrow while bad credit risks are still willing to borrow. Because of the resulting increase in adverse selection, lenders will no longer want to make loans. The substantial decline in lending will lead to a substantial decline in investment and aggregate economic activity.

An increase in interest rates also leads to higher interest payments and a decline in firms' **cash flow,** the difference between its cash receipts and the cash it must pay out to cover its costs, including its borrowing. If it has sufficient cash flow, a firm can finance its projects internally, and there is no asymmetric information because it knows how good its own projects are. (Indeed, American businesses fund around two-thirds of their investments with internal funds.) With less cash flow, the firm has fewer internal funds and must raise funds from an external source, say a bank, which does not know the firm as well as its owners or managers know it. The bank cannot be sure if the firm will invest in safe projects or instead take on big risks and

---

[6]Although those of us in the United States have not experienced any financial crises since the Great Depression, we have had several close calls—the October 1987 stock market crash, for example. An important reason why we have escaped financial crises is the timely action of the Federal Reserve to prevent them during episodes like that of October 1987 (Chapter 8).

then be unlikely to pay back the loan. Because of this increased adverse selection and moral hazard, the bank may choose not to lend even firms with good risks the money to undertake investments, even though they would have been profitable for the firms and the bank. We thus see that, when cash flow drops as a result of an increase in interest rates, adverse selection and moral hazard problems become more severe, again curtailing lending, investment, and economic activity. The cash flow channel provides an additional reason why sharp increases in interest rates can be an important factor leading to financial crises.

Increases in Uncertainty A dramatic increase in uncertainty in financial markets, due perhaps to the failure of a prominent financial or nonfinancial institution, a recession, or a stock market crash, makes it harder for lenders to screen good from bad credit risks. The resulting inability of lenders to solve the adverse selection problem makes them less willing to lend, which leads to a decline in lending, investment, and aggregate economic activity.

Asset Market Effects on Balance Sheets The state of firms' balance sheets has important implications for the severity of asymmetric information problems in the financial system. A sharp decline in the stock market is one factor that can cause a serious deterioration in firms' balance sheets. In turn, this deterioration can increase adverse selection and moral hazard problems in financial markets and provoke a financial crisis. A decline in the stock market means that the net worth of corporations has fallen, because share prices are the valuation of a corporation's net worth. The decline in net worth as a result of a stock market decline makes lenders less willing to lend because, as we have seen, the net worth of a firm plays a role similar to that of collateral. When the value of collateral declines, it provides less protection to lenders, meaning that losses on loans are likely to be more severe. Because lenders are now less protected against the consequences of adverse selection, they decrease their lending, which in turn causes investment and aggregate output to decline. In addition, the decline in corporate net worth as a result of a stock market decline increases moral hazard by providing incentives for borrowing firms to make risky investments, as they now have less to lose if their investments go sour. The resulting increase in moral hazard makes lending less attractive—another reason why a stock market decline and resultant decline in net worth leads to decreased lending and economic activity.

In economies in which inflation has been moderate, which characterizes most industrialized countries, many debt contracts are typically of fairly long maturity with fixed interest rates. In this institutional environment, unanticipated declines in the aggregate price level also decrease the net worth of firms. Because debt payments are contractually fixed in nominal terms, an unanticipated decline in the price level raises the value of firms' liabilities in *real* terms (increases the burden of the debt) but does not raise the real value of firms' assets. The result is that net worth in *real* terms (the difference between assets and liabilities in *real* terms) declines. A sharp drop in the price level therefore causes a substantial decline in real net worth and an increase in adverse selection and moral hazard problems facing lenders. An unanticipated decline in the aggregate price level thus leads to a drop in lending and economic activity.

Because of uncertainty about the future value of the domestic currency in developing countries (and in some industrialized countries), many nonfinancial firms, banks, and governments in these countries find it easier to issue debt denominated in foreign currencies. This can lead to a financial crisis in a similar fashion to an unanticipated decline in the price level. With debt contracts denominated in foreign currency, when there is an unanticipated decline in the value of the domestic currency, the debt burden of domestic firms increases. Since assets are typically denominated in domestic currency, there is a resulting deterioration in firms' balance sheets and a decline in net worth, which then increases adverse selection and moral hazard problems along the lines just described. The increase in asymmetric information problems leads to a decline in investment and economic activity.

Problems in the Banking Sector Banks play a major role in financial markets because they are well positioned to engage in information-producing activities that facilitate productive investment for the economy. The state of banks' balance sheets has an important effect on bank lending. If banks suffer a deterioration in their balance sheets and so have a substantial contraction in their capital, they will have fewer resources to lend, and bank lending will decline. The contraction in lending then leads to a decline in investment spending, which slows economic activity.

If the deterioration in bank balance sheets is severe enough, banks will start to fail, and fear can spread from one bank to another, causing even healthy banks to go under. The multiple bank failures that result are known as a **bank panic.** The source of the contagion is asymmetric information. In a panic, depositors, fearing for the safety of their deposits (in the absence of deposit insurance) and not knowing the quality of banks' loan portfolios, withdraw their deposits to the point that the banks fail. The failure of a large number of banks in a short period of time means that there is a loss of information production in financial markets and a direct loss of banks' financial intermediation.

The decrease in bank lending during a financial crisis decreases the supply of funds available to borrowers, which leads to higher interest rates. The outcome of a bank panic is an increase in adverse selection and moral hazard problems in credit markets: These problems produce an even sharper decline in lending to facilitate productive investments and lead to an even more severe contraction in economic activity.

Government Fiscal Imbalances In emerging market countries (Argentina, Brazil, and Turkey are recent examples), government fiscal imbalances may create fears of default on the government debt. As a result, the government may have trouble getting people to buy its bonds and it might force banks to purchase them. If the debt then declines in price—which, as we have seen in Chapter 5, will occur if a government default is likely—bank balance sheets will weaken and their lending will contract for the reasons described earlier. Fears of default on the government debt can also spark a foreign exchange crisis in which the value of the domestic currency falls sharply because investors pull their money out of the country. The decline in the domestic currency's value will then lead to the destruction of the balance sheets of firms with large amounts of debt denominated in foreign currency. These balance sheet problems lead to an increase in adverse selection and moral hazard problems, a decline in lending, and a contraction of economic activity.

CASE

Financial Crises in the United States

The United States has a long history of banking and financial crises. Such crises occurred every 20 years or so in the nineteenth and early twentieth centuries—in 1819, 1837, 1857, 1873, 1884, 1893, 1907, and 1930–1933. Our analysis of the factors that lead to a financial crisis can explain why these crises took place and why they were so damaging to the U.S. economy.

study guide

To understand fully what took place in a U.S. financial crisis, make sure that you can state the reasons why each factor—increases in interest rates, increases in uncertainty, asset market effects on balance sheets, and problems in the banking sector—increases adverse selection and moral hazard problems, which in turn lead to a decline in economic activity. To help you understand these crises, you might want to refer to Figure 15.2, a diagram that traces the sequence of events in a U.S. financial crisis.

As shown in Figure 15.2, most financial crises in the United States have begun with a deterioration in banks' balance sheets, a sharp rise in interest rates (frequently stemming from increases in interest rates abroad), a steep stock market decline, and an increase in uncertainty resulting from a failure of major financial or nonfinancial firms (the Ohio Life Insurance & Trust Company in 1857, the Northern Pacific Railroad and Jay Cooke & Company in 1873, Grant & Ward in 1884, the National Cordage Company in 1893, the Knickerbocker Trust Company in 1907, and the Bank of United States in 1930). During these crises, deterioration in banks' balance sheets, the increase in uncertainty, the rise in interest rates, and the stock market decline increased the severity of adverse selection problems in credit markets. The stock market decline, the deterioration in banks' balance sheets, and the rise in interest rates (which decreased firms' cash flow) also increased moral hazard problems. The rise in adverse selection and moral hazard problems then made it less attractive for lenders to lend, which led to a decline in investment and aggregate economic activity.

Because of the worsening business conditions and uncertainty about their bank's health (perhaps banks would go broke), depositors began to withdraw their funds from banks, which led to bank panics. The resulting decline in the number of banks raised interest rates even further and decreased the amount of financial intermediation by banks. Worsening of the problems created by adverse selection and moral hazard led to further economic contraction.

Finally, there was a sorting out of firms that were **insolvent** (had a negative net worth and hence were bankrupt) from healthy firms by bankruptcy proceedings. The same process occurred for banks, often with the help of public and private authorities. Once this sorting out was complete, uncertainty in financial markets declined, the stock market underwent a recovery, and interest rates fell. The overall result was that adverse selection and moral hazard problems diminished and the financial crisis subsided. With the financial markets able to operate well again, the stage was set for the recovery of the economy.

If, however, the economic downturn led to a sharp decline in prices, the recovery process was short-circuited. In this situation, shown in Figure 15.2, a process

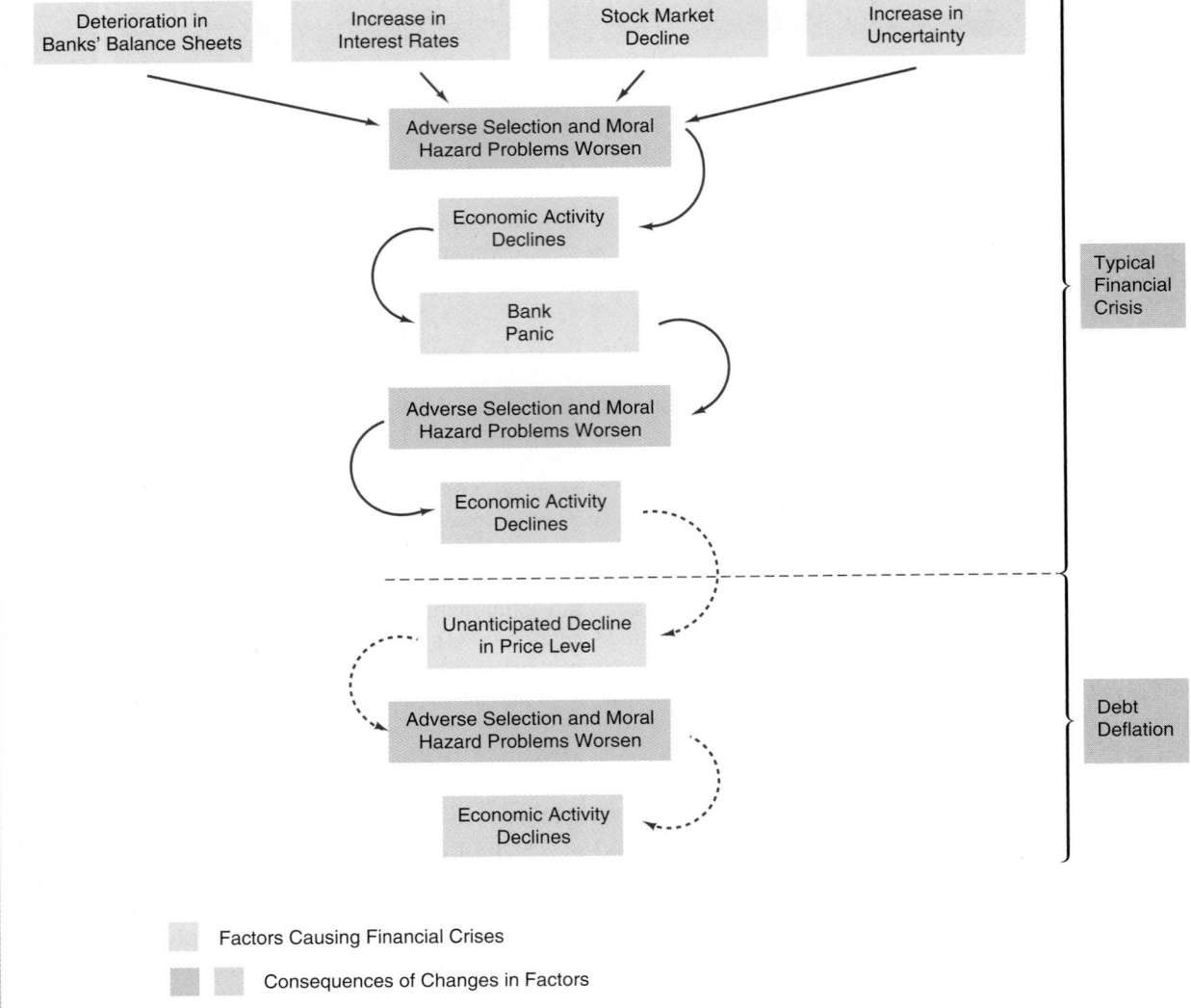

Figure 15.2 Sequence of Events in U.S. Financial Crises

The solid arrows trace the sequence of events in a typical financial crisis; the dotted arrows show the additional set of events that occur if the crisis develops into a debt deflation.

go online

www.amatecon.com/
gd/gdtimeline.html
A time line of the Great
Depression.

called **debt deflation** occurred, in which a substantial decline in the price level set in, leading to a further deterioration in firms' net worth because of the increased burden of indebtedness. When debt deflation set in, the adverse selection and moral hazard problems continued to increase so that lending, investment spending, and aggregate economic activity remained depressed for a long time. The most significant financial crisis that included debt deflation was the Great Depression, the worst economic contraction in U.S. history (see the Mini-Case box, "Case Study of a Financial Crisis: The Great Depression").

mini-case

Case Study of a Financial Crisis: The Great Depression

In 1928 and 1929, prices doubled in the U.S. stock market. Federal Reserve officials viewed the stock market boom as excessive speculation. To curb it, they pursued a tight monetary policy to raise interest rates; the Fed got more than it bargained for when the stock market crashed in October 1929, falling by more than 60%.

Although the 1929 crash had a great impact on the minds of a whole generation, most people forget that by the middle of 1930, more than half of the stock market decline had been reversed. What might have been a normal recession turned into something far different, however, with adverse shocks to the agricultural sector, a continuing decline in the stock market after the middle of 1930, and a sequence of bank collapses from October 1930 until March 1933 in which more than one-third of the banks in the United States went out of business.

The continuing decline in stock prices after mid-1930 (by mid-1932 stocks had declined to 10% of their value at the 1929 peak) and the increase in uncertainty from the unsettled business conditions created by the economic contraction made adverse selection and moral hazard problems worse in the credit markets. The loss of one-third of the banks reduced the amount of financial intermediation.

This intensified adverse selection and moral hazard problems and decreased the ability of financial markets to channel funds to firms with productive investment opportunities. As our analysis predicts, the amount of outstanding commercial loans fell by half from 1929 to 1933, and investment spending collapsed, declining by 90% from its 1929 level.

The short-circuiting of the process that kept the economy from recovering quickly, which it does in most recessions, occurred because of a fall in the price level by 25% in the 1930–1933 period. This huge decline in prices triggered a debt deflation in which net worth fell because of the increased burden of indebtedness borne by firms. The decline in net worth and the resulting increase in adverse selection and moral hazard problems in the credit markets led to a prolonged economic contraction in which unemployment rose to 25% of the labor force. The financial crisis in the Great Depression was the worst ever experienced in the United States, and it explains why this economic contraction was also the most severe one ever experienced by the nation.*

---

*See Ben Bernanke, "Nonmonetary Effects of the Financial Crisis in the Propagation of the Great Depression," *American Economic Review* 73 (1983): 257–276, for a discussion of the role of asymmetric information problems in the Great Depression period.

CASE

Financial Crises in Emerging-Market Countries: Mexico, 1994–1995; East Asia, 1997–1998; and Argentina, 2001–2002

In recent years, many emerging-market countries have experienced financial crises, the most dramatic of which were the Mexican crisis, which started in December 1994; the East Asian crisis, which started in July 1997; and the Argentine crisis, which started in 2001. An important puzzle is how a developing country can shift dramatically from a path of high growth before a financial crisis—as was true for Mexico and particularly the East Asian countries of Thailand, Malaysia, Indonesia, the Philippines, and South Korea—to a sharp decline in economic activity. We can apply our asymmetric information analysis of financial crises to explain this puzzle and to understand the Mexican, East Asian, and Argentine financial situations.[7]

Because of the different institutional features of emerging-market countries' debt markets, the sequence of events in the Mexican, East Asian, and Argentine crises differs from that occurring in the United States in the nineteenth and twentieth centuries. Figure 15.3 diagrams the sequence of events that occurred in Mexico, East Asia, and Argentina.

An important factor leading up to the financial crises in Mexico and East Asia was the deterioration in banks' balance sheets because of increasing loan losses. When financial markets in these countries were deregulated in the early 1990s, a lending boom ensued in which bank credit to the private nonfinancial business sector accelerated sharply. Because of weak supervision by bank regulators and a lack of expertise in screening and monitoring borrowers at banking institutions, losses on the loans began to mount, causing an erosion of banks' net worth (capital). As a result of this erosion, banks had fewer resources to lend, and this lack of lending eventually led to a contraction in economic activity.

Argentina also experienced a deterioration in bank balance sheets leading up to its crisis, but the source of this deterioration was quite different. In contrast to Mexico and the East Asian crisis countries, Argentina had a well-supervised banking system, and a lending boom did not occur before the crisis. On the other hand, in 1998 Argentina entered a recession that led to some loan losses. However, it was the fiscal problems of the Argentine government that led to severe weakening of bank balance sheets. Again, in contrast to Mexico and the East Asian countries before their crises, Argentina was running substantial budget deficits that could not be financed by foreign borrowing. To solve its fiscal problems, the Argentine government coerced banks into absorbing large amounts of government debt. When investors lost confidence in the ability of the Argentine government to repay this debt, the price of this debt plummeted, leaving big holes in banks' balance sheets. This weakening helped lead to a contraction of economic activity, as in Mexico and East Asia.

Consistent with the U.S. experience in the nineteenth and early twentieth centuries, another precipitating factor in the Mexican and Argentine (but not East Asian) financial crises was a rise in interest rates abroad. Before the Mexican crisis, in February 1994, and before the Argentine crisis, in mid-1999, the Federal Reserve began a cycle of raising the federal funds rate to head off inflationary pressures. Although the monetary policy moves by the Fed were successful in keeping inflation in check in the United States, they put upward pressure on interest rates in both Mexico and Argentina. The rise in interest rates in Mexico and Argentina directly added to increased adverse selection in their financial markets because, as discussed earlier, it was more likely that the parties willing to take on the most risk would seek loans.

Also consistent with the U.S. experience in the nineteenth and early twentieth centuries, stock market declines and increases in uncertainty occurred prior to, and contributed to, full-blown crises in Mexico, Thailand, South Korea, and Argentina. (The stock market declines in Malaysia, Indonesia, and the Philippines, on the other

---

[7]This chapter does not examine two other recent crises, those in Brazil and Russia. Russia's financial crisis in August 1998 can also be explained with the asymmetric information story here, but it is more appropriate to view it as a symptom of a wider breakdown in the economy—and this is why we do not focus on it here. The Brazilian crisis in January 1999 has features of a more traditional balance-of-payments crisis (see Chapter 14), rather than a financial crisis.

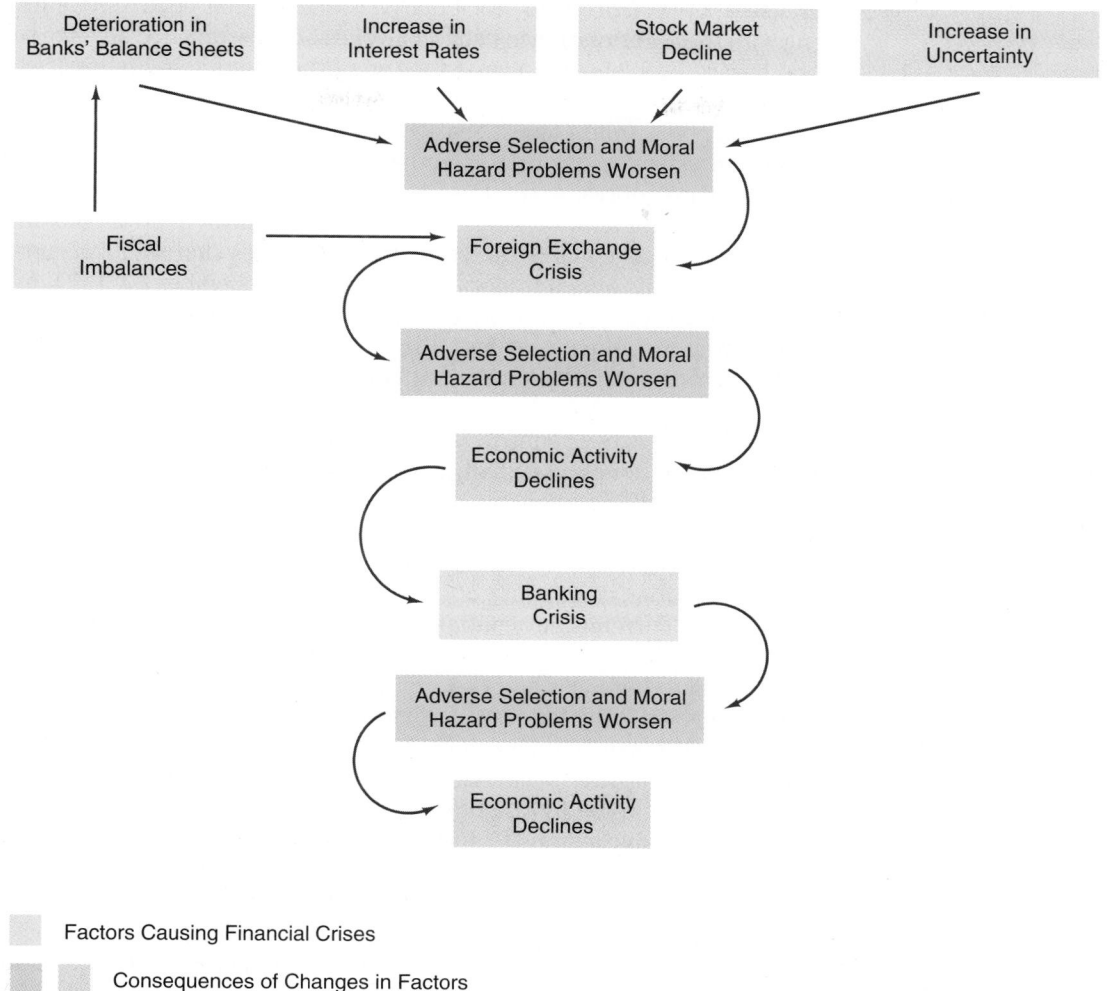

Factors Causing Financial Crises

Consequences of Changes in Factors

Figure 15.3 Sequence of Events in the Mexican, East Asian, and Argentine Financial Crises

The arrows trace the sequence of events during the financial crisis.

hand, occurred simultaneously with the onset of the crisis.) The Mexican economy was hit by political shocks in 1994 (specifically, the assassination of the ruling party's presidential candidate and an uprising in the southern state of Chiapas) that created uncertainty, while the ongoing recession increased uncertainty in Argentina. Right before their crises, Thailand and South Korea experienced major failures of financial and nonfinancial firms that increased general uncertainty in financial markets.

As we have seen, an increase in uncertainty and a decrease in net worth as a result of a stock market decline increase asymmetric information problems. It becomes harder to screen out good from bad borrowers, and the decline in net worth decreases the value of firms' collateral and increases their incentives to make risky investments because there is less equity to lose if the investments are unsuccessful. The increase in uncertainty and stock market declines that occurred before the crisis, along with the deterioration in banks' balance sheets, worsened adverse selection and moral hazard problems (shown at the top of the diagram in Figure 15.3) and made the economies ripe for a serious financial crisis.

At this point, full-blown speculative attacks developed in the foreign exchange market, plunging these countries into a full-scale crisis. With the Colosio assassination, the Chiapas uprising, and the growing weakness in the banking sector, the Mexican peso came under attack. Even though the Mexican central bank intervened in the foreign exchange market and raised interest rates sharply, it was unable to stem the attack and was forced to devalue the peso on December 20, 1994. In the case of Thailand, concerns about the large current account deficit and weakness in the Thai financial system, culminating with the failure of a major finance company, Finance One, led to a successful speculative attack that forced the Thai central bank to allow the baht to float downward in July 1997. Soon thereafter, speculative attacks developed against the other countries in the region, leading to the collapse of the Philippine peso, the Indonesian rupiah, the Malaysian ringgit, and the South Korean won. In Argentina, a full-scale banking panic began in October–November 2001. This, along with realization that the government was going to default on its debt, also led to a speculative attack on the Argentine peso, resulting in its collapse on January 6, 2002.

The institutional structure of debt markets in Mexico and East Asia now interacted with the currency devaluations to propel the economies into full-fledged financial crises. Because so many firms in these countries had debt denominated in foreign currencies like the dollar and the yen, depreciation of their currencies resulted in increases in their indebtedness in domestic currency terms, even though the value of their assets remained unchanged. When the peso lost half its value by March 1995 and the Thai, Philippine, Malaysian, and South Korean currencies lost between a third and half of their value by the beginning of 1998, firms' balance sheets took a big negative hit, causing a dramatic increase in adverse selection and moral hazard problems. This negative shock was especially severe for Indonesia and Argentina, which saw the value of their currencies fall by more than 70%, resulting in insolvency for firms with substantial amounts of debt denominated in foreign currencies.

The collapse of currencies also led to a rise in actual and expected inflation in these countries, and market interest rates rose sky-high (to around 100% in Mexico and Argentina). The resulting increase in interest payments caused reductions in households' and firms' cash flow, which led to further deterioration in their balance sheets. A feature of debt markets in emerging-market countries, like those in Mexico, East Asia, and Argentina is that debt contracts have very short durations, typically less than one month. Thus, the rise in short-term interest rates in these countries meant that the effect on cash flow and hence on balance sheets was substantial. As our asymmetric information analysis suggests, this deterioration in households' and firms' balance sheets increased adverse selection and moral hazard problems in the credit markets, making domestic and foreign lenders even less willing to lend.

Consistent with the theory of financial crises outlined in this chapter, the sharp decline in lending helped lead to a collapse of economic activity, with real GDP growth falling sharply.

As shown in Figure 15.3, further deterioration in the economy occurred because the collapse in economic activity and the deterioration in the cash flow and balance sheets of both firms and households led to worsening banking crises. The problems of firms and households meant that many of them were no longer able to pay off their debts, resulting in substantial losses for the banks. Even more problematic for the banks was that they had many short-term liabilities denominated in foreign currencies, and the sharp increase in the value of these liabilities after the devaluation led to a further deterioration in the banks' balance sheets. Under these circumstances, the banking system would have collapsed in the absence of a government safety net—as it did in the United States during the Great Depression—but with the assistance of the International Monetary Fund, these countries were in some cases able to protect depositors and avoid a bank panic. However, given the loss of bank capital and the need for the government to intervene to prop up the banks, the banks' ability to lend was nevertheless sharply curtailed. As we have seen, a banking crisis of this type hinders the ability of the banks to lend and also makes adverse selection and moral hazard problems worse in financial markets, because banks are less capable of playing their traditional financial intermediation role. The banking crisis, along with other factors that increased adverse selection and moral hazard problems in the credit markets of Mexico, East Asia, and Argentina, explains the collapse of lending and hence economic activity in the aftermath of the crisis.

Following their crises, Mexico began to recover in 1996, while the crisis countries in East Asia tentatively began their recovery in 1999, with a stronger recovery later. Argentina was still in a severe depression in 2003, but subsequently the economy bounced back. In all these countries, the economic hardship caused by the financial crises was tremendous. Unemployment rose sharply, poverty increased substantially, and even the social fabric of the society was stretched thin. For example, after the financial crises, Mexico City and Buenos Aires became crime-ridden, while Indonesia experienced waves of ethnic violence.

SUMMARY

1. There are eight basic facts about U.S. financial structure. The first four emphasize the importance of financial intermediaries and the relative unimportance of securities markets for the financing of corporations; the fifth recognizes that financial markets are among the most heavily regulated sectors of the economy; the sixth states that only large, well-established corporations have access to securities markets; the seventh indicates that collateral is an important feature of debt contracts; and the eighth presents debt contracts as complicated legal documents that place substantial restrictions on the behavior of the borrower.

2. Transaction costs freeze many small savers and borrowers out of direct involvement with financial markets. Financial intermediaries can take advantage of economies of scale and are better able to develop expertise to lower transaction costs, thus enabling their savers and borrowers to benefit from the existence of financial markets.

3. Asymmetric information results in two problems: adverse selection, which occurs before the transaction, and moral hazard, which occurs after the transaction. Adverse selection refers to the fact that bad credit risks are the ones most likely to seek loans, and moral hazard refers to the risk of the borrower's engaging in activities that are undesirable from the lender's point of view.

4. Adverse selection interferes with the efficient functioning of financial markets. Tools to help reduce the adverse selection problem include private production and sale of information, government regulation to increase information, financial intermediation, and collateral and net worth. The free-rider problem occurs when people who do not pay for information take advantage of information that other people have paid for. This problem explains why financial intermediaries, particularly banks, play a more important role in financing the activities of businesses than securities markets do.

5. Moral hazard in equity contracts is known as the principal–agent problem, because managers (the agents) have less incentive to maximize profits than stockholders (the principals). The principal–agent problem explains why debt contracts are so much more prevalent in financial markets than equity contracts. Tools to help reduce the principal–agent problem include monitoring, government regulation to increase information, and financial intermediation.

6. Tools to reduce the moral hazard problem in debt contracts include collateral and net worth, monitoring and enforcement of restrictive covenants, and financial intermediaries.

7. Financial crises are major disruptions in financial markets. They are caused by increases in adverse selection and moral hazard problems that prevent financial markets from channeling funds to people with productive investment opportunities, leading to a sharp contraction in economic activity. The five types of factors that lead to financial crises are increases in interest rates, increases in uncertainty, asset market effects on balance sheets, problems in the banking sector, and government fiscal imbalances.

KEY TERMS

agency theory, *p. 371*
audits, *p. 373*
bank panic, *p. 388*
cash flow, *p. 386*
collateral, *p. 368*
costly state verification, *p. 378*
creditors, *p. 384*
debt deflation, *p. 390*
equity capital, *p. 376*
financial crises, *p. 386*
free-rider problem, *p. 372*

incentive compatible, *p. 380*
insolvent, *p. 389*
net worth (equity capital), *p. 376*
pecking order hypothesis, *p. 375*
principal–agent problem, *p. 377*
restrictive covenants, *p. 368*
secured debt, *p. 368*
state-owned banks, *p. 384*
unsecured debt, *p. 368*
venture capital firm, *p. 378*

QUESTIONS

1. How can economies of scale help explain the existence of financial intermediaries?

2. Describe two ways in which financial intermediaries help lower transaction costs in the economy.

3. Would moral hazard and adverse selection still arise in financial markets if information were not asymmetric? Explain.

4. How do standard accounting principles help financial markets work more efficiently?

5. Do you think the lemons problem would be more severe for stocks traded on the New York Stock Exchange or those traded over-the-counter? Explain.

6. Which firms are most likely to use bank financing rather than to issue bonds or stocks to finance their activities? Why?

7. How can the existence of asymmetric information provide a rationale for government regulation of financial markets?

8. Would you be more willing to lend to a friend if she put all of her life savings into her business than you would if she had not done so? Why?

9. Rich people often worry that others will seek to marry them only for their money. Is this a problem of adverse selection?

10. "The more collateral there is backing a loan, the less the lender has to worry about adverse selection." Is this statement true, false, or uncertain? Explain your answer.

11. How does the free-rider problem aggravate adverse selection and moral hazard problems in financial markets?

12. Explain how the separation of ownership and control in American corporations might lead to poor management.

13. Is a financial crisis more likely to occur when the economy is experiencing deflation or inflation? Explain.

14. How can a stock market crash provoke a financial crisis?

15. How can a sharp rise in interest rates provoke a financial crisis?

QUANTITATIVE PROBLEMS

1. You are in the market for a used car. At a used car lot, you know that the blue book value for the cars you are looking at is between $20,000 and $24,000. If you believe the dealer knows *as much* about the car as you, how much are you willing to pay? Why? Assume that you only care about the expected value of the car you buy and that the car values are symmetrically distributed.

2. Now, you believe the dealer knows *more* about the cars than you. How much are you willing to pay? Why? How can this be resolved in a competitive market?

3. You wish to hire Ricky to manage your Dallas operations. The profits from the operations depend partially on how hard Ricky works, as follows.

	Probabilities	
	Profit = $10,000	**Profit = $50,000**
Lazy	60%	40%
Hard worker	20%	80%

If Ricky is lazy, he will surf the internet all day, and he views this as a zero cost opportunity. However, Ricky would view working hard as a "personal cost" valued at $1,000. What fixed percentage of the profits should you offer Ricky? Assume Ricky only cares about his expected payment less any "personal cost."

4. You own a house worth $400,000 that is located on a river. If the river floods moderately, the house will be completely destroyed. This happens about once every 50 years. If you build a seawall, the river would have to flood heavily to destroy your house, which only happens about once every 200 years. What would be the annual premium for an insurance policy that offers full insurance? For a policy that only pays 75% of the home value, what are your expected costs with and without a seawall? Do the different policies provide an incentive to be safer (i.e., to build the seawall)?

WEB EXERCISES

Why Do Financial Institutions Exist?

1. In this chapter we discuss the lemons problem and its effect on the efficient functioning of a market. This theory was initially developed by George Akerlof. Go to **http://www.nobelprize.org/nobel_prizes/ economics/articles/akerlof/index.html**. This site reports that Akerlof, Spence, and Stiglitz were awarded the Nobel prize in economics in 2001 for their work. Read this report down through the section on George Akerlof. Summarize his research ideas in one page.

2. This chapter discusses how an understanding of adverse selection and moral hazard can help us better understand financial crises. The greatest financial crisis faced by the United States was the Great Depression, from 1929 to 1933. Go to **www .amatecon.com/greatdepression.html**. This site contains a brief discussion of the factors that led to the Great Depression. Write a one-page summary explaining how adverse selection and moral hazard contributed to the Great Depression.

CHAPTER

16

What Should Be Done About Conflicts of Interest? A Central Issue in Business Ethics

Preview

Since the end of the stock market boom in 2000, financial markets have been jolted by one corporate scandal after another. The cycle began in December 2001 with the spectacular bankruptcy of Enron Corporation (once valued as the seventh-largest corporation in the United States) and the indictment of Enron's auditor, Arthur Andersen, one of the "Big Five" accounting firms. Subsequently, revelations of misleading accounting statements at numerous other corporations, including WorldCom, Tyco Industries, and Fannie Mae, have increased investors' doubts about the quality of information coming from the corporate sector. Criminal cases have been filed against all of the top investment banks (Morgan Stanley, J. P. Morgan, Merrill Lynch, Lehman Brothers, and Goldman Sachs, among others) that encouraged their stock analysts to hype dubious stocks, which later proved to be disastrous investments.

These scandals have attracted tremendous public attention for several reasons. First, the resulting bankruptcies cost employees of these firms their jobs, their pensions, or both. Second, these activities may have been a factor in the massive stock market decline that occurred from March 2000 to September 2002; during this downturn, the value of the S&P 500 index declined by 50% and NASDAQ's value declined by 75%. Third, the scandals have created doubts about the ethics of those working in the financial service industry.

go online

http://stockcharts.com/charts/historical/

To review the timing of the stock market declines, this Web site graphs a variety of stock market indexes for easy viewing.

Conflicts of interest, a type of moral hazard problem that occurs when a person or institution has multiple objectives (interests) and as a result has conflicts between them, may be responsible for the recent scandals. In each case, people who were supposed to act in the investing public's best interests by providing investors with reliable information had incentives to deceive the public and thereby benefit both themselves and their corporate clients. What are these conflicts of interest, and how serious are they? Where do they occur, and why have they been the source of the recent woes in financial markets? What can, and should, we do about them?

This chapter provides a framework for answering these questions. It first explains what conflicts of interest are, why we should care about them, and why they raise ethical issues. It then surveys the different types of conflicts of interest that have arisen in the financial industry and discusses policies to remedy them.[1]

What Are Conflicts of Interest and Why Are They Important?

In Chapter 15, we saw how financial institutions play a key role in the financial system. Specifically, their expertise in interpreting signals and collecting information from their customers gives them a cost advantage in the production of information. Furthermore, because they collect, produce, and distribute this information, financial institutions can use the information over and over again in as many ways as they would like, thereby realizing economies of scale. By providing multiple financial services to their customers, they can also realize **economies of scope**—that is, they can lower the costs of information production for each service by applying one information resource to many different services. A bank, for example, can evaluate the creditworthiness of a corporation when making a loan to it, which then helps the bank decide whether it would be easy to sell the bonds of this corporation to the public. Additionally, by providing multiple financial services to their customers, financial institutions can develop broader and longer-term relationships with firms. These relationships further reduce the cost of producing information and, therefore, enhance economies of scope.

Although economies of scope may substantially benefit financial institutions, they also create potential costs in the form of conflicts of interest. Although conflicts of interest arise in almost all aspects of our lives, we need to be precise about the conflicts of interest that concern us here. Given the crucial role of information in financial markets, we focus on those conflicts of interest that arise when financial service firms or their employees have the opportunity to serve their own interests, rather than the interests of their customers, by misusing information, providing false information, or concealing information.

---

[1]The analysis in this chapter is based on Andrew Crockett, Trevor Harris, Frederic S. Mishkin, and Eugene N. White, *Conflicts of Interest in the Financial Services Industry: What Should We Do About Them?* Geneva Reports on the World Economy 4 (Geneva and London: International Center for Monetary and Banking Studies and Centre for Economic Policy Research, 2003).

Conflicts of interest may occur within financial institutions that provide a specialized service, but they are most problematic when an institution provides multiple financial services to a given client or to many clients. The competing interests of these services may lead employees or a department of a financial institution to conceal information or disseminate misleading information to financial markets. Combinations of services that bring together any group of depository intermediaries, nondepository intermediaries, and brokers, or that allow any of these groups to invest directly in a business, are most likely to lead to conflicts of interest.

Why Do We Care About Conflicts of Interest?

Conflicts of interest can substantially reduce the quality of information in financial markets, thereby increasing asymmetric information problems. In turn, asymmetric information prevents financial markets from channeling funds into productive investment opportunities and causes financial markets and the economy to become less efficient.

Ethics and Conflicts of Interest

Conflicts of interest raise ethical dilemmas for those engaged in the financial service business by generating incentives for financial service firms or their employees to conceal or provide misleading information, thereby hurting the customers for whom they work. The growing economies of scope in the financial industry that have led financial institutions to offer more services under one roof have increased conflicts of interest and, not surprisingly, led to more unethical behavior. One way to limit unethical behavior is to make those working in the financial industry aware of the ethical issues that arise when they exploit conflicts of interest; with this awareness, employees are less likely to engage in unethical behavior. To address this need to limit unethical behavior, business schools are now bringing the discussion of ethics into the classroom and firms are establishing policies (discussed later in this chapter) that make it harder for individuals to exploit conflicts of interest.

Types of Conflicts of Interest

Four areas of financial service activities harbor the greatest potential for generating conflicts of interest that ultimately reduce the amount of information available in financial markets:

- Underwriting and research in investment banking
- Auditing and consulting in accounting firms
- Credit assessment and consulting in credit-rating agencies
- Universal banking

Underwriting and Research in Investment Banking

Investment banks perform two tasks: They *research* corporations issuing securities, and they *underwrite* these securities by selling them to the public on behalf of the issuing corporation. Investment banks often combine research and underwriting because the information synergies created may lead to economies of scope. In other words, information that is produced for one task is also useful for another task. A conflict of interest arises between research and underwriting because the investment bank attempts to serve the needs of two client groups—the firms for which it is issuing the securities and the investors to whom it sells these securities.

These client groups have different information needs: Issuers benefit from optimistic research, whereas investors desire unbiased research. Due to economies of scope, however, both groups will receive the same information. When the potential revenues from underwriting greatly exceed brokerage commissions, the investment bank has a strong incentive to alter the information provided to both types of clients so as to favor the issuing firms' needs. If the information provided is not favorable to the issuing firm, it might take its business to a competitor that is willing to put out more positive information and thereby entice more people to buy the newly issued stock. For example, an internal Morgan Stanley memo excerpted in the *Wall Street Journal* on July 14, 1992, stated: "Our objective . . . is to adopt a policy, fully understood by the entire firm, including the Research Department, that we do not make negative or controversial comments about our clients as a matter of sound business practice."

Because of directives like this one, analysts in investment banks might be persuaded to distort their research to please the underwriting department of their bank and the corporations issuing the securities. Of course, such actions undermine the reliability of the information that investors use to make their financial decisions and, as a result, diminish the efficiency of securities markets. A similar chain of events precipitated the tech boom of the 1990s (see the Conflicts of Interest box, "The King, Queen, and Jack of the Internet").

Another practice that exploits conflicts of interest is **spinning.** Spinning occurs when investment banks allocate hot, but underpriced, **initial public offerings (IPOs),** shares of newly issued stock, to executives of other companies that may potentially have business with the investment bank (see the Conflicts of Interest box, "Frank Quattrone and Spinning"). Because hot IPOs typically rise immediately in price after they are first purchased by investors, spinning is a form of kickback to other firms' executives, luring them to use that investment bank. When the executive's company plans to issue its own securities, he or she will be more likely to use as an underwriter the investment bank that gave the executive the hot IPO shares, which is not necessarily the investment bank that could get the highest price for the firm's securities This action may raise the cost of capital for the firm, and therefore hinder the efficiency of the capital market.

Auditing and Consulting in Accounting Firms

Traditionally, an auditor reduces the information asymmetry between a firm's managers and its shareholders by checking the firm's books and monitoring the quality of the information the firm produces. Auditors play an important role in financial markets because they can reduce the inevitable information asymmetry between the firm's managers and its shareholders.

Threats to truthful reporting in an audit arise from several potential conflicts of interest. The conflict of interest that has received the most attention in the media occurs when an accounting firm provides its client with auditing services and nonaudit consulting services—commonly known as **management advisory services**—such as advice on taxes, accounting or management information systems, and business strategies. Accounting firms that provide multiple services enjoy economies

conflicts of interest

The King, Queen, and Jack of the Internet

The King, Queen, and Jack of the Internet are the nicknames of a trio of bullish technology analysts who were very influential during the tech boom of the late 1990s: Henry Blodgett at Merrill Lynch, Jack Grubman at Salomon Smith Barney (Citigroup), and Mary Meeker at Morgan Stanley. Their stories reveal a lot about how conflicts of interest may have influenced analysts' recommendations during this heady period.*

In late 1998, Henry Blodgett, then at Oppenheimer and Company, recommended a price target of $400 per share for Amazon.com. At the time, most analysts believed that Amazon.com was overvalued at $240 per share. In particular, Jonathan Cole of Merrill Lynch indicated that $50 was a more reasonable price. When the price of Amazon.com stock rose above $400 per share, Blodgett was hailed as a guru and hired by Merrill Lynch, while Cole left the firm. Clearly, Blodgett saw that he could reap benefits by hyping tech stocks. A subsequent investigation by the New York Attorney General's office found that Blodgett issued very positive reports on certain Internet stocks while privately deriding them in e-mails. Blodgett was accused of issuing favorable research reports for InfoSpace because he knew that it was planning to buy Go2Net, one of Merrill Lynch's clients. Similarly, Blodgett was alleged to have maintained a positive recommendation for GoTo.com, even though it was not doing well, at a time when Merrill Lynch was competing to manage a new stock issue for the company. He downgraded GoTo.com's rating only after it chose Credit Suisse First Boston as its underwriter instead.

The New York Attorney General's office accused Jack Grubman of engaging in similarly questionable

behavior. Although he expressed doubts in private, Grubman made wildly bullish recommendations about several telecom companies—including WorldCom, Global Crossing, and Winstar Communications—that were spiraling toward bankruptcy. In 1999, he upgraded his rating of AT&T when Salomon Smith Barney was competing for a new issue of AT&T's spin-off of its cellular division. Six months after his firm, along with Goldman Sachs and Merrill Lynch, was awarded AT&T's business, Grubman downgraded AT&T's rating.

Blodgett and Grubman have faced criminal charges for their actions, whereas Mary Meeker has not. Like Blodgett and Grubman, Mary Meeker kept her ratings of tech stocks high after their prices plummeted. However, unlike Blodgett and Grubman, there was no evidence that Meeker did not believe her ratings, and she did discourage many Internet issues when the companies had poor outlooks. Morgan Stanley argued on her behalf that "research analysts helped screen out IPO candidates such that Morgan Stanley rejected five Internet IPOs for every one the firm underwrote. Mary Meeker was an integral part of this screening process, which benefited the firm's investor clients." Despite the New York Attorney General's office's criticisms of some of Morgan Stanley practices, Mary Meeker was not subjected to criminal charges because she did provide some screening and no exploitation of conflicts of interest was evident.

*For more detail, see Andrew Crockett, Trevor Harris, Frederic S. Mishkin, and Eugene N. White, *Conflicts of Interest in the Financial Services Industry: What Should We Do About Them?* Geneva Reports on the World Economy 4 (Geneva and London: International Center for Monetary and Banking Studies and Centre for Economic Policy Research, 2003).

of scale and scope, but have two potential sources of conflicts of interest. First, clients may pressure auditors into skewing their judgments and opinions by threatening to take their accounting and management services business to another accounting firm. Second, if auditors are analyzing information systems or examining tax and financial advice put in place by their nonaudit counterparts within the accounting firm, they may be reluctant to criticize the advice or systems. Both types of conflicts may potentially lead to biased audits. With less reliable information available to investors, it becomes more difficult for financial markets to allocate capital efficiently.

conflicts of interest

Frank Quattrone and Spinning

Frank Quattrone of Credit Suisse First Boston was a highly regarded investment banker specializing in technology companies. But his reputation took a big hit in March 2003, when the National Association of Securities Dealers (NASD) filed a complaint against him for improperly pressuring his analysts to provide favorable coverage in an effort to solicit customers for his firm. Allegedly, Quattrone linked his analysts' bonuses to their investment banking work and permitted executives of companies whose stock he handled to make changes in his staff's draft research reports.

NASD also accused Quattrone of spinning because he maintained more than 300 "Friends of Frank" accounts for executives of technology companies that were active or prospective clients of the bank. These "friends" were allocated hot shares at

his discretion. Spinning was not isolated to Quattrone's firm; it was actually quite common on Wall Street. Salomon Smith Barney also allocated hard-to-get IPO shares to a number of executives, including Bernard Ebbers of WorldCom, Philip Anshutz and Joe Nacchio of Qwest, Stephen Garfalo of Metromedia, and Clark McLeod of McLeodUSA. The bank claimed that it issued shares to these executives because they were among the firm's best individual customers and not because it wanted to persuade these executives to channel their companies' investment banking business to Salomon Smith Barney. This claim was deemed dubious, at best. Quattrone was convicted in 2004 of obstructing the investigation into his activities and was sentenced to eighteen months in prison, but the conviction was later overturned.

A third type of conflict of interest arises when an auditor provides an overly favorable audit in an effort to solicit or retain audit business. The unfortunate collapse of Arthur Andersen—once one of the five largest accounting firms in the United States—suggests that this may be the most dangerous conflict of interest (see the Conflicts of Interest box, "The Collapse of Arthur Andersen").

Credit Assessment and Consulting in Credit-Rating Agencies

go online

www.moodys.com/cust/default.as

Moody's is a major rating agency for company debt. To view the Moody's Web site and learn more about how it evaluates company credit, you must register to view Moody's Web materials.

Investors use credit ratings (e.g., Aaa or Baa) that reflect the probability of default to determine the creditworthiness of particular debt securities. As a consequence, debt ratings play a major role in the pricing of debt securities and in the regulatory process. Conflicts of interest can arise when multiple users with divergent interests (at least in the short term) depend on the credit ratings. Investors and regulators are seeking a well-researched, impartial assessment of credit quality; the issuer needs a favorable rating. In the credit-rating industry, the issuers of securities pay a rating firm such as Standard and Poor's or Moody's to have their securities rated (see the Mini-Case box). Because the issuers are the parties paying the credit-rating agency, investors and regulators worry that the agency may bias its ratings upward to attract more business from the issuer.

Other conflicts of interest may arise when credit-rating agencies also provide ancillary consulting services. Debt issuers often ask rating agencies to advise them on how to structure their debt issues, usually with the goal of securing a favorable rating. In this situation, the credit-rating agencies would be auditing their own work and would experience a conflict of interest similar to the one found in accounting firms

conflicts of interest

 ### The Collapse of Arthur Andersen

In 1913, Arthur Andersen, a young accountant who had denounced the slipshod and deceptive practices that enabled companies to fool the investing public, founded his own firm. Until the early 1980s, auditing was the most important source of profits for this firm. By the late 1980s, however, the consulting part of the business began to experience high revenue growth with high profit margins, even as the audit profits slumped in a more competitive market. Consulting partners began to assume more power within the firm, and the resulting internal conflicts split the firm in two. Arthur Andersen (the auditing service) and Andersen Consulting were established as separate companies in 2000.

During the period of increasing conflict before the split, Andersen's audit partners had faced increasing pressure to focus on boosting revenue and profits from audit services. Many of Arthur Andersen's clients that later went bust—Enron, WorldCom, Qwest, and Global Crossing—were also the largest clients in Arthur Andersen's regional offices. The com-

bination of intense pressure to generate revenue and profits from auditing and the fact that some clients dominated the business of regional offices translated into tremendous incentives for regional office managers to provide favorable audit stances for these large clients. The loss of a client such as Enron or WorldCom would have been devastating for a regional office and its partners, even if that client contributed only a small fraction of the overall revenue and profits for Arthur Andersen as a whole.

The Houston office of Arthur Andersen, for example, ignored many problems in Enron's reporting. Arthur Andersen was indicted in March 2002 and then convicted in June 2002 for obstruction of justice for impeding the SEC's investigation of the Enron collapse. (The conviction was overturned by the Supreme Court in May 2005.) Its conviction—the first ever against a major accounting firm—barred Arthur Andersen from conducting audits of publicly traded firms and so effectively put it out of business.

that provide both auditing and consulting services. Furthermore, credit-rating agencies may deliver favorable ratings to garner new clients for the ancillary consulting business. The possible decline in the quality of credit assessments issued by rating agencies could increase asymmetric information in financial markets, thereby diminishing their ability to allocate credit.

Universal Banking

Commercial banks, investment banks, and insurance companies were orginally created as distinct financial institutions that offered separate and distinct services. These institutions soon recognized, however, that combining these activities and services would provide economies of scope. In 1933, the Glass-Steagall Act halted the development of universal banking in the United States by banning the consolidation of these services under one organization. When the Glass-Steagall Act was repealed by Congress in 1999, universal banking reappeared. Given that the divisions within universal banks serve multiple clients, many potential conflicts of interest exist. If the potential for revenues in one department increases, employees in that department will have an incentive to distort information (or to pressure employees in another department to distort information) to the advantage of their clients and the profit of their department.

mini-case

Why Do Issuers of Securities Pay to Have Their Securities Rated?

Prior to the 1970s, credit-rating agencies earned revenues by having subscribers pay to receive information about securities ratings. In the early 1970s, however, the major rating agencies switched to having issuers of securities pay for their ratings. Why would they do this, given that it appears to set up an obvious conflict of interest?

The answer is provided by the asymmetric information framework discussed in Chapter 15. By the early 1970s, technological changes, such as the advent of cheap photocopying, made it easier to disseminate information. Market participants were able to readily get information on securities ratings without paying for it. The free-rider problem became more widespread. As a result, the credit-rating agencies were no longer able to earn enough revenues by selling ratings information. The solution was to have the issuers of securities pay for the ratings, and this is the business model that we see currently.

Several types of conflicts of interest can arise in universal banks:

- Securities issuers served by the underwriting department (and the underwriting department itself) will benefit from aggressive sales of the securities issue to customers of the bank, whereas the customers expect unbiased investment advice.
- A bank manager may push the issuing firm's securities to the disadvantage of the customer or may limit losses from a poor IPO by selling the firm's securities to the bank's managed trust accounts.
- A bank with an outstanding loan to a firm whose credit or bankruptcy risk has increased has private knowledge that may encourage the bank to use its underwriting department to sell bonds to the unsuspecting public, thereby paying off the loan and earning a fee.
- A bank may make loans to a firm on overly favorable terms to obtain fees from it for performing activities such as underwriting the firm's securities.
- To sell its insurance products, a bank may try to influence or coerce a borrowing or investing customer.

All of these conflicts of interest may decrease the amount of accurate information production by the universal bank, thereby hindering its ability to promote efficient credit allocation. Although there have not been any recent banking scandals involving conflicts of interest, they did surface in the aftermath of the stock market crash of 1929 (see the Conflicts of Interest box, "Banksters").

Can the Market Limit Exploitation of Conflicts of Interest?

Conflicts of interest become a problem for the financial system when they lead to a decrease in the flow of reliable information, either because information is concealed or because misleading information is disseminated. The decline in the flow of reliable

conflicts of interest

 **Banksters**

Just as in the aftermath of the collapse of the tech bubble in 2000, the stock market crash of 1929 prompted many investors to question why they had been encouraged to purchase so many securities that declined in value so quickly. The public blamed the universal banks for hyping securities, and bankers were pejoratively referred to as "banksters" to equate them with gangsters. Public pressure led the Senate Banking and Currency Committee to hold hearings to investigate potential abuses by the universal banks. These hearings, which became known as the Pecora hearings after the chief counsel who led them, were as famous in their day as the Watergate hearings that led to President Nixon's resignation in 1974 or the hearings of the 9/11 Commission in 2004.

The Pecora hearings turned up several cases of apparently severe abuses of conflicts of interest in the banking industry. An affiliate of National City Bank (the precursor to Citibank) was accused of selling "unsound and speculative securities" to the bank's customers, particularly bonds from the Republic of Peru that went into default. Chase National Bank and National City Bank were accused of converting bad loans to companies such as General Theaters and Equipment and the General Sugar Company into securities that were sold to the public and investment trusts managed by these banks. The president of National City Bank, Charles E. Mitchell, and the head of Chase National Bank, Albert H. Wiggin, were accused of setting up *pool operations*, in which resources from the banks were used to prop up their stock price for the benefit of these executives and their associates.

The resulting scandals led to passage of the Glass-Steagall Act in 1933, which eliminated the possibility of these conflicts of interest by mandating complete separation of commercial banking from investment banking activities. It was not until 1999 that this act was repealed by Congress to enable banks to be more competitive.

information makes it harder for the financial system to solve adverse selection and moral hazard problems, which can slow the flow of credit to parties with productive investment opportunities.

Even though conflicts of interest exist, they do not necessarily reduce the flow of reliable information because the incentives to exploit the conflict of interest may not be very high. When an exploitation of a conflict of interest is visible to the market, it can punish a financial service firm by denying it business. Given the importance of maintaining and enhancing a financial firm's reputation, exploiting any conflicts of interest would decrease the firm's future profitability because it would have greater difficulty selling its services. In this way, the firm has incentives *not* to exploit a conflict of interest. These incentives limit conflicts of interest in the long run, but they may not be effective in the short run depending on structural factors within the firm, such as a lack of transparency and inappropriate monetary incentives.

One enlightening example of how the market can limit exploitation of conflicts of interest occurs in credit-rating agencies. At first glance, the fact that rating agencies are paid by the firms issuing securities to produce ratings for these securities looks like a serious conflict of interest. Rating agencies would seem to have powerful incentives to gain business by providing security-issuing firms with higher credit ratings than they deserve, making it easier for the firms to sell their securities at higher prices. In reality, little evidence suggests that rating agencies take advantage of this conflict of interest, despite prominent examples such as Enron.[2] Much research has shown that a reasonably close correlation exists between ratings and default probabilities. Ratings agencies do not exploit the conflict of interest because giving higher credit ratings to firms that pay for the ratings would lower the credibility of the ratings, making them less valuable to the market. The market is able to assess the quality of biased ratings because it can observe poorer performance by individual securities. Furthermore, credit-rating agencies themselves provide evidence on the relationship between their ratings and subsequent default history. If a rating agency continually gave high ratings to firms that eventually defaulted, investors in the market would no longer trust its ratings, its reputation would become tarnished, and good, nondefaulting firms would go elsewhere for their ratings. For this reason, the rating agency has an incentive not to exploit this conflict of interest and overrate the bonds of its customers.

Similarly, commercial banks that underwrote securities prior to the enactment of the Glass-Steagall Act do not appear to have exploited this conflict of interest. When a commercial bank underwrites securities, the bank may have an incentive to market the securities of financially troubled firms to the public because the firms will then be able to pay back the loans they owe to the bank, while at the same time the bank earns fees from the underwriting services. The evidence suggests that in the 1920s, markets found securities underwritten by bond departments within a commercial bank to be less attractive than securities underwritten in separate affiliates where the conflict of interest was more transparent. To maintain the bank's reputation, commercial banks shifted their underwriting to separate affiliates over time, with the result that securities underwritten by banks became valued as highly as those underwritten by independent investment banks.[3] When affiliates were unable to certify the absence of conflicts, they focused on underwriting securities from well-known firms, for which less of an information asymmetry existed and conflicts of interest were less pronounced. Again, the market provided incentives to control potential conflicts of interest. However, it is important to note that the market solution was not immediate, but took some time to develop.

The responsiveness of the market is also evident in the apparent conflict of interest present in investment banks when underwriters who have incentives to favor issuers over investors pressure research analysts to provide more favorable assessments of issuers' securities. Analysts at an investment bank that is underwriting particular IPOs tend to make more "buy" recommendations for these IPOs than do

---

[2]See the survey in Bank for International Settlements, "Credit Ratings and Complementary Sources of Credit Quality Information," Basel Committee on Banking Supervision Working Papers No. 3, August 2000, and the discussion in Andrew Crockett, Trevor Harris, Frederic S. Mishkin, and Eugene N. White, *Conflicts of Interest in the Financial Services Industry: What Should We Do About Them?* Geneva Reports on the World Economy 4 (Geneva and London: International Center for Monetary and Banking Studies and Centre for Economic Policy Research, 2003).

[3]See Randall S. Kroszner and Raghuram G. Rajan, "Is the Glass-Steagall Act Justified? A Study of the US Experience with Universal Banking Before 1933," *American Economic Review* 84 (1994): 810–832; Randall S. Kroszner and Raghuram G. Rajan, "Organization, Structure, and Credibility: Evidence from Commercial Bank Securities Activities Before the Glass-Steagall Act," *Journal of Monetary Economics* 39 (1997); James S. Ang and Terry Richardson, "The Underwriting Experience of Commercial Bank Affiliates Prior to the Glass-Steagall Act," *Journal of Banking and Finance* 18 (March 1994): 351–395; and Manu Pari, "Commercial Banks in Investment Banking: Conflict of Interest or Certification Role?" *Journal of Financial Economics* 40 (1996): 373–401.

analysts at other investment banks, and the market takes account of this tendency in pricing these securities. Over a two-year period, the performance of other analysts' recommended securities was 50% better than the performance of securities recommended by analysts at the investment banks that underwrote these IPOs. The market appears to recognize the difference in the quality of information when the potential for a conflict of interest exists.[4]

Fewer empirical studies have examined how the market addresses conflicts of interest that arise in accounting firms, but the limited evidence available does suggest that the market adjusts securities' prices to account for potential conflicts of interest. The evidence suggests that clients, who are concerned about the conflicts of interest that arise from the joint provision of auditing and management advisory services, ascribe less value to audit opinions and limit their nonaudit purchases from the accounting firms that have these conflicts of interest.[5]

Although the market can sometimes ameliorate the effects of conflicts of interest in financial service firms, it cannot always constrain the incentives to exploit conflicts of interest. For the market to prevent this type of exploitation, it needs to have enough information to assess whether an exploitation of conflicts of interest is actually occurring. In some cases, parties who want to take advantage of conflicts of interest will try to hide this information from the market. In other cases, alerting the market to potential conflicts of interest would reveal proprietary information that would help a financial firm's competitors, thus reducing the firm's incentives to reveal its true position.

The recent scandals described in this chapter demonstrate that the exploitation of a conflict of interest often leads to large gains for some members of the financial firm even while it reduces the value of the firm as a whole. Inappropriately designed compensation plans (the result of poor management), for example, may produce conflicts of interest that not only reduce the flow of reliable information to credit markets but also end up destroying the firm. Indeed, the collapse of Arthur Andersen illustrates how the compensation arrangements for one line of business, such as auditing, can create serious conflicts of interest. In the Arthur Andersen case, the partners in regional offices had incentives to please their largest clients even if their actions were detrimental to the firm as a whole. The conflict of interest problem can become even more hazardous when several lines of business are combined and the returns from one of the activities—such as underwriting or consulting—are very high for only a brief amount of time. Also, a compensation scheme that works reasonably well in the short term might become poorly aligned over time.

The extraordinary surge in the stock market created huge temporary rewards, making it possible for well-positioned analysts, underwriters, and audit firm partners to exploit the conflicts before incentives could be realigned. Often, these conflicts of interest were not readily visible to the market, and they may have been invisible even to the top management of a firm. In the most severe cases, opportunistic individuals were able to capture the firm's **reputational rents,** profits that the firm earns because it is trusted by the marketplace. The exploitation of conflicts of interest clearly damaged the reputation of such investment banks as Merrill Lynch, Salomon

[4]Rani Micaela and Kent L. Womack, "Conflict of Interest and the Credibility of Underwriter Analyst Recommendations," *Review of Financial Studies* 12 (Special Issue 1999): 653–686.

[5]Mohinder Parkas and Carol F. Venable, "Auditee Incentives for Auditor Independence: The Case of Non Audit Services," *Accounting Review* 68 (1993): 113–133.

Smith Barney of Citigroup, and Credit Suisse First Boston—and perhaps the credibility of analysts in general. Audit firms have lost much of their nonaudit business, while Arthur Andersen was destroyed.

What Has Been Done to Remedy Conflicts of Interest?

Two major policy measures have been implemented to deal with conflicts of interest in financial markets: the Sarbanes-Oxley Act and the Global Legal Settlement.

Sarbanes-Oxley Act of 2002

go online

www.sarbanes-oxley.com/
A Web site devoted to
discussion and dissemination
of information about the
Sarbanes-Oxley Act.

In 2002, the public outcry over the corporate and accounting scandals led to the passage of the Public Accounting Reform and Investor Protection Act, more commonly referred to as the Sarbanes-Oxley Act after its two principal authors in Congress. This act has four major components.

1. The act increases supervisory oversight to monitor and prevent conflicts of interest:
   - It establishes a Public Company Accounting Oversight Board (PCAOB), overseen by the SEC, to supervise accounting firms and ensure that audits are independent and controlled for quality.
   - It increases the SEC's budget to supervise securities markets.
2. Sarbanes-Oxley also directly reduces conflicts of interest:
   - The act makes it unlawful for a registered public accounting firm to provide any nonaudit service to a client contemporaneously with an impermissable audit (as determined by the PCAOB).
3. Sarbanes-Oxley provides incentives for investment banks not to exploit conflicts of interests:
   - It beefs up criminal charges for white-collar crime and obstruction of official investigations.
4. Sarbanes-Oxley also has measures to improve the quality of information in the financial markets:
   - It requires a corporation's chief executive officer (CEO) and chief financial officer (CFO) to certify that periodic financial statements and disclosures of the firm (especially regarding off-balance-sheet transactions) are accurate.
   - It requires members of the audit committee (the subcommittee of the board of directors that oversees the company's audit) to be "independent"—that is, they cannot be managers in the company or receive any consulting or advisory fee from the company.

Global Legal Settlement of 2002

The second policy arose out of a lawsuit brought by New York Attorney General Eliott Spitzer against the ten largest investment banks (Bear Stearns, Credit Suisse First Boston, Deutsche Bank, Goldman Sachs, J. P. Morgan, Lehman Brothers, Merrill Lynch, Morgan Stanley, Salomon Smith Barney, and UBS Warburg). Spitzer alleged that these firms allowed their investment banking departments to have inappropriate influence over their research analysts, thereby creating a conflict of interest. On December 20, 2002, the SEC, the New York Attorney General, NASD, NASAA, NYSE, and state regulators reached a global agreement with these investment banks. The agreement includes three key elements:

1. Like Sarbanes-Oxley, the Global Legal Settlement directly reduces conflicts of interest:
   - It requires investment banks to sever the links between research and securities underwriting.
   - It bans spinning.
2. The Global Legal Settlement provides incentives for investment banks not to exploit conflicts of interests:
   - It imposes $1.4 billion of fines on the accused investment banks.
3. The Global Legal Settlement has measures to improve the quality of information in financial markets:
   - It requires investment banks to make public their analysts' recommendations.
   - It requires investment banks for a five-year period to contract with no fewer than three independent research firms that would provide research to their brokerage customers.

A Framework for Evaluating Policies to Remedy Conflicts of Interest

The information view of conflicts of interest developed in this chapter provides a framework for evaluating whether conflicts of interest require public policy actions to eliminate or reduce them. Some combination of financial service activities may result in incentives for agents to conceal information, but they may also result in synergies that make it easier to produce information. Thus, preventing the combination of activities to eliminate the conflicts of interest may actually make financial markets less efficient. This reasoning suggests that two propositions are critical to evaluating what should be done about conflicts of interest:

1. *The existence of a conflict of interest does not mean that it will have serious adverse consequences.* Even though a conflict of interest exists, the incentives to exploit the conflict of interest may not be very high. An exploitation of a conflict of interest that is visible to the market will typically tarnish the reputation of the financial firm where it takes place. Given the importance of maintaining and enhancing its reputation, exploiting the conflict of interest would decrease the firm's future profitability because the firm would have greater difficulty selling its services. As a consequence, firms try to structure their salary and reward systems so as to include incentives to avoid the exploitation of the conflict of interest. Hence, the marketplace may be able to control conflicts of interest because a high value is placed on financial firms' reputations. When evaluating the need for remedies, this proposition raises the issue of whether the market has adequate information and incentives to control conflicts of interest.

2. *Even if incentives to exploit conflicts of interest remain strong, elimi-nating the economies of scope that create the conflicts of interest may be harmful because it will reduce the flow of reliable information.* Thus, in evaluating possible remedies, we need to examine whether imposing the remedy will do more harm than good by curtailing the flow of reliable information in financial markets.

Approaches to Remedying Conflicts of Interest

In thinking about remedies for specific problematic situations, it is worthwhile to discuss five generic approaches to reconciling conflicts of interest. These approaches are discussed in the order of their intrusiveness, from least intrusive to most intrusive.

Leave It to the Market This approach has a powerful appeal to many economists and may be a sufficient response in many cases. Market forces can work through two mechanisms. First, they can penalize the financial service firm if it exploits a con-flict of interest. For example, a penalty may be imposed by the market in the form of higher funding costs or lower demand for the firm's services, in varying degrees, even to the point of forcing the demise of the firm. Second, market forces can pro-mote new institutional means to contain conflicts of interest. For example, they can generate a demand for information from nonconflicted organizations. This is exactly what happened in the United States in the 1920s, when security affiliates took pre-eminence over in-house bond departments in universal banks.

One advantage of market-driven solutions is that they can hit where it hurts the most, through pecuniary penalties. Moreover, they may help avoid the risk of over-reaction. It can be hard to resist the temptation to adopt nonmarket solutions to appease a public outcry that may reduce information production in financial markets. Conversely, market-based solutions may not always work if the market cannot obtain sufficient information to appropriately punish financial firms that are exploiting conflicts of interest. Memories may be short in financial markets, as is suggested by the new field of behavioral finance discussed in Chapter 6. Once a triggering event has faded from memory, conflicts may creep back in unless reforms have been "hard-wired" into the system.

go online
www.sec.gov/
The SEC is primarily responsible for preventing fraud in the securities markets. Click on "What We Do" to learn what role the SEC envisions for itself in the securities industry.

Regulate for Transparency A competitive market structure does not always ade-quately reduce information asymmetries. The gathering of information is costly, and any individual economic agent will gather information only if the private benefit outweighs the cost. When the information collected becomes available to the mar-ket immediately, the free-rider problem may reach serious levels. Information has the attribute of a public good, which will be undersupplied in the absence of some pub-lic intervention. To some extent, mandatory information disclosure can alleviate infor-mation asymmetries and is a key element of regulation of the financial system.

When mandatory disclosure of information reveals whether a conflict of inter-est exists, the market is able to discipline the financial firm that fails to ameliorate conflicts of interest. In addition, if a financial institution is required to provide infor-mation about potential conflicts of interest, the user of the institution's information services may be able to judge how much weight to place on the information this insti-tution supplies.

At the same time, mandatory disclosure could create problems if it reveals so much proprietary information that the financial institution is unable to profitably engage in the information production business. The result could then be less information production, rather than more. Also, mandatory disclosure may not work if financial firms can successfully avoid the regulation and continue to hide relevant information about potential conflicts of interest. The free-rider problem might likewise result in insufficient monitoring of conflicts of interest because the benefits of monitoring and constraining these conflicts accrue only partially to the monitors. Finally, complying with regulations requiring information disclosure may be costly for financial firms—possibly exceeding the costs due to conflicts of interest.

Supervisory Oversight If mandatory disclosure does not work because firms continue to hide relevant information, because the free-rider problem is severe, or because mandatory disclosure would reveal proprietary information, supervisory oversight can come to the rescue and contain conflicts of interest. Supervisors can observe proprietary information about conflicts of interest without revealing it to a financial firm's competitors so that the firm can continue to profitably engage in information production activities. Armed with this information, the supervisor can take actions to prevent financial firms from exploiting conflicts of interest. As part of this supervisory oversight, standards of practice can be developed, either by the supervisor or by the firms engaged in a specific information production activity. Enforcement of these standards would then be placed in the hands of the supervisor.

As we will see in Chapter 20, supervisory oversight of this type is very common in the banking industry. In recent years, bank supervisors have sharpened their focus on risk management. They now examine banks' risk management procedures to ensure that the appropriate internal controls on risk taking have been established at the bank. In a similar fashion, supervisors can examine banks' internal procedures and controls to restrict conflicts of interest. When they find weak internal controls, they can require the financial institution to modify them so that incentives to exploit conflicts of interest are eliminated.

Although supervisory oversight has proved successful in improving internal controls in financial firms in recent years, if the incentives to exploit conflicts of interest are sufficiently strong, financial institutions may still be able to hide conflicts of interest from the supervisors. Furthermore, supervisors have not always done their job well.

Separation of Functions Where the market cannot obtain sufficient information to constrain conflicts of interest—because there is no satisfactory way of inducing information disclosure by market discipline or supervisory oversight—the incentives to exploit conflicts of interest may be reduced or eliminated by regulations enforcing separation of functions. Several degrees of separation are possible. First, activities may be separated into different in-house departments with firewalls between them. Second, the firm may restrict different activities to separately capitalized affiliates. Third, regulations may prohibit the combination of activities in any organizational form.

The goal of separation of functions is to ensure that agents are not placed in the position of responding to multiple principals. Moving from relaxed to more stringent separation of functions, conflicts of interest are reduced to an increasing degree. Of course, more stringent separation of functions also reduces synergies of information collection, thereby preventing financial firms from taking advantage of economies of scope in information production. The resulting increased cost of producing information could, in turn, lead to a decreased flow of reliable information because it becomes more expensive to produce it. Deciding on the appropriate amount of separation therefore involves a trade-off between the benefits of reducing conflicts of interest and the cost of reducing economies of scope in producing information.

Socialization of Information Production The most radical response to conflicts generated by the existence of asymmetric information is the socialization of the provision or the funding source of the relevant information. For example, much macroeconomic information is provided by publicly funded agencies, because this particular public good is likely to be undersupplied if left to private provision. It is conceivable that other information-providing functions—for example, credit ratings and auditing— could also be publicly supplied. Alternatively, if the information-generating services are left to the private sector, they could be funded by public sources or by a publicly mandated levy to help ensure that information production is not tainted by obligations to fee-paying entities with special interests.

Of course, the problem with this approach is that a government agency or publicly funded entity may not have the same strong incentives as private financial institutions to produce high-quality information. Forcing information production to be conducted by a government or quasi-government entity—although it may diminish conflicts of interest—may reduce the flow of reliable information to financial markets. Furthermore, government agencies may have difficulty paying the market wages required to attract the best people. This problem may become even more serious if economies of scope are affected. For example, analysts in an investment banking firm are likely to receive additional compensation when their research has multiple uses. By contrast, a government agency that is interested in only one use of research may not provide a level of compensation sufficient to produce high-quality information. In addition, the government might not provide sufficient funds for information collection. Indeed, government provision of important series of macroeconomic data has already been discontinued because of a lack of funding.

CASE

Evaluating Sarbanes-Oxley and the Global Legal Settlement

Using the analytic framework discussed earlier, we now can turn to evaluating the Sarbanes-Oxley Act and the Global Legal Settlement.

We have seen that policies that regulate conflicts of interest can help to increase the amount of information in financial markets. Sarbanes-Oxley does exactly this when it requires that the CEO and the CFO certify the periodic financial statements and disclosures of the firm. It increases the likelihood that these statements will provide reliable information. In addition, Sarbanes-Oxley requires disclosure of off-balance-sheet transactions and other relationships with special-purpose entities. Again, this step can help increase information in the marketplace because these off-balance-sheet transactions were often used, as in the Enron case, to hide what was going on inside the firm.

However, the costs of complying with the new regulations imposed by Sarbanes-Oxley are not cheap. Complaints about high costs have focused particularly on the act's Section 404 requirements that firms and auditors review and test the quality of firms' internal risk control systems. Weaknesses in these systems that might lead to financial misstatements must be disclosed, giving firms strong incentives to incur costs to strengthen their control systems and thereby increase the reliability of the information they provide financial markets.[6] Small firms are hit particularly hard: The estimated costs of complying with Sarbanes-Oxley exceed $800,000 for smaller firms with revenues of less than $100 million, which amounts to nearly 1.5% of their sales. Sarbanes-Oxley might severely hurt such companies' profitability and make it harder for them to make productive investments.

Fortunately, there are signs that compliance costs are coming down for both large and small firms. A poll of chief financial officers at 200 large companies (with average revenues of $6.8 billion) showed that average compliance costs fell to $2.9 million in 2006, down 23% from 2005. It appears that complying with Sarbanes-Oxley involves high start-up costs but also a learning curve of greater efficiency as time passes. Relief is also on the way for small firms: In 2007 the SEC relaxed some of the guidelines for implementing Section 404, which will allow firms' managers and auditors to focus on specific areas of information reporting where risk of fraud or error is greatest. Auditors can concentrate on the end result, whether a company's system of financial controls works, rather than prepare a detailed (and costly) evaluation of the process that produces that result. These changes could help reduce firms' auditing expenses by as much at 50%.[7]

We have also seen that the market is often able to constrain conflicts of interest when it has sufficient information to do so. The Global Legal Settlement includes a provision that requires investment banking firms to make their analysts' recommendations public. This policy will help the market to assess whether the analysts are acting in good faith. The SEC also requires increased disclosure by investment analysts, credit-rating agencies, and auditors, forcing them to reveal any interests they have in the firms they analyze. Provision of this information makes it more likely that financial institutions will develop internal rules to ensure that conflicts of interest are minimized, so that their reputations remain high and the firms profitable.

Of course, disclosure may not be enough to get markets to control conflicts of interest, because firms still have incentives to hide information so that they can profitably exploit conflicts of interest. Disclosure may also reveal so much proprietary information that the financial institution is unable to profitably engage in the information production business. In addition, some of the most damaging conflicts of interest have resulted from poorly designed internal compensation mechanisms, which are difficult for markets to observe. Supervisory oversight can focus on exactly these issues.

---

[6]Indeed, Sarbanes-Oxley might create incentives for firms to strengthen their financial controls *too much* (and thus incur even greater costs). This occurs because top executives may face personal liability for damages that result from financial misinformation about their firm. This may lead them to approve spending to strengthen the firm's accounting control systems even when the reduction in the likelihood of misinformation that results is slight relative to the cost of the improvement. This is an example of the principal–agent problem: The firm's top executives (the agents) choose a level of spending on financial controls that is higher than the firm's stockholders (the principals) desire. This occurs because the objective of the top executives, to minimize their legal liability, differs from the stockholders' objective of maximum profits. See John C. Coates IV, "The Goals and Promise of the Sarbanes-Oxley Act," *Journal of Economic Perspectives*, 21 (2007): 91–116, for a discussion of this and other effects of the Sarbanes-Oxley Act.

[7]"Five Years Under the Thumb," *The Economist*, July 28, 2007:73–74.

Increased supervisory oversight is a key feature of the Sarbanes-Oxley Act. First, the act establishes the PCAOB to supervise accounting firms. The PCAOB monitors compensation mechanisms to verify that they are in accord with the best practices to control conflicts of interest. Second, Sarbanes-Oxley provides substantially more resources for the SEC. A supervisory agency cannot do its job properly without adequate resources. Indeed, one reason why the SEC may have failed to provide adequate supervisory oversight during the boom of the 1990s is because it was starved for resources. A similar problem occurred for the supervisors of the savings and loan industry, and it helped lead to scandals and a bailout that cost taxpayers more than $100 billion.

By keeping the audit committee independent of management, Sarbanes-Oxley eliminates the conflict of interest that occurs when the management of a firm hires its auditor. The PCAOB will be instrumental in writing the regulations to ensure that auditors will report to, be hired by, and be compensated by an independent audit committee that is supposed to represent shareholders other than management.

The Global Legal Settlement also directly eliminates one Wall Street practice that led to obvious conflicts of interest—spinning, in which executives received hot IPO shares in return for their companies' future business with the investment bank underwriting the new issue. The Global Legal Settlement punished investment banks that exploited conflicts of interest by imposing a fine of more than $1.4 billion. This tough punishment, along with the harsher criminal penalties established by Sarbanes-Oxley, provides incentives for investment banking firms to avoid taking advantage of conflicts of interest in the future.

The more radical parts of Sarbanes-Oxley and the Global Legal Settlement involve separation of functions and socialization of information. Sarbanes-Oxley makes it illegal for accounting firms to provide nonaudit consulting services to their audit customers. This law will potentially reduce the economies of scope available to auditing firms that also offer consulting services. It is unlikely that the proscription of nonauditing services in this situation, as envisioned by Sarbanes-Oxley, would have prevented the recent audit failures. However, greater transparency about the nature and role of nonaudit services would be a valuable aid to control a firm's temptation to exploit this conflict of interest. Similarly, the Global Legal Settlement requires investment banking firms to sever the link between research and investment banking. This divestiture also has the potential to eliminate economies of scope in information production. After all, analysts may be able to obtain much more information on firms they cover when the investment banking arm of the firm can share information with them.

The Global Legal Settlement requires that for a five-year period, brokerage firms contract with independent research firms to provide information to their customers. In addition, part of the $1.4 billion fine paid by the investment banks will be used to fund independent research and investor education. While it remains to be seen how the terms of this agreement will be implemented, there are both potentially positive and potentially negative features. Independent research may produce unbiased information. However, by socializing research, firms can no longer compete for customers on the basis of the quality of their research. Because they are being taxed to fund independent research, firms may decrease their investment in their own research analysis. Indeed, this is exactly what has already happened, with research budgets at the seven largest securities firms being cut almost in half since 2000. If the investment banks do not control the information that they are being forced to acquire, the analysis produced may be of a lower quality.

SUMMARY

1. Conflicts of interest arise when financial service firms or their employees serve multiple interests and develop incentives to misuse or conceal information needed for the effective functioning of financial markets. If taking advantage of conflicts of interest substantially reduces the amount of reliable information in financial markets, asymmetric information increases and prevents financial markets from channeling funds to those firms with the most productive investment opportunities.

2. Four types of financial service activities have the greatest potential for conflicts of interest that reduce reliable information in financial markets: (1) underwriting and research in investment banking, (2) auditing and consulting in accounting firms, (3) credit assessment and consulting in credit-rating agencies, and (4) universal banking.

3. Even though conflicts of interest may exist, they do not necessarily have to reduce the flow of reliable information, because the market provides strong incentives for financial service firms to avoid damaging their reputations. The evidence suggests that the market often succeeds in constraining the incentives to exploit conflicts of interest. However, conflicts of interest still pose a threat to the efficiency of financial markets.

4. Two major policy measures deal with conflicts of interest: the Sarbanes-Oxley Act of 2002 and the Global Legal Settlement arising from the lawsuit by the New York Attorney General against the 10 largest investment banks.

5. Two basic propositions are critical to evaluating what should be done about conflicts of interest: (1) The fact that a conflict of interest exists does not mean that the conflict will necessarily have serious adverse consequences. (2) Even if incentives to exploit conflicts of interest remain strong, eliminating the conflict of interest may be harmful if it destroys economies of scope, thereby reducing the flow of reliable information. Five approaches to remedying conflicts of interest, going from least intrusive to most intrusive, have been suggested: (1) leave it to the market, (2) regulate for transparency, (3) provide supervisory oversight, (4) mandate separation of functions, and (5) require socialization of information.

6. Sarbanes-Oxley and the Global Legal Settlement help increase the flow of reliable information in financial markets by requiring the CEO and CFO to certify financial statements, corporations to disclose off-balance-sheet transactions and entities, and investment banks to make public their analysts' recommendations, and by requiring increased disclosure of potential conflicts of interest. Sarbanes-Oxley increases supervisory oversight by establishing the Public Company Accounting Oversight Board (PCAOB) and by increasing the resources available to the SEC. The act also reduces conflicts of interest in auditing by making the audit committee independent of management. The Global Legal Settlement eliminates the conflict of interest inherent in spinning. The $1.4 billion fine and harsher criminal penalties imposed by Sarbanes-Oxley provide incentives for investment banks not to exploit conflicts of interest in the future. The more radical parts of Sarbanes-Oxley and the Global Legal Settlement, which involve separation of functions (research from underwriting, and auditing from nonaudit consulting) and socialization of research information, may ultimately reduce the information available in financial markets.

KEY TERMS

conflicts of interest, *p. 400*
economies of scope, *p. 400*
initial public offerings (IPOs), *p. 402*

management advisory services, *p. 402*
reputational rents, *p. 409*
spinning, *p. 402*

QUESTIONS

1. Why can the provision of several types of financial services by one firm lead to a lower cost of information production?

2. How does the provision of several types of financial services by one firm lead to conflicts of interest?

3. How can conflicts of interest make financial markets less efficient?

4. How can conflicts of interest lead to unethical behavior?

5. Describe two conflicts of interest that occur when underwriting and research are provided by a single investment banking firm.

6. How does spinning lead to a less efficient financial market?

7. Describe two conflicts of interest that occur in accounting firms.

8. Some commentators have attributed the demise of Arthur Andersen to the combination of auditing and consulting activities in the firm. Is this assessment correct?

9. Describe two conflicts of interest that occur in credit-rating agencies.

10. Describe two conflicts of interest that occur in universal banks.

11. "Conflicts of interest always reduce the flow of reliable information." Is this statement true, false, or uncertain? Explain your answer.

12. Give two examples of conflicts of interest that do not seem to have been exploited and thus did not lead to a reduction of reliable information in the financial markets.

13. When is it more likely that conflicts of interest will be exploited?

14. How can compensation schemes in financial service firms lead to conflicts of interest?

15. What are the advantages and disadvantages of mandatory disclosure in dealing with conflicts of interest?

16. How can supervisory oversight help reduce conflicts of interest?

17. What are the disadvantages of separating financial activities into different firms in an effort to avoid conflicts of interest?

18. What are the advantages and disadvantages of government provision of information as a solution to the problems created by conflicts of interest?

19. Which provisions of the Sarbanes-Oxley Act do you think are beneficial, and which are not?

20. Which provisions of the Global Legal Settlement do you think are beneficial, and which are not?

WEB EXERCISES

What Should Be Done About Conflicts of Interest?

1. Go to **www.SOX-online.com**. This site tracks issues and news related to the Sarbanes-Oxley Act. Click on "SOX Basics."

   a. Summarize in two or three sentences the primary reason for passage of the Sarbanes-Oxley Act.

   b. Under "Special Collections," click on "News Articles." Summarize one of the articles discussed under "Google News." Address how this article relates to conflicts of interest in the financial industry.

2. Go to **www.sec.gov/** and click on "Press Releases."

   a. Summarize the major types of issues that the SEC addresses in these press releases.

   b. Review the last three months of releases, and count how many appear to be enforcement actions aimed at firms or individuals who have violated SEC regulations. From this review, does the SEC appear to be active in its effort to prevent fraud and misrepresentation in the securities industry?

PART 6

The Financial Institutions Industry

CHAPTER 17

Banking and the Management of Financial Institutions

Preview

Because banking plays such a major role in channeling funds to borrowers with productive investment opportunities, this financial activity is important in ensuring that the financial system and the economy run smoothly and efficiently. In the United States, banks (depository institutions) supply more than $6 trillion in credit annually. They provide loans to businesses, help us finance our college educations or the purchase of a new car or home, and provide us with services such as checking and savings accounts.

In this chapter, we examine how banking is conducted to earn the highest profits possible: how and why banks make loans, how they acquire funds and manage their assets and liabilities (debts), and how they earn income. Although we focus on commercial banking because this is the most important financial intermediary activity, many of the same principles are applicable to other types of financial intermediation.

The Bank Balance Sheet

go online

www.bankofamerica.com/
investor/index.cfm?
section=700
Click on Annual Reports to
view the balance sheet.

To understand how banking works, we start by looking at the bank **balance sheet,** a list of the bank's assets and liabilities. As the name implies, this list balances; that is, it has the characteristic that

$$\text{total assets} = \text{total liabilities} + \text{capital}$$

A bank's balance sheet is also a list of its *sources* of bank funds (liabilities) and *uses* to which the funds are put (assets). Banks obtain funds by borrowing and by issuing other liabilities such as deposits. They then use these funds to acquire assets such as securities and loans. Banks make profits by

TABLE 17.1 Balance Sheet of All Commercial Banks (items as a percentage of the total, end of 2007)

Assets (Uses of Funds)*		Liabilities (Sources of Funds)	
Reserves and cash items	3%	Checkable deposits	6%
Securities		Nontransaction deposits	
U.S. government and agency	12	Small-denomination time deposits	
State and local government and		(<$100,000 + savings deposits)	40
other securities	11	Large-denomination time deposits	19
Loans		Borrowings	26
Commercial and industrial	12	Bank capital	9
Real estate	34		
Consumer	7		
Interbank	4		
Other	9		
Other assets (for example, physical capital)	8		
Total	100	Total	100

*In order of decreasing liquidity.
Source: www.federalreserve.gov/releases/h8/current/.

charging an interest rate on their asset holdings of securities and loans that is higher than the interest and other expenses on their liabilities. The balance sheet of all commercial banks at the beginning of 2007 appears in Table 17.1.

Liabilities

A bank acquires funds by issuing (selling) liabilities, such as deposits, which are the *sources of funds* the bank uses. The funds obtained from issuing liabilities are used to purchase income-earning assets.

Checkable Deposits Checkable deposits are bank accounts that allow the owner of the account to write checks to third parties. Checkable deposits include all accounts on which checks can be drawn: non-interest-bearing checking accounts (demand deposits), interest-bearing NOW (negotiable order of withdrawal) accounts, and money market deposit accounts (MMDAs). Introduced with the Depository Institutions Act in 1982, MMDAs have features similar to those of money market mutual funds and are included in the checkable deposits category. However, MMDAs are not subject to reserve requirements (discussed later in the chapter) as checkable deposits are. Table 17.1 shows that the category of checkable deposits is an important source of bank funds, making up 6% of bank liabilities. Once, checkable deposits were the most important source of bank funds (more than 60% of bank liabilities in 1960), but with the appearance of new, more attractive financial instruments, such as money market deposit accounts, the share of checkable deposits in total bank liabilities has shrunk over time.

Checkable deposits and money market deposit accounts are payable on demand; that is, if a depositor shows up at the bank and requests payment by making a withdrawal, the bank must pay the depositor immediately. Similarly, if a person who receives a check written on an account from a bank, presents that check at the bank, it must pay the funds out immediately (or credit them to that person's account).

A checkable deposit is an asset for the depositor because it is part of his or her wealth. Because the depositor can withdraw funds and the bank is obligated to pay, checkable deposits are a liability for the bank. They are usually the lowest-cost source of bank funds because depositors are willing to forgo some interest to have access to a liquid asset that can be used to make purchases. The bank's costs of maintaining checkable deposits include interest payments and the costs incurred in servicing these accounts—processing, preparing, and sending out monthly statements, providing efficient tellers (human or otherwise), maintaining an impressive building and conveniently located branches, and advertising and marketing to entice customers to deposit their funds with a given bank. In recent years, interest paid on deposits (checkable and nontransaction) has accounted for around 30% of total bank operating expenses, while the costs involved in servicing accounts (employee salaries, building rent, and so on) have been approximately 50% of operating expenses.

Nontransaction Deposits Nontransaction deposits are the primary source of bank funds (59% of bank liabilities in Table 17.1). Owners cannot write checks on nontransaction deposits, but the interest rates paid on these deposits are usually higher than those on checkable deposits. There are two basic types of nontransaction deposits: savings accounts and time deposits (also called certificates of deposit, or CDs).

Savings accounts were once the most common type of nontransaction deposit. In these accounts, to which funds can be added or from which funds can be withdrawn at any time, transactions and interest payments are recorded in a monthly statement or in a passbook held by the owner of the account.

Time deposits have a fixed maturity length, ranging from several months to over five years, and assess substantial penalties for early withdrawal (the forfeiture of several months' interest). Small-denomination time deposits (deposits of less than $100,000) are less liquid for the depositor than passbook savings, earn higher interest rates, and are a more costly source of funds for the banks.

Large-denomination time deposits (CDs) are available in denominations of $100,000 or more and are typically bought by corporations or other banks. Large-denomination CDs are negotiable; like bonds, they can be resold in a secondary market before they mature. For this reason, negotiable CDs are held by corporations, money market mutual funds, and other financial institutions as alternative assets to Treasury bills and other short-term bonds. Since 1961, when they first appeared, negotiable CDs have become an important source of bank funds (19%).

Borrowings Banks also obtain funds by borrowing from the Federal Reserve System, the Federal Home Loan banks, other banks, and corporations. Borrowings from the Fed are called **discount loans** (also known as *advances*). Banks also borrow reserves overnight in the federal (fed) funds market from other U.S. banks and financial institutions. Banks borrow funds overnight to have enough deposits at the Federal Reserve to meet the amount required by the Fed. (The *federal funds* designation is somewhat confusing, because these loans are not made by the federal government or by the Federal Reserve, but rather by banks to other banks.) Other sources of borrowed funds are loans made to banks by their parent companies (bank holding companies), loan arrangements with corporations (such as repurchase agreements), and borrowings of Eurodollars (deposits denominated in U.S. dollars residing in foreign banks or foreign branches of U.S. banks). Borrowings have become a more important source of bank funds over time: In 1960, they made up only 2% of bank liabilities; currently, they are 26% of bank liabilities.

Bank Capital The final category on the liabilities side of the balance sheet is bank capital, the bank's net worth, which equals the difference between total assets and liabilities (9% of total bank assets in Table 17.1). Bank capital is raised by selling new equity (stock) or from retained earnings. Bank capital is a cushion against a drop in the value of its assets, which could force the bank into insolvency (having liabilities in excess of assets, meaning that the bank can be forced into liquidation).

Assets

A bank uses the funds that it has acquired by issuing liabilities to purchase income-earning assets. Bank assets are thus naturally referred to as *uses of funds*, and the interest payments earned on them are what enable banks to make profits.

Reserves All banks hold some of the funds they acquire as deposits in an account at the Fed. **Reserves** are these deposits plus currency that is physically held by banks (called **vault cash** because it is stored in bank vaults overnight). Although reserves currently do not pay any interest, banks hold them for two reasons. First, some reserves, called **required reserves,** are held because of **reserve requirements,** the regulation that for every dollar of checkable deposits at a bank, a certain fraction (10 cents, for example) must be kept as reserves. This fraction (10% in the example) is called the **required reserve ratio.** Banks hold additional reserves, called **excess reserves,** because they are the most liquid of all bank assets and can be used by a bank to meet its obligations when funds are withdrawn, either directly by a depositor or indirectly when a check is written on an account.

Cash Items in Process of Collection Suppose that a check written on an account at another bank is deposited in your bank and the funds for this check have not yet been received (collected) from the other bank. The check is classified as a cash item in process of collection, and it is an asset for your bank because it is a claim on another bank for funds that will be paid within a few days.

Deposits at Other Banks Many small banks hold deposits in larger banks in exchange for a variety of services, including check collection, foreign exchange transactions, and help with securities purchases. This is an aspect of a system called *correspondent banking*.

Collectively, reserves, cash items in process of collection, and deposits at other banks are referred to as *cash items*. In Table 17.1, they constitute only 3% of total assets, and their importance has been shrinking over time: In 1960, for example, they accounted for 20% of total assets.

Securities A bank's holdings of securities are an important income-earning asset: Securities (made up entirely of debt instruments for commercial banks, because banks are not allowed to hold stock) account for 23% of bank assets in Table 17.1, and they provide commercial banks with about 10% of their revenue. These securities can be classified into three categories: U.S. government and agency securities, state and local government securities, and other securities. The U.S. government and agency securities are the most liquid because they can be easily traded and converted into cash with low transaction costs. Because of their high liquidity, short-term U.S. government securities are called **secondary reserves.**

Banks hold state and local government securities because state and local governments are more likely to do business with banks that hold their securities. State and local government and other securities are both less marketable (less liquid) and riskier than U.S. government securities, primarily because of default risk: There is some possibility that the issuer of the securities may not be able to make its interest payments or pay back the face value of the securities when they mature.

Loans Banks make their profits primarily by issuing loans. In Table 17.1, some 66% of bank assets are in the form of loans, and in recent years they have generally produced more than half of bank revenues. A loan is a liability for the individual or corporation receiving it, but an asset for a bank, because it provides income to the bank. Loans are typically less liquid than other assets, because they cannot be turned into cash until the loan matures. If the bank makes a one-year loan, for example, it cannot get its funds back until the loan comes due in one year. Loans also have a higher probability of default than other assets. Because of the lack of liquidity and higher default risk, the bank earns its highest return on loans.

As you saw in Table 17.1, the largest categories of loans for commercial banks are commercial and industrial loans made to businesses, and real estate loans. Commercial banks also make consumer loans and lend to each other. The bulk of these interbank loans are overnight loans lent in the federal funds market. The major difference in the balance sheets of the various depository institutions is primarily in the type of loan in which they specialize. Savings and loans and mutual savings banks, for example, specialize in residential mortgages, while credit unions tend to make consumer loans.

Other Assets The physical capital (bank buildings, computers, and other equipment) owned by the banks is included in this category.

Basic Banking

Before proceeding to a more detailed study of how a bank manages its assets and liabilities to make the highest profit, you should understand the basic operation of a bank.

In general terms, banks make profits by selling liabilities with one set of characteristics (a particular combination of liquidity, risk, size, and return) and using the proceeds to buy assets with a different set of characteristics. This process is often referred to as *asset transformation.* For example, a savings deposit held by one person can provide the funds that enable the bank to make a mortgage loan to another person. The bank has, in effect, transformed the savings deposit (an asset held by the depositor) into a mortgage loan (an asset held by the bank). Another way this process of asset transformation is described is to say that the bank "borrows short and lends long" because it makes long-term loans and funds them by issuing short-dated deposits.

The process of transforming assets and providing a set of services (check clearing, record keeping, credit analysis, and so forth) is like any other production process in a firm. If the bank produces desirable services at low cost and earns substantial income on its assets, it earns profits; if not, the bank suffers losses.

To make our analysis of the operation of a bank more concrete, we use a tool called a **T-account.** A T-account is a simplified balance sheet, with lines in the form of a T, that lists only the changes that occur in balance sheet items starting from some initial balance sheet position. Let's say that Jane Brown has heard that the First National Bank provides excellent service, so she opens a checking account with a $100 bill. She now has a $100 checkable deposit at the bank, which shows up as a $100 liability on the bank's balance sheet. The bank now puts her $100 bill into its vault so that the bank's assets rise by the $100 increase in vault cash. The T-account for the bank looks like this:

First National Bank			
Assets		Liabilities	
Vault Cash	+$100	Checkable deposits	+$100

Because vault cash is also part of the bank's reserves, we can rewrite the T-account as follows:

Assets		Liabilities	
Reserves	+$100	Checkable deposits	+$100

Note that Jane Brown's opening of a checking account leads to *an increase in the bank's reserves equal to the increase in checkable deposits.*

If Jane had opened her account with a $100 check written on an account at another bank, say, the Second National Bank, we would get the same result. The initial effect on the T-account of the First National Bank is as follows:

Assets		Liabilities	
Cash items in process of collection	+$100	Checkable deposits	+$100

Checkable deposits increase by $100 as before, but now the First National Bank is owed $100 by the Second National Bank. This asset for the First National Bank is entered in the T-account as $100 of cash items in process of collection because the First National Bank will now try to collect the funds that it is owed. It could go directly to the Second National Bank and ask for payment of the funds, but if the two banks are in separate states, that would be a time-consuming and costly process. Instead, the First National Bank deposits the check in its account at the Fed, and the Fed collects the funds from the Second National Bank. The result is that the Fed transfers $100 of reserves from the Second National Bank to the First National Bank, and the final balance sheet positions of the two banks are as follows:

First National Bank				Second National Bank			
Assets		Liabilities		Assets		Liabilities	
Reserves	+$100	Checkable deposits	+$100	Reserves	−$100	Checkable deposits	−$100

The process initiated by Jane Brown can be summarized as follows: When a check written on an account at one bank is deposited in another, the bank receiving the deposit gains reserves equal to the amount of the check, while the bank on which the check is written sees its reserves fall by the same amount. Therefore, ***when a bank receives additional deposits, it gains an equal amount of reserves; when it loses deposits, it loses an equal amount of reserves.***

study guide

T-accounts are used to study various topics throughout this text. Whenever you see a T-account, try to analyze what would happen if the opposite action were taken; for example, what would happen if Jane Brown decided to close her $100 account at the First National Bank by writing a $100 check and depositing it in a new checking account at the Second National Bank?

Now that you understand how banks gain and lose reserves, we can examine how a bank rearranges its balance sheet to make a profit when it experiences a change in its deposits. Let's return to the situation when the First National Bank has just received the extra $100 of checkable deposits. As you know, the bank is obliged to keep a certain fraction of its checkable deposits as required reserves. If the fraction (the required reserve ratio) is 10%, the First National Bank's required reserves have increased by $10, and we can rewrite its T-account as follows:

First National Bank

Assets		Liabilities	
Required reserves	+$10	Checkable deposits	+$100
Excess reserves	+$90		

Let's see how well the bank is doing as a result of the additional checkable deposits. Because reserves pay no interest, it has no income from the additional $100 of assets. But servicing the extra $100 of checkable deposits is costly, because the bank must keep records, pay tellers, pay for check clearing, and so forth. The bank is taking a loss! The situation is even worse if the bank makes interest payments on the deposits, as with NOW accounts. If it is to make a profit, the bank must put to productive use all or part of the $90 of excess reserves it has available. One way to do this is to invest in securities. The other is to make loans; as we have seen, loans account for approximately two-thirds of the total value of bank assets (uses of funds). Because lenders are subject to the asymmetric information problems of adverse selection and moral hazard (discussed in Chapter 15), banks take steps to reduce the incidence and severity of these problems. Bank loan officers evaluate potential borrowers using what are called the "five C's": character, capacity (ability to repay), collateral, conditions (in the local and national economies), and capital (net worth) before they agree to lend. (Chapter 24 provides a more detailed discussion of the methods banks use to reduce the risk involved in lending.)

Let us assume that the bank chooses not to hold any excess reserves but to make loans instead. The T-account then looks like this:

Assets		Liabilities	
Required reserves	+$10	Checkable deposits	+$100
Loans	+$90		

The bank is now making a profit because it holds short-term liabilities such as checkable deposits and uses the proceeds to buy longer-term assets such as loans with higher interest rates. As mentioned earlier, this process of asset transformation is frequently described by saying that banks are in the business of "borrowing short and lending long." For example, if the loans have an interest rate of 10% per year, the bank earns $9 in income from its loans over the year. If the $100 of checkable deposits is in a NOW account with a 5% interest rate and it costs another $3 per year to service the account, the cost per year of these deposits is $8. The bank's profit on the new deposits is then $1 per year (a 1% return on assets).

General Principles of Bank Management

Now that you have some idea of how a bank operates, let's look at how a bank manages its assets and liabilities to earn the highest possible profit. The bank manager has four primary concerns. The first is to make sure that the bank has enough ready cash to pay its depositors when there are **deposit outflows**—that is, when deposits are lost because depositors make withdrawals and demand payment. To keep enough cash on hand, the bank must engage in **liquidity management,** the acquisition of sufficiently liquid assets to meet the bank's obligations to depositors. Second, the bank manager must pursue an acceptably low level of risk by acquiring assets that have a low rate of default and by diversifying asset holdings (**asset management**). The third concern is to acquire funds at low cost (**liability management**). Finally, the manager must decide the amount of capital the bank should maintain and then acquire the needed capital (**capital adequacy management**).

To understand bank and other financial institution management fully, we must go beyond the general principles of bank asset and liability management described next and look in more detail at how a financial institution manages its assets. Chapter 24 provides an in-depth discussion of how a financial institution manages **credit risk,** the risk arising because borrowers may default, and how it manages **interest-rate risk,** the riskiness of earnings and returns on bank assets that results from interest-rate changes.

Liquidity Management and the Role of Reserves

Let us see how a typical bank, the First National Bank, can deal with deposit outflows that occur when its depositors withdraw cash from checking or savings accounts or write checks that are deposited in other banks. In the example that follows, we assume that the bank has ample excess reserves and that all deposits have the same required reserve ratio of 10% (the bank is required to keep 10% of its time and checkable deposits as reserves). Suppose that the First National Bank's initial balance sheet is as follows:

Assets		Liabilities	
Reserves	$20 million	Deposits	$100 million
Loans	$80 million	Bank capital	$ 10 million
Securities	$10 million		

The bank's required reserves are 10% of $100 million, or $10 million. Given that it holds $20 million of reserves, the First National Bank has excess reserves of $10 million. If a deposit outflow of $10 million occurs, the bank's balance sheet becomes

Assets		Liabilities	
Reserves	$10 million	Deposits	$90 million
Loans	$80 million	Bank capital	$10 million
Securities	$10 million		

The bank loses $10 million of deposits *and* $10 million of reserves, but because its required reserves are now 10% of only $90 million ($9 million), its reserves still exceed this amount by $1 million. In short, ***if a bank has ample excess reserves, a deposit outflow does not necessitate changes in other parts of its balance sheet.***

The situation is quite different when a bank holds insufficient excess reserves. Let's assume that instead of initially holding $10 million in excess reserves, the First National Bank makes additional loans of $10 million, so that it holds no excess reserves. Its initial balance sheet would be

Assets		Liabilities	
Reserves	$10 million	Deposits	$100 million
Loans	$90 million	Bank capital	$ 10 million
Securities	$10 million		

When it suffers the $10 million deposit outflow, its balance sheet becomes

Assets		Liabilities	
Reserves	$ 0 million	Deposits	$90 million
Loans	$90 million	Bank capital	$10 million
Securities	$10 million		

After $10 million has been withdrawn from deposits and hence reserves, the bank has a problem: It has a reserve requirement of 10% of $90 million, or $9 million, but it has no reserves! To eliminate this shortfall, the bank has four basic options. One is to acquire reserves to meet a deposit outflow by borrowing them from other banks in the federal funds market or by borrowing from corporations.[1] If the First National Bank acquires the $9 million shortfall in reserves by borrowing it from other banks or corporations, its balance sheet becomes

Assets		Liabilities	
Reserves	$ 9 million	Deposits	$90 million
Loans	$90 million	Borrowings from other	$ 9 million
Securities	$10 million	banks or corporations	
		Bank capital	$10 million

The cost of this activity is the interest rate on these borrowings, such as the federal funds rate.

---

[1]One way that the First National Bank can borrow from other banks and corporations is by selling negotiable certificates of deposit. This method for obtaining funds is discussed in the section on liability management.

A second alternative is for the bank to sell some of its securities to help cover the deposit outflow. For example, it might sell $9 million of its securities and deposit the proceeds with the Fed, resulting in the following balance sheet:

Assets		Liabilities	
Reserves	$ 9 million	Deposits	$90 million
Loans	$90 million	Bank capital	$10 million
Securities	$ 1 million		

The bank incurs some brokerage and other transaction costs when it sells these securities. The U.S. government securities that are classified as secondary reserves are very liquid, so the transaction costs of selling them are quite modest. However, the other securities the bank holds are less liquid, and the transaction cost can be appreciably higher.

A third way that the bank can meet a deposit outflow is to acquire reserves by borrowing from the Fed. In our example, the First National Bank could leave its security and loan holdings the same and borrow $9 million in discount loans from the Fed. Its balance sheet would be

Assets		Liabilities	
Reserves	$ 9 million	Deposits	$90 million
Loans	$90 million	Borrowings from the Fed	$ 9 million
Securities	$10 million	Bank capital	$10 million

The cost associated with discount loans is the interest rate that must be paid to the Fed (called the **discount rate**).

Finally, a bank can acquire the $9 million of reserves to meet the deposit outflow by reducing its loans by this amount and depositing the $9 million it then receives with the Fed, thereby increasing its reserves by $9 million. This transaction changes the balance sheet as follows:

Assets		Liabilities	
Reserves	$ 9 million	Deposits	$90 million
Loans	$81 million	Bank capital	$10 million
Securities	$10 million		

The First National Bank is once again in good shape because its $9 million of reserves satisfies the reserve requirement.

However, this process of reducing its loans is the bank's costliest way of acquiring reserves when there is a deposit outflow. If the First National Bank has numerous short-term loans renewed at fairly short intervals, it can reduce its total amount of loans outstanding fairly quickly by *calling in* loans—that is, by not renewing some loans when they come due. Unfortunately for the bank, this is likely to antagonize the customers whose loans are not being renewed because they have not done anything to deserve such treatment. Indeed, they are likely to take their business elsewhere in the future, a very costly consequence for the bank.

A second method for reducing its loans is for the bank to sell them off to other banks. Again, this is very costly because other banks do not personally know the customers who have taken out the loans and so may not be willing to buy the loans at their full value (This is just the lemons adverse selection problem described in Chapter 15.)

The foregoing discussion explains why banks hold excess reserves even though loans or securities earn a higher return. When a deposit outflow occurs, holding excess reserves allows the bank to escape the costs of (1) borrowing from other banks or corporations, (2) selling securities, (3) borrowing from the Fed, or (4) calling in or selling off loans. ***Excess reserves are insurance against the costs associated with deposit outflows. The higher the costs associated with deposit outflows, the more excess reserves banks will want to hold.***

Just as you and I would be willing to pay an insurance company to insure us against a casualty loss such as the theft of a car, a bank is willing to pay the cost of holding excess reserves (the opportunity cost, the earnings forgone by not holding income-earning assets such as loans or securities) to insure against losses due to deposit outflows. Because excess reserves, like insurance, have a cost, banks also take other steps to protect themselves; for example, they might shift their holdings of assets to more liquid securities (secondary reserves).

study guide

Bank management is easier to grasp if you put yourself in the banker's shoes and imagine what you would do in the situations described. To understand a bank's possible responses to deposit outflows, imagine how you as a banker might respond to two successive deposit outflows of $10 million.

Asset Management

Now that you understand why a bank has a need for liquidity, we can examine the basic strategy a bank pursues in managing its assets. To maximize its profits, a bank must simultaneously seek the highest returns possible on loans and securities, reduce risk, and make adequate provisions for liquidity by holding liquid assets. Banks try to accomplish these three goals in four basic ways.

First, banks try to find borrowers who will pay high interest rates and are unlikely to default on their loans. They seek out loan business by advertising their borrowing rates and by approaching corporations directly to solicit loans. It is up to the bank's loan officer to decide if potential borrowers are good credit risks who will make interest and principal payments on time (i.e., engage in screening to reduce the adverse selection problem). Typically, banks are conservative in their loan policies; the default rate is usually less than 1%. It is important, however, that banks not be so conservative that they miss out on attractive lending opportunities that earn high interest rates.

Second, banks try to purchase securities with high returns and low risk. Third, in managing their assets, banks must attempt to lower risk by diversifying. They accomplish this by purchasing many different types of assets (short- and long-term, U.S. Treasury, and municipal bonds) and approving many types of loans to a number of customers. Banks that have not sufficiently sought the benefits of diversification often come to regret it later. For example, banks that had overspecialized in making loans to energy companies, real estate developers, or farmers suffered huge losses in the 1980s with the slump in energy, property, and farm prices. Indeed, many of these banks went broke because they had "put too many eggs in one basket."

Finally, the bank must manage the liquidity of its assets so that it can satisfy its reserve requirements without bearing huge costs. This means that it will hold liquid securities even if they earn a somewhat lower return than other assets. The bank must decide, for example, how much in excess reserves must be held to avoid costs from a deposit outflow. In addition, it will want to hold U.S. government securities as secondary reserves so that even if a deposit outflow forces some costs on the bank, these will not be terribly high. Again, it is not wise for a bank to be too conservative. If it avoids all costs associated with deposit outflows by holding only excess reserves, the bank suffers losses because reserves earn no interest, while the bank's liabilities are costly to maintain. The bank must balance its desire for liquidity against the increased earnings that can be obtained from less liquid assets such as loans.

Liability Management

Before the 1960s, liability management was a staid affair: For the most part, banks took their liabilities as fixed and spent their time trying to achieve an optimal mix of assets. There were two main reasons for the emphasis on asset management. First, more than 60% of the sources of bank funds were obtained through checkable (demand) deposits that by law could not pay any interest. Thus, banks could not actively compete with one another for these deposits by paying interest on them, and so their amount was effectively a given for an individual bank. Second, because the markets for making overnight loans between banks were not well developed, banks rarely borrowed from other banks to meet their reserve needs.

Starting in the 1960s, however, large banks (called **money center banks**) in key financial centers, such as New York, Chicago, and San Francisco, began to explore ways in which the liabilities on their balance sheets could provide them with reserves and liquidity. This led to an expansion of overnight loan markets, such as the federal funds market, and the development of new financial instruments such as negotiable CDs (first developed in 1961), which enabled money center banks to acquire funds quickly.[2]

This new flexibility in liability management meant that banks could take a different approach to bank management. They no longer needed to depend on checkable deposits as the primary source of bank funds and as a result no longer treated their sources of funds (liabilities) as given. Instead, they aggressively set target goals for their asset growth and tried to acquire funds (by issuing liabilities) as they were needed.

For example, today, when a money center bank finds an attractive loan opportunity, it can acquire funds by selling a negotiable CD. Or, if it has a reserve shortfall, it can borrow funds from another bank in the federal funds market without incurring high transaction costs. The federal funds market can also be used to finance

---

[2]Because small banks are not as well known as money center banks and so might be a higher credit risk, they find it harder to raise funds in the negotiable CD market. Hence, they do not engage nearly as actively in liability management.

loans. Because of the increased importance of liability management, most banks now manage both sides of the balance sheet together in an *asset–liability management (ALM) committee.*

The greater emphasis on liability management explains some of the important changes over the past three decades in the composition of banks' balance sheets. While negotiable CDs and bank borrowings have greatly increased in importance as a source of bank funds in recent years (rising from 2% of bank liabilities in 1960 to 45% by the end of 2007), checkable deposits have decreased in importance (from 61% of bank liabilities in 1960 to 6% by the end of 2007). Newfound flexibility in liability management and the search for higher profits have also stimulated banks to increase the proportion of their assets held in loans, which earn higher income (from 46% of bank assets in 1960 to 66% by the end of 2007).

Capital Adequacy Management

Banks have to make decisions about the amount of capital they need to hold for three reasons. First, bank capital helps prevent *bank failure,* a situation in which the bank cannot satisfy its obligations to pay its depositors and other creditors and so goes out of business. Second, the amount of capital affects returns for the owners (equity holders) of the bank. Third, a minimum amount of bank capital (bank capital requirements) is required by regulatory authorities.

How Bank Capital Helps Prevent Bank Failure Let's consider two banks with identical balance sheets, except that the High Capital Bank has a ratio of capital to assets of 10% while the Low Capital Bank has a ratio of 4%.

High Capital Bank				Low Capital Bank			
Assets		Liabilities		Assets		Liabilities	
Reserves	$10 million	Deposits	$90 million	Reserves	$10 million	Deposits	$96 million
Loans	$90 million	Bank capital	$10 million	Loans	$90 million	Bank capital	$ 4 million

Suppose that both banks get caught up in the euphoria of the telecom market, only to find that $5 million of their telecom loans became worthless later. When these bad loans are written off (valued at zero), the total value of assets declines by $5 million. As a consequence, bank capital, which equals total assets minus liabilities, also declines by $5 million. The balance sheets of the two banks now look like this:

High Capital Bank				Low Capital Bank			
Assets		Liabilities		Assets		Liabilities	
Reserves	$10 million	Deposits	$90 million	Reserves	$10 million	Deposits	$96 million
Loans	$85 million	Bank capital	$ 5 million	Loans	$85 million	Bank capital	−$ 1 million

The High Capital Bank takes the $5 million loss in stride because its initial cushion of $10 million in capital means that it still has a positive net worth (bank capital) of $5 million after the loss. The Low Capital Bank, however, is in big trouble. Now the value of its assets has fallen below its liabilities, and its net worth is now

−$1 million. Because the bank has a negative net worth, it is insolvent: It does not have sufficient assets to pay off all holders of its liabilities. When a bank becomes insolvent, government regulators close the bank, its assets are sold off, and its managers are fired. Because the owners of the Low Capital Bank will find their investment wiped out, they would clearly have preferred the bank to have had a large enough cushion of bank capital to absorb the losses, as was the case for the High Capital Bank. We therefore see an important rationale for a bank to maintain a sufficient level of capital: *A bank maintains bank capital to lessen the chance that it will become insolvent.*

How the Amount of Bank Capital Affects Returns to Equity Holders Because owners of a bank must know whether their bank is being managed well, they need good measures of bank profitability. A basic measure of bank profitability is the **return on assets (ROA),** the net profit after taxes per dollar of assets:

$$\text{ROA} = \frac{\text{net profit after taxes}}{\text{assets}}$$

The return on assets provides information on how efficiently a bank is being run, because it indicates how much profits are generated on average by each dollar of assets.

However, what the bank's owners (equity holders) care about most is how much the bank is earning on their equity investment. This information is provided by the other basic measure of bank profitability, the **return on equity (ROE),** the net profit after taxes per dollar of equity (bank) capital:

$$\text{ROE} = \frac{\text{net profit after taxes}}{\text{equity capital}}$$

There is a direct relationship between the return on assets (which measures how efficiently the bank is run) and the return on equity (which measures how well the owners are doing on their investment). This relationship is determined by the **equity multiplier (EM),** the amount of assets per dollar of equity capital:

$$\text{EM} = \frac{\text{assets}}{\text{equity capital}}$$

To see this, we note that

$$\frac{\text{net profit after taxes}}{\text{equity capital}} = \frac{\text{net profit after taxes}}{\text{assets}} \times \frac{\text{assets}}{\text{equity capital}}$$

which, using our definitions, yields

$$\text{ROE} = \text{ROA} \times \text{EM} \tag{1}$$

The formula in Equation 1 tells us what happens to the return on equity when a bank holds a smaller amount of capital (equity) for a given amount of assets. As we have seen, the High Capital Bank initially has $100 million of assets and $10 million of equity, which gives it an equity multiplier of 10 (=$100 million/$10 million). The Low Capital Bank, by contrast, has only $4 million of equity, so its equity multiplier is higher, equaling 25 (=$100 million/$4 million). Suppose that these banks have been equally well run so that they both have the same return on assets, 1%. The return on equity for the High Capital Bank equals 1% × 10 = 10%, while the return on equity for the Low Capital Bank equals 1% × 25 = 25%. The equity holders in the Low Capital Bank are clearly a lot happier than the equity holders in the High Capital Bank because they are earning more than twice as high a return. We now see why owners of a bank may not want it to hold too much capital. ***Given the return on assets, the lower the bank capital, the higher the return for the owners of the bank.***

Trade-off Between Safety and Returns to Equity Holders We now see that bank capital has both benefits and costs. Bank capital benefits the owners of a bank in that it makes their investment safer by reducing the likelihood of bankruptcy. But bank capital is costly because the higher it is, the lower will be the return on equity for a given return on assets. In determining the amount of bank capital, managers must decide how much of the increased safety that comes with higher capital (the benefit) they are willing to trade off against the lower return on equity that comes with higher capital (the cost).

In more uncertain times, when the possibility of large losses on loans increases, bank managers might want to hold more capital to protect the equity holders. Conversely, if they have confidence that loan losses won't occur, they might want to reduce the amount of bank capital, have a higher equity multiplier, and thereby increase the return on equity.

Bank Capital Requirements Banks also hold capital because they are required to do so by regulatory authorities. Because of the high costs of holding capital for the reasons just described, bank managers often want to hold less bank capital relative to assets than is required by the regulatory authorities. In this case, the amount of bank capital is determined by the bank capital requirements. We discuss the details of bank capital requirements and their important role in bank regulation in Chapter 20.

THE PRACTICING MANAGER

Strategies for Managing Bank Capital

Mona, the manager of the First National Bank, has to make decisions about the appropriate amount of bank capital. Looking at the balance sheet of the bank, which like the High Capital Bank has a ratio of bank capital to assets of 10% ($10 million of capital and $100 million of assets), Mona is concerned that the large amount of bank capital is causing the return on equity to be too low. She concludes that the bank has a capital surplus and should increase the equity multiplier to increase the return on equity.

To lower the amount of capital relative to assets and raise the equity multiplier, she can do any of three things: (1) She can reduce the amount of bank capital by buying back some of the bank's stock. (2) She can reduce the bank's capital by paying out higher dividends to its stockholders, thereby reducing the bank's retained earnings. (3) She can keep bank capital constant but increase the bank's assets by acquiring new funds—say, by issuing CDs—and then seeking out loan business or purchasing more securities with these new funds. Because the manager thinks that it would enhance her position with the stockholders, she decides to pursue the second alternative and raise the dividend on the First National Bank stock.

Now suppose that the First National Bank is in a similar situation to the Low Capital Bank and has a ratio of bank capital to assets of 4%. The bank manager now might worry that the bank is short on capital relative to assets because it does not have a sufficient cushion to prevent bank failure. To raise the amount of capital relative to assets, she now has the following three choices: (1) She can raise capital for the bank by having it issue equity (common stock). (2) She can raise capital by reducing the bank's dividends to shareholders, thereby increasing retained earnings that it can put into its capital account. (3) She can keep capital at the same level but reduce the bank's assets by making fewer loans or by selling off securities and then using the proceeds to reduce its liabilities. Suppose that raising bank capital is not easy to do at the current time because capital markets are tight or because shareholders will protest if their dividends are cut. Then Mona might have to choose the third alternative and decide to shrink the size of the bank.

In past years, many banks experienced capital shortfalls and had to restrict asset growth, as Mona might have to do if the First National Bank were short of capital. The important consequences of this for the credit markets are discussed in the case that follows.

CASE

Did the Capital Crunch Cause a Credit Crunch in the Early 1990s?

During the 1990–1991 recession and the year following, there occurred a slowdown in the growth of credit that was unprecedented in the post–World War II era. Many economists and politicians have claimed that there was a "credit crunch" during this period in which credit was hard to get, and as a result the performance of the economy in 1990–1992 was very weak. Was the slowdown in credit growth a manifestation of a credit crunch, and if so, what caused it?

Our analysis of how a bank manages bank capital suggests that a credit crunch was likely to have occurred in 1990–1992 and that it was caused at least in part by the capital crunch, in which shortfalls of bank capital led to slower credit growth.

The period of the late 1980s saw a boom and then a major bust in the real estate market that led to huge losses for banks on their real estate loans. As our example of how bank capital helps prevent bank failures demonstrates, the loan losses caused a substantial fall in the amount of bank capital. At the same time, regulators were raising capital requirements (a subject discussed in Chapter 20). The resulting capital shortfalls meant that banks had to either raise new capital or restrict their asset growth by cutting back on lending. Because of the weak economy at the time, raising new capital was extremely difficult for banks, so they chose the latter course. Banks did restrict their lending, and borrowers found it harder to obtain loans, leading to complaints from banks' customers. Only with the stronger recovery of the economy in 1993, helped by a low-interest-rate policy at the Federal Reserve, did these complaints subside.

Off-Balance-Sheet Activities

Although asset and liability management has traditionally been the major concern of banks, in the more competitive environment of recent years banks have been aggressively seeking out profits by engaging in off-balance-sheet activities.[3] **Off-balance-sheet activities** involve trading financial instruments and generating income from fees and loan sales, activities that affect bank profits but do not appear on bank balance sheets. Indeed, off-balance-sheet activities have been growing in importance for banks: The income from these activities as a percentage of assets has nearly doubled since 1980.

Loan Sales

One type of off-balance-sheet activity that has grown in importance in recent years involves income generated by loan sales. A **loan sale,** also called a *secondary loan participation*, involves a contract that sells all or part of the cash stream from a specific loan and thereby removes the loan from the bank's balance sheet. Banks earn profits by selling loans for an amount slightly greater than the amount of the original loan. Because the high interest rate on these loans makes them attractive, institutions are willing to buy them, even though the higher price means that they earn a slightly lower interest rate than the original interest rate on the loan, usually on the order of 0.15 percentage point.

Generation of Fee Income

Another type of off-balance-sheet activity involves the generation of income from fees that banks receive for providing specialized services to their customers, such as making foreign exchange trades on a customer's behalf, servicing a mortgage-backed security by collecting interest and principal payments and then paying them out, guaranteeing debt securities such as banker's acceptances (by which the bank promises to make interest and principal payments if the party issuing the security cannot), and providing backup lines of credit. There are several types of backup lines of credit. The most important is the **loan commitment,** under which for a fee the bank agrees to provide a loan at the customer's request, up to a given dollar amount, over a specified period of time. Credit lines are also now available to bank depositors with "overdraft privileges"—these bank customers can write checks in excess of their deposit balances and, in effect, write themselves a loan. Other lines of credit for which banks get fees include standby letters of credit to back up issues of commercial paper and other securities and credit lines (called *note issuance facilities*, NIFs, and *revolving underwriting facilities*, RUFs) for underwriting Euronotes, which are medium-term Eurobonds.

Off-balance-sheet activities involving guarantees of securities and backup credit lines increase the risk a bank faces. Even though a guaranteed security does not appear on a bank balance sheet, it still exposes the bank to default risk: If the issuer of the security defaults, the bank is left holding the bag and must pay off the security's

---

[3]Other financial intermediaries, such as insurance companies, pension funds, and finance companies, also make private loans, and the credit risk management principles we outline here apply to them as well.

owner. Backup credit lines also expose the bank to risk because the bank may be forced to provide loans when it does not have sufficient liquidity or when the borrower is a very poor credit risk.

Trading Activities and Risk Management Techniques

As we will see in Chapter 25, banks' attempts to manage interest-rate risk have led them to trading in financial futures, options for debt instruments, and interest-rate swaps. Banks engaged in international banking also conduct transactions in the foreign exchange market. All transactions in these markets are off-balance-sheet activities because they do not have a direct effect on the bank's balance sheet. Although bank trading in these markets is often directed toward reducing risk or facilitating other bank business, banks may also try to outguess the markets and engage in speculation. This speculation can be a very risky business and indeed has led to bank insolvencies, the most dramatic being the failure of Barings, a British bank, in 1995.

Trading activities, although often highly profitable, are dangerous because they make it easy for financial institutions and their employees to make huge bets quickly. A particular problem for management of trading activities is that the principal–agent problem, discussed in Chapter 15, is especially severe. Given the ability to place large bets, a trader (the agent), whether she trades in bond markets, in foreign exchange markets, or in financial derivatives, has an incentive to take on excessive risks: If her trading strategy leads to large profits, she is likely to receive a high salary and bonuses, but if she takes large losses, the financial institution (the principal) will have to cover them. As the Barings Bank failure in 1995 so forcefully demonstrated, a trader subject to the principal–agent problem can take an institution that is quite healthy and drive it into insolvency very rapidly (see the Conflicts of Interest box).

To reduce the principal–agent problem, managers of financial institutions must set up internal controls to prevent debacles like the one at Barings. Such controls include the complete separation of the people in charge of trading activities from those in charge of the bookkeeping for trades. In addition, managers must set limits on the total amount of traders' transactions and on the institution's risk exposure. Managers must also scrutinize risk assessment procedures using the latest computer technology. One such method involves the value-at-risk approach. In this approach, the institution develops a statistical model with which it can calculate the maximum loss that its portfolio is likely to sustain over a given time interval, dubbed the value at risk, or VAR. For example, a bank might estimate that the maximum loss it would be likely to sustain over one day with a probability of 1 in 100 is $1 million; the $1 million figure is the bank's calculated value at risk. Another approach is called "stress testing." In this approach, a manager asks models what would happen if a doomsday scenario occurs; that is, she looks at the losses the institution would sustain if an unusual combination of bad events occurred. With the value-at-risk approach and stress testing, a financial institution can assess its risk exposure and take steps to reduce it.

U.S. bank regulators have become concerned about the increased risk that banks are facing from their off-balance-sheet activities, and, as we will see in Chapter 20, are encouraging banks to pay increased attention to risk management. In addition, the Bank for International Settlements is developing additional bank capital requirements based on value-at-risk calculations for a bank's trading activities.

conflicts of interest

Barings, Daiwa, Sumitomo, and Allied Irish: Rogue Traders and the Principal–Agent Problem

The demise of Barings, a venerable British bank more than a century old, is a sad morality tale of how the principal–agent problem operating through a rogue trader can take a financial institution that has a healthy balance sheet one month and turn it into an insolvent tragedy the next.

In July 1992, Nick Leeson, Barings's new head clerk at its Singapore branch, began to speculate on the Nikkei, the Japanese version of the Dow Jones stock index. By late 1992, Leeson had suffered losses of $3 million, which he hid from his superiors by stashing the losses in a secret account. He even fooled his superiors into thinking he was generating large profits, thanks to a failure of internal controls at his firm, which allowed him to execute trades on the Singapore exchange *and* oversee the bookkeeping of those trades. (As anyone who runs a cash business, such as a bar, knows, there is always a lower likelihood of fraud if more than one person handles the cash. Similarly for trading operations, you never mix management of the back room with management of the front room; this principle was grossly violated by Barings's management.)

Things didn't get better for Leeson, who by late 1994 had losses exceeding $250 million. In January and February 1995, he bet the bank. On January 17, 1995, the day of the earthquake in Kobe, Japan, he lost $75 million, and by the end of the week had lost more than $150 million. When the stock market declined on February 23, leaving him with a further loss of $250 million, he called it quits and fled Singapore. Three days later, he turned himself in at the Frankfurt airport. By the end of his wild ride, Leeson's losses, $1.3 billion in all, ate up Barings's capital and caused the bank to fail. Leeson was subsequently convicted and sent to jail in Singapore for his activities. He was released in 1999 and apologized for his actions.

Our asymmetric information analysis of the principal–agent problem explains Leeson's behavior and the danger of Barings's management lapse. By letting Leeson control both his own trades and the back room, it increased asymmetric information, because it reduced the principal's (Barings's) knowledge about Leeson's trading activities. This lapse increased the moral hazard incentive for him to take risks at the bank's expense, as he was now less likely to be caught. Furthermore, once he had experienced large losses, he had even greater incentives to take on even higher risk because if his bets worked out, he could reverse his losses and keep in good standing with the company, whereas if his bets soured, he had little to lose because he was out of a job anyway. Indeed, the bigger his losses, the more he had to gain by bigger bets, which explains the escalation of the amount of his trades as his losses mounted. If Barings's managers had understood the principal–agent problem, they would have been more vigilant at finding out what Leeson was up to, and the bank might still be here today.

Unfortunately, Nick Leeson is no longer a rarity in the rogue traders' billionaire club, those who have lost more than $1 billion. Over 11 years, Toshihide Iguchi, an officer in the New York branch of Daiwa Bank, also had control of both the bond trading operation and the back room, and he racked up $1.1 billion in losses over the period. In July 1995, Iguchi disclosed his losses to his superiors, but the management of the bank did not disclose them to its regulators. The result was that Daiwa was slapped with a $340 million fine and the bank was thrown out of the country by U.S. bank regulators.

Yasuo Hamanaka is another member of the billionaire club. In July 1996, he topped Leeson's and Iguchi's record, losing $2.6 billion for his employer, the Sumitomo Corporation, one of Japan's top trading companies. John Rusnak lost *only* $691 million for his bank, Allied Irish Banks, over the period from 1997 until he was caught in February 2002.

The moral of these stories is that management of firms engaged in trading activities must reduce the principal–agent problem by closely monitoring their traders' activities, or the rogues' gallery will continue to grow.

Measuring Bank Performance

To understand how well a bank is doing, we need to start by looking at a bank's income statement, the description of the sources of income and expenses that affect the bank's profitability.

Bank's Income Statement

The end-of-year 2006 income statement for all federally insured commercial banks appears in Table 17.2.

TABLE 17.2 Income Statement for All Federally Insured Commercial Banks, 2006

	Amount ($ billions)		Share of Operating Income or Expenses (%)
Operating Income			
Interest income		548.0	71.6
Interest on loans	411.6		53.8
Interest on securities	79.0		10.3
Other interest	57.4		7.5
Noninterest income		217.4	28.4
Service charges on deposit accounts	35.7		4.7
Other noninterest income	181.7		23.7
Total operating income		765.4	100.0
Operating Expenses			
Interest expenses		263.1	45.5
Interest on deposits	173.1		29.9
Interest on fed funds and repos	34.5		6.0
Other	55.5		9.6
Noninterest expenses		290.2	50.1
Salaries and employee benefits	133.3		23.0
Premises and equipment	35.9		6.2
Other	121.0		20.9
Provisions for loan losses		25.5	4.4
Total operating expense		578.8	100.0
Net Operating Income		186.6	
Gains (losses) on securities		(1.3)	
Extraordinary items, net		2.6	
Income taxes		−59.5	
Net Income		128.4	

Source: http://www2.fdic.gov/SDI/main.asp.

Operating Income **Operating income** is the income that comes from a bank's ongoing operations. Most of a bank's operating income is generated by interest on its assets, particularly loans. As we see in Table 17.2, in 2006 interest income represented 71.6% of commercial banks' operating income. Interest income fluctuates with the level of interest rates, and so its percentage of operating income is highest when interest rates are at peak levels. That is exactly what happened in 1981, when interest rates rose above 15% and interest income rose to 93% of total bank operating income.

Noninterest income, which made up 28.4% of operating income in 2006, is generated partly by service charges on deposit accounts, but the bulk of it comes from the off-balance-sheet activities mentioned earlier, which generate fees or trading profits for the bank. The importance of these off-balance-sheet activities to bank profits has been growing in recent years. Whereas in 1980 other noninterest income from off-balance-sheet activities represented only 5% of operating income, it reached 23.7% in 2006.

Operating Expenses **Operating expenses** are the expenses incurred in conducting the bank's ongoing operations. An important component of a bank's operating expenses is the interest payments that it must make on its liabilities, particularly on its deposits. Just as interest income varies with the level of interest rates, so do interest expenses. Interest expenses as a percentage of total operating expenses reached a peak of 74% in 1981, when interest rates were at their highest, and fell to 45.5% in 2006 as interest rates moved lower. Noninterest expenses include the costs of running a banking business: salaries for tellers and officers, rent on bank buildings, purchases of equipment such as desks and vaults, and servicing costs of equipment such as computers.

The final item listed under operating expenses is provisions for loan losses. When a bank has a bad debt or anticipates that a loan might become a bad debt in the future, it can write up the loss as a current expense in its income statement under the "provision for loan losses" heading. Provisions for loan losses are directly related to loan loss reserves. When a bank wants to increase its loan loss reserves account by, say, $1 million, it does this by adding $1 million to its provisions for loan losses. Loan loss reserves rise when this is done because by increasing expenses when losses have not yet occurred, earnings are being set aside to deal with the losses in the future.

Provisions for loan losses have been a major element in fluctuating bank profits in recent years. The 1980s brought the third-world debt crisis; a sharp decline in energy prices in 1986, which caused substantial losses on loans to energy producers; and a collapse in the real estate market. As a result, provisions for loan losses were particularly high in the late 1980s, reaching a peak of 13% of operating expenses in 1987. Since then, losses on loans have begun to subside, and in 2006 provisions for loan losses dropped to only 4.4% of operating expenses.

Income Subtracting the $578.8 billion in operating expenses from the $765.4 billion of operating income in 2006 yields net operating income of $186.6 billion. Net operating income is closely watched by bank managers, bank shareholders, and bank regulators because it indicates how well the bank is doing on an ongoing basis.

Two items, gains (or losses) on securities sold by banks ($1.3 billion) and net extraordinary items, which are events or transactions that are both unusual and infrequent (insignificant), are added to the $186.6 billion net operating income figure to get the $187.9 billion figure for net income before taxes. Net income before taxes is more commonly referred to as profits before taxes. Subtracting the $59.5 billion of income taxes then results in $128.4 billion of net income. Net income, more commonly referred to as profits after taxes, is the figure that tells us most directly how well the bank is doing because it is the amount that the bank has available to keep as retained earnings or to pay out to stockholders as dividends.

Measures of Bank Performance

Although net income gives us an idea of how well a bank is doing, it suffers from one major drawback: It does not adjust for the bank's size, thus making it hard to compare how well one bank is doing relative to another. A basic measure of bank profitability that corrects for the size of the bank is the return on assets (ROA), mentioned earlier in the chapter, which divides the net income of the bank by the amount of its assets. ROA is a useful measure of how well a bank manager is doing on the job because it indicates how well a bank's assets are being used to generate profits. At the beginning of 2007, the assets of all federally insured commercial banks amounted to $10,090.4 billion, so using the $128.4 billion net income figure from Table 17.2 gives us a return on assets of

$$\text{ROA} = \frac{\text{net income}}{\text{assets}} = \frac{128.4}{10,090.4} = 0.013 = 1.3\%$$

Although ROA provides useful information about bank profitability, we have already seen that it is not what the bank's owners (equity holders) care about most. They are more concerned about how much the bank is earning on their equity investment, an amount that is measured by the return on equity (ROE), the net income per dollar of equity capital. At the beginning of 2007, equity capital for all federally insured commercial banks was $1,030.18 billion, so the ROE was therefore

$$\text{ROE} = \frac{\text{net income}}{\text{capital}} = \frac{128.4}{1,030.18} = 0.125 = 12.5\%$$

Another commonly watched measure of bank performance is called the **net interest margin (NIM),** the difference between interest income and interest expenses as a percentage of total assets:

$$\text{NIM} = \frac{\text{interest income} - \text{interest expenses}}{\text{assets}}$$

As we have seen earlier in the chapter, one of a bank's primary intermediation functions is to issue liabilities and use the proceeds to purchase income-earning assets. If a bank manager has done a good job of asset and liability management such that the bank earns substantial income on its assets and has low costs on its liabilities, profits will be high. How well a bank manages its assets and liabilities is affected by the spread between the interest earned on the bank's assets and the interest costs on its liabilities. This spread is exactly what the net interest margin measures. If the bank is able to raise funds with liabilities that have low interest costs and is able to acquire assets with high interest income, the net interest margin will be high, and the bank is likely to be highly profitable. If the interest cost of its liabilities rises relative to the interest earned on its assets, the net interest margin will fall, and bank profitability will suffer.

Recent Trends in Bank Performance Measures

Table 17.3 provides measures of return on assets (ROA), return on equity (ROE), and the net interest margin (NIM) for all federally insured commercial banks from 1980 to 2007. Because the relationship between bank equity capital and total assets for all commercial banks remained fairly stable in the 1980s, both the ROA and ROE measures of bank performance move closely together and indicate that from the early to the late 1980s, there was a sharp decline in bank profitability. The rightmost column,

TABLE 17.3 Measures of Bank Performance, 1980–2007

Year	Return on Assets (ROA) (%)	Return on Equity (ROE) (%)	Net Interest Margin (NIM)(%)
1980	0.77	13.38	3.33
1981	0.79	13.68	3.31
1982	0.73	12.55	3.39
1983	0.68	11.60	3.34
1984	0.66	11.04	3.47
1985	0.72	11.67	3.62
1986	0.64	10.30	3.48
1987	0.09	1.54	3.40
1988	0.82	13.74	3.57
1989	0.50	7.92	3.58
1990	0.49	7.81	3.50
1991	0.53	8.25	3.60
1992	0.94	13.86	3.89
1993	1.23	16.30	3.97
1994	1.20	15.00	3.95
1995	1.17	14.66	4.29
1996	1.19	14.45	4.27
1997	1.23	14.69	4.21
1998	1.18	13.30	3.47
1999	1.31	15.31	4.07
2000	1.19	14.02	3.95
2001	1.15	13.09	3.90
2002	1.30	14.08	3.96
2003	1.38	15.05	3.73
2004	1.28	13.20	3.54
2005	1.30	12.73	3.50
2006	1.28	12.31	3.31
2007*	1.21	11.44	3.32

*"Projected by FDIC.
Source: http://www2.fdic.gov/qbp/2007mar/all1a.html.

net interest margin, indicates that the spread between interest income and interest expenses remained fairly stable throughout the 1980s and even improved in the late 1980s and early 1990s, which should have helped bank profits. The NIM measure thus tells us that the poor bank performance in the late 1980s was not the result of interest-rate movements.

The explanation of the weak performance of commercial banks in the late 1980s is that they had made many risky loans in the early 1980s that turned sour. The resulting huge increase in loan loss provisions in that period directly decreased net income and hence caused the fall in ROA and ROE. (Why bank profitability deteriorated and the consequences for the economy are discussed in Chapters 18 and 20.)

Beginning in 1992, bank performance improved substantially. The return on equity rose to nearly 14% in 1992 and remained above 12% in the 1993–2006 period. Similarly, the return on assets rose from the 0.5% level in the 1990–1991 period to well over the 1% level in 1993–2006. The performance measures in Table 17.3 suggest that the banking industry has returned to health.

SUMMARY

1. The balance sheet of commercial banks can be thought of as a list of the sources and uses of bank funds. The bank's liabilities are its sources of funds, which include checkable deposits, time deposits, discount loans from the Fed, borrowings from other banks and corporations, and bank capital. The bank's assets are its uses of funds, which include reserves, cash items in process of collection, deposits at other banks, securities, loans, and other assets (mostly physical capital).

2. Banks make profits through the process of asset transformation: They borrow short (accept deposits) and lend long (make loans). When a bank takes in additional deposits, it gains an equal amount of reserves; when it pays out deposits, it loses an equal amount of reserves.

3. Although more liquid assets tend to earn lower returns, banks still desire to hold them. Specifically, banks hold excess and secondary reserves because they provide insurance against the costs of a deposit outflow. Banks manage their assets to maximize profits by seeking the highest returns possible on loans and securities while at the same time trying to lower risk and making adequate provisions for liquidity. Although liability management was once a staid affair,

large (money center) banks now actively seek out sources of funds by issuing liabilities such as negotiable CDs or by actively borrowing from other banks and corporations. Banks manage the amount of capital they hold to prevent bank failure and to meet bank capital requirements set by the regulatory authorities. However, they do not want to hold too much capital because by so doing they will lower the returns to equity holders.

4. Off-balance-sheet activities consist of trading financial instruments and generating income from fees and loan sales, all of which affect bank profits but are not visible on bank balance sheets. Because these off-balance-sheet activities expose banks to increased risk, bank management must pay particular attention to risk assessment procedures and internal controls to restrict employees from taking on too much risk.

5. A bank's net operating income equals operating income minus operating expenses. Adding gains (or losses) on securities and net extraordinary items to net operating income and then subtracting taxes yields net income (profits after taxes). Additional measures of bank performance include the return on assets (ROA), the return on equity (ROE), and the net interest margin (NIM).

KEY TERMS

asset management, *p. 428*
balance sheet, *p. 421*
capital adequacy management, *p. 428*
credit risk, *p. 428*
deposit outflows, *p. 428*
discount loans, *p. 423*
discount rate, *p. 430*
equity multiplier (EM), *p. 434*
excess reserves, *p. 424*
interest-rate risk, *p. 428*
liability management, *p. 428*
liquidity management, *p. 428*
loan commitment, *p. 437*
loan sale, *p. 437*

money center banks, *p. 432*
net interest margin (NIM), *p. 442*
off-balance-sheet activities, *p. 437*
operating expenses, *p. 441*
operating income, *p. 441*
required reserve ratio, *p. 424*
required reserves, *p. 424*
reserve requirement, *p. 424*
reserves, *p. 424*
return on assets (ROA), *p. 434*
return on equity (ROE), *p. 434*
secondary reserves, *p. 425*
T-account, *p. 426*
vault cash, *p. 424*

QUESTIONS

1. Rank the following bank assets from most to least liquid:
   a. Commercial loans
   b. Securities
   c. Reserves
   d. Physical capital

2. If the president of a bank told you that the bank was so well run that it has never had to call in loans, sell securities, or borrow as a result of a deposit outflow, would you be willing to buy stock in that bank? Why or why not?

3. If the bank you own has no excess reserves and a sound customer comes in asking for a loan, should you automatically turn the customer down, explaining that you don't have any excess reserves to loan out? Why or why not? What options are available for you to provide the funds your customer needs?

4. Why has the development of overnight loan markets made it more likely that banks will hold fewer excess reserves?

5. If you are a banker and expect interest rates to rise in the future, would you want to make short-term or long-term loans?

6. "Bank managers should always seek the highest return possible on their assets." Is this statement true, false, or uncertain? Explain your answer.

7. "Banking has become a more dynamic industry because of more active liability management." Is this statement true, false, or uncertain? Explain your answer.

8. Why has noninterest income been growing as a source of bank operating income?

9. Which components of operating expenses experience the greatest fluctuations? Why?

10. Why do equity holders care more about ROE than about ROA?

11. What does the net interest margin measure, and why is it important to bank managers?

12. If a bank doubles the amount of its capital and ROA stays constant, what will happen to ROE?

13. If a bank finds that its ROE is too low because it has too much bank capital, what can it do to raise its ROE?

14. What are the benefits and costs for a bank when it decides to increase the amount of its bank capital?

15. If a bank is falling short of meeting its capital requirements by $1 million, what three things can it do to rectify the situation?

QUANTITATIVE PROBLEMS

1. The balance sheet of TriBank starts with an allowance for loan losses of $1.33 million. During the year, TriBank charges off worthless loans of $0.84 million, recovers $0.22 million on loans previously charged off, and charges current income for a $1.48 million provision for loan losses. Calculate the end-of-year allowance for loan losses.

2. X-Bank reported an ROE of 15% and an ROA of 1%. How well capitalized is this bank?

3. Wiggley S&L issues a standard 30-year fixed rate mortgage at 7.8% for $150,000. Thirty-six months later, mortgage rates jump to 13%. If the S&L sells the mortgage, how much of a loss is incurred?

4. Refer to the previous question. In 1981, Congress allowed S&Ls to sell mortgages at a loss and to amortize the loss over the remaining life of the mortgage. If this were used for the previous question, how would the transaction have been recorded? What would be the annual adjustment? When would that end?

5. For the upcoming week, Nobel National Bank plans to issue $25 million in mortgages and purchase $100 million 31-day T-bills. New deposits of $35 million are expected, and other sources will generate $15 million in cash. What is Nobel's estimate of funds needed?

6. A bank estimates that demand deposits are, on average, $100 million with a standard deviation of $5 million. The bank wants to maintain a minimum of 8% of deposits in reserves at all times. What is the highest expected level of deposits during the month? What reserves do they need to maintain? Use a 99% confidence level.

The remaining questions relate to the first month's operations of NewBank.

7. NewBank started its first day of operations with $6 million in capital. $100 million in checkable deposits is received. The bank issues a $25 million commercial loan and another $25 million in mortgages, with the following terms:

   - Mortgages: 100 standard 30-year fixed-rate mortgages with a nominal annual rate of 5.25% each for $250,000

   - Commercial loan: 3-year loan, simple interest paid monthly at 0.75% per month

   If required reserves are 8%, what does the bank balance sheets look like? Ignore any loan loss reserves.

8. NewBank decides to invest $45 million in 30-day T-bills. The T-bills are currently trading at $4,986.70 (including commissions) for a $5000 face value instrument. How many do they purchase? What does the balance sheet look like?

9. On the third day of operations, deposits fall by $5 million. What does the balance sheet look like? Are there any problems?

10. To meet any shortfall in the previous question, NewBank will borrow the cash in the federal funds market. Management decides to borrow the needed funds for the remainder of the month (now 29 days). The required yield on a discount basis is 2.9%. What does the balance sheet look like after this transaction?

11. The end of the month finally arrives for NewBank, and it receives all the required payments from its mortgages, commercial loans, and T-bills. How much cash was received? How are these transactions recorded?

12. NewBank also pays off its federal funds borrowed. How much cash is owed? How is this recorded?

13. What does the month-end balance sheet for NewBank look like? Calculate this before any income tax consideration.

14. Calculate NewBank's ROA and NIM for its first month. Assume that net interest equals EBT, and that NewBank is in the 34% tax bracket.

15. Calculate NewBank's ROE and final balance sheet, including its tax liabilities.

16. If NewBank were required to establish a loan loss reserve at 0.25% of the loan value for commercial loans, how would this be recorded? Recalculate NewBank's ROE and final balance sheet, including its tax liabilities.

17. If NewBank's target ROE is 4.5%, how much net fee income must it generate to meet this target?

18. After making payments for three years, one of the mortgage borrowers defaults on the mortgage. NewBank immediately takes possession of the house and sells it at auction for $175,000. Legal fees amount to $25,000. If no loan loss reserve was established for the mortgage loans, how is this event recorded?

WEB EXERCISES

Banking and the Management of Financial Institutions

1. Table 17.1 reports the balance sheet of all commercial banks based on aggregate data found in the Federal Reserve *Bulletin*. Compare this table to the balance sheet reported by Wachovia in its latest annual report, which can be found at **www.wachovia .com/inside/page/0,,133_202_257,00.html**. Does Wachovia have more or less of its portfolio in loans than the average bank? Which type of loan is most common?

2. It is relatively easy to find up-to-date information on banks because of their extensive reporting requirements. Go to **www2.fdic.gov/qbp/**. This site is sponsored by the Federal Deposit Insurance Corporation. You will find summary data on financial institutions. Go to the most recent Quarterly Banking Profile. Scroll down and open Table 1-A.

   a. Have banks' return on assets been increasing or decreasing over the last few years?

   b. Has the core capital been increasing, and how does it compare to the capital ratio reported in Table 17.1 in the text?

   c. How many institutions are currently reporting to the FDIC?

CHAPTER 18

Commercial Banking Industry: Structure and Competition

Preview

The operations of individual banks (how they acquire, use, and manage funds to make a profit) are roughly similar throughout the world. In all countries, banks are financial intermediaries in the business of earning profits. When you consider the structure and operation of the banking industry as a whole, however, the United States is in a class by itself. In most countries, four or five large banks typically dominate the banking industry, but in the United States there are on the order of 7,500 commercial banks.

Is more better? Does this diversity mean that the American banking system is more competitive and therefore more economically efficient and sound than banking systems in other countries? What in the American economic and political system explains this large number of banking institutions? In this chapter we try to answer these questions by examining the historical trends in the commercial banking industry and its overall structure.

We start by examining the historical development of the banking system and how financial innovation has increased the competitive environment for the banking industry and is causing fundamental changes in it. We then go on to look at the commercial industry in detail. In addition to looking at our domestic banking system, we also examine the forces behind the growth in international banking to see how it has affected us in the United States. Finally, we examine how financial innovation has increased the competitive environment for the banking industry and is causing fundamental changes in it.

Historical Development of the Banking System

The modern commercial banking industry in the United States began when the Bank of North America was chartered in Philadelphia in 1782. With the success of this bank, other banks opened for business, and the American banking industry was off and running. (As a study aid, Figure 18.1 provides a time line of the most important dates in the history of American banking before World War II.)

A major controversy involving the industry in its early years was whether the federal government or the states should charter banks. The Federalists, particularly Alexander Hamilton, advocated greater centralized control of banking and federal chartering of banks. Their efforts led to the creation, in 1791, of the Bank of the United States, which had elements of both a private bank and a central bank, a government institution that has responsibility for the amount of money and credit supplied in the economy as a whole. Agricultural and other interests, however, were quite suspicious of centralized power and hence advocated chartering by the states. Furthermore, their distrust of moneyed interests in the big cities led to political pressures to eliminate the Bank of the United States, and in 1811 their efforts met with success, when its charter was not renewed. Because of abuses by state banks and the clear need for a central bank to help the federal government raise funds during the War of 1812, Congress was stimulated to create the Second Bank of the United States in 1816. Tensions between advocates and opponents of centralized banking power were a recurrent theme during the operation of this second attempt at central banking

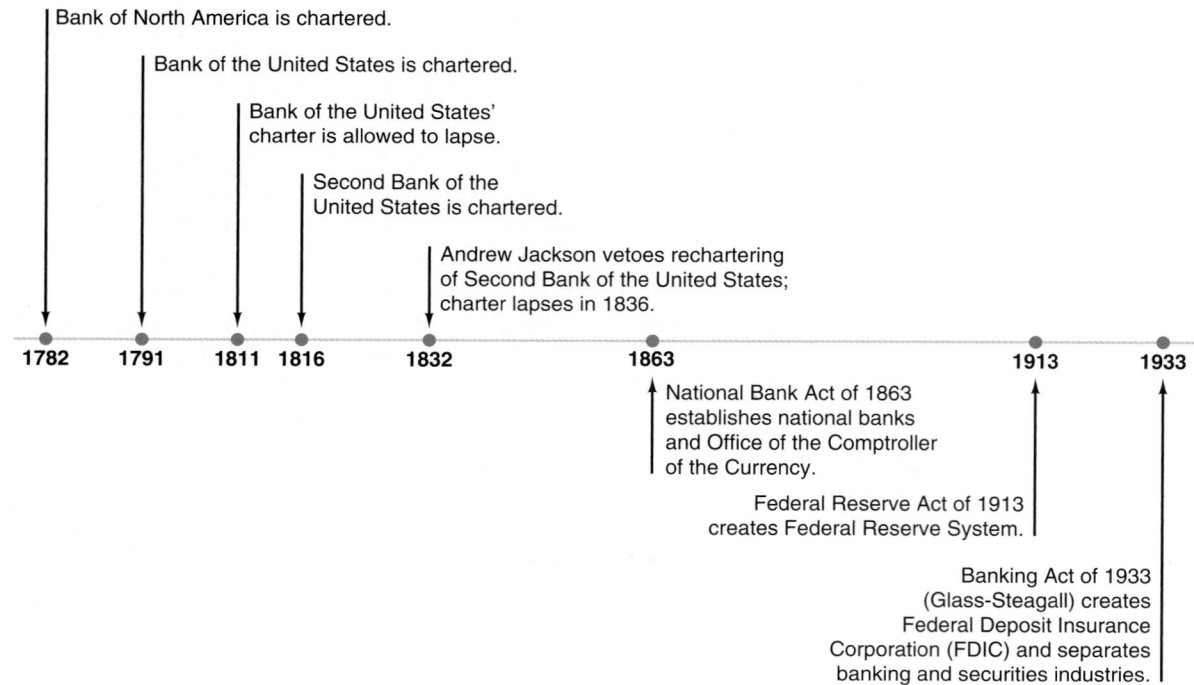

Figure 18.1 Time Line of the Early History of Commercial Banking in the United States

in the United States, and with the election of Andrew Jackson, a strong advocate of states' rights, the fate of the Second Bank was sealed. After the election in 1832, Jackson vetoed the rechartering of the Second Bank of the United States as a national bank, and its charter lapsed in 1836.

Until 1863, all commercial banks in the United States were chartered by the banking commission of the state in which each operated. No national currency existed, and banks obtained funds primarily by issuing *banknotes* (currency circulated by the banks that could be redeemed for gold). Because banking regulations were extremely lax in many states, banks regularly failed due to fraud or lack of sufficient bank capital; their banknotes became worthless.

To eliminate the abuses of the state-chartered banks (called **state banks**), the National Bank Act of 1863 (and subsequent amendments to it) created a new banking system of federally chartered banks (called **national banks**), supervised by the Office of the Comptroller of the Currency, a department of the U.S. Treasury. This legislation was originally intended to dry up sources of funds to state banks by imposing a prohibitive tax on their banknotes while leaving the banknotes of the federally chartered banks untaxed. The state banks cleverly escaped extinction by acquiring funds through deposits. As a result, today the United States has a **dual banking system** in which banks supervised by the federal government and banks supervised by the states operate side by side.

Central banking did not reappear in this country until the Federal Reserve System (the Fed) was created in 1913 to promote an even safer banking system. All national banks were required to become members of the Federal Reserve System and became subject to a new set of regulations issued by the Fed. State banks could choose (but were not required) to become members of the system, and most did not because of the high costs of membership stemming from the Fed's regulations.

go online
www.fdic.gov/bank/
The FDIC gathers data about individual financial institutions and the banking industry.

During the Great Depression years 1930–1933, some 9,000 bank failures wiped out the savings of many depositors at commercial banks. To prevent future depositor losses from such failures, banking legislation in 1933 established the Federal Deposit Insurance Corporation (FDIC), which provided federal insurance on bank deposits. Member banks of the Federal Reserve System were required to purchase FDIC insurance for their depositors, and non–Federal Reserve commercial banks could choose to buy this insurance (almost all of them did). The purchase of FDIC insurance made banks subject to another set of regulations imposed by the FDIC.

Because investment banking activities of the commercial banks were blamed for many bank failures, provisions in the banking legislation in 1933 (also known as the Glass-Steagall Act) prohibited commercial banks from underwriting or dealing in corporate securities (though allowing them to sell new issues of government securities) and limited banks to the purchase of debt securities approved by the bank regulatory agencies. Likewise, it prohibited investment banks from engaging in commercial banking activities. In effect, the Glass-Steagall Act separated the activities of commercial banks from those of the securities industry.

Under the conditions of the Glass-Steagall Act, which was repealed in 1999, commercial banks had to sell off their investment banking operations. The First National Bank of Boston, for example, spun off its investment banking operations into the First Boston Corporation, now part of one of the most important investment banking firms in America, Credit Suisse First Boston. Investment banking firms typically discontinued their deposit business, although J. P. Morgan discontinued its investment banking business and reorganized as a commercial bank; however, some senior officers of J. P. Morgan went on to organize Morgan Stanley, another one of the largest investment banking firms today.

Multiple Regulatory Agencies

Commercial bank regulation in the United States has developed into a crazy quilt of multiple regulatory agencies with overlapping jurisdictions. The Office of the Comptroller of the Currency has the primary supervisory responsibility for the 1,850 national banks that own more than half of the assets in the commercial banking system. The Federal Reserve and the state banking authorities have joint primary responsibility for the 900 state banks that are members of the Federal Reserve System. The Fed also has regulatory responsibility over companies that own one or more banks (called **bank holding companies**) and secondary responsibility for the national banks. The FDIC and the state banking authorities jointly supervise the 4,800 state banks that have FDIC insurance but are not members of the Federal Reserve System. The state banking authorities have sole jurisdiction over the fewer than 500 state banks without FDIC insurance. (Such banks hold less than 0.2% of the deposits in the commercial banking system.)

If you find the U.S. bank regulatory system confusing, imagine how confusing it is for the banks, which have to deal with multiple regulatory agencies. Several proposals have been raised by the U.S. Treasury to rectify this situation by centralizing the regulation of all depository institutions under one independent agency. However, none of these proposals has been successful in Congress, and whether there will be regulatory consolidation in the future is highly uncertain.

Financial Innovation and the Evolution of the Banking Industry

go online

www.financialservicefacts
.org/financial
Learn about the number of employees and the current profitability of commercial banks and saving institutions.

To understand how the banking industry has evolved over time, we must first understand the process of financial innovation, which has transformed the entire financial system. Like other industries, the financial industry is in business to earn profits by selling its products. If a soap company perceives that there is a need in the marketplace for a laundry detergent with fabric softener, it develops a product to fit the need. Similarly, to maximize their profits, financial institutions develop new products to satisfy their own needs as well as those of their customers; in other words, innovation—which can be extremely beneficial to the economy—is driven by the desire to get (or stay) rich. This view of the innovation process leads to the following simple analysis: *A change in the financial environment will stimulate a search by financial institutions for innovations that are likely to be profitable.*

Starting in the 1960s, individuals and financial institutions operating in financial markets were confronted with drastic changes in the economic environment: Inflation and interest rates climbed sharply and became harder to predict, a situation that changed demand conditions in financial markets. The rapid advance in computer technology changed supply conditions. In addition, financial regulations became more burdensome. Financial institutions found that many of the old ways of doing business were no longer profitable; the financial services and products they had been offering to the public were not selling. Many financial intermediaries found that they were no longer able to acquire funds with their traditional financial instruments, and without these funds they would soon be out of business. To survive in the new economic environment, financial institutions had to research and develop new products and services that would meet customer needs and prove profitable, a process referred to as **financial engineering.** In their case, necessity was the mother of innovation.

Our discussion of why financial innovation occurs suggests that there are three basic types of financial innovation: responses to changes in demand conditions, responses to changes in supply conditions, and avoidance of regulations. Now that we have a framework for understanding why financial institutions produce innovations, let's look at examples of how financial institutions in their search for profits have produced financial innovations of the three basic types.

Responses to Changes in Demand Conditions: Interest Rate Volatility

The most significant change in the economic environment that altered the demand for financial products in recent years has been the dramatic increase in the volatility of interest rates. In the 1950s, the interest rate on three-month Treasury bills fluctuated between 1.0% and 3.5%; in the 1970s, it fluctuated between 4.0% and 11.5%; in the 1980s, it ranged from 5% to more than 15%. Large fluctuations in interest rates lead to substantial capital gains or losses and greater uncertainty about returns on investments. Recall that the risk that is related to the uncertainty about interest-rate movements and returns is called *interest-rate risk*, and high volatility of interest rates, such as we saw in the 1970s and 1980s, leads to a higher level of interest-rate risk.

We would expect the increase in interest-rate risk to increase the demand for financial products and services that could reduce that risk. This change in the economic environment would thus stimulate a search for profitable innovations by financial institutions that meet this new demand and would spur the creation of new financial instruments that help lower interest-rate risk. Two examples of financial innovations that appeared in the 1970s confirm this prediction: the development of adjustable-rate mortgages and financial derivatives.

Adjustable-Rate Mortgages Like other investors, financial institutions find that lending is more attractive if interest-rate risk is lower. They would not want to make a mortgage loan at a 10% interest rate and two months later find that they could obtain 12% in interest on the same mortgage. To reduce interest-rate risk, in 1975 savings and loans in California began to issue adjustable-rate mortgages; that is, mortgage loans on which the interest rate changes when a market interest rate (usually the Treasury bill rate) changes. Initially, an adjustable-rate mortgage might have a 5% interest rate. In six months, this interest rate might increase or decrease by the amount of the increase or decrease in, say, the six-month Treasury bill rate, and the mortgage payment would change. Because adjustable-rate mortgages allow mortgage-issuing institutions to earn higher interest rates on mortgages when rates rise, profits remain high during these periods.

This attractive feature of adjustable-rate mortgages has encouraged mortgage-issuing institutions to issue adjustable-rate mortgages with lower initial interest rates than on conventional fixed-rate mortgages, making them popular with many households. However, because the mortgage payment on a variable-rate mortgage can increase, many households continue to prefer fixed-rate mortgages. Hence, both types of mortgages are widespread.

Financial Derivatives Given the greater demand for the reduction of interest-rate risk, commodity exchanges such as the Chicago Board of Trade recognized that if they could develop a product that would help investors and financial institutions to protect themselves from, or **hedge,** interest-rate risk, then they could make profits by selling this new instrument. **Futures contracts,** in which the seller agrees to provide a certain standardized commodity to the buyer on a specific future date at an agreed-on price, had been around for a long time. Officials at the Chicago Board of Trade realized that if they created futures contracts in financial instruments, which are called **financial derivatives** because their payoffs are linked to (*i.e.*, derived from) previously issued securities, they could be used to hedge risk. Thus, in 1975, financial derivatives were born.

Responses to Changes in Supply Conditions: Information Technology

The most important source of the changes in supply conditions that stimulate financial innovation has been the improvement in computer and telecommunications technology. This technology, called *information technology,* has had two effects. First, it has lowered the cost of processing financial transactions, making it profitable for financial institutions to create new financial products and services for the public. Second, it has made it easier for investors to acquire information, thereby making it easier for firms to issue securities. The rapid developments in information technology have resulted in many new financial products and services that we examine here.

Bank Credit and Debit Cards Credit cards have been around since well before World War II. Many individual stores (Sears, Macy's, Goldwater's) institutionalized charge accounts by providing customers with credit cards that allowed them to make purchases at these stores without cash. Nationwide credit cards were not established until after World War II, when Diners Club developed one to be used in restaurants all over the country (and abroad). Similar credit card programs were started by American Express and Carte Blanche, but because of the high cost of operating these programs, cards were issued only to selected persons and businesses that could afford expensive purchases.

A firm issuing credit cards earns income from loans it makes to credit card holders and from payments made by stores on credit card purchases (a percentage of the purchase price, say 5%). A credit card program's costs arise from loan defaults, stolen cards, and the expense involved in processing credit card transactions.

Seeing the success of Diners Club, American Express, and Carte Blanche, bankers wanted to share in the profitable credit card business. Several commercial banks attempted to expand the credit card business to a wider market in the 1950s, but the cost per transaction of running these programs was so high that their early attempts failed.

In the late 1960s, improved computer technology, which lowered the transaction costs for providing credit card services, made it more likely that bank credit card programs would be profitable. The banks tried to enter this business again, and this time their efforts led to the creation of two successful bank credit card programs: BankAmericard (originally started by the Bank of America but now an independent organization called Visa) and MasterCharge (now MasterCard, run by the Interbank Card Association). These programs have become phenomenally successful; more than 200 million of their cards are in use. Indeed, bank credit cards have been so profitable that nonfinancial institutions such as Sears (which launched the Discover card), General Motors, and AT&T have also entered the credit card business.

Consumers have benefited because credit cards are more widely accepted than checks to pay for purchases (particularly abroad), and they allow consumers to take out loans more easily.

The success of bank credit cards has led these institutions to come up with a new financial innovation, *debit cards.* Debit cards often look just like credit cards and can be used to make purchases in an identical fashion. However, in contrast to credit cards, which extend the purchaser a loan that does not have to be paid off immediately, a debit card purchase is immediately deducted from the card holder's bank account. Debit cards depend even more on low costs of processing transactions, because their profits are generated entirely from the fees paid by merchants on debit card purchases at their stores. Debit cards have grown extremely popular in recent years.

Electronic Banking The wonders of modern computer technology have also enabled banks to lower the cost of bank transactions by having the customer interact with an electronic banking (e-banking) facility rather than with a human being. One important form of an e-banking facility is the **automated teller machine (ATM),** an electronic machine that allows customers to get cash, make deposits, transfer funds from one account to another, and check balances. The ATM has the advantage that it does not have to be paid overtime and never sleeps, thus being available for use 24 hours a day. Not only does this result in cheaper transactions for the bank, but it also provides more convenience for the customer. Because of their low cost, ATMs can be put at locations other than a bank or its branches, further increasing customer convenience. The low cost of ATMs has meant that they have sprung up everywhere and now number more than 250,000 in the United States alone. Furthermore, it is now as easy to get foreign currency from an ATM when you are traveling in Europe as it is to get cash from your local bank.

With the drop in the cost of telecommunications, banks have developed another financial innovation, *home banking.* It is now cost-effective for banks to set up an electronic banking facility in which the bank's customer is linked up with the bank's computer to carry out transactions by using either a telephone or a personal computer. Now a bank's customers can conduct many of their bank transactions without ever leaving the comfort of home. The advantage for the customer is the convenience of home banking, while banks find that the cost of transactions is substantially less than having the customer come to the bank. The success of ATMs and home banking has led to another innovation, the **automated banking machine (ABM),** which combines in one location an ATM, an Internet connection to the bank's Web site, and a telephone link to customer service.

With the decline in the price of personal computers and their increasing presence in the home, we have seen a further innovation in the home banking area, the appearance of a new type of banking institution, the **virtual bank,** a bank that has no physical location but rather exists only in cyberspace. In 1995, Security First Network Bank, based in Atlanta but now owned by Royal Bank of Canada, became the first virtual bank, offering an array of banking services on the Internet—accepting checking account and savings deposits, selling certificates of deposits, issuing ATM cards, providing bill-paying facilities, and so on. The virtual bank thus takes home banking one step further, enabling the customer to have a full set of banking services at home 24 hours a day. In 1996, Bank of America and Wells Fargo entered the virtual banking market, to be followed by many others, with Bank of America now

Will "Clicks" Dominate "Bricks" in the Banking Industry?

With the advent of virtual banks ("clicks") and the convenience they provide, a key question is whether they will become the primary form in which banks do their business, eliminating the need for physical bank branches ("bricks") as the main delivery mechanism for banking services. Indeed, will stand-alone Internet banks be the wave of the future?

The answer seems to be no. Internet-only banks such as Wingspan (owned by Bank One), First-e (Dublin-based), and Egg (a British Internet-only bank owned by Prudential) have had disappointing revenue growth and profits. The result is that pure online banking has not been the success that proponents had hoped for. Why has Internet banking been a disappointment?

There are several strikes against Internet banking. First, bank depositors want to know that their savings are secure, and so are reluctant to put their money into new institutions without a long track record. Second, customers worry about the security of their online transactions and whether their transactions will truly be kept private. Traditional banks are viewed as being more secure and trustworthy in terms of releasing private information. Third, customers may prefer services provided by physical branches. For example, banking customers seem to prefer to purchase long-term savings products face-to-face. Fourth, Internet banking has run into technical problems—server crashes, slow connections over phone lines, mistakes in conducting transactions—that will probably diminish over time as technology improves.

The wave of the future thus does not appear to be pure Internet banks. Instead it looks like "clicks and bricks" will be the predominant form of banking, in which online banking is used to complement the services provided by traditional banks. Nonetheless, the delivery of banking services is undergoing massive changes, with more and more banking services delivered over the Internet and the number of physical bank branches likely to decline in the future.

---

being the largest Internet bank in the United States. Will virtual banking be the predominant form of banking in the future (see the E-Finance box, "Will 'Clicks' Dominate 'Bricks' in the Banking Industry?")?

Electronic Payment The development of inexpensive computers and the spread of the Internet now make it very cheap for banks to allow their customers to make bill payments electronically. Whereas in the past you had to pay your bills by mailing a check, now banks provide a Web site in which you just log on, make a few clicks, and your payment is transmitted electronically. You not only save the cost of the stamp, but paying bills now becomes (almost) a pleasure, requiring little effort. Electronic payment systems provided by banks now even allow you to avoid the step of having to log on to pay the bill. Instead, recurring bills can be automatically deducted from your bank account without your having to do a thing. Providing these services increases profitability for banks in two ways. First, payment of a bill electronically means that banks don't need people to process what would have otherwise been a paper transaction. Estimates of the cost savings for banks when a bill is paid electronically rather than by a check exceed one dollar. Second, the extra convenience for you, the customer, means that you are more likely to open an account with the bank. Electronic payment is thus becoming far more common in the United States, but Americans are far behind Europeans, particularly Scandinavians, in their use of electronic payments (see the E-Finance box "Why Are Scandinavians So Far Ahead of Americans in Using Electronic Payments and Online Banking?").

e-finance

Why Are Scandinavians So Far Ahead of Americans in Using Electronic Payments and Online Banking?

Americans are the biggest users of checks in the world. Close to 100 billion checks are written every year in the United States, and over three-quarters of noncash transactions are conducted with paper. In contrast, in most countries of Europe, more than two-thirds of noncash transactions are electronic, with Finland and Sweden having the greatest proportion of online banking customers of any countries in the world. Indeed, if you were Finnish or Swedish, instead of writing a check, you would be far more likely to pay your bills online, using a personal computer or even a mobile phone. Why do Europeans and especially Scandinavians so far outpace Americans in the use of electronic payments?

First, Europeans got used to making payments without checks even before the advent of the personal computer. Europeans have long made use of *giro* payments, in which banks and post offices transfer funds for customers to pay bills. Second, Europeans—and particularly Scandinavians—are much greater users of mobile phones and the Internet than are Americans. Finland has the highest per capita use of mobile phones in the world, and Finland and Sweden lead the world in the percentage of the population that accesses the Internet. Maybe these usage patterns stem from the low population densities of these countries and the cold and dark winters that keep Scandinavians inside at their PCs. For their part, Scandinavians would rather take the view that their high-tech culture is the product of their good education systems and the resulting high degree of computer literacy, the presence of top technology companies such as Finland's Nokia and Sweden's Ericsson, and government policies promoting the increased use of personal computers, such as Sweden's tax incentives for companies to provide their employees with home computers. The wired populations of Finland and Sweden are (percentage-wise) the biggest users of online banking in the world.

Americans are clearly behind the curve in their use of electronic payments, which has imposed a high cost on the U.S. economy. Switching from checks to electronic payments might save the U.S. economy tens of billions of dollars per year, according to some estimates. Indeed, the U.S. federal government is trying to switch all its payments to electronic ones by directly depositing them into bank accounts, in an effort to reduce its expenses. Can Americans be weaned from paper checks and fully embrace the world of high-tech electronic payments?

E-Money Electronic payments technology can not only substitute for checks but can, in the form of **electronic money** (or **e-money**), money that exists only in electronic form, substitute for cash as well. The first form of e-money is a stored-value card. The simplest form of a stored-value card is purchased for a preset dollar amount that the consumer spends down. The more sophisticated stored-value card is known as a **smart card.** It contains its own computer chip so that it can be loaded with digital cash from the owner's bank account whenever needed. Smart cards can be loaded either from ATM machines, personal computers with a smart card reader, or from specially equipped telephones.

A second form of electronic money is often referred to as **e-cash,** and it is used on the Internet to purchase goods or services. A consumer gets e-cash by setting up an account with a bank that has links to the Internet and then has the e-cash transferred to her PC. When she wants to buy something with e-cash, she surfs to a store on the Web, clicks the "buy" option for a particular item, whereupon the e-cash is automatically transferred from her computer to the merchant's computer. The merchant can then have the funds transferred from the consumer's bank account to his before the goods are shipped.

e-finance

Are We Headed for a Cashless Society?

Predictions of a cashless society have been around for decades, but they have not come to fruition. For example, *Business Week* predicted in 1975 that electronic means of payment "would soon revolutionize the very concept of money itself," only to reverse itself several years later. Pilot projects in recent years with smart cards to convert consumers to the use of e-money have not been a success. Mondex, one of the widely touted, early stored-value cards that was launched in Great Britain in 1995, is only used on a few British university campuses. In Germany and Belgium, millions of people carry bank cards with computer chips embedded in them that enable them to make use of e-money, but very few use them. Why has the movement to a cashless society been so slow in coming?

Although e-money might be more convenient and may be more efficient than a payments system based on paper, several factors work against the disappearance of the paper system. First, it is very expensive to set up the computer, card reader, and telecommunications networks necessary to make electronic money

the dominant form of payment. Second, electronic means of payment raise security and privacy concerns. We often hear media reports that an unauthorized hacker has been able to access a computer database and to alter information stored there. Because this is not an uncommon occurrence, unscrupulous persons might be able to access bank accounts in electronic payments systems and steal funds by moving them from someone else's accounts into their own. The prevention of this type of fraud is no easy task, and a whole new field of computer science has developed to cope with security issues. A further concern is that the use of electronic means of payment leaves an electronic trail that contains a large amount of personal data on buying habits. There are worries that government, employers, and marketers might be able to access these data, thereby encroaching on our privacy.

The conclusion from this discussion is that although the use of e-money will surely increase in the future, to paraphrase Mark Twain, "The reports of cash's death are greatly exaggerated."

Given the convenience of e-money, you might think that we would move quickly to the cashless society in which all payments were made electronically. However, this hasn't happened, as discussed in the E-Finance box "Are We Headed for a Cashless Society?"

Junk Bonds Before the advent of computers and advanced telecommunications, it was difficult to acquire information about the financial situation of firms that might want to sell securities. Because of the difficulty in screening out bad from good credit risks, the only firms that were able to sell bonds were very well-established corporations that had high credit ratings.[1] Before the 1980s, then, only corporations that could issue bonds with ratings of Baa or above could raise funds by selling newly issued bonds. Some firms that had fallen on bad times, known as *fallen angels*, had previously issued long-term corporate bonds that now had ratings that had fallen below Baa, bonds that were pejoratively dubbed "junk bonds."

With the improvement in information technology in the 1970s, it became easier for investors to acquire financial information about corporations, making it easier

---

[1]The discussion of adverse selection problems in Chapter 15 provides a more detailed analysis of why only well-established firms with high credit ratings were able to sell securities.

to screen out bad from good credit risks. With easier screening, investors were more willing to buy long-term debt securities from less well-known corporations with lower credit ratings. With this change in supply conditions, we would expect that some smart individual would pioneer the concept of selling new public issues of junk bonds, not for fallen angels but for companies that had not yet achieved investment-grade status. This is exactly what Michael Milken of Drexel Burnham Lambert, an investment banking firm, started to do in 1977. Junk bonds became an important factor in the corporate bond market, with the amount outstanding exceeding $200 billion by the late 1980s. Although there was a sharp slowdown in activity in the junk bond market after Milken was indicted for securities law violations in 1989, it heated up again in the 1990s and 2000s.

Commercial Paper Market *Commercial paper* is a short-term debt security issued by large banks and corporations. The commercial paper market has undergone tremendous growth since 1970, when there was $33 billion outstanding, to over $2.2 trillion outstanding at the end of 2006. Indeed, commercial paper has been one of the fastest-growing money market instruments.

Improvements in information technology also help provide an explanation for the rapid rise of the commercial paper market. We have seen that the improvement in information technology made it easier for investors to screen out bad from good credit risks, thus making it easier for corporations to issue debt securities. Not only did this make it easier for corporations to issue long-term debt securities in the junk bond market, but it also meant that they could raise funds by issuing short-term debt securities such as commercial paper more easily. Many corporations that used to do their short-term borrowing from banks now frequently raise short-term funds in the commercial paper market instead.

The development of money market mutual funds has been another factor in the rapid growth in the commercial paper market. Because money market mutual funds need to hold liquid, high-quality, short-term assets such as commercial paper, the growth of assets in these funds to around $1.9 trillion has created a ready market in commercial paper. The growth of pension and other large funds that invest in commercial paper has also stimulated the growth of this market.

Securitization An important example of a financial innovation arising from improvements in both transaction and information technology is securitization, one of the most important financial innovations in the past two decades. **Securitization** is the process of transforming otherwise illiquid financial assets (such as residential mortgages, auto loans, and credit card receivables), which have typically been the bread and butter of banking institutions, into marketable capital market securities. As we have seen, improvements in the ability to acquire information have made it easier to sell marketable capital market securities. In addition, with low transaction costs because of improvements in computer technology, financial institutions find that they can cheaply bundle together a portfolio of loans (such as mortgages) with varying small denominations (often less than $100,000), collect the interest and principal payments on the mortgages in the bundle, and then "pass them through" (pay them out) to third parties. By dividing the portfolio of loans into standardized amounts, the financial institution can then sell the claims to these interest and principal payments to third parties as securities. The standardized amounts of these securitized loans make them liquid securities, and the fact that they are made up of a bundle of loans helps diversify risk, making them desirable. The financial institution selling the securitized loans makes a profit by servicing the loans (collecting the interest and principal payments and paying them out) and charging a fee to the third party for this service.

Avoidance of Existing Regulations

The process of financial innovation we have discussed so far is much like innovation in other areas of the economy: It occurs in response to changes in demand and supply conditions. However, because the financial industry is more heavily regulated than other industries, government regulation is a much greater spur to innovation in this industry. Government regulation leads to financial innovation by creating incentives for firms to skirt regulations that restrict their ability to earn profits. Edward Kane, an economist at Boston College, describes this process of avoiding regulations as "loophole mining." The economic analysis of innovation suggests that when the economic environment changes such that regulatory constraints are so burdensome that large profits can be made by avoiding them, loophole mining and innovation are more likely to occur.

Because banking is one of the most heavily regulated industries in America, loophole mining is especially likely to occur. The rise in inflation and interest rates from the late 1960s to 1980 made the regulatory constraints imposed on this industry even more burdensome, leading to financial innovation.

Two sets of regulations have seriously restricted the ability of banks to make profits: reserve requirements that force banks to keep a certain fraction of their deposits as reserves (vault cash and deposits in the Federal Reserve System) and restrictions on the interest rates that can be paid on deposits. For the following reasons, these regulations have been major forces behind financial innovation.

1. *Reserve requirements.* The key to understanding why reserve requirements led to financial innovation is to recognize that they act, in effect, as a tax on deposits. Because the Fed does not pay interest on reserves, the opportunity cost of holding them is the interest that a bank could otherwise earn by lending the reserves out. For each dollar of deposits, reserve requirements therefore impose a cost on the bank equal to the interest rate, i, that could be earned if the reserves could be lent out times the fraction of deposits required as reserves, r. The cost of $i \times r$ imposed on the bank is just like a tax on bank deposits of $i \times r$ per dollar of deposits.

    It is a great tradition to avoid taxes if possible, and banks also play this game. Just as taxpayers look for loopholes to lower their tax bills, banks seek to increase their profits by mining loopholes and by producing financial innovations that allow them to escape the tax on deposits imposed by reserve requirements.

2. *Restrictions on interest paid on deposits.* Until 1980, legislation prohibited banks in most states from paying interest on checking account deposits, and through Regulation Q, the Fed set maximum limits on the interest rate that could be paid on time deposits. To this day, banks are not allowed to pay interest on corporate checking accounts. The desire to avoid these **deposit rate ceilings** also led to financial innovations.

    If market interest rates rose above the maximum rates that banks paid on time deposits under Regulation Q, depositors withdrew funds from banks to put them into higher-yielding securities. This loss of deposits from the banking system restricted the amount of funds that banks could lend (called **dis-intermediation**) and thus limited bank profits. Banks had an incentive to get around deposit rate ceilings, because by so doing, they could acquire more funds to make loans and earn higher profits.

We can now look at how the desire to avoid restrictions on interest payments and the tax effect of reserve requirements led to two important financial innovations.

Money Market Mutual Funds Money market mutual funds issue shares that are redeemable at a fixed price (usually $1) by writing checks. For example, if you buy 5,000 shares for $5,000, the money market fund uses these funds to invest in short-term money market securities (Treasury bills, certificates of deposit, commercial paper) that provide you with interest payments. In addition, you are able to write checks up to the $5,000 held as shares in the money market fund. Although money market fund shares effectively function as checking account deposits that earn interest, they are not legally deposits and so are not subject to reserve requirements or prohibitions on interest payments. For this reason, they can pay higher interest rates than deposits at banks.

The first money market mutual fund was created by two Wall Street mavericks, Bruce Bent and Henry Brown, in 1971. However, the low market interest rates from 1971 to 1977 (which were just slightly above Regulation Q ceilings of 5.25% to 5.5%) kept them from being particularly advantageous relative to bank deposits. In early 1978, the situation changed rapidly as inflation rose and market interest rates began to climb over 10%, well above the 5.5% maximum interest rates payable on savings accounts and time deposits under Regulation Q. In 1977, money market mutual funds had assets of less than $4 billion; in 1978, their assets climbed to close to $10 billion; in 1979, to more than $40 billion; and in 1982, to $230 billion. Currently, their assets are around $2 trillion. To say the least, money market mutual funds have been a successful financial innovation, which is exactly what we would have predicted to occur in the late 1970s and early 1980s when interest rates soared beyond Regulation Q ceilings.

Sweep Accounts Another innovation that enables banks to avoid the "tax" from reserve requirements is the **sweep account.** In this arrangement, any balances above a certain amount in a corporation's checking account at the end of a business day are "swept out" of the account and invested in overnight securities that pay interest. Because the "swept out" funds are no longer classified as checkable deposits, they are not subject to reserve requirements and thus are not "taxed." They also have the advantage that they allow banks in effect to pay interest on these checking accounts, which otherwise is not allowed under existing regulations. Because sweep accounts have become so popular, they have lowered the amount of required reserves to the degree that most banking institutions do not find reserve requirements binding: In other words, they voluntarily hold more reserves than they are required to.

The financial innovation of sweep accounts is particularly interesting because it was stimulated not only by the desire to avoid a costly regulation, but also by a change in supply conditions—in this case, information technology. Without low-cost computers to process inexpensively the additional transactions required by these accounts, this innovation would not have been profitable and therefore would not have been developed. Technological factors often combine with other incentives, such as the desire to get around a regulation, to produce innovation.

THE PRACTICING MANAGER

Profiting from a New Financial Product: A Case Study of Treasury Strips

We have seen that the advent of high-speed computers, which lowered the cost of processing financial transactions, led to such financial innovations as bank credit and debit cards. Because there is money to be made from financial innovation, it is important for managers of financial institutions to understand the thinking that goes into producing new, highly profitable financial products that take advantage of computer technology. To illustrate how financial institution managers can figure out ways to increase profits through financial innovation, we look at Treasury strips, a financial instrument first developed in 1982 by Salomon Brothers and Merrill Lynch. (Indeed, this innovation was so successful that the U.S. Treasury copied it when they issued STRIPS in 1985, as discussed in Chapter 10.)

One problem for investors in long-term coupon bonds, even when investors have a long holding period, is that there is some uncertainty in their returns arising from what is called *reinvestment risk*. Even if an investor holding a long-term coupon bond has a holding period of 10 years, the return on the bond is not certain. The problem is that coupon payments are made before the bond matures in 10 years, and these coupon payments must be reinvested. Because the interest rates at which the coupon payments will be reinvested fluctuate, the eventual return on the bond fluctuates as well. In contrast, long-term zero-coupon bonds have no reinvestment risk because they make no cash payments before the bond matures. The return on a zero-coupon bond if it is held to maturity is known at the time of purchase. The absence of reinvestment risk is an attractive feature of zero-coupon bonds, and as a result, investors are willing to accept a slightly lower interest rate on them than on coupon bonds, which do bear some reinvestment risk.

The fact that zero-coupon bonds have lower interest rates, along with the ability to use computers to create so-called hybrid securities, which are securities derived from other underlying securities, gave employees of Salomon Brothers and Merrill Lynch a brilliant idea for making profits. They could use computers to separate ("strip") a long-term Treasury coupon bond into a set of zero-coupon bonds. For example, a $1 million 10-year Treasury bond might be stripped into ten $100,000 zero-coupon bonds, which, naturally enough, are called *Treasury strips*. The lower interest rates on the more desirable Treasury strip zero-coupon bonds would mean that the value of these bonds would exceed the price of the underlying long-term Treasury bond, allowing Salomon Brothers and Merrill Lynch to make a profit by purchasing the long-term Treasury bond, separating it into Treasury strips, and selling them off as zero-coupon bonds.

To see in more detail how their thinking worked, let's look more closely at a $1 million 10-year Treasury bond with a coupon rate of 10% whose yield to maturity is also 10%, so it is selling at par. The cash payments for this bond are listed in the second column of Table 18.1. To make things simple, let's assume that the yield curve is absolutely flat so that the interest rate used to discount all the future cash payments is the same. Because zero-coupon bonds, which have no reinvestment risk, are more desirable than the 10-year Treasury coupon bond, the interest rate on the zero-coupon bonds is 9.75%, a little lower than the 10% interest rate on the coupon bond.

TABLE 18.1 Market Value of Treasury Strip Zero-Coupon Bonds Derived from a $1 Million 10-Year Treasury Bond with a 10% Coupon Rate and Selling at Par

(1)	(2)	(3)	(4)
Year	Cash Payment ($)	Interest Rate on Zero-Coupon Bond (%)	Present Discounted Value of Zero-Coupon Bond ($)
1	100,000	9.75	91,116
2	100,000	9.75	83,022
3	100,000	9.75	75,646
4	100,000	9.75	68,926
5	100,000	9.75	62,802
6	100,000	9.75	57,223
7	100,000	9.75	52,140
8	100,000	9.75	47,508
9	100,000	9.75	43,287
10	100,000	9.75	39,442
10	1,000,000	9.75	394,416
Total			$1,015,528

How would Fran, a smart and sophisticated financial institution manager, figure out if she could make a profit from creating and selling the Treasury strips? Her first step is to figure out what the zero-coupon Treasury strips would sell for. She would find this easy to do if she had read Chapter 3 of this book: Using Equation 1 in that chapter, she would figure out that each of the Treasury strip zero-coupon bonds would sell for its present discounted value:

$$\frac{\text{Cash payment in year } n}{(1 + 0.0975)^n}$$

The results of this calculation for each year are listed in column (4) of Table 18.1. When Fran adds up the values of the collection of the Treasury strip zero-coupon bonds, she gets a figure of $1,015,528, which is greater than the $1 million purchase price of the Treasury bond. As long as it costs less than $15,528 to collect the payments from the Treasury and then pass them through to the owners of the zero-coupon strips, which is likely to be the case since computer technology makes the cost of conducting these financial transactions low, the zero-coupon strips will be profitable for her financial institution. Fran would thus recommend that her firm go ahead and market the new financial product. Because the financial institution can now generate much higher profits by selling substantial numbers of Treasury strips, it would amply reward Fran with a spanking new red BMW and a $100,000 bonus!

Financial Innovation and the Decline of Traditional Banking

The traditional financial intermediation role of banking has been to make long-term loans and to fund them by issuing short-term deposits, a process of asset transformation commonly referred to as "borrowing short and lending long." Here we examine how financial innovations have created a more competitive environment for the banking industry, causing the industry to change dramatically, with its traditional banking business going into decline.

In the United States, the importance of commercial banks as a source of funds to nonfinancial borrowers has shrunk dramatically. As we can see in Figure 18.2, in 1974, commercial banks provided close to 40% of these funds; by 2006, their market share was down to below 30%. The decline in market share for thrift institutions has been even more precipitous, from more than 20% in the late 1970s to around 5% today. Another way of viewing the declining role of banking in traditional financial intermediation is to look at the size of banks' balance sheet assets relative to those of other financial intermediaries. Commercial banks' share of total financial intermediary assets has fallen from about 40% in the 1960–1980 period to 30% by the end of 2006. Similarly, the share of total financial intermediary assets held by thrift institutions has declined even more from the 20% level of the 1960–1980 period to about 6% by 2005.

Clearly, the traditional financial intermediation role of banking, whereby banks make loans that are funded with deposits, is no longer as important in our financial system. However, the decline in the market share of banks in total lending and total financial intermediary assets does not necessarily indicate that the banking indus-

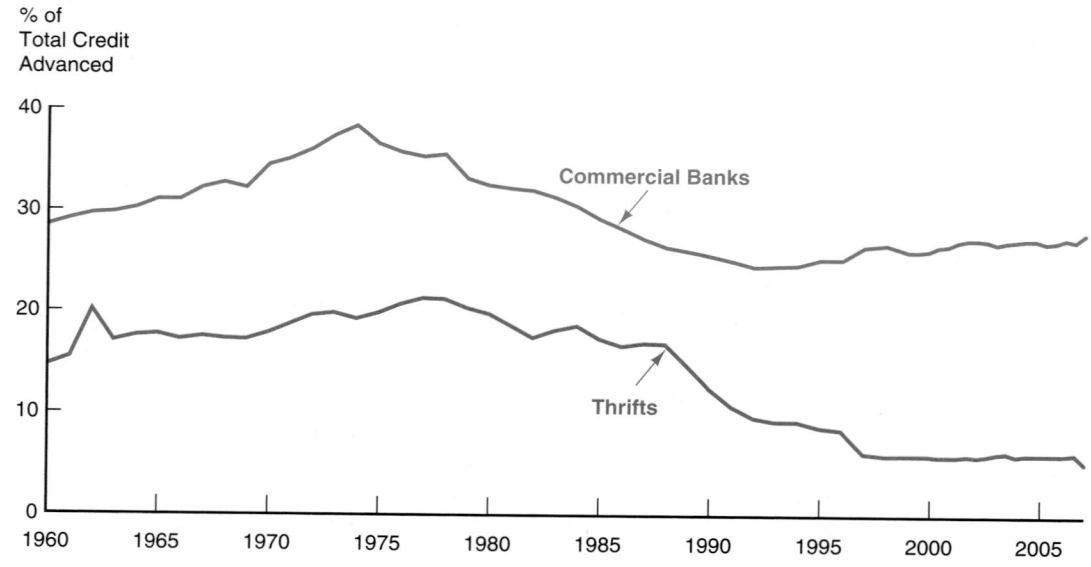

Figure 18.2 Bank Share of Total Nonfinancial Borrowing, 1960–2006

Source: Federal Reserve Flow of Funds Accounts; Federal Reserve Bulletin.

try is in decline. There is no evidence of a declining trend in bank profitability. However, overall bank profitability is not a good indicator of the profitability of traditional banking, because it includes an increasing amount of income from nontraditional off-balance-sheet activities, discussed in Chapter 17. Noninterest income derived from off-balance-sheet activities, as a share of total banking income, increased from around 7% in 1980 to more than 45% of total bank income today. Given that the overall profitability of banks has not risen, the increase in income from off-balance-sheet activities implies that the profitability of traditional banking business has declined. This decline in profitability explains why banks have been reducing their traditional business.

To understand why traditional banking business has declined in both size and profitability, we need to look at how the financial innovations described earlier have caused banks to suffer declines in their cost advantages in acquiring funds—that is, on the liabilities side of their balance sheet—while at the same time they have lost income advantages on the assets side of their balance sheet. The simultaneous decline of cost and income advantages has resulted in reduced profitability of traditional banking and an effort by banks to leave this business and engage in new and more profitable activities.

Decline in Cost Advantages in Acquiring Funds (Liabilities) Until 1980, banks were subject to deposit rate ceilings that restricted them from paying any interest on checkable deposits and (under Regulation Q) limited them to paying a maximum interest rate of a little more than 5% on time deposits. Until the 1960s, these restrictions worked to the banks' advantage because their major source of funds (in excess of 60%) was checkable deposits, and the zero interest cost on these deposits meant that the banks had a very low cost of funds. Unfortunately, this cost advantage for banks did not last. The rise in inflation beginning in the late 1960s led to higher interest rates, which made investors more sensitive to yield differentials on different assets. The result was the *disintermediation* process, in which people began to take their money out of banks, with their low interest rates on both checkable and time deposits, and began to seek out higher-yielding investments. At the same time, attempts to get around deposit rate ceilings and reserve requirements led to the financial innovation of money market mutual funds, which put the banks at an even further disadvantage because depositors could now obtain checking account-like services while earning high interest on their money market mutual fund accounts. One manifestation of these changes in the financial system was that the low-cost source of funds, checkable deposits, declined dramatically in importance for banks, falling from more than 60% of bank liabilities to less than 10% today.

The growing difficulty for banks in raising funds led to their supporting legislation in the 1980s that eliminated Regulation Q ceilings on time deposit interest rates and allowed checkable deposit accounts that paid interest. Although these changes in regulation helped make banks more competitive in their quest for funds, it also meant that their cost of acquiring funds had risen substantially, thereby reducing their earlier cost advantage over other financial institutions.

Decline in Income Advantages on Uses of Funds (Assets) The loss of cost advantages on the liabilities side of the balance sheet for American banks is one reason that they have become less competitive, but they have also been hit by a decline in income advantages on the assets side from the financial innovations we discussed earlier—junk bonds, securitization, and the rise of the commercial paper market.

We have seen that improvements in information technology have made it easier for firms to issue securities directly to the public. This has meant that instead of going to banks to finance short-term credit needs, many of the banks' best business customers now find it cheaper to go instead to the commercial paper market for funds. The loss of this competitive advantage for banks is evident in the fact that before 1970, nonfinancial commercial paper equaled less than 5% of commercial and industrial bank loans, whereas the figure has risen to over 11% today. In addition, this growth in the commercial paper market has allowed finance companies, which depend primarily on commercial paper to acquire funds, to expand their operations at the expense of banks. Finance companies, which lend to many of the same businesses that borrow from banks, have increased their market share relative to banks: Before 1980, finance company loans to business equaled about 30% of commercial and industrial bank loans; currently, they are 64%.

The emergence of the junk bond market has also eaten into banks' loan business. Improvements in information technology have made it easier for corporations to sell their bonds to the public directly, thereby bypassing banks. Although *Fortune* 500 companies started taking this route in the 1970s, now lower-quality corporate borrowers are using banks less often because they have access to the junk bond market.

We have also seen that improvements in computer technology have led to securitization, whereby illiquid financial assets such as bank loans and mortgages are transformed into marketable securities. Computers enable other financial institutions to originate loans because they can now accurately evaluate credit risk with statistical methods, while computers have lowered transaction costs, making it possible to bundle these loans and sell them as securities. When default risk can be easily evaluated with computers, banks no longer have an advantage in making loans. Without their former advantages, banks have lost loan business to other financial institutions even though the banks themselves are involved in the process of securitization. Securitization has been a particular problem for mortgage-issuing institutions such as S&Ls, because most residential mortgages are now securitized.

Banks' Responses In any industry, a decline in profitability usually results in exit from the industry (often due to widespread bankruptcies) and a shrinkage of market share. This occurred in the banking industry in the United States during the 1980s via consolidations and bank failures (discussed in Chapter 20).

In an attempt to survive and maintain adequate profit levels, many U.S. banks face two alternatives. First, they can attempt to maintain their traditional lending activity by expanding into new and riskier areas of lending. For example, U.S. banks increased their risk taking by placing a greater percentage of their total funds in commercial real estate loans, traditionally a riskier type of loan. In addition, they increased lending for corporate takeovers and leveraged buyouts, which are highly leveraged transaction loans. The decline in the profitability of banks' traditional business may thus have helped lead to the crisis in banking in the 1980s and early 1990s that we discuss in the next two chapters.

The second way banks have sought to maintain former profit levels is to pursue new off-balance-sheet activities that are more profitable. U.S. commercial banks did this during the early 1980s, more than doubling the share of their income coming from off-balance-sheet, non-interest-income activities. This strategy, however, has generated concerns about what activities are proper for banks and whether nontraditional activities might be riskier and, therefore, result in excessive risk taking by banks.

The decline of banks' traditional business has thus meant that the banking industry has been driven to seek out new lines of business. This could be beneficial because by so doing, banks can keep vibrant and healthy. Indeed, bank profitability has been high in recent years, and nontraditional, off-balance-sheet activities have been playing an important role in the resurgence of bank profits. However, there is a danger that the new directions in banking could lead to increased risk taking, and thus the decline in traditional banking requires regulators to be more vigilant. It also poses new challenges for bank regulators, who, as we will see in Chapter 20, must now be far more concerned about banks' off-balance-sheet activities.

Decline of Traditional Banking in Other Industrialized Countries Forces similar to those in the United States have been leading to the decline of traditional banking in other industrialized countries. The loss of banks' monopoly power over depositors has occurred outside the United States as well. Financial innovation and deregulation are occurring worldwide and have created attractive alternatives for both depositors and borrowers. In Japan, for example, deregulation has opened a wide array of new financial instruments to the public, causing a disintermediation process similar to that in the United States. In European countries, innovations have steadily eroded the barriers that have traditionally protected banks from competition.

In other countries, banks have also faced increased competition from the expansion of securities markets. Both financial deregulation and fundamental economic forces in other countries have improved the availability of information in securities markets, making it easier and less costly for firms to finance their activities by issuing securities rather than going to banks. Further, even in countries where securities markets have not grown, banks have still lost loan business because their best corporate customers have had increasing access to foreign and offshore capital markets, such as the Eurobond market. In smaller economies, like Australia, which still do not have well-developed corporate bond or commercial paper markets, banks have lost loan business to international securities markets. In addition, the same forces that drove the securitization process in the United States are at work in other countries and will undercut the profitability of traditional banking in these countries as well. The United States is not unique in seeing its banks face a more difficult competitive environment. Thus, although the decline of traditional banking occurred earlier in the United States than in other countries, the same forces are causing a decline in traditional banking abroad.

Structure of the U.S. Commercial Banking Industry

There are approximately 7,500 commercial banks in the United States, far more than in any other country in the world. As Table 18.2 indicates, we have an extraordinary number of small banks. A remarkable 43.5% of the banks have less than $100 million in assets. Far more typical is the size distribution in Canada or the United Kingdom, where five or fewer banks dominate the industry. In contrast, the 10 largest commercial banks in the United States (listed in Table 18.3) together hold just 52% of the assets in their industry.

Most industries in the United States have far fewer firms than the commercial banking industry; typically, large firms tend to dominate these industries to a greater

TABLE 18.2 Size Distribution of Insured Commercial Banks, March 31, 2007

Assets	Number of Banks	Share of Banks (%)	Share of Assets Held (%)
Less than $100 million	3,212	43.5	1.7
$100 million–$1 billion	3,672	49.8	10.4
$1 billion or more	496	6.7	87.9
Total	7,380	100.00	100.00

Source: http://www2.fdic.gov/sdi/main.asp.

TABLE 18.3 Ten Largest U.S. Banks, September 30, 2007

Bank	Assets ($ millions)	Share of All Commercial Bank Assets (%)
1. J. P. Morgan Chase, Columbus, OH	1224	12.1
2. Bank of America Corp., Charlotte, NC	1204	11.9
3. Citibank, New York, NY	1077	10.6
4. Wachovia Corp., Charlotte, NC	519	5.1
5. Wells Fargo, Sioux Falls, SD	397	3.9
6. U.S. Bancorp, Cincinnati, OH	220	2.2
7. SunTrust Bank, Atlanta, GA	185	1.8
8. HSBC Bank US, Wilmington, DE	169	1.7
9. FIA CARD, Wilmington, DE	139	1.4
10. Regions BK, Birmingham, AL	133	1.3
Total	5267	52.0

Source: www.federalreserve.gov/releases/lbr/current/lrg_bnk_1st.txt.

extent than in the commercial banking industry. (Consider the computer software industry, which is dominated by Microsoft, or the automobile industry, which is dominated by General Motors, Ford, Toyota, and Honda.) Does the large number of banks in the commercial banking industry and the absence of a few dominant firms suggest that commercial banking is more competitive than other industries?

Restrictions on Branching

The presence of so many commercial banks in the United States actually reflects past regulations that restricted the ability of these financial institutions to open **branches** (additional offices for the conduct of banking operations). Each state had its own regulations on the type and number of branches that a bank could open. Regulations on both coasts, for example, tended to allow banks to open branches throughout a state; in the middle part of the country, regulations on branching were more restrictive. The McFadden Act of 1927, which was designed to put national banks and state banks on an equal footing (and the Douglas Amendment of 1956, which closed a loophole in the McFadden Act), effectively prohibited banks from branching across state lines and forced all national banks to conform to the branching regulations in the state of their location.

The McFadden Act and state branching regulations constituted strong anti-competitive forces in the commercial banking industry, allowing many small banks to stay in existence, because larger banks were prevented from opening a branch nearby. If competition is beneficial to society, why have regulations restricting branching arisen in America? The simplest explanation is that the American public has historically been hostile to large banks. States with the most restrictive branching regulations were typically ones in which populist antibank sentiment was strongest in the nineteenth century. (These states usually had large farming populations whose relations with banks periodically became tempestuous when banks would foreclose on farmers who couldn't pay their debts.) The legacy of nineteenth-century politics was a banking system with restrictive branching regulations and hence an inordinate number of small banks. However, as we will see later in this chapter, branching restrictions have been eliminated, and we are heading toward nationwide banking.

Response to Branching Restrictions

An important feature of the U.S. banking industry is that competition can be repressed by regulation but not completely quashed. As we saw earlier in this chapter, the existence of restrictive regulation stimulates financial innovations that get around these regulations in the banks' search for profits. Regulations restricting branching have stimulated similar economic forces and have promoted the development of two financial innovations: bank holding companies and automated teller machines.

Bank Holding Companies A holding company is a corporation that owns several different companies. This form of corporate ownership has important advantages for banks. It has allowed them to circumvent restrictive branching regulations, because the holding company can own a controlling interest in several banks even if branching is not permitted. Furthermore, a bank holding company can engage in other activities related to banking, such as the provision of investment advice, data processing and transmission services, leasing, credit card services, and servicing of loans in other states.

The growth of the bank holding companies has been dramatic over the past three decades. Today, bank holding companies own almost all large banks, and more than 90% of all commercial bank deposits are held in banks owned by holding companies.

Automated Teller Machines Another financial innovation that avoided the restrictions on branching is the automated teller machine (ATM). Banks realized that if they did not own or rent the ATM, but instead let it be owned by someone else and paid for each transaction with a fee, the ATM would probably not be considered a branch of the bank and thus would not be subject to branching regulations. This is exactly what the regulatory agencies and courts in most states concluded. Because they enable banks to widen their markets, a number of these shared facilities (such as Cirrus and NYCE) have been established nationwide. Furthermore, even when an ATM is owned by a bank, states typically have special provisions that allow wider establishment of ATMs than is permissible for traditional "brick and mortar" branches.

As we saw earlier in this chapter, avoiding regulation was not the only reason for the development of the ATM. The advent of cheaper computer and telecommunications technology enabled banks to provide ATMs at low cost, making them a profitable innovation. This example further illustrates that technological factors often combine with incentives such as the desire to avoid restrictive regulations like branching restrictions to produce financial innovation.

Bank Consolidation and Nationwide Banking

As we can see in Figure 18.3, after a remarkable period of stability from 1934 to the mid-1980s, the number of commercial banks began to fall dramatically. Why has this sudden decline taken place?

The banking industry hit some hard times in the 1980s and early 1990s, with bank failures running at a rate of over 100 per year from 1985 to 1992 (more on this later in the chapter and in Chapter 20). But bank failures are only part of the story. In the years 1985–1992, the number of banks declined by 3,000—more than double the number of failures. And in the period 1992–2006, when the banking industry returned to health, the number of commercial banks declined by a little over 3,500, less than 5% of which were bank failures, and most of these were of small banks. Thus, we see that bank failures played an important, though not predominant, role in the decline in the number of banks in the 1985–1992 period and an almost negligible role in the decline in the number of banks since then.

So what explains the rest of the story? The answer is bank consolidation. Banks have been merging to create larger entities or have been buying up other banks.

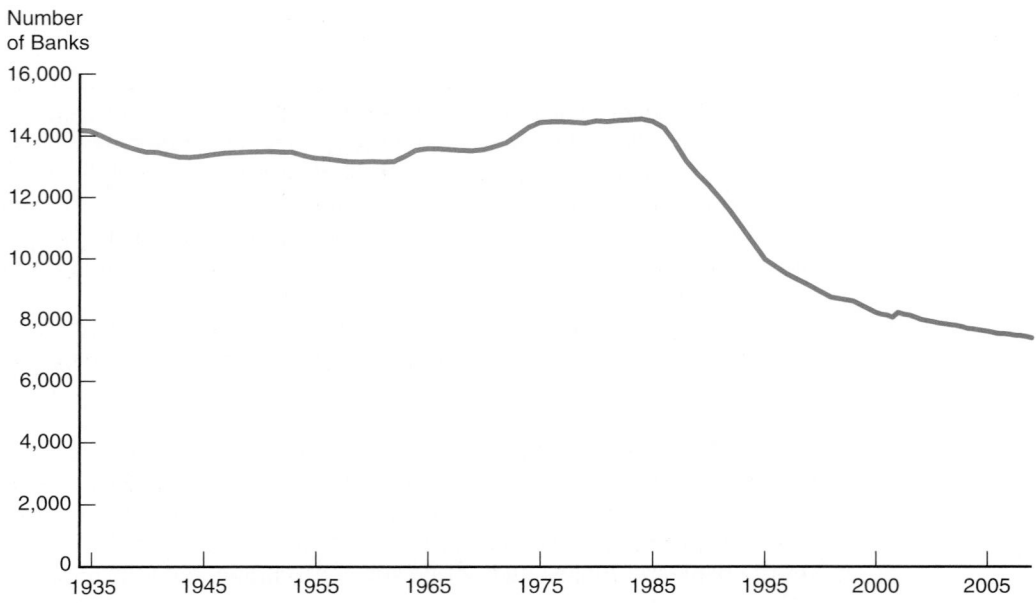

Figure 18.3 Number of Insured Commercial Banks in the United States, 1934–2006

Source: www2.fdic.gov/qbp/qbpSelect.asp?menuitem=STAT.

This gives rise to a new question: Why has bank consolidation been taking place in recent years?

As we have seen, loophole mining by banks has reduced the effectiveness of branching restrictions, with the result that many states have recognized that it would be in their best interest if they allowed ownership of banks across state lines. The result has been the formation of reciprocal regional compacts in which banks in one state are allowed to own banks in other states in the region. In 1975, Maine enacted the first interstate banking legislation that allowed out-of-state bank holding companies to purchase banks in that state. In 1982, Massachusetts enacted a regional compact with other New England states to allow interstate banking, and many other regional compacts were adopted thereafter until by the early 1990s, almost all states allowed some form of interstate banking.

With the barriers to interstate banking breaking down in the early 1980s, banks recognized that they could gain the benefits of diversification because they would now be able to make loans in many states rather than just one. This gave them the advantage that if one state's economy was weak, another state in which they operated might have a strong economy, thus decreasing the likelihood that loans in different states would default at the same time. In addition, allowing banks to own banks in other states meant that they could increase their size through out-of-state acquisition of banks or by merging with banks in other states. Mergers and acquisitions explain the first phase of banking consolidation, which has played such an important role in the decline in the number of banks since 1985. Another result of the loosening of restrictions on interstate branching is the development of a new class of banks, the **superregional banks,** bank holding companies that have begun to rival the money center banks in size but whose headquarters are not in one of the money center cities (New York, Chicago, and San Francisco). Examples of these superregional banks are Bank of America of Charlotte, North Carolina, and Banc One of Columbus, Ohio.

Not surprisingly, the advent of the Web and improved computer technology is another factor driving bank consolidation. Economies of scale have increased, because large up-front investments are required to set up many information technology platforms for financial institutions (see the E-Finance box, "Information Technology and Bank Consolidation"). To take advantage of these economies of scale, banks have needed to get bigger, and this development has led to additional consolidation. Information technology has also been increasing **economies of scope,** the ability to use one resource to provide many different products and services. For example, details about the quality and creditworthiness of firms not only inform decisions about whether to make loans to them, but also can be useful in determining at what price their shares should trade. Similarly, once you have marketed one financial product to an investor, you probably know how to market another. Business people describe economies of scope by saying that there are "synergies" between different lines of business, and information technology is making these synergies more likely. The result is that consolidation is taking place not only to make financial institutions bigger, but also to increase the combination of products and services they can provide. This consolidation has had two consequences. First, different types of financial intermediaries are encroaching on each other's territory, making them more alike. Second, consolidation has led to the development of what the Federal Reserve has named **large, complex banking organizations (LCBOs).** This development has been facilitated by the repeal of the Glass-Steagall restrictions on combinations of banking and other financial service industries discussed in the next section.

Information Technology and Bank Consolidation

Achieving low costs in banking requires huge investments in information technology. In turn, such enormous investments require a business line of very large scale. This has been particularly true in the credit card business in recent years, in which huge technology investments have been made to provide customers with convenient Web sites and to develop better systems to handle processing and risk analysis for both credit and fraud risk. The result has been substantial consolidation: As recently as 1995, the top five banking institutions issuing credit cards held less than 40% of total credit card debt, while today this number is more than 60%.

Information technology has also spurred increasing consolidation of the bank custody business. Banks hold the actual certificate for investors when they purchase a stock or bond and provide data on the value of these securities and the amount of risk an investor is facing. Because this business is also computer-intensive, it also requires very large-scale investments in computer technology for the bank to offer these services at competitive rates. The percentage of assets at the top 10 custody banks has therefore risen from 40% in 1990 to more than 90% today.

The increasing importance of e-finance, in which the computer is playing a more central role in delivering financial services, is bringing tremendous changes to the structure of the banking industry. Although banks are more than willing to offer a full range of products to their customers, they no longer find it profitable to produce all of them. Instead, they are contracting out the business, a practice that will lead to further consolidation of technology-intensive banking businesses in the future.

The Riegle-Neal Interstate Banking and Branching Efficiency Act of 1994

Banking consolidation was given further stimulus by the passage in 1994 of the Riegle-Neal Interstate Banking and Branching Efficiency Act. This legislation expands the regional compacts to the entire nation and overturns the McFadden Act and Douglas Amendment's prohibition of interstate banking. Not only does this act allow bank holding companies to acquire banks in any other state, notwithstanding any state laws to the contrary, but bank holding companies can also merge the banks they own into one bank with branches in different states. States also have the option of opting out of interstate branching, a choice only Texas has made.

The Riegle-Neal Act finally established the basis for a true nationwide banking system. Although interstate banking was accomplished previously by out-of-state purchase of banks by bank holding companies, until 1994 interstate branching was virtually nonexistent, because very few states had enacted interstate branching legislation. Allowing banks to conduct interstate banking through branching is especially important, because many bankers feel that economies of scale cannot be fully exploited through the bank holding company structure, but only through branching networks in which all of the bank's operations are fully coordinated.

Nationwide banks are now emerging. With the merger in 1998 of Bank of America and NationsBank, which created the first bank with branches on both coasts, consolidation in the banking industry has led to banking organizations with operations in almost all of the 50 states.

What Will the Structure of the U.S. Banking Industry Look Like in the Future?

go online

www2.fdic.gov/SDI/SOB

Visit this Web site to gather statistics on the banking industry.

Now that true nationwide banking in the United States is a reality, the benefits of bank consolidation for the banking industry have increased substantially, driving the next phase of mergers and acquisitions and accelerating the decline in the number of commercial banks. With great changes occurring in the structure of this industry, the question naturally arises: What will the industry look like in 10 years?

One view is that the industry will become more like that in many other countries and we will end up with only a couple of hundred banks. A more extreme view is that the industry will look like that of Canada or the United Kingdom, with a few large banks dominating the industry. Research on this question, however, comes up with a different answer. The structure of the U.S. banking industry will still be unique, but not to the degree it once was. Most experts predict that the consolidation surge will settle down as the U.S. banking industry approaches several thousand, rather than several hundred, banks.[2]

Banking consolidation will result not only in a smaller number of banks, but as the mergers between Chase Manhattan Bank and Chemical Bank and between Bank of America and NationsBank suggest, a shift in assets from smaller banks to larger banks as well. Within 10 years, the share of bank assets in banks with less than $100 million in assets is expected to halve, while the amount at the megabanks, those with more than $100 billion in assets, is expected to more than double. Indeed, the United States now has several trillion-dollar banks (e.g., Citibank, J. P. Morgan Chase, and Bank of America).

Are Bank Consolidation and Nationwide Banking Good Things?

Advocates of nationwide banking believe that it will produce more efficient banks and a healthier banking system less prone to bank failures. However, critics of bank consolidation fear that it will eliminate small banks, referred to as *community banks*, and that this will result in less lending to small businesses. In addition, they worry that a few banks will come to dominate the industry, making the banking business less competitive.

Most economists are skeptical of these criticisms of bank consolidation. As we have seen, research indicates that even after bank consolidation is completed, the United States will still have plenty of banks. The banking industry will thus remain highly competitive, probably even more so than now, considering that banks that have been protected from competition from out-of-state banks will now have to compete with them vigorously to stay in business.

---

[2]For example, see Allen N. Berger, Anil K. Kashyap, and Joseph Scalise, "The Transformation of the U.S. Banking Industry: What a Long, Strange Trip It's Been," *Brookings Papers on Economic Activity* 2 (1995): 55–201; and Timothy Hannan and Stephen Rhoades, "Future U.S. Banking Structure, 1990–2010," *Antitrust Bulletin* 37 (1992) 737–798. For a more detailed treatment of the bank consolidation process taking place in the United States, see Frederic S. Mishkin, "Bank Consolidation: A Central Banker's Perspective," in *Mergers of Financial Institutions,* ed. Yakov Amihud and Geoffrey Wood (Boston: Kluwer Academic Publishers, 1998), pp. 3–19.

It also does not look as though community banks will disappear. When New York state liberalized its branching laws in 1962, there were fears that community banks upstate would be driven from the market by the big New York City banks. Not only did this not happen, but some of the big boys found that the small banks were able to run rings around them in the local markets. Similarly, California, which has had unrestricted statewide branching for a long time, continues to have a thriving population of community banks.

Economists see some important benefits from bank consolidation and nationwide banking. The elimination of geographic restrictions on banking will increase competition and drive inefficient banks out of business, increasing the efficiency of the banking sector. The move to larger banking organizations also means that there will be some increase in efficiency because they can take advantage of economies of scale and scope. The increased diversification of banks' loan portfolios may lower the probability of a banking crisis in the future. In the 1980s and early 1990s, bank failures were often concentrated in states with weak economies. For example, after the decline in oil prices in 1986, all of the major commercial banks in Texas, which had been very profitable, found themselves in trouble. At that time, banks in New England were doing fine. However, when the 1990–1991 recession hit New England hard, some New England banks started failing. With nationwide banking, a bank could make loans in both New England and Texas and would thus be less likely to fail, because when loans go sour in one location, they would likely be doing well in the other. Thus, nationwide banking is seen as a major step toward creating a banking system that is less vulnerable to banking crises.

Two concerns remain about the effects of bank consolidation—that it may lead to a reduction in lending to small businesses and that banks rushing to expand into new geographic markets may take increased risks leading to bank failures. The jury is still out on these concerns, but most economists see the benefits of bank consolidation and nationwide banking as outweighing the costs.

Separation of the Banking and Other Financial Service Industries

Another important feature of the structure of the banking industry in the United States until recently was the separation of the banking and other financial services industries—such as securities, insurance, and real estate—mandated by the Glass-Steagall Act of 1933. As pointed out earlier in the chapter, Glass-Steagall allowed commercial banks to sell new offerings of government securities but prohibited them from underwriting corporate securities or from engaging in brokerage activities. It also prevented banks from engaging in insurance and real estate activities. In turn, it prevented investment banks and insurance companies from engaging in commercial banking activities and thus protected banks from competition.

Erosion of Glass-Steagall

Despite the Glass-Steagall prohibitions, the pursuit of profits and financial innovation stimulated both banks and other financial institutions to bypass the intent of the Glass-Steagall Act and encroach on each other's traditional territory. Brokerage firms engaged in the traditional banking business of issuing deposit instruments with the development of money market mutual funds and cash management accounts. After the Federal Reserve used a loophole in Section 20 of the Glass-Steagall Act in 1987 to allow bank holding companies to underwrite previously prohibited classes of securities, banks began to enter this business. The loophole allowed affiliates of approved commercial banks to engage in underwriting activities as long as the revenue didn't exceed a specified amount, which started at 10% but was raised to 25% of the affiliates' total revenue. After the U.S. Supreme Court validated the Fed's action in July 1988, the Federal Reserve allowed J. P. Morgan, a commercial bank holding company, to underwrite corporate debt securities (in January 1989) and to underwrite stocks (in September 1990), with the privilege later extended to other bank holding companies. The regulatory agencies also allowed banks to engage in some real estate and some insurance activities.

The Gramm-Leach-Bliley Financial Services Modernization Act of 1999: Repeal of Glass-Steagall

Because restrictions on commercial banks' securities and insurance activities put American banks at a competitive disadvantage relative to foreign banks, bills to overturn Glass-Steagall appeared in almost every session of Congress in the 1990s. With the merger in 1998 of Citicorp, the second-largest bank in the United States, and Travelers Group, an insurance company that also owned the third-largest securities firm in the country (Salomon Smith Barney), the pressure to abolish Glass-Steagall became overwhelming. Legislation to eliminate Glass-Steagall finally came to fruition in 1999. This legislation, the Gramm-Leach-Bliley Financial Services Modernization Act of 1999, allows securities firms and insurance companies to purchase banks, and allows banks to underwrite insurance and securities and engage in real estate activities. Under this legislation, states retain regulatory authority over insurance activities, while the Securities and Exchange Commission continues to have oversight of securities activities. The Office of the Comptroller of the Currency has the authority to regulate bank subsidiaries engaged in securities underwriting, but the Federal Reserve continues to have the authority to oversee the bank holding companies under which all real estate and insurance activities and large securities operations will be housed.

Implications for Financial Consolidation

As we have seen, the Riegle-Neal Interstate Banking and Branching Efficiency Act of 1994 has stimulated consolidation of the banking industry. The financial consolidation process will be further hastened by the Gramm-Leach-Bliley Act of 1999, because the way is now open to consolidation in terms not only of the number of banking institutions, but also across financial service activities. Given that information technology is increasing economies of scope, mergers of banks with other financial service firms like that of Citicorp and Travelers should become increasingly common, and more mega-mergers are likely to be on the way. Banking institutions are becoming not only larger, but also increasingly complex organizations, engaging in the full gamut of financial service activities.

Separation of Banking and Other Financial Services Industries Throughout the World

Not many other countries in the aftermath of the Great Depression followed the lead of the United States in separating the banking and other financial services industries. In fact, in the past this separation was the most prominent difference between banking regulation in the United States and in other countries. Around the world, there are three basic frameworks for the banking and securities industries.

The first framework is *universal banking,* which exists in Germany, the Netherlands, and Switzerland. It provides no separation at all between the banking and securities industries. In a universal banking system, commercial banks provide a full range of banking, securities, real estate, and insurance services, all within a single legal entity. Banks are allowed to own sizable equity shares in commercial firms, and often they do.

The *British-style universal banking system,* the second framework, is found in the United Kingdom and countries with close ties to it, such as Canada and Australia, and now the United States. The British-style universal bank engages in securities underwriting, but it differs from the German-style universal bank in three ways: Separate legal subsidiaries are more common, bank equity holdings of commercial firms are less common, and combinations of banking and insurance firms are less common.

The third framework features some legal separation of the banking and other financial services industries, as in Japan. A major difference between the U.S. and Japanese banking systems is that Japanese banks are allowed to hold substantial equity stakes in commercial firms, whereas American banks cannot. In addition, most American banks use a bank-holding-company structure, but bank holding companies are illegal in Japan. Although the banking and securities industries are legally separated in Japan under Section 65 of the Japanese Securities Act, commercial banks are increasingly being allowed to engage in securities activities and, like U.S. banks, are becoming more like British-style universal banks.

International Banking

In 1960, only eight U.S. banks operated branches in foreign countries, and their total assets were less than $4 billion. Currently, around 100 American banks have branches abroad, with assets totaling more than $1.3 trillion. The spectacular growth in international banking can be explained by three factors.

First is the rapid growth in international trade and multinational (worldwide) corporations that has occurred since 1960. When American firms operate abroad, they need banking services in foreign countries to help finance international trade. For example, they might need a loan in a foreign currency to operate a factory abroad. And when they sell goods abroad, they need to have a bank exchange the foreign currency they have received for their goods into dollars. Although these firms could use foreign banks to provide them with these international banking services, many of them prefer to do business with the U.S. banks with which they have established long-term relationships and which understand American business customs and practices. As international trade has grown, international banking has grown with it.

Second, American banks have been able to earn substantial profits by being very active in global investment banking, in which they underwrite foreign securities. They also sell insurance abroad, and they derive substantial profits from these investment banking and insurance activities.

Third, American banks have wanted to tap into the large pool of dollar-denominated deposits in foreign countries known as Eurodollars. To understand the structure of U.S. banking overseas, let us first look at the Eurodollar market, an important source of growth for international banking.

Eurodollar Market

Eurodollars are created when deposits in accounts in the United States are transferred to a bank outside the country and are kept in the form of dollars. For example, if Rolls-Royce PLC deposits a $1 million check, written on an account at an American bank, in its bank in London—specifying that the deposit is payable in dollars—$1 million in Eurodollars is created.[3] More than 90% of Eurodollar deposits are time deposits, more than half of them certificates of deposit with maturities of 30 days or more. The total amount of Eurodollars outstanding is on the order of $5.2 trillion, making the Eurodollar market one of the most important financial markets in the world economy.

Why would companies such as Rolls-Royce want to hold dollar deposits outside the United States? First, the dollar is the most widely used currency in international trade, so Rolls-Royce might want to hold deposits in dollars to conduct its international transactions. Second, Eurodollars are "offshore" deposits—they are held in countries that will not subject them to regulations such as reserve requirements or restrictions (called *capital controls*) on taking the deposits outside the country.[4]

The main center of the Eurodollar market is London, a major international financial center for hundreds of years. Eurodollars are also held outside Europe in locations that provide offshore status to these deposits—for example, Singapore, the Bahamas, and the Cayman Islands.

The minimum transaction in the Eurodollar market is typically $1 million, and approximately 75% of Eurodollar deposits are held by banks. Plainly, you and I are unlikely to come into direct contact with Eurodollars. The Eurodollar market is, however, an important source of funds to U.S. banks, whose borrowing of these deposits is more than $700 billion. Rather than using an intermediary and borrowing all the deposits from foreign banks, American banks decided that they could earn higher profits by opening their own branches abroad to attract these deposits. Consequently, the Eurodollar market has been an important stimulus to U.S. banking overseas.

Structure of U.S. Banking Overseas

U.S. banks have most of their foreign branches in Latin America, the Far East, the Caribbean, and London. The largest volume of assets is held by branches in London, because it is a major international financial center and the central location for the Eurodollar market. Latin America and the Far East have many branches because of the importance of U.S. trade with these regions. Parts of the Caribbean (especially the Bahamas and the Cayman Islands) have become important as tax havens, with minimal taxation and few restrictive regulations. In actuality, the bank branches in the Bahamas and the Cayman Islands are "shell operations" because they function primarily as bookkeeping centers and do not provide normal banking services.

An alternative corporate structure for U.S. banks that operate overseas is the **Edge Act corporation,** a special subsidiary engaged primarily in international banking. U.S. banks (through their holding companies) can also own a controlling

---

[3]Note that the London bank keeps the $1 million on deposit at the American bank, so the creation of Eurodollars has not caused a reduction in the amount of bank deposits in the United States.

[4]Although most offshore deposits are denominated in dollars, some are denominated in other currencies. Collectively, these offshore deposits are referred to as Eurocurrencies. A Japanese yen-denominated deposit held in London, for example, is called a Euroyen.

interest in foreign banks and in foreign companies that provide financial services, such as finance companies. The international activities of U.S. banking organizations are governed primarily by the Federal Reserve's Regulation K.

In late 1981, the Federal Reserve approved the creation of **international banking facilities (IBFs)** within the United States that can accept time deposits from foreigners but are not subject to either reserve requirements or restrictions on interest payments. IBFs are also allowed to make loans to foreigners, but they are not allowed to make loans to domestic residents. States have encouraged the establishment of IBFs by exempting them from state and local taxes. In essence, IBFs are treated like foreign branches of U.S. banks and are not subject to domestic regulations and taxes. The purpose of establishing IBFs is to encourage American and foreign banks to do more banking business in the United States rather than abroad. From this point of view, IBFs were a success: Their assets climbed to nearly $200 billion in the first two years, and were $1.0 trillion at the end of 2004.

Foreign Banks in the United States

The growth in international trade has not only encouraged U.S. banks to open offices overseas, but has also encouraged foreign banks to establish offices in the United States. Foreign banks have been extremely successful in the United States. Currently, they hold more than 11% of total U.S. bank assets and do a large portion of all U.S. bank lending, with nearly a 16% market share for lending to U.S. corporations.

Foreign banks engage in banking activities in the United States by operating an agency office of the foreign bank, a subsidiary U.S. bank, or a branch of the foreign bank. An agency office can lend and transfer funds in the United States, but it cannot accept deposits from domestic residents. Agency offices have the advantage of not being subject to regulations that apply to full-service banking offices (such as requirements for FDIC insurance). A subsidiary U.S. bank is just like any other U.S. bank (it may even have an American-sounding name) and is subject to the same regulations, but it is owned by the foreign bank. A branch of a foreign bank bears the foreign bank's name and is usually a full-service office. Foreign banks may also form Edge Act corporations and IBFs.

Before 1978, foreign banks were not subject to many regulations that applied to domestic banks: They could open branches across state lines and were not expected to meet reserve requirements, for example. The passage of the International Banking Act of 1978, however, put foreign and domestic banks on a more equal footing. The act stipulated that foreign banks could open new full-service branches only in the state they designate as their home state or in states that allow the entry of out-of-state banks. Limited-service branches and agency offices in any other state are permitted, however, and foreign banks are allowed to retain any full-service branches opened before the act was ratified.

The internationalization of banking, both by U.S. banks going abroad and by foreign banks entering the United States, has meant that financial markets throughout the world have become more integrated. As a result, there is a growing trend toward international coordination of bank regulation, one example of which is the 1988 Basel Accord to standardize minimum bank capital requirements in industrialized countries, discussed in Chapter 20. Financial market integration has also encouraged bank consolidation abroad, culminating in the creation of the first trillion-dollar bank with the proposed merger of the Industrial Bank of Japan, Dai-Ichi Kangyo Bank, and

TABLE 18.4   Ten Largest Banks in the World, 2006

Bank	Assets (U.S. $ millions)
1. Barclays Bank, U.K.	1,586,879
2. Mitsubishi UFJ Financial Group, Japan	1,585,277
3 UBS, Switzerland	1,563,223
4. HSBC, U.K.	1,498,773
5. Citigroup, U.S.	1,494,037
6. BNP Paribas, France	1,483,968
7. Group Credit Agricole, France	1,380,486
8. Royal Bank of Scotland, U.K.	1,333,608
9. Bank of America, U.S.	1,294,312
10. Mizuho Financial Group, Japan	1,268,012

Source: www.forbes.com/2005/03/30/05f2000land.html; *Euromoney,* August 2006, vol. 37 (448), p. 78–84.

Fuji Bank, announced in August 1999, but which took place in 2002. Another development has been the importance of foreign banks in international banking. As is shown in Table 18.4, in 2006, eight of the ten largest banking groups in the world were foreign.

SUMMARY

1. The history of banking in the United States has left us with a dual banking system, with commercial banks chartered by the states and the federal government. Multiple agencies regulate commercial banks: the Office of the Comptroller, the Federal Reserve, the FDIC, and the state banking authorities.

2. A change in the economic environment will stimulate financial institutions to search for financial innovations. Changes in demand conditions, especially an increase in interest-rate risk; changes in supply conditions, especially improvements in information technology; and the desire to avoid costly regulations have been major driving forces behind financial innovation. Financial innovation has caused banks to suffer declines in cost advantages in acquiring funds and in income advantages on their assets. The resulting squeeze has hurt profitability in banks' traditional lines of business and has led to a decline in traditional banking.

3. Restrictive state branching regulations and the McFadden Act, which prohibited branching across state lines, led to a large number of small commercial banks. The large number of commercial banks in the United States reflected the past *lack* of competition, not the presence of vigorous competition. Bank holding companies and ATMs were important responses to branching restrictions that weakened the restrictions' anticompetitive effect.

4. Since the mid-1980s, bank consolidation has been occurring at a rapid pace. The first phase of bank consolidation was the result of bank failures and the reduced effectiveness of branching restrictions. The second phase has been stimulated by information technology and the Riegle-Neal Interstate Banking and Branching Efficiency Act of 1994, which establishes the basis for a nationwide banking system. Once banking consolidation has settled down, we are likely to be left with a banking system with several thousand banks. Most economists believe that the benefits of bank consolidation and nationwide banking will outweigh the costs.

5. The Glass-Steagall Act separated commercial banking from the securities industry. Legislation in 1999, however, repealed the Glass-Steagall Act, removing the separation of these industries.

6. With the rapid growth of world trade since 1960, international banking has grown dramatically. United States banks engage in international banking activities by opening branches abroad, owning controlling interests in foreign banks, forming Edge Act corporations, and operating international banking facilities (IBFs) located in the United States. Foreign banks operate in the United States by owning a subsidiary American bank or by operating branches or agency offices in the United States.

KEY TERMS

automated banking machine (ABM), *p. 455*
automated teller machine (ATM), *p. 455*
bank holding companies, *p. 452*
branches, *p. 468*
deposit rate ceilings, *p. 460*
disintermediation, *p. 461*
dual banking system, *p. 451*
e-cash, *p. 457*
economies of scope, *p. 471*
electronic money (e-money), *p. 457*
Edge Act corporation, *p. 477*
financial derivatives, *p. 454*

financial engineering, *p. 452*
futures contracts, *p. 454*
hedge, *p. 454*
international banking facilities (IBFs), *p. 478*
large, complex banking organizations (LCBOs), *p. 471*
national banks, *p. 451*
securitization, *p. 459*
smart card, *p. 457*
state banks, *p. 451*
superregional banks, *p. 471*
sweep account, *p. 461*
virtual bank, *p. 455*

QUESTIONS

1. Why was the United States one of the last of the major industrialized countries to have a central bank?

2. Which regulatory agency has the primary responsibility for supervising the following categories of commercial banks?

   a. National banks

   b. Bank holding companies

   c. Non–Federal Reserve member state banks

   d. Federal Reserve member state banks

3. "The commercial banking industry in Canada is less competitive than the commercial banking industry in the United States because in Canada only a few large banks dominate the industry, while in the United States there are around 7,500 commercial banks." Is this statement true, false, or uncertain? Explain your answer.

4. Why did new technology made it harder to enforce limitations on bank branching?

5. Why has there been such a dramatic increase in bank holding companies?

6. What incentives have regulatory agencies created to encourage international banking? Why have they done this?

7. How could the approval of international banking facilities (IBFs) by the Fed in 1981 have reduced employment in the banking industry in Europe?

8. If the bank at which you keep your checking account is owned by Saudi Arabians, should you worry that your deposits are less safe than if the bank were owned by Americans?

9. If reserve requirements were eliminated in the future, as some economists advocate, what effects would this have on the size of money market mutual funds?

10. Why have banks been losing cost advantages in acquiring funds in recent years?

11. "If inflation had not risen in the 1960s and 1970s, the banking industry might be healthier today." Is this statement true, false, or uncertain? Explain your answer.

12. Why have banks been losing income advantages on their assets in recent years?

13. "The invention of the computer is the major factor behind the decline of the banking industry." Is this statement true, false, or uncertain? Explain your answer.

14. How did competitive forces lead to the repeal of the Glass-Steagall Act's separation of the banking and the securities industries?

15. What will be the likely effect of the Gramm-Leach-Bliley Act on financial consolidation?

WEB EXERCISES

Commercial Banking Industry: Structure and Competition

1. Go to **www2.fdic.gov/SDI/SOB**. Select "Historical Statistics on Banking," then "Commercial Bank Reports." Finally, choose "Number of Institutions, Branches and Total Offices." Looking at the trend in bank branches, does the public appear to have more or less access to banking facilities? How many banks were there in 1934 and how many are there now? Does the table indicate that the trend toward consolidation is continuing?

2. Despite the regulations that protect banks from failure, some do fail. Go to **www2.fdic.gov/hsob/**. Select the tab labeled "Bank and Thrift Failures." How many bank failures occurred in the United States during the most recent complete calendar year? What were the total assets held by the banks that failed? How many banks failed in 1937?

CHAPTER **19**

Savings Associations and Credit Unions

Preview

Suppose that you are a typical middle-class worker in New York in 1820. You work hard and earn fair wages as a craftsman. You are married and about to have a child, so you decide that you would like to own your own home. There are many commercial banks in the city, but as their name implies, these institutions exist to serve commerce, not the working class, because that is where the profits are. Where could you go to borrow the money to buy a home? Your options at that time would have been very limited. Later in the century, however, a new institution emerged that opened the possibility of home ownership to more than the very wealthy. That institution was the savings and loan association.

The middle class also had problems finding financial institutions willing to offer small consumer-type loans. Again, banks had determined that loans to these customers were not profitable. Another type of institution, the credit union, emerged at about the same time as savings and loans to service the borrowing needs of this segment of the economy.

In Chapters 17 and 18 we discussed commercial banks, the largest of the depository institutions. Though smaller, savings and loan associations, mutual savings banks, and credit unions, collectively called thrift institutions or thrifts, are important to the servicing of consumer borrowing needs. Thrifts are primarily concerned with lending to individuals and households, as opposed to banks, which still tend to be more concerned with lending to businesses. We begin our discussion by reviewing the history of the thrift industry. We then describe the nature of the industry today and project where it might be in the future.

Mutual Savings Banks

The first pure savings banks were established by philanthropists in Scotland and England to encourage saving by the poor. The founders of the institutions would often provide subsidies that allowed the institution to pay interest rates above the current market level. Because of the nature of the savings banks' customers, the institutions were very conservative with their funds and placed most of them in commercial banks. The first savings banks in the United States were chartered by Congress and founded in the Northeast in 1816. These institutions quickly lost their distinction of being strictly for the poor and instead became a popular place for members of the middle class to store their excess money.

Savings banks were originally organized as **mutual banks,** meaning that the depositors were the owners of the firm. This form of ownership led to a conservative investment posture, which prevented many of the mutual savings banks from failing during the recession at the end of the nineteenth century or during the Great Depression in the 1930s. In fact, between 1930 and 1937, deposits in mutual savings banks grew while those in commercial banks actually shrank. Following World War II, savings banks made mortgage lending their primary business. This focus made them similar to savings and loans.

Mutual ownership means that no stock in the bank is issued or sold; the depositors own a share of the bank in proportion to their deposits. There are currently 367 mutual savings banks, primarily concentrated on the eastern seaboard. Most are state chartered. (Federal chartering of savings banks did not begin until 1978.) Because they are state chartered, they are regulated and supervised by the state as well as the federal government.

The mutual form of ownership has both advantages and disadvantages. On the one hand, since the capital of the institution is contributed by the depositors, more capital is available because all deposits represent equity. This leads to greater safety in that mutual savings banks have far fewer liabilities than other banking organizations. On the other hand, the mutual form of ownership accentuates the principal-agent problem that exists in corporations. In corporations, managers are hired by the board of directors, who are in turn elected by the shareholders. Because most shareholders do not own a very large percentage of the firm, when there is a disagreement with management, it makes more sense to sell shares than to try to change policy. This problem also exists for the mutual form of ownership. Most depositors do not have a large enough stake in the firm to make it cost-effective for them to monitor the firm's managers closely.

The corporation, however, has alternative methods of aligning managers' goals with those of shareholders. For example, managers can be offered a stake in the firm, or stock options can be part of their compensation package. Similarly, managers of corporations are always under the threat of takeover by another firm if they fail to manage effectively. These alternatives are not available in the mutual form of ownership. As a result, there may be less control over management.

An advantage to the mutual form of ownership is that managers are more risk-averse than in the corporate form. This is because mutual managers gain nothing if the firm does very well, since they do not own a stake in the firm, but they lose everything if the firm fails. This incentive arrangement appeals to the very risk-averse investor, but its importance has diminished now that the government provides deposit insurance.

Savings and Loan Associations

go online

Information about savings institutions is available online; for example, the Wisconsin Department of Financial Institutions' Web site, **www.wdfi.org/fi/**, gives lists of savings institutions, statutes, rules, and financial data of the institutions.

In the early part of the nineteenth century, commercial banks focused on short-term loans to businesses, so it was very difficult for families to obtain loans for the purchase of a house. In 1816, Congress decided that home ownership was part of the American dream, and to make that possible, Congress passed regulations creating savings and loans and mutual savings institutions. Congress chartered the first savings and loans 15 years after the first mutual savings banks received their charters. The original mandate to the industry was to provide a source of funds for families wanting to buy a home.

These institutions were to aggregate depositors' funds and use the money to make long-term mortgage loans. The institutions were not to take in demand deposits but instead were authorized to offer savings accounts that paid slightly higher interest than that offered by commercial banks.

There were about 12,000 savings and loans in operation by the 1920s. Mortgages accounted for about 85% of their total assets. The rest of their assets were usually deposited in commercial banks. One of every four mortgages in the country was held by a savings and loan institution, making S&Ls the single largest provider of mortgage loans in the country.

go online

www2.fdic.gov/qbp/ provides a source for tools and charts related to savings and loans. Most current data in this chapter comes from this source.

Despite the large number of separate savings and loan institutions, they were not an integrated industry. Each state regulated its own S&Ls, and regulations differed substantially from state to state. In 1913, Congress created the Federal Reserve System to regulate and help commercial banks. No such system existed for savings and loans.

Before any significant legislation could be passed, the Great Depression caused the failure of thousands of thrift institutions. In response to the problems facing the industry and to the loss of $200 million in savings, Congress passed the **Federal Home Loan Bank Act of 1932.** This act created the **Federal Home Loan Bank Board (FHLBB)** and a network of regional home loan banks, similar to the organization of the Federal Reserve System. The act gave thrifts the choice of being state or federally chartered. In 1934, Congress continued its efforts to support savings and loans by establishing the **Federal Savings and Loan Insurance Corporation (FSLIC),** which insured deposits in much the same way as the FDIC did for commercial banks.

Savings and loans were successful, low-risk businesses for many years following these regulatory changes (see Chapter 20). Their main source of funds was individual savings accounts, which tended to be stable and low-cost, and their primary assets (about 63% of their total assets) were mortgage loans (see Figure 19.1). Since real estate secured virtually all of these loans and since real estate values increased steadily through the mid-1970s, loan losses were very small. Thrifts provided the fuel for the home-building boom that for almost half a century, from 1934 to 1978, was the centerpiece of America's domestic economy.

Mutual Savings Banks and Savings and Loans Compared

Mutual savings banks and savings and loan associations are similar in many ways; however, they do differ in ways other than ownership structure.

- Mutual savings banks are concentrated in the northeastern United States; savings and loans are located throughout the country.

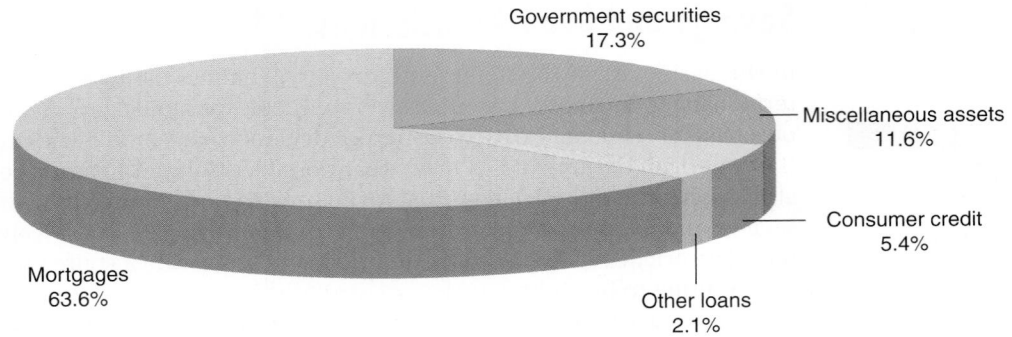

Government securities
17.3%

Miscellaneous assets
11.6%

Consumer credit
5.4%

Other loans
2.1%

Mortgages
63.6%

Figure 19.1 Distribution of Savings and Loan Assets, 2006

Source: http://www2.fdic.gov/qbp/2006mar/sav2.html.

- Mutual savings banks may insure their deposits with the state or with the Federal Deposit Insurance Corporation; S&Ls may not.
- Mutual savings banks are not as heavily concentrated in mortgages and have had more flexibility in their investing practices than savings and loans.

Because the similarities between mutual savings banks and savings and loans are more important than the differences, the focus of this chapter will be more on savings and loans.

Savings and Loans in Trouble: The Thrift Crisis

As part of the regulatory changes following the Great Depression, Congress imposed a cap on the rate of interest that savings and loans could pay on savings accounts. The theory was that if S&Ls obtained funds at a low cost, they could make loans to home borrowers at a low cost. The interest-rate caps became a serious problem for savings and loans in the 1970s when inflation rose. Chapters 17 and 18 provide an in-depth discussion of the capital adequacy and interest-rate problems depository institutions faced at that time.

By 1979, inflation was running at 13.3%, but savings and loans were restricted to paying a maximum of 5.5% on deposits. These rates did not even maintain depositors' purchasing power with inflation running almost 8% higher than their interest return—in effect, the real interest rate they were earning was −7.8%. They were actually losing spending power leaving money in savings and loans.

At this same time, securities houses began offering a new product that circumvented interest-rate caps. *Money market accounts* paid market rates on short-term funds. Though not insured, the bulk of the cash placed in money market funds was in turn invested in low-risk securities such as Treasury securities or commercial paper. Because the savings and loan customers were not satisfied with the low returns they were earning on their funds, they left S&Ls in droves for the high returns these accounts offered.

Financial innovation and deregulation in the permissive atmosphere of the 1980s led to expanded powers for the S&L industry that led to several problems. First, many S&L managers did not have the required expertise to manage risk appropriately in these new lines of business. Second, the new expanded powers meant that there was a rapid growth in new lending, particularly to the real estate sector. Even if the required expertise was available initially, rapid credit growth might outstrip the available information resources of the banking institution, resulting in excessive risk taking. Third, these new powers of the S&Ls and the lending boom meant that their activities were expanding in scope and were becoming more complicated, requiring an expansion of regulatory resources to monitor these activities appropriately. Unfortunately, regulators of the S&Ls at the Federal Savings and Loan Insurance Corporation (FSLIC) had neither the expertise nor the resources that would have enabled them to monitor these new activities sufficiently. Given the lack of expertise in both the S&L industry and the FSLIC, the weakening of the regulatory apparatus, and the moral hazard incentives provided by deposit insurance, it is no surprise that S&Ls took on excessive risks, which led to huge losses on bad loans.

In addition, the incentives of moral hazard were increased dramatically by a historical accident: the combination of the sharp increases in interest rates from late 1979 until 1981 and a severe recession in 1981–1982, both of which were engineered by the Federal Reserve to bring down inflation. The sharp rises in interest rates produced rapidly rising costs of funds for the savings and loans that were not matched by higher earnings on the S&Ls' principal asset, long-term residential mortgages (whose rates had been fixed at a time when interest rates were far lower). The 1981–1982 recession and a collapse in the prices of energy and farm products hit the economies of certain parts of the country, such as Texas, very hard. As a result, there were defaults on many S&Ls' loans. Losses for savings and loan institutions mounted to $10 billion in 1981–1982, and by some estimates over half of the S&Ls in the United States had a negative net worth and were thus insolvent by the end of 1982.

Later Stages of the Crisis: Regulatory Forbearance

At this point, a logical step might have been for the S&L regulators—the Federal Home Loan Bank Board and its deposit insurance subsidiary, the Federal Savings and Loan Insurance Fund (FSLIC), both now abolished—to close the insolvent S&Ls. Instead, these regulators adopted a stance of **regulatory forbearance:** They refrained from exercising their regulatory right to put the insolvent S&Ls out of business. To sidestep their responsibility to close ailing S&Ls, they adopted irregular regulatory accounting principles that in effect substantially lowered capital requirements. For example, they allowed S&Ls to include in their capital calculations a high value for intangible capital, called *goodwill*.

There were three main reasons why the Federal Home Loan Bank Board and FSLIC opted for regulatory forbearance. First, the FSLIC did not have sufficient funds in its insurance fund to close the insolvent S&Ls and pay off their deposits. Second, the Federal Home Loan Bank Board was established to encourage the growth of the savings and loan industry, so the regulators were probably too close to the people they were supposed to be regulating. Third, because bureaucrats do not like to admit that their own agency is in trouble, the Federal Home Loan Bank Board and the FSLIC preferred to sweep their problems under the rug in the hope that they would go away.

Regulatory forbearance increases moral hazard dramatically because an operating but insolvent S&L (nicknamed a "zombie S&L" by Edward Kane of Ohio State University because it is the "living dead") has almost nothing to lose by taking on great risk and "betting the bank": If it gets lucky and its risky investments pay off, it gets out of insolvency. Unfortunately, if, as is likely, the risky investments don't pay off, the zombie S&L's losses will mount, and the deposit insurance agency will be left holding the bag.

This strategy is similar to the "long bomb" strategy in football. When a football team is almost hopelessly behind and time is running out, it often resorts to a high-risk play: the throwing of a long pass to try to score a touchdown. Of course, the long bomb is unlikely to be successful, but there is always a small chance that it will work. If it doesn't, the team is no worse off, since it would have lost the game anyway.

Given the sequence of events we have discussed here, it should be no surprise that savings and loans began to take huge risks: They built shopping centers in the desert, bought manufacturing plants to convert manure to methane, and purchased billions of dollars of high-risk, high-yield junk bonds. The S&L industry was no longer the staid industry that once operated on the so-called *3–6–3 rule*: You took in money at 3%, lent it at 6%, and played golf at 3 PM. Although many savings and loans were making money, losses at other S&Ls were colossal.

Another outcome of regulatory forbearance was that with little to lose, zombie S&Ls attracted deposits away from healthy S&Ls by offering higher interest rates. Because there were so many zombie S&Ls in Texas pursuing this strategy, above-market interest rates on deposits at Texas S&Ls were said to have a "Texas premium." Potentially healthy S&Ls now found that to compete for deposits, they had to pay higher interest rates, which made their operations less profitable and frequently pushed them into the zombie category. Similarly, zombie S&Ls in pursuit of asset growth made loans at below-market interest rates, thereby lowering loan interest rates for healthy S&Ls, and again made them less profitable. The zombie S&Ls had actually taken on attributes of vampires—their willingness to pay above-market rates for deposits and take below-market interest rates on loans was sucking the lifeblood (profits) out of healthy S&Ls.

Competitive Equality in Banking Act of 1987

Toward the end of 1986, the growing losses in the savings and loan industry were bankrupting the insurance fund of the FSLIC. The Reagan administration sought $15 billion in funds for the FSLIC, a completely inadequate sum considering that many times this amount was needed to close down insolvent S&Ls. The legislation passed by Congress, the Competitive Equality in Banking Act (CEBA) of 1987, did not even meet the administration's requests. It allowed the FSLIC to borrow only $10.8 billion through a subsidiary corporation called Financing Corporation (FICO) and, what was worse, included provisions that directed the Federal Home Loan Bank Board to continue to pursue regulatory forbearance (allow insolvent institutions to keep operating), particularly in economically depressed areas such as Texas.

The failure of Congress to deal with the savings and loan crisis was not going to make the problem go away, and consistent with our analysis, the situation deteriorated rapidly. Losses in the savings and loan industry surpassed $10 billion in 1988 and approached $20 billion in 1989. The crisis was reaching epidemic proportions. The collapse of the real estate market in the late 1980s led to additional huge loan losses that greatly exacerbated the problem.

Political Economy of the Savings and Loan Crisis

Although we now have a grasp of the regulatory and economic forces that created the S&L crisis, we still need to understand the political forces that produced the regulatory structure and activities that led to it. The key to understanding the political economy of the S&L crisis is to recognize that the relationship between voter-taxpayers and the regulators and politicians creates a particular type of moral hazard problem, discussed in Chapter 15: the *principal-agent problem,* which occurs when representatives (agents) such as managers have incentives that differ from those of their employer (the principal) and so act in their own interest rather than in the interest of the employer.

Principal-Agent Problem for Regulators and Politicians

Regulators and politicians are ultimately agents for voter-taxpayers (principals) because in the final analysis, taxpayers bear the cost of any losses by the deposit insurance agency. The principal-agent problem occurs because the agent (a politician or regulator) does not have the same incentives to minimize costs to the economy as the principal (the taxpayer).

To act in the taxpayer's interest and lower costs to the deposit insurance agency, regulators have several tasks, as we have seen. They must set tight restrictions on holding assets that are too risky, must impose high capital requirements, and must not adopt a stance of regulatory forbearance, which allows insolvent institutions to continue to operate. However, because of the principal-agent problem, regulators have incentives to do the opposite. Indeed, as our sad saga of the S&L debacle indicates, they have at times loosened capital requirements and restrictions on risky asset holdings and pursued regulatory forbearance. One important incentive for regulators that explains this phenomenon is their desire to escape blame for poor performance by their agency. By loosening capital requirements and pursuing regulatory forbearance, regulators can hide the problem of an insolvent bank and hope that the situation will improve. Edward Kane characterizes such behavior on the part of regulators as "bureaucratic gambling."

Another important incentive for regulators is that they want to protect their careers by acceding to pressures from the people who most influence their careers. These people are not the taxpayers but the politicians who try to keep regulators from imposing tough regulations on institutions that are major campaign contributors. Members of Congress have often lobbied regulators to ease up on a particular S&L that contributed large sums to their campaigns (as we see in the following case). Regulatory agencies that have little independence from the political process are more vulnerable to these pressures.

In addition, both Congress and the presidential administration promoted banking legislation in 1980 and 1982 that made it easier for savings and loans to engage in risk-taking activities. After the legislation passed, the need for monitoring the S&L industry increased because of the expansion of permissible activities. The S&L regulatory agencies needed more resources to carry out their monitoring activities properly, but Congress (successfully lobbied by the S&L industry) was unwilling to allocate the necessary funds. As a result, the S&L regulatory agencies became so shortstaffed that they actually had to cut back on their on-site examinations just when these were needed most. In the period from January 1984 to July 1986, for example, several hundred S&Ls were not examined even once. Worse yet, spurred on by the intense lobbying efforts of the S&L industry, Congress passed the Competitive Equality in Banking Act of 1987, which provided inadequate funding to close down the insolvent S&Ls and also hampered the S&L regulators from doing their job properly by including provisions encouraging regulatory forbearance.

As these examples indicate, the structure of our political system has created a serious principal-agent problem: Politicians have strong incentives to act in their own interests rather than in the interests of taxpayers. Because of the high cost of running campaigns, American politicians must raise substantial contributions. This situation may provide lobbyists and other campaign contributors with the opportunity to influence politicians to act against the public interest, as we see in the following case.

CASE

Principal-Agent Problem in Action: Charles Keating and the Lincoln Savings and Loan Scandal

We see that the principal-agent problem for regulators and politicians creates incentives that may cause excessive risk taking on the part of banking institutions, which then causes substantial losses to the taxpayer. The scandal associated with Charles H. Keating Jr. and the Lincoln Savings and Loan Association provides a graphic example of the principal-agent problem at work. As Edwin Gray, a former chairman of the Federal Home Loan Bank Board, stated, "This is a story of incredible corruption. I can't call it anything else."[1]

Charles Keating was allowed to acquire Lincoln Savings and Loan of Irvine, California, in early 1984, even though he had been accused of fraud by the SEC less than five years earlier. For Keating, whose construction firm, American Continental, planned to build huge real estate developments in Arizona, the S&L was a gold mine: In the lax regulatory atmosphere at the time, controlling the S&L gave his firm easy access to funds without being scrutinized by outside bankers. Within days of acquiring control, Keating got rid of Lincoln's conservative lending officers and internal auditors, even though he had promised regulators he would keep them. Lincoln then plunged into high-risk investments such as currency futures, junk bonds, common stock, hotels, and vast tracts of desert land in Arizona.

Because of a shortage of savings and loan examiners at the time, Lincoln was able to escape a serious examination until 1986, whereupon examiners from the Federal Home Loan Bank of San Francisco discovered that Lincoln had exceeded the 10% limit on equity investments by $600 million. Because of these activities and some evidence that Lincoln was deliberately trying to mislead the examiners, the examiners recommended federal seizure of the bank and all its assets. Keating was not about to take this lying down; he engaged hordes of lawyers—eventually 77 law

---

[1]Quoted in Tom Morganthau, Rich Thomas, and Eleanor Clift, "The S&L Scandal's Biggest Blowout," *Newsweek*, November 6, 1989, p. 35.

firms—and accused the bank examiners of bias. He also sued unsuccessfully to overturn the 10% equity limit. Keating is said to have bragged that he spent $50 million fighting regulators.

Lawyers were not Keating's only tactic for keeping regulators off his back. After receiving $1.3 million of contributions to their campaigns from Keating, five senators—Dennis De Concini and John McCain of Arizona, Alan Cranston of California, John Glenn of Ohio, and Donald Riegle of Michigan (subsequently nicknamed the "Keating Five")—met with Edwin Gray, the chairman of the Federal Home Loan Board, and later with four top regulators from San Francisco in April 1987. They complained that the regulators were being too tough on Lincoln and urged the regulators to quit dragging out the investigation. After Gray was replaced by M. Danny Wall, Wall took the unprecedented step of removing the San Francisco examiners from the case in September 1987 and transferred the investigation to the bank board's headquarters in Washington. No examiners called on Lincoln for the next ten months, and as one of the San Francisco examiners described it, Lincoln dropped into a "regulatory black hole."

Lincoln Savings and Loan finally failed in April 1989, with estimated costs to taxpayers of $2.6 billion, making it possibly the most costly S&L failure in history. Keating was convicted for abuses (such as having Lincoln pay him and his family $34 million), but after serving four and a half years in jail, his conviction was overturned in 1996. Wall was forced to resign as head of the Office of Thrift Supervision because of his involvement in the Keating scandal. As a result of their activities on behalf of Keating, the Keating Five senators were made the object of a congressional ethics investigation, but given Congress's propensity to protect its own, they were subjected only to minor sanctions.

Savings and Loan Bailout: Financial Institutions Reform, Recovery, and Enforcement Act of 1989

go online
The Office of Thrift Supervision Web site, **www.ots.treas.gov/**, contains quarterly industry information, statistical reports, and laws and regulations. The OTS 2006 Fact Book, **www.ots.treas.gov/docs/ 4/480967.pdf**, offers a statistical profile of the thrift industry.

Immediately after taking office, the Bush administration proposed new legislation to provide adequate funding to close down the insolvent S&Ls. The resulting legislation, the **Financial Institutions Reform, Recovery, and Enforcement Act (FIRREA),** was signed into law on August 9, 1989. It was the most significant legislation to affect the thrift industry since the 1930s. FIRREA's major provisions were as follows: The regulatory apparatus was significantly restructured without the Federal Home Loan Bank Board and the FSLIC, both of which had failed in their regulatory tasks. The regulatory role of the Federal Home Loan Bank Board was relegated to the Office of Thrift Supervision (OTS), a bureau within the U.S. Treasury Department, whose responsibilities are similar to those that the Office of the Comptroller of the Currency has over the national banks. The regulatory responsibilities of the FSLIC were given to the FDIC, and the FDIC became the sole administrator of the federal deposit insurance system with two separate insurance funds: the Bank Insurance Fund (BIF) and the Savings Association Insurance Fund (SAIF). Another new agency, the **Resolution Trust Corporation (RTC),** was established to manage and resolve insolvent thrifts placed in conservatorship or receivership. It was made responsible for selling more than $450 billion of real estate owned by failed institutions. After seizing the assets of about 750 insolvent S&Ls, over 25% of the industry, the RTC sold over 95% of them, with a recovery rate of over 85%. After this success, the RTC went out of business on December 31, 1995.

Initially, the total cost of the bailout was estimated to be $159 billion over the ten-year period through 1999, but more recent estimates indicated that the cost would be far higher. Indeed, the General Accounting Office placed a cost for the bailout at more than $500 billion over 40 years. However, as pointed out in Chapter 3, this estimate was misleading because, for example, the value of a payment 30 years from now is worth much less in today's dollars. The present value of the bailout cost actually ended up being on the order of $150 billion. The funding for the bailout came partly from capital in the Federal Home Loan Banks (owned by the S&L industry) but mostly from the sale of government debt by both the Treasury and the Resolution Funding Corporation (RefCorp).

To replenish the reserves of the Savings Association Insurance Fund, insurance premiums for S&Ls were increased from 20.8 cents per $100 of deposits to 23 cents and can rise as high as 32.5 cents. Premiums for banks immediately rose from 8.3 cents to 15 cents per $100 of deposits and were raised further to 23 cents in 1991.

FIRREA also imposed new restrictions on thrift activities that in essence reregulated the S&L industry to the asset choices it had before 1982. S&Ls can no longer purchase junk bonds and had to sell their holdings by 1994. Commercial real estate loans are restricted to four times capital rather than the previous limit of 40% of assets, and so this new restriction is a reduction for all institutions whose capital is less than 10% of assets. S&Ls must also hold at least 70%—up from 60%—of their assets in investments that are primarily housing-related. Among the most important provisions of FIRREA was the increase in the core capital leverage requirement from 3% to 8% and the eventual adherence to the same risk-based capital standards imposed on commercial banks.[2]

FIRREA also enhanced the enforcement powers of thrift regulators by making it easier for them to remove managers, issue cease and desist orders, and impose civil penalties. The Justice Department was also given $75 million per year for three years to uncover and prosecute fraud in the banking industry, and maximum fines rose substantially.

As a result of the failure of savings and loans and the passage of FIRREA, the total assets of savings and loans fell between 1988 and 1998. Figure 19.2 shows the total assets of savings and loans between 1979 and 2006; note the rapid decrease between 1988 and 1992. Since 1997, the assets of S&Ls have been increasing slowly.

The Savings and Loan Industry Today

Despite the problems and turmoil surrounding the industry in the 1980s, the savings and loan industry managed to survive, although somewhat changed. In this section we review the current state of the industry.

---

[2]Thrifts are now prohibited from accepting brokered deposits, short-term large-denomination deposits placed in thrifts by funds managers. Brokered deposits are discussed further in Chapter 20.

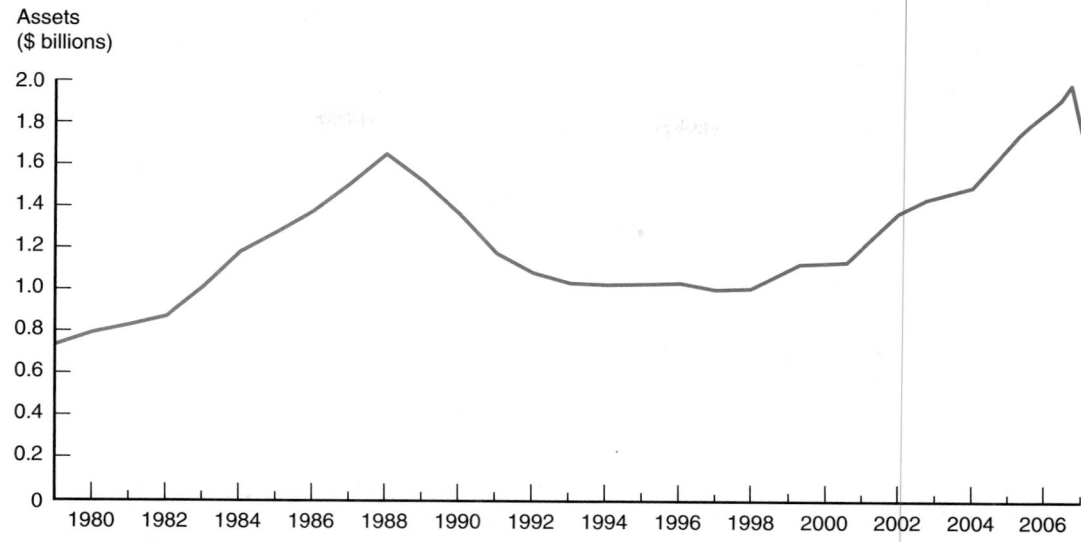

Figure 19.2   Total Assets of Savings and Loan Associations, 1979–2007

Source: http://www2.fdic.gov/qbp/2007mar/qbpsav.html.

Number of Institutions

The savings and loan industry has witnessed a substantial reduction in the number of institutions. Many failed or were taken over by the RTC; others merged with stronger institutions to avoid failure. The number of S&Ls declined by nearly two-thirds between the end of 1986, when there were 3,600 of them, and 2006, when there were only 1,279. As shown in Figure 19.3, the number of savings institutions continues to decline. Although new S&Ls continue to open, existing ones convert to commercial banks or credit unions or merge with other savings banks. It is interesting to note that consolidation in the savings industry has not been as dramatic as in commercial banking in recent years.

S&L Size

Figure 19.4 shows the average total assets for savings and loans since 1984. When viewed along with Figure 19.3, the graph indicates that the industry has consolidated in recent years. Between 1988 and 1991, the average size of S&Ls fell. This was likely due to the 1989 passage of FIRREA, which required S&Ls to increase their capital-to-asset ratio. Many institutions met the new standard by decreasing their assets rather than by increasing their capital. From 1992 to 2005, total S&L assets generally increased, even though the number of institutions decreased. The result is fewer but larger institutions.

A second point to note about Figure 19.4 is that the average size of savings and loans is now very close to that of commercial banks. Recall from Chapter 18 that the growth of commercial banks was often constrained by restrictive banking regulations.

Figure 19.3 Number of Savings and Loans in the United States, 1993–2007

Source: http://www2.fdic.gov/qbp/2007mar/sav1.html.

As a result, the average size of commercial banks at the end of 2006 was over $1.3 billion in assets. Thus, the size of the average commercial bank is about the same as that of the average savings and loan.

S&L Assets

Table 19.1 provides a consolidated balance sheet for the savings and loan industry. Let us first discuss the assets side.

The 1982 reforms allowed S&Ls to make consumer and commercial loans. The intent of this legislation was to give S&Ls a source of assets with short maturities. The problem was that commercial loans are far riskier and require lending expertise that many S&Ls did not possess. FIRREA severely curtailed S&Ls' commercial lending. In the four years following passage of the law, the number of loans made for commercial purposes dropped by about 50%. Currently, nearly 90% of all S&L loans are secured by real estate, and 62% are for residential mortgages. Clearly, the industry has returned to its original mandate of financing home ownership.

Savings and loans are subject to reserve requirements, just like banks. Recall from Chapter 17 that reserve requirements are cash deposits that must be held in the vault or at the Federal Reserve in non-interest-bearing accounts. The purpose of reserve requirements is to limit the expansion of the money supply and to ensure adequate liquidity for the institutions. About 4% of total S&L assets are kept in cash.

Assets
($ millions)

Figure 19.4 Average Assets per Savings and Loan Association, 1984–2007

Source: http://www2.fdic.gov/qbp/2007mar/qbpsav.html.

TABLE 19.1 Consolidated Balance Sheet for Savings and Loan Associations
($ billions, fourth quarter, 2006)

Savings and Loan Associations

Assets		Liabilities	
Cash and reserves	47.4	Deposits	1091.4
Securities	281.6	Other borrowed funds	287.2
Mortgage loans	1073.9	All other liabilities	221.4
Commercial loans	67.5	Equity	114.5
Consumer credit	95.5	Total liabilities and equities	1,714.5
Corporate equities	24.9		
Miscellaneous	123.7		
Total assets	1,714.5		

Sources: Flow of Funds, Table L114 and www.federalreserve.gov/releases/z1.

In addition to cash, savings and loans hold securities, such as corporate, Treasury, and government agency bonds. Unlike reserve deposits, these assets earn interest. The 1982 legislation allowed savings and loans to hold up to 11% of their assets in junk bonds. S&Ls were a major source of funds during the mid-1980s for corporations looking for capital to use in acquiring other firms. In 1989, the FIRREA required that savings and loans divest themselves of these high-risk securities. Currently, only relatively safe securities can be purchased.

S&L Liabilities and Net Worth

Now let's look at the right-hand side of the balance sheet in Table 19.1. The primary liabilities of savings and loans are deposits and borrowed funds.

The largest liability of savings and loans are customer funds held on deposit. In the past, the bulk of the deposits were from **passbook savings accounts,** interest-bearing savings accounts. In the past, banks issued small books to savers to use for keeping track of their savings balances. The customer would present this book to the teller every time a deposit or withdrawal was made, and the teller would validate the entry. The physical passbook has almost been phased out over the years and replaced with computerized record keeping.

The second major liability is *borrowings*, funds obtained in either the money or capital markets. Since savings and loan deposits are typically short-term, one way to lengthen their average maturity is to borrow long-term funds. Borrowed funds have become a major source of funds for savings and loans, now accounting for over 18% of total assets, up from 11% in 1990.

Capital

The capital of financial institutions is often measured by the *net worth ratio*, total equity (also known as *net worth*) divided by total assets. This figure is closely watched by regulators for indications that a financial institution may be undercapitalized. The average net worth-to-assets ratio was about 3% in 1984. Many institutions had a negative net worth at this time. Since 1989, the average net worth ratio has improved. At the end of 2003, it stood at 7.6%. This is now about the same as the 6% average net worth ratio for commercial banks. One reason for the improvement in the capital of savings and loans is that FIRREA mandated that it be increased. (We discussed the importance of capital in the functioning of a financial institution in Chapter 17.)

The accounting for savings and loans permitted extensive use of goodwill, an asset account on the balance sheet that supposedly reflects the value of a firm's good name and reputation. For example, in 1987, goodwill accounted for $29.6 billion of savings and loan assets. This represented more than half of the $53.8 billion in total capital. If we removed goodwill from capital before calculating the net worth-to-assets ratio in 1987, we find that the ratio is only 1.6%, not the 3.7% it was when including goodwill. The value of goodwill fell steadily since its high that year. Listing large amounts of goodwill as an asset was another way that savings and loans were able to hide the fact that they were insolvent.

Profitability and Health

One indication that the health of savings and loans has improved in recent years is that their earnings have increased. From 1987 through 1990, the industry suffered net losses. But in 1991, net after-tax income for the industry was $859 million, and by 2000, it had reached $10.7 billion (see Figure 19.5).

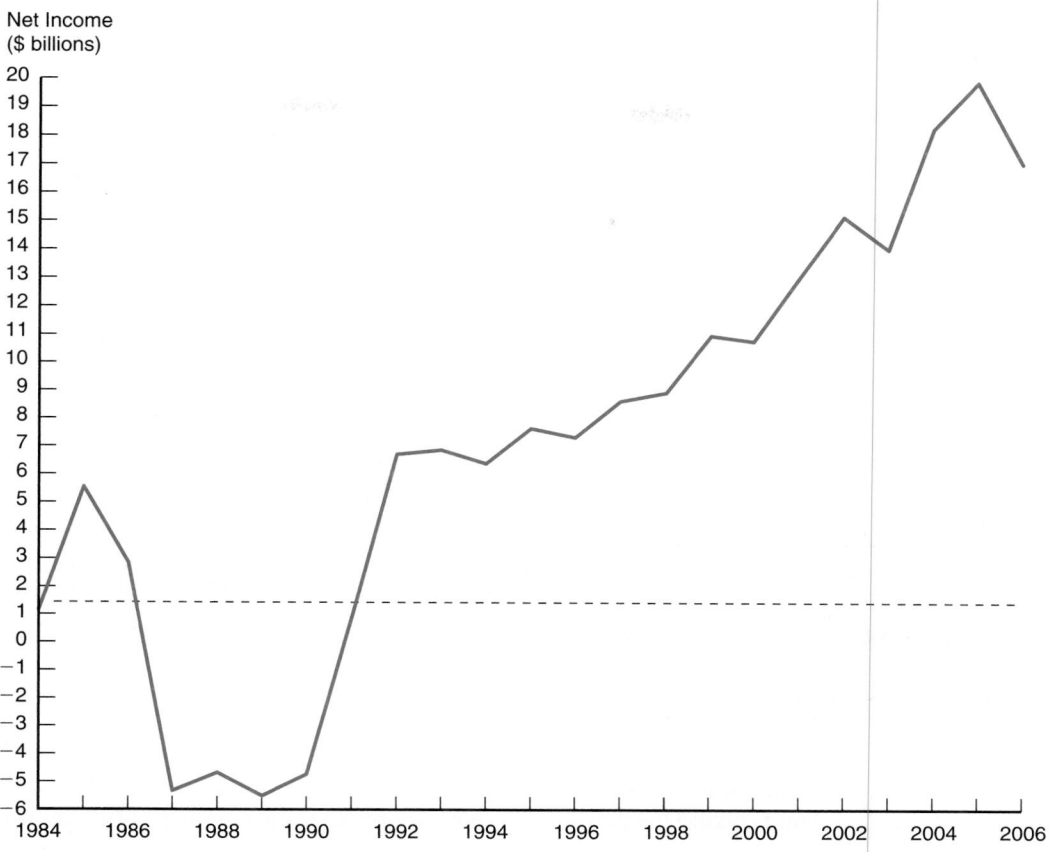

Figure 19.5   Net Income of Savings and Loan Associations, 1984–2006

Source: http://www2.fdic.gov/qbp/2007mar/sav2.html.

A better measure of a firm's health than net income is its return on equity (ROE). Figure 19.6 shows that there was a steady increase in S&Ls' ROE from 1993 to 2003, when it was over 12%. S&L profits for 2003 were the highest ever reported by the industry. Over 94% of all S&Ls were profitable. Part of this income was due to the sale of mortgage loans that had increased in value when interest rates fell.

Only 2 S&Ls have failed since 2002. Furthermore, the number of "problem" thrifts is down to 7, compared to 146 in 1993. The percentage of loans being charged off as losses is also at a low 0.33%.

In summary, savings institutions, which were in grave condition a decade ago, have returned to robust health. They are providing fair returns to their shareholders and are not in any danger of causing additional taxpayer losses. The industry's equity-to-capital ratio is now the highest it has ever been.

The Future of the Savings and Loan Industry

One issue that has received considerable attention in recent years is whether the savings and loan industry is still needed. Observers who favor eliminating S&L charters altogether point out that there is now a large number of alternative mortgage

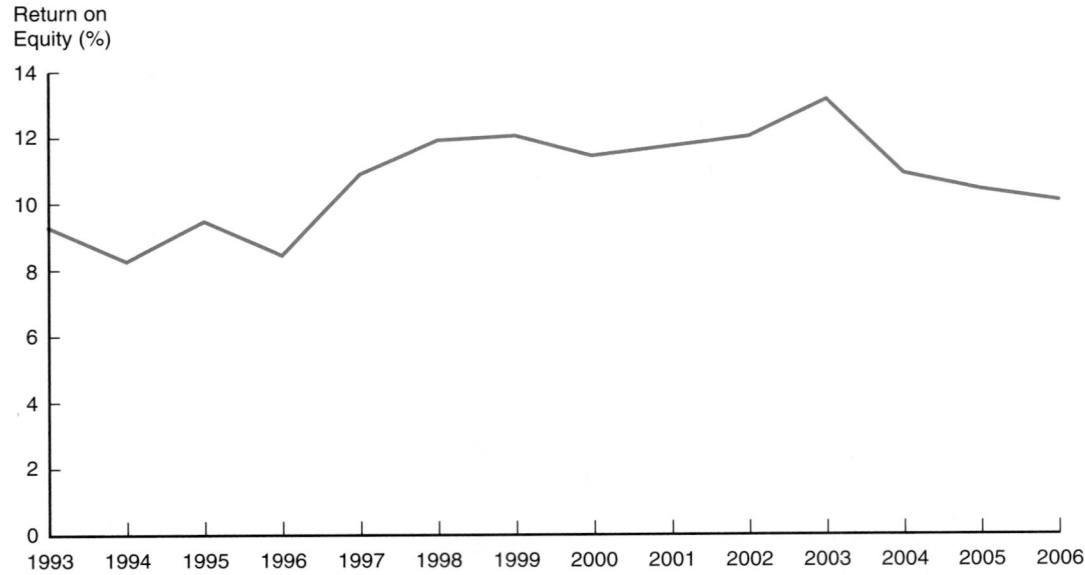

Figure 19.6 Average Return on Equity for Savings and Loan Institutions, 1993–2006

Source: http://www2.fdic.gov/qbp/2007mar/sav1.html.

loan outlets available for home buyers. In Chapter 12 we introduced the securitized mortgage. This new instrument has provided the majority of the funds needed by the mortgage market. A reasonable question to ask is whether there is a need for an industry dedicated exclusively to providing a service efficiently provided elsewhere in the financial system.

Let us review the history of the savings and loan industry for a moment. S&Ls were established to provide mortgages to home buyers. The industry was healthy until interest rates increased and they were stuck holding low-interest fixed-rate mortgages financed with high-cost funds. Congress attempted to provide relief by giving S&Ls a great deal of flexibility in their capital structure and lending functions. Due to abuses, poor market conditions, inadequate supervision by FSLIC, and fraud, tremendous losses accrued. Finally, Congress reregulated the industry and again required that its primary business be mortgage lending. The only trouble now is that mortgage loans are available from many other sources (see Chapter 12).

Just as efficient markets develop new securities and services when the need for them arises, efficient markets should eliminate unneeded institutions when they are no longer required. Many industry analysts expect the savings and loan industry to disappear, perhaps by existing savings and loans being acquired by other institutions or by commercial banks. We can examine the evidence to see if this is beginning to happen.

We noted earlier that the number of savings and loans has decreased by 56% since its high in 1986. There were fewer S&Ls in 2004 than in 1994. However, the drop in the number of institutions could be due to consolidation within the industry, much like what is happening in commercial banking. A better indication of the future of the industry may be provided by the trend in total assets. Figure 19.2 shows that the total assets of savings and loans have increased since 1993. This suggests that there is at least not a rapid trend to eliminate these institutions. It may be that they will continue to be a provider of mortgage loans along with a number of other sources.

Congress will be pressured again to deregulate the industry to allow S&Ls to perform more of the functions allowed by commercial banks. Although this may happen, the losses sustained as a result of the last attempt at deregulation are still fresh in the minds of regulators. It is unlikely that we will again witness an attempt at rapid deregulation. Instead, we can expect to see gradual changes in the industry that will continue to blur the distinction between savings and loans and commercial banks.

Credit Unions

The third type of thrift institution is the **credit union,** a financial institution that focuses on servicing the banking and lending needs of its members. These institutions are also designed to service the needs of consumers, not businesses, and are distinguished by their ownership structure and their "common bond" membership requirement. Most credit unions are relatively small.

History and Organization

In the early 1900s, commercial banks focused most of their attention on the business borrower. This left the small consumer without a ready source of funds. Because Congress was concerned that commercial banks were not meeting the needs of consumers, it established savings banks and savings and loan associations to help consumers obtain mortgage loans. In the early 1900s, the credit union was established to help consumers with *other* types of loans. A secondary purpose was to provide a place for small investors to place their savings.

The concept behind credit unions originated in Germany in the nineteenth century. A group of consumers would pool their assets as collateral for a loan from a bank. The funds so raised were then loaned to the members of the group, and each member of the group was personally liable for repayment of the loan. Defaults were very rare because members knew one another well.

The first two credit unions in the United States were established in Massachusetts in 1910. The Massachusetts Credit Union (MCU) was organized in 1914 as a functioning credit union but with the additional purpose of encouraging the formation of additional credit unions. The MCU evolved into a kind of central credit union facility. In 1921, the MCU was reorganized as the **Credit Union National Extension Bureau (CUNEB),** which worked to have credit unions established in every state. In 1935, CUNEB was replaced by the **Credit Union National Association (CUNA).**

In 1934, Congress passed the **Federal Credit Union Act,** which allowed federal chartering of credit unions in all states. Prior to this, most credit unions were chartered by the state in which they operated. Currently, about 40% of credit unions have state charters and 60% have federal charters.

One reason for the growth of credit unions has been the support they received from employers. They realized that employee morale could be raised and time saved if banking-type facilities were readily available. In many cases, employers donated space on business property for the credit union to operate. The convenience of this institution soon attracted a large number of customers.

Mutual Ownership Credit unions are organized as *mutuals*; that is, they are owned by their depositors. A customer receives shares when a deposit is made. Rather than earning interest on deposited funds, the customer earns dividends. The amount of the dividend is not guaranteed, like the interest rate earned on accounts at banks. Instead, the amount of the dividend is estimated in advance and is paid if at all possible.

Each depositor has one vote, regardless how much money he or she may have with the institution. Depositors vote for directors, who in turn hire managers to run the credit union.

Because credit unions are cooperative businesses, they are managed somewhat differently from other businesses. For example, many credit unions make extensive use of volunteer help to reduce their costs. Since any cost reductions are passed on to the depositors, volunteers feel that they are working for the common good. Similarly, as noted, operating facilities may be donated.

Common Bond Membership The single most important feature of credit unions that distinguishes them from other depository institutions is the common bond member rule. The idea behind **common bond membership** is that only members of a particular association, occupation, or geographic region are permitted to join the credit union. A credit union's common bonds define its field of membership.

The most frequent type of common bond applies to employees of a single occupation or employer. For example, most state employees are eligible to join their state credit union. Similarly, the Navy Credit Union is open to all U.S. Navy personnel. Other credit unions accept members from the same religious or professional background.

One problem with the common bond membership rule is that it prevents credit unions from diversifying their risk. If most of a credit union's members are employed by one business and that business is forced to lay off workers, it is likely that the credit union will have high default rates on loans. A recent trend among credit unions has been for several to merge, a move that helps reduce the risk of having all members linked by a single bond. To make mergers easier, regulators have interpreted the common bond requirement less strictly. For example, most credit unions now let members of the immediate family of an eligible member join, and many credit unions have adopted a "once a member, always a member" policy. In 1982, regulators ruled that credit unions could accept members from several employee groups instead of just one. In 1988, regulators determined that the bond between members of the American Association of Retired People was sufficient and authorized the organization to open its own credit union. The American Automobile Association, however, was rejected.

The commercial bank lobby violently disagrees with relaxed membership rules for credit unions that in some instances have allowed them to admit virtually everyone in a community. Commercial banks view credit unions as unfair competitors due to the government support they receive in the form of tax advantages (to be discussed shortly). Many bankers feel that the threat posed by credit unions could cause more vulnerable banks to fail.

To curb this threat, a group of Tennessee bankers sued to change the regulators' stance that federal law allows multiple occupational groups, each of which independently shares a common bond, to join a single credit union. In April 1997, an appeals court ruled in favor of the bankers, saying that the restrictions on common bond membership should be left intact.

On February 24, 1997, the U.S. Supreme Court reviewed a different lower court ruling on the AT&T Family Federal Credit Union that placed sharp limits on membership in federally chartered credit unions. It ruled that bankers have the right to sue about the field-of-membership issue and that the credit union regulator, the National Credit Union Administration, can no longer allow federal credit unions to expand outside of their original memberships.

This ruling resulted in intense congressional lobbying by credit union supporters that led to the passage of the Credit Union Membership Access Act on August 7, 1998. The intent of this law was to preserve the right of all consumers to choose the credit union alternative. It maintains the concept of common bond membership but allows for the combining of groups with different common bonds in a single credit union. This act became effective on January 1, 1999.

Nonprofit, Tax-Exempt Status The Federal Credit Union Act of 1934 contained the provision that credit unions were to be nonprofit and consequently exempt from federal taxation. All of the income earned by the institutions is to be spent on their members. Credit unions are currently the only financial institutions that are tax-exempt. This makes it easier for them to accumulate retained earnings than it is for other institutions. Banks and S&Ls are questioning this tax-exempt status as credit unions become larger and more significant competitors. Savings and loans lost their tax-exempt status in 1951. The American Bankers Association estimates that the subsidy reduces the cost of funds to credit unions by almost 2.5% and gives them a cost advantage of $1 billion per year. The credit unions dispute this number and assign their cost advantage to their use of volunteer help. It remains a question how long the favorable tax treatment for credit unions can be maintained.

Partly as a result of being nonprofit and partly due to the cost advantage of being tax-exempt, credit union fees tend to be lower than those of banks.

Regulation and Insurance The **National Credit Union Act of 1970** established the **National Credit Union Administration (NCUA).** This independent federal agency is charged with the task of regulating and supervising federally chartered credit unions and state-chartered credit unions that receive federal deposit insurance. The remaining credit unions are regulated by state credit union or banking departments, which generally follow federal practices.

The National Credit Union Act of 1970 also established the **National Credit Union Share Insurance Fund (NCUSIF),** to be controlled by the NCUA. This fund insures the deposits of all nationally chartered credit unions and most state-chartered credit unions for up to $100,000 per account. The remaining state-chartered credit unions are insured by one of the state insurance systems. Since the savings and loan crisis, most states are eager to get out of the insurance business. It is likely that in the future, all credit union deposit insurance will be provided by the NCUSIF.

Central Credit Unions Because many credit unions are small and have very little diversification, they are often susceptible to seasonal cash flow problems. Most credit unions also lack the size needed to support large administrative staffs. One way they overcome these problems is with "state central" or "corporate" credit unions, which service the credit unions in their area by providing computer and financial assistance. There are currently 44 state central credit unions, which provide a number of valuable services, including these:

- They may help with member institutions' credit needs. The state central can invest excess funds and make loans to cover short-term shortages.

go online
The National Credit Union Administration Web site, www.ncua.gov/, includes general information about credit unions and credit union data.

- They can invest excess funds with the **U.S. Central Credit Union,** which in turn can invest in the financial markets.
- They can hold clearing balances.
- They can provide educational services.

The U.S. Central Credit Union was organized in 1974 to act as a central bank for credit unions. It is chartered as a commercial bank in Kansas, and its primary function is to provide banking services to the 44 state central credit unions. It allows these institutions access to the money markets and to long-term capital markets. Most individual credit unions and even most state central credit unions lack sufficient size and transaction volume to operate efficiently in these wholesale markets.

In 1978, the **Financial Institutions Reform Act** created the **Central Liquidity Facility (CLF)** as the lender of last resort for credit unions. This agency provides many of the same functions for credit unions that the Federal Reserve provides for commercial banks. Although most day-to-day liquidity needs of credit unions are met by the state central organizations, in the event of a national liquidity crisis, a federal agency can raise far more funds. For example, in a crisis, the CLF can borrow directly from the Federal Reserve.

Membership in the CLF is voluntary, and any state or federally chartered credit union may join the CLF by pledging 0.5% of capital. Most of the funds in the CLF are borrowed from the federal government.

Credit Union Size   Credit unions are small relative to other depository financial institutions. The industry accounts for only about 10% of all consumer deposits and about 15% of all consumer loans. One reason for credit unions' limited size is the common bond restraint. Because credit unions can enroll only members who satisfy the common bond, their growth potential is severely restricted. Nevertheless, some credit unions have grown quite large. The Navy Credit Union dwarfs the others, with over $19 billion in total assets. However, most credit unions have less than $1 billion in assets, and many have less than $5 million. Table 19.2 lists the largest credit unions.

TABLE 19.2   Ten Largest Federally Insured Credit Unions, December 31, 2006

Current Rank	Name of Credit Union	Rank 1 Year Ago	City	State	Year Chartered	Assets ($)
1	Navy	1	Merrifield	VA	1947	27,121,892,092
2	State Employees'	2	Raleigh	NC	1937	13,957,758,286
3	Pentagon	3	Alexandria	VA	1935	9,339,663,044
4	Boeing Employees	5	Tukwila	WA	1935	7,186,332,339
5	Orange County Teachers	6	Santa Ana	CA	1934	6,815,129,855
6	The Golden 1	4	Sacramento	CA	1933	6,179,177,609
7	Suncoast Schools	7	Tampa	FL	1978	5,464,096,272
8	Alliant	8	Chicago	IL	1935	4,441,518,046
9	American Airlines	9	Ft. Worth	TX	1982	4,142,654,170
10	Security Service	10	San Antonio	TX	1956	3,992,718,842

Source: http://www.ncua.gov/ReportsAndPlans/statistics/YearEnd2006.pdf.

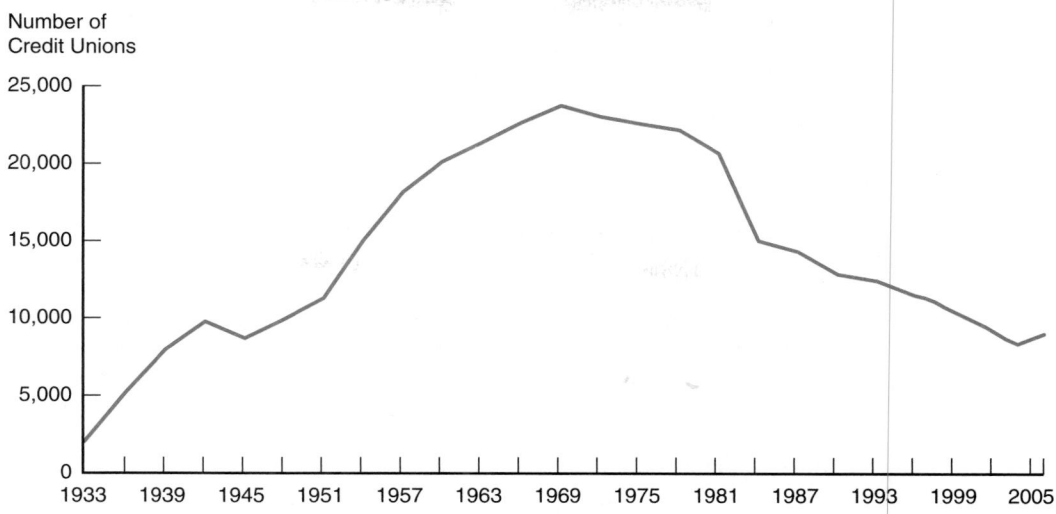

Figure 19.7 Number of Credit Unions, 1933–2006

Source: http://www.ncua.gov/ReportsAndPlans/statistics/YearEnd2006.pdf.

As discussed earlier, mergers between credit unions help them capture economies of scale and diversify their risk. This trend has resulted in fewer but larger credit unions. Figure 19.7 reports the number of credit unions active from 1933 to 2006. The number has fallen steadily since 1970 as credit unions merged.

Trade Associations Because credit unions are so small, they often lack the economies of scale necessary to service their customers at competitive costs. For example, a credit union with only $5 million of deposits cannot afford the costs of maintaining a computer center for processing checks and sending out statements. Similarly, most credit unions cannot afford to maintain their own automated teller machine network. One solution to this problem is the use of **trade associations,** groups of credit unions that have organized together. These associations provide services to large numbers of credit unions.

The largest of the trade associations is the Credit Union National Association. CUNA has a number of affiliations that provide specific services:

- CUNA Service Group provides new products for credit unions.
- CUNA Supply, Inc., provides for bulk purchases of supplies to lower supply costs.
- ICU Services, Inc., provides various investment options, automated payment services, credit card programs, and IRA plans.
- CUNA Mortgage provides a liquidity facility for mortgage lending by credit unions.

In addition to using trade associations, many credit unions contract with commercial banks for data processing services. Checks written by credit union customers are automatically routed to the bank, which takes the funds out of a credit union account. The bank then provides a transaction history in electronic form that is given to the credit union. The tie-in with the servicing bank may be so close that the credit union's teller terminals are linked to the bank's computer system, just like the bank's own teller terminals. The credit union customer may never be aware that a bank is involved in the process.

Sources of Funds

Over 73% of credit union funds come from customer savings and share draft accounts. Unlike commercial banks, credit unions seldom purchase funds in the capital or money markets. Four main types of accounts are offered by credit unions: regular share accounts, share certificates, share draft accounts, and money market accounts. Figure 19.8 shows the distribution of funds among the share accounts.

Regular Share Accounts Regular share accounts are savings accounts. Customers cannot write checks against these accounts, although they can withdraw funds without giving prior notice or incurring any penalties. These accounts make up about 30% of total deposits. Customers do not receive interest on these accounts. Instead they receive dividends that are not guaranteed in advance but are estimated. The credit union tries to pay the estimated amount.

Share Certificates Share certificates are comparable to CDs offered by commercial banks. The customer agrees to leave the funds on deposit with the credit union for a specified length of time and in exchange receives a higher return.

Share Draft Accounts Share drafts were first developed in 1974 and made legal nationally in 1980. They are virtually identical to the checks written by customers of commercial banks. Share draft accounts usually pay interest and permit depositors to write share drafts against them. These accounts represent about 12% of credit union liabilities.

Capital Credit union capital cannot be measured in the usual way because credit union share accounts are in fact equity accounts. A more meaningful approach is

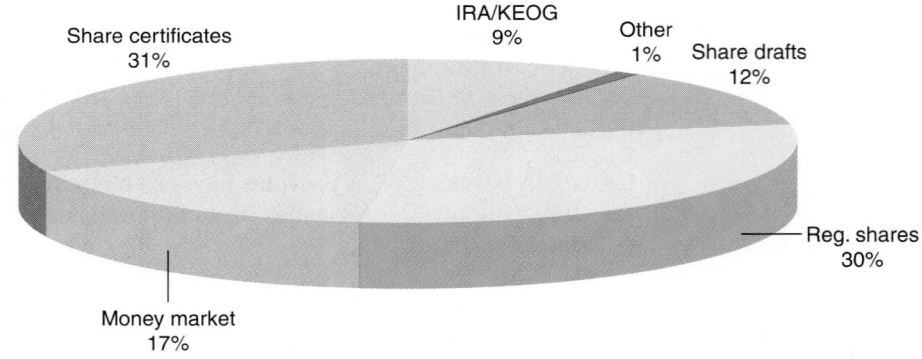

Figure 19.8 Share Distribution

Source: http://www.ncua.gov/ReportsAndPlans/statistics/YearEnd2006.pdf.

to measure capital as the difference between total assets and total liabilities, where liabilities include all share accounts. Using this approach, the average capital-to-asset ratio was 11.5% in December 2006. One reason for this strong capital position is that regulations require a capital-to-loan ratio of at least 10% for credit unions.

Uses of Funds

In December 2006, 70% of credit union assets were invested in loans. Most credit union loans are relatively small. For example, the average credit union loan in 2006 was $12,147. This is in keeping with the mission of credit unions to provide loans to small borrowers. Credit union loan losses are usually quite small. The average ratio of delinquent loans to total loans was under .68% in 2006, the lowest rate ever. This compares closely to the loan loss ratio for commercial banks. The rate of charged off loans was .45% in 2006.

The mix of loans made by credit unions demonstrates that credit unions are indeed providing a service directed at consumers. Figure 19.9 shows the loan distribution of the industry. We see that auto loans make up about 36% of the total loans volume.

The balance of credit union assets are in cash, government securities, deposits at other institutions, and fixed assets. Credit unions tend not to make risky investments and are limited by regulations to certain types of investment securities that assure low risk.

Advantages and Disadvantages of Credit Unions

Figure 19.10 traces the membership in credit unions from 1933 to 2006. The steady increase is expected to continue because credit unions enjoy several advantages over other depository institutions. These advantages have contributed toward their growth and popularity.

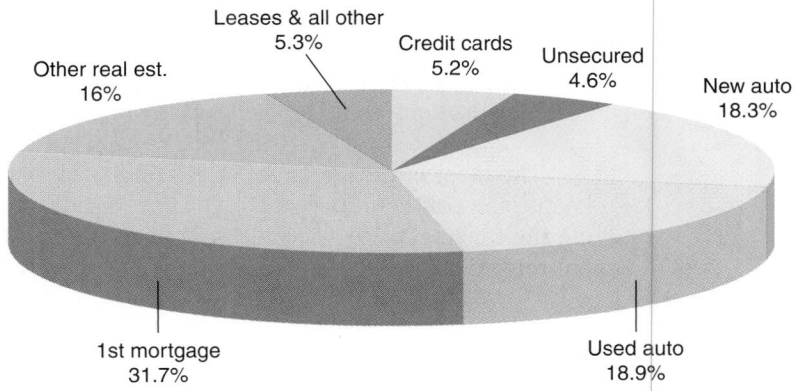

Figure 19.9 Loan Distribution

Source: http://www.ncua.gov/ref/statistics/midyear2006.pdf.

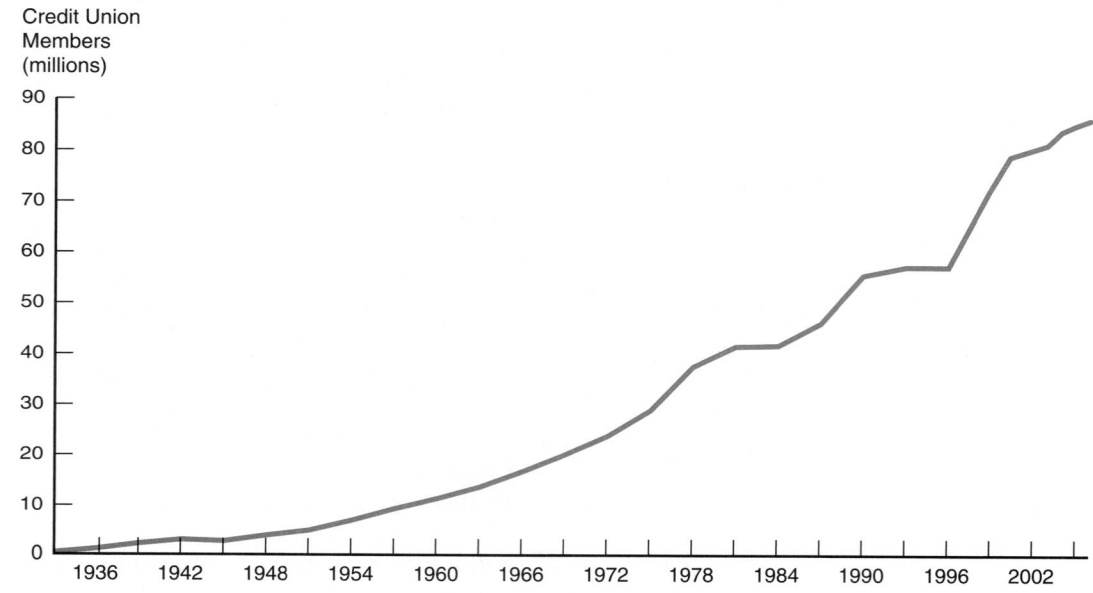

Figure 19.10 Credit Union Membership, 1933–2006

Source: http://www.ncua.gov/ReportsAndPlans/statistics/YearEnd2006.pdf.

- *Employer support.* Many employers recognize that it is in their own best interest to help their employees manage their funds. This motivates the firm to support the employee credit union. Businesses will frequently provide free office space, utilities, and other help to the credit unions.
- *Tax advantage.* Because credit unions are exempt from paying taxes by federal regulation, this savings can be passed on to the members in the form of higher dividends or lower account-servicing costs.
- *Strong trade associations.* Credit unions have formed many trade associations, which lower their costs and provide the means to offer services the institutions could not otherwise offer.

The main disadvantage of credit unions is that the common bond requirement keeps many of them very small. The cost disadvantage can prevent them from offering the range of services available from larger institutions. This disadvantage is not entirely equalized by the use of trade associations.

The Future of Credit Unions

Credit unions are well positioned to continue their growth as a significant provider of financial services to consumers. Figure 19.11 shows that credit union assets increased from $282 billion in 1993 to $709.9 billion in 2006, a 7.4% compounded annual growth rate. Though credit unions are likely to remain small compared to other financial institutions, their cost advantages give them a competitive edge that will continue to attract consumer business.

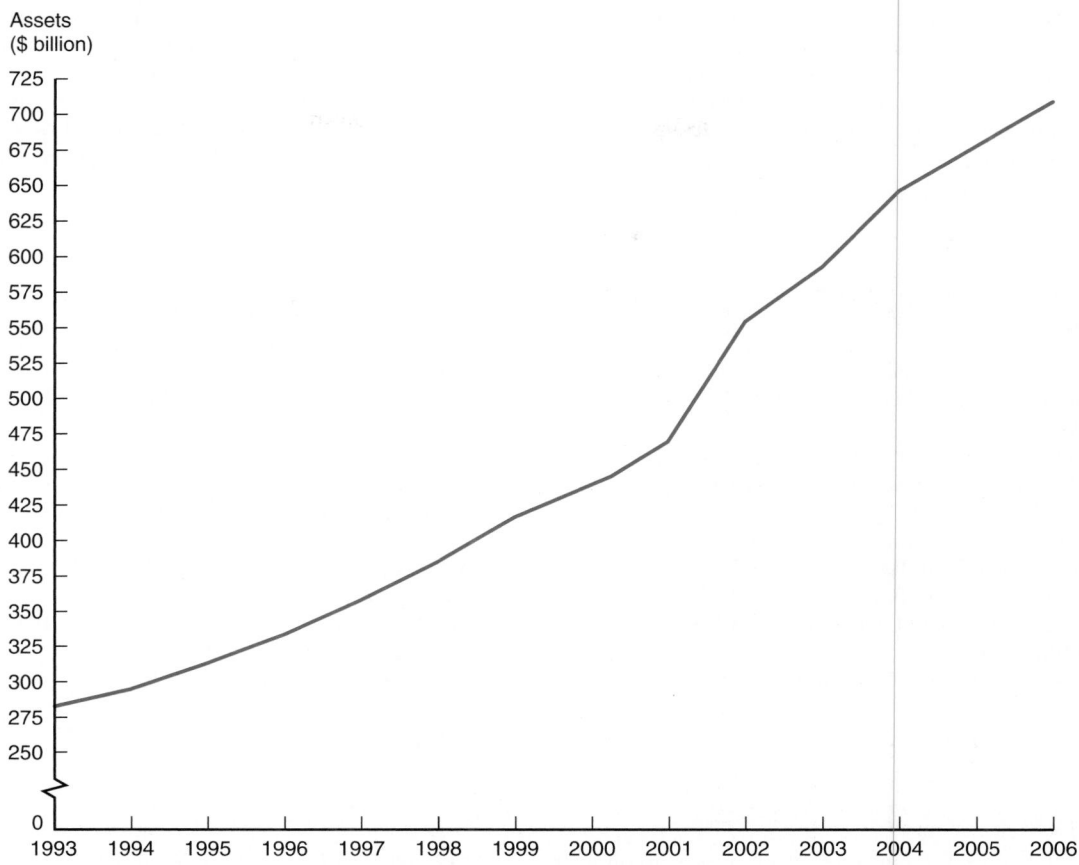

Figure 19.11 Credit Union Assets, 1993–2006

Source: http://www.ncua.gov/ReportsAndPlans/statistics/YearEnd2006.pdf.

SUMMARY

1. Congress mandated that savings and loans and mutual savings banks provide mortgage loan opportunities for consumers. For most of the twentieth century, they profitably satisfied this need.

2. In the late 1970s and the 1980s, savings and loans lost money because interest rates on their deposits rose while the return on their mortgage portfolios was fixed. These losses initially led to deregulation. Savings and loans continued to lose money despite regulatory reform.

3. Due to mounting losses among savings and loans the industry was reregulated in 1987. It has since recov-

ered in terms of both profitability and net worth. The industry continues to consolidate, though total assets are remaining about constant. It is too early to determine whether the industry will simply merge with commercial banks or remain independent.

4. Credit unions were established to serve the public's demand for consumer-type loans. They are unique because members must satisfy a common bond requirement to join. This common bond requirement has restricted the growth of credit unions. Most are small compared to savings and loans and commercial banks.

5. Because of their small size, credit unions have benefited by forming cooperative organizations. These coops, such as CUNA, provide technical, liquidity, mortgage, and insurance services that would be impossible for the individual credit unions to have otherwise.

6. Credit unions enjoy several advantages that should keep them viable in the future. First, as nonprofit organizations, they are exempt from federal taxation. Second, many have strong support from a sponsoring company or business, which lowers the operating cost of the institution. The use of volunteers also helps keep costs low.

KEY TERMS

Central Liquidity Facility (CLF), *p. 502*
common bond membership, *p. 500*
credit union, *p. 499*
Credit Union National Association (CUNA), *p. 499*
Credit Union National Extension Bureau (CUNEB), *p. 499*
Federal Credit Union Act, *p. 499*
Federal Home Loan Bank Act of 1932, *p. 485*
Federal Home Loan Bank Board (FHLBB), *p. 485*
Federal Savings and Loan Insurance Corporation (FSLIC), *p. 485*
Financial Institutions Reform Act, *p. 502*

Financial Institutions Reform, Recovery, and Enforcement Act (FIRREA), *p. 491*
mutual banks, *p. 484*
National Credit Union Act of 1970, *p. 501*
National Credit Union Administration (NCUA), *p. 501*
National Credit Union Share Insurance Fund (NCUSIF), *p. 501*
passbook savings accounts, *p. 496*
regulatory forbearance, *p. 487*
Resolution Trust Corporation (RTC), *p. 491*
trade associations, *p. 503*
U.S. Central Credit Union, *p. 502*

QUESTIONS

1. How does the mutual form of ownership differ from the typical corporate form of ownership?

2. What is the primary disadvantage of the mutual form of ownership?

3. What are the primary assets of savings and loan institutions?

4. Name three factors that led to the thrift crisis.

5. Why did depositors not object to the risky loans and investments made by savings and loans in the early and mid-1980s?

6. How was the thrift crisis ended?

7. What is the most common measure of the capital adequacy of a financial institution?

8. What has been the trend in S&L net income since the mid-1990s?

9. What type of customers are credit unions focused on servicing?

10. What is the purpose of the Credit Union National Association (CUNA)?

11. Describe the common bond membership rule.

12. Why does the commercial banking lobby object to the nonprofit, tax-exempt status enjoyed by credit unions?

13. Are most credit unions larger or smaller than commercial banks? Why?

14. What are share accounts, share certificates, and share drafts?

15. What are the primary advantages enjoyed by credit unions?

16. Why is regulatory forbearance a dangerous strategy for a deposit insurance agency?

17. Why did the S&L crisis not occur unitl the 1980s?

18. The FIRREA legislation in 1989 is the most comprehensive thrift legislation since the 1930s. Describe its major features.

19. Some advocates of campaign finance reform believe that government funding of political campaigns and restrictions on campaign financing might reduce the principal-agent problem in our political system. Do you agree?

20. How can the S&L crisis be blamed on the principal-agent problem?

WEB EXERCISES

Savings Associations and Credit Unions

1. Like banks, thrifts provide a great deal of summary information to the public. One of the most extensive sites for thrift information is at **http://www.ots .treas.gov/**. Select "Industry Performance" under "Data and Research" on the left margin of the site. Now go to "Thrift Industry Selected Indicators" on the site to answer the following questions.

   a. What is the return on average assets for the most recent time period?

   b. What is the return on average equity for the most recent time period?

   c. How many thrift institutions are reporting to the OTS during the most recent time period?

2. Go to **http://www.ncua.gov/**. This is the home page of the National Credit Union Administration. Click on "About NCUA" on the left margin of the site and then click on History of Credit Unions.

   a. According to the NCUA, what features define a credit union?

   b. What was the name of the first credit union opened in the United States in 1909?

   c. In what year was the Federal Credit Union Act signed into law?

20

Banking Regulation

Preview

As we have seen in the previous chapters, the financial system is among the most heavily regulated sectors of the economy, and banks are among the most heavily regulated of financial institutions. In this chapter, we develop an economic analysis of why regulation of banking takes the form it does.

Unfortunately, the regulatory process may not always work very well, as evidenced by recent crises in the banking systems, not only in the United States but in many countries throughout the world. Here, we also use our analysis of banking regulation to explain the worldwide crises in banking and to consider how the regulatory system can be reformed to prevent future disasters.

Asymmetric Information and Banking Regulation

go online
www.ny.frb.org/banking/
supervisionregulate.html
View bank regulation
information.

go online
www.federalreserve.gov/
Regulations/default.htm
Access regulatory publications
of the Federal Reserve Board.

In earlier chapters, we have seen how asymmetric information—the fact that different parties in a financial contract do not have the same information—leads to adverse selection and moral hazard problems that have an important impact on our financial system. The concepts of asymmetric information, adverse selection, and moral hazard are especially useful in understanding why government has chosen the form of banking regulation we see in the United States and in other countries. There are eight basic categories of banking regulation: the government safety net, restrictions on bank asset holdings, capital requirements, chartering and bank examination, assessment of risk management, disclosure requirements, consumer protection, and restrictions on competition.

Government Safety Net: Deposit Insurance and the FDIC

As we saw in Chapter 15, banks are particularly well suited to solving adverse selection and moral hazard problems because they make private loans that help avoid the free-rider problem. However, this solution to the free-rider problem creates another asymmetric information problem, because depositors lack information about the quality of these private loans. This asymmetric information problem leads to two reasons why the banking system might not function well.

go online
www.fdic.gov/bank/
historical/bank/index.html
Search for data on bank
failures in any year.

First, before the FDIC started operations in 1934, a bank failure (in which a bank is unable to meet its obligations to pay its depositors and other creditors and so must go out of business) meant that depositors would have to wait to get their deposit funds until the bank was liquidated (until its assets had been turned into cash); at that time, they would be paid only a fraction of the value of their deposits. Unable to learn if bank managers were taking on too much risk or were outright crooks, depositors would be reluctant to put money in the bank, thus making banking institutions less viable. Second, depositors' lack of information about the quality of bank assets can lead to bank panics, which, as we saw in Chapter 15, can have serious harmful consequences for the economy. To see this, consider the following situation. There is no deposit insurance, and an adverse shock hits the economy. As a result of the shock, 5% of the banks have such large losses on loans that they become insolvent (have a negative net worth and so are bankrupt). Because of asymmetric information, depositors are unable to tell whether their bank is a good bank or one of the 5% that are insolvent. Depositors at bad *and* good banks recognize that they may not get back 100 cents on the dollar for their deposits and will want to withdraw them. Indeed, because banks operate on a "sequential service constraint" (a first-come, first-served basis), depositors have a very strong incentive to show up at the bank first, because if they are last in line, the bank may run out of funds and they will get nothing. Uncertainty about the health of the banking system in general can lead to runs on banks both good and bad, and the failure of one bank can hasten the failure of others (referred to as the *contagion effect*). If nothing is done to restore the public's confidence, a bank panic can ensue.

Indeed, bank panics were a fact of American life in the nineteenth and early twentieth centuries, with major ones occurring every 20 years or so in 1819, 1837, 1857, 1873, 1884, 1893, 1907, and 1930–1933. Bank failures were a serious problem even during the boom years of the 1920s, when the number of bank failures averaged around 600 per year.

A government safety net for depositors can short-circuit runs on banks and bank panics, and by providing protection for the depositor, it can overcome reluctance to put funds in the banking system. One form of the safety net is deposit insurance, a guarantee such as that provided by the Federal Deposit Insurance Corporation (FDIC) in the United States in which depositors are paid off in full on the first $100,000 they have deposited in a bank no matter what happens to the bank. With fully insured deposits, depositors don't need to run to the bank to make withdrawals—even if they are worried about the bank's health—because their deposits will be worth 100 cents on the dollar no matter what. From 1930 to 1933, the years immediately preceding the creation of the FDIC, the number of bank failures averaged more than 2,000 per year. After the establishment of the FDIC in 1934, bank failures averaged fewer than 15 per year until 1981.

The FDIC uses two primary methods to handle a failed bank. In the first, called the *payoff method*, the FDIC allows the bank to fail and pays off deposits up to the

$100,000 insurance limit (with funds acquired from the insurance premiums paid by the banks who have bought FDIC insurance). After the bank has been liquidated, the FDIC lines up with other creditors of the bank and is paid its share of the proceeds from the liquidated assets. Typically, when the payoff method is used, account holders with deposits in excess of the $100,000 limit get back more than 90 cents on the dollar, although the process can take several years to complete.

In the second method, called the *purchase and assumption method*, the FDIC reorganizes the bank, typically by finding a willing merger partner who assumes (takes over) all of the failed bank's deposits so that no depositor loses a penny. The FDIC may help the merger partner by providing it with subsidized loans or by buying some of the failed bank's weaker loans. The net effect of the purchase and assumption method is that the FDIC has guaranteed *all* deposits, not just those under the $100,000 limit. The purchase and assumption method was the FDIC's most common procedure for dealing with a failed bank before new banking legislation in 1991.

Deposit insurance is not the only way in which governments provide a safety net for depositors. In other countries, governments have often stood ready to provide support to domestic banks when they face runs even in the absence of explicit deposit insurance. This support is sometimes provided by lending from the central bank to troubled institutions and is often referred to as the "lender of last resort" role of the central bank. In other cases, funds are provided directly by the government to troubled institutions, or these institutions are taken over by the government and the government then guarantees that depositors will receive their money in full. However, in recent years, government deposit insurance has been growing in popularity and has spread to many countries throughout the world. Whether this trend is desirable is discussed in the Global box, "The Spread of Government Deposit Insurance Throughout the World: Is This a Good Thing?"

Moral Hazard and the Government Safety Net Although a government safety net has been successful at protecting depositors and preventing bank panics, it is a mixed blessing. The most serious drawback of the government safety net stems from moral hazard, the incentives of one party to a transaction to engage in activities detrimental to the other party. Moral hazard is an important concern in insurance arrangements in general because the existence of insurance provides increased incentives for taking risks that might result in an insurance payoff. For example, some drivers with automobile collision insurance that has a low deductible might be more likely to drive recklessly, because if they get into an accident, the insurance company pays most of the costs for damage and repairs.

Moral hazard is a prominent concern in government arrangements to provide a safety net. With a safety net, depositors know that they will not suffer losses if a bank fails, so they do not impose the discipline of the marketplace on banks by withdrawing deposits when they suspect that the bank is taking on too much risk. Consequently, banks with a government safety net have an incentive to take on greater risks than they otherwise would, with taxpayers paying the bill if the bank subsequently goes belly up. Banks have been given the following bet: "Heads I win, tails the taxpayer loses."

Adverse Selection and the Government Safety Net A further problem with a government safety net like deposit insurance arises because of adverse selection, the fact that the people who are most likely to produce the adverse outcome insured against (bank failure) are those who most want to take advantage of the insurance. For example, bad drivers are more likely than good drivers to take out automobile collision

The Spread of Government Deposit Insurance Throughout the World: Is This a Good Thing?

For the first 30 years after federal deposit insurance was established in the United States, only six countries emulated the United States and adopted deposit insurance. However, this began to change in the late 1960s, with the trend accelerating in the 1990s, when the number of countries adopting deposit insurance topped 70. Government deposit insurance has taken off throughout the world because of growing concern about the health of banking systems, particularly after the increasing number of banking crises in recent years (documented at the end of this chapter). Has this spread of deposit insurance been a good thing? Has it helped improve the performance of the financial system and prevent banking crises?

The answer seems to be no under many circumstances. Research at the World Bank has found that, on average, the adoption of explicit government deposit insurance is associated with less banking sector stability and a higher incidence of banking crises.* Furthermore, on average, it seems to retard financial development. However, the negative effects of deposit insurance appear only in countries with weak institutional environments: an absence of rule of law, ineffective regulation and supervision of the financial sector, and high corruption. This is exactly what might be expected because, as we will see later in this chapter, a strong institutional environment is needed to limit the moral hazard incentives for banks to engage in the excessively risky behavior encouraged by deposit insurance. The problem is that developing a strong institutional environment may be very difficult to achieve in many emerging market countries. This leaves us with the following conclusion: Adoption of deposit insurance may be exactly the wrong medicine for promoting stability and efficiency of banking systems in emerging market countries.

*See World Bank, *Finance for Growth: Policy Choices in a Volatile World* (Oxford: World Bank and Oxford University Press, 2001).

insurance with a low deductible. Because depositors protected by a government safety net have little reason to impose discipline on the bank, risk-loving entrepreneurs might find the banking industry a particularly attractive one to enter—they know that they will be able to engage in highly risky activities. Even worse, because protected depositors have so little reason to monitor the bank's activities, without government intervention outright crooks might also find banking an attractive industry for their activities because it is easy for them to get away with fraud and embezzlement.

"Too Big to Fail" The moral hazard created by a government safety net and the desire to prevent bank failures have presented bank regulators with a particular quandary. Because the failure of a very large bank makes it more likely that a major financial disruption will occur, bank regulators are naturally reluctant to allow a big bank to fail and cause losses to its depositors. Indeed, consider Continental Illinois, one of the 10 largest banks in the United States when it became insolvent in May 1984. Not only did the FDIC guarantee depositors up to the $100,000 insurance limit, but it also guaranteed accounts exceeding $100,000 and even prevented losses for Continental Illinois bondholders. Shortly thereafter, the Comptroller of the Currency (the regulator of national banks) testified to Congress that 11 of the largest banks would receive a similar treatment to that of Continental Illinois. Although the Comptroller did not use the term "too big to fail" (it was actually used by Congressman McKinney in those hearings), this term is now applied to a policy in which the government provides guarantees of repayment of large uninsured creditors of the largest banks, so that no depositor or creditor suffers a loss, even when they are not automatically entitled to this guarantee. The FDIC would do this by using the purchase and assumption method, giving the insolvent bank a large infusion of capital and then finding a willing merger partner to take over the bank and its deposits. The too-big-to-fail policy was extended to big banks that were not even among the 11 largest. (Note that "too big to fail" is somewhat misleading because when a bank is closed or merged into another bank, the managers are usually fired and the stockholders in the bank lose their investment.)

One problem with the too-big-to-fail policy is that it increases the moral hazard incentives for big banks. If the FDIC were willing to close a bank using the payoff method, paying depositors only up to the $100,000 limit, large depositors with more than $100,000 would suffer losses if the bank failed. Thus, they would have an incentive to monitor the bank by examining the bank's activities closely and pulling their money out if the bank was taking on too much risk. To prevent such a loss of deposits, the bank would be more likely to engage in less risky activities. However, once large depositors know that a bank is too big to fail, they have no incentive to monitor the bank and pull out their deposits when it takes on too much risk: No matter what the bank does, large depositors will not suffer any losses. The result of the too-big-to-fail policy is that big banks might take on even greater risks, thereby making bank failures more likely.[1]

Financial Consolidation and the Government Safety Net With financial innovation and the passage of the Riegle-Neal Interstate Banking and Branching and Efficiency Act of 1994 and the Gramm-Leach-Bliley Financial Services Modernization Act in 1999, financial consolidation has been proceeding at a rapid pace, leading to both larger and more complex banking organizations. Financial consolidation poses two challenges to banking regulation because of the existence of the government safety net. First, the increased size of banks as a result of financial consolidation increases the too-big-to-fail problem, because there will now be more large institutions whose failure would expose the financial system to systemic (systemwide) risk. Thus, more banking institutions are likely to be treated as too big to fail, and the increased moral hazard incentives for these large institutions to take on greater risk can then increase the fragility of the financial system. Second, financial consolidation of banks with other financial services firms means that the government safety net may be extended to new activities, such as securities underwriting, insurance, or real estate activities, thereby increasing incentives for greater risk taking in these activities that can also weaken the fabric of the financial system. Limiting the moral hazard incentives for the larger, more complex financial organizations that have arisen as a result of recent changes in legislation will be one of the key issues facing banking regulators in the future.

Restrictions on Asset Holdings and Bank Capital Requirements

As we have seen, the moral hazard associated with a government safety net encourages too much risk taking on the part of banks. Bank regulations that restrict asset holdings and bank capital requirements are directed at minimizing this moral hazard, which can cost the taxpayers dearly.

[1]Evidence reveals, as our analysis predicts, that large banks took on riskier loans than smaller banks and that this led to higher loan losses for big banks; see John Boyd and Mark Gertler, "U.S. Commercial Banking: Trends, Cycles and Policy," *NBER Macroeconomics Annual*, 1993, pp. 319–368.

Even in the absence of a government safety net, banks still have the incentive to take on too much risk. Risky assets may provide the bank with higher earnings when they pay off; but if they do not pay off and the bank fails, depositors are left holding the bag. If depositors were able to monitor the bank easily by acquiring information on its risk-taking activities, they would immediately withdraw their deposits if the bank was taking on too much risk. To prevent such a loss of deposits, the bank would be more likely to reduce its risk-taking activities. Unfortunately, acquiring information on a bank's activities to learn how much risk the bank is taking can be a difficult task. Hence, most depositors are incapable of imposing discipline that might prevent banks from engaging in risky activities. A strong rationale for government regulation to reduce risk taking on the part of banks therefore existed even before the establishment of federal deposit insurance.

Bank regulations that restrict banks from holding risky assets such as common stock are a direct means of making banks avoid too much risk. Bank regulations also promote diversification, which reduces risk by limiting the amount of loans in particular categories or to individual borrowers. Requirements that banks have sufficient bank capital are another way to reduce the bank's incentives to take on risk. When a bank is forced to hold a large amount of equity capital, the bank has more to lose if it fails and is thus more likely to pursue less risky activities.

Bank capital requirements take two forms. The first type is based on the **leverage ratio,** the amount of capital divided by the bank's total assets. To be classified as well capitalized, a bank's leverage ratio must exceed 5%; a lower leverage ratio, especially one below 3%, triggers increased regulatory restrictions on the bank. Through most of the 1980s, minimum bank capital in the United States was set solely by specifying a minimum leverage ratio.

In the wake of the Continental Illinois and savings and loans bailouts, regulators in the United States and the rest of the world have become increasingly worried about banks' holdings of risky assets and about the increase in banks' **off-balance-sheet activities,** activities that involve trading financial instruments and generating income from fees, which do not appear on bank balance sheets but nevertheless expose banks to risk. An agreement among banking officials from industrialized nations set up the **Basel Committee on Banking Supervision** (because it meets under the auspices of the Bank for International Settlements in Basel, Switzerland), which has implemented the **Basel Accord** that deals with a second type of capital requirements, risk-based capital requirements. The Basel Accord, which required that banks hold as capital at least 8% of their risk-weighted assets, has been adopted by more than 100 countries, including the United States. Assets and off-balance-sheet activities were allocated into four categories, each with a different weight to reflect the degree of credit risk. The first category carries a zero weight and includes items that have little default risk, such as reserves and government securities issued by the Organization for Economic Cooperation and Development (OECD—industrialized) countries. The second category has a 20% weight and includes claims on banks in OECD countries. The third category has a weight of 50% and includes municipal bonds and residential mortgages. The fourth category has the maximum weight of 100% and includes loans to consumers and corporations. Off-balance-sheet activities are treated in a similar manner by assigning a credit-equivalent percentage that converts them to on-balance-sheet items to which the appropriate risk weight applies. The 1996 Market Risk Amendment to the Basel Accord set minimum capital requirements for risks in banks' trading accounts.

Over time, limitations of the Basel Accord have become apparent, because the regulatory measure of bank risk as stipulated by the risk weights can differ substantially from the actual risk the bank faces. This has resulted in **regulatory arbitrage,** a practice in which banks keep on their books assets that have the same risk-based capital requirement but are relatively risky, such as a loan to a company with a very low credit rating, while taking off their books low-risk assets, such as a loan to a company with a very high credit rating. The Basel Accord could thus lead to increased risk taking, the opposite of its intent. To address these limitations, the Basel Committee on Bank Supervision has released proposals for a new capital accord, often referred to as Basel 2, but it is not clear if it is workable (see the Global box, "Basel 2: How Well Will It Work?").

The Basel Committee's work on bank capital requirements is never-ending. As the banking industry changes, the regulation of bank capital must change with it to ensure the safety and soundness of the banking institutions.

---

global

Basel 2: How Well Will It Work?

Starting in June 1999, the Basel Committee on Banking Supervision released several proposals to reform the original 1988 Basel Accord. These efforts have culminated in what bank supervisors refer to as Basel 2, which is based on three pillars. Pillar 1 intends to link capital requirements for large, internationally active banks more closely to actual risk. It does so by specifying many more categories of risk with different weights in its standardized approach. Alternatively, it allows sophisticated banks to pursue instead an internal ratings-based approach that permits banks to use their own models of credit risk. Pillar 2 focuses on strengthening the supervisory process, particularly in assessing the quality of risk management in banking institutions and in evaluating whether these institutions have adequate procedures to determine how much capital they need. Pillar 3 focuses on improving market discipline through increased disclosure of details about the bank's credit exposures, its amount of reserves and capital, the officials who control the bank, and the effectiveness of its internal ratings system.

Although Basel 2 makes great strides toward limiting excessive risk taking by internationally active banking institutions, it has come at a cost of greatly increasing the complexity of the accord. The document describing the original Basel Accord was 26 pages, while the second draft of Basel 2 issued in January 2001 exceeded 500 pages. The original timetable called for the completion of the final round of consultation by the end of May 2001, with the new rules taking effect by 2004. However, criticism from banks, trade associations, and national regulators led to several postponements. The final draft was not published until June 2004 and Basel 2 was then scheduled to be implemented at the beginning of 2008. European banks began testing computer models in January 2007 to determine how the new standards will affect their capital levels and should meet the 2008 implementation date.

U.S. bank regulators delayed implementation of Basel 2 because of concern that required capital levels at the largest U.S. banks might fall under the new standards. The FDIC in particular was worried about the possibility that the new capital standards would provide inadequate protection against unexpected market shocks and credit risks. This would subject the banks to greater risk of failure and the FDIC's insurance fund to greater probability of loss. In mid-2007, regulators from the FDIC, the Federal Reserve, the Comptroller of the Currency, and the Office of Thrift Supervision agreed on a set of safeguards to minimize adverse impacts on bank capital levels that might accompany adoption of the new standards. U.S. banks using Basel 2 will test its effects on capital levels beginning in 2008 and should be ready to adopt it in 2009. Only the dozen or so largest U.S. banks will be subject to Basel 2; all others will be allowed to use a simplified version of the standards it imposes.

Because of its complexity, Basel 2 has been a long time coming. Now the question is how well will it work?

Bank Supervision: Chartering and Examination

Overseeing who operates banks and how they are operated, referred to as **bank supervision** or more generally as **prudential supervision,** is an important method for reducing adverse selection and moral hazard in the banking business. Because banks can be used by crooks or overambitious entrepreneurs to engage in highly speculative activities, such undesirable people would be eager to run a bank. Chartering banks is one method for preventing this adverse selection problem; through chartering, proposals for new banks are screened to prevent undesirable people from controlling them.

Regular on-site bank examinations, which allow regulators to monitor whether the bank is complying with capital requirements and restrictions on asset holdings, also function to limit moral hazard. Bank examiners give banks a *CAMELS rating.* The acronym is based on the six areas assessed: capital adequacy, asset quality, management, earnings, liquidity, and sensitivity to market risk. With this information about a bank's activities, regulators can enforce regulations by taking such formal actions as *cease and desist orders* to alter the bank's behavior or even close a bank if its CAMELS rating is sufficiently low. Actions taken to reduce moral hazard by restricting banks from taking on too much risk help reduce the adverse selection problem further, because with less opportunity for risk taking, risk-loving entrepreneurs will be less likely to be attracted to the banking industry. Note that the methods regulators use to cope with adverse selection and moral hazard have their counterparts in private financial markets (see Chapters 15 and 24). Chartering is similar to the screening of potential borrowers, regulations restricting risky asset holdings are similar to restrictive covenants that prevent borrowing firms from engaging in risky investment activities, bank capital requirements act like restrictive covenants that require minimum amounts of net worth for borrowing firms, and regular bank examinations are similar to the monitoring of borrowers by lending institutions.

A commercial bank obtains a charter either from the Comptroller of the Currency (in the case of a national bank) or from a state banking authority (in the case of a state bank). To obtain a charter, the people planning to organize the bank must submit an application that shows how they plan to operate the bank. In evaluating the application, the regulatory authority looks at whether the bank is likely to be sound by examining the quality of the bank's intended management, the likely earnings of the bank, and the amount of the bank's initial capital. Before 1980, the chartering agency typically explored the issue of whether the community needed a new bank. Often a new bank charter would not be granted if existing banks in a community would be hurt by its presence. Today, this anticompetitive stance (justified by the desire to prevent failures of existing banks) is no longer as strong in the chartering agencies.

Once a bank has been chartered, it is required to file periodic (usually quarterly) *call reports* that reveal the bank's assets and liabilities, income and dividends, ownership, foreign exchange operations, and other details. The bank is also subject to examination by the bank regulatory agencies to ascertain its financial condition at least once a year. To avoid duplication of effort, the three federal agencies work together and usually accept each other's examinations. This means that, typically, national banks are examined by the Office of the Comptroller of the Currency, the state banks that are members of the Federal Reserve System are examined by the Fed, and insured nonmember state banks are examined by the FDIC.

Bank examinations are conducted by bank examiners, who sometimes make unannounced visits to a bank (so that nothing can be "swept under the rug" in anticipation of their examination). The examiners study a bank's books to see whether it is complying with the rules and regulations that apply to its holdings of assets. If a bank is holding securities or loans that are too risky, the bank examiner can force the bank to get rid of them. If a bank examiner decides that a loan is unlikely to be repaid, the examiner can force the bank to declare the loan worthless (to write off the loan, which reduces the bank's capital). If, after examining the bank, the examiner feels that it does not have sufficient capital or has engaged in dishonest practices, the bank can be declared a "problem bank" and will be subject to more frequent examinations.

Assessment of Risk Management

Traditionally, on-site bank examinations have focused primarily on assessment of the quality of the bank's balance sheet at a point in time and whether it complies with capital requirements and restrictions on asset holdings. Although the traditional focus is important for reducing excessive risk taking by banks, it is no longer felt to be adequate in today's world, in which financial innovation has produced new markets and instruments that make it easy for banks and their employees to make huge bets easily and quickly. In this new financial environment, a bank that is healthy at a particular point in time can be driven into insolvency extremely rapidly from trading losses, as forcefully demonstrated by the failure of Barings in 1995 (discussed in Chapter 17). Thus, an examination that focuses only on a bank's position at a point in time may not be effective in indicating whether a bank will, in fact, be taking on excessive risk in the near future.

This change in the financial environment for banking institutions has resulted in a major shift in thinking about the bank supervisory process throughout the world. Bank examiners are now placing far greater emphasis on evaluating the soundness of a bank's management processes with regard to controlling risk. This shift in thinking was reflected in a new focus on risk management in the Federal Reserve System's 1993 guidelines to examiners on trading and derivatives activities. The focus was expanded and formalized in the Trading Activities Manual issued early in 1994, which provided bank examiners with tools to evaluate risk management systems. In late 1995, the Federal Reserve and the Comptroller of the Currency announced that they would be assessing risk management processes at the banks they supervise. Now bank examiners give a separate risk management rating from 1 to 5 that feeds into the overall management rating as part of the CAMELS system. Four elements of sound risk management are assessed to come up with the risk management rating: (1) the quality of oversight provided by the board of directors and senior management, (2) the adequacy of policies and limits for all activities that present significant risks, (3) the quality of the risk measurement and monitoring systems, and (4) the adequacy of internal controls to prevent fraud or unauthorized activities on the part of employees.

This shift toward focusing on management processes is also reflected in recent guidelines adopted by the U.S. bank regulatory authorities to deal with interest-rate risk. These guidelines require the bank's board of directors to establish interest-rate risk limits, appoint officials of the bank to manage this risk, and monitor the bank's risk exposure. The guidelines also require that senior management of a bank develop formal risk management policies and procedures to ensure that the board of directors' risk limits are not violated and to implement internal controls to monitor interest-rate risk and compliance with the board's directives. Particularly important is the implementation of *stress testing*, which calculates losses under dire scenarios, or value-at-risk (VAR) calculations, which measure the size of the loss on a trading portfolio that might happen 1% of the time—say, over a two-week period. In addition to these guidelines, bank examiners will continue to consider interest-rate risk in deciding the bank's capital requirements.

Disclosure Requirements

The free-rider problem described in Chapter 15 indicates that individual depositors and other bank creditors will not have enough incentive to produce private information about the quality of a bank's assets. To ensure that there is better information for depositors and the marketplace, regulators can require that banks adhere to certain standard accounting principles and disclose a wide range of information that helps the market assess the quality of a bank's portfolios and the amount of the bank's exposure to risk. More public information about the risks incurred by banks and the quality of their portfolios can better enable stockholders, creditors, and depositors to evaluate and monitor banks and so act as a deterrent to excessive risk taking. This view is consistent with a position paper issued by the Eurocurrency Standing Committee of the G-10 Central Banks, which recommends that estimates of financial risk generated by firms' own internal risk management systems be adapted for public disclosure purposes.[2] Such information would supplement disclosures based on traditional accounting conventions by providing information about risk exposure and risk management that is not normally included in conventional balance sheet and income statement reports.

Consumer Protection

The existence of asymmetric information also suggests that consumers may not have enough information to protect themselves fully. Consumer protection regulation has taken several forms. First is "truth in lending," mandated under the Consumer Protection Act of 1969, which requires all lenders, not just banks, to provide information to consumers about the cost of borrowing, including a standardized interest rate (called the *annual percentage rate*, or *APR*) and the total finance charges on the loan. The Fair Credit Billing Act of 1974 requires creditors, especially credit card issuers, to provide information on the method of assessing finance charges and requires that billing complaints be handled quickly. Both of these acts are administered by the Federal Reserve System under Regulation Z.

Congress has also passed legislation to reduce discrimination in credit markets. The Equal Credit Opportunity Act of 1974 and its extension in 1976 forbid discrimination by lenders based on race, gender, marital status, age, or national origin. It is administered by the Federal Reserve under Regulation B. The Community Reinvestment Act (CRA) of 1977 was enacted to prevent "redlining," a lender's refusal to lend in a particular area (marked off by a hypothetical red line on a map). The Community Reinvestment Act requires that banks show that they lend in all areas in which they take deposits, and if banks are found to be in noncompliance with the act, regulators can reject their applications for mergers, branching, or other new activities.

Restrictions on Competition

Increased competition can also increase moral hazard incentives for banks to take on more risk. Declining profitability as a result of increased competition could tip the incentives of bankers toward assuming greater risk in an effort to maintain former

[2]See Eurocurrency Standing Committee of Central Banks of Group of Ten Countries (Fisher Group), "Discussion Paper on Public Disclosure of Markets and Credit Risks by Financial Intermediaries," September 1994, and a companion piece to this report, Federal Reserve Bank of New York, "A Discussion Paper on Public Disclosure of Risks Related to Market Activity," September 1994.

profit levels. Thus, governments in many countries have instituted regulations to protect banks from competition. These regulations have taken two forms in the United States in the past. First were restrictions on branching, such as those described in Chapter 18, which reduced competition between banks, but were eliminated in 1994. The second form involved preventing nonbank institutions from competing with banks by engaging in banking business, as embodied in the Glass-Steagall Act, which was repealed in 1999.

Although restricting competition propped up the health of banks, restrictions on competition also had serious disadvantages: They led to higher charges to consumers and decreased the efficiency of banking institutions, which did not have to compete as vigorously. Thus, although the existence of asymmetric information provided a rationale for anticompetitive regulations, it did not mean that they would be beneficial. Indeed, in recent years, the impulse of governments in industrialized countries to restrict competition has been waning. Electronic banking has raised a new set of concerns for regulators to deal with. See the E-Finance box for a discussion of this challenge.

e-finance

Electronic Banking: New Challenges for Bank Regulation

The advent of electronic banking has raised new concerns for banking regulation, specifically about security and privacy. Worries about the security of electronic banking and e-money are an important barrier to their increased use. With electronic banking, you might worry that criminals can access your bank account and steal your money by moving your balances to someone else's account. Indeed, a notorious case of this happened in 1995, when a Russian computer programmer got access to Citibank's computers and moved funds electronically into his and his conspirators' accounts. Private solutions to deal with this problem have arisen with the development of more secure encryption technologies to prevent this kind of fraud. However, because bank customers are not knowledgeable about computer security issues, there is a role for the government in regulating electronic banking to make sure that encryption procedures are adequate. Similar encryption issues apply to e-money, so requirements that banks make it difficult for criminals to engage in digital counterfeiting make sense. To meet these challenges, bank examiners in the United States assess how a bank deals with the special security issues raised by electronic banking and also oversee third-party providers of electronic banking platforms. Also, because consumers want to know that electronic banking transactions are executed correctly, bank examiners assess the technical skills of banks in setting up electronic banking services and the bank's capabilities for dealing with problems. Another security issue of concern to bank customers is the validity of digital signatures. The Electronic Signatures in Global and National Commerce Act of 2000 makes electronic signatures as legally binding as written signatures in most circumstances.

Electronic banking also raises serious privacy concerns. Because electronic transactions can be stored on databases, banks are able to collect a huge amount of information about their customers—their assets, creditworthiness, purchases, and so on—that can be sold to other financial institutions and businesses. This potential invasion of our privacy rightfully makes us very nervous. To protect customers' privacy, the Gramm-Leach-Bliley Act of 1999 has limited the distribution of these data, but it does not go as far as the European Data Protection Directive, which prohibits the transfer of information about online transactions. How to protect consumers' privacy in our electronic age is one of the great challenges our society faces, so privacy regulations for electronic banking are likely to evolve over time.

go online

www.fdic.gov/regulations/
laws/important/index.html

Describes the most important
laws that have affected
the banking industry in the
United States.

study guide

Because so many laws regulating banking have been passed in the United States, it is hard to keep track of them all. As a study aid, Table 20.1 lists the major banking legislation in the twentieth century and its key provisions.

TABLE 20.1 Major Banking Legislation in the United States in the Twentieth Century

Federal Reserve Act (1913)	Created the Federal Reserve System
McFadden Act of 1927	Effectively prohibited banks from branching across state lines Put national and state banks on equal footing regarding branching
Banking Acts of 1933 (Glass-Steagall) and 1935	Created the FDIC Separated commercial banking from the securities industry Prohibited interest on checkable deposits and restricted such deposits to commercial banks Put interest-rate ceilings on other deposits
Bank Holding Company Act and Douglas Amendment (1956)	Clarified the status of bank holding companies (BHCs) Gave the Federal Reserve regulatory responsibility for BHCs
Depository Institutions Deregulation and Monetary Control Act (DIDMCA) of 1980	Gave thrift institutions wider latitude in activities Approved NOW and sweep accounts nationwide Phased out interest-rate ceilings on deposits Imposed uniform reserve requirements on depository institutions Eliminated usury ceilings on loans Increased deposit insurance to $100,000 per account
Depository Institutions Act of 1982 (Garn–St. Germain)	Gave the FDIC and the FSLIC emergency powers to merge banks and thrifts across state lines Allowed depository institutions to offer money market deposit accounts (MMDAs) Granted thrifts wider latitude in commercial and consumer lending
Competitive Equality in Banking Act (CEBA) of 1987	Provided $10.8 billion to the FSLIC Made provisions for regulatory forbearance in depressed areas
Financial Institutions Reform, Recovery, and Enforcement Act (FIRREA) of 1989	Provided funds to resolve S&L failures Eliminated the FSLIC and the Federal Home Loan Bank Board Created the Office of Thrift Supervision to regulate thrifts Created the Resolution Trust Corporation to resolve insolvent thrifts Raised deposit insurance premiums Reimposed restrictions on S&L activities

Federal Deposit Insurance Corporation Improvement Act (FDICIA) of 1991	Recapitalized the FDIC
	Limited brokered deposits and the too-big-to-fail policy
	Set provisions for prompt corrective action
	Instructed the FDIC to establish risk-based premiums
	Increased examinations, capital requirements, and reporting requirements
	Included the Foreign Bank Supervision Enhancement Act (FBSEA), which strengthened the Fed's authority to supervise foreign banks
Riegle-Neal Interstate Banking and Branching Efficiency Act of 1994	Overturned prohibition of interstate banking
	Allowed branching across state lines
Gramm-Leach-Bliley Financial Services Modernization Act of 1999	Repealed Glass-Steagall and removed the separation of banking and securities industries
Federal Deposit Insurance Reform Act of 2005	Merged the Bank Insurance Fund and the Savings Association Insurance Fund
	Increased deposit insurance on individual retirement accounts to $250,000 per account
	Allowed for future automatic adjustments to the insurance limits based on inflation
	Authorized FDIC to revise its system of risk-based premiums

International Banking Regulation

Because asymmetric information problems in the banking industry are a fact of life throughout the world, bank regulation in other countries is similar to that in the United States. Banks are chartered and supervised by government regulators, just as they are in the United States. Deposit insurance is also a feature of the regulatory systems in most other developed countries, although its coverage is often smaller than in the United States and is intentionally not advertised. We have also seen that bank capital requirements are in the process of being standardized across countries with agreements like the Basel Accord.

Problems in Regulating International Banking

Particular problems in bank regulation occur when banks are engaged in international banking and thus can readily shift their business from one country to another. Bank regulators closely examine the domestic operations of banks in their country, but they often do not have the knowledge or ability to keep a close watch on bank operations in other countries, either by domestic banks' foreign affiliates or by foreign banks with domestic branches. In addition, when a bank operates in many countries, it is not always clear which national regulatory authority should have primary responsibility for keeping the bank from engaging in overly risky activities. The difficulties inherent in regulating international banking were highlighted by the collapse of the Bank of Credit and Commerce International (BCCI) in 1991. BCCI, which was operating in more than 70 countries, including the United States and the United Kingdom, was supervised by Luxembourg, a tiny country unlikely to be up to the task. When massive fraud was discovered, the Bank of England closed BCCI down, but not before depositors and stockholders were exposed to huge losses. Cooperation among regulators in different countries and standardization of regulatory requirements provide potential solutions to the problems of regulating international banking. The world has been moving in this direction through agreements like the Basel Accord and oversight procedures announced by the Basel Committee in July 1992, which require a bank's worldwide operations to be under the scrutiny of a single home-country regulator with enhanced powers to acquire information on the bank's activities. Also, the Basel Committee ruled that regulators in other countries can restrict the operations of a foreign bank if they feel that it lacks effective oversight. Whether agreements of this type will solve the problem of regulating international banking in the future is an open question.

Summary

Asymmetric information analysis explains what types of banking regulations are needed to reduce moral hazard and adverse selection problems in the banking system. However, understanding the theory behind regulation does not mean that regulation and supervision of the banking system are easy in practice. Getting bank regulators and supervisors to do their job properly is difficult for several reasons. First, as we learned in the discussion of financial innovation in Chapter 18, in their search for profits, financial institutions have strong incentives to avoid existing regulations by loophole mining. Thus, regulation applies to a moving target: Regulators are continually playing cat-and-mouse with financial institutions—financial institutions think up clever ways to avoid regulations, which then causes regulators to modify their regulation activities. Regulators continually face new challenges in a dynamically changing financial system, and unless they can respond rapidly to change, they may not be able to keep financial institutions from taking on excessive risk. This problem can be exacerbated if regulators and supervisors do not have the resources or expertise to keep up with clever people in financial institutions who think up ways to hide what they are doing or to get around the existing regulations.

Bank regulation and supervision are difficult for two other reasons. In the regulation and supervision game, the devil is in the details. Subtle differences in the details may have unintended consequences; unless regulators get the regulation and supervision just right, they may be unable to prevent excessive risk taking. In addition, regulators and supervisors may be subject to political pressure to not do their jobs properly. For all these reasons, there is no guarantee that bank regulators and supervisors will be successful in promoting a healthy financial system. Indeed, as we will see, bank regulation and supervision have not always worked well, leading to banking crises in the United States and throughout the world.

The 1980s U.S. Banking Crisis

Before the 1980s, federal deposit insurance seemed to work exceedingly well. In contrast to the pre-1934 period, when bank failures were common and depositors frequently suffered losses, the period from 1934 to 1980 was one in which bank failures

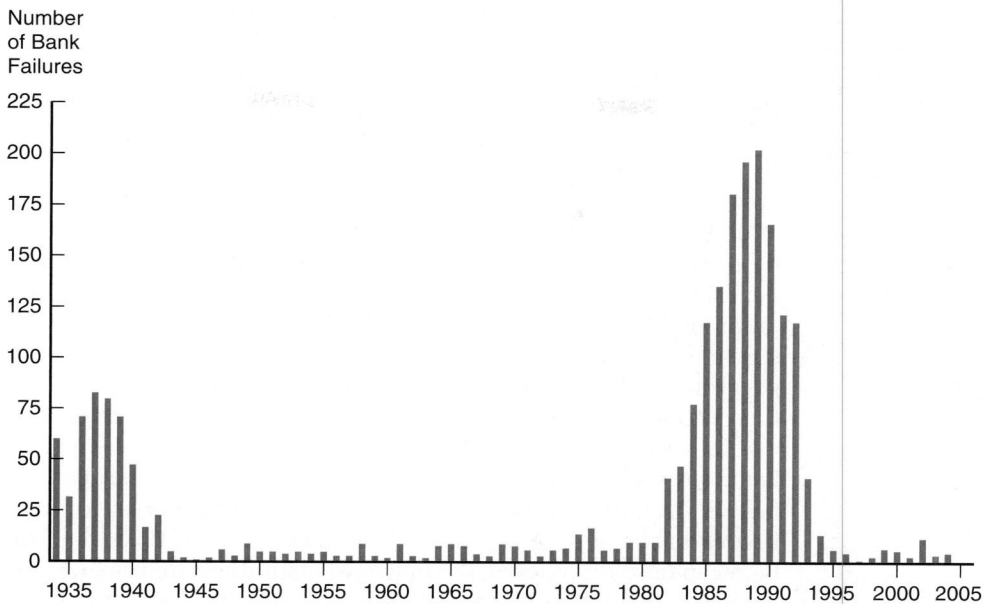

Figure 20.1   Bank Failures in the United States, 1934–2006

Source: www2.fdic.gov/book/hsob/selectrpt.asp?entrytyp=30.

were a rarity, averaging 15 per year for commercial banks and fewer than five per year for savings and loans. After 1981, this rosy picture changed dramatically. Failures in both commercial banks and savings and loans climbed to levels more than 10 times greater than in earlier years, as can be seen in Figure 20.1. Why did this happen? How did a deposit insurance system that seemed to be working well for half a century find itself in so much trouble?

The story starts with the burst of financial innovation in the 1960s, 1970s, and early 1980s. As we saw in Chapter 18, financial innovation decreased the profitability of certain traditional lines of business for commercial banks. Banks now faced increased competition for their sources of funds from new financial institutions, such as money market mutual funds, even as they were losing commercial lending business to the commercial paper market and securitization.

With the decreasing profitability of their traditional business, by the mid-1980s commercial banks were forced to seek out new and potentially risky business to keep their profits up, by placing a greater percentage of their total loans in real estate and in credit extended to assist corporate takeovers and leveraged buyouts (called *highly leveraged transaction loans*).

The existence of deposit insurance increased moral hazard for banks because insured depositors had little incentive to keep the banks from taking on too much risk. Regardless of how much risk banks were taking, deposit insurance guaranteed that depositors would not suffer any losses.

Adding fuel to the fire, financial innovation produced new financial instruments that widened the scope for risk taking. New markets in financial futures, junk bonds, swaps, and other instruments made it easier for banks to take on extra risk—making the moral hazard problem more severe.

In addition, the Depository Institutions Deregulation and Monetary Control Act (DIDMCA) of 1980 increased the mandated amount of federal deposit insurance from $40,000 per account to $100,000 and phased out Regulation Q deposit-rate ceilings. Banks and S&Ls that wanted to pursue rapid growth and take on risky projects could now attract the necessary funds by issuing larger-denomination insured certificates of deposit with interest rates much higher than those being offered by their competitors. Without deposit insurance, high interest rates would not have induced depositors to provide the high-rolling banks with funds because of the realistic expectation that they might not get the funds back. But with deposit insurance and widespread use of the purchase and assumption method to handle failed banks, the government was guaranteeing that the deposits were safe, so depositors were more than happy to make deposits in banks with the highest interest rates.

As a result of these forces, commercial banks did take on excessive risks and began to suffer substantial losses. The outcome was that bank failures rose to a level of 200 per year by the late 1980s. The resulting losses for the FDIC meant that it would have depleted its Bank Insurance Fund by 1992, requiring that this fund be recapitalized. Although the Financial Institutions Reform, Recovery, and Enforcement Act (FIRREA) of 1989 (described in Chapter 19) did not focus on the underlying adverse selection and moral hazard problems created by deposit insurance, it did, however, mandate that the U.S. Treasury produce a comprehensive study and plan for reform of the federal deposit insurance system. After this study appeared in 1991, Congress passed the Federal Deposit Insurance Corporation Improvement Act (FDICIA), which engendered major reforms in the bank regulatory system.

Federal Deposit Insurance Corporation Improvement Act of 1991

FDICIA's provisions were designed to serve two purposes: to recapitalize the Bank Insurance Fund of the FDIC and to reform the deposit insurance and regulatory system so that taxpayer losses would be minimized.

FDICIA recapitalized the Bank Insurance Fund by increasing the FDIC's ability to borrow from the Treasury and also mandated that the FDIC assess higher deposit insurance premiums until it could pay back its loans and achieve a level of reserves in its insurance funds that would equal 1.25% of insured deposits.

The bill reduced the scope of deposit insurance in several ways, but the most important one is that the too-big-to-fail doctrine has been substantially limited. The FDIC must now close failed banks using the least costly method, thus making it far more likely that uninsured depositors will suffer losses. An exception to this provision, whereby a bank would be declared too big to fail so that all depositors, both insured and uninsured, would be fully protected, would be allowed only if not doing so would "have serious adverse effects on economic conditions or financial stability." Furthermore, to invoke the too-big-to-fail policy, a two-thirds majority of both the Board of Governors of the Federal Reserve System and the directors of the FDIC, as well as the approval of the Secretary of the Treasury, are required. Furthermore, FDICIA requires that the Fed share the FDIC's losses if long-term Fed lending to a bank that fails increases the FDIC's losses.

Probably the most important feature of FDICIA is its prompt corrective action provisions, which require the FDIC to intervene earlier and more vigorously when a bank gets into trouble. Banks are now classified into five groups based on bank capital. Group 1, classified as "well capitalized," are banks that significantly exceed minimum capital requirements and are allowed privileges, such as the ability to do some securities underwriting. Banks in group 2, classified as "adequately capitalized," meet minimum capital requirements and are not subject to corrective actions but are not allowed the privileges of the well-capitalized banks. Banks in group 3, "undercapitalized," fail to meet capital requirements. Banks in groups 4 and 5 are "significantly undercapitalized" and "critically undercapitalized," respectively, and are not allowed to pay interest on their deposits at rates that are higher than average. In addition, for group 3 banks, the FDIC is required to take prompt corrective actions, such as requiring them to submit a capital restoration plan, restrict their asset growth, and seek regulatory approval to open new branches or develop new lines of business. Banks that are so undercapitalized as to have equity capital less than 2% of assets fall into group 5, and the FDIC must take steps to close them down.

FDICIA also instructed the FDIC to come up with risk-based insurance premiums. The system the FDIC put in place did not work very well, however, because it resulted in more than 90% of the banks, with over 95% of the deposits, paying the same premium. The Federal Deposit Insurance Reform Act of 2005 attempts to remedy this by requiring banks that take on more risk to pay higher insurance premiums regardless of the overall soundness of the banking system or level of the insurance fund relative to insured deposits. Under this act, premiums paid by the riskiest banks will be 10 to 20 times greater than the least-risky banks will pay. (Other provisions of FDICIA and the Federal Deposit Insurance Reform Act of 2005 are listed in Table 20.1 earlier in this chapter.)

FDICIA was an important step in the right direction because it increased the incentives for banks to hold more capital and decreased their incentives to take on excessive risks. Concerns that FDICIA did not adequately address risk-based premiums have been dealt with. Remaining concerns about the too-big-to-fail problem and other issues related to deposit insurance mean that economists and regulators will continue to search for further reforms that might help promote the safety and soundness of the banking system.[3]

Banking Crises Throughout the World

Because misery loves company, it may make you feel better to know that the United States has by no means been alone in suffering a banking crisis. Indeed, as Table 20.2 and Figure 20.2 illustrate, banking crises have struck a large number of countries throughout the world, and many of them have been substantially worse than ours. We will examine what took place in several of these other countries and see that the same forces that produced a banking crisis in the United States have been at work elsewhere, too.

---

[3]A further discussion of how well FDICIA has worked and other proposed reforms of the banking regulatory system appears in an appendix to this chapter that can be found on this book's Web site at www.prenhall.com/mishkin_eakins.

TABLE 20.2 The Cost of Rescuing Banks in Several Countries

Date	Country	Cost as a Percentage of GDP
1980–1982	Argentina	55
1997–2002	Indonesia	55
1990s–ongoing	China	47
1996–2000	Jamaica	44
1981–1983	Chile	42
1997–2002	Thailand	35
1993–1994	Macedonia	32
2000–ongoing	Turkey	31
1977–1983	Israel	30
1997–2002	South Korea	28
1988–1991	Cote d'Ivoire	25
1991–ongoing	Japan	24
1994–1995	Venezuela	22
1998–2001	Ecuador	20
1994–2000	Mexico	19
1997–2001	Malaysia	16
1992–1994	Slovenia	15
1998–ongoing	Philippines	13
1994–1999	Brazil	13
1995–2000	Paraguay	13
1989–1991	Czech Republic	12
1997–1998	Taiwan	12
1991–1994	Finland	11
1989–1990	Jordan	10
1991–1995	Hungary	10
1990–1993	Norway	8
1991–1994	Sweden	4
1988–1991	United States	3

Source: Gerard Caprio, Daniela Klingebiel, Luc Laeven, and Guillermo Noguera, *Banking Crises Database* (updated October 2003), http://www1.worldbank.org/finance/html/database_sfd.html.

Scandinavia

As in the United States, an important factor in the banking crises in Norway, Sweden, and Finland was the financial liberalization that occurred in the 1980s. Before the 1980s, banks in these Scandinavian countries were highly regulated and subject to restrictions on the interest rates they could pay to depositors and on the interest rates they could earn on loans. In this noncompetitive environment, and with artificially low rates on both deposits and loans, these banks lent only to the best credit risks,

Figure 20.2 Banking Crises Throughout the World Since 1970

Source: Gerard Caprio and Daniela Klingebiel, "Episodes of Systemic and Borderline Financial Crises" mimeo., World Bank, October 1999.

and both banks and their regulators had little need to develop expertise in screening and monitoring borrowers. With the deregulated environment, a lending boom ensued, particularly in the real estate sector. Given the lack of expertise in both the banking industry and its regulatory authorities in keeping risk taking in check, banks engaged in risky lending. When real estate prices collapsed in the late 1980s, massive loan losses resulted. The outcome of this process was similar to what happened in the savings and loan industry in the United States. The government was forced to bail out almost the entire banking industry in these countries in the late 1980s and early 1990s on a scale that was even larger relative to GDP than in the United States (see Table 20.2).

Latin America

The Latin American banking crises typically show a pattern similar to those in the United States and in Scandinavia. Before the 1980s, banks in many Latin American countries were owned by the government and were subject to interest-rate restrictions as in Scandinavia. Their lending was restricted to the government and other low-risk borrowers. With the deregulation trend that was occurring worldwide, many of these countries liberalized their credit markets and privatized their banks. We then see the same pattern we saw in the United States and Scandinavia—a lending boom in the face of inadequate expertise on the part of both bankers and regulators. The result was again massive loan losses and the inevitable government bailout.

The Argentine banking crisis of 2001, which is ongoing, differed from those typically seen in Latin America. Argentina's banks were well supervised and in relatively good shape before the government coerced them into purchasing large amounts of Argentine government debt to help solve the government's fiscal problem. However, when market confidence in the government plummeted, spreads between Argentine government debt and U.S. Treasuries soared to more than 2,500 basis points (25 percentage points), leading to a sharp fall in the price of these securities. The losses on their holdings of government debt and rising bad loans because of the ongoing severe recession increased doubts about the solvency of the banking system.

A banking panic erupted in October and November 2001, with the Argentine public rushing to withdraw their deposits. On December 1, after banks had lost more than $8 billion of deposits, the government imposed a $1,000 monthly limit on deposit withdrawals. Then, with the collapse of the peso and the requirement that the banks must pay back their dollar deposits at a higher exchange value than they would be paid back on their dollar loans, banks' balance sheets went even further in the hole. The cost of the recent Argentine banking crisis is not yet clear, but it could very well be as large as the previous banking crisis in Argentina in the 1980–1982 period listed in Table 20.2 and exceed 50% of GDP.

What is particularly striking about the Latin American experience is that the cost of the bailouts relative to GDP dwarfs that in the United States. The cost to the taxpayer of the government bailouts in Latin America has been anywhere from around 20% to more than 50% of GDP, in contrast to the 3% figure for the United States.

Russia and Eastern Europe

Before the end of the Cold War, in the communist countries of Eastern Europe and the Soviet Union, banks were owned by the state. With the downfall of communism in 1990, banks in these countries had little expertise in screening and monitoring loans. Furthermore, a bank regulatory and supervisory apparatus that could rein in the banks and keep them from taking on excessive risk barely existed. Given the lack of expertise on the part of regulators and banks, not surprisingly substantial loan losses ensued, resulting in the failure or government bailout of many banks. For example, in the second half of 1993, eight banks in Hungary with 25% of the financial system's assets were insolvent, and in Bulgaria, an estimated 75% of all loans in the banking system were estimated to be substandard in 1995.

On August 24, 1995, a bank panic requiring government intervention occurred in Russia when the interbank loan market seized up and stopped functioning because of concern about the solvency of many new banks. This event was not the end of troubles in the Russian banking system. On August 17, 1998, the Russian government announced that Russia would impose a moratorium on the repayment of foreign debt because of insolvencies in the banking system. In November, the Russian central bank announced that nearly half of the country's 1,500 commercial banks might go under; the cost of the bailout was on the order of $15 billion.

Japan

Japan was a latecomer to the banking crisis game. Before 1990, the vaunted Japanese economy looked unstoppable. Unfortunately, it has recently experienced many of the same pathologies that we have seen in other countries. Before the 1980s, Japan's financial markets were among the most heavily regulated in the world, with very strict restrictions on the issuing of securities and interest rates. Financial deregulation and innovation produced a more competitive environment that set off a lending boom, with banks lending aggressively in the real estate sector. As in the other countries we have examined here, financial disclosure and monitoring by regulators did not keep pace with the new financial environment. The result was that banks could and did take on excessive risks. When property values collapsed in the early 1990s, the banks were left holding massive amounts of bad loans. For example, Japanese banks decided to get into the mortgage lending market by setting up *jusen*, home mortgage lending companies that raised funds by borrowing from banks and then lent these funds out to households. Seven of these *jusen* became insolvent, leaving banks with $60 billion or so of bad loans.

As a result, the Japanese experienced their first bank failures since World War II. In July 1995, Tokyo-based Cosmo Credit Corporation, Japan's fifth-largest credit union, failed. On August 30, 1995, the Osaka authorities announced the imminent closing of Kizu Credit Cooperative, Japan's second-largest credit union. (Kizu's story is remarkably similar to that of many U.S. savings and loans. Kizu, like many American S&Ls, began offering high rates on large time deposits and grew at a blistering pace, with deposits rising from $2.2 billion in 1988 to $12 billion by 1995 and real estate loans growing by a similar amount. When the property market collapsed, so did Kizu.) On the same day, the Ministry of Finance announced that it was liquidating Hyogo Bank, a midsize Kobe bank that was the first commercial bank to fail. Larger banks now began to follow the same path. In late 1996, the Hanwa Bank, a large regional bank, was liquidated, followed in 1997 by a government-assisted restructuring of the Nippon Credit Bank, Japan's seventeenth-largest bank. In November 1997, Hokkaido Takushoku Bank was forced to go out of business, making it the first city bank (a large commercial bank) to be closed during the crisis.

The Japanese went through a cycle of regulatory forbearance similar to the one that occurred in the United States in the 1980s. The Japanese regulators in the Ministry of Finance enabled banks to meet capital standards and to keep operating by allowing them to artificially inflate the value of their assets. For example, they were allowed to value their large holdings of equities at historical value, rather than market value, which was much lower. Inadequate amounts were allocated for recapitalization of the banking system, and the extent of the problem was grossly underestimated by government officials. Furthermore, until the closing of the Hokkaido Takushoku Bank, the bank regulators in the Ministry of Finance were unwilling to close down city banks and impose any losses on stockholders or any uninsured creditors.

By the middle of 1998, the Japanese government began to take some steps to attack these problems. In June, supervisory authority over financial institutions was taken away from the Ministry of Finance and transferred to the Financial Supervisory Agency (FSA), which reports directly to the prime minister. This was the first instance in half a century in which the all-powerful Ministry of Finance was stripped of some of its authority. In October, the parliament passed a bailout package of 60 trillion yen ($500 billion). Immediately after the 1998 banking law was passed, one of the ailing city banks, Long-Term Credit Bank of Japan, was taken over by the government and declared insolvent. In December 1998, the Nippon Credit Bank was finally put out of its misery and closed down by the government. After this event, the cleanup process stalled. Disbursement of the funds depended on the voluntary cooperation of the banks: The law did not require insolvent banks to close or to accept the funds. Indeed, acceptance of the funds required the bailed-out bank to open its books and reveal its true losses, and thus many banks remained very undercapitalized. Burdened with bad loans and poor profitability, the banking sector in Japan thus remained in very poor shape. Indeed, many private sector analysts estimate that bad loans peaked at a level of more than $1 trillion. Japan's weak economy, averaging an anemic 1% growth rate over the period 1991 to 2002, contributed to weakness in its banking sector.

Finally, progress started to be made. A new, reform-oriented prime minister, Junichiro Koizumi, who pledged to clean up the banking system, came into office in 2001. Nevertheless, the Japanese government was slow to come to grips with the banking problems; indeed, the amount of nonperforming loans was still estimated to exceed $1 trillion in 2003. That year, the country's fifth-largest bank, Resona, was kept afloat only with a 23 trillion yen ($17 billion) bailout, and a large regional bank, Ashigara, was declared insolvent and nationalized. With the pickup of the Japanese economy in 2003, however, the number of bad loans in Japanese banks finally began to decline. These are no longer a problem, at least for Japan's largest banks. These banks also have paid back most of the government money lent to keep them afloat. The crisis now seems to be over, and Japan's banks are shifting their focus from mere survival to a return to profitability.

China

Despite its rapid economic growth (nearly 10% per year), China has also had a severe banking problem. Estimates of nonperforming loans are currently around $500 billion. In 1998, the Chinese government injected $30 billion into the country's four largest banks (the "Big Four"), all state-owned—Industrial and Commercial Bank of China, Agricultural Bank of China, Bank of China, and China Reconstruction Bank—with another $170 billion injection in 2000–2001. In 2004, the Chinese government entered into its third bailout, handing out a capital injection of more than $100 billion (which is expected to grow to as much as $200 billion).

The state-owned banks have gotten into trouble because they have lent massively to unprofitable state-owned enterprises and are notoriously inefficient: The Big Four have more than one million employees and more than 100,000 branches. The government hopes that its third try at a bailout will be a charm, and is attempting to handle this one differently. The new bailout is part of a plan to prepare the Big Four to become partially privatized by having them issue shares overseas. These banks are being encouraged to speed up their disposal of nonperforming loans, to close unprofitable branches, and to lay off unproductive employees. The Chinese government is aware that it needs to reform the banking sector so that capital can be allocated to private borrowers with good investment opportunities rather than to inefficient state-owned enterprises, but this is a daunting task. How successful the Chinese government will be in this endeavor remains far from clear.

East Asia

We discussed the banking and financial crisis in the East Asian countries (Thailand, Malaysia, Indonesia, the Philippines, and South Korea) in Chapter 15. Due to inadequate supervision of the banking system, the lending booms that arose in the aftermath of financial liberalization led to substantial loan losses, which became huge after the currency collapses that occurred in the summer of 1997. An estimated 15% to 35% of all bank loans turned sour in Thailand, Indonesia, Malaysia, and South Korea, and the cost of the bailout for the banking system was more than 15% of GDP in these countries and more than 50% of GDP in Indonesia. The Philippines fared somewhat better, with the cost being 13% of GDP.

"Déjà Vu All Over Again"

What we see in banking crises in these different countries is that history keeps repeating itself. The parallels between the banking crisis episodes in all these countries are remarkably similar, leaving us with a feeling of déjà vu. Although financial liberalization is generally a good thing because it promotes competition and can make a financial system more efficient, as we have seen in the countries examined here, it can lead to an increase in moral hazard, with more risk taking on the part of banks if there is lax regulation and supervision; the result can then be banking crises. However, these episodes do differ in that deposit insurance has not played an important role in many of the countries experiencing banking crises. For example, the size of the Japanese equivalent of the FDIC, the Deposit Insurance Corporation, was so tiny relative to the FDIC that it did not play a prominent role in the banking system and exhausted its resources almost immediately with the first bank failures. This means that deposit insurance is not to blame for some of these banking crises. However, what is common to all the countries discussed here is the existence of a government safety net, in which the government stands ready to bail out banks whether deposit insurance is an important feature of the regulatory environment or not. It is the existence of a government safety net, and not deposit insurance per se, that increases moral hazard incentives for excessive risk taking on the part of banks.

SUMMARY

1. The concepts of asymmetric information, adverse selection, and moral hazard help explain the eight types of banking regulation that we see in the United States and other countries: the government safety net, restrictions on bank asset holdings, capital requirements, chartering and bank examination assessment of risk management, disclosure requirements, consumer protection, and restrictions on competition.

2. Because asymmetric information problems in the banking industry are a fact of life throughout the world, bank regulation in other countries is similar to that in the United States. It is particularly problematic to regulate banks engaged in international banking because they can readily shift their business from one country to another.

3. Because of financial innovation and deregulation, adverse selection and moral hazard problems increased

in the 1980s and resulted in a banking crisis in the United States.

4. The Federal Deposit Insurance Corporation Improvement Act (FDICIA) of 1991 recapitalized the Bank Insurance Fund of the FDIC and included reforms for the deposit insurance and regulatory system so that taxpayer losses would be minimized. This legislation limited the use of the too-big-to-fail policy, mandated prompt corrective action to deal with troubled banks, and instituted risk-based deposit insurance premiums. These provisions have helped reduce the incentives of banks to take on excessive risk and so should help reduce taxpayer exposure in the future.

5. The parallels between the banking crisis episodes that have occurred in other countries are striking, indicating that similar forces are at work.

KEY TERMS

bank supervision, *p. 518*
Basel Accord, *p. 516*
Basel Committee on Banking Supervision, *p. 516*
leverage ratio, *p. 516*

off-balance-sheet activities, *p. 516*
prudential supervision, *p. 518*
regulatory arbitrage, *p. 517*

QUESTIONS

1. Give one example each of moral hazard and adverse selection in private insurance arrangements.

2. If casualty insurance companies provided fire insurance without any restrictions, what kind of adverse selection and moral hazard problems might result?

3. What bank regulation is designed to reduce adverse selection problems for deposit insurance? Will it always work?

4. What bank regulations are designed to reduce moral hazard problems created by deposit insurance? Will they completely eliminate the moral hazard problem?

5. What are the costs and benefits of a too-big-to-fail policy?

6. What special problem do off-balance-sheet activities present to bank regulators, and what have they done about it?

7. Why does imposing bank capital requirements on banks help limit risk taking?

8. What forms does bank supervision take, and how does it help promote a safe and sound banking system?

9. What steps were taken in the FDICIA legislation of 1991 to improve the functioning of federal deposit insurance?

10. Why has the trend in bank supervision moved away from a focus on capital requirements to a focus on risk management?

11. How do disclosure requirements help limit excessive risk taking by banks?

12. Do you think that eliminating or limiting the amount of deposit insurance would be a good idea? Explain your answer.

13. Do you think that removing the impediments to a nationwide banking system will be beneficial to the economy? Explain.

14. How could higher deposit insurance premiums for banks with riskier assets benefit the economy?

15. How could market-value accounting for bank capital requirements (discussed in the Web appendix to this chapter) benefit the economy? How difficult would it be to implement?

QUANTITATIVE PROBLEMS

1. Consider a failing bank. A deposit of $150,000 is worth how much if the FDIC uses the *payoff* method? The *purchase and assumption* method? Which is more costly to taxpayers?

2. Consider a bank with the following balance sheet:

Assets		Liabilities	
Required		Checkable	
Reserves	$8 million	Deposits	$100 million
Excess		Bank Capital	$6 million
Reserves	$3 million		
T-bills	$45 million		
Mortgages	$40 million		
Commercial			
Loans	$10 million		

Calculate the bank's risk-weighted assets.

3. Consider a bank with the following balance sheet:

Assets		Liabilities	
Required		Checkable	
Reserves	$8 million	Deposits	$100 million
Excess		Bank Capital	$6 million
Reserves	$3 million		
T-bills	$45 million		
Commercial			
Loans	$50 million		

The bank commits to a loan agreement for $10 million to a commercial customer. Calculate the bank's capital ratio before and after the agreement. Calculate the bank's risk-weighted assets before and after the agreement.

Problems 4 through 11 relate to a sequence of transactions at Oldhat Financial.

4. Oldhat Financial started its first day of operations with $9 million in capital. $130 million in checkable deposits are received. The bank issues a $25 million commercial loan and another $50 million in mortgages, with the following terms:

   • Mortgages: 200 standard 30-year, fixed-rate with a nominal annual rate of 5.25% each for $250,000.

   • Commercial loan: Three-year loan, simple interest paid monthly at 0.75% per month.

   If required reserves are 8%, what does the bank balance sheet look like? Ignore any loan loss reserves. How well capitalized is the bank?

5. Calculate the risk-weighted assets and risk-weighted capital ratio after Oldhat's first day.

6. The next day, terrible news hits the mortgage markets, and mortgage rates jump to 13%. What is the market value of Oldhat's mortgages? What is Oldhat's "market value" capital ratio?

7. Bank regulators force Oldhat to sell its mortgages to recognize the fair market value. What is the accounting transaction? How does this affect its capital position?

8. Congress allowed Oldhat to amortize the loss over the remaining life of the mortgage. If this technique was used in the sale, how would the transaction have been recorded? What would be the annual adjustment? What does Oldhat's balance sheet look like? What is the capital ratio?

9. Oldhat decides to invest the $77 million in excess reserves in commercial loans. What will be the impact on its capital ratio? Its risk-weighted capital ratio?

10. The bad news about the mortgages is featured in the local newspaper, causing a minor bank run. $6 million in deposits is withdrawn. Examine the bank's condition after this occurs.

11. Oldhat borrows $5.5 million in the overnight federal funds market to meet its resources requirement. What is the new balance sheet for Oldhat? How well capitalized is the bank?

Banking Regulation

1. Go to **www.fdic.gov/regulations/laws/important/index.html**. This site reports on the most significant pieces of legislation affecting banks since the 1800s. Summarize the most recently enacted bank regulation listed on this site.

2. The Office of the Comptroller of the Currency is responsible for many of the regulations affecting bank operations. Go to **www.occ.treas.gov/**. Click on "Law and Regulations" in the far right column under Legal & Licensing. Now click on the 12 CFR Parts 1 to 199. What does Part 1 cover? How many parts are there in 12 CFR? Open Part 18. What topic does it cover? Summarize its purpose.

WEB APPENDICES

Please visit our Web site at **www.prenhall.com/mishkin_eakins** to read the Web appendix to Chapter 20:

• **Appendix:** Evaluating FDICIA and Other Proposed Reforms of the Banking Regulatory System

The Mutual Fund Industry

Preview

Suppose that you decide that you want to begin investing for retirement. You would probably want to hold some money in a diversified portfolio of stocks. You might want to put some money in bonds. You might even want to hold stock in some foreign companies. Now suppose your budget will only let you invest $25 per week. How are you going to build this retirement fund? You will probably not want to buy individual stocks, and with only $25 to spend at a time, you will not be able to buy bonds. The solution to your problem is to invest in mutual funds.

Mutual funds pool the resources of many small investors by selling them shares in the fund and use the proceeds to buy securities. Through the asset transformation process of issuing shares in small denominations and buying large blocks of securities, mutual funds can take advantage of volume discounts on brokerage commissions and can purchase diversified portfolios of securities. Mutual funds allow small investors to obtain the benefits of lower transaction costs in purchasing securities and to take advantage of a reduction in risk by diversifying their portfolios.

In this chapter we will study why mutual funds have become so popular in recent years, the types of mutual funds, how mutual funds are regulated, and finally, how conflicts of interest in the mutual fund industry have led to many scandals, fines, and indictments since 2001.

The Growth of Mutual Funds

Mutual funds have become the investment vehicle of choice for many investors. At the beginning of 2007, nearly 16% of all assets in intermediaries were held by mutual funds. Twenty-five percent of the entire retirement market was

go online

The mutual fund fact book found at www.ici.org/stats/latest/2007_factbook.pdf provides extensive statistics on the mutual fund industry.

invested in mutual funds by the beginning of 2007, and almost 50% of all U.S. households held stock in them. Given the pervasive nature of those intermediaries, we should wonder exactly what service they provide that has caused them to grow from $292 billion in assets to more than $10 trillion in assets over just the last 20 years.

The First Mutual Funds

The origins of mutual funds can be traced back to the mid to late 1800s in England and Scotland. Investment companies were formed that pooled the funds of investors with modest resources and used the money to invest in a number of different securities. These investment companies became more popular when they began investing in the economic growth of the United States, mostly by purchasing American railroad bonds.

The first fund in which new shares were issued as new money was invested—the dominant structure seen today—was introduced in Boston in 1824. This fund allowed for continuous offering of shares, the ability to cash out of the fund at any time, and a set of restrictions on investments aimed at protecting investors from losses.

The stock market crash of 1929 set mutual fund growth back for several decades because small investors distrusted stock investments generally and mutual funds in particular. The Investment Company Act of 1940, which required much more disclosure of fees and investment policies, reinvigorated the industry, and mutual funds began a steady growth.

Benefits of Mutual Funds

There are five principal benefits that attract investors to mutual funds:

1. Liquidity intermediation
2. Denomination intermediation
3. Diversification
4. Cost advantages
5. Managerial expertise

Liquidity intermediation means that investors can convert their investments into cash quickly and at a low cost. If you buy a CD or a bond, there can be early redemption penalties or transaction fees imposed if you need your funds before the securities mature. Additionally, if you bought a $10,000 CD, you must redeem the whole security even if you only require $5,000 to meet your current needs. Mutual funds allow investors to buy and redeem at any time and in any amount. Some funds are designed especially to meet short-term transaction requirements and have no fees associated with redemption, whereas others are designed for longer-term investment and may have redemption fees if they are held only a short time.

Denomination intermediation allows small investors access to securities they would be unable to purchase without the mutual fund. For example, in Chapter 9 we learned that most money market securities are only available in large denominations, often in excess of $100,000. By pooling money, the mutual fund can purchase these securities on behalf of investors.

Diversification is an important advantage to investing in mutual funds. As we learned in Chapter 4, your risk can be lowered by holding a portfolio of diversified securities rather than a limited number. Small investors buying stocks individually may find it difficult to acquire enough securities in enough different industries to capture this benefit. Additionally, mutual funds provide a low-cost way to diversify into foreign stocks. It can be difficult and expensive to invest in a foreign security not listed on U.S. exchanges. The net assets in world equity funds totaled $1.35 trillion in 2007, representing over 13% of all U.S. mutual fund investments.

Significant *cost advantages* may accrue to mutual fund investors. Institutional investors negotiate much lower transaction fees than are available to individual investors. Additionally, large block trades of 100,000 shares or more trade according to a different fee structure than do smaller trades. By buying securities through a mutual fund, investors can share in these lower fees.

One of the main features that has driven mutual fund growth has been access to *managerial expertise*. Despite the fact that research discussed in Chapter 6 has consistently demonstrated that mutual funds do not outperform a random pick from the market, many investors prefer to rely on professional money managers to select their stocks. The failure of mutual funds to post greater-than-average returns should not come as a surprise given our discussion of market efficiency. Still, the financial markets remain something of a mystery to a large number of investors. These investors are willing to pay fees to let someone else choose their stocks.

The increase in the number of defined-contribution pension plans has also been a factor in mutual fund growth. In the past, most pension plans either invested on behalf of the employee and guaranteed a return or required employees to invest in company stock. Now, most new pension plans require the employee to invest his or her own pension dollars. With pension investments being made every payday, the mutual fund provides the perfect pension conduit. Currently, over 22% of all pension dollars are invested in mutual funds. This amount is likely to grow as more pension plans convert to the defined-contribution structure.

Table 21.1 shows the total net assets, number of funds, and number of mutual funds accounts since 1970. There are currently over 8,700 separate mutual funds for investors to choose from. It is interesting to note that this means there are more separate mutual funds than there are stocks trading on the New York, American, and NASDAQ stock exchanges combined.

In 33 years the amount invested in mutual funds has increased from $47 billion to over $10.4 trillion. To put this figure in perspective, this is about the same as the total assets of all commercial banks in the United States at the beginning of 2004.

Ownership of Mutual Funds

An estimated 54.9 million, or 48%, of households own mutual funds. By the beginning of 2007, 80% of mutual fund shares were owned by households, with the rest held by fiduciaries and other business organizations. This represents a tremendous increase since 1980, when only 5.7% of households held mutual fund shares (see Figure 21.1). The median mutual fund investor is middle class, 48 years old, married, employed, and possesses financial assets of $125,000. About 25% are retired, and fully 92% cite preparing for retirement as one of their main reasons for holding shares.

Mutual funds accounted for $4.1 trillion, or 25%, of the $16.4 trillion U.S. retirement market at the beginning of 2007. This represents 39% of all mutual fund assets.

Deposits into retirement mutual funds come from two sources: employer-sponsored defined-contribution plans, especially 401(k) plans, and individual retirement accounts (IRAs). Figure 21.2 shows the average asset allocation of all 401(k) mutual fund accounts. The bulk of retirement assets are in equity funds, followed by guaranteed investment contracts, bond funds, and company stock.

TABLE 21.1 Total Industry Net Assets, Number of Funds, and Number of Shareholder Accounts

Year	Net Assets (millions)	Number of Funds	Number of Accounts (thousands)
1970	47,618	361	10,690
1971	55,045	392	10,901
1972	59,830	410	10,635
1973	46,518	421	10,330
1974	35,776	431	10,074
1975	45,874	426	9,876
1976	51,276	452	9,060
1977	48,936	477	8,692
1978	55,837	505	8,658
1979	94,511	524	9,790
1980	134,760	564	12,087
1981	241,365	665	17,499
1982	296,678	857	21,448
1983	292,985	1,026	24,604
1984	370,680	1,241	28,268
1985	495,385	1,527	34,762
1986	715,667	1,835	46,012
1987	769,171	2,312	54,421
1988	809,370	2,708	54,676
1989	980,671	2,900	58,135
1990	1,065,194	3,081	61,948
1991	1,393,189	3,405	68,334
1992	1,642,543	3,826	79,932
1993	2,070,023	4,538	93,217
1994	2,155,396	5,330	114,388
1995	2,811,484	5,728	131,231
1996	3,526,270	6,254	150,176
1997	4,468,200	6,684	170,521
1998	5,525,209	7,314	193,854
1999	6,846,339	7,791	226,872
2000	6,965,249	8,171	243,518
2001	6,974,950	8,305	248,809
2002	6,390,360	8,244	251,224
2003	7,414,080	8,126	260,650
2004	8,107,000	8,420	269,468
2005	8,905,000	8,454	275,479
2006	10,414,000	8,726	289,971

Source: Investment Company Institute, *2007 Mutual Fund Fact Book,* 47th ed. (Washington, DC: ICI), p. 105. www.icifactbook.org/index.html.

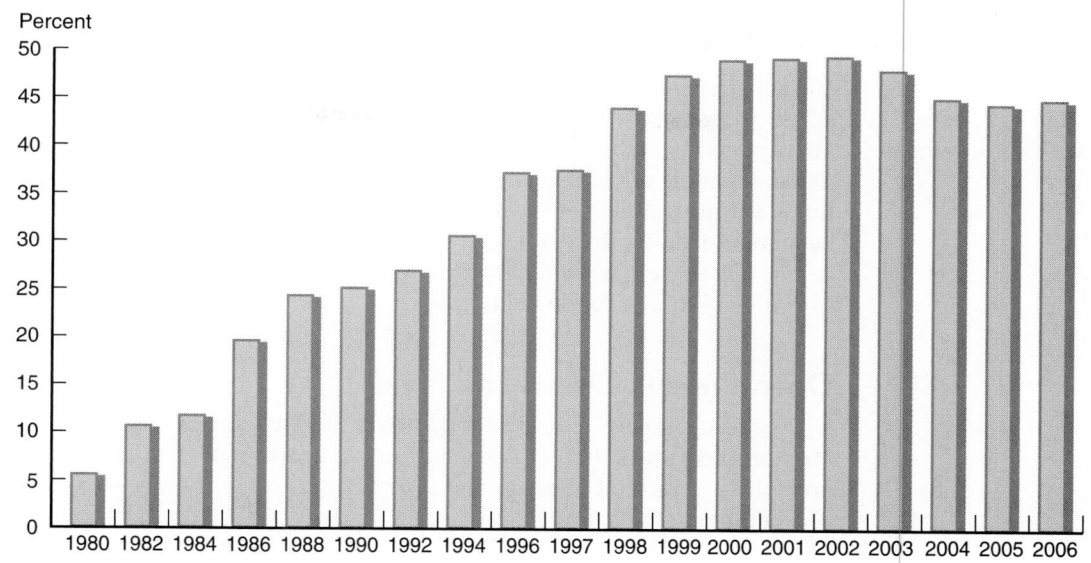

Figure 21.1 Household Ownership of Mutual Funds, 1980–2006

Source: Investment Company Institute, *2007 Mutual Fund Fact Book,* 47th ed. (Washington, DC: ICI), p. 105. www.icifactbook.org/index.html.

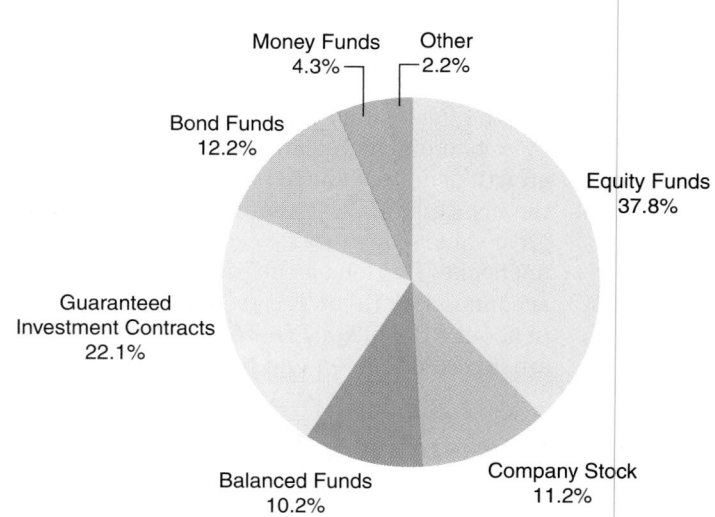

Figure 21.2 Average Asset Allocation for All 401(k) Plan Balances

Source: Investment Company Institute, *2007 Mutual Fund Fact Book,* 47th ed. (Washington, DC: ICI), p. 105. www.icifactbook.org/index.html.

Mutual Fund Structure

Mutual fund companies frequently offer a number of separate mutual funds. They are called *complexes* and are defined as a group of funds under substantially common management, composed of one or more families of funds. The advantage to investors of fund complexes is that investments can usually be transferred among different funds within a family very easily and quickly. Additionally, account information can be summarized by the complex to help investors keep their assets organized.

In this section we will look at how mutual funds are structured and at the types of investments the funds hold.

Open- Versus Closed-End Funds

Mutual funds are structured in two ways. The first funds were what are now called **closed-end funds.** In a closed-end fund, a fixed number of nonredeemable shares are sold at an initial offering and are then traded in the over-the-counter market like common stock. The market price of these shares fluctuates with the value of the assets held by the funds. The market value of the shares may be above or below the value of the assets held by the fund, depending on the market's assessment of how likely managers are to pick stocks that will increase fund value.

The problem with closed-end funds is that once shares have been sold, the fund cannot take in any more investment dollars. Thus, to grow the fund managers must start a whole new fund. The advantage of closed-end funds to managers is that investors cannot make withdrawals. The only way investors have of getting money out of their investment in the fund is to sell shares.

Today, the closed-end fund has been largely replaced with the **open-end fund.** Investors can contribute to an open-end fund at any time. The fund simply increases the number of shares outstanding. Another feature of open-end funds is that the fund agrees to buy back shares from investors at any time. Each day the fund net asset value is computed based on the number of shares outstanding and the net assets of the fund. All shares bought and sold that day are traded at the same net asset value. See the Case for a complete discussion of computing the net asset value.

Open-end mutual funds have a couple of advantages that have contributed to the growth of mutual funds. First, because the fund agrees to redeem shares at any time, the investment is very liquid. As discussed earlier, this liquidity intermediation has great value to investors. Second, the open-end structure allows mutual funds to grow unchecked. As long as investors want to put money into the fund, it can expand to accommodate them. For example, the Vanguard S&P 500 index fund has holdings of about $123 billion. These advantages explain why 97% of all mutual fund dollars are invested in open-end funds.

Organizational Structure

Regardless of whether a fund is organized as a closed- or an open-end fund, it will have the same basic organizational structure. The investors in the fund are the shareholders. In the same way that shareholders of corporations receive the residual income of a company, the shareholders of a mutual fund receive the earnings, after expenses, of the mutual fund.

The board of directors oversees the fund's activities and sets policy. They are also responsible for appointing the investment advisor, usually a separate company, to manage the portfolio of investments and a principal underwriter, who sells the fund shares. SEC regulation requires that a majority of the directors be independent of the mutual fund.

The investment advisers manage the fund in accordance with the fund's stated objectives and policies. The investment advisors actually pick the securities that will be held by the fund and make both buy and sell decisions. It is their expertise that determines the success of the fund.

CASE

Calculating a Mutual Fund's Net Asset Value

If you invest in a mutual fund, you will receive periodic statements summarizing the activity in your account. The statement will show funds that were added to your investment balance, funds that were withdrawn, and any earnings that have accrued. One term on the statement that is critical to understanding the investment's performance is the **net asset value (NAV).** The net asset value is the total value of the mutual fund's stocks, bonds, cash, and other assets minus any liabilities such as accrued fees, divided by the number of shares outstanding. An example will make this clear.

Suppose that a mutual fund has the following assets and liabilities:

Stock (at current market value)	$20,000,000
Bonds (at current market value)	$10,000,000
Cash	$ 500,000
Total value of assets	$30,500,000
Liabilities	−$ 300,000
Net worth	$30,200,000

The net asset value is computed by dividing the net worth by the number of shares outstanding. If 10 million shares are outstanding, the net asset value is $3.02 ($30,200,000/10,000,000 = $3.02).

The net asset value rises and falls as the value of the underlying assets changes. For example, suppose that the value of the stock portfolio held by the mutual fund rises by 10% and the value of the bond portfolio falls by 2% over the course of a year. If the cash and liabilities are unchanged, the new net asset value will be

Stock (at current market value)	$22,000,000
Bonds (at current market value)	$9,800,000
Cash	$ 500,000
Total value of assets	$32,300,000
Liabilities	−$ 300,000
Net worth	$32,000,000

$$\text{NAV} = \frac{\$32,000,000}{10,000,000} = \$3.20$$

The yield on your investment in the mutual fund is then

$$\text{Yield} = \frac{\$3.20 - \$3.02}{\$3.02} = \frac{\$0.18}{\$3.02} = 5.96\%$$

When you buy and sell shares in the mutual fund, you do so at the current NAV.

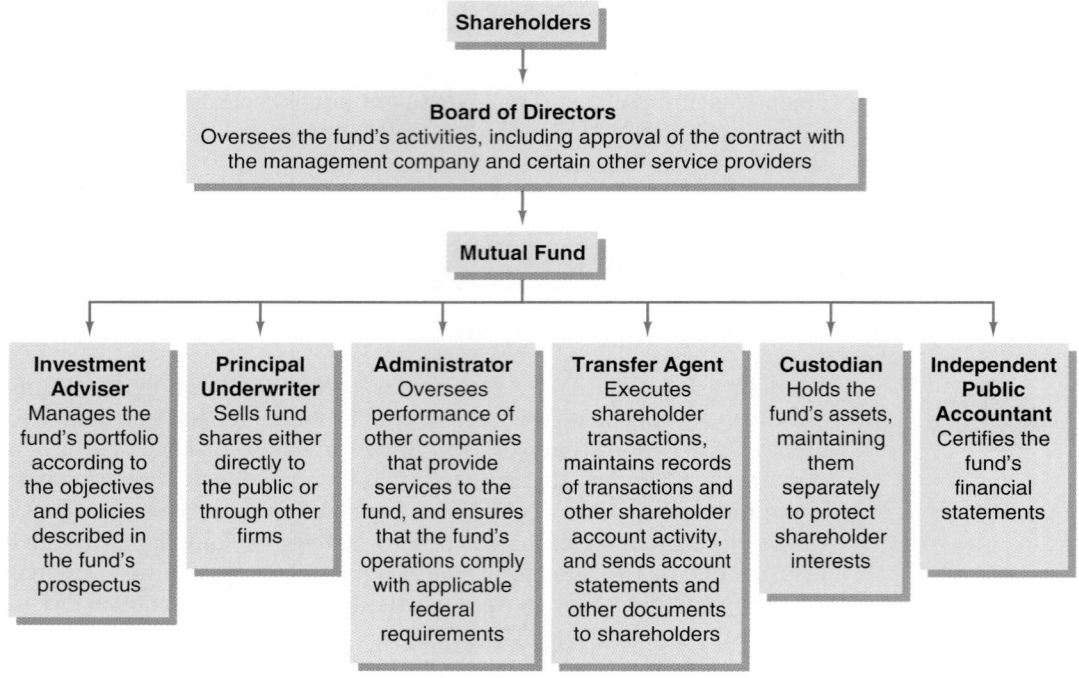

Figure 21.3 The Organizational Structure of a Mutual Fund

Source: Investment Company Institute, www.ici.org.

In addition to the investment advisors, the fund will contract with other firms to provide additional services. These will include underwriters, transfer agents, and custodians. Contracts will also be arranged with an independent public accountant. Large funds may arrange for some of these functions to be done in-house, whereas other funds will use all outside companies. Figure 21.3 shows the organizational structure of a mutual fund.

Investment Objective Classes

Four primary classes of mutual funds are available to investors. They are (1) stock funds (also called equity funds), (2) bond funds, (3) hybrid funds, and (4) money market funds. Figure 21.4 shows the distribution of assets among these types of funds at the beginning of 2007. The largest class is the equity funds, followed by the money market, bond, and hybrid funds.

Equity Funds

Equity funds share a common theme in that they all invest in stock. After that, they can have very different objectives. The three classes reported by the Investment Company Institute are capital appreciation funds, world funds, and total return funds. Capital appreciation funds are the largest, with about 25% of all mutual fund assets.

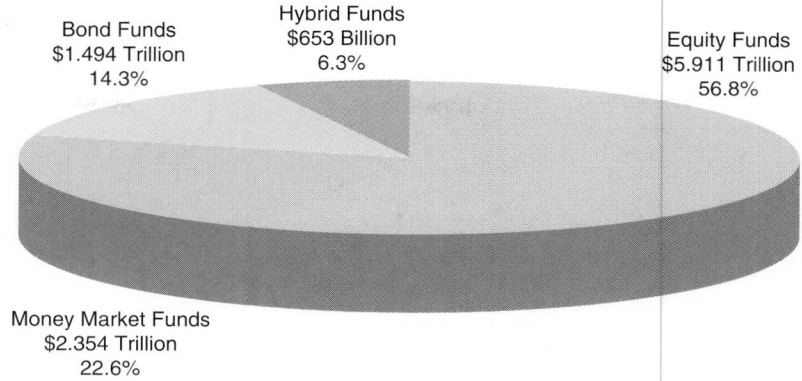

Figure 21.4 Distribution of Assets Among Types of Mutual Funds, 2007

Source: Investment Company Institute, *2007 Mutual Fund Fact Book,* 47th ed. (Washington, DC: ICI), p. 105. www.icifactbook.org/index.html.

These funds seek rapid capital appreciation (increases in share prices) and are not concerned with dividends. Many of these funds are relatively risky in that the fund managers are attempting to select companies incurring rapid growth. For example, many capital appreciation mutual funds invested heavily in high technology and Internet stocks during the 1990s.

Total return funds represent about 19% of total mutual fund assets. The goal of these funds is to seek a combination of current income and capital appreciation. They will include both mature firms that are paying dividends and growth companies that are expected to post large stock price increases. Total return funds are expected to be less risky than capital appreciation funds since they will include more large established firms. This was borne out in 2000 when capital appreciation funds lost 16.5% of their assets and total return funds only lost 5.7%.

World equity funds invest primarily in stocks of foreign companies. These funds allow investors easy access to international diversification. Many financial planners recommend that investors hold at least a small portion of their investments in foreign stocks. These world funds provide the primary vehicle.

The three types of equity funds presented here oversimplify the range of stock mutual funds available to investors. For example, the Vanguard family of mutual funds offers 62 different stock funds. Each one differs in its stated goals. Some hold stock from specific industries; others hold stock with certain historical growth rates. Others are chosen by their PE ratio. Mutual fund companies try to offer a fund that will appeal to every investor's needs.

Bond Funds

Figure 21.5 shows the major types of bond funds tracked by the Investment Company Institute. Strategic income bonds are the most popular and invest in a combination of U.S. corporate bonds to provide a high level of current income. The quality of the bonds in these funds will often be lower than in some other classes, but their yields will be higher. Investors are trading safety for greater returns. Corporate bond funds, the next most popular fund type, invest primarily in high-grade corporate bonds.

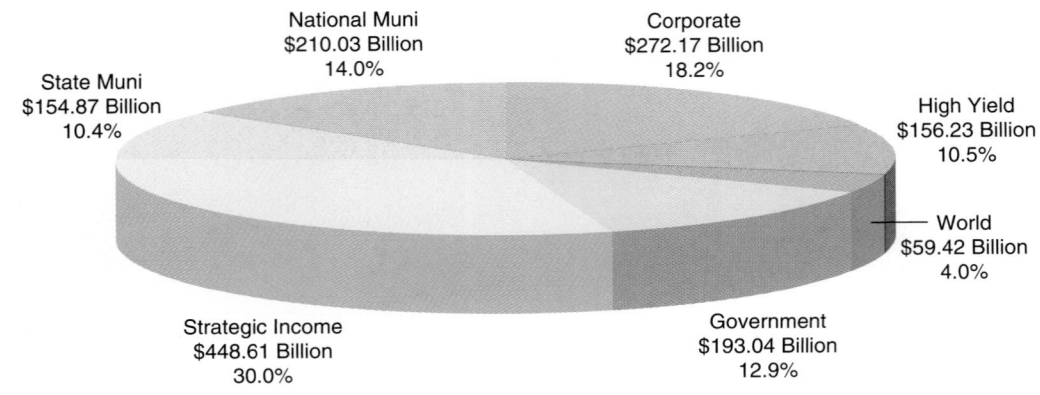

Figure 21.5 Assets Invested in Different Types of Bond Mutual Funds

Source: Investment Company Institute, *2007 Mutual Fund Fact Book,* 47th ed. (Washington, DC: ICI), p. 105. www.icifactbook.org/index.html.

Government bonds are also popular. These are essentially default risk free, but will have relatively low returns. The state and national municipal (muni) bonds are tax free.

Bonds are not as risky as stocks, and so it is not usually as important that investors diversify across a large number of different bonds. Additionally, it is relatively easy to buy and sell bonds through the secondary market. As a result, it is not surprising that bond mutual funds hold only about a fourth of the assets held by stock mutual funds. Still, many investors value the liquidity intervention and automatic reinvestment features provided by bond mutual funds.

Hybrid Funds

Hybrid funds combine stocks and bonds into one fund. The idea is to provide an investment that diversifies across different types of securities as well as across different issuers of a particular type of security. Thus, if an investor found a hybrid fund that held the percentage of stocks and bonds he wanted, he could own just one fund instead of several. Despite this apparent convenience, most investors still prefer to choose separate funds. Only about 6% of all mutual fund accounts are hybrid accounts.

Money Market Funds

Money market mutual funds (MMMFs) have existed since the early 1970s; however, the low market interest rates before 1977 (which were either below or just slightly above the Regulation Q ceiling of 5.25% to 5.5%) kept them from being particularly advantageous relative to bank deposits. In 1978, Merrill Lynch recognized that it could provide better service to its customers if it offered an account that customers could use to warehouse money. Prior to the introduction of MMMFs as a small-investor account, customers had to bring in checks to the brokerage house when they wanted to invest and had to pick up checks when they sold securities. Customers who had MMMF accounts, however, could simply direct the broker to take funds out of this

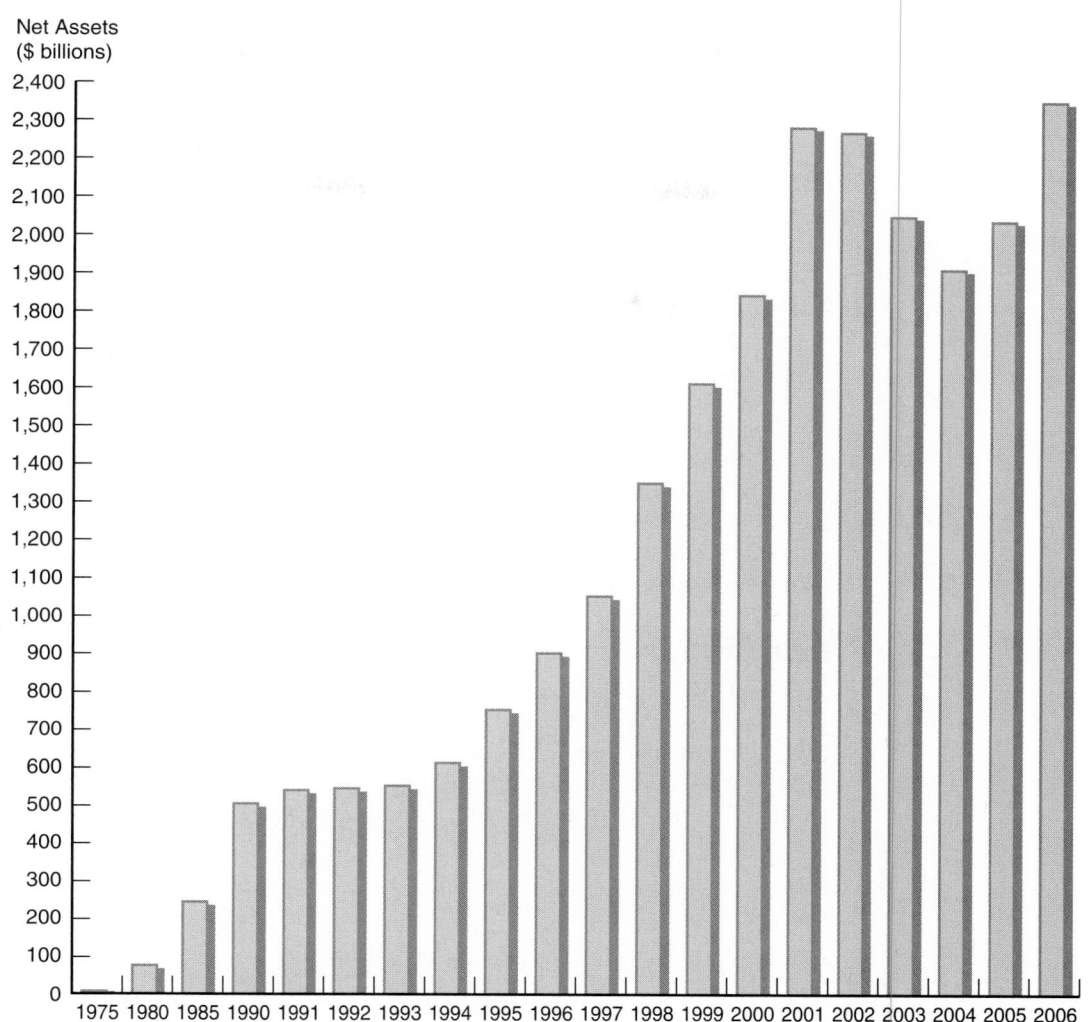

Net Assets
($ billions)

Figure 21.6   Net Assets of Money Market Mutual Funds, 1975–2006

Source: Investment Company Institute, *2007 Mutual Fund Fact Book,* 47th ed. (Washington, DC: ICI), p. 105.
www.icifactbook.org/index.html.

go online

The most recent statistics on the net assets of money market mutual funds can be found at **www.ici.org/stats/index.html** by clicking on "Mutual Fund Statistics" and then on Money Market Mutual Fund Assets for the most current date.

account to buy stocks or to deposit funds in this account when they sold securities. Initially, Merrill Lynch did not look on the MMMF as a major source of income.

In the early 1980s, inflation and interest rates skyrocketed. Regulation Q restricted banks from paying more than 5.25% in interest on savings accounts. With interest rates in the money markets exceeding 15%, investors flocked to MMMFs. Figure 21.6 shows the growth of MMMFs since 1975.

All MMMFs are open-end investment funds that invest only in money market securities. Most funds do not charge investors any fee for purchasing or redeeming shares. The funds usually have a minimum initial investment of $500 to $2,000. The funds' yields depend entirely on the performance of the securities purchased.

An important feature of MMMFs is that many have check-writing privileges. They often do not charge a fee for writing checks or have any minimum check amount as long as the balance in the account is above the stated level. This convenience, along with market interest rates, makes the accounts very popular with small investors.

Investors often take their money out of federally insured banks and thrifts and put it into uninsured MMMFs. An important question is why they are so willing to take this extra level of risk. The reason is that the extra risk is really very small. The money invested in MMMFs is in turn invested in money market instruments. Commercial paper is by far the largest component of these funds, followed by U.S. Treasury securities and repurchase agreements. Figure 21.7 shows the distribution of money market fund assets. Because the risk of default on these securities is very low, the risk of MMMFs is very low. Investors recognize this and so are willing to abandon the safety of banks for higher returns.

Legislation in 1980 and 1982 removed most of the restrictions on bank interest-rate ceilings. These changes were aimed at reducing the flow of funds out of banks and into brokerage houses. Currently, investors earn 0.5% to 1% higher return by investing in MMMFs than by putting their money in banks. While MMMFs are still very popular, the low interest rates in recent years have slowed their growth. Any significant increase in short-term rates would likely reverse this trend.

Index Funds

A special kind of mutual fund that does not fit any of the classes discussed previously, yet which represents an alternative investment style, is the index fund. Traditional funds employ investment managers who select stocks and bonds for the fund's portfolio. If we believe the lessons about market efficiency discussed in Chapter 6, we would conclude that investment managers are not likely to pick stocks any better

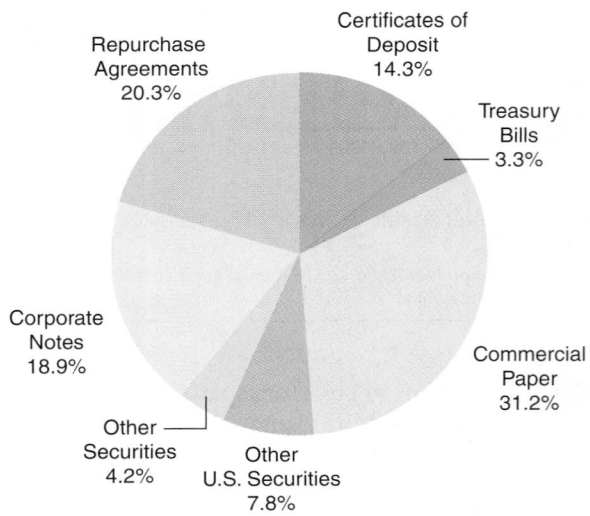

Figure 21.7 Average Distribution of Money Market Fund Assets, 2007

Source: Investment Company Institute, *2007 Mutual Fund Fact Book*, 47th ed. (Washington, DC: ICI), p. 105. www.icifactbook.org/index.html.

than could a dart thrown at the stock pages of the *Wall Street Journal*. If investment managers are not superior stock pickers, then we might ask why one should pay them a fee to provide a service that may not have any marginal benefit.

Many investors want the benefits of mutual fund investing without the cost of paying for investment manager services. The answer is the index fund. An index fund contains the stocks in an index. For example, the mammoth Vanguard S&P 500 index fund contains the 500 stocks in that index. The stocks are held in a proportion such that changes to the fund value closely match changes to the index level. There are many other index funds available that mimic the behavior of various stock and bond indexes.

Index funds do not require managers to choose securities. As a result, these funds tend to have far lower fees than other actively managed funds. Some financial experts even argue that these funds will outperform most fund managers because they will ignore the fads, trends, emotions, and hysteria that often cloud investment adviser and individual investor judgment. In an interesting admission, the recently retired founder and former CEO of the Vanguard Group of mutual funds, John Bogle, stated he was an "index investor."[1]

Fee Structure of Investment Funds

Originally, most shares of mutual funds were sold by brokers who received a commission for their efforts. Because this commission was paid at the time of the purchase and immediately subtracted from the redemption value of the shares, these funds were called **load funds.** If the fee is charged when the funds are deposited, it is a front-end load. Most front-end loads are between 1% to 2%, but some exceed 6%. If a fee is charged when funds are taken out (usually a declining fee over five years), it is a **deferred load.** The primary purpose of loads is to provide compensation for sales brokers. An alternative motivation, especially for deferred-load funds, is to discourage early withdrawal of deposits.

Beginning in the 1980s, funds that did not charge a direct load (or fee) appeared. These are called **no-load funds.** Most no-load funds can be purchased directly by individual investors, and no middleman is required. Currently about 55% of equity funds and 65% of bond funds are no load. Many investors have realized that when the initial deposit is immediately reduced, it can take a long time to catch up to the returns offered by no-load funds. The shares of front-end loaded funds are termed Class A shares. Shares in deferred-load funds are termed Class B shares. Class C shares are issued for no-load funds.

Regardless whether a load is charged, all mutual fund accounts are subject to a variety of fees. One of the primary factors that an investor should consider before choosing a mutual fund is the level of fees the fund charges. The fees are taken out of portfolio income before it is passed on to the investor. Since the investor is not directly charged the fees, many will not realize that they have even been subtracted. The usual fees charged by mutual funds are the following:

- A *contingent deferred sales charge* imposed at the time of redemption is an alternative way to compensate financial professionals for their services. This fee typically applies for the first few years of ownership and then disappears.

---

[1]Keynote speech by John Bogle, founder and former CEO of the Vanguard Group, before the American Business Editors and Writers Personal Finance Workshop, Denver, Colorado, October 27, 2003.

- A *redemption fee* is a back-end charge for redeeming shares. It is expressed as a dollar amount or a percentage of the redemption price.
- An *exchange fee* may be charged when transferring money from one fund to another within the same fund family.
- An *account maintenance fee* is charged by some funds to maintain low balance accounts.
- *12b-1 fees*, if any, are deducted from the fund's assets to pay marketing and advertising expenses or, more commonly, to compensate sales professionals. By law, 12b-1 fees cannot exceed 1% of the fund's average net assets per year.

Clearly, there are many opportunities for mutual fund managers to charge investors for the right to invest. Investors should very carefully evaluate a mutual fund's fee structure before investing, since these fees can range from 0.25% to as much as 8% per year. No research supports the argument that investors get better returns by investing in funds that charge higher fees. On the contrary, most high-fee mutual funds fail to do as well, after expenses, as low-fee funds.

Over the last 20 years, competition within the mutual fund industry has produced substantially lower costs. Between 1980 and 2006, the average total shareholder cost of equity mutual funds decreased by more than 50%. The cost of bond funds dropped by 59%. One factor undoubtedly contributing to this reduction is the requirement by the SEC that mutual funds clearly disclose all fees and costs that investors will incur. The SEC further requires mutual funds to include in their prospectus a standardized sample account where $10,000 is invested for one, three, five, and ten years. The analysis shows investors exactly what fees they will be subject to if they choose the fund. The fee disclosure requirement makes it very easy for investors to compare funds, and therefore increases competition among them.

Regulation of Mutual Funds

Mutual funds are regulated under four federal laws designed to protect investors. The Securities Act of 1933 mandates that funds make certain disclosures. The Securities Exchange Act of 1934 set out antifraud rules covering the purchase and sale of fund shares. The Investment Company Act of 1940 requires all funds to register with the SEC and to meet certain operating standards. Finally, the Investment Advisers Act of 1940 regulates fund advisers.

As part of this government regulation, all funds must provide two types of documents free of charge: a prospectus and a shareholder report. A mutual fund's prospectus describes the fund's goals, fees and expenses, and investment strategies and risks; it also gives information on how to buy and sell shares. The SEC requires a fund to provide a full prospectus either before an investment or together with the confirmation statement of an initial investment.

Annual and semiannual shareholder reports discuss the fund's recent performance and include other important information, such as the fund's financial statements. By examining these reports, an investor can learn if a fund has been effective in meeting the goals and investment strategies described in the fund's prospectus.

In addition, investors are sent a yearly statement detailing the federal tax status of distributions received from the fund. Mutual fund shareholders are taxed on the fund's income directly, as if the shareholders held the underlying securities themselves. Similarly, any tax-exempt income received by a fund is generally passed on to the shareholders as tax-exempt.

Investment funds are run by brokerage houses and by institutional investors, who now control over 50% of the outstanding stock in the United States. Over 70% of the total daily volume in stocks is due to institutions initiating trades. Many of the mutual funds are run by brokerage houses; others are run by independent investment advisers. Because of the volume of stock controlled by these investors, there is tremendous competition for their business. This has led to significant cost cutting and to the proliferation of alternative methods of trading. For example, computerized trading that eliminates the broker from the transaction accounts for a growing percentage of the activity in stocks.

Mutual funds are the only companies in America that are required by law to have independent directors. The SEC believes that independent directors play a critical role in the governance of mutual funds. In January 2001, the SEC adopted substantive rule amendments designed to enhance the independence of investment company directors and provide investors with more information to assess directors' independence. These rules require that:

- Independent directors constitute at least a majority of the fund's board of directors,
- Independent directors select and nominate other independent directors, and
- Any legal counsel for the fund's independent directors be an independent legal counsel.

In addition, SEC rules require that mutual funds publish extensive information about directors, including their business experience and fund shares held. This system of overseeing the interests of mutual fund shareholders has helped the industry avoid systemic problems and contributed significantly to public confidence in mutual funds.

Hedge Funds

Hedge funds are a special type of mutual fund that have received considerable attention recently, due to the near collapse of Long Term Capital Management. In Chapter 24 we discuss how financial markets can use hedges to reduce risk in a wide variety of situations. These risk-reducing strategies should not be confused with hedge funds. Although hedge funds often attempt to be market-neutral, protected from changes in the overall market, they are not riskless.

To illustrate a typical type of transaction conducted by hedge funds, consider a trade made by Long Term Capital Management in 1994. The fund managers noted that $29\frac{1}{2}$-year U.S. Treasury bonds seemed cheap relative to 30-year Treasury securities. The managers figured that the value of the two bonds would converge over time. After all, these securities have nearly identical risk since the maturity risk difference between $29\frac{1}{2}$-year securities and 30-year securities is insignificant. To make money from the temporary divergence of the bond prices, the fund bought $2 billion of the $29\frac{1}{2}$-year bonds and sold short $2 billion of the 30-year bonds. (Selling short means that the fund borrowed bonds it did not own and sold them. Later the fund must cover its short position by buying the bonds back, hopefully at a lower price.) The net investment by Long Term Capital was $12 million. Six months later,

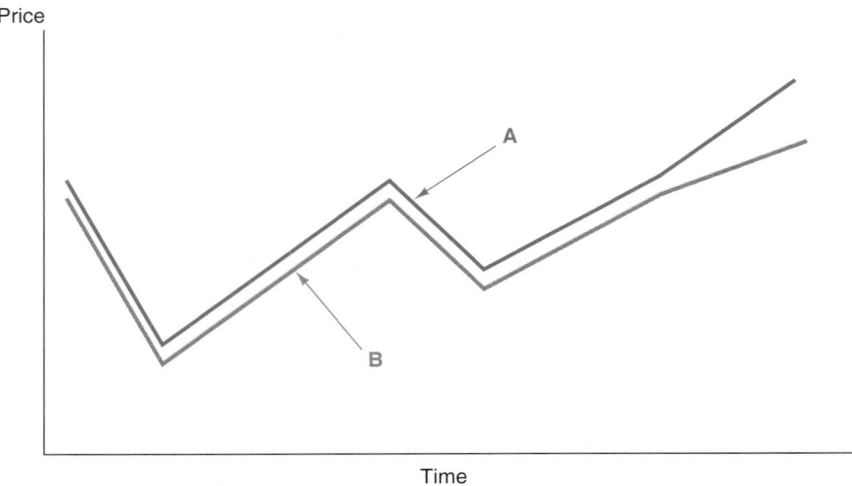

Figure 21.8 *The Price of Two Similar Securities*

Hedge funds search for related securities that historically move in lockstep but have temporarily diverted. In this example, the hedge fund would sell security A short and buy security B.

the fund covered its short position by buying 30-year bonds and sold its $29\frac{1}{2}$-year bonds. This transaction yielded a $25 million profit.[2]

In the transaction, the managers did not care whether the overall bond market rose or fell. In this sense, the transaction was market-neutral. All that was required for a profit was that the prices of the bonds converge, an event that occurred as predicted. Hedge fund managers scour the world in their search for pricing anomalies between related securities. Figure 21.8 shows a situation where hedge funds could invest. Securities A and B move in lockstep over time. At some point they diverge, creating an opportunity. The hedge fund would buy security B, because it is expected to increase relative to A, and would sell A short. The fund managers hope that the gain on security B will be greater than the loss on security A. At times, the search for opportunities leads hedge funds to adopt exotic approaches that are not easily available elsewhere, from investing in distressed securities to participating in venture-capital financing.

In addition to investing money contributed by individuals and institutions, hedge funds often set up lines of credit to use to leverage their investments. For instance, in our example, Long Term Capital earned $25 million on an investment of $12 million, a 108% return [($25 million − $12 million)/$12 million = 1.08 = 108%]. Suppose that half of the $12 million had been borrowed funds. Ignoring interest cost, the return on invested equity would then be 317% ($25 million − $6 million/$6 million = 3.17 = 317%). Long Term Capital advertised that it was leveraged 20 to 1; however, by the time of the crisis, the figure was actually closer to 50 to 1. The Mini-Case box discusses how Long Term Capital eventually required a private rescue plan to prevent its failure.

---

[2]*Wall Street Journal*, November 16, 1998, p. A18.

mini-case

The Long Term Capital Debacle

Long Term Capital Management was a hedge fund managed by a group that included two Nobel Prize winners and 25 other Ph.D.s. It made headlines in September 1998 because it required a private rescue plan organized by the Federal Reserve Bank of New York.

The experience of Long Term Capital Management demonstrates that hedge funds are not risk-free, despite their being market-neutral. Long Term Capital expected that the spread between long-term Treasury bonds and long-term corporate bonds would narrow. Many stock markets around the world plunged, causing a flight to quality. Investors bid up the price of Treasury securities while the price of corporate securities fell. This is exactly the opposite of what Long Term Capital Management had predicted. As losses mounted, Long Term Capital's lenders required that the fund increase its equity position.

By mid-September, the fund was unable to raise sufficient equity to meet the demands of its creditors. Faced with the potential collapse of the fund, together with its highly leveraged investment portfolio consisting of nearly $80 billion in equities and over $1 trillion of notional value in derivatives, the Federal Reserve stepped in to prevent the fund from failing. The Fed's rationale was that a sudden liquidation of the Long Term Capital Management portfolio

would create unacceptable systemic risk. Tens of billions of dollars worth of illiquid securities would be dumped on an already jittery market, causing potentially huge losses to numerous lenders and other institutions. A group consisting of banks and brokerage firms contributed $3.6 billion to a rescue plan that prevented the fund's failure.

The Fed's involvement in organizing the rescue of Long Term Capital is controversial, despite no public funds being expended. Some critics argue that the intervention increases moral hazard by weakening the discipline imposed by the market on fund managers. However, others say that the tremendous economic damage the fund's failure would have caused was unacceptable.

Hedge funds have continued to fail in the years since the Long Term Capital bailout. In September, 2006, Amaranth Advisors lost its bet on natural gas futures and dropped $6 billion in one week. This is currently the largest hedge fund collapse in history. Other funds have suffered significant losses for their investors, including Advanced Investment Management (lost $415 million), Bayou Management, LLC (lost $450 million) and Lipper Convertibles (lost $315 million). Hedge funds are a high risk game for well-heeled investors.

Hedge funds accumulate money from many people and invest on their behalf, but several features distinguish them from traditional mutual funds. First, hedge funds have a minimum investment requirement of between $100,000 and $20 million, with the typical minimum investment being $1 million. Long Term Capital Management required a $10 million minimum investment. Most hedge funds are set up as limited partnerships. Federal law limits hedge funds to no more than 99 limited partners with steady annual incomes of $200,000 or more or a net worth of $1 million, excluding their homes. Funds may have up to 499 limited partners if each has $5 million in invested assets. All of these restrictions are aimed at allowing hedge funds to exist largely unregulated, on the theory that the rich can look out for themselves. Many of the 4,000 funds are domiciled offshore to escape all regulatory restrictions.

Second, hedge funds are unique in that they usually require that investors commit their money for long periods of time, often several years. The purpose of this requirement is to give managers breathing room to attempt long-range strategies.

Hedge funds often charge large fees to investors. The typical fund charges a 1% annual asset management fee plus 20% of profits. Some charge significantly more. For example, Long Term Capital Management charged investors a 2% management fee and took 25% of profits.

Despite the argument that the wealthy do no need regulatory protection from the risk incurred by hedge fund investments, the SEC passed regulation in 2006 requiring that hedge fund advisers register. The SEC cited two concerns prompting the new move. First, they were concerned about the growing incidence of fraudulent conduct by hedge fund advisers. Second, they expressed concern that more investors were participating in hedge funds through "retailization," and that this justified increased oversight. By requiring advisers to register, the SEC can conduct on-site examinations. The SEC argues these examinations are necessary to protect the nation's securities market as well as hedge fund investors.

Conflicts of Interest in the Mutual Fund Industry

In Chapter 16 we discussed conflicts of interest in the financial industry. We concluded that many of the corporate governance breakdowns observed recently were due to the principal-agent relationship. This section extends that discussion to mutual funds, which have been subject to scandals, fines, and indictments. Several top mutual funds managers and CEOs have even been sentenced to jail time.

Investor confidence in the stability and integrity of the mutual fund industry is critical. A large portion of the population is now responsible for planning their own retirement, and most of these investments are being funneled into various funds. If these funds take advantage of investors or fail to provide the returns they should, people will find themselves unable to retire or having to scale back their retirement plans. No one argues that mutual funds can or should guarantee any specific return. They should, however, treat all investors equally and accurately disclose risk and fees. They must also follow the policies and rules they publish as governing the management of each fund.

Sources of Conflicts of Interest

Conflicts of interest arise when there is asymmetric information and the principal's and agent's interests are not closely aligned. The governance structure of mutual funds creates such a situation. Investors in a mutual fund are the shareholders. They elect directors, who are supposed to look out for their interest. The directors in turn select investment advisors, who actually run the mutual fund. However, given the large number of shareholders in the typical fund, there is a free-rider problem that prevents them from monitoring either the directors or the investment advisers.

Shareholders depend on directors to monitor investment advisors. Unfortunately, recent evidence demonstrates that directors' efforts have not been sufficient to prevent abuses. The incentive structure for compensating investment advisers does not assure that they will be motivated to maximize shareholder wealth. In the absence of monitoring, investment advisers will attempt to increase their own fees and income, even at the expense of shareholders. For example, suppose an institutional investor offers to make a large deposit into the fund in exchange for special trading privi-

Many Mutual Funds Are Caught Ignoring Ethical Standards

Some of the best-known names in the mutual fund industry have come under attack by the New York attorney general's office and the SEC. Over 300 lawsuits against 18 different firms were filed and consolidated in federal court in Baltimore. The mutual funds are eager to settle the suits and to get the bad publicity behind them. Nine firms agreed to pay $1.6 billion in restitution to investors and an additional $855 million in fee reductions. Among the larger settlements were the following:

- The Alliance Capital Management Corp. was charged with allowing traders to engage in market timing. The firm will cut fees by $350 million and pay $250 million in fines and restitution to shareholders.
- Bank of America, which was implicated along with Canary Capital Partners in late trading and

market timing, agreed to fee reductions of $160 million and fines and restitution of $375 million.
- Janus Capital Management LLC will reduce fees by $125 million and pay fines and restitution of $100 million.
- Putnam Investments, the fifth-largest family of funds, agreed to pay $10 million in fee reductions and $100 million in fines and restitution.

In addition to the fines, restitution, and fee reductions, some individual investment managers were charged with criminal activity. The vice-chairperson of Fred Alger & Company, James Connelly Jr., was sentenced to one to three years in jail for his involvement in preferential treatment and self-dealing in the mutual fund.

Source: Wall Street Journal, July 14, 2004, p. C1.

leges not afforded other investors. Since investment advisors are compensated as a percentage of the funds under management, they may choose to provide the special treatment because it increases their income. The recent negative publicity about mutual funds is due to this type of misaligned interest. The Conflicts of Interest box above discusses some of the better-known mutual fund scandals.

Mutual Fund Abuses

Until 2001, the mutual fund industry could brag that it had been "untainted by major scandal for more than 60 years."[3] This changed when the New York attorney general began investigating tips that mutual funds were engaging in various activities that undermined their fiduciary duty to shareholders, violated their own policies, and in some cases broke SEC laws. Most of the abuses centered around two activities: late trading and market timing, both of which take advantage of the structure of open-end mutual funds that provide daily liquidity to shareholders by marking all trades to the NAV as of the close of business at 4:00 PM.

1. *Late trading.* Late trading refers to the practice of allowing trades that are received after 4:00 PM to trade at the 4:00 price when they should trade at the next day's price. Suppose that on Wednesday at 4:00 PM the NAV for a technology fund is $20. Now suppose that news is received by traders at 6:00 PM

[3]Terry Glenn, head of the mutual funds industry's Investment Company Institute, quoted in the *Wall Street Journal*, September 4, 2003, p. C1.

that HP, Intel, and Microsoft have reported their income surged 50% over the last quarter. Traders, knowing the industry impact this will have, may want to enter buy orders for the fund at the $20 price. They are sure the NAV on Thursday will be substantially higher and they can earn a quick profit. A late trader can trade at the stale 4:00 PM price and buy or sell the funds the next day at a profit.

The attorney general reported in hearings before Congress that "late trading is like betting on a horse race after the horses have crossed the finish line." It is illegal under SEC regulations. The reason it went undetected for many years is that certain late trades were regularly accepted and were legal. If a broker received a buy order from a client at 2:00, the order might not get consolidated with other orders and transmitted to the fund by 4:00. Since the investor placed the order before the market closed, the investor could not benefit from the late trade. Late trades were simply an opportunity to catch up with order processing. It was when large investors took advantage of their special arrangements at the expense of other shareholders that the legal line was crossed.

2. *Market timing.* Market timing, though technically legal, is considered unethical and is expressly forbidden by virtually all mutual funds' policy standards. Market timing involves taking advantage of time zone differences that allow arbitrage opportunities, especially in foreign stocks. Mutual funds will set their 4:00 closing NAV using the most recent available foreign prices. However, these prices may be very stale. Japan, for example, closes nine hours earlier. If news is released in Japan that is not reflected in their closing prices, arbitrage opportunities exist by buying at the stale prices embedded in the NAV.

Most mutual funds have fees that are supposed to discourage these kinds of rapid in-and-out trades. However, if an investor such as Bank of America places large deposits in the fund, these fees can be waived. This is exactly what Edward J. Stern and his hedge fund Canary Capital Partners LLC did. In September 2003, Stern settled with the attorney general for $40 million in fines for allowing both late trading and market timing by Bank of America.

To better understand how shareholders in mutual funds are hurt by market timing and late trading, suppose a technology fund holds stock in various firms with a total current market value of $350. Further suppose you own one of ten shares outstanding in the fund. The NAV of the fund will be $35 per share ($350/10). Now suppose that after the market closes the tech industry announces better-than-expected earnings that everyone agrees will drive the value of shares held by the fund to $400 when the market opens the next morning. The NAV of your share would be $40 ($400/10). However, if another investor with special privileges is allowed to buy a share in the fund for $35 after hours, your NAV will be diluted. The $35 received by the fund from the privileged investor will have to be held as cash since the market is closed and no additional stock can be purchased by the fund. As a result, the value of the fund's assets the next morning will be $435 ($400 in stock and $35 in cash). The NAV will be $435/11 = $39.54 instead of $40. All of the original investors in the fund will have lost $0.46 per share, while the privileged investor will have gained $4.54 ($39.54 − $35.00).

The costs to investors of market timing and late trading are very hard to estimate since no reliable statistics are available on how frequently these abuses were prac-

conflicts of interest

SEC Survey Reports Mutual Fund Abuses Widespread

When the New York attorney general announced that his office was going to indict a number of mutual fund managers in September 2003, he caught many regulators off guard. Their focus had been on security abuses by corporations. The revelation that the mutual fund industry might also be dirty resulted in rapidly called hearings before Congress. At these hearings Stephen Cutler, the chief of enforcement for the SEC, presented results that showed that illegal trading in mutual funds was more widespread than anyone had imagined. In a sample of the largest 88 mutual fund companies, which represented 90% of the industry's assets, the SEC said that about 25% of the broker-dealers were allowed to make illegal late trades. Additionally, half the funds let some privileged shareholders engage in market timing trades. Finally, the research showed that more than 30% of the funds admitted that their managers had shared sensitive portfolio information with favored shareholders.

ticed. Recent academic studies have estimated the losses to long-term investors to be as high as $4.9 billion.[4] See the Conflicts of Interest box above for a discussion of how widespread mutual fund abuses may be.

Government Response to Abuses

Arthur Levitt, former chairman of the SEC, admitted, "I believe this is the worst scandal we have seen in 50 years and I can't say that I saw it coming."[5] In fact the SEC, which is supposed to watch the mutual fund industry, was not the agency that initially investigated the abuses. It was New York State Attorney General Eliot Spitzer who caught the SEC unaware by filing indictments against many of the major players in the mutual fund industry. Now that the issues are commonly recognized, both the SEC and Congress are attempting to assure the safety of these funds.

- *More independent directors.* By January 2006, funds were required to have an independent board chairman and 75% of the board must be independent. In addition, the independent board members must hold annual executive sessions outside the presence of fund managers. The legislation also requires that these independent board members have authority to hire staff to support their oversight efforts.
- *Hardening of the 4:00 PM valuation rule.* By more strictly enforcing the rule that trades received after 4:00 be traded at the next day's NAV rather than at the stale NAV, late trading activities should be prevented. These proposals, however, are controversial because they penalize investors whose trades do not get completed due to trading backlogs. They also fail to prevent market timing arbitrage across time zones.

---

[4]See Eric Zitzewitz, *Journal of Law, Economics & Organization* 19, no. 2 (2003): 245–280; Jason Greene and Charles Hodges, *Journal of Financial Economics* 65 (2002): 131–158; and Goetzmann, Ivkovic, and Rouwenhorst, *Journal of Financial and Quantitative Analysis* 36, no. 3 (September 2001): 287–309.

[5]*New York Times*, November 16, 2003, p. A1.

- *Increased and enforced redemption fees.* Most funds already have a policy against market timing and have a redemption fee that is imposed for shares that are sold within 60 or 90 days of purchase. These fees are usually discretionary and were waived in the cases where abuses occurred. The problem with mandatory fees is that they may penalize the investor who needs to make an unexpected withdrawal due to an emergency. This penalty makes mutual funds less attractive and, critics contend, would reduce their popularity. As a result of this argument, in March 2005, a voluntary redemption fee rule was adopted. The rule requires that the board consider whether they should impose the fee to protect shareholders from market timing abuses.

- *Increased transparency.* Other regulations follow the most common approach taken by the SEC—increased disclosure of operating practices to the public. Directors are required to more clearly and openly reveal any relationships that exist between fund owners or investment managers. Investment managers are required to more clearly disclose compensation arrangements and how fees are charged. Additionally, more information is required about compensation arrangements between the mutual fund and sales brokers. This strategy leaves it to the market to discipline any firms that seek to exploit any conflicts of interest.

SUMMARY

1. Mutual funds have grown rapidly over the last two decades. The growth has been partly fueled by the increase in the number of investors who are responsible for managing their own retirement. Increased liquidity and diversification, among other factors, have also been important. There are currently over 8,700 separate mutual funds with over $10 trillion in net assets.

2. Mutual funds can be organized as either open- or closed-end funds. Closed-end funds issue stock in the fund at an initial offering and do not accept additional funds. Most new funds are organized as open-end funds and issue additional shares when new money is received. The net asset value (NAV) of the shares is computed each day. All trades conducted that day are at the NAV.

3. The primary classes of mutual funds are stock funds, bond funds, hybrid funds, and money market funds. Stock and bond funds can be either actively managed by investment managers or can be structured as index funds that contain the securities in some index, such as the S&P 500.

4. Hedge funds attempt to earn returns by trading on deviations between historical security relationships and current market conditions.

5. The mutual fund industry has been subject to widely publicized scandals for violating SEC regulations and internal policy. Most abuses centered on market timing and late trading by investors receiving privileged treatment in exchange for large deposits with the funds. Conflicts of interest created by fee structures that reward investment managers more for total assets than for returns are partly responsible.

KEY TERMS

closed-end funds, *p. 542*
deferred load, *p. 549*
diversification, *p. 538*
hedge funds, *p. 551*

load funds, *p. 549*
net asset value (NAV), *p. 543*
no-load funds, *p. 549*
open-end fund, *p. 542*

1. What features of mutual funds and the investment environment have led to mutual funds' rapid growth in the last two decades?

2. What is meant by liquidity intermediation?

3. Considering the discussion of market efficiency from Chapter 6, discuss whether you should be willing to pay high fees to mutual fund investment managers.

4. Distinguish between an open- and closed-end mutual fund.

5. Discuss why a mutual fund family may find it beneficial to offer 50 or 60 different stock mutual funds.

6. How does an index fund differ from an actively managed fund?

7. What is a load fund?

8. How are deferred loads usually structured?

9. What distinguishes a hedge fund from other types of mutual funds?

10. What prompted the growth of money market mutual funds?

11. What do 12b-1 fees pay and what is the maximum amount these fees can be?

12. What is the primary source of the conflict of interest between shareholders and investment managers?

13. What is *late trading* when referred to by mutual funds?

14. What is *market timing* when referred to by mutual funds?

15. What regulatory changes have been adopted or are being considered to deal with abuses in the mutual fund industry?

1. On January 1, the shares and prices for a mutual fund at 4:00 PM are as follows:

Stock	Shares owned	Price
1	1,000	$1.92
2	5,000	$51.18
3	2,800	$29.08
4	9,200	$67.19
5	3,000	$4.51
Cash	n.a.	$5,353.40

Stock 3 announces record earnings, and the price of stock 3 jumps to $32.44 in after-market trading. If the fund (illegally) allows investors to buy at the current NAV, how many shares will $25,000 buy? If the fund waits until the price adjusts, how many shares can be purchased? What is the gain to such illegal trades? Assume 5,000 shares are outstanding.

2. A mutual fund charges a 5% upfront load plus reports an expense ratio of 1.34%. If an investor plans on holding a fund for 30 years, what is the average annual fee, as a percent, paid by the investors?

3. A mutual fund offers "A" shares, which have a 5% upfront load and an expense ratio of 0.76%. The fund also offers "B" shares, which have a 3% back-end load and an expense ratio of 0.87%. Which shares make more sense for an investor looking over an 18-year horizon?

4. A mutual fund reported year-end total assets of $1,508 million and an expense ratio of 0.90%. What total fees is the fund charging each year?

5. A $1 million fund is charging a back-end load of 1%, 12b-1 fees of 1%, and an expense ratio of 1.9%. Prior to deducting expenses, what must the fund value be at the end of the year for investors to break even?

Questions 6–12 trace a sequence of transactions involving a single mutual fund.

6. On January 1, a mutual fund has the following assets and prices at 4:00 PM.

Stock	Shares owned	Price
1	1,000	$1.97
2	5,000	$48.26
3	1,000	$26.44
4	10,000	$67.49
5	3,000	$2.59

Calculate the net asset value (NAV) for the fund. Assume that 8,000 shares are outstanding for the fund.

7. An investor sends the fund a check for $50,000. If there is no front-end load, calculate the new number of shares and price per share. Assume the manager purchases 1,800 shares of stock 3, and the rest is held as cash.

8. On January 2, the prices at 4:00 PM are as follows:

Stock	Shares owned	Price
1	1,000	$2.03
2	5,000	$51.37
3	2,800	$29.08
4	10,000	$67.19
5	3,000	$4.42
Cash	n.a.	$2,408.00

Calculate the net asset value (NAV) for the fund.

9. Assume the new investor then sells the 420 shares. What is his profit? What is the annualized return? The fund sells 800 shares of stock 4 to raise the needed funds. Assume 250 trading days per year.

10. To discourage short-term investing in its fund, the fund now charges a 5% upfront load and a 2% back-end load. The same investor decides to put $50,000 back into the fund. Calculate the new number of shares outstanding. Assume the fund manager buys back as many round-lot shares of stock 4 with the cash.

11. On January 3, the prices at 4:00 PM are as follows:

Stock	Shares owned	Price
1	1,000	$1.92
2	5,000	$51.18
3	2,800	$29.08
4	9,900	$67.19
5	3,000	$4.51
Cash	n.a.	$5,353.40

Calculate the new NAV.

12. Unhappy with the results, the new investor then sells the 389.09 shares. What is his profit? What is the new fund value?

WEB EXERCISES

Investment Banks, Brokerage Firms, and Mutual Funds

1. Morningstar is the best-known company that specializes in analysis and review of mutual funds. There are a number of Web sites that report Morningstar's results. Go to **www.quicken.com/investments/ mutualfunds/finder**. Perform the EasyStep Search according to your own preferences for investment. Can you find funds that provide the return you want with the expense ratio you are willing to pay?

2. The mutual fund industry publishes a fact book containing exhaustive data on the historic and current state of mutual funds. Go to **www.ici.org/stats/ latest/2007_factbook.pdf**.

a. Section 1 provides an overview of the mutual fund industry. Select and report on one statistic not reported in this textbook.

b. Section 2 reports on trends in the mutual fund industry. Discuss the relationship between the return on equity and flows to equity mutual funds.

c. According to Chapter 4, what percentage of mutual funds assets are currently owned by households?

d. According to Chapter 4, what is the average annual income of an investor in mutual funds?

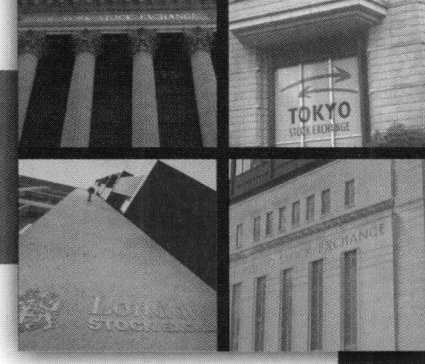

Insurance Companies and Pension Funds

Preview

In this chapter we continue our discussion of financial institutions by looking at two nonbank institutions: insurance companies and pension funds. Insurance is an important industry in the United States. Most people hold one or more types of insurance policies (health, life, homeowners, automobile, disability, and so on), and the annual revenues of insurance companies exceed $600 billion. Insurance companies are also a major employer, especially of business majors. Figure 22.1 shows the number of persons employed by the insurance industry between 1960 and 2005. The numbers rose rapidly during the 1960s, 1970s, and early 1980s. (Currently, well over 2 million Americans are employed in the insurance industry.) In recent years, the rate of growth has slowed, however. There are a couple of possible explanations for this. First, technology has streamlined claims processing so that fewer back-office workers are needed. Second, competition by other financial institutions such as commercial banks and brokerage houses may be cutting into some of the business traditionally reserved for insurance companies.

One major competitor to insurance has been the private, company-sponsored pension plan. Better-educated and longer-lived workers are putting more money into pension funds than ever before. Over 65 million individuals are now invested in a private pension fund. These plans are also reviewed in this chapter.

Insurance companies and pension funds are considered financial intermediaries for several reasons. First, they receive investment funds from their customers. For example, when a person buys a whole life insurance policy, the person receives a life insurance benefit and accumulates a cash balance. Many people use insurance companies as their primary investment avenue. Similarly, private pension funds also take in investment dollars from their customers. Second, both of these institutions place their money in a variety of money-earning investments. Insurance companies and pension funds make large commercial mortgage loans, invest in stocks, and buy bonds. Thus, these institutions are financial intermediaries in that they take in funds from one sector and invest it in another.

Insurance Companies

Insurance companies are in the business of assuming risk on behalf of their customers in exchange for a fee, called a *premium*. Insurance companies make a profit by charging premiums that are sufficient to pay the expected claims to the company plus a profit. Why do people pay for insurance when they know that over the lifetime of their policy, they will probably pay more in premiums than the expected amount of any loss they will suffer? Because most people are risk-averse: They would rather pay a **certainty equivalent** (the insurance premium) than accept the gamble that they will lose their house or their car. Thus, it is because people are risk-averse that they prefer to buy insurance and know with certainty what their wealth will be (their current wealth minus the insurance premium) than to incur the risk and run the chance that their wealth may fall.

Consider how people's lives would change if insurance were not available. Instead of knowing that the insurance company would help if an emergency occurred, everyone would have to set aside reserves. These reserves could not be invested long-term

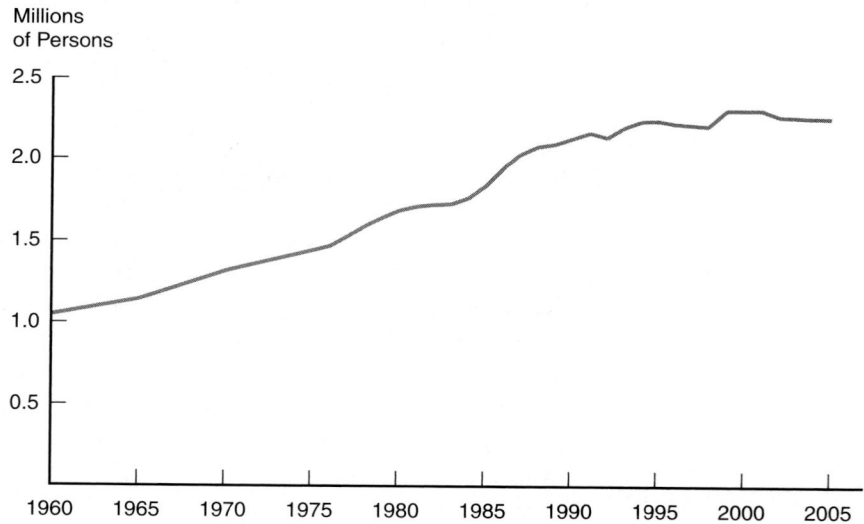

Figure 22.1 Number of Persons Employed in the U.S. Insurance Industry, 1960–2005

Source: Life Insurance Fact Book, 2006 (American Council of Life Insurers); http://www.acii.com/ACLI/Tools/Industry+Facts/Life+Insurers+Fact+Book/FB06.htm.

but would have to be kept in an extremely liquid form. Furthermore, people would be constantly worried that their reserves would be inadequate to pay for catastrophic events such as the loss of their house to fire, the theft of their car, or the death of the family breadwinner. Insurance allows us the peace of mind that a single event can have only a limited financial impact on our lives.

Fundamentals of Insurance

Although there are many types of insurance and insurance companies, all insurance is subject to several basic principles.

1. There must be a relationship between the *insured* (the party covered by insurance) and the *beneficiary* (the party who receives the payment should a loss occur). In addition, the beneficiary must be someone who may suffer potential harm. For example, you could not take out a policy on your neighbor's teenage driver because you are unlikely to suffer harm if the teenager gets into an accident. The reason for this rule is that insurance companies do not want people to buy policies as a way of gambling.
2. The insured must provide full and accurate information to the insurance company.
3. The insured is not to profit as a result of insurance coverage.
4. If a third party compensates the insured for the loss, the insurance company's obligation is reduced by the amount of the compensation.
5. The insurance company must have a large number of insureds so that the risk can be spread out among many different policies.
6. The loss must be quantifiable. For example, an oil company could not buy a policy on an unexplored oil field.
7. The insurance company must be able to compute the probability of the loss occurring.

The purpose of these principles is to maintain the integrity of the insurance process. Without them, people may be tempted to use insurance companies to gamble or speculate on future events. Taken to an extreme, this behavior could undermine the ability of insurance companies to protect persons in real need. In addition, these principles provide a way to spread the risk among many policies and to establish a price for each policy that will provide an expectation of a profitable return. Despite following these guidelines, insurance companies suffer greatly from the problems of asymmetric information that we first described in Chapter 2.

Adverse Selection and Moral Hazard in Insurance

Recall that adverse selection occurs when the individuals most likely to benefit from a transaction are the ones who most actively seek out the transaction and are thus most likely to be selected. In Chapter 2 we discussed adverse selection in the context of borrowers with the worst credit being the ones who most actively seek loans. The problem also occurs in the insurance market. Who is more likely to apply for health insurance, someone who is seldom sick or someone with chronic health problems? Who is more likely to buy flood insurance, someone who lives on a mountain or someone who lives in a river valley? In both cases, the party more likely to suffer a loss is the party likely to seek insurance. The implication of adverse selection is that loss probability statistics gathered for the entire population may not accurately reflect the loss potential for the persons who actually want to buy policies.

The adverse selection problem raises the issue of which policies an insurance company should accept. Because someone in poor health is more likely to buy a supplemental health insurance policy than someone in perfect health, we might predict that insurance companies should turn down anyone who applies. Since this does not happen, insurance companies must have found alternative solutions. For example, most insurance companies require physical exams and may examine previous medical records before issuing a health or life insurance policy. If some previous illness is found to be a factor in the person's health, the company may issue the policy but exclude this preexisting condition. Insurance firms often offer better rates to insure groups of people, such as everyone working at a particular business, because the adverse selection problem is then avoided.

In addition to the adverse selection problem, moral hazard plagues the insurance industry. Moral hazard occurs when the insured fails to take proper precautions to avoid losses because losses are covered by insurance. For example, moral hazard may cause you not to lock your car doors if you will be reimbursed by insurance if the car is stolen. When Hurricane Ernesto approached the North Carolina coast in 2006, many yacht owners did not take down their old canvas covers because they hoped the covers would be destroyed by the hurricane, in which case the owners could file a claim with the insurance company and get money to buy new covers.

One way that insurance companies combat moral hazard is by requiring a **deductible**. A deductible is the amount of any loss that must be paid by the insured before the insurance company will pay anything. For example, if new canvas yacht covers cost $5,000 and the yacht owner has $1,000 deductible, the owner will pay the first $1,000 of the loss and the insurance company will pay $4,000. In addition to deductibles, there may be other terms in the insurance contract aimed at reducing risk. For example, a business insured against fire may be required to install and maintain a sprinkler system on its premises to reduce the loss should a fire occur.

Although contract terms and deductibles help with the moral hazard problem, these issues remain a constant difficulty for insurance companies. The insurance industry's reaction to moral hazard and adverse selection are discussed in greater detail in "The Practicing Manager" later in this chapter.

Selling Insurance

Another problem common to insurance companies is that people often fail to seek as much insurance as they actually need. Human nature tends to cause people to ignore their mortality, for example. For this reason, insurance, unlike many banking services, does not sell itself. Instead, insurance companies must hire large sales forces to sell their products. The expense of marketing may account for up to 20% of the total cost of a policy. A good sales force can convince people to buy insurance coverage that they never would have pursued on their own yet may need.

Insurance is unique in that agents sell a product that commits the company to a risk. The relationship between the agent and the company varies: *Independent agents* may sell insurance for a number of different companies. They do not have any particular loyalty to any one firm and simply try to find the best product for their customer. There are in excess of 60,000 independent agents in the United States. *Exclusive agents* sell the insurance products for only one insurance company.

mini-case

Insurance Agent: The Customer's Ally

An underwriter working for Prudential Insurance was responsible for a number of agents selling property insurance in Southern California in 1985. One agent sold a large number of fire insurance policies and was always careful to document clearly when a fire hydrant was on the property by including it in a photograph attached to the policy application. The agent made a mistake on one policy, however, when he included his car in a picture of a different view of the property. The picture showed a plastic fire hydrant lying in the open trunk of his car. He had been putting this fire hydrant on property for years when he needed to give a low quote to get business.

The agent was neither fired nor sued. He was simply advised to halt the practice, and his policies continued to be accepted by the company.

Most agents, whether independent or exclusive, are compensated by being paid a commission. The agents themselves are usually not at all concerned with the level of risk of any one policy because they have little to lose if a loss occurs. (Rarely are commissions influenced by the claims submitted by an agent's customers.) To keep control of the risk that agents are incurring on behalf of the company, insurance companies employ **underwriters**, people who review and sign off on each policy an agent writes and who have the authority to turn down a policy if they deem the risk unacceptable. If underwriters have questions about the quality of customers, they may order an independent inspector to review the property being insured or request additional medical information. A final decision to accept the policy may depend on the inspector's report (see the Mini-Case box above).

Growth and Organization of Insurance Companies

Figure 22.2 shows the number of life insurance companies from 1950 to 2005. There was a steady increase in the number until 1988. Since then the number has fallen steadily. Another interesting point to note about Figure 22.2 is that insurance companies can be organized as either *stock* or *mutual* firms. A **stock company** is owned by stockholders and has the objective of making a profit.

Mutual insurance companies are owned by the policyholders. The objective of mutual insurance firms is to provide insurance at the lowest possible cost to the insured. Policyholders are paid dividends that reflect the surplus of premiums over costs. Because the policyholders share in reducing the cost of insurance, there may be some reduction in the moral hazard that most insurance companies face. A unique feature of mutual insurance dividends is that they are not taxed like dividends received from other types of corporations. The Internal Revenue Service regards the dividends as refunds of overcharges on insurance premiums.

Most new insurance companies organize as stock corporations. As Figure 22.2 shows, at the end of 2005, only 135 of 1,119 insurance companies were organized as mutuals.

Number of
Life Insurance
Companies

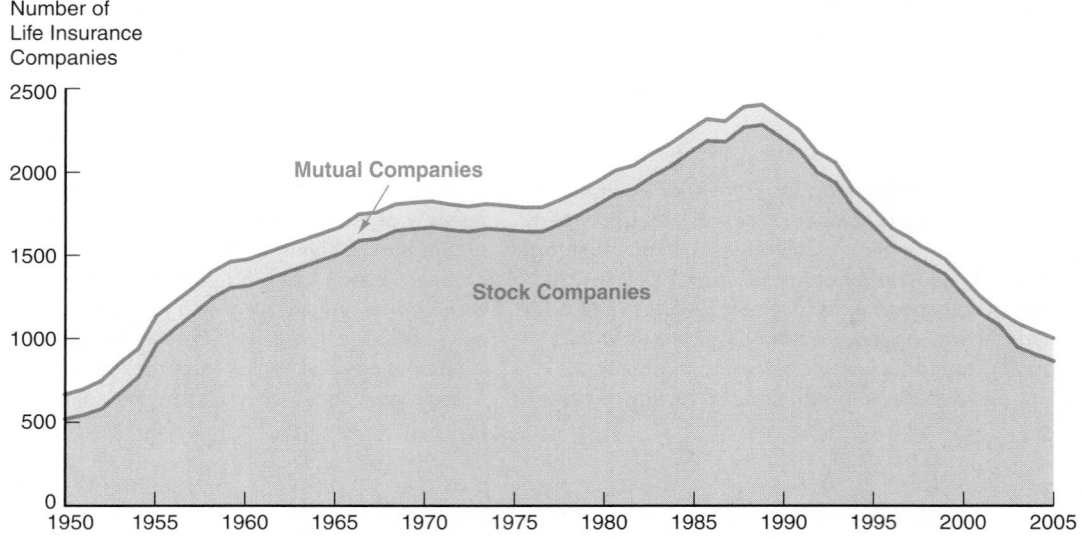

Figure 22.2 Number of Life Insurance Companies in the United States, 1950–2005

Source: Life Insurance Fact Book, 2005, 2006, Table 1.1 (American Council of Life Insurers); http://www.acii.com/ACLI/Tools/Industry+Facts/Life+Insurers+Fact+Book/FB06.htm.

Types of Insurance

Insurance is classified by which type of undesirable event is insured. The most common types are life insurance and property and casualty insurance. In its simplest form, life insurance provides income for the heirs of the deceased. Many insurance companies offer policies that provide retirement benefits as well as life insurance. In this case, the premium combines the cost of the life insurance with a savings program. The cost of life insurance depends on such factors as the age of the insured, average life expectancies, the health and lifestyle of the insured (whether the insured smokes, engages in a dangerous hobby such as skydiving, and so on), and the insurance company's operating costs.

Property and casualty insurance protects property (houses, cars, boats, and so on) against losses due to accidents, fire, disasters, and other calamities. Marine insurance, for example, which insures against the loss of a ship and its cargo, is the oldest form of insurance, predating even life insurance. Property and casualty policies tend to be short-term contracts subject to frequent renewal. Another significant distinction between life insurance policies and property and casualty policies is that the latter do not have a savings component. Property and casualty premiums are based simply on the probability of sustaining the loss. That is why car insurance premiums are higher if a driver has had speeding tickets, has caused accidents, or lives in a high-crime area. Each of these events increases the likelihood that the insurance company will have to pay a claim.

Life Insurance

Life is assumed to unfold in a predictable sequence: You work for a number of years while saving for retirement; then you retire, live off the fruits of your earlier labor, and die at a ripe old age. The problem is that you could die too young and not have time to provide for your loved ones, or you could live too long and run out of retirement assets. Either option is very unappealing to most people. The purpose of life insurance is to relieve some of the concern associated with either eventuality. Although insurance cannot make you comfortable with the idea of a premature death, it can at least allow you the peace of mind that comes with knowing that you have provided for your heirs. Life insurance companies also want to help people save for their retirement. In this way, the insurance company provides for the customer's whole life.

The basic products of life insurance companies are life insurance proper, disability insurance, annuities, and health insurance. Life insurance pays off if you die, protecting those who depend on your continued earnings. As mentioned, the person who receives the insurance payment after you die is called the *beneficiary* of the policy. Disability insurance replaces part of your income should you become unable to continue working due to illness or an accident. An **annuity** is an insurance product that will help if you live longer than you expect. For an initial fixed sum or stream of payments, the insurance company agrees to pay you a fixed amount for as long as you live. If you live a short life, the insurance company pays out less than expected. Conversely, if you live unusually long, the insurance company may pay out much more than expected.

Notice one curiosity among these various types of insurance: Although predicting any one individual's life expectancy or probability of being disabled is very difficult, when many people are insured, the actual amount to be paid out by the insurance company can be predicted very accurately. Insurance companies collect and analyze statistics on life expectancies, health claims, disability claims, and other relevant matters.

For example, a life insurance company can predict with a high degree of accuracy when death benefits must be paid by using *actuarial tables* that predict life expectancies. Table 22.1 lists the expected life of persons at various ages. A 25-year-old female can expect to live another 55.7 years; a 25-year-old male, however, can expect to live only another 50.9 years.

The **law of large numbers** says that when many people are insured, the probability distribution of the losses will assume a normal probability distribution, a distribution that allows accurate predictions. This distribution is important: Because insurance companies insure so many millions of people, the law of large numbers tends to make the company's predictions quite accurate and allows companies to price the policies so that they can earn a profit.

Life insurance policies protect against an interruption in the family's stream of income. The broad categories of life insurance products are *term, whole life*, and *universal life*.

Term Life The simplest form of life insurance is the *term insurance policy*, which pays out if the insured dies while the policy is in force. This form of policy contains no savings element. Once the policy period expires, there are no residual benefits.

As the insured ages, the probability of death increases, so the cost of the policy rises. For example, Table 22.2 shows the estimated premiums for a 40-year-old

TABLE 22.1 Life Expectancy at Various Ages in the United States, 2006

Age	Male	Female	Total Population
0	74.4	79.8	77.2
1	74.0	79.3	76.7
5	70.1	75.4	72.8
15	60.2	65.5	62.9
25	50.9	55.7	53.4
35	41.5	46.0	43.9
45	32.5	36.6	34.7
55	24.0	27.7	26.0
65	16.4	19.4	18.1
75	10.2	12.3	11.5
85	5.7	6.9	6.5
100	2.5	2.8	2.7

Source: Life Insurance Fact Book, 2006, Table 11.2 (American Council of Life Insurers).

TABLE 22.2 Typical Annual Premiums on a $100,000 Term Policy for a 40-Year-Old Male Nonsmoker

Age of Insured	Cost ($)
40	134
41	147
42	153
45	192
50	286
55	461
60	810

male nonsmoker for $100,000 of term life insurance from a major insurance company. The premium for the first year is $134. This rises to $147 when the insured is 41 years old, $153 when the insured is 42, and so on. By the time the insured is 60 years old, $100,000 of life insurance costs $810 per year. Of course, rates vary among insurance companies, but these sample rates demonstrate how the annual cost of a term policy rises with the age of the insured.

Some term policies fix the premiums for a set number of years, usually five or ten. Alternatively, *decreasing term policies* have a constant premium, but the amount of the insurance coverage declines each year.

Term policies have been historically hard to sell because once they expire, the policyholder has nothing to show for the premium paid. This problem is solved with whole life policies.

Whole Life   A *whole life insurance* policy pays a death benefit if the policyholder dies. Whole life policies usually require the insured to pay a level premium for the duration of the policy. In the beginning, the insured pays more than if a term policy had been purchased. This overpayment accumulates as a cash value that can be borrowed by the insured at reasonable rates.

Survivorship benefits also contribute to the accumulated cash values. When members of the insured pool die, any remaining cash values are divided among the survivors. If the policyholder lives until the policy matures, it can be surrendered for its cash value. This cash value can be used to purchase an annuity. In this way, the whole life policy is advertised as covering the insured for the duration of his or her life.

Universal Life   In the late 1970s, whole life policies fell into disfavor because the rates of return earned on the policy premiums were well below rates available on other investments. For example, say that an investor bought a term policy instead of a whole life policy and invested the difference in the premiums. If she did this each year for the term of the whole life policy, she would be able to pay for term insurance and still have a much greater amount in her investment account than if she had initially purchased the whole life policy. Investment advisers and insurance agents began steering customers away from whole life policies. The sales pitch became "buy term and invest the difference." Because the agents were also selling other investments, they did not suffer from this change in insurance plans. To combat the flow of funds out of their companies, insurance firms introduced the *universal life policy*.

Universal life policies combine the benefits of the term policy with those of the whole life policy. The major benefit of the universal life policy is that the cash value accumulates at a much higher rate.

The universal life policy is structured to have two parts, one for the term life insurance and one for savings. One important advantage that universal life policies have over many alternative investment plans is that the interest earned on the savings portion of the account is tax-exempt until withdrawn. To keep this favorable tax treatment, the cash value of the policy cannot exceed the death benefit.

Universal life policies were introduced in the early 1980s when interest rates were at record high levels. They immediately became very popular and by 1984 accounted for 32% of the volume of life insurance sold. Later, as interest rates fell, their popularity ebbed.

Annuities   If we think of term life insurance as insuring against death, the annuity can be viewed as insuring against life. As we noted earlier, one risk people have is outliving their retirement funds. If they live longer than they projected when they initially retired, they could spend all of their money and end up in poverty. One way to avoid this outcome is by purchasing annuities. Once an annuity has been purchased for a fixed amount, it makes payments as long as the beneficiary lives.

Annuities are particularly susceptible to the adverse selection problem. When people retire, they know more about their life expectancy than the insurance company knows. People who are in good health, have a family history of longevity, and have attended to their health all of their lives are more likely to live longer and hence to want to buy an annuity more than people in poor or average health. To avoid this problem, insurance companies tend to price individual annuities expensively. Most annuities are sold to members of large groups where all employees covered by a particular pension plan automatically receive their benefit distribution by purchasing an annuity from the insurance company. Because the annuity is automatic, the adverse selection problem is eliminated.

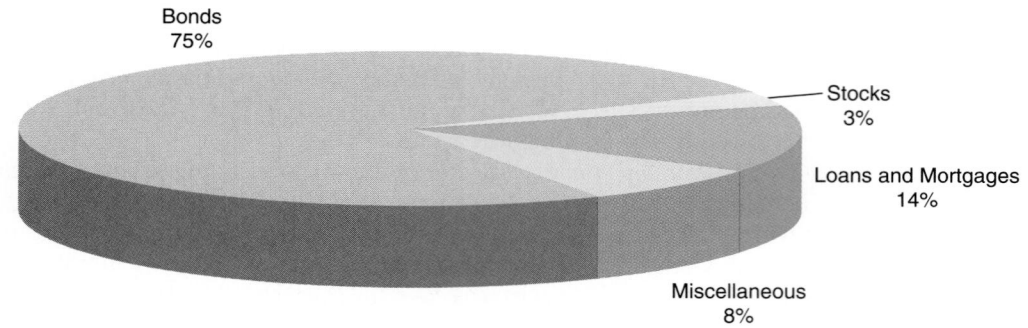

Figure 22.3   Distribution of Life Insurance Company Assets (2005)

Source: Life Insurance Company Fact Book, 2006, Table 2.2 (American Council of Life Insurers).

Assets and Liabilities of Life Insurance Companies Life insurance companies derive funds from two sources. First, they receive premiums that represent future obligations that must be met when the insured dies. Second, they receive premiums paid into pension funds managed by the life insurance company. These funds are long-term in nature.

Since life insurance liabilities are predictable and long-term, life insurance companies can invest in long-term assets. Figure 22.3 shows the distribution of assets of the average life insurance company at the beginning of 2005. Most of the assets are in long-term investments such as bonds.

Insurance companies have also invested heavily in mortgages and real estate over the years. In 2006, about 6.5% of life insurance assets were invested either in mortgage loans or directly in real estate. This percentage is down substantially from historic levels. Figure 22.4 displays the percentage of assets invested in mortgages from 1920 to 2006. The decline in mortgage investment, which represents a shift to lower-risk assets, has been offset by increased investment in corporate bonds and government securities.

The shift to less risky securities may be the result of losses suffered by some insurance companies in the late 1980s. As insurance companies competed against mutual funds and money market funds for retirement dollars, they found that they needed higher-return investments. This led some insurance companies to invest in real estate and junk bonds. Deteriorating real estate values brought on by over-building during the 1980s caused some firms to suffer large losses. The combination of large real estate losses and junk bond investment contributed to the failure of several large firms in 1991, including Executive Life, with assets of $15 billion, and Mutual Benefit Life, with assets of $14 billion.

Health Insurance

Individual health insurance coverage is very vulnerable to adverse selection problems. People who know that they are likely to become ill are the most likely to seek health insurance coverage. This causes individual health insurance to be very expensive. Most policies are offered through company-sponsored programs in which the company pays all or part of the employee's policy premium.

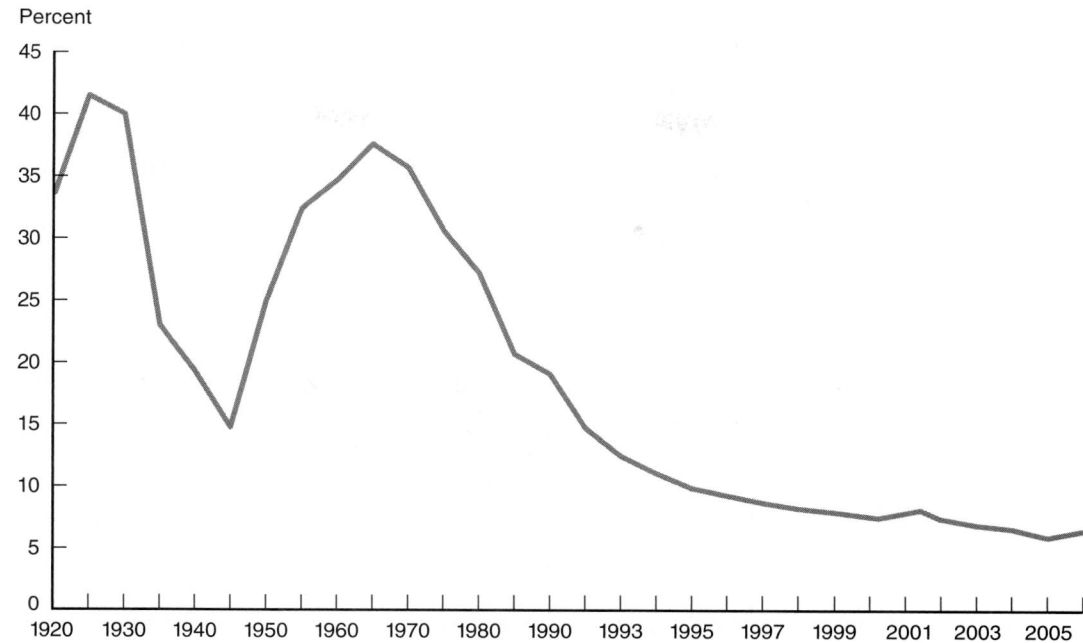

Figure 22.4 Percentage of Life Insurance Company Assets Invested in Mortgages, 1920–2006

Source: Federal Reserve Flow of Funds Accounts, Table L117; http://www.federalreserve.gov/releases/z1/Current/z1.pdf.

Most life insurance companies also offer health insurance. Health insurance premiums account for about 24% of total premium income. Life insurance companies compete with Blue Cross and Blue Shield organizations, nonprofit firms that are sponsored by hospitals. Blue Cross usually covers hospital care, and Blue Shield, doctors' services. One national agency coordinates and monitors the 73 Blue Cross/Blue Shield organizations.

The government is also involved in health insurance through Medicare and Medicaid. Medicare provides medical coverage for the elderly, and Medicaid provides coverage for people on welfare.

Health insurance was a major political issue in the 1992 presidential election and continues to be the subject of regulation and debate. In 1996, Congress passed legislation making it more difficult for insurance companies to refuse to insure a person with a preexisting medical problem.

One reason for the extensive debate over medical insurance has been the spiraling costs of health care. For most of the past decade, the cost of health care has risen much faster than the cost of living and real wages. One factor contributing to this increase is the more sophisticated and expensive treatments constantly being offered. For example, studies have shown that cholesterol-reducing drugs can reduce the likelihood of cardiovascular trouble across a broad portion of the population. These drugs cost about $3 per day and did not even exist 20 years ago. Insurance companies have dealt with these rising costs in a number of ways. For example, today the risk of most company-sponsored plans is borne by the company, with the insurance company administering the plan and covering catastrophic expenses. This increases the sponsoring company's incentive to maintain a healthy workforce and to encourage responsible use of medical facilities by its employees. For example, many large firms have found it cost-effective to employ physician assistants on site to reduce medical fees and absenteeism.

Another way that insurance companies are attempting to deal with increased medical costs is by controlling them. This is done by negotiating contracts with physician groups to provide services at reduced cost and through *managed care*, where approval is required before services can be rendered. *Health maintenance organizations (HMOs)* shift the risk from the insurance company to the provider. The insurance company pays the HMO a fixed payment per person covered in exchange for medical services. One problem many people find with the HMO form of health care is that the provider has an incentive to limit medical services. Regulation was required, for example, to ensure mothers at least 48 hours in the hospital following a delivery.

Though it appears that a national health insurance overhaul is not going to come out of Congress any time soon, the attention focused on the problem has prompted many changes at the state and local levels. These changes are likely to continue in the future, due largely to pressure from insurance companies.

Property and Casualty Insurance

Property and casualty insurance was the earliest form of insurance. It began in the Middle Ages when merchants sent ships off to foreign ports to trade. A merchant, though willing to accept the risk that the trading might not turn a profit, was often unwilling to accept the risk that the ship might sink or be captured by pirates. To reduce such risks, merchants began to band together and insure each other's ships against loss. The process became more sophisticated as time went on, and insurance policies were written that were then traded in the major commercial centers of the time.

In 1666, the Great Fire of London did much to advance the case for fire insurance. The first fire insurance company was founded in London in 1680. In the United States, the first fire insurance company was formed by a group led by Benjamin Franklin in 1752. By the beginning of the nineteenth century, the assets of property and casualty insurance firms exceeded even those of commercial banks, making these firms the most important financial intermediary. The invention of the automobile did a great deal to spur the growth of property and casualty insurance companies during the twentieth century.

Property and Casualty Insurance Today Property and casualty insurance protects against losses from fire, theft, storm, explosion, and even neglect. **Property insurance** protects businesses and owners from the impact of risk associated with owning property. This includes replacement and loss of earnings from income-producing property as well as financial losses to owners of residential property. **Casualty insurance** (or **liability insurance**) protects against liability for harm the insured may cause to others as a result of product failure or accidents. For example, part of your car insurance is property insurance (which pays if your car is damaged), and part is casualty insurance (which pays if you cause an accident).

Property and casualty insurance is different from life insurance. First, policies tend to be short-term, usually for one year or less. Second, whereas life insurance is limited to insuring against one event, property and casualty companies insure against many different events. Finally, the amount of the potential loss is much more difficult to predict than for life insurance. These characteristics cause property and casualty companies to hold more liquid assets than those of life insurance companies. The wide range of losses means that property and casualty firms must maintain substantial liquidity.

Property insurance can be provided in either **named-peril policies** or **open-peril policies.** Named-peril policies insure against loss only from perils that are specifically named in the policy, whereas open-peril policies insure against all perils except those specifically excluded by the policy. For example, many homeowners in low-lying areas are required to buy flood insurance. This insurance covers only losses due to flooding, so it is a named-peril policy. A homeowner's insurance policy, which protects the house from fire, hurricane, tornado, and other damage, is an example of an open-peril policy.

Casualty or liability insurance protects against financial losses because of a claim of negligence. Liability insurance is bought not only by manufacturers who might be sued because of product defects but also by many types of professionals, including physicians, lawyers, and building contractors. Whereas the risk exposure in property insurance policies is relatively easy to predict, since it is usually limited to the value of the property, liability risk exposure is much more difficult to determine.

Liability risk exposure can have long lag times (often referred to as "tails"). This means that a liability claim may be filed long after the policy expires. Consider liability claims filed against the manufacturers of light airplanes. In the 1950s, 1960s, and 1970s, Cessna and Piper produced airplanes that are still being used today. The companies often get sued when one of these 30- or 40-year-old planes crashes. Insurance premiums grew so large in the 1980s due to the extensive lag time that both Cessna and Piper had to stop producing private airplanes. The cost of the liability insurance put the price of the planes out of reach of most private pilots.

There has been extensive publicity about high liability awards given by juries. These awards have often been well above what the insurance companies could have predicted. Liability insurance premiums continue to rise as a result. Some states have attempted to limit liability awards in an effort to contain these insurance costs.

Reinsurance One way that insurance companies may reduce their risk exposure is to obtain **reinsurance.** Reinsurance allocates a portion of the risk to another company in exchange for a portion of the premium. Reinsurance allows insurance companies to write larger policies because a portion of the policy is actually held by another firm.

About 10% of all property and casualty insurance is reinsured. Smaller insurance firms obtain reinsurance more frequently than large firms. You can think of it as insurance for the insurance company.

Since the originator of the policy usually has more to lose than the reinsurer, the moral hazard and adverse selection problems are small. This means that little specific information about the risk being reinsured is required. As a result of the simplified information requirements, the reinsurance market consists of relatively standardized contracts. One problem with the market is the risk that the reinsurer can fail. For example, in 1990, insurance firms were owed about $20 billion in unrecovered reinsurance.

Terrorism Risk Insurance Act of 2002 The September 11, 2001, terrorist attacks led the insurance industry to rethink its exposure to losses that could potentially destroy even the best-capitalized insurance company. Following an intensive lobbying effort by the insurance industry, new legislation was passed on November 26, 2002, limiting the amount insurance firms would be required to pay out in the event of future attacks. The Terrorism Risk Insurance Act of 2002 is limited to acts of international terrorism in which losses exceed $5 million. Should an act of terrorism occur, as defined in the legislation, the government will pay 90% of the losses. Losses in excess of $100 billion are not covered.

Insurance Regulation

Insurance companies are subject to less federal regulation than many other financial institutions. In fact, the McCarran-Ferguson Act of 1945 explicitly exempts insurance from federal regulation. The primary federal regulator is the Internal Revenue Service, which administers special taxation rules.

Most insurance regulation occurs at the state level. Not only must an insurance company follow the standards set by the state in which it is chartered, but it must also comply with the regulations set in any state in which it does business. New York requires that any insurance company doing business in the state comply with its investment standards. Because New York is such a big market, virtually every company complies. This makes the New York State regulations almost the same as national regulations.

---

conflicts of interest

 Insurance Behemoth Charged with Conflicts of Interest Violations

In October 2004, New York Attorney General Eliot Spitzer charged Marsh & McLennan Cos. (MMC), a $12 billion financial-services company, with fraud related to its insurance brokerage business. This initial attack is likely to have far-reaching effects on an industry that has so far remained removed from the scandals that have plagued other financial service firms.

Companies hire insurance brokers to help them control risk in a cost-effective manner. An insurance broker is hired to use its expertise and influence to search for the best possible prices from the insurance industry. The broker receives a fee for providing this service.

In the complaint filed against MMC, Spitzer charges that the insurance firm engaged in bid-rigging and accepted payoffs from insurance companies in exchange for directing business their way. In practicing bid-rigging, MMC required some insurance companies to submit abnormally high bids. This allowed another favored insurer to receive the business at a price fixed by MMC. The insurance companies were told by MCC that if they did not follow MMC's directions they would lose future business.

MMC also required insurers to pay contingent commissions—payments to MMC for steering clients to them. These pay-to-play revenues amounted to $800 million per year to MMC, or about half of the firm's 2003 net income. An email Spitzer obtained from a senior MMC executive reads, "We need to place our business in 2004 with those that . . . pay us the most." MMC, along with other major insurance brokerage firms Aon and Willis Group Holdings, has halted all contingent commissions.

In the aftermath of these conflicts of interest scandals, Chairman and CEO Jeffery Greenberg and four other top executives left the firm. A number of other insurance firms and insurance brokerage companies have come under further scrutiny. In the past, the insurance industry has been largely self-regulated. It is likely that the abuses uncovered by the attorney general and their clear costs to consumers will result in additional regulation and oversight.

The purpose of most regulations is to protect policyholders from losses due to the insolvency of the company. To accomplish this, insurance companies are restricted as to their asset composition and minimum capital ratio. All states also require that insurance agents and brokers obtain state licenses to sell each kind of insurance: life, property and casualty, and health. These licenses are to ensure that all agents have a minimum level of knowledge about the products they sell.

See the Conflicts of Interest box on this spread for a discussion of recent scandals affecting a major insurance broker. Such scandals could result in increased insurance industry regulation.

THE PRACTICING MANAGER

Insurance Management

Insurance companies, like banks, are in the financial intermediation business of transforming one type of asset into another for the public. Insurance companies use the premiums paid on policies to invest in assets such as bonds, stocks, mortgages, and other loans; the earnings from these assets are then used to pay out claims on the policies. In effect, insurance companies transform assets such as bonds, stocks, and loans into insurance policies that provide a set of services (for example, claim adjustments, savings plans, friendly insurance agents). If the insurance company's production process of asset transformation efficiently provides its customers with adequate insurance services at low cost and if it can earn high returns on its investments, it will make profits; if not, it will suffer losses.

In Chapters 2 and 15 the concepts of adverse selection and moral hazard allowed us to understand why financial intermediaries such as insurance companies are important in the economy. Here we use the adverse selection and moral hazard concepts to explain many management practices specific to the insurance industry.

In the case of an insurance policy, moral hazard arises when the existence of insurance encourages the insured party to take risks that increase the likelihood of an insurance payoff. For example, a person covered by burglary insurance might not take as many precautions to prevent a burglary because the insurance company will reimburse most of the losses if a theft occurs. Adverse selection holds that the people most likely to receive large insurance payoffs are the ones who will want to purchase insurance the most. For example, a person suffering from a terminal disease would want to take out the biggest life and medical insurance policies possible, thereby exposing the insurance company to potentially large losses. Both adverse selection and moral hazard can result in large losses to insurance companies because they lead to higher payouts on insurance claims. Minimizing adverse selection and moral hazard to reduce these payouts is therefore an extremely important goal for insurance companies, and this goal explains the insurance practices we discuss here.

Screening

To reduce adverse selection, insurance companies try to screen out poor insurance risks from good ones. Effective information collection procedures are therefore an important principle of insurance management.

When you apply for auto insurance, the first thing your insurance agent does is ask you questions about your driving record (number of speeding tickets and accidents), the type of car you are insuring, and certain personal matters (age, marital status). If you are applying for life insurance, you go through a similar grilling, but you are asked even more personal questions about such things as your health, smoking habits, and drug and alcohol use. The life insurance company even orders a medical evaluation (usually done by an independent company) that involves taking blood and urine samples. The insurance company uses the information you provide to allocate you to a risk class—a statistical estimate of how likely you are to have an insurance claim. Based on this information, the insurance company can decide whether to accept you for the insurance or to turn you down because you pose too high a risk and thus would be an unprofitable customer for the insurance company.

Risk-Based Premium

Charging insurance premiums on the basis of how much risk a policyholder poses for the insurance company is a time-honored principle of insurance management. Adverse selection explains why this principle is so important to insurance company profitability.

To understand why an insurance company finds it necessary to have risk-based premiums, let's examine an example of risk-based insurance premiums that at first glance seems unfair. Harry and Sally, both with no accidents or speeding tickets, apply for auto insurance. Harry, however, is 20 years old, while Sally is 40. Normally, Harry will be charged a much higher premium than Sally. Insurance companies do this because young males have a much higher accident rate than older females. Suppose, though, that one insurance company did not base its premiums on a risk classification but rather just charged a premium based on the average combined risk for those it insures. Then Sally would be charged too much and Harry too little. Sally could go to another insurance company and get a lower rate, while Harry would sign up for the insurance. Because Harry's premium isn't high enough to cover the accidents he is likely to have, on average the company would lose money on Harry. Only with a premium based on a risk classification, so that Harry is charged more, can the insurance company make a profit.[1]

Restrictive Provisions

Restrictive provisions in policies are another insurance management tool for reducing moral hazard. Such provisions discourage policyholders from engaging in risky activities that make an insurance claim more likely. One type of restrictive provision keeps the policyholder from benefiting from behavior that makes a claim more likely. For example, life insurance companies have provisions in their policies that eliminate death benefits if the insured person commits suicide. Restrictive provisions may also require certain behavior on the part of the insured that makes a claim less likely. A company renting motor scooters may be required to provide helmets for renters in order to be covered for any liability associated with the rental. The role of restrictive provisions is not unlike that of restrictive covenants on debt contracts described in Chapter 15: Both serve to reduce moral hazard by ruling out undesirable behavior.

---

[1]You may recognize that the example here is in fact an example of the lemons problem described in Chapter 15.

Prevention of Fraud

Insurance companies also face moral hazard because an insured person has an incentive to lie to the company and seek a claim even if the claim is not valid. For example, a person who has not complied with the restrictive provisions of an insurance contract may still submit a claim. Even worse, a person may file claims for events that did not actually occur. Thus, an important management principle for insurance companies is conducting investigations to prevent fraud so that only policyholders with valid claims receive compensation.

Cancellation of Insurance

Being prepared to cancel policies is another insurance management tool. Insurance companies can discourage moral hazard by threatening to cancel a policy when the insured person engages in activities that make a claim more likely. If your auto insurance company makes it clear that if a driver gets too many speeding tickets, coverage will be canceled, you will be less likely to speed.

Deductibles

The deductible is the fixed amount by which the insured's loss is reduced when a claim is paid off. A $250 deductible on an auto policy, for example, means that if you suffer a loss of $1,000 because of an accident, the insurance company will pay you only $750. Deductibles are an additional management tool that helps insurance companies reduce moral hazard. With a deductible, you experience a loss along with the insurance company when you make a claim. Because you also stand to lose when you have an accident, you have an incentive to drive more carefully. A deductible thus makes a policyholder act more in line with what is profitable for the insurance company; moral hazard has been reduced. And because moral hazard has been reduced, the insurance company can lower the premium by more than enough to compensate the policyholder for the existence of the deductible.

Another function of the deductible is to eliminate the administrative costs of small losses by forcing the insured to bear these losses.

Coinsurance

When a policyholder shares a percentage of the losses along with the insurance company, their arrangement is called **coinsurance**. For example, some medical insurance plans provide coverage for 80% of medical bills, and the insured person pays 20% after a certain deductible has been met. Coinsurance works to reduce moral hazard in exactly the same way that a deductible does. A policyholder who suffers a loss along with the insurance company has less incentive to take actions, such as going to the doctor unnecessarily, that involve higher claims. Coinsurance is thus another useful management tool for insurance companies.

Limits on the Amount of Insurance

Another important principle of insurance management is that there should be limits on the amount of insurance provided, even though a customer is willing to pay for more coverage. The higher the insurance coverage, the more the insured person can gain from risky activities that make an insurance payoff more likely and hence the greater the moral hazard. For example, if Zelda's car were insured for more than its true value, she might not take proper precautions to prevent its theft, such as making sure that the key is always removed or putting in an alarm system. If her car were stolen, she comes out ahead because the excessive insurance payoff would allow her to buy an even better car. By contrast, when the insurance payment is lower than the value of her car, she will suffer a loss if it is stolen and will thus take the proper precautions to prevent this from happening. Insurance companies must always make sure that their coverage is not so high that moral hazard leads to large losses.

Summary

Effective insurance management requires several practices: information collection and screening of potential policyholders, risk-based premiums, restrictive provisions, prevention of fraud, cancellation of insurance, deductibles, coinsurance, and limits on the amount of insurance. All of these practices reduce moral hazard and adverse selection by making it harder for policyholders to benefit from engaging in activities that increase the amount and likelihood of claims. With smaller benefits available, the poor insurance risks (those who are more likely to engage in the activities in the first place) see less benefit from the insurance and are thus less likely to seek it out.

Pensions

A **pension plan** is an asset pool that accumulates over an individual's working years and is paid out during the nonworking years. Pension plans represent the fastest-growing financial intermediary. There are a number of reasons for this rapid growth.

As the United States became more urban, people realized that they could not rely on their children to care for them in their retirement. In a rural culture, families tend to stay together on the farm. The property passes from generation to generation with an implicit understanding that the younger generations will care for the older ones. When families became more dispersed and moved off farms, both the opportunity for and the expectation of extensive financial support of the older generations declined.

A second factor contributing to the growth of pension plans is that people are living longer and retiring younger. Again, in the rural setting, people often remained productive well into their retirement years. Many companies in urban America, however, encourage older workers to retire. They are often earning high wages as a result of seniority, yet may be less productive than younger workers. The result of this trend toward younger retirement and longer lives is that the average person can expect to spend more years in retirement. These years must be funded somehow, and the pension plan is often the vehicle of choice.

Types of Pensions

Pension plans can be categorized in several ways. They may be defined-benefit or defined-contribution plans, and they may be public or private.

Defined-Benefit Pension Plans

Under a **defined-benefit plan,** the plan sponsor promises the employees a specific benefit when they retire. The payout is usually determined with a formula that uses the number of years worked and the employee's final salary. For example, a pension benefit may be calculated by the following formula:

Annual payment = 2% × average of final 3 years' income × years of service

In this case, if a worker had been employed for 35 years and the average wages during the last three years were $50,000, the annual pension benefit would be

$$0.02 \times \$50,000 \times 35 = \$35,000 \text{ per year}$$

The defined-benefit plan puts the burden on the employer to provide adequate funds to ensure that the agreed payments can be made. External audits of pension plans are required to determine whether sufficient funds have been contributed by the company. If sufficient funds are set aside by the firm for this purpose, the plan is **fully funded.** If more than enough funds are available, the plan is **overfunded.** Often, insufficient funds are available and the fund is **underfunded.** For example, if Jane Brown contributes $100 per year into her pension plan and the interest rate is 10%, after ten years, the contributions and their interest earnings would be worth $1,753.[2] If the defined benefit on her pension plan is $1,753 or less after ten years, the plan is fully funded because her contributions and earnings will cover this payment in full. But if the defined benefit is $2,000, the plan is underfunded because her contributions and earnings do not cover this amount. Underfunding is most common when the employer fails to contribute adequately to the plan. Surprisingly, it is not illegal for a firm to sponsor an underfunded plan. The companies of the S&P 500, for example, have an estimated aggregate pension deficit of about $150 billion.

Defined-Contribution Pension Plans

As the name implies, instead of defining what the pension plan will pay, **defined-contribution plans** specify only what will be contributed to the fund. The retirement benefits are entirely dependent on the earnings of the fund. Corporate sponsors of defined-contribution plans usually put a fixed percentage of each employee's wages into the pension fund each pay period. In some instances, the employee also contributes to the plan. An insurance company or fund manager acts as trustee and invests the fund's assets. Frequently, employees are allowed to specify how the funds in their individual accounts will be invested. For example, an employee who is a conservative investor may prefer government securities, while one who is a more aggressive investor may prefer to have his or her retirement funds invested in corporate stock. When the employee retires, the balance in the pension account can be transferred into an annuity or some other form of distribution.

Defined-contribution pension plans are becoming increasingly popular. Many existing defined-benefit plans are converting to this form, and virtually all new plans

---

[2]The $100 contributed in year 1 would become worth $100 × (1 + 0.10)^{10} = $259.37 at the end of 10 years; the $100 contributed in year 2 would become worth $100 × (1 + 0.10)^9 = 235.79; and so on until the $100 contributed in year 10 would become worth $100 × (1 + 0.10) = $110. Adding these together, we get the total value of these contributions and their earnings at the end of 10 years as $1,753.

are established as defined-contribution. One reason the defined-contribution plan is becoming so popular is that the onus is put on the employee rather than the employer to look out for the pension plan's performance. This reduces the liability of the employer.

One problem is that plan participants may not understand the need to diversify their holdings. For example, many firms actively encourage employees to invest in company stock. The firm's motivation is to better align employee interest with that of stockholders. The downside is that employees suffer twice should the firm fail. First, they lose their jobs, and second, their retirement portfolios evaporate. The collapse of Enron Inc. brought this issue forcibly to the public's attention.

Another problem with defined-contribution plans is that many employees are not familiar enough with investments to make wise long-term choices. For example, only 3.7% of plan participants choose to put any more than half of their investment in stocks, even though long-term growth potential is greatest in the stock market.

Private and Public Pension Plans

Private pension plans, sponsored by employers, groups, and individuals, have grown rapidly as people have become more concerned about the viability of Social Security and more sophisticated about preparing for retirement. In the past, private pension plans invested mostly in government securities and corporate bonds. Although these instruments are still important pension plan assets, corporate stocks, mortgages, open market paper, and time deposits now play a significant role. Figure 22.5 shows the distribution of private pension plan assets. They are now the largest institutional investor in the stock market. This makes pension plan managers a potentially powerful force if they choose to exercise control over firm management (see the Mini-Case box).

An alternative to privately sponsored pension plans is the public plans, though in many cases there is very little difference between the two. A **public pension plan** is one that is sponsored by a governmental body.

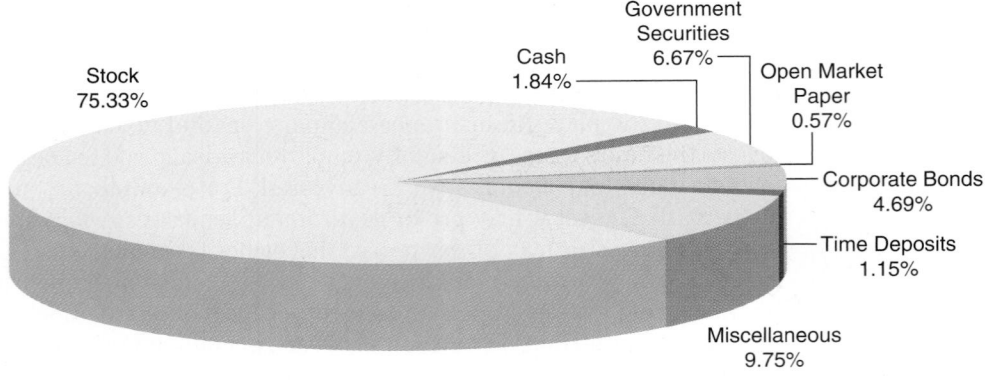

Figure 22.5   Distribution of Private Pension Plan Assets (end of 2006)

Source: http://www.federalreserve.gov/releases/21/current/21.pdf, Table L118.

mini-case

Power to the Pensions

One ramification of the growth of pension plans and other institutional investors is that the managers of these funds have the ability to exercise substantial control over corporate management. Clearly, when a pension fund manager, who controls many thousands of shares, calls a corporate officer, the officer is going to listen. Evidence suggests that fund managers actively apply the power they have to influence corporate management. For example, pension funds recently defeated management-sponsored antitakeover proxy proposals at Honeywell. And Texaco agreed to name a director from candidates submitted by the huge California Public Employees Retirement System. In addition, the stated mission of the Council of Institutional Investors is to "encourage trustees to take an active role in assuring that corporate actions are not taken at the expense of shareholders." It is possible that these actions will work to benefit shareholders, who do not individually wield enough clout to exert control. However, the clout shareholders wield when their shares are placed into a fund manager's hands may be sufficient to improve corporate management significantly.

go online

Information on your Social Security benefits is available at www.ssa.gov/.

The largest of the public plans is the Federal Old Age and Disability Insurance Program (often called simply Social Security). This pension plan was established in 1935 to provide a safety net for aging Americans and is a "pay-as-you-go" system—money that workers contribute today pays benefits to current recipients. Future generations will be called on to pay benefits to the individuals who are currently contributing. Many people fear that the fund will be unable to meet its obligations by the time they retire. This fear is based on problems that the fund encountered in the 1970s and on the realization that a large number of people from the baby boom generation (born between 1946 and 1964) will swell the ranks of retirees in the rapidly approaching future.

The amount of the Social Security benefits a retiree receives is based on the person's earnings history. Workers contribute 6.2% of wages up to a current maximum wage of $97,500 (as of 2007). Employers contribute the same amount. There is a certain amount of redistribution in the benefits, with low-income workers receiving a relatively larger return on their investment than high-income workers. One way to evaluate the amount of the benefits of a pension plan is to determine how the monthly benefits compare to preretirement income. This replacement ratio ranged from 49% for someone earning $15,000 a year to 24% for someone earning $53,400.

Figure 22.6 shows that the total assets in the Social Security fund decreased in the late 1970s and early 1980s at the same time that the number of insured people was increasing. This situation led to a restructuring that included raising the program's contributions and reducing the program's benefits. To build public confidence, the Social Security system has started accumulating reserves to be used when the baby boom generation begins retiring.

The problem is that the 77 million baby boomers born between 1946 and 1964 will begin reaching their normal retirement ages in 2011. Meanwhile, the number of workers supporting each one of those retirees will fall from 3.3 to 2 by 2041. The government predicts that the Social Security trust fund, built up over the years with

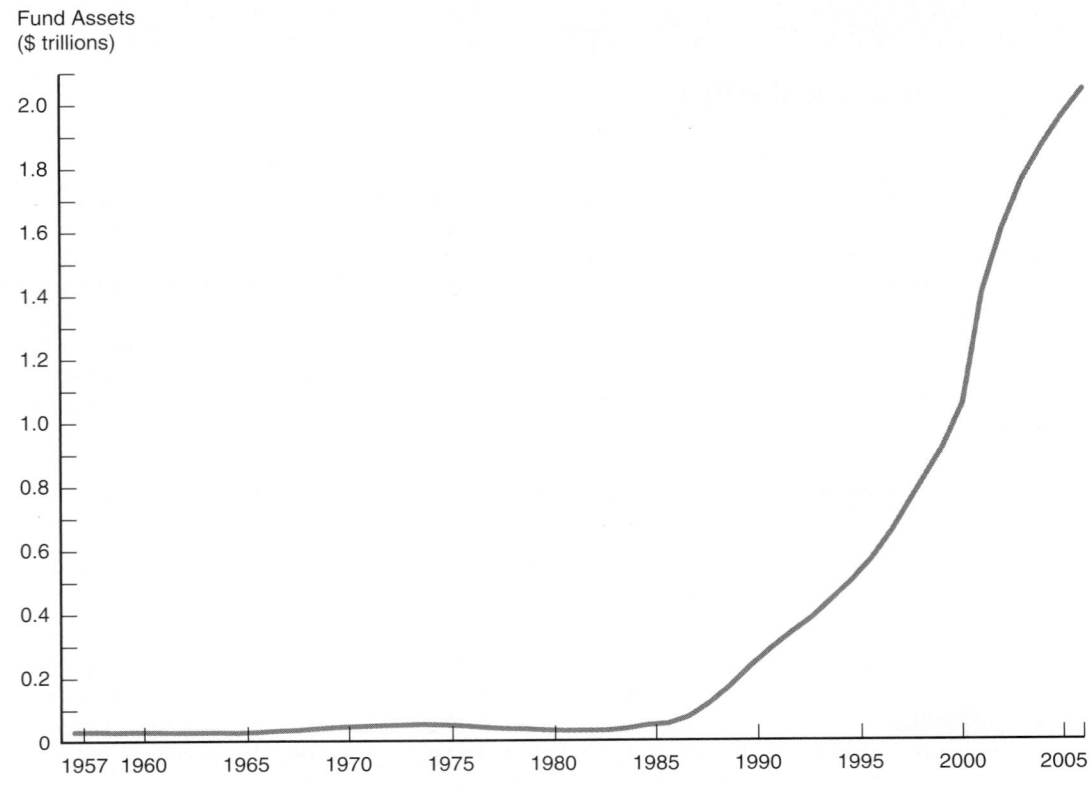

Fund Assets
($ trillions)

Figure 22.6   Social Security Fund Assets, 1957–2006

Source: http://www.ssa.gov/oact/stats/table4a2.html.

go online

www.ssab.gov is the Web
site for the Social Security
advisory board. This site will
report the most current
estimates for when the trust
fund will be depleted.

excess payroll taxes, will be depleted by that date (see Figure 22.7). After that, taxes would cover only 75% of benefits. Some experts argue that the crisis will arrive much earlier, as soon as 2018. This is because in 2018 the program will have to start redeeming the trust fund's special Treasury bonds that represent the Social Security surplus. The trouble is that money to redeem these bonds is being spent to run the federal government. By 2030, Social Security will have to redeem $750 billion worth of bonds. "Whether that's a crisis for Social Security, it certainly is a crisis for whoever is around trying to come up with $750 billion," says Michael Tanner, director of the Cato Institute's Project on Social Security Privatization.

A number of proposals are being considered to help keep Social Security viable for the future. The idea that AARP polling finds as the least objectionable is to raise the cap on the maximum amount that workers have to pay into the fund in any given year. The maximum wage that was taxed in 2007 was $97,500, which represents only 85% of all income. This is down from a tax on 90% of income in 1983. It is likely that this will be one area for change.

Another possible change concerns the minimum age when one can start receiving benefits. This was changed in 1984 to gradually rise so that those born after 1960 cannot start receiving full benefits until they are age 67. The original retirement

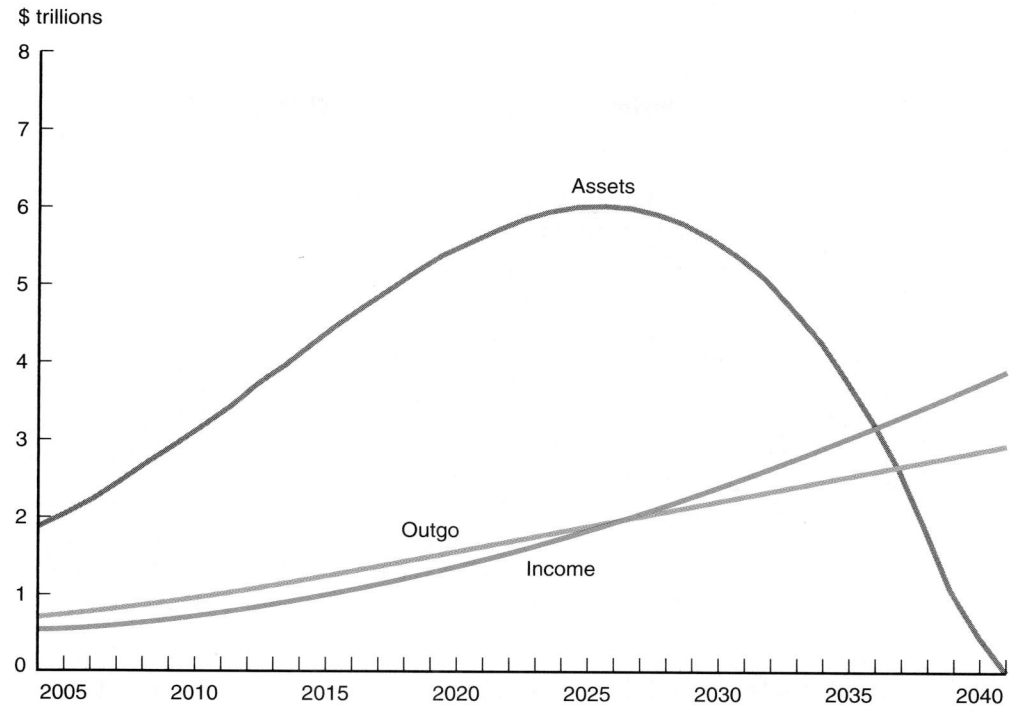

$ trillions

Figure 22.7 Projected Social Security Trust Fund Assets

Source: http://www.ssab.gov/documents/whyactionshouldbetakensoon.pdf.

age of 65 dates back to 1874, when a railroad company established a pension plan. The basis of this decision was that 65 was considered to be the maximum age at which one could safely operate a train. This rule was later incorporated into the Federal Railroad Retirement Act of 1934, which was used to support that retirement age when the Social Security Act was written. Since few Americans are required to operate trains any more, there is some justification for reevaluating the retirement age. The good news is that relatively small changes to the retirement age have a large impact on the Social Security fund balance.

In 2004, Alan Greenspan, then chairman of the Federal Reserve, suggested altering the way that cost of living adjustments to Social Security payments were calculated. Currently the benefit payments are adjusted annually based on the consumer price index (CPI). Greenspan argued that this overstated true inflation because it ignored consumers' switching to less expensive alternatives. While admitting some validity to this, critics argue that the CPI underestimates the increase in medical costs, which make up a large portion of retirees' budgets.

Still another suggestion is to recognize that beneficiaries are living longer than in the past and to adjust benefit payments to stretch them over a longer period of time.

Prior to the stock market falling in 2000, many investors were calling for the privatization of Social Security. The biggest obstacle to privatization is that funds diverted into private accounts would not be available to pay current retirees' benefits. This exacerbates the looming problem rather than solving it. Analysts estimate that the cost of transitioning to a fully funded privatized plan would be enormous—about $100 billion. Over time, analysts argue, privatization would gradually transform Social Security from an unfunded, pay-as-you-go system to a fully funded pension with real assets. Workers who retired 20 years ago received all that they paid in, plus interest and much more. But those who retire today will get only about a 2.2% return, adjusted for inflation. A 30-year-old worker will lose money in absolute terms upon retirement. However, falling stock prices in 2000–2002 have reduced support for all privatization options.

In the short term, Social Security reform is more likely to take the form of an increase in tax, a reduction in benefits, a delay in receiving benefits, or all three. For example, the age at which benefits begin is already scheduled to increase from 65 to 67. Some plans suggest delaying benefits until age 70.

If no funding reforms take place and the current estimates regarding the depletion of the Social Security fund are accurate, the payroll tax rate would have to be increased from 12.4% to 18%.

We must remember that these estimates are based on current facts as they are known. Many factors can change to cause the estimates to change. For example, research on cures for cancer has received a great deal of publicity recently. If a cure for any major cause of death is found, the fund will be in greater trouble than currently thought.

It is extremely difficult to make accurate estimates on the health of the social security system. In 1995, for example, the Social Security Administration estimated that the fund would be depleted by 2029, 12 years earlier than currently projected. Many factors affect the fund balance including life expectancies, birth rates, and even the rate of legal and illegal immigration. While it would be political disaster for the government to allow the program to fail, current workers should realize that they should not rely on it to provide the majority of their retirement cash flow. In the future, the proportion of pre-retirement income it replaces may well continue to decrease.

Regulation of Pension Plans

For many years, pension plans were relatively free of government regulation. Many companies provided pension benefits as rewards for long years of good service and used the benefits as an incentive. Frequently, pension benefits were paid out of current income. When the firm failed or was acquired by another firm, the benefits ended. During the Great Depression, widespread pension plan failures led to increased regulation and to the establishment of the Social Security system.

A major U.S. Supreme Court decision in 1949 established that pension benefits were a legitimate part of collective bargaining, the negotiation of contracts by unions. This decision led to a great increase in the number of plans in existence as unions pressured employers to establish such plans for union members.

Employee Retirement Income Security Act

The most important and most comprehensive legislation affecting pension funds is the **Employee Retirement Income Security Act (ERISA),** passed in 1974. ERISA set certain standards that must be followed by all pension plans. Failure to follow the provisions of the act may cause a plan to lose its advantageous tax status. The motivation for the act was that many workers who had contributed to plans for many years were losing their benefits when plans failed. The principal features of the act are the following:

- ERISA established guidelines for funding.
- It provided that employees switching jobs may transfer their credits from one employer plan to the next.
- It said that plans must have minimum vesting requirements. *Vesting* refers to how long an employee must work for the company to be eligible for pension benefits. The maximum permissible vesting period is seven years, though most plans allow for vesting in less time. Employee contributions are always immediately vested.
- It increased the disclosure requirements for pension plans, providing employees with more ample information about the health and investments of their pension plans.
- It assigned the responsibility of regulatory oversight to the Department of Labor.

go online

www.pbgc.gov provides additional information about the Pension Benefit Guarantee Corporation.

go online

www.pbgc/gov/docs/ 2005databook.pdf provides extensive statistics on the health of PBGC.

ERISA also established the **Pension Benefit Guarantee Corporation** (PBGC or simply called **Penny Benny**), a government agency that performs a role similar to that of the FDIC. It insures pension benefits up to a limit (currently just over $49,500 per year per person) if a company with an underfunded pension plan goes bankrupt or is unable to meet its pension obligations for other reasons. Penny Benny charges pension plans a premium to pay for this insurance, but it can also borrow funds up to $100 million from the U.S. Treasury. Penny Benny currently pays benefits to about 700,000 retirees whose pension plans failed.

Over 66% of defined-benefit pension plan assets are invested in stocks. When the market prices were high, most defined-benefit pension plans were adequately funded. However, the market fall in 2000 along with low interest rates and a weak economy have put many pension plans in jeopardy. As a result, in 2006 PBGC was in the red by $18.1 billion. According to PBGC, there is another $85 billion in pension deficits on the books of weak companies that could end up pushing this deficit far higher.

The accounting for pension plans makes it very difficult to accurately access whether a fund is over- or underfunded. The assumptions behind such calculations are subject to constant revision and argument. Cash-strapped firms have tremendous incentive to underfund their pension plans, and Congress is reluctant to enforce higher payments that could put a firm at greater risk of failure.

The Pension Benefit Guaranty Corporation is rapidly facing a funding crisis that could have far-reaching effects. Many defined-benefit pension funds are in severe trouble due to the increasing life spans of their pensioners, increased medical costs, and weak corporate income that has made it difficult to keep up with funding obligations. Currently, the airline and steel industries are responsible for the bulk of PBGC's claims. For example, United Airlines terminated its defined benefit program in 2005. Since then, PBGC has paid over $7.6 billion in claims to 122,000 vested United participants. Figure 22.8 shows annual payments made since 1980 to failed plan participants. In PBGC's 2005 data book, they say the plan has never been under greater stress.

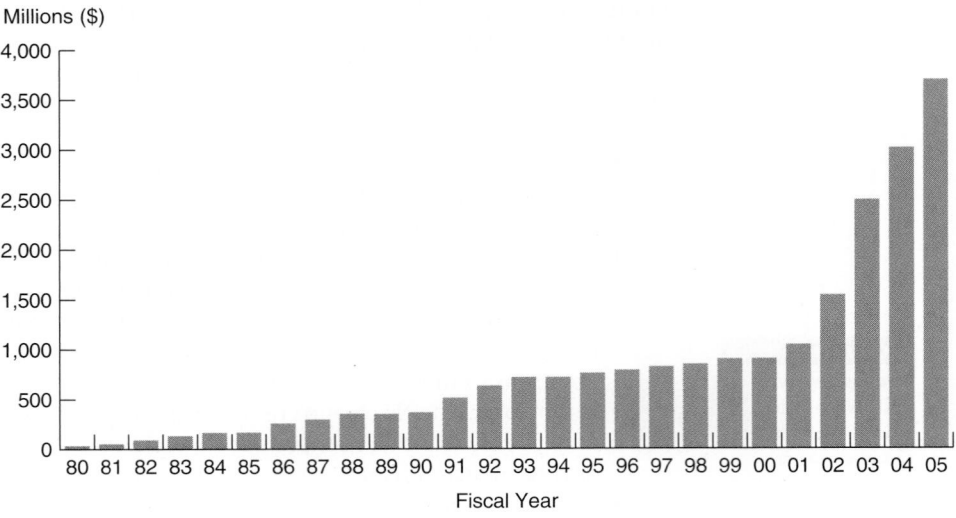

Millions ($)

Figure 22.8 Total PBGC Benefit Payments

Source: http://www.pbgc.gov/docs/2005databook.pdf.

Many firms with defined-benefit plans find it hard to compete against firms with much lower cost defined-contribution plans. This competitive disadvantage increases the likelihood that the firms may not survive to pay down their deficits. For example, General Motors' profit margin per car is about 0.5%. Without the burden of pension and retiree health care costs, the margin would be about 5.5%. Morgan Stanley estimates that the benefits cost is $1,784 per car for GM, while it is only $200 per car for Toyota.

Firms often fail when they face a cost disadvantage. Due to higher costs, including pension obligations, Bethlehem Steel, LTV, and National Steel all filed for bankruptcy in 2002 and terminated their pension plans. PBGC is now paying over 200,000 former steel workers' benefits. International Steel Group Inc. (ISG) has acquired the mills of these old steel companies and is now the largest steel producer in the country. Its defined-contribution cost for employees is about $45 million. Prior to its bankruptcy, Bethlehem Steel alone was paying out $500 million a year in pension benefits.

If firms with defined benefit plans continue to fail, PBGC will be forced to assume their pension funds' liabilities. These obligations could quickly surpass the financial resources available to PBGC if the economy remains weak. In that event, taxpayers may be called upon to make up the difference.

The government is not strictly responsible for backing up PBGC; however, most observers feel it could not politically allow pensioners to lose their benefits. The temporary fix is to allow firms to use a higher interest rate in their pension calculations so that their pension liability is reduced. The hope is that the economy will continue to revive, stocks will rise, and interest rates increase. Recall from Chapter 19 that this same technique (called regulatory forbearance) was used to prolong the savings and loan crisis. We can only hope it works better this time.

The Pension Protection Act of 2006 was passed to address the growing problem with underfunded and failing pension plans. This legislation provides for stronger pension funding rules, greater transparency, and a stronger pension insurance system.

Individual Retirement Plans

The Pension Reform Act of 1978 updated the Self-Employed Individuals Tax Retirement Act of 1962 to authorize **individual retirement accounts (IRAs).** IRAs permitted people (such as those who are self-employed) who are not covered by other pension plans to contribute into a tax-deferred savings account. Legislation in 1981 and 1982 expanded the eligibility of these accounts to make them available to almost everyone. IRAs proved extremely popular, to the extent that their use resulted in significant losses of tax revenues to the government. That led Congress to include provisions in the Tax Reform Act of 1986 sharply curtailing eligibility.

Keogh plans are a retirement savings option for the self-employed. Funds can be deposited with a depository institution, life insurance company, or securities firm. The owner of the Keogh is often allowed some discretion as to how the funds will be invested.

On January 1, 1997, the Small Business Protection Act of 1996 went into effect. This act created simplified retirement plans with so-called SIMPLE IRAs and 401(k) plans for businesses with 100 or fewer employees. SIMPLE retirement plans are becoming significantly more popular, especially among the smallest businesses.

The Future of Pension Funds

We can expect that pension funds will continue their growth and popularity as the population continues to grow and age. Workers in their early years of employment often find discussions of retirement investing creeping into their conversations. This heightened attention to providing for the future will result in an increased number of pension funds as well as a greater variety of pension fund options to choose among. We can also expect to see pension funds gain increased power over corporations as they control increasing amounts of stock.

SUMMARY

1. Insurance companies exist because people are risk-averse and prefer to transfer risk away from themselves. Insurance benefits people's lives by reducing the size of reserves they would have to maintain to cover possible loss of life or property.

2. Adverse selection and moral hazard are problems inherent to the insurance business. Many of the provisions of insurance policies—including deductibles, application screening, and risk-based premiums—are aimed at reducing their effects.

3. Insurance is usually divided into two primary types, life insurance and property and casualty insurance. Many life insurance products also serve as savings vehicles. Property and casualty insurance usually has a much shorter term than most life insurance.

4. Because life insurance liabilities are very predictable, these insurers are able to invest in long-term assets. Property and casualty insurance companies must keep their assets more liquid to pay out on unexpected losses.

5. Pension plans are rapidly growing as a longer-lived generation plans for early retirement.

6. There are two primary types of pension plans: defined-benefit and defined-contribution. Defined-benefit plans pay benefits according to a formula that is established in advance. Defined-contribution plans specify only how much is to be saved; benefits depend on the returns generated by the plans.

7. The largest public pension plan is Social Security, which is a pay-as-you-go system. Current retirees receive payments from current workers. Many people are concerned that as the number of retirees increases, the amount paid in to the Social Security system will not be sufficient to cover the sums being paid out.

8. Most private pension plans are insured by the Pension Benefit Guarantee Corporation, which pays benefits when a plan's sponsor goes bankrupt or is otherwise unable to make payments.

KEY TERMS

annuity, *p. 567*
casualty (liability) insurance, *p. 572*
certainty equivalent, *p. 562*
coinsurance, *p. 577*
deductible, *p. 564*
defined-benefit plan, *p. 579*
defined-contribution plan, *p. 579*
Employee Retirement Income Security Act
  (ERISA), *p. 584*
fully funded, *p. 579*
individual retirement accounts (IRA), *p. 587*
law of large numbers, *p. 567*
mutual insurance companies, *p. 565*

named-peril policies, *p. 573*
open-peril policies, *p. 573*
overfunded, *p. 579*
Pension Benefit Guarantee Corporation
  (Penny Benny), *p. 585*
pension plan, *p. 578*
private pension plans, *p. 580*
property insurance, *p. 572*
public pension plan, *p. 580*
reinsurance, *p. 573*
stock company, *p. 565*
underfunded, *p. 579*
underwriters, *p. 565*

QUESTIONS

1. Why do people choose to buy insurance even if their expected loss is less than the payments they will make to the insurance company?

2. Why do insurance companies not allow people to buy insurance on personally unrelated risks?

3. What is information asymmetry, and how does it affect insurance companies?

4. Distinguish between adverse selection and moral hazard as they relate to the insurance industry.

5. How do insurance companies protect themselves against losses due to adverse selection and moral hazard?

6. Distinguish between independent agents and exclusive agents.

7. Are most insurance companies organized as mutuals or stock companies?

8. How are insurance companies able to predict their losses from claims accurately enough to let them price their policies such that they will make a profit?

9. What is the difference between term life insurance and whole life insurance?

10. What risks do property and casualty insurance policies protect against?

11. What is the purpose behind reinsurance?

12. Distinguish between defined-benefit and defined-contribution pension plans.

13. Why have private pension plans grown rapidly in recent years?

14. What is a pay-as-you-go pension plan?

15. Why is Social Security in danger of eventually going bankrupt?

QUANTITATIVE PROBLEMS

1. Research indicates that the 1,000,000 cars in your city experience unrecoverable losses of $250,000,000 per year from theft, collisions, etc. If 30% of premiums are used to cover expenses, what premium must be charged to car owners?

2. Assume that life expectancy in the United States is normally distributed with a mean of 73 years and a standard deviation of 9 years. What is the probability that you will live to be over 100 years old?

3. Your rich uncle dies, leaving you a life insurance policy worth $100,000. The insurance company also offers you an option to receive $8,225 per year for 20 years, with the first payment due today. Which option should you use?

4. A home products manufacturer estimates that the probability of being sued for product defects is 1% per year per product manufactured. If the firm currently manufactures 20 products, what is the probability that the firm will experience no lawsuits in a given year?

5. Kio Outfitters estimated the following losses and probabilities from past experience:

Loss	Probability (%)
$30,000	0.25
$15,000	0.75
$10,000	1.50
$5,000	2.50
$1,000	5.00
$250	15.00
$0	75.00

What is the probability Kio will experience a loss of $5,000 or greater? If an insurance company offers a loss policy with $1,500 deductible, what is the most Kio will pay?

6. A client needs assistance with retirement planning. Here are the facts:
   - The client, Dave, is 21 years old. He wants to retire at 65.
   - Dave has disposable income of $2,000 per month.
   - The IRA Dave has chosen has an average annual return of 8%.

   If Dave contributes half of his disposable income to the account, what will it be worth at 65? How much would he need to contribute to have $5,000,000 at 65?

7. When opening an IRA account, investors have two options. With a regular IRA account, funds added are not taxed initially, but are taxed when withdrawn. With a Roth IRA, the funds are taxed initially, but not when withdrawn. If an investor wants to contribute $15,000 before taxes to an IRA, what will be the difference after 30 years between the two options? Assume that the investor is currently in the 25% tax bracket, and that the IRA will earn 6% per year.

8. An employee contributes $200 a year (at the end of the year) to her pension plan. What would be the total contributions and value of the account after five years? Assume that the plan earns 15% per year over the period.

9. Paul's car slid off the icy road, causing $2,500 in damage to his car. He was also treated for minor injuries, costing $1,300. His car insurance has a $500 deductible, after which the full loss is paid. His health insurance has a $100 deductible and covers 75% of medical cost (total). What were Paul's out-of-pocket costs from the incident?

WEB EXERCISES

Insurance Companies and Pension Funds

1. There are many sites on the Web to help you compute whether you are properly preparing for your retirement. One of the better is offered by Quicken. You will find it at **http://cgi.money.cnn.com/tools/ retirementplanner/retirementplanner.jsp**.

   Have you set aside enough retirement money to last your lifetime? The earlier you start, the easier it will be.

In general, your retirement funds will come from four sources:
   - Pension plans
   - Social Security
   - Tax-deferred savings
   - Basic (taxable) savings

Use the Retirement Planner to predict the income from the first two, and to determine how much you will need to save to make up the balance for your retirement goals.

2. The Internet offers many calculators to help consumers estimate their needs for various financial services. When using these tools, you must remember that they are usually sponsored by financial intermediaries that hope to sell you products. Visit one such site at **www.finaid.org/calculators/lifeinsuranceneeds.phtml** and calculate how much life insurance you need. Do you have another life insurance policy? Use the calculator to see if that policy is large enough.

CHAPTER 23

Investment Banks, Security Brokers and Dealers, and Venture Capital Firms

Preview

If you decide to take advantage of that hot stock tip you just heard about from your roommate, you may need to interact with a securities company. Similarly, as the new CFO of WWCF, a candy manufacturer, you may need a securities company if you are asked to coordinate a bond sale or to issue additional stock. If your grandfather decides to sell his firm to the public, you may need to help him by working with investment bankers at that securities company. Finally, if you are looking for capital to grow a small, but successful, start-up company, you may need the help of a venture capital firm.

The smooth functioning of securities markets, in which bonds and stocks are traded, involves several financial institutions, including securities brokers and dealers, investment banks, and venture capital firms. None of these institutions were included in our list of financial intermediaries in Chapter 2 because they do not perform the intermediation function of acquiring funds by issuing liabilities and then using the funds to acquire financial assets. Nonetheless, they are important in the process of channeling funds from savers to spenders.

To begin our look at how securities markets work, recall the distinction between primary and secondary securities markets discussed in Chapter 2. In a **primary market,** new issues of a security are sold to buyers by the corporation or government agency ultimately using the funds. A **secondary market** then trades the securities that have been sold in the primary market (and so are secondhand). Investment banks assist in the initial sale of securities in the primary market; securities brokers and dealers assist in the trading of securities in the secondary markets. Finally, venture capital firms provide funds to companies not yet ready to sell securities to the public.

591

Investment Banks

Investment bankers were called "Masters of the Universe" in Tom Wolfe's *The Bonfire of the Vanities.* They are the elite on Wall Street. They have earned this reputation from the types of financial services they provide. Investment banks are best known as intermediaries that help corporations raise funds. However, this definition is far too narrow to accurately explain the many valuable and sophisticated services these companies provide. (Despite its name, an investment bank is not a bank in the ordinary sense; that is, it is not a financial intermediary that takes in deposits and then lends them out.) In addition to underwriting the initial sale of stocks and bonds, **investment banks** also play a pivotal role as deal makers in the mergers and acquisitions area, as intemediaries in the buying and selling of companies, and as private brokers to the very wealthy. Some well-known investment banking firms are Morgan Stanley, Merrill Lynch, Salomon Brothers, First Boston Corporation, and Goldman, Sachs.

One feature of investment banks that distinguishes them from stockbrokers and dealers is that they usually earn their income from fees charged to clients rather than from commissions on stock trades. These fees are often set as a fixed percentage of the dollar size of the deal being worked. Because the deals frequently involve huge sums of money, the fees can be substantial. The percentage fee will be smaller for large deals, in the neighborhood of 3%, and much larger for smaller deals, sometimes exceeding 10%.

Background

In the early 1800s, most American securities had to be sold in Europe. As a result, most securities firms developed from merchants who operated a securities business as a sideline to their primary business. For example, the Morgans built their initial fortune with the railroads. To help raise the money to finance railroad expansion, J. P. Morgan's father resided in London and sold Morgan railroad securities to European investors. Over time, the profitability of the securities businesses became evident and the securities industry expanded.

Prior to the Great Depression, many large, money center banks in New York sold securities and simultaneously conducted conventional banking activities. During the Depression, about 10,000 banks failed (about 40% of all commercial banks). This led to the passage of the **Glass-Steagall Act,** which separated commercial banking from investment banking.

The Glass-Steagall Act made it illegal for a commercial bank to buy or sell securities on behalf of its customers. The original reasoning behind this legislation was to insulate commercial banks from the greater risk inherent in the securities business. There were also concerns that conflicts of interest might arise that would subject commercial banks to increased risk. For example, suppose that an investment banker working at a commercial bank makes a mistake pricing a new stock offering. After promising the customer that he can sell the stock for $20, no sales materialize. The investment banker might be tempted to go down the hall to the commercial bank's investment department and talk them into bailing him out. This would subject depositors to the risk that the bank could lose money on poor investments.

Regulators thought another problem existed. Suppose the investment banker still cannot sell all of that $20 stock issue. He could call up bank customers and offer to loan them 100% of the funds needed to buy a portion of the stock issue. This would not cause a problem if the stock price rose in the future, but if it fell, the value of the securities would be less than the amount of the loan and the customer might not feel a great obligation to repay the loan. Many industry observers felt that this practice was partially to blame for some of the bank failures that occurred during the Depression. However, bank lobbyists currently argue that although only large banks were involved in issuing securities, most banks that actually failed were small. There is no evidence that security abuses led directly to any bank failures.

When the Glass-Steagall Act separated commercial banking from investment banking, new securities firms were created, many of which currently offer both investment banking services (selling new securities to the public) as well as brokerage services (selling existing securities to the public).

The legal barriers between commercial and investment banks have been decaying rapidly since the 1980s. One significant trend has been the acquisition of investment banks by commercial banks. For example, in 1997, Bankers Trust acquired Alex Brown, the oldest investment bank in the nation. Bankers Trust was subsequently acquired by Deutsche Banks, which has been spending enormous amounts of money establishing its own investment banking arm. Bank of America bought Roberson Stephens & Co., while NationsBank acquired Montgomery Securities. Subsequent mergers among banks are continuing the consolidation.

Underwriting Stocks and Bonds

When a corporation wants to borrow or raise funds, it may decide to issue long-term debt or equity instruments. It then usually hires an investment bank to facilitate the issuance and subsequent sale of the securities. The investment bank may underwrite the issue. The process of underwriting a stock or bond issue requires that the securities firm *purchase* the entire issue at a predetermined price and then resell it in the market. There are a number of services provided in the process of underwriting.

Giving Advice Most firms do not issue capital market securities very frequently. Over 80% of all corporate expansion is financed using profits retained from prior-period earnings. As a result, the financial managers at most firms are not familiar with how to proceed with a new security offering. Investment bankers, since they participate in this market daily, can provide advice to firms contemplating a sale. For instance, a firm may not know if it should raise capital by selling stocks or by selling bonds. The investment bankers may be able to help by pointing out, for example, that the market is currently paying high prices for stocks in the firm's industry (historically high PE ratios), while bonds are currently carrying relatively high interest rates (and therefore low prices).

Firms may also need advice as to *when* securities should be offered. If, for example, competitors have recently released earnings reports that show poor profits, it may be better to wait before attempting a sale: Firms want to time the market to sell stock when it will obtain the highest possible price. Again, because of daily interaction with the securities markets, investment bankers should be able to advise firms on the timing of their offerings.

Possibly the most difficult advice an investment banker must give a customer concerns at what *price* the security should be sold. Here the investment banker and the issuing firm have somewhat differing motives. First, consider that the firm wants to sell the stock for the highest price possible. Suppose you started a firm and ran it well for 20 years. You now wish to sell it to the public and retire to Tahiti. If 500,000 shares are to be offered and sold at $10 each, you will receive $5 million for your company. If you can sell the stock for $12, you will receive $6 million.

Investment bankers, however, do not want to overprice the stock because in most underwriting agreements, they will buy the entire issue at the agreed price and then resell it through their brokerage houses. They earn a profit by selling the stock at a slightly higher price than they paid the issuing firm. If the issue is priced too high, the investment bank will not be able to resell, and it will suffer a loss.

Pricing securities is not too hard if the firm has prior issues currently selling in the market, called **seasoned issues.** When a firm issues stock for the first time, called an **initial public offering (IPO),** it is much more difficult to determine what the correct price should be. All of the skill and expertise of the investment banking firm will be used to determine the most appropriate price. If the issuing firm and the investment banking firm can come to agreement on a price, the investment banker can assist with the next stage, filing the required documents.

Filing Documents In addition to advising companies, investment bankers will assist with making the required **Securities and Exchange Commission (SEC)** filings. The activities of investment banks and the operation of primary markets are heavily regulated by the SEC, which was created by the Securities and Exchange Acts of 1933 and 1934 to ensure that adequate information reaches prospective investors. Issuers of new securities to the general public (for amounts greater than $1.5 million in a year and with a maturity longer than 270 days) must file a **registration statement** with the SEC. This statement contains information about the firm's financial condition, management, competition, industry, and experience. The firm also discloses what the funds will be used for and management's assessment of the risk of the securities. The issuer must then wait 20 days after the registration statement is filed with the SEC before it can sell any of the securities. The SEC will review the registration statement, and if it does not object during a 20-day waiting period, the securities can then be sold.

The SEC review in no way represents an endorsement of the offering by the SEC. Their approval merely means that all of the required statements and disclosures are included in the statement. Nor does SEC approval mean that the information is accurate. Inaccuracies in the registration statement open the issuing firm's management up to lawsuits if it incurs losses. In extreme cases, inaccuracies could result in criminal charges.

A portion of the registration statement is reproduced and made available to investors for review. This widely circulated document is called a **prospectus.** By law, investors must be given a prospectus before they can invest in a new security.

While the registration document is in the process of being approved, the investment banker has other chores to attend to. For issues of debt, the investment banker must:

- Secure a credit rating from one or more of the credit review companies, such as Standard and Poor's or Moody's.
- Hire a bond counsel who will issue a statement attesting to the legality of the issue.
- Select a trustee who is responsible for seeing that the issuer fulfills its obligations as stated in the security's contract.
- Have the securities printed and prepared for distribution.

For equity issues, the investment banker may arrange for the securities to appear on one of the stock exchanges. Clearly, the investment banker can be of great assistance to an issuer well before any securities are actually offered for sale.

Underwriting Once all of the paperwork has been completed, the investment banker can proceed with the actual underwriting of the issue. At a prespecified time and date, the issuer will sell all of the stock or bond issue to the investment banking firm at the agreed price. The investment banker must now distribute this issue to the public at a greater price to earn its fee. (The 10 largest underwriters in the United States are listed in Table 23.1.)

By agreeing to underwrite an issue, the investment banking firm is certifying the quality of the issue to the public. We again see how asymmetric information helps justify the need for an intermediary. Investors do not want to put in weeks and weeks of hard technical study of a firm before buying its stock. Nor can they trust the firm's insiders to accurately report its condition. Instead, they rely on the ability of the investment bank to collect information about the firm in order to accurately establish the firm's value. They trust the investment bank's assessment, since it is backing up its opinion by actually purchasing securities in the process of underwriting them. Investment bankers recognize the responsibility they have to report information accurately and honestly, since once they lose investors' confidence, they will no longer be able to market their deals.

The investment banking firm is clearly taking a huge risk at this point. One way that it can reduce the risk is by forming a **syndicate.** A syndicate is a group of investment banking firms, each of which buys a portion of the security issue. Each firm in the syndicate is then responsible for reselling its share of the securities. Most securities issues are sold by syndicates because it is such an effective way to spread the risk among many different firms.

Investment banks advertise upcoming securities offerings with ads in the *Wall Street Journal.* The traditional advertisement is a large block ad in the financial

TABLE 23.1 Top Ten U.S. Underwriters of Global Debt and Equity Issues, 3/31/07

Underwriter	Market Share (%)
1. Citigroup	9.5
2. J.P. Morgan	8.2
3. Deutsche Bank	7.4
4. Merrill Lynch	6.6
5. Morgan Stanley	5.7
6. Lehman Brothers	5.3
7. Barclays Capital	4.8
8. Goldman Sachs & Co	4.7
9. Credit Suisse	4.5
10. UBS	4.4
Total	61.1

Source: http://www.thomson.com/solutions/financial/investbank/leaguetable_home/.

following the financial news

New Securities Issues

24,636,659 Shares

Initial Public Offering of Class A Common Stock
(par value $0.001 per share)

_____

Expected Price Range: $108 to $135 per share

You may obtain an electronic copy of the preliminary prospectus from any of the underwriters listed below.

_____

Joint Book-Running Managers

Morgan Stanley   **Credit Suisse First Boston**

_____

Goldman, Sachs & Co.	**Citigroup**
Lehman Brothers	**Allen & Company LLC**
JPMorgan	**UBS Investment Bank**
WRHambrecht+Co	**Thomas Weisel Partners LLC**

Ameritrade	**M.R. Beal & Company**	**William Blair & Company**
Blaylock & Partners, L.P.	**Cazenove Inc.**	**Deutsche Bank Securities**

E*TRADE Securities Inc.   **Epoch Securities, Inc.**   **Fidelity Capital Markets**   **HARRIS**direct
(distributed by Charles Schwab & Co., Inc.)   (a division of National Financial, LLC, a Fidelity Investments company)

Lazard   **Needham & Company, Inc.**   **Piper Jaffray**   **Ramirez & Co., Inc.**

Muriel Siebert & Co., Inc.   **Utendahl Capital**   **Wachovia Securities**   **Wells Fargo Securities, LLC**

The offering referred to above constitutes a new financing for the company. 14,142,135 of the shares will be issued and sold by Google and 10,494,524 of the shares will be sold by the selling stockholders. A registration statement relating to these securities has been filed with the Securities and Exchange Commission but has not yet become effective. These securities may not be sold nor may offers to buy be accepted prior to the time the registration statement becomes effective. This communication shall not constitute an offer to sell or the solicitation of an offer to buy nor shall there be any sale of these securities in any state in which such offer, solicitation or sale would be unlawful prior to the registration or qualification under the securities laws of any such state.

Information about new securities being issued is presented in distinctive advertisements published in the *Wall Street Journal* and other newspapers. These advertisements, called "tombstones" because of their appearance, are typically found in the "Money and Investing" section of the *Journal*.

The tombstone shown here indicates the number of shares of stock being issued (24,636,659 shares for Google) and the investment banks involved in selling them.

Source: Wall Street Journal, August 2, 2004 p. C5.

section of the paper. These ads are called **tombstones** because of their shape, and they list all of the investment banking firms included in the syndicate. Review the tombstone reproduced in the Following the Financial News box. The ad states that this is neither an offer to sell nor will offers to buy be accepted. The actual offer to sell can only be made in the prospectus. Also note the different investment banking firms involved in the syndicate.

The longer the investment banker holds the securities before reselling them to the public, the greater the risk that a negative price change will cause losses. One way that the investment banking firm speeds the sale is to solicit offers to buy the securities from investors prior to the date the investment bankers actually take ownership. Then, when the securities are available, the orders are filled and the securities are quickly transferred to the final buyers.

Most investment bankers are attached to larger brokerage houses (multifunction securities firms) that have nationwide sales offices. Each of these offices will be contacted prior to the issue date, and the sales agents will contact their customers to see if they would like to review a prospectus on the new security. The goal is to **fully subscribe** the issue. A fully subscribed issue is one where all of the securities available for sale have been spoken for before the issue date. Security issues may also be **undersubscribed.** In this case, the sales agents have been unable to generate sufficient interest in the security among their customers to sell all of the securities by the issue date. An issue may also be **oversubscribed,** in which case there are more offers to buy than there are securities available.

It is tempting to assume that the best alternative is for an issue to be oversubscribed, but in fact this will alienate the investment banker's customers. Suppose you were issuing a security for the first time and had negotiated with your investment banker to sell the issue of 500,000 shares of stock at $20. Now you find out that the issue is oversubscribed. You would feel that the investment banker had set the price too low and that you had lost money as a result. Maybe the stock could have sold for $25 and you could have collected an extra $2.5 million [($25 − $20) × 500,000 = $2,500,000]. You, as well as other issuing firms, would be unlikely to use this investment banker in the future.

It is equally serious for an issue to be undersubscribed, since it may be necessary to lower the price below the price the investment bankers paid to the issuer in order to sell all of the securities to the public. The investment banking firm stands to lose extremely large amounts of money because of the volume of securities involved. For example, review the tombstone shown in the Following the Financial News box once more. There are over 24 million shares being offered for sale. If the price must be lowered by even $.25 per share, over $6,000,000 would be lost. The high risk taken by investment bankers explains why they tend to be the most elite and highest-paid professionals on Wall Street, many earning in the millions of dollars per year.

Best Efforts An alternative to underwriting a securities offering is to offer the securities under a *best efforts agreement*. In a best efforts agreement, the investment banker sells the securities on a commission basis with no guarantee regarding the price the issuing firm will receive. The advantage to the investment banker of a best efforts transaction is that there is no risk of mispricing the security. There is also no need for the time-consuming task of establishing the market value of the security. The investment banker simply markets the security at the price the customer asks. If the security fails to sell, the offering can be canceled.

Private Placements An alternative method of selling securities is called the *private placement*. In a private placement, securities are sold to a limited number of investors rather than to the public as a whole. The advantage of the private placement is that the security does not need to be registered with the SEC as long as certain restrictive requirements are satisfied. Investment bankers are also often involved in private placement transactions. While investment bankers are not required for a private placement, they often facilitate the transaction by advising the issuing firm on the appropriate terms for the issue and by identifying potential purchasers.

The buyers of private placements must be large enough to purchase large amounts of securities at one time. This means that the usual buyers are insurance companies, commercial banks, pension funds, and mutual funds. Private placements are more common for the sale of bonds than for stocks. Goldman Sachs is the most active investment banking firm in the private placement market.

The process of taking a security public is summarized in Figure 23.1.

Equity Sales

Another service offered by investment banks is to help with the sale of companies or corporate divisions. For example, in 1984, Mattel was dangerously close to having its bank loans called when its electronics subsidiary incurred significant losses. Mattel enlisted the help of the investment banking firm Drexel Burnham Lambert. The first step in the firm's restructuring was to sell off all of its nontoy businesses. Mattel returned to health until it again ran into problems in 1999 due to the acquisition of a software company. In 2000, Mattel again used the services of investment bankers to sell this subsidiary.

The first step in any equity sale will be the seller's determination of the business's worth. The investment banker will provide a detailed analysis of the current market for similar companies and apply various sophisticated models to establish company value. Unlike a box of detergent or bar of candy, a going concern has no set price. The company value is based on the use the buyer intends to make of it. If a buyer is only interested in the physical assets, the firm will be worth one amount. A buyer

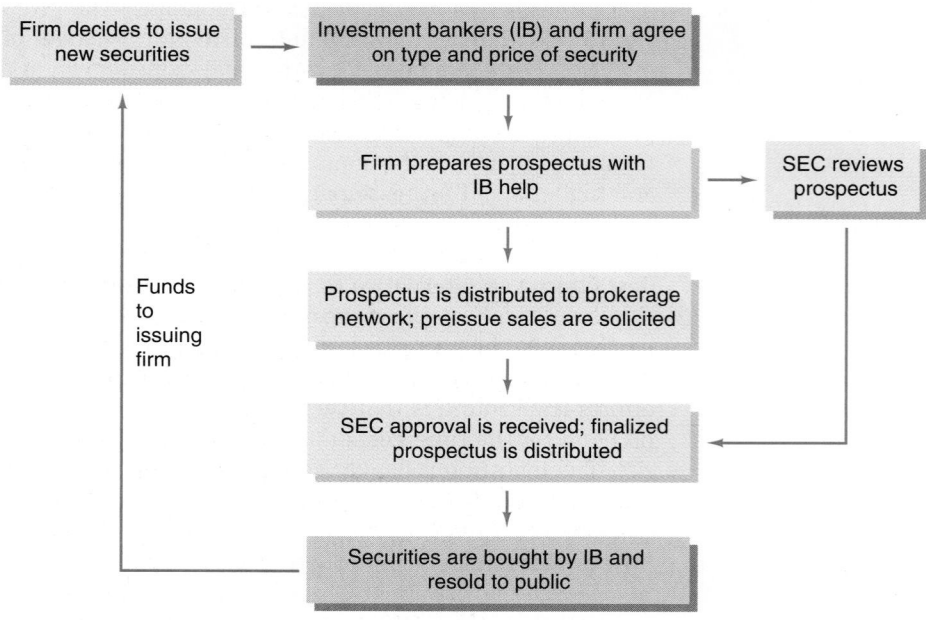

Figure 23.1   Using Investment Bankers to Distribute Securities to the Public

who sees the firm as an opportunity to take advantage of synergies between this firm and another will have a very different price. Despite the elasticity of the yardstick, investment bankers have developed a number of tools to give business owners a range of values for their firms.

How much cash flows will have to be discounted depends very much on who will be bidding on the firm. Again, investment bankers help. They may make discreet inquiries to feel out who in the market may be interested. Additionally, they will prepare a **confidential memorandum** that presents the detailed financial information required by prospective buyers to make an offer for the company. All prospective buyers must sign a confidentiality agreement stipulating that they will not use the information to compete or share it with third parties. The investment bank will screen prospects to ensure that the information goes only to qualified buyers.

The next step in an equity sale will be the **letter of intent** issued by a prospective buyer. This document signals a desire to go forward with a purchase and outlines preliminary terms. The investment banker will negotiate the terms of the sale on the seller's behalf and will help to analyze and rank competing offers. The investment banker may even help structure financing in order to obtain a better offer.

Once the letter of intent has been accepted by the seller, the **due diligence** period begins. This 20- to 40-day period is used by the buyer to verify the accuracy of the information contained in the confidential memorandum. The findings shape the terms of the **definitive agreement.** This agreement converts information gathered during the due diligence period and the results of subsequent negotiations into a legally binding contract.

As this discussion demonstrates, a wide variety of skills are required to move a typical corporate sale forward. To meet these needs, investment banks often send in multidisciplined teams of experts to work with clients on their projects. These teams include attorneys, financial analysts, accountants, and industry experts.

Mergers and Acquisitions

Investment banks have been active in the **mergers and acquisitions market** since the 1960s. A merger occurs when two firms combine to form one new company. Both firms support the merger, and corporate officers are usually selected so that both companies contribute to the new management team. Stockholders turn in their stock for stock in the new firm. In an acquisition, one firm acquires ownership of another by buying its stock. Often this process is friendly, and the firms agree that certain economies can be captured by combining resources. At other times, the firm being purchased may resist. Resisted takeovers are called *hostile.* In these cases, the acquirer attempts to purchase sufficient shares of the target firm to gain a majority of the seats on the board of directors. Board members are then able to vote to merge the target firm with the acquiring firm.

Investment bankers serve both acquirers and target firms. Acquiring firms require help in locating attractive firms to pursue, soliciting shareholders to sell their shares in a process called a *tender offer*, and raising the required capital to complete the transaction. Target firms may hire investment bankers to help ward off undesired takeover attempts.

The mergers and acquisitions markets requires very specialized knowledge and expertise. Investment bankers involved in this market are highly trained (and, not incidentally, highly paid). The best known investment banker involved in mergers and acquisitions was Michael R. Milken, who worked at Drexel Burnham Lambert, Inc.

Milken is credited with inventing the junk bond market, which we discussed in Chapter 10. *Junk bonds* are high-risk, high-return debt securities that were used primarily to finance takeover attempts. By allowing companies to raise large amounts of capital, even small firms could pursue and take over large ones. During the 1980s, when Milken was most active in this market, merger and acquisition activity peaked. On February 13, 1990, Drexel Burnham Lambert filed for bankruptcy due to rising default rates on its portfolio of junk bonds, a slow economy, and regulations that forced the savings and loan industry out of the junk bond market. Milken pled guilty to securities fraud and was sent to prison.

As a result of the collapse of Drexel and the junk bond market, merger and acquisitions activity slowed during the early 1990s. A healthy economy and regulatory changes caused a resurgence, especially among commercial banks, in the mid and late 1990s. Mergers and acquisitions again slowed during the recession in 2001.

Securities Brokers and Dealers

Securities brokers and dealers conduct trading in secondary markets. *Brokers* are pure middlemen who act as agents for investors in the purchase or sale of securities. Their function is to match buyers with sellers, a function for which they are paid brokerage commissions.

In contrast to brokers, dealers link buyers and sellers by standing ready to buy and sell securities at given prices. Therefore, dealers hold inventories of securities and make their living by selling these securities for a slightly higher price than they paid for them—that is, on the *spread* between the *bid price,* the price that the broker pays for securities they buy for their inventory, and the *ask price,* the price they receive when they sell the securities. This is a high-risk business because dealers hold securities that can rise or fall in price; in recent years, several firms specializing in bonds have collapsed. Brokers, by contrast, are not as exposed to risk because they do not own the securities involved in their business dealings.[1]

Brokerage Services

Securities brokers offer several types of services.

Securities Orders If you call a securities brokerage house to buy a stock, you will speak with a broker who will take your order. You have three primary types of transactions available: market orders, limit orders, and short sells.

The two most common types of securities orders are the market order and the limit order. When you place a **market order,** you are instructing your agent to buy or sell the security at the current market price. When placing a market order, there is a risk that the price of the security may have changed significantly from what it was when you made your investment decision. If you are buying a stock and the price falls, no harm is done, but if the price goes up, you may regret your decision. The most notable occasion when prices changed between when orders were placed and when

---

[1]It is easy to remember the distinction between dealers and brokers if you relate to auto dealers and real estate brokers. Auto *dealers* take ownership of the cars and resell them to the public. Real estate *brokers* do not take ownership of the property; they just act as go-betweens.

they were filled was during the October 19, 1987, stock crash. Panicked investors told their brokers to sell their stocks, but the transaction volume was so great that day that many orders were not filled until hours after they were placed. By the time they were filled, the price of the stocks had often fallen far below what they were at the time the original orders were placed.

An alternative to the market order is the **limit order.** Here buy orders specify a *maximum* acceptable price, and sell orders specify a *minimum* acceptable price. For example, you could place a limit order to sell your 100 shares of IBM at $100. If the current market price of IBM is less than $100, the order will not be filled. Unfilled limit orders are reported to the stock specialist who works that particular stock on the exchange. When the stock price moves in such a way that limit orders are activated, the stock specialist initiates the trade.

The **stop loss order** is similar to the limit order, but is for stocks you already own. This order tells your broker to sell your stock when it reaches a certain price. For example, suppose you buy a stock for $20 per share. You do not want to suffer a major loss on this stock, so you enter a stop loss order at $18. In the event the stock price falls to $18 the broker will sell the stock. The stop loss order received a great deal of attention in the highly publicized Martha Stewart trial. She was suspected of trading on insider information about ImClone stock. She argued that the reason for the stock sale was because she had a stop loss order on ImClone at $60. Her conviction suggests that the court did not believe this order was truly in place.

When investors believe that the price of a stock will rise in the future, they buy that stock and hold it until the increase occurs. They can then sell at a profit and capture a gain for their effort. What can be done if an investor is convinced that a stock will *fall* in the future? The solution is to sell short. A **short sell** requires that the investor borrow stocks from a brokerage house and sell them today, with the promise of replacing the borrowed stocks by buying them in the future. Suppose that you just tried out the new Apple notebook computer and decided that it would sell poorly (in fact, in 1995, Apple had to recall all of its Powerbook computers to fix problems). You might believe that as the rest of the market learned of the poor product, the price of Apple's stock could decline. To take advantage of this situation, you might instruct your broker to short Apple 100 shares. The broker would then borrow 100 shares from another investor on your behalf and sell them at current market prices. You do not own those shares, of course. They are borrowed and at some point in the future, you would be required to purchase those 100 shares at the new market price to replace them. If you were right and the price of Apple declined, you would buy the shares at a lower price than you received for their earlier sale and would earn a profit. Of course, if you are wrong and the price rises, you will suffer a loss.

Market and limit orders allow you to take advantage of stock price *increases,* and short sells allow you to take advantage of stock price *decreases.* Analysts track the number of short positions taken on a stock as an indicator of the number of investors who feel that a stock's price is likely to fall in the future.

Other Services In addition to trading in securities, stockbrokers provide a variety of other services. Investors typically leave their securities in storage with the broker for safekeeping. If the securities are left with the broker, they are insured against loss by the Securities Investor Protection Corporation (SIPC), an agency of the federal government. This guarantee is not against loss in value, only against loss of the securities themselves.

Brokers also provide **margin credit.** Margin credit refers to loans advanced by the brokerage house to help investors buy securities. For example, if you are certain that Intel Corporation stock is going to rise rapidly when its latest computer chip is introduced, you could increase the amount of stock you can buy by borrowing from the brokerage house. If you had $5,000 and borrowed an additional $5,000, you could buy $10,000 worth of stock. Then, if the price goes up as you predict, you could earn nearly twice as much as without the loan. The Federal Reserve sets the percentage of the stock purchase price that brokerage houses can lend. Interest rates on margin loans are usually 1 or 2 percentage points above the prime interest rate (the rate charged large, creditworthy corporate borrowers).

As noted in Chapter 18, the forces of competition have led brokerage firms to offer services and engage in activities traditionally conducted by commercial banks. In 1977, Merrill Lynch developed the cash management account (CMA), which provides a package of financial services that includes credit cards, immediate loans, check-writing privileges, automatic investment of proceeds from the sale of securities in a money market mutual fund, and unified record keeping. CMAs were adopted by other brokerage firms and spread rapidly. Many of these accounts allow check-writing privileges and offer ATM and debit cards. In these ways, they compete directly with banks.

As a result of CMAs, the distinction between banking activities and the activities of nonbank financial institutions has become blurred. Walter Wriston, former head of Citicorp (the largest bank holding company in the country), has been quoted as saying, "The bank of the future already exists, and it's called Merrill Lynch."[2]

The advantage of brokerage-based cash management accounts is that they make it easier to buy and sell securities. The stockbroker can take funds out of the account when an investor buys a security and put the money into the account when the investor sells securities.

Full-Service Versus Discount Brokers Prior to May 1, 1975, virtually all brokerage houses charged the same commissions on trades. Brokerage houses distinguished themselves primarily on the basis of their research and customer relations. In May 1975, Congress determined that fixed commissions were anticompetitive and passed the Securities Acts Amendment of 1975, which abolished fixed commissions. Now brokerage houses may charge whatever fees they choose. This has resulted in two distinct types of brokerage firms: full-service and discount.

Full-service brokers provide research and investment advice to their customers. Full-service brokers will often mail weekly and monthly market reports and recommendations to their customers in an effort to encourage them to invest in certain securities. For example, when the investment banking department of the brokerage house has an initial public offering available, brokers will contact customers they feel may be interested and offer to send a prospectus. Full-service brokers attempt to establish long-term relationships with their customers and to help them assemble portfolios that are consistent with their financial needs and risk preferences. Of course, this extra attention is costly and must be paid for by requiring higher fees for initiating trades. Merrill Lynch is the biggest of the full-service brokers.

Discount brokers simply execute trades on request. If you want to buy a particular security, you call the discount broker and place your request. No advice or

---

[2]"Banking "Takes a Beating," *Time*, December 3, 1984, p. 50.

research is typically provided. Because the cost of operating a discount brokerage firm is significantly less than the cost of operating a full-service firm, lower transaction costs are charged. These fees may be a fraction of the fees charged by a full-service broker. Charles Schwab Corp. is the best-known discount broker. Many discount brokerage firms are owned by large commercial banks, which have historically been prohibited from offering full-service brokerage services.

Regardless of which type of brokerage firm you choose, it will be a member of the major exchanges and have computer links to the NASDAQ (National Association of Security Dealers Automated Quotation System). Suppose that you place an order for 100 shares of IBM with your local Merrill Lynch office. Your broker will send an electronic message to the Merrill Lynch traders who work on the floor of the New York Stock Exchange (NYSE) to buy 100 shares of IBM in your name. On the floor of the NYSE, there are circular work areas where specialists in each security that is traded on the exchange stand. Each specialist is responsible for several stocks. The Merrill Lynch floor trader will know where the IBM specialist is and will approach that person to fill your buy order. Confirmation of the purchase will then be communicated back to your local broker, who will inform you that the trade has been completed (see the Mini-Case box).

Example of Using the Limit-Order Book

Suppose a trader on the New York Stock Exchange was a specialist responsible for Circuit City stock. The limit-order book might look like the following:

Unfilled Circuit City Limit Orders

Buy Orders		Sell Orders	
37	100		
37.12	300		
37.25	100		
		37.37	200
		37.50	500
		37.62	100

Listed under Buy Orders are the highest prices investors are willing to pay to buy the stock. Listed under Sell Orders are the lowest prices investors holding Circuit City are willing to accept to sell. Currently, no transactions occur because there are no cross-over or common prices. In other words, there is currently no one willing to sell Circuit City at a price anyone is willing to pay.

Now suppose the specialist receives a new 200-share market order to buy, an order to be filled at the best market price currently available. The specialist will consult the Sell Orders column and fill the order at 37.37.

Next, the specialist receives a 300-share limit order to sell at 37.12. Again, the specialist will consult the book, but this time will look under the Buy Orders column. The limit order will be filled with 100 shares at 37.25 and 200 shares at 37.12.

Next, suppose that a limit order to buy 500 shares at 36.88 is received. Since there is no sell order for this amount, the order is added to the book, which looks as follows at this point:

Unfilled Circuit City Limit Orders

Buy Orders		Sell Orders	
36.88	500		
37	100		
37.12	100		
		37.50	500
		37.62	100

Securities Dealers

Securities dealers hold inventories of securities, which they sell to customers who want to buy. They also hold securities purchased from customers who want to sell.

It is impossible to overemphasize the importance of dealers to the smooth functioning of the U.S. financial markets. Consider what an investor demands before buying a security. In addition to requiring a fair return, the investor wants to know that the investment is *liquid*—that it can be sold quickly if it no longer fits into the investor's portfolio. Consider a small, relatively unknown firm that is trying to sell securities to the public. An investor may be tempted to buy the firm's securities, but if these securities cannot be resold easily, it is unlikely that the investor will take a chance on them. This is where the dealers become crucial. They stand ready to make a market in the security at any time—that is, they make sure that an investor can always sell or buy a security. For this reason, dealers are also called **market makers.** When an investor wishes to sell a thinly traded stock (one without an active secondary market), it is unlikely that another investor is simultaneously seeking to buy that security. This nonsynchronous trading problem is solved when the dealer buys the security from the investor and holds it in inventory until another investor is ready to buy it. The knowledge that dealers will provide this service encourages investors to buy securities that would be otherwise unacceptable. In countries with less well developed financial markets, where dealers will not make a market for less popular securities, it is extremely difficult for small, new, or regional firms to raise funds. Securities market dealers are largely responsible for the health and growth of small businesses in the United States.

Regulation of Securities Firms

Many financial firms engage in all three securities market activities, acting as brokers, dealers, and investment bankers. The largest in the United States is Merrill Lynch; other well-known firms include Paine Webber, Morgan Stanley Dean Witter, and Salomon Smith Barney. The SEC not only regulates the firms' investment banking operations but also restricts brokers and dealers from misrepresenting securities and from trading on *insider information,* unpublicized facts known only to the management of a corporation.

When discussing regulation, it is important to recognize that the public's confidence in the integrity of the financial markets is critical to the growth of our economy and the ability of firms to continue using the markets to raise new capital. If the public believes that there are other powerful players with superior information who can take advantage of smaller investors, the market will be unable to attract funds from these smaller investors. Ultimately, the markets could fail entirely.

The lemons problem introduced in Chapter 15 also applies to the securities markets. Due to asymmetric information, investors will not know as much about securities being offered for sale by firms as firm insiders will. If an average price is set for all securities based on this lack of information, good securities would be withdrawn and only poor and overpriced securities would remain for sale. With only these securities offered, the average price would fall. Now any securities worth more than this new average would be withdrawn. Eventually, the market would fail as the average security offered drops in quality and market prices fall as a result. One solution to the lemons problem is for the government to regulate full disclosure so that asymmetric information is reduced.

The securities laws were designed with two goals: to protect the integrity of the markets and to restrict competition among securities firms so that they would be less likely to fail. Two acts passed in 1933 and 1934 provide the primary basis for regulation of today's securities markets. These acts were passed shortly after the Great Depression and were largely responding to abuses that many people at the time felt were partly responsible for the economic troubles the country was suffering. The principal provisions of the 1933 and 1934 acts are as follows:

- To establish the Securities and Exchange Commission (SEC), which is charged with administering securities laws
- To require that issuers register new securities offerings and that they disclose all relevant information to potential investors
- To require that all publicly held corporations file annual and semiannual reports with the SEC; publicly held corporations must also file a report whenever any event of "significant interest" to investors occurs
- To require that insiders file reports whenever shares are bought or sold
- To prohibit any form of market manipulation

go online

The Securities and Exchange Commission Web site, **www.sec.gov**, contains regulatory actions, concept releases, interpretive releases, and more.

Prior to the passage of these acts, the market was subject to much abuse. For example, a study conducted in 1933 showed evidence of 127 "investment pools" operating during 1932 alone. An investment pool is formed to manipulate the market. A group of investors band together and spread false but damaging rumors about the health of a firm. These rumors drive the price of the firm's stock down. When the price is depressed, the members of the pool buy the stock. Once they all hold shares purchased at artificially low prices, the members of the pool release good news about the company so that the price of the stock rises. Obviously, the members of the pool stand to earn huge profits. Small, uninformed investors lose. Practices such as these were outlawed by the securities acts of 1933 and 1934.

As noted in our discussion of private placements, not all securities issues are subject to SEC oversight. SEC registration is not required if less than $1.5 million in securities is issued per year, if the securities mature in less than 270 days, or if the securities are issued by the U.S. government or most municipalities.

Other legislation of significance to securities firms include the Glass-Steagall Act of 1933, which separated commercial and investment banking (mostly repealed by Gramm-Leach-Bliley Act); the Investment Advisers Act of 1940, which required investment advisers to register with the SEC; and the Securities Protection Corporation Act of 1970, which established the Securities Investor Protection Corporation, which insures customers of securities firms from losses to their cash accounts up to $100,000 and from losses of securities documents up to $500,000. Other regulations related specifically to banks but of interest to securities firms are discussed in Chapter 20.

Relationship Between Securities Firms and Commercial Banks

For many years, commercial banks have lobbied for legislative relief to enable them to compete with securities firms. Consider how the business of banking has been eroded. Prior to the introduction of cash management accounts at Merrill Lynch, the only source of checking accounts was a bank. The Merrill Lynch account not only provided low-cost checking but also paid interest that was higher than the law permitted banks to pay. Securities firms were allowed to make loans, offer credit and debit cards, provide ATM access, and, most important, sell securities. In addition, securities firms could sell some types of insurance. It is not hard to understand why bankers were frustrated. Regulations prevented them from competing with securities firms, but no laws restricted securities firms from competing with banks.

Commercial banks clamored on Capitol Hill for a "level playing field." As noted in Chapter 20, regulatory relief in 1980 and 1982 substantially slowed the movement of funds from commercial banks to securities firms; however, banks were still not permitted to sell securities. This is gradually changing.

Private Equity Investment

When you talk about investing, you are usually discussing stocks and bonds. Both of these securities are sold to the public and have oversight by the SEC. The vast majority of the volume handled by brokers and dealers is in these publicly held securities. However, there is an alternative to public equity investing, which is private equity investing. With private equity investing, instead of raising capital by selling securities to the public, a limited partnership is formed that raises money from a small number of high-wealth investors. Within the broad universe of private equity sectors, the two most common are venture funds and **capital buyouts.** In many cases, the same firms are active in both arenas. Major investors in this industry include KKR (Kohlberg, Kravis, Roberts & Co.), Bain Capital, and Blackstone Group.

Venture Capital Firms

Suppose that you develop and market a new process that you think has a great chance of being a success. However, since it is new and unproven, you cannot get funding from conventional sources. Commercial banks will not loan you money since there is no established cash flow to use to repay the loan. It will be hard to sell stock to the public through investment bankers because the company is so new and has not yet proven that it can be successful. In the absence of alternative sources of funds, your great idea may not have a true chance to be developed. Venture capital firms provide the funds a start-up company needs to get established.

Description of Industry Venture capital is usually defined as money supplied to young, start-up firms. This money is most frequently raised by limited partnerships and invested by the general partner in firms showing promise of high returns in the future.

Since the mid-1940s, venture capital firms have nurtured the growth of America's high-technology and entrepreneurial communities. Their activities have resulted in job creation, economic growth, and international competitiveness. Venture capitalists backed many of the most successful high-technology companies during the 1980s and 1990s, including Apple Computer, Cisco Systems, Genentech, Microsoft, Netscape, and Sun Microsystems. A number of service firms, such as Staples, Starbucks, and TCBY, also benefited from venture financing. Indeed, much of the growth experienced through the 1980s and 1990s can be traced back to the funding provided by the venture capital industry. Table 23.2 shows the explosive growth in venture cap-

TABLE 23.2   Venture Capital Investments Made from 1990–2006

Year	Number of Companies Funded	Investment Total ($ millions)
1990	1,317	3,376.21
1991	1,088	2,511.43
1992	1,294	5,177.56
1993	1,151	4,962.87
1994	1,191	5,351.18
1995	1,327	5,608.30
1996	2,078	11,278.60
1997	2,536	14,903.00
1998	2,974	21,090.60
1999	4,411	54,203.70
2000	6,342	104,986.80
2001	3,787	40,686.70
2002	2,617	21,824.00
2003	2,414	19,678.30
2004	2,571	22,117.40
2005	2,646	22,765.80
2006	2,869	25,504.80

Source: http://www.vx.thomsonib.com.

ital funding witnessed during the 1990s and the rapid drop in activity after the market fell in 2000.

Venture Capitalists Reduce Asymmetric Information Uncertainty and information asymmetries frequently accompany start-up firms, especially in high-technology communities. Managers of these firms may engage in wasteful expenditures, such as leasing expensive office space, since the manager may benefit disproportionately from them but does not bear their entire cost. The difficulty outside investors have in tracking early-stage high-technology companies leads to other types of costs. For example, a biotechnology company founder may invest in research that brings personal acclaim but little chance for significant returns to investors. As a result of these informational asymmetries, external financing may be costly, difficult, or even impossible to obtain.

Venture capital firms can alleviate the information gap and thus allow firms to receive financing they could not obtain elsewhere. First, as opposed to bank loans or bond financing, venture capital firms hold an equity interest in the firm. The firms are usually privately held, so the stock does not trade publicly. Equity interests in privately held firms are very illiquid. As a result, venture capital investment horizons are long-term. The partners do not expect to earn any return for a number of years, often as long as a decade. In contrast, most investors in stocks are anxious to see annual returns through either stock appreciation or dividend payouts.

They are often unwilling to wait years to see if a new idea, process, innovation, or invention will yield profits. Similarly, most investors in bonds are not going to wait years for revenues to grow to a point where interest payments become available. Venture capital financing thus fills an important niche left vacant by alternative sources of capital.

As a second method of addressing the asymmetric information problem, venture capital usually comes with strings attached, the most noteworthy being that the partners in a venture capital firm take seats on the board of directors of the financed firm. Venture capital firms are not passive investors. They actively attempt to add value to the firm through advice, assistance, and business contacts. Venture capitalists may bring together two firms that can complement each other's activities. Venture capital firms will apply their expertise to help the firm solve various financing and growth-related problems. The venture capital partners on the board of directors will carefully monitor expenditures and management to help safeguard the investment in the firm.

One of the most effective ways venture capitalists have of controlling managers is to disburse funds to the company in stages only as the firm demonstrates progress toward its ultimate goal. If development stalls or markets change, funds can be withheld to cut losses.

Implicit to venture capital financing is an expectation of high risk and large compensating returns. Venture capital firms will search very carefully among hundreds of companies to find a few that show real growth potential. Despite this exhaustive search effort, the selected firms usually have little to show initially other than a unique and promising idea. Venture capitalists mitigate the risk by developing a portfolio of young companies within a single fund. Additionally, many venture capital partnerships will manage multiple funds simultaneously. By diversifying the risk among a number of start-up firms, the risk of loss is significantly lowered.

Origins of Venture Capital The first true venture capital firm was American Research & Development (ARD), established in 1946 by MIT president Karl Compton and local business leaders. The bulk of their success can be traced to one $70,000 investment in a new firm, the Digital Equipment Company. This seed money grew in value to $355 million over the next three decades.[3]

During the 1950s and 1960s, most venture capital funding was for the development of real estate and oil fields. By the late 1960s, a shift occurred toward financing technology start-ups. High technology remains the dominant area for venture capital funding.

The source of venture capital funding has shifted from wealthy individuals to pension funds and corporations. In 1979, the U.S. Department of labor clarified the **prudent man rule,** which restricted pension funds from making risky investments, to explicitly allow investment in some high-risk assets. This resulted in a surge of pension fund dollars going into venture projects.

Corporate funding of venture capital projects increased when many companies reduced their investment in their own in-house R&D in favor of outside start-up companies. If the project was successful, the company could acquire the start-up. This change was fueled by evidence that many of the best ideas from in-house centralized

---

[3]Part of this discussion is based on "The Venture Capital Revolution," by Paul Gompers and Josh Lerner, *Journal of Economic Perspectives,* Number 2, Spring 2001, pp. 145–168.

R&D languished unused or were commercialized in new firms started by defecting employees. Salaried employees tend not to be as motivated as entrepreneurs who stand to capture a large portion of the profits a new idea may generate. By investing in start-up firms, corporations can benefit from new discoveries while supporting the entrepreneurial spirit.

Structure of Venture Capital Firms   Most early venture capital firms were organized as closed-end mutual funds. A closed-end mutual fund sells a fixed number of shares to investors. Once all of the shares have been sold, no additional money can be raised. Instead, a new venture fund is established. The advantage of this organizational structure is that it provides the long-term money required for venture investing. Investors cannot pull money out of the investment as they could from an open-end mutual fund.

In the 1970s and 1980s, venture capital firms began organizing as limited partnerships. This organizational structure is exempt from securities regulations, including the burdensome disclosure requirements of the Investment Security Act of 1940. While both organizational forms continue to be used, currently most venture capital firms are limited partnerships.

The Life of a Deal   Most venture capital deals follow a similar life cycle that begins when a limited partnership is formed and funds are raised. In the second phase, the funds are invested in start-up companies. Finally, the venture firm exits the investment.

Next, we take a more detailed look at this process.

Fundraising   A venture firm begins by soliciting commitments of capital from investors. As discussed above, these investors are typically pension funds, corporations, and wealthy individuals. Venture capital firms usually have a portfolio target amount that they attempt to raise. The average venture fund will have from just a few investors up to 100 limited partners. Because the minimum commitment is usually so high, venture capital funding is generally out of reach of most average individual investors.

Once the venture fund begins investing, it will "call" its commitments from the limited partners. These capital calls from the limited partners to the venture fund are sometimes called "takedowns" or "paid-in-capital." Venture firms typically call their capital on an as-needed basis.

The limited partners understand that investments in venture funds are long-term. It may be several years before the first investment starts to pay. In many cases, the capital may be tied up for seven to ten years. The illiquidity of the investment must be carefully considered by the potential investor.

Investing   Once commitments have been received, the venture fund can begin the investment phase. Venture funds may either specialize in one or two industry segments or may generalize, looking at all available opportunities. It is not uncommon for venture funds to focus investments in a limited geographical area to make it easier to review and monitor the firms' activities.

Frequently, venture capitalists invest in a firm before it has a real product or is even clearly organized as a company. This is called **seed investing.** Investing in a firm that is a little further along in its life cycle is known as **early-stage investing.** Finally, some funds focus on **later-stage investing** by providing funds to help the company grow to a critical mass to attract public financing.

Typically, about 60% of venture capital funds go into seed investments, 25% into early-stage investments, and 15% into later-stage investments.

Exiting The goal of a venture capital investment is to help nurture a firm until it can be funded with alternative capital. Venture firms hope that an exit can be made in no more than seven to ten years. Later-stage investments may take only a few years. Once an exit is made, the partners receive their share of the profits and the fund is dissolved.

There are a number of ways for a venture fund to successfully exit an investment. The most glamorous and visible is through an initial public offering. At the public stock offering, the venture firm is considered an insider and receives stock in the company, but the firm is regulated and restricted in how that stock can be sold or liquidated for several years. Once the stock is freely tradable, usually after two years, the venture fund distributes the stock to its limited partners, who may then hold the stock or sell it. Over the last 25 years, over 3,000 companies financed by venture funds have had initial public offerings. During the peak years, there were 258 venture-backed initial public offerings.

While not as visible, an equally common type of successful exit for venture investments is through mergers and acquisitions. In these cases, the venture firm receives stock or cash from the acquiring company. These proceeds are then distributed to the limited partners. The number of venture-backed merger and acquisition deals peaked at 269 in 2000.

Venture Fund Profitability Venture investing is extremely high-risk. Most start-up firms do not succeed. Despite the careful monitoring and advice provided by the venture capital firm, there are innumerable hurdles that must be jumped before a new concept or idea yields profits. If venture investing is high-risk, then there must also be the possibility of a high return to induce investors to continue supplying funds.

Historically, venture capital firms have been very profitable, despite their high risk. The 20-year average return is 16.5%. Seed investing is the most profitable, with a 20-year average return of 20.4% compared to about 13.5% for later-stage investing. The 1990s were a wonderful time to be a venture capitalist. The ten-year average return was 30%. From 1995 to 2000, the average return soared to over 50%.

In the late 1990s, venture capital returns continued to be extraordinary. For example, returns exceeded 165% in 1999. Unfortunately, as the market cooled to technology, so too did venture capital returns. By 2000, average returns were 37.5%, and in 2001, venture firms reported a first quarter loss of 8.9%. These losses are likely to extend for a number of years while venture capital firms recover from excessive investment in Web-based technology companies. The E-Finance box discusses possible explanations for the losses suffered by venture capital firms.

Private Equity Buyouts

In the last section, we learned that new startup companies often fund their growth by raising capital from venture capital firms. The private company is allow to mature, then, with profitability assured, it sells shares to the public. In a **private equity buyout,** instead of a private company going public, a public company goes private.

In a typical private equity buyout, the publicity trades shares of a company are purchased by a limited partnership formed for that purpose. Since the public shares are then retired, the firm is no longer subject to the controls and oversight required of publicly held companies, nor does it have to answer to diverse stockholders.

e-finance

Venture Capitalists Lose Focus with Internet Companies

Table 23.2 shows that there was a tremendous surge in funds available for venture capitalists in the last half of the 1990s. Much of the investing focus was on the financing of dot-com companies. There are two serious ramifications that result. First, it is likely that there are only a certain number of worthy projects to finance at any one time. When too much money is chasing too few deals, firms are going to obtain financing that would be rejected at other times. As result, the average quality of venture fund portfolios falls.

A second problem caused by the surge of money into venture funds is that the ability of the partners to provide quality monitoring is reduced. Consider the case of Webvan, an Internet grocer that received more than $1 *billion* in venture financing. Even though it was backed by a group of experienced financiers, including Goldman Sachs and Sequoia Capital, its business plan was fundamentally flawed. In its short life, Webvan spent more than $1 billion building automated warehouses and pricey tech gear. This high overhead made it impossible to compete in the grocery business, where average margins are about 1%. Had the investment bankers been actively monitoring the activities of Webvan, they might have balked at developing an infrastructure that required 4,000 orders per day per warehouse just to break even. Not surprisingly, Webvan declared bankruptcy in July 2001.

Advantages to Private Equity Buyouts

Private equity partners and the managers of privately held firms cite a number of advantages to the private equity ownership structure. First, as private companies they are not subject to the controversial regulations included in the 2002 Sarbanes-Oxley Act. Many managers and CEOs complain that meeting the requirements of Sarbanes-Oxley is frustrating and takes valuable time away from more productive activities.

Second, CEOs of publicly held firms often feel under pressure to produce quarterly profits. In a private equity scenario, CEOs frequently have more time and flexibility to enact the changes needed to turn around sub-par companies. Instead of trying to convince thousands of diverse investors of the wisdom of a particular course of action, the CEO of a privately held company only need convince the managing partners of the private equity firm. This increased freedom has attracted some of the best known corporate leaders in the country, such as Jack Welch (former CEO of GE), Michael Eisner (Former CEO of Disney), Louis Gerstner (former CEO of IBM), and Millard Drexler (former CEO of Ann Taylor and Gap Inc.). One reason top CEOs have been attracted to privately held firms is that they can be compensated more easily with an ownership interest in the firms. Typically, executives are recruited with a small cash salary and an opportunity to invest their own money in the firm, often taking as much as a 20% ownership position. Some believe this more closely aligns the executive's interest with those of the private equity partnership.

Investors in private equity partnerships are well compensated for taking the risk of purchasing poorly performing companies. Partners typically earn a 1.5% fee for managing the equity fund investments. In addition, they get a share of the profits, usually pegged at 20%, when the firm is sold or taken back public. An additional perk is that the profits for both CEOs and the partners are taxed at the 15% capital gains rate, rather than the 35% rate they would suffer if the income was received as salary.

Life Cycle of the Private Equity Buyout

In a typical private equity buyout, a partnership is formed and private equity investors are contacted to pledge participation. Each investor usually pledges at least $1 million of capital and agrees to leave the funds under the partnerships control for an extended period of time, often five years or more.

The partnership now identifies an under-performing company that it believes can be turned around by new management. Using the equity contributed by the partners, the firm buys the outstanding public shares of the troubled company. A new CEO and board is elected to run the company. The managing partners tend to be active participants in the management of the firm.

Once the company is revived and showing improved revenues and profitability, it will be either sold to another firm or taken public in an IPO. This is where the investors in the private buyout earn their return. Because the company is now stronger, it is expected to sell for much more than it did when initially purchased and taken private.

Implications of the Private Equity Ownership Structure

There are both high risk and high returns to investors in private equity buyouts. Figure 23.2 shows the average returns earned over the last 20 years in both venture and buyout private equity markets. The NASDAQ and S&P 500 returns are included for comparison. Over the last 20 years, private equity investing has earned a 14% return, compared to 9.7% for investors in the S&P 500. Along with the higher returns are higher risks. As the market for under performing companies becomes

Fund Type	1 Yr	3 Yr	5 Yr	10 Yr	20 Yr
Early Seed VC	2.90	5.50	−5.40	38.30	20.50
Balanced VC	10.70	12.80	1.80	16.80	14.60
Later Stage VC	27.80	10.50	2.70	9.40	13.90
All Venture	**10.80**	**9.40**	**−1.00**	**20.50**	**16.50**
Small Buyouts	11.30	9.40	5.00	6.00	25.20
Med Buyouts	37.20	12.30	6.10	10.90	15.30
Large Buyouts	23.10	16.10	8.30	8.30	12.40
Mega Buyouts	23.40	16.20	10.10	8.90	11.60
All Buyouts	**23.60**	**15.60**	**9.20**	**8.80**	**13.20**
All Private Equity	**19.00**	**13.20**	**5.90**	**11.20**	**14.00**
NASDAQ	5.50	7.80	8.70	7.10	11.40
S&P 500	9.70	9.90	5.20	7.50	9.70

Figure 23.2 Investment Horizon Performance Through 09/30/2006

Source: http://www.thomson.com/pdf/financial/news_release_pdfs/Q306_PE_performance.

more competitive, it will likely become more difficult and costly to locate and buy firms that can be easily turned around. If private equity firms compete with each other to purchase firms, prices will rise and it will be much more challenging to continue achieving the results private equity investors have come to expect.

SUMMARY

1. Investment banks are firms that assist in the initial sale of securities in the primary market and, as securities brokers and dealers, assist in the trading of securities in the secondary markets, some of which are organized into exchanges. The Securities and Exchange Commission regulates the financial institutions in the securities markets and ensures that adequate information reaches prospective investors.

2. Underwriting involves the investment banking firm's taking ownership of the stock issue by purchasing all of the shares from the issuer and then reselling them in the market. Issues may be oversubscribed, undersubscribed, or fully subscribed, depending on whether the price is set correctly.

3. Investment bankers assist issuing firms by providing advice, filing documents, and marketing issues. Investment bankers often assist in mergers and acquisitions and in private placements as well.

4. Securities brokers act as go-betweens and do not usually own securities. Securities dealers do buy and sell securities and by doing so make a market. By always having securities to sell and by always being willing to

purchase securities, dealers guarantee the liquidity of the market.

5. Investors may place an order, called a *market order,* to buy a security at the current market price. They may also set limits to the lowest price at which they will sell their security or the highest price they will pay for a security. Orders of this type are called *limit orders.*

6. Some brokerage houses provide research and investment advice in addition to conducting trades on behalf of customers. These are called *full-service brokers. Discount brokers* simply place orders. Brokerage houses also store securities, advance loans to buy securities, and offer cash management accounts.

7. Private equity investments include both venture fund investing and capital buyouts of public companies. A typical venture fund investment includes pooling funds from investors to use to support a new company until it is able to go public. In a capital buyout, investors funds are again pooled, but this time they are used to buy a controlling interest in a public company that is then taken private.

KEY TERMS

capital buyout, *p. 606*
confidential memorandum, *p. 599*
definitive agreement, *p. 599*
due diligence, *p. 599*
early-stage investing, *p. 609*
fully subscribe, *p. 597*
Glass-Steagall Act, *p. 592*
initial public offering (IPO), *p. 594*
investment banks, *p. 592*
later-stage investing, *p. 609*
letter of intent, *p. 599*
limit order, *p. 601*
margin credit, *p. 602*
market makers, *p. 604*
market order, *p. 600*
mergers and acquisitions market, *p. 599*

oversubscribed, *p. 597*
primary market, *p. 591*
private equity buyout, *p. 610*
prospectus, *p. 594*
prudent man rule, *p. 608*
registration statement, *p. 594*
seasoned issues, *p. 594*
secondary market, *p. 591*
Securities and Exchange Commission (SEC), *p. 594*
seed investing, *p. 609*
short sell, *p. 601*
stop loss order, *p. 601*
syndicate, *p. 595*
tombstone, *p. 596*
undersubscribed, *p. 597*

QUESTIONS

1. What was the motivation behind legislation separating commercial banking from investment banking?

2. What law separated investment banking from commercial banking?

3. What does it mean to say that investment bankers *underwrite* a security offering? How is this different from a best-efforts offering?

4. What are the primary services that an investment banker will provide a firm issuing securities?

5. Does the fact that a security has passed an SEC review mean that investors can buy the security without having to worry about taking a loss on the investment?

6. Why do investment banking firms often form syndicates for selling securities to the public?

7. Is it better for a security issue to be fully subscribed or oversubscribed?

8. Why would an investment banker advise a firm to issue a security using best efforts rather than underwriting?

9. What is the difference between a hostile takeover and a merger?

10. What valuable service do dealers provide that facilitates transaction trading and keeping the markets liquid?

11. What is the difference between a market order and a limit order?

12. Is it possible to make money if you know that the price of a security will *fall* in the future? How?

13. Why do commercial banks object to brokerage houses being allowed to offer many of the same services traditionally reserved for banks?

14. What are the principle advantages often cited as motivation for a private equity buyout?

QUANTITATIVE PROBLEMS

Amazon.com issued an initial public offering in May of 1997. Prior to its IPO, the following information on shares outstanding was listed in the final prospectus:

Name and Address	Number of Shares Beneficially Owned	Percentage of Shares Outstanding	
		Prior to Offering	After Offering
Jeffrey P. Bezos c/o Amazon.com, Inc. 1516 Second Avenue, 4th Floor Seattle, WA 98101	9,885,000	47.5%	41.4%
L. John Doerr Kleiner Perkins Caufield & Byers 4 Embarcadero Center, Suite 3520 San Francisco, CA 94111	3,401,376	16.4	14.3
Tom A. Alberg	195,000	*	*
Scott D. Cook	75,000	*	*
Patricia Q. Stonesifer	75,000	*	*
All directors and executive officers as a group (14 persons)	15,688,925	72.5	63.5
Total shares outstanding	20,858,702	100.0	—.—

In the IPO, the firm issued 3,000,000 new shares. The initial price was $18.00/share with investment bankers retaining $1.26 as fees. The final first-day closing price was $23.50.

1. What were the total proceeds from this offering? What part was retained by Amazon? What part by the investment bankers? What percent of the offering is this?

2. Mr. Doerr of Kleiner Perkins Caufield & Byers owned a significant number of shares. What was the market value of these shares at the end of the first day of trading?

3. What was the market value of Amazon.com following its first day as a publicly held company?

4. Refer back to the IPO of eBay presented in the problems for Chapter 11. What were the fees for eBay as a percent of funds raised? Does a pattern emerge?

5. To verify this further, examine the IPO for Blue Nile, Inc. It can be found on the SEC's site at **http://www .sec.gov/Archives/edgar/data/1091171/00008916 1804001024/v97093b4e424b4.htm**. What was the offering price? What percent was retained by the underwriter?

6. For Blue Nile, Inc., what are the expected proceeds to the company? Is this certain? What assumptions are you making? How would you verify this?

7. You want to buy 100 shares of a stock currently trading at $50 per share. Your brokerage firm allows margin sales with a 50% opening margin and a maintenance margin of 25%. What does this mean? If you close your position with the shares at $53.50, what is your return?

8. The limit order book for a security is as follows:

Unfilled Limit Orders			
Buy Orders		**Sell Orders**	
25.12	100		
25.20	500		
25.23	200		
		25.36	300
		25.38	200
		25.41	200

The specialist receives the following, in order:

- Market order to sell 300 shares
- Limit order to buy 100 shares at 25.38
- Limit order to buy 500 shares at 25.30

How, if at all, are these orders filled? What does the limit order book look like after these orders?

WEB EXERCISES

Investment Banks, Security Brokers and Dealers, and Venture Capital Firms

1. In initial public offerings (IPOs), securities are sold to the public for the first time. Go to **http://ipohome .com**. This site lists various statistics regarding the IPO market.

   a. What was the largest IPO offered recently, ranked by amount raised?

   b. What is the next IPO that will be offered to the public?

   c. How many IPOs were priced in each of the last four years?

2. The Securities and Exchange Commission is responsible for regulating securities firms. Go to **www.sec .gov**. This is the official home page of the SEC. Use this page to answer the following.

   a. What is EDGAR?

   b. What is the stated purpose of the SEC?

   c. Provide a one-sentence summary of the most recently proposed SEC regulation.

PART 7

The Management
of Financial
Institutions

CHAPTER 24

Risk Management in Financial Institutions

Preview

Managing financial institutions has never been an easy task, but in recent years it has become even more difficult because of greater uncertainty in the economic environment. Interest rates have become much more volatile, resulting in substantial fluctuations in profits and in the value of assets and liabilities held by financial institutions. Furthermore, as we have seen in Chapter 5, defaults on loans and other debt instruments have also climbed dramatically, leading to large losses at financial institutions. In light of these developments, it is not surprising that financial institution managers have become more concerned about managing the risk their institutions face as a result of greater interest-rate fluctuations and defaults by borrowers.

In this chapter we examine how managers of financial institutions cope with credit risk, the risk arising because borrowers may default on their obligations, and with interest-rate risk, the risk arising from fluctuations in interest rates. We will look at the tools that these managers use to measure risk and the strategies that they employ to reduce it.

go online

The Web site of the Risk Management Association, **www.rmahq.org**, offers useful information such as annual statement studies, on-line publications, and more.

Managing Credit Risk

A major part of the business of financial institutions, such as banks, insurance companies, pension funds, and finance companies, is making loans. In order for these institutions to earn high profits, they must make successful loans that are paid back in full (and so have low credit risk). The concepts of adverse selection and moral hazard (discussed in Chapters 2 and 15) provide a framework for understanding the principles that financial institution managers must follow to minimize credit risk and make successful loans.

Adverse selection in loan markets occurs because bad credit risks (those most likely to default on their loans) are the ones who usually line up for loans; in other words, those who are most likely to produce an *adverse* outcome are the most likely to be *selected.* Borrowers with very risky investment projects have much to gain if their projects are successful, so they are the most eager to obtain loans. Clearly, however, they are the least desirable borrowers because of the greater possibility that they will be unable to pay back their loans.

Moral hazard exists in loan markets because borrowers may have incentives to engage in activities that are undesirable from the lender's point of view. In such situations, it is more likely that the lender will be subjected to the *hazard* of default. Once borrowers have obtained a loan, they are more likely to invest in high-risk investment projects—projects that pay high returns to the borrowers if successful. The high risk, however, makes it less likely that they will be able to pay the loan back.

To be profitable, financial institutions must overcome the adverse selection and moral hazard problems that make loan defaults more likely. The attempts of financial institutions to solve these problems help explain a number of principles for managing credit risk: screening and monitoring, establishment of long-term customer relationships, loan commitments, collateral and compensating balance requirements, and credit rationing.

Screening and Monitoring

Asymmetric information is present in loan markets because lenders have less information about the investment opportunities and activities of borrowers than borrowers do. This situation leads to two information-producing activities by financial institutions—screening and monitoring.

Screening Adverse selection in loan markets requires that lenders screen out the bad credit risks from the good ones so that loans are profitable to them. To accomplish effective screening, lenders must collect reliable information from prospective borrowers. Effective screening and information collection together form an important principle of credit risk management.

When you apply for a consumer loan (such as a car loan or a mortgage to purchase a house), the first thing you are asked to do is fill out forms that elicit a great deal of information about your personal finances. You are asked about your salary, your bank accounts and other assets (such as cars, insurance policies, and furnishings), and your outstanding loans; your record of loan, credit card, and charge account repayments; the number of years you've worked and who your employers have been. You also are asked personal questions such as your age, marital status, and number of children. The lender uses this information to evaluate how good a credit risk you are by calculating your "credit score," a statistical measure derived from your answers that predicts whether you are likely to have trouble making your loan payments. Deciding on how good a risk you are cannot be entirely scientific, so the lender must also use judgment. The loan officer, whose job is to decide whether you should be given the loan, might call your employer or talk to some of the personal references you supplied. The officer might even make a judgment based on your demeanor or your appearance.

The process of screening and collecting information is similar when a financial institution makes a business loan. It collects information about the company's profits and losses (income) and about its assets and liabilities. The lender also has to evaluate the likely future success of the business. So in addition to obtaining information on such items as sales figures, a loan officer might ask questions about the company's future plans, the purpose of the loan, and the competition in the industry. The officer may even visit the company to obtain a firsthand look at its operations. The bottom line is that, whether for personal or business loans, financial institutions need to be nosy.

Specialization in Lending One puzzling feature of lending by financial institutions is that they often specialize in lending to local firms or to firms in particular industries, such as energy. In one sense, this behavior seems surprising, because it means that the financial institution is not diversifying its portfolio of loans and thus is exposing itself to more risk. But from another perspective, such specialization makes perfect sense. The adverse selection problem requires that the financial institution screen out bad credit risks. It is easier for the financial institution to collect information about local firms and determine their creditworthiness than to collect comparable information on firms that are far away. Similarly, by concentrating its lending on firms in specific industries, the financial institution becomes more knowledgeable about these industries and is therefore better able to predict which firms will be able to make timely payments on their debt.

[handwritten margin note: MITIGATION OF ADVERSE SELECTION THROUGH SPECIALIZATION]

Monitoring and Enforcement of Restrictive Covenants Once a loan has been made, the borrower has an incentive to engage in risky activities that make it less likely that the loan will be paid off. To reduce this moral hazard, financial institutions must adhere to the principle for managing credit risk that a lender should write provisions (restrictive covenants) into loan contracts restricting borrowers from engaging in risky activities. By monitoring borrowers' activities to see whether they are complying with the restrictive covenants and by enforcing the covenants if they are not, lenders can make sure that borrowers are not taking on risks at their expense. The need for financial institutions to engage in screening and monitoring explains why they spend so much money on auditing and information-collecting activities.

[handwritten margin note: MITIGATION OF MORAL HAZARD]

Long-Term Customer Relationships

An additional way for financial institution managers to obtain information about their borrowers is through long-term customer relationships, another important principle of credit risk management.

If a prospective borrower has had a checking or savings account, or other loans with a financial institution over a long period of time, a loan officer can look at past activity on the accounts and learn quite a bit about the borrower. The balances in the checking and savings accounts tell the loan officer how liquid the potential borrower is and at what time of year the borrower has a strong need for cash. A review of the checks the borrower has written reveals the borrower's suppliers. If the borrower has borrowed previously from the financial institution, the institution has a record of the loan payments. Thus, long-term customer relationships reduce the costs of information collection and make it easier to screen out bad credit risks.

The need for monitoring by lenders adds to the importance of long-term customer relationships. If the borrower has borrowed from the financial institution before, the institution has already established procedures for monitoring that customer. Therefore, the costs of monitoring long-term customers are lower than those for new customers.

[handwritten margin note: COST SAVINGS TO INSTITUTION]

Long-term relationships benefit the customers as well as the financial institution. A firm with a previous relationship will find it easier to obtain a loan at a low interest rate because the financial institution has an easier time determining if the prospective borrower is a good credit risk and incurs fewer costs in monitoring the borrower.

A long-term customer relationship has another advantage for the financial institution. No financial institution manager can think of every contingency when the institution writes a restrictive covenant into a loan contract; there will always be risky borrower activities that are not ruled out. However, what if a borrower wants to preserve a long-term relationship with the financial institution because it will be easier to get future loans at low interest rates? The borrower then has the incentive to avoid risky activities that would upset the financial institution, even if restrictions on these risky activities are not specified in the loan contract. Indeed, if the financial institution manager doesn't like what a borrower is doing even when the borrower isn't violating any restrictive covenants, the manager has some power to discourage the borrower from such activity: She can threaten not to let the borrower have new loans in the future. Long-term customer relationships therefore enable financial institutions to deal with even unanticipated moral hazard contingencies.

Loan Commitments

Banks have a special vehicle for institutionalizing a long-term customer relationship called a **loan commitment.** A loan commitment is a bank's commitment (for a specified future period of time) to provide a firm with loans up to a given amount at an interest rate that is tied to some market interest rate. The majority of commercial and industrial loans from banks are made under the loan commitment arrangement. The advantage for the firm is that it has a source of credit when it needs it. The advantage for the bank is that the loan commitment promotes a long-term relationship, which in turn facilitates information collection. In addition, provisions in the loan commitment agreement require that the firm continually supply the bank with information about the firm's income, asset and liability position, business activities, and so on. A loan commitment arrangement is a powerful method for reducing the bank's costs for screening and information collection.

Collateral

Collateral requirements for loans are important credit risk management tools. Loans with these collateral requirements are often referred to as **secured loans.** Collateral, which is property promised to the lender as compensation if the borrower defaults, lessens the consequences of adverse selection because it reduces the lender's losses in the case of a loan default. It also reduces moral hazard because the borrower has more to lose from a loan default. If a borrower defaults on a loan, the lender can sell the collateral and use the proceeds to make up for its losses on the loan. Collateral requirements thus offer important protection for financial institutions making loans, and that is why they are extremely common in loans made by financial institutions.

Compensating Balances

One particular form of collateral required when a bank makes commercial loans is called **compensating balances:** A firm receiving a loan must keep a required minimum amount of funds in a checking account at the bank. For example, a business getting a $10 million loan may be required to keep compensating balances of at least $1 million in its checking account at the bank. This $1 million in compensating balances can then be taken by the bank to make up some of the losses on the loan if the borrower defaults.

Besides serving as collateral, compensating balances help increase the likelihood that a loan will be paid off. They do this by helping the bank monitor the borrower and consequently reduce moral hazard. Specifically, by requiring the borrower to use a checking account at the bank, the bank can observe the firm's check payment practices, which may yield a great deal of information about the borrower's financial condition. For example, a sustained drop in the borrower's checking account balance may signal that the borrower is having financial trouble, or account activity may suggest that the borrower is engaging in risky activities; perhaps a change in suppliers means that the borrower is pursuing new lines of business. Any significant change in the borrower's payment procedures is a signal to the bank that it should make inquiries. Compensating balances therefore make it easier for banks to monitor borrowers more effectively and are another important credit risk management tool.

Credit Rationing

Another way in which financial institutions deal with adverse selection and moral hazard is through **credit rationing:** refusing to make loans even though borrowers are willing to pay the stated interest rate or even a higher rate. Credit rationing takes two forms. The first occurs when a lender refuses to make a loan *of any amount* to a borrower, even if the borrower is willing to pay a higher interest rate. The second occurs when a lender is willing to make a loan but restricts the size of the loan to less than the borrower would like.

At first, you might be puzzled by the first type of credit rationing. After all, even if the potential borrower is a credit risk, why doesn't the lender just extend the loan but at a higher interest rate? The answer is that adverse selection prevents this solution. Individuals and firms with the riskiest investment projects are exactly those that are willing to pay the highest interest rates. If a borrower took on a high-risk investment and succeeded, the borrower would become extremely rich. But a lender wouldn't want to make such a loan precisely because the credit risk is high; the likely outcome is that the borrower will *not* succeed and the lender will not be paid back. Charging a higher interest rate just makes adverse selection worse for the lender; that is, it increases the likelihood that the lender is lending to a bad credit risk. The lender would therefore rather not make any loans at a higher interest rate; instead, it would engage in the first type of credit rationing and would turn down loans.

Financial institutions engage in the second type of credit rationing to guard against moral hazard: They grant loans to borrowers, but not loans as large as the borrowers want. Such credit rationing is necessary because the larger the loan, the greater the benefits from moral hazard. If a financial institution gives you a $1,000 loan, for example, you are likely to take actions that enable you to pay it back because you don't want to hurt your credit rating for the future. However, if the financial institution lends you $10 million, you are more likely to fly down to Rio to celebrate. The larger your loan, the greater your incentives to engage in activities that make it less likely that you will repay the loan. Because more borrowers repay their loans if the loan amounts are small, financial institutions ration credit by providing borrowers with smaller loans than they seek.

Managing Interest-Rate Risk

With the increased volatility of interest rates that occurred in the 1980s, financial institution managers became more concerned about their exposure to interest-rate risk, the riskiness of earnings and returns that is associated with changes in interest rates. Indeed, the S&L debacle, described in Chapter 19, made clearer the dangers of interest-rate risk when many S&Ls went out of business because they had not managed interest-rate risk properly. To see what interest-rate risk is all about, let's take a look at the balance sheet of the First National Bank:

(handwritten margin note: INTEREST-RATE RISK DEFINED)

First National Bank				
Assets		**Liabilities**		
Reserves and cash items	$5 million	Checkable deposits		$15 million
Securities		Money market deposit		
Less than 1 year	$5 million	accounts		$5 million
1 to 2 years	$5 million	Savings deposits		$15 million
Greater than 2 years	$10 million	CDs		
Residential mortgages		Variable-rate		$10 million
Variable-rate	$10 million	Less than 1 year		$15 million
Fixed-rate (30-year)	$10 million	1 to 2 years		$5 million
Commercial loans		Greater than 2 years		$5 million
Less than 1 year	$15 million	Fed funds		$5 million
1 to 2 years	$10 million	Borrowings		
Greater than 2 years	$25 million	Less than 1 year		$10 million
Physical capital	$5 million	1 to 2 years		$5 million
		Greater than 2 years		$5 million
		Bank capital		$5 million
Total	$100 million	Total		$100 million

The first step in assessing interest-rate risk is for the bank manager to decide which assets and liabilities are rate-sensitive, that is, which have interest rates that will be reset (repriced) within the year. Note that rate-sensitive assets or liabilities can have interest rates repriced within the year either because the debt instrument matures within the year or because the repricing is done automatically, as with variable-rate mortgages.

For many assets and liabilities, deciding whether they are rate-sensitive is straightforward. In our example, the obviously rate-sensitive assets are securities with maturities of less than one year ($5 million), variable-rate mortgages ($10 million), and commercial loans with maturities less than one year ($15 million), for a total of $30 million. However, some assets that look like fixed-rate assets whose interest rates are not repriced within the year actually have a component that is rate-sensitive. For example, although fixed-rate residential mortgages may have a maturity of 30 years, homeowners can repay their mortgages early by selling their homes or repaying the mortgage in some other way. This means that within the year, a certain percentage of these fixed-rate mortgages will be paid off, and interest rates on this amount will be repriced. From past experience the bank manager knows that 20% of the fixed-rate residential mortgages are repaid within a year, which means that $2 million of these mortgages (20% of $10 million) must be considered rate-sensitive.

The bank manager adds this $2 million to the $30 million of rate-sensitive assets already calculated, for a total of $32 million in rate-sensitive assets.

The bank manager now goes through a similar procedure to determine the total amount of rate-sensitive liabilities. The obviously rate-sensitive liabilities are money market deposit accounts ($5 million), variable-rate CDs and CDs with less than one year to maturity ($25 million), federal funds ($5 million), and borrowings with maturities of less than one year ($10 million), for a total of $45 million. Checkable deposits and savings deposits often have interest rates that can be changed at any time by the bank, although banks often like to keep their rates fixed for substantial periods. Thus, these liabilities are partially but not fully rate-sensitive. The bank manager estimates that 10% of checkable deposits ($1.5 million) and 20% of savings deposits ($3 million) should be considered rate-sensitive. Adding the $1.5 million and $3 million to the $45 million figure yields a total for rate-sensitive liabilities of $49.5 million.

Now the bank manager can analyze what will happen if interest rates rise by 1 percentage point, say, on average from 10% to 11%. The income on the assets rises by $320,000 (= 1% × $32 million of rate-sensitive assets), while the payments on the liabilities rise by $495,000 (= 1% × $49.5 million of rate-sensitive liabilities). The First National Bank's profits now decline by $175,000 = ($320,000 − $495,000). Another way of thinking about this situation is with the net interest margin concept described in Chapter 17, which is interest income minus interest expense divided by bank assets. In this case, the 1% rise in interest rates has resulted in a decline of the net interest margin by 0.175% (= − $175,000/$100 million). Conversely, if interest rates fall by 1%, similar reasoning tells us that the First National Bank's income rises by $175,000 and its net interest margin rises by 0.175%. This example illustrates the following point: ***If a financial institution has more rate-sensitive liabilities than assets, a rise in interest rates will reduce the net interest margin and income, and a decline in interest rates will raise the net interest margin and income.***

Income Gap Analysis

One simple and quick approach to measuring the sensitivity of bank income to changes in interest rates is **gap analysis** (also called **income gap analysis**), in which the amount of rate-sensitive liabilities is subtracted from the amount of rate-sensitive assets. This calculation, GAP, can be written as

$$GAP = RSA - RSL \tag{1}$$

where RSA = rate-sensitive assets
              RSL = rate-sensitive liabilities

In our example, the bank manager calculates GAP to be

$$GAP = \$32 \text{ million} - \$49.5 \text{ million} = -\$17.5 \text{ million}$$

Multiplying GAP times the change in the interest rate immediately reveals the effect on bank income:

$$\Delta I = GAP \times \Delta i \tag{2}$$

where ΔI = change in bank income
              Δi = change in interest rates

example 24.1 Income Gap Analysis

Using the −$17.5 million gap calculated using Equation 1, what is the change in income if interest rates rise by 1%?

Solution

The change in income is −$175,000.

$$\Delta I = GAP \times \Delta i$$

where

$$GAP = RSA - RSL \qquad = -\$17.5 \text{ million}$$
$$\Delta i = \text{change in interest rate} = 0.01$$

Thus,

$$\Delta I = -\$17.5 \text{ million} \times 0.01 = -\$175,000$$

The analysis we just conducted is known as *basic gap analysis,* and it suffers from the problem that many of the assets and liabilities that are not classified as rate-sensitive have different maturities. One refinement to deal with this problem, the *maturity bucket approach,* is to measure the gap for several maturity subintervals, called maturity buckets, so that effects of interest-rate changes over a multiyear period can be calculated.

example 24.2 Income Gap Analysis

The manager of First National Bank notices that the bank balance sheet allows him to put assets and liabilities into more refined maturity buckets that allow him to estimate the potential change in income over the next one to two years. Rate-sensitive assets in this period consist of $5 million of securities maturing in one to two years, $10 million of commercial loans maturing in one to two years, and an additional $2 million (20% of fixed-rate mortgages) that the bank expects to be repaid. Rate-sensitive liabilities in this period consist of $5 million of one- to two-year CDs, $5 million of one- to two-year borrowings, $1.5 million of checkable deposits (the 10% of checkable deposits that the bank manager estimates are rate-sensitive in this period), and an additional $3 million of savings deposits (the 20% estimate of savings deposits). For the next one to two years, calculate the gap and the change in income if interest rates rise by 1%.

Solution

The gap calculation for the one- to two-year period is $2.5 million.

$$GAP = RSA - RSL$$

where

$$RSA = \text{rate-sensitive assets} \quad = \$17 \text{ million}$$
$$RSL = \text{rate-sensitive liabilities} = \$14.5 \text{ million}$$

Thus,

$$GAP = \$17 \text{ million} - \$14.5 \text{ million} = \$2.5 \text{ million}$$

If interest rates remain 1% higher, then in the second year income will improve by $25,000.

$$\Delta I = GAP \times \Delta i$$

where

$GAP = RSA - RSL$ = $2.5 million

Δi = change in interest rate = 0.01

Thus,

$$\Delta I = \$2.5 \text{ million} \times 0.01 = \$25,000$$

By using the more refined maturity bucket approach, the bank manager can figure out what will happen to bank income over the next several years when there is a change in interest rates.

Duration Gap Analysis

The gap analysis we have examined so far focuses only on the effect of interest-rate changes on income. Clearly, owners and managers of financial institutions care not only about the effect of changes in interest rates on income but also about the effect of changes in interest rates on the market value of the net worth of the financial institution.[1]

An alternative method for measuring interest-rate risk, called **duration gap analysis,** examines the sensitivity of the market value of the financial institution's net worth to changes in interest rates. Duration analysis is based on Macaulay's concept of *duration,* which measures the average lifetime of a security's stream of payments (described in Chapter 3). Recall that duration is a useful concept because it provides a good approximation, particularly when interest-rate changes are small, of the sensitivity of a security's market value to a change in its interest rate using the following formula:

$$\%\Delta P \approx -DUR \times \frac{\Delta i}{1 + i} \tag{3}$$

where $\%\Delta P = (P_{t+1} - P_t)/P_t$ = percent change in market value of the security

DUR = duration

i = interest rate

After having determined the duration of all assets and liabilities on the bank's balance sheet, the bank manager could use this formula to calculate how the market value of each asset and liability changes when there is a change in interest rates and then calculate the effect on net worth. There is, however, an easier way to go about doing this, derived from the basic fact about duration we learned in Chapter 3:

---

[1]Note that accounting net worth is calculated on a historical-cost (book-value) basis, meaning that the value of assets and liabilities is based on their initial price. However, book-value net worth does not give a complete picture of the true worth of the firm; the market value of net worth provides a more accurate measure. This is why duration gap analysis focuses on what happens to the market value of net worth, and not on book value, when interest rates change.

Duration is additive; that is, the duration of a portfolio of securities is the weighted average of the durations of the individual securities, with the weights reflecting the proportion of the portfolio invested in each. What this means is that the bank manager can figure out the effect that interest-rate changes will have on the market value of net worth by calculating the average duration for assets and for liabilities and then using those figures to estimate the effects of interest-rate changes.

To see how a bank manager would do this, let's return to the balance sheet of the First National Bank. The bank manager has already used the procedures outlined in Chapter 3 to calculate the duration of each asset and liability, as listed in Table 24.1.

TABLE 24.1 Duration of the First National Bank's Assets and Liabilities

	Amount ($ millions)	Duration (years)	Weighted Duration (years)
Assets			
Reserves and cash items	5	0.0	0.00
Securities			
Less than 1 year	5	0.4	0.02
1 to 2 years	5	1.6	0.08
Greater than 2 years	10	7.0	0.70
Residential mortgages			
Variable-rate	10	0.5	0.05
Fixed-rate (30-year)	10	6.0	0.60
Commercial loans			
Less than 1 year	15	0.7	0.11
1 to 2 years	10	1.4	0.14
Greater than 2 years	25	4.0	1.00
Physical capital	5	0.0	0.00
Average duration			2.70
Liabilities			
Checkable deposits	15	2.0	0.32
Money market deposit accounts	5	0.1	0.01
Savings deposits	15	1.0	0.16
CDs			
Variable-rate	10	0.5	0.05
Less than 1 year	15	0.2	0.03
1 to 2 years	5	1.2	0.06
Greater than 2 years	5	2.7	0.14
Fed funds	5	0.0	0.00
Borrowings			
Less than 1 year	10	0.3	0.03
1 to 2 years	5	1.3	0.07
Greater than 2 years	5	3.1	0.16
Average duration			1.03

For each asset, the manager then calculates the weighted duration by multiplying the duration times the amount of the asset divided by total assets, which in this case is $100 million. For example, in the case of securities with maturities of less than one year, the manager multiplies the 0.4 year of duration times $5 million divided by $100 million to get a weighted duration of 0.02. (Note that physical assets have no cash payments, so they have a duration of zero years.) Doing this for all the assets and adding them up, the bank manager gets a figure for the average duration of the assets of 2.70 years.

The manager follows a similar procedure for the liabilities, noting that total liabilities excluding capital are $95 million. For example, the weighted duration for checkable deposits is determined by multiplying the 2.0-year duration by $15 million divided by $95 million to get 0.32. Adding up these weighted durations, the manager obtains an average duration of liabilities of 1.03 years.

example 24.3 **Duration Gap Analysis**

The bank manager wants to know what happens when interest rates rise from 10% to 11%. The total asset value is $100 million, and the total liability value is $95 million. Use Equation 3 to calculate the change in the market value of the assets and liabilities.

Solution

With a total asset value of $100 million, the market value of assets falls by $2.5 million ($100 million × 0.025 = $2.5 million).

$$\%\Delta P = -DUR \times \frac{\Delta i}{1 + i}$$

where

$$DUR = \text{duration} \qquad\qquad = 2.70$$
$$\Delta i = \text{change in interest rate} = 0.11 - 0.10 = 0.01$$
$$i = \text{interest rate} \qquad\qquad = 0.10$$

Thus,

$$\%\Delta P \approx -2.70 \times \frac{0.01}{1 + 0.10} = -0.025 = -2.5\%$$

With total liabilities of $95 million, the market value of liabilities falls by $0.9 million ($95 million × 0.009 = -$0.9 million).

$$\%\Delta P \approx -DUR \times \frac{\Delta i}{1 + i}$$

where

$$DUR = \text{duration} \qquad\qquad = 1.03$$
$$\Delta i = \text{change in interest rate} = 0.11 - 0.10 = 0.01$$
$$i = \text{interest rate} \qquad\qquad = 0.10$$

Thus,

$$\%\Delta P \approx -1.03 \times \frac{0.01}{1 + 0.10} = -0.009 = -0.9\%$$

The result is that the net worth of the bank would decline by $1.6 million (−$2.5 million − (−$0.9 million) = −$2.5 million + $0.9 million = −$1.6 million).

The bank manager could have obtained the answer even more quickly by calculating what is called a *duration gap*, which is defined as follows:

$$DUR_{gap} = DUR_a - \left(\frac{L}{A} \times DUR_l \right) \qquad (4)$$

where
$$DUR_a = \text{average duration of assets}$$
$$DUR_l = \text{average duration of liabilities}$$
$$L = \text{market value of liabilities}$$
$$A = \text{market value of assets}$$

example 24.4 **Duration Gap Analysis**

Based on the information provided in Example 24.3, use Equation 4 to determine the duration gap for First National Bank.

Solution
The duration gap for First National Bank is 1.72 years.

$$DUR_{gap} = DUR_a - \left(\frac{L}{A} \times DUR_l \right)$$

where

$$DUR_a = \text{average duration of assets} \quad = 2.70$$
$$L = \text{market value of liabilities} \quad = 95$$
$$A = \text{market value of assets} \quad = 100$$
$$DUR_l = \text{average duration of liabilities} = 1.03$$

Thus,

$$DUR_{gap} = 2.70 - \left(\frac{95}{100} \times 1.03 \right) = 1.72 \text{ years}$$

To estimate what will happen if interest rates change, the bank manager uses the DUR_{gap} calculation in Equation 4 to obtain the change in the market value of net worth as a percentage of total assets. In other words, the change in the market value of net worth as a percentage of assets is calculated as

$$\frac{\Delta NW}{A} \approx -DUR_{gap} \times \frac{\Delta i}{1 + i} \qquad (5)$$

---

example 24.5 **Duration Gap Analysis**

What is the change in the market value of net worth as a percentage of assets if interest rates rise from 10% to 11%? (Use Equation 5.)

Solution

A rise in interest rates from 10% to 11% would lead to a change in the market value of net worth as a percentage of assets of -1.6%.

$$\frac{\Delta NW}{A} = -DUR_{gap} \times \frac{\Delta i}{1 + i}$$

where

$$DUR_{gap} = \text{duration gap} \qquad\qquad = 1.72$$
$$\Delta i = \text{change in interest rate} = 0.11 - 0.10 = 0.01$$
$$i = \text{interest rate} \qquad\qquad = 0.10$$

Thus,

$$\frac{\Delta NW}{A} = -1.72 \times \frac{0.01}{1 + 0.10} = -0.016 = -1.6\%$$

With assets totaling $100 million, Example 24.5 indicates a fall in the market value of net worth of $1.6 million, which is the same figure that we found in Example 24.3.

As our examples make clear, both income gap analysis and duration gap analysis indicate that the First National Bank will suffer from a rise in interest rates. Indeed, in this example, we have seen that a rise in interest rates from 10% to 11% will cause the market value of net worth to fall by $1.6 million, which is one-third the initial amount of bank capital. Thus, the bank manager realizes that the bank faces substantial interest-rate risk because a rise in interest rates could cause it to lose a lot of its capital. Clearly, income gap analysis and duration gap analysis are useful tools for telling a financial institution manager the institution's degree of exposure to interest-rate risk.

---

study guide

To make sure that you understand income gap and duration gap analyses, you should be able to verify that if interest rates fall from 10% to 5%, the First National Bank will find its income increasing and the market value of its net worth rising. For even more practice with these concepts, do some of the problems at the end of this chapter.

Example of a Nonbanking Financial Institution

So far we have focused on an example involving a banking institution that has borrowed short and lent long so that when interest rates rise, both income and the net worth of the institution fall. It is important to recognize that income gap and duration gap analyses apply equally to other financial institutions. Furthermore, it is important for you to see that some financial institutions have income gaps and duration gaps that are opposite in sign to those of banks, so that when interest rates rise, both income and net worth rise rather than fall. To get a more complete picture of income gap and duration gap analyses, let us look at a nonbank financial institution, the Friendly Finance Company, which specializes in making consumer loans.

The Friendly Finance Company has the following balance sheet:

<table>
<tr><th colspan="4">Friendly Finance Company</th></tr>
<tr><th colspan="2">Assets</th><th colspan="2">Liabilities</th></tr>
<tr><td>Cash and deposits</td><td>$3 million</td><td>Commercial paper</td><td>$40 million</td></tr>
<tr><td>Securities</td><td></td><td>Bank loans</td><td></td></tr>
<tr><td> Less than 1 year</td><td>$5 million</td><td> Less than 1 year</td><td>$3 million</td></tr>
<tr><td> 1 to 2 years</td><td>$1 million</td><td> 1 to 2 years</td><td>$2 million</td></tr>
<tr><td> Greater than 2 years</td><td>$1 million</td><td> Greater than 2 years</td><td>$5 million</td></tr>
<tr><td>Consumer loans</td><td></td><td>Long-term bonds and</td><td></td></tr>
<tr><td> Less than 1 year</td><td>$50 million</td><td> other long-term debt</td><td>$40 million</td></tr>
<tr><td> 1 to 2 years</td><td>$20 million</td><td>Capital</td><td>$10 million</td></tr>
<tr><td> Greater than 2 years</td><td>$15 million</td><td></td><td></td></tr>
<tr><td>Physical capital</td><td>$5 million</td><td></td><td></td></tr>
<tr><td>   Total</td><td>$100 million</td><td>Total</td><td>$100 million</td></tr>
</table>

The manager of the Friendly Finance Company calculates the rate-sensitive assets to be equal to the $5 million of securities with maturities of less than one year plus the $50 million of consumer loans with maturities of less than one year, for a total of $55 million of rate-sensitive assets. The manager then calculates the rate-sensitive liabilities to be equal to the $40 million of commercial paper, all of which has a maturity of less than one year, plus the $3 million of bank loans maturing in less than a year, for a total of $43 million. The calculation of the income gap is then

$$GAP = RSA - RSL = \$55 \text{ million} - \$43 \text{ million} = \$12 \text{ million}$$

To calculate the effect on income if interest rates rise by 1%, the manager multiplies the *GAP* of $12 million times the change in the interest rate to get the following:

$$\Delta I = GAP \times \Delta i = \$12 \text{ million} \times 1\% = \$120,000$$

Thus, the manager finds that the finance company's income will rise by $120,000 when interest rates rise by 1%. The reason that the company has benefited from the interest-rate rise, in contrast to the First National Bank, whose profits suffer from the rise in interest rates, is that the Friendly Finance Company has a positive income gap because it has more rate-sensitive assets than liabilities.

Like the bank manager, the manager of the Friendly Finance Company is also interested in what happens to the market value of the net worth of the company when interest rates rise by 1%. So the manager calculates the weighted duration of each item in the balance sheet, adds them up as in Table 24.2, and obtains a duration for the assets of 1.16 years and for the liabilities of 2.77 years. The duration gap is then calculated to be

$$DUR_{gap} = DUR_a - \left(\frac{L}{A} \times DUR_l\right) = 1.16 - \left(\frac{90}{100} \times 2.77\right) = -1.33 \text{ years}$$

Since the Friendly Finance Company has a negative duration gap, the manager realizes that a rise in interest rates by 1 percentage point from 10% to 11% will increase

TABLE 24.2 Duration of the Friendly Finance Company's Assets and Liabilities

	Amount ($ millions)	Duration (years)	Weighted Duration (years)
Assets			
Cash and deposits	3	0.0	0.00
Securities			
Less than 1 year	5	0.5	0.05
1 to 2 years	1	1.7	0.02
Greater than 2 years	1	9.0	0.09
Consumer loans			
Less than 1 year	50	0.5	0.25
1 to 2 years	20	1.5	0.30
Greater than 2 years	15	3.0	0.45
Physical capital	5	0.0	0.00
Average duration			1.16
Liabilities			
Commercial paper	40	0.2	0.09
Bank loans			
Less than 1 year	3	0.3	0.01
1 to 2 years	2	1.6	0.04
Greater than 2 years	5	3.5	0.19
Long-term bonds and other long-term debt	40	5.5	2.44
Average duration			2.77

the market value of net worth of the firm. The manager checks this by calculating the change in the market value of net worth as a percentage of assets:

$$\frac{\Delta NW}{A} = -DUR_{gap} \times \frac{\Delta i}{1 + i} = -(-1.33) \times \frac{0.01}{1 + 0.10} = 0.012 = 1.2\%$$

With assets of $100 million, this calculation indicates that net worth will rise in market value by $1.2 million.

Even though the income gap and duration gap analyses indicate that the Friendly Finance Company gains from a rise in interest rates, the manager realizes that if interest rates go in the other direction, the company will suffer a fall in income and market value of net worth. Thus, the finance company manager, like the bank manager, realizes that the institution is subject to substantial interest-rate risk.

Some Problems with Income Gap and Duration Gap Analyses

Although you might think that income gap and duration gap analyses are complicated enough, further complications make a financial institution manager's job even harder.

One assumption that we have been using in our discussion of income gap and duration gap analyses is that when the level of interest rates changes, interest rates on all maturities change by exactly the same amount. That is the same as saying that we conducted our analysis under the assumption that the slope of the yield curve remains unchanged. Indeed, the situation is even worse for duration gap analysis because the duration gap is calculated assuming that interest rates for all maturities are the same—in other words, the yield curve is assumed to be flat. As our discussion of the term structure of interest rates in Chapter 5 indicated, however, the yield curve is not flat, and the slope of the yield curve fluctuates and has a tendency to change when the level of the interest rate changes. Thus, to get a truly accurate assessment of interest-rate risk, a financial institution manager has to assess what might happen to the slope of the yield curve when the level of the interest rate changes and then take this information into account when assessing interest-rate risk. In addition, duration gap analysis is based on the approximation in Equation 3 and thus only works well for small changes in interest rates.

A problem with income gap analysis is that, as we have seen, the financial institution manager must make estimates of the proportion of supposedly fixed-rate assets and liabilities that may be rate-sensitive. This involves estimates of the likelihood of prepayment of loans or customer shifts out of deposits when interest rates change. Such guesses are not easy to make, and as a result, the financial institution manager's estimates of income gaps may not be very accurate. A similar problem occurs in calculating durations of assets and liabilities because many of the cash payments are uncertain. Thus, the estimate of the duration gap might not be accurate either.

Do these problems mean that managers of banks and other financial institutions should give up on gap analysis as a tool for measuring interest-rate risk? Financial institutions do use more sophisticated approaches to measuring interest-rate risk, such as scenario analysis and value-at-risk analysis, which make greater use of computers to more accurately measure changes in prices of assets when interest rates change. Income gap and duration gap analyses, however, still provide simple frameworks to help financial institution managers to get a first assessment of interest-rate risk, and thus they are useful tools in the financial institution managers' toolkit.

THE PRACTICING MANAGER

Strategies for Managing Interest-Rate Risk

Once financial institution managers have done the income gap and duration gap analyses for their institutions, they must decide which alternative strategies to pursue. If the manager of the First National Bank firmly believes that interest rates will fall in the future, he or she may be willing to take no action knowing that the bank has more rate-sensitive liabilities than rate-sensitive assets and so will benefit from the expected interest-rate decline. However, the bank manager also realizes that the First National Bank is subject to substantial interest-rate risk because there is always a possibility that interest rates will rise rather than fall, and as we have seen, this outcome could bankrupt the bank. The manager might try to shorten the duration of the bank's assets to increase their rate sensitivity either by purchasing assets of shorter maturity or by converting fixed-rate loans into adjustable-rate loans. Alternatively, the bank manager could lengthen the duration of the liabilities. With these adjustments to the bank's assets and liabilities, the bank would be less affected by interest-rate swings.

For example, the bank manager might decide to eliminate the income gap by increasing the amount of rate-sensitive assets to $49.5 million to equal the $49.5 million of rate-sensitive liabilities. Or the manager could reduce rate-sensitive liabilities to $32 million so that they equal rate-sensitive assets. In either case, the income gap would now be zero, so a change in interest rates would have no effect on bank profits in the coming year.

Alternatively, the bank manager might decide to immunize the market value of the bank's net worth completely from interest-rate risk by adjusting assets and liabilities so that the duration gap is equal to zero. To do this, the manager can set DUR_{gap} equal to zero in Equation 4 and solve for DUR_a:

$$DUR_a = \frac{L}{A} \times DUR_l = \frac{95}{100} \times 1.03 = 0.98$$

These calculations reveal that the manager should reduce the average duration of the bank's assets to 0.98 year. To check that the duration gap is set equal to zero, the calculation is

$$DUR_{gap} = 0.98 - \left(\frac{95}{100} \times 1.03 \right) = 0$$

In this case, using Equation 5, the market value of net worth would remain unchanged when interest rates change. Alternatively, the bank manager could calculate the value of the duration of the liabilities that would produce a duration gap of zero. To do this would involve setting DUR_{gap} equal to zero in Equation 4 and solving for DUR_l:

$$DUR_l = DUR_a \times \frac{A}{L} = 2.70 \times \frac{100}{95} = 2.84$$

This calculation reveals that the interest-rate risk could also be eliminated by increasing the average duration of the bank's liabilities to 2.84 years. The manager again checks that the duration gap is set equal to zero by calculating

$$DUR_{gap} = 2.70 - \left(\frac{95}{100} \times 2.84 \right) = 0$$

study guide

To see if you understand how a financial institution manager can protect income and net worth from interest-rate risk, first calculate how the Friendly Finance Company might change the amount of its rate-sensitive assets or its rate-sensitive liabilities to eliminate the income gap. You should find that the income gap can be eliminated either by reducing the amount of rate-sensitive assets to $43 million or by raising the amount of rate-sensitive liabilities to $55 million. Also do the calculations to determine what modifications to the duration of the assets or liabilities would immunize the market value of Friendly Finance's net worth from interest-rate risk. You should find that interest-rate risk would be eliminated if the duration of the assets were set to 2.49 years or if the duration of the liabilities were set to 1.29 years.

One problem with eliminating a financial institution's interest-rate risk by altering the balance sheet is that doing so might be very costly in the short run. The financial institution may be locked into assets and liabilities of particular durations because of its field of expertise. Fortunately, recently developed financial instruments, such as financial futures, options, and interest-rate swaps, help financial institutions manage their interest-rate risk without requiring them to rearrange their balance sheets. We discuss these instruments and how they can be used to manage interest-rate risk in the next chapter.

SUMMARY

1. The concepts of adverse selection and moral hazard explain the origin of many credit risk management principles involving loan activities, including screening and monitoring, development of long-term customer relationships, loan commitments, collateral, compensating balances, and credit rationing.

2. With the increased volatility of interest rates that occurred in recent years, financial institutions became more concerned about their exposure to interest-rate risk. Income gap and duration gap analyses tell a financial institution if it has fewer rate-sensitive assets than liabilities (in which case a rise in interest rates will reduce income and a fall in interest rates will raise it) or more rate-sensitive assets than liabilities (in which case a rise in interest rates will raise income and a fall in interest rates will reduce it). Financial institutions can manage interest-rate risk by modifying their balance sheets and by making use of new financial instruments.

KEY TERMS

compensating balances, *p. 622*
credit rationing, *p. 623*
duration gap analysis, *p. 627*

gap analysis (income gap analysis), *p. 625*
loan commitment, *p. 622*
secured loans, *p. 622*

QUESTIONS

1. Can a financial institution keep borrowers from engaging in risky activities if there are no restrictive covenants written into the loan agreement?

2. Why are secured loans an important method of lending for financial institutions?

3. "If more customers want to borrow funds at the prevailing interest rate, a financial institution can increase its profits by raising interest rates on its loans." Is this statement true, false, or uncertain? Explain your answer.

4. Why is being nosy a desirable trait for a banker?

5. A bank almost always insists that the firms it lends to keep compensating balances at the bank. Why?

6. "Because diversification is a desirable strategy for avoiding risk, it never makes sense for a financial institution to specialize in making specific types of loans." Is this statement true, false, or uncertain? Explain your answer.

QUANTITATIVE PROBLEMS

1. A bank issues a $100,000 variable-rate 30-year mortgage with a nominal annual rate of 4.5%. If the required rate drops to 4.0% after the first six months, what is the impact on the interest income for the first 12 months?

2. A bank issues a $100,000 fixed-rate 30-year mortgage with a nominal annual rate of 4.5%. If the required rate drops to 4.0% immediately after the mortgage is issued, what is the impact on the value of the mortgage?

3. Calculate the duration of a $100,000 fixed-rate 30-year mortgage with a nominal annual rate of 7.0%. What is the expected percentage change in value if the required rate drops to 6.5% immediately after the mortgage is issued?

4. The value of a $100,000 fixed-rate 30-year mortgage falls to $89,537 when interest rates move from 5% to 6%. What is the approximate duration of the mortgage?

5. Calculate the duration of a commercial loan. The face value of the loan is $2,000,000. It requires simple interest yearly, with an APR of 8%. The loan is due in four years. The current market rate for such loans is 8%.

6. A bank's balance sheet contains interest-sensitive assets of $280 million and interest-sensitive liabilities of $465 million. Calculate the income gap.

7. Calculate the income gap for a financial institution with rate-sensitive assets of $20 million and rate-sensitive liabilities of $48 million. If interest rates rise from 4% to 4.8%, what is the expected change in income?

8. Calculate the income gap given the following items:
- $8 million in reserves
- $25 million in variable-rate mortgages
- $4 million in checkable deposits
- $2 million in savings deposits
- $6 million of two-year CDs

9. The following financial statement is for the current year. From the past, you know that 10% of fixed-rate mortgages prepay each year. You also estimate that 10% of checkable deposits and 20% of savings accounts are rate-sensitive.

What is the current income gap for Second National Bank? What will happen to the bank's current net interest income if rates fall by 75 basis points?

Second National Bank			
Assets		**Liabilities**	
Reserves	$1,500,000	Checkable deposits	$15,000,000
Securities		Money market	
< 1 year	$6,000,000	deposits	$5,500,000
1 to 2 years	$8,000,000	Savings accounts	$8,000,000
> 2 years	$12,000,000	CDs	
Residential mortgages		Variable-rate	$15,000,000
Variable-rate	$7,000,000	< 1 year	$22,000,000
Fixed-rate	$13,000,000	1 to 2 years	$5,000,000
Commercial loans		> 2 years	$2,500,000
< 1 year	$1,500,000	Federal funds	$5,000,000
1 to 2 years	$18,500,000	Borrowings	
> 2 years	$30,000,000	< 1 year	$12,000,000
Buildings, etc.	$2,500,000	1 to 2 years	$3,000,000
		> 2 years	$2,000,000
		Bank capital	$5,000,000
Total	$100,000,000	Total	$100,000,000

10. Chicago Avenue Bank has the following assets:

Asset	Value	Duration (in years)
T-bills	$100,000,000	0.55
Consumer loans	$40,000,000	2.35
Commercial loans	$15,000,000	5.90

What is Chicago Avenue Bank's asset portfolio duration?

11. A bank added a bond to its portfolio. The bond has a duration of 12.3 years and cost $1,109. Just after buying the bond, the bank discovered that market interest rates are expected to rise from 8% to 8.75%. What is the expected change in the bond's value?

12. Calculate the change in the market value of assets and liabilities when the average duration of assets is 3.60, the average duration of liabilities 0.88, and interest rates increase from 5% to 5.5%.

13. Springer County Bank has assets totaling $180 million with a duration of five years, and liabilities totaling $160 million with a duration of two years. If interest rates drop from 9% by 75 basis points, what is the change in the bank's capitalization ratio?

14. The manager for Tyler Bank and Trust has the following assets to manage:

Asset	Value	Duration (in years)
Bonds	$75,000,000	9.00
Consumer loans	$875,000,000	2.00
Commercial loans	$700,000,000	5.00

Liability	Value	Duration (in years)
Demand deposits	$300,000,000	1.00
Saving accounts	??	0.50

If the manager wants a duration gap of 3.00, what level of saving accounts should the bank raise? Assume that any difference between assets and liabilities is held as cash (duration = 0).

15. The financial statement below is for the current year. After you review the data, calculate the duration gap for the bank.

	Assets	Duration (in years)		Liabilities	Duration (in years)
					Second National Bank

	Assets		Duration (in years)		Liabilities		Duration (in years)
Reserves		$5,000,000	0.00	Checkable deposits		$15,000,000	2.00
Securities				Money market deposits		5,000,000	0.10
< 1 year		5,000,000	0.40	Savings accounts		15,000,000	1.00
1 to 2 years		5,000,000	1.60	CDs			
> 2 years		10,000,000	7.00	Variable-rate		10,000,000	0.50
Residential mortgages				< 1 year		15,000,000	0.20
Variable-rate		10,000,000	0.50	1 to 2 years		5,000,000	1.20
Fixed-rate		10,000,000	6.00	> 2 years		5,000,000	2.70
Commercial loans				Interbank loans		5,000,000	0.00
< 1 year		15,000,000	0.70	Borrowings			
1 to 2 years		10,000,000	1.40	< 1 year		10,000,000	0.30
> 2 years		25,000,000	4.00	1 to 2 years		5,000,000	1.30
Buildings, etc.		5,000,000	0.00	> 2 years		5,000,000	3.10
				Bank capital		5,000,000	
Total		$100,000,000		Total		$100,000,000	

For Problems 16–23, assume that the First National Bank initially has the balance sheet shown on page 624 and that interest rates are initially at 10%.

16. If the First National Bank sells $10 million of its securities with maturities greater than two years and replaces them with securities maturing in less than one year, what is the income gap for the bank? What

will happen to profits next year if interest rates fall by 3 percentage points?

17. If the First National Bank decides to convert $5 million of its fixed-rate mortgages into variable-rate mortgages, what happens to its interest-rate risk? Explain with income gap and duration gap analyses.

18. If the manager of the First National Bank revises the estimate of the percentage of fixed-rate mortgages that are repaid within a year from 20% to 10%, what will be the revised estimate of the interest-rate risk the bank faces? What will happen to profits next year if interest rates fall by 2 percentage points?

19. If the manager of the First National Bank revises the estimate of the percentage of checkable deposits that are rate-sensitive from 10% to 25%, what will be the revised estimate of the interest-rate risk the bank faces? What will happen to profits next year if interest rates rise by 5 percentage points?

20. Given the estimates of duration in Table 24.1, what will happen to the bank's net worth if interest rates rise by 10 percentage points? Will the bank stay in business? Why or why not?

21. If the manager of the First National Bank revises the estimates of the duration of the bank's assets to four years and liabilities to two years, what is the effect on net worth if interest rates rise by 2 percentage points?

22. Given the estimates of duration in Problem 21, how should the bank alter the duration of its assets to immunize its net worth from interest-rate risk?

23. Given the estimates of duration in Problem 21, how should the bank alter the duration of its liabilities to immunize its net worth from interest-rate risk?

For Problems 24–29, assume that the Friendly Finance Company initially has the balance sheet shown on page 632 and that interest rates are initially at 8%.

24. If the manager of the Friendly Finance Company decides to sell off $10 million of the company's consumer loans, half maturing within one year and half maturing in greater than two years, and uses the resulting funds to buy $10 million of Treasury bills, what is the income gap for the company? What will happen to profits next year if interest rates fall by 5 percentage points? How could the Friendly Finance Company alter its balance sheet to immunize its income from this change in interest rates?

25. If the Friendly Finance Company raises an additional $20 million with commercial paper and uses the funds to make $20 million of consumer loans that mature in less than one year, what happens to its interest-rate risk? In this situation, what additional changes could it make in its balance sheet to eliminate the income gap?

26. Given the estimates of duration in Table 24.2, what will happen to the Friendly Finance Company's net worth if interest rates rise by 3 percentage points? Will the company stay in business? Why or why not?

27. If the manager of the Friendly Finance Company revises the estimates of the duration of the company's assets to two years and liabilities to four years, what is the effect on net worth if interest rates rise by 3 percentage points?

28. Given the estimates of duration found in Problem 27, how should the Friendly Finance Company alter the duration of its assets to immunize its net worth from interest-rate risk?

29. Given the estimates of duration in Problem 27, how should the Friendly Finance Company alter the duration of its liabilities to immunize its net worth from interest-rate risk?

WEB EXERCISES

Risk Management in Financial Institutions

1. This chapter discussed the need financial institutions have to control credit risk by lending to credit-worthy borrowers. If you allow your credit to deteriorate, you may find yourself unable to borrow when you need to. Go to **http://www.quicken.com/cms/viewers/article/banking/39654** and assess your own creditworthiness. What can you do to improve your appeal to lenders?

2. The FDIC is extremely concerned with risk management in banks. High-risk banks are more likely to fail and cost the FDIC money. The FDIC regularly examines banks and rates them using a system called CAMELS. Go to **http://www.fdic.gov/regulations/safety/manual/index.html**. What does the acronym CAMELS stand for? Go to Part II. 7.1 and review the discussion of Market Risk. Summarize the FDIC interest-rate risk-measurement methods.

CHAPTER 25

Hedging with Financial Derivatives

Preview

Starting in the 1970s and increasingly in the 1980s and 1990s, the world became a riskier place for financial institutions. Swings in interest rates widened, and the bond and stock markets went through some episodes of increased volatility. As a result of these developments, managers of financial institutions have become more concerned with reducing the risk their institutions face. Given the greater demand for risk reduction, the process of financial innovation described in Chapter 18 came to the rescue by producing new financial instruments that help financial institution managers manage risk better. These instruments, called **financial derivatives,** have payoffs that are linked to previously issued securities and are extremely useful risk reduction tools.

In this chapter we look at the most important financial derivatives that managers of financial institutions use to reduce risk: forward contracts, financial futures, options, and swaps. We examine not only how markets for each of these financial derivatives work but also how each can be used by financial institution managers to reduce risk.

Hedging

Financial derivatives are so effective in reducing risk because they enable financial institutions to **hedge,** that is, engage in a financial transaction that reduces or eliminates risk. When a financial institution has bought an asset, it is said to have taken a **long position,** and this exposes the institution to risk if the returns on the asset are uncertain. On the other hand, if it has sold an asset that it has agreed to deliver to another party at a future date, it is said to have taken

HEDGE DEFINED

LONG POSITIONS DEFINED

641

Basic Principle for Hedging

go online

www.rmahq.org

The Web site of the Risk Management Association reports useful information such as annual statement studies, on-line publications, and so on.

a **short position,** and this can also expose the institution to risk. Financial derivatives can be used to reduce risk by invoking the following basic principle of hedging: ***Hedging risk involves engaging in a financial transaction that offsets a long position by taking an additional short position, or offsets a short position by taking an additional long position.*** In other words, if a financial institution has *bought* a security and has therefore taken a long position, it conducts a hedge by contracting to *sell* that security (take a short position) at some future date. Alternatively, if it has taken a short position by *selling* a security that it needs to deliver at a future date, then it conducts a hedge by contracting to *buy* that security (take a long position) at a future date. We first look at how this principle can be applied using forward contracts.

Forward Markets

Forward contracts are agreements by two parties to engage in a financial transaction at a future (forward) point in time. Here we focus on forward contracts that are linked to debt instruments, called **interest-rate forward contracts;** later in the chapter we discuss forward contracts for foreign currencies.

Interest rate forward contracts are linked to debt instruments

Interest-Rate Forward Contracts

4 components of interest rate forward contracts

Interest-rate forward contracts involve the future sale or purchase of a debt instrument and have several dimensions: (1) specification of the actual debt instrument that will be delivered at a future date, (2) amount of the debt instrument to be delivered, (3) price (interest rate) on the debt instrument when it is delivered, and (4) date on which delivery will take place. An example of an interest-rate forward contract might be an agreement for the First National Bank to sell to the Rock Solid Insurance Company, one year from today, $5 million face value of the 6s of 2029 Treasury bonds (coupon bonds with a 6% coupon rate that mature in 2029) at a price that yields the same interest rate on these bonds as today's, say, 6%. Because Rock Solid will buy the securities at a future date, it has taken a long position, while the First National Bank, which will sell the securities, has taken a short position.

THE PRACTICING MANAGER

Hedging Interest-Rate Risk with Forward Contracts

To understand why the First National Bank might want to enter into this forward contract, suppose that you are the manager of the First National Bank and have previously bought $5 million of the 6s of 2029 Treasury bonds, which currently sell at par value and so their yield to maturity is also 6%. Because these are long-term bonds, you recognize that you are exposed to substantial interest-rate risk and worry that if interest rates rise in the future, the price of these bonds will fall, resulting in a substantial capital loss that may cost you your job. How do you hedge this risk?

Knowing the basic principle of hedging, you see that your long position in these bonds must be offset by an equal short position for the same bonds with a forward contract. That is, you need to contract to sell these bonds at a future date at the current par value price. As a result, you agree with another party, in this case, Rock Solid Insurance Company, to sell them the $5 million of the 6s of 2029 Treasury bonds at par one year from today. By entering into this forward contract, you have locked in the future price and so have eliminated the price risk First National Bank faces from interest-rate changes. In other words, you have successfully hedged against interest-rate risk.

Why would the Rock Solid Insurance Company want to enter into the forward contract with the First National Bank? Rock Solid expects to receive premiums of $5 million in one year's time that it will want to invest in the 6s of 2029 but worries that interest rates on these bonds will decline between now and next year. By using the forward contract, it is able to lock in the 6% interest rate on the Treasury bonds (which will be sold to it by the First National Bank).

Pros and Cons of Forward Contracts

The advantage of forward contracts is that they can be as flexible as the parties involved want them to be. This means that an institution like the First National Bank may be able to hedge completely the interest-rate risk for the exact security it is holding in its portfolio, just as it has in our example.

However, forward contracts suffer from two problems that severely limit their usefulness. The first is that it may be very hard for an institution like the First National Bank to find another party (called a *counterparty*) to make the contract with. There are brokers to facilitate the matching up of parties like the First National Bank with the Rock Solid Insurance Company, but there may be few institutions that want to engage in a forward contract specifically for the 6s of 2029. This means that it may prove impossible to find a counterparty when a financial institution like the First National Bank wants to make a specific type of forward contract. Furthermore, even if the First National Bank finds a counterparty, it may not get as high a price as it wants because there may not be anyone else to make the deal with. A serious problem for the market in interest-rate forward contracts, then, is that it may be difficult to make the financial transaction or that it will have to be made at a disadvantageous price; in the parlance of the financial world, this market suffers from a *lack of liquidity*. (Note that this use of the term *liquidity* when it is applied to a market is somewhat broader than its use when it is applied to an asset. For an asset, liquidity refers to the ease with which the asset can be turned into cash, whereas for a market, liquidity refers to the ease of carrying out financial transactions.)

The second problem with forward contracts is that they are subject to default risk. Suppose that in one year's time, interest rates rise so that the price of the 6s of 2029 falls. The Rock Solid Insurance Company might then decide that it would like to default on the forward contract with the First National Bank because it can now buy the bonds at a price lower than the agreed price in the forward contract. Or perhaps Rock Solid may not have been rock solid and will have gone bust during the year and so is no longer available to complete the terms of the forward contract. Because there is no outside organization guaranteeing the contract, the only recourse is for the First National Bank to go to the courts to sue Rock Solid, but this process will be costly. Furthermore, if Rock Solid is already bankrupt, the First National Bank will suffer a loss; the bank can no longer sell the 6s of 2029 at the price it had agreed with Rock Solid but instead will have to sell at a price well below that because the price of these bonds has fallen.

The presence of default risk in forward contracts means that parties to these contracts must check each other out to be sure that the counterparty is both financially sound and likely to be honest and live up to its contractual obligations. Because this is a costly process and because all the adverse selection and moral hazard problems discussed in earlier chapters apply, default risk is a major barrier to the use of interest-rate forward contracts. When the default risk problem is combined with a lack of liquidity, we see that these contracts may be of limited usefulness to financial institutions. Although there is a market for interest-rate forward contracts, particularly in Treasury and mortgage-backed securities, it is not nearly as large as the financial futures market, to which we turn next.

Financial Futures Markets

Given the default risk and liquidity problems in the interest-rate forward market, another solution to hedging interest-rate risk was needed. This solution was provided by the development of financial futures contracts by the Chicago Board of Trade starting in 1975.

Financial Futures Contracts

A **financial futures contract** is similar to an interest-rate forward contract in that it specifies that a financial instrument must be delivered by one party to another on a stated future date. However, it differs from an interest-rate forward contract in several ways that overcome some of the liquidity and default problems of forward markets.

To understand what financial futures contracts are all about, let's look at one of the most widely traded futures contracts, that for Treasury bonds, which are traded on the Chicago Board of Trade. (An illustration of how prices on these contracts are quoted can be found in the Following the Financial News box, "Financial Futures.") The contract value is for $100,000 face value of bonds. Prices are quoted in points, with each point equal to $1,000, and the smallest change in price is one thirty-second of a point ($31.25). This contract specifies that the bonds to be delivered must have at least 15 years to maturity at the delivery date (and must also not be callable, that is, redeemable by the Treasury at its option, in less than 15 years). If the Treasury bonds delivered to settle the futures contract have a coupon rate different from the 6% specified in the futures contract, the amount of bonds to be delivered is adjusted to reflect the difference in value between the delivered bonds and the 6% coupon bond. In line with the terminology used for forward contracts, parties who have bought a futures contract and thereby agreed to buy (take delivery) of the bonds are said to have taken a *long position,* and parties who have sold a futures contract and thereby agreed to sell (deliver) the bonds have taken a *short position.*

To make our understanding of this contract more concrete, let's consider what happens when you buy or sell one of these Treasury bond futures contracts. Let's say that on February 1, you sell one $100,000 June contract at a price of 115 (that is, $115,000). By selling this contract, you agree to deliver $100,000 face value of the long-term Treasury bonds to the contract's counterparty at the end of June for $115,000. By buying the contract at a price of 115, the buyer has agreed to pay

following the financial news

Financial Futures

The prices for financial futures contracts for debt instruments are published daily. In the *Wall Street Journal*, these prices are found in the "Commodities" section under the "Interest Rate" heading of the "Futures Prices" columns. An excerpt is reproduced here.

			Interest Rate			
		Treasury Bonds (CBT)-$100,000; pts. 32nds of 100%				
	OPEN	HIGH	LOW	SETTLE	CHANGE	OPEN INTEREST
Sept	106-28	107-28	106-26	107-24	31	994,358
Dec	107-02	107-18	106-26	107-18	31	2,068

Information for each contract is presented in columns, as follows. (The Chicago Board of Trade's contract for delivery of long-term Treasury bonds in September 2007 is used as an example.)

Open: Opening price; each point corresponds to $1,000 of face value—106 28/32 is $106,875 for the September contract

High: Highest traded price that day—107 28/32 is $107,875 for the September contract

Low: Lowest traded price that day—106 26/32 is $106,812.50 for the September contract

Settle: Settlement price, the closing price that day—107 24/32 is $107,750 for the September contract

Chg: Change in the settlement price from the previous trading day—+31/32 is +$968.75 for the September contract

Open Interest: Number of contracts outstanding—994,358 for the September contract, with a face value of $99.4 billion (994,358 × $100,000)

$115,000 for the $100,000 face value of bonds when you deliver them at the end of June. If interest rates on long-term bonds rise so that when the contract matures at the end of June the price of these bonds has fallen to 110 ($110,000 per $100,000 of face value), the buyer of the contract will have lost $5,000 because he or she paid $115,000 for the bonds but can sell them only for the market price of $110,000. But you, the seller of the contract, will have gained $5,000 (less commission and expenses) because you can now sell the bonds to the buyer for $115,000 but have to pay only $110,000 for them in the market.

It is even easier to describe what happens to the parties who have purchased futures contracts and those who have sold futures contracts if we recognize the following fact: ***At the expiration date of a futures contract, the price of the contract converges to the price of the underlying asset to be delivered.*** To see why this is the case, consider what happens on the expiration date of the June contract at the end of June when the price of the underlying $100,000 face value Treasury bond is 110 ($110,000). If the futures contract is selling below 110, say, at 109, a trader can buy the contract for $109,000, take delivery of the bond, and immediately sell it for $110,000, thereby earning a quick profit of $1,000. Because earning this profit involves no risk, it is a great deal that everyone would like to get in on. That means that everyone will try to buy the contract, and as a result, its price will rise. Only when the price rises to 110 will the profit opportunity cease to exist and the buying pressure disappear. Conversely, if the price of the futures contract is above 110, say, at 111, everyone will want to sell the contract. Now the sellers get $111,000 from selling the futures contract but have to pay only $110,000 for the Treasury bonds that they must deliver to the buyer of the contract, and the $1,000 difference is their profit. Because this profit involves no risk, traders will continue to sell the futures contract until its price falls back down to 110, at which price there are no longer any profits to be made. The elimination of riskless profit opportunities in the futures market is referred to as **arbitrage,** and it guarantees that the price of a futures contract at expiration equals the price of the underlying asset to be delivered.[1]

Armed with the fact that a futures contract at expiration equals the price of the underlying asset, it is even easier to see who profits and loses from such a contract when interest rates change. When interest rates have risen so that the price of the Treasury bond is 110 on the expiration day at the end of June, the June Treasury bond futures contract will also have a price of 110. Thus, if you bought the contract for 115 in February, you have a loss of 5 points, or $5,000 (5% of $100,000). But if you sold the futures contract at 115 in February, the decline in price to 110 means that you have a profit of 5 points, or $5,000.

THE PRACTICING MANAGER

Hedging with Financial Futures

As the manager of the First National Bank, you can also use financial futures to hedge the interest-rate risk on its holdings of $5 million of the 6s of 2029.

To see how to do this, suppose that in March 2009, the 6s of 2029 are the long-term bonds that would be delivered in the Chicago Board of Trade's T-bond futures contract expiring one year in the future, in March 2010. Also suppose that the interest rate on these bonds is expected to remain at 6% over the next year so that both the 6s of 2029 and the futures contract are selling at par (i.e., the $5 million of bonds is selling for $5 million and the $100,000 futures contract is selling for $100,000). The basic principle of hedging indicates that you need to offset the long position in these bonds with a short position, so you have to sell the futures contract. But how many contracts should you sell? The number of contracts required to hedge the interest-rate risk is found by dividing the amount of the asset to be hedged by the dollar value of each contract, as is shown in Equation 1 below.

$$NC = VA/VC \qquad (1)$$

where
NC = number of contracts for the hedge
VA = value of the asset
VC = value of each contract

---

[1]In actuality, futures contracts sometimes set conditions for the timing and delivery of the underlying assets that cause the price of the contract at expiration to differ slightly from the price of the underlying assets. Because the difference in price is extremely small, we ignore it in this chapter.

example 25.1 Hedging with Interest-Rate Futures

The 6s of 2029 are the long-term bonds that would be delivered in the CBT T-bond futures contract expiring one year in the future in March 2010. The interest rate on these bonds is expected to remain at 6% over the next year so that both the 6s of 2029 and the futures contract are selling at par. How many contracts must First National sell to remove its interest-rate risk exposure from its $5 million holdings of the 6s of 2029?[2]

Solution

$VA = \$5$ million

$VC = \$100,000$

Thus,

$$NC = \$5 \text{ million}/\$100,000 = 50$$

You therefore hedge the interest-rate risk by selling 50 of the Treasury bond futures contracts.

Now suppose that over the next year, interest rates increase to 8% due to an increased threat of inflation. The value of the 6s of 2029 the First National Bank is holding will then fall to $4,039,640 in March 2010.[3] Thus, the loss from the long position in these bonds is $960,360, as shown below:

Value in March 2010 @ 8% interest rate	$4,039,640
Value in March 2009 @ 6% interest rate	−$5,000,000
Loss	−$ 960,360

However, the short position in the 50 futures contracts that obligate you to deliver $5 million of the 6s of 2029 in March 2010 has a value equal to the $5 million of these bonds on that date, after the interest rate has risen to 8%. This value is $4,039,640, as we have seen above. Yet when you sold the futures contract, the buyer was obligated to pay you $5 million on the maturity date. Thus, the gain from the short position on these contracts is also $960,360, as shown below:

Amount paid to you in March 2010, agreed in March 2009	$5,000,000
Cost of bonds delivered in March 2010 @8% interest rate	−$4,039,640
Gain	$ 960,360

Therefore, the net gain for the First National Bank is zero, showing that the hedge has been conducted successfully.

The hedge just described is called a **micro hedge** because the financial institution is hedging the interest-rate risk for a specific asset it is holding. A second type of hedge that financial institutions engage in is called a **macro hedge,** in which

---

[2]In the real world, designing a hedge is somewhat more complicated than the example given here because the bond that is most likely to be delivered might not be a 6s of 2029.

[3]The value of the bonds can be calculated using a financial calculator as follows: FV = $5,000,000, PMT = $300,000, I = 8%, N = 19, PV = $4,039,640.

the hedge is for the institution's entire portfolio. For example, if a bank has more rate-sensitive liabilities than assets, we have seen in Chapter 24 that a rise in interest rates will cause the value of the bank to decline. By selling interest-rate future contracts that will yield a profit when interest rates rise, the bank can offset the losses on its overall portfolio from an interest-rate rise and thereby hedge its interest-rate risk.[4]

Organization of Trading in Financial Futures Markets

Financial futures contracts are traded in the United States on organized exchanges such as the Chicago Board of Trade, the Chicago Mercantile Exchange, the New York Futures Exchange, the MidAmerica Commodity Exchange, and the Kansas City Board of Trade. These exchanges are highly competitive with one another, and each organization tries to design contracts and set rules that will increase the amount of futures trading on its exchange.

The futures exchanges and all trades in financial futures in the United States are regulated by the Commodity Futures Trading Commission (CFTC), which was created in 1974 to take over the regulatory responsibilities for futures markets from the Department of Agriculture. The CFTC oversees futures trading and the futures exchanges to ensure that prices in the market are not being manipulated, and it also registers and audits the brokers, traders, and exchanges to prevent fraud and to ensure the financial soundness of the exchanges. In addition, the CFTC approves proposed futures contracts to make sure that they serve the public interest. The most widely traded financial futures contracts listed in the *Wall Street Journal* and the exchanges where they are traded (along with the number of contracts outstanding, called **open interest,** on July 1, 2007) are listed in Table 25.1.

Given the globalization of other financial markets in recent years, it is not surprising that increased competition from abroad has been occurring in financial futures markets as well.

Globalization of Financial Futures Markets

Because American futures exchanges were the first to develop financial futures, they dominated the trading of financial futures in the early 1980s. For example, in 1985, all of the top 10 futures contracts were traded on exchanges in the United States. With the rapid growth of financial futures markets and the resulting high profits made by the American exchanges, foreign exchanges saw a profit opportunity and began to enter this business. By the 1990s, Eurodollar contracts traded on the London International Financial Futures Exchange, Japanese government bond contracts and Euroyen contracts traded on the Tokyo Stock Exchange, French government bond contracts traded on the Marché à Terme International de France, and Nikkei 225 contracts traded on the Osaka Securities Exchange. All became among the most widely traded futures contracts in the world. Even developing countries are getting into the act. In 1996, seven developing countries (also referred to as *emerging market countries*) established futures exchanges, and this number is expected to double within a few years.

---

[4]For more details and examples of how interest-rate risk can be hedged with financial futures, see the appendix to this chapter which can be found on the book's Web site at www.prenhall.com/mishkin_eakins.

TABLE 25.1 Widely Traded Financial Futures Contracts

Type of Contract	Contract Size	Exchange*	Open Interest (July 1, 2007)
Interest-Rate Contracts			
Treasury bonds	$100,000	CBT	994,358
Treasury notes	$100,000	CBT	2,773,695
Five-year Treasury notes	$100,000	CBT	1,566,050
Two-year Treasury notes	$200,000	CBT	958,036
Thirty-day Fed funds	$5 million	CBT	117,942 (July)
One-month LIBOR	$3 million	CME	30,373 (Aug)
Eurodollar	$1 million	CME	1,613,379 (March 08)
Stock Index Contracts			
Standard & Poor's 500 Index	$250 × index	CME	585,978
DJ Industrial	$ 10 × index	CBT	32,106
NASDAQ 100	$100 × index	CME	60,099
Russell 1000	$500 × index	NYBOT	7,177
Currency Contracts			
Yen	¥12,500,000	CME	310,679
Euro	E125,000	CME	185,905
Canadian dollar	C$100,000	CME	141,074
British pound	£62,500	CME	153,338
Swiss franc	SF 125,000	CME	107,682
Mexican peso	N$ 500,000	CME	70,675

*Exchange abbreviations: CBT, Chicago Board of Trade; CME, Chicago Mercantile Exchange; NYBOT, New York Board of Trade.
Source: Wall Street Journal, June 29, 2007, p. C12. Republished by permission of Dow Jones, Inc. via Copyright Clearance Center, Inc. ©2007 Dow Jones and Company, Inc. All Rights Reserved Worldwide.

Foreign competition has also spurred knockoffs of the most popular financial futures contracts initially developed in the United States. These contracts traded on foreign exchanges are virtually identical to those traded in the United States and have the advantage that they can be traded when the American exchanges are closed. The movement to 24-hour-a-day trading in financial futures has been further stimulated by the development of the Globex electronic trading platform, which allows traders throughout the world to trade futures even when the exchanges are not officially open. Financial futures trading has thus become completely internationalized, and competition between U.S. and foreign exchanges is now intense.

Explaining the Success of Futures Markets

The tremendous success of the financial futures market in Treasury bonds is evident from the fact that the total open interest of Treasury bond contracts was 962,139 on July 21, 2007, for a total value of over $96 billion (962,139 × $100,000). There are several differences between financial futures and forward contracts and in the organization of their markets that help explain why financial futures markets, like those for Treasury bonds, have been so successful.

Several features of futures contracts were designed to overcome the liquidity problem inherent in forward contracts. The first feature is that, in contrast to forward contracts, the quantities delivered and the delivery dates of futures contracts are standardized, making it more likely that different parties can be matched up in the futures market, thereby increasing the liquidity of the market. In the case of the Treasury bond contract, the quantity delivered is $100,000 face value of bonds, and the delivery dates are set to be the last business days of March, June, September, and December. The second feature is that after the futures contract has been bought or sold, it can be traded (bought or sold) again at any time until the delivery date. In contrast, once a forward contract is agreed on, it typically cannot be traded. The third feature is that in a futures contract, not just one specific type of Treasury bond is deliverable on the delivery date, as in a forward contract. Instead, any Treasury bond that matures in more than 15 years and is not callable for 15 years is eligible for delivery. Allowing continuous trading also increases the liquidity of the futures market, as does the ability to deliver a range of Treasury bonds rather than one specific bond.

Another reason why futures contracts specify that more than one bond is eligible for delivery is to limit the possibility that someone might corner the market and "squeeze" traders who have sold contracts. To corner the market, someone buys up all the deliverable securities so that investors with a short position cannot obtain from anyone else the securities that they contractually must deliver on the delivery date. As a result, the person who has cornered the market can set exorbitant prices for the securities that investors with a short position must buy to fulfill their obligations under the futures contract. The person who has cornered the market makes a fortune, but investors with a short position take a terrific loss. Clearly, the possibility that corners might occur in the market will discourage people from taking a short position and might therefore decrease the size of the market. By allowing many different securities to be delivered, the futures contract makes it harder for anyone to corner the market because a much larger amount of securities would have to be purchased to establish the corner. Corners are more than a theoretical possibility, as the Mini-Case box "The Hunt Brothers and the Silver Crash" indicates, and are a concern to both regulators and the organized exchanges that design futures contracts.

Trading in the futures market has been organized differently from trading in forward markets to overcome the default risk problems arising in forward contracts. In both types, for every contract there must be a buyer who is taking a long position and a seller who is taking a short position. However, the buyer and seller of a futures contract make their contract not with each other but with the clearinghouse associated with the futures exchange. This setup means that the buyer of the futures contract does not need to worry about the financial health or trustworthiness of the seller, or vice versa, as in the forward market. As long as the clearinghouse is financially solid, buyers and sellers of futures contracts do not have to worry about default risk.

To make sure that the clearinghouse is financially sound and does not run into financial difficulties that might jeopardize its contracts, buyers or sellers of futures contracts must put an initial deposit, called a **margin requirement,** of perhaps $2,000 per Treasury bond contract into a margin account kept at their brokerage firm. Futures contracts are then **marked to market** every day. What this means is that at the end of every trading day, the change in the value of the futures contract is added to or subtracted from the margin account. Suppose that after buying the Treasury bond contract at a price of 115 on Wednesday morning, its closing price at the

mini-case

The Hunt Brothers and the Silver Crash

In early 1979, two Texas billionaires, W. Herbert Hunt and his brother, Nelson Bunker Hunt, decided that they were going to get into the silver market in a big way. Herbert stated his reasoning for purchasing silver as follows: "I became convinced that the economy of the United States was in a weakening condition. This reinforced my belief that investment in precious metals was wise . . . because of rampant inflation." Although the Hunts' stated reason for purchasing silver was that it was a good investment, others felt that their real motive was to establish a corner in the silver market. Along with other associates, several of them from the Saudi royal family, the Hunts purchased close to 300 million ounces of silver in the form of either actual bullion or silver futures contracts. The result was that the price of silver rose from $6 an ounce to over $50 an ounce by January 1980.

Once the regulators and the futures exchanges got wind of what the Hunts were up to, they decided to take action to eliminate the possibility of a corner by limiting to 2,000 the number of contracts that any single trader could hold. This limit, which was equivalent to 10 million ounces, was only a small fraction of what the Hunts were holding, and so they were

forced to sell. The silver market collapsed soon afterward, with the price of silver declining back to below $10 an ounce. The losses to the Hunts were estimated to be in excess of $1 billion, and they soon found themselves in financial difficulty. They had to go into debt to the tune of $1.1 billion, mortgaging not only the family's holdings in the Placid Oil Company but also 75,000 head of cattle, a stable of thoroughbred horses, paintings, jewelry, and even such mundane items as irrigation pumps and lawn mowers. Eventually both Hunt brothers were forced into declaring personal bankruptcy, earning them the dubious distinction of declaring the largest personal bankruptcies ever in the United States.

Nelson and Herbert Hunt paid a heavy price for their excursion into the silver market, but at least Nelson retained his sense of humor. When asked right after the collapse of the silver market how he felt about his losses, he said, "A billion dollars isn't what it used to be."

Source: G. Christian Hill, "Dynasty's Decline: The Current Question About the Hunts of Dallas: How Poor Are They?" *Wall Street Journal,* November 14, 1984, p. C28. Republished by permission of Dow Jones, Inc. via Copyright Clearance Center, Inc. © 1984 Dow Jones and Company, Inc. All Rights Reserved Worldwide.

end of the day, the *settlement price,* falls to 114. You now have a loss of 1 point, or $1,000, on the contract, and the seller who sold you the contract has a gain of 1 point, or $1,000. The $1,000 gain is added to the seller's margin account, making a total of $3,000 in that account, and the $1,000 loss is subtracted from your account, so you now only have $1,000 in your account. If the amount in this margin account falls below the maintenance margin requirement (which can be the same as the initial requirement but is usually a little less), the trader is required to add money to the account. For example, if the maintenance margin requirement is also $2,000, you would have to add $1,000 to your account to bring it up to $2,000. Margin requirements and marking to market make it far less likely that a trader will default on a contract, thus protecting the futures exchange from losses.

A final advantage that futures markets have over forward markets is that most futures contracts do not result in delivery of the underlying asset on the expiration date, whereas forward contracts do. A trader who sold a futures contract is allowed to avoid delivery on the expiration date by making an offsetting purchase of a futures contract. Because the simultaneous holding of the long and short positions means that the trader would in effect be delivering the bonds to itself, under the exchange rules the trader is allowed to cancel both contracts. Allowing traders to cancel their contracts in this way lowers the cost of conducting trades in the futures market relative to the forward market in that a futures trader can avoid the costs of physical delivery, which is not so easy with forward contracts.

THE PRACTICING MANAGER

Hedging Foreign Exchange Risk with Forward and Futures Contracts

As we discussed in Chapter 13, foreign exchange rates have been highly volatile in recent years. The large fluctuations in exchange rates subject financial institutions and other businesses to significant foreign exchange risk because they generate substantial gains and losses. Luckily for financial institution managers, the financial derivatives discussed in this chapter—forward and financial futures contracts—can be used to hedge foreign exchange risk.

To understand how financial institution managers manage foreign exchange risk, let's suppose that in January, the First National Bank's customer Frivolous Luxuries, Inc., is due a payment of 10 million euros in two months for $10 million worth of goods it has just sold in Germany. Frivolous Luxuries is concerned that if the value of the euro falls substantially from its current value of $1, the company might suffer a large loss because the 10 million euro payment will no longer be worth $10 million. So Sam, the CEO of Frivolous Luxuries, calls up his friend Mona, the manager of the First National Bank, and asks her to hedge this foreign exchange risk for his company. Let's see how the bank manager does this using forward and financial futures contracts.

Hedging Foreign Exchange Risk with Forward Contracts

Forward markets in foreign exchange have been highly developed by commercial banks and investment banking operations that engage in extensive foreign exchange trading and so are widely used to hedge foreign exchange risk. Mona knows that she can use this market to hedge the foreign exchange risk for Frivolous Luxuries. Such a hedge is quite straightforward for her to execute. Because the payment of euros in two months means that at that time Sam would hold a long position in euros, Mona knows that the basic principle of hedging indicates that she should offset this long position by a short position. Thus, she just enters a forward contract that obligates her to sell 10 million euros two months from now in exchange for dollars at the current forward rate of $1 per euro.[5]

---

[5]The forward exchange rate will probably differ slightly from the current spot rate of $1 per euro because the interest rates in Europe and the United States may not be equal. In that case, as we saw in Equation 2 in Chapter 13, the future expected exchange rate will not equal the current spot rate and neither will the forward rate. However, since interest differentials have typically been less than 6% at an annual rate (1% bimonthly), the expected appreciation or depreciation of the euro over a two-month period has always been less than 1%. Thus, the forward rate is always close to the current spot rate, and so our assumption in the example that the forward rate and the spot rate are the same is a reasonable one.

In two months, when her customer receives the 10 million euros, the forward contract ensures that it is exchanged for dollars at an exchange rate of $1 per euro, thus yielding $10 million. No matter what happens to future exchange rates, Frivolous Luxuries will be guaranteed $10 million for the goods it sold in Germany. Mona calls up her friend Sam to let him know that his company is now protected from any foreign exchange movements, and he thanks her for her help.

Hedging Foreign Exchange Risk with Futures Contracts

As an alternative, Mona could have used the currency futures market to hedge the foreign exchange risk. In this case, she would see that the Chicago Mercantile Exchange has a euro contract with a contract amount of 125,000 euros and a price of $1 per euro. To do the hedge, Mona must sell euros as with the forward contract, to the tune of 10 million euros of the March futures.

example 25.2 **Hedging with Foreign Exchange Futures Contracts**

How many of the Chicago Mercantile Exchange March euro contracts must Mona sell in order to hedge the 10 million euro payment due in March?

Solution
Using Equation 1:

VA = 10 million euros

VC = 125,000 euros

Thus,

$$NC = 10 \text{ million}/125{,}000 = 80$$

Mona does the hedge by selling 80 of the CME euro contracts.

Given the $1 per euro price, the sale of the contract yields 80 × 125,000 euros = $10 million. The futures hedge thus again enables her to lock in the exchange rate for Frivolous Luxuries so that it gets its payment of $10 million.

One advantage of using the futures market is that the contract size of 125,000 euros, worth $125,000, is quite a bit smaller than the minimum size of a forward contract, which is usually $1 million or more. However, in this case, the bank manager is making a large enough transaction that she can use either the forward or the futures market. Her choice depends on whether the transaction costs are lower in one market than in the other. If the First National Bank is active in the forward market, that market would probably have the lower transaction costs, but if First National rarely deals in foreign exchange forward contracts, the bank manager may do better by sticking with the futures market.

Stock Index Futures

go online

www.usafutures.com/
stockindexfutures.htm

Detailed information about
stock index futures.

As we have seen, financial futures markets can be useful in hedging interest-rate risk. However, financial institution managers, particularly those who manage mutual funds, pension funds, and insurance companies, also worry about **stock market risk,** the risk that occurs because stock prices fluctuate. Stock index futures were developed in 1982 to meet the need to manage stock market risk, and they have become among the most widely traded of all futures contracts. The futures trading in stock price indexes is now controversial (see the Mini-Case box below) because critics assert that it has led to substantial increases in market volatility, especially in such episodes as 1987's stock market crash.

Stock Index Futures Contracts

To understand stock index futures contracts, let's look at the Standard & Poor's 500 Index futures contract (shown in the Following the Financial News box, "Stock Index Futures"), the most widely traded stock index futures contract in the United States. (The S&P 500 Index measures the value of 500 of the most widely traded stocks.) Stock index futures contracts differ from most other financial futures contracts in that

---

mini-case

Program Trading and Portfolio Insurance: Were They to Blame for the Stock Market Crash of 1987?

In the aftermath of the Black Monday crash on October 19, 1987, in which the stock market declined by over 20% in one day, trading strategies involving stock price index futures markets have been accused (especially by the Brady Commission, which was appointed by President Reagan to study the stock market) of being culprits in the market collapse. One such strategy, called program trading, involves computer-directed trading between the stock index futures and the stocks whose prices are reflected in the stock price index. Program trading is a form of arbitrage conducted to keep stock index futures and stock prices in line with each other. For example, when the price of the stock index futures contract is far below the prices of the underlying stocks in the index, program traders buy index futures, thereby increasing their price, and sell the stocks, thereby lowering their price. Critics of program trading assert that the sharp fall in stock index futures prices on Black Monday led to massive selling in the stock market to keep stock prices in line with the stock index futures prices.

Some experts also blame portfolio insurance for amplifying the crash because they feel that when the

stock market started to fall, uncertainty in the market increased, and the resulting increased desire to hedge stocks led to massive selling of stock index futures. The resulting large price declines in stock index futures contracts then led to massive selling of stocks by program traders to keep prices in line.

Because they view program trading and portfolio insurance as causes of the October 1987 market collapse, critics of stock index futures have advocated restrictions on their trading. In response, certain brokerage firms, as well as organized exchanges, have placed limits on program trading. For example, the New York Stock Exchange has curbed computerized program trading when the Dow Jones Industrial Average moves by more than 50 points in one day. However, some prominent finance scholars (among them Nobel laureate Merton Miller of the University of Chicago) do not accept the hypothesis that program trading and portfolio insurance provoked the stock market crash. They believe that the prices of stock index futures primarily reflect the same economic forces that move stock prices—changes in the market's underlying assessment of the value of stocks.

following the financial news

 ## Stock Index Futures

The prices for stock index futures contracts are published daily. In the *Wall Street Journal,* these prices are found in the section "Futures Prices" under the "Index" heading. An excerpt from this listing is reproduced here.

Index					
S&P 500 Index (CME) $250 × Index					
OPEN	HIGH	LOW	SETTLE	CHANGE	OPEN INTEREST
Sept 1489.10	1489.50	1468.50	**1476.60**	−13.00	515,527
Dec 1493.50	1495.00	1482.00	**1489.70**	−13.20	139,860

Information for each contract is given in columns, as follows. (The September S&P 500 Index contract is used as an example.)

Open: Opening price; each point corresponds to $250 times the index—1489.10; that is, 1489.1 × $250 = $372,275 per contract
High: Highest traded price that day—1489.50, or $372,375 per contract
Low: Lowest traded price that day—1468.50, or $367,125 per contract

Settle: Settlement price, the closing price that day— 1476.60, or $369,150 per contract
Chg: Change in the settlement price from the previous trading day—−13.00 points, or −$3,250 per contract
Open Interest: Number of contracts outstanding— 515,527, or a total value of $190 billion (=515,527 × $369,150).

Source: *Wall Street Journal,* Sept. 6, 2007, p. C12. Republished by permission of Dow Jones, Inc. via Copyright Clearance Center, Inc. © 2007 Dow Jones and Company, Inc. All Rights Reserved Worldwide.

they are settled with a cash delivery rather than with the delivery of a security. Cash settlement gives these contracts the advantage of a high degree of liquidity and also rules out the possibility of anyone's cornering the market. In the case of the S&P 500 Index contract, at the final settlement date, the cash delivery due is $250 times the index, so if the index is at 1,000 on the final settlement date, $250,000 would be the amount due. The price quotes for this contract are also quoted in terms of index points, so a change of 1 point represents a change of $250 in the contract's value.

To understand what all this means, let's look at what happens when you buy or sell this futures contract. Suppose that on February 1, you sell one June contract at a price of 1,000 (that is, $250,000). By selling the contract, you agree to a delivery amount due of $250 times the S&P 500 Index on the expiration date at the end of June. By buying the contract at a price of 1,000, the buyer has agreed to pay $250,000 for the delivery amount due of $250 times the S&P 500 Index at the expiration date at the end of June. If the stock market falls so that the S&P 500 Index declines to 900 on the expiration date, the buyer of the contract will have lost $25,000 because he or she has agreed to pay $250,000 for the contract but has a delivery amount due of $225,000 (900 × $250). But you, the seller of the contract, will have a profit of $25,000 because you agreed to receive a $250,000 purchase price for the contract but have a delivery amount due of only $225,000. Because the amount payable and due are netted out, only $25,000 will change hands; you, the seller of the contract, receive $25,000 from the buyer.

THE PRACTICING MANAGER

Hedging with Stock Index Futures

Financial institution managers can use stock index futures contracts to reduce stock market risk.

example 25.3 **Hedging with Stock Index Futures**

Suppose that in March 2010, Mort, the portfolio manager of the Rock Solid Insurance Company, has a portfolio of stocks valued at $100 million that moves percentagewise one-for-one with the S&P Index. Suppose also that the March 2011 S&P 500 Index contracts are currently selling at a price of 1,000. How many of these contracts should Mort sell so that he hedges the stock market risk of this portfolio over the next year?

Solution
Because Mort is holding a long position, using the basic principle of hedging, he must offset it by taking a short position in which he sells S&P futures. To calculate the number of contracts he needs to sell, he uses Equation 1.

$VA = \$100 \text{ million}$

$VC = \$250 \times 1,000 = \$250,000$

Thus,

$$NC = \$100 \text{ million}/\$250,000 = 400$$

Mort's hedge therefore involves selling 400 S&P March 2011 futures contracts.

If the S&P Index falls 10% to 900, the $100 million portfolio will suffer a $10 million loss. At the same time, however, Mort makes a profit of $100 \times \$250 = \$25,000$ per contract because he agreed to be paid $250,000 for each contract at a price of 1,000, but at a price of 900 on the expiration date he has a delivery amount of only $225,000 (900 × $250). Multiplied by 400 contracts, the $25,000 profit per contract yields a total profit of $10 million. The $10 million profit on the futures contract exactly offsets the loss on Rock Solid's stock portfolio, so Mort has been successful in hedging the stock market risk.

Why would Mort be willing to forego profits when the stock market rises? One reason is that he might be worried that a bear market was imminent, so he wants to protect Rock Solid's portfolio from the coming decline (and so protect his job).[6]

---

[6]For more details of how stock market risk can be hedged with futures options, see the appendix to this chapter which can be found on the book's Web site at www.prenhall.com/mishkin_eakins.

Options

Another vehicle for hedging interest-rate and stock market risk involves the use of options on financial instruments. **Options** are contracts that give the purchaser the option, or *right,* to buy or sell the underlying financial instrument at a specified price, called the **exercise price** or **strike price,** within a specific period of time (the *term to expiration*). The seller (sometimes called the *writer*) of the option is *obligated* to buy or sell the financial instrument to the purchaser if the owner of the option exercises the right to sell or buy. These option contract features are important enough to be emphasized: The *owner* or buyer of an option does not have to exercise the option; he or she can let the option expire without using it. Hence, the *owner* of an option is *not obligated* to take any action but rather has the *right* to exercise the contract if he or she so chooses. The *seller* of an option, by contrast, has no choice in the matter; he or she *must* buy or sell the financial instrument if the owner exercises the option.

Because the right to buy or sell a financial instrument at a specified price has value, the owner of an option is willing to pay an amount for it called a **premium.** There are two types of option contracts: **American options** can be exercised *at any time up to* the expiration date of the contract, and **European options** can be exercised only *on* the expiration date.

Option contracts are written on a number of financial instruments. Options on individual stocks are called **stock options,** and such options have existed for a long time. Option contracts on financial futures called **financial futures options,** or, more commonly, **futures options,** were developed in 1982 and have become the most widely traded option contracts.

You might wonder why option contracts are more likely to be written on financial futures than on underlying debt instruments such as bonds or certificates of deposit. As you saw earlier in the chapter, at the expiration date, the price of the futures contract and of the deliverable debt instrument will be the same because of arbitrage. So it would seem that investors should be indifferent about having the option written on the debt instrument or on the futures contract. However, financial futures contracts have been so well designed that their markets are often more liquid than the markets in the underlying debt instruments. Investors would rather have the option contract written on the more liquid instrument, in this case the futures contract. That explains why the most popular futures options are written on many of the same futures contracts listed in Table 25.1.

The regulation of option markets is split between the Securities and Exchange Commission (SEC), which regulates stock options, and the Commodity Futures Trading Commission (CFTC), which regulates futures options. Regulation focuses on ensuring that writers of options have enough capital to make good on their contractual obligations and on overseeing traders and exchanges to prevent fraud and ensure that the market is not being manipulated.

Option Contracts

A **call option** is a contract that gives the owner the right to *buy* a financial instrument at the exercise price within a specific period of time. A **put option** is a contract that gives the owner the right to *sell* a financial instrument at the exercise price within a specific period of time.

Profits and Losses on Option and Futures Contracts

To understand option contracts more fully, let's first examine the option on the February Treasury bond futures contract in the following table.

Strike Price	CALLS-SETTLE			PUTS-SETTLE		
	Feb	Mar	Apr	Feb	Mar	Apr
110	1-39	1-52	1-29	0-02	0-15	0-49
111	0-45	1-05	0-57	0-08	0-32	1-13
112	0-09	0-34	0-32	0-36	0-61	...
113	0-02	0-13	0-16	1-28	1-40	...
114	0-01	0-04	0-07	...	2-31	...
115	0-01	0-01	0-03	...	3-28	...

Options on Treasury Bond Futures Contract
$100,000; points and 64ths of 100%

If you buy this futures contract at a price of 115 (that is, $115,000), you have agreed to pay $115,000 for $100,000 face value of long-term Treasury bonds when they are delivered to you at the end of February. If you sold this futures contract at a price of 115, you agreed, in exchange for $115,000, to deliver $100,000 face value of the long-term Treasury bonds at the end of February. An option contract on the Treasury bond futures contract has several key features: (1) It has the same expiration date as the underlying futures contract, (2) it is an American option and so can be exercised at any time before the expiration date, and (3) the premium (price) of the option is quoted in points that are the same as in the futures contract, so each point corresponds to $1,000. If, for a premium of $2,000, you buy one call option contract on the February Treasury bond contract with an exercise price of 115, you have purchased the right to buy (call in) the February Treasury bond futures contract for a price of 115 ($115,000 per contract) at any time through the expiration date of this contract at the end of February. Similarly, when for $2,000 you buy a put option on the February Treasury bond contract with an exercise price of 115, you have the right to sell (put up) the February Treasury bond futures contract for a price of 115 ($115,000 per contract) at any time until the end of February.

Futures option contracts are somewhat complicated, so to explore how they work and how they can be used to hedge risk, let's first examine how profits and losses on the call option on the February Treasury bond futures contract occur. In November, our old friend Irving the Investor buys, for a $2,000 premium, a call option on the $100,000 February Treasury bond futures contract with a strike price of 115. (We assume that if Irving exercises the option, it is on the expiration date at the end of February and not before.) On the expiration date at the end of February, suppose that the underlying Treasury bond for the futures contract has a price of 110. Recall that on the expiration date, arbitrage forces the price of the futures contract to converge to the price of the underlying bond, so it, too, has a price of 110 on the expiration date at the end of February. If Irving exercises the call option and buys the futures contract at an exercise price of 115, he will lose money by buying at 115 and selling at the lower market price of 110. Because Irving is smart, he will not exercise the option, but he will be out the $2,000 premium he paid. In such a situation, in which the price of the underlying financial instrument is below the exercise price, a call option is said to be "out of the money." At the price of 110 (less than the exercise price), Irving thus suffers a loss on the option contract of the $2,000 premium he paid. This loss is plotted as point A in panel (a) of Figure 25.1.

On the expiration date, if the price of the futures contract is 115, the call option is "at the money," and Irving is indifferent to whether he exercises his option to buy the futures contract or not, since exercising the option at 115 when the market

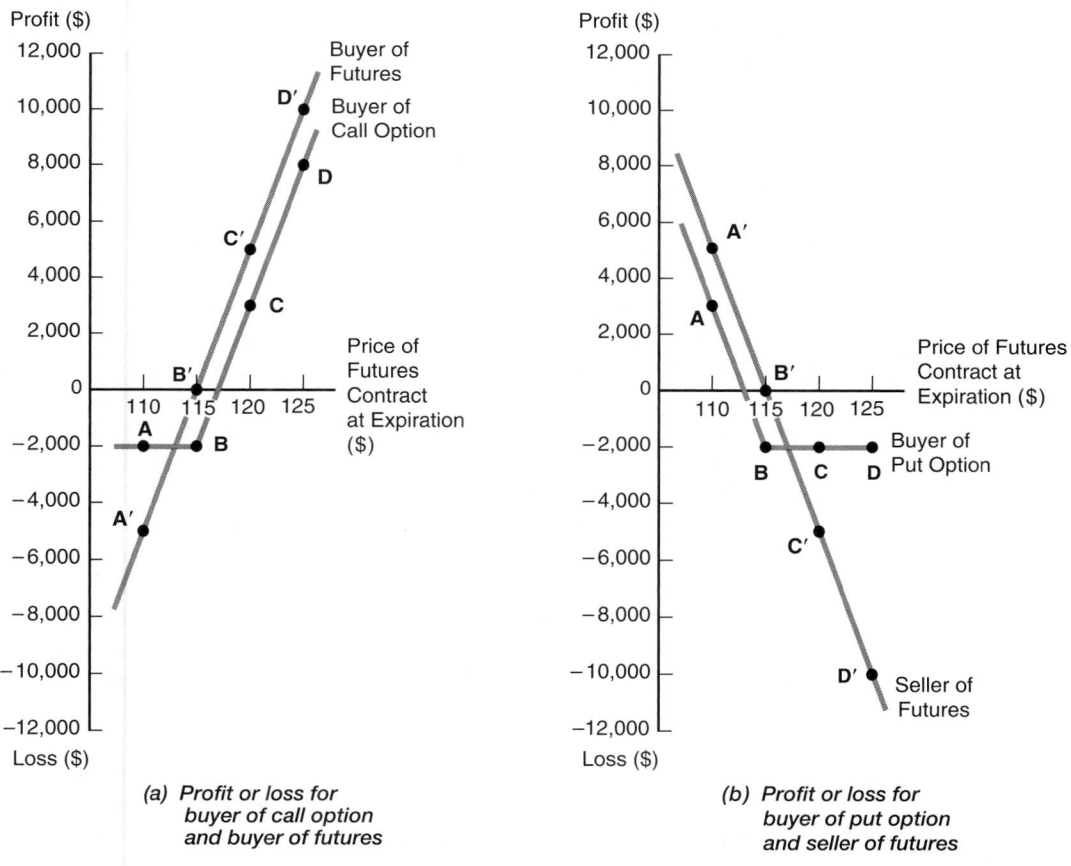

(a) *Profit or loss for buyer of call option and buyer of futures*

(b) *Profit or loss for buyer of put option and seller of futures*

Figure 25.1   Profits and Losses on Options Versus Futures Contracts

The futures contract is the $100,000 February Treasury bond contract, and the option contracts are written on this futures contract with an exercise price of 115. Panel (a) shows the profits and losses for the buyer of the call option and the buyer of the futures contract, and panel (b) shows the profits and losses for the buyer of the put option and the seller of the futures contract.

price is also at 115 produces no gain or loss. Because he has paid the $2,000 premium, at the price of 115 his contract again has a net loss of $2,000, plotted as point B.

If the futures contract instead has a price of 120 on the expiration day, the option is "in the money," and Irving benefits from exercising the option: He would buy the futures contract at the exercise price of 115 and then sell it for 120, thereby earning a 5% gain ($5,000 profit) on the $100,000 Treasury bond contract. Because Irving paid a $2,000 premium for the option contract, however, his net profit is $3,000 ($5,000 − $2,000). The $3,000 profit at a price of 120 is plotted as point C. Similarly, if the price of the futures contract rose to 125, the option contract would yield a net profit of $8,000 ($10,000 from exercising the option minus the $2,000 premium), plotted as point D. Plotting these points, we get the kinked profit curve for the call option that we see in panel (a).

Suppose that instead of purchasing the futures *option* contract in November, Irving decides instead to buy the $100,000 February Treasury bond *futures* contract at the price of 115. If the price of the bond on the expiration day at the end of February declines to 110, meaning that the price of the futures contract also falls to 110, Irving suffers a loss of 5 percentage points, or $5,000. The loss of $5,000 on the futures contract at a price of 110 is plotted as point A′ in panel (a). At a price of 115 on the expiration date, Irving would have a zero profit on the futures contract, plotted as point B′. At a price of 120, Irving would have a profit on the contract of 5 percentage points, or $5,000 (point C′), and at a price of 125, the profit would be 10 percentage points, or $10,000 (point D′). Plotting these points, we get the linear (straight-line) profit curve for the futures contract that appears in panel (a).

Now we can see the major difference between a futures contract and an option contract. As the profit curve for the futures contract in panel (a) indicates, the futures contract has a linear profit function: Profits grow by an equal dollar amount for every point increase in the price of the underlying financial instrument. By contrast, the kinked profit curve for the option contract is highly nonlinear, meaning that profits do not always grow by the same amount for a given change in the price of the underlying financial instrument. The reason for this nonlinearity is that the call option protects Irving from having losses that are greater than the amount of the $2,000 premium. In contrast, Irving's loss on the futures contract is $5,000 if the price on the expiration day falls to 110, and if the price falls even further, Irving's loss will be even greater. This insurance-like feature of option contracts explains why their purchase price is referred to as a premium. Once the underlying financial instrument's price rises above the exercise price, however, Irving's profits grow linearly. Irving has given up something by buying an option rather than a futures contract. As we see in panel (a), when the price of the underlying financial instrument rises above the exercise price, Irving's profits are always less than that on the futures contract by exactly the $2,000 premium he paid.

Panel (b) plots the results of the same profit calculations if Irving buys not a call but a put option (an option to sell) with an exercise price of 115 for a premium of $2,000 and if he sells the futures contract rather than buying one. In this case, if on the expiration date the Treasury bond futures have a price above the 115 exercise price, the put option is "out of the money." Irving would not want to exercise the put option and then have to sell the futures contract he owns as a result of exercising the put option at a price below the market price and lose money. He would not exercise his option, and he would be out only the $2,000 premium he paid. Once the price of the futures contract falls below the 115 exercise price, Irving benefits from exercising the put option because he can sell the futures contract at a price of 115 but can buy it at a price below this. In such a situation, in which the price of the underlying instrument is below the exercise price, the put option is "in the money," and profits rise linearly as the price of the futures contract falls. The profit function for the put option illustrated in panel (b) of Figure 25.1 is kinked, indicating that Irving is protected from losses greater than the amount of the premium he paid. The profit curve for the sale of the futures contract is just the negative of the profit for the futures contract in panel (a) and is therefore linear.

Panel (b) of Figure 25.1 confirms the conclusion from panel (a) that profits on option contracts are nonlinear but profits on futures contracts are linear.

---

study guide

To make sure you understand how profits and losses on option and futures contracts are generated, calculate the net profits on the put option and the short position in the futures contract at prices on the expiration day of 110, 115, 120, and 125. Then verify that your calculations correspond to the points plotted in panel (b) of Figure 25.1.

Two other differences between futures and option contracts must be mentioned. The first is that the initial investment on the contracts differs. As we saw earlier in the chapter, when a futures contract is purchased, the investor must put up a fixed amount, the margin requirement, in a margin account. But when an option contract is purchased, the initial investment is the premium that must be paid for the contract. The second important difference between the contracts is that the futures contract requires money to change hands daily when the contract is marked to market, whereas the option contract requires money to change hands only when it is exercised.

Factors Affecting the Prices of Option Premiums

There are several interesting facts about how the premiums on option contracts are priced. The first fact is that when the strike (exercise) price for a contract is set at a higher level, the premium for the call option is lower and the premium for the put option is higher. For example, in going from a contract with a strike price of 112 to one with 115, the premium for a call option for the month of March might fall from 1 45/64 to 16/64, and the premium for the March put option might rise from 19/64 to 1 54/64.

Our understanding of the profit function for option contracts illustrated in Figure 25.1 helps explain this fact. As we saw in panel (a), a lower price for the underlying financial instrument (in this case a Treasury bond futures contract) relative to the option's exercise price results in lower profits on the call (buy) option. Thus, the higher the strike price, the lower the profits on the call option contract and the lower the premium that investors like Irving are willing to pay. Similarly, we saw in panel (b) that a lower price for the underlying financial instrument relative to the exercise price raises profits on the put (sell) option, so that a higher strike price increases profits and thus causes the premium to increase.

The second fact is that as the period of time over which the option can be exercised (the term to expiration) gets longer, the premiums for both call and put options rise. For example, at a strike price of 112, the premium on a call option might increase from 1 45/64 in March to 1 50/64 in April and to 2 28/64 in May. Similarly, the premium on a put option might increase from 19/64 in March to 1 43/64 in April and to 2 22/64 in May. The fact that premiums increase with the term to expiration is also explained by the nonlinear profit function for option contracts. As the term to expiration lengthens, there is a greater chance that the price of the underlying financial instrument will be very high or very low by the expiration date. If the price becomes very high and goes well above the exercise price, the call (buy) option will yield a high profit; if the price becomes very low and goes well below the exercise price, the losses will be small because the owner of the call option will simply decide not to exercise the option. The possibility of greater variability of the underlying financial instrument as the term to expiration lengthens raises profits on average for the call option.

Similar reasoning tells us that the put (sell) option will become more valuable as the term to expiration increases, because the possibility of greater price variability of the underlying financial instrument increases as the term to expiration increases. The greater chance of a low price increases the chance that profits on the put option will be very high. But the greater chance of a high price does not produce substantial losses for the put option, because the owner will again just decide not to exercise the option.

Another way of thinking about this reasoning is to recognize that option contracts have an element of "Heads, I win; tails, I don't lose too badly." The greater variability of where the prices might be by the expiration date increases the value of both kinds of options. Because a longer term to the expiration date leads to greater variability of where the prices might be by the expiration date, a longer term to expiration raises the value of the option contract.

The reasoning that we have just developed also explains another important fact about option premiums. When the volatility of the price of the underlying instrument is great, the premiums for both call and put options will be higher. Higher volatility of prices means that for a given expiration date, there will again be greater variability of where the prices might be by the expiration date. The "Heads, I win; tails, I don't lose too badly" property of options then means that the greater variability of possible prices by the expiration date increases average profits for the option and thus increases the premium that investors are willing to pay.

Summary

Our analysis of how profits on options are affected by price movements for the underlying financial instrument leads to the following conclusions about the factors that determine the premium on an option contract:

1. The higher the strike price, everything else being equal, the lower the premium on call (buy) options and the higher the premium on put (sell) options.
2. The greater the term to expiration, everything else being equal, the higher the premiums for both call and put options.
3. The greater the volatility of prices of the underlying financial instrument, everything else being equal, the higher the premiums for both call and put options.

The results we have derived here appear in more formal models, such as the Black-Scholes model, which analyze how the premiums on options are priced. You might study such models in other finance courses.

THE PRACTICING MANAGER

Hedging with Futures Options

Earlier in the chapter, we saw how a financial institution manager like Mona, the manager of the First National Bank, could hedge the interest-rate risk on its $5 million holdings of 6s of 2029 by selling $5 million of T-bond futures (50 contracts). A rise in interest rates and the resulting fall in bond prices and bond futures contracts would lead to profits on the bank's sale of the futures contracts that would exactly offset the losses on the 6s of 2029 the bank is holding.

As panel (b) of Figure 25.1 suggests, an alternative way for the manager to protect against a rise in interest rates and hence a decline in bond prices is to buy $5 million of put options written on the same Treasury bond futures. Because the size of the options contract is the same as the futures contract ($100,000 of bonds), the number of put options contracts bought is the same as the number of futures contracts sold, that is, 50. As long as the exercise price is not too far from the current price as in panel (b), the rise in interest rates and decline in bond prices will lead to profits on the futures and the futures put options, profits that will offset any losses on the $5 million of Treasury bonds.

The one problem with using options rather than futures is that the First National Bank will have to pay premiums on the options contracts, thereby lowering the bank's profits in order to hedge the interest-rate risk. Why might the bank manager be willing to use options rather than futures to conduct the hedge? The answer is that the option contract, unlike the futures contract, allows the First National Bank to gain if interest rates decline and bond prices rise. With the hedge using futures contracts, the First National Bank does not gain from increases in bond prices because the profits on the bonds it is holding are offset by the losses from the futures contracts it has sold. However, as panel (b) of Figure 25.1 indicates, the situation when the hedge is conducted with put options is quite different: Once bond prices rise above the exercise price, the bank does not suffer additional losses on the option contracts. At the same time, the value of the Treasury bonds the bank is holding will increase, thereby leading to a profit for the bank. Thus, using options rather than futures to conduct the micro hedge allows the bank to protect itself from rises in interest rates but still allows the bank to benefit from interest-rate declines (although the profit is reduced by the amount of the premium).

Similar reasoning indicates that the bank manager might prefer to use options to conduct the macro hedge to immunize the entire bank portfolio from interest-rate risk. Again, the strategy of using options rather than futures has the disadvantage that the First National Bank has to pay the premiums on these contracts up front. By contrast, using options allows the bank to keep the gains from a decline in interest rates (which will raise the value of the bank's assets relative to its liabilities) because these gains will not be offset by large losses on the option contracts.

In the case of a macro hedge, there is another reason why the bank might prefer option contracts to futures contracts. Profits and losses on futures contracts can cause accounting problems for banks because such profits and losses are not allowed to be offset by unrealized changes in the value of the rest of the bank's portfolio. Consider the case when interest rates fall. If First National sells futures contracts to conduct the macro hedge, then when interest rates fall and the prices of the Treasury bond futures contracts rise, it will have large losses on these contracts.

Of course, these losses are offset by unrealized profits in the rest of the bank's portfolio, but the bank is not allowed to offset these losses in its accounting statements. So even though the macro hedge is serving its intended purpose of immunizing the bank's portfolio from interest-rate risk, the bank would experience large accounting losses when interest rates fall. Indeed, bank managers have lost their jobs when perfectly sound hedges with interest-rate futures have led to large accounting losses. Not surprisingly, bank managers might shrink from using financial futures to conduct macro hedges for this reason.

Futures options, however, can come to the rescue of the managers of banks and other financial institutions. Suppose that First National conducted the macro hedge by buying put options instead of selling Treasury bond futures. Now if interest rates fall and bond prices rise well above the exercise price, the bank will not have large losses on the option contracts because it will just decide not to exercise its options. The bank will not suffer the accounting problems produced by hedging with financial futures. Because of the accounting advantages of using futures options to conduct macro hedges, option contracts have become important to financial institution managers as tools for hedging interest-rate risk.[7]

Interest-Rate Swaps

In addition to forwards, futures, and options, financial institutions use one other important financial derivative to manage risk. **Swaps** are financial contracts that obligate each party to the contract to exchange (swap) a set of payments it owns for another set of payments owned by another party. There are two basic kinds of swaps: **Currency swaps** involve the exchange of a set of payments in one currency for a set of payments in another currency. **Interest-rate swaps** involve the exchange of one set of interest payments for another set of interest payments, all denominated in the same currency. We focus on interest-rate swaps.

Interest-Rate Swap Contracts

Interest-rate swaps are an important tool for managing interest-rate risk, and they first appeared in the United States in 1982 when, as we have seen, there was an increase in the demand for financial instruments that could be used to reduce interest-rate risk. The most common type of interest-rate swap (called the *plain vanilla swap*) specifies (1) the interest rate on the payments that are being exchanged; (2) the type of interest payments (variable or fixed-rate); (3) the amount of **notional principal,** which is the amount on which the interest is being paid; and (4) the time period over which the exchanges continue to be made. There are many other more complicated versions of swaps, including forward swaps and swap options (called *swaptions*), but here we will look only at the plain vanilla swap. Figure 25.2 illustrates an interest-rate swap between the Midwest Savings Bank and the Friendly Finance Company. Midwest Savings agrees to pay Friendly Finance a fixed rate of 5% on $1 million of notional principal for the next 10 years, and Friendly Finance agrees

---

[7]For more details of how interest-rate risk can be hedged with futures options, see the appendix to this chapter which can be found on the book's Web site at www.prenhall.com/mishkin_eakins.

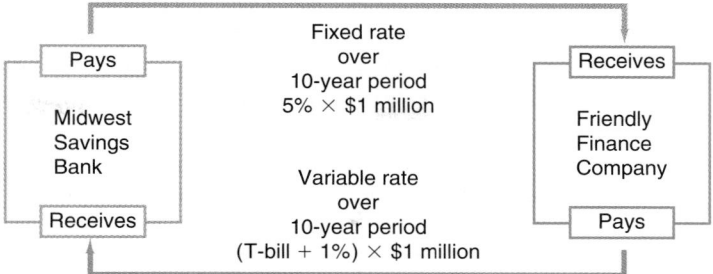

Figure 25.2 Interest-Rate Swap Payments

In this swap arrangement, with a notional principal of $1 million and a term of 10 years, the Midwest Savings Bank pays a fixed rate of 5% × $1 million to the Friendly Finance Company, which in turn agrees to pay the one-year Treasury bill rate plus 1% × $1 million to the Midwest Savings Bank.

to pay Midwest Savings the one-year Treasury bill rate plus 1% on $1 million of notional principal for the same period. Thus, as shown in Figure 25.2, every year, the Midwest Savings Bank would be paying the Friendly Finance Company 5% on $1 million while Friendly Finance would be paying Midwest Savings the one-year T-bill rate plus 1% on $1 million.

THE PRACTICING MANAGER

Hedging with Interest-Rate Swaps

You might wonder why the managers of the two financial institutions find it advantageous to enter into this swap agreement. The answer is that it may help both of them hedge interest-rate risk.

Suppose that the Midwest Savings Bank, which tends to borrow short-term and then lend long-term in the mortgage market, has $1 million less of rate-sensitive assets than it has of rate-sensitive liabilities. As we learned in Chapter 24, this situation means that as interest rates rise, the rise in the cost of funds (liabilities) is greater than the rise in interest payments it receives on its assets, many of which are fixed-rate. The result of rising interest rates is thus a shrinking of Midwest Savings' net interest margin and a decline in its profitability. As we saw in Chapter 24, to avoid this interest-rate risk, the manager of the Midwest Savings would like to convert $1 million of its fixed-rate assets into $1 million of rate-sensitive assets, in effect making rate-sensitive assets equal to rate-sensitive liabilities, thereby eliminating the gap. This is exactly what happens when she engages in the interest-rate swap. By taking $1 million of its fixed-rate income and exchanging it for $1 million of rate-sensitive Treasury bill income, she has converted income on $1 million of fixed-rate assets into income on $1 million of rate-sensitive assets. Now when interest rates increase, the rise in rate-sensitive income on its assets exactly matches the rise in the rate-sensitive cost of funds on its liabilities, leaving the net interest margin and bank profitability unchanged.

The manager of the Friendly Finance Company, which issues long-term bonds to raise funds and uses them to make short-term loans, finds that he is in exactly the opposite situation to Midwest Savings: He has $1 million more of rate-sensitive assets than of rate-sensitive liabilities. He is therefore concerned that a fall in interest rates, which will result in a larger drop in income from its assets than the decline in the cost of funds on its liabilities, will cause a decline in profits. By doing the interest-rate swap, the manager eliminates this interest-rate risk because he has converted $1 million of rate-sensitive income into $1 million of fixed-rate income. Now the manager of the Friendly Finance Company finds that when interest rates fall, the decline in rate-sensitive income is smaller and so is matched by the decline in the rate-sensitive cost of funds on its liabilities, leaving profitability unchanged.[8]

Advantages of Interest-Rate Swaps

To eliminate interest-rate risk, both the Midwest Savings Bank and the Friendly Finance Company could have rearranged their balance sheets by converting fixed-rate assets into rate-sensitive assets, and vice versa, instead of engaging in an interest-rate swap. However, this strategy would have been costly for both financial institutions for several reasons. The first is that financial institutions incur substantial transaction costs when they rearrange their balance sheets. Second, different financial institutions have informational advantages in making loans to certain customers who may prefer certain maturities. Thus, adjusting the balance sheet to eliminate interest-rate risk may result in a loss of these informational advantages, which the financial institution is unwilling to give up. Interest-rate swaps solve these problems for financial institutions because in effect they allow the institutions to convert fixed-rate assets into rate-sensitive assets without affecting the balance sheet. Large transaction costs are avoided, and the financial institutions can continue to make loans where they have an informational advantage.

We have seen that financial institutions can also hedge interest-rate risk with other financial derivatives such as futures contracts and futures options. Interest-rate swaps have one big advantage over hedging with these other derivatives: They can be written for very long horizons, sometimes as long as 20 years, whereas financial futures and futures options typically have much shorter horizons, not much more than a year. If a financial institution needs to hedge interest-rate risk for a long horizon, financial futures and option markets may not do it much good. Instead it can turn to the swap market.

Disadvantages of Interest-Rate Swaps

Although interest-rate swaps have important advantages that make them very popular with financial institutions, they also have disadvantages that limit their usefulness. Swap markets, like forward markets, can suffer from a lack of liquidity. Let's return to looking at the swap between the Midwest Savings Bank and the Friendly Finance Company. As with a forward contract, it might be difficult for the Midwest

---

[8]For more details and examples of how interest-rate risk can be hedged with interest-rate swaps, see the appendix to this chapter which can be found on the book's Web site at www.prenhall.com/mishkin_eakins.

Savings Bank to link up with the Friendly Finance Company to arrange the swap. In addition, even if the Midwest Savings Bank could find a counterparty like the Friendly Finance Company, it might not be able to negotiate a good deal because it couldn't find any other institution to negotiate with.

Swap contracts also are subject to the same default risk that we encountered for forward contracts. If interest rates rise, the Friendly Finance Company would love to get out of the swap contract because the fixed-rate interest payments it receives are less than it could get in the open market. It might then default on the contract, exposing Midwest Savings to a loss. Alternatively, the Friendly Finance Company could go bust, meaning that the terms of the swap contract would not be fulfilled.

It is important to note that the default risk of swaps is not the same as the default risk on the full amount of the notional principal because the notional principal is never exchanged. If the Friendly Finance Company goes broke because $1 million of its one-year loans default and it cannot make its interest payment to Midwest Savings, Midwest Savings will stop sending its payment to Friendly Finance. If interest rates have declined, this will suit Midwest Savings just fine because it would rather keep the 7% fixed-rate interest payment, which is at a higher rate, than receive the rate-sensitive payment, which has declined. Thus, a default on a swap contract does not necessarily mean that there is a loss to the other party. Midwest Savings will suffer losses from a default only if interest rates have risen when the default occurs. Even then, the loss will be far smaller than the amount of the notional principal because interest payments are far smaller than the amount of the notional principal.[9]

Financial Intermediaries in Interest-Rate Swaps

As we have just seen, financial institutions do have to be aware of the possibility of losses from a default on swaps. As with a forward contract, each party to a swap must have a lot of information about the other party to make sure that the contract is likely to be fulfilled. The need for information about counterparties and the liquidity problems in swap markets could limit the usefulness of these markets. However, as we saw in Chapter 15, when informational and liquidity problems crop up in a market, financial intermediaries come to the rescue. That is exactly what happens in swap markets. Intermediaries such as investment banks and especially large commercial banks have the ability to acquire information cheaply about the creditworthiness and reliability of parties to swap contracts and are also able to match up parties to a swap. Hence, large commercial banks and investment banks have set up swap markets in which they act as intermediaries.

Credit Derivatives

In recent years, a new type of derivatives has come on the scene to hedge credit risk. Like other derivatives, **credit derivatives** offer payoffs linked to previously issued securities, but ones that bear credit risk. In the past 10 years, the markets in credit derivatives have grown at an astounding pace and the notional amounts of these derivatives now number in the trillions of dollars. These credit derivatives take several forms.

---

[9]The actual loss will equal the present value of the difference in the interest payments that the bank would have received if the swap were still in force as compared to interest payments it receives otherwise.

Credit Options

Credit options work just like the options discussed earlier in the chapter: For a fee, the purchaser gains the right to receive profits that are tied either to the price of an underlying security or to an interest rate. Suppose you buy $1 million of General Motors bonds but worry that a potential slowdown in the sale of SUVs might lead a credit-rating agency to *downgrade* (lower the credit rating on) GM bonds. As we saw in Chapter 5, such a downgrade would cause the price of GM bonds to fall. To protect yourself, you could buy an option for, say, $15,000, to sell the $1 million of bonds at a strike price that is the same as the current price. With this strategy, you would not suffer any losses if the value of the GM bonds declined because you could exercise the option and sell them at the price you paid for them. In addition, you would be able to reap any gains that occurred if GM bonds rose in value.

A second type of credit option ties profits to changes in an interest rate such as a credit spread (the interest rate on the average bond with a particular credit rating minus the interest rate on default-free bonds such as those issued by the U.S. Treasury). Suppose that your company, which has a Baa credit rating, plans to issue $10 million of one-year bonds in three months and expects to have a credit spread of 1 percentage point (i.e., it will pay an interest rate that is 1 percentage point higher than the one-year Treasury rate). You are concerned that the market might start to think that Baa companies in general will become riskier in the coming months. If this were to happen by the time you are ready to issue your bonds in three months, you would have to pay a higher interest rate than the 1 percentage point in excess of the Treasury rate and your cost of issuing the bonds would increase. To protect yourself against these higher costs, you could buy for, say, $20,000 a credit option on $10 million of Baa bonds that would pay you the difference between the average Baa credit spread in the market minus the 1 percentage point credit spread on $10 million. If the credit spread jumps to 2 percentage points, you would receive $100,000 from the option (=[2% − 1%] × $10 million), which would exactly offset the $100,000 higher interest costs from the 1 percentage point higher interest rate you would have to pay on your $10 million of bonds.

Credit Swaps

Suppose you manage a bank in Houston called Oil Drillers' Bank (ODB), which specializes in lending to a particular industry in your local area, oil drilling companies. Another bank, Potato Farmers Bank (PFB), specializes in lending to potato farmers in Idaho. Both ODB and PFB have a problem because their loan portfolios are not sufficiently diversified. To protect ODB against a collapse in the oil market, which would result in defaults on most of its loans made to oil drillers, you could reach an agreement to have the loan payments on, say, $100 million worth of your loans to oil drillers paid to the PFB in exchange for PFB paying you the loan payments on $100 million of its loans to potato farmers. Such a transaction, in which risky payments on loans are swapped for each other, is called a **credit swap.** As a result of this swap, ODB and PFB have increased their diversification and lowered the overall risk of their loan portfolios because some of the loan payments to each bank are now coming from a different type of loans.

Another form of credit swap is, for arcane reasons, called a **credit default swap,** although it functions more like insurance. With a credit default swap, one party who wants to hedge credit risk pays a fixed payment on a regular basis, in return for a contingent payment that is triggered by a *credit event* such as the bankruptcy of a particular firm or the downgrading of the firm's credit rating by a credit-rating agency. For example, you could use a credit default swap to hedge the $1 million of General Motors bonds that you are holding by arranging to pay an annual fee of $1,000 in exchange for a payment of $10,000 if the GM bonds' credit rating is lowered. If a credit event happens and GM's bonds are downgraded so that their price falls, you will receive a payment that will offset some of the loss you suffer if you sell the bonds at this lower price.

Credit-Linked Notes

Another type of credit derivative, the **credit-linked note,** is a combination of a bond and a credit option. Just like any corporate bond, the credit-linked note makes periodic coupon (interest) payments and a final payment of the face value of the bond at maturity. If a key financial variable specified in the note changes, however, the issuer of the note has the right (option) to lower the payments on the note. For example, General Motors could issue a credit-linked note that pays a 5% coupon rate, with the specification that if a national index of SUV sales falls by 10%, then GM has the right to lower the coupon rate by 2 percentage points to 3%. In this way, GM can lower its risk because when it is losing money as SUV sales fall, it can offset some of these losses by making smaller payments on its credit-linked notes.

CASE

Are Financial Derivatives a Worldwide Time Bomb?

With the bankruptcies of Orange County in 1994 (see the Conflicts of Interest box) and the Barings Bank in 1995 (discussed in Chapter 17)—both of which involved trades in financial derivatives—politicians, the media, and regulators have become very concerned about the dangers of derivatives. Indeed, Warren Buffet has called financial derivatives "financial weapons of mass destruction." This concern is international and has spawned a slew of reports issued by such organizations as the Bank for International Settlements (BIS), the Bank of England, the Group of Thirty, the Office of the U.S. Comptroller of the Currency (OCC), the Commodity Futures Trading Commission (CFTC), and the Government Accounting Office (GAO). Particularly scary are the notional amounts of derivatives contracts—over $100 trillion worldwide—and the fact that banks, which are subject to bank panics, are major players in the derivatives markets. As a result of these fears, some politicians have called for restrictions on banks' involvement in the derivatives markets. Are financial derivatives a time bomb that could bring down the world financial system?

There are three major concerns about financial derivatives. First is that financial derivatives allow financial institutions to increase their leverage; that is, they can in effect hold an amount of the underlying asset that is many times greater than the amount of money they have had to put up. Increasing their leverage enables them to take huge bets on currency and interest-rate movements, which if they are wrong can bring down the bank, as was the case for Barings in 1995. This concern is valid. As we saw earlier in the chapter, the amount of money placed in margin accounts

conflicts of interest

The Orange County Bankruptcy

Orange County, California, one of the richest counties in the United States, was forced to declare bankruptcy on December 6, 1994, in the largest municipal bankruptcy filing ever. Orange County's downfall was the investment activities of its treasurer, Robert Citron, who was in charge of the $7.8 billion investment fund, which had not only $4.7 billion of funds from Orange County agencies but also $3.1 billion from 180 other municipalities and local government agencies. For years, the Orange County fund looked like a good investment, with the annual returns averaging 10% over the 15-year period to 1994. Unfortunately, these high returns were obtained with a highly leveraged strategy in which the fund purchased amounts of medium- to long-term bonds several times the value of the fund by borrowing with repurchase agreements. Everything was fine until interest rates began to rise in late 1993 and early 1994 and bond prices declined, leaving the fund with large losses.

We have already seen in our discussion of the Barings collapse how the principal-agent problem becomes especially severe once a trader or a manager of a fund starts to experience sizable losses. Once in the hole, the manager of the fund knows that his or her future depends on reversing these losses promptly. In this situation, the fund manager has a strong moral hazard incentive to take excessive risks. This is exactly what Citron did in late 1993 and early 1994 when he began buying large amounts of "inverse floaters," highly risky derivative securities that have high payoffs if long-term bond rates decline. Unfortunately for Citron, interest rates

continued to rise, and the fund slipped deeper in the hole. When Peter Swan, the president of the Irvine Ranch Water District, became suspicious about the financial situation of the fund in November 1994 and asked to redeem $400 million, the jig was up for Citron because the fund did not have the cash to meet this redemption. Finally, on December 5, Citron was forced to resign, and the following day, Orange County declared bankruptcy. When bankruptcy was declared, the fund had estimated losses of $1.5 billion, and was found to have $20 billion of securities, $8.5 billion of which were derivatives, a risky portfolio indeed.

Although the role of derivatives in the Orange County debacle has often been emphasized, the problem here was really one of leverage and the principal-agent problem at work. Indeed, an important reason that Citron was able to get away with such a risky strategy, particularly after the fund sustained large losses, was that disclosure requirements were not as strong as they could be for municipal investment funds in the state of California. In contrast to other states, which require monthly or even daily disclosure of the market value of their municipal investment funds, California required this disclosure only once a year. If California had stricter disclosure requirements, investors in Citron's fund would have found out more quickly the risks he was taking, making it more likely that they would have pulled out their funds. This might have prevented Citron from taking on the risks that he did, and the Orange County bankruptcy would have been avoided.

is only a small fraction of the price of the futures contract, meaning that small movements in the price of a contract can produce losses that are many times the size of the initial amount put in the margin account. Thus, although financial derivatives can be used to hedge risk, they can also be used by financial institutions to take on excessive risk.

The second concern is that financial derivatives are too sophisticated for managers of financial institutions because they are so complicated. Although it is true that some financial derivatives can be so complex that some financial managers are not sophisticated enough to use them—a possibility in the Orange County case—this seems unlikely to apply to the big international financial institutions that are the major players in the derivatives markets. Indeed, in the Barings case, the bank was brought down not by trades in complex derivatives but rather by trades in one of the simplest of derivatives, stock index futures. (Recall from Chapter 17 that Barings's problem was more a lack of internal controls at the bank than a problem with derivatives per se.)

A third concern is that banks have holdings of huge notional amounts of financial derivatives, particularly swaps, that greatly exceed the amount of bank capital, and so these derivatives expose the banks to serious risk of failure. Banks are indeed major players in the financial derivatives markets, particularly the swaps market, where our earlier analysis has shown that they are the natural market-makers because they can act as intermediaries between two counterparties who would not make the swap without their involvement. However, looking at the notional amount of swaps at banks gives a very misleading picture of their risk exposure. Because banks act as intermediaries in the swap markets, they are typically exposed only to credit risk—a default by one of their counterparties. Furthermore, swaps, unlike loans, do not involve payments of the notional amount but rather the much smaller interest payments based on the notional amounts. For example, in the case of a 7% interest rate, the payment is only $70,000 for the $1 million swap. Estimates of the credit exposure from swap contracts indicate that they are on the order of only 1% of the notional value of the contracts and that credit exposure at banks from derivatives is generally less than a quarter of their total credit exposure from loans. Banks' credit exposure from their derivatives activities are thus not out of line with other credit exposures they face. Furthermore, an analysis by the GAO indicates that actual credit losses incurred by banks in their derivatives contracts have been very small, on the order of 0.2% of their gross credit exposure.

The conclusion is that financial derivatives do have their dangers for financial institutions, but some of these dangers have been overplayed. The biggest danger occurs in trading activities of financial institutions, and as discussed in Chapter 20, regulators have been paying increased attention to this danger and have issued new disclosure requirements and regulatory guidelines for how derivatives trading should be done. The credit risk exposure posed by derivatives, by contrast, seems to be manageable with standard methods of dealing with credit risk, both by managers of financial institutions and their regulators.

SUMMARY

1. Interest-rate forward contracts, which are agreements to sell a debt instrument at a future (forward) point in time, can be used to hedge interest-rate risk. The advantage of forward contracts is that they are flexible, but the disadvantages are that they are subject to default risk and their market is illiquid.

2. A financial futures contract is similar to an interest-rate forward contract in that it specifies that a debt instrument must be delivered by one party to another on a stated future date. However, it has advantages over a forward contract in that it is not subject to default risk and is more liquid. Forward and futures contracts can be used by financial institutions to hedge against (protect) interest-rate risk.

3. Stock index futures are financial futures whose underlying financial instrument is a stock market index like the Standard and Poor's 500 Index. Stock index futures can be used to hedge stock market risk by reducing systematic risk in portfolios or by locking in stock prices.

4. An option contract gives the purchaser the right to buy (call option) or sell (put option) a security at the exercise (strike) price within a specific period of time. The profit function for options is nonlinear—profits do not always grow by the same amount for a given change in the price of the underlying financial instrument. The nonlinear profit function for options explains why their value (as reflected by the premium paid for them) is negatively related to the exercise price for call options, positively related to the exercise price for put options, positively related to the term to expiration for both call and put options, and positively related to the volatility of the prices of the underlying financial instrument for both call and put options. Financial institutions use futures options to hedge interest-rate risk in a similar fashion to the way they use financial futures and forward contracts. Futures options may be preferred for macro hedges because they suffer from fewer accounting problems than financial futures.

5. Interest-rate swaps involve the exchange of one set of interest payments for another set of interest payments and have default risk and liquidity problems similar to those of forward contracts. As a result, interest-rate swaps often involve intermediaries such as large commercial banks and investment banks that make a market in swaps. Financial institutions find that interest-rate swaps are useful ways to hedge interest-rate risk. Interest-rate swaps have one big advantage over financial futures and options: They can be written for very long horizons.

6. Credit derivatives are a new type of derivatives that offer payoffs on previously issued securities that have credit risk. These derivatives—credit options, credit swaps, and credit–linked notes—can be used to hedge credit risk.

7. There are three concerns about the dangers of derivatives: They allow financial institutions to more easily increase their leverage and take big bets (by effectively enabling them to hold a larger amount of the underlying assets than the amount of money put down), they are too complex for managers of financial institutions to understand, and they expose financial institutions to large credit risks because the huge notional amounts of derivative contracts greatly exceed the capital of these institutions. The second two dangers seem to be overplayed, but the danger from increased lever-age using derivatives is real.

KEY TERMS

American options, *p. 657*

arbitrage, *p. 646*

call option, *p. 657*

credit default swap, *p. 668*

credit derivatives, *p. 667*

credit-linked note, *p. 669*

credit options, *p. 668*

credit swap, *p. 668*

currency swaps, *p. 664*

European options, *p. 657*

exercise price (strike price), *p. 657*

financial derivatives, *p. 641*

financial futures contract, *p. 644*

financial futures options (futures options), *p. 657*

forward contracts, *p. 642*

hedge, *p. 641*

interest-rate forward contracts, *p. 642*

interest-rate swaps, *p. 664*

long position, *p. 641*

macro hedge, *p. 647*

margin requirement, *p. 650*

marked to market, *p. 650*

micro hedge, *p. 647*

notional principal, *p. 664*

open interest, *p. 648*

options, *p. 657*

premium, *p. 657*

put option, *p. 657*

short position, *p. 642*

stock market risk, *p. 654*

stock options, *p. 657*

swaps, *p. 664*

QUESTIONS

1. Why does a lower strike price imply that a call option will have a higher premium and a put option a lower premium?

2. If the finance company you manage has a gap of +$5 million (rate-sensitive assets greater than rate-sensitive liabilities by $5 million), describe an interest-rate swap that would eliminate the company's income gap.

QUANTITATIVE PROBLEMS

1. If the pension fund you manage expects to have an inflow of $120 million six months from now, what forward contract would you seek to enter into to lock in current interest rates?

2. If the portfolio you manage is holding $25 million of 6s of 2029 Treasury bonds with a price of 110, what forward contract would you enter into to hedge the interest-rate risk on these bonds over the coming year?

3. If at the expiration date, the deliverable Treasury bond is selling for 101 but the Treasury bond futures contract is selling for 102, what will happen to the futures price? Explain your answer.

4. If you buy a $100,000 February Treasury bond contract for 108 and the price of the deliverable Treasury bond at the expiration date is 102, what is your profit or loss on the contract?

5. Suppose that the pension you are managing is expecting an inflow of funds of $100 million next year and you want to make sure that you will earn the current interest rate of 8% when you invest the incoming funds in long-term bonds. How would you use the futures market to do this?

6. How would you use the options market to accomplish the same thing as in Problem 5? What are the advantages and disadvantages of using an options contract rather than a futures contract?

7. If you buy a put option on a $100,000 Treasury bond futures contract with an exercise price of 95 and the price of the Treasury bond is 120 at expiration, is the contract in the money, out of the money, or at the money? What is your profit or loss on the contract if the premium was $4,000?

8. Suppose that you buy a call option on a $100,000 Treasury bond futures contract with an exercise price of 110 for a premium of $1,500. If on expiration the futures contract has a price of 111, what is your profit or loss on the contract?

9. Explain why greater volatility or a longer term to maturity leads to a higher premium on both call and put options.

10. If the savings and loan you manage has a gap of −$42 million, describe an interest-rate swap that would eliminate the S&L's income risk from changes in interest rates.

11. If your company has a payment of 200 million euros due one year from now, how would you hedge the foreign exchange risk in this payment with 125,000 euros futures contracts?

12. If your company has to make a 10 million euros payment to a German company in June, three months from now, how would you hedge the foreign exchange risk in this payment with a 125,000 euros futures contract?

13. Suppose that your company will be receiving 30 million euros six months from now and the euro is currently selling for 1 euro per dollar. If you want to hedge the foreign exchange risk in this payment, what kind of forward contract would you want to enter into?

14. A hedger takes a short position in five T-bill futures contracts at the price of 98 5/32. Each contract is for $100,000 principal. When the position is closed, the price is 95 12/32. What is the gain or loss on this transaction?

15. A bank issues a $100,000 variable-rate 30-year mortgage with a nominal annual rate of 4.5%. If the required rate drops to 4.0% after the first six months, what is the impact on the interest income for the first 12 months? Assume the bank hedged this risk with a short position in a 181-day T-bill future. The original price was 97 26/32, and the final price was 98 1/32 on a $100,000 face value contract. Did this work?

16. Laura, a bond portfolio manager, administers a $10 million portfolio. The portfolio currently has a duration of 8.5 years. Laura wants to shorten the duration to 6 years using T-bill futures. T-bill futures have a duration of 0.25 years and are trading at $975 (face value = $1,000). How is this accomplished?

17. Futures are available on three-month T-bills with a contract size of $1 million. If you take a long position at 96.22 and later sell the contracts at 96.87, how much would the total net gain or loss be on this transaction?

18. Chicago Bank and Trust has $100 million in assets and $83 million in liabilities. The duration of the assets is 5.9 years, and the duration of the liabilities is 1.8 years. How many futures contracts does this bank need to fully hedge itself against interest-rate risk? The available Treasury bond futures contracts have a duration of 10 years, a face value of $1,000,000, and are selling for $979,000.

19. A bank issues a $3 million commercial mortgage with a nominal APR of 8%. The loan is fully amortized over ten years, requiring monthly payments. The bank plans on selling the loan after two months. If the required nominal APR increases by 45 basis points when the loan is sold, what loss does the bank incur?

20. Assume the bank in the previous question partially hedges the mortgage by selling three 10-year T-note futures contracts at a price of 100 20/32. Each contract is for $1,000,000. After two months, the futures contract has fallen in price to 98 24/32. What was the gain or loss on the futures transaction?

21. Springer County Bank has assets totaling $180 million with a duration of five years, and liabilities totaling $160 million with a duration of two years. Bank management expects interest rates to fall from 9% to 8.25% shortly. A T-bond futures contract is available for hedging. Its duration is 6.5 years, and it is currently priced at 99 5/32. How many contracts does Springer need to hedge against the expected rate change? Assume each contract has a face value of $1,000,000.

22. From the previous question, rates do indeed fall as expected, and the T-bond contract is priced at 103 5/32. If Springer closes its futures position, what is the gain or loss? How well does this offset the approximate change in equity value?

23. A bank issues a $100,000 fixed-rate 30-year mortgage with a nominal annual rate of 4.5%. If the required rate drops to 4.0% immediately after the mortgage is issued, what is the impact on the value of the mortgage? Assume the bank hedged the position with a short position in two 10-year T-bond futures. The original price was 64 12/32 and expired at 67 16/32 on a $100,000 face value contract. What was the gain on the futures? What is the total impact on the bank?

24. A bank customer will be going to London in June to purchase £100,000 in new inventory. The current spot and futures exchange rates are as follows:

Exchange Rates (Dollars/Pound)

Period	Rate
Spot	1.5342
March	1.6212
June	1.6901
September	1.7549
December	1.8416

The customer enters into a position in June futures to fully hedge her position. When June arrives, the actual exchange rate is $1.725 per pound. How much did she save?

25. Consider a put contract on a T-bond with an exercise price of 101 12/32. The contract represents $100,000 of bond principal and had a premium of $750. The actual T-bond price falls to 98 16/32 at the expiration. What is the gain or loss on the position?

26. Consider a put contract on a T-bond with an exercise price of 101 12/32. The contract represents $100,000 of bond principal and has a premium of $750. The actual T-bond price is currently 100 1/32. How can you arbitrage this situation?

27. A banker commits to a two-year $5,000,000 commercial loan and expects to fulfill the agreement in 30 days. The interest rate will be determined at that time. Currently, rates are 7.5% for such loans. To hedge against rates falling, the banker buys a 30-day interest-rate floor with a floor rate of 7.5% on a notional amount of $10,000,000. After 30 days, actual rates fall to 7.2%. What is the expected interest income from the loan each year? How much did the option pay?

28. A trust manager for a $100,000,000 stock portfolio wants to minimize short-term downside risk using Dow put options. The options expire in 60 days, have a strike price of 9,700, and a premium of $50. The Dow is currently at 10,100. How many options should she use? Long or short? How much will this cost? If the portfolio is perfectly correlated with the Dow, what is the portfolio value when the option expires, including the premium paid?

29. A swap agreement calls for Durbin Industries to pay interest annually based on a rate of 1.5% over the one-year T-bill rate, currently 6%. In return, Durbin receives interest at a rate of 6% on a fixed-rate basis. The notional principal for the swap is $50,000. What is Durbin's net interest for the year after the agreement?

30. North-Northwest Bank (NNWB) has a differential advantage in issuing variable-rate mortgages, but does not want the interest income risk associated with such loans. The bank currently has a portfolio of $25,000,000 in mortgages with an APR of prime + 150 basis points, reset monthly. Prime is currently 4%. An investment bank has arranged for NNWB to swap into a fixed interest payment of 6.5% on a notional amount of $25,000,000 in return for its variable interest income. If NNWB agrees to this, what interest is received and given in the first month? What if prime suddenly increased 200 basis points?

Hedging with Financial Derivatives

1. We have discussed the various stock markets in detail throughout this text. Another market that is less well known is the New York Mercantile Exchange. Here, contracts on a wide variety of commodities are traded on a daily basis. Go to **www.nymex.com/aindex .aspx** and read the discussion explaining the origin and purpose of the mercantile exchange. Write a one-page summary discussing this material.

2. The following site can be used to demonstrate how the features of an option affect the option's prices. Go to **www.intrepid.com/~robertl/option-pricer4 .html**. What happens to the price of an option under each of the following situations?

   a. The strike price increases.

   b. Interest rates increase.

   c. Volatility increases.

   d. The time until the option matures increases.

Please visit our Web site at **www.prenhall.com/mishkin_ eakins** to read the Web appendix to Chapter 25:

- **Appendix:** More on Hedging with Financial Derivatives

Glossary

advances: See *discount loans.*

adverse selection: The problem created by asymmetric information before a transaction occurs: the people who are the most undesirable from the other party's point of view are the ones who are most likely to want to engage in the financial transaction. 27

agency theory: The analysis of how asymmetric information problems affect economic behavior. 371

American depository receipts (ADR): A receipt for foreign stocks held by a trustee. The receipts trade on U.S. stock exchanges instead of the actual stock. 275

American option: An option that can be exercised at any time up to the expiration date of the contract. 657

amortized: Paid off in stages over a period of time. Each payment on a loan consists of the accrued interest and an amount that is applied to repay the principal. When all of the payments have been made, the loan is paid off (fully amortized). 282

anchor currency: The currency to which a country fixes its exchange rate. 343

annuity: An insurance product that provides a fixed stream of payments. 567

appreciation: Increase in a currency's value. 307

arbitrage: Elimination of a riskless profit opportunity in a market. 130, 646

ask price: The price market makers sell the stock for. 263

asset: A financial claim or piece of property that is a store of value. 4, 71

asset management: The acquisition of assets that have a low rate of default and diversification of asset holdings to increase profits. 428

asset market approach: Determining asset prices using stocks of assets rather than flows. 79

asset transformation: The process by which financial intermediaries turn risky assets into safer assets for investors by creating and selling assets with risk characteristics that people are comfortable with and then use the funds they acquire by selling these assets to purchase other assets that may have far more risk. 27

asymmetric information: The inequality of knowledge that each party to a transaction has about the other party. 27

audits: Certification by accounting firms that a business is adhering to standard accounting principles. 373

automated banking machine (ABM): An electronic machine that combines in one location an ATM, an Internet connection to the bank's website, and a telephone link to customer service. 455

automated teller machine (ATM): An electronic machine that allows customers to get cash, make deposits, transfer funds from one account to another, and check balances. 455

balance of payments: A bookkeeping system for recording all payments that have a direct bearing on the movement of funds between a country and all other countries. 342

balance-of-payments crisis: A foreign exchange crisis stemming from problems in a country's balance of payments. 351

balance sheet: A list of the assets and liabilities of a bank (or firm) that balances: total assets equal total liabilities plus capital. 421

balloon loan: A loan on which the payments do not fully pay off the principal balance, meaning that the final payment must be larger than the rest. 282

bank holding companies: Companies that own one or more banks. 452

bank panic: The simultaneous failure of many banks, as during a financial crisis. 388

bank supervision: Overseeing who operates banks and how they are operated. 518

banker's acceptance: A short-term promissory note drawn by a company to pay for goods on which a bank guarantees payment at maturity. Usually used in international trade. 227

banks: Financial institutions that accept deposits and make loans (such as commercial banks, savings and loan associations, and credit unions). 8

Basel Accord: An agreement that requires that banks hold as capital at least 8% of their risk-weighted assets. 516

Basel Committee on Banking Supervision: A committee that meets under the auspices of the Bank for International Settlements in Basel, Switzerland, and that sets bank regulatory standards. 516

bearer instrument: A security payable to the holder or "bearer" when presented. No proof of ownership is required. 224

behavioral finance: The field of study that applies concepts from other social sciences, such as anthropology, sociology, and particularly psychology, to understand the behavior of securities prices. 142

beta: A measure of sensitivity of an asset's return to changes in the value of the market portfolio, which is also a measure of the asset's marginal contribution to the risk of the market portfolio.

bid price: The price market makers pay for the stocks. 263

Board of Governors of the Federal Reserve System: A board with seven governors (including the chairman) that plays an essential role in decision making within the Federal Reserve System. 149

bond: A debt security that promises to make payments periodically for a specified period of time. 4

bond indenture: Document accompanying a bond that spells out the details of the bond issue, such as covenants and sinking fund provisions. It states the lender's rights and privileges and the borrower's obligations. 244

book entry: A system of tracking securities ownership where no certificate is issued. Instead, the security issuer keeps records, usually electronically, of who holds outstanding securities. 221

branches: Additional offices of banks that conduct banking operations. 468

Bretton Woods system: The international monetary system in use from 1945 to 1971 in which exchange rates were fixed and the U.S. dollar was freely convertible into gold (by foreign governments and central banks only). 344

brokered deposits: Deposits that enable depositors to circumvent the $100,000 limit at each bank so that the total amount deposited is fully insured.

brokers: Agents for investors who match buyers with sellers. 21

bubble: A situation in which the price of an asset differs from its fundamental market value. 141

call option: An option contract that provides the right to buy a security at a specified price. 657

call provision: A right, usually included in the terms of a bond, that gives the issuer the ability to repurchase outstanding bonds before they mature. 246

capital: Wealth, either financial or physical, that is employed to produce more wealth. 19

capital account: An account that describes the flow of capital between the United States and other countries. 343

capital adequacy management: Managing the amount of capital the bank should maintain and then acquiring the needed capital. 428

capital call: A requirement of limited partners in a venture capital agreement to supply funds per their commitment with the partnership. 609

capital market: A financial market in which longer-term debt (maturity of greater than one year) and equity instruments are traded. 22

capital mobility: A situation in which foreigners can easily purchase a country's assets and the country's residents can easily purchase foreign assets. 316

captive finance company: A finance company that is owned by a retailer and makes loans to finance the purchase of goods from the retailer.

cash flow: The difference between cash receipts and cash expenditures. 42, 386

casualty (liability) insurance: Protection against financial losses because of a claim of negligence. 572

central bank: The government agency that oversees the banking system and is responsible for the amount of money and credit supplied in the economy; in the United States, the Federal Reserve System. 8

Central Liquidity Facility (CLF): The lender of last resort for credit unions, created in 1978 by the Financial Institutions Reform Act. 502

certainty equivalent: An amount that will be received or spent with certainty. An insurance payment is a certainty equivalent since it removes the risk that unexpected amounts will need to be spent. 562

closed-end fund: A mutual fund that sells a fixed number of shares of stock and does not continue to accept investments. 542

coinsurance: An insurance policy under which the policyholder bears a percentage of the loss along with the insurance company. 577

collateral: Property that is pledged to the lender to guarantee payment in the event that the borrower should be unable to make debt payments. 368

collateralized mortgage obligation (CMO): Securities classified by when prepayment is likely to occur. Investors may buy a group of CMOs that are likely to mature at a time that meets the investors' needs. 298

common bond membership: A requirement that all members of credit unions share some common bond, such as working for the same employer. 500

common stock: A security that gives the holder an ownership interest in the issuing firm. This ownership interest includes the right to any residual cash flows and the right to vote on major corporate issues. 5, 277

compensating balance: A required minimum amount of funds that a firm receiving a loan must keep in a checking account at the bank. 622

competitive bidding: Competing in an auction against other potential buyers of Treasury securities. 220

confidential memorandum: A document that presents detailed financial information required by prospective buyers prior to making an offer to acquire a firm. 599

conflicts of interest: A manifestation of moral hazard in which one party in a financial contract has incentives to act in its own interest, rather than in the interests of the other party. 28, 400

conventional mortgages: Mortgage contracts originated by banks and other mortgage lenders that are not guaranteed by the FHA or the VA. They are often insured by private mortgage insurance. 290

costly state verification: Monitoring a firm's activities, an expensive process in both time and money. 378

coupon bond: A credit market instrument that pays the owner a fixed interest payment every year until the maturity date, when a specified final amount is paid. 44

coupon rate: The dollar amount of the yearly coupon payment expressed as a percentage of the face value of a coupon bond. 44

credit-rating agencies: Investment advisory firms that rate the quality of corporate and municipal bonds in terms of the probability of default. 102

credit default swap: A transaction in which one party who wants to hedge credit risk pays a fixed payment on a regular basis, in return for a contingent payment that is triggered by a credit event such as the bankruptcy of a particular firm, or the downgrading of the firm's credit rating by a credit rating agency. 668

credit derivatives: Derivatives that have payoffs to previously issued securities, but ones which bear credit risk. 667

credit-linked note: A type of credit derivative which is a combination of a bond and a credit option. 669

credit options: Options in which for a fee, the purchaser has the right to get profits that are tied either to the price of an underlying risky security or to an interest rate. 668

credit rationing: A lender's refusing to make loans even though borrowers are willing to pay the stated interest rate or even a higher rate or restricting the size of loans to less than the amount being sought. 623

credit risk: The risk arising from the possibility that the borrower will default. 428

credit swap: A transaction in which risky payments on loans are swapped for each other. 668

credit union: A financial institution that focuses on servicing the banking and lending needs of its members, who must be linked by a common bond. 499

Credit Union National Association (CUNA): A central credit union facility that encourages establishing credit unions and provides information to its members. 499

Credit Union National Extension Bureau (CUNEB): A central credit union facility established in 1921 that was later replaced by the Credit Union National Association. 499

creditor: A lender or holder of debt. 384

currency board: A monetary regime in which the domestic currency is backed 100% by a foreign currency (say, dollars) and in which the note-issuing authority, whether the central bank or the government, establishes a fixed exchange rate to this foreign currency and stands ready to exchange domestic currency at this rate whenever the public requests it. 348

currency swap: A swap that involves the exchange of a set of payments in another currency. 664

current account: An account that shows international transactions involving currently produced goods and services. 342

current yield: An approximation of the yield to maturity that equals the yearly coupon payment divided by the price of a coupon bond. 51, 250

dealers: People who link buyers with sellers by buying and selling securities at stated prices. 21

debt deflation: A situation in which a substantial decline in the price level sets in, leading to a further deterioration in firms' net worth because of the increased burden of indebtedness. 390

deductible: An amount of any loss that must be paid by the insured before the insurance company will pay anything. 564

deep markets: Markets where there are many participants and a great deal of activity, thus ensuring that securities can be sold rapidly at fair prices. 220

default: A situation in which the party issuing a debt instrument is unable to make interest payments or pay off the amount owed when the instrument matures. 100

default-free bonds: Bonds with no default risk, such as U.S. government bonds. 100

default risk: The risk that a loan customer may fail to repay a loan as promised.

defensive open market operations: Open market operation intended to offset movements in other factors that affect reserves and the monetary base. 177

deferred load: A fee on a mutual fund investment that is charged only if the investment is withdrawn. The amount of the deferred load usually falls the longer the investment is left in the fund. 549

defined-benefit plan: A pension plan in which the benefits are stated up front and are paid regardless of how the investments perform. 579

defined-contribution plan: A pension plan in which the contributions are stated up front but the benefits paid depend on the performance of the investments. 579

definitive agreement: A legally binding contract that details the terms and conditions for an acquisition of one firm by another. 599

demand curve: A curve depicting the relationship between quantity demanded and price when all other economic variables are held constant. 75

demand deposit: A deposit held by a bank that must be paid to the depositor on demand. Demand deposits are more commonly called *checking accounts.* 224

deposit facility: The European Central Bank's standing facility in which banks are paid a fixed interest rate 100 basis points below the target financing rate. 184

deposit outflows: Losses of deposits when depositors make withdrawals or demand payment. 428

deposit rate ceilings: Restrictions on the maximum interest rates payable on deposits. 460

depreciation: Decrease in a currency's value. 307

devaluation: Resetting of the par value of a currency at a lower level. 347

direct placement: An issuer's bypassing the dealer and selling the security directly to the investor. 226

dirty float: An exchange rate regime in which exchange rates fluctuate from day to day, but central banks attempt to influence their countries' exchange rate by buying and selling currencies.

discount: When the bond sells for less than the par value. 254

discount bond: A credit market instrument that is bought at a price below its face value and whose face value is repaid at the maturity date; it does not make any interest payments. Also known as a *zero-coupon bond.* 44

discount loans: A bank's borrowings from the Federal Reserve System. Also known as *advances.* 423

discount points: Percentage of the total loan paid back immediately when a mortgage loan is obtained. Payment of discount points lowers the annual interest rate on the debt. 283

discount rate: The interest rate that the Federal Reserve charges banks on discount loans. 170, 430

discount window: The Federal Reserve facility at which discount loans are made to banks. 179

discount yield: See *yield on a discount basis*.

discounting: Reduction in the value of a security at purchase such that when it matures at full value, the investor receives a fair return. 218

disintermediation: A reduction in the flow of funds into the banking system that causes the amount of financial intermediation to decline. 461

diversification: Investing in a collection (portfolio) of assets whose returns do not always move together, with the result that overall risk is lower than for individual assets. 27, 538

dividends: Periodic payments made by equities to shareholders. 20

dollarization: A monetary strategy in which a country abandons its currency altogether and adopts that of another country, typically the U.S. dollar. 348

down payment: A portion of the original purchase price that is paid by the borrower so that the borrower will have equity (ownership interest) in the asset pledged as collateral. 286

dual banking system: The system in the United States in which banks supervised by the federal government and banks supervised by the states operate side by side. 451

dual mandate: A central bank mandate in which there are two co-equal objectives, price stability and maximum employment. 189

due diligence period: A 20- to 40-day period used by the buyer of a firm to verify the accuracy of the information contained in the confidential memorandum. 599

duration: The average lifetime of a debt security's stream of payments. 61

duration gap analysis: A measurement of the sensitivity of the market value of a bank's assets and liabilities to changes in interest rates. 627

dynamic open market operations: Open market operations intended to change the level of reserves and the monetary base. 177

early-stage investing: Investment by a venture capital firm in a company that is in the very beginning stage of its development. 609

e-cash: A second form of electronic money used on the Internet to pay for goods and services. 457

econometric model: A model whose equations are estimated using statistical procedures. 92

economies of scale: Savings that can be achieved through increased size. 26

economies of scope: Increased business that can be achieved by offering many products in one easy-to-reach location. 400, 471

Edge Act corporation: A special subsidiary of a U.S. bank that is engaged primarily in international banking. 477

effective exchange rate index: An index reflecting the value of a basket of representative foreign currencies. 328

efficient market hypothesis: The hypothesis that prices of securities in financial markets fully reflect all available information. 128

e-finance: A new means of delivering financial services electronically. 9

electronic money (or e-money): Money that exists only in electronic form and substitutes for cash as well. 459

Employee Retirement Income Security Act (ERISA): A comprehensive law passed in 1974 that set standards that must be followed by all pension plans. 584

equities: Claims to share in the net income and assets of a corporation (such as common stock). 20

equity capital: See *net worth*.

equity multiplier: The amount of assets per dollar of equity capital. 434

Eurobonds: Bonds denominated in a currency other than that of the country in which they are sold. 22

Eurocurrencies: Foreign currencies deposited in banks outside the home country. 23

Eurodollars: U.S. dollars that are deposited in foreign banks outside of the United States or in foreign branches of U.S. banks. 23

European option: An option that can be exercised only at the expiration date of the contract. 657

excess demand: A situation in which quantity demanded is greater than quantity supplied. 78

excess reserves: Reserves in excess of required reserves. 171, 424

excess supply: A situation in which quantity supplied is greater than quantity demanded. 78

exchange rate: The price of one currency in terms of another. 7, 305

exchange rate overshooting: A phenomenon whereby the exchange rate changes by more in the short run than it does in the long run when the money supply changes. 327

exchanges: Secondary markets in which buyers and sellers of securities (or their agents or brokers) meet in one central location to conduct trades. 21

exercise price: The price at which the purchaser of an option has the right to buy or sell the underlying financial instrument. Also known as the *strike price*. 657

expectations theory: The theory that the interest rate on a long-term bond will equal an average of the short-term interest rates that people expect to occur over the life of the long-term bond. 109

expected return: The return on an asset expected over the next period. 71

face value: The specified final amount repaid at the maturity date of a coupon bond. Also called *par value*. 44

factoring: The sale of accounts receivable to another firm, which takes responsibility for collections.

Federal Credit Union Act: Law passed in 1934 that allowed federal chartering of credit unions in all states. 499

federal funds: Short-term deposits bought or sold between banks. 222

federal funds rate: The interest rate on overnight loans of deposits at the Federal Reserve. 173

Federal Home Loan Bank Act of 1932: Law that created the Federal Home Loan Bank Board and a network of regional home loan banks. 485

Federal Home Loan Bank Board (FHLBB): Agency responsible for regulating and controlling savings and loan institutions, abolished by FIRREA in 1989. 485

Federal Open Market Committee (FOMC): The committee that makes decisions regarding the conduct of open market operations; composed of the seven members of the Board of Governors of the Federal Reserve System, the president of the Federal Reserve Bank of New York, and the presidents of four other Federal Reserve banks on a rotating basis. 149

Federal Reserve banks: The 12 district banks in the Federal Reserve system. 149

Federal Reserve System (the Fed): The central banking authority responsible for monetary policy in the United States. 8

Federal Savings and Loan Insurance Corporation (FSLIC): An agency that provided deposit insurance to savings and loans similar to the Federal Deposit Insurance Corporation which insured banks. FSLIC was eliminated in 1989. 485

FICO scores: A credit history of a potential borrower by lenders to determine a borrowers' credit worthiness. 287

financial crisis: A major disruption in financial markets, characterized by sharp declines in asset prices and the failures of many financial and nonfinancial firms. 386

financial derivatives: Instruments that have payoffs that are linked to previously issued securities and are extremely useful risk reduction tools. 454, 641

financial engineering: The process of researching and developing new financial products and services that would meet customer needs and prove profitable. 452

financial futures contract: A futures contract in which the standardized commodity is a particular type of financial instrument. 644

financial futures options: Options in which the underlying instrument is a futures contract. Also called *futures options*. 657

financial guarantee: A contract that guarantees that bond purchasers will be paid both principal and interest in the event the issuer defaults on the obligation. 250

Financial Institutions Reform Act: Law passed in 1978 that created the Central Liquidity Facility as the lender of last resort for credit unions. 502

Financial Institutions Reform, Recovery, and Enforcement Act: Law passed in 1989 to stop losses in the savings and loan industry. It reversed much of the deregulation included in the Garn–St Germain Act of 1982. 491

financial instrument: See *security*.

financial intermediaries: Institutions (such as banks, insurance companies, mutual funds, pension funds, and finance companies) that borrow funds from people who have saved and then make loans to others. 8

financial intermediation: The process of indirect finance whereby financial intermediaries link lender-savers and borrower-spenders. 24

financial markets: Markets in which funds are transferred from people who have a surplus of available funds to people who have a shortage of available funds. 4

financial panic: The widespread collapse of financial markets and intermediaries in an economy. 34

Fisher effect: The outcome that when expected inflation occurs, interest rates will rise; named after economist Irving Fisher. 87

fixed exchange rate regime: Policy under which central banks buy and sell their own currencies to keep their exchange rates fixed at a certain level. 343

fixed-payment loan: A credit market instrument that provides a borrower with an amount of money that is repaid by making a fixed payment periodically (usually monthly) for a set number of years. 44

floating exchange rate regime: An exchange rate regime in which the value of currencies are allowed to fluctuate against one another. 344

foreign bonds: Bonds sold in a foreign country and denominated in that country's currency. 22

foreign exchange intervention: An international financial transaction in which a central bank buys or sells currency to influence foreign exchange rates. 337

foreign exchange market: The market in which exchange rates are determined. 6, 305

foreign exchange rate: See *exchange rate.*

forward contract: An agreement by two parties to engage in a financial transaction at a future (forward) point in time. 642

forward exchange rate: The exchange rate for a forward (future) transaction. 307

forward rate: The interest rate predicted by pure expectations theory of the term structure of interest rates to prevail in the future. 121

forward transaction: An exchange rate transaction that involves the exchange of bank deposits denominated in different currencies at some specified future date. 307

free reserves: Excess reserves in the banking system minus the volume of discount loans.

free-rider problem: The problem that occurs when people who do not pay for information take advantage of the information that other people have paid for. 372

fully amortized loan: A fixed payment loan in which the lender provides the borrower with an amount of funds that must be repaid by making the same payment every period, consisting of part of the principal and interest for a set number of years. 44

fully funded: Describing a pension plan in which the contributions to the plan and their earnings over the years are sufficient to pay out the defined benefits when they come due. 579

fully subscribed: Describing a security issue for which all of the securities available have been spoken for before the issue date. 597

futures contract: A contract in which the seller agrees to provide a certain standardized commodity to the buyer on a specific future date at an agreed-on price. 454

futures options: See *financial futures options.*

gap analysis: A measurement of the sensitivity of bank profits to changes in interest rates, calculated by subtracting the amount of rate-sensitive liabilities minus rate-sensitive assets. Also called *income gap analysis.* 625

general obligation bonds: Bonds that are secured by the full faith and credit of the issuer, which includes the taxing authority of municipalities. 243

generalized dividend model: Calculates that the price of stock is determined only by the present value of the dividends. 266

Glass-Steagall Act: Law that made it illegal for commercial banks to underwrite securities for sale to the public. 592

goal independence: The ability of the central bank to set the goals of monetary policy. 157

goodwill: An accounting entry to reflect value to the firm of its having special expertise or a particularly profitable business line. 487

Gordon growth model: A simplified model to compute the value of a stock by assuming constant dividend growth. 266

hedge: To protect oneself against risk. 454, 641

hierarchical mandate: A mandate for the central bank which puts the goal of price stability first, but as long as it is achieved other goals can be pursued. 189

hybrid funds: A mutual fund that is composed of both stocks and bonds. 551

incentive-compatible: Aligning the incentives of both parties to a contract. 380

income gap analysis: See *gap analysis.*

index fund: A mutual fund that is composed only of securities that are included in some popular stock index, such as the S&P 500. The fund is designed to mimic the returns generated by the underlying index. 548

indexed bonds: Bonds whose interest and principal payments are adjusted for changes in the price level and whose interest rate thus provides a direct measure of a real interest rate. 55

individual retirement account (IRA): Retirement account in which pretax dollars can be invested by individuals not covered by some other retirement plan. 587

inflation targeting: A monetary policy strategy that involves public announcement of a medium-term numerical targets for inflation. 194

initial public offering (IPO): A corporation's first sale of securities to the public. 238, 402, 594

insolvent: A situation in which the value of a firm's or bank's assets have fallen below its liabilities; bankrupt. 389

installment credit: A loan that requires the borrower to make a series of equal payments over some fixed length of time.

instrument independence: The ability of the central bank to set monetary policy instruments. 157

insured mortgage: Mortgages guaranteed by either the Federal Housing Administration or the Veterans Administration. These agencies guarantee that the bank making the loan will not suffer any losses if the borrower defaults. 289

interest parity condition: The observation that the domestic interest rate equals the foreign interest rate plus the expected appreciation in the foreign currency. 316

interest rate: The cost of borrowing or the price paid for the rental of funds (usually expressed as a percentage per year). 4

interest-rate forward contracts: Forward contracts that are linked to debt instruments. 642

interest-rate risk: The possible reduction in returns that is associated with changes in interest rates. 59, 255, 428

interest-rate swap: A financial contract that allows one party to exchange (swap) a set of interest payments for another set of interest payments owned by another party. 664

intermediate target: Any number of variables, such as monetary aggregates or interest rates, that have a direct effect on employment and the price level and that the Fed seeks to influence. 200

intermediate-term: With reference to a debt instrument, having a maturity of between one and ten years. 20

international banking facilities (IBFs): Banking establishments in the United States that can accept time deposits from foreigners but are not subject to either reserve requirements or restrictions on interest payments. 478

International Monetary Fund (IMF): The international organization created by the Bretton Woods agreement whose objective is to promote the growth of world trade by making loans to countries experiencing balance-of-payments difficulties. 344

international policy coordination: Agreements among countries to enact policies cooperatively.

international reserves: Central bank holdings of assets denominated in foreign currencies. 338

inverted yield curve: A yield curve that is downward-sloping. 107

investment banker: A securities dealer who facilitates the transfer of securities from the original issuer to the public. 592

investment banks: Firms that assist in the initial sale of securities in the primary market. 21

January effect: An abnormal rise in stock prices from December to January. 136

junk bonds: Bonds rated lower than BBB by bond-rating agencies. Junk bonds are not investment grade and are considered speculative. They usually have a high yield to compensate investors for their high risk. 102, 248

large, complex banking organizations (LCBOs): Large companies that provide banking as well as many other financial services. 471

later-stage investing: Investment by a venture capital firm in a company to help the firm grow to a critical mass needed to attract public financing. 609

law of large numbers: The observation that when many people are insured, the probability distribution of the losses will assume a normal probability distribution. 567

law of one price: The principle that if two or more countries produce an identical good, the price of this good should be the same no matter which country produces it. 309

leasing: An arrangement whereby one party obtains the right to use an asset for a fee paid to another party for a predetermined length of time.

lender of last resort: Provider of reserves to financial institutions when no one else would provide them to prevent a financial crisis. 180

letter of intent: A document issued by a prospective buyer that signals a desire to go forward with a purchase and that outlines the preliminary terms of the purchase. 599

leverage ratio: A bank's capital divided by its assets. 516

liabilities: IOUs or debts. 18

liability management: The acquisition of funds at low cost to increase profits. 428

lien: A legal claim against a piece of property that gives a lender the right to foreclose or seize the property if a loan on the property is not repaid as promised. 285

limit order: An order placed by a customer to buy stock that specifies a maximum price or an order to sell stock that places a minimum acceptable price. 601

liquid: Easily converted into cash. 21

liquid market: A market in which securities can be bought and sold quickly and with low transaction costs. 220

liquidity: The relative ease and speed with which an asset can be converted into cash. 72

liquidity management: The decision made by a bank to maintain sufficient liquid assets to meet the bank's obligations to depositors. 428

liquidity preference framework: A model developed by John Maynard Keynes that predicts the equilibrium interest rate on the basis of the supply of and demand for money.

liquidity premium theory: The theory that the interest rate on a long-term bond will equal an average of short-term interest rates expected to occur over the life of the long-term bond plus a positive term (liquidity) premium. 114

liquidity risk: The risk that a firm may run out of cash needed to pay bills and to keep the firm operating.

liquidity services: Services that make it easier for customers to conduct transactions. 26

load fund: A mutual fund that charges a fee when money is added to or withdrawn from the fund. 549

loan commitment: A bank's commitment (for a specified future period of time) to provide a firm with loans up to a given amount at an interest rate that is tied to some market interest rate. 437, 622

loan sale: The sale under a contract (also called a *secondary loan participation*) of all or part of the cash stream from a specific loan, thereby removing the loan from the bank's balance sheet. 437

loanable funds: The quantity of loans. 80

loanable funds framework: Determining the equilibrium interest rate by analyzing the supply of and demand for bonds (loanable funds). 81

London interbank bid rate (LIBID): The rate of interest large international banks charge on overnight loans among themselves. 229

London interbank offer rate (LIBOR): The interest rate charged on short-term funds bought or sold between large international banks. 229

long position: A contractual obligation to take delivery of an underlying financial instrument. 641

long-term: With reference to a debt instrument, having a maturity of ten years or more. 20

longer-term refinancing operations: A category of open market operations by the European Central Bank which are similar to the Fed's outright purchase of securities. 184

macro hedge: A hedge of interest-rate risk for a financial institution's entire portfolio. 647

main refinancing operations: Operations which involve weekly reverse transactions (purchase or sale of eligible assets under repurchase agreements or credit operations against eligible assets as collateral) that are reversed within two weeks and are the primary monetary policy tool of the European Central Bank. 184

managed float regime: The current international financial environment in which exchange rates fluctuate from day to day, but central banks attempt to influence their countries' exchange rates by buying and selling currencies. Also known as a *dirty float*. 344

management advisory services: Auditing and non-auditing consulting services that accounting firms sometimes provide to their clients. 402

margin credit: Loans advanced by a brokerage house to help investors buy securities. 602

margin requirement: A sum of money that must be kept in an account (the margin account) at a brokerage firm. 650

marginal lending facility: The European Central Bank's standing lending facility in which banks can borrow (against eligible collateral) overnight loans from the national central bank at a rate 100 basis points above the target financing rate. 184

marginal lending rate: The interest rate charged by the European Central Bank for borrowing at its marginal lending facility. 184

marked to market: Repriced and settled in the margin account at the end of every trading day to reflect any change in the value of the futures contract. 650

market equilibrium: A situation occurring when the quantity that people are willing to buy (demand) equals the quantity that people are willing to sell (supply). 78

market fundamentals: Items that have a direct impact on future income streams of the security. 131

market maker: Dealers who buy or sell securities from their own inventories, thereby ensuring that there is always a market in which investors can buy or sell their securities. 604

market order: An order placed by a customer to buy stock at the current market price. 600

market segmentation theory: A theory of the term structure that sees markets for different-maturity bonds as completely separated and segmented such that the interest rate for bonds of a given maturity is determined solely by supply and demand for bonds of that maturity. 113

matched sale-purchase transaction: An arrangement whereby the Fed sells securities and the buyer agrees to sell them back to the Fed in the near future; sometimes called a reverse repo. 179

maturity: Time to the expiration date (maturity date) of a debt instrument. 20

mean reversion: The phenomenon that stocks with low returns today tend to have high returns in the future, and vice versa. 137

mergers and acquisitions market: An informal and unorganized market where firms are bought, sold, or merged with other firms. 599

micro hedge: A hedge for a specific asset. 647

monetary base: The sum of the Fed's monetary liabilities (currency in circulation and reserves) and the U.S. Treasury's monetary liabilities (Treasury currency in circulation, primarily coins). 170

monetary neutrality: A proposition that in the long run, a percentage rise in the money supply is matched by the same percentage rise in the price level, leaving unchanged the real money supply and all other economic variables such as interest rates. 326

monetary policy: The management of the money supply and interest rates. 8

monetary targeting: A monetary policy strategy in which the central bank announces that it will achieve a certain value (the target) of the annual growth rate of a monetary aggregate. 190

money: Anything that is generally accepted in payment for goods or services or in the repayment of debts. Also called *money supply*. 8

money center banks: Large banks in key financial centers. 432

money market: A financial market in which only short-term debt instruments (maturity of less than one year) are traded. 22

money market mutual funds: Funds that accumulate investment dollars from a large group of people and then invest in short-term securities such as Treasury bills and commercial paper.

money market securities: Securities that have an original maturity of less than one year, such as Treasury bills, commercial paper, banker's acceptances, and negotiable certificates of deposit. 217

money supply: See *money*.

moral hazard: The risk that one party to a transaction will engage in behavior that is undesirable from the other party's point of view. 28

mortgage: A long-term loan secured by real estate. 282

mortgage-backed security: A security that is collateralized by a pool of mortgage loans. Also called a *securitized mortgage*. 296

mortgage pass-through: A security that has the multiple borrowers' mortgage payments pass through a trustee before being disbursed to the investors. 296

mutual bank: A bank owned by the depositors. 484

mutual insurance company: An insurance company that is owned by the policyholders and has the objective of providing insurance for the lowest possible price. 565

named-peril policy: Insurance policy that protects against loss from perils that are specifically named in the policy. 573

National Association of Securities Dealers Automated Quotation System (NASDAQ): A computerized network that links dealers around the country together and provides price quotes on over-the-counter securities. 262

national banks: Federally chartered banks. 451

National Credit Union Act of 1970: Law that established the National Credit Union Administration (NCUA), an independent agency charged with the task of regulating and supervising federally chartered credit unions and state-chartered credit unions that receive federal deposit insurance. 501

National Credit Union Share Insurance Fund (NCUSIF): Agency established by the National Credit Union Act of 1970 that is controlled by the National Credit Union Administration and insures the deposits in credit unions for $100,000 per account. 501

natural rate of unemployment: The rate of unemployment consistent with full employment at which the demand for labor equals the supply of labor. 187

negotiable certificates of deposit: A bank-issued short-term security that is traded and documents a deposit and specifies the interest rate and the maturity date.

net asset value: The total value of a mutual fund's assets minus any liabilities, divided by the number of shares outstanding. 543

net interest margin (NIM): The difference between interest income and interest expense as a percentage of assets. 442

net worth: The difference between a firm's assets (what it owns or is owed) and its liabilities (what it owes). Also called *equity capital*. 376

no-load fund: A mutual fund that does not charge a fee when funds are added to or withdrawn from the fund. 549

nominal anchor: A nominal variable such as the inflation rate, an exchange rate, or the money supply that monetary policymakers use to tie down the price level. 185

nominal interest rate: An interest rate that is not adjusted for inflation. 52

nonbank banks: Limited-service banks that either do not make commercial loans or do not take in deposits. 631

noncompetitive bidding: Offering to buy Treasury securities without specifying a price; the securities are ultimately sold at the weighted average of the competitive bids accepted at the same auction. 220

notional principal: The amount on which interest is being paid in a swap arrangement. 664

off-balance-sheet activities: Bank activities that involve trading financial instruments and the generation of income from fees and loan sales, all of which affect bank profits but are not visible on bank balance sheets. 437, 516

official reserve transactions balance: The current account balance plus items in the capital account. 343

open-end fund: A mutual fund that accepts investments and allows investors to redeem shares at any time. The value of the shares is tied to the value of investment assets of the fund. 542

open interest: The number of contracts outstanding. 648

open market operations: The buying and selling of government securities in the open market that affect both interest rates and the amount of reserves in the banking system. 152, 171

operating expenses: The expenses incurred from a bank's ongoing operations. 441

operating income: The income earned on a bank's ongoing operations. 441

operating instrument: A variable that is very responsive to the central bank's tools and indicates the stance of monetary policy (also called a *policy instrument*). 200

operating target: Any of a set of variables, such as reserve aggregates or interest rates, that the Fed seeks to influence and that are responsive to its policy tools.

opportunity cost: The amount of interest (expected return) sacrificed by not holding an alternative asset.

options: Contracts that give the purchaser the option (right) to buy or sell the underlying financial instrument at a specified price, called the *exercise price* or *strike price*, within a specific period of time (the *term to expiration*). 657

overfunded: Describing a pension plan that has assets greater than needed to make the projected benefit payments owed by the plan. 579

oversubscribed: Having received more offers to buy than there are securities available for sale. 597

over-the-counter (OTC) market: A secondary market in which dealers at different locations who have an inventory of securities stand ready to buy and sell securities to anyone who comes to them and is willing to accept their prices. 21

overnight cash rate: The interest rate for very-short-term interbank loans in the euro area. 183

passbook savings account: An interest-bearing savings account held at a commercial bank. 496

pecking order hypothesis: The hypothesis that the larger and more established is a corporation, the more likely it will be to issue securities to raise funds. 375

Pension Benefit Guarantee Corporation (Penny Benny): A government agency that performs a role similar to that of the FDIC, insuring pension benefits up to a limit if a company with an underfunded pension plan goes bankrupt. 585

pension plan: An asset pool that accumulates over an individual's working years and is paid out during the nonworking years. 578

perpetuity: A perpetual bond with no maturity date and no repayment of principal that makes periodic fixed payments forever. 49

policy instrument: A variable that is very responsive to the central bank's tools and indicates the stance of monetary policy (also called an *operating intrument*). 200

political business cycle: A business cycle caused by expansionary policies before an election. 164

portfolio: A collection of assets. 27

preferred stock: Stock on which a fixed dividend must be paid before common dividends are distributed. It often does not mature and usually does not give the holder voting rights in the company. 261

premium: The amount paid for an option contract. 254, 657

present discounted value: See *present value.*

present value: Today's value of a payment to be received in the future when the interest rate is *i*. Also called *present discounted value.* 42

price earnings ratio (PE): A measure of how much the market is willing to pay for $1 of earnings from a firm. 268

price stability: Low and stable inflation. 185

primary dealers: Government securities dealers, operating out of private firms or commercial banks, with whom the Fed's open market desk trades. 178

primary market: A financial market in which new issues of a security are sold to initial buyers. 20, 591

principal-agent problem: A moral hazard problem that occurs when the managers in control (the agents) act in their own interest rather than in the interest of the owners (the principals) due to differing sets of incentives. 377

private equity buyout: When a public company becomes private. 610

private mortgage insurance (PMI): Insurance that protects the lender against losses from defaults on mortgage loans. 286

private pension plan: A pension plan sponsored by an employer, group, or individual. 580

property insurance: Insurance that protects against losses from fire, theft, storm, explosion, and neglect. 572

prospectus: A portion of a security registration statement that is filed with the Securities and Exchange Commission and made available to potential purchasers of the security. 594

prudent man rule: This rule states that those with the responsibility of investing money for others should act with prudence, discretion, intelligence, and regard for safety of capital as well as income. 608

public pension plan: A pension plan sponsored by a government body. 580

put option: An option contract that provides the right to sell a security at a specified price. 657

quotas: Restrictions on the quantity of foreign goods that can be imported. 312

random walk: The movements of a variable whose future changes cannot be predicted because, given today's value, the variable is just as likely to fall as to rise. 132

rate of capital gain: The change in a security's price relative to the initial purchase price. 57

rate of return: See *return.*

rational expectations: Expectations that reflect optimal forecasts (the best guess of the future) using all available information.

real interest rate: The interest rate adjusted for expected changes in the price level (inflation) so that it more accurately reflects the true cost of borrowing. 53

real terms: Terms reflecting actual goods and services one can buy. 53

registered bonds: Bonds requiring that their owners register with the company to receive interest payments. Registered bonds have largely replaced bearer bonds, which did not require registration. 245

registration statement: Information about a firm's financial condition, management, competition, industry, and experience that must be filed with the Securities and Exchange Commission prior to the sale to the public of any security with a maturity of more than 270 days. 594

Regulation Z: The requirement that lenders disclose the full cost of a loan to the borrower; also known as the "truth in lending" regulation.

regulatory arbitrage: An attempt to avoid regulatory capital requirements by keeping assets on banks' books that have the same risk-based capital requirement but are relatively risky, while taking off their books low-risk assets. 517

regulatory forbearance: Refraining from exercising a regulatory right to put insolvent savings and loans out of business. 487

reinsurance: Allocating a portion of the risk to another company in exchange for a portion of the premium. 573

reinvestment risk: The interest-rate risk associated with the fact that the proceeds of short-term investments must be reinvested at a future interest rate that is uncertain. 60

repossession: The taking of an asset that has been pledged as collateral for a loan when the borrower defaults.

repurchase agreement: A form of loan in which the borrower simultaneously contracts to sell securities and contracts to repurchase them, either on demand or on a specified date. 179

required reserve ratio: The fraction of deposits that the Fed requires to be kept as reserves. 171, 424

required reserves: Reserves that are held to meet Fed requirements that a certain fraction of bank deposits be kept as reserves. 171, 424

reserve account: An account used to make insurance and tax payments due on property securing a mortgage loan. A portion of each monthly loan payment goes into the reserve account. 294

reserve currency: A currency such as the U.S. dollar that is used by other countries to denominate the assets they hold as international reserves. 345

reserve for loan losses: An account that offsets the loan accounts on a lender's books that reflects the lender's projected losses due to default.

reserve requirements: Regulations making it obligatory for depository institutions to keep a certain frac-tion of their deposits in accounts with the Fed. 173, 424

reserves: Banks' holding of deposits in accounts with the Fed, plus currency that is physically held by banks (vault cash). 170, 424

Resolution Trust Corporation (RTC): A temporary agency created by FIRREA that was responsible for liquidating the assets of failed savings and loans. 491

restrictive covenants: Provisions that specify certain activities that a borrower can and cannot engage in. 246, 368

return: The payments to the owner of a security plus the change in the security's value, expressed as a fraction of its purchase price; more precisely called the *rate of return*. 55

return on assets (ROA): Net profit after taxes per dollar of assets. 434

return on equity (ROE): Net profit after taxes per dollar of equity capital. 434

revaluation: Resetting of the par value of a currency at a higher level. 347

revenue bonds: Bonds for which the source of income that is used to pay the interest and to retire the bonds is from a specific source, such as a toll road or an electric plant. If this revenue source is unable to make the payments, the bonds can default, despite the issuing municipality's being otherwise healthy. 243

reverse transactions: Purchase or sale of eligible assets by the European Central Bank under repurchase agreements or credit operations against eligible assets as collateral that are reversed within two weeks. 184

risk: The degree of uncertainty associated with the return on an asset. 27, 72

risk premium: The spread between the interest rate on bonds with default risk and the interest rate on default-free bonds. 100

risk sharing: The process by which financial intermediaries create and sell assets with risk characteristics that people are comfortable with and then use the funds they acquire by selling these assets to purchase other assets that may have far more risk. 27

risk structure of interest rates: The relationship among the various interest rates on bonds with the same term to maturity. 99

roll over: To renew a debt when it matures.

seasoned issues: Securities that have been trading publicly long enough to have let the market clearly establish their value. 594

secondary market: A financial market in which securities that have previously been issued can be resold. 20, 591

secondary reserves: U.S. government and agency securities held by banks. 425

secured debt: Debt guaranteed by collateral. 368

secured loan: A loan guaranteed by collateral. 622

securitization: The process of transforming illiquid financial assets into marketable capital market instruments. 459

securitized mortgage: See *mortgage-backed security.* 299

security: A claim on the borrower's future income that is sold by the borrower to the lender. Also called a *financial instrument.* 4

seed investing: Investment by a venture capital firm in a company before it has a real product or is even clearly organized as a company. 609

Separate Trading of Registered Interest and Principal Securities (STRIPS): Securities that have their periodic interest payments separated from the final maturity payment and the two cash flows are sold to different investors. 242

share draft account: Accounts at credit unions that are similar to checking accounts at banks.

shelf registration: An arrangement with the Securities and Exchange Commission that allows a single registration document to be filed that permits multiple securities issues.

short position: A contractual obligation to deliver an underlying financial instrument. 642

short sale: An arrangement with a broker to borrow and sell securities. The borrowed securities are replaced with securities purchased later. Short sales let investors earn profits from falling securities prices. 142, 601

short-term: With reference to a debt instrument, having a maturity of one year or less. 20

simple loan: A credit market instrument providing the borrower with an amount of funds that must be repaid to the lender at the maturity date along with an additional payment (interest). 42

sinking fund: Fund created by a provision in many bond contracts that requires the issuer to set aside each year a portion of the final maturity payment so that investors can be certain that the funds will be available at maturity. 246

smart card: A more sophisticated stored-value card that contains its own computer chip so that it can be loaded with digital cash from the owner's bank account whenever needed. 457

special drawing rights (SDRs): A paper substitute for gold issued by the International Monetary Fund that functions as international reserves. 320

spinning: When an investment bank allocates hot, but underpriced, initial public offerings (IPOs), shares of newly issued stock, to executives of other companies in return for their companies' future business with the investment banks. 402

spot rate: The interest rate at a given moment. 121

spot exchange rate: The exchange rate for the immediate (two-day) transaction. 307

spot transaction: The immediate exchange of bank deposits denominated in different currencies. 307

standard deviation: A statistical indicator of an asset's risk. 73

standing lending facility: A lending facility in which healthy banks are allowed to borrow all they want from a central bank. 179

state banks: Banks chartered by the states. 451

state-owned banks: Banks that are owned by governments. 384

sterilized foreign exchange intervention: A foreign exchange intervention with an offsetting open market operation that leaves the monetary base unchanged. 340

stock: A security that is a claim on the earnings and assets of a corporation. 5

stock company: An insurance company that issues stock and has the objective of making a profit for its shareholders. 565

stock market risk: The risk associated with fluctuations in stock prices. 654

stock option: An option on an individual stock. 657

stop loss order: An order placed with a broker to buy or sell when a certain price is reached; designed to limit an investor's loss on a security position. 601

strike price: See *exercise price.*

subprime loans: Loans made to borrowers who do not qualify for loans at the usual rate of interest due to poor credit rating or too large of a loan. 299

superregional banks: Bank holding companies similar in size to money center banks whose headquarters are not based in one of the money center cities (New York, Chicago, San Francisco). 471

supply curve: A curve depicting the relationship between quantity supplied and price when all other economic variables are held constant. 77

swap: A financial contract that obligates one party to exchange (swap) a set of payments it owns for a set of payments owned by another party. 664

sweep account: An arrangement in which any balances above a certain amount in a corporation's checking account at the end of a business day are "swept out" of the account and invested in overnight repos that pay the corporation interest. 461

syndicate: A group of investment banks that come together for the purpose of issuing a security. The syndicate spreads the risk of the issue among the members. Each participant attempts to market the security and shares in losses. 595

systematic risk: The component of an asset's risk that cannot be eliminated by diversification.

T-account: A simplified balance sheet with lines in the form of a T that lists only the changes that occur in a balance sheet starting from some initial balance sheet position. 426

target financing rate: The European Central Bank's target for the overnight cash rate, the interest rate for very-short-term interbank loans in the euro area. 183

tariffs: Taxes on imported goods. 312

term security: A security with a specified maturity date. 224

term structure of interest rates: The relationship among interest rates on bonds with different terms to maturity. 99

theory of efficient capital markets: The theory that prices of securities in financial markets fully reflect all available information. 128

theory of purchasing power parity (PPP): The theory that exchange rates between any two currencies will adjust to reflect changes in the price levels of the two countries. 310

thrift institutions (thrifts): Savings and loan associations, mutual savings banks, and credit unions. 29

time-inconsistency problem: The problem that occurs when monetary policymakers conduct monetary policy in a discretionary way and pursue expansionary policies that are attractive in the short run but lead to bad long-run outcomes. 185

tombstone: A large notice placed in financial newspapers announcing that a security will be offered for sale by an underwriter or group of underwriters. 596

trade association: A group of credit unions organized to provide a variety of services to a large number of credit unions. 503

trade balance: The difference between merchandise exports and imports. 342

transaction costs: The time and money spent trying to exchange financial assets, goods, or services. 25

Treasury bills (T-bills): Securities sold by the federal government with initial maturities of less than one year. They are often considered the lowest-risk security available. 218

underfunded: Describing a pension plan in which the contributions and their earnings are insufficient to pay out the defined benefits when they come due. 579

undersubscribed: Having received fewer offers to buy than there are securities available for sale. 597

underwriters: Investment banks that guarantee prices on securities to corporations and then sell the securities to the public. 565

underwriting: Guaranteeing prices on securities to corporations and then selling the securities to the public. 21

unexploited profit opportunity: A situation in which an investor can earn a higher-than-normal return. 130

unsecured debt: Debt not guaranteed by collateral. 368

unsterilized foreign exchange intervention: A foreign exchange intervention in which a central bank allows the purchase or sale of domestic currency to affect the monetary base. 339

U.S. Central Credit Union: A central bank for credit unions that was organized in 1974 and provides banking services to the state central credit unions. 502

usury: Charging an excessive or inordinate interest rate on a loan.

vault cash: Currency that is physically held by banks and stored in vaults overnight. 424

venture capital firm: A financial intermediary that pools the resources of its partners and uses the funds to help entrepreneurs start up new businesses. 378

virtual bank: A bank that has no building but rather exists only in cyberspace. 455

wealth: All resources owned by an individual, including all assets. 71

wholesale market: Market where extremely large transactions occur, as for money market funds or foreign currency. 212

World Bank: The International Bank for Reconstruction and Redevelopment, an international organization that provides long-term loans to assist developing countries in building dams, roads, and other physical capital that would contribute to their economic development. 344

World Trade Organization (WTO): The organization that monitors rules for the conduct of trade between countries (tariffs and quotas). 345

yield curve: A plot of the interest rates for particular types of bonds with different terms to maturity. 107

yield on a discount basis: The measure of interest rates by which dealers in bill markets quote the interest rate on U.S. Treasury bills. Also known as the *discount yield.*

yield to maturity: The interest rate that equates the present value of payments received from a credit market instrument with its value today. 45

zero-coupon bond: See *discount bond.*

zero-coupon securities: See *Separate Trading of Registered Interest and Principal Securities (STRIPS).*

Index

Note: Page numbers followed by letters *f*, *n*, and *t* refer to figures, notes, and tables, respectively.

Greenland

Godthab

Reykjavik
Iceland

Trondheim
Norway
Bergen
Oslo
Aberdeen
Copenhagen
Stockholm
Denmark
United Kingdom
Dublin
Manchester
Ireland
Berlin
London
Germany
Paris
France
Italy
Rome
Portugal
Spain
Naples
Lisbon
Madrid
Tunis
Algiers
Athens
Rabat
Tripoli
Morocco

Sweden
Finland
Tampere
Helsinki
St. Petersburg
Moscow
Minsk
Belarus
Warsaw
Kiev
Poland
Ukraine
Odesa
Bucharest
Istanbul
Ankara
Turkey
Syria
Tehran
Baghdad
Shiraz
Iran

Russia
Perm'
Yekaterinburg
Kostroma
Ryazan'
Omsk
Voronezh
Oufa
Chelyabinsk
Astana
Kazakhstan
Novosibirsk
Bishkek
Tashkent
Uzbekistan
Ashgabat
Turkmenistan
Kabul
Afghanistan
China
Islamabad
Lahore
Ludhiana
Pakistan
New Delhi
Kathmandu
Nepal
Bhopal
Calcutta
India
Bombay
Ahmadabad
Karachi
Bangalore
Hyderabad
Chennai
Madurai
Colombo
Sri Lanka

Western Sahara
(Occupied by Morocco)
Algeria
Libya
Cairo
Egypt
Riyadh
Saudi Arabia
Muscat
Jeddah
San'a
Yemen
Mali
Nouakchott
Mauritania
Niger
Chad
Khartoum
Sudan
Addis Ababa
Ethiopia
Somalia
Mogadishu
Bamako
Niamey
Nigeria
Abuja
N'Djamena
Senegal
Guinea-Bissau
Guinea
Sierra Leone
Liberia
Côte d'Ivoire
Bangui
Central African Republic
Yaounde
Kampala
Kenya
Nairobi
Libreville
Gabon
Congo
Brazzaville
Dem. Rep.
of Congo
Rwanda
Burundi
Dodoma
Dar es Salaam
Tanzania
Kinshasa
Luanda
Angola
Zambia
Lusaka
Zimbabwe
Harare
Mozambique
Antananarivo
Mauritius
Namibia
Windhoek
Botswana
Gaborone
Pretoria
Johannesburg
Swaziland
South Africa
Cape Town
Port Elizabeth
Madagascar

Cape Verde

St. John's
Montreal
Halifax
New York
Philadelphia
Washington

Bahamas
Dom. Rep.
Caracas
Trinidad & Tobago
Venezuela
Guyana
Georgetown
Paramaribo
French Guiana
Belem

Recife
Brazil
La Paz
Bolivia
Brasilia
Belo Horizonte
Rio De Janeiro
Paraguay
Asuncion
Sao Paulo
Porto Alegre
Cordoba
Argentina
Uruguay
Buenos Aires
Montevideo
Salvador

multinational
management

A Strategic Approach 5e

multinational
management

A Strategic Approach 5e

John B. **Cullen**
Amsterdam Business School

K. Praveen **Parboteeah**
University of Wisconsin, Whitewater

SOUTH-WESTERN
CENGAGE Learning

Australia • Brazil • Japan • Korea • Mexico • Singapore • Spain • United Kingdom • United States

SOUTH-WESTERN
CENGAGE Learning

Multinational Management:
A Strategic Approach, Fifth Edition
John B. Cullen, K. Praveen Parboteeah

Vice President of Editorial, Business:
Jack W. Calhoun

Editor-in-Chief: Melissa Acuna

Senior Acquisitions Editor: Michele
Rhoades

Developmental Editor: Jennifer King

Senior Editorial Assistant: Ruth Belanger

Marketing Manager: Clinton Kernen

Senior Marketing Communications
Manager: Jim Overly

Senior Content Project Manager:
Kim Kusnerak

Media Editor: Danny Bolan

Senior Frontlist Buyer, Manufacturing:
Sandee Milewski

Production Service: MPS Limited,
A Macmillan Company

Compositor: MPS Limited, A Macmillan
Company

Senior Art Director: Tippy McIntosh

Internal Designer: c miller design

Cover Designer: Imbue Design

Cover Image: © iStock

Permissions Acquisition Manager—Text:
Mardell Glinski Schultz

Permissions Acquisition Manager—Images:
John Hill

For product information and technology assistance, contact us at
Cengage Learning Customer & Sales Support, 1-800-354-9706
For permission to use material from this text or product,
submit all requests online at **www.cengage.com/permissions**
Further permissions questions can be emailed to
permissionrequest@cengage.com

Library of Congress Control Number: 2009941169

ISBN-13: 978-1-4390-8065-8

ISBN-10: 1-4390-8065-8

South-Western Cengage Learning
5191 Natorp Boulevard
Mason, OH 45040
USA

Cengage Learning products are represented in Canada by Nelson Education, Ltd.

For your course and learning solutions, visit
www.cengage.com

Purchase any of our products at your local college store or at our preferred online store **www.CengageBrain.com**

Printed in the United States of America
2 3 4 5 6 7 13 12 11

To les deux

J & J

and

to Kyong, Alisha, and Davin

BRIEF CONTENTS

CONTENTS

ix

part two   Strategy Content and Formulation for Multinational
             Companies 169

part three   Management Processes in Strategy Implementation: Design Choices for Multinational Companies   289

part four

Strategy Implementation for Multinational Companies: Human Resource Management   435

Defining the nature of today's business are the globalization of markets, financial institutions, and companies; the growing importance of the emerging markets of Brazil, China, India, and Russia (the BRIC markets); and the global impact of financial crises, wars, terrorism, and even disease. Developing and making strategic choices are the mainstays of successful decision making in this increasingly complex global environment. To help students develop the essential skills needed to formulate and implement successful strategic moves in the new competitive and interlaced global environment, this fifth edition of *Multinational Management: A Strategic Approach* continues its tradition of providing a thorough review and analysis of the latest research on international management. In addition, by using a strategic perspective as a unifying theme to explore the global economy and the impact of managerial decisions, we bring a distinctive method to the teaching and learning of international management. This text was the first international management text to use this critical emphasis on strategic decision making as the cornerstone of its approach, and each subsequent edition has built on this tradition.

After reading this text, students will understand that successful multinational managers view the world as an integrated market where competition and collaboration evolve from almost anywhere and anyone. At the same time, these future managers must appreciate the wide array of differences that exist in cultures and social institutions. This text considers how cultural differences affect strategies and operations and gives the student an appreciation of how social institutions such as the economic system, the polity, the educational system, and religion play an important role in any multinational operation. As such, the reader is not limited to understanding multinational management from the perspective of any one nation or group.

New to This Edition

The entire text has been updated to reflect current research and examples from the field of international management. All chapters have new boxed features to reflect the latest trends. Additionally, most of the statistics reported in the chapters reflect the latest numbers. Many of the new updates pertain to the opportunities presented by the emerging markets such as Brazil, China, India, and Russia, and the text recognizes the emergence of the class of emerging market competitors. Finally, chapters were written keeping in mind the economic crisis of 2008–2009, while acknowledging that, as most experts predict, emerging markets will recover much more quickly than developed nations.

Among many changes, some specific revisions to the text material include the following:

New Cases

All chapters and each major section of the text have their own cases with specific case-based discussion questions. Around 75 percent of the cases in this edition are new to this edition. Specifically, 17 new cases have been added and others have been updated. Case topics reflect the current global environment and cover most of the world's continents.

- Some cases pertain to companies operating in the world's biggest markets, such as India and China. Two new cases deal with Tata Motors in India, providing valuable insights into the Indian markets and the emergence of this potential world competitor.

- Cases include companies in the Czech Republic and Poland to reflect the challenges faced as these countries transition to market-based economies.

- Cases on Asian economies, such as South Korea and Japan, illustrate some of the difficulties encountered as these countries deal with an environment that is counter to collectivist values.

- The case on Kimberly-Clark in Latin American illustrates some of the unique challenges multinationals experience in this region of the world.

- Other cases, such as Google in China and Alibaba versus Yahoo, reflect some of the challenges and the opportunities of e-commerce strategies.

- Many new cases on international ethics and corporate social responsibility (e.g., Yahoo and Customer Privacy, Procter and Gamble and Safe Drinking Water, Shell in Nigeria, Micro-credit in Armenia) have been added to reflect the increasingly crucial importance of this area.

- Case material on Europe and Canada show that these places also represent particular difficulties for multinationals.

New Topical Areas

All chapters include the latest developments in the international management field.

- ***Chapter 1—Multinational Management in a Changing World*** has been thoroughly updated to reflect the latest trends in the field. A significant emphasis in the chapter pertains to the emergence of powerful new competitors from emerging markets. The chapter details the reasons why these new competitors are emerging and how they are drastically influencing strategies of the well-established multinationals.

- ***Chapter 2—Culture and Multinational Management*** has been updated and remains one of the most balanced presentations of culture, including the popular Hofstede framework and the most recent GLOBE framework. Readers are also alerted to the dangers of relying too much on culture.

- ***Chapter 3—The Institutional Context of Multinational Management*** has been updated and now emphasizes important information on social inequality and its impact on multinational management.

- ***Chapter 6—Multinational and Participation Strategies: Content and Formulation*** now emphasizes the section on political risk and what companies can do to mitigate it. The chapter includes more discussion of the new emerging market competitors.

- ***Chapter 8—Organizational Designs for Multinational Companies*** continues the extensive discussion of knowledge management, adding a timely and interesting topic to the traditional discussion of multinational organizational structures. This reflects the growing importance to multinationals of knowledge management systems.

- ***Chapter 10—Multinational E-Commerce: Strategies and Structures*** is included in this fifth edition making it one of the only texts with a chapter on this important topic. More detail is now provided on the growing importance of multinational e-commerce security and the many aspects of IT security.

- ***Chapters 11 and 12—International Human Resource Management*** continues the strong tradition of considering human resource management issues for both expatriates and other employees. Special emphasis is placed on emerging markets and the more sustained difficulty of finding and retaining qualified workers.

- ***Chapter 15—Leadership and Management Behavior in Multinational Companies*** continues the examination of leadership in a global context and integrates the latest GLOBE research on leadership in over 60 nations.

Current Data

All chapters have been updated to include the latest research, examples, and statistics in multinational management, creating the most accurate and current presentation possible:

- Current multinational management examples in the Case in Point and other chapter features, including Multinational Management Briefs, Multinational Management Challenges, and Multinational Management Skill Builders.

- Updated tables and figures using recent findings on multinational leadership from *GLOBE: The Global Leadership and Organizational Behavior Effectiveness Research Program.*

- Updated tables and figures using recent findings on organizational behavior issues from the *World Values Survey* and the *International Social Survey Program.*

- Updated tables and figures using recent publications from the latest World Bank's *World Trade Report*, other critical information from the United Nations Conference on Trade and Development (UNCTAD), and the United Nation's *World Investment Report.*

- Prepublication information from the authors' own research on the effects of social institutions on work values and international recruiting.

- A large selection of new cases.

Pedagogical Approach

In addition to providing a thorough review and analysis of multinational management, *Multinational Management: A Strategic Approach*, fifth edition, includes several unique pedagogical learning tools:

- ***Strategic viewpoint:*** This viewpoint provides a unifying theme that guides the reader through the material. It highlights for students the process that multinational companies engage in when deciding to compete in the global economy and the management consequences of these strategic choices.

- ***Comparative management issues:*** Multinational managers must understand the strengths, weaknesses, and strategies of competitors from anywhere in the world. In addition, they must know when and how to adapt their organizational practices to accommodate local situations. Where applicable, the comparative sections of the text assist students in understanding the complexities of the cultures and business practices of other nations.

- **_Review of management principles:_** The text contains several chapters that assume some background knowledge in management, specifically strategic management, organizational design, human resource management, and organizational behavior. For students with limited previous coursework in management, or for those who need a review, each chapter provides background primers with brief explanations of key concepts and ideas.

- **_Small business and entrepreneurship applications:_** Unlike most international management texts, this book explains the multinational activities of small businesses. An entire chapter focuses specifically on the problems and prospects for entrepreneurs and small businesses looking to become multinational competitors.

- **_Application based:_** Each chapter gives the learner three different opportunities to apply the knowledge gained from reading the chapter: Multinational Management Skill Builders, chapter Internet Activities (located on the book Web site, www.cengage.com/management/cullen), and end-of-chapter cases. These exercises simulate the challenges that practicing multinational managers encounter on the job.

Key Features

- **_Chapter Cases and Multinational Management Skill Builders:_** End-of-chapter projects include cases and activities, which give the learner the opportunity to apply the text material to real-life managerial problems.

- **_Integrating Cases:_** Each major section offers at least one full-length case that requires the integration of material from all preceding chapters. These cases were chosen to challenge the reader with the complexities of the global environment.

- **_Extensive examples:_** Throughout the text, many examples enhance the text material by showing actual multinational management situations. These examples are illustrated in six different formats:

  - *Preview Case in Point:* These brief cases open each chapter and focus the reader's interest on the chapter content.

  - *Focus on Emerging Markets:* This edition strengthens a feature that was introduced in the fourth edition and that focuses on the growing importance of the BRIC emerging markets in Asia, Latin America, and Europe. Each chapter discusses the many opportunities and threats presented by emerging markets in the context of the chapter. Furthermore, many of these examples emphasize the two dominant emerging markets, India and China.

  - *Case in Point:* These real-life examples of multinational companies discuss relevant topics in each chapter.

  - *Multinational Management Challenge:* These cases explore challenging situations faced by multinational managers in actual companies and situations.

  - *Multinational Management Brief:* Brief examples elaborate on an issue discussed in the text.

- *Comparative Management Brief:* These examples show how a unique cultural or social institutional setting can influence management decisions.
- **Models as examples:** The authors created numerous models to act as visual aids for students as they study key principles.
- **Learning aids:** The Multinational Management Electronic Study Tools for students, product support Web site, and supporting video make learning easy and fun while exposing the learner to the complex issues of multinational management. In addition, included on the product support Web site are Internet Activities that challenge students to use Internet resources in locating international business information. The Web site also contains an extensive selection of Internet links to resources and information that are updated regularly.

Contents

The text is structured into five major parts. Part One is divided into four chapters: three introductory chapters that provide essential background on the nature of multinational management and a fourth on international ethics. These chapters address the challenges facing managers in the new global economy, how national cultures affect management, the institutional context of multinational companies, and the ethical challenges these firms encounter.

Part Two includes three chapters that review how multinational companies formulate successful strategies to compete internationally. Chapter 5 provides a broad overview of strategic management with global implications. Chapter 6 focuses on the strategies required to "go international." Chapter 7 applies the concepts from the previous two chapters to the unique problems faced by small, entrepreneurial organizations.

Part Three addresses the management systems used to implement multinational strategies. Specifically, Chapter 8 considers how multinational companies design and structure their organizations to implement their strategies. Chapter 9 examines the management and design issues involved in building global strategic alliances. Chapter 10 considers how companies can use e-commerce in multinational operations.

Part Four contains two chapters dealing with the human resource management issues related to implementing strategy. Topics considered include international human resource practices and the adaptation of these practices across cultures.

Finally, Part Five continues to examine strategy implementation at the level of the individual in the organization. Chapters consider international negotiation and cross-cultural communication, motivating people in different nations, and leadership challenges in multinational companies.

Ancillary Materials

Multinational Management: A Strategic Approach, fifth edition, offers a highly intensive learning and teaching package of ancillary tools for both students and instructors. These supplements give students and instructors many options for learning and teaching.

For Instructors

- ***Instructor's Manual:*** The Instructor's Manual offers instructional materials, case solutions, and questions. For this fifth edition, we continue to provide case solutions for each chapter in a consistent format. Instructors are provided with a list of suggested questions and solutions, along with a synopsis and case objectives that show the academic value of each case.
- ***PowerPoint® Slide Presentations:*** The authors have created more than 450 slides illustrating the concepts of each chapter.
- ***ExamView:*** ExamView Computerized Testing Software, located on the Instructor's Resource CD-ROM, contains all of the questions in the test bank, which are available on the instructor's companion Web site. This program is an easy-to-use test creation software, compatible with Microsoft Windows. Instructors can add or edit questions, instructions, and answers, and select questions by previewing them on the screen, selecting them randomly, or selecting them by number.
- ***Instructor's Resource CD-ROM:*** This CD-ROM includes the key instructor support materials—Instructor's Manual, ExamView Test Bank, and PowerPoint® Slides—and provides instructors with a comprehensive capability for customizing lectures and presentations.
- ***Web Sites:*** Visitors to the Web site (www.cengage.com/management/ cullen) will find these teaching ancillaries available for download in the password-protected Instructor Resources section. The student companion Web site provides key instructional materials, and a Premium Web site for students features additional Internet-based learning activities related to international business for each chapter.
- ***DVD:*** The DVD to accompany *Multinational Management: A Strategic Approach,* fifth edition, offers video clips featuring real-world companies and illustrating the international business concepts outlined in the text. Focusing on both small and large businesses, the video clips help students apply the theories presented in the book to actual situations and issues that global corporations face. A set of video case-based discussion questions and answers are included in the Instructor's Manual.

For Students

- ***SSO Premium Web Site:*** The SSO Premium Web site features valuable learning aids, such as online games and self-evaluation quizzes, tied to each chapter.
- ***Student Companion Web Site:*** The student companion Web site— available to all students—offers essential learning tools, such as learning objectives and flash cards.
- ***World Map:*** Included inside the text cover is a full-color world map.

Acknowledgments

Most of all, we must thank our families for giving us the time and quiet to accomplish this task. Numerous individuals helped make this book possible. Jean Johnson, professor of marketing at the Amsterdam Business School, an experienced internationalist and John's wife read and commented on all chapters. Her insights were invaluable, as was her suggestion to organize the book around the strategic management perspective. Kyong Pyun, Praveen's wife, was very patient during the revision process. She stayed calm and collected as Praveen worked on two different text projects. Praveen's eight-year-old daughter, Alisha, continues to be fascinated with the text revision. However, she now no longer wants to be a professor and would rather work as a vet. Davin continues to bother the family, typical of three-year-old boys!

This text would not be possible without the support of a team of professionals at Cengage Learning. Our initial thanks go to John Szilagyi, former executive editor of South-Western's management list, who encouraged us to write earlier editions of this book, as well as Senior Acquisitions Editor Michele Rhoades. The commitment of the marketing staff, including Clinton Kernen and Sarah Rose, make possible the continued success of this book. Developmental Editor Jennifer King worked diligently and with patient tact to keep us on track. Our thanks also go to the numerous other professionals who made this text possible, including Media Editor Danny Bolan and Art Director Tippy McIntosh. We also appreciate the hard work of individuals involved on the production side, particularly Senior Content Project Manager Kim Kusnerak.

Several colleagues who read and offered insightful comments on this and previous editions include the following:

Len J. Trevino, *Washington State University*

William Y. Jiang, *San Jose State University*

Manjula Salimath, PhD, *University of North Texas*

Carol Sanchez, *Grand Valley State University*

Raffaele DeVito, *Emporia State University*

David F. Martin, *Murray State University*

Anthony J. Avallone Jr., *Point Loma Nazarene University*

Gerry N. Muuka, *Murray State University*

Maru Etta-Nkwelle, *Howard University*

Gary Baker, *Buena Vista University*

Douglas M. Kline, *Sam Houston State University*

Michael J. Pisani, *Texas A&M International University*

Tracy A. Thompson, *University of Washington, Tacoma*

Bonita Barger, *Tennessee Technological University*

Dave Flynn, *Hofstra University*

Songpol Kulviwat, *Hofstra University*

Joan C. Hubbard, *University of North Texas*

Manisha Singal, *Virginia Tech*

Mike Giambattista, *University of Washington*

Kamala Gollakota, *University of South Dakota*

Stephen Jenner, *California State University, Dominguez Hills*

John A. Kilpatrick, *Idaho State University*

Richard Lovacek, *North Central College*

Scott L. Boyar, *University of South Alabama*

Carl R. Broadhurst, *Campbell University*

Linda L. Blodgett, *Indiana University South Bend*

Joseph Peyrefitte, *University of Southern Mississippi*

Lawrence A. Beer, *Arizona State University*

Janet S. Adams, *Kennesaw State University*

The following authors deserve special recognition for contributing their cases to this book: Thomas A. Fruscello and Jenny Mead: Yahoo! and Customer Privacy; Krystyna Joanna Zaleska: Organizational and National Cultures in a Polish/U.S. Joint Venture; Prahar Shah: Google in China; Klaus Meyer: Ethics of Offshoring: Novo Nordisk and Clinical Trials in Emerging Economies; Isaiah A. Litvak: Royal Dutch Shell in Nigeria: Operating in a Fragile State; Laura P. Hartman, Justin Sheehan, and Jenny Mead: Procter & Gamble: Children's Safe Drinking Water; James W. Bronson and Graham Beaver: Harley-Davidson and the International Market for Luxury Goods; Rua-Huan Tsaih and Darren Meister: Polaris 2008; Marlene Reed: AREGAK Micro-Credit Organization in Armenia; Prashant Salwan: Tata Motors; Marlene Reed and Rochelle R. Brunson: The Fleet Sheet; Mikolaj Jan Piskorski and Alessandro L. Spadini: Procter & Gamble: Organization 2005; Jordan Mitchell and Brian Hohl: Fiat's Strategic Alliance with Tata; Katherine Xin, Winter Nie, and Vladimir Pucik: Alibaba versus eBay: Competing in the Chinese C2C Market; Sonia Ferencikova: Transition at Whirlpool Tatramat: From Joint Venture to Acquisition; Sandeep Krisnamurthy: The Failure of Boo.com; Gareth Evans: The Road to Hell; Preeti Goyal: People Management, The Mantra for Success: The Case of Singhania and Partners; Debi S. Saini: People Management Fiasco in Honda Motorcycles and Scooters India Ltd.; Markus Pudelko, Brian Stewart, Sally Stewart, and Xunyi Xu: Cross-Cultural Negotiation: Americans Negotiating a Contract in China; Brian J. Hall and Nicole S. Bennett: Insulting Andrew; Asianweek.com and Sang-Hun Choe: Old Corporate Ways Fade as New Korean Generation Asserts Itself; Stephen Ko: Cheung Yan: China's Paper Queen; Megan Anderson: Kimberly-Clark Andean Region: Creating a Winning Culture

John B. Cullen
K. Praveen Parboteeah

John B. Cullen

John Cullen is professor of strategy at the Amsterdam Business School, where he teaches courses on international management, organizational theory, strategic management, and business ethics. He has also taught on the faculties of Washington State University, the University of Nebraska, the University of Rhode Island, Waseda and Keio Universities in Japan (as a Fulbright lecturer), and the Catholic University of Lille in France. He received his PhD from Columbia University. He consults regularly with U.S. and Japanese organizations regarding international strategic alliances and the management of ethical behavior.

Professor Cullen is the author or coauthor of four books and over 60 journal articles, which have appeared in journals such as *Administrative Science Quarterly, Journal of International Business Studies, Academy of Management Journal, Organization Science, Journal of Management, Organizational Studies, Management International Review, Journal of Vocational Behavior, American Journal of Sociology, Organizational Dynamics, Journal of Business Ethics,* and the *Journal of World Business.* He also has given over 100 presentations at national and regional meetings. His major research interests include the effects of national culture and social institutions on managers and workers, the management of trust and commitment in international strategic alliances, ethical climates in multinational organizations, and the dynamics of organizational structure. Professor Cullen serves or has served on various editorial boards including the *Academy of Management Journal* and *Advances in International Management* and reviews for major journals in management and international business.

K. Praveen Parboteeah

K. Praveen Parboteeah is professor of international management in the Department of Management, University of Wisconsin–Whitewater. He received his PhD from Washington State University and holds an MBA from California State University–Chico and a BSc (Honors) in management studies from the University of Mauritius.

Parboteeah's research interests include international management, ethics, and technology and innovation management. He has been actively involved in developing alternative models to national culture to explain cross-national differences in individual behaviors. He has published over 25 articles in journals such as the *Academy of Management Journal, Organization Science, Journal of International Business Studies, Decision Sciences, Human Relations, Small Group Research, Journal of Business Ethics, Management International Review, Journal of World Business, Journal of Engineering and Technology Management,* and *Journal of Product Innovation Management.*

Parboteeah has received numerous awards for his research. He was the 2005 Western Academy of Management Ascendant Scholar. He recently won the University of Wisconsin–Whitewater Award for Outstanding Research. He has won the Research Award from the College of Business for four consecutive years.

Parboteeah has been involved in many aspects of international education at the University of Wisconsin–Whitewater. He chaired the International Business Committee, helping create criteria to evaluate strategic alliances with other universities for exchanges. He is the coordinator for exchanges with two French xxviii

universities, namely ESC Rouen and the Burgundy School of Business in Dijon. He has also lectured in many countries, including Mexico, South Korea, Taiwan, Trinidad and Tobago, and the U.K. He now regularly lectures at Germany's leading business school, the Otto Beisheim School of Management, and Sun Yat-Sen University in Taiwan.

Of Indian ancestry, Parboteeah grew up on the African island of Mauritius and speaks English, French, and Creole. He currently lives in Whitewater, Wisconsin, with his South Korean wife Kyong, daughter Alisha, and son Davin.

multinational
management

A Strategic Approach 5e

Foundations of Multinational Management

part one

1 Multinational Management in a Changing World

Preview CASE IN POINT

Emerging Market Multinationals

The latest trend in global business is the rise of new multinationals hailing from emerging markets such as India, China, Brazil, and Russia. These new multinationals are using innovative strategies to compete effectively with their established counterparts from developed countries. Often, these emerging market multinationals use their local markets for testing before deploying their products to Western markets.

Take the cases of companies based in India and South America. In 2008 Tata Motors, one of India's biggest industrial conglomerates, acquired the British automakers Jaguar and Land Rover and began developing cars for these prestigious companies. Furthermore, the firm even launched the Tata Nano, a car that sells for about $2,500. Consider also that the world's leading maker of regional jets is based in Brazil. Embraer, a Brazilian company, has taken advantage of its local engineering experience to innovate at a global level. It now manufactures small, sleek, fast jets for the international market.

Multinationals from developed nations are also paying attention to emerging companies from China and Mexico. For example, Chery International, China's leading car exporter, has plans to build plants in the Middle East, Africa, and Eastern Europe. Cemex, one of the world's largest suppliers of cement, is based in Mexico and has improved on its local business model to go international.

Recent trends also suggest that new multinationals are emerging in Africa. Safaricom, Kenya's most popular mobile phone company, listed its shares on the Nairobi Stock Exchange and was able to raise over $800 million in one of the biggest initial public offerings in sub-Saharan Africa. In fact, Goldman Sachs even recently published a report on Africa's emergence, noting about 500 companies with capitalization over $100 billion. Furthermore, this report excluded trends in South Africa.

The overwhelming agreement among experts is that emerging market countries and their multinationals are expected to become or have already become major players in world trade. As examples, India and China experienced a 6 percent gross domestic product (GDP) growth rate between the beginning of 2009 and the end of March 2009.

Sources: Based on Economist. 2008. *"The new champions." September 20, p. 53;* Economist. 2008. *"The challengers—Emerging market multinationals." January 12, p. 61;* Economist. 2009. *"Not so Nano; Emerging market multinationals." March 28, pp. 20–22;* Economist. 2009. *"Not just straw men." June 20, pp. 63–64.*

A s the examples in the Preview Case in Point show, businesses and individuals, whether from the old or the new economy, increasingly see the entire world as a source of business opportunities. The world is becoming one connected economy in which companies conduct business and compete anywhere and with anyone, regardless of national boundaries. New multinationals with the clout to compete effectively against established multinationals are emerging worldwide. In a global economy, any company or individual from any country can become a competitor. The Internet crosses national boundaries with the click of a mouse, allowing even the smallest businesses to go global immediately. Consequently, companies can no longer afford the luxury of assuming that success in their home markets equates to long-term profitability—or even survival. Furthermore, although the integrated global economy presents challenges and threats such as terrorism, war, and recession, there are significant opportunities for most companies. Consider the next Focus on Emerging Markets.

What does this trend mean to the student of international business? With companies increasingly looking at global rather than domestic markets, managers will have little choice in the future but to be multinational in outlook and strategies. Consequently, all students of business should have at least a basic background in multinational management. **Multinational management** is the formulation of strategies and the design of management systems that successfully take advantage of international opportunities and that respond to international threats. Successful multinational managers are executives with the ability and motivation to meet and beat the challenges of multinational management.

To provide you with a basic background in multinational management, this book introduces you to the latest information on how managers throughout the world respond to the challenges of globalization. You will see how businesses, both large and small, deal with the complexities of national differences in cultures, economies, and political systems. You will learn how multinational managers use their understanding of these national differences to formulate strategies to maximize their companies' success in globalizing industries. But, because having good strategies is not enough to succeed in today's economy, you will learn how multinational managers carry out their global strategies.

To give you insights into the real world of multinational management, you will find several features in this and the following chapters.

- The *Preview Case in Point* shows you examples of how multinational companies deal with a key issue discussed in the chapter.
- *Cases in Point* give information on how actual multinational companies handle other issues raised in the course of the chapter.
- *Multinational Management Briefs* give you further details and examples that extend the discussion.

Multinational management
The formulation of strategies and the design of management systems that successfully take advantage of international opportunities and that respond to international threats.

Growing Opportunities

As mentioned in the Preview Case in Point, emerging markets are providing the base for the development of a new breed of powerful competitors. However, emerging markets also provide established companies with significant opportunities. As of 2009, while much of the developed world reeled from the economic recession, emerging markets were proving able to weather the storm. The ability to grow despite the recession has largely been due to healthy demand in local markets. For example, although car sales in the developed markets fell during the recession, they were predicted to increase by 10 percent in China by 2010. Furthermore, while market shares steadily fell in most developed markets, they rose by over 345 percent in Brazil, by 390 percent in India, and by 639 percent in Russia between November 2001 and September 2008.

Such upward trends are likely to continue. In fact, Goldman Sachs predicts that the global middle class is growing by over 70 million a year and is expected to continue growing. By 2030, it is expected that over two billion people will have joined the middle-class group. Such trends suggest tremendous opportunities for multinationals worldwide.

Sources: Economist. 2008. "The new champions." September 20, p. 53; Economist. 2009. "Not so Nano; Emerging market multinationals." March 28, pp. 20–21.

- *Multinational Management Challenges* describe problems and dilemmas that real multinational managers face and for which there are no easy answers.
- *Comparative Management Briefs* provide examples of management issues that are influenced by a unique cultural or social institutional setting.
- Finally, the *Focus on Emerging Markets* feature reflects the sustained importance of emerging markets in world trade.

Multinational management takes place within the multinational company. What is a multinational company? The next section gives a definition and brief introduction to the major players in multinational competition.

The Nature of the Multinational Company

Multinational company (MNC)
Any company that engages in business functions beyond its domestic borders.

The **multinational company (MNC)** is broadly defined as any company that engages in business functions beyond its domestic borders. This definition includes all types of companies, large and small, that engage in international business. Most multinational companies, however, are multinational corporations; that is, the companies are publicly owned through stocks. Usually, when you see references to MNCs in the popular business press, the reference is to multinational corporations. The largest multinationals are all public corporations.

Exhibit 1.1 lists the top 20 multinational corporations ranked by sales revenue. As the exhibit shows, many of the largest corporations are in the petroleum industry—not surprisingly, given the increase in oil prices in 2008–2009. However, out of the top ten companies, some are automotive companies and big *consumers* of the oil industry. Wal-Mart is the only retailer, and a few of the remaining companies are from the financial and insurance industries.

EXHIBIT 1.1 Largest Companies in the World

Rank	Company	Main Industry	Headquarter's Country	Revenues ($ million)
1	Wal-Mart Stores	Retailing	United States	378,799
2	Exxon Mobil	Petroleum	United States	372,824
3	Royal Dutch Shell	Petroleum	Netherlands	355,782
4	BP	Petroleum	U.K.	291,438
5	Toyota Motor	Automotive	Japan	230,201
6	Chevron	Petroleum	United States	210,783
7	ING Group	Insurance	Netherlands	210,516
8	Total	Petroleum	United States	182,347
9	General Motors	Automotive	United States	182,347
10	ConocoPhilips	Petroleum	United States	178,558
11	Daimler	Automotive	Germany	177,167
12	General Electric	Electronics	United States	176,656
13	Ford Motor	Automotive	United States	176,656
14	Fortis	Insurance	Belgium, Netherlands	164,877
15	AXA	Insurance	France	162,762
16	Sinopec	Petroleum	China	159,620
17	Citigroup	Finance	United States	159,229
18	Volkswagen	Automotive	Germany	149,054
19	Dexia Group	Finance	Belgium	147,648
20	HSBC Holdings	Finance	U.K.	146,500

Source: Adapted from Fortune 2009. *"Fortune Global 500." http://www.fortune.com/fortune/global500.*

Where are most of the global multinationals located? Exhibit 1.2 lists selected countries with higher numbers of Fortune Global 500 companies. As you can see, global multinationals are concentrated not just in major Western cities. Prominent new competitors can be found in countries such as China, South Korea, Brazil, and Mexico. As of 2008, the United States had about 153 global multinationals, with Japan having the next highest number at 64. This exhibit also shows that global companies can be located anywhere in the world and are not confined to European or U.S. cities. Furthermore, the presence of China, Taiwan, and South Korea in the list is evidence of the increased importance of Asia in global trade.

What kinds of business activities might make a company multinational? The most apparent activity, of course, is international sales. When a company produces in its own country and sells in another country, it engages in the simplest form of multinational activity. However, as you will see in much more detail, crossing national borders opens up more options than simply selling internationally.

To introduce some of these options, consider the following hypothetical U.S. company that produces and sells men's shirts. As a domestic-only company, it could buy the dye, make the fabric, cut and sew the garment, and sell the shirt all in the United States. However, the firm might not be able to compete successfully using this approach. The U.S. market may be stagnant, with competitive pricing and decreased profit margins. Competitors might find higher-quality fabric or dye from overseas suppliers. Competitors might find lower production costs in low-wage countries, allowing them to offer lower prices. What can this company do?

As a multinational company, the firm might sell its shirts to overseas buyers with less competition and at higher prices. Several other multinational activities

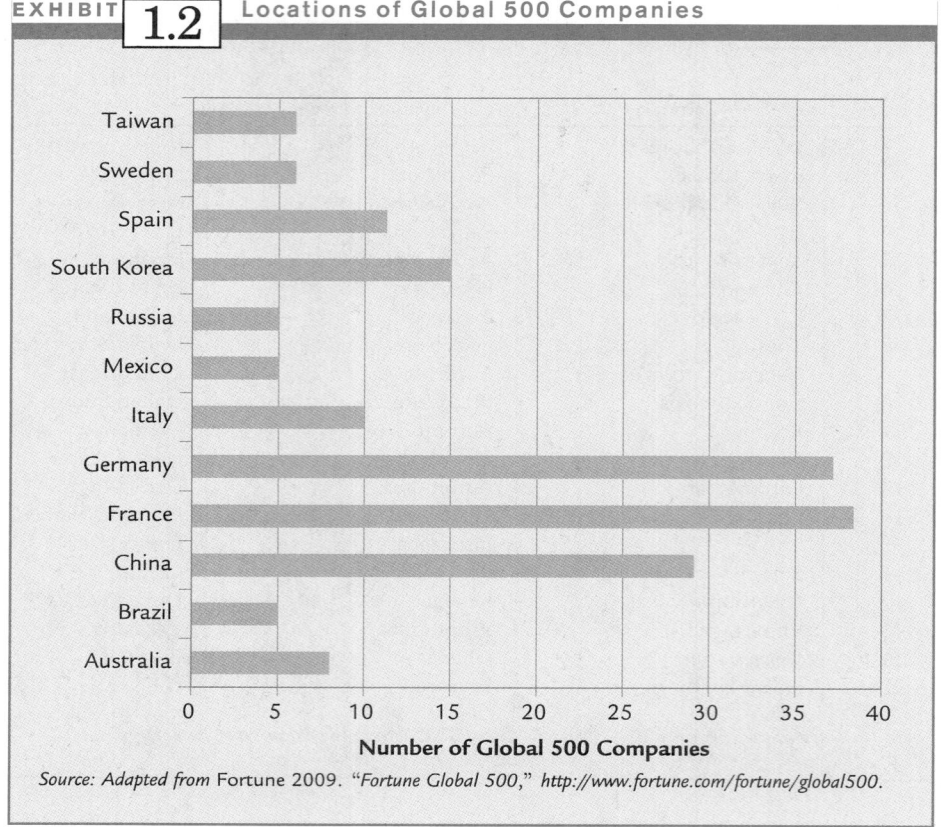

EXHIBIT 1.2   Locations of Global 500 Companies

Source: Adapted from Fortune 2009. *"Fortune Global 500," http://www.fortune.com/fortune/global500.*

might also increase its competitive strength. For example, the shirtmaker might locate any of the steps in obtaining raw materials or completing production in another country. It might buy the highest-quality dye from Italy, use low-cost, high-quality fabric producers in Hong Kong, and have the cutting and sewing done in Vietnam with its very low labor costs. For any of these steps, the company might contract with local companies in another country, or it may own its own factories in the other country. As you will see in later chapters, multinational companies must develop strategies and systems to accomplish all or some of the multinational business tasks of this hypothetical U.S. firm.

Next, we will consider the forces that drive the new economic reality that faces the next generation of multinational managers and multinational companies.

The Globalizing Economy: A Changing (but Not Always Stable) Environment for Business

Trade barriers are falling, and, in the first decade of this century, world trade among countries in goods and services has grown faster than domestic production. Money is flowing more freely across national borders, allowing companies to seek the best rates for financing—and allowing investors to look for the best returns—anywhere in the world. All these processes represent a trend known as **globalization**, which is the trend of the world's economies to become borderless and interlinked. Companies are no longer limited by their domestic boundaries and may conduct any kind of business activity anywhere in the world. Globalization means that companies are more likely to compete anywhere, source their raw material or research and development (R&D) anywhere, and produce their products anywhere.

Globalization, however, is not a uniform evolutionary process, and not all economies of the world are benefiting or participating equally in it. Terrorism, wars, and, at times, a worldwide economic stagnation have limited or in some cases even reversed some aspects of globalization. Additionally, globalization is producing such worrisome effects as natural resource scarcity, environmental pollution, negative social impacts, and increased interdependence of the world's economies.[1] Furthermore, some even argue that globalization is widening the gap between rich and poor countries.

However, others see globalization as beneficial to the world's economies. For instance, globalization is resulting in lower prices in many countries as multinationals become more efficient. Lower prices give consumers more for their money while encouraging local productivity through competition.[2] Furthermore, globalization is clearly benefiting many emerging markets such as India and China because these countries enjoy greater availability of jobs and better access to technology. Globalization has been the major reason why many new companies from countries such as Mexico, Brazil, China, India, and South Korea are among the new dominant global competitors.

Several key trends drive the globalization of the world economy and, in turn—even with shakeups to the world economy—force businesses to become more multinational to survive and prosper. Some of the most important trends include falling borders, growing cross-border trade and investment, the rise of global products and global customers, the growing use of the Internet and sophisticated information technology (IT), privatizations of formerly government-owned companies, the emergence of new competitors in the world market, and the rise of global standards for quality and production.

Before discussing the key globalization trends that affect multinational managers and their companies, it is useful to look at some commonly used classifications of the world's countries. The classifications roughly indicate a country's GDP and its growth in GDP. The classifications are not exact, but they simplify discussions of world trade and investments.

Countries of the World: The Arrived, the Coming, and the Struggling

Exhibit 1.3 shows some divisions of the world's economies based roughly on classifications used by the United Nations and *The Economist*. **Developed countries** have mature economies with substantial per-capita GDPs and international trade and investments. **Developing countries**, such as Hong Kong, Singapore, South Korea, and Taiwan, have economies that have grown extensively over the past two decades yet have sometimes struggled, especially during the setbacks of the Asian crisis in the late 1990s. Other developing economies to watch are what the UN calls the **transition economies** of Central and Eastern Europe, such as the Czech Republic, Hungary, Poland, and Russia. Transition economies are countries that have changed from government-controlled, mostly Communist economic systems to free market or capitalistic systems. The former systems relied on state-controlled organizations and centralized government control to

Globalization
The worldwide trend of cross-border economic integration that allows businesses to expand beyond their domestic boundaries.

Developed countries
Countries with mature economies, high GDPs, and high levels of trade and investment.

Developing countries
Countries with economies that have grown extensively in the past two decades.

Transition economies
Countries in the process of changing from government-controlled economic systems to capitalistic systems.

EXHIBIT **1.3**   **Selected Economies of the World**

Developed Economies	Developing Economies	Transition Economies	Emerging Markets
Australia	Hong Kong	Czech Republic	Argentina
Austria	Singapore	Hungary	Brazil
Belgium	South Korea	Poland	China
Britain	Taiwan	Russia	Chile
Canada	Malaysia		Colombia
Denmark	Indonesia		India
France	Thailand		Mexico
Germany			Philippines
Italy			South Africa
Ireland			Turkey
Japan			Venezuela
Netherlands			
Spain			
Sweden			
Switzerland			
United States			

Sources: Adapted from Economist. 2003. *"Markets and data, weekly indicators." http://www.economist.com, June 7;* Economist. 2006. *"Emerging markets and interest rates." August 5, p. 65;* Economist. 2009. *"Not so Nano; Emerging market multinationals." March 28, pp. 20–21.*

run the economy. In the transition to free market and capitalistic systems, many government-owned companies were converted to private ownership. From that point, the market, not the government, determined the success of companies. Several of these transition economies, such as Hungary, Poland, Slovakia, and the Czech Republic, have developed market economies and are now members of the European Union (EU).

Finally, **emerging markets** are currently between developed and developing countries and are rapidly growing. Although it is difficult to determine the exact list of emerging markets, prominent countries such as India, China, Brazil, and Russia are considered to be emerging. Furthermore, some of the emerging markets also show up on the transition economies list.

The term *emerging markets,* coined by the World Bank around 25 years ago, represents markets that present tremendous opportunities for all multinationals.[3] In fact, emerging markets have about five-sixths of the world's population with only half of the output. Furthermore, the purchasing power in many emerging markets has been increasing steadily. It is therefore not surprising to see that emerging markets now account for 30 percent of exports compared to only 20 percent in 1970. Recent trends also show that developed countries' trade with emerging markets has been growing twice as much compared to trade with each other.[4]

Less developed countries (LDCs) have yet to show much progress in the evolving global economy. They are the poorest nations and are often plagued with unstable political regimes, high unemployment, and unskilled workers. Most of these countries are located in Central and South America, Africa, and the Middle East. However, recent trends suggest that LCDs are experiencing significant growth in their share of world trade, with sharp increases in 2006–2009.[5] Furthermore, developed country markets are becoming less

Emerging markets
Countries that are currently between developed and developing countries and are rapidly growing.

Less developed countries (LDCs)
The poorest nations, often plagued with unstable political regimes, high unemployment, and low worker skills.

important to LCDs for exports. China has been very aggressive in promoting trade with LCDs and now accounts for one-third of all exports from LCDs.

With this overview of the major economies of the world, we can now look more closely at the driving forces of the new world economy. Exhibit 1.4 illustrates these important forces. Each of these driving forces will be discussed.

Disintegrating Borders: The World Trade Organization and Free Trade Areas

In 1947, several nations began negotiating to limit worldwide tariffs and encourage free trade. At that time, worldwide tariffs averaged 45 percent. Seven rounds of tariff negotiations reduced the average worldwide tariffs on manufactured goods from 45 percent to less than 7 percent. These negotiations were known as the **General Agreement on Tariffs and Trade (GATT)**.

Negotiations in Uruguay began in 1986 and ended in 1993 with agreements to reduce tariffs even further, to liberalize trade in agriculture and services, and to eliminate some nontariff barriers to international trade, such as excessive use of health regulations to keep out imports.[6] The Uruguay talks also established the **World Trade Organization (WTO)** to succeed GATT. The WTO provides a formal structure for continued negotiations and for settling trade disputes

General Agreement on Tariffs and Trade (GATT) Tariff negotiations among several nations that reduced the average worldwide tariff on manufactured goods.

World Trade Organization (WTO) A formal structure for continued negotiations to reduce trade barriers and a mechanism for settling trade disputes.

EXHIBIT 1.4   The Globalizing Economy

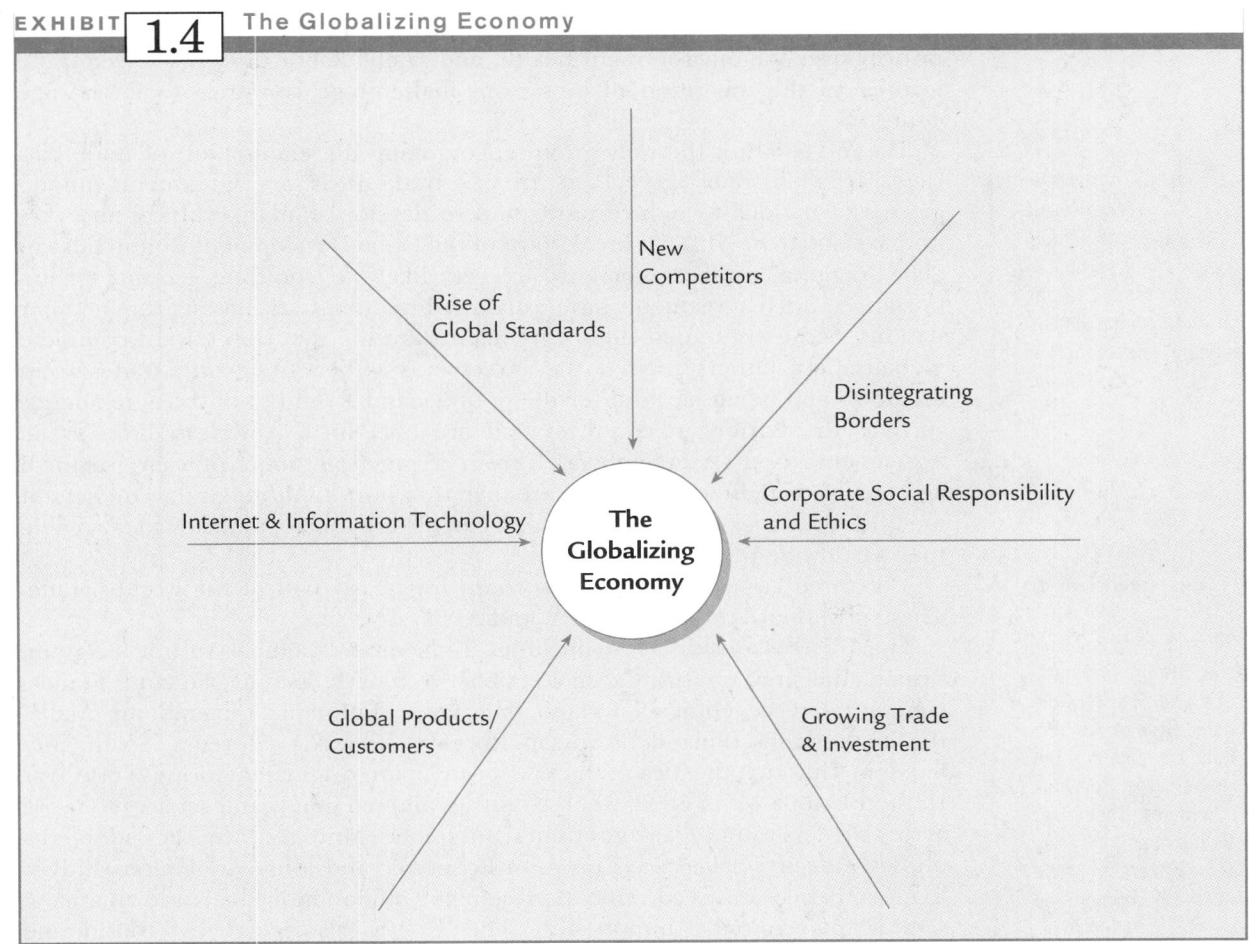

among nations. There are now more than 150 nations in the WTO, up from 92 when the 1986 GATT talks began, including 29 of the UN-classified least developed countries. Thirty other countries, including Russia, seek WTO membership. Since 1995, tariffs on industrial products have fallen from an average of 6.3 percent to 3.8 percent.[7]

In March 1997, trade ministers from countries representing 92 percent of world trade in IT products agreed to end tariffs on trade in software, computer chips, telecommunications equipment, and computers by the year 2005. The immediate result was that, with tariffs eliminated, high-tech exports to Europe from Asia and the United States doubled. Developing countries, even those not party to the agreement, also benefited as prices began to go down on products, such as phones, faxes, and computers, produced in tariff-free locations.[8]

Is free trade working? The WTO thinks so, and the data seems to support its conclusion. Since the early GATT agreements, world trade has grown at more than four times the output of the world's gross domestic product. This suggests that the world's economies are increasingly more intertwined and mutually stimulated.

There are, however, critics. Some argue that the WTO favors the developed nations because it is more difficult for poorer nations to compete in a non-regulated world. Environmentalists note that free trade encourages large multinational companies to move environmentally damaging production to poorer and often environmentally sensitive countries; that is, commercial interests have priority over the environment, health, and safety. Labor unions see free trade leading to the migration of jobs from higher-wage countries to lower-wage countries.

The WTO is not the only group encouraging the elimination of trade barriers. **Regional trade agreements**, or free trade areas, are agreements among groups of nations to reduce tariffs and to develop similar technical and economic standards. With the breakdown of the Doha Development Round talks in 2008, regional trade agreements are very likely to continue growing in importance.[9] Such agreements have usually led to more trade among the member nations. Some argue that these agreements are the first step toward complete globalization. Others criticize the agreements as benefiting only trade group members and being harmful for the poorer nations left out of the agreements, such as the Caribbean countries that are not North American Free Trade Agreement (NAFTA) members.[10] From a practical point of view, regional agreements benefit world trade more than they hurt it. Although they do benefit member countries the most, such agreements are more politically manageable than worldwide trade agreements.[11]

The three largest agreements account for nearly half of the world's trade. These groups are the EU, NAFTA, and APEC.

The **EU (European Union)** includes 27 members, namely Austria, Belgium, Britain, Bulgaria, Cyprus, Czech Republic, Denmark, Estonia, Finland, France, Germany, Greece, Hungary, Ireland, Italy, Latvia, Lithuania, Luxembourg, Malta, the Netherlands, Poland, Portugal, Romania, Slovakia, Slovenia, Spain, and Sweden. Although the idea of the European Union originated during World War II, the EU took off in 1992, when countries allowed goods and services to move across borders without customs duties and quotas. More recently, they adopted a unified currency called the European Economic and Monetary Union (EMU). EU member countries currently represent 450 million individuals and an area of significant economic importance. The EU is also currently considering

Regional trade agreements
Agreements among nations in a particular region to reduce tariffs and develop similar technical and economic standards.

European Union (EU)
Austria, Belgium, Bulgaria, Britain, Denmark, Finland, France, Germany, Greece, Ireland, Italy, Luxembourg, the Netherlands, Portugal, Romania, Spain, and Sweden, plus Norway and Switzerland in the related European Free Trade Area.

applications for membership from countries such as Croatia, Macedonia, and Turkey. You can check the current status of the EU at http://europa.eu.

The **North American Free Trade Agreement (NAFTA)** links the United States, Canada, and Mexico in an economic bloc that allows the relatively free exchange of goods and services. After the agreement went into effect in the early 1990s, all three countries saw immediate increases in trade. However, the Mexican economy soon went into a tailspin, with inflation running as high as 45 percent.[12] Emergency loans from the United States helped stabilize the situation, and by 1996 Mexico had paid back the loans—before the due date. The next step for NAFTA may be FTAA, or the Free Trade Area of Americas. This group will include not only the United States, Canada, and Mexico, but also most of the other Caribbean, Central American, and South American nations.

Compared with the EU or NAFTA, the **Asia-Pacific-Economic Cooperation (APEC)** is a loose confederation of 21 nations with less specific agreements on trade facilitation. However, its ultimate goals call for total free trade in the Pacific region by 2020.[13] Some of the major players in APEC include China, the United States, Japan, Taiwan, South Korea, Hong Kong, Australia, Singapore, Thailand, and Malaysia. Exhibit 1.5 shows all the major regional trade agreements and their member countries.

Sell Anywhere, Locate Anywhere: Trade and Foreign Investment Are Growing but Setbacks Are Part of the Challenge

World trade among countries (imports and exports) grew at an average rate of 6.5 percent per year between 1990 and 2000,[14] slowed to 4 percent by 2004, and grew again to 6 percent in 2005.[15] It grew by 8.5 percent in 2006. However, the latest available figures suggest that trade then slowed down because of the economic recession. The deceleration of demand from the United States, Europe, and Japan was a large contributor to the decline (see the WTO Web site for current information).

Exhibit 1.6 shows the leading exporting and importing countries based on data published by the WTO. Note that the combined countries of the EU now lead the United States in exporting. Exhibit 1.6 also shows that nearly half of the more than $5 trillion in world trade takes place among the European Union, the United States, and Japan. This trading group is sometimes called the **TRIAD**. However, China is now in second place in exports and third in imports, and it is rapidly gaining on the TRIAD countries.

A few other trends in world trade are worth noting. First, Brazil, China, and India have seen major surges in world exports; such trends confirm the emerging nature of these economies. Second, China's surge in exports has been among the biggest. Since it joined the World Trade Organization in 2001, China's exports have grown almost fourfold. Third, the number of least developed countries participating in world trade has increased over the past five years. In many least developed economies, the ratio of trade to gross domestic product continues to grow. Finally, the growth of trade in services has surpassed trade in goods for the first time in five years. China and India saw the biggest surges in the growth of commercial services.

Multinational companies not only trade across borders with exports and imports but also build global networks that link R&D, supply, production, and sales units around the globe. The result is that cross-border ownership, called foreign direct investment, is on the rise, more than doubling between 1998 and 2001.[16] **Foreign direct investment (FDI)** occurs when a multinational company from

North American Free Trade Agreement (NAFTA) A multilateral treaty that links the United States, Canada, and Mexico in an economic bloc that allows freer exchange of goods and services.

Asia-Pacific-Economic Cooperation (APEC) A confederation of 19 nations with less specific agreements on trade facilitation in the Pacific region.

TRIAD The world's dominant trading partners: the European Union, the United States, and Japan.

Foreign direct investment (FDI) Multinational firm's ownership, in part or in whole, of an operation in another country.

EXHIBIT 1.5   Regional Trade Agreements around the World

Andean Common Market
- Bolivia
- Colombia
- Ecuador
- Peru
- Venezuela

ASEAN (Association of Southeast Asian Nations)
- Brunei Darussalam
- Cambodia
- Indonesia
- Lao People's Democratic Republic
- Malaysia
- Myanmar
- Philippines
- Singapore
- Thailand
- Vietnam

Baltic Countries
- Estonia
- Latvia
- Lithuania

CEPGL (Economic Community of the Great Lakes Countries)
- Burundi
- Democratic Republic of the Congo
- Rwanda

APEC (Asia-Pacific Economic Cooperation)
- Australia
- Brunei Darussalam
- Canada
- Chile
- China
- Hong Kong, China
- Indonesia
- Japan
- Malaysia
- Mexico
- New Zealand
- Papua New Guinea
- Peru
- Philippines
- Republic of Korea
- Russian Federation
- Singapore
- Taiwan
- Thailand
- United States of America

UEMOA (West African Economic and Monetary Union)
- Benin
- Burkina Faso
- Côte d'Ivoire
- Guinea-Bissau
- Mali
- Niger
- Senegal
- Togo

CARICOM (Caribbean Community)
- Antigua and Barbuda
- Bahamas
- Barbados
- Belize
- Dominica
- Grenada
- Guyana
- Jamaica
- Montserrat
- Saint Kitts and Nevis
- Saint Lucia
- Saint Vincent and the Grenadines
- Suriname
- Trinidad and Tobago

ECO (Economic Cooperation Organization)
- Afghanistan
- Azerbaijan
- Islamic Republic of Iran
- Kazakhstan
- Kyrgyzstan
- Pakistan
- Tajikistan
- Turkey
- Turkmenistan
- Uzbekistan

EU (European Union)
- Austria
- Belgium
- Denmark
- Finland
- France
- Germany
- Greece
- Ireland
- Italy
- Luxembourg
- Netherlands
- Portugal
- Spain
- Sweden
- United Kingdom

UMA (Arab Maghreb Union)
- Algeria
- Libya
- Mauritania
- Morocco
- Tunisia

CIS (Commonwealth of Independent States)
- Armenia
- Azerbaijan
- Belarus
- Georgia
- Kazakhstan
- Kyrgyzstan
- Moldova
- Russian Federation
- Tajikistan
- Turkmenistan
- Ukraine
- Uzbekistan

OECS (Organization of Eastern Caribbean States)
- Anguilla
- Antigua and Barbuda
- British Virgin Islands
- Dominica
- Grenada
- Montserrat
- Saint Kitts and Nevis
- Saint Lucia
- Saint Vincent and the Grenadines

FTAA (Free Trade Area of the Americas)

Antigua and Barbuda, Argentina, Bahamas, Barbados, Belize, Bolivia, Brazil, Canada, Chile, Colombia, Costa Rica, Dominica, Dominican Republic, Ecuador, El Salvador, Grenada, Guatemala, Guyana, Haiti, Honduras, Jamaica, Mexico, Nicaragua, Panama, Paraguay, Peru, Saint Kitts and Nevis, Saint Lucia, Saint Vincent and the Grenadines, Suriname, Trinidad and Tobago, United States of America, Uruguay, Venezuela

GCC (Gulf Cooperation Council)

Bahrain, Kuwait, Oman, Qatar, Saudi Arabia, United Arab Emirates

EU (European Union and Accession Countries)

Member states: Austria, Belgium, Denmark, Finland, France, Germany, Greece, Ireland, Italy, Luxembourg, Netherlands, Portugal, Spain, Sweden, UK

New Member states: Cyprus, Czech Republic, Estonia, Hungary, Latvia, Lithuania, Malta, Poland, Slovakia, Slovenia

Ascension States: Romania, Slovakia, Turkey

ECOWAS (Economic Community of West African States)

Benin, Burkina Faso, Cape Verde, Côte d'Ivoire, Gambia, Ghana, Guinea, Guinea-Bissau, Liberia, Mali, Niger, Nigeria, Senegal, Sierra Leone, Togo

MERCOSUR (Southern Cone Common Market)

Argentina, Brazil, Paraguay, Uruguay

SAARC (South Asian Association for Regional Cooperation)

Bangladesh, Bhutan, India, Maldives, Nepal, Pakistan, Sri Lanka

ECCAS (Economic Community of Central African States)

Angola, Burundi, Cameroon, Central African Republic, Chad, Congo, Democratic Republic of the Congo, Equatorial Guinea, Gabon, Rwanda, Sao Tome and Principe

Source: Adapted from UNCTAD (UN Conference on Trade and Development). 2003. "Prospects for global and regional FDI inflows, UNCTAD's worldwide survey of investment promotion agencies." Research Note, May 14.

EXHIBIT **1.6**

Who's Selling, Who's Buying: The World's Leading Exporters and Importers ($ billion): (a) Exports and (b) Imports

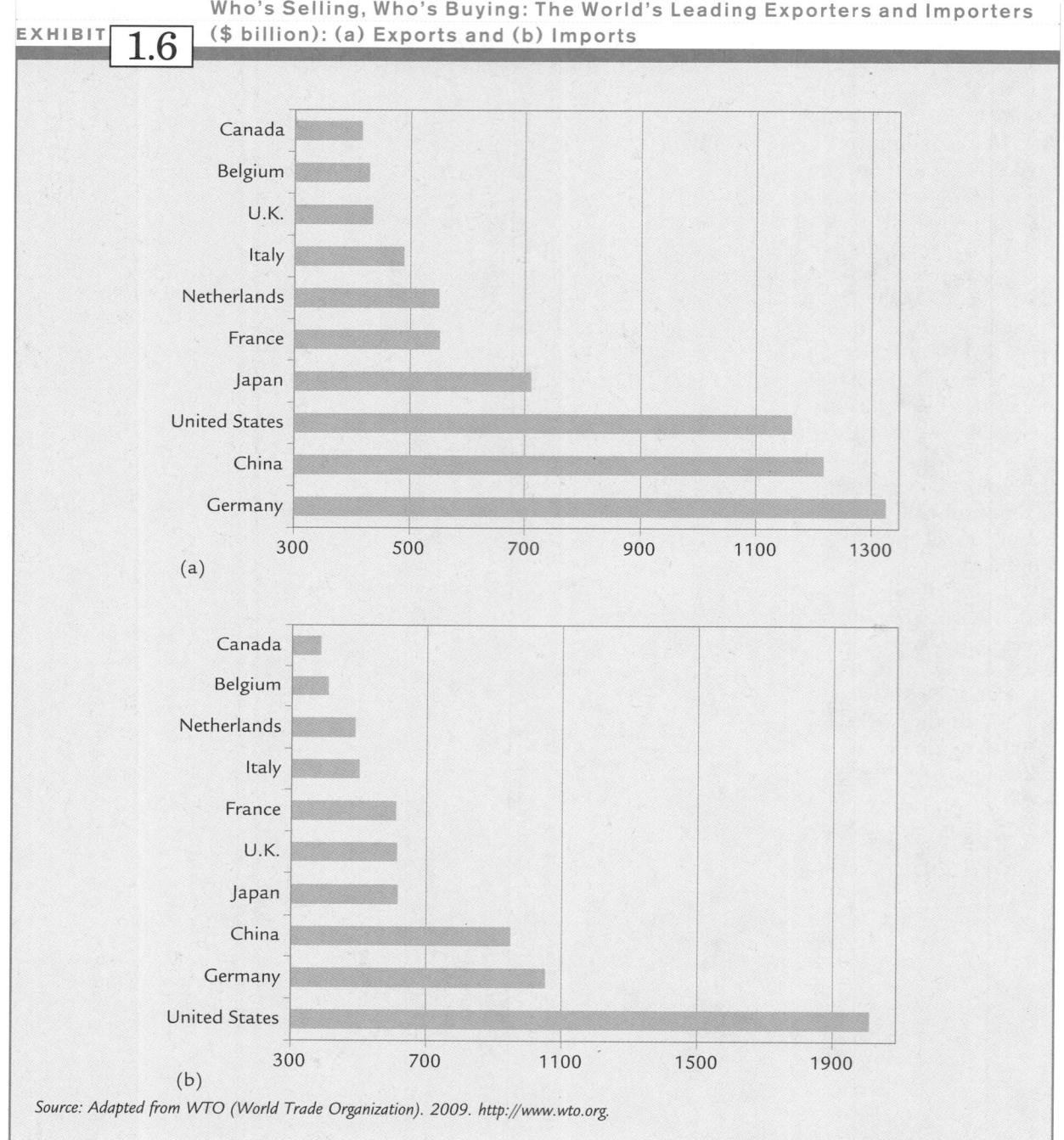

(a)

(b)

Source: Adapted from WTO (World Trade Organization). 2009. http://www.wto.org.

one country has an ownership position in an organizational unit located in another country. Fueled by cross-border mergers and acquisitions, such as the merger of Chrysler and Daimler-Benz, cross-border ownership was especially high in the late 1990s, up to the year 2000.

Foreign direct investment soared by more than 36 percent between 1996 and 2000 and reached a record of more than $1.5 trillion in 2000.[17] Following a pattern similar to international trade, however, FDI declined to $735 billion in

2001, less than half of the previous year, and declined another 25 percent in 2002. The global environment for FDI seems to be declining significantly. According to the 2008 statistics provided by the Organization for Economic Co-operation and Development Web site, countries in the OECD group saw declines in foreign direct investment for both incoming investment (35 percent) and outgoing investment (19 percent). Furthermore, projections suggested that these trends would accelerate in 2010.

Another important indicator of FDI is the extent of mergers and acquisitions (M&A), in which the data also reflects a decline. Statistics reported in the OECD Investment Report suggested that the OECD countries would see a decline of almost 60 percent in both inward and outward M&As from the record reached in 2007.

Despite these declines, the importance of emerging markets is reflected in the growth of FDI in these economies. Exhibit 1.7 shows the percentage change of FDI in a few selected OECD developed countries. As you can see, some economies, such as Greece, Hungary, and Portugal, saw increases in incoming FDI. Most importantly, the OECD predicts that cross-border M&A in the emerging economies, such as Brazil, Russia, India, Indonesia, and China, will most likely increase. Furthermore, India and China now account for a large percentage of international investment in other emerging economies. Both countries accounted for 65 percent of all inward international investment into the largest emerging economies.

What does this mean for individual companies? Trends suggest that, despite the slowdown, FDI will probably resume its steady growth and stay steady, with mergers and acquisitions playing an important role in these markets. Perhaps the most important implication is that multinational companies now manufacture and sell anywhere.

Although the TRIAD countries dominate the bulk of world FDI and will continue to do so in the immediate future, astute multinational managers are looking to other areas of the world for future investments. Specifically,

EXHIBIT 1.7

FDI Growth/Decline in Selected Markets (% change 2007–2008)

Country	FDI Inflows	FDI Outflows
Australia	7	113
Canada	–59	30
France	–7	18
Germany	–56	–13
Hungary	17	–50
Iceland	–100	–100
Japan	4	74
Mexico	–20	–88
Poland	–30	–40
Portugal	33	–62
Sweden	83	6
U.K.	–48	–60
United States	16	–17

Sources: Adapted from Organisation for Economic Co-operation and Development. 2009. http://www.oecd.org.

emerging markets will continue to attract significant inflows of FDI. As we will see throughout the text, many countries such as India, China, Brazil, Russia, and others will continue to present tremendous opportunities. However, succeeding in these markets will not be easy. Consider the next Case in Point. Despite these challenges, multinationals will likely continue to invest in these markets, but Western-based multinationals will have to be very creative to succeed and beat local companies. As the Case in Point suggests, a good knowledge of the local market is necessary for any company to succeed. In addition, multinationals will have to develop strategies that local companies cannot easily copy.

Additionally, although developing countries may provide great opportunities for multinational companies, they are also among the most risky locations in the world. We usually think of two types of risks in multinational business: economic and political. As you will see in more detail in Chapter 5, political risk is anything a government might do (or not do) that might adversely affect a company. In extreme circumstances—and now very rarely—governments have expropriated or taken over foreign firms with little or no compensation. More often, though, a government's instability and the uncertainty of its reactions to foreign investment are the most important considerations. Economic risk considers all factors of a nation's economic climate that may affect a foreign investor. Government policies affect some of these factors such as mandating artificially high or low interest rates. Other factors, such as a volatile exchange rate, may respond to economic forces from outside the country.

CASE IN POINT

Succeeding in Emerging Markets

It is not easy to succeed in emerging markets, which often present significant challenges that may discourage the most well-intentioned companies. For instance, the roads in some emerging markets may still be impassable, or local products may be sold at prices well below the cost of production. Other markets have local products with intensely loyal customers. How can multinationals succeed in such markets? A recent study of successful multinationals suggests some common best practices. Successful multinationals:

- *Enter the mass market to achieve economies of scale.* Although multinationals in the past would target only premium segments, it is becoming increasingly evident that the mass market presents significant opportunities.

- *Localize as much as possible.* If companies take the time to understand local market needs, they increase their chance of succeeding. Consider the case of Procter & Gamble and its reformulated toothpaste Crest in fruit and tea flavors with herbal elements. Such localization gives the product a very local flavor.

- *Develop a good-enough mentality.* Rather than focusing on the upscale or low-end target, successful multinationals develop products that are of better quality than those of the low end but not in the premium category. Such products then become more affordable to the local population.

- *Hire local managers rather than expatriates.* Local managers have better knowledge of the local market.

- *Make acquisitions that have strong business fit.* Consider the case of Gillette (owner of Duracell) and its acquisition of Fujian Nanping Nanfu Battery in China. By acquiring the company, Gillette not only acquired its main competitor but also got access to a state-of-the-art manufacturing company and a network of three million retailers.

Source: Based on Shankar, S., C. Ormiston, N. Bloch, R. Schaus, and V. Viswhwanath. 2008. "How to win in emerging markets." MIT Sloan Management Review, 49(3), pp. 19–23.

The Internet and Information Technology Are Making It All Easier

The explosive growth in the Internet, as well as in the capabilities of information technology, increases the multinational company's ability to deal with a global economy. The Internet makes it easy for companies to go global because anyone in the world can access any Web site. Thus, companies and individuals can shop and sell anywhere. Because of the growing importance of e-commerce, Chapter 10 discusses the impact of the Internet on multinational management in detail.

Electronic communication vehicles, such as e-mail and the World Wide Web, allow multinational companies to communicate with company locations around the world, and information technology expands the global reach of an organization. Multinational companies can now monitor worldwide operations to an extent never before possible. Text and graphic information can flow to any part of the world nearly instantaneously. Headquarters, R&D, manufacturing, or sales can be located anywhere there is a computer. Because employees, suppliers, and customers are geographically dispersed, organizations are becoming virtual— linked by networks of computers. Information technology makes it all happen.

Information technology is also spurring a borderless financial market. Investors are going global, and companies of the future will get their financing not in local stock or bond markets but in global markets that seek the best companies worldwide. Consider this *Business Week* comment, which captures the feel of financial markets of the next century:

> *It's January 20, 2015, a fine summer day in Sydney. You stroll up to a Citibank automated-teller machine and, after the eye retina scan log on, a computer in Bombay greets you, and you get down to business. First, you shift 10,000 Euros into today's special—a NAFTA-dollar certificate of deposit issued by GEC Capital in Rome. Equities are looking good, so you punch in an order for 500 shares of Telefonos de Mexico on the New York Stock Exchange. Then, at the press of a button, an account officer in Singapore comes onto the screen to answer your questions about a loan for your factory in Argentina.*[18]

As we will see in Chapter 7, information technologies are allowing small companies to get very easy access to resources worldwide (capital, human resources, and machinery).

Information technologies make available many new tools that facilitate business operations. For instance, Voice-Over-Internet Protocol (VOIP) companies, such as Skype, now allow employees to communicate worldwide at very low costs. WIKI companies allow companies to set up collaborative networks at very low cost. Instant messaging through such services as MSN Messenger and AOL also allow employees to stay in constant communication. Finally, increasingly sophisticated search engines like Google allow anyone to find crucial information. Many small companies typically use such searches to find suppliers or manufacturers in emerging markets, such as India or China.

Information technology is thus presenting multinationals with many new opportunities. Consider the next Multinational Management Brief.

The use of information technology and the Internet is also speeding up another globalization driver. Because many companies now use the Web to search for suppliers, being a global customer is much easier than it used to be.

The Rise of Global Products and Global Customers

Although large differences still exist among countries in terms of national cultures and political and economic systems, the needs of customers around the

Multinational Management **Brief**

Information Technology Opportunities in India

As more Indian multinationals take advantage of the opportunities presented by IT, multinationals are rushing to provide products and services. Experts predict that Indian companies will spend over Rs 110,000 crores (or roughly $23 billion) for their IT requirements in 2008. Companies like Dell and IBM are seeking ways to gain market share.

Computer maker Dell has recently achieved the $1 billion mark after being in India for only three years. Dell has even gone from a 0 percent to 10 percent market share in the government sector while looking to play an important role in the private sector.

IBM has also been successful in cornering the services market. As more Indian companies and the government start investing in IT to improve their operations, IBM has been in the lead in that segment. The firm has entered into many contracts with large companies in the telecommunication, financial services, and consumer goods sectors, targeting both large and small companies as customers. IBM sees great potential in dealing with small enterprises, bidding for contracts as small as $10,000.

Source: Based on Sachitanand, R., and K. Mitra. 2008. "Giants on the prowl; Foreign information technology giants aren't just dominating the domestic market, they're opening up new segments and setting the agenda for some categories." Business Today, November 2.

world for many products and services are growing more similar. For example, the products offered by fast-food chains like McDonald's, aircraft manufacturers like Boeing, and automakers like Toyota are quite similar and successful no matter where they are sold in the world. In industries where customers' needs are similar across national boundaries, global competition is more likely.[19]

Along with the rise of worldwide customer needs, a new type of customer is increasingly common: the global customer. Global customers search the world for their supplies without regard for national boundaries. Price and quality affect the purchase decision more than nationality. At present, most global customers are companies making industrial purchases. This explains why 70 percent of the global e-commerce comes from business-to-business transactions. However, with the globalization of mail order businesses and the increased use of Web stores for purchasing consumer goods, including everything from athletic equipment to PCs, soon anyone can be a global customer.

Similar customer needs and globally minded customers link economies because companies can produce one product for everybody, and anyone can buy anything from anywhere. These trends will continue as developing nations become more than sources of cheap production and turn into the areas of the greatest consumer growth.

New Competitors Are Emerging

The free market reforms in emerging countries are creating a potential group of new competitors around the world. As you have seen in this chapter, experts now recognize the existence of powerful emerging market competitors that are using many new techniques and strategies to compete successfully in their local markets. In many cases, these new competitors had to survive brutal competition in their domestic markets to become successful. By competing every day with both domestic rivals and Western multinationals, they were able to develop strategies to generate profits at very low prices. How do these competitors survive? Consider the next Case in Point.

C A S E   I N   P O I N T

Emerging Market Competitors

Although emerging markets present tremendous opportunities to multinationals, succeeding in these markets is not easy. Many local companies have been able to successfully fend off competition from larger, better established multinationals. In Brazil, for example, Grupo Positivo has a larger market share of the PC market than either HP or Dell. In China, many local companies are excelling. For instance, the use of the local search engine Baidu exceeds Google by a large margin. In Mexico, Grupo Elektra has formed one of the largest retailers, and they are trying to fend off Wal-Mart.

Why are these local companies so successful? Experts suggest a number of reasons.

- First, local companies often have better knowledge of the local market and can thus customize their products to satisfy local needs. For instance, Tencent is the market leader in China for Internet services because it figured out that the Chinese prefer instant messaging over e-mails. It has 70 to 80 percent of the instant messaging market because of its free messenger and its "cute" penguin mascot, which appeals to young users.

- Second, local companies are able to develop business models to surmount local challenges. For instance, many of the major videogame companies such as Microsoft have not really succeeded in

China because of software piracy. However, a local company developed an online multiplayer system that makes software piracy irrelevant. Furthermore, it also developed a payment system whereby players can buy prepaid tickets from local merchants.

- Finally, local companies are often more likely to use the latest technologies. Being new means that these local companies are not burdened by previous investments in old technologies. For instance, the Gurajat Cooperative Milk Marketing Federation (GCMMF) is now able to collect 6.5 million liters of fresh milk daily from farmers in almost 13,000 villages in the Indian Western state of Gujarat. Competitors then take the milk to a central facility for fat content analysis and weighing, and farmers have to wait for over a week for payment. GCMMF employees at collection centers, however, can assess fat content and weight within five minutes and pay farmers right away. GCMMF is also taking advantage of the latest satellite technologies to coordinate its operations. Such investments have allowed the company to become a formidable competitor in both urban and rural markets.

Source: Based on Bhattacharya, A., and D. C. Michael. 2008. "How local companies keep multinationals at bay." Harvard Business Review March, pp. 85–95.

Global trade has two important effects in developing new competitors. First, when the large multinationals use developing countries as low-wage platforms for high-tech assembly, they facilitate the transfer of technology. Workers and companies in developing countries often learn new skills when the large multinationals use them for low-cost production and assembly. In countries where the workers are well educated and motivated, the former assemblers often become the creators rather than the builders of advanced technologies. Second, aggressive multinational companies from emerging market countries are also expanding beyond their own borders.

The Rise of Global Standards

Increasingly, especially in technical industries, global product standards are common. For example, you can buy a AA battery anywhere in the world, and it will fit into your flashlight. A driving factor is that, when a product standard is accepted globally or regionally, companies can make one or only a few versions of a product for the world market. This is much cheaper than making 100 different versions for 100 different countries. Component makers also benefit because they can take advantage of the same efficiencies with fewer product designs.

Certainly there are still many diverse technical standards throughout the world. For example, Europe and North America have different formats for TVs and VCRs. Differences in electrical currents and plugs are common examples of difficulties that international travelers face. However, many electronic devices are now smart enough to overcome these differences. Power sources for computers, for example, often can adjust automatically for differences in voltage.

As new products are introduced into the world market, there is increasing competitive pressure to save money by developing one product for everyone. Thus, the company that can establish its standard as dominant, either regionally or worldwide, has a tremendous strategic advantage. For example, Motorola of the United States is locked in a fierce competitive battle with Finland's Nokia and Sweden's Ericsson over setting the standard for the next generation of digital cell phone technology.

Consistency in quality also has become a requirement for doing business in many countries. The International Organization for Standardization (ISO) in Geneva, Switzerland, has developed a set of technical standards known originally as ISO 9000 and now called the ISO 9001:2000 series (International Standards Organization 2006). There are also environmental protection standards known as ISO 14000.

> **ISO 9001:2000**
> The current name for the technical and quality standards of the International Organization for Standardization.

> **ISO 14000**
> The current name for the environmental protection standards of the International Organization for Standardization.

In 1992, ISO compliance became part of product safety laws in many European countries. Many large European multinationals, such as Germany's Siemens, now require suppliers to be ISO certified. As a result, in order to do business in the EU, the pressure is increasing for the United States and other countries to adopt ISO quality requirements and standardization.[20]

Complying with global standards has been beneficial to companies. Consider the next Multinational Management Brief.

Corporate Social Responsibility and Business Ethics

Multinationals are facing increased pressure to be socially responsible. Although, because of their size, many multinationals have significant clout and power to influence local governments, these firms are now under the increased

---

Multinational Management **Brief**

Metro Cash and Carry and Process Standardization

Metro Cash and Carry is part of the Metro Group, a German retailer that ranks among the top three in the world. It has operations around the world and is the global market leader in wholesale cash and carry. The retailer is reputed for its ability to deliver fresh meat, fruits, and vegetables around the world. How did it achieve such competence in delivering freshness? An important factor is that the company has strictly standardized procedures with respect to how it deals with its supply chain around the world. At a minimum, Metro's 90,000 employees are required to satisfy strict international professional standards in whatever they are doing. This standardized process has allowed the company to keep all employees, departments, and subsidiaries around the world on the same page.

Source: Dziobaka-Spitzhorn, A. 2006. "From West to East." Performance Improvement, 45(6), pp. 41–47.

scrutiny of both the media and the public. As a result, many multinationals are now very cognizant of the impact of their actions on the societies and countries in which they operate. Such companies need to pay attention to climate change, environmental degradation and pollution, sweatshop conditions, and bribery, to name only a few issues, because ignoring business ethics and corporate social responsibility issues can be perilous. Such multinationals can face significant backlash at home and in the international markets, suffering significant losses in terms of both reputation and finance.

Proactive multinationals are therefore paying strong attention to such issues. Consider the examples in the next Case in Point. As shown there, multinationals are finding ways to become more ethical. This issue is so important we devote an entire chapter (Chapter 4) to understanding business ethics in the global environment.

Other evidence of the importance of business ethics to multinationals is the appearance of rankings on ethics. In that context, Covalence, a Geneva-based

CASE IN POINT

Corporate Social Responsibility and Multinationals

Multinationals worldwide are working hard to implement corporate social responsibility programs to show their approach to how they manage social responsibility and business ethics issues. Consider the following initiatives:

- A British nonprofit organization, Carbon Disclosure Project, is coordinating an important project to help major multinationals curb greenhouse gas emissions. Companies such as Cadbury Schweppes, Dell, Nestlé, Pepsi, Procter & Gamble, and Tesco are working closely with their suppliers to identify sources of carbon emissions in their supply chain. These companies intend then to work together to identify ways to gradually reduce carbon emissions.

- According to a recent climate report, a 2–3° Celsius increase in global temperatures would make water scarce for around 3.2 billion people. The European council therefore established the European Water Directive to start regulating the global water supply. In their latest report, the Ethical Corporation Institute has identified companies such as Rio Tinto, SAB Miller, Coca-Cola, Intel, Johnson & Johnson, and IKEA as leaders in ethical water management. This new ranking will most likely motivate other multinationals to assess their water use.

- Many multinationals are now abandoning tax havens as a way to ward off future government regulation. Most governments have been strong critics of leading multinationals with addresses in tax haven

countries because these companies avoid paying taxes in countries that do not have treaties with the tax havens. For example, in 2008, Accenture changed its location from Bermuda to Dublin.

- Some multinationals are creating separate local social enterprises to tackle local problems. Consider the case of Indian chulas, which are wood-burning ovens made from mud. Although the chulas are very cheap to operate, they can often cause burns because of uncontrolled flames. Furthermore, the smoke can frequently fill the users' rooms, creating a sooty film in the kitchen and making breathing difficult. The electronics giant Royal Philips Electronics decided to partner with local chula users to find a better design. Only a year later, users were using the model designed by Philips. Rather than using a single length of pipe as a chimney, Philips devised a three-part chimney that can be easily disassembled for cleaning. Chula users now breathe much more easily. Philips is also obtaining tremendous in-depth knowledge of product preferences.

Sources: Based on BusinessWire. 2008. "Multinationals and water: New ethical corporation report examines how Rio Tinto, SABMiller, Coca-Cola, Intel, Johnson & Johnson, IKEA and Molson Coors are tackling the issue of water scarcity." December 23; Capell, K., and N. Lakshman. 2008. "Philanthropy by design." BusinessWeek, September 22, p. 66; Houlder, V. 2009. "Focus on image excises fondness for tax havens." Financial Times, June 15, p. 12; New York Times. 2008. "Multinationals fight climate change." January 21, p. C5.

EXHIBIT 1.8   The Top 25 Most Ethical Companies

Rank	Company	Country	Industry
1	Intel Corp	United States	Technology
2	HSBC Holdings	U.K.	Banks
3	IBM	United States	Technology
4	Unilever	Netherlands	Food and beverages
5	Marks & Spencer	U.K.	Retail
6	Alcoa Inc	United States	Basic resources
7	Dell Inc	United States	Technology
8	Xerox	United States	Technology
9	Cisco Systems	United States	Technology
10	General Electric	United States	Industrial goods and services
11	DuPont de Nemours	United States	Chemicals
12	Procter & Gamble	United States	Personal and household goods
13	Rio Tinto	U.K.	Basic resources
14	Starbucks	United States	Beverages
15	Honda Motor	Japan	Automobiles and parts
16	BASF	Germany	Chemicals
17	Nissan Motor	Japan	Automobiles and parts
18	Ericsson	Sweden	Technology
19	Diageo	U.K.	Food and beverages
20	Kraft Foods	United States	Food and beverages
21	Sun Microsystems	United States	Technology
22	Bristol Myers Squibb	United States	Health care
23	Vodafone Group PLC	U.K.	Telecommunication
24	Barclays Bank	U.K.	Banks
25	Microsoft	United States	Technology

Source: Adapted from Covalence. 2009. http://www.covalence.ch.

knowledge resource firm, is conducting an annual survey to produce a ranking of the world's most ethical corporations. The company uses 45 criteria based on issues such as working conditions, impact of the multinational's production, impact of the multinational's products, and institutional impact. Covalence uses sources like media monitoring and the Internet to collect information on the various criteria. Exhibit 1.8 shows the list of the top 25 most ethical companies.

The next section discusses the next generation of multinational managers by describing some of their characteristics.

The Next Generation of Multinational Managers

Consider what the experts say about the need for multinational managers and leaders:

> It takes more than a lot of frequent flyer miles to become a global leader. Today's cosmopolitan executive must know what to do when competitive advantage is fleeting, when change becomes chaos, and when home base is the globe.[21]
>
> We need global leaders at a time when markets and companies are changing faster than the ability of leaders to reinvent themselves. We have a shortage of global leaders at a

time when international exposure and experience are vital to business success. And we need internationally minded, globally literate leaders at a time when leadership styles are in transition around the world.[22]

To become global leaders and to keep pace with the dizzying rate of globalization, most managers will need additional strengths to meet the related challenges. According to some experts, the next generation of successful multinational managers must have the following characteristics:[23]

- *A global mindset:* A person with a **global mindset** understands that the world of business is changing rapidly and that the world is more interdependent in business transactions. A global mindset requires managers to think globally but act locally. Managers must see similarities in the global market while being able to adapt to local conditions in any country. A global mindset is necessary for all employees, from the CEO to the rank and file, if a company is to support and implement a global strategic vision.

- *Emotional intelligence:* There is growing evidence that being able to manage one's emotions, or emotional intelligence, is a crucial requirement for the multinational manager. Previous research has shown that emotional intelligence prepares the manager to better adjust to and deal with new cultures and people.

- *A long-range perspective:* A short-term view seldom succeeds in the new global economy. Credited with responsibility for turning Motorola into a global player, former CEO Robert W. Galvin put a representative in Beijing more than ten years ago. Now Motorola is the largest U.S. investor in China. Successful companies must be persistent if they are to overcome the complexities of dealing with the international environment.

- *The talent to motivate all employees to achieve excellence:* The ability to motivate has always been a hallmark of leadership. In the next generation of organizations, the leader will face additional challenges of motivation. Employees may come from any country and may live in any country. Leaders will face the motivational challenge of having employees identify with the organization rather than with their country. Leaders also will need to develop motivational strategies that transcend cultures.

- *Accomplished negotiating skills:* All business transactions require negotiation. However, leaders in the global economy will spend considerably more time negotiating cross-culturally. Such skills will be more challenging to acquire and more necessary to apply.

- *The willingness to seek overseas assignments:* The next generation of leaders will have significant international experience. They will demonstrate management skills and success in more than one cultural environment.

- *An understanding of national cultures:* In spite of the pressures of globalization to treat the world as one market, large differences still exist among national cultures. No multinational leader or business can succeed without a deep understanding of the national cultures in which they do business. Multinational managers often will be required to learn two or more additional languages as well as the nuances of local cultural differences.

Can you develop the skills necessary to be a successful multinational manager? One of the first tasks is to learn all you can about multinational management and international business. In the next section, we will discuss how this text can contribute to this goal.

Global mindset
Mindset that requires managers to think globally, but act locally.

Multinational Management: A Strategic Approach

Why should you study multinational management? In today's Internet-connected world, you may have little choice but to be a multinational manager. Foreign competition and doing business in foreign markets are daily facts of life for today's managers. The study of multinational management helps you prepare for dealing with this evolving global economy and for developing the skills necessary to succeed as a multinational manager. This text will introduce some of the basic requisite skills.

Competing successfully in the global economy takes a strategic approach to multinational management, particularly how multinational managers formulate and implement such strategies. **Strategy** is defined here as the maneuvers or activities that managers use to sustain and increase organizational performance. **Strategy formulation** is the process of choosing or crafting a strategy. **Strategy implementation** encompasses all the activities that managers and an organization must perform to achieve strategic objectives.

From the perspective of the multinational company and managers, strategies must include maneuvers that deal with operating in more than one country and culture. Thus multinational strategy formulation takes on the added challenges of dealing with opportunities and competition located anywhere in the world. Similarly, multinational strategy implementation carries added challenges, including the need to develop complex management systems to carry out strategies that reach beyond domestic boundaries.

The rules of competition are constantly evolving. Today's multinationals face an environment that is drastically different from the environment that multinationals faced in the past. A company can be a dominant player but can lose its competitive edge rapidly. As we examine international management from a strategic perspective, it is important to understand these trends that will shape the future business environment. These include:[24]

- **Blurring of industry boundaries:** Information and other communication technologies have made industry boundaries less clear. For instance, the South Korean company Samsung now produces products ranging from televisions to cell phones to microprocessors. This blurring of boundaries makes it much harder to identify and understand competitors.

- **Flexibility matters more than size:** Recent failure of large companies suggest that being big may no longer be useful. Consider that many giants such as GM, Microsoft, Dell, and IBM have all hit market caps. As outsourcing, alliances, and partnering gather steam, companies are finding that they can convert many fixed costs into variable costs. Such changes make scale less useful.

- **Finding your niche:** Multinationals have traditionally strived to be the leader in their respective industries. However, such thinking is now changing. Kim and Mauborgne's Blue Ocean Strategy suggests that finding those uncontested niches also leads to success. In fact, many companies are finding that they can do well by finding niches and satisfying the needs in that niche.[25]

- **Hypercompetition:** The new environment is characterized by intense competition coming from companies located in all parts of the world. Businesses cannot expect to be stable and be around for a long time. For instance, consider that Haier, a Chinese company that entered the U.S. market in

Strategy
The maneuvers or activities that managers use to sustain and increase organizational performance.

Strategy formulation
Process by which managers select the strategies to be used by their company.

Strategy implementation
All the activities that managers and an organization must perform to achieve strategic objectives.

1999, is now the top-selling brand of dorm fridges. It also is the market leader in home wine coolers and ranks third in freezers.

- ***Emphasis on innovation and the learning organization:*** Successful companies are going to those that can draw on local knowledge to innovate and compete globally. For instance, many of the successful South Korea and Japanese companies were able to use their domestic markets as tests to improve and launch their products globally. To achieve such success, any multinational will need to develop the appropriate mechanisms and systems to integrate the local knowledge to produce value for the company.

Given these requirements, a fundamental assumption of this book is that successful multinational management requires managers to understand their potential competitors and collaborators.[26]

When you understand your competitors and yourself, you will always win.

—Sun Tzu, The Art of War

Multinational companies and managers must be prepared to compete with other firms from any country. In addition, they must be prepared to collaborate with companies and people from anywhere in the world as suppliers, alliance partners, and customers. Accomplishing these tasks means that multinational managers must understand more than the basics of national culture. They must understand how people from different nations view organizational strategies and organizations. To provide such a background, this text devotes several chapters to comparative management—the comparison of management practices used by people from different nations.

Summary and Conclusions

This chapter provided you with key background information that supports the study of multinational management, defining multinational management and the multinational company. You saw examples of the world's largest multinationals. However, as the Preview Case in Point showed, companies of all sizes can be multinational.

Because we exist in a globalizing world, considerable attention has been devoted to the forces that drive globalization. These are key environmental issues that affect every multinational company and its managers. World trade and investments are growing rapidly, but not always consistently, making all economies more linked and creating both opportunities and threats for both domestic and multinational companies. New competitors, strong and motivated, are coming from developing nations in Asia, the Americas, and the transitioning economies of Eastern Europe. Customers, products, and standards are becoming more global. The increasing sophistication and lower cost of information technology fuel the development of global companies that can more easily manage worldwide operation.

Multinational managers of the next generation will need skills not always considered necessary for domestic-only managers. This chapter described key characteristics of successful multinational managers as identified by several experts. Perhaps the most encompassing characteristic is the global mindset. Managers with such a mindset understand the rapidly changing business and economic environment. They can see the world as an integrated market, yet appreciate and understand the wide array of differences in the world cultures and social institutions.

The next two chapters in this section will begin building the foundation of your global mindset. You will see how cultural differences affect business practices. You will see not only how understanding national culture is crucial to your success as a multinational manager but also how social institutions, such as religion and law, influence multinational management. This combination of national culture and social institutions is called the national context.

After reading this text, you should have the foundation for understanding the latest challenges and practices of multinational management. However, the field is dynamic, and your learning will never be complete. Successful multinational managers will view the understanding of their field as a lifelong endeavor.

Discussion Questions

1. Discuss how any company can become a multinational company. What are some of the options available to companies that allow them to use international markets and locations competitively?

2. Discuss some reasons why reductions in world trade barriers are driving the world toward a global economy.

3. Consider how things such as wars, terrorist activities, and bird flu might alter the progression of globalization. What should a multinational manager do to deal with such situations?

4. Discuss the differences between foreign trade and foreign direct investment.

5. Discuss some of the advantages and disadvantages of setting up production in developing nations.

Consider the benefits of market growth versus the risk of the venture. Consider the position of Motorola discussed in the text. If you were the CEO, would you think that Motorola made the right move?

6. Look at the information on developing economies and competition discussed in the text. Where do you think the next generation of world-class competitors will come from? Why?

7. Discuss the characteristics of a next-generation multinational manager. How can you develop those characteristics through education and experience?

8. What are some of the new rules of competition? How are these new rules going to affect global trade?

Multinational Management **Skill Builder**

Interview a Multinational Manager

Step 1. As a member of a team or as an individual, contact a current or former multinational manager. Where can you find such a manager? Perhaps some are close by. In a business college, many graduate students and professors have work experience as multinational managers. Also, the parents of many students are similarly experienced. Most likely, however, you will need to contact a company and ask to speak with the individual in charge of international operations. Do not overlook small companies. Although it may not be a full-time responsibility, international sales may be the responsibility of someone in many companies.

Step 2. Set up an appointment for an interview.

Step 3. Arrive on time, professionally dressed with a list of prepared questions. Some possible questions are:

What circumstances led you to assume a position with international responsibilities?

What are the major challenges in the international part of your job?

How would you describe the international strategy of your company?

How important is international work to advancement in your company?

How do you deal with and prepare for cultural differences?

Do you ever have to manage employees from other countries directly? If so, what are the challenges in doing that?

How are people selected for international assignments?

Do you face any unique ethical situations in your job?

Endnotes

1 Lamy, Pascale. 2006. "Humanizing globalization." *International Trade Forum*, 1, pp. 5–6.

2 *Economist*. 2006. "The future of globalization," July 29, p. 11.

3 *Economist*. 2006. "Climbing back," January 21, p. 69.

4 Ibid.

5 WTO (World Trade Organization). 2006. *World Trade Report 2006*. Geneva: World Trade Organization.

6 *Economist*. 1996. "All free traders now?" December 7, pp. 23–25.

7 *Economist*. 2003. "Heading east." http://www.economist.com, March 27.

8 WTO (World Trade Organization). 2009. *http://www.wto.org*.

9 *Economist*. 2006. "In the twilight of Doha," July 29, pp. 69–70.

10 *Economist*. 1996. "Spoiling world trade." December 7, pp. 15–16.

11 Lubbers, R. F. M. 1996. "Globalization: An exploration." *Nijenrode Management Review*, p. 1.

[12] Boscheck, Ralph. 1996. "Managed trade and regional preference." In IMD, *World Competitiveness Yearbook 1996*, pp. 333–334. Lausanne, Switzerland: Institute for Management Development.

[13] *Economist*. "Spoiling world trade."

[14] WTO (World Trade Organization). *World Trade Organization: Trading into the Future* (2002) Geneva: World Trade Organization.

[15] WTO (World Trade Organization), *World Trade Report. 2009*.

[16] Organisation for Economic Co-operation and Development. 2009. http://www.oecd.org.

[17] UNCTAD (UN Conference on Trade and Development). 2000. *World Investment Report*. New York and Geneva: United Nations; UNCTAD (UN Conference on Trade and Development). 2000. "World FDI flows exceed US$ 1.1 trillion in 2000." UNCTAD Press Release, December 7.

[18] Javetski, Bill, and William Glasgall. 1994. "Borderless finance: Fuel for growth." *BusinessWeek*, November 18, pp. 40–50.

[19] Yip, George S. 2002. *Total Global Strategy II*. Englewood Cliffs: Prentice Hall.

[20] Levine, Jonathan B. 1992. "Want EC business? You have two choices." *BusinessWeek*, October 19, pp. 58–59.

[21] Rhinesmith, Steven H., John N. Williamson, David M. Ehlen, and Denise S. Maxwell. 1989. "Developing leaders for the global enterprise." *Training and Development Journal*, April, pp. 25–34.

[22] Rosen, Robert H., Patricia Digh, Mashall Singer, and Carl Phillips. 1999. *Global Literacies: Lessons on Business Leaders and National Cultures*. Riverside, NJ: Simon & Schuster.

[23] Beamish, Allen, J. Morrison, Andrew Inkpen, and Philip Rosenzweig. 2003. *International Management*. New York: McGrawHill-Irwin; Gabel, Racheli Shmueli, Shimon L. Dolan, and Jean Luc Cerdin. 2005. "Emotional intelligence as predictor of cultural adjustment for success in global assignments." *Career Development International*, 10(5), pp. 375–395; Moran, Robert T., and John R. Riesenberger. 1994. *The Global Challenge*. London: McGraw-Hill.

[24] Hitt, Michael A., Barbara W. Keats, and Samuel M. DeMarie. 1998. "Navigating in the new competitive landscape: Building strategic flexibility and competitive advantage in the 21st century." *Academy of Management Executive*, 12(4), pp. 22–42; Kim, Chan W., and Renee Mauborgne. 2005. "Value innovation: A leap into the blue ocean." *The Journal of Business Strategy*, 26(4), pp. 22–28; Morris, Betsy. 2006. "The new rules." *Fortune*, July 24, pp. 70–87.

[25] Kim and Mauborgne, "Value innovation: A leap into the blue ocean."

[26] Hamel, Cary, and C. K. Prahalad. 1989. "Strategic intent." *Harvard Business Review*, May–June, pp. 63–76.

Yahoo! and Customer Privacy (A)

I n the summer of 2004, the People's Republic of China asked Yahoo!'s Chinese subsidiary for the name and address associated with username "houyan1989@yahoo.com.cn." The government gave no explanation of why it needed this information or what it intended to do with it. Yahoo!'s privacy policy stated it would not divulge a customer's personal information unless officially requested via a court order or some other legal means. This was new and unexplored territory, however. U.S. customers were highly sensitive about privacy issues, but China was a far different environment politically and culturally. There was the potential for a seemingly small issue to become a bigger problem. Given the lack of detail in the government's request, the immediate question appeared to be whether to ask for further information to evaluate against Yahoo!'s privacy policy, or to simply hand over the information as requested.

Yahoo!

One of the Internet's earliest and biggest success stories, Yahoo! began in early 1994 as a side project of David Filo and Jerry Yang, two PhD students at Stanford. The Internet was just beginning to explode with Web sites on a seemingly infinite number of topics, so Filo and Yang cataloged the sites they liked and made the list available on their own Web page. Their well-organized directory was immensely popular, and in 1995 they incorporated their business as Yahoo!, took it public, and became multimillionaires.

From the beginning the founders had ambitious plans to harness and organize the still-developing Internet by creating "the only place in the world that anyone would have to go to find, and get connected to, anything or anybody."[1] To this end they hired an experienced management team and set out on an aggressive campaign to grow the business quickly. The company executed a series of acquisitions that expanded its service offerings to include Internet radio, e-mail, news, business-to-business commerce, auctions, and more. Some acquisitions were quite large, including $3.7 billion to acquire GeoCities in 1998 and $5 billion to acquire http://www.broadcast.com in 1999. The company also expanded geographically, starting with Yahoo! Japan and Yahoo! Europe in 1996, followed by Yahoo! Korea in 1997.

Yahoo! also established a quirky corporate image that reflected the personality of the founders and was typical of the "new business" Internet era. The theme was edgy and offbeat, as evidenced by its catchy and highly successful commercials with the tag line "Do you Yahoo?" The management analysis section of the 1999 Annual Report was printed on postcards, seemingly emphasizing that shareholders had ventured into new frontiers and should tell others about it. The company also sought to preserve the original identity and creativity of its founders by defining "what we value" and "what we don't value," complete with smiley-face "emoticons" (Exhibit 1).

By 2003, the combination of experienced management, avant-garde positioning, and an aggressive growth strategy had generated more than $1.6 billion in revenue (a 71% increase over 2002) and almost

---

EXHIBIT 1

Excerpts from Yahoo!'s Mission and Corporate Values

As expressed under the heading "What We Value," Yahoo!'s mission was "to be the most essential global Internet service for consumers and businesses." This mission was shaped by a set of core values, or "the standards that guide interactions with fellow Yahoos!, the principles that direct how we service our customers, the ideals that drive what we do and how we do it." The mission statement also referred to the creation of these values "by two guys in a trailer some time ago," as well as values that were put into practice as the company grew.

These values included Excellence, Innovation, Customer Fixation, Teamwork, Community, and Fun.

Yahoo! was also quite clear about what the company didn't value. Among many other things (a full page and a half on the Yahoo! Web site) was "bureaucracy," "same ol' same ol'," "shoulda coulda woulda," "head in the sand," and "a stick in the eye."

Source: http://docs.yahoo.com/info/values (accessed 12 November 2007).

$238 million in profits, and company leadership was seeking ways to continue the trend. Its total of users was approximately 263 million, 23% more than in 2002, with around 133 million registered users (logging in with a user name and password at least once a month), a figure that was up more than 30% from the previous year.[2]

China

By the early 21st century, China had emerged as a highly lucrative, but unpredictable and controversial, market. One of the world's oldest civilizations, mainland China had been a significant economic player in the 19th century, at one time representing 33% of global gross domestic product (GDP); but political turmoil throughout much of the 20th century had reduced the economy to less than 2% global GDP by 1990.[3] By 2004, however, that poor output was a thing of the past, with vigorous economic growth in 2003 and a GDP that had climbed to 9.1% in that year.[4] This growth, coupled with a massive population and government signals of openness, created tremendous potential for the Chinese economy and for western companies.

The People's Republic of China (PRC), in existence since 1949, had experienced several radical shifts in political, social, and economic policy in its brief history. After several infamous state-managed programs, including "The Great Leap Forward" and "The Cultural Revolution" under Chairman Mao Zedong, the PRC adopted a new approach in the late 1970s under Deng Xiaoping. After 30 years of tight control, the government focused on economic reforms using a pragmatic, experimental approach. Rather than implementing a massive nationwide policy such as "The Great Leap Forward," government would consider practical solutions, test them on a local level, and expand them if they worked. Under this incremental approach, which Deng labeled "socialism with Chinese characteristics," the PRC government slowly began releasing its grip on the economy by granting new freedoms in agriculture, trade, and foreign investment.

Although this incremental approach produced significant improvements in China's economy, concerns about social freedoms and basic human rights remained. These pressures, both within and outside China, strongly contributed to the unstable, uncertain, and risky environment exemplified by the April 1989 Tiananmen Square protests by students and workers critical of the government. The Chinese government's crackdown—declaring martial law on May 20 and resorting to military action in the square on June 4—was widely covered by the media, and many people worldwide blasted the Chinese government for its use of force on seemingly peaceful demonstrators. "Tiananmen Square," to many, became synonymous with lack of human rights in China.

In subsequent years, China cautiously continued economic reforms and its economy grew at an average rate of 10% annually, the highest in the world. Deng continued his socialism with Chinese characteristics with additional reforms, and by the late 1990s China was actively pursuing membership in the World Trade Organization (WTO). Membership would require China not only to lower the tariff and regulation trade barriers, but also to force key trading partners to remove quotas on Chinese goods. China's slow, but steady, reform trend was making it more enticing for companies to test the economic waters. Deng died in 1997 and was succeeded by Jiang Zemin, who immediately legalized private enterprise and unveiled a plan to privatize Communist China's state-owned enterprises. In December 2001, after 15 years of diplomatic wrangling and negotiating, China became the 143rd country to join the WTO. In return for its spot in the organization, China agreed that it would "undertake a broad series of reforms that will open its market to multinational corporations and open many of its industries to foreign investment. The changes are expected to put increased pressure on already troubled sectors of the economy, even as it draws foreign capital into the country."[5]

In 2002, Zemin resigned and Hu Jintao succeeded him in the first peaceful transition of power in China since 1949. Little known outside of China (and to a certain extent within the country), Hu Jintao was a fairly inexperienced politician and lacked both charisma and factional support but was known as a consensus-builder. Born in 1942, he had studied engineering at Qinghua University, worked his way up within the Communist Party's rank and file, and had an "urbane, unassuming, controlled ... and immaculate"[6] personal style. Some believed, however, that, given his role in bringing reforms to the Communist Youth Corps, Jintao could possibly be China's Gorbachev and "finally free the world's next superpower from its Leninist strait-jacket."[7] By 2004, Jintao had defeated these expectations by pushing aside any rivals and cracking down on dissidents, activism, and criticism of the government. At the same time, Jintao showed a more compassionate side, promising to assist those whose lives had not been helped by economic advances and even journeying to the poorer areas of the country. He advocated openness in the media when the SARS crisis hit, argued for "sustainable development," and began to reign in the frenzy of construction in China's larger towns and investigate alleged corruption.[8]

Particularly attractive to businesses both within and outside China was the burgeoning number of Internet users in the country. With a rapidly growing economy, more people were able to buy computers and thus go online. Although the market was problematic in that it was highly fragmented and dominated by local companies, Internet usage was "mouth-wateringly high across the region," as one business reporter characterized it, and international heavy-hitters such as Yahoo!, Google, and MSN were "understandably frantic to make an impression in Asia" and keep up with the "lift-off of the world's fastest-growing medium in the world's fastest-growing advertising region."[9] By 2004, China had 80 million online users, 22 million of whom had emerged in 2003, making it second only to the United States in the number of users.[10] China was projected to surpass the United States in 2006, with 153 million users.[11] The Internet also provided for many a way to skirt, with mixed results, the tight government censorship of China. (See Exhibit 2 for Asian Internet statistics.)

Although the Asian Internet market was enormously attractive to outside companies, not all Internet behemoths had navigated their way in successfully, and some had chafed under tight restrictions when they did. Lycos had withdrawn from many of the Asian markets in 2003, and AOL struggled, somewhat unsuccessfully, to gain a foothold. Other companies such as Time Warner had chosen to walk away from China altogether. In 2002, [AOL] announced a $200 million joint venture with Chinese company Legend to set up AOL in China, but later abandoned the idea, in part out of concern over the government's demands that AOL block certain content.[12] AOL also had significant problems with software piracy that undermined its CD-ROM marketing campaign.

Yahoo! China

In September 1999, Yahoo! cofounder Jerry Yang had declared "I am Chinese" in Mandarin to announce a joint venture with Beijing Founder Electronics.[13] The Taiwanese-born Yang caught industry analysts by surprise because his announcement came only one week after Wu Jiquan, head of China's Ministry of Information Industry, publicly stated that China's ban on foreign investment by Internet service providers also included search engines and Web portals such as Yahoo!. A few days later, ministry officials seemingly backtracked and stated more explicit regulations regarding Internet investment could be written by year's end.[14] Yahoo! opted to launch the new site from Hong Kong, allowing the company to benefit from the "one country, two systems" policy crafted by Deng Xiaopeng. By doing so, Yahoo! would not necessarily have to follow the laws and regulations of mainland China, including those of the Ministry of Information Industry. Yahoo! later opened an office in Beijing once regulations were clearly written and endorsed by the government.

China's regulation of Internet content presented a much bigger challenge (Exhibit 3). The government introduced regulations in 1995 and continuously added laws as Internet usage increased. But the rules were very broad and vague:

Units and individuals engaging in international networking shall observe relevant state laws and administrative rules and regulations, and strictly implement a security and classified information protection system; they are not allowed to use international networking to harm national security, leak state secrets, and engage in law-breaking

EXHIBIT 2   Internet Markets in Asia (2003 statistics)

Market	Internet Penetration (percentage)	Internet Users (millions)	Population (millions)	Broadband Penetration (percentage)	User Growth 2000–2004 (percentage)
South Korea	55.3	26.3	47.6	73.2	61
Singapore	51.3	2.3	4.5	23.2	78
Japan	44.9	57.0	127.4	21.0	42
Australia	42.6	8.4	19.7	3.7	102
Taiwan	38.2	8.6	22.0	32.3	8.5
Malaysia	28.6	6.5	22.7	0.4	134
Thailand	7.7	4.8	62.4	0.1	203
China	4.6	60.0	1,300.0	3.0	287
Indonesia	1.7	4.0	231.0	0.3	304
India	1.6	16.6	1,050.0	0.02	270

Source: Rob Gray, Haymarket Publishing Services Ltd., "Pan-Asian Media—Asia Online," Special Report, 19 November 2004, http://www.brandrepublic.com/News/228666 (accessed 8 August 2007).

EXHIBIT 3 Internet Society of China Public Pledge of Self-Regulation and Professional Ethics for China Internet Industry (revised July 19, 2002)

Chapter I General

Article 1 This pledge is made in accordance with the basic principle of "to develop vigorously, improve administration, go for its benefits while steering clear of its undesirables and use it to our benefit, in order to establish a self-regulating mechanism for China's Internet Industry, improve the conduct of Internet Industry Participants, and promote and ensure the sound development of the Internet Industry consistent with the law.

Article 2 The term "Internet Industry" as used herein refers to all the activities related to Internet businesses including operation, application, information, development and production of network products and information resources, scientific research, education, and customer services.

Article 3 The basic principles of Self-regulation and Professional Ethics for Internet the Industry are being patriotic observance of law, equitableness, trustworthiness, and honesty.

Article 4 All Participants are called upon to accede to and actively implement this Pledge on Self-regulation and Professional Ethics and create a favorable environment for the development of Internet businesses consistent with the fundamental interests of the nation and the entire Internet Community.

Article 5 The Internet Society of China, is the self-enforcement agency for purposes of this Pledge, and shall be responsible for its implementation.

Chapter II Provisions of Self-Regulation and Professional Ethical Conduct

Article 6 We pledge that in promoting the development of professional ethics of the Internet sector, the state laws, regulations, and policies governing the development and administration of the Internet shall be observed consistent with and to carry forward the rich cultural tradition of the Chinese nation and the moral code of socialist spiritual civilization.

Article 7 We pledge to encourage lawful, equitable, and orderly competition, and we pledge to oppose unfair competitive practices.

Article 8 We pledge to respect the lawful rights and interests of consumers and we shall protect the confidentiality of their information. We pledge not to use the information provided by users for any activity other than those as promised to users, and no technology or any other advantage may be used to infringe upon the lawful rights and interests of the consumers or users.

Article 9 We Internet information-service providers pledge to abide by the state regulations on Internet information-service management conscientiously and shall fulfill the following disciplinary obligations in respect of Internet information service:

1. Refraining from producing, posting or disseminating pernicious information that may jeopardize state security and disrupt social stability, contravene laws and regulations, and spread superstition and obscenity. Monitor the information publicized by users on Web sites according to law and remove the harmful information promptly;

2. Refraining from establishing links to the Web sites that contain harmful information so as to ensure that the content of the network information is lawful and healthy;

3. Observing laws and regulations concerning intellectual property rights in the course of producing, posting, and propagating information on Internet;

4. Encouraging people to use the Internet in an ethical way, to enhance the Internet ethical sense, and reject the spread of harmful information on the Internet.

5. If the Internet service provider discovers information which is inconsistent with the law on its Web site, it will remove it.

Article 10 We Internet access service providers pledge to inspect and monitor information on domestic and foreign Web sites when it provides access to those sites and refuse access to those Web sites that disseminate harmful information.

continued

EXHIBIT | **3** | *Continued*

Article 11 We Operators of Internet access venues pledge to use our best efforts to take effective measures to create a healthy and civilized environment for Internet usage and to assist the users, especially the teenagers to use the Internet in a healthy manner.

Article 12 We Producers of Internet information and network products pledge to respect the intellectual property rights of others and to refrain from producing products that contain harmful information or infringe upon the intellectual property right of others.

Article 13 All the Participants who sign this Pledge to work together to prevent malicious "hacking" and introducing damaging computer code and disruptive programs from spreading on the Internet. We pledge to oppose production and dissemination of computer programs that are capable of malicious attack against computer networks and the computer information systems of others and oppose illegal intrusion into and damaging computer information systems of others.

Article 14 We pledge to use our best efforts to strengthen communication and collaboration, study and formulate strategies for the development of Internet businesses in China and to encourage policy and legislative recommendations for the establishment, development, and management of Internet businesses.

Article 15 We pledge to support and encourage effective measures to collaborate in areas such as research, production, and service in the Internet industry and to create a favorable environment for Internet development.

Article 16 We pledge to encourage enterprises, research, education, and other institutions as well as individuals to develop computer software, hardware, and various network products and to protect self-owned intellectual property rights as well as to encourage "open source development" so as to provide strong support to the further development of China's Internet industry.

Article 17 We pledge to actively participate in international cooperation and exchanges, involving in the development of international rules and standards for the Internet industry and to observe the international rules to which China has acceded.

Article 18 We pledge to accept supervision and criticism over the Internet industry from the public and to jointly resist and correct unethical practices in the Internet industry.

Chapter III Implementation of the Pledge

Article 19 The Internet Society of China shall be responsible for organizing the implementation and administering this Pledge, communicating to the member organizations the information related to Internet laws, policies, and industry self-regulation, reporting to the competent authority of the government the wishes and requirements of our members, upholding their lawful interests, organizing the implementation of Internet Industry self-regulation and ethical conduct and supervise and inspect the implementation of this Pledge by our members.

Article 20 We pledge to abide by and comply with the various self-self regulation and ethical principles embodied in this Pledge.

Article 21 In the event that dispute arises among the parties to this Pledge, they shall try to seek solutions to the dispute through consultation according to the principle of mutual understanding and compromise, or they may refer the dispute to the administering agency for mediation, with the purpose of safeguarding the industrial unity and the overall interests of the entire industry and the Internet community

Article 22 If any party to this Pledge violates the provisions of this Pledge, any other party may report the violations to the administrating agency promptly and may require the administering agency investigate. The administering agency may also conduct investigations directly and shall make public the findings of such investigations to all the member organizations.

Article 23 Where violations of this Pledge are found to be true by the administering agency and to have a negative impact then the administering agency will announce its findings to the member organizations. In addition the administering agency may revoke the Participant's membership, in light of specific circumstances.

Article 24 All the parties to this Pledge may monitor the fairness and impartiality of the ladministering agency in implementing this Pledge and may report violations of this Pledge by the agency or its staff to a higher-level department of the agency.

Article 25 The administering agency and its member organizations must abide by state laws land regulations in the course of implementing this Pledge.

Chapter IV Supplementary Provisions

Article 26 This Pledge shall become effective after being signed by the legal persons or the representatives of the first group member organizations and each signor shall be made public by Internet Society of China within 30 days after the member's pledge becomes effective.

   Article 27 In the effective period, this Pledge can be amended only when such amendments are proposed by the administering agency or one-tenth or above of the member organizations and supported by two-thirds or above of the member organizations.

   Article 28 The Internet Industry Participants of China that accept the self-regulation and Code of Professional and Ethical Conduct and the related disciplinary rules can apply for accession to this Pledge; the parties to this Pledge may also secede from this Pledge and shall notify the administering agency of such accordingly; and the executing agency shall publish the list of the members that accede to or secede from this Pledge on periodic basis.

   Article 29 The member organizations of this Pledge may reach self-regulation and ethical conduct agreements specific to different segments of the Internet industry under the general framework of this Pledge and may publish for implementation such agreements as attachments to this Pledge with the agreement of its member organizations.

   Article 30 The right of interpretation of this Pledge lies with Internet Society of China.

   Article 31 This Pledge shall be implemented as of the date of its promulgation.

Beijing ICP Record No.363
Undertaken by Chinanetizen & Cnii

Source: http://www.isc.org.cn/20020417/ca102762.htm (accessed 12 November 2007).

---

criminal activities; and they are not allowed to produce, read, duplicate, or circulate information hampering public security and obscene pornographic information.[15]

Although general categories were clearly unlawful, such as transmitting state secrets, there was no clear definition of how to identify unlawful content—for example, what was and was not a state secret.

In 2002, Yahoo! and 120 other companies signed a Public Pledge of Self-Regulation and Professional Ethics, created by the Internet Society of China. The pledge carried no legal weight and listed no specific requirements not already defined by law. Even so, Yahoo! drew sharp criticism from human rights activists, such as Kenneth Roth, executive director of Human Rights Watch: "If it implements the pledge, Yahoo! will become an agent of Chinese law enforcement. It will switch from being an information gateway to an information gatekeeper."[16]

Competition

Despite the risks and difficulties of working in China, other major companies such as Microsoft, Cisco, and Google had also set their sights on Asia. The "first mover advantage"[17] was significant in the young Internet industry and the thought of gaining a foothold in China struck both excitement and fear in the hearts of executives. But they were also finding challenges in the Chinese market. In August 2002, Google's search engine stopped working for Chinese Internet surfers and remained unavailable for two weeks. Even after the site was restored Internet users found certain search topics no longer produced results. Google denied making any changes, creating speculation that the government was actively blocking content. By 2004, Google took an active role when it launched a Chinese news service and voluntarily excluded information from sites the government considered subversive.[18] Still, the company was unsure how to proceed in the precarious Chinese market without going against its "do no evil" philosophy.

Nonetheless, Yahoo! China was feeling the pressure from its competitors, primarily Google. In early 2004, Yahoo!, in an effort to build its profile, launched a Chinese Internet search Web site modeled on that of Google. Called Yisou, or "one search," this site used the "uncluttered and simpler user search interface" that Google had created and that had been imitated by Baidu, China's largest Internet search provider. The competitive threat had only increased the previous year, when Google had moved closer to taking a minority stake in Baidu. The seriousness of Yahoo!'s efforts to dominate the market was underscored by Yahoo!'s decision not to use paid advertising or links on the site. The company's ultimate plan was to have a search engine that was not only more "international" than Baidu's, but also "better adapted to the local market" than Google's.[19] In 2003, Yahoo! had acquired 3721

Network Software, a Chinese language search developer, for $120 million.

Yahoo!'s Experience with Privacy

The laws and precedents concerning customer privacy were still evolving in the young Internet industry, and Yahoo! already had some experience with these issues. In 2000, a company called AnswerThink filed a defamation lawsuit against a Yahoo! user who had posted derogatory comments about AnswerThink on a chat room. The company served Yahoo! with a subpoena to reveal the user's name, and Yahoo! complied. The user then sued Yahoo!, claiming the company had violated his privacy by inappropriately sharing his information with a third party without first notifying him or validating the subpoena.[20] The case was ultimately settled out of court. In another privacy case, Yahoo! refused to hand over the e-mails of a U.S. marine to his father after the soldier was killed in Iraq. The family sued and won, and Yahoo! complied with the court order, saying it was glad to do so under the legal process.[21]

The company also faced international challenges. In 2000, a French court ordered Yahoo! to block access for French users to its auctions that included Nazi and other similar memorabilia, because such items were outlawed for display or sale in France. Yahoo! fought the suit, saying that it already excluded items from its French site, www.yahoo.fr, but that France had no jurisdiction to restrict content of its U.S. site, www.yahoo.com, which was also available to Internet users in France. Yahoo! attorney Christophe Pecnard stated: "The question put before this court is whether a French jurisdiction can make a decision on the English content of an American site, run by an American company ... for the sole reason that French users have access via the Internet."[22]

What Do You Do, Yahoo!?

There were several possibilities open to Yahoo!, but none was simple. The company could just comply with the Chinese request. In the United States, such a request for information would likely have been more explicit as to why the information was needed, or might even be in the form of a subpoena that the company could formally investigate and confirm. Since the request was from the Chinese government, it seemed to have sufficient official authority to meet Yahoo!'s criteria for when to divulge customer information. Working with the Chinese government certainly was a different experience than working in the United States. If the user in question was committing crimes, such as kidnapping or murder, surely it would be easy for the

government to share that, but if the case involved more nebulous political issues, Yahoo! could find itself in an uncomfortable situation.

Saying no to the government could be difficult, and the government's tight reign over business could put the company's Chinese operations at risk. Resisting the request could prod the government into divulging more information, or perhaps its intentions, but there was some risk of offending officials. Rumors of human rights abuses abounded, but without more information it was difficult to know if this was such a case.

Searching for alternatives to compliance held some promise, but was difficult and fraught with risk, as exemplified by Chinese media tycoon Liu Changle. Liu's Phoenix Satellite television, China's only private television network, was the only station to mention the death of former Communist Party Leader Zhao Ziyang who had been punished for his opposition to the government's response to Tiananmen Square. When provincial governments began blocking his TV signal, however, Liu stopped broadcasting the story of Ziyang's death and quickly started apologizing. He explained his actions: "We walk on a tightrope...If we do everything the government wants, people will treat us with contempt. If we follow the people completely, the government will wipe us out.... It can be very uncomfortable."[23] Liu believed, as did other business leaders, that while China should move towards a more democratic system, it could only do so in a gradual and orderly manner.[24]

The various issues of legality and confidentiality seemed overwhelming, but the bottom line was that Yahoo! had to decide exactly what to do with "houyan1989@yahoo.com.cn."

CASE DISCUSSION QUESTIONS

1. If you were the CEO of Yahoo! and were presenting an opinion to the board of directors whether or not to release information to the Chinese government regarding a subscriber to Yahoo!'s e-mail, what would you say is more important—penetrating the Chinese market or adhering to Yahoo!'s principles regarding privacy protection?
2. One of the challenges of setting up a business in a foreign country is how much to adapt your product or service and company policies to local conditions. Make a case that companies must adapt to local tastes, traditions, and laws in order to survive.
3. One strategy Yahoo! could use to deal with the Chinese government is to allow its local joint venture partner, Beijing Founder Electronics, to deal with the Chinese government. What are the benefits and risks of doing so?

4. A multinational company deals with many constituents. How should Yahoo! respond to the criticisms from Human Rights Watch?

CASE CREDIT

This case was prepared by Thomas A. Fruscello (MBA '06) and Senior Ethics Research Associate Jenny Mead under the direction of Andrew C. Wicks, Associate Professor of Business Administration, R. Edward Freeman, Elis and Signe Olsson Professor of Business Administration, and Patricia H. Werhane, Ruffin Professor of Business Ethics. It was written as a basis for class discussion rather than to illustrate effective or ineffective handling of an administrative situation.

CASE NOTES

1. Yahoo! 1997 Annual Report, 9.

2. Yahoo! 2003 Annual Report, Chairman and CEO's Report, http://www.shareholder.com/shared/dynamicdoc/YHOO/626/YHOO_626.pdf (accessed 30 July 2007)

3. Meeker Mary. *The Internet in China*, Morgan Stanley.

4. The GDP was (Chinese yuan) CNY11,669.4 billion, the equivalent of approximately (U.S. dollars) USD1.5 billion.

5. "China Joins WTO." 2001. *New York Times*, 12 December.

6. Luard Tim. 2005. "China's Leader Shows His Stripes," *BBC News*, January 11, http://news.bbc.co.uk/go/pr/fr/-/2/hi/asia-pacific/4165209.stm (accessed 25 February 2008).

7. Luard

8. Luard.

9. Rob Gray, "Pan-Asian Media—Asia Online," Special Report, Haymarket Publishing Services Ltd., 19 November 2004, 40, http://www.brandrepublic.com/News/228666 (accessed 8 August 2007).

10. Bruce Einhorn, "China.Net," *Business Week* (15 March 2004): 22.

11. This growth was even more astonishing in light of the 1999 Chinese Internet statistics, compiled by the China Internet Network Information Center: There were 4 million Internet users,

representing a 240% increase over the previous year and a mere 0.3% penetration of China's 1.2 billion population. Furthermore, more than 75% of users were under the age of 30, a highly attractive market.

12. Jason Dean and Kevin J. Delaney, "Limited Search: As Google Pushes Into China, It Faces Clashes With Censors; Executives Wrestled With Issue As Others Took the Lead; Now, It's Charging Ahead; What 'Don't Be Evil' Means," *Wall Street Journal*, 16 December 2005, A-1.

13. "Yahoo! hits China amid uncertainty," *Advertising Age International*, October 1999, 1.

14. William J. McMahon, "Yahoo!'s Yang Walks Portal/ICP Line in China," *ChinaOnline News* (29 September 1999).

15. State Council Decree No. 195 of the People's Republic of China, Article 13.

16. Human Rights Watch, "Yahoo! Risks Abusing Rights in China," 9 August 2002, http://www.hrw.org/press/2002/08/yahoo080902.htm (accessed 25 February 2008).

17. A strong, often insurmountable advantage gained by the first *significant* (as opposed to simply the first) company to move into a new market. For example, though eBay may not have been the first on-line auction Web site, it was the first significant one and therefore had "first mover advantage."

18. Jason Dean and Kevin J. Delaney, "Limited Search: As Google Pushes into China, It Faces Clashes With Censors; Executives Wrestled With Issue as Others Took the Lead; Now, It's Charging Ahead; What 'Don't Be Evil' Means," *Wall Street Journal*, 16 December 2005, A-1.

19. Mure Dickie, "Yahoo's China Site Modeled on Google's," *Financial Times*, 22 June 2004, 31.

20. According to U.S. law, AnswerThink was required to notify the defendant about the suit, and if unable to do so, it had to request permission from the court to issue a subpoena or post public notice about the lawsuit. Because AnswerThink had not sought permission to issue the subpoena, the user contended that his rights had been violated, and that Yahoo! was party to this. Source: Dan Bischof, "Through Accusations of Defamation, Companies Are Starting to Unmask Anonymous Online Critics," *News Media & the Law*, 1 January 2001.

21. Stephanie Olsen, "Yahoo Releases E-Mail of Deceased Marine," *News.com*, 21 April 2005, http://news.com.com/2100-1038_3-5680025.html (accessed 12 November 2007).

22. "France Bans Internet Nazi Auctions," *BBC News*, 23 May 2000, http://news.bbc.co.uk/1/hi/world/europe/760782.stm (accessed 12 November 2007).

23. Philip P. Pan, "Media Tycoon Stirs Up China's Airwaves," *Wall Street Journal Asia*, 20 September 2005.

24. Pan.

2 Culture and Multinational Management

Preview CASE IN POINT

Different and the Same: Explorations in Culture

The poem "We and They" by Rudyard Kipling captures some of the feelings associated with intercultural experiences.

Father, Mother, and Me
Sister and Auntie say
All the people like us are We,
And everyone else is They.
And They live over the sea
While we live over the way,
But—would you believe it?—They look upon We
As only a sort of They!

We eat pork and beef
With cow-horn-handled knives.
They who gobble Their rice off a leaf
Are horrified out of Their lives;
While They who live up a tree,
Feast on grubs and clay,
(Isn't it scandalous?) look upon We
As a simply disgusting They!

We eat kitcheny food.
We have doors that latch.
They drink milk and blood
Under an open thatch. We have doctors to fee.
They have wizards to pay.
And (impudent heathen!) They look upon We
As a quite impossible They!

All good people agree,
And all good people say,
All nice people, like us, are We

And everyone else is They:
But if you cross over the sea,
Instead of over the way,
You may end by (think of it!) looking on We
As only a sort of They!

Source: Kipling, Rudyard., "We and They." 1923. In Craig Storti, 1990. The Art of Crossing Cultures. *Yarmouth, ME: Intercultural Press, pp. 92–91.*

The Preview Case in Point shows the feelings that many individuals have when they meet people from other cultures. They see behavior that they have trouble understanding. They see, hear, smell, and taste things that are strange and unpredictable. However, in today's business world, these seemingly strange people are often your customers, employees, suppliers, and business partners.

To remain competitive and to flourish in the complex and fast changing world of multinational business, multinational managers look worldwide not only for potential markets but also for sources of high-quality and less expensive raw materials and labor. Even managers who never leave their home country must deal with markets and workforces whose cultural backgrounds are increasingly diverse. Managers with the skills to understand and adapt to different cultures are better positioned to succeed in these endeavors and to compete successfully in the world market.

Throughout this text you will be exposed to numerous cultural differences in management practices from countries around the world. To help you better understand these cultural underpinnings of management, this chapter considers two basic questions: (1) What is culture? and (2) How does culture affect management and organizations? Culture will be revisited in most other chapters to show how an understanding of cultural differences in management practices can contribute to the more effective management of multinational organizations.

What Is Culture?

Culture is a concept borrowed from cultural anthropology. Anthropologists believe that cultures provide solutions to problems of adaptation to the environment. Culture helps people become attached to their society. It tells us who we are and to what groups we belong. Culture provides mechanisms for the continuation of the group. For example, culture determines how children are educated and tells us when and whom to marry. Culture pervades most areas of our life, determining, for example, how we should dress and what we should eat.

Anthropologists have numerous and subtle different definitions of culture.[1] However, for the purposes of this book, with its focus on multinational management, **culture** is defined as the pervasive and shared beliefs, norms, and values that guide the everyday life of a group. These beliefs, norms, and values are expressed to current group members and passed on to future group members through cultural rituals, stories, and symbols.

Culture
The pervasive and shared beliefs, norms, and values that guide the everyday life of a group.

Cultural norms
Prescribed and pro-
scribed behaviors, tell-
ing us what we can do
and what we cannot do.

Cultural values
Values that tell us such
things as what is good,
what is beautiful, what
is holy, and what are
legitimate goals in life.

Cultural beliefs
Our understandings
about what is true.

Cultural symbols
These may be physical,
such as national flags
or holy artifacts. In the
workplace, office size
and location can serve
as cultural symbols.

Cultural stories
These include such
things as nursery
rhymes and traditional
legends.

Cultural rituals
Ceremonies such as
baptism, graduation, the
tricks played on a new
worker, or the pledge to
a sorority or fraternity.

Pervasive
The idea that culture
affects almost every-
thing we do, everything
we see, and everything
we feel and believe.

**Shared cultural
values, norms, and
beliefs**
The idea that people in
different cultural groups
have similar views of
the world.

Cultural norms both prescribe and proscribe behaviors; that is, they tell us what we can and cannot do. For example, norms prescribe when and whom we can marry and what clothes we can or cannot wear to a funeral or to the office. **Cultural values** tell us such things as what is good, what is beautiful, what is holy, and what are legitimate goals in life. **Cultural beliefs** represent our understandings about what is true. For example, most people in the United States accept the scientific method as a valid way of discovering facts. In contrast, other cultures may have the belief that facts can be revealed only by God.

Cultural symbols, **stories**, and **rituals** communicate the norms, values, and beliefs of a society or a group to its members. Each generation passes its culture to the next generation by symbols, stories, and rituals. A particular culture is continuously reinforced when people see symbols, hear stories, and engage in rituals.

Rituals include ceremonies such as baptism and graduation, as well as the tricks played on a new worker or the pledge to a sorority or fraternity. Stories include such things as nursery rhymes, proverbs, and traditional legends (such as the U.S. legend that George Washington could not tell a lie). Symbols may be physical, such as national flags or holy artifacts. In the workplace, office size and location can serve as a cultural symbol. North American managers, for example, use large offices with physical barriers such as outer offices as symbols to communicate their power. In contrast, Japanese managers avoid physical barriers. They prefer instead to locate their desks at the center of communication networks, where their desks are surrounded by coworkers.

Culture is **pervasive** in societies. It affects almost everything we do, see, feel, and believe. Pick any aspect of your life, and it is likely affected by your culture. What you sleep on, what you eat, what clothes you wear, how you address your family members and boss, whether you believe that old age is good or bad, what your toilet looks like, all relate to cultural differences. In each of these areas, societies develop pervasive cultural norms, values, and beliefs to assist their members in adapting to their environments.

Because culture affects so many aspects of our lives, many of the core values, norms, and beliefs about what should happen in everyday life are taken for granted. People do not consciously think about how culture affects their behaviors and attitudes. They just do what they believe is "right and natural" (see the Preview Case in Point). Even the society members themselves may not fully understand why they behave as they do.

Another key component of the definition of culture is that cultural values, norms, and beliefs must be **shared** by a group of people: The group must accept that, for the most part, the norms, values, and beliefs of their group are correct and compelling.[2] The phrase "correct and compelling" means that, although people in any culture do not all behave the same way all the time, behaviors are predictable most of the time. Imagine, for example, the chaos that would exist if we did not have norms to guide our driving. For example, when driving on two-lane roads in Ireland, drivers routinely pass slower vehicles even when faced with oncoming traffic. Unlike in the United States, oncoming drivers expect this tactic and routinely move to the breakdown lane. Although this norm makes driving different from that in the United States, the majority of people in Ireland manage to drive without running into each other. The next Case in Point discusses a particular cultural value in France and how this value is changing.

For the multinational manager, the importance of understanding and dealing with cultural differences is unavoidable. To succeed cross-culturally,

CASE IN POINT

Lunch in France

The French are well-known for their cuisine. It is part of French cultural values and norms to spend significant time preparing and eating good food. In fact, French people have traditionally taken the time to sit down for lunch at local restaurants. Such activities are seen as characteristic of being French.

However, recent changes seem to be affecting these cultural values. Older generations are finding that younger generations often prefer to eat sandwiches at their desks rather than taking time for proper sit-down lunches. Women also prefer sandwiches because they can then use the lunch hour for other activities. The French have actually seen sandwich sales jump by about 28 percent between 2003 and 2008.

Source: Based on Economist. *2009. "Sandwich courses," February 7, p. 44.*

---

multinational managers must learn as much as they can about the important cultural norms, values, and beliefs of the societies in which they work. They also must learn to recognize the important symbols, values, and rituals of a culture. Such knowledge helps the multinational manager understand the "why" behind the behavior of their customers, workers, and colleagues.

The next Case in Point shows the challenges caused by a lack of cultural sensitivity to local cultural values.

The next section expands our discussion of culture by looking at how the various levels of culture affect the multinational manager in the business world.

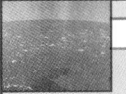

CASE IN POINT

Cultural Misunderstandings

- You negotiate extensively with a Chinese company to enter into an alliance to penetrate the Chinese market. After agreeing on the alliance, you visit the Chinese company and present management with an extremely meticulous document discussing the details of the agreement. You then find that the Chinese are reluctant to establish the alliance. Why? The Chinese are more interested in developing a relationship than in signing a contract.

- You spend considerable time preparing for your meeting in Tokyo. Your meeting goes well, and you are able to answer everyone's questions about the proposed joint venture without hesitation. However, you do not hear from your contacts when you get back to the United States. Why? During your proposal, you crossed your ankle over your knee, a posture that is considered rude in Japan.

- Your meeting with your Chinese counterparts goes very well. After the negotiations end, you exchange gifts with your Chinese hosts. However, your gift is met with looks of disapproval. Why? Although your gift was an expensive clock with the corporate logo, clocks tend to be reminders of funerals in China.

- You are in charge of training managers in China, and the training program seems to be going smoothly. However, you find the trainees very unresponsive after you start using the participants' first names. You also feel some discomfort after praising an individual in the class. You then find that you embarrassed the individual by singling her out. You also find that the Chinese culture tends to be very formal and that it is better to use last names.

Sources: Based on Llorente, Elizabeth. 2006. "A little cultural savvy can go a long way toward sealing a deal: Avoid faux pas that can cost business." The Record, February 7, p. X28; Penzner, Betty. 2006. "The art of Chinese business etiquette: Ancient traditions form the basis of strategy." AFP Exchange, May, 26(4), pp. 61–63; Orkin, Nei. 2008. "Focus on China." Training, 45(6), p. 18.

Levels of Culture

The international businessperson needs to be aware of three levels of culture that may influence multinational operations: national culture, business culture, and the occupational and organizational cultures. Exhibit 2.1 shows the levels of culture that affect multinational management.

National Culture

National culture is the dominant culture within the political boundaries of the nation-state. The dominant national culture usually represents the culture of the people with the greatest population or the greatest political or economic power. Formal education is generally taught, and business is usually conducted in the language of the dominant culture.

Political boundaries, however, do not necessarily reflect cultural boundaries. Many countries, such as Canada and Singapore, have more than one major cultural group within their political boundaries. Even states with relatively homogeneous cultures have subcultures, representing regional and rural/urban cultural differences that affect business transactions.

Most business takes place within the political boundaries of the nation-state. As a result, the dominant culture of the nation-state has the greatest effect on international business. In particular, the dominant national culture usually influences not only the language of business transactions but also the nature and types of laws that govern businesses.

Business Culture

To a large degree, when multinational managers express concern with the impact of culture on international operations, they focus on how national cultures influence business operations. They ask, "How do the [Germans, Indians, Japanese, Koreans, South Americans, Africans, Israelis, etc.] do business?" What concerns these managers is the business culture. More than cultural differences in business etiquette, business culture represents norms, values, and beliefs that pertain to all aspects of doing business in a culture.[3] Business cultures tell people the correct, acceptable ways to conduct business in a society.

EXHIBIT 2.1   Levels of Culture in Multinational Management

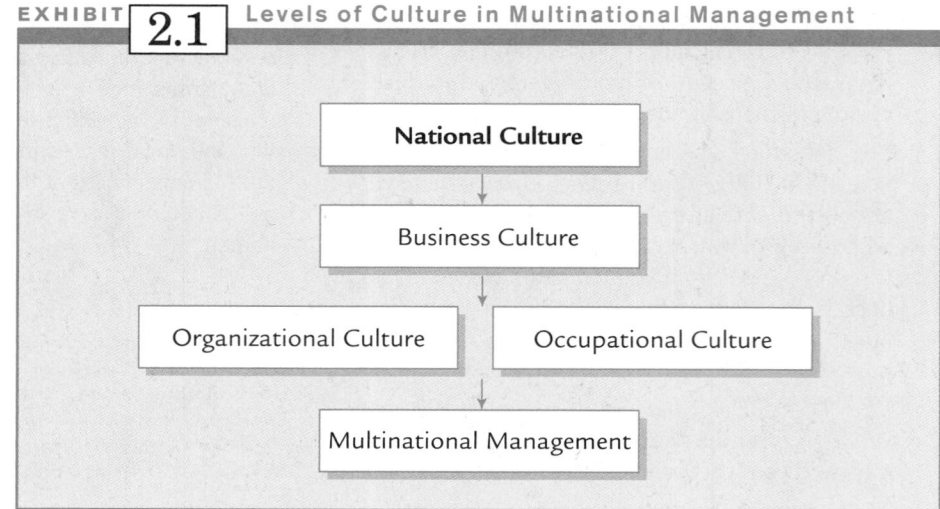

Each national culture produces its own business culture. As such, business cultures are not separate from the broader national culture. Rather, the more pervasive national culture constrains and guides the development of business culture in a society. In any society, business closely interweaves with the broader culture's values, norms, and beliefs. Examples are the priorities given to age and seniority, the role expectations for women with their families, and expectations concerning how superiors should behave toward subordinates.

Focus on Emerging Markets

Business Culture in China

China's business culture is undergoing dramatic and constant change. China's Cultural Revolution actually sent many young professionals to work in rural areas while denying education to others. Also, because most Chinese enterprises were state owned, most Chinese did not have the opportunity to study business-related areas to help craft the Chinese business culture. However, over the past two decades, more Chinese have had the chance to pursue business education and careers, and they are helping to define the Chinese business culture.

Although Chinese business culture is rapidly evolving, a number of key issues need to be addressed when doing business in China:

- *Understand that business moves slowly:* Business happens at a much slower pace in China than in the United States. Companies wanting to do business may need to visit China numerous times before purchasing or negotiating anything.

- *Know the organizational hierarchy:* Chinese companies remain very hierarchical, and it helps to know the highest individuals at the negotiating table because they are most likely the decision makers.

- *Get it in writing:* Chinese companies are reluctant to say no, and what may seem to have been agreed upon may not necessarily be what has been agreed upon. It is therefore important to get as much of an agreement in writing as possible for future consideration.

- *Respect Chinese business etiquette:* Individuals hoping to do business with Chinese companies should respect the many aspects of Chinese business etiquette. For instance, dressing conservatively and arriving promptly for appointments are strongly advised. The negotiator is also expected to present business cards with both hands. It is advantageous to carry business cards in English on one side and in Chinese on the other. Because of the emphasis on formality, it is also advisable to use last names unless asked to do otherwise. Chinese companies also treat their visitors with lavish banquets, and negotiators should expect to participate in some form of drinking.

- *Value harmony and order:* The Chinese value harmony and order. You therefore do not want to highlight individual performances or to praise members of a group. It is typically better to focus on the group performance.

Sources: Based on Hannon, David. 2006. "Dos and DON'Ts of doing business in China." Purchasing, May 18, 135(8), pp. 52–54; Orkin, Neil. 2008. "Focus on China." Training, July–August, 45(6): p. 18; Penzner, Betty. 2006. "The art of Chinese business etiquette: Ancient traditions form the basis of strategy." AFP Exchange, May, 26(4), pp. 61–63.

At a very broad level, business culture, as a reflection of national culture, influences all aspects of work and organizational life. This includes how managers select and promote employees, lead and motivate their subordinates, structure their organizations, select and formulate their strategies, and negotiate with other businesspeople. Much of what you read in this text will help you understand how national and business cultures affect organizations and management. Consider the Focus on Emerging Markets on the previous page, which explores the evolving business culture in China.

Business culture also guides everyday business interactions, and the business cultures of different nations vary widely in the codes of conduct that represent proper business etiquette. As we saw in the last Focus on Emerging Markets, what to wear to a meeting, when and how to use business cards, and how to treat members of a group are examples of business etiquette that vary according to national cultures.

Understanding the basic business etiquette of a business culture is a minimal requirement for the multinational manager. In Germany, "Show up half an hour late [for a business meeting] and it makes no matter how bad the traffic and how tight your schedule. You've likely lost the appointment and may have a tough time getting another."[4]

Occupational Culture and Organizational Culture

Although differences in national and business cultures usually present challenges to the multinational manager, other types of distinct cultures develop around work roles and organizations. These cultures are called occupational and organizational cultures.

Different occupational groups, such as physicians, lawyers, accountants, and craftspeople, have distinct cultures called occupational cultures. Occupational cultures are the norms, values, beliefs, and expected ways of behaving for people in the same occupational group, regardless of their organizational employer.

In spite of the importance of national and business cultures, the multinational manager cannot ignore differences in occupational cultures. To demonstrate this point, a study by Hofstede, which included more than 40 different national cultures, found that people with similar jobs often had very similar cultural values. Moreover, the people from different occupational groups were often more similar to one another than to people from their own national cultures.

The existence of an occupational culture is more prevalent for professional and technical occupations, such as physicians. This distinction occurs because professionals have similar educational backgrounds and have access to the free flow of technical information across national boundaries.

During the last decade, managers and academics realized that the concept of culture also applies to individual organizations. Differences in organizational cultures seemed to answer questions such as why two organizations with similar structures and strategies have different performance levels and why the merger of two otherwise successful companies fails. In particular, the idea of an organizational culture helps us understand how organizations are affected by more than their formally designed systems, such as the organizational structure.

Vijay Sathe defined organizational culture as "the set of important understandings (often unstated) that members of a community share in common." Edgar Schein of MIT added that these assumptions, values, and beliefs concerning the organization are discovered and created when members learn to cope with external and internal problems, such as developing a strategy or the criteria for allocating organizational rewards. When coping strategies—such as

Occupational cultures
Distinct cultures of occupational groups such as physicians, lawyers, accountants, and craftspeople.

Organizational culture
The norms, values, and beliefs concerning the organization that are shared by members of the organization.

Hewlett-Packard's "management by wandering around"—work successfully, they are taught to new members as "the correct way to perceive, think, and feel in relation to those problems."

Seldom do organizations have only one organizational culture, nor perhaps should they. Because organizational subunits (i.e., divisions, departments) all face different situations, most subunits develop distinct subcultures. Subunits may retain many of the overall characteristics of the parent company, but, for example, few would expect an R&D department to have the same culture as a manufacturing plant.

Although various parts of the organization may have different organizational cultures, it is important to note that organizational cultures may also have as important an influence on employees as the national culture does. For instance, consider that many U.S. companies promote the use of first names as a way to encourage employees to bond and feel comfortable with each other. Such practices may not work well in more hierarchical societies such as Germany and France, where it is important to respect titles and hierarchy. However, organizational cultures in smaller firms may actually make the use of first names more acceptable because smallness encourages employees to be more familiar with each other. Consequently, it is critical for the multinational manager to understand the influences of the various levels of culture on employees. In the next section, we discuss some of the more popular national culture frameworks.

Cultural Differences and Basic Values: Three Diagnostic Models to Aid the Multinational Manager

Multinational managers face a complex array of cultures that challenge their ability to manage. To be successful in various cultures, multinational managers must understand the important ways in which national and business cultures differ. The following sections therefore describe three popular cultural models.

The Dutch scientist Geert Hofstede introduced the first model in the early 1980s and continued his research on national culture for over two decades.[5] Management scholars now use Hofstede's work extensively as a way of understanding cultural differences. We call his model the Hofstede model of national culture. Hofstede developed his cultural model primarily based on differences in values and beliefs regarding work goals. It has easily identifiable implications for business by providing a clear link between national and business cultures. It also serves an important role as a basis for extensive research on cross-cultural management.[6] You will see later in the text numerous examples of Hofstede's ideas providing the background for understanding differences in management practices.

The second model, the most recent development of a national culture framework, is represented by the Global Leadership and Organizational Behavior Effectiveness (GLOBE) project.[7] This model, based heavily on Hofstede's national culture model, involves nine cultural dimensions. Seven of the nine dimensions are directly related to the five Hofstede dimensions, while only two of those nine dimensions are developed independently of the Hofstede model. We will therefore focus our discussion of the GLOBE national culture model on these two dimensions.

Finally, the third model, created by Fons Trompenaars, is called the 7d culture model because it represents seven dimensions of culture. This model

Hofstede model of national culture A cultural model mainly based on differences in values and beliefs regarding work goals.

Global Leadership and Organizational Behavior Effectiveness (GLOBE) project Recent large-scale project based on Hofstede's model to determine nine cultural dimensions of 62 countries.

7d culture model Seven-dimension cultural model based on beliefs regarding how people relate to each other, how people manage time, and how people deal with nature.

comes from extensive and continuing cross-national research by Fons Trompenaars and his colleagues.[8]

All three models equip managers with the basic tools necessary to analyze the cultures in which they do business. Furthermore, these approaches also provide useful terms to help you understand the complexities of different cultural values. By using these models, you will develop an initial understanding of important cultural differences and key cultural traits.

The next section provides more detail on the Hofstede model, followed by a briefer section describing the GLOBE model. The section concludes with Trompenaars' 7d model.

Hofstede's Model of National Culture

To describe national cultures, Hofstede[9] uses five dimensions of basic cultural values:

1. *Power distance:* Expectations regarding equality among people.
2. *Uncertainty avoidance:* Typical reactions to situations considered different and dangerous.
3. *Individualism:* Relationship between the individual and the group in society.
4. *Masculinity:* Expectations regarding gender roles.
5. *Long-term orientation:* Basic orientation toward time.

Hofstede's framework was based on 116,000 surveys from 88,000 employees of IBM subsidiaries around the world. Although the original sample included 72 countries, Hofstede used only the countries that had more than 50 responses.[10] Hofstede thus identified four of these cultural value dimensions in the reduced sample of 40 countries.[11] However, the database was later expanded to include 10 additional countries from three regions: Arab countries and East and West Africa. Later research by Hofstede and others added to the number of countries studied and introduced the fifth dimension, long-term orientation.[12]

Research on the long-term orientation dimension was unique. Rather than using survey questions developed by Western researchers, Michael Bond and several Chinese colleagues designed a new survey based on questions developed by Asian researchers reflecting Confucian values. Hofstede and Bond have related the long-term orientation to the recent economic growth in the mini-dragons (e.g., Singapore, South Korea) of the rising Asian economies.[13]

Hofstede's Cultural Model Applied to Organizations and Management

The following section defines Hofstede's dimensions of national culture.[14] It also adapts and extends this work to show how cultural values affect numerous management practices in different cultures. The management practices considered in the discussion of Hofstede's model are:

1. *Human resources management:*
   a. Management selection: How people are chosen for jobs.
   b. Training: What the focus of job training is.
   c. Evaluation and promotion: What counts to get ahead.
   d. Remuneration: What accounts for differences in pay.
2. *Leadership styles:* How leaders behave.

3. *Motivational assumptions:* Beliefs regarding how people respond to work.

4. *Decision making and organizational design:* How managers structure their organizations and make decisions.

5. *Strategy:* Effects of culture on selecting and implementing strategies.

Power Distance

Power distance is concerned with how cultures deal with inequality. It focuses on (1) the norms that tell superiors (bosses, leaders) how much they can determine the behavior of their subordinates and (2) the values and beliefs that superiors and subordinates are fundamentally different kinds of people.

High-power-distance countries have norms, values, and beliefs such as the following:[15]

- Inequality is fundamentally good.
- Everyone has a place; some are high, some are low.
- Most people should be dependent on a leader.
- The powerful are entitled to privileges.
- The powerful should not hide their power.

Power distance Expectations regarding equality among people.

Organizations in countries high on power distance use management systems and processes that reflect a strong concern with hierarchy. As shown later in the chapter in Exhibit 2.7, Latin American, Latin European, and Far Eastern countries demonstrate the highest levels of power distance.

The concern for hierarchy and inequality in organizations is rooted in early socialization in the family and school. In high-power-distance cultures, children are expected to be obedient to parents and elders. This deference continues as long as parents are alive. When children enter school, teachers assume the role of dominance. Children must show extreme respect and seldom challenge a teacher's authority. Later in life, organizations assume many of the roles of parents and teachers.

In high-power-distance countries, the ideal people for a managerial job have either come from a high social class or graduated from an elite university. These characteristics define the person as having the intrinsic or built-in qualities of a leader. Who you are in terms of elite associations is more important than past performance. Leaders and subordinates expect large wage differences between management and workers.

The basic motivational assumption in high-power-distance countries is that people dislike work and try to avoid it. Consequently, managers believe that they must adopt a Theory X leadership style; that is, they must be authoritarian, must force workers to perform, and must closely supervise their subordinates. Similarly, employee training emphasizes compliance (following orders) and trustworthiness.

Organizational structures and systems match the assumptions regarding leadership and motivation. Decision making is centralized. Those at the top make most of the decisions. The close supervision of workers requires many supervisors and a tall organizational pyramid (an organization with many levels). Strategic decisions in high-power-distance countries are influenced by the need to maintain and support those in power.

Comparative Management **Brief**

Respect and Power in Mexico versus Respect and Fair Play in the United States

In describing Mexican business culture, a high-power-distance culture, Marc J. Erlich, a psychologist who works with U.S. businesses in Mexico, noted:

> Within Mexican society, there is a tendency to respect those in power. The boss's respectability is manifested by maintaining a definite social distance, through an unwillingness to delegate.
>
> Fair play, shared responsibility, and playing by the rules are characteristics of respect for the [North] American. Respect is earned, not given. North of the border, the ability to be one of the team reflects responsibility.
>
> The U.S. executive frequently perceives Mexican submission to authority as a lack of resolve and an unfortunate passivity. The Mexican will typically view the U.S. executive's insistence on fair play and desire to delegate as an inability to accept the power associated with position.
>
> The power distance is also reflected in Mexican organizations, which are hierarchical. Top management uses and is expected to use power. This organizational structure results in many layers of management and slow decision making. Building trust is thus a key component of Mexican business culture and can speed up decision making for foreign firms. However, impatience is perceived as a weakness in Mexican culture; so foreign multinational managers should avoid moving too quickly.

Source: Based on Executive Planet. 2009. http://www.executiveplanet.com; Erlich, Mark J. 1993. "Making sense of the bicultural workplace." Business Mexico, August, p. 18.

The above Comparative Management Brief describes how differences in power distance affect specific U.S. and Mexican business practices.

Exhibit 2.2 gives a summary of the managerial implications for power distance. The next section considers uncertainty avoidance.

Uncertainty Avoidance

Uncertainty avoidance relates to norms, values, and beliefs regarding a tolerance for ambiguity. A higher-uncertainty-avoidance culture seeks to structure social systems (politics, education, and business) where order and predictability are paramount, and rules and regulations dominate. In such a culture, risky situations create stress and upset people. Consequently, people avoid behaviors such as changing jobs.

High-uncertainty-avoidance countries have norms, values, and beliefs such as the following:[16]

- Conflict should be avoided.
- Deviant people and ideas should not be tolerated.
- Laws are very important and should be followed.
- Experts and authorities are usually correct.
- Consensus is important.

The business cultures in countries high on uncertainty avoidance have management systems and processes that make organizations and employees

EXHIBIT 2.2   Management Implications of Power Distance

Management Processes	Low Power Distance	High Power Distance
Human resources management		
Management selection	Educational achievement	Social class; elite education
Training	For autonomy	For conformity/obedience
Evaluations/promotion	Performance	Compliance; trustworthiness
Remuneration	Small wage difference between management and worker	Large wage difference between management and worker
Leadership styles	Participative; less direct supervision	Theory X; authoritarian, with close supervision
Motivational assumptions	People like work; extrinsic and intrinsic rewards	Assume people dislike work; coercion
Decision making/organizational design	Decentralized; flat pyramids; small proportion of supervisors	Tall pyramids; large proportion of supervisors
Strategy issues	Varied	Crafted to support the power elite or government

Sources: Adapted from Hofstede, Geert. 1980. Culture's Consequences: International Differences in Work-Related Values. *London: Sage; Hofstede, Geert. 1991.* Cultures and Organizations: Software of the Mind. *London: McGraw-Hill; and Hofstede, Geert. 1993. "Cultural dimensions in people management." In Vladimir Pucik, Noel M. Tichy, and Carole K. Barnette,* Globalizing Management. *Hoboken, NJ: Wiley, pp. 139–158.*

dependable and predictable. People in such cultures react with stress and anxiety when the rules of behavior are not clear in organizational settings. Generally, Nordic and Anglo countries are low on uncertainty avoidance, whereas Latin European and Latin American countries are high. As the next Case in Point shows, Belgian students have little uncertainty when deciding whether to enter their professors' offices.

In high-uncertainty-avoidance cultures, entry-level people are chosen for their potential fit with and loyalty to the organization. Managers follow the logic, "If people are like me, come from my town or my family, then I understand them and trust them more." This minimizes interpersonal conflict, reduces potential employee turnover, and makes people more predictable.

In some cultures, uncertainty regarding employees is further reduced by selecting and promoting people with specialized expertise. Employers seek out people who will be loyal and committed to them and to the organization. Later, seniority, long-term commitment to the organization, and expertise in the area of management become the prime bases for promotion and payment. Both managers and employees believe that loyalty to the organization is a virtue and that conflict and competition should be avoided.

Task-directed leaders give clear and explicit directions to subordinates. This reduces ambiguity regarding job expectations. The boss tells workers exactly what to do. Task-directed leaders are the preferred leaders in high-uncertainty-avoidance cultures. Such leaders make subordinates less anxious, because subordinates know exactly what is expected of them. Similarly, organizations in these cultures have many written rules and procedures. Like the situation produced by the task-directed leader, extensive rules and procedures tell employees exactly what the organization expects of them. Consequently, employees believe that these rules should not be broken.

In contrast, leaders in low-uncertainty-avoidance cultures favor more flexibility and allow subordinates more choices on the job. The design of their

Uncertainty Avoidance in a Belgian University and in Corruption

Belgium ranks in the top 10 percent (91st percentile) on Hofstede's uncertainty avoidance dimension. As a result, one expects Belgian organizations to have many of the characteristics for high uncertainty avoidance, as shown in Exhibit 2.3. This seems true even for Belgium's universities.

At the University of Leuven, an old Belgian university, three lights stand over a professor's door: green, yellow, and red. Students wishing to see their professor must ring a bell and wait for an appropriate response. Green means come in, yellow means wait a few minutes, and red means go away. There is no ambiguity in these situations. Students do not have to interpret the situation to see whether the professor is busy. In contrast, most students from the United States, a low-uncertainty-avoidance country (21st percentile), would probably find this degree of formality impersonal at best and perhaps even insulting.

Uncertainty avoidance also has an impact on the level of corruption in a country. Research suggests that countries with high levels of uncertainty avoidance tend to have high levels of corruption. Because of the prevalence of strict rules and regulations in high-uncertainty-avoidance countries, people often find it unnecessary to use informal channels to achieve their personal objectives. It is therefore more likely for officials to seek or accept bribes. Furthermore, the bureaucratic structures of high uncertainty societies also often encourage managers to behave unethically.

Sources: Based on Gannon, Martin J., and Associates. 1994. Understanding Global Cultures. Thousand Oaks, CA: Sage Publications; McGinnis, A. Seleim, and N. Bontis. 2009. "The relationship between culture and corruption: A cross-national study." Journal of Intellectual Capital, 10(1), pp. 165–184.

organizations also builds in more freedom, with fewer rules and regulations. There are also more subordinates per manager, which results in less supervision and greater autonomy for workers.

People in high-uncertainty-avoidance cultures do not like risk, and they often fear failure. As decision makers, they are conservative. Thus, it is unlikely that individual managers will choose risky strategies for their organizations. Hofstede[17] notes, however, that neither low nor high uncertainty avoidance necessarily relates to success. Innovations may be more likely in low-uncertainty-avoidance countries like the United States, but the implementation of innovations may be more likely in high-uncertainty-avoidance countries such as Japan.

Exhibit 2.3 summarizes the managerial implications of uncertainty avoidance.

Individualism/Collectivism

Individualism
Relationship between the individual and the group in society.

The values, norms, and beliefs associated with individualism focus on the relationship between the individual and the group. Individualistic cultures view people as unique. People are valued in terms of their own achievements, status, and other unique characteristics.

Collectivism
Set of cultural values that views people largely through the groups to which they belong.

The cultural values associated with individualism are often discussed with the opposing set of values, called collectivism. Collectivist cultures view people largely in terms of the groups to which they belong. Social groups such as family, social class, organization, and team all take precedence over the individual.

Countries high on individualism have norms, values, and beliefs such as the following:[18]

- People are responsible for themselves.
- Individual achievement is ideal.
- People need not be emotionally dependent on organizations or groups.

EXHIBIT **2.3** Management Implications of Uncertainty Avoidance

Management Processes	High Uncertainty Avoidance	Low Uncertainty Avoidance
Human resources management		
Management selection	Seniority; expected loyalty	Past job performance; education
Training	Specialized	Training to adapt
Evaluation/promotion	Seniority; expertise; loyalty	Objective individual performance data; job switching for promotions
Remuneration	Based on seniority or expertise	Based on performance
Leadership styles	Task-oriented	Nondirective; person-oriented; flexible
Motivational assumptions	People seek security, avoid competition	People are self-motivated, competitive
Decision making/organizational design	Larger organization; tall hierarchy; formalized; many standardized procedures	Smaller organizations; flat hierarchy, less formalized, with fewer written rules and standardized procedures
Strategy issues	Averse to risk	Risk taking

Sources: Adapted from Hofstede, Geert. 1980. Culture's Consequences: International Differences in Work-Related Values. *London: Sage; Hofstede, Geert. 1991.* Cultures and Organizations: Software of the Mind. *London: McGraw-Hill; and Hofstede, Geert. 1993. "Cultural dimensions in people management." In Vladimir Pucik, Noel M. Tichy, and Carole K. Barnette,* Globalizing Management. *Hoboken, NJ: Wiley, pp. 139–158.*

In contrast, collectivist countries have norms, values, and beliefs like the following:[19]

- One's identity is based on group membership.
- Group decision making is best.
- Groups protect individuals in exchange for their loyalty.

Countries with low individualism have collectivist norms, values, and beliefs that influence a variety of managerial practices. Organizations in collectivist cultures tend to select managers who belong to favored groups. Usually, the favored group is the extended family and friends of the extended family. Being a relative or someone known by the family becomes more important than an individual's personal qualifications. In contrast, people in highly individualistic societies, such as the United States (the most individualistic society by Hofstede's measurement), often view favoritism toward family and friends as unfair and perhaps illegal. In such societies, most people believe that job selection should be based on universalistic qualification, which means that the same qualifications apply universally to all candidates. The cultural belief is that open competition allows the most qualified individual to get the job.

Organizations in collectivist cultures base promotions mostly on seniority and age. People tend to move up the organizational hierarchy by being promoted with their age cohort (people of the same age). People feel that a major reward for working is being taken care of by their organizations, a type of organizational paternalism. The senior managers in the organization act as father figures. Unlike individualistic societies, where people expect extrinsic rewards such as money and promotions, managers in collectivist societies use "a call to duty" as an emotional appeal to work for the good of the group.

Multinational Management **Brief**

Asian Countries and Collectivism

Chinese businesspeople outside the People's Republic of China, whom Hofstede calls "the overseas Chinese," have developed highly performing businesses in Taiwan, Hong Kong, and Singapore, as well as throughout the world. Many of their organizations, however, lack all the trappings of modern management. They tend to be feudal (i.e., dominated by the entrepreneurial father), family owned, and small, and they have few if any professional managers. Most focus on only one product, and cooperation with networks of other small organizations is based on personal family friendships.

There are seldom any formal systems within or between organizations—only networks of people guided roughly by Confucian ethics. For example, in the father-dominated family firm, Confucian ethics dictate that the son must show respect and obedience to the father and that the father must protect and show consideration for the son. In a practical sense, this means that the father will dominate organizational decision making. As the son gets older, he may be given considerations such as managing a new firm venture. However, on inheriting the family firm, brothers may engage in more horizontal decision making because their family obligations are less vertical.

This family aspect to business is not unique to China. Japan and South Korea are also collectivistic societies, and how businesses operate is also determined by collectivism. For instance, many Western-based companies are readily willing to sever relationships with suppliers in an effort to cut cost. However, this practice is not acceptable in Japan, where collectivism encourages Japanese companies to hold long-term and often personal relationships with suppliers.

However, as you will see later, although many Asian countries are collectivistic, they are not necessarily similar. For instance, Japanese companies, as a display of collectivism, are well-known for providing lifetime employment. In contrast, Chinese companies do not necessarily offer such benefits. Furthermore, although Japanese employees may not address salary inequities with their supervisors, Chinese employees are likely to discuss salary with each other and their supervisors.

Sources: Based on Dvorak, Phred. 2006. "Managing: Making U.S. ideas work elsewhere: Firms work to adapt management theory to local practices." Wall Street Journal, May 22, p. 31; Hofstede, Geert. 1993. "Cultural constraints in management theories." Academy of Management Executive, 7, p. 1; Li, Xinjian, and Martin Puettrill. 2007. "Strategy implications of business culture differences between Japan and China," Business Strategy Series, 8(2), pp. 148–154; and Syu, Agnes. 1994. "A linkage between Confucianism and the Chinese family firm in the Republic of China." In Dorothy Marcic and Sheila M. Puffer, eds. Management International. Minneapolis, MN: West.

The effects of collectivism on aspects of various Asian countries are described in the above Multinational Management Brief.

Exhibit 2.4 summarizes the managerial implications of high individualism versus collectivist (low individualism) norms, values, and beliefs.

Masculinity

Different cultural expectations for men and women occur in all societies. In all cultures, men and women receive different socialization and usually perform

EXHIBIT **2.4**   Management Implications of Individualism

Management Processes	Low Individualism	High Individualism
Human resources management		
Management selection	Group membership; school or university	Universalistic based on individual traits
Training	Focus on company-based skills	General skills for individual achievement
Evaluation/promotion	Slow, with group; seniority	Based on individual performance
Remuneration	Based on group membership/ organizational paternalism	Extrinsic rewards (money, promotion) based on market value
Leadership styles	Appeals to duty and commitment	Individual rewards and punishments based on performance
Motivational assumptions	Moral involvement	Calculative; individual cost/benefit
Decision making/organizational design	Group; slow; preference for larger organization	Individual responsibility; preference for smaller organizations
Strategy issues	Incremental changes with periodic revolutions	Aggressive

Sources: Adapted from Hofstede, Geert. 1980. Culture's Consequences: International Differences in Work-Related Values. London: Sage; Hofstede, Geert. 1991. Cultures and Organizations: Software of the Mind. London: McGraw-Hill; and Hofstede, Geert. 1993. "Cultural dimensions in people management." In Vladimir Pucik, Noel M. Tichy, and Carole K. Barnette, Globalizing Management. Hoboken, NJ: Wiley, pp. 139–158.

different roles. A variety of studies shows that, in most—but certainly not all—cultures, male socialization has a greater emphasis on achievement, motivation, and self-reliance. In contrast, the socialization of women emphasizes nurturance and responsibility.[20]

As a cultural dimension, masculinity represents the overall tendency of a culture to support the traditional masculine orientation; that is, higher masculinity means that the business culture of a society takes on traditional masculine values, such as emphasis on advancement and earnings. However, within each culture, there remain gender differences in values and attitudes.

Masculinity Tendency of a society to emphasize traditional gender roles.

High-masculinity countries have norms, values, and beliefs such as the following.[21]

- Gender roles should be clearly distinguished.
- Men are assertive and dominant.
- Machismo or exaggerated maleness in men is good.
- People—especially men—should be decisive.
- Work takes priority over other duties, such as family.
- Advancement, success, and money are important.

In highly masculine societies, jobs are clearly defined by gender. There are men's jobs and women's jobs. Men usually choose jobs that are associated with long-term careers. Women usually choose jobs that are associated with short-term employment, before marriage and children. However, smaller families, delayed childbirth, pressure for dual-career earnings, and changing national cultural values may be eroding the traditional views of masculinity. Consider the cases for working women in Japan and Sweden, as described in the next Comparative Management Brief.

Comparative Management **Brief**

Working Women in Japan and Sweden: Contrasts in Cultural Masculinity

Japan is currently the highest-ranking masculine culture. For instance, it ranks 106 among 189 countries in terms of the percentage of female lawmakers in its House of Representatives. It nevertheless now faces a challenge to its traditional cultural values regarding masculinity and the role of women. Traditionally, Japanese companies expected most women, even college graduates, to quit their jobs by the age of 25. Women occupy most of the part-time jobs and have less access to the fabled lifetime employment than do men. However, with the slowdown in the Japanese economy, many women are not leaving as expected. The popular Japanese press now has many stories about companies that "have problems with their women." Such phraseology reflects the conflict of changing values regarding masculinity in Japan. Although there are traditional cultural expectations about what women "should" do regarding work and family, there is no legal or accepted way to force Japanese women to leave their jobs when they choose to remain employed.

Perhaps because of strong norms of equality, the Nordic countries rank lowest in masculinity. In contrast to masculine Japan, where support for working women, such as day care, is rare, the Swedish government provides day care to all who need it. Since more than 85 percent of Swedish women work outside the home, day care is essential. In addition, with the birth of a child, one year of parental leave is available for both parents. Approximately 20 percent of the men take this option.

Sources: Based in part on Gannon, Martin J., and Associates. 1994. Understanding Global Cultures. *Thousand Oaks, CA: Sage; Nagata, K. 2009. "Women still largely absent from politics: Japan ranks 106th in female participation in national legislature," Mc-Clatchy Tribune Business News, Japan Times, January 29.*

In addition to clear work-related roles based on gender, work in masculine cultures tends to be very central and important to people, especially men. In cultures like Japan, men often take assignments for over a year in other cities or other countries while other family members remain at home.

In the high-masculinity-culture, recognition on the job is considered a prime motivator. People work long hours, often work more than five days a week, and take short vacations. In most low-masculinity-countries, work typically has less centrality. People take more time off, take longer vacations, and emphasize the quality of life. There are, however, some exceptions. In the highly masculine Mexican culture, for example, gender differences are strong but work is less central. The cultural value is that people "work to live."

In masculine cultures, managers act decisively. They avoid the appearance of intuitive decision making, which is often regarded as feminine. They prefer to work in large organizations, and they emphasize performance and growth in strategic decision making.

Exhibit 2.5 shows the major effects of high masculinity on work and organizations.

The next section deals with the impact of long-term orientation on work and organizations.

Long-Term Orientation

Long-term (Confucian) orientation
An orientation toward time that values patience.

Because we have data on the **long-term (Confucian) orientation** for only a few countries, Hofstede and others have produced less research on how this

EXHIBIT 2.5   Management Implications of Masculinity

Management Processes	Low Masculinity	High Masculinity
Human resources management		
Management selection	Independent of gender, school ties less important; androgyny	Jobs gender identified; school performance and ties important
Training	Job-oriented	Career oriented
Evaluation/promotion	Job performance, with less gender-based assignments	Continues gender-tracking
Remuneration	Less salary difference between levels; more time off	More salary preferred to fewer hours
Leadership styles	More participative	More Theory X; authoritarian
Motivational assumptions	Emphasis on quality of life, time off, vacations; work not central	Emphasis on performance and growth; excelling to be best; work central to life; job recognition important
Decision making/organizational design	Intuitive/group; smaller organizations	Decisive/individual; larger organization preferred
Strategy issues	Preference for consistent growth	Aggressive

Sources: Adapted from Hofstede, Geert. 1980. Culture's Consequences: International Differences in Work-Related Values. *London: Sage; Hofstede, Geert. 1991.* Cultures and Organizations: Software of the Mind. *London: McGraw-Hill; and Hofstede, Geert. 1993. "Cultural dimensions in people management." In Vladimir Pucik, Noel M. Tichy, and Carole K. Barnette,* Globalizing Management. *Hoboken, NJ: Wiley, pp. 139–158.*

orientation relates to work and organizations. Consequently, the discussion is more speculative on this issue than on others.

Because of the need to be sensitive to social relationships, managers in cultures high on long-term orientation are selected based on the fit of their personal and educational characteristics to the company. A prospective employee's particular skills have less importance in the hiring decision than they do in cultures with short-term orientation. Training and socialization for a long-term commitment to the organization compensate for any initial weaknesses in work-related skills. Organizations in cultures with short-term orientation, in contrast, must focus on immediately usable skills. Managers do not assume that employees will remain with the company for an extended time. They cannot be assured of a return on any investment in employee training and socialization.

In short-term-oriented cultures, leaders use quick rewards that focus on pay and rapid promotion. Employees in long-term-oriented cultures value security, and leaders work on developing social obligations.

Hofstede notes that Western cultures,[22] which tend to have short-term orientations, value logical analysis in their approach to organizational decisions. Managers believe in logically analyzing the situation for their company and following up with a solid game plan. In contrast, Eastern cultures, which rank the highest on long-term orientation, value synthesis in organizational decisions. Synthesis is not a search for the correct answer or strategy. Rather, synthesis takes apparently conflicting points of view and logic and seeks practical solutions. Not surprisingly, organizations in short-term-oriented cultures are designed and managed purposefully to respond to immediate pressures from the environment. Managers often use quick layoffs of "excess" employees to adjust to shrinking demand for products. Organizations in long-term-oriented cultures are designed first to manage internal social relationships. The assumption is that good social relationships eventually lead to successful organizations. The difference between long- and short-term-oriented cultures is apparent in the goals that companies set in strategic decision making. Managers in countries such as the United States want immediate financial returns. They are the most comfortable with fast, measurable success. Countries with more long-term orientations do not ignore financial objectives, but they prioritize growth and long-term paybacks. The long time horizons allow managers to experiment and seek success by developing their "game plans" as they go along.

Exhibit 2.6 summarizes the managerial implications of long-term (Confucian) orientation.

To apply Hofstede's model to specific countries, look at Exhibit 2.7, which displays the percentile ranks of selected countries on five of Hofstede's dimensions of national culture. To interpret this exhibit, you need to understand percentiles. The percentile for each country tells you the percentage of other countries that rank below it. For example, the United States has the highest scores on individualism, so its percentile rank tells you that 100 percent of the countries are equal to or below the United States on individualism. A percentile rank of 75 percent tells you that 75 percent of the other countries have equal or lower ranks on a cultural dimension.

Country clusters
Groups of countries with similar cultural patterns.

To simplify generalizations from Hofstede's data, the table groups countries by country clusters.[23] **Country clusters** are groups of countries, such as Anglo, Latin American, and Latin European, with roughly similar cultural patterns. Although cultures differ within these broad classifications, such summaries are useful for condensing cultural information. They are also useful to predict likely cultural traits when specific information is not available.

EXHIBIT 2.6   Management Implications of Long-Term Orientation

Management Processes	Short-Term Orientation	Long-Term Orientation
Human resources management		
Management selection	Objective skill assessment for immediate use to company	Fit of personal and background characteristics
Training	Limited to immediate company needs	Investment in long-term employment skills
Evaluation/promotion	Fast; based on skill contributions	Slow; develop skills and loyalty
Remuneration	Pay, promotions	Security
Leadership styles	Use of incentives for economic advancement	Building social obligations
Motivational assumptions	Immediate rewards necessary	Immediate gratification subordinate to long-term individual and company goals
Decision making/organizational design	Logical analyses of problems; design for logic of company situation	Synthesis to reach consensus; design for social relationships
Strategy issues	Fast; measurable payback	Long-term profits and growth; incrementalism

Sources: Adapted from Hofstede, Geert. 1980. Culture's Consequences: International Differences in Work-Related Values. London: Sage; Hofstede, Geert. 1991. Cultures and Organizations: Software of the Mind. London: McGraw-Hill; and Hofstede, Geert. 1993. "Cultural dimensions in people management." In Vladimir Pucik, Noel M. Tichy, and Carole K. Barnette, Globalizing Management. Hoboken, NJ: Wiley, pp. 139–158.

Percentile Ranks for Hofstede's Cultural Dimensions for Selected
Countries by Cultural Cluster (100 = highest, 50 = middle)

EXHIBIT **2.7**

Cultural Group/ Country	Power Distance	Uncertainty Avoidance	Individualism	Masculinity	Long-Term Orientation
Anglo:					
Australia	25	32	98	72	48
Canada	28	24	93	57	19
Great Britain	21	12	96	84	27
United States	30	21	100	74	35
Arab:					
Arab countries	89	51	52	58	n/a
Far Eastern:					
China	89	44	39	54	100
Hong Kong	73	8	32	67	96
Singapore	77	2	26	49	69
Taiwan	46	53	19	41	92
Germanic:					
Austria	2	56	68	98	n/a
Germany	21	47	74	84	48
Netherlands	26	36	93	6	65
Switzerland	17	40	75	93	n/a
Latin America:					
Argentina	35	78	59	63	n/a
Colombia	70	64	9	80	n/a
Mexico	92	68	42	91	n/a
Venezuela	92	61	8	96	n/a
Latin European:					
Belgium	64	92	87	60	n/a
France	73	78	82	35	n/a
Italy	38	58	89	93	n/a
Spain	43	78	64	31	n/a
Near Eastern:					
Greece	50	100	45	67	n/a
Iran	46	42	57	35	n/a
Turkey	67	71	49	41	n/a
Nordic:					
Denmark	6	6	85	8	n/a
Finland	15	42	70	13	n/a
Norway	12	30	77	4	n/a
Sweden	12	8	82	2	58
Independent:					
Brazil	75	61	52	51	81
India	82	17	62	63	71
Israel	4	66	66	47	n/a
Japan	32	89	55	100	n/a

Sources: Adapted from Hofstede, Geert. 1980. Culture's Consequences: International Differences in Work-Related Values. London: Sage; Hofstede, Geert. 1991. Cultures and Organizations: Software of the Mind. London: McGraw-Hill; Hofstede, Geert. 1993. "Cultural dimensions in people management." In Vladimir Pucik, Noel M. Tichy, and Carole K. Barnette, Globalizing Management. Hoboken, NJ: Wiley, pp. 139–158; Ronen, S., and O. Shenkar. 1985. "Clustering countries on attitudinal dimensions: A review and synthesis." Academy of Management Review, September.

Next, we consider the GLOBE model of culture.[24] This model is heavily based on Hofstede's dimensions, and we focus mainly on the two dimensions unique to the model.

GLOBE National Culture Framework

The GLOBE project involves 170 researchers who collected data on 17,000 managers from 62 countries around the world.[25] Using the Hofstede model as the base, the GLOBE researchers conceptualized and developed nine cultural dimensions. Of the nine dimensions, only two are independent of the Hofstede model. The seven GLOBE dimensions that are similar to Hofstede's model are:

- Assertiveness orientation and gender egalitarianism (similar to masculinity-femininity).
- Institutional and family collectivism (similar to individualism-collectivism).
- Future orientation (similar to long-term orientation).
- Power distance.
- Uncertainty avoidance.[26]

Given the GLOBE project dimensions' similarity with Hofstede's, many of the implications discussed earlier for Hofstede's cultural dimensions apply for the corresponding GLOBE dimensions. However, we focus on the two dimensions unique to the GLOBE project: performance orientation and humane orientation.

Performance orientation refers to the degree to which a society encourages its members to innovate, to improve their performance, and to strive for excellence. This dimension is similar to Weber's Protestant work ethic and reflects the desire for achievement in society.[27] Countries such as the United States and Singapore have high scores on performance orientation, whereas countries such as Russia and Greece have low scores on that dimension. Javidan, Dorfman, de Luque, and House argue that countries with high performance orientation scores tend to favor training and development, whereas in countries low on performance orientation, family and background are more important.[28] In societies with high performance orientation, people are rewarded for taking initiative and for performing with the belief that one can succeed by trying hard. In contrast, low-performance-oriented societies reward harmony with the environment, emphasizing loyalty and integrity while regarding assertiveness as unacceptable. Exhibit 2.8 summarizes some of the management implications of performance orientation.

Humane orientation is an indication of the extent to which individuals are expected to be fair, altruistic, caring, and generous. In high-humane-oriented societies, the need for belongingness and affiliation is emphasized more than needs such as material possessions, self-fulfillment, and pleasure. Less humane-oriented societies are more likely to value self-interest and self-gratification.[29]

Countries such as Malaysia and Egypt score highly on humane orientation, whereas France and Germany have low scores. As such, companies in high-humane-oriented countries such as Egypt are generally expected to be caring and offer benefits that seem unusual for U.S. companies. For instance, companies may offer tuition assistance to employees' children, paid family vacations, or even home appliances.[30] Exhibit 2.9 lists some of the management implications of humane orientation.

Performance orientation
The degree to which the society encourages societal members to innovate, to improve their performance, and to strive for excellence.

Humane orientation
An indication of the extent to which individuals are expected to be fair, altruistic, caring, and generous.

EXHIBIT **2.8**   Management Implications of Performance Orientation

Management Processes	High Performance Orientation	Low Performance Orientation
Human resources management		
Management selection	Based on individual achievement and merit	Emphasis on seniority and experience
Training	Value training and development	Value societal and family relationships
Evaluation/promotion	Based on merit and achievement	Based on age
Remuneration	Pay, promotions	Tradition
Performance appraisal	Systems emphasize results	Systems emphasize integrity and loyalty
Leadership styles	Have can-do attitude	Emphasize loyalty and belongingness
Motivational assumptions	Value bonuses and rewards	Value harmony with environment and quality of life
Communication	Value direct and to-the-point communication	Value subtlety and ambiguity in communication

Source: Adapted from House, R., P. Hanges, M. Javidan, P. Dorfman, and V. Gupta. 2004. Culture, Leadership and Organizations: The GLOBE Study of 62 Societies. Thousand Oaks, CA: Sage Publications.

EXHIBIT **2.9**   Management Implications of Humane Orientation

Management Processes	High Humane Orientation	Low Humane Orientation
Relationships	Importance of others (i.e., family, friends, and community)	Emphasis on self-interest
Leadership styles		
Style	More consideration-oriented leadership	Less consideration-oriented leadership
Concern for subordinates	Individualized/holistic consideration	Standardized/limited consideration
Approach	More benevolent	Less benevolent
Relationship with subordinates	More personal and less informal	More informal and less personal
Motivational assumptions	Need for belongingness	Motivation by power and material possessions
Company role	Support for employees	Expectation of people to solve problems on their own

Source: Adapted from House, R., P. Hanges, M. Javidan, P. Dorfman, and V. Gupta. 2004. Culture, Leadership and Organizations: The GLOBE Study of 62 Societies. Thousand Oaks, CA: Sage Publications.

The GLOBE data shows that countries can be categorized by ten clusters and that these clusters differ with respect to the nine cultural dimensions. Clusters in the GLOBE project include Anglo, Confucian Asia, Eastern Europe, Germanic Europe, Latin America, Latin Europe, Middle East, Nordic Europe, Southern Asia, and Sub-Saharan. Exhibit 2.10 shows the various clusters and the corresponding cultural scores. Refer to Exhibit 15.7 in Chapter 15 to see which countries are included in each cluster. Many of the management implications of Hofstede's cultural dimensions can be used for the seven GLOBE dimensions that are similar to Hofstede's.

EXHIBIT 2.10 The GLOBE Model of Culture

Cluster	Performance Orientation	Assertiveness	Future Orientation	Humane Orientation	Institutional Collectivism	In-Group Collectivism	Gender Egalitarianism	Power Distance	Uncertainty Avoidance
Anglo	High	Medium	Medium	Medium	Medium	Low	Medium	Medium	Medium
Confucian Asia	High	Medium	Medium	Medium	High	High	Medium	Medium	Medium
Eastern Europe	Low	High	Low	Medium	Medium	High	High	Medium	Low
Germanic Europe	High	High	High	Low	Low	Low	Medium	Medium	High
Latin America	Low	Medium	Low	Medium	Low	High	Medium	Medium	Low
Latin Europe	Medium	Medium	Medium	Low	Low	Medium	Medium	Medium	Medium
Middle East	Medium	Medium	Low	Medium	Medium	High	Low	Medium	Low
Nordic Europe	Medium	Low	High	Medium	High	Low	High	Low	High
Southern Asia	Medium	Medium	Medium	High	Medium	High	Medium	Medium	Medium
Sub-Saharan Africa	Medium	Medium	Medium	High	Medium	Medium	Medium	Medium	Medium

Source: Based on Javidan, Mansour, Peter W. Dorfman, Mary Sully de Luque, and Robert J. House. 2006. "In the eye of the beholder: Cross cultural lessons in leadership for project GLOBE." The Academy of Management Perspectives, February, 20(1), pp. 67–90.

Next we consider the model developed by Trompenaars and his colleagues. You will see that this model is also similar in some respects to Hofstede's, but it contains more dimensions and deals with a broader array of countries.

7d Cultural Dimensions Model

The 7d cultural model builds on traditional anthropological approaches to understanding culture. Anthropologists argue that culture comes into existence because all humans must solve basic problems of survival.[31] These challenges include how people relate to others, such as family members, supervisors, friends, and fellow workers; how people deal with the passage of time; and how people relate to their environment. All cultures develop ways to confront these basic problems, but the solutions are not the same, which is why cultures differ significantly.

Five of the seven dimensions of the 7d cultural model deal with the challenges of how people relate to each other. Each dimension is a continuum or range of cultural differences. The five dimensions that deal with relationships among people are:

1. *Universalism versus particularism:* The choice of dealing with other people based on rules or based on personal relationships.
2. *Collectivism versus individualism:* The focus on group membership versus individual characteristics.
3. *Neutral versus affective:* The range of feelings outwardly expressed in the society.
4. *Diffuse versus specific:* The types of involvement people have with each other, ranging from all aspects of life to specific components.
5. *Achievement versus ascription:* The assignment of status in the society based on performance (e.g., college graduation) versus assignment based on heritage.

The two final dimensions deal with how a culture manages time and how it deals with nature:

6. *Past, present, future, or a mixture:* The orientation of the society to the past, present, or future or some combination of the three.
7. *"Control of" versus "accommodation with" nature:* Nature viewed as something to be controlled versus something to be accepted.

Exhibit 2.11 gives a summary of the 7d model and the issues addressed by each dimension. The following sections define the dimensions and show their managerial applications.

Universalism versus Particularism

Universalism and particularism pertain to how people from a culture treat each other based on equally applied rules rather than personal relationships. In a universalistic culture, how people are treated is based on abstract principles such as the rules of law, religion, or cultural principles (e.g., "Do unto others as you would have them do unto you"). Thus, universalism suggests that there are rules or appropriate and acceptable ways of doing things, and we look to those precise guides in all situations.

In contrast, in particularistic cultures, rules represent only a rough guide to life. Each judgment represents a unique situation and the "right" way of behaving must take into account who the person is and his or her relationship to

Universalism
Dealing with other people based on rules.

Particularism
Dealing with other people based on personal relationships.

EXHIBIT **2.11** The 7d Model of Culture

Cultural Dimension	Critical Question
Relationships with people:	
Universalism versus particularism	Do we consider rules or relationships more important?
Individualism versus collectivism	Do we act mostly as individuals or as groups?
Specific versus diffuse	How extensively are we involved with the lives of other people?
Neutral versus affective	Are we free to express our emotions, or are we restrained?
Achievement versus ascription	Do we achieve status through accomplishment, or is it part of our situation in life (e.g., gender, age, social class)?
Perspective on time:	
Sequential versus synchronic	Do we do tasks in sequence or several tasks at once?
Relationship with the environment:	
Internal versus external control	Do we control the environment, or does it control us?

Source: Adapted from Trompenaars, Fons, and Charles Hampden-Turner. 1998. Riding the Waves of Culture: Understanding Cultural Diversity in Global Business. *New York: McGraw-Hill.*

the one doing the judging. In particularistic cultures, rules may be in place and fully recognized, but people expect exceptions to be made for friends, family relations, and others. The focus is on situation-to-situation judgments and on the exceptional nature of changing circumstances.[32]

In developing his 7d model, Trompenaars uses dilemmas that show the contrasts in cultural values. Consider the following dilemma and the different cultural assumptions that people use to make the "right" choice.

One of the dilemmas used to show differences between universalistic and particularistic cultures concerns the story of a motorist hitting a pedestrian while going 35 miles per hour in a 20-mile-per-hour zone. The driver's lawyer notes that, if a witness says the driver was going only 20 miles per hour, the judge will be lenient. The question is this: Should a friend who is a witness be expected to—or feel obligated to—testify to the lower speed? In universalistic cultures such as the United States and Switzerland, more than 93 percent say no: The principle of telling the truth supersedes friendship. In particularistic cultures such as South Korea, Nepal, and Venezuela, close to 40 percent say yes: Friendship supersedes the law.[33]

No culture is purely universalistic or particularistic. However, the tendency to lean in one direction or the other influences business practices and relationships between business partners from different cultures. In particular, more universalistic cultures tend to use contracts and law as a basis for business. Managers from such cultures are often uncomfortable when written documents are ignored and the personal relationships between partners become paramount. Consequently, managers from universalistic cultures doing business in particularistic cultures must be sensitive to building relationships. However, managers from particularistic cultures must make efforts to realize that the

EXHIBIT **2.12**   Universalism versus Particularism: Differences and Managerial Implications

Universalism ←————————————————————————————————→ Particularism

| USA | U.K. | Czech Rep. | Nigeria | Mexico | South Korea |

Differences

Focus on rules	Focus on relationships
Contracts difficult to break	Contracts easy to modify
Trustworthy people honor their word	Trustworthy people adapt to each other's needs based on trust
Belief is in only one reality	Reality is relative to each person's situation
"Deals" are obligations	"Deals" are flexible to the situation and the person

Managerial Implications

Use procedures applied to all	Use informal networks to create understanding
Formalize business practices	Make changes subtly and privately
Treat all cases similarly	Treat each case based on its unique circumstances
Announce changes publicly	Keep only insiders informed

Sources: Adapted from Economides, A. A. 2008. "Culture-aware collaborative learning." Multicultural and Technology Journal, 2(4), *pp, 243–267; Trompenaars, Fons, and Charles, Hampden-Turner. 1998.* Riding the Waves of Culture: Understanding Cultural Diversity in Global Business. *New York: McGraw-Hill.*

emphasis on law and contract does not mean a distrust of the business partner in a universalistic culture.

Exhibit 2.12 gives a brief description of universalism and particularism as cultural dimensions and shows the managerial implications for doing business in each.

Individualism versus Collectivism

In the preceding sections, we examined Hofstede's view of individualism and collectivism. The 7d model considers the same distinctions. Although the 7d view of individualism is similar to Hofstede's in concept, the rankings of countries do not match exactly. One explanation for this difference may be that Trompenaars' ranking comes from more recent data. Another reason is that the 7d model uses a different methodology from Hofstede's model and captures more subtle aspects of the individualism-collectivism continuum.

One of the questions that Trompenaars used to look at cultural differences in individualism asked about typical organizations in each country. One choice represented organizations where individual work and individual credit were common. The other choice represented group work and group credit. In the more collectivist societies such as India and Mexico, fewer than 45 percent of the workers said that their jobs involved individual work with individual credit. Somewhat surprising was the finding that the former Eastern Bloc countries of the Czech Republic, Russia, Hungary, and Bulgaria were the most individualistic in their organizations, ranking ahead of the United States.

Exhibit 2.13 gives a brief description of the individualistic and collectivistic cultural dimensions and the managerial implications of doing business in each.

EXHIBIT **2.13**   Individualism versus Collectivism: Differences and Managerial Implications

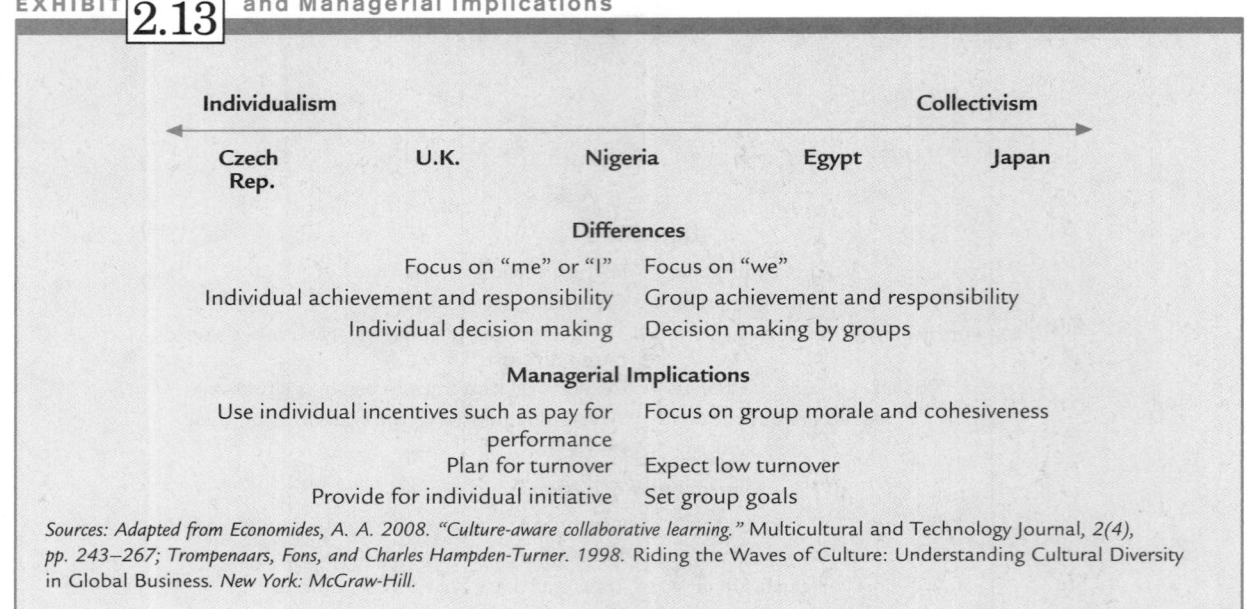

Individualism ←————————————————————————————————→ Collectivism

| Czech Rep. | U.K. | Nigeria | Egypt | Japan |

Differences

Focus on "me" or "I"	Focus on "we"
Individual achievement and responsibility	Group achievement and responsibility
Individual decision making	Decision making by groups

Managerial Implications

Use individual incentives such as pay for performance	Focus on group morale and cohesiveness
Plan for turnover	Expect low turnover
Provide for individual initiative	Set group goals

Sources: Adapted from Economides, A. A. 2008. "Culture-aware collaborative learning." Multicultural and Technology Journal, 2(4), pp. 243–267; Trompenaars, Fons, and Charles Hampden-Turner. 1998. Riding the Waves of Culture: Understanding Cultural Diversity in Global Business. New York: McGraw-Hill.

Neutral versus Affective

Neutral versus affective
The acceptability of expressing emotions.

The **neutral versus affective** dimension of the 7d model concerns the acceptability of expressing emotions. In cultures with a more neutral orientation, people expect that interactions are objective and detached. The focus is more on the task and less on the emotional nature of the interaction. People emphasize achieving objectives without the messy interference of emotions. In contrast, in cultures with a more affective orientation, all forms of emotion are appropriate in almost every situation. Expressions of anger, laughter, gesturing, and a range of emotional outbursts are considered normal and acceptable. The natural and preferred way is to find an immediate outlet for emotions.[34]

You can test yourself on this dimension by responding to one of Trompenaars' dilemmas. How would you respond in a negotiation if your partner called your proposal insane? People from neutral cultures attempt to hide their emotional reactions to this insult. Revelation of the hurt would show weakness and vulnerability. People from affective cultures would react immediately. They realize that such a reaction shows that they are insulted, but they believe that their partner should know this. This is expected behavior and is not viewed negatively by people in an affective culture.[35]

Exhibit 2.14 gives a brief description of the neutral versus affective cultural dimensions and the managerial implications of doing business within each.

Specific versus Diffuse

Specific versus diffuse
The extent to which all aspects of an individual's life are involved in his or her work relationships.

The **specific versus diffuse** cultural dimension addresses the extent to which an individual's life is involved in his or her work relationships. In a specific-oriented culture, business is segregated from other parts of life. People in business-exchange and work relationships know each other, but the knowledge is very limited and shared for only very specific purposes. In such societies, written contracts frequently prescribe and delineate such relationships. Conversely, in diffuse-oriented cultures, business relationships are more encompassing and inclusive.

EXHIBIT **2.14**   Neutral versus Affective: Differences and Managerial Implications

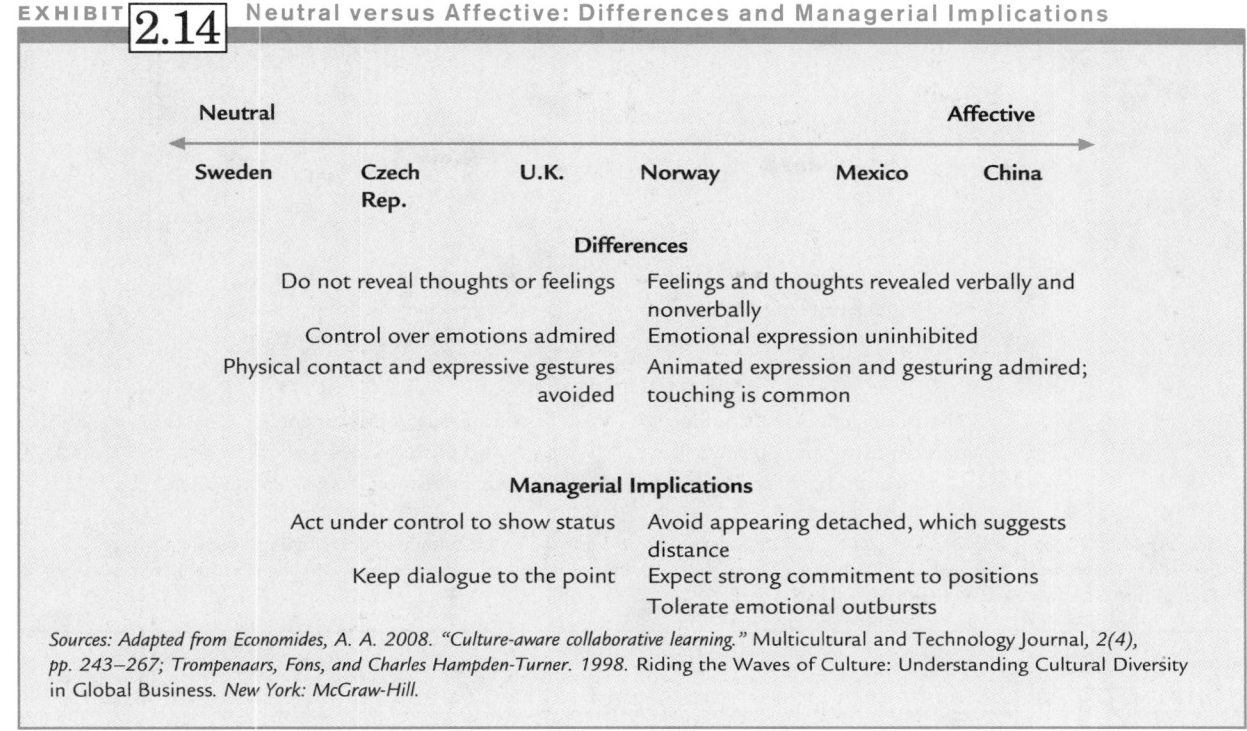

Neutral					Affective
Sweden	Czech Rep.	U.K.	Norway	Mexico	China

Differences

Do not reveal thoughts or feelings	Feelings and thoughts revealed verbally and nonverbally
Control over emotions admired	Emotional expression uninhibited
Physical contact and expressive gestures avoided	Animated expression and gesturing admired; touching is common

Managerial Implications

Act under control to show status	Avoid appearing detached, which suggests distance
Keep dialogue to the point	Expect strong commitment to positions
	Tolerate emotional outbursts

Sources: Adapted from Economides, A. A. 2008. "Culture-aware collaborative learning." Multicultural and Technology Journal, 2(4), pp. 243–267; Trompenaars, Fons, and Charles Hampden-Turner. 1998. Riding the Waves of Culture: Understanding Cultural Diversity in Global Business. New York: McGraw-Hill.

The preference is to involve multiple areas and levels of life simultaneously; truly private and segregated spaces in life are quite small. In doing business, the parties come to know each other personally and more thoroughly, and they become acquainted with each other across a variety of life's dimensions and levels.[36]

The example Trompenaars uses to test the differences between specific and diffuse cultures concerns a boss who asks a subordinate to help him paint his house. In specific cultures, most people believe that the worker has no obligation to help because the boss has no authority outside work. In diffuse cultures, people feel an obligation to help the boss in any way possible even if the help is beyond the job's requirements.[37]

Exhibit 2.15 gives a brief description of the specific versus diffuse cultural dimensions and the managerial implications of doing business in each.

Achievement versus Ascription

The dimension identified as achievement versus ascription addresses how a particular society accords or gives status. In achievement-oriented cultures, people earn status by their performance and accomplishments. In contrast, when a culture bases status on ascription, one's inherent characteristics or associations define status. For example, ascription-oriented societies often assign status based on the schools or universities attended or on age. Ascribed status does not require any justification. It simply exists. In such cultures, titles and their frequent usage play a large part in interactions.[38]

Exhibit 2.16 gives a brief description of the achievement versus ascription cultural dimensions and the managerial implications of doing business in each.

To better understand this cultural dimension, consider the next Multinational Management Challenge. It describes culture clash for a young woman manager from an achievement-oriented society who is working in an ascription-oriented society.

Achievement versus ascription
How a society grants or gives status.

EXHIBIT 2.15   Specific versus Diffuse: Differences and Managerial Implications

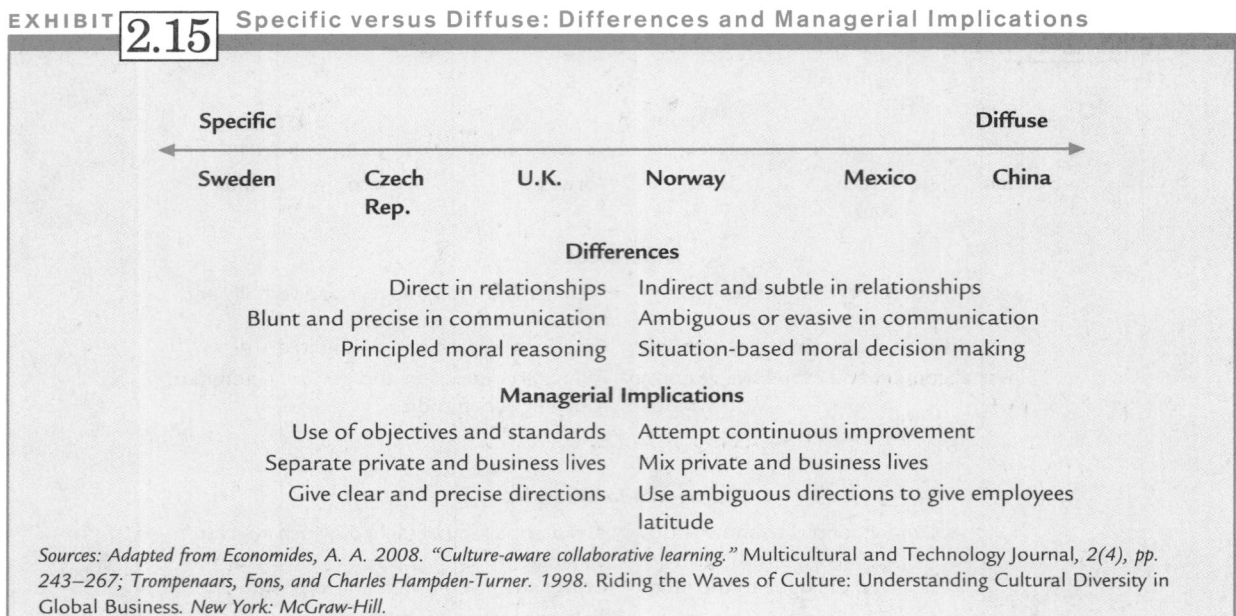

Sources: *Adapted from Economides, A. A. 2008. "Culture-aware collaborative learning."* Multicultural and Technology Journal, *2(4), pp. 243–267; Trompenaars, Fons, and Charles Hampden-Turner. 1998.* Riding the Waves of Culture: Understanding Cultural Diversity in Global Business. *New York: McGraw-Hill.*

EXHIBIT 2.16   Achievement versus Ascription: Differences and Managerial Implications

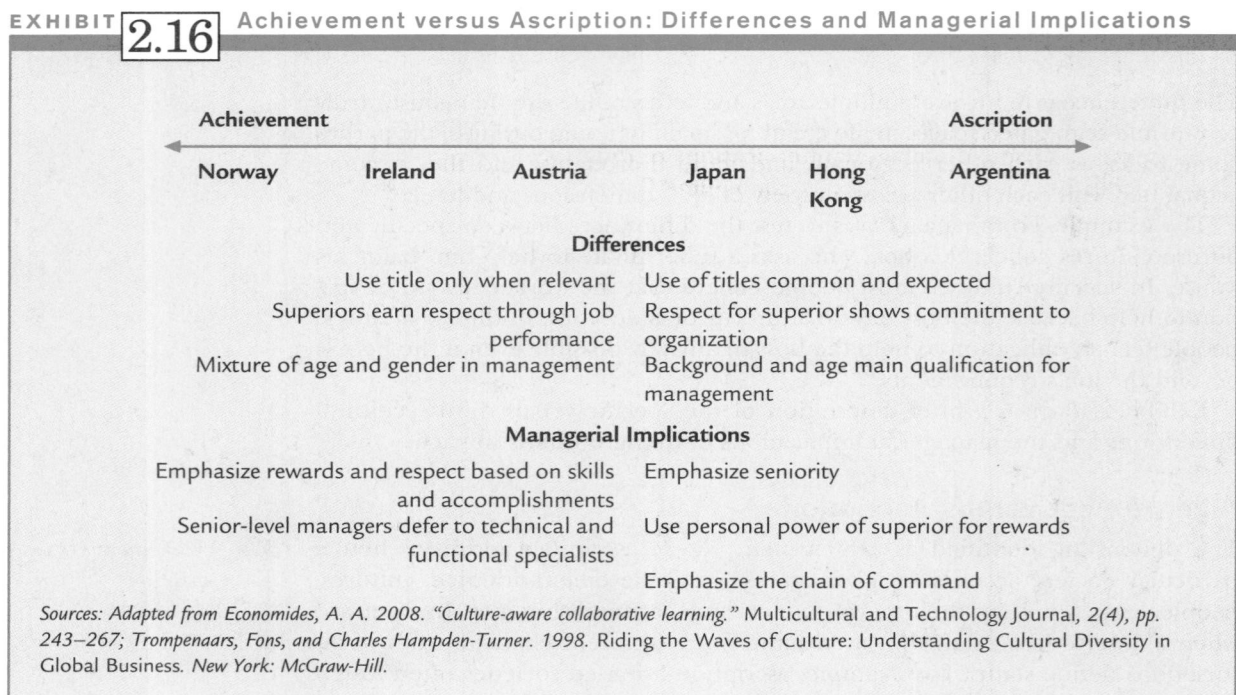

Sources: *Adapted from Economides, A. A. 2008. "Culture-aware collaborative learning."* Multicultural and Technology Journal, *2(4), pp. 243–267; Trompenaars, Fons, and Charles Hampden-Turner. 1998.* Riding the Waves of Culture: Understanding Cultural Diversity in Global Business. *New York: McGraw-Hill.*

Time Orientation

Time horizon
The way cultures deal with the past, present, and future.

To coordinate any business, managers must have a shared understanding of time. Experts on culture find vast differences in how people deal with time, and these differences become apparent when people from different cultures engage in business exchanges. One dimension of time that is important to managers is the time horizon. The **time horizon** concerns how cultures deal with the past, present, and future, as well as the boundaries among these time zones. Mexicans

Multinational Management **Challenge**

Achievement-Based Management in an Ascription-Based Culture

What happens when young and previously successful managers from achievement-oriented Western societies find themselves in an ascription-based culture? Ms. Moore, a successful 34-year-old female manager from a U.S. company, takes a promotion as director of marketing in Ankara, Turkey. She has international experience in Britain and is confident that she can replicate her success at winning the support and trust of her subordinates and colleagues in Turkey.

Within a few months, Ms. Moore finds her authority eroding. Hasan, a 63-year-old Turk, is gradually and consciously taking over her authority as the boss and is becoming the driving force behind marketing projects. Although everyone recognizes that Ms. Moore's marketing knowledge is much greater than Hasan's, her attempts to fulfill her function meet with increased resistance. The company follows Hasan's direction even though the results are not satisfactory. Later, Ms. Moore learns that her predecessor, a U.S. man her age, was fired for "failure to command local managers."

If you were sending a young, female manager to this assignment, what strategies would you recommend?

Source: Based on Trompenaars, Fons, and Charles Hampden-Turner. 1998. Riding the Waves of Culture: Understanding Cultural Diversity in Global Business. *New York: McGraw-Hill.*

and Chinese, for example, have long time horizons and distinct boundaries among the time zones.[39]

Exhibit 2.17 summarizes the cultural characteristics of different time horizons. It also gives some managerial implications of differing time orientations.

In future-oriented societies, such as the United States, organizational change is considered necessary and beneficial. The static organization is the dying organization. However, in past-oriented societies, people often assume that life follows a preordained course based on traditions or the will of God. As a result, strategic planning has little importance for the organization. A changing organization is suspicious to both employees and society. Stability is revered. Within these organizations, senior people are thought to make the best decisions because they have the authority and wisdom to know the right way. Symbols and rituals dominate the organizational culture.

To consider your own time horizon, ask yourself how long ago your past started and ended, how long ago your present started and ended, and when your future will start and end. Trompenaars uses similar questions to measure the time horizons of different cultural groups.[40]

Internal versus External Control

The cultural dimension of **internal versus external control** concerns beliefs regarding control over one's fate. This cultural dimension is perhaps best reflected in how people interact with their natural environment. Does nature dominate us, or do we dominate nature?

To measure this dimension, Trompenaars and his colleagues presented managers with the following options: "It is worthwhile trying to control important natural forces like the weather" and "Nature should take its course, and we just have to accept it the way it comes and do the best we can."[41] Managers in Arabic countries, such as Bahrain, Egypt, and Kuwait, are the most fatalistic, with

Internal versus external control Beliefs regarding whether one controls one's own fate.

EXHIBIT 2.17   Time Horizon: Differences and Managerial Implications

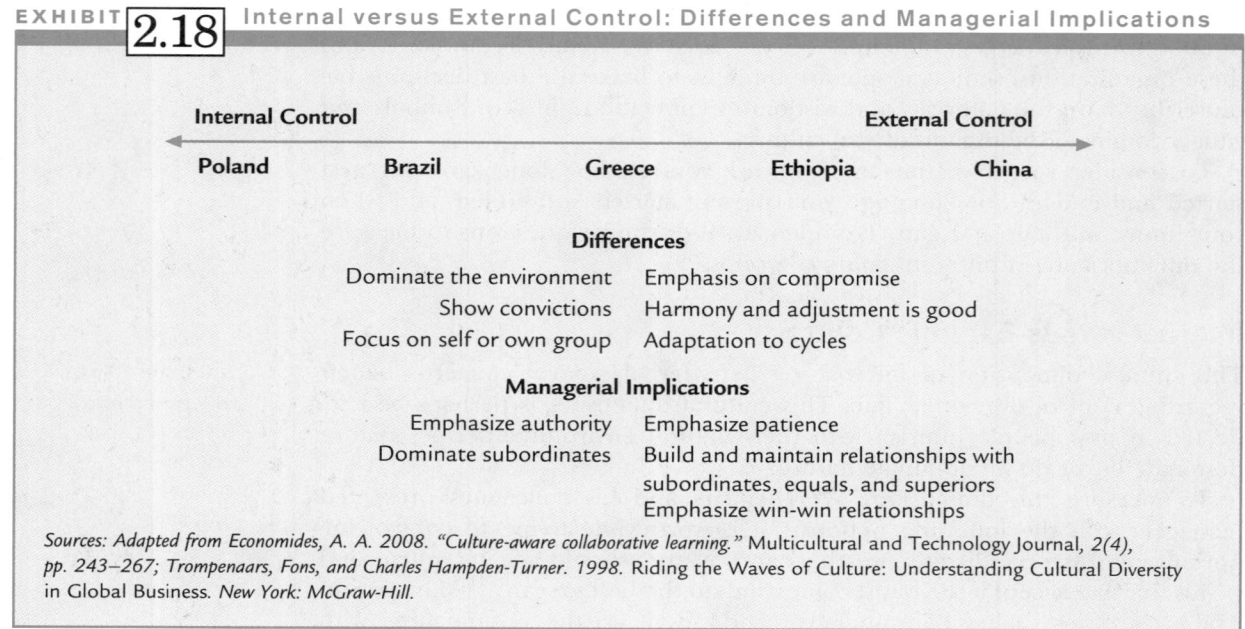

Past/Present				Future
Hong Kong	Israel	Russia	Korea	Hong Kong

Differences

Past	Present	Future
Communication references history and origins of country, business, and family	Enjoy the moment	Communication refers to potential achievements
Respect for past glory and elder	Planning seldom results in execution	Planning important
History provides a context for present actions	Immediate impact most important	Potential for future advantage emphasized

Managerial Implications

Past and Present	Future
Emphasize and be sensitive to history and tradition	Motivate by emphasis on opportunities
Avoid strict deadlines for completion of tasks	Set specific deadlines

Sources: Adapted from Economides, A. A. 2008. "Culture-aware collaborative learning." Multicultural and Technology Journal, *2(4), pp. 243–267; Trompenaars, Fons, and Charles Hampden-Turner. 1998.* Riding the Waves of Culture: Understanding Cultural Diversity in Global Business. *New York: McGraw-Hill.*

fewer than 20 percent of them choosing the option of control over nature. This contrasts with more than 50 percent of the managers from Spain and Cuba who choose the option of control over nature.

Exhibit 2.18 summarizes the internal versus external cultural dimensions and their managerial implications.

EXHIBIT 2.18   Internal versus External Control: Differences and Managerial Implications

Internal Control				External Control
Poland	Brazil	Greece	Ethiopia	China

Differences

Dominate the environment	Emphasis on compromise
Show convictions	Harmony and adjustment is good
Focus on self or own group	Adaptation to cycles

Managerial Implications

Emphasize authority	Emphasize patience
Dominate subordinates	Build and maintain relationships with subordinates, equals, and superiors
	Emphasize win-win relationships

Sources: Adapted from Economides, A. A. 2008. "Culture-aware collaborative learning." Multicultural and Technology Journal, *2(4), pp. 243–267; Trompenaars, Fons, and Charles Hampden-Turner. 1998.* Riding the Waves of Culture: Understanding Cultural Diversity in Global Business. *New York: McGraw-Hill.*

Cultural values regarding relationships with nature can affect how organizations and managers approach strategic and operational problems. In cultures where nature is believed to dominate people, managers are likely to be fatalistic. They believe that situations must be accepted and reacted to rather than changed. In such cultures, people do not emphasize planning and scheduling. Work schedules must adjust to other priorities, such as family.

In contrast, where cultural values support the notion that people dominate nature, managers tend to be proactive. They believe that situations can be changed. Strategic plans and operations reflect the assumption that obstacles can be conquered. What works is what is important. Organizations focus on using concrete data that suggests the best way to solve problems.

This section concludes our examination of the 7d view of culture. As Exhibit 2.7 did for the Hofstede model, Exhibit 2.19 gives percentile rankings for these dimensions in selected countries.

From the sections on cultural models, you should have acquired two skills. First, you can now apply the models to diagnose and understand the basic cultural values of a society. Second, you can apply this information to assess how the characteristics of a particular culture affect business operations. Later chapters will build on your knowledge of culture and on the concepts introduced here. However, developing an in-depth understanding of any culture goes beyond the simple application of cultural models. The successful multinational manager will seek information continually from all sources. Consider, for example, how Exhibit 2.20 shows that proverbs provide less formal insights into national cultures.

The chapter concludes with some cautions for all who venture into international operations.

Caveats and Cautions

Although understanding the cultures of people and organizations is crucial for international business success, multinational managers in particular must realize that cultures provide only broad guidelines for behavior. For instance, although the United States scores very highly on individualism, it has the highest percentage of charity giving in the world (clearly a collectivistic behavior). Similarly, whereas many Latin American cultures prefer warm interpersonal relationships, researchers were surprised to find that Costa Ricans preferred automatic tellers over human tellers.[42] These are examples of **cultural paradoxes**, where individual situations seem to contradict cultural prescriptions. However, if one assumes that all people within a culture behave, believe, feel, and act the same, it is known as **stereotyping**.

Using the cultural stereotype—the typical way people act—to understand a culture is not necessarily wrong if done carefully. Broad generalizations about a culture can serve as a starting point for understanding the complexities of cultural differences. Most books that explain how to do business with the _____ [name a culture] use stereotypical cultural generalizations. Such books are helpful in understanding a culture as a whole, not in perceiving the variations within it. After considering such information, however, the multinational manager must realize that organizational and occupational cultures differ within the national context and that individuals vary widely within each level of culture. Consequently, management functions such as planning, organizational design, and personnel management must account not only for differences in national culture, but also for those in occupational and organizational cultures. Similarly,

Cultural paradoxes When individual situations seem to contradict cultural prescriptions.

Stereotyping When one assumes that all people within a culture behave, believe, feel, and act the same.

EXHIBIT 2.19   Percentile Ranks for the 7d Model Cultural Dimensions in Selected Countries

	Universalism	Individualism	Neutral	Specific	Achievement	Past Orientation	Future Orientation	Internal Control
Argentina	n/a	n/a	21	n/a	8	n/a	n/a	59
Australia	n/a	71	69	73	84	32	n/a	78
Austria	n/a	n/a	90	60	3	n/a	n/a	63
Belgium	n/a	52	46	n/a	n/a	n/a	n/a	43
Brazil	n/a	19	46	n/a	34	18	n/a	73
Bulgaria	n/a	84	81	n/a	29	n/a	n/a	20
Canada	95	74	77	80	92	n/a	47	88
China	26	26	85	3	58	82	89	2
Cuba	n/a	n/a	4	n/a	11	n/a	n/a	98
Czech Rep.	16	100	56	37	45	n/a	84	n/a
Denmark	n/a	61	33	70	82	n/a	n/a	80
Egypt	n/a	10	2	n/a	n/a	n/a	n/a	n/a
Ethiopia	n/a	n/a	100	97	37	n/a	n/a	24
Finland	n/a	58	50	63	76	n/a	n/a	39
France	63	n/a	25	53	71	77	74	90
Germany	n/a	35	35	n/a	61	64	53	34
Greece	42	32	38	40	55	n/a	n/a	51
Hong Kong	n/a	n/a	92	87	13	100	100	29
Hungary	79	94	58	23	47	n/a	n/a	n/a
India	21	16	83	27	18	9	39	27
Indonesia	47	n/a	85	17	n/a	36	39	32
Ireland	84	48	23	n/a	95	n/a	n/a	71

Italy	n/a	n/a	31	n/a	66	n/a	16	43
Japan	58	6	98	57	53	59	63	n/a
Kenya	n/a	n/a	n/a	n/a	26	n/a	n/a	17
Malaysia	n/a	29	25	43	n/a	n/a	n/a	n/a
Mexico	n/a	13	50	n/a	63	n/a	n/a	n/a
Netherlands	n/a	55	63	93	n/a	41	32	54
Nigeria	53	81	69	13	n/a	n/a	n/a	76
Norway	n/a	n/a	44	50	100	23	n/a	95
Pakistan	n/a	42	n/a	n/a	n/a	n/a	n/a	n/a
Philippines	n/a	n/a	15	33	21	n/a	n/a	n/a
Poland	37	87	96	90	39	27	n/a	100
Portugal	n/a	39	67	n/a	74	n/a	n/a	46
Romania	68	90	n/a	n/a	n/a	n/a	n/a	n/a
Russia	5	97	17	10	42	50	11	12
Korea	11	n/a	n/a	n/a	24	91	79	61
Singapore	32	23	69	47	68	73	5	10
Spain	n/a	68	4	n/a	32	55	n/a	93
Sweden	89	45	63	100	79	86	68	22
Switzerland	100	n/a	29	67	50	68	58	49
Thailand	n/a	n/a	58	n/a	16	n/a	n/a	56
U.K.	74	65	n/a	83	87	45	26	68
United States	n/a	77	54	77	97	14	21	66
Russia	5	97	17	10	42	50	11	12

Source: Computed from data reported in Trompenaars, Fons, and Charles Hampden-Turner. 1998. Riding the Waves of Culture: Understanding Cultural Diversity in Global Business. New York: McGraw-Hill.

EXHIBIT 2.20   Proverbs: Windows into National Cultures

Cultural Belief/ Value	Country or Culture	Proverb
Time	United States	Time is money.
	China	Drips of water wear through stone.
Directness	Mexico	Only little children and drunks always tell the truth.
	Arab	If I have regretted my silence once, I have regretted my chatter many times.
Modesty	Japan	The nail that sticks up gets pounded down.
	Korea	A barking dog is never a good hunter.
Collectivism	Arab	My brother and I against my cousin. My cousin and I against the stranger.
	Indonesia	Both a light burden and a heavy burden should be carried together.
Value of age	Turkey	Beauty passes, wisdom remains.
	Nigeria	The elders of a community are the voice of God.
Power distance	Romania	There is no good accord where every man would be a lord.
	China	When you are an anvil, hold still. When you are a hammer, strike at will.
Fate	Arab	Man does not attain everything he desires; winds don't always blow as the vessels wish.
	China	A wise person adapts to circumstances as water conforms to the jar that contains it
Risk	Korea	Even if it is a stone bridge, make sure it is safe.
	Arab	Only a fool tests the depth of water with both feet.

Source: Wederspahn, Cary M. 2003. "Proverbs: Windows into other cultures." Executive Planet, October 4, 2002. http://www.executiveplanet.com/ business-culture.

successful leadership, motivation, and the development of individual employees must further adjust for expectations based on the unique characteristics of each employee.

Perhaps the greatest cultural danger facing the multinational manager is **ethnocentrism**, which occurs when people from one culture believe that theirs consists of the only correct norms, values, and beliefs. The ethnocentric person may look down on people from other cultures and may even consider them backward, dirty, weird, or stupid. The multinational manager can offset the ethnocentric tendency and truly understand another culture—many anthropologists believe—only by adopting the mindset of **cultural relativism**. This is the philosophical stance that all cultures, no matter how different, are correct and moral for the people of those cultures.

Few multinational managers, however, are so ethnocentric that they fail to realize that people from other cultures just do things differently. Rather, the danger is a subtle form of ethnocentrism; that is, managers may find it difficult to remain entirely neutral in response to other cultures. For example, things such as the variations in the pace of work in other countries, the unwillingness of subordinates to take responsibility, or practices such as bribery often frustrate North American managers. Especially when first assigned overseas, managers must be wary of judging subordinates in terms of their own cultural values. A common ethnocentric reaction is, "Why don't they do it right, as we do?"

Given the complexities and subtleties associated with national cultures, multinational managers have to work diligently to adequately understand any culture. Often this process can take years of living and working in the new

Ethnocentrism
When people from one culture believe that theirs are the only correct norms, values, and beliefs.

Cultural relativism
A philosophical position arguing that all cultures, no matter how different, are correct and moral for the people of those cultures.

country. Chapter 11 discusses how multinational firms can provide cultural training to their managers who are about to take foreign assignments in new cultures.

The goal of the multinational manager is ultimately to become culturally intelligent. Researchers such as Crowe define **cultural intelligence** as the ability to interact effectively in multiple cultures.[43] A culturally intelligent manager is able to understand diverse cultural situations and to act appropriately. For instance, the culturally savvy and intelligent manager can be proactive and avoid many of the cultural misunderstandings discussed earlier in the first Case in Point in this chapter (page 39).

How can managers become culturally intelligent? Research by Crowe suggests that exposure to new cultural experiences in other countries heightens cultural intelligence. A multinational company may therefore send its employees on foreign trips for this kind of exposure. Crowe's research also points to the importance during one's education of studying abroad and seeking foreign internships as a means to start developing cultural intelligence. Crowe's research also suggests that the depth of exposure increases cultural intelligence. Multinationals may therefore benefit from sending their employees on frequent and different foreign assignments.

> **Cultural relativism**
> A philosophical position arguing that all cultures, no matter how different, are correct and moral for the people of those cultures.

Summary and Conclusions

After completing this chapter you should know that a variety of cultural levels affect multinational managers and organizations. However, the descriptions and examples of cultural effects on management are broad illustrations. No one book or chapter can do justice to the immense variety of cultures that exist in the world. This chapter hopes only to sensitize readers to the extremely complex and subtle influences that culture has on management and organizations.

The models of cultural values proposed by the GLOBE researchers, Hofstede and Trompenaars and his colleagues provide basic concepts for analyzing cultural differences. They are tools to help you understand a culture and adjust your business practices to various cultural environments.

The most successful multinational managers realize that understanding a different culture is a never ending learning process. They will prepare for their international assignments by studying all that they can about the country in which they will work, including more than business etiquette. Understanding the national culture as well as important historical, social, esthetic, political, and economic trends builds a foundation. They will study the language. Few can really get behind the front stage of culture without speaking the local language. Finally, they will be sensitive and observant, continually adjusting their behavior to what works locally.

This chapter presents only a brief introduction. As you read later chapters, especially those with a comparative focus, you will broaden your understanding of cultural differences. You also will learn to seek advantage in differences and to avoid looking at culture as a potential obstacle.

Discussion Questions

1. Identify five cultural rituals, stories, or symbols from your native culture. Examples might include national holidays, the country's flag, nursery rhymes, childhood traditional stories, and sayings, such as "A stitch in time saves nine." Discuss how each of these communicates cultural values, norms, and beliefs.

2. Define and contrast backstage and front stage culture. Discuss how someone not familiar with your culture could misunderstand a front stage behavior.

3. Discuss several ways that stereotyping and ethnocentrism limit successful multinational management.

4. Define levels of culture, and discuss the interrelationships among the levels.

5. Compare and contrast Hofstede's model of culture with the 7d model. Which model do you think is more valuable for managers? Why?

6. Compare and contrast the GLOBE model with the 7d model.

7. Pick three countries from Exhibits 2.7 and 2.19. Summarize and discuss the managerial implications

of cultural differences by applying the Hofstede and 7d models.

8. What are cultural paradoxes? How can a manager prepare for such paradoxes?

Multinational Management **Skill Builder**

A Briefing Paper

Step 1. Read the following scenario.

You are a recent college graduate and a junior-level executive in a midsize multinational firm. Your CEO will depart next week on a one-month business trip to meet potential joint venture partners in Saudi Arabia, Poland, Hong Kong, Germany, Greece, and Brazil. Because of your expertise in international business, the CEO has asked you to prepare a cultural brief dealing with the national and business cultures she will be visiting. She does not want to make any cultural faux pas. She expects a high-quality oral and written presentation. Because this is your first major assignment, it is important that you perform well. First impressions are lasting, and your job may depend on it.

Step 2. Your instructor will divide the class into six groups and assign each group at least one country.

Step 3. Using sources on the World Wide Web and in the library, research general cultural issues such as (but not limited to) basic cultural norms, values, and beliefs that may affect work (e. g., attitudes toward work in general, the role of the family in work, food and diet, the role of religion, language). Research specific business cultural issues such as expectations regarding dress, appointments, business entertaining, business cards, titles and forms of address, greetings, gestures, gift giving, the language of business, interaction styles, the timing for closing deals, and the potential reactions to a woman executive.

Step 4. Present your findings to the class.

Endnotes

1. Kroeber, A. L., and C. Kluckhohn. 1952. "Culture: A critical review of concepts and definitions." *Papers of the Peabody Museum of American Archaeology and Ethnology,* 47, p. 1.

2. Terpstra, Vern, and Kenneth David. 1991. *The Cultural Environment of International Business.* Cincinnati, OH: South-Western.

3. Ibid.

4. *Craighead's International Business, Travel, and Relocation Guide 2000.* Detroit: Gale Research.

5. Hofstede, Geert. 2001. *Culture's Consequences: International Differences in Work-Related Values,* 2nd ed. Thousand Oaks, CA: Sage Publications.

6. Ibid.

7. House, R., P. Hanges, M. Javidan, P. Dorfman, and V. Gupta. 2004. *Culture, Leadership and Organizations: The GLOBE Study of 62 Societies.* Thousand Oaks, CA: Sage Publications.

8. Trompenaars, Fons, and Charles, Hampden-Turner. 1998. *Riding the Waves of Culture: Understanding Cultural Diversity in Global Business.* New York: McGraw-Hill. 2000. http://www.7d-culture.nl/.

9. Hofstede, *Culture's Consequences.*

10. Kirkman, Bradley L., Kevin B. Lowe, and Cristina B. Gibson. 2006. "A quarter century of Culture's Consequences: A review of empirical research incorporating Hofstede's cultural values framework." *Journal of International Business Studies,* 10(4), pp. 1–36.

11. Hofstede, *Culture's Consequences.*

12. Hofstede, Geert. 1991. *Cultures and Organizations: Software of the Mind.* London: McGraw-Hill; Hofstede, Geert and Michael Harris Bond. 1988. "The Confucian connection: From cultural roots to economic growth." *Organizational Dynamics,* 16, pp. 4, 4–21.

13. Hofstede and Bond.

14. Ibid.

15. Hofstede, *Culture's Consequences.*

16. Ibid.

17. Ibid.

18. Ibid.

19. Ibid.

20. Ibid.

21. Ibid.

22. Hofstede, *Cultures and Organizations.*

23. Ronen, S., and O. Shenkar. 1985. "Clustering countries on attitudinal dimensions: A review and synthesis." *Academy of Management Review,* September, pp. 435–454.

24. House et al.

25. Ibid.

26. Leung, Kwok, Rabi S. Bhagat, Nancy R. Buchan, and Cristina B. Gibson. 2005. "Culture and international business: Recent advances and their implications for future research." *Journal of International Business Studies,* 36, pp. 357–378.

27 House et al.

28 Javidan, Mansour, Peter W. Dorfman, Mary Sully de Luque, and Robert J. House. 2006. "In the eye of the beholder: Cross cultural lessons in leadership for project GLOBE." *The Academy of management Perspectives,* February, 20(1), pp. 67–90.

29 House et al.

30 Javidan et al.

31 Kluckhohn, Florence, and F. L Strodtbeck. 1961. *Variations in Value Orientations.* New York: Harper & Row.

32 Trompenaars et al.

33 Ibid.

34 Ibid.

35 Ibid.

36 Ibid.

37 Ibid.

38 Ibid.

39 Ibid.

40 Ibid.

41 Ibid.

42 Osland, Joyce S., Allan, Bird, June, Delano, and Mathew, Jacob. 2000. "Beyond sophisticated stereotyping: Cultural sensemaking in context." *The Academy of Management Executive,* February, 14(1), pp. 65–79.

43 Crowe, K. A. 2008. "What leads to cultural intelligence." *Business Horizons,* 51, pp. 391–399.

Organizational and National Cultures in a Polish–U.S. Joint Venture

This case looks at differences in the cultural values and beliefs of Polish and U.S. managers employed in a joint venture in Poland. The case comes from data collected from interviews with Polish and expatriate U.S. managers.

Background

The U.S./Polish Company The company was a joint venture with a Polish partner and a wholly owned subsidiary of a U.S. multinational corporation located in Poland. The U.S. company started operations in Poland in 1990. The joint venture started two years later.

The joint venture was a small, nonbureaucratic organization with 140 employees. Everybody knew each other and a family type of relationship existed among the managers. Both local Polish managers and U.S. expatriates reported a friendly work climate even though all top managerial positions were held by the U.S. expatriates.

Polish Attitudes Regarding U.S. Management

When asked why they chose to work for this company, Polish managers often described U.S. business as "real," "healthy," "tough," "honest," and "fair," even though they had never had the opportunity to work with U.S. Americans. In addition, they felt that the features of Polish national culture such as "ability to work in difficult situations" and "experience of struggle with hardship of communism" combined well with American management expertise. In addition, Polish managers reported that working for a U.S. company was a major bonus for their future success and careers. Multinational corporations give employment security because they have a low risk of bankruptcy. In comparison with state-owned companies, the organization was perceived as having a very efficient organizational design dedicated to efficiency and profit making. Reflecting on his experience in state-owned operations, a Polish manager from the customer service operation unit noted:

The basic difference between state companies and this company is that the organization of U.S. firms contains many necessary and indispensable elements. Whereas, in Polish companies, many elements were not needed and, even in some cases, disturbed the effective functioning of the company as a whole. Profit was not a major goal, only apparent activities. Many jobs and even whole companies were created when they were not needed. They were unproductive. Here we have only jobs and departments which help the company to function effectively.

The Polish managers expressed a great deal of enthusiasm and excitement for learning U.S. business know-how. Polish managers felt that they learned something new each day, not only from formal training but also from on-the-job training. Often Polish managers compared the company to a university. For the first time since entering a market economy, they felt they had the opportunity to learn business functions such as marketing, distribution, and logistics. These pro-American attitudes created an eagerness among the Polish managers to accept expatriate ideas concerning new work priorities. The attitudes also worked to legitimize the power and leadership of the U.S. Americans in the company.

The Polish managers believed that, unlike under the previous communist system, the new organization encouraged the development of the individual. They believed that the U.S. system of management inspired self-expression and achievement, respecting individuals and their unique personalities. There was a strong belief that hard work would bring success. Talented people who were willing to work could advance and succeed.

These organizational values were quite new for the Polish managers. In their previously state-controlled organizations, competence and good performance were not the main bases for a promotion and compensation. Party membership was the key to a successful managerial career. Rewards and promotions depended on fulfilling a political role rather than on achieving economic goals.

The Cultural Conflicts

In spite of the very positive attitudes of the Polish managers toward a U.S. management style, there were still many conflicts between expectations based on Polish cultural traditions and an organizational culture based on the national culture of the United States.

Managerial Selection Many Polish employees wanted to be hired immediately as managers, without any experience in basic business functions. They associated the magic word *manager* with a higher status and success. U.S. managers, however, felt that "you had to earn your spurs first." The U.S. expatriate district manager recalled:

> People applying for positions in the sales department do not want to do basic business first, to be a sales representative, they want to be immediately managers. People that I interview want to be only managers. How you can manage sales representatives if you don't know what they do? They lack a concrete answer for my question.

Merit, Age, and Seniority The corporate culture encouraged rewards primarily based on competence in key skills and performance against objective criteria. Both local and expatriate managers believed that individuals were appointed and promoted based on their knowledge and professional expertise. This situation often resulted in much younger managers having older subordinates. As one U.S. manager from the finance department stated:

> The company gives a lot of authority to young people very quickly. You never know, the guy who is looking younger than you could be a vice president already.

Although Polish managers appreciated promotions based on competence, the issue of age presented some adjustment problems. Traditional expectations hold that, when one is young, it is impossible to be knowledgeable and to have the necessary experience and competence to manage successfully. As a Polish assistant manager from the marketing department admitted:

> I prefer to have an older boss because it would be very stupid if I have a boss younger than me. He has less life experience and a shorter marriage. He is younger and he is not authority to me. I would prefer someone who has more life experience. I realize that it is a very Polish thing that I find this to be a problem.

The Salary System Polish managers expressed difficulty in adjusting to the confidentiality of the new salary system. The Polish and U.S. managers differed in their beliefs regarding what kind of information was personal and what kind should be public. Polish managers wanted to know as much about each other's salaries as possible. They had no problems asking another employee about exactly how much they were paid. To the Polish managers, this served as a means of establishing their relative status. As a Polish assistant brand manager indicated:

> I like this system but I would like to know how I am in comparison with the others. If I knew that the person who works together with me had a higher salary than me, I would be very unhappy.

For the expatriate U.S. Americans, however, it was not part of the company culture to reveal explicit salary information. Salary information was considered personal and confidential. Most felt that revealing salary information disrupted the family climate of the organization. Instead, the Americans expressed faith in the system of assessment and reward allocation. As the expatriate head of the finance department noted:

> Poles make mistakes when they say: "Americans don't share salaries in this system." I would say it is not that straightforward at all. In the American system, in our company's system, we don't share specifics on what any one person makes. We try very hard to share the system by which you make more salary. We make it very clear that your salary is based on your performance. If you perform well you will make a lot of money.

Team Goals Working not only for your own interests but also for the success of the team or the whole company was a challenge for many Polish managers, especially for those who had their initial managerial experiences in a state-controlled economy. One Polish manager noted:

> Americans want to hire the best, because the organization will gain from them and you as a boss should be not afraid if you hire a person who is more clever than you. You will benefit from it because the company will benefit. In state companies you had to protect yourself by not cooperating—a new, better employee was your potential enemy.

Another Polish assistant marketing manager mentioned:

> In a state company, if somebody has a problem, he or she solves it with their own interests in mind. Here we are thinking in terms of the benefit of the whole company. I made a mistake and I regarded it as my mistake because I was responsible for it.

But the problem was judged [by the Americans] as a problem and loss for all of us. This is a different way of thinking, and this is the attitude of this company. Success belongs to everybody and so does failure. This is better than making one person responsible for it.

The Psychological Contract In the eyes of the Polish managers, the organization required them to accept a new psychological contract between the organization and the individual. On the one hand, they felt positive about the degree of personal involvement and responsibility in the daily activities of company affairs. On the other hand, they were confused where to draw the line between professional and private lives. Many of the Polish managers felt that, for them to succeed as employees, the organization demanded too much of their private lives. As the Polish marketing manager said:

Americans look differently at the firm. They associate themselves very closely with it. They are part of the firm. In the past I never felt such a relationship with the firm.

Another Polish district manager mentioned:

This new way of thinking, that you have to have a strong psychological connection with the firm, surprised me. You have to show you are interested. In the past you escaped from your job as quickly as possible.

Trust A U.S. cultural trait that surprised Polish employees was the perception of an underlying good faith in people. Both the company culture and the expatriate managers had positive valuations regarding the intentions of people within the organization. As a Polish accountant stated:

What was new for me was that Americans have the assumption that you are acting for the good of the firm and that you are honest and that people are good. If you go to a restaurant for a business meal, nobody will tell you that you are nasty and that you used the company money and did it for a bad purpose.

A Polish assistant brand manager added:

A positive attitude toward people, trust in people— this is a basis for everything. Americans don't wait to catch you in a mistake. We are more suspicious of people. Our immediate assumption is that a person wants to do something bad.

Polish managers expressed much more negative attitudes regarding the nature of people. These were evidenced in many aspects of the daily business life of the organization: subordinate–superiors ("My boss wants to harm me"), employee–peers ("My colleagues would only criticize me"), customer–product ("Americans are trying to sell us bad products"), employee–product ("I don't believe in the value of this product"). A U.S. expatriate brand manager, describing the Polish managers, indicated:

I have never met a group of people that was more skeptical of the future and more distrusting. Everyone we do business with is convinced that we are dumping a less quality product on the market. The Polish customer is very skeptical. They don't believe that they can get products as good as anybody else in the world.

Distrust, fear, and a disbelief that the boss wishes well for the employees were common attitudes observed by the U.S. expatriates. One U.S. expatriate from customer service operations remarked:

Sometimes they [the Polish managers] don't understand that the company is trying to do the right things for individuals. Sometimes there will be questions which assume that the employer is going to take advantage of them and is going to treat locals badly. It is not a good assumption that the company and manager are not trying to help them if they have a problem.

Informality U.S. managers valued blunt and direct speaking. Saying exactly what you mean was considered a virtue, and the U.S. managers had a low tolerance for ambiguity. Therefore, expatriate managers took most explanations at face value. Reacting to this, Polish managers often described Americans as very "open," "direct," "spontaneous," and "natural" during communication. However, this style of communication clashed with the indirect communication habits of Polish employees. As the American head of the marketing department stated:

Communication with Polish employees is difficult, especially when an employee has a problem. There is a general unwillingness to talk directly about oneself and one's problems. Poles will gladly talk about somebody else. They will not talk about their own needs. They don't like direct questions about things which are important to them. Perhaps it is considered impolite, too bold, or inappropriate for them.

Polish managers adapted to the U.S. directness by developing an informal network of communication among themselves, which served as a buffer between the U.S. and Polish managers. To deal with their U.S. superiors, Polish managers first talked among themselves. Then one person would become responsible for going to a U.S. manager and telling him or her about someone else's problems. Expatriate managers found it unusual when subordinates who needed to communicate problems resorted to this informal channel. However, this buffer in communication provided a comfort zone for the Polish managers. As the Polish assistant marketing manager noted:

Poles more easily criticize things among themselves, but it is difficult for them to criticize things in the presence of Americans. It is as if they don't believe in their strengths, and are afraid that their opinions are either untrue or irrational. They are afraid of being funny.

Americans also introduced an informal style of communication by addressing everyone in the office on a first-name basis. Expatriates expressed the belief that their organizational culture provides an opportunity to "lead by competence, not by formality in relationships between superiors and subordinates." They were proud of their openness and equality in forming business relations. To the expatriates, the Polish managers who resisted the informality appeared to be cold and distrusting. Expatriates interpreted it as the "director syndrome" or as an example of an attitude from the communist-controlled past. The expatriate head of the sales department described it as follows:

I respect their history. I respect the cultural aspects. Every time they call me "Mister Director" I remind them to call me by my first name. I am constantly telling them that I have a culture, too. This company has a culture, one that I want to build here. I don't like the environment that formality fosters and the environment that it creates. It is a barrier for effective communication. You almost have too much respect, and then you stop talking to me, soon you stop coming and saying, "I have a problem."

The majority of Polish managers adjusted to the norm of a first-name basis very quickly in dealing with the Americans. However, this did not mean that they wished to be on a first-name basis when speaking among Polish managers, especially with their Polish subordinates. Using first names for older people or for superiors is not a Polish norm. Some Polish managers were afraid that they would lose the ability to lead by being so informal. They believed that distance between superiors and subordinates helped them in the direct management of lower staff. The Polish head of the human resource department said:

There are some people in the firm with whom I will never be on a first-name basis. I am on a first-name basis with some people and on a Ms./Mr. basis with others. I don't know why, but I will not change that.

Informality also contrasted with Polish views that managers should symbolically show their status and success. Polish managers gave much value to formality, titles, and signs of status, such as having a good make of car. Superiors were expected to have these trappings as a demonstration of their authority over subordinates. In contrast, the U.S. expatriates regarded many of these status symbols as counterproductive and meaningless. A U.S. brand manager mentioned:

Poles are passionate about getting ahead in status. People are looking for examples of badges to wear for the rest of the populace to know that you have made it. My boss must be in a big car. "What car are you going to drive?" I was asked by a Pole in the first meeting in Poland.

Positive Feedback on the Job There were significant differences between Polish managers and expatriate Americans in the type of feedback given on the job. Consistent with their views of management practices, the U.S. managers were quick to recognize achievements publicly and privately. Polish managers were generally positive about this approach and perceived it as motivating. However, in spite of this reaction, positive feedback was not a popular management technique among the Polish managers. They preferred to give criticism and generally negative feedback in front of subordinates and peers. Reacting to the U.S. approach, a Polish district manager described the situation:

If you are good, Americans can send you a congratulatory letter. Once I had got such a letter from an American colleague of mine even though he had no particular responsibility for my job. He was not my boss. I would never think of doing so. It was so spontaneous.

Conclusions

Coming from a culture that lacked experience and contact with U.S. businesses before 1989, Polish managers generally had positive but stereotypical views of U.S. business practices. In the short term, such attitudes played a highly motivating role in attracting managers to the joint venture. In the long term, however, despite the initial enthusiasm, basic cultural differences may lead to disillusionment among Polish managers.

CASE DISCUSSION QUESTIONS

1. What are some important cultural differences between the Poles and the U.S. expatriates?

2. Using Hofstede's and the 7d cultural dimension models, explain some of the cultural differences noted in the case.

3. What are some institutional explanations for how the Polish workers are reacting to U.S. management style?

4. How can the joint venture take advantage of the initial enthusiasm of the Polish managers to build a stronger organization?

5. What cultural adaptations would you suggest to the U.S. expatriate managers regarding their management styles?

CASE CREDIT

This case was prepared by Krystyna Joanna Zaleska of the Canterbury Business School, University of Kent, Canterbury, England, while a postgraduate student at the Central European University, Prague. Reprinted with permission of the author.

The Institutional Context of Multinational Management

3

Preview CASE IN POINT

Entrepreneurship in the United States and Europe

As of 2009, the United States still leads the world in the creation of new businesses. Between 1996 and 2004, it is reported that about 550,000 new businesses were created every month. In contrast, the number of new businesses created in Europe and Japan remains much smaller.

Why is the United States creating new businesses at such a high rate? Experts agree that the United States enjoys a number of important characteristics that facilitate entrepreneurship. For instance, the country has a very flexible labor market that allows companies to freely hire and fire workers. Also, its educational system has long promoted close cooperation between higher education and industry. Universities such as Stanford and Harvard place a strong emphasis on entrepreneurship. Finally, the United States presents companies with a fairly flexible immigration system.

The European environment, in contrast, is not seen as conducive to entrepreneurship. For instance, the tax system is seen as much higher and thus less likely to promote new businesses. The legal and patent requirements are very complex and daunting. Small businesses find it very expensive and time-consuming to navigate such barriers successfully. Furthermore, in contrast to the United States, where entrepreneurs such as Bill Gates are celebrated, not all Europeans view entrepreneurs in such a positive light. Many universities view industry with skepticism and have been reluctant to establish partnerships. In general, businesses tend to be viewed more suspiciously.

Will things change? Experts note that Europeans are increasingly adopting the U.S. model. Further, many European universities are establishing stronger links with industry. The success of Skype is a good example of European entrepreneurial effort. So the future is likely to see more and more new businesses coming from Europe.

Source: Based on Economist. *2009. "The United States of Entrepreneurs. Special Report on Entrepreneurship," March 14, pp. 9–13.*

I n Chapter 2, we discussed some of the ways societies can be compared in terms of their national cultures. However, as the Preview Case in Point shows, other elements of a society besides national culture, such as education and the legal system, can affect important business-related differences among societies. In that case, you saw how such factors as the legal, education, and tax systems were all important in explaining differences in entrepreneurial output between the United States and Europe. These factors are critical in how businesses are conducted in societies, and some of them may even encourage individuals to adopt values that are not consistent with their national cultures. It is therefore important to understand the dominant institutional context of any society and to appreciate its influence on both individuals and organizations.

Specifically, understanding the institutional context is extremely critical to effective multinational management. At a basic level, a manager cannot completely understand any society without examining the national culture and the institutional context.[1] Both are key elements of societies, and both have important influences on issues related to strategic multinational management. Exhibit 3.1 shows a model of how the national context (i.e., institutional context, national culture, and business culture) leads to national differences that have implications for the business environment of a country.

EXHIBIT | **3.1** | **The National Context and Multinational Companies**

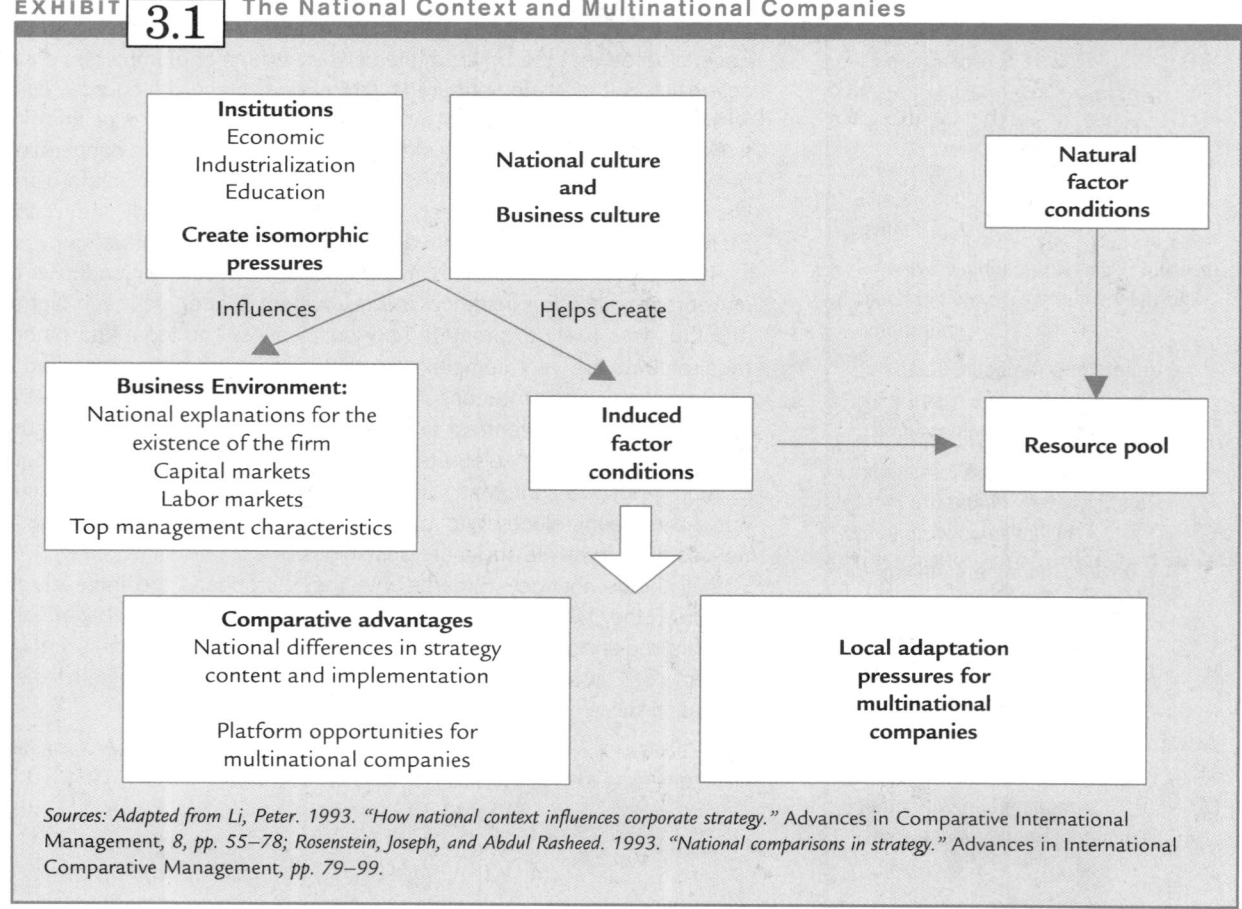

Sources: Adapted from Li, Peter. 1993. "How national context influences corporate strategy." Advances in Comparative International Management, *8, pp. 55–78; Rosenstein, Joseph, and Abdul Rasheed. 1993. "National comparisons in strategy."* Advances in International Comparative Management, *pp. 79–99.*

The **national context** is made up of the respective national cultures and social institutions of a society. As we saw in Chapter 2, the national culture of a society shapes its important norms, values, and beliefs. These cultural components exert important influences on the business culture and on acceptable and correct ways of doing business. However, closely intertwined with national cultural forces are social institutions such as the economic system, religion, and education. As we will see later in this chapter and in other chapters, they also represent a significant influence on people's norms, values, and beliefs and have implications for the business culture.

This chapter thus provides a basic understanding of the institutional context of societies. In the next section, we discuss briefly the main elements of a country's institutional environments: social institutions and how they influence society. In subsequent sections, we discuss each of these social institutions in depth and their implications for multinational strategic management. We conclude this chapter by looking at some of the ways social institutions are connected to later chapters.

Social Institutions and Their Influence on Society

A **social institution** can be defined as "a complex of positions, roles, norms, and values lodged in particular types of social structures and organizing relatively stable patterns of human resources with respect to fundamental problems in . . . sustaining viable societal structures within a given environment."[2] In addition to national culture, social institutions have profound effects on people's life conditions and provide the context for psychological differences among people. Similar to national culture, social institutions provide boundaries and norms that prescribe how people will behave; that is, they provide people with behavioral guides when facing different social situations.

We consider three key social institutions that are the most likely to influence the business environment: the economic system (e.g., capitalism or socialism), the level of industrialization, and the types of religion. We also briefly consider the educational system and the level of social inequality because both have been linked to a lesser degree with the business environment.

Economic Systems

The **economic system** is the "interrelated network or system of beliefs (concerning work, property, constructs, and wealth), activities (extraction, production, and distribution), organizations (business firms, labor unions, consumer associations, regulatory agencies), and relationships (ownership, management, employment, sales) that provide the goods and services consumed by the members of a society."[3] Economic systems are usually reflected in their governments' influence, specifically in terms of whether productive activities are state owned or privately owned.

Economic systems can be typified by the extremes of capitalism and socialism, with mixtures of elements of both in the mixed economy. The **capitalist or market economy** refers to an economic system where production activities are "decentralized to private-property-rights holders (or their agents) who carry out these activities for the purpose of making profits in a competitive market."[4] In contrast, the **socialist or command economy** is one where production resources

---

National context
National culture and social institutions that influence how managers make decisions regarding the strategies of their organizations.

Social institution
A complex of positions, roles, norms, and values organizing relatively stable patterns of human resources with respect to sustaining viable societal structures within a given environment.

Economic system
System of beliefs (concerning work, property, and wealth), activities (extraction, production, and distribution), organizations (business firms, labor unions), and relationships (ownership, management) that provide the goods and services consumed by the members of a society.

Capitalist or market economy
System where production is decentralized to private owners who carry out these activities to make profits.

Socialist or command economy
Production resources are owned by the state and production decisions are centrally coordinated.

CASE IN POINT

Socialism and Venezuela

Venezuela is an example of a socialist economy. The government, led by Hugo Chavez, has strived to intervene in many industries to take hold of production in the interests of the poor. This approach worked well when the price of oil was relatively high because oil represents about 90 percent of Venezuela's exports. The significant inflow of cash allowed Chavez to fund many social programs to keep the population content. However, the fall in oil prices in 2008 weakened government finances, making it harder to maintain such programs.

To minimize economic worries—and remain consistent with socialist principles—the government started taking over private companies. For instance, the government seized a rice plant belonging to Cargill, as well as plants owned by Venezuela's most powerful conglomerates.

Rice is an important staple for Venezuelans, and disruption in its supply could trigger unrest. When Venezuela experienced a significant rice shortage, the rice companies argued that they were operating at loss because of price controls. The Venezuelan government then took control of the rice plants to enforce price-controlled production.

Source: Based on Economist. 2009. *"Socialism in Venezuela. Feeding frenzy," March 14, p. 40.*

are owned by the state and production decisions are centrally coordinated.[5] The ideal socialist economies pursue collective goals such as social equality and solidarity. Consider the above Case in Point.

Finally, the **mixed economy** combines aspects of the capitalist and socialist economic systems. In such economies, certain sectors of the economy are left to private ownership while the state runs others, such as health care and education. The state determines that private interests cannot run some sectors of the economy and thus takes control of such sectors, making resource allocation and production decisions. Countries such as Sweden, France, Denmark, Italy, and India are examples of mixed economies.

Although it is impossible to cover all their possible business implications, economic systems have two major implications for strategic multinational management:

1. Dominant market type.
2. Market transitions.

Mixed economy
Combines aspects of capitalist and socialist economies.

Dominant Market Type

At a basic level, decisions to operate in a country can be made based on the dominant economic type. For instance, to operate relatively freely from governmental interference, a multinational may want to set up operations in a capitalist society like the United States or Britain. However, if multinationals expect to do business in mixed economies like France and Italy, they should expect to subordinate their economic goals and respect social objectives. Emerging markets also present peculiar challenges for investors. Consider the next Focus on Emerging Markets.

The Focus on Emerging Markets clearly shows the impact of governmental interference on a multinational's operations. As a rough guide, multinational managers may want to consider a country's **index of economic freedom** to determine the extent of its governmental intervention. Since 1995, the Heritage Foundation, a U.S.-based research foundation, has been constructing the index.

Index of economic freedom
Determines the extent of governmental intervention in a country.

Focus on Emerging Markets

Governmental Interference in China

Research by Luo shows how companies deal with difficulties when forming joint ventures in China. Specifically, the international joint venture contract, which governs how many joint ventures are operated, incorporates three important components: (1) term specificity (the degree to which contractual terms are clearly specified), (2) contingency adaptability (the degree to which companies can adapt to changing situations), and (3) contractual "obligatoriness" (the degree to which companies are bound by the contract). Using surveys from 110 executives involved in international joint ventures, Luo showed that the more the respondents experienced governmental interference, the more highly they rated the need for contingency adaptability in the contract. In other words, the more governmental interference, the more the contract needs to leave room for adaptation to new situations. Luo also found that governmental interference had a negative impact on contract specificity because the more the government intervened, the less possible it was to specify the contract clearly. Such research provides some important guidelines regarding how companies need to structure their contracts to counteract Chinese local and central governmental interventions.

Other events point to the role played by the Chinese government in other cases. For instance, Coca-Cola attempted to buy China Huiyan, China's largest juice company, offering $2.4 billion, an amount that represented about three times the value of the company. For the privately run company, the offer was very appealing, but the Chinese government rejected the offer. Many experts see the move as an effort to prevent foreign companies from dominating the Chinese market. Although Coca-Cola controls half of the market for soft drinks, the juice market is highly fragmented. The successful acquisition of China Huiyan would have given Coca-Cola control of 20 percent of the market. Other industries, such as aviation, banking, and automaking, are seeing significant governmental control through nationalization.

Sources: Based on Economist. *2009. "Business in China. So much for capitalism," March 7, p. 72;* Economist. *2009. "Coca-Cola and China. Hard to swallow," March 21, pp. 68–69; Luo, Yadong. 2005. "Transactional characteristics, institutional environment and joint venture contracts."* Journal of International Business Studies, *36, pp. 209–230.*

It defines the index as "the absence of government coercion or constraint on the production, distribution, or consumption of goods and services beyond the extent necessary for citizens to protect and maintain liberty itself." The index includes ten indicators, ranging from trade freedom (i.e., the degree to which the government hinders free trade through tariffs), taxation policies, and the level of governmental intervention in the economy, to property rights (freedom to accumulate private property) and business freedom (i.e., ease of obtaining a business license). The foundation assigns scores of 0 through 100, with 100 being the perfect degree of economic freedom. Exhibit 3.2 shows selected top and bottom ten countries on the 2009 assessment.

The indices shown in Exhibit 3.2 are not surprising. Capitalist societies such as Canada, Australia, the United Kingdom, Singapore, and Hong Kong figure prominently in the list of top ten countries. Communist societies such as Cuba and North Korea are in the bottom ten. Additionally, countries with repressive governments such as Zimbabwe and Libya are also in the bottom ten.

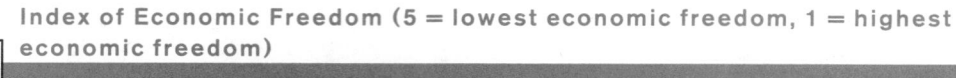

EXHIBIT 3.2

Index of Economic Freedom (5 = lowest economic freedom, 1 = highest economic freedom)

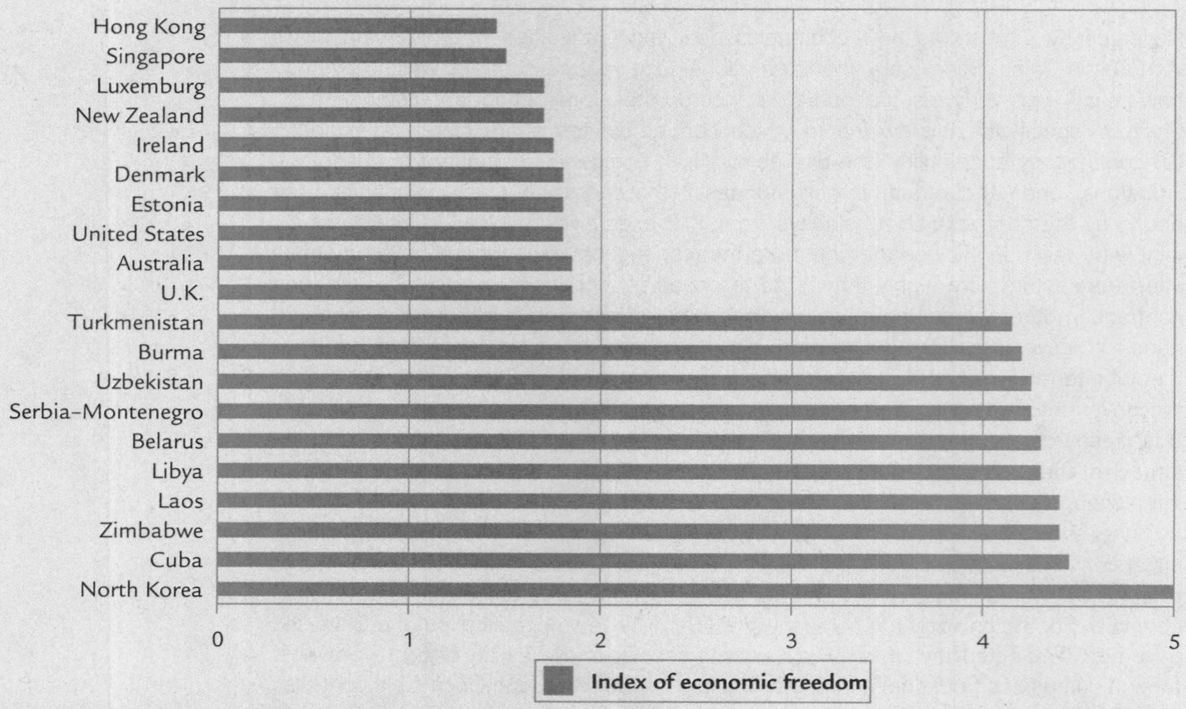

Source: Adapted from Heritage Foundation. 2009. http/www.heritage.org.

Market Transitions

Market transitions
Changes that societies go through as they move from socialism toward a market-based economy.

The second economic system implication involves **market transitions**, which are the changes that many societies go through as they move from socialism toward a market-based system. The post-1980s saw a large number of countries in Russia, Eastern Europe, and Asia (i.e., China and Vietnam) undergo marked attempts by the governments to infuse heavy doses of capitalism. For most multinationals, such open market policies have presented incredible opportunities because they represent new markets and access to skilled but relatively cheaper labor. An important aspect of this transition for many multinationals has been an increase in international strategic alliances with local companies, as described in Chapter 9.

For most multinationals, an important component of market transitions has been to understand socialism and its effects on both people and organizations in order to better understand the workers' reactions to market mechanisms. Under socialism, most enterprises were mere factories, with no need for cost control.[6] Often these enterprises did not have any strategic planning, accounting, or marketing departments. Furthermore, central planners guaranteed the survival of these firms—despite their inefficiencies—by setting up prices that were not accurate reflections of costs. Instead, prices were sometimes kept low to encourage the heavy consumption of goods manufactured on the orders of the central planners. Banks also were managed according to the needs of central planners. Loans were often made on the basis of connections and personal relationships rather than creditworthiness.

It is not difficult to understand, then, what multinationals experience in facilitating the transition to a market economy. Drastic measures have to be taken to turn inefficient companies into firms that can perform essential business functions. Additionally, managers' thinking has to be changed completely so that they understand management functions and the necessity to be cost-effective. Finally, the financial system, the firms, and prices have to be left unregulated to more accurately reflect the needs of the market rather than to satisfy the needs of central planners.

Multinationals also have to be aware of the effects of socialism on workers. Pearce provides a good understanding of what workers go through in socialist societies.[7] In socialist societies the government is considered as nonfacilitative because it does not provide the structure to ensure that people can depend on interpersonal trust. Government officials are actually more likely to have the power to distribute rewards and to make important salary decisions. For

---

Comparative Management **Brief**

Human Resource Management Challenges in China

As companies strive to learn how to do business in China, they have to contend with governmental interference, but employees also pose a challenge. The 1950s Iron Rice Bowl policy was based on the notion that workers had the right to lifetime employment and a wide range of social programs, such as housing, schools, and medical care. Thereafter, the long isolation under communism resulted in the complete elimination of the human resource management function. China now is transitioning to a market economy, and companies are finding that they are facing major challenges as they try to adapt market-based approaches to this function.

In face-to-face interviews with ten individuals closely linked to private firms in China, a number of significant challenges were described. For instance, because the old system emphasized personal networks and ties, private firms found that Chinese managers tend to hire relatives and friends and to overstaff. Additionally, Chinese workers in these firms were not accustomed to do more than what was specified in their job description, and they were often risk averse. Finally, job appraisals and rewards were very difficult to manage, especially when good relations with workers and government officials had to be maintained.

In addition to these challenges, research suggests that the Chinese contextual environment has resulted in other problems. For instance, the planned economy and the Cultural Revolution emphasized loyalty at the expense of initiative among workers. Furthermore, the lack of business education in the past means that China is currently suffering from a severe shortage of qualified professionals. As a result, the workforce is very mobile, and employees do not hesitate to change jobs frequently to take advantage of high demand for qualified individuals. Multinationals also find it risky to bring Chinese employees to train in Europe because such training makes the employees more attractive to other firms when they return to China.

Sources: Based on Bruton, Garry D., David A. Ahlstrom, and Eunice S. Chan. 2000. "Foreign firms in China: Facing human resources challenges in a transitional economy." SAM Advanced Management Journal, *Autumn, pp. 4–36; Jaussaud, Jacques, and Xueming Liu. 2006. "La GRH des personnels locaux dans les enterprises etrangeres en Chine: Une approche exploratoire."* Revue de Gestion des Ressources Humaines, *59, pp. 60–71; Economist. 2009. "Business in China. So much for capitalism," March 7, p. 72.*

instance, Walder,[8] in a study of Chinese companies, discusses how supervisors were responsible for writing character reports on workers, which were then relayed to the central party. Such information was then used in responding to workers' requests for housing and other scarce consumer items. Workers could not rely on meritocracy but instead had to rely on the personal relationships with their supervisors and party officials. Consequently, they tended to develop a severe distrust of each other because they were all competing for the same limited rewards. Additionally, they focused their energies on refining their personal networks rather than on performance because networks were more likely to help with success.

Multinationals have incredible challenges as they hire employees in former socialist societies. At a basic level, they need to train these workers to trust each other. As multinationals start up team-based approaches to designing work, they are finding that workers are reluctant to cooperate and work with each other. Furthermore, multinationals also need to change the mentality that personal relationships are key components of success. As they introduce more open systems based on meritocracy, they sometimes face significant opposition from these employees. Consider the Comparative Management Brief on the previous page, showing the various challenges private firms have faced with regard to human resource policies in China and their response to these challenges.

Clearly, economic systems have important implications for the strategic management of multinationals, impacting relationships among companies and how these companies are structured. Specifically, the transition of many former socialist countries to a market-based approach presents significant challenges for multinationals. However, economic systems also affect individuals, specifically how workers view work and even how they justify ethical behaviors, as we will see in subsequent chapters.

In the next section, we consider another critical social institution: the levels of economic development through different degrees of industrialization.

Industrialization

The application of the steam engine to the gathering and production processes is largely used to explain the Industrial Revolution in Europe.[9] The machine eliminated the excessive reliance on animal power and allowed the building and use of new machines and equipment that were very effective in resource use. This new ability to gather and transform resources led to the rapid development in many Western societies of large factories with large numbers of workers assembled around networks of machines. Such changes dramatically influenced all aspects of society.

Industrialization refers to the cultural and economic changes that are brought about by fundamental changes in how production is organized and distributed in society. Industrialization can be categorized in several ways. In a **preindustrial society**, agriculture dominates and shapes the economic environment. Religious norms and tradition are emphasized, and social mobility is discouraged.[10] Occupational placement tends to be based on ascription (family background), and social status is largely determined through inheritance. An **industrial society** tends to be characterized by the dominance of the manufacturing or secondary sector. Such societies reflect the prevalence of technological development that makes rapid economic growth possible. Industrial societies tend to require wider ranges of skills in their workforce relative to preindustrial societies. Occupational placement is based on universalistic

Industrialization
Cultural and economic changes that occur because of how production is organized and distributed in society.

Preindustrial society
Characterized by agricultural dominance and shaping of the economic environment.

Industrial society
Characterized by the dominance of the secondary or manufacturing sectors.

criteria, such as achievement. Finally, the **postindustrial society** emphasizes the service sector. The dominance of employment by the service sector leads to a drastic expansion of the role of formal education due to the need for highly trained workers with specialized skills. Exhibit 3.3 shows selected countries and the distribution of employment by primary, secondary, and tertiary sectors.

The level of industrialization has important implications for strategic multinational management. Consider the next Case in Point.

What does the Case in Point mean in terms of international management? There is a direct correspondence between the level of economic development and industrialization, so preindustrial societies tend to be the least economically developed. Multinational companies can use such indicators to determine the feasibility of doing business in preindustrial societies. Given that the long-term prospect of a business in any country depends on market size and income, preindustrial societies tend to provide fewer opportunities. However, preindustrial societies also provide relatively cheap labor compared to industrialized societies, so, not surprisingly, many companies tend to locate their plants in preindustrial countries. Also, preindustrial societies tend to have poor infrastructure and business support. Operating in such countries may be more costly because the multinational company may have to provide its own infrastructure and support services. Many African countries unfortunately fall into this preindustrial category, and multinationals have generally shunned most of them because of political instability. However, as the Case in Point, "What Does the Future Hold for Africa," shows, the future for some African countries is bright, and multinationals have to be aware of the role they can play in such developments.

As technological development makes it possible to shift production to the manufacturing sector, important changes in a society's economic environment

Postindustrial society
Characterized by emphasis on the service sectors.

EXHIBIT 3.3   Distribution of Production Activities by Sector

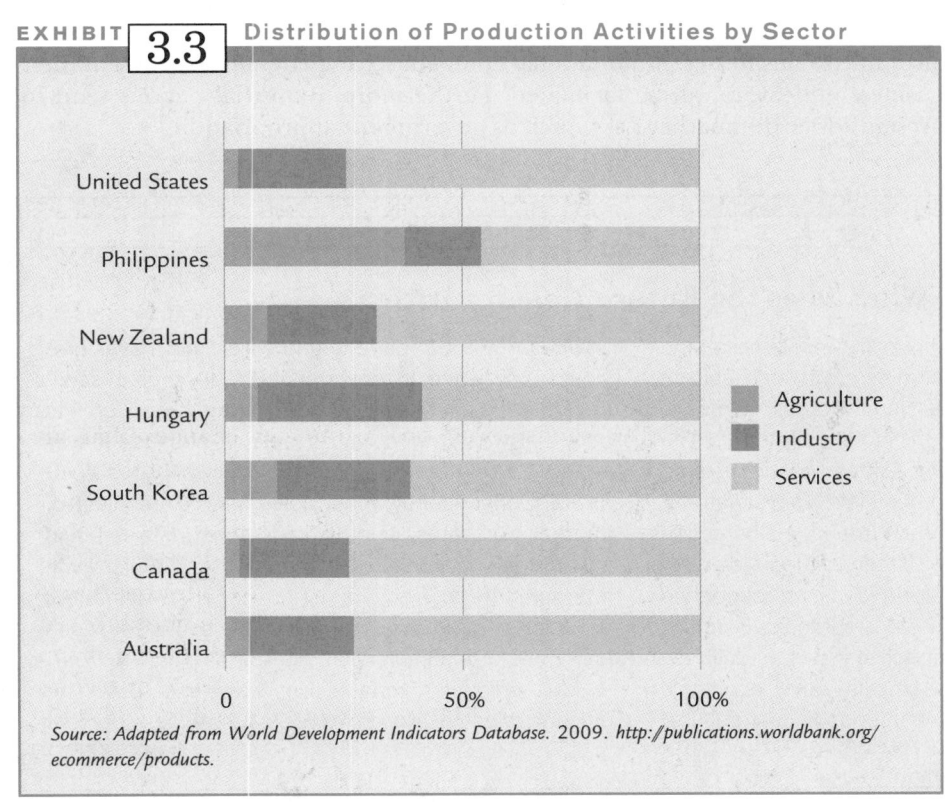

Source: Adapted from World Development Indicators Database. 2009. http://publications.worldbank.org/ecommerce/products.

Industrialization and India

India is currently experiencing tremendous changes because of industrialization. Even though a significant percentage of the population remains in poverty, India has nevertheless seen a growing middle class with the rise of service companies, such as Infosys. Such experiences are bringing major changes that will likely affect the future work environment in that country.

One of the many changes has been a new celebration of entrepreneurial success. Many Indians are now willing to leave or turn their backs on jobs at well-known companies to start their own businesses. Such efforts are also spurred by new entrepreneurship

competitions, such as the National Entrepreneurship Network's competition to find India's hottest start-ups.

One company shortlisted for the competition is Sammaan ("dignity"). Irfan Alam came up with the idea when he was sitting in a rickshaw on a hot summer day. He asked the rickshaw puller for a drink of water and realized that rickshaws cover over six miles a day. He realized that the rickshaw pullers could supplement their meager income by selling water and even advertising on their rickshaws. He thus sells ads through the rickshaws.

Source: Economist. *2008. "Start-Ups in India. A suitable business,"* December 20, pp. 111–112.

affect strategic management. Instead of emphasizing tradition and communal obligations that are heavily influenced by the religious norms typical of preindustrial societies, industrial societies tend to favor innovation and individualism. Economic achievement becomes the top priority for industrial societies, and discipline and achievement-oriented norms predominate.[11] Industrial societies tend to present significant opportunities for multinational companies. Multinational companies have access to an environment that is very favorable to businesses and a labor force that is often educated and motivated. Additionally, industrialized societies tend to have governments that are usually favorable to businesses. Multinational companies can generally expect that their business endeavors will be facilitated. Furthermore, industrial nations tend to present lower nonmarket risks, such as government appropriation.

What Does the Future Hold for Africa?

With the exception of nations like Botswana and Mauritius, few African economies have been able to sustain growth in real per-capita gross domestic product, one indicator of industrialization. The reality is that African nations have been growing much more slowly than other developing nations. Why have most African countries been left behind in terms of industrialization? It is often argued that, after many African nations experienced independence from the three major colonizers (France, Belgium, and Great Britain), their respective elites established one-party rule "promising stability and economic development in return for a monopoly on political

power." However, these countries did not have previous experience in governing and in capital accumulation. Furthermore, any outward-oriented growth potential was viewed with suspicion because it was seen as foreign interference from the previous colonizers. Consequently, most governments, because of internal pressures, engaged in more state-led and inward-looking industrialization efforts. Coupled with internal strife and governments' response to interest groups, African nations have not achieved much economic progress.

Multinational companies nevertheless have significant roles to play in Africa's future development

continued

and growth. Africa has sizable physical and human resources, and it represents significant market opportunities. As the continent wrestles with the failings of most autocratic regimes, many of these countries are gradually moving toward multiparty regimes with an emphasis on political stability. As more and more of them gain political freedom, the economic environment will become more conducive to capital accumulation and growth. Eventually, multinational companies will have a significant role to play as investors. As a rough guide for investment decisions, multinational companies may want to consider liberal democracy indices, that is, the extent to which a political system enables political liberties and democratic rule. The following exhibit shows the political democracy indices for selected African countries.

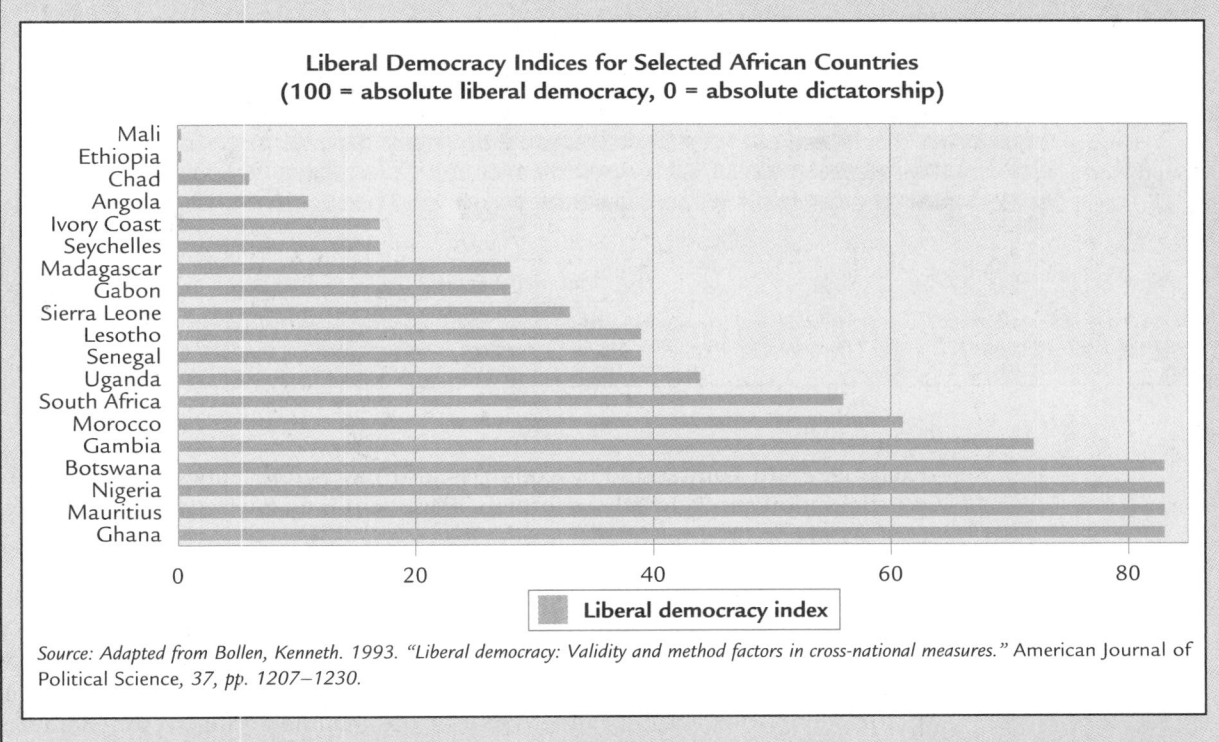

Liberal Democracy Indices for Selected African Countries
(100 = absolute liberal democracy, 0 = absolute dictatorship)

Source: Adapted from Bollen, Kenneth. 1993. "Liberal democracy: Validity and method factors in cross-national measures." American Journal of Political Science, 37, pp. 1207–1230.

Exhibit 3.4 shows the materialist scores of selected countries. These scores indicate how much societies value such goals as economic growth and maintaining discipline, both indicators of the degree of industrialization. As the exhibit shows, many countries that are currently undergoing industrialization (e.g., China, Hungary, India, and Brazil) have high rankings on the materialist index, suggesting that individuals in such societies are achievement oriented and favor material gains. The emphasis on economic achievement implies that multinational companies are well advised to motivate employees with monetary rewards.

In addition to shaping norms for individuals, industrialization also has implications for how industries are shaped. Industrialization can therefore take many forms and have various effects based on the conditions in the society. In some cases, industrialization efforts can be inward oriented, where local industries are promoted to satisfy the domestic market and preserve foreign

EXHIBIT 3.4   Materialist Values for Selected Countries

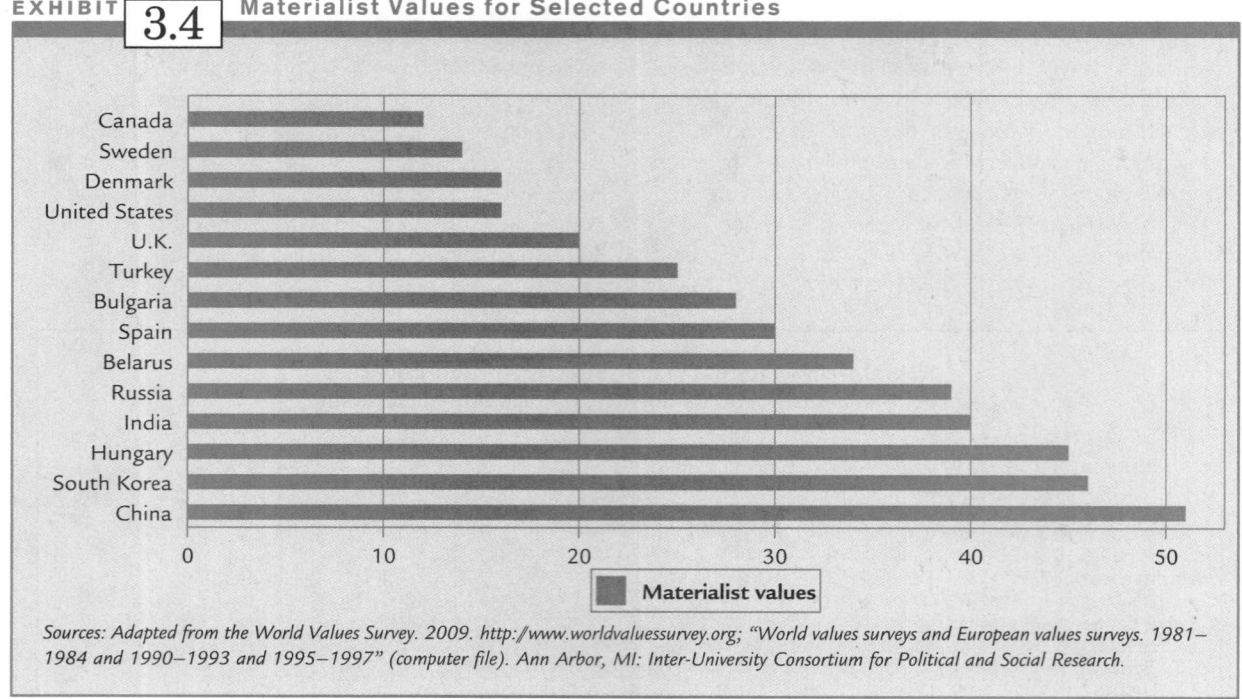

Sources: Adapted from the World Values Survey. 2009. http:/www.worldvaluessurvey.org; "World values surveys and European values surveys. 1981–1984 and 1990–1993 and 1995–1997" (computer file). Ann Arbor, MI: Inter-University Consortium for Political and Social Research.

exchange.[12] In contrast, some countries also have more outward-oriented industrialization strategies where foreign investment is encouraged and exporting is heavily promoted.

A postindustrial society is characterized by the domination of the service sectors in production activities.[13] In such a society, productivity and growth tend to come from the generation of knowledge as applied to all economic sectors through information processing. Countries transitioning from an industrial to a postindustrial society experience an almost complete demise of the agricultural sector, along with a significant decline in the manufacturing sector. Because services delivery becomes prevalent, there is a significant rise of information-rich occupations, such as managerial, professional, and technical jobs. As societies become more postindustrial, more jobs require increased skills and advanced educational achievements.

Postindustrialization is leading to a postmodern shift in many societies. Inglehart et al.[14] argue that the disciplined and achievement-oriented norms and values typical of industrialized societies have reached a peak. In postindustrial societies, the "emphasis on economic achievement as the top priority is now giving way to an increasing emphasis on the quality of life."[15] As a result, people are more likely to espouse individual expression values and a movement toward a more humane society.

Exhibit 3.5 shows selected countries and their scores on the postmaterialist scale. As the exhibit shows, many of the most developed societies have high postmaterialist scores. Multinational companies operating in such countries have to be aware of the changing needs of workers in these countries. Specifically, people are likely to value jobs over which they have the most control. Such workers also are more likely to prefer noneconomic incentives rather than monetary rewards. Companies should strive to find ways to satisfy such needs.

EXHIBIT 3.5   Postmaterialist Values for Selected Countries

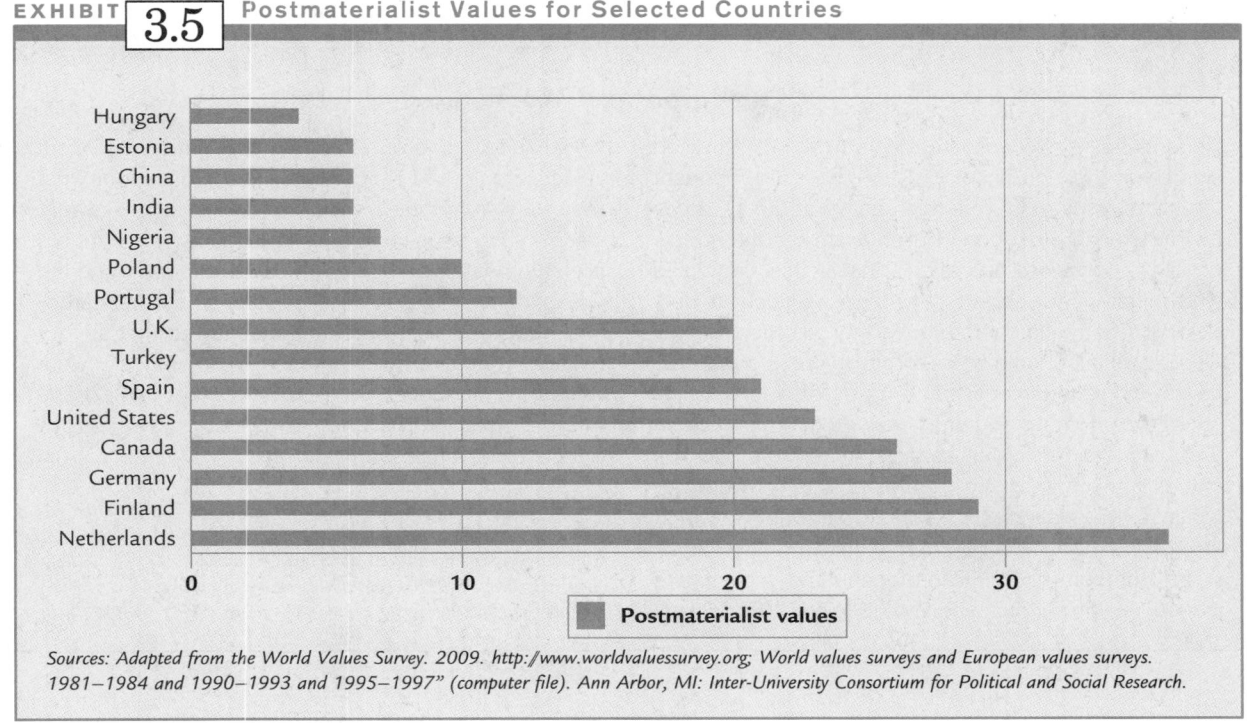

Sources: Adapted from the World Values Survey. 2009. http://www.worldvaluessurvey.org; World values surveys and European values surveys. 1981–1984 and 1990–1993 and 1995–1997" (computer file). Ann Arbor, MI: Inter-University Consortium for Political and Social Research.

In this section, we described some of the possible effects of industrialization on societies. Specifically, we looked at industrialization levels and how they affect individuals as well as organizations. In the next section, we consider another critical social institution: religion.

Religion

A **religion** can be defined as a shared set of beliefs, activities, and institutions based on faith in supernatural forces. Religions continue to be an important aspect of most societies. The reemergence of Christianity in the United States, the rise of Islamic fundamentalism in the Middle East, the rapid growth of Protestantism in Latin America, and the religious devotion in the former Soviet Union and Eastern Europe all signal that religions continue to be pervasive and important.[16]

Religion, work, and their interrelationships form the very foundations of human society.[17] In fact, the link between religion and how societal systems are structured for economic purposes forms the basis of Max Weber's famous formulation of the Protestant work ethic.[18] Weber, a famous German sociologist, proposed that the domination of Protestant religions led to the emergence of modern capitalism in Western Europe. He argued that Protestant beliefs emphasize hard work, the creation of wealth, and frugality. This combination of values allowed individuals to work hard to accumulate wealth. However, because Protestant beliefs encouraged believers to reinvest the wealth rather than spend it, they formed the basis of the Western European capitalist expansion.

Religion
Shared set of beliefs, activities, and institutions based on faith in supernatural forces.

CASE IN POINT

Religion and Work

Understanding how religion affects work has attracted significant attention, but only recently have the important effects of religion on work been demonstrated. A study by Parboteeah, Hoegl, and Cullen examined the effects of religion on work obligations, that is, the degree to which individuals believe they have a societal duty to work. The researchers argued that all religions view work as an important obligation and, more important, as having religious dimensions. Analysis of a large-scale set of data from 45 countries showed that the belief in God and the behavioral aspects of religion, such as church attendance, have positive effects on work obligations. Multinationals may therefore want to weigh religion in determining how their employees view work.

In another study, Parboteeah and colleagues looked at how four specific religions (Buddhism,

Christianity, Hinduism, and Islam) influence work values. Employees typically have preferences for what they want from their work. Some prefer extrinsic work values, such as income and job security, while others prefer intrinsic work values, such as autonomy and the use of initiative at work. Analysis of another large-scale data set from 40 countries showed that all four religions have positive influences on intrinsic work values. Furthermore, the results show that three of the four religions (Christianity excluded) have positive effects on extrinsic work values.

Sources: Based on Parboteeah, K. P., Y. Paik, and J. B. Cullen. 2009. "Religious groups and work values." International Journal of Cross Cultural Management, 9(1), pp. 51–67; Parboteeah, K. P, M. Hoegl, and J. B. Cullen. 2009 "Religious dimensions and work obligations: A country institutional profile approach." Human Relations, 62(1), pp. 119–148.

Religions have important influences on society, providing its members with a way of dealing with issues that reflect individual wishes and activities.[19] However, religions also affect business and other organizational procedures. Consider that Islam, as discussed later in this chapter, has productivity implications during the Ramadan months or that Christianity has obvious consumer behavior implications during Christmastime.[20] As we will see, for instance, in Chapter 4 on ethics, religions have important influences on how people do business in different parts of the world, as the above Case in Point demonstrates.

As the Case in Point shows, clearly religion has profound influences on work. As multinationals conduct operations in foreign locales, they need to be sensitive to religion. We therefore consider various aspects of religion in this section.

Despite a great variety of religions around the world, only four are practiced by a large percentage of the world's population. In the next few sections, we look at Christianity, Islam, Hinduism, and Buddhism, along with their implications for multinational strategic management. Exhibit 3.6 shows the distribution of religions around the world, both in percentage of the world population and in number of followers. As the exhibit shows, Christianity, Hinduism, Islam, and Buddhism are followed by almost 71 percent of the world's population; of the remaining 29 percent, approximately 20 percent are considered nonreligious.

Christianity
Religion based on the life and teachings of Jesus.

"Christianity is a faith based on the life, teachings, death, and resurrection of Jesus"[21] and is clearly the most practiced religion around the world. Christianity started with the birth of Jesus Christ approximately 2,000 years ago and has evolved considerably into different forms because of many internal feuds and divisions. A major separation occurred in 1054 when the Roman Catholic Church split from the Eastern Orthodox Church. The majority of Orthodox Christians today live in Russia, Serbia, Bulgaria, Romania, Albania, Poland, and the Czech Republic, and most Roman Catholics live in Western Europe and the Americas. In 1517, yet another major division occurred in Christian history. Disillusioned with the Roman Catholic Church's authority and practices, Martin

EXHIBIT **3.6**

Religion by Percentage of World Population and Number of Followers

Religion	Percentage of World Population Following Religion (%)	Number of Followers (000)
Christians	33.60	1,900,174
Nonreligious	20.50	1,163,189
Muslims	18.25	1,033,453
Hindus	13.50	764,000
Others	7.33	414,725
Buddhists	5.99	338,621
Sikhs	0.36	20,204
Jews	0.24	13,451
Confucians	0.10	6,334
Jains	0.07	3,951
Shintoists	0.06	3,387

Sources: Adapted from Fisher, Mary P. 2007. Living Religions, 7th ed. Upper Saddle River, N.J.: Prentice-Hall.

Luther, a German monk and priest, initiated different interpretations of the Bible that led to the Protestant branch of Christianity.

Despite the many divisions among Christianity, Christians all share the belief that Jesus is the incarnation of God who was sent to cleanse the sinfulness of humanity. Jesus is often associated with love and allows humans to connect with God through penance, confessions of their sins, self-discipline, and purification.

The impact of Protestantism on the development of capitalism is seen as major evidence of the link between religion and economic structuring of societies. Because Protestantism emphasized wealth and hard work for the glory of God, it allowed the focus on goals related to economic development and wealth accumulation. In contrast, Catholics were more likely to question the pursuit and accumulation of wealth. This difference explains the sustained development of capitalism in Western Protestant societies.

In general, Christians agree "on the value and dignity of human life, labor, and happiness."[22] There is a general support for the freedom to accumulate wealth and possessions. However, human greed and selfishness are nevertheless viewed with contempt, and attempts are made to ensure equality of opportunity and fairness for the less fortunate. Additionally, Christianity, through the Ten Commandments, provides the basis for what are considered ethical behaviors. Although not all individuals follow these commandments, they are nevertheless seen as norms guiding behaviors with respect to such things as theft ("You shall not steal"), murder ("You shall not kill"), and protection of private property ("You shall not covet your neighbor's house or anything that is his"). Multinational companies therefore have access to environments that are conducive to conducting business.

The essence of Islam, as described in the *Qur'an,* is the submission to the will of Allah (God). Islam can be traced back to Muhammad, a prophet born in 570 CE. However, unlike the Christian view that the founder Jesus was divine, Muslims do not ascribe divinity to Muhammad. Rather, he is seen as the messenger of Allah's revelations and the last in a line of prophets starting with Adam, through Moses, Jesus, and Abraham.[23] Islam is currently the second

Islam
Religion based on the submission of the will to Allah (God).

largest of the world's religions and has adherents in Africa, the Middle East, China, Malaysia, and the Far East. It continues to grow rapidly in many countries, especially in Europe.

Muslim society is heavily influenced by Islamic standards and norms. Islam provides encompassing guidance in all spheres of life, both social and economic. Those who serve Allah and accept the reality and oneness of Allah go to paradise in the afterlife.[24] Muslims also believe that Allah wants them to live according to the *Shari'ah* (Law). The *Shari'ah* requires Muslims to follow five pillars: Confession, Prayer, Alms Giving, Fasting, and Pilgrimage to Mecca.[25]

These pillars have important implications for multinational strategic management. First, a multinational company operating in a Muslim country has to accommodate the Muslim's need to pray five times a day. Muslims need to pray in the early morning, noon, midafternoon, sunset, and evening.[26] Furthermore, during the Ramadan, a month of fasting, multinational companies face some decline in productivity. During that month, Muslims are not allowed to eat, drink, smoke, and even take medicines from dawn till dusk. As such, multinational managers are advised to take steps to ensure that business activities are not disrupted. The month is also considered very spiritual, and multinational companies should expect their workers to be more concerned with sacred matters and a heightened spiritual atmosphere.

The alms-giving pillar also has critical implications for multinational strategic management and how Islam views business. In general, the *Qur'an* is supportive of entrepreneurship and the earning of profits through legitimate business activities. The *Qur'an* also allows the accumulation and protection of private property. However, Muslims are naturally concerned with issues of social justice and fairness, and they are likely to condemn the pursuit of profits through the exploitation of others. Multinational companies thus have to ensure that their business activities are conducted in a socially just manner and that some form of alms giving is practiced. Muslims (and organizations) are required to share their accumulated wealth by charitable giving to the poor. This practice is seen as necessary to decrease social inequalities and personal greed. Multinational companies may be well-served by participating in such donations.

An important consequence of Islam's condemnation of the exploitation of others is that Muslims may not pay or receive interest. Islam regards the payment or acceptance of interest as a serious sin. Such beliefs are not just ideals but are actually put into practice in many countries, including Pakistan. In such countries, governments have instituted financial laws declaring interest illegal. For a multinational company operating in a Muslim country, the prohibition of interest presents a serious challenge. However, many Muslim societies have been working in profit-sharing plans to avoid the payment or receipt of interest. For instance, if a multinational company borrows money from a bank in a Muslim country, it should expect to be asked to share the profits from the investment as an alternative to paying interest. Multinational companies should thus be prepared to formulate creative but acceptable ways to manage their finances.

Multinational firms are likely to be presented with significant opportunities in the Muslim countries in years to come. For instance, it has been estimated that the Middle East alone has approximately 300 infrastructure projects representing $45–$60 billion of possible private investment [27] and it is likely that multinational companies will have to provide significant financing for these projects. The challenges of financial exchanges, therefore, will become more urgent and will have to be dealt with. Consider the next Comparative Management Brief on the challenges of Islamic laws.

Comparative Management **Brief**

Islamic and Financial Operations

In an effort to revitalize its economy after the Gulf War, the Kuwaiti government embarked on a strategy of attracting foreign investment to make up for the deficits incurred in reconstruction. However, Kuwait is an Islamic society and has to respect the *Shari'ah,* or religious law, which prohibits receiving or paying interest. In addition to this well-known financial requirement of Islam, the *Shari'ah* also prohibits uncertainty and gambling, and it stresses honesty in business and monetary transactions. As a consequence, all contracts have to be specified in great detail. Additionally, because futures and options have speculative natures, they are regarded as gambling and are illegal. Such prohibitions represent significant challenges for international capital providers.

The EQUATE (Ethylene Products from Kuwait) project was a joint venture between Petrochemical Industries Company, a subsidiary of the Kuwaiti national oil company, and Union Carbide Corporation. The joint venture, formed to finance the construction and operation of a $2 billion petrochemical plant, faced a number of significant financing challenges. For instance, the venture participants wanted part of the financing to come from Islamic banks in an effort to involve Kuwaiti citizens and investors. However, the Islamic banks could not loan the money directly; they had to be involved directly in the venture so that they could share in the profits instead of earning interest. Eventually, the Islamic banks purchased assets and leased them to the joint venture.

Compared to a regular loan, these financial arrangements present significant challenges. With the ownership of assets in a company comes ownership risk. For instance, how much should the Islamic banks be liable for if the plant causes serious environmental damage? This problem was addressed by placing the assets in a special-purpose vehicle with limited liability. Another challenge pertained to the leasing aspect of the financial arrangement: the Islamic banks owned the assets while the venture was the actual user. As with any lease agreement, the Islamic banks are responsible for maintaining the assets of the plant and for insuring against losses that may occur should the assets break down. A major expectation for the venture was therefore to ensure that the Islamic banks took such insurance and maintenance precautions. Another challenge dealt with the application of the law in the event of default: Should Islamic or other law apply to the contract? Additionally, the Islamic investors were at a great disadvantage if payments were late because of their inability to collect penalty interest, which would have to be donated to charities. Finally, in the event of a bankruptcy, the Islamic bank still owned the assets and would be able to claim them from the venture. However, such actions would destroy the ongoing value of the project and reduce any chance of recovery.

Sources: Based on Al-Kashif, A. M. 2009. "Shari'ah's normative framework as to financial crime and abuse." Journal of Financial Crime, *16(1), pp. 86–98; Esty, Benjamin C. 2000. "The EQUATE project: An introduction to Islamic project finance."* Journal of Project Finance, *5, pp. 7–20.*

A final multinational strategic management implication of Islam pertains to the role of women in Muslim countries. Although the *Qur'an* puts men and women on an equal footing as individuals, the guidelines for the roles of men and women differ.[28] While the man's role is to work and support the family, the woman's role is to provide care and stability to the family in the home. Not surprisingly, many Muslim societies are strictly divided by gender. Multinational companies have to be aware of the effects of their business actions based on gender roles. For instance, given the dominance of the male sector, it is not advisable for multinational companies to post women in executive positions in Muslim countries. Additionally, human resource management practices need to take into consideration the limited role of women in such societies. Although there has been much progress in many Muslim societies regarding gender roles, respecting such roles is clearly important for any multinational firm operating in a Muslim country.

Hinduism is a broad and inclusive religion encompassing individuals who respect and accept the ancient traditions of India, "especially the Vedic scriptures and the social class structure with its special respect for *Brahmans* (the priestly class)."[29] Unlike Christianity and Islam, Hinduism has no specific founder, and Hindus place no special significance on historical events or on the sequence of events. Rather, Hinduism, through the Vedic scriptures, is seen as timeless and eternal. Currently about 760 million Hindus reside in India, Malaysia, Nepal, Suriname, and Sri Lanka. Many of the Hindus outside of India typically share ancestors from India.

The quest for *Brahman* is the ultimate goal for most Hindus. *Brahman* refers to the ultimate reality and truth, the "sacred power that pervades and maintains all things."[30] However, to discover the *Brahman,* one needs to look into one's *atma,* or soul. Hinduism generally believes in the reincarnation of the *atma* based on one's *karma,* or the effects of one's past actions. Whoever tries hard to live life according to the principles of *dharma,* or principles of righteousness and moral order, will be reincarnated in successively more favorable *atmas* until one reaches *Brahman.*

One aspect of Hinduism that is most likely to have implications for multinational companies in India is the caste system, which is the ordering of Indian society into four occupational groups. The highest caste includes the priests, followed by the kings and warriors, and then merchants and farmers. The fourth caste includes the manual laborers and artisans. Although the caste system seems unfair and is illegal in India, its original purpose was to create a higher law that would subordinate individual interests to the collective good. The system remains a dominant feature of life in India today, and multinational companies operating in India have to be aware of it. For instance, having a lower caste member supervise higher caste individuals can be problematic. Additionally, members of lower castes may face promotion ceilings in organizations because of their caste membership. Finally, at meetings, it is important to consider how the various castes interact.

Consider the experience of FoodWorld supermarket chains in India.[31] While opening new retail supermarkets in India, the firm had to hire and train managers. However, being a retail manager is not seen as having a high social status in India, and only members of the lower caste were willing to take the jobs. Given the pervasiveness of the caste system in India, these workers felt that they had significantly lower status. Training programs therefore had to be designed to emphasize confidence in the workers in order to get them to perform their duties adequately. Another major challenge was to find ways to alleviate the concerns of traditional Indian customers who may not want to make contact with someone from a lower caste.

Some, however, argue that the caste system is slowly dying. The next Case in Point provides evidence of fundamental changes in Indian society and how it views the caste system.

Hinduism
Acceptance of the ancient traditions of India that are based on the Vedic scriptures

CASE IN POINT

Is the Caste System Dying?

The villagers of Seetanagaram were tired of their water pumps breaking down frequently. Despite their complaints to local officials, the pumps were seldom repaired. The women would then have to walk two hours to get water from the Sarada River, and the water would often make them sick. Things changed when Mr. Rao, a 23-year-old resident, was sent to attend the pump repair training program offered by a British charity, Water Aid. After he attended the training, his services were much in demand. However, Mr. Rao is a member of the *Dalit* caste, or untouchable, a fifth class below the other four castes. Furthermore, Seetanagaram is a very segregated village, where the upper castes live in a separate colony and exclude the *Dalits* even from participation in marriages and festivals. At first, the upper-caste members were reluctant to interact with the *Dalits*. However, faced with the possibility of nonfunctioning pumps, the upper castes gradually accepted the idea of a *Dalit* helping them fix the pumps. Such programs, like Water Aid's efforts to train 490 lower-caste villagers, are slowly eroding the caste-based prejudice systems.

The political environment also shows some evidence that the caste system is slowly dying. At the time of writing, Kumari Mayawait, a 53-year-old former school teacher and member of the *Dalit* caste, was running for prime minister, and some experts believed she had a chance to win. Furthermore, India was considering extending quotas in various occupations to ensure that the lower castes get a fair representation. Indian companies were also implementing voluntary plans to increase the numbers of lower castes in the workforce. Some companies were thinking about offering better educational and training opportunities, while others were investigating coaching classes to encourage lower castes to achieve higher education. The Indian government was at the same time considering tax breaks for companies offering employment to lower-caste people in poor areas.

Sources: Based on Economist. 2006. "Asia: Caste and cash," April 29, p. 67; Harding, Luke. 2002. "Indian villagers given a taste of equality: Lower-caste Dalits trained to fix pumps gain clean water and modicum of respect." Guardian, December 7, p. 20; Waldman, Amy. 2003. "Mayawati embodies outcasts' political rise; She is India's first Dalit chief minister." Seattle Times, May 4, p. A26; Westhead, R. 2009. "Can 'untouchable' be India's PM? Born into lower caste, Kumari Mayawati is trying to make history as she stirs controversy." Toronto Star, March 26, p. A15.

Hinduism's teachings and philosophies have other implications for multinational strategic management. The religion provides clear guidelines on ethical behaviors, among which performing one's duty and respect for one's parents are prominent. In connection with the caste system, most people have clearly defined paths that they should be engaged in. Multinational companies would be well-advised to take such guidelines into consideration. The Hindu's respect for parents also has business implications. Multinationals will often find that families run Indian businesses and that the elder males in the business typically make the major decisions. As such, multinational companies should be ready to accept parental influence even when dealing with younger family members. Finally, Hindus believe that they should aim for four goals in life: spiritual achievement, material prosperity, pleasure, and liberation, although the aims vary depending on the stage of life.[32] Nevertheless, multinational firms should be aware that Hinduism does not condemn the pursuit of material possessions; they can generally expect an environment that is conducive to business and wealth accumulation.

Buddhism is the broad and multifaceted religious tradition that focuses primarily on the reality of worldly suffering and on the ways one can be freed from it. Gautama Buddha, the founder of Buddhism, was born as a prince in the sixth century BCE in India. Buddhist accounts of his life suggest that his father tried to protect him from seeing suffering to prepare him as a king. Buddha was,

Buddhism
Religious tradition that focuses primarily on the reality of world suffering and the ways one can be freed from suffering.

however, dissatisfied with the impermanence of life, and, when he turned 29, he abandoned all riches to become "a wandering ascetic, searching for truth."[33] Today, Buddhism is very popular in Europe and the United States, although most of its followers are found in countries such as Cambodia, China, Japan, Korea, Laos, Sri Lanka, and Thailand.

The essence of Buddhism is that craving and desires inevitably produce suffering. It is, however, possible to reach a state where there is no longer any suffering. Buddha proposed that, to remove suffering, one had to follow the Eightfold Path of right understanding, right intention, right speech, right action, right livelihood, right effort, right mindfulness, and right concentration. Buddhists also believe that the way to end suffering is to meditate in order to train and soothe the mind and ultimately reach enlightenment, or *Nirvana*.

Nanayakkara's interpretations of Buddha's teachings suggest that he saw poverty as the major reason for the decline of ethical behavior in society.[34] Buddhism therefore prescribed a work ethic that encouraged workers to engage in their best efforts and that promoted qualities such as taking initiative, persistence, and hard work. Laziness is seen as a very negative quality and is heavily discouraged. Buddhist workers may be expected to have a generally positive view of work, but multinational managers must be aware that Buddhism proposes a work ethic that emphasizes teamwork and ethical means to achieve success. Multinational companies would be well-advised to provide environments that take advantage of such values.

Given Buddhism's strong emphasis on compassion and love, some have suggested that Western profit-oriented companies should adopt Buddhist principles. In that context, Gould proposes that employees (and multinational managers) engage in a number of exercises to enhance their ethical orientation to business.[35] For instance, if everyone is considered as a mother, father, brother, or sister, one is more careful about the consequences of one's actions on others. Furthermore, the compassion and love inherent in considering others as close relatives may be helpful in dealing with the employee diversity of multinational companies. Another Buddhist principle is the acknowledgment that the positive action of others makes life possible. Hence, if multinational managers recognize the efforts of their workers through ethical treatment, they are likely to enjoy long-term benefits. Finally, although work is a key component of life, other areas need to be balanced. Multinational companies can respect a balanced work design for their workers.

These descriptions of the four major world religions show that they all have implications for how the economic environment is shaped.

In this section, we looked at four of the world's main religions and examined the implications for multinational strategic management. In the next section, we look at two final social institutions: education and social inequality. Both are key in most societies, even though their effects on multinational strategic management may not be as great as that of the other three social institutions.

Education

Education Organized networks of socialization experiences that prepare individuals to act in society.

Education consists of the "organized networks of socializing experiences which prepare individuals to act in society" and "is also a central element in the table of organization of society, constructing competencies and helping create professions and professionals."[36] Education is seen as a critical path to economic development and progress. Most countries want to achieve universal educational enrollment[37] because education enables society to instill the skills, attitudes, behaviors, and knowledge that allow people to demand more and give more to society. Such exchanges enhance the societal expansion and modernization.

Education has obvious implications for multinational strategic management. For one thing, educational levels indicate the skill and productivity of workers.[38] The more educated workers are, the more skills they possess, and the more likely they are to contribute to a country's production, both in products and services. As you will see in Chapters 11 and 12, educational systems have implications for how labor force issues are approached and how policies are implemented. Educational systems determine the nature of the workforce, and having an abundant supply of well-educated individuals allows countries to facilitate the absorption of technology from developed countries. Multinational companies can thus gauge the educational levels of various countries to determine what to expect from workers. Specifically, multinational companies can look at the mean years of education or educational attainment scores to get an idea of the human capital potential in a society. To estimate the availability of service-oriented multinationals, multinational companies can look at the percentage of population enrolled in tertiary education. Exhibit 3.7 shows, for a selected number of countries, the percentages of individuals within the relevant age groups enrolled in tertiary education. The scores reported in Exhibit 3.7 give a very rough estimate of educational potential.

Nevertheless, the focus of education varies widely. As you will see in Chapter 11, some societal educational systems value only academic education, while others, like Germany, have a balance between the academic and vocational components of the workforce. Multinational companies may therefore be interested in the skills and experience to be gained from a country's educational system by considering the test scores of students on internationally comparable tests. For instance, the test scores on mathematics and science, as conducted by the International Evaluation of Educational Achievement and International Assessment of Educational Progress, provide a good idea of the quality of a workforce and the educational system's preference for specific areas. Furthermore, if a multinational company is engaged in high-level R&D, it may find that

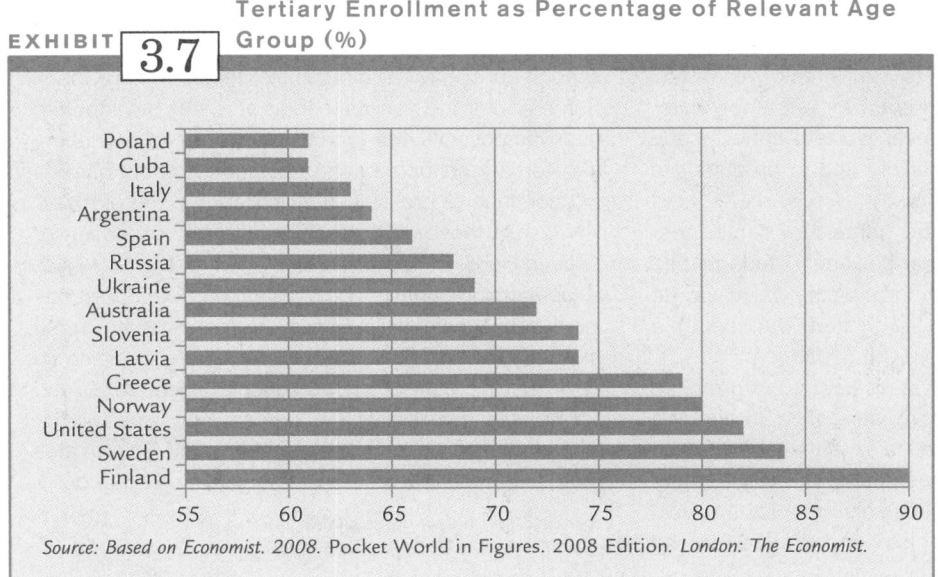

EXHIBIT 3.7 Tertiary Enrollment as Percentage of Relevant Age Group (%)

Source: Based on Economist. 2008. Pocket World in Figures. 2008 Edition. London: The Economist.

EXHIBIT **3.8**   Total Expenditures on R&D as Percentage of GDP (%)

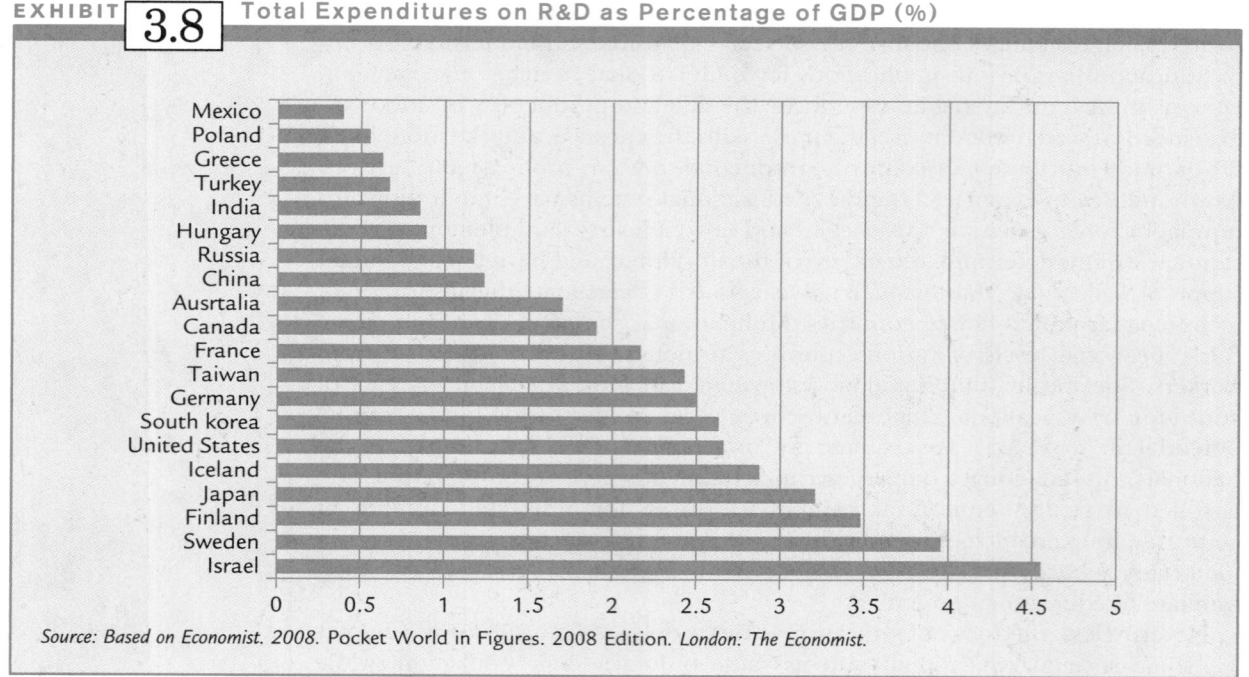

Source: Based on Economist. 2008. Pocket World in Figures. 2008 Edition. *London: The Economist.*

locating in countries with high research and development may be necessary. Exhibit 3.8 shows the percentage of GDP that goes to research and development in selected countries.

C A S E I N P O I N T

Research and Development in Asia

China is currently struggling with efforts to redesign its educational system. For decades, its system was based on rote learning; both parents and teachers would encourage students to memorize brutal amounts of information and cram for extremely competitive examinations. However, current critics argue that the system stifles creativity and is producing a very unhappy student force. A survey conducted in 2002 found that about 50 percent of senior secondary students and first-year university students had actually considered committing suicide as a way to cope with the difficulties associated with being a student.

The nature of the changes has been to reformulate textbooks to make them more interesting, integrating practical situations to theoretical explanations. Instead of merely memorizing facts, students are encouraged to see how facts relate to solutions to practical problems. Students are also encouraged to be imaginative and to view texts as the foundation for learning rather than as sacred books.

These reforms, however, cost money, and many schools are having difficulties implementing them. Some also argue that, as long as students have to take nearly impossible entrance examinations to secondary and tertiary schools based on memorization, parents will continue to pressure their children in the old way.

Despite these difficulties, the future looks bright for Asian nations. Observations show that research and development in countries like China and South Korea has increased substantially. For example, Samsung spent more on R&D in 2007 than IBM. Corporate spending on R&D in China grew 23 percent between 2001 and 2006, while it grew only 1–2 percent in Europe and the United States. Other statistics show that Taiwan has more high-tech researchers than the United Kingdom.

Sources: Based on Economist. 2009. *"Rising in the East," January 3, p. 47;* Economist. 2003. *"Roll over, Confucius," January 25, pp. 40–41.*

As Exhibit 3.8 shows, an important issue is the extent to which educational systems actually encourage students to be innovative and creative. In that context, many Asian societies have been grappling with the redesign of educational systems that are extremely competitive at the secondary level but that rely heavily on rote learning. Nevertheless, some of these societies have been extremely successful in research and development. Consider the Case in Point on the previous page, which shows that, in many Asian societies, students may go through extreme hardship to succeed. Multinational companies have to be aware that their workers have gone through schooling experiences based sometimes on rote memorization. However, the evidence also suggests that Asia will play a key role in the future with regard to innovation.

This section has explained that education has important effects on how societies are structured economically. In the next and final section, we look at social inequality.

Social Inequality

Social inequality is the degree to which people have privileged access to resources and positions within societies.[39] In high-social-inequality societies, a few individuals have the ability to control and use important resources as sources of control. This access to resources also enables the select few to use this power to gain access to even more power and to use it, in turn, to perpetuate inequality. Additionally, the level of inequality is typically taken for granted by people as the various socialization agents, such as schools and parents, tend to teach their children to justify such social stratification.

Social inequality
Degree to which people have privileged access to resources and positions within societies.

C A S E   I N   P O I N T

Gender Inequality and Chiquita Bananas

Multinational companies involved in trading bananas have been under intense pressure to improve the labor conditions of both their workers and their suppliers' workers. Chiquita, for example, has developed a comprehensive corporate social responsibility policy. A major component of this policy is a voluntary code of conduct, which both Chiquita and its independent producers must implement. However, a survey of Nicaraguan women banana workers revealed that the code of conduct has not made much difference in their lives.

Why has the code been less effective for Nicaraguan women and women in other countries? Prieto-Carron argues that, among other factors, structural gender inequalities have mitigated the effectiveness of such codes. The banana industry employs approximately 482,000 women in countries such as Guatemala, Honduras, Nicaragua, Colombia, and Ecuador. However, most of these women are involved in very low-paying, high-hour packing jobs. They face significant inequalities compared to their male counterparts. Additionally, they are employed in a very seasonal industry, and many more women workers are usually available to perform these jobs. Coupled with a social context where domestic violence and the negative perception of women are common, women workers have faced much harder working conditions than men because of such inequalities.

What can Chiquita do to reduce gender inequalities? Most experts agree that improving the conditions of women is a challenging task. However, local governments and companies can work to provide equal pay for equal work. Furthermore, gender awareness training may be useful to encourage male workers to change their perception of female counterparts. Additionally, more female supervisors can be hired to reduce cases of sexual harassment, and systems can be implemented so that women can safely report incidents and violators can be sanctioned. Finally, companies can be proactive and work to provide a better environment for maternity rights.

Source: Based on Prieto-Carron, Marina. 2006. "Corporate social responsibility in Latin America." Journal of Corporate Citizenship, 21, pp. 85–94.

Social inequality has important implications for multinational management. As you will see in the next chapter on international ethics, multinational companies are subject to significant criticism for their operations in countries with high social inequalities. Many firms endure negative publicity for paying low wages or using child labor, and the high levels of social inequality only magnify the publicity. As a result, many multinational companies are realizing that it is sometimes in their interest to be socially active to mitigate social inequalities. Consider the previous Case in Point, which considers social inequality from a gender perspective.

As the Case in Point implies, social inequality can have important implications for location decisions. Many multinational companies now actively avoid countries with high inequalities to prevent potential negative publicity. As we will see in Chapter 4, many key ethical issues arise in countries with high forms of social inequalities. For that reason, multinational companies can consider the GINI index as an indicator of the degree of social inequality. The GINI index measures the degree to which people's income deviates from a perfectly equal income distribution. Exhibit 3.9 shows the GINI indices for selected countries.

Few cross-cultural studies have examined the effect of social inequality on work-related variables. However, in an innovative study of 30,270 individuals from 26 nations, Parboteeah and Cullen showed that social inequality negatively impacts the degree to which people are attached to work.[40] Social inequality provides job opportunities only to some highly placed individuals. Furthermore, high levels of social inequality may result in more demoralized workers who are suspicious of their "exploiters." It is therefore less likely that people in high-social-inequality societies see work as more important in their lives. In fact, high levels of social inequality likely result in a less favorable work environment.

This study clearly shows the importance of social inequality and its potential impact on multinational companies.

EXHIBIT 3.9

GINI Index for Selected Countries (0 = perfect equality; 100 = perfect inequality)

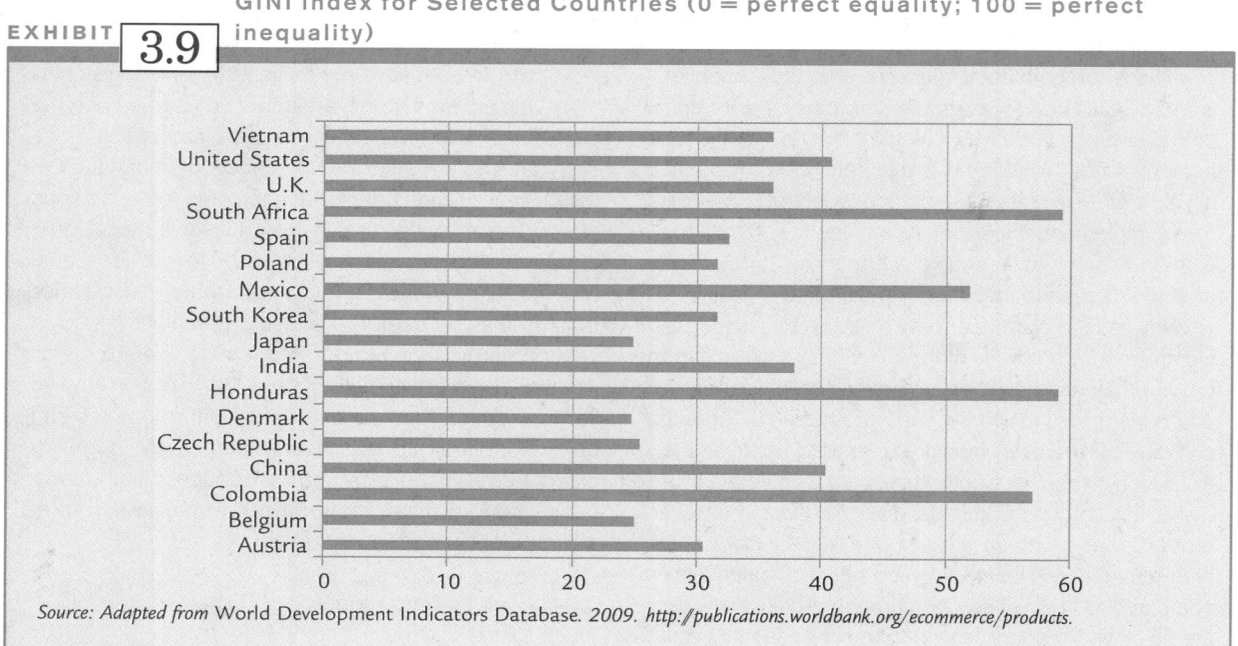

Source: Adapted from World Development Indicators Database. *2009. http://publications.worldbank.org/ecommerce/products.*

Summary and Conclusions

To get a full understanding of any society, it is essential to understand both national culture and the institutional context. We first looked at a model to examine how both national culture and social institution combine to form the national context that influences the business culture of a society. The chapter then complemented Chapter 2 by providing more specific background information on four important social institutions and their implications both for companies and for the people they employ.

First, the chapter defined social institutions and provided an explanation of how social institutions affect individuals and organizations. The chapter then described economic systems, especially their extreme types. It was shown that in societies arranged along socialist systems, the government owns the systems of production, whereas in capitalist systems private individuals make production decisions. Lodged between these two extremes is the mixed economy. Two major implications of economic systems for multinational strategic management were then discussed: the extent of governmental intervention in the business arena and the transition from a socialist economy to a free-market economy.

The institutional context includes industrialization. In that context, the chapter discussed preindustrial, industrial, and postindustrial societies and their implications for multinational strategic management. Preindustrial societies are typically less developed and thus present

significant challenges for multinational companies. In contrast, industrial societies tend to be more economically advanced, with the manufacturing sector dominating the economic environment. Finally, in the postindustrial society, services become the dominant sector, and people start shifting from achievement values to more quality-of-life values.

Religion is also an important social institution in most societies. We discussed four of the major religions around the world: Christianity, Islam, Hinduism, and Buddhism. The chapter also outlined the important business implications for each.

Educational systems have important implications regarding the available skills and experiences of the workforce in a society. However, other aspects of educational systems, such as the emphasis on sciences and mathematics, were also discussed.

Finally, we saw that social inequality can have important implications for multinational companies. The chapter concludes with the theme that social institutional differences are important now and will continue to be important in the future. We concluded by arguing that successful multinational managers are the ones who can properly assess the institutional context of the society in which they operate and who can design work environments that fit the institutional context.

Discussion Questions

1. What are the three major types of economic systems? What are the effects of economic systems on how organizations are structured in societies?

2. What are some implications of the market transition that many formerly communist societies are experiencing? What are some major challenges companies are facing in such societies as they try to motivate workers?

3. Why has Africa lagged behind other countries in economic development? What can multinational companies do to encourage economic progress on that continent?

4. What are the major philosophies of each of the world's four major religions? Pick two religions, and discuss how they affect the business environment.

5. Discuss specific Buddhist principles and how they can be applied to help multinational managers become more ethical.

6. How does the educational system influence the business environment in a country?

7. What is social inequality? What important areas of business can social inequality impact?

Multinational Management **Skill Builder**

A Briefing Paper

You have just been informed that your company has agreed to a joint venture with a company in the Czech Republic. You not only will provide new technology to

manufacture lightbulbs but also will have to provide your managerial expertise to manage and motivate workers. Your understanding is that you will take over the managerial aspects of the joint venture at the beginning and gradually train Czechs in management positions.

Using the World Wide Web and the library, research general issues such as Czech culture, Czech workers' attitudes toward work, the appropriateness for Czech partners of Western-based motivational practices typically used in your company, and the managerial potential of Czech workers. Identify key challenges you will face as you make the merger work. Discuss some potential solutions to these challenges. Discuss some of the training methods you may want to use as you train Czechs to become managers. What are some challenges you may face when you try to train Czechs to become managers?

Present your findings to the class.

Endnotes

1. Schooler, C. 1996. "Cultural and socio-cultural explanations of cross-national psychological differences." *Annual Review of Sociology*, 22, pp. 323–319.

2. Turner, J. H. 1997. *The Institutional Order.* New York: Addison-Wesley p. 6.

3. Olsen, M. E. 1991. *Societal Dynamics: Exploring Macrosociology* Englewood Cliffs, NJ: Prentice-Hall p. 35.

4. Tsoukas, Haradimos. 1994. "Socio-economic systems and organizational management: An institutional perspective on the socialist firm." *Organization Studies*, 15, pp. 21–45.

5. Ibid.

6. Healey, Nigel M. 1996. "Economic transformation in Central and Eastern Europe and the commonwealth of independent states: An interim report." *Contemporary Review*, 268, pp. 229–236.

7. Pearce, Jones L. 2001. *Organization and Management in the Embrace of Government.* Mahwah, NJ: Lawrence Erlbaum Associates.

8. Walder, A. G. 1986. *Communist Neo-Traditionalism.* Berkeley: University of California Press.

9. Turner, *The Institutional Order.*

10. Blau, Peter, and Otis Duncan. 1967. *The American Occupational Structure.* Hoboken, NJ: Wiley.

11. Inglehart, Ronald, Miguel Basanez, and Alejandro Moreno. 1998. *Human Values and Beliefs: A Cross-Cultural Sourcebook.* Ann Arbor: University of Michigan Press.

12. Gereffi, Garry, and Donald L Wyman. 1990. *Manufacturing Miracles: Paths of Industrialization in Latin America and East Asia.* Princeton, NJ: Princeton University Press.

13. Kuruvilla, Sarosh. 1996. "Linkages between industrialization strategies and industrial relations/human resource policies: Singapore, Malaysia, the Philippines, and India." *Industrial and Labor Relations Review*, 49, pp. 635–657.

14. Ibid., p. 652.

15. Bell, Daniel. 1973. *The Coming of Postindustrial Society.* New York: Basic Books.

16. Stark, Rodney, and William S. Bainbridge. 1985. *The Future of Religion.* Berkeley: University of California Press.

17. Iannaconne, Laurence R. 1998. "Introduction to the economics of religion." *Journal of Economic Literature*, 36, pp. 1465–1496.

18. Harpaz, Itzhak. 1998. "Cross-national comparison of religious conviction and the meaning of work." *Cross-Cultural Research*, 32, pp. 143–170.

19. Weber, Max. 1958. *The Protestant Ethic and the Spirit of Capitalism.* Translated by T. Parsons. New York: Scribner's.

20. Terpstra, V., and K. David. 1991. *The Cultural Environment of International Business.* Cincinnati, OH: South-Western.

21. Harpaz.

22. Fisher, Mary P. 1999. *Living Religions*, 7th ed. Upper Saddle River, NJ: Prentice Hall p. 273.

23. Ludwig, Theodore M. 2001. *The Sacred Paths*, 3rd ed. Upper Saddle River, NJ: Prentice Hall, p. 425.

24. Fisher.

25. Ibid.

26. Ludwig.

27. Esty, Benjamin C. 2000. "The EQUATE project: An introduction to Islamic project finance." *Journal of Project Finance*, 5, pp. 7–20.

28. Ludwig.

29. Ibid., 64.

30. Ibid., 84.

31. Wylie, David. 1996. "FoodWorld supermarkets in India." In A. A. Thompson and A. J. Strickland, *Strategic Management*, 11th ed. Boston: Irwin/McGraw-Hill.

32. Ludwig.

33. Ibid., p. 117.

34. Nanayakkara, S. 1992. *Ethics of Material Progress: The Buddhist Attitude.* Colombo, Sri Lanka: The World Fellowship of Buddhist Activities Committee.

35. Gould, Stephen J. 1995. "The Buddhist perspective on business ethics: Experiential exercises for exploration and practice." *Journal of Business Ethics*, 14, pp. 63–70.

36. Meyer, John W. 1977. "The effects of education as an institution." *American Journal of Sociology*, 83, pp. 55–77.

37. Meyer, John W., Francisco O. Ramirez, and Yasemin N. Soysal. 1992. "World expansion of mass education, 1870–1980." *Sociology of Education*, 65, pp. 128–149.

38. Barro, Robert J., and Jong-Wha Lee. 2000. "International data on educational attainment: Updates and implications." Working Papers, Center for International Development at Harvard University.

39. Olsen.

40. Parboteeah, K. Praveen, and John B. Cullen. 2003. "Social institutions and work centrality: Explorations beyond national culture." *Organization Science*, 14(2), pp. 137–148.

Google in China[1]

Richard Ivey School of Business
The University of Western Ontario

IVEY | Institute for Entrepreneurship

Prahar Shah wrote this case under the supervision of Professor Deborah Compeau solely to provide material for class discussion. The authors do not intend to illustrate either effective or ineffective handling of a managerial situation. The authors may have disguised certain names and other identifying information to protect confidentiality.

Ivey Management Services prohibits any form of reproduction, storage or transmittal without its written permission. Reproduction of this material is not covered under authorization by any reproduction rights organization. To order copies or request permission to reproduce materials, contact Ivey Publishing, Ivey Management Services, c/o Richard Ivey School of Business, The University of Western Ontario, London, Ontario, Canada, N6A 3K7; phone (519) 661-3208; fax (519) 661-3882; e-mail cases@ivey.uwo.ca.

In less than 10 years of existence, Google had truly become a global success story. The Internet giant had experienced unprecedented growth, wooed highly acclaimed talent from rival Microsoft and other competitors to join the company—including the "father of the internet," Vinton Cerf—and entered new markets across the world at a rapid pace. The company prided itself on its philosophy of "Do No Evil"—something that had served them well while operating in North America. However, in early 2006, they faced an ethical dilemma that put this philosophy to the test. According to some, Google's decision to censor search results in China left their motto "in smithereens."[2] The company faced intense international criticism and a backlash that made them question if their decision had been the right one.

The Birth of the Search Engine

Throughout the 1990s and into the new millennium, the world had seen the creation of a new "communications superhighway" which changed the way

people accessed resources and shared knowledge. Perhaps the fastest-growing and farthest-reaching creation since the telephone, the Internet and the World Wide Web had forever changed the way people communicated and delivered information, products, and services without any international boundaries. By 2005, almost 14.6 percent of the world's population—close to one billion people—accessed it.[3]

During this time, as the Web blossomed so did the need for a tool that enabled users to quickly and efficiently search the hundreds and thousands of isolated Web pages available online. Computer engineers and developers all over the World attempted to create a search engine that indexed these Web sites, and in 1990 the first tool to search the Internet, nicknamed "Archie," was introduced by McGill University student Alan Emtage. The program downloaded directory listings of all the files located on a File Transfer Protocol (FTP) site into a searchable database. Shortly thereafter, Mark McCahill and a team from the University of Minnesota launched "Gopher"—the first search engine that organized and enabled access to plain text files from across the Web.[4]

As it became clear that this tool could quickly become a backbone of the Internet, investors and developers began simplifying, streamlining and marketing online search engines. Competition within the industry was intense, and with minimal barriers to entry and minimal capital required to launch a successful search engine, competitive advantage was not easily sustained. Between 1990 and 1997, dozens of Internet search engines were created, including Excite, Galaxy, Yahoo, WebCrawler, Lycos, Infoseek, AltaVista, Inktomi, Overture, AskJeeves, and MSN Search. They each had their own algorithm of organizing, ranking, and displaying search results and serviced a multitude of users. In 1998, two students at Stanford University—as part of a research project—launched Google, using a new and unique method of inbound links to rank sites.[5]

Google.Com

Co-founders Larry Page, president of products, and Sergey Brin, president of technology, brought Google to life in September 1998. By 2006, the company had grown to more than 5,000 employees worldwide, with a management team representing some of the most experienced technology professionals in the industry.

Dr. Eric Schmidt joined Google as chairman and chief executive officer in 2001 while Vinton Cerf joined in 2005 as Google's vice-president and chief Internet evangelist.[6] While Page, Brin and Schmidt were largely responsible for the company's day-to-day operations and developing sustainable longer-term strategies, Cerf focused primarily on developing new ideas to launch products and find new sources of revenue apart from its search engine business. See Exhibit 1 and 2 for Google Inc.'s 2004 and 2005 financial statements.

Google's Business Model Google's search engine used a pay-per-click (PPC) method to earn advertising revenue and provide companies with a vehicle to promote their products and services. According to wikipedia:

Pay-per-click is often used to kick-start website visibility when a new website or page is promoted, and is basically a bidding system for advertisers who pay a fee to the promotion vehicle (search engine or directory) whenever a surfer clicks on their advertisement. The more the customer pays, the higher the bid, and the more highly placed— prominent—the advertisement appears. Advertisers specify the words that should trigger their ads and the maximum amount they are willing to pay per click. When a user searches Google's search engine on www.google.com, ads for relevant words are shown as "sponsored link" on the right side of the screen, and sometimes above the main search results.[7]

Consolidated Statements of Income (in thousands, except per share amounts)

EXHIBIT 1

| | Year Ended December 31, | | |
	2003	2004	2005
Revenues	$1,465,934	$3,189,223	$6,138,560
Costs and expenses:			
Cost of revenues	625,854	1,457,653	2,571,509
Research and development.	91,228	225,632	483,978
Sales and marketing	120,328	246.300	439,741
General and administrative	56,699	139.700	335,345
Stock-based compensation*	229,361	278,746	200,709
Contribution to Google Foundation	—	—	90,000
Non-recurring portion of settlement of disputes with Yahoo	—	201,000	—
Total costs and expenses	1,123,470	2,549,031	4,121,282
Income from operations.	342,464	640,192	2,017,278
Interest income and other, net	4,190	10,042	124,399
Income before income taxes	346,654	650,234	2,141,677
Provision for income taxes	241,006	251,115	676,280
Net income	$ 105,648	$ 399,119	$1,465,397
Net income per share:			
Basic.	$ 0.77	$ 2.07	$ 5.31
Diluted	$ 0.41	$ 1.46	$ 5.02
Number of shares used in per share calculations:			
Basic	137,697	193,176	275,844
Diluted	256,638	272,781	291,874

| | Year Ended December 31, | | |
	2003	2004	2005
Cost of revenues	$ 8,557	$ 11,314	$ 5,579
Research and development	138,377	169,532	115,532
Sales and marketing	44,607	49,449	28,411
General and administrative	37,820	48,451	51,187
	$ 229,361	$ 278,746	$ 200,709

Stock-based compensation is allocated as follows.
Source: Google Inc. Annual Report 2005

EXHIBIT **2** Consolidated Balance Sheets (in thousands, except par value)

	December 31,	
	2004	2005
Assets		
Current assets:		
Cash and cash equivalents	$ 426,873	$ 3,877,174
Marketable securities	1,705,424	4,157,073
Accounts receivable, net of allowances of $3,962 and $14,852	311,836	687,976
Income taxes receivable	70,509	-
Deferred income taxes, net	19,463	49,341
Prepaid revenue share, expenses and other assets	159,360	229,507
Total current assets	2,693,465	9,001,071
Property and equipment, net	378,916	961,749
Goodwill	122,818	194,900
Intangible assets, net	71,069	82,783
Deferred income taxes, net, non-current	11,590	–
Prepaid revenue share, expenses and other assets, non-current	35,493	31,310
Total assets	$ 3,313,351	$10,271,813
Liabilities and Stockholders' Equity		
Current liabilities:		
Accounts payable	$ 32,672	$ 115,575
Accrued compensation and benefits	82,631	198,788
Accrued expenses and other current liabilities	64,111	114,377
Accrued revenue share	122,544	215,771
Deferred revenue	36,508	73,099
Income taxes payable	—	27,774
Current portion of equipment leases	1,902	—
Total current liabilities	340,368	745,384
Deferred revenue, long-term	7,443	10,468
Liability for stock options exercised early long-term	5,982	2,083
Deferred income taxes, net	—	35,419
Other long-term liabilities	30,502	59,502
Commitments and contingencies		
Stockholders' equity:		
Class A and Class B common stock, $0.001 per value: 9,000,000 shares authorized at December 31, 2004 and December 31, 2005, 266,917, and 293,027 shares issued and outstanding, excluding 7,605 and 3,303 shares subject to repurchase	267	293
Additional paid-in capital	2,582,352	7,477,792
Preferred stock-based compensation	(249,470)	(119,015)
Accumulated other comprehensive income	5,436	4,019
Retained earnings	590,471	2,055,868
Total stockholders' equity	2,929,056	9,418,957
Total liabilities and stockholders' equity	$ 3,313,351	$10,271,813

Source: Google Inc. Annual Report 2005

The technology Google used to accomplish this was called AdWords. AdWords used a combination of pricing and relevance to place ads. If an ad was clicked through frequently, it would be displayed more prominently. An ad which fell below a threshold click-through rate would be deemed not relevant, and thus would be removed from that particular search. The key benefit of Google's approach was its targeting of ads.

Ads were served in the places where they would be of most relevance to users, which had the dual effect of minimizing user frustration with advertising and optimizing clickthrough rates for advertisers.

Google's AdSense technology was created based on the success of AdWords. Google recognized a much more vast marketing opportunity and released a system for webmasters and site owners to publish Google advertisements on their Web sites. Essentially, a Web site owner could choose to have Google ads served up on its pages using the same process as Google used for its own sites. When users clicked through these ads, Google and the referring site shared the revenue.

Other Google Products The AdWords promotional engine had catapulted the company's commercial worth into the multi-billion dollar league and funded development of spin-off search technology such as their desktop search. It had also led to further marketing opportunities for businesses as the search engine giant expanded into such areas as e-mail and map marketing. In 2004, Google launched its first beta version of Google Desktop, a free downloadable application for locating one's personal computer files (including e-mail, work files, Web history and instant message chats) using Google-quality search. It also introduced Gmail in 2004, an e-mail application service that received world-wide publicity during its launch. Gmail offered a powerful built-in search function, messages grouped by subject line into conversations and enough free storage to hold years' worth of messages.[8] Using AdSense technology, Gmail was designed to deliver relevant ads adjacent to mail messages, giving recipients a way to act on this information. By early 2006, Google offered a range of products (see Exhibit 3).

Google in China

On July 19, 2005, Google announced the opening of a product research and development center in China, to be led by renowned computer scientist and industry pioneer Dr. Kai-Fu Lee. Dr. Lee served as the company's first president and hoped to exploit China's thriving economy, excellent universities and multitude of talent to help Google develop new products and expand its international business operations. "The opening of a research and development (R&D) center in China will strengthen Google's efforts in delivering the best search experience to our users and partners worldwide," said Alan Eustace, vice-president of engineering at Google. "Under the leadership of Dr. Lee, with his proven track record of innovation and his passion for technology and research, the Google China R&D center will enable us to develop more innovative products and technologies for millions of users in China and around the world."[9]

One of the company's goals was to revitalize the Google Web site and offer a search engine catered specifically to the Chinese population. As Andrew McLaughlin, senior policy counsel for Google, explained in January of 2006:

> *Google users in China today struggle with a service that, to be blunt, isn't very good. Google.com appears to be down around 10 per cent of the time. Even when users can reach it, the website is slow, and sometimes produces results that when clicked on, stall out the user's browser. Our Google News service is never available; Google Images is accessible only half the time. At Google we work hard to create a great experience for our users, and the level of service we've been able to provide in China is not something we're proud of. This problem could only be resolved by creating a local presence, and this week we did so, by launching our website for the People's Republic of China.[10]*

Google.cn The launch of the new Web site and search engine, Google.cn, enabled the company to create a greater presence in the growing Chinese market and offered a customized region-specific tool with features (such as Chinese-language character inputs) that made the Chinese user experience much simpler. It also sparked the greatest controversy in the company's history. In order to gain the Chinese government's approval and acceptance, it agreed to self-censor and purge any search results of which the government disapproved. Otherwise, the new Web site risked being blocked in the same way the previous Google.com was blocked by the Chinese authorities. Google conceded. Type in "Falun Gong" or "Tiananmen Square" on Google.com and thousands of search results will appear; however, when typed into Google.cn all the links will have disappeared. Google will have censored them completely. Google's decision did not go over well in the United States. In February 2006, company executives were called into Congressional hearings and compared to Nazi collaborators. The company's stock fell, and protesters waved placards outside the company's headquarters in Mountain View, California.

Google's Defense Google defended its position, insisting that while the decision was a difficult one, it served the greater advantage to the greatest number of people.

> *We know that many people are upset about this decision, and frankly, we understand their point of view. This wasn't an easy choice, but in the end, we believe the course of action we've chosen will prove to be the right one.*

Alerts

— a service which provides e-mails of news and search results for a particular topic area

Answers

— a service where users can post queries for which they are willing to pay others to do research; the user sets the price they are willing to pay

Blogs

— Google's own blog site is "blogger"

— also provide a blog search utility

Book & catalog search

— allows users to search the full text of books and to search and browse online catalogs for mail order businesses

Images and Video

— Google's sites for searching pictures on the Web and videos

Google Earth & Google Maps

— global maps and driving directions

— also includes the capability to search for various businesses etc. within a map and display the results graphically

Google Scholar

— allows users to search academic papers

Google Groups

— a site to allow users to create mailing lists and discussion groups

Google Desktop Search

— uses Google's search technology to track information on the user's PC

GMail

— Google's mail application

For a complete listing of Google products and services, see http://www.google.ca/intl/en/options/index.html.

Launching a Google domain that restricts information in any way isn't a step we took lightly. For several years, we've debated whether entering the Chinese market at this point in history could be consistent with our mission and values. Our executives have spent a lot of time in recent months talking with many people, ranging from those who applaud the Chinese government for its embrace of a market economy and its lifting of 400 million people out of poverty to those who disagree with many of the Chinese government's policies, but who wish the best for China and its people. We

ultimately reached our decision by asking ourselves which course would most effectively further Google's mission to organize the world's information and make it universally useful and accessible. Or, put simply: how can we provide the greatest access to information to the greatest number of people?

Filtering our search results clearly compromises our mission. Failing to offer Google search at all to a fifth of the world's population, however, does so far more severely. Whether our critics agree with our decision or not, due to the severe quality problems faced by users trying to access Google.com from within China, this is precisely the choice we believe we faced. By launching Google.cn and making a major ongoing investment in people and infrastructure within China, we intend to change that.

No, we're not going to offer some Google products, such as Gmail or Blogger, on Google.cn until we're comfortable that we can do so in a manner that respects our users' interests in the privacy of their personal communications. And yes, Chinese regulations will require us to remove some sensitive information from our search results. When we do so, we'll disclose this to users, just as we already do in those rare instances where we alter results in order to comply with local laws in France, Germany and the U.S.

Obviously, the situation in China is far different than it is in those other countries; while China has made great strides in the past decades, it remains in many ways closed. We aren't happy about what we had to do this week, and we hope that over time everyone in the world will come to enjoy full access to information. But how is that full access most likely to be achieved? We are convinced that the Internet, and its continued development through the efforts of companies like Google, will effectively contribute to openness and prosperity in the world. Our continued engagement with China is the best (perhaps only) way for Google to help bring the tremendous benefits of universal information access to all our users there.

We're in this for the long haul. In the years to come, we'll be making significant and growing investments in China. Our launch of Google.cn, though filtered, is a necessary first step toward achieving a productive presence in a rapidly changing country that will be one of the world's most important and dynamic for decades to come. To some people, a hard compromise may not feel as satisfying as a withdrawal on principle, but we believe it's the best way to work toward the results we all desire.[11]

Dr. Lee, a Chinese citizen, also defended Google's decision to censor the search results for Google.cn, stating that the Chinese students he meets and employs "do not hunger for democracy." He claims that,

People are actually quite free to talk about the subject (of democracy and human rights in China). I don't think they care that much. I think people would say: "Hey, U.S. democracy, that's a good form of government. Chinese government, good

and stable, that's a good form of government. Whatever, as long as I get to go to my favorite web site, see my friends, live happily." Certainly, the idea of personal expression, of speaking out publicly, had become vastly more popular among young Chinese as the Internet had grown and as blogging and online chat had become widespread. But I don't think of this as a political statement at all. I think it's more people finding that they can express themselves and be heard, and they love to keep doing that.[12]

Google's management team, although publicly supporting their decision, were disturbed nonetheless by the growing anti-censorship campaign targeting Google. Led by groups such as the "Students for a Free Tibet" and Amnesty International, mass public rallies and demonstrations were staged outside Google offices, more than 50,000 letters were sent to Google CEO Eric Schmidt demanding the removal of search filters, and the company received intense negative publicity in the media.[13]

The web is a great tool for sharing ideas and freedom of expression. However, efforts to try and control the Internet are growing. People are persecuted and imprisoned simply for criticizing their government, calling for democracy and greater press freedom, or exposing human rights abuses, online.

But Internet repression is not just about governments. IT companies have helped build the systems that enable surveillance and censorship to take place. Yahoo! has supplied email users' private data to the Chinese authorities, helping to facilitate cases of wrongful imprisonment. Microsoft and Google have both complied with government demands to actively censor Chinese users of their services.

Freedom of expression is a fundamental human right. It is one of the most precious of all rights. We should fight to protect it.[14]

As the debate continued, Google executives realized that statements such as "We actually did an evil scale and decided that not to serve at all was worse evil"[15] made by Schmidt were not resonating with the public. It wondered what the immediate and longer-term implications of their action would be, and whether they really were staying true to their motto "Don't Be Evil."

CASE DISCUSSION QUESTIONS

1. What immediate and longer-term issues does Google's censorship decision create?

2. Prior to the launch of Google.cn, what factors should Google have considered in reaching their decision to comply with Chinese government censorship laws?

3. Assess Dr. Schmidt's statement, "We actually did an evil scale and decided that not to serve at all was worse evil." Was Google being evil?

4. Using Thomas Donaldson's *Ethical Algorithm,* assess the censorship issue and determine whether Google could be said to have acted ethically based on this model. Is the Ethical Algorithm model adequate when making ethical decisions outside of the company's home country?

5. It has been said that "[in the U.S. Constitution] the First Amendment does not reflect universal values. There is very little to say in favor of a single global standard of speech." Do you agree/disagree with this statement, and how would you relate it to this case?

6. What should Google do?

CASE NOTES

1. This case has been written on the basis of published sources only. Consequently, the interpretation and perspectives presented in this case are not necessarily those of Google Inc. or any of its employees.

2. "Google move 'black day' for China," http://news.bbc.co.uk/2/hi/technology/4647398.stm, accessed August 2006.

3. Brin, Sergey and Lawrence Page. 1998. "The anatomy of a large-scale hypertextual Web search engine." Stanford University, accessed August 2006.

4. Ibid.

5. http://en.wikipedia.org/wiki/Search_engine, accessed August 2006.

6. "Vint Cerf: Google's new idea man," http://www.wired.com/news/business/0,1367,68808,00.html, accessed August 2006.

7. Ad Words, http://en.wikipedia.org/wiki/AdWords, accessed August 2006.

8. http://www.google.com/corporate/history.html, accessed August 2006.

9. http://news.bbc.co.uk/2/hi/technology/4647398.stm, accessed August 2006.

10. http://googleblog.blogspot.com/2006/01/google-in-china.html, accessed August 2006.

11. http://googleblog.blogspot.com/2006/01/google-in-china.html, accessed August 2006.

12. Google – New York Times, http://www.nytimes.com/2006/04/23/magazine/23google.html?ei=5090&en=972002761056363f&ex=1303444800.&adxnnl=1&adxnnlx=1156925160-KvHRNCAA/InAFCXMUlz/+g, accessed August 2006.

13. http://politics.slashdot.org/politics/06/02/20/0238233.shtml, accessed August 2006.

14. http://irrepressible.info/about, accessed August 2006.

15. http://www.rfa.org/english/news/technology/2006/02/01/china_google, accessed August 2006.

4 Managing Ethical and Social Responsibility Challenges in Multinational Companies

Learning Objectives

After reading this chapter you should be able to:

- Know the definitions of international business ethics and social responsibility.

- Understand some basic principles of ethical philosophy relevant to business ethics.

- Understand how social institutions and national culture affect ethical decision making and management.

- Understand the implications of using ethical relativism and ethical universalism in ethics management.

- Identify the basic principles and consequences of the U.S. Foreign Corrupt Practices Act.

- Understand how international agreements affect international business ethics.

- Understand the differences among economic, legal, and ethical analyses of business problems.

- Develop skills in international decision making with ethical consequences.

Preview CASE IN POINT

The Growing Responsibility of Multinationals

How responsible are multinational managers for working conditions and the use of child labor in overseas production facilities? For example, should the U.S. shoe or garment manufacturer be concerned if its goods are produced by subcontractors (at the lowest competitive cost) using child labor sweatshops in Asia? Is it the duty of retailers to worry about where and how the goods they sell were produced? Increasingly, such issues are becoming important to multinational companies that source their production in the lowest-cost areas of the world. Such issues also attract public and governmental attention.

In response to these issues, a growing number of U.S. multinational companies—Levi Strauss, Nordstrom, Wal-Mart, and Reebok International—actively monitor wages, working conditions, workers' rights, and safety in their production facilities. Levi Strauss is among the most active. The company routinely sends inspectors to Southeast Asia to inspect working conditions in factories from Indonesia to Bangladesh. Even over the objections of some senior managers and board members, Levi CEO Robert D. Haas took action. He dropped two of the cheapest labor sites, China and Burma, from its manufacturing locations because of unsatisfactory working conditions.

Levi Strauss even went further with its plants in Bangladesh. When the company discovered that two sewing subcontractors employed young children, it was faced with a dilemma. Children without jobs frequently beg or engage in prostitution. Consequently, Levi, did not want to have these children fired. The solution that won the company great praise was to ask the subcontractors to remove these children from the factory, and Levi would continue to pay their wages while they attended school full-time. These children were then guaranteed their jobs back when they reached maturity at age 14.

The Swedish furniture maker IKEA also takes social responsibility very seriously. As IKEA moved its supply chain to low-cost countries, it faced a number of societal and environmental challenges, such as those connected with child labor. IKEA has joined forces with UNESCO and the Save the Children organization to work on child labor issues. Many multinationals respond to child labor problems by suddenly pulling out, but then the children often have to resort to other means, such as prostitution, to make money. Rather than pulling out, IKEA has made long-term commitments to address child labor issues in the countries in which it operates.

Sources: Based on Davids, Meryl. 1999. "Global standards, local problems." Journal of Business Strategy, January–February, pp. 38–43; Marion, Vivian. 1996. "What's fit to buy?" Lewiston Morning Tribune, June 30, pp. 1e, 5e; Maher, Kris. 2004. "Global companies face reality of instituting ethics program. "Wall Street Journal, November 9, p. b8; Strand, R. 2009. "Corporate responsibility in Scandinavian supply chains." Journal of Business Ethics, 85, pp. 179–185; Zachary, G. Pascal. 1994. "Levi tries to make sure contract plants in Asia treat workers well." Wall Street Journal, July 28, pp. A1, A5.

The Preview Case in Point shows how multinational firms are facing growing ethical issues. This chapter will present an overview of business ethics and build on this knowledge to discuss ethical and social responsibilities unique to multinational management. Consider other examples in the Case in Point below.

Managers at all levels face ethical issues every day. "If I fire a poorly performing employee, what will happen to his children?" "If we can get cheap child labor overseas, and it is legal there, should we use it because our competitors do?" "Should we refuse to give a bribe to an underpaid government official and lose the contract to our competitor's weaker product?" "Should we dump our waste in the river, knowing well that it would pose pollution risks although it is acceptable in the country?"

Why is so much attention being paid to ethical issues in multinational companies? Woods argues that approximately 60,000 multinationals are operating across country borders today but that an overwhelming majority of them and their 500,000 subsidiaries are based in developing countries.[1] Multinational

CASE IN POINT

International Ethics in Various Global Companies

Many global multinationals have been involved in actions that have resulted in major international ethics scandals.

Satyam, one of India's biggest software and services companies, is now considered India's Enron. For several years, Satyam's founder and chairman, Mr. Raju, was involved in many actions that resulted in fraud amounting to more than $1.47 million. For instance, he inflated profits while reporting cash and earned interest that never existed. Furthermore, the company overstated the amount of money it was owed. The pattern of deception finally crashed when the company tried to buy two other firms owned by members of the family. Shareholders revolted and the

deal was aborted. However, the scheme was discovered, leading to major questions for India's corporations to answer.

Similarly, Siemens, Germany's powerhouse and one of Europe's largest engineering firms, had to face a major bribery scandal. For decades, Siemens had three "cash desks," where employees could bring suitcases to be filled with cash, which was then used to bribe individuals to win contracts. Reportedly, over $850 million was paid to foreign officials to help Siemens win contracts around the world.

Sources: Based on Economist. 2008. "Bavarian baksheesh," December 20, pp. 112–113; Economist. 2009. "India's Enron," January 10, pp. 56–57.

firms have access to vast financial, capital, and human resources, and such access provides power that limits the ability of the developing countries' governments to regulate these companies. In some cases, the governments of developing countries are not willing to regulate because they are competing for foreign investment.

This chapter will provide some of the background and skills required to deal with the ethical situations faced by multinational managers.

What Are International Business Ethics and Social Responsibility?

Before you can understand the ethical dilemmas faced by multinational managers, you need a working definition of business ethics. Most experts consider business ethics as an application of the broader concern for all ethical behavior and reasoning, which pertains to behaviors or actions that affect people and their welfare. A decision by managers to knowingly sell a useful but dangerous product is an ethical decision. Ethics deal with the "oughts" of life—that is, the rules and values that determine the goals and actions people "ought" to follow when dealing with other human beings.[2]

Although economic logic (i.e., making money) dominates business decision making, most business decisions have consequences for people (workers, suppliers, customers, and society). Thus, ethical decision making permeates organizational life. For example, decisions such as those regarding product safety, layoffs, closing or relocating a plant, or the truthfulness of an advertisement have consequences for people. When managers make such decisions, they make decisions with ethical consequences—whether consciously or not.

However, ethical questions seldom have clear or unambiguous answers that all people accept. For example, producing automobiles that are safer than those currently on the market is possible. However, if such vehicles were required by law, they would be extremely expensive (only the rich could drive), they would probably result in smaller automobile production plants (putting people out of work), they would likely require larger engines (increasing oil consumption and pollution), and they would likely reduce profits (violating the ethical responsibilities of the managers to stockholders). So automobile manufacturers always deal with an ethical dilemma of whether a vehicle is sufficiently safe versus sufficiently affordable.

International business ethics pertain to the unique ethical problems faced by managers conducting business operations across national boundaries. International business ethics differ from domestic business ethics on two accounts. First, and perhaps most important, international business is more complex because business is conducted cross-nationally. Different cultural values and institutional systems necessarily mean that people may not always agree on what one "ought" to do. Expatriate managers may face situations where local business practices violate their culturally based sensibilities or home country laws. Second, the very large multinational companies often have powers and assets that equal those of some foreign governments. Managers in these large and powerful multinationals may encounter challenging ethical dilemmas regarding how to use this power. Consider the next Case in Point, which shows that international business ethics issues may affect multinationals located anywhere in the world.

Closely related to business ethics is the concept of corporate social responsibility, which is the idea that businesses have a responsibility to society beyond

International business ethics Unique ethical problems faced by managers conducting business operations across national boundaries.

Corporate social responsibility Idea that businesses have a responsibility to society beyond making profits.

C A S E I N P O I N T

Social Responsibility in Various Global Companies

Social responsibility usually means going beyond complying with ethical standards. For instance, although it is ethical not to hire children, it is socially responsible to pay for the education of workers' children. The Zero Hunger program in Brazil is a good example of social responsibility. Multinational companies such as IBM, Ford, Bayer A.G., and Unilever are all working with the Zero Hunger program to eradicate poverty in Brazil.

Ford recently became the first automaker in Brazil to set up a social responsibility department. It is donating 440 pounds of food for every truck sold and is now working with unions on adult literacy programs. Ford has also donated spare cars and spare parts to a mechanics school for underprivileged adolescents.

Similarly, Asea Brown Boveri (ABB) has partnered with the World Wide Fund for Nature to direct some of its donations toward rural electrification in Africa. The partnership chose the remote village of Ngrambe in Tanzania to install a diesel-based generator to supply electricity. ABB also has trained numerous technicians in the village, hoping that the villagers will be able to develop a business model so that they can financially support the project.

Finally, some companies are even requiring their suppliers to be socially responsible. Novo Nordisk, a Danish company leading in diabetes care, has instituted many new practices to ensure that suppliers abide by certain principles. Novo Nordisk has developed a series of supplier engagement and assessment tools. The firm clearly communicates expectations regarding suppliers' environmental and societal performance and even provides guidelines as to how suppliers can best meet these expectations. Such efforts have resulted in Novo Nordisk's being named best in class in the health care sector on the Dow Jones Sustainability Indexes.

Sources: Based on Egels, Niklas. 2005. "CSR in electrification of rural Africa." Journal of Corporate Citizenship, 18, pp. 75–85; Smith, Tony. 2003. "In Brazil, companies help poor: Da Silva makes battle on poverty popular." International Herald Tribune, April 1, p. 1; Strand, R. 2009. "Corporate responsibility in Scandinavian supply chains." Journal of Business Ethics, 85, pp. 179–185.

making profits. Corporate social responsibility means that a company must take into account the welfare of other constituents (e.g., customers, suppliers) in addition to stockholders. While business ethics usually concern the ethical dilemmas faced by managers as individuals, corporate social responsibility is usually associated with the ethical consequences of a company's policies and procedures. Monitoring the working conditions of your suppliers, paying for the education of the children of workers, and donating money to the local community are examples of corporate social responsibility in action. Consider the Case in Point above.

In practice, ethics and social responsibility are not easily distinguished. Usually, procedures and policies in a company regarding social responsibility reflect the ethical values and decisions of the top management team.[3] For example, as shown in the Preview Case in Point, Levi's decision to engage in the socially responsible action of monitoring the working conditions of its suppliers reflects the ethical beliefs of Levi CEO Robert D. Haas regarding these issues.

The ethical and social responsibility issues faced by multinational companies are complex and varied. Exhibit 4.1 identifies some of the stakeholders in the multinational company and shows typical problems that multinational companies face and that affect the stakeholders. As the exhibit shows, multinational companies are faced both with primary and secondary stakeholders. Primary stakeholders are directly linked to a company's survival and include customers, suppliers, employees, and shareholders. In contrast, secondary stakeholders are less directly linked to the company's survival and include the media, trade associations, and special interest groups.[4] Although secondary stakeholders may seem to have less potential

Primary stakeholders
Groups or entities directly linked to a company's survival, including customers, suppliers, employees, and shareholders.

Secondary stakeholders
Groups or entities less directly linked to a company's survival, including the media, trade associations, and special interest groups.

EXHIBIT
4.1
Areas of Ethical and Social Responsibility Concerns
for the Multinational Company (MNC)

Stakeholder Affected	Ethical/Social Responsibility Issue	Example problems for the MNC
Customers	Product safety	Should an MNC delete safety features to make a product more affordable for people in a poorer nation?
	Fair price	Should a sole supplier in a country take advantage of its monopoly?
	Proper disclosures and information	Should an MNC assume the cost of translating all its product information into other languages?
Stockholders	Fair return on investment	If a product is banned because it is unsafe in one country, should it be sold in countries where it is not banned to maintain profit margins?
		What should a company do if it is found that the corporate executives have been involved in accounting scandals? What protection measures should be taken to protect shareholders' interests?
		How much should CEOs be paid? Should shareholders ignore extremely generous severance packages?
	Fair wages	Should a company pay more than market wages when such wages result in other people living in poverty?
	Safety of working conditions	Should a company be responsible for the working conditions of its suppliers' employees?
Employees	Child labor	Should an MNC use child labor if it is legal in the host country?
	Discrimination by sex, race, color, or creed	Should a company assign a woman to a country where women are expected to remain separate from men in public?
	Impact on local economies	Should an MNC use transfer pricing and other internal accounting measures to reduce its actual tax base in a foreign country?
Host country	Following local laws	Should an MNC follow local laws that violate home country laws against discrimination?
	Impact on local social institutions	Should an MNC require its workers to work on religious holidays?
	Environmental protection	Is an MNC obligated to control its hazardous waste to a degree higher than local laws require?
Society in general	Raw material depletion	Should MNCs deplete natural resources in countries that are willing to let them do so?

impact on multinational companies, recent examples show that they are as important as primary shareholders in terms of their effect. Consider, for example, that Shell Oil has been forced to acknowledge its relationship with a corrupt government in Nigeria. Similarly, the agricultural giant Monsanto has been forced to deal with secondary stakeholders such as Greenpeace and Friends of the Earth as it tries to develop agricultural biotechnology products.[5] Such examples show that addressing the needs of both groups of shareholders is critical.

How can international managers deal with the constant ethical challenges such as those in Exhibit 4.1? To succeed and be profitable in a socially responsible fashion, multinational company managers must weigh and balance the economic, legal, and ethical consequences of their decisions. The next sections discuss how managers must analyze situations with ethical consequences. The first section presents an overview of basic ethical philosophies used by managers as guides for ethical decision making. The second section deals with national differences in business ethics and social responsibility. The third considers the development of transnational business ethics—an ethical system for the multinational company that does not rely on the ethical principles and philosophies of any one country. In the final section, we consider the practical considerations of balancing the needs of the company and managerial actions with ethical consequences.

Ethical Philosophy

In this section, we examine two ways to approach ethical decision making. The first comes from traditional ethical philosophy. The second is a contemporary philosophical view of how we can think about ethics.

Traditional Views

Two basic systems of ethical reasoning dominate ethical philosophy: the teleological and the deontological systems.

In teleological ethical theories, the morality of an act or practice comes from its consequences. The most popular teleological theory is utilitarianism. Utilitarianism argues that what is good and moral comes from acts that produce the greatest good for the greatest number of people. For example, from a utilitarian perspective, one might argue that stealing a loaf of bread to feed a hungry family is moral because eating the bread is crucial for the family's survival. Many multinational economic decisions are based on utilitarianism. For instance, a multinational company can choose a plant location among a number of candidate countries by doing a cost-and-benefit analysis, which represents one of the most popular applications of utilitarianism.

In contrast to teleological ethical theories, deontological ethical theories do not focus on consequences. Rather, actions by themselves have a good or bad morality regardless of their outcomes. For example, a person who chooses not to steal a loaf of bread because stealing is immoral, even if people starve because of this action, behaves ethically according to the deontological argument. In this case, the moral principle forbidding stealing, common in many religious doctrines, takes precedence over a bad outcome. Similarly, deontologists argue that closing a plant is unethical because workers are not being treated with dignity.

Some deontological ethical philosophers argue that morality is intuitive and self-evident; that is, moral people just know what is right because how an ethical person should behave is obvious. Other deontologists argue that we cannot rely on intuition. Instead, we should follow an essential moral principle or value, such as the Golden Rule or a concern for justice. Still others argue for a more comprehensive set of moral principles or rules that can guide our behavior, such as the Ten Commandments, the *Qur'an,* or the *Bible.*[6]

Moral Languages

A more contemporary way of looking at ethics, favored by Thomas Donaldson, an expert on international business ethics, broadens the rough distinction between the teleological and deontological ethical theories. Donaldson argues that international business ethics is best understood by focusing on the

---

Teleological ethical theory
Theory that suggests that the morality of an act or practice comes from its consequences.

Utilitarianism
Argument that what is good and moral comes from acts that produce the greatest good for the greatest number of people.

Deontological ethical theory
Focus on actions that, by themselves, have a good or bad morality regardless of their outcomes.

Moral languages
Descriptions of the basic ways that people use to think about ethical decisions and to explain their ethical choices.

"language of international corporate ethics."[7] According to Donaldson, **moral languages** describe the basic ways that people use to think about ethical decisions and to explain their ethical choices. The six basic ethical languages identified by Donaldson are:[8]

1. *Virtue and vice:* This language identifies a person's good or virtuous properties and contrasts them with vices. For example, temperance might be contrasted with lust. People or groups who exhibit or who have virtuous characteristics are seen as ethical. It is not important what results from an action, but rather the virtuous intent of the action.

2. *Self-control:* This language emphasizes achieving perfection at controlling thoughts and actions, such as passion. It is apparent in the Buddhist and Hindu views of the world but also appears in many Western traditions, such as in the philosophy of Plato and in the control of "appetites."

3. *Maximizing human welfare:* This is the basic language of the utilitarian view, emphasizing the greatest good for the greatest number of people. For example, using this language of ethical thought, one might argue that exposing a few people to dangerous chemicals is okay if most people in the society benefit.

4. *Avoiding harm:* Like the emphasis on the greatest good for the greatest number, this language of ethics also sees good or bad in terms of consequences. However, rather than maximizing benefits, it focuses on avoiding unpleasant outcomes or consequences. For example, one might argue, "If it doesn't hurt anyone, it's okay."

5. *Rights and duties:* This language focuses on principles that guide ethical behaviors. The principles specify required duties, such as the duties of a parent to care for a child. The principles also specify the rights of people, such as the right to free speech. According to Donaldson, the language of rights and duties fits well in a legal context.

6. *Social contract:* The social contract language structures ethics as a form of agreement among people. These agreements need not be written but may be taken for granted by all parties. In this sense, what is ethical is what the people in our culture or in our organization have come to agree is ethical.

Ethical philosophies provide a language or structure for thinking about ethical decisions and dilemmas. They help managers understand the philosophical bases for their decision making and for the company's ethical or social responsibility policies. International managers face the additional challenge of understanding the unfamiliar cultural and institutional contexts surrounding their ethical decision making. The next section shows how culture and social institutions come into play in the complexities of ethical decision making.

National Differences in Business Ethics and Social Responsibility

As with most multinational business practices, national culture and social institutions play a role; in this case they affect how businesses manage ethical behavior and social responsibility. Exhibit 4.2 presents a simple model of the relationships among national culture, social institutions, and business ethics. As explained in Chapter 2, national culture, by means of cultural norms and values, influences important business practices, such as how women and minorities are treated on the job, attitudes toward gift giving and bribery, and expectations

EXHIBIT 4.2 A Model of Institutional and Cultural Effects on Business
Ethics Issues and Management

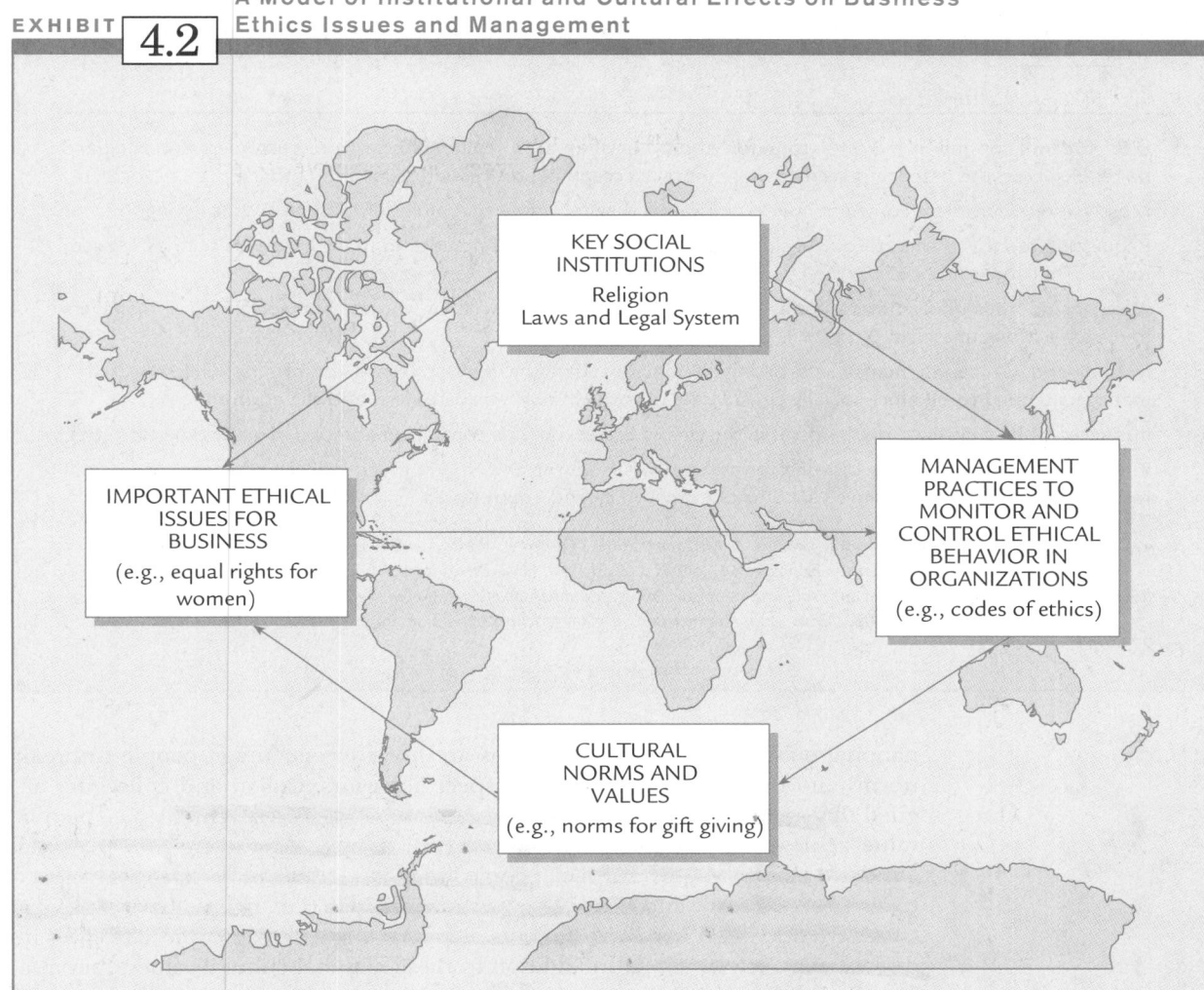

regarding conformity to written laws. Similarly, the social institutions described
in Chapter 3, such as religion and the legal system, are probably the key institutions that affect what ethical issues are important in a society and how they
are typically managed.

Although there are significant differences in how people view ethics, Forsyth,
O'Boyle Jr., and McDaniel argue that some actions are universally condemned
from an ethical standpoint.[9] For instance, lying to others, harming or killing
innocent children, failing to keep one's promises, and taking valuables from
others are all often morally condemned. However, despite these universals,
other actions are viewed with significantly more variation. Consider Exhibit 4.3,
which clearly shows that there are significant differences in how actions with
moral consequences are viewed.

How can such differences be explained? Although no comprehensive body of
knowledge identifies exactly how national culture and social institutions affect
business ethics and under what conditions, work by Cullen, Parboteeah, and
Hoegl suggests possible applications to multinational ethics.[10] Basing their study
on Messner and Rosenfeld's institutional anomie theory,[11] they argue that specific

---

Results of Cross-Cultural Studies

- U.S. students consider it morally wrong for employees of an auto repair shop to lie to customers about repairs done. However, the practice is seen as more morally acceptable to Russian students.

- Most Westerners violate copyright laws even though they recognize that violation of such laws is wrong.

- Requesting money to smooth out business transactions is standard practice in many countries such as Mexico, Russia, Thailand, and Haiti. In the United States, such practices are frowned upon.

- Austrians do not find it immoral for a male boss to promote only women who see him socially. U.S. managers find such actions unethical.

- Muslim and Caucasian managers working in Malaysia had the highest regard for profits, while Australian managers tended to be more socially considerate toward employees, customers, and the environment.

- It is acceptable to evaluate one's bosses in the United States, but it is considered immoral in many other societies.

- In a study comparing whistle-blowing forms, students from the U.K. had a much higher preference for internal forms of whistle-blowing relative to students from Turkey and South Korea.

Sources: Based on Forsyth, D. R., E. H. Boyle Jr., and M. A. McDaniel. 2008. "East meets West: A meta-analytic investigation of cultural variations in idealism and relativism." Journal of Business Ethics, 83(4), pp. 813–833; Park, H., J. Blenkinsopp, M. K. Oktem, and U. Omurgonulsen. 2008. "Cultural orientation and attitudes toward different forms of whistleblowing: A comparison of South Korea, Turkey and the U.K." Journal of Business Ethics, 82, pp. 929–929; Yong, A. 2008. "Cross-cultural comparisons of managerial perceptions on profit." Journal of Business Ethics, 82, pp. 775–791.

---

national culture and social institutions are likely to encourage people to break norms and thereby justify ethically suspect behaviors. Cullen and colleagues argued that societies with national cultural values of high achievement (i.e., people value achievement), high individualism (i.e., people value their own personal freedom), high universalism (i.e., people are more ambitious because they expect to be treated fairly), and high pecuniary materialism (i.e., people have high materialist tendencies) are likely to have a greater number of people engaging in deviant acts such as crime. In addition to these national cultural values, they also specified that social institutions, such as industrialization, the type of economic system, family, and education, should be related to the breaking of norms. They suggest that societies with relatively high levels of industrialization, capitalist systems, low degrees of family breakdown, and easily accessible education should encourage more deviance. Testing their theory on 3,450 managers from 28 countries, the researchers found support for most of their hypotheses. Multinational managers can use this theory to understand how people approach ethics. However, managers can often use only their own knowledge of a country's social institutions and culture to make inferences about which ethical issues are important and how they are best managed.

Other research has been done on how the national institutional context affects business ethics. For example, Seleim and Bontis examined how the cultural dimensions of the GLOBE studies (Chapter 2) influence corruption.[12] They found that countries that rate high on future orientation have relatively low levels of corruption. Possibly the focus on future-oriented behaviors, such as strategic planning and creating vision statements, discourages corruption. The researchers also found that societies high on institutional collectivism practices also tend to have low levels of corruption. The high levels of integration and bonding of people in such societies very likely reinforce ethical standards.

Among other results, the study found that societies high on in-group collectivism have relatively high levels of corruption. Such results suggest that people in these societies engage in actions that will benefit their own groups and friends rather than the wider good, thereby encouraging corruption.

With its extensive legal control over the management of ethical behaviors, the United States is unique in the world. The next section discusses a major law governing ethical behavior in international business that has possibly the greatest impact of all legislation on U.S. multinational companies.

Questionable Payments and Bribery

In addition to the many possible ethical issues presented in Exhibit 4.1, a particular ethical difficulty for many multinational companies relates to bribery, or what some call questionable payments. In many societies, people routinely offer bribes or gifts to expedite government actions or to gain advantage in business deals. Even the major German multinational Siemens was involved in a major bribery scandal. "Grease money" can speed up the import or export of goods or get customs agents to look the other way. A gift or a kickback may be expected for a purchasing agent to select your company's product over another. Words for these types of actions exist in all countries. For example, in Mexico the bribe is known as *mordida*, the bite; in France, the *pot-de-vin*, jug of wine; in Germany, the "N.A.," an abbreviation of *nützliche Abagabe*, the useful contribution; and in Japan, the *jeitinho*, the fix.[13]

Corruption and bribery can have devastating effects on societies. Compte, Lambert-Mogiliansky, and Verdier argue that companies typically make up for bribery by increasing the contract price by the amount of the bribe.[14] As such, many developing countries suffer because they are charged higher prices. However, companies also routinely use poorer-quality products or materials to make up for the bribe, thus putting out inferior products. Furthermore, corruption can also result in collusion among firms, resulting in even higher prices. As a result, corruption and bribery usually result in higher public spending, lower-quality projects, undermined competition, and the inefficient allocation of resources. Additionally, some argue that corruption discourages entrepreneurship because bribery becomes a form of taxation.[15] Such impediments to entrepreneurship affect investment growth and development, leading to lessened economic performance.[16]

To understand the level of corruption in countries, multinational companies can rely on the corruption perception index (CPI). The CPI, developed by Transparency International, is a rating of the perceived levels of corruption in a country. Exhibit 4.4 shows the CPI for selected countries where high CPIs indicate the least corruption.

Another important index, shown in Exhibit 4.5, reflects estimates of the extent of bribery that public officials have accepted from companies doing business in the leading exporting countries. To create the Bribe Payers Index, Transparency International surveyed business leaders in key economies and asked,[17] "In the business sectors with which you are familiar, please indicate whether companies from the following countries are very likely, quite likely, or unlikely to pay bribes to win or retain business in this country."

For further insights into bribery in emerging markets, consider the next Focus on Emerging Markets.

As in the United States, most countries have formal laws forbidding corrupt practices. However, because of wide differences among countries in legal traditions, enforcement differs greatly. The accepted amounts of gift giving and

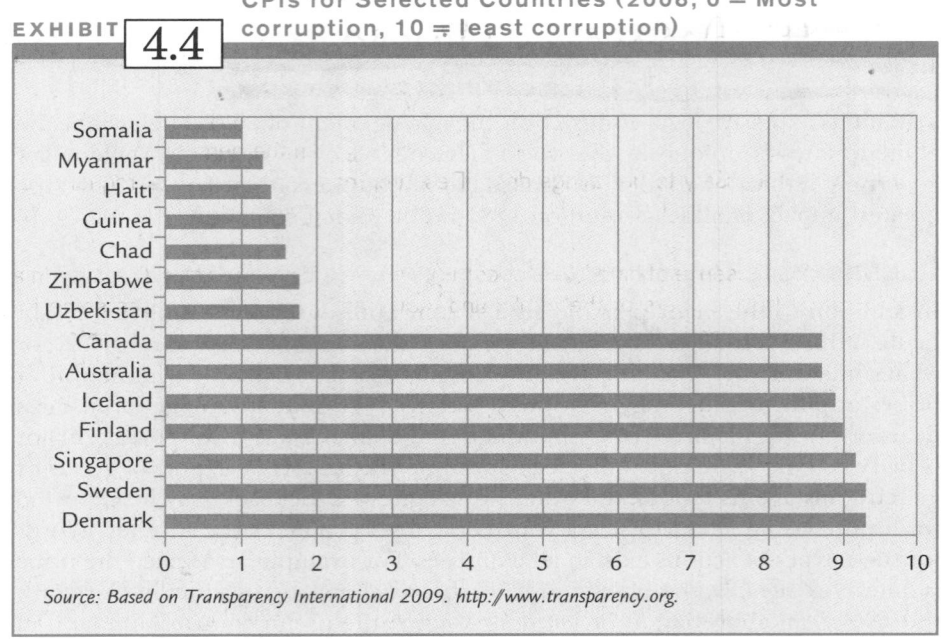

EXHIBIT 4.4

CPIs for Selected Countries (2008; 0 = Most corruption, 10 = least corruption)

Source: Based on Transparency International 2009. http://www.transparency.org.

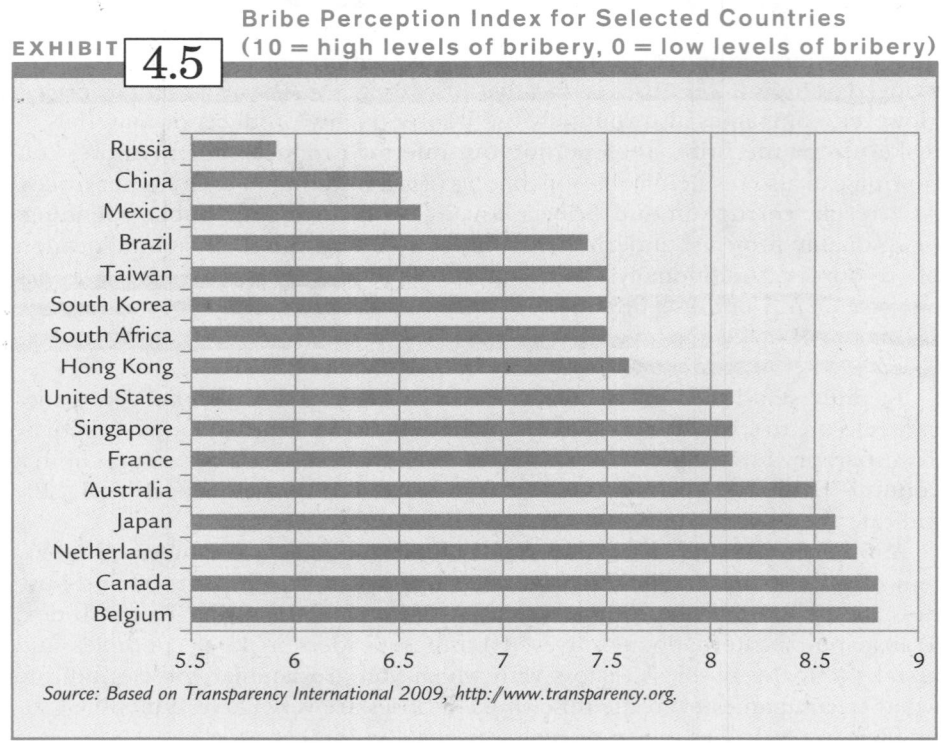

EXHIBIT 4.5

Bribe Perception Index for Selected Countries (10 = high levels of bribery, 0 = low levels of bribery)

Source: Based on Transparency International 2009, http://www.transparency.org.

entertainment associated with business transactions vary enormously. For example, even for academic research grants, Japanese professors will budget as a legitimate expense about 20 percent of the grant for entertainment costs—something unheard of in U.S. academic research.

Focus on Emerging Markets

Corruption and Corruptibility in Post-Communist Europe

People in post-communist European countries suffer from the perception that bribes are always necessary to get things done. Research has shown that the frequent bureaucratic encounters between citizens and officials actually reveal that individuals make extensive use of contacts, presents, and bribes to navigate the bureaucracies. But does the presence of high levels of corruption reflect the values of individuals? In a study of 6,000 members of the public and 1,300 officials, Miller provides some insights on corruption in the Czech Republic, Slovakia, Bulgaria, and the Ukraine. The findings suggest that a majority of the public and officials in these countries abhor the use of presents and bribes to influence officials. However, more that half of these officials were willing to accept some small gift or were willing to justify others' acceptance of small payments. The following exhibit illustrates some of these findings.

As the exhibit shows, most individuals in these societies condemn bribes, suggesting that bribes are inconsistent with their values. However, they are also willing to give or accept bribes, suggesting that they are corruptible. Such findings indicate that external pressures play a big role in encouraging people to accept or give bribes. These findings are also noteworthy in that bribery might be reduced in the long run through the reduction of such external pressures.

Source: Based on Miller, William L. 2006. "Corruption and corruptibility." World Development, 34(2), pp. 371–380.

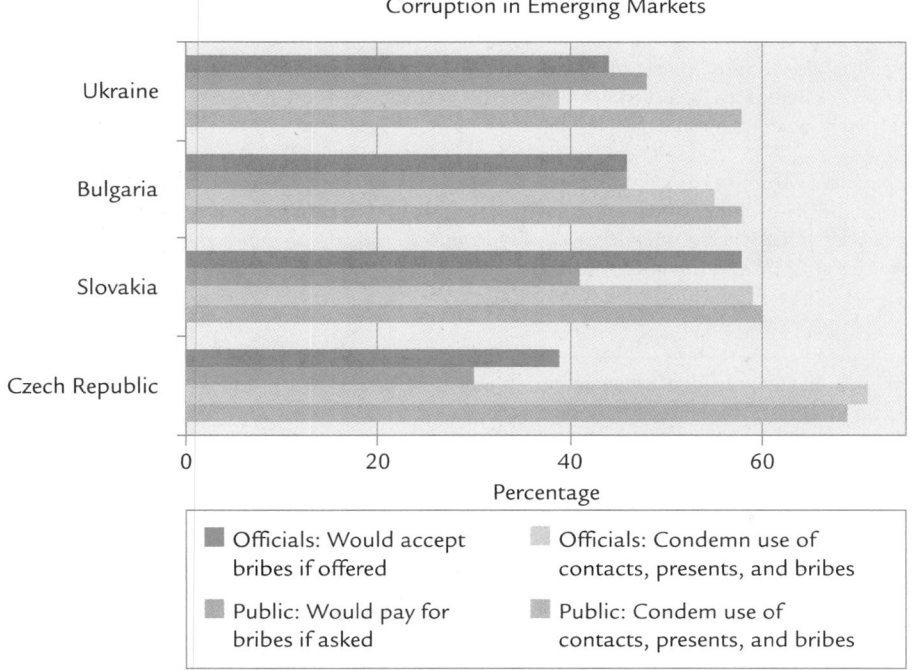

Corruption in Emerging Markets

Legend:
- Officials: Would accept bribes if offered
- Officials: Condemn use of contacts, presents, and bribes
- Public: Would pay for bribes if asked
- Public: Condem use of contacts, presents, and bribes

Source: Adapted from Miller, William L. 2006. "Corruption and corruptibility." World Development, 34(2), pp. 371–380.

In 1977, in response to several investigations by U.S. government agencies, President Jimmy Carter signed the **Foreign Corrupt Practices Act (FCPA)**.[18] Exhibit 4.6 shows excerpts taken directly from the FCPA.

The FCPA forbids U.S. companies from making or offering payments or gifts to foreign government officials for the sake of gaining or retaining business. However, the act does not prohibit some forms of payments that may occur in international business. Payments made under duress to avoid injury or violence are acceptable. For example, in an unstable political environment, a company may pay local officials "bribes" to avoid harassment of its employees. Small payments that merely encourage officials to do their legitimate and routine jobs are legal. Payments made that are lawful in a country are also acceptable. These "grease" payments must not seek illegal ends but just speed up or make possible normal business functions, such as necessary paperwork.

EXHIBIT 4.6   Excerpts from the Foreign Corrupt Practices Act

Prohibited Foreign Trade Practices

It shall be unlawful for *any domestic concern* or for any officer, director, employee, or agent of such domestic concern or any stockholder thereof acting on behalf of such domestic concern, to make use of the mails or any means or instrumentality of interstate commerce corruptly in furtherance of an offer, payment, promise to pay, or authorization of the payment of any money, or offer, gift, promise to give, or authorization of the giving of anything of value to any foreign official for purposes of—

A. influencing any act or decision of such foreign official, political party, party official, or candidate in his or its official capacity, or

B. inducing such foreign official, political party, party official, or candidate to do or omit to do any act in violation of the lawful duty of such foreign official, political party, party official, or candidate, or

C. inducing such foreign official, political party, party official, or candidate to use his or its influence with a foreign government or instrumentality thereof to affect or influence any act or decision of such government or instrumentality, in order to assist such issuer in obtaining or retaining business for or with, or directing business to, any person.

Also prohibited is any offer, payment, promise to pay, or authorization of the payment of any money, or offer, gift, promise to give, or authorization of the giving of anything of value *when given to any person, while knowing* that all or a portion of such money or thing of value will be offered, given, or promised, directly or indirectly, to any foreign official, to any foreign political party or official thereof, or to any candidate for foreign political office, for purposes of A through C above.

Definitions

1. The term *"domestic concern"* means any individual who is a citizen, national, or resident of the United States; and any corporation, partnership, association, joint-stock company, business trust, unincorporated organization, or sole proprietorship which has its principal place of business in the United States, or which is organized under the laws of a State of the United States or a territory, possession, or commonwealth of the United States.

2. The term *"foreign official"* means any officer or employee of a foreign government or any department, agency, or instrumentality thereof, or any person acting in an official capacity for or on behalf of any such government or department, agency, or instrumentality.

3. A person's state of mind is *"knowing"* with respect to conduct, a circumstance, or a result if—

   (i) such person is aware that such person is engaging in such conduct, that such circumstance exists, or that such result is substantially certain to occur; or

   (ii) such person has a firm belief that such circumstance exists or that such result is substantially certain to occur. Knowledge is established if a person is aware of a high probability of the existence of such circumstance, unless the person actually believes that such circumstance does not exist.

continued

4. The term *"routine government action"* means only an action which is ordinarily and commonly performed by a foreign official in such cases as obtaining permits, licenses, or other official documents to qualify a person to do business in a foreign country. The term "routine governmental action" does not include any decision by a foreign official whether, or on what terms, to award new business to or to continue business with a particular party, or any action taken by a foreign official involved in the decision-making process to encourage a decision to award new business to or continue business with a particular party.

5. The term *"interstate commerce"* means trade, commerce, transportation, or communication among the several States, or between any foreign country and any State or between any State and any place or ship outside thereof.

Exceptions

A. Facilitating or expediting payment to a foreign official, political party, or party official the purpose of which is to expedite or *to secure the performance of a routine governmental action* by a foreign official, political party, or party official.

B. The payment, gift, offer, or promise of anything of value that was made, *was lawful under the written laws and regulations of the foreign official's, political party's, party official's, or candidate's country;* or

C. The payment, gift, offer, or promise of anything of value that was made, was a *reasonable and bona fide expenditure,* such as travel and lodging expenses, incurred by or on behalf of a foreign official, party, party official, or candidate and was directly related to the promotion, demonstration, or explanation of products or services; or the execution or performance of a contract with a foreign government or agency thereof.

Penalties

1. Any domestic concern that violates this section shall be fined not more than $2,000,000 and shall be subject to a civil penalty of not more than $10,000 imposed in an action brought by the Attorney General.

2. Any officer or director of a domestic concern, or stockholder acting on behalf of such domestic concern, who willfully violates this section shall be fined not more than $100,000, or imprisoned not more than 5 years, or both.

3. Any employee or agent of a domestic concern who is a United States citizen, national, or resident or is otherwise subject to the jurisdiction of the United States (other than an officer, director, or stockholder acting on behalf of such domestic concern), and who willfully violates this section, shall be fined not more than $100,000, or imprisoned not more than 5 years, or both.

4. Any officer, director, employee, or agent of a domestic concern, or stockholder acting on behalf of such domestic concern, who violates this section shall be subject to a civil penalty of not more than $10,000 imposed in an action brought by the Attorney General.

5. *Whenever a fine is imposed upon any officer, director, employee, agent, or stockholder of a domestic concern, such fine may not be paid, directly or indirectly, by such domestic concern.*

Source: U.S. Code, Title 15—Commerce and Trade, Chapter 2B—Securities Exchanges, Section 78dd–1.

A tricky component of the FCPA for U.S. companies is the law's reason-to-know provision. This provision means that a firm is liable for bribes or questionable payments made by agents hired by the firm, even if members of the firm did not actually make the payments or see them being made. To take advantage of a local person's knowledge of "how to get things done" in a country, U.S. multinational managers often use local people as agents to conduct business. If it is common knowledge that these agents use part of their fees to bribe local officials to commit illegal acts, then the U.S. firm is breaking the law. If, however, the U.S. firm has no knowledge of the behavior of the agent and no reason to expect illegal behavior by the agent, then the firm has no liability under the FCPA. The term "knowing" means that the person actually knows an illegal bribe will be given, knows that the circumstances surrounding the situation make it likely that an illegal bribe will be given, or is aware of the high probability that an illegal act will occur. Exhibit 4.6 states the types of penalties included in the FCPA. Note that the penalties apply to individuals as well as to companies and that individual fines cannot be paid by the company.

Toward Transnational Ethics

Globalization dramatically increases contact among people from different ethical and cultural systems. This contact is creating pressure for ethical convergence and for the development of transnational agreements among nations to govern business practices. The next Case in Point shows that the battle is on against corrupt relationships between business and government.

Next, we review some of the trends toward ethical convergence and transnational ethical agreements.

C A S E   I N   P O I N T

Corruption Attacked Around the World

No nation is free from ethical violations in business practices. However, there are wide differences in how national legal systems prosecute ethical violations and in the degree to which the public tolerates violations. For instance, a common joke in Asia is that it is futile to pursue contracts without a sizable checkbook because bribery is a normal part of doing business. However, some evidence now suggests that there is a worldwide trend to clean up business practices, especially unethical business relationships with government. The growing power of shareholders challenges the once cozy relationships between business and government, from Paris to Seoul to Mexico City. Ordinary citizens, prosecutors, and the press are challenging the corporate elite and clamoring for ethical corporate governance.

For example, investigators in Korea found that 35 Korean *chaebols* (conglomerates) gave approximately $369 million in bribes to former President Roh Tae Woo. Leading the bribery list were the chairmen of giant *chaebols* Samsung (with $32 million) and Daewoo (with $31 million in bribes). The chairman of Hyundai is also facing prosecution in another bribery scandal. Both the chairman and his son are accused of creating slush funds to bribe South Korean public officials.

At the international level, the World Bank and the International Monetary Fund have stopped lending or have threatened to stop lending to countries such as Kenya, Nigeria, and Indonesia, where corruption and

bribery have stifled economic growth. Twenty-nine members of the Organisation for Economic Co-operation and Development and five nonmembers signed a bribery convention, which, like the U.S. Foreign Corrupt Practices Act, requires each country to make it a crime to bribe a foreign office to win or retain business.

U.S. multinationals and the U.S. government are also taking corruption more seriously than ever. For instance, Morgan Stanley recently fired a high-level executive in China after finding out that the executive may have been involved in a bribery scandal. Although the executive was instrumental in helping Morgan Stanley's real estate business take off in China, the firm did not show any hesitation in the firing.

The U.S. government is also actively pursuing companies in violation of the FCPA. For example, engineering and oil services company KBR (formerly Haliburton) has settled charges over violation of the FCPA and has agreed to pay fines of $579 million.

Sources: Based on Barboza, D. 2009. "Morgan Stanley fires executive in China on suspicions of bribery." Wall Street Journal, February 13, p. B6; Brull, Steven, and Margaret Dawson. 1995. "Why Korea's cleanup won't catch on." BusinessWeek Online, International Edition, December 18; Economist. 1999. "A global war against bribery." Economist.com, January 16, Story_1D=18208; Financial Times. 2009. "Battling bribery," February 16, p. 8; Rossant, John. 1995. "Dirty money." BusinessWeek Online, International Edition, December 18; Woods, Walter. 2006. "Hyundai scandal delays 2nd plant." Atlanta Journal-Constitution, April 25, p. C4.

Pressures for Ethical Convergence

In spite of the wide differences in cultures and in social institutions, there are growing pressures for multinational companies to follow the same rules in managing ethical behavior and social responsibility. This trend is called **ethical convergence**. There are four basic reasons for ethical convergence:

1. The growth of international trade and trading blocs, such as NAFTA (North American Free Trade Agreement) and the European Union, creates pressures to have common ethical practices that transcend national cultures and institutional differences. Predictable interactions and behaviors among trading partners from different countries make trade more efficient. Furthermore, many of these trade organizations and other international associations are developing measures to reduce corruption.

2. Interaction between trading partners puts the pressure on for imitating the business practices of other countries. As the people from different cultural backgrounds increase their interactions, exposure to varying ethical traditions encourages people to adjust to, imitate, and adopt new behaviors and attitudes.

3. Companies that do business throughout the world have employees from varied cultural backgrounds who need common standards and rules regarding how to behave. As such, multinational companies often rely on their corporate culture to provide consistent norms and values that govern ethical issues.

4. An increasing number of business watchdogs, such as ethical investment companies and nongovernmental organizations, also are encouraging multinational companies to be ethical.

In addition to moral pressure to eliminate corrupt activity, there is increasing financial pressure. Extensive corruption costs money, makes businesses less competitive internationally, and risks embarrassing and costly scandals.

Ethical convergence
The growing pressures for multinational companies to follow the same rules in managing ethical behavior and social responsibility.

Prescriptive Ethics for the Multinational

Donaldson argues that the three moral languages of avoiding harm, rights and duties, and the social contract should guide multinational companies. He advocates **prescriptive ethics for multinationals**; that is, multinational companies should engage in business practices that avoid negative consequences to their stakeholders (e.g., employees, the local environment). Although multinationals retain basic rights, such as seeking a fair profit, these rights imply duties, such as providing a fair wage to local employees. The multinational company also has a social contract with its stakeholders, which, even if taken for granted, defines the nature of the relationships. For example, when a multinational company enters a country, it accepts the social contract to follow local laws.

These three moral languages are the easiest of ethical systems to specify in written codes, such as contracts and international laws. Donaldson believes that these moral languages are the most appropriate for managing ethical behaviors among culturally heterogeneous multinationals; that is, regardless of their national culture, companies can agree with their stakeholders on the basic rules of moral behavior.[19]

For Donaldson's ideas to work, there must be a code of conduct to guide multinational companies that is independent of national boundaries. The code must include prescriptive and proscriptive rules to guide multinational behavior. Prescriptive rules tell multinational managers and companies what they should do, whereas proscriptive rules tell them what they may not do.

Prescriptive ethics for multinationals
Suggested guidelines for the ethical behavior of multinational companies.

Some scholars argue that such ethical guides currently exist in various international agreements and in the codes of international governing bodies, such as the United Nations and the International Labor Office.[20]

Exhibit 4.7 summarizes ethical stipulations for the multinational company derived from the following international sources:

- The United Nations Universal Declaration of Human Rights
- The United Nations Code of Conduct on Transnational Corporations
- The European Convention on Human Rights
- The International Chamber of Commerce Guidelines for International Investment
- The Organization for Economic Cooperation and Development Guidelines for Multinational Enterprises
- The Helsinki Final Act
- The International Labor Office Tripartite Declarations of Principles Concerning Multinational Enterprises and Social Policy

The principles in the code of conduct for the multinational company shown in Exhibit 4.7 have two supporting rationales. The first rationale comes from the basic deontological principles dealing with human rights, such as the right to work and the right to be safe. To a large degree, the international agreements specify the rights and duties of multinational companies that are presumed to be transcultural; that is, the basic ethical principles apply to all, regardless of a company's country of origin or its current business location. The second rationale comes from the history of experiences in international business interactions.[21] For example, because multinational companies often ignore the environmental impact of their operations in other countries, several international agreements specify their duties regarding the environment.

Although such agreements are diverse and not always enforceable, they are useful in that they provide a safe guide to ethical management for multinational managers. It is likely that, if managers follow the code of conduct shown in Exhibit 4.7, both in individual behavior and in guiding a company, they will generally be on safe ethical and legal ground in nearly all situations.

The next Multinational Management Brief discusses Cisco's efforts to change the corporate culture to become more ethical.

The next section concludes this chapter with a focus on ethical decision making for the individual multinational manager.

The Ethical Dilemma in Multinational Management: How Will You Decide?

The potentially wide differences in ethical systems and in how ethics are managed create dilemmas for multinational managers. This section looks first at the issue of which ethical system you should use—your own country's or that of the host country. It concludes with a description of an ethical decision model for the multinational manager.

Ethical Relativism versus Ethical Universalism

The extensive effects of cultural value differences on all areas of management are never more apparent than when multinational companies have to determine

EXHIBIT 4.7   A Code of Conduct for the Multinational Company

Respect Basic Human Rights and Freedoms

- Respect fundamental human rights of life, liberty, security, and privacy.
- Do not discriminate on the basis of race, color, gender, religion, language, ethnic origin, or political affiliation.
- Respect personal freedoms (e.g., religion, opinion).

Maintain High Standards of Local Political Involvement

- Avoid illegal involvement in local politics.
- Don't pay bribes or other improper payments.
- Do not interfere in local government internal relations.

Transfer Technology

- Enhance the transfer of technology to developing nations.
- Adapt technologies to local needs.
- Conduct local R&D when possible.
- Grant fair licenses to use technology.

Protect the Environment

- Follow local environmental-protection laws.
- Actively protect the environment.
- Repair damage to the environment done by company operations.

- Help develop local standards.
- Provide accurate assessments of environmental impact of the company.
- Provide complete disclosure of the environmental effects of operations.
- Develop standards to monitor environmental effects.

Consumer Protection

- Follow local consumer-protection laws.
- Ensure accurate and proper safety disclosures.

Employment Practices

- Follow relevant policies and employment laws of host nation.
- Help create jobs in needed areas.
- Increase local employment opportunities and standards.
- Provide local workers stable employment and job security.
- Promote equal employment opportunities.
- Give priority to local national residents when possible.
- Provide training opportunities at all levels for local employees.
- Promote local nationals to management positions.
- Respect local collective-bargaining rights.
- Cooperate with local collective-bargaining units.
- Give notice of plant closings.
- Do not use threat of leaving country in collective-bargaining dealings.
- Provide income protection to terminated workers.
- Match or improve local standards of employment.
- Protect employees with adequate health and safety standards.
- Provide employees information on job-related health hazards.

Sources: Adapted from Getz, Kathleen A. 1990. "International codes of conduct: An analysis of ethical reasoning." Journal of Business Ethics, 9, pp. 567–578; HR Focus. 2008. "Why global ethics count and how HR can help." October, 85(10), pp. 13–15; Frederick, William C. 1991. "The moral authority of transnational corporate codes. Journal of Business Ethics," 10, pp. 165–177.

how to deal with ethical differences among the countries in which they do business. Do you impose your own country's ethical system everywhere, or do you follow the maxim, "When in Rome, do as the Romans do"?

Recall the concept of cultural relativism (Chapter 2), the philosophical position in anthropology that all cultures are legitimate and viable as a means for people to guide their lives. In other words, what people consider right or wrong, pretty or ugly, good or bad all depends on their cultural norms and values.

A similar concept in business ethics is called ethical relativism, which means that a multinational manager considers each society's view of ethics as legitimate and ethical. For example, if the people in one country believe something like assisted suicide is morally wrong, then for them it is morally wrong. If, on the other hand, people in another country believe that assisted suicide is morally correct, then for them it is moral. For multinational companies, ethical relativism means that managers need only follow local ethical conventions. Thus, for example, if bribery is an accepted way of doing business in a country, then it is okay for a multinational manager to follow local examples, even if it would be illegal at home. Consider the next Comparative Management Brief.

The opposite of ethical relativism is ethical universalism, which holds that basic moral principles transcend cultural and national boundaries. All cultures, for example, have rules that prohibit murder, at least of their own people.

The difficulty in using ethical universalism as a guide for multinational business practices is that there is little agreement on which moral principles exist in all cultures. Moreover, even when the same principles are used, there is no guarantee that all societies use the principles in the same way. For example, two societies may prohibit murder. However, for the group to have a better chance of surviving at a time when food resources are marginal, the aged might be obliged to commit suicide or newborn girls might be killed. The members of the society

Ethical relativism
Theory that each society's view of ethics must be considered legitimate and ethical.

Ethical universalism
Theory that basic moral principles transcend cultural and national boundaries.

Comparative Management **Brief**

Chinese Guanxis: Are They Ethical?

Most experts agree that the Chinese economy will continue experiencing tremendous growth and that the opportunities for business in China will likely stay strong. However, doing business will also become more complex and challenging. Experts agree that having personal connections is often better than having business acumen to do business in China.

Consider the case of *guanxis,* which are special relationships among Chinese companies that rely on trust, favor, and interdependence. Companies that are within the same network, or *guanxi,* are bound by expectations of reciprocal obligations and are expected to give preferential treatments to other members within the network. Western companies have often argued that such arrangements lead to unethical behaviors, bribery, and corruption. In the absence of a good legal infrastructure, *guanxis* lead to unethical behaviors because members within the same network engage in under-the-table dealings and give preferential treatment to each other.

However, for the Chinese, a *guanxi* network is indispensable for efficiently doing business and is therefore ethical. *Guanxis* substitute for the poorly developed legal and distribution systems in China. For instance, Chinese export companies are faced with dealing with complicated administrative procedures regarding distribution involving complex customs clearance rules and difficulties with securing raw materials and finished goods. These companies are more likely to develop special relationships with local customs officials and other trading firms to ensure a smooth and speedy delivery. Similarly, the Chinese are more likely to engage in conflict resolution based on trust within their network rather than relying on the poorly developed commercial laws.

For the ethical relativist, *guanxis* are acceptable because they represent the legitimate views of Chinese business society. Furthermore, most foreign companies find that they need to rely on these personal connections to do business. However, ethical universalists most likely view *guanxis* as unethical because they violate transparency norms.

Sources: Based on Chan, Ricky, Y.K. Louis, T. W. Cheng, and Ricky W.F. Szeto. 2002. "The dynamics of guanxi and ethics for Chinese executives." Journal of Business Ethics, 41, pp. 327–336; Kissel, M. 2009. "A web of connections." Wall Street Journal, March 10, p. C4; Su, Chenting, M. Joseph Sirgy, and James L. Littlefield, 2003. "Is guanxi orientation bad, ethically speaking? A study of Chinese enterprises." Journal of Business Ethics, 44, pp. 303–312.

certainly do not consider such practices to be murder, but rather an ethical way to ensure the survival of the group. Most societies tolerate some form of killing, such as in executions of criminals or in wars. Even though people die by human action, these acts are not defined as murder but as legitimate acts of society.

For the multinational company, however, practical problems come with following either ethical relativism or ethical universalism. Some ethicists argue that cultural relativism, while a necessary condition for conducting unbiased anthropological research, cannot be applied to ethics. Thomas Donaldson, for example, argues that multinational companies have a higher moral responsibility than ethical relativism.[22] He notes that, at the extreme, ethical relativism can become convenient relativism. Convenient relativism occurs when companies use the logic of ethical relativism to behave any way they please, using differences in cultures as an excuse. Donaldson gives the example of child labor in

Convenient relativism
What occurs when companies use the logic of ethical relativism to behave any way they please, using the excuse of differences in cultures.

developing countries. In some cases, children as young as seven years of age work for a pittance wage producing products that eventually are used by large multinational companies.

Extreme moral universalism also has its pitfalls. The assumption that one can identify universal ethics that all people should follow can lead to a type of ethnocentrism that Donaldson calls cultural imperialism. Managers who assume that they know the correct and ethical ways of behaving can easily view the moral systems of foreign cultures as inferior or immoral. This is particularly dangerous when the multinational is a big and financially powerful company with subsidiaries located in the developing world.

Individual Ethical Decision Making for the Multinational Manager

Although companies develop policies, procedures, organizational cultures, and business practices that have ethical consequences, individual managers ultimately must make decisions.

The first duty of a manager is to consider whether a decision makes business sense. This is called economic analysis. In economic analysis, the prime interest is in making the best decision for a company's profits. However, if profits alone guide ethical decision making, managers could worry little about how their decisions affect anyone except the owners of the company. Some argue that this type of decision making is not ethics at all because businesses could engage in deceptive and dangerous practices with only the marketplace to control their actions.

Economic analysis
Of an ethical problem, focuses on what is the best decision for a company's profits.

After considering the business impact of a decision, multinational managers must consider the legal and ethical consequences of their actions.[23] Exhibit 4.8 shows a decision flowchart illustrating the issues that multinational managers must consider beyond profits when confronted with ethical decisions.

In the legal analysis of an ethical problem, managers focus first on complying with the laws of the country in which their company is operating and, if required, the laws of their home country. Should the law not forbid something, it is ethical. In a combination of pure economic and legal analyses, managers should seek to maximize profits within the confines of the letter of the law. The law in this sense provides the rules of the game by which companies and people compete. Because legal systems vary from country to country, multinational managers who use only a legal analysis of an ethical problem are free to behave within the law in each country, provided their own country does not have other requirements. Some scholars, such as the Nobel Laureate Milton Friedman, believe that profit maximization—within the rules of the game of open and free competition—is the main ethical responsibility of business.[24] Many multinational managers also believe that the legal analysis includes not only a test of whether behaviors or their consequences meet legal standards in the home and host countries, but also a comparison against international standards. These standards come from the international agreements among nations and the resulting code, summarized in Exhibit 4.7.

Legal analysis
Of an ethical problem, focuses only on meeting legal requirements of host and parent countries.

An important piece of legislation that pertains to business behavior with ethical implications is the 2002 Sarbanes-Oxley Act. The act requires multinational companies to hold their executives and senior management accountable for ethical conduct. Additionally, the legislation addresses the auditor–client relationship. This act was proposed by the Securities Exchange Commission in reaction to the accounting scandals at companies like Enron and

EXHIBIT 4.8   **Decision Points for Ethical Decision Making in Multinational Management**

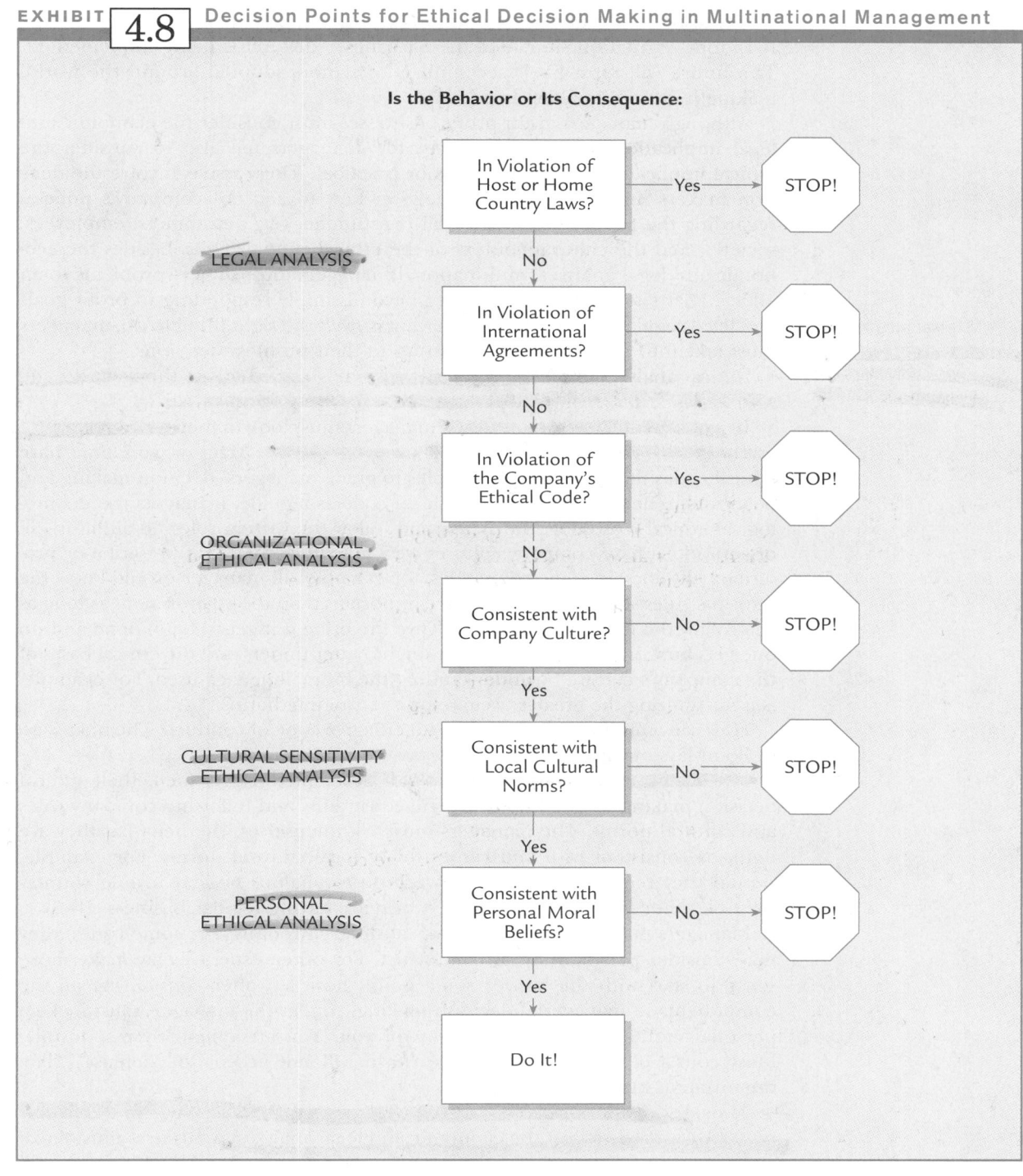

Is the Behavior or Its Consequence:

LEGAL ANALYSIS

In Violation of Host or Home Country Laws? — Yes → STOP!

No

In Violation of International Agreements? — Yes → STOP!

No

ORGANIZATIONAL ETHICAL ANALYSIS

In Violation of the Company's Ethical Code? — Yes → STOP!

No

Consistent with Company Culture? — No → STOP!

Yes

CULTURAL SENSITIVITY ETHICAL ANALYSIS

Consistent with Local Cultural Norms? — No → STOP!

Yes

PERSONAL ETHICAL ANALYSIS

Consistent with Personal Moral Beliefs? — No → STOP!

Yes

Do It!

WorldCom. However, as we saw at the beginning of the chapter, U.S. companies are not alone in being affected by accounting scandals. European and Asian companies have also engaged in numbers manipulation, usually to inflate profits. As multinational companies get more involved in businesses in other countries, executives around the world are facing increasing pressure to operate legally, especially regarding accounting issues. Even in Canada and the United Kingdom, legislation similar to the Sarbanes-Oxley Act is being implemented. The future will most likely see similar legislation adopted around the world, making it groundbreaking legislation.

Although managers in for-profit businesses must consider the economic and legal implications of their decisions, few managers fail also to consider the ethical implications of their actions or practices. These issues involve the decision makers' individual moral beliefs on how to act, the company's policies regarding the proper way to treat all constituents (e.g., customers, employees, society), and the cultural context of the ethical issue.[25] Thus, besides the economic and legal analyses, multinational managers must subject problems to an **ethical analysis**; that is, they must go beyond simply responding to profit goals and legal regulations. To determine what is *really* the right thing to do, managers must take into account additional issues in their business decisions.

Ethical analysis has three components: one's organization, the national culture in which the business operates, and personal ethical beliefs.

In organizational ethical analysis, managers must look to their written codes of ethics and the unwritten norms of the company culture. Many organizations have ethical codes that specify the principles to guide managers' decision making and behaviors. When referring to the ethical code as a guide, managers use deontological ethical reasoning; they know and follow the written rules. In addition, all organizations have company cultures with unwritten rules that prescribe or proscribe behaviors. In some companies, for example, all managers would know the informal rules such as, "Profit is more important than the environment as long as you follow the letter of the law" or "Give the bribe if it gets the job done and no one gets hurt or caught." A manager might better understand the ethical bases of the company's culture by understanding the moral language used. For example, is it maximizing the greatest welfare or is it avoiding harm?

How can a multinational develop an effective code of conduct? The next Case in Point lays out some of the key steps.

Multinational managers are guests in other nations. As such, their ethical decision making must go beyond legal constraints and following company rules and cultural norms. The managers must ask themselves whether what they are doing is consistent with and respectful of local cultural norms. For example, should they require employees to work on a religious holiday in one country because other units throughout the world are having regular business days?

Managers may begin these analyses at different points. For some issues, they may consider personal moral beliefs first. For other issues, it may make more sense to start with the law. At some point, however, after considering all the components in managerial decision making, you, as the manager, must make a personal moral judgment. Is it right for you? You are ultimately responsible. Most courts of law throughout the world will not accept the defense, "The organization made me do it."

Thus, for the multinational manager, the purely ethical issues in a decision must be weighed against the economic and legal analyses. A business must make a profit to survive, people don't want to go to jail or be fined, and most people want to behave ethically. Often there is no easy answer. For example, should a manager move a factory to a country with a cheap labor force, even if the move hurts the people who will lose their jobs? Should a multinational company sell potentially dangerous but useful products to a Third World country because the people in that country cannot afford the higher-priced, safer products? Should a multinational company ignore the use of child labor by some of its suppliers

Ethical analysis
One that goes beyond focusing on profit goals and legal regulations.

CASE IN POINT

Creating a Code of Conduct for a Multinational

As the chapter explains, there are cultural variations regarding how ethics are viewed in different countries. For instance, the French privacy watchdog did not allow McDonald's to enact its whistle-blower initiatives because the group said it was against French privacy law. How, then, can a multinational develop an enforceable code of conduct for its many subsidiaries? Experts suggest the following:

- *Involve the human resources management department:* Rather than turning to the legal department, experts suggest making use of the human resources management department. This department can help with developing a values-based approach to ethics rather than just a compliance- or legal-based approach.

- *Create an international advisory board:* Involve employees who are knowledgeable about the cultural demands of the regions they work in. Avoid

using expatriates, who may not have as much in-depth cultural knowledge.

- *Draft a contents list and ensure that the code is culturally neutral:* The advisory board can get input from its different subsidiaries to determine the areas the code should address. Drafting of the contents should be done in as culturally neutral a way as possible.

- *Finalize contents:* Hold focus groups in the different areas to finalize the contents. Address any cultural discrepancies.

- *Translate the code of conduct:* Translate the code of conduct to the native languages of all employees. This will ensure maximal comprehension of the document.

Source: Based on HR Focus. *2008. "Why global ethics count and how HR can help," October, 85(10), pp. 13—15.*

because the children's families desperately need the money and their competitors will use these suppliers anyway?

When faced with such complex conflicts among economics, law, and ethics, how do managers know whether they are behaving ethically? Although not every ethical dilemma faced by every individual in every culture has a resolution, one aid to ethical decision making is to approach decisions using philosophical ethical theories. Unfortunately, there is no single accepted ethical theory or system that managers can use as a guide when they face difficult ethical problems. Philosophers have debated for millennia the merits of various systems. Nevertheless, managers can make use of generally accepted ethical theories to help them understand ethical problems and the nature of their ethical decisions.

Although an ethical analysis like the one suggested in Exhibit 4.8 does not provide the "right" answer to an ethical problem, it does help to clarify the reasons behind ethical choices. It also raises the businessperson's awareness of the ethical nature of business decisions.

Summary and Conclusions

The multinational manager faces ethical challenges similar to the domestic manager, but the challenges are magnified by the complexity of working in different countries and cultures. Part of this chapter provided essential background information on business ethics

that is useful for ethics management in all settings. The chapter proposes a starting point for understanding international business ethics: understanding the relationship between ethics and social responsibility; how ethical philosophies underlay much of our ethical reasoning; and the differences among financial, legal, and ethical analyses.

Unlike the domestic-only manager, multinational managers must be able to assess how a country's social institutions and culture will affect their ability to manage ethical behavior. The examples showed that differences in legal and religious institutions and in basic cultural values often lead to different perceptions of what is ethical in business. Although there is some evidence of a convergence in business ethics due to the increase in international trade and investment, a multinational manager can never be too sensitive to issues as important as moral behavior in another culture.

Besides understanding the cultural setting in which they operate, multinational managers can never ignore their home country laws. In this regard, the U.S. manager probably faces the strictest constraints. The FCPA constrains U.S. managers from behaving in ways that, while accepted in other societies, are off limits to U.S. managers. All multinational managers, regardless of national origin, should be aware of the international agreements to which their country is party. Following the summary of these agreements, as shown in Exhibit 4.7, will likely help managers avoid legal and ethical difficulties in their international operations.

The chapter concluded with a decision model for making ethical decisions in a multinational setting. Although the model does not tell you what to do, it does provide a variety of issues that a manager should consider. Managing ethically in the international environment is not always easy, and certainly the challenges will continue to grow with increasing interactions among nations.

Discussion Questions

1. Discuss some of the issues that make international business ethics more complex than domestic business ethics.

2. What is ethical relativism? What are some of the dangers of using ethical relativism to justify all ethical decisions?

3. How do legal and ethical analyses differ? Give examples. Can a manager behave ethically just by following the host country's laws? Explain.

4. Discuss the difference between teleological and deontological theories of ethics. Give examples of how an international manager might appeal to

either type of theory when faced with the opportunity to offer a bribe.

5. How do social institutions and culture affect the practice of business ethics in different countries? How do these differences affect managers who take the moral positions of ethical relativism and ethical universalism?

6. Discuss the arguments regarding whether businesses from other nations should follow the United States' FCPA.

7. Discuss reasons for the trend toward a universal code of business ethics.

Multinational Management **Skill Builder**

Rex Lewis's Ethical Dilemma

Step 1.   Reread the section on Thomas Donaldson's views on moral languages.

Step 2.   Read the following scenario: Rex Lewis is a 25-year-old manager for ICS Corp., a small U.S. manufacturer of dietary supplements. After graduation, Mr. Lewis worked at company headquarters in Lexington, Nebraska, in a variety of positions. As an international business major, Mr. Lewis jumped at the chance to take a position as country manager in Matinea. Mr. Lewis studied the Matinean language for four years and visited the country for a summer while an undergraduate. He feels confident that he can handle this position because he has both the managerial and cultural experience.

ICS's major product is SUPALL, a dietary supplement that is inexpensive to produce and that can provide children with all of their basic nutritional needs. This product is very attractive to poor countries such as Matinea, where agricultural production is not sufficient to feed the population and recent droughts have made the situation even worse. Although cheaper than a well-rounded basic diet, one child's monthly supply of SUPALL costs about one-quarter of an average worker's salary at current prices, and most families are quite large.

In his first week in Matinea, Mr. Lewis makes a variety of startling discoveries. In spite of the relatively high price of SUPALL, demand in the Matinean market is strong. Moreover, ICS is making a 50 percent return on the product! Now Mr. Lewis realizes why the revenues from SUPALL have been able to support his company's crucial R&D research on other products. When he worked back in the United States, the CEO told him personally that if ICS doesn't come up with new products soon, the big companies will soon have a SUPALL-type product, and the price will fall drastically.

Mr. Lewis, who considers himself a good Christian, begins to wonder whether the price is fair for the Matineans. The price of SUPALL is cheaper than food, but it takes virtually all of a family's income to buy it. Yet ICS needs the profits to survive. Mr. Lewis has the authority to set prices in the country, but he must justify his decision to headquarters back in the United States.

Step 3.   Divide the class into six teams, one for each moral language. Each team represents a version of the ICS Corp. but with a corporate culture dominated by one of the moral languages.

Step 4.   As a team, review Exhibit 4.7 and conduct the relevant analyses. Come to a consensus and give a recommendation to Rex Lewis.

Step 5.   Present and discuss your findings with the entire class.

Endnotes

1   Woods, Walter. 2006. "Hyundai scandal delays 2nd plant." *The Atlanta Journal-Constitution*, April 25, p. C4.

2   Buchholz, Rogene A. 1989. *Fundamental Concepts and Problems in Business Ethics*. Englewood Cliffs, NJ: Prentice Hall.

3   Cullen, John B., Bart Victor, and Carroll Stephens. 1989. "An ethical weather report: Assessing the organization's ethical climate." *Organizational Dynamics*, 18, pp. 50–62.

4   Ferrell, O. C., John Fraedrich, and Linda Ferrell. 2005. *Business Ethics*. New York: Houghton Mifflin.

5   Hall, Jeremy, and Harrie Vredenburg. 2005. "Managing stakeholder ambiguity." *MIT Sloan Management Review*, 47(1), pp. 11–13.

6   Buchholz.

7   Donaldson, Thomas. 1992. "The language of international corporate ethics." *Business Ethics Quarterly*, 2, pp. 271–281.

8   Ibid.

9   Foryth, Donelson R., Ernest H. O'Boyle, and Michael A. McDaniel. 2008. "East meets West: A meta-analytic investigation of cultural variations in idealism and relativism." *Journal of Business Ethics*, 83 (4), pp. 813–833.

10 Cullen, J. B., K. Praveen Parboteeah, and Martin Hoegl. 2004. "Cross-national differences in managers' willingness to justify ethically suspect behaviors: A test of institutional anomie theory." *Academy of Management Journal*, 47(3), pp. 410–421.

11 Messner, S. F., and R. Rosenfeld. 2001. *Crime and the American Dream*. Belmont, CA: Wadsworth.

12 Seleim, A., and N. Bontis. 2009. "The relationship between culture and corruption: A cross–national study." *Journal of Intellectual Capital*, 10(1), pp. 165–184.

13 Mendenhall, Mark E., Betty Jane Punnet, and David Ricks. 1994. *Global Management*. Cambridge, MA: Blackwell.

14 Comte, O., A. Lambert-Mogiliansky, and T. Verdier. 2005. "Corruption and competition in procurement actions." *The Rand Journal of Economics*, 36(1), pp. 1–15.

15 Bayar, Guzin. 2005. "The role of intermediaries in corruption." *Public Choice*, 122, pp. 277–298.

16 Soon, Lim Ghee. 2006. "Macro-economic outcomes of corruption: A longitudinal empirical study." *Singapore Management Review*, 28(1), pp. 63–72.

17 Transparency International. 2006. "2005 bribe payers index." http://www.transparency.org/cpi/, accessed October 16, 2009.

18 Gleich, Oren, and Ryan Woodward. 2005. "Foreign corrupt practices act." *The American Criminal Law Review*, 42(2), pp. 545–571.

19 Donaldson, Thomas. 1989. *The Ethics of International Business*. New York: Oxford University Press; Donaldson.

20 Frederick, William C. 1991. "The moral authority of transnational corporate codes." *Journal of Business Ethics*, 10, pp. 165–177; Getz, Kathleen A. 1990. "International codes of conduct: An analysis of ethical reasoning." *Journal of Business Ethics*, 9, pp. 567–578.

21 Frederick.

22 Donaldson, Thomas. 1992. "Can multinationals stage a universal morality play?" *Business and Society Review*, 81, pp. 51–55.

23 Hosmer, Larue Tone. 1987. *The Ethics of Management*. Homewood, IL: Irwin.

24 Friedman, Milton. 1970. "The social responsibility of business is to increase its profits." *New York Times Magazine*, September 13, pp. 122–126.

25 Victor, Bart, and John B. Cullen. 1988. "The organizational bases of ethical work climates." *Administrative Science Quarterly*, 33, pp. 101–125.

Ethics of Offshoring: Novo Nordisk and Clinical Trials in Emerging Economies

On a warm day in early spring 2008, the telephone is ringing in the office of Anders Dejgaard, chief medical officer of Novo Nordisk, a leading developer and manufacturer of insulin and related products. A business journalist of the Danish national newspaper *Berlingske Tidende* is on the line and asking for an interview. Dejgaard knows her from several conversations relating to business practices in the pharmaceutical industry.

The journalist is investigating the offshoring of clinical trials by Danish companies. A report recently published in the Netherlands alleges that multinational pharmaceutical companies routinely conduct trials in developing countries under allegedly unethical conditions. Also, the Danish National Committee on Biomedical Research Ethics has expressed concerns because Danish pharmaceutical companies are not obtaining ethical reviews in Denmark for such trials despite the offer from this committee. Thus, she wants to discuss Novo Nordisk's position on these issues.

Dejgaard reflects on how to react. Several articles on ethical aspects related to medical research in the Third World had appeared in the Danish press in recent months, creating an atmosphere of suspicion toward the industry.[1] Should he meet with the journalist and if so, what should he tell her? Or should he rather focus on his forthcoming business trip to new production facilities and send Novo Nordisk's press officer to meet the journalist? In his mind flashes the possibility of derogatory headlines in the tabloid press. As a company emphasizing corporate responsibility, the interaction with the media presents both opportunities and risks to Novo Nordisk.

Novo Nordisk[2]

Novo Nordisk A/S had been created in 1989 through a merger between two Danish companies, Novo Industri A/S and Nordisk Gentofte A/S. Both had been established in the 1920s as manufacturers of insulin, a crucial medication for diabetes. Over decades of fierce competition, they had become leading providers of insulin and related pharmaceutical products. Novo Industri had been pursuing an internationally oriented strategy from the outset, and by 1936 was supplying insulin to 40 countries. A significant step in the internationalization of the company was a major push into the U.S. market in 1979. At the time, Food and Drug Administration (FDA) regulations required Novo Industri to replicate its clinical studies in the United States to obtain the approval of the marketing of their new products. In 1989, the two companies merged and in 2000 the merged company spun off the enzyme business "Novozymes."

In 2008, Novo Nordisk presents itself as a focused company within the healthcare industry and a world leader in diabetes care. It claims the broadest and most innovative diabetes product portfolio in the industry, including the most advanced insulin delivery systems. In addition, Novo Nordisk holds leading positions in areas such as haemostasis management, growth hormone therapy, and hormone replacement therapy. Sales reached DKr41.8 billion (about US$8 billion) in 2007, of which DKr30.5 billion were in diabetes care and DKr11.4 billion were in biopharmaceuticals.

Innovation is considered pivotal to the success of Novo Nordisk, as it was to its predecessor companies. Continuous innovations allow the development of more refined, and thus more effective, insulin preparations, and new delivery systems, such as Novopen, that facilitate the administration of the treatment, including self-administration by patients. In 2008, about 18 percent of employees are working within research and development.

In 2008, Novo Nordisk holds market shares for insulin of about 56 percent in Europe, 41 percent in North America and 73 percent in Japan and employs about 26,000 people, of whom 12,689 are located in Denmark, 3,411 in the rest of Europe, 3,940 in North America, and the remainder in Asia Pacific and the rest of the world. Production facilities are located in six countries and products are marketed in 179 countries.

The shares of Novo Industri were first listed on the Copenhagen Stock Exchange in 1974 and on the London Stock Exchange in 1981 as the first Scandinavian company to be listed in London. In 2008, Novo Nordisk's B shares are listed on the stock exchanges in both Copenhagen and London, while its American depositary receipts (ADRs) are listed on the New York Stock Exchange.

Novo Nordisk emphasizes corporate social responsibility as part of its image, pursing a triple bottom line approach: environmental and social responsibility along with economic viability. This commitment is demonstrated through its values and its environmental and social responsibility policies that are reported on its Web site (see Appendix 1).

Appendix 1   Corporate Sustainability at Novo Nordisk (Extracts)

At Novo Nordisk, we refer to corporate sustainability as companies' ability to sustain and develop their business in the long-term perspective, in harmony with society. This implies a more inclusive view of business and its role; one in which engagements with stakeholders are not just used to legitimise corporate decisions, but rather the foundation for how a company conducts and grows its business. It is about innovation, opportunity and planning for the long term.

The Triple Bottom is the principle behind our way of doing business. The company's Articles of Association state that it 'strives to conduct its activities in a financially, environmentally and socially responsible way.' This is a commitment to sustainable development and balanced growth, and it has been built into corporate governance structures, management tools and methods of assessing and rewarding individuals' performance. . . .

The stakeholder dimension: Novo Nordisk needs to stay attuned to emerging trends and 'hot issues' on the global agenda in order to respond and to contribute to the debate. Stakeholder engagement is an integrated part of our business philosophy. We have long-standing engagements with stakeholders that are vital for building trust and understanding of a variety of issues. By involving stakeholders in the decision-making processes, decisions are better founded and solutions more likely to succeed. Stakeholders are defined as any individual or group that may affect or be affected by a company's activities.

Translating commitment to action: Corporate sustainability has made a meaningful difference to our business, and we believe it is a driver of our business success. This is best illustrated in three examples:

Business ethics: Surveys indicate that ethical behaviour in business is today the number one driver of reputation for pharmaceutical companies. Any company that is not perceived by the public as behaving in an ethical manner is likely to lose business, and it takes a long time to regain trust. While the Novo Nordisk Way of Management is a strong guide to our behaviour, we decided we needed more detailed guidance in the area of business ethics. In 2005 we therefore framed a new business ethics policy, in line with universally accepted high standards, backed by a set of procedures. Since then we have trained managers and employees, held workshops and offered e-learning on the new policy.

Climate change: We need to act to put a brake to human-induced climate change. While the implications of climate change pose major business risks, there are also opportunities. We have partnered with the WWF [World Wildlife Fund] in the Climate Savers programme and set an ambitious target to achieve a 10% reduction in our company's CO_2 emissions by 2014, compared with 2004 emission levels. This will occur through optimised production, energy savings, and greater use of renewable energy supplies.

continued

Appendix 1   Continued

The diabetes pandemic: Today, diabetes is recognised as a pandemic. Novo Nordisk responds to this major societal challenge by working in partnerships with many others to rally the attention of policy-makers and influencers to change diabetes. We have made a promise of **Changing Diabetes**® and have framed **a strategy for inclusive access to diabetes care.** We established the **World Diabetes Foundation**, and have made several initiatives to advocate for change and build evidence of diabetes developments. **The National Changing Diabetes**® programme and **DAWN** are examples of education and awareness programmes implemented by Novo Nordisk affiliates in their respective countries. Our **Changing Diabetes**® Bus that promotes Novo Nordisk's global **Changing Diabetes**® activities had reached 86,000 people by the end of 2007 during its world tour. Its primary goal is to support the **UN Resolution on diabetes**, which was passed in December 2006.

Source: www.novonordisk.com, accessed November 2008.

Critical milestones in Novo Nordisk's ambition to be recognized as a leader of corporate sustainability include the publication in 1994 of its Environmental Report. It was the first company in Denmark and one of the first in the world to do so. This was followed in 1999 by the first annual Social Report. In 2001, Novo Nordisk established the World Diabetes Foundation, a charity aiming to improve diabetes care in developing countries, where diabetes is becoming an epidemic as it had in Europe and North America a few decades earlier.

In recognition of its sustainability engagement, Novo Nordisk had been included in the Dow Jones Global Sustainability Indices, where it was ranked as "best in class" in the healthcare category in 2007. At home, Novo Nordisk is frequently ranked as having the most highly regarded corporate image by Danish magazines *Berlingske Nyhedmagasin, Børsen,* and *Ingeniøren.*

New Medications: Development and Approval

Novo Nordisk, like other pharmaceutical and medical companies, heavily invests in the development of new medications offering more effective, safe, and user-friendly treatments. New product development involves the creation of new drugs or modifications in their use, for instance their dosage and the form of administration.

To bring new drugs or medical devices to market, they must be approved by the relevant authorities—the FDA in the United States and European Medicines Agency (EMEA) in the European Union. The approval of drugs and medical devices requires proof of their efficacy and their safety. Efficacy refers to scientific evidence that the drug improves patients' conditions as claimed by the manufacturer. Safety refers to the absence of substantive negative side-effects. Thus, to obtain approval, pharmaceutical companies have to provide scientific evidence that the drug improves the conditions of patients and is free of disproportional side-effects.

This evidence has to be based on, among other data, clinical trials in which the drug has been tested on actual patients. The clinical trials are normally conducted in four stages. Phase 1 involves a small number of healthy volunteers and serves to assess the kinetic properties and tolerability of the drug. Phase 2 is performed on larger groups of patients to assess how well the drug works and to establish the doses that give the desired effect and to continue its safety assessment. Phase 3 trials often involve thousands of patients and aims to provide a definitive assessment of how effective and safe the drug is. All data generated in the three phases form an essential part of submissions to the regulatory authorities (FDA, EMEA, and their counterparts in other countries) for drug approval. With this approval, the drug can then be marketed for the approved indications. Further trials, in phase 4, may be required to obtain permission to extend the labeling of a drug to new indications (e.g. a different disease) or specific groups, such as children or pregnant women.

Phase 3 and 4 trials require a large number of patients with the specific disease that the drug is to improve. A typical approval process conducted by Novo Nordisk might require six to eight different phase 3 trials with different patient groups or combinations of the drug component, each involving about 400 to 800 patients. Such trials are often conducted as multinational studies involving up to 15 countries. With increasing requirements for patient exposure for approval and increasing numbers of drugs being tested, the recruitment of patients is often a major challenge. Typically, trials are conducted at multiple hospitals that all must follow the same trial protocol to ensure the consistency of data and compliance with existing "good clinical practice" (GCP) guidelines. Multi-site trials also facilitate the recruitment of patients with diverse backgrounds, for instance different ethnicities and diets, while helping to demonstrate their universal properties. Doctors and nurses but not patients are normally paid for this work and hospitals often find it attractive to participate in trials that allow access to new medications and front line research. Clinical trials, especially phase 3, are a major cost factor in the development of new medications and they often take many years to conduct (on average eight years).

In the early 2000s, major pharmaceutical industries increasingly moved parts of their trials, especially phases 3 and 4, to countries outside their traditional areas of operations, especially to Eastern Europe, South America, India, and China. Hospitals in these areas provide access to qualified medical staff and larger numbers of patients with the specific conditions, while potentially being able to administer a trial at lower costs. Moreover, the efficacy of drugs may also vary across contexts, for instance due to genetic, dietary, climatic, or other environmental conditions. In such cases, multi-site trials help to establish the efficacy of medications across contexts. Some countries, such as Japan, India, and China, in fact require that trials are at least in part conducted locally to approve a new medication in the respective countries. However, the conduct of clinical trials in these areas also raises a range of ethical issues.

Ethical Issues in Medical Research[3]

Ethical issues in the pharmaceutical industry have received considerable media attention over several decades, as the industry has failed to live up to the expectations of some interest groups. In particular, clinical trials raise a number of widely recognized issues. Medical professionals, and with them many NGOs and media, focus on the medical ethics grounded in the Hippocratic oath that commits doctors to treat each patient to the best of their abilities, never to cause intentional harm, and to maintain patient confidentiality. Scientists and approval authorities have been concerned about the scientific rigor of the tests to provide solid evidence of the effects of a new drug, and thus to protect potential future users of the drug. At the same time, pharmaceutical companies have to operate with limited financial resources and to satisfy shareholders and thus cannot spend more resources than expected future revenues would justify. Accordingly, the industry has been accused of performing trials in developing countries with lower attention to ethical principles—"ethical bribing," with patients acting as guinea pigs that do not understand and/or care about the risk involved but just want to get free medication and with investigators not meeting the competence requirements, etc. Allegedly, all this just

serves to generate documentation for compounds that are to be sold only in developed countries.

Medical (Hippocratic) ethics concern primarily the individual patients that are participating in any experiment. The relationship between the doctor and the subject participating in a trial is thus governed by the doctor's responsibility to care for his or her patient. Past incidences where this principle had been violated continue to affect popular perceptions of medical research. Most infamously, the Tuskegee syphilis study left 400 impoverished and unwitting African-American men in Macon County, Alabama, untreated to study how they developed the disease—an experiment initiated in 1932 and terminated only in the 1970s.

To prevent such scandals, professional medical organizations have developed guidelines and principles of ethics to guide their research, notably the Helsinki Declaration of the World Medical Association (see Appendix 2). These widely accepted ethical principles aim to protect subjects, e.g., patients, participating in such research. These include:

- *Voluntary informed consent:* Each patient has to agree voluntarily to participate in the research based on being fully informed about the purposes of the study and potential risks for the individual. Sponsors and local site investigators thus normally write an "informed consent" document that informs potential subjects of the true risks and potential benefits, which is signed by each patient or their legal guardian before any trial procedure.

- *Respect of patients:* The privacy of the subject should be protected and they should be free to withdraw from the experiment at any time without reasoning. The doctor's professional responsibility to the patient should take precedence over any other considerations.

- *Independent review:* Any medical and pharmacological research has to be assessed on its scientific merits and ethicality by an independent review board (IRB) that is independent from those involved in or sponsoring the research.

Scientific ethics are concerned about the validity of the results of the scientific inquiry and thus the methodological rigour of the study. Thus, a study has to use valid measurements and statistical techniques and samples that are unbiased and sufficiently large that they can generate trustworthy and valid results.

Such scientific rigor is important to anyone who may in the future use an approved drug or medical device. Awareness of the need for rigorous tests prior to launching new medications had been triggered by various scandals of the 1960s, notably the Thalidomide

Appendix 2 Helsinki Declaration of the World Medical Association (Excerpts)

10. It is the duty of the physician in medical research to protect the life, health, privacy, and dignity of the human subject.

13. The design and performance of each experimental procedure involving human subjects should be clearly formulated in an experimental protocol. This protocol should be submitted for consideration, comment, guidance, and where appropriate, approval to a specially appointed ethical review committee, which must be independent of the investigator, the sponsor or any other kind of undue influence. This independent committee should be in conformity with the laws and regulations of the country in which the research experiment is performed. The committee has the right to monitor ongoing trials. The researcher has the obligation to provide monitoring information to the committee, especially any serious adverse events. The researcher should also submit to the committee, for review, information regarding funding, sponsors, institutional affiliations, other potential conflicts of interest and incentives for subjects.

14. The research protocol should always contain a statement of the ethical considerations involved and should indicate that there is compliance with the principles enunciated in this Declaration.

15. Medical research involving human subjects should be conducted only by scientifically qualified persons and under the supervision of a clinically competent medical person. The responsibility for the human subject must always rest with a medically qualified person and never rest on the subject of the research, even though the subject has given consent.

16. Every medical research project involving human subjects should be preceded by careful assessment of predictable risks and burdens in comparison with foreseeable benefits to the subject or to others. This does not preclude the participation of healthy volunteers in medical research. The design of all studies should be publicly available.

17. Physicians should abstain from engaging in research projects involving human subjects unless they are confident that the risks involved have been adequately assessed and can be satisfactorily managed. Physicians should cease any investigation if the risks are found to outweigh the potential benefits or if there is conclusive proof of positive and beneficial results.

18. Medical research involving human subjects should only be conducted if the importance of the objective outweighs the inherent risks and burdens to the subject. This is especially important when the human subjects are healthy volunteers.

19. Medical research is only justified if there is a reasonable likelihood that the populations in which the research is carried out stand to benefit from the results of the research.

20. The subjects must be volunteers and informed participants in the research project.

21. The right of research subjects to safeguard their integrity must always be respected. Every precaution should be taken to respect the privacy of the subject, the confidentiality of the patient's information and to minimize the impact of the study on the subject's physical and mental integrity and on the personality of the subject.

22 In any research on human beings, each potential subject must be adequately informed of the aims, methods, sources of funding, any possible conflicts of interest, institutional affiliations of the researcher, the anticipated benefits and potential risks of the study and the discomfort it may entail. The subject should be informed of the right to abstain from participation in the study or to withdraw consent to participate at any time without reprisal. After ensuring that the subject has understood the information, the physician should then obtain the subject's freely-given informed consent, preferably in writing. If the consent cannot be obtained in writing, the non-written consent must be formally documented and witnessed.

23 When obtaining informed consent for the research project the physician should be particularly cautious if the subject is in a dependent relationship with the physician or may consent under duress. In that case the informed consent should be obtained by a well-informed physician who is not engaged in the investigation and who is completely independent of this relationship.

29   The benefits, risks, burdens and effectiveness of a new method should be tested against those of the best current prophylactic, diagnostic, and therapeutic methods. This does not exclude the use of placebo, or no treatment, in studies where no proven prophylactic, diagnostic or therapeutic method exists.

   Note of clarification on paragraph 29 of the WMA Declaration of Helsinki

   The WMA hereby reaffirms its position that extreme care must be taken in making use of a placebo-controlled trial and that in general this methodology should only be used in the absence of existing proven therapy. However, a placebo-controlled trial may be ethically acceptable, even if proven therapy is available, under the following circumstances:

   • Where for compelling and scientifically sound methodological reasons its use is necessary to determine the efficacy or safety of a prophylactic, diagnostic or therapeutic method; or

   • Where a prophylactic, diagnostic or therapeutic method is being investigated for a minor condition and the patients who receive placebo will not be subject to any additional risk of serious or irreversible harm.

   All other provisions of the Declaration of Helsinki must be adhered to, especially the need for appropriate ethical and scientific review.

30   At the conclusion of the study, every patient entered into the study should be assured of access to the best proven prophylactic, diagnostic and therapeutic methods identified by the study.

   Note of clarification on paragraph 30 of the WMA Declaration of Helsinki

   The WMA hereby reaffirms its position that it is necessary during the study planning process to identify post-trial access by study participants to prophylactic, diagnostic and therapeutic procedures identified as beneficial in the study or access to other appropriate care. Post-trial access arrangements or other care must be described in the study protocol so the ethical review committee may consider such arrangements during its review.

Source: www.wma.net/e/policy/b3.htm, accessed October 2008.

scandal involving a pain killer used by women to ease sleep problems and pregnancy sickness. Due to side-effects of this medication, thousands of children worldwide were born with incomplete arms or legs, before the drug was withdrawn. In consequence to this and other scandals, the licensing and approval procedures for drugs have been tightened to ensure that only drugs with scientifically proven efficacy and safety are marketed.

Ethical businesses have to balance activities done in the interest of the wider society with their pursuit of profits. The late Nobel prize-winning economist Milton Friedman famously declared that the primary social responsibility of business is to make profits.[4] Under efficient markets, which he firmly believed in, this would generate the most mutually beneficial outcome. Thus, he argued, firms ought to give precedence to shareholders over any other interest groups.

Others argue that firms should engage in corporate social responsibility because it can be expected to benefit their bottom line in the long run, for instance through reputation effects. Yet others argue that firms have an intrinsic, normative responsibility to use their influence to do good for society and to aspire to the highest moral standards, independent of the profit motive. However, even so, their financial resources will be limited. Like organizations in the governmental or non-profit sector, businesses have to make critical decisions about how best to use their scarce resources.

Ethics of Placebo Experiments[5]

Particular concerns have arisen for placebo trials, that is, trials where a control group of patients receives a treatment without any active ingredient for the disease. The purpose of placebo trials is, normally, to provide evidence of product efficacy by showing statistically significant improvements of the conditions of patients receiving the active treatment, compared to those receiving a placebo treatment.

Placebo trials are especially important for diseases that are affected by the so-called placebo effect, that is, patients' conditions improving because of the positive effect of receiving a form of treatment rather than the specific medication. This has been shown to be quite substantive, for instance, for schizophrenia and other psychiatric conditions. Both American and European authorities thus often require placebo trials as prerequisite for the approval of new medications.

Alternatives to placebo trials include the use of active controls, in which the control groups receive a previously marketed medication with known properties. Yet these types of trials are often not sufficient to provide the required rigorous evidence regarding the efficacy of the medication.[6] Placebo trials may create risks for patients in the placebo group, in particular when patients are denied a treatment that is known to improve their condition. The Helsinki Declaration therefore requires avoiding placebo experiments unless very special reasons require them or no alternative treatment of the illness is available (see Appendix 2, item 29). Ethics review boards have become very restrictive in permitting placebo trials. There have been arguments from some groups that one reason for the pharmaceutical industry to place studies in developing countries is the possibility of performing placebo trials that otherwise can be difficult to get approval for in developed countries.

Novo Nordisk generally avoids placebo trials. Usually, they are used only in phase 1 trials in healthy volunteers when new drug candidates are being developed. These trials are normally located near its main research centers in Europe and rarely in non-Western countries.

Media Spotlights

In February 2008, a report from the Dutch NGO SOMO raised public awareness of placebo trials conducted by major pharmaceutical companies in developing countries.[7] The report was critical of trials that had been submitted to the FDA and the EMEA for drug approval. Its primary concern was that key information about ethical aspects of these clinical trials was not available to it as an external observer and it found incidences where patients suffered serious harm after receiving a placebo in a trial.

The report focused on three case studies of clinical trials for recently approved drugs conducted in Eastern Europe and Asia, based on publicly available information. It concluded that

> trial subjects in these countries are more vulnerable and their rights are less secured than in high income countries. Conditions such as poverty, illiteracy, poor health systems and inadequate research ethics committees result in international ethical standards not being met. Current EU legislation requires that results from unethical clinical trials . . . not be accepted for marketing authorization. With three case studies on recently approved drugs in the EU (Abilify, Olmetec, and Seroquel), SOMO demonstrates that this principle is being violated. European authorities devote little to no attention to the ethical aspects of the clinical trials submitted, and they accept unethical trials as well as trials of poor quality.[8]

In its conclusions, the report alleges that local regulation and the enforcement of ethical principles are less strict, partly because local independent review boards are less qualified and partly because they are less keen on restricting what is potentially a revenue earner. The authors thus advocate global harmonization of ethical criteria along the principles currently used by ethics committees in Europe: ". . . there must be no discrepancy between the ethical criteria used to approve research protocols in Western Europe and in low and middle income economies to avoid the creation of 'easy countries.'"[9]

The media picked up, in particular, the case of a schizophrenic patient committing suicide while participating in a trial of the anti-schizophrenia medicine Seroquel by Astra-Zeneca. Moreover, media reported that 10 percent of recipients in the placebo group had to be hospitalized because of worsening conditions. Careful reading of the original report suggests that 8.3 percent (p. 64) of a group of 87 patients (p. 62) were affected, which adds up to seven persons. No assessment of the likelihood of such incidents under alternative medication available at the time had been included in the report.

Concerns have also been raised by the Danish National Committee on Biomedical Research Ethics.[10] In particular, the committee criticizes the industry for not accepting the committee's offer to provide independent ethical reviews before submitting to local ethics committees as a service to the industry. The chairperson for the committee, Johannes Gaub, chief medical officer at Odense Hospital, told the media:

> Like production companies locate their factories in low wage areas, the medical industry is outsourcing its scientific experiments in the same way. The costs of conducting medical trials in developing countries are only a fraction of what they are in the West because of the low wages . . . In the USA it costs about DKr 150,000 to move one patient through a trial. In Denmark, it costs DKr 80,000. I don't really know the price in developing countries, but it is a fraction of that.

Gaub also rejects the concern of the industry that hospitals in Denmark would not be able to conduct trials of the necessary scale, given the growing requirements worldwide to provide clinical trial data for approvals around the world:

> We have considerable spare capacity in Denmark. Despite the high costs we have a well-functioning health system. We have data about patients because of our national identity number system, and there are many clinical researchers in the hospitals who would be happy to participate in the trials of

new medications . . . It is actually worrying that we do not receive more applications in Denmark. We need clinical research to maintain the high level of health science that we so far have had in the country.[11]

Danish politicians also joined the debate. In a statement to the health committee of the national parliament, the minister for health emphasized that E.U. regulation for the approval of new medicines requires that trials conducted outside the European Union have been implemented in accordance with the European Union's own rules as well as with ethical principles such as the Helsinki Declaration. The minister thus concluded:

I find no reason to take initiatives to constrain research projects by the Danish medical industry outside the EU. In this context, I consider it important to emphasize that all clinical trials that shall be used as a basis for applications for approval of marketing of a medication in the EU must comply with the EU's laws on good clinical practice and the ethical principles regarding medical research with human subjects.[12]

Also, other politicians joined the debate. For example, Member of Parliament Birgitte Josefsen (V)[13] urged Danish pharmaceutical companies to hold the ethical flag high: "The medical industry ought to be very careful about whom they use as test persons. That should be people who have resources to say 'no'. A poor Indian mother with three children is not the right one to become a test person."[14]

Novo Nordisk's Position on Clinical Trials

Anders Dejgaard is pondering the complexity of the ethical issues. As corporate sustainability features highly on Novo Nordisk's agenda, the ethically appropriate handling of clinical trials is important to the company. It conducts clinical trials globally to test the safety and efficacy of new drug candidates in order to obtain global marketing authorization. These trials always follow a common protocol and thus the same standards at all trials sites. Trials sites are selected based on a variety of criteria, including the quality of regulatory authorities, ethical review processes, and medical practices. Moreover, drugs have to be tested on the types of patients who will later become users of the drug and trial subjects should have access to the drugs after the process has been completed. In addition, Novo Nordisk will only conduct trials in countries where it has affiliates with the necessary competence to arrange and monitor

the trials. In 2008, these criteria were met in about 65 countries worldwide.

Novo Nordisk has adapted the global guidelines and recommendations by all the professional bodies and publishes its policies on clinical trials on its Web site (see Appendix 3). This includes enhanced global exposure of investigated products through its own Web site as well as Web sites sponsored by the FDA (see Appendix 3). Novo Nordisk conducts research in therapies that require global trials and the inclusion of different ethnic populations. The company also anticipates a need to increase the number of clinical trials due to an expanding pipeline and more extensive global and local regulatory requirements. Its ethical principles and standard operating procedures, which apply globally, are designed to ensure due respect for the safety, rights, integrity, dignity, confidentiality, and well-being of all human beings participating in Novo Nordisk–sponsored trials. Novo Nordisk is auditing 10 percent of all trials, while at the same time the American and European authorities, FDA and EMEA, are making random checks of about 1 percent of Novo Nordisk's clinical trials. These random checks have never identified ethical problems in clinical trials in developing countries. Since trials are normally conducted in multiple countries, the same standards are applied everywhere, for both ethical and scientific reasons (consistency of results).

At the same time, Dejgaard is irritated about the request for an additional ethics approval by the Danish National Committee on Biomedical Research Ethics. He estimates that it would add three months to the preparation of each new trial. In his own experience, the ethical reviews in those locations he worked in are as rigorous as in Western countries and he does not recognize an added benefit, as the Danish committee would be no better in assessing a trial than a local ethics committee. On the contrary, he finds the suggestion more appropriate for a colonial empire. Moreover, specific local issues, such as ethnic or religious minorities, would be better understood by local committees.

Yet various issues come to mind. Is Novo Nordisk doing its research and development in an appropriate manner or are there issues that could be done better in view of Novo Nordisk's triple bottom line commitments? Are Novo Nordisk's standard operating procedures being properly implemented in all developing countries that participate in the programs and how is such compliance to be monitored? How should Novo Nordisk manage its simultaneous relationships with various regulatory authorities, independent review boards at various sites, and with the Danish National Committee on Biomedical Research Ethics?

Appendix 3   Clinical Trials: Novo Nordisk's Position

- Clinical trials sponsored by Novo Nordisk will always be conducted according to the Helsinki Declaration, which describes human rights for patients participating in clinical trials, and similar international ethical guidelines such as the Nuremberg code, the Belmont report and CIOMMS, and the International Conference of Harmonisation (ICH) guidelines for current good clinical practice (cGCP).

- The above guidelines and regulations are the foundation for our clinical Standard Operating Procedures (SOPs) including the SOP on the 'principles of clinical trials'. These standards are laid out to ensure the safety, rights, integrity, confidentiality, and well-being of persons involved in Novo Nordisk trials globally.

- Novo Nordisk will apply the same procedures wherever we sponsor clinical trials. This means that all subjects enrolled in Novo Nordisk trials are protected by the same rights, high ethical standards, and regulations irrespective of location of the study.

- The interest and well-being of the trial subject should always prevail over the interest of science, society, and commerce.

- Novo Nordisk will not conduct clinical trials for drug development in countries where we do not intend to market the investigational drug. In any country where we do undertake clinical trials we will ensure that a proper internal organisation and a proper regulated external environment exist.

- Clinical trials should only be done if they can be scientifically and medically justified, and all Novo Nordisk-sponsored trials should be based on sound scientific methodology described in a clear and detailed protocol. Placebo will only be used as comparator when scientifically and ethically justified.

- No trial activity in Novo Nordisk–sponsored trials will start before approval is obtained from external local ethics committees and health authorities.

- We will always ensure that investigators involved in Novo Nordisk clinical trials are skilled in the therapeutic area and are trained in GCP. No procedure involving a person undergoing clinical trial activities will take place before the appropriate freely given informed consent is obtained based on proper information on potential risk of participation in the trial. A patient can at any time withdraw from a clinical trial without giving any reason. In cases where trial subjects are incompetent, physically or mentally incapable of giving consent, or if the person is a minor, Novo Nordisk will follow local regulations for obtaining consent.

- Products used in Novo Nordisk–sponsored clinical trials will be manufactured and controlled according to international and local regulations and laws. Novo Nordisk will conduct frequent site monitoring to ensure that the study is executed according to the study protocol, and that data used in statistical analysis and reporting reflects the data obtained from the involved patients during the trial. Safety information from any Novo Nordisk trial will be monitored on a continuous basis and appropriate actions will be taken if risks of the investigational product outweigh the potential benefits.

- Patients participating in Novo Nordisk-sponsored clinical trials will always be offered best available and proven treatment after study termination. The treatment will be offered at the discretion of the responsible physician. If study medication is not marketed the responsible physician can apply for medication on a named patient basis. Post-study medication will be described in the protocol and informed consent.

- Novo Nordisk will ensure proper indemnification of trial subjects in case a trial product or procedures in a Novo Nordisk-sponsored trial cause bodily harm to a trial subject.

- Novo Nordisk strives to have all clinical trial results published according to accepted international guidelines, and we will always ensure transparency of our studies by publishing protocol synopses on the external Web site: **www.clinicaltrials.gov**. Study results from trials involving marketed drugs can be accessed via **www.clinicalstudyresults.org**. Furthermore, Novo Nordisk has its own online repository for clinical trials activities: **novonordisk-trials.com**. Novo Nordisk is collating all information about bioethics in the R&D area on **www.novonordisk.com/R&D/bioethics**.

Source: www.novonordisk.com, accessed November 2008.

Most pressing is the decision on how to handle the journalist. Should he meet her in person, send a public relations person, or not meet at all and reply in writing, citing the corporate Web site? If he is to meet her, what should be the key messages that he should get across and how should he prepare himself for any questions she might raise during the meeting?

CASE DISCUSSION QUESTIONS

The case is written from the perspective of Anders Dejgaard, chief medical officer. Assignment questions thus may take his perspective.

1. Considering both economic and ethical aspects, is it appropriate for companies like Novo Nordisk to conduct clinical trials in, for example, India? What exactly are the principles that should guide such a decision?

2. If trials are conducted in an emerging economy, how should they be managed, and which standards should apply?

3. What interest groups are joining the public debate and why? How should businesses handle them? What is the role, respectively, of Danish, European, American, and host country authorities and ethics committees in this process?

4. How should Anders Dejgaard react when the journalist calls to discuss Novo Nordisk's practices? What is the most effective way to communicate with the public?

CASE NOTES

1 See in particular Alfter, B. 2008. "De fattige er verdens nye forsøgskaniner. Krav om kontrol med medicinalindustrien," Information, Feb. 26, pp. 4–5, and Lambeck, B. and S.G. Jensen. 2007. "Halvdelen af al medicin afprøves i den tredje verden," Politiken, October 6.

2 This section draws on the company Web site, www.novonordisk.com, and an undated (circa 2002) document, "Novo Nordisk History," available via this Web site.

3 This section draws in particular on Emanuel, E.J., D. Wendler, and C. Grady. 2000. "What makes clinical research ethical?" Journal of the American Medical Association, 283:20, pp. 2701–2711, and

Michael A. Santoro and Thomas M. Gorrie, Ethics and the Pharmaceutical Industry, Cambridge University Press, 2005.

4 Friedman M. 1970. "The social responsibility of business is to increase profits," The New York Times Magazine, September 13; reprinted in Meyer, K.E. 2009. Multinational Enterprises and Host Economies, Elgar, Cheltenham.

5 This section draws on contemporary discussions in the medical literature, in particular Emanuel, E.J. and F.G. Miller. 2001. "The ethics of placebo-controlled trials: A middle ground." New England Journal of Medicine, 345:12, pp. 915–919, and Temple, R. and S.S. Ellenberg. 2000. "Placebo-controlled trials and active-controlled trials in the evaluation of new treatments," Annals of Internal Medicine, 133:6, pp. 455–463.

6 An active-control trial infers efficacy from non-significant differences of performance compared to the active-control drug. Such non-significance, however, can be caused by a number of other influences. Moreover, this test is problematic if the active-control drug is subject to large placebo effects varying with study designs. On the merits and concerns of active-control trials, see e.g., Temple, [FI] and [FI] Ellenberg. 2000. "Placebo-controlled trials and active-controlled trials in the evaluation of new treatments," and Walsh, B.T., S.N. Seidman, R. Sysko and M. Gould. 2002. "Placebo response in studies of major depression: Variable, substantial and growing," Journal of the American Medical Association, 287:14, pp. 1840–1847.

7 Schipper, I. and F. Weyzing. 2008. "Ethics for drug testing in low and middle income countries: Considerations for European market authorisation," Stichting Onderzoek Multinationale Ondernemingen (SOMO), http://somo.nl/publications-en/Publication_2472, accessed October 2008.

8 Ibid., abstract on the cover page.

9 Ibid., p. 68.

10 For further information on the Danish National Committee on Biomedical Research Ethics, seewww.cvk.im.dk/cvk/site.aspx?p=119.

11 Both citations are from Erhardtsen, B. 2008. "Medicinalindustrien dropper frivillig etisk blåstempling," Berlingske Tidende, April 5, Inland section, pp. 6-7 (case author's translation).

12 Nielsen, J.K. 2008. Besvarlse af spørgsmal nr. 20 (alm. del) som Folketingets Sundhedsudvalg har stillet til indenrigs - og sundhedsministeren (Written reply to a question in the health committee of the Danish parliament), January 9. (Archives of the Danish government: Indenrigs or Sundhedministeriet, Lægemiddlekontoret, J.nr. 2007-13009-599, Sagsbeh: nhj) (case author's translation).

13 (V) refers to Venstre, one of the parties of the minority government at the time.

14 Berlingske Tidende Web site. 2008. www.berlingske.dk/article/20080403/danmark/704030057, April 3, accessed October 2008 (case author's translation).

Royal Dutch Shell in Nigeria: Operating in a Fragile State

Richard Ivey School of Business
The University of Western Ontario   **IVEY** | Institute for Entrepreneurship

In July 2005, Benjamin Aaron, a distinguished conflict resolution and public policy consultant, received a folio of materials from one of his most important and demanding clients, the chief executive officer (CEO) of a leading European-based, multinational mining corporation with a major operating presence in Africa, the Middle East, and Central Asia. Aaron was aware that his client had recently been approached about joining the board of Royal Dutch Shell. The covering memo included the following:

Will be meeting with some friends in late September to discuss Shell's Niger Delta situation. Want you to develop some approaches on how Royal Dutch Shell might best handle its actions and performance in Nigeria. Ben, "think outside the box." Shell is doing a commendable job in Nigeria, but, alas, public perceptions differ markedly from the facts. Royal Dutch Shell has a significant investment stake in Nigeria; it faces continuing political risks, and the level of criticism at the local and global levels is increasing the political costs of doing business in many of its other key regions of operations. Enclosed are some materials as background reading. You probably are familiar with this material. There is much more. Don't get bogged down. I want your creative input! Confident you will come up with some solid insights and helpful suggestions. Look forward to getting your brief in four weeks' time. Diana will call you to arrange a suitable meeting time so that we may explore your views and thoughts. Cheers!

Matt

Corporate Stigma

Aaron attended the January 26, 2005, "Public Eye on Davos" press conference at which the Shell Petroleum Development Company of Nigeria (SPDC) was named villain of the Nigerian environment. The unwelcome award was made on the opening day of the World Economic Forum (WEF).

Friends of the Earth, a non-governmental organization (NGO), charged:

the Shell Company has laid its fangs and maintained a firm grip on the politics and economy of Nigeria thereby distorting its core values and impoverishing the people . . .

A former Nigerian Minister of Petroleum Resources, Dan Etete, in frustration decried that Shell and the other oil companies in Nigeria were short-changing the government and people of Nigeria.[1]

To be named an irresponsible company was a bit hard to take, given the stakeholder consultative actions Royal Dutch Shell in Nigeria had taken in recent years so as to be seen and in fact to have behaved as a socially responsible corporation. It was especially frustrating for Royal Dutch Shell board members and corporate executives that the unwelcome award announcement was being played out on an international stage before the world's media, given the attendance of the world's most powerful political and business leaders, in addition to the many NGO representatives.

The Royal Dutch Shell Group took great pride in its corporate history and was flummoxed by its Nigerian travails. At the June 28, 2004, Annual General Meetings of Royal Dutch Petroleum Company and the Shell Transport and Trading Company, p.l.c., management acknowledged that:

The Niger Delta is a very difficult and sometimes violent place in which to operate. So, as well as investing to develop Nigeria's resources, we are working with others to support community development and promote a safer and more peaceful environment. We don't always succeed. But we do keep trying.[2]

Shell's goal was not altruistic. Shell's Nigerian investment, operations, and future prospects loomed large in its overall quest for competitive sustainability and profitability in the oil industry. Conducting business in zones of conflict was difficult at best of times, and the 2005 situation in the Niger Delta was hardly a peaceful operating environment.

The past year had been especially challenging for the Royal Dutch Shell Group. Sir Philip Watts, chairman of the company, was pressured into resigning on March 3, 2004, after an internal organization investigation revealed that the Royal Dutch Shell Group overstated its oil and natural gas reserves by 20 percent. Criticism from investors over the discrepancy and especially over the company's handling of the restatement was severe. Walter van de Vijver, the chief executive of the Group's exploration and production and potential successor to Sir Philip Watts, also submitted his resignation.

Certain industry, financial, and investment circles viewed the Royal Dutch Shell Group's corporate organization structure as byzantine, one that fostered a conservative and less than transparent management approach to business, including relations with shareholders and stakeholders generally:

The recalculation was also a result of overstating reserves in Nigerian on-shore oil projects. Analysts and investors said that was unusual because estimating on-shore reserves is generally a much more exact science than determining those off-shore. Sir Philip [Watts] was chief executive of Shell's Nigerian operations from 1991 to 1994.[3]

On June 28, 2005, investors in the Hague and London voted in support of the unification of the Royal Dutch Petroleum Company and Shell Transport and Trading. The newly created Anglo-Dutch group became known as Royal Dutch Shell p.l.c. A major effect of the merger was its impact on the group's corporate governance structures. Most importantly, Royal Dutch Shell moved to the more traditional single-board structure with one chairman and one chief executive. This new structure replaced the dual-board arrangements based in Britain and the Netherlands. The single board of directors was to be chaired by a non-executive chairman. The first chief executive officer was Jeroen van der Veer, (formerly President of Royal Dutch Petroleum) and Jorma Ollila, chairman and CEO of Nokia, was appointed as the company's non-executive chairman.

At the time the Royal Dutch Shell Group was undergoing a change in leadership, SPDC was being drawn into a local political quagmire of violence and abuses around Warri in the oil-rich Niger Delta. The clashes involved the Ijaw and Itsekiri communities and members of the government security forces. Shell employees and contractors were also among the victims of the Warri clashes.

On April 7, 2003, Human Rights Watch, a major NGO, appealed in letters to the managing directors of the three main oil-operating companies in the area, Royal Dutch Shell, ChevronTexaco and TotalFinaElf:

> to publicly state that the response of government security forces must not be disproportionate to the threat . . . that their operation should be conducted in a manner that ensures respect for due process and fundamental human rights. . . . Such a statement would be consistent with the commitments the company has made under the Voluntary Principles on Security and Human Rights in the Extractive Industries. . . .[4]

Shell viewed itself as being in the vanguard of multinational corporations (MNCs) when it came to advancing and practicing sound principles of corporate social responsibility (CSR), specifically with respect to human rights:

> In 1996, the Shell Group publicly stated its support for the Universal Declaration of Human Rights. The Declaration had existed since 1948. It addresses "all organs of society" which obviously includes business. But Shell was the first energy company and one of the first multinationals to take a public stand in support of it. . . .[5]

Military Dictatorships and Human Rights

Nigeria came into existence in 1914 when Britain amalgamated two colonial protectorates into one territorial unit, the Colony and Protectorate of Nigeria. This form of nation creation was not uncommon in Africa. Europe's former colonial powers formed countries out of territories where the population included numerous distinct ethnic and political groups, each with its own language, culture, customs, and traditional types of government.

Nigerian nationalism and demands for independence pressured Britain into granting the country full independence in October 1960. Three years later, in October 1963, Nigeria altered its relationship with the United Kingdom by proclaiming itself a federal republic and promulgated a new constitution.

Nigeria's history was one of successive military dictatorships, secessionist pressures, civil war (Biafra), violations of human rights, and failed attempts at holding democratic elections. Probably the most corrupt and worst of the military governments was headed by Sani Abacha (1993–1998) who assumed power on November 17, 1993, by forcing the resignation of Ernest Shonekan, a prominent businessman. It was Abacha's government that prosecuted prominent author, journalist, and Ogoni political activist Ken Saro-Wiwa and others for their alleged roles in the killings of four prominent Ogoni politicians in May 1994. "Saro-Wiwa and 14 others pleaded not guilty to charges that they procured and counseled others to murder the politicians."[6] The trial was seen as a sham by many in Nigeria and in the West. The Ogoni Civil Disturbances Special Tribunal, established by the Abacha administration, sentenced Saro-Wiwa and eight others to death by hanging. The sentence was carried out on November 10, 1995.[7]

The Saro-Wiwa episode was a major blight on Shell's corporate reputation. The controversy surrounding Saro-Wiwa's execution and the alleged complicity involving Royal Dutch Shell in Nigeria, specifically its support of, if not acquiescence to, the brutal Abacha dictatorship was a millstone around Shell's corporate neck in oil-rich Ogoni and Nigeria generally.

Indeed, Friends of the Earth, in advance of the 10-year remembrance of the execution of Ken Saro-Wiwa and eight others, issued a press release signaling their intention to protest "Shell's record of human rights abuses and environmental damage around the world,"[8] at Shell's June 28, 2005 annual general meeting. At what was described as a heated meeting, Shell attempted to fend off criticism by the Friends of the Earth, who had flown in community leaders from countries including Nigeria, South Africa, and the Philippines. They "attacked Shell for not doing enough to clear up pollution."[9] Friends of the Earth documented their case in a report entitled, "Lessons Not Learned: The Other Shell Report 2004," released on June 28, 2005.[10]

The Saro-Wiwa cause célèbre was being kept alive in U.S. courts as well. Under a little known American law, the Alien Tort Claims Act (ATCA), a suit was filed against Shell [Ken and Owens Wiwa v. Royal Dutch Petroleum Company].

> *The plaintiffs, including non governmental organization Earthrights International, have alleged that the defendant, Royal Dutch/Shell, was complicity [sic] involved in an effort by the Nigerian government to try and ultimately execute Mr. Saro–Wiwa for his actions relating to organizing protests against Shell/Nigeria's business activities in the mid 1990s. Royal Dutch/Shell has consistently denied the plaintiffs' allegations. . . .*
>
> *In effect, the defendants have argued that the action should not be heard in a U.S. court. However, in a major victory for the plaintiffs, on Feb. 28, 2002, U.S. Federal District Court Judge Kimba Wood, ruled that the plaintiffs' allegations met the requirements of the ATCA in that the alleged actions of Royal Dutch/Shell "constituted participation in crimes against humanity, torture, summary execution, arbitrary detention, cruel, inhuman, and degrading treatment, and other violations of international law."[11]*

General Abdusalami Abubakar assumed control upon General Abacha's death in June 1998. During his short tenure, Abubakar allowed for an increase in freedoms, paving the way for local, federal, and presidential elections. The presidential election was won by former military head of state Olusegun Obasanjo, who ran as a civilian candidate. Obasanjo was released from prison by Abubakar. Not surprisingly for Nigeria, irregularities marred the vote. In spite of the irregularities, the Obasanjo administration ushered in a "comparatively" democratic government in May 1999, after 16 years of consecutive military rule.

However, communal violence, ethnic conflict, and private and public sector corruption were still pervasive in Nigeria. Despite the magnitude of the problems, the Obasanjo administration was viewed as an improvement over previous military regimes. Obasanjo's win in 1999 marked the first relatively successful election of a civilian government since 1960 when Nigeria gained independence from the United Kingdom.[12] In 2003, Olusegun Obasanjo was re-elected president.

President Obansanjo in February 2005 initiated a "national political reform conference" with the goal of addressing tensions, frequently violent that characterize the geographic, ethnic, cultural, and religious differences among the various Nigerian communities. These differences collided when delegates from the oil-producing Niger Delta walked out of the June conference. This action was taken when other delegates, especially from Nigeria's Muslim-dominated north, balked at concessions that would allow for an increase in the proportion of oil revenues to be transferred to the Delta State governments.[13]

Another significant initiative by President Olusegun Obasanjo was to appoint, in May 2005, Father Matthew Hassan Kukah as facilitator of the Ogoni reconciliation, which was to be a structured process involving the Rivers State government and the Movement for the Survival of the Ogoni People.

> *Basil Omiyi, managing director of Shell Petroleum Development Company of Nigeria Limited, said: "We warmly welcome the statements today by the President, the Rivers State Governor, and the Movement for the Survival of the Ogoni People. We will continue to do everything we can to ensure that a lasting reconciliation amongst and between Ogonis and Shell is achieved, to the benefit of all stakeholders. We look forward to working with Father Kukah, the federal and state governments, and Ogoni leaders in making the president's vision of reconciliation a reality."*

Shell was forced out of Ogoniland in January 1993 following threats to its staff and contractors.[14]

Shell Companies in Nigeria

Nigeria was Africa's largest oil producer and the eleventh largest in the world. In spite of its oil wealth, Nigeria was one of the world's poorest countries with more than 70 percent of the population living in abject poverty. The country's economy was heavily dependent on oil-sector revenues, which represented nearly 80 percent of Nigerian government revenues and 95 percent of its export earnings. Europe and the United States were Nigeria's major trading partners. Nigeria's oil resources were estimated at almost 32 billion barrels. Nigeria also had major gas reserves even greater than the country's oil reserves when translated into energy-equivalent terms.

The Royal Dutch Group of companies, one of the world's largest oil and gas multinationals, had sales of approximately $265 billion in 2004 and a workforce of some 112,000.[15] The company's vision for its Nigerian operations was "to be one of the world's leading oil and gas operating companies contributing to the sustained development of Nigeria and its people."[16] Its mission statement was "To find, produce and deliver hydrocarbons safely, responsibly and economically for the benefit of all stakeholders."[17]

Shell had pioneered the Nigerian oil and gas industry, having proven more than 50 percent of the country's oil and gas reserves. Shell had operated in Nigeria for more than 60 years, since pre-independence, and employed more than 10,000 people, 95 percent of whom were Nigerian. As the major multinational company in Nigeria's oil and gas industry, Shell recognized that it played a key role in the Nigerian economy and was committed to describing its operations in full, to all its stakeholders, and to providing evidence of its commitment to the sustainable development of Nigeria's energy resources.

Most of the oil in Nigeria came from the Niger Delta. There were five major oil companies. The largest was operated by Shell Petroleum Development Company of Nigeria Ltd., (SPDC). It was majority-owned by the Nigerian National Petroleum Corporation (NNPC) and produced nearly half of Nigeria's crude oil, with average daily production of approximately 1.1 million barrels per day. The others included ExxonMobil, ChevronTexaco, Agip, and TotalFinaElf. All operations were joint ventures with the government holding a majority share of between 55 and 60 percent. NNPC and its subsidiaries were senior partners in all major upstream ventures. In addition to its extensive downstream domestic operations, NNPC owned large reserves of oil and gas, and enjoyed a monopoly in refining and petrochemicals.[18]

Shell companies included Shell Petroleum Development Company of Nigeria Ltd. (SPDC), Shell Nigeria Exploration and Production Company Ltd. (SNEPCO), Shell Nigeria Gas Ltd. (SNG), Shell Nigeria Oil Products Ltd. (SNOP), and Nigeria Liquefied Natural Gas Company Ltd. (NLNG).[19]

SPDC

SPDC was the operator of a joint venture involving the NNPC, which held 55 percent, Shell (30 percent), TotalFinaElf (10 percent), and Agip (five percent). The partners funded the operations in proportion to their shareholdings. The company's operations were concentrated in the Niger Delta and the adjoining shallow offshore, where it operated in an oil-mining lease area of about 31,000 square kilometres. It had more than 6,000 kilometres of pipelines and flowlines, 87 flowstations, eight gas plants, and more than 1,000 producing wells.

Shell Nigeria Exploration and Production Company Ltd. (SNEPCO)

SNEPCO was established in 1993, and later that year it signed production sharing contracts with the NNPC to operate two deep-water and three onshore licenses. SNEPCO made the first major deep-water discovery (Bonga) in Nigeria in 1995.

Shell Nigeria Gas Ltd. (SNG)

This company was incorporated in March 1998 to promote gas utilization as a cheaper, more reliable, and cleaner fuel alternative and feedstock for industry. SNG was driven by the vision that natural gas would overtake liquid fuel as the fuel of first choice for Nigerian industries by 2010.

Shell Nigeria Oil Products Ltd. (SNOP)

SNOP was incorporated in Nigeria during the last quarter of 2000. The company was expected to develop and maintain the market for Shell-branded products and services to customers in Nigeria. The company's vision was to become the largest supplier of refined petroleum products in the country.

Nigeria Liquefied Natural Gas Company Ltd. (NLNG)

Shell had a 25.6 percent shareholding in NLNG and was also the technical adviser. Its partners in this company were NNPC (49 percent), TotalFinaElf (15 percent) and Agip (10.4 percent). The company supplied liquefied natural gas to markets in Europe and the United States.

Shell Companies in Nigeria (SCiN)

Shell Companies in Nigeria (SCiN) were part of the Shell Group. While SCiN enjoy significant autonomy, they shared a set of "Business Principles" enunciated worldwide. "The core values of the Shell Group as laid out in our Business Principles were honesty, integrity and respect for people."[20] According to Shell, meeting the expectations of Nigerian society, in an honest and transparent way was essential to its mode of operations. "We adhere to the group's Business Principles as the bedrock of our business dealings and are enforcing zero tolerance of bribery, corruption and unfair trade and competition."[21] But to do so realistically, Shell acknowledged "it has to do business in the real world with all its complexities."[22]

The Niger Delta, where Shell's operations were mainly situated, covered an area of 70,000 square kilometres. Shell Companies in Nigeria used approximately 400 square kilometres of this land, which was acquired in accordance with the law, in negotiation with the land-owning families and communities or their accredited representatives. While most of this land was acquired for long-term use, some was required only on a short-term basis. The population of the Niger Delta was estimated to be seven million. According to Shell's management, "To ensure that our operations have a positive impact on the people whose lives we touch, we engage in continuous dialogue with the communities of the Niger Delta region and with many other important groups at an international, national, and local level."[23]

Corruption and Threats

Multinational corporations operating in zones of conflict and/or emerging economies tended to underestimate the challenges and costs of conducting business in such environments. Local politics were frequently characterized by shifting coalitions involving community leaders, political parties, union leaders, and tribal leaders. Religious and ethnic rivalries, warlords, and local bullies were known to seize on opportunities in such circumstances to advance their own goals. This was certainly the case in Nigeria. As a broad generalization, power vacuums tended to create potentially lethal uncertainty, especially when the rule of law and legal order was absent. What made the Nigerian situation even more troublesome was the inability or unwillingness of the national government to provide the necessary protection to its citizenry and economic enterprises.

Transparency International's (TI's) Corruption Perception Index 2004 ranked a record 146 countries. The list was publicly released on October 20, 2004, in London. TI declared that "most oil-producing countries are prone to high corruption" and urged Western governments "to oblige their oil companies to publish what they pay in fees, royalties and other payments to host governments and state oil companies." TI Chairman Peter Eigen believed that "access to this vital information will minimize opportunities for hiding the payment of kickbacks to secure oil tenders, a practice that has blighted the oil industry in transition and post war economies." Eigen acknowledged:

> *Many of the areas in which the issues of sustainability are neglected are areas where it is more expensive for companies to behave in a socially responsible manner. It is, for example, expensive to give up corruption when everybody else is bribing in a certain market. It is more expensive and if there are not enabling environments which force governments and enterprises alike to live up to these standards of social responsibility, then it becomes a prisoner's dilemma, facing many companies because they know if they are the first ones to behave better than their competitors they will lose business and could go bankrupt. In that sense, unfortunately, there is an [incentive] for many companies driven by shareholder value to violate these ethical standards.[24]*

Nigeria was ranked on the TI index as one of the most corrupt countries of the world, well ahead, on the corruption scale, of other oil-rich corrupt countries such as Angola, Azerbaijan, Chad, Ecuador, Indonesia, Iran, Iraq, Kazakhstan, Libya, Russia, Sudan, Venezuela, and Yemen.[25] Not surprisingly, Shell's Nigerian companies faced a bewildering range of challenges and threats.

Shell Admits Fueling Corruption[26]

On June 11, 2004, BBC News reported that Shell "admitted it inadvertently fed conflict, poverty and corruption through its oil activities in Nigeria." The news headline emerged out of a report commissioned by Shell, which was carried out by three internationally known conflict resolution experts. The report "warned that Shell could eventually be forced to withdraw from the West African country if violence in the Niger Delta escalates." To address the issues, Emmanuel Etomi, Shell's community development manager in Nigeria stated:

> *Government and local communities must take the lead [but] as part of an industry inadvertently contributing to the problem, we are prepared to help.*

The company acknowledged that operating with integrity in zones of conflict was challenging. Dismissal of career and contract staff for corrupt practices was not unusual. Another Shell spokesperson, London-based Simon Buerk, on the issue of corruption, explained:

> *To prevent money earmarked for community projects being siphoned off, Shell's Nigerian operations introduced "13 Big Rules" to tighten internal spending controls. . . . When we go to a community and offer development projects, some actually demand cash instead. Obviously once you put cash into a community it's hard to know where it goes.*

Other contentious issues identified included those related to the need to clean up oil spills, and the charge that Shell supports corrupt regimes. Chris Finlayson, chairman of Shell Companies in Nigeria, observed "We recognize that our development activities in the past have been less than perfect." The findings of the commissioned report were incorporated into The SPDC 2003 Annual Report, *People and the Environment* (April 2004). The "13 Big Rules" and Shell's sustainable community development strategies were listed in its 2003 Annual Report (see Exhibit 1).

Challenges

Shell was beset with increasing challenges. It was being challenged on two fronts: operational viability and institutional legitimacy. Labor unrest triggered by rising domestic fuel prices certainly aggravated the situation. On October 11, 2004, Nigerian unions declared a four-day strike to protest against rising fuel prices. The unions described this development as a warning strike, one the government had to address by cutting fuel prices or face a nationwide strike. Adams Oshiomhole, head of the Nigerian Labour Congress (NLC), met with Nigerian President, Olusegun Obasanjo, to try to resolve the fuel price issue in order to stave off a national strike, which potentially could have had a deleterious impact on the Nigerian economy. The fuel price increase resulted from the removal of fuel price subsidies as part of the government's economic reform package.

The major multinational company oil producers had contingency plans to allow oil to flow should a national strike materialize. The "warning strike" contributed to student unrest and militancy in Lagos, the commercial capital of Nigeria. Many businesses were shuttered. Various segments of the local population heeded the unions' warnings to stay home. Of special import, the warning strike was yet another major blow to Nigeria's oil industry.

During September, fighting between Nigerian troops and ethnic militia in the Niger Delta forced many oil workers to evacuate, negatively affecting daily oil production. The relationship between the NLC and the government was a confrontational one, so much so that the government tabled a law to outlaw the NLC. On October 21, 2004, Nigeria's union leaders declared Royal Dutch Shell "to be an enemy of the Nigerian people." Adams Oshiomhole charged that Shell sided with the Nigerian government, "a government intent on oppressing

MESSAGE FROM THE CHAIRMAN

. . . of major concern is the level of violence in the Niger Delta region. The availability of arms, the theft of crude oil, inter-communal conflicts, social disintegration and other factors have contributed to the level of insecurity and tension in the area. As this state of affairs does not present a safe environment for our staff, our contractors and the communities in and amongst whom we work, we are committed to seeking ways by which, with other stakeholders, we can contribute towards promoting peace and reducing conflict in the area.

We remain committed to corporate social responsibility, one aspect of which is our contribution towards the development of the Niger Delta and the reduction of poverty, but recognise that our development activities in the past may have been less than perfect. Our community development spend has gone down this year for various reasons. But we are committed to improving our processes for delivering future projects, examining our impact on communities and the environment in which we operate and taking corrective action. We believe that one way of improving the delivery of community development projects is through partnership, which will allow the sharing of resources and knowledge, the harnessing of expertise and should lead to the achievement of better results...

There are many ways in which businesses can contribute to sustainable development. For SPDC, and other Shell companies in Nigeria, our most significant contribution comes from carrying out our direct business activities efficiently, profitably and to high standards. It also comes from the sizeable investments we make. These create wealth for the nation, through the substantial amounts of taxes and royalties generated...

PARTNERING FOR COMMUNITY DEVELOPMENT

New Directions

Meeting basic developmental needs is a huge challenge. SPDC's approach initially reflected a traditional philanthropic or grant-making approach and concentrated on education (scholarships), agriculture, infrastructure-type projects, and health care. But by mid-1997, an internal review reported that though the majority of these projects were functional, some were poorly executed, poorly maintained and lacked sustainability...

Sustainable Community Development

During 2003, we began to lay the groundwork for a further major shift in our CD strategy. This followed another comprehensive review of our community interface activities (that is, CD and community relations) conducted in 2002. The review concluded that, whilst our current CD approach demonstrates a number of best practices, there were also critical shortcomings in some areas of our interaction with communities. In particular, it identified the need for a coordinated approach to enhance community ownership and sustainability of CD programmes, and recommended the development of strategies to address current and emerging issues in a manner that will:

- Promote sustainable social and economic development of the communities
- Partner and work with government, NGOs and development agencies in capacity building efforts
- Improve our internal processes related to CD
- Secure SPDC's licence to operate and grow, and ultimately, maximise Nigeria's oil and gas development revenues.

Based on these recommendations and subsequent preliminary work, we established in April a new Sustainable Community Development (SCD) strategy, aimed at improving the management of all community interfaces within Shell. A team was also established to undertake the detailed study, design and development of the new strategy. The team completed its work in December, following which SCD is now the next phase in our journey from CA to sustainable social development...

The SCD strategy places greater emphasis on partnerships, not just with the communities themselves, but also with government and strategic local and international development organisations and non-governmental organisations (NGOs). Such partnerships complement our own efforts, and enable solutions to be developed that we may not be able to achieve on our own, thereby accelerating developmental and employment-generating opportunities across the region. Two such partnerships were entered into during the year: with USAID—a five-year $20 million agreement that will develop Nigerian capacity in agriculture, health and business enterprise; and with Africare—a three-year $4.5 million partnership that will focus on reducing deaths from malaria . . .

SCD Policy

In order to improve the quality of life and maintain a mutually beneficial relationship with communities in the Niger Delta, SCiN shall:

- operate an efficient and cost-effective sustainable community development programme which applies world standard of practice to serve communities in its area of operations.
- enhance partnerships with all segments of the community and where appropriate with governments, donors, non-governmental organisations, and other relevant stakeholders.
- encourage full participation and ownership of projects by communities through participation in planning, implementation, monitoring and evaluation.
- develop and maintain communication with all segments of the communities in order to integrate their concerns and contributions and bring these to the attention of the appropriate authorities.
- identify and promptly manage issues arising from company operations in communities in accordance with approved procedures and statutory provisions.
- focus intervention on sustainable community development programmes that have high impact and broad benefits for the wider population...

SUSTAINABLE COMMUNITY DEVELOPMENT "BIG RULES"

Big Rules are defined and agreed as clear principles for managing community interfaces in SCiN.[27] These rules form the key to, and basis of, leadership commitment and role modelling for SCD's operating and compliance framework. The Big Rules are the basis for the prescription and documentation of processes to effect the SCD strategy. Deviation from the Big Rules will have undesired consequences on both external and internal stakeholders and jeopardise the legitimacy of the SCD operating model. They must be adhered to, to ensure commitment, integrity and accountability of all parties.

The BIG RULES are:

1. SCD sets the corporate direction and strategy of community interactions and manages corporate CD activities in the SciN.
2. All community development projects/programmes must be in accordance with the agreed/approved five-year rolling SCiN community development plan, which is aligned to the Niger Delta master plan where appropriate.
3. All community budget and expenditure must be approved and accounted for in accordance with SCD procedures.
4. SCD programmes/projects must have a sustainability plan and exit strategies and must be subjected to independent verification.
5. All new projects must have a baseline community survey and all existing projects must have a social evaluation review.
6. All community MoUs must conform to SCD guidelines and be approved by the Asset and SCD Managers.
7. Area teams are accountable for the implementation of SCD projects in line with agreed plans and SCD guidelines.
8. There shall be **no** payments to communities other than those specified for legitimate business reasons.
9. No payment for ghost workers or stand-by employment.
10. Contractors/sub-contractors working under contract with SCiN must strictly adhere to the SCD policy and procedures for community interaction.
11. SCiN must deliver on SCD commitments.
12. SCiN will strictly adhere to SCD guidelines/policies at all times, even when operational continuity is threatened.
13. The Sustainable Community Development Controls Committee (SCDCC) must approve any deviation from the above rules.

Source: 2003 Annual Report, http://www.shell.com/static/nigeria/downloads/pdfs/annualreport_2003.pdf, accessed April 17, 2005.

its own people." This development was proof enough for the NLC to accuse Royal Dutch Shell of interfering in the internal politics of Nigeria. A union threat to call a general strike was in the offing.

Disputes and conflicts between multinational corporations, governments, and communities in the Niger Delta were an ongoing problem. This vast region pumped most of Nigeria's 2.3 million barrels a day. Armed conflict, occupations, hostage taking, extortion, and sabotage were not uncommon. In early December 2004, for example, hundreds of Kula residents, including women and children, took control of three oil platforms operated by Royal Dutch Shell and ChevronTexaco, cutting off oil supplies and briefly trapping more than 100 workers. The Kula residents were peaceful protesters, however similar situations have been known to turn violent because of the opportunistic involvement of armed pirates and ethnic militants.

The Nigerian government managed to contain the dispute by promising to send a high-powered delegation to help resolve the issue. The issue that led to the protest was a long simmering one; namely, the Kula people's concern with the need for local jobs and development. The Kula people, much like other Niger Delta villagers, contended they received few benefits from the significant oil wealth being pumped from their traditional tribal lands. The Nigerian government contended that the state and local governments in the Niger Delta in fact were provided with a larger share of oil revenues than neighboring regions because of their larger contribution to the Nigerian economy. Then why the difference in perspective? Certain NGOs and civil society groups had complained that the Niger Delta region's leaders were known to be looting the money rather than allocating the funds for the purpose of enhancing local services and infrastructure, which would have benefited the local population. Human Rights Watch, an NGO, released a briefing paper that examined the violence in Nigeria's oil-rich region and presented a number of recommendations to interested parties and stakeholders on how they might best address the problems and issues (see Exhibit 2).

In December 2004, SPDC suspended exports totaling 114,000 barrels of oil per day (another 20,000 barrels involved ChevronTexaco) due to unrest in the Niger Delta. Royal Dutch Shell declared a "force majeure," informing customers it would not be able to meet export contracts from its Bonny Terminal. A Shell spokesperson voiced the view that restarting production and lifting the "force majeure" probably would not take place until the more central dispute between the Kula community and Nigerian authorities was addressed. "Political and ethnic strife in the Niger Delta region, including violence, kidnapping, sabotage and the seizure of oil facilities, often disrupts Nigerian oil production."[28]

Brokering talks to convince Kula protesters to vacate Shell facilities merely tackled a symptom. The much deeper problem had to do with the allocation and distribution of the foreign direct investment benefits in the oil industry, and the less than transparent, equitable, and socially responsible behavior of Nigerian government authorities, local Niger Delta government officials and community leaders.

Battering Shell in Nigeria was an ongoing pre-occupation. Local organizations, groups, tribal leaders, politicians, lawmakers, and guerrilla leaders who had differences with one another became united when it came to targeting Shell. Not surprisingly, Shell expatriates suffered from a siege mentality and perceived their company and themselves as scapegoats for whatever ailed Nigeria. In 2004, for example, the Nigerian senate demanded Shell pay US$1.5 billion in damages for polluting Niger Delta communities. In addition, there

THE EMERGENCE OF ARMED GROUPS IN RIVERS STATE

Since oil exploration began in Nigeria in the 1950s, the nine states that constitute the Niger Delta have been sites of intense violence, from the Biafran war of succession in the 1960s to the Ogoni uprising in the early 1990s. From 1997, Delta State, primarily in and around the capital Warri, has been the main site of violence in the delta. In late 2003, the center of violence shifted to Rivers State, principally in and around the "oil capital" of Port Harcourt.

Although the violence across the Niger Delta has manifested in different forms—in Warri it is seen as a conflict between Ijaw and Itsekeri ethnic militias, in Rivers State as a battle between Ijaw groups—it is essentially a fight for control of oil wealth and government resources. The violence in Port Harcourt has been perpetrated by two rival armed groups and their affiliates who battled to control territory and lucrative oil bunkering routes. Oil bunkering is the illegal tapping directly into oil pipelines, often at manifolds or well-heads, and the extraction of crude oil which is piped into river barges that are hidden in small tributaries. The crude is then transported to ships offshore for sale, often to other countries in West Africa but also to other farther destinations.

Both Asari's NDPVF and Tom's NDV are primarily comprised of young Ijaw men from Port Harcourt and nearby villages. In addition to these two groups, there are, according to the state government, more than 100 smaller armed groups, locally known as "cults." Many of these "cult" groups, with names such as the Icelanders, Greenlanders, KKK, Germans, Dey Gbam, Mafia Lords, and Vultures, were originally formed in the early 1990's as university fraternities, but later largely evolved into criminal gangs. In late 2003, in an effort to increase their access to weapons and other resources, many of the "cult" groups formed alliances with either Asari's or Tom's armed group as the two leaders fought for control of oil bunkering routes. Although the smaller groups retained their names and leadership structures, Asari and Tom assumed command and control responsibilities over the militant actions of these smaller groups.

The militarization of what started out as non-violent youth and "cult" groups in the 1990's and the later emergence of large, well organized armed groups like the NDPVF and NDV can be attributed to several key factors:

Violence In Nigeria's Oil Rich Rivers State in 2004

1. The manipulation of youth groups by local politicians

2. Payments made to communities by multinational oil companies and their impact on fomenting conflict over traditional leadership positions

3. Poverty, underdevelopment and widespread youth unemployment

4. The use of youth groups by conglomerates involved in the illegal theft and sale of crude oil, or illegal oil bunkering

5. Widespread availability of small arms and other weapons

6. The prevailing culture of impunity in Nigeria

The Agreement to End the Violence in Rivers State

The federal government initiative, headed by President Obasanjo to bring Asari and Tom to the negotiating table resulted in the signing of the October 1, 2004 agreement between the two armed groups. This agreement called for an immediate ceasefire, the "disbandment of all militias and militant groups" and total disarmament. Since then there have been several meetings between government officials, leaders of the various armed factions, and civil society representatives. The parties drafted a more comprehensive agreement which addressed two major issues: the disarmament of Asari's NDPVF, Tom's NDV, and their affiliated "cult" and youth group members, and the re-integration of these groups into society. In addition, numerous local committees have been established to monitor progress on these issues and examine the underlying causes of violence....

Human Rights Watch commends the government's effort to address the violence that dramatically escalated in 2004 but two issues of concern remain about the agreement:

1. The granting of amnesty to individuals responsible for serious human rights abuses, including killings, will contribute to the culture of impunity and jeopardize the prospects for peace in Rivers State. To effectively establish the rule of law and ensure lasting peace, all individuals, including government officials, responsible for murder and other serious crimes must be held fully accountable.

continued

2. The agreement fails to address the root causes of the violence, in particular the sponsorship and manipulation of youth groups by political leaders, traditional elites, and networks of "oil bunkerers," as well as the tensions created by the impact of oil company payments to communities. As the 2007 elections draw closer and local politicians jostle for positions, it is likely that frustrated youth will be easily re-mobilized unless these underlying issues are addressed.

RECOMMENDATIONS

To the Nigerian Federal and Rivers State Governments:

- Promptly investigate the 2003–2004 violence around Port Harcourt by the NDPVF and the NDV, including allegations of the role of state government officials in sponsoring armed groups. Independent investigations must also be undertaken into alleged abuses and excessive use of force by state security forces. Prosecute any individuals alleged to be responsible for serious human rights abuses, including murder and wanton destruction of property, in accordance with international fair trial standards.

- Take prompt and effective measures to ensure that families who suffered loss of lives and property as a result of human rights violations committed by government agents, including government complicity in abuses committed by the armed groups, receive appropriate reparation. Work with international donors and multinational oil companies to obtain financial and logistical assistance to assist all those who have been internally displaced, and had homes and property destroyed during the violence in late 2003 and 2004.

- Deploy adequate numbers of police in Rivers State, in particular to the riverine communities, to protect the local population from potential acts of violence by armed groups. Ensure that members of the police force deployed act professionally, impartially and in accordance with international standards.

- Take measures to stop the flow of small arms into the Niger Delta, such as the strengthening of controls over government-controlled weapons and the improvement of border security with neighbouring countries. Take the lead in pressing for the implementation of a binding regional convention on small arms to replace the ECOWAS small arms moratorium. Establish more robust mechanisms for monitoring the disarmament process.

- Provide to the public, reports on payments of oil companies to the government and government revenues derived from the extractive industries sector, as recommended by the Extractive Industries Transparency Initiative, signed onto by the Nigerian government in 2003.

- Establish a comprehensive strategy for investigating illegal oil bunkering activities, and for ensuring that such investigations and resulting arrests and prosecutions are not affected by political considerations. Explore the possibility of oil certification as a means of eliminating the role of illegal oil bunkering in fuelling the violence, by reducing the income that can be made from the illegal sale of oil.

To donor governments and international financial institutions:

- Urge the federal and state government to investigate responsibility for the 2003 and 2004 violence around Port Harcourt and to hold perpetrators of serious human rights abuses accountable.

- Provide assistance for government and civil society initiatives to assist internally displaced persons.

- Provide technical and financial assistance for initiatives to curb the flow of small arms in the Niger Delta and the wider sub-region.

- Encourage full implementation by the Nigerian government of the Extractive Industries Transparency Initiative and support the international campaign—commonly known as the "Publish What You Pay" campaign—calling for the mandatory disclosure of all taxes, fees, royalties and other payments made by companies to governments for the extraction of natural resources.

To intergovernmental institutions, including the United Nations, the African Union and ECOWAS:

- Urge the federal and state government to investigate responsibility for the 2003 and 2004 violence around Port Harcourt and to hold perpetrators of serious human rights abuses accountable.

- Take measures to stop the flow of small arms into the Niger Delta, such as the improvement of border security with neighbouring countries. Press for the implementation of a binding regional convention on small arms to replace the ECOWAS small arms moratorium.

To oil companies operating in the Niger Delta:

- Publicly and privately urge the federal and state government to investigate responsibility for the 2003 and 2004 violence around Port Harcourt and to hold perpetrators of serious human rights abuses accountable.

- Encourage full and swift implementation by the Nigerian government of the Extractive Industries Transparency Initiative.

- Publish details of all fees, royalties, contracts and other payments made to all levels of the Nigerian government and to local communities, including compensation payments and community development funding.

- Ensure credible third party audits of community development assistance, including payments that are given to community representatives to disburse or spend on community projects and employment agreements with local communities. Results of such audits should be made public to ensure that all funds are used for their stated and intended purpose.

- Explore the possibility of oil certification as a means of stopping illegal oil bunkering.

Source: Human Rights Watch website, http://hrw.org/backgrounder/africa/nigeria0205/2.htm, accessed August 19, 2005.

were many outcries resulting from violent outbreaks that involved militant protesters and armed gangs who stormed and seized Shell facilities and were met by armed Nigerian military called in to protect the Shell platforms.

Underlying the charges and grievances was the deeper issue that, in spite of the oil wealth, the minority tribes in the delta waterways—Ijaw, Ekwere, Ogoni, Itsekiri and others—continued to live in extreme poverty. There was massive unemployment among the young, and many villagers lacked such basic amenities as clean water and electricity.

Nigeria's Oil Industry Roller Coaster Ride

CNN reported on January 14, 2005, that Shell's dispute with the Kula community was resolved on January 4, 2005. Shell facilities were reopened in Nigeria, including pipelines damaged by vandalism at Egbema and at the Odeama flowstations. However, stability in the Nigerian oil industry and Shell's operations was short-lived. Some 12 days later, CNN reported that labor unrest was again threatening Nigeria's oil industry.[29]

Indeed, it would not be an exaggeration to describe operating in Nigeria's oil industry as an economic-politico-socio roller coaster experience. The Nigerian operating environment was highly complex, threatening, and generally explosive. But at the same time, its oil and gas resources were too rich for Shell to walk away from, or for that matter too tempting not to further explore and commercialize (i.e. exploit). In this context, Shell was no different from other major foreign oil companies in Nigeria, be they private or state-controlled, and headquartered in Europe, the United States or the People's Republic of China, for example.

Shell's participation in the Bonga Deepwater Project in the Niger Delta was indicative of the company's long–term commitment in Nigeria. "Bonga lies 120 kilometres south–west of the Niger Delta, in water more than 1,000 metres deep. The areal extent of the Bonga field is some 60 square kilometres. After acquiring and processing 3-D seismic in 1993/94, the first Bonga discovery well was drilled between September 1995 and January 1996. Recoverable reserves have been put at 600 million barrels (bbl) of oil."[30] Shell Nigeria Explorations and Production Ltd. held a 55 percent share in the joint venture. The other partners were Esso

(20 percent), TotalFinaELF (12.5 percent) and Agip (12.5 percent). The US $3.9 billion development was Shell's first deepwater offshore project in Nigeria, with Shell's investment share totaling US$2.1 billion. The estimated output was more than 200,000 barrels of oil and 150 million standard cubic feet (SCF) of natural gas per day.[31] Production was projected to begin in 2004, but because of operational delays, industry analysts had moved the date to 2006. Cost overruns had also swelled the Bonga budget.[32]

The Task at Hand

Benjamin Aaron's task was a formidable one, and he could not help but be amused by the irony of the consulting assignment. Royal Dutch Shell, after all, pioneered and was a major advocate of the system of scenario planning that was designed to anticipate dramatic changes. During his January 2005 participation at the World Economic Forum in Davos, he attended the new Shell Global Scenario 2005 presentation by Dr. Albert Bressand, vice president, Royal Dutch Shell Group of Companies. Exploring the future and collaborating on public interests was a stated commitment and mainstay of Shell's strength, akin to a core competency. One of the more interesting Shell pieces of information received from Matt was entitled "Case Study: Nigeria."

The material included the following information:

- The Nigerian government and Shell are leading supporters of the U.K. Government's Extractive Industries Transparency Initiative (EITI) that encourages public disclosure of the revenues received from natural resources.

- In 2003, [SPDC] became the first company to disclose the revenues it paid the Nigerian government. The publication of these figures, for the years 2001 and 2002 in the company's annual People and the Environment report, was made with the permission and full support of the Nigerian government.

- SPDC (operator of a joint venture involving [NNPC], Shell, Total, and Agip) in 2003 contributed US$1.2 billion in petroleum profit tax, US$668 million in royalties, and paid a signature bonus of $210 million.

- Nigeria is one of a number of developing countries that have already agreed to join the EITI initiative. Speaking at the 10th birthday celebrations of Transparency International, Olusegun Obasanjo, president of Nigeria, said: "The administration will seek to encourage a private sector and civil society check on the exercise of power by government, by providing information about its actions, receipts and expenditures in the oil sector."

- The position as of today is that Nigeria is resolutely committed to the "Publish What You Pay" and "Publish What You earn [sic]" initiative.

- The Nigerian government, with the assistance of the World Bank, launched the initiative with a multi-stakeholder conference in February 2004 that involved participants from government, civil society, and industry. A multi-stakeholder steering committee has been appointed to agree the practical steps necessary for full disclosure from both the government and the oil companies (including the state oil company: the [NNPC]). Shell is committed to supporting this process.[33]

The World Bank's involvement was consistent with its Low Income Countries Under Stress (LICUS) initiative that sought a new approach to engage fragile states such as Nigeria—countries sharing a specific set of development challenges linked to weak policies, weak institutions and poor governance. These challenges were particularly apparent in the Nigerian oil industry where local activists viewed the foreign multinationals not only as visible symbols of economic wealth and political power, but as convenient proxies for a federal government that was distant and insensitive to local needs and exploited local resources for its own benefit and gain.

CASE DISCUSSION QUESTIONS

1. Shell has been in Nigeria for more than 60 years. What has made Shell's operations in Nigeria more at risk and simultaneously more valuable?
2. What political risks does Shell face in Nigeria?
3. Does Shell have the option to pull out of Nigeria?
4. How do the roles of the government and the multi-national companies differ?
5. What underlying assumptions, observations, and re-commendations should Benjamin Aaron include in his brief?

CASE NOTES

[1] Ojo, G. 2005. "The Public Eye Award 2005 in the category Environment goes to: Royal Dutch/Shell Group," Friends of the Earth, Davos, January 26. http://www.evb.ch/publiceyeondavos.htm, accessed April 17.

[2] van der Veer, J. 2004. Speech, Annual General Meetings of Royal Dutch Petroleum Company and the "Shell" Transport and Trading Company, p.l.c., June 28, p. 2.

[3] Timmons, H. 2004. "UK: Shell's top executive is forced to step down." *New York Times*, March 4. http://www.corpwatch.org/article.php?id=10248, accessed April 17, 2005.

[4] Letter from Arvind Ganesan, executive director, Business and Human Rights and Peter Takirambudde, director, Africa Division to Ron van den Berg, managing director, Shell Petroleum Development Company of Nigeria, Ltd, Shell Petroleum Development Company of Nigeria, April 7, 2003.

[5] Letter from Robin Aram, vice-president External Relations, Policy and Social Responsibility, Shell International Limited, to Mr. Dzidek Kedzia, chief, Research and Right to Development Branch, United Nations High Commissioner for Human Rights, September 24, 2004.

[6] U.S. State Department. "Background Note: Nigeria." p. 5. http://www.state.gov/r/pa/ei/bgn/2836.htm, assessed August 1, 2005.

[7] Ibid.

[8] Friends of the Earth. 2005. "Shell faces community rebellion at AGM." Press Release, June 28. http://www.foe.co.uk/resource/press_releases/shell_faces_community_ rebe_27062005.html, accessed August 16, 2005.

[9] Macalister, T. 2005. "Rowdy meeting mnds Shell's 100-year split." *The Guardian*, June 29. http://www.guardian.co.uk/oil/story/0,11319,1517070,00.html#article_continue, accessed August 18, 2005.

[10] Friends of the Earth. 2005. "Lessons not learned: The other shell report 2004." June. http://www.foe.co.uk/resource/reports/lessons_not_learned.pdf, accessed August 18, 2005.

[11] 2003. "Human rights violations based on U.S. alien tort claims act may subject multinationals to liability in U.S. Courts." *International Journal of Corporate Sustainability*, March, pp. 6-3, 6-4. http://www.cesjournal.com/pages/alerts/ref/100306003s.pdf, accessed May14, 2005.

[12] U.S. State Department. pp. 6–7.

[13] *Economist.* "Nigeria: A troubled but lingering president." August 6–12, p. 38.

[14] Shell Nigeria Press Release. 2005. "Shell welcomes progress in Ogoni reconciliation process." May 31. http://www.shell.com/home/Framework?siteId=nigeria&FC2=/nigeria/html/iwgen/news_and_library/press_releases/2005/zzz_lhn.html&FC3=/nigeria/html/iwgen/news_and_library/press_releases/2005/2005_3105_31051718.html, accessed July 16, 2005.

[15] http://www.hoovers.com/free/co/factsheet, accessed April 18, 2005.

[16] Shell Nigeria Web site. "Shell's role in the Nigerian oil and gas industry." http://www.shell.com/home/Framework?siteId=nigeria&FC2=&FC3=/nigeria/html/iwgen/about_shell/what_we_do/dir_what_we_do.html, accessed April 18, 2005.

[17] Ibid.

[18] "Nigeria country analysis brief." http://www.eia.doe.gov, accessed April 18, 2005.

[19] Shell Petroleum Development Company of Nigeria Ltd., Annual Report 2003, People and the Environment, May 2004, p. 32.

[20] Shell Nigeria Web site.

[21] Ibid.

[22] Ibid.

[23] Ibid.

[24] Eigen, P. panelist. 2004. "Competition and cooperation—The State and 'Foreign Policy' by companies and NGOs," in Beyond the State?, 21st Sinclair House Debate, Herbert-Quandt-Siftung, Bad Homburg v.d. Ho he, August, p. 35.

[25] Transparency International, Corruption Perception Index 2004, p. 5. http://www.icgg.org/corruption.cpi_2004.html.

[26] Material drawn from BBC News. 2004. "Shell admits fuelling corruption," June 11. http://news.bbc.co.uk/1/hi/business/3796375.stm, accessed February 18, 2005.

[27] Shell Web site. "Case study: Nigeria," http://www.shell.com/home/Framework?siteId=royal-en...FC2=...FC3=/royal-en/html/iwgen/environment_and_society/key_issues_and_topics/issues/payments_to_governments/nigeria_case_study_05072005.html, accessed December 23, 2005.

[28] Shell Companies in Nigeria (SciN).

[29] "Nigeria country analysis brief." p. 5.

[30] Material drawn from, *CNNMoney.* 2005. "All Shell facilities reopen in Nigeria." January 14. http://money.cnn.com/2005/01/14/news/international/nigeria_shell.reut; CNN.com 2005. "Labor unrest threatens Nigeria's oil industry." January 26. http://www.cnn.com/2005/world/AFRICA/01/26/nigeria.oil. unrest.ap, accessed January 30, 2005.

[31] Shell Off-Shore Technology Web site. "Bonga deepwater project, Niger delta; Nigeria." http://www.offshore-technology.com/projocuftngal, accessed March 11, 2005.

[32] Ibid.

[33] Mortished, C. 2005. "Shell's woes mount as it admits cost overruns, and delays," *Times Online.* July 29. http://business.timesonline.co.uk/article/O„9072-1712974,00.html, accessed August 3, 2005.

Procter & Gamble: Children's Safe Drinking Water (A)

In 1995, Procter & Gamble (P&G) scientists began researching methods of water treatment for use in communities facing water crises. P&G, one of the world's largest consumer products companies, was interested in bringing industrial-quality water treatment to remote areas worldwide, because the lack of clean water, primarily in developing countries, was alarming.[1] In the latter half of the 1990s, approximately 1.1 billion (out of a worldwide population of around 5.6 billion)[2] people lacked access to clean drinking water or sanitation facilities. An estimated 6 million children died annually from diseases, including diarrhea, hookworm, and trachoma, brought about by contaminated water.[3] One report estimated that "about 400 children below age five die per hour in the developing world from waterborne diarrheal diseases"[4] and that, "at any given time, about half the population in the developing world is suffering from one or more of the six main diseases associated with water supply and sanitation."[5]

Procter & Gamble[6]

The Procter & Gamble company dated back to 1837, in Cincinnati, Ohio, when William Procter and James Gamble, married to sisters, started a soap and candle business with $3,596.47 each. By 1859, P&G sales reached $1 million, the company had 80 employees, and it was supplying the Union Army during the Civil War. Gamble's son, a trained chemist, created an inexpensive white soap in 1879 that they named "Ivory" from the biblical phrase "out of ivory palaces." Ivory soap became one of the first nationally advertised products. In the late 1880s, during a time of labor unrest throughout the country, P&G developed a pioneering profit-sharing program for factory workers, giving them a stake in the company. By 1890, P&G sold more than 30 different types of soap. The company also set up one of the first product research laboratories in the United States. In 1911, P&G developed Crisco, the first all-vegetable shortening, less expensive and considered healthier than butter.

In 1915, P&G built its first manufacturing facility outside the United States, in Canada, and established its chemicals division to formalize research procedures

Source: This case was prepared by DePaul University Professor of Business Ethics Laura P. Hartman, DePaul University's, Institute for Business and Professional Ethics Project Developer Justin Sheehan, and the Darden School's Olsson Center Senior Ethics Research Associate Jenny Mead under the supervision of Patricia H. Werhane, Ruffin Professor of Business Ethics. It was written as a basis for class discussion rather than to illustrate effective or ineffective handling of an administrative situation.

and develop new products. In 1919, Procter revised its articles of incorporation to include the directive that the "interests of the Company and its employees are inseparable." The 1920s saw several marketing innovations: P&G's Crisco was the sponsor of radio cooking shows; the company created a market research department to study consumer preferences and buying habits; and the company developed a brand management system.

As the 20th century progressed, P&G rolled out a number of new and eventually successful products and expanded its product lines through regular acquisitions of well-known and long-standing consumer brands as well as lesser-known products that showed considerable development potential. Products included: Camay (1926); Dreft, the first synthetic detergent intended for household use (1933); Drene, the first detergent-based shampoo (1934); Tide detergent and Prell shampoo (1946); Crest, the first toothpaste with fluoride (1955); Charmin toilet paper (a 1957 acquisition); Downy fabric softener (1960); Pampers (1961); Folgers coffee (a 1963 acquisition); Pringles Potato Crisps, named for a street in Cincinnati (1968); Bounce fabric softener sheets (1972); Always feminine protection (1983); Liquid Tide (1984); Vicks and Oil of Olay (separate 1985 acquisitions); Pert, a combination shampoo/conditioner (1986); Ultra Pampers and Luvs Super Baby Pants, thinner than traditional diapers (1986); Noxell, whose products were CoverGirl, Noxzema, and Clarion (a 1989 acquisition); Febreze, Dryel, and Swiffer, introduced and distributed globally in 18 months (1998); Iams canine products (a 1999 acquisition); and ThermaCare air-activated HeatWraps (2002).

Along the way, P&G celebrated its 100th anniversary in 1937 with sales of $230 million, then its 150th anniversary in 1987 as the second-oldest company among the 50 largest *Fortune* 500 companies. P&G created its first division, drug products, in 1943, and in 1978, introduced its first pharmaceutical product, Didronel (etidronate disodium)—a treatment for Paget's disease. P&G was also a leader in environmental and solid waste prevention practices. In 1988, Germany's retail grocers called P&G's refill packs for liquid products, which reduced packaging by 85%, the invention of the year. In the early 1990s, the company began using recycled plastic for more and more of its products, and in 1992, it received the World Environment Center Gold Medal for International Corporate Environmental Achievement. P&G was also recognized for its affirmative action programs by the U.S. Department of Labor, in 1994, with its Opportunity 2000 Award for commitment to instituting equal employment opportunities and creating a diverse work force. In 1998, P&G began to implement Organization 2005, designed to "push the often slow-moving P&G to innovate, to move fast with product development and marketing and with this, grow revenues, earnings, and shareholder value."[7]

The Global Water Crisis

As the 20th century came to a close, there was general agreement that the characteristics of a developed country included "[i]mproved longevity, reduced infant mortality, health, productivity, and material well-being."[8] But none of these was easily attainable unless the country had a supply of safe, drinkable water and a successful means of disposing of the household and industrial waste that often contaminated the drinking supply in developing countries.

Many of the deaths attributed to contaminated water were preventable, if a product that sanitized water was paired with effective systems of education and distribution. Most of the communities without access to clean water sources lacked the infrastructure to build large municipal water treatment facilities; often, if these facilities existed, they were hard to maintain. Inhabitants of these areas used wells or local surface water for bathing, drinking, and cooking. In addition, animals (both domesticated livestock and those that were wild) frequented the water sources, contaminating them with their feces. Heavily populated areas in some countries were susceptible to natural disaster, which often produced safe-drinking-water crises. Floods, monsoons, and earthquakes often led to the contamination of local water sources when "large runoffs of silt and clay [ran] into the catchment areas of municipal water supplies, which overwhelmed] routine sedimentation and filtration methods"[9] and overwhelmed efforts to obtain and then to distribute safe water.

The metal contaminants in water could impair the mental development of children who drank it. The main diseases that resulted from contaminated water included:

- Diarrhea, which occurred when microbial and viral pathogens existed in either food or water. Diarrheal diseases were the big killer and, if they did not result in death, brought about malnutrition and stunted growth in children, because the diseases left the body unable to absorb important nutrients long past the period of the actual diarrhea.
- *Ascaris, Dracunculisis,* Hookworm, and *Schistosomiasis* were caused by infestations of different kinds of worms. Ultimately, people suffering from them experienced disability, morbidity, and occasionally, death.
- Trachoma, which was caused by bacteria and often resulted in blindness.

In addition to the deaths and physical illnesses caused by unsafe drinking water, there were larger economic consequences. These included "economic and health costs of about 10 million person-years of time and effort annually, mostly by women and girls, carrying water from distant, often polluted sources."[10] Entire households suffered financially when the primary breadwinner became ill. Boiling water as a purification technique was time-consuming, often eating up hours each day that could better be spent raising crops as food or, for children, attending school. In short, a shortage of safe drinking water could stunt the growth of a community just as it could stunt the growth of sick and malnourished children.

The Search for a Solution

In the mid-1990s, a number of companies, such as Mioxx Corporation, Innova Pure Water, Pall, CUNO, Millipore, Ionics, and Clorox's Brita, were already in the water-purification business. Their products covered a range of needs, including household, municipal, and military. As the global water access crisis grew, however, there was greater pressure to address the needs of developing countries through new water sanitation products and the alteration of existing technology. Crucial to the success of any water purification program was developing effective models for distribution and combining them with effective education about the use of potential products. A successful program would feature a product that could offer:

- inexpensive, on the spot, or "point-of-use" treatment;
- ease of use, requiring no more than simple educational demonstrations;

• potential to fit into a long-term, sustainable distribution system flexible enough to be utilized in disaster relief efforts.

With a long history of scientific research and innovation in health, hygiene, and nutrition, P&G, with more than 200 scientists, considered ways the company could address the safe-drinking-water crisis as the millennium approached. The United Nations was drafting its Millennium Development Goals, which would be presented for resolution by the General Assembly in 2000. Included in the draft document was a 2015 goal to cut by half the world population that currently did not have access to safe drinking water. Although P&G had a vast array of successful products, the company did not offer anything that involved water purification, either domestically or in developing countries where poverty, lack of infrastructure, and inaccessibility of remote communities made the prospect of cleaning up the water more difficult.

CASE DISCUSSION QUESTIONS

1. P&G is at cross-roads and has to decide whether they want to invest in developing safe drinking water for children in poor countries. Use utilitarianism as discussed in the book to show how P&G can defend its decision to invest in the venture.

2. What are some benefits P&G can gain from developing safe drinking water for children? What are some of the costs?

3. P&G will obviously get free publicity for its efforts. Some critics of large corporations argue that companies like P&G only undertake activities that have potential to bring them goodwill and profits. Do you think that is the case with P&G? Should companies engage in charitable activities only if they have the potential to gain from the activities?

4. What should P&G do? Should they invest in the technology to develop a method to purify water? Why or why not?

CASE NOTES

[1] P&G Health Sciences Institute. "Safe drinking water." http://www.pghsi.com/pghsi/safewater, accessed 15 February 2008.

[2] U.S. Census Bureau, International Data Base. 2007. "Total midyear population for the world: 1950–2050," 16 July. http://www.census.gov/ipc/www/idb/worldpop.html, accessed 28 February, 2008.

[3] Hawkes, N. and N. Nuttall. 1995. "Seeds offer hope of pure water for the developing world." *The Times* (London), 15 September.

[4] Gadgil, A. 1998. "Drinking water in developing countries." *Annual Review of Energy and the Environment* 23, November, 254.

[5] Ibid.

[6] P&G Web site. "Our history." http://www.pg.com/company/who_we_are/ourhistory.jhtml, accessed February 15, 2008.

[7] Nugent, M. 1999. "P&G CEO sees transformation in five years." Reuters News Service, October 12.

[8] Gadgil, 264.

[9] Ibid.

[10] Ibid., 256.

Strategy Content and Formulation for Multinational Companies

5 Strategic Management in the Multinational Company: Content and Formulation

Learning Objectives

After reading this chapter you should be able to:

- Define the generic strategies of differentiation and low cost.

- Understand how low-cost and differentiation strategists make money.

- Recall multinational examples of the use of the generic strategies.

- Understand competitive advantage and the value chain and how it applies to multinational operations.

- Understand how multinational firms use offensive and defensive strategies.

- Understand the basics of multinational diversification.

- Understand how to apply the traditional strategy formulation techniques, industry and competitive analysis, and company situation analysis to the multinational company.

- Realize that the national context affects both convergence and divergence in the strategies used by multinational companies.

Preview CASE IN POINT

Fiat's Turnaround

When CEO Sergio Marchionne arrived at Fiat in 2004, the famed Italian automaker was in dire straits. Sales were down, Fiat had lost a large percentage of its European market share, and employee morale was low. Furthermore, customers did not see Fiat cars as reliable. In fact, some saw Fiat as standing for "Fix it again, Tony." However, over the next five years, Marchionne undertook a most dramatic turnaround. As soon as he arrived, he got rid of the so-called Great Man model of leadership, where senior executives waited for the boss's approval to make decisions. He appointed many young executives and now boasts that its Alfa Romeo and Fiat divisions are run by individuals in their early forties. He laid off people who were entrenched in the old way of doing things at Fiat. He also gave senior management more responsibility but also demanded more accountability. Experts also argue that Fiat's success is due to the use of common platforms for many of its new products. Using these common platforms allows Fiat to produce new cars quickly.

The results have been dramatic. Fiat is now doing very well compared to its main rivals. The company ended 2008 with $1 billion profit made from selling 2.2 million cars; that was more than GM made from selling 8 million cars. Furthermore, the company has a lineup of many new products that are selling very well, and the Retro 500 is exceeding expectations.

A further testament to Fiat's turnaround is its bid to acquire both Chrysler and Opel. Marchionne sees Chrysler as complementary to Fiat's operations. Both companies sell in the mass market, and Marchionne sees the possibility of merging with Chrysler to achieve scale efficiencies. Marchionne also believes Opel can give Fiat access to GM's market in Europe.

Sources: Based on Brown, S. 2007. "Platforms key to Fiat turnaround," Just-Auot, July, pp. 11–12; Irish Times. 2009. "Fix it again Sergio—and then fix the rest of 'em," May 6, p. 2; Kahn, G., and K. Maxwell. 2006. "Fiat's turnaround gains traction." Wall Street Journal, July 25, p. 3; Vlasic, B., and N. D. Schwartz. 2009. "In Fiat, Chrysler sees a more simpatico partner." International Herald Tribune, May 6, p. 14.

The Preview Case in Point indicates how rapidly firms can adjust their strategies in the new competitive landscape. Although Fiat seemed to be in a terrible market position, its fortunes improved quickly because of major alterations in its strategy. Successful companies like Fiat will be able to accurately predict and be prepared for quick changes in the business landscape. Furthermore, the environment facing companies has never been more complex. Companies now face global competition, extremely unpredictable environments, rapid technological change, hypercompetitive markets, and an increasing emphasis on price and quality by demanding customers.[1] In such a highly competitive environment, multinational managers must craft the competitive strategies to guide their companies toward profitability and long-term success. This chapter introduces the basic strategies that all multinational managers must be prepared to face and to master.

To develop an understanding of these strategies, this chapter presents the major components of the strategic management process in three main sections. The first section provides background on basic strategic content, as applied to the multinational firm, including the available strategic options. The second section reviews the principles of strategic formulation with applications for the multinational company, including the processes by which managers analyze their industries and companies to select a strategy.

After reading this chapter, you should understand how the basic elements of the strategic management process apply to multinational operations. You also should understand how the multinational manager is faced with more complex challenges than those a domestic-only manager encounters.

Basic Strategic Content Applied to the Multinational Company

What is a strategy? Hambrick and Fredrickson argue that statements such as "Our strategy is to be the low-cost provider" or "Our strategy is to provide excellent customer service" are not really strategies.[2] These statements represent only elements of strategies. Rather, a **strategy** is the central, comprehensive, integrated, and externally oriented set of choices of how a company will achieve its objectives. Ideally, a strategy needs to address important areas such as which businesses a company wants to be in, what the company will use to create presence in a market, and how the company will win customers.[3] For a multinational company's strategy, a major question is to decide which country to enter at what time or what products to produce. Consider the next Case in Point.

Multinational companies use many of the same strategies practiced by domestic companies, for which we present an overview next. For students with coursework in strategic management, this will serve as a partial review. However, the discussion illustrates specifically how multinational companies use basic strategies. In particular, the Cases in Point show how real multinational firms use basic strategic options in international business. After this introductory chapter, the text focuses on the strategic options that are unique to the multinational company.

Competitive Advantage and Multinational Applications of Generic Strategies

Generic strategies represent very basic ways in which both domestic and multinational companies achieve and sustain competitive advantage. **Competitive advantage** occurs when a company can outmatch its rivals in attracting and

---

Strategy
The central, comprehensive, integrated, and externally oriented set of choices of how a company will achieve its objectives.

Generic strategies
Basic ways that both domestic and multinational companies keep and achieve competitive advantage.

Competitive advantage
When a company can outmatch its rivals in attracting and maintaining its targeted customers.

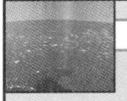

CASE IN POINT

Airbus and Boeing: Product Sequencing

In 2009, Airbus and Boeing were developing dramatically different commercial airplanes, each hoping its assumptions about the market were correct. Airbus developed the A380, believing that airlines would want an airplane that could carry 550 or more passengers between hubs, from which travelers would then transfer to smaller planes going to their final destinations. The A380 outdid Boeing's 747 as the world's largest commercial jet. In contrast, Boeing assumed that passengers would be willing to pay a premium to fly long distances. It was therefore developing the Dreamliner, the company's first new plane in ten years, which could fly 8,000 miles nonstop, or 2,000 miles more than any other plane at the time. The Dreamliner has a lightweight structure and new engines, making it

20 percent more efficient than similar planes carrying more than 200 passengers.

Both companies had their share of delays with their planes. Although Airbus received many orders for the A380, manufacturing difficulties have created many delays. Boeing is also facing similar difficulties with its Dreamliner. To make matters worse, many airlines began delaying plane orders with both Boeing and Airbus. Experts predicted that both airlines would have to cut future production significantly.

Sources: Based on Betts, P. 2009. "Boeing and Airbus fly in face of industry's tailspin." FT.com, April 20; Daily Mail. 2006. "Setback for Boeing's Dreamliner," June 20, p. 68; Michaels, Daniel. 2006. "Leading the news: Airbus scrambles to fix wiring problems; Effort aims to put production, delivery of 380 back on track." Wall Street Journal Asia, June 26, p. 3.

maintaining its targeted customers. Porter identifies the two primary generic strategies that companies use to gain competitive advantage as differentiation and low cost.[4]

Differentiation strategy
Strategy based on finding ways to provide superior value to customers.

Companies that adopt a **differentiation strategy** find ways to provide superior value to customers. Superior value comes from sources such as exceptional product quality, unique product features, rapid innovation, or high-quality service. For example, BMW competes in the world market by providing customers with very high-quality and high-performance sport touring cars. Caterpillar competes worldwide in its heavy construction equipment business by offering not only high-quality machinery but also, more important, after-sales service committed to delivering spare parts anywhere in the world.

Low-cost strategy
Producing products or services equal to those of competitors at a lower cost.

In contrast, companies that adopt a **low-cost strategy** produce or deliver products or services equal to those of their competitors, but they find a way to produce their products or to deliver their services more efficiently than the competition. In other words, they lower costs without sacrificing the level of quality that is acceptable to customers. The cost savings may occur anywhere from the creation of the product to its final sale: finding sources of cheaper raw materials, employing cheaper labor, using more efficient production methods, or using more efficient delivery methods. Porter notes, for example, that Korean steel and semiconductor firms often perform well against U.S. and Japanese firms, using low-cost strategies.[5] The Korean firms save money with low-cost and productive labor, combined with advanced and efficient production methods.

How Do Low-Cost and Differentiation Firms Make Money?

Differentiation leads to higher profits because people often pay a higher price for the extra value of a superior product or service. Levi's jeans have relatively high prices in the world market because of the special appeal of the Levi's brand. The Swiss firm Tobler/Jacobs can charge more for its specially produced chocolate than Hershey can for its mass-produced product. Tobler/Jacobs uses higher-quality ingredients, a longer processing time, and specialized distribution channels. These factors produce a high-quality product that commands a high price.[6]

High quality, service, and other unique characteristics of a differentiated product usually increase costs; that is, it takes more expensive labor or higher-quality materials to make a differentiated product or to provide a differentiated service. In addition, to make customers aware of the special value of their products or services, firms must spend more on marketing. Consequently, to maintain an acceptable profit margin, the differentiating company must increase prices to offset its additional costs.

Low-cost firms produce products or services similar to their competitors in price and value. Their competitive advantage and their additional profits come from cost savings. Every dollar, mark, or yen they save contributes to the bottom line by increasing their profit margins. Exhibit 5.1 shows how the relationships among costs, prices, and profits work for the differentiator and the low-cost strategists, compared to the average competitor. As the exhibit shows, both the differentiator and the low-cost strategist have higher profits than those of the average competitor. The next Multinational Management Brief on Ryanair shows how a low-cost competitor is gaining market share over its competitors.

Porter identifies another competitive issue regarding the two basic generic strategies, called the **focus strategy**, which is the application of a differentiation or low-cost strategy to a narrow market.[7] Focus strategy is based on **competitive scope**, which represents how broadly a firm targets its products or services. For example, companies with a narrow competitive scope may focus only on limited products, certain types of buyers, or specific geographical areas. Companies with a broad competitive scope may have many products targeted at a wide range of buyers. Auto manufacturers such as BMW target a high-income market with a few models, whereas most U.S. and Japanese auto manufacturers target a broad-income market with many models. Exhibit 5.2 shows the four subdivisions of Porter's generic strategies, including the basic differentiation and cost-leadership strategies with their broad-market or narrow-market options.

Focus strategy
Applying a differentiation or low-cost strategy to a narrow market.

Competitive scope
How broadly a firm targets its products or service.

EXHIBIT 5.1   Costs, Prices, and Profits for Differentiation and Low-Cost Strategies

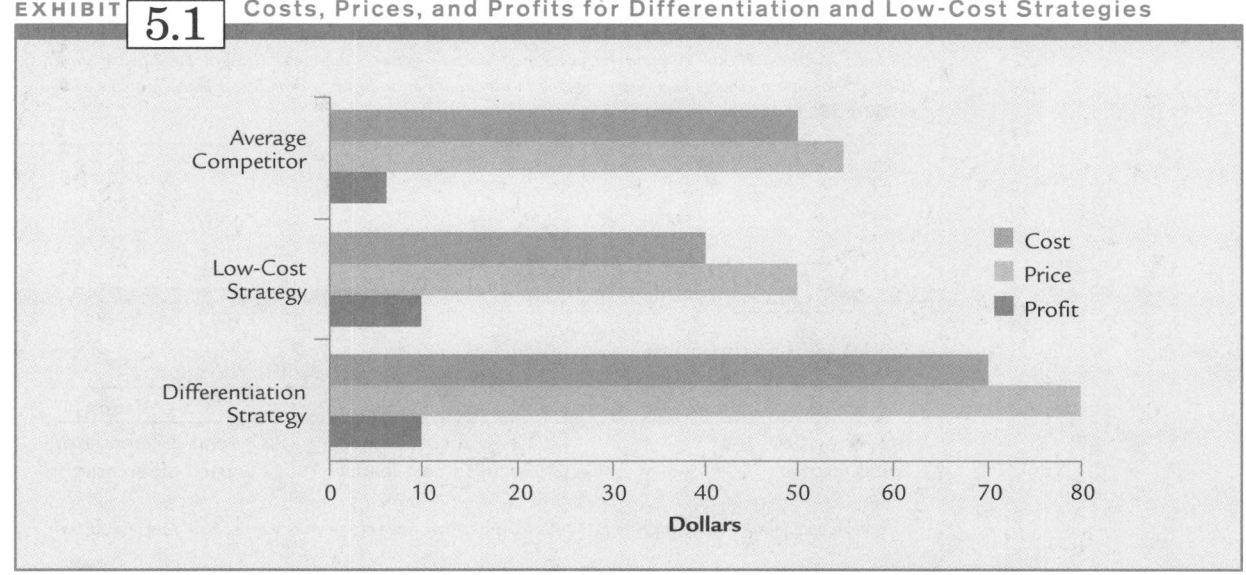

Multinational Management **Brief**

Ryanair: Taking Cost Leadership to the Next Level

Ryanair has become one of Europe's most popular and profitable airlines. While other European airlines struggled, Ryanair's obsessive commitment to keeping costs low resulted in an impressive 12 percent increase between April 2008 and April 2009. Ryanair's similarity to Southwest Airlines is not coincidental. Michael O'Leary, the company CEO, went to Dallas to meet Southwest Airlines executives to learn some lessons that could be used in Ireland. Similar to Southwest Airlines, Ryanair uses a single type of aircraft and focuses on smaller and cheaper airports. Passengers are offered open seating, meaning that Ryanair does not need to maintain complicated seating systems. However, Ryanair has also found other innovative ways to cut costs. For instance, it decided to remove all seat-back pockets in its airplanes. This move reduces not only weight, resulting in better fuel efficiency, but also cleaning expenses.

However, Ryanair seems to be taking the cost-leadership approach to the next level. While it works tirelessly to reduce operational costs, it is finding new ways to get more revenue from each traveler. For instance, Ryanair charges passengers for all amenities on the plane, and, last year, in-flight beverages generated $61 million in revenues. Similarly, Ryanair started charging $3.50 per bag for checked-in luggage and expects to save $36 million in fuel and handling costs. Ninety-eight percent of Ryanair's customers buy their tickets online, making its Web site the largest travel site in Europe. This has enabled Ryanair to use its site for marketing purposes while getting commissions on other items such as car rentals or hotel room bookings. Ryanair also sells advertising opportunities when repainting the exterior of the planes. The company is even charging consumers £1 for using the lavatories on the aircraft. While passengers have reacted to the news with incredulity, this intense focus on finding new sources of revenue and on reducing costs is indicative of Ryanair's financial success.

Ryanair's goal is to offer the ultimate in cost leadership: free air travel. Will it be successful? Some think that the company can achieve that goal. Consider that it already offers free travel for more than a quarter of its passengers.

Sources: Adapted from M2 Presswire. 2009. "Ryanair's 5.3 April passengers double those of British Airways," May 6; Maier, Matthew. 2006. "A radical fix for airlines: Make flying free." Business 2.0, April, pp. 32–34; Smyth, C. 2009. "Ryanair may charge passengers 1 pound to use lavatories on flights." Wall Street Journal, online edition February 28.

EXHIBIT 5.2   Porter's Generic Strategies

Scope of Competitive Target	Source of Competitive Advantage	
	Lower Cost	Differentiation
Broad market	General cost leader	General differentiator
Niche market	Focused cost leader	Focused differentiator

Source: Adapted from Porter, Michael E. 1990. Competitive Advantage of Nations. New York: Free Press.

Competitive Advantage and the Value Chain

A firm can gain a competitive advantage over other firms by finding sources of lower cost or differentiation in any of its activities—from getting the necessary raw materials, through production, to sales, and eventually to follow-up with after-sales service. For example, a company may save cost by obtaining cheap raw materials or cheap labor in other countries. A multinational company may base its differentiation on the excellent R&D of its subsidiary in a country where high-quality engineering talent is cheap. Many multinational software design companies, for example, take advantage of the very high number of quality engineers in India and Singapore.

A convenient way of thinking about a firm's activities is in terms of the **value chain**. According to Michael Porter, the term "value chain" represents all the activities that a firm uses "to design, produce, market, deliver, and support its product."[8] The value chain consists of areas where a firm can create value for customers. Better designs, more efficient production, and better service all represent value added in the chain. Ultimately, the value a company produces represents what customers will pay for a product or service. Exhibit 5.3 shows a picture of the value chain. Later, you will see that the value chain provides a useful way of thinking about how multinational companies operate.

Porter divides the value chain into primary and support activities. These activities represent (1) the processes of creating goods or services and (2) the organizational mechanisms necessary to support the creative activities. *Primary activities* involve the physical actions of creating (or serving), selling, and providing after-sale service of products. Early activities in the value chain, such as R&D and dealing with suppliers, are called *upstream*. Later value chain activities, such as sales and dealing with distribution channels, represent *downstream* activities. *Support activities* include systems for human resources management (e.g., recruitment and selection procedures), organizational design and control (e.g., structural form and accounting procedures), and a firm's basic technology.

The utility of the value chain is that it enables companies to determine its internal cost structure by assessing the cost levels associated with the different

Value chain
All the activities that a firm uses to design, produce, market, deliver, and support its product.

EXHIBIT 5.3   The Value Chain

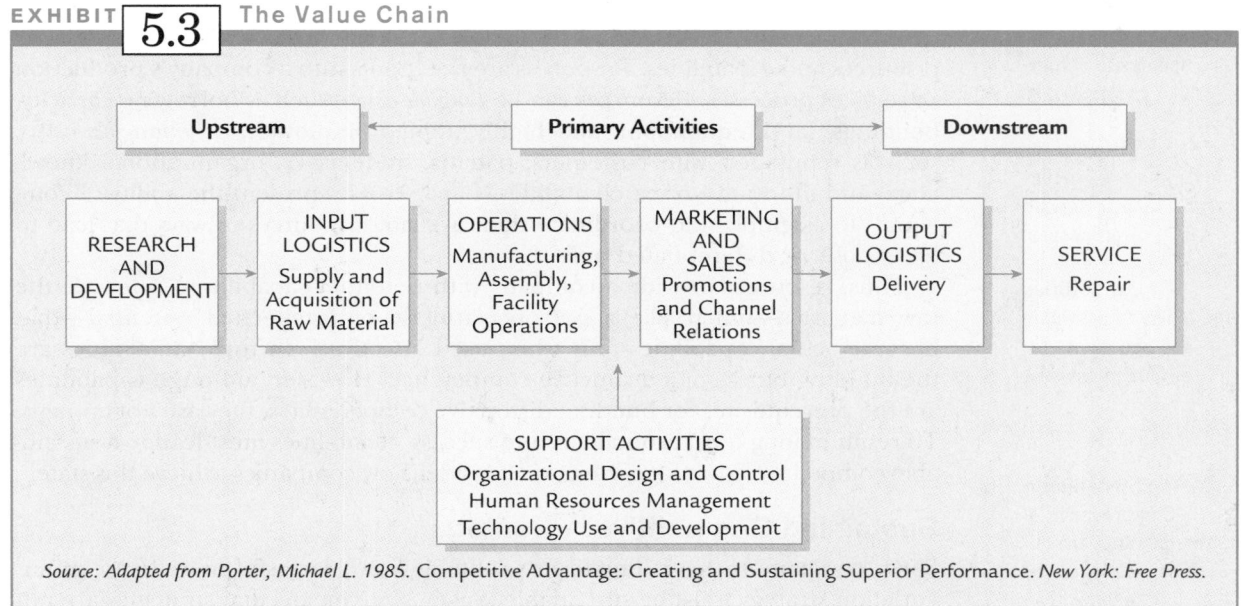

Source: Adapted from Porter, Michael L. 1985. Competitive Advantage: Creating and Sustaining Superior Performance. New York: Free Press.

activities.[9] Comparing internal cost structure against the industry or other competitors provides the multinational company with information about the relative efficiency of its internal activities. This benchmarking exercise also provides important guidance on which activities are sources of internal cost advantage or disadvantage. To become more competitive, most multinational firms need to find ways to correct cost disadvantages.

Of all the ways to correct internal cost disadvantages, one of the most popular and controversial is outsourcing, which is the deliberate decision to have outsiders or strategic allies perform certain activities in the value chain.[10] Merrifield argues that, if current trends continue, about half of U.S. manufacturing jobs will be outsourced to more than 28 emerging countries over the next ten years.[11] However, outsourcing is not limited to manufacturing. Consider that 28 developing, low-wage countries currently offer about 4.3 million engineers with the skills to work for U.S. multinational companies and that within the next few years about 10 percent of U.S. service jobs may be outsourced.[12]

When should a multinational company outsource? In general, outsourcing makes sense if an outsider can perform a value chain task better or more cheaply.[13] However, outsourced tasks should be ones that are not crucial to the company's ability to achieve competitive advantage. For example, functions of low strategic value (e.g., billing services, maintenance services, benefits management) are frequently outsourced.

Many multinational companies are considering shifting manufacturing to emerging markets such as China because of the cost savings. Consider the next Focus on Emerging Markets regarding outsourcing to China.

The value chain thus identifies the areas in the input, throughput, and output processes where multinational companies can find sources of differentiation or lower costs. In the search for those sources, the company must take advantage of the distinctive competencies in its value chain. What distinctive competencies are and where they come from are the topics of the next section.

Distinctive Competencies

Distinctive competencies are the strengths anywhere in the value chain that allow a company to outperform rivals in areas such as efficiency, quality, innovation, or customer service.[14] Distinctive competencies come from two related sources: resources and capabilities. Resources are the inputs into a company's production or services processes. Resources can be *tangible assets,* such as borrowing capacity, buildings, land, equipment, and highly trained employees, or *intangible assets,* such as reputation with customers, patents, trademarks, organizational knowledge, and innovative research abilities. Capabilities represent the ability of companies to assemble and coordinate their available resources in ways that lead to lower costs or differentiated output.

Thus, resources provide a company with potential capabilities. They are the raw materials—much like a person's athletic or intellectual potential—that become actual capabilities only when used effectively. In turn, capabilities are the building blocks of a distinctive competence. However, although capabilities are the prerequisites for building distinctive competencies, they are not enough. To result in long-term profitability and success, capabilities must lead to a sustainable competitive advantage. Next, we consider how companies achieve this state.

Sustaining Competitive Advantage

For a company to have long-term profitability, a successful low-cost or differentiation strategy must be sustainable. Sustainable means that strategies are not

---

Outsourcing
The deliberate decision to have outsiders or strategic allies perform certain activities in the value chain.

Distinctive competencies
Strengths that allow companies to outperform rivals.

Resources
Inputs into the production or service processes.

Capabilities
The ability to assemble and coordinate resources effectively.

Sustainable
Characteristic of strategies that are not easily defeated by competitors.

Focus on Emerging Markets

Outsourcing to China

China's recent economic growth and its easing of rules and regulations mean that more companies are outsourcing manufacturing to China. However, before making any outsourcing commitment, multinational companies' management must understand some key issues:

- *The local business environment:* China is a big country with great variations in business conditions and customs, and it is important to understand and adapt to such differences.
- *Availability and cost of resources:* Management cannot assume that labor is inexpensive everywhere in China. Interior provinces, such as Sichuan and Anhui, do provide cheap labor, but the coastal areas, such as Shanghai and Guandong, are experiencing skilled labor shortages. Energy supply also varies greatly from location to location.
- *Local contacts:* Companies need to respect local officials if they want to be successful. Having face-to-face meetings to build such respect and relationships is essential.
- *Local laws:* Navigating the legal environment in China can be challenging. The levels of government and inconsistencies in application of laws and regulations can frustrate outsourcing plans.

Nevertheless, with the economic crisis of 2008–2009 and the consequent drop in manufacturing, China began working to boost its services sector to encourage outsourcing. It has promised relocating services companies such perks as tax breaks, financial support, subsidies, and intellectual property rights. China hopes to benefit from this effort.

Sources: Adapted from Business Wire. 2009. "China's service outsourcing emerging amidst economic recession." April 14, online; Pan, Alexander. 2006. "Manufacturing in China? Key facts for getting started." Financial Executive, April, 22(3), p. 19.

---

easily neutralized or attacked by competitors.[15] Sustainability is traced to the nature of a company's capabilities. Capabilities that lead to competitive advantage must have four characteristics:[16] They must be valuable, rare, difficult to imitate, and nonsubstitutable.

Valuable capabilities create demand for a company's services or products or give companies cost advantages.

Rare capabilities are those that a company has but that are possessed by no competitor or by only a few competitors. For example, Boeing and Airbus are two companies with the rare technological capability to design and manufacture large commercial aircraft.

As we've seen, either providing customers superior value or delivering products or services at lower cost results in increased profit margins. Competitors seek high profits by imitating or substituting for these capabilities. Thus, for a competitive advantage to be sustainable or long-term, a company's capabilities must be not only valuable and rare, but also difficult to imitate or nonsubstitutable.

Difficult-to-imitate capabilities are not easily copied by competitors. One of the most imitated sources of lower costs in the international marketplace is cheap labor. Competitors with access to the same international labor pools quickly duplicate the cost advantage of locating manufacturing facilities in countries with cheap labor. In addition, wage rates in countries with cheap labor often rise faster than productivity, gradually undermining those cost advantages.

Nonsubstitutable capabilities leave no strategic equivalent available to competitors. For example, many early e-commerce companies, such as Amazon.com, developed capabilities to conduct business over the Internet. Not only have these models been easy to copy, but competitors have also substituted for these capabilities by outsourcing such procedures as Web site building and translation. In contrast, consider the example of Toyota in the next Case in Point, which shows how Toyota uses strategic capabilities that competitors have found difficult to copy or for which competitors have been unable to create substitutes.

Exhibit 5.4 summarizes the relationships among resources, capabilities, distinctive competencies, and eventual profitability.

C A S E   I N   P O I N T

Toyota's Distinctive Competencies Along the Value Chain: Strategic Capabilities in Cost Reductions, Quality, and Service

Although Toyota seemed to be suffering from the global economic crisis of 2008–2009, it remained Japan's number one automaker and went on to become the world's number one car manufacturer. Its competitive advantages over other automakers from Japan, Europe, and the United States are the firm's distinctive competencies in cost reduction and high-quality materials and service. Using techniques such as just-in-time production and lean manufacturing, Toyota has transformed itself from a small car manufacturer to a global giant.

How did it achieve such a feat? Upstream in the value chain, to bring new models to market more quickly and cheaply, Toyota combines manufacturing and production engineering, thereby eliminating mistakes in production design and reducing cost. Toyota designs cars with the objectives of using fewer parts, tying up fewer production machines, and reducing production times. For example, the company's redesigned Corolla model had 25 percent fewer parts, was 10 percent lighter, and was more fuel efficient than previous models. Of the $1 billion necessary to design a new model and build the plants to produce it, tools and machinery can account for three-quarters of the cost.

The mastery of *kanban*, the just-in-time production system, provides a basis of cost reduction and customer service. Not only do suppliers deliver materials just in time, as now happens for many U.S. manufacturers, but the whole value chain also works just in time.

Downstream, in the marketing and sales component of the value chain, Toyota dealers use online computers to order models directly from the factory. A built-to-order car can be delivered in as few as five days using its virtual production system. The system precisely calculates the types and timing of parts to arrive on the assembly line exactly when needed for a particular production mix. Even with this design flexibility, Toyota uses only 14 person-hours to assemble a car, compared with 22 for Honda and Ford. However, Toyota also has distinctive competencies in developing engines that are more fuel efficient than those of the American Big Three automakers. This manufacturing efficiency also translates into bigger profits, with Toyota's average profit margin per vehicle at 9.4 percent compared to GM's 3 percent. Thus Toyota has the advantage not only of being the cost leader but also of being perceived by consumers as being among the highest-quality manufacturers.

Sources: Based on Bunkley, Nick. 2006. "Gas prices stall U.S. sales of big vehicles: Detroit's Asian rivals benefit, helped by fuel-efficiency reputation." International Herald Tribune, June 5, p. 11; Jiji Press English News Service. 1999. "Toyota shrinks car production time to 5 days." August 6; Norton, L. P. 2009. "Toyota hits a roadblock." Barron's, April 27, 89(17), p. M9; Peterson, Thane. 2000. "Toyota's Fujio Cho: Price competition will be brutal." April, http://www.businessweek .com; Pande, S. 2009. "Lean manufacturing, just-in-time are hallmark manufacturing philosophies that have dominated production practices since the 1950s." Business Today, April 19; and Williams, Chambers G. III. 2003. "Toyota strategy includes San Antonio expansion." Knight Ridder Tribune Business News, February 7.

EXHIBIT **5.4**   How Distinctive Competencies Lead to Successful Strategies

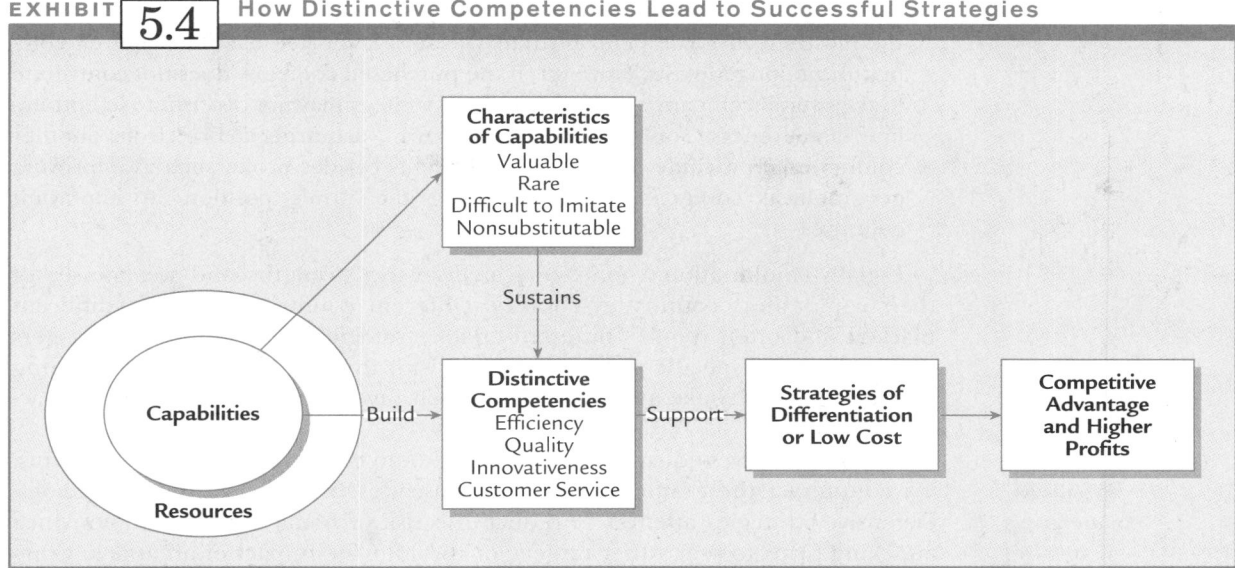

Companies also develop strategies that directly target rival firms, some of which the following section reviews from the vantage point of the multinational company.

Offensive and Defensive Competitive Strategies in International Markets

Besides using basic generic strategies in their operations, multinational companies use several strategic moves called **competitive strategies**. Competitive strategies can be offensive or defensive. In *offensive* strategies, companies directly target rivals from whom they wish to capture market share. For example, an attacking company may suddenly drop its prices or add new features to its products that compete with its rival's products. In *defensive* strategies, companies seek to beat back or discourage their rivals' offensive strategies. For example, a firm might match a rival's lower prices or give distributors volume discounts to discourage customers from shifting to a rival's products.

Examples of **offensive competitive strategies** include direct attacks, end-run offensives, preemptive strategies, and acquisitions.[17]

- *Direct attacks:* Direct attacks include price cutting, adding new features, comparison advertisements that show lesser quality in a competitor's products, or going after neglected or poorly served market segments.

- *End-run offensives:* Companies try to avoid direct competition and seek unoccupied markets. In international competition, unoccupied markets are usually countries ignored or underserved by competitors.

- *Preemptive competitive strategies:* These strategies involve being the first to gain a particular advantageous position. Advantages might include getting the best suppliers of raw material, buying the best locations, or getting the best customers. In international markets, being the first company with a global strategy can bring great advantages. For example, a multinational company can seek the best raw material anywhere in the world, or it can work to become the first company to have its brand recognized worldwide.

Competitive strategies
Moves multinational firms use to defeat competitors.

Offensive competitive strategies
Direct attacks, end-run offensives, preemptive strategies, and acquisitions.

- *Acquisitions:* In this type of acquisition, a firm buys its competitor. This can be the most effective competitive strategy against rivals because the acquired competitor no longer exists. However, if the purchased company does not contribute to the overall company's performance, the strategy may not contribute to bottom-line effectiveness. For the multinational firm, acquiring a firm from another country might include other strategic benefits besides profit, such as improving geographical coverage or strengthening the firm's position in important countries.

Usually, multinational managers analyze the strengths and weaknesses of their competitors country by country. Different countries represent different markets and often require different attack strategies. Consequently, managers develop country-specific plans for dealing with their competitors and deciding whether to attack, take an end-run approach (avoid direct competition), or acquire the rivals.

In a competitive industry, all managers should expect attacks from rival firms. To counteract these attacks, companies use **defensive competitive strategies**. Defensive strategies attempt to reduce the risk of being attacked, to convince attacking firms to seek other targets, or to blunt the impact of an attack. Companies may defend themselves at several points on the value chain. For example, a firm may sign exclusive contracts with the best suppliers, thus blocking competitors' access to raw materials. A company can introduce new models and match its competitors' lower prices. A firm may get exclusive contracts with distributors or provide better warranties or after-sales service. To scare off potential challengers, firms may make public announcements about their willingness to fight. Rivals then realize that an attack will be costly, and they often decide it is not worth the risk. Attacked firms can also **counterparry**, a popular strategy for multinationals. In international markets, the counterparry fends off a competitor's attack in one country by attacking it in another country, usually the competitor's home country. This strategy draws resources from the competitor and weakens its attack. The tactic is most successful when the rival firm is forced to protect its established home markets. Kodak used this strategy to defend against Fuji. When Fuji attacked Kodak in the U.S. market, Kodak countered by attacking Fuji in Japan. Goodyear used the same strategy against Michelin. When Michelin attacked Goodyear with low prices in the United States, Goodyear countered by attacking Michelin in Europe.

Next, we discuss how multinational companies use diversification in the international marketplace.

Multinational Diversification Strategy

Most of the strategic options discussed so far pertain to the operation of a single business, and they are called **business-level strategies**. However, many corporations have more than one type of business. Strategies for multibusiness companies are called **corporate-level strategies**, which concern how companies choose their mix of different businesses. When a company moves from a single type of business into two or more businesses, this type of move is called diversification. There are two types of diversification: related and unrelated.

In **related diversification**, companies start or acquire businesses that are similar in some way to their original or core business. These similarities can exist all along the value chain. Firms choose related diversification for three basic reasons: sharing activities, transferring core competencies, and developing market power.[18] *Sharing activities* along the value chain can include the common

---

Defensive competitive strategies
Attempts to reduce the risks of being attacked, to convince an attacking firm to seek other targets, or to blunt the impact of any attack.

Counterparry
Fending off a competitor's attack in one country by attacking in another country, usually the competitor's home country.

Business-level strategies
Those for a single business operation.

Corporate-level strategies
How companies choose their mixture of different businesses.

Related diversification
A mix of businesses with similar products and markets.

purchasing of similar raw material, the common production of similar components, and the sharing of sales forces, advertising, and distribution activities. Companies such as Honda *transfer core competencies* across units by using similar technologies in their internal combustion engines for motorcycles and lawn mowers. Nike transferred its core competency in brand recognition when it added a clothing line to its athletic shoe operations. Firms use related diversification to build *market power* by attacking rivals with multipoint competition or with competition in more than one area and by vertical integration Vertical integration allows firms to internalize supply (e.g., coffee growing for a company like Starbucks) or other downstream components of their value chain (e.g., direct sales). Integration can result in greater profits if it leads to lower costs or to improved bases of diversification.

In **unrelated diversification**, firms acquire businesses in any industry, and their main concern is only whether an acquisition is a good financial investment.[19] Businesses can be acquired as long-term investments. If so, the acquired firm has potential for growth, but it does not have the financial or other resources necessary to grow without help. To reach its potential, the acquired company needs the parent company's financial or managerial resources. Businesses can also be acquired as short-term investments. In this case, the parent company hopes to sell off the acquired firm's assets for more than the cost of acquisition. In addition, some firms look for businesses in industries with different economic cycles. In this way, the parent firm can remain profitable even if one industry is in an unprofitable economic cycle.

> **Unrelated diversification**
> A mix of businesses in any industry.

Like domestic companies, multinational firms also pursue diversification strategies. Acquiring a business in another country is a quick way to gain a presence and often a recognized brand name. The multinational company with related diversification can also coordinate and use resources, such as R&D from different businesses located anywhere in the world, to gain competitive advantages. It can more easily establish global brand names for different but related products. Diversified multinational companies can cross-subsidize, both across countries and across companies, to attack rivals in different countries. Cross-subsidization means that money generated in one country or from one company of a corporation provides resources to sister organizations in other countries or other companies to undercut their local competition.

However, diversification is not without its costs, and multinationals need to balance its benefits with the added costs. For instance, companies diversifying into new countries face the liability and related costs of newness and foreignness (i.e., being new and foreign in a country) and the coordination and administration costs of managing a more complex organization. Recent research by Quian, Li, Li, and Quian suggests that multinationals can benefit tremendously by diversifying on a regional basis up to some point.[20] Diversification into regions allows the multinational to enter markets that are fairly similar, reducing costs associated with the diversification efforts. However, beyond a certain point, higher levels of diversification actually hurt a multinationals' profits. Multinationals that operate in a moderate number of regions optimize their performance. Exhibit 5.5 shows a selection of Global Fortune 500 diversified multinational companies with their major lines of businesses.

Strategy Content: Brief Conclusions

The first section of this chapter provided an overview of the content or makeup of basic strategies: generic, competitive, and diversified. Like solely domestic firms, multinational companies use these strategies to achieve and maintain

EXHIBIT 5.5 Examples of Diversified Multinationals

Company (headquarters location)	Major Lines of Business	Countries	Revenues ($ million)	Profits ($ million)	Number of employees
GE (U.S.)	Aircraft engines, aerospace, appliances, communications and services, electrical distribution and control, financial services, industrial and power systems, lighting, medical systems, motors, NBC, plastics, transportation	100+	176,656.00	22,208.00	327,000
Siemens (Germany)	Automation and drives, automotive systems, computers, industrial projects and technical services, mobile information and communication, information and communication networks, medical engineering, power distribution and transmission, power generation, production and logistics system, building technologies, business services, design and exhibition, financial services, real estate management, transportation systems	190	106,440.00	5,062.60	386,200
Samsung (South Korea)	Mobile phones, television sets, camcorders, MP3 players, computers and related products, semiconductors, business telephone systems, networking, home appliances, fiber optics	50+	106,006.50	7,958.50	144,000
Nestlé (Switzerland)	Drinks, dairy products, chocolate and confectionery, culinary products, frozen food and ice cream, food service products, hotels and restaurants, instant food and dietetic products, pet foods, pharmaceutical products and cosmetics, refrigerated products	113	89,630.00	8,874.50	276,000
Procter & Gamble (U.S.)	Health, beauty care, industrial chemicals, beverages and food, laundry and cleaning detergents, food services and lodging, paper	140	64,760.00	10,340.00	138,000
Mitsui (Japan)	Iron and steel, nonferrous metals, property, service, construction, machinery chemicals, energy, foods, textiles, general merchandise	88	50,252.30	3,590.70	144,000

Sources: Based on Fortune. 2009. Global 500. http://money.cnn.com; Siemens. 2009. http://www.siemens; Mitsui. 2009. http://www.mitsui.co.jp; Procter & Gamble. 2006. http://www.pg.com; Samsung. 2009. http://www.samsung.com; and General Electric. 2009. http://www.ge.com.

competitive advantage over rivals. The next section reviews traditional strategy formulation techniques as applied to the multinational company.

Strategy Formulation: Traditional Approaches

Managers use several common techniques as aids in formulating their strategies. In general, **strategy formulation** is the process by which managers select the strategies to be used by their company.

In this section, we review some of the popular types of analyses that provide managers with the information to formulate successful strategies. These analyses help managers understand: (1) the competitive dynamics of their industry, (2) their company's competitive position in the industry, (3) the opportunities and threats faced by their company, and (4) their organization's strengths and weaknesses. This information allows managers to choose strategies that best fit their firm's unique situation.

Strategy formulation
Process by which managers select the strategies to be used by their company.

Industry and Competitive Analyses

Companies compete within industries, meaning that industries are the main competitive arenas of a company's business activities. To formulate effective strategies, managers must understand their industries well. They must know the forces affecting the industry, its economic characteristics, and the driving forces of change and competition within it.

Porter's five forces model is a popular technique that can help a multinational manager understand the major forces at work in the industry and the industry's degree of attractiveness.[21] The first important force to consider is the degree of competition in the industry. For instance, there is a high degree of global competition among auto manufacturers, and such competition has a significant influence on the profitability of the industry and on the strategic moves of the players.

Porter's five forces model
A popular technique that can help a multination firm understand the major forces at work in the industry and its degree of attractiveness.

The second force to evaluate is the threat of new entrants. Companies need to consider the degree to which they may face new competitors in their industry. The threat of new entrants is generally dependent on barriers to entry, as shown in the next Case in Point.

The third force in Porter's model is the bargaining power of buyers, which is the degree to which buyers of the industry's products can influence competitors within the industry. Most experts argue that buyers are becoming increasingly sophisticated globally and will have an ever growing influence on most industries. To remain competitive, therefore, most companies will have to create innovative products and services at low prices.[22]

To understand any industry, multinational companies must also look at the bargaining power of suppliers, the fourth force. Suppliers tend to have high power if they can exert significant influence on competitors within the industry. DeBeers, for example, controls a significant proportion of the supply of diamonds and has significant influence on the global diamond market.

The final force is the threat of substitutes: the extent to which competitors are confronted with alternatives to their products. For instance, Netflix, the company that pioneered Web-based DVD rental, along with other competitors like Blockbuster and Amazon.com, is threatened by substitutes in the form of Web-based movies on demand.[23] In such industries, the threat of substitutes is high.

C A S E   I N   P O I N T

Barriers to Entry in the Computer Industry

Many of the computer giants are facing antitrust lawsuits and problems. For instance, in 2009 the European Union was set to rule on whether to impose a billion-Euro fine on Intel. Microsoft, IBM, and Google have all faced lawsuits, both within the United States and around the world. Microsoft will soon face the European Union in Brussels to defend itself against accusations that it bundled its Web browser with its operating system to discourage competition. Why are these companies constantly dealing with antitrust lawsuits?

A big factor is that the industry is dominated by a few companies that benefit from maintaining significant barriers to entry. Consider the microprocessor industry. The market is now controlled by two major competitors: Intel and AMD, with Intel clearly the dominant player. To enter that industry, new players

will have to invest massive amounts of capital to develop products that can effectively compete against the existing products. Furthermore, both Intel and AMD have strong followings, and any new company will have to fight the branding inertia. Finally, the companies within an industry can create barriers to entry. For instance, Intel has been criticized for offering rebates and discounts to retailers who sell a limited number of PCs running on AMD. Similarly, Microsoft has been accused of stifling competition by bundling its Web browser with Windows. The European Union is expected to ask Microsoft to include rival browsers and to give consumers the choice of their preferred browsers when buying a PC.

Source: Based on Economist. *2009. "Technology and antitrust. Here we go again," May 9, pp. 63–64.*

Although Porter's five forces model is a powerful technique to understand domestic competition, multinational firms can use it to examine their industries in other countries. The model allows multinational firms to determine the attractiveness of their industries and to ascertain which forces require attention. Such analyses can be very helpful as strategies are crafted.

The next important step in understanding an industry is to assess its dominant economic characteristics, which affect how strategies work. Issues that influence strategy selection include market size, ease of entry and exit, and whether there are economies of scale in production.[24] For example, markets with high growth rates often attract new competitors, and companies in such industries must be prepared to execute defensive strategies against the new rivals. Michael Porter argues that strategists must also monitor several driving forces of change in an industry.[25] These forces include the speed of new product innovations, technological changes, and changing societal attitudes and lifestyles. For example, rapidly changing technology creates the risk of being quickly overtaken by competitors; firms must respond by emphasizing innovation. Industries are also affected by the extent of competition. Competition is increased by such forces as the power of key suppliers and buyers or the threat of potential new entries into the industry.[26] Knowing your industry can be the key to strategic survival.

An analysis of an industry helps the manager identify the characteristics of companies and of their products or services that lead to competitive success. For example, in some industries, speed to market with a new product might be the key. Intel maintains dominance in the microprocessor industry by continually beating its rivals to the market with the next generation of computer chips. In other industries, high-quality designs may be critical for competitive success.

The factors that lead to success in an industry are called **key success factors** (**KSFs**). Each factor can have a different degree of importance in various industries or within the same industry at different points in time. Possible KSFs are:[27]

Key success factors (KSFs) Important characteristics of a company or its product that lead to success in an industry.

- Innovative technology or products.
- A broad product line.
- Effective distribution channels.
- Price advantages.
- Effective promotion.
- Superior physical facilities or skilled labor.
- Experience of the firm in business.
- The cost position for raw materials.
- The cost position for production.
- R&D quality.
- Financial assets.
- Product quality.
- The quality of human resources.

A knowledge of industry dynamics and KSFs helps both multinational and domestic managers formulate strategies to achieve their key goals. With an understanding of what drives competition in the industry and what the successful firms do to achieve and maintain their profitability, managers can formulate strategies that have the best chance of success for their firms. The next Case in Point shows how South African Breweries uses a knowledge of KSFs to defend its monopoly in the South African beer market.

Understanding an industry and identifying KSFs represent only some of the analysis necessary to formulate successful strategies. Managers must also understand and anticipate their competitors' strategies. One technique used to assess rivals is a **competitor analysis**, which is a profile of a competitor's strategies and objectives. It can help you select an offensive or defensive competitive strategy based on the current or anticipated actions of your rivals.

Competitor analysis
Profile of a competitor's strategies and objectives.

The competitor analysis has four steps:

1. *Identifying the basic strategic intent of competitors:* Strategic intent consists of the broad strategic objectives of the firm, such as to be the market share leader or to be a company known for its technological innovation.

2. *Identifying the generic strategies used and anticipated to be used by competitors (e. g., producing at the lowest cost):* This information helps managers determine which KSFs are currently the most important to competitors and the most likely to be important in the future. For example, cheap labor cost might be an important KSF for a competitor's low-cost strategy.

3. *Identifying the offensive and defensive competitive strategies currently used or anticipated to be used by rivals.*

4. *Assessing the current positions of competitors:* An example is identifying the market leader or the companies losing market share.

Understanding current and anticipated competitive moves by rival firms allows managers to plan offensive or defensive strategies for their own firms. For example, if a competitor uses a differentiation strategy based on high-quality products, a company may attack by matching or exceeding that quality at a lower price.

To formulate their competitive strategies, multinational companies use a country-by-country competitive analysis. In this way, a company can make competitive moves based on a specific competitive strategy for each competitor

Mastery of Local KSFs: SABMiller (South African Breweries Miller) Defends Its Local Markets

SABMiller is touted as one of South Africa's major multinationals, growing from a small local brewery to the world's second largest. Having merged with Coors and Miller, it now has 86 breweries in 31 countries. How has it become so strong?

One of SABMiller's key success factors is its mastery of local markets. It is one of the dominant players in the South African alcoholic beverages market with a 97 percent market share in beer and more than 60 percent of the liquor market. However, SABMiller dominates the South African market not because its beers have a unique taste or quality but rather because the company has the distinctive competency to meet the complex demands of the local market.

The key success factor for selling beer in South Africa is mastery of the distribution channel. In South Africa, most beer is sold through *shebeens,* unlicensed pubs left over from the time of apartheid, when the sale of alcohol to blacks was illegal. Although most *shebeens* are in poor and rural areas with bad roads and an unstable supply of electricity, the government allows them to exist to discourage the use of potentially lethal home brews.

SABMiller does not sell directly to the illegal pubs but works through local distributors and independent truck drivers. Loyal to SAB, many of the truck drivers are former employees who started their delivery businesses with help from SAB. In remote towns and villages, SAB provides refrigerators and generators to make sure their beer is cold. SAB is also a cost leader with very efficient production, allowing it to reduce prices by more than 50 percent over the last decade and to serve poor, price-sensitive customers.

Foreign brewers often consider trying to break SAB's monopoly in South Africa, as Diageo did when it launched Smirnoff Ice in 1999. SAB, however, countered with a similar product named Brutal Fruit, which is now one of the best-selling flavored alcoholic drinks. Like Diageo, foreign companies would have to develop the competency to build a competitive distribution channel in this unique region.

Despite its merger with U.S.-based Miller, SABMiller is trying to stay close to its roots. The firm is heavily involved in affirmative action and in other socially responsible programs in South Africa. Furthermore, although the company's headquarters moved to London, six of the eight members of the executive committee and the chief executive are all South African nationals.

Sources: Based on Mawson, N. 2009. "SABMiller grows from 'dusty operation' into a global giant." BusinessDay, March 27; Reed, John. 2005. "How SAB Miller stayed dominant at home while aiming to go global." Financial Times, October, 12.

in each country. Exhibit 5.6 shows hypothetical competitive profiles of four companies in different countries. Using this hypothetical illustration, a multinational manager might decide to avoid attacking Bronson, Inc., the dominant leader, in its home market. Bronson has threatened retaliation.

Company-Situation Analysis

Each company faces a unique situation in the competitive business world. Managers must understand what *their* particular company can and cannot do best, realistically assessing their company's resources and strategic capabilities. In addition, they must identify any opportunities for or threats to their company's unique position in the industry.

The most common tool for a company-situation analysis is called the SWOT, an acronym for strengths, weaknesses, opportunities, and threats. The SWOT has an internal component, which focuses on an organization's *strengths* and *weaknesses,* and an external component, which focuses on *opportunities* or *threats* from the environment.

SWOT
The analysis of an organization's internal strengths and weaknesses and the opportunities or threats from the environment.

EXHIBIT 5.6   Hypothetical Country-by-Country Competitive Analysis of Rivals

Rivals	Strategic Issues	Canada	Mexico	France	Taiwan
Bronson, Inc. (United States)	Strategic Intent	Dominant leader	Maintain position	Dominant leader	Move into the top five
	Generic Strategies	Low cost	Low cost	Low cost	Differentiation based on foreign image
	Competitive Strategies	Defensive based on threat of retaliation	None	Offensive price cutting	Offensive price cutting
	Current Position	Market leader	Middle of the pack	Increasing share: No. 2	New entry
Leroux (Belgium)	Strategic Intent	Overtake the leader	Move up a notch	Dominant leader	Survive
	Generic Strategies	Differentiation based on brand name	Differentiation based on brand name	Differentiation based on brand name	Differentiation based on brand name
	Competitive Strategies	Price cutting based on counter-parry	Price cutting based on counter-parry	Provide resources for counter-parries	Price cutting based on counter-parry
	Current Position	Holding at No. 3	Market leader	New entry; too early to tell	Holding at No. 2
Shin, Ltd. (Singapore)	Strategic Intent	Gain and hold market share	Gain and hold market share	Gain and hold market share	Gain and hold market share
	Generic Strategies	Differentiation based on high quality	Differentiation based on high quality	Differentiation based on high quality	Differentiation based on high quality
	Competitive Strategies	Offensive by comparative advertisements	Offensive by comparative advertisements	Defensive, lock in long-term contracts	Defensive, lock in long-term contracts
	Current Position	Middle of the pack	Middle of the pack, but rising	Market leader	Market leader
Keio, Ltd. (Japan)	Strategic Intent	New entry, rising fast	New entry, rising fast	Expected to enter this year	New entry, rising fast
	Generic Strategies	To catch and pass the leaders	To catch and pass the leaders	To catch and pass the leaders	To catch and pass the leaders
	Competitive Strategies	Low cost based on cheap labor	Low cost based on cheap labor	Low cost based on cheap labor	Low cost based on cheap labor
	Current Position	Heavy discounts based on volume purchases	Heavy discounts based on volume purchases	Heavy discounts based on volume purchases	Heavy discounts based on volume purchases

A *strength* is a distinctive capability, resource, skill, or other advantage of an organization relative to its competitors. Strengths may come from technological superiority, innovative products, high efficiencies and low costs, human resource capabilities, marketing and promotional strengths, or other factors.

A *weakness* is any competitive disadvantage of a company relative to its competitors. To identify relevant strengths or weaknesses, managers must assess their organizations' distinctive competencies that can lead to sustainable competitive advantage when matched with an appropriate strategy. Relevant strengths and weaknesses are often industry specific and depend on the KSFs in a company's industry. Companies attempt to build their strategies on their strengths. For example, if you can produce at lower costs, you can underprice your rivals. If you can innovate quickly, you can be first to market with a new product.

Opportunities are favorable conditions in a firm's environment. *Threats* are unfavorable conditions in the environment. Threats come from any changes that challenge a company's position in its industry: for example, new competitors, such as Korean electronics makers in the United States; technological change; political change; or changes in import regulations. Opportunities often come from the same sources as threats. Hence, a threat for one company may seem like an opportunity for another. For example, Honda, Toyota, and Nissan view Europe as the next opportunity after the United States for their luxury models Acura, Lexus, and Infinity. BMW and Mercedes, however, view their Japanese rivals' moves into the upscale European car market as a major threat. New markets often constitute important opportunities. Consider the next Multinational Management Brief on emerging markets and opportunities.

Multinational Management **Brief**

Emerging Markets and Opportunities

As more and more multinationals look for new markets, China is becoming increasingly attractive, but opportunities are not always in the big cities. In larger cities such as Shanghai and Fuzhou, retail space per household exceeds that of many more developed countries. Yet, although retail space is readily available, the high real estate and advertising costs in these cities are pushing multinationals to look for opportunities in the 300 so-called Tier-2 cities with populations over a million. Tier-2 cities, such as Yantai, Shaoxing, and Wuix, now represent over 88 percent of China's GDP. Furthermore, the middle class has been growing at almost the same rate as in Tier-1 cities for the last decade. Companies like France's Carrefour and L'Oreal and U.S.-based Wal-Mart are targeting these smaller cities. Of the 30 stores Wal-Mart opened in China in 2007, only two were in big cities (Shanghai and Beijing), and Carrefour opened its first store in one of the Tier-2 cities in 2007.

Banks are going even further to find new markets. The rural areas in China are often seen as impoverished and backward. However, these rural areas represent the financial needs of over 750 million farmers and a very large number of vibrant small- and medium-sized enterprises. Furthermore, the lending rate ceilings are not as strict in these areas as in others, and banks can make wider profit margins. HBSC has acquired banking licenses to operate in the rural district in the Hubei province. Citibank and Standard Chartered have similar plans to enter the rural Chinese financial industry.

Sources: Based on Lannes, B., and L. Zhu. 2009. "Hunting for fortune in postcrisis China." Far Eastern Economic Review, *172(1), pp. 45–48; Ong, L. 2009. "Gold in China's rural hills."* Far Eastern Economic Review, *172(1), pp. 48–51.*

The SWOT analysis for the multinational company is more complex than for the domestic company, especially for assessing opportunities and threats. Multinational companies face more complex general and operating environments because they compete in two or more countries. Each country provides its own national context, which may present its particular opportunities or threats. Import or export barriers may make shipping products or bringing in supplies prohibitively expensive. Volatile exchange rates may make an otherwise attractive business environment threatening. Local inflation may play havoc with prices for the international market. Changes in government policies may affect the ability to repatriate earnings (i.e., get the company's money out of the country). In conducting a SWOT, therefore, multinational managers must conduct an extremely thorough analysis of the business environment in each country, and a country-by-country SWOT is probably the most prudent approach.

Corporate Strategy Selection

A diversified corporation has a portfolio (a selection) of businesses, with the primary goal of investing in profitable businesses. The major strategic question is which businesses in the portfolio are targets for growth and investment and which are targets for divestment or harvesting. Targets for growth and investment receive additional corporate resources because managers anticipate high returns. Targets for divestment are businesses that managers decide to sell or liquidate. Targets for harvesting are usually mature and profitable businesses that managers see as sources of cash for other investments.

One way of assessing a corporate business portfolio is through a matrix analysis. While several consultants and companies have developed their own business matrix systems to assess business portfolios, a popular one is the growth-share matrix of the Boston Consulting Group (BCG). This matrix is used to decide how much of its resources a corporation should devote to any unit. The BCG growth-share matrix divides businesses into four categories based on the industry growth rate and the relative market share of the business in question. The most attractive businesses are those in fast growing industries in which the business has a relatively large market share compared to the most successful firm in the industry. Businesses in this category are called *stars*. In contrast, *dogs* are businesses with relatively low market shares in low-growth industries. *Cash cows* are businesses in slow-growth industries where the company has a strong market share. *Problem children* are businesses in high-growth industries where the company has a poor market share. For each type of business, the growth-share matrix has a suggested strategy, as shown in Exhibit 5.7.

Another popular portfolio matrix is the GE portfolio matrix. This matrix contains nine cells based on high, medium, and low levels of industry attractiveness and on strong, average, and weak levels of a business's competitive position in the industry. Some indicators of industry strength are market size and growth rate. Competitive position is based on the strategic capabilities of a business, such as lower costs for production. The matrix is used to determine the competitive position of a business in its industry.

For the diversified multinational company, the portfolio assessment becomes more complex because market share and industry growth are seldom the same in all the countries in which a multinational competes. Thus, as illustrated in Exhibit 5.7 showing a cross-country BCG analysis, portfolio analyses must be conducted for each business in each country or region of operation.

This is only a brief review of some of the analytical techniques used to formulate strategy for the multinational company. The challenge for the

EXHIBIT **5.7**   **BCG Growth-Share Matrix for a Diversified Multinational Company**

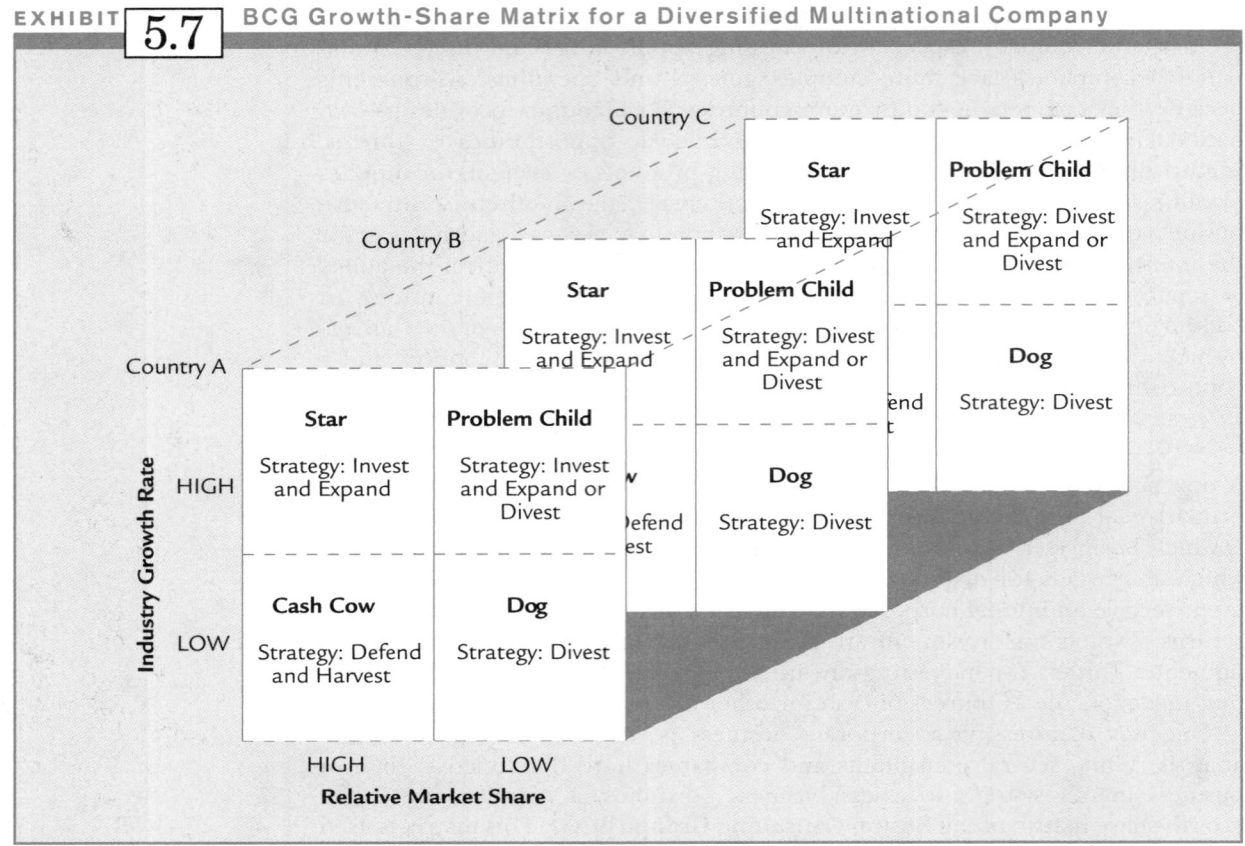

multinational manager is to use these and other techniques in the highly complex and evolving world of international competition.

The next section shows how broad institutional forces can affect the choice of strategies for the multinational company and its competitors. Specifically, the final section presents an overview of how the national context leads to country-by-country differences in strategic management practices.

The National Context and Organizational Strategy: Overview and Observations

The national context—the immediate environment where firms compete—directly affects organizational strategy and design. These environments provide firms with nation-specific opportunities and threats; that is, the specific combinations of opportunities and threats in any given nation are different from those in other nations. As a result, the varieties of national contexts enable different industries to flourish and different strategies to be effective.

The national context affects organizational design and strategy formulation and content through the following processes:

• The social institutions and national and business cultures encourage or discourage certain forms of businesses and strategies in each nation. There are generally acceptable and unacceptable ways of conducting business.

- Each nation must rely on its available factor conditions for developing industries and the firms within industries. Factor conditions play a role in shaping each country's unique resource base, and local firms have easy access to local resources. Consequently, local firms are likely to favor similar strategies that take advantage of their unique bundle of local resources.

- Social institutions and culture determine which resources are used, how they are used, and which resources are developed. The resource base limits the strategic options available to multinational companies.

These points provide a general picture of the processes by which national context affects strategic management. Multinational managers can go on to generalize and apply these ideas in order to understand the actions of rivals or alliance partners in any country where their firms do business.

Summary and Conclusions

The business environment becomes increasingly global each day. Few students who read this book will work in industries untouched by global competition, and many will work for multinational companies or their subsidiaries. Consequently, managers need to have a good understanding of multinational business strategy. This chapter provides a foundation and the basic terminology to understand the strategic issues facing the multinational manager.

To formulate strategies, multinational managers use many of the same tools available to domestic managers. Differing from the solely domestic firm, however, the multinational company always faces more complex situations. Basic strategies that work in one country may not work in another. Competitive strategies must be considered on a country-by-country basis. The multinational company and its rivals are seldom in the same competitive positions in all the countries in which they compete. Although there are global trends of convergence in strategies, the institutional and cultural conditions favor different strategies by competitors from different nations. Multinational managers must be aware

of these differences because they affect both collaborators and competitors. Because of these complexities and those of a multicountry economic and political environment, the multinational manager faces continuous challenges in strategy formulation.

The multinational manager also must realize that strategy is a combination of planned intent and adaptive reactions to changing circumstances. The techniques discussed in this and the following chapters refer to the planned aspects of strategy: what managers determine is the best game plan given the nature of their companies and of the competitive and general environments. Modifying or changing strategies in response to new opportunities and new threats is a necessity in today's world of rapid cross-border competition.

Beyond the traditional strategic questions facing all managers, the multinational manager must confront other issues related to strategy. Chapter 6 will deal directly with these issues and introduce the global-local dilemma facing multinational companies. Chapter 6 will also present an array of strategies that multinational companies use to participate in different markets.

Discussion Questions

1. Discuss how a multinational firm might use a low-cost strategy in one country while using a differentiation strategy in another country.

2. Identify examples of how multinational companies have used the offensive competitive strategies discussed in the chapter.

3. How can a multinational competitor such as Wal-Mart attack multinational rivals using the counterparry?

4. Discuss the advantages that multinational companies might have over domestic rivals in sustaining competitive advantage.

5. Identify and discuss the KSFs that are most likely to vary by national context. Explain your answer.

Multinational Management **Skill Builder**

Identifying Distinctive Competencies and Generic Strategies

Step 1. Choose a global industry, such as the automobile industry or the cell phone industry, and identify two to four major competitors in the industry.

Step 2. Research the selected companies in the popular business press, and make a list of the unique capabilities of each company. Identify where on the value chain these capabilities exist.

Step 3. For each company, write a one-page analysis showing how these capabilities lead to distinctive competencies.

Step 4. For each company, write a one-page analysis showing how the company attempts to use its distinctive competencies to successfully implement a generic strategy. Note whether companies have different generic strategies for different products or for different market segments.

Endnotes

1 Hitt, Michael A., B. W. Keats, and S. M. DeMarie. 1998. "Navigating in the new competitive landscape: Building competitive advantage and strategic flexibility in the 21st century." *Academy of Management Executive*, 12, pp. 22–42.

2 Hambrick, Donald C., and James W. Fredrickson. 2005. "Are you sure you have a strategy?" *Academy of Management Executive*, 19 (4), pp. 51–62.

3 Ibid.

4 Porter, Michael E. 1990. *Competitive Advantage of Nations*. New York: Free Press.

5 Ibid.

6 Ibid.

7 Ibid.

8 Porter, Michael E. 1985. *Competitive Advantage: Creating and Sustaining Superior Performance*. New York: Free Press.

9 Thompson, Arthur A. Jr., A. J. Strickland III, and John E. Gamble. 2007. *Crafting and Executing Strategy*. Homewood, IL: McGraw-Hill Irwin.

10 Ibid.

11 Merrifield, Bruce. 2006. "Make outsourcing a core competency." *Research Technology Management*, May–June, 49(3), pp. 10–13.

12 Ibid.

13 Kakumanu, Prasad, and Anthony Portanova. 2006. "Outsourcing: Its benefits, drawbacks and other related issues. *Journal of American Academy of Business*, September, 9(2), pp. 1–7.

14 Hill, Charles, W. L. Jones, and Gareth R. Jones. 2001. *Strategic Management Theory*. Houghton Mifflin: Boston, p. 137.

15 Aaker, David A. 1989. "Managing assets and skills: The key to sustainable competitive advantage." *California Management Review*, 31, pp. 91–106.

16 Barney, J. B. 1991. "Firm resources and sustained competitive advantage." *Journal of Management*, 17, pp. 99–120.

17 Thompson, Strickland, and Gamble; Yip, George S. 2002. *Total Global Strategy II*. NJ: Prentice Hall: Englewood Cliffs.

18 Ibid.

19 Thompson, Strickland, and Gamble.

20 Qian, G., L. Li, J. Li, and Z. Qian. 2008. "Regional diversification and firm performance. *Journal of International Business Studies*, 39, pp. 197–214.

21 Thompson, Strickland, and Gamble.

22 Hitt, Keats, and DeMarie.

23 Heilemann, John. 2005. "Showtime for Netflix." *Business 2.0*, March, pp. 36–38.

24 Thompson, Strickland, and Gamble.

25 Porter, Michael E. 1980. *Competitive Strategy: Techniques for Analyzing Industries and Competitors*. New York: Free Press.

26 Porter, Michael E. 1979. "How competitive forces shape strategy." *Harvard Business Review*, 57, March–April, pp. 137–145.

27 Pearce, John A. II, and Richard B. Robinson Jr. 1994. *Strategic Management: Formulation, Implementation, and Control*. Burr Ridge, IL: Irwin; Thompson, Strickland, and Gamble.

Harley-Davidson, Inc.: Troubled Times Increase H-D's Reliance on International Sales

James W. Bronson, University of Wisconsin–Whitewater
Margaret L. Kuchan, University of Wisconsin–Whitewater

2009 Mission Statement, as stated on the company Web site: We inspire and fulfill dreams around the world through Harley-Davidson motorcycling experiences.

2007 Mission Statement: We fulfill dreams through the experience of motorcycling, by providing to motorcyclists, and to the general public, an expanding line of motorcycles, branded products, and services in selected market segments.

Harley-Davidson, the over-100-year-old manufacturer of motorcycles, turned a corner in 2008–2009, but it was largely the wrong corner. Total sales for 2008 were down 4 percent from the company's 2006 high. Sales in North America, the company's dominant market, were off 17 percent, and the company estimated its total sales would be down an additional 10–13 percent in 2009. Part of the problem could be attributed to selling a luxury good during a recession, but Harley-Davidson (H-D) had also made some notable tactical errors.

Harley-Davidson's Financial Services (HDFS) had financed the sale of motorcycles to buyers of questionable financial means. These motorcycle loans were resulting in a high default rate. H-D's questionable loans and high default rate closely paralleled the 2008–2009 bank crisis brought on by subprime mortgages. H-D wrote off $80 million in loans in 2008, and 2009 is expected to be worse. Where H-D had been a Wall Street darling since the early 1990s, as of mid-2009 it is on many sell lists.

The most damaging aspect of loan default was not the loss on the loans, but the thousands of used H-D motorcycles that entered the marketplace at bargain prices. Traditionally, used H-D motorcycles had retained their value, and value retention was a major selling point. However, the glut of used H-D motorcycles not only eroded the sales of new H-D motorcycles but significantly reduced the value of H-D owners' investments.

H-D had been touted as a model for favorable labor relations management for many years. This era may have come to an end in 2008 when H-D announced the layoff of up to 1,500 employees, or about 15 percent of the company's workforce. While the labor force was being reduced as the result of declining domestic sales and diminished profits, outgoing CEO James Ziemer's pay jumped from $4,447,713 in 2007 to $5,625,595 in 2008, a 26.5 percent increase.

The bright spot for H-D was international sales. Between 2006 and 2008 H-D's international revenue increased by 49 percent. During the same period the number of motorcycles sold in international markets grew 28 percent, while the domestic market decreased 25 percent.

H-D produces and sells only heavyweight motorcycles under the H-D brand. These motorcycles, showcasing chrome and flawless paint, are intended to make a statement for their owners. It can be an expensive statement; 2009 base prices ranged from $6,999 for the smallest model, the venerable Sportster, to over $29,999 for the massive Tri Glide Ultra Classic. Accessories, shipping, import tariffs, and other duties and licenses can more than double the factory price in offshore markets. The company also manufactures about 13,000 motorcycles a year under the Buell brand.

The company has defined the heavyweight segment as motorcycles with engines displacing a minimum of 651 cc. Following a decade of short supply, the production of H-D heavyweight motorcycles rose markedly in the first six years of the twenty-first century. A portion of the rise in production was attributable to a nontraditional design, the V-Rod or VRSC. Introduced for the 2002 model year, H-D's VRSC model merged engineering from German auto manufacturer Porsche with H-D's classic design. Increased production capacity and a slowing domestic market were driving H-D's increased focus on international markets.

International Market for Luxury Goods

Economists define luxury goods and services as goods for which demand increases more than proportionally

H-D Units Sold	2008	Percentage Change (%)	2007	Percentage Change (%)	2006	Percentage Change (%)	2005	Percentage Change (%)	2004
Domestic	206,309	−15	241,539	−12	273,312	3	266,507	2	260,607
International	97,170	9	89,080	17	75,984	22	62,510	10	56,682
Total	303,479	−8	330,619	5	349,196	6	329,017	4	317,289

Harley-Davidson: Motorcycle Sales in Units: Domestic and International Markets

as income rises. From a sociocultural perspective, a luxury good is seen as a product at the highest end of the market in terms of design, quality, durability, performance, and price. The definition of luxury is not solely objective; it is also subjective as a function of the buyers' personal circumstances and the status the good conveys. The concept of luxury evolves constantly with the ever shifting economic, demographic, sociocultural, and geopolitical climate. Classic luxury goods include haute couture items such as clothing, perfume, and luggage. Most products and services have a luxury segment, such as cars, hotels, and even chocolate. Bain and Company, consultants, put the value of the global market for luxury goods at $201 billion. Estimates of this market can vary widely depending on the goods and services included and range up to $1 trillion. What does not vary widely are estimates of the global decline in the luxury good market, about 10 percent for 2009. The decline will be even higher in the United States, where sales are expected to be off 15 percent. Not all markets for luxury goods are expected to contract; China should be up 7 percent. Whether sold in the domestic or international market, H-D motorcycles fall into the highest end of the market in terms of price, quality, and finish—the luxury segment of the motorcycle market.

North and South America The United States consumes roughly 25 percent of the world's luxury goods, with the remainder of North and South America consuming an additional 8 percent. In the United States, four million households have an income of more than $1 million. This population defines the luxury sector through its patronage. There are an additional 18 million households in the U.S. with incomes over $100,000. Although the purchase of luxury goods is less frequent in these 18 million households, their collective purchase of luxury goods is a significant share of the market. The purchasers of luxury goods are not price resistant, but they do want to know what they get for their money. Thus, companies must demonstrate that not only are their products luxurious but that they will also add value to the consumer's lifestyle.

Europe The estimates for the size of the European luxury good market is currently 38 percent of the global

market. Europe is the spiritual home of luxury goods and the originator of many traditional brands, such as Chanel, Louis Vuitton, and Ferrari. European demographics bear many similarities to those in the United States. However, in Europe income growth has been more evenly distributed across the population. Europe also has doubled the population of seniors. Those seniors control more wealth and are more likely to spend that wealth on luxury goods.

Japan Japan is the home of the largest Louis Vuitton store, a fact that seems appropriate given that 94 percent of Tokyo women in their 20s own something from Louis Vuitton. Japanese luxury goods retailers account for 12 percent of the global market, and they often charge 40 percent more than in the European market. Prestige is valued in Japanese culture, and external signs of status are evident.

China China, together with India and Russia, is part of what is seen as the so-called golden triangle of the newly wealthy who are thirsty for luxury goods. These growth markets are attractive to Western luxury goods businesses, whose sales efforts have traditionally been concentrated on the United States, Europe, and Japan. China currently accounts for 3 percent of the global market for luxury goods. China is expected to pass Japan to become the world's second-largest purchaser of luxury goods by 2015. Consumers are status conscious, increasingly wealthy, hungry for brand image, and fanatical about shopping. A recent survey of young urbanites on the Chinese mainland found that over 60 percent of them are prone to buying high-end consumer goods. On the average, luxury goods consumption accounts for 4 percent of consumer spending, but in China the proportion is estimated to be as high as 40 percent.

India Of all Indian households, 1.6 million spend an average of $9,000 a year on luxury items. India has the highest wage growth in Asia. Multi-income families and increasing international exposure are driving a sociocultural transition from saving to spending. Sales of luxury products have risen by 20 percent per year, and consumers want the latest models and exclusive editions. India's luxury car market has tripled in the past five years despite import duties of about 100 percent.

Russia Russia accounts for 5 percent of the global luxury goods market. The country is producing today's most determinedly conspicuous consumers and may rival China as the fastest growing market for luxury goods. A lot of this spending is abroad, as more than 23 million Russians travel outside the country each year. While the luxury market continues to develop in Russia, it is not yet saturated and the demand for exclusive and prestigious brands continues.

Consumption of luxury goods reflects a movement to a single luxury esthetic that incorporates influences from every corner of the globe. This means that a brand's ethnicity is no longer an indicator of where its owners are from, where the goods are produced, or who buys them, but rather a matter of buyer preference—for anyone who can pay the price.

The International Heavyweight Motorcycle Market

In the United States, H-D clearly trades on its image and nostalgia to sell its traditional bikes. While Harley's quality and engineering are excellent, the technology of the company's traditional bikes lags behind that of competitors. The technology gap is largely intentional; customers are paying for an American icon. H-D relies on something other than nostalgia for an American icon to sell motorcycles in the international market, however. That something consists of the image and status conveyed by a luxury good. Like the traditional styling and dated mechanical movement of a Rolex watch, the value of an H-D motorcycle is in its status and image and not in its technology.

Heavyweight bikes constituted 55 percent of the U.S. motorcycle market in 2008. H-D has led the motorcycle industry in domestic unit sales of heavyweight bikes for 20 straight years. In 2008 H-D manufactured 46 percent of the heavyweight motorcycles sold in the United States. In the face of recession, the company's domestic unit sales decreased 10 percent from 2004 to 2008. The company faces a challenge in balancing motorcycle availability to ensure high markups for itself and its dealers, while maintaining market share in the face of stiff competition.

Traditionally, a maximum of 20 percent of the production of H-D's traditional motorcycles has been shipped offshore. This policy ensured that the supply of new motorcycles favored domestic dealers. The company broke this unwritten policy in 2006 when it exported 22 percent of production, and by 2008 the export percentage had reached 32 percent. In 2008 the company's combined market share in the heavyweight motorcycle segment for the United States and Europe was 31 percent.

The European market is a particularly difficult one for H-D, and the company's market share hovers around 10 percent. The market is an attractive one, however, because European heavyweight motorcycle sales are 83 percent of those in the U.S. market. Unlike the U.S. market, in Europe the H-D image and nostalgia don't sell many bikes. Seventy percent of the European market is comprised of performance bikes, a market segment in which the traditional H-D offerings are not competitive. Harley-Davidson's newest design, the V-Rod or VRSC, with its Porsche-designed engine, competes in this market segment. Europeans differ in their tastes on a regional and national basis. Those that favor Italian flair have the option of the racy Ducati and similar bikes, while those who like Teutonic thoroughness can opt for the highly refined BMW. H-D would like to double its European market share over the next few years. In 2008, H-D acquired an Italian manufacturer of motorcycles, MV Agusta. The MV Agusta acquisition appears to have been made to advance H-D's pursuit of the European market.

In 2008 H-D sold over 14,600 motorcycles in Japan through a network of 81 dealers. The VRSC model is popular with Japan's 20-something thrill junkies. Overall motorcycle ownership in Japan peaked in the mid-1980s and has been in a slow decline since then. However, the decline in ownership has been largely limited to motorcycles less than 250 cc. Japanese law

H-D: Motorcycle Retail Unit Sales by International Market (1,000 motorcycles)

	2008	Percentage Change (%)	2007	Percentage Change (%)	2006	Percentage Change (%)	2005	Percentage Change (%)	2004
United States	218.9	−13.0	251.8	−6.2	268.4	5.9	253.4	4.2	243.2
Canada	16.5	11.7	14.8	9.4	13.5	15.9	11.7	4.1	11.2
Europe	40.7	4.8	38.9	15.0	33.8	14.6	29.5	19.9	24.6
Japan	14.6	6.5	13.8	3.6	13.3	16.3	11.4	11.1	10.3
Other markets	23.1	25.0	18.5	23.7	15.0	34.3	11.2	19.4	9.3
Total	313.8	−7.1	337.8	−1.8	344.0	8.5	317.2	6.2	298.6

currently does not allow a motorcycle driver to carry a passenger.

China and India offer large and fast growing motorcycle markets. In both countries motorcycles meet the basic transportation needs of millions of families and businesses. Each country currently consumes about six million new motorcycles each year with almost all bikes displacing 250 cc or less. Price is the competitive issue, and joint ventures between domestic companies and international motorcycle manufacturers like Honda and Kawasaki produce affordable motorcycles of good quality. H-D has an agreement with China's Zonshen Motorcycle Group to develop the Chinese market, and a H-D dealership was opened on the outskirts of Beijing in 2006. Trade barriers at all levels remain a problem in the Chinese market, and motorcycles are banned from a large portion of Beijing. Import tariffs are also onerous in India, running over 90 percent for a heavyweight motorcycle. India's emission standards for bikes over 500 cc are exceedingly rigorous and exclude H-D's current products. H-D has engaged in talks with the government of India, but there is little reason to think India will change its regulations to permit the import of H-D motorcycles. Despite the vagaries of Indian regulations, Suzuki and Kawasaki have enjoyed modest success selling performance motorcycles in India.

Australia and New Zealand continue to be strong markets for H-D motorcycles. Australia in particular has roads and landscapes similar to those found in United States. H-D is seen as a symbol of the freedom of the open road and has a loyal and passionate following. The growth segment in the Australian motorcycle market is off-road or dirt bikes with 40 percent of the market. H-D operates a wheel manufacturing plant in Adelaide, Australia. Other significant markets for H-D include Canada, Brazil, and Mexico. H-D opened its first dealership in Moscow, Russia, in 2005.

Competitors

According to H-D:

> Competition in the heavyweight motorcycle market is based upon a number of factors, including price, quality, reliability, styling, product features, customer preference, and warranties.... The Company emphasizes quality, reliability and styling in its products and offers a two-year warranty .... (2008 Form 10-K).

All of H-D's major competitors have their headquarters outside the United States. Most of the major competitors are operating units of large diversified companies like Honda, Yamaha, Kawasaki, Suzuki, and

BMW. At least one of H-D's major competitors, Honda, manufactures its largest motorcycles in the United States. A major exception to the large diversified company rule is Ducati, an Italian company that is a leader in the European performance market. In addition to offshore competition, H-D faces domestic competitors. These companies include relatively new brands like Big Dog and Polaris, and a number of small custom shops that cater to the ultrahigh-end motorcycle market.

Ducati Motor Holdings Ducati is representative of H-D's European competition and is listed on both the Milan and New York stock exchanges. Ducati has adopted a cyberspace model selling motorcycles, accessories, and clothing online. The company promotes its cyberspace model through participation in motorcycle racing where Ducati has dominated the world Superbike Championships for over ten years. Unlike H-D, Ducati does not build bikes on the basis of nostalgia and comfort; rather Ducati sells style and performance based on technologically advanced designs. Ducatis are race-proven bikes, sold for use on the street—the ultimate café racer. Like H-D, Ducati employs a premium pricing strategy, even though its customers tend to be younger and somewhat less affluent. Unlike most of its competitors, Ducati's sales were up 22 percent in 2008. H-D's V-Rod appears to be aimed squarely at the high end of Ducati's customer base.

BMW BMW's focus is on putting their best efforts into a small range of products, a policy that makes their products unique in quality, style, and performance. Their motorcycle production concentrates on three different series, each stressing superior quality. BMW's strategy is based on premium pricing and building the best motorcycle that money can buy by setting the standard in technology, environment, and safety in all of their product offerings. Each of their motorcycles portrays the traditional motorcycle image; however, BMW also includes elements of sophistication and class in their products. All of BMW's motorcycles have high resale values; however, their high purchase price limits their market share.

Honda Honda is the world leader in motorcycle manufacturing with 17 percent of the North American market, 22 percent of the European market, and 23 percent of the Asian-Pacific market. In 2008, Honda and its affiliated companies sold over four million motorcycles in India alone. Honda combines excellent engineering and quality with highly automated manufacturing to achieve significant economies of scale. Honda has been able to leverage its low-cost advantage into global leadership.

Honda is a diversified company that at one time surpassed Toyota in sales to become the third-largest automobile company in the United States. In addition to motorcycles and automobiles, Honda manufactures all-terrain vehicles (ATVs), outboard motors, generators, lawn care equipment, and other power products. Honda has a presence in the financial services industry, providing financing options for motorcycle and automobile dealers and consumers. Honda's niche in the U.S. motorcycle market is touring bikes. With up to 1,500 cc water-cooled engines, Honda's touring bikes are high quality, refined, comfortable, and fuel efficient. Honda encourages creativity and is widely regarded as being the global leader in four-cycle gasoline engine technology.

Kawasaki Kawasaki is a world leader in the transportation equipment and industrial goods industries with diverse product lines in each category. Kawasaki motors is focused on motorcycles, ATVs, jet ski watercraft, utility vehicles, rail cars, wheels, robots, and engines for consumer products such as lawnmowers. Kawasaki is well-known for providing a wide range of products that offer high-performance and low-maintenance attributes. Kawasaki offers multiple models of motorcycles, making them competitive in many different facets of the industry, including touring bikes, sport bikes, off-road bikes, dual-purpose bikes, street bikes, and police bikes.

Kawasaki has a large international presence with production facilities in Southeast Asia, China, Europe, and the United States. They hold the third-largest motorcycle market share in North America at 10 percent, the fourth-largest share in the Asian-Pacific market at 19 percent, and the fifth largest share in European markets at 12 percent.

Suzuki Suzuki manufactures automobiles, commercial vehicles, outboard motors, and ATVs. Suzuki is the third largest manufacturer of motorcycles, lagging behind only Honda and Yamaha. Motorcycles comprise 19 percent of the company's total sales. Suzuki motorcycles have a significant international presence with sales in over 190 countries. Eighty percent of Suzuki's total motorcycle sales are in offshore markets. Suzuki began using joint manufacturing efforts in foreign countries in 1993 and uses direct sales subsidiaries to reach customers. The joint manufacturing efforts require constant and dynamic technical cooperation between groups using cost-reduction activities to achieve their ongoing goal of providing a low-cost product. Efficiency is the backbone of Suzuki's low-cost position in the industry.

Yamaha Yamaha has manufacturing facilities, distribution, and R&D operations in many international markets. Yamaha focuses on tailoring its products to local market conditions. Yamaha Motor Company has a diverse product line including outboard motors, boats, personal watercraft, generators, golf carts, ATVs, snowmobiles, outdoor power equipment, race kart engines, accessories, apparel, and motorcycles. Yamaha produces a full line of motorcycles, ranging from scooters to heavyweights; however, their competitive advantage focuses on speedy and high-performance racing bikes. Yamaha's motorcycle sales are strong globally; they currently hold the fifth largest market share in North America, the third largest in Asia-Pacific, and the second largest in Europe. Their target market throughout the world is the young and thrill-seeking consumer who sees riding as a sport.

The H-D Company in 2008

H-D is an American icon with a loyal customer following that has been described as cult-like. The company has to be careful not to offend its traditional customers by going too far, too fast. With one notable exception, H-D's line of motorcycles are engineered and designed to evoke an earlier age. Although the company has continuously been in business since 1903, today's company is the result of a leveraged buyout in 1981. The 1980s proved to be a difficult time, and the company was often on the brink of failure. The 1990s brought a complete reversal in H-D's fortunes with the demand for the company's motorcycles far outstripping supply. During this period it was not unusual for a buyer to have to wait as long as two years to take delivery on the company's most popular models. Profits soared and H-D became the darling of Wall Street. By 2005 management had narrowed the gap between demand and supply. By carefully managing growth, the company ensures that its bikes are not too easy to come by. Starting in 2007, the company was forced to cut back on manufacturing to avoid oversupplying the market. Managing the supply of H-D motorcycles maintains high prices and permits H-D to avoid having to offer promotions and discounts to sell its product. Promotions and discounts are practices that are inconsistent with a luxury good.

H-D's premium pricing limits the number of young buyers. Two-thirds of its customers are between the ages of 35 and 54 years. H-D has redesigned some of its bikes to better accommodate female riders. The percentage of female buyers has reached 12 percent and continues to move slowly upward. H-D also offers motorcycle driver education courses, where 40 percent of the participants are women.

For the most part, the company has failed in its attempts to diversify into related industries. The economic downturn of 2007–2008 negatively impacted Harley-Davidson Financial Services (HDFS). HDFS's primary business is to provide financing and insurance to H-D dealers and buyers. In 1998 H-D moved to expand its presence within the motorcycle industry when it acquired the outstanding shares of the Buell Motorcycle Company. While sharing components and technology with H-D, the performance-oriented Buell is intended to attract younger and nontraditional riders to the H-D family. In 2008 H-D acquired the European motorcycle manufacturer, MV Agusta, which includes the MV Agusta and Cagiva brand names. MV Agusta products emphasize design and performance and feature a liquid-cooled, four-cylinder engine design. Cagiva products are lightweight sport bikes featuring 125-cc air-cooled engines.

H-D Strategy In 2008 H-D's strategy incorporated three objectives, at least two of which are a direct result of the economy: (1) investing in the H-D brand, (2) restructuring operations and reducing the cost structure, and (3) obtaining funding for HDFS.

The first objective, investing in the brand, is to be achieved through a two-pronged approach. First, the company intends to increase its market base by reaching out to nontraditional rider groups, including women and minorities. The second prong is directed at its traditional rider group, and product innovation is the vehicle of choice for reaching this group.

The second objective, restructuring operations, is to be accomplished by plant closing and outsourcing. The company will close two engine and transmission plants in Milwaukee and move their operations to a third plant in Menomonee Falls, Wisconsin. Paint and frame operations in York, Pennsylvania, will be combined with other operations at that site. A distribution facility in Franklin, Wisconsin, that handles parts and accessories will be closed and its operations outsourced. Finally, the company's trucking operation will be terminated and its activities outsourced. It is expected that restructuring and reduced product demand will result in the loss of 1,500 hourly and salaried positions.

The third objective, obtaining funding for HDFS will be the most problematic and includes:

- Accessing the unsecured debt capital markets.
- Increasing asset-backed credit.
- Renewing existing lines of credit.
- Accessing the asset-backed securitization market through the U.S. Federal Reserve programs.

H-D has found it difficult to sell motorcycles without providing a source for financing. Consequently, the company's well-being hinges on the liquidity of HDFS.

H-D Human Resources Management H-D prides itself on open communication with its union and non-union employees and on its team-based culture. Employees are involved in goal setting, and this practice facilitates a shared vision of the company's direction. Self-directed work groups are the norm. Departmental differences are minimized through a focus on cross-functional communications. These types of personnel practices are known as partnering at H-D; partnering results include increased employee motivation and a reduced need for supervision.

The company developed its Performance Effectiveness Process to foster both employee performance and career development. Employees are rated on a form that includes over 90 descriptors, which include: (1) values diversity in the workforce, (2) does what he/she says he/she will do, and (3) responds in a positive manner to criticism. The performance evaluation was tested and refined on managers before it was used on the workforce. H-D takes career development seriously and has formalized all the company's learning, training, and development initiatives under its Leadership Institute. Each year over a third of the company's employees attend the institute's courses. Management believes these courses improve the company's competitiveness, while giving employees the knowledge and skills needed for advancement and personal growth. H-D prefers to promote from within the company to give employees opportunities for advancement and to demonstrate the company's commitment to retaining talent. This is why they also have an extensive tuition reimbursement program, including undergraduate and graduate programs offered through Marquette University and Milwaukee Area Technical College. H-D even developed a program to assist its distributors. Classes offered at H-D University (HDU) help distributors improve customer satisfaction, store layout, and merchandising.

An emphasis for HDU is teaching dealers how to market and sell motorcycles. Until 2005–2006, the H-D's dealers functioned as order takers. Demand for H-D motorcycles exceeded manufacturing capacity, and most buyers had to wait a few months before receiving their bikes. During the transition from the 2005 to the 2006 model years, supply briefly exceeded demand. For the first time in the memory of most dealers, unsold motorcycles were sitting on the showroom floor. The fact that dealers simply didn't know how to handle this situation became painfully evident when sales trended downward in 2007. HDU stepped in to help H-D dealers learn what every successful car dealership already knows: how to sell your product.

In 2008 the company employed approximately 9,000 employees in the manufacture of motorcycles. As a function of their geographical location, unionized employees are represented by one of two unions. H-D had incurred only one previous strike since the AMF buyout in 1981 when in 2007 the employees at the York, Pennsylvania, plant went on strike for three weeks. The bones of contention were pay, a tiered wage system, and copay for medical benefits. In the end workers received a 12 percent wage increase over three years, and the company received a lower starting wage for new employees. The tiered wage system flew in the face of Harley's compensation structure, which had traditionally been driven by two guidelines: (1) make a larger portion of the employee's pay at risk or variable and (2) compensate all employees in the same manner. An example of a bonus compensation system used for employees is giving equal percentage bonuses, based on 15 percent of sales. It is believed that this practice minimizes differences in employee pay and promotes teamwork and lessens jealousy among employees. H-D generally evokes a deep commitment from employees. Building consensus with union employees is H-D's standard practice. Resolving the occasional union grievance is left to the employee's filing the grievance, the union steward, the work group, and the work group's advisor (manager). The grievance resolution is considered binding by the union and the company.

Harley has a time-tested device for keeping up with customer demands and ensuring product quality. Half of the company's 9,000 employees ride a H-D, yet every employee, including the CEO, must go through a dealer to get a bike. This is just a testament to H-D being a company driven by the human resources function. Fairness and equality are driving this company into the future with a workforce that believes they are part of something special.

H-D Operations H-D has an ongoing production strategy of increasing the supply of its motorcycles, but at a rate less than that demanded by the market. To this end, the company expanded its manufacturing capacity through 2006. The company tries to position its product development staff in proximity to its manufacturing operations in order to ensure that new product and model changes are coordinated prior to and during ramp-up.

A company operation in South America imports parts and subassemblies from the United States for final assembly in Brazil. Assembling the bikes in Brazil reduces duties and taxes, thus reducing the selling price and increasing the company's market. However, the volume of this facility remains under 1,000 units per year. Bikes for all other international markets are exported from the United States.

H-D actively practices lean manufacturing and quality management. The company continuously strives to improve the quality of its operations while controlling costs. Quality management practices include statistical process control, employee involvement in operations-related decisions, supplier participation, just-in-time inventory control, and partnerships with the company's unions. H-D trains its employees in the use of statistical methods and problem solving through its Leadership Institute courses. The company is proud of its relationship with employees and encourages employee involvement, emphasizing a highly flexible and participative workforce. The company employs this flexibility in cross-functional teams that review every aspect of the production process.

H-D strives to establish long-term mutually beneficial relationships with its suppliers. The company involves suppliers in the design and manufacturing of its products and quality improvement programs. Harley requires that its suppliers be committed to annual cost reductions even when labor and material costs are rising. The company believes that vendor involvement results in improved products, the adoption of new technologies, and the smoother introduction of new products and product changes. Supplier involvement is not without its costs and has led to an increase in the number of purchasing engineers from 4 to 30 in the 1990s. The involvement of suppliers has resulted in improvements in productivity and product quality, and a four- to five-day component inventory, all of which translates into an estimated savings of over $10 million per year.

In conjunction with its just-in-time inventory and assembly controls, H-D has introduced an automated

Harley-Davidson Manufacturing Facilities

Facility	Size (sq. ft.)	Part(s) Supplied
Wauwatosa, Wisconsin	430,000	Powertrain
Menomonee Falls, Wisconsin	881,000	Powertrain
Tomahawk, Wisconsin	211,000	Fiberglass parts and painting
York, Pennsylvania	1,331,000	Parts fabrication, painting, and assembly
Kansas City, Missouri	450,000	Sportster assembly, V-Rod powertrain
East Troy, Wisconsin (Buell)	40,00	Buell assembly
Manaus, Brazil	82,000	Office and subassembly for local markets
Varese, Italy	1,378,000	MV Agusta facilities
Adelaide, Australia	485,000	Motorcycle wheels

electrified monorail (AEM) system in its two Wisconsin engine assembly plants. The AEM systems have increased productivity, improved ergonomics and increased the speed of changeover between different assemblies, while freeing up space on the factory floor. Similarly, the company's parts and accessories distribution centers have been highly automated leading to increased speed of delivery and a 99.7 percent level of accuracy.

H-D Marketing August 2003 saw the culmination of H-D's hundredth anniversary celebration when an estimated 200,000 people participated in events in and around Harley's hometown of Milwaukee, Wisconsin. Riders came from every state and from every inhabited continent. H-D's anniversary was one of the biggest—some said the biggest—events in Milwaukee's history. H-D's public exposure from the carefully orchestrated event was beyond price, but events and promotions are the norm for H-D. Countless features in the media focus on the company, its bikes, and the image of Harley riders. The company has a long history of successful promotion, and its bikes have costarred in numerous major film productions.

The 130,000-square-foot H-D Museum opened in Milwaukee in 2008. The museum, showcasing both historic and current motorcycles, is intended to strengthen the company's bonds with riders and the general public. The museum includes a restaurant, café, retail , and meeting spaces. The company will use the space to host special events for the Harley Owners Group (HOG®).

The company's traditional advertising and promotional venues include dealer promotions and cooperative programs, magazine and direct mail advertising, and its famous HOG customer events. The annual gathering in Sturgis, South Dakota, has been the subject of public television documentaries. H-D's Web site offers an interactive and exhaustive online catalog. Customers can order accessories and customize bikes with hundreds of options. It wasn't until 2002 that Harley-Davison felt the need to advertise its products on television. The result of the company's marketing actions is that Harley-Davison ranks near the top among iconic brands, along with Disney and Apple Computer.

Formed in 1983, the company-sponsored HOG had over 1.1 million members worldwide in 2008. The group sponsors events, including national rides and rallies, and the company sponsors racing activities. Harley's buyers are not locked into any social class. You are just as likely to find a CEO on a Harley as a worker off the assembly line. Harley owners are loyal, with 90 percent of buyers reporting the intention of purchasing another Harley bike. Clearly image sells to this demographic, Harley ranks near the 100th

percentile on the Brand Asset Valuator scale for such qualities as authentic, rugged, daring, dynamic, distinctive, and high performance. As one Harley owner put it, "What Harley-Davidson appeals to me is that we all think we're cooler than we really are." (*Milwaukee Journal Sentinel,* August 24, 2003)

A creative tool in H-D's marketing program is its Authorized Rental and Tour program. Operated in the United States and overseas, this program puts riders on factory-maintained Harleys for guided tours. Included in the tour are some meals, lodging, and a support vehicle to carry the heavy luggage and take care of any mechanical malfunctions. A lot of development ideas come from bike-riding employees and from employee attendance at the Harley rallies that are held around the country. Harley riders traditionally customize their bikes, and this practice led H-D to offer custom bikes in 1998. This ongoing product group allows buyers to alter their factory bikes with a wide range of accessories and paint. With an average of $9,000 in extras, these bikes go for more than $27,000 and carry a 40 percent profit margin. Delivery time for the factory-custom bikes can run up to year. The company's marketing efforts were recognized when H-D was inducted into the 2001 Marketing Hall of Fame. Their selection was based on "an outstanding job of building and sustaining their brand through smart marketing" (http://proquest.umi.com). The honor recognized what Harley followers have known for years: Brand equity plus superior manufacturing has positioned H-D as the elite manufacturer in the North American motorcycle market.

H-D Distribution H-D products are sold through a network of 686 independently owned full-service dealerships in the United States. The company maintains a European headquarters in England. Dealerships can be found in 36 European, Middle Eastern, and African countries, in 8 Asian countries, and in 15 Latin America countries. Most dealerships sell only H-D and Buell products.

Uke's H-D/Buell dealership in Kenosha, Wisconsin, is fairly typical of Harley dealers. Uke's recently completed a new 54,000-square-foot facility alongside I-94. What may be unique to Uke's is a six-story glass tower that displays custom bikes like jewels in a showcase. The new building features a 15,000-square-foot showroom and a 10,000-square-foot service area. The basement is given over to the winter storage of customer's bikes, while the second-floor mezzanine houses a museum and art gallery. The architectural firm of Kubala Washatko of Cedarburg, Wisconsin, designed the new facility. Kubala Washatko has designed dozens of Harley dealerships around the United States.

H-D Research and Development H-D believes research and development is a key component of its ability

Harley-Davidson Dealership Locations in 2007	
Country/Region	H-D/Buell Dealerships
United States	684
Canada	74
Europe	370
All other	240
Total	1,368

to lead the touring bike market. The company maintains a 409,000-square-foot product development center and a separate 79,000-square-foot development center for the Buell product line. The product development centers are staffed with employees from styling, purchasing, and manufacturing, as well as supplier representatives. The practice is consistent with H-D's commitment to quality management and results in seamless product development. Due to the increasing prevalence of environmental and safety regulations, the product development centers are staffed with professionals specializing in the regulatory process. The company has sought to be proactive in meeting environmental and safety regulations in both its products and facilities. The company spent $163.5 million in 2008, $185.5 million in 2007, and $177.7 million in 2006 on product development.

The company's products are in compliance with all current federal and state emission and noise standards. H-D has made the investment necessary to comply with the Environmental Protection Agency's tailpipe emission standards that became effective in 2010. A more pressing problem for H-D may come from more stringent noise standards in the European Union and Japan. Such standards may interfere with one of Harley's most sacred traditions: the bike's distinctive, and loud, exhaust.

H-D Motorcycle Unit According to H-D:

The total on-highway motorcycle market, including the heavyweight portion of the market, is comprised of the following four segments:

- *standard (emphasizes simplicity and cost)*
- *performance (emphasizes handling and acceleration)*
- *custom (emphasizes styling and individual owner customization)*
- *touring (emphasizes comfort and amenities for long-distance travel) (2008 Form 10-K)*

The company currently addresses all categories with its offerings from the MV Agusta line in the performance segment, with the Buell lineup in the standard and performance segments, and with H-D offerings in the standard, performance, touring, and custom segments. The larger displacement custom and touring models are the most profitable for the company.

The company's motorcycle unit consists of H-D Motor Company, the Buell Motorcycle Company, and MV Agusta. The motorcycle unit designs, manufactures, and markets primarily heavyweight bikes, as well as motorcycle parts, accessories, and merchandise. The company is the only major U.S. manufacturer of motorcycles and has led the heavyweight market since going public in 1986. The Motorcycle Industry Council figures give H-D a 45.5 percent share of the domestic heavyweight market for 2008. For some years the motorcycle unit generated about 80.0 percent of the total net sales of Harley-Davidson, Inc.

Harley's heavyweight bikes are, by the company's own definition, more than 650 cc of engine displacement. The company currently markets 33 models of performance, touring, and custom bikes with suggested retail prices up to $29,999 for a limited-edition factory-customized model. These bikes are built on five basic chassis designs (Softail, Sportster, Dyna Glide, Touring, and the VRSC, or V-Rod) and are powered by one of four 45-degree V-twin air-cooled engines ranging from 883 cc to a huge 1803-cc brute (the V-Rod utilizes a liquid-cooled engine). The company pioneered the touring heavyweight motorcycle, and this segment includes well-equipped bikes with fairings, windshields, and luggage carriers. The custom segment includes the retro-look bikes that are typically highly customized through the use of chrome, paint, and accessories. These bikes sell for prices that are about 50 percent higher than competitors' comparable models.

The V-Rod or VRSC model is the first in a new series of bikes aimed at the performance café racer market. The VRSC shares nothing with existing bikes and is equipped with the Porsche-designed, liquid-cooled, 60-degree V-twin, 1130-cc, 110+-hp, Revolution engine. It is the most expensive development project in the company's history, but H-D has not revealed the numbers. The VRSC model has met grudging acceptance at best with H-D's traditional buyers, but has done well with nontraditional buyers and the international market. Harley's previous foray into the performance segment with its Buell line of motorcycles has met with only limited success.

H-D manufactured and shipped 303,479 motorcycles in 2008 down from 330,619 in 2007. About half of all bikes on the road are Harley's big street cruisers, like the Softail, that sell for about $18,000. Around 30 percent are the true heavyweight touring machines; equipped with fiberglass saddlebags, CD players, radios, and cruise control, these bikes sell for $20,000 or more. The remaining bikes are mostly the $7,000-or-more

Sportsters; with ongoing cosmetic upgrades, the Sportster remains Harley's oldest and most affordable model.

H-D Parts and Accessories Parts and accessories include genuine H-D replacement parts and cosmetic bike accessories. Parts and accessories comprised 15.4 percent of sales in the motorcycle segment in 2008. This segment includes general merchandise, an area encompassing such items as clothes and collectibles. Around the country are 80 dealerships with shops that feature H-D clothes and collectibles, as well as an additional 52 Harley stores in malls, airports, and vacation destinations and another 20 seasonal shops. General merchandise constitutes 5.6 percent of sales in the motorcycle segment. While general merchandise is a small entry on H-D's income statement, it is an important form of advertising and a major player in the company's quest to turn the brand into a lifestyle. H-D licenses its name and logo for such items as T-shirts, jewelry, and toys. The company believes that licensing is a useful tool for promotion and routinely polices the unauthorized use of its name and logo. Royalty revenues totaled $45.4 million in 2008. While royalties are not great, the margins are high.

H-D Financial Services Unit The 700 employees of HDFS engage in the financing of dealer inventories and retail consumer installment sales contracts. The growth area in this market appears to be in the financing of new motorcycles. During 2008, 53.5 percent of all new H-D motorcycles retailed in the United States were financed by HDFS, up from 40 percent in 2004. H-D also reports that it provided financing to 95 percent of its dealers in 2008. Operating income from financial services was $82,765,000 in 2008, down 61 percent from 2007. While most of its business is directed at H-D dealers and the dealer's customers, Financial Services also provides financing for non-commercial aircraft, as well as broker's insurance and service contracts for motorcycle owners.

H-D Financial Statements

In the face of the 2008–2009 recession, H-D's net profit remained strong but significantly off the 2006 high of $1,043,153. Profits in 2008 were $654,718, down 37 percent from 2006. The company has relatively little debt. Needless to say, H-D is no longer the darling of investors and the financial press. The board of directors has authorized the company to repurchase shares of the company's common stock. Under these plans, large blocks of stock have been repurchased by the company in recent years and have helped to keep H-D's stock price up in an often down market. Nonetheless, the company's stock value has declined

markedly. The high value in the first quarter of 2007 was $74.03 per share, which may be contrasted against a low value of $11.54 per share in the fourth quarter of 2008.

H-D has taken steps to reduce its exposure to fluctuations in the international financial markets. The company made $95 million on foreign exchange adjustments in 2008, largely due to the decline in the dollar. The company expects to lose on foreign exchange adjustments in 2009. To reduce foreign exchange risks, the company selectively uses financial instruments. Forward foreign exchange contracts are used to hedge the effect of earnings fluctuation on the dollar. H-D is also exposed to loan defaults and interest rate fluctuations through its financial services division. To minimize its risk, HDFS packages and resells most of its loans. Harley's pension and SERPA benefit obligation has increased from $963,824 in 2005 to $1,178,283 in 2008. The postretirement health care liability went from $298,340 to $372,631 in 2005 and 2006, respectively. These liabilities will need to be closely monitored in the years to come.

CASE DISCUSSION QUESTIONS

1. Which of Porter's generic strategies is H-D using? Will this strategy work for all of the countries described in the case? Why or why not?
2. What does a Porter's five forces analysis reveal about the strategies H-D has employed in recent years?
3. How does H-D compare to its competitors?

CASE CREDIT

Harley-Davidson, Inc., 3700 West Juneau Avenue, Milwaukee, Wisconsin 53208. http://www.harley-davidson.com. SIC: 3751—Motorcycles, bicycles & parts.

CASE NOTES

1 Barrett, R. 2009. "New Harley CEO brings the chops." *Milwaukee Journal Sentinel*, April 12.
2 Barrett, R. 2009. "Job cuts, outsourcing questioned at Harley shareholders meeting." *Milwaukee Journal Sentinel*, April 26.
3 Barrett, R. 2009. "Job auction services, tent sales market repossessed bikes." *Milwaukee Journal Sentinel*, April 26.
4 Carpenter, S. 2008. "Bumpy road ahead for industry." *Los Angeles Times*, January 23.
5 Content, T. 2003. "Harley looks to a new breed of bike for growth." *Milwaukee Journal Sentinel*, August 24.
6 Half-yearly report of Ducati Motor Holding S.p.A. as of June 30, 2008.
7 Hamner, Susanna. 2009. "Harley, you're not getting any younger." *New York Times*, March 22.
8 Harley Davidson, Inc., Form 10-K, December 31, 2004.
9 Ibid., 2005.
10 Ibid., 2006.
11 Ibid., 2007.

12 Ibid., 2008.

13 *PR Newswire*, "Harley-Davidson and Staples elected to the 2001 Marketing Hall of Fame." April, p. 1.

14 *Journal of Business and Design.* 2002. "Harley-Davidson: Marketing an American icon." January 05. http://www.cdf.org/cdf/atissue/vol2_1/harley/harley.html.

15 *Economist.* 2004. "Luxury's new empire," June 17. http://www.economist.com/business/displaystory.cfm?story_id=2771531.

16 Narayan, S. 2006. "India's lust for Luxe." *Time: Asia*, April. http://www.time.com/time/asia/magazine/printout/0,13675,501060410-1179415,00.html.

17 O'Connell, V. 2009. "Sales of luxury goods seen falling by 10 percent" WSJ.com, April 11.

18 Spivak, C. 2009. "Earning their keep?" *Milwaukee Journal Sentinel*, May 24.

19 Steverman, B. 2009. "Harley-Davidson: Cruising on recovery road." *Business Week Online*, April 20.

20 Teerlink, R., and L. Ozley. 2000. *More than a motorcycle: The leadership journey at Harley-Davidson.* Harvard Business School Press Boston, MA: Harvard Business School Press.

21 Teerlink, R. 2000. "Harley's leadership U-turn." *Harvard Business Review*, July–August, pp. 43–48.

22 Tortoiella, R., S. Kessler, E. Kolb, C. Montevirgen, and M. Basham. 2009. "S&P picks and pans: GE, Google, Harley-Davidson, AMD, Microsemi, Chipotle." *Business Week Online*, January 26.

23 Weisman, K. 2005. "America's take on new luxury." *International Herald Tribune*, December 5.

24 Windle, C. 2005. "China luxury industry prepares for boom." *BBC News*, September 27. http://news.bbc.co.uk/2/hi/business/4271970.stm.

25 http://www.harley-davidson.com.

26 http://www.hoovers.com.

27 Zielinski, G. 2003. "Milwaukee gears up for motorcycle mania." *Milwaukee Journal Sentinel*, August 24.

6

Multinational and Participation Strategies: Content and Formulation

Preview CASE IN POINT

BMW: Success in Selling Premium Cars

By automotive industry standards, BMW is a small auto manufacturer. While automotive giants such as Toyota or GM are selling cars by the tens of millions, BMW sold only 1.7 million cars in 2008. However, even though BMW is often seen as too small, too exclusive, and too Eurocentric to achieve success in the U.S. market, the carmaker has been extremely successful. Although it suffered along with other car manufacturers in the recent economic downturn, it nevertheless posted a smaller fall in sales in 2008, compared to other competitors. How has BMW become such a successful seller of premium cars?

A look at its strategic approaches provides some answers. Because BMW is a small company, many expect its orientation to be dominated by marketers. However, four of the last five BMW CEOs have been manufacturing experts, and BMW has always been guided by manufacturing excellence. Furthermore, this zeal for manufacturing performance has encouraged the company to constantly strive for efficiency. For instance, both the 1 and 3 series share about 60 percent of their parts. Similarly, both the 5 and 6 series are going to be built on the 7 series architecture. Such efficiencies allow BMW to have excellent returns, allowing them to remain independent. Also, the German car manufacturer has a plant in South Carolina, thereby demonstrating its commitment to efficiency by locating plants close to the market.

However, BMW is clearly considered a premium car manufacturer and cannot rely solely on efficiency to remain successful. A big component of BMW's success has had to do with technology. In fact, one of BMW's major current challenges is to understand the demand for green cars and customer expectations for them. While BMW can charge premium prices for its zippier cars, it probably cannot do the same with green cars. The CEO is therefore dedicating a cross-functional staff of 80 to 100 staff members to study and understand the green market. Called Project I, the team is working hard to develop a green vehicle with the potential to succeed. One of the most immediate goals of the project team is to develop a battery-powered Mini Cooper. BMW hopes that it will be able to understand changes in the market and continue selling premium cars.

Source: Based on Taylor III, Alex. (2009). "Bavaria's next top model." Fortune, March 30, pp. 100–105.

T he Preview Case in Point describes BMW and the many facets of its strategy. Whether BMW is deciding on which market to enter or where to build its next factory or which car to build next, it relies on many aspects of strategy to make the best decisions. In this chapter you will find a review of the essential strategies that multinationals use to bring their companies to international markets and to compete successfully in them.

This chapter contains three major sections. The first section introduces general strategies for multinational operations. The second section explains the specific techniques that multinationals use to enter markets. The final section provides an understanding of the political risk, an important risk that many multinational companies face.

Multinational Strategies: Dealing with the Global-Local Dilemma

Multinational companies face a fundamental strategic dilemma when competing internationally: the global-local dilemma. On one hand, there are pressures to respond to the unique needs of the markets in each country in which a company does business. When a company chooses this option, it adopts the **local-responsiveness solution**. On the other hand, there are efficiency pressures that encourage companies to deemphasize local differences and to conduct business similarly throughout the world. Companies that lean in this direction choose the **global integration solution**.

The solution for the so-called **global-local dilemma**—the choice between local responsiveness or global integration—forms the basic strategic orientation of a multinational company.[1] This strategic orientation affects the design of organization and management systems as well as of supporting functional strategies in areas such as production, marketing, and finance. Here we consider only the strategic implications. In later chapters, you will see how this fundamental problem influences other areas of multinational management, such as human resources management and the choice of an organizational design.

Companies that lean toward the local-responsiveness solution stress customizing their organizations and products to accommodate country-related or regional differences, with the focus on satisfying local customer needs by tailoring products or services. Forces that favor a local-responsiveness solution come primarily from national or cultural differences in consumer tastes and variations in customer needs, as well as from how industries work and political pressures. For example, government regulations can require a company to share ownership with a local firm, and some governments require companies to produce their products in the countries in which they sell.[2]

Multinational companies that lean toward a global integration solution reduce costs, to the largest degree possible, by using standardized products,

Local-responsiveness solution
Responding to differences in the markets in all the countries in which a company operates.

Global integration solution
Conducting business similarly throughout the world and locating company units wherever there is high quality and low cost.

Global-local dilemma
Choice between a local-responsiveness or global approach to a multinational's strategies.

promotional strategies, and distribution channels in every country. Such globally oriented multinational firms seek sources of lower costs or higher quality anywhere in their value chain and anywhere in the world. For example, in such companies, headquarters, R&D, production, or distribution centers may be located anywhere they can obtain the best value added while maintaining quality or lowering cost.[3] However, a company can also use a global approach in how it manages its international operations. Consider the next Case in Point.

As you will see, Hyundai is struggling with its global approach. In fact, neither responding to local customer needs nor selling the same product worldwide is a guarantee of success. For each product or business, multinational firms must choose carefully how globally or locally to orient their strategies. Later in the chapter, you will see some of the questions that managers must answer before selecting an appropriate multinational strategy. Before that, however, we will review the broad strategic choices for the multinational manager dealing with the global-local dilemma.

Four broad multinational strategies offer solutions to this dilemma: multidomestic, transnational, international, and regional. The multidomestic and transnational strategies represent the bipolar reactions to one side of the global-local dilemma. The international and regional strategies reflect compromises that attempt to balance these conflicting drives.

Multidomestic Strategy

Multidomestic strategy
Emphasizing local-responsiveness issues.

The **multidomestic strategy** gives top priority to local responsiveness. The multidomestic strategy is in many respects a form of differentiation strategy. The company attempts to offer products or services that attract customers by closely satisfying their cultural needs and expectations. For example, advertisements, packaging, sales outlets, and pricing are adapted to local standards.

As with most types of differentiation, it usually costs more for multinational companies to produce and sell unique or special products for different countries than to standardize. There are extra costs to adapt each product to local

---

CASE IN POINT

Hyundai and the U.S. Market

Kia and its parent company, Hyundai, have been successful in conquering the U.S. market. Although both brands entered the market as sellers of low-cost cars, both companies are now striving to move upscale. Hyundai has been fairly successful, doubling sales since 2000. However, in running its U.S. operations, Hyundai has adopted a global approach; it uses its South Korean business philosophy by applying the management practices in the United States. The company is well-known for taking a build-factories-now-and-worry-about-sales-later approach. The global approach has also manifested itself in a top-down management system where the top managers run the company in an extremely authoritarian manner. In fact, American employees have found this system to be very different from what they are used to. Hyundai top managers prefer micromanaging details and seldom listen to local managers and frown upon disagreements.

The application of this global approach to its U.S. operations has resulted in challenges for Hyundai. The approach of building cars and finding customers later has resulted in increased inventories. Many American top managers have also been fired because they fail to adapt to Hyundai's management philosophy. Furthermore, Hyundai has also been reluctant to leave its fate in the hands of U.S. marketers, and the company hopes to play a bigger role in communicating the message.

Source: Based on Welch, D., D. Kiley, and M. Ihlwan. 2008. "My way or the highway at Hyundai." BusinessWeek, March 17, pp. 48–51.

requirements, such as different package sizes and colors. Thus, to succeed, a multidomestic strategy usually requires the company to charge higher prices to recoup the costs of tailoring products. Customers will pay the higher prices if they perceive an extra value in having a company's products adapted to their tastes, distribution systems, and industry structures.[4]

A multidomestic strategy is not limited to large multinational companies that can afford to set up overseas subsidiaries. Even a small firm that exports only its products may use a multidomestic strategy by extensively adapting its product line to different countries and cultures. However, for larger organizations, with production and sales units in many countries, using a multidomestic strategy often means treating foreign subsidiaries as independent businesses. Headquarters focuses on the bottom line, viewing each country as a profit center. Each country's subsidiary is free to manage its own operations as necessary, but it must generate a profit in order to receive resources. Besides having its own local production facilities, marketing strategy, sales staff, and distribution system, the subsidiary of the multidomestic company often uses local sources for raw materials and employs mostly local people.

Transnational Strategy

The **transnational strategy** gives two goals top priority: seeking location advantages and gaining economic efficiencies from operating worldwide.[5] Using **location advantages** means that the transnational company disperses or locates its value chain activities (e. g., manufacturing, R&D, and sales) anywhere in the world where the company can "do it best or cheapest" as the situation requires. For example, many U.S. and Japanese multinational companies have production facilities in Southeast Asian countries where labor is currently cheap. Michael Porter argues that, for global competition, firms must look at countries not only as potential markets but also as what he calls global platforms.[6] A **global platform** is a country location where a firm can best perform some, but not necessarily all, of its value chain activities.

Historically, international firms took advantage of their nations' comparative advantages—such as, for example, the United States' abundant natural resources—to compete on the world market. However, the comparative advantage of a nation no longer gives competitive advantages only to domestic firms; that is, the induced or natural resources available in different nations provide the transnational firm with the global platforms for location-based competitive advantages in costs and quality. For the most part, these resources support upstream activities in the value chain, such as R&D and production. Thus, a transnational strategy enables a company to base activities upstream in its value chain not only on lower costs but also on the potential for creating additional value for its products or services.

Location advantages can also exist for other value chain activities, such as being close to cheap manufacturing, key customers, and the most demanding customers. Location in the Japanese market, for example, usually requires a firm to maintain a product quality level that is acceptable to the whole world. The next Case in Point shows how several multinational automobile manufacturers use Thailand as a global platform for production and sales.

Often costs or quality advantages associated with a particular nation are called national **comparative advantage**. This is different from *competitive* advantage, which refers to the advantages of individual firms over other firms. *Comparative* advantage refers to advantages of *nations over other nations*. For example, a country with cheaper and better educated labor has a comparative advantage

Transnational strategy
Seeking location advantages and gaining economic efficiencies from operating worldwide.

Location advantages
Dispersing value chain activities anywhere in the world where the company can do them best or cheapest.

Global platform
Country location where a firm can best perform some, but not necessarily all, of its value chain activities.

Comparative advantage
That arising from cost, quality, or resource advantages associated with a particular nation.

C A S E   I N   P O I N T

Bangkok: "Welcome to the Detroit of the East"

Thailand remains the destination of choice for manufacturing. Toshiba recently picked Thailand as a hard disk drive manufacturing hub, and many firms involved in computer-related products have chosen Taiwan as the manufacturing base for export to other Asian countries. However, Thailand may not seem like the premier choice for the auto industry until one sees the sign at the gate of the Eastern Seaboard Industrial Estate in Bangkok. The sign reads, "Welcome to the Detroit of the East." Bangkok is the site of manufacturing units of Ford and General Motors, and the name "Detroit" on the sign reflects the fact that these two companies account for almost one-third of region-leading Thailand's vehicle exports. Thailand represents Ford's largest investment in Asia, but Toyota, Honda, Mitsubishi, and Isuzu also manufacture there. In fact, Honda plans to make Thailand its regional auto manufacturing hub.

Manufacturing in Thailand is not just for the local market, even though the total market size for the Association of Southeast Asian Nations (ASEAN) is expected to be more than 2.5 million by 2010. Rather, Thailand is a manufacturing platform for both global and regional distribution. Isuzu and Mitsubishi use Thailand as the global manufacturing platform for pickup trucks. BMW sees three phases of development for its new plant. First, build cars only for Thailand. Second, start exporting to other countries in the ASEAN regional trade association. Third, go transnational and source from or export to anywhere in the world.

One attraction of Thailand and other Third World nations is low labor costs. Wages are often less than one-tenth of those in home countries. In fact, in the 1990s, many automakers spent billions of dollars

developing state-of-the-art manufacturing facilities in the developing nations with the hope of a growing local demand. For the most part, demand has not reached expectations, and the automakers are looking to use this excess capacity worldwide. Honda now uses its plant in Thailand to supply its home market in Japan, the first Japanese manufacturer to try that strategy on the fickle Japanese market. Ford's most efficient factory in the world is in Brazil, and the new plant is the planned manufacturing site of a mini-sport utility vehicle for the U.S. market. BMW produces its 3 series car in South Africa for shipment to the United States and Japan. The plant matches German quality standards and gets an extra bonus due to U.S. import duty exemptions as the result of a law intended to increase trade with African countries.

Although well-established car companies have had operations in Thailand for a long time, new Chinese car companies also intend to create a presence in Thailand. In fact, Chery Automobile recently announced its intention of starting car production in Thailand.

Sources: Based on Bangkok Post. *2008. "Honda picks Thailand for regional technology role," November 20;* Bangkok Post. *2009. "Toshiba picks Thailand as HDD hub after buyout," May 11; Phoosuphanusorn, Srisamorn. 2002. "Ford aims to double turnover in Thailand."* Knight Ridder Tribune Business News, *October 16; Shirouzu, Norihiko. 2003. "Ford sees tough road for core unit: Projections are disclosed for North American business as 4th-period loss narrowed."* Wall Street Journal, *January 22, p. A3; Santivimolnat, S. 2009. "Local production of Chery possible."* Bangkok Post, *March 17; Shirouzu, Norihiko. 2003. "Ford aims to speed up process of new-vehicle development."* Wall Street Journal, *February 20, p. B8; Zaun, Todd, Gregory L. White, Norihiko Shirouzu, and Scott Miller. 2002. "A global report—two-way street: Automakers get even more mileage from third world—low-cost plants abroad start to supply home markets, as quality picks up steam—elephants white and rented."* Wall Street Journal, *July 31, p. A1.*

over other nations. Comparative advantage is important to organizations because they can use their nation's comparative advantages to gain competitive advantages over rivals from other nations.

Traditionally, scholars viewed comparative advantage as something that benefited only the indigenous or local organizations in world competition. Many Japanese and Korean organizations, for example, built their early competitive advantages on the cheap, high-quality, and motivated labor available in their countries. However, the transnational strategy has made this view somewhat out of date. The transnational firm views *any country* as a global platform where it can perform *any value-chain activity*. Thus, the comparative advantage of a nation is no longer just for locals. With increasingly free and open borders, any firm, regardless of its nation of ownership, can turn any national advantage into a competitive advantage—if the firm has the flexibility and willingness to locate anywhere.

Location advantages provide the transnational company with cost or quality gains for different value chain activities. To reduce costs even further, transnationalist firms strive for uniform marketing and promotional activities throughout the world; these companies use the same brand names, advertisements, and promotional brochures wherever they sell their products or services. The soft drink companies, such as Coca-Cola, have been among the most successful in taking their brands worldwide. When a company can do things similarly throughout the world, it can take advantage of economies of scale. Thus, for example, it is most efficient to have one package of the same color and size produced worldwide in centralized production facilities.

International Strategy

Companies pursuing international strategies, such as Toys "R" Us, Boeing, and IBM, take a compromise approach to the global-local dilemma. Like transnational strategists, firms pursuing international strategies attempt to sell global products and use similar marketing techniques worldwide. Adaptation to local customs and culture, if any, is limited to minor adjustments in product offerings and marketing strategies. However, international strategist firms differ from transnational companies in that they choose not to locate their value chain activities anywhere in the world. In particular, upstream and support activities remain concentrated at home country headquarters. The international strategist hopes that the concentration of its R&D and manufacturing strengths at home brings greater economies of scale and quality than the dispersed activities of the transnational. For example, Boeing in the United States keeps most of its production and development at home while selling planes such as the 757 worldwide with the same sales force. Its marketing approach focuses on price and technology, and even the prices and payments are quoted and made in U.S. currency.

Many companies in emerging markets have used the international strategy to enter new markets. Consider the next Focus on Emerging Markets.

When necessary for economic or political reasons, companies with international strategies frequently set up sales and production units in major countries of operation. However, the home country headquarters retains control of local strategies, marketing, R&D, finances, and production. Local facilities become only scaled-down replicas of production and sales facilities at home.[7]

> **International strategies**
> Selling global products and using similar marketing techniques worldwide.

Regional Strategy

The regional strategy is another compromise strategy. It attempts to balance the economic efficiency and location advantages of the transnational and international strategies with some of the local-adaptation advantages of the multidomestic strategy. Rather than having worldwide products and a worldwide value chain, the regional strategist manages raw material sourcing, production, marketing, and some support activities within a particular region. For example, a regional strategist might have one set of products for North America and another for Mexico and South America. This strategy not only allows some cost savings similar to those of the transnational and international strategists but also gives the firm flexibility for regional responsiveness. Managers have the

> **Regional strategy**
> Managing raw material sourcing, production, marketing, and support activities within a particular region.

Focus on Emerging Markets

China's Hisense

According to a Boston Consulting Group report, many new emerging market companies are going global and are succeeding. Experts argue that part of their approach is to use an international strategy. Hisense, a $3.3 billion consumer electronics group, which emerged in China in 1994, now sells over 10 million TVs and 3 million air conditioners in more than 40 countries. It is even the leading seller of flat screen TVs in France. How did Hisense achieve this enviable position in such a short time?

Part of the answer may be that many of the emerging market companies present local companies with important advantages. Many emerging markets are extremely competitive, and the ones that survive have managers with honed skills to thrive in a hypercompetitive environment. Furthermore, the rapid growth of the local markets has provided emerging market multinational companies with ample cash to invest in overseas markets. For instance, with access to 10 percent of the TV market share in China, Hisense has been able to use the Chinese market to perfect its product and marketing approach. Furthermore, the Chinese market provides the company with a cheap and reliable manufacturing base. Adding strong design and world-class R&D enables a company to catapult over established competitors in more developed nations. It is predicted that the world will see many more successful emerging market multinationals.

Source: Based on Economist. *2008. "The challengers—Emerging market multinationals." January 12, pp. 61–62.*

---

opportunity to deal regionally with regional problems, such as competitive position, product mix, promotional strategy, and sources of capital.[8]

Regional trading blocs, such as the European Union (EU) and North American Free Trade Agreement (NAFTA), have led to relative uniformity of customer needs and expectations within member nations. Trading blocs also reduce differences in government- and industry-required specifications for products. As a result, companies within the trading bloc can use regional products and regional location advantages for all value chain activities. The rise of trading blocs has also forced some former multidomestic strategists, especially in Europe and the United States, to adopt regional strategies. For example, Procter & Gamble and DuPont have combined their subunits in Mexico, the United States, and Canada into one regional organization. With this strategy, these companies gain some of the advantages of both local adaptation and transnationalization.

A Brief Summary and Caveat

Students of multinational management should realize that all these strategies are general descriptions of multinational strategic options and that companies seldom adopt any of them in pure form. Companies with more than one business may adopt a different multinational strategy for each. Even single-business companies may alter strategies to adjust for product differences. In addition, governmental regulations regarding trade, historical evolution of the company, and the cost of switching strategies may prevent a firm from fully implementing any given strategy.

Exhibit 6.1 summarizes the content of the four basic multinational strategies. As the exhibit shows, the array of multinational strategic options means that managers must carefully analyze the situation for their companies when formulating or choosing a strategy. Which strategy works best? Different companies

EXHIBIT 6.1   Multinational Strategy Content

Strategy Content	Transnational Strategy	International Strategy	Multidomestic Strategy	Regional Strategy
Worldwide markets	Yes, as much as possible, with flexibility to adapt to local conditions	Yes, with little flexibility for local adaptation	No, each country treated as a separate market	No, but major regions treated as similar market (e.g., Europe)
Worldwide location of separate value chain activities	Yes, anywhere, based on best value to company—lowest cost for highest quality	No, or limited to sales or local production replicating headquarters	No, all or most value chain activities located in country of production and sales	No, but region can provide some different country location of activities
Global products	Yes, to the highest degree possible, with some local products if necessary; reliance on worldwide brand recognition	Yes, to the highest degree possible, with little local adaptation; companies rely on worldwide brand recognition	No, products made in and tailored to the country of location to best serve needs of local customers	No, but similar products offered throughout a major economic region
Global marketing	Yes, similar strategy to global product development	Yes, to the highest degree possible	No, marketing focuses on local country customers	No, but region is often treated similarly
Global competitive moves	Resources from any country used to attack or defend	Attacks and defenses in all countries, but resources must come from headquarters	No, competitive moves planned and financed by country units	No, but resources from region can be used to attack or defend

use different approaches to suit their needs. Consider LG Electronics' successful localized approach in its various markets in the next Focus on Emerging Markets.

The following section presents diagnostic questions that multinational managers can use to select a strategy appropriate for their company. These diagnostic questions guide multinational companies in resolving the global-local dilemma.

Resolving the Global-Local Dilemma: Formulating a Multinational Strategy

The selection of a transnational, multidomestic, international, or regional strategy depends to a large degree on the globalization of the industry in which a company competes. Multibusiness companies need to consider the degree of globalization within all the industries in which they compete.

What makes an industry global? George Yip calls the trends that globalize an industry the globalization drivers. **Globalization drivers** are conditions in an industry that favor the more globally oriented transnational or international strategies over the locally oriented multidomestic or regional strategies.[9]

Globalization drivers Conditions in an industry that favor transnational or international strategies over multilocal or regional strategies.

Focus on Emerging Markets

LG Electronics' Success in Emerging Markets

LG Electronics is currently the world's top producer of air conditioners and is among the top three producers in other appliances, such as washing machines, microwave ovens, and refrigerators. It is the dominant player in emerging markets like India in nearly every appliance and electronics category. It has a 40 percent market share of plasma TVs in the Middle East and Africa. Furthermore, although it is a relative newcomer in the Chinese market, LG has been successful and has achieved sales of $8 billion in China.

LG uses an in-depth localized strategy. It tries to understand the realities and subtleties of the local market by establishing local research, manufacturing, and marketing facilities. Such efforts come easily to LG, which pioneered the kimchi refrigerator in South Korea. Kimchi, which is made from fermented cabbage seasoned with garlic and pepper, is used with most meals in South Korea. However, it has a strong smell that can overpower other items when placed in a regular refrigerator. About 20 years ago, LG introduced a special refrigerator with a separate compartment for kimchi. This product has been very successful, encouraging competitors like Samsung to introduce similar products.

LG's localization strategy in India provides a good understanding of its approach. To meet local Indian needs, LG offers refrigerators with large compartments for vegetables and water storage and with surge-resistant power supplies to deal with frequent power outages. LG even customizes its products to suit local customers' color preferences, selling red refrigerators in the south and green in Kashmir. It offers microwave ovens with dark interiors to mask staining from curries. Additionally, to take advantage of the Indian passion for cricket, LG offers televisions that come with cricket video games.

LG's localization strategy in the Middle East is also noteworthy. It has developed the *Qur'an* TV with the entire text of the *Qur'an* installed on screen. Viewers can also have the Holy Book narrated to them. LG has already incorporated Bluetooth connectivity to its plasma TVs because more consumers want that connectivity. For instance, consumers can use their TVs to directly view pictures taken on their mobile phones.

LG's localization approach in emerging markets has been successful because it realized that customers in emerging markets generally do not yet have strong brand loyalties. By offering products adapted to the local needs, LG can start to build its own brand. For example, LG's research in other markets has resulted in products such as microwaves with preset shish kebab heat settings in Iran and refrigerators with special compartments to store dates in the Middle East. Research in Russia revealed that people are more likely to entertain indoors during the harsh winters. LG then developed a karaoke phone that can hold more than 100 Russian songs. The phone has been very popular, and LG sold more than 220,000 handsets in 2004.

Sources: Based on Esfahani, Elizabeth. 2005. "Thinking locally, succeeding globally." Business 2.0, December, pp. 96–98; Middle East Company News. 2009. "LG—A plasma powerhouse in Korea, Middle East and Africa," April 27.

The globalization drivers fall into four categories: markets, costs, governments, and competition. Associated with each of these areas are key diagnostic questions that strategists must answer in selecting the degree of globalization of their multinational strategies. The more positive the answer to each of these questions, the more likely it is that the company should select a global transnational or international strategy.

Global Markets

- *Are there common customer needs?* Increasingly, in many industries, such as automobiles, pharmaceuticals, and consumer electronics, customer needs are converging. However, in industries where cultural differences, income, and physical climate are important, common customer needs are less likely.

- *Are there global customers?* Global customers are usually organizations (not individual consumers) that search the world market for suppliers. PC manufacturers usually become global customers for PC components.

- *Can you transfer marketing?* If you can use the same brand name, advertising, and channels of distribution, the industry is more global.

Costs

- *Are there global economies of scale?* In some industries, such as the disposable syringe industry, no one country's market is sufficiently large to buy all the products of efficient production runs. To be cost-competitive, firms in this industry must go global and sell worldwide.

- *Are there global sources of low-cost raw materials?* If so, it pays to source your raw materials in those countries with this advantage. If not, it is probably cheaper to produce the product at home and avoid the additional costs of shipping and administration.

- *Are there cheaper sources of highly skilled labor?* If so, as in the case of raw materials, the strategic push is for companies to manufacture in foreign locations. The move of many U.S. manufacturing operations to Mexico and the use of manufacturing plants in Eastern Europe by German companies are examples of the many companies seeking global sources of lower costs.

Governments

- *Do the targeted countries have favorable trade policies?* Government trade policies differ by industry and product. Import tariffs, quotas, and subsidized local companies are examples of policies that restrict global strategies. For example, import restrictions and heavy subsidies of rice farmers in other countries keep foreign competition out of Japan and maintain domestic prices that often approach four times the world market price. Trade agreements such as the World Trade Organization and trading blocs such as NAFTA and the EU encourage global strategies by lowering governmental trade restrictions, at least among member nations.

- *Do the target countries have regulations that restrict operations?* Restrictions on foreign ownership, on advertising and promotional content, and on the extent of expatriate management present barriers to full implementation of a transnational or international strategy.

Competition

- *What strategies do your competitors use?* If transnational or international companies successfully attack the markets of multidomestic companies, then the multidomestics may have to become more global.

- *What is the volume of imports and exports in the industry?* A high volume of trade suggests that companies see advantages in more global strategies.

Caution

The increasingly popular strategy of going global by making uniform products for the world market can sometimes backfire. Cultural and national differences still exist, and even transnational and international strategists must adjust to key differences in national or regional needs. However, managing the degree of local adaptation can also be a challenge. The next Multinational Management Challenge shows how McDonald's is searching for the right mix.

Next, we discuss how the globalization drivers push some firms toward the transnational strategy and others toward the international strategy.

Some firms may have competitive strengths in downstream activities, such as customer service, but compete in industries with strong globalization drivers. Other companies may produce high-quality products efficiently but compete in

Multinational Management **Challenge**

Find the Right Level of Local Adjustment

At one time, McDonald's was the quintessential model of international growth and success. At the peak of its international expansion in 1996, McDonald's opened 2,000 stores. When it opened its first store in Kuwait City, the drive-through line stretched for seven miles. However, the number of new store openings is now falling.

The McDonald's business model is based on rigid standards for cleanliness, speed, and uniformity of the eating experience, if not uniformity of all its products. Consistency in serving cheap food in familiar settings, whether it is Moscow, Idaho, or Moscow, Russia, was the recipe for expansion. Although the form of its restaurant is a global product, McDonald's has always shown an ability to adapt locally. It has veggie burgers in India, beer in most European stores, and even a drive-through for snow-mobiles in Sweden.

The debate is whether the global product setting with some local adaptation is still a viable model for international competition. Some analysts note that the more McDonald's becomes local, the less it can position its product as an American experience. Without that mystique, McDonald's quick-and-cheap strategy is subject to attack by local competitors, who can often provide fast food at lower prices. For instance, in India, McDonald's had to be very local from the day the first store was opened. It had to develop recipes from scratch and had to get these new items approved by the appropriate authorities. Care had to be taken to avoid beef and pork altogether to be sensitive to India's Muslim and Hindu customers. Furthermore, McDonald's had to devise a system to completely separate vegetarian items from nonvegetarian items across all activities in the value chain. Similarly, in France, McDonald's is becoming even more local. In some markets, gone are the trademark golden arches from restaurants that do not resemble the classic cookie-cutter model. Facing increased competition from fast baguettes, McDonald's remodeled nearly 1,000 French stores for a more upscale and not so uniform image. Early signs show that the strategy is working, but whether McDonald's can use the same model worldwide remains a question.

Sources: Based on Dutta, Devangshu. 2005. "The perishable food chain in India: Opportunities and issues." Just-Food, September, pp. 22–28; Ghazvinian, John, and Karen Lowry Miller. 2002. "Hold the fries: Mighty McDonald's has long been the epitome of Pax Americana. Lately the multinational giant has stumbled. Here's why." Newsweek, December 30, pp. 16–20; Leung, Shirley. 2002. "McHaute cuisine: Armchairs, TVs and espresso—is it McDonald's—burger giant's makeover in France boosts sales; big changes for fast food—some franchisees have a beef." Wall Street Journal, August 30, p. A1; McDonald's. 2009. http://www.mcdonalds.com.

industries with strong pressures for local adaptation. In such circumstances, multinational companies often compromise and select a regional strategy. For the firm with upstream competitive strengths, such as high-quality R&D, the regional strategy allows some downstream adaptation of products to regional differences. For the firm with downstream competitive strengths, such as after-market service, the regional strategy allows some of the economies of scale produced by activities such as centralized purchasing and uniform products.

Exhibit 6.2 shows how these factors and the pressures for globalization and local responsiveness combine to suggest different multinational strategies.

Transnational or International: Which Way for the Global Company?

In globalized industries, companies with global strategies tend to perform better than multidomestic or regional strategists because they can usually offer cheaper or higher-quality products or services. How do companies choose between these two approaches to globalization—the transnational and the international?

To select a transnational over an international strategy, the multinational manager must believe that the benefits of dispersing activities worldwide offset the costs of coordinating a more complex organization. For example, a company may do R&D in one country, parts manufacturing in another, final assembly in another, and sales in a fourth. Coordination of these activities across national borders and in different parts of the world is costly and difficult.

In contrast to the transnational strategist, the international strategist believes that centralizing key activities such as R&D reduces coordination costs and gives economies of scale. The cost savings from these economies of scale then offset the lower costs or high-quality raw materials or labor that the transnationalist can find by locating worldwide.

Once multinational managers choose their basic internationalization strategic approach—that is, their multinational strategy—they must also select the operational strategies necessary to enter different countries. Strategic operations are discussed in detail next.

Participation Strategies: The Content Options

Regardless of their choice of a general multinational strategy (e.g., multidomestic or transnational), companies must also choose exactly how they will enter each international market. For example, multinational managers must decide whether to export only or to build a manufacturing plant in the target country. The strategies that deal with how to enter foreign markets and countries are called **participation strategies**. This section reviews several popular participation strategies, including exporting, licensing, strategic alliances, and foreign direct investment.

Participation strategies
Options multinational companies have for entering foreign markets and countries.

EXHIBIT 6.2   Multinational Strategies, Value Chain Locations of Competitive Advantages, and Pressures for Globalization or Local Responsiveness

Global/Local Responsiveness Pressures	Primary Source of Competitive Advantage in Value Chain	
	Upstream	Downstream
High pressures for globalization	Transnational strategy or international strategy	Regional strategy compromise
High pressures for local responsiveness	Regional strategy compromise	Multilocal strategy

Exporting

Exporting is the easiest way to sell a product in the international market. The effort can be as simple as treating and filling overseas orders like domestic orders, often called **passive exporting**. At the other extreme, a multinational company can put extensive resources into exporting with a dedicated export department or division and an international sales force. The export options beyond passive exporting are discussed next.

Although exporting is often the easiest participation strategy, it is an important one. In the United States, most export sales, as measured in dollars, go to large companies. The aircraft manufacturer Boeing, for example, receives over half of its revenues from exports. However, most U.S. exporters are small companies. As we will see in the next chapter, exporting is often the only strategy available to small businesses.

Most governments understand the importance of exports to the economy. In the United States, several federal agencies work closely with states to provide assistance to small companies interested in exporting.

Export Strategies

Once a company moves beyond passive exporting, they can adopt two general export strategies: indirect and direct exporting.

Small firms and new exporters usually find indirect exporting the most viable option. In **indirect exporting**, intermediary or go-between firms provide the knowledge and contacts necessary to sell overseas. Indirect exporting provides a company with an export option without the risks and complexities of going it alone.

The most common intermediary types are the export management company (EMC) and the export trading company (ETC). An **export management company (EMC)** usually specializes in a particular type of product or in a particular country or region, and it may have both product and country specializations. Usually for a commission, it provides a company with ready-made access to an international market. For example, a U.S. apple producer who wished to export to Japan would seek an EMC specializing in fruit products for the Asian market. Good EMCs have established networks of foreign distributors and know their products and countries very well. An **export trading company (ETC)** is similar to an EMC and provides many of the same services. The ETC, however, usually takes title to the product before exporting; that is, the ETC first buys the goods from the exporter and then resells them overseas. The most important advantage of an EMC or an ETC is that a company can quickly get into a foreign market at a low cost in terms of management and financial resources.

In contrast to indirect exporting, **direct exporting** is a more aggressive strategy in which exporters take on the duties of the intermediaries; that is, the exporters make direct contact with companies located in the foreign market. Direct exporters often use foreign sales representatives, foreign distributors, or foreign retailers to get their products to end users in foreign markets. At the highest level of investment, direct exporters may set up their own branch offices in foreign countries.

Foreign sales representatives use the company's promotional literature and samples to sell the company's products to foreign buyers. Sales representatives do not take title to products, nor are they employed by the direct exporters. Rather, sales representatives have contracts with companies that define their commissions, their assigned territories, the length of agreements, and other

Passive exporting Treating and filling overseas orders like domestic orders.

Indirect exporting Intermediary or go-between firms provide the knowledge and contacts necessary to sell overseas.

Export management company (EMC) Intermediary specializing in particular types of products or particular countries or regions.

Export trading company (ETC) Intermediary similar to EMC, but it usually takes title to the product before exporting.

Direct exporting Exporters take on the duties of intermediaries and make direct contact with customers in the foreign market.

details. Unlike foreign sales representatives, foreign distributors buy products from domestic sellers at a discount and resell the products in a foreign market at a profit. Typically, the foreign distributor is an intermediary selling to foreign retailers rather than to end users.

Licensing

International **licensing** is a contractual agreement between a domestic licenser and a foreign licensee. A licenser usually has a valuable patent, technological know-how, a trademark, or a company name that it provides to the foreign licensee. In return, the foreign licensee provides royalties to the domestic licenser. Licensing provides one of the easiest, lowest-cost, and least risky mechanisms for companies to go international. Licensing, however, is not just for small companies or for companies with limited capital. Even the giant multinationals use licensing when the conditions are right. The next Case in Point shows how Disney is licensing its characters for use in European supermarkets.

Exhibit 6.3 shows the contents of a typical licensing agreement. The licensing agreement or contract provides the legal specifications of the relationship between the licensee and the licensor. These contracts can be quite complex. They deal with everything from specific descriptions of the licensed product or technology to how the licensing agreement will end. Usually specialized attorneys from both countries work to prepare a document that is valid in both countries.

> **Licensing**
> Contractual agreement between a domestic licenser and a foreign licensee. (Licenser usually has a valuable patent, technological know-how, a trademark, or a company name that it provides to the foreign licensee.)

Some Special Licensing Agreements

Many international firms enter foreign markets using agreements similar to the basic licensing agreement. Like the more general forms of licensing, these agreements allow firms to operate in foreign countries without extensive capital investments.

International franchising is a form of comprehensive licensing agreement. The franchisor grants to the franchisee the use of a whole business operation, usually including trademarks, business organization, technologies and know-how, and training. Some worldwide franchisors, such as McDonald's, even

> **International franchising**
> Comprehensive licensing agreement where the franchisor grants to the franchisee the use of a whole business operation.

C A S E   I N   P O I N T

Disney and Licensing

In 2009, Disney had very ambitious plans for its licensing divisions. It anticipated licensing its characters for products such as toys, clothing, food, and consumer electronics. It was working closely with many of the large retailers, such as U.K.-based Tesco, French-based Carrefour, and U.S.-based Wal-Mart and Target, to increase its licensing arrangements with many of the retailers' own brand products. It had even signed a licensing agreement with Lego, which would start making kits for the many Disney Pixar films, such as *Toy Story* and *Cars.*

Disney also planned to become more closely associated with healthy foods for children. The company did not renew its ten-year global promotional contract with McDonald's. Instead, it was working to license its characters to encourage children to eat healthy food. For instance, British-based Tesco started selling satsumas, a citrus fruit, with stickers of "collectible" characters based on the Winnie the Pooh stories. Children were encouraged to transfer these stickers to a sticker book. Disney planned to extend these licensing agreements to other fruits such as bananas and apples. In fact, it launched more than 300 new products during 2005, and it was continually working to extend licenses to other products.

Sources: Based on Marketing Week. 2009. "Disney signs licensing deal with Lego," February 19, p. 9; Wiggins, Jenny. 2006. "Disney banks on Winnie formula." Financial Times, June 8, p. 20–22.

EXHIBIT 6.3   Content of a Licensing Agreement

What Is Licensed	Conditions of Use	Compensation	Other Provisions
Know-how; Special knowledge or technology	*Who:* Which companies can use the licensed property (and whether the use is exclusive)	*Currency:* In what currency	*Termination:* How to end the agreement
Patents: The right to use inventions	*Time:* How long the license lasts	*Schedule:* When payments must be made	*Disputes:* What type of dispute resolution mechanism will be used
Trademarks: Brand names, such as Levi's	*Where:* In what countries the license can or cannot be used	*Method:* Payments may be lump-sum, installments, royalties as a percentage of profits	*Language:* What the official language of the contract will be
Designs: The right to copy the design or production of final products	*Confidentiality:* Provisions to protect trade secrets or designs	*Minimum payments:* Agreements regarding minimum royalty	*Law:* What country's contract law will apply
Copyrights: the use of intellectual property, such as book material or CDs	*Performance:* What exactly the licensee has to do	*Other:* Fees for technical assistance, product improvements, training, etc.	*Penalties:* What penalties are in place for lack of performance by either party
	Improvements: Rights of the licensee and licenser regarding improvements in licensed property		*Reports:* What and when the licensee must report
			Inspections and audits: The rights of the licenser

Sources: Adapted from Beamish, Paul J., Peter Killing, Donald J. Lecraw, and Allen J. Morrison. 1994. International Management. Burr Ridge, IL: Irwin; Doherty, A. M. 2009. "Market and partner selection process in international retail franchising." Journal of Business Research, 62, pp. 528–534; Root, Franklin R. 1994. Entry Strategies for International Markets. New York: Lexington Books.

provide company-owned stores. To standardize operations, franchisees agree to follow strict rules and procedures. The franchisor, in turn, receives royalties and other compensation, usually based on sales revenue. U.S. companies, such as Holiday Inn, McDonald's, 7-Eleven, and Kentucky Fried Chicken, dominate the use of franchising as an international participation strategy.[10] The next Case in Point gives some background on worldwide franchising strategy.

An international company sometimes contracts with local foreign firms to produce its products overseas. Similar to the licensing agreement, the foreign companies use the international firm's technology and specifications to make products for their local market or for other markets. However, unlike the typical licensing agreement, the international firm still sells the products and controls marketing. This form of agreement is called **contract manufacturing**. It represents another means of quick, low-cost entry, especially for small markets not warranting direct investment.[11]

In **turnkey operations**, the international company makes a project fully operational before turning it over to the foreign owner. It is called turnkey because the multinational firm builds the project and trains local workers and managers on how to operate it. After this, the multinational firm gives the owners an operational project, which they start simply by "turning the key."

Turnkey operations occur usually in public construction projects done by multinational companies for host governments. For example, an international

Contract manufacturing
Producing products for foreign companies following the foreign companies' specifications.

Turnkey operations
Multinational company makes a project fully operational and trains local managers and workers before the foreign owner takes control.

C A S E   I N   P O I N T

Franchising Worldwide

Franchising is a popular way for global multinationals to expand their presence in other countries. For example, the British hypermarket operator Tesco is considering expanding to Malaysia through franchising in the convenience store market. It is already a market leader in the large-format stores but is considering franchising convenience stores to compete against the already established French rival, Carrefour, which already runs Carrefour Express in Malaysia.

The popularity of Japanese food in other Asian countries, such as China, Thailand, and Taiwan, is the major factor behind the surge in Japanese restaurants in these countries. However, most of this growth is originating in franchising efforts led by Japanese multinationals. For instance, Kazokutei Inc. which runs soba and udon noodle stores, plans on opening 200 to 300 franchises across China between 2009 and 2014. Similarly, other Japanese restaurant chains, such as Sato Restaurant, Marche Co., and Ootoya Co., have either opened new franchises or anticipate starting chains in other Asian countries.

Sources: Based on Daily Yomiuri. *2009. "Japanese restaurants spreading across Asia,"* March 14; Ganeshan, V. 2009. *"Tesco to consider Franchised stores."* New Straits Times, *March 10, p. 1.*

construction company, such as Bechtel, might build a hydroelectric power plant for a Middle Eastern government. Besides building the plant, the construction company would provide training for workers and management to make certain that the plant is fully operational in the hands of local people.

International Strategic Alliances

International strategic alliances are cooperative agreements between two or more firms from different countries to participate in business activities. These activities may include any value chain activity, from R&D to sales and service.

Gaining increasing popularity during the last decade, international strategic alliances have become one of the dominant participation strategies for multinational firms. Even firms such as IBM and General Motors, which have resources for and traditions of operating independently, have turned increasingly to international strategic alliances as basic participation strategies.[12] Thus, because of the importance of strategic alliances, a separate chapter is devoted to these issues. We will therefore discuss strategic alliance in Chapter 9.

> **International strategic alliance** Agreement between two or more firms from different countries to cooperate in any value chain activity from R&D to sales.

Foreign Direct Investment

Although international joint ventures (IJVs) are a special form of direct investment (i.e., ownership is involved), usually **foreign direct investment (FDI)** means that a multinational company owns, in part or in whole, an operation in another country. Unlike the IJV, a new firm is not created by parent companies. FDI reflects the highest stage of internationalization.

Multinational companies can use FDI to set up, from scratch, any kind of subsidiary (R&D, sales, manufacturing, etc.) in another country, or they can use FDI to acquire existing companies in another country. According to the *World Investment Report,*[13] cross-border mergers and acquisitions (M&As) are a major driving force affecting FDI. From 1996 to 2000, cross-border M&As increased by an average of 49.8 percent. In spite of the post-9/11 recession, which hit the developed nations hard, resulting in a 47.5 percent decline in M&As, the total

> **Foreign direct investment (FDI)** Multinational firm's ownership, in part or in whole, of an operation in another country.

Greenfield investments
Starting foreign operations from scratch.

value of mergers and acquisitions was still greater in 2001 than in 1998. Unlike **greenfield investments**, which involve starting your own foreign company from scratch, M&As provide speed and access to propriety assets. According to the *World Investment Report*,[14] the rapid pace of technological change and the liberalization of foreign investment policies by numerous countries are the major driving factors leading to more M&As as a form of FDI. Exhibit 6.4 illustrates the driving forces behind cross-border M&A activity based on a United Nations report of worldwide levels of FDI.

Reports by the Organisation for Economic Co-operation and Development (OECD) also suggest that foreign direct investment reached record levels in 2007.[15] Direct investment in OECD countries actually increased to $791 billion in 2007. Foreign direct investment outflows increased to around $1,150 billion. The main recipient of FDI in 2007 were the G7 countries. The United States, France, the U.K., and Canada were the main recipients of this foreign direct investment boom. Furthermore, FDI is playing an integration role because there are significant inflows to Eastern European countries, and these inflows have actually increased by 23 percent each year. China is also playing a critical role in foreign direct investment. Since 2000, China's outward flow of FDI has increased 19-fold, with most of these investments dominated by China's state-owned enterprises. These Chinese foreign direct investments are likely to flow to developing countries, such as those in Africa, rather than to industrialized nations.

EXHIBIT 6.4   **The Driving Forces of Cross-Border M&As**

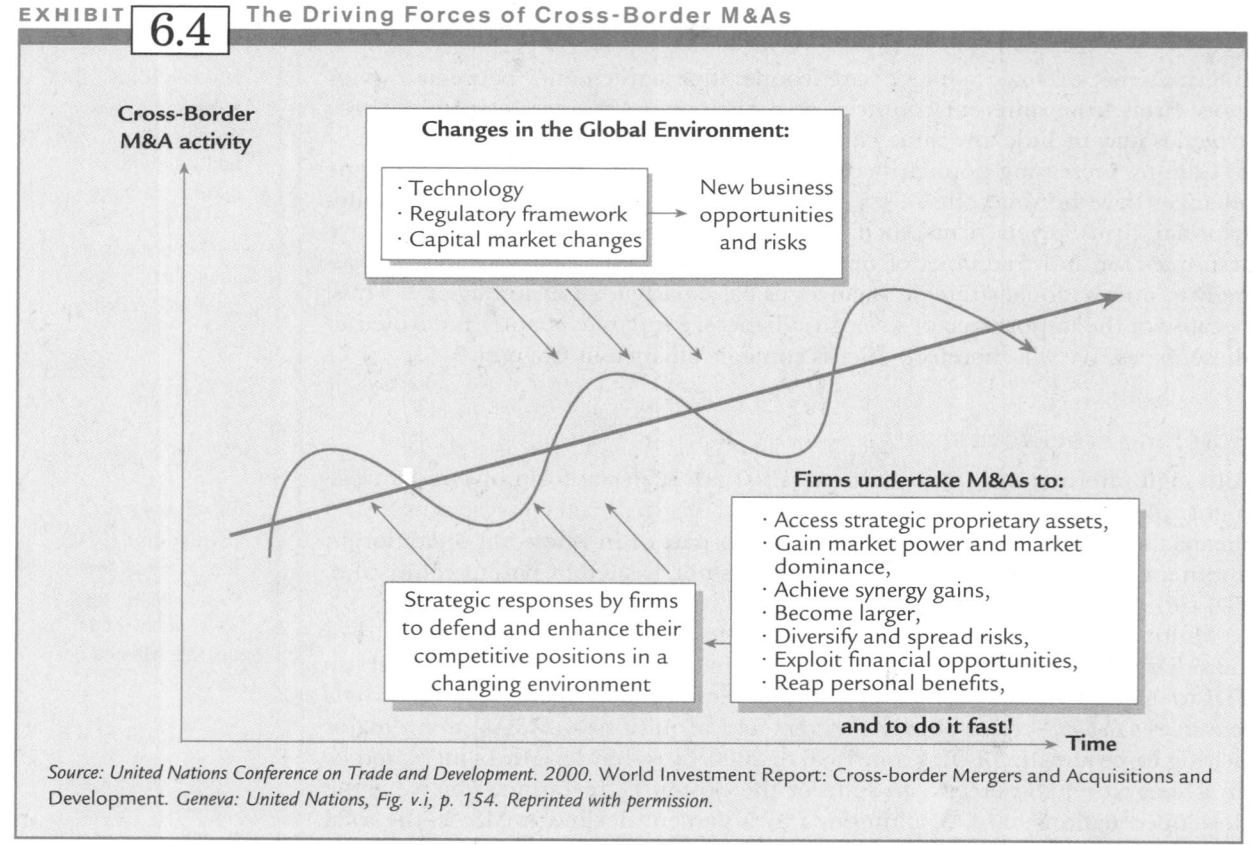

Source: United Nations Conference on Trade and Development. 2000. World Investment Report: Cross-border Mergers and Acquisitions and Development. Geneva: United Nations, Fig. v.i, p. 154. Reprinted with permission.

Some multinational companies set up foreign operations only to extract raw materials to support their production at home. This type of backward vertical integration is common in the steel, aluminum, and petroleum industries. Other companies set up foreign operations primarily to find low-cost labor, components, parts, or finished goods. Finished products or components are then shipped home or to other markets. Ford, for example, assembles some automobiles in Mexico and Thailand, primarily for export. Market penetration, however, is the major motivation to invest abroad. Companies invest in foreign subsidiaries to have a base for production or sales in their target countries.[16]

The scale of FDI often changes as firms gain greater returns from their investments or perceive less risk in running their foreign operations. For example, a multinational manufacturing firm may begin with only a sales office, later add a warehouse, and still later build a plant or acquire a local company with the capacity just to assemble or package its product. Ultimately, at the highest scale of investment, the firm can build or acquire its own full-scale production facility.[17]

Despite the importance of FDI, most experts agreed that the economic downturn of 2008–2009 would see falls in FDI levels. As economies contracted, most companies and countries were likely to reduce the amount of their investments overseas.

Although multinational companies have many options regarding how to participate internationally, the difficult questions focus on choosing the right participation strategy for a company and its products. The next section addresses these questions in detail.

Formulating a Participation Strategy

As with any strategy, formulating a participation strategy must take into account several issues, including the basic functions of each participation strategy; general strategic considerations regarding the company and its strategic intent, products, and markets; and how best to support the company's multinational strategy. We will next deal with each of these issues in turn.

Basic Functions of Participation Strategies

Deciding on an Export Strategy

Exporting is the easiest and cheapest participation strategy, although it may not always be the most profitable. However, it is a way to begin to internationalize or to test new markets. Most companies will continue to export even as they adopt more sophisticated participation strategies. However, a company must answer this question: Which form of exporting should it choose?

Each export strategy has some advantages and some drawbacks. As with most business decisions, the relatively great potential profits of direct exporting are offset by the commensurate financial risk and the need to commit resources.[18] In addition, there are considerations regarding the needs and capabilities of the company. The following diagnostic questions can help multinational managers select the best export strategy for their companies:[19]

* *Does management believe it must control foreign sales, customer credit, and the eventual sale of the product to the customer?* If yes, choose a form of direct exporting.

* *Does the company have the financial and human resources for creating an organizational position or department to manage export operations?* If not, choose a form of indirect exporting.

- *Does the company have the financial and human resources to design and execute international promotional activities (for example, international trade shows and foreign language advertisements)?* If not, rely on the expertise of intermediaries; choose a form of indirect exporting.

- *Does the company have the financial and human resources to support extensive international travel or possibly an expatriate sales force?* If yes, choose a form of direct exporting.

- *Does the company have the time and expertise to develop its own overseas contacts and networks?* If not, rely on the expertise of intermediaries; choose a form of indirect exporting.

- *Will the time and resources required for the export business affect domestic operations?* If not, favor direct exporting.

When Should a Company License?

The decision to license is based on three factors: the characteristics of the product selected for licensing, the characteristics of the target country in which the product will be licensed, and the nature of the licensing company.

The Product   The best products to license use a company's older or soon-to-be-replaced technology. Companies that license old technologies avoid giving potential competitors their newest innovations while using the license to profit from earlier investments.

Often, licensed products no longer have domestic sales potential, perhaps because the domestic market is saturated or domestic buyers anticipate new technologies. However, old technologies may remain attractive to the international market for several reasons. First, in countries where there are no competitors with recent technology, strong demand may still exist for the licensed product, even if it is based on old technology. Second, the foreign licensees may not have production facilities capable of producing the latest technology. Third, from the licensee firm's point of view, it may still have an opportunity to learn production methods or other information from a licensor's old technology.[20]

The Target Country   The situation in the target country may make licensing the only viable participation strategy. Factors that add costs to a product often make licensing more attractive than exporting. Trade barriers, such as tariffs or quotas, add costs to finished goods that can make exporting unprofitable. In this situation, rather than transferring a physical product, a company can transfer the intangible know-how through a license. For example, a brewing company that exports kegs of beer may face stiff import tariffs. However, by licensing the brewing process to a local brewer, know-how is transferred, and tariffs or import quotas are avoided.

Other issues associated with the target country affect the licensing decision. Sometimes it is the only option. For some military and high-technology products, local governments require that the production be done locally. In other situations, licensing is the low-risk option. Political instability or the threat of a government takeover of companies in the industry can make the lower risks of licensing more attractive. Because a firm neither contributes equity nor transfers products to the host country, it only risks losing the licensing income in an unstable environment. Finally, the market may simply be too small to support any investment larger than licensing.[21]

The Company Some companies lack adequate financial, technical, or managerial resources to export or to invest directly in foreign operations. With licensing, however, the company does not have to manage international operations. There is no need for an export department, a foreign sales force, or an overseas manufacturing site. The company's managers do not need to know much about operations in the foreign country or how to adapt their product to local needs. The licensee assumes these chores and responsibilities. Thus, licensing is a low-cost option. It does not demand much from the licensing company, and it often is the most attractive option for small companies.[22]

Having more than one product makes it more advantageous for a company to license. Multiproduct companies can license their more peripheral or sideline products but not their key or most important products. This protects their core technologies from potential competitors but still allows additional profits from licensing.[23]

Some Disadvantages of Licensing Although a low-cost and low-risk strategy, licensing presents four major drawbacks.[24]

First and most important, licensing *gives up control*. Once an agreement is signed and the trademark, technology, or know-how is transferred, there is little the licensor can do to control the behavior of the licensee, short of revoking the agreement. For example, a licensee may not market the product adequately or correctly.

Second, a company may create a *new competitor*. The licensee may use the licensor's technology to compete against it not only in the licensee's country but elsewhere in the world market. Even though a contract may prohibit future use of the technology or its use in other countries, local laws may not support this type of clause in the licensing agreement. In addition, even with the protection of local laws, the cost of foreign litigation may make enforcement too costly to pursue.

Third, *low income* generally results. Royalty rates seldom exceed 5 percent. Often licensees are less motivated to sell a licensed product with its shared profits than to sell its own, homegrown products.

Fourth, there are *opportunity costs* to licensing. The licensee removes the opportunity to enter the country through other means, such as exporting or direct investment. Usually the licensing contract grants licensees the exclusive right to use trademarks or technologies in their countries, excluding even the licensor.

Why Do Companies Seek Strategic Alliances?

Given the importance of strategic alliances to multinational companies, we consider them separately in Chapter 9.

Some Advantages and Disadvantages of FDI

All but the most experienced international firms usually try other forms of participation strategies before they select direct investment. Exporting, licensing, or alliances can prepare a firm for FDI and can minimize the chances of failure. In any case, however, the advantages and disadvantages of FDI must be weighed. Exhibit 6.5 summarizes the advantages and disadvantages of FDI.

Choosing a Participation Strategy: General Strategic Considerations

Once a multinational manager considers the general merits of each possible participation strategy, there are several broader strategic issues for multinational

EXHIBIT **6.5**   Advantages and Disadvantages of FDI

Advantages	Disadvantages
Greater control of product marketing and strategy	Increased capital investment
Lower costs of supplying host country with the firm's products	Drain on managerial talent to staff FDI or to train local management
Avoiding import quotas on raw material supplies or finished products	Increased costs of coordinating units dispersed worldwide over long distances
Greater opportunity to adapt products to the local markets	Greater exposure of the investment to local political risks as expropriation
Better local image of the product	Greater exposure to financial risks
Better after-market service	
Greater potential profits	

Source: Adapted from Root, Franklin R. 1994. Entry Strategies for International Markets. *New York: Lexington Books.*

managers to consider: (1) their company's strategic intent regarding profits versus learning, (2) the capabilities of their company, (3) local government regulations, (4) the characteristics of the target product and market, (5) geographic and cultural distance between the home country and target country, and (6) the tradeoff between risk and control.[25]

The strategic intent of a multinational will likely determine its participation strategy. If it is interested in short-term profit, the costs and benefits of the various participation strategies can be compared and the most profitable one used. However, many companies enter international markets with a low emphasis on short-term profit. Other goals—such as being first in a market with potential or learning a new technology—often motivate their internationalization efforts. For example, many firms have entered China and the former Eastern bloc countries with the knowledge that profits will be possible only in the distant future.

The multinational has to assess its capabilities to determine its extent of internationalization. For many companies, exporting is the only viable option, but companies should also consider human resource issues. Do they have the managers who can run a wholly owned subsidiary, transfer to a joint venture, or even supervise an export department? Production capabilities may be important if the company needs to adapt its products to foreign markets.

The product targeted for the international market affects the participation decision in several ways. For example, products that spoil quickly or that are difficult to transport might be poor candidates for exporting, whereas products that need little adaptation to local conditions might be good candidates for licensing, joint ventures, or direct investment. Another key issue relates to how and where the product is sold. This means that a company must address the question of how to get the product to market. Can the firm use local channels of distribution? If not, it might explore exporting or joint ventures. If it can develop its own channels of distribution, direct investment might be the best strategy.

Geographic or cultural distance plays an important role. Physical distance raises several issues. When the producing country is far from the consuming country, exporting may be limited by excessive transportation costs. Even with direct investment for production, sometimes components or raw materials have to be shipped to the producing country. However, cultural distance can often be just as important—if not more so. Cultural distance is the extent that national cultures differ on fundamental beliefs, attitudes, and values. Usually, when two countries have distinctly different cultures, the foreign company initially avoids direct investment. Instead, joint ventures, for example, are attractive because they allow local partners to deal with the many local cultural issues. Licensing and exporting further remove the foreign company from direct dealings with the local culture.

Next we discuss the control-versus-risk tradeoff.

The Control-Versus-Risk Tradeoff: The Need for Control

A company going international must determine how important it is to monitor and control overseas operations. Key areas for concern over control are product quality in the manufacturing process, product price, advertising and other promotional activities, where the product is sold, and after-market service. Companies, such as McDonald's, that use uniform product quality for competitive advantage often have high needs for control. FDI usually provides the greatest control.

Usually, participation choices that increase control entail greater risk. For example, exporting and licensing are low-risk ventures, but they surrender control over the product or service to another party. The various forms of FDI allow firms to maximize control, but they also expose the firm to the greatest financial and political risks. Exhibit 6.6 shows the tradeoffs between risk and control for common international participation strategies.

EXHIBIT 6.6   **Risk-Versus-Control Tradeoff**

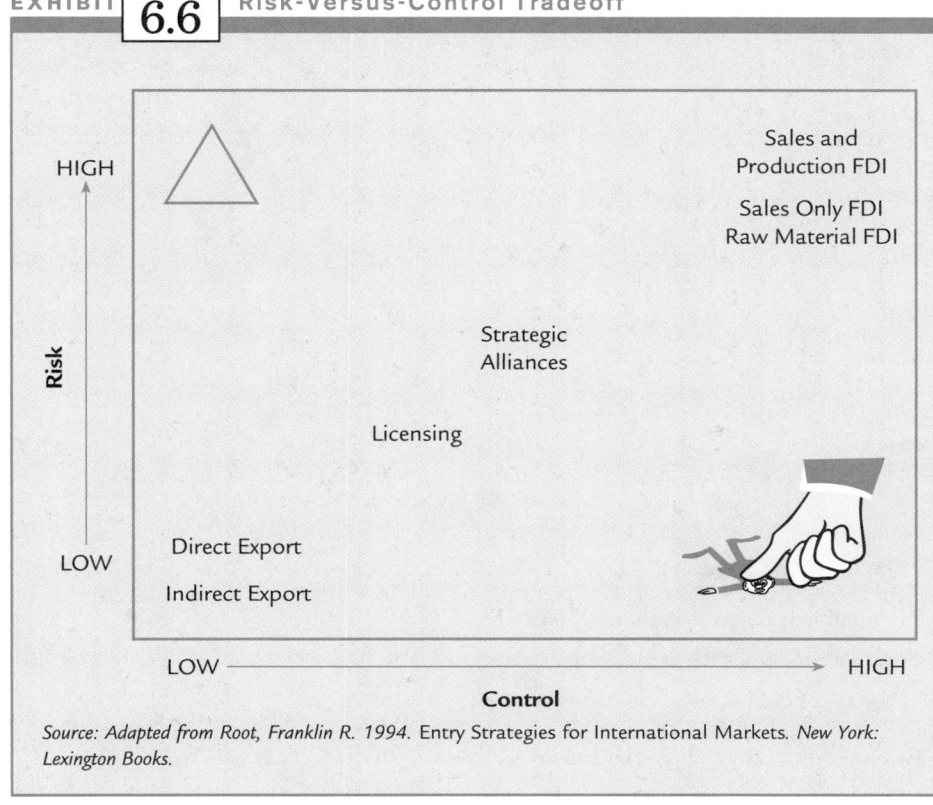

Source: Adapted from Root, Franklin R. 1994. Entry Strategies for International Markets. New York: Lexington Books.

Exhibit 6.7 summarizes the preferred participation strategies for companies facing different conditions. Ultimately, and perhaps most important, participation strategies must align with the multinational strategy, a subject that the next section addresses.

Participation Strategies and the Multinational Strategies

Should a transnational strategist use mostly FDI? Should an international strategist use mostly exporting? There are no simple answers to these questions.

Why a company is in a host country dictates its choice of a general multinational strategy. Transnationalists seek location advantages and may be in any

EXHIBIT 6.7   Decision Matrix for Formulating Participation Strategies

Company Situation		Participation Strategies				
		INDIRECT EXPORT	DIRECT EXPORT	LICENSING AND CONTRACTS	IJVs AND OTHER ALLIANCES	FDI
STRATEGIC INTENT	Learn the market			👍	👍👍	👍👍👍
	Immediate profit	👍👍👍	👍👍👍	👍👍	👍	👍
COMPANY RESOURCES	Strong financial position				👍👍	👍👍👍
	International expertise				👍👍👍	👍👍👍
LOCAL GOVERNMENT PRODUCT	Favorable regulations		👍	👍	👍👍	👍👍
	Difficult to transport			👍👍	👍👍	👍👍
	Easy to adapt	👍👍	👍👍	👍	👍	👍
GEOGRAPHY	Long distance between markets			👍👍	👍👍	👍👍
CULTURE	Large differences between cultures	👍👍	👍	👍	👍👍	👍
NEED FOR CONTROL	High				👍	👍👍👍
RISK	Low	👍👍👍	👍👍	👍	👍	👍

👍 = Favorable conditions for participation strategy

👍👍 = More favorable conditions for participation strategy

👍👍👍 = Most favorable conditions for participation strategy

Source: Adapted in part from Root, Franklin R. 1994. Entry Strategies for International Markets. *New York: Lexington Books.*

country for any value chain activity. Multidomestics seek local adaptation, and they must determine whether this is best done by modifying home country exports or by locating the entire value chain from R&D to service in each country. Thus, the basic diagnostic question for the multinational manager is which participation strategy best serves the firm's objectives for being in the country or region. In this sense, participation strategies represent the nuts and bolts of how a company is actually going to use international markets and country locations to carry out its more general multinational strategies. Exhibit 6.8 describes how companies with various multinational strategies might use the different participation options.

EXHIBIT 6.8   Participation Strategies and the Multinational Strategies

Participation Strategies	Multinational Strategies			
	Multidomestic	**Regional**	**International**	**FDI**
Exporting	Export uniquely tailored products to different countries	Export similar products to each region served	Export home-produced global products worldwide	Export global products made in the most advantageous locations to any other country
Licensing	License local companies to produce products with flexibility to adapt to local conditions	License local companies to produce product with flexibility to adapt to regional conditions	License only when export barriers or other local requirements preclude imports from the home country	License only when export barriers or other local requirements preclude imports from optimal production locations or when local risk factors or other barriers preclude FDI
Strategic cooperative alliances	Use when partner's knowledge is required for local adaptation of product or service	Use when partner's knowledge is required for regional adaptation of product or service	Use alliances for upstream value chain activities when required by own resources (e.g., investment cost); use down-stream alliance under same conditions as licensing	Use alliance for upstream value chain activities when required by own resources (e.g., investment cost or knowledge); use downstream alliance under same conditions as licensing
FDI	Own full value chain activities in each country—from raw materials to service	Own full value chain activities in regions—distribute activities within regions for location advantages	Use for down-stream sales and after-market services	Invest anywhere in the world for location advantages in sourcing, R&D, production, or sales

Political Risk

In the previous section, we looked at some of the ways in which companies can participate in international markets. However, events early in this century suggest that multinationals have to assess and deal with political risk when making entry decisions. Terrorist activities and wars are making political risk a more crucial factor than ever in investment decisions today. Furthermore, while emerging markets present significant potential, many of them suffer from high degrees of political risk. In this final section, we look at political risk and what multinational companies can do to offset it.

Political risk is the impact of political decisions or events on the business climate in a country, such that a multinational's profitability and feasibility of its global operations are negatively affected.[26] For example, consider Russia's politically motivated jailing of Mikhail Khodorkovsky, the business tycoon;[27] the Ukraine's disputed recent elections resulting in presidential uncertainties;[28] the Brazilian government's insistence that both government agencies and private citizens use only open source software; and the turmoil in countries like Iran, Lebanon, and Sudan. In such cases, government actions or related incidents raise uncertainties in the business climate, and multinational firms have to carefully consider whether those uncertainties might constrain their investments.

Why should a multinational company be concerned about political risk? Historically, many multinational companies have understood that political risk can have a serious impact on profitability. In fact, for companies like Royal Dutch/Shell, political risk is so important that they dedicate whole departments to assessing it. However, changes in the global situation have accentuated the need for an increased understanding of political risk. For instance, although many multinational companies find that outsourcing production to locations such as India or Kenya can reduce costs, they also are discovering that workers in such locations often work in very harsh conditions that can greatly exacerbate the risk of social unrest.[29] Furthermore, the world is dependent on energy sources in locations with high political risk (e.g., Venezuela, Saudi Arabia, Nigeria), and political instability in these societies can have dramatic effects on multinational firms. Additionally, because the world is so connected, political uncertainties in one country can have substantial reverberations around the world. Consider the next Case in Point.

As the Case in Point will demonstrate, given the importance of political risk, it is useful to understand some of the factors that influence political risk in any society. Bremmer argues that all the factors that can politically stabilize or destabilize a country play important roles in political risk assessments.[30] Some of the most common factors are changes in the government, a sudden shift in governmental policies or ideology, social volatility, the passage of new laws, leadership changes and the related potential for unrest, and the level of corruption.[31] How can a multinational company assess these various factors? The next Multinational Management Brief lists some important questions that a multinational company must ask before it decides to invest in a country.

Not all companies can afford to dedicate departments to understanding political risk, as Royal Dutch/Shell does. In these cases, various agencies can provide risk assessment ratings to multinational companies, which can consult them in making decisions about the appropriateness of investment decisions. One of the most popular such companies is the Economist Intelligence Unit, which offers risk ratings to multinational firms.

Political risk
The impact of political decisions or events on the business climate in a country such that a multinational's profitability and feasibility of its global operations are negatively affected.

C A S E   I N   P O I N T

Political Risk in Russia

Multinationals operating in Russia have had to face significant political risk. Consider the case of BP's joint venture with Russia's TNK-BP. When the multibillion-dollar joint venture was created in 2003, the then Russian president hosted a reception to toast the agreement. However, BP is now facing a lawsuit and the danger of losing its significant investment. The lawsuit originated with TNK-BP's shareholders, who claimed that BP did not operate the joint venture in their interests. In January of 2008, visas for 148 BP expatriates were not renewed, and in March the offices of both BP and TNK-BP were raided.

Political risk in Russia is of concern not only to foreign multinationals, but also to local companies. In fact, about 8,000 companies annually face lawsuits, often initiated by rivals who want to stop the companies' operation or take them over. The corrupt legal system allows competitors to bribe the police to start rival company investigations, which can range from criminal investigations to office raids and even to favorable court rulings.

Source: Based on Samara, J. B. 2008. "Russia's raiders." BusinessWeek, June 16, pp. 67–71.

Another indicator is the index of democracy, which is a measure of the extent of freedom in a society. Exhibit 6.9 shows the ratings for selected countries. High degrees of freedom suggest that companies may have a freer operating environment.

Given the impact of political risk on operations and profitability, multinational companies must take the appropriate steps to assess and manage it. Several options are available. Some private organizations offer political risk insurance, and the governmental agency Overseas Private Investment Corporation (OPIC) provides insurance against various risks such as political violence,

Multinational Management **Brief**

Political Risk Assessment

Political risk assessment is a very subjective and difficult task. However, experts suggest that asking a number of key questions can provide preliminary insights into the political risk of a market that a multinational firm is choosing to enter:

* How durable and resilient is the political system?
* How peaceful have governmental transitions been in the past?
* What roles do other nongovernmental organizations, such as trade unions, churches, and the press, play in the country's political stability?
* Could internal factors, such as social, ethnic, or religious tensions, result in social unrest or civil war?
* What is the level of corruption?
* How reliable is the rule of law?
* What is the likelihood that the country can be hit by natural disasters such as tsunamis or earthquakes?

Sources: Based on Bremmer, Ian. 2005. "Managing risk in an unstable world." Harvard Business Review, June, pp. 51–60; Wade, Jared. 2005. "Political risk in Eastern Europe." Risk Management Magazine, March, 52(3), pp. 24–29.

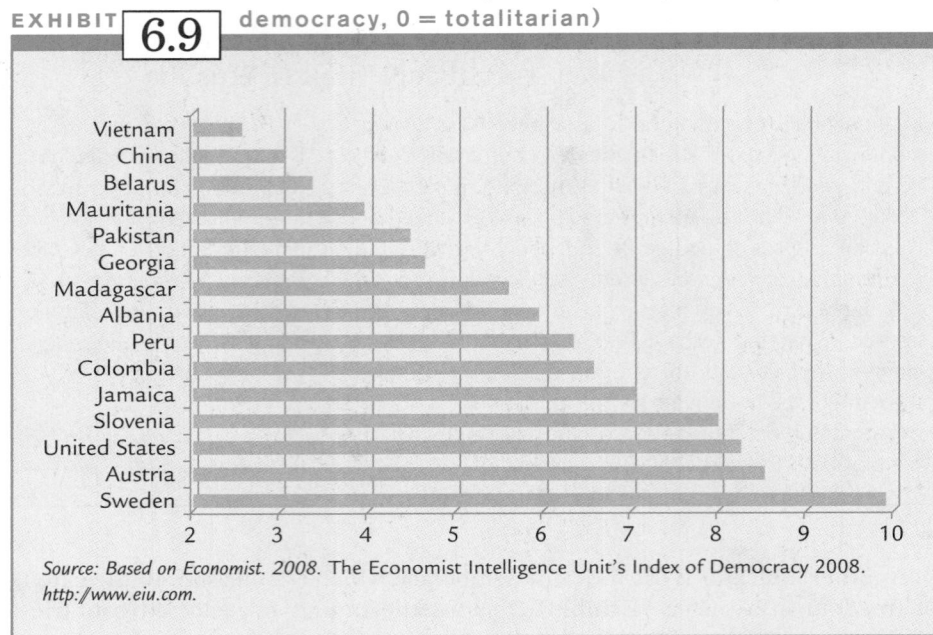

EXHIBIT **6.9**   Index of Democracy (2008; 10 = perfect democracy, 0 = totalitarian)

Source: Based on Economist. 2008. The Economist Intelligence Unit's Index of Democracy 2008. http://www.eiu.com.

foreign currency inconvertibility, expropriation, and other types of interference with business operations. However, the insurance can be expensive because it may not always be easy to quantify the risks, and, for some forms of insurance, insurers may not be able to offer protection at all. For example, many insurance underwriters are now hesitant to insure foreign-owned natural-resource-extraction companies operating in Latin American countries such as Bolivia, Ecuador, and Venezuela.[32] In such countries, recent government actions have greatly constrained the business operations of multinational firms.

Multinational companies can also rely on local partners to mitigate political risks. For instance, Japan's Sumito Chemical entered into a $4.3 billion joint venture with Saudi Arabia's Aramco to build a major petrochemical plant in Saudi Arabia.[33] Such ventures may help a company deal with local political risk. Furthermore, in a case study of various international firms, Lankova and Katz showed that multinational companies often can take a high-involvement strategy by developing a network of government, business, and public partners to help them face local political risks.[34]

Multinational companies clearly will continue to invest in countries with high levels of political risk. Many of the emerging markets with the highest potential (e.g., Egypt, Colombia, Jordan) have high levels of political risk,[35] but such markets usually present tremendous potential. Furthermore, as Bremmer argues,[36] some of these markets may be so unstable that further instability does not have much influence. Political risk assessment is a very subjective exercise and can vary greatly by region or industry. Consequently, multinational firms must adequately assess political risk and then devise the appropriate measures to manage it.

Summary and Conclusions

The multinational manager faces an array of complex strategic issues. In the previous chapter, you saw how basic strategic management issues apply to the situations faced by multinational firms. In this chapter, you built on that knowledge to see how multinational managers confront strategic issues unique to the multinational situation.

All multinational managers, in both large and small companies, must deal with the dilemma of local responsiveness versus the global solution. The choice of a solution to this dilemma was called the multinational strategy, and each such strategy has its costs and benefits.

There are benefits to favoring local responsiveness, a form of differentiation. Through either the multidomestic or the regional strategy, the multinational company can meet the needs of customers by country or region. Tailoring products or services for each country, the pure multidomestic strategy is the most costly, but it allows the company to deal specifically with differences in culture, language, and political and legal systems. The regional strategy, however, goes only part of the way toward local adaptation. Regional adaptation is balanced against the efficiencies of doing things similarly in a whole region.

International and transnational strategists see the world as one market. They try to have global products with global marketing. The goal is to produce high-quality products as efficiently as possible. The transnational strategist differs from the international strategist primarily by using worldwide locations or platforms to maximize efficiency and quality. The transnational will do anything anywhere.

For the multinational company, participation in the international market may occur anywhere in the value chain. At some point, all multinational firms must choose participation strategies that focus on the downstream activities of selling their products or services. All participation strategies, from exporting to FDI, can be used for sales. Exporting focuses just on sales, although there may be other strategic benefits, such as learning about the market. However, the other participation strategies, including licensing, strategic alliances, and FDI, serve other value chain activities, including sales. For example, a multinational company might use a strategic alliance for R&D and sales in one country and FDI for production and sales in another country.

In a globalizing world, the complexities of choosing multinational and participation strategies present significant challenges to multinational managers. For example, the nature of the product, the government and political systems where the company locates, the risk of the investment, and the needs of the company to control operations (to name only a few issues) come into play in formulating strategic choices for the multinational company. The Cases in Point showed how practicing managers faced and responded to the challenge of formulating multinational and participation strategies.

Finally, political risk is becoming an increasingly important component of investment decisions. The final section discussed some of the components of political risk and the ways in which multinational firms can manage it.

Discussion Questions

1. Discuss the conditions in which a transnational or international firm is likely to perform better than a multidomestic or regional strategist. Contrast this with the opposite situation, where the multidomestic firm is more likely to be successful.

2. Contrast the transnational and international strategies in their approach to location advantages.

3. Pick a product and analyze its globalization potential, using Yip's diagnostic questions.

4. How might a small manufacturing company become a global marketer?

5. You work for a small company that has an innovative, low-cost production method for laser disks. A Chinese firm approaches your CEO to license the technology. The CEO asks you to write a report detailing the potential risks and benefits of this deal.

6. You work for a small company that has an innovative, low-cost production method for laser disks. A Belgian firm approaches your CEO to form a joint venture with your company. The CEO asks you to write a report detailing the risks and potential benefits of this deal.

7. Discuss some key issues to consider when choosing a participation strategy.

8. What is political risk? How can a multinational company manage political risk?

Multinational Management **Skill Builder**

Step 1. You have been contacted by a local company, which is a major producer of soy, an agricultural component that can be used for many purposes. Research the major products produced using soy.

Step 2. The CEO of the company wants to go international. The company is fairly small and has limited resources. Discuss the many options available to the company. Provide a rationale for which method would work the best.

Step 3. Research some more to find which countries import the most soy. Prepare a report discussing which countries would be best for the local company to sell to and the way that they should go about entering the market(s).

Endnotes

1 Humes, Samuel. 1993. *Managing the Multinational: Confronting the Global-Local Dilemma.* New York: Prentice Hall.

2 Ghoshal, Sumatra. 1987. "Global strategy: An organizing framework." *Strategic Management Journal*, 8, pp. 424–440.

3 Doz, Yves L. 1980. "Strategic management in multinational companies." *Sloan Management Review*, 21, pp. 2, 27–16; Porter, Michael E. 1986. "Changing patterns of international competition." *California Management Review*, 28, p. 2; Porter, Michael E. 1990. *Competitive Advantage of Nations.* New York: Free Press.

4 Ghoshal.

5 Bartlett, C. A., and S. Ghoshal. 2002. *Managing Across Borders: The Transnational Solution.* Boston: Harvard Business School Press.

6 Porter.

7 Hill, Charles W. L. *International Business.* Burr Ridge, IL: Irwin.

8 Morrison, Allen J., David A. Ricks, and Kendall Roth. 1991. "Globalization versus regionalization: Which way for the multinational?" *Organizational Dynamics*, Winter, pp. 17–29.

9 Yip, George S. 1995. *Total Global Strategy.* Upper Saddle River, NJ.: Prentice Hall.

10 Root, Franklin R. 1994. *Entry Strategies for International Markets.* New York: Lexington Books.

11 Ibid.

12 Beamish, Paul J., Allen J. Morrison, Philip M. Rosenzweig, and Andrew Inkpen. 2002. *International Management.* Burr Ridge, IL: Irwin.

13 United Nations Conference on Trade and Development (UNCTAD). 2002. *World Investment Report: Transnational Corporations and Export Competitiveness.* New York: United Nations.

14 United Nations Conference on Trade and Development (UNCTAD). 2000. *World Investment Report: Cross-Border Mergers and Acquisitions and Development.* New York: United Nations.

15 Organisation for Economic Co-operation and Development (OECD). 2008. Investment news, OECD. http://www.oecd.org/dataoecd/28/10/40283257.pdf.

16 Root.

17 Beamish et al.

18 Wolf, Jack S. 1992. *Export Profits: A Guide for Small Business.* Dover, NH: Upstart Publishing Company.

19 Ibid.

20 Beamish et al.

21 Ibid.

22 Root.

23 Beamish et al.

24 Root.

25 Ibid.

26 Clilck, Reid W. 2005. "Financial and political risks in US direct foreign investment." *Journal of International Business Studies*, 36, pp. 559–575.

27 Ibid.; Wade, Jared. 2005. "Political Risk in Eastern Europe." *Risk Management Magazine*, March, 52(3), pp. 24–29.

28 Bremmer, Ian. 2005. "Managing risk in an unstable world." *Harvard Business Review*, June, pp. 51–60.

29 Wade.

30 Bremmer.

31 Ibid.

32 Ceniceros, Roberto. 2006. "Political risk insurers leery of Latin America." *Business Insurance*, May 29, 40(22), pp. 21–22.

33 Baker, Greg. 2006. "Peace Dividends." *Financial Management*, March, pp. 16–18.

34 Lankova, Elena, and Jan, Katz. 2003. "Strategies for political risk mediation by international firms in transition economies: The case of Bulgaria." *Journal of World Business*, August 38(3), p. 182.

35 Davis, Chris. 2006. "Emerging markets still a good bet despite recent volatility: Long-term outlook remains strong but be careful, investors told." *South China Morning Post*, May 28, p. 15.

36 Bremmer.

Polaris 2008

Professors Rua-Huan Tsaih and Darren Meister wrote this case solely to provide material for class discussion. The authors do not intend to illustrate either effective or ineffective handling of a managerial situation. The authors may have disguised certain names and other identifying information to protect confidentiality.

Ivey Management Services prohibits any form of reproduction, storage or transmittal without its written permission. Reproduction of this material is not covered under authorization by any reproduction rights organization. To order copies or request permission to reproduce materials, contact Ivey Publishing, Ivey Management Services, c/o Richard Ivey School of Business, The University of Western Ontario, London, Ontario, Canada, N6A 3K7; phone (519) 661-3208; fax (519) 661-3882; e-mail cases@ivey.uwo.ca.

The 2008 Chinese New Year was still a few days off, but Polaris Financial Group (Polaris) Chairman Wayne Pai had already set off some fireworks. At the security firm's weekly management meeting, Pai had announced the approval of Polaris's investment plans in Singapore, Vietnam, and Abu Dhabi by the Financial Supervisory Commission (the highest administrative commission for Taiwan's banking, securities, and insurance sectors) of the Executive Yuan (Taiwan's highest administration office). This approval launched the further globalization of the Polaris Financial Group, a rapidly growing firm with operations in Taiwan and Hong Kong.

In Taiwan's securities exchange market, Wayne Pai's—and Polaris's—name was synonymous with innovation and entrepreneurship. Pai had led Polaris Securities Co. Ltd. (Polaris Securities) to a stand-out position in Taiwan's securities exchange market by launching online stock trading with a remarkable synergy of complementary assets. Pai had then transferred the business model to Polaris Securities (Hong Kong) Ltd. (Polaris Securities [HK]), including innovative information technology, affluent financial

experiences and good customer services. Past successes aside, after the meeting, Pai and the rest of the senior leadership team contemplated whether Polaris's Taiwan and Hong Kong models could be duplicated to Singapore, Vietnam, and Abu Dhabi. These new markets would likely demand new investments in some areas and provide opportunities to further leverage their existing assets.

Polaris Securities' Background

On July 22, 1988, Pai established Polaris Securities Co. Ltd. as a stock brokerage firm, with capital of NT$200 million.[1] Two years later, in June 1990, Polaris Securities obtained a license from the governing agency to be a full-service securities firm. In 1996, it was listed as an over-the-counter firm, and on September 16, 2002, its stock was approved for listing on the Taiwan Stock Exchange. By early 2008, total paid-in capital of Polaris Securities exceeded NT$19 billion, making it the major source of revenue for the Polaris Financial Group (see Exhibit 1 for Polaris Securities' major business operations; see Exhibit 2 for Polaris Securities' organizational chart). In 2008, total asset value of the Polaris Financial Group totaled more than NT$300 billion.

Pai had not only solidly established the securities firm but under his leadership, the Polaris Financial Group had swiftly reformed and restructured several times within the competitive Taiwan environment. For example, Pai had taken the initiative and merged three other securities firms—Da-Shun, Shi-Dai, and Hua-Yu — with Polaris Securities. Polaris had also purchased the Central Insurance Company in Taiwan, worked with the world's biggest futures company to set up Polaris MF Global Futures Co., Ltd. and purchased the Overseas Bank in Taiwan, which was later sold to Citigroup.

The stated business goal of the Polaris Financial Group was to help investors obtain more wealth management information and conduct their financial transactions. Polaris offered customers various financial and investment products and services, including margin purchases, assistance in issuing initial public offerings (IPOs), firm underwriting public subscriptions, financial consulting, corporate restructuring, securities and futures services, and other related professional investment services.

The major entities that comprised the Polaris Financial Group included Polaris Securities Co. Ltd.,

---

EXHIBIT 1   **Major Business Operations of Polaris Securities**

1. Consignment trading of securities in a centralized securities exchange market.

2. General trading of securities in a centralized securities exchange market.

3. Underwriting securities.

4. Consignment trading of securities in an over-the-counter market.

5. General trading of securities in an over-the-counter market.

6. Related agent services of securities.

7. Margin purchase and short sale of securities.

8. Futures introducing broker.

9. Consignment trading of foreign securities.

10. Securities firms to do futures dealing.

11. Short-term bill business.

12. Other related securities activities approved by a competent government agency.

Source: The Polaris Financial Group

Polaris MF Global Futures Co., Ltd., Polaris Securities Investment Trust, Polaris Pu-Tai Investment Consulting, Polaris Futures Co., Ltd., Polaris Holdings (Cayman) Ltd., Polaris Insurance Agent Co., Ltd., Bao-Ju Insurance Agent Co., Ltd., and other companies in which Polaris owned more than 50 percent of the shares (see Exhibit 3).

Although Polaris was a large company with 1,930 employees, its founder and president, Wayne Pai, who strongly believed in resourcefulness and entrepreneurial skills, dominated its management style. Polaris, for example, had revolutionized online trading in Taiwan and had grown its overall market presence through this initiative. Pai also believed that expanding globally would make Polaris an important company on the world's financial services' stage; leveraging Polaris's information technology assets was part of Pai's plan to support this expansion.

The History of Online Trading in Taiwan

Growth of Taiwan's securities market had been very strong prior to 1998, with many mid- and small-sized Taiwanese firms setting up as many branch offices as possible to compete for market share. After mid-1997, however, Taiwan's security firms found that opening branches did not acquire new customers but increased the operating costs. By 2000, the daily trading volume on the Taiwan Stock Exchange averaged NT$120 billion, and 1,100 security firm branch offices were operating in and around Taiwan.[2]

At the same time, online trading was becoming an important force in the United States and other economies. The Taiwanese company Da-Xin Securities (later Ji-Xiang Securities) realized the increased cost of branch offices could be countered by following the U.S. trend, although Taiwan's government had not yet approved online transactions. Da-Xin Securities introduced online stock trading on June 6, 1997, and on October 17, 1997, the Taiwanese government formally approved online stock trading, revising Taiwan's related regulations on November 6, 1997.

Similar to the situation for many U.S. firms, online stock trading did not immediately become a business success in Taiwan. Initially, some major Taiwanese securities firms, such as Yuan-Ta and Ri-Sheng, did not actively promote the online business because their securities brokers, who were worried about the possibility of decreasing commissions, were reluctant to cooperate. By the end of 1997, only four securities firms had embarked on online stock trading. In addition to brokers' objections, the introduction of online stock trading had led to security concerns being voiced by investors. Moreover, without profit guarantees, the boards of directors of Taiwanese securities firms were reluctant to support these investments.

Polaris Securities and Online Trading

At Polaris, however, a different story was unfolding. Pai believed in online trading and, because he owned

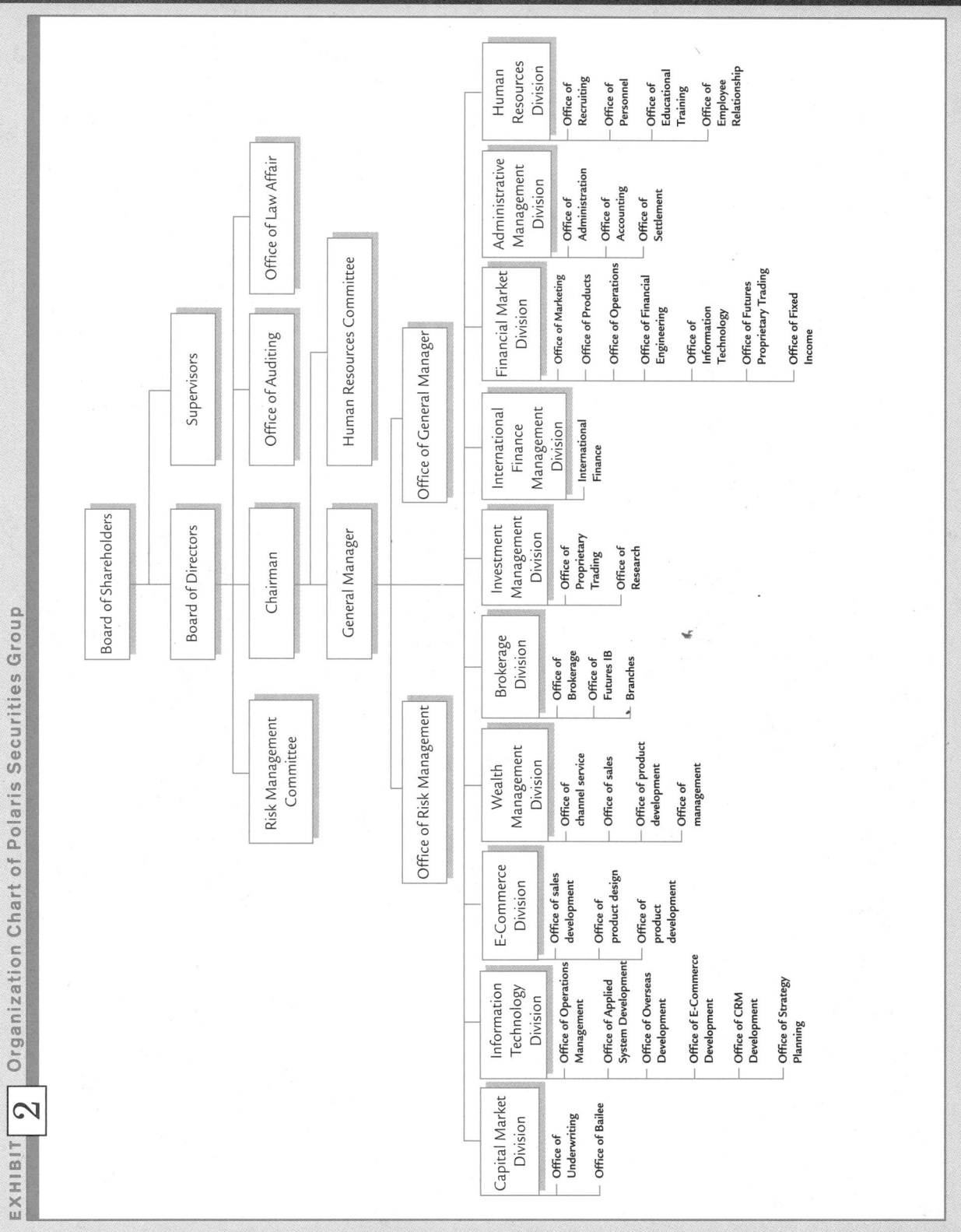

EXHIBIT 2   Organization Chart of Polaris Securities Group

EXHIBIT 3   Polaris Financial Group

Investment Company	Subsidiary	Business Type	% of Share Holding
Polaris Securities Co., Ltd.	Polaris MF Global Future Co., Ltd.	Futures	52.58%
	Polaris Securities Investment Trust	Investment & Trust	52.07%
	Polaris Pu-Tai Investment Consulting	Investment Consulting	99.91%
	Polaris Futures Co., Ltd.	Futures Management	100.00%
	Polaris Holdings (Cayman) Ltd.	Investment	100.00%
	Polaris Insurance Agent Co., Ltd.	Assets Insurance Agent	100.00%
	Bao-Ju Insurance Agent Co., Ltd.	Life Insurance Agent	100.00%
Polaris Holdings (Cayman) Ltd.	Polaris Securities (HK)	Securities	100.00%
	Polaris Capital (Asia) Ltd.	Securities	98.50%
	GC Structured Products Ltd.	Securities	98.62%
	Polaris Investment Management (Cayman) Ltd.	Investment	100.00%

Source: The Polaris Financial Group

20 percent of Polaris Securities' stock, his influence led the Polaris board of directors to unanimously authorize an online trading project to be launched in December 1997.

Pai insisted on a combination of tangible and virtual transactions, meaning that Polaris did not set up a new online stock trading department, but required securities brokers to engage in both traditional trading and online trading at the same time. Pai envisioned Polaris Securities' brokers as the seed team to launch online transactions. In 1997, Pai scrupulously interviewed and recruited a seed team and asked them to distribute information flyers on the streets to introduce the public to online stock trading.[3] Moreover, Pai used the following example to encourage his brokers:

> Once, one of our brokers was seriously ill and stayed in the hospital for eight days. However on the third day, his sale performance ranked 3rd in our Office of Brokerage. How did he do it? Most of his clients trade through the Internet and telephone. Consequently, his sales performance still ranked 3rd even though he was sick in the hospital.

Major securities customers were generally hesitant to engage in online stock trading because of perceived risks to their personal information. In 1997, to guarantee online transaction security and therefore win customer confidence, Polaris Securities and the Institute for Information Industry in Taiwan jointly developed "a golden key" with a secret design and digital signature. In 1999, Polaris Securities worked with RSA Security to launch a security passport that changed the secret code every 60 seconds.

Vertical Value-added Chain and Online Trading Systems

Chairman Pai has absolute decision power and employees do not object to his decisions. However, he also values employees' good ideas and responds to them quickly. Accordingly, Polaris Securities welcomes ideas and suggestions from the bottom up.

– Chang-Xueng Li[4]

Before launching online stock trading, Polaris had developed a complete vertical value-added chain and a well-designed trading platform. Specifically, Pai had established two affiliate companies—Russell Information Systems Co., Ltd. (Russell) and APEX International (APEX)—to form a vertical value-added chain. Russell, in the upstream, was responsible for collection, management, and analysis of original data. APEX, in the midstream, applied the information to develop financial models. Finally, Polaris utilized the information and models to offer various investment consulting services and financial products to its customers. As chairman, Pai requested that Polaris's trading platform cover operational activities among the front desk, middle office, and back office. Pai's goal was that not only software design in the front desk could offer customers investment consulting services and financial products but information technology systems in the middle office, and back office could properly match, confirm, clear, and settle related business activities (see Exhibit 4).

Pai also insisted on utilizing information technology to help innovate trading systems and offer other financial services.[5] For example, Polaris continued improving the

EXHIBIT 4   System Infrastructure of Polaris Financial Group

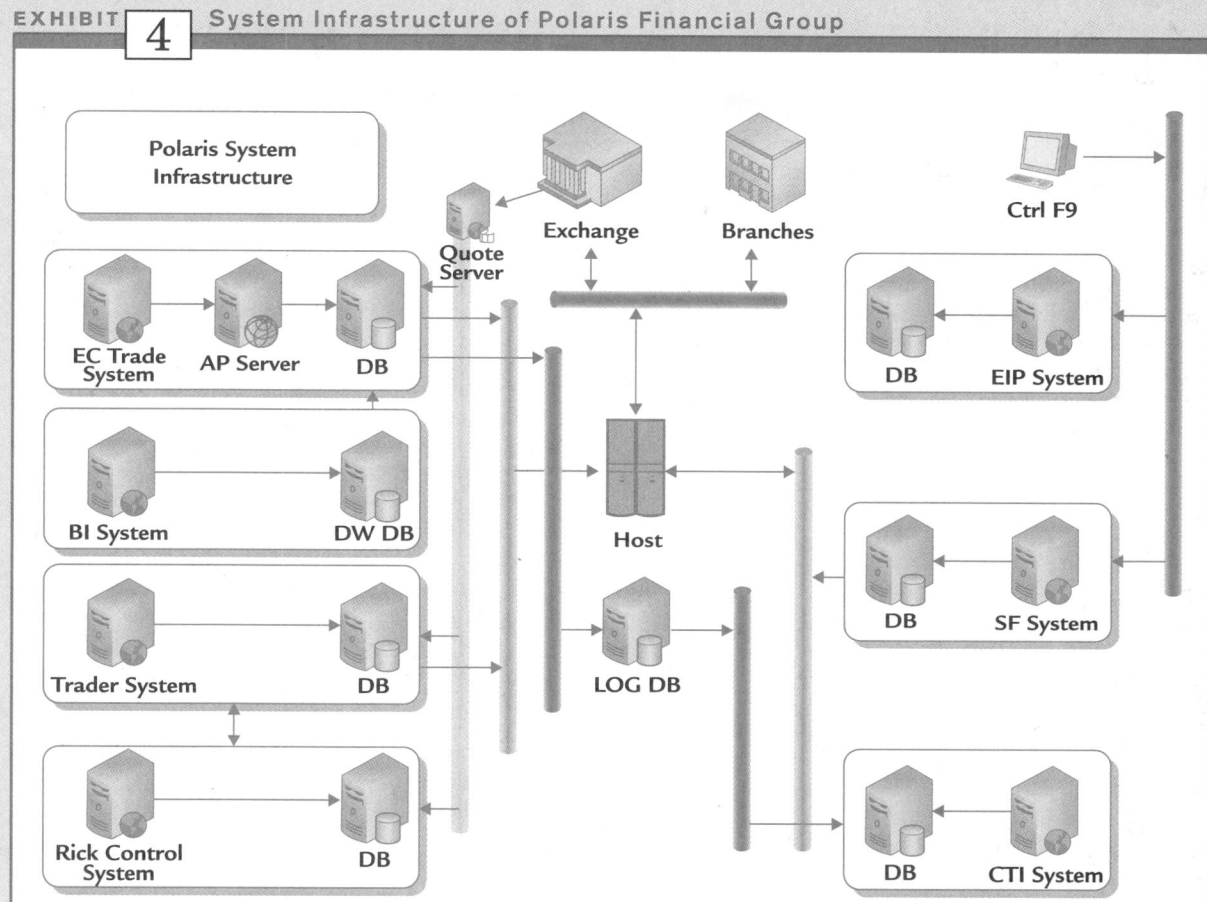

The abbreviation explanations are as follows: DB: Database; AP Server: Application Server; SF: Sales front Desk; EIP: Enterprise Information Portal; Ctrl F9: Content Provider/Content Collator; BI: Business intelligence; DW: Data warehouse.

Source: The Polaris Securities Group.

trading platform to meet customer needs, introducing changes every two or three years. In May 1999, Polaris Securities introduced the "Blue Wizard," which is a freeware of an online stock trading system enabling users to promptly keep an eye on the stock market fluctuation. Thanks to Internet information technology, the Blue Wizard successfully attracted huge numbers of customers. Polaris Securities' trading volume exceeded more than NT$20 billion at the releasing month, outperforming other securities companies. In 2001, Polaris Securities launched the first Chinese version of a multinational trading platform called "Polaris Financial Airport," which linked with 11 major stock exchanges in six regions of the world, offering investors 24-hour trading services. This trading platform brought about a large-scale business increase in the Polaris Securities overseas plural commission business,[6] ranking Polaris as one of the top three firms in the Taiwan securities market. Furthermore, Polaris Securities worked with the Central News Agency, offering large amounts of financial news to investors. Because the Central News Agency frequently updated its news content, the financial information offered by Polaris Financial Airport was always up-to-the-minute.

By the end of 2002, Polaris led the market. Key to its competitive victory was Polaris's introduction of the first electrified options trading platform called "Options Lotto Online Trading Platform." This pioneering platform led to Taiwan's options market growing by 13 times the following year. This growth also increased the options trading volume of Polaris Securities by more than 11 times.[7] Accordingly, Taiwan became one of the top 20 futures exchange centers in the world. In 2003, Polaris Securities developed a wealth management software, Polaris EWinner, through which investors could obtain all stock market information free of charge, save considerable transmission fees, access an unlimited self-selected stock-reporting system and obtain stock market analyses and forecasts. This software allowed investors to master the current stock market situation and easily make orders. In 2004, Polaris Securities and Da-Xin Securities, a leading Korean online trading company, signed an agreement to jointly develop a flexible and speedy customized Home Trading System, offering investors multifunctional trading services. In 2005, Polaris Securities introduced a powerful arbitrage profit trading system, Polaris BT Trade System, which helped investors set their own parameters, combined simulation analysis, monitored the market and responded according to an automatically determined arrangement and schedule. In 2006, Polaris Securities combined wealth management banking services to introduce the Smart FP Polaris Wealth Navigation System, the first wealth management online trading platform. Later, other securities firms followed Polaris's steps by launching related businesses.

After introducing online stock trading in 1998, Polaris Securities offered investors various trading channels and promoted its services to more potential clients, leading to online transactions accounting for more than 15 percent of the total securities market.[8] As of 2008, Polaris ranked first in the Taiwan financial market in terms of market shares of online stock trading, online futures and online options trading.

Beyond its innovative trading platform, the Polaris Financial Group had actively introduced new financial products to Taiwan. Following development experiences in other countries and trends in foreign financial markets, Pai believed that one of Polaris's competitive advantages should be the research capabilities and sales abilities for introducing derivative products to investors in Taiwan. Accordingly, Polaris had worked with local well-known universities in the early 1990s, making personnel and academic connections in the fields of finance and information technology. Therefore, when the Taiwanese government lifted restrictions on issuing warrants in 1997, Polaris became the first securities firm in Taiwan to issue Polaris 01 real estate warrants.[9] Moreover, Polaris launched Taiwan's first exchanged-traded fund (ETF) in 2003, known as the Polaris Taiwan Excellence 50 Fund. Within five months,

Polaris took the ETF public, breaking a world record for taking an ETF public.[10] The Polaris Financial Group, based on its financial capabilities, was good at designing customized financial products structured on the New Taiwanese dollar to boost the profit return. Polaris's structured products had also outperformed the market. Polaris further worked with the Russell Investment Group, the world's biggest investment consulting and pension management institute, to introduce a multi-manager fund that helped investors with well-rounded asset allocation management.[11]

The Hong Kong Experience Based on the advantages of financial innovation and online transaction, the Polaris Financial Group had not only outperformed other Taiwan financial groups[12] but had displayed outstanding performance abroad as well. Polaris had copied its Taiwan experience in innovative information technology and affluent financial experiences and exported it successfully to Hong Kong. When Polaris first entered Hong Kong in 2004, Polaris Securities (HK) ranked 150th in securities companies in the local market. Currently, the Polaris Financial Group, with its excellent performance, ranked 37th in Hong Kong. Accordingly, it was awarded "The Excellent Service Award of Best Securities Firm"[13] (see Exhibit 5 for a list of other honors and awards).

Since Taiwan's entry into the World Trade Organization in 2002, the Taiwanese financial services industry had faced increased globalization. Taiwan's manufacturing industry had already internationalized, with offices and factories established in China and other countries. Taiwan's financial services industry needed to follow in the steps of these manufacturers and establish branch offices offering related financial services in other countries. Opening branch offices in the neighborhood of Taiwanese manufacturers' overseas offices would give Taiwanese financial services firms a better understanding of how businesses operated in China and other countries, which would lead them to offer the appropriate financial services. The Polaris Financial Group was aware of this need and had been actively reaching for foreign markets.[14]

The Polaris Financial Group was looking to expand into the Greater China region.[15] As an initial step, in 1993, Polaris had established an office in Hong Kong, the most prosperous of the cities on the two sides of the Taiwan Strait and the ideal place, it seemed, to boost Polaris's influence among Asia's Chinese population. Polaris Securities (HK) had obtained several authorizations to practice in Hong Kong: an asset management license and other licenses specifically for dealing and advising in securities and for dealing in futures and commodities. Polaris Securities (HK) had

EXHIBIT 5   **Honors and Awards of Polaris Financial Group**

Polaris Securities Co., Ltd.

- Golden Goblet Award for Outstanding Talents in Business Leadership
- 2006 - Outstanding Financial Institution in Risk Management Award, *Asia Risk* magazine
- 2006 - Award for 2006 Annual Outstanding Trading in Taiwan, *The Asset* magazine
- 2005 - Golden Goblet Award for Outstanding Talents in Securities Industry
- 2005 - Golden Goblet Award for Outstanding Talents in Futures Industry
- 2004 - The Benchmark Enterprise in Securities Industry, *CommonWealth Magazine*
- 2003 - Golden Goblet Award for Outstanding Talents in Securities Industry
- 2003 - Outstanding Securities Firm in Taiwan, *AsiaMoney* magazine
- 2003 - Golden Goblet Award for Special Contribution

Polaris Securities Investment Trust

- Golden Goblet Award for Outstanding Financial Products Innovation
- Outstanding Assets Management Company in Taiwan, *Asia Investor* magazine
- Golden Goblet Award for Outstanding Talents in Investment Consulting
- 2004 - Outstanding Assets Management Company in Taiwan, *Asia Investor* magazine
- 2003 - Award for Best Product Innovation, *Asia Asset Management* magazine
- 2003 - Golden Goblet Award for Outstanding Talents in Investment Trust and Investment Consulting

Polaris MF Global Future Co., Ltd.

- Golden Goblet Award for Outstanding Talents on Futures Industry
- Ranked 1st in Revenues Earned by Securities Firms in Domestic and Foreign Markets
- Ranked 1st in Market Share of Securities Firms in Domestic and Foreign Markets
- 2004 - Ranked 1st in Clearing Awarded by Taiwan Securities Exchange
- 2003 - Ranked 1st in Clearing Awarded by Taiwan Securities Exchange
- 2003 - Golden Goblet Award for Outstanding Talents in Futures Industry

APEX International Financial Engineering Co., Ltd.

- 2006 - Ranked 11th among the Top 1000 Service Industries with high growth in net profits after tax, *Business Weekly* magazine
- 2006 - Ranked 19th among Fast 50 hi-tech companies with high profits in Taiwan, Deloitte & Touche
- 2002 - Financial award for innovation and technology R&D plan from Hsin-Chu Science Park
- 2002 - Financial award for New Financial Products and Risk Management Techniques by the Taiwanese Ministry of Economic Affairs
- 2001 - Financial award for Intelligent Assists Management Techniques by the Taiwanese Ministry of Economic Affairs

Source: The Polaris Financial Group.

also become a participant in the Hong Kong Stock Exchange with four trading seats.

To expand its corporate scope, Polaris Securities (HK) had adapted Taiwan Polaris's innovative information technology, financial experiences, trading platform, and customer services to the Hong Kong market. For example, Polaris Securities (HK) launched in Hong Kong a simplified Chinese version of the Polaris EWinner, trading software that facilitated investors in their online transactions. Because the language interface was a simplified Chinese version, investors in both Hong Kong and China could use it. Polaris Securities (HK) also worked with the Credit Suisse Group to introduce a back office trading system that offered investment products in seven markets around the world, including the United States, Japan, Hong Kong, Singapore, Taiwan, China and South Korea. The trading system offered investors a trading mechanism, trading information, a financial mechanism and trading opportunities. Polaris Securities (HK), through trading systems in Taipei and Hong Kong, set up a trading center across both sides of the Taiwan Strait. Trading center transactions dealt with a range of financial products, including securities, futures, options, structured products, Euro convertible bonds, and Global Depositary Receipts. The trading center offered its customers 24-hour cross-country multifunctional financial services, operated through a back office clearing and settlement system among different companies, markets, products, and foreign currencies.

Time for Decision-making

The past does not amount to the future. People cannot live on past successful experiences. The best choice is to proceed forward.

— Wayne Pai

The Polaris Financial Group expected to apply Polaris Securities' experiences to overseas markets. The firm's reasons for exploring individual markets varied. For example, the Hong Kong market gave Polaris the opportunity to collect international capital and acted as a stepping stone for entering China, which was enjoying remarkable growth in its financial market. Many Taiwanese manufacturers had established factories in Vietnam, and because many of these manufacturers trusted compatriot services, Polaris was eager to set up offices there to offer related financial services. Exploring the Singapore market involved obtaining an issuing license for emerging stocks in Singapore while learning about Singapore's financial development. Although Abu Dhabi was an off-shore financial center offering a platform for international capital flow, the city

allowed the Polaris Financial Group to easily collect capital for later development.

The Challenge

Developments in Vietnam, Singapore, Abu Dhabi, and other emerging markets posed a challenge for Polaris. Although the experiences of Polaris Securities and Polaris Securities (HK) provided a valuable background for the strategic initiatives in these countries, each market was characterized by its own laws and regulations, investors' habits, information technology infrastructure, and front, middle, and back office systems. Pai wondered how best to proceed. He knew he had to not only cope with individual market differences but also leverage Polaris's existing assets and experiences.

CASE DISCUSSION QUESTIONS

1. What critical success factors led to Polaris's launch of online stock trading and online transactions in Taiwan?
2. How did Polaris transfer its Taiwanese success to Hong Kong?
3. What advice would you give Wayne Pai?

CASE NOTES

[1] The exchange rate in 1988 is approximately US$1= NT$1.27.

[2] Ya-wei Lin. 1999. Gong-Cheng, Polaris, and Da-Xin are the top three electronic securities firms. *Business Weekly*, 599, May 17, pp.102–103.

[3] Mei-zhen Ren. 1999. Polaris heads all firms in on-line stock trading. *Business Weekly*, 610, August 2, pp. 126–128.

[4] Chang-Xueng, Li. 1999. Polaris securities and the electrification of financial service industry—To engage in continuous innovation in commercial models and to put emphasis on employees' core competence. *An Industry EB Model Case Study—Research Results in the Scientific and Technological Plan*, Taipei: Institute for information industry, pp. 2.26–2.35.

[5] Ibid.

[6] The overseas plural commission business, through domestic securities firms, helped domestic investors with an overseas commission business license to purchase and sell securities and financial products in overseas markets.

[7] Zi-Qiao Lin 2007. Wayne Pai, a pioneer in Taiwan finance market, leads Polaris' overseas expansion. *Capital CEO Magazine*, Hong Kong: South China Media 44, November, pp. 24–31.

[8] Ya-chin Huang 2002. Securities firms fighting for online trading business. *Win-Win Weekly*, 309, November 25, pp. 82–83.

[9] Xian-Da Si-Tu 2003. *Analysis on Strategic Management Case Studies: Concepts and Cases*. Taipei: Zhi-Sheng Culture, p. 164.

[10] Zi-Qiao Lin.

[11] Jun-hui Lin 2007. Multi-functional manager in fund management sweeps the market. *Timing Financial and Economic Network*, February 1, http://www.yi123.com.tw/forum_1494.html, accessed November 17.

[12] See Exhibit 5.

[13] Zi-Qiao Lin.

[14] Jie-zhi Wu 2001. Polaris securities explore its business in China with low profile. *Win-Win Weekly*, 225, April 8, pp. 110–111.

[15] *Greater China* is a term referring collectively to both the territories administered by the People's Republic of China (including Hong Kong and Macau) and territories administered by the Republic of China (Taiwan and some neighboring islands). This term is most commonly used in the investment and economics community, referring to their growing economic interaction and integration.

Small Businesses and International Entrepreneurship: Overcoming Barriers and Finding Opportunities

Learning Objectives

After reading this chapter you should be able to:

- Understand the basic definitions of small business and entrepreneurship.

- Explain how small businesses can begin as global start-ups or follow the stages of internationalization.

- Understand how small businesses can overcome barriers to internationalization.

- Identify when a small business or entrepreneur should consider going international.

- Describe how small businesses or entrepreneurs can find customers, partners, or distributors abroad.

- Understand how new venture wedge strategies can be used in foreign markets.

- Explain the factors driving entrepreneurship at an international level.

Preview CASE IN POINT

Small Businesses in China

China's economic success has been primarily due to small businesses. Whereas most of the economic output was coming from poorly run state-owned enterprises a decade ago, small businesses now contribute almost 60 percent of China's output. According to rough estimates, Chinese small businesses employ almost 75 percent of the urban work force. These small companies have often thrived on the business of a few clients or by selling large quantities of small-margin products.

The ongoing economic crisis has had a serious impact on these dynamic Chinese small businesses. Almost 62,400 companies shut down in the Guangdong province. In all of China, many companies closed, laying off millions of people. For instance, Ye Jianquing, a Chinese entrepreneur, saw a rapid decline in orders from his European and U.S. customers. His small business, which manufactures sunglasses, has seen orders decline by 80 percent from 2007 to 2008. He is now branching out to other products, such as key rings and prescription glasses, hoping to survive.

Experts predicted that the Chinese economy's performance would be heavily dependent on how its small businesses deal with the economic slowdown. The government recently recognized their importance, and government officials have actually requested that banks lend more money to them.

Source: Based on Chao, L., and A. Batson. 2009. "China's small factories struggle." Wall Street Journal, January 31, p. A6.

Small businesses contribute significantly to most national economies. As the Preview Case in Point shows, China has become an economic power primarily due to its small businesses, which support the economy by contributing to the economic output and providing jobs for millions of workers. Even in the developed nations of Europe, North America, and Japan, more than 98 percent of all businesses are small. In these countries, small businesses employ more than 50 percent of the workforce and produce nearly 50 percent of the countries' GNPs.

The U.S. economy is also very dependent on its small businesses. In fact, during the periods of downsizing by large firms in the United States, small companies created more than two-thirds of the new jobs.[1] How important are small businesses to the U.S. economy? Consider the following facts regarding American small businesses:[2]

- Small businesses represent 99.7 percent of all employing firms, employing about half of all private employees.
- Small businesses generate about 60 to 80 percent of all new jobs annually.
- Small businesses employ almost 41 percent of all high-tech workers.
- Small businesses pay almost 45 percent of the private payroll.
- Small businesses represent 97 percent of identified exporters, producing 29 percent of export value in 2007.
- Small businesses have generated 13 to 14 times more patents per employee than large patenting firms.

Given the importance of small businesses to the growth of most national economies and to the increasing globalization of business, it is not surprising that small businesses seek opportunities outside their national boundaries, just as their larger brother and sister firms do. When going international, small businesses can use the same participation strategies and multinational strategies available to larger businesses. They can export, form a joint venture, license, and engage in FDI. Small businesses can also act like multidomestic strategists in product adaptation, or they can develop transnational networks for supply, manufacturing, and distribution. In Korea, for example, small businesses account for approximately 40 percent of exports and 65 percent of Korean manufacturing FDI.[3]

Because they are small and often controlled by their entrepreneurs or founders, small businesses face circumstances different from those of larger multinational corporations. This chapter presents examples and reviews the barriers that small businesses face and must overcome in internationalization. It also shows how basic entrepreneurial strategies can serve small businesses in taking their products or services to the global marketplace.

What Is a Small Business?

There are many definitions of a **small business**. The United Nations and Organization for Economic Cooperation and Development (OECD) define small- and medium-size businesses as those having fewer than 500 employees.[4] The popular press usually considers small businesses as those with fewer than 100 employees. The U.S. Small Business Administration (SBA) has a more complex definition. Its definition of small varies by industry and uses both sales revenue and the number of people as indicators of size. For example, to be classified as small by the SBA, annual receipts cannot exceed $17 million in the general construction

Small business
UN definition: fewer than 500 employees. Popular press definition: fewer than 100 employees. The U.S. Small Business Administration's definition varies by industry and uses both sales revenue and the number of employees.

industry but may range up to $22 million in wholesale trade industries. In manufacturing industries, the maximum number of employees for small businesses ranges between 500 and 1,500, depending on the specific industry.[5]

Internationalization and the Small Business

Small business stage model
Incremental process of internationalization followed by many small businesses.

Global start-up/ born-global firm
Company that begins as a multinational company.

How do small businesses go international? This section examines two ways. First, some organizations follow the stages of international involvement, with each stage leading to greater involvement. This incremental approach to internationalization is called the **small business stage model**. Second, organizations can begin as global companies. They begin international operations at the same time they start up domestically. Going global from day one of the company's life is called a **global start-up** or **born-global firm**.

The next two sections discuss these processes.

The Small Business Stage Model of Internationalization

Traditionally, small business internationalization follows the stage model; that is, small companies take an incremental approach. These companies begin as passive exporters, filling international orders but not actively seeking such sales. It is assumed that these companies typically consider exporting only after they have a strong domestic base.[6] However, later they may add an export department or an international division, with a more proactive approach to international sales. Joint ventures and other forms of direct investment follow. The stage model probably applies to the majority of small business efforts at internationalization. Most but not all small businesses do not have the managerial and financial resources for immediate globalization.

The typical stages of internationalization for a small entrepreneurial business are:[7]

- *Stage 1—Passive exporting:* The company fills international orders but does not seek export business. At this stage, many small business owners do not realize that they have an international market.

- *Stage 2—Export management:* The CEO or a designated manager specifically seeks export sales. Because of resource limitations, most small businesses at this stage rely on the indirect channel of exporting (see Chapter 6). However, this stage is often a major change in orientation for the entrepreneur or small business manager. Exporting is seen as an opportunity for new business.

- *Stage 3—Export department:* The company uses significant resources to seek increased sales from exporting. Managers no longer see exporting as a prohibitive risk. The key for most small businesses is finding a good local partner for distribution.

- *Stage 4—Sales branches:* High demand for the company's product in a country or region justifies setting up a local sales office. Small businesses must have the resources to transfer home managers to expatriate assignments or to hire and train local managers and workers to run the operations.

- *Stage 5—Production abroad:* Production moves a company beyond downstream value chain activities. It allows companies to gain local advantages, such as easy local product adaptation or production efficiencies. Companies may use licensing, joint ventures, or direct investment. This is often a very difficult stage for a small business because the cost of a failed direct investment can put the survival of the whole company at risk.

- *Stage 6—The transnational:* Small size does not preclude a business from developing a globally integrated network that characterizes the transnational corporation. As we will see, some entrepreneurs begin their small businesses as transnationals.

Many small and some large companies find the incremental process of internationalization adequate for their strategic position. Following the stage model allows companies to minimize their exposure to risk and to develop their international expertise gradually. In contrast, other entrepreneurial companies have products that often require them to go international immediately or to move rapidly through the internationalization stages. In the next section, we discuss the growing phenomenon of global start-ups to show how rapidly some beginning businesses become global operations.

Small Business Global Start-Up, or Born-Global Firms

Global start-ups occur when companies begin as multinational companies. In fact, by definition, the born-global company must pursue a global vision from inception and globalize rapidly.[8] Impossible? Not in today's international marketplace. The next Multinational Management Challenge shows how one company was able to go global from its founding.

Multinational Management **Challenge**

Can You Go Global from Day One? Surftech Did.

Surftech is a small manufacturer of molded surfboards. Fifty-year-old entrepreneur Larry French has turned his passion into a transnational business.

With boards that cost around $800, Surftech targets the high end of the surfing market. However, its boards are manufactured in molds unlike the typical high-end product, which is handcrafted and shaped by skilled artisans. After demonstrating that his boards could perform equally as well as handmade types, French convinced 25 of the top shapers in the world to make molds for his products. With an innovative manufacturing process and top designers on board, he needed a production platform that could produce the boards in quantity. Like many transnational cousins, he found it—not in his native California, but in Thailand with a company skilled in producing sailboards.

Designers (shapers) from around the world produce masters. Then a mold is built, and, four months later, boards ship from Thailand to warehouses in the United States (Florida, Hawaii, and California), Australia, Japan, New Zealand, and the United Kingdom.

Surftech sold only 75 boards during its first year of business. However, French consistently pursued the world's top surfers. The company now has the endorsement of most of these individuals and sold between 18,000 and 20,000 boards in 2006.

"It's funny," French says. "We're running a sophisticated global business, but we're probably earning as much as the corner 7-Eleven. It's just not a business where you can have a machine churning out 200 parts an hour."

Sources: Based on Pitta, Julie. 2003. "Kowabunga! A surfin' safari supply chain." http://www.worldtrademag.com; Surftech. 2009. http://www.surftech.com.

Born-globals are critical to the international business environment. In fact, some have even argued that traditional multinationals have a lot to fear from born-globals. Born-globals are often very flexible and fast moving, especially in high-technology areas, because born-globals tend to be very knowledge intensive.[9] Such born-globals are thus often able to introduce innovations that may change the business environment.

How do companies following the small business model compare with born-global firms? Exhibit 7.1 shows some of the major differences.

Although not always possible for a new venture, the global start-up is an increasingly popular choice for many new companies—when the conditions are right. Although all entrepreneurial ventures are risky, global start-ups are riskier than domestic ventures. Nevertheless, even with the increased risk and complexity of immediately going international, global start-ups may offer the only avenue of success for new ventures in rapidly globalizing industries.

Small-Business E-Commerce

To a large extent, technology has helped to level the playing field for small companies. Today, a small business in rural Maine can export machine parts to 38 countries, using the Internet. A woman in Mississippi can export food products to Canada. Handcrafted bowls from Colorado can be sold in Japan.[10]

Regardless of whether a small business uses a stage development model or a global start-up model of going international, a Web site configured for e-commerce is a low-cost and quick way to sell products across national borders. However,

EXHIBIT 7.1   Comparison of Small Business Model Firms and Born-Global Firms

Attribute	Born-Global Firm	Small-Business Model
Managerial vision	Global from founding	International market developed after solid domestic market base
Previous global experience	Significant among founders	Low degree of previous global experience
Networking	Strong use of personal and business networks at both domestic and international level	Looser network with only foreign distributors playing a key role in internationalization efforts
International market knowledge	High from founding of firm	Low and slowly accumulating based on domestic market knowledge
Degree of innovation	High, though product differentiation based on leading-edge technology and technological innovativeness	Less innovative approach
Nature of international strategy	Niche-oriented and proactive international strategy to gain market share in key markets around the world	Broader market approach and more reactive strategic approach
Environmental approach	Fast and flexible	Less flexible
Nature of relationship with foreign customers	Strong customer orientation and close or direct customer relationships	Indirect relationships through intermediaries at early stages of internationalization

Sources: Based on Rialp, Alex, Josep Rialp, David Urbano, and Yancy Vaillant. 2005. "The born-global phenomenon: A comparative case study research." Journal of International Entrepreneurship, 3, pp. 133–171; Vapola, T. J., P. Tossavainen, and M. Gabrielsson. 2008. "The battleship strategy: The complementing role of born globals in MNC's new opportunity creation." Journal of International Entrepreneurship, 6, pp. 1–21.

besides the use of a Web site, the Internet provides small companies with the ability to undertake many other activities. Consider the next Case in Point.

As the Case in Point shows, small companies can be easily created using the power of today's Internet technology. Chapter 10 provides a longer treatment of the challenges associated with cross-border e-commerce. However, some of the major benefits follow.[11]

Advantages

- Ability of small firms to compete with other companies both locally, nationally, and internationally.
- Possibility and opportunity for more diverse people to start a business.
- Convenient and easy way of doing business transactions (not restricted to certain hours of operation; open 24 hours a day, seven days a week).
- An inexpensive way (compared to the cost of paper, printing, and postage prior to the Internet) for small businesses to compete with large companies.
- Availability of domestic products in other countries.

However, in spite of the expanding opportunities for small businesses to internationalize, psychological and resource-related barriers remain in place. The next section reviews some of the obstacles that often prevent small businesses from going international.

Overcoming Small Business Barriers to Internationalization

Conventional wisdom argues that small businesses face many barriers that prevent them from becoming multinational companies. Small size often means limited financial and personnel resources to dedicate to international activities.

CASE IN POINT

Global Hosted Operating System

Zvi Schreiber, born and educated in the U.K., came up with the idea of accessing personal documents from multiple computers after watching his daughter laboriously e-mail files to herself. He then decided to form Global Hosted Operating System (G.ho.st). G.ho.st is based in Ramallah, Palestine, and CEO Schreiber lives in Jerusalem. In fact, he has never visited the company headquarters in Ramallah because he is Israeli. How did he form the small business?

Schreiber used the many opportunities offered by the Internet. When he came up with the idea, he decided to hire Palestinians as a way to further his peace ambition and to create jobs for Palestinians. He Googled for "Palestinian software executives," and Google led him to Murad Tahboub, who runs an

IT-outsourcing company in Ramallah. Tahboub agreed to help start G.ho.st. and now about 30 Palestinian software engineers work in Ramallah. While CEO Schreiber and his three Israeli workers work in West Jerusalem, the rest of the engineers work in Ramallah, a town ten miles from Jerusalem, with the two towns separated by a concrete barrier.

Schreiber then organized a meeting where all of the employees met. Although the meeting seemed like a company picnic, it was the first time that both the Palestinian and Israeli employees of G.ho.st. met to talk about their families and a new product launch.

Source: Based on Lev-Ram, M. "A fighting chance." Fortune Small Business, March 19, 2, 62–63.

Small size can also mean a lack of sufficient scale to produce goods or services as efficiently as larger companies. Small companies often have top managers with limited international experience and possibly negative attitudes toward becoming multinational. Such managers view international ventures as too risky and not potentially profitable. Negative managerial attitudes and past success at home lead to organizational cultures with a strong domestic orientation.

Although many barriers to internationalization seem internal, small businesses also have to face contextual and other environmental issues that magnify the difficulties pertaining to international operations. These difficulties are particularly salient in many of the emerging markets in Central and Eastern Europe. Consider the next Focus on Emerging Markets.

In spite of the difficulties with internationalization, many small companies aggressively enter international markets and succeed. Next, we consider examples of how small businesses and entrepreneurs have overcome the barriers to establish successful multinational operations.

Developing a Small-Business Global Culture

Global culture
Managerial and worker values that view strategic opportunities as global and not just domestic.

A **global culture** occurs when an organization has managerial and worker values that view strategic opportunities as global and not just domestic. At all levels of the organization, members share a common language to describe international operations. This common language gives organizational employees a framework to interpret and understand their company's actions in the international arena.[12]

Generally, increased international competition and exposure to international markets have forced large companies, such as those in the automobile industry, to develop more of a global culture. The need for survival made it necessary for top executives of all nationalities to respond to global competition. Small businesses, however, often ignore international opportunities because key decision makers, given the culture of their organizations, see only their domestic competition. In a truly global culture, entrepreneurial owners develop an international mindset for themselves and for their companies. Thinking globally permeates everything that happens in the company. People believe that national boundaries are not so relevant and that the company can do business and conduct value chain operations (e.g., R&D, manufacturing, raising capital) anywhere in the world.

Several characteristics of the key decision makers in an organization affect the development of a global culture:[13]

- *Perceived psychological distance to foreign markets:* This is the extent to which managers believe that foreign markets are "just too different" for involvement. As the Focus on Emerging Markets feature illustrates, Australian small businesses found the psychic distance from the Central and European markets to be a significant constraint.[14] However, when key managers overcome this belief, a global culture can then develop.

- *International experience:* Managers with little training in foreign languages and little international travel often resist internationalization. However, managers with previous international experiences, even if just from personal travel and sightseeing, have a greater propensity to recognize global opportunities. Often even a chance meeting during a foreign vacation can trigger an international small business venture.

- *Risk aversion:* Managers who are unwilling to take risks have difficulty supporting internationalization. Going international requires an entrepreneurial spirit and thus the willingness to face risks.

Focus on Emerging Markets

Small Business Barriers in the Transitional Economies in Central and Eastern Europe

Small businesses face significant barriers when going international. However, the barriers are even more challenging when small companies try to take advantage of emerging markets. In interviews with the management of Australian small businesses involved in markets in Central and Eastern Europe, Freeman and Reid identified the following major constraints, which are often beyond the control of management.[15]

- *Geographic distance:* The strongest constraint facing small business owners in Australia was the geographic distance from their markets in Poland and the Czech Republic. Unlike larger firms that have more managers to send to negotiate or manage foreign operations, small businesses often rely on a few individuals, who therefore have to travel more often. Having to travel frequently to meet geographically dispersed partners can take a toll on the small business.

- *Lack of Central and Eastern European managers with decision-making authority:* Small firms in Australia often had to deal with the existing Central and Eastern European staff's inability to make decisions. Such slow decision making can be very costly because time is very critical for small businesses.

- *Psychological distance:* Small business managers often have a hard time understanding local market conditions, culture, and business etiquette. For example, they may not have access to the training and other resources needed to gain such market and cultural knowledge. This challenge is very significant given that most of the interviewees in the study agreed that a small company's global venture will likely fail if no effort is made to understand and adapt to such differences.

- *Central and Eastern European middle managers' mindsets:* Although large companies may be able to hire local middle managers, train them, and wait until they acquire modern management techniques, many small businesses have to contend with middle managers who have worked under communism for many years. It is very challenging for small business owners to deal with such managers.

- *Finding reliable suppliers:* Small businesses often find it challenging to locate local suppliers. Decades of state-ownership of businesses have not encouraged private enterprises to flourish. Small businesses face the challenge of having to find committed suppliers, and dealing with such suppliers and distributors can be difficult and sometimes unethical.

- *Bureaucracy and regulations:* Understanding and addressing governmental regulations and the accompanying bureaucracy can be especially challenging for a small business. Whereas large companies may have the resources to address such issues, small companies often have to contend with government regulations that have not changed much to address the needs of a market-based economy.

Sources: Based Freeman, Susan, and Imogen Reid. 2006. "Constraints facing small Western firms in transitional markets." European Business Review, 18(3), pp. 187–213; Kanter, J. 2009. "'Significant' barriers blocking SMEs from public sector work." Supply Management, December 11, p. 11.

- *Overall attitudes toward international strategies:* Some managers simply find the idea of international strategies too threatening to the status quo. Others see international opportunities as beneficial to the company and to their careers. A global culture will develop when the owner/entrepreneur promotes company values that support and reward the search for international opportunities.

Furthermore, as Exhibit 7.1 showed, born-global firms likely have global cultures. In such companies, the founders or top managers already have very high levels of international experience,[16] and they use that experience to influence all facets of operations. The next Case in Point shows how the CEO's influence is critical in creating a global culture.

Changing Attitudes of Key Decision Makers

Both the stage model and the global start-up model depend on the attitudes of the primary decision makers in small and medium-size businesses. For companies that internationalize their business in stages, each stage demonstrates the key executives' increasing commitment to internationalization. Early in this process, managers perceive foreign markets as risky, with high costs to enter and low potential benefits. Because of these negative attitudes toward internationalization, most international sales for small- and medium-size businesses come from countries that are close in culture and in geography. For example, most Canadian companies begin exporting first to their geographically and culturally similar neighbor to the south. These cautious early moves help top managers overcome initial skepticism regarding international markets. In the later stages, these attitudes change, with the international market often perceived as more profitable than the domestic market.[17] Exhibit 7.2, for example, shows that exporters and nonexporters in the U.S. industrial equipment industry have quite different attitudes regarding internationalization.

Positive attitudes toward overseas markets are perhaps more necessary for global start-ups than for companies that move slowly into the international

C A S E   I N   P O I N T

G24i: Basing a Solar Power Business in Rainy Wales

Bob Hertzberg, a former California politician, is the founder of G24i, which manufactures silicon-free solar strips. Unlike most other companies, which produce silicone solar panels for the developed world, G24i is focused on producing solar products for the Third World. Hertzberg argues that many solar companies have concentrated on rich countries, thereby benefiting consumers only from rich countries. He wants to change that and has contracts with local companies in India, Kenya, Rwanda, and Nigeria. The solar strips that G24i produces can be fitted on backpacks, in purses, and in other carriers, yet provide enough charging power for cell phones and other gadgets.

G24i has been very successful largely because of the founder's influence on the company. Hertzberg is seen as the green contrarian in the industry. Although

some experts see his strategy of dealing with Third World countries as risky, he believes that it is the right way to do business.

When he was setting up the business, he met with many bureaucratic regulations in California. He found that Europe had fewer regulations and decided to investigate a European location for his start-up. He heard about a plant that Acer commissioned in Wales but decided to cut back. He quickly flew to Wales and made a very attractive proposal to the government. Today, G24i has 66 employees and is making important strides toward meeting its goal of providing affordable solar power to Third World countries.

Source: Based on Power, Carla. 2009. "Green contrarian." Fortune Small Business, 19(1), pp. 76–79.

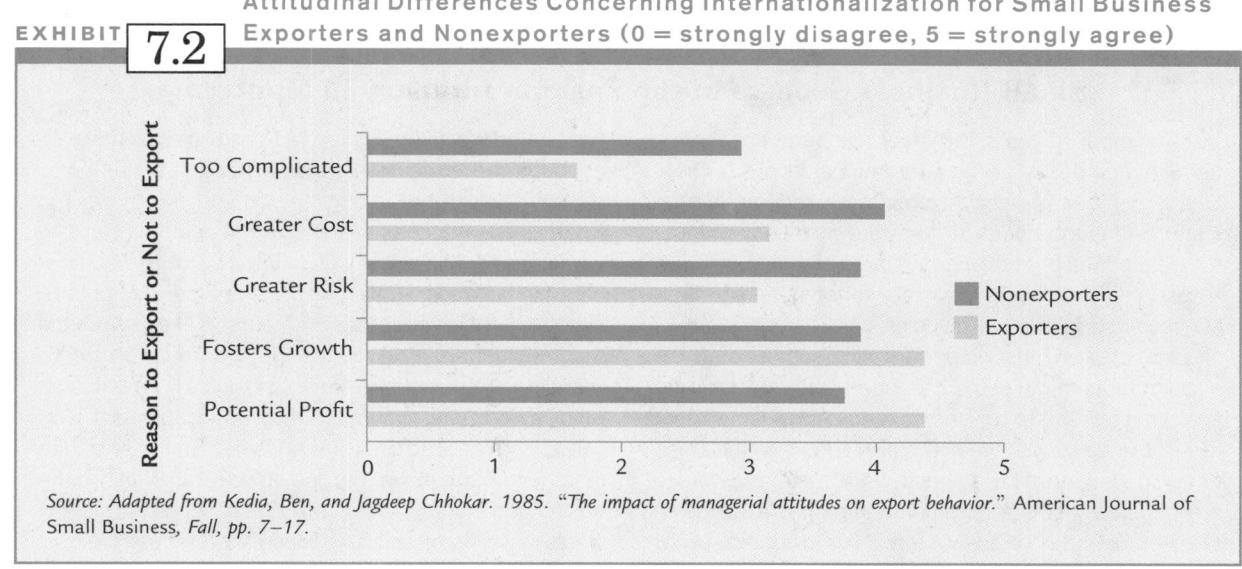

EXHIBIT 7.2   Attitudinal Differences Concerning Internationalization for Small Business Exporters and Nonexporters (0 = strongly disagree, 5 = strongly agree)

Source: Adapted from Kedia, Ben, and Jagdeep Chhokar. 1985. "The impact of managerial attitudes on export behavior." American Journal of Small Business, Fall, pp. 7–17.

marketplace. Experts argue that successful global start-ups require the founders to communicate an appropriate vision to everyone in the organization.[18] Managers use their global vision to help their companies become multinational from birth.

Gaining Experience: Duties and the Personal Life of the Small-Business CEO

The effects of internationalization on the personal life and duties of the CEO may play a more important role in the international activities of small and medium-size companies than in larger firms. As the Case in Point showed, Hertzberg's drive had an important influence on G24i's ability to succeed. The owner of a small business is often the CEO and the driving entrepreneurial force in the business. Running a small business is always extremely time-consuming and challenging, even when the firm is involved only in the domestic market.[19] However, internationalization demands significantly more commitment, and, when the internationalization effort affects the CEO, it threatens the whole fabric of the organization.[20]

For a small firm, opening new markets is often the CEO's personal responsibility. Although small company CEOs spend only 20 percent of their time managing export and other international functions, they must be willing to incur more than economic costs for the venture.[21] They must be ready to pay social and business costs because their responsibilities for the new international venture often entail increased travel and stress. Many CEOs feel that these activities adversely affect family life, and they dislike being away from the daily management of their businesses.[22] Consider the next Case in Point.

In addition, the job of the small business CEO may change when the company becomes multinational. A study of Canadian manufacturers that had recently begun exporting found that more than 50 percent of the CEOs felt that their duties had changed since going international. The impact seemed to affect CEOs more than the workers. Only slightly more than 20 percent of the

Small Business Success in the Fashion Industry in Montreal

For a number of years, Montreal has been developing its fashion industry at the international level. Montreal has a number of small companies working in that sector. Although some of them are succeeding, most have faced major challenges related to being small. In a case study of five of them, the reasons behind their success and failure are discussed.

One of the most important findings is that the successful companies had founders who were willing to commit themselves and to dedicate a consistent level of energy over time to make sure that the business succeeded. The owner's work ethic and values are especially critical in small companies involved in the fashion industry because the founders often provide the creative input necessary to produce the clothing. One of the five companies, Angelo Bucaro Design, disappeared because the founder was no longer willing to keep up the required level of energy.

The founder's values changed, and she decided to abandon the professional responsibilities of the company in favor of her family.

Business success at the international level is also very dependent on the CEO. Only two of the companies in the case study had international aspirations. However, for both companies (Rugby North America and Minimome), the desire of the founder to investigate new markets was the primary impetus in both going international. The two founding CEOs carefully expanded first in the United States and then in other countries in Europe and Asia. Without the desire and hard work of the CEO, neither company would have been able to succeed in the international fashion market.

Source: Based on Tremblay, M., and F. Seguin. 2009. "La croissance des P.M.E de design de mode: Les lecons a tirer." Gestion, 33(4), pp. 22–32.

employees in the same companies had their jobs restructured and needed retraining due to the firms' international business.[23]

As new multinational managers, the Canadian CEOs also believed that they needed skill upgrading for international business. Exhibit 7.3 shows key skills that the CEOs felt they needed.

Is Size a Barrier for Small Business Internationalization?

Large firms tend to enter export markets more than small companies. They have more resources to absorb the risk of exporting and often have a greater incentive to export when domestic markets become saturated.[24] As the Emerging Markets Feature made clear, large firms have other advantages, such as access to more qualified individuals with the ability to negotiate with geographically dispersed partners.[25] In contrast, small businesses often have to rely on a few individuals, who become involved in grueling travel. Large firms have more resources to invest in cross-cultural training to better understand the countries in which they operate, with its local business and national culture. Such training tends to be less likely for small firms with limited resources.

Many academic researchers and small business managers thus argue that only large companies have the resources to become multinationals.[26] In fact, most studies find that the larger the business, the more likely the firm exports its products.[27] Even among exporting firms, the large companies tend toward committed exporting and the smaller ones tend toward passive exporting. Large firms also serve more national markets. For example, one study of Canadian firms found that companies with total sales of more than $50 million exported on average to 27 markets, while smaller firms averaged only slightly more than 12.[28]

These statistics show that small companies do suffer from the **liabilities of smallness**; in other words, compared to large firms, small businesses find it more

Liabilities of smallness
The challenges facing small businesses in getting access to necessary resources to internationalize.

EXHIBIT | 7.3

Training and Knowledge Needs of Small Firm CEOs Entering Internationalization

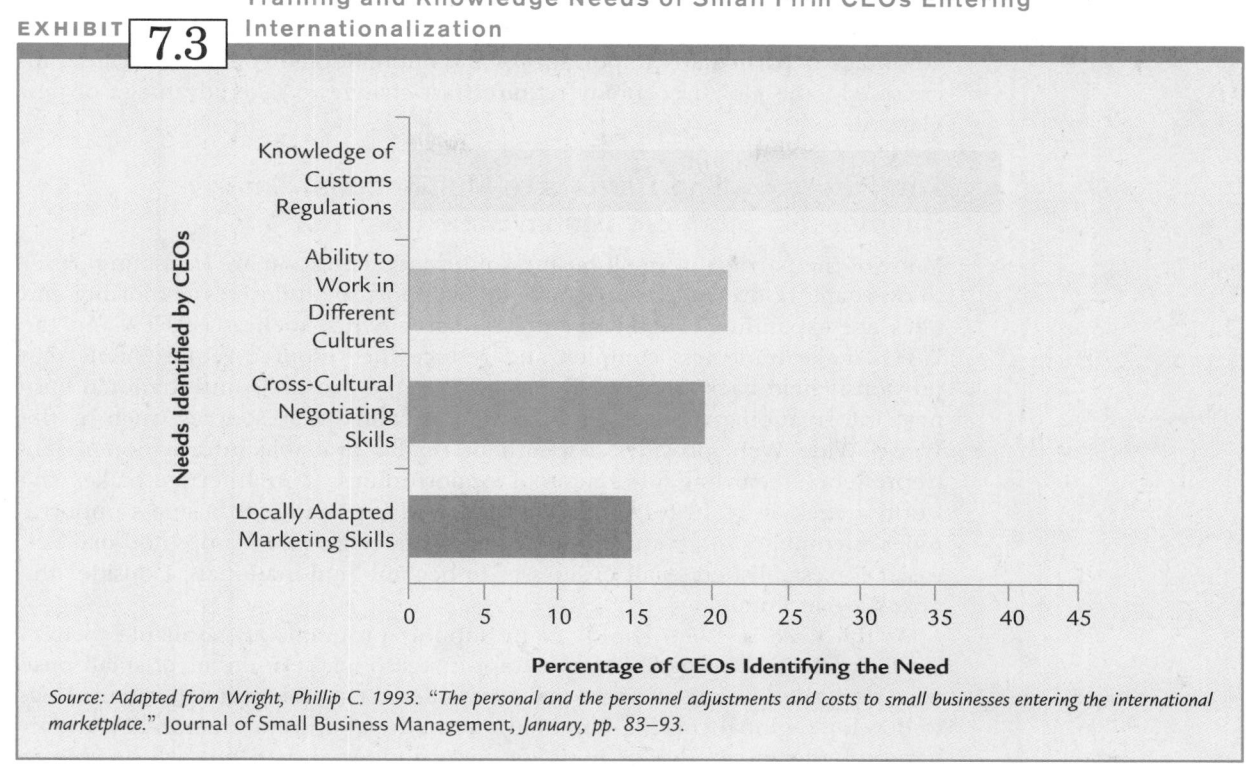

Source: Adapted from Wright, Phillip C. 1993. "The personal and the personnel adjustments and costs to small businesses entering the international marketplace." Journal of Small Business Management, January, pp. 83–93.

challenging to obtain and secure the necessary resources they need to internationalize.[29]

However, the liabilities of smallness may exist only during the initial internationalization stage. Large size makes it easier for a company to begin exporting or making direct investments, but once firms choose to take on an international venture, experts suggest that the international sales intensity of small firms equals or may even exceed that of large firms.[30] **International sales intensity** is the amount of international sales divided by the total sales of the company. Once involved in international ventures, small multinational companies often gain sales revenues proportionally equal to or greater than those of large multinational companies.[31]

International sales intensity
Amount of international sales divided by total sales of the company.

Using the Small Business Advantage

In spite of some barriers to internationalization, the small business has some advantages over large and often entrenched organizations. In fact, the trend-spotting author of *The Global Paradox,* John Naisbitt, predicts that small multinational businesses will have even greater advantages in the increasingly global economy. He argues that small companies can change products and internal operations faster to take advantage of evolving technologies. In contrast, large organizations often must overcome extensive bureaucratic procedures when adopting new products or new management operations. The bureaucratic procedures of large organizations slow down decision making, often leading to missed opportunities in the international marketplace.

Speed is therefore the **small business advantage**. When large companies are slow to react to rapidly changing conditions, fast-moving entrepreneurs can use

Small business advantage
Fast moving entrepreneurs can use their competitive advantage of speed. Being first to market, they can capture significant sales before large competitors react.

their competitive advantage of speed. Being first to market, they can capture significant sales before the large competitors can react.[32] The small business advantage is particularly important for the multinational company because, increasingly, the global economy requires fast change to take advantage of new markets.

The Future: Falling Barriers to Multinational Small Businesses and More Global Start-Ups

Many of the barriers to small business internationalization are becoming easier to overcome. Government programs that support small business exporting and sales are expanding. High-impact trade agreements, such as NAFTA and the WTO, make trade less complex and reduce the resource requirements that previously held back many small firms. The rapid growth of international business information produced by governments and other sources, such as the World Wide Web, provides a wealth of readily available information to entrepreneurs regarding international opportunities. The Internet makes the world a click away. In turn, this knowledge of international business opportunities encourages more entrepreneurs to consider global start-ups and makes it easier for established small businesses to become multinationals. Consider the next Case in Point.

As the Case in Point shows, many support programs are available to help small businesses succeed. The resultant increase in the number of small businesses engaged in international activities will make it easier for other businesses to develop a global culture. Potential international entrepreneurs will not only have a better knowledge of business opportunities abroad but will be able to copy the cultures of other successful small multinational companies. In addition, as managers gain experience in international business, negative attitudes among small business owners and entrepreneurs toward international sales will decrease.

Overall, therefore, going international should become easier for the small firm. In fact, many experts suggest that the only way a small firm can survive and

---

CASE IN POINT

Support for Small Businesses

Most governments understand the importance of small businesses generating income, which helps the economy. It is therefore not surprising to see strong government-sponsored support programs for small businesses in many countries. In China, most banks are naturally inclined to lend to large firms, but then most small businesses would have to seek capital overseas. As a result, the Chinese government established a new growth enterprise board, which is similar to a stock exchange for small- and medium-size companies looking to raise money from the capital market. Similar programs exist in other countries, such as Britain, Singapore, and the United States.

Large multinationals are also taking steps to help small companies. Avis offered 1,500 free car rentals to their small business customers in the U.K. British Airways provides close to £15 million worth of free flights to small- and medium-size companies to encourage small company owners to visit trade fairs and meet with customers, all in an effort to help them boost exports.

Sources: Based on Poulter, S., and O. Koster. 2009. "Now Avis joins the drive to help small businesses." Daily Mail, April 29, p. 12; Xinhua News Agency. 2009. "China's growth enterprise board to shore up small businesse," April 1.

grow is by going international. Consider that exporting, the first phase in internationalization, can bring several important long-term advantages for the small business.[33] Exporting allows the small firm to increase sales volumes and income, thereby providing much needed cash flow. More important, exporting allows the small firm to better understand global markets through contact with new cultures and the development of new contacts. Such activities can help the small firm's future foray into new markets and its competitive advantage.

The next section provides a series of diagnostic questions that can help small business owners and managers make the internationalization decision. The section after that describes how small businesses can make the contacts with customers and potential partners necessary to succeed in foreign sales.

When Should a Small Business Go International?

The small business must respond to many of the same questions as the large business does when considering multinational options. However, the limited number of products or services—and the limited resources—of most small firms make certain drivers of internationalization more important for them.

Affirmative answers to the following questions suggest that a small business is ready to become a multinational company:

- *Do we have a global product or service?* A global product or service can be sold worldwide with minimal changes for each country. Because small businesses seldom have the resources to adapt a product to local needs, producing a standard worldwide product makes globalization easier. As discussed in Chapter 6, if customers have similar needs or if customers seek a product or service from anywhere in the world, then an opportunity for globalization exists.[34]

- *Do we have the managerial, organizational, and financial resources to internationalize?* Internationalization, even with the more simple participation strategies, requires significant availability of financial and personnel resources. Exhibit 7.4 gives some of the questions concerning resource requirements that a small business needs to address.

- *Even if we do have the resources, are we willing to commit them and face the risks of internationalization?* Small company managers must view internationalization as they would start-up ventures. For the right company, with the right products, the eventual returns from a new international venture may exceed the investment and make the exposure to risk worthwhile. To seek the potential returns, managers must overcome the related psychological and cultural boundaries.

- *Is there a country in which we feel comfortable doing business?* Without the resources to understand the cultural and business practices in many countries, small business managers often first seek international opportunities in national cultures similar to their own.

- *Is there a profitable market for our product or service?* Even with good products or services, a key question focuses on which countries to enter. For example, research by managers at Ekkwill Tropical Fish Farm indicated that collecting fish was a popular hobby in many countries. One-third of its production now goes to markets in Asia, Latin America, Canada, and the West Indies.[35]

EXHIBIT 7.4   Questions to Consider in the Small Business Decision to Go International

Management Objectives
- What is the reason for going international?
- How committed is top management to the internationalization decision?
- How quickly does management expect the internationalization effort to pay off?

Management Experience and Resources
- What in-house international expertise does the firm have (international sales experience, language capabilities, etc.)?
- Who will be responsible for the international organizational component of the company (e.g., export department)?
- How much senior management time should be allocated?
- What organizational structure is required?

Production Capacity
- How is the present capacity being used?
- Will international sales hurt domestic sales?
- What will be the cost of additional production at home or in a foreign location?
- What modifications of the product or service are required?

Financial Capacity
- What amount of capital can be committed to international production and marketing?
- What level of operating costs for international operations can be supported?
- What other financial requirements may compete with the internationalization efforts?

Source: Adapted from U.S. Department of Commerce. 2009. Basic Guide to Exporting. Washington, DC: Government Printing Office.

- *Which country should we enter?* A thorough strategic analysis is required. Firms need to identify potential threats and opportunities by country. For example, current and future demand for a product may vary by country. Each country also has different competitors and barriers to entry (e.g., tariffs, complex distribution systems). Exhibit 7.5 summarizes the steps that small businesses can follow to find customers abroad.

- *Do we have a unique product or service that is not easily copied by large multinational companies or local entrepreneurs?* Although small firms may have the advantage of speed to market, large multinationals may use their advantage of economies of scale to imitate an innovation, using a lower-priced product. To maintain their competitive advantage over large firms, small multinational companies must have rare (i.e., not easily copied) and valuable resources—factors that allow the company to produce a product or service valued by customers. These rare and valued resources may include technical superiority, innovation, or high quality.[36]

- *Do location advantages exist upstream in the value chain?* Internationalization of a small firm need not be just a downstream activity, such as marketing. When there are advantages of lower cost or higher quality in supply or manufacturing, small multinational companies can seek the same location advantages available to large companies by sourcing raw materials or manufacturing in other countries.

EXHIBIT 7.5   Steps in Picking a Foreign Market

1. Screen potential markets:

• Get statistics that show the extent of the relevant products exported to or produced in potential countries.

• Identify five to ten countries with large and fast-growing markets for the products. Examine the trends in the market in past years and in different economic circumstances.

• Identify additional countries with small, newly emerging markets, which may provide first mover advantages.

• Target three to five of the most promising markets. Mix established markets with emerging markets, depending on management's tolerance for risk.

2. Assess targeted markets:

• Examine market trends for the company's products or services and for related products or services that could affect demand.

• Identify demographic trends (e.g., income, age, education, population, and so on) that identify the users of the company's products or services.

• Estimate the overall consumption of the product or service and the supply provided by foreign and domestic producers.

• Identify sources of competition from domestic producers and other foreign competitors, including price, quality, features, and service.

• Identify local channels of distribution.

• Assess what modifications of the product or service are required.

• Identify cultural differences that may influence participation strategies.

• Identify any foreign barriers to exporting or other participation options (e.g., tariffs, limitations on percentage of ownership, home country export controls, etc.).

• Identify any foreign or home country incentives to enter the market.

3. Draw conclusions and make the choice.

Source: Adapted from U.S. Department of Commerce. 2009. Basic Guide to Exporting. Washington, DC: Government Printing Office.

• *Can we afford not to be a multinational?* Several factors, even for the small business, may make becoming a multinational company necessary for survival. A shrinking home market may require a firm to internationalize to maintain sales revenue. Finding international sources of lower costs of raw material or production facilities may be necessary to match competitors' prices and to maintain profit margins. Small multinational companies may find the positive image of being a multinational firm necessary for attracting new customers and investors.

The next section reviews the participation strategies available to the small multinational company.

Getting Connected to the International Market

Participation Strategies

Small- and medium-size multinational companies have the same participation options as do large firms, including exporting, licensing, joint ventures, and foreign direct investment. Usually, however, the small business turns to exporting as its major international participation strategy. For the small firm without knowledge of potential foreign customers or sufficient resources to set up an overseas sales office, indirect exporting makes the most sense. These firms use the services of ETCs or EMCs to get their products to the international market.

Finding Customers and Partners

To go international, small businesses must find ways to reach their foreign customers, either by direct contact or by teaming up with foreign partners (distributors, joint venture partners, or licensees) who deal with the ultimate customers. As with large multinational companies, there is no set formula for finding partners or customers. Much depends on the nature of the product, the countries involved, and the nature and resources of the company. However, some standard techniques are readily available to small multinational companies. In this section, we show some of these common **customer contact techniques**.

Customer contact techniques
Trade shows, catalog expositions, international advertising agencies and consulting firms, government-sponsored trade missions, and direct contact.

- *Trade shows:* National and international trade shows give small businesses inexpensive mechanisms to contact potential customers or business partners. Trade shows give businesses the opportunity to set up displays of their products and to provide brochures and other documents that describe their product or service. Businesses may rent space at the shows individually or as part of a large group. The U.S. Commerce Department runs a virtual trade show, and the Web site offers constant access to U.S. suppliers and international buyers. The Web site shows product descriptions, photos, and videos.[37]

- *Catalog expositions:* Catalog expositions are similar to trade shows except that a business does not have its product or people at the show, but rather, product catalogs, sales brochures, and other graphic presentations of a firm's goods or services. Some U.S. embassies and consulates provide catalog expositions for U.S. goods. Because a company need only send printed matter, catalog expositions provide a low-cost way of testing international markets.

- *International advertising agencies and consulting firms:* International advertising agencies and consulting firms have offices throughout the world, often with specialists in different products or services. International advertising agencies can provide advertising and promotional services geared to a local national environment. Consulting firms often have a good knowledge of local regulations, competitors, and distribution channels, but a business that uses these services can expect to pay significant compensation. However, local market expertise and contacts may make the expenditure worthwhile.

- *Government-sponsored trade missions:* To foster growth in international trade, governments often sponsor trade missions, which represent companies or industries looking to open new markets in the countries visited. Host governments usually provide introductions to potential local sales representatives, distributors, and end users.

- *Direct contact:* Although the option is often more difficult and costly, small business entrepreneurs and managers can seek channel partners, joint venture partners, and end users directly. If the managers/entrepreneurs can find key intermediaries—that is, potential alliance partners or distributors—or can directly access potential customers, then direct contact may work best.

Beyond these methods, the Web also provides access to prospective customers. Consider the next Multinational Management Brief.

Exhibit 7.6 shows some of the sources on the World Wide Web that any multinational company can access to find trade leads.

Multinational Management Brief

Using the Web to Find New Customers: Alibaba.com

Alibaba.com is a prominent Chinese Web site, positioning itself as the virtual intermediary between Chinese exporters and foreign buyers. It was founded in 1999 by Jack Ma, a former English teacher. He saw where the Chinese economy was headed and created Alibaba.com to take advantage of the related opportunities. Alibaba.com has grown rapidly and provides numerous services to its customers. Chinese users, which make up most of Alibaba.com's customer base, pay a service fee to have their products listed on their Web sites. Alibaba.com provides other assistance, such as photo displays or videos, and anyone in the world can access these products for a fee.

As another important service, Alibaba.com supplies product listings and translation services to foreign customers interested in importing from China. For a fee, foreign buyers can view product listings and decide on which company they want to do business with. Alibaba.com thus provides a very efficient way to meet new customers. Rather than attending trade shows in China or using an actual intermediary, firms can use the Web service, which provides a very efficient and quick way to find new suppliers and customers.

Source: Based on Chao, L. 2009. "How Alibaba.com keeps growing." Wall Street Journal, *April 24, p. 16.*

EXHIBIT 7.6

International Trade Leads: A Web Sampler of International Import-Export Trade Leads

WorldBidMiddleEast: An international, business-to-business marketplace that focuses on international trade within the Middle East

Busytrade: A well-organized trade lead Web site that offers a large collection of trade leads, products, company listings, and trade show announcements

ChinaBusinessWorld.com: Listings of Chinese and foreign-based suppliers, buyers, and products, all classified into categories, as well as a listing of the most recent buying trade leads

ECeurope: A business-to-business trading bulletin board that serves small- to medium-size companies in accessing trade leads

FoodTrader: Geared toward the agricultural and food sectors, providing products available for purchase and sale

Tradeinindia: Dedicated to India, offers news briefs, country export-import opportunity listings, a bulletin board, and importer and exporter company directories

BuyKorea: Offers free trade leads and customized tender notification service

Nudeal: A Canadian-based company that offers both local and international trade leads and company directory listings

OpenRussia: Buy/sell offers from Russian companies, as well as information relating to customs clearance and the documents required for foreign trade activities

Taiwantrade: An online trading hub designed for business-to-business contact for small and medium-size enterprises, with the aim of using the latest Web technology to link buyers and sellers around the world to conduct business online

Wbiz.net: A trading place for exporters and importer, features business offers, product listings, and company directories

Source: Michigan State University. http://globaledge.msu.edu/ibrd/. 2009. Used with permission.

Ready to Go and Connected: A Synopsis

The preceding sections provided the diagnostic questions that small business owners can ask in order to decide when to take their businesses international. These questions focused first on whether a firm has the right products and adequate resources to go international. They then prompted entrepreneurs to consider the competition and the country environments where they hope to do business.

If the company is ready to go international and the foreign opportunities are attractive, then a variety of mechanisms are popular among small multinational businesses to make international contacts for customer and partners. The previous section reviewed many of the readily available sources. However, an enterprising small businessperson will find that many more sources exist and that detailed research *will* increase the likelihood of the international venture's success. Finding the right overseas partner may be the most crucial decision of all.

Even with the right company, the right product, and a potential customer, a small business needs a wedge to break into a new market. The next section shows how small businesses can use traditional entrepreneurial wedge strategies in starting and building an international venture.

New Venture Strategies for Small Multinational Companies

New ventures, whether global start-ups or new international operations for an ongoing business, need some type of entry wedge to gain an initial position in a new market. Karl Vesper, the renowned expert on new ventures, defines the **entry wedge** as "a strategic competitive advantage for breaking into the established pattern of commercial activity."[38] In this section, the chapter examines how some of the common entrepreneurship entry wedges work for the small multinational business. The section also includes numerous examples of small businesses using entry wedges for their multinational activities.

New Product or Service and First Mover Advantage

A basic entrepreneurial wedge strategy that focuses on being the first to introduce a new product or service is the **first mover advantage**,[39] whereby the entrepreneur moves quickly into a new venture and establishes the business before other firms can react. To succeed, the new product or service must be not only innovative but also comprehensive. "Comprehensive" means that the product must meet customer expectations in areas such as warranty, customer service, and expected components. Without a comprehensive introduction, the new product or service is easy for competitors to imitate.

Technological leadership provides the most common source of first mover advantage. The first company to use or introduce a new technology often has the best understanding of how to make a product, having done the initial research and development and having the greatest familiarity with the product's characteristics. Such firms can build on this knowledge to keep ahead of competition by using their head start to introduce new product developments and innovations.

Several other situations give first movers an advantage. They may have initial access to natural and social resources, such as mining rights and close relationships with research universities. The first movers can choose the best locations not only for raw materials but also for proximity to customers. Finally, and perhaps more important in international business, first movers can have the best

Entry wedge
Company's competitive advantage for breaking into the established pattern of commercial activity.

First mover advantage
That of the entrepreneur who moves quickly into a new venture and establishes the business before other companies can react.

Technological leadership
Being first to use or introduce a new technology.

access to social relationships. Social relationships lead to the personal contacts necessary to build effective channels of distribution and to trust and commitment from business partners and customers.

The final advantage of being first comes from switching costs, which a customer incurs in turning to a competitor's products. Customers become familiar with products, and they often invest time and effort learning to use them. For example, many people do not switch between Apple- and Windows-based computers because they already know one operating system. In addition, because of brand loyalty, many customers may not want to undergo the discomfort of switching to another brand of a product or service.

Switching costs
Expenses incurred when a customer switches to a competitor's products.

Copycat Businesses

Copycat businesses follow the me-too strategy, adopting existing products or services. Competitive advantage comes from varying the nature of product or service characteristics or from how the company provides the product or service.[40] Successful copycats do not copy existing businesses identically. They find a niche or a slight innovation to attract customers away from existing businesses. Sometimes the innovation can be as simple as a new location that is more convenient for customers. How can companies find their niche and follow copycat strategy? Here are some suggestions to copycat successfully:[41]

Copycat businesses
Those following the me-too strategy, whereby they adopt existing strategies for providing products or services.

- *Be the first to change to a new standard:* New standards of quality or internationally recognized specification standards offer powerful entry wedges for new competitors.

- *Go after the toughest customers:* Often established firms shy away from some customer groups. Highly price- or quality-sensitive customers may constitute an opportunity for a niche market.

- *Play to minor differences in customer needs:* Established firms often ignore minor differences in customer needs and leave the door open to a competitor who will cater to such differences.

- *Transfer the location:* A business that works in one part of the country may work equally well in another part of a country or in another country. The success of U.S. franchises like McDonald's throughout the world shows that this strategy is viable for creating a new business.

- *Become a dedicated supplier or distributor:* A dedicated supplier finds a firm that needs the vendor's goods or services and focuses all its efforts on that major customer. For example, a small firm in the state of Washington provides cargo containers for Boeing airplanes. This small company serves Boeing directly and sells indirectly to users of Boeing jets throughout the world.

- *Seek abandoned or ignored markets:* The major players in any industry do not always serve every market fully and well.

- *Acquire existing business:* Acquiring an existing business is a common start-up strategy for small businesses in domestic markets, but opportunities also exist in foreign countries to acquire businesses. In particular, formerly state-controlled businesses in Eastern Europe provide potentially good acquisition targets for entrepreneurs from around the world.

As you may have realized, entrepreneurship plays a big role in small business creation. In the final section, we consider some key aspects of international entrepreneurship.

International Entrepreneurship

Entrepreneur
Person who creates new ventures that seek profit and growth.

New ventures
Entering a new market; offering a new product or service; or introducing a new method, technology, or innovative use of raw materials.

International entrepreneurship
The discovery, evaluation, and exploitation of market opportunities.

An **entrepreneur** creates new ventures that seek profit and growth. An entrepreneur deals with the risk and uncertainty of new and untested business. **New ventures** exist when a company enters a new market, offers a new product or service, or introduces a new method, technology, or innovative use of raw materials. Risk results from new ventures because their possible outcomes, such as survival and profitability, are variable. Some companies survive and others die. Some companies make a profit and grow, and others remain small. Uncertainty results because the founder can never fully predict which outcome will befall the new company.[42]

International entrepreneurship refers to the "discovery, evaluation and exploitation of international market opportunities."[43] Why should an international management student be concerned about international entrepreneurship? Most experts consider entrepreneurship the driving force of all small businesses. Without the entrepreneurial spirit, few small businesses would exist anywhere in the world. If we want to fully understand the small businesses in any nation, we need to examine the level of entrepreneurship there. In any country, at some point the local entrepreneurs have to face the risk and uncertainty of starting up the business. Entrepreneurship is therefore the driver of innovation and economic development anywhere.[44] For instance, countries like the United States and the United Kingdom underwent rapid industrialization because their country context allowed entrepreneurial activities to flourish, not only creating new jobs but also generating new wealth and growth. Today, many individuals around the world are becoming entrepreneurs to solve social problems. Consider the next Case in Point.

Another important reason for understanding international entrepreneurship is that many multinational firms rely on small businesses and their owners to do business when entering a new country. Small businesses can often provide

---

CASE IN POINT

Entrepreneurship and Doing Good

Entrepreneurship is drastically changing how philanthropy is viewed today. In fact, many people seek not only to make money by being entrepreneurial but also to solve social problems. Entrepreneurship plays an important role in the voluntary sector.

- Riders for Health was created in Africa when motorbike enthusiasts found that vehicles used by health care providers were not being properly maintained. The organization now helps to provide health care to more than 1 million individuals in inaccessible places, often using a motorbike.

- Shane Immelman was appalled to see that many poor school children in South Africa did not have desks. He invented a lap desk that provides a stable surface on the child's lap. By featuring

advertisements on the laps, he has been able to supply the lapdesks for free. However, better-off people have been buying them, and exports to other less developed countries have also started.

- Vinod Kapur's dream is to feed India's rural poor. He has therefore dedicated most of his life to breeding a "superchicken," and he has developed one that is resistant to disease, capable of surviving on farm scrap, and strong enough to fight predators. Most importantly, the chicken provides twice as much meat and five times as many eggs as other breeds. Kapur has also built an important supply chain to make sure that the chickens are accessible to people.

Source: Based on Economist. 2009. "Saving the world." March 14, Special Report on Entrepreneurship, p. 19–20.

critical products or services, thereby facilitating entry. Consider the challenges facing Handango when it entered the Japanese market.[45] Handango discovered that Japanese consumers do not use credit cards for purchases, and it had to partner with a local small business to provide alternative payment options for its Japanese consumers. Low, Henderson, and Weiler[46] argue that entrepreneurs play a very important role in bringing new ideas and innovations to the marketplace; so small businesses can assist multinational companies in developing or offering new products. For example, Pixalert, a small Dublin-based company, developed innovative image recognition software that can alert a company when employees are viewing inappropriate pictures online.[47] Viewing inappropriate images on the job results in a significant drop in productivity and creates a potential corporate liability in the context of sexual harassment issues. Whereas traditional filters cannot detect images installed from flash drives or other means, such as instant messaging, Pixalert's system can monitor any image viewing through image analysis.[48]

Finally, multinational companies may make location decisions based on how entrepreneurial a country's inhabitants are. In that context, Global Entrepreneurship Monitor (GEM) is an ongoing study of entrepreneurship activity around the world. The GEM research team has developed several measures of entrepreneurship and studies the cultural and institutional conditions supporting the driving forces of contemporary economies. Exhibit 7.7 shows the total entrepreneurial activity (TEA) ratings for selected countries.[49] The TEA represents the number of entrepreneurs (measured by start-ups) per 100 members of the population in a country.

EXHIBIT 7.7   Total Entrepreneurial Activity (TEA) Ratings for Selected Countries

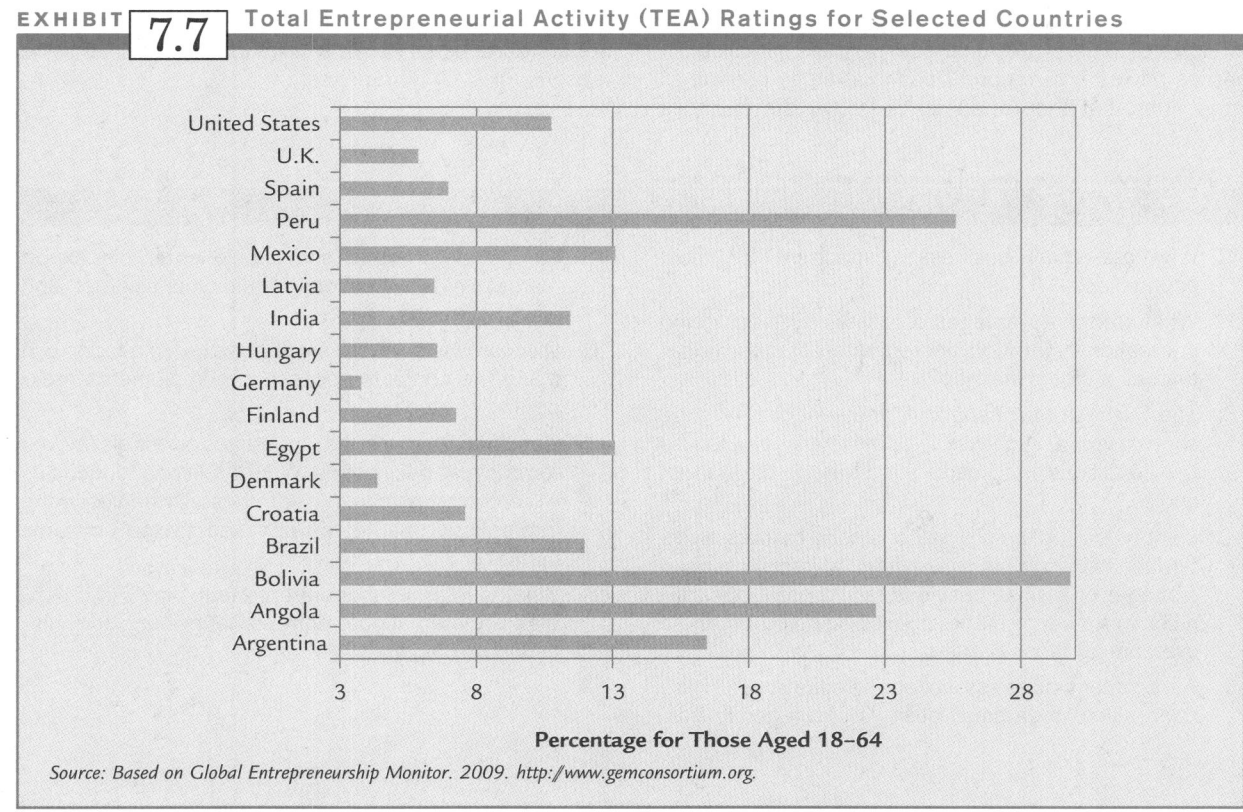

Percentage for Those Aged 18–64

Source: Based on Global Entrepreneurship Monitor. 2009. http://www.gemconsortium.org.

Summary and Conclusions

Small businesses are important to the economies of all nations. Often they provide the most jobs, the greatest economic growth, and the best innovation. Increasingly, small businesses must face the challenges of becoming multinational companies and entering the international marketplace. Small businesses do, however, encounter unique problems and prospects when entering global competition. In this chapter, we have extended the study of multinational and participation strategies to focus on situations with particular application to small multinational companies.

After defining the basic characteristics of a small business and entrepreneurship, we reviewed the processes by which small businesses go international: through stages or through global start-ups. Increasingly, global start-ups are replacing stages of internationalization, especially for high-tech entrepreneurial companies in fast changing industries.

A small business must overcome the traditional barriers to its internationalization. The chapter discussed how small businesses develop a global culture, change the attitudes of key decision makers, gain crucial international experience, and overcome the size-related barrier. The chapter also presented the diagnostic questions that a small businessperson can ask in deciding when the company is ready to go global.

Crucial to a small business is finding ways to access foreign customers and business partners. Small businesses have the same participation strategy options as large firms, but they often do not have the in-house resources to identify or go directly to foreign customers. Fortunately, many public and private resources are available to businesses wishing to become multinational. This chapter provided an overview of some of the pertinent resources available from the government and private sector. Increasingly, electronic media, such as the World Wide Web, provide easy and quick access to information on markets throughout the world. Exhibit 7.6 provided just a small sample from this growing source of multinational business information.

For the small business, entering the international market is an entrepreneurial venture, and entrepreneurial ventures require successful entry wedge strategies to have any chance of success. Traditionally, books on entrepreneurship consider entry wedge strategies only in terms of the domestic market. This chapter, however, showed how such strategies could work in the global marketplace. Several Cases in Point showed how actual entrepreneurs used the strategies to compete successfully with large international rivals.

A full appreciation of small businesses is not possible without also understanding international entrepreneurship. Entrepreneurship is important to a country because it generates jobs and wealth. It is also critical to multinational companies because small businesses can provide large companies with new ideas, as well as crucial products and services. The degree to which countries are entrepreneurial varies, and we looked at some of the reasons for such differences.

Discussion Questions

1. Why are small businesses important for most economies?

2. What are the advantages of a small business going international through incremental stages rather than as a global start-up?

3. The Surftech Multinational Management Challenge showcased a successful global start-up. Discuss the conditions that made this strategy the correct choice.

4. Identify two or three small business barriers to internationalization. If you were a recently hired manager of a small business facing great opportunities in a foreign market, how would you go about overcoming these barriers?

5. As a recent business college graduate, you have been asked by a small business manager to help her decide whether she should enter the export market. What questions would you ask her and why?

6. Discuss ways that a small business manager can make the contacts necessary to implement an exporting strategy.

7. Consider three of the suggested strategic moves for copycat businesses. What additional difficulties will a company face in using these strategies in the international market as opposed to the domestic market?

8. What is international entrepreneurship? What benefits do international entrepreneurs bring to multinational companies?

Multinational Management Skill Builder

Take a Product International

Step 1. Your instructor will divide the class into groups.

Step 2. Select an agricultural or industrial product produced in your region of the country. If possible, interview a small businessperson concerning his or her perspectives on the international opportunities for the company's product. In the United States, one way of finding a potential business owner is through the small business development centers attached to many U.S. universities. Your instructor may assign you a business or product.

Step 3. Using the steps shown in Exhibit 7.5 and information from World Wide Web sources (such as those in Exhibit 7.6) and your library, identify a foreign market or markets for the product or products.

Step 4. Using Web sources (such as those in Exhibit 7.6), identify potential trade shows, trading partners, or other intermediaries (e.g., ETCs) that would help you get the product to the international marketplace.

Step 5. Present your findings to your class, and to the small businessperson, if possible.

Endnotes

1 Organization for Economic Cooperation and Development (OECD). 2002. *OECD Small and Medium Enterprise Outlook*. Paris: OECE Publication Services.

2 U.S. Small Business Administration. 2009. "Advocacy: The voice of small business in government." June. http://www.sba.gov/advo.

3 OECD.

4 Ibid.

5 Scarborough, Norman M., and Thomas W. Zimmer. 1996. *Effective Small Business Management*. Upper Saddle River, NJ: Prentice Hall.

6 Rialp, Alex, Josep Rialp, David Urbano, and Yancy Vaillant. 2005. "The born-global phenomenon: A comparative case study research." *Journal of International Entrepreneurship*, 3, pp. 133–171.

7 Dollinger, Marc J. 1995. *Entrepreneurship*. Burr Ridge, IL: Irwin.

8 Vapola, T. J., Tossavainen, P., and Gabrielsson, M. 2008. "The battleship strategy: The complementing roles of born globals in MNC's new opportunity creation." *Journal of International Entrepreneurship*, 6, pp. 1–21.

9 Ibid.

10 U.S. Small Business Administration. 1999. *E-Commerce: Small Businesses Venture Online*. Washington, DC: Government Printing Office.

11 Ibid.

12 Caprioni, Paula J., Stefanie Ann Lenway, and Thomas P. Murtha. 1994. "Understanding internationalization: Sense-making process in multinational corporations." In Tamir Agmon and Richard Drobnick, eds. *Small Firms in Global Competition*, New York: Oxford University Press, pp. 27–36.

13 Dichtl, Drwin, Hans-Georg Koeglmayr, and Stefan Mueller. 1990. "International orientation as a precondition for export success." *Journal of International Business Studies*, 1st quarter, pp. 23–40.

14 Freeman, Susan, and Imogen Reid. 2006. "Constraints facing small western firms in transitional markets." *European Business Review*, 18(3), pp. 187–213.

15 Ibid.

16 Rialp et al.

17 Calof, Jonathan L., and Wilma Viviers. 1995. "Internationalization behavior of small- and medium-sized South African enterprises." *Journal of Small Business Management*, October, pp. 71–79; Miesenbock, Kurt J. 1988. "Small business and internationalization:

A literature review." *International Small Business Journal*, 6, pp. 42–61.

18 Oviatt and McDougall.

19 Dalin, Shera. 2005. "Owning a business isn't a 9-to-5 job." *St. Louis Post-Dispatch*. October 30, p. E6.

20 Wright, Phillip C. 1993. "The personal and the personnel adjustments and costs to small businesses entering the international market place." *Journal of Small Business Management*, January, pp. 83–93.

21 Beamish P. W., and H. J. Munro. 1987. "Exporting for success as a small Canadian manufacturer." *Journal of Small Business and Entrepreneurship*, 4, pp. 38–43.

22 Wright.

23 Ibid.

24 Bonacorsi, Andrea. 1992. "On the relationships between firm size and export intensity." *Journal of International Business Studies*, 4th quarter, pp. 605–633.

25 Freeman and Reid.

26 Bonacorsi.

27 Christensen, C., Angela da Rocha, and Rosane Gertner. 1987. "An empirical investigation of the factors influencing export success of Brazilian firms." *Journal of International Business Studies*, Fall, pp. 61–78.

28 Calof, Jonathan L. 1993. "The impact of size on internationalization." *Journal of Small Business Management*, October, pp. 60–69.

29 Lu, Jane W., and Paul W. Beamish. 2006. "Partnering strategies and performance of SMEs' international joint ventures." *Journal of Business Venturing*, 21, pp. 461–486.

30 Calof.

31 Bonacorsi.

32 Scarborough and Zimmer.

33 Hilton, Gregory. 2005. "Knocking down export barriers to smaller firms." *Business and Economic Review*, July–September, 51(4), pp. 18–20.

34 Yip, George S. 2001. *Total Global Strategy*. Englewood Cliffs, NJ: Prentice Hall.

35 Knowlton, Christopher. 1988. "The new export entrepreneurs." *Fortune*, June, pp. 6, 98.

[36] Barney, J. B. 1991. "Firm resources and sustained competitive advantage." *Journal of Management*, 17. pp. 99–120.

[37] Barry, Doug. 2000. "From Appalachia to India: U.S. small businesses are going global." *Business Credit*, 102(6), pp. 49–50.

[38] Vesper. Karl M. 1980. *New Venture Strategies*. Englewood Cliffs, NJ: Prentice Hall.

[39] Dollinger.

[40] Vesper.

[41] Dollinger.

[42] Ibid.

[43] Baker, Ted, Eric Gedajlovic, and Michel Lubatkin. 2005. "A framework for comparing entrepreneurship processes across nations." *Journal of International Business Studies*, 36, pp. 492–504.

[44] Busenitz, Lowell W., Carolina Gomez, and Jennifer W. Spence. 2000. "Country institutional profiles: Unlocking entrepreneurial phenomena." *Academy of Management Journal*, October, 43(5), pp. 994–1003.

[45] Bright, Beckey. 2005. "How do you say 'Web'? Planning to take your online business international? Beware; E-commerce can get lost in translation." *Wall Street Journal*, May 23, p. R11.

[46] Low, Sarah, Jason Henderson, and Stephan Weiler. 2005. "Gauging a region's entrepreneurial potential." *Economic Review–Federal Reserve Bank of Kansas City*, 3rd quarter, 90(3), pp. 61–89.

[47] Hosford, Christopher. 2006. "Selling strategies for small business." *Sales and Marketing Management*, April, 158(3), pp. 30–33.

[48] Ibid.

[49] Minniti, Maria, William D. Bygrave, and Erkko Autio. 2005. "Global Entrepreneurship Monitor 2005 executive report." *GEM*, pp. 1–67.

Aregak Micro-Credit Organization in Armenia

Mariam Yesayan, executive director of Aregak Micro-Credit, crossed Yerevan's Republic Square, walked a few steps down Abovyan Street, and turned in at Arami Street, heading toward her office next to the Georgian Embassy. She reviewed in her mind the events of the last nine years since she had launched Aregak to provide small loans to low-income women in several small villages in Armenia. The loans were designed to assist them in starting up small entrepreneurial ventures. The nongovernmental organization (or NGO, the term often used to describe nonprofit organizations internationally) had met all of her expectations, but it was now 2006 and she knew she must decide whether to remain an NGO or apply to the Armenian government to be a licensed and regulated for-profit organization.

Background on Mariam Yesayan

Mariam Yesayan was a native Armenian who grew up in Yerevan, the capital of Armenia. Mariam was well-educated, having received her education in the Armenian public school system as well as attending Yerevan State University where she got a degree in education. She also studied at the Gorki Institute of World Literature in Moscow, Russia, and received a degree in journalism. As was required during Soviet times, Mariam started working immediately. At the age of 21, she was well on her way—touching lives in Armenia. That year she began teaching at the Yerevan State University.

It was not until the collapse of the Soviet Union that NGOs started arriving in Armenia. The first two that Mariam worked for were ASDI/VOCA (Agency for Promoting Sustainable Development Initiatives) and the Save the Children organization. The main purpose of ASDI was to educate and train individuals so that they could make a living for themselves. Save the Children was worldwide, and Mariam worked for them in many different areas of Armenia. The organization strived to create short-term employment for families with the help of community involvement.

After ten years of working for the same NGO, Mariam felt she needed a radical change in her career. She yearned for more practical work and more benefits for her family; so she began the search for a position that would help her meet those needs. Her quest ultimately led to her changing jobs every two years until she found

one to her satisfaction. The jobs she had all dealt with U.S./AID programs and community development. Along the way, Mariam worked with companies like the World Bank and UMCOR (United Methodist Committee on Relief), which was the parent of the organization that she would later initiate.

Aregak Micro-Credit Organization

In 1996, Mariam Yesayan began working for UMCOR in Armenia. By the fall of 1997, she had established the Aregak Micro-Credit Organization to provide small loans to economically challenged women in three small villages north of Yerevan.

Her rationale in beginning this program was to supplant the aid programs that came into Armenia after the collapse of communism, which had become permanent handouts. Many of these programs, Mariam believed, made the people dependent long term and psychologically vulnerable. She believed that it was important to the self-worth of the individual women to be empowered to become self-sustaining.

Armenians at this time were very depressed because of the earthquake of 1988 that killed 28,000 people and left many more homeless; by the embargo by Turkey and Azerbaijan, which stopped the flow of all oil and gas supplies into the country; and by the unemployment rate, which had reached 80 percent shortly after the fall of communism.[1] After the earthquake, there was no electricity throughout the country for a long period of time, leaving the people in darkness and heightening their sense of being cut off from the rest of the world.

In her earlier work with the United Nations, Mariam had done research on sustainable projects to support vulnerable population groups, and this was her first acquaintance with microfinance programs. Bank loans at this time were neither accessible nor affordable.

The Process for Developing Clients Mariam began the organization by applying for loans from UMCOR to fund small loans to prospective women entrepreneurs. She got three people to help her, and they all drove up to three small villages north of Yerevan.

To make the women feel comfortable, they wore some of their oldest clothes and began conversations with the women to try to change their attitude about being dependent on other people or aid agencies. They found that the best way to meet large groups of women in these villages was to show up at someone's business or home who had a television set and had women crowded around it, watching Brazilian or American soap operas such as *Santa Barbara*. In these places, they knew they had a captive audience.

The psychological work with clients at this stage of development was important because the people faced depression about the high unemployment rate in the country, and they believed there was no longer light at the end of the tunnel—unless it was a train barreling toward them. The large Armenian eyes all looked vacant and without hope. Mariam and her coworkers began to talk to the women about developing small, sustainable businesses with the money Aregak would lend them. They were attempting to promote self-confidence and a belief in personal success among the women. Mariam would say to the women, "We can create opportunities together." Soon the women began to believe and filled out the papers to apply for a loan.

When the women began to ask about what they would have to put up as collateral for the loan, Mariam replied that they would not need collateral; their own good name and character would be the only collateral they needed. One client said to Mariam, "If I use my car as collateral for a bank loan and I can't pay the loan back, I may lose my car, but I can do without it for a while and finally get another one. But if I lose my good character by not paying back the Aregak loan, I can never get that back." The loans were negotiated at an interest rate between 20 and 25 percent, which was consistent with bank loan rates at the time.

Outcome of the Program Mariam could hardly wait for a month to pass until the time arrived for her and her coworkers to return to the villages where they had given loans to the women to collect the portion of the principal and interest that was due. She wondered how many would be there to pay on their loan; so she arrived two hours early and waited. To her great joy, all of the women who had received loans came on time to repay that month's portion. Mariam would later discover that the default on the Aregak loans was only 2 percent over the entire nine years of operation. This was encouraging because the people to whom Aregak had made loans did not have to pledge any collateral for their credit.

Soon Aregak began offering assistance with business planning and credit consulting, which were programs the Armenian banks could not offer at that time. By 2006, the number of employees at Aregak had increased to 180; there were 27 service centers in Armenia and Nagorno Karabakh (a piece of Armenia cut off in Ajerbaijan); Aregak had developed over

21,000 clients (mostly but not exclusively women), they had over $9 million in their outstanding portfolio of loans, over 450 communities were being served, and approximately 35 scholarships of $350 each were being offered to talented children of the entrepreneurs they had funded.

Alternative Sources of Financing in Armenia

In the early 1990s in Armenia, there was a crisis in the banking sector. This was shortly after the time that the state bank had been abolished and private commercial banks were being established. The newly privatized banking sector was still underdeveloped and fragile. Because many citizens had been financially hurt by the failure of the Soviet banking system and a later currency collapse, they were mistrustful of all lending institutions. In addition, many of the private citizens who established commercial banks did not know how to give loans, and the people did not know how to apply for them.

Only in the late 1990s did banks start to operate independently and give loans, but they were still charging very high interest rates. In the late 1990s, banks were charging 40 percent interest per year. By early 2003, the rate had dropped to 24 percent, and then by October of 2003 it finally dropped to 20 percent per year.

In addition to high interest rates, individuals and companies who applied for a bank loan were required to secure the loan with collateral. They might have to pledge their house or car to secure the financing for their business. This meant that they could lose these valuable assets if they defaulted on their loans. It was very difficult for an Armenian man to get a bank loan at this time, and it was almost impossible for a woman who possessed few assets.

By 2003, more than half of the private capital of Armenian banks belonged to foreign investors, and this percentage continued to increase. This trend indicated that the Union of Armenian Banks was becoming a regional financial center. Armenian financial legislation also assisted in the process by no longer hindering currency circulation inside and outside the country, and there was no limitation on the free sale of currency. The downside was that domestic as well as foreign money was going abroad because it was difficult to make investments in such a risky country as Armenia had become.

The Microfinance Industry

Microfinance is said to have evolved as an economic development approach intended to benefit low-income women and men. Included in microfinance are both financial and social improvements. Many industries provide education in financial literacy to their clients, training and investing in client confidence development, and teaching on entrepreneurship and management techniques. So "microfinance is not simply banking, it is a development tool."[2]

Although the exact number of microfinance institutions remains a mystery, researchers are able to conclude that the number of such institutions in the early years of the twenty-first century was in the thousands, if not millions. In 2005, there were more than 600,000 institutions in Indonesia alone.[3] The Microcredit Summit Campaign (MCS) annually published a collection of data, providing an analysis on the current position of the microfinance fight against poverty. According to the Microcredit Summit Campaign Report of 2005, 3,164 microcredit institutions were reported to be serving over 92 million clients, the majority of which lived in Asia. Of those 92 million, nearly 67 million were among the world's poorest populations when they took their first loan. The poorest population was defined by the MCS as "those who are in the bottom half of those living below their nation's poverty line, or any of the 1.2 billion [people] who live on less than US$1 a day adjusted for purchasing power parity (PPP)."[4] As of 2004, it was estimated that approximately 333 million people were indirectly affected by the microfinance loans made to some of the world's poorest populations, a number equivalent to the combined populations of Norway, the United Kingdom, Switzerland, the Netherlands, Spain, France, Germany, and Italy.[5] Some of the largest and most developed microfinance programs included the Grameen Bank, ACCION, FINCA, Opportunity International, and PreCredit.[6]

The Consultative Group to Assist the Poor (CGAP), a donor consortium connected with the World Bank, said that in 2004 large development aid agencies promised about $1 billion to the microfinance industry. Additionally, many large amounts were provided by private donors. Other costs, such as technical support, were generally sought after at low or even zero cost (*The Economist*, November 2005).[7] Typically, donors focused their support on microfinance institutions with goals to achieve financial sustainability and strong outreach. The industry began in the 1980s and has grown significantly in revenue, market share, and client population.

Remaining steady amid industry changes, however, clients continued to invest newly acquired funds and previously established talents into a new trade. Clients could be found in both rural and urban areas, in both developed and developing countries. Generally, clients were self-employed, with work ranging from farming to cutting hair, repairing shoes to sewing handbags, street vending to craft making. Seeking to avoid government regulations and stipulations, many microfinance institutions have remained self-regulated, nonprofit organizations in an effort to remain versatile. Their mission has been to show seemingly hopeless people that someone believed in them. For Mariam Yesayan and Aregak, this mission had been the source of motivation for service to their clients—far beyond profit or recognition. Often it was this simple confidence lenders received that made them successful in doing something for which they had great talent. However, many struggling institutions have been forced to seek funding from the government, despite the fact that this freedom of a mission focus was at risk of being regulated. This was one of the difficult decisions Aregak faced.

Industry Service: Women and Men More than 66 million people among the world's poorest have been served by a microfinance institution. Of those, nearly 56 million were women, a total of 83.5 percent. Microcredit programs have generally marketed their services to female entrepreneurs. One reason for this has been that men in developing countries, or even developed countries, have been more likely to find employment without third-party assistance. Some organizations, such as Pro Mujer, are solely "dedicated to women's development through provision of credit."[8] However, many institutions have also offered loans and financial assistance to men, even in developed nations such as the United States.

NGOs and For-Profit Operations Many nongovernmental organizations (NGO) specializing in microfinance have been faced with a major decision: to seek government funding and be under its regulations or to forego state assistance and remain self-regulating. Some organizations have remained nonprofit, while others have chosen to become for-profit entities. In some cases, a nation's government has required all microfinance institutions in that country to become regulated for-profit entities. In nations where this is not a requirement (such as Armenia), organizations have still chosen to exchange their nongovernmental status for any or several reasons. The first such reason was the opportunity to mobilize savings. Most unregulated nongovernmental microfinance institutions around the world and in the United States have been unable to collect savings in order to prevent consumers from fraudulent activity. Second, most regulated microcredit programs have been able to tap into formal capital markets, including commercial banks and global investment funds, which normally would not contribute to unregulated or nongovernmental microcredit institutions. Finally, submitting to the government's operational regulations supported governmental efforts to prevent scamming and poorly practiced programs from developing.

Government restrictions against NGOs typically included, but were not limited to, laws against nonprofits conducting financial transactions or a requirement for all money lending agencies to be state owned. The controlling officials have indirectly chosen to change the mission of the organization from a service-oriented enterprise into a for-profit firm. Whether an organization became government regulated or not determined the path of the organization.

Microfinance in Developed Countries versus Developing Countries Microfinance institutions have not only existed in developing countries, but their market in developed nations has been fairly substantial as well. The Microcredit Summit Report 2005 stated that 3,044 microcredit programs reported doing work in the developing world, serving a total of more than 92 million clients. The 120 institutions that reported work in the industrialized, developed world claimed to reach almost 233,000 people. Armenia fell into the "Europe and NIS (Newly Independent States)" category, which was said to have 72 programs at work. Approximately 3.5 million of the world's poorest families, according to Microcredit Summit Campaign Report 2005 statistics, lived within Europe and the Newly Independent States, yet only 60,000 of these families are reached by microcredit projects. In other words, only 1.7 percent of the poorest families living in Europe and the Newly Independent States, including Armenia, have been reached by established microfinance institutions.[9] According to Mariam Yesayan, Aregak controlled about half of Armenia's microfinance market, reaching about 10,000 clients.

The Decision

Mariam Yesayan walked past the Georgian Embassy next to her office and entered Aregak's headquarters at 42 Arami Street. She waved to the person sitting at the reception desk on the right and then began climbing the stairs on the left to the third floor. After reaching her office on the third floor, she put the materials she had worked on at home down on her desk and sat in her desk chair. She immediately continued the thoughts she had begun while walking across Republic Square. She knew she must decide soon whether to let Aregak retain the status it had held as a nonprofit organization for the past nine years or file papers to let it become a for-profit organization regulated by the government. She knew the decision was important because it would shape the strategy of the organization in the future.

CASE DISCUSSION QUESTIONS

1. Summarize the process Mariam Yesayan used in approaching women about loan opportunities through Aregak.
2. Compare opportunities for funding for women entrepreneurs through the commercial banking system in Armenia with funding opportunities available to them through the Aregak program in the late 1990s.
3. Explain the reason for a default rate on loans of only 2 percent with Aregak in spite of the fact that their loans were not collaterized.
4. Discuss the importance of microfinance programs in the progress of developing nations.
5. In what way might Mariam Yesayan be considered a "social entrepreneur"?
6. Debate the issue of whether Mariam Yesayan should take steps to license Aregak as a nonprofit organization in Armenia, which would bring with it regulation by the government, or remain an NGO (nongovernmental organization) as it had been originally structured.

CASE NOTES

[1] Benedetto, Joe. 2002. "Where will the jobs be?" *Design Engineering*, April, 48(3), p. 14.

[2] Ledgerwood, J. 1999. *Microfinance Handbook: An Institutional and Financial Perspective*. Washington, DC: World Bank.

[3] Daley-Harris, S. (2005). Microcredit Summit Campaign Report 2005. http://www.microcreditsummit.org.

[4] Ibid.

[5] Ibid.

[6] *Economist*. 2005. "The hidden wealth of the poor: A survey of microfinance" and "From Charity to Business."

[7] Ibid.

[8] Pro Mujer. http://www.promujer.org.

[9] Daley-Harris.

Tata Motors

Introduction

Economically lower-class Indians felt empowered when they walked into a Tata Motors (TML) showroom in Mumbai, India, on April 21, 2009 and booked their first family car for Rs 1,00000 crores (US $2,000). In that month, India was under the spell of two global influencing acts. The first was the holding of general elections in which the world's largest democracy was going to the polls. The second was the opening of booking for the world's cheapest car. No one had thought it possible to sell a car with all the required safety features and design for just under US $2,000. Tata Motors, a company that changed the basic automotive business model, had products ranging from the costliest—Jaguar and Land Rover—to the world's cheapest car, Nano. Tata Motors is the only automobile company in the world offering products from the smallest car, through middle-level cars, to the luxury segment.

The success of Tata Motors lies in its international growth strategy (Appendix I), which was "to consolidate position in the domestic market and expand international footprint through development of new products by:

• Leveraging inhouse capabilities.

• Acquisitions and strategic collaborations to gain complementary capabilities."

Appendix I   Growth Strategy of TML
1984 : India's first LCV (407 truck)
1996 : India's first SUV (Safari)
1998 : India's first passenger car—Indica
2004 : Acquisition of Tata Daewoo, Korea
2005 : India's first mini-truck (Ace)
2005 : Acquisition of stake in Hispano, Spain
2007 : Formed an industrial JV with Fiat
2007 : JV in India with Marcopolo of Brazil
2007 : JV in Thailand with Thonburi
2008 : People's car—Tata Nano
2008 : Acquisiton of Jaguar Land Rover

EXHIBIT 1   International Markets for Tata Motors

Passenger Vehicle International Markets	Commercial Vehicle International Markets
Venezuela	Chile
Senegal	Algeria
Ghana	Nigeria
Congo	Ghana
South Africa	Zambia
Ethiopia	Angola
Tanzania	Mozambique
Kenya	Uganda
Russia	Mauritius
Ukraine	Australia
Spain	Turkey
Italy	Egypt
Poland	Russia
Turkey	Ukraine
SAARC	Spain
Thailand	Italy
Malaysia	Poland
Middle east	SAARC
	Thailand
	Malaysia
	Middle east
	Senegal
	Ghana
	Congo
	South Africa
	Ethiopia
	Tanzania
	Kenya

In 2009 Tata Motors had operations in 35 countries around the world. (Exhibit 1), and it was on the 100 New Global Challengers list released by Boston Consulting Group. TML became the largest player in the 8-ton heavy truck segment in South Africa and the second-largest player in the 2- to 4-ton segment in South Africa. TML is the largest player in light buses and the second-largest in light trucks. The story of global expansion of Tata Motors started in 2004.

Domestic Economy

The Indian economy in the year 2004 had a growth rate of 8.0 percent. Indian gross domestic product (GDP) grew by 4.4 percent in fiscal year (FY) 2001, by 5.8 percent in FY 2002, and by 4.3 percent in FY 2003, with an expected future growth rate of 7.0 percent in FY 2005 and 9 percent in 2006 and 11 percent in 2007. However, according to Goldman Sachs, India will have the highest growth rate in GDP in comparison with other emerging economies until 2045–2050.

Governmental Initiation

The government of India in the years 2002–2003 invested heavily in infrastructure, implementing the following six-point strategy:

1. Strengthening and four-laning of high-density corridors.

2. Golden Quadrilateral (5,846 kilometers).

3. NSEW Corridor (7,300 kilometers).

4. Road connectivity to major ports.

5. Private sector participation in financing construction and maintenance.

6. Improvement, maintenance, and augmentation of the existing national highways network.

This investment was expected to enhance commercial vehicle penetration in India. Furthermore, in 2008, India became the:

- Second-largest two-wheeler market in the world.

- Fourth-largest commercial vehicle market in the world.

- Eleventh-largest passenger car market in the world and is expected to be the seventh-largest market by 2016.

Demographic Shift in India

It was expected that, by 2009, 60 percent of India's population will be 25 years of age and less. The consumption of food and beverage, which was 62.5 percent in the years 1970–1971, came down to 44.5 percent in 2001 and was trending toward further reductions. The consumption of transportation was 2.8 percent in the years 1970–1971 and grew to 13.5 percent in the year 2000–2001. The increasing per-capita disposable income is leading to a subsequent decline in the proportion of spending on basic necessities and an increasing proportion on transportation. Transportation became the second-largest spend category in 2002.

Domestic Automobile Industry

According to Goldman Sachs' BRIC Team, there will be a significant increase in the middle-class population in India, coupled with an increase in per-capita GDP (in terms of purchasing power parity, PPP), and the team expects India to hit the "sweet spot of car ownership" between 2015 and 2025.

These structural changes have totally changed the commercial vehicle market because there will be a structural shift toward heavy commercial vehicles (HCV). The demand for buses will increase substantially, especially for large, luxury buses.

International Automobile Market

Global Automobile Trends

International automobile markets are at a crossroad. Factors like consumer preferences, competitive dynamics, and the cyclical nature of product design, environmental factors, and regionalism are all factors affecting the global strategy of automobile giants.

Motorization and population increases are the two most influential factors in automakers' strategic product management. In countries where population is increasing but motorization is saturated, auto companies have to consolidate their present position as well as launch new products to attract new, young customers. In areas where both factors are increasing, they have to invest in services, supply chain, and new product launches.

In United States, Western Europe, Japan, and South Korea, there was an average sales reduction of 20 percent from 2007 to 2009. The sales growth was unaffected in China and grew in India and Eastern Europe.

The global automobile industry is varied not only in strategic orientation but also in customer preferences. For example, for an American automaker, styling means boxiness, a large nose/deck, and an emphasis on size. For a European, it can mean roundness, a short nose/deck, and emphasis on aerodynamics and space efficiency. The engine body, from an American point of view, will be large and powerful engine, a heavy body with slow response. For a Japanese car, the engine can be small, with a light body; the emphasis is on fuel economy and sharp response. In terms of value added, a European wants total balance, and the Japanese want options and many features as standard equipment. The overall image for an American vehicle is that of an all-purpose road cruiser—large, comfortable, powerful—and for a European the automobile is a driving machine—responsive, precise, sophisticated.

The automobile companies make more profit in selling luxury cars rather than in selling small cars. The revenue shares for participants in the automobile value chain are as follows: Suppliers have a 60 percent share of the recommended retail price, assemblers have 10 percent, marketing logistics another 10 percent, and dealers 20 percent. Vehicle manufacturers in mature markets derive about 20 percent of revenues and 40 percent of operating profits from sales of spare parts.

Tata Group

Tata Group has been one of the largest and most respected industrial houses of India, with a pioneering track record of 130 years. In FY 2004 Tata Group had over 80 companies with leadership presence in most of the sectors. Its revenues were approximately Rs 615 billion (US $13.4 billion, equivalent to 2.6 percent of India's GDP at current prices), and its net profit was Rs 57 billion (US $1.3 billion).

Tata Motors

In the year 2004 Tata Motors was India's largest automotive company in terms of revenue. Tata Motors was the market leader in commercial vehicles and the second-largest player in passenger vehicles. In 1954, it began manufacturing vehicles. The firm has demonstrated very strong R&D skill sets with the capability of developing vehicle platforms indigenously at a relatively low cost. In 2003 Tata Motors had three manufacturing facilities in Jamshedpur, Pune, and Lucknow. In 2004 it acquired Daewoo Motors and added the Gunsan plant in South Korea, its first outside India. It had the widest range of product offerings in the Indian market, consisting of commercial vehicles, multiutility vehicles, and passenger cars.

International Business Initiatives by Tata Motors in 2004

In 2004, exports were 15 percent of revenues, and Tata Motors made a target of increasing the exports by 20 percent in 2006.

Mr. Ravi Kanth, Managing Director TML, thought that the best strategy for Tata Motors was focused positioning and marketing in selected countries.

- *South Africa*: In South Africa the market was 360,000 units annually and was comprised of passenger cars and pickup trucks. Tata Motors positioned itself as a seller of a "value for money" product there. The production plan was to make the products in India and ship them to South Africa in 2005. The initial target was 2,000 or more by the third quarter of that year.

- *Sri Lanka*: The commercial vehicle volume was approximately 13,800, primarily medium to heavy commercial vehicles (MHCVs) and light commercial vehicles (LCVs). The competition in Sri Lanka was from secondhand imports of Japanese vehicles. Tata Motors had to cut the Japanese market in Sri Lanka. The plan was to export around 700 vehicles in the third quarter of 2005 and approximately 1,800 units in 2005.
- *Russia and East Europe*: Targeting the LCV truck market in Russia, Tata Motors started operations in 2004 in the Ukraine through bus assembly.

Tata Motors replicated these strategies in other key markets of Southeast and South Asia, Southern Europe, the Middle East, and Africa.

Organic Growth Strategies of Tata Motors

To develop and sustain a competitive advantage, Tata Motors developed a two-pronged strategy. First, it expanded its capacity. In 2004 the utilization was around 75 percent for commercial vehicles (CVs) and utility vehicles (UVs) and 100 percent for the Indica plant, which made passenger cars (PCs). Indica's PC capacity was expanded by 50 percent by the end of 2005. In the same year, CV capacity was expanded and new products were developed (small pickups and intercity and intracity buses). By 2006–2007, new platforms were started up for global trucks, a new utility vehicle, and compact cars. For the people's car, there were new engine offerings and commensurate expansion in R&D capability. The goal was for expansion into new markets and product categories, both domestically and internationally.

Inorganic Growth Planning of Tata Motors in 2004

Tata Motor's philosophy of inorganic growth was as follows:

- Acquiring an international company for (a) access to markets, (b) access to new technology and R&D capability, and (c) growth in international business.
- Marketing tie-ins for (a) distribution and (b) cobranding.
- Asset purchases for (a) new products, (b) new technology, and (c) new capacities.
- Strategic alliances for (a) product swaps and (b) R&D alliances.

There were further challenges for Tata Motors, such as cost pressures on input materials like steel, engineering plastics, aluminum, copper, and so on. As of April 2005, the company also felt the impact of emission compliance measures. Eleven cities in India have migrated to Euro III, while the rest of the country will migrate to Euro II emission norms. The cost of meeting the emission standards may lead to an increase in price, leading to sluggish demand conditions in 2006. Fuel price increases are also a factor.

Furthermore, the automotive business model was changing. Automobile manufacturers were making money not only by selling cars but also by maintaining them and selling accessories.

Tata Motors acquired Daewoo Commercial Vehicle Co. (DWCV) of Korea and made it a 100 percent subsidiary on March 30, 2004. The HCV was a product segment of DWCV and a complementary product for Tata. The acquisition gave Tata access to assembly technology for high-end trucks, the potential for leading the domestic market in high-end trucks, and an entry to the South Korea market for medium and intermediate commercial vehicles. Tata had a market share of 25 percent as well as an additional annual production capacity of 20,000 units. The purchase was a very profitable venture, earning Tata US $5.4 million on a turnover of US $222 million in fiscal year 2003 on a 21 percent of Daewoo's capacity utilization.

Positioning of Tata Motors in the Global Markets

Mr. Ravi Kant, Tata's Managing Director, had to decide on a positioning strategy for Tata Motors in the global markets. Tata Motors aspired to be among the top global manufacturers in the product group of medium and heavy trucks. In pickup trucks, Tata Motors had to establish a presence in the global segment and couple that with a high domestic demand potential. Tata Motors also targeted the niche global markets in the compact car segment.

Enhancing Capabilities: Partnering with World-Class Players

Tata Motors is no stranger to global partnering:

1. In a joint venture with Marcopolo (Tata Motors, 51 percent; Marcopolo, 49 percent), the goal was to take advantage of product development and participation in mass transport opportunities in Indian and international markets. The target is, using India's low-cost advantage, to produce 150,000 buses (24- to 54-seaters) in five years.

2. In an alliance with Fiat, (a) Fiat distributes products in India, and (b) the two companies engage in a joint manufacturing venture (Tata Motors, 50 percent; Fiat, 50 percent) in India. Tata gained access to world-class car engine technology. Both companies gained access to a production capacity of 100,000 cars and 250,000 units of engines and transmissions for use globally.

3. To capitalize on the regional trading block ASEAN and local country competencies, Tata formed a joint venture in Thailand with Thonburi Thailand (Tata Motors, 70 percent; Thonburi, 30 percent). In Phase I, the production capacity was 12,500 units per annum. In March 2008, Xenon was launched in Thailand, and an eco car project started.

4. To deal with customs in South Africa, Tata Motors formed a subsidiary (Tata Motors, 60 percent; Tata Africa, 40 percent). The products manufactured will be passenger and commercial vehicles.

Despite this track record, the whole world was shocked when Tata Motors acquired Jaguar Land Rover for US $2.3 billion. Watching a developing country company acquire a developed country's largest brands was a very painful experience for many. Tata had its reasons for the purchase: (a) the opportunity to participate in two fast growing auto segments (premium and small cars) and to build a comprehensive product portfolio with an immediate global footprint; (b) to increase business diversity across markets and product segments; (c) to get a unique opportunity to move into a premium segment with access to world-class iconic brands; (d) to fit Land Rover naturally above Tata's utility/sport utility/crossover offerings for the 4×4 premium category and to broaden the brand portfolio with Jaguar's performance/luxury vehicles; and (e) to enjoy long-term benefits from component sourcing, low-cost engineering, and design services.

For any company to survive, its organizational structure must be excellent and coupled with a suitable business model, effective cost control mechanisms, appropriate products and services, ample resource capabilities, process, and quality, as well as with organic and inorganic growth strategies.

CASE DISCUSSION QUESTIONS

1. What are some of the features of the Indian market that make it an attractive domestic market to TATA?
2. Prepare a SWOT analysis for Tata Motors.
3. What does a five forces model look like for TATA in the global automotive market?
4. What are the key success factors for a global automobile major?
5. As mentioned in the case, the international success strategies for Tata Motors were "to consolidate position in the domestic market and expand international footprint through development of new products by leveraging in house capabilities, acquisitions, and strategic collaborations to gain complementary capabilities." Did TATA achieve these goals? Please elaborate your answers with examples from the case.
6. Mr. Ravi Kanth Managing Director TML said that the success internationally will be through focused positioning and marketing in selected countries. Do you agree with his viewpoint?

The Fleet Sheet

Marlene M. Reed/Professor, School of Business,
Samford University, Birmingham, Alabama
Rochelle R. Brunson/Department Chair, Management Development
Alvin Community College, Alvin, Texas

A t precisely 8:00 A.M. on Monday, April 3, 2000, faxes began printing out simultaneously in the offices of English-speaking companies all over the Czech Republic. Among the news of the Czech Republic translated into English that day was an interesting political insight gleaned from two newspapers:

> "The Washington Post *wrote that Madeleine Albright is the weakest U.S. Secretary of State since the early 1970s and is now only popular in Prague. Euro quips that that's not so bad: The only place Vaclav Havel* is now taken seriously is in Washington."[1]

It was this kind of honest, straightforward evaluation of the Czech economy and government that had made the *Fleet Sheet* so popular to foreign companies and their managers. For Erik Best, founder of the *Fleet Sheet,* there were many decisions to be made concerning the future of the company as well as his own future.

He had begun the business on February 22, 1992, because of a perceived short-term need by Western companies rushing into Czechoslovakia after the Velvet Revolution for economic and political information that they could understand. He had envisioned that in a few years these companies would train Czech nationals to take over their operations in the country, and the English-speaking Westerners would withdraw. That had not happened, and he now wondered if he had a "going concern" that lacked a sound organizational and legal structure to survive into the future. He also wondered how long an operation such as his would continue to be a viable venture because of rapidly-changing technology and greater access to news through the Internet. Erik was now 37 years old, and he knew he needed to make some decisions for the future.

Erik's Education and Early Work Experience

Erik was born in North Carolina, and when he was 11 years old, his family moved to Montana. He went to high school there and wrote for the high school newspaper. He also became a part-time staff sports writer for the *Missoulian*—the local newspaper. Near the end of his Senior year in high school, Erik was offered a journalism scholarship to Vanderbilt University; however, he turned it down because at that time he was not sure he wanted to be a journalist. In the back of his mind, he had thought for some time that he wanted to be involved in business or politics or perhaps both. He decided to attend Georgetown University, and he received a degree in Foreign Service from Georgetown in 1985.

In the summers while working on his undergraduate degree at Georgetown, he also studied the Russian language at Middlebury College in Vermont, a school well known for its concentration on international affairs. He subsequently received a Master's Degree in Russian from Middlebury in the Summer of 1985. Perhaps the educational experience that had the greatest impact upon Erik's life was a required four months' stint in Moscow. When he had completed his degree at Middlebury, he entered the M.B.A. program at the University of North Carolina at Chapel Hill and received his M.B.A. degree in 1987.

The Move to Prague

Erik Best, a fluent speaker of the Russian language and one conversant in other Slavic languages, became enamored with the historic changes taking place in Eastern Europe. Never in the 20th Century had the opportunity existed to be a part of such a great transformation. Never before in history had countries formerly living under a Socialist government with centrally planned economies tried to make the transition to a free market economy where Adam Smith's "Invisible Hand" would be responsible for moving resources into their most advantageous usage.

Therefore, when the offer was made to Erik by the M.B.A. Enterprise Corps to join them in their work in Czechoslovakia, he quickly accepted. In February of 1991, Erik packed his bags and moved to Prague. He immediately fell in love with the country and found the Czech language very similar to Russian. In explaining his love of Prague to others, Erik would state, "I have always loved music, and there is no city in the world so rich with music as Prague. There are classical concerts daily in concert halls, churches, town squares, on the breathtaking Charles Bridge, private chambers, large public halls and under street arches. There are violinists and accordianists playing on street corners and in Metro stations. I have heard that there are more musicians per capita in the Czech Republic than anywhere else in the world. After all, it was in Prague that Mozart wrote the opera *Don Giovanni* and found greater acclaim than in his own Austria. It was also the home of composers Dvorak and Smetana. This is one of the reasons I feel at home in this city."

The Situation in Eastern Europe

In the early 1990s, the breakup of centralized Socialist economies was occurring all over Eastern Europe. Simultaneously, there was a rapid growth of the private sector in Russia and the surrounding countries of Poland, Czechoslovakia, and Hungary. One of the challenges in the burgeoning market economies was creating small businesses out of large enterprises and also launching entirely new ventures where none had been before. In fact, the development of the small business sector had been the most successful manifestation of the movement to a market economy. Small businesses had also been the greatest success story in the privatization process. Auctions of small businesses and the restitution of property in these countries had led to the restoration of some family businesses.

However, numerous problems beset these newly-created companies. In some cases, the venture was merely additional work added to one or two other jobs to keep the entrepreneur afloat with increasingly higher inflation rates and increasingly stagnant wage rates. Many small businesses were forced into operating illegitimately to deal with unfair and cumbersome legal procedures in the regulatory environment, or to avoid the attention of the Mafia or corrupt officials. It became very difficult to work out a secure contract for lease of property, and the banking system was not equipped to deal with the needs of small business.[2]

Another serious problem was the lack of experience in running private businesses that existed in Eastern Europe. Most hopeful entrepreneurs had lived all of their lives in a Socialist economy and had no training or knowledge related to the way in which one becomes an entrepreneur. It was into this environment that many organizations from the West sent consultants to assist with the revitalization of the economy as a free market. The M.B.A. Enterprise Corps was one such operation.

Origination of Idea for the *Fleet Sheet*

After working in Prague for a year, it became clear to Erik that international companies that had established offices and operations in the Czech Republic had difficulty in obtaining accurate and timely information on political and economic trends in the country upon which to make business decisions. From his work as a management consultant, he knew that decision makers in companies are very busy, and those operating in the Czech Republic would need information that was very concise and written in English. At the time, no such product was available in the country. It occurred to him that a 1-page faxed bulletin would be the best format for such a paper. The fax was also an inexpensive medium to use. He knew that in the beginning there would not be much news to report, and a 1-page sheet of paper would probably hold all he needed to print.

By early 1992, he had worked out all of the details to begin the business, and on February 22nd he published the first issue. Erik believed that if he had 4 or 5 subscribers in the first month, the product would be successful. In fact, approximately 15 to 20 subscribers signed up in the first month of operations. By early Spring of 2000, there were somewhere in the neighborhood of 1,000 subscribers receiving the *Fleet Sheet* on a regular basis.

Believing that the life cycle of his product would be relatively short, Erik took little thought to establishing a permanent structure for his business. He set it up as a sole proprietorship, and did not bother with a business plan since the operations of the company were uncomplicated and easy to establish. By 2000, he had 8 staff members in the company. Some of the staff came in the very early morning to review newspapers and begin translating the news from Czech to English. Other members of the staff came in around 7:30 A.M. and were involved in distribution and client support. Erik assumed the major responsibility for picking out the most important news to be translated and distributed in the *Fleet Sheet*. He believed a key competitive advantage of the *Fleet Sheet* was its emphasis on a quality product that reported useful Czech economic and political news. Occasionally, the *Sheet* had made a person unhappy by interpreting something incorrectly. However, if Erik agreed with the person's argument, he would admit it and print a retraction. He had found it important to listen to customer complaints and recognize the needs of the customer. He attempted to treat his readers as equal partners. The name for his paper came from the fact that it was issued in a timely manner, and also in reference to Fleet Street in London where all of the major newspapers once resided before moving to the Docklands.

The Pricing Strategy

Erik realized immediately that the major publication constraint would be the number of people he could physically fax copies of the *Fleet Sheet* to in a short period of time. This was primarily due to the fact that he knew there would be a limitation on the number of telephone lines that he could get. He also knew that another constraint was the budget of the companies and when they needed to have the news. The larger multinational companies, he speculated, would be willing to pay a higher price to get the information very early in the morning. On the other hand, smaller companies beset with fewer complicated decisions would probably be willing to pay a lower price to have the information later in the day. Some businesses might need the information only once a week.

On the basis of this assessment, Erik constructed a pricing structure that averaged $3 to $4 per day for the customer who wanted the *Fleet Sheet* faxed to the him or her early in the morning, and for the smaller companies who needed the *Fleet Sheet* faxed to them only once a week, the price would drop to $.50 to $.75 an issue. There would be intermediate pricing between the two end points. Therefore, the large companies and lawyers for whom "time is money," could have access to all of the Czech political and economic news early in the morning so that they could make astute and timely decisions based upon realistic information. The companies that did not need information in a timely manner could enjoy the benefit of a discounted price for the information. The graduated pricing strategy would also make the distribution of the paper manageable. It seemed to be an effective pricing strategy: Pricing based upon when the subscriber receives the news. The attractiveness of the pricing strategy was that anyone could afford the *Fleet Sheet*.

In order to insure the timeliness of the paper, Erik initially guaranteed the larger companies that if they did not receive their fax of the *Fleet Sheet* before 9:00 A.M. each day, it would be free. However, the fax was never late, and Erik simply dropped this guarantee since no one worried about getting a fax late.

Marketing of the *Fleet Sheet*

The marketing of the *Fleet Sheet* was multi-pronged. The first thing that Erik did was to advertise in English-language publications such as the *Prague Post, Business Central Europe* (published by *The Economist*), *The American Chamber of Commerce Newsletter* and in the Czech press in very select publications read by the elite. He was surprised that his subscribers had been not only people from English-speaking countries, but also the Dutch, French, German, and even some Czech companies that realized having the news abbreviated for them saved valuable time.

The company also engaged in direct marketing. They found out about new companies moving to town from the American Chamber of Commerce, people Erik met, personal contacts, and by word of mouth. With all new contacts, the company immediately apprised them of the product they were offering. Erik found that his satisfied subscribers let other people know about the service, and many new customers came from referrals. One reason his subscribers had been well satisfied was because Erik made an effort to dig into the important issues facing businesses in the Czech Republic. He also attempted to give people analysis rather than a simple reporting of the news. He found that clients read the *Fleet Sheet* because of the selection of articles that were covered.

A more recent addition to his marketing activities had been using e-mail to whet the appetite of potential subscribers. (See Exhibit 1, "e-mail Synopsis of *Fleet Sheet*.") Whenever anyone e-mailed him, Erik immediately added their name to a list of people who receive a summary of the day's *Fleet Sheet* articles twice a week. The purpose of this was to acquaint them with the value of subscribing to the *Fleet Sheet* for daily faxes. Understanding the animosity some people have to receiving "junk e-mails," Erik added a notice at the bottom of the e-mail that explained:

If you do not wish to receive such messages in the future, please simply let us know and we will remove your name from our list.

EXHIBIT 1   E-Mail Synopsis of Fleet Sheet

Subj: **In today's Fleet Sheet**
Date: 11/20/00 12:43:19 AM Central Standard Time
From: info@fleet.cz (Fleet Sheet/E.S. Best)
To: info@fleet.cz
From today's Fleet Sheet:

(MFD/1) The four-party coalition won a big victory in the Senate elections yesterday, gaining seats in 16 of the 19 races in which it had candidates. ODS and CSSD lost their Senate majority and will not be able to elect the chairman of the Senate or push through constitutional changes on their own. The top position in the Senate is now held by Libuse Benesova of ODS, but she lost to Helena Rognerova of the 4C. ODS won just eight of the 27 Senate seats at stake, and CSSD managed only one victory. An independent candidate won the final seat. The communists (KSCM) failed to win any seats. One seat had been decided in the first round in favor of the 4C. Of the 81 total Senate seats, the 4C now has 39, to 22 for ODS, 15 for CSSD, three for KSCM and two for independents. Voter turnout was less than 20%. Vaclav Klaus responded to this by saying the Senate should be reformed so that its elections become part of the regional elections. (MFD/8) Jiri Leschtina of MFD says it will be interesting to see whether the Senate results lead anyone from within ODS and CSSD to break the loyalty pact and take a firm stance against Klaus and Zeman.
*
(HN/2) The results of the Senate elections reduce the chance that Vaclav Klaus will succeed Vaclav Havel as President. The results suggest that a candidate close to the 4C and Havel has a better chance. The results also make it unlikely that the constitutional amendment to reduce the powers of the President will win approval. If passed, the President's power to pick Bank Board members would be limited.
*
(HN/3) CEO Jaroslav Mil of CEZ said that if price were the top priority, the sale of the state's stakes in âEZ and the regional electricity distributors could bring Kc 200–300bn in privatization. If synergies were sought with the natural-gas distributors, he said, the amount could be higher. However, if things such as maintaining employment and coal output play a role, this amount cannot be expected, he said. In this respect, he said he could imagine a requirement that a certain amount of output be guaranteed by the buyer. He also said he sees no reason why one Czech company should not be able to offer gas, water, and electricity. He also indicated that he expects more use of nuclear power in the future. (HN/P9) CEZ's stock hit a low for the year of Kc 85 and might fall more.
*
(MFD/2) Klaus got a bit touchy at ODS campaign headquarters yesterday after the first results of the Senate elections were announced. When an MFD photographer made a call during Klaus' live interview on Czech TV, Klaus grabbed the man's cellphone out of his hand and tossed it into the corner."How can he dare (talk on the phone) while I'm being interviewed?" Klaus asked. (MFD/3) Milos Zeman, for his part, refused to face defeat and didn't even show up at CSSD campaign headquarters.

Few people ever asked to have their names removed, and many signed up as regular subscribers. This was probably because the e-mail was only sent to individuals whom Erik believed would have an interest in Czech news.

In the late 1990s, Erik developed a Web site for his company. The Web address was http://www.fleet.cz.(See Exhibit 2, "*Fleet Sheet*" Home Page and Final Word) He believed that the Web site had enormous market potential for his

---

EXHIBIT 2 · *Fleet Sheet* Home Page and Final Word

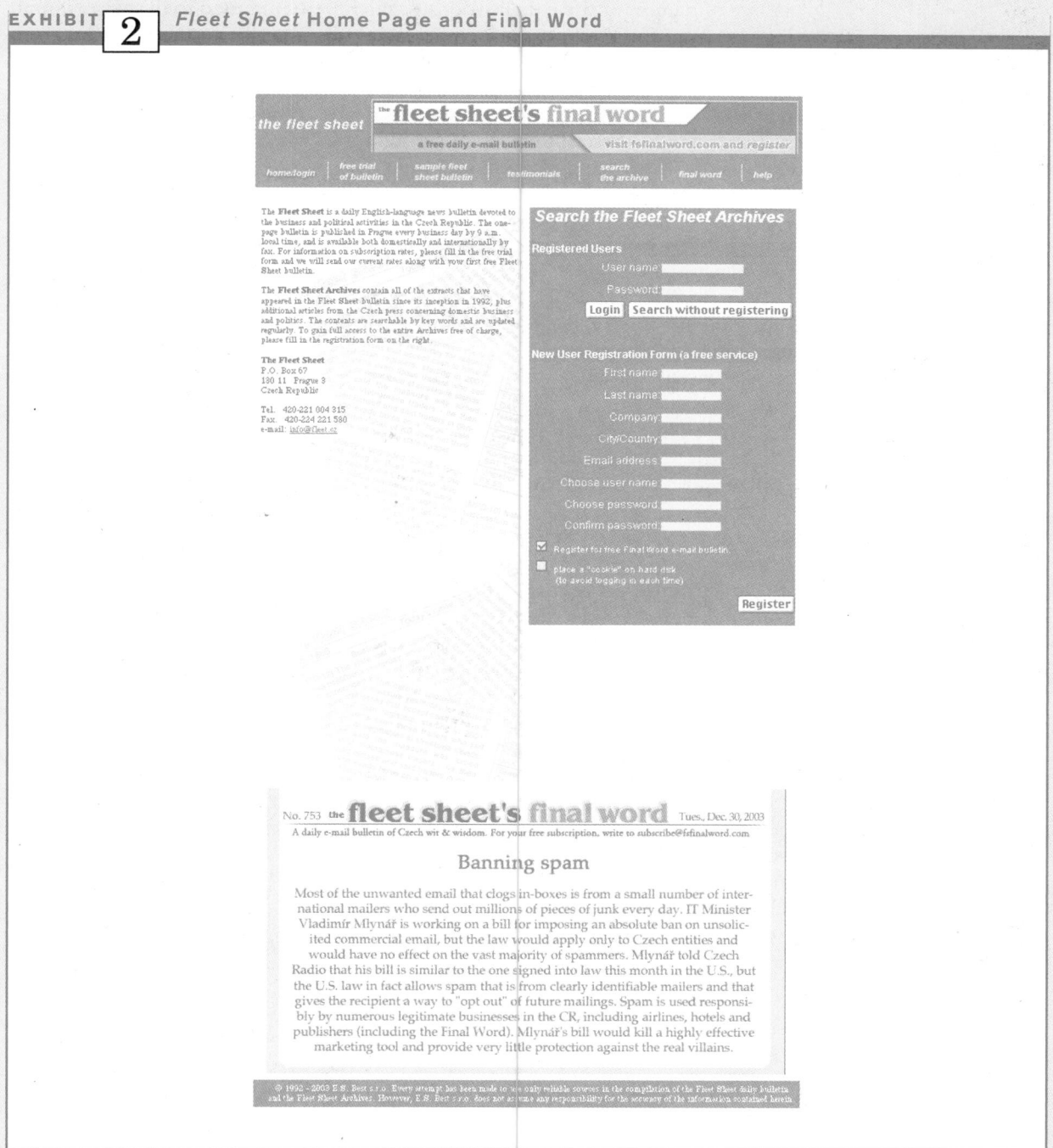

company. It would now be possible for the company to place a page on the Web site that was a sampling of the *Fleet Sheet* for interested individuals and companies. Erik believed this had the potential to generate an even greater number of subscribers than did the e-mail synopses.

In the past, Erik had offered the entire archives on disk. A company would pay about $500 a year to subscribe to the service. However, he decided to put all of his archives from the past 8 years on the Web site. The service was free, but one had to register to have access to it. This registry began to generate a good source of names for the e-mail synopses which were intended to develop enough interest from the reader to cause him or her to subscribe to the fax service.

Erik hoped that his Web site would be of sufficiently high quality for people to continue to read it. He was gambling on the belief that a company could make more money in the long run by using its archives as a marketing tool to generate more subscriptions than by selling the archives as some companies such as the *Wall Street Journal* had done.

People occasionally asked Erik why he didn't go to e-mail entirely as the medium for publishing and distributing the *Fleet Sheet*. His response was, "There is the problem of protecting intellectual property. Unless you can encrypt it, you may have a copyright infringement of your material. In fact, Stephen King's most recent story which was published originally on the Internet was encrypted, but someone broke the code. Another problem with encryption is that the message can only be sent to a specific person—not a company. Therefore, there are some real problems with encrypting the information on the Internet."

Hurdles for the Business

Unlike most start-up businesses, the *Fleet Sheet* was profitable from the very beginning. Erik made an early decision to rent office space and computers initially. Whenever it became clear that the *Fleet Sheet* was a viable business, he did invest in some assets for the company such as necessary equipment.

Concerning the success of the company, Erik mused, "The revenues of the company have grown every year because the Czech Republic was seen early as the darling of the West, and they also received a great deal of media attention. Under more realistic conditions, many of the companies would not have come here." However, in the last couple of years of the 1990s, there had been a decline in subscribers. Erik often contemplated how recent world economic events might be affecting the circulation of the *Fleet Sheet*.

As to the last hurdle, Erik commented, "We have had to fend off 6 or 7 competitors who began to offer the same service that we were offering—a faxed bulletin with important political and economic news. It was a blatant rip-off of our product. The success of the *Fleet Sheet* drew other companies into the market."

Erik speculated:

The drastic price reduction the competition offered in the beginning served to lower the overall revenue size of the market. I have often wondered if there is a big enough market to support ONE such publication over the long run, much less numerous competitors in a smaller revenue pool.

However, he also observed:

The reason we survived was due to the overall quality of the paper. Business people know quality when they see it, and they immediately know that the Fleet Sheet is professionally done.

Government regulations which had been devastating to many businesses in the Czech Republic had been minimal for the *Fleet Sheet*. The company did not require a large number of licenses or drug approvals as did the large pharmaceutical companies operating in the country. However, they had been faced with government bureaucracy—especially in the distribution of their product. The Government informed them that they had to send the *Fleet Sheet* to hundreds of libraries at the company's own expense. This, of course, would have made the company non-profitable and no one would have read the paper anyway. They decided to take a risk and send the paper to only selected libraries where they believed there was a greater chance of someone actually reading the *Fleet Sheet*. Fortunately, the regulation was changed in the early part of 2000 so that the company would no longer be required to distribute the paper in this manner.

In the late 1990s, Erik decided to add an advertisement to the *Fleet Sheet*. The ad was priced at $400 a day and was rotated among 4 or 5 different companies' ads. (See Exhibit 3, "*Fleet Sheet* with Ad.") If he should decide to add another advertisement, Erik would probably have to add another page to the fax. Faxing charges are minimal, the primary cost would be additional staff to prepare another page. However, he wondered if the primary focus of the paper—relevant information in a concise format—would be maintained. People don't mind taking the time to read 1 page of the most concise political and economic news of the day, but would they read 2 pages?

In the Spring of 2000, there were around 800 subscribers to the *Fleet Sheet* paying an average of $2.50 each per day to receive the publication. In addition, each additional subscriber brought in 90% in profits and only 10% in variable costs. Erik speculated about whether a new format with two pages would actually reduce—rather than increase—subscribers.

Erik had always used Adobe Acrobat to format the paper, and the faxed paper was very easy to read. If he went to an e-mail publication of the paper altogether, there could be a text format that would not be limited to one or two pages. But he wondered if that would affect the integrity of the product. They had done so well in the past with the concise format of a 1-page fax. Would people actually sit at their computers and read through a lengthy e-mail the way they read through a newspaper or fax that they can hold in their hands? Erik speculated, "If you could produce the same experience of reading a newspaper on the Internet, it would be good. However, our present computer monitors prevent this from occurring." Erik also wondered how a company could build a brand name and attract a loyal readership over the Internet. On the Internet, one must click through so many pages to get to the desired material that the opportunity cost of one's time becomes very expensive.

When Erik began his venture in 1992, he firmly believed it would be a short-term operation bridging the gap until a new economy was established and other sources of information became available. With that in mind, he had spent little time pondering an appropriate legal structure for the business. He had initially set the business up as a sole proprietorship, but now he wondered if he should have established it as an LLC. He would also have developed a long-term strategy for the company. He wondered if it was too late to develop a business plan for the *Fleet Sheet* and alter its legal structure. He knew he would have to fill out some forms and notify the United States Government of his actions, but perhaps he should do that. Erik wondered if a change in the legal structure of the organization would have capital gains tax implications if he decided to sell the business. He never assumed the business would last this long or he might have spent more time in planning rather than starting the business up in two weeks.

EXHIBIT 3   *Fleet Sheet* with Ad

the fleet sheet

No. 2999   *Today's news, today* Prague, Tues., Dec. 30, 2003

Business

(MFD/1) A poll by SC&C found that many Czechs associate EU accession next year with higher prices. Some price increases will take effect immediately in Jan., while others will be timed to coincide with EU accession on May 1. Consumers are stocking up on such things as gasoline, alcohol and prepaid phone cards at the old prices. The SC&C poll found that 26.8% of respondents fear price increases next year, compared to 16.7% who fear losing their job and 9.9% who fear accession. Most respondents consider 2003 to be an average year. Most young respondents thought it was a good year, while older respondents and low wage-earners tended to be more pessimistic. (MFD/B4) EU entry will mean higher prices for imports from some non-EU countries of such things as bananas, rice, tuna, bicycles and CDs. (MFD/6) MFD pictures Klaus in a cartoon working on his New Year's address. "Bad things come in threes," he says. "First the floods, then the drought, then EU entry."

(MFD/7) Oskar said it expects a single-digit decrease in calling levels during the first months of next year, due to the sharp VAT increase. T-Mobile said it expects calling traffic to return to its previous level after a few months. Český Telecom expects about 100,000 people to give up their fixed lines because of the higher tax.

(HN/1) Some building & loans have been unable to handle all the customers seeking to sign contracts by the end of the year, before the state subsidy declines next year. ČMSS said that it expects to serve as many as 10,000 customers a day this week. About 2m new contracts are expected this year. Next year, though, this should drop to just six figures, according to ČMSS. Building & loans will use the promise of loans to attract new customers next year. (LN/6) Some clients are using very high target savings levels - such as Kč 1m - as a way to guarantee the higher state subsidies for many years to come.

(HN/13) Pre-Christmas internet sales quadrupled this year. Czech shoppers bought more-expensive items on line, such as DVD players and digital cameras.

(HN/18) Landowners claim that a planned new law for specifying the price and length of their leases of land to farmers is unconstitutional. One version of the bill would allow farmers to continue to pay today's artificially low rates. Farmers welcome the law and favor long lease periods.

(MFD/9) Škoda Auto is offering bonuses of up to Kč 90,000 on Octavias. (EU/62) Škoda does not expect its planned new Octavia to cannibalize its sister brands.

(HN/1) The terms for reserving and paying for tickets to next year's hockey championships were so tight that many people risk losing their reservations. Tickets went on sale shortly before Christmas and had to be paid for within seven days. Due to the holidays, payment orders needed to be submitted many days in advance. Sazka said it will wait an extra day or two and will then put any tickets that have not been paid for on sale in early Jan. (MFD/D1) Some people are threatening to sue Sazka for not honoring ticket reservations that were made in the summer. Sazka blamed the situation on the Hockey Union.

(HN/13) The CR attracted 40 investments this year into IT and service centers, from companies such as Accenture, DHL, Honeywell and ExxonMobil. Investment into the 15 largest of them will exceed Kč 17bn. (DHL accounts for Kč 16bn of this, and HN gives no figure for Accenture, Honeywell and ExxonMobil.) These 15 investments are expected to lead to 4,386 new jobs. (EU/62) Separately, Škoda Auto Chairman Vratislav Kulhánek said the decade-long tax breaks given to foreign investors are "perverse." Many of the companies would come anyway, he said, and CzechInvest pays no attention to whether the new investments will threaten the existence of thriving businesses. CzechInvest's policies in general need to be examined, he said.

(HN/17) One of the pillars of Český Telecom's strategy is to remain in a business only if it is No. 1 or No. 2 on the market, according to HR Director Imrich Gombar. Layoffs will be closely linked to this. Job cuts are planned preliminarily for the end of each of the first three quarters of 2004. On average, employees will get about eight months' wages as severance pay.

(HN/2) Charges are expected to be filed early next year in what HN calls the biggest corruption affair since 1989. Karel Srba, Pavel Jaroš, Alex Šatánek and other former top-level employees of the foreign ministry are suspected of profiting from state contracts. [HN's article was written by Sabina Slonková. Srba has already been found guilty of conspiring to kill her.]

(HN/17) Czech Railways chose Kapsch again to supply a GSM-R network.... Due to changes in U.S. rules, large PR agencies active here will no longer disclose their annual results.... Ruhrgas will shift its 24% stake in Pražská plynárenská Holding to E.ON. (EU/8) The SEC launched a Kč 100m computer system for detecting trading fraud. (MFD/5) On Jan. 10, Mountfield will launch discounts of "up to 100%" on garden tools and swimming pools.

Politics

(P/1) Stanislav Gross said KDU-ČSL Chair Miroslav Kalousek should join the cabinet. Kalousek said he is willing to enter into talks with ČSSD and US-DEU about a fourth cabinet seat for KDU. He ruled out any reshuffling of KDU's three seats.

(MFD/2) Czech TV will air a taped three-minute toast by Václav Havel at midnight on New Year's Eve. Václav Klaus will give his live New Year's address 13 hours later. (MFD/4) Separately, architect Bořek Šípek said he will wait for Klaus' term to expire to carry through with his idea of erecting 25 small buildings in the Castle grounds for representing EU countries. The project is supported by Havel but has been rejected by the current Castle administration.

(HN/4) Jiří Svoboda, who led the Communist Party for three years in the early 1990s, said the shift of voters away from ČSSD to the Communists is due mainly to two things. First, ČSSD makes one decision as a party and another on the cabinet level (such as in the case of the Iraq war), and this confuses voters. Second, voters perceive that the use of "repressive elements," such as wiretaps, is on the rise, and this reminds them of pre-1989 days.

(HN/3) Interior Minister Stanislav Gross said he has the feeling that Viktor Kožený does not meet the conditions set forth in the election law for running for office. Kožený has said that he plans to run for the European Parliament next year.

Society

(MFD/4) Two youths shot by security guards while allegedly trying to force their way into a nightclub in Most have died, and a third was charged with disorderly conduct. The guards have so far not been charged. A police car was called to the scene, but the officers reportedly remained in the vehicle while the shots were fired.

(MFD/1) Another flu epidemic is expected after New Year's, and it could be worse than the pre-Christmas epidemic. MFD quotes an epidemiology official from Ústí nad Labem as saying that anyone with a fever should seek medical attention.

(HN/13) About 25,000 Czechs are spending the holidays at the beach, up 25% from last year. Accommodations are cheap, income is up, the weather at the beach is warm, and there isn't much snow in the mountains. Favored destinations include Egypt, the Canary Islands and Thailand.

Published by 9 a.m. Mon-Fri, except holidays by E.S. Best s.r.o., P.O. Box 67, 130 11 Prague 3. Tel. 420 221 004 315 Fax 420 224 221 580 info@fleet.cz Unauthorized use or copy prohibited. © 2003
MK ČR E 6106 MIČ 46553 ISSN 1210-5279 69/K2 www.fleet.cz

Euro (fixing)	32.505	-0.015
Dollar	26.009	-0.235
Pound	46.168	-0.125
Slovak crown 100	79.011	-0.036
3-month Pribor	2.07	0.00
Dow Jones	10450.0	+1.2%
DAX	3952.7	+1.3%
Nikkei	10500.6	+0.8%
České Radiokom.	345.50	+0.6%
Český Telecom	287.50	-0.3%
ČEZ	145.25	+1.7%
Erste Bank	3210.0	+1.9%
Komerční banka	2414.00	+1.2%
Philip Morris ČR	15398.0	+1.6%
Unipetrol	66.39	+1.9%
PX 50	656.9	+1.15%

Erik's Dilemma

Erik wondered if this business could survive indefinitely into the future. He also wondered what factors would have an impact on its remaining as a "going concern." Some foreign companies had already begun to close their offices in the Czech Republic because of the difficulties of doing business there, and the German banks were beginning to focus on Germany and not other countries. Even if the multinationals decided to stay in the country and there continued to be a market for the *Fleet Sheet,* he wondered what format it might take in the future. And then there was the question of the Internet. Would people have such quick access to data on the Internet that a service such as his would become obsolete?

Erik also thought about future competition. Would other companies try to offer the service he was offering at a lower price? Would subscribers be enticed by lower prices even though the quality of the product might be inferior?

When Erik had first begun his business, he was not making what he considered an adequate salary; and he often speculated that it would be very easy to close the business and go to work somewhere else. However, by the Spring of 2000, the business was doing so well that he was making a very good salary that might be difficult to duplicate somewhere else. Erik thought it humorous to contemplate all of the problems that one encounters when a business becomes successful.

CASE DISCUSSION QUESTIONS

1. What are the potential difficulties of starting a business in a transition economy?
2. Prepare a SWOT analysis for the *Fleet Sheet.*
3. What are the key success factors of *Fleet Sheet*?
4. What is the relationship between education, experience, personal skill, and entrepreneurship for Erik Best?
5. What did you learn about entrepreneurship from this case?
6. Erik Best did not prepare a business plan for starting *Feet Sheet.* What type of operation would benefit most from a business plan?

CASE CREDIT

Used with permission of the authors, Professor Marlene M. Reed, Samford University and Rochelle R. Brunson, Alvin Community College. Exhbits used courtesy of Erik Best and The Fleet Sheet.

CASE NOTES

[1] Vaclav Havel was the gifted writer who was elected the first President of Czechoslovakia after the dissolution of Communism and was serving his last term in office.

[2] Lyapura, Stanislav, and Allan A. Gibb. 1996. "Creating small businesses out of large enterprises." *Small Business in Transition Economies*. London: Intermediate Technology Publications, Ltd. pp. 34–50.

Management Processes in Strategy Implementation: Design Choices for Multinational Companies

part three

8 Organizational Designs for Multinational Companies

Learning Objectives

After reading this chapter you should be able to:

- Understand the components of organizational design.
- Know the basic building blocks of organizational structure.
- Understand the structural options for multinational companies.
- Know the choices multinational companies have in the use of subsidiaries.
- See the links between multinational strategies and structures.
- Understand the basic mechanisms of organizational coordination and control.
- Know how multinational companies use coordination and control mechanisms.
- Understand the need for knowledge management systems within organizations.

Preview CASE IN POINT

Takeda's Global Centers of Excellence

Takeda is a global research-based pharmaceuticals company. It is Japan's largest pharmaceuticals company and considered a global leader in the industry. The firm produces drugs to treat common ailments, such as diabetes and hypertension, but has products for treating other diseases, such as peptic ulcers and cancer.

In 2009, the company announced important changes in its corporate structure. It streamlined executive reporting relationships by creating new corporate-level functions. Takeda is creating a new R&D center of excellence, to be run by a newly appointed chief scientific officer, along with a new international operations role. The individuals appointed to these new positions all have executive reporting relationships directly to the president. Furthermore, Takeda is moving its development headquarters from Osaka, Japan, to Deerfield, Illinois.

These changes were motivated by the company's desire to become a global company with highly integrated operations. The company hopes that these changes will allow it to maximize the company's international product potential and presence. Additionally, the headquarters move is seen as the means for Takeda to optimize its development functions.

Source: Based on PR Newswire. 2009. "Takeda to create Global Centers of Excellence." March 30; Takeda. 2009. http://www.takeda.com/.

The best multinational strategies do not ensure success. Implementation of a multinational business strategy requires that managers build the right type of organization—that is, managers must try to design their organizations with what they believe are the best mechanisms to carry out domestic and multinational strategies. As shown in the Preview Case in Point, the global pharmaceuticals company Takeda hopes that its organizational changes will provide the right support for their global strategies in the next decade. In this chapter, you will see other design choices and consider the complexities of organizing for international competition.

This chapter discusses the organizational design options available to implement multinational strategies. What is organizational design? **Organizational design** is how organizations structure their subunits and use mechanisms for coordination and control to achieve their strategic goals. This chapter shows how having the right organizational design is crucial to multinational companies' achieving their multinational strategic goals.

The choices regarding how to set up an organization are complex and varied. Each organizational design has costs and benefits regarding the best way to deliver a product or service to the domestic or international customer. Some organizational designs for multinational companies favor flexibility; these designs provide managers with the organizational tools to deliver products adapted to different national or regional markets or to take advantage of resources located in various regions of the world. Other organizational designs favor efficiency. These designs provide managers with organizations best suited to deliver low-cost products worldwide.

The chapter first presents a survey of organizational design and a summary of basic background knowledge on organizational structure. Building on this information, the chapter then discusses the organizational structures used by multinational companies. Because organizational structure effectively breaks the business down into logical entities, it is necessary to implement coordination and control mechanisms to integrate the entities, and the chapter summarizes the mechanisms available to do that. Finally, most experts agree that knowledge is crucial in today's increasingly competitive and ambiguous environment. In the final section of the chapter, we look at knowledge management as it relates to design issues.

> **Organizational design**
> How organizations structure subunits and use coordination and control mechanisms to achieve their strategic goals.

The Nature of Organizational Design

The two basic questions in designing an organization are: (1) How shall we divide the work among the organization's subunits? (2) Then how shall we coordinate and control the efforts of the units we create?[1]

In very small organizations, everyone does the same thing and does everything. There is little reason to divide the work. However, as organizations grow, managers divide work first into specialized jobs; people perform different tasks. Later, when many people are doing the same tasks and a supervisor is required, managers divide their organizations into specialized subunits. In small organizations, the subunits are usually called departments. In large organizations, divisions or subsidiaries become the major subunits.

Once an organization has specialized subunits, managers must develop mechanisms to coordinate and control their efforts. For example, a manufacturing company must make sure that the production department produces the goods to be available when the marketing department promised the customers. Similarly, a multinational company must ensure that its foreign operations support the parent company's strategic goals. Some companies monitor their subunits very closely; they *centralize* decision making at company headquarters to make certain that the production and delivery of products or services conform to rigid standards. Other companies give subunits greater flexibility by *decentralizing* decision making. Later in the chapter, we will discuss why multinational companies might choose tight or loose control.

Why should multinational companies be concerned about organizational design? In today's world, characterized by hypercompetition and ambiguous industry boundaries, it has never been more crucial to pay attention to organizational design issues. Many companies, such as GM, IBM, Sears, and Kodak, suffered major setbacks and saw their profits fall dramatically in the last couple of decades because of their poor organizational designs. While global competition demanded flexibility and speed, these companies had very bloated bureaucratic structures that made it difficult to adapt rapidly to a changing environment.[2] A properly aligned organizational design allows a multinational company to respond quickly to altered conditions.

A Primer on Organizational Structures

Before you can understand the organizational structures necessary to implement multinational strategy, you need a basic knowledge of organizational structure. To provide this background, the next section gives a brief summary of the fundamental structural options available to managers in designing their organizations. Students who have had course work on organizational design will find this a review.

Organizations usually divide work into departments or divisions based on functions, geography, products, or a combination of these criteria. Each way of organizing has its advantages and disadvantages. A company's choice of subunit forms is based on management's beliefs concerning the best structure or structures to implement the chosen strategies. In this chapter, some of the advantages and disadvantages of each choice will be explained.

The Basic Functional Structure

Functional structure
Has departments or subunits based on separate business functions, such as marketing or manufacturing.

In a **functional structure**, departments perform separate business functions such as marketing or manufacturing. The functional structure is the simplest of organizations and typical of small businesses. However, even large organizations often have functional subunits. Because most organizations use charts to display their organizational structures, the chapter shows each type of organization using exhibits of hypothetical or real organizational charts. Exhibit 8.1 shows an organizational chart for a generic functional structure.

EXHIBIT 8.1 Basic Functional Structure

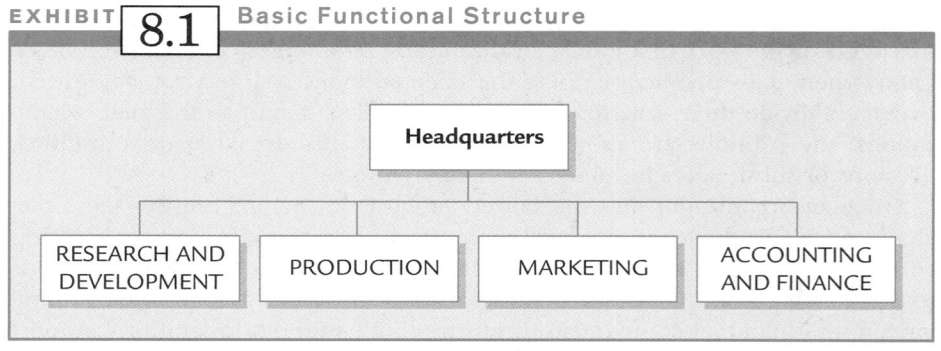

Organizations choose a functional structure primarily for efficiency. The functional structure gets its efficiency from economies of scale in each function because there are cost savings when a large number of people do the same job in the same place. For example, the organization can locate all marketing or all manufacturing people in one subunit, with one staff support group, one telephone system, and one management system. However, because functional subunits are separated from each other and serve functional goals, coordination among them can be difficult, and responses to changes in the environment can be slow. The functional structure works best, therefore, when organizations have few products, few locations, or few types of customers. It also works best when the organization faces a stable environment in which the need for adaptation is minimal.[3]

A variety of situations can undermine the effectiveness of the functional structure. It can lose effectiveness and efficiency when organizations have many products, serve different customer groups, or locate in widely dispersed geographical areas. The most common reaction by managers to these situations is to organize departments or divisions by product or geography.

The Basic Product and Geographic Structures

The structural arrangements for building a department or subunit around a product or a geographic area are called the product structure and the geographic structure, respectively. Exhibits 8.2 and 8.3 show simple product and geographic structures.

Product or geographic organizations must still perform the functional tasks of a business (e.g., marketing, accounting). In contrast to functionally structured firms, however, organizations structured around products or geographic locations do not concentrate functions in dedicated subunits. Instead, functional tasks are duplicated for each product or geographic-area department. The duplication of these functional tasks usually requires more managers and more people.

The duplication of functions also suggests the greatest weakness of product or geographic structures: the loss of economies of scale. These organizations are usually less efficient than the purely functional organization.

Product structure
Has departments or subunits based on different product groups.

Geographic structure
Has departments or subunits based on geographical regions.

EXHIBIT 8.2   **Basic Product Structure**

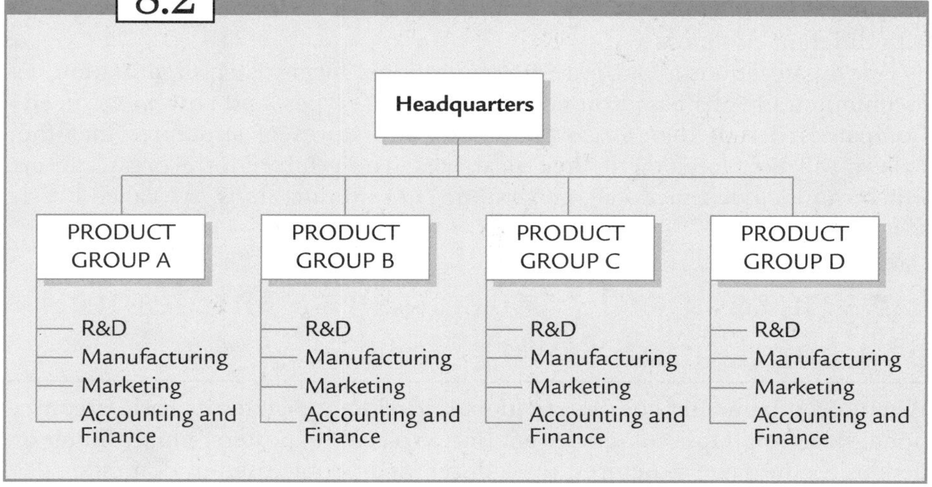

EXHIBIT **8.3**   Basic Geographic Structure

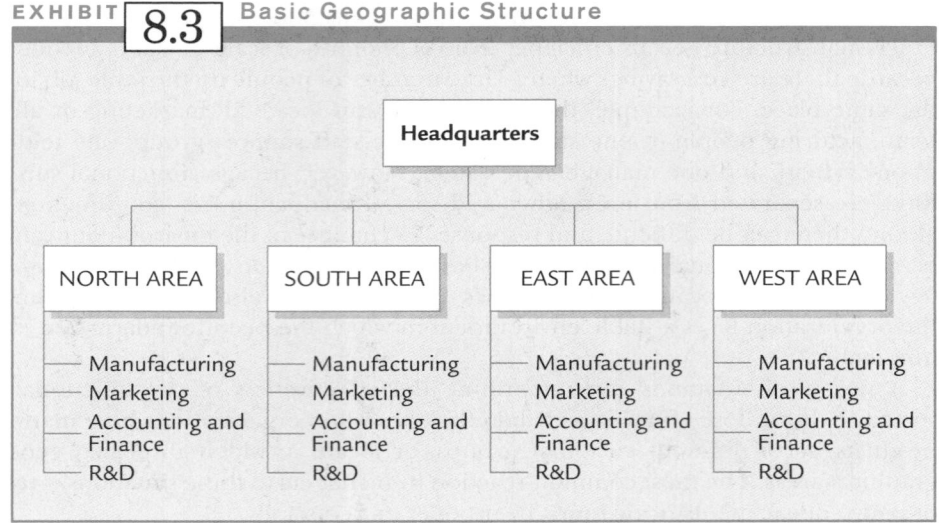

Managers accept the loss of functional efficiencies for two reasons. First, as customer groups and products proliferate, the cost of coordination and control across functions grows, offsetting basic functional efficiencies. Second, even for small organizations, product and geographic organizations can have competitive advantages over the more efficient functional structure.

Organized by region or some other geographic unit, geographic structure allows a company to serve customer needs that vary by region; that is, the business sets up a minifunctional organization in each region. Rather than having one large, functional organization serve all customers, the small, regional subunit focuses all its activities on serving the unique needs of the local customer. Because the subunits concentrate on specific customer groups, managers can more easily and quickly identify customer needs and adapt products accordingly.

Managers choose product structures when they believe that a product or a group of products is unique enough to require specialized functional efforts. This structure creates strong coordination across the functional areas to support the product group. Driving the selection of product structures are the products' unique or changing technologies or the association of distinct customer groups with different products.

Few organizations adopt purely organizational forms. Each organization has its unique trade-offs based on efficiency, product types, and customers' needs. Companies design their organizations with mixtures of structures that they believe will best implement their strategies. These mixed-form organizations, which can include functional, geographic, and product units, are called **hybrid structures**.

Hybrid structures
Mixes functional, geographic, and product units.

Organizational Structures to Implement Multinational Strategies

When a company first goes international, it seldom changes its basic organizational structure. Most companies act first as passive exporters, simply filling orders using the same structures, procedures, and people used in domestic sales.

Even with greater involvement in exporting, companies often avoid fundamental organizational changes. Instead, they use other companies to provide them with international expertise and to run their export operations. As explained in Chapter 6, export management companies and export trading companies manage exporting for companies that do not have the resources or skills to run their own export operations.

Similarly, the choice of licensing as a multinational participation strategy has little impact on domestic organizational structures. The licensor need only negotiate a contract and collect the royalties. The licensor's corporate attorneys may negotiate the licensing contract, and its managers may monitor the licensing contract. However, the licensee's organization must deal with most of the organizational problems of bringing a product or service to the foreign market.

When international sales become more central to a firm's success, then sophisticated multinational and participation strategies usually become a significant part of a company's overall business strategy. As a result, companies must restructure themselves appropriately to manage their multinational operations and implement their multinational strategies. The following sections focus on the options for such companies.

The Export Department

When exports contribute a significant percentage of sales and the company wishes to increase its control over export operations, managers often create a separate **export department**. Consider the next Case in Point, which shows that many small companies—in this case, those involved in green exports—are likely to establish an export department.

By having an export department, top management shows its belief that the investment of human and financial resources in exporting is necessary to sustain and build international sales. The export department deals with all international customers for all products. Managers in the export department often control the pricing and promotion of products for the international market,

Export department
Coordinates and controls a company's export operations.

C A S E   I N   P O I N T

Green Exports

Green technologies are an important component of today's global economy. Many countries are encouraging their consumers to switch to alternative energy sources, such as solar or wind. According to experts, the global environmental market is valued at about $729 billion. In the United States, the export of products based on alternative energy doubled between 2002 and 2007. Clearly, companies involved in this industry will have many opportunities in the future.

One of the downsides for such businesses, however, is that they are often small and lack capital. Many of them strive to establish export departments as their exports grow because an export department makes

the company better able to manage the export process and customers.

The U.S. governmental organization Ex-Im Bank provides help to companies. In fact, this independent federal agency is now dedicated to helping small businesses export environmentally friendly products. For instance, it provided financial support to Powerlight Corp. to export solar tracking technologies to Germany and South Korea. Powerlight hopes that it can grow and eventually establish an export department.

Source: Based on Conlin, L. M. 2008. "Banking on green exports." Journal of Commerce, *November 10.*

and the people within it may have particular country or product expertise. Export department managers have the responsibility to deal with export management companies, with foreign distributors, and with foreign customers. When the company uses a direct exporting strategy, sales representatives located in other countries may also report to the export department management. Exhibit 8.4 shows a hypothetical organization with a functional structure and an export department.

As companies evolve beyond the initial participation strategies of exporting and licensing, they need more sophisticated structures to implement the necessary complex multinational strategies. These more complex structures include the international division, the worldwide geographic and products structures, the worldwide matrix structure, and the transnational network structure.

Before discussing these structures in detail, some background is necessary on the types of subunits multinational companies set up in foreign countries.

Foreign Subsidiaries

The more complex multinational organizational structures support participation strategies that include direct investments in a foreign country, which requires setting up an overseas subunit of the parent firm. These subunits are called **foreign subsidiaries**. Foreign subsidiaries are subunits of the multinational company located in countries other than that of the parent company's headquarters. Foreign subsidiaries are a growing component of international business. For example, the United Nations estimates worldwide that there are more than 65,000 multinational corporations with more than 850,000 foreign subsidiaries employing nearly 25 million people.[4] Siemens, the German giant, reported 900 fully owned and 400 majority-owned subsidiaries in its 2005 statements. Other multinational organizations such as Total and Asea Brown Boveri (ABB) report associations with more than 1,000 entities each, and General Electric reports ownership in more than 8,000 subsidiaries.[5]

Foreign subsidiaries Subunits of the multinational company located in another country.

EXHIBIT 8.4   **Functional Structure with an Export Department**

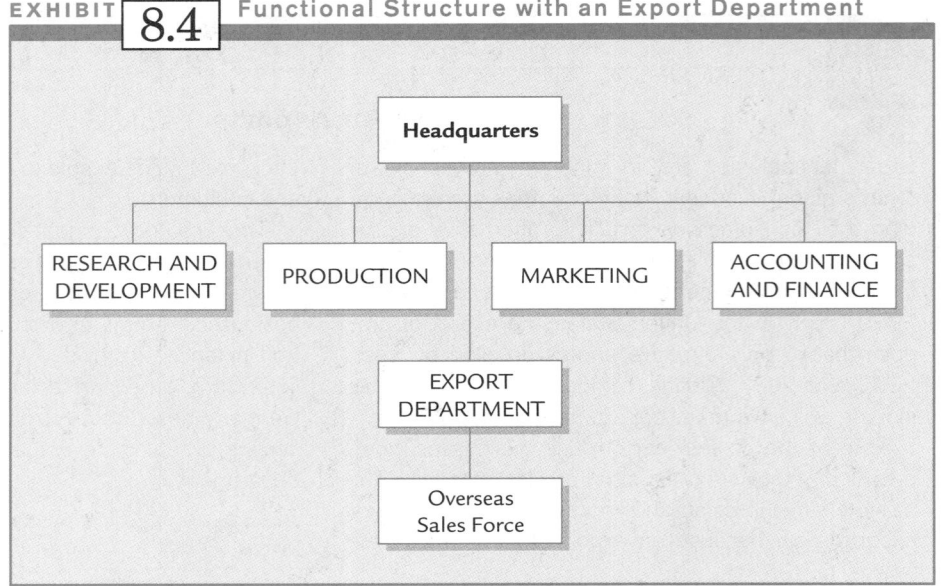

Subsidiaries

Multinational firms vary their control over their subsidiaries.[6] Some retain control by maintaining a board that is active in subsidiary management. Such forms of control tend to be typical of joint ventures in emerging markets in India and China where the multinational firm wants to control the subsidiary's activities. Another form of control is the rubber stamp board, which tends to be required by law. Such boards are more likely to be formal, and they merely approve the subsidiary's activities. However, most multinational companies use a third form of control by which the multinational firm avoids managing the local subsidiary and leaves management decisions up to it. The latter arrangement is seen as necessary to ensure that local subsidiaries stay as lean and mean as possible.

Multinational companies use several types of foreign subsidiaries. For companies pursuing a multidomestic strategy, the foreign subsidiary often becomes a scaled-down version of the parent company.[7] This type of subsidiary is called the **minireplica subsidiary**. It uses the same technology and produces the same products as the parent company, but it runs on a smaller scale. By producing products or services strictly for the local market, the minireplica can adapt to local conditions and support the multidomestic strategy.

Minireplicas use few expatriate managers. Local managers run the organization, often with little influence from headquarters. Because of its autonomy from headquarters, the minireplica is usually a profit center. In a profit center, corporate headquarters evaluates local managers based on the unit's profitability, using financial performance information such as return on investment. Seldom do minireplicas contribute to corporation-wide goals such as providing R&D or manufacturing for other locations around the world.

At the opposite end of the spectrum from the minireplica is the **transnational subsidiary**. This type of subsidiary supports a multinational firm strategy based on location advantages. The transnational subsidiary has no company-wide form or function. Each subsidiary contributes what it does best for corporate goals.

To respond to local conditions, a transnational subsidiary may make products that it adapts to the local tastes. Multinational companies often make consumer goods locally. Products such as laundry detergents need adjustments for cultural preferences, washing techniques, and characteristics of the water supply. To contribute to overall corporate efficiency, transnational subsidiaries may also produce products for sale in the worldwide market. To increase organizational learning, transnational subsidiaries can provide information to the parent company about local markets, help solve problems for another unit elsewhere in the world, or develop new technologies. For instance, the Dutch company Philips had its first stereo color TV developed by its Australian subsidiary.[8]

To implement transnational strategies based on location advantages, multinational companies may place subsidiaries in different countries to take advantage of factor costs (e.g., cheap labor or raw materials), to capitalize on other resources (e.g., an educated workforce or unique skills), or to gain access to the country. For example, DuPont gives worldwide control of its Lycra business to its Swiss subsidiary to benefit from its concentration of unique production and management skills.

Some foreign subsidiaries begin as only sales offices and later take on other functions. Before manufacturing a product in another country, companies frequently test the market by opening a foreign sales office. If the market looks promising, companies invest in the plant and equipment to manufacture locally. In contrast, other subsidiaries begin as and remain suppliers of raw materials for the parent company or other subsidiaries. These units often have no manufacturing or sales capacities. For example, major oil companies such as British

Minireplica subsidiary
Scaled-down version of the parent company, using the same technology and producing the same products as the parent company.

Transnational subsidiary
Has no company-wide form or function; each subsidiary does what it does best or most efficiently anywhere in the world.

Petroleum use many of their subsidiaries only to supply raw material. Finally, some multinational companies use their subsidiaries as offshore production or assembly plants for export back to the headquarters' country.

Most subsidiaries are neither pure minireplicas nor pure transnationals. Rather, foreign subsidiaries take many forms and have many functions. Multinational companies choose the mix of functions for their foreign subsidiaries based on several issues, including (1) the firm's multinational strategy or strategies, (2) the subsidiaries' capabilities and resources, (3) the economic and political risk of building and managing a subunit in another country, and (4) how the subsidiaries fit into the overall multinational organizational structure.

Foreign subsidiaries are the structural building blocks for running multinational operations; that is, once companies move beyond simple exporting, foreign subsidiaries become key parts of the organizational designs that multinational companies use to implement their multinational strategies. With the background knowledge of the nature of foreign subsidiaries, we will now consider how multinational companies use organizational structures to implement their multinational strategies.

International Division

International division
Responsible for managing exports, international sales, and foreign subsidiaries.

As companies increase the size of their international sales force and set up manufacturing operations in other countries, the export department often grows into an international division. The international division differs from the export department in several ways; it is usually larger and has greater responsibilities. Besides managing exporting and an international sales force, this division oversees foreign subsidiaries that perform a variety of functions. Although usually the subsidiaries are sales units, units that procure raw material and produce the company's products are also common. The international division has more extensive staff with international expertise. Top management expects the international people to perform functions such as negotiating licensing and joint venture agreements, translating promotional material, or providing expertise on different national cultures and social institutions.

Exhibit 8.5 gives an example of an international division in a domestic product structure. In this example, the division handles all products, controls foreign subsidiaries in Europe and Japan, and manages a general sales force in the rest of Asia.

The international division structure has declined in popularity among the large multinational companies.[9] For multiproduct companies operating in many countries, it is not considered an effective multinational structure.[10] However, for companies of moderate size with a limited number of products or country locations, the international division remains a popular and potentially effective organizational firm.

To deal with the shortcomings of the international division structure, multinational companies have several options: the worldwide product structure, the worldwide geographic structure, the matrix structure, and the transnational network structure. The following section discusses the worldwide geographic and product structures.

Worldwide Geographic Structure and Worldwide Product Structure

Worldwide geographic structure
Has geographical units representing regions of the world.

In the worldwide geographic structure, regions or large-market countries become the geographic divisions of the multinational company. Consider the next Multinational Management Brief.

EXHIBIT | **8.5** |
International Division in a Domestic Product Structure

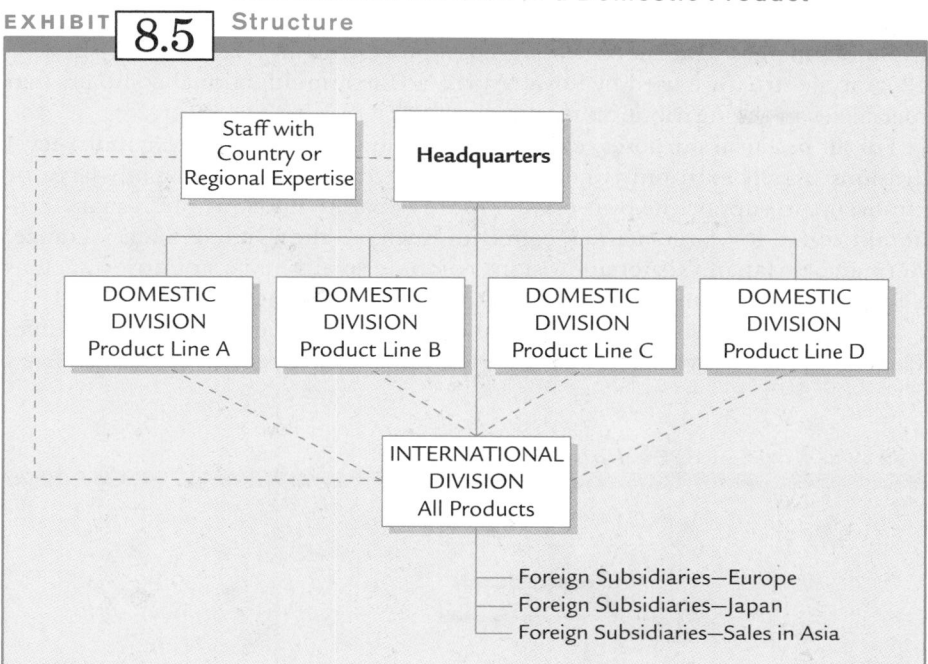

As the Multinational Management Brief shows, the primary reason to choose a worldwide geographic structure is to implement a multidomestic or regional strategy, which requires a company to differentiate its products or services by country or region and therefore to have an organizational design with maximum geographic flexibility. The semiautonomous regional or country-based subunits of the worldwide geographic structure provide the flexibility to tailor or

Multinational Management **Brief**

Cooper-Standard Automotive

Cooper-Standard Automotive is a leading global automotive supplier headquartered in Michigan. It employs about 18,000 people located in approximately 70 countries. The company manufactures products such as body sealing systems and other fluid handling systems.

Cooper-Standard was originally organized along its product lines, but in 2009 it began changing to a geographic structure. Rather than have the company divided along product lines, the firm will operate two divisions. One division (North America) will cater to the North American market, and the International Division will be in charge of Europe, South America, and Asia. The company is also discontinuing its body and chassis and fluid system divisions.

Cooper-Standard hopes that these changes will allow it to keep its global products while better responding to the needs of its customers.

Source: Based on PR Newswire. 2009. "Cooper-Standard Automotive reorganizes operations into geographic structure." March 26.

develop products that meet the particular needs of local or regional markets. Often differences in an area's product or service needs or in channels of distribution increase the need for a geographic structure. Exhibit 8.6 shows a geographic structure used by Royal Vopak, a Dutch multinational company that specializes in the distribution of chemicals.

For all practical purposes, even given a multidomestic strategy, country-level divisions usually exist only when a country's market size is sufficiently large or important to support its own organization. Separate divisions often make economic sense for large-market countries such as the United States, France, Germany, or Japan. Regional divisions combine small similar countries, such as a Southern European division for Italy, Spain, and Portugal.

For the regional strategist, combinations of countries are as large as possible. The combinations are based on similarities in customer requirements, balanced

EXHIBIT 8.6   Royal Vopak's Worldwide Geographic Structure

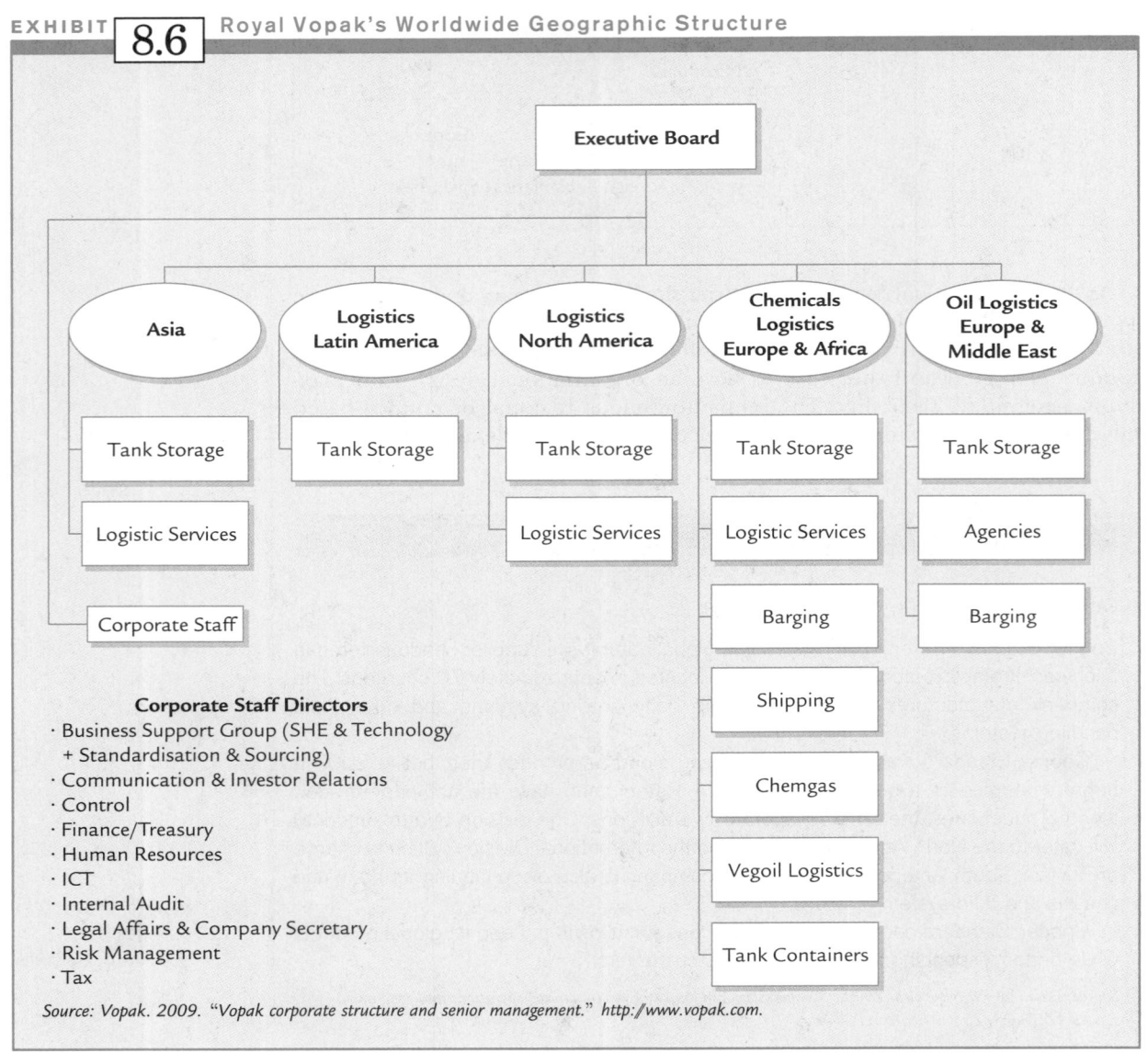

Source: Vopak. 2009. "Vopak corporate structure and senior management." http://www.vopak.com.

against the efficiencies of uniform products. However, interestingly, Toyota made some important changes to its geographic structure. Both its sales operations and planning operations groups had been organized by region (domestic and overseas), but then the company decided to integrate both operations by combining the domestic and overseas divisions.[11] As a global company, Toyota wanted more coordination among the various regions, including Japan, to implement the most appropriate growth strategy from a global perspective.

However, as emerging markets gain importance, some companies are shifting their attention to these markets. Consider the next Focus on Emerging Markets.

Product divisions form the basic units of worldwide product structures, as shown in Exhibit 8.7. Each product division assumes responsibility for producing and selling its products or services throughout the world. The product structure therefore supports strategies that emphasize the production and sales of worldwide products. It is usually considered the ideal structure to implement an international strategy, in which the company attempts to gain economies of scale by selling worldwide products with most of the upstream activities based at home.

The worldwide product structure supports international strategies because it provides an efficient way to organize and centralize the production and sales of similar products for the world market. This type of structure sacrifices regional or local adaptation strengths derived from a geographic structure to gain economies of scale in product development and manufacturing. For example, Ford Motor Company implemented its Ford 2000 strategy by scrapping Ford of

Worldwide product structure
Gives product divisions responsibility to produce and sell their products or services throughout the world.

Focus on Emerging Markets

Cisco and Emerging Markets

Cisco's organizational structure was traditionally geographic, or what Cisco calls theatres. These theatres included the United States, Americas International, Europe, the Middle East and Africa, Asia Pacific, and Japan. This organization made sense for Cisco because these regions had sufficient demand and need for product adaptation that required being in their own theatres. However, the recent explosion in the emerging markets for Cisco and changes to other markets led to the creation of a new geographic structure to include an Emerging Markets Theatre, a European markets theater, and a U.S. and Canada theater.

Cisco's restructuring was necessary because of geographic developments. For instance, Cisco realized that the emerging markets represented by countries in Latin America, the Caribbean, the Middle East and Africa, and Russia and Eastern Europe have tremendous potential because they invest heavily in new networking capabilities. By creating the Emerging Markets Theatre, Cisco is hoping to be able to apply the appropriate processes and resources to meet the unique needs of these new markets. Cisco feels that the many regions in the Emerging Markets Theatre have similar needs and that, by creating a special division devoted to the region, it can apply knowledge learned across the markets to deliver tailored local solutions. Cisco also hopes that, by creating the new division, it can show its commitment to these new emerging markets and create demand and growth for the future.

Sources: Based on Business Wire. 2005. "Cisco System announces three new geographic theatres: New 'emerging markets' theatre created to drive growth." June 6; Cisco. 2009. http://www.cisco.com.

EXHIBIT **8.7**   Worldwide Product Structure

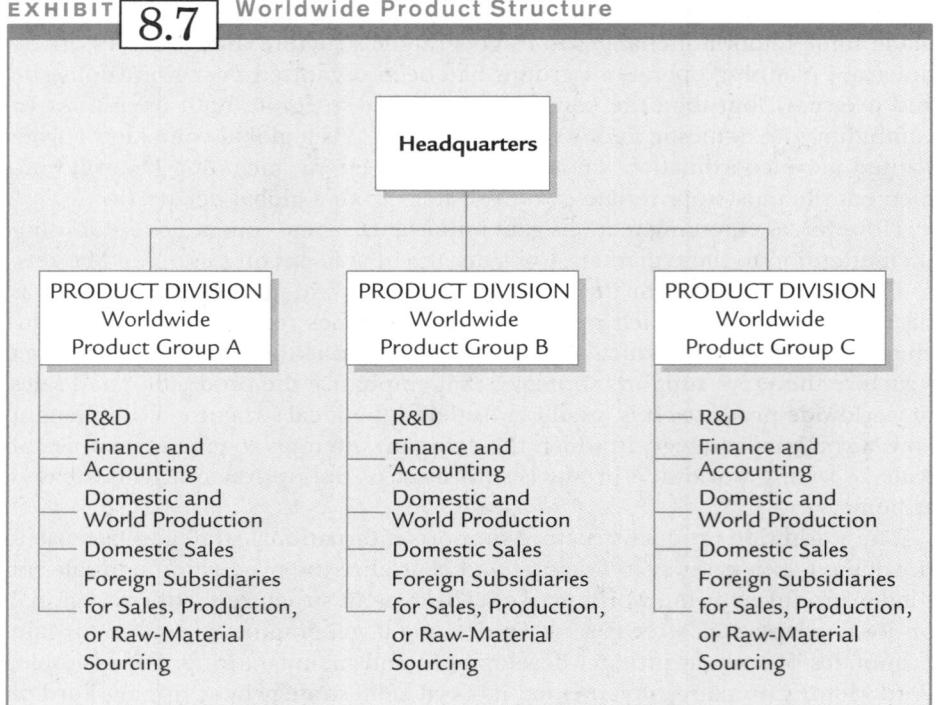

Europe and centralizing product engineering and design in Detroit. It created product groups, called Vehicle Centers, that had worldwide responsibility to develop new trucks and cars. This product-oriented design resulted in substantial cost savings from using fewer global suppliers and eliminating duplication in product development.[12] However, the current view is that, with its worldwide product organization, Ford lost touch with local customers in Europe.[13] A danger for Ford—or any other company that emphasizes product over geography—is that the cost savings from efficient production may not offset revenue losses when products fail to please the local market.

Foreign subsidiaries in the worldwide product structure may produce worldwide products/components, supply raw materials, or specialize only in local sales. However, they serve product goals directed from the product division headquarters. Production or supply subsidiaries often have little concern for their local markets. The sales subsidiaries exercise minimal local adaptation of the headquarters-directed worldwide marketing strategy. Manufacturing subsidiaries in the product structure may produce component products for the global market and export them back to the division's home country for final assembly. In this case, sister sales subsidiaries may then reimport the finished product for local sales.[14] For example, the U.S. aircraft manufacturer Boeing produces many of its aircraft components outside the United States. Its subsidiaries return these components to the United States for final assembly. Later, airlines in many of the producing countries buy the completed Boeing planes.

Hybrids and Worldwide Matrix Structures

Both the worldwide product structure and the worldwide geographic structure have advantages and disadvantages for multinational strategy implementation. The product structure best supports strategies that emphasize global products and rationalization (worldwide products using worldwide, low-cost sources of raw materials, and worldwide marketing strategies). The geographic structure best supports strategies that emphasize local adaptation (managers are often local nationals and are sensitive to local needs). Most multinational companies, however, adopt strategies that include concerns both for local adaptation and for the economic and product development benefits of globalization. Consequently, most large multinationals have hybrid structures, or mixtures of product and area units. The nature of the product determines whether the emphasis is given to the product or geographic side of the company (how global the products are) and the nature of the markets (how complex and different the major markets are).

At Sony Corporation headquarters, for example, worldwide product group managers exercise broad oversight over their businesses. However, Sony also focuses on regional needs by dividing global operations into four zones: Japan, North America, Europe, and the rest of the world. The consumer products giant, Unilever PLC, has a regional structure with local managers in three areas: Africa/Middle East, Latin America, and East Asia/Pacific. However, managers in Europe and North America report to worldwide product coordinators.[15] Similarly, Unilever gives the greatest power to the global product units when customers have similar needs worldwide. When customer needs vary by country or region, the company emphasizes geographic unit power with product groups under local management.[16]

To balance the benefits of geographic and product structures and to coordinate a mix of product and geographic subunits, some multinationals create a worldwide matrix structure. Unlike hybrid organizations, the **worldwide matrix structure**, shown in Exhibit 8.8, is a symmetrical organization, with equal lines of authority for product groups and for geographic divisions. Consider the next Multinational Management Brief.

Ideally, the matrix provides the structure for a firm to pursue both local and global strategies at the same time. Geographic divisions focus on national responsiveness, and product divisions focus on finding global efficiencies. The matrix structure works well only when there are nearly equal demands from the environment for local adaptation and for product standardization, with its associated economies of scale. Without these nearly equal demands, the organization tends to evolve into a product or geographic structure, based on which side is more important for competitive advantage.

In theory, the matrix produces quality decisions because two or more managers reach consensus on how to balance local and worldwide needs. Managers who hold positions at the intersection of product and geographic divisions are called two-boss managers because they have a boss from the product side and a boss from the geographic side of the organization. Product bosses tend to emphasize goals such as efficiency and using worldwide products, whereas geographic bosses tend to emphasize local or regional adaptation. The conflict in these interests is intended to balance globalization and localization pressures. As such, for managers at all levels, the matrix requires continual compensation for product and geographic needs.

To succeed at balancing the inherent struggles between global and local concerns, the matrix requires extensive resources for communication among the managers. Middle- and upper-level managers must have good human relations skills to deal with inevitable personal conflicts originating from the competing interests of product and geography. Middle-level managers must also learn to deal with two bosses, who often have competing interests. Upper-level

Worldwide matrix structure Symmetrical organization, usually with equal emphasis on worldwide product groups and regional geographical divisions.

EXHIBIT **8.8**   Worldwide Matrix Structure

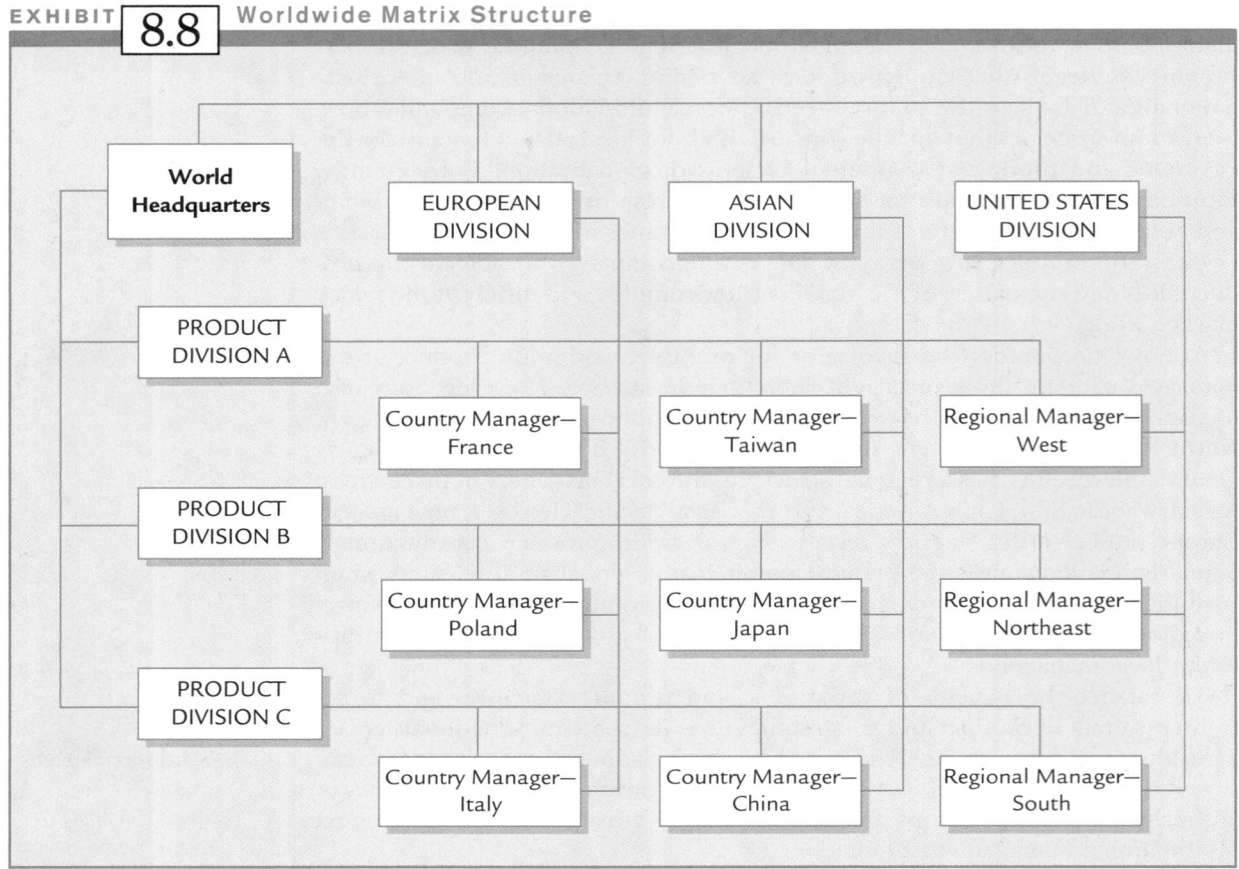

Multinational Management **Brief**

Montreal's CAE and the Matrix Organization

CAE, based in Montreal, is a world leader in providing simulation and other training technologies for the civil aviation industry. It currently has more than 6,000 employees in approximately 75 offices worldwide. Through its 27 aviation centers, it trains more than 75,000 individuals yearly. Ninety percent of its $1 billion (Canadian) is derived from its international operations.

    CAE uses both functional and project matrices. For instance, when it is building simulators, CAE uses a functional matrix whereby a project manager works closely with the different functional engineers to complete the project. For more complex projects, CAE uses a project-based matrix whereby a project manager shares authority with a functional manager to get the project done.

    For CAE, a matrix organization has tremendous benefits because it allows the company to bring the products to market faster, but it also creates difficulties. Conflict can occur between project and functional managers, and the temporary assignment to projects can also create uncertainty for employees regarding their future. Despite these difficulties, CAE has found that the matrix is the best structure for them.

Sources: Based on Appelbaum, S., D. Nadeau, and M. Cyr. 2008. "Performance evaluation in a matrix organization: A case study (Part One)." Industrial and Commercial Training, *40(5), pp. 236–241; Appelbaum, S., D. Nadeau, and M. Cyr. 2008. "Performance evaluation in a matrix organization: A case study (Part Two)."* Industrial and Commercial Training, *40(6), pp. 295–299.*

managers, in turn, must be prepared to resolve conflicts between geographic and product managers.

Is the matrix worth the effort? During the 1980s, the matrix structure was a popular organizational solution to the global-local dilemma. More recently, however, the matrix has come under fire because consensus decision making between product and geographic managers has proved to be slow and cumbersome. In many organizations, the matrixes became too bureaucratic, with too many meetings and too much conflict. Some organizations, such as the Royal Dutch/Shell Group (see the next Case in Point), abandoned their matrixes and returned to product structures. Other organizations have redesigned their matrix structures to be more flexible, with speedier decision making. In the more flexible matrixes, management centralizes key decisions in the product side or the geographic side of the matrix, depending on the need. For example, geographic areas with unique characteristics may require the freedom to tailor strategies. Facing such a situation, AT&T and Owens-Corning Fiberglas Corp. created highly autonomous units in China. They believe that the local Chinese and Asian markets are so dynamic that local managers (both Chinese and expatriates) need a great deal of freedom to seek opportunities.[17]

The evolving intensity and complexity of competition in international business have led to the evolution of strategies beyond geography and product foci. We saw earlier that this resulted in the transnational strategy. To carry out a transnational strategy effectively, a new organizational form has also arisen: the transnational network structure.

CASE IN POINT

Change at Shell and Philips

In 1995, Cornelius A. J. Herkstruter, chair of the Royal Dutch/Shell Group, announced a radical restructuring of his company. In a speech delivered simultaneously to corporate headquarters in London and The Hague, he declared that the matrix was out. Instead, global product divisions, such as exploration, production, and chemical, will report to teams of senior executives. These executives will have centralized decision-making power, no longer sharing it with country or functional managers.

Shell's old matrix was quite complex. For the multinational firm, most matrix structures combine two organizational designs, usually geography and product. Shell's matrix was three dimensional, with some managers having functional, product, and area bosses! For example, a finance executive could have a functional boss (e.g., chief financial officer), a country-level boss, and a product boss (e.g., chemical products).

Herkstruter believed that, over the years, Shell's complex matrix resulted in too much bureaucracy. The matrix required too many managers. In addition, the meetings and consensus process of the matrix slowed decision making. To remain competitive in the oil industry, Shell had to cut many management positions and be quicker to identify business opportunities.

Philips, the Dutch electrical giant, was one of the earliest multinational companies to use the matrix structure, which combined product and country divisions. For instance, the head of the washing machine division in Italy had to report both to the head of that division and to the top washing machine head in the Netherlands. This created major difficulties for Philips, and there were continuous accountability problems. For instance, it was not easy to determine whether the country head or product head was responsible for profits and losses in a country. As a result, Philips reorganized into a number of units around the company's main businesses, and the national offices are now held accountable for these units.

Sources: Based on Dwyer, Paula, and Heidi Dawley. 1995. "The passing of the Shell man: An era ends as Royal Dutch/Shell vows to centralize power." BusinessWeek Online. International Edition, April 17; Economist. 2006. "Survey: The matrix master." January 21.

The Transnational Network Structure

Transnational network structure
Network of functional, product, and geographic subsidiaries dispersed throughout the world, based on the subsidiaries' location advantages.

The **transnational network structure** is the newest solution to the complex demands of being locally responsive while taking advantage of global economies of scale and seeking location advantages, such as host country sources of knowledge. Like the matrix, the transnational network tries to gain all the advantages of the various structural options, combining functional, product, and geographic subunits. However, unlike the symmetrical matrix structure, the transnational network has no basic form. It has no symmetry or balance between the geographic and product sides of the organization. Instead, the network links different types of transnational subsidiaries throughout the world. Nodes, the units at the center of the network, coordinate product, functional, and geographic information. Product group units and geographic area units have different structures, and often no two subunits are alike. Rather, transnational units evolve to take advantage of resources, talent, and market opportunities wherever they exist in the world. Resources, people, and ideas flow in all directions.

The Dutch multinational Philips Electronics N.V. is only one example of a transnational network.[18] Working in 60 different countries, the company makes products as diverse as defense systems and light bulbs. There are eight product divisions with more than 60 subgroups based on product similarity. The product divisions have subsidiaries throughout the world, and the subsidiaries may focus on only one product or on an array of products. Subsidiaries can specialize in R&D, manufacturing, or marketing for world or regional markets. Some subsidiaries engage only in sales. Some units are highly independent of headquarters while headquarters tightly controls other units.

In terms of geography, Philips divides the world into three groups. So-called key countries' such as the Netherlands and the United States, produce for local and world markets and control local sales. Large countries, such as Mexico and Belgium, have some local and worldwide production facilities and local sales. Local business countries are smaller nations that are primarily sales units and that import products from the product divisions' worldwide production centers in other countries. All these design choices attempt to optimize efficiency, organizational learning, and local responsiveness.[19]

Exhibits 8.9 and 8.10 show two different perspectives on how one can look at Philips' very complex transnational network structure. One exhibit views geographic links among locations, and the other looks at the functions of different locations. Another company often considered to have the prototypical transnational structure is ABB. The next Case in Point discusses the transnational network structure of ABB, termed a "loose matrix" by its former CEO.

The basic structural framework of the transnational network consists of three components: dispersed subunits, specialized operations, and interdependent relationships.[20] The transnational network structure uses the flexible transnational subsidiary as the basic structural unit. **Dispersed subunits** are subsidiaries located anywhere in the world where they can benefit the company. Some subsidiaries take advantage of low factor costs (e.g., low labor costs); other units provide information on new technologies, new strategies, and consumer trends. All subunits try to tap worldwide managerial and technical talent.

Dispersed subunits
Subsidiaries located anywhere in the world where they can most benefit the company.

Specialized operations
Subunits specializing in particular product lines, research areas, or marketing areas.

Specialized operations are operations that subunits can specialize in, whether it is in product lines, research areas, or marketing areas. Specialization builds on the diffusion of subunits by tapping local expertise or other resources anywhere and everywhere in the company's subsidiaries. Philips, for example, has eight research labs located in six countries. Some units have broad mandates, such as

EXHIBIT 8.9   Geographic Links in the Philips Transnational Structure

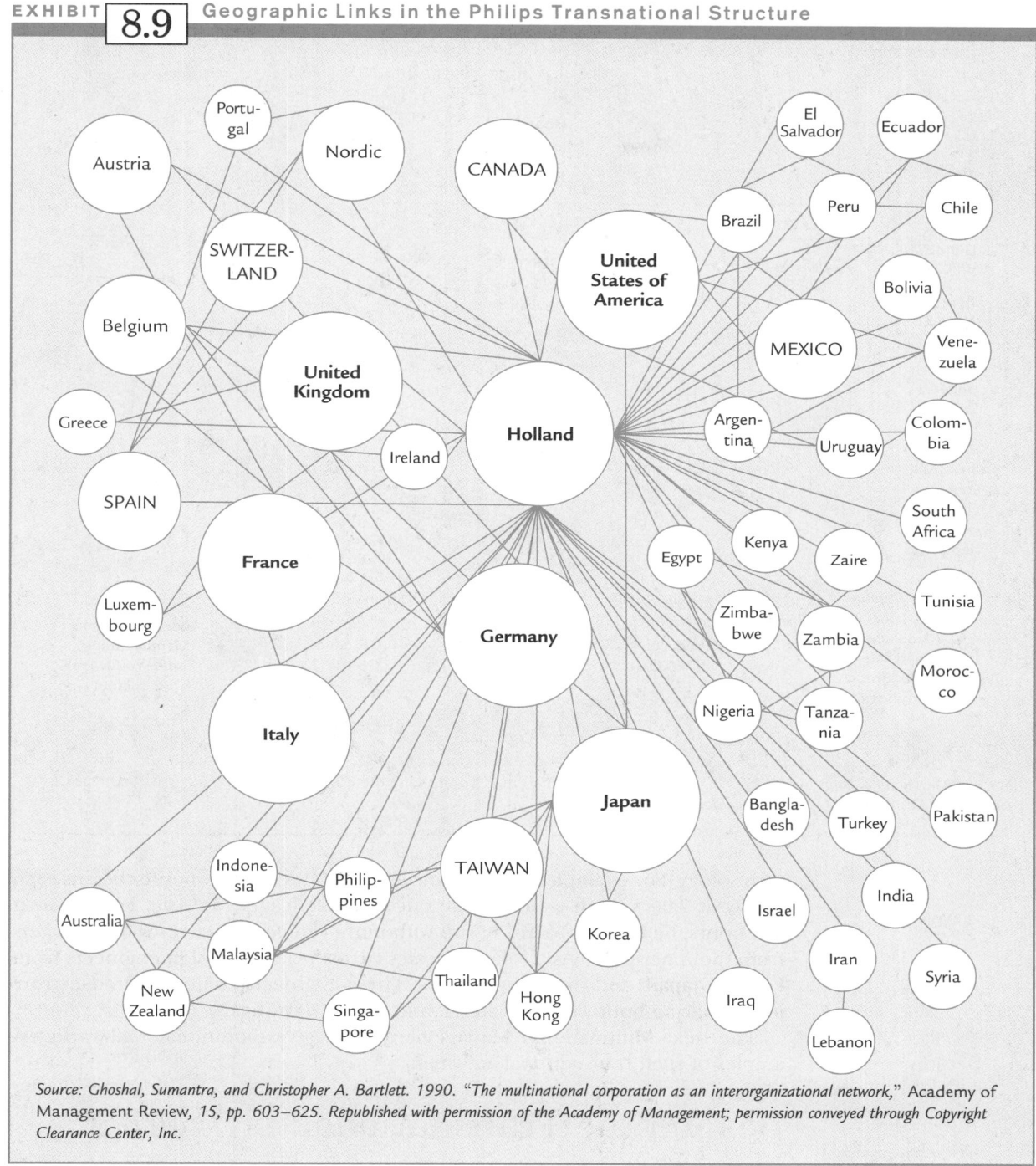

Source: Ghoshal, Sumantra, and Christopher A. Bartlett. 1990. "The multinational corporation as an interorganizational network," Academy of Management Review, 15, pp. 603–625. Republished with permission of the Academy of Management; permission conveyed through Copyright Clearance Center, Inc.

Philips' central laboratory in Eindhoven. Other units focus on specific areas, such as the laboratories for solid-state electronics work at Redhill in the United Kingdom.[21]

Interdependent relationships must exist to manage the dispersed and specialized subunits, and units share information and resources continuously. To do this, transnationals usually build communication systems based on the latest

Interdependent relationships Continuous sharing of information and resources by dispersed and specialized subunits.

EXHIBIT 8.10   Product Links in the Philips Transnational Structure

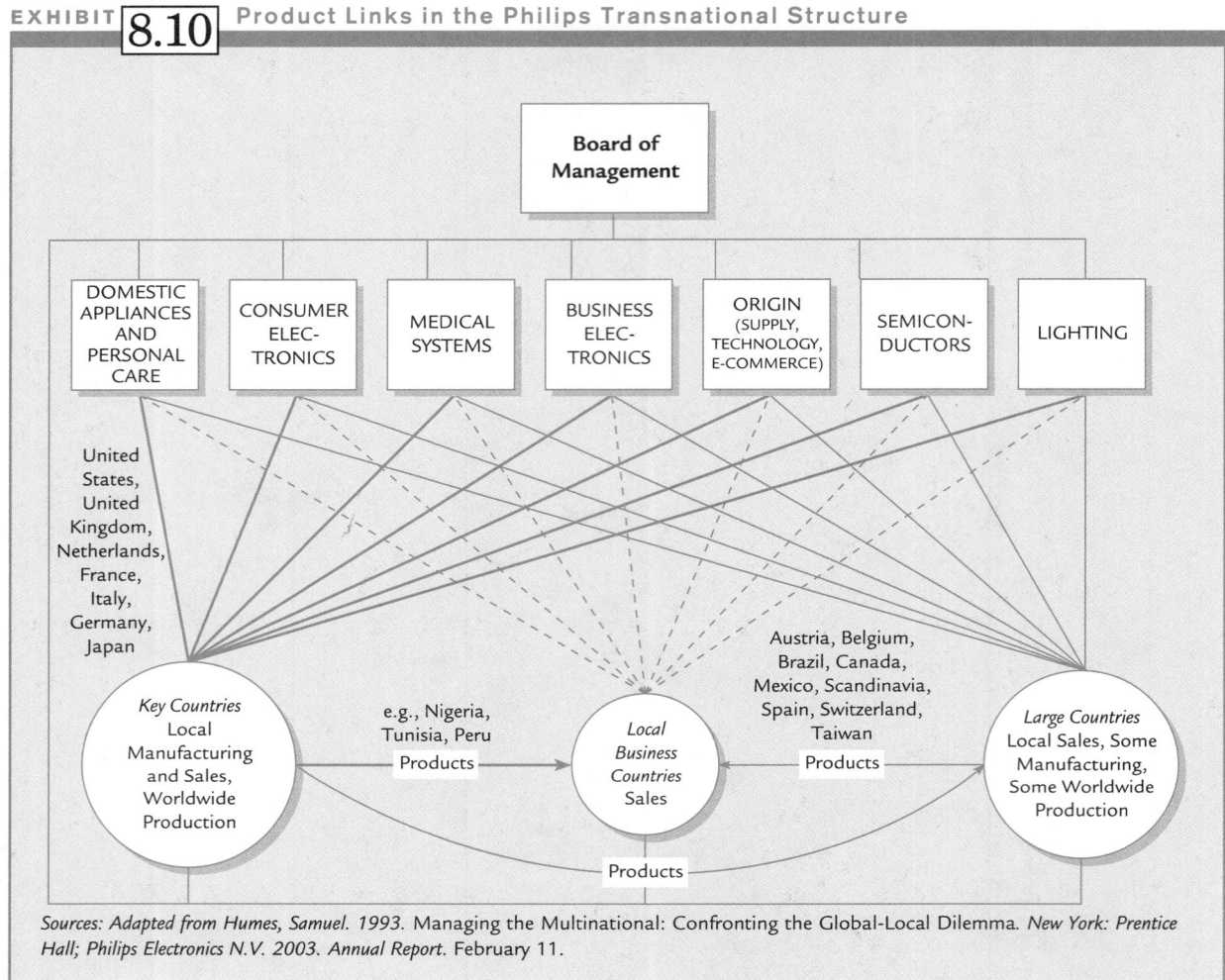

Sources: Adapted from Humes, Samuel. 1993. Managing the Multinational: Confronting the Global-Local Dilemma. New York: Prentice Hall; Philips Electronics N.V. 2003. Annual Report. February 11.

technology. For example, GE Appliances' CEO J. Richard Stonesifer begins each Friday at 7:00 a.m. in a videoconference with colleagues in Asia. For the next five hours, he follows the rising sun with more videoconferences with managers from the Americas to Asia.[22] Ford creates virtual teams of design engineers from Europe, Japan, and the United States. These engineers communicate electronically, sharing both written material and design drawings.

The next Multinational Management Brief gives additional real-world examples of such transnational activities.

Beyond the Transnational: Is There a New Structure for the Multinational?

Metanational structure

An evolution of the transnational network structure that develops extensive systems to encourage organizational learning and entrepreneurial activities.

Some evidence suggests that the transnational network is not the end of the evolution of the multinational's structure. Professor Yves Doz and his colleagues argue that a new structure is emerging called the **metanational**.[23] The metanational company is "a large, entrepreneurial multinational firm that is able to tap into hidden pockets of innovation, technology, and market now scattered around the world, especially in emerging markets."[24]

C A S E   I N   P O I N T

ABB: An Organization with Matrix and Transnational Qualities

Asea Brown Boveri (ABB) is a Swiss-based electrical equipment company that is bigger than Westinghouse and that hopes to take on GE. Although headquartered in Zurich, Switzerland, the company's 13 top managers speak only English at their meetings. English is the common language, but it is a second language to all but one manager. The choice of meeting language personifies the global culture of ABB.

ABB's organization is a loose and decentralized matrix, according to Percy Barnevik, ABB's former CEO. ABB has about 100 country managers, most of whom come from the host country. Sixty-five global managers head product divisions from a number of product segments: transportation, process automation, environmental devices, financial services, electrical equipment, and electric power generation, transmission, and distribution. The matrix calls for two-boss managers at some 1,100 local companies. These local company managers must deal with their country-level boss on local responsiveness and with their global manager on worldwide efficiency.

The organization is transnational because the matrix is not balanced and the functions of the subunits are not uniform. Depending on the situation, either country or global product bosses may have control. The organizational culture of ABB encourages sharing technology and products within product lines. For example, ABB's U.S. steam turbine business uses techniques developed in Switzerland to repair the machines built with U.S. technology. There is no bias against things "not invented here." Management expects even locally run factories to participate in global coordination. For example, 31 power transformer factories, located in 16 countries, share all their performance data monthly through the global segment headquarters in Mannheim, Germany. If even one factory has a problem, global headquarters expects solutions from all factories.

Sources: Based on Taylor, William. 1991. "The logic of global business: An interview with ABB's Percy Barnevik." Harvard Business Review, March–April, pp. 91–105; Rapoport, Carla. 1992. "A tough Swede invades the U.S." Fortune, June 29, pp. 76–79; Ferner, Anthony. 2000. "Being local worldwide: ABB and the challenge of global management." Relations Industrielles, Summer, pp. 527–529.

In many ways the metanational structure is like the transnational network. The metanational is a networked organization with different types of platforms around the world, and, like the transnational, it is a centerless organization that reduces hierarchy and places critical decision making in the peripheral units or nodes throughout the world. The difference with the metanational is its overriding objective to learn from anywhere in the world and to share this knowledge with the rest of the company. The metanational organization uses the latest in virtual connectivity to link team members worldwide.

The characteristics of the metanational structure are:[25]

- Nonstandard business formulas for any local activity.
- Looking to emerging markets as sources of knowledge and ideas, not just for local labor.
- Creating a culture and an advanced communication systems that support global learning.
- The extensive use of strategic alliances to gain knowledge for varied sources.
- High levels of trust between partners to encourage knowledge sharing.
- A centerless structure that moves strategic functions away from headquarters and to major markets.
- A decentralization of decision making away from headquarters and to the managers who serve the key customers and strategic partners.

Multinational Management Brief

Transnational Activities

Because the transnational model has no fixed organizational components and activities, consider how the following companies include transnational activities in their organizational designs.

- *Flattened hierarchies for quick decision making:* ABB operates in more than 140 countries but still has only one layer of management between the top ranks and the business units.

- *Decentralized R&D for short product life cycles:* Nokia, the Finnish cell phone maker, puts R&D at the plant level at five factories around the world. Concurrent engineering takes place, and the culture supports sharing any valuable engineering information with plants in all country locations.

- *Finding global products:* Texas Instruments created a team with the mandate to search the company worldwide for possible global products.

- *Tapping worldwide talent:* ABB designs locomotives in Switzerland and tilting trains in Sweden. Singapore engineers designed a new pager for Motorola.

- *Integrating the workforce:* To build a collaborative culture between workers in Singapore and workers in their sister plant in the United States, Motorola brought the workers to a Colorado resort for Outward Bound–style team-building games.

- *Using e-mail, information systems, Voice-Over-Internet Protocol, and WIKIs (server software that allows users to create or change Web site content):* Unilever PLC has 31,000 employees worldwide communicating by e-mail or Lotus Notes. The Mexican company Cemento Mexicanos can tell with one keystroke the energy use in an oven from its Spanish subsidiary.

- *Using Web-based collaboration systems, such as WebEx or Lotus Notes:* Dallas-based Fluor, a publicly owned engineering services company has more than 46,000 employees worldwide with major offices in eight countries and operations in 50 international locations. It uses various Web-based collaboration systems such as Lotus Notes and SkillSoft for collaboration and online learning. Aperian GlobeSmart's cultural diversity training tool can be helpful to provide culture training.

Sources: Based on Bolch, M. 2008. "Going global." Training 45(4), pp. 28–29; BusinessWeek Online. 1994. "Grabbing markets from the giants," November 18; BusinessWeek Online. 1994. "Tearing up today's organization chart," November 18; Copeland, Michael V. 2006. "The mighty micro-multinational." Business 2.0, July, pp. 107–114; Forteza, Jorge H., and Gary L. Neilson. 1999. "Multinationals in the next decade." Strategy & Business, 16, 3rd quarter, pp. 1–11.

Multinational Strategy and Structure: An Overview

Exhibit 8.11 shows the relationship between various multinational strategies and the types of organizational structure. The connections between the boxes show typical ways that multinational structures evolve.

Strategies of national or regional responsiveness (i.e., the multidomestic or regional strategies discussed in Chapter 6) suggest the use of geographic structures. Given an international strategy, managers should consider a product organization and have worldwide products.

EXHIBIT 8.11 Multinational Strategy, Structure, and Evolution

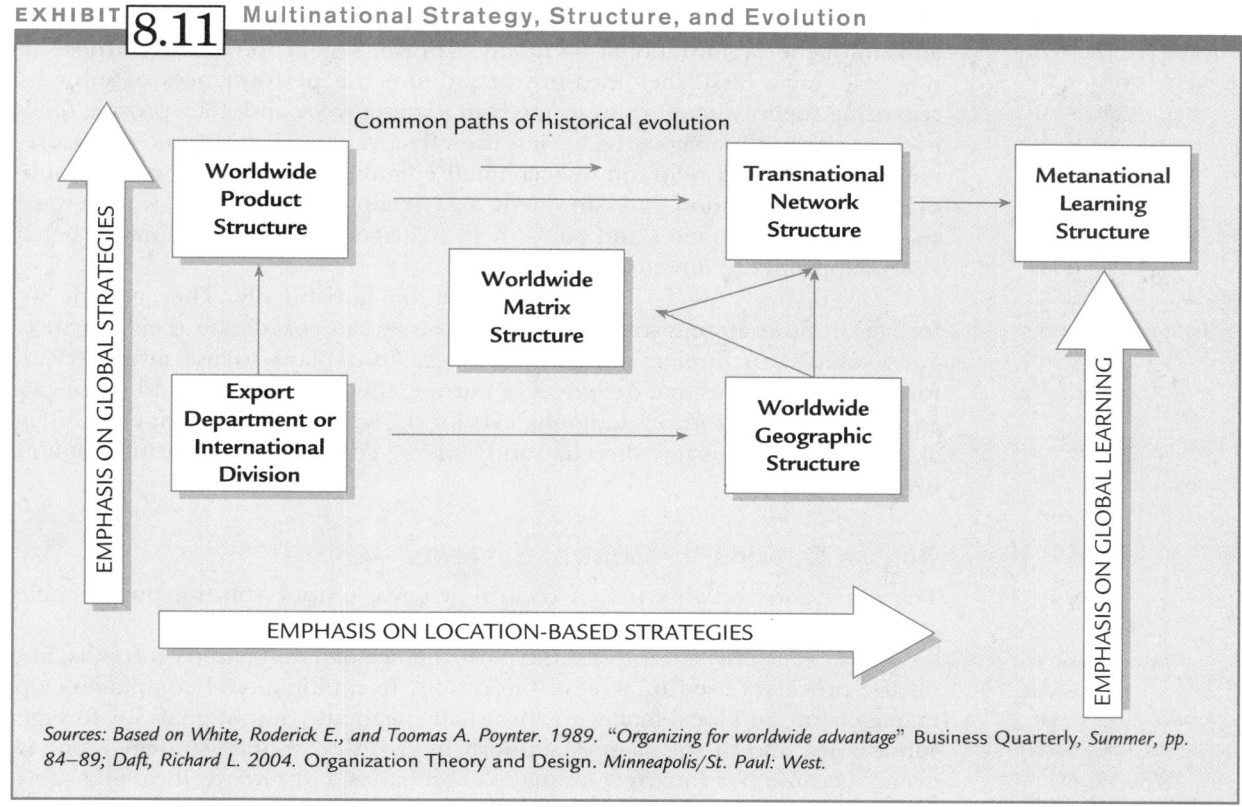

Sources: Based on White, Roderick E., and Toomas A. Poynter. 1989. "Organizing for worldwide advantage" Business Quarterly, Summer, pp. 84–89; Daft, Richard L. 2004. Organization Theory and Design. Minneapolis/St. Paul: West.

Most companies support their early internationalization with export departments or international divisions. Later, as Exhibit 8.12 suggests, and depending on the globalization of their strategy, companies evolve into worldwide product or geographic structures. After this, because of the dual demands of local adaptation pressures and globalization, many companies move toward a matrix or transnational network structure. Most companies, however, never quite reach the pure matrix, transnational, or metanational state. Instead, they typically adopt hybrid structures with some matrix and some transnational qualities. With the globalization of ever more products and the competitive efficiencies they bring, large multinational companies are giving product divisions increased power and creating more transnational subsidiaries.

Up to this point, we have discussed how to divide the organization into units that best support the chosen strategies. Next, we will see how these units are brought together to accomplish organizational goals.

Control and Coordination Systems

In addition to selecting different types of subunits to perform specialized tasks and responsibilities, top managers must design organizational systems to control and coordinate the activities of these subunits. This is a difficult task. Foreign subsidiaries differ widely by geographic location, local markets, cultures, and legal systems, as well as by the talents and resources available to the subsidiary.[26] This section reviews such systems.

For multinational companies, organizational control consists of the procedures used to focus the activities of subsidiaries in directions that support the

Control system
Vertical organizational links, up and down the organizational hierarchy.

company's strategies. **Control systems** help link the organization vertically, up and down the organizational hierarchy. Control systems serve this purpose in two basic ways: First, they measure or monitor the performances of subunits regarding their assigned roles in the firm's strategy. Second, they provide feedback to subunit managers regarding the effectiveness of their units. Measurement and feedback help top management communicate strategic goals to subordinates. In addition, measurement and feedback—combined with reward systems (e.g., promotion and pay)—help managers direct subordinates' behavior in appropriate directions.

Coordination system
Horizontal organizational links.

Coordination systems link the organization horizontally. They provide information flows among subsidiaries so that they can coordinate their activities. For example, in implementing its strategy, Ford plans to use advanced information systems so that designers in Europe, the United States, and Japan can coordinate their efforts in designing cars for the world market. Engineers will be able to communicate directly and share complex design information instantaneously.

Design Options for Control Systems

There are four broad types of control systems: output control, bureaucratic control, decision-making control, and cultural control.

Output control system
Assesses the performance of a unit based on results, not on the processes used to achieve the results.

Output control systems assess the performance of a unit based on results, not on the processes used to achieve the results. In multinational companies, top management and local management usually negotiate output goals for foreign subsidiaries, and the goals must support the overall corporate strategy. Control occurs because headquarters evaluates subsidiaries and rewards local managers depending on how well the subsidiaries achieve the output goals.

Profit center
Unit controlled by its profit or loss performance.

Responsibility for profit is the most common output control. As already noted, a **profit center** is the name given to a unit controlled on the basis of profit or loss. Companies compare such units by looking at each profit center's profit or loss. The minireplica subsidiary is often a profit center. Profit center subsidiaries usually set their own strategies, hire local workers, and act independently from the multinational company's headquarters. Top managers judge the success of the unit and its managers on the basis of the profits generated for the parent company.

Besides profit, other outcomes—such as market share, developing new technologies, and supplying high-quality raw materials—provide performance targets used to control multinational subsidiaries. For example, companies with transnational strategies and structures may evaluate each of their subsidiaries differently. One subsidiary may be evaluated based on its development of worldwide products, and another subsidiary may be evaluated on its market penetration by capturing market share.

Bureaucratic control system
Focuses on managing organizational processes through budgets, statistical reports, standard operations procedures, and centralization of decision making.

Bureaucratic control systems focus on managing behaviors, not outcome, within the organization. Typical bureaucratic control mechanisms include budgets, statistical reports, standard operating procedures, and centralization of decision making.[27] These systems work as follows:

- *Budgets set financial targets for expenditures during specific time periods.* Budgets control subsidiary behavior by providing rules that limit how much the subsidiary can spend on an activity. They focus on controlling costs and usually emphasize efficiency goals; that is, efficient subunits produce more output (service or products) on a fixed budget than inefficient subunits.

- *Statistical reports provide information to top management on non-financial outcomes.* For example, a service organization might report on the number of customer complaints each week. A manufacturing organization might report on the number of units produced or the number of units rejected by quality control.
- *Standard operating procedures (SOPs) provide the rules and regulations that identify the approved ways of behaving.* For example, SOPs might prescribe that all subsidiaries should follow a standard practice for personnel evaluations.

Decision-making control represents the level in the organizational hierarchy where managers have the authority to make decisions. Upper management seldom makes all the decisions in the organization. In decentralized organizations, lower-level managers make a large number of important decisions. In centralized organizations, higher-level managers make most of the important decisions. In most worldwide product structures, control over the functional and strategic activities (i.e., production, finance, marketing, and product strategies) is centralized in the product division headquarters. Local country-level subsidiary managers deal only with local administrative, legal, and financial affairs.[28] In contrast, decentralized decision making is more common in worldwide area structures; local country or regional subsidiaries have considerable autonomy from headquarters. Transnational network structures do not exhibit a tendency for decision-making control in one direction or the other. The transnational company has several headquarters, each controlling different types of decisions depending on local expertise and the strategic situation. Depending on the strengths of a subsidiary, decision making may be centralized in the headquarters' nodes or passed down to lower levels.

Cultural control systems use the organizational culture (Chapter 2) to control employees' behaviors and attitudes. Strong organizational cultures develop shared norms, values, beliefs, and traditions among workers. Such cultures encourage high levels of commitment and support for the organization. Workers and managers understand management goals and direct their efforts in support of them. Many experts now argue that a strong organizational culture may be the only way to link a dispersed multinational company with managers from many different national cultures.

Cultural control is the favored control mechanism for transnational network structures. Although transnational organizations use bureaucratic and output-control mechanisms, the uncertainties and complexities of the international environment make these relatively formal mechanisms less effective than culture. For example, budgets or output goals set at the Paris headquarters may not be timely for changing situations in Budapest or Singapore. Instead, headquarters relies on local managers' commitment to corporate goals and trusts that they will adjust appropriately to local conditions.

Multinational companies use all these control mechanisms to varying degrees, depending on their structure. Exhibit 8.12 shows the relationships between the control mechanisms and the basic multinational organizational structures.

Design Options for Coordination Systems

There are six basic horizontal coordination systems: textual communication (memos or reports in electronic or paper form), direct contact, liaison roles, task forces, full-time integrators, and teams.[29] We discuss first the mechanisms

Decision-making control
Level in the organizational hierarchy where managers have the authority to make decisions.

Cultural control system
Uses organizational culture to control the behaviors and attitudes of employees.

EXHIBIT **8.12**   Use of Control Mechanisms in Multinational Organizational Structures

Multinational Structures	Control Systems			
	Output-Control	Bureaucratic Control	Decision-Making Control	Cultural Control
International division	Most likely to be profit center	Must follow company policies	Some centralization possible	Treated like other divisions
Worldwide geographic	Profit center most common	Some policies and procedures necessary	Local units have autonomy	Local subsidiary culture often more important
Worldwide product	Unit output for supply; sales volume for sales	Tight process controls for product quality and consistency	Centralized at product division headquarters	Possible for some companies but not always necessary
Matrix	Shared profit responsibility with product and geographic units	Less important	Balanced between geographic product units	Culture must support shared decision making
Transnational Network	Used for supplier units and some independent profit centers	Less important	Few decisions centralized at headquarters; more decisions centralized in key network nodes	Organizational culture transcends national cultures; supports sharing and learning; the most important control mechanism

that provide the least amount of coordination and then continue to the mechanisms that offer the greatest amount of coordination.

All organizations use textual communication, such as e-mail, memos, and reports, to coordinate the activities of subunits. Units report on their activities, keeping other units aware of problems, output levels, innovations, or any other important information. With the increased availability of low-cost computer equipment, most memos and reports no longer appear on paper. Companies use e-mail or postings to local Web sites. Such electronic communication is particularly popular for multinational companies because they need rapid interaction over long distances and across many time zones.

Direct contact
Face-to-face interaction of employees.

Direct contact means that managers or workers interact face to face. For multinational companies, direct contact often requires sophisticated videoconferencing and knowledge of a common language. For example, GE Medical Systems uses nearly 1,000 hours of teleconferencing in a year. Ford has computer-aided design and manufacturing links between two continents to allow its engineers in Europe and the United States to communicate design and engineering ideas.[30]

Liaison roles
Part of a person's job in one department to communicate with people in another department.

Liaison roles are the specific job responsibilities of a person in one department to communicate with people in another department. A liaison role is only part of a manager's job responsibilities. For example, in a multinational company, one manager in each country subsidiary might be given the responsibility of coordinating marketing efforts within a region.

Full-time integrators are similar to liaison roles, but coordination is their sole job responsibility. Often product managers are full-time integrators. Product managers coordinate the development of their products with design teams, their production with the manufacturing departments, and their sales and promotion with marketing. In the multinational company, product managers often serve as links between the production units and local country operations.

Task forces are temporary teams, usually linking two or more departments, created to solve a particular organizational problem, such as entering a new market. For example, to take advantage of new market opportunities in China, Unilever assembled a group of Chinese-speaking troubleshooters selected from its 100 country operations and sent them to China. The troubleshooters built plants, planned strategy and organization, and returned to their home countries when they had completed their task.[31]

Teams are the strongest coordination mechanisms. Unlike task forces, which have a short life, teams are permanent units of the organization. Teams come from several organizational subunits to specialize in particular problems. For example, a team doing new product development might include a scientist from R&D and managers from production and marketing. In a multinational example, Texas Instruments uses permanent special-project teams, called Nomads, to set up chip fabrication plants anywhere in the world—from Italy to Singapore.[32]

As with the control options, most multinational companies use several if not all of the coordination mechanisms at one time or another. However, matrix and transnational network structures have very high needs for coordination. In these types of organizations, one sees a great use of the more elaborate control mechanisms of task forces, full-time integrators, and teams. For transnational networks, with their extensive geographic dispersion of subunits, teams are increasingly virtual units, with members seldom meeting face to face. As such, given the importance of teams coordination mechanisms, we consider them in more depth.

Teams

As multinational companies strive to meet both local and global customer needs by integrating the design and development expertise from around the world, they are making increased use of teams.[33] Teams give global companies the ability to better coordinate the work and expertise of widely dispersed individuals, to develop and launch new products, and to become more flexible. For example, International Truck and Engine Corporation created cross-functional project teams of employees located in Canada, the United States, and Mexico to develop its new products.[34] By incorporating the top employees in engineering, manufacturing, finance, and project management in these cross-functional teams, International Truck and Engine Corporation hopes to find ways to bring products to market more rapidly while increasing productivity. Furthermore, the new global workplace is seeing an increased use of **global virtual teams**, which are groups of people from different parts of the world who work together by using information and communication technologies such as intranets, Web meetings, WIKIs, e-mails, and instant messaging.[35]

Although global teams are popular, they face significant challenges, many of which are associated with having team members with diverse cultural backgrounds located in different parts of the world. Previous surveys and empirical research identify several challenges such as the diversity of languages and

Full-time integrator
Cross-unit co-ordination is the main job responsibility.

Task force
Temporary team created to solve a particular organizational problem.

Team
Permanent unit of the organization designed to focus the efforts of different subunits on particular problems.

Global virtual team
Groups of people from different parts of the world who work together by using information and communication technologies such as intranets, Web meetings, WIKIs, e-mails, and instant messaging.

cultural differences of the members.[36] Such challenges often make it difficult for the teams to collaborate.

Despite these challenges, multinational companies can take steps to ensure that their global teams collaborate to function effectively:[37]

- *Build relationships and trust:* Important steps have to be taken to encourage global team members to get to know each other and build trust. For instance, initial face-to-face meetings should be organized not only to let team members learn about each other but also to set project goals and roles. Some even suggest that the first meeting should last at least three days. However, if traveling is too expensive, conference calls or other means can be used regularly. It is advisable to use the time at the start of such meetings to encourage global team members to get to know each other personally. This can be done by assigning a full-time communication specialist who can plan and manage both information flows and communication across teams. For instance, a communication specialist may request team members to provide more extensive feedback when necessary or educate them about the pros and cons of the various forms of communication, such as e-mail and videoconferencing.

- *Pay attention to project planning and hold project progress meetings regularly:* Ensuring that projects are completed on schedule and on budget is difficult enough with domestic teams. However, the added complexity of having team members located around the world suggests that multinational companies need to devote significant resources to planning the project. All team members should be made aware of the goals and time line of the project, and the project leader should send clear messages about the key issues and how they relate to the strategic objective. Furthermore, regular team meetings should be held to inform team members of progress. Corrective actions can also be implemented as necessary.

- *Cultural, language, and active-listening training:* Global teams can function only if team members are all on the same wavelength. Multinational companies need to devote resources to train global team members appropriately and to assess their level of cultural competency. Language training may also be appropriate for a level of language commonality among all team members. For instance, the prescriptions discussed in Chapter 13 on international negotiation regarding communication with non-native speakers may be helpful. Also, global teams may fail because they consider lengthy discussions a waste of time. Group members must be trained to be sensitive to different communication styles and to practice active listening to avoid overlooking important issues.

This section completes our consideration of organizational design by showing how managers can control and coordinate subunits. In the final section, we look at knowledge management, a design issue that is becoming crucial for most multinational companies.

Knowledge Management

In Chapter 7, we saw that most multinational companies face a very chaotic and unfocused environment. Industry boundaries are ambiguous, and companies are facing intense competition. Product life cycles are being increasingly compressed, and most multinational companies are experiencing severe information overload.[38] To face such challenges, companies must make optimal use of the available knowledge—that is, the filtered information of value to a company—to build an innovative culture. Knowledge is the most important source of sustainable competitive advantage as multinational companies face shifting markets, rapid product cycles, and hypercompetition.[39] Companies must therefore implement systems to manage knowledge.

In this final section, we examine some of the critical design issues related to knowledge management.

Knowledge management consists of the systems, mechanisms, and other design elements of an organization to ensure that the right form of knowledge is available to the right individual at the right time.[40] Consider the next Case in Point.

Why is it so critical for companies to manage their knowledge closely? For domestic companies, adequately managing existing knowledge can be instrumental in generating new knowledge, which can then lead to innovation and value creation.[41] However, as the Case in Point demonstrates, for multinational companies, knowledge management is even more critical because they face unique challenges. Many multinationals now have to face forces for both international integration and local differentiation while achieving global innovation. Multinational companies therefore need to be able to implement systems that are capable of combining worldwide local knowledge in order to innovate and then to transfer the innovation to new products for international markets.

> **Knowledge management**
> Systems and mechanisms to ensure that the right form of knowledge is available to the right individual at the right time.

C A S E   I N   P O I N T

Knowledge Management in Various Multinationals

Knowledge management systems are keys to the success of multinationals. Telenor Mobile of Norway was one of the world's pioneers in mobile phones, introducing the world's first automatic cellular service as far back as the 1980s. Its entry strategy was to develop joint ventures with local telecommunication companies. In many cases, Telenor was buying into companies at the start-up stage, proving its technical expertise as the basis for the joint ventures. However, as mobile phone technology became more standardized, it was losing its competitive advantage based on technical expertise.

Telecommunication companies like Telenor realized that the only way to succeed was to develop systems that could identify the best practices in the markets they were operating in and spread those practices across their operations. Telenor therefore devised a knowledge management system whereby local best practices were identified and collected in a central system. Local affiliates identified best practices, and Telenor then attempted to implement the practices in other locations. Without such a knowledge management system, Telenor would not have been able to benefit from the knowledge from its many foreign partners.

The insurance industry also benefits tremendously from knowledge management systems. DKVA is a German insurance company responsible for health care claims by German citizens living in other parts of the European Union. It processes about 1.2 million claims per year and has to deal with a 10 to 15 percent dispute rate. DKVA designed a knowledge management system to help with its claims. It selected a Process360 optimization solution whereby users can find out where all their claims and payments are. The system also allows DKVA to find out the stage of a dispute, as well as print invoices and retrieve other critical documents. Most importantly, the system is flexible enough to accommodate the frequent changes in health coverage and payment rules that characterize the European Union.

Sources: Based on Britt, P. 2008. "KM reaps benefits worldwide for insurers." KMWorld, October, pp. 20, 26; Goodermam, P. N., and S. Ulset. 2007. "Telenor's third way." European Business Forum, Winter, 31, pp. 46–48.

Appropriately managing knowledge can give multinational companies the means to create the global flexibility they will need to survive and prosper.[42]

To develop an effective knowledge management system, the first step is to identify potential barriers to knowledge sharing within the organization. Barriers can exist at various levels, including the individual and organizational levels.[43] Sharing knowledge across companies located in different parts of the world introduces a number of cross-cultural and geographic distance-related challenges. Exhibit 8.13 summarizes some of the most important individual, organizational, and cross-cultural problems.

The next step is for multinational companies to assess the degree to which these barriers exist and implement appropriate actions to reduce their effects. For instance, the multinational firm can take the appropriate steps to communicate to employees about the necessity to share knowledge. Individual employees should be motivated and encouraged to capture and disseminate the appropriate knowledge to others in the organization as needed, and they should be rewarded when they do so.[44] Furthermore, the organizational structure should be aligned with the need for knowledge management. Tall, hierarchical structures are obvious barriers to information flow, and important steps need to be taken toward a flatter and more fluid structure. Finally, an important aspect of knowledge management is the use of computer-based technology.[45] Computer and Web-based technologies allow multinational companies to create simple data repositories of explicit knowledge (i.e., knowledge that can be

EXHIBIT 8.13   Knowledge Management Barriers

Individual barriers:

- Lack of time or interest to share knowledge.
- Lack of understanding of importance of sharing knowledge.
- Lack of trust in others.
- Use of hierarchical position or power to encourage sharing of explicit rather than tacit knowledge.
- Poor communication skills.

Organizational barriers:

- Lack of communication of importance of knowledge management.
- No strategic alignment between organization's mission and objectives and knowledge-sharing strategy and initiatives.
- Lack of sufficient mechanisms (both online and face to face) to share knowledge.
- Lack of reward systems to foster and encourage knowledge sharing.
- Communication flows restricted to one direction as reflected in the organizational hierarchy.
- Internal strife and conflict among business units.

Cross-cultural barriers:

- Language barriers.
- Cultural differences.
- Time zone and other geographic distance-related challenges.

Sources: Based on Riege, Andreas. 2005. "Three-dozen knowledge-sharing barriers managers must consider." Journal of Knowledge Management, *9(3), pp. 18–35; Voelpel, Sven C., and Zheng Han. 2005. "Managing knowledge sharing in China: The case of Siemens ShareNet."* Journal of Knowledge Management, *9(3), pp. 51–63.*

stored and shared), and they enable firms to use their tacit knowledge through such tools as networking, collaborative commerce, and other decision support systems. DuPont uses Lotus Notes to allow its R&D personnel to collaborate and consult with other inhouse and outside experts.[46] So it is important for multinational companies to invest in building the integrative platform for individuals located around the world.

Summary and Conclusions

Good strategies by themselves will never guarantee successful multinational operations. Good implementation is equally important. Perhaps the most important part of strategy implementation is having the right organizational design to carry out strategic intents, goals, and objectives. This chapter provided a review of how multinational companies use organizational designs to implement multinational strategies. Organizational design entails the choice of subunits (how to divide work) and the choice of coordination and control mechanisms (how to focus the efforts of the subunits).

The chapter reviewed the basics of organizational structure. Functional, product-oriented, and geographic structures were described and pictured. They also were compared and contrasted for their strengths and weaknesses. A knowledge of these basic structures is necessary because function, product, and area structures are the building blocks for the organizational structures used by multinational companies.

As companies internationalize their strategies, they usually progress from using an export department or international division to more complex organizational structures. More complex structures call for foreign subsidiaries to conduct value chain activities (e.g., manufacturing) in other countries. Some of these subsidiaries are minireplicas—small reproductions of the home country organization. Other subsidiaries are transnational; they can do anything or be anywhere depending on the local strengths and the parent company's needs. Companies use different types of subsidiaries depending on the structures they choose.

If companies adopt a multidomestic or regional multinational strategy, they usually favor a worldwide geographic structure, which emphasizes responding to local markets. In contrast, the worldwide product structure supports an international strategy; it facilitates building and selling global products. Hybrid and matrix structures support companies with mixtures of strategies for different products and businesses. These structures combine some of the benefits of both the geographic and the product structures. The transnational network structure goes beyond the matrix and hybrid. It has no set form, and its subsidiaries respond uniquely to global efficiency pressures, company learning needs, or local needs, as the strategic situation dictates. The step beyond the transnational network structure is the metanational structure, whose organizational learning and virtual information sharing become the drivers of the organization.

Organizational designs are not complete without integration mechanisms. These mechanisms link subunits and coordinate their activities. Control systems, such as bureaucratic and cultural controls, link the organization vertically. Coordination mechanisms, such as task forces and teams, link the organization horizontally. Multinational organizations use all these integration mechanisms, but, for the multinational company, cultural control is often considered most important. A strong organizational culture helps the multinational company bridge the national cultures of its employees.

Finally, an important component of today's multinational companies consists of knowledge management systems. Knowledge management systems allow the multinational company to encourage the sharing of valuable expertise of individuals located around the world. To implement such systems successfully, the multinational organization must assess barriers to knowledge sharing and implement knowledge networks.

Discussion Questions

1. You work for a company with three major products, and your CEO has decided to sell these products in the international marketplace. She asks your advice in setting up an organizational structure. What issues would you discuss with her regarding the company's international strategy before making any recommendations?

2. What are the advantages of a worldwide product structure over a worldwide area structure? What type of company would most likely choose each type?

3. What are the costs and benefits of having a matrix structure?

4. What transnational activities might be possible for a small company with only an export department or an international division?

5. Identify some areas in multinational companies where cultural control might work better than bureaucratic control.

6. What cultural values must a metanational company encourage so that alliance partners and dispersed subsidiaries share knowledge?

7. What are virtual teams? What benefits can virtual teams bring to multinational companies?

8. What are some of the typical problems multinationals face when using teams as integration mechanisms? What can multinational companies do to address these problems?

9. What are knowledge management systems? How can they be appropriately designed?

Multinational Management **Skill Builder**

Build an Organization Structure for P&G

Step 1. Procter & Gamble (P&G) is a major multinational corporation headquartered in the United States. Review the popular business press (e.g., *Wall Street Journal, Fortune, Economist, BusinessWeek,* etc.) over the last year for articles on P&G's operations around the globe.

Step 2. Given this background information, design a multinational structure that you think can best implement P&G's strategies for different products. Exhibits 8.14 and 8.15 show an overview of P&G's geographic locations and major global products.

Step 3. Prepare a written or oral report showing your design and providing a rationale for your structural choices.

EXHIBIT 8.14   P&G's Worldwide Locations and Starting Dates of Operations

Algeria, 2001	Denmark, 1992	Indonesia, 1970	Panama, 2000	Tanzania, 1997
Argentina, 1991	Egypt, 1986	Ireland, 1980	Peru, 1956	Thailand, 1985
Australia, 1985	El Salvador, 1988	Israel, 2001	Philippines, 1935	Turkey, 1987
Austria, 1966	Estonia, 1995	Italy, 1956	Poland, 1991	Uganda, 1995
Azerbaijan, 1998	Federal Republic of	Japan, 1973	Portugal, 1989	Ukraine, 1993
Bangladesh, 1995	Yugoslavia, 1996	Kazakhstan, 1996	Puerto Rico, 1947	United Arab
Belarus, 1995	Federation of Bosnia-	Kenya, 1985	Romania, 1994	Emirates, 2001
Belgium, 1955	Herzegovina, 1998	Korea, 1988	Russia, 1991	United Kingdom,
Brazil, 1988	Finland, 1971	Latvia, 19995	Saudi Arabia, 1957	1930
Bulgaria, 1994	Former Yugoslav	Lebanon, 1959	Singapore, 1969	United States,
Canada, 1915	Republic of Macedonia,	Lithuania, 1997	Slovak Republic,	1837
Caribbean Islands,	1998	Malaysia, 1969	1993	Uzbekistan, 1996
1986	France, 1954	Mexico, 1948	Slovenia, 1996	Venezuela, 1950
Chile, 1983	Germany, 1960	Morocco, 1958	South Africa, 1994	Vietnam, 1994
China, 1988	Ghana, 1998	Netherlands, 1964	Spain, 1968	Yemen, 1995
Colombia, 1982	Greece, 1960	New Zealand, 1985	Sri Lanka, 1996	
Costa Rica, 1995	Guatemala, 1985	Nicaragua, 1985	Sweden, 1969	
Croatia, 1991	Honduras, 1985	Nigeria, 1992	Switzerland, 1953	
Czech Republic,	Hong Kong, 1969	Norway, 1993	Syria, 1998	
1991	Hungary, 1991	Pakistan, 1989	Taiwan, 1984	

Source: Adapted from Procter & Gamble. 2003. Facts About P&G 2002–2003 Worldwide. *Cincinnati: Procter & Gamble.*

EXHIBIT 8.15   **P&G's Global Product Groups and Product Types**

Product Groups	Product Types	Net Sales ($ millions)
Baby, feminine, and family care	Baby diapers, baby wipes, baby bibs, baby change and bed mats	11.9
	Toilet tissue, paper towels, and facial tissue	
	Feminine protection pads, pantiliners, and tampons	
Beauty care	Cosmetics	11.6
	Deodorants	
	Fragrances	
	Hair coloring	
	Skin care	
Fabric and home care	Bleach	8.1
	Care for special fabrics	
	Dish care	
	Fabric conditioners	
	Household cleaners	
	Laundry detergent	
	P&G chemicals	
	Cosmetics	
Food and beverage	Beverages	3.8
	Snacks	
Health care	Oral and personal care	5.0
	Pet health and nutrition	
	Prescription drugs	
	Water filtration	

Source: Adapted from Procter & Gamble. 2003. Facts About P&G 2002–2003 Worldwide. Cincinnati: Procter & Gamble.

Endnotes

1 Jones, Gareth R. 2009. *Organizational Theory, Design and Change.* Upper Saddle River, NJ: Pearson-Prentice Hall.

2 Ibid.

3 Duncan, Robert. 1979. "What is the right organization structure? Decision tree analysis provides the answer." *Organizational Dynamics*, Winter.

4 United Nations Conference on Trade and Development (UNCTAD). 2003. *World Investment Report.* New York and Geneva: United Nations.

5 Brellochs, Jochen, and Ulrich Steger. 2006. "Most multinationals now derive most of their value from subsidiaries. So, why do so few have robust systems in place to ensure that principles of governance are applied consistently across their organizational networks?" *Financial Times*, June, 2, p. 4.

6 Ibid.

7 Beamish, Paul W., J. Peter Killing, Donald J. Lecraw, and Allen J. Morrison. 1994. *International Management.* Burr Ridge, IL: Irwin.

8 Bartlett, Christopher A., and Sumantra Ghoshal. 1989. *Managing Across Borders: The Transnational Solution.* Boston: Harvard University Press.

9 Humes, Samuel. 1993. *Managing the Multinational: Confronting the Global-Local Dilemma.* New York: Prentice Hall.

10 Stopford, J. M., and L. T. Wells Jr. 1972. *Managing the Multinational Enterprise.* New York: Basic Books.

11 Toyota. 2006. "Toyota announces board of directors and organizational changes." June 23. http://www.toyota.co.jp.

12 *BusinessWeek Online.* 1994. "Borderless management: Companies strive to become truly stateless." May 23; Treece, James B., Kathleen Kerwin, and Heidi Dawley. 1995. "Ford: Alex Trotman's daring global strategy." *BusinessWeek Online*, April 3.

13 *Economist.* 2000. "Ford in Europe: in the slow lane." October 7; *Economist.* 2002. "From baron to hotelier." May 9; Lublin, Joann. 2001. "Division problem—place vs. product: It's tough to choose a management model—Exide tore up system based on countries for one on centered battery lines—rolling over European fiefs." *Wall Street Journal* (Eastern edition). June 27, p. A1.

14 Beamish et al.

15 *BusinessWeek Online*. 1994. "Borderless management: Companies strive to become truly stateless," May 23.

16 *Economist*. "From baron to hotelier."

17 *BusinessWeek Online*. 1994. "High-tech jobs all over the world." November 18.

18 *Economist*. 2006. "Survey: The matrix master," January 21.

19 Ghoshal, Sumantra, and Christopher A. Bartlett. 1990. "The multinational corporation as an interorganizational network." *Academy of Management Review*, pp. 15, 603–625; Humes, S. *Managing the Multinational: Confronting the Global-Local Dilemma*; Philips Electronics N.V. 2003. *Annual Report*. February 11.

20 Ghoshal and Bartlett.

21 Ibid.

22 *BusinessWeek Online*. "High-tech jobs all over the world."

23 Doz, Yves, J., Jose Santos, and Peter Williamson. 2001. *From Global to Metanational: How Companies Win in the Knowledge Economy*. Boston: Harvard Business School Press.

24 Fisher, Lawrence M. 2002. "STMicroelectronics: The metaphysics of a metanational pioneer." *Strategy & Business*, 19, 3rd quarter pp. 2–10.

25 Ibid.

26 Cray, David. 1984. "Control and coordination in multinational corporations." *Journal of International Business Studies*, Fall, pp. 85–98.

27 Daft, Richard L. 2004. *Organization Theory and Design*. Minneapolis/St. Paul: West; Jones.

28 Beamish et al.

29 Daft.

30 *BusinessWeek Online*. "Borderless management: Companies strive to become truly stateless."

31 *Business Week Online*. "Tearing up today's organization chart." November 18.

32 *Business Week Online*. "High-tech jobs all over the world."

33 Barczak, Gloria, Edward F. McDonough III, and Nicholas Athanassiou. 2006. "So you want to be a global project leader?" *Research Technology Management*, May–June, 49(3), pp. 28–35.

34 Rosswurm, Gretchen, and Patricia Bayerlein. 2004–2005. "Overcoming barriers to global success at International." *Strategic Communication Management*, December–January, 9(1), pp. 14–17.

35 Brake, Terence. 2006. "Leading global virtual teams." *Industrial and Commercial Training*, 38(3), pp. 116–121.

36 Barczak, Gloria, and Edward F. McDonough III. 2003. "Leading global product development teams." *Research Technology Management*, November–December, 46(6), pp. 14–18; Barczak, McDonough III, and Athanassiou, "So you want to be a global project leader?"; Rosswurm and Bayerlein.

37 Barczak, McDonough III, and Athanassiou, "So you want to be a global project leader?"; Kumar, Janaki Mythily. 2006. "Working as a designer in a global team." *Interactions*, March–April, pp. 25–27; Rosswurm and Bayerlein.

38 Davis, Joseph G., Eswaran Subrahmanian, and Arthur W. Westerberg. 2005. "The 'global' and the 'local' in knowledge management." *Journal of Knowledge Management*, 9(1), pp. 101–112.

39 Ibid.

40 Wang, Junxia, Hans Peter Peters, and Jiancheng Guan. 2006. "Factors influencing knowledge productivity in German research groups: Lessons for developing countries." *Journal of Knowledge Management* 10(4), pp. 113–126.

41 Voelpel, Sven C., and Zheng Han. 2005. "Managing knowledge sharing in China: The case of Siemens ShareNet." *Journal of Knowledge Management*, 9(3), pp. 51–63.

42 Davis, Subrahmanian, and Westerberg.

43 Riege, Andreas. 2005. "Three-dozen knowledge-sharing barriers managers must consider." *Journal of Knowledge Management*, 9(3), pp. 18–35.

44 Ibid.

45 Holsapple, Clyde W. 2005. "The inseparability of modern knowledge management and computer-based technology." *Journal of Knowledge Management*, 9(1), pp. 42–52.

46 Davis, Subrahmanian, and Westerberg.

Procter & Gamble: Organization 2005 (A)

MIKOLAJ JAN PISKORSKI

ALESSANDRO L. SPADINI

When [Lafley] took over in June 2000, on the same day as CEO Durk Jager's sudden resignation, the company was the sort of ink-stained mess you'd find in a Tide commercial. It had slammed four profit warnings into two quarters. . . . Its stock had dropped by half in the previous six months—losing a crushing $70 billion in market value. And the combative Jager, whose 17 volatile months on the job had made his the shortest CEO tenure in Procter & Gamble's grand 165-year history, had left the company unsure of its footing. The day Lafley got the keys, no one had high hopes.[1]

Fortune, *September 2002*

A. G. Lafley (MBA 77) did not have much time to decide how to turn around Procter & Gamble (P&G). His predecessor, Durk Jager, had introduced an aggressive restructuring program—Organization 2005—designed to generate bolder innovations and accelerate their global rollout in order to double P&G sales to $70 billion by 2005 and achieve annual earnings growth of 13–15 percent. At the core of the program lay a radical new organizational design. In the past, P&G's chain of formal command put geography first, followed by product, and then by function. In the new design, P&G was structured as three interdependent global organizations, one organized by product category, one by geography, and one by business process. The early results of the reorganization had been abysmal: flat sales and negative core earnings growth had caused P&G to issue four profit warnings. Lack of immediate results coupled with substantial job reductions—an integral part of the Organization 2005 restructuring—contributed to sagging employee morale. In a short time, Lafley had to decide whether or not to put an end to this new design and return to the previous organizational structure that had worked well in the past.

The organizational problems were aggravated by strategic concerns. Many analysts questioned whether it made sense for P&G, a $38 billion multinational consumer-products company, to compete in over 50 categories, ranging from toilet paper to pharmaceuticals, with more than 300 brands.[2] Though traditionally P&G could rely on its marketing and R&D expertise to justify its presence across multiple markets, in the previous couple of years focused competitors had been steadily taking away market share in many product lines and regions, suggesting perhaps that the corporate advantage had withered away. As Lafley contemplated his organizational decision, he also had to decide whether he could create more value by splitting the company into sets of stand-alone businesses.

Procter & Gamble History, 1837–1948

The Procter & Gamble Company was founded in Cincinnati, Ohio by an English immigrant William Procter and James Gamble, an immigrant from Ireland. Both men had arrived in Cincinnati separately, forced to stop there to tend to illnesses while on their way West. Each independently decided to settle to found a business. Procter became a candlemaker and Gamble a soapmaker. After marrying sisters, they formed a partnership in 1837.[3] At that time, Cincinnati, nicknamed "Porkopolis", was the country's largest meatpacking center allowing for inexpensive access to animal fat—a primary raw material for candles and soap. This attracted many new entrants, such that by 1845 P&G had to compete with as many as 14 other local manufacturers of unbranded soaps and candles.[4] To differentiate itself P&G embarked on an aggressive investment strategy building a large factory in the 1850s despite rumors of impending civil war. During the war P&G operated day and night to supply the Union armies, and by the war's end sales had more than quintupled to over $1 million.[5] When soldiers returned home carrying its high-quality products, distinguished by their characteristic moon-and-stars packaging, P&G quickly developed a national reputation.[6] Rapid growth and a series of innovations in human-resource management, R&D, distribution, marketing, and organizational design soon followed.

From its inception, P&G focused on product innovation. In 1879, Gamble's son James Norris Gamble, a trained chemist, developed *Ivory*, the first American soap comparable to fine European imports. James transformed P&G's soap- and candle-making processes from an art to a science by soliciting help from chemistry professors. *Ivory,* first marketed nationally in 1882 for its superior purity, transformed P&G into a branded-goods producer. Mass-scale production of *Ivory* began at an enormous new plant, Ivorydale, in 1887 to meet rapidly growing national demand. P&G simultaneously instituted one of the first profit-sharing programs to maintain harmony with its workforce. The company started paying dividends in 1890 and has done so continuously ever since.[7] The same year, P&G established one of the first centralized R&D labs in industry.[8] R&D ultimately led to diversification into many other chemistry-based consumer industries, including cooking oils, laundry detergents, personal-care products, paper products, and even pharmaceuticals (see Exhibit 1).[9] P&G also innovated by establishing a direct sales force in 1919, disintermediating wholesalers. Direct distribution to stores enhanced P&G's insight into retail customers and enabled the company to tie production more closely to demand. P&G established one of the first market-research departments in 1924 and invented the soap opera in 1933. "Guiding Light," which first aired as a 15-minute radio serial in 1937, is still being produced by a P&G-owned production studio and appears daily on CBS.[10]

Throughout the 1920s brand managers were encouraged to be entrepreneurial and to manage brands as individual companies. Competitive brand management was institutionalized in 1931, formally empowering each brand manager to target different consumer segments. The organization started forming around product lines so that quicker and more consumer-focused business decisions could be made by brand managers at lower levels in the corporate hierarchy. In 1943 P&G created its first product-category division, the drug-products department, focused on a growing line of personal-care products. Strong centralized functions were retained, however, in areas such as R&D and manufacturing. *Tide,* a revolutionary synthetic detergent launched in 1946, was developed by R&D against the wishes of brand management through a secret 5-year program known as "Project X." Upper management eventually fast-tracked the project; *Tide* captured market leadership in just 4 years (and still held it over 50 years later), validating R&D's independence.[11]

Diverging Organizational Structures (1948–1987)

In 1948, P&G established its first international sales division to manage its rapidly growing foreign businesses.[12] Over the next forty years P&G would steadily build its foreign presence, while carefully managing its U.S. operations. The two types of operations led to two very different modes of organizational architectures. The United States, with a large homogenous market, lent itself to nationwide brand and product division management. Western Europe, which represented the lion's share of P&G's overseas division, was a heterogeneous market with different languages, cultures, and laws, and therefore adopted a decentralized hub-and-spoke model.

United States

Product Division Management In 1954, P&G created individual operating divisions to better manage growing lines of products, each with its own line and staff organizations (see Diagram 1). Within this model, the organization developed along two key dimensions: functions and brands. Brand managers bore responsibility for profitability and could focus on matching company strategy with product-category dynamics. Brand managers in the same product division competed in the marketplace but shared access to strong divisional functions. Those divisional functions transferred best practices and talent across many brands, fostering leading-edge competencies in R&D, manufacturing, and market research in a rapidly developing consumer-products industry. A corporate basic-research department helped to make innovative connections across divisions, leading to inventions like fluoride toothpaste in 1955.

Advent of Matrix In 1987, the United States made a historic shift away from the competitive brand-management system put in place in 1931; brands would now be managed as components of category portfolios by category general managers. At the same time, product categories were beginning to require more differentiated functional activities. Thus 39 U.S. category business units were created, each run by a general manager to whom both brand and dedicated functional managers would report (see Diagram 2).[13] Each category business unit had its own sales, product-development, manufacturing, and finance functions. To retain functional strengths, a matrix reporting structure was set up whereby functional leaders reported directly to their business leadership and also had a dotted-line reporting relationship to their functional leadership. For example, all sales employees' dotted-line reporting relationships would ultimately filter up to the Vice President of Sales for the United States.

Western Europe

Geographic Management In Europe, the P&G organization developed along three dimensions: country,

EXHIBIT 1   Research-&-Development-Driven Category Diversification

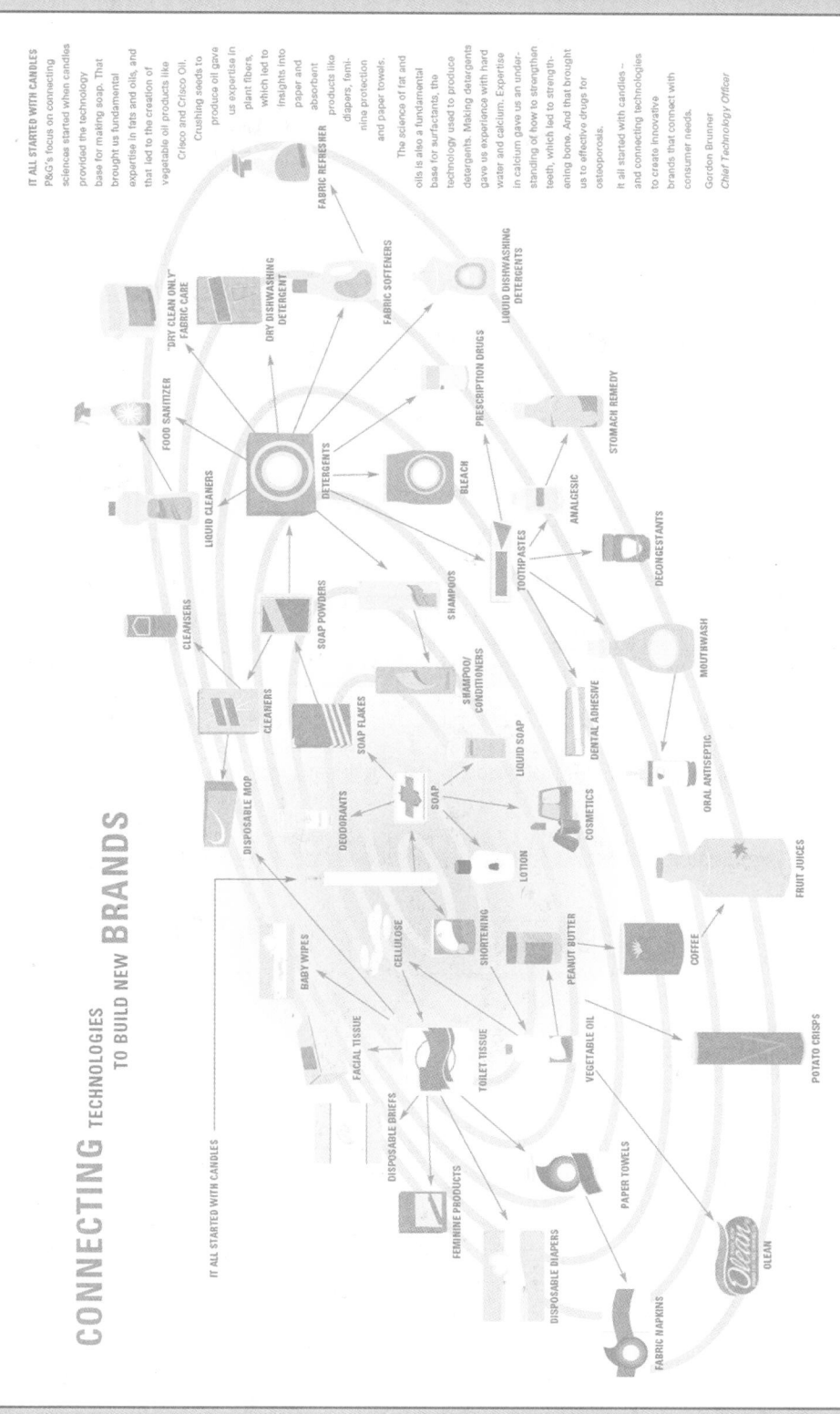

Source: Procter & Gamble. 1999 Annual Report (Cincinnati: Procter & Gamble, 1999), pp. 3-5, http://www.pg.com/investors/annualreports.jhtml, accessed March 2006.

DIAGRAM **1**   **U.S. Divisional Structure in 1955**

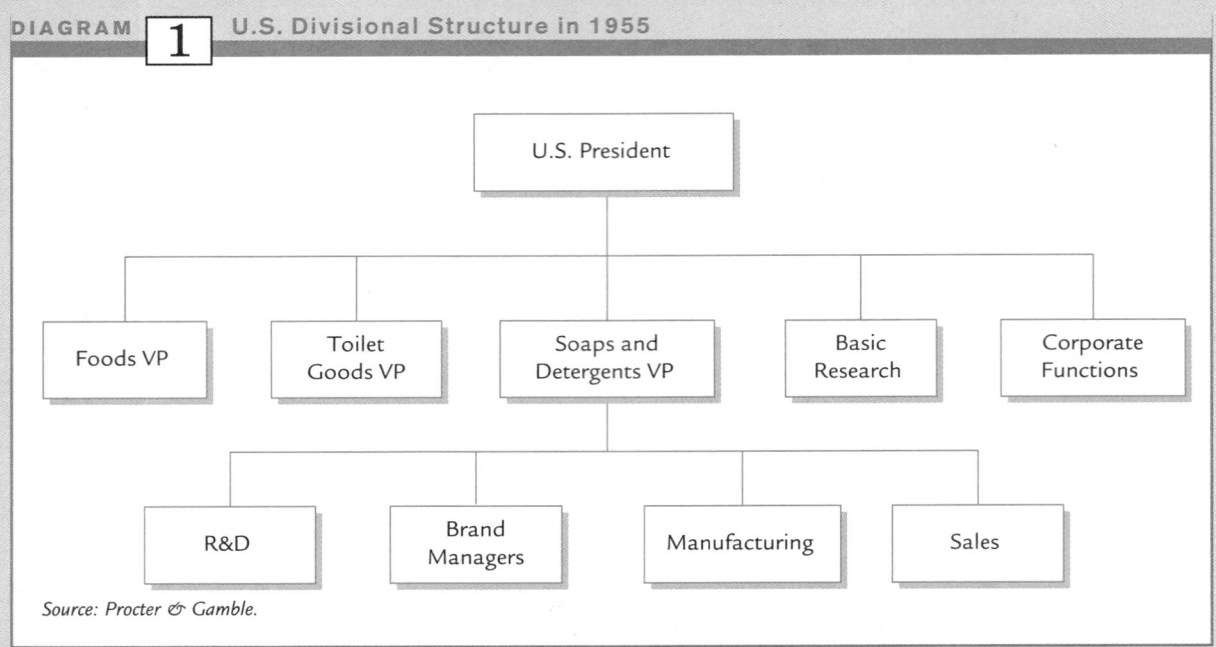

Source: *Procter & Gamble.*

function, and brand (see Diagram 3). "P&G began expanding globally after World War II," explained former P&G CEO John Pepper, "but the company created 'mini-U.S.es' in each country."[14] In fact, P&G's first president of overseas operations, Walter Lingle, established this model to tailor products and processes to local tastes and norms. The result was a portfolio of self-sufficient subsidiaries led by country general managers (GMs) who adapted P&G technology and marketing expertise to local markets.[15] New product technologies were sourced from U.S. R&D labs in Cincinnati and then qualified, tested, and adapted by

DIAGRAM **2**   **U.S. Matrix Category/Function Business Unit Structure, 1987**

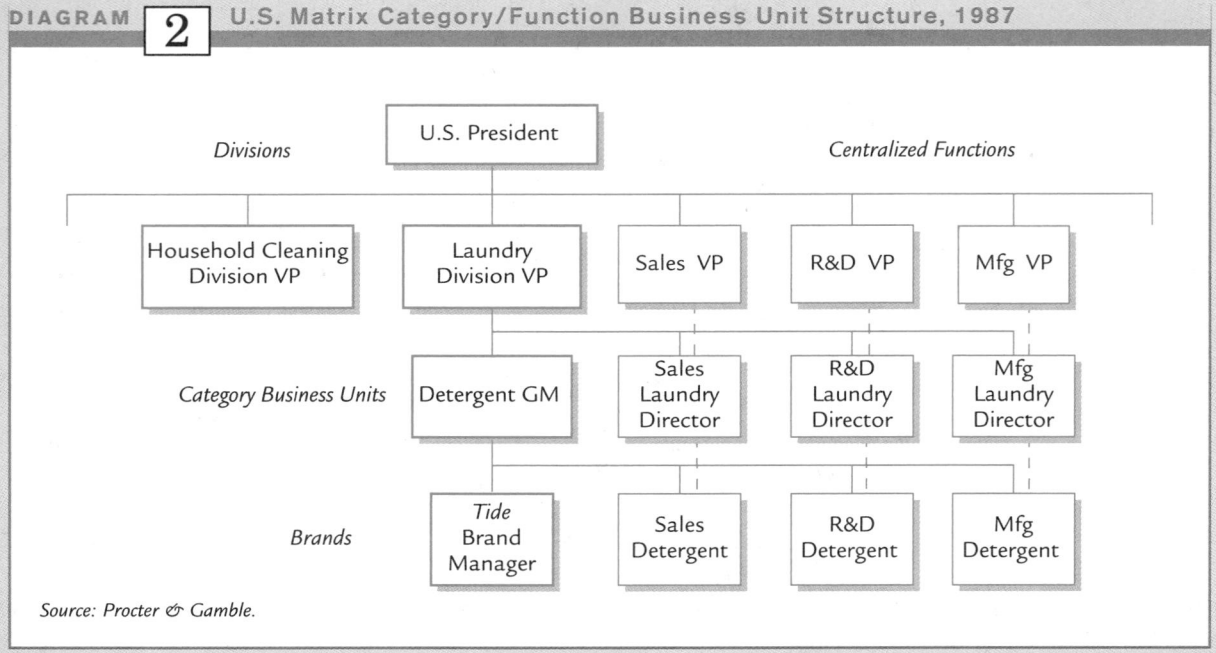

Source: *Procter & Gamble.*

DIAGRAM **3** **Initial European Organizational Design**

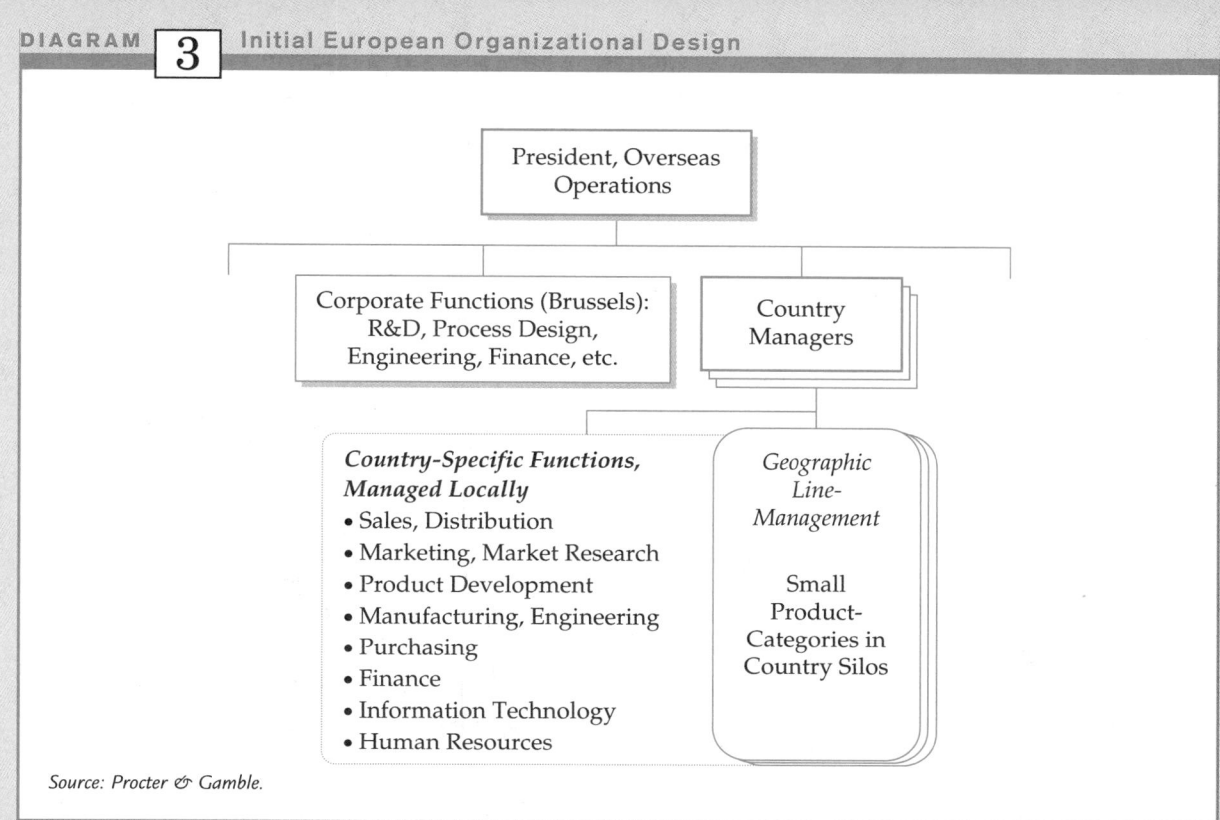

Source: Procter & Gamble.

local R&D and manufacturing organizations in each country. In 1963, the European Technical Center (ETC) in Brussels was inaugurated to house a European corporate R&D and process-engineering function. ETC developed products and manufacturing processes that country managers could choose to adapt to and launch in their own countries.

In this model country managers, not brand managers, had responsibility for profitability and market strategy. The Brussels regional headquarters was very hands-off, serving mostly as a legal, tax-accounting, and public-relations entity. This structure ultimately led to a situation in which innovations and brands could take more than 10 years to globalize.[16] *Pampers,* for example, was launched in the United States in 1961, in Germany in 1973, and in France not until 1978.[17] Not only were European functional organizations embedded in country silos, but European corporate functions were also completely disconnected from the U.S. operation. Corporate R&D in Europe, for example, had little contact with labs in Cincinnati. Furthermore, focus on product categories and brands was fragmented by country, virtually precluding region-wide category or branding strategies.

Advent of Category Management By the early 1980s P&G operated in 27 countries and derived a quarter of its $11 billion in revenues from overseas operations. At that scale, it was becoming clear that the European globalization model was not very effective.[18] Unstandardized and subscale manufacturing operations in each country were expensive and unreliable. Products were tweaked unnecessarily, creating pack-size and formulation variations that added no value for the consumer but significant cost and complexity to the supply chain. Country R&D labs were expensive to maintain and reinvented the wheel with each new product initiative. Therefore, beginning in the early 1980s, Europe attempted to promote cross-border cooperation across functions and to shift focus from country management to product-category management. Headquarters in Brussels encouraged the formation of regional committees composed of large-country managers and corporate functional leaders to eliminate needless product variations, coordinate marketing communications, prioritize product launches, and orchestrate competitive responses across the region. Unsurprisingly, many small-country managers objected that there was no "typical" European consumer and that this initiative

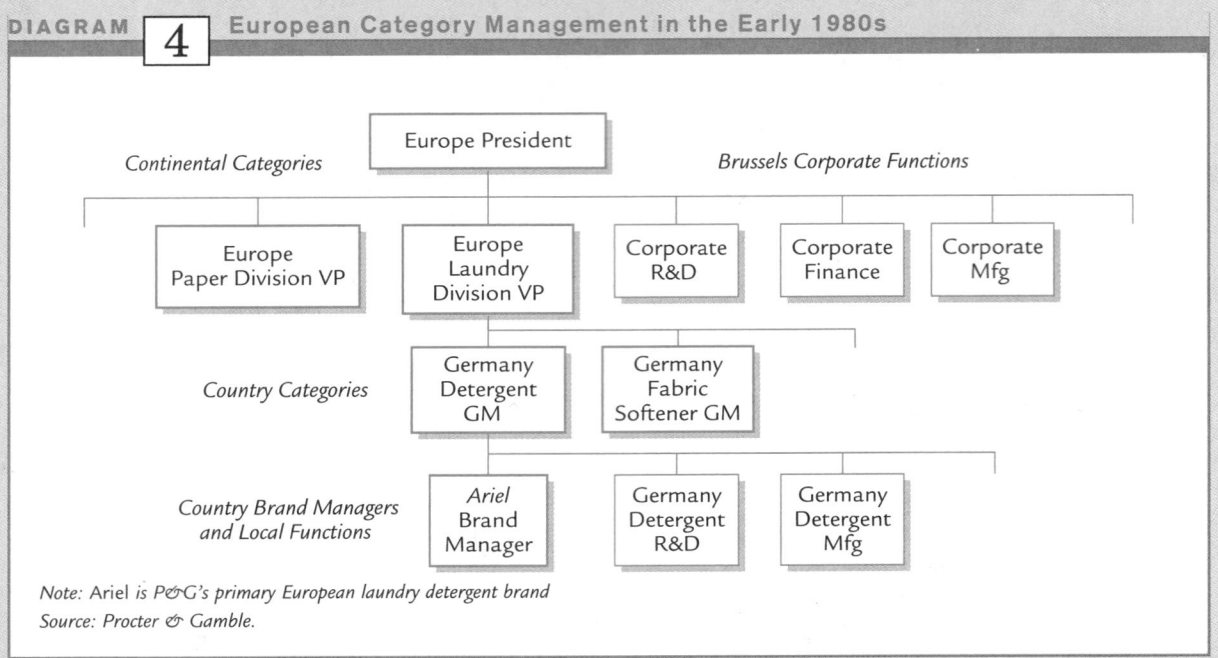

DIAGRAM **4** **European Category Management in the Early 1980s**

Note: Ariel *is P&G's primary European laundry detergent brand*
Source: *Procter & Gamble.*

would lead to neglect of local consumer preferences. The strategy eventually proved successful, however, and Europe was split into three subregions whose leaders were given secondary responsibilities for coordinating particular product categories across the entire continent. In the early 1980s, Europe was fully restructured around product categories. Product-category division VP positions were established and assigned continent-wide divisional profit-and-loss responsibility. Country GMs were replaced with multiple-country product-category GMs who reported to the division VPs. Thus, for example, the GM responsible for marketing and selling laundry detergents in Germany would report to the VP of laundry for Europe (see Diagram 4).

Global Matrix (1987–1995)

In the late 1980s, attractive expansion opportunities in Japan and developing markets led P&G to question its globalization model, particularly in anticipation of the new challenge of appealing to more diverse consumer tastes and income levels. In Europe, increased focus on cross-border category management had proven successful, but corporate functions in Brussels still lacked direct control of country functional activities. Therefore, P&G started migrating to a global matrix structure of categories and functions. First, Europe's country functions were consolidated into continental functions characterized by dotted-line reporting through functional leadership and direct reporting through the regional

business managers (see Diagram 5). Global functional senior vice presidencies were created to manage functions across all regions. Then, in 1989, to better coordinate category and branding strategies worldwide, P&G created global category presidencies reporting directly to the CEO.[19] All country category GMs had dotted-line reporting to their global category president; however, career progression and promotion remained in the hands of regional line management. Global category presidents were given direct responsibility for managing a fully globalized corporate R&D function, subdivided by category rather than region. Global R&D vice presidencies were established to manage R&D for a given product division worldwide; they reported directly to global category presidents and were dotted-line reports to the global SVP of R&D. This structure allowed for the creation of global technical centers in different regions, each with a core competency in a specific product category. Together, the global category presidents and R&D VPs developed product-category platform technologies that could be applied to global branding strategies. In 1995 this structure was extended to the rest of the world through the creation of four regions—North America, Latin America, Europe/Middle East/Africa, and Asia—each of which had its own president with responsibility for profit and loss.

P&G's matrix organizational structure facilitated tremendous top-and bottom-line improvements (see Exhibits 2, 3, and 4). The creation of powerful and independent global functions promoted the pooling

DIAGRAM 5 Global Matrix Structure Partial Organization Chart, 1995–1998

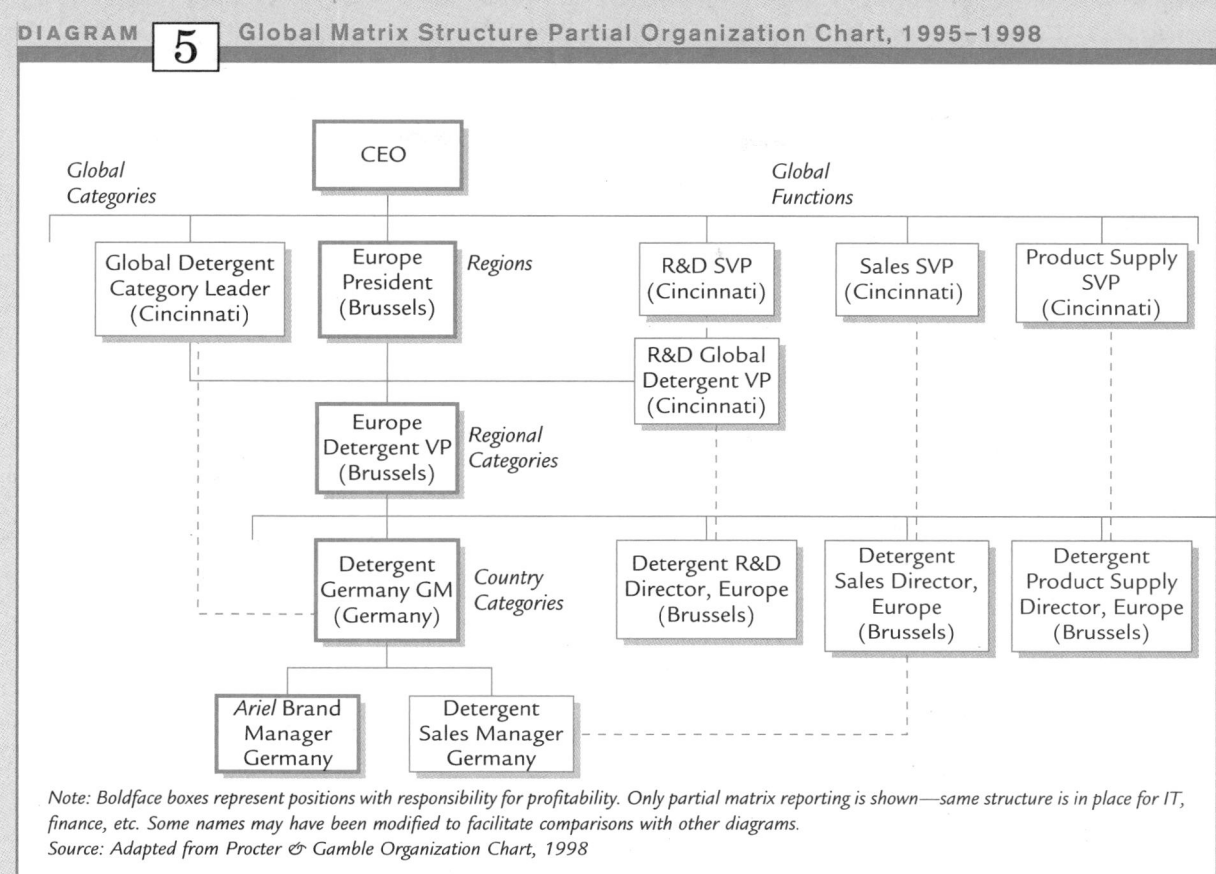

Note: Boldface boxes represent positions with responsibility for profitability. Only partial matrix reporting is shown—same structure is in place for IT, finance, etc. Some names may have been modified to facilitate comparisons with other diagrams.
Source: Adapted from Procter & Gamble Organization Chart, 1998

of knowledge, transfer of best practices, elimination of intraregional redundancies, and standardization of activities. The new matrix organization also allowed for manufacturing, purchasing, engineering, and distribution to be integrated, in 1987, into one global product-supply function, which managed the supply chain from beginning to end. Regionally managed product-supply groups could extract massive savings by consolidating country manufacturing plants and distribution centers into higher-scale regional facilities. In 1993, as part of the massive "Strengthening Global Effectiveness" (SGE) restructuring program, the product-supply organization integrated the supply chain of a string of acquisitions that P&G had made, primarily in beauty care. Standardization allowed for quick rationalization of acquired assets and smooth integration into the existing manufacturing-and-distribution network; 30 of 147 plants were eliminated.[20] Meanwhile a stronger global sales organization with regional leadership was transformed into the Customer Business Development (CBD) function. CBD developed closer global relationships with big customers, one result of which was the

unprecedented step of co-locating with Wal-Mart in Bentonville, Arkansas, to pursue joint strategic planning. Coupled with its early supply-chain initiatives, this undertaking allowed P&G to be a first mover in electronic integration with customers, leading to disproportionate share growth with mass discounters. Finally, significant initial standardization in IT systems was made possible by a globally managed IT organization. By 1997, financial and accounting information storage had been consolidated at three global data-storage centers.

Global category management also generated impressive benefits. Global category managers developed close relationships with strong global R&D product-category organizations, helping to standardize and accelerate global product launches. By the early 1990s, it took only four years, on average, to globalize a new initiative. This advance allowed P&G to quickly inject new technologies into recently acquired beauty care brands like *Pantene, Olay,* and *Old Spice.* For example, two-in-one shampoo-and-conditioner technology was developed at the Sharon Woods beauty-care global technical center in Cincinnati in the mid-1980s. The

EXHIBIT 2   Procter & Gamble Net Sales, 1985–2000

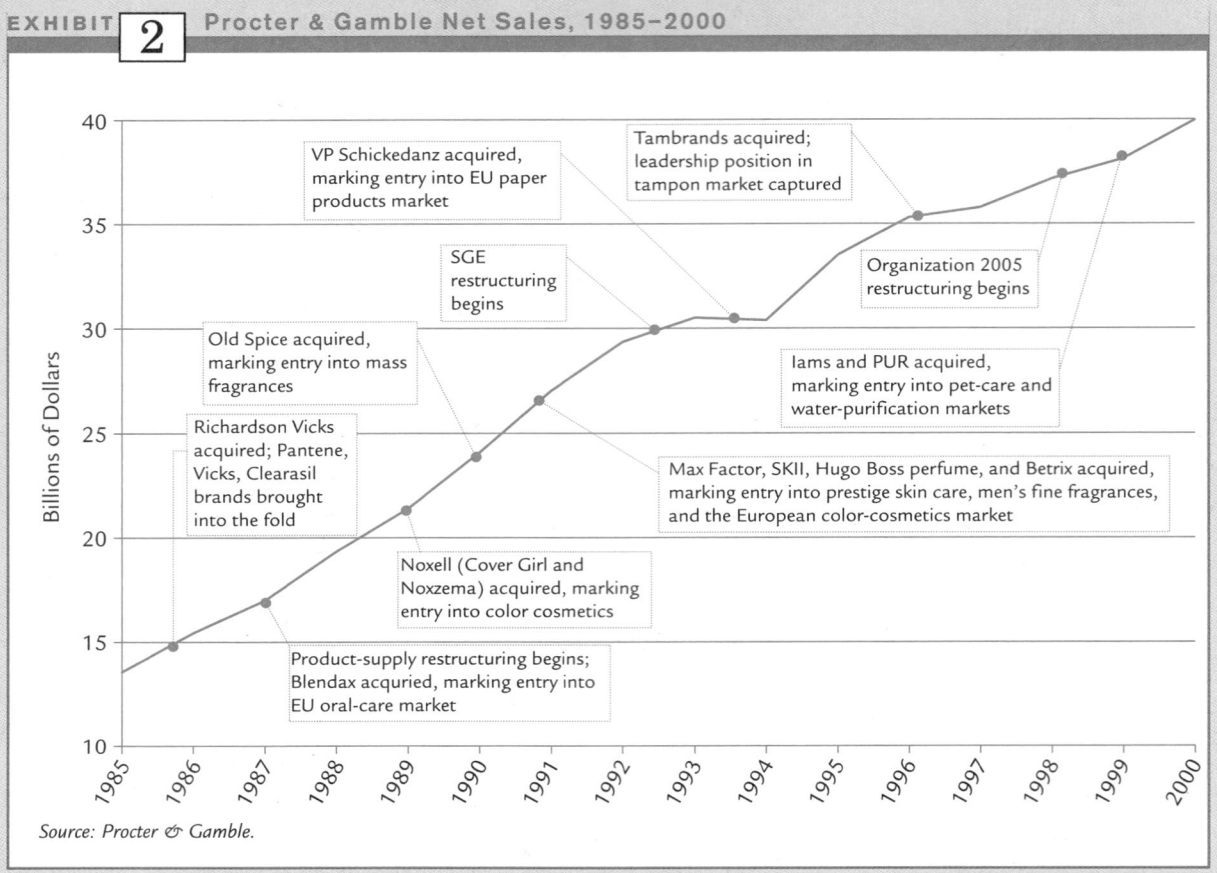

Source: Procter & Gamble.

EXHIBIT 3   P&G Income Statement, Fiscal Years 1992-2000

	1992	1993	1994	1995	1996	1997	1998	1999	2000
Net Sales	29,362	30,433	30,385	33,482	35,284	35,764	37,154	38,125	39,951
Cost of Goods Sold	17,324	17,683	17,338	19,561	20,938	20,510	20,896	21,027	21,018
Gross Profit	**12,038**	**12,750**	**13,047**	**13,921**	**14,346**	**15,254**	**16,258**	**17,098**	**18,933**
Total SG&A	9,171	9,589	9,377	9,677	9,531	9,766	10,203	10,845	12,165
Advertising Expense*	*2,693*	*2,973*	*2,996*	*3,284*	*3,254*	*3,466*	*3,704*	*3,639*	*3,793*
R&D Expense*	*861*	*956*	*964*	*1,148*	*1,399*	*1,469*	*1,546*	*1,726*	*1,899*
Operating Income	**2,867**	**3,161**	**3,670**	**4,244**	**4,815**	**5,488**	**6,055**	**6,253**	**6,768**
Net Interest Expense	(510)	(552)	(482)	(488)	(221)	(239)	(347)	(650)	(722)
Other non-op Income	425	404	158	244	120	-	-	235	304
Restructuring Charges	-	(2,705)	-	-	-	-	-	-	(814)
Other Items	103	41	-	-	(45)	-	-	-	-
Income Tax Expense	1,013	80	1,135	1,355	1,623	1,834	1,928	2,075	1,994
Net Income from Cont. Ops.	**1,872**	**269**	**2,211**	**2,645**	**3,046**	**3,415**	**3,780**	**3,763**	**3,542**
Employees ('000)	*106*	*103.5*	*96.5*	*99.2*	*103*	*106*	*110*	*110*	*110*

Source: Procter & Gamble Annual Reports.

EXHIBIT 4   P&G Cash Flow Statements, Fiscal Years 1992–2000

	1992	1993	1994	1995	1996	1997	1998	1999	2000
Net Income	1,872	269	2,211	2,645	3,046	3,415	3,780	3,763	1,872
Depreciation	1,051	1,140	1,134	1,253	1,358	1,487	1,598	2,148	2,191
Asset Writedowns	-	2,705	-	-	-	-	-	-	-
Other Operating Activities	125	(1,065)	196	181	328	(26)	(101)	(60)	463
Change in Working Capital	(23)	289	108	(511)	(574)	1,006	(392)	(307)	(1,521)
Cash from Op. Activities	**3,025**	**3,338**	**3,649**	**3,568**	**4,158**	**5,882**	**4,885**	**5,544**	**4,675**
Capital Expenditure	(1,911)	(1,911)	(1,841)	(2,146)	(2,179)	(2,129)	(2,559)	(2,828)	(3,018)
Sale of PP&E	291	725	105	310	402	520	555	434	419
Cash Acquisitions	(1,240)	(138)	(295)	(623)	(358)	(150)	(3,269)	(137)	(2,967)
Invest. In Marketable Sec.	-	(306)	23	96	(331)	(309)	63	356	221
Cash from Investing	**(2,860)**	**(1,630)**	**(2,008)**	**(2,363)**	**(2,466)**	**(2,068)**	**(5,210)**	**(2,175)**	**(5,345)**
Net Change in Debt	1,019	(215)	(664)	(490)	(38)	(660)	2,853	1,341	3,030
Net Purch. Of Com. Stock	(49)	(55)	(14)	(115)	(432)	(1,652)	(1,929)	(2,533)	(1,430)
Total Dividends Paid	(788)	(850)	(949)	(1,062)	(1,202)	(1,329)	(1,462)	(1,626)	(1,796)
Other Financing Activities	71	77	36	67	89	134	158	212	-
Cash from Financing	**253**	**(1,043)**	**(1,591)**	**(1,600)**	**(1,583)**	**(3,507)**	**(380)**	**(2,606)**	**(196)**
FX Rate Adj.	(26)	(119)	1	50	(63)	(31)	(96)	(18)	(13)
Net Change in Cash	**392**	**546**	**51**	**(345)**	**46**	**276**	**(801)**	**745**	**(879)**

Source: Procter & Gamble Annual Reports.

hair-care global category president then helped roll it out globally under the *Pantene* brand name with a consistent worldwide marketing message and identity. In just over a decade, increased global focus on product categories helped P&G's beauty-care division to grow from a $600 million orphan to a highly strategic $7 billion business.

Matrix Runs into Problems (1995–1998)

Strong regional functions had produced extraordinary competitive advantages, but as the organization entered the mid-1990s they appeared to create gridlock. The matrix management structure had never been symmetrical. Though most functions nominally had straight-line reporting through regional management and only dotted-line reporting through functional management, the function retained a high degree of de-facto control because it determined career paths and promotion for its employees. Ultimately each function developed its own strategic agenda, which largely revolved around maximizing its own power within the company rather than cooperating with other functions and business units to win in the marketplace. Management by functional conflict initially served as an effective system of checks and balances but eventually led to poor strategic alignment throughout the

company. For example, while product supply made global efforts to reduce the number of chemical suppliers for P&G products, R&D sought out high-performance ingredients to enhance product performance, no matter where they came from. Neither sought an optimal tradeoff between performance and cost; each tried to maximize its particular parameter. It was very difficult for regional managers focused on particular countries to address these global functional conflicts. If, for example, product supply wanted to use a less expensive replacement surfactant in laundry formulations, it could demonstrate huge potential savings that a lone country manager would be hard-pressed to dispute.

It also became clear that the matrix structure had not fully resolved the tension between regional and product-category management. Regional managers still had sole responsibility for financial results, and thus it was they who ultimately chose whether or not to launch initiatives made available by the global category-management organizations. R&D divisions and global category leaders were aligned globally by product category, and therefore fought hard to globalize new technological and brand innovations quickly. But they still had to obtain agreement from each regional manager, and sometimes even from large-country managers, to launch a product in a given area. Regional managers would often hesitate to launch a particular product even if it made sense for the company strategically because it could weaken their upcoming profit and loss statement. As a result, the company's track record of globalizing innovation and brands had stagnated and seemed to be falling behind that of more focused rivals. For example, *Cover Girl,* a U.S. cosmetics brand that P&G had acquired in 1989, still had not been globalized by 1997. By contrast *Maybelline,* acquired by L'Oreal in 1996, was globalized in just a few years and was on its way to becoming a billion-dollar brand.

To make matters worse, competitors were catching up quickly. P&G had been a first mover in supply-chain consolidations and integration with customers, but by the latter half of the decade over 200 other vendors had opened "embassies" to Wal-Mart in Bentonville. As a result P&G's shares in big-box discount stores had fallen by 3.3 percent since 1993 in categories representing roughly two-thirds of the business.[21] As a result, sales grew only 2.6 percent in 1997 and 1998 by contrast to 8.5 percent on average in the 1980s. Ultimately, the question was whether the matrix organizational structure was internally coherent or scalable over the long term. Full accountability for results could not really be assigned to regional profit centers because they couldn't fully manage functional strategy and resource allocation. Many believed that this scenario had created a culture of risk aversion and avoidance of failure above all else. With over 100 profit centers, it just seemed like there were "too many cooks in the kitchen." Furthermore, as P&G diversified, an ever-increasing number of country product-category GM positions would have to be created. By the mid-1990s, for example, Germany alone had roughly a dozen category GMs.

Organization 2005

In September 1998, P&G announced a six-year restructuring plan—Organization 2005. The company estimated that the plan would cost $1.9 billion over five years and would achieve $900 million in annual after-tax cost savings by 2004. It called for voluntary separations of 15,000 employees by 2001, with almost 10,500 overseas.[22] Forty five percent of all job separations would result from global product-supply consolidations and a quarter from exploitation of scale benefits arising from more standardized business processes.[23] The plan also called to eliminate six management layers, reducing the total from 13 to 7.[24] The second part of Organization 2005 entailed dismantling the matrix organizational structure and replacing it with an amalgam of interdependent organizations: Global Business Units with primary responsibility for product, Market Development Organizations with primary

responsibility for markets, and a Global Business Services unit responsible for managing internal business processes. This radically new organizational design, described in detail below, was designed to improve the speed with which P&G innovated and globalized its innovations. Many at the company expected that, once in place, Organization 2005 should generate consistent sales growth of 6–8 percent and profit growth of 13–15 percent per year.

Global Business Units (GBUs) Global Business Units were responsible for product development, brand design, business strategy and new business development. Each operated autonomously focusing on a different product category, such as Fabric and Home Care or Tissue and Towel (see the middle section of Exhibit 5). In total, there were seven GBUs each with complete profit responsibility, and benchmarked against focused product-category competitors. Each GBU was led by a president, who reported directly to the CEO and was a member of the global leadership council that determined overall company strategy. At a GBU level, Vice Presidents of Marketing, R&D, Product Supply, New Business Development, and support functions such as IT implementation reported to the GBU President (see the middle section of Diagram 6). The new business development function of GBUs was managed separately from the rest of the GBU. To assure that the R&D divisions of different GBUs would share technological innovations, a technology council composed of the GBU R&D VPs would be formed to cross-pollinate ideas. This structure would increase agility and reduce costs through accelerated global standardization of manufacturing processes and better coordination of marketing activities across countries. Organizing product supply by product category rather than geography, for example, would allow for global standardization of diaper-manufacturing processes, which were still on 12 different regional platforms.[25] Combined with elimination of the arduous process of obtaining launch approval from regional managers, this scenario would finally allow for systematically faster global rollouts of innovations and new brands.

Market Development Organizations (MDOs) Market Development Organizations (MDOs) were designed to take responsibility for "tailoring the company's global programs to local markets and [for using] their knowledge of local consumers and retailers to help P&G develop market strategies to guide the entire business."[26] Customer Business Development functions previously dispersed among various business units would be consolidated regionally and converted into the line functions in each MDO. Consumer Market

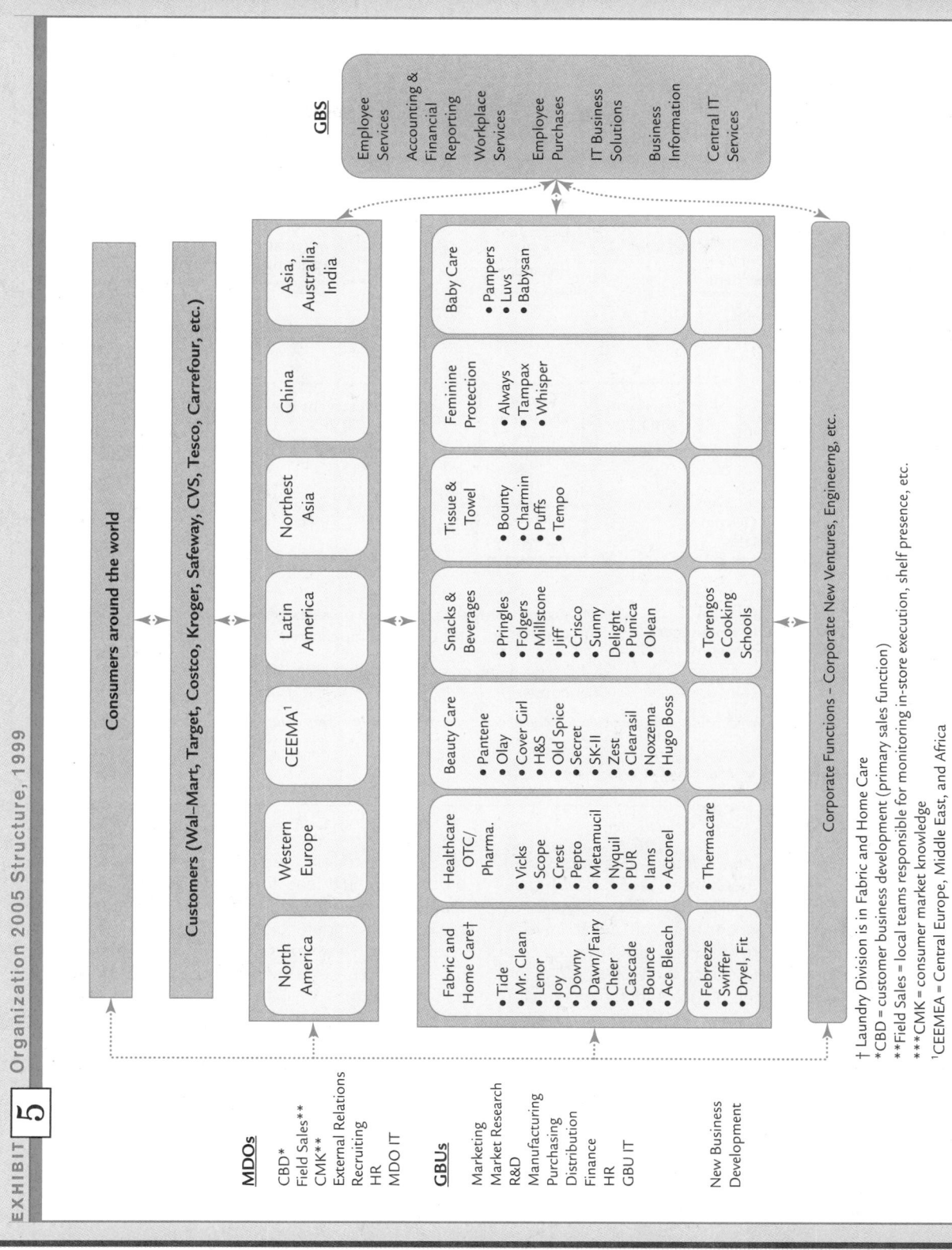

EXHIBIT 5 Organization 2005 Structure, 1999

Consumers around the world

Customers (Wal-Mart, Target, Costco, Kroger, Safeway, CVS, Tesco, Carrefour, etc.)

GBS
- Employee Services
- Accounting & Financial Reporting
- Workplace Services
- Employee Purchases
- IT Business Solutions
- Business Information
- Central IT Services

MDOs
- North America
- Western Europe
- CEEMA[1]
- Latin America
- Northest Asia
- China
- Asia, Australia, India

MDOs
- CBD*
- Field Sales**
- CMK**
- External Relations
- Recruiting
- HR
- MDO IT

GBUs
- Marketing
- Market Research
- R&D
- Manufacturing
- Purchasing
- Distribution
- Finance
- HR
- GBU IT

Fabric and Home Care†
- Tide
- Mr. Clean
- Lenor
- Joy
- Downy
- Dawn/Fairy
- Cheer
- Cascade
- Bounce
- Ace Bleach

Healthcare OTC/Pharma.
- Vicks
- Scope
- Crest
- Pepto
- Metamucil
- Nyquil
- PUR
- Iams
- Actonel

Beauty Care
- Pantene
- Olay
- Cover Girl
- H&S
- Old Spice
- Secret
- SK-II
- Zest
- Clearasil
- Noxzema
- Hugo Boss

Snacks & Beverages
- Pringles
- Folgers
- Millstone
- Jiff
- Crisco
- Sunny Delight
- Punica
- Olean

Tissue & Towel
- Bounty
- Charmin
- Puffs
- Tempo

Feminine Protection
- Always
- Tampax
- Whisper

Baby Care
- Pampers
- Luvs
- Babysan

- Febreeze
- Swiffer
- Dryel, Fit

- Thermacare

- Torengos
- Cooking Schools

New Business Development

Corporate Functions – Corporate New Ventures, Engineerng, etc.

† Laundry Division is in Fabric and Home Care
*CBD = customer business development (primary sales function)
**Field Sales = local teams responsible for monitoring in-store execution, shelf presence, etc.
***CMK = consumer market knowledge
[1]CEEMA = Central Europe, Middle East, and Africa

Source: Adapted from Procter & Gamble organization charts, 1999

DIAGRAM $\boxed{6}$ **Initial Design of Organization 2005, Partial Organization Chart, 1999**

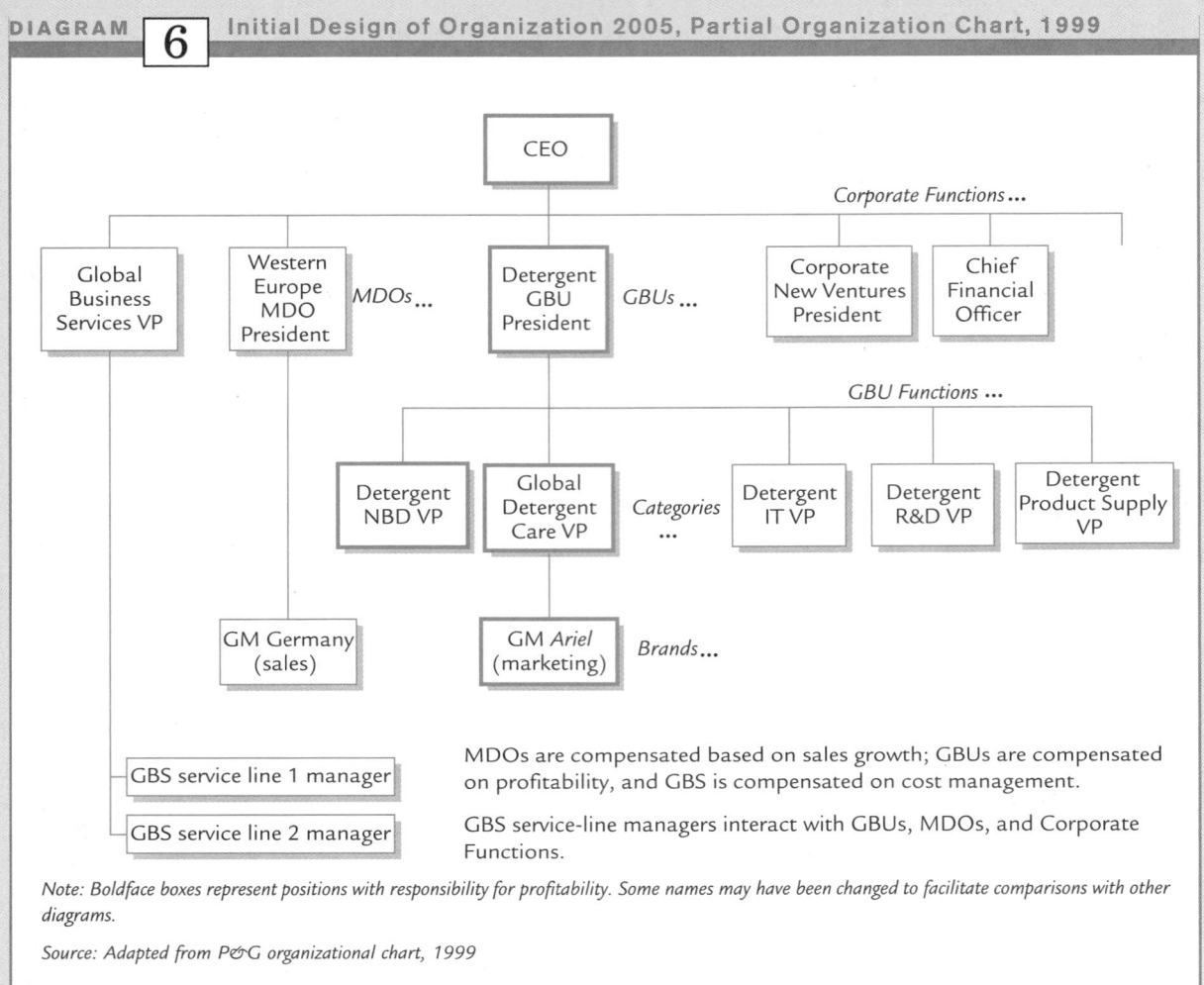

MDOs are compensated based on sales growth; GBUs are compensated on profitability, and GBS is compensated on cost management.

GBS service-line managers interact with GBUs, MDOs, and Corporate Functions.

Note: Boldface boxes represent positions with responsibility for profitability. Some names may have been changed to facilitate comparisons with other diagrams.

Source: Adapted from P&G organizational chart, 1999

Knowledge, field sales, and support functions would report to CBD. In total, there were seven MDOs (see the top part of Exhibit 5). Unlike the GBUs, they did not have complete profit responsibility, but were instead compensated on sales growth. Each MDO was led by a president who reported directly to the CEO and, like the GBU presidents, sat on the global leadership council.

Global Business Services (GBS) The third leg of the new organizational structure, Global Business Services (GBS) unit was given an ambitious plan to standardize, consolidate, streamline, and ultimately strengthen business processes and IT platforms across GBUs and MDOs around the world. Before GBS, business services, and IT systems for processes like accounting transactions, payroll processing, and facilities management were duplicated and performed differently across

regions. Centralizing responsibility for managing these processes could lead to economies of scale, while at the same time allowing GBUs and MDOs to focus on their core competencies. GBS was organized as a cost center. The head of GBS reported directly to the CEO, but was not a member of the global leadership council.

The first task of GBS was to move the entire company onto a single shared SAP software system, which would require re-engineering 70 percent of the company's IT systems. In total, 72 systems across 70 countries had to be standardized and globalized. Then a set of "service lines" (see the right side of Exhibit 5) for business and employee support were created and managed centrally by business-process directors. GBS established three "follow-the-sun" service centers, in Costa Rica, England, and the Philippines, to perform business-process work 24 hours a day. This arrangement allowed GBS to achieve critical mass in business-process execution and to take advantage of wage arbitrage.

Routines and HR policies In addition to changes in the formal architecture, Organization 2005 sought to change the routines in the organization. Many decisions that had once been made by committee were now assigned to individuals. As a result, many business tasks that had taken months, such as obtaining advertising-copy approvals, could now be accomplished in days. Budgeting processes were also streamlined, integrating formerly separate marketing, payroll, and initiative budgets into a single business-planning process whereby all budget elements could be reviewed and approved jointly.[27] Finally, P&G also overhauled its incentive system, while maintaining the promote-from-within policy. The performance-based portion of compensation for upper-level executives increased from 20 percent (10 percent up or down) to 80 percent (40 percent up or down) of base pay.[28] Stock-option compensation, formerly limited to 9,000 employees, was extended to 100,000.[29]

Organization 2005 in action

To implement the extensive restructuring program, on January 1, 1999, the P&G board installed a new CEO, Durk Jager. A long time P&G employee, Jager had been a key player in developing the plans for Organization 2005 while occupying the position of COO. He hoped to use Organization 2005 to change P&G's risk-averse regionally managed structure so that it could launch new blockbuster brands based on new technologies rather than incremental improvements of existing products.[30] To this end, he allocated a large share of P&G's resources to GBU NBD groups and a Corporate New Ventures function (see Exhibit 6). This led to the development of several new categories and brands such as *Febreze, Swiffer,* and *Dryel.* To drive his vision, Jager frequently scrutinized P&G's R&D portfolio and personally stewarded new technologies through the pipeline that he felt were promising.

In October 1999, P&G's fiscal first quarter results showed immediate acceleration in business performance. Sales were up 5 percent over the previous year, a marked improvement over the 2.6 percent annual revenue growth P&G had experienced the previous two years. Core net earnings, excluding restructuring costs, increased by 10 percent. Though these numbers fell short of the long-term goals, they were quite respectable for the first full quarter of any restructuring program. As a consequence, P&G's stock appreciated

significantly (see Exhibit 7). The stock price reached an all-time high of $118.38, when the next quarterly report came out on January 30, 2000, stating that sales grew an impressive 7 percent and core net earnings increased 13 percent (see Exhibits 8 and 9)

Yet, the situation deteriorated drastically on March 7, 2000, when P&G announced that instead of the expected 8 percent increase in quarterly earnings, the core earnings would be 10 percent lower than the 1999 January-March quarter, despite an increase in revenue. Higher-than-expected raw-material costs, delays in FDA approvals, and particularly intense international competition were blamed for the situation. That day the company's stock lost 30 percent of its value, closing at $57.25, less than a half of what it traded at in January. Jager told analysts:

> *We've had a track record of meeting our bottom-line commitments [and] have learned that we simply can't focus on the top line to make the bottom line grow. We are getting more innovations to market faster because of our Organization 2005 structure and culture changes.[31] This has been a transition year. Going forward we are going to focus on P&G basics—hard-nosed cost management as well as accelerating sales growth.[32]*

Other executives noted that the company had 50 new products in the pipeline, including *Impress,* a patented food wrap that formed a water-tight seal with the application of pressure. The growing sales of *Febreze, Swiffer,* and *Dryel* were also expected to help reverse the crisis quickly. Yet, the situation became even worse when P&G announced its official quarterly numbers on April 25, 2000. Core net earnings excluding restructuring costs had fallen 18 percent while sales increased 6 percent despite a 2 percent hit from exchange-rate changes. "We are redoubling our efforts to manage costs," Jager told analysts.[33] The stock lost 10 percent of its value, giving back some gains to close in the mid-60s.[34]

Despite executives' promises, P&G disappointed once again on June 8, 2000. Fourth-quarter profits were flat, against the expectations of 15–17 percent increase. P&G also lowered its future quarterly sales growth estimates to 2–3 percent, casting doubt on whether Organization 2005 was even lifting the top line. Increased competition, lower volume growth and negative currency effects were again blamed for the disappointing results. Market-research companies confirmed P&G's poor competitive position citing its loss of U.S. market share in 16 out of 30 categories since the preceding year.[35] P&G stock lost 7 percent, falling to $57 after the announcement; it had been the

EXHIBIT 6 Jager's Vision for Organization 2005

BREADTH OF BUSINESSES PROVIDES
ADVANTAGE

The first key to faster growth, greater business vitality, is increasing the pace of innovation at P&G. This has been true for us in the past and is just as true today.

P&G is unique when it comes to innovation. We compete in nearly 50 product categories – laundry products, toothpaste, paper towels, personal cleansing, cough and cold, bone disease therapies, snacks, diapers, cosmetics – and many others.

Some people argue that such a diversity of categories leads to a lack of focus. We see it differently. The breadth of our business enables us to connect technologies from seemingly unrelated businesses in unexpected ways.

We don't leave these connections to chance. Our Technology Council brings together R&D leaders from our existing product categories to more quickly transfer technologies from one business to another. Even as the Company grows bigger and bigger, the Technology Council accelerates the exchange of ideas much like the discussions that happened over the lunch table when we were much, much smaller.

Our Innovation Leadership Team, which I chair, is fueling our growth in new product categories. It funds promising ideas that fall outside our businesses, from seed-level investment all the way through test market. Previously, these kinds of ideas would often go undeveloped.

INVESTING IN R&D With an investment of $1.7 billion this year, P&G is the 21st largest U.S.-based and 52nd largest global investor in research and development. We invest to drive clear product superiority in our core businesses and to acquire new technologies and fund entrepreneurial programs that create big, discontinuous product innovation. Ten years ago, our investment in R&D was 2.9% of net sales. Today it represents 4.8% of net sales. www.pg.com/about/md

P&G'S R&D INVESTMENT AS A PERCENTAGE OF NET SALES

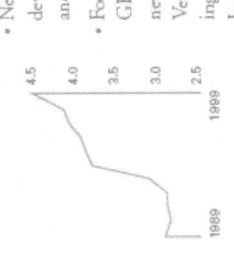

Connections create breakthroughs. Last year, for example, we were granted more U.S. patents than any of our competitors. We hold over 25,000 patents worldwide, and this technology base is paying off.

We are launching more new-to-the-world products than at any other time in our history – products like Febreze, our fabric refresher; Swiffer, our disposable mop; and Dryel, our home care product for dry-cleanables.

We are also introducing an unprecedented number of major improvements on established brands such as Pampers Rash Guard, the first diaper specifically designed to protect against diaper rash, and a new Tide with Bleach that kills 99.9% of bacteria.

CONNECTIONS CREATE
BREAKTHROUGHS

Today, we have tapped only a portion of our innovation capacity. With Organization 2005, we are making changes to unleash this capability and to capitalize on the new marketplace in which we compete.

UNLEASHING INNOVATION

- New Global Business Units (GBUs) leverage our scale. We will develop products and plans globally, to better utilize our technology and get products to the world faster.

- Focus on new business will increase our innovative output. Each GBU has a dedicated New Business Development unit to create new brands in related categories. In addition, our Corporate New Ventures group focuses on big ideas that don't fit neatly within existing businesses – and helps commercialize ideas funded by the Innovation Leadership Team.

Source: Excerpted from Procter & Gamble, 1999 Annual Report (Cincinnati: Procter & Gamble, 1999), pp. 3–5, http://www.pg.com/investors/annualreports.jhtml, accessed March 2006.

EXHIBIT 7   Procter & Gamble Share Price History, 1997–2000

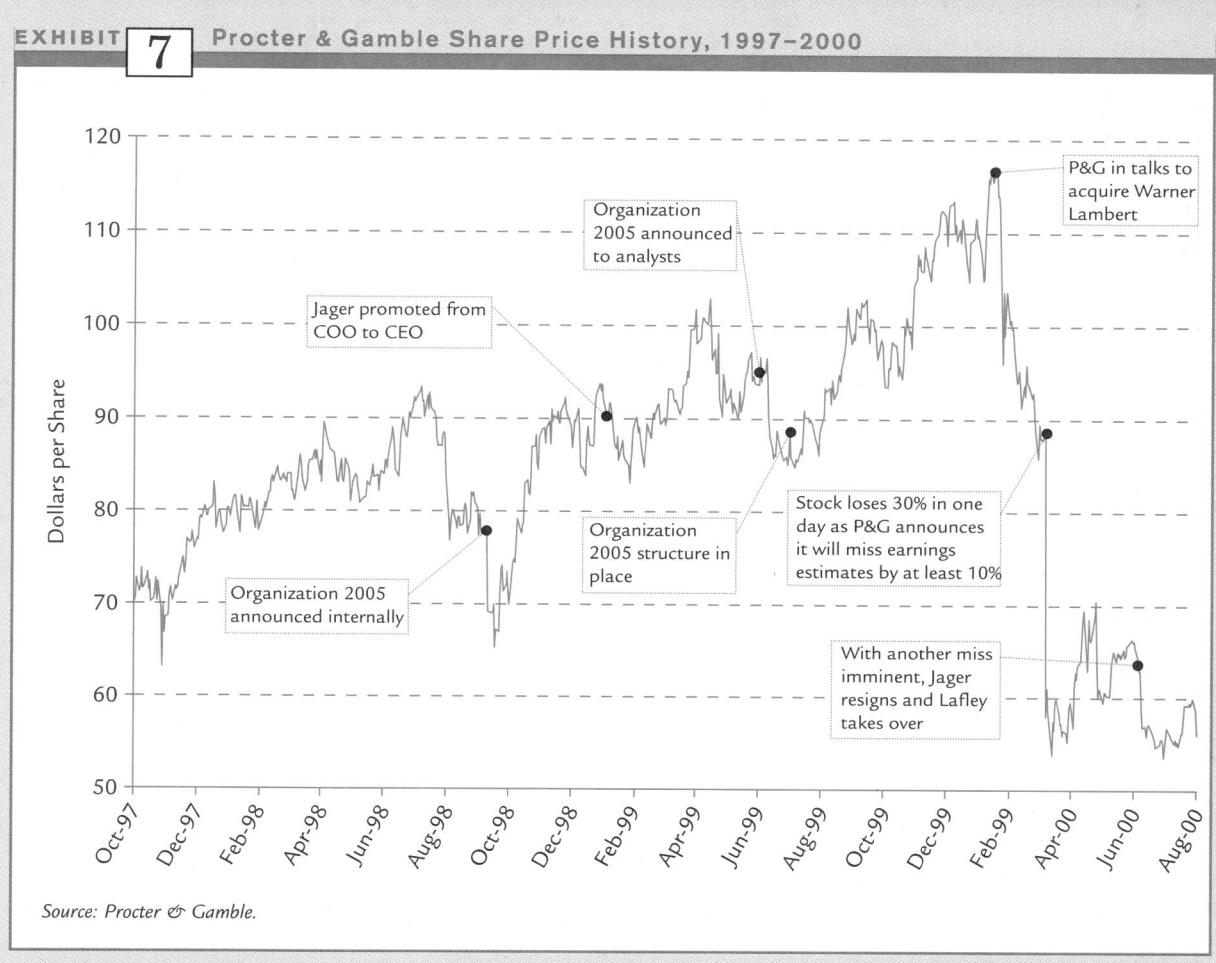

Source: *Procter & Gamble.*

worst-performing component of the Dow over the previous six months.[36] Jager had no choice but to resign.

Appendix: Selected Competitors of P&G

Unilever Unilever was founded in 1930 through a merger of a Dutch margarine company Margarine Unie with British soap company Lever Brothers. In 2000 Unilever generated $44 billion in revenues and employed 261,000 people, making it the second-largest consumer products company, after $50bn Nestlé. Fifty percent of Unilever's sales came from foods, 22 percent from home care and 26 percent from personal care.[37] Unilever managed 1600 brands, with a quarter of them generating 91 percent of revenue.[38] Unilever's products were extremely diverse, including *Lipton* tea, *Ben & Jerry's* ice cream, *Calvin Klein* fragrances, *Dove* personal cleansers, *Axe* deodorants, *I Can't Believe It's*

Not Butter margarine, *Slim-Fast* diet foods, *Q-Tips,* *Domestos* toilet cleaner, and *Vaseline* petroleum jelly. Unilever was one of the most diversified consumer-products companies—largely by acquiring hundreds of small to medium-sized local companies. Unilever wanted to expand its share of revenues from developing countries from 33 percent to 50 percent by 2010. Unilever considered itself a "truly multilocal multinational," and utilized a highly decentralized organizational structure in which geographic organizations bore sole responsibility for financial performance and full control over resource allocation across brands and product categories.[39] Functional organizations such as manufacturing, R&D, marketing, and sales were managed regionally, and often by country, for maximum responsiveness to local needs.

In February 2000 Unilever announced a restructuring plan—*Path to Growth*—aimed at annual sales growth of 5 percent and operating margins of 15 percent within

EXHIBIT 8   P&G GBU Financial Data, 1998–2000 Fiscal Years

	Fabric & Home Care*			Paper			Beauty Care			Health Care			Food & Beverage		
	1998	1999	2000	1998	1999	2000	1998	1999	2000	1998	1999	2000	1998	1999	2000
Net Sales	11,019	11,415	12,157	11,685	12,190	12,044	7,469	7,376	7,389	2,889	2,876	3,909	4,620	4,655	4,634
EBIT	2,240	2,417	2,318	1,772	2,195	1,817	1,379	1,457	1,393	381	372	540	477	528	566
Depreciation	295	293	354	611	638	664	198	198	194	105	107	159	135	149	153
Net Earnings	1,406	1,497	1,450	990	1,278	1,069	845	917	894	232	242	335	294	328	364
Total Assets		5,047	5,477		8,184	8,415		3,754	3,497		1,556	2,229		2,598	2,611
CapEx		638	807		1,327	1,282		285	310		143	195		237	235
Key Brands	Tide, Ariel, Downy, Lenor			Pampers, Always Charmin, Bounty			Pantene, Olay, Covergirl, SK-II			Vics, Actonel			Folgers, Pringles, Jiff, Crisco		

*Fabric and Home Care includes Laundry Division.

Note: All numbers in Millions of 2000 U.S. dollars. The difference between GBU totals and the corporate is attributable to corporate eliminations, or corporate level assets.

Source: Procter & Gamble, 2000 Annual Report (Cincinnati: Procter & Gamble, 2000), p. 40, http://www.pg.com/investors/annualreports.jhtml, accessed March 2006.

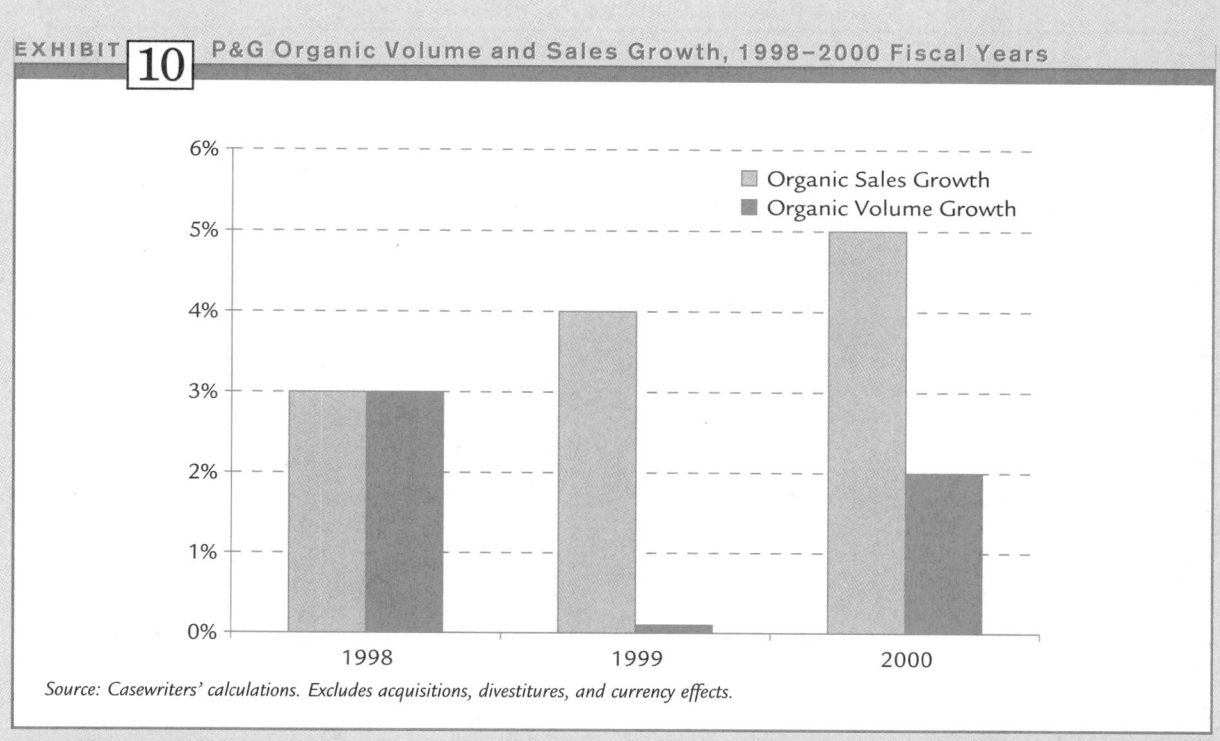

EXHIBIT **9** P&G Regional Sales/Profit Breakdowns, 2000 Fiscal Year

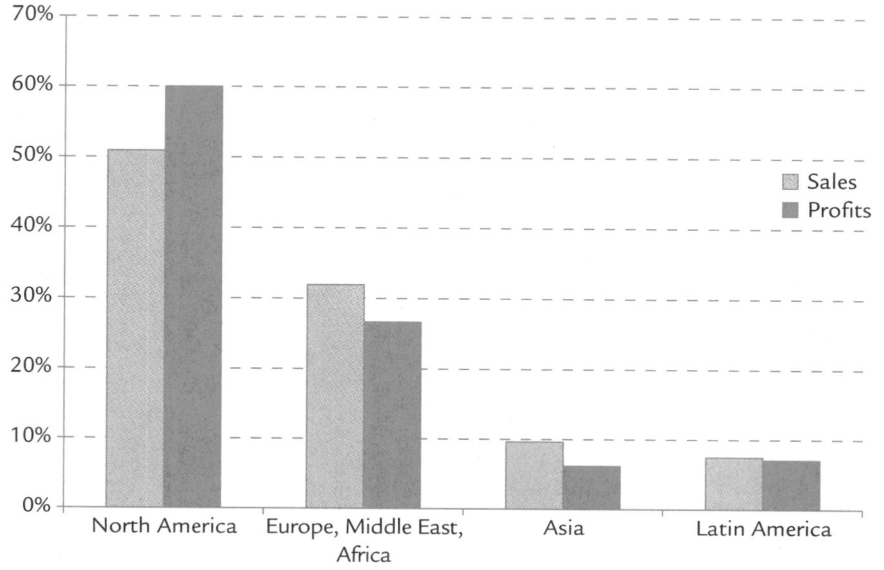

Source: Procter & Gamble, 2000 Annual Report (Cincinnati: Procter & Gamble, 2000), http://www.pg.com/investors/annualreports.jhtml, accessed March 2006.

EXHIBIT **10** P&G Organic Volume and Sales Growth, 1998–2000 Fiscal Years

Source: Casewriters' calculations. Excludes acquisitions, divestitures, and currency effects.

EXHIBIT 11   Financial Comparisons with Key Competitors

2000 Fiscal Year Income Statement (In Millions of 2000 Dollars)

	Unilever	Colgate	Kimberly-Clark	L'Oreal
Net Sales	44,254	9,358	13,982	11,709
Cost of Goods Sold		4,000	7,607	
Gross Profit		5,358	6,375	
SG&A		3,300	3,113	
Operating Income		2,058	3,262	1,780
Depreciation		338	673	356
Operating Profit	2,981	1,720	2,589	1,424
Net Interest Expense		204	243	101
Other Non-Operating Inc (Exp)		73	275	-100
Special Items		9	1	0
Pre-Tax Earnings	2,396	1,598	2,622	1,223
Income Tax Expense		503	759	451
Minority Interest		33	63	
Earnings from Cont. Ops.	1,017	1,062	1,800	954

2000 Fiscal Year Supplemental Items

	Unilever	Colgate	Kimberly-Clark	L'Oreal
Advertising Expense	6,144	551	349	ND
R&D Expense	1,114	176	277	360
Capital Expenditures	1,249	367	1,170	444
Employees	261,000	38,300	66,300	48,200

Average Rates of Growth, 1999 and 2000 Fiscal Years

	Unilever	Colgate	Kimberly-Clark	L'Oreal
Sales Growth	2%	7%	10%	13%
Volume Growth	2%	6%	9%	ND

Source: Procter & Gamble Annual Reports.

four years. The 1,200 brands that together generated only 9 percent of revenue were to be eliminated, as were 25,000 jobs and a quarter of manufacturing plants. The remaining brands would receive additional $400 million in advertising and promotional spend in addition to $320 million that would otherwise go to the marginal brands. Supply-chain information-technology systems would be standardized and improved to optimize this new fully integrated network of manufacturing plants and distribution facilities. Purchasing was to be further automated and centralized to reduce costs. The program was expected to cost $3.2 billion through 2004, including asset writedowns. To align management with the new growth targets, performance-based pay would increase from 40 percent to 100 percent of base pay. Once this first-stage streamlining of brands and supply-chain systems

was completed, further reduction in overheads would become possible through significant business simplification. Beginning in 2004, some financial processes would be consolidated into a small number of shared service centers around the world.[40]

To aid the new plan, Unilever unveiled its new organizational structure in April 2000. Each regional organization would be split into two divisions: foods and home and personal care (HPC). Each division would possess its own sales, marketing, and regional innovation functions. Regional presidents would retain profit responsibility but would manage the two divisions as separate entities. In pursuit of a more global focus on products and brands, each regional president would serve on either a foods or an HPC executive committee. Each executive committee would be chaired by a divisional director whose compensation would be based on global divisional performance. The R&D and supply-chain functions would then be globally consolidated by product division. This arrangement would allow the individual foods and HPC supply chains to develop platform manufacturing and distribution solutions across regions. Large global technical centers would focus on core technologies that would ultimately be adapted regionally in smaller regional innovation centers.[41] Just as Path to Growth got under way, Unilever made its largest-ever acquisition, Bestfoods, for $24.4 billion, bringing the large global brands Hellmann's and Knorr into the fold along with an array of U. S. favorites like Skippy peanut butter and Mazola cooking oil.

Colgate-Palmolive In 2000 Colgate-Palmolive (CP) generated $9.4 billion in revenues and employed 38,000 people. Since 1990, revenues had been growing at 5 percent compound rate, while net profits soared at 13 percent per annum. Seventy-five percent of Colgate's sales came from roughly 25 global brands, with *Colgate* toothpaste being a multibillion-dollar brand in its own right. CP enjoyed global share leadership in oral care, where its namesake dentifrice brand had literally become the word for toothpaste in many languages. Colgate also had an almost 40 percent share of the global dishwashing-liquid market and a leadership share in the global high-end pet-nutrition market. Oral care, personal care, and pet nutrition had rapidly grown share in the preceding five years.[42]

CP managed its business through four regional reporting subsidiaries. Each subsidiary had two product-category divisions: oral/personal/household care and pet nutrition. In a matrix reporting structure similar to P&G's, general managers of regions were balanced by heads of product-category divisions. R&D was an almost purely corporate function, with major global technical centers delivering platform technologies to be commercialized around the world. Manufacturing used large regional focused factories, purchasing was being centralized regionally, and SAP already ran 80 percent of Colgate's systems worldwide.[43]

Kimberly-Clark Kimberly-Clark (KC), the world's largest tissue manufacturer, focused its $14-billion, 64,000-employee business almost entirely on paper products. Fifty-five percent of sales came from North America, 15 percent from Europe, and 30 percent from the rest of the world. KC had the highest operating margin of any paper company (nearly 18 percent, versus the second-highest, P&G Paper, at just over 12 percent).[44] *Kleenex* and *Huggies* were global billion-dollar brands, and KC had number-one or number-two market share in over 80 countries. *Huggies* had surpassed the category creator, Pampers, in the United States in 1992 and currently held a commanding 15 percent share advantage.[45] KC had averaged 6–8 percent sales growth and double-digit earnings growth for 15 years.[46] In Europe, KC was in the process of shifting from a country-based sales force to a customer-based sales force; each of KC's 32 main customers was assigned a dedicated sales force.[47]

L'Oreal L'Oreal was the largest beauty company in the world in 2000, with sales of $12.8 billion in 150 countries and 48,000 employees. L'Oreal's sales were concentrated primarily in 15 global brands. The *L'Oreal* brand alone had global sales of over $4 billion; the largest luxury brand, *Lancôme*, had global sales of nearly $2 billion. Excluding changes in financial reporting, L'Oreal's sales had increased by over 150 percent since 1996, largely through acquisition and rapid globalization of strong local brands.[48] L'Oreal managed its business by distribution channel and geography. Brands were typically slotted into one of the following divisions: consumer (grocery, pharmacy, and mass discounter), luxury (department-store counters, specialty retail, or L'Oreal-owned retail stores), professional (salons), and active cosmetics (dermatologists). Global brand teams were based on the brand's continent of origin, along with dedicated R&D resources. These teams developed the global "brand key," or essence of the brand, along with formulations, packaging, and strategy. Regional brand teams negotiated with global brand teams to fine-tune execution locally. Interestingly, brands were managed as if they were separate businesses; cooperation was minimal, even within categories. This approach was meant to engender competition and to maintain distinctive offerings. L'Oreal prided itself on its R&D capabilities, spending 3 percent of sales on R&D in 2000.

CASE DISCUSSION QUESTIONS

1. Why did the U.S. organizational structure shift from product grouping in the 1950s to a matrix in the 1980s? Why did the European organizational structure shift from geographic grouping in the 1950s to category management in the 1980s? Why were the two structures integrated into a global cube in the 1990s?

2. What are the key distinguishing features of Organization 2005? Why did P&G adopt this structure?

3. Should Lafley make a strong commitment to keeping Organization 2005, or should he plan to dismantle the structure?

CASE CREDIT

Professor Mikoaj Jan Piskorski and Alessandro L. Spadini (MBA 2006) prepared the original version of this case, "Procter & Gamble: Organization 2005 (A)," HBS No. 707-401, which is being replaced by this version prepared by the same authors. HBS cases are developed solely as the basis for class discussion. Cases are not intended to serve as endorsements, sources of primary data, or illustrations of effective or ineffective management.

Copyright © 2007 President and Fellows of Harvard College. To order copies or request permission to reproduce materials, call 1-800-545-7685, write Harvard Business School Publishing, Boston, MA 02163, or go to http://www.hbsp.harvard.edu. No part of this publication may be reproduced, stored in a retrieval system, used in a spreadsheet, or transmitted in any form or by any means— electronic, mechanical, photocopying, recording, or otherwise— without the permission of Harvard Business School.

CASE NOTES

1 Brooker, Katrina. 2002. "P&G's un-CEO." *Fortune*, September 16. http://faculty.msb.edu/homak/HomaHelpSite/WebHelp/P&G_s_Un-CEO_Fortune_9-16-02.htm, accessed May 2005.

2 Gingrich, Jim. 2000. *The P&G Train Has Left the Station—Is It Too Late to Hop On?* Sanford C. Bernstein & Company, October 9.

3 Procter & Gamble. "A company history, 1837–today," Procter & Gamble Web site, www.pg.com/translations/history_pdf/english_history.pdf, accessed April 2006.

4 "Why pigs?" Big Pig Gig Web site, http://www.bigpiggig.com/contact/news/news.php?id=31, accessed March 2005.

5 Dyer, Davis, Fredrick Dalzell, and Rowena Olegario. 2004. *Rising Tide*. Boston, MA: Harvard Business School Press, p. 18.

6 Procter & Gamble. "A company history, 1837–today."

7 Ibid.

8 Ibid.

9 Procter & Gamble. 1999. *1999 Annual Report*. Cincinnati: Procter & Gamble, pp. 5–6.

10 Procter & Gamble. "A company history, 1837–today."

11 Dyer, Dalzell, and Olegario, pp. 68–73.

12 Procter & Gamble. "A company history, 1837–today."

13 Dyer, Dalzell, and Olegario, p. 198.

14 Larkin, Patrick. 1998. "P&G plan: Sweeping changes," *The Cincinnati Post*, September 10. http://www.cincypost.com/business/1998/pg091098.html, accessed August 2005..

15 Bartlett, Christopher A. 2004. "P&G Japan: The SK-II globalization project," HBS No. 303–003. Boston: Harvard Business School Publishing, p. 2.

16 Ibid.

17 Vedpuriswar, A.V. "Procter & Gamble," http://www.vedpuriswar.org/book/Procter%20&%20Gamble.htm, accessed June 2005.

18 Ibid., p. 2.

19 Ibid., p. 293.

20 Ibid., p. 289.

21 McQulling, Andrew. 2000. *Procter & Gamble*. UBS Warburg, July 28.

22 Ibid.

23 Ibid.

24 Larkin.

25 Bartlett, p. 6.

26 Procter & Gamble. "Linking opportunity with responsibility sustainability report." Procter & Gamble Web site, www.pg.com/translations/sustainability_pdf/english_sustainability.pdf, accessed October 2005.

27 Bartlett, p. 5.

28 Ibid.

29 Larkin.

30 Alexander, Garth. 1998. "P&G gambles on shake-up to beat crisis." *The Sunday Times*, September 18.

31 Max, Kevin. 2000. "Procter & Gamble gets slammed after earnings warning." The Street.com Web site, March 7, 2000, http://www.thestreet.com/pf/brknews/consumer/896216.html, accessed April 2006.

32 Isidore, Chris and Martha Slud. 2000. "P&G warning hurts Dow," *CNN Money* Web site, March 7, 2000, http://money.cnn.com/2000/03/07/companies/procter, accessed April 2006.

33 "P&G earnings tumble." *CNN Money* Web site, http://money.cnn.com/2000/04/25/companies/procter/, accessed April 2006.

34 Ibid.

35 Berner, Robert. "What's driving P&G's executive spin cycle?" *BusinessWeek Online*, http://www.businessweek.com/bwdaily/dnflash/june2000/nf00608h.htm, accessed April 2006.

36 "P&G CEO quits amid woes." *CNN Money* Web site, http://money.cnn.com/2000/06/08/companies/procter/, accessed April 2006.

37 Unilever. "Charts 1995–2005," Unilever Web site, http://www.unilever.com/ourcompany/investorcentre/financial_reports/charts_1995.asp, accessed April 2006.

38 Lorenz, Andrew. 2000. "Unilever crosses the Rubicon." *The Sunday Times*, February 7..

39 Unilever. "Unilever's approach to corporate responsibility." Unilever Web Site, http://www.unilever.com/Images/2001%20Social%20Review%20of%202000%20Data_tcm13-5331.pdf, accessed May 2006.

40 Unilever. "Unilever plans for faster growth." Unilever Web site, http://www.unilever.com/ourcompany/newsandmedia/pressreleases/2000/growth.asp, accessed May 2006.

41 Unilever. "Realignment of senior management structure at Unilever," Unilever Web site, http://www.unilever.com/ourcompany/newsandmedia/pressreleases/2000/management.asp, accessed May 2006.

42 Colgate-Palmolive Company. 1999. *2000 Annual Report*. New York: Colgate-Palmolive Company.: New York: http://investor.colgate.com/annual/annual.cfm, accessed April 2006.

43 Ibid.

44 Shore, Andrew. 2004. *Kimberly-Clark Corporation: Cry no More*, Deutsche Bank. February 2, 2004.

45 Ibid.

46 Kimberly-Clark Company. 2001. *2001 Annual Report*. Dallas:: Kimberly-Clark, pp. 1–30.

47 Ibid., p. 13.

48 L'Oreal SA. 2000. *2000 Annual Report*. Paris: L'Oreal SA, pp. 1–19.

International Strategic Alliances: Design and Management

9

Learning Objectives

After reading this chapter you should be able to:

- Know the steps for implementing successful international strategic alliances.

- Describe how multinational companies link value chains in international strategic alliances.

- Understand the importance of choosing the right partners for alliances.

- Know the important characteristics to look for in potential alliance partners.

- Distinguish between equity-based international joint ventures and other types of international cooperative alliances.

- Know the basic components of an international strategic alliance contract.

- Understand the control systems and management structures used in alliance organizations.

- Appreciate the unique problems in human resource management faced by managers in alliance organizations.

- Realize the importance of interfirm commitment and trust for building successful international strategic alliances.

- Understand how multinational companies assess the performance of their international strategic alliances.

- Know when companies should continue or dissolve their alliances.

Preview CASE IN POINT

Strategic Alliances in Emerging Markets

Emerging markets such as India, China, Russia, Brazil, and South Africa continue to enjoy good health largely due to maturing economic policies. Many of the emerging markets have taken steps to control potentially damaging economic factors such as inflation while maintaining strict monetary and fiscal policies. These emerging markets present tremendous potential for multinational companies because multinational companies take advantage of the significant cost benefits and the rising middle classes in these countries. Consider that, in the next decade, more than 800 million people in China, India, Russia, and Brazil will qualify as members of the middle class with more than $1 trillion to spend on products.

Many multinational companies also find that, if they want to take advantage of such markets, they need to form strategic alliances with local companies. For example, McDonald's signed a significant deal with the Chinese company Sinopec, which runs almost 30,000 gas stations and is growing by about 500 stations annually. McDonald's is hoping to create thousands of drive-through restaurants at many of Sinopec's locations. It anticipates that the alliance will give it a powerful means to attract the young and affluent Chinese who are more likely to drive.

Similarly, GE Drivetrain Technologies signed a joint venture agreement with A-Power Generation System of China, the largest provider of power generation systems in that country. A-Power has entered the wind power energy market, and GE Drivetrain agreed to provide 900 2.7-megawatt gearboxes beginning in 2010. Also under the agreement, GE Drivetrain and A-Power are jointly building a wind turbine gearbox assembly plant. This alliance serves A-Power by providing it with access to GE Drivetrain's technology and expertise. For GE Drivetrain, the alliance gains the firm access to the Chinese market and surrounding Southeast Asian nations.

Sources: Based on Litterick, David. 2006. "Fast food McDonald's takes meals on wheels to China." The Daily Telegraph, June 21, p. 1; PR Newswire. 2009. "GE Drivetrain Technologies signs LOIS with A-Power to establish joint venture." January 12; Van Arnum, Patricia. 2006. "Asian producers raise their profiles in the global pharmaceutical value chain." Pharmaceutical Technology, May, 30(5): pp. 70–76.

A s the Preview Case in Point shows, emerging markets will likely continue to enjoy good economic health and provide tremendous potential for multinational companies. Because strategic alliances are fast and flexible ways to gain complementary resources, they are increasingly among the most popular strategies that companies use to develop new products and to expand into these new geographic areas or markets. In fact, a recent worldwide study by Accenture (formerly Andersen Consulting) found that major multinational companies expect alliances to account for up to 40 percent of company value in the next five years.[1] However, the same study found that only 30 percent of the alliances were considered outright successes by top management.

Why do alliances fail to meet expectations? The most common reason is a poorly designed or managed alliance organization—not a poor strategic choice in entering the alliance. Increasingly, strategic alliances involve companies from two or more nations. Foreign partners often have the most attractive resources or skills that make them the partners of choice. However, partnering with a company from a different nation only compounds the management difficulties. As a result, the student of multinational management needs an understanding of international strategic alliance operations and management.

Although strategic alliances are attractive for a variety of reasons, they are inherently unstable and entail significant management challenges. Estimates of failure rates range from 30 to 60 percent. Partners may fail to deliver, partners may disagree on how to run the business, and even profitable alliances can be torn by conflict. Successful alliances must make strategic sense, but they also require good implementation. In this chapter, you will see the steps necessary to implement a successful strategic alliance. In our discussion, we will follow the model of these steps presented in Exhibit 9.1.

Where to Link in the Value Chain

The many benefits of strategic alliances include gaining access to a local partner's knowledge of the market, meeting government requirements, sharing risks, sharing technology, gaining economies of scale, and accessing lower-cost raw materials or labor. The objectives a firm hopes to achieve determine where multinational companies link in the value chain.

Exhibit 9.2 shows two value chains and the areas in which companies commonly link to gain strategic benefits.

Alliances that combine the same value chain activities often do so to gain efficient scales of operations, to merge compatible talents, or to share risks. These alliances are attractive when no one company is big enough, has the necessary talent, or is willing to take on an enormously risky venture. In R&D alliances, for example, high-tech multinational companies often use joint research and development to merge different technical skills or to share the risks of developing new or costly technologies. The alliance of IBM, Toshiba, and Siemens illustrates these points. These companies bring together the engineering talent from three nations with the hope of discovering the next generation of computer chips. Why not do it alone? R&D in computer chips is a highly risky and expensive venture, which no one company wants to attempt by itself. Just the costs of chip design and fabrication run in the billions.

In operations alliances, multinational companies often combine manufacturing or assembly activities to achieve a profitable volume of activity. For

EXHIBIT 9.1   Implementing a Strategic-Alliance Strategy

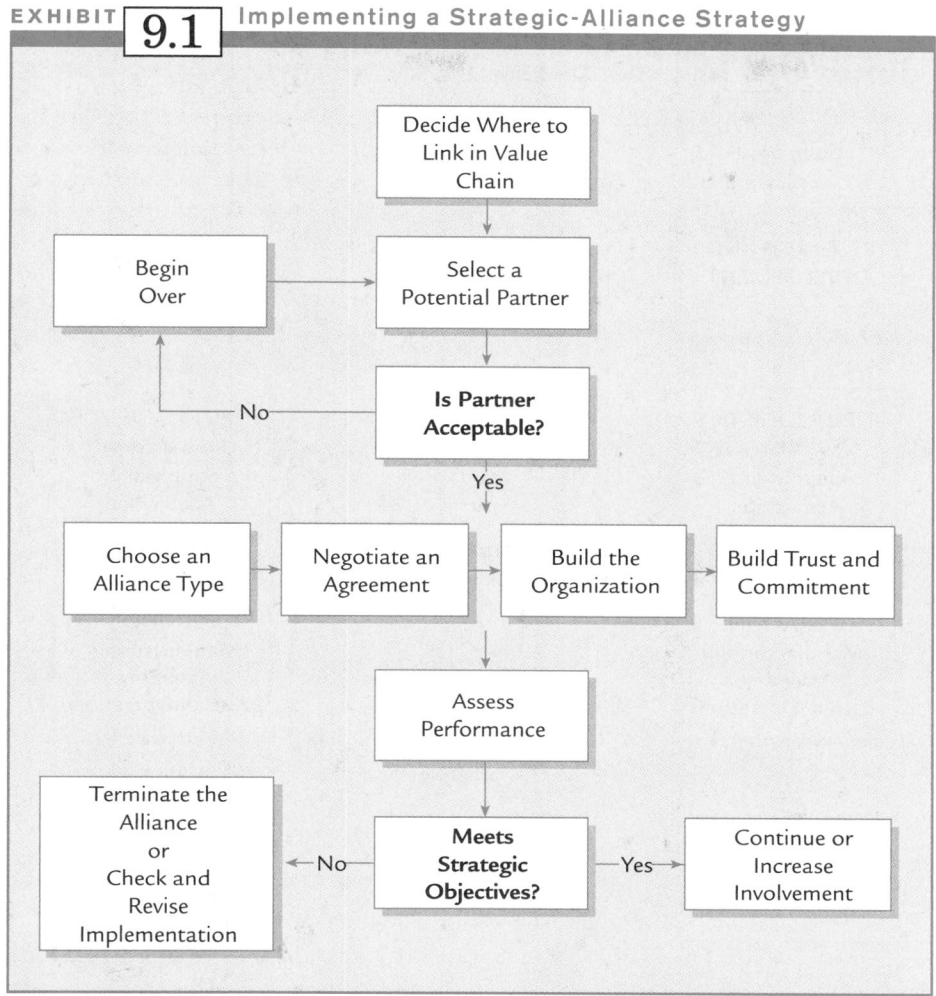

example, General Motors of the United States and Renault SA of France have an alliance to develop and market pickup trucks and vans targeted at the light commercial truck market.[2] These companies intend to work together to produce light commercial trucks for the European market. Leadership skills and a focus on results and values have made this alliance between GM and Renault a success.[3]

Marketing and sales alliances allow multinational companies to increase the scope and number of products sold and to share distribution systems. Sometimes partners even share logos. In the KLM/Northwest Airlines alliance, the companies share advertising that notes their joint reservation-and-route systems. In the automobile industry, alliance partners often share each other's dealer systems. Consider the next Case in Point.

Output alliances deliver a service and are perhaps the most popular in the airline industry. International alliances—such as those between KLM and Northwest, Swissair and Delta Airlines, and British Airways and USAir—deliver their services jointly through a process called code sharing (the sharing of reservation codes). In this way, passengers can buy an international ticket in one

EXHIBIT 9.2 Examples of Linking Value Chains in Strategic Alliances

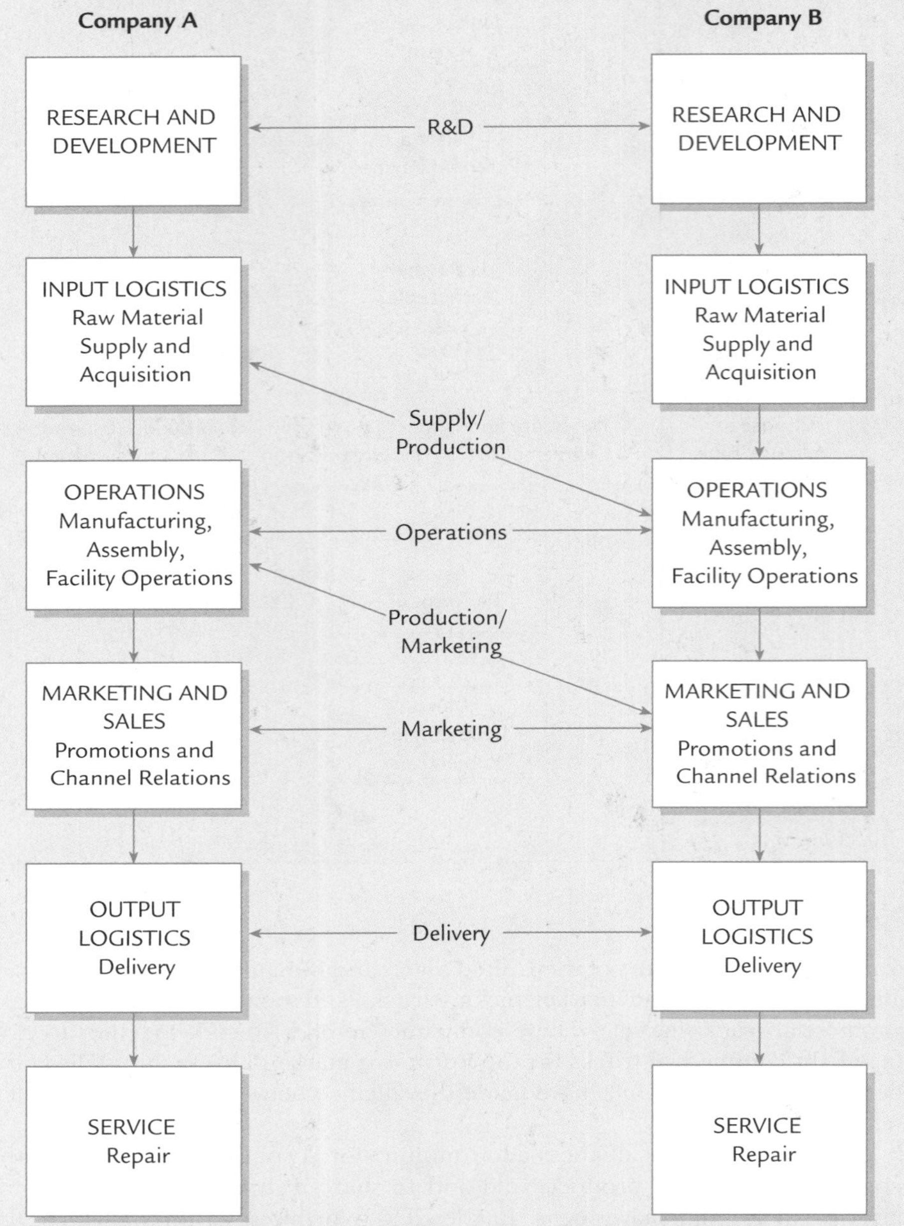

Source: Adapted from Lorange, Peter, and Johan Roos. 1992. Strategic Alliances. Cambridge, MA: Blackwell.

airline's country, fly to the partner's country, and get continuing flights with the same ticket on the partner's airline.

Alliances linking upstream and downstream components of the value chain can serve the objectives of low-cost supply or manufacturing. In some supply/

CASE IN POINT

Swisscom and Verizon Strategic Alliance

Swisscom, the leader in the delivery of enterprise communication services in the Swiss market, entered into a strategic alliance with Verizon. Swisscom supports its corporate customers with planning, implementation, and operation of its IT and other communications products. In contrast, Verizon is recognized as a global market leader for its extensive global networks and its capability of providing communications and IT-related products for large multinationals. With this strategic alliance, Swisscom is able to access Verizon's global network to provide services to its multinational customers. For Verizon, the strategic alliance gives the company access to the Swiss market.

Why is the Swiss market so attractive? Switzerland has a very high density of multinational headquarters. Having access to this market means that Verizon can provide the globally integrated solutions that these multinationals require. As these Swiss-based multinationals strive to develop systems that integrate distant locations and operations, the alliance will be able to improve services based on Swisscom's deep knowledge of the market and customers and on Verizon's global network.

Source: Based on PR Newswire. *2008. "Swisscom and Verizon Business enter strategic alliance," May 28.*

operations alliances, one partner provides low-cost sources of supply or components, and the other partner does the manufacturing. Operations/marketing links can work similarly. One company trades a source of low-cost manufacturing for another company's eventual sales. For example, because of increasing wages in their own countries, many Japanese and Korean companies formed production/marketing alliances with low-wage Southeast Asian companies. Production and assembly occur at the low-cost site, and the Japanese and Korean companies do the downstream marketing and sales.

For U.S. companies, the majority of international strategic alliances occur in operations. Exhibit 9.3 shows the mixture of value chain links for the nearly 800 publicly announced international strategic alliances created by U.S. multinational companies during a four-year period.[4]

The links discussed so far and illustrated in Exhibits 9.2 and 9.3 are only some of those possible for international strategic alliances. In building alliances, each company must determine which of its value chain activities can be enhanced by the relationships, thereby helping the firm achieve its strategic objectives. Having made that selection, management faces what is generally considered the most important step in implementing a strategic alliance: choosing the right partner.

Choosing a Partner: The Most Important Choice?

Most experts attribute the success or failure of strategic alliances to how well the partners get along. Especially early in the relationship, each party must believe that it has a good partner who can deliver on promises and be trusted. The next Case in Point shows some of the difficulties that can occur when a company makes mistakes in partner selection.

CASE IN POINT

Picking the Wrong Partner

In 2000, Kuwait's state-run Petrochemical Industries Company (PIC) signed a deal to pay Dow Chemicals $7.5 billion for 50 percent ownership in several chemical plants. Unfortunately for Dow, PIC had second thoughts about the deal and decided not to honor the agreement. Members of the Kuwaiti government argued that the deal might not have been feasible given the economic conditions in the years following the agreement. Furthermore, some politicians claimed that the deal was overpriced.

Picking the wrong partner had major consequences for Dow, which had planned to use the funds to acquire Rohm and Haas, a rival. With PIC's breaking of the agreement, Dow no longer had access to the funds and became engaged in several legal battles. The firm is suing PIC for $2.5 billion for breaking the agreement. Furthermore, it is staring down a Rohm and Haas lawsuit to force Dow to complete its agreed acquisition. Dow shares fell 22 percent after news that the Kuwaitis would not honor their agreement.

Sources: Based on Sieb, C. 2008. "Kuwait decision to quit joint venture puts Dow Chemical's Expansion in jeopardy." The Times, December 30, pp. 39; Westervelt, R. 2009. "Dow launches arbitration proceedings against PIC." Chemical Week, 171, p. 7.

EXHIBIT 9.3 Value Chain Links in U.S. International Strategic Alliances

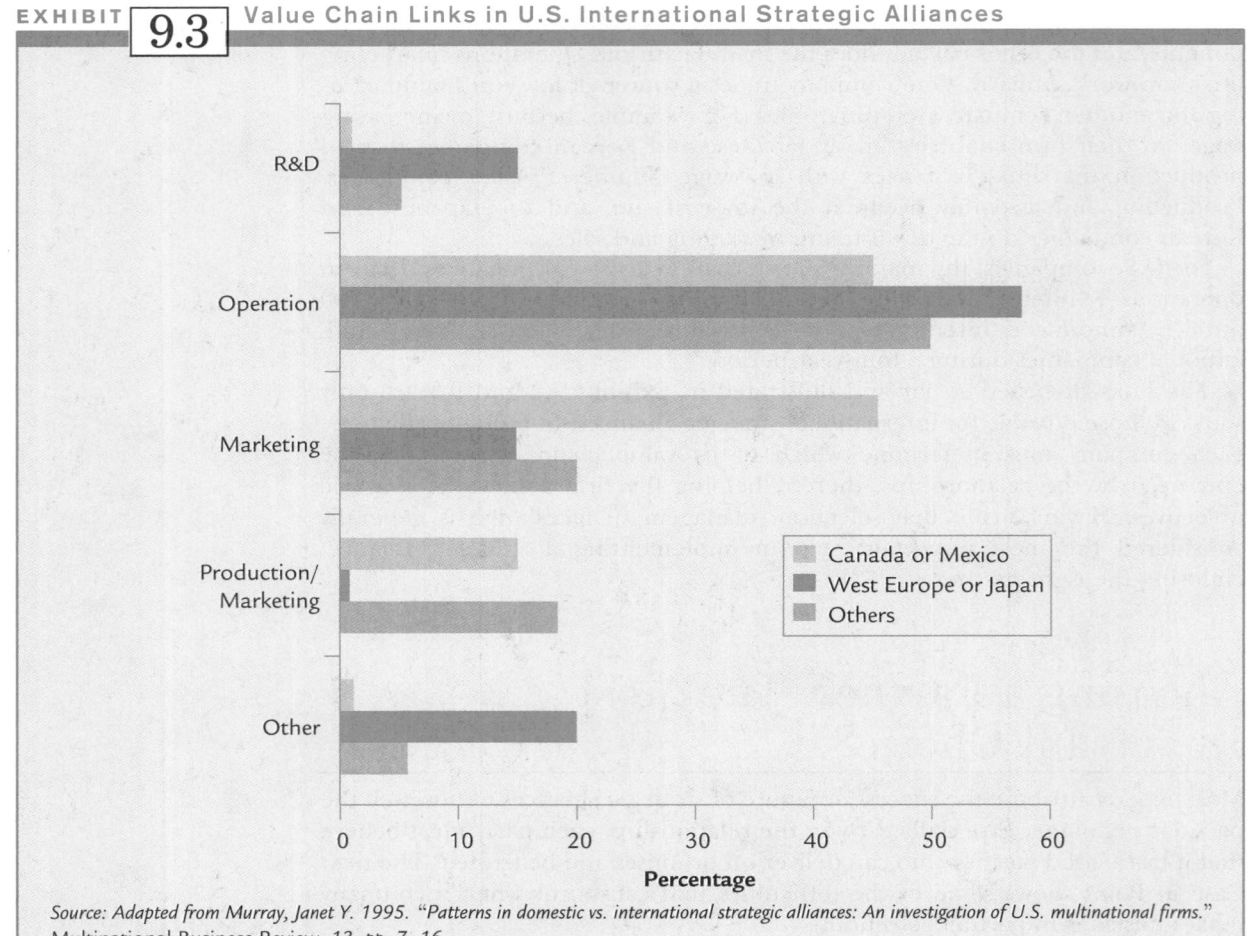

Source: Adapted from Murray, Janet Y. 1995. "Patterns in domestic vs. international strategic alliances: An investigation of U.S. multinational firms." Multinational Business Review, 13, pp. 7–16.

Experts identify several key criteria for picking an appropriate alliance partner:[5]

- *Seek **strategic complementarity***: Before forming the strategic alliance, prospective partners must have a good understanding of each other's strategic objectives for the venture. Each should know what the other hopes to achieve, both in the short term and in the long term. It is not necessary, however, that partners have the same objectives. Although similar strategic objectives, such as rapid growth, are beneficial, objectives can be complementary. For example, a U.S. or Japanese firm may have an advanced technology for manufacturing computer components that is attractive to a Chinese firm. The Chinese firm may dominate the Chinese market and could provide a potential powerful sales and distribution outlet for a partner. These companies have complementary strategic objectives. The U.S. or the Japanese company desires growth in its Chinese market share, and the Chinese company seeks access to the other side's technology.

  > **Strategic complementarity**
  > The alliance partners' strategies are complementary.

- *Pick a partner with **complementary skills:*** Partners must contribute more than money to the venture. Each partner must contribute some skills or resources that complement those of the other partner. J. Michael Geringer asserts that technical complementarity is the most important criterion.[6] A typical complementary alliance, for example, occurs when one company (usually the foreign country) contributes technical skills and another company (usually a host country company) contributes marketing skills. Another recommendation is to find partners with similar but not identical products or markets, thus avoiding the difficulties of working with direct competitors.[7]

  > **Complementary skills**
  > One that enhances but does not necessarily duplicate an alliance partner's skills.

- *Seek out companies with compatible management styles:* Lord Weinstock, the managing director for 27 years of Britain's General Electric Company (GEC, not related to the U.S. company GE), is a strategic alliance expert. He has seen many alliances succeed and fail. One recent failure, an alliance of GEC with Germany's Siemens, flopped. Consultants noted that Siemens is an engineers' company, consistent with many values in German business culture, and GEC is a financiers' company. The managers simply didn't get along. Weinstock noted that for alliances to succeed, "You have to suppress the ego—it's absolute poison in a joint venture."[8]

- *Seek a partner that will provide the right level of mutual dependency:* As in any marriage, mutual dependency means that companies must rely on each other to contribute to the relationship. With a good match, partners feel a mutual need to supply their unique resources or capabilities to the alliance. Both partners see their contribution as critical to the success of the relationship and ultimately to the success of the alliance. The best level of mutual dependency is balanced, wherein both companies feel equally dependent on the outcome of the venture. Geringer suggests maintaining this mutual dependency by building safeguards into the agreement, such as types of "alimony" payments and restrictions on entering the same business over a specified period.[9] The alimony payments would require payments to the partner if the relationship breaks up before a specified period.

- *Avoid the so-called anchor partner:* **Anchor partners** hold back the development of a successful strategic alliance because they cannot or will not provide their share of the funding. Prospective partners should study carefully each other's financial position and investment plans. A potential partner with a weak division or expansion in other areas may drain financial support

  > **Anchor partners**
  > A partner that holds back the development of a successful strategic alliance because it cannot or will not provide its share of the funding.

from the alliance. If a potential partner is financially weak but still attractive for other reasons, precautions are advised. For example, a contract might specify that the division of the alliance's profits (or other alliance outputs) among the partners will vary in proportion to their financial contributions.

Elephant-and-ant complex
Occurs in strategic alliances when two companies are greatly unequal in size.

- *Be cautious of the elephant-and-ant complex:* The **elephant-and-ant complex** occurs when two companies are greatly unequal in size. In such cases, serious potential problems can result. First, the larger firm may dominate the smaller one, controlling the strategies and management of the alliance. Second, the corporate cultures probably differ significantly. For example, bureaucracy and slower decision making usually characterize large, old companies. Small companies are often more entrepreneurial and informal. Thus, because of cultural differences, a small firm's executives may see the large firm's managers as ignoring immediate problems. The large partner's executives may see the small firm's managers as less professional. For instance, an analysis of the strategic alliance between Telia and Telenor, Sweden's and Norway's largest telecommunication companies, shows that the elephant-and-ant complex may have played a role in its failure.[10] A close look at the alliance shows that Norwegian nationalistic feelings emerged when the country's largest telecom company, Telenor, was being treated poorly by Sweden's Telia. The elephant-and-ant complex was reflected in the perception that a big country company (Sweden, the elephant) was bullying a small country company (Norway, the ant). In spite of these potential problems, however, elephant-and-ant alliances do succeed. When other factors exist, such as complementary skills, managers find ways to overcome size differences. Exhibit 9.4 contrasts some of the incentives and concerns for small businesses in elephant-and-ant international strategic alliances.

- *Assess operating policy differences with potential partners:* Marriage partners need to work out how to squeeze the toothpaste, when to have dinner, who makes the beds, who cleans the house, and all the other operational details of running a household. Similarly, would-be partners in a strategic alliance likely have operational differences in how their companies are run

EXHIBIT 9.4 International Strategic Alliances for Small Multinational Companies: Incentives and Concerns

Incentives	Concerns
• Gain legitimacy Act as a seal of approval	• Relative level of contribution Must commit relatively more assets than large firm
• Develop links in distribution channel Use large firm's existing channels	• Entering a large scale of operations Lack of experience with large-scale operations
• Access to resources Sped-up access to market	• Risk of unequal proprietary information disclosure Easier access to small firm's information
• Diversification of risk Sharing risk with richer partner	• Mismatch of interacting managers Small-firm entrepreneur with large-firm functional or product specialists
	• Loss of control Concerns of large firm's dominating relationship

Sources: Adapted from Ghisi, F. A., J. A. G. da Silveria, T. Kristensen, M. Hingley, and A. Lindgreen. 2008. "Horizontal alliances amongst small retailers in Brazil." British Food Journal, 110(4/5), pp. 514–538; Peridis, Theodoros. 1992. "Strategic alliances for smaller firms." Research in Global Strategic Management, 3, pp. 129–142.

on a day-to-day basis. Accounting policies, human resource management policies, financial policies, reporting policies, and the like may all differ because of organizational or cultural differences. For example, potential European partners may want to shut down operations during certain holiday periods, or Japanese partners may want the strategic alliance to respect the age hierarchy of management. For the strategic alliance to function smoothly and before the strategic alliance comes into operation, partners should agree on mutually satisfactory operational policies.

• *Assess the difficulty of cross-cultural communication with a likely partner:* Even if partners speak each other's languages, cross-cultural communication is never as easy as it is within one's own culture or organization. Managers must expect slower communication and more errors of understanding. For example, in a joint venture between a Japanese company and the U.S. aircraft manufacturer Boeing, the agreement required that fuselage panels have a "mirror finish." The Japanese workers interpreted this specification literally. They polished the metal to a mirror finish. The result was excessively high labor costs and the need for further discussion to resolve the meaning of "mirror finish."[11]

The next Multinational Management Brief discusses some of the key questions to ask when picking a partner.

Multinational Management **Brief**

Picking an Alliance Partner

Picking an alliance partner is a very important task, but it can be a difficult one. In fact, some experts see choosing a partner as one of the key factors that can determine the success or failure of an alliance. However, Jagersma, in extensive interviews with 106 chief executives and top managers from 89 global companies, suggests that multinational companies need to ask a number of questions about the potential partner. These questions are regarded as "make-or-break." The interview participants advised companies to avoid the cross-border alliance if the potential partner answers no to any of the following questions:

• Can the partner deliver as required to make the alliance successful?
• Can both partners agree on clear goals and objectives for the strategic alliance?
• Have there been attempts to minimize potential for competition and friction with the partner? Does the potential partner have any alliances with your competitors?
• Does the potential partner share with you a vision about how the cross-border strategic alliance might evolve?
• Is the partner willing and able to contribute the necessary skills and resources to ensure that the alliance is successful?
• Does the partner have a history of success with previous strategic alliances?
• Have you compared the potential partner with other partners in terms of value creation?
• Does the cross-border alliance fit with your vision of your future alliance network?

Sources: Based on Holmberg, S. R. and J. L. Cummings. 2009. "Building successful alliances." Long Range Planning, *42, pp. 164–193; Jagersma, Peter Klaas. 2005. "Cross-border alliances: Advice from the executive suite."* Journal of Business Strategy, *26(1), pp. 41–50.*

After finding potentially satisfactory partners, multinational managers from all companies involved must decide on the form of the alliance. Next, we consider the popular choices in types of international strategic alliances.

Choosing an Alliance Type

There are three main types of strategic alliances:[12] informal international cooperative alliances, formal international cooperative alliances (ICAs), and international joint ventures (IJVs). Exhibit 9.5 outlines the major differences among the types. We consider each of these next.

Informal and Formal International Cooperative Alliances

Informal international cooperative alliances are agreements between companies from two or more countries that are not legally binding. They can be agreements of any kind and can provide links between companies anywhere on their value chains. For example, a local company might agree informally to market and sell a foreign firm's products in exchange for exclusive distribution rights. Although neither firm is legally bound to continue the relationship, the companies might use the informal agreement as a test of their ability to work together in future, more formal agreements. If the informal alliance does not work, it can be ended at any time.

Because the contract offers no legal protection, managers usually limit the scope of their involvement with the other company. They are usually reluctant to dedicate sizable resources to the relationship, such as product changes for the partner's benefit. In addition, multinational companies in informal alliances resist revealing a company's proprietary information, that is, information that a

Informal international cooperative alliance
A nonlegally binding agreement between companies to cooperate on any value chain activity.

EXHIBIT 9.5   Types and Characteristics of International Strategic Alliances

Alliance Type	Degree of Involvement	Ease of Dissolution	Visibility to Competitors	Contract Required	Legal Entity
Informal international cooperative alliance	Usually limited in scope and time; a marriage of convenience	Easy, at the convenience of either side	Often unknown to competitors	No	None
Formal international cooperative alliance	Deeper involvement requiring exchange of proprietary company knowledge and resources	More difficult to dissolve before end of contract because of legal obligations and commitment of resources by companies	Often visible to competitors through announcements in business press but details can be secure	Yes	None
International joint venture	Deep involvement requiring exchange of financial, proprietary company knowledge, and managerial resources	Most difficult to dissolve because companies invest significant resources and have ownership in a separate legal entity	High visibility because joint venture company is a separate legal entity	Yes	Yes, separate company

firm considers its own and wants to keep secret from competitors. An example might be special manufacturing processes.

The **formal international cooperative alliance (ICA)** calls for a high degree of involvement among partners. This type of alliance usually requires a formal contract specifying exactly what each company must contribute, which could be managers, technical specialists, factories, information or knowledge, or money. To achieve a strategic gain that a single company cannot attain by itself, companies must usually share some knowledge, skill, or specialized resources through a formal ICA. This sharing of proprietary information or knowledge raises the level of involvement of the partners. Both companies must give away something valuable to the partner to get something in return. In addition, in combination with the obligations specified in the contract, the sharing of proprietary knowledge makes backing out of a formal alliance more difficult than for alliances with informal agreements.

Formal ICAs are very popular in some high-tech industries, particularly the semiconductor industry, because of the high costs and risks of R&D.

International Joint Ventures

An **international joint venture (IJV)** is a self-standing legal entity owned by parent companies from different countries; the participating companies have an equity or ownership position in an independent company. The simplest IJV occurs when two parent companies have 50/50 ownership of the venture. International joint ventures are becoming increasingly popular as a means for global companies to join forces by sharing resources.[13]

Not all joint ventures have only two partners, even though two-partner joint ventures are probably the most common. When a large number of companies form a joint venture, the resulting legal entity is often called a consortium. Airbus Industries, for example, is a consortium that includes Aerospatiale from France, Messerschmitt Boklow Blohm from Germany, British Aerospace, and Construcciones Aeronauticas from Spain.

Companies need not have equal ownership to form a joint venture. Often one partner has a majority ownership. In some countries, the law requires the local partner to be the dominant owner. In such cases, for example, in a two-company venture, the foreign company cannot own more than 49 percent of the IJV's stock. Companies may also increase or decrease their ownership shares; agreements may require a foreign company to surrender its ownership after a specified time. The first McDonald's in Russia, for example, was a joint venture designed to revert eventually to sole Russian ownership. Some parent companies also increase or decrease ownership depending on the IJV's performance or the parent company's strategic goals. One company may buy out its partner and take over the joint venture as a wholly owned subsidiary.

One difficulty in determining the initial ownership of a joint venture arises from equity contributions other than cash. Companies may contribute equal monetary shares to a venture to have equal equity positions, but they may also bring nonfinancial resources. If the partners accept that the contributed resources have an economic value, then the resources become part of a firm's equity contribution. For example, one parent company in a 50/50 joint venture may contribute only its advanced technology, whereas the other partner may furnish all of the financing.

Even when a joint venture is created as a 50/50 partnership, there is no guarantee that the partners have equal influences on the venture. Consider the next Case in Point.

Formal international cooperative alliance (ICA)
A nonequity alliance with formal contracts specifying what each company must contribute to the relationship.

International joint venture (IJV)
A separate legal entity in which two or more companies from different nations have ownership positions.

C A S E   I N   P O I N T

The TNK–BP Joint Venture

In 2003, BP joined forces with several Russian tycoons to create the multibillion-dollar joint venture of TNK–BP. BP took over 50 percent of TNK's assets, and the joint venture had access to exploit over 5.2 billion barrels of oil. The merger was approved by the Russian authorities.

Despite the official welcome of the joint venture, events proved problematic for BP. BP's expatriates' work visas were declared invalid, preventing critical employees from working. The Moscow police raided the offices of the venture. One of the TNK–BP managers was arrested for allegedly spying. TNK's Russian shareholders claimed that the venture ignored their needs and that BP is blocking TNK's international expansion plans. The venture is also being blamed for spending too much money on foreign employees rather than on Russians.

As all this shows, a 50/50 venture does not guarantee 50/50 influence. In fact, Russian authorities have had a major influence on how the venture is progressing. The problems with authorities escalated and for a while, the joint venture's chief, Robert Dudley, was not even allowed to work in Russia. He was accused of failing to obey immigration laws and was in hiding.

Sources: Based on Hotten, R. 2008. "BP to appeal Russia's work bank on joint venture chief." Daily Telegraph, August 15; Bush, J. 2008. "BP: Roughed up in Russia." BusinessWeek, June 16, p. 69.

Formal ICAs and IJVs require formal agreements. Next you will see some of the issues considered by multinational managers in negotiating alliance agreements.

Negotiating the Agreement

For an IJV or a formal ICA, contractual agreements have to be negotiated and signed. Similar to licensing agreements, alliance contracts are the legal documents that bind partners together. The formal agreements, however, are never as important as the ability of managers to get along. Exhibit 9.6 shows some of the questions that must be addressed as **IJV negotiation issues**.

IJV negotiation issues
Points such as equity contributions, management structure, and "prenuptial" agreements regarding the dissolution of the relationship.

In general, experts recommend that negotiation teams with technical and negotiation experience handle an alliance agreement. This cross-cultural negotiation follows the steps explained in Chapter 13.

Once a firm has a partner and an agreement, it must build the organization to run the alliance, a process that includes organizational design and human resource management issues. First, we consider structure and design.

Building the Organization: Organizational Design in Strategic Alliances

Design depends on the type of alliance chosen. Informal ICAs often require no formal design, and managers from the participating companies cooperate without formal control. Formal ICAs may require a separate organizational unit housed in one of the companies, with employees from all the parents. The IBM/Toshiba/Siemens alliance, located in New York, is an example of an organizational unit setup for an ICA. However, some formal ICAs may share information or products with minimal organizational requirements. For example, two

EXHIBIT **9.6**

Selected Questions for a Strategic Alliance Agreement

For Both ICAs and IJVs:

- What products or services does the alliance produce?
- Where is the new alliance located?
- Under which country's law does the agreement operate?
- What are the basic responsibilities of each partner? The responsibilities in question might include which company provides the production technology, the plant location, the training of the workforce, the marketing expertise.
- What are the partners' contributions of senior managers?
- What are the partners' contributions of other employees?
- How will royalties or profits be divided?
- How should the company be controlled?
- How is the company organized?
- Who owns new products or technology developed by the new company?
- To whom and where will the strategic alliance sell its products?
- Is a prenuptial agreement needed?
- How can the alliance be dissolved?

Primarily for IJVs:

- What is the name of the new IJV company?
- What are the equity contributions of each partner?
- What is the makeup of the IJV's board of directors?

airlines may book each other's routes but need no common organizational entity. IJVs, however, are separate legal entities, and they require a separate organization to carry out the alliance's objectives.

In this section, we consider two key issues in managing an alliance organization: decision-making control and the management structure. These design issues are applicable mostly to IJVs but also to formal ICAs that require organizational settings. For example, the IBM/Toshiba/Siemens alliance created an organization headquartered at an IBM location but managed by a Toshiba engineer.

Decision-Making Control

Parent companies must consider two major areas of decision making when designing their alliance organizations: operational decision making and strategic decision making. Operational decisions include management decisions associated with the day-to-day running of the organizations, such as the size of production runs and the hiring of assembly line workers. Strategic decisions focus on issues that are important to the long-term survival of the alliance organization, such as opening a new plant and introducing a new product.

Majority ownership of an IJV does not necessarily mean that the parent company controls its operational and strategic decision making. Similarly, providing the location for a formal ICA does not entitle a partner to such control.

Depending on each partner's skills, parent companies may agree to distribute the managerial decision-making duties among partners.

In the IJV, strategic decision making usually takes place at the level of the IJV's board of directors or the top management team. So, to gain more control over strategic decision making, some IJV parent companies place more of their managers on the board of directors or top management team. IJV parent companies that wish to control the IJV's operational decision making usually have most of their people serving as mid- to lower-level managers.

In nonequity ICAs, strategic decision making usually remains with the parent companies. Alliance managers focus on operational decision making related to delivering the product or to knowledge from the parent companies.

Management Structures

The mix of strategic and operational decision-making control among alliance partners is often complex and unique. However, to formalize the decision-making control, partners must choose a management structure that formally specifies the division of control responsibilities among partners. Multinational companies typically use five management control structures for their ICAs or IJVs:[14]

Dominant parent
Majority owner or contributor who controls or dominates the strategic and operational decision making of the alliance.

Shared management structure
Occurs when both parent companies contribute approximately the same number of managers to the alliance organization.

Split-control management structure
Partners usually share strategic decision making but split functional-level decision making.

Independent management structure
Alliance managers act like managers from a separate company.

- *Dominant parent:* The **dominant parent** is usually the majority owner of an IJV or, in some cases (especially when majority ownership is not possible), the major contributor of critical resources to an ICA. In this structure, one parent controls or dominates strategic and operational decision making. Its managers hold most of the important positions in the IJV or ICA organization. For IJVs, the dominant parent treats the IJV as if it were just another one of its subsidiaries.

- *Shared management:* In the **shared management structure**, both parents contribute approximately the same number of managers to positions such as the board of directors, the top management team, and the functional areas of management (e.g., production or marketing).

- *Split control:* The **split-control management structure** is similar to the shared management structure in that partners usually share strategic decision making. However, at the functional level (e.g., marketing, production, and R&D), partners make decisions independently. Often one partner has a unique skill or technology that it does not want to share completely, and so it insists on independent decision making in these protected areas.

- *Independent management:* In the **independent management structure**, the alliance managers act more like managers from separate companies. This structure is characteristic of mature IJVs—which must be legally separate organizations—and seldom occurs in ICAs. Especially for operational decisions, IJV managers have nearly complete decision-making autonomy. Because of their independence, IJVs with this structure often recruit managers and other employees from outside the parent companies' organizations.

- *Rotating management:* Managers from the various partners rotate through the key positions in the management hierarchy. For example, the alliance's top manager or management team may change each year, with each partner appointing its own managers. The rotating management structure is popular with alliance partners from developing countries. It serves to train local management and technical talent and to transfer the expertise to the developing country.[15]

Choosing a Strategic Alliance Management Structure

Many characteristics of the alliance relationship influence the choice of a management structure. Usually, a parent that has a dominant equity position or contributes the most important resources to the alliance favors a dominant management structure, at least for strategic decision making. Alliance partners with equal ownership shares (for IJVs) or equal resource contributions (for ICAs) tend to avoid the dominant management structure. Instead, they adopt one of the more balanced managerial control systems, such as the shared, split, or rotating structures.

Management structures can change as companies' needs or contributions to the alliance change. When an Italian motorcycle helmet manufacturer found that inexperienced Belarussian managers had difficulty running the operation, the IJV faced a serious challenge to its viability. The next Multinational Management Challenge shows how the company solved the problems. How would you react?

Multinational Management **Challenge**

Finding the Right Management Structure

AGV is a small but highly successful Italian manufacturer of motorcycle helmets. Although the firm has only 190 employees, it is the second leading producer of helmets in the world. AGV exports to more than 30 countries and has nearly 2,000 sales outlets in a number of countries.

Seeking a presence in the former Soviet republics and a cheaper source of raw materials, AGV formed a joint venture with Steklovolokno, a fiberglass producer located in Belarus. AGV took a 40 percent ownership share in the joint venture company called Agv Polspo.

Management control problems surfaced quickly. As the minority owner, AGV was forced to use the local managers from its Belarussian partner. The Italian side discovered that these managers, trained and developed in a formerly state-run organization, had no concept of marketing or of the need to meet deadlines in production. To solve the problem, AGV first attempted retraining. It brought 30 managers to Italy for training in the AGV management methods. However, the Belarussian managers were reluctant to change their old practices, and the program was eventually abandoned.

To gain dominant management control of the venture, AGV bought an additional 20 percent of Agv Polspo. It then installed an Italian CEO and Italian managers in sales and production. Because of the cost and difficulty of hiring and maintaining expatriate managers in Belarus, AGV saw this as only an intermediate step. It recruited and trained mostly young Belarussian managers, who eventually filled the positions held by Italian expatriate managers. Agv Polspo is now a successful company exporting its helmets to 17 countries.

However, not all joint ventures work well with dominant parent structures. A case study of product development alliances indicated that one of the major success factors is equality in decision making. In such cases, it is probably more advantageous to go with a shared management structure.

Sources: Based on Olsen, J. R., H. Harnsen, and A. Friis. 2008. "Product development alliances: Factors influencing formation and success." British Food Journal, 110(45), pp. 430–443; United Nations Economic Commission for Europe and ILO. 1993. "The management challenge in Belarus: The case of AGV-Polotsk." In Management Development in East-West Joint Ventures *New York: United Nations, pp. 33–36; Agv Polspo. 2003. http://www.agvpolspo.narod.ru/.*

Additional considerations in the choice of a management structure relate to the strategic and organizational characteristics of the parent companies and the nature of their industry; that is, parent company and industry characteristics make certain management structures more effective or more attractive to the companies involved.[16] A summary of alliance research summarized several of the factors that multinational managers take into account when designing a management structure for their international strategic alliances:[17]

- If partners have *similar* technologies or know-how and they contribute this knowledge *equally* to the alliance, they prefer a shared management structure.
- If partners have *different* technologies or know-how and they contribute this knowledge *equally* to the alliance, they prefer split management structures.
- If the alliance has more strategic importance to one partner, a dominant management structure is likely.

For joint ventures in particular:

- Mature joint ventures move to independent structures as the IJV's management team gains expertise.
- Joint ventures in countries with a high degree of government intervention produce IJVs with local partner dominance.
- Independent management structures are likely when the market is expanding, the venture does not require much capital, or the venture does not require much R&D input from its parents.

A strategic alliance is like a marriage. Without mutual trust and commitment, the relationship will fail. We now examine how these issues are handled in strategic alliances.

Commitment and Trust: The Soft Side of Alliance Management

A common theme among managers from both failed and successful strategic alliances is the importance of building mutual trust and commitment among partners. No matter how beneficial and logical the venture may seem at its start, without trust and commitment, the alliance will either fail entirely or fail to reach its strategic potential.[18]

The Importance of Commitment and Trust

Commitment in a strategic alliance means taking care of each other and putting forth extra effort to make the venture work. **Attitudinal commitment** means that partners are committed and willing to dedicate resources and effort and to face risks to make the venture work. Formally, attitudinal commitment is the psychological identification with the relationship and a pride of association with the partner and with the alliance. Attitudinal commitment in international strategic alliances is demonstrated in many ways: a fair financial commitment; a commitment to support the partner's strategic goals; a commitment to the partner's employees; and a commitment to understand the culture, politics, and economics of the partner's country. If all partners involved in the alliance demonstrate this kind of commitment, the venture develops based on the principle of **fair exchange**;[19] that is, all partners believe that they receive benefits from the relationship that equal their contributions.

Commitment
In a strategic alliance, when partners take care of each other and put forth extra effort to make the venture work.

Attitudinal commitment
The willingness to dedicate resources and efforts and to face risks to make the alliance work.

Fair exchange
In a strategic alliance, when partners believe that they receive benefits from the relationship equal to their contributions.

Why is commitment important? The marriage of two or more distinct companies from different cultures creates a strong potential for conflict and mistrust. Without a sense of mutual obligation to each other and to the alliance, partners often fail to work out problems. Instead, they retreat to their own companies or cultures, leaving issues unresolved and often feeling that the venture is not worth the effort. As Henry Lane and Paul Beamish point out,[20] "A successful relationship requires constant attention and nurturing. As one executive explained, 'Good local partners have to be cherished and taken care of.'"

Commitment also has a practical side. **Calculative commitment** comes from the evaluations, expectations, and concerns about the future potential for gaining rewards in a relationship. Businesses require tangible outcomes for a relationship to continue. A study of commitment in IJVs suggests that commitment increases when both partners achieve their strategic goals, which may be financial or related to market entry or learning a new technology. However, it is not necessary that partners have the same strategic goals for the relationship to endure or grow in commitment.[21] Perhaps, like any marriage, if partners select each other carefully, it is easier to develop complementary strategic goals and the eventual commitment to the relationship.

Trust and commitment usually go hand in hand. As with commitment, there are two forms of trust. **Credibility trust** is the confidence that the partner has the intent and ability to meet its obligations and make its promised contributions. **Benevolent trust** is the confidence that the partner will behave with goodwill and with fair exchange.[22]

The development of trust between alliance partners may take time. Partners often begin a relationship suspicious of each other's motives. Fears and questions are typical: Do they want to steal my technology? Are they trying to take me over? Am I building a new competitor? Am I giving away too much? Will they or can they provide what we agreed on? Such initial suspicions make trust difficult.

Most experts on trust believe that it develops in what are called trust cycles. Just like people in relationships, partners in IJVs and ICAs often feel vulnerable. This early vulnerability makes partners tentative in their involvement in the relationship and reluctant to reveal true motives, business know-how, or technology. Gradually, as each side deals repeatedly with the other, suspicion declines and reciprocal trust grows.[23] Exhibit 9.7 illustrates the trust and commitment cycle in strategic alliances.

Why is trust important? Successful cooperation requires alliance participants to contribute quality inputs into the alliance organization. When partners do not trust each other, they hold back information or take unfair advantage of each other, given the opportunity. In such cases, the alliance seldom produces all the expected mutual benefits. Recall the alliance between Telia and Telenor, Norway's and Sweden's largest telecommunication companies. The lack of trust was so critical that it led to the breakdown of the alliance. Although the CEOs had trust in each other during the prealliance phase, it did not carry over to the individuals involved in the implementation.[24]

Trust is also necessary because formal contracts can never identify all the issues that arise in strategic alliances. It is impossible to write a contract with sufficient detail to cover every foreseeable situation. Much of what happens between alliance partners develops informally as the alliance matures. In addition, the technology and know-how of organizations entail tacit knowledge, which includes rules, procedures, and ways of doing things that are parts of the organization's culture. Tacit knowledge is not written down, and often people are

Calculative commitment Alliance partner's evaluations, expectations, and concerns regarding the potential rewards from the relationship.

Credibility trust The confidence that the partner has the intent and ability to meet promised obligations and commitments.

Benevolent trust The confidence that the partner will behave with good will and with fair exchange.

EXHIBIT 9.7   **Trust/Commitment Cycle**

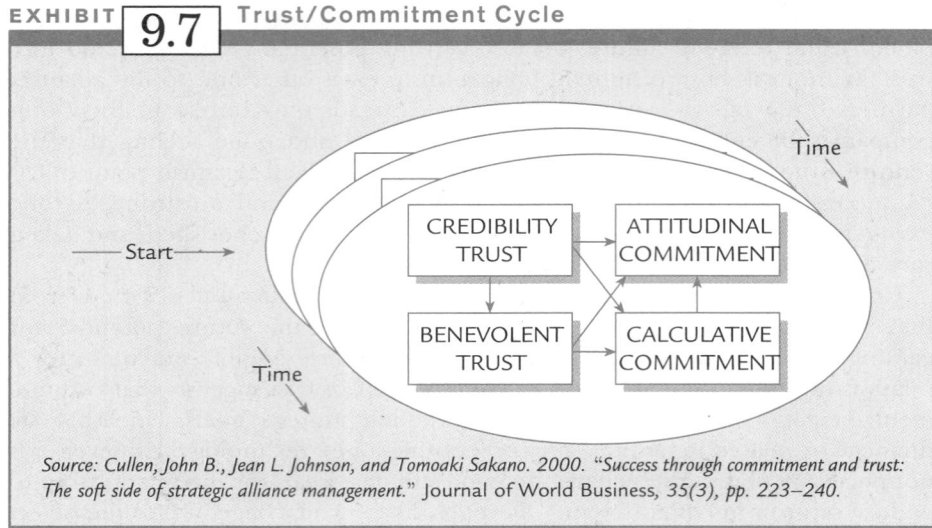

Source: Cullen, John B., Jean L. Johnson, and Tomoaki Sakano. 2000. "Success through commitment and trust: The soft side of strategic alliance management." Journal of World Business, 35(3), pp. 223–240.

not aware that it exists. As a result, for two organizations to share sensitive knowledge and go beyond the details of a formal contract, trust must exist. What happens if trust is lost and evolves into a distrust cycle? Consider the next Multinational Management Challenge, which shows some of the difficulties Pepsi faced with its joint venture partner in China.

Building and Sustaining Trust and Commitment

Multinational managers need to consider several key factors to build and sustain commitment and trust in international strategic alliances:[25]

- *Pick your partner carefully:* Picking a partner must include consideration of more than potential strategic complementarity and resource contributions. Alliance partners must believe that they can trust each other, and they must believe that mutual commitment is possible.

- *Know your strategic goals and those of your partner:* Mutual revelations of strategic goals build a crucial step in the trust cycle and allow partners to realize early in the relationship whether they can commit to each other's goals. However, alliance partners must realize that strategic goals for the ICA or IJV may change.

- *Seek win-win situations:* To achieve and maintain mutual commitment in an alliance, each side must gain something of importance from the relationship. Although the outcomes from the alliance need not be the same, both sides must perceive them as a fair exchange if commitment and trust are to evolve.

- *Go slowly:* Participants in international strategic alliances must realize that problems arise and take time to work out. Trust and commitment develop in cycles, not necessarily all at once.

- *Invest in cross-cultural training:* As in all international ventures, managers with cross-cultural sensitivity and language competence will likely have more success in understanding their partner's needs and interests. Quality cross-cultural interactions between partners' employees enable them to avoid conflict and misunderstandings, leading to greater trust and commitment.

Multinational Management **Challenge**

Pepsi Seeks a Divorce

Divorce is not a pleasant thing; you only go through it where there is no alternative. We have found them impossible to work with. They have totally destroyed any basis for cooperation.

— Wah-Hui Chu, president of Pepsi's China regarding a local IJV partner

The attraction of gaining access to a city of ten million led Pepsi to create a joint venture with Sichuan Radio and Television Industrial Development Co., a subsidiary of the province's Bureau of Radio, Film, and Television. Although the Chinese company had no knowledge of the beverage industry, most foreign investments in China require local partners; so Pepsi saw this as a way to gain local government favor. Pepsi's Chu noted, "They came to us and said they could secure government approval to set up the business, and off we went. It wasn't a pure commercial decision. You could call it an arranged marriage." Pepsi invested $20 million into the factory, which resulted in only 27 percent ownership. However, it retained the right to 50 percent of the board.

Although the assembly line is still pumping out bottles of cola, the international joint venture between Pepsi and the Sichuan provincial government in China, Sichuan Pepsi-Cola Beverages Co., has deteriorated. Once a symbol of China's economic reforms, the IJV is now an embarrassment for both partners. How could such a promising venture go into the distrust cycle?

Pepsi's side:

- The partner looted the company, using funds for fancy vacations and cars. Managers submitted multiple copies of receipts to pad reimbursements.
- The general manager of the IJV, appointed by the local partner, did not follow company policies regarding sales areas.
- The partner changed the ownership structure.
- The partner blocked Pepsi's auditors from looking at factory books.

The local side:

- Managers dismissed talks of the improper use of company monies.
- We must sell outside the markets assigned by Pepsi to make a profit; managers' bonuses depend on it.
- Pepsi's accusations are exaggerations of long unresolved conflicts designed to lead to the replacement of the factory's management.
- Pepsi is practicing "commercial hegemonism."

In what amounts to a public admission of failure, Pepsi filed papers to dissolve the partnership. An international arbitrator considered the case in Stockholm with Chinese arbitrators. In 2005, the arbitrators ruled in favor of Pepsi and ordered the partnership be dissolved. However, with a market of 70 million people in Sichuan province, Pepsi intends to stay and will seek other partners or go it alone without a partner.

Sources: Based on Ambler, T., M. Witzel, and C. Xi. 2009. Doing business in China. New York: Routledge. Goodman, Peter S. 2002. "Pepsi seeks 'divorce' in China: Subsidiary seeks to dissolve partnership that runs bottling plant in Sichuan Province." Washington Post, September 28, p. E01.

- *Invest in direct communication:* To overcome national, business, and organizational cultural differences, alliance partners are more successful at building trust and commitment when they deal with issues face to face.
- *Find the right level of trust and commitment:* Exhibit 9.8 shows the trade-off between the vulnerability that comes with trust and commitment and their benefits.

Companies form IJVs or ICAs for benefits in the short term, in the long term, or both. Consequently, companies must assess whether the alliance is living up to expectations. In the next section, we consider the complex problems of assessing the performance of international strategic alliances.

Assessing the Performance of an International Strategic Alliance

Like all business ventures, strategic alliances should contribute eventually to their parents' profitability. When the strategic intent of the alliance is to produce immediate results, assessment of the alliance's performance is not difficult. Standard financial and efficiency measures of performance, such as profit, sales revenue, or number of units produced, are common. Often such alliances, particularly IJVs, become stand-alone profit centers that provide direct financial benefits to the parents. Profit center alliances produce and sell their own products on the open market. Parents evaluate such alliances as they would their

EXHIBIT 9.8   The Right Level of Trust and Commitment

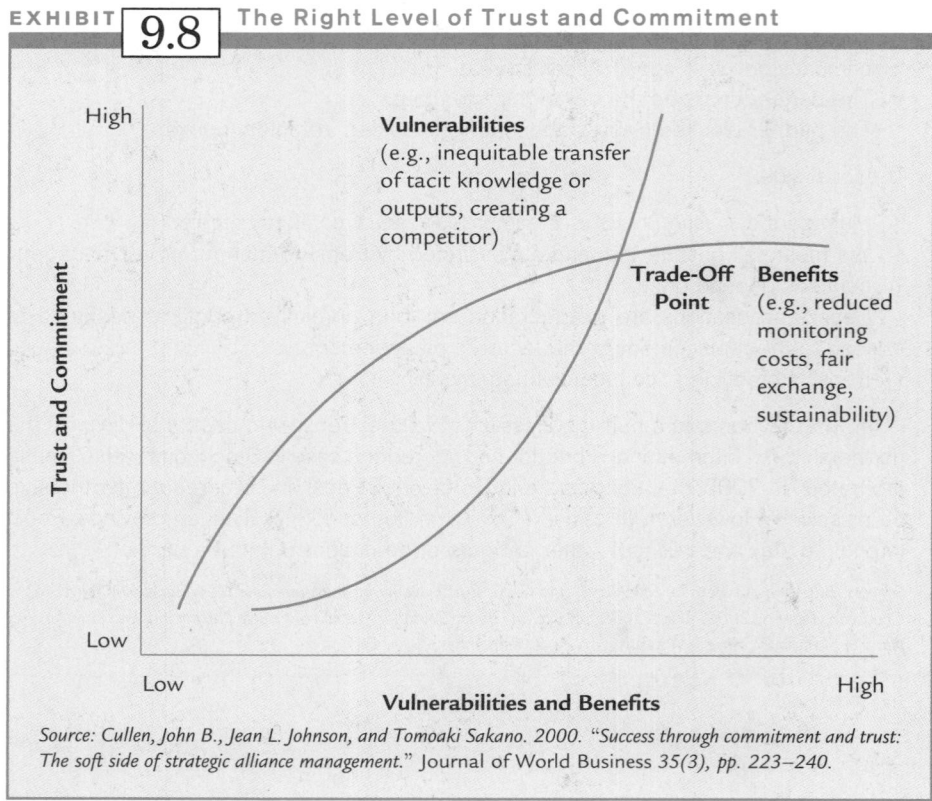

Source: Cullen, John B., Jean L. Johnson, and Tomoaki Sakano. 2000. "Success through commitment and trust: The soft side of strategic alliance management." Journal of World Business 35(3), pp. 223–240.

other corporate divisions, based on traditional financial profitability ratios, such as return on investment.

Other types of strategic alliances provide mostly indirect strategic contributions to parents, and the alliance organizations may never generate profits. Instead, they produce other valued outputs, such as new technologies with potential benefits for their parents. Indirect benefits from strategic alliances may come from penetrating risky markets, learning new markets or technologies, developing new technologies, overcoming local political barriers, developing a presence in a market, or supporting other competitive tactics.[26] Consider the next Multinational Management Brief.

Eventually, all companies hope to make money from their ICA or IJV investments. The alliance itself may not produce the profit, but the knowledge gained may allow the parents to succeed in the future. In the meantime, however, how can upper management assess the performance of a strategic alliance and of the managers responsible for it? **What is distinctive about IJV and ICA performance criteria?**

Financial measures alone are seldom good indicators of performance for strategic alliances created for indirect strategic benefits. Depending on the unique objectives of the alliances, parent companies must develop more subjective performance criteria, such as creating harmony among the partners, identifying product adaptations for a new market, or capturing market share to gain first-mover advantages over their competitors.[27]

Research emphasis on the relational aspects of alliances has spurred interest in other forms of alliance performance measures.[28] For instance, some have proposed "alliance satisfaction" as a measure of performance, and others emphasize measures like goal accomplishment. Still others have argued for alternatives to more direct measures of performance, such as duration of the alliance

IJV and ICA performance criteria
Often must include other than financial criteria, such as organizational learning.

Multinational Management **Brief**

Performance Criteria in a Strategic Alliance

Oxford Bio Therapeutics (OBT) and pharmaceuticals giant GlaxoSmithKline (GSK) entered into a strategic alliance. OBT is focused on the development of innovative cancer-fighting drugs through antibody-based approaches. Because of its expertise in the development of such drugs, GSK has entered into the alliance to benefit from OBT's expertise in drug development. In exchange for up-front payments and other financial support that may add up to about $370 million, OBT will develop drugs up to the clinical proof of concept. GSK will then use its own expertise to take the drug through the clinical testing phase and eventual commercialization. In return, OBT will then receive royalties on sales of the product.

The success of this alliance therefore depends on the development of new and financially rewarding drugs, but it cannot be measured directly, such as in terms of profit. To ensure that the alliance progresses smoothly, GSK has devised milestones and will compensate OBT as it reaches the milestones: a specified discovery, development, regulatory compliance, and commercialization. Success for both GSK and OBT is measured in terms of these milestones, with the hope that the new drug will be a commercial success.

Source: Based on PR Newswire. 2009. "Oxford Bio Therapeutics and GlaxoSmithKline form strategic alliance to develop novel cancer therapeutic antibodies," May 18.

with early termination suggesting failure.[29] However, most measures are problematic, and the best measure depends on the nature of the alliance. For instance, duration may not be an appropriate measure because most alliances are formed with the explicit notion that they will be dissolved once the goals have been achieved. Early termination may imply that the goals have been achieved sooner than expected.

Assessing the performance of all types of alliances demands that parents match the alliances' strategic objectives with the measures used for assessment. If immediate profit is the strategic goal, then profit must be in the assessment. If the goals are long term, such as learning a new market or technology, then immediate profit must be deemphasized in favor of other performance measures.

Exhibit 9.9 shows a list of potential performance measures that parent companies use to evaluate their strategic alliances.

Not all alliances achieve their strategic intent. The next section addresses how managers must plan for handling a nonperforming alliance.

If the Alliance Does Not Work

If the alliance fails to meet strategic goals, managers have two basic choices (see Exhibit 9.1). Providing that they keep their same strategic intent, they can negotiate an end to the agreement or improve their implementation.

The art of managing strategic alliances is in knowing when to quit and when to invest more time and resources in building the relationship. There are really no hard-and-fast rules, and each case is unique. Often, the personal

EXHIBIT 9.9   Selected Performance Criteria for Strategic Alliances

Management Processes	Competitive
Good partner relationships; no conflict or handled well High worker morale Meeting goals of social responsibility Development of human resources Dealing with the local government	Gaining market share Minimizing knowledge leakage to partners (knowledge not intended for partners) Affecting competitors (e.g., preventing them from gaining a foothold in the country)
Organizational Learning	**Marketing**
Understanding a new market Learning a new technology Improving R&D cycle times Developing new management techniques Developing innovative technologies Generating other potential opportunities	Total sales Customer satisfaction Insights into customer needs Facilitating the sale of other products
	Financial
	Return on investment (return on assets) Return on assets

Sources: Adapted from Anderson, Erin. 1990. "Two firms, one frontier: On assessing joint venture performance." Sloan Management Review, Winter, pp. 19–30; Gomes-Casseres, Ben. 1998. "Strategy before structure." Alliance Analyst, August.

relationships among alliance managers become the key for turning around a nonperforming alliance.

A particular danger in all questionable alliance relationships is the **escalation of commitment**,[30] which means that managers continue in relationships longer than necessary because of past financial and emotional investments. Consider the next Multinational Management Brief in terms of the possibility of the escalation of commitment.

Improving the implementation means going over each step in the implementation process to determine what, if any, changes can be made. Perhaps, for example, partners failed to develop an appropriate design for the alliance organization or chose a weak alliance manager. Of course, if one side decides that it just has the wrong partner, it must dissolve the relationship and, if necessary, seek another.

A recommended strategy of alliance formation is to plan for the end of the alliance from its beginning. Alliance contracts can contain a kind of prenuptial agreement that specifies how the alliance can be dissolved. This agreement describes the procedures to end the alliance and states the periods during which both sides must agree to keep the alliance alive. It may also specify penalties for early termination by either side. The advantage of including such an agreement up front, before the alliance begins, is that negotiations occur in a positive and friendly stage of the relationship, not later when there is often conflict between the partners and a high level of distrust.

The death of a strategic alliance should not be confused with a failed relationship. Many alliances are intended to be short term. Once partners achieve

> **Escalation of commitment**
> Companies continue in an alliance relationship longer than necessary because of past financial and emotional investments.

Multinational Management **Brief**

Escalation of Commitment and Shell

Shell, the Anglo-Dutch oil company, is making one of its largest investments in a very large plant in the country of Qatar. It is entering into a strategic alliance with Pearl GTL, the state-run Qatar petroleum company. With its $18 billion investment, Shell hopes to transform natural gas into clean-burning synthetic diesel, a process known as gas-to-liquid (GSL).

The project presents significant potential benefits to both companies. It enables Pearl GTL to diversify by transforming Qatar's huge reserves of natural gas into value-added fuel and lubricants. For Shell, the alliance has the potential of allowing it to reduce its dependence on oil-based products. As supplies of oil product are depleted, this outcome may be very advantageous to Shell.

However, for Shell, the project presents several dangers related to the escalation of commitment. Many oil experts are already arguing that the project may not be financially feasible. It costs about $40 to $90 dollars to produce a barrel of GSL. If gas prices are lower than $90, the project may fail. Furthermore, the construction cost of the plant is already much higher than originally thought when the project was proposed in 2002. Shell will have to determine whether it wants to forge ahead with the project despite the negative information regarding the project's potential to succeed and its initial cost. Only the future will show whether Shell was prone to escalation of commitment.

Source: Based on Chazan, G. 2009. "Shell's gamble in Qatar: Company is betting on new technology to get diesel fuel." Wall Street Journal, February 9, p. 8.

their strategic goals, they both go their own ways. For example, an alliance may end after a new technology is developed, a new market is penetrated, or a temporary product gap is remedied. In addition, IJVs are often acquired by one of the partners and move to the next level of direct investment.

Next we consider the role of the parent company in managing a portfolio of international joint ventures.

Learning to Partner: Building a Dedicated Strategic Alliance Unit and Key Lessons from Cross-Border Alliances

Alliances are so common in today's global business environment—the Global 500 companies average 60 each—that companies are developing specialized units to manage their design. These specialized units provide processes and procedures that, for example, help managers identify the need for an alliance, evaluate partners, negotiate agreements, structure the alliance organizations, and develop specific performance indicators.

Experienced multinational companies that have had many alliances are taking the experience of what has worked and what has failed and developing templates of successful practices. For example, a recent study showed that multinational companies with alliance-management units, such as HP and Lucent Technologies, outperform companies without them.[31] However, alliance management units do not work for all companies. Typically, only the very large multinational companies have enough alliances to dedicate the resources necessary to create such a specialized unit.

As we saw in this chapter, strategic alliances are likely to become more crucial in the future as multinational companies take advantage of emerging markets as well as try to lower costs. To conclude this chapter, we look at some key lessons learned from successful cross-border alliances based on Peter Jagersma's interview and survey of key individuals involved in successful cross-border alliances:[32]

- *Understand and appreciate business and cultural differences:* Successful cross-border alliances can be possible only if the partners recognize cultural and business differences and adapt to them.

- *Keep strong executive support:* Successful cross-border alliances consistently retain strong executive support. Involvement of the executive shows commitment and support of the alliance.

- *Communicate:* Communication is crucial to the cross-border alliance's success. Nothing is worse than two partners having different visions for the alliance.

- *Commitment, trust, and dedication:* In successful cross-border alliances, the partners are committed to the alliance and willing to commit the resources and personnel (including senior management time) to make it work.

- *Have checkpoint as the alliance is being implemented:* Build in go/no-go checkpoints to ensure that the partners are informed and satisfied with progress and development.

- *Review the alliance's viability:* Multinational companies need to review any alliance frequently to determine whether the alliance is viable and beneficial.

Summary and Conclusions

The use of international strategic alliances as a major participation strategy continues to grow in the global business environment. Implementing this strategy demands a sound knowledge of the problems and prospects associated with alliance management. This chapter provided a basic understating of the related issues, including where to link in the value chain, how to select a partner, how to design an alliance organization, HRM practices in an alliance, how to build trust and commitment, how to assess performance, and what to do if the alliance fails.

Perhaps the most important decision in managing successful strategic alliances is picking the right partner. Choosing a compatible partner with the appropriate skills determines the eventual fate of most alliances.

Strategic alliances have no set structure for ownership, decision-making control, or management control. Partners must negotiate structures that support their mutual strategic goals. Most experts also consider trust and commitment as making up the foundation for IJV or ICA success, second only to picking the right partner. Commitment and trust take on such importance because not everything can be stated in a contract. For long-term success, partner companies must trust each other to deliver the agreed-upon outputs and to not take advantage of partners in the relationship.

Because alliances' strategic goals are varied and subtle, the performance of an IJV or ICA is often difficult to determine. Usually, companies expect a strategic alliance to generate more than short-term financial returns. Other objectives, such as organizational learning and market penetration, often figure strongly in performance assessment.

Strategic alliances are inherently unstable and many will fail. Consequently, when an international strategic alliance fails to meet strategic goals, multinational managers must be prepared to improve their implementation efforts or to abandon the alliance. However, many strategic alliances die natural deaths when they meet their strategic objectives or are bought out by one of the parent companies.

International strategic alliances are now so common among the major multinational companies that many have formalized the process of implementing them and their organizations. Eli Lilly, for example, calls its unit the Office of Alliance Management.

Discussion Questions

1. What are the characteristics of a good partner in a strategic alliance? How do these partner traits help make an alliance successful?

2. Which of the alliance contract issues explained in the text do you think are most important? Why?

3. Discuss some costs and benefits of the different management structures. Under what conditions should a firm choose a particular structure?

4. What types of personnel are usually assigned to strategic alliances? For each type of personnel, what kind of impact does the IJV assignment have on future careers?

5. What are some of the difficulties of assessing IJV or ICA performance? How do these differ for companies with different strategic goals?

6. Why are trust and commitment so important to strategic alliances? How can a partner demonstrate trust and commitment to a joint venture?

Multinational Management Skill Builder

Compare and Contrast International Joint Venture Contracts

Most multinational companies have many joint ventures or strategic alliances. Your task is to identify the alliances of a company you select.

Step 1. Go to http://contracts.corporate.findlaw.com/ and search for joint venture or alliance contracts. Many are available and include well-known companies.

Step 2. Select two contracts for alliances in the same industry, and make a summary list of the major points covered.

Step 3. Compare and contrast these contracts regarding inclusiveness and detail of points covered versus the flexibility of the relationship.

Step 4. Search the Web and see if the venture still exists.

Endnotes

1 Accenture. 2009. http://www.accenture.com.

2 Kimberley, William. 2001. "Renault and GM target the light truck market." *Automotive Design and Production*. December. http://www.autofieldguide.com, accessed 2001.

3 *Strategic Direction*. 2006. "Create successful international mergers and alliances," 22(1), pp. 25–28.

4 Murray, Janet Y. 1995. "Patterns in domestic vs. international strategic alliances: An investigation of U.S. multinational firms." *Multinational Business Review*, 13, pp. 7–16.

5 Geringer, J. Michael. 1988. *Joint Venture Partner Selection.* Westport, CT: Quorum Books.

6 Ibid.

7 Main, Jeremy. 1990. "Making global alliances work." *Fortune*, December 17, pp. 121–126.

8 Ibid.

9 Geringer.

10 *Strategic Direction.*

11 Geringer.

12 Lorange, Peter, and Johan Roos. 1992. *Strategic Alliances.* Cambridge, MA: Blackwell.

13 Kealey, Daniel L., David R. Protheroe, Doug MacDonald, and Thomas Vulpe. 2006. "International projects: Some lessons on avoiding failure and maximizing success." *Performance Improvement*, March, 45(3), p. 38.

14 Gray, Barbara, and Aimin Yan. 1992. "A negotiations model of joint venture formation, structure, and performance: Implications for global management." *Advances in International Comparative Management*, 7, pp. 41–75; Killing, J. P. 1988. "Understanding alliances: The role of task and organizational complexity." In F. J. Contractor and P. Lorange, eds. *Cooperative Strategies in International Business*, pp. 241–245. Lexington, MA: Lexington Books.

15 Vernon, R. 1977. *Storm over Multinationals*. Cambridge, MA: Harvard University Press.

16 Ibid.

17 Ibid.

18 Taylor, Andrew. 2005. "An operations perspective on strategic alliance success factors: An exploratory study of alliance managers

in the software industry." *International Journal of Operations & Production Management*, 25(5/6), pp. 469–490.

19 Lane, Henry W., and Paul W. Beamish. 1990. "Cross-cultural cooperative behavior in joint ventures in IDCs." *Management International Review*, 30, Special Issue, pp. 87–102.

20 Ibid.

21 Cullen, John B., Jean L. Johnson, and Tomoaki Sakano, "Success through commitment and trust: The soft side of strategic alliance management." Cullen, John B., Jean L. Johnson, and Tomoaki Sakano. 1995. "Japanese and local partner commitment to IJVs: Psychological consequences of outcomes and investments in the IJV relationship." *Journal of International Business Studies*, 26(1), pp. 91–116.

22 Johnson, Jean L., John B. Cullen, Tomoaki Sakano, and Hideyuki Takenouchi. 1996. "Setting the stage for trust and strategic integration in Japanese–U.S. cooperative alliances." *Journal of International Business Studies*, 27, pp. 981–1004.

23 Ibid.; Ring, Peter Smith, and Andrew, H. Van De Ven. 1992. "Structuring cooperative relationships between organizations." *Strategic Management Journal* 13, pp. 483–498.

24 *Strategic Direction.*

25 Cullen, Johnson, and Sakano, "Success through commitment and trust."

26 Lei, David. 1993. "Offensive and defensive uses of alliances." *Long Range Planning* 26, pp. 32–44.

27 Anderson, Erin. 1990. "Two firms, one frontier: On assessing joint venture performance." *Sloan Management Review*, Winter, pp. 19–30.

28 Rahman, Noushi. 2006. "Duality of alliance performance." *Journal of American Academy of Business*, September, 10(1), pp. 305–311.

29 Ibid.

30 Cullen, Johnson, and Sakano, "Japanese and local partner commitment to IJVs."

31 Dyer, Jeffrey H., Prashant Kale, and Harbir Singh. 2001. "How to make strategic alliances work." *Sloan Management Review*, 42, pp. 37–44.

32 Jagersma, Peter Klaas. 2005. "Cross-border alliances: Advice from the executive suite." *Journal of Business Strategy*, 26(1), pp. 41–50.

Tata Motors and Fiat Auto: Joining Forces

"This is the beginning of what promises to be a far-reaching, long-term relationship between Fiat and Tata." [1]

— Ratan Tata, Chairman, Tata Motors, in 2006.

"While Tata Motors will get technology to develop economically priced small cars and entry-level sedans and an entry into untapped markets, Fiat India can continue to have a presence in the Indian market without much investment." [2]

— Kalpesh Parekh, Auto analyst, ASK Raymond James,[3] in 2006.

Introduction

In July 2006, major Italian automaker Fiat Auto S.p.A. (Fiat Auto), and the Indian automaker Tata Motors (TM), signed a Memorandum of Understanding (MoU) to form a joint venture to produce passenger cars, engines, and transmissions in India. These products were intended both for the Indian and the international market. Earlier, in January 2006, the two companies had signed a marketing and distribution agreement under which TM marketed select models of Fiat cars through a few of its dealers. The joint venture was seen as a major development in the Indian automobile industry.

Both TM and Fiat Auto had a long history in automobile manufacturing. Until the 1990s, TM was mostly a manufacturer of commercial vehicles. It entered the passenger car market in the 1990s with the *Indica*, a 1400 cc small car with a diesel engine,[4] which went on to become a success and placed TM among the top three passenger vehicle manufacturers in India. However, in 2002, because of a fall in the demand for commercial vehicles, TM reported a loss. As a part of its turnaround strategy, it improved its internal efficiencies and also decided to focus on overseas markets to reduce the impact of demand fluctuations in the domestic market. In 2003, TM returned to profitability. By 2005, it had a market presence in Thailand, Senegal, South Africa, Turkey, Europe, and West Asia. However, in spite of its impressive growth, TM was still a small player at the global level.

Fiat Auto, which built its first car in 1899, also had an illustrious history in the automobile world. After World War II, it became a major manufacturer of small cars in Italy, and later on in Europe. Until the 1990s, Fiat Auto dominated the small car market in Europe and other parts of the world.[5] In India, Fiat cars were imported even as far back as 1905. In the 1950s, the Fiat Group entered into a license agreement with India-based Premier Automobiles Ltd. (PAL) to manufacture its cars.[6] Fiat Auto formally entered the Indian market in 1997 through a joint venture with PAL.

In the early 2000s, Fiat Auto ran into losses as it was slow in adapting to the changed economic environment in Italy in particular and Europe in general.[7] Its market share in the Italian and European car markets declined. Around the same period, Fiat Auto's share in the Indian automobile market also fell drastically. In 2002, the company adopted a turnaround strategy which included several measures like cutting costs, restructuring debts, launching new models, increasing advertising spend, and focusing on markets where the demand for small cars was high. India being a major market for small cars, Fiat Auto decided to revive its operations in the Indian market. And the joint venture with TM was a step in that direction.

Most analysts were of the opinion that the joint venture would benefit both parties; TM would gain in terms of better accessibility to technology, design, and global markets, while for Fiat Auto, it would mean a larger presence in India, one of the world's fastest growing auto markets, without heavy investments. However, there were others who felt that the joint venture would end in brand dilution and product cannibalization for both parties. Also, with Honda, Toyota, GM, Mitsubishi, M&M/Renault, Nissan, Skoda, etc., chalking out plans to enter the small car segment, especially the premium small car segment, it seemed likely that the TM-Fiat Auto joint venture would face intense competition in the coming years.

Tata Motors

TM had its origins in Tatanagar Shops,[8] which was acquired by Tata Sons Ltd.[9] on June 1, 1945, from the Government of India (GoI). Tata Sons renamed the company Tata Locomotive and Engineering Company

Ltd. Initially, the company produced steam locomotive boilers and later graduated to producing complete locomotives and other engineering products. From 1960 onward, it was referred to as Telco (Tata Engineering and Locomotive Company Ltd.).

Telco began production of medium commercial vehicles in 1954. The company gradually grew under the leadership of J.R.D. Tata (Chairman between 1945 and 1973) and Sumant Moolgaokar (Moolgaokar) (Chairman between 1973 and 1988). Telco set up a second factory in Pune in the 1970s. The company started manufacturing heavy commercial vehicles in 1983 and light commercial vehicles in 1986. Telco also increased its exports over the years. In 1988, Ratan Tata replaced Moolgaokar as Telco's Chairman. Under Ratan Tata, the company stepped into the passenger car segment. Telco began to test several indigenously developed car models in the late 1980s and the early 1990s.

Until 1990, India had a licensing and regulatory regime that stifled competition in the automobile industry. Due to this, the automobile market was a seller's market, with customers having to endure long waiting periods while purchasing new vehicles.

However, all this changed with the liberalization of the Indian economy in 1991. The seller's market was transformed into a buyer's market. The 1990s saw the entry of several major global automobile manufacturing companies into India. In 1991, Ratan Tata took over as Chairman of the Tata Group.

In 1991, the first utility vehicle (described as a cross between a truck and a car) under the Tata marquee called the *Sierra* was launched. This was followed by the *Estate* in 1992. In the same year, Telco opened a new factory at Lucknow. In 1994, the company entered into a joint venture agreement with Daimler-Benz AG for the manufacture of Mercedes Benz passenger cars in India,[10] an agreement which continued until 2001. The same year, it also launched a multi-utility vehicle (MUV) called the *Sumo*.

In 1998, Telco launched the *Safari*, India's first sports utility vehicle (SUV). The same year, the company also introduced the *Indica*,[11] a small hatchback with an indigenously developed diesel engine.[12] The launch of the *Indica* was a defining moment for Telco as it was not only the company's first small car, but also India's first indigenously developed small car.[13]

At the time of launch of the *Indica*, the small car market in India was dominated by the *Maruti 800*, a small hatchback manufactured by Maruti Udyog Ltd. (MUL).[14] The *Indica* was priced aggressively to attract *Maruti 800* customers. This forced MUL to lower the retail price of the *Maruti 800*, which made small cars more affordable to the Indian middle class and consequently expanded the market for small cars. Telco

changed the rules of the game in the Indian automobile market by providing customers of the *Indica* with options like air conditioning, power steering, alloy wheels, and electric windows features which until then had been available only in premium cars.

By 1999, with 115,000 bookings, it was clear that the *Indica* was a success. Even as the car was a commercial success, Telco received several complaints from customers on aspects such as excessive tire wear, engine vibration, and problems with gears. Telco then re-engineered the car totally and launched it as the *Indica V2* (or version 2). This version fixed most of the technical problems that had plagued the *Indica* and it went on to become very popular with customers.

Even though Telco was making impressive inroads into the passenger car market, the year 2001 saw the company recording a net loss of about Rs. 5 billion—its first loss in 57 years. This was attributed to the Indian commercial vehicles market contracting by about 40 percent during the year. As Telco was the market leader in the commercial vehicles (light and heavy) segment with a market share of 74 percent (in 2001), the impact of this on the company was particularly severe.

As part of a turnaround strategy, Telco focused on improving internal efficiencies and restructuring its debts. It also took measures to increase productivity. These efforts helped it to cut costs by Rs. 9.60 billion within two years (Telco was able to reduce the cost of raw materials by 65 percent and of interest costs by 25 percent). "Our turnaround initiatives during the past two years were focused on aggressive cost reduction, right-sizing the organization, financial restructuring, gains in volume and market share, re-engineering processes, organizational transformation, and launching new products,"[15] said Praveen Kadle (Kadle), executive director (Finance), Telco.

The company improved its overall efficiency, which allowed it to break even at a much lower level of capacity utilization than before (31 percent for commercial vehicles and 48 percent for cars). It adopted the platform-sharing system, where different vehicle models shared the same manufacturing system and some key components, which cut down costs as well as the time-to-market. In 2002, it launched the *Indigo*, a mid-size three-box car which shared a platform with the *Indica*.

In 2002–2003, Telco registered a net profit of Rs. 3 billion. In this period, the company worked out a two-pronged strategy for growth and to protect itself from future downturns in markets. The first component of the strategy was to enter and establish itself in overseas markets. This, in addition to aiding growth, was expected to help the company ride out demand fluctuations in the domestic market. "The international markets mitigate risk and provide a growth opportunity,"[16] said

Kadle. The second part of the strategy was to produce new products in new segments and to increase the focus on small passenger vehicles.

The Growth Strategy

Going Global In December 2002, Telco signed a manufacturing and supply agreement with the UK-based MG Rover Group.[17] Under the agreement, Telco was to supply the *Indica,* suitably modified to meet the applicable regulatory standards, to MG Rover, which would then sell it in the UK and in Continental Europe as the *City Rover.* Telco also planned to simultaneously market the *Indica* in Europe through its own distribution network. Ratan Tata said, "This agreement will enhance the volume throughput of the Indica plant [at Pune] significantly. More importantly, we look at it as an endorsement by a major international company of Tata Engineering's [Telco] capabilities in general, and the world-class acceptability of the Indica in particular."[18]

In keeping with its global aspirations, Telco was renamed as Tata Motors (TM) in September 2003. "It's all about growth and a bit of international aspiration. We are driving a change in mindset through this new name, embarking on a journey that will be increasingly global," [19] said a Tata spokesperson.

In October 2003, TM won a US$ 19 million tender for the supply of 500 buses to Senegal. It then set up a bus assembly unit in Thies, Senegal.

In 2004, TM set up a regional office and a special sales team in the UAE to boost its commercial vehicles business in West Asia. In March 2004, TM acquired Korea-based Daewoo's commercial vehicles business. One of the reasons for this acquisition was to gain an entry into the high-volume Chinese market. "About 60 percent of Daewoo's total exports goes to China, and it is already working with a company there to make trucks in China for the local market. So we would use Daewoo as leverage to strengthen our position in the Chinese market,"[20] said Kadle.

TM had been selling its medium commercial vehicles and buses in the South African market through Tata Automobile Corporation South Africa (TACSA) since 1997. In 2004, the company invested Rs. 40 million in a bus assembly unit in Johannesburg. TM also launched its passenger cars–the *Indica* and the *Indigo*–in the South African market that year. The cars were sold through a network of 20 dealers. According to reports, TM aimed to capture 7 percent of the South African passenger vehicle market by 2007–08.

TM was listed on the New York Stock Exchange (NYSE) in September 2004.[21] "We are confident that the company will benefit from the capital market access that this listing provides,"[22] said Ratan Tata.

By the end of 2004, TM's agreement with MG Rover came under a cloud with Rover selling far fewer *City Rovers* than expected. Eventually, the agreement came to an end in April 2005, when Rover was shut down because of financial problems.

However, TM continued to scout for new opportunities overseas. In March 2005, it acquired a 21 percent stake in Hispano Carrocera SA,[23] a Spanish bus manufacturing company, giving it controlling rights in the company and an option to buy the remaining stake at a later date. "This strategic alliance with Hispano Carrocera will give us access to its design and technological capabilities to fully tap the growing potential of this segment in India and other export markets. Besides, it provides us with a foothold in developed European markets,"[24] said Ravi Kant (Kant), executive director (commercial vehicle business unit), TM.

In February 2005, TM launched the *Indica* in Turkey through a network of 16 dealers.

In September 2005, TM entered into an agreement with Thai Rung Union Car Plc., Thailand's largest pick-up truck modifier,[25] to set up a manufacturing unit for pick-ups in Thailand. Thailand was the largest manufacturing base for utility vehicles after the United States and a major market for utility vehicles.[26] With this venture, TM also hoped to gain access to the ASEAN region.[27] TM also made known its plans to set up a production base for hybrid and low-cost small cars in this region in the future.

New Product Initiatives Alongside its global forays, TM launched several new products, some of which created new categories in the Indian market. In 2004, it unveiled plans to launch the *Indiva,* a seven-seater multipurpose vehicle (MPV). In September 2004, TM launched the *Indigo Marina,* a station wagon, positioned as a premium car that combined the luxury of a sedan with the convenience of an MPV. "We believe that the Indigo Marina will create a new segment in the market. Tata Motors has always endeavored to grow the market by prying open new segments,"[28] said Dr V. Sumantran, executive director, engineering research centre and passenger car business unit, TM. The same year, it also launched an improved version of the *Indica V2* and the *Sumo Victa,* an improved version of the *Sumo.*

At the Geneva Motor Show in March 2005, TM unveiled the *Xover,* a concept car which was a fusion of a car and a SUV. After gauging customer reactions, TM planned to take a decision regarding the commercial launch of the car in Europe, India, and some other markets.

In May 2005, TM launched the *Ace,* a sub-one ton mini-truck that was uniquely positioned between three-wheeled cargo carriers and light commercial vehicles. The vehicle generated intense interest as it offered more load carrying capacity than the three-wheeled vehicles, and at a reasonable price. Moreover, the *Ace* catered to a segment of the auto industry that was believed to be less cyclical than the light, medium, and heavy commercial vehicles segments. In this period, TM also launched the *Safari Dicor,* the *Indigo SX series* (a luxury variant of the *Indigo*), the *Indica V2 Turbo Diesel,* the *TL 4X4* (India's first Sports Utility Truck), and the *Novus* (a range of commercial vehicles).

In September 2005, TM announced plans to launch a Rs. 100,000 car within three years.[29] "The vehicle would seat four to five people and have a rear engine. It will not be a scooter, three-wheeler or an auto-rickshaw made into a car,"[30] said Ratan Tata. The product was to be positioned between two-wheelers and the existing entry-level cars.

At the end of 2005, TM continued to be the market leader in the US$ 5 billion Indian commercial vehicle market (truck and bus) with about 58 percent market share (*See Exhibit I for the market share of TM in commercial vehicles market in India*). The company was the world's sixth largest commercial vehicle manufacturer,[31] and the third biggest car maker in India after MUL and Hyundai (*See Exhibit II for the market share of TM in the Indian passenger vehicles market*). International business, including exports, accounted for 18 percent of its revenues (in 2005–06).

Fiat Auto

Fiat came into existence on July 11, 1899.[32] The company was established by Giovanni Agnelli (Giovanni) together with a group of investors. The first Fiat car manufacturing facility was opened in 1900 in Corso Dante, Italy. Giovanni became the managing director of the company in 1902. In 1908, the company started exporting cars to the United States, France, Australia, and the U.K.

By 1911, the Fiat Group had diversified into the production and marketing of commercial vehicles, marine engines, trucks, and trams and by 1925, it had entered the steel, railways, power, and public transportation businesses.

The Fiat Group's auto division used mass production to keep production costs low. By the late 1950s, the Group had set up several new manufacturing plants abroad for automobiles as well as for farm machinery. In 1966, Gianni Agnelli (Agnelli), the grandson of Giovanni, became the Chairman of the Fiat Group. In later years, the Group expanded its operations into areas such as aerospace and telecommunications with varying degrees of success. In 1967, in its first acquisition, the Fiat Group purchased Autobianchi.[33] In 1969,[34] it purchased controlling interests in Ferrari and Lancia.[35]

In 1976, the Fiat Group's auto division entered the automobile market in Brazil. It also established production facilities in the country. Later, it entered the Argentinean automobile market. Over the years, the Group invested heavily in these two markets.

In the 1970s, the Fiat Group's numerous operations were spun off as independent companies. In 1979, the automobile division of the Group (consisting of Fiat, Lancia, Autobianchi, Abarth,[36] and Ferrari) was incorporated as an independent company called Fiat Auto S.p.A. By the late 1970s, Fiat Auto had plants in Italy, Poland, Brazil, and Argentina. In 1986, Fiat Auto took over Alfa Romeo,[37] a sports car manufacturer. In 1993, it acquired Maserati,[38] another sports car manufacturing company.

By the late 1980s, Fiat Auto was facing severe competition from Japanese auto manufacturers in several markets. During this period, Fiat Auto withdrew from the American and Australian markets.

In the early 1990s, Agnelli was made a senator for life in recognition of his role in developing Italy's economy. At that time, the Fiat Group accounted for almost 5 percent of Italy's Gross Domestic Product (GDP) and was also Italy's biggest employer and something of a national icon.

Fiat India

The Fiat Group's association with the Indian automobile market goes back to 1905, when it appointed Bombay Motor Cars Agency as the sales agent for its cars in India. In the 1950s, the Fiat Group entered into a license and service agreement with PAL, which allowed PAL to manufacture the *Fiat 500* in 1951, the *Millicento* in 1954, and the *Fiat 1100* in 1964. The Fiat 1100 model was later marketed in India as the *Premier Padmini.* The *Premier Padmini,* launched in 1968, went on to become very popular in India. PAL manufactured and marketed the *Premier Padmini* until 2000. PAL also launched the 118 NE which combined the body shell of the Fiat 124 with a Nissan engine. This model was not very successful.

In 1995, Fiat Auto established a wholly-owned subsidiary in India—Fiat India Auto Ltd (FIAL). FIAL entered into a 51:49 joint venture with PAL to form Ind Auto Ltd. The joint venture company manufactured the *Uno,* a small hatchback, at a plant in Kurla, Mumbai. The production of the *Uno* started in 1996. In 1997, FIAL increased its stake in the joint venture to 97 percent, took over the Kurla plant, and created a new dealer network. Ind Auto Ltd. was renamed as Fiat India Pvt. Ltd. (Fiat India). In 1998, Fidis S.p.A., Fiat Auto's subsidiary in the auto finance business, entered into a joint venture with Sundaram Finance Ltd.,[39] to form Fiat Sundaram Auto Finance Ltd. (FISAF) to finance Fiat cars.

EXHIBIT I

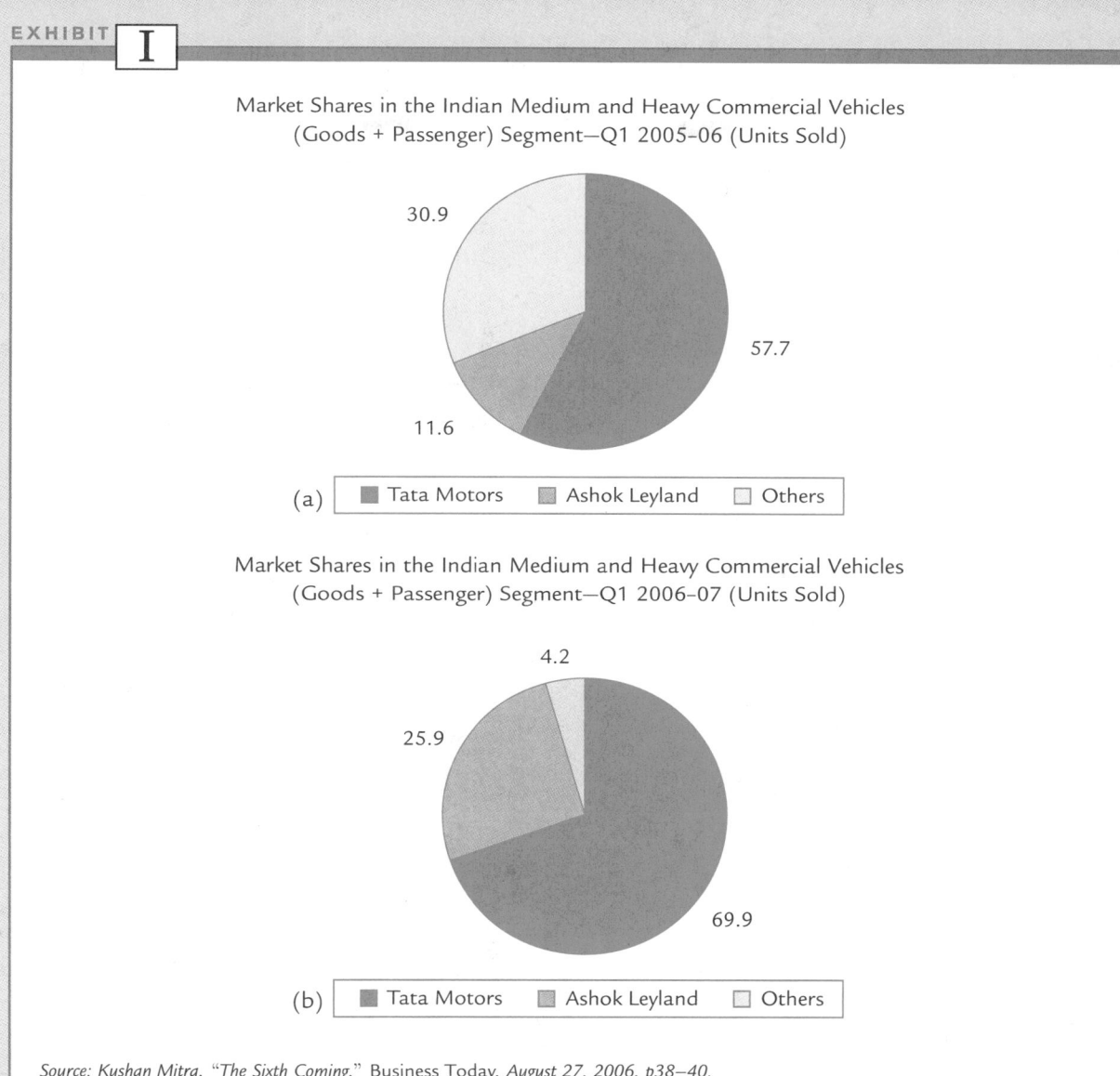

Market Shares in the Indian Medium and Heavy Commercial Vehicles (Goods + Passenger) Segment—Q1 2005–06 (Units Sold)

30.9

57.7

11.6

(a) ■ Tata Motors   ■ Ashok Leyland   □ Others

Market Shares in the Indian Medium and Heavy Commercial Vehicles (Goods + Passenger) Segment—Q1 2006–07 (Units Sold)

4.2

25.9

69.9

(b) ■ Tata Motors   ■ Ashok Leyland   □ Others

Source: Kushan Mitra, "The Sixth Coming," Business Today, August 27, 2006, p38–40.

Though the *Uno* received favorable reviews for its design and was considered to be a car that offered good value for money, it was not a commercial success. Reportedly customer interest in the product declined over a period of time due to poor customer service and promotion. Fiat India launched the *Siena* in 1999 and the *Palio* in 2001.

Financial Problems at Fiat Auto

By the late 1990s, Fiat Auto was in deep trouble. Its problems had been building up for years. One of the main reasons for its problems was that, over the years, it had failed to move beyond the small car segment to the segments for bigger cars, where margins were higher. Italy's adoption of the Euro, the common currency of the European Union, also had an adverse effect on Fiat Auto. The Italian government's decisions to withdraw the concessions and subsidies given to the company, and at the same time, give foreign auto companies free access to the Italian market, severely affected the company's revenues and profitability. "The terrible story of Fiat [Fiat Auto] reflects the protectionism, ineffectiveness, corruption, and compromise

EXHIBIT **II**

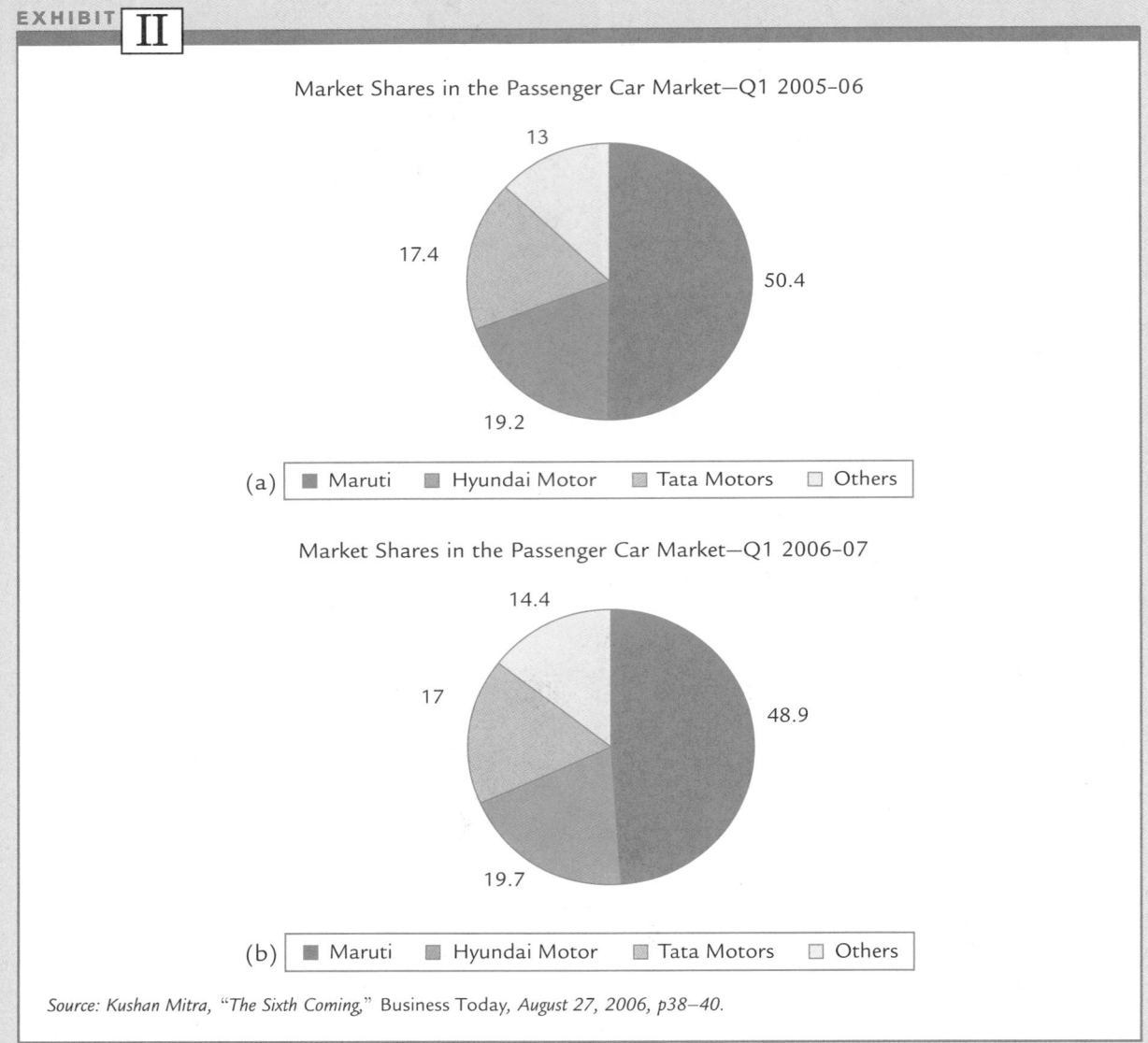

Market Shares in the Passenger Car Market—Q1 2005–06

13

17.4

50.4

19.2

(a) ■ Maruti ■ Hyundai Motor ▦ Tata Motors ☐ Others

Market Shares in the Passenger Car Market—Q1 2006–07

14.4

17

48.9

19.7

(b) ■ Maruti ■ Hyundai Motor ▦ Tata Motors ☐ Others

Source: Kushan Mitra, "The Sixth Coming," Business Today, August 27, 2006, p38–40.

typical of the way Italy has done business for the past 30 years,"[40] said an Italian entrepreneur. However, as much as to the macro-economic factors, auto analysts attributed the decline of Fiat Auto to the poor quality and performance of its cars.

Apart from increasing foreign competition, the late 1990s also saw the demand for cars falling in Italy and some other European countries. The European car industry was burdened with excess capacity, and Fiat Auto started incurring losses in its European operations because of falling sales and increasing costs. Other auto companies too were affected and some of them

even shut down their plants in Europe. Fiat Auto, which had invested heavily in expanding the markets in Latin America, suffered another blow when the region faced a financial crisis in 1998–99. Due to all these developments, the company found itself in deep financial trouble.

Paolo Fresco (Fresco) became chairman of Fiat Auto in 1998, by which time its market share in Italy had fallen to 41 percent from around 62 percent in 1984. In 2000, the Fiat Group entered into a joint venture agreement with General Motors (GM).[41] While GM took a 20 percent share in Fiat Auto, the Italian company took a

6 percent share in GM. The deal included a put option, valid between January 2004 and July 2009, which required GM to acquire the Group's auto business, failing which GM would have to pay a penalty of US$ 2 billion to the Fiat Group.

By 2002, Fiat Auto had accumulated losses of US$ 2.5 billion, including a loss of $1.3 billion in 2001. The Fiat Group as a whole had debts of almost € 33.4 billion (in 2002).

In 2002, Fiat Auto's market share was down to 28 percent in Italy, and a mere 7 percent in Europe.[42] Its share price had also fallen by almost 50 percent over a ten-year period. In the same year, the company embarked on a restructuring program to deal with the crisis caused by declining sales, increasing losses, and rising levels of debt.

The crisis at Fiat Auto prompted the Italian government to consider buying a stake in the company. However, private banks, which were the major creditors of the Fiat Group, preferred a market-guided restructuring for the company. The Fiat Group received about € 3 billion in credit from the private banks with a requirement to either sell or turn around its auto

business. The Group also transferred a major share in Fidis Retail Italia (FRI),[43] a subsidiary in the auto finance business, to the banks.[44]

In an effort to cut costs, Fiat Auto announced its intention to trim its workforce. The proposal met with stiff resistance not only from the labor unions but also from the Italian government. However, the company went ahead and in 2002, cut more than 8,100 jobs at its factories in Italy. It also increased investment in R&D and new product development.[45]

The Fiat Group also sold some of its industrial assets to pay off loans. In 2003, the Group sold its insurance and aviation businesses and in February 2004, its engineering and power businesses (*See Exhibit III for the corporate structure of the Fiat Group*).

Through the early 2000s, Fiat Auto saw the entry and exit of four chief executives. These frequent changes in leadership had their impact on the restructuring process. In June 2004, Sergio Marchionne (Marchionne) became the CEO of Fiat Auto. He initiated further cost-cutting measures, and fired managers whose performance was unsatisfactory. He also drew up a schedule for new model launches,

EXHIBIT III **Corporate Structure of the Fiat Group**

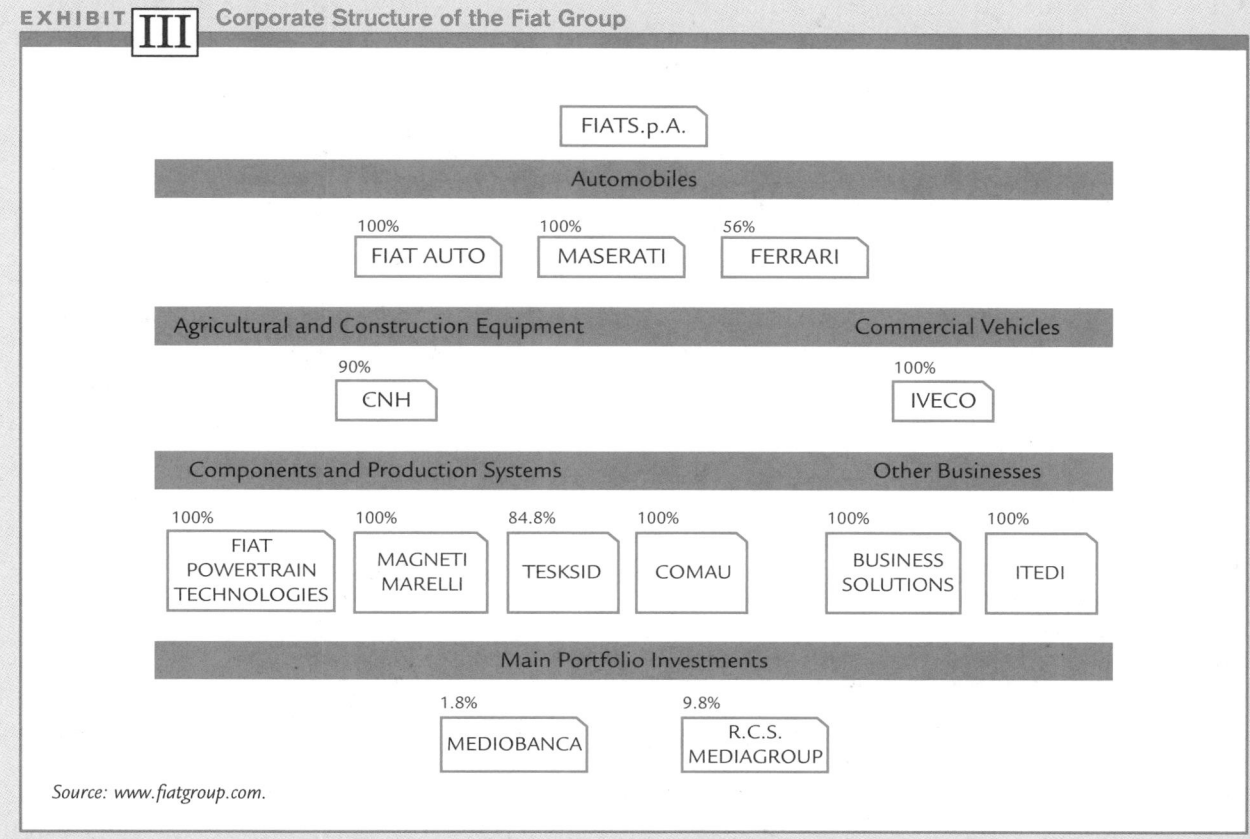

Source: www.fiatgroup.com.

refurbished Fiat Auto's European showrooms, and increased advertising expenditure. In this period, Fiat Auto also adopted a strategy to develop new feature-rich models, which could be sold at higher prices.

These measures were taken to revive the fortunes of Fiat Auto so that the Group would not have to sell the company to GM. However, with losses mounting, the Fiat Group was forced to consider the put option. GM, whose European operations (which primarily consisted of the *Opel* and *Vauxhall* brands) were themselves making losses, was not keen to acquire yet another loss-making car manufacturer. Therefore, it started negotiations with the Fiat Group to extricate itself from the deal. On May 13, 2005, the agreement between GM and the Fiat Group was dissolved and GM paid the Group US\$ 2 billion (€ 1.55 billion) as penalty. GM also returned its stake (10 percent) in Fiat Auto to the Fiat Group.

Amidst the growing consolidation in the global auto industry, Fiat Auto's market share continued to shrink rapidly. Fierce competition and high levels of over-capacity in the developed countries made Fiat Auto look to markets in developing countries, especially India and China. Fiat Auto's expertise in small cars gave it an advantage in these markets, where small, cheap cars were in great demand. Also, generally, the cars sold in developing countries were much simpler (in that they offered fewer features as options, and used less complex technology) than those sold in mature markets, resulting in lower product development costs.

However, in the mid-2000s, Fiat Auto's Indian operations were faring badly, even though the company had, over the years, invested more than Rs. 20 billion. The *Palio* was initially very successful, and Fiat India even started work on a second manufacturing facility at Ranjangaon, Maharashtra. However, the car's popularity waned very quickly. Fiat India's other products—the *Siena* (later relaunched as the *Petra*), and the *Palio Adventure* also fared badly. The company faced a situation where its sales declined and its plant was underutilized. To add to its problems, the Kurla plant (which had an annual capacity of 60,000 cars) was severely damaged by floods in the middle of 2005, bringing production at the plant to a halt.[46]

In March 2005, Paulo Castagna (Castagna) was appointed as the managing director of Fiat India. Around this time, several Indians were appointed to top management positions. In June 2005, Fiat India initiated a 12-month revival plan. "India is a strategic market for Fiat [Auto] and we will take all measures to make it profitable for us. We are taking a long-term view of the market and hope to turn around the current position,"[47] said Castagna.

In 2005, Fiat Auto made a fresh infusion of about Rs. 2 billion into its Indian operations. The company also made efforts to rationalize the dealer and service network, removing non-performers. "We are concentrating from the commercial side. . . . restructuring and deepening relations with the dealer,"[48] said Castagna. The company also announced plans to introduce new models in India in the near future.

As a part of its initiative to cut costs and reduce risks, Fiat Auto was also working with other major auto makers on product development, market development, etc. The company had entered into partnerships with global auto manufacturers like Ford Motor Co., PSA Peugeot Citroen, etc. In the second half of 2005, there were reports that Fiat Auto was considering teaming up with TM.

Tata Motors and Fiat Auto: Joining Forces

On September 22, 2005, TM announced that it was signing a Memorandum of Understanding (MoU) with Fiat Auto to explore the possibility of cooperation across different areas in the passenger car market. The two auto makers were examining the possibility of joint product development, manufacturing, sourcing, and distribution of products, aggregates, and components.

A 15-member joint team consisting of senior officials from both organizations was set up to study the viability and the specifics of the nature of cooperation, both in the short and the long term. "If found feasible, the two companies will enter into definitive agreements in the course of the coming months,"[49] said an official statement.

Both companies appeared optimistic about the possibilities from the alliance. "We are delighted to be in dialogue with the Fiat Group on the range of possibilities between the two corporations,"[50] said Ratan Tata. For Fiat Auto, this alliance was in keeping with its global strategy. "The possible strategic cooperation agreement with Tata Group represents another step in our clearly defined strategy that calls for targeted alliances across the automobile value chain. It is consistent with successful ventures established with premier partners,"[51] said Marchionne.

In October 2005, Giovanni De Filippis was appointed as managing director of Fiat India in place of Castagna.

In January 2006, the TM-Fiat Auto alliance moved another step forward, with the announcement of a shared dealer network in 11 Indian cities, representing 70 percent of Fiat India's market. Under the deal, TM dealers would sell Fiat cars from March 2006. Moreover, the two companies also examined synergies in overseas distribution so that Fiat Auto could give marketing support to TM through its retail network in Europe. "The two big companies have come together looking at opportunities not confined to India but spreading to other places of the world,"[52] said Ratan Tata.

The new TM-Fiat Auto India dealer network consisted of 25 TM dealers and three Fiat India dealers. The 28 dealers were to sell Fiat's *Palio* and *Palio Adventure* in addition to all TM passenger cars–the *Indica, Indigo, Indigo Marina, Sumo,* and *Safari*–through 44 outlets. These dealers were to offer service and spare parts for both Fiat and TM cars. Moreover, the co-operation extended to vehicle finance as well. According to the deal, Fiat cars were to be financed through Tata Motor Finance, the finance division of TM.

The two companies also announced that discussions were on to identify new areas for co-operation. Officials said that new agreements would be reached as and when their feasibility was established. It was also announced that Fiat Auto would give TM access to its technology and there was also a possibility of the two companies sharing platforms in the future. "This is not a joint venture, but this is the start of a relationship which could go beyond even a joint venture. It is a relationship which is beginning to form. We want to give it time,"[53] Ratan Tata said.

Fiat Auto's alliance with TM took place against the backdrop of a revival in sales in Europe. The company earned a quarterly trading profit for the first time in nearly four years in the last quarter of 2005. This came about mostly because of the high sales of its new model–the *Grande Punto* (*Refer to Exhibit IV for a photo of the model*). In the first half of 2006, Fiat Auto earned an operating profit of US$ 184 million from revenues of US$ 14.8 billion (*See Exhibit V for financials of Fiat Group and revenues by sector*).

Meanwhile, TM continued with its forays into international markets. In May 2006, the company entered into a 51:49 joint venture with Brazil-based Marcopolo to build buses and coaches for the Indian as well as the overseas markets,[54] at a production facility to be set up in India at an investment of Rs. 1.5–2 billion.

In mid-2006, Fiat India began using the paint booth facility at its Kurla complex for painting the *Tatamobile 207*, TM's pickup. This was done to increase the utilization of Fiat India's facilities. "We are painting 3,000–4,000 bodies of the Tatamobile on a monthly basis, thus optimizing the paint booth facility. The idea is to be self-sufficient through internal means and the paint booth plays an instrumental role in sourcing revenue for the company,"[55] said Filippis. Around this time, the alliance between the two companies was further strengthened by Ratan Tata joining the board of Fiat S.p.A.[56]

In July 2006, TM signed another MoU with Fiat Auto for setting up a joint venture in India to manufacture passenger vehicles, engines and transmissions. The joint venture was to manufacture both TM and Fiat vehicles for the Indian and overseas markets. Fiat India transferred its facility at Ranjangaon, where 100,000 cars and 250,000 engines and transmissions were to be produced, to the joint venture. The two companies were expected to jointly build Fiat cars in the B and C segments (The *Fiat Grande Punto* and a new Fiat sedan) and its successful small diesel engine for Indian as well as export markets. "Fiat [Auto] has technology . . . and the opportunities are endless,"[57] said Ratan Tata. The joint venture was expected to commence production in late 2007 or early 2008.

Fiat Auto and TM also commissioned a 60-day study aimed at exploring industrial and commercial cooperation in Latin America. The study was to examine the prospect of using Fiat Auto's production units in Cordoba, Argentina, to manufacture Tata vehicles, especially utility vehicles and pick-ups, and market them in South America and other markets.

EXHIBIT IV   **The Grande Punto**

Source: www.fiat.com.

EXHIBIT V

Fiat Group Financials 2004–05 *(in millions of euros)*

Particulars	2005	2004	2003	2002
Net Revenues	46,544	45,637	47,271	55,649
Trading Profit	1,000	50	–	–
Operating Result	2,215	(585)	(510)	(762)
Income/(loss) before taxes	2,264	(1,629)	(1,298)	(4,817)
Net Income/(loss) before interest	1,420	(1,579)	(1,948)	(4,263)
Group interest in net income/(loss)	**1,331**	**(1,634)**	–	–

Source: www.fiatgroup.com.

Fiat Group's Revenues by Sector *(in millions of euros)*

Particulars	2005	2004
Fiat Auto	19,533	19,695
Maserati	533	409
Ferrari	1,289	1,175
Fiat Powertrain Technologies	1,966	-
Agricultural and Construction Equipment (CNH Global)	10,212	9,983
Trucks and Commercial Vehicles (Iveco)	9,489	9,047
Components (Magneti Marelli)	4,033	3,795
Metallurgical Products (Teksid)	1,036	910
Production Systems (Comau)	1,573	1,711
Services (Business Solutions)	752	976
Publishing and Communications (Itedi)	397	407
Holding Companies, Other Companies and Eliminations	(4,269)	(2,741)
Total for the Group	**46,544**	**45,637**

Source: www.fiatgroup.com.

The July MoU was an indication of the growing commitment and co-operation between the two companies to work together and use their combined strengths to capture key markets. "Both companies have complementary strengths, convergent objectives, and shared values. Together, we can meaningfully address markets in India and other select geographies, combining technologies, products, and human skills of both organizations,"[58] said Ratan Tata.

The companies also had plans to expand the dealership network in India. Though the two companies did not reveal their investments in the venture, analysts estimated that it would be around of Rs. 2.2 billion.

Moreover, the Fiat Group intended to take TM's assistance in establishing a market for its truck unit Iveco in India.[59] Iveco earlier had a stake in Ashok Leyland (the second largest commercial vehicle manufacturer in India), through which it had sold its cargo range of trucks in India. However, with sales being less than satisfactory, the range was phased out within a few years of its launch. TM and Fiat were also looking for other areas where they could partner. "There will be additional alliances that we will disclose as they are concluded,"[60] said Marchionne.

Advantages of the Alliance

Even though Fiat India had been present in India for close to a decade, it had the lowest market share among the 11 players—including later entrants like Skoda India—in the growing car market.[61] Though the company's cars like the *Palio* were initially quite successful, Fiat's image suffered due to its dealers. Fiat customers were reported to have faced problems because of the non-availability of spare parts and lackadaisical customer service. Such problems had an adverse impact on the company's image, and it struggled to compete effectively in the Indian automobile market. The alliance with TM was expected to improve its dealership network and customer service without the company having to make significant investments. The goodwill enjoyed by TM, and the company's reach were expected to improve Fiat's image in India. "This alliance enables us to increase our customer base in India and also provide superior service and facilities to our existing customers,"[62] said Marchionne.

Through the alliance, Fiat India also planned to source spare parts for its vehicles from TM. The Tata Group was a cost effective supplier of auto components and had several manufacturing companies under the TACO Group.[63] Fiat Auto also had plans to increase the level of component sourcing for its overseas operations from India to US$ 10 million in 2006. Component sourcing was expected to be a major area of cooperation between the two companies.

According to auto analysts, while the alliance was expected to cut manufacturing costs for Fiat India (since the manufacturing at the Ranjangaon facility would use the cost efficient production processes of TM), TM was also expected to improve efficiency. "The tie-up between Tata Motors and Fiat will provide better synergy for both the companies in terms of operational efficiency and better utilization of resources,"[64] said HC Raveendra of KR Choksey, a Mumbai-based broking firm.

Though TM was a force to reckon with in the diesel passenger car segment of the Indian auto market, it did not possess the latest in diesel engine technology. In contrast, Fiat Auto's expertise in diesel engine technology, specifically in the common rail technology,[65] was world-renowned. The joint venture was expected to strengthen TM's position in the diesel passenger car segment. Among the engines to be made under the joint venture was the 1.3 liter next-generation JTDi diesel engine.[66] Fiat Auto also announced that it would introduce a small diesel engine in India. Auto analysts expected this to be used in the Rs. 100,000 small car that TM was planning to launch in 2008.

Though TM was the leader in the diesel segment of the Indian auto market, its presence in the petrol segment was limited. TM's *Indica* petrol version contributed only 5 percent to its total car sales. The company was therefore keen on upgrading its petrol engine technology. "We are looking at getting a larger piece of the petrol market than we have and that is something we must also do. We cannot only be dependent on the diesel when the proliferation of diesel products is greater than ours alone,"[67] said Ratan Tata. Through the alliance with Fiat Auto, TM expected to gain access to next generation petrol powertrains.[68] According to auto industry sources, the TM-Fiat Auto joint venture was set to produce two petrol engines called the 'Fire' range.[69] Both engines were expected to be used in future models from TM and Fiat.

The joint venture also planned to co-develop new car models. This was expected to help TM to learn and benefit from Fiat Auto's expertise, gained through years of producing small cars and sedans. "The alliance with Fiat [Auto] could help Tata get technologies and designs for new models in future. It's a win-win deal for both,"[70] said Kalpesh Parekh, an analyst with ASK Raymond James.

The Ranjangaon plant was expected to add to TM's production capacity. The new capacity was being added at a critical time for the company as its manufacturing facility at Pune had been working at full capacity.

India was one of the fastest growing car markets in the world, with most of the growth taking place in the small car segment. In the 2000s, car sales in India had grown by almost 20 percent annually. In addition, in 2005–06, the GoI had announced a cut in excise duty on small cars which was expected to make India the world's manufacturing hub for small or compact cars. The joint venture was expected to help TM and Fiat Auto (*See Exhibit VI for photographs of some Fiat cars*) compete effectively against MUL and Hyundai Motor Company (Hyundai)—who were aggressively increasing their production capacities—and to capture a larger share of the small car market in India.

The joint venture was expected to improve TM's competitiveness in global automobile markets, as the company would be able to sell its cars in several regions of Europe, through Fiat Auto's distribution network. After the termination of the agreement with the Rover group, TM had been selling the *Indica* in Europe on its own. Fiat Auto was expected to take up the distribution of the car in Europe through its outlets, reciprocating the distribution of Fiat cars by TM in India. Since Europe was a major market for small cars, TM expected to gain substantial benefits from the arrangement. "We live in a boundary-less world. We hope to grow beyond the shores of India,"[71] Ratan Tata said.

Fiat Auto also had a very strong market presence in Brazil and Argentina, whereas TM had almost no presence in Latin America. "Fiat [Auto] has plants in various parts of the world like eastern Europe and Latin America. Both are areas that we would like to be in and where they have ideal capacity presence, that is another opportunity of working together,"[72] said Ratan Tata. If the talks were successful, models like the *Sumo* and the *Tatamobile 207* would be marketed in South America and in other overseas markets.

Threats

Even though both firms gained several advantages by co-operating, they also faced significant threats. The TM-Fiat Auto alliance was expected to face intense competition from other automobile manufacturers in India, some of who were in the midst of forming their own alliances.

EXHIBIT **VI**   **New Models of Fiat Auto**

(a) Fiat Ducato

Source: www.fiatautopress.com.

(b) Fiat Stilo

Source: www.whatcar.com.

In February 2005, Renault SA formed a 49:51 joint venture with Mahindra & Mahindra Ltd. The alliance was to launch the *Logan,* a sedan, which would compete against TM's *Indigo.* Toyota Motor Corp. and its subsidiary Daihatsu Motor Co. Ltd., had plans to launch a new small car for the Indian market.

More significantly, MUL was all set to challenge TM's diesel supremacy, by entering the diesel car market in a big way. It was planning to invest Rs. 32 billion to set up a new car plant and diesel engine production facility. In 2006, MUL announced that it would launch three new small car models in the next five years. Also, Nissan and Suzuki (which owned 54.2 percent percent of MUL) had entered into an alliance in June 2006. Under this alliance, MUL was to produce a small car (the Nissan *Moco*). There were also reports that Nissan had plans to enter the Indian small car market on its own.

Another potential threat came from GM India. In 2005 and 2006, GM India was able to improve its market share in India, with successful launches of the *Chevrolet Optra* and the *Chevrolet Aveo.* It planned to launch the *Chevrolet Spark,* a small car, in India, in mid-2007.

There were reports that Hyundai planned to launch diesel variants of its popular models—the *Getz* and the *Santro.* It also had plans to launch a new small car by the end of 2007. Honda Motor Co. planned to launch a small hatchback car, for which it was to build a new production facility. Hindustan Motors had plans to launch the Mitsubishi *iCar* in India in 2007.[73] Similarly, while Volkswagen was expected to announce its India plans in late 2006, the Indian arm of its Czech subsidiary, Skoda India, which had already made a mark in the premium sedan market in India, was toying with the idea of launching the *Roomster,* a compact five-seater.

TM's ambitions in the highly competitive European automobile market were also fraught with difficulties. Even though the company had demonstrated its ability to compete effectively against global players in the Indian domestic market, this did not imply that its major export product, the *Indica,* was of high quality. The *Indica* was believed to have succeeded in India primarily because of the price advantage it offered over other models. However, in the European markets, quality was a far more significant issue than in the Indian market.

Another worrisome consequence of the plans for joint production and distribution was the prospect of brand dilution for both companies.[74] TM felt that the joint venture would strengthen its global expansion initiatives without adversely affecting its market share in India. "Fiat [India] operations are small when compared to ours . . . We will have access to their technology, new aggregates and we will market some of their products,"[75] said Ratan Tata.

TM did recognize the threat from Fiat Auto's *Petra* to its *Indigo* model and planned not to offer the *Petra* through its dealers. The *Petra,* though priced higher than the *Indigo,* reportedly offered better ride quality and other benefits.[76] A TM spokesman gave the reason for the exclusion of the *Petra* as, "The combined portfolio had been picked keeping in mind the need for complementary products and models that contributed best to strengthening the Fiat brand in the local market."[77]

Outlook

India was one of the fastest growing automobile markets in the world, with passenger car sales forecast to reach two million units per annum by 2010. As of 2006, small cars made up more than two-thirds of India's passenger car market. Even in the future, at least in the short to medium term, the small car segment was expected to remain the largest segment of the market. Therefore, in spite of the intense competition, the TM-Fiat Auto joint venture was aiming to make an impact in this high-volume segment. "Obviously Tata-Fiat [Auto] JV is entering an over-crowded and a price sensitive segment. But this [small car] segment which contributes to more than 60 percent of the total car sales will remain a key segment in the Indian car market for many years,"[78] said an auto analyst. Also, the fact that

EXHIBIT VII   Tata Motors: Financials

(In millions of Rupees) As on (Months)	31-Mar-06(12)	31-Mar-05(12)	31-Mar-04(12)
Profit/Loss Statement			
Net Sales	200,374.90	171,539.80	128,955.50
Operating Income (OI)	204,880.70	172,658.20	131,273.00
OPBDIT	20,793.20	19,470.30	17,894.50
OPBDT	18,529.70	17,928.80	16,279.20
OPBT	13,320.30	13,427.20	11,936.80
Non-Operating Income	7,217.80	3,097.30	1,067.90
Extraordinary/Prior Period	-1,421.50	-511.30	-3,935.80
Tax	3,827.80	3,643.70	965.50
Profit after tax(PAT)	15,288.80	12,369.50	8,103.40
Cash Profit	20,498.20	16,871.10	12,445.80
Dividend-Equity	4,979.40	4,521.90	2,821.10

Source: www.myiris.com.

EXHIBIT VIII   Tata Motors: Sales

Unit Sales	2005–06	2004–05	% Change
Medium & HCV	136,964	135,337	1.2
LCV	108,084	74,253	45.6
Utility Vehicles	39,783	37,032	7.4
Passenger Cars	169,512	152,943	10.8
Total	454,343	399,565	13.7

Source: Kushan Mitra, "The Sixth Coming," Business Today, August 27, 2006, p38–40.

only eight in a thousand Indians owned a car meant that there was a huge potential for growth.

As of 2006, both TM and Fiat Auto were financially sound (*See Exhibit VII for the financials of TM*). Fiat Auto reported a 56 percent rise in second-quarter (April–June 2006) profits partly due to the encouraging sales of its new model–the *Grande Punto*. The *Grande Punto* had increased Fiat Auto's market share in Western Europe to 7.9 percent from 6.6 percent a year earlier. The company also intended to launch several new models in 2007, like the next generation *Stilo* and *Ducato*. Fiat Auto had also formed partnerships with some of the other global car majors. For example, it announced new industrial ventures in Russia with Severstal Auto and in China with SAIC Motor Corporation Ltd. TM also saw a rise in sales and exports during this period (*see Exhibit VIII for the sales of TM*).[79]

Fiat Auto aimed to increase its market share in India to 5 percent by 2010. In August 2006, Fiat India shut down its Kurla plant. It planned to completely relocate its manufacturing operations to Ranjangaon.

In September 2006, there were newspaper reports that Fiat Auto was evaluating whether it could share the *Indica* platform for a new low-cost car it intended to sell in Europe and in other markets–a proposal that went even beyond the scope of the July 2006 MoU. "It will be in the short term as they [TM] have already done most of the work. We will add our know-how, and maybe the money,"[80] said Marchionne. There were also reports that Fiat Auto might invest in TM's Rs. 100,000 car project, and that TM might build cars for some of Fiat Auto's luxury marquees like Alfa Romeo. (*See Exhibit IX for the all models of Fiat Auto.*) Kant said, "Nothing is ruled out and that includes Fiat [Auto]'s top-end models like the Alfa Romeo."[81] The new developments indicated the potential in the joint venture, and the possibilities that remained to be explored.

CASE DISCUSSION QUESTIONS

1. What is Fiat's current situation in India?
2. What is the business opportunity in India? Do you think that Fiat needs a partner?
3. Do you think Fiat and Tata make for good partners? Compare the Fiat-GM relationship with the Fiat-Tata relationship.
4. Is the business case convincing for the joint venture? Back your answer up with a financial analysis.
5. How would you assess the negotiation process between Fiat and Tata?
6. What would you recommend for the alliance to be successful?

REFERENCES AND SUGGESTED READING

1 Lou Ann Hammond, "Who owns whom," www.carlist.com, *September 07, 2006.*
2 Lijee Philip & Nandini Sen Gupta, "La dolce deal?" www .economictimes.indiatimes.com, *August 04, 2006.*
3 "Tata Motors, Fiat chart a winning formula," www.economictimes .indiatimes.com, *July 27, 2006.*
4 Gail Edmondson, "Fiat's comeback - Is it for real?", www .businessweek.com, July 26, 2006.
5 "Tata Motors, Fiat in 50:50 JV for cars, engines," www .finanacialexpress.com, July 26, 2006.
6 Razib Ahmed, "Tata Motors made good profit but not enough!" www.southasiabiz.com, *May 19, 2006.*
7 "Car makers beware, the Tata-Fiat tag team is here," www.rediff .com, January 14, 2006.

EXHIBIT IX   Fiat Group: Automobile Models

	Marquee	Models
1	Fiat	Panda, Idea, Stilo, Grande Punto, Mutipla, Croma, and Sedici.
2	Lancia	Ypsilon, Musa, Thesis, Lybra, and Phedra.
3	Alfa Romeo	Alfa 147 GTA, Alfa 156, Alfa 159, Alfa 166, Alfa GT, Alfa Sportwagon, Alfa Spider, and Brera.
4	Maserati	Quattroporte, Gransport, Gransport Spyder, GT, Cambiocorsa, and MC12.
5	Ferrari	F430, F430 Spider, 599 GTB Fiorano, and 612 Scaglietti.

Source: Compiled from various sources.

8 Sudhakar Shah, "Tata partnership with Fiat would play to strengths," www.wardsauto.com, September 28, 2005.

9 "Rs 1 lakh car in 3 yrs: Tata," www.indiacar.net, September 01, 2005.

10 Raghuvir Srinivasan, "Tata Motors: India's own wheels," www.thehindubusinessline.com, January 28, 2004.

11 "The new and improved Tata twins," www.tata.com, November 09, 2003.

12 S. Muralidhar, "More wheels in each segment," www.thehindubusinessline.com, July 27, 2003.

13 "What now for Fiat?" www.bbc.co.uk, January 24, 2003.

14 Biswajit Chowdhury, "An auto giant in distress," www.flonnet.com, December 21, 2002.

15 "Comeback kid," www.tata.com, June 24, 2002.

16 "Ciao, Paolo," www.economist.com, June 13, 2002.

17 Sudipta Basu, "Riding the global wave," www.tata.com.

18 "Crisis at Fiat Auto worsens," www.eiro.eirofound.eu.int.

19 www.tata.com.

20 www.thehindubusinessline.com.

21 www.fiat.com.

22 www.indiacar.net.

23 www.siam.com.

24 www.autocarindia.com.

CASE CREDIT

This case was written by **Namratha V.Prasad** and **Sachin Govind**, under the direction of **S.S. George**, ICMR Center for Management Research (ICMR). It was compiled from published sources, and is intended to be used as a basis for class discussion rather than to illustrate either effective or ineffective handling of a management situation.

©2007, ICMR. All rights reserved.

To order copies, call 0091-40-2343-0462/63 or write to ICMR, Plot # 49, Nagarjuna Hills, Hyderabad 500 082, India or e-mail info@icmrindia.org.

www.icmrindia.org

CASE NOTES

1 "Fiat and Tata announce joint venture in India," www.detnews.com, July 26, 2006.

2 "La dolce deal?" www.economictimes.indiatimes.com, August 04, 2006.

3 ASK Raymond James Securities India Pvt. Ltd. (ASK RJ) is a joint venture between ASK Investment and Financial Consultants Ltd. (India), Raymond James Financial Inc. of the US, and Bharat Shah, an investor. It offers portfolio management services and investment advisory services.

4 A small car, in the Indian context, is a car of length not exceeding 4,000 mm and with an engine capacity not exceeding 1,500 cc for diesel cars and not exceeding 1,200 cc for petrol cars. They are the most fuel-efficient cars available in both diesel and petrol variants, and also the cheapest.

5 In 1968, Fiat surpassed Volkswagen as the largest carmaker outside the United States, with 157,000 employees producing 1.75 million cars a year. Fiat continued to expand through much of the 1970s and 1980s. (Source: www.time.com)

6 Premier Automobiles Ltd. (PAL) was established by Walchand Hirachand in 1942. In 1946, in association with U.S.-based Chrysler, the company assembled De Soto and Plymouth cars. As of 2006, the company was making auto components.

7 In the early 2000s, the European Union's new requirements for open competition came into force. This and the dismantling of protectionist measures changed the economic environment for businesses in the EU region.

8 Tatanagar is a part of the city of Jamshedpur. The East Indian Railway had a locomotive manufacturing facility at that place called the Singhbhum Shops or the Tatanagar Shops.

9 Tata Sons Ltd., a holding company, is a successor to the first trading company founded by Jamsetji Tata (the founding father of the Tata business empire). The Tata Sons Ltd. board is made up of the chairmen or CEOs of major operating Tata Group companies, and the elected chairman of the board of Tata Sons Ltd. is recognized as the Group Chairman. The company is based in Mumbai.

10 Daimler-Benz AG, founded in 1926 in Germany, was a leading manufacturer of automobiles, motor vehicles, and engines. In 1998, it merged with U.S.-based Chrysler Corp. to form DaimlerChrysler AG. It sells passenger cars/SUVs under Mercedes-Benz, Maybach, Smart, Chrysler, Dodge, and Jeep brands and commercial vehicles under Fuso, Sterling, Orion, Setra, Freightliner, Mercedes-Benz, Thomas, and Western Star brands.

11 A type of automobile design wherein the passenger cabin included additional cargo space accessed through a hatch tail gate or a flip up window.

12 The engine design was based on the TUD5 Peugeot engine. Telco claimed to have further refined and optimized the engine to deliver higher standards of efficiency and emission.

13 Telco paid for services to develop technology in accordance with its specifications. Styling was sourced from Italy, engine design from France, and instrumentation from Japan. But the design process and implementation of the manufacturing and supply lines was done by Telco. The *Indica* was launched within three years of conception, at a development cost of about $400 million as against the international norm of $1.2 billion required to develop a new car.

14 Maruti Udyog Ltd. was established through an Act of the Indian parliament in February 1981. In 1982, it entered into a license and joint venture agreement with Suzuki Motor Company (later renamed as Suzuki Motor Corp.). In 1992, SMC raised its stake to 50% and in 2002, to 54.2%. With this, MUL became a subsidiary of SMC.

15 "The new and improved Tata twins," www.tata.com, November 09, 2003.

16 Ibid.

17 Rover Company Ltd. (Rover), an automobile manufacturer, was set up in 1904. Over its 100-year history it changed hands several times. It was taken over by BMW, a German automobile company, in 1994. In 2000, BMW sold it to the Phoenix Corporation. MG (a sports car manufacturing company) was then merged with Rover to form the MG Rover Group. It was taken over by China-based Nanjing Automobile Group, a Chinese automobile company, in July 2005.

18 "Tatas to ship Rover-branded Indicas," www.blonnet.com, December 21, 2002.

19 "Rechristened thus," www.tata.com, September 28, 2003.

20 "Fencing with the West," www.cfoasia.com, April 2004.

21 The company listed its depository shares on NYSE through the conversion of its existing international Global Depository Shares (GDSs) into American Depository Shares (ADSs). The company's symbol on the NYSE is 'TTM'. Citibank NA was the depository. With the listing, the company was required to publish its financial results annually under both the US GAAP and the Indian GAAP.

22 "Tata Motors drives into Wall Street," www.tata.com, September 28, 2004.

23 The Spanish company had a market share of 25% in the bus market in Spain, and sold its buses in Europe and several other countries outside Europe. It had its own in-house product development facility for buses and coaches.

24 "Tata Motors to acquire 21 per cent stake in Hispano Carrocera," www.tata.com, February 25, 2005.

25 A modifier alters the specifications of a vehicle to suit his client's special needs. Most governments prescribe the standards for modification so that the 'modified' vehicle adheres to safety and other norms.

26 "Can India become a global sourcing hub for small cars?" www.thehindubusinessline.com, May 09, 2004.

27 The Association of Southeast Asian Nations (ASEAN) is a political and economic organization of countries located in Southeast Asia. The members of ASEAN include Brunei, Cambodia, Indonesia, Laos, Malaysia, Myanmar, Philippines, Singapore, Thailand, and Vietnam.

28 "Tata Indigo Marina set for launch on September 15, 2004," www.tata.com, September 14, 2004.

29 Tata Motors had first mentioned that it was working on a Rs. 100,000 car project at the 2003 Geneva Motor Show. However, in September 2005, the company made an official announcement regarding the project and indicated a time frame for its implementation.

30 " Tatas' Rs 1-lakh car to be gearless," www.rediff.com, August 31, 2005.

31 According to www.tatamotors.com.

32 Fabbrica Italiana Automobili Torino or Italian car factory of Turin.

33 Bianchi (later renamed Autobianchi) was established by Edoardo Bianchi in 1899. The cars were built for the luxury segment with great attention to detail. It produced a very small number of successful small cars. Autobianchi later came under the control of Lancia.

34 Ferrari was founded by Enzo Ferrari in 1929 to manufacture race cars. Ferrari S.p.A. was established in 1946 to produce street legal cars. The Fiat Group acquired a 50% stake in Ferrari in 1969, which went up to 90% in 1988. In 2002, the Group sold 34% of its stake to Mediobanca, a bank. As of 2006, the Fiat Group had expressed its intention to acquire the bank's stake.

35 Lancia was an Italian automobile manufacturer founded in 1906 by Vincenzo Lancia. Lancia was famous for many innovations in the automobile industry, including the first full-production V6 engine (in the 1950 Aurelia), V8 and V12 engine configurations, etc.

36 Karl Abarth was a car enthusiast who remodeled cars. Fiat entered into an agreement with Abarth in the mid-1950s, where Fiat supplied partly constructed cars and Abarth would finish them at his workshop. The remodeled cars were sold as Fiat Abarths. The first car under the Fiat-Abarth brand was the 750 Berlina, based on the Fiat 600.

37 Alfa Romeo was established in 1907 as Darracq Italiana. It was renamed as ALFA (Anonima Lombarda Fabbrica Automobili) around 1909 and then as Alfa Romeo in 1920. It came under Fiat Auto in 1986.

38 Maserati was an Italian manufacturer of racing cars and sports cars established by six Maserati brothers in 1914. It was acquired by the Fiat Group in 1993. In 1997, as part of a restructuring effort, Maserati was brought under Ferrari. In 2005, Maserati was brought back as a direct subsidiary of Fiat S.p.A., the flagship company of the Fiat Group.

39 Sundaram Finance Ltd., part of the TVS Group, was established in 1954. It is involved in car and commercial vehicle finance, home loans, software solutions, tire finance, deposits and mutual funds, etc.

40 "Fiat: Running on empty," www.businessweek.com, May 13, 2002.

41 General Motors was the world's largest automaker. It was established in 1908 in United States.

42 Fiat had a 14 percent share in the European car market and a 60 percent market share in the Italian car market in the early 1990s. (www.time.com)

43 The Fiat Group sold 51 percent of its stake in FRI to four banks—Capitalia, Banca Intesa, San-Paolo-ISI, and UniCredito—for € 370 million.

44 "Fiat agrees sale of Fidis to banks," www.italiaspeed.com, March 14, 2003.

45 In 2004, Fiat Auto announced that it would invest US$ 4.92 billion on R&D over four years (2008).

46 Production resumed only in the first half of 2006.

47 "Fiat works on 12 month revival plan," www.indiacar.com, September 01, 2005.

48 Ibid.

49 "Tata Motors, Fiat tie up to explore cooperation in passenger car segment," www.thehindubusinessline.com, September 23, 2005.

50 Ibid.

51 Ibid.

52 "Pact with Fiat our window to the world: Tata," www.tata.com, January 14, 2006.

53 "Tata Motors, Fiat in joint drive—Marketing tie-up is first step towards deeper relationship," www.thehindubusinessline.com, January 14, 2006.

54 Marcopolo, founded in 1949 in Brazil, manufactured bodies for a whole range of coaches, e.g. microbuses, and inter-city and touring coaches. It had manufacturing plants in Brazil, Argentina, Colombia, Mexico, Portugal, and South Africa. It also exported its coaches to more than 60 countries of the world.

55 "Fiat paints Tatamobile bodies at its plant," www.blonnet.com, June 28, 2006.

56 Fiat S.p.A. is the holding company in the Fiat Group.

57 "Fiat and Tata plan India venture," www.news.moneycentral.msn.com, July 24, 2006.

58 "Tata-Fiat JV to make passenger cars," www.indianexpress.com, July 26, 2006.

59 Iveco, a subsidiary company in the Fiat Group, was a leading manufacturer of trucks and buses in Europe.

60 "Fiat and Tata plan India venture," www.news.moneycentral.msn.com, July 24, 2006.

61 Apart from TM and Fiat India, MUL, Hyundai, Ford, GM, Mahindra & Mahindra, Skoda, Mercedes Benz, Honda, and Toyota were the other players in India. BMW was also setting up a factory in India and was to begin sales in 2007.

62 "Tatas, Fiat tie up to sell vehicles," www.tribuneindia.com, January 13, 2006.

63 TACO was established in 1995 by the Tata Group. The group includes Tata Autocomp Systems Ltd., joint ventures with several global auto manufacturing players and two subsidiaries (plastics and stampings).

64 "Tata Motors, Fiat in 50:50 JV for cars, engines," www.finanacialexpress.com, July 26, 2006.

65 Common rail is a modern variant of direct fuel injection system for diesel engines.

66 This engine won the Engine of the Year Award in 2005.

67 "Tata's grand vision," www.tata.com, January 15, 2006.

68 The powertrain for a vehicle consists of all the components, including the engine, transmission, driveshafts, differentials, and

the final drive (drive wheels, caterpillar track, propeller, etc), that produce power and help the vehicle travel over road, water, or in air.

[69] The first was a 1.2 liter, 8 valve, 75 horsepower engine and the other was a 1.4 liter, 16 valve, 95 horsepower petrol engine.

[70] "Tata Motors in pact with Fiat," www.newstodaynet.com, January 17, 2006.

[71] "Tata, Fiat to share car dealer networks," www.expressindia.com, January 13, 2006.

[72] "Tata's grand vision," www.tata.com, January 15, 2006.

[73] Hindustan Motors was making Mitsubishi brand cars including the popular *Lancer* since 1998 under a tie-up with Mitsubishi Motor Corporation, Japan.

[74] Brand dilution happens when products that are not a natural fit are offered in the market place under a particular company's corporate identity. This also affects the company's brand positioning when the new product gives out messages which differ from the company's own communications.

[75] "Tata Motors-Fiat alliance gets ready for a long drive," www.telegraphindia.com, December 07, 2006.

[76] "Turnaround artist," www.bsmotoring.com, August 07, 2004.

[77] "Tata Motors, Fiat India to share dealer network," www.thehindubusinessline.com, March 07, 2006.

[78] "La dolce deal?"www.economictimes.indiatimes.com, August 04, 2006.

[79] Tata Motors exported 4,257 vehicles in February compared with 3,290 vehicles in the same month in the previous year, representing an increase of 29.4 percent. The cumulative sales from exports in the current period amounted to 44,031 vehicles, a growth of 66 percent over the corresponding period in the previous year.

[80] Parvathy Ullatil, "Fiat, Tata mull platform sharing," *The Economic Times*, September 06, 2006.

[81] "Tata Motors plans big push," www.economictimes.com, September 09, 2006.

10 Multinational E-Commerce: Strategies and Structures

Learning Objectives

After reading this chapter you should be able to:

- Define the forms of e-commerce.
- Appreciate the growing presence of e-commerce in the global economy.
- Understand the structure of the Internet economy.
- Identify the basic component of a successful e-commerce strategy.
- Know the basic multinational e-commerce business models.
- Identify the practicalities of running a multinational e-commerce business.
- Understand the function of enablers in multinational e-commerce operations.

Preview CASE IN POINT

The Global Internet Economy

The Internet and electronic commerce (e-commerce) are seen as drastically changing how international business is done. The Internet allows any company to create a virtual and global presence to conduct operations around the world, and it allows a multinational company to dramatically alter the way it presents and communicates with global customers. Web presence can give any company the ability to advertise and present useful information that is seen as critical in influencing purchasing decisions. In fact, product-based Web sites are becoming increasingly important as an advertising medium. Furthermore, the Internet enables companies to analyze their value chain to become more efficient and competitive by implementing e-commerce initiatives all along it.

It is predicted that this trend will accelerate in the future. Consider the following facts regarding the Internet economy and e-commerce:

- Online consumer sales increased to 126 billion yuan in China in 2008 from about 16 billion in 2005. About one-third of the 253 million Internet users in China shopped online in 2006.

- The figures in the U.K. suggest that e-commerce grew by 25 percent for each of the last five years. Furthermore, approximately 55 percent of all Internet users aged 16 and older had made online purchases in 2008, and that percentage is predicted to grow.

- Online purchases in the United States are expected to grow to $275 billion in 2010 from $170 billion in 2006. There are many successful U.S. online retailers. For instance, Apple's Itunes has sold more than 5 billion songs since 2003. Online music sales are expected to grow to $5.5 billion in 2010.

- Broadband, which is considered one of the fastest modes of Internet connection, continues to grow at a rapid pace.

- There are about 542 million hosts connected to the Internet in 2008—13 times more than in 1999.

- In Iceland, Finland, Switzerland, Denmark, and Japan, over 98 percent of businesses with 10 or more employees use the Internet.
- Over 2006–2007, broadband speed increased by 29 percent while prices went down by 19 percent.
- On average, 57 percent of Internet users in the Organization for Economic Co-operation and Development (OECD) countries used the Internet to send e-mail or to make telephone calls in 2007.
- South Korea had the highest percentage of households with access to the Internet (94 percent), followed by Iceland (84 percent) and the Netherlands (83 percent).

Sources: Cavanes, S. 2008. "Alibaba raises bet on Taobao site." Wall Street Journal Asia, October 9, p. 6; Fletcher, M. 2008. "E-commerce." Revolution, December, pp. 52–55; Organisation for Economic Cooperation and Development. 2009. "The future of the Internet economy." http://www.oecd.org; Shareowner. 2009. "Opportunities in the Internet sector." May 22, 5, pp. 9–10.

Although still small in comparison to the traditional economy, the Internet economy is booming and growing faster than any other business trend in history. As shown in the Preview Case in Point, the Internet economy is growing exponentially and has become a worldwide phenomenon. Consequently, multinational managers must be knowledgeable in all aspects of e-commerce and prepared to use the Internet as a global platform for multinational business transactions.

Earlier chapters discussed many of the intricacies involved in developing multinational strategies and building the organizations to implement them. This chapter will show that new opportunities exist for companies to expand their multinational operations via the Web and the Internet.

Many of the issues involved in doing multinational business over the Web are similar to those faced by traditional multinational companies. However, the next generation of multinational managers must address unique challenges in formulating and implementing multinational strategies for the Internet economy.

This chapter will provide essential background on the nature of e-commerce and the Internet economy. First, it considers basic e-commerce strategies, structures, and operations. Second, it discusses issues unique to the multinational company, including the costs and benefits of globalizing via the Internet, basic multinational e-commerce models, and practical issues associated with multinational e-commerce such as Web site design. After reading this chapter and considering the array of multinational management issues considered earlier, you should gain a sound understanding of and appreciation for the e-commerce challenges multinational companies must face now and in the near future.

The Internet Economy

What Is E-Commerce?

E-commerce is the selling of goods or services over the Internet. These goods or services include those delivered offline, such as UPS shipping a book purchased through Amazon.com to a customer anywhere in the world, and those delivered online, such as downloaded computer software. When most people talk about e-commerce, they focus on two types of transactions. The first type is business-to-consumer transactions, such as buying toys from eToys. The acronym **B2C** is

E-commerce
The selling of goods or services over the Internet.

B2C
Business-to-consumer transactions.

commonly used to refer to these transactions. The second type consists of the buying and selling done among businesses, or business-to-business transactions. This is the **B2B** component of e-commerce. B2B transactions make up 70 to 85 percent of current e-commerce business. The high proportion of B2B relative to B2C is expected to continue in the future.[1]

One of the most important reasons for the significance of B2B e-commerce comes from the revolution in supply chain management made possible by electronic links between businesses and suppliers. Information sharing between business customers and suppliers allows vendors to know what their customers want and enables businesses to know price, availability, and product characteristics immediately.

For example, Ericsson, the Swedish mobile phone giant, has gone to paperless procurement. It uses the company's local network, or intranet, to find approved suppliers. The intranet provides links to the suppliers' Web sites, and a purchase is made within predefined levels. Prior to this system, Ericsson spent an average of $100 on every order processed. The reduction in paperwork has reduced the average transaction cost to $15.[2] Similarly, Microsoft uses an intranet procurement process called Microsoft Market that reduced its business purchase transaction costs from $60 to $5.[3] Exhibit 10.1 shows how e-commerce activities work along the value chain.

Longitudinal research in the United States confirms the pervasiveness of Internet usage. A large number of firms were studied, and the most interesting finding showed that all companies experienced increased Internet use all along the value chain. The companies surveyed were making increased use of the Internet to facilitate such value chain activities as human resources, sales, advertising, and other operations.[4] This study showed that we will likely see more e-commerce in all these activities.

In addition to these e-commerce models, the Internet has spawned other forms of business transactions. eBay is a global player in the **C2C** (consumer-to-consumer) business of auctions. Anyone can sell something online and/or place

B2B
Business-to-business transactions.

C2C
Consumer-to-consumer transactions.

EXHIBIT 10.1   E-Commerce Value Chain

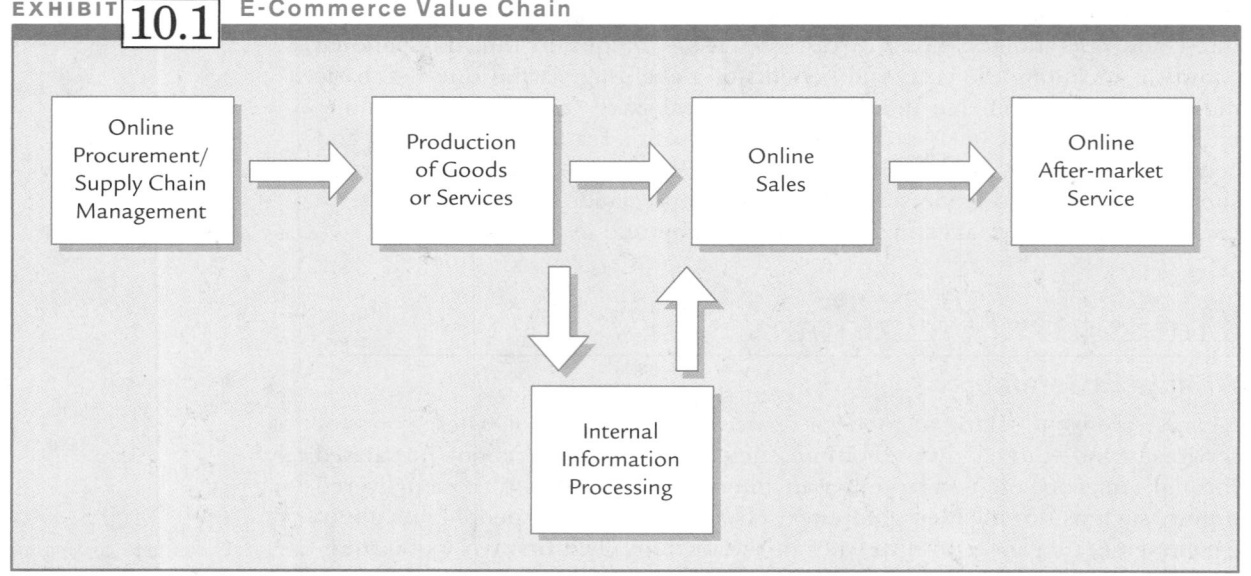

bids for items. Other forms of business transactions to consider are **C2B** (consumer-to-business), such as price comparison Web sites like AddALL, which searches online bookstores throughout the world to provide price comparisons and shipping and delivery information.

What is the current global presence of e-commerce? Recent reports from the OECD use two indicators.[5] One is the number of secure servers. A **secure server** is an Internet host that allows users to send encrypted data so that those outside the connection cannot see the information. Such servers are necessary for e-commerce to thrive because they encourage users to send credit card information over the Internet. A second indicator of the presence of e-commerce is the number of **Internet hosts**. Any computer connected to the Internet with its own Internet Protocol address is considered a server in OECD statistics. An Internet Protocol address is a unique address that a computer has on the Web so that other Internet users can access the public information there.

OECD countries dominate the Internet,[6] with 309 million hosts in 2006. These countries represent most of the developed economies in the world, although China is not a member. The number of OECD country Internet hosts doubled between 2000 and 2006, and OECD countries had the majority of secure Web servers, a necessity for conducting e-commerce. Exhibit 10.2 shows the secure server and Internet host rankings for selected countries in the OECD. Projections are that the U.S. dominance in Internet use will decline gradually over the next decade.

The growth in the use of the Internet, or the World Wide Web, for e-commerce is so dramatic that its impact is difficult to estimate. Some say that the Internet will have more impact on the world than the industrial revolution. Exhibit 10.3 shows the trend in the number of households with Internet access in different parts of the world, according to recent estimates.[7] Such consistent growth suggests tremendous opportunities for multinational companies to use the Internet as a tool for conducting business worldwide at any point in the value chain, from the procurement of raw materials to the eventual sale. China also presents companies with significant opportunities. Consider the next Focus on Emerging Markets.

C2B
Consumer-to-business transactions.

Secure server
Internet host that allows users to send and receive encrypted data.

Internet hosts
Computer connected to the Internet with its own Internet Protocol address.

EXHIBIT 10.2   Internet Hosts in OECD Countries (per thousand inhabitants)

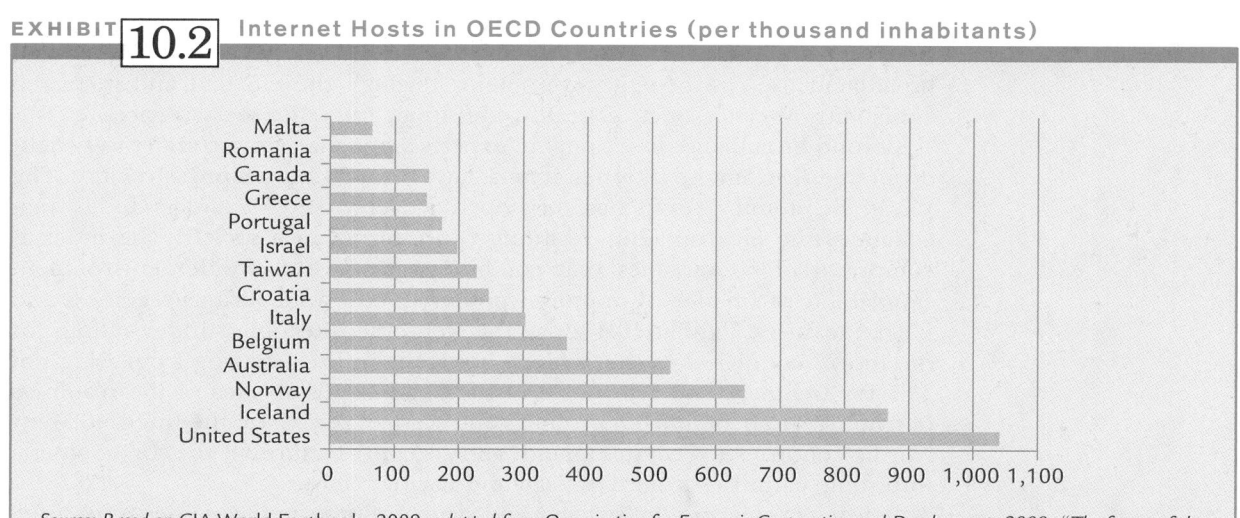

Source: Based on CIA World Factbook—2009; adapted from Organisation for Economic Cooperation and Development. 2009. "The future of the Internet economy." http://www.oecd.org.

EXHIBIT **10.3**   Percentage of Households with Internet Access

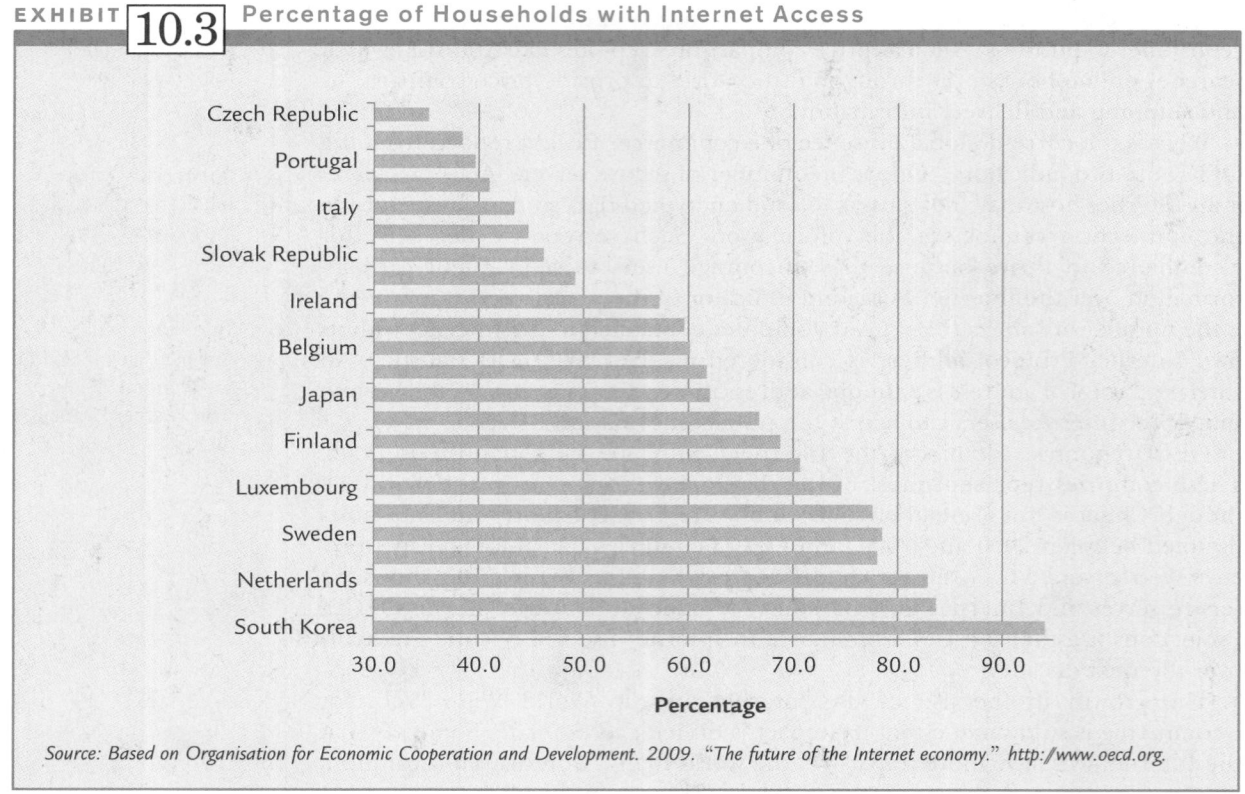

Source: Based on Organisation for Economic Cooperation and Development. 2009. "The future of the Internet economy." http://www.oecd.org.

The OECD sees broadband development as a critical aspect of the Internet and e-commerce.[8] Broadband is a combination of digital technologies that enables data and other digital services to be transmitted rapidly, often simultaneously. It is seen as a major reason why people access information and technology products and services. The OECD believes that, in turn, such use can result in economic growth, facilitating social and cultural development and even innovation. Broadband also allows small- and medium-sized firms to benefit from heightened efficiency through sped-up information exchanges. The OECD also argues that broadband use can benefit governments through the efficient and increased availability of services such as health, education, and other social services.[9]

Beyond broadband development, experts agree that, for a country to benefit economically from the Internet, it must have a good Internet infrastructure. The World Economic Forum has developed a Networked Readiness Index that examines the environment regarding the Internet in a society. The index is comprised of 68 variables that combine aspects of the wider environment (availability of finances, innovation potential, etc.) with various readiness and usage measures. Exhibit 10.4 shows the Networked Readiness Index ratings for the top 25 countries. As the exhibit shows, the index—ranging from a high of 5.85 for Denmark and a low of 2.44 for Chad—gives an idea of the readiness of countries to benefit from products and services relying on the Internet. Many Nordic countries (Sweden, Finland, and Iceland) feature on the top 25, along with some countries from the Asian and Pacific regions.

Before considering the strategy and structure of using e-commerce in multinational business, the chapter next provides background material on the nature of the Internet economy.

EXHIBIT 10.4   Networked Readiness Index Ratings (2008–2009)

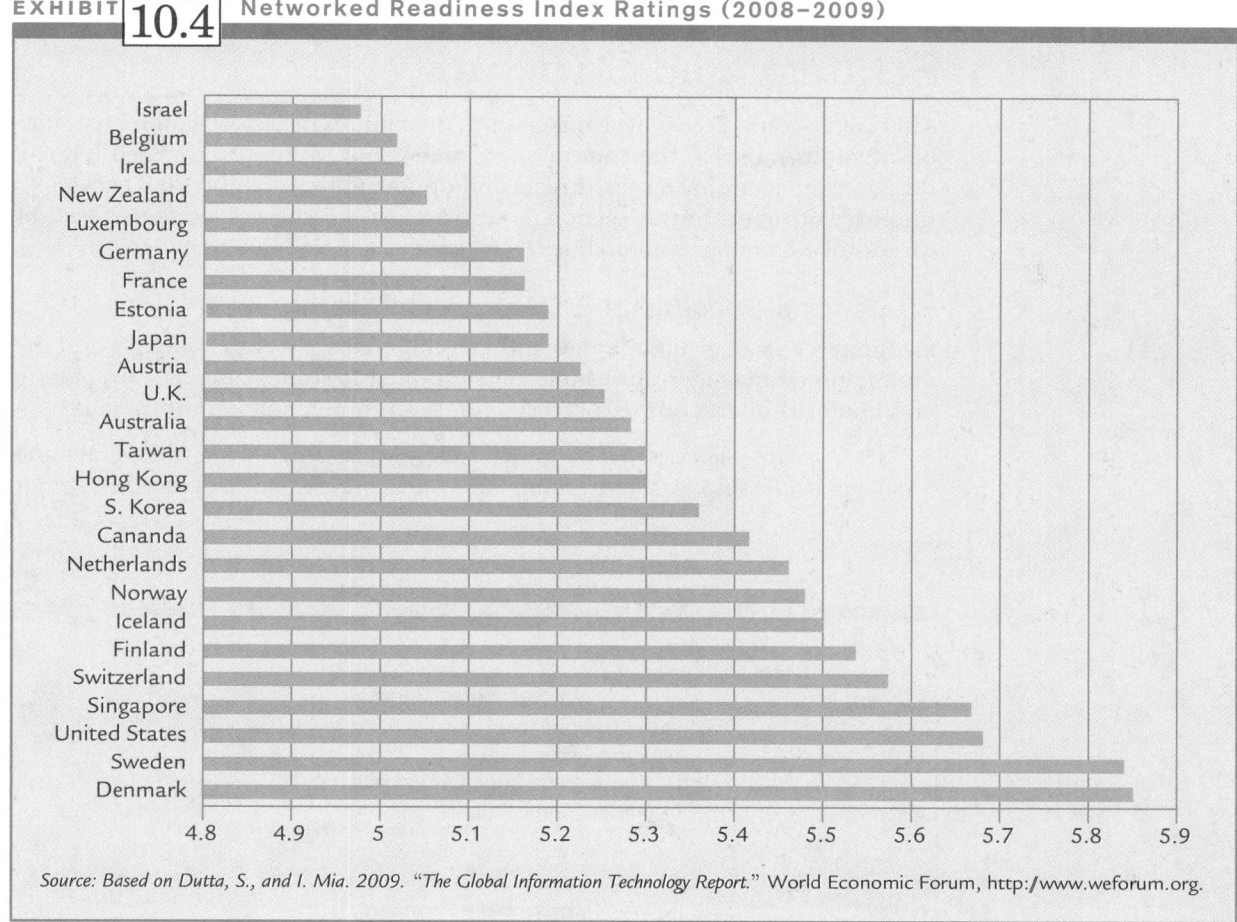

Source: Based on Dutta, S., and I. Mia. 2009. "The Global Information Technology Report." World Economic Forum, http://www.weforum.org.

Focus on Emerging Markets

The Internet in China

China has seen tremendous growth in Internet use. It is estimated that in 2006, China had approximately 110 million Web surfers, second only to the United States. The Chinese government estimates that the 2006 online revenues were valued at nearly $69 billion, representing a growth of 58 percent over 2005. It is predicted that online consumer sales in 2008 will increase to 126 billion yuan. Analysts predict that China will have the world's leading online commerce by 2010. Furthermore, about a third of China's Internet users have shopped online. China thus presents tremendous opportunities.

Even so, multinationals have to contend with challenges. China's Web is constantly being monitored by more than 30,000 people who filter and delete prohibited phrases. The Chinese Web is also being targeted by scam artists and criminals ready to take advantage of naive customers through phishing and spamming.

Sources: Adapted from Barboza, David. 2006. "110 million surfers can buy sex and drugs, but Reform is still illicit." New York Times, March 8, p. C1; Cavanes, S. 2008. "Alibaba raises bet on Taobao site." Wall Street Journal, October 9, p. 6.

Fundamentals of E-Commerce Strategy and Structure

Although e-commerce is evolving quickly, the failures of many e-commerce start-ups demonstrate that the Internet economy is not without risks. Each layer of the Internet economy has its threats and opportunities. Exhibit 10.5 provides a summary of them. In this section, you will learn the current strategies used by successful e-commerce companies to overcome some of these challenges.

Steps for a Successful E-Commerce Strategy

E-commerce strategizing is a new and evolving management challenge, and the multinational manager must build on sound, basic strategizing as a prelude to multinational operations. Experts suggest seven fundamental requirements:[10]

1. *Leadership:* Successful e-commerce is possible only through dynamic and strong leadership. At a minimum, CEO and senior executives should strongly

EXHIBIT 10.5   E-Commerce Business Models: Openings and Barriers for Going Global

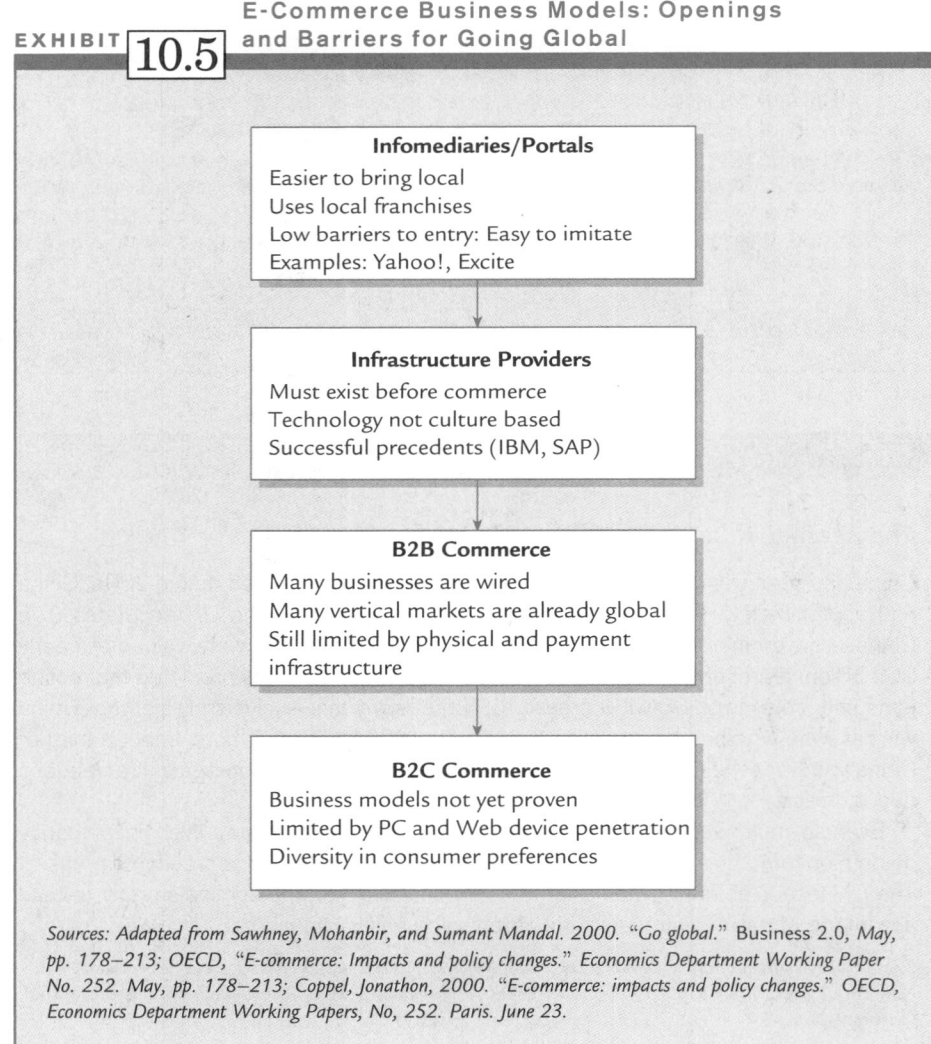

Infomediaries/Portals
Easier to bring local
Uses local franchises
Low barriers to entry: Easy to imitate
Examples: Yahoo!, Excite

Infrastructure Providers
Must exist before commerce
Technology not culture based
Successful precedents (IBM, SAP)

B2B Commerce
Many businesses are wired
Many vertical markets are already global
Still limited by physical and payment infrastructure

B2C Commerce
Business models not yet proven
Limited by PC and Web device penetration
Diversity in consumer preferences

Sources: Adapted from Sawhney, Mohanbir, and Sumant Mandal. 2000. "Go global." Business 2.0, May, pp. 178–213; OECD, "E-commerce: Impacts and policy changes." Economics Department Working Paper No. 252. May, pp. 178–213; Coppel, Jonathon, 2000. "E-commerce: impacts and policy changes." OECD, Economics Department Working Papers, No, 252. Paris. June 23.

believe in the benefits of an e-commerce approach. They should also have expertise to objectively assess the company's position on e-commerce in order to craft the most appropriate e-commerce strategy.

2. *Build on current business models and experiment with new e-commerce models:* Search for ways to use the e-commerce business to reduce costs or to enhance traditional services. E-commerce transactions can be cheap, yet they can add value to customers. Customers can get timely updates like the American Airlines Alert, an e-mail service to notify customers of changes in schedules.

3. *Meet the challenge of developing an e-commerce organization:* The basic choice involves the distinction between a separate autonomous entity for e-commerce business and a seamless integration into the current model. The integrated model works best when the customer finds it difficult to separate e-commerce from the existing form of business. The integrated model also requires senior management's commitment to using the Internet aggressively as part of the company's strategy, and the entire firm must be prepared to embrace the e-commerce model, as did Egghead Software when it moved entirely to a Web-based business.

4. *Allocate resources:* A successful e-commerce strategy must commit financial, human, and technological resources to developing e-commerce capabilities. If these capabilities do not exist within the organization, then selected e-commerce operations are outsourced to third parties or to strategic alliance partners. Consider the next Multinational Management Brief about the critical need to commit resources to an e-commerce venture.

5. *Have an e-commerce strategy:* Companies should not implement e-commerce haphazardly. The company can use some of the strategic management techniques discussed in Chapter 5 to implement a strong strategic e-commerce plan. Some of the most recent experiences suggest that a well-positioned brand name is very critical for repeat purchases. However, companies need to ensure that they offer reliable customer service because that is often seen as more critical than a strong brand. It is also not always necessary

Multinational Management Brief

Alibaba, Taobao, and Resources

Alibaba.com is currently the world's leading business-to-business e-commerce service provider. It provides its small- and medium-sized business customers with a platform to sell their products. However, Alibaba.com also owns Taobao, China's market leader in online auctions. When Taobao entered the market in 2003, it severely undermined eBays' market position in China. Taobao did not require that customers pay a listing fee, and eBay eventually had to leave the market because all its customers migrated to Taobao. However, Taobao is facing new competition from Baidu.com, which is challenging Taobao's position as the market leader in online auctions. As a result, Alibaba.com has decided that it needs to invest more resources. Alibaba Group will therefore be investing about $725 million over the next five years, hoping that the investment will help it keep its market dominance.

Sources: Based on Cavanes, S. 2008. "Alibaba raises bet on Taobao site." Wall Street Journal Asia, October 9, p. 6; Perez, B. 2009. "Alibaba steers small producers to home market." South China Morning Post, May 19, p. 5.

to offer the same products online as in physical locations. Companies such as Office Depot typically offer more products online, whereas others, such as Costco, have smaller and more specialized product offerings.

6. *Develop appropriate e-commerce systems:* To fully benefit from e-commerce, there has to be a cultural transformation in how information flows through the organization. The company has to work hard to remove traditional barriers and to ensure increased coordination and information flows among the various functional areas, such as manufacturing, sales, service, and shipping. Any company that is serious about e-commerce must also align human resource policies and compensation with the e-commerce goals.

7. *Measure success:* Companies need to have metrics in place to measure e-commerce success. Obvious output success measures include Web site hits, the number of new e-commerce customers, e-commerce revenue, and the number of customers learning about new products to purchase through other channels. Companies also can assess process success measures, such as the degree of top management commitment to e-commerce and e-commerce integration across internal and external operations.

The Internet economy has spawned numerous new companies. At the same time, it has provided opportunities for traditional companies to use this evolving business tool. Next, you will see one of the major issues faced by traditional companies when they engage in e-commerce.

E-Commerce Structure: Integrated or Autonomous

Each company needs to decide how e-commerce fits into its existing organizational design and management systems. Writing in the *Harvard Business Review,* Ranjay Gulati of Northwestern University and Jason Garino of the Boston Consulting Group call this the "right mixture of bricks and clicks."[11] They mean that companies must decide how much to integrate their evolving Internet operations into their traditional business operations. In the evolving e-commerce jargon, traditional business operations are often called the **brick-and-mortar** part of the company.

Brick-and-mortar
Traditional or nonvirtual business operation.

The degree of integration between brick-and-mortar operations and the Internet business can occur anywhere in the value chain from the procurement of raw material to after-sales service. Additionally, the degree of integration can range from the nearly seamless operation of an Office Depot to the mostly independent operations of Barnes & Noble and Barnesandnoble.com.

Each choice has its benefits. The independent operation can move faster and be more entrepreneurial when freed from corporate bureaucracy. It can seek funding from the deep pockets of venture capitalists willing to invest in e-commerce companies. The integrated operation, on the other hand, can benefit from the cross-promotion of shared products, shared customer information, increased large-quantity purchasing leverage, and economies of scale by using the same distribution channels.[12]

The choice between seamless integration and a fully autonomous unit is not simple and seldom is clear-cut. The best option for most companies is something in between. As with most strategy implementation issues, managers must evaluate their company's situation to make an informed decision. Exhibit 10.6 shows a decision model with the questions that managers must consider when choosing the best level of integration for the e-commerce unit.

EXHIBIT 10.6 Key Decisions in Web Business Integration

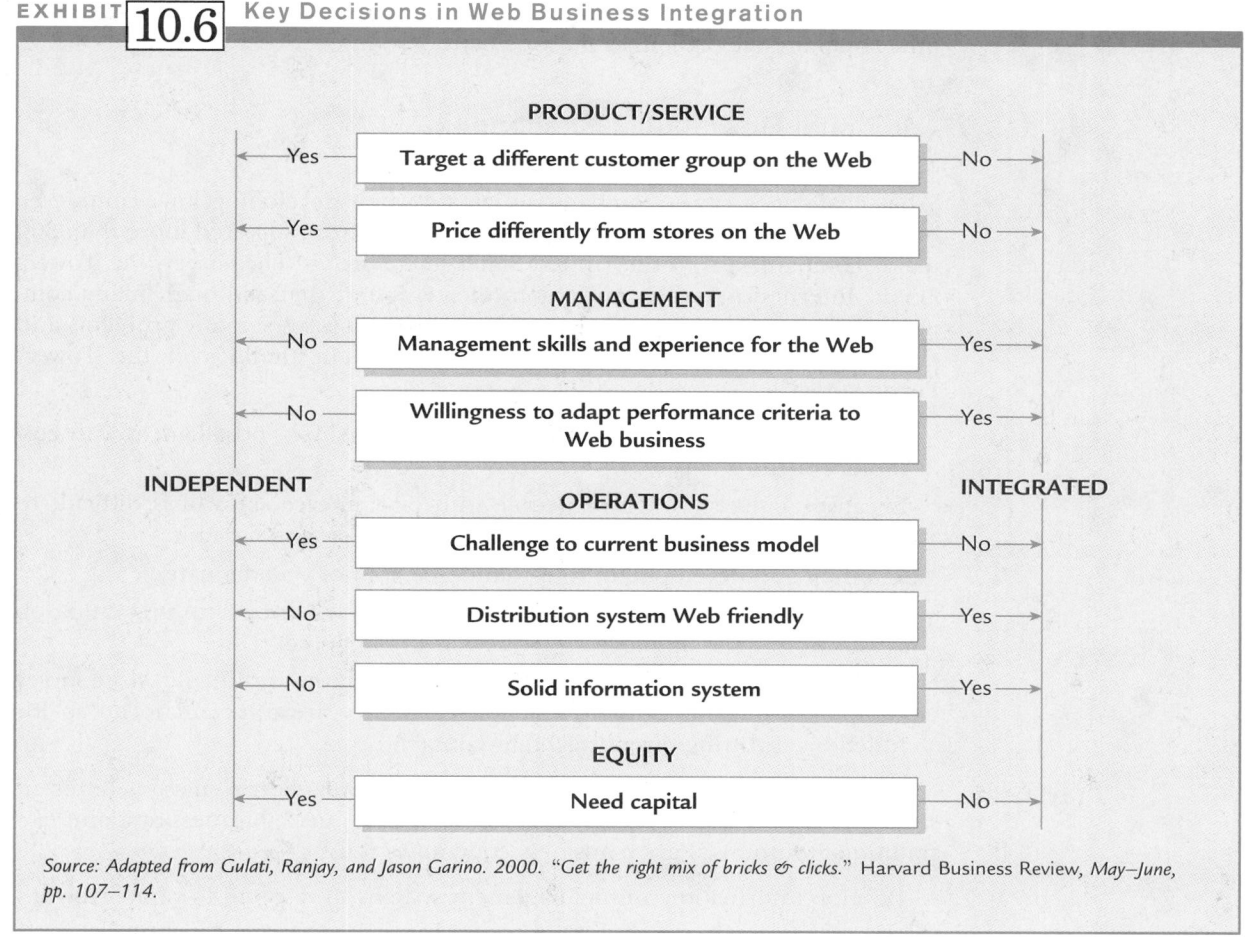

PRODUCT/SERVICE

Yes ← Target a different customer group on the Web → No

Yes ← Price differently from stores on the Web → No

MANAGEMENT

No ← Management skills and experience for the Web → Yes

No ← Willingness to adapt performance criteria to Web business → Yes

INDEPENDENT **OPERATIONS** INTEGRATED

Yes ← Challenge to current business model → No

No ← Distribution system Web friendly → Yes

No ← Solid information system → Yes

EQUITY

Yes ← Need capital → No

Source: Adapted from Gulati, Ranjay, and Jason Garino. 2000. "Get the right mix of bricks & clicks." Harvard Business Review, May–June, pp. 107–114.

Although Exhibit 10.6 provides useful guidance regarding the appropriate level of integration, experience suggests that more companies in the United States are taking steps to integrate their online and offline channels.[13] Customers are getting more sophisticated about their purchases and often use channels that offer the best prices. These customers get frustrated if they are not informed of appropriate pricing or inventory differences between a retailer's online and offline offerings. Here are some of the ways companies can integrate their online and offline operations:[14]

- *Keep customers informed:* Most retailers find it impossible to maintain the same pricing and inventories on their Web sites and in their stores. However, this discrepancy does not have to be a source of frustration for consumers. Companies often find that their customers appreciate being informed of such differences.

- *Share customer data across channels:* Companies are realizing the benefits of sharing customer data across channels. For instance, retailers can send tailored product e-mails based on store purchases. Segmentation campaigns can be compared across channels (online versus in the store) to get better insights into customer purchasing behaviors.

Although the level of e-commerce integration is a crucial decision, numerous other operational challenges must be considered.

Additional Operational Challenges for an E-Commerce Business

What challenges can a company anticipate when developing an e-commerce business? Towers Perrin, the New York consulting firm, surveyed more than 300 major companies from the United States and Europe. The survey, the Towers Perrin Internetworked Organization Survey, found that, although many companies see the advantages of e-commerce, they also foresee many problems and challenges. This section summarizes the important findings of the Towers Perrin survey.

- Many companies have difficulty finding partnerships and alliances with customers or third parties.
- Because of the shortage of people with e-commerce skills, it is difficult to attract, retain, and, develop employees in the e-commerce unit.
- Training and development in e-commerce are not yet adequate.
- Finding ways to provide individuals with growth opportunities and job satisfaction drives employee retention in e-commerce.
- Deciding which e-commerce functions to outsource is difficult. Most survey companies outsource many functions, but they are reluctant to do so for functions involving direct customer contact.

How can companies meet these challenges? Towers Perrin suggests different strategies depending on whether the company is a pure e-business or a unit of a traditional business. Pure e-business companies must:

- Develop information and management systems to respond to rapid growth.
- Maintain rapid decision making, creativity, innovation, and flexibility.
- Build external relationships with e-commerce support companies and customers.
- Attract and retain e-commerce-capable talent.
- Develop an effective management team.

Traditional companies with e-commerce units must:

- Build a common vision and commitment to the e-commerce operation throughout the organization.
- Change the organizational structure to emphasize quick reconfiguration of assets and capabilities.
- Change the organizational culture to create a supporting environment for e-commerce.
- Attract and retain e-commerce-skilled employees.
- Alter HR programs to suit the different skill requirements of e-commerce employees.

E-commerce security Degree to which customers feel that their private and personal information is safeguarded by companies collecting it.

Exhibit 10.7 shows the organizational changes multinational companies are making to implement their e-commerce strategies.

As companies and institutions take advantage of e-commerce and its applications, they face a new and important challenge: **e-commerce security**,[15] which

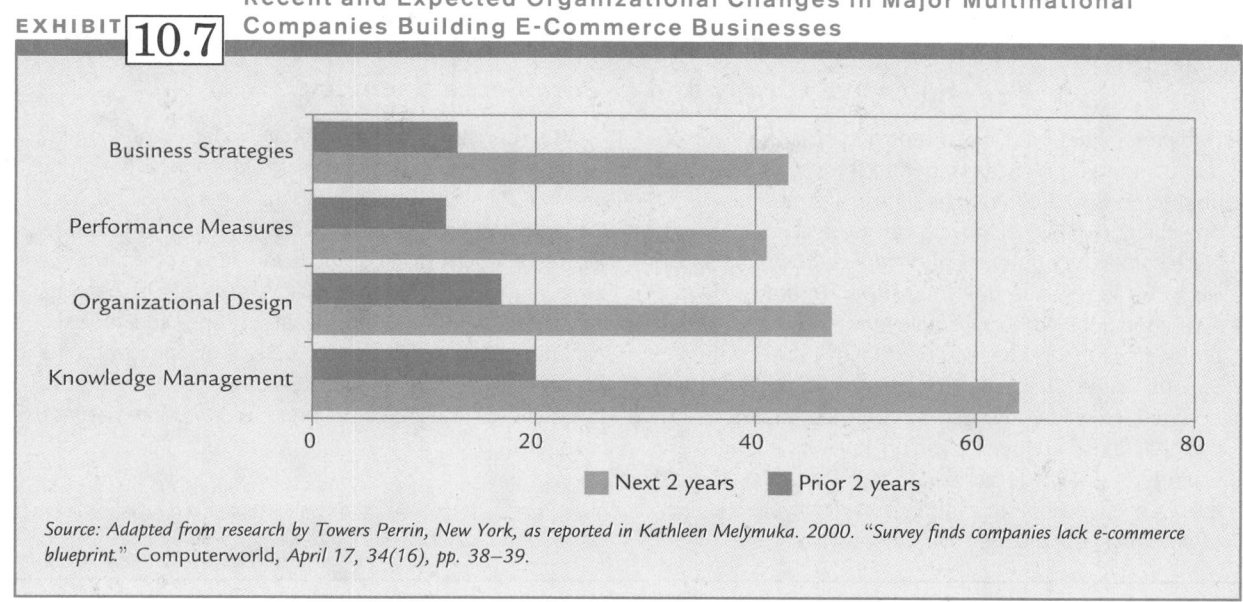

EXHIBIT 10.7   Recent and Expected Organizational Changes in Major Multinational Companies Building E-Commerce Businesses

Source: Adapted from research by Towers Perrin, New York, as reported in Kathleen Melymuka. 2000. "Survey finds companies lack e-commerce blueprint." Computerworld, April 17, 34(16), pp. 38–39.

is the degree to which customers feel that their private, personal information is safe in the hands of online companies collecting it. Hundreds of millions of people around the world provide personal information on the Internet as they browse or purchase products and services online.[16] How such information is collected and stored and what is done with it are sources of concern for most Internet users. Furthermore, attacks on popular Web sites are increasing rapidly, resulting in the theft of credit card numbers of thousands of customers. Specific industries, such as online banking, are suffering significant Internet attacks through phishing and Trojan horses.[17] Banking regulators suggest that online bank frauds may drain from 2 to 5 percent of a bank's overall revenue. Furthermore, recent observations suggest that cyber criminals are becoming increasingly sophisticated.[18] Instead of attacking operating systems and Internet services on the Web, cyber criminals now focus on applications and network operating systems. Cyber-criminals are also emphasizing specific vulnerabilities within certain companies. In this respect, e-commerce security is at risk for a not so obvious reason: software piracy. Consider the next Case in Point.

As the Internet becomes a crucial medium of international trade and commerce, countries are being urged to improve Internet security. The European Union and ASEAN (Association of South East Asian Countries, including Singapore, Thailand, Malaysia, and Indonesia) are being encouraged not only to improve Internet security, but also to minimize abuse because many online scams and phishing tend to originate in some of these member countries.

Multinationals are also being encouraged to beef up their Internet security. Specifically, most companies need to be concerned about a number of information security issues:[19] (1) confidentiality (making sure that private information is protected), (2) availability (ensuring that information is accessible to authorized users), (3) integrity (ensuring that the information collected is accurate and reliable), and (4) authentication (having systems in place to ensure that persons using the systems are legitimate). Companies are also under increased pressure

Software Piracy and E-Commerce Security

Software piracy—the illegal copying of software—has many important disadvantages to the e-commerce industry. Software companies incur revenue losses, for one thing. Research shows that for every $1 of software sold in a country, local IT service companies lose $3 to $4 in revenue due to spillover. Pirated software also costs jobs for local employees. One of the worst problems is the increased potential of cyber crime and security issues. Legally acquired software is regularly updated. However, the users of pirated copies do not get the latest updates, allowing hackers to take advantage of new vulnerabilities. In fact, the proliferation of the Conficker virus was attributed mostly to the lack of automatic updates for pirated software.

Where is software piracy most problematic? Research suggests that the lowest-piracy countries are the United States, Japan, New Zealand, and Luxembourg, with about a 20 percent piracy rate. However, countries such as Bangladesh and Armenia have among the highest piracy rates at 90 percent. Countries in Central and East Europe and in Latin America have piracy rates up to 66 percent. The European Union and North American regions have the lowest rates at 35 percent and 21 percent, respectively.

Source: Based on U.S. Newswire. 2009. "A fifth of PC software in the US is pirated." May 12, http:/www.bsa.org.

to protect the privacy of individuals as more and more personal information is being collected, stored, and shared by companies in industries such as health care, banking and finance, travel, and the government.[20]

Experts thus suggest the use of (1) firewalls,[21] antivirus protection software,[22] (2) data encryption and several levels of authentication for users,[23] and (3) abiding by privacy rules to address internet security issues.[24]

The preceding sections reviewed the basic strategies, structures, and challenges managers face when developing an e-commerce business. The following sections will discuss some of the additional challenges faced when companies choose to go multinational with their e-commerce operations.

Globalizing Through the Internet

The increase in information exchanges and efficiency due to the Internet and e-commerce has made it possible for companies to reach customers worldwide. However, the Internet also makes possible the emergence of a new form of multinational, the born-global firms.[25] From the day they are created, born-global firms are able to obtain a significant portion of their revenues from sales in international markets (see Chapter 7).

Although a Web site immediately gives the entire world access to a company's products or services, many of the challenges of globalization faced by traditional brick-and-mortar companies remain. A company still must solve the global-local dilemma (Chapter 6). Managers must decide whether the company's products or services are global in content and delivery or require localization at the national or regional level. E-commerce companies also must address the traditional multinational business problems relating to national and business cultures and national institutional contexts (e.g., currencies/payments, local laws, and infrastructure for delivery or procurement). Other chapters will consider these issues in more detail. This section adds to the understanding of multinational strategy formulation and implementation by considering some issues unique to the e-commerce operation.

Multinational E-Commerce Strategy Formulation: The Nature of the Business

What kind of e-business is easiest to take global? To a large degree, the kind of company depends on the types of products or services offered through e-commerce. Consider the next Case in Point. The next section reviews the distinguishing features.

According to e-commerce experts, Mohanbir Sawhney and Sumant Mandal,[26] e-commerce companies work in three areas: (1) Some move bits of computerized information; (2) others move money in payment flows; (3) still others move physical products. Each type of operation requires an infrastructure to support the transaction. Telecommunications infrastructures support moving bits. A payment infrastructure allows the movement of money. Moving physical goods requires physical infrastructure. The ease of taking e-commerce international depends mostly on the mix of infrastructures required.

Sawhney and Mandal argue that there is a hierarchy of difficulty in e-commerce depending on infrastructure requirements. Portals and infomediaries provide gateways to the Internet. Portals are primarily search engines to locate Web sites, and infomediaries go a step further by providing not only links but also information, such as current news. They were also the first e-business forms to have a global presence.

At the next level are businesses such as travel services, digital music, and software vendors. Although they do not move physical objects, they still must rely on local infrastructure to take payments for their products. The technical and managerial challenge comes from dealing with issues such as credit card payments (fraud and the lack of use in some areas), currency conversion, and a bewildering array of tax jurisdictions. Most difficult to globalize are e-commerce businesses that rely on a physical infrastructure. Like their brick-and-mortar counterparts, these businesses must ship goods to fulfill customer orders and manage their supply chains located throughout the world. In addition, they must deal with the challenges of receiving payments through a variety of payment infrastructures.

For e-businesses that require a physical infrastructure in host countries, large multinational firms with an existing global presence often have an advantage as

---

C A S E I N P O I N T

Casual Male: Going Global

Casual Male is a specialty retailer offering a wide array of sportswear, dress clothing, and footwear. All of Casual Male's customers have distinct physical characteristics. The typical customer has a waist size of 42 inches and is about 6 feet 2 inches tall. Casual Male targets the big-and-tall segment of the apparel market.

Most retailers strive to find new sources of customers, particularly during economic downturns. Casual Male is going global by launching six new e-commerce sites targeting the European Union. Rather than venture into unknown territories in emerging markets such as India or China, Casual Male has decided to rely on available customer information to enter the European market. Furthermore, they have decided that they would much rather launch online initiatives than invest in relatively unreliable real estate to establish actual stores in the European Union. Casual Male will soon launch six separate online stores in France, Germany, Italy, the Netherlands, Spain, and the U.K.

Source: Based on Amato-McCoy, D. M. 2008. "Going global." Retail Technology Quarterly, July, pp. 42–44.

they enter into e-commerce. They have in place either brick-and-mortar units or the resources to establish physical bases and localized Web sites. Small firms and firms new to the complexities of multinational commerce face more challenges in establishing an international presence.

Basic Opportunities and Threats of Multinational E-Commerce

In deciding whether to globalize their e-commerce operations—either as an existing brick-and-mortar company or as a pure e-commerce company—managers need to weigh the attractions and deterrents of international e-commerce.[27] Again, this is a traditional strategy formulation problem: Managers must consider the opportunities and threats before deciding on a strategy. However, the e-commerce environment has some unique characteristics. Consider the following.[28]

The major attractions of e-commerce globalization are:

- *Cost reduction:* Reaching international customers via the Web can be relatively inexpensive.
- *Technology:* The technology to reach anyone with an Internet-linked computer is readily available.
- *Efficiencies:* Electronic communication and processes can be very efficient.
- *Convenience:* The Web is in operation seven days a week and 24 hours a day, regardless of location.
- *Speed of access:* Once a Web site is running, a company's products or services can be accessed immediately from anywhere in the world.

Some deterrents include:

- *The return/receipt burden and cost of delivery:* If the pattern follows catalog sales, businesses should expect a 30 to 40 percent return rate for online purchases.[29]
- *Costs of site construction, maintenance, upgrades:* Web site construction and maintenance in multiple languages, currencies, and tax locations can cost companies millions of dollars per year.
- *Channel conflicts:* Distributors and retailers that sell a company's products may be undermined by competition from a company's Web site that sells directly to end users—a major fear of many automobile dealers if the manufacturers were to sell directly. Consider what is happening to travel agents as more people buy tickets online directly from the airline companies.
- *Easily copied models:* Local competitors can easily see and copy a multinational's product, service, or business model if it is displayed on the Web.
- *Cultural differences:* Understanding global customers and overcoming cultural barriers and language differences can be difficult on the Web. Web sites not only must be multilingual, but they must also present a format that is culturally appropriate.
- *Traditional cross-border transaction complexities:* These issues include pricing for exchange rates, varying taxes, and government regulations.
- *Standard or local Web sites:* Companies must decide whether to standardize Web sites or tailor them to the local context.

- *Customer trust and satisfaction:* Companies must determine whether customers abroad will trust and be satisfied with e-commerce in general and with their Web sites in particular.

The next Case in Point gives an example of how one company overcame cultural differences to succeed in Japan.

Picking a Market

Clay Shirky suggests that Web entrepreneurs should target countries based on two factors.[30] First, attractive markets for e-commerce are those with market inefficiencies. Shirky claims that many formerly state-controlled markets have suboptimal economic performance. In these markets, e-commerce shopping allows buyers to obtain better quality and lower prices because they are free from state control. Second, target markets with attractive demographic characteristics. These include locations with an Internet population of at least 5 percent, a high literacy rate (to predict the future growth of the Internet population), a country that participates in at least one free trade agreement, and a government with a viable legal system.

In Shirky's opinion, e-commerce potential is great in South America because of the Mercosur trade group and in Southeast Asian countries with membership in the ASEAN trade group. He also suggests that the European Union is the next boom area for e-commerce because many countries such as France, Italy, and Germany retain market inefficiencies from pre-Union days. The open borders and common currency in the EU should make for fertile ground for e-commerce growth.

Not all countries are equally e-commerce ready. The population must have access to computers and infrastructure links to the Internet. Governments and financial institutions must be ready to protect and process e-commerce

---

C A S E   I N   P O I N T

Adapting E-Commerce to Cultural Differences

Most experts agree that using the Internet to go international can be a good way to gain access to new markets. Selling online allows a company to weather slowdowns in local markets while diversifying into new territories. However, going global through the Internet means more than just offering Web sites in local languages. Multinationals need to take into consideration other factors, such as the culture, customs, and technical sophistication, while adapting their products to meet local needs. Research shows that 52 percent of online buyers will buy only from Web sites using their own language. Thus, although experts agree that Internet access is spreading and more consumers are becoming comfortable with e-commerce, significant cultural differences pose serious challenges to e-commerce.

Consider the case of Handango, which decided to expand into Japan after it noticed that Japanese customers were purchasing from its U.S. Web sites. Although the company was encouraged to find that there are no shipping restrictions for its products, it quickly faced significant barriers. For instance, Japanese consumers prefer to make online payments using a method called *konbini*, which requires consumers to go to a local convenience store to make a cash payment. The clerk then transfers the money to the vendor's online account. Handango decided to form a partnership with a local consumer electronics company to handle marketing and sales.

Sources: Adapted from Bright, Becky. 2006. "E-commerce: How do you say 'Web'? Planning to take your online business international." Wall Street Journal, May 23, p. R11; Murphy, S. 2008. "A touch of local flavor." Chain Store Age, May, p. 144.

transactions. Exhibit 10.8 shows a ranking of the e-commerce readiness of selected countries. The e-commerce readiness scale is developed by the Economist Intelligence Unit and is based on a number of factors that determine how suitable a market is to Internet-based opportunities.[31]

The enormous growth in global e-commerce shows that its benefits clearly outweigh the risks, as firms increasingly use the Internet to globalize operations. In the rapidly growing Internet environment, however, the competition is heating up. Achieving sustainable competitive advantage is difficult when competitors can easily copy business models.

Multinational E-Commerce Strategy Implementation

Successful implementation of a multinational e-commerce strategy requires building an appropriate organization and developing the necessary technical capabilities to conduct electronic transactions. The following sections provide an overview of the options available to multinational managers.

The Multinational E-Commerce Organization

How is a multinational e-business organized? Amazon.com and Yahoo! provide the most likely models.[32] These organizations are three-tiered, mixing global and local functions.

1. Corporate headquarters represents the global core that supplies the vision, strategy, and leadership driving the electronic marketing of worldwide products or services.

2. Headquarters also provides shared services, such as the network infrastructure. Managers at headquarters and in the shared functional areas have worldwide responsibility for their operations.

EXHIBIT $\boxed{10.8}$ E-Readiness Index (10 = perfect e-readiness)

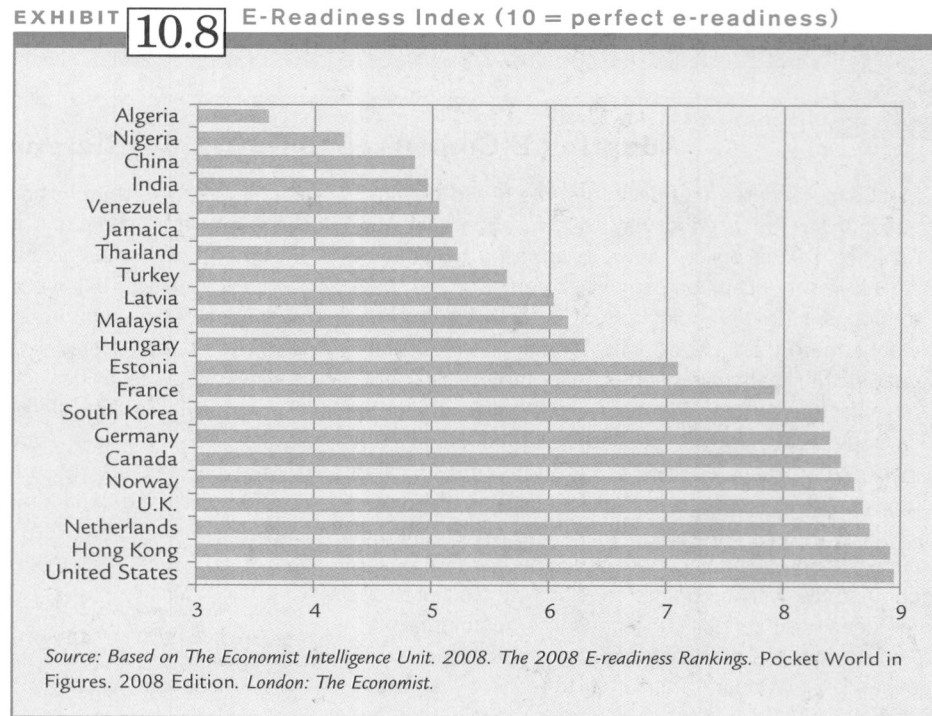

Source: Based on The Economist Intelligence Unit. 2008. The 2008 E-readiness Rankings. Pocket World in Figures. 2008 Edition. London: The Economist.

3. Local subsidiaries, which actually deliver the goods, take charge of functions that are better done locally, such as managing the supply chain and dealing with regulations. These organizations try to solve the global-local dilemma with the integration of similar technical functions, such as Web server design, while making necessary adaptations such as Web site translations.[33] Exhibit 10.9 illustrates the levels and functions of this type of organization.

Technical Capabilities and Implementation Options for Multinational E-Commerce

Components of a successful multinational online presence require electronic capabilities and support throughout the value chain.[34] Such capabilities are:

- Software to process pricing in multiple currencies. (The most sophisticated software not only supports payment processing systems that show prices in multiple currencies but also accepts payment in the customer's preferred currency.)

- Systems that calculate and show purchase information on international shipping, duties, and local taxes such as the VAT (value-added tax common in Europe).

- Systems that check regulatory compliance with local and international laws.

- The ability to give support in multilingual service centers.

EXHIBIT 10.9   **Organizational Structures of the Multinational E-Corporation**

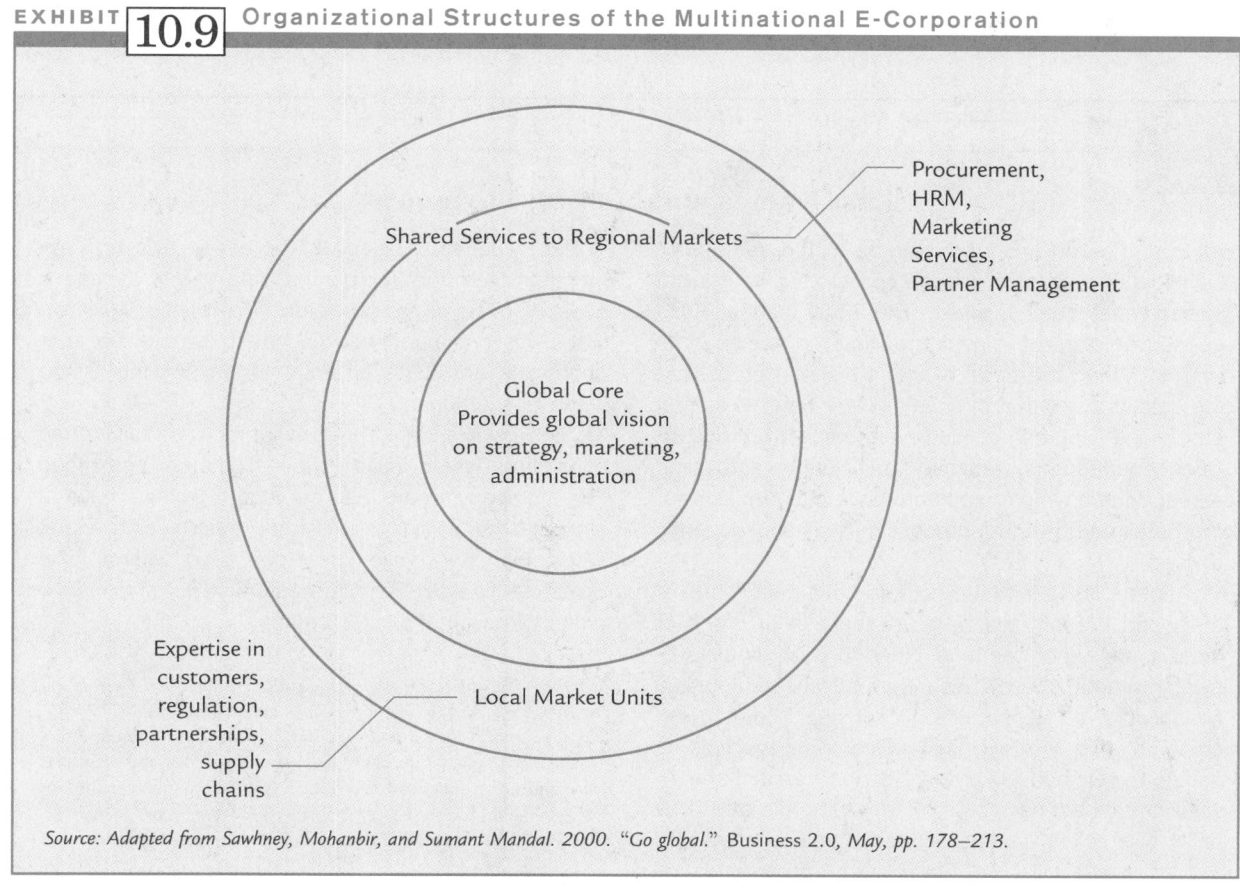

Shared Services to Regional Markets — Procurement, HRM, Marketing Services, Partner Management

Global Core
Provides global vision on strategy, marketing, administration

Expertise in customers, regulation, partnerships, supply chains — Local Market Units

Source: Adapted from Sawhney, Mohanbir, and Sumant Mandal. 2000. "Go global." Business 2.0, May, pp. 178–213.

- Fraud protection.
- Electronic payment models in addition to credit cards (not used as commonly as in the United States).

In addition, local realities influence how a multinational approaches its international markets. Many areas of the world do not process data the same way. In some countries, for instance, last names may actually come first. Similarly, not all countries use credit and debit cards—a significant problem for e-commerce. The next Case in Point shows how 7-Eleven and other companies manage their electronic payment model without the use of credit cards.

Web Sites: Localize or Standardize?

As more and more multinationals use product-based Web sites and corporate Web sites to present, sell, and communicate with the public and their consumers, the issue of Web site adaptation is becoming critical.[35] As in the local-global dilemma, multinationals have to decide whether they want a **standardized Web site** (the company's Web sites are fairly similar in layout and design around the world) or a **localized Web site** (the values, appeals, symbols, and even themes in the communication content are adapted to the local culture).[36]

For some companies, the localization of Web sites is minimal. Dell Computer has Web sites in 50 countries using 21 different languages, but it uses the same layout for the sites in all countries. In contrast, Chipshot.com, which sells golf equipment online, tailors its sites to local cultural needs. In Japan, to take advantage of the Japanese golfer's sensitivity to brand names, the Chipshot site

Standardized Web site
Web site that is similar in design and layout around the world.

Localized Web site
Web site that is adapted to the local cultures.

CASE IN POINT

Last Names and Making Payments

All countries do not process data in the same way. Consider the case of a large conference held in an international hotel in Asia. The hotel had all 200 guests registered but could not find the names in its system. When the hotel examined how it processed the data, it found that the names were entered as first name and last name. However, many of the conference attendees went by family name and given name. Such a simple problem was a major hassle for the hotel, and the data processing was subsequently revised.

Another issue is that e-commerce in many parts of the world is restricted because the use of credit or debit cards is not common. How do you pay electronically without a card? Even in an advanced industrial nation such as Japan, credit card use is much less common than in the United States. For example, in Japan, fewer than 10 percent of the transactions involve credit card payments. In Japan, people often pay utility bills at convenience stores. Thinking creatively,

7-Eleven Japan took advantage of the existing payment structure for Web purchase payments. Japanese users of 7dream.com can select "Payment at 7-Eleven Store" as an option, allowing them to pick up their purchases and pay for them at any of the 8,000 7-Elevens in Japan.

Similarly, Handango found that many of its German consumers would leave in the middle of their order. The company soon learned that Germans have a strong cultural bias against debt and using credit cards. Handango eventually partnered with a local company to allow German customers to wire money directly from their bank accounts.

Sources: Adapted from Bright, Becky. 2006. "E-commerce: How do you say 'Web'? Planning to take your online business international." Wall Street Journal, May 23, p. R11; Litchy, T. R., and R. A. Barra. 2008. "International issues of the design and usage of websites for e-commerce: Hotel and airline examples." Journal of Engineering and Technology Management, 25, pp. 93–111; Sawhney, Mohanbir, and Sumant Mandal. 2000. "Go global." Business 2.0, May, pp. 178–213.

shows brand names conspicuously and emphasizes the availability of custom-made clubs. By comparison, the U.S. site appeals to the more cost-conscious U.S. customers by emphasizing the 50-percent discount.[37]

Should companies standardize or localize? The practitioners and academic literature are fairly silent on the subject, but studies are starting to provide some guidance on the question. Consider the next Case in Point examining McDonald's Web sites around the world. The study in that case provides evidence of the influence of cultural factors on Web site design and layout.

Developing a global Web site entails challenges to organizations beyond cultural sensitivity and language differences. Many firms discover that they need to adapt their organizations to the information flow and customer demands created by Web locations accessed from anywhere in the world. The resultant changes in organizational structure and in internal information systems make the company more globally integrated.

The results of the Forrester Research survey, reported in Exhibit 10.10, suggest that organizational challenges are among the most important issues affecting Web site globalization.

To Build or Outsource Technical Capabilities?

Similar to companies' choosing an export strategy (directly or indirectly, with the aid of export management companies), e-commerce companies seeking to globalize their operations have two basic options. They can run all the e-commerce functions themselves, or they can outsource them to e-fulfillment specialists, called **e-commerce enablers**. Enablers provide services and software that translate Web sites and calculate shipping, value-added taxes, duties, and

> **E-commerce enablers**
> Fulfillment specialists that provide other companies with services such as Web site translation.

C A S E   I N   P O I N T

McDonald's Web Sites around the World

McDonald's multinational corporation currently operates more than 31,000 restaurants serving 58 million people daily in 118 nations. Given McDonald's effort to customize its products to meet local needs, the company not surprisingly tailors its Web sites to satisfy local preferences. In an interesting study, Wurtz compared McDonald's Web sites in high-context cultures (i.e., where communication is not direct but includes implicit messages contained in body language and silence) and in low-context cultures (i.e., where communication occurs primarily through explicit statements, such as text and speech). Comparing high-context countries such as Japan, India, and South Korea with low-context countries such as Denmark, Germany, Finland, Norway, and the United States, Wurtz found strong evidence of McDonald's Web site adaptation to local cultures. For instance, the author found more animation centered on people in the Web sites of

high-context cultures, showing a preference for complexity in communication, while low-context Web sites are more static and use less animation. Navigation on low-context Web sites tends to be more linear, while on high-context Web sites more new browser windows open with less transparent guidance. The author also examined some aspects of Hofstede's cultural dimensions and how they influence Web design. For instance, the highly individualistic Swiss and German Web sites display images of individuals listening to music and relaxing (a very individual activity). In contrast, the Indian Web site shows a man running with a child in a shopping cart, emphasizing the family ties and group approach typical of collectivistic societies.

Sources: McDonald's. 2009. http://www.mcdonalds.com; Wurtz, Elizabeth. 2005. "A cross-cultural analysis of Websites from high-context cultures and low-context cultures." Journal of Computer Mediated Communications, 11, pp. 25–43.

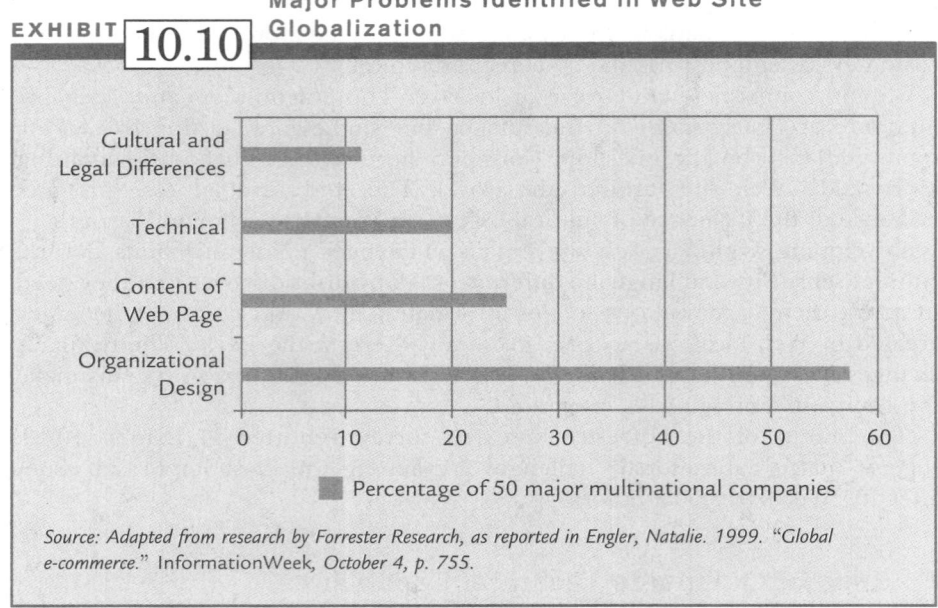

EXHIBIT 10.10   **Major Problems Identified in Web Site Globalization**

Percentage of 50 major multinational companies

Source: Adapted from research by Forrester Research, as reported in Engler, Natalie. 1999. "Global e-commerce." InformationWeek, October 4, p. 755.

other charges unique to each country. They take on functions such as receiving the customers' purchased goods, storing, packing, and eventual shipping to the customer. As with good export management firms, successful order fulfillment enablers understand local business culture and know how to comply with taxation and regulatory requirements.[38]

Enablers exist because many companies—from small to quite large—do not have the internal resources or capabilities to conduct all the required e-commerce functions. In addition, in such a rapidly changing, competitive environment, few companies have the time to develop such strategic capabilities. For example, Forrester Research estimates that 85 percent of U.S. e-retailers cannot fill international orders because they do not have the capability to deal with the complexities of shipping across borders. Even some very large companies, such as Nike and Blockbuster, outsource to enablers.

Many enablers specialize in helping companies globalize their e-commerce. Companies such as Global Site and Idion help create multilingual versions of Web sites for their customers. These companies have automated the translation process so that updates to Web sites can occur rapidly. This type of service has become so popular that Forrester Research expects a 50 percent per year increase in it.

The next Multinational Management Brief gives an overview of the services offered by NextLinx, one of the first global e-commerce enablers, and E4X, another enabler.[39]

In addition to e-commerce enablers that provide transaction services, numerous companies offer Web translations, some of which have automated the translation process. A challenge of translation is to keep up with the frequent, often costly changes in global Web sites. Culturally sensitive enablers go beyond simple translations. Like any advertisement or promotion in different countries, the Web site must be sensitive to cultural and religious differences. Colors,

Multinational Management Brief

Looking at a Global E-Commerce Enablers' Services

NextLinx has identified long-term obstacles to international business that can be simplified by its services:

- Export and import regulations and duties.
- Complex border crossings.
- Multiregional/country-related expertise needed.
- Extensive documentation required.
- Coordination of multiple transportation legs.
- Often unknown total landed cost until after the shipment is delivered.

The NextLinx software reduces the global e-commerce transaction to three phases on a Web site. In the preclick phase, the buyer reviews transportation options and costs and gets import duties, VAT, excise taxes, and other governmental charges to determine the total landed cost. In the click phase, the buyer orders and determines door-to-door shipping. This phase also screens for customers with denied access and checks to determine whether a license is required. In the postclick phase, documentation is printed and tracking of the shipment begins until it reaches the destination.

The NextLinx system covers 100 exporting and importing countries and all 99 chapters of the Harmonized Tariff Schedule (HTS), including all its headings and subheadings. (There are more than 19,000 HTS export and import codes.) The software calculates customs duty rates, including all trade preferential programs. It also calculates governmental charges such as VAT, excise taxes, merchandise processing fees (MPF), and port charges. NextLinx can host the technology on its Web site for a company, or it can provide software and technical support to clients who use their own servers.

E4X also provides e-commerce enabling software. For instance, in the past, international consumers of Saks or Overstock.com had to log onto another site after making their purchases. E4X provides international storefronts with multicurrency localization. International customers can now access a global checkout window that loads up in the company's site when a customer logs out.

Sources: Adapted from Management Dynamics, Inc. 2009. http://www.nextlinx.com; Minnick, F. 2008. "Global as local." Stores, December, 90(2), p. 31.

---

symbols, pictures, and variance in the local use of the same language may cause undesirable reactions depending on locale.

How will e-commerce and the Internet evolve for multinationals? Many experts agree that the explosion of discussion forums, blogs, and social networking sites is creating tremendous new opportunities for companies.[40] Consumers are using user-generated content (UGC) such as product reviews to make purchasing decisions. Multinationals will be well-advised to understand and accommodate this new medium. Many multinationals are already using UGC to their advantage, and this trend is bound to continue.

Summary and Conclusions

This chapter introduced the concepts of e-commerce in general and of multinational e-commerce in particular. It discussed the basic forms of e-commerce, including B2C, B2B, C2C, and C2B. Presently, B2B dominates the Internet economy, but B2C is expected to gain a major share of e-commerce transactions. Overall, e-commerce is expanding geometrically. Although the United States currently dominates e-commerce, statistics show that other areas of the world are quickly catching up.

The fundamentals of e-commerce strategy emphasize building on traditional business models and experimenting with cost reductions and areas of differentiation that Internet use might provide. There is no easy formula for building a successful e-commerce business. Innovative and creative managers will find ways to use e-commerce tools to improve their firms' cost leadership or differentiation strategies. Because the World Wide Web makes e-commerce models transparent and easy to copy, only the most innovative and rapidly moving companies are likely to survive.

Companies conducting multinational operations via the Internet face most of the same challenges as brick-and-mortar multinational companies. The problems remain of the global-local dilemma and of conducting business in different cultural and institutional environments. The Web, however, provides instant access to the world for all companies willing to navigate the e-commerce world. It will probably become one of the most important drivers of globalization in the future.

Discussion Questions

1. Define e-commerce and discuss the types of e-commerce transactions.
2. Identify and discuss the levels of the Internet economy. How has the Internet created new types of businesses?
3. Compare and contrast the costs and benefits of a fully integrated brick-and-mortar and e-commerce company.
4. What are the advantages of e-commerce businesses over traditional brick-and-mortar businesses when taking their operations global? What are the disadvantages?
5. Discuss the advantages and disadvantages of outsourcing global e-commerce activities to enablers.
6. Discuss the characteristics of a successful multinational Web page.

Multinational Management Skill Builder

Build a Web Store

Step 1. Your instructor will divide the class into groups.

Step 2. Select an agricultural or industrial product produced in your region of the country. If possible, interview a small business person concerning his or her perspectives on the international opportunities for the product. In the United States, one way of finding a potential business owner is through the small business development centers attached to many U.S. universities. Your instructor may assign you a business or product.

Step 3. Using the steps shown in Exhibit 7.5 (Chapter 7), information from Web sources, and your library, identify a foreign market or markets for the product or products.

Step 4. Build a simulated or actual Web site in your own language that shows the company's products or services. If you have the technical capabilities and are working with a real business, you can build a Web store. Simple, no-cost or low-cost versions of Web storefronts can be downloaded from sources such as http://www.authstores.com/. Periodically search the Web for additional free e-commerce sources because new sites frequently become available.

Step 5. Translate your Web site into the language(s) of your target country or countries. Use the free translation software available on the Web at Google or others.

Step 6. Test your translation and site layout with native speakers. If it is a real site, wait for orders.

Step 7. Present your site and its performance to your class and to the small business person, if possible.

Endnotes

1. Andersen, Poul Houman. 2005. "Export intermediation and the Internet: An activity-unbundling approach." *International Marketing Review*, 22(2), pp. 147–164.

2. ebusinessforum.com. 2000. "Ericsson: The promise of purchasing cards." December 18. http://www.ebusinessforum.com.

3. Neff, Dale. 2001. *e-Procurement*. Upper Saddle River, NJ: Prentice-Hall.

4. Koh, Chang E., and Kyungdoo "Ted" Nam. 2005. "Business use of the Internet: A longitudinal study from a value chain perspective." *Industrial Management + Data Systems*, 105(1/2), pp. 82–95.

5. Coppel, Jonathan. 2000. "E-commerce: Impacts and policy challenges." *OECD, Economics Department Working Papers*, No. 252. June 23. Paris.

6. Organization for Economic Cooperation and Development (OECD). 2009. *Measuring the Internet Economy 2008*. Paris: Organization for Economic Cooperation and Development.

7. Ibid.

8. Ibid.

9. Ibid.

10. Epstein, Marc J. 2005. "Implementing successful e-commerce initiatives." *Strategic Finance*, March, 86(9), pp. 22–29; Venkatraman, N. 2000. "Five steps to a dot-com strategy: How to find your footing on the Web." *Sloan Management Review*, Spring, pp. 15–28.

11. Gulati, Ranjay, and Jason Garino. 2000. "Get the right mix of bricks & clicks." *Harvard Business Review*, May–June, pp. 107–114.

12. Ibid.

13. Beasty, Colin. 2006. "Retail's 2 worlds: Tips on integrating online and offline channels." *Customer Relationship Management*, March, 10(3), pp. 30–35.

14. Ibid.

15. Kim, Hyunwoo, Younggoo Han, Sehun Kim, and Myeonggil Choi. 2005. *Journal of Information Systems Education*, Spring, 16(1), pp. 55–64.

16. Peslak, Alan R. 2006. "Internet privacy policies of the largest international companies." *Journal of Electronic Commerce in Organizations*, 4(3), pp. 46–62.

17. Grimes, Roger. 2006. "E-commerce in crisis: When SSL isn't safe." *InfoWorld*, May 1, 28(18), p. 26.

18. Claburn, Thomas. 2005. "New path of attack." *InformationWeek*, No. 1066. November 28.

19. Gordon, Lawrence, and Martin P. Loeb. 2006. "Budgeting process for information security expenditures." *Communications of the ACM*, January, 49(1), pp. 121–125.

20. Karat, Clare-Marie, Carolyn Brodie, and John Karat. 2006. "Usable privacy and security for personal information management." *Communication of the ACM*, January, 49(1), pp. 56–57.

21. Fahmy, Dalia. 2005. "Making financial data more secure." *Institutional Investor*, December, p. 1; Grimes.

22. Chandra, Akhilesh, and Thomas Calderon. 2005. "Challenges and constraints to the diffusion of biometrics in information systems." *Communications of ACM*, December, 48(12), pp. 101–106.

23. Mientka, Matt. 2006. "Behavioral biometric to improve e-commerce security." *AFP Exchange*, January–February, pp. 32–33.

24. Peslak.

25. Knight, Gary A., and Tamer Cavusgil. 2005. "A taxonomy of born-global firms." *Management International Review*, 45, pp. 15–35.

26. Sawhney, Mohanbir, and Sumant Mandal. 2000. "Go global." *Business 2.0*, May, pp. 178–213.

27. Rosen, Kenneth T., and Amanda L. Howard. 2000. "E-retail: Gold rush or fool's gold?" *California Management Review*, Spring, 42(3), pp. 72–100.

28. Cyr, Dianne, Carole Bonanni, John Bowes, and Joe Ilsever. 2005. "Beyond trust: Web site design preferences across cultures." *Journal of Global Information Management*, October–December, 13 (4), pp. 25–54; Singh, Nitish, George Fassot, Hongxin Zhao, and Paul D. Boughton. 2006. "A cross-cultural analysis of German, Chinese and Indian consumers' perception of Web site adaptation." *Journal of Consumer Behavior*, 5, pp. 56–68; Singh, Nitish, Olivier Furrer, and Massimiliano Ostinelli. 2004. "To localize or standardize on the web: Empirical evidence from Italy, India, Netherlands, Spain and Switzerland." *Multinational Business Review*, 12(1), pp. 69–87.

29. Rosen and Howard.

30. Shirky, Clay. 2000. "Go global or bust." *Business 2.0*, March 1, pp. 145–146.

31. The Economist Intelligence Unit. 2008. *The 2008 E-readiness Rankings*. Pocket World in Figures. 2008 Edition. *London: The Economist*.

32. Sawhney and Mandal.

33. Ibid.

34. Hudgins, Christy. 1999. "International e-commerce." *Network Computing*, November 15, 10(23), pp. 75–50.

35. Singh, Furrer, and Ostinelli.

36. Singh, Furrer, and Ostinelli.

37. Engler, Natalie. 1999. "Global e-commerce," *InformationWeek*, October 4, p. 755.

38. Wilkerson, Phil. 2000. "Enabling global e-commerce." *Discount Store News*, April 17, 39(8), pp. 15–16.

39. Ghosh, Chandrani. 2000. "E-trade routes," *Forbes*, August 7, p. 108.

40. *Retailing Today*. 2008. "UGC, CGC: The hot new buzz words both online and off," December, p. 5.

Alibaba versus Ebay: Competing in the Chinese C2C Market (A)

Professors Katherine Xin, Winter Nie, and Vladimir Pucik prepared this case as a basis for class discussion rather than to illustrate either effective or ineffective handling of a business situation.

In April 2003 Jack Ma, the 39-year-old CEO of Alibaba–the leading business-to-business (B2B) e-commerce company in China–was worried. According to the latest market data, eBay, the global leader in online auctions had reached almost total dominance of the local consumer-to-consumer (C2C) market–only about a year after its entry into China. While Alibaba was not active in the Chinese C2C market, and eBay's expansion did not impact its current business, looking forward, there was cause for concern. What if eBay decided to use its C2C power to attack Alibaba in its traditional B2B domain? Jack wondered if anything could be done to prevent this from happening?

Background

Jack Ma founded Alibaba in February 1999. Born in the city of Hangzhou, he graduated from Hangzhou Normal University in 1988 and became a lecturer in English and International Trade at the same university. Before establishing Alibaba, he was head of the Infoshare division of the China International Electronic Commerce Center, owned by the Ministry of Commerce.

Alibaba's B2B Web site primarily served small- and medium-sized enterprises by connecting global businesses with Chinese manufacturers. Alibaba's initial financing of $4.5 million came primarily from Goldman Sachs in October 1999. By mid-2000, Alibaba had attracted $25 million in venture capital from Softbank, Goldman Sachs, and others.

By early 2003 Alibaba.com had 1.8 million registered users from more than 200 countries and regions, and RMB 60 billion (US$7.3 billion) in trade. Alibaba.com was named "Best of the Web: B2B" by *Forbes* magazine for three years in a row (2000–2002).[1] It described itself as "the world's largest marketplace for global trade, and a leading provider of online marketing services for importers and exporters."

Globalization of eBay

Founded in September 1995 as an online auction, eBay grew quickly to become the world's biggest C2C online transaction platform. eBay's business model was to provide a trading platform for individual buyers and sellers. The company did not take possession of the goods exchanged on the auction site, but it charged the seller listing fees, final value fees, and some value-added service fees (window display, shopping classification, homepage recommendation, etc.). It also charged subscription fees for power sellers (who had to reach certain transaction volumes).

In 2003 the company had 94.9 million registered users, $2.165 billion in revenue, with margins of 78.44% gross and 20.4% net. eBay's success was often attributed to the strength of its community, positive customer experiences, quirky charm, and community feel. Meg Whitman, CEO of eBay, once said:

> *We wake up every morning trying to figure out how to make it safer and more fun, with more features and a better user experience.*[2]

eBay began its global outreach in June 1999 when it bought Alando.de, Germany's largest online auction site. By the fall of 2001, eBay was the leading online auction site in 16 of the 17 markets in which it competed.

The 17th market was Japan, the 2nd biggest internet market in the world. In February 2000, five months after Yahoo Japan launched its auction site, eBay entered the Japanese online auction market. The major difference between these two sites was that Yahoo Japan was free and eBay charged fees. A year later, eBay had only 4,000 listings (fourth in the Japanese market) compared with Yahoo Japan's 2 million, and eBay decided to pull out of the Japanese market. In retrospect, industry analysts offered a number of explanations for why eBay had failed there: Its site lacked local color such as horoscopes, newsletters, and other features that Japanese users expected; while Yahoo Japan advertised heavily, eBay did little media promotion; eBay was slow to react to market developments, since it tried to make key decisions from the United States while Yahoo gave managers in Japan authority to respond quickly to market demands.[3]

The setback in Japan did not deter eBay from further expansion in Asia. In 2001 the company entered the Korean market by buying a majority stake in InternetAuctionCo for $120 million, and by 2003 it was firmly established as market leader. In March 2002 eBay entered Taiwan by acquiring a local online auction site. Adjusting to local market expectations, eBay did not charge for its auction service here or in Hong Kong or Singapore—the only three markets in which it did not do so. China was the natural next step—being among the fastest-growing internet markets in the world and potentially the largest.

eBay in China

eBay entered the Chinese market in March 2002 by acquiring a share in the most popular Chinese auction site, EachNet. EachNet.com was founded by two young Chinese HBS graduates who transported the eBay concept to China in 1999. It had built a registered user base of 3.5 million, with a transaction volume of RMB 780 million ($97.8 million) and a C2C market share of about 90% before eBay invested $30 million to buy a 33% stake.[4] According to Meg Whitman, China held a strategic importance in eBay's global strategy and the company was ready to invest for a long term—pay back on its investment in 5 to 10 years would be sufficient.[5]

EachNet's sole revenue was commodity listing fees. Six months after the acquisition, eBay EachNet started collecting final value fees from its users. In June 2003 eBay invested another $150 million to buy the remaining EachNet shares. Soon after, eBay EachNet began collecting subscription fees for power sellers. In 2003 eBay EachNet almost monopolized China's C2C market with 90% market share. When Alibaba saw the budding of the B2C platform on eBay, it feared that eBay would eventually venture into its B2B domain.

Taobao: "Hunt for Treasure"

In April 2003 Jack Ma convened a secret meeting with seven employees at his private lakeside villa in Hangzhou with the mandate to create a C2C e-commerce Web site. These seven people, with an average age of 25, became the founders of Taobao.com (taobao means hunt for treasure in Chinese), a company created to compete with eBay. The 37-year-old Alibaba veteran Toto Sun, with a background in advertising and foreign trade, was appointed as the new company CEO.

Jack Ma's expectations for Taobao were clear: C2C market share, rather than profit, as a goal. So, from day one, the target was eBay EachNet. In the first one or two months of operations, the seven founders worked more than 10 hours every day carefully studying eBay EachNet's site, debating its strengths and weaknesses, totally isolated from the outside world with no access to phones or e-mail.

The start-up team believed that the Taobao site needed to be unique and have a Chinese feel. Following an in-depth study of eBay EachNet and other auction Web sites, they were confident that they could launch an online auction site that would be fun for Chinese consumers to use. However, they did not know how Chinese color would translate into a Web auction experience and they were unsure whether users would appreciate the local flavor sufficiently. They were also concerned whether small improvements would be enough to lure customers.

The fundamental issue facing Toto Sun and his team was how to compete with eBay EachNet, which already had a 90% market share. Toto Sun outlined the questions that they needed to answer:

- On which dimension should Taobao compete? Should we use the same business model, with listing fees, final value fees, and value-added service fees?
- How can we reach customers? How can we attract sellers to put goods up for sale on our site? How can we attract buyers and assure them that it is safe to buy on our site given Chinese consumers' inherent distrust of strangers?
- How can we build an organization that is not afraid of competing with a giant? What culture should Taobao instill in this new organization?

CASE DISCUSSION QUESTIONS

1. On which dimension should Taobao compete? Should we use the same business model, with listing fees, final value fees, and value-added service fees?
2. How can we reach customers? How can we attract sellers to put goods up for sale on our site? How can we attract buyers and assure them that it is safe to buy on our site given Chinese consumers' inherent distrust of strangers?
3. How can we build an organization that is not afraid of competing with a giant? What culture should Taobao instill in this new organization?

CASE CREDIT

CASE NOTES

[1] *Forbes* magazine also selected Alibaba.com as "Best of the Web: B2B" in 2003 and 2004.

[2] Cohen, Adam. 2002. *The Perfect Store*, p.168.

[3] Mangalindan, Mylene. 2005, "Hot Bidding: In a challenging China market, eBay confronts a big new rival." August 12. http://online .wsj.com/PA2VJBNA4R/article_print/SB1123805104865114 59.html.

[4] http://tech.sina.com.cn/i/c/2002-03-18/107177.shtml.

[5] Beijing Youth Newspaper's interview with Meg Whitman in April 2002, http://news.chinabyte.com/41/1604541_1.shtml.

Transition at Whirlpool Tatramat: From Joint Venture to Acquisition

T his case gives a description of the evolution of Whirlpool's participation strategy in Slovakia. Beginning first with a joint venture, Whirlpool eventually takes control of the whole operation.

The Joint Venture Partners

Whirlpool Corporation

Whirlpool Corporation is one of the world's leading manufacturers and marketers of home appliances, such as washing machines, refrigerators, and kitchen ranges. Its growth, from a domestic manufacturer in the United States to a firm with worldwide presence, is the result of a strategic decision taken in the mid-1980s.

Unable to find adequate growth potential in the United States appliance market, the company began its global expansion. By 1998, the company manufactured products in 13 countries and marketed them in approximately 170 countries. It employed over 59,000 people worldwide, and its net sales reached $10.5 billion.[1] Over ten years, the company had doubled the number of its brands, its employees, and its revenues, and had tripled the number of countries in which it had manufacturing sites (Table 1).

Whirlpool's Western European operations started in 1989, when Whirlpool and N.V. Philips of the Netherlands formed a joint venture, Whirlpool Europe B.V. (WEBV). Its mission was to manufacture and market appliances in Europe. Originally, Whirlpool held a 53 percent stake in the joint venture; in 1991, it became the sole owner through the acquisition of the remaining shares.

Whirlpool Europe B.V. soon became the third largest household appliance producer in Europe, behind the Swedish company AB Electrolux and the

TABLE 1 A Decade of Whirlpool's Internationalization, 1988 and 1998

Item	1988	1998
Countries with manufacturing sites	4	13
Brands	14	25
Employees	29,100	59,000
Revenues (billions of dollars)	4.4	10.5

Source: Whirlpool Corporation. 1998. Vision, 1, 2 (March–April) and information provided by Whirlpool Slovakia.

German joint venture Bosch-Siemens Hausgerate GmbH. After its acquisition of Philips's shares, Whirlpool began production in several European countries (France, Italy, Germany, and Sweden). These sites achieved economies of scale by producing a minimum of 600,000 pieces per year per factory. However, the Western European market soon experienced a recession, which was reflected in disappointing sales and profits, unlike at that time those in the United States.

After the fall of the Berlin wall and the revolutionary wave in Central and Eastern European (CEE) countries, WEBV started looking for opportunities in the transition economies of Eastern Europe. Given the competitive pressure in Western Europe, as well as pressures on manufacturing costs, WEBV capitalized on the idea of opening new markets as well as using the low-cost competitive advantage of CEE by investing in Poprad, Slovakia.

Whirlpool Europe not only ranked as the third largest producer and marketer in Western Europe, but it also was the leader in CEE, where it had one manufacturing center (in Poprad, Slovakia) and ten sales offices. Whirlpool's strategy for Europe has evolved over time. During the 1990s, Whirlpool focused on closing the "value gap" between the costs of appliances relative to consumers' disposable income in Western Europe as compared to other major world markets, such as North America. That strategy was by and large successful, although at that time the whole industry was under cost pressures, as economic growth in Europe stagnated and consumers turned to lower-cost, less featured products.

Through new products, the company undertook a dramatic restructuring of its entire line during the second half of the 1990s. Using extensive consumer and trade customer research, new products were introduced in every appliance category. In 1997, an estimated 60 percent of revenues came from these new products. In February 1998, Whirlpool CEO David Whitman commented on the situation in Europe: "Europe proved to be a bright spot for us in 1997, following two years of turbulent times. Our performance in Europe has consistently improved, quarter after quarter, following cost-reduction and productivity improvement efforts begun in 1996. Additionally, we continued to expand our business in Central Europe and other emerging markets by drawing from our expertise throughout our other European operations. As a result, Whirlpool remains the leading brand across the whole region."[2]

Tatramat

Karol Scholz founded Tatramat in 1845 as a producer of nails and currycombs for grooming horses. After World War I, the company switched to producing domestic kitchen goods; after World War II, the company was nationalized. Under the 45 years of socialism, the company expanded to produce zinc-coated and painted barrels, water heaters, electric ovens, and automatic washing machines. It began production of automatic top-loading washing machines (under license with VIVA of France) in 1969, and front-loading washing machines in cooperation with Elektronska Industrija of Yugoslavia in 1972. In Czechoslovakia, it was the number one manufacturer of automatic washing machines (202,500 units in 1990) and domestic water heaters (146,900 units). At the beginning of the 1990s, Tatramat employed approximately 2,300 people. It controlled 88 percent of the automatic washing machine market in Czechoslovakia, a near monopoly. The company derived about 12 percent of its revenues from exports. In 1990, its sales reached $48 million. The operating profit was about $3.2 million, resulting in an operating margin of 6.8 percent. Tatramat's washing machines were designed to meet the requirements of the Czechoslovak market.

In the late 1980s, Western brands were often too expensive, too complicated, or simply too large to appeal to the average Czechoslovak buyer. Tatramat also had an established distribution and servicing network in Czechoslovakia. This, along with a wide spread of the brand, meant cheaper distribution costs, cheaper servicing costs, and lower advertising costs relative to imported brands. In addition, there was an untapped market for washing machines in Czechoslovakia. At the beginning of the 1990s, the penetration level for washing machines was only 58 percent. It was expected to rise to the levels of Western Europe (approximately 90 percent) within a decade. The demand for major consumer appliances was expected to increase gradually in Czechoslovakia and in neighboring countries as the region reoriented itself toward a market economy.

After the Velvet Revolution in 1989 in Czechoslovakia, Tatramat, as well as other Czech and Slovak companies, went through major changes. The communist government was overthrown and Czechoslovakia began to build a democratic society and a market economy. Although restructuring was difficult, and the year of 1990 was particularly hard, Czechoslovakia was considered to be among the leading and most successful countries in transition. Martin Ciran, the director of Tatramat and, subsequently, Whirlpool Slovakia, described the situation of Tatramat at that time as follows:

> After 1988, State export subsidies that covered the difference between high domestic costs and low prices on foreign markets were gradually abolished in our country. It hit the sales of our main export article, frontloaded washing machines very strongly. At that time we realized that our products were not competitive on the open European market. We concentrated on top loaded washing machines because our main customers were all interested in top-loaders and we were able to increase the production of only one product at a time. Obviously, top-loaders and front-loaders were produced using different technology. In 1989–1990, we introduced abroad our new product, the MINI, fully designed by Tatramat. It was a failure because of its low quality and high price. It was simply an old concept; a new machine, but an old concept. Afterwards, we started to think about how to increase the competitiveness of our products. We considered the purchase of technology or licensed production. In 1989, prior to the revolution, I began looking for partners to supply technology for top-loading washing machines. We received bids from Philips, Thompson, and Zanussi. We intended to improve the technical standards of our production as well as to increase production capacity. We realized that it was not enough to produce only 200,000 units per year, because studies showed us that we had to produce more than 300,000 per year to achieve scale economies.

Martin Ciran and other managers of the company visited the leading manufacturers of white goods in Western Europe and saw that even 300,000 washing machines per year were probably not enough. The best companies produced 600,000 to 1 million units per year. They decided hence to change their products, to increase production, to share costs, and to cut unit costs for the company to survive. Martin Ciran went on:

> In the meantime, the COMECON market collapsed. We totally lost our foreign markets for washing machines and boilers; domestic demand also went down as a result of the difficulties of the first years of transition. There were fewer apartments built, fewer weddings.... People had other troubles and preferences than the purchase of a washing machine. We lost markets, we lost customers. In 1990, we fired about 100 people; in 1991, we fired 900, from an original of 2,300. We were lucky, because such a major lay-off did not lead to any special discontent. Employees got good compensation according to the law and some of them started to run their own small private businesses, which had not been allowed under socialism. It was also a time of so-called small privatization—the privatization of small shops, services, etc. formerly owned by the State, which attracted some of our employees, too.

One of the primary challenges in the Czechoslovak transition and in the shift toward a market economy was privatization. On October 1, 1990, the Slovak Ministry of Economy transformed Tatramat from a state enterprise into a state joint stock company. At that time, ownership of assets, in the form of shares, was transferred to the National Assets Fund, under the administration of the Slovak Ministry of Privatization. As a joint stock company, the intention was to privatize Tatramat through vouchers. Companies owned by the National Assets Funds could establish joint ventures with foreign investors only after approval by the Slovak Ministry of Privatization.

Martin Ciran recalled:

We were transformed from a State-owned company into a State-owned joint stock company, one of the first companies in Czechoslovakia. In the meantime, the separate Czech and Slovak Governments became much stronger and federal Czechoslovak Government lost most of its power. It meant that our superior authorities were no longer the federal authorities in Prague but the Slovak authorities in Bratislava. The change of the form of the company also resulted in more power in the hands of management. We started to have a real feeling for new responsibilities, and we could do a lot of things without the approval from the State or State authorities. Although short of ownership, we had more competence and power. We could, for example, negotiate with foreign companies. After we recognized that the price for a license or a new technology was very high, we started thinking about capital investment or about a partner for a joint venture. It took us half to three-quarters of a year to understand that it would not be enough to produce new machines without access to markets. Under the new conditions brought by the revolution, it was possible to think about other forms of cooperation or alliance with foreign companies, not only about licensing. At that time, Volkswagen was preparing a deal with Skoda in the Czech Republic and with BAZ in the Slovak Republic, with the assistance of Credit Suisse First Boston. We also prepared a memorandum about us, followed by an offer for cooperation. This memorandum was sent in January 1991 to all prospective investors known worldwide, all leading companies in white goods. I cannot say that all the people in the company were eager for such cooperation with Western companies as I and my closest team were, but everybody felt it was necessary to do something.

After receiving the memorandum, Whirlpool, Electrolux, Bosch-Siemens, and Thompson all declared their interest in possible cooperation. It is to be recalled that, at the end of the 1980s and at the beginning of the 1990s, Tatramat produced about 200,000 washing machines per year: 100,000 top-loading washing machines (the so-called MINI, 95 percent sold in the Czechoslovak market) and 100,000 front-loading machines (25 percent for the Czechoslovak market, 75 percent for exports, primarily to the socialist countries of Poland, Bulgaria, Yugoslavia, and the German Democratic Republic; only 5,000 were sold in Western markets). At that time, various problems surfaced in the factory and its environment: high fixed costs, low productivity and quality, backward technology, products unsuitable for foreign markets, the abolition of state export subsidies, the collapse of the COMECON market, and a drop in demand on the domestic market. Tatramat sales dropped from around 350,000 units in 1988 to around 220,000 units in 1991 (Table 2). Finally, the devaluation of the Czechoslovak crown in 1990 tripled production costs.

At that time, Tatramat's management realized that a single purchase of technology would not solve all its problems. Market access was needed, as well as a partner who would be able to guarantee it. Tatramat's idea shifted from a purchase of technology or licensed production to capital investment or a joint venture. During the search for the right partner, it was realized that Whirlpool was the firm most interested in improving Tatramat's management and including Tatramat in its global network.

TABLE 2　Tatramat Sales, 1988–1991 (thousand units)

Item	1988	1989	1990	1991
Washing machines	200.0	199.1	210.6	144.1
Water heaters	151.8	143.7	133.3	76.2

Source: Information provided by Tatramat.

Motivations for an Alliance Between Whirlpool Europe B.V. and Tatramat

In 1990, the managers of WEBV realized that the changes in CEE brought about new opportunities and challenges for their company. They were attracted by the possibility of gaining new markets, as well as obtaining production facilities and a skilled labor force. Their facilities were not efficient, but they were low cost in comparison to Western Europe. The privatization of state-owned factories opened the way for potential ownership and control. However, WEBV was not driven only by external reasons. It was also forced to look at new opportunities because of its internal problems: more limited success in Western Europe than expected, disappointing operating margins, and the need to decrease costs.

Strategic Options for Whirlpool

To solve some of these problems, WEBV could use various strategic options: exporting, joint venture, acquisition, or greenfield investment in CEE. Every option had some advantages and disadvantages:

Exporting

- *Advantages:* Sales would increase, without assuming high risks.
- *Disadvantages:* Production costs would not be reduced; tariff barriers would remain.

Joint venture

- *Advantages:* Access would be had to an existing facility, an existing brand, an existing labor force, an established market share, existing distribution facilities, an established local supplier base; low production costs; contact with authorities through the local partner; the potential to increase ownership control at a later stage.
- *Disadvantages:* Control would be shared, relationships and trust need to be built, labor force training would need to change local attitudes, need to overcome negative attitude toward the local brand name.

Acquisition

- *Advantages:* Full control plus all advantages of a joint venture.
- *Disadvantages:* More resistance from the target firm and local government. In Czechoslovakia, takeovers had no precedence, resulting in more prejudice and in less motivation or cooperation by the local partner; the facility and the labor force would be more difficult to change.

Greenfield

- *Advantages:* New facility, full control, own trained labor force, low costs.
- *Disadvantages:* No labor force at hand, more training needed, local competition, more obstacles from the government and local authorities, more

expatriate staff would be needed, no inherited market share, no previous brand name recognition.

A takeover would have been the best choice for Whirlpool. However, the legal system of Czechoslovakia and the resistance of the local managers as well as the Government did not allow going for this form immediately. Therefore, the most realistic choice for Whirlpool from a strategic point of view was a joint venture, with the possibility of a gradual increase in investment until a final takeover.

Strategic Options for Tatramat

Tatramat's reasons for entering into the joint venture could be summarized as follows: drop in domestic demand, collapse of export markets in CEE, high and growing costs, obsolete technology, risk of massive layoffs, and a need to increase production to reach scale economies. To solve its problems, Tatramat had to choose between two strategic options: licensing or joint venture. Both options had some advantages and disadvantages:

Licensing

- *Advantages:* New technology, no partner to be accommodated, full control, access to training in technology, continued production of both washing machines and water boilers under Tatramat's control.
- *Disadvantages:* No market access, possibly high technology and license fees, no other know-how or skills inflow, no capital inflow.

Joint venture

- *Advantages:* Technology, capital, training capacity, know-how, and market access.
- *Disadvantages:* Profits and control to be shared, eventually leading to a loss of control over the enterprise.

A joint venture seemed to be a better choice in comparison to a licensing agreement. Because the potential partners wanted only the washing machine unit, Tatramat's contribution could be only this part of production. The main question that remained was what to do with the water boiler segment. Other problems could be solved through gradually selling Tatramat's ownership to Whirlpool or by becoming a supplier to the joint venture.

Form of the Deal

As seen from this analysis, the most suitable form for both partners was a joint venture. Tatramat was nevertheless concerned by the three conditions set by Whirlpool: the possibility of a gradual increase of Whirlpool's share in the joint venture, Whirlpool's unwillingness to include water boiler operations in the joint venture, and the call for an increase in the tariff protection of the local washing machine market. Tatramat was in a weak position vis-á-vis Whirlpool, and it decided to accept fully the first two conditions. It even managed to lobby for import tariffs.

Anatomy of the Deal: Main Problems and Outcomes

After complex negotiations, the contractual basis for the joint venture was created at the end of 1991, and it began operations in May 1992. Whirlpool contributed know-how in technology, production, and marketing to the joint

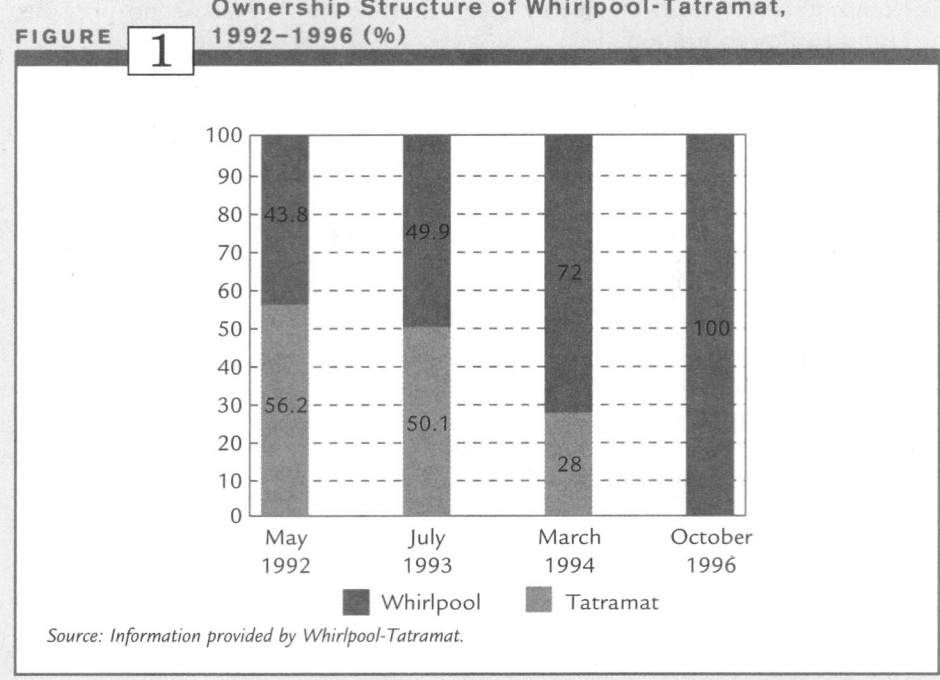

FIGURE **1**

Ownership Structure of Whirlpool-Tatramat, 1992–1996 (%)

Source: Information provided by Whirlpool-Tatramat.

venture, and also bought 43.8 percent of the shares for $6 million (Figure 1). Tatramat's nonfinancial contribution consisted of intellectual property rights in the area of washing machine production, goodwill, buildings, machinery, land, and contracts. It kept 56.2 percent of the shares of the joint venture. The original agreement was signed for ten years.

With Whirlpool's investment, the original Tatramat company split into three separate entities: (1) the joint venture Whirlpool-Tatramat became the number one washing machine producer in both the Slovak and Czech Republics; (2) Tatramat itself continued to produce water heaters; and (3) Tatramat-Quasar, a small joint venture with an Italian partner, continued to produce vending machines.

Whirlpool-Tatramat became a separate organization with its own sales staff and after-sales service. Whirlpool-Tatramat produced two types of top-loading washing machines: the old Tatramat MINI (under Tatramat's brand name), and the Whirlpool T-12 (under the Whirlpool-Philips brand name). The first T-12 rolled off the line in October 1992. Even though results improved over time, the number of units produced in 1993 (59,000 MINIs and 39,000 T-12s) was below expectations.

Not only quantity but also quality became a critical problem in Poprad. As WEBV envisaged broadening Poprad's role to an international production platform for Western markets, the quality of Poprad's products had to meet the strict demands of Whirlpool and its customers. Quality had improved at Poprad during the years 1992 and 1993 but not enough, forcing them to sell to mostly Czech and Slovak customers.

Employment levels significantly dropped after the establishment of the joint venture. Initially, 550 employees were transferred from Tatramat to the joint venture, and the remaining 750 employees stayed on the payroll of the Slovak parent company. In the case of management staff, Tatramat did not want to lose its best employees to Whirlpool-Tatramat, and therefore any transfer of white-collar workers was subject to its approval.

By 1993, employment at the joint venture was down to 219.[3] However, productivity increased from 153 units per employee in 1992 to 199 units in 1993.

In July 1993 Whirlpool transferred $1.5 million to the joint venture, increasing its share in the joint venture to 49.9 percent (Figure 1). This amount was invested into a partial transfer of "hard" technology.

The external conditions of the joint venture also experienced a drastic change. In 1993, as a consequence of the division of Czechoslovakia, the local market for Whirlpool-Tatramat, with its location in Slovakia, diminished by two-thirds with the loss of the Czech Republic. However, Tatramat's brand name still enjoyed high name recognition in the Czech Republic, and the company maintained distribution facilities there. To catch up with the political changes, including new borders, and to avoid losses resulting from worsened operational conditions, Whirlpool-Tatramat established its own affiliate in the Czech Republic in May 1993.

Despite the loss of about $1.5 million in the first full year of operations, Whirlpool increased its share in the joint venture to 72 percent in February 1994 (Figure 1). Before Whirlpool's stake reached two-thirds of the joint venture, Tatramat had the right to nominate the chairperson of the board of directors and two other board members, compared to two seats for Whirlpool. After having obtained the two-thirds majority, Whirlpool got the chairpersonship plus two additional seats. Moreover, as soon as Whirlpool reached two-thirds in the joint venture, the joint venture agreement allowed it to decide, without the approval of Tatramat, on most important issues, such as plans, major contracts, and financing. As Martin Ciran, managing director of Whirlpool-Tatramat since the beginning of its operations, recalled: "We were aware of the necessity of performance improvement, but we did not want to have our hands tied up by Tatramat, which faced big economic troubles at that time."

In 1994, production experienced moderate growth, with the production of T-12 more than doubling to 95,000 units (Table 3). The joint venture also produced the 11,000 MINIs that year, but it was the last year that the model was manufactured. The MINI was abandoned due to poor design, quality, declining sales, and thin margins. Initially, in 1992 and 1993, the Whirlpool-Tatramat assembled washing machines from kits imported from Amiens, France, where the T-12 was also made. The joint venture produced only the T-12 in 1995 and 1996.

In October 1996, Whirlpool bought out the remaining shares and became the sole owner of the company (Figure 1). The name was changed to Whirlpool

TABLE 3   Whirlpool-Tatramat's and Whirlpool Slovakia's Production, 1992–2000 (thousand units)

Type	Brand	1992	1993	1994	1995	1996	1997	1998	1999	2000
MINI	Tatramat	74	59	16	–	–	–	–	–	–
TL*	Whirlpool Ignis	5	39	93	8,149	267	349	381	495	585
FL	Whirlpool Ignis	–	–	–	–	–	1	140	275	360
Total		79	98	111	219	267	350	521	770	945

Note: TL: top-loaders, FL: front-loaders. The model T-12 has been produced since the beginning. In 1998, other top-loaders (Kireco and Alliance) were introduced.

Source: Information provided by Whirlpool Slovakia.

Slovakia, and its headquarters and national sales office were moved from Poprad to the capital city, Bratislava. The following year the company exceeded, for the first time, the production targets outlined in the original joint venture agreement. A new front-loading model, the Tatry, was introduced in 1997 and production reached over half a million washing machines in 1998 and nearly one million by the year 2000. Although the capacity at Poprad made it the smallest of Whirlpool's European manufacturing centers, it remains the lowest-cost production facility.

Operational Issues

Since 1994, Poprad has begun to integrate vertically, producing more of its components in-house in an effort to reduce its reliance on the expensive Amiens components. Components account for 80 percent of a machine's costs. This, together with transport distance, customs regulations, and problems with timely delivery from the Amiens site, led to a decision to source as much as possible locally. While local content was only 3 percent in the first year, it reached 12 percent in 1994, 37 percent by the end of 1995, and 60 percent by the middle of 1997. This share has been maintained since then. In the mid-1990s, the plant had only 14 local suppliers; by 2000, it had 35.

With the creation of a local supplier network, the company succeeded in increasing production flexibility, reducing costs, and avoiding import restrictions such as duty and import surcharges.

The total equity investment of Whirlpool, including the initial investment and the equity increases, reached about $11 million (including technology capitalized at $3 million) by 1996. The joint venture invested $14 million into production in 1992 to 1995. In the years 1996 through 1998, the company planned significant investments into new front-loading machines (the so-called Delta). This project was supposed to introduce a completely new front-loading machine for the European market. Later, Project Delta was changed to Project Tatry, with less investment and different technology, producing low-end front-loading washing machines. Investment into this model reached about $10 million by 1997. To prepare for the launching of this product, changes had to be made to production areas and technology, and a semirobotic line for assembling was installed.

The total amount of Whirlpool investment into the Poprad plant reached $36 million by the year 2000. In comparison to hard technology, soft technology transfer has been more pronounced. Whirlpool introduced its management and incentive structures in Poprad. The company stressed the importance of communication with workers. Face-to-face meetings with management took place, explaining human resources practices previously unknown to the employees. After the first shock from Western management style in 1992 and 1993, employment gradually grew.

The human resources department adopted new policies, such as performance evaluation, pay for performance, a "recognition policy" to reward hard work and innovation, and gain-sharing schemes in which additional wages were linked to company profits. It also emphasized the need for improving inter- and intradepartmental communication and for training on specialized topics, such as teamwork, decision making, and individual thinking.

White-collar workers were trained in basic business skills, market economics, quality management, supplier quality, ISO 9000, English, computer skills, and Whirlpool philosophy and corporate culture. These training programs were intended to increase managers' commitment to the firm and to spread the new corporate philosophy among workers. People were taught how to communicate, organize their workplace, and increase productivity and the quality of work.

Additionally, the human resources department provided introductory courses on the Whirlpool Excellence System (WES). These courses were popular among Whirlpool Slovakia employees. According to the managers, it became a valuable tool for improving the work of the company. The region of Poprad had an unemployment rate of about 17 percent, and for Whirlpool this meant the possibility to ensure flexible work practices.

The human resources department received 400–500 job applications annually. Seventy percent of the candidates completed high school education. Currently, workers' wages consist of a fixed part (73 percent on average) and a collective bonus (27 percent), depending on productivity, flexibility, quality, and the level of absenteeism. A collective bonus was chosen as a way of encouraging cooperation among employees to work more efficiently at a lower level of absenteeism.

Since work there is considered to be intense, most employees at the Poprad plant are young, with an average age of 28 years. The average manager is 38 years old, which is also considered to be young. This may reflect the fact that only young people were willing to join a terra incognita—a joint venture—when the joint venture was established in 1992. They were trained by Whirlpool and were able to take their new positions quickly. In comparison to the Slovak average, they are well paid: During the first six years of Whirlpool's operations in Slovakia, only one employee had left the company. Currently, there is only one expatriate in Slovakia, an Italian national who serves as plant director in Poprad.

The joint venture was established with the aim to reach the productivity levels that were typical of other Whirlpool plants in Europe. The productivity in Poprad's plant increased significantly from 153 pieces per employee in 1992 to 199 in 1993 and to 323 in 1994. It reached 927 pieces per employee in 1997, which is far above the expectation and levels in similar plants (Table 3). Product quality has been a critical aspect of production at Poprad. As WEBV intended to expand Poprad's role as an international production center to serve Western markets, Poprad's products had to meet Whirlpool's global quality requirements. Quality improvements in Poprad have been attributed to the training of employees in quality concepts, in-process checks, and vertical integration, including greater internal control over the quality of components. During production, every machine is tested electronically, and 10 percent are taken off the assembly line and tested for 50 cycles. Additionally, 3 percent out of the 10 percent taken from the line are taken to the factory reliability lab where they are run through 250 cycles (corresponding to one year's usage) or 2,500 cycles (ten year's usage).

During the two first years (1992–1993), the company operated only in the Czech and Slovak markets because product quality at that time was too low to guarantee exports. In 1994, the company started to sell in Poland, Hungary, and Argentina. In 1995, it entered into the Western European market. In 2000, about 90 percent of the output of Poprad was exported through the corporate distribution network. On balance, Whirlpool-Tatramat proved to be successful. Its performance has gradually improved. Its WES score rose from 238 in 1993 to 702 in 1997. Even the best Whirlpool plant in Europe managed to score only slightly better in 1997 (850). According to Whirlpool managers, the performance of Poprad has remained at the same high level since then.

Reasons for the Takeover of the Joint Venture by Whirlpool

The following reasons for the full takeover of the joint venture by Whirlpool could be identified:

- *The global strategy of Whirlpool.* Whirlpool and Tatramat were two unequal partners with two different goals: Since the beginning, the goal of Whirlpool was a gradual increase of its share in the joint venture with the aim of taking it over. It is consistent with its worldwide strategy of acquisitions and global control.

- *The economic problems of Tatramat.* Tatramat was not able to keep its share in the joint venture. In 1993, when it was time for the first significant investment to increase productivity, Tatramat was unable to contribute. This situation propelled a gradual increase in the share of Whirlpool in the joint venture. Under the worsened conditions, the goals of Tatramat to continue washing machine production and to survive the transition could be reached only at the expense of losing control over the joint venture. The hopes of Tatramat's management to obtain the dividends from a profitable joint venture and to improve its own difficult economic situation were not realized.

At the beginning of its operations, the joint venture was in the red, and the only way for Tatramat to get some cash was to sell its shares to the other partner. With this deal, each party nevertheless satisfied at least some of their needs: Whirlpool established production in a low-cost country, benefited from the local skilled labor force, reached a new market, and created a new export base for other countries. Tatramat avoided going into bankruptcy and received cash and knowledge in various areas, including marketing, management, and production.

Factors of Success at Whirlpool Slovakia

A Manager's Point of View

According to Martin Ciran:

> The very comprehensive and detailed joint venture agreement consisting of 30 pages and four appendices worked out by English lawyers from the Scadden Arps Company was one of the reasons for the success of the company. In each case of a misunderstanding, we referred to this agreement, and it really showed us the way out. On the other hand, you have several cases in Slovakia where a joint venture broke up because of a non-qualified agreement. After the collapse of the centrally run economy, the establishment of joint ventures was marked by a lack of hands-on experience on the Slovak side. Due to a shortage of reputable and experienced law firms, we chose a foreign company to draft the agreement and it was really worthwhile.

There is still more to that story. Martin Ciran described other success factors:

> Based on the joint venture agreement and the follow-up development of the ownership structure, the parent company Whirlpool practically had full managing and decision-making power in the company. Its approach has been very transparent and we got all the necessary knowledge and skills through training and technology transfer. On the other hand, Whirlpool's headquarters in Italy had agreed to the use and application of this knowledge. I would say mutual trust has been one of the basic points of our success. Furthermore, our people have been eager to learn and to apply new procedures. It was also essential that top management of the joint venture was young

and not "afflicted by socialist working practices." It identified very quickly with the Whirlpool philosophy and corporate culture. The managers have transferred these values to other employees. We have implemented a new management system known as the Whirlpool Excellence System, quickly and successfully. In my opinion, the greatest change since the Tatramat days has not been in technological innovation or investment but in employee attitudes. The new thinking of our employees and their accomplishments in improving the working conditions at the facility and in making the production lines more flexible set the company apart from most of the other firms in Slovakia today. On top of that, the next very important success factor has been "not over investing." In other words, our company has a big cost advantage in comparison to Western European producers because of low debts. With high investment we would lose this advantage.

A Broader Approach to Success Factors

Even though Martin Ciran mentioned many success factors, it is necessary to add that the story started with the investment of Whirlpool into a local monopoly producer. Hence, an immediate market share was guaranteed for the joint venture. This was important especially at the beginning of the operations when it was not possible to export products abroad due to their low quality. The monopoly position was also guaranteed in the joint venture agreement stipulating a noncompetition clause. It did not allow the Slovak parent company to produce washing machines and excluded competition between affiliates and parent companies. Whirlpool could also realize classical first mover advantages. The combination of a monopoly position, low-cost production, and first mover advantages has contributed to the success of Whirlpool Slovakia. It is interesting to note that Whirlpool insisted on market protection, but this was automatically abolished in the Czech Republic after the split of Czechoslovakia and did not play any special role in Slovakia. The firm maintained its market share simply because imported goods were too expensive for the average Slovak costumer at the beginning of the 1990s. There were no other classical incentives (such as tax holidays) provided to Whirlpool.

The Performance of the Slovak Parent Company

The managers of Whirlpool were satisfied with the evolution of Whirlpool-Tatramat and later Whirlpool Slovakia. However, the situation in the Slovak parent company, Tatramat, has proved to be more complex. With the creation of the joint venture Whirlpool-Tatramat and the splitting of the old Tatramat into washing machines and boilers production, the parent company Tatramat entered into a period of difficulties. The parent company Tatramat tried to adjust to its joint ventures with foreign partners. At the beginning of the 1990s, in addition to Whirlpool-Tatramat, it established Tatramat-Quasar, which produced vending machines with an Italian partner. At a later stage, it also established Scame-Tatramat with an Italian partner to produce plastic parts. As activities moved out from the parent firm into the joint ventures, Tatramat experienced a large decline in its labor force, especially in the first half of the 1990s, and at one point even faced bankruptcy. As initially expected, the sense of rivalry, jealousy, and competition between Whirlpool-Tatramat and its Slovak parent company evolved during the first year of operations: Tatramat, located in the neighborhood of Whirlpool, has become its main local supplier. According to the Slovak managers of Whirlpool, Whirlpool's orders placed in Tatramat and its ventures created employment for about 200 persons there. Besides that, they argued that Whirlpool contributed to the creation of 400 more jobs in other Slovak companies. This means that one workplace established in Whirlpool created another job in supplier, service, or distribution companies doing business with or for Whirlpool.

In the end, Tatramat survived its period of transition. In 2000, it reported a turnover of about $11 million, of which 75 percent came from export sales. It recorded a pretax profit of $0.15 million (compared with a loss of $0.6 million in 1997) with 520 employees.

Conclusions

The acquisition of Tatramat by Whirlpool is only one example out of many: Since the middle of the 1990s, the strategy of investors in Slovakia has changed, especially among large multinational corporations (MNCs). The new trend is characterized by incremental takeovers. In several instances in the late 1990s, MNCs (including the biggest investor in manufacturing, Volkswagen) steadily increased their equity shares in joint ventures in Slovakia. There are a number of reasons for this new trend:

- The global strategies of MNCs.
- The weak, unequal position of the local partners in comparison to their foreign partners.
- The conflicts between the Slovak and foreign partners over the joint venture strategy.
- Conflicts over the control of key or common services such as energy, telecommunications, and security (joint ventures are usually situated in the former plants of Slovak parent companies).
- Conflicts over pricing and transferring profits abroad.
- A lack of experience by local companies in how to deal with these issues (under socialism, cooperation with Western companies was not permitted).
- The inability or unwillingness of the Slovak partners to maintain their shares in the joint ventures.
- Financial difficulties of the Slovak partners, forcing them to sell their shares in the joint ventures to their foreign partners.
- The success of MNCs in establishing their own communication channels with the authorities, in building positive public relations and in finding local managers for top positions, resulting in less reliance on local partners in these areas.
- The recognition by MNCs that the transition process is irreversible and thus risk sharing with local partners was no longer necessary.

Most multinational companies that first established a joint venture with local partners in Slovakia have, in the meantime, moved into the acquisition of shares (Whirlpool-Tatramat, Volkswagen-BAZ, Alcatel SELTesla, Henkel-Palma, Hoechst-Biotika, etc.). There are only a few exceptions, usually based on legal constraints, such as state participation in the telecommunication industry. Moreover, this situation is typical not only for Slovakia, but also for many other transition economies in CEE.

Like the best-known examples in Slovakia (Whirlpool and Volkswagen), similar developments occurred, for example, in Hungary with General Electric-

Tungsram, in Poland with Gerber, and in the Czech Republic with Philip Morris. As soon as multinational companies became sole owners, they tended to invest more into technology (however, they usually tried not to "over invest," i.e., not to lose the cost advantage and not to replace cheap labor by machinery). Most governments seem to have no policy to prevent an "incremental takeover." Moreover, entry into the European Union and the acceptance of its legal framework may further limit the possibilities to block such acquisitions.

Epilogue: Whirlpool Slovakia in the New Century

At the turn of the century (years 1999, 2000, 2001), Whirlpool Slovakia produced around 1 million units yearly. In 2002 the production reached 1.2 million units, half of that top-loaders and another half front-loaders. In 2003 production reached 1.5 million pieces and the company employed more than 800 employees. Since 2004 Whirlpool Europe decided to shift all the production of washing machines in the group to Slovakia (e.g., 300,000 units from Amiens, 150,000 from Polar), and the capacity was removed from Neukirchen to Poprad.

From 2004 until 2008, Whirlpool Slovakia produced almost 2 million units each year (slightly more top-loaders than front-loaders every year); for example, in 2008 the total production was 1.97 million washing machines. In 1998 the company produced the millionth piece in its history, and in 2008 the 15 millionth washing machine produced in Poprad ran off the production line.

In 2004–2008, the company employed about 1,200 people directly, and about 1,800 employees worked in the Poprad area for the suppliers of Whirlpool Slovakia (such as Tatramat, Pascal, Sagit, Cima, AZD). Three to four percent of the yearly production is sold on the domestic market; about 96–97 percent of the production is shipped to Africa, Asia, Latin America—to almost 30 countries.

Planned yearly capacity for Whirlpool Slovakia is 2.2 million units; some managers even talked about 4 million units in the future.

Plainly, the operation of Whirlpool has changed from a market-seeking to a fully low-cost-seeking operation.

The year 2008 meant a new landmark in the history of Whirlpool Slovakia: The company has opened a new central warehouse of 24,000 square meters in Lozorno in Western Slovakia, to which the Whirpool products from nine European factories and China are shipped and from where about 1.5 million of Whirlpool white appliances for Czech, Slovak, Hungarian, and Austrian markets are distributed.

There is an interesting story related to the acquisition of Polar in Poland: Polar was on the radar screen of Whirlpool Europe early in the nineties, but at that time the top management decided not to engage the company because of the strong trade unions and low willingness of the then Polish management to work with a foreign investor. Later, Thomson Electric, a French company, acquired Polar, but the deal ended up in economic problems: When Whirlpool Europe was buying Polar, it had the value $28 million and was $14 million in debt; so the company put itself for sale for $42 million. At that time Whirlpool Europe was trying to find a company in Central and Eastern Europe where it could localize refrigerators production for all of Europe (based on a very good experience from Slovakia, where a major production site for washing machines was created).

There was a cheap refrigerator company for sale in Slovakia, the former Calex company whose value decreased after an unsuccessful joint venture with

Samsung. The local Slovak management, led by Martin Ciran, was trying to persuade Whirlpool Europe to buy it. Even though the success of Whirlpool in Slovakia was undeniable and the country at that time had a very progressive government introducing many market-oriented reforms and one of the best business environments in Europe, Whirlpool Europe decided to buy a much more expensive Polish facility instead. The reasons may be seen in risk diversification and the relatively big size of the Polish market.

Plainly, Central and Eastern Europe has become more and more attractive for big MNCs as a location of production for the whole European market. The advantages of the CEE countries, such as relatively cheap and skilled labor, even increased since 2004 when Poland and Slovakia (together with other CEE countries) entered the European Union.

Since that time many producers, especially from outside of the EU (the United States, Asia), established their major European production and distribution centers in CEE (e.g., Sony, Samsung, Hundayi, Kia, Panasonic).

CASE DISCUSSION QUESTIONS

1. Would you have recommended a greenfield investment strategy for Whirlpool Slovakia rather than a joint venture? Explain your answer.
2. Would you have recommended a direct acquisition of Tatramat for Whirlpool rather than a joint venture? Explain your answer.
3. How would you assess the control versus risk trade-off by Whirlpool?

CASE CREDIT

Sonia Ferencikova. 2002. "Transition at Whirlpool-Tatramat: From joint venture to acquisition." *Transnational Corporations*, 1, 1, pp. 69–98. Used with permission of the author.

CASE NOTES

[1] Whirlpool Corporation. 1996. *Annual Report 1996*. Benton Harbor, MI: Whirlpool Corporation.

[2] Whirlpool Corporation. 1998. *Annual Report* 1997. Benton Harbor, MI: Whirlpool Corporation, p. 4.

[3] William Davidson Institute. 1994. *Whirlpool Tatramat, a.s.* Mimeo. Ann Arbor, MI: William Davidson Institute, University of Michigan School of Business Administration.

[?] Maruca, Regina Fazio. 1994. "The right way to go global: Interview with the Whirlpool CEO David Whitman." *Harvard Business Review*, 72, March–April, pp. 135–145.

[?] Steinmetz, Greg and Carl Quintanilla. 1998. "Tough target." *Wall Street Journal Europe*, 16, 50, p. 1.

[?] Whirlpool Corporation. 1998. Vision, 1, 2 (March–April).

[?] Whirlpool Corporation. 1999. *Annual Report 1998*. Benton Harbor, MI: Whirlpool Corporation.

The Failure of Boo.com

Introduction

Boo.com was one of the most anticipated e-tailing sites around the world. The company was attempting to become a fashion merchandise seller in several different markets, with the dream of creating a global brand.

Surprisingly, after a glitzy launch at the end of 1999, Boo.com announced in mid-May 2000 that it had put the company's assets up for liquidation. During a period of one year, the company had spent $135 million with spectacularly poor results.[1] By April 1999, gross sales were only $500,000 a month, and Boo.com was spending $1 million more than it was earning every week. Only $500,000 of the initial investment remained.[2]

The demise of Boo.com stands as a spectacular landmark in the history of e-commerce. AOL vice president of e-commerce, Patrick Gates, said,[3] "Boo.com was one of the big reality checks for everyone. I don't think any of us were surprised specifically. I sensed that there would be some issues there based on the product mix and sort of high-flying technology. But that one made a lot of people look back and go, 'Wow.'"

The event contributed in large measure to dire predictions about B2C commerce and to widespread pessimism about the dot-com revolution. Soon after the closure of Boo.com, the Gartner Group, for example, announced that up to 95% of e-tailers could go out of business by mid-2001.[4] Similarly, Price Waterhouse Coopers announced that one in four British online firms would run out of cash by 2000.[5] Boo.com's failure also led to a widespread sentiment that selling apparel on the Web would not succeed, which forced even online retailers that had made steady progress, such as Dressmart.com, to fold.[6]

In addition to its historic significance, an analysis of Boo.com offers rich insights into everything that should be avoided when launching an e-tailing business. Analyzing the company reveals serious flaws on many fronts—from its Web site design to its promotion to its grandiose strategic ambition.

Background

Boo.com was founded by two Swedish entrepreneurs: Kajsa Leander, a fashion model, and Ernst Malmsten. Before Boo.com, they had created the Swedish Internet bookstore bokus.com in 1997 and sold it the following year. Boo.com was backed by Paris-based Europ@web, the private investment company of LVMH Chairman Bernard Arnault; 21 Investimenti of Italy, the private investment company of the Benetton family; Bain Capital Inc. of Boston; and the New York investment firm Goldman Sachs & Co.[7]

Boo.com first announced that it would launch by the end of May 1999; however, due to software problems, the Web site actually launched in November

1999. The company failed to meet its sales targets by January 2000. It fired 100 staff members and reduced its product prices by up to 40%. In May 2000, Rob Shepherd quit as chief technology officer, the third high-level personnel loss in a month. Finally, on May 17, 2000, after failed attempts at selling the site to other retailers and trying to get more funding from the shareholders, Boo.com announced that it was shutting down.

The rights to the name Boo.com were acquired by Fashionmall.com for 250,000 British pounds.[8] In February 2001, Boo.com recast itself as a fashion and style portal that provided fashion advice and reviews. It also provided links to small boutiques where customers could go to buy the products.[9] The new site was also less data intensive making downloading easier.[10]

An Analysis of Firm Strategy

Ernst Malmsten, a cofounder, said, "We have been too visionary."[11] As implausible as it may sound, this statement may provide us a glimpse at the flaw in the firm's strategy.

Boo.com believed in the big-splash theory of firm strategy. The firm wanted to be a global fashion super retailer. The company hoped to have a major presence in multiple prominent fashion markets—at one point, it had offices in London, New York, Munich, Stockholm, Paris, and Amsterdam.[12] It aimed to leverage the power of the Internet by serving brands that were local powerhouses or global superstars to the consumers in these markets. And it intended to provide access to consumers in different multiple languages and transact business in multiple currencies.

The vision for the firm can be summarized in one word: grandiose. Although this strategy can be faulted on many counts, envisioning a global reach is not in itself a mistake. It is, however, problematic to hope to achieve that all at once. Because the company's Web site was launched simultaneously in several countries, the firm had to ensure that it had an effective presence in all of those countries. As a result, its resources were spread thin. The company may have been better served by starting small and spreading out over time.

The company also failed to consider those companies with strong brand names (e.g., Land's End, Nordstrom) that had already established strong presences in the markets that they wished to attack. Many of these companies had a long history in these markets due to catalog or bricks-and-mortar operations. Consequently, they had an advantage in resources, as well as in brand name.

Boo.com furthermore chose a product category, fashion goods, that is hard to sell on the Internet. Individuals like to touch and feel the fabric, try on a dress, and experience the product firsthand before buying it. In spite of these challenges, companies such as Land's End are successfully selling apparel online today by using systems such as virtual dressing rooms. Although Boo.com had a lot of functionality on its Web site, it did not adequately focus on the functionality that could best help its consumers.

The global vision for the company led to several execution problems. An ex-employee described a few.[13]

Multiple Currencies

If you want to trade globally, you can't only offer US dollars. As a result, you need to figure out a way to handle multiple currencies ranging from dollars to pounds to liras to francs, to deutschmarks, to kroners, etc. . . . If you are planning on doing this well, you have to peg your prices to a particular value. However, you have to realize that prices are not the same in every country and what may seem expensive in the US can be seen as cheap in other countries. This is where you have to make a decision as to whether you want to set a fixed price in the local currency or set a more dynamic price that is affected by currency exchanges and other fluctuations. It's a fascinating problem in and of itself but it's one that we discovered to be a big pain to deal with. In the end, Boo built a system that allowed us to set a different price for each country or set a single price for all countries and have that price be translated in the proper currency based on a set exchange rate. It was a bit of a kludge but it worked and, to this day, I haven't seen an e-commerce shop with a similar system.

A global e-tailer must worry about optimally setting prices in multiple markets. One price is not valid across all markets; the price must be set for each market in terms of the buying power of the market, its market size, and so forth. In addition, e-tailers must worry about the signals that the prices send. Price signals quality in the fashion business, and maintaining a consistent position across nations is certainly an important objective. All in all, developing a system that allowed them to set prices in multiple ways across countries was certainly one achievement of Boo.com.

Multiple Languages

First of all, forget translation software packages. They are still relatively immature and there is (at this point anyway) little hope that they will mature much beyond their current point in the near future. If you've taken any linguistics course, you know that grammatical rules can hardly be standardized for several languages. For example, something as simple as a verb can become a whole new set of problems. In English, there is a relatively small set of basic rules. The verb "to want" breaks down into "I want, you want, he wants, we want, you want, they want." Notice that there are only two basic variations here. In French, the same verb "vouloir" breaks down as follows: "Je veux, tu veux, il veut, nous voulons, vous voulez, ils veulent." In this case, there are 5 different variations. In Spanish, it's six . . . and so on. Take that problem and try to automate it and you are building a system that is bound to fail. The way we worked around it at Boo was to create a system where the copy was translated by hand by people who were fluent in the language. Unfortunately, another problem cropped up: British English and American English are EXTREMELY different. Considering that the assumption was that one version of each language was sufficient, problems cropped up and some of the perfectly normal British English stuff ended up being very offensive in the US. THAT was a major problem.

On the one hand, to be accepted by markets in different countries, the content has to be in different languages. Moreover, the language and product selection must be sensitive to the local cultures in order to truly appeal. Boo.com may have underestimated the cost of achieving this on the Web.

On-the-Fly Tax Calculation

This one almost killed me. In the US, it's relatively easy to deal with taxation. For the most part, the only taxes you have to pay are for states in which you have a physical presence. Where it gets tricky is when your servers are located in one area and your offices are in another. Technically, that is two locations. In the case of Boo, it got worse. For example, a sale to France was taxed three ways. Why? Quite simply because the company had offices in Paris, its servers were located in London, UK, and its distribution center was in Cologne, Germany. However, the interesting part of the problem was that we were making a sale but not delivering a good in the UK, delivering a good but not making a sale in Germany, and making a sale and delivering a good in France. This was just one example. Multiply that by the number of countries the company was doing business in and it soon got VERY complicated. Add to that the fact that certain goods were coming from China or Taiwan and the picture got so clouded that we had to bring in tax attorneys to help us on the details.

The Web has certainly complicated the matters of international taxation. To this day, there is no consistent set of global rules on taxation and the laws in this area are still emerging. Clearly, international coordination is necessary to solve some of these problems. Boo.com's vision was perhaps premature.

Integration with Multiple Fulfillment Partners

The main issue here was dealing with different file formats for DeutschePost (the European fulfillment company) and UPS (the company that did fulfillment for the US). What we ended up doing was create an EDI link to those guys (DeutschePost was not web-enabled yet) and create a set of filters for each of them. A simple answer to a simple problem but this little answer cost about 150 man hours of work as the content had to be migrated from the old (untagged) setup to the new one. Because the original database was originally set up wrong, we had to totally reorganize the schema and refit the content into it.

Working with multiple fulfillment partners can lead to new levels of complexity because the company has to work with different systems and cultures.

Perhaps the most telling sign of what went wrong can be found in a statement made by cofounder, Ms. Leander,[14] "We kind of forgot about the consumer." In other words, the company's grandiose vision was not put in place with the explicit intention of serving consumers and providing them value—that was a secondary purpose! Businesses often fail when they forget the consumer.

Problems with the Web Site

Boo.com had spectacular problems with its Web site when it first launched. The site was designed with excessive graphics, movies, audio, and video. Examples of such features included short movies that featured the brands for sale and a personal shopping assistant called Miss Boo, who made remarks to assist shoppers. They tended to see Miss Boo as an annoyance because of the irrelevance of her comments. For example, when a user clicked on the Acupuncture Deep Greco Fashion Velcro shoe, Miss Boo popped up exclaiming: "Tie me up, tie me down in a shoe that looks like it's been attacked by Gulliver's Lilliputians."[15]

Every product on the Boo.com Web site had a 3-D image. Photographing the products to create these images cost up to half a million dollars a month.[16]

A company spokesperson explained, saying, "We realize we're selling clothing. But we're selling a lifestyle item, not a commodity, so we wanted to build a different type of experience. Some of it is around rich graphics, some of it is around rich elements of design. In some cases, this was not ideal for the customer experience. So we're taking this information and trying to make it better."[17] However, an analyst for Forrester Research rightly points out[18] that this was the wrong strategy for Web site design at the time because "99% of European and 98% of US homes lacked the high-bandwidth access needed to fully benefit from the site." The company rolled out a site for low-bandwidth users in February 2000, but the target market had already been alienated. Moreover, Boo.com was built using Macromedia's Flash program, which at the point of the launch, was loaded on the computers of only a small proportion of the population.

The initial response to the Web site was awful. An article in the *Wall Street Journal* reported:[19]

> On Day 1, according to Boo, only 50% of consumers who typed in the address www.Boo.com actually made it onto the site. There were a variety of reasons: The site didn't run on some combinations of browser software and hardware, particularly Macintoshes. The abundance of graphics and animation made it extremely slow, even for customers with high-speed connections. Many of those with low-bandwidth connections found it impossible to access the site, or simply gave up, Boo says. And, worst of all, those who did manage to make it onto the site were unable to purchase anything because of a glitch in the checkout process that unexpectedly returned customers to the opening screen just before the transaction was completed.

A Web site reviewer for the *Wall Street Journal* coined a new term, "Boo rage." She reported that she had spent three hours attempting to order a skirt.[20] Also, "the first 17 times I tried to submit my order, my browser crashed. I also endured pages that took forever to download, was randomly tossed off of the site, and was besieged by a ridiculous number of questions when registering."

The Web usability guru Jakob Nielsen wrote this scathing review in December 1999:[21]

> Boo.com takes itself too seriously. Instead of making it easy to shop, the site insists on getting in your face with a clumsy interface. It's as if the site is more intent on making you notice the design than on selling products. Boo should be congratulated, though, on running a site that supports 18 countries equally well in terms of both language and shipping.

Screen Pollution

> Boo insists on launching several of its own windows. My own browser window is left with the message "Nothing happens on this page, except that you may want to bookmark it." Fat chance, especially since the windows forced upon me are frozen and can't be adapted to my window or font preferences.
>
> This site is simply slow and unpleasant. All product information is squeezed into a tiny window, with only about one square inch allocated to the product description. Since most products require more text than will fit in this hole, Boo requires the user to use a set of non-standard scroll widgets to expose the rest of the text, 20 words at a time. Getting to a product requires precise manipulation of hierarchical menus followed by pointing to minuscule icons and horizontal scrolling. Not nice.

Miss Boo, the Shopping Assistant

> She is prettier than Microsoft's Bob but just as annoying. Web sites do need personality, but in the form of real humans with real opinions and real advice. I prefer the interactive content experiments in the site's magazine section, such as a feature on the similarities between stone-age living and some current fashion products.

What's a Boobag?

> It's a shopping cart, actually, and unlike other carts it contains miniature photos of your products. It is also possible to drape the items on a mannequin to see how they look as an outfit, though too much dragging and low-level interface manipulation is required.

In general, Boo.com became a victim of Internet time. Businesses move faster in Internet time; e-tailing systems take much longer to develop. In this case, the

Web site was not fully designed when it was launched, which meant changes had to be made in public, reducing consumer confidence.

The Badly Designed Advertising Campaign

Another problem faced by Boo.com was that it overspent on advertising early on. It created a great deal of consumer interest, but then the Web site launch was delayed by about five months, during which time, consumers finally got fed up.

Anticipating a May 1999 launch, Boo.com announced a two-year $65 million advertising budget after hiring the London ad agency BMP DDB. The agency created a campaign showing geeky kids playing sports in cool clothes that would be available from Boo.com.[22]

According to Marina Galanti, the second marketing director, when the launch got delayed, the ad campaign was modified to make it "more about mood and attitude and less about sports." The launch was rescheduled for July and teaser ads began running in magazines. However, teaser ad campaigns work only when the firm knows exactly when the final product is going to be available. In this case, the tease campaign backfired because the site did not launch until November 1999. It also placed the spotlight on the company while it was still tinkering with the Web site.

The company believed in going on an all-out blitz rather than building the business gradually. As described in a *Wall Street Journal* article,[23] "the company launched press, television, cinema and outdoor campaigns in six countries and expanded to nine others, spending about $25 million—much of it still owed to the agencies that created and executed the ads."

After setting grandiose expectations, Boo.com seemed to have faltered in its marketing strategy. Panicked by low sales, the company abandoned its image as a high-end retailer and started offering huge discounts—but without modifying its advertising.[24]

It seemed to some that the company had simply not catered to its target market and had failed to make a connection. Simon Mathews, managing director of Optimedia International, a media planning firm, said, "Boo.com's advertising strategy was emblematic of what was wrong with its business." The focus was on showboating instead of selling a product with clear substance. They never gave people a real reason to buy their clothes."[25]

Poor Management Quality

Boo.com has also been criticized for poor management quality. The firm had few management controls and many of the personnel were consultants with little relevant business experience.[26] The company is also said to have been too enamored with the fashion industry: Senior managers were rewarded with five-star hotels and first-class airline tickets to attend fashion shows in cities such as Paris and Milan. Early employees were also rewarded with Palm Pilots and other perks.[27]

But the poor management went further than simple extravagance, as an ex-employee recounts:[28]

When I joined the company in August, the launch was behind schedule by three months and we had ten weeks to the Xmas season. The first thing I asked to see was the project plan. It didn't exist. People were working on bits and pieces of the project without communicating with other people they were affecting. Within a week, we put together a MS-project chart and things started to move properly.

Lack of communications to and from the top was definitely a problem as well as a lack of understanding of Internet time....

Boo.com set out to do too many things and ended up doing none of them. The site was designed to create an immersive online retailing experience, but most users did not have broadband connectivity to benefit from it. The ad campaign built traffic to the site when it was not up. The management quality was poor and in the end, Boo's failure did not particularly surprise anyone who had worked for or with the company. Future attempts at building a global online apparel retailer will surely learn from the experiences of Boo.

The Future

Boo.com failed to create an immersive retailing experience online. The question for the future is will it ever be possible? Some studies now show that online users respond more to text than to pictures, which seems to support the approach taken by Amazon.com. But the jury is still out on this question.

CASE DISCUSSION QUESTIONS

1. Was Boo.com doomed more by its faulty strategy or by its poor implementation?
2. Can apparel ever be sold successfully on the Web? How about other fashion products such as jewelry and perfume?
3. What can the Web add to apparel sales that a catalog cannot?
4. What is the appropriate way to use graphics when designing a Web site?
5. Was Boo.com just ahead of its time? Will there ever be a global online retailer?
6. Will the impending broadband revolution help sites that want to create an immersive retail experience online?

CASE CREDIT

Krishnamurthy Sandeep, 2003. *E-Commerce Management*. Mason: Ohio: South-Western, pp. 129–135. Used with permission.

CASE NOTES

[1] Regan, Keith and Nora Macaluso. 2000. "Boo.com saga ends with asset sale." *E-commerce Times*, May 30.
[2] Glick, Bryan. 2000. "Boo.com's fall makes realism the fashion." http://www.vnunet.com/Analysis/1102339, May 24.
[3] Weisman, John. 2000. "The making of E-Commerce: 10 Key Moments, Part II." http://www.ecommercetimes.com/news/articles2000/000823-1.shtml, August 23.
[4] Ibid.
[5] Glick.
[6] Brady, Mick. 2000. "The Web's touchy-feely fashion challenge." http://www.ecommercetimes.com/perl/story/4131.html, August 28.
[7] Corcoran, Cate T. 2000. "E-Commerce (A special report). Industry by Industry—More than style: Fashion sites need to be exciting and stylish; And, as this tale of two ventures shows, They also need to be practical." *Wall Street Journal*. April 17, R 68.
[8] Holloway, Karen. 2000. "Boo.com reborn as lifestyle portal." http://www.karenholloway.com/boo.htm, October 30.
[9] Parker, John. 2001. "Boo.com reborn." *Traffic World*, 265(9), 23.
[10] Tillett, Scott. 2000. "It's back from the dead: Boo.com." *Internet Week*, 834, 11.
[11] Weisman.
[12] Portanger, Erik and Stephanie Gruner. 2000. "Boo.com to move into receivership as funds dry up." *Wall Street Journal*, p.B16.
[13] Tristan, Louis. 2000. "What i learned at Boo.com." http://www.tnl.net/newsletter/2000/boobust.asp. May 19 .
[14] Corcoran.
[15] Ibid.
[16] Glick.
[17] Corcoran.
[18] Cassy, John and Mary O'Hara. 2000. "It all ends in tears at Boo.com." http://www.shoppingunlimited.co.uk/newsandviews/story/0,5804,222624,00.html, May 19.
[19] Corcoran.
[20] Petersen, Andrea. 1999. "Watching the Web: Buzzkill." *Wall Street Journal*, November 11.
[21] Nielsen, Jakob. 2000. "Boo's Demise," http://www.useit.com/alertbox/20000528_boo.html, May.
[22] Ellison, Sarah. 2000. "Boo.com: Buried by badly managed buzz." *Wall Street Journal*, May 23, p. B10.
[23] Ibid.
[24] Ibid.
[25] Ibid.
[26] Cassy and O'Hara.
[27] Portanger and Gruner.
[28] Tristan.

Strategy Implementation for Multinational Companies: Human Resource Management

part four

11 International Human Resource Management

Learning Objectives

After reading this chapter you should be able to:

- Know the basic functions of human resource management.
- Define international human resource management.
- Understand how international human resource management differs from domestic human resource management.
- Know the types of workers that multinational companies use.
- Explain how and when multinational companies decide to use expatriate managers.
- Know the skills necessary for a successful expatriate assignment.
- Understand how expatriate managers are compensated and evaluated.
- Appreciate the issues regarding expatriate assignments for female managers.
- Know what companies can do to make the expatriate assignment easier for their female expatriates.
- Understand the relationship between choice of a multinational strategy and international human resource management.

Preview CASE IN POINT

Fast-Track Global Multinationals

U.S. companies and other multinationals around the world are increasingly relying on their expatriates to run their overseas operations. As these companies search for new customers and markets abroad, they have a growing need for managers with the necessary skills for global assignments. In fact, studies and surveys suggest that, despite the economic crisis of 2008–2009, an increasing number of multinationals are relying on expatriate assignments to achieve their goals. Clearly, properly managing expatriates presents both significant opportunities and challenges.

Companies with serious ambitions to become key global competitors are devoting significant resources to manage international assignments. Consider the expatriate management program of DuPont, which routinely sends its employees on international assignments. For example, engineers from Mexico and the United States may be sent to work in a chemical plant in China. Such international assignments pose challenges because DuPont has to deal with multiple nationalities within the same assignment. Instead of allowing each country or division to set its own policies, DuPont is finding that having a standardized international assignment policy works well for its 300 to 400 international assignments each year. DuPont's Global Transfer Center of Expertise manages all aspects of the program, from preparing the candidates for the international assignment to finding educational opportunities for the candidates' children.

IBM is another example of a multinational with a large number of expatriates—more than 375,000 employees worldwide in over 160 countries. As you will read later in the chapter, the big challenge for IBM has been to integrate its worldwide operations to ensure that each project gets the best talent.

Sources: Based on Hamm, S. 2008. "International isn't just IBM's first name." BusinessWeek, Janaury 28, pp. 36–40; Minton-Eversole, T. 2009. "Overseas assignments keep pace." HR Magazine, pp. 72–74.

The Preview Case in Point shows that more and more multinationals are seeking internationally experienced managerial talent to run their operations in the global market. This emphasis on building such talent comes from the increasing popularity of multinational strategies in response to a globalizing world economy. However, there are many challenges. A key ingredient of implementing any successful multinational strategy includes using compatible human resource management (HRM) policies. Multinationals will have to get creative to manage the workforce adequately.

The chapter first presents a basic definition of international human resource management and shows how it differs from its strictly domestic counterpart. The chapter then discusses how multinational companies must choose a mixture of employees and managers with different nationalities to set up operations overseas. Particular attention is given to the role, selection, training, and evaluation of multinational managers in international assignments. Also explained are issues regarding women with international postings and the particularly difficult conditions that female expatriates face. The chapter concludes with a discussion of the four basic orientations to international human resource management and how each supports multinational strategies.

International Human Resource Management Defined

Business organizations necessarily combine physical assets (e.g., buildings and machines) and financial assets, as well as technological and managerial processes, to perform work. However, without people, the organization would not exist. Managing and developing human assets are the major goals of human resource management (HRM), which deals with the overall relationship of the employee with the organization. The basic HRM functions are recruitment (identification of qualified individuals for a vacant position), selection (choosing an individual for the position), training (providing opportunities to help the individual perform), performance appraisal (assessing the individual's performance), compensation (providing the adequate reward package), and labor relations (the relationship between the individual and the company).[1]

> **Human resource management (HRM)**
> Recruitment, selection, training and development, performance appraisal, compensation, and labor relations.

International Human Resource Management and International Employees

When applied to the international setting, the HRM functions make up international human resource management (IHRM). When a company enters the international arena, all the basic HRM activities remain, but they take on added complexity, for two reasons. First, the employees of multinational organizations include a mixture of workers of different nationalities. Second, multinational managers must decide how necessary it is to adapt the company's HRM policies to the national cultures, business cultures, and social institutions where the company is doing business.

> **International human resource management (IHRM)**
> All the HRM functions, adapted to the international setting.

Types of Employees in Multinational Organizations

IHRM must take into account several types of employees in the multinational organization. Expatriate employees come from a country that is different from the one in which they are working. Expatriate employees who come from the parent firm's home country are called home country nationals.

> **Expatriate**
> Employee who comes from a country that is different from the one in which they working.

> **Home country national**
> Expatriate employee who comes from the parent firm's home country.

Third country nationals
Expatriate workers who come from neither the host nor home country.

Host country nationals
Local workers who come from the host country where the unit (plant, sales unit, etc.) is located.

Inpatriate
Employees from foreign countries who work in the country where the parent company is located.

Flexpatriates
Employees who are sent on frequent but short-term international assignments.

International cadre
Managers who specialize in international assignments.

Expatriate workers who come from neither the host nor the home country are called **third country nationals**. Local workers who come from the host country where the unit (plant, sales unit, etc.) is located are **host country nationals**. Usually, home country and third country expatriates belong to the managerial and professional staff rather than to the lower-level workforce. The globalization of the workforce also is breeding a special type of expatriate called the **inpatriate**. Inpatriates are employees from foreign countries who work in the country where the parent company is located. Recent trends also suggest a new breed of workers known as **flexpatriates**.[2] Flexpatriates are employees who are sent on frequent short-term international assignments. Finally, multinational companies have created a separate group of managers who specialize in international assignments, called the **international cadre**, or *globals*. Members of the international cadre have permanent international assignments. They are recruited from any country and are sent to worldwide locations to develop cross-cultural skills and to give the company a worldwide perspective.[3]

Given the high costs of expatriates, more and more companies are relying flexpatriates on more short-term international assignments. Consider the following Focus on Emerging Markets.

Focus on Emerging Markets

Rotational Assignments in Asia-Pacific

Surveys have shown that companies are increasingly relying on short-term intensive international assignments because of the excessive costs of full expatriate programs. For example, a KPMG survey in the United States revealed that over 49 percent of the 348 human resources managers felt that international assignments took too much time and effort to manage. Thus, because of the intense competition for skilled professionals in China and in many emerging Asian countries, companies are using short-term rotational assignments to quickly develop and retain these skilled individuals. The rotations involve moving flexpatriates from position to position in different countries.

Such rotation has many advantages for companies. Short-term rotational assignments tend to be more cost-efficient than full expatriate programs. Furthermore, by working for shorter durations in different countries, participants can accelerate learning by developing the necessary communication, team-building, and decision-making skills to function in the global environment. Companies such as General Electric and Procter & Gamble use rotational assignments to develop their future leaders. They devise assignments tailored to their workers' abilities and potential.

Although many companies are sending expatriates on short assignments, their experiences suggest that many important issues need to be addressed to ensure that such programs work. For instance, because of the short-term nature of the assignment, it is better to send expatriates to countries with cultures similar to their own. Companies are finding that the transfer of learning to China tends to work better if rotations are in other Asian countries. Companies also are still expected to be ready to address family, compensation, and performance appraisal issues.

*Sources: Based on Fallon, M. 2006. Maximizing rotational assignments in Asia Pacific. China Staff, 1(12), pp. 3;
PR Newswire. 2008. "Globalization forces companies to reexamine international assignments," January 8; and
Tahvanainen, M. D. Welch, and V. Worm. 2005. "Implications of short-term international assignments."
European Management Journal, 23(6), pp. 663–673.*

Multinational Managers: Expatriate or the Host Country

U.S. companies employ more than seven million people outside the United States. Although most of these employees are lower-level workers, they require a significant number of managers. When are the management positions filled by expatriates? When are they filled by host country nationals? Deciding how many expatriates or local managers to use depends mostly on a company's multinational strategy. Transnational strategists see their managerial recruits as employable anywhere in the world. Multidomestic strategists tend to favor local managers or use expatriates only for short-term assignments. Regardless of multinational strategy, management teams usually contain a mixture of expatriate and host country nationals. For a particular position, a firm might approach its staffing decisions by answering questions like the following:[4]

- *Given our strategy, what is our preference for this position (host country, home country, or third country national)?* For example, a company with a regional strategy may favor the use of third country nationals as country-level managers.

For expatriate managers (parent country or third country nationals):

- *Is there an available pool of managers with the appropriate skills for the position?* To use expatriate managers, a company must have qualified and available managers within its own ranks, or it must be able to recruit qualified parent company or third country managers to fill open positions.
- *Are these managers willing to take expatriate assignments?* Not all managers will take assignments abroad. Some managers believe that international assignments can hurt their advancement at home. Increasing numbers of managers have employed spouses, making it impossible to take international assignments.
- *Do any laws affect our assignments of expatriate managers?* Some countries have strict restrictions on foreigners taking employment. Temporary work visas may be difficult or impossible for employees to obtain.

For host country managers:

- *Do our host country managers have the expertise for the position?* To use host country managers, the local labor pool must have available managers with the training and expertise to fill open positions. Host country managers often lack the expertise of managers from multinational companies.
- *Can we recruit managers with the desired skills from outside our firm?* Even if qualified managerial talent exists in a country, a foreign multinational might not have the reputation or the local connections to attract host country managerial talent. For example, in Japan, many college graduates are reluctant to work for foreign multinationals because they do not provide the security of Japanese companies.

Is the Expatriate Worth It?

IHRM decisions regarding the use of expatriate managers must take into account the costs of the assignments. The total compensation of expatriate managers often is three to four times higher than home-based salaries and benefits. Extremely costly locations such as China can be even higher. In China, for example, a bilingual senior U.S. executive can expect a base salary approaching $400,000, hardship allowances as high as 35 percent of salary, two free houses (one in Hong Kong for the weekends and one in China), and chauffeur-driven cars.[5] An expatriate manager with a base salary of $100,000 and a family of four can cost as much as $360,000 in Tokyo, $275,000 in Hong Kong, $210,000 in Singapore, and $250,000 in London. Consider that a Pacific Northwest manufacturing company was spending about $500,000 for its expatriate's salary.[6] As the next Case in Point shows, expatriate assignments can sometimes carry unusual compensation packages.

The compensation packages of expatriates depend on the cost of living in the host country. Mercer Human Resources Consulting has developed a cost-of-living index that companies routinely use to determine how much to pay their expatriates. The index uses New York as a base and compares prices in the host country by weighting price ratios in the expenditure patterns of the expatriate. The index is a measure of the cost-of-living of American employees assigned to a foreign country. Exhibit 11.1 shows additional data on the cost-of-living index in 15 selected cities. As the exhibit shows, of the 50 cities surveyed by Mercer Human Resources Consulting, Tokyo is the most expensive city for multinational companies to send expatriates.

Even with such high costs, the success of an expatriate assignment is not guaranteed. U.S. companies in particular have poor records of expatriate success when compared with European and Japanese multinational companies. Surveys show that U.S. multinationals often have failure rates for managers in overseas assignments ranging from 10 to 40 percent[7] while other international surveys reveal that 83 percent of companies surveyed experienced expatriate failure.[8] A more recent study shows that 21 percent of companies surveyed had

C A S E I N P O I N T

Unusual Expatriate Expenses

As more multinationals extend their operations into remote locations around the world, they have to provide significant benefits to encourage expatriates to go there. Here are some unusual benefits given to expatriates:

- In countries with extreme temperatures, expatriates are provided with clothing allowances. For instance, British expatriates in Russia often find that their wardrobe is not suitable for the freezing winters.

- Expatriates sent on assignment in South America rainforest areas are provided with suitable safari-style clothing.

- In parts of Sweden and Canada, where it snows almost year round, expatriates are given allowances to have snow regularly cleared off their roofs.

- Expatriates sent to non-English-speaking countries often are given allowances for Internet and other benefits, such as global news channels.

- Expatriates sent to remote regions of China are given allowances to take shopping trips to big cities.

- Expatriates sent to countries affected by war or other natural disasters increasingly are provided with extensive insurance coverage and with special emphasis on accidental death and disability to deal with catastrophic situations.

- Companies having difficulties luring expatriates to polluted Mexico City offer pollution-escape trips to the Pacific or Gulf coasts.

- To prevent kidnapping in Brazil, executive-level expatriates are offered chauffeured, bulletproof cars, followed by vehicles with bodyguards.

Sources: Based on Employee Benefits. 2005. "International and unusual perks: Cases of the weird and wonderful," March, pp. S11; McGregor, J. 2008. "The right perks." BusinessWeek, January 28, pp. 42–43; Mueller, S. 2006. "Shoring up protection for overseas employees." Risk Management, 53(3), pp. 38–41.

EXHIBIT **11.1** Cost-of-Living Indexes (2008; New York, U.S. = 100)

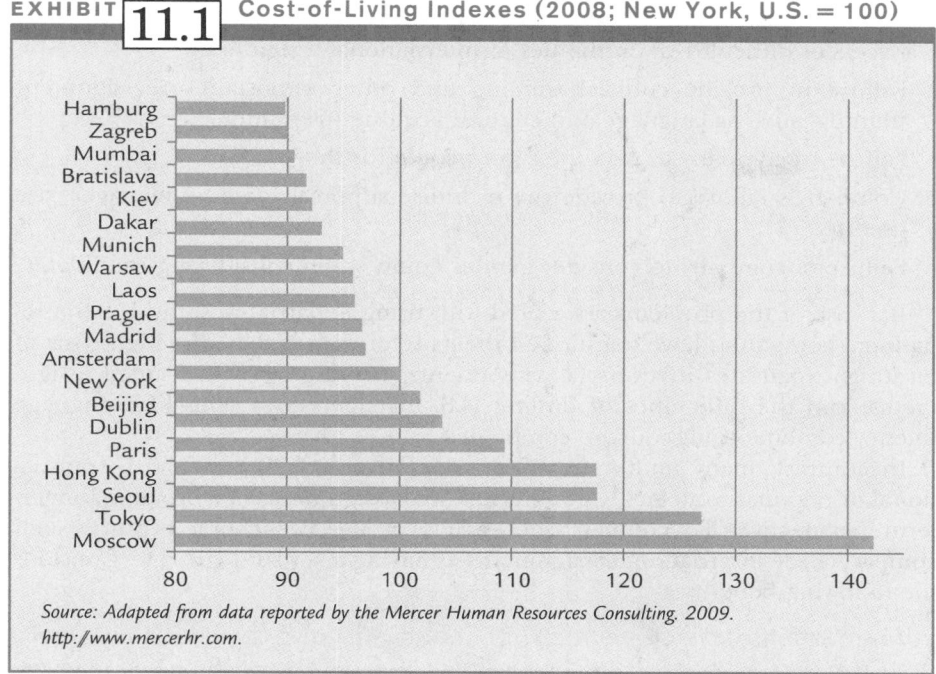

Source: Adapted from data reported by the Mercer Human Resources Consulting. 2009. http://www.mercerhr.com.

expatriates leave in the middle of their international assignments.[9] Clearly, ensuring expatriate success is a major challenge for companies.

Although it has been traditionally assumed that expatriates fail because they are not adequately prepared for their foreign assignments, other factors come into play. Often, failures occur because companies don't have human resource management policies compatible with expatriate policies.[10] Many organizations tend to neglect appropriate human resource practices when they send their employees overseas. Failure can take many other forms.[11] Some expatriates may be reassigned to the home country for poor performance. Others may choose to return because of their own or their family's difficulties adjusting to the local culture. Expatriates may willingly choose to return because they find themselves ineffective in their jobs. Some companies also see their expatriates end their assignments prematurely to take jobs with other companies.

Thus, typical reasons for U.S. expatriate failure include individual, family, cultural, and organizational factors:[12]

Individual

- Personality of the manager.
- Lack of technical proficiency.
- No motivation for international assignment.

Family

- Spouse or family members fail to adapt to local culture or environment.
- Family members or spouses do not want to be there.

Cultural

- Manager fails to adapt to local culture or environment.
- Manager fails to develop relationships with key people in the new country because of the complexities of cultivating networks with diverse people.

Organizational

- Excess of difficult responsibilities of international assignment.
- Failure to provide cultural training and other important preassignment training, such as language and cultural acquisition training.
- Failure of company to pick the right people for the job.
- Company's failure to provide the technical support domestic managers are used to.
- Failure of company to consider gender equity when considering candidates.

Because of the problems associated with using expatriates, some U.S. multinational companies have questioned their use of expatriates. The high costs of locating expatriates in overseas assignments, the high costs of failed assignments, and the difficulties of finding U.S. managers with skills like language fluency combine to discourage companies.

In contrast, many multinational companies, especially those with transnational or regional strategies, view international assignments in a broader, longer-term perspective. To compete successfully in the twenty-first century, such companies see international assignments as having a key strategic role. Consider the following benefits:

- *International assignments help managers acquire the skills necessary to develop successful strategies in a global context:* Strategic management in the coming decades will require managers who understand global competition, customers, suppliers, and markets. Seldom can managers make

Multinational Management **Brief**

Importance of International Assignments

IBM is now a global multinational with over 375,000 employees worldwide. Although it still has about 127,000 employees in the United States, it also has a sizable number of employees in countries such as Japan (25,000), India (75,000), Brazil (13,000), Britain (20,000), and France (11,000) among many others. Since 2004, IBM has been transforming itself into a truly globally integrated enterprise. Prior to this transformation, IBM was operating its subsidiaries in 160 countries like mini-IBMs. However, this system was very costly because IBM was not taking advantage of its global workforce. Its philosophy now is that it will get the job done where the job can best be done.

To achieve this global integration, IBM has realized that it is crucial to send its employees on international assignments to transmit the corporate values. Consider the case of IBM Brazil. When resources are tight there, the Brazilians favored projects from local customers, and IBMers from other countries pushed for their own clients in those other countries. American Robert Payne was sent to address this conflict. IBM sent the 22-year IBM executive to facilitate the global integration process. By encouraging the employees to think of the company's interests in the long term, he was able to reduce some of the conflict. IBM has sent other expatriates to other key subsidiaries to help integrate the company's operations.

Source: Based on Hamm, S. 2008. "International isn't just IBM's first name." BusinessWeek, January 28, pp. 36–40.

effective strategic decisions without considering worldwide implications. Without international management experience, the future top managers may not develop talents, such as understanding foreign customers or foreign governments. Recognizing such challenges, companies like Colgate-Palmolive provide a variety of international assignments, both for high-potential managers and for managers who recently have graduated from college.[13] Consider the Multinational Management Brief on the previous page.

- *Expatriate assignments help a company coordinate and control operations that are dispersed geographically and culturally:* Expatriates with a shared vision and objectives for the corporation serve as links to communicate corporate needs and values to culturally and geographically diverse local subsidiaries. Expatriates also have firsthand knowledge of local situations and communicate local needs and strategic information to headquarters. In contrast, an overuse of host country managers may create employees who identify primarily with the host country subunit rather than with the global organization.[14]

- *Global assignments provide important strategic information:* Because of the length of typical expatriate assignments (two to five years), compared with short visits from headquarters, expatriate managers have sufficient time to gather complex information.[15] For example, in politically risky countries, an experienced expatriate manager can provide the top management of the parent company with critical and timely information, which might include key trends in the host country's political, economic, and financial environments.[16]

- *Global assignments provide crucial detailed information about local markets:* Expatriates have incredible in-depth knowledge of local markets.[17] This information needs to be part of the strategic planning of companies because it can be extremely critical for companies with a wide geographic presence. For instance, Colgate-Palmolive's expatriates' detailed knowledge of local markets enabled them to determine that small sachets of detergent sell better in Africa than the typical 64-ounce bottle sold in the United States. Similarly, interviews of 16 Austrian expatriates in Polish banks revealed that the bankers acquired significant knowledge of local market conditions such as the legal system.[18]

- *Global assignments provide important network knowledge:* Because expatriates meet many people, such as clients, suppliers, and people within the subsidiary, they create an important network in the host country. Because they are the main contacts between the host and the parent companies, they also may develop a new network at the home company. Such networks can be very useful because they can create new business opportunities and help the subsidiary function smoothly.[19]

Next, the chapter considers how to use the expatriate manager to maximize strategic advantage.

The Expatriate Manager

Once a company makes the decision to use expatriate managers or to develop a full-time international cadre, successful multinational organizations develop IHRM policies that maximize their effectiveness. This section discusses the effective selection, training and development, performance appraisal, compensation, and repatriation of the expatriate multinational manager.

Selecting Expatriate Managers

Selecting the wrong person for any job can lead to failure and can be a major expense for the company.[20] It is even more pronounced for expatriates because a failed expatriate assignment can cost the company from two to five times the assignee's annual salary.[21] In fact, it is estimated that each expatriate failure through early departure can cost a company more than $1 million.[22] Furthermore, it has even been argued that improperly selected employees who cannot perform adequately but who remain on assignment can be more damaging to the company than those who leave prematurely.[23] Companies are therefore becoming more aware of the strategic need to select the right person for the job the first time. Consider the examples in the next Case in Point.

Traditionally, multinational companies have assumed that domestic performance predicts expatriate performance. This assumption leads companies to search for job candidates with the best technical skills and professional competence. When these factors become the major, if not the only, selection criteria for international assignments, companies often overlook other important

---

CASE IN POINT

Selecting the Right Person for the Assignment

More and more companies are realizing that it is critical for their success to send the right person abroad for the assignment. A key aspect of any successful selection program is advanced planning. To ensure successful selection, companies are involving their human resource department in the process. Consider the following examples:

- At Kellogg, managers are asked to select possible candidates for foreign assignments. HR and senior management members then review the list and select individuals whom they consider to be ideal candidates. These candidates are then interviewed and surveyed based on their potential to do well on overseas assignments. The findings of the surveys, emphasizing potential risks and areas of concerns, are then presented to the candidates and their spouses. These candidates can then determine their chances of succeeding in the assignments.

- Apache Corporation, a natural gas and oil company with operations in Egypt, China, and Poland, has implemented a formal system to identify candidates for expatriate assignments, and employees are surveyed to determine interested candidates. Location managers are requested to report on their

hiring needs for the coming year. The company can then easily determine potential matches between employees and future open positions and whether they need to hire from outside.

- DuPont has developed a centralized expatriate program to take care of all human resource functions regarding expatriates. This program has allowed DuPont to better select and treat its 300 to 400 annual expatriates around the world.

- Key Equipment Finance, a leasing company based in Colorado, used to select the best overall employees, who often had long-term career goals incompatible with international assignments. However, Key recently changed its selection procedures to find workers who had other skill sets but who were willing to relocate. When these expatriates return, they still have time for growth managing domestic markets.

Sources: Based on Micciche, T. 2009. "Preparation and data management are key for a successful expatriate program." Employment Relations Today, Spring, pp. 35–39; Poe, Andrea C. 2002. "Welcome back." HRMagazine, 45(3), pp. 94–101; Schoeff, Mark Jr. 2006. "International assignments best served by unified policy." Workforce Management, February 13, p. 36; Tyler, Kathryn. 2006. "Retaining repatriates." HRMagazine, March, 51(5), pp. 97–102.

criteria.[24] What other criteria are important for selecting the best people for expatriate assignments?

Several experts on international HRM have identified **key success factors for expatriate assignments.**[25] In addition to professional and technical competence, these factors are relational abilities, family situation, motivation, and language skills.

- *Technical and managerial skills:* Often an expatriate assignment gives managers more tasks and greater responsibilities than similar-level assignments at home. Additionally, the geographical distance from headquarters can result in the manager's having more decision-making autonomy. Only managers with excellent technical, administrative, and leadership skills have a strong likelihood of success in such positions.

- *Personality traits:* A foreign assignment inevitably comes with a host of unexpected problems and new situations. To be able to deal with such uncertainties and novelty, the expatriate has to be flexible, be willing and eager to learn new things, be able to deal with ambiguity, have an interest in other people and cultures, and have a good sense of humor. Extraversion also is critical to success.[26] Extraverts are more likely to be sociable, talkative, and thus motivated to communicate and develop relationships with locals. Relationships with locals can not only help expatriates adjust better in the new country but also provide access to important information regarding appropriate behavior.

- *Relational abilities:* Relational abilities help employees avoid a major pitfall of international assignments: the failure to adapt to different cultures. People with good relational skills have the ability to adapt to strange or ambiguous situations. They are culturally flexible and sensitive to cultural norms, values, and beliefs. They also have the ability to modify their own behaviors and attitudes to fit in with a new culture. They favor collaborative negotiation styles and avoid direct confrontation.

- *Family situation:* Selection for an international assignment also must weigh the potential expatriate's family situation. An overseas assignment affects the spouse and children as much as the employee, so a family situation favorable to the assignment is crucial for expatriate success. Key factors to consider are the spouse's willingness to live abroad, the impact of the potential posting on the spouse's career and the children's education, and the spouse's relational skills. Because of the increasing number of dual-career couples, multinational companies may need to offer two positions or compensation for the spouse's lost income to ensure a successful assignment.

- *Stress tolerance:* Adapting to a new culture and work environment can be extremely stressful. The ability to tolerate stress is a crucial quality that can help an expatriate succeed on an international assignment.[27] Expatriates who can maintain their composure in the face of extreme stressors are more likely to succeed in their new assignments.

- *Language ability:* The ability to speak, read, and write the host country language enhances many of the other key success factors. Managers with good language skills are well prepared to apply their technical and managerial skills. They have heightened success in dealing with local colleagues, subordinates, and customers. Knowledge of the local language also increases the understanding of the local culture and reduces the stress of adapting to a new cultural environment.

- *Emotional intelligence:* Research suggests that emotional intelligence is a crucial success factor.[28] Emotional intelligence is the ability of being aware of oneself, understanding and relating to others, and being empathetic and managing one's emotions. Expatriates inevitably need to relate to others and manage their own presence. Those with high emotional intelligence are likely to be able to relate to locals and show the appropriate emotions when adjusting locally.

Selecting an expatriate manager with the appropriate array of skills demands more effort than selecting domestic managers. There are more key success factors to consider than in domestic assignments. Most successful multinationals use a combination of selection techniques to identify people with the appropriate talent for an expatriate posting. Some popular techniques are interviews, standardized tests of intelligence or technical knowledge, assessment centers (testing centers where candidates solve simulated managerial problems), biographical data, work samples, and references. Scholarship suggests the use of assessment to measure cross-cultural intelligence, as shown in the next Case in Point.

Exhibit 11.2 shows some of the key success factors and selection techniques used in the expatriate selection process.

The importance of the expatriate success factors is not the same for all expatriate job assignments. Each factor has a different priority depending on four assignment conditions:[29] assignment length, cultural similarity, required communication with host country nationals, and job complexity and responsibility. Each of these conditions affects the selection criteria:

- *Assignment length:* The amount of time an expatriate expects to remain in the host country may range from short postings of a month or less to several

CASE IN POINT

Assessing Cross-Cultural Social Intelligence

Experts agree that a key success factor for expatriates is cross-cultural social intelligence. Building on the concept of social intelligence, scholars argue that cross-cultural intelligence is the ability of an individual to gauge and understand verbal and nonverbal cues from a variety of cultures. An accurate assessment of such clues implies that the individual can make accurate social inferences from the cultural situation and can behave in the appropriate way to address those cues.

Given its importance, how can multinationals assess their international assignment candidates' degree of cross-cultural social intelligence? Experts suggest the use of scenario-based vignettes in which candidates can select from different ways to deal with the situation. The scenarios and alternatives were developed after extensive interviews of 29 expatriates from a variety of countries.

Consider a scenario in which an employee who came to the United States a month ago from China is having trouble with how meetings are conducted. Because of cultural differences, the Chinese employee does not feel comfortable with the U.S. style of meetings and feels that the team is not getting her best ideas. In contrast, her manager thinks that she is participating actively and is making her contribution. She finally confronts the manager, saying how difficult it is for her. Participants in the assessment are then offered four alternative responses, ranging from "This is the way to do things" to "I realize that your culture is not used to this kind of meeting." Cross-cultural intelligence can be assessed by asking how potential candidates for expatriate positions will respond to such situations.

Source: Based on Ascalon, M. E., D. J Schleicher, M. P. Born. 2008. "Cross-cultural social intelligence: An assessment for employees working in cross-national contexts." Crosscultural Management, 15(2), 109–130.

EXHIBIT 11.2   Expatriate Success Factors and Selection Methods

Key Success Factors	Selection Methods					
	Interviews	Standardized tests	Assessment centers	Biographical data	Work samples	References
Professional/technical skills						
➤ Technical skills	✔	✔		✔	✔	✔
➤ Administrative skills	✔		✔	✔	✔	✔
➤ Leadership skills						
Relational abilities						
➤ Ability to communicate	✔		✔			✔
➤ Cultural tolerance and empathy	✔	✔	✔			
➤ Tolerance for ambiguity	✔		✔			
➤ Flexibility to adapt to new behaviors and attitudes	✔		✔			✔
➤ Stress adaptation skills	✔		✔			
International motivation						
➤ Willingness to accept expatriate position	✔			✔		
➤ Interest in culture of assignment location	✔					
➤ Commitment to international mission	✔					
➤ Fit with career development stage	✔			✔		✔
Family situation						
➤ Spouse's willingness to live abroad	✔					
➤ Spouse's relational abilities	✔	✔	✔			
➤ Spouse's career goals	✔					
➤ Children's educational requirements	✔					
Language skills						
➤ Ability to communicate in local language	✔	✔	✔	✔		✔

Sources: Adapted from Black, J. Stewart, Hal B. Gregersen, and Mark E. Mendenhall. 1992. Global Assignments. San Francisco: Jossey-Bass; Ronen, Simcha. 1986. Comparative and Multinational Management. Hoboken, NJ: Wiley.

years. Selection for short-term assignments usually focuses primarily on technical and professional qualifications.

• *Cultural similarity:* Cultures vary widely, but certain cultures are similar to each other. The cultural similarity of Japan and Korea, for example, is higher than that of the United States and Taiwan or France and Saudi Arabia. Thus, finding the right French or U.S. expatriate for an assignment in the Middle East or Asia requires more emphasis on family factors, relational skills, and language skills. Managers from similar cultures usually find adaptation much easier.

• *Required interaction and communication:* Some jobs require a lot of interaction and communication with host country nationals, such as subordinates, suppliers, customers, and joint venture partners. Increased relational skills and knowledge of the host country language and culture become important in such situations.

- *Job complexity and responsibility:* In jobs with complex tasks and great responsibilities, the personal abilities of the manager often have significant effects on the success of projects. For this reason, even though professional and technical skills are important, the more important the job is to the organization, the more the candidate's skills and previous success in related work will count in the selection decision.

Exhibit 11.3 summarizes issues to consider in setting priorities in the expatriate selection process. Each factor is more or less important depending on the expatriate's job assignment conditions.

The efforts to ensure the best chance of the expatriate manager's success do not end with the selection. Expatriates need training and development, which we consider next.

Training and Development

Cross-cultural training
Increases the relational abilities of future expatriates and, in some cases, of their spouses and families.

Strong evidence shows that predeparture **cross-cultural training** reduces expatriate failure rates and increases job performance.[30] The main objective of cross-cultural training is to increase the relational abilities of the future expatriate and, when possible, of the spouse and family. The techniques used and the rigor of the training depend on the anticipated situations in the assignment.

In spite of the evidence that cross-cultural training contributes to successful expatriate assignments, many multinational companies do not invest heavily in it.[31] This situation may be changing. U.S. multinational firms like American Express, Colgate-Palmolive, and General Electric continually upgrade their international training. A recent survey of 264 multinational companies, with a total worldwide expatriate population of 74,709, was conducted by the consulting firm Windham International,[32] which found that approximately 63 percent of the firms had cross-cultural training prior to expatriate assignments.

Training rigor
Extent of effort by both trainees and trainers to prepare the expatriate.

Training rigor is the extent of effort by both trainees and trainers to prepare the expatriates.[33] Low rigor means that training lasts for a short period and includes techniques such as lectures and videos on the local culture and briefings concerning company operations. High-rigor training may last more than a month. It contains more experiential learning and extensive language training

EXHIBIT **11.3** Selecting Expatriates: Priorities for Success Factors by Assignment Characteristics

Expatriate Success Factors	Assignment Characteristics			
	Longer duration	More cultural dissimilarity	Greater interaction and communication requirements with locals	More complex or responsible job
Professional/technical skills	High	Neutral	Moderate	High
Relational abilities	Moderate	High	High	Moderate
International motivation	High	High	High	High
Family situation	High	High	Neutral	Moderate
Language skills	Moderate	High	High	Neutral

Sources: Adapted from Black, J. Stewart, Hall B. Gregersen, and Mark E. Mendenhall. 1992. Global Assignments. San Francisco: Jossey-Bass; Tung, Rosalie L. 1981. "Selection and training of personnel for overseas assignments." Columbia Journal of World Business, 16(1), pp. 68–78.

and often interactions with host country nationals. Exhibit 11.4 shows various training techniques and their objectives as the rigor of the cross-cultural training grows.

Training vigor depends on the same conditions as the prioritizing of expatriate success factors. Increases in the length of the assignment, the cultural dissimilarity between home and host country, the amount of required interaction and communication with local people, and job complexity/responsibility all suggest a need for increased training rigor.[34] See Exhibit 11.5. Because a major reason for expatriate failure relates to family situations, training for a long assignment in a dissimilar culture may include all family members, not just the expatriate.

As the Multinational Management Brief shows, training cannot fully prepare expatriates to face life in the new country. Many companies are now relying on mentor and buddy programs to facilitate integration in the host country.

Once expatriates are on assignment, IHRM does not stop. Multinational managers must have appropriate performance appraisal techniques.

Performance Appraisal for the Expatriate

Conducting a reliable and valid performance appraisal of expatriate managers poses one of the greatest IHRM challenges for the international company. Seldom can a company transfer the same performance criteria and measures to a

EXHIBIT 11.4 Building Cross-Cultural Training Rigor: Techniques and Objectives

Training Rigor (High → Low)

Techniques: Field trips to host country, meetings with managers experienced in host country, meetings with host country nationals, intensive language training.
Objectives: Develop comfort with host country national culture, business culture, and social institutions.

Techniques: Intercultural experiential learning exercises, role-playing, simulations, case studies, survival language training.
Objectives: Build general and specific knowledge of host country culture, reduce ethnocentrism.

Techniques: Lectures, videotapes, reading background material.
Objectives: Provide background information on host country business and national cultures, basic information on company operations.

Sources: Adapted from Black, J. Stewart, Hal B. Gregersen, and Mark E. Mendenhall. 1992. Global Assignments. San Francisco: Jossey-Bass; Ronen, Simcha. 1986. Comparative and Multinational Management. Hoboken, NJ: Wiley.

Training Needs and Expatriate Assignment

EXHIBIT **11.5** Characteristics

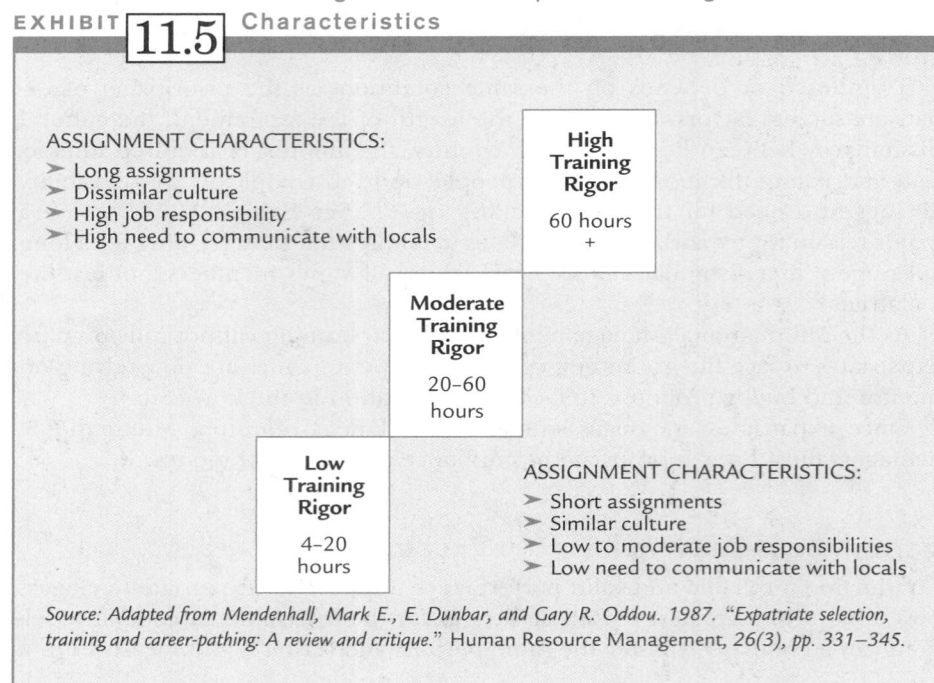

ASSIGNMENT CHARACTERISTICS:

➤ Long assignments
➤ Dissimilar culture
➤ High job responsibility
➤ High need to communicate with locals

High Training Rigor

60 hours +

Moderate Training Rigor

20–60 hours

Low Training Rigor

4–20 hours

ASSIGNMENT CHARACTERISTICS:

➤ Short assignments
➤ Similar culture
➤ Low to moderate job responsibilities
➤ Low need to communicate with locals

Source: Adapted from Mendenhall, Mark E., E. Dunbar, and Gary R. Oddou. 1987. "Expatriate selection, training and career-pathing: A review and critique." Human Resource Management, 26(3), pp. 331–345.

host country operation. Here are some of the issues that make expatriate performance appraisals difficult:[35]

- *Fit of international operation in multinational strategy:* As discussed in Chapter 6, companies often enter international markets for strategic reasons other than immediate profit. Learning about a new market and challenging an international competitor may be strategic goals that put a subsidiary in the red but still serve a useful purpose for the organization. In these cases, local managers might look quite ineffective to a company that uses economic performance measures such as return on investment (ROI).

- *Unreliable data:* Data used to measure local subunit performance may not be comparable with the home unit's data or data from other international operations. For example, local accounting rules can alter the meaning of financial data, or production efficiency can look bad because local laws require full employment rather than the occasional use of overtime.

- *Complex and volatile environments:* The international environment is complex and unstable. Economic and other environmental conditions can change rapidly and often in ways unanticipated by managers back in the home country headquarters. Consequently, reasonable and achievable performance objectives that are developed early can quickly become impossible.

- *Time differences and distance separation:* Although decreasing in importance with more rapid communication and travel options, the separation of local organizations from the home office by geography and time differences remains a problem for evaluating local managers. Often out of sight and out of mind, expatriate and local managers lack the frequency and intensity of communication to keep home office staff adequately informed.

Multinational Management Brief

Mentorship and Expatriate Buddy Programs

According to surveys, some of the major challenges faced by expatriates when they start their assignments are such things as choosing schools for their children, finding housing, opening bank accounts, finding grocery stores, getting a driver's license, and learning about the community. Unfortunately, many of these challenges cannot be easily addressed in predeparture training. Expatriates usually must deal with such challenges as they start their foreign assignments. Experts thus suggest mentorship and even buddy programs.

In a recent study of 299 expatriates, researchers examined the effectiveness of mentorship programs on key aspects of assignments. The researchers examined the effects of both home country mentors and host country mentors. They found that having a host country mentor positively impacts the expatriates' organizational knowledge, job performance, promotability, and teamwork. They also found that home country mentors were beneficial but had a positive impact only on the expatriates' organizational knowledge, job performance, and promotability.

Given the importance of host country mentors, many global companies, such as KPMG International and Balfour Beatty, have implemented buddy programs to help expatriates adjust to their new surroundings and deal with the challenges. In these programs, expatriates are assigned buddies in their host location. At Balfour Beatty, buddies receive cultural awareness training prior to the expatriates' arrival. Once they arrive, they go through more cultural training with their buddies. Buddies also get time off work to help the newly arrived expatriates shop for houses and select schools. At KPMG, the buddies play an important networking role. They typically invite the expatriates to dinners and help them get adjusted socially. Small companies motivate their expatriates through cash incentives to join local trade and social clubs. In general, global companies are finding that such buddy programs are useful to ensure that the expatriates adjust smoothly in their host locations.

Sources: Carraher, S. M., S. E. Sullivan, and M M. Crocitto. 2008. "Mentoring across global boundaries: An empirical examination of home- and host-country mentors on expatriate career outcomes." Journal of International Business Studies, 39, pp. 1310–1326; Krell, Eric. 2006, "Budding relationships." HRMagazine, 50(6), pp. 114–118.

Without intensive and direct contact, performance appraisals can fail to demonstrate a comprehensive understanding of an expatriate manager's situation.

To overcome the difficulty of conducting performance appraisals of international managers and other employees, experts suggest several steps:[36]

- *Fit the evaluation criteria to strategy:* For example, if the objective is to enter a market for long-term position, it does not make sense to use short-term financial performance measures.
- *Fine-tune the evaluation criteria:* Senior managers need to consider carefully all their objectives for the international operation. They need to visit local sites to understand the problems and situations faced by expatriate and local managers. Recently repatriated managers also can furnish excellent knowledge about local circumstances.

- *Use multiple sources of evaluation with varying periods of evaluation:* The complexity of the international situation demands more information than at-home appraisals, and high-level management should rely on several sources of information. Exhibit 11.6 shows several common components of expatriate performance appraisals, which include sources of evaluation information, evaluation criteria, and evaluation periods.

The next question is: How do multinational companies determine the fair and adequate compensation of expatriate managers?

Expatriate Compensation

Expatriate compensation presents significant challenges to companies. On the one hand, companies are being pressured to control the ever-growing costs associated with expatriate assignments with the knowledge that failure can reach exorbitantly high levels.[37] On the other hand, companies need to provide an appropriate compensation package not only to entice expatriates to relocate, but also to retain and motivate expatriate employees.

Compensation packages tend to have many common factors:[38]

- *Local market cost of living:* One of the most important factors in determining expatriate compensation is the cost of living in the host country. Often, companies try to adjust compensation levels so that the expatriate suffers no loss from relocation. As an example, expatriates sent to Japan may have close to 50 percent added to their home pay as services and goods allowances.

- *Housing:* Many multinationals tend to provide some form of housing allowance, with many companies providing free housing. Providing comparable housing is much more difficult than offering cost-of-living allowances because there are major differences in the acceptable sizes of houses. For instance, an American expatriate may move from a 3,000-square-foot house in the United States to a smaller 1,200-square-foot apartment in London.

- *Taxes:* Expatriates may face double taxation because they are taxed in the host country as well as in the home country. Although there are some exceptions, U.S. citizens and residents are taxed on their worldwide income.[39]

EXHIBIT 11.6   Evaluation Sources, Criteria, and Time Periods for Expatriate Evaluation

Evaluation Sources	Criteria	Periods
Self-evaluation	Meeting objectives ● Management skills ● Project successes	Six months and at the completion of a major project
Subordinates	Leadership skills ● Communication skills ● Subordinates' development	After completion of major project
Peer expatriate and host country managers	Team building ● Interpersonal skills ● Cross-cultural interaction skills	Six months
On-site supervisor	Management skills ● Leadership skills ● Meeting objectives	At the completion of significant projects
Customers and clients	Service quality and timeliness ● Negotiation skills ● Cross-cultural interaction skills	Yearly

Source: Adapted from Black, J. Stewart, Hal B. Gregersen, and Mark E. Mendenhall. 1992. Global Assignments. San Francisco: Jossey-Bass.

Some multinationals therefore have to cover the payment of taxes to ensure that their employees do not experience double taxation.

- *Benefits:* Benefits such as pension and health care remain an important aspect of compensation packages.[40] Many expatriates tend to be frustrated with their benefit packages when they are in the host country. Often, the benefits are not similar to the home situation or they are inadequate in the host country. As a result, companies need to find better ways to provide benefits to their expatriates. Current events around the world also suggest the need for emergency benefits.

Providing the appropriate compensation package can evidently be a daunting task. Some of the methods used to determine the level of benefits are discussed next.

The Balance Sheet Approach

More than 85 percent of U.S. multinational companies commonly apply the **balance sheet method** for determining expatriate compensation.[41] This method provides a compensation package that attempts to equate or balance an expatriate's purchasing power in the host country with his or her purchasing power in the home country.[42] The basic aim is that the expatriate should not be in a better or worse position financially as a result of the assignment. To balance the compensation received for the international assignment with compensation received in the home country, multinational companies usually provide additional salary, which includes adjustments for differences in taxes, housing costs, and the costs of basic goods and services. Goods and services are items such as food, recreation, personal care, clothing, education, home furnishing, transportation, and medical care.[43] Exhibit 11.7 provides a simple view of how the balance sheet approach works.

Besides matching the expatriate's purchasing power, companies often provide other allowances and extra benefits, called perquisites. These benefits cover the initial logistics of the international move (such as hotel costs while getting settled), compensation for lifestyle differences between the home and host country, and incentives to take the assignment. Here are some of these additional allowances and perquisites:[44]

- *Foreign-service premiums:* Multinational companies often provide 10 to 20 percent of base pay for accepting the individual and family difficulties associated with an overseas assignment. Approximately 78 percent of major U.S. multinational companies pay this premium.
- *Hardship allowance:* This allowance provides extra money for a particularly difficult posting due to issues such as high risk or poor living conditions.
- *Relocation allowances:* Along with the basic costs of moving a family to an international assignment, many companies pay a flat amount equal to one month's salary at the beginning and end of the assignment to cover miscellaneous costs of relocating.
- *Home leave allowances:* These allowances provide transportation costs for expatriates and their families to return to their home country once or twice a year.

Other Approaches

The high cost of expatriate compensation and the trend for multinational companies to have workers anywhere in the world have resulted in modifications of the traditional balance sheet approach. Some companies simply pay home

Balance sheet method
Attempts to equate purchasing power in the host country with purchasing power in the expatriate's home country.

EXHIBIT 11.7   A Balance Sheet Approach to Expatriate Compensation

Domestic Assignment: Expenses and Spendable Income:			Expatriate Assignment: Expenses and Balanced Spendable Income + Allowances:
Base Salary		+	Base Salary
		=	
Taxes		=	Taxes
		+	
Goods and Services		=	Goods and Services
		+	
Housing		=	Housing
		+	
Spendable Income		=	Spendable Income

■ Allowances as an incentive to take position, foreign service premium, hardship pay, R&R

■ Allowances to balance extra tax payments

■ Allowances to cover cost-of-living differences, housing, children's education, medical costs, automobile, recreation, home leave travel

□ Allowances for moving expenses, settling-in expenses, initial housing costs, and furnishing allowances

Headquarters-based compensation system
Paying home country wages regardless of location.

Host-based compensation system
Adjusting wages to local lifestyles and costs of living.

Global pay system
Worldwide job evaluations, performance appraisal methods, and salary scales are used.

country wages regardless of location. This approach, called the **headquarters-based compensation system**, works well when home country wages are high compared with the local assignment's cost of living.[45] However, it can be a problem in high-cost locations such as Paris or Tokyo.

Many experts recommend that companies wean expatriates gradually from dependence on perks and allowances that allow them to maintain their home country lifestyles or sometimes to live better overseas.[46] These companies assume that there is nothing special about being an expatriate, especially for longer assignments.[47] After an initial period on assignment, firms reduce allowances, using local or regional markets to determine compensation. Such companies expect the expatriate to become an efficient consumer by adjusting to local lifestyles and costs of living. This approach is called the **host-based compensation system**.

The international cadre presents different compensation problems. To address the question of compensation for multiple and continual global assignments, companies develop **global pay systems**, which are worldwide job evaluation and performance appraisal methods designed to assess the worth of jobs to the company and then equitably reward subordinates. To some extent, global pay systems resemble the balance sheet system. Allowances still exist for differences in expenses such as cost of living, taxes, settling in, and housing. However, the system does not balance compensation to produce parity with lifestyles in the home country. Rather, companies use a worldwide standard of compensation and make only necessary adjustments to that standard. The objectives are to reduce waste from expatriate perquisites, to eliminate the steep differences in compensation, and to maintain compensation equity for all long-term international cadre managers.[48]

Although international cadre managers are not expected to come home, most other types of expatriate managers return to their parent company in their home country. Returning home is not always as easy as many managers expect, and multinational companies often face the so-called repatriation problem.

The Repatriation Problem

Bringing expatriate employees home and back into full participation in the company is a difficult problem for many organizations. For example, studies of North American companies found that 25 percent of managers completing foreign assignments wanted to leave the firm.[49] Turnover may range from 33 percent to as high as 50 percent within two years after return.[50] A recent Cendant Mobility study showed that approximately half of the companies surveyed had no repatriation program. This finding is especially troubling because U.S. employers often spend as much as $1 million to send an expatriate on an overseas assignment. It is therefore imperative for companies to retain returned expatriates.

The difficulties that managers face in coming back to their home countries and reconnecting with their old job constitute the **repatriation problem**. However, these difficulties can be solved with proper preparation and planning by the expatriate and the company.

Expatriates face at least three basic cultural problems when coming home.[51] Many of these problems relate to the phenomenon called reverse culture shock, whereby people must relearn the subtleties of their own cultural norms, values, and beliefs. First, the expatriate must adapt to what is often a new work environment and the organizational culture of the home office, leading to low work performance or turnover after the assignment. Second, expatriates and their families must relearn to communicate with friends and coworkers in the home and organizational cultures. Often, as a result of having adpated to their former host cultures, expatriates are unaware that they now use different communication patterns. Third, although surprising for people who have lived most of their lives in their home country, many expatriates need time to adapt to the basic living environment, such as school, food, and weather.

Even when repatriation is not a concern, there are other organizational problems for the expatriate and the company. One survey reported that 61 percent of expatriates felt they were not given the chance to use their international experience. After years in challenging international postings, three-quarters of expatriates reported that their present jobs were demotions. Often, there were no planned career paths for expatriates after returning home.[52] Three months after their return home, one-third of the former expatriates were still in temporary jobs.[53] Finally, expatriates also get used to the autonomy abroad and may no longer feel challenged when they return.

Repatriation problem Difficulties that managers face in coming back to their home countries and reconnecting with their home organizations.

A variety of strategies allow companies to successfully repatriate their managers:[54]

- *Provide a strategic purpose for the repatriation:* Use the expatriate's experiences to further organizational goals. Expatriates often provide excellent sources of information and experiences that companies should plan to use.

- *Establish a team to aid the expatriate:* The HRM department and the expatriate's supervisor can help plan for the expatriate's return. The returning expatriates can be provided with counseling so that they are aware of the challenges of repatriation as well as how business has changed at the local office. The team also can look for obvious reverse culture shock symptoms (boredom, fatigue, withdrawal, frustration, and isolation from coworkers) and provide help as needed.

- *Provide parent company information sources:* Many companies assign mentors or sponsors who keep the expatriate informed of current changes in the company, including job opportunities.

Multinational Management **Brief**

Repatriation Programs and Promotions

During the economic downturn of 2008–2009, many multinationals recalled expatriates early to cut costs. However, the returning expatriates are facing very dire situations upon their return. In addition to having to deal with individual repatriation problems, these individuals are encountering very difficult conditions at home. Consider that only 42.1 percent of companies surveyed by Mercer were able to guarantee jobs to returning expatriates.

Furthermore, although repatriation programs can have a significant long-term impact on companies, surveys show that they are the least developed areas of expatriate programs. The 2004 Cendant Mobility survey showed that only 49 percent of companies had repatriation programs. Even companies with repatriation programs often fail to consider one critical aspect: what to do when expatriates come back. The 2005 Geodesy survey revealed that almost one quarter of expatriates resigned within a year of returning to the home country. Such departures can represent significant losses for companies that have made substantial investments in those employees.

The most dooming factor for repatriation is that most companies fail to recognize that expatriates expect to be promoted when they return. However, the 2005 Geodesy survey showed that only 33 percent of expatriates are promoted, and about 27 percent are not even guaranteed positions.

To ensure that valuable expatriates are retained, some experts suggest that companies conduct postassignment career planning even before the expatriates leave. This career planning will ensure that the expatriates know how they will be treated when they return. It also allows the expatriate to develop skills that may be needed upon repatriation. However, for as long as the downturn continues, these efforts are likely to be abandoned as multinationals look for ways to cut costs.

Sources: Based on PriceWaterhouseCoopers. 2005. "International assignments: Global policy and practice. Key trends 2005." http:/www.pwc.com; Tyler, Kathryn. 2006. "Retaining repatriates." HRMagazine, March, 51(5), pp. 97–102; Rafer, M. V. 2009. "Return trip for expats." Workforce Management, March 16, pp. 1, 3.

- *Provide training and preparation for the return:* This preparation can begin as early as six months before the return. Visits home and specific training for the next assignment help ease transition difficulties.

Even if companies have strong repatriation programs, the economic downturn of 2008–2009 means that the repatriation effort in many multinationals will suffer.[55] Furthermore, multinational companies sometimes neglect an important aspect of an international assignment. Consider the previous Multinational Management Brief.

Traditionally, in most multinational companies, international assignments have been male dominated. The previous section discusses the reasons for this tendency, whether the practice is ongoing, and several issues that arise when women take on international assignments.

International Assignments for Women

The most striking fact about women in international assignments is their rarity. Estimates are that only 12 percent of expatriate managers are women.[56] In North America, it is estimated that 14 percent of global assignees are women while women represent 45 percent of management in general.[57] In the U.K. it is estimated that only 9 percent of the expatriate population are women.[58] This data shows that, although multinational companies are willing to promote women domestically, they are reluctant to post them overseas.[59] Personnel managers believe foreigners would be prejudiced against women managers.[60] In addition, of the women who do get international assignments, very few have top management positions.[61] These findings are even more striking when one considers that North American companies use more women in international positions than do Asian or European companies.[62] All this has led some researchers to suggest that women managers face not only a glass ceiling at home but also an **expatriate glass ceiling**.[63] In other words, multinationals are reluctant to give international assignments to female managers.

Why are the barriers so strong against women gaining international positions, even in countries such as the United States where nearly half of the business school graduates are women?

Culturally based gender role expectations for women and men enter into many selection decisions. Some managers question whether family problems, a known predictor of expatriate failure, will be greater for women. They doubt whether women will be willing to take the time away from their families that is necessary to handle an expatriate position. They ask: How will the spouse fit in? What will happen if there are dual careers? Some even voice the concern that women are not tough enough to face the physical hazards, isolation, and loneliness of some international postings.[64]

However, the data tends to prove these prejudices wrong. Nancy Adler, a leading expert on women in international management, notes two important myths that lead HR executives and top-line managers to overlook qualified and motivated women for international postings:[65]

- *Myth 1: Women do not wish to take international assignments.* In a survey of women graduating with MBAs, more than three-quarters said that they would choose an international position at some time during their career.
- *Myth 2: Women will fail in international assignments because of the foreign culture's prejudices against local women.* To address this

Expatriate glass ceiling
The organizational and structural barriers preventing female managers from receiving international assignments.

myth, Adler surveyed more than 100 women managers with international postings for North American companies. More than 95 percent of them reported successful expatriate assignments, well above the average success rate for men.

Successful Women Expatriates: Foreign, Not Female

In a classic article, subtitled "A *Gaijin,* Not a Woman," Nancy Adler debunked one of the key myths regarding women as expatriates.[66] *Gaijin* is the Japanese word for foreigner. From her research, Adler concluded that it is a mistake to assume that people from foreign cultures, even traditionally patriarchal Asian cultures, apply the same gender role expectations to foreign women that they apply to local women. It seems that people from even very traditional cultures can view foreign businesswomen so differently from how they view local women that gender becomes irrelevant for business purposes. For example, one businesswoman working in the Sudan was surprised by the behavior of her Sudanese host. She asked him how it was possible that he could serve her food, give her a cushion to sit on, and wash her arms after the meal? Men never do these things for women according to traditional Sudanese gender role expectations. The Sudanese host reasoned, "Oh, it's no problem. Women do not do business; therefore, you are not a woman."[67] After establishing a business relationship, according to Adler, the real issues that arise in cross-cultural interactions depend more on how host country people react to people of another nationality than on how they react to an expatriate's gender.

The next Case in Point describes a situation where a woman's business status determined how Japanese men responded to her.

The Woman's Advantage and Disadvantage

Some studies suggest that women may have some advantages in expatriate positions, especially in Asia.[68] Being unique has its benefits. Because so few women have expatriate assignments, women who take them report being more visible. Local businesspeople were more likely to remember them and often sought them out more than the women's male colleagues. North American

---

C A S E   I N   P O I N T

The Gender-Free *Meishi*

The Japanese and many other Asian cultures exchange business cards (*meishi* in Japanese) during introductions. *Meishi* serve to define status with one's company and determine how one should interact with business associates, including the use of polite forms of language.

Two U.S. professors, a husband-and-wife team working on a research project in Japan, observed how the *meishi* determined the pattern of interaction with the woman. If the man was introduced first or the two were introduced as a married couple, Japanese businessmen and professors would focus attention on the man and treat the wife, politely but obviously, as *oksuma* (wife). However, if the woman also produced her *meishi* at the same time as the husband did, the role of wife was ignored, and the Japanese responded to the woman in terms of her professional rank. She was *sensei* (a polite form of address for professors), and gender or marital status became irrelevant. It seemed particularly important, however, to establish professional rank initially. The Japanese seemed to have more difficulty moving a woman to professional status after they perceived her initially as a wife.

expatriate women also report that local businessmen from traditional cultures assume that the woman is the best person for the job, reasoning, "Why else would the organization send a woman?"

Women may be more likely to excel in relational skills, a major factor in expatriate success. Women report that local male managers can be more open in communication with a woman than with a man. Local men, even from traditional cultures, can talk at ease with a woman about an array of subjects that includes issues outside the domain of traditional male-only conversations. Consequently, being both a businessperson and female gives expatriate women a wider range of interaction options than those available to expatriate men or to local women.[69]

Despite the many obvious advantages women expatriates enjoy, the situation is nevertheless bleak for many of them. In-depth interviews with 50 European female expatriates revealed that they faced much worse situations than their male counterparts.[70] Female expatriates are more likely to:

- *Face the glass ceiling:* Women expatriates have more difficulty being taken seriously in the early stages of their career. They are more likely to face isolation and loneliness.[71] They must work harder than their male counterparts, and they constantly need to prove themselves. Studies have shown that, in some cases, women have to be at much higher positions than their male counterparts before they are assigned international positions.

- *Need to balance work and family responsibilities:* Because of socialization and childhood experiences, research suggests that women expatriates may have a higher burden than their male counterparts to balance family and home responsibilities. There is evidence that female expatriates may be more likely to have to choose between having an international career and having a family, often because of very little support from the partner. Not surprisingly, women managers are less likely to be married and more likely to remain childless than their male counterparts.[72]

- *Need to worry about accompanying spouse:* Many female expatriates felt that they could be successful only if the career of their spouse became secondary. However, because of societal norms, it is still difficult for male partners to accept that their spouses have the primary career. It has been found that female expatriates are more likely to have partners with professional careers and that it is more difficult for the company to accommodate the needs of the male partner because of visa regulations and other host country work policies.[73]

Furthermore, even in societies where women may have advantages because they are viewed differently (e.g., *gaijin* in Japan), they still face significant barriers. For instance, although research found that Western women had some advantages because they were seen as foreigners rather than as women, it also found that these women faced significant barriers, influencing their ability to adjust to the Japanese environment and to perform well in their jobs.[74] However, a more recent study argued that Western women should have an easier time in Japan.[75] It reasoned that Japan has experienced many institutional changes, such as a more flexible market, growth of foreign multinational presence, growth of women in the workforce, and Japan's 1986 Equal Opportunity Act. These changes should result in some convergence between Western and Japanese attitudes toward women and make for a better environment for women. However, results show that many of the barriers found in a similar study a decade ago are still formidable. Foreign women managers still face cultural barriers, making it harder for them to adjust to their new jobs, perform well, and become accepted in Japan.

The next section explains that women are an ever-growing segment of the expatriate population and companies can implement programs to ensure that they have an opportunity to flourish.

What Can Companies Do to Ensure Female Expatriate Success?

Despite the disadvantages women face, the opportunities for them as expatriate managers are expected to grow, particularly with global companies. Scholars see several factors leading to more women in international assignments.

Many global and multinational companies face an acute shortage of high-quality multinational managers.[76] At the same time, perhaps because of the rise in dual-career couples, fewer men are willing to take the assignments.[77] One solution is to tap the available population of women managers. Freed from local cultural barriers that restrict the use of women managers, multinational companies can select the best people for the job regardless of gender. Because of potentially stronger relational skills, women managers often may be better qualified for international positions than their male colleagues.

Because women expatriates are likely to increase in number and are as motivated and willing to take international assignments as men, companies must take the necessary steps to ensure that their female expatriates are successful. Companies should provide other mentors[78] and also offer opportunities for networking with other working women.[79] Finally, multinationals also need to ensure that they can identify and remove barriers.[80]

Multinational Strategy and IHRM

Multinational companies have several options in developing the appropriate IHRM policies for the implementation of multinational strategies. One way to ascertain a company's approach to IHRM is to examine its IHRM orientation or philosophy. Experts identify four IHRM orientations, which are discussed next, followed by a consideration of how these orientations support the implementation of multinational strategies.

IHRM Orientations

IHRM orientation
Company's basic tactics and philosophy for coordinating IHRM activities for managerial and technical workers.

The four **IHRM orientations** reflect a company's basic tactics and philosophy for coordinating its IHRM activities for managerial and technical workers. The four basic types are ethnocentric, polycentric, regiocentric, and global. Exhibit 11.8 shows how the IHRM orientations relate to some of the basic HRM functions.

Ethnocentric IHRM Orientation

Ethnocentric IHRM
All aspects of HRM for managers and technical workers tend to follow the parent organization's home country HRM practices.

Given an **ethnocentric IHRM** orientation, all aspects of HRM for managers and technical workers tend to follow the parent organization's home country HRM practices. In recruitment, key managerial and technical personnel come from the home country. Local employees fill only lower-level and supporting jobs. Past performance at home and technical expertise govern the selection criteria for overseas assignments in the ethnocentric IHRM company.[81]

EXHIBIT **11.8**   IHRM Orientation and IHRM Practices for Managers and Technical Workers

IHRM Practice	IHRM Orientation			
	Ethnocentric	Polycentric	Regiocentric	Global
Recruitment and selection	Home country nationals for key positions selected by technical expertise or past home country performance; host country nationals for lowest levels of management only	Home country nationals for top management and technical positions; host country nationals for mid level management positions; selection of home country nationals similar to ethnocentric; selection of host country nationals based on fit with home country culture, e.g., home country language ability	Home country nationals for top management and technical positions; regional country nationals for mid level management and below	World wide throughout the company; based on best qualified for position
Training for cross-cultural adaptation	Very limited or none; no language requirements	Limited for home country nationals; some language training.	Limited to moderate training levels for home country nationals; home and host country nationals use language of business, often English	Continuous for cultural adaptation and multilingualism
Management development effects of international assignments	May hurt career	May hurt career of home country nationals; host country nationals' advancement often limited to own country	Neutral to slightly positive career implications; international assignments of longer duration	International assignments required for career advancement
Evaluation	Home standards based on contribution to corporate bottom line	Host standards based on contribution to unit bottom line	Regional standards based on contribution to corporate bottom line	Global standards based on contribution to corporate bottom line
Compensation	Additional pay and benefits for expatriate assignments	Additional pay and benefits for expatriate assignments; host country compensation rates for host country nationals	Due to longer assignments, less additional compensation for expatriate assignments	Similar pay and benefit packages globally with some local adjustments

Sources: Adapted from Adler, Nancy J., and Fariborz Ghadar. 1990. "International strategy from the perspective of people and culture: The North American context." Research in Global Business Management, 1, pp. 179–205; Heenan, D. A., and H. V. Perlmutter. 1979. Multinational Organization Development. Reading, MA: Addison Wesley.

Consistent with the use of home country nationals for management and technical positions, evaluations and promotions use parent country standards. The company assesses managers' performances using the same criteria and measures used for home country units. Because of national context variations, companies may be forced to use different approaches for the evaluation and promotion of host country managers. Such local adaptations, however, often have little effect on the ethnocentric company's procedures for promotions beyond the lowest levels of management. When an ethnocentric IHRM company uses expatriates, training for the international assignment is often limited or nonexistent. Except for top country-level or region-level positions, most international assignments last only a short time, often only for marketing and sales contacts. The use of home company evaluation and promotion standards, the lack of training, and the often short periods of expatriate assignments limit and discourage cultural adjustments for expatriates. Seldom, for example, do expatriate managers from the parent country know the host country's language.

Here are some of the benefits and costs of ethnocentric IHRM policies:

Benefits[82]

- *Little need to recruit qualified host country nationals for higher management:* Local employees will hold only lower-level jobs or midlevel management jobs. Often a glass ceiling limits the advancement of host country nationals.
- *Greater control and loyalty of home country nationals:* These employees know that the home culture drives their careers. They seldom identify with the local country subsidiaries.
- *Little need to train home country nationals:* Managers look to headquarters for staffing and evaluation and follow headquarters' policies and procedures.
- *Key decisions centralized:* Personnel decisions are made at headquarters.

Costs

- *Possibly limited career development for host country nationals:* High-potential host country nationals may never get beyond the glass ceiling, and talent is wasted.
- *Host country nationals may never identify with the home company:* Host country nationals are governed by local HRM practices, and they often realize that the glass ceiling exists. Therefore, they typically have more allegiance to the local company than to the home company.
- *Expatriate managers are often poorly trained for international assignments and make mistakes:* Training is not valued and assignments are usually short.

Regiocentric IHRM
Regionwide HRM policies are adopted.

Polycentric IHRM
Firm treats each country-level organization separately for HRM purposes.

Regiocentric and Polycentric IHRM Orientations

Firms with **regiocentric** or **polycentric IHRM** orientations are more responsive to the host country differences in HRM practices. These orientations are similar in that they emphasize adaptation to cultural and institutional differences among countries. They differ only in that the polycentric company adapts IHRM practices to countries while the regiocentric company adapts to regions. Given their similarity in IHRM philosophy, they are discussed together in this section.

Companies with polycentric IHRM orientations treat each country-level organization separately for HRM purposes. The home company headquarters ordinarily lets each country-level subsidiary follow local HRM practices. The regiocentric organization tends to adopt region-wide HRM policies. Consistent with these orientations, companies recruit and select their managers mostly from host countries or regions. Regiocentric companies may also look within the home company for key people who have mastered the cultures and languages of the countries in their regional locations. Qualifications for managers from the host country follow local or regional practices. However, to communicate with the multinational's headquarters, host country managers usually must be able to speak and write in the home company's national language.

Polycentric and regiocentric multinationals usually place home country nationals in top-level management or technical positions. These home country managers are used to control overseas operations or to transfer technology to host country production sites.[83] As with the ethnocentric IHRM companies, HRM home country policies are applied to expatriates. In addition, unless headquarters values country- or region-specific international experiences, there remains a tendency for international assignments to have negative effects on the managerial careers of home country nationals.[84]

Some benefits and costs of polycentric and regiocentric IHRM policies are as follows:[85]

Benefits

* *Reduced training expenses:* Using mostly host country nationals or third country nationals from the region reduces the costs of training expatriate managers from headquarters: Successful expatriate assignments, especially in a widely different culture, require heavy investments in training.

* *Fewer language and adjustment issues:* The use of host country and third country nationals limits the number of home country expatriate employees who face language barriers and adjustment problems: Local managers speak their area's language. Third country nationals from the region usually come from a similar culture and are more likely to have local language skills. Consequently, no investment in language training is necessary. The multinational company also faces fewer problems in managing expatriate adjustments to local cultures and in bringing home company expatriates back into the headquarters organization.

* *Lessened hiring and relocation costs:* Host country employees and third country nationals from the region are often less expensive than home country expatriates: The costs of expatriates are usually quite high.

Costs

* *Coordination problems with headquarters based on cultural, language, and loyalty differences:* Even when host country or regional managers speak the language of the multinational's headquarters, communication can be difficult and misunderstandings can result. Host country managers may have more loyalty to their local organization than to the multinational parent.

* *Limited career path opportunities for host country and regional managers:* As with ethnocentric HRM practices, host country and regional managers may face a glass ceiling on promotions, that is, limited to advancement within a country or region.

- *Limited international experience for home country managers:* Because international experience often is not valued or rewarded, it does not always attract the best managers. Companies with limited managerial talent in international operations often face difficulties if their industry becomes global, requiring a step-up in international operations.

Global IHRM Orientations

Global IHRM
Recruiting and selecting worldwide, and assigning the best managers to international assignments regardless of nationality.

Organizations with truly **global IHRM** orientations assign their best managers to international assignments.[86] Recruitment and selection take place worldwide, in any country where the best-quality employees can be found. The fit of the manager to the requirements of the job far outweighs any consideration of the individual's country of origin or of job assignment. Capable managers adapt easily to different cultures and are usually bilingual or multilingual. In addition, the international assignment becomes a prerequisite for a successful managerial career in companies with global orientations.

In companies with global orientations, managers are selected and trained to manage cultural diversity inside and outside the company. Employees inside their organization have culturally diverse backgrounds, and the company's multiple country locations provide culturally diverse customers and suppliers.[87] Besides confronting issues of cultural diversity, global managers must meet the coordination and control needs of corporate headquarters.[88] To meet these challenges successfully, managers need continual training in cultural adaptation and in the skills needed to balance local needs with overall company goals.[89]

As with other IHRM orientations, a global IHRM has its costs and benefits:[90]

Benefits

- *Bigger talent pool:* The available talent pool of managers and technical specialists is not limited by nationality or geography.
- *High international expertise:* Multinational companies develop a large group of experienced international managers.
- *Development of transnational organizational cultures:* Managers identify with the organizational culture more than with any national culture.

Costs

- *Difficulty in importing managerial and technical employees:* Host countries often have immigration laws that limit the use of foreign nationals or that make their use very costly.
- *Added expense:* Training and relocation costs are expensive. Expatriate compensation is higher than for host country employees.

Summary and Conclusions

This chapter introduced the basic HRM practices of recruitment, selection, training and development, performance appraisal, compensation, and labor relations. When these practices are applied to a company's international operations, they become IHRM, or international human resource management. Besides basic HRM functions, two key issues in IHRM are the mixture of expatriate and host country managers and knowing how to adapt home company HRM practices to the host country's situation. This chapter focused on HRM practices for expatriate employees. The next chapter reviews the differences in national HRM practices. Knowledge of these national differences helps multinational managers adapt IHRM to local conditions.

Expatriate managers present challenges and opportunities to multinational companies. They are costly, often costing two to three times as much as host country managers. They need special training to succeed even though they are not always successful. However, expatriate managers are loyal to the home organization, and they often have skills that are impossible to find in host country managers. It is important for multinational companies to find ways to properly manage their expatriates to fully benefit from the expatriates' experience.

As companies face a global shortage of managers, they will increasingly rely on their women managers to take on expatriate responsibilities. Multinationals therefore must heighten their awareness of the significant barriers their women managers face in taking international assignments, and they must do what is necessary to facilitate the female expatriates' experience.

Successful IHRM presents one of the most important challenges to multinational companies in the twenty-first century. Many globalization trends—the development of large-scale trading blocs, the opening of national boundaries for trade, and the increasing prevalence of international strategic alliances—offer multinational companies the opportunity to use human resources unrestrained by political, linguistic, and cultural boundaries. Companies, large and small, that exploit international human resources the most effectively will have strong competitive advantages in an increasingly global economy.

Discussion Questions

1. Identify the components of HRM and describe how they differ for IHRM.

2. Describe the types of nationals employed by multinational firms. Note likely situations when each type would be used.

3. Using the basic components of HRM as a guide, describe the likely practices used by a transnational firm.

4. Contrast the positive and negative issues for using short-term international cadre. Consider both the organization's perspective and the career implications for the individual manager.

5. Discuss the options available for expatriate compensation. Consider how these options might be used for a transnational and a multidomestic company.

6. Discuss how multinational companies can deal with the repatriation issue.

7. How can companies benefit from using women expatriates? Discuss some of the advantages women expatriates have over their male counterparts.

8. Discuss some of the major problems facing women expatriates. What can companies do to make their expatriate experience successful?

Multinational Management Skill Builder

A Presentation

You are the vice president of the human resource management department of a large multinational company. Your company has decided to expand overseas. It is possible that you may send expatriates around the world, including countries such as Australia, Japan, Mexico, Malaysia, India, South Africa, and Chile. You just came back from an important meeting with other VPs and the CEO. The major emphasis during the meeting was deciding which countries to expand into and how to ensure the expatriates' satisfaction with their overseas assignments and overall cost reductions because of efficiency pressures. You have been instructed to report some solutions to these pressing problems. As you prepare your presentation, you know that you need to address the following issues:

Step 1. Using as many sources of information as possible, prepare a list of types of information/issues that you can use to show the costs and benefits of sending the expatriates to the the preceding countries.

Step 2. Demonstrate the types of information and sources you can use for them.

Step 3. Demonstrate how capturing the various types of information can be beneficial to the company; and how such information can be used.

Step 4. Recommend one or a few countries.

Step 5. Present your findings to the class.

Endnotes

1 Milkovich, George T., and Jerry Newman. 1993. *Compensation*, 4th ed. Homewood, IL: Irwin; Bohlander, George W., Scott Snell, and Arthur W. Sherman Jr. 2001. *Managing Human Resources*, 12th ed. Cincinnati, OH: South-Western.

2 Mayerhofer, Helene, Linley C. Hartmann, and Anne Herbert. 2004. "Career management issues for flexpatriate international staff." *Thunderbird International Business Review*, November–December, 46(6), pp. 647–666.

3 Quelch, John A., and Helen Bloom. "Ten steps to a global human resources strategy." *Strategy & Business*, 1st quarter, pp. 2–13.

4 Black, J. Stewart, Hal B. Gregersen, and Mark E. Mendenhall. 1992. *Global Assignments*. San Francisco: Jossey-Bass; Quelch and Bloom; Tung, Rosalie L. 1981. "Selection and training of personnel for overseas assignments." *Columbia Journal of World Business*, 16 (1), pp. 68–78.

5 Melvin, Sheila. 1997. "Shipping out." *The China Business Review*, 24, pp. 30–35.

6 Rafer, M. V. 2009. "Return trip for expats." *Workforce Management*, March 16, pp. 1, 3.

7 Ashamalla, Maali H. 1998. "International human resource management practices: The challenge of expatriation." *Competitiveness Review*, 8(2), pp. 54–65.

8 McFarland, Jean. 2006. "Culture shock." *Benefits Canada*, January 30, 1, p. 31.

9 *Business Wire*. 2006. "International job assignment: Boon or bust for an employee's career?" March 13, p. 1.

10 Harzing, Anne-Wil, and Claus Christensen. 2004. "Think piece: Expatriate failure: Time to abandon the concept?" *Career Development International*, 9(6/7), pp. 616–626.

11 McCaughey, Deirdre, and Nealia S. Bruning. 2005. "Enhancing opportunities for expatriate job satisfaction: HR strategies for foreign assignment success." *HR Human Resources Planning*, 28 (4), pp. 21–29.

12 Ashamalla, Maali H. 1998. "International human resource management practices: The challenge of expatriation." *Competitiveness Review*, 8(2), pp. 54–65; Harzing and Christensen; McCall, Morgan W, and George P. Hollenbeck. 2002. "Global fatalities: When international executives derail." *Ivey Business Journal*, May–June, pp. 74–78; McCaughey and Bruning; Poe, Andrea C. 2002. "Welcome back." *HRMagazine*, 45(3), pp. 94–101; Tung, Rosalie L. 1987. "Expatriate assignments: Enhancing success and minimizing failure." *Academy of Management Executive*, 1(2), pp. 117–126.

13 Fink, Gerhard, Sylvia Meierewert, and Ulrike Rohr. 2005. "The use of repatriate knowledge in organizations." *HR Human Resources Planning*, 28(4), pp. 30–36; Gregersen, Hal B. 1999. "The right way to manage expats." *Harvard Business Review*, March–April, pp. 52–61; Lublin, Joann S. 1992. "Younger managers learn global skills." *Wall Street Journal*, March 3, p. B1; O'Connor, Robert. 2002. "Plug the expat knowledge drain." *HRMagazine*, October, pp. 101–107.

14 Korbin, Stephen J. 1988. "Expatriate reduction and strategic control in American multinational corporations." *Human Resource Management*, 27(1), pp. 63–75.

15 Gregersen.

16 Boyacigiller, Nakiye A. 1991. "The international assignment reconsidered." In Mark Mendendhall and Gary Oddou, eds. *Readings and Cases in International Human Resource Management*. Boston: PWS-Kent, pp. 148–155.

17 O'Connor.

18 Fink, Meierewert, and Rohr.

19 Ibid.

20 Micciche, T. 2009. "Preparation and data management are key for a successful expatriate program." *Employment Relations Today*, Spring, pp. 35–39.

21 Poe.

22 Sims, Robert H., and Mike Schraeder. 2005. "Expatriate compensation: An exploratory review of salient contextual factors and common practices." *Career Development International*, 10(2), pp. 98–108.

23 Selmer, J. 2002. "Practice makes perfect? International experience and expatriate adjustment." *Management International Review*, January, 42(1), pp. 71–87.

24 Tung, "Selection and training of personnel for overseas assignments."

25 Gregersen; Halcrow. Allan. 1999. "Expats: The squandered resource." *Workforce*, July, 3, pp. 28–30; Mendenhall, Mark, and Gary Oddou. 1985. "The dimensions of expatriate acculturation: A review." *Academy of Management Review* 10, pp. 39–47; Poe; Tung, "Selection and training of personnel for overseas assignments."

26 Tye, Mary G., and Peter Y. Chen. 2005. "Selection of expatriates: Decision-making models used by HR professionals." *HR Human Resource Planning*, 28(4), p. 15.

27 Ibid.

28 Gabel, Racheli Shmueli, Shimon L. Dolan, and Jean Luc Cerdin. 2005. "Emotional intelligence as predictor of cultural adjustment for success in global assignments." *Career Development International*, 10(5), pp. 375–395.

29 Tung, "Selection and training of personnel: Decision-making models used by HR professionals."

30 Black, J. Stewart, and Mark E. Mendenhall. 1990. "Cross-culture training effectiveness: A review and theoretical framework for future research." *Academy of Management Review*, 15, pp. 113–36; Forster, Nick. 2000. "Expatriates and the impact of cross-cultural training." *Human Resource Management Journal*, 10, pp. 63–78.

31 Forster.

32 Winham International. 2000. "Survey highlights." http://www.windhamint.com.

33 Black, Gregersen, and Mendenhall.

34 Mendenhall, Mark, and Gary Oddou. 1988. "Acculturation profiles of expatriate managers: Implications for cross-cultural training programs." *Columbia Journal of World Business* 21, pp. 73–79; Tung, "Selection and training of personnel for overseas assignments."

35 Dowling, Peter J., Denice E. Welch, and Randall S. Schuler. 1999. *International Human Resource Management*. Cincinnati, OH: Southwestern.

36 Black, Gregersen, and Mendenhall.

37 Sims and Schraeder.

38 Ibid.; *Employee Benefits*. 2006. "Sending perks overseas." February 10, p. S10.

39 Davis, Debra A. 2005. "Paying the piper: Taxation of global employees." *Journal of Pension Benefits*, Autumn, 13(1), p. 85.

40 Frazee, Valerie. 1998. "Is the balance sheet right for your expats?" *Workforce*, 3, pp. 19–23.

41 Overman, Stephenie. 2000. "In sync." *HRMagazine*, 45(3), pp. 86–92.

42 Sims and Schraeder.

43 Dowling, Welch, and Schuler.

44 Black, Gregersen, and Mendenhall.

45 Ibid.

46 Frazee; Overman.

47 Sims and Schraeder.

48 Overman.

49 Gregersen.

50 Klaff, Leslie G. 2002. "The right way to bring expats home." *Workforce*, July, pp. 40–44; Poe.

51 Black, Gregersen, and Mendenhall.

52 Klaff.

53 Gregersen.

54 Klaff; Gregersen; Black, Gregersen, and Mendenhall; Tyler, Kathryn. 2006. "Retaining repatriates." *HRMagazine*, March, 51(5), pp. 97–102

55 Rafer, M.V. 2009. "Return trip for expats." *Workforce Management*, March 16, pp. 1, 3.

56 Lancaster, Hal. 1999. "To get shipped abroad, women must overcome prejudice at home." *Wall Street Journal*, June 29, p. B1.

57 Caligiuri, P. M. and R. Tung. 1999. "Comparing the success of male and female expatriates from a US based company." *International Journal of Human Resource Management*, 10(5), pp. 163–179.

58 Harris, Hillary. 2002. "Think international manager, think male: Why are women not selected in international management assignments?" *Thunderbird International Business Review*, 44(2), pp. 175–203.

59 Linehan, Margaret. 2000. *Senior female international managers: Why so few.* Ashgate, UK: Aldershot.

60 Jelinek, Mariann, and Nancy J. Adler. 1988. "Women: World-class managers for global competition." *Academy of Management Executive*, 11(1), pp. 11–19; Stroh, Linda K., Arup Varma, and Stacy J. Valy-Durbin. 2000. "Why are women left at home: Are they unwilling to go on international assignments?" *Journal of World Business*, 35, pp. 241–255.

61 Izraeli, Dafna, and Yoram Zeira. 1993. "Women managers in international business: A research review and appraisal." *Business and the Contemporary World*, Summer, pp. 35–46.

62 Linehan.

63 Inshc, G. S., N. McIntyre, and N. Napier. 2008. "The expatriate glass ceiling: The second layer of glass." *Journal of Business Ethics*, 83, pp. 19–28.

64 Adler, Nancy J. 1993. "Women managers in a global economy." *HRMagazine*, September, pp. 52–55.

65 Ibid.

66 Adler, Nancy J. "Pacific basin managers: A *gaijin*, not a woman." *Human Resource Management*, 26(2), pp. 169–191.

67 Solomon, Julie. 1989. "Women, minorities and foreign postings." *Wall Street Journal*, June 2, p. B1.

68 Adler, "Pacific basin managers: A *gaijin*, not a woman."

69 Adler, "Women managers in a global economy."

70 Linehan, Margaret, and Hugh Scullion. 2001. "European female expatriate careers: critical success factors." *Journal of European Industrial Training*, 25(8), pp. 392–418.

71 O'Leary, V. E., and J. L Johnson. 1991. "Steep ladder, lonely climb." *Women in Management Review and Abstracts*, 6(5), pp. 10–16.

72 Parasuraman, S. J., and J. H. Greenhaus. 1993. "Personal portraits: The lifestyle of the woman manager." In E. A. Fagenson, ed. *Women in Management: Trends, Issues and Challenges in Management Diversity.* London: Sage, pp. 186–211.

73 Davidson, M. J., and C. L. Cooper. 1983. *Stress and the Woman Manager.* London: Martin Robertson.

74 Adler, "Pacific basin managers: A *gaijin*, not a woman."

75 Volkmar, John, and Kate L. Westbrook. 2005. "Does a decade make a difference? A second look at western women working in Japan." *Women in Management Review*, 20(7), pp. 464–477.

76 Thaler-Carter, Ruth E. 1999. "Vowing to go abroad." *HRMagazine*, 44(12), pp. 90–96.

77 Izraeli and Zeira.

78 Linehan and Scullion.

79 Davidson and Cooper.

80 Inshc, McIntyre, and Napier.

81 Mendenhall, Mark E., E. Dunbar, and Gary R. Oddou. 1987. "Expatriate selection, training and career-pathing: A review and critique." *Human Resource Management*, 26(3), pp. 331–345.

82 Dowling, Peter J., and Denice E. Welch. 1988. "International human resource management: An Australian perspective." *Asia Pacific Journal of Management*, 6(1), pp. 39–65; Reynolds, Calvin. 1997. "Strategic employment of third country nationals." *Human Resource Planning*, 20(1), pp. 33–39.

83 Adler, Nancy J., and Fariborz Ghadar. 1990. "International strategy from the perspective of people and culture: The North American context." *Research in Global Business Management*, 1, pp. 179–205; Bohlander, Snell, and Sherman.

84 Adler and Ghadar.

85 Dowling and Welch; Reynolds.

86 Quelch and Bloom.

87 Ibid.

88 Bartlett, Christopher A., and Sumantra Ghoshal. 1998. *Managing Across Borders*, 2nd ed. Boston: Harvard Business School Press.

89 Quelch and Bloom.

90 Dowling and Welch.

The Road to Hell

John Baker, chief engineer of the Caribbean Bauxite Company of Barracania in the West Indies, was making his final preparations to leave the island. His promotion to production manager of Keso Mining Corporation near Winnipeg—one of Continental Ore's fast expanding Canadian enterprises—had been announced a month before, and now everything had been tidied up except the last vital interview with his successor, the able young Barracanian, Matthew Rennalls. It was vital that this interview be a success and that Baker should leave his office uplifted and encouraged to face the challenge of his new job. A touch on the bell would have brought Rennalls walking into the room, but Baker delayed the moment and gazed thoughtfully through the window, considering just exactly what he was going to say and, more particularly, how he was going to say it.

John Baker, an English expatriate, was forty-five years old and had served his twenty-three years with Continental Ore in many different places: in the Far East, in several countries of Africa, in Europe, and, for the last two years, in the West Indies. He hadn't cared much for his previous assignment in Hamburg and was delighted when the West Indian appointment came through. Climate was not the only attraction. Baker had always preferred working overseas (in what were termed the developing countries) because he felt he had an innate knack—more than most other expatriates working for Continental Ore—of knowing just how to get on with regional staff. After only twenty-four hours in Barracania, however, he realized that he would need all of his innate knack if he was going to deal effectively with the problems that awaited him.

At that time, in his first interview with Hutchins, the production manager, the whole problem of Rennalls and his future were discussed. It was made quite clear to Baker that one of his most important tasks would be the grooming of Rennalls as his successor. Hutchins had pointed out that not only was Rennalls one of the brightest Barracanian prospects on the staff of Caribbean Bauxite—at London University he had taken first-class honors in the B.Sc. engineering degree—but also, as the son of the minister of finance and economic planning, he had no small political pull.

The company managers had been particularly pleased when Rennalls decided to work for them rather than for the government in which his father had such a prominent post. They ascribed his decision to the effect of their vigorous and liberal regionalization program, which, since World War II, had produced 18 Barracanians at midmanagement level and had given Caribbean Bauxite a good lead in this respect over all other international concerns operating in Barracania. The success of the regionalization policy led to excellent relations with the government—a relationship that was given added importance when Barracania, three years later, became independent, an occasion that encouraged a critical and challenging attitude toward the role foreign interests would have to play in the new Barracania. Hutchins had therefore little difficulty in convincing Baker that the successful career development of Rennalls was of primary importance.

The interview with Hutchins was now two years old, and Baker, leaning back in his office chair, reviewed just how successful he had been in grooming Rennalls. What aspects of the latter's character had helped and what had hindered? Baker reflected on his own personality. How had that helped or hindered? The first item to go on the credit side would, without question, be Rennalls's ability to master the technical aspects of his job. From the start he had shown keenness and enthusiasm and had often impressed Baker with his ability in tackling new assignments and with the constructive comments he invariably made in departmental discussions. He was popular with all ranks of Barracanian staff and had an ease of manner that stood him in good stead when dealing with his expatriate seniors. These were all assets.

But what about the debit side? First and foremost, there was his racial consciousness. His four years at London University had accentuated this feeling and made him sensitive to any sign of condescension on the part of expatriates. It may have been to give expression to this sentiment that, as soon as he returned home from London, he threw himself into politics on behalf of the United Action Party, which was later to win the preindependence elections and provide the country with its first prime minister.

The ambitions of Rennalls—and he certainly was ambitious—did not, however, lie in politics. As staunch a nationalist as he was, he saw that he could serve himself and his country best (for was not bauxite responsible for nearly half the value of Barracania's export trade?) by putting his engineering talent to the highest use possible. On this account, Hutchins found that he had an unexpectedly easy task in persuading Rennalls to give up his political work before entering the production department as an assistant engineer.

Baker knew that Rennalls's well-repressed sense of race consciousness had prevented their relationship from being as close as it should have been. On the surface, nothing could have seemed more agreeable. Formality between the two men was at a minimum. Baker was delighted to find that his assistant shared his own peculiar "shaggy dog" sense of humor so that they continually exchanged jokes; they entertained each other at their houses and often played tennis together. Yet the barrier remained invisible, indefinable, but ever present. The existence of this screen between them was a constant source of frustration to Baker because it indicated a weakness that he was loath to accept. If he could be successful with all other nationalities, why not with Rennalls?

But at least he had managed to break through to Rennalls more than any other expatriate. In fact, it was the young Barracanian's attitude—sometimes overbearing, sometimes cynical—toward other company expatriates that had been one of the subjects Baker had raised last year when he discussed Rennalls's staff report with him. He knew, too, that he would have to raise the same subject again in the forthcoming interview because Jackson, the senior draftsman, had complained only yesterday about Rennalls's rudeness. With this thought in mind, Baker leaned forward and spoke into the intercom. "Would you come in Matt, please? I'd like a word with you." When Rennalls came in, he said, "Do sit down," proffering the box. "Have a cigarette." He paused while he held out his lighter and then went on.

"As you know, Matt, I'll be off to Canada in a few days' time, and before I go, I thought it would be useful if we could have a final chat together. It is indeed with some deference that I suggest I can be of help. You will shortly be sitting in this chair doing the job I am now doing, but I, on the other hand, am ten years older, so perhaps you can accept the idea that I may be able to give you the benefit of my longer experience."

Baker saw Rennalls stiffen slightly in his chair as he made this point; so he added in explanation. "You and I have attended enough company courses to remember those repeated requests by the personnel manager to tell people how they are getting on as often as the convenient moment arises and not just the automatic 'once a year' when, by regulation, staff reports have to be discussed."

Rennalls nodded his agreement; so Baker went on. "I shall always remember the last job performance discussion I had with my previous boss back in Germany. He used what he called the plus and minus technique. His firm belief was that when a senior, by discussion, seeks to improve the work performance of his staff, his prime objective should be to make sure that the latter leaves the interview encouraged and inspired to improve. Any criticism must therefore be constructive and helpful. He said that one very good way to encourage a person—and I fully agree with him—is to tell him about his good points—the plus factors—as well as his weak ones—the minus factors. So I thought, Matt, it would be a good idea to run our discussion along these lines."

Rennalls offered no comment; so Baker continued: "Let me say right away that, as far as your own work performance is concerned, the plus far outweighs the minus. I have, for instance, been most impressed with the way you have adapted your considerable theoretical knowledge to master the practical techniques of your job—that ingenious method you used to get air down to the fifth shaft level is a sufficient case in point—and at departmental meetings I have invariably found your comments well-taken and helpful. In fact, you will be interested to know that only last week I reported to Mr. Hutchins that, from the technical point of view, he could not wish for a more able man to succeed to the position of chief engineer."

"That's very good indeed of you, John," cut in Rennalls with a smile of thanks. "My only worry now is how to live up to such a high recommendation."

"Of that I am quite sure," returned Baker, "especially if you can overcome the minus factor, which I would like now to discuss with you. It is one which I have talked about before so I'll come straight to the point. I noticed that you are more friendly and get on better with your fellow Barracanians than you do with Europeans. In point of fact, I had a complaint only yesterday from Mr. Jackson, who said you had been rude to him—and not for the first time either.

"There is, Matt, I am sure, no need for me to tell you how necessary it will be for you to get on well with expatriates because until the company has trained up sufficient people of your caliber, Europeans are bound to occupy senior positions here in Barracania. All this is vital to your future interests, so can I help you in any way?"

While Baker was speaking on this theme, Rennalls had sat tensed in his chair, and it was some seconds before he replied. "It is quite extraordinary, isn't it, how one can convey an impression to others so at variance with what one intends? I can only assure you once again that my disputes with Jackson—and you may remember also Godson—have had nothing at all to do with the color of their skin. I promise you that if a Barracanian had behaved in an equally peremptory manner I would have reacted in precisely the same way. And again, if I may say it within these four walls, I am sure I am not the only one who has found Jackson and Godson difficult. I could mention the names of several expatriates who have felt the same. However, I am really sorry to have created this impression of not being able to get on with Europeans. It is an entirely false one, and I quite realize that I must do all I can to correct it—and must do so as quickly as possible. On your last point, regarding Europeans holding senior positions in the company for some time to come, I quite accept the situation. I know that Caribbean Bauxite—as it has been doing for many years now—will promote Barracanians as soon as their experience warrants it. And, finally, I would like to assure you, John—and my father thinks the same too—that I am very happy in my work here and hope to stay with the company for many years to come."

Rennalls had spoken earnestly and, although not convinced by what he had heard, Baker did not think he could pursue the matter further except to say, "All right, Matt, my impression may be wrong, but I would like to remind you of that old saying, 'What is important is not what is true but what is believed.' Let it rest at that."

But suddenly Baker knew that he didn't want to "let it rest at that." He was disappointed once again at not being able to break through to Rennalls and having yet again to listen to his bland denial that there was any racial prejudice in his makeup. Baker, who had intended ending the interview at this point, decided to try another tack.

"To return for a moment to the plus-and-minus technique I was telling you about just now, there is another plus factor I forgot to mention. I would like to congratulate you not only on the caliber of your work but also on the ability you have shown in overcoming a challenge which I, as a European, have never had to meet."

"Continental Ore is, as you know, a typical commercial enterprise—admittedly a big one—which is a product of the economic and social environment of the United States and Western Europe. My ancestors have all been brought up in this environment for the past two or three hundred years, and I have therefore been able to live in a world in which commerce (as we know it today) has been part and parcel of my being. It has not been something revolutionary and new which has suddenly entered my life. In your case," Baker went on, "the situation is different because you and your forebears have only had some fifty or sixty years' experience with this commercial environment. You have had to face the challenge of bridging the gap between fifty and two or three hundred years. Again, Matt, let me congratulate you—and people like you—once again on

having so successfully overcome this particular hurdle. It is for this very reason that I think the outlook for Barracania—and particularly Caribbean Bauxite—is so bright."

Rennalls had listened intently and, when Baker finished, replied, "Well, once again, John, I have to thank you for what you have said, and, for my part, I can only say that it is gratifying to know that my own personal effort has been so much appreciated. I hope that more people will soon come to think as you do."

There was a pause, and for a moment Baker thought hopefully that he was about to achieve his long awaited breakthrough, but Rennalls merely smiled back. The barrier remained unbreached. There remained some five minutes' cheerful conversation about the contrast between the Caribbean and Canadian climates and whether the West Indies had any hope of beating England in the Fifth Test before Baker drew the interview to a close. Although he was as far as ever from knowing the real Rennalls, he was nevertheless glad that the interview had run along in this friendly manner and particularly that it had ended on such a cheerful note.

This feeling, however, lasted only until the following morning. Baker had some farewells to make, so he arrived at the office considerably later than usual. He had no sooner sat down at his desk than his secretary walked into the room with a worried frown on her face. Her words came fast. "When I arrived this morning, I found Mr. Rennalls already waiting at my door. He seemed very angry and told me in quite a peremptory manner that he had a vital letter to dictate which must be sent off without any delay. He was so worked up that he couldn't keep still and kept pacing about the room, which is most unlike him. He wouldn't even wait to read what he had dictated. Just signed the page where he thought the letter would end. It has been distributed and your copy is in your in tray."

Puzzled and feeling vaguely uneasy, Baker opened the envelope marked "Confidential" and read the following letter:

From: Assistant Engineer
To: The Chief Engineer, Caribbean Bauxite
Limited
*14th August, 196_*

ASSESSMENT OF INTERVIEW
BETWEEN MESSRS.
BAKER AND RENNALLS

It has always been my practice to respect the advice given me by seniors, so after our interview, I decided to give careful thought once again to its main points and so make sure that I had understood all that had been said. As I promised you at the time, I had every intention of putting your advice to the best effect.

It was not, therefore, until I had sat down quietly in my home yesterday evening to consider the interview objectively that its main purport became clear. Only then did the full enormity of what you said dawn on me. The more I thought about it, the more convinced I was that I had hit upon the real truth—and the more furious I became. With a facility in the English language which I—a poor Barracanian—cannot hope to match, you had the audacity to insult me (and through me every Barracanian worth his salt) by claiming that our knowledge of modern living is only a paltry fifty years old whilst yours goes back 200–300 years. As if your materialistic commercial environment could possibly be compared with the spiritual values of our culture. I'll have you know that if much of what I saw in London is representative of your most boasted culture, I hope fervently that it will never come to Barracania. By what right do you have the effrontery to condescend to us? At heart, all you Europeans think us barbarians, or, as you say amongst yourselves, we are "just down from the trees."

Far into the night I discussed this matter with my father, and he is as disgusted as I. He agrees with me that any company whose senior staff think as you do is no place for any Barracanian proud of his culture and race—so much for all the company "clap-trap" and specious propaganda about regionalization and Barracania for the Barracanians.

I feel ashamed and betrayed. Please accept this letter as my resignation, which I wish to become effective immediately.

c.c. Production Manager
Managing Director

CASE DISCUSSION QUESTIONS

1. What are the strengths and weaknesses of the performance review technique used by Baker?
2. Should Baker have anticipated Rennalls's reaction to his performance review? Why?
3. What issues of cultural sensitivity are germane for understanding the case? Was it the performance review or Baker's interaction style that prompted Rennalls's resignation?
4. Why was Baker's extensive international experience not helpful in dealing with Rennalls?
5. If you were Baker, what would you do now?

CASE CREDIT

Prepared by Gareth Evans for Shell-BP Development Co. of Nigeria Ltd., Intercollegiate Case Clearing House, Soldiers Field, Boston, MA 02163.

Learning Objectives

After reading this chapter you should be able to:

- Have a basic understanding of how the national context affects HRM practices.

- Describe how recruitment and selection practices differ among national contexts.

- Identify possible host adaptations in recruitment and selection practices for a multinational company.

- Explain how training and development techniques are used in different countries.

- Name sources of high-quality workers in different nations.

- Understand how training must be adapted to host country workers.

- Identify how performance evaluation and compensation practices differ in various national contexts.

- Discuss possible host country adaptations in performance evaluation and compensation practices for a multinational company.

- Understand how labor costs vary among nations.

- Appreciate how the national context and historical conditions affect the relationship of management and labor in different countries.

Preview CASE IN POINT

Following Local Traditions

The United States is the only industrialized country without government-mandated vacation time. Employees in U.S. firms average just two weeks of vacation per year. In contrast, their European counterparts receive an average of five to six weeks of vacation annually. Countries such as Italy, France, Germany, Spain, Sweden, and others have regulations that guarantee workers at least a month of paid annual vacation. It is therefore not surprising that U.S workers are likely to work about 250 more hours a year than workers in Western Europe. Although many U.S. managers see the European vacation as excessive, European managers counter that U.S. organizations have misplaced goals.

When Nokia decided to open a new plant, it chose Cluj, a city of 400,000 in Romania. Why Cluj? Nokia found that it is difficult to recruit and retain skilled workers in many emerging cities in India and China. In fact, experts argue that, although both India and China have an increasing number of qualified graduates, recruiting quality staff is becoming increasingly difficult. In contrast, Cluj has a plentiful supply of workers who are very eager to get these jobs. However, because one of the major success factors in the mobile phone business is maximum productivity, Nokia realizes that it had to respect local customs and give workers the appropriate incentives to make the plant succeed. Nokia planned to give workers free food, a gym, and even playing fields. Furthermore, as a show of respect for the local culture, foreign staffers will have to study Romanian.

Sources: Based on Beacham, W. 2009. "Competition for talent is still fierce." ICIS Chemical Business, February 2, 8, p. 5; Ewing, J. 2008. "Nokia's new home in Romania." Business-Week, Janaury 28, pp. 41–42; Poe, Andrea C. 1999. "When in Rome . . . European law and tradition back generous vacation policies." HRMagazine, p. 44; HR Magazine Online Archive, http://www.my.SHRM.org; Simmers, Tim. 2005. "Workers in U.S. labor longer with less vacation than others." Business Writer, December 10, p. 1.

The Preview Case in Point shows several issues that can affect how multinational companies conduct business in a host country. Similar critical questions might be: How do you hire a worker in Mexico? What educational background can you expect from German workers? Can you lay off workers in Denmark? What would happen in Japan if you promoted a 30-year-old to supervise 40-year-old employees? What kind of relationships should you expect with unions in South Africa?

To avoid costly mistakes in human resource management, multinational companies need to consider several key questions regarding local employees such as:[1]

- How can we identify talented local employees?
- How can we attract the prospective employees to apply for jobs?
- Can we use our home country's training methods with local employees?
- What types of appraisal methods are customary?
- What types of rewards do local people value (e.g., security, pay, benefits)?
- Do any local laws affect staffing, compensation, and training decisions?

To show the impact of the national context (national and business cultures and social institutions) on human resource management, this chapter illustrates varied practices from the United States and other countries. The chapter builds on your understanding of international human resource management (IHRM), discussed in Chapter 11. Reading both chapters will help you, the multinational manager, select and implement appropriate human resource management policies and, when necessary, adapt the policies to the local environment.

Why Do Nations Differ in HRM?

Cross-national differences in HRM and the pressures to adapt to local conditions arise from the array of factors that make each nation unique. As we saw in Chapter 3, these factors are called the **national context** and include such things as the national culture, the country's available labor and other natural resources, the characteristics of political and legal institutions, the types of managers available to firms, social institutions, national and business culture, factor conditions, and their combined effects on the business environment. Thus, the national context provides the unique setting for each nation in which managers make HRM decisions. Exhibit 12.1 shows a model of how the national context leads to national differences in HRM policies and practices.

National context
National culture and social institutions that influence how managers make decisions regarding the strategies of their organizations.

Chapters 2 and 3 showed that the values and norms associated with national and business cultures result in preferred ways of doing business. These preferences influence all aspects of the organization: strategies, organizational design, and human resource practices. Basic norms and values regarding gender, age, and family and friends influence HRM practices from recruitment to performance appraisal.

Because countries' social institutions differ widely, multinational managers must select and implement HRM practices that meet the demands of a society's social institutions. Just as social institutions relate to how relationships are structured among people, they help define the correct ways of doing business in a country. In the United States, for example, antidiscrimination laws, part of the legal social institution, prohibit many recruitment practices common in Japanese and Korean companies. In Japan, the family system relies on women raising children so that men can work long hours at night or be away from home for

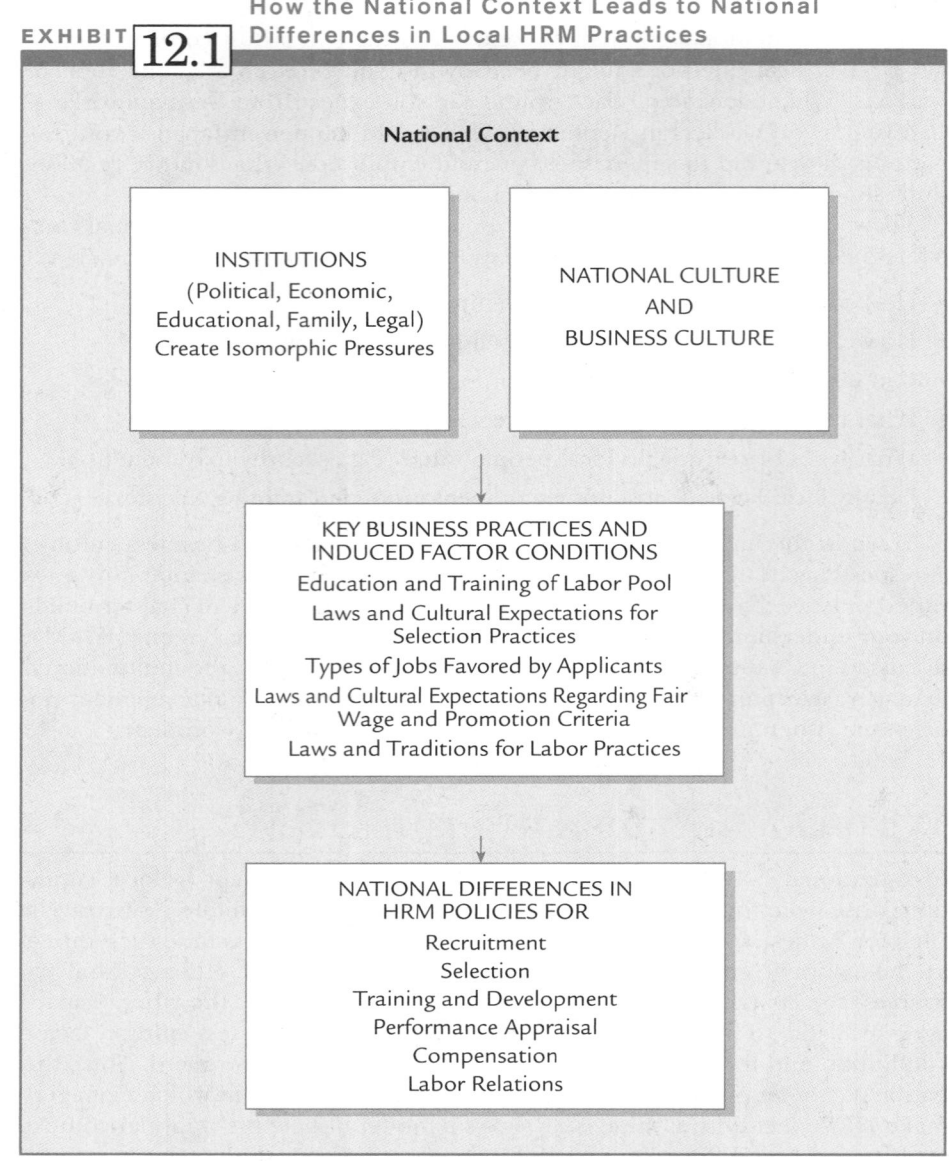

EXHIBIT 12.1   How the National Context Leads to National Differences in Local HRM Practices

National Context

INSTITUTIONS
(Political, Economic,
Educational, Family, Legal)
Create Isomorphic Pressures

NATIONAL CULTURE
AND
BUSINESS CULTURE

KEY BUSINESS PRACTICES AND
INDUCED FACTOR CONDITIONS

Education and Training of Labor Pool

Laws and Cultural Expectations for
Selection Practices

Types of Jobs Favored by Applicants

Laws and Cultural Expectations Regarding Fair
Wage and Promotion Criteria

Laws and Traditions for Labor Practices

NATIONAL DIFFERENCES IN
HRM POLICIES FOR

Recruitment
Selection
Training and Development
Performance Appraisal
Compensation
Labor Relations

extended periods. As such, there are unwritten biases against women holding managerial positions after they have children.

The national context also includes the pool of resources available for firms. The **resource pool** represents all the human and physical resources available in a country. Examples are the quality of labor, the availability of scientific laboratories, and sources of fuel. If all countries had access to the same resources, there would be fewer differences across nations in management practices. Regardless of nationality, if firms could access the same resources, they would copy the strategies and organizations of the most successful competitors in the world. However, the national endowments of physical resources (e.g., supply of raw materials) and other resources (e.g., culturally based motivations to work, educational systems) are unique to each country.

Resource pool
All the human and physical resources available in a country.

The resource pool represents the factor conditions associated with a country. Five key factors influence the resource pool and, in turn, the management practices favored by firms in a given nation:[2]

1. *The quality, quantity, and accessibility of raw material:* For example, the extensive tracts of fertile land in the United States enable U.S. agricultural firms to compete with low prices and high quality on the world market.

2. *The quantity, quality, and cost of personnel available:* Germany, for example, has large pools of technically trained workers who support the development of industries and firms where high-quality differentiation strategies abound. In contrast, however, German workers are among the most highly paid in the world, thus making low-cost strategies difficult.

3. *The scientific, technical, and market-related knowledge available to firms:* Both Japan and the United States, for example, have abundant stores of scientific and technical knowledge from universities and industry-based R&D. Additionally, in countries like China and Taiwan, the government is taking an active role in reshaping the educational system in order to encourage people to get trained in more knowledge-oriented sectors.[3]

4. *The cost and amount of capital available to firms for operations and expansion:* This factor addresses the question of how firms get financing to run their operations. For example, during the double-digit expansion of the Korean economy, Korean *chaebol* (conglomerates) relied mostly on heavy debt financing from government-controlled banks. In a post-1998 Korean economy, reeling from the shock of failing *chaebol* and a weakened currency, Korean banks were less likely to loan money to debt-ridden companies.

5. *The type, quality, and costs of supporting institutions such as the systems of communication, education, and transportation:* Nations differ widely in the supporting resources necessary to run a business. Trained workers are a critical resource, but factors such as reliable phones and the ability to transport goods cheaply and predictably are also important.

Some resources, called **natural factor conditions**, occur naturally. For example, countries with extensive coal and gas reserves favor the development of industries and firms that require high energy consumption. Canada has abundant sources of the water necessary for the efficient production of aluminum.

Natural factor conditions
National resources that occur naturally, such as abundant water supply.

Other resources, called **induced factor conditions**, arise from cultural and institutional pressures. For example, the high cultural value placed on education in many Asian societies helps create a well-trained workforce for countries like Singapore and Korea. Social institutions such as the government can affect induced factor conditions. For example, the knowledge base available to the Japanese robotics industry is facilitated by the more than 180 Japanese universities that created robotics laboratories and the $20 million a year contributed to program development by the Japanese Ministry of International Trade and Industry.[4]

Induced factor conditions
National resources created by a nation, such as a superior educational system.

As the model shows, the national and business cultures combine with social institutions to affect the business environment and certain factor conditions. In turn, this national context determines a company's management practices and policies and eventually its types of HRM adaptations. This chapter outlines the major national context characteristics that affect HRM, which are as follows:

- *Education and training of the labor pool:* The type and quality of labor available to companies is a key issue in HRM. A country's educational system provides the raw human resource material for companies. Later you will see how the German system of specialized training dominates key aspects of German HRM.

- *Laws and cultural expectations of selection practices:* The laws of a country and people's expectations tell managers the "right" way to find new employees. In some nations, for example, you are expected to hire your relatives. In other nations, it might be against a company's policies to do so. Sometimes it is considered common and necessary to ask women job applicants if they plan to get married soon, but asking a job applicant such a question in the United States would be illegal and discriminatory.

- *Types of jobs favored by applicants:* Japanese college graduates prefer to be hired by big companies. They are attracted by the security of working for a large company. Most Chinese businesses are family dominated, and family members expect to work for and with other family members. These examples illustrate cultural values and norms regarding the "best" and "right" places to work.

- *Laws and cultural expectations regarding fair wages and promotion criteria:* Should older workers make more money than younger workers? Should men be promoted faster than women? Should people who enter the company together make the same salary and be promoted together? Should a worker's family situation influence his or her salary? Due to cultural expectations and institutional pressures, the answers to such questions vary according to national context. Values, norms, and institutional expectations influence compensation decisions and the relationship between performance appraisals and compensation. For example, U.S. multinational managers often find that the link between compensation and performance, considered legal and fair in U.S. companies, is considered less important in other nations.

Multinational Management Brief

Kidnappings in France

France has always had contentious labor relations. Its laws and traditions empower employees to have strong unions and to fight for their rights. Furthermore, the French population has very little sympathy for businesses, seeing them as the root of many problems. Experts are therefore not surprised to see many top-level executives being held hostage by workers who are trying to get better working conditions or better severance packages as they get laid off. In fact, several major companies, such as Sony and Michelin, have had top-level executives held hostage after announcing impending layoffs. Serge Foucher, the head of Sony in France, was released the next day after agreeing to pay better severance packages. The French tire manufacturer Michelin saw two of its top-level executives locked up after it announced plans to close a plant.

Although executive kidnapping is fairly popular in France, workers in other countries typically use less drastic measures to fight for their rights. For instance, sit-ins are very popular in the United States. However, some experts believe that executive kidnappings could easily happen in other countries as workers deal with rashes of layoffs in an economic downturn.

Source: Based on Economist. *2009. "Kidnapped," March 21, p. 68.*

• *Laws and traditions regarding labor practices:* The legal position and power of unions and the historical relationships between management and labor have profound influences on HRM practices in labor relations. For example, in some nations labor-management conflict has long-term historical precedents. However, labor conflict and the popularity of unions among workers differ by national context. Consider the previous Multinational Management Brief.

The remainder of this chapter illustrates the impact of national context on HRM practices in several nations. These examples only hint at the extent of differences among national HRM practices. To understand a particular host country's HRM practices, multinational managers must pay careful attention to the relevant values, norms, and laws.

For comparison purposes, each basic task of HRM is treated by contrasting the dominant practices in the United States with those of other nations. The tasks considered are recruitment, selection, training and development, performance appraisal, compensation, and labor relations.

Recruitment

Exhibit 12.2 summarizes the major steps in recruitment. First, managers determine that there are vacancies, which may occur in anticipation of expansion or as the result of workers leaving the organization. Second, employers determine the types of people and skills necessary for the job. Third, employers generate a pool of applicants.

Recruitment strategies to generate the applicant pool include:

• Walk-ins or unsolicited applications.

• Advertisements placed in newspapers or on the Internet.

• Company Web site job postings—listings of vacant positions on the firm's Web site.

• Internal job postings—company listings of vacant jobs targeted at current employees.

EXHIBIT 12.2   Steps in the Recruiting Process

- Jobs open
- Applicant characteristics identified
- Recruitment strategies applied
    - Walk-ins
    - Newspaper and other advertising (e.g., Internet)
    - Job positions posted in organization
    - State and private employment services
    - Educational institutions
    - Employee referrals
- Applications received

Sources: Adapted from Bohlander, George W., and Scott, Snell. 2009. Managing Human Resources; *Cincinnati, OH: South-Western; Werther, William B., and Keith, Davis. 1993.* Human Resources and Personnel Management. *New York: McGraw-Hill.*

- Public and private personnel agencies.
- Placement services of educational institutions.
- Current employee recommendations.

Managers hope that one or more of these recruitment strategies will generate a pool of applicants who are qualified for the vacant job.

Most national differences in recruitment occur in the preferences for types of strategies. National and business cultures determine the "right way" to find employees, but the norms of organizational and occupational cultures also affect recruitment. For example, firms such as Procter & Gamble in the United States have strong norms favoring recruitment from within the firm. Social institutions such as educational systems also affect recruitment. In Japan, for example, personal contacts between university professors and managers are often a prerequisite for university students getting good jobs in big companies.

Recruitment in the United States

U.S. companies use all types of recruiting strategies, but U.S. managers do not judge all recruitment strategies to be equally effective. Exhibit 12.3 shows the

EXHIBIT 12.3   Effectiveness of Recruiting Sources for U.S. Companies by Job Category

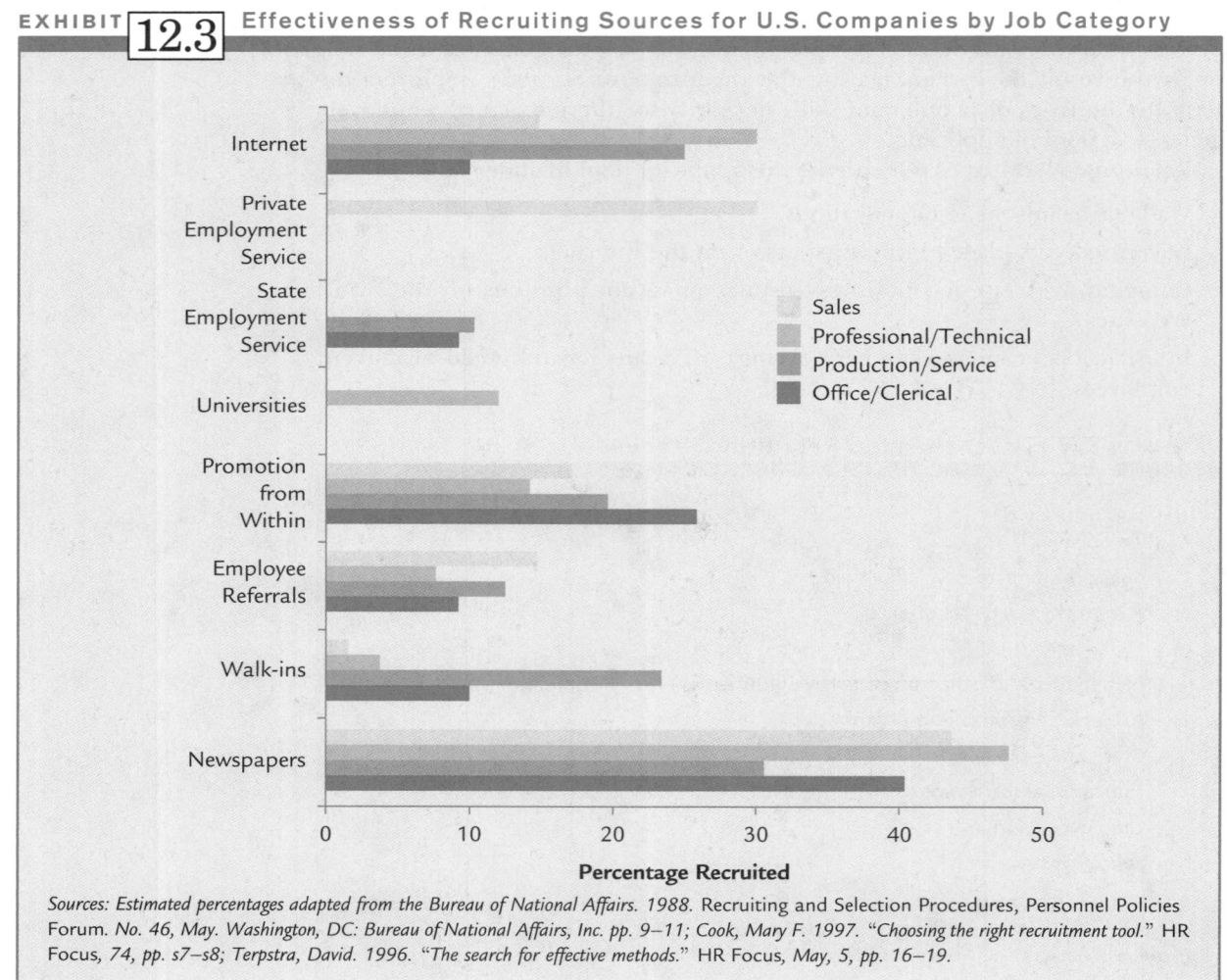

Sources: Estimated percentages adapted from the Bureau of National Affairs. 1988. Recruiting and Selection Procedures, Personnel Policies Forum. No. 46, May. Washington, DC: Bureau of National Affairs, Inc. pp. 9–11; Cook, Mary F. 1997. "Choosing the right recruitment tool." HR Focus, 74, pp. s7–s8; Terpstra, David. 1996. "The search for effective methods." HR Focus, May, 5, pp. 16–19.

relative effectiveness of recruitment strategies in the United States for four job categories.

As you can see from Exhibit 12.3, for all types of positions, U.S. managers see advertising—whether it be online or in print—as one of the most effective recruitment channels. College or university recruitment was judged among the most effective only for professional and technical jobs.

Managers believe that employee referrals produce only marginal success. There is some concern in the United States that employee referrals result in the recruitment of only employees with similar backgrounds to current workers. There is also a fear that recruitment by personal contacts (common in many other nations) may result in potential biases against certain groups, such as women and minorities.[5]

The belief in the United States that open and public advertisements are the most effective recruiting strategy reflects U.S. individualistic cultural values. Managers in the United States and in other individualistic societies view prospective workers as unique combinations of skills, and these skills are purchased by the company on the labor market. Public advertisements of jobs maximize the pool of available talent and, from the workers' point of view, support egalitarian norms that all can compete for open jobs. Consider the next Multinational Management Brief regarding recruitment in Mexico.

Recruitment

Whereas the United States favors open forms of recruitment, recruitment in collectivist societies tends to focus on the in-group, such as the family and friends of those already in the organization. South Korea, for example, ranks moderately low on Hofstede's individualism scale (21st percentile) and has HRM practices that are representative of collectivist cultures. Recruitment in South Korea originated from a mixture of Confucian values and Western pragmatism. Most Korean companies recruit blue-collar workers by **backdoor recruitment**, a form of employee referral; that is, prospective employees are

Backdoor recruitment
Prospective employees are friends or relatives of those already employed.

Multinational Management **Brief**

Recruitment in Mexico

An important recruitment practice in the United States is to avoid any form of discriminatory language in job advertisements. For instance, it is illegal to advertise jobs expressing preferences for specific ages, gender, physical appearance, or marital status. However, not all societies share this emphasis on equality. In fact, inequality is very prevalent in Mexico and in many Latin American countries. In such societies, it is acceptable to advertise jobs reflecting preferences for gender, age, physical appearance, and marital status.

To compare recruitment practices between the United States and Mexico, a study looked at job advertisements of U.S. multinationals operating in Mexico and of Mexican companies. The study found that U.S. multinationals operating in Mexico are less likely than Mexican companies to use discriminatory language. Such results show the influence of the U.S. recruitment practices on U.S.-based multinationals.

Source: Based on Daspro, E. 2009. "An analysis of U.S. multinationals' recruitment practices in Mexico." Journal of Business Ethics, 87, pp. 221–232.

friends or relatives of those already employed. From the company's perspective, friends and relatives represent a good pool of candidates. If prospective employees are relatives or friends, then someone can vouch for their trustworthiness and industriousness. Small companies and those in rural areas tend to rely more on backdoor recruitment rather than on open recruitment.

Like the Japanese system, the South Korean recruitment of managers emphasizes looking for candidates at prestigious universities. Also like the Japanese, Korean companies prefer recent graduates to managers with experience. Companies assume that young people will adapt more easily to fit the company's culture. However, a form of backdoor recruitment occurs at this level, primarily through old school ties. A company tends to favor graduates of a particular university, from which a disproportionate number of the firm's managers might come.

In addition to companies' preference for recruitment strategies, individuals located around the world prefer ways to find jobs. These preferences evolve most likely from the norms associated with the national culture and social institutions. For instance, Korean workers looking for jobs know that many Korean firms prefer forms of backdoor recruitment, and so they are likely to resort to friends and family to find jobs.

To provide additional information on cross-cultural differences in preference for appropriate ways to find jobs, we analyzed data collected through the International Social Survey Program (ISSP), provided by the Inter-University Consortium for Political and Social Research.[6] The ISSP is a cross-national collaboration dedicated to the collection of important data related to work and work orientations.

The ISSP asked respondents who were looking for jobs to indicate what means they were using: registering with public and private agencies, advertising in the newspaper, responding to advertisements, applying directly to employers, and asking relatives or friends. Comparisons of the forms of recruitment confirm that both national culture and social institutions influence recruitment practices by encouraging people in a given society to prefer various ways to look for jobs.

Exhibit 12.4 illustrates, for selected countries, whether individuals were registered with a public or a private agency in their job-seeking efforts. As the exhibit shows, individuals from, for instance, Sweden, Norway, Hungary, and France were more likely to register with a public agency as one way to find a job. Such findings are not surprising considering that the governments of these countries are actively involved in the day-to-day operation of the country. Both former communist societies (e.g., Hungary, Slovenia) and socialist societies (e.g., Sweden, Spain) are heavily influenced by governmental regulations and policies. It is therefore natural that individuals from these societies rely on their governments as a way to find a new job. In contrast, individuals in countries where governments play a lesser role (i.e., United States, United Kingdom, and New Zealand) are more likely to rely on private agencies. Such results clearly demonstrate the influence of social institutions on preferences for ways to find jobs.

Exhibit 12.5 shows which countries have the highest preference for advertising in newspapers or responding to newspaper advertisements. Both advertising in newspapers and responding to them reflect very open recruitment forms. In both cases, potential employees depend on open competition in the labor market and on how their skills and qualifications compare to others'. Not surprisingly, many individualistic countries (e.g., United Kingdom, United States, New Zealand) are found on that list. Individuals in such societies prefer open

12.4   Preferred Ways to Look for a New Job: Public versus Private Agency

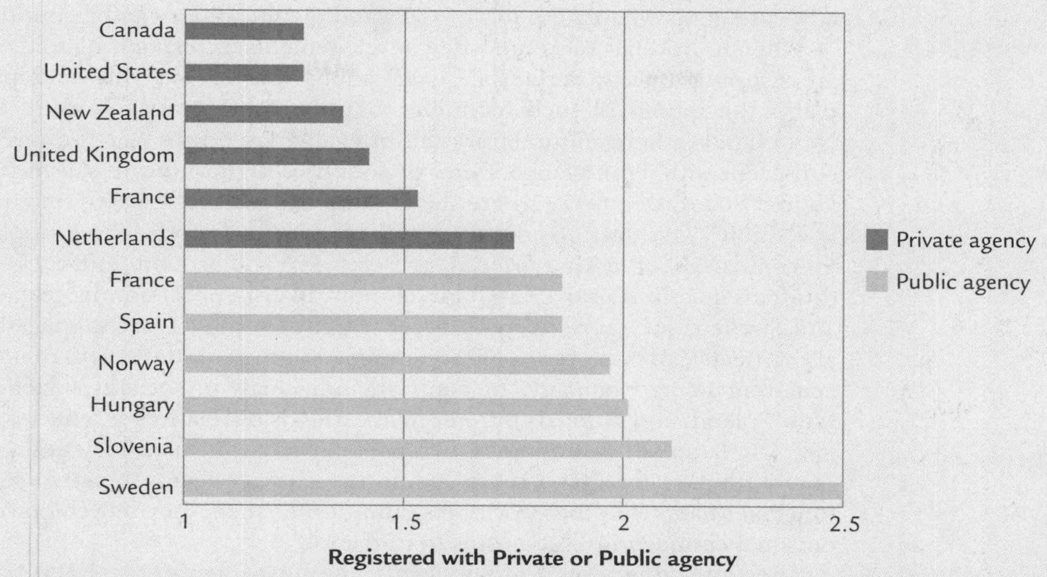

Registered with Private or Public agency

Source: Adapted from International Social Survey Program (ISSP). 2009–1999/2000. "International social survey program: Work orientations II, 1997" (computer file).

12.5   Preferred Ways to Look for a New Job: Answered Advertisements versus Advertised in Newspaper

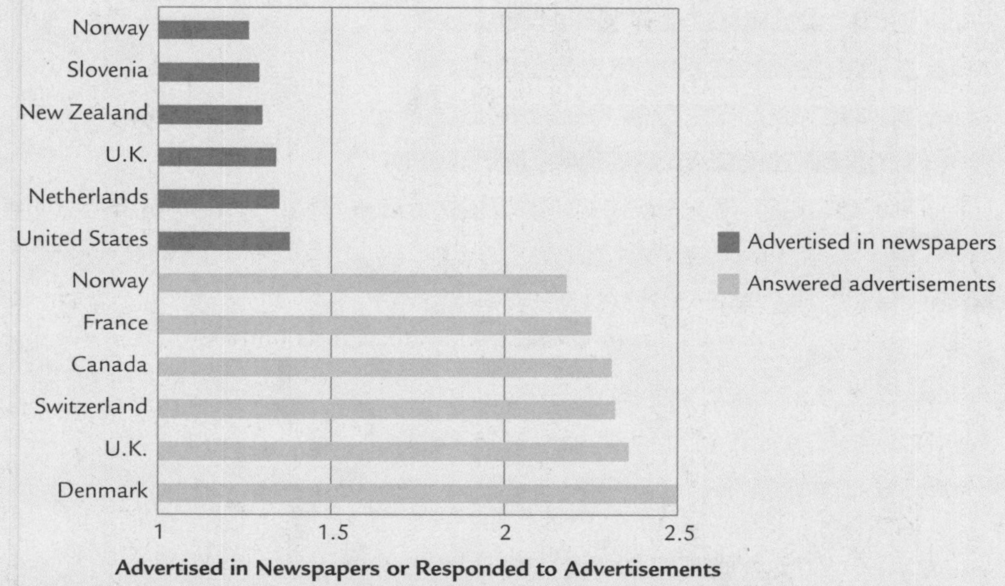

Advertised in Newspapers or Responded to Advertisements

Source: Adapted from International Social Survey Program (ISSP). 2009–1999/2000. "International social survey program: Work orientations II, 1997" (computer file).

means because these are the preferred recruitment methods—societies high on individualism favor hiring the best person with the right skills for the job. One of the most likely ways to ensure that the best person is hired is through open advertisements where all pools of skills and qualifications can be considered.

When individuals rely on posting advertisements or responding to them, they are assuming that universalistic qualifications apply to all. This assumption explains the ratings of such feminine countries as Denmark, Norway, and the Netherlands, where cultural norms favor egalitarian norms. Such results are also consistent with Trompenaar's view of countries high on universalism (Canada, United States, Denmark) where the cultural expectation is based on equality.[7]

Exhibit 12.6 shows, by country, whether individuals prefer direct applications to companies or asking friends or relatives. The exhibit indicates that individuals in countries that are high on individualism or femininity (e.g., Canada and Sweden) are more likely to apply directly for jobs. Direct applications are also reflective of open forms of recruitment and the cultural norms of individual achievement and equality. In contrast, individuals in socialist societies (e.g., Italy, Poland, and Hungary) prefer to ask friends or relatives as a means to get a job. The latter is not surprising because individuals in such societies rely more on friends, relatives, and other connections (i.e., relationships) for work advancement and for other work opportunities. As such, they rely chiefly on their personal connections as a means to find a job.

After attracting a pool of applicants, the next stage in the HRM process is selection.

EXHIBIT 12.6   Preferred Ways to Look for a New Job: Direct Application versus Asking Friends or Relatives

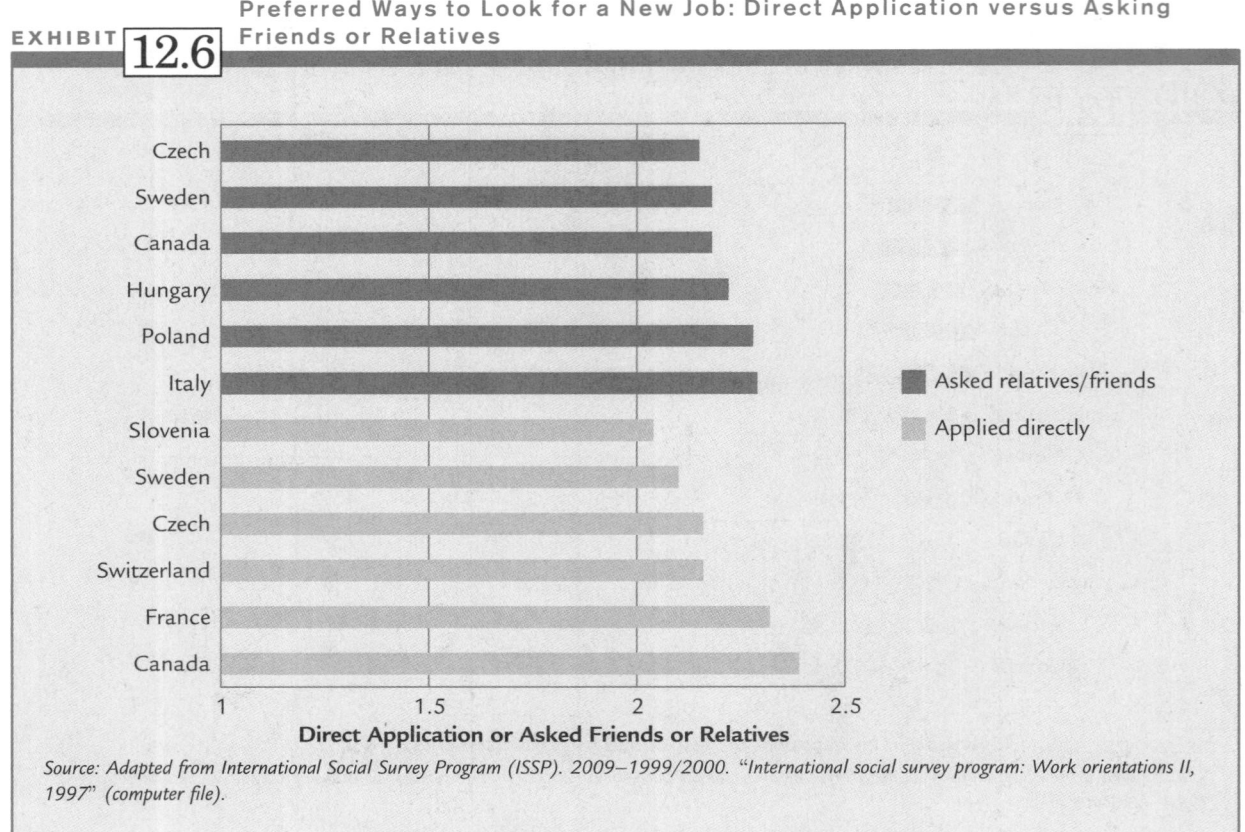

Source: Adapted from International Social Survey Program (ISSP). 2009–1999/2000. "International social survey program: Work orientations II, 1997" (computer file).

Selection

Selection in the United States

U.S. experts on human resource management identify a series of steps in the selection process.[8] Exhibit 12.7 shows these steps, from the initial application to the final hiring.

The aim of typical U.S. selection practices is to gather quality information on a candidate's job qualifications. The ideal selection then results in a match between the applicant's skills and the job requirements. As in the recruitment process, an individual is seen as a bundle of skills that the organization can purchase. The individualistic culture in the United States promotes a focus on a person's achievements (e.g., education, natural ability, experience), not on group affiliations such as the family. As a result, many U.S. companies have prohibitions against nepotism—the hiring of relatives—and have policies forbidding managers to supervise family members.

EXHIBIT 12.7   Typical Steps in U.S. Personnel Selection

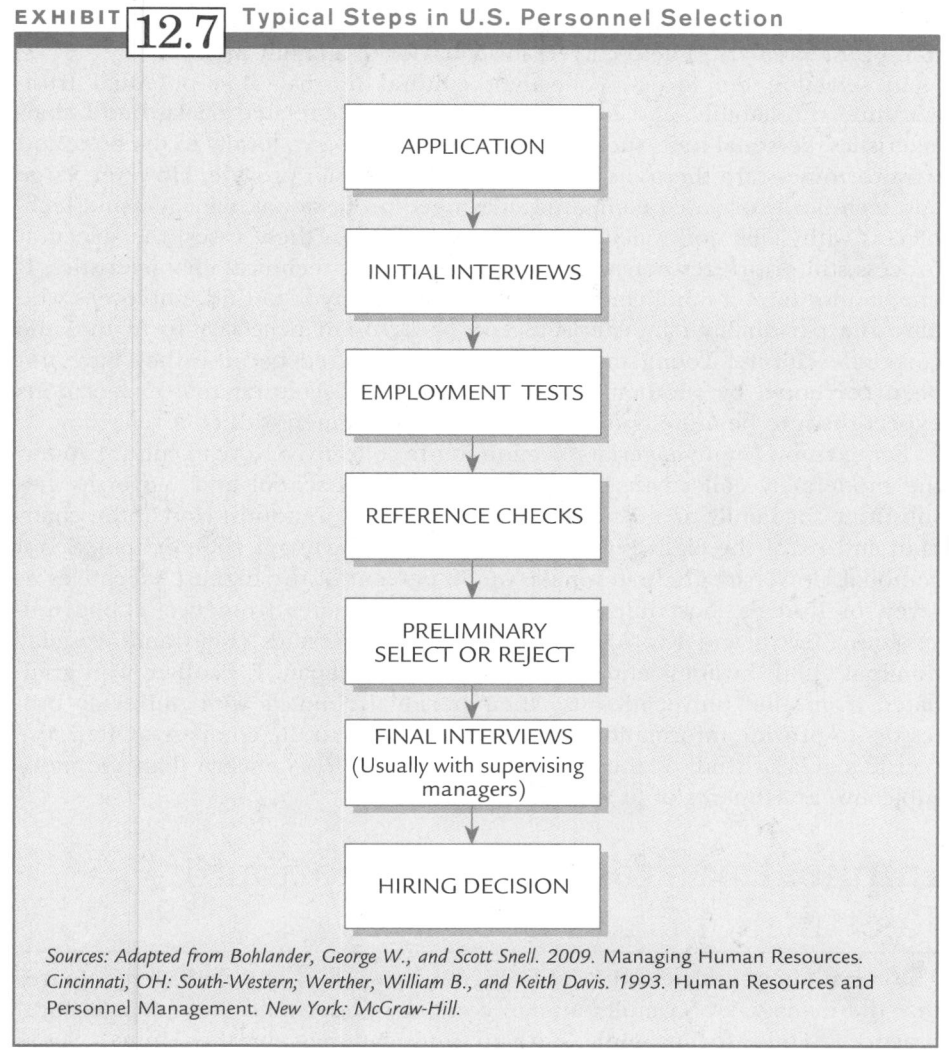

APPLICATION

INITIAL INTERVIEWS

EMPLOYMENT TESTS

REFERENCE CHECKS

PRELIMINARY SELECT OR REJECT

FINAL INTERVIEWS (Usually with supervising managers)

HIRING DECISION

Sources: Adapted from Bohlander, George W., and Scott Snell. 2009. Managing Human Resources. *Cincinnati, OH: South-Western; Werther, William B., and Keith Davis. 1993.* Human Resources and Personnel Management. *New York: McGraw-Hill.*

Previous work experience, performance on tests, and perceptions of qualifications in interviews help inform HRM personnel or hiring managers about the applicant's qualifications. To avoid discrimination or favoritism, laws and cultural norms in the United States prescribe that the information gathered during the selection process must be valid; that is, the information gathered from prospective employees must relate to performance on the job. Job qualification tests must predict job performance. For example, lifting 100 pounds would not be a valid selection test for most clerical jobs. Personal information gathered during the selection process, such as height and weight, must also be relevant to the job.

Next, we consider contrasting selection practices in collectivist national cultures.

Selection in Collectivist Cultures

Hofstede captures the essence of hiring in collectivist cultures:[9] "The hiring process in a collectivist society always takes the in-group into account. Usually preference is given to hiring relatives, first of the employer, but also of other persons already employed by the company. Hiring persons from a family one already knows reduces risks. Also relatives will be concerned about the reputation of the family and help correct misbehavior of a family member."

In selecting employees, collectivist cultural norms value potential trustworthiness, reliability, and loyalty over performance-related background characteristics. Personal traits such as loyalty to the company, loyalty to the boss, and trustworthiness are the traits that family members can provide. However, large and technically oriented companies may need professional managers and technicians with skills not available inside the family. In these cases, the selection process still prioritizes personal characteristics over technical characteristics. If one cannot have a family member, then the priority is to find employees who have the personality characteristics and background necessary to fit into the corporate culture. Young male recruits are preferred because they have not been corrupted by another company's values, and cultural role expectations expect them to be more dedicated to work than women with children.

For example, in managerial selection in the collectivist Korean culture and in the moderately collectivist Japanese culture, high school and university ties substitute for family membership. At Daewoo Corporation in Korea, the chairman and six of the eight top executives attended Kyunggi High School. Seoul National University graduates make up 62 percent of the highest executives in seven of Korea's most important *chaebol*.[10] Graduates from two public universities (Tokyo and Kyoto) and two private universities (Keio and Waseda) dominate both business and public leadership in Japan. Executives who graduated from elite universities use their personal contacts with university professors to provide information on a recruit's worth to the company. Often, the recruit's area of study at the university is of much less concern than the more subjective assessments of fit with the company.

Implications for the Multinational: Recruitment and Selection

The recruitment and selection of host country workers and managers requires that the managers of a multinational company understand and adapt to local practices. Thus, for example, foreign multinationals in the United States probably have the most success using the typical U.S. recruitment practices: advertising in newspapers and going to college campuses. In other countries, the multinational manager will also need to discover and use local recruitment and selection practices.

Adaptation to local recruitment and selection practices may not always be easy. In societies where backdoor or personal contacts are acceptable recruitment strategies, foreign multinational managers may not have access to the appropriate recruitment channels. In Japan, for example, most foreign multinational companies do not have the personal contacts with Japanese professors that they need to attract the best managerial talent. For U.S. companies, such recruitment methods may violate ethical codes that require competitive access to all open jobs.

What happens when a company does not follow local norms in recruitment and selection? First, it may not get the best employees. Second, it may offend local cultural norms or break host country laws. Thus, multinational managers must always assess the trade-off between following home practices that get what they believe are the "right" people for the job and the costs and benefits of following local traditions.

Many companies are now making use of electronic human resources (e.HR) to manage their human resources. The use of e.HR has also proved to be very useful for the recruitment function. Consider the next Case in Point discussing e.HR for recruitment.

After identifying a pool of applicants and selecting those to be hired, the next step in the HRM process is the training and development of the employees.

Training and Development

Within a country, training and development needs vary widely, affected by different industries, technologies, strategies, organizational structures, and local labor market conditions. However, broad national differences in training and development do exist.

The cross-national differences in training and development are most associated with institutional differences in national educational systems, which create large differences in recruits' qualifications in basic skills and in attitudes toward work. For example, more than 90 percent of the 25- to 34-year-olds in Norway, Japan, and Korea finish secondary school. Turkey and Portugal have only 24 percent.[11] For another example, consider Germany, which has a strong technical education program and an apprenticeship system that originated with the guild system of the Middle Ages.

Cross-cultural training and development differences are also associated with the degree of emphasis placed by the national governments.[12] For instance, the Australian government requires companies above a certain size to spend 1.5 percent of their payroll expenses on training. The Chinese government is also heavily involved in training; companies are encouraged to train their workers before they are offered full-time jobs. The Taiwanese have gone even further by establishing 13 public vocational training institutes for those who do not have access to higher education. Cultural values regarding types of educational credentials and other personnel practices, such as lifetime employment, also affect training and development needs. For example, though threatened by economic practicalities and often maligned as inefficient, the Japanese retain the ideal of long-term employment. For companies like Ricoh, which continues to avoid layoffs at all cost, long-term employment allows management training and

CASE IN POINT

Using e.HR for Recruitment

Many companies are now relying on electronic human resources (e.HR) because they see important benefits to using such systems. For instance, electronic human resources can provide employees with ways to access their payroll and other critical employment information. In fact, global companies like Nike, KPN, and Siemens are all using e.HR systems to manage their human resource functions around the world. Consider that Nike's European, Middle Eastern, and Asian headquarters gets almost 800 job applications a month for approximately 100 to 120 positions. Nike's policy is that each applicant is a potential employee and customer and that each has to be treated as such. However, before e.HR was implemented, there was tremendous stress on the HR department to quickly process the resumes to make hiring decisions. Unfortunately, reviews of the system showed that mistakes were made and that the cost of hires needed to be reduced while the level of talent needed to increase.

The new e.HR system at Nike has been helpful in addressing many of the problems. All applicants can now apply for specific jobs or for future job opportunities through the Nike Web site, which is linked to other external recruiting sites that enable more potential applicants to be aware of job opportunities. Furthermore, for each new job position, the online system makes the first cut and matches the candidates with the job requirements. As such, Nike managers have access to a candidate short list rather than the large number of hard-copy resumes of the previous system. Th e.HR system has enabled Nike to improve the quality of the candidates it considers. Furthermore, applicants are encouraged to update their resume every six months to show their continued interest in the company. Nike has a constantly growing list of applicants for future positions. The database now contains about 8,500 resumes.

Nike has seen tremendous benefits with the implementation of the e.HR system. The company has saved close to 50 percent of recruitment costs. Furthermore, with the regular resume updates, the company has relied less on external recruiters because it always has qualified applicants on hand. The system's ability to provide short lists based on job requirements also has improved the quality of hires, and the time to fill vacancies has dropped from 62 to 42 days.

Sources: Based on MacLellan, J. 2009. "Electronic solutions a greener option." Canadian HR Reporter, 22(8), p. 8; Pollitt, David. 2005. "Recruiting the right project managers at Siemens Business Services." Human Resources Management International Digest, 13(7), pp. 28–30; 2005. "E-recruitment gets the Nike tick of approval." Human Resources Management International Digest, 13(2), pp. 33–35; 2006. "E-HR brings everything together at KPN." Human Resources Management International Digest, 14(1), pp. 34–35.

development to take place slowly, through extensive job rotations. Managers learn by doing, with many different job assignments early in their careers.

Exhibit 12.8 gives an overview of work-related training systems in use throughout the world, and Exhibit 12.9 presents some specific detail about training in a number of countries.

Next, as a detailed example, we will discuss training and development differences between the voluntary system of the United States and the cooperative system of Germany.

Training and Development in the United States

U.S. companies with more than 100 employees invest more than $60 billion in training.[13] Exhibit 12.10 shows the types of skills taught to employees. The most popular training topics are management development and computer skills. However, other types of training, such as those needed for new methods and procedures, reach more people on all levels of the organization. In spite of the billions of dollars invested, training in the United States does not reach all workers. Estimates are that U.S. employers provide training to only 1 out of every 14 workers.[14] Because of perceived weaknesses in U.S. secondary education, the

EXHIBIT 12.8   Training Systems around the World

Type	Example Countries	Features and Sources of Institutional Pressures
Cooperative	Austria, Germany, Switzerland, and some Latin American countries	Legal and historical precedents for cooperation among companies, unions, and the government.
Company-based voluntarism/ high labor mobility	United States and U.K.	Lack of institutional pressures to provide training. Companies provide training based on own cost benefits.
Voluntarism/low labor mobility	Japan	Low labor turnover encourages investment in training without institutional pressure.
State-driven incentive provider	Hong Kong, Korea, Singapore, Taiwan, China, Australia	Government identifies needs for skills and uses incentives to encourage companies to train in chosen areas.
Supplier	Developing countries in Asia and Africa, transition economies	No institutional pressures for companies to train. Government provides formal training organizations.

Source: Adapted from International Labor Organization (ILO). 1999. World Employment Report 1998–99. Geneva: International Labor Office.

pressure on U.S. businesses to supplement basic educational training will increase. Thirty percent of U.S. students do not finish high school, and many of the graduates do not have sufficient reading and mathematical skills for current and future jobs.[15] For example, 40 percent of the companies in Exhibit 12.11 already see the need to provide remedial and basic education.

The shift in emphasis of the U.S. economy from manufacturing to service is predicted to be an important issue in the future. The service sector tends to be very capital and skill intensive and requires employees to have not only the appropriate technical skills but also critical thinking skills, team-building skills, and learning abilities.[16] This prediction suggests that there may be a widening gap between what companies emphasize in their training programs and the skills required for the future. Compounding the problem are pressures to cut costs, which have resulted in more U.S. companies outsourcing their training needs. Unfortunately, as training is moved out of the organizations, its relevance and applicability to the companies' needs is lessened.

Predictions of high needs for training have resulted in some calls from business and government for German-style apprentice programs. In such programs, the government requires industry to provide vocational training to workers in exchange for tax benefits. However, in the United States, training that is not specifically tailored to a company is often viewed as something that the employee may eventually take to a competitor. This fear makes some companies reluctant to invest in training without a more immediate and positive cost-benefit analysis regarding their own bottom line.[17]

Next we describe perhaps the most acclaimed model of vocational training.

Training and Vocational Education in Germany

German companies are renowned worldwide for their high-quality technical products. A sophisticated and standardized national system of vocational education and training provides a major human resource for German industry.

Key Specific Training and Development Characteristics of Selected Countries

EXHIBIT **12.9**

Australia
- Government-introduced 1990 Training Guarantee Act, requires companies to spend 1.5% of annual payroll expenses on training.
- More training provided at managerial level than blue-collar level.
- Not enough initiatives are yet available to assess effectiveness of training programs.

Canada
- Because of NAFTA, companies are facing increasing pressures to cut costs, and HR departments are being disproportionately affected.
- Use of outside consultants for training purposes is becoming increasingly prevalent.
- Only half of corporate HRM departments are involved in training.

China
- High degree of governmental intervention to encourage companies to train.
- Heavy emphasis is on training and development of managers.
- Training programs are more likely to emphasize corporate values and interpersonal skills.
- Many multinationals (ABB, Ericcson, Procter & Gamble, Motorola) have established state-of-the-art campus training centers.

Japan
- Training and development is planned and executed in disciplined manner at all levels of the organization.
- Training for white-collar and blue-collar workers is fairly similar.
- Skills in coordination and communication are considered as important as technical skills in training programs.

Korea
- Emphasis is on molding current and future managers and workers to fit the corporate culture.
- Loyalty, dedication, and team spirit are emphasized rather than job skills.
- The Asian crisis has forced companies to cut down on training costs.
- Governmental policies require companies with more than 150 employees to establish training centers.

Mexico
- Increased levels of training are driven by standards established by international investors and other trade agreements (North American Free Trade Agreement, MERCOSUR).
- Major emphasis on on-the-job training and skill development of lower-level employees. Training is seen as becoming increasingly important because often business and cultural practices collide on a variety of manufacturing and other techniques (i.e., JIT).
- Training methods such as on-the-job training are used to familiarize workers with job requirements.

Taiwan
- Government has built a vast educational system and established 13 vocational training schools. New curricula stressing creativity and free thought are replacing traditional educational approaches based on memorization and job-specific skills.
- Taiwanese companies are seeing the importance of training as the country shifts to more knowledge-intensive sectors.
- Among different training practices, job rotation is perceived as most effective, followed by in-house and outside training.
- Emphasis is on managerial rather than technical training.

Sources: Adapted from Cantu de la Torre, I., and L. Cantu Licon. 2009. "Focus on Mexico." Training, February, 46(2), p. 20; Drost, Ellen A., Colette A. Frayne, Kevin B. Lowe, and J. Michael Geringer. 2002. "Benchmarking training and development practices: A multicountry analysis." Human Resource Management, 41(1), pp. 67–86.

Dual system
A form of vocational education in Germany that combines in-house apprenticeship training with part-time vocational school training and that leads to a skilled worker certificate.

There are two forms of vocational education in Germany. One consists of general and specialized vocational schools and professional and technical colleges. The other form, called the **dual system**, combines in-house apprenticeship training with part-time vocational school training, leading to a skilled worker certificate. This training can be followed by the *Fachschule,* a college giving advanced vocational training. Ultimately, one can achieve the status of a **Meister,** or master technician.

EXHIBIT **12.10**   Skills Taught by U.S. Organizations

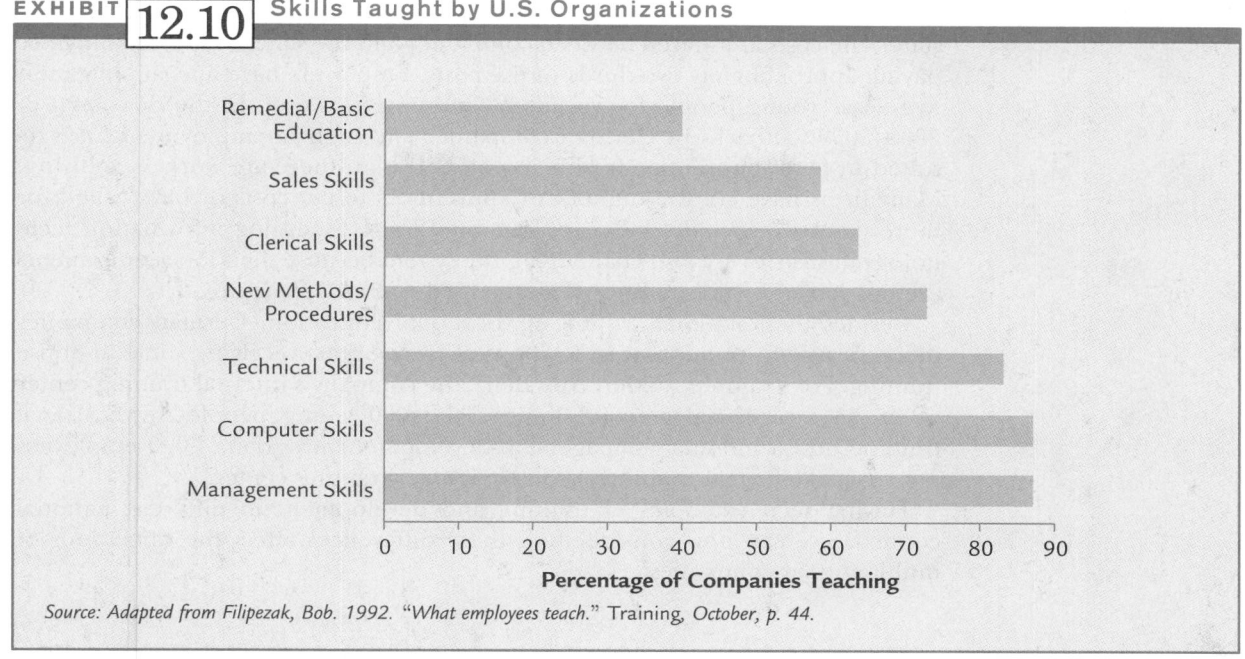

Source: Adapted from Filipezak, Bob. 1992. "What employees teach." Training, October, p. 44.

The dual system is probably the most important component of German vocational training. The training and certificate qualifications are standardized throughout the country. This produces a well-trained national labor force with skills that are not company specific. Apprenticeships exist not only for manual occupations but also for many technical, commercial, and managerial occupations. Apprenticeships are not limited to the young. Older workers often seek apprenticeships and the resulting certificates to enhance their development. There are nearly 400 nationally recognized vocational certificates.[18] Unions, organizations, and the government are now identifying new groups of certificates to represent qualifications for high-tech jobs in the new economy.

Meister
In Germany, a master technician.

EXHIBIT **12.11**   Germany's Apprenticeship Program Under Pressure

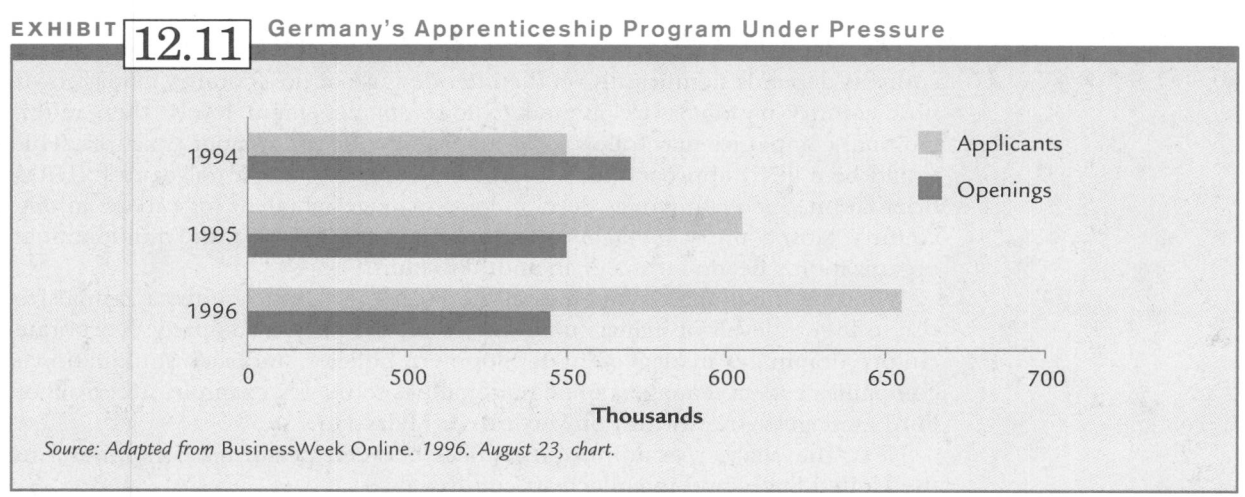

Source: Adapted from BusinessWeek Online. 1996. August 23, chart.

The dual system results from a collaboration of employers, unions, and the state. The costs are shared between companies and the state, with the companies paying approximately two-thirds of the costs. Employers have a legal obligation to release young people for vocational training. However, in the downturn of 2008–2009, cutbacks by German companies and high unemployment have resulted in fewer apprenticeships being offered than there are workers applying. Many firms have cut the number of apprentices to cut costs or have called for more company-specific skills (see Exhibit 12.11). Emerging information technology industries are also challenging the system because their job requirements are not served by the traditional German educational structure.[19]

Besides their national system of vocational education, German companies invest heavily in training, with four out of five workers receiving some in-house training. For example, at Mercedes Benz, the company's internal training center offers 180 vocational courses. Besides the 600 young people in vocational training and a modular management-development program, 4,000 employees per year take formal training at the company's training center.[20]

Having seen examples of training and development in different national contexts, we can now consider how these differences affect the operations of multinational companies.

Implications for the Multinational: Training and Development

Before setting up operations in a host foreign country, multinational managers must consider the quality of the workers and sometimes of the managers in the host country. They must also examine the feasibility of exporting their company's training techniques to the host country. For example, a transnational company might need workers with basic skills in mathematics and science to staff future plants. Rather than invest in basic education to train a low-cost workforce, the company can locate in countries with the best educational systems. Thus, for example, a multinational company with a requirement for technical workers might examine which educational systems produce the best students in mathematics and science.

Regardless of the basic talent of host country workers, training is an important component of the HR strategy. The next Case in Point describes efforts by multinational companies to increase diversity training among their employees.

The adaptation of management-development practices to different national contexts depends significantly on the intended use of host country managers. If host country nationals are limited to lower management levels, then multinational companies may follow local management-development practices. This would be a likely approach for a multilocal company with a polycentric IHRM orientation. Such companies develop local managerial talent for careers in one country. Host country managers often never expect to work at the multinational organization's headquarters or in another country.

When multinational companies allow and expect host country nationals to rise to higher levels of management, however, the parent company's corporate culture dominates management-development policies, and such multinational companies expect managers of all nationalities to be, for example, Motorola or Ford managers—not British or Mexican or Malaysian.

Next, the chapter examines differences between performance appraisal in the United States and in collectivist cultures.

C A S E I N P O I N T

Diversity Training

Most multinational companies are finding that diversity training is essential if they want to compete globally. Consider the attempt by the Chinese computing giant Lenovo to implement diversity training programs to unify its culturally and geographically diverse workforce. The company sees potential for competitive advantage in its workforce and is striving to find ways to take advantage of the diversity. Lenovo employees go through intensive programs focused on training employees from different nationalities and backgrounds to work effectively together. Such training is also being positioned as crucial to long-term success rather than the usual approach—that it is the right thing to do.

Many other companies are also implementing diversity training and see it as crucial not only to integrate the workforce integration but also to ensure fairness to all races, genders, and sexual orientations around the world. For instance, IBM believes that the way to deliver superior products is to have an environment where diverse employees can contribute without having to fear harassment or discrimination. Some of these companies are going as far as hiring diversity officers who report directly to the CEO. These companies are also taking deliberate steps to measure the effectiveness of such training and often are linking compensation to diversity goals.

Sources: Based on Egodigwe, Laura. 2005. "Workplace-diversity training gets a new mandate; Touchy-feely approach gives way to fomenting cross-cultural strategies." Asian Wall Street Journal, November 14, p. 38; Childs, J. T. (Ted) Jr. 2005. "Managing workforce diversity at IBM: A global HR topic that has arrived." Human Resources Management, 44(1), pp. 73–77.

Performance Appraisal

Regardless of the national setting, all companies at some point must deal with the human resource problems of identifying people to reward, promote, demote, develop and improve, retain, or terminate. Not everyone can move up the ladder of the organizational pyramid. Not everyone can be a leader. Not everyone will perform at acceptable levels. Even in countries like Japan, with its high value for lifetime employment, the survival of the company often requires layoffs.

The fundamental assumption in the West, and in particular, in individualistic cultures, is that performance appraisal systems provide rational and fair solutions to these human resource problems. In other words, ideally, appraisal systems provide management with objective, honest, and fair data on employee performance. Consequently, human resource decisions, such as pay or promotion, can be based on this data. Although issues regarding seniority, experience, and security are not ignored, the cultural ideal is a meritocracy, where good performers get more rewards.

Performance Appraisal in the United States

The U.S. performance appraisal system represents cultural values that espouse links among individual rights, duties, and rewards, as well as a legal system that promotes equal opportunity. Thus, the ideal U.S. system is highly rational, logical, and legal. The textbook view of it contains four elements: performance standards, performance measures, performance feedback, and human resource decisions related to remuneration, promotion, or termination.[21]

- *Performance standards* reflect management's goals regarding the acceptable quality and quantity of work output: work-related knowledge, quality, volume, and initiative. For example, a secretary may be expected to type a certain number of words per minute.

- *Performance measures* are techniques intended for the objective and often comparative assessment of employees on the performance standards. The most popular measures use some form of rating scale.[22] The employee is rated on a variety of traits (e.g., work quality), usually by managers but occasionally by peers or subordinates. Teacher evaluations by class members and peer evaluations of contributions to a student group project are examples of performance ratings.

- *Performance feedback* usually occurs in a formal interview between superior and subordinate. Three methods are common in the United States.[23] First, in the tell-and-sell method, the supervisor gives feedback and explains the evaluation. Second, in the tell-and-listen method, the supervisor gives feedback and listens to the subordinate's reactions. Third, in the problem-solving method, the supervisor and subordinate work to identify problems and propose solutions for improvement.

- *Human resource decisions* related to the performance appraisal system, in most U.S. organizations, are compensation decisions. Other major but less common uses include performance improvement, feedback, documentation, and promotion.[24]

Because of the concern in the United States that human resource decisions be fair and equitable for all individuals, performance appraisal systems must follow **U.S. legal requirements for appraisals** that ensure fairness by regulating performance evaluation practices.

The U.S. performance appraisal system is rooted in an individualistic culture and an institutional system that aspire to protect equal rights and equal opportunities. Cultural stories like the American dream of rags to riches support the idea that all can achieve wealth and success through their own efforts.

Next, we will see how the institutional systems and cultural values of other nations result in the valuing and evaluation of quite different aspects of work performance.

U.S. legal requirements for appraisals
Regulating performance evaluation practices to ensure their fairness.

Performance Appraisals around the World

Although performance-appraisal practices vary widely among countries, they are undertaken with the common purpose of devising ways to control employees so that they give maximum performance.[25] However, while appraisals are based on similar notions in many countries, there are wide variations in terms of what they are used for. In that context, the Best International Human Resource Management Practices Project[26] provides extensive evidence on cross-national differences in performance appraisal purposes in Australia, Canada, Indonesia, Japan, South Korea, Latin America, Mexico, China, Taiwan, and the United States.

Exhibit 12.12 shows the top five countries for each performance appraisal purpose. The project asked respondents to rate the importance of 12 purposes of performance appraisals, and the results revealed significant differences among countries. However, the most striking finding is that Australia, Canada, and the United States are among the top five countries for all performance appraisal purposes—not surprisingly because these countries are very high on individualism, where there is heavy emphasis on the development of the individual. As such, performance appraisals are seen as the most effective method to gauge how well an employee is doing and how that person's performance can

EXHIBIT 12.12

Cross-National Differences in Purposes of Performance Appraisals: Top Five Countries and Regions for Each Category

Performance Appraisal Purpose	Countries				
Determine pay	Taiwan	Canada	United States	China	Japan
Document performance	Australia	United States	Taiwan	Latin America	Canada
Plan development activities	Australia	Latin America	Canada	Taiwan	Mexico
Salary administration	Latin America	Taiwan	United States	Canada	Indonesia
Recognize subordinate	Australia	Taiwan	United States	Canada	China
Discuss improvement	Australia	Latin America	Canada	United States	Taiwan
Discuss subordinate views	Australia	Canada	Taiwan	United States	Mexico
Evaluate goal achievement	Australia	Latin America	Taiwan	Canada	Japan
Identify strengths and weaknesses	Latin America	Australia	United States	Canada	Taiwan
Let subordinate express feelings	Australia	Taiwan	Canada	China	United States
Determine promotion potential	Korea	Latin America	Taiwan	Australia	Japan

Source: Adapted from Geringer, J. Michael, Colette A. Frayne, and John F. Milliman. 2002. "In search of 'best practices' in international human resource management: Research design and methodology." Human Resource Management, 41(1), pp. 5–30.

be improved. However, it is also interesting to see countries and regions such as Taiwan and Latin America figure prominently on the list. Their presence suggests the possible effects of social institutions such as the government and the trade agreements. Because these countries are emulating Western-based systems to satisfy trade agreements and other competitiveness requirements, they are perhaps seeing performance appraisal systems as critical.

It also is interesting to note that the collectivist societies surveyed (e.g., China, Japan, Korea, Indonesia) were very unlikely to be among the top five countries for each performance appraisal purpose. This suggests that performance appraisals may not be seen as important in such societies. Consider the next Multinational Management Brief.

In collectivist cultures, age and in-group memberships (usually family or social status) make up a large component of the psychological contract with the organization; that is, the employer and employee accept as correct and fair that human resource decisions should take into account personal background characteristics more than achievement. Since who you are and how old you are may count more than how you perform, the usefulness of a Western-style performance appraisal system is less clear. For example, if only family members are eligible for promotion, it makes little sense to evaluate all employees for management potential.

None of this implies, however, that information regarding performance is not communicated to people in collectivist cultures. Members of work groups often know the best and the worst performers. Because it is important to work for the benefit of the group, members may subtly praise or punish other workers based on their performance. Managers also may work indirectly to discourage poor performance. Behaviors such as withdrawing normal favors or working through intermediaries (who are often relatives) are common. For the Japanese, the supervisor can communicate negative feedback for poor work performance simply by ignoring his subordinate. Thus, even without formal appraisal systems, feedback occurs indirectly.

According to Hofstede,[27] managers in collectivist societies often avoid direct performance appraisal feedback. An open discussion of performance may clash with the society's norm of harmony, which takes precedence. For example, during the first eight to ten years of their careers, Japanese managers may never encounter the appraisal system. Even if one exists, it is often secret and lacks direct feedback to the employee. Instead, all beginning managers get the same salary and promotions, based on age and seniority. Reducing competition among managers and maintaining harmony among the group are higher-priority values than identifying or developing high performers.

Steers, Shin, and Ungson point out that the preference for seniority-based promotions is even stronger among Koreans.[28] They note that while job performance is important and most companies have appraisal systems, seniority is the most important factor for advancement. This follows "from the Confucian tradition that strives to preserve harmony (since it is unseemly for younger employees to supervise older ones). It is also easier to use seniority to make promotion decisions than to rely on imprecise personnel evaluation methods to discriminate between a group of high achievers."[29]

Perhaps because of the long-term orientation of Korean culture, Korean performance appraisal systems focus on evaluating and developing the so-called whole man for the long-term benefit of the company. They evaluate sincerity, loyalty, and attitude on an equal footing with job performance. Only for senior management, where the logic of an organizational pyramid dictates a small number of top positions, does the performance evaluation focus on actual performance and contribution to the company.[30]

Regardless, at least from the individualistic societies' perspective, performance appraisals provide the information necessary for promotion and compensation decisions.

Next, we will see how compensation practices in other national contexts differ from the U.S. model.

Compensation

Compensation includes wages and salaries, incentives such as bonuses, and benefits such as retirement contributions. There are wide variations both among countries and among organizations concerning how to compensate workers. A country's economic development, cultural traditions, legal institutions, and the role of labor unions all affect compensation. Consider these examples:

- Japanese workers earn more than three times the wages of workers in other East Asian countries such as Taiwan, Singapore, and Korea.[31]

- Although not required by law, South Korean and Japanese workers expect bonuses at least twice a year.

- In Denmark, more than 80 percent of employees belong to unions, and agreements between unions and employers' associations determine minimal and normal pay.[32]

- In the European Union, there is a statutory minimum of four weeks of vacation. As an example, France has a law that guarantees workers five weeks of paid vacation on an annual basis.[33]

Compensation Practices in the United States

Conditions external and internal to the company affect the wages and salaries of workers and managers.[34] External factors include local and national wage rates, government legislation, and collective bargaining. Internal factors include the importance of the job to the organization, the affluence of the organization or its ability to pay, and the employee's relative worth to the business (merit).

Taking into account these external and internal factors, most U.S. companies develop formal and systematic policies to determine wages and salaries. The Personnel Policies Forum, a group of personnel managers representing companies of all sizes and from all industries, found that 75 percent of their member companies had formal written policies for wage and salary administration.[35] What are these policies? Consider the following additional results from the Personnel Policies Forum study.

To establish that their companies' wages and salaries are competitive in the labor market, the Personnel Policies Forum study showed that 94 percent of U.S. companies used data from comparative wage and salary surveys to determine compensation. Comparative wage and salary surveys tell companies how their compensation packages match up with those of competitors. Two-thirds of the companies check on comparative wage and salary data at least once a year. Nearly 40 percent assess their competitive wage and salary position more than seven times a year.

Perhaps more than any other society, the highly mobile U.S. labor market requires this hefty concern with external equity (i.e., do we pay at or above market level?). The individualistic U.S. culture views careers as private and personal, and mobility, advancement, and higher wages often require leaving a company. Thus, unlike in countries such as Japan and Korea, where company loyalty often prevails over opportunities for higher remuneration, U.S. companies must rely on competitive wages to maintain a quality workforce.

Most U.S. companies also develop procedures to establish that people receive equitable pay for the types of jobs they perform. Seventy-five percent of the companies surveyed by the Personnel Policies Forum have formal systems to evaluate how much particular jobs (independent of the people doing them) contribute to the company.[36] A variety of methods help to establish a hierarchy of jobs based on their worth to the company. Issues such as responsibility, skill requirements, and the importance of the job's tasks to the organization contribute to the worth of a job. Those who occupy the higher-ranked jobs are paid more.

Although the worth of a job to the company largely determines the base pay assigned to a certain position, raises in pay are determined mostly by merit.[37] As discussed in more detail in the following section, this is particularly unlike the seniority-based systems of Korea and Japan.

As part of the total compensation package, benefits have grown substantially in the United States during the last few decades. Major employee benefits in the United States include pension plans, health care benefits, insurance coverage, vacation pay, sick leave, and paid holidays. Social Security insurance, unemployment insurance, family leave, and workers' compensation insurance for work-related accidents are required by law. However, as the next Multinational Management Brief shows, U.S. benefits still lag behind those that a multinational company should expect to pay in Europe.

Next we will look at one of the most comprehensive studies on compensation practices and the perceived trend toward convergence.

Compensation around the World

Compensation packages vary widely among countries. The Best International Human Resource Management Practices Project represents one of the most extensive cross-national studies of compensation practices to date.[38] The researchers investigated cross-national variations in nine compensation practices in ten countries or regions (Australia, Canada, China, Indonesia, Japan,

---

Multinational Management **Brief**

A Comparison of Some Benefits around the World

Country	Average Salary (Head of Sales and Marketing) (US $)	Expected Days off	Local Perks
Brazil	$208,691	40	Chauffeured bulletproof cars followed by bodyguards for top-level employees
China	$ 92,402	23	Contribution to housing fund to help employees buy houses
France	$188,771	40	Use of company-owned ski chalets and beachhouses
Hong Kong	$149,905	26	Traditional Chinese medicine health coverage in addition to regular health insurance
India	$ 56,171	31	Compensation for health care of aging parents of employees
Japan	$148,899	35	Family allowances on top of salary
Mexico	$163,591	23	Before Mother's Day weekend, getting the day or half day off to take mothers out to lunch
Philippines	$ 95,286	19	"Rice" allowances that they can convert to perks such as free cell phones
United States	$229,300	25	Access to financial planners for top-level employees
Russia	$117,135	39	Company-sponsored mortgages

Sources: Based on McGregor, J. 2008. "The right perks." BusinessWeek, January 28, pp. 42–43; Mercer. 2009. http://www.mercer.com.

Korea, Latin America, Mexico, Taiwan, and the United States). Respondents were asked a number of questions pertaining to these compensation practices, both in terms of their assessment of the current state of practice and also the extent to which they felt that these practices should be used in the future.

Results of the study revealed some convergence of compensation practices. For instance, managers of all countries and regions felt that it was necessary that all but one of the nine compensation practices (that pay incentives should be important, pay should be contingent on group/organizational performance, incentives should be a significant amount of pay, job performances should be the basis of pay raises, benefits should be important, benefits should be more generous, and pay should be based on long-term results) be used more in the future.[39] These managers also felt that less emphasis should be placed on using seniority as a determinant of pay decisions. Additionally, all managers felt that a properly designed compensation plan is key to harnessing employee performance and therefore to organizational effectiveness.

These results are particularly striking given that the countries studied have wide variations in terms of both the national culture and social institutions, but they provide some practical guidelines for practicing managers. In general, it is suggested that managers make more effective use of the preceding nine compensation practices. For instance, given that the respondents felt that job performance should become more prevalent as the basis for pay raises, it is essential for HRM managers to implement systems that provide a stronger link between job performance and pay raises.

Despite the evidence of convergence in many areas, the study also revealed surprising results. For instance, the researchers expected that the collectivist countries would have higher ratings for the compensation practice "pay is contingent on group or organizational performance." However, findings show that there were no major differences between collectivistic and individualistic countries on that point. Yet another perplexing result is that there were no significant variations among countries in terms of the compensation practice of using seniority as the basis for pay decisions.

This study suggests that there may be some convergence pressures on compensation practices. As further evidence of convergence, we will see an example of the changing compensation system in Japan. In response to competition, ten years of recession, and the globalization of Japanese organizations, Japanese firms are moving toward a Western style of compensation management. However, it still differs from the U.S. approach in its emphasis on age and group harmony.

Compensation in Japan

As with U.S. firms, Japanese companies determine base salaries to a large degree by the classification of positions. Positions have skill and educational requirements. Those who occupy the more demanding positions receive higher wages and bonuses.

Seniority has two effects on the Japanese compensation system. First, besides educational qualifications, each position has minimum age requirements. As the Japanese worker gains in seniority he, and less often she, becomes eligible to move up to more valued and more highly paid positions. Second, seniority factors into pay decisions, but at a declining rate; that is, seniority counts more for pay raises earlier in one's career and diminishes after age 45. The logic of this system is that more money is required early, when family responsibilities, such as buying a home or paying for children's education, are highest. These responsibilities decrease after middle age. In fact, early in a career it is not uncommon for marital status and family size to affect wages or salary.

In more recent times, merit (as the Japanese interpret it) affects pay raises to a greater degree than under the traditional position/seniority system. Even though the Japanese view of merit does not match exactly the Western view, stressing attitudes as much as job performance, experts on Japanese personnel policies predict that merit and achievement—at least Japanese style— will continue to have a greater impact on Japanese compensation and promotions.[40] Exhibit 12.13 shows the traditional compensation formula as it is being modified for pay raises in many Japanese companies today. The major shift is the weight given to merit over seniority.

Economic pressures on the Japanese compensation system are growing,[41] partly due to the increasing costs of compensating a large management staff recruited from the Baby Boomer Generation. As a result, some Japanese companies are taking the radical approach of basing management compensation only on merit. Honda was among the first to introduce this type of system, called the **nenpo system**, in 1992. At Honda, there are no cost-of-living raises, housing allowances, family allowances, or automatic pay raises. Instead, superiors determine a manager's pay by yearly performance evaluations that emphasize goals.[42] Although seniority remains important for holding certain positions, trends in Japanese human resource practices show a convergence with practices used in the United States and other Western nations. A recent survey shows that 90 percent of Japanese companies have or plan to introduce performance into their pay and promotion systems.[43]

Along with raises based on age, promotions, and merit, a significant component of Japanese compensation is the **bonus system**. Many Korean companies use similar systems. Bonuses come twice a year, usually during traditional gift-giving seasons. During the high of the Japanese boom economy, employees often received up to 30 percent of their base salary in the form of bonuses. Successful large companies paid up to 100 percent of base salaries in bonuses in particularly good years. However, with the current economic situation in Japan, such levels are now infrequent.

Nenpo system
New Japanese compensation system based on yearly performance evaluations that emphasize goals, although goals are not always the same as in Western companies.

Bonus system
In Japan, employees often receive as much as 30 percent of their base salary, usually given twice a year during traditional gift-giving seasons.

Implications for the Multinational: Performance Evaluation and Compensation

As with recruitment and selection, multinational companies must match their performance evaluation system to their multinational strategies. For example, top U.S. managers for Japanese companies in the United States often report that

EXHIBIT 12.13   The Japanese Pay Raise Formula: Changing the Balance

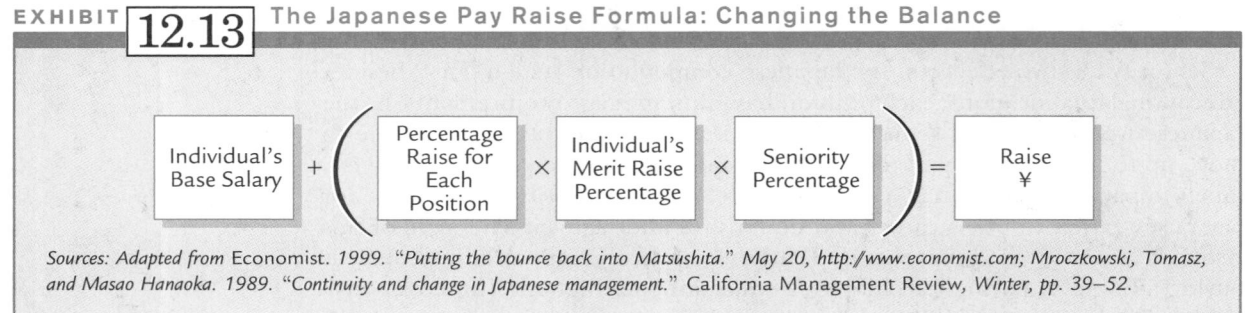

$$\text{Individual's Base Salary} + \left(\text{Percentage Raise for Each Position} \times \text{Individual's Merit Raise Percentage} \times \text{Seniority Percentage} \right) = \text{Raise ¥}$$

Sources: Adapted from Economist. 1999. *"Putting the bounce back into Matsushita."* May 20, http:/www.economist.com; Mroczkowski, Tomasz, *and Masao Hanaoka. 1989. "Continuity and change in Japanese management."* California Management Review, Winter, pp. 39–52.

they must adjust to the HRM practices of their Japanese parents; they are uncomfortable with ill identified career paths and the lack of specialization. Moreover, many U.S. managers working in Japan believe that headquarters management posts are blocked by the glass ceiling. As Bill Bsand, executive vice president for Hitachi America, notes: "There are very few Americans who work for Hitachi in Japan and usually at a very low level."[44]

A multinational company with locations in several nations may therefore need several compensation systems for host country nationals. For each host country, worker compensation levels must match wage levels in the local labor market. Country-level comparative compensation data is available from many government, private, and international sources. Information on compensation laws is usually available from host country governments. However, multinational managers must also consider regional differences within countries. Both labor costs and regional government laws may be different.

The relatively low cost of labor, managers, and engineers in Eastern European countries and India shows why many multinational companies seek location advantages in these countries. Children from these countries also score well in cross-national comparisons of ability in mathematics and science. These locations will probably provide excellent future workers in technical occupations. However, multinational companies are also finding that it is harder to retain talented workers in India. Consider the next Focus on Emerging Markets.

Some experts argue that competitive advantages based on wage rates are only short term. They cite the many Japanese, South Korean, and Taiwanese companies that based their early competitive advantages on their own high-quality, low-cost labor. Most of them have moved plants to cheaper locations in China or Southeast Asia. The implication for multinational companies is that, when local wage rates rise, the company will be forced either to keep pace or to seek another low-cost location.

In the next section, the chapter looks at labor relationships.

A Comparative View of Labor Relations

The variations of labor relations arise not only from cultural differences but also from the unique national histories of unionization.[45] Historical factors, such as the state of technological development during early unionization and the point at which governments recognized the legality of unions, influence current union structure and activities. Some unions were developed for ideological reasons, such as overthrowing the capitalist system or representing religious values. Others developed simply to improve wages and working conditions. Management views of unions also differ from country to country. Astute multinational managers should be well-versed in the history, structure, and ideology of unions in the countries in which their companies operate. Consider some of the difficulties of labor relations in India, as shown in the next Case in Point.

A major HRM issue is the popularity of unions, as indicated by what is called union membership density.

Union Membership Density

A strong indicator that multinational managers can use to tell how much unions influence companies is the **union membership density**. Union membership

Union membership density
Proportion of workers in a country who belong to unions.

Focus on Emerging Markets

Compensation Plans in Indian Multinational Companies

Although India boasts a plentiful supply of skilled labor, cultivating loyalty to retain valuable workers has proved to be a difficult challenge. As local and multinational companies expand their presence in India, demand for talented employees is becoming fierce. Employees are becoming very willing to leave their companies to start new positions. Because it is predicted that many sectors will face future shortages, many companies are starting to work harder to design compensation plans to retain their workers.

A survey by the Grow Talent Company shows that companies that are successful at retaining their employees show respect for them through compensation and benefits. For instance, these companies use HR strategies such as bring-your-spouse-to-the-office days, or they have big budgets to celebrate birthdays or weddings. Other companies are finding that engaging their workers' families also strikes a good work-family balance. Yet other multinational companies are finding that offering the possibility of attaining a masters in business administration or some form of global experience cultivates loyalty.

Infosys, India's famous technology services firm, has been able to retain employees through the Employee Relations Program, which typifies Infosys's commitment to work-life balance. The program includes counseling services, athletic competitive events, the celebration of important cultural events, and even health fairs open to the employees' families. The company also supports the strong family ties inherent in Indian culture by inviting family members to visit its campus. This program has allowed Infosys not only to enjoy a very low attrition rate of 10 percent but also to prevent competitors such as IBM and Oracle from taking its trained employees.

Both domestic and multinational organizations are finding that good HR practices have important benefits. Often, the buzz about employers with good HR practices spreads rapidly through the labor market grapevine. As a result, these companies are able not only to retain their workforce but also to attract more applicants for future positions.

Sources: Based on Hamm, S. 2008. "Young and impatient in India." BusinessWeek, *January, pp. 45–46; Merchant, Khozem. 2006. "Companies in India offer a taste of the sweet life: Keeping skilled workers is a challenge in the buoyant Indian jobs market and businesses are offering an ever-growing range of perks to keep them happy."* Financial Times, *February 2; Workforce Management. 2006. "The 10 most forward-thinking leaders in workforce management," March 13.*

density refers to the proportion of workers who belong to unions in a country. Estimates of union membership density are always approximate because some reports do not consider white-collar workers or professional unions.

Union membership in the United States has declined considerably over the last 30 years. Some decline worldwide is due to the end of compulsory union membership in the transition economies of Eastern Europe. However, European and other industrialized countries still have high proportions of workers who are union members. In major industrialized countries, union membership is declining but still averages greater than 50 percent. In countries such as South Africa, with the opening of unions to the formerly barred black population, unions have more than doubled in size.[46] Exhibit 12.14 summarizes unionization density in various parts of the world.

Dealing with Unions in India

India's free market reforms have attracted multinational firms General Electric, Otis Elevator Co., and Unilever, to name only a few. However, these firms are encountering a national context in which strong institutional pressures give power to unions and encourage union militancy.

India has a rich trade union history. The first trade union was created by a social worker when he discovered the exploitative working conditions of workers. Today, India has more than 45 overlapping, sometimes conflicting, and often confusing major labor laws. These laws allow unions to be formed by as few as seven people, and some companies must deal with as many as 50 different labor groups. The laws also make it difficult to fire employees or to close money-losing operations. A company with more than 10 workers needs government permission to fire employees—something almost never given. In fact, Indian labor laws tend to be highly protective of labor, and they have encouraged a very inflexible labor market.

How are multinational companies adapting? Siemens AG, Whirlpool Corp., and Philips Electronics NV are using golden handshakes to buy out workers. Rather than confronting unions directly, these companies offer workers voluntary retirement and payoffs. For example, with little fanfare, Siemens shed 1,300 of 7,500 employees from its bloated Indian operation for a maximum payout of $16,160 per person—low by European standards but high for India. Many multinational managers sense that unions are ignoring such practices because of a growing realization that Indian businesses must be more efficient to compete internationally.

Given the high prevalence of strikes and lockouts, some are arguing that Indian labor laws need to be revised to improve productivity and to make industries more profitable. They point to the experiences of China, which has transitioned from extreme job security to major reform in the labor laws. Currently, China has a relatively mobile labor market, and surveys show that Chinese workers have benefited from such changes. These experiences may be useful to India as it considers reforms.

Sources: Based on Amjad, Ali. 2001. Labour Legislation and Trade Unions in Pakistan. *Karachi: Oxford University Press; Bhowmik, S. K. 2009. "India—Labor searching for a direction."* Work and Occupation, *36(2), pp. 126–144; Economist. 2003. "Two systems, one grand rivalry." June 21, pp. 21–23; Hindu. 2006. "Needed: Labour reforms." February 28, p. 1; Rai, Saritha. 2006. "Airport workers across India strike to protest plan for privatizations."* New York Times, *February 2, p. C5; Karp, Jonathan, and Michael Williams. 1997. "Firms in India use buyouts to skirt layoff rules."* Wall Street Journal, *October 13, p. A16.*

Some Historical and Institutional Differences

Historical conditions during the early days of unionization and the unions' relationships with social institutions like the government tend to influence the activities of contemporary unions. Consider the differences among British, German, French, U.S., Asian, and Indian unions observed by Professor Christel Lane.[47]

British unions began early in the nineteenth century, corresponding to the rise of major factory-based industries. Ignored early on by government, British unions developed without government interference. Not until the 1980s was there much legal control of management–labor conflict. If the union went on strike, neither the company nor the workers had any legal obligation to solve the conflict, such as honoring the workers' right to return to work. According to Lane,[48] the lack of government intervention led management and workers to develop strong adversarial relationships that remain in existence today in Britain. Lane characterizes the British situation as fragmented and highly conflictual.

Perhaps because German culture ranks high on uncertainty avoidance, labor relationships have a more orderly tradition. The government recognized the union movement in the mid-1880s. The strong role of the state served to

EXHIBIT 12.14 **Union Density in Selected Countries**

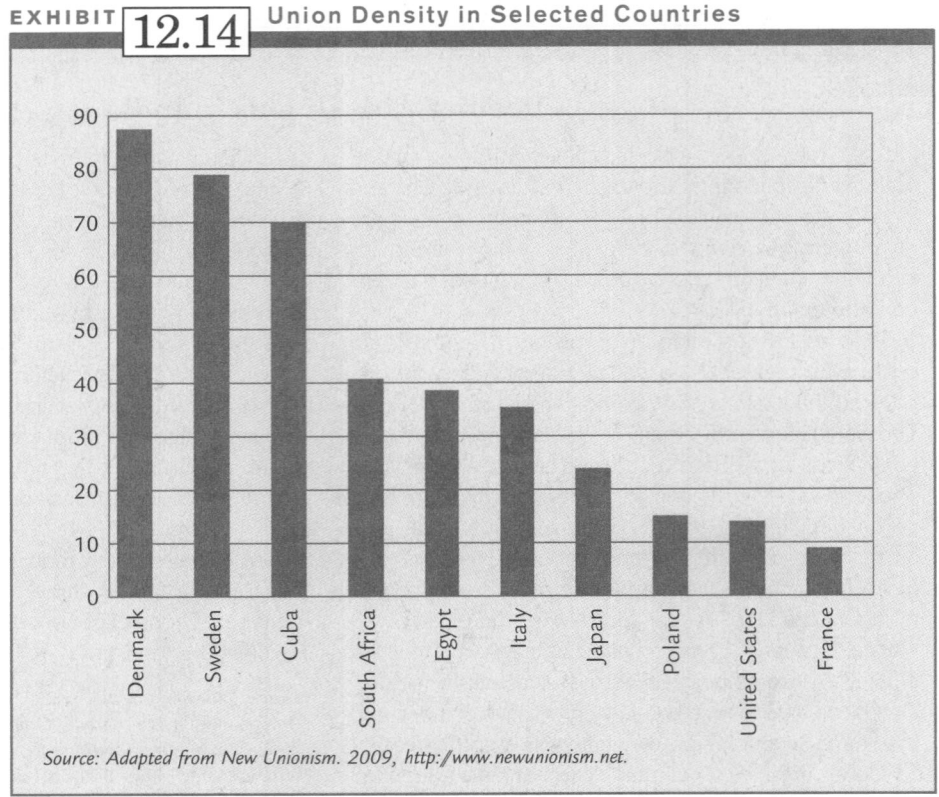

Source: Adapted from New Unionism. 2009, http://www.newunionism.net.

develop more harmonious relationships between labor and management. The result in today's Germany is a formalized, legalistic, low-conflict situation with centralized bargaining between large unions and large corporations. Lane argues that the government serves as an intermediary between unions and management.

French unions began much later and developed more slowly than did British or German unions. According to Lane,[49] there were many small companies, and this fragmentation of businesses retarded union growth. In some industries, legal recognition of the right to bargain collectively occurred as late as 1969. The lack of legal protection of French workers and the difficulties of unionization led to highly militant unions. French unions often have strong ideological orientations, and they adopt anticapitalistic stances based on a belief in the unavoidability of class conflicts between owners and workers. The French ideological unions tend to compete for union members within the same organizations, the consequence of which sometimes has favored management. In many cases, management simply ignores the unions.

In the United States before 1926, there was little legal support for union activity. The Wagner Act, passed in 1935, provided the most important legal protection for unions and granted federal protection of the right to organize and bargain collectively. U.S. unions tended early on to focus on the bread-and-butter issues of wages, benefits, and working conditions. They never developed the ideological orientations of the French unions or the formal union–management cooperation of the Germans. Union membership peaked soon after the Wagner Act, during the 1940s. However, with the decline of many traditionally unionized industries and the movement offshore of U.S. manufacturing, union strength in the United States has continually weakened.

In Asia, unionization has taken several different paths. As described in more detail later, formerly militant Japanese unions were absorbed into the corporate structure and now largely support management. However, Korean unions have developed a more conflictive relationship with industry and government. For example, recent Korean labor legislation introduced more freedom for companies to fire workers. This led to student unrest and strikes, costing more than $2 billion in lost output in just one month.[50] In tightly controlled economies such as Singapore's, where unionization has gained little, there were no days lost to industrial disputes between 1992 and 1994.[51]

In India, the first union was formed in 1918. B. P. Wadia, a social worker, created the union as a response to ongoing worker exploitation. However, that union was short-lived because the courts agreed with the companies that the actions of the union were illegal. Mahatma Gandhi was also closely associated with the creation of a textile union. After independence from Britain in 1947, India adopted a socialist model leading to the strengthening of the unions and a strong public sector. Only recently has the government started liberalizing the economy.[52]

Reflecting their particular ideologies and orientations, unions from different countries tend to adopt different structures. Next, you will see a summary of such structures in use today.

Union Structures

The type and structure of unions reflect the institutional pressures and historical traditions surrounding unionization. Several major types exist:

- **Enterprise unions** represent all the people in an organization, regardless of occupation or location.
- **Craft unions** represent people from one occupational group, such as plumbers.
- **Industrial unions** represent all the people in an industry regardless of occupational type.
- **Local unions** usually represent one occupational group in one company, but they are often affiliated with larger craft or industrial unions.
- **Ideological unions** represent all workers based on an ideology (e.g., communism) or religious orientation.
- **White-collar or professional unions** represent occupational groups.

Exhibit 12.15 shows selected countries and the popular unions in them.

The nature of union structures, in turn, influences the collective bargaining process and the general relationship between management and workers.

Enterprise unions are most often associated with Japanese labor relations, although they are not the only unions that exist now or that have existed in Japan. However, most radical Japanese ideological and industrial unions were effectively crushed during the first half of the twentieth century and were replaced by enterprise unions. Sometimes critically called company unions, these unions have close associations with management. In fact, one-sixth of the executives in major Japanese companies were previously union executives.[53] Not surprisingly, there is often close cooperation between union and management, with unions viewing management goals as their own.

Enterprise union
Represents all the people in one organization, regardless of occupation or location.

Craft union
Represents people from one occupational group, such as plumbers.

Industrial union
Represents all people in an industry, regardless of occupational type.

Local union
Represents one occupational group in one company.

Ideological union
Represents all types of workers based on an ideology (e.g., communism) or religious orientation.

White-collar or professional union
Represents an occupational group, similar to craft union.

EXHIBIT **12.15**   Popular Form of Unions in Selected Countries

Country	Craft	General	Industrial	White-Collar	Professional	Enterprise
Australia	✓	✓	✓	✓	✓	
Belgium			✓		✓	
Canada	✓					
Denmark	✓			✓		
England	✓			✓		✓
Finland				✓	✓	
Germany				✓	✓	
Japan						✓
Netherlands		✓		✓		
Norway	✓		✓			
Sweden	✓		✓	✓		
Switzerland	✓		✓	✓		
United States			✓	✓		

Source: Adapted from Poole, M. 1986. Industrial Relations: Heritage and Adjustment. *Oxford: Oxford University Press.*

Works council
In Germany, employee group that shares plant-level responsibility with managers regarding issues such as working conditions.

German unions favor the industrial form of organization. There are 17 major industrial unions, and collective bargaining generally takes place between the unions and employer associations (groups of employers). At the plant level, an elected **works council** negotiates working conditions directly with the employer, and industry unions negotiate wages at the national or regional level. The next Multinational Management Brief shows how the works council is integrated into management decision making in Germany and is globalizing its influence in tandem with the globalization of German companies.

Given that the most common objective of French unions is to organize along ideological lines, union structure does not necessarily follow industry, occupational, or enterprise categorization. Instead, one union will represent a variety of workers who adhere to the same ideological beliefs. Any one company may have several of these groups organizing workers.

In the United States, the local union remains the major structural feature. Most locals associate with some craft, industry, or mixed national union. There are approximately 170 national unions in the United States. Local craft unions tend to represent workers in a local region while local industrial unions tend to represent workers at plant level. Although most collective bargaining takes place at the local level, in some instances, such as in the automobile industry, unions attempt to make company-wide or industry-wide agreements.

Implications for the Multinational:
The Search for Harmony

When they use local workers, multinational companies have no choice but to deal with local labor practices, traditions, and laws that must be considered in any strategic decision regarding locating in another country. Consider these examples. In the United States, Japanese companies have avoided locations in the more union-friendly Northern states, favoring instead Southern locations with less union activism. The militant unions in Western Europe have led some

Multinational Management **Brief**

Globalization of the Works Council

Codetermination (*Mitbestimmung* in German) means that management surrenders to workers a share of the control of the organization reserved traditionally for management and owners. In Germany, codetermination exists at two levels. At the plant level, workers elect the works council, which has certain prerogatives supported by law and which shares some decisions with management, such as selection criteria. Some management decisions can be vetoed, such as reassignment. Finally, management must consult and inform the works council on other decisions, such as accident protection. These rights are detailed in the exhibit.

At the enterprise level, industrial democracy in Germany gives many workers equal representation on the board of directors with those elected by the shareholders. In practice, however, most of these arrangements include policies that favor owners and managers in tight votes. For example, one of the worker-selected representatives must be a manager.

For the Volkswagen Group, the works council has followed its globalization with the formation of the World Works Council in 1999. Although the World Works Council does not have the participatory rights granted German groups by Germany's Industrial Constitution Law, it is funded out of corporate operations and has some powers to influence the group's worldwide strategic decisions.

The Hoppmann Company, a car dealer and repair shop in Sigen, Germany, has taken codetermination beyond the legal requirement. The company has given workers more power and participation. For example, Hoppmann shares profits 50/50 with its employees. Furthermore, the Hoppmann owner has also transferred all property rights of his company to a foundation, that makes decisions regarding the company and to which profits are routinely transferred. Workers also have full say in major decisions affecting the company.

Codetermination
Surrender by management to workers of a share of control of the organization, traditionally reserved for management and owners.

Examples of Decisions and Levels of Participation by German Works Councils

Codetermined with Management	Veto Power over Management	Consulted or Provided Information by Management
Compensation system	Selection criteria	Major business plans
Piecework rates	Training	Introducing new technology
Job design	Recruitment	Introducing new equipment
Holiday planning	Dismissal	Financial information
Accident prevention	Reassignment	

Sources: Based on Jochmann-Doll, A., and H. Wachter. 2008. "Democracy at work—revisited." Management Review, 19, pp. 274–290; Lane, Christel. 1989. Management and Labour in Europe. Aldershot, UK: Edward Elgar; International Labor Organization (ILO). 2000. "Globalization of works council activities." World of Work, 36, http://www.ilo.org/public/english/bureau/inf/magazine/36/.

multinational companies to look for locations in countries like the Czech Republic, where not only wages but also labor conflict are lower. The country's labor relations situation is thus an important factor in designing a multinationals' IHRM policies.

Summary and Conclusions

This chapter highlighted fundamental national differences in the HRM processes of recruitment, selection, training and development, performance appraisal, compensation, and labor relations. The chapter also showed how multinational operations are affected by the HRM practices prevalent in host countries.

To understand why HRM practices differ, the chapter presented a model of how the national context affects HRM practices—national culture, business culture, and key social institutions, such as education and the legal system.

To show how the model works in different national contexts, the chapter provided numerous illustrations that contrasted U.S. HRM practices with those of other nations. Countries with collectivist cultures were often chosen for comparisons because of their cultural distances from the highly individualistic United States. The contrasts purposefully showed large differences in HRM practices, giving some sense of the variety of HRM practices around the world. However, no one chapter or book could explain adequately all the worldwide differences in human resource management. Thus, the examples given serve only to sensitize multinational managers to the complexity of their task in the HRM area.

The chapter compared U.S. recruitment and selection practices with those in collectivist societies. In contrast to managers used to working with the more public and legalistic U.S. practices, managers from collectivist societies believe that personal contact is the best method to recruit and identify the best employees.

The chapter noted that the training of entry-level workers depends largely on the institutional structure of the educational system. U.S. managers are increasingly concerned that workers do not have the basic educational skills necessary to succeed in complex jobs. In contrast, Germany has perhaps the best system of technical training, based on a collaboration of companies, unions, and the government. Many other countries, including some of the transitioning economies and developing countries, have educational systems that produce workers with good mathematical and science skills.

We also saw that management-development practices are embedded in cultural expectations regarding the relationship of managers with their organizations. U.S. companies face the dilemma of investing to develop top management talent and then risking that they will go to another company. In collectivist national cultures, such as Japan and Korea, managers have a commitment to remain with the organization (they often have little choice). Companies can therefore take a long-term view of investing in extensive management development and training.

To avoid the legal ramifications of race, gender, and age biases, U.S. performance evaluation systems tend to be formal and public. In collectivist societies, in contrast, performance appraisal tends to be informal and relatively secret. In the United States, rewards—in particular, compensation—are linked to the results of performance appraisals. In collectivist societies, factors such as age, family situation, loyalty to the company, and the relationship to the owners often influence rewards more than performance does.

Most multinational companies are attracted to production sites in countries where the wages are low but the talent pool is strong, and so they tend to adopt the host country's wage and salary levels. Numerous sources of information can provide guidance on appropriate compensation strategies. In general, multinational companies need to adapt their practices to be consistent with local norms and customs.

Confronting and dealing with differences in traditions and the volatility of labor relationships are unavoidable activities in running overseas operations. Multinational companies can seldom change a country's traditions of labor relations. Consequently, the volatility of host country labor often becomes a key factor in choosing locations.

Whether a company establishes a joint venture or sets up wholly owned operations in another country, a detailed study of the HRM practices of the local environment is required. Each nation's history, tradition, culture, and social institutions (education and legal and government systems) create unique HRM practices. Moreover, even countries that are similar culturally often have different historical and traditional patterns of labor relations. Thus, a successful multinational manager comes prepared not only with knowledge of the local culture but also with an understanding of how HRM practices evolved to become part of a host country's business environment.

Discussion Questions

1. Describe and discuss the major factors in the national context that affect a nation's HRM practices.
2. Compare and contrast recruitment and selection strategies in the United States and in nations with collectivist cultures. Discuss legal and cultural problems that multinational managers might face using a collectivist approach to recruitment and selection in the United States and using a U.S. approach in collectivist cultures.

3. Some U.S. politicians have called for the development of a German-type apprenticeship training system in the United States. If you were a manager of a U.S. Fortune 500 multinational company, how would you respond to this proposal and why?

4. Discuss the advantages and disadvantages of a permanent employment system for managers. Discuss how this system might work for non-Asian countries other than the United States.

5. You have been given the assignment of setting up a training program for first-level managers in a formerly government-owned Eastern European company. How would you go about developing a curriculum? Why?

6. Compare and contrast the appraisal and compensation systems in the United States and collectivist culture nations. Discuss legal and cultural problems that multinational managers might face using a collectivist approach to these systems in the United States and using a U.S. approach in collectivist cultures.

7. Contrast the different types of unions, and discuss the challenges each type might pose to a multinational manager.

Multinational Management **Skill Builder**

The HRM Component in a Multinational Company's Location Decision

Step 1. Read the following multinational problem:

You are now a vice president for human resources for the XYZ Company located in the United States. Your company manufactures components for industrial robots. Employees need U.S. high-school-level ability in reading and mathematics to maintain job skills.

You have just come from a meeting where the CEO has asked all functional area vice presidents to prepare a report concerning the location advantages or disadvantages of country _____. Marketing and production VPs will look at issues such as potential market size, the availability of raw materials, and supply and sales distribution channels. Your job is to consider the nature of the labor force should your company decide to set up operations in the overseas location. You will need to plan for a host country national workforce of 200 production workers, 10 first-line managers, and 2 midlevel managers.

Step 2. Picking teams and countries.

Your instructor will divide you into teams of three to five people. Each team will choose a different country for a prospective location. Your team will act in the role of the vice president for human resources and will prepare the report called for in Step 1. Your instructor may also require that you work within a specific industry.

This is a library research project. Your instructor may provide you with general data sources. You may also use information from the text.

Step 3. Prepare reports.

Reports may be written, oral, or both. A typical report analyzes the implications of economic, cultural, and institutional factors as they might affect all of the HRM functions discussed in this chapter. Following are some key topics that must be addressed. Your instructor may assign additional topics.

- *Economic considerations:*

  Comparative wage and salary levels of this country with other countries

  Employment levels, including workforce participation of women and youth

  Employer-provided benefits

  Characteristics of labor relations (e.g., likelihood of work stoppages)

- *Institutional conditions:*

  Availability of educated workers

  Extent of government intervention in employment—wage levels, benefit requirements, policies for layoffs, mandated holidays, other labor legislation

  Legal power of unions

- *National and business cultures:*

  Effects of dominant religion and language on labor relations

  Cultural effects of the relationship of the employee with the organization—long term, family dominated, preference for large or small organizations, etc.

  Traditions regarding union types and labor

- *Analysis:*

  Costs and benefits of locating in this country

  Solutions for potential problems

  Recommendation to the president

Step 4. Present your findings.
Oral reports for this exercise will take between 1 and 2 hours, depending on your instructor's requirements.

Source: Adapted from Balfour, Alan. 1988–1989. "A beginning focus for teaching international human resources administration." Organizational Behavior Teaching Review, 13(2), pp. 79–89.

Endnotes

1 Black, J. Stewart, Hal B. Gregersen, and Mark E. Mendenhall. 1992. *Global Assignments.* San Francisco: Jossey-Bass; Reynolds, Calvin. 1997. "Strategic employment of third country nationals." *Human Resource Planning*, 20(1), pp. 33–39.

2 Porter, Michael E. 1990. *The Competitive Advantage on Nations.* New York: Free Press.

3 *Economist.* 2003. "Roll over, Confucius." January 25, p. 40.

4 Porter.

5 Bohlander, George W., Scott Snell, and Arthur W. Sherman Jr. 2001. *Managing Human Resources.* Cincinnati: South-Western.

6 International Social Survey Program (ISSP). 1999–2000. "International social survey program: Work orientations II, 1997" (computer file).

7 Trompenaars, Fons. 1994. *Riding the Waves of Culture: Understanding Diversity in Global Business.* Chicago: Irwin.

8 Bohlander, Snell, and Sherman; Werther, William B., and Keith Davis. 1993. *Human Resources and Personnel Management.* New York: McGraw-Hill.

9 Hofstede, Geert. 1991. *Cultures and Organizations: Software of the Mind.* London: McGraw-Hill.

10 Steers, Richard M., Yoo Keun Shin, and Gerardo R. Ungson. 1989. *The Chaebol: Korea's New Industrial Might.* New York: HarperBusiness.

11 Organisation for Economic Co-operation and Development (OECD). 2000. *Education at a Glance: OECD Indicators.* Paris, France: OECD.

12 Drost, Ellen A., Colette A. Frayne, Kevin B. Lowe, and J. Michael Geringer. 2002. "Benchmarking training and development practices: A multicountry analysis." *Human Resource Management*, 41(1), pp. 67–86.

13 Van Buren, Mark E., and Stephen B. King. 2000. "ASTD's annual accounting of worldwide patterns in employer-provided training." *Training & Development*, Supplement, The 2000 ASTD International Comparisons Report, pp. 1–24.

14 Cook, Mary F. 1993. *The Human Resources Yearbook 1993/1994 Edition.* Englewood Cliffs, N.J.: Prentice Hall.

15 Ibid.

16 Drost et al.

17 Bondreau, John W. 1991. "Utility analysis in human resource management decision." In M. D. Dunnette and Latta M. Hough, eds. *Handbook of Industrial and Organizational Psychology*, 2nd ed. Palo Alto, CA: Consulting Psychology Press, pp. 1111–1143.

18 Arkin, Anat. 1992. "Personnel management in Denmark: The land of social welfare." *Personnel Management*, March, pp. 32–35; International Labor Organization (ILO). 1999. *World Employment Report 1998–99.* Geneva: International Labor Office.

19 *BusinessWeek Online.* 1996. August 23, chart; International Labor Organization (ILO).

20 Arkin.

21 Werther and Davis.

22 Locher, Alan H., and Kenneth S. Teel. 1988. "Appraisal trends." *Personnel Journal,* 67(9), pp. 139–145.

23 Bohlander, Snell, and Sherman.

24 Ibid.

25 Milliman, John, Stephen Nason, Cherrie Zhu, and Helen De Cieri. 2002. "An exploratory assessment of the purposes of performance in North and Central America and the Pacific Rim." *Human Resource Management*, 41(1), pp. 87–102.

26 Geringer, Frayne, and Milliman.

27 Hofstede.

28 Steers, Shin, and Ungson.

29 Ibid, p. 101.

30 Ibid.

31 U.S. Department of Labor. 1995. *Hourly Compensation Costs for Production Workers, June 1995.* Washington, DC: U.S. Government Printing Office.

32 International Labor Organization (ILO). 1997. *World Employment Report 1996–97.* Geneva: International Labor Office.

33 Simmers, Tim. 2005. "Workers in U.S. labor longer with less vacation than others." *Business Writer*, December 10, p. 1.

34 Bohlander, Snell, and Sherman.

35 Bureau of National Affairs. 1988. *Recruiting and Selection Procedures, Personnel Policies Forum.* No. 46, May. Washington, DC: Bureau of National Affairs, Inc., pp. 9–11.

36 Ibid.

37 Hansen, Fay. 1998. "Incentive plans are now commonplace in large firms." *Compensation and Benefits Review*, 30, p. 8.

38 Geringer, Frayne, and Milliman.

39 Lowe, Kevin B., John Milliman, Helen De Cieri, and Peter J. Dowling. 2002. "International compensation practices: A ten-country comparative analysis." *Human Resource Management*, 41(1), pp. 45–66.

40 Macharzina, Klaus. 2000. "Editorial: The Japanese model—out of date?" *Management International Review*, 40, pp. 103–106.

41 *Economist*, 2006. "Greying Japan the downturn," January 9. http://www.economist.com.

42 Takahashi, Shunsuke. 1993. "New trends on human resource management in Japan." In Mary F. Cook, ed. *The Human Resource Yearbook 1993/1994.* Upper Saddle River, NJ: Prentice Hall, pp. 1.37–1.38; Schmidt, Richard. 1997. "Japanese management, recession style." *Business Horizons*, 39, pp. 70–75.

43 *Economist.* 1999. "Putting the bounce back into Matsushita." May 20, http://www.economist.com.

44 Lancaster, Hal. 1996. "How you can learn to feel at home in a foreign-based firm." *Wall Street Journal,* June 4, p. B1.

45 International Labor Organization (ILO). *World Employment Report 1998–99.* Geneva: ILO; Poole, M. 1986. *Industrial Relations: Heritage and Adjustment.* Oxford: Oxford University Press.

46 International Labor Organization (ILO). *World Employment Report 1996–97;* International Labor Organization (ILO). 1997. *World Labour Report 1997–98.* Geneva: International Labor Office.

47 Lane, Christel. 1989. *Management and Labour in Europe.* Aldershot, England: Edward Elgar.

48 Ibid.

49 Ibid.

50 *Economist.* 1997. "The trouble with South Korea." January 18, pp. 59–60.

51 IMD. 1996. *The World Competitiveness Yearbook 1996.* Lausanne, Switzerland: IMD.

52 Bhowmik, S. K. 2009. "India—Labor searching for a direction." *Work and Occupations*, 36(3), pp. 126–144.

53 Abegglen, James C. and Stalk Jr, George *Kaisha: The Japanese Corporation.* New York: Basic Books.

People Management, The Mantra for Success: The Case of Singhania and Partners

It was 9:15am on 25 April 2006. An article published in that day's *Economic Times,* a leading Indian financial daily, had attracted the attention of both Mr Ravi Singhania and Ms Manju Mohotra. Singhania was the founder and managing partner of Singhania and Partners,[1] one of the largest full-service national law firms in India; Mohotra was its chief executive. The Indian legal services industry had been booming since the country's economic liberalization, which had started in the 1990s. The exponential growth of this industry was accompanied by an acute talent crunch. The ability to hire and retain talent was becoming a source of competitive advantage, a mantra for success. The news article Singhania and Mohotra read was about the movement of partners between legal services firms. It was yet another testimony to the high attrition rate in the Indian legal services industry. Sitting in Mohotra's office, the article provoked both Singhania and Mohotra to reflect on the adequacy of their firm's people practices.

Indian Legal Services Industry

"The legal services market includes practitioners of law operating in every sector of the legal spectrum. These include commercial, criminal, legal aid, insolvency, labor/industrial, family and taxation law."[2] Before 1992, a vast majority of Indian lawyers worked in small practices as Indian law mandated that law firms could neither have more than 20 partners nor could they advertise their services.[3] Additionally, Indian corporations preferred in-house legal advisors as they were more economical compared to external counsels,[4] further rendering the creation of large legal firms less likely. The legal services industry had competitive pricing and legal firms were mostly fragmented and competed in niche domains.

With the liberalization of the Indian economy, beginning in the early 1990s, came the foreign investors and multinational corporations. Indian law firms soon realized the importance of providing legal services to these new arrivals. But, only a few Indian legal firms had the expertise to handle commercial work for multinational corporations.[5] Combined with this paucity of expertise was the high demand for it, created by the fact that the legal system in India was very slow and companies preferred arbitration over going to court in settling disputes. These two factors combined to create an explosive demand for legal services in India.

In spite of the country's accession to the World Trade Organization in 1995, the Indian legal services market remained closed to foreign players. Various political parties were opposed to the idea of opening up this sector to outsiders. Hence the Indian legal services industry was protected—the practice of law was restricted to Indian nationals only.[6] Under the Indian Advocates Act of 1961, foreign law firms were not allowed to open offices in India[7] and were "prohibited from giving any legal advice that could constitute practising Indian law."[8] This prevented foreign lawyers and law firms from establishing offices in India. International law firms were "allowed to function only as liaison offices, or foreign legal consultants."[9]

Law firms were people-intensive organizations and their key capability was the skill, knowledge, and capacity of their employees. The high demand for lawyers that came with the liberalization of the Indian economy, together with the continued shortage of good quality lawyers in many areas of law, meant that the industry faced an acute shortage of legal professionals. With ample employment opportunities in the industry, attrition became a real concern. Effective human resource management became essential for law firms. The increasingly competitive labor market required firms to develop creative approaches to the recruitment and reward of employees. It also brought significant retention challenges. Firms had to find ways of holding on to their employees and of ensuring that they continued to be motivated. It was a challenge for firms to create a legal practice which met both the needs of clients for a high quality service and the needs of lawyers for a sustainable work–life balance. Typically, firms increased profits by reducing the number of employees and increasing the workload of the remaining employees.

Global spending on legal services in 2005 was over US$390 billion, and was forecast to grow to over US$480 billion by 2010, with the United States accounting for around 49 percent of the global value.[10] Thanks to the highly qualified, low-cost legal workforce, fast-growing economies such as India were likely to become outsourcing destinations, occupying a significant portion of this market.[11] This area of work opened up new avenues for Indian legal professionals, creating even more opportunities for an already scarce high-quality legal workforce. The main focus of legal process outsourcing ("LPO") was in the areas of "legal transcription," "document review," "litigation support," "legal research," "intellectual property," "contract related services," and "secretarial and legal publishing services."[12] The Indian LPO space was divided into captive centers, third party niche service providers and third party multiservice providers, with third party service providers dominating the space. The growth strategy for most service providers was to begin with low value services and gradually move up the value chain by acquiring and exhibiting domain expertise.[13] The largely untapped LPO sector was in its nascent stages, providing vast business opportunities in high volume services like document review and legal publishing, and in high end services such as intellectual property and contract services.[14]

Regional competitors like China, Korea, etc. were increasingly liberalising their legal services sectors.[15] The Indian government, though concerned by this decision of its regional competitors, had yet to make any formal decisions about the liberalization of Indian legal services. If the proposed liberalization of the legal services sector were to go through, and the restrictions on nationality in order to practice in India were removed, it was expected that India would witness the entry of many foreign law firms and legal consultants. Meanwhile, even more foreign investors and multinational corporations were expected to enter India in 2006. This would further increase competition and legal expertise requirements in areas such as foreign direct investment, intellectual property rights, infrastructure financing, human rights, environmental law, etc.[16]

Singhania and Partners

Singhania grew up surrounded by his father's corporate law and litigation practice in New Delhi, India. From his formative years, Singhania knew that he was going to be a lawyer and have his own practice one day. In 1987, while going to law school, he started his legal career with his father's firm—Singhania & Company.[17] He worked on various cases and helped manage the practice with offices all over India. During these years, Singhania became well versed with the nuts and bolts of the legal services business. His most important lessons were that customer is king and that Singhania's employees were his biggest asset.

Singhania was able to capitalize on the demand for legal services created by the liberalization of the Indian economy. A lot of work came to the firm from overseas clients, particularly from the east coast of the United States. During 1996–1997, Singhania & Company felt that in order to effectively serve clients and gain a competitive advantage, it would be valuable to establish an overseas office; New York City was the chosen location. In October 1997, Singhania moved to New York to set up Singhania & Company's office. Through his interactions with other law firms, he became conversant with the Western style of legal services management, which had a significant impact on his own management style. In November 1999, Singhania moved back to New Delhi to set up his own corporate law and litigation practice under the name of Singhania and Partners—a name very similar to his father's firm. Singhania's father encouraged his decision and advised him to take on Mohotra, who had worked with Singhania & Company, to meet the new challenge of setting up a law firm.

In the beginning, it was Singhania, an associate lawyer and Mohotra in a small office in New Delhi. While Singhania managed the core legal services aspects of the business, Mohotra took responsibility for managing the overall business [see Figure 1] and the assignment of personnel to various projects based on their competencies and availability, in consultation with senior management. The marketing activities were handled jointly by both Singhania and Mohotra. Singhania's father sought approval from clients already working with Singhania & Company to move them over to Singhania and Partners. The first few clients that moved to the firm were America Online, Fedders Corporation, Standard & Poor's, and McGraw Hill.

Although the firm did not have any litigation work in hand, Singhania, realizing the potential of a litigation practice, hired Arvind, a litigation lawyer, in early 2000. Sure enough, soon after Arvind came on board, Daewoo approached the firm with a litigation case, giving the firm's litigation practice a boost. In an effort to better serve its clients, between 1999 and 2002 the firm moved to a bigger office in the same building in New Delhi and set up offices in Bangalore, Mumbai, and Hyderabad. At the same time, it also formed affiliations with counsels across several Indian states in order to meet its clients' need to interact with one face for legal services across the country. The firm grew from two lawyers in 1999 to 50 lawyers in 2006, eight of whom were partners. The firm's practice areas included tax, corporate and commercial law, intellectual property, as well as arbitration and litigation. After the onset of the outsourcing wave, the firm had been approached by potential clients for legal process

FIGURE   1   Singhania and Partners' Organization Chart

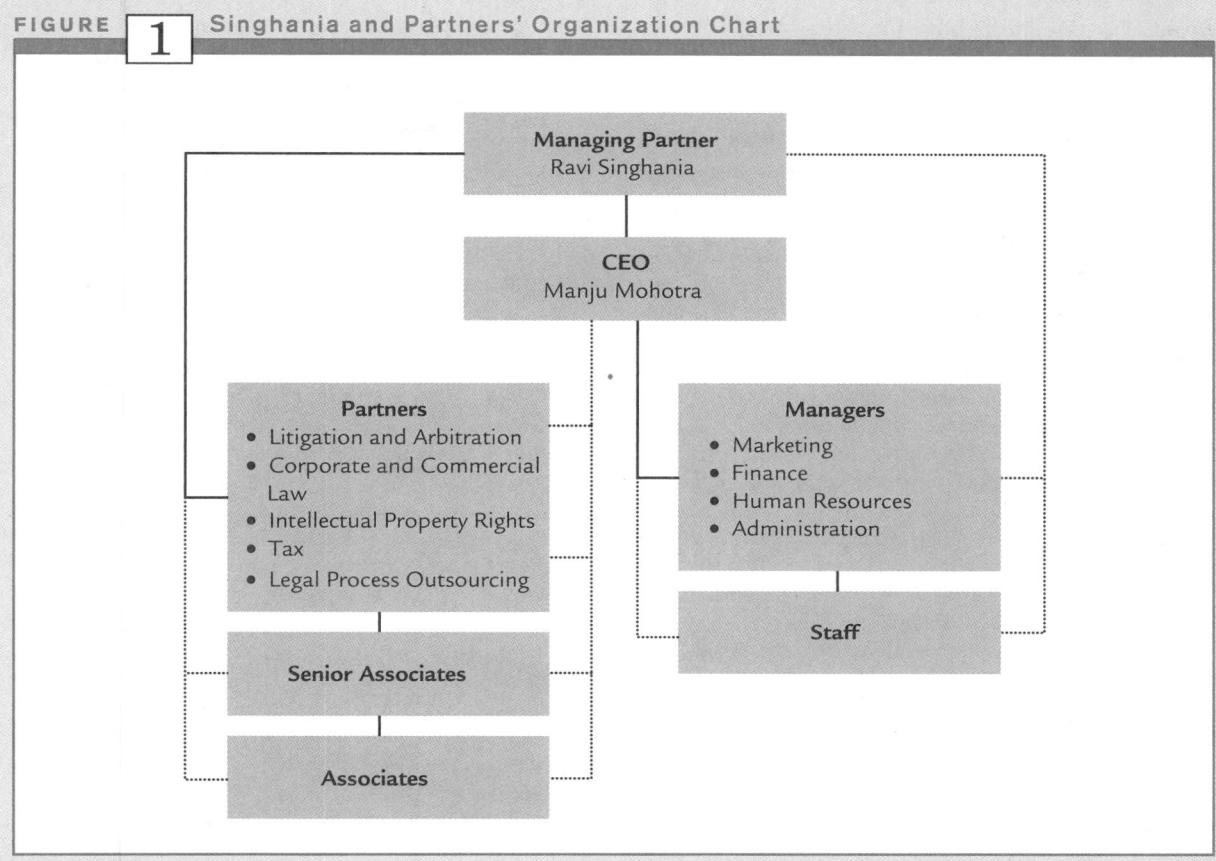

outsourcing. While Singhania and Mohotra agreed that this was a booming industry, they knew that this was not their core competence and were not sure if they should try to make it one. So although Singhania and Partners did enter this domain, it did so with great caution and was extremely selective about the quality of work it picked up.

The firm gained considerable experience in cross-border transactions in the areas of mergers and acquisitions, joint ventures, due diligence, technology transfer, as well as in assisting its clients in establishing wholly owned subsidiaries in India. The practice was built in ways so as to ensure that the clients could realize value from the firm's services. Turnaround time, accessibility to senior members in the firm, meeting deadlines, and providing services in a cost effective manner were all important to clients and formed the core values of the firm. The firm's systems, in turn, revolved around these core values.

Since Indian law prohibited legal services firms to directly market their services through any means other than the yellow pages, Singhania and Partners increased business by getting work through referrals. Singhania knew that this could only happen by providing exceptional services to clients. He put systems and processes in place and used technology to provide state-of-the-art infrastructure to serve clients effectively. In order to institutionalize the systems put in place, the firm sought an ISO 9002[18] certification in 1999, which they got in 2000. Foreseeing tremendous growth in the infrastructure and information technology sectors in India, in 2001 Singhania and Partners began focusing on these two sectors. In that same year, India witnessed mega infrastructure deals, with the golden quadrangle project[19] being announced by the government of India. The National Highways Authority of India[20] was at the forefront of these projects, and Singhania and Partners, emerging from intense competition, was appointed its legal counsel.

Are We at Risk?

When Singhania walked into Mohotra's room, she was engrossed in reading an article in that day's *Economic*

Times. She asked if he had read the article. "The one about J. Sagar?" he asked.

"Yes, attrition seems to be becoming a monster in the industry," said Mohotra and started reading the news out aloud. "'Corporate lawyers Dina Wadia, a former partner of Little & Co.; Nitin Potdar, former partner of Amarchand Mangaldas; and Akshay Chudasama, former partner of AZB and Partners and Lex Inde have signed up with national law firm J. Sagar Associates.' Do you think we need to worry about our people?"

Singhania exclaimed, "I'd rather look at this now than wait for it to become a problem and then address it!"

Mohotra, answering her own question, said, "I don't think we need to be concerned about our people. I don't think anybody in the industry can provide a better environment to work in than us. We have always thought of our people as our core asset and have treated them accordingly. After all, it's our people who make us a market leader by providing quality service to clients. And accordingly we do everything to retain talent."

"You are right. When we were looking at outsourcing, the important criteria in accepting processes was our people—we absolutely refused to do processes that required form-filling sort of work because it would not stimulate our lawyers," said Singhania. "You do think they remain intellectually stimulated, don't you?"

"We try our best. Apart from the regular work, in the bi-weekly open house we have small presentations on different topics from different legal areas. Even our junior-most lawyers are encouraged to present. It's a great opportunity to learn, build confidence, and grow with the organization!

"And if there were any dissatisfaction, I would hope for it to come out in the weekly senior management meeting or the bi-weekly open house. We encourage these forums to be utilised for voicing opinions, suggestions, ideas . . . Moreover, given our open door policy, anybody can walk in to any senior management's cabin for discussions," continued Mohotra.

Singhania said, "And the career growth is all merit based. A good example is our first litigation lawyer who started as an associate and is now a partner. Moreover, we don't just rely on annual performance reviews for increments; it is done on an as-and-when-needed basis. And, again, it is all merit based! In fact I remember that recently we increased a new employee's salary by 50 percent even before he got his first pay check, purely because we felt he provided that kind of value to the firm. He seemed happy."

Mohotra pondered further, "Talking of happiness, I can't forget the staff's excitement when we go for the annual firm retreats. The first year when we went to Naukuchiyatal,[21] it was 3 days full of fun. We played games, had picnics; it was total unwinding time. It was a great time to bond! And at our most recent camping retreat to Dhanaulti,[22] everybody had a great time. I am already being asked where we will be going this year!"

Singhania contemplated, "Do you think we're paying them enough?" Without waiting for a reply, he continued, "I do believe that we are among the best paymasters in the industry and the year-end bonuses are substantial. And like you said, it is all merit based. All the same, Seth did leave us for more money without even talking to us about it. And he was a good performer."

"You are right, but again, we try our best. We try not to overwork our lawyers. For projects that require five lawyers, we assign seven whereas others in the industry would like to assign only three. This is because we feel family life is most important. We have also been able to provide a stress free environment to work in."

Both of them felt much better than they had felt at the beginning of their conversation. Just then Mohotra's phone rang It was Seth. Putting the call on speaker, Mohotra replied, "Good morning Seth. How are you?"

"Fine thanks. Do you have a few minutes?"

"Sure."

"Well, it's a little awkward, but I'll be straightforward. Would you be open to bringing me back on board?"

Singhania and Mohotra silently agreed. "We could talk about it, but I would like to understand the reasons for your decision."

"Well, the foremost reason is that I miss the environment of Singhania and Partners. And . . . could we meet to discuss?"

"Ummm. . .I am traveling this week, so, would you like to come to the office sometime next week and we can chat about it? Say sometime next Tuesday?" replied Manju.

"Sure Ma'am. Is 10:00 am convenient?"

Referring to her diary, Manju replied, "Yes it is. All right, I'll see you Tuesday, 1st May at 10:00 am then."

"Thank you, ma'am. See you then," said Seth, concluding the conversation.

Mohotra and Singhania looked at each other and smiled. Preparing to leave, Singhania thought out aloud, "We seem to be fine for today, but what about tomorrow . . . especially with all the talk about the entry of foreign law firms into India?"

CASE DISCUSSION QUESTIONS

1. Discuss Singhania and Partners' HR practices.
2. Evaluate the adequacy of the firm's HR practices. Use the PCMM for this evaluation. What level does it appear to be at?
3. If the organization wants to improve its PCMM level, what steps should it take?

CASE CREDIT

(©) 2008 by the Asia Case Research Centre, The University of Hong Kong. Preeti Goyal prepared this case for class discussion.

CASE NOTES

[1] Singhania and Partners' Web site, http://www.singhania.net, accessed June 20, 2006.

[2] *Business Wire*. 2007. "New report helps you to spot future trends and developments in the global legal services players." March 29.

[3] RocSearch Ltd. 2006. *Indian Legal Services Market: An Analysis*. February.

[4] Ibid.

[5] Ibid.

[6] Ibid.

[7] Ibid.

[8] Sengupta, Reena. 2005. "India's legal market on the cusp of inevitable change LAW SERVICES IN ASIA PART I: Outsourcing and f", *The Financial Times*.

[9] RocSearch Ltd.

[10] *Datamonitor. 2005. "Global Legal Services—Industry Profile"*. December

[11] RocSearch Ltd.

[12] ValueNotes. 2006. *Offshoring Legal Services to India*. December

[13] *Business Wire*. 2007. "An In-Depth Analysis of the Indian Vendor Space along with Profiles of All Major Industry Players". July 10.

[14] Ibid.

[15] RocSearch Ltd.

[16] Ibid.

[17] Singhania and Company's Web site, http://www.singhania.com, accessed June 24, 2006.

[18] ISO 9002 is a model for quality assurance for production, installation and servicing developed and maintained by the International Organization for Standardization, or ISO.

[19] The golden quadrangle project would link the four metropolitan cities of India—Delhi, Mumbai, Chennai and Calcutta—via a national highway.

[20] The National Highways Authority of India was constituted by the Indian Parliament and is responsible for the development, maintenance and management of national highways in India.

[21] Naukuchiyatal is a lake resort in the northern Indian state of Uttranchal.

[22] Dhanaulti is a camp resort in the northern Indian state of Uttranchal.

People Management Fiasco in Honda Motorcycles and Scooters India Ltd

At the onset of 2006, the president of Honda Motorcycles and Scooters India Ltd. (HMSI), who was also its chief executive officer, had to make some radical decisions on a number of issues confronting the company following the July 2005 altercations with its workers. Not only did he have to repair the damage to the company's image, but he also had to develop a strategy for long-term cooperation with its employees. As he reflected upon the bitter memories of the last twelve months, he wondered if the company could achieve targets laid out in the aggressive expansion plan developed before the unrest. This included tripling the Gurgaon plant's production capacity to 0.6 million motorcycles and 1.2 million two-wheelers by the end of fiscal 2007–2008.

Neither he, nor perhaps any of the members in his managerial team, could have imagined that workers' seemingly minor grievances would turn into a warlike situation, as they did in July 2005. The company, despite all its efforts, had not been able to prevent the union formation, that too with an affiliation to All India Trade Union Congress (AITUC), which was the trade union wing of the Communist Party of India. With the events taking a nasty violent overtone, the adverse publicity might have done perhaps irreparable harm to the public image of the company. In addition, the drop in the company's sales was also worrying. The company had suffered a production decline resulting in a loss of Rs 1.3 billion[1] as a consequence of the strike and go-slow tactics by the workers, especially during the months of May and June 2005. But there was much more at stake than just the monetary loss. While choosing the company's logo of the wings, the company had aimed to fly high by taking a dominant role in the Indian two-wheeler. Industry, simultaneously taking advantage of the rapidly growing Indian economy. Given the unexpected turn of events, would the CEO be able to successfully implement strategies that would not only wash away past wounds but would also lay the foundations of a soaring future?

Dr. Debi S. Saini, professor and chairperson, HRM at Management Development Institute (MDI), Gurgaon, India, prepared this case for class discussion. This case is not intended to show effective or ineffective handling of decision or business processes.

The author thanks the many people who helped in construction of this case. The three union office bearers of the HMSI union who visited MDI at his request twice to give interviews; Mr. M. R. Patlan, the Deputy Labour Commissioner of Gurgaon, and his staff, who shared information and provided other help to reconstruct some of the nuances of the case; some anonymous persons who also shared useful information that facilitated cross-checking of the claims of the HMSI union and in building several new formulations. The author also thanks Rakhi Sehgal, a doctoral scholar in sociology, American University, Washington, for helping him establish contacts with many respondents.

HMSI: Products and Workforce

HMSI was a wholly-owned subsidiary of Honda Motor Company Limited (HMCL), Japan. The Tokyo-headquartered HMCL was one of the world's leading manufacturers of automobiles and power products. With more than 120 manufacturing facilities in 30 countries, it was also the largest manufacturer of two-wheelers in the world. HMCL was known to have excelled in the adoption of the post-Fordist production system (also called the Toyota Production System).

HMSI was established on October 20, 1999 with an aim to produce world-class scooters and motorcycles in India. The state of the art HMSI factory, located in Gurgaon, was spread over 52 acres. The initial installed capacity was 100,000 scooters per year, which was scheduled to reach 600,000 scooters by the end of 2005. HMSI operated on the principles that were followed by all Honda companies worldwide. Maintaining a global viewpoint, HMSI was dedicated to supplying products of the highest quality, yet at a reasonable price to ensure complete customer satisfaction. These two-wheelers, manufactured with Honda-tested technology, were backed with after-sales service in line with Honda's global standards. Instead of being just vehicles for transportation, HMSI's products were intended to be vehicles for change: change in the way people worked, the way they travelled, and the way they lived.

HMSI had about 3,000 employees in all; of these 2,000 were in the worker category,[2] 1,300 were confirmed workers while 700 were contract workers. The other 1,000 employees belonged to the supervisory and managerial staff. In addition, 700 persons were working as trainees and 300 were apprentices under the Apprentices Act 1960. Almost every worker or trainee held a certificate from an Industrial Training Institute (ITI) in India. All trainees, after completion of their training, normally got absorbed into the regular workforce, whereas only about 15% of the apprentices were able to get a job with the company after their apprenticeship. Considering the region-cum-industry averages, HMSI had the reputation of being a comparatively good paymaster. In October 2005, monthly wages for workers ranged from Rs 8,150 for unskilled workers to Rs 11,200 for skilled workers, which included a Rs 2,000 allowance for home rental.[3]

Human Resource Policies at HMSI

The human resource (HR) policies of HMSI were in alignment with the philosophy of its parent company, HMCL. The latter considered itself a unique organization, having adopted some distinctive employment and production practices. It also had certain fundamental beliefs, which, among others, included the value of each individual. HMSI's philosophy advocated two fundamental beliefs: respect for individual differences, and the "Three Joys" that it wanted to promote for all organizational members.

Respect for the individual stemmed from initiative, equality, and trust. The company believed that it was the contribution of each employee that was responsible for a company's success, and which would take the company into the future. Based on its philosophy, respect for the individual translated into independence of spirit and freedom, equality and mutual trust of human beings who worked for or came in contact with the company. The company claimed that its policies focused on developing each individual's capacity to think, to reason, and, most importantly, to dream.

In line with its parent Honda's philosophy, HMSI conducted all its daily activities in pursuit of the Three Joys: the joy of buying (ie, the joy of using world-class products), the joy of selling (ie, the joy of selling world-class products), and the joy of manufacturing (ie, the joy of producing high-quality products). In addition, as an extension of its key mission, the company had imbibed the "joy of creating" as an important value for itself. The management believed that the joy of creating, which helped staff derive happiness from their daily work, thrilled its employees the most.

The company also promoted association among different categories of employees through provision of similar uniforms and common canteen facilities for all. In fact, all employees were called associates. The induction program of HMSI involved, among others, acclimatizing the employees to the Honda philosophy, which was a clear written statement. The company also talked of a "Honda way" which was not a written statement but was expected to run through the company. It was commonly understood that the Honda way meant 'human behavior or way of thinking based on Honda philosophy.' For example, one of the prominent Honda ways was perseverance to ensure safety and quality in all aspects. The HR department was expected to organize training programs and facilitate internalization of culture-building so as to promote the Honda way among the employees. Apart from training in Honda philosophy, the company organized other types of training, such as TQM (total quality management) training, training for building team leaders, ISO 9000 training, and 5S training.[4]

The company also published a six-page quarterly newsletter, "Dream Team." Its focus, among others, was on covering the company's achievement in terms of awards, contracts, recognitions, quality certification, new dealers, and kaizen activity. Employee-related matters were restricted to sports competition results and announcements of marriages and childbirths.[5]

Performance Appraisal System

HMSI had a performance appraisal system for all its employees, including those in the worker category. Appraisal was performed by the section head and the shift in charge, who graded the employee on a rating scale. From this grade, workers were divided into five categories with increments ranging from Rs 400 to 1,400 per month. The company announced all appraisal results and salary-hikes immediately on the end of the fiscal year. Thus on April 1 of each year, all employees would receive their pay-hike or promotion letters. The promotion opportunities for workers ranged from worker to sub-leader to assistant executive to executive. Since almost no employee was covered by the Payment of Bonus Act, 1961, the company had institutionalized a policy of giving an *ex gratia* of one month's gross pay to every employee as incentive pay around the Diwali festival.[6]

Works Committee

Since April 1, 2004, the company had constituted a works committee under the Industrial Disputes Act, 1947 (IDA), consisting of 15 workers and 5 management representatives.[7] The management had also constituted some other committees consisting of workers and management representatives. Some of these were the canteen committee, the transport committee, the health committee, and the sports committee. Nominations to these committees were done by the management based on the perceived interest of different persons.

Employee Welfare

In line with its HR policies, all employees at HMSI, including the managers, wore similar uniforms. The company provided two sets of uniforms, one company cap and one pair of shoes to each employee every year. HMSI had also taken several initiatives in the area of employee welfare, which ranged from subsidised canteen facilities to attractive hospitalization reimbursement for all employees. Besides the canteen, another key initiative in this regard was transport facilities to and from workers' residences, provided at subsidised rates. The company also had a sports club for employees' use at Sukhrali village in Gurgaon, which had facilities for both outdoor and indoor games. Workers used these facilities to organize matches with employees of other companies in a variety of sports including football, volleyball, table tennis, chess, carom board, badminton, tug of war, high jump, and long jump. In the initial years, the company used to invite workers' families to celebrate the foundation day, but as the size of the workforce increased, the practice was discontinued.[8]

Most of the HMSI workers did not qualify for the Employees State Insurance scheme under the ESI Act, 1948, as their salaries had crossed the maximum salary limit for coverage. The company covered such employees under the Paramount Health Care facility. In addition to out-patient department facilities, this scheme provided re-imbursement for hospitalisation expenses. Untill September 2005, a worker and his or her spouse and up to two children were covered for Rs 75,000 each for hospitalisation insurance, while the worker's mother and father were covered for Rs 150,000 each per annum.[9] In addition, to provide support to an associate at times of financial need, the company had a policy of paying, in cash, Rs 2,100 for the birth of a child (limited to a maximum number of two children) and Rs 3,100 on an employee's marriage. Rs 5,000 was given to the family of an employee on his or her death and Rs 3,000 on the death of an associate's spouse, child, or parent. The company also met its liabilities under various labor laws.

Seeds of Unionization and After

For a couple of years after commencement of production, things ran smoothly. However, despite all the HR initiatives, it seemed all was not as it had appeared. The first signs of acrimony were voiced in November 2004, when workers expressed resentment at receiving Diwali gifts valued at Rs 600 apiece. Union leaders were quoted to have said, "in the past years also, the value of the Diwali gift was of about Rs 400 to Rs 500. Looking at the stature that our company enjoys in the global market, we all felt belittled at this small gift." A manager added that the perception of unfairness among workers was exacerbated by additional rumors that Hero-Honda,[10] a competitor of HMSI, was giving a refrigerator each to its workers as a Diwali gift. In the end, 99 percent of the HMSI workers refused to accept the Diwali gift, and the company took it back. As an alternative, it offered a coupon of Rs 600, with which workers could buy any gift item of their choice from certain specified dealers, but that too was turned down by the workers. Ten days after Diwali, this money was transferred to their bank accounts.

Other resentments were also festering among the workers. They were made to sign a "movement sheet" whenever they took a break to go to the toilet or drink water. In a much-cited incident, a worker was once denied permission to go to the toilet. When he could no longer bear it, he pulled the line chain to stop the conveyor belt and rushed to relieve himself. When he returned some minutes later, he was dismissed. Also, as in the post-Fordist production system, workers were often required to attend to more than one machine simultaneously; this increased stress levels on the shop floor. The company was also very strict in granting leave. Even when a worker's close relative was seriously ill or circumstances were otherwise serious, leave would not be granted. Apparently, while denying the leave, managers would lecture the employees. Sometimes they would be told to leave the company permanently if they could not perform up to expectations. If a worker wanted to change a shift temporarily for some obligatory reason, it was almost never granted. Almost every day, some worker or another would get a threat of termination. Because there was considerable fear of management's authority, nobody dared to speak up or seek a grievance redressal.

Workers also perceived that many managers showed partiality in matters related to job postings. Their favorites were posted in jobs outside the production line. Production-line jobs were far more exerting than any other postings. The enormity of the problem took on serious proportions, and led to considerable bickering among workers. It seemed that while this practice was in place since the beginning, the Japanese top management knew little about it. The Indian managers would not let the workers meet the top management to share their grievances, but rather encouraged the scenario, as it prevented workers from uniting. Union leaders reinforced this view and claimed that managers did so to create friction amongst the common workers. They wanted these postings to be done on the basis of seniority.

At the same time, workers were also unhappy with the idiosyncratic attitude of the vice-president of manufacturing (a Japanese national), who was a strict Honda disciplinarian. Known for his unpredictability, he had a reputation for saying anything to anybody at any time. He was often seen patrolling the shop floor with a 14-foot-long stick that was used for measuring the heights of trolleys. Most workers took a dim view of him and cracked jokes about him behind his back. Once, a worker returned two minutes late from the teatime break. To show his disapproval, the VP kicked this worker in the leg, albeit in a friendly manner. At the time, neither the concerned worker nor the other workers around him reacted at all. However, by evening, the news had spread amongst the others and slogans were raised against the VP. The next day, the VP apologised in front of the workers' gathering. Subsequently, the Indian managers asked some 15 workers to have a meeting with them on the issue. The incident resulted in production stopping for a day and a half. A similar incident occurred when a Sikh officer of the company was wearing a different-coloured cap and not the usual company cap.[11] The VP gave a push to his cap, knocking it off him. Although the official concerned felt insulted, he kept quiet.

Although the errant VP was later sent back to Japan, no other action was taken against him. Not satisfied with a mere apology from the VP, in the last week of March 2005 the workers came out with a charter consisting of more than 50 demands. These included: an increase of Rs 2,500 per month in wages; a 20 percent annual increment in wages; house rent allowance to be pegged at 70 percent of wage; conveyance allowance of Rs 1,500 per month; a 20 percent bonus on wage plus a dearness allowance; provision for free distribution of one kilogram of milk and ½ kilogram of *gur* (jaggery) per worker everyday; provision for a union office on the company premises along with all incidental facilities including a telephone; a loan of Rs 200,000 for marriage of a sibling or child; provision of a library on the company premises, and the abolition of the policy of overstay (if the production target for the day was not achieved, workers were required to compulsorily stay back until the target was achieved). Reluctantly, on April 1st 2005, the management offered the workers a compensation package comprising an increment of Rs 3,000 per month, on the condition that the workers not form a union. They refused to accept the management's offer.

When the management did not yield, the workers started collecting money for funding union activities. HMSI management suggested that the workers form an internal committee instead. When workers declined this suggestion, many were individually called into a manager's room and exhorted not to join the union. Letters were sent to certain workers' homes, claiming that they were indulging in undesirable activities. The management allegedly hired some outsider toughs to frighten the workers if they formed a union. But their resolve was too strong. With the help of local union leaders (affiliated with political parties), HMSI workers began making efforts to form a union, and subsequently moved an application for registration of the union to the registrar of trade unions in Chandigarh.[12] The management, not wanting the formation of a union in the organization, tried its best to stop the union registration. It resorted to various means like lobbying with the government of Haryana to help prevent the formation and subsequent registration of the union. As a result, the registrar allegedly denied registration of the union on the ground that the proposed workers' action was initiated in bad taste. The registrar also claimed that it would result in disharmony of relations between the industry and workers in the region at large and would prove detrimental to the growth and development of the industrial belt in and around Manesar.[13]

Consequent to this, the workers resorted to a slowdown of work (go-slow) and refused to put in overtime to complete production targets. The management viewed the new stand of the workers as a serious breach of discipline and suspended four workers on charges of insubordination, tampering with the quality of output, adopting a go-slow policy, indiscipline, and unrest. During the same period, the management also refused to absorb some trainees who had completed their two years of internship. These actions of the management led to widespread discontent among the workers. Most workers, whether permanent or trainees, collected together under the leadership of the suspended workers and started raising slogans. They also *gheraoed* the management within the offices located at the factory premises.[14] During this *gherao,* one person from senior management was manhandled and beaten up. The entire incident of the *gherao* and resulting violence resulted in production being shut down for 30 minutes. The management saw this as a grave and acute case of breach of discipline. It retorted by suspending 50 workers and dismissing the previously suspended four workers without any inquiry. This made the situation in the company still more explosive. Interestingly, in regard to the importance of local laws, the global philosophy of Honda stated as follows:

> *Honda is committed to providing a work environment that is free from unlawful discrimination, including harassment that is based on any legally protected status. Honda will not tolerate any form of harassment that violates this policy. This policy forbids any unwelcome conduct that is based on an individual's age, race, colour, religion, sex, national origin, ancestry, marital status, sexual-orientation . . . or any other basis protected by state, federal or local law.*

In view of the resistance from the management, the registration of the proposed HMSI union was further delayed by more than a month. It was only when the cause of the workers and their application for registration was supported by a letter from AITUC chief Gurudas Dasgupta, a member of Indian Parliament, that the HMSI labor union registration finally took place. This letter, dated May 20, 2005, was addressed to the chief minister of Haryana and requested that he look into the matter to secure early registration of the proposed union. The newly-formed union, while adopting the demands raised earlier, also added additional demands to their charter.

Conciliation Failure and the Intensity of Workers' Action

Eventually, the dispute landed itself for conciliation. Conciliation proceedings were initiated on May 26, 2005 by the deputy labor commissioner of Gurgaon, who served as the conciliation officer in the Gurgaon region for all general-demands disputes. For conciliating matters related to individual disputes, the Gurgaon area was divided into four regions, each headed by a labor-cum-conciliation officer. Six conciliation meetings were held on June 3, 17, 28, and July 8, 14, and 19, 2005. The HMSI management was represented by two managers belonging to the company's HR department. They remained quiet almost throughout the proceedings. The only contention the management raised was that the company was not required on any ground, whether legal or equitable, to raise the wages of the workers since it was already paying more than the region-cum-industry standards. The representatives of the union, however, chose to stick to their demands. The commissioner thought that the conciliation proceedings failed due to "the uncompromising stand adopted by both the union as well as the management representatives." He submitted a confidential failure report to the Haryana government under section 12 (4) of the Industrial Disputes Act, 1947 (IDA) on July 19, 2005.

Concurrently, pending the outcome of the conciliation proceedings, the management asked the workers to sign a statement of good conduct. This statement stipulated that the workers return to work unconditionally and remain disciplined while on the factory premises. The statement also contained a clause stipulating non-pursuance of union activities by the workers while at work. It was this clause that became contentious and which compelled workers not to sign the statement. The management, in retaliation, refused to let the workers enter the factory premises without their signatures on the good-conduct bond.

In order to maintain production schedules, the management hired some temporary workers from its vendor companies. These temporary workers were asked to stay in the factory premises and requisite facilities were provided to them within the factory. Eventually, in June 2005, the management and the union reached an agreement whereby the management agreed to allow the workers to enter the premises of the company and work only under the condition that the terminated staff would not be taken back or reinstated. Furthermore, it was decided that the workers would be allowed entry into the factory premises in batches of 400 and that too only if they signed good conduct bonds. However, further apprehensions continued to plague the management. A few years prior at Hero-Honda Motorcycles Ltd, Dharuhera,[15] a similar situation had arisen and temporary workers from vendor companies were called in to continue the production. The management of Hero-Honda Motorcycles Ltd, under circumstances similar to those faced by HMSI, had entered into an agreement with their employees and allowed batches of 400 workers to enter the premises and resume work. However, after entering the premises, these workers disrupted the work done by the temporary workers from the vendor companies and brought production to a halt. The management at HMSI feared similar consequences at their factory.

While the workers agreed to the management proposition, on the following day, they put up the union flag at the factory gate. HMSI management became cautious and decided to allow only batches of 100 workers to enter the factory premises. Later, the management further retracted and announced that it would take back workers in batches of no more than 50. Anguished workers agreed yet again, but the management eventually decided not to allow any worker to enter the factory. The management also requested and received a good degree of police protection. The potentially explosive situation in the factory resulted in a fear in the minds of the temporary workers who had come from the vendor companies. Many of these workers fled from the factory premises. On June 18, 2005, only 38 temporary workers reported to work. At 1:30 p.m., the management was forced to shut down production for the day.

All these disruptions, in addition to the go-slow tactics adopted by the workers after the union registration, severely affected daily production at the plant. During the months of May, June, and July 2005, production dropped to a mere 10 percent of normal levels, from 2,000 scooters per day to around 200. This was a grave cause for concern to the management, causing HMSI to place a newspaper advertisement for the recruitment of new workers.

The Dance of Violence and its Aftermath

On July 25, 2005, workers from HMSI and some from neighboring industries staged a rally at offices of the district authorities to press their demands for reinstatement of their dismissed and suspended colleagues. The police prohibited the workers from entering the Civil Lines area, which housed the offices of all major government functionaries of the district, including the district collector. At this point, several masked men began throwing stones. The protesters attacked the deputy superintendent of police, who was beaten mercilessly. They also set fire to the vehicle belonging to the sub-divisional magistrate. Eventually, the police succeeded in controlling the mob. The incident was covered by the television media and generated a great deal of public sympathy for the police. The identity of the masked men was not confirmed, and HMSI workers denied that anyone from their ranks was among them.

After this much-publicized clash, a message was sent to the workers that the administration would meet them and accept their memorandum. They were asked to assemble at the lawns of the secretariat. Once inside the enclosure, on some slight provocation, the police resorted to the use of brute force against the unarmed workers, reportedly in retaliation for the earlier attack on the police. The constabulary forced workers indiscriminately to kneel holding their ears while they were thrashed. The number of workers injured was initially claimed to be 700. While most workers were discharged after first-aid, 70 of them suffered severe injuries. Later on, the police arrested a number of workers and booked them under different sections of the Indian Penal Code. The Haryana police also booked the legal counsel of the HMSI union on charges of attempt to murder. The media reported that this use of the worst possible police brutality on the workers, though inexcusable, was not exactly unprovoked [see Exhibit 1 for media pictures of the event]. The television images of the savagery exhibited by the police in their attack on the workers brought to many minds the savagery of General Dyer's army at Jalianwala Bagh, perpetrated in the interest of their British masters. P. Sainath, a journalist for the *Hindu,* an English language daily, wrote:

> The scenes from Gurgaon gave us more than just a picture of labor protest, police brutality or corporate tyranny . . . The streets of Gurgaon gave us a glimpse of something larger than a single protest. Bigger than a portrait of the Haryana police.

Greater than Honda. Far more complex than the "image of India" as an investment destination. It presented us a microcosm of the new and old Indias. Of private cities and gated communities. Of different realities for different classes of society. Of ever-growing inequality.

P. Sainath, journalist for the Hindu

While it was admitted that some police officers were beaten by the mob before the police responded with its brutality, the HMSI union maintained that it was done by outsiders. Violence continued on the next day, reportedly sparked off by enraged members of the public who turned up at the civil

EXHIBIT **1**   **Press Images of the July 2005 Union Incident**

Picture 1: Police beating HMSI workers on July 25, 2005

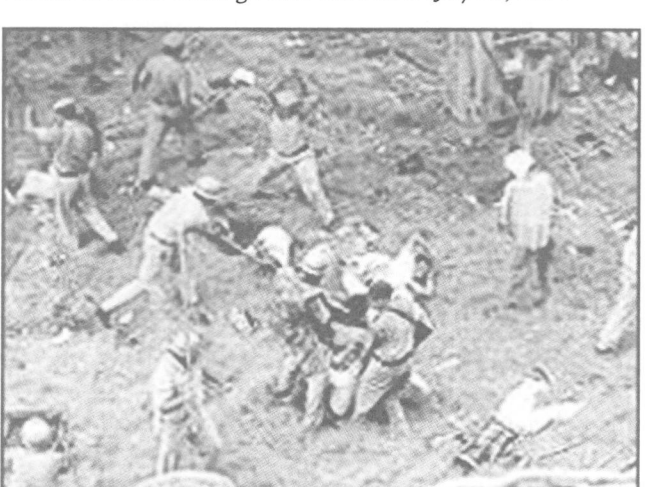

Picture 2: An angry relative of an injured worker attempting to hit a policeman for his role in beating HMSI workers

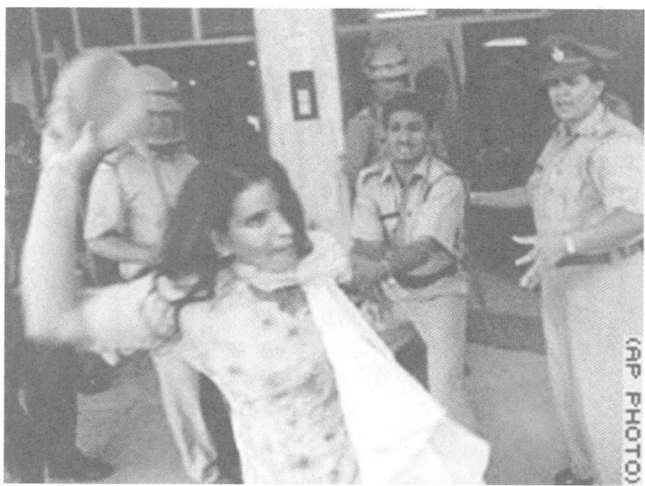

(AP PHOTO)

continued

EXHIBIT   **1**   Continued

Picture 3: HMSI union leaders meet Mrs. Sonia Gandhi,
president of the ruling Congress Party, to seek help
against the police action

hospital and could not find their relatives. Some of these were whisked away by
the police and were charged with the previous day's violence. This inflamed
matters even further. The police action on workers was severely protested by the
print and television media and by politicians in and outside the Parliament. As a
result, the inspector-general of police conceded that the incident was an act of
gross negligence on the part of the police. The deputy superintendent of police
and the sub-divisional magistrate concerned claimed that out of the 375-odd
persons arrested after the incident, 79 had nothing to do with the strike at
HMSI. This was later verified by the records of HMSI.

On July 26, 2005, the day after the unprecedented violence, HMSI closed operations for half a day, but it did not declare a lockout. Consequent to severe
protests in different circles, on July 27, the Haryana chief minister ordered a court
of enquiry to investigate the violent incident, to be conducted by a retired judge
of the Punjab and Haryana High Court.[16] The terms of reference provided for,
among others: completing the inquiry within a period of three months;
examining the role of outsiders in the incident; examining whether the force
used by the police was justified or excessive; and whether the means available to
the police were adequate to control the crowd. The Haryana chief minister was
also directed by Congress president Sonia Gandhi to hold discussions with the
HMSI management and its workers. For more than two weeks, 61 workers
remained in jail. They were subsequently released on August 11, 2005.

The Truce and the Role of the State

On July 30, 2005, an agreement arbitrated by the Haryana chief minister was arrived at between the workers and the management of HMSI. Of course, technically this was a conciliated settlement and not a case of arbitration under the IDA. The agreement stated that the striking workers would resume duty from Monday, August 1, 2005, and that they would not raise any new demands during the next one year. The trade union, which was the bone of contention between the workers and management would, however, continue to operate. The agreement also stated that the 50 suspended workers would be reinstated, as well as the four union leaders whose services had been previously terminated. However, the employees would be reinstated only after they had submitted an unconditional letter of apology. The four terminated workers were also required to submit a separate assurance letter to the top management. The settlement contained a clause stipulating that the workers promised not to engage in any act of indiscipline and assure normal production. However, the management retained the right to conduct an inquiry into the reasons for termination of the aforementioned four employees and, if the employees were found guilty, the management had the right to transfer them to any other department other than the manufacturing department. The agreement also provided for termination of any employee of HMSI who was convicted in any of the court cases that had been initiated against them by the city administration in connection with the July 25, 2005 incident. The workers were awarded full salary for the months of May and June, 2005. However, from June 27 onwards, the principal of "no work, no pay" would be implemented.[17] It was also provided that the injured workers who were not able to work immediately would be given paid leave.

About the workers' demand to absorb the trainees as permanent employees after the completion of their internship, it was decided that a proper test and a detailed appraisal form would be administered for evaluating their performance before inducting them as permanent staff. Finally, it was decided that the agreement be considered as final conciliation in respect to all demands raised by the workers and that, in the future, both the parties would maintain cordial relations.

Union–Management Dynamics in the Post-Violence Scenario

The union office-bearers felt that a good degree of change could be seen in the attitude of the managers in the post-July 25 scenario. The management allowed concessions on several fronts. On the day of the tripartite agreement, the management wanted to terminate the services of some 200 contract workers even though the tripartite agreement provided for reinstatement of all workers. But the union was able to convince the management that the company should stick to the agreement. No domestic inquiry proceedings were started against the four dismissed workers who had been taken back, nor were they transferred to other departments as envisaged in the tripartite agreement.

The management had also informally allotted a temporary room to the union leaders, though it was not sufficiently big, and promised them a proper union office after some time. There was also an informal understanding that the union leaders would have the freedom not to work on the shop floor as long as several industrial relations issues were still pending. For example, police had registered cases against

63 workers, including all the seven union office-bearers, for the July 25 violence. This necessitated running around contacting different people to build a sound defence. Meanwhile, the injured workers had their own problems, requiring the intervention of the union. Of the 50 workers who had suffered major injuries, 15 cases were very serious and involved head injuries, multiple fractures, damage to knee caps, etc. The company showed all these injured as absent, and was hesitant to pay them their salaries. According to union leaders, they "had to struggle to ensure that their salaries are paid regularly."

They also had to monitor the worker–supervisor relations closely to see that workers were treated better. Another area of the union leaders' involvement was the issue of absorption of trainees into regular positions. Even as the absorption of all persons who had completed their training into regular service formed part of the tripartite settlement, the management was initially refusing to take most of them on different pretexts. As these trainees had supported the workers' struggle, the union got all of them absorbed into regular jobs. Speaking of the change, S.K. Shafi, the secretary of the union, observed:

> Now, when a worker asks for leave, managers speak with much restraint; their response being far more positive. Workers are able to adjust a half-day shift within the next day with negligible hassles. The number of memos that workers get is negligible. The workers wanted four days' leave on Diwali in November 2005, and consequently closure of the factory for four days. This meant three days' compensatory working on Sunday and/or holidays; the management has hesitantly agreed to this proposal. Further, most factories in Gurgaon were working on 29th September, 2005 when some of the major Indian trade union federations gave a call for industrial strike all over the country in protest against the Central Government's economic policies. Our union, however, observed the day as strike. Though the management felt bad to know its decision, the union compensated the loss by working on a Sunday
>
> *S.K. Shafi, secretary of the HMSI workers' union*

Another major achievement by the union was the hike in the coverage of the workers and their family members under the medical insurance scheme. This was a result of negotiations following an incident in September 2005, when the hospitalization expense of a worker's wife cost him Rs 135,000. Although the worker was in extreme distress over the death of his wife, the management refused to pay the excess of the coverage limit. Earlier, nobody would have dared to talk about such an incident with the management. In the changed circumstances, the union negotiated the issue and made the management agree to a family floater coverage scheme of Rs 175,000. This overall limit could be utilized by one or more or all the family members. If the expenses still exceeded this amount, the company agreed to pay up to Rs 100,000. This agreement was reached not through any written settlement with the union, but by way of a change in management policy at the insistence of the union, and came into effect on October 1, 2005.

Another new development was that, whenever there was a workers-related problem or issue, the management invited all seven of the union office-bearers for discussion. This had never been done earlier. For example, the management faced a problem of increasingly stressed workers who had to work overtime to meet the production targets. Overtime was being paid at the rate of double the basic wage rate. Workers found it somewhat attractive to work overtime and make extra money. But this had led to, among others, medical problems. Workers never felt fresh while at work, thus hampering overall productivity. The union's help was sought and a decision was taken to scrap overtime completely, except under exceptional circumstances.

In a landmark incident on September 9, 2005, the "A-shift" in assembly achieved its target of 1,000 scooters for the first time after the union formation. Prior to the unrest, the target was achieved in almost every shift. Union leaders said that the targets could not be achieved due to various interruptions. However, they could not satisfactorily explain why these interruptions had not affected the target achievement earlier. On hearing the target achievement that day, the vice-president of manufacturing, along with the general manager of production, came to the shop floor during the lunch time and commended the achievement of the workers. The next day, sweets were distributed to all workers.

The scheme of inviting workers' families on the founders' day had been stopped as the number of employees had increased, and the practice was becoming unmanageable in view of the fact that Honda workers were from more than 20 different states of India. This practice was revived in late September 2005. Thereafter, family members were invited to the factory at the company's expense in batches and were shown the conditions under which their loved ones worked.

The Diwali gift for the year 2005 was also settled through negotiations. Each employee was given a gift of Rs 2,000 and an incentive bonus in the form of a bank account credit of Rs 4,000. This included all managerial staff. Ironically, unlike the one month's gross pay disbursed for the year 2004, the bonus money for the year 2005 was smaller. The management was able to convince the union that the factory had suffered huge losses and thus the *ex gratia* bonus had to be cut down. The biggest sufferers from this agreement were the managerial employees, who received substantially less than their one month of gross salary in previous years.

Despite these developments, there were still some odd incidents reminiscent of the previous unrest. One took place on September 2, 2005, when two supervisors in the aluminium machine shop treated workers authoritatively and in a provocative manner, just as they had done before. The workers of this department reacted. Some 150 of them came to the union leaders seeking their intervention. When the union leaders went to settle the issue with the senior manager concerned, he spoke angrily with the union leaders too. Workers of the whole shift halted work for around 15 minutes. A union leader later said, "we went to all the departments to exhort the workers to start the work; we did not want work to be interrupted. That day most senior managers had gone to Chandigarh for some work. After they came back, the next day they all felt sorry for the incident and appreciated our intervention in the matter."

Expatiating on the dynamics involved, C.D. Tikar, the general secretary of the union, observed:

We are committed to the company. We consider it as ours, and always want to do our best for it. The respect for the individual and the joys that the company claims to be practicing are merely in the book. Some of the senior managers want to see a big distance between the top management and the workers. The HR manager never wants that we meet the Japanese top management, as he feels that if he is asked to become transparent in his working, this will prevent him from realizing his hidden objectives including favouring his chosen few. Only some 20 per cent of the managers treat us with the dignity that we expect as members of the company; most others have big egos. The managers as well as the workers need to change. You know, the problems always emanate at the shop floor, but nobody bothers about analyzing their causes and possible solutions in a more practical and acceptable manner. The worker always wants fair and just working of the company. When this does not happen, he reacts.

C.D. Tikar, general secretary of the HMSI workers' union

Looking Back and Planning for the Future

The company had been performing extremely well since beginning, and had shown promising results on several fronts [see Exhibit 2]. The TNS Automotive Dealers Satisfaction Study, 2004 ranked HMSI as the leader in the two-wheeler category in India with 108 points, followed by Hero-Honda with 96 points. The company also received several recognitions in other spheres. But in the post-July 25 scenario, the company took quite some time to absorb the shock of what had happened. The management wanted to know what had gone wrong and where, and how things could be improved. Some of the issues at hand that needed attention were summarized by an anonymous manager of HMSI as follows:

The company had a total lack of direction on the people front, which to a great extent is still persisting. Management does not know what to do to overcome the shock of July 25 and its aftermath. Japanese were conversant dealing with the Japanese unions, which were known to be much more tolerant. The company also has a lot of problems of hierarchy consciousness. The present GM–Operations came from Maruti (a Suzuki-controlled automobile company), where he could successfully tackle somewhat similar discontent among workers. The Japanese do not understand the workers' language also. The Director–General Affairs, who also is responsible for overall HR management, came with a lot of ideas, but he could not understand the organisational working from the employees' point of view. When workers had

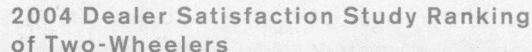

EXHIBIT 2   **2004 Dealer Satisfaction Study Ranking of Two-Wheelers**

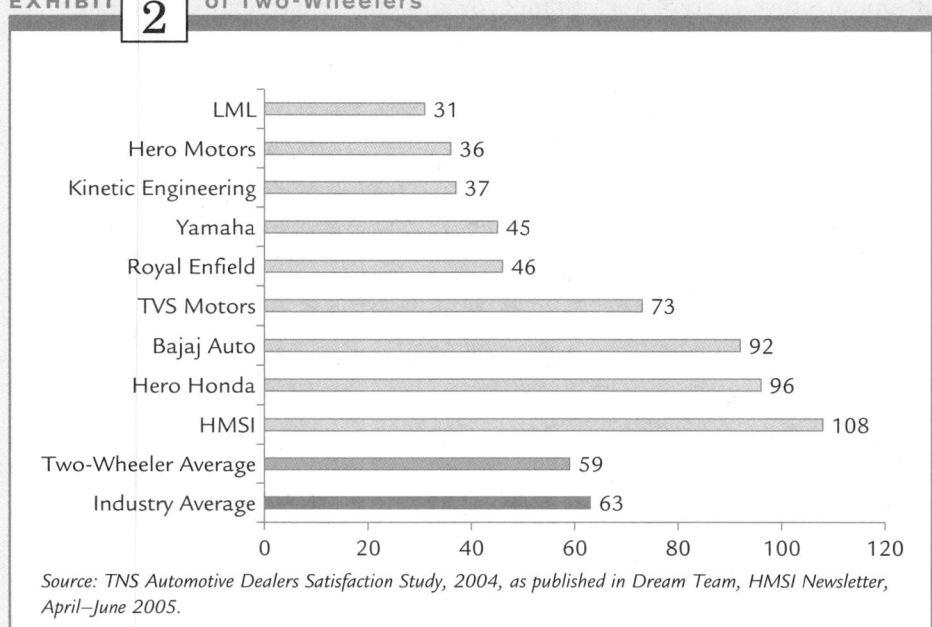

Source: TNS Automotive Dealers Satisfaction Study, 2004, as published in Dream Team, HMSI Newsletter, April–June 2005.

resorted to go-slow, Japanese managers did not know what to do. On the other hand, Indian managers were specialists in production; they did not understand how to handle industrial relations (IR) issues. If D.P. Singh [who was HR chief till some time ago, and had left HMSI, commanded respect among most workers] had not left, perhaps the problems may never have arisen. He had a good rapport with the workers. Another problem was that the Japanese had not given Indian managers much power to take major initiatives in different dimensions. Things have, however, somewhat improved in this regards now after July 25.

As one of the direct consequences of the unrest, the company revamped and intensified its training function. Managers were sent out to attend management development programs (organized by, among others, the Confederation of Indian Industry and the All India Management Association). Training areas included inter-personal skills, negotiation skills, team-building and conflict management, and leadership building. Interestingly, however, the position of assistant manager of training remained vacant.

In view of the damage done to the company's reputation, HSMI was also busy in an image-building exercise. Earlier, the managers were under the impression that Honda products would sell because of the company's image as a global brand. Now it had come to realise that, following the July 25 violence, its advertisements were no longer effective. The company was forced to consider new ways of enhancing their market image. In an innovative attempt, a week-long drive was organized during which henna tattoos of the HMSI logo were applied on women's hands.[18] In its endeavour to reach the far-flung masses across the country, HMSI also ran road shows of two of its popular two-wheeler models, Eterno and Unicorn.

A strategic meeting of the top management and the department heads took place at a country resort to decide the future course of action. They were well aware that, in addition to the assistant manager of training position, the posts of senior manager of industrial relations and senior manager of administration were also lying vacant. An outcome of the meeting was the decision to appoint a new person as the senior manager for both these functions. In September 2005, all union office-bearers were trained by the HR department on building co-operative industrial relations. External trainers were also invited to participate in this program. The company also nominated a committee consisting of seven worker representatives who would bring the workers' grievances to the notice of the management and the union leaders.

The short but bitter history of industrial relations of HMSI had shaken the company's top management. Its CEO was wondering what impact this would have on the ambitious expansion plans that he had drawn out just a few months before the July 25 violence. In preparation for the move forward, he was looking for ways to undo the bitter feelings among the workers, while at the same time deliberating what steps he should implement, not only to repair the damage to the company's image, but also to maintain and enhance productivity.

C A S E   D I S C U S S I O N   Q U E S T I O N S

1. Identify and discuss the key factors that led to the breakdown of industrial relations at HMSI.
2. Discuss the failures on the part of the Japanese and Indian managers that contributed to the present situation.
3. What HRM strategy was being pursued by the management, and what factors led to its failure?
4. Discuss the provisions of Indian industrial relations law that may have been violated by the HMSI management.

5. How should HMSI go about attending to the issues in people management systems and processes? What HR strategy should it adopt and implement for making lasting improvement in industrial relations?

CASE NOTES

1. US$1 = 45 INR on May 1, 2005.

2. Under the Factories Act 1948, a worker is "a person employed directly or by or through any agency (including a contractor) ... in any manufacturing process or in cleaning any part of the machinery or premises used for a manufacturing process or in any other kind of work incidental to, or connected with, the manufacturing process ...."

3. In the state of Haryana, India, the minimum wage rates for unskilled, semi-skilled, skilled, and highly skilled workers in the month of May 2005 were Rs 2,360, Rs 2,470, Rs 2,615, and Rs 2,920 respectively.

4. The training department, which was a part of its human resource department, was supposed to be headed by an assistant manager; but this position lay vacant for a long time.

5. A perusal of the past issues of the newsletter revealed that its focus was on targets, safety, exhortations related to, and announcement of, achievements concerning quality, safety, and training programs on defensive and safe driving of two-wheelers. Very few employee-related matters were covered. Nor was there any scope for workers' expression through any letter to the editor related to issues that concerned them.

6. Diwali is the most important and most widely observed festival of Hindus, who constitute more than 80 percent of the Indian population. Festivities include gift exchanges and purchases of new clothes and household items. The exact date of the festival is decided according to the Hindu calendar, normally falling in the month of November, and, on occasion, in the last week of October.

7. After the union came into being, the works committee had become merely symbolic.

8. The practice was reinstated in late September 2005 after union negotiations.

9. Subsequently, after the union intervention these rates were enhanced.

10. Hero-Honda is an Indian company, which is a joint venture between the Hero group of companies and HMCL. It is a separate entity and has no connection with HMSI. Hero-Honda also produces motorcycles and scooters. It has two plants, one at Gurgaon (Haryana) and the other at Dharuhera (Haryana). While there is no union in the Gurgaon plant, the Dharuhera plant is unionised.

11. Sikhs, as a part of their religion wear turbans as a part of their normal daily attire.

12. Gurgaon falls in the Indian state of Haryana. Chandigarh is the capital city of Haryana, which houses all state offices.

13. Manesar is an industrial belt of Haryana which includes sections of Gurgaon.

14. *Gherao* is a Hindi word. It means to encircle. It is often used by employees against managers or officers as a pressure tactic. Persons indulging in a *gherao* surround the person concerned (usually one or more managers) and do not let him/them move at all. Technically, it is illegal as it violates the provisions of the Indian law of crime. It leads to illegal confinement of the person *gheraoed*. But in case any other violence is not practiced, normally no action is taken against those indulging in a *gherao* in the interest of industrial peace.

15. See footnote number 9.

16. Punjab and Haryana are two Indian states which share the Union Territory of Chandigarh as their capital.

17. In accordance with an earlier ruling of the supreme court of India in the case of "Bank of India v. T.S. Kelawala" (1990), *Labour law Reporter*, 313.

18. The application of henna tattoos is a popular Indian ritual undertaken by women on happy occasions such as weddings or festivals.

Strategy Implementation for Multinational Companies: Interaction Processes

part five

13 International Negotiation and Cross-Cultural Communication

Learning Objectives

After reading this chapter you should be able to:

- Understand the basics of verbal and nonverbal communication that may influence cross-cultural management and negotiation.

- Describe the basic international negotiation processes from preparation to closing the deal.

- Explain the basic tactics of international negotiation.

- Recognize and respond to "dirty tricks" in international negotiations.

- Know the differences between the problem-solving and competitive approaches to international negotiation.

- Identify the personal characteristics of the successful international negotiator.

Preview CASE IN POINT

Deals That Failed

During the recent economic crisis, many companies sought various kinds of mergers and acquisitions. In Brazil, the two food giants, Perdigao and Sadia, were in discussions to create a merger. Similarly, in Japan, electronics company Panasonic started talks to buy its rival, Sanyo. However, at the time of writing, the degree of success of both potential mergers will depend a lot on the negotiation skills of the companies. If these companies approach the process without the requisite skills, the negotiations could end and any hopes of merger or acquisition abandoned. Consider the following negotiation mishaps.

When Kiel AG, a Swiss multinational conglomerate, discovered that Georgia-based Edwards Engineering Inc. (EEI) was for sale, Kiel's management felt that they had found the right company to acquire in the United States. There was a construction boom in the Southeastern United States that Kiel viewed as a strategic opportunity. Moreover, EEI was a successful company, whose founder, Tom Edwards, was close to retirement and willing to sell.

Kiel made an initial offer close to the asking price, and the outlook for the purchase looked positive. Kiel president Herbert Kiel even came to the United States to conduct the negotiations personally. However, after four difficult days of negotiations, the Kiel team went home and talks ended.

What happened? In a typical U.S. American way, Edwards was open and friendly in the negotiations. He was eager to sell the business. He was direct and forthright about the strengths and weaknesses of his business. He made every effort to provide information requested and to adjust his proposals to Kiel's positions. But the U.S. style didn't work.

Edwards confused the Swiss. They approached the negotiations in a formal and measured way. They perceived Edwards' openness as dangerous and untrustworthy. They responded by asking to review documents and by hiring a major U.S. accounting firm to audit the EEI books. Edwards, on the other hand, found the audit insulting and time-consuming. He was annoyed by Kiel's continuously polite but unresponsive answers to his proposals. Ultimately, neither side played the negotiation game the way the other expected. Distrust grew, and an otherwise good deal ended in failure.

Sources: Based on Bryan, Robert M., and Peter C. Buck. 1989. "When customs collide: The pitfalls of international acquisitions." Financial Executive, 5, pp. 43–46; Goman, Carol Kinsey. 2002. "Cross-cultural business practices." Communication World, February–March, pp. 22–25; Copeland, L., and L. Griggs. 1985. Going International. New York: Random House; Regalado, A., and K. Rapoza. 2009. "Brazil food giants discuss merger." Wall Street Journal, May 18, p. B4; Tudor, A., and H. Tabuchi. 2008. "Panasonic enters talks to buy Sanyo." Wall Street Journal, November 3, p. B3; Whately, Arthur. 1994. "International negotiation case." In Dorothy Marcic and Sheila Puffer, eds., Management International, St. Paul, MN: West, pp. 73–74.

I nternational negotiation is the process of making business deals across national and cultural boundaries, and it precedes any multinational business project. However, as shown in the Preview Case in Point, without successful negotiation and the accompanying cross-cultural communication, there are seldom successful business transactions.[1]

Consider some of the following examples where the successful outcome of the business opportunity depends on successful international negotiations. Companies that sell overseas must negotiate with foreign distributors and sales organizations. Companies that participate in an international joint venture must negotiate a contract to establish the alliance. Companies that receive raw materials from overseas sources must negotiate with local suppliers to provide raw materials at an acceptable cost. Companies that set up manufacturing operations in other countries often must negotiate with foreign governments to get necessary permissions. Finally, as in the Preview Case in Point, companies that wish to acquire businesses in other countries must negotiate successfully with the current owners.

As the world's market becomes increasingly global, companies will need to become adept at conducting international negotiations. Consider, for example, the possibility that, over the next 20 years, the economic "center of gravity" of the world markets is going to shift to the emerging markets of China, Brazil, Turkey, India, and Mexico.[2] These countries also are expected to show strong technology-driven growth and provide major opportunities for U.S. organizations. However, understanding how the significant cultural differences between the United States and these countries affect international negotiations will be increasingly crucial if the U.S. multinational companies want to capitalize on such opportunities.

This chapter provides a survey of the basic processes that guide international negotiation: successful preparation, building relationships with foreign partners, using persuasion tactics, gaining concessions, and reaching a final agreement. We will also consider how to identify and avoid the common dirty tricks of negotiators and what personal characteristics make a good international negotiator.

The Basics of Cross-Cultural Communication

Successful international negotiation requires successful cross-cultural communication. Negotiators must understand (or have interpreted) not only the written and oral language of their counterparts but also other components of culturally different communication styles. Mistakes in this area often go unnoticed by the communicator, but they can do damage to international relationships and negotiations. Mistakes or misinterpretations of the subtle gestures of hand and face, the use of silence, what is said or not said, and the intricacies of dealing with age and status often prove to be pitfalls for the multinational businessperson.

To help you negotiate and communicate more successfully in your role as a multinational manager, we will review some of the major issues in cross-cultural communication: the relationship between language and culture, differences between high- and low-context cultures, cultural differences in communication styles, nonverbal communication through body movements and the use of personal space, when and how to use interpreters, how to speak to nonnative speakers of your language, and how to avoid cross-cultural communication errors based on faulty attributions.

Language and Culture

There are approximately 3,000 basic languages in the world, with many dialects.[3] Language is so essential to culture that many consider linguistic groups synonymous with cultural groups. Multinational managers should also note that many countries—Canada and Belgium, for example—have more than one national language. Even within political boundaries, these national languages often represent diverse cultural groups regarding communication and negotiation styles. In addition, the choice of the wrong language may touch on areas of extreme cultural sensitivity.

The interrelationship between language and culture is so strong that some experts suggest that a society's language determines the nature of its culture. This is known as the **Whorf hypothesis**, developed by the anthropologist and linguist Benjamin Lee Whorf.[4] Whorf argued that words provide the concepts for understanding the world. According to Whorf, all languages have limited sets of words. These restricted word sets, in turn, constrain the ability of the users to understand or conceptualize the world. Because language structures the way we think about what we see, it determines cultural patterns.

In his famous and at the time futuristic novel *1984*, George Orwell used Whorf's premise that those who controlled the available vocabulary would control the world. Not all experts agree with Whorf, and some argue the opposite: Culture comes first and requires the development of certain concepts and thus certain words. However, no one debates that there is a close interrelationship between language and culture. Most experts agree that the twenty-first-century global leader must necessarily have language skills to bridge cultural differences.[5]

High- and Low-Context Languages

The anthropologist Edward T. Hall identified an important distinction among the world's languages based on whether communication is explicit or implicit.[6] Hall focused on how different cultures use the context or the situation in which communication takes place to understand what people are saying. Languages in which people state things directly and explicitly are called **low context**. The words provide most of the meaning, and you do not have to understand the situation. Languages in which people state things indirectly and implicitly are called **high context**. Communications have multiple meanings that one can interpret only by reading the situation. So important are the ideas of high and low context that many people refer to the entire culture as being high or low context.

Most Northern European languages, including German, English, and the Scandinavian, are low context. People use explicit words to communicate direct meaning. Thus, for example, if a German manager says "Yes," she means yes. In addition, most Western cultures attach a positive value to clear and direct communication. This inclination is particularly apparent in negotiations, where low-context languages allow clear statements concerning what a negotiator wants out of the relationship.

In contrast, Asian and Arabic are among the highest-context languages in the world. In Asian languages, often what is left unsaid is just as important as what is said. Silent periods and the use of incomplete sentences require a person to read the situation in order to interpret what the communicator does not say. Arabic introduces interpretation into the language with an opposite tack. Extensive imprecise verbal and nonverbal communication produces an interaction where reading the situation is necessary for understanding. Exhibit 13.1 shows a ranking of languages by their degrees of high and low context.

Communication between high- and low-context people is a challenge. Translated words that have explicit meanings to a low-context speaker may have

EXHIBIT 13.1   Country Differences in High- and Low-Context Communication

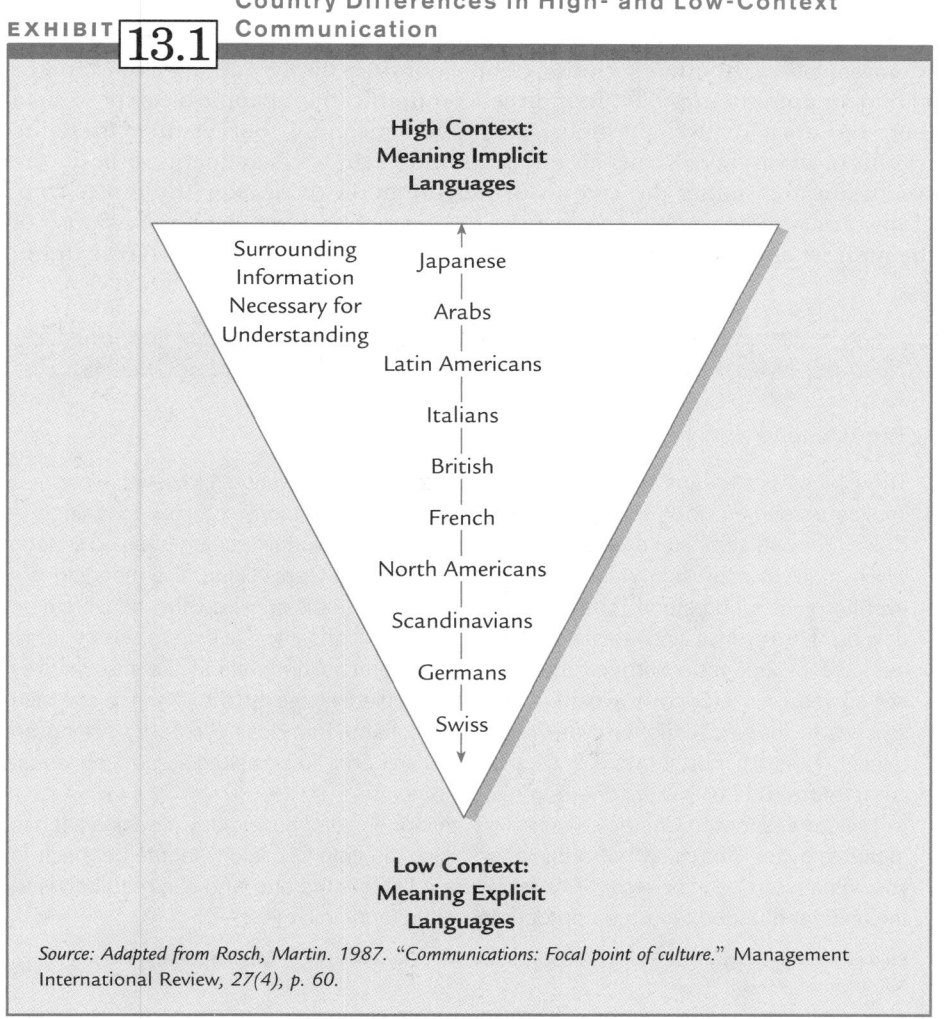

Source: Adapted from Rosch, Martin. 1987. "Communications: Focal point of culture." Management International Review, 27(4), p. 60.

a multitude of meanings to a high-context speaker. For example, Japanese speech is full of words that encourage a speaker to continue and to repeat the message, often in a slightly different way. One of these words, *hai*—literally "yes" in English—means yes in the English sense only if other components of the situation also mean yes. *Hai* can also mean: "Yes, I hear you," "Yes, say it again," "Yes, give me more information," "Yes, please continue with the conversation," or "Yes, I don't really want to say no, but it should be obvious to you that the answer is no." Consider the next Multinational Management Brief.

Such difficulties in translation suggest that, when negotiations take place between high- and low-context cultures, both sides must realize that communication may have errors. Moreover, even good translations may require contextual interpretations for effective communication.

Differences in languages can have other effects on international negotiations. Consider the next Case in Point.

Basic Communication Styles

In addition to high- and low-context language use, other cultural differences in communication can influence cross-cultural interactions and negotiations. In some cultures, people speak very directly; they tend to state opinions and ask questions that come right to the point and lack ambiguity. This is called **direct communication**. In other societies, people consider directly asking a question or stating an opinion impolite. In indirect communication, people attempt to state their opinions or ask questions by implied meaning. Successful and polite communication allows the receiver to understand a statement without the communicator stating directly his or her intentions. Consider the direct communicator who asks, "Will we reach a deal tonight?" Consider the response of the indirect communicator who says, "Tonight we will go to a superb restaurant,

> **Direct communication**
> Communication that comes to the point and lacks ambiguity.

Multinational Management **Brief**

The Chinese and *Yes*

The Chinese often answer yes to negotiators asking a question. However, while *yes* implies agreement in Western culture, it can carry many more complex meanings in China. *Yes* can sometimes be used to make sure that the conversation goes on. In fact, when there is confusion, many believe that if people keep talking, the meaning will eventually be understood. *Yes* is thus used as a means to keep the conversation flowing. However, it can also be a way for the Chinese to save face. Sometimes, because of language barriers, the Chinese pretend to understand the meaning by saying yes. This is done to avoid feeling embarrassed. However, the Chinese can also say yes in these situations to prevent the negotiator from losing face by asking an unclear question. Furthermore, it is considered an honor to be asked something, and it is therefore rude or bad manners to reject someone.

In sum, *yes* for the Chinese can be very ambiguous and have many meanings. It can mean "maybe," "back up," "I'm thinking," "give me time to think," "let me get back to you with an answer," or "yes." The astute negotiator is the one who can read between the lines and understand the appropriate understanding of *yes*.

Source: Based on Doucet, M. 2008. "What part of Yes don't you understand?" Mechanical Engineering, November, pp. 46–47.

C A S E   I N   P O I N T

Differences between the Chinese and English Languages

As companies try to take advantage of the tremendous opportunities presented by China, they will have to deal with the challenges of language comprehension. Almost a quarter of the world's population, including Chinese, Japanese, and Korean speakers, read logographic characters that represent meanings rather than sound. In contrast, in many other languages, such as those using Latin alphabets (English, Spanish), Arabic, and Hindi, the words represent sounds rather than meaning. This difference in reading process has been shown to have important implications for how people remember things or even how they process thoughts.

The difference also has important implications for how U.S. negotiators approach presentations to their Chinese counterparts. For instance, research shows that Chinese individuals are likely to respond more positively to visual cues, such as font selection, whereas U.S. Americans are more likely to respond to the speaker's voice. As such, it is important for U.S. negotiators to use as many visual stimuli as they can to make their presentation more effective. Other research shows that Chinese subjects were more likely to remember brands and to associate brand names with logos when information was presented visually. U.S. negotiators are thus encouraged to rely on visual information if they want their Chinese counterparts to remember aspects of their presentation. Instead of focusing on the presentation style of the negotiator, it may be more beneficial to improve the content.

Sources: Based Kambil, Amit, Victor Wei-the Long, and Clarence Kwan. 2006. "The seven disciplines for venturing in China." MIT Sloan Management Review, Winter, 47(2), pp. 85–89; Lieberthal, Kenneth, and Geoffrey Lieberthal 2003. "The great transition." Harvard Business Review, October, pp. 13–27; Tavassoli, Nader T., and Jin K. Han. 2002. "Auditory and visual brand identifiers in Chinese and English." Journal of International Marketing, 10, pp. 13–28.

which best represents our national cuisine." This answer usually means, "I am not ready to do business with you until I get to know you better." Exhibit 13.2 shows a ranking of direct communication styles for several countries.

Another cultural trait of communication style that often affects or surprises those communicating with U.S. Americans is the lack of **formal communication** expected. As you can see in Exhibit 13.2, U.S. Americans are among the least formal in communication. The casual use of first names, informal dress, and the dispensing of titles characterize U.S. communication styles. Most other cultures communicate, especially in business settings, with more formality. They take care to acknowledge rank and titles when addressing each other. There is also more formality of dress for men and women, as well as sensitivity to ceremony and procedures in social interactions. In many countries, for example, adult men never wear short pants unless engaged in an exercise or sport activity.

At several points, we have noted that communication consists of more than verbal interaction. Multinational managers and negotiators must be aware of cultural differences in both verbal and nonverbal communications. The next section provides background on nonverbal communication.

> **Formal communication**
> Communication that acknowledges rank, titles, and ceremony in prescribed social interaction.

Nonverbal Communication

Nonverbal communication means communicating without words. Often it is not necessary to speak to communicate with someone. People gesture, they smile, they gaze into another's eyes, they hug, they kiss—they engage in a whole array of behaviors that supplement or enhance spoken communication. How important are nonverbal signs? Consider the next Multinational Management Brief.

> **Nonverbal communication**
> Face-to-face communication that is not oral.

EXHIBIT 13.2   Cultural Differences in Communication Styles

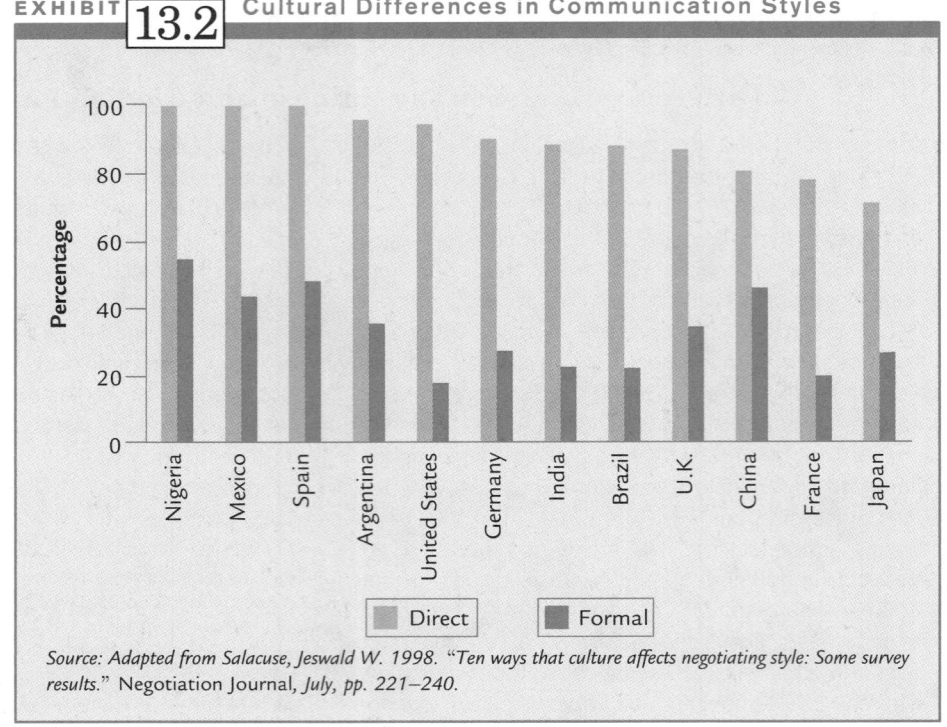

Source: Adapted from Salacuse, Jeswald W. 1998. "Ten ways that culture affects negotiating style: Some survey results." Negotiation Journal, July, pp. 221–240.

The types of nonverbal communication we consider here are body movements (kinesics), the use of personal space (proxemics), and forms of communication that rely on senses, such as touching (haptics), eye contact (oculesics), and smell (olfactics).

Multinational Management **Brief**

Nonverbal Communication

As more employees increasingly interact with their counterparts from foreign locales, understanding nonverbal communication is becoming even more critical. A classic study reveals that only 7 percent of the total impact of a message is based on the words used. The rest is based on the tone of voice (38 percent) and various other types of nonverbal communication aspects (facial expressions, body language, etc.— 57 percent).

Clearly, it is critical for multinationals to appreciate the complexities involved in nonverbal communication. Consider the case of a CEO who showed up at an oil refinery in an expensive suit to address rank-and-file employees dressed in their blue overalls. Before starting his speech, he took his watch off and placed it in front of the lectern. Although he started the speech with "I am happy to be with you today," the nonverbal signs communicated, "I don't like coming to dirty places, and I have only 20 minutes to spend with you." Multinational negotiators should thus be very cognizant of nonverbal communication and use appropriate body language and other nonverbal signs.

Source: Based on Gorman, C.K. 2008. "Lost in translation." Communication World, July/August, 25, 31–33.

Kinesics

Kinesics means communicating through body movements. Every culture uses body posture, facial expressions, hand gestures, and movement to communicate nonverbally. Most Asian cultures, for example, use bowing to indicate respect for older people or people of higher status. The person of lesser status must bow at a lower angle than the person of higher status.

It is easy to misinterpret the meanings of body movements in another culture. Like oral communication, there is no universal code for what body movements mean in all societies. For example, U.S. Americans communicate a relaxed atmosphere by putting their feet up. The manager with feet on the desk is saying, "I am relaxing, and you can too." However, people from many other cultures consider such behavior rude or even insulting. Most German managers would consider putting one's feet up on the desk uncivilized. Showing the soles of the feet is among the most outrageous insults to most Arabs.[7]

Facial expressions occur in every human interaction. People smile, frown, squint, sneer, and engage in a range of facial movements. Some scholars argue that certain facial expressions are biological and do not vary across cultures. For example, the quick raising and lowering of eyebrows when people greet each other seems to occur in many different cultural settings.[8] In addition, people born deaf or blind have most of the common facial expressions, suggesting that at least some are inborn.[9]

Body posture relates to the way people stand, walk, and sit. Each culture encourages and discourages different body postures depending on the situation. A trip on a Japanese subway, for example, quickly reveals the proper way of sitting—straight forward, legs together, head slightly down, and (for women) handbag placed squarely on the lap. Cultural norms determine whether people slouch, stand, or sit erect, as well as the speed and cadence of the walking gait.

All cultures use hand gestures to embellish and add emphasis to oral communication. Some cultures use expressive gestures, and others use subtle gestures. The same gestures often mean different things from one society to another, a common source of embarrassment for international communicators. For example, the gesture with the thumb and forefinger joined in a circle means "okay" in North America and money in Japan, but it is obscene in Brazil. The thumbs-up gesture means everything is going well for North Americans and many Europeans, but it is a rude gesture in West Africa. Even the "V" for victory sign made with two fingers held upward, popularized by the British prime minister Winston Churchill during World War II, has a rude meaning for the British and the French if the palm is facing inward. Nodding the head means yes in most of the world, but it means no in Bulgaria.[10]

The important point to remember for international negotiators and multinational managers is that it is easy to misinterpret gestures. A safe communication strategy is to minimize their use. You should use only the gestures that you understand well. Eventually, as you get to know a culture better, acceptable and appropriate gestures will become second nature.

Proxemics

Proxemics focuses on how people use space to communicate. According to some experts, the basic senses of sight, smell, hearing, and touch allow people to perceive and sense differences in space.[11] Naturally, there are large cultural differences in how people react to the sounds, sights, smells, and personal contact. Each culture has appropriate distances for various levels of

Kinesics
Communication through body movements.

Proxemics
The use of space to communicate.

communication, and most people are uncomfortable if those distances are ignored. Violations of space may even be considered offensive

The personal bubble of space around each individual may range from 9 inches to more than 20 inches. North Americans are most comfortable with 20 inches, whereas groups from Latin and Arab cultures generally prefer a closer spacing. It is not uncommon to see a North American continuously backing up to maintain a comfortable 20 inches when interacting with someone from the Middle East or Latin America.

Personal space may also affect the design of offices. In the next Multinational Management Brief, the exhibit shows a typical Japanese office, where the desks are in contact and managers work closely together. In contrast, Germans are even more protective of their personal office space than North Americans. They prefer heavy office furniture that people cannot move to get too close. A

Multinational Management **Brief**

The Typical Japanese Office

In the typical Japanese office, space is shared so that the workers and managers are all within hearing distance of each other. Unlike the typical U.S. office, the Japanese version has no separate rooms or partitions that divide the work area. Standard office desks are placed back to back and side by side. Workers often share the same phone and computer.

This closeness with colleagues provides a feeling of comfort for the Japanese that many Westerners find unnerving. Unlike most Westerners, the Japanese see no need for privacy during phone conversations or discussions with coworkers or when concentrating on their work. In the reverse cultural situation, many Japanese salarymen who have expatriate assignments in the United States or Europe find the compartmentalization of buildings very uncomfortable.

The exhibit shows the layout of a typical Japanese office with the placement of a manager (*kachoo*), first-line supervisors, and workers.

Seating in a Typical Japanese Office

German newspaper editor stationed in the United States was highly intolerant of the U.S. American habit of moving chairs closer in certain social situations. He finally reacted by having his visitor's chair bolted to the floor, keeping people at a comfortable and "proper" distance.[12]

Haptics or Touching, Oculesics, and Olfactics

Nonverbal communication also can occur through touching, smelling, and seeing. **Haptics** or touching is communication through body contact. **Oculesics** refers to communication through eye contact or gazing. **Olfactics** is the use of smells as a means of nonverbal communication.

Haptics is related to proxemics and is a basic form of human interaction. In greeting one another, people may shake hands, embrace, or kiss. In routine interaction, people may touch or pat each other in a variety of ways. The type of touching deemed appropriate is deeply rooted in cultural values. For example, Russian men often kiss other men outside their family as a form of greeting. Brazilian men hug in greeting. Japanese schoolgirls routinely walk holding hands with other girls, although touching among strangers is less accepted. In some cultures, people expect a firm handshake, whereas in other cultures, the handshake is limp. Generally, Latin European and Latin American cultures accept more touching than do Germanic, Anglo, or Scandinavian cultures. Axtell has classified the degree of touching among countries into categories,[13] such as no touching (e.g., Japan, United States, England, and many Northern European countries), moderate touching (e.g., Australia, China, Ireland, and India), and touching (e.g., Latin American countries, Italy, and Greece).

The degree of comfort with gaze and eye contact (oculesics) also varies significantly around the world. In some countries like the United States and Canada, people are very comfortable and expect eye contact to be maintained for a short moment during conversations. In contrast, in countries like China and Japan, eye contact is considered very rude and disrespectful; in fact, the way to show respect in such societies is by avoiding eye contact. Yet in other societies like France and the Middle East, maintaining eye contact for long periods of time is socially acceptable.

To avoid blunders, negotiators must be aware of a society's degree of comfort with eye contact. For instance, U.S. negotiators should know that a prolonged stare from the French is not rude or hostile but rather shows interest. Similarly, when negotiating with the Chinese, it is important to avoid direct gazing or eye contact so as not to place the Chinese negotiators in an uncomfortable position.

Finally, different countries have different views of smell (olfactics). Societies like the United States and United Kingdom tend to be very uncomfortable with body odors. In fact, U.S. Americans find such body odor offensive and will avoid talking to someone who has body odor. However, in contrast, Arabs are much more accepting of body odors and consider them natural.[14] Negotiators need to be aware of such diverse perspectives on smell and accept and adapt to them.

This section concludes our discussion of the basic forms of nonverbal communication. The following section deals with three practical issues in cross-cultural business communications: when to use interpreters, how to speak with someone whose language is not your own, and how to recognize and avoid incorrectly applying your own cultural assumptions to people's motivations.

Practical Issues in Cross-Cultural Business Communication

Cross-cultural negotiations and communications nearly always face a language barrier because one or both parties must communicate in a foreign language.

Haptics or touching
Basic form of human interaction, including shaking hands, embracing, or kissing when greeting one another.

Oculesics
Communication through eye contact or gaze.

Olfactics
Use of smells as a means of nonverbal communication.

International managers are always at an advantage if they speak more than one language fluently. U.S. Americans are among the worst when it comes to learning a second language, whereas Europeans are much more likely to be bilingual or multilingual. U.S. businesspeople are fortunate that English is the most common language of business. However, even if English is the local business language and you negotiate in English, communication and understanding of the local culture always improve if you speak the local language. An important preparation for any international assignment, therefore, is gaining at least rudimentary skills in the language of the country.

Using Interpreters

Interpreter's role
To ensure the accuracy and common understanding of written and oral agreements.

To make sure that all parties understand agreements, international negotiation often requires the use of interpreters. The **interpreter's role** is to provide a simultaneous translation of a foreign language while a person speaks. This role requires greater linguistic skills than speaking a language or translating written documents. Good interpreters not only are bilingual, but also have the specialized knowledge and vocabulary to deal with technical details of business transactions.

Even if some of the negotiators understand or speak both languages, it is often a good idea to use interpreters. It detracts from a negotiation team member's negotiation task if he or she must also serve as the team's interpreter. In addition, even if all members of the negotiating team are competent speakers of both languages, professional interpreters can be present to ensure the accuracy and common understanding of written and oral agreements.

However, even with interpreters, the intended message is not always conveyed efficiently. It is therefore important for any negotiator to meet and work with the interpreter to ensure that talks proceed smoothly. For instance, U.S negotiators are well-advised to have interpreters review their notes and other information they intend to share with the other party. Such proactive efforts may greatly help the U.S. negotiators anticipate problems. Axtell,[15] Chaney, and Martin suggest the following tips:[16]

- Spend time with the interpreter so that he or she gets to know your accent and general approach to conversations.

- Go over technical and other issues with the interpreter to make sure that they are properly understood.

- Insist on frequent interruptions for translations rather than at the end of statements.

- Learn about appropriate communication styles and etiquette from the interpreter.

- Look for feedback and comprehension by watching the listener's eyes.

- Discuss the message beforehand with the interpreter if it is complex.

- Request that your interpreter apologizes for your inability to speak in the local language.

- Confirm through a concluding session with the interpreter that all key components of the message have been properly comprehended.

To simplify the increasing diversity of languages in business organizations, some multinational companies use one language as the corporate tongue. Increasingly, this language is English because it is the most common second language. Examples of companies using English are Philips Electronics and DHL

Worldwide Express. Using English allows these companies a more consistent corporate culture while dealing with the linguistic diversity of their employees and customers. Yet even these major multinational companies have permanent translators on staff to manage such issues as interaction with the international press, the translation of local product information, and negotiations with other companies.

Although the use of company-wide languages simplifies some of the multinational's communication problems, it creates other linguistic challenges. One of the greatest challenges is communicating with nonnative speakers. The next section gives practical suggestions on how to do that.

Communication with Nonnative Speakers

In the multinational organization, it is very likely that you will be speaking with and writing to employees, customers, and business associates in their second or even third language. In this situation, communications scholars recommend several techniques that make communication easier and more accurate:[17]

- *Use the most common words with their most common meanings:* A good source of these words is a book for a beginning language course.
- *Select words with few alternative meanings:* If this is impossible, use the word with its most common meaning.
- *Strictly follow the basic rules of grammar:* Follow the rules more than you would with native speakers.
- *Speak with clear breaks between words:* It is often difficult for a nonnative speaker to hear distinct words, especially amid background noise.
- *Avoid "sports" words or words borrowed from literature:* In U.S. English, for example, phrases such as "he struck out" should be avoided.
- *Avoid words or expressions that are pictures:* Some words or expressions, such as "knee deep in the big muddy" in U.S. English, require listeners to have a mental image of the picture.
- *Avoid slang:* Slang is often based on age and region, and the nonnative speaker may have learned the language from people from other regions. For example, British English slang is quite different from U.S. English slang.
- *Mimic the cultural flavor of the nonnative speaker's language:* For example, use more flowery communication with Spanish-speaking listeners than with Germans.
- *Summarize:* Paraphrase and repeat basic ideas.
- *Test your communication success:* Do not ask, "Did you understand?" Instead, ask your listener what he or she heard. Ask the listener to paraphrase what you said.
- *When your counterpart does not understand:* Repeat the basic ideas using different words. Use more common nouns and verbs.
- *Confirm important aspects in writing:* Make sure all important information is written to avoid any misunderstanding or confusion.

Sensitivity to cross-cultural communication provides a solid foundation for a multinational negotiator. Next, the chapter provides you with the essential background to develop your knowledge of international negotiations and to prepare you for negotiating in the global business environment.

International Negotiation

International negotiation is more complex than domestic negotiation. Differences in national cultures and in political, legal, and economic systems often separate potential business partners. Consequently, most international businesspeople find it necessary to modify the negotiation styles of their home country. If they wish to succeed in the multinational arena, they must develop a style of negotiation based on the flexible application of sound principles. This section develops your understanding of those principles by describing the steps in a successful international negotiation.

Steps in International Negotiations

Most experts recognize that international negotiation requires a number of steps.[18] Although each negotiation is unique and may combine two or more steps or repeat some, the process involves five steps leading to the final step, an agreement. (See Exhibit 13.3, which shows a seventh step, postagreement, discussed later in the chapter.) The **negotiation steps** are preparation, building the relationship, exchanging information and the first offer, persuasion, concessions, and the agreement. The most important step in international negotiation is preparation, and the culturally naive negotiator almost always fails to bring home an adequate agreement.

Step 1: Preparation

A winning international negotiating strategy requires significant preparation. Prior to the negotiations, the well-prepared international negotiator gathers

Negotiation steps
Preparation, building the relationship, exchanging information, first offer, persuasion, concessions, agreement, and postagreement.

EXHIBIT 13.3   Steps in International Negotiations

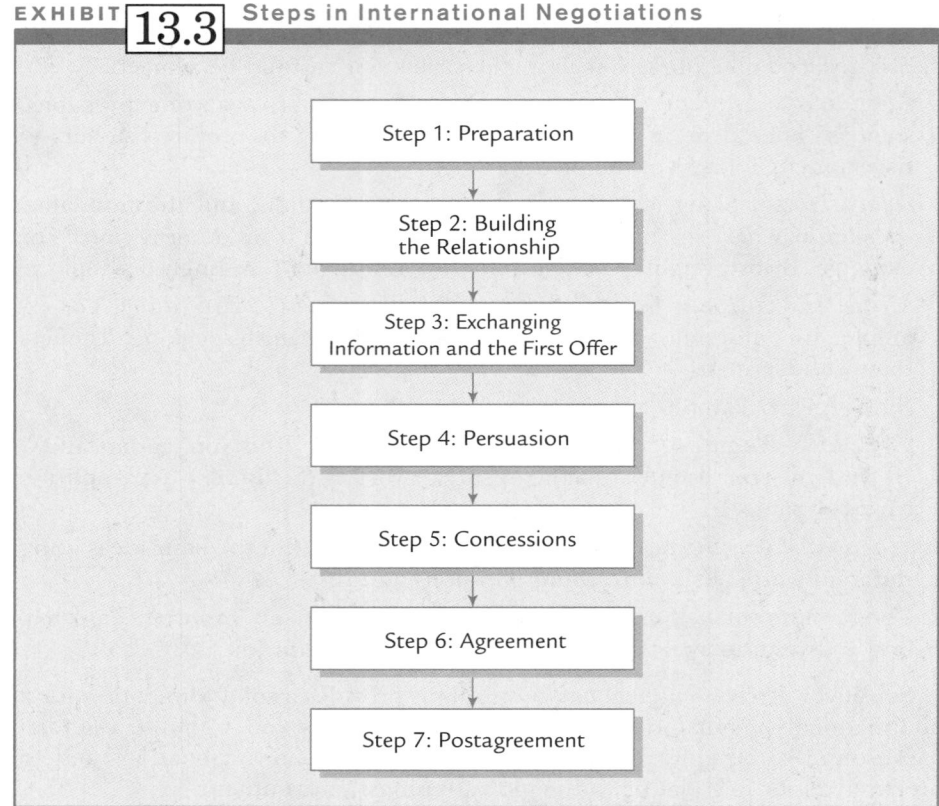

Step 1: Preparation

Step 2: Building the Relationship

Step 3: Exchanging Information and the First Offer

Step 4: Persuasion

Step 5: Concessions

Step 6: Agreement

Step 7: Postagreement

extensive information on the negotiation issues, on the setting in which the negotiation will take place, and on the firm and people involved. In this stage, you must answer questions such as, "Where do I stand?" in order to understand your company's position in the negotiation process. However, after you understand your own position, you also want to understand your counterpart's position by answering questions such as, "What do they want?" or "What is important to them?"

Experts on international negotiation identify numerous essential questions and issues to consider before the negotiation:[19]

- *Determine if the negotiation is possible:* To begin the negotiation process, you must believe that you have at least some areas of agreement with your negotiating counterparts.

- *Know exactly what your company wants from the negotiation:* What does the company hope to achieve in the negotiation? What are the minimally acceptable conditions of an agreement? Make a list of your specific needs or demands. Which specific demands have more negotiating power?

- *Be aware of what can be compromised:* It is very unlikely that you will get everything you want from the negotiation. Think in advance about the compromise and concessions that you can make. By thinking ahead, you reduce the likelihood of giving up too much or making concessions on the wrong issues.

- *Know the other side:* What does the other side bring to the situation? Can the other organization deliver what your company wants? What are the goals of the other side? Are they dealing with competitors, and do the competitors have any advantages? What are they willing to negotiate? How badly do they want the deal?

- *Send the proper team:* Do the negotiators have the appropriate knowledge of the technical details, sufficient experience in negotiations, language abilities, and knowledge of the country and its culture? Have they prepared as a team? What authority do they have?

- *Agenda:* Is there an agreed-upon agenda? Can it lead somewhere the company does not want to go?

- *Prepare for a long negotiation:* Avoid being rushed to accept a disadvantageous solution. Know when you must leave, but don't tell the other side. Be willing to walk away if you can't negotiate a deal that you both agree on. Furthermore, avoid making a deal for the deal's sake. Desperation usually results in poor judgment and unfavorable decisions.

The successful international negotiator not only prepares for the substance of the negotiation (e.g., technical details, company needs) but also does extensive research on the nature and negotiation styles of the foreign culture. For example, a study of successful U.S. negotiations with the Japanese found that careful preparations led to high-quality results. Preparations that improved negotiations included reading books on Japanese business culture, hiring experts to train the negotiation teams, and practicing in simulated negotiations.[20]

The economic situation of 2008–2009 has affected negotiations in such a way that emphasizes the need for adequate preparation. Consider the next Case in Point.

Although it is impossible to understand the negotiating styles of all the world's cultures, managers can anticipate certain key differences among cultures. This section identifies some of those common differences: in the goals of

CASE IN POINT

Negotiations and Risk

The economic situation of 2008–2009 provided many multinationals the opportunity to acquire companies that were previously out of reach. In fact, negotiation teams felt increased pressure to complete the deal of a lifetime. However, without adequate preparation, such acquisitions can be very risky. Experts agree that the implementation of a merger is as critical as getting the deal signed. For instance, what should a multinational do as customers reduce purchases or suppliers go bankrupt? Unfortunately, negotiators often downplay or ignore such risks to get the deal signed as soon as possible. Multinational negotiators are therefore encouraged to take the time to prepare and to get as much information as possible so they can ask the important questions regarding risk:

- Treat risk as an integral part of the discussion rather than avoiding it.
- Break the risk into components to show how solutions can be devised to address these issues.
- Understand that risks and problems can be addressed jointly.
- Allow the counterparties to express their concerns.

Rather than hurry the negotiating along, multinationals are well-advised to prepare adequately to fully address problematic issues that may arise.

Source: Based on Ertel, D. 2009. "Negotiating the risk or risky negotiations?" Financial Executive, April, pp. 40–42.

the negotiation, in the personal styles of the negotiators, in the communication styles of the negotiators, in the negotiators' sensitivity to timing and pacing of the negotiation, in the forms of agreement typical in the society, and in the common types of negotiating team organization. The examples from different countries discussed next show the extreme differences in these areas,[21] but keep in mind that many countries fall between these cases.[22]

- *Negotiation goal—signing the contract or forming a relationship:* Most Chinese and Japanese businesspeople consider as the prime objective of negotiation the formation of relationships. A negotiation may produce signed agreements, but the signed paper represents only the formal expression of the relationship between the companies and sometimes of the personal relationships between the individual negotiators. The contract exists only as an initial step in the relationship, one that may lead to longer-term mutual benefits. In legalistic societies, such as the United States, the detailed, signed contract is the most important goal of the negotiation. Commitment is less personally binding but relies instead on the force of law. The sanctity of the contract is a valued legal principle in U.S. courts.

- *Formal or informal personal communication style:* Business cultures differ widely on the acceptability of informal styles. Australians, like U.S. Americans, easily adapt to using first names and having informal conversations. As shown in Exhibit 13.2, however, Nigerian, Spanish, and Chinese negotiators react negatively to the informality of using first names among short-term business acquaintances.

- *Direct or indirect communication style:* We saw in the section on communication that the extent to which communication is direct and verbal, rather than indirect and nonverbal, varies widely by culture. The rules of politeness and styles of interaction in different cultures encourage or restrict the ability of negotiators to come directly to the point. For example, the Japanese will seldom say "No" directly. Instead, if something is "very difficult," it is probably impossible. Conversely, a speaker of a more explicit language might interpret such aversion to direct speech as an effort to hide something.

- *Sensitivity to time—low or high:* The pace of negotiation and the time given to each phase of it intertwine with the objective of the negotiation. Cultures place different values on how much time is devoted to the pursuit of goals. For U.S. Americans, closing the deal means signing a contract, and time is money. As a result, Americans tend to get down to business as soon as they can. In contrast, Asian cultures place value on creating a relationship rather than simply signing a contract. These cultures tend to want to take time to get to know the other parties better to determine whether a long-term relationship is worthwhile. Attempts to speed up negotiations tend to be viewed with suspicion that the other party may be trying to hide something.

- *Forms of agreement—specific or general:* A negotiated agreement may consist of general principles or of very detailed documents that attempt to anticipate all possible outcomes of the relationship. In many countries, such as Japan, the preferred contract states only general principles, not detailed rules and obligations. The Japanese argue that, because it is impossible to foresee all possible contingencies, a detailed agreement is dangerous and unnerving. The contract may obligate someone to do something that eventually becomes impossible due to unforeseen circumstances. In contrast, broad agreements, preferably based on strong personal relationships, allow for fair adjustments if circumstances change. Pressing for legalistic, detailed coverage of all contingencies, as U.S. Americans typically do, leads many people from other cultures to believe that their U.S. partners have little trust in the relationship. Exhibit 13.4 shows the differences among nations in cultural preferences for a broad agreement.

- *Team organization—a team or one leader:* The senior U.S. negotiator often has, within specified boundaries, the final authority to make commitments for his or her company and to close the deal. This style of organization

EXHIBIT 13.4   Cultural Differences in Preference for Broad Agreements

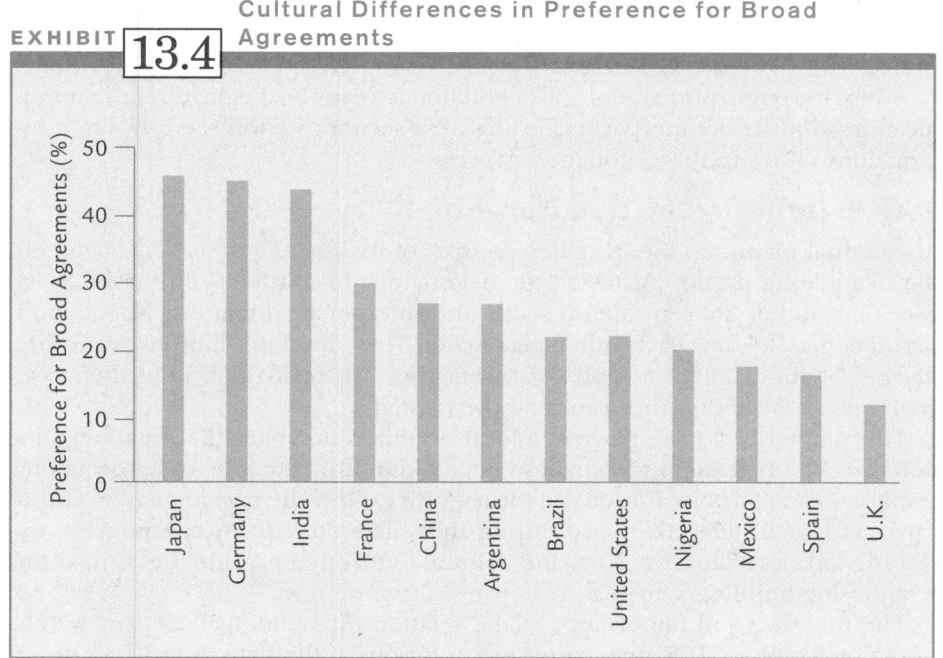

fits the U.S. mode of rapid negotiations and the goal of reaching a signed contract. In international negotiations, a small U.S. negotiation team with one leader faces a much larger team, where the true decision maker might not be present or, if present, might say very little. Russians, Japanese, and Chinese prefer large teams and rely chiefly on consensus decision making.

- *Attitude toward negotiation—win-lose or win-win:* Because of the role of culture, different nationalities tend to approach the negotiation with their own mindsets. Some cultures view the process as one in which both parties can benefit (win-win), and others see it as a necessity that one side wins while the other loses (win-lose). For instance, Salacuse reports that 100 percent of Japanese approached negotiations with a win-win mindset,[23] whereas only 33 percent of the Spanish executives surveyed had the same view. By understanding the approach, you can be aware of your situation.

- *High or low emotions:* As we saw in Chapter 2, societies differ in terms of the acceptability and appropriateness of emotional displays. For instance, Latin Americans and the Spanish are said to usually show their emotions through negotiations, whereas the Japanese and Germans tend to be reserved. Knowing the appropriateness of emotional display is also necessary to ensure that the negotiation progress smoothly.

Lack of preparation for cultural differences in international negotiations can lead to many problems. For example, the negotiating style typical of the highly individualistic U.S. culture seldom works well in collectivist cultures. Both U.S. managers and managers from other cultures who are negotiating with a U.S. firm should prepare to avoid some of the pitfalls of the U.S. negotiating style. Exhibit 13.5 contrasts some common U.S. negotiating characteristics with those from other national cultures. U.S. negotiators have what John Graham and Roy Herberger call the "John Wayne" style of negotiation.[24] As Exhibit 13.5 shows, U.S. negotiators are independent, aggressive, and direct. Although this style makes sense in the individualistic U.S. culture, it contrasts sharply with the negotiating styles from nations with other cultural values and norms. The next Multinational Management Brief shows what to expect in negotiations with Arabs.

After thorough preparation, a negotiator is ready to begin direct communication with the counterparties. In the next section, we will see how these interactions evolve in the negotiation process.

Step 2: Building the Relationship

Building a relationship
The first stage of the actual negotiation process, when negotiators concentrate on social and interpersonal matters.

After initial planning, the next step consists of **building a relationship** between the negotiating parties. At this stage, negotiators do not focus on the business issues but rather concentrate on social and interpersonal matters. Negotiation partners get to know each other personally. They develop opinions regarding the personalities of the negotiators: what they are really like, what their real goals are, and whether they can really be trusted.

This phase often takes place at a location different from the formal negotiation site. The first step in a Japanese negotiation, for example, often occurs by drinking tea in a room outside the formal office. Only the exchange of business cards and small talk take place during this encounter. In most countries, including Japan, restaurants, bars, and cultural tours often provide the context for relationship-building activities.

The duration and importance of the relationship-building stage vary widely by national culture. U.S. negotiators are notorious in their attempts to get down

EXHIBIT **13.5**   Preparation: Understanding Negotiators from Other Countries

U.S. Negotiation Style	Rationale	Contrasting Negotiation Style	Rationale
"I can go it alone."	Why spend the money for more people than necessary?	Bring a team.	More people provide social pressure.
"Just call me John."	Formalities are unnecessary.	Be extremely formal.	Rank and status count in language.
"Pardon my French."	Why bother? English is the international language.	Understand English but use interpreters anyway.	Gives extra time to listen and formulate responses.
"Get to the point."	Why beat around the bush?	Build the personal relationship and exchange information first.	Personal relationships and trust are more important than contracts.
"Lay your cards on the table."	Give and expect honest information up front.	Don't reveal the real position at first.	A bit of trickery or avoiding saying "No" is okay.
"Don't just sit there, speak up."	Long periods of silence are unacceptable.	Long periods of silence are acceptable, especially in response to an impasse.	Time is necessary to react.
"One thing at a time."	A final agreement is a sum of agreements on each issue.	A holistic approach leaves all points open for discussion until the end.	Issues are always interconnected.
"A deal is a deal."	A commitment is final down to the last detail.	Today's commitment can be voided if tomorrow's circumstances are different.	Negotiation partners must understand that absolutes are impossible and things change.
"I don't need to check with the home office."	Negotiators should have the authority to make the deal.	I must check with the home office first.	To complete the negotiation, you have to convince not only me but also my boss on another continent.

Source: Adapted from Graham, John L., and Roy A. Herberger Jr. 1983. "Negotiators abroad—Don't shoot from the hip." Harvard Business Review, 61, pp. 160–168.

to business after brief and perfunctory socializing.[25] German negotiators also get to the point quickly. When foreign negotiators bring up issues not related directly to the negotiation objective, U.S. negotiators often view this as a waste of time and an inefficient use of company resources. The pressure on U.S. managers is to get to the point, make the deal, and come home—particularly when they are overseas. International travel and hotels are costly, and many U.S. companies believe that a manager's time is better spent at home, getting on with implementing the negotiated deal.

The goal of U.S. negotiators is to get the details of the agreement on a written contract, with specific requirements and due dates. From this perspective, there is little need to develop personal relationships. In the U.S. legalistic view, "The partner must agree to a legally binding document." Other legal systems, however, do not see the contract as binding in its detail. For example, for many Chinese managers, a contract provides only the foundation on which to build the relationship, with details to be worked out later. As with most Asian societies, the Chinese believe that investing the time to build personal relationships must come first. Consider the Multinational Management Brief on page 551.

Multinational Management **Brief**

What to Expect When Negotiating with Arabs

While most of the world reeled from the recession of 2008–2009, many of the Middle Eastern Arab states weathered it fairly well. For instance, many of the governments of the Gulf Cooperation Council, an alliance of six Arab states in the gulf region, created large financial reserves. These countries took advantage of the high oil prices to add to wealth funds. Experts thus predicted that more Western multinationals would be negotiating with Arab states to take advantage of opportunities that they offer.

There are five key characteristics of negotiations with people from Arab nations:

1. *A subjective view:* Arabs look at the world as subjective. Reality is based on perception, not on facts. A common frustration for Westerners is that logical flaws in arguments have less impact than expected. If the facts do not fit someone's beliefs, then that person may reject the facts and consider only his or her own view of the situation. In particular, personal honor is more important than fact.

2. *The type of relationship expected:* A good personal relationship is the most important foundation for doing business with Arabs.

3. *Information on family and connections:* Social connections and networks are crucial in the highly personalized Arab societies. This should not be interpreted as useless information, but rather it may represent the key to finalizing a business deal.

4. *Persuasion:* For Arab negotiators, personalized arguments are more effective than logical arguments. Emphasis on friendship and personal appeals for consideration are common. Showing emotion by raising the voice, repeating points with enthusiasm, or even pounding the table is acceptable. An emotional argument shows the sincerity of the concern.

5. *The time required to complete the process:* From the perspective of Western businesspeople, negotiations with Arabs take considerable time. Time is not fixed for Arabs. There are no fixed beginnings and endings of events. Everyone expects delays.

Sources: Based on Canadian Business. *2009. "The United Arab Emirates: Gateway to the Gulf," Summer, 82, pp. 143–144; Nydell, Margaret K. 1997.* Understanding Arabs: A Guide for Westerners. *Yarmouth, ME: Intercultural Press.*

Building a good relationship among the negotiating parties provides a foundation for working out an eventual deal. As illustrated in the Multinational Management Brief, in many Asian societies, it is extremely important to build trust and relationships. Even in individualistic societies such as the United States, personal trust among negotiators is important. However, a business negotiation must eventually specify who is going to do what, when, and for what price. The next section shows how negotiators begin to address these issues.

Step 3: Exchanging Information and the First Offer

At this stage, both parties exchange information on their needs for the agreement. This so-called **task-related information** pertains to the actual details of the proposed agreement. Typically, both sides make a formal presentation of what they desire out of the relationship, such as the quantity, characteristics, and price of a product. Both sides usually present their **first offer**, which is their first proposal of what they expect from the agreement.

Task-related information
Actual details of the proposed agreement.

First offer
First proposal by parties of what they expect from the agreement.

Multinational Management **Brief**

Negotiating with the Chinese: The Need for Cooperation

Chinese negotiators are known to prefer to take time to develop a relationship rather than merely focusing on the negotiation. The Chinese are more apt to work with the other party to explore contradictions and ambiguities. Additionally, the negotiation may be just the beginning of a long-term relationship. In contrast, for the U.S. negotiators, the emphasis is on completing the negotiations, a task-oriented focus that minimizes the importance of relationships.

The Chinese regard relationships differently. Researchers had four foreign managers communicate with 120 Chinese participants. The foreign managers communicated either with warmheartedness or indifference, and they proposed either mutual or independent rewards for the negotiation. Results showed that participants who interacted with the managers displaying warmheartedness were more likely to feel that they had cooperative goals and were more confident in future collaboration. The employees who dealt with the managers with mutual rewards were more likely to find that the managers' ideas were reasonable.

These results suggest that foreign managers negotiating in China should display warmheartedness, which can take the form of listening carefully, understanding non-verbals, and showing interest by asking caring questions. It is also recommended that negotiators communicate their interest through sincere conversations, smiles, and using soft voices. Outcomes of the negotiations should also be structured so that they are win-win.

Source: Based on Yinfeng, N. C., D. Tjosvold, and W. Peiguan. 2008. "Effects of warm-heartedness and reward distribution on negotiation." Group Decision Negotiation, 17, pp. 79–96.

At this stage, national and business cultures influence what information is given and requested, how the information is presented, and how close the initial offer is to the actually expected or hoped-for specifications in the agreement. Exhibit 13.6 shows a comparison among nations regarding information exchange and first offer strategies. Note, for example, the difference between the typical U.S. initial negotiation point (off the real goal by 5 to 10 percent) and the more extreme starting points used by Arab negotiators.

EXHIBIT 13.6   Information Exchange and First Offer Strategies

	Arabs	Japanese	Mexicans	Russians	U.S. Americans
Information exchange	Focus is on information about the relationship and less on technological details.	Extensive requests are made for technical information.	Focus is on information about the relationships and less on technical details.	Great attention is paid to detail.	Information is given directly and briefly, often with a multimedia presentation.
First offer or counteroffer	20% to 50% of goal	10% to 20% of goal	Fair for both parties and close to goal	Extreme and purposefully unfair	5% to 10% of goal

Sources: Adapted from Chaney, Lillian H., and Jeanette S. Martin. 1995. Intercultural Business Communication. Upper Saddle River, NJ: Prentice Hall; Yale; Richmond, B. 1992. From Nyet to Da: Understanding the Russians. Yarmouth, ME: Intercultural Press.

In the information presentation stage, the negotiator must properly understand the audience and adapt the presentation to the audience's needs. There is some evidence that cultures have different preferences for the type of information being presented and that some countries in both Asia and Europe value depth.[26] Negotiators must know the negotiation aspects in depth. If they display ignorance, the other party may be offended. In contrast, some cultures, such as the Arab and Mexican cultures, may focus more on relationships. In such cases, presenters may need to focus more on the relational aspects of the presentation. If the information presented is too technical or difficult to understand, the other party may feel intimidated and more reluctant to make a deal,[27] so presenters must make sure that appropriate information is presented.

Negotiators need also to be attentive to the emotional aspect of the offer. Consider the next Multinational Management Brief.

After the first offer, the core of the negotiation begins. Negotiators move beyond first offer strategies and attempt to reach accord on the actual nature of the agreement. The next section outlines some of the tactics used in the next step.

Step 4: Persuasion

In the **persuasion stage**, each side in the negotiation attempts to get the other side to agree to its position. This is at the heart of the negotiation process. Numerous tactics are available to international negotiators. Although all negotiators use somewhat similar tactics to argue for their side, their emphasis and mix of tactics vary according to their cultural background.

Persuasion stage
Stage when each side in the negotiation attempts to get the other side to agree to its position.

Multinational Management **Brief**

Emotions and Negotiation Offers

Displays of emotions play a big role in terms of creating first impressions and the eventual acceptance of an offer. For instance, for Asians, saving face is a key aspect of negotiations. Negotiators who display emotions consistent with saving face are more likely to be viewed in a positive light. One of the key requirements for saving face is respect. For East Asians, respect can be shown through humility, deference to authority, and minimal disagreement. In contrast, emotions that show lack of respect, such as arrogance, direct confrontation, and open disagreements, are not likely to show respect for face.

In an interesting study, Hong Kong and Israeli negotiators were presented with positive emotions (humility and minimal disagreement) and negative emotions (arrogance and direct confrontation). Consistent with cultural expectations, the East Asian negotiators were more likely to accept offers from the individuals displaying positive emotions, who were viewed in a better light because they were acting consistently with normative expectations. In contrast, the Israeli culture values directness and in-your-face argumentation. Unlike the Hong Kong negotiators, the Israeli negotiators were indifferent to the displayed emotions and were as likely to accept offers from negotiators displaying both positive and negative emotions.

Clearly, culture affects how emotions are interpreted in negotiations. Multinationals need to ensure that people sent to negotiate display the appropriate emotion whenever possible.

Sources: Based on Canadian Business. *2009. "The United Arab Emirates: Gateway to the Gulf." Summer, 82, pp. 143–144; Kopelman, S., and A. S. Rosette. 2008. "Cultural variation in response to strategic emotions in negotiations."* Group Decision Negotiation, *17, pp. 65–77.*

We will review two general types of tactics: (1) standard verbal and nonverbal negotiation tactics and (2) some dirty tricks.

Verbal and Nonverbal Negotiation Tactics   John L. Graham, an expert on international negotiations, identifies several **verbal negotiation tactics** common in international negotiations:[28]

- *Promise:* If you do something for me, I will do something for you.
- *Threat:* If you do something I don't like, I will do something you don't like.
- *Recommendation:* If you do something I desire, good things will happen to you (e.g., people will buy your product).
- *Warning:* If you do something I don't like, bad things will happen to you (e.g., other companies will know you cannot do business here).
- *Reward:* I am going to do something beneficial for you (without conditions).
- *Punishment:* I am going to do something you will dislike—without conditions (e.g., end the negotiations immediately).
- *Normative appeal:* This is the way we do or do not do business here (e.g., "You must learn the Japanese way").
- *Commitment:* I agree to do something specific (e.g., meet a delivery date).
- *Self-disclosure:* I will tell you something about myself or my company to show you why we need to close the deal.
- *Question:* I ask you something about your company or yourself.
- *Command:* This is an order that you must follow.
- *Refusal:* Just saying no.
- *Interruption:* I talk when you talk.

> **Verbal negotiation tactics**
> Promises, threats, recommendations, warnings, rewards, punishments, normative appeals, commitments, self-disclosures, questions, commands, saying no (refusals), interruptions.

Exhibit 13.7 shows examples of cultural differences in these tactics among Japanese, U.S., and Brazilian negotiators.

EXHIBIT 13.7   Frequencies of Verbal Negotiating Behaviors: A Comparison of Brazilian, U.S., and Japanese Negotiators

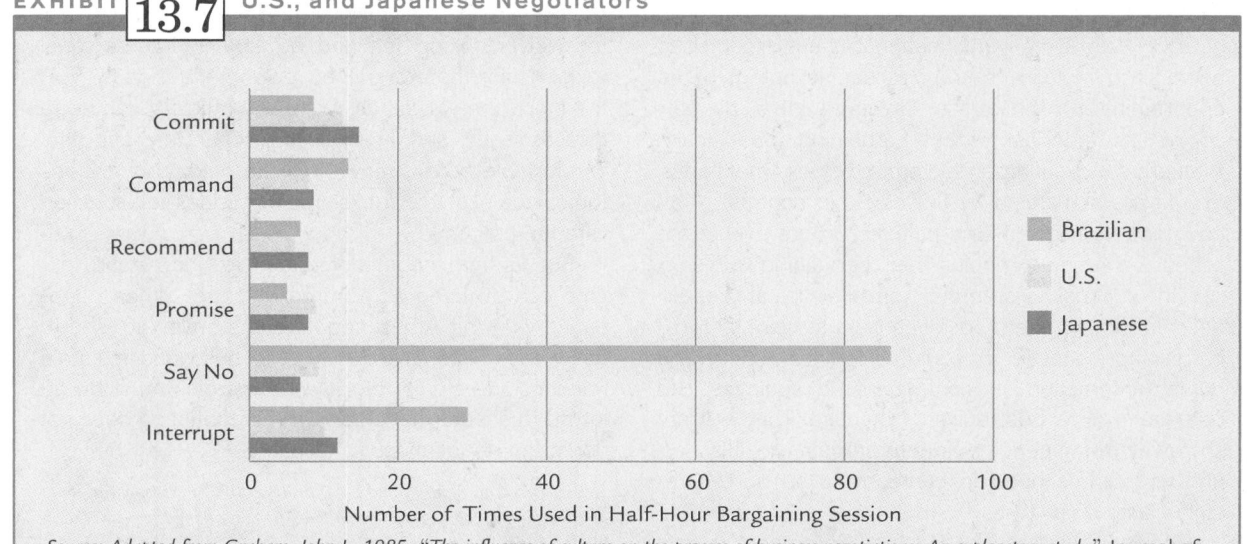

Source: Adapted from Graham, John L. 1985. "The influence of culture on the process of business negotiations: An exploratory study." Journal of International Business Studies, 26, pp. 81–96.

Cultural differences in nonverbal communication styles also influence negotiations. Nonverbal communication, through such things as body posture, facial expression, hand gestures, and the use of personal space, is a natural part of any international negotiation. For example, a hand gesture or a facial expression might be a subtle way to indicate agreement or disagreement. In addition, foreign nonverbal communication might also create (purposely or not) situations that make a negotiator uncomfortable. For example, people from cultures with a comfortable speaking distance of 1 meter (about 3 feet) might have difficulty concentrating on negotiations when someone stands inside their comfort range.

As explained earlier in this chapter, the interpretation of nonverbal communication is tricky for people of different cultural backgrounds. For example, in dealings with the Japanese, a proposal might be met with downcast eyes and no response, a reaction that U.S. negotiators often interpret as a rejection. The Japanese, however, take whatever time they need to think and formulate a proper response. Unlike most U.S. negotiators, they feel no pressure to fill the gaps in conversation. Stressed by the silence, U.S. negotiators may continue to talk, causing the Japanese to hesitate even more. Feeling that their position is rejected, U.S. negotiators often offer unnecessary concessions.[29]

Although many Asian societies use silence to communicate that they are still deliberating, other cultures allow hardly any time for introspection. One study found that, in 30 minutes of negotiation, the Japanese had more than five periods of complete silence of ten seconds or longer, nearly twice as many as U.S. negotiators. Brazilians, on the other hand, were never silent for more than ten seconds.[30] Yet another aspect of the persuasion stage is time. Consider the next Case in Point about possible bargaining tactics with Arabs.

The more direct tactics of negotiation are often supplemented by tactics that not all people consider fair. The next section shows you some of them and possible responses.

C A S E   I N   P O I N T

Time and Impact on Negotiations

As the Arabic countries fared well during the recession of 2008–2009, many multinationals were expected to begin negotiations with Arabs to take advantage of the opportunities in the region. However, the Arab perception of time can affect bargaining. Specifically, Western culture is organized around clock time; that is, events are scheduled by the clock. In contrast, Arab countries have event-time cultures, where events are scheduled around people. Their bargaining and persuasion process is different from the typical Westerner's. In fact, Western societies tend to want to avoid bargaining because it requires significant time and human interaction. In contrast, Arab societies see bargaining as a trust-building exercise. They will not shy away from spending time to bargain on all issues, and negotiators need to be ready to spend the required amount of time.

Consider the case of Bechtel Corporation negotiating with the Kuwait Oil Company to rebuild Kuwaiti oil fields. The Kuwaitis preferred to socialize extensively, drinking tea and developing interpersonal relationships before getting down to business. Furthermore, the Kuwait Oil Company officials wanted to discuss each and every issue separately and feel comfortable before moving to the next. Negotiations took place over 15 weeks, and both sides felt satisfied with the outcome.

So Western negotiators need to understand that time can be used as a bargaining tool. When negotiating with the Arabs, negotiators are well-advised to be willing to commit the time to build and maintain relationships. Furthermore, wide margins must be allowed to ensure that clock-event negotiating does not doom the negotiations to failure.

Source: Based on Alon, I., and J. M. Brett. 2007. "Perceptions of time and their impact on negotiations in the Arabic-speaking Islamic world." Negotiation Journal, 23, pp. 55–73.

Dirty Tricks in International Negotiations In both international and domestic negotiations, people can use many tactics to gain an upper hand. All negotiators want to get the best deal for their company, and they use a range of ploys or tactics to get what they want. However, people from different cultures consider some negotiating tactics **dirty tricks**, which are negotiation tactics that pressure opponents to accept unfair or undesirable agreements or concessions.[31]

The nature of cross-cultural negotiation makes the perception of dirty tricks almost unavoidable. Cultures differ on the norms and values that determine acceptable strategies for negotiation. As compared to U.S. Americans, Brazilians, for example, expect more deception and truth-stretching during the initial stages of negotiation.[32] It is therefore also critical that to pay special attention to the presenters to detect whether information is being presented truthfully.

In many countries, unlike the typical situation for U.S. negotiators, the negotiating team lacks the authority to complete a contract. Just when one party believes the deal is final, the other party responds by saying that a higher authority must approve the contract before the deal is complete. The agreement often comes back with modifications, psychologically pressuring the other side to accept numerous minor modifications.

Here are some examples of common ploys in international negotiations (that some may consider dirty tricks), with possible response tactics:[33]

- *Deliberate deception or bluffing:* Negotiators present flagrant untruths either in their facts or in their intentions for the negotiation. For example, one foreign negotiating team spent a week in a hotel pursuing a deal, only to find out later that they were part of a dirty trick being played by the local company. The local company was already negotiating in earnest with another foreign company and had brought in the second foreign company only to scare the negotiators.
  Possible response: Point out directly what you believe is happening.

- *Stalling:* Negotiators wait until the last minute before the international negotiating team plans to go home. They then push for quick concessions to close the deal.
  Possible responses: Do not reveal when you plan to leave. When asked, say that you plan to stay as long as it takes. Alternatively, state when you will leave, with or without the deal.

- *Escalating authority:* Negotiators make an agreement but then reveal that it must be approved by senior managers or the government. The objective is to put the other team under psychological pressure to make more concessions.
  Possible response: Clarify decision-making authority early in the negotiating process.

- *Good-guy, bad-guy routine:* One negotiator acts agreeable and friendly while a partner makes outrageous or unreasonable demands. The good guy suggests that only a small concession will appease the unreasonable bad guy.
  Possible response: Do not make any concessions. Ignore the ploy and focus on the mutual benefits of the potential agreement.

- *You are wealthy, and we are poor:* Often used by negotiators from developing countries, this tactic attempts to make concessions seem trivial. Small companies may also use this tactic when dealing with larger companies.
  Possible response: Ignore the ploy and focus on the mutual benefits of potential agreement.

Dirty tricks
Negotiation tactics that pressure opponents to accept unfair or undesirable agreements or concessions.

- *Old friends:* Negotiators act as if the companies and their negotiators have long-enduring friendships. They feign hurt feelings if their counterparts disagree or do not agree to their requests.
  Possible response: Keep a psychological distance that reflects the true nature of the relationship.

Successful international negotiators recognize and deal with dirty tricks and other ploys. Besides the suggested strategies, experts recommend other general responses to dirty tricks.[34] First, stick to your standards and avoid using the tricks yourself. This encourages negotiating counterparts to be more forthright. Second, point out the dirty tricks or ploys when they are used. This discourages their use later in the negotiation. Third, try to avoid fighting back directly. Fourth, be ready to walk out of the negotiation if the other side fails to play fairly. This may involve some cost, but it is probably better than a bad deal for your company. Finally, realize that ethical systems differ by culture, and understand that your opponents may not feel that they are really doing something wrong or immoral.

Although negotiators use a variety of tactics to argue their points, the goal remains to make a business deal. In the next section, we will examine the final steps in negotiation that bring the process to a successful conclusion.

Steps 5 and 6: Concessions and Agreement

Final agreement
Signed contract, agreeable to all sides.

Successful negotiations result in the **final agreement**, which is the signed contract, agreeable to all sides. The agreement must be consistent with the chosen legal system or systems. The safest contracts are legally binding in the legal systems of all the signers. Most important, people from different national and business cultures must understand the contract in principle. Partners must have a true commitment to it, beyond the legal stipulations.

Concession making
Process requiring each side to relax some of its demands to meet the other party's needs.

For most negotiations to reach a final agreement, each side must make some concessions. **Concession making** requires that each side relax certain demands to meet the other party's needs. It usually means giving in on the points of less importance to you to achieve your major objectives.

Sequential approach
Each side reciprocates concessions made by the other side.

Styles of concession making differ among cultures, and none are necessarily the most successful. Experts point out that North American negotiators take a **sequential approach**.[35] Each side reciprocates the concessions made by the other side. North Americans have a norm of reciprocity, which means that one party should meet a concession made by the counterparty by making a concession. In many cultures, however, people consider a concession as a sign of giving in, of weakness, and an encouragement to extract more concessions. In addition, in the typical U.S. negotiating strategy, partners consider each issue as a *separate* point. Negotiators expect each side to give and take on the individual issues in sequence, and they complete the agreement when the sequential concession making resolves all issues.

Holistic approach
Each side makes very few, if any, concessions until the end of the negotiation.

In contrast, a **holistic approach** is common in Asia. The parties make very few, if any, concessions during discussions of each point. Only after all the participants discuss all the issues can concession making begin. When dealing with holistic negotiators, North Americans are often perplexed to learn that a point that they believed was negotiated arises again in the discussion of the overall package.

To illustrate cross-national differences in concession-making styles, Hendon, Roy, and Ahmed surveyed 10,424 executives from more than 21 countries over a 15-year period (1985–1999).[36] They presented the executives with seven different patterns in a hypothetical situation: They are negotiating and have to distribute $100 within one hour, and their counterparts are unaware that they will give away the $100. The executives also have to make distribution decisions at the end of each of the four 15-minute periods in an hour, at the end of which they have to have given away exactly $100. The seven patterns presented to the executives are as follows:

- *Pattern 1:* Give away $25 at the end of each of the four 15-minute periods.
- *Pattern 2:* Give away $50 at the end of each of the first two 15-minute periods, leaving no concession for the last two 15-minute periods in the hour.
- *Pattern 3:* Give away $100 at the end of the negotiation, with no concessions during the first three 15-minute periods.
- *Pattern 4:* Give away $100 at the end of the first 15-minute period, with no concessions for the remaining three 15-minutes periods.
- *Pattern 5:* Give away increasing amounts in the order of $10, $20, $30, and $40 at the end of each of the 15-minute periods, in that order.
- *Pattern 6:* Give away decreasing amounts in the order of $40, $30, $20, and $10 for the end of each of the 15-minute periods, in that order.
- *Pattern 7:* Give away $50 at the end of the first 15-minute period, $30 at the end of the second 15-minute period, $25 at the end of the third 15-minute period, and take back $5 at the end of the negotiation.

Results of the study showed that the various regions studied agreed on Patterns 4 and 7 as being their least favorite concession patterns. Executives from the 21 regions represented by the five regions of North America, British Commonwealth (e.g., the United Kingdom, Australia, South Africa), more developed Southeast Asian countries (i.e., Taiwan, Singapore, and Malaysia), less developed nations of South East Asia (i.e., Philippines, Papua, New Guinea), and Latin America overwhelmingly agreed that they disliked these patterns. Pattern 4 is known as the naive negotiating style, where the bottom line is revealed at the beginning of the negotiation; practitioners do not recommend it because it makes the negotiator vulnerable—the bottom line is revealed too fast. Pattern 7, known as the renegotiation style, is also discouraged because it signals that the negotiator gave away too much.

However, the results were more interesting in that the preferred concession patterns among these regions varied widely. For instance, the North Americans seemed to prefer Pattern 3 the most, whereas none of the other regions liked this pattern. Pattern 3 is known as the tough hard-nosed concession style and is consistent with the macho culture of the individualist societies of North America. Concessions are made only at the end when everything else has failed. This strategy is, however, discouraged because concessions need to be made occasionally to break deadlocks and to keep the negotiation progressing.

The less developed Southeast Asian region preferred Pattern 5, known as the escalating pattern, in which increasing levels of concession are made as the negotiation progresses. Although this seems to be a popular style, practitioners nevertheless discourage its use. The major problem with this style is that the negotiating counterparty may get greedy and expect more and more concessions or even prolong negotiations in order to get more.

The British Commonwealth, advanced Asian, and Latin American nations all preferred Pattern 6. This is known as the de-escalation pattern; the negotiator is sending the message that fewer and fewer concessions can be made. However, the experienced negotiating counterparty may try to get as much as possible early in the negotiations.

These preference patterns suggest that negotiators can be better prepared by understanding the styles of their counterparty. Such knowledge can be invaluable because the appropriate strategies can be adopted to get the maximum advantage from the concession-making style.

Approaches to the negotiating steps vary not only by culture but also by a general philosophy regarding negotiating strategy. The next section discusses two approaches to negotiation, along with their implications for international negotiations.

Basic Negotiating Strategies

There are two basic negotiating strategies: competitive negotiating and problem-solving negotiating.[37] The competitive negotiator views the negotiation as a win-lose game. One side's gain must result in the other side's loss. Problem-solving negotiators, in contrast, search for possible win-win situations wherein the outcome of the negotiation is mutually satisfactory to both sides.

In **competitive negotiation**, each side tries to give as little as possible. They begin with high and often unreasonable demands. They make concessions only grudgingly. Competitive negotiators use dirty tricks and any plot that leads to their advantage. They spend more energy defending their positions while attempting to get the other side to make all the concessions.

Competitive negotiation seldom leads to long-term relationships built on mutual trust and commitment. Additionally, starting from inflexible positions often leads to outcomes that satisfy neither side. Thus, both sides develop negative attitudes toward each other, and often the losers seek revenge, reneging on the agreement when the opportunity arises.

The foremost tenet of **problem-solving negotiation** is separating positions from interests.[38] Negotiators do not think of defending their company's position as the major goal of the negotiation. Rather, they seek mutually satisfactory ground that is beneficial to both companies. Problem-solving negotiators avoid dirty tricks and use objective information whenever possible. They often find that actively seeking to please both sides results in the discovery of new ways to achieve mutual gains.

Exhibit 13.8 summarizes and contrasts how the competitive negotiator and the problem-solving negotiator differ in their approaches.

In international negotiations, there are three important points regarding the use of competitive or problem-solving strategies.

First, in cross-cultural bargaining, the ease of misreading the other side's negotiation strategy increases dramatically. For example, the formal politeness used by many Asian negotiators may look like problem solving to U.S. negotiators. The tendency of Brazilian negotiators to talk or to exaggerate may look like competitive bargaining to people from cultures with ritual politeness. However, in either of the examples, culturally based rules of social interaction can mask either a highly inflexible position or a true openness to problem solving.

Second, cultural norms and values may predispose some negotiators to one of the approaches. Exhibit 13.9 shows some recent evidence from a cross-national study on cultural differences in the preference for a problem-solving negotiation style.

Third, most experts on international bargaining recommend a problem-solving negotiating strategy. They believe that problem solving leads to better long-term contracts and relationships. Problem solving is more likely to achieve the multinational's goals of mutual benefits from international trade. In contrast, competitive negotiations exacerbate the inevitable conflicts and misunderstandings that occur in cross-cultural interaction.

Competitive negotiation Each side tries to give as little as possible and tries to win for its side.

Problem-solving negotiation Negotiators seek mutually satisfactory ground that is beneficial to both companies.

EXHIBIT 13.8   Competitive and Problem-Solving Negotiation

Stages in Negotiation	Competitive Negotiating Strategy	Problem-Solving Negotiating Strategy
Preparation	Identify the economic or other benefits that the company needs from the deal. Know the position to defend.	Define the interests of the company. Prepare to overcome cross-cultural barriers to defining interests.
Relationship building	Look for weaknesses in the other side. Find out as much as possible about your competition. Reveal as little as possible.	Separate the people in the negotiation from the problem. Change negotiators if necessary. Adapt to the other side's culture.
Information exchange and first offer	Give as little as possible. Give only task-related information. Make your position explicit.	Give and demand objective information that clarifies interests. Accept cultural differences in speed and type of information needs.
Persuasion	Use dirty tricks and any ploys that you think will work. Use pressure tactics.	Search for and invent new options that benefit the interests of both sides.
Concession	Begin with high initial demands. Make concessions slowly and grudgingly.	Search for mutually acceptable criteria. Accept cultural differences in the starting positions and in how and when concessions are made.
Agreement	Sign only if you win and get an iron-clad contract.	Sign when the interests of your company are met. Adapt to cultural differences in contracts.

Sources: Adapted from Adler, Nancy J. 1991. International Dimensions of Organizational Behavior, *2nd ed. Boston: PWS-Kent; Kublin, Michael. 1995.* International Negotiating. *New York: International Business Press.*

EXHIBIT 13.9   Cultural Differences in Preference for a Problem-Solving Negotiation Strategy

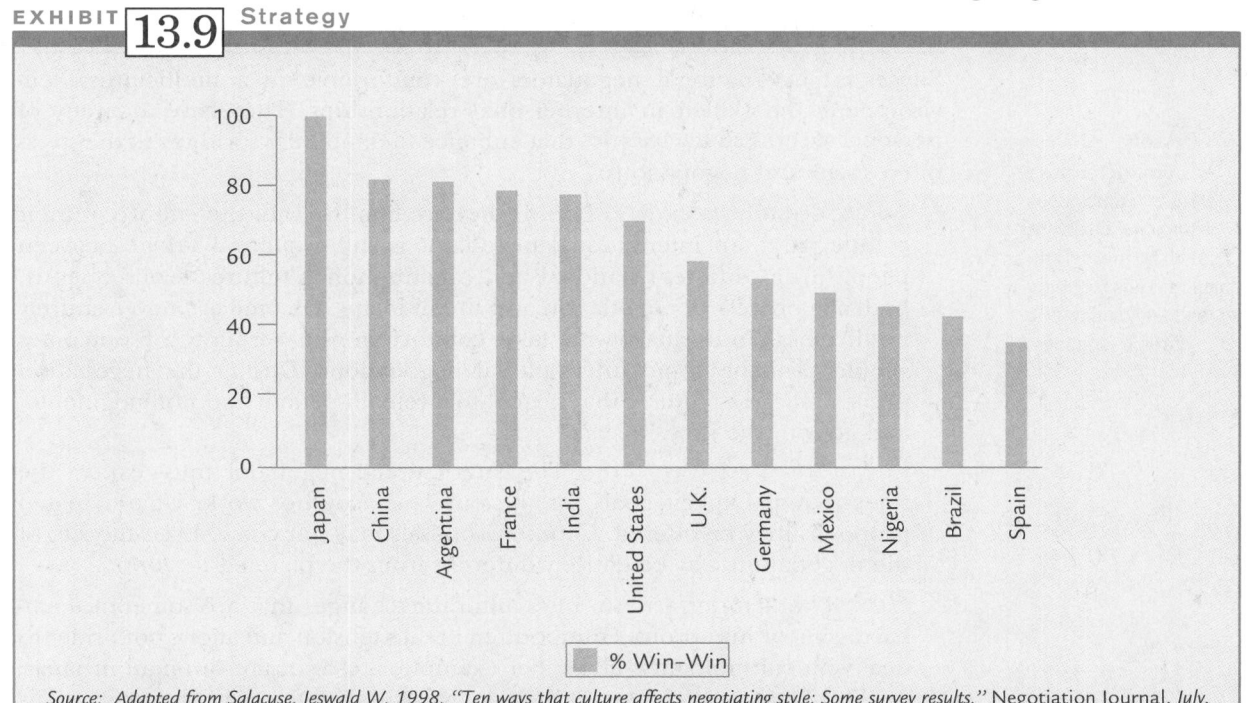

% Win–Win

Source: Adapted from Salacuse, Jeswald W. 1998. "Ten ways that culture affects negotiating style: Some survey results." Negotiation Journal, *July, pp. 221–240.*

Step 7: Postagreement

Postagreement
Consists of an evalua-
tion of the success of a
completed negotiation.

A commonly ignored step by U.S. negotiators is the postagreement phase, which consists of an evaluation of the success of a completed negotiation. Because of their inherent task orientation, negotiators tend to ignore the benefits of postagreement as they get ready to move on to the next deal. Additionally, the short-term and impatient nature of U.S. negotiators also encourages them to ignore engaging in a postagreement session.[39]

The postagreement stage can be very beneficial because it allows the garnering of valuable insights into the strengths and weaknesses of the approach used during the negotiation. Such knowledge can be very important for organizational learning and for success in future negotiations. By analyzing each step, the negotiators can determine where things went well and where improvements are needed. However, beyond information critical to learning, postagreement analysis can enable members of a negotiating team to develop a closer relationship with their counterpart. As more U.S. companies increasingly negotiate with Asian countries, taking a long-term relationship approach is necessary. For instance, for the Chinese, agreement on a deal is not the end of the negotiation but rather the beginning of an opportunity to develop trust and the relationship. U.S. negotiators will need to become more adept at postagreement work in order to further enhance their relationship-building skill.

Superior products or services, combined with good negotiating, lead to sound multinational business relationships. However, people must do the negotiating. In the next section, we will consider the characteristics of the successful international negotiator.

The Successful International Negotiator: Personal Characteristics

**Personal success
characteristics**
Tolerance of ambiguous
situations, flexibility,
creativity, humor, sta-
mina, empathy, curios-
ity, and knowledge of a
foreign language.

Successful international negotiators are comfortable in a multicultural environment and skilled in interpersonal relationships. They have a variety of personal success characteristics that enhance their abilities to adjust to the stress of cross-cultural negotiations:[40]

• *Tolerance of ambiguity:* Even if they are familiar with the culture of their counterparty, an international negotiator is still a cultural bridge between people from different national and organizational cultures. Consequently, both the process of negotiation and the ultimate outcome are never entirely predictable. Individuals who take comfort in the certainty of outcomes should probably avoid international negotiations. During the negotiation process, success requires that negotiators remain patient and nonjudgmental and go with the flow.

• *Flexibility and creativity:* The international negotiator must expect the unexpected. Explicit goals for the outcome may not work. Unanticipated proposals may be offered. Counterproposals may not come. Even the site of the negotiation may be entirely different from the planned location.

• *Humor:* Situations arise in intercultural exchanges that are sometimes embarrassing or humorous. Humor often breaks tension and allows both sides to deal with cultural ambiguities. For example, a U.S. businesswoman in Japan was shocked to see a lobster, which she was eating at the time, demonstrate its freshness by attempting to walk off the plate. Her Japanese hosts were much amused at her shock. She joined in their laughter as they teased her about eating "active" food.

- *Stamina:* Long travel times, jet lag, different foods, different climates, hotel living, and culture shock stress the physical stamina of even experienced international negotiators. Negotiators must overcome these physical challenges and still listen, analyze, observe, and socialize during the negotiation exchange. Only negotiators with a strong constitution succeed.

- *Empathy:* Empathy means putting yourself in the place of your foreign colleagues—understanding the world from their perspective. This does not mean that a negotiator must agree with all counterparties on all issues, but rather to have a sincere concern for their feelings and perspectives. Empathy facilitates the negotiation because it softens the impact of interpersonal errors and cultural misunderstandings.

- *Curiosity:* Curiosity opens the door to new information. Managers with a genuine curiosity and respect concerning other cultures often discover subtleties that a task-oriented negotiator misses.

- *Bilingualism:* Knowing the counterparty's language is an asset. However, sometimes linguistic ability alone is not enough. Even people who speak a language fluently may not understand significant aspects of a country's business culture. In particular, a good negotiator needs to understand how the business culture affects styles of negotiation.

Summary and Conclusions

In this chapter, we examined the negotiating process and elements of cross-cultural communication in international business. The negotiating process involves preparation, building relationships with counterparts, persuading others to accept your reasonable goals through verbal and nonverbal negotiating tactics, making concessions, and finally reaching an agreement. Successful negotiators prepare well and understand the steps in negotiation. They also avoid the use of dirty tricks and competitive negotiating strategies.

The people who become successful negotiators are bilingual and have good cross-cultural communication skills. In addition, they are tolerant, flexible, empathic, and curious. They react to the stress of international negotiations with humor and stamina.

Oral cross-cultural communication demands that one learn the language or use interpreters, especially in complex negotiations. High-context languages also require that people learn to interpret situations that may not be apparent from analysis of the spoken component.

Nonverbal communications through body movements, proxemics, and touching vary widely among cultural groups. International negotiators and managers must learn to interpret these behaviors in sensitive and empathic ways. This often requires looking at the world through the prism of the other culture.

Avoiding attribution errors is a key to cross-cultural communication. International managers need sensitivity to their own behaviors and to the behaviors of their foreign counterparties to avoid misinterpreting the meanings surrounding their forms of communication. For example, a dirty trick in one culture may be a perfectly acceptable tactic in another.

Discussion Questions

1. Identify the steps in the negotiating process.
2. How does the U.S. John Wayne style of negotiation influence the steps in the negotiating process?
3. Pick two countries and discuss the cultural differences in how people might use verbal negotiating tactics.
4. What is an attribution? How do attributions influence cross-cultural communication?
5. How can attributions influence the perception of dirty tricks?
6. Identify some cultural differences in body movements. How might these influence a negotiating session?
7. How might a manager successfully influence his or her subordinates in a high-context culture?
8. Discuss each of the seven stages of negotiation. Which stage do you feel is the most important? Why?

Multinational Management **Skill Builder**

Negotiating an International Contract: A Simulation

Step 1. (1 minute) Read the following scenario.

This exercise simulates an international negotiation between Sportique Shoes, a North American manufacturer of athletic shoes, and Tong Ltd., a shoe manufacturer from the fictitious Southeast Asian country of Poreadon. Both countries are members of the World Trade Organization. Because of increasing price competition in the shoe industry, Sportique Shoes is seeking a low-cost manufacturing facility overseas. In preliminary correspondence, Tong Ltd. has offered the lowest price. It is also common knowledge that Poreadon has a high-quality and motivated workforce.

A negotiating team from Sportique Shoes, charged with the task of beginning negotiations, arrives today to negotiate with the Tong Ltd. management team for a contract to manufacture Sportique's shoes for the next year.

Step 2. (10 minutes) Your instructor will divide the class into two teams. One team will represent the management of Sportique Shoes. The other team will represent the management team of Tong Ltd. Go to separate rooms or separate parts of one classroom.

Independently of the two teams, four people will be assigned the roles of World Bankers (two) and Administrators (two). These four people do not participate in the negotiation; rather, they observe, keep time, manage the finances, and take notes on the progress of the negotiation.

The objective of both the Sportique Shoes team and the Tong Ltd. team is to achieve the best contract for their company.

Step 3. (15 minutes) Each team will receive a packet of materials from the instructor. Read the Timeline, Negotiation Tasks, Cultural Background, and Negotiation Roles at this time. Decide who will play which roles.

Step 4. (10 minutes) Read the general rules for the following simulation:

A. The contract must cover four points:
   1. Delivery dates for product shipments.
   2. Quantity to be delivered at each shipment.
   3. Price per 100 shoes manufactured.
   4. Penalties for lateness.

B. Finances
   1. Each team member must contribute $1.00 to each company's Capital Account. Your instructor may change or eliminate this requirement, depending on the circumstances of your course. The Capital Account is managed by each team's CFO.
   2. The CFO delivers 40 percent of each company's Capital Account to the World Bank, which will finance future operations and requires this payment as an indication of good faith negotiations. The World Bank calls this money your Good Faith Account.
   3. Forty percent of your Good Faith Account will be returned to each team after a successful contract is signed and delivered to your instructor. Should you fail to reach an accord in the time allocated, you will forfeit your entire Good Faith Account to the World Bank. (It will be donated to a local charity.) You may recover the additional 60 percent of your Good Faith Account by meeting certain objectives as stated in the Contract Negotiation Objectives.

C. General Contract Objectives and Financial Implications
   1. Each team should try to negotiate a contract that is consistent with its cultural values and economically favorable for its company.
   2. Long-term financial gains and losses can result from what you negotiate. As in real life, these are not completely certain during the negotiation. However, the closer you are to reaching your objectives, the more likely it is that you will gain in the negotiations. For each point of negotiation, there are ranges of possible outcomes; some are neutral and both teams win, and some result in financial gain for one or the other side. After you negotiate your contract, your instructor will inform you of the economic results of your negotiations. For each point on which a team gains a favorable outcome, the other team will contribute 10 percent of its remaining Capital Account to the other team's Capital Account. For each

point on which the contract results in balanced outcomes (you both win), the World Bank will contribute a flat fee of $1.00 to each company's Capital Account.

Step 5. (10 minutes) Read the Contract Negotiation Objectives provided by your instructor.

Step 6. (20 minutes) Plan a negotiation strategy with your team members.

Step 7. (10 minutes) Make a first offer.

Step 8. (60 minutes) Negotiate!

Step 9. (30 minutes) World Bankers and Administrators balance accounts between teams. Entire group debriefs.

Endnotes

1. Hise, Richard T., Roberto Solano-Mendez, and Larry G. Gresham. 2003. "Doing business in Mexico." *Thunderbird International Business Review* 45, pp. 211–224.

2. De Mattos, Claudio, Stuart Sanderson, and Pervez Ghauri. 2002. "Negotiating alliances in emerging markets—Do partner's contributions matter?" *Thunderbird International Business Review*, 44, pp. 710–728.

3. Terpstra, Vern, and Kenneth David. 1991. *The Cultural Environment of International Business*. Cincinnati, OH: South-Western.

4. Whorf, Benjamin Lee. 1965. *Language, Thought, and Reality*. Hoboken, NJ: Wiley.

5. Babanoury, Claire. 2006. "Collaborative company research projects: A blueprint for language. *The Journal of Language for International Business*, 17(1), pp. 15–28.

6. Hall, Edward T. 1976. *Beyond Culture*. Garden City, NY: Anchor Press.

7. Ferraro, Gary P. 1994. *The Cultural Dimension of International Business*. Upper Saddle River, NJ: Prentice Hall.

8. Eibel-Eibesfeldt, I. 1971. "Similarities and differences between cultures in expressive movement." In Robert E. Hinde, ed. *Behavior and Environment: The Use of Space by Animals and Men*. London: Cambridge University Press, pp. 297–312.

9. Ferraro.

10. Axtell, R. E. 1998. *Gestures*. Hoboken, NJ: Wiley; Chaney, Lillian H., and Jeanette S. Martin. 2005. *Intercultural Business Communication*, 4th ed. Upper Saddle River, NJ: Prentice Hall.

11. Hall, Edward T., and Mildred Reed Hall. 1990. *Understanding Cultural Differences*. Yarmouth, ME: Intercultural Press.

12. Ferraro.

13. Axtell.

14. Chaney and Martin.

15. Axtell.

16. Chaney and Martin.

17. Harris, Philip R., and Robert T. Moran. 1991. *Managing Cultural Differences*. Houston, TX: Gulf.

18. Adler, Nancy J., and Allison Gundersen. 2007. *International Dimensions of Organizational Behavior*, 4th ed. Boston: PWS-Kent; Graham, John L., and Roy A. Herberger Jr. 1983. "Negotiators abroad—Don't shoot from the hip." *Harvard Business Review*, 61, pp. 160–168.

19. Copeland, L., and L. Griggs. 1985. *Going International*. New York: Random House; Dolan, John Patrick. 2005. "Strategies to negotiate any sale." *Agency Sales*, January, 35(1), p. 24; Dolan, John Patrick. 2005. "How to prepare for any negotiation session." *Business Credit*, March, 107(3), p. 18; Salacuse, Jeswald W. 1991. *Making Global Deals*. Boston: Houghton Mifflin.

20. Tung, Rosalie L. 1984. "How to negotiate with the Japanese." *California Management Review*, 26, pp. 62–77.

21. Salacuse.

22. Ibid; Salacuse, Jeswald W. 2005. "Negotiating: The top ten ways that culture can affect your negotiation." *Ivey Business Journal Online*, March–April, pp. 1–6.

23. Salacuse, "Negotiating: The top ten ways that culture can affect your negotiation.

24. Graham and Herberger Jr.

25. Salacuse, "Negotiating: The top ten ways that culture can affect your negotiation."

26. Chaney and Martin.

27. Inman, William. 2006. "What are you talking about?" *Industrial Engineer*, January, 38(1), pp. 36–39.

28. Graham, John L 1985. "The influence of culture on the process of business negotiations: An exploratory study." *Journal of International Business Studies*, 26, pp. 81–96.

29. Adler and Gundersen.

30. Graham.

31. Adler and Gundersen.

32. Graham, "The influence of culture on the process of business negotiations: An exploratory study."

33. Adler and Gundersen; Elahee, Mohammad N., Susan L. Kirby, and Ercan Nasif. 2002. "National culture, trust, and perceptions about ethical behavior in intra- and cross-cultural negotiations: An analysis of NAFTA countries." *Thunderbird International Business Review* 44, pp. 799–818; Fisher, Roger, and William Ury. 1981. *Getting to Yes*. New York: Penguin; Kublin, Michael. 1995. *International Negotiating*. New York: International Business Press.

34. Adler and Gundersen; Dolan, "How to prepare for any negotiation session.

35. Adler and Gundersen; Kublin.

36. Hendon, Donald W., Matthew H. Roy, and Zafar U. Ahmed. 2003. "Negotiation concession patterns: A multi-country multiperiod study." *American Business Review*, January, pp. 75–83.

37. Kublin.

38. Bazerman, Max H., and Margaret A. Neale. 1991. *Negotiating Rationally*. New York: Free Press.

39. Palich, Leslie E., Gary R. Carinini, and Linda P. Livingstone. 2002. "Comparing American and Chinese negotiating styles: The influence of logic paradigms." *Thunderbird International Review*, 44, pp. 777–798.

40. Kublin.

Cross-Cultural Negotiation: Americans Negotiating a Contract in China

MARKUS PUDELKO, TÜBINGEN UNIVERSITY

This comprehensive fictitious case covers the essential aspects and facets of a cross-cultural negotiation, in this case between an American and a Chinese company. The difficulties, problems, and misunderstandings both sides are facing are particularly stressed. In addition, the case's unique contribution is in presenting cross-cultural negotiation from both perspectives, the American and the Chinese. The presentation of both perspectives is structured in the same way, facilitating a direct comparison. This multi-perspective approach is rather distinctive in so far as cross-cultural negotiation tends to be regarded in most texts of Western origin exclusively from the angle of the Western side. However, it is only through a better understanding of the respective 'other' party that performance in cross-cultural negotiation can be significantly improved.

In order to facilitate group work, the various aspects covered in this case are clearly divided into various sections. This allows the class to be split up into different groups, which can each discuss specific sections in more detail and subsequently present their results to the entire class.

The case should be useful in all courses that cover cross-cultural negotiation, that is mainly in Management Across Cultures and International Business courses. The case has been written primarily for business students at the MBA level and for participants in executive education programs. However, students in advanced undergraduate classes should also benefit substantially from this case.

Introduction

Mr. Jones: I had just come back to our headquarters in Alabama from two months of negotiations in Shanghai. We hoped to set up a Joint Venture (JV) with a Chinese state owned vehicle component company. It was our intention to outsource some of our production to China to reduce our costs. When I was assigned to lead our negotiation team, I realized this could substantially boost my career and I was determined to bring these negotiations to a successful end.

Of course I was aware of the fact that the Chinese are known for being tough negotiators, but so what I thought, we Americans are certainly tough as well when it comes to business. And I was probably chosen because I have a reputation for my no-nonsense, straightforward, and sometimes even aggressive way of negotiating. What I had subsequently to discover however was that the Chinese are not tough, which would have been fine with me, they just don't know how business is done these days and they just try to cheat and play unfair games wherever possible. They still have a lot to learn if they want to be successful on the world markets. Anyway, we decided to pull out of the negotiations. You just can't trust them.

Mr. Wang: We were negotiating over the last two months with a major vehicle component company from Alabama, USA. We hoped to set up a JV which would have allowed us to improve substantially our technological knowledge base. Of course we knew about Americans always being direct to the point of rudeness and indeed we had to put up with a lot of just uncivilized behavior. Anyway, we did our best to build up a long-term relationship. And after many difficulties we were almost there, but then the Americans lost their nerve and pulled out. You just can't trust them.

Preparing for the Negotiations

Mr. Jones: Before flying over to Shanghai we did our homework very thoroughly. We made inquiries about the Chinese company and had a pretty good picture about their production facilities, product quality, and their amazingly low production costs. We thought about each little detail and knew exactly what specific information we needed. So, all that we wanted from our Chinese counterparts at the start of the negotiations were specific answers to specific questions and once we had all the missing numbers we could have simply put them into our equations and come up with a proposal which would be fair for both sides.

I stress fairness because successful negotiations are essentially a positive sum game. You learn that in every MBA program. We should all know each other's interests and viewpoints and as adults we should be able after some tough negotiations to come to a mutually satisfactory solution. All that it takes is a little bit of trust, openness, frankness, and transparency. But, as it turns out, these are terms which apparently don't exist in Chinese.

Mr. Wang: Before the Americans came over we had done our homework very thoroughly. We made inquiries about the American company and had a pretty good picture about their overall business philosophy, their corporate culture, the people running the company, and their sophisticated production technology from which we could learn much. We were keen to get to know them and hoped to enter a long-term partnership built on mutual trust. We prepared their arrival carefully, arranging meetings with everyone whom they should meet. Business is in the end about people and for people to get to know each other it takes time and we were willing to invest this time. But as it turns out, Americans don't care for people and trust, all they care about is the bottom line.

Upon Arrival

Mr. Jones: Upon arrival we were very impressed and positively surprised by the reception we received. A delegation was waiting for us already at Pudong Airport and once we arrived at the company's headquarters a huge banner across the gate was put up to welcome us. In the consecutive days, we had many meetings, not just with people from the Chinese company but even with local government officials. So, we felt greatly honored. And in the evenings we had one banquet after the other.

While appreciating the hospitality of our hosts, we were kept completely ignorant about the schedule and agenda: we had no idea what we would be doing the next day, whom we were going to meet and talk to, or even when the official negotiation would start. And we became increasingly impatient, also because my boss back home called me every day to find out where we were with the negotiations and every time I had to tell him that we hadn't even started yet.

Then we noticed that during all this friendly chit-chat with our hosts, they dropped from time to time and in seemingly casual ways questions about our business plan. In order to maintain the good atmosphere we were quite willing to answer openly. But whenever we asked questions the topic quickly changed again to the quality of Chinese food or the "long-established" friendship between China and America.

Mr. Wang: In order to show our guests how much we valued their visit, we invested a lot of time and effort to make them feel welcome. We took them out to lavish dinners, organized meetings with government and party officials, so that they could report home that they were treated with great honor. Being introduced to people with high rank and influence increases your own status and opens doors and what matters than status and access to important people?

In their ignorance and short-sightedness, all they could think of was their business presentation and kept asking when we would start the negotiations, and even got quite annoyed by some changes of agenda, without any understanding that sometimes we ourselves didn't have the detailed schedule either. This was decided by our bosses. By openly showing their annoyance and asking us questions about the agenda we didn't know the answers to, they made us lose face. How rude!

And what was this talk about when to start negotiations? As far as we were concerned the negotiations started with the first hand-shake. By the time we formally sat down for formal discussions we had already learned a lot about them and their actual intentions. But for the Americans only facts and figures presented in formal presentations or written down in documents seem to count. And if they felt increasingly under time pressure, which they naively even openly admitted, well that's part of the game.

General Principles

Mr. Jones: Fortunately, after more than a week the first real business meeting was scheduled. It was with the CEO, Mr. Chen, of the company. He is of a much higher rank and may be twenty years older than I am so I rehearsed my entire presentation carefully, in order not to make any mistakes. But then again, the whole meeting didn't touch upon any material content of our contract, instead we wasted time discussing the history of Chinese civilization and the promising business environment in China.

Finally the CEO stressed the important purpose of this meeting was to reach an agreement upon the general principles between both partners. And when I tried to raise some detailed issues, Mr. Chen just laughed and referred to Chairman Mao's meeting with US Secretary of State, Henry Kissinger. At Kissinger's mere mention of political issues, Chairman Mao stopped him in courtesy, saying "You can talk about any detail with Prime Minister Zhou later on, but with me only about general principles."

I didn't quite understand what this talk of "general principles" was all about, but I just went along. So, Mr. Chen highlighted the importance of mutual understanding, good-will, trust, a long-term relationship, the importance for the Chinese side to learn from us technological know-how, and so on and so forth. I said yes to everything, but also mentioned our interests. Later on a communiqué was even drafted. I noticed that our interests were hardly mentioned, but in the interest of keeping a good atmosphere I was happy to sign the document, after all it was just a legally non-binding statement of some intentions.

As I found out later, that was a huge mistake. Much later on in our negotiation of concrete details, whenever we refused to make any more concessions, the Chinese would refer to these general principles, pointing out our failure to understand the spirit of those general principles which were clearly spelled out and warned us not to jeopardize our mutual understanding. How they managed to build up the connection between every detail of the contract and these non-binding wishy-washy general principles was just far beyond any of us.

Mr. Wang: After one week we invited Mr. Jones and his delegation to see our CEO, Mr. Chen. We were not overly impressed that the American CEO did not fly over for this meeting. After all this was the meeting where the "general principles" for the JV were to be agreed upon: the most important part of the negotiations. This was for us a sign of disrespect and insincerity, but in order not to spoil the atmosphere we didn't mention it at all.

Apparently, Mr. Jones yet again failed to understand the importance of this meeting and foolishly agreed to everything we suggested. And when he refused to make concessions later on in the negotiations and we referred back to what he himself agreed upon when discussing the "general principles," he made it clear to us that he didn't care much about them. But these mutually approved principles constituted the foundation of our entire cooperation. How can you trust someone who ignores general principles which are based on trust? All that mattered for the Americans were the details of the actual contract. Only those with bad intentions hide behind paragraphs of some contract.

Patience

Mr. Jones: When it finally came down to negotiating the details of our contract, it appeared that our Chinese counterparts always controlled the pace of the negotiations, using delays very purposefully to put us under pressure. The Chinese never missed any chance to ask for concessions, and it seems the only thing they're willing to sacrifice is time. Whenever we thought we had made some progress, the Chinese had to double-check with their superiors and even government and party officials and that could take forever. And when we asked to resume the talks, they replied that consistent with the general principles of "mutual understanding", we should make more efforts to understand the slowness of Chinese bureaucracy.

However, whenever we had to get advice from our headquarters back in the States and the response took a bit longer than foreseen, then this was unacceptable to the Chinese. They thought that, as we were from such an efficient and advanced capitalist country, there could be no other reason for delays than some malice intentions. So much for the principle of mutual understanding!

Mr. Wang: We actually felt quite annoyed and almost insulted by the insistence of the Americans on discussing specific details, coming to an agreement, and moving on. What is the point of hurrying and discussing some details of a contract if you haven't even got to know the people well with whom you will actually have to implement the contract. That matters much more than some details which would need to be adapted over time anyway, because things just develop and change. And how can you adapt if there is no mutual understanding?

Also we can't just take decisions at the negotiating table, as we often need approval, not only from our superiors but also from certain government agencies and this takes time. Of course we can't always admit to this openly, it makes us lose face, but they should have understood that negotiating teams in China don't have the autonomy Americans have. Decisions in Chinese companies are often taken by people in the background.

Friendship, Trust, Harmony, and Contracts

Mr. Jones: One thing we felt really strange about was the constant insistence on friendship and long-term trust relationships between the two sides throughout the negotiation process. Whenever the Chinese "offered" something we considered as a matter of course anyway, they made a big story out of it, implying that it was only because of our friendship that they "offered" us this "favor." And whenever they wanted something we considered as out of question they tried to pressure us with the hint that refusing would endanger our friendship. As far as I am concerned, I never considered these Chinese (or for that matter any other persons I ever negotiated with) as friends. We have common interests to start negotiations, during the negotiations themselves we certainly have more opposite interests and to sort this out is a question of professionalism, not of friendship.

Another of their constantly repeated buzz-words is harmony. In the beginning we were always very polite, soft spoken, and even tolerated some attempts from the Chinese side to take advantage of us. But the more we gave them, the more they wanted and so we became increasingly direct in communicating where our limits were. And at times that included some outburst and door slamming. But the next day it was all forgotten and we moved on.

With all their talk about trust, one thing the Chinese never seemed to fully trust was what has been written in a contract. They constantly asked to whom they should turn if something went wrong. But if "something went wrong," that can only mean that one of the two parties broke the contract, and that should be solved by required legal procedure. But the Chinese insisted on adding some clauses about arbitration through a third party into the contract, again with the emphasis on mutual understanding and trust. But how can you trust someone who apparently already thinks about breaking the contract before it is actually signed?

Mr. Wang: We Chinese do business on the basis of personal relationships, friendship, and trust and not on the basis of some written document. We give ourselves a long time before doing business with someone, but once we believe we can enter a business relationship, then we stick to it and we would never give it up, only because, say, someone would offer us for some deal a better price.

Although it didn't seem at all a problem for the Americans, they behaved at times quite rudely. Even if you don't agree with the other side, you should always control your anger and maintain harmony. How can the Americans still get along when they just had a furious argument the day before? To keep harmony is our way to express intention to build up long-term relationship. We wouldn't mind taking more time and patience when problem arises, so long as both sides remain calm and discuss in a peaceful way. However, the Americans only cared for speed in the negotiation.

Then the Americans who were always so interested in the specifics of the contract, were very reluctant to introduce arbitration clauses in case some changes occur which need to be taken into consideration. They said: "If something goes wrong, we have to go to court." How can you trust someone who wants to sue you if a problem comes up? If you really are interested in a long-term business relationship, no contract in the world can foresee all eventualities. It's like a marriage. Its success is based on trust, not on a contract.

Guanxi

Mr. Jones: If one thing is known to Westerners about Chinese business culture it is the concept of *guanxi*. Of course all over the world connections and networks do matter in business, but the Chinese take it to an extreme and apply it to virtually every aspect in society. In order to get planning permission for the plant we intended to build, our Chinese partner encouraged us to take the senior officials of the local planning approval commission out for a luxurious dinner. Building up good

connections might shorten the application process from several months to just a couple of weeks. However, what our Chinese business partners labeled as building up connections, sounded to us very much like corruption. It is our company's strict policy not to engage in any kind of such activities, no matter where in the world.

Apparently, also the recruitment and promotion policy of our Chinese business partner was mainly determined by *guanxi*. Sons and daughters of business partners and influential bureaucrats clearly received preferential treatment. Once engaged in the JV we would have had to make an end to all that to make sure that only the best candidates got recruited or promoted. What a mess, to clean all this up!

Mr. Wang: As always the Americans only thought about business in terms of abstract concepts. We don't dispute the validity of these concepts, but we take a more holistic approach and don't forget that business is done in the end by people, and people have to get along with each other. Everything comes down to give and take and what matters is that in the end there is a balance between the favors you receive and do. We like to do someone a favor, as we know the person will feel morally obliged to return the favor at one point. Therefore we also like to repay a favor as soon as possible, so that we don't feel indebted anymore.

Moral obligations are much smoother, flexible, and adaptable than contractual obligations. We don't like to sue each other which seems to be a national sport in the United States. If you go to court, all parties involved lose face. And a system which is built on moral obligations can only work if a high degree of ethical standards are observed. That is why we get so upset, if the Americans equal *guanxi* with corruption. I freely admit that we have the problem of corruption in China, but this is because of the abuse of power by bureaucrats, not because of the importance we attach to mutual obligations which go back to Confucius. Why do you think, overseas Chinese are so successful in so many countries? It is because of trust and sense for obligation, in short because of *guanxi*.

America might be at the moment the most powerful country in the world, but their values are not as universal as they might think. And our American business partners, with their usual combination of arrogance and ignorance, did not follow our advice to build up *guanxi* with the planning commission and I am sure they would still be waiting today for approval.

Overseas Chinese

Mr. Jones: Considering the difficulty we anticipated to have in communicating with our Chinese counterparts, we had a fellow in our negotiation team who was of Chinese origin. We thought that his fluency in Chinese and his deeper understanding of the Chinese way of doing things would be useful. And indeed, we benefited greatly from his accurate interpretation and prediction of responses from the Chinese. Even though both sides had professional interpreters, his role was appreciated also by the Chinese, as he was able to better interpret conflicting standpoints and mediate between both sides.

However, it didn't take long before we ran into problems. Whenever there was some dispute over the contract details, our Chinese counterparts began to pressure him to sort out things in their favor. Never mind that he was born in the United States, was an American citizen and was working for an American company, they just saw him as one of theirs and couldn't grasp that he represented the other side. This was not China against America, this was a negotiation between two companies and he was an employee of our company, so what did they expect? It's completely ridiculous that the Chinese felt entitled to ask so much from him just because he was of Chinese origin.

Mr. Wang: There was this U.S.-born Chinese guy on the American negotiation team, and we interpreted his presence as a sign of sincerity and goodwill on the part of the Americans and their wish to establish a good relationship with us. Finally someone who would appreciate how business is done here. So we focused on trying to make him understand our position. But instead of acting like a bridge between the two sides, he showed no sympathy whatsoever for us. He was coming from rich America and should have had more consideration for our situation. And when he overheard us discussing in Chinese, he must have passed on what he heard to his bosses. So, the man we thought of as a friend was nothing but a spy. Not exactly the right way to establish trust.

Honesty

Mr. Jones: Our Chinese partners constantly stressed the values of trust and harmony in business. But how can you expect to be trusted if you are not completely honest. And the Chinese were the masters of deception and game play. Of course no one puts his cards on the table, but there is a difference between holding back some crucial information and telling stories which are not true. Overall we were quite frank with what we wished to see to come out of the negotiation, because we were convinced we were in a win-win situation and we wanted to build up trust. But we didn't get anything back for our honesty. In the end I think they considered our honesty as a weakness.

Mr. Wang: Life in society would not be possible without honesty. You should never lie to your parents, relatives or close friends. But in a business negotiation you have to act strategically. To our great surprise, the Americans turned out unbelievably naïve with being overly honest. With all their money and technological know-how they might think they can afford to be completely honest, but if you start out at the weaker end, one needs to compensate for this by being cleverer. At one point the American negotiation leader even called us dishonest. What an insult! Only because we were cleverer by not revealing everything, we are not dishonest. And what the Americans mistook for honesty and frankness was often nothing but impolite and rude behavior.

Face/Shame

Mr. Jones: The Chinese concept of "saving face" soon began driving us mad. In a business negotiation you have to think logically, you need to be objective and look at the facts. In the interest of the project you have to be able to criticize and accept criticism. Once we were discussing the optimal way of setting up machines in the factory. It was a purely technical detail. The head of the Chinese negotiation team, Mr. Wang, made a proposal which simply didn't make sense. We had it all figured out and based on our calculations. I calmly but firmly explained to him that what he suggested was simply nonsense. He became angry and left the meeting. What is this? First not getting the maths right and then getting upset? If we hadn't picked up on this, we could have incurred lots of costs which would have been of no interest to anyone. I might have been more diplomatic, but I wasn't putting him down, I only made my point.

Still, I apologized later on and he replied I shouldn't worry there was no problem. But the following day when I just confused two figures, he corrected me like a teacher would a school boy, looking triumphantly to his team. Apparently, he tried to regain face by shaming me. What childish behavior! What we never could quite comprehend when communicating with the Chinese is how much they care about the formal way of communication, instead of its actual content. No problem to tell a blunt lie, if you only do it with a polite smile!

Mr. Wang: Being completely fixated on profits and efficiency, our American counterparts showed no respect to people. Once I made a point which was probably not well thought through. It was just a detail, no reason fighting over. But instead of just leaving it for the moment and telling me later on, Mr. Jones lectured me for 10 minutes about why I was wrong, thus causing me embarrassment in front of my entire team. I think he was not even aware of the fact that I lost face, but that is even worse: the Americans always seem to think that their way of behavior represents the universal standard and everything else are just folkloristic oddities which should be abandoned for the sake of the only right (American) way. And in addition, Mr. Jones is ten years younger than I am, how dare he treat me with so little respect!

Haggling

Mr. Jones: What amazed us quite a lot was the fact that the Chinese adopt exactly the same strategy in business negotiation as in shopping on the street market. The seller demands an unreasonably high price, followed by some intense haggling which usually ends at around half of the initial asking price. In the end, both parties feel happy, even though they could have settled for half the price right away without wasting all the time on fierce negotiation. It took us quite a while to realize what satisfaction the Chinese take from asking and receiving concessions. The bargaining ability is something the Chinese take pride in, and they enjoy practicing it no matter if it is for obtaining better conditions in a multi-million contract or for getting cheaper vegetables for dinner. At each item on the agenda, our Chinese counterparts started out with some totally unacceptable conditions, waited for our counter-offer which was much closer to a realistic solution and then continued asking us for concessions with an unbearable patience.

Before coming to China an expert on Chinese business suggested to me to read *The Art of War*, written by Sun Tzu more than 2000 years ago. At that point I laughed at this advice, but it turned out I should have taken it more seriously, as the Chinese themselves interpret negotiation as psychological warfare and use the war metaphor quite frequently when talking about negotiations. Chinese just don't understand the concept of a positive sum game. They only think in terms of losing or winning. How can you enter a JV if you are always perceived as the rival and not as the partner?

Mr. Wang: We are surprised how little negotiation skills the Americans had. They always were so upfront with their real intentions that we could easily get concessions when we pushed the right buttons. And we could read from the expressions on their faces like an open book. I thought the Americans were so good at poker, but apparently not. In negotiation you should never reveal what you think.

Also, the Americans reacted always so nervously if there was a delay in the negotiation. Whenever we agreed on something important we told them we needed approval from our superiors which was also often the case. We just don't have the decision making authority the Americans are used to. Anyway, as they often reacted so impatiently, we delayed sometimes the process on purpose. And in particular when they became irrationally agitated and furious we always got the concession we wanted.

Skillful negotiation is about ascertaining the genuine intention of the other side, and preparing responding strategies so as to reap the most benefits from the final result. This is what real negotiation encompasses, which is far more than "haggling" as the Americans refer to our tactics. Of course, for a long-term partnership both sides need to be satisfied, but it is always good to be a little more satisfied than the other side.

Strategic Behavior

Mr. Jones: Negotiating with the Chinese feels almost like walking in complete darkness—you never know what their next move will be, you can't even figure out whether they are content with your proposal or not. Always seemingly modest and courteous, we never knew what they were thinking. Whenever we suggested something and explained in detail why this should be good for both sides, they never contradicted, always nodded, frequently said "yes," but in the end, they often just ignored what we just laid out or said they needed to refer this to their superiors and come back to us which they never did.

And every time they pushed us for another concession, they started by emphasizing the importance of looking at the long-term benefits, as if we were just myopic and unwise not to agree with the conditions more favorable to them. And when asked what these long-term benefits would be, they usually vaguely described them as the possibility of much more lucrative contracts in the "near future." Whatever that means.

Mr. Wang: One of the most crucial criteria in our society to judge a person's social status and social skills, is the ability to control one's own emotions. The more someone plainly shows satisfaction or irritation, the more people will regard this person as shallow, undignified, and inexperienced. Americans with their noisy directness and openness will never understand this. This has put us into an advantageous position, as we always knew where we were with them, but they had no clue about our position. As a result, they also felt less and less confident and more willing to compromise.

Americans like to feel dominant. They like to talk a lot and explain this and that. So we let them talk, we listen and nod encouragingly. The more you listen the more you learn, but the more you talk the more you reveal your position. At the end of a negotiation day, our

American friends were happy, because they felt they were in charge and we were happy because we understood their intentions better.

What Means "Yes" and "No"

Mr. Jones: What frustrated us most was the fact the Chinese negotiators were never prepared to give a definitive answer, everything remained "subject to approval" of their superiors. And even if we got what we thought was a definite agreement, the Chinese were not the slightest embarrassed to reopen a subject we thought to have settled. So, a "yes" could mean anything, including "no."

While we often got a "yes" without knowing what it meant, we never got a clear "no." Only after a while we understood that phrases such as "it's possible, so long as..." or "this would be very difficult" were equivalent to "forget it." In short, you never knew what was going on. When we said "yes" we meant it and they could count on it. And also when we said "no," we meant it as well, but the Chinese never took "no" for an answer. Sometimes I felt like being in a kindergarten!

Mr. Wang: Reality is just too complex for simple "yes" or "no" answers. Everything depends on everything else and everything is in flow, so what matters is the overall picture. The Americans are always so proud of their analytical approach. But to "analyze," means to "take apart" and you simply can't just tear things apart and treat them as independent from each other. This is for us a sign of an immature view of the complexities of reality. We don't analyze reality, we take a holistic view, in order to comprehend the totality of the problem. Therefore, we could never comprehend how upset the Americans became when we asked to revise a certain point. Negotiations are a circular and iterative process, not a linear and sequential one!

Chinese Lack of Technological Know How

Mr. Jones: Another point we were never able to comprehend was the following: Often we detected a certain feeling of cultural superiority with the Chinese who appeared to look down on us. But then, at times, they fully surprised us by putting themselves down to the verge of self-humiliation. This was specifically the case when the negotiation touched upon technology and R&D. Here the Chinese openly admitted how backwards their technological standards were, which was all due to foolish Chinese politics in the past. Now they had to catch up and so our Chinese partners expressed straightforward their admiration for our advanced technology and their willingness to "learn from the Americans," pleading for our help. Deeply impressed by the Chinese ambitions, we felt it, to certain extent, as our moral duty to contribute with our technology to the development of this amazing country.

However, things soon went completely wrong when, after exploring the possibilities of our cooperation on the technology level, we moved on to the estimated costs of R&D, licensing fees, and others. What shocked us was that the Chinese refused to even consider paying for anything, and said they were truly disappointed at our intention to charge them for our technological know-how which was in clear opposition to the spirit of trust and good relations. They argued that it wouldn't cost us anything to just provide them with the know-how, as we already had the technology. Besides we are from a rich company and a rich country, while they were from a poor state-owned company in a still developing country. The fact that we had spent hundreds of millions of dollars on R&D and that our company is fiercely competing with other big corporations on the world market and that we have to act in the best interest of our shareholders and can therefore not just give away technology for free was incomprehensible to our Chinese partners.

I think they somehow still had this notion in the back of their mind that for centuries foreigners traveled from all parts of the world to China, bringing with them their knowledge and goods which they freely offered as tribute and sign of respect to the Chinese who perceived themselves as the only real civilization on earth and the center of the world. Well, not with us!

Mr. Wang: We were deeply disappointed with the Americans' attitude about passing on technological know-how. We very much admire the American ingenuity to develop new products and we were eager to learn from them. But they apparently only wanted to engage in the JV to use cheap Chinese labor. And when we discussed technology transfer and expressed our interest in learning from them, they asked for outrageously high fees which we would never have been able to pay. We are from a still poor country and the Americans shouldn't try to take advantage of this and exploit us. I think they were acting very selfishly and immorally.

Criticism

Mr. Jones: The Chinese never accepted any constructive criticism, however well intended. I admit, we Americans might be more direct than the Chinese and this might cause some friction, but why is it that we always have to adapt to them?

Mr. Wang: We were just tired of the Americans lecturing us all the time. They kept making critical comments about everything, about our interpreter who had a strong accent which made it difficult to understand him, about people in the streets who seldom obey traffic rules, about air pollution in the cities, and so on. At one point they even touched upon sensitive issues such as democracy, human rights, and Taiwan. How dare they mingle into our internal affairs. That's none of their business.

Conclusion

Mr. Jones: Despite all the obstacles and everything we had to put up with, we were almost there! We had gone through all points and agreed with much difficulty on each item. The day for the formal signature of the contract was set and our CEO planned to fly in for this event. We were all enthusiastic to finally go back home. At this point the Chinese negotiation leader came to us, apologized to us and said that some "little points" still had to be revisited on the request of his superiors. And it turned out that these "little points" were absolutely fundamental and purely unacceptable to us. I was absolutely furious and called him a dishonest game player. He realized that he might have gone too far, but it was too late. I told him that the deal was off. The next day we flew home. With people who behave in this way one can't do any business.

Mr. Wang: For us Chinese a negotiation starts with the first hand-shake and hasn't finished until the contract is signed. But the Americans seemed to be all content to have gone through their check list with all their little items and only thought about going home. For us, however, it makes sense to leave everything open to further possible adjustment up to the very final stage, so that we can always re-consider earlier agreements. We can't just say "yes" or "no" to a little issue and then move on until you reached the end of the agenda. This is just a sign of naivety and immaturity.

And of course it is standard tactical negotiation behavior to try to score some final points at the very end,

taking advantage of the tiredness of your negotiation partners. One of the advantages to negotiate on your home turf is that at the end the others are eager to return home and often willing to make some last minute concessions. Of course I didn't expect the Americans to fully agree to my proposals, but just a little concession would have been sufficient. They are rich enough to make one more compromise and I would have been regarded by my superiors as a clever negotiator to obtain some last minute concessions. Mr. Jones should have known that. But instead, he became all angry, shouted at me and thus completely lost face. It is very unfortunate, but even in the future we cannot take up the negotiations again. With people who behave in this way one can't do any business.

CASE DISCUSSION QUESTIONS

1. What are the different approaches both parties take toward business negotiations?
2. What are the mistakes both parties have committed in this cross-cultural negotiation process, and what should they have done better?
3. What are the key characteristics of a successful cross-cultural negotiator?
4. How could both sides have prepared better to anticipate the problems faced in the negotiation?

CASE CREDIT

This case was written by Markus Pudelko, now Professor of International Business at Tübingen University, with assistance from Brian Stewart, former diplomat in China and from 1981 to 1998 adviser to American and British companies entering the Chinese market; from Sally Stewart, former Head of Department of Management at the University of Hong Kong; and from Xunyi Xu, student of Economics at Fudan University.

14 Motivation in Multinational Companies

Learning Objectives

After reading this chapter you should be able to:

- Recognize how people from different nations perceive the basic functions of working.
- Explain how people from different nations view the importance of working.
- Understand how the national context affects the basic processes of work motivation.
- Apply common theories of work motivation in different national contexts.
- Design jobs for high motivational potential in different national cultures.

Preview CASE IN POINT

Motivating Workers in China and India

Many experts predict that the emerging countries, such as India and China, were, at the time of writing, weathering the 2008–2009 recession well. However, as more multinationals moved into China and India, they created an intense competition for good workers. These multinational companies are finding it no easy task to attract the upwardly mobile Chinese and Indian professional with strong technical and international management skills. As domestic companies reform their operations, they are pursuing these same individuals. In China, where the average wage is $250 a year, money talks, especially in recruitment and retention. Skilled secretaries get monthly salaries that match or even double the yearly national average. When companies don't match the local market wages, job performance drops and turnover increases.

However, recent trends show that pay is no longer the best motivator for Chinese workers. As many of the safety nets of the centrally controlled government (e.g., low-cost housing, health care, guaranteed jobs) have disappeared, budgeting for such items is slowly eating away at people's incomes. Additionally, corruption has become rampant. Chinese workers are becoming disenchanted with the uncertainties inherent in a capitalist society, and many job seekers are applying for civil servant or other government jobs to benefit from job security.

Other surveys suggest that multinational companies have to become more creative to motivate their talented Chinese workers. As salary levels between cities and increases start to level off, multinational companies need to go beyond pay to motivate their workers. Some companies are finding that they need to provide adequate training programs, and others are refining their performance management systems, incorporating stronger pay-for-performance philosophies. A recent survey by Watson Wyatt showed that Chinese workers are increasingly looking for safer and healthier work environments where the organization shows genuine concern for their professional development.

Multinationals in India are experiencing similar circumstances. Unlike their parents, young Indian professionals do not necessarily value security and stability in a job. Rather, they grew up in an age of economic optimism and thus demand more of their employers. Multinationals need to develop plans to ensure that these new workers' energies are harnessed. However, these new employees come with high expectations. If they feel that their employers are not treating them well in terms of salary or advancement, they do not hesitate to find work in other companies or change careers. Multinationals thus have to devise appropriate plans to retain and motivate these new Indian employees.

Sources: Based on Dominic, B. 2009. "Asia's future and the financial crisis." McKinsey Quarterly, 1, pp. 102–105; Chen, Kathy. 2006. "Free market rattles Chinese; Economists' ties' questioned; Job seekers eye state positions." Wall Street Journal, January 26, p. A9; Hamm, S. 2008. "Young and impatient in India." Business Week, January 28, pp. 45–48; Johnson, Mike. 1998. "Beyond pay: What rewards work best when doing business in China." Compensation and Benefits Review, 30, pp. 51–56; Leininger, Jim. 2004. "The key to retention: Committed employees." China Business Review, January–February, 31, pp. 16–17, 38–39.

A ll managers must motivate their subordinates to accomplish organizational goals. However, as the Preview Case in Point showed, motivational techniques present significant challenges for companies. The motivational methods based on pay used previously by multinational companies in China or India are no longer working. New trends suggest that multinational companies need to constantly be aware of what workers seek in their work environment and adjust rapidly to satisfy those needs. As more multinational companies and domestic companies compete for the same talented workers, they are encountering increased pressure to find new ways to motivate and retain workers.

To provide the background necessary to understand how to motivate workers in multinational organizations, this chapter reviews differences in work values and in the meaning of work, discusses major theories of motivation and their multinational applications, and reviews U.S. and European views of designing jobs to produce high levels of motivation.

Work Values and the Meaning of Work

Before we can understand how to motivate or lead people from different national cultures, we must have some knowledge about what work means to people from different societies. Two basic questions need to be answered: How important is work in people's lives? What do people value in work?

How Important Is Work in People's Lives?

To answer this question, a number of major international research projects studied thousands of workers from several countries. These studies included workers in all types of occupations: professional, managerial, clerical, service, and production.[1] The most recent study, the World Values Surveys and European Values Surveys (WVS/EVS),[2] contains information on people's attitudes toward work and life from the 50 countries that include the majority of the world's population.

One question addressed in the Meaning of Work study is the degree to which people are attached to work. **Work centrality** is "the degree of general

Work centrality
Overall value of work in a person's life.

importance that working has in the life of an individual at any given point in time."[3] Work centrality represents the importance of work in a person's life when compared with other activities, including leisure, family, community, and religion.

Few studies have examined the country-level factors that lead to cross-national differences in work centrality. However, Parboteeah and Cullen used a combination of national culture (Chapter 2) and social institutions (Chapter 3) to examine work centrality differences in 26 nations.[4] They examined five social institutions, namely the extent of socialism, the degree of industrialization, the degree of union strength, the accessibility of education, and the extent of social inequality, and they found that all five social institutions had negative effects on work centrality. In addition, the study also looked at three of Hofstede's national culture dimensions.[5] Results showed that uncertainty avoidance and masculinity had negative effects on work centrality. In contrast, the cultural dimension of individualism had positive effects on work centrality.

The study showed that the traditional attachment to work typical of most industrialized societies may be changing. Such changes are consistent with Inglehart, Basanez, and Moreno's observation of a postmodern shift in many industrialized societies.[6] They argue that industrialized societies have long thrived on values that encouraged work centrality, economic achievement, individualism, and innovation but that these values have now reached their limits. In the postindustrialized societies, people are now more concerned with quality-of-life issues and individual self-expression.

Multinational Management **Brief**

Karoushi and *Karojisatus:* Sudden Death or Suicide from Overwork

In Japanese, *karoushi* translates in English as "sudden death from overwork." *Karojisatus* is suicide from overwork. As we saw in Chapter 12, the Japanese work more hours than people from most other countries do. They also have the highest work-centrality score.

This psychological and time commitment to working probably accounts for some of the Japanese economic growth. However, there is some indication that the benefits may have physical and psychological costs. As most of the managers who led Japan through its period of growth reach later middle age, the costs to them of long working hours and other Japanese business practices (long hours of drinking and smoking with colleagues after work) may be taking its toll. Early evidence suggests that death from work-related stress is on the rise. Police estimate the number of work-related suicides at 1,300 annually, but they have no official classification for this type of death. Some lawyers representing surviving family members put the estimate higher.

However, besides death from overwork, Japan is also facing worker suicides caused by overwork. According to Japanese officials, 81 cases of worker suicides were attributed to stress over the 2007–2008 fiscal year. Over 40 percent of these deaths involved workers in their 20s and 30s. Japanese officials are alarmed because suicides will probably increase as the work environment incorporates more temporary workers who are more likely to commit suicide.

Sources: Based on Economist. 2006. "*Greying Japan—The downturn,*" January 7; Caryl, Christian. 2006. "*Turningun–Japanese.*" Newsweek, February 20; Jiji Press English News Service. 2008. "*Worker suicides keep increasing in Japan.*" August 4; Tubbs, W. 1993. "*Karoushi: Stress-death and the meaning of work.*" Journal of Business Ethics, *12, pp. 869–877.*

Higher levels of work centrality are closely correlated with the average number of hours worked per week in the country (Chapter 12): People from countries with great work centrality usually work long hours. The average Japanese worker, for example, puts in more hours than his or her counterpart in most other industrialized nations. Hence, managers may be able to apply management techniques that favor job-related incentives in order to motivate workers in societies with high work centrality.

In general, high levels of work centrality may lead to dedicated workers and effective organizations. However, as the previous Multinational Management Brief shows, high levels of work centrality can also have adverse effects on workers. Evidence suggests that the number of hours worked by the Japanese is declining and that many workers are complaining of burnout, perhaps indicating a change in work centrality for this country.[7]

In addition to work centrality, the levels of **work obligation norms** are important. In general, societies with high work obligation norms expect their citizens to view work as an obligation or a duty. These societies are more likely to have individuals who work longer hours. Exhibit 14.1 shows the levels of work obligations in various societies surveyed by the World Values Survey.[8] As the exhibit shows, many of the emerging economies, such as India, Turkey, Poland, and Bulgaria, show very high levels of work obligation norms. Such findings are encouraging for multinational companies with substantial investments in these

Work obligation norms
Degree to which work is seen as an obligation or duty to society.

EXHIBIT 14.1   Work Obligations Norms for Selected Countries

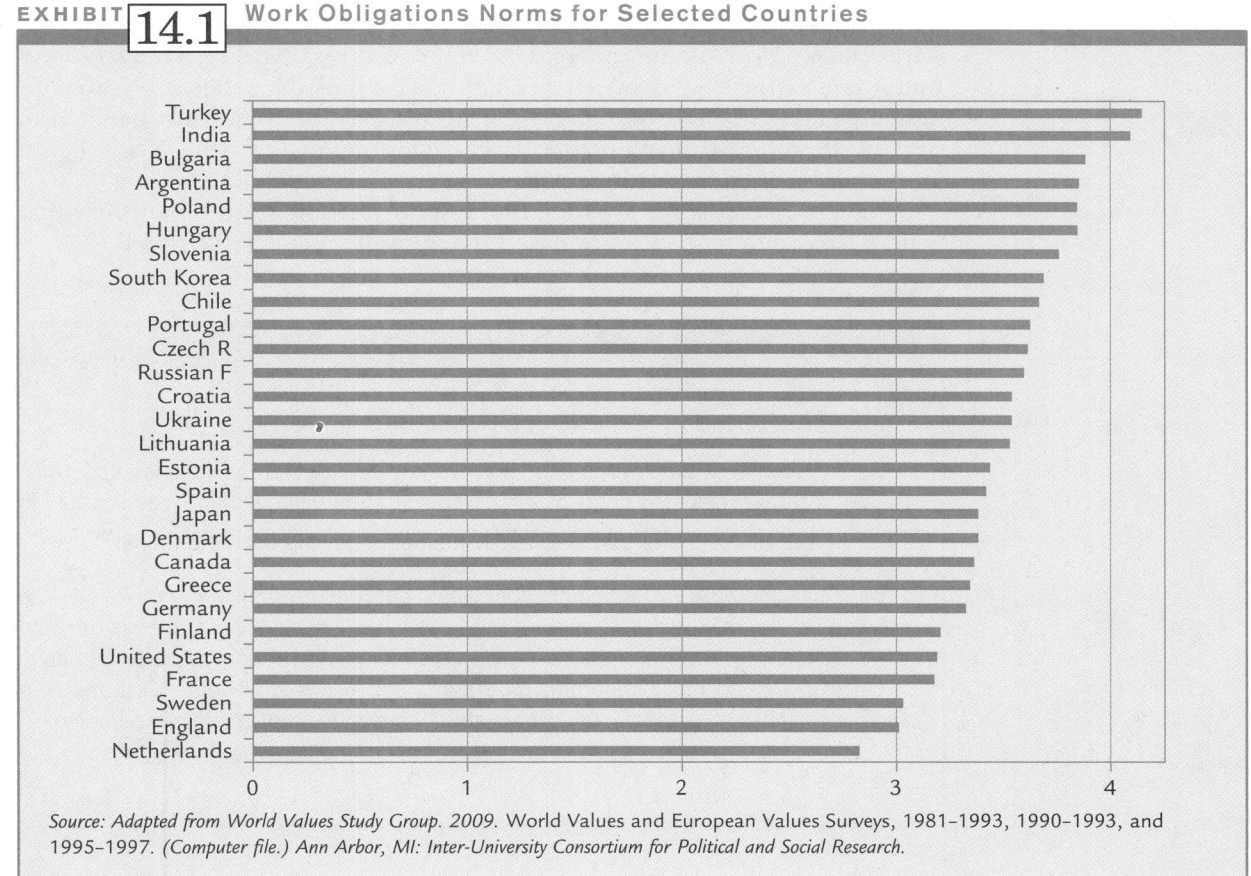

Source: Adapted from World Values Study Group. 2009. World Values and European Values Surveys, 1981–1993, 1990–1993, and 1995–1997. (Computer file.) Ann Arbor, MI: Inter-University Consortium for Political and Social Research.

countries. Many of these emerging economies now have much stricter monetary and fiscal policies and more stable financial systems.[9] The high work obligation norms, coupled with a more structurally sound financial environment, suggest that multinational companies will face a workforce with a very favorable view of work.

Exhibit 14.1 also shows that more developed economies, such as the Netherlands, the United States, and Germany, have much lower work obligation norms. Such results are consistent with Inglehart, Basanez, and Moreno's post-industrialization shift.[10] Decades of prosperity have reduced the importance of a strong work ethic, and individuals in these societies no longer view work as a duty.

What Do People Value in Work?

The WVS/EVS study also looked at work values: what people expect from work. Two important work values are extrinsic work values and intrinsic work values. Individuals with **extrinsic work values** express a preference for security from their jobs, with such aspects as income, job security, and less demanding work. In contrast, workers with **intrinsic work values** express preferences for openness to change, the pursuit of autonomy, growth, creativity, and the use of initiative at work. Consider the next Multinational Management Brief.

Exhibits 14.2 and 14.3 show the extrinsic and intrinsic work values for selected countries of the World Values Survey.[11]

As Exhibit 14.2 shows, the most important finding is that people from different nations did not express the same preference for extrinsic and intrinsic work values. Most of the emerging economies (e.g., Turkey, Hungary, and India) rate extrinsic work values very highly. This probably reflects the situation in many of these countries where the security aspect of work is instrumental to survival. In contrast, many of the developed societies (e.g., the Netherlands, France, the United States) rate extrinsic work values much lower.

Similar to extrinsic work values, findings for intrinsic work values show that people from different societies have varying preferences (see Exhibit 14.3). A

Extrinsic work values
Preference for the security aspects of jobs, such as income and job security.

Intrinsic work values
Preference for openness-to-change job aspects, such as autonomy, being able to take initiative and be creative.

Multinational Management **Brief**

Employee Motivation in the Greek Public Sector

Understanding what employees expect in work is very useful for multinationals. Motivation can take place through extrinsic motivators (salary, working conditions, job security) and intrinsic motivators (opportunities for creativity, opportunities to use initiative, and how others perceive the job).

By satisfying work expectations, companies can ensure that their employees are motivated to do their best. In a study of the Greek public sector, researchers were able to determine the key motivators. The surveyed employees were asked what they perceive to be the most important motivators, and the researchers found that the employees felt that extrinsic work motivators were more motivating. This finding, at least according to one research stream, is similar to findings about companies in the private sector.

Source: Based on Human Resource Management International Digest. *2008. "Does the board know whether it is the money, or the love?" 16(3), pp. 14–16.*

EXHIBIT 14.2 **Preference for Extrinsic Work Values**

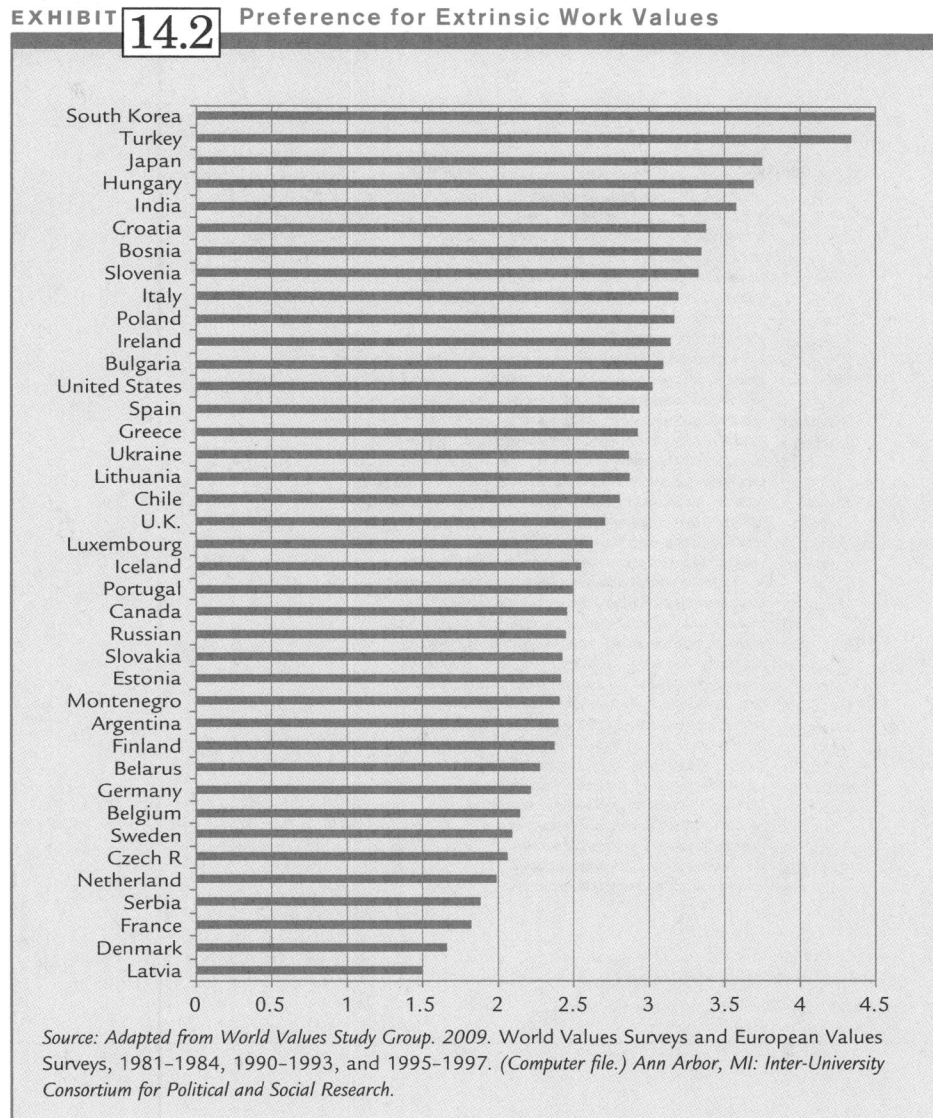

Source: Adapted from World Values Study Group. 2009. World Values Surveys and European Values Surveys, 1981-1984, 1990-1993, and 1995-1997. (Computer file.) Ann Arbor, MI: Inter-University Consortium for Political and Social Research.

surprising finding, however, is that many of the countries that rated extrinsic work values highly also rated intrinsic work values highly. This suggests that many of the emerging economies may view all work aspects positively while people of the developed nations do not see work in a positive light. Consequently, when crafting their motivational strategies for a local workforce, multinational managers must not assume that people from different nations express the same preferences for work values.

The WVS/EVS research team asked workers to note what characteristics of a job they believe are important. As shown in Exhibit 14.4, the priorities given to different job characteristics vary by country. Note, for example, that Japan and Russia differ from the world trend of giving a high priority to holidays. In spite of pay being a dominant function of work for many of the transition and developing nations, no country rated pay as the most important work characteristic.

EXHIBIT 14.3   Preference for Intrinsic Work Values

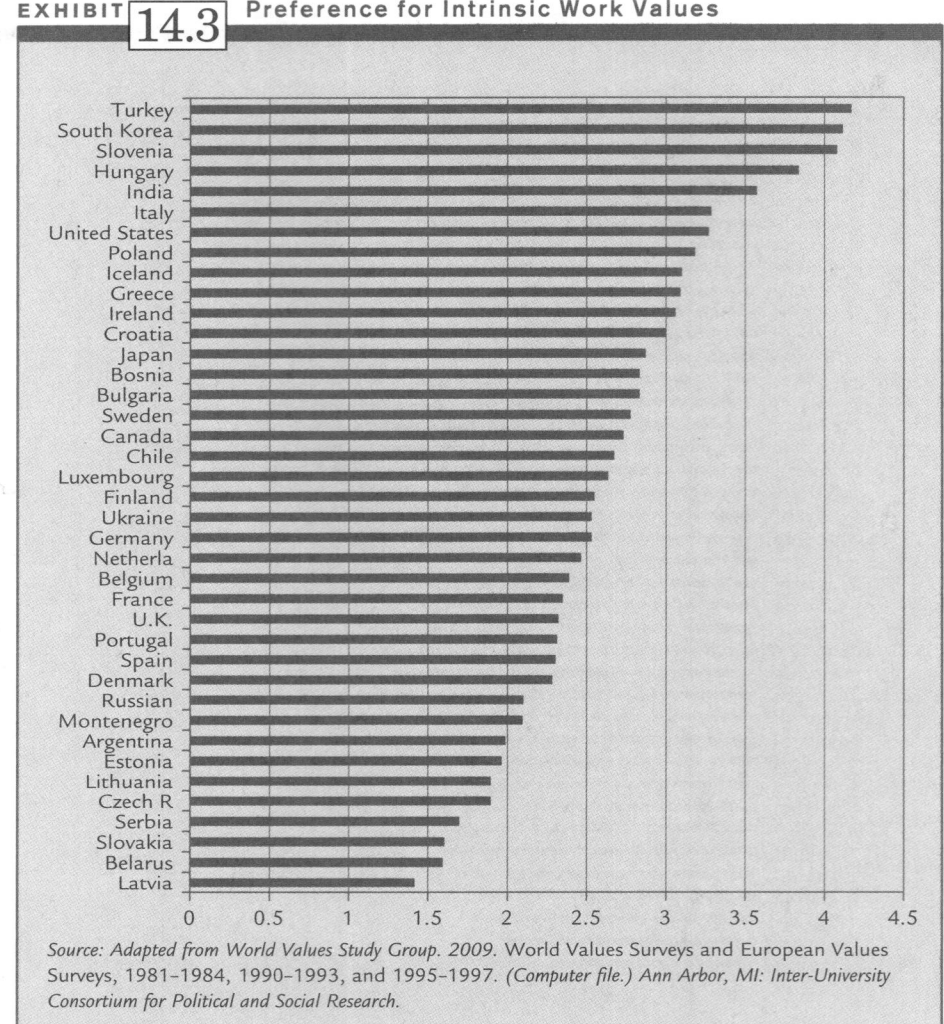

Source: Adapted from World Values Study Group. 2009. World Values Surveys and European Values Surveys, 1981–1984, 1990–1993, and 1995–1997. *(Computer file.) Ann Arbor, MI: Inter-University Consortium for Political and Social Research.*

The Meaning of Work study and the more current WVS/EVS study give us a good beginning picture of how work values differ in national contexts. They suggest the following conclusions:

- In some societies, work is central and absorbs much of a person's life. People in such societies willingly work long hours and have a strong commitment to succeeding at work. However, in many industrialized countries that have traditionally been seen as valuing high work centrality (e.g., the United States and Japan), people may be changing their views of work. In contrast, less developed societies may have a workforce that places significant importance on the role of work in their lives.

- All people hope to receive certain benefits from work. Regardless of national context, money is a necessity, but it is not enough. Other emotional and practical benefits derived from work may have higher priorities. The benefits people hope to get from their jobs vary by national context.

EXHIBIT 14.4 Importance Rankings of Work Characteristics in Nine Countries

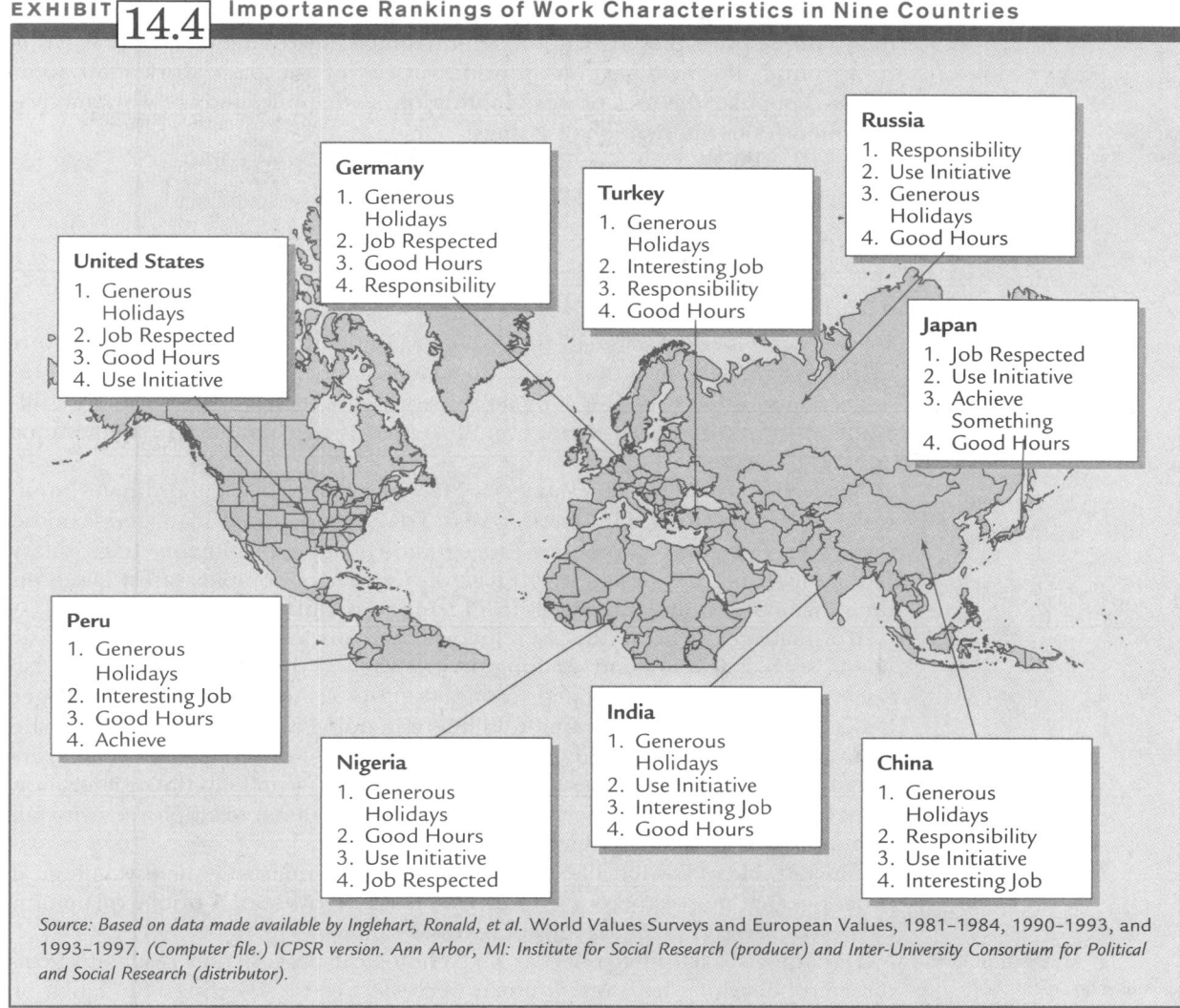

Russia
1. Responsibility
2. Use Initiative
3. Generous Holidays
4. Good Hours

Germany
1. Generous Holidays
2. Job Respected
3. Good Hours
4. Responsibility

Turkey
1. Generous Holidays
2. Interesting Job
3. Responsibility
4. Good Hours

United States
1. Generous Holidays
2. Job Respected
3. Good Hours
4. Use Initiative

Japan
1. Job Respected
2. Use Initiative
3. Achieve Something
4. Good Hours

Peru
1. Generous Holidays
2. Interesting Job
3. Good Hours
4. Achieve

Nigeria
1. Generous Holidays
2. Good Hours
3. Use Initiative
4. Job Respected

India
1. Generous Holidays
2. Use Initiative
3. Interesting Job
4. Good Hours

China
1. Generous Holidays
2. Responsibility
3. Use Initiative
4. Interesting Job

Source: Based on data made available by Inglehart, Ronald, et al. World Values Surveys and European Values, 1981–1984, 1990–1993, and 1993–1997. (Computer file.) ICPSR version. Ann Arbor, MI: Institute for Social Research (producer) and Inter-University Consortium for Political and Social Research (distributor).

- Societies differ in the degree to which they regard work as an obligation to society. Societies that have high work obligation norms are more likely to have individuals working longer to conform to such duties.

- Many of the emerging economies that value extrinsic work values such as income and job security also place a high value on intrinsic work values. Multinational companies need to provide jobs that not only provide adequate compensation but also provide job satisfaction.

- The first key to successful motivational strategies in multinational companies is understanding the differences among countries in the functions of work, work centrality, and the priorities given to different job characteristics.

Multinational managers must understand that people from different countries often have their own reasons for working and priorities regarding the important attributes of their jobs. Although this knowledge is important to have, is it all a manager needs to motivate and manage a multinational workforce successfully? Probably not. To use the knowledge of national differences in work attitudes for motivational purposes, the manager needs to understand how basic motivational principles work in the multinational environment. To give you this background, the next sections provide reviews of the basic work motivation process, popular theories of work motivation, and applications of work motivation theories to multinational settings.

Work Motivation and the National Context

The Basic Work Motivation Process

Why do some people set goals that are more difficult and put forth more effort to achieve them than others? Why do some students seek A's while other students feel satisfied with C's? Why do some workers seek jobs that are more difficult and work harder at them, even if the pay is not higher? These questions address the issue of motivation.

Motivation concerns all managers. Managers want their subordinates motivated to achieve organizational goals. Toward this end, managers choose incentives (e.g., pay, promotion, recognition) and punishments (e.g., salary reduction), and they design work (e.g., with simple or complex tasks) based on their assumptions and knowledge concerning what motivates people.

If a manager believes that her subordinates work only to meet their basic needs, such as feeding and clothing themselves and their families, she may use wages and bonuses as her major motivational tool. Alternatively, if a manager believes that people work to find fulfillment in doing a challenging job well, she might assign subordinates complex, varied, and interesting tasks. Managers usually respond positively to people (e.g., with raises) who help the organization achieve its goals and negatively (e.g., with bad evaluations) to employees who fail to help the organization achieve its goals.

The left side of Exhibit 14.5 presents a picture summarizing the psychological processes that most experts use to explain work motivation. A brief explanation of these underlying psychological processes follows.

Psychologists see **motivation** as a psychological process that results in goal-directed behaviors that satisfy human needs. A **need** is a feeling of a deficit or lacking that all people experience at some time. Although needs differ for individuals and for cultural groups, all people seek to satisfy them. A need might be very basic, such as being hungry for the next meal. A need might be more complex, such as the need to be the best at something. To satisfy the hunger need, you may go to work to earn money to buy food. To satisfy an achievement need, you might practice ice skating daily with the ultimate goal of becoming an Olympic champion. In each case, a person uses **goal-directed behaviors** (i.e., work or practice) to satisfy unfulfilled or unsatisfied needs (i.e., hunger or the need for achievement). Goal-directed behaviors are behaviors that people use with the intention of satisfying a need.

Although satisfying needs is a general condition for human motivation, people use the work setting to satisfy many needs. For example, for most people, work is necessary to provide food and shelter. In addition, as you saw from the WVS/EVS study, working provides people with an opportunity to satisfy needs such as affording leisure, having interesting things to do, having responsibility, having a chance to use initiative, and developing relationships with other people. Many theories of work motivation have a basic assumption that people will work harder if they can satisfy more of their needs on the job.

Motivation
A psychological process resulting in goal-directed behavior that satisfies human needs.

Need
Feeling of deficit or lacking that all people experience at some time.

Goal-directed behavior
One that people use with the intention of satisfying a need.

EXHIBIT 14.5   The Basic Work Motivation Process and the National Context

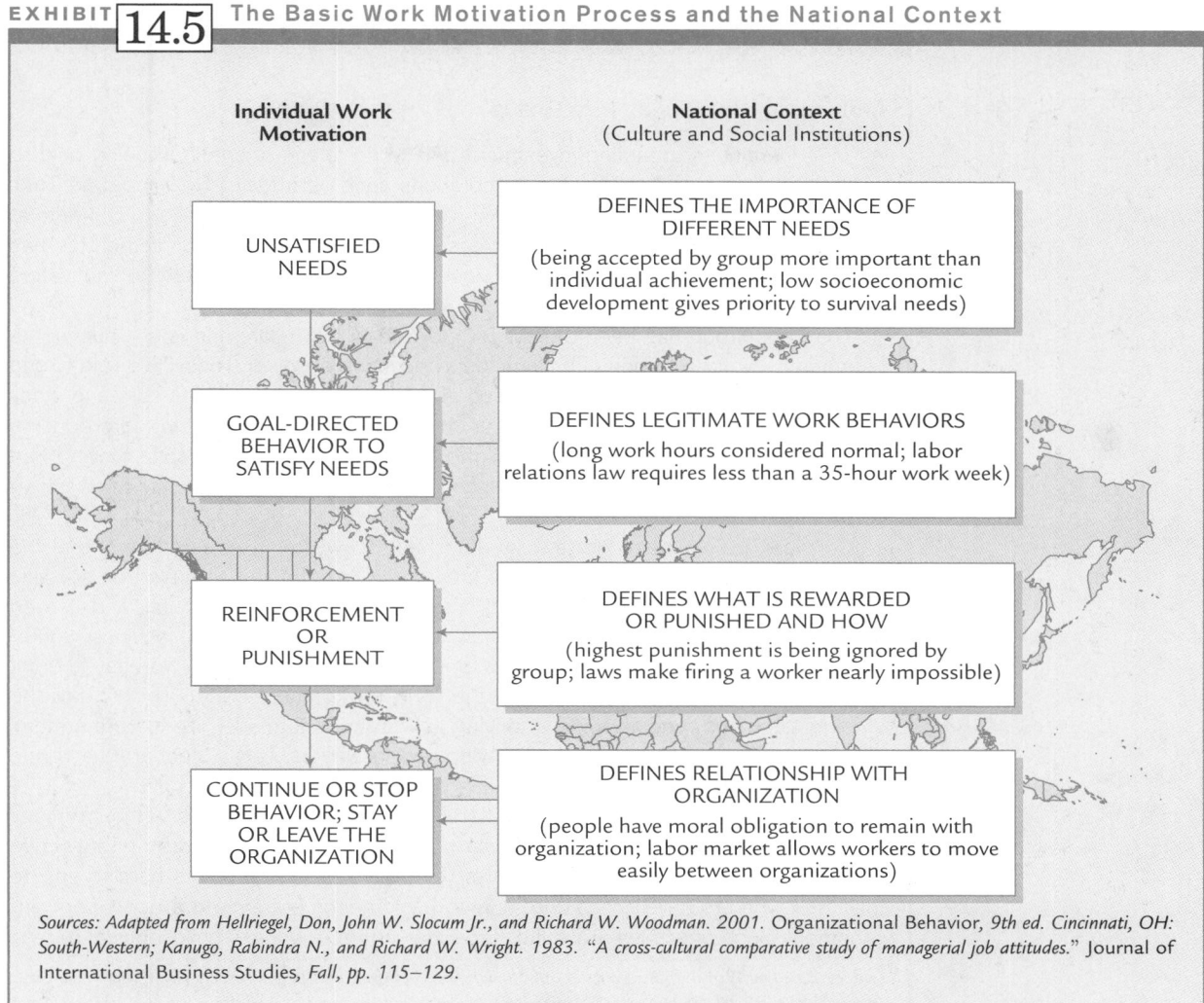

Individual Work Motivation	National Context (Culture and Social Institutions)
UNSATISFIED NEEDS	DEFINES THE IMPORTANCE OF DIFFERENT NEEDS (being accepted by group more important than individual achievement; low socioeconomic development gives priority to survival needs)
GOAL-DIRECTED BEHAVIOR TO SATISFY NEEDS	DEFINES LEGITIMATE WORK BEHAVIORS (long work hours considered normal; labor relations law requires less than a 35-hour work week)
REINFORCEMENT OR PUNISHMENT	DEFINES WHAT IS REWARDED OR PUNISHED AND HOW (highest punishment is being ignored by group; laws make firing a worker nearly impossible)
CONTINUE OR STOP BEHAVIOR; STAY OR LEAVE THE ORGANIZATION	DEFINES RELATIONSHIP WITH ORGANIZATION (people have moral obligation to remain with organization; labor market allows workers to move easily between organizations)

Sources: Adapted from Hellriegel, Don, John W. Slocum Jr., and Richard W. Woodman. 2001. Organizational Behavior, 9th ed. Cincinnati, OH: South-Western; Kanugo, Rabindra N., and Richard W. Wright. 1983. "A cross-cultural comparative study of managerial job attitudes." Journal of International Business Studies, Fall, pp. 115–129.

The next Focus on Emerging Markets shows how the world-class Indian conglomerate Tata Motors uses both satisfaction of needs and the work setting to motivate its workers.

Because most goal-directed behaviors take place in a social context, motivation includes more than satisfying needs; that is, when we do things that affect others, people react positively or negatively. In reinforcement theory, we call these reactions reinforcement and punishment. **Reinforcement** means that the consequences that follow a person's behavior encourage the person to continue the behavior. **Punishment** means that the consequences that follow a person's behavior encourage the person to stop the behavior. In the work setting, for example, managers use reinforcement, such as bonus pay, to encourage certain behaviors, such as increased daily output. Managers also use punishment, such as docking pay, to discourage behaviors, such as missing days of work. Based on whether they meet their needs at work and how managers react to their behaviors at work, employees may put more or less effort into work, feel satisfied or dissatisfied, or stay with or leave the organization.

Reinforcement
Reactions to a person's behavior that encourage the person to continue the behavior.

Punishment
Consequences of a person's behavior that discourage the behavior.

Focus on Emerging Markets

Motivating Workers at Tata Group

As India continues attracting investment and world talent, attention is being paid to some of India's most well-known corporations such as Infosys, Reliance, and Tata. These local companies show that they can produce goods and services to compete at the highest world-class level. This increased attention on Indian conglomerates has brought some interest in the Tata Group and its unique approach to motivating workers.

The Tata Group has been around for more than 130 years and is still pursing its nineteenth-century mission of making India an industrial power. Today, the Tata Group is a family conglomerate that is involved in such business sectors as cars and steel, software and consulting, and even luxury hotels. Tata has recently started producing one of the cheapest cars in the world, the Tata Nano. However, despite thriving in a brutal global economy, the Tata Group has stayed true to its liberal roots of first taking care of its workers.

Consider, for example, the town of Jamshedpur, which was created by one of the founders of Tata. When the town was created in Calcutta, it was based on socialist principles. The company built schools, churches, parks, and a hospital, and it even provided housing to workers. In addition to satisfying many of the obvious worker needs, the company provided generous employee benefits. It cut the workday to eight hours and undertook efforts to make the work environment better. To this day, the steel mill and surrounding town is thriving as Tata tries to modernize it. Furthermore, although India is generally prone to having regular strikes, Tata's steel arm has gone decades without one.

This concern for workers is similar across all of Tata's businesses. Although many of the company's executives have Western MBAs, they are very aware of Tata's mission and view layoffs and downsizing as very "un-Tata." Tata works hard to ensure that their workers have access not only to basic needs but also to a good work environment. Such principles are still based today on the founder's philosophical beliefs.

Sources: Based on Birmingham Post. 2009. *"Indian firms in driving seat to give best staff new Tata Nano car," April 27, p. 27; Patel, Vibhuti. 2005. "India, Inc.: No longer just an outsourcing hub for low-level jobs, India is luring American talent and unprecedented new investments by tech giants Microsoft and Intel."* Newsweek, *Dec. 19, http://www.msnbc.msn.com/id/10455090/site/newsweek; Wehrfritz, George, and Ron Moreau. 2006. "A new kind of company: Tata coddles workers, not managers, keeps its distance from Wall Street—yet thrives in brutal global industries as a uniquely Indian kind of multinational."* Newsweek, *http://www.msnbc.msn.com/id/8359069/site/newsweek.*

National Context and Work Motivation: A Brief Introduction

Although certain basic needs are common to all humans (e.g., the need for food and shelter), the national context (culture and the social institutions) influences all steps of the motivational process. The right side of Exhibit 14.5 shows the effects of the national context on the work-motivation process. Each box contains two examples. One example shows an effect of national culture on the motivation process. The other example shows an effect of social institutions on the motivational process. More explanation and examples follow.

Cultural values, norms, and supporting social institutions—important aspects of any society's business context—influence the priority that people attach to work in general and the types of needs that people hope to satisfy at work. For example, early education and childhood games encourage people in collectivist societies to develop a need to belong to groups. The national context also helps to define the behaviors that provide legitimate ways to satisfy needs. For example, in countries such as Japan, where work is central to a person's status and self-image, seeking a job in the largest and most prestigious company satisfies a need for achievement.

The national context influences reactions to goal-directed behaviors at work. For example, if a Japanese worker brags about her performance, she is likely to be sanctioned by her work group. The Japanese have a saying: "The nail that stands out gets hammered down." Finally, national culture and social institutions influence the levels of satisfaction workers expect to receive in an organization and how committed they are to their organization and its goals. For example, in countries where labor is well-organized and militant, resistance to increases in work productivity is considered legitimate. Consider the next Case in Point, in which clearly the national cultural context influences the techniques that can be used to motivate Thai workers.

C A S E I N P O I N T

Motivating Thais: Cultural Influences

As multinational companies increase their investments in Thailand, being able to understand and motivate Thai workers is becoming crucial. In fact, recent trends suggest that Thailand continues to be a destination of choice for many countries, including the United States. For example, the Ford–Mazda AutoAlliance Thailand assembly plant manufactures cars and pickup trucks for sale in more than 130 markets. Toyota is also seriously pursuing efforts to open a gearbox plant in Thailand. Between 2004 and 2007, imports from Thailand grew by more than 15 percent, as U.S companies extended their supply chains into Thailand to take advantage of high productivity and low cost.

A Hofstede study revealed that Thailand has a high score on collectivism, moderately high scores on uncertainty avoidance, and a low score on masculinity. Motivational do's and don'ts garnered from practical experience in Thailand suggest that cultural influences may be very helpful in determining what works and what does not.

The high score on collectivism suggests that Thais are very attentive to the needs of in-groups. They generally function better in groups, and harmonious relationships are preferred. Not surprisingly, care must be taken not to criticize individual employees openly. Furthermore, senior Thais deserve *hai-kiat* (respect), and arguing with them in front of junior staff can be devastating. *Sia nah* (losing face) is the ultimate humiliation and has to be avoided.

The moderately high score on uncertainty avoidance implies that Thais prefer structure in their jobs and organizations to make things more certain and predictable. Unclear instructions or an organizational structure without clear lines of communications can be very demotivating. Managers are thus advised to provide clear structure.

Finally, the low score on masculinity, or more feminine nature of the culture, suggests a preference for family and quality of life as opposed to work. It is imperative to understand Thais' appreciation of work and to avoid training on weekends or expecting Thais to invest their personal time in the company. Motivational practices should focus on integration of the family.

Sources: Based on Field, A. M. 2009. "Fall from grace." Journal of Commerce, February 9, pp. 56–60; Hofstede, Geert. 2001. Culture's Consequences: International Differences in Work-Related Values, 2nd ed. London: Sage; M2 Presswire, 2006. "Research and markets: An analysis of the latest happenings in the automotive manufacturing industry from around the world," January 11; Niratpattanasai, Kriengsak. 2002. "How to make work miserable." Bangkok Post, November 22, p. 1; Sawyer, Christopher A. 2006. "Ford making Tracs for Thailand." Automotive Design & Production, February, p. 28; Thapanachai, Somporn. 2006. "Oldest Californian firm picks Saraburi." Bangkok Post, February 21, p. 1.

This brief overview of work motivation and the effects of the national context provide only an introduction to the complexities of motivating international workers. Next, the chapter expands on the basic model of work motivation. In the following sections, we will review several motivation theories and discuss how the national context influences the application of each motivation theory and how the multinational manager can use the theory.

Theories of Work Motivation in the Multinational Context

Work-motivation theories attempt to show how basic motivational processes apply to a work setting. Managers can use the theories to develop systematic approaches to motivating employees on the job. There are two basic types of motivational theories: need theories and process theories. The following section summarizes the major need theories of motivation, which have the most international applications. A later section considers process theories.

The Need Theory of Motivation

The **need theory** of motivation rests on the assumption that people can satisfy basic human needs in the work setting; that is, people are motivated to work because their jobs satisfy both basic needs, such as money for food and shelter, and higher-level needs, such as personal growth.

There are four popular need theories of motivation:

1. Maslow's hierarchy of needs.
2. ERG theory.
3. Motivator-hygiene theory.
4. Achievement motivation theory.

This section briefly reviews each theory. You can find more detailed reviews of these and other theories of motivation in courses and texts in organizational behavior. Exhibit 14.6 gives a summary and comparison of these four theories and also shows the characteristics of jobs that can satisfy the types of needs identified by them.

Maslow's Hierarchy of Needs

The psychologist Abraham Maslow offered perhaps the most famous need theory of motivation.[12] The **hierarchy of needs theory** states that people have five basic types of needs: physiological, security, affiliation, esteem, and self-actualization. Physiological needs include basic survival such as food, water, air, and shelter. Security needs include safety and the avoidance of pain and life-threatening situations. Affiliation needs include being loved, having friendship, and belonging to a human group. Esteem needs focus on respect, recognition by others, and feelings of self-worth. Self-actualization needs, the highest level in Maslow's theory, are those associated with maximizing personal achievement.

Maslow believed that the five basic needs follow a hierarchy from the lower to the higher levels. First, people seek to satisfy lower-level needs, such as the physiological need for food and shelter. After they fulfill these lower-level needs, people seek to satisfy higher-level needs, such as the need for esteem. According to Maslow, once a need is satisfied, it no longer motivates. Thus, for example, if your base pay is adequate for survival, it has no motivational value. Then other

Need theory
Of motivation, assumes that people can satisfy basic human needs in the work setting.

Hierarchy of needs theory
States that people have five basic types of needs: physiological, security, affiliation, esteem, and self-actualization.

EXHIBIT **14.6**   Need Theories of Motivation

Source of Need Satisfaction on the Job	Maslow's Needs Hierarchy	ERG Theory	Motivator-Hygiene Theory	Achievement Motivation
• Advancement • Use of ability • Meaningful work • Achievement • Interesting job	Self-actualization	Growth	Motivators • Advancement • Growth • Achievement	Need for achievement
• Recognition • Influence • Esteem	Esteem			Need for power
• Coworker support • Supervisor support • Social interaction	Affiliation	Relatedness	Hygiene factors • Working conditions • Job security • Salary	Need for affiliation
• Work conditions • Benefits • Security	Security	Existence		
• Base pay	Physiological			

Sources: Adapted from Daft, Richard L. 1991. Management, *2nd ed. Chicago: Dryden; Gordon, Judith R. 1987.* A Diagnostic Approach to Organizational Behavior. *Boston: Allyn &; Bacon; Hellriegel, Don, John W. Slocum Jr., and Richard W. Woodman. 2001.* Organizational Behavior, *9th ed. Cincinnati, OH: South-Western.*

characteristics of the work situation, such as working in teams to meet affiliation needs, become motivational.

The current opinion on Maslow's approach suggests that, while there are two groups of needs representing higher- and lower-level needs, the need hierarchy does not work in sequence. Moreover, not all available jobs in a country provide the activities required to meet all levels of needs.[13]

Alderfer's ERG Theory

Clay Alderfer developed **ERG theory** as a simplified hierarchy of needs having only three levels (see Exhibit 14.6 for a comparison with Maslow's theory):[14] growth needs, relatedness needs, and existence needs. Growth needs are similar to Maslow's self-actualization and esteem needs. Work is motivating when it provides the opportunity for personal growth, such as by using one's creativity. Relational needs are similar to Maslow's affiliation needs. Getting support from one's work group satisfies relational needs. Existence needs are lower-level needs and represent basic survival needs.

> **ERG theory**
> Simplified hierarchy of needs: growth needs, relatedness needs, and existence needs.

In ERG theory, the frustration of a need motivates behavior to satisfy the need. In addition, a person who cannot satisfy a higher-level need will seek to satisfy lower-level needs. For example, if the satisfaction of growth needs is impossible on the job, satisfaction of relational needs becomes the prime motivator.

Motivator-Hygiene Theory

Proposed by Frederick Herzberg, the **motivator-hygiene theory** assumes that a job has two basic characteristics, motivators and hygiene factors.[15] Motivating

> **Motivator-hygiene theory**
> Assumption that a job has two basic characteristics: motivators and hygiene factors.

factors are the characteristics of jobs that allow people to fulfill higher-level needs. For example, a challenging job might allow someone to meet his or her need for heightened levels of achievement. Hygiene factors are characteristics of jobs that allow people to fulfill lower-level needs, such as when good benefits and working conditions satisfy security needs.

Motivating factors arise from the content or the actual tasks that people perform on the job. Hygiene factors focus on the context or the setting in which the job takes place. Thus, for example, tasks that allow you to use your abilities are motivators. However, the size of your desk and the color of your office are context or hygiene factors. Unlike other need theories, which assume that the desire to satisfy any type of need can motivate, Herzberg argued that satisfying lower-level needs at work (i.e., the hygiene factors) brings people only to a neutral state of motivation. To move employees beyond just a neutral reaction to the job, managers must build motivators into the context of a job (e.g., provide interesting tasks). Thus, only the opportunity to satisfy higher-level needs increases motivation.

Achievement-Motivation Theory

The psychologist David McClelland identified three key needs as the basis of motivation:[16] achievement, affiliation, and power (see Exhibit 14.6). However, most of McClelland's influential work focused on achievement motivation. **Achievement-motivation theory** suggests that some people (approximately 10 percent in the United States) have the need to win in competitive situations or to exceed a standard of excellence. High achievement-motivated people like to set their own goals. They seek challenging situations but avoid goals that they feel are too difficult. Because they like to achieve success in their goals, high achievers desire immediate feedback. They like to know how they are performing at every step leading to a goal.

McClelland believed that achievement motivation is fixed in early childhood and that different cultures have different levels of achievement motivation. Some evidence supports McClelland's contention of different levels of achievement motivation in different cultures. However, there is no clear evidence regarding whether nations with more achievement-motivated people have better economic performance.[17]

Needs and the National Context

There are both similarities and divergence in the needs that people from different nations seek to satisfy by working. Similarities of needs across cultures occur because people tend to group needs into similar clusters or categories;[18] that is, regardless of national background, people see their work-related needs *grouped* in ways that match the broad groups proposed by need theories of motivation.

However, national groups vary in two ways on how people see needs being satisfied at work. First, people from different nations do not give the same priorities to the needs that might be satisfied at work. For example, as shown in Exhibit 14.7, Hungarians give a high priority to satisfying physiological needs through higher base pay. This is not true for people from some other countries, such as China or Holland. Second, even if workers from different countries have similar needs, they may not give the same level of importance to satisfying these needs. For example, one cross-national comparison found that interesting work (something that satisfies growth needs) ranked as the most important work goal for Japanese, British, and Belgian workers. However, interesting work was still

Achievement-motivation theory Suggestion that only some people have the need to win in competitive situations or to exceed a standard of excellence.

Rankings of the Importance of Job-Related Sources of Need Satisfaction for Seven Countries (H = upper third, M = middle third, L = bottom third, 1 = highest rank)

EXHIBIT 14.7

Job-Related Sources of Satisfaction for:	China	Germany	Holland	Hungary	Israel	Korea	United States
Self-actualization needs							
• Advancement	M	M	H	L	H	H	H
• Use of ability	H	H	H	H	M	H	H
• Meaningful work	M	H	M	M	M	M	M
• Achievement	1	M	H	H'	1	1	H
• Interesting job	H	1	1	H	H	H	1
Esteem needs							
• Recognition	M	L	M	H	M	M	M
• Influence	M	L	M	L	L	L	L
• Esteem	H	M	M	M	H	L	H
Affiliation needs							
• Coworker support	M	H	H	M	M	H	L
• Supervisor support	M	H	M	#1	H	H	M
• Interaction	L	L	M	M	L	L	L
Security needs							
• Work conditions	L	L	L	M	L	M	L
• Benefits	L	H	L	M	M	M	M
• Security	L	H	M	M	L	H	M
Physiological needs							
• Base pay	L	M	L	H	M	M	L

Source: Adapted from Elizur, Dov, Ingwer Borg, Raymond Hunt, and Istvan Magyari Beck. 1991. "The structure of work values: A cross cultural comparison." Journal of Organizational Behavior, 12, pp. 21–38.

relatively more important for Belgian workers than it was for Japanese and British workers.[19]

Can multinational managers use need satisfaction as a motivational tool? Yes, it can serve as a motivational tool, if multinational managers take into account the particular needs that people in a nation seek to satisfy in the work setting. Consider the following Case in Point, which gives examples of companies that increased motivation by linking organizational goals to the local employees' needs.

What differences in need satisfaction might multinational managers expect to find in different countries? Exhibit 14.7 illustrates some of the differences in the priorities given to job-related sources of need satisfaction by people from a group of nations.[20] The exhibit divides the rankings of job-related sources of need satisfaction into three groups: high (H) for the top third, middle (M) for the middle third, and low (L) for the bottom third. Exhibit 14.7 also shows the job-related sources of need satisfaction in terms of Maslow's need hierarchy. For cross-referencing to other need theories, see Exhibit 14.6, which shows how Maslow's need hierarchy relates to other need theories.

As Exhibit 14.7 shows, people from different nations do not necessarily prioritize their sources of need satisfaction at work as suggested by need theories. For example, although most need theories suggest that higher-level needs (e.g., self-actualization) should be most important regardless of national

CASE IN POINT

Finding the Right Needs in Central Eastern Europe

Central and Eastern European countries remain attractive destinations for foreign investment. Most major foreign investors coming from neighboring Germany and Austria, as well as U.S. investors, see these growing markets as very lucrative. However, despite being in the region for a decade, foreign investors still face challenges.

For instance, taking over a formerly state-owned firm in Poland turned out to be a motivational challenge for the Finnish paper and power equipment firm Ahlstrom Fakop. Morale and sales were low, and the new management searched for ways to improve the situation. The first try, offering incentive pay, produced no results. As workers recently jettisoned into a market economy, the East European employees of Ahlstrom Fakop had needs other than money. Decades of communism had ingrained an expectation of a guaranteed job. When told that their jobs were secure if sales and productivity targets were met, workers responded positively with increases in both. It seems that the anxiety produced by the transition to a market economy made keeping a job more important than bonuses for productivity.

When Dow Chemical took over a crumbling chemical plant in the former East Germany, it inherited a bloated workforce and the knowledge that it would need to lay off 400 workers. To ease the culture shock of the transition to a market-based company and to increase productivity, Dow built a motivational system based on trust and individual initiative. Many workers adapted well to the system, using the newfound independence to achieve heightened levels of performance and promotions. However, some floundered, confused by managers who did not watch their every move and a distrust of those with power.

Trends suggest that many multinational companies are now facing a challenge of a new kind. After being in the former East Germany for a decade, many companies are finding that the pool of inexpensive talent is slowly drying up. Local companies have made substantial progress and are competing with foreign companies for the same local talent. As a consequence, attracting and retaining talented employees are becoming the most important challenges. Such trends suggest that properly understanding Eastern European workers will become even more critical in the future.

Sources: Based on Dougherty, Carter. 2006. "Eastern Europe at cross-roads." International Herald Tribune, January 19; Dougherty, Carter. 2006. "Europe's young economies grow up but retain appeal: Even as costs rise, investors keep going east." International Herald Tribune, January 18; Fargher, S., S. Kesting, T. Lange, and G. Pacheco. 2009. "Cultural heritage and job satisfaction in Eastern and Western Europe." International Journal of Manpower, 29(7), pp. 630–650; Jacob, Rahul. 1995. "Secure jobs trump higher pay." Fortune, March 20, p. 24; Warren, Susan. 2000. "Five-year mission: For Dow, a dirty job in Germany presented a chance to clean up—to court eastern Europe, it wrestled a dinosaur from the Communist era—Razing 'the glittering hall.'" Wall Street Journal, May 19, p. A1.

background, many sources of satisfying self-actualization needs had only moderate importance. Only the need for interesting work fell into the top third classification for all seven countries. High levels of potential need satisfiers on the job were found at all levels of the need hierarchy. In Germany, for example, perhaps because of the social institutional support for labor, job characteristics that could satisfy security and affiliation needs were as important as those related to self-actualization needs.

Many multinational managers work in emerging or formerly state-controlled economies, where there is little available information on the often evolving employee attitudes toward work. How can the manager anticipate need differences in such countries? In these cases, skillful managers must anticipate worker needs based on cultural norms and values and institutional conditions. Hofstede's work gives some additional hints on how a multinational manager might do this.[21] Exhibit 14.8 shows some of the motivators at work, as identified by Hofstede, for different types of national cultures (see Chapter 2). Hofstede's

EXHIBIT 14.8 **and Motivators at Work**

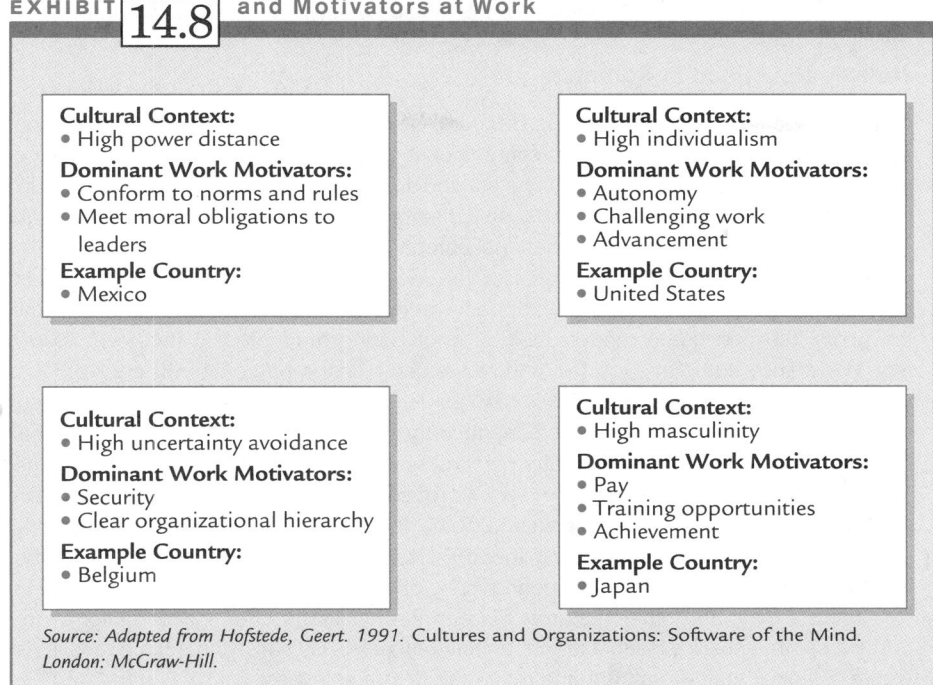

Cultural Context:
• High power distance
Dominant Work Motivators:
• Conform to norms and rules
• Meet moral obligations to leaders
Example Country:
• Mexico

Cultural Context:
• High individualism
Dominant Work Motivators:
• Autonomy
• Challenging work
• Advancement
Example Country:
• United States

Cultural Context:
• High uncertainty avoidance
Dominant Work Motivators:
• Security
• Clear organizational hierarchy
Example Country:
• Belgium

Cultural Context:
• High masculinity
Dominant Work Motivators:
• Pay
• Training opportunities
• Achievement
Example Country:
• Japan

Source: Adapted from Hofstede, Geert. 1991. Cultures and Organizations: Software of the Mind. *London: McGraw-Hill.*

work suggests that satisfying high-level needs at work may apply better to highly individualistic cultures. In addition, he cautions that need satisfaction may not be a motivator at all in some high-power-distance countries dominated by norms of service to the elite.

Applying Need Theories in Multinational Settings

Here are some points to consider in adapting need theories of motivation to the international context:

• *Identify the basic functions of work in the national or local culture:* Where work is not central, people may satisfy their needs outside the work setting, limiting the manager's use of need satisfaction as a motivational tool.

• *Identify the needs considered most important by workers in the national or local culture:* The evidence presented in this chapter shows that need priorities differ by national context. Managers should identify cultural differences in potential need satisfiers at work and focus on providing jobs that satisfy them. Consider the next Multinational Management Brief.

• *Sources of need fulfillment may differ for the same needs:* Even if people from different cultures have the same needs, they may find different sources of fulfillment on the job. For example, people from different cultures may consider interesting work the most important need, but they may have quite different ideas about what is interesting work. Hofstede's work suggests that individualism and power distance represent important dimensions of national culture that affect how people find need satisfaction at work.

Multinational Management Brief

Nokia's New Plant in Romania

Nokia decided to close its factory in Bochum, Germany, because it was becoming too expensive. When looking for a replacement location, it considered several places in the usual emerging markets, such as China and India, but it chose Cluj, Romania. Why Cluj? Nokia found that Cluj had a plentiful supply of eager workers looking to take advantage of opportunities offered by a multinational company. Nokia could not expand its facility in Komarom, Hungary, because most of the local workforce was already tapped. In contrast, Cluj still had a largely untapped workforce, and it is home to a technical university that provides a ready supply of engineering graduates. In fact, over 8,000 individuals showed up at a job fair, and Nokia had plans to hire only 500 people.

Nokia expects to keep most of its new employees in Cluj by satisfying local needs. Most of the Cluj inhabitants are emerging from poverty as a result of the dictatorial regime. Nokia expects that it can satisfy workers by providing competitive wages, but the firm wants to look beyond cost and work to retain these employees. As multinationals have dealt with similar issues in India and China, they found that wages can rise quickly and workers are then quickly willing to work for the highest offer. To ensure that the employees are retained, Nokia is offering many other perks at the plant: a cafeteria with free food, a gym, and other features. Furthermore, Nokia is offering international opportunities not usually available in Romanian companies. By satisfying such needs in its workers, Nokia hopes to attract and retain the best employees.

Source: Based on Ewing, J. 2008. "Nokia's new home in Romania." BusinessWeek, *January 28, pp. 40–42.*

• *Understand the limitations of available jobs to satisfy needs:* Although satisfying higher-level needs is possible in most industrialized countries, the same may not be true in many developing nations. Existing jobs may provide only the satisfaction of basic needs for survival.

To increase the motivation of host-country workers or to solve other motivational problems, multinational managers can consider approaches to motivation other than need theories. Next, the chapter will provide reviews of additional theories of motivation and their applications to multinational settings.

Process and Reinforcement Theories of Motivation

Process theories
Of motivation, arising from needs and values combined with an individual's beliefs regarding the work environment.

In this section, we briefly review the process theories of motivation known as expectancy theory, equity theory, and goal-setting theory. More complex than need theories, **process theories** assume that motivation arises from needs and values *combined* with an individual's beliefs regarding the work environment. Besides the popular versions of these theories, this section reviews reinforcement theory and its application to multinational settings. These approaches to motivation receive fewer applications in the international setting than do need theories. However, we can draw some tentative conclusions regarding how they work in national settings. For a complete review of these theories, students should consult any current organizational behavior textbook.

Expectancy Theory

Expectancy theory
Assumption that motivation includes people's desire to satisfy their needs and their beliefs regarding how much their efforts at work will eventually satisfy their needs.

Victor Vroom proposed a view of motivation that is more complex than simple need satisfaction.[22] This theory and its later variants are known as **expectancy theory**. Vroom proposed that work motivation is a function not only of an individual's needs or values but also of an individual's beliefs regarding what happens if you work hard. Expectancy theory assumes that part of motivation is an individual's desire to satisfy his or her needs. However, the level of motivation also depends on people's beliefs regarding how much, or if, their efforts at work will eventually satisfy their needs.

The three factors that make up expectancy theory are expectancy, valence, and instrumentality. The theory often is presented in the form of the following equation:

$$\text{Motivation} = \text{Expectancy} \times \text{Valence} \times \text{Instrumentality}$$

Expectancy is an individual's belief that his or her effort will lead to some result. For example, if you believe that intensive study over a weekend will lead to a high grade, you have a high expectancy in that situation. *Valence* is the value you attach to the outcome of your efforts. For example, a student may value a high grade in a class compared to the pleasure of going skiing over a weekend. *Instrumentality* refers to the links between early and later results of the work effort. For example, there is a link between one outcome of studying, a grade on a test, and a later outcome, a final grade for a course. If the test was worth only 1 percent of the final grade, instrumentality would be low; that is, how one performs on a minor test has little effect on a final grade.

Thus, in expectancy theory, motivation is much more than the value people attach to work outcomes. Beliefs regarding whether an effort will lead to success and whether the results of effort will lead eventually to valued outcomes also come into play.

Some suggest that expectancy theory serves best as a diagnostic tool to determine why workers are motivated or not motivated.[23] The manager must ask three questions: First, do workers believe that their efforts will lead to the successful performance of a task? Second, do workers believe that present success at some task (e.g., no defects for a week) will lead to success at some future valued outcome (e.g., getting a raise)? Third, do employees value the outcomes that follow from their efforts at work?

Applying Expectancy Theory in Multinational Settings   There are two key issues in applying expectancy theory in the multinational company. The first is to identify which outcomes people value in a particular national or local cultural setting; that is, the multinational manager must find and use rewards with positive valence for employees. The second is to find culturally appropriate ways of convincing employees that their efforts will lead to desirable ends.

In the Case in Point on page 588, we saw that the workers from a former Eastern Bloc country had a higher valence for secure jobs than they did for bonus pay. When managers from the Finnish parent company recognized this, they promised job security (the workers' ultimate goal) in return for the workers' putting more effort into productivity. As expectancy theory would predict, when the workers became convinced that their efforts would lead to their valued goal of security, their motivation increased.

Equity Theory

Equity theory focuses on the fairness that people perceive in the rewards that they receive for their efforts at work, which can include pay, benefits, recognition, job perquisites, and prestige. Under this theory, the "efforts" people put into the job are not only the quality and quantity of their work but also such factors as their age, educational qualifications, seniority, and social status.[24]

Equity theory
Proposal that people perceive the fairness of their rewards vis-á-vis their inputs based on how they compare themselves to others.

Equity theory proposes that people have no absolute standards for fairness in the input/output (effort/reward) equation. Rather, people perceive the fairness of their rewards relative to their inputs, based on how they compare themselves to others. For example, if two people have the same experience, do the same job, but do not have the same pay, then one is in overpayment inequity and the other is in underpayment inequity. Equity theory predicts that workers who believe that they are underrewarded reduce their contribution to the company (e.g., take longer breaks). Workers in an inequitable situation produced by overrewards increase their work input, at least in the short run.

How does equity theory apply to the international setting? Consider the next Case in Point.

Applying Equity Theory in Multinational Settings The first issue to consider in the multinational applications of equity theory is the importance of equity norms in a society. Developing reward systems based on equity norms may not be motivating when other norms for rewarding people have more importance than equity.

Psychologists identify three principles of allocating rewards whose use varies in different cultural settings: the principle of equity (based on contributions), the principle of equality (based on equal division of rewards), and the principle

---

CASE IN POINT

Equity and Expatriates

Nowhere is inequity more apparent than when local workers compare their salaries to those of expatriates. The significant gap is due to the practice of paying expatriates home market rates while local employees are paid according to local labor market. Research has provided ample evidence of the perceived inequity and injustices associated with this large gap. Multinationals are thus very wary of this gap and its effects on local employee productivity, and they are looking for ways to minimize the perception.

Chen, Choi, and Chi's study of international joint ventures and compensation disparities provides some insight into the applications and subtleties of equity theory in an international context. The study examined Chinese employees' perception of fairness compared with that of their expatriate counterparts in international joint ventures. As expected, it was found that local Chinese employees perceived less fairness when comparing their incomes with expatriates than when comparing them with other locals. However, the study also showed that other factors can neutralize part of the felt inequity. For instance, it was found that the local employees' perception of fairness increased if they were paid more than local employees in other

international joint ventures. Additionally, if the employees endorsed ideological explanations that expatriates are necessary and important to the Chinese economy and position in the global environment, their perception of fairness toward expatriates was higher. Finally, the study also showed that employees who perceived that expatriates were interpersonally sensitive and nice to them perceived higher fairness with regard to these expatriates' compensation packages.

A more recent study shows that the perceived inequity can be reduced if expatriates are seen as more trustworthy. While adjusting the salary of locals to reduce the gap may not always be realistic, multinationals can find other ways to reduce the effect of the perceived wage inequity. For instance, if foreign plants can implement practices to enhance expatriate trustworthiness, local employees feel less inequity.

Sources: Based on Chen, C.C., Choi, J. and Chi, S.C. 2002. "Making justice sense of local expatriate compensation disparity: Mitigation by local referents, ideological explanations, and interpersonal sensitivity in China-foreign joint ventures." Academy of Management Journal, 45, pp. 807–817; Leung, K., X. Zhu and G. Ge. 2009. "Compensation disparity between locals and expatriates: Moderating the effects of perceived injustice in foreign multinationals in China." Journal of World Business, 44, pp. 85–93.

of need (based on individual needs).[25] A review of cross-national reports on the three principles of reward allocation suggests the following:

- *Equity norms prevail in individualistic cultures:* In particular, managerial practices in the United States such as bonus pay, management by objectives, and most U.S. performance appraisal systems use the equity norm. Rewards are based on performance. Good work deserves good pay.[26] In contrast, in societies where status comes from group membership rather than achievement, rewards based on performance may not make sense. High-status groups are expected to get higher rewards regardless of their performance levels.

- *Equality norms prevail over equity norms in collectivist cultures:* In societies with strong equality norms, at least for the members of one's group or team, group members prefer equal rewards for all. For example, one study of an Israeli company found that 40 percent of the workers perceived a bonus system as unfair even though it increased their income. They suggested that fair rewards should go to the team instead of to individuals.[27]

  However, as the Chen et al. study shows, in some collectivistic societies like China, equity may be potentially becoming more important.[28] As China has adopted a more open-door, market-oriented economic approach, it is possible that employees are beginning to prefer equitable situations based on their performance. Managers must carefully assess local conditions to determine if equity is preferred.

- *The principle of need may prevail over equity in certain conditions:* One study found, for example, that Indian managers preferred rewards based on need over rewards based on either equality or equity.[29] Collectivist cultures in particular may place more value on other people's needs than on one's own contributions.

Exhibit 14.9 shows an example of how the fairness of equity or equality rewards can affect even students' responses to grades relative to contributions. The information comes from a study in which Korean, Japanese, and U.S. students assigned peer evaluation grades for contributions to group projects. Although some equity norms seemingly worked for all students, U.S. students clearly linked rewards to performance much more than did the students from the two Asian societies.[30] Clearly, U.S. students were more likely to get rewards for high performance from their peers.

The final issue to consider in applying equity theory is the cultural differences in beliefs regarding the sources of a person's contributions to work. In some cultures, age, social status, and family membership may be more important inputs to work than the actual effort and performance on the job. In many Asian countries, for example, most people would consider it very unfair if a young worker received more pay than an older worker—particularly if the two did the same job. Research suggests that, in addition to performance criteria, collectivist cultures judge pay fairness based on factors such as seniority, education, and family size.[31]

Goal-Setting Theory

Goal-setting theory assumes that people want to achieve goals. When they meet or exceed a goal, people feel competent and satisfied. When they fail to meet a goal, they feel dissatisfied. Thus, the mere existence of a goal is motivating.[32]

Goal-setting theory
Assumption that the mere existence of a goal is motivating.

EXHIBIT 14.9   **Rewards from Peers for Contributions to a Student Group Project**

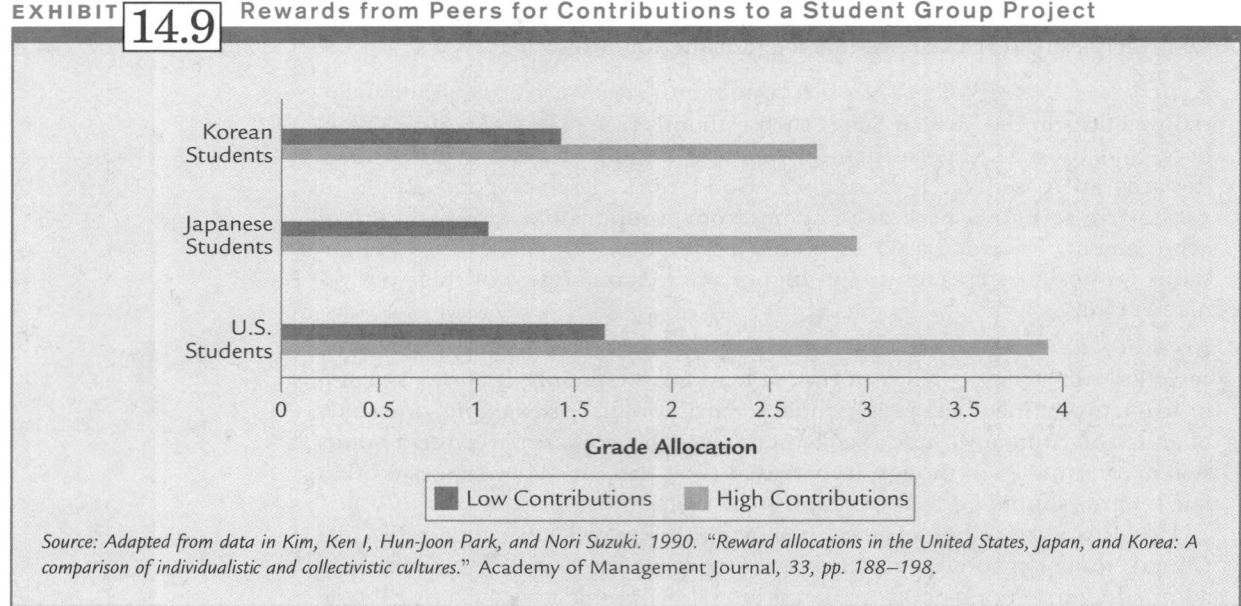

Source: Adapted from data in Kim, Ken I, Hun-Joon Park, and Nori Suzuki. 1990. "Reward allocations in the United States, Japan, and Korea: A comparison of individualistic and collectivistic cultures." Academy of Management Journal, 33, pp. 188–198.

Goal-setting theory has several principles,[33] and the theory's proponents argue that managers who follow these principles can motivate employees to meet organizational objectives:

- *Set clear and specific goals:* Employees need to know and understand what management expects them to accomplish.

- *Assign difficult but achievable goals:* If goals are too difficult, there is little incentive to try to achieve them. If goals are too easy, employees may not take them seriously.

- *Increase employee acceptance of goals:* At least in the United States, studies tell us that employees who participate in goal setting have a greater acceptance of managerial goals.[34]

- *Provide incentives to achieve goals:* Tying rewards (e.g., salary, bonuses) to goal achievement increases the acceptance of the goals.[35]

- *Give feedback on goal attainment:* To be motivated and to achieve their goals, people must understand how well they are doing.

Applying Goal-Setting Theory in Multinational Settings   Some experts believe that goal setting works to some degree regardless of location.[36] Setting goals does affect behavior in a positive direction. However, cultural expectations vary regarding whether subordinates should participate with managers in setting the goals and whether it is better to set goals for groups or for individuals.

In individualistic cultures, such as in the United States, setting individual goals may prove more effective than setting goals for a work group. People from individualistic cultures do not easily share responsibility for group outcomes. Thus, they do not find goals assigned to groups as motivating as goals assigned to them personally. In contrast, workers in collectivist cultures may respond better to high levels of participation in goal setting than people from individualistic cultures, such as the United States. In societies with cultural values supporting the necessity of belonging to a group, participation may have a greater chance of enhancing the worker's ownership and commitment to goals.

Finally, in cultures high on power distance, worker participation in setting goals may not produce any positive effects. Workers expect the leader to set the goals and tell them what to do.[37]

Exhibit 14.10 demonstrates some of the outcomes that can occur when people from different cultures have varying degrees of participation in the goal-setting process. This exhibit is based on a study of U.S. and Israeli university students.[38] Three groups of students performed simulated job tasks. For the first group, goals were assigned. For the second group, a representative from the group expressed the students' opinions on goals to the leader. For the third group, all members participated in setting goals. Because Israeli culture is more collectivist and lower on power distance than U.S. culture, the experimenters expected that goal assignment would not work very well for the Israeli students.

Participation in goal setting improved the performance of all groups. However, perhaps because U.S. students come from a highly individualistic and moderate-power-distance national culture, they performed almost as well with assigned goals as they did when given the opportunity to participate in goal setting. This was not true for the Israeli students, who come from a more collectivist and lower power culture. The Israeli students did much better with participation. The implication is that subordinate participation in goal setting is an effective motivational tool in collectivist nations, but it is less important in individualistic or high-power-distance national cultures.

Reinforcement Theory

Most managerial applications of reinforcement theory focus on **operant conditioning**, which represents a basic way people learn. The famous psychologist B. F. Skinner identified most of the principles underlying operant conditioning.[39]

The operant conditioning model proposes that behavior is a function of its consequences. If a pleasurable consequence follows a behavior, the behavior will continue. If an unpleasant consequence follows a behavior, the behavior will stop.[40] Unlike most other theories of motivation, operant conditioning focuses

Operant conditioning
Model proposes that if a pleasurable consequence follows a behavior, the behavior will continue, whereas if an unpleasant consequence follows a behavior, the behavior will stop.

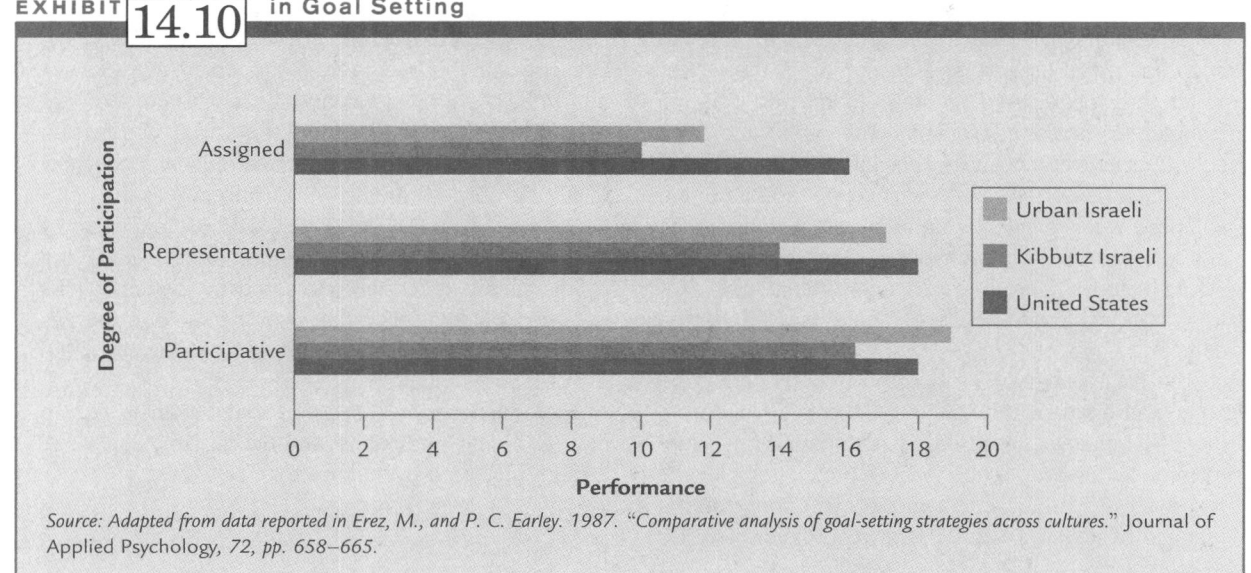

EXHIBIT 14.10   **Cultural Effects on Performance by the Degree of Participation in Goal Setting**

Source: Adapted from data reported in Erez, M., and P. C. Earley. 1987. "Comparative analysis of goal-setting strategies across cultures." Journal of Applied Psychology, 72, pp. 658–665.

on observable behavior and not on the psychological processes (e.g., meeting needs) that affect people's motivation. Consider the next Case in Point

The operant-conditioning model has three steps, as are shown in Exhibit 14.11 with a managerial example. The antecedent comes first and stimulates behavior. The behavior follows the antecedent, and the pleasant or unpleasant consequences follow the behavior. The exhibit shows a simple example based on work attendance. In the antecedent, management sets an attendance goal. The employee behaves by either coming to work or missing work. Management then provides pleasant or unpleasant consequences for the behavior.

Positive reinforcement occurs when management responds with a rewarding consequence, but the consequence is deemed rewarding only if it increases the desired behavior. Not all people respond to the same positively intended consequences in the same way. Although often confused with punishment, negative reinforcement increases desired behavior by eliminating some negative consequence; that is, people behave in a certain way to avoid something unpleasant. For example, you may put on a heavy coat to avoid the pain of extreme cold. Punishment occurs when something unpleasant occurs after a behavior. The exhibit shows that docking pay is an unpleasant consequence that follows the behavior of not coming to work. Extinction occurs when a manager ignores a behavior, but managers must be careful to avoid extinction when other rewards (e.g., a paid day off) may be operating.

In most management applications of reinforcement theory, positive reinforcement is used to encourage the desired behaviors, and managers have an array of organizational rewards. These include material rewards (e.g., pay), benefit rewards (e.g., company car), status rewards (e.g., prestigious office), and social rewards (e.g., praise).[41]

CASE IN POINT

The Japanese Salaryman and Reinforcement Theory

It is widely believed that the Japanese salary is a major reason why Japan has been able to experience such sustained growth. The salaryman is the white-collar employee who is fully dedicated to the company. In fact, the salaryman was part of the managerial class who chose to work for a company rather than for a career. As a fresh university graduate, the company would inculcate the employee with its values and provide training, perks, and other benefits that would historically provide for a comfortable life. In return, the employee would dedicate his life to the company.

The salaryman's ongoing commitment to the company was ensured through many types of reinforcement. If employees conformed to norms, they were rewarded. However, if norms were broken, employees faced severe negative consequences. Consider the practice of drinking late into the night a few times a week. Most employees feel obliged to go along with such activities to avoid retribution for not participating. Drinking with the boss is seen as a way to show loyalty and to build camaraderie, and those who conform are given a positive reward. Another practice involves the use of holidays. Most salarymen take only a fraction of their paid holidays to show their devotion to the company. Those who take longer holidays are punished by being denied pay raises and promotions. Finally, a salaryman works for only one company. Switching jobs is close to impossible because many factors, such as seniority-based wages and the loss of pension, make moving jobs difficult.

Experts nevertheless agree that Japan is seeing new economic conditions wherein the traditional salaryman may be a dying breed.

Source: Based on Economist. *2008. "Sayonara, salaryman." January 5, pp. 68–70.*

EXHIBIT **14.11**   Management Example of Operant Conditioning Process and Types of Consequences

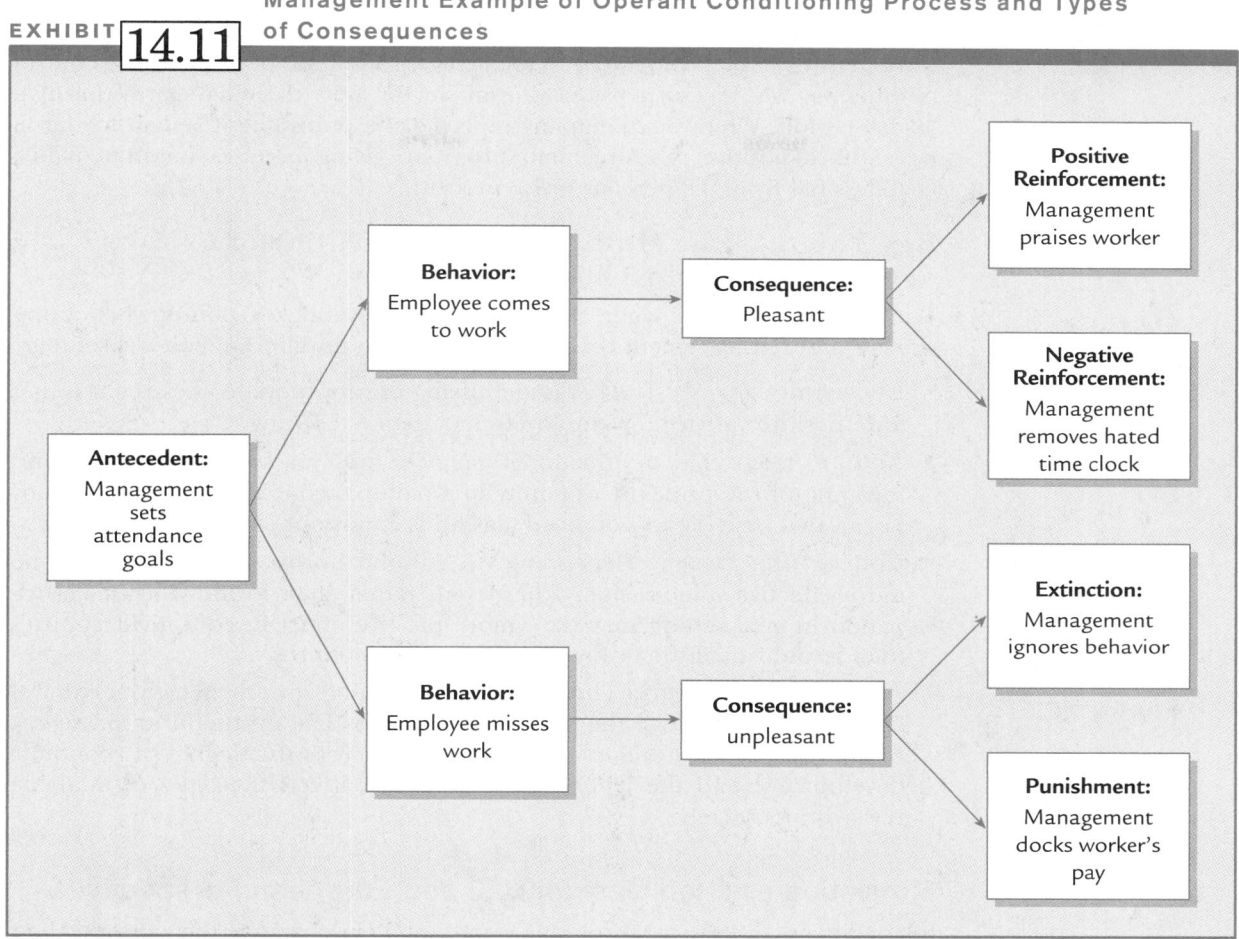

Applying Reinforcement Theory in Multinational Settings For behaviors that are easily observable and measurable, such as attendance, the evidence from most U.S. studies suggests that positive reinforcement works.[42] However, finding appropriate organizational reinforcers remains a major difficulty in applying reinforcement theory to diverse national groups. Given that people from various nations expect different rewards from work, groups may respond to different reinforcers. Furthermore, managers must be able to determine whether it is always necessary to use certain forms of punishment for observable behaviors such as absences.

The challenge for the multinational manager is not only to understand how work values influence potential rewards but also to identify the organizational rewards available in a national setting. National cultures and social institutions define acceptable and legitimate rewards. Consider these two examples. In highly unionized countries such as Germany, pay and benefits are fixed nationally and are not available as organizational rewards targeted to specific behaviors. In Japan, employees often consider public praise embarrassing; it implies that one is somehow better than his or her colleagues. This embarrassment and the potential ostracism by the work group would result not in a reward but in punishment, unintended by the culturally ignorant manager.

Evidence exists, however, that when multinational managers can find culturally and institutionally appropriate reinforcers, reinforcement theory works. For example, companies in Mexico City often use punishment to control tardiness—a one-day suspension without pay for every three days tardy during a 30-day period. When one company replaced the punishment system for tardiness with a positive reinforcement program, giving bonuses for punctuality, tardiness fell from 9.8 percent to 1.2 percent.[43]

Key Points in the Multinational Application of Process and Reinforcement Theories

The multinational manager should consider several key points when using process and reinforcement theories of motivation in different cultural settings:

- *Expectancy theory:* The key is identifying the appropriate work rewards that have positive valence for employees in a national setting.
- *Equity theory:* The multinational manager must assess the importance and meaning of the principle of equity in a national context. Equality norms or norms that base rewards on need may be as important or more so than equity.
- *Goal-setting theory:* Depending on cultural norms, goal setting may be more effective when assigned to groups rather than to individuals. Participation in goal setting may have more positive effect in collectivist cultures than in individualistic or high-power-distance cultures.
- *Reinforcement theory:* The rewards people value at work, in a given cultural context, may influence the types of reinforcers that are useful to managers. In addition, the institutional environment, such as the degree of economic development and the labor relations system, affects the types of available rewards in a society.

Motivation and Job Design: U.S. and European Perspectives

Job design attempts to make jobs more motivating by changing the nature of their functions and tasks. Early theories of job design focused primarily on making jobs more efficient through procedures such as time and motion studies. The objective was to make a job as fast and as efficient as possible, with little concern for the psychological state of the worker. Contemporary views of job design take into account the psychological effects on the worker produced by the types of tasks associated with a job. Theories on ways to design jobs for high motivation focus on how job characteristics allow a worker to meet or satisfy motivating needs.

A U.S. Approach: The Job Characteristics Model

Job characteristics model

Suggests that work is more motivating when managers enrich core job characteristics, such as by increasing the number of skills a job requires.

Although there are several approaches to redesigning work for increased motivation, one of the most popular in the United States is the **job characteristics model.**[44] This model suggests that work is more motivating when managers enrich core job characteristics, such as requiring more than one skill. In turn, these core job characteristics affect the psychological states of a worker that are critical to motivation. For example, one such psychological state is whether the worker believes the job is meaningful. Proponents of the job characteristics model argue that, if the core job characteristics lead to appropriate psychological reactions, then jobs have a high potential to motivate workers.

The job characteristics model sees three critical psychological states as motivating. First, a person must believe that the job is meaningful. A meaningful job is perceived as important or valuable. Second, a person must believe that he or she is responsible or accountable for the outcome of the work. Third, a person must understand how well he or she has performed.

Core job characteristics that lead to motivating psychological states are:

- *Skill variety:* A job with skill variety requires the use of different abilities and activities.
- *Task identity:* Task identity increases when a person can complete a whole piece of work from beginning to end.
- *Task significance:* Task significance increases when a job has important effects on other people.
- *Autonomy:* People control their own schedules and job procedures.
- *Feedback:* Feedback occurs when the job allows timely information on a person's performance.

Not all people respond positively to jobs with enriched job characteristics. The model suggests that jobs with high motivational potential work best for people who have a strong need for personal growth and who have the appropriate knowledge and skills to perform the job well. Exhibit 14.12 gives a picture of how the model works when a job has a high potential for motivating workers.

EXHIBIT 14.12   A Motivating Job in the Job Characteristics Model

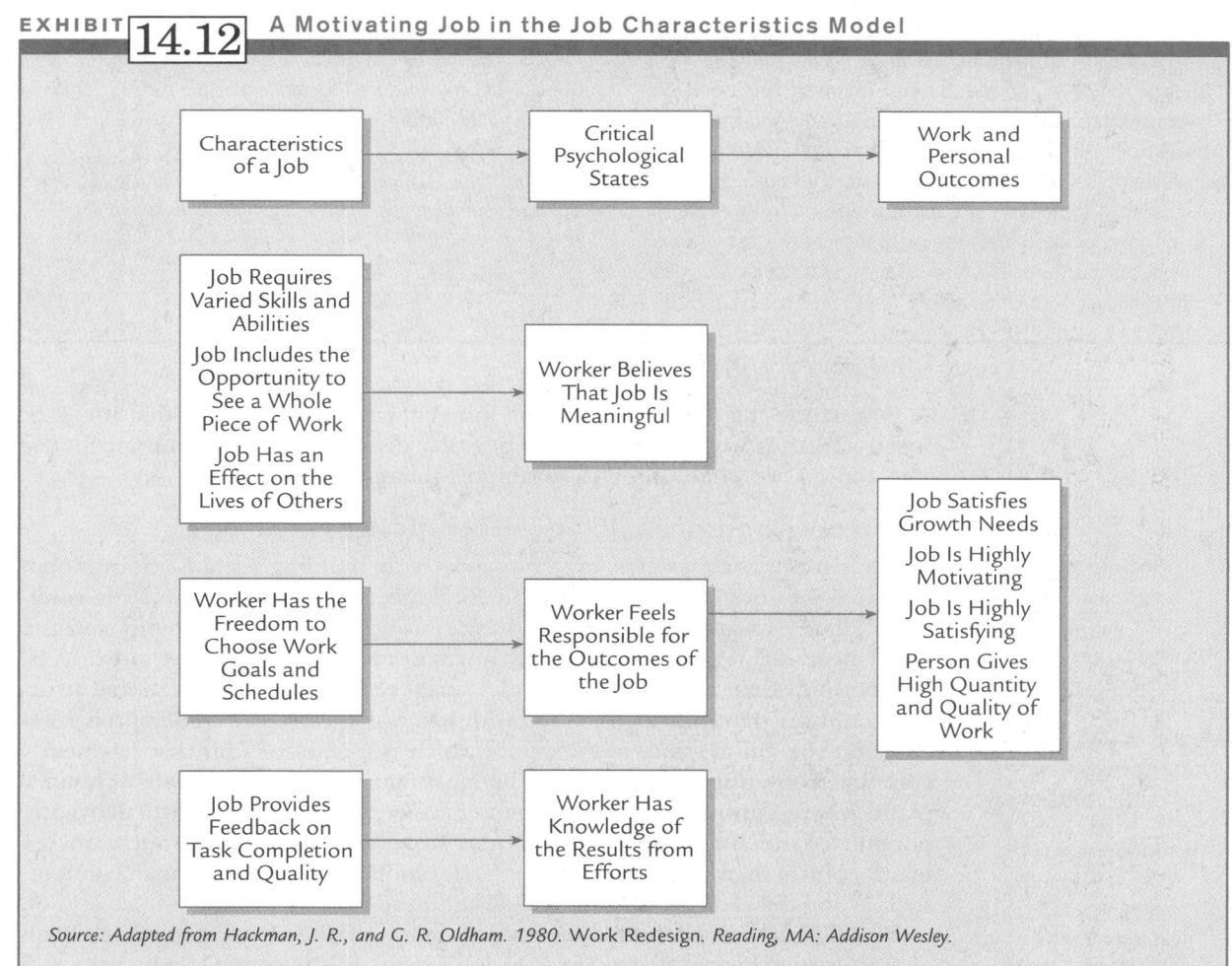

Source: Adapted from Hackman, J. R., and G. R. Oldham. 1980. Work Redesign. Reading, MA: Addison Wesley.

The Job Characteristics Model: A Comparison of Mauritian and Australian Hotel Workers

Mauritius, a small island off the east coast of Madagascar, has a vibrant tourism sector. Many of the world's leading hotel groups, such as One & Only Resorts, Club Med, and Hilton Hotels, have world-class resorts on the island. The tourism sector employs a significant number of Mauritians, and these hotels work hard to motivate their employees.

In an innovative study, Lee-Ross provides some insights into application of the job characteristics model when comparing Mauritian and Australian hotel workers. The author argues that because Mauritian workers have higher power distance, higher uncertainty avoidance, and lower individualism than their Australian counterparts, they are less likely to be given jobs that display high levels of core job characteristics. For instance, the author argues, Mauritian workers are not likely to be given work that requires taking initiative or becoming involved in decision making because high power distance means that they are less likely to disagree with their supervisors. High uncertainty avoidance also implies that they are not very comfortable with situations involving high levels of autonomy. Because of their cultural attributes, therefore, Mauritian workers are less likely to be given jobs with high core job characteristics. The study supports this argument, showing that Australian workers perceive higher levels of core job characteristics than their Mauritian counterparts.

However, although the job characteristics model suggests that people with high levels of core job characteristics are likely to be motivated (i.e., the Australians), the study showed that both Mauritian and Australian workers had similar levels of motivation. The authors suggest that the high power distance of Mauritians encourages them to agree with authority and even to be deferential to customers. This allows Mauritian workers to satisfy their predisposed cultural obligations of deference to those in positions of authority. By behaving consistently with their cultural predispositions, Mauritian hotel employees experience levels of motivation similar to their Australian counterparts.

Such results show that the job characteristics model is clearly culture dependent and needs to be adapted to fit cultural predispositions.

Sources: Based on Lee-Ross, Darren. 2005. "Perceived job characteristics and internal work motivation. An exploratory cross-cultural analysis of the motivational antecedents of hotel workers in Mauritius and Australia." Journal of Management Development, *24, pp. 253–266; Stott, Bridget. 2006. "Mauritius ready to open doors to paradise." Observer, February 19, p. 21.*

One of the major criticisms of the job characteristics model is that it is U.S. based and thus works only for societies that display similar cultural attributes. The above Case in Point seems to support that criticism.

A European Approach: Sociotechnical Systems

Sociotechnical systems (STS) approach
Focuses on designing motivating jobs by blending the social system (i.e., organizational structure, culture) with technologies.

Autonomous work group
Team or unit that has nearly complete responsibility for a task.

The **sociotechnical systems (STS) approach** to building a job's motivational potential was originally developed in England and some Scandinavian countries.[45] The STS approach attempts to mesh both modern technology and the social needs of workers, but it does not consider workers just as individuals. Rather, individual workers are part of a social system (i.e., organizational structure, culture) that must be blended with technologies.[46] The STS approach focuses on the **autonomous work group**, which is a team or unit that has nearly complete responsibility for a task. The most famous example is Volvo's Kalmar plant, where autonomous work groups have responsibility for particular components of the automobile (e.g., doors). In autonomous work groups, worker teams control many aspects of their jobs traditionally governed by management, such as the tasks assigned to individuals and the pace of work.[47]

The STS approach builds into a job many of the same motivational job characteristics proposed by the U.S. job characteristic model. However, in a crucial difference with the U.S. approach, the team's tasks become the focus of job enrichment, not the individual worker's tasks.[48] The team decides individual task assignments and thus increases skill variety. The team makes autonomous decisions on a variety of matters related to its job, such as which task to complete first. The team has task identity by producing a whole product. And the team gets feedback from its work, often by conducting its own quality inspections.

Choosing Job Enrichment Techniques in Multinational Settings

How can a multinational manager choose the best techniques to design motivating work? Some experts suggest that the choice should depend on whether the culture is individualistic and collectivist.[49] Approaches created in the United States tend to focus on how the *individual* reacts to core job characteristics. They have a cultural bias in favor of individualistic cultures. Approaches designed in collectivist cultures, including the sociotechnical systems approach and the quality circles popular in Japan, focus on the job characteristics of the *team*. They have a cultural bias in favor of collectivist cultures. Although proponents of both forms of enrichment can point to success stories in several nations, experts recommend a team focus for job enrichment in collectivist cultures and an individual focus in individualistic cultures.

One explanation of why team-based job enrichment may not work well in individualistic cultures is that people from individualistic cultures just do not work as well in groups. Exhibit 14.13 gives an example of this phenomenon. It

EXHIBIT 14.13

Comparing the Performance of Chinese, U.S., and Israeli Managers Working Alone and in Groups

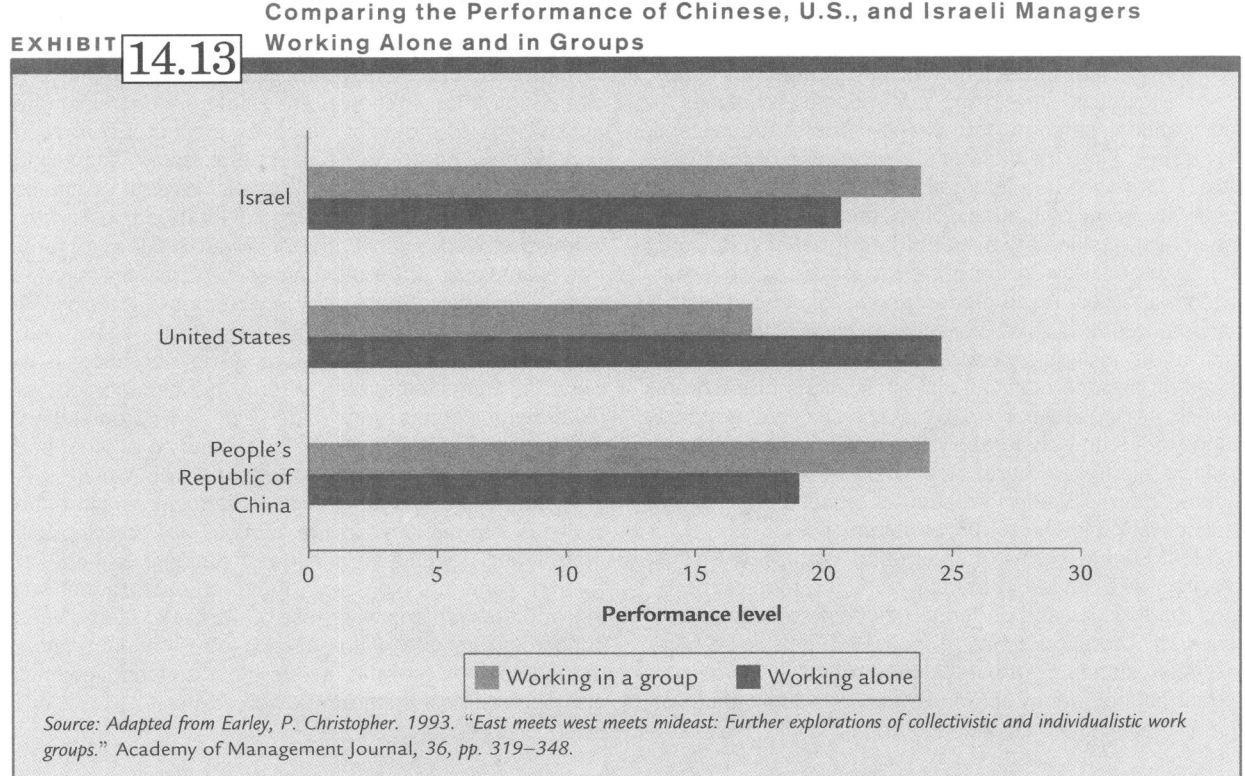

Source: Adapted from Earley, P. Christopher. 1993. "East meets west meets mideast: Further explorations of collectivistic and individualistic work groups." Academy of Management Journal, 36, pp. 319–348.

shows a comparison of three culturally diverse groups of managers working in groups or alone. As you can see, unlike the managers from the collectivist cultures, U.S. managers performed much worse in groups than they did alone.

Why does performance drop off with the use of teamwork in individualistic cultures? Some experts explain this by noting that people from individualistic cultures often engage in social loafing; that is, people put out less effort when they work in groups. They do this for three reasons. First, working in groups, people do not feel responsible for group outcomes and feel less pressure to perform. Second, workers in groups often believe that the group will make up for any slack in their personal efforts. Third, especially in highly individualistic cultures such as the United States, people give their own work and interests priority over the group's. However, in individualistic cultures, social loafing has less of a detrimental effect on a group's performance when individuals rather than the groups are held accountable for performance.[50]

Social loafing
People put out less effort when they work in groups.

Summary and Conclusions

Motivating workers in diverse cultural settings is a constant challenge for multinational managers. As companies both large and small become more global and transnational in their strategic and human resource orientations, the challenge of increasing worker motivation in multinational settings will become even greater. For a multinational company to remain competitive in the global environment, each company and its managers must find ways to motivate an increasingly diverse workforce.

As a guide to developing motivational techniques in multinational settings, this chapter addressed several key issues. First, the chapter showed some of the available information on international differences in work centrality, work obligation norms, and extrinsic and intrinsic work values in several different nations. Second, the chapter reviewed the basic processes of work motivation and how these processes are influenced by the national context. Third, it reviewed classic theories of motivation (including need, process, and reinforcement theories) and the multinational applications of each approach. In these sections were specific and practical suggestions on how to apply these theories in different national contexts. Fourth, and finally, the chapter considered both U.S. and European approaches to designing jobs with high motivational potential.

Most of the views of motivation discussed in this chapter were "made in the U.S.A." U.S. academics created the theories and performed much of the supporting research. The approaches to motivation discussed here are also standard fare in U.S. university courses in organizational behavior. However, the dominance of the United States as the country of origin for many

motivational theories does not invalidate their multinational applications—if a manager makes appropriate adjustments for national contexts and various subcultures. Many of the psychological theories that underlie common U.S. approaches to motivation have culture-free assumptions and research support; that is, they attempt to explain human behavior independently of cultural setting.

However, even if psychological processes that underlie motivational theories are culture independent, the applications of motivation theories are not. Even when people respond to work using the same underlying psychological processes, the national context continues to influence other factors, such as what people find rewarding at work and what people feel is fair and moral. For example, a U.S. American and a Brazilian may respond similarly to the psychological process of positive reinforcement; their behaviors increase when consequences are pleasant. But they do not necessarily view the same reinforcers offered by management as rewarding. Nations vary widely in their predominant views regarding the functions and meaning of work and in the rewards that people hope to get from work.

A brief discussion of motivation can only sensitize the multinational manager to the subtleties of applying any motivational technique in a given national setting. Although managers may begin their approach to motivating workers with an awareness of the broad stereotypes concerning national cultures, each job situation requires an understanding of the unique organizational, regional, and occupational cultures as well as the individual differences of each employee.

Discussion Questions

1. Compare the job characteristics approach to job design and the sociotechnical systems approach. Pick a national culture with which you are familiar (besides your own), and discuss which approach would most likely succeed and why.

2. How might a country's educational and political systems affect the effectiveness of redesigning work as a motivational tool?

3. Discuss differences in the attributes of work considered the most important in different nations. How might these differences influence the application of expectancy theory and reinforcement theory to the work setting?

4. Discuss the differences between the need and process theories of motivation. Which type do you think is more applicable to multinational management and why?

5. Discuss the three principles of fairness of rewards. Do you think that equity theory could work in societies where other principles besides equity operate? If so, how would you apply equity theory as a manager in these countries?

6. Under what conditions would you recommend involving groups in setting goals? Discuss the cultural influences on goal setting using Hofstede's original four dimensions of national culture.

Multinational Management **Skill Builder**

Planning Motivational Strategies for Different Countries

Step 1. Read the following multinational problem.

You have just completed your first year as a management trainee for the XYZ company. Your company manufactures components for industrial robots. You have just come from a meeting with the vice president for personnel. She has told you that XYZ has decided to open a manufacturing plant in the country of_____. Because of your background in international business, top management has chosen you to be the new plant manager. The VP tells you that this is a significant opportunity and challenge since you would have to wait at least five more years to get this level of responsibility at home. Personnel experts are already in_____, working on recruitment, selection, and training. Your major job will be to motivate the local workers to reach the plant's full capacity as soon as possible. Given your knowledge of the local culture and social institutions, the VP asks you to prepare a report specifying the motivational strategies that you might use on your new assignment.

Step 2. Pick teams and countries.

Your instructor will divide you into teams of three to five people. Each team will choose or be assigned a different country for a plant location. Your team will act in the role of the new expatriate plant manager. If your instructor chooses, this may also be an individual assignment. This project may be a library research project or an in-class assignment based on information from the text.

Step 3. Prepare reports.

Reports may be written, oral, or both. They are to analyze the likely effectiveness of motivational approaches given different economic, cultural, and institutional factors in the country in question

Each report must discuss the strengths and weaknesses of applying the following motivational theories in the selected country:
- Need theory.
- Expectancy theory.
- Goal-setting theory.
- Equity theory.
- Reinforcement theory.
- Job design.

Step 4. Present your findings to the class.

Step 5. Class discussion.

Alternative approach: The whole class works with one country, and each team deals with one approach to motivation.

Endnotes

[1] Meaning of Work International Research Team. 1987. *The Meaning of Working: An International Perspective*. New York: Academic Press.

[2] World Values Study Group. 1994. *World Values Surveys and European Values Surveys, 1981–1984, 1990–1993, and*

1995–1997. (Computer file.) Ann Arbor, MI: Inter-University Consortium for Political and Social Research.

[3] Meaning of Work International Research Team.

[4] Parboteeah, K. Praveen, and John B. Cullen. 2003. "Social institutions and work centrality: Explorations beyond national culture." *Organization Science*, 14, pp. 137–148.

[5] Hofstede, Geert. 2001. *Culture's Consequences: International Differences in Work-Related Values*, 2nd ed. London: Sage.

[6] Inglehart, Ronald, Miguel Basanez, and Alejandro Moreno. 1998. *Human Values and Beliefs: A Cross-Cultural Sourcebook.* Ann Arbor, MI: University of Michigan Press.

[7] Grant, Linda. 1997. "Unhappy in Japan." *Fortune*, January 13, p. 142.

[8] World Values Study Group.

[9] *Economist.* 2006. "Emerging economies—Climbing back." January 21.

[10] Inglehart, Basanez, and Moreno.

[11] World Values Study Group.

[12] Maslow, A. 1970. *Motivation and Personality.* New York: Harper & Row.

[13] Pinder, C. C. 1984. *Work Motivation.* Glenview, IL: Scott, Foresman.

[14] Alderfer, C. P. 1972. *Existence, Relatedness and Growth: Human Needs in Organizational Settings.* New York: Free Press.

[15] Herzberg, F., B. Mausner, and B. B. Snyderman. 1959. *The Motivation to Work.* Hoboken, NJ: Wiley.

[16] McClelland, David C. 1961. *The Achieving Society.* Princeton, NJ: Van Nostrand Reinhold.

[17] Ronen, Simcha. 1986. *Comparative and Multinational Management.* Hoboken, NJ: Wiley.

[18] Ronen, Simcha. 1994. "An underlying structure of motivation need taxonomies: A cross-cultural confirmation." *Handbook of Industrial and Organizational Psychology*, 4, pp. 241–269.

[19] Harpaz, Itzhak. 1990. "The importance of work goals: An international perspective." *Journal of International Business Studies*, 1st quarter, pp. 75–93.

[20] Elizur, Dov, Ingwer Borg, Raymond Hunt, and Istvan Magyari Beck. 1991. "The structure of work values: A cross cultural comparison." *Journal of Organizational Behavior*, 12, pp. 21–38.

[21] Hofstede, Geert. 1991. *Cultures and Organizations: Software of the Mind.* London: McGraw-Hill.

[22] Vroom, Victor H. 1964. *Work and Motivation.* Hoboken, NJ: Wiley.

[23] Gordon, Judith R. 1996. *Organizational Behavior.* Upper Saddle River, NJ: Prentice Hall.

[24] Adams, J. S. 1963. "Toward an understanding of inequity." *Journal of Abnormal and Social Psychology*, 67, pp. 422–436.

[25] Erez, Miriam. 1994. "Toward a model of cross-cultural industrial and organizational psychology." *Handbook of Industrial and Organizational Psychology*, 4, pp. 559–607.

[26] Gluskinos, U. M. 1988. "Cultural and political consideration in the introduction of western technologies: The Mekorot Project." *Journal of Management Development*, 6, pp. 34–36.

[27] Ibid.

[28] Chen, C.C., Choi, J. and Chi, S.C. 2002. "Making justice sense of local expatriate compensation disparity: Mitigation by local referents, ideological explanations, and interpersonal sensitivity in China–

foreign joint ventures." *Academy of Management Journal*, 45, pp. 807–817.

[29] Berman, J. J., and P. Singh. 1985. "Cross-cultural similarities and differences in perceptions of fairness." *Journal of Cross-Cultural Psychology*, 16, pp. 55–67.

[30] Kim, Ken I., Hun-Joon Park, and Nori Suzuki. 1990. "Reward allocations in the United States, Japan, and Korea: A comparison of individualistic and collectivistic cultures." *Academy of Management Journal*, 33, pp. 188–198.

[31] Hundley, Greg, and Jooyup Kim. 1997. "National culture and the factors affecting perceptions of pay fairness in Korea and the United States." *International Journal of Organizational Analysis*, 5(4), pp. 325–341.

[32] Locke, E. A., and G. P. Latham. 1990. *A Theory of Goal Setting and Task Performance.* Upper Saddle River, NJ: Prentice Hall.

[33] Hellriegel, Don, and John W. Slocum Jr. 2007. *Organizational Behavior*, 11th ed. Cincinnati, OH: South-Western.

[34] Erez, M., P. C. Earley, and C. L. Hulin. 1987. "The impact of participation on goal acceptance and performance: A two-step model." *Academy of Management Journal*, 12, pp. 265–277.

[35] Locke, E. A., G. P. Latham, and M. Erez. 1988. "The determinants of goal commitment." *Academy of Management Review*, 13, pp. 23–39.

[36] Erez, M., and P. C. Earley. 1987. "Comparative analysis of goal-setting strategies across cultures." *Journal of Applied Psychology*, 72, pp. 658–665.

[37] Erez.

[38] Erez and Earley.

[39] Skinner, B. F. 1938. *The Behavior of Organisms: An Experimental Analysis.* New York: D. Appleton-Century.

[40] Luthans, Fred, and Robert Kreitner. 1985. *Organizational Behavior Modification.* Glenview, IL: Scott, Foresman.

[41] Hellriegel and Slocum.

[42] Luthans and Kreitner.

[43] Herman, J. 1973. "Effects of bonuses for punctuality on the tardiness of industrial workers." *Journal of Applied Behavioral Analysis*, 6, pp. 563–570.

[44] Hackman, J. R., and G. R. Oldham. 1980. *Work Redesign.* Reading, MA: Addison-Wesley.

[45] Trist, E., and H. Murry. 1993. *The Social Engagement of Social Science: An Anthology, Vol. II: The Socio-Technical Perspective.* Philadelphia: University of Pennsylvania Press; Thorsrud, E. 1984. "The Scandinavian model: Strategies of organizational democracy." In B. Wilpert and A. Sorge, eds. *International Perspectives on Organizational Democracy.* Hoboken, NJ: Wiley, pp. 337–370.

[46] Cummings, T. G. 1978. "Self-regulating work groups: A socio-technical synthesis." *Academy of Management Review*, 3, pp. 625–634.

[47] Gordon.

[48] Erez, M., and P. C. Earley. 1993. *Culture, Self-Identity and Work.* New York: Oxford University Press.

[49] Ibid.

[50] Earley, P. Christopher. 1989. "Social loafing and collectivism: A comparison of the United States and the People's Republic of China." *Administrative Science Quarterly*, 34, pp. 565–581.

Insulting Andrew

"This is our guy . . ." was all the text message from the CEO said. Joseph Rogers, head of HR for Ayoub Companies (AC), received the one-line note just as Yusef Ayoub, CEO of the Dubai-based conglomerate, was finishing his interview with Andrew Yard, a candidate to take over the company's struggling Retail business. The text message was soon followed by a phone call from Ayoub explaining that he had so enjoyed the interview with Yard that they had decided to stretch it into a long dinner meeting. At the end of the evening, Ayoub—knowing that the rest of the executive team had already endorsed Yard—offered him the job on the spot. Ayoub told his trusty HR head to put together an offer for Yard and to close the deal as soon as possible. They had finally found the leader they had been looking for.

Company Background

Ayoub Companies (AC) was one of the largest, privately-owned companies in the Middle East. With operations in 40 countries, it was a multi-billion dollar conglomerate with more than 20 businesses organized into several major business groups ranging from automotive sales and services, consumer credit, manufacturing of construction products, distribution of fast-moving consumer goods and a retail group that included home furnishings, electronics, and home construction products. The company's revenues were concentrated in Dubai, and operations spanned the Gulf Region and in Southeast Asia, where growth had been very strong in recent years. Since Yusef Ayoub (HBS 1998) had taken over the CEO role from his father in 2002, he had launched a major growth strategy centered on recruiting and retaining top talent and on building a highly meritocratic culture. Five years later, growth by any measure—profits, employees, revenues—had nearly tripled, and it appeared to be accelerating. During this time, the company's capabilities at the center—finance, IT, HR, and business development, the last of which had only been added 18 months earlier—had all been dramatically upgraded.

Ayoub had built the company into a diversified firm that would attract the best talent from around the world, where operational excellence would combine with a hard-driving performance-oriented culture that focused on operational excellence during his first five years as CEO. More recently, the focus of the company had been on growth. Ayoub had a strong and diverse

executive team—his ten direct reports alone represented seven different nationalities. With promising growth opportunities in many of the businesses, the Business Development team had identified the largest growth potential in retail, the business group that was struggling most. The most recent numbers from the retail business, which was anchored by consumer electronics and home furnishings, showed that the progress was stalled. Ayoub and Rogers believed that the problems stemmed from weak leadership—there was a desperate need for a major overhaul throughout the top management in the group; currently, the vacant top spot was being managed on an interim basis by the COO.

Andrew Yard

When Rogers interviewed Andrew Yard, he was hopeful that this candidate would finally clear the bar. The difficult search had lasted nearly a year. Finding an appropriate, experienced candidate who was willing to relocate to the Middle East was a major challenge. Currently heading up international expansion of AJW, a large British furniture retailer, into East Asia, Yard had broad retail expertise in both home goods and in electronics. Furthermore, he had great experience managing diverse teams in international locations. According to the background references pulled together by Egon Zehnder, Yard's coworkers, subordinates and superiors described him as "a first class retailer—one of the best in the industry" who had demonstrated consistent success at rolling out large numbers of retail chains quickly and effectively over several regions—from Korea and China to Turkey and the Czech Republic. Yard was further described as "tough and sometimes blunt . . . the ultimate professional. Not the most charismatic of people, but widely respected for his knowledge and achievements" and able to "engender great loyalty from his people."

With such a strong endorsement from Egon Zehnder, Rogers had been eager to meet Yard and had not been disappointed. Yard was every bit as good as advertised by the headhunter and all the top managers who met with him had come away very impressed. Now it was time for Rogers to step up for the more delicate part: negotiating the package.

During his career, Rogers had negotiated hundreds of packages. Relocating to the Middle East from Hong

Kong would be difficult for Yard and his family and Yard had explained that he was worried about the transition. After some back and forth on the pay, they came to an agreement that represented a considerable bump in pay and bonus: 600K salary plus 75 percent bonus along with a significant equity award in the company's phantom stock plan, plus standard benefits such as health coverage, life insurance, car, housing, and relocation.

Although the deal had been agreed upon, the start date was the only remaining sticking point. Yard had made it clear during the interviews that he would not be able to leave his current position immediately—he had a contracted six-month notice period with his current employer and it was important to him that he tie up his current projects and leave on good terms. Although AC knew about this issue from the beginning of the interview process, they had not realized how firm Yard's six month commitment was from his perspective. Furthermore, during the long search process, the urgency to find a leader for the business had intensified; if Yard served the whole six-months, he could not move to Dubai until the end of July. The COO's recent emails to the team showed that the retail business was at a critical juncture: "We're putting out fires daily over here. I'm having trouble doing my day job as COO while managing these." Meanwhile, the business development group was constantly identifying new growth opportunities for retail. In a meeting with the CEO, Ayoub pressured Rogers to speed up the process: "We need to get him on board as soon as possible. Every week of mismanagement in retail is a huge cost to the company, and those losses are nothing compared to the cost of missing out on these opportunities bus-dev is finding."

Rogers carefully considered how to work through this problem with Yard—if Yard broke his contract with AJW he would be sacrificing a potentially large piece of equity in that company. During the negotiations, Rogers had offered to make him whole on anything left behind, within reason, but Yard balked at the idea saying that it would be too hard to calculate counterfactuals. While Yard was contractually obligated to stay, it was common in these situations for departing employees to be able to negotiate an early release. However, there was often ambiguity about departure packages in terms of unvested equity and long-term bonus plans.

Because of this ambiguity, the precise loss would be difficult for Yard, let alone Rogers, to calculate, but Rogers suspected that it was significant and was certainly contributing to Yard's reluctance to come sooner. Nevertheless, Rogers needed to find some way to induce Yard to negotiate himself out of his current contract. Rogers came up with the idea of offering a signing bonus, or, more accurately, a "join-soon bonus." The size of the bonus would be tied to how early Yard could join, since an early start date would be valuable to the company. Rogers called Yard to explain the idea:

I know that we already hammered out the details and you've already agreed to the deal, but I wanted to let you know that we've added an extra bonus in the contract you'll be getting soon. It would be really valuable to us if you could find a way to join us earlier than August—the earlier the better. August is just such a long time away and six months is pretty unusual. Additionally, we'd like to show you how excited we are to have you join, so we'd like to give you a signing bonus with heavy weighting for starting early. The bonus can be worth up to 200,000 at maximum, and will decline by 40K per month. So, if you were to join any time within the next month—which we know is unlikely—it would be 200K; if you start during the next month, it's 160, and so on. This keeps falling until the end of July, when it's 40; and six months from now, on August 1, it falls to 0. We know you weren't expecting this add on, but I hope that you don't mind if we threw it in at the last minute. Yard seemed surprised by the offer, but mentioned that it sounded reasonable and offered a polite thanks.

Three days later, Rogers and Yard were on a scheduled call to discuss progress on the searches to fill the open positions on Yard's new team. Yard seemed a little uncomfortable, however, and at the end of the conversation, he said:

There's just one other thing, Joseph. With regard to the signing bonus, I've been thinking about that and thanks. But I also thought you should know that I found it slightly insulting. It seems to imply that it takes a bunch of money to get me to join quickly, and that I might not hurry without money to motivate me—I would work hard to join quickly in any case. It's not the money that is keeping me at my current job longer, it's just that I feel like I have a duty to do a good job here during the transition and to leave the business and my team in good shape.

Yard paused for a few seconds and continued, "That is where my head is at. I thought I should tell you."

Caught off guard, Rogers tried to figure out how to respond. The awkward silence got louder....

CASE DISCUSSION QUESTIONS

1. Motivating top talent to work in difficult international assignments is a major challenge for top international managers. What might be more important than money to make this work?

2. Why do you think that Andrew Yard was insulted by the surprise bonus offered by Rogers to have him take the job early?

3. If you were Rogers, how would you respond to Yard's reaction finding the signing bonus "slightly insulting?" You would have to think fast.

4. Ayoub Companies had developed "a hard-drive performance-oriented culture" that attracted top executives from many nationalities. Given this unique group of employees, what strategies would you use to motivate them to continue at such a high performance level?

CASE CREDIT

Professor Brian J. Hall and Research Associate Nicole S. Bennett prepared this case. Certain details have been disguised. HBS cases are developed solely as the basis for class discussion. Cases are not intended to serve as endorsements, sources of primary data, or illustrations of effective or ineffective management.

Preview CASE IN POINT

Same Problem, Different Styles

Consider the fictional example of the leadership styles of two CEOs of pharmaceutical companies, one in the United States and the other in Japan. They must lead their subordinates in dealing with a crisis regarding a potentially deadly batch of headache medicine produced by one of their overseas subsidiaries. Although the characters and companies are fictional, the styles are based on real leaders.

Ms. Moore, a U.S. American CEO	Sakano-san, a Japanese CEO
7:00 Ms. Moore, CEO of Thorndike Pharmaceuticals, leaves for work with her daughter.	Sakano-san, CEO of Kobe Pharmaceuticals, eats a breakfast of a raw egg and rice. Sakano-san's wife wakes their two children in enough time for their 45-minute subway ride to school.
7:30 Ms. Moore leaves her daughter at a private junior high school for girls.	
7:45 Ms. Moore receives a cell phone call from the Thorndike Pharmaceuticals European area manager to tell her of a death and the nonfatal poisoning of several people in France as a result of their taking tainted headache medication produced by their company. The European area manager asks what he should do. Moore says she will get back to him.	
8:00 Ms. Moore calls her executive secretary and tells him to plan for an 8:30 videoconference with relevant U.S. and European managers and legal staff.	Sakano-san exchanges a polite bow with his driver and begins his limousine ride to Kobe Pharmaceuticals.

Ms. Moore, a U.S. American CEO	Sakano-san, a Japanese CEO
8:30 Ms. Moore has a videoconference with the management team and briefs its members on the crisis.	
8:45 Corporate attorneys brief Ms. Moore and the top management team on legal options and liabilities.	
9:00 The director of public relations calls Moore, asking how she can deal with the press.	
9:05 The plant manager of the French facility that produced the tainted drug calls and asks what he should do about the protesters outside the gate.	
9:45 Fearing further deaths and injury, the VP of European operations temporarily shuts down all production of the tainted drug and recalls all drugs produced after a certain date.	Sakano-san meets with executives from Bayer to discuss an international joint venture.
10:00 Ms. Moore asks the finance and accounting department to figure out how much this is going to cost.	Around this time, a trusted midlevel manager, a student of Sakano-san's old Tokyo University professor, informs Sakano-san discreetly that a problem exists and that staff members are developing a solution. Sakano-san nods his understanding. Staff members engage in consensus building *(nemawashi)* to develop a plan of action to deal with the crisis.
10:05 Top management and legal staff meet with Ms. Moore to give her an update.	
10:30 Ms. Moore gives an interview to the press.	
11:30 Ms. Moore has a hurried lunch at her desk. She takes calls from the legal department and from the VP for European operations while eating.	Subordinates formally brief Sakano-san on the problem and their plan to deal with it. He acknowledges the information and thanks them for their quick work.
For the remainder of the day and to well after 8:00 p.m., Ms. Moore continues at this hectic pace of meetings and phone calls. She calls her husband at 4:00, reminding him to pick up their daughter at school.	With the knowledge that his staff is working on dealing with the crisis, Sakano-san continues his regular business day: a two-hour luncheon meeting with government officials to discuss long-term R&D goals for the industry. He ends his day talking with a chemical supply company CEO at 1:00 a.m. in a private bar in Tokyo's entertainment district, Ropongi.

Source: Based on the format in a fictional story in Doktor, Robert H. 1990. "Asian and American CEOs: A comparative study." Organizational Dynamics, Winter, pp. 46–56.

Leadership

Ability of an individual to influence, motivate, and enable others to contribute toward the effectiveness and success of the organizations of which they are members.

What is **leadership**? The Western-based view defines leadership as the influencing of group members to achieve organizational goals. However, it is important to understand whether this definition is acceptable in most cultures. In that respect, the Global Leadership and Organizational Behavior Effectiveness project (GLOBE, described in more detail later) sheds some light on the issue. The project gathered about 200 researchers from 60 countries, and, after hours of discussion, the GLOBE's universal definition of leadership emerged. The researchers agreed that leadership is "the ability of an individual to influence, motivate, and enable others to contribute toward the effectiveness and success of the organizations of which they are members."[1]

The European Foundation for Quality Management,[2] an important association dedicated to fostering quality in European companies, has also attempted to define leadership within the European context. It sees leadership as the process by which individuals "develop and facilitate the achievement of the mission and vision, develop values required for long-term success and implement these via appropriate actions and behaviors, and are personally involved in ensuring that the organization's management system is developed and implemented."[3]

As we see from the GLOBE and EFQM definitions, leadership is more than simply holding a management position. Improving one's leadership skills in a domestic company is a difficult enough challenge, but becoming an excellent leader in a multinational company is an even greater one. This chapter shows that successful multinational leaders choose effective leadership styles based on an understanding of how national culture and a country's social institutions affect leadership. The chapter covers two important areas. First, it provides a summary of theories of leadership offered by experts from different countries. Second, it offers key examples of how leaders of different national backgrounds behave in their home cultures. As the Preview Case in Point shows and as the chapter will point out, managers working in different cultures may achieve similar goals using widely different leadership styles.

Global Leadership: The New Breed

Global leader

One who has the skills and abilities to interact with and manage people from diverse cultural backgrounds.

The rise of transnational companies and the dependence of even the smallest companies on international trade create a need for a new type of leader. This **global leader** must have the skills and abilities to interact with and manage people from the diverse cultural backgrounds that populate his or her multinational company. Consider the next Case in Point.

Let us consider some of the characteristics of this new breed of leader. According to experts on managing cultural differences, the successful global leader is:[4]

- *Cosmopolitan:* Sufficiently flexible to operate comfortably in pluralistic cultural environments.
- *Skilled at intercultural communication:* Knowledgeable of at least one foreign language and understands the complexities of interaction with people from other cultures.
- *Culturally sensitive:* Experienced in different national, regional, and organizational cultures needed to build relationships with culturally different people while understanding his or her own culture and cultural biases.
- *Capable of rapid acculturation:* Rapidly acculturated or adjusted to strange or different cultural settings.

> ### C A S E I N P O I N T
>
> ## Vodafone Group and the Global Leader
>
> U.K.-based Vodaphone is the world's largest mobile operator, with operations in more than 25 countries and about 60,000 employees. It recently won Chief Executive's 20 Best Companies for Leaders. Vodaphone's CEO, 53-year-old Arun Sarin, epitomizes the global leader. Sarin was born in India, has U.S. citizenship, and is now based in the U.K. He clearly believes that the leaders of tomorrow's multinationals will need global expertise. For instance, at Vodaphone, he manages a very diverse workforce, with more than five nationalities represented among his top ten executives. Sarin believes that his global leadership perspective has helped Vodaphone enormously, and he considers his experience as invaluable in understanding global markets.
>
> Born in India, Sarin lived there for 20 years. He then moved to the United States, where he lived for 30 years. Now he lives in the U.K. He is adamant that these experiences have helped him tremendously in his job as CEO at Vodaphone. Such global perspectives allow Sarin to be sensitive to cultural imperatives. For instance, he recognizes that U.S. managers prefer to make quicker decisions than do Europeans, who want more debate. Accordingly, Sarin typically slows down discussions in Europe to accommodate this need. Furthermore, his experiences and global leadership perspectives enable Vodaphone to better operate in the marketplace. Vodaphone considers itself German in Germany, Indian in India, and so on around the world.
>
> *Source: Based on Pellet, J. 2008. "Global, mobile and growing." Chief Executive, March, p. 232.*

- *A facilitator of subordinates' intercultural performance:* Understanding cultural differences in work and living and able to prepare subordinates for successful overseas experiences.
- *A user of cultural synergy:* Takes advantage of cultural differences by finding a synergy that combines the strengths of each cultural group and by using performance standards understandable across cultural groups, resulting in increased levels of organizational performance than that produced by culturally homogeneous companies.
- *A promoter and user of the growing world culture:* Understands, uses, and takes advantage of the international advances in media, transportation, and travel that support the globalization of business.
- *Emotionally intelligent:*[5] Able to accurately perceive his or her emotions and to use them to solve problems and to relate to others.

How can multinationals train global leaders? Consider the next Multinational Management Brief.

The remainder of this chapter provides a background on leadership. Few managers will reach the levels and experience of truly global managers, but all managers can benefit by gaining a better understanding of leadership, thereby developing the strengths of a global leader.

Three Classic Models: A Vocabulary of Leadership

The three basic models of leadership entail leadership traits, leader behavior, and contingency leadership. Knowledge of these views of leadership will help you understand the terms used to describe leadership options in a multinational setting.

Multinational Management **Brief**

Intel's Leadership Training Program

Intel, the Silicon Valley–based semiconductor giant, obtains 70 percent of its revenues from outside the United States. It currently has more than 91,000 employees located in more than 48 nations. Given the global nature of its operations, Intel places crucial importance on the ability of its managers to deal with cross-cultural differences. In that context, it has a very innovative leadership program that requires all of its midlevel leaders to be exposed to other cultures.

The design of the leadership training program is the result of substantial co-operation among employees from places such as China, Russia, the United States, and Israel. Intel expects about 800 of its nearly 2,300 midlevel managers to attend the week-long seminar in a location other than their home base. To ensure that the managers get cross-cultural training, Intel also requires that 30 percent of the attendees come from other regions.

The program incorporates seminars emphasizing the development of leadership skills, such as setting pace and implementing business plans. Although the seminars do not necessarily include cultural training, the program requires teams of six to nine midlevel leaders from various regions to create new product proposals at the end of the training. In doing so, Intel forces the participants to consider cultural differences by working with individuals from many different societies. Such experiences ensure that attendees have a chance to deal with cultural variations as they work on the project.

Sources: Based on Fraueheim, Ed. 2005. "Crossing cultures." Workforce Management, *November, p. 1; Hamm, S. 2008. "Young and impatient in India."* BusinessWeek, *January 28, pp. 45–48; Thomke, Stefan H. 2006. "Capturing the real value of innovation tools."* MIT Sloan Management Reviews, *Winter, 47, pp. 24–32; Time of India. 2009. "RMSI, Intel among best work places in India," June 10.*

Like the motivation theories discussed in Chapter 14, most, but not all, of these leadership models originate in North America. However, this chapter focuses on the multinational applicability of leadership models, not just on their North American applications.

Leadership Traits

Trait models of leadership evolved from the debate regarding whether leaders are born or made. Early leadership theorists looked at successful leaders in business, politics, religion, and the military, such as Alexander the Great and Muhammad. They concluded that such leaders were born with unique characteristics that made them quite different from other people. This view of leadership is known as the **great person theory**.

Although leadership theorists never identified an exact list of leadership traits, decades of research has uncovered some differences between leaders and their subordinates.[6] At least in the United States, successful leaders exhibit the following traits: high intelligence and self-confidence, great initiative, assertiveness and persistence, a great desire for responsibility and the opportunity to influence others, and a high awareness of the needs of others. However, unlike the great person theory of leadership, contemporary views of leadership traits do not assume that leaders are born. Although leaders are different, aspiring leaders can achieve this difference through training and experience.

Great person theory
Leaders are born with unique characteristics that make them quite different from ordinary people.

Leadership Behaviors
U.S. Perspectives on Leadership Behaviors

Although leaders have different traits than their subordinates, North American studies of leadership traits have concluded that traits alone do not make a leader. The *behaviors* leaders use to manage their employees may be more important. Classic studies of leadership behaviors in the United States came from two U.S. universities: Ohio State University and the University of Michigan. Based on hundreds of studies of North American managers, these teams of researchers identified two major types of leadership behaviors.[7] One includes behaviors that focus on completing tasks by initiating structure. Leaders who have a principal concern for initiating structure are called task-centered leaders. A **task-centered leader** gives specific directions to subordinates so that they can complete tasks. This type of leader establishes standards, schedules work, and assigns employees tasks. A second type of leader, a **person-centered leader**, focuses on meeting the social and emotional needs of employees. Such consideration behaviors include showing a concern for subordinates' feelings and taking subordinates' ideas into account.

The distinction between person-centered and task-centered leader behaviors also applies to how leaders make decisions. Leaders who adopt an **autocratic leadership** style make all major decisions themselves. Those who employ a **democratic leadership** style include subordinates in the decision making. Most experts accept that a range of leadership behaviors exists between the authoritarian leader, who makes all decisions, and the purely democratic leader, who delegates all decision making to the group.[8] For example, the **consultative or participative leadership** style often falls midway between the autocratic and democratic leadership styles. Do some cultures prefer specific leadership decision making styles? Consider the next Case in Point.

Taking a somewhat broader perspective than just leadership behavior, Rensis Likert, a famous management and leadership theorist, identified four styles of management that reflect a similar distinction between the task and the person.[9] These patterns are exploitative/authoritative, benevolent/authoritative, consultative, and participative. Exhibit 15.1 shows how each management style

Task-centered leader One who gives subordinates specific standards, schedules, and tasks.

Person-centered leader One who focuses on meeting employees' social and emotional needs.

Autocratic leadership Leaders make all major decisions themselves.

Democratic leadership Leader includes subordinates in decision making.

Consultative or participative leadership Leader's style falls midway between autocratic and democratic styles.

CASE IN POINT

South Korea and Leadership Decision-Making Style

Many South Korean companies have traditionally been run autocratically. This is not surprising given the paternalistic rule that corporations play in South Korea. Consider the case of Hyundai, one of South Korea's powerhouses. Chung Mong Koo, Hyundai's chairman, and his team of executives have managed the firm using a very autocratic style. It has been claimed that the executive team micromanages details and seldom listens to advice. Furthermore, the executives do not display much tolerance for disagreement. This style is nevertheless running into major problems in U.S. operations. Both Hyundai and its sister company, Kia,

have fired many American executives. Critics argue that the very autocratic style has frustrated American executives, who are used to a participative leadership style. For instance, Hyundai and Kia both have South Korean coordinators whose role is to monitor decision making and other results. This system is resented by American managers because they have to get the approval of the South Korean coordinators whether making big or small decisions. This has resulted in many top executives getting fired.

Source: Based on Welch, D., D. Kiley, and M. Ihlwan. 2008. "My way or the highway at Hyundai." BusinessWeek, March 17, pp. 48–51.

EXHIBIT 15.1   Likert's Four Styles of Management

Management Behaviors	Exploitative Authoritative (System 1)	Benevolent Authoritative (System 2)	Consultative (System 3)	Participative (System 4)
General leadership style	Autocratic, top-down	Paternalistic but still autocratic	Less autocratic, more attention to employees	Employee centered
Motivation techniques	Punishments, some rewards	More rewards, but still punishment dominated	Reward dominated	Employees set own goals and appraise results
Communication style	Downward, little use of teamwork	Downward, with some limited teamwork	Employees give opinions	Extensive multiway communication both laterally and vertically
Decision-making style	Decisions made at top of organization	Management sets boundaries	Management consults but makes final decision	Group or team makes most decisions
Control mechanisms	Process and output managed from the top	Management sets boundaries	More output control than process	Team appraises results

Source: Adapted from Likert, R., and Jane Likert. 1976. New Ways of Managing Conflict. New York: McGraw-Hill.

relates to a general leadership orientation, preferred motivational techniques, communication style, decision-making style, and controlling style.

Based on the early studies of U.S. workers, we can conclude that leaders choose behaviors that focus on initiating structure for task completion or on meeting the social and emotional needs of workers. Which style of leader behavior is best? Perhaps it all depends on the situation. In later sections, you will see that contemporary U.S. leadership theories challenge the assumption that one style of leadership behavior fits all situations. Before considering that issue, however, we will look at leadership as perceived in Japan.

Japanese Perspectives on Leader Behaviors

Performance-maintenance (PM) theory
Japanese perspective on balancing task- and person-centered leader behaviors.

The **performance maintenance (PM) theory** of leadership represents a Japanese perspective on leader behavior. Created in Japan but similar to many U.S. leadership theories, PM theory has two dimensions.[10] The performance function (P) is similar to task-centered leadership; the manager guides and pressures subordinates to achieve increasing levels of group performance. The performance (P) side of PM leadership has two components. First, the leader works for or with subordinates to develop work procedures, called the planning component. Second, the leader pressures employees to put forth the effort and to do good work; this is the pressure component. The maintenance function (M) is similar to person-centered leadership. It represents behaviors that promote group stability and social interaction.

One key difference exists between the Japanese PM approach and the U.S. perspective on task- and person-centered leadership. The Japanese PM leader focuses on influencing groups. The U.S. task- or person-centered leader focuses on influencing individuals.

PM theory suggests that groups perform best when both P and M are present. That is, a leader can pressure a group to increase levels of performance as long as the leader also supports the social interaction needs of the group, the M function. The theory suggests that the positive effects of combining the P and M leadership components should work in all cultural settings. However, in adapting to national differences, many Japanese companies use modified versions of PM theory to manage their overseas operations.[11]

The next section presents an overview of a more complex view of leadership, called contingency theory. It shows the historical progression of leadership theory beyond the simple trait and behavior models.

Contingency Theories

The early models of leadership tended to look for leadership universals: Managers and researchers wanted to know which leadership traits or behaviors defined excellent leadership in all situations. After years of study, experts concluded that "it all depends"; no one leadership style works best for all situations. This conclusion led to an approach to leadership known as **contingency theory**, which assumes that the appropriate type of styles and leaders depends on the situation. To lead successfully, managers must choose different leadership styles in different situations.

How does contingency theory work? Consider the next Multinational Management Brief.

The next section reviews two important North American contingency theories of leadership: Fiedler's theory of leadership and path-goal theory. These identify several factors that influence the effectiveness of certain leadership styles in different situations. They also provide the basic framework that multinational managers can use to adapt their leadership styles to work in different

Contingency theory Assumption that different styles and leaders are appropriate for various situations.

Multinational Management **Brief**

Management at LG

The preference of South Korean multinationals for autocratic styles of leadership is consistent with the Confucian-influenced Korean culture: "Father knows best." However, other multinationals, such as LG, are making changes to this approach. LG, a major electronics multinational, used to be one of the most Korean of South Korea's conglomerates, or *chaebols*. The chief executive, Nam Yong, believes that changing the decision-making style is critical in enabling LG to succeed in its global markets. Unlike other South Korean multinationals, LG has been steadily hiring foreigners to diversify its managers. Foreign executives and top managers now represent over 25 percent of the company's leadership, and the new executives are gradually changing the leadership styles at LG. However, Nam Yong's recent comments reflect his contingency style approach to leadership. He recently wrapped up a stormy strategy meeting where tempers flared—a very rare occurrence in a culture that values agreement and consensus. Nam Yong told his chief marketing officer, Dermot Boden, an Irishman working in Seoul, "You know, we argue a lot. Why don't we argue more often?"

Sources: Based on Ihlwan, M. 2008. "The foreigners at the top of LG." BusinessWeek, December 22, pp. 56–58; Welch, D., D. Kiley, and M. Ihlwan. 2008. "My way or the highway at Hyundai." BusinessWeek, March 17, pp. 48–51.

national contexts. For additional reviews of other contingency theories of leadership, consult standard organizational behavior textbooks.

Fiedler on Leadership Effectiveness

Fred Fiedler, an expert on leadership, developed one of the most popular early contingency views of leadership.[12] **Fiedler's theory of leadership** proposes that managers tend to be either task- or person-centered leaders. The success of these leadership styles depends on three contingencies, or characteristics, of the work situation: the relationships between the leader and subordinates (e.g., the degree to which the subordinates trust the leader), the degree to which subordinates' tasks are easily and clearly defined (e.g., tasks for assembly line work usually are clearly defined), and the officially granted organizational power of the leader (e.g., the formal power of a position, such as a ship's captain).

As with all contingency theories, effective leadership occurs when the style matches the situation. What situations suggest a task- or person-centered leadership style? Exhibit 15.2 shows the predicted effectiveness of task- and person-centered leadership in different conditions. Task-centered leadership works best when the work situation includes a positive relationship between the leader and subordinates, highly structured tasks, and high levels of organizational power. It also works best in just the opposite conditions, such as when the job requirements are unclear. Person-centered leadership is required in mixed conditions, such as when a leader has low formal power but good relationships with subordinates.

The theory's logic suggests that task-centered leadership works best in situations that are favorable or unfavorable for a leader. In favorable situations, the leader does not need to worry about the psychological needs of subordinates. They already feel positive about their work, the tasks are clear, and the leader is powerful. The leader tells people what to do, and they do it willingly. In unfavorable situations, such as when job requirements are unclear or subordinates are uncooperative, the leader must focus on getting subordinates to complete the job. In mixed situations, however, employee commitment and satisfaction become more important, and a successful leader must focus time on people rather than on just getting tasks done.

Path-Goal Theory

Another popular contingency theory, **path-goal theory**, identifies four types of leadership styles that a manager might choose depending on the situation:

Fiedler's theory of leadership
Proposal that success of task- or person-centered leader depends on relationships between the leader and subordinates, the degree that subordinates' tasks are easily and clearly defined, and the officially granted organizational power of the leader.

Path-goal theory
Four types of leadership styles that a manager might choose depending on the situation.

EXHIBIT 15.2   **Predictions of Leader Effectiveness under Different Conditions**

Leadership Style	Leader Effectiveness		
Person-centered	Ineffective	Effective	Ineffective
Task-centered	Effective	Ineffective	Effective
Contingency conditions	Good relations between leader and group Structured tasks Low power in leader's position (generally favorable for the leader)	Mixed	Poor relations between leader and group Unclear job requirements Low power in leader's position (generally unfavorable for the leader)

Source: Adapted from Fiedler, F. 1978. "Contingency model and the leadership process." In L. Berkowitz, ed. Advances in Experimental Social Psychology, 11th ed. New York: Academic Press, pp. 60–112.

- *Directive style:* Give subordinates specific goals, schedules, and procedures.
- *Supportive style:* Show a concern for satisfying subordinates' needs and establishing good relationships.
- *Participative style:* Consult with subordinates, ask for suggestions, encourage participation in decision making.
- *Achievement-oriented style:* Set goals, reward goal accomplishment.

In path-goal theory, the key contingency or situational factors that determine the choice of the best leadership styles are the nature of the subordinates and the characteristics of the subordinates' tasks. Exhibit 15.3 presents a simplified overview of path-goal theory.

The path-goal theory projects many outcomes from the complex interactions between leadership and the contingencies. So a complete review of path-goal theory is beyond the scope of this chapter. However, here are some key leadership suggestions based on path-goal theory:[13]

- When subordinates have high achievement needs, successful leaders adopt the achievement-oriented style.
- Subordinates with high social needs respond best to the supportive leadership style.
- When the subordinates' job is unstructured, the theory suggests using a directive style (the leader details very specific job tasks and requirements) or an achievement-oriented style (the leader gives subordinates responsibility to discover solutions).

EXHIBIT 15.3   A Simplified Model of Path-Goal Theory

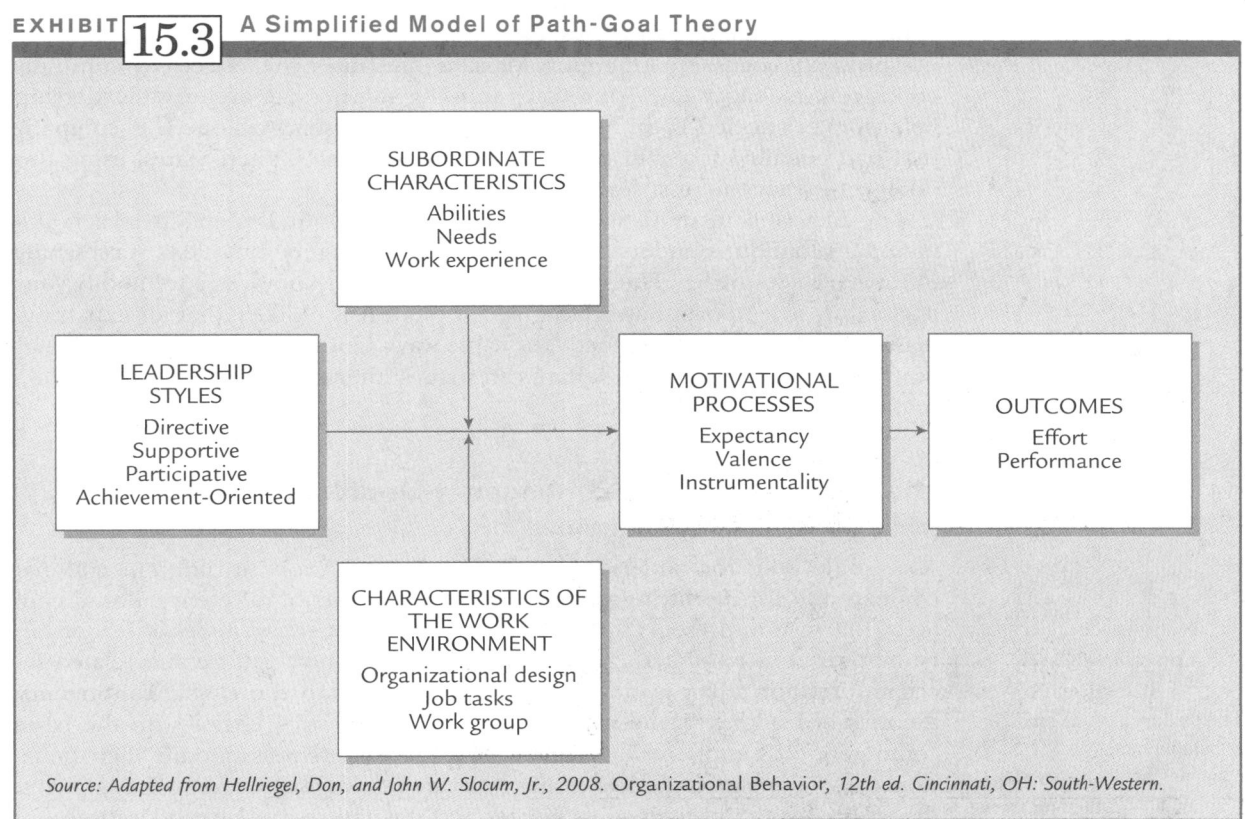

Source: Adapted from Hellriegel, Don, and John W. Slocum, Jr., 2008. Organizational Behavior, 12th ed. Cincinnati, OH: South-Western.

Traits, Behaviors, and Contingencies

Given our review of North American and Japanese views of leadership traits, behaviors, and contingency theory, we know that leaders have different characteristics than their subordinates. However, it seems that leaders can develop the required characteristics if they do not come naturally. Leaders have a variety of behaviors that they can use to get the job done. These range from a task- to a person-centered style and include decision-making styles from autocratic to democratic.

Most experts now believe that no one leadership trait or behavior works in all situations. The contingency theory of leadership suggests that a successful leader must diagnose the situation and pick the behaviors or develop the leadership traits that fit best.

The next sections will explain how national culture and social institutions, such as the educational system, affect the choice of an appropriate leadership style.

National Context as a Contingency for Leadership Behaviors

Most experts on leadership in multinational companies argue that a contingency perspective is required;[14] that is, successful leadership in multinational companies requires that managers adjust their leadership style to fit the situation. This adjustment must occur in response not only to traditional contingency factors, such as subordinates' characteristics, but also to the cultural and institutional contexts of the country locations.

The next Focus on Emerging Markets illustrates the effects of culturally contingent management behavior by showing some of the preferred leadership behaviors in selected Latin American countries. It also shows one U.S. company that had equally successful plants in Mexico and the United States, using two different management styles.

The first step in understanding how to adjust your leadership to a multinational situation is understanding what local managers do to lead successfully in their own countries. The second step is using that knowledge to modify your leadership style appropriately; that is, although it is unlikely that an expatriate manager can ever lead in exactly the same way as local managers, knowledge of how successful local leaders behave can suggest the necessary modifications in a multinational leader's behavior.

The National-Context Contingency Model of Leadership: An Overview

National-context contingency model of leadership
Shows how culture and related social institutions affect leadership practices.

As a guide both for understanding leadership behaviors in different national contexts and for modifying your leadership behaviors in different cultural contexts, this section presents the **national-context contingency model of leadership** (summarized in Exhibit 15.4). This model explains how culture and related social institutions affect leadership practices. Similar to the classic contingency theories of leadership, the model shown in Exhibit 15.4 begins with the basic contingency assumption that to be successful, leaders must modify their behaviors or develop particular leadership traits, depending on two key contingencies: the characteristics of their subordinates and the nature of their work setting.

Focus on Emerging Markets

Leadership Styles in Latin America and Mexico

In 2008–2009, trends suggested that many Latin America countries were facing difficult economic situations because of the recession but that some of them would be able to weather the storm. Experts suggested that these economies still presented many opportunities. For instance, Brazil's economy seemed to improve significantly in 2008, while banks were offering other Latin American countries loans. Such changes were likely to continue, encouraging more investments. As multinational companies begin operations in Latin America, they need to adapt their leadership styles to the cultural demands of employees.

Many Latin American countries share a cultural heritage because of their common Spanish colonial history. As a result, many Spanish institutional traditions, such as authoritarianism and paternalism, are strong today. Hofstede also found that many Latin American countries share high power distance, high uncertainty avoidance, and high masculinity. These historical and cultural facts have implications for leaders.

The traditional Latin American leader, *el patron,* is expected to be autocratic and directive, seldom delegating work or using teams. Such leaders use the formal top-down organizational hierarchy to communicate, are relationship oriented, and are expected to be aggressive and assertive. An exploratory study in Argentina, Chile, the Dominican Republic, Mexico, Peru, Puerto Rico, and Venezuela confirms that the leaders in these countries were more likely to adhere to *el patron* behaviors.

Other studies suggest that appropriate leadership behaviors and styles are dependent on the culture. In a study using two plants of a U.S. manufacturer, one in the United States and the other in Mexico, two researchers from the University of San Diego found that different leadership styles produced the same level of success. The exhibit shows their results based on the classification of management styles developed by Likert. Neither plant used a participative management style. The U.S. plant achieved success with a consultative management style. The Mexican plant succeeded with a management style falling into the authoritative range on all of Likert's management behaviors. The equally effective performances of the plants suggest that national culture may be an important contingency factor in choosing a leadership or management style. Furthermore, the results confirm the suitability of authoritative leadership styles and behaviors in Latin American countries.

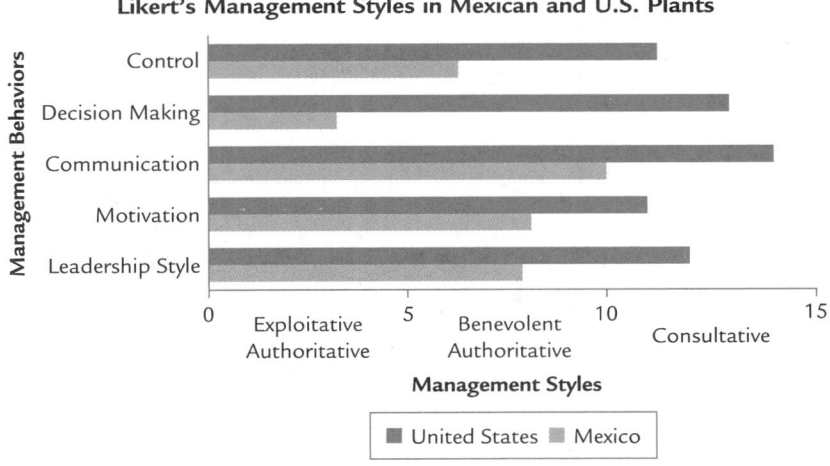

Sources: Based on Davis, B. 2008. "International groups offer Latin America more loans." Wall Street Journal, October 14, p. A4; Economist Intelligence Unit Viewswire. 2009. "Brazil economy; Industrial output picks up," June 10; Morris, Tom, and Cynthia M. Pavett. 1992. "Management style and productivity in two cultures." Journal of International Business Studies, 1st quarter, pp. 169–179; Romero, Eric J. 2004. "Latin American leadership: El patron & el lider moderno." Cross Cultural Management, 11(3), p. 25.

EXHIBIT 15.4 A National-Context Contingency Model of Leadership

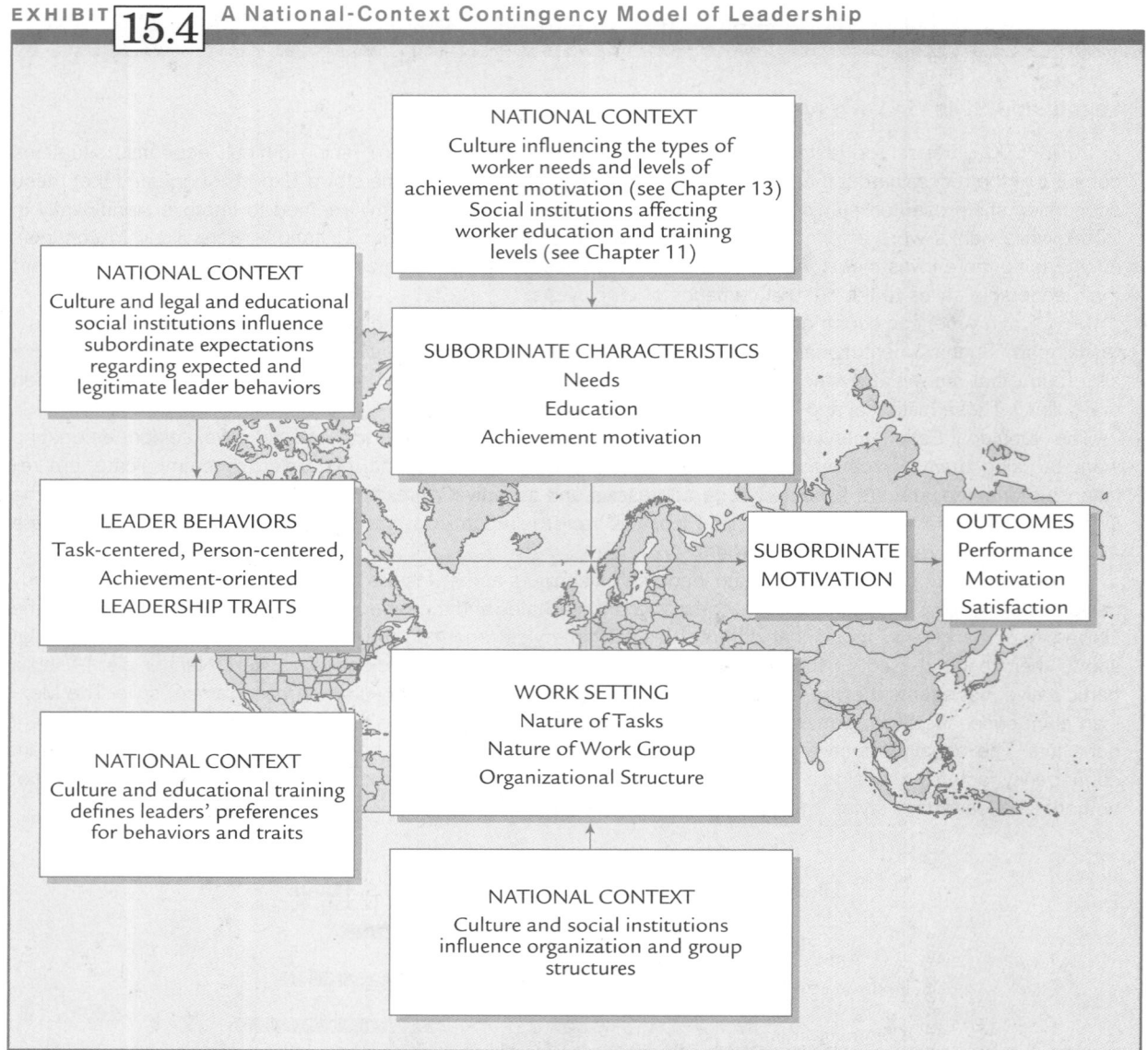

In the multinational setting, however, the components of the contingency leadership model (leader behavior and traits, subordinates' characteristics, and the work setting) are affected by the national context (the national culture, business culture, and social institutions). Here is how the national context affects leadership behaviors, traits, and contingencies:

• *Leader behaviors and traits:* National culture, business culture, and social institutions define the array of preferred and acceptable leader behaviors and traits for managers. Consider the following examples. In high-power-distance countries, leaders and subordinates expect the manager to act with authority. Educational systems like the French *grandes écoles* train managers to believe that they should act as an elite social class. If the host country's legal system gives power to unions to participate in management decisions, then managers must adjust their leadership behaviors to this situation (Chapter 12).

- *Subordinates' characteristics:* National and business cultures influence workers' needs and levels of achievement motivation (Chapter 14). Additionally, a country's socioeconomic development and institutional support for education affect the quality and availability of training and education for workers (Chapter 12). Consequently, leaders must modify their style to fit the types of workers in a given nation.

- *Work setting:* Culture and social institutions affect the choices managers make in designing organizations and subunits. The organizational characteristics, in turn, affect the leader's options in the work setting; that is, task characteristics, such as routine work, and organizational characteristics, such as formalized jobs, constrain leadership options. In fact, the organizational context can be so powerful that, in some situations, certain leader behaviors may not even be necessary.[15] For example, a highly formalized organization may not require much direct leader supervision.

The next sections expand on the cultural contingency model of leadership. They provide more examples and detail on how national culture, business culture, and social institutions affect the choice of leader behaviors or traits.

Leadership Traits and Behaviors in the National Context

There is considerable evidence that people prefer certain traits and behaviors in their leaders depending on their cultural backgrounds. The many cultures in the world have different images of what distinguishes successful leaders. However, there is also evidence that some leader behaviors and traits are cultural universals; that is, they are endorsed or accepted by almost all people. The following section provides more detail on cross-national differences in leadership. Following that presentation, you will see some of the traits and behaviors that seem successful in numerous national contexts.

Dorfman suggests that leadership has different evaluation connotations from one society to another.[16] The United States places a very important premium on leadership, which is seen as a desirable quality having a positive connotation. In contrast, other societies seem to place less emphasis on leadership. In Japan, for example, CEOs typically attribute organizational success to their subordinates rather than to their own leadership. In Holland, where people are mostly preoccupied with consensus and equality, the concept of leadership is thought to be overemphasized.

In addition to differences in the evaluation of leadership, Hofstede points out that the attributes and characteristics of leaders do not necessarily translate well into other national contexts.[17] In Germany, for example, the engineer, not the manager, is the cultural hero. Doctorate degrees are more important than business degrees. In France, the distinction between management and worker reflects social class distinctions between *cadres* and *noncadres*. Becoming a member of the *cadre* requires graduating from one of the *grandes écoles* and, usually, coming from the correct social class. In the Netherlands, a desired leadership trait is modesty, in contrast to the trait of assertiveness usually valued in the United States. In the Chinese family business, the leader is the patriarch, the oldest male head of the family.

The very latest research on cross-national differences in leadership is the project called GLOBE (Global Leadership and Organizational Behavior Effectiveness). The GLOBE study (Chapter 2) contains insights that can help the multinational manager develop a leadership style to navigate successfully the maze of cultural settings. Led by Robert House, nearly 200 researchers from

60 countries are looking at what makes a leader successful and to what extent leader behaviors and traits are contingent on the national context.[18] Prior to this comprehensive study, we had studies that considered leadership in only a few countries at a time.

The GLOBE research team assembled a list of more than 100 leader behaviors and traits. They asked people—from countries representing the majority of the world's population and from every continent—whether these traits or behaviors inhibit a person's leadership or contribute to leadership success. The first task of the team was to see which leadership traits and behaviors are "culturally endorsed," that is, considered best for a leader in a particular national context. The GLOBE team found that most people, regardless of cultural background, believe that some traits and behaviors lead to outstanding leadership whereas other traits and behaviors prevent managers from leading successfully. We consider these traits and behaviors cultural universals because they seem to work for everyone regardless of cultural or national background. Exhibit 15.5 shows a list of the universally acceptable or disliked behaviors and traits identified by the GLOBE study. The implication for the multinational manager is that one can adopt these traits or behaviors and behave within cultural expectations almost anywhere in the world.

Another way of looking at the leadership traits and behaviors is to consider groups of them that represent different leadership styles. Earlier in the chapter you saw the classic distinctions among leadership styles focusing on the person versus the task leader and on the degree of participation. The GLOBE research team identified leadership styles that are particularly relevant to leadership in other cultural settings. Some are similar to the classic leadership style distinctions. We consider five here: team-oriented, self-protective, participative, humane, and autonomous.

The team-oriented style characterizes a leader who is an integrator, who is diplomatic and benevolent, and who works collaboratively with the team. The self-protective leader is self-centered, status conscious, procedural, and a face-saver. The participative leader is a delegator and encourages subordinate participation in decisions. The humane style characterizes leaders who have modesty and a compassionate orientation. Finally, the autonomous leader—individualistic, independent, and unique—is expected to act in a self-interested fashion.

EXHIBIT 15.5 Culture-Free Positively and Negatively Regarded Leadership Traits and Behaviors from 60 Countries

Positively Regarded Traits and Behaviors		Negatively Regarded Traits Behaviors
Trustworthy	Dependable	Loner
Just	Intelligent	Asocial
Honest	Decisive	Not cooperative
Plans ahead	Effective bargainer	Nonexplicit
Encouraging	Win-win problem solver	Egocentric
Positive	Skilled administrator	Ruthless
Dynamic	Communicator	Dictatorial
Motivator	Informed	
Confidence builder	Team builder	

Source: Adapted from Den Hartog, Deanne N., Robert J. House, Paul J. Hanges, Peter W. Dorfman, S. Antonio Ruiz-Quintanna, and 170 associates. 1999. "Culture specific and cross-culturally generalizable implicit leadership theories: Are attributes of charismatic/transformational leadership universally endorsed?" Leadership Quarterly, 10, pp. 219–256.

To compare leadership behaviors, we use the GLOBE's study grouping of countries by clusters,[19] which are convenient to summarize information regarding how countries are similar as well as how they differ.[20] We consider ten clusters: the Anglo cluster, the Confucian Asia cluster, the East Europe cluster, the Germanic Europe cluster, the Latin America cluster, the Latin Europe cluster, the Middle East cluster, the Nordic Europe cluster, the Southern Asia cluster, and the Sub-Saharan cluster.

Exhibit 15.6 shows the countries included in each cluster, and Exhibit 15.7 shows how each style varies across clusters representing a large sample of nations representing Asia, Africa, Europe, the Middle East, and North America. As shown in the exhibits, there are differences in the various leadership styles based on cultural differences. For instance, it is not surprising to find that team-oriented leaders are preferred in Latin European, East European, and Southern Asian societies. Latin European societies have had a history of socialist governments, corresponding with collectivism rather than individualism.[21] Similarly, Southern Asian societies are high on collectivism, and leaders who are willing to be collaborative and diplomatic and who respect the group and the collective are likely to succeed.[22] Surprisingly, East European societies prefer high team-oriented leaders. However, these societies have had long periods of communism when people have had to rely on each other to satisfy basic needs. It is also possible that the presence of many multinational companies in these countries and the use of teams are gradually encouraging East Europeans to view team-oriented leaders in a better light.

The participative leader delegates and encourages subordinates to participate in decisions. Exhibit 15.8 shows that the Anglo, Nordic European, and Germanic European clusters have the highest score on this dimension. Germanic and Nordic European countries all have systems that emphasize economic developments through cooperation between workers and employers rather than

EXHIBIT 15.6   GLOBE's Study Clusters and Countries Included in Each

Anglo	Eastern Europe	East Europe	Latin America	Confucian Asia
Australia	Israel	Albania	Argentina	China
Canada	Italy	Georgia	Bolivia	Hong Kong
Ireland	Portugal	Greece	Brazil	Japan
New Zealand	Spain	Hungary	Colombia	Singapore
South Africa (White)	France	Kazakhstan	Costa Rica	South Korea
United Kingdom	Switzerland (French)	Poland	El Salvador	Taiwan
United States		Russia	Guatemala	
		Slovenia	Mexico	
			Venezuela	

Nordic Europe	Germanic Europe	Sub-Saharan Africa	Middle East	Southern Asia
Denmark	Austria	Namibia	Qatar	India
Finland	Switzerland	Nigeria	Morocco	Indonesia
Sweden	Netherlands	South Africa (Black)	Turkey	Philippines
	Germany (former East)	Zambia	Egypt	Malaysia
	Germany (former West)	Zimbabwe	Kuwait	Thailand
				Iran

Source: Adapted from Gupta, Vipin, Paul J. Hanges, and Peter Dorfman. 2002. "Cultural clusters: Methodology and findings." Journal of World Business, 37, pp. 11–15.

confrontational means.[23] This desire for cooperation and harmony between labor and capital means that effective leaders are seen as those who are willing to listen to their subordinates and accept their input. Anglo cultures tend to be very individualistic, and individualism is synonymous with people valuing their

EXHIBIT 15.7   Culturally Contingent Beliefs Regarding Effective Leadership Styles

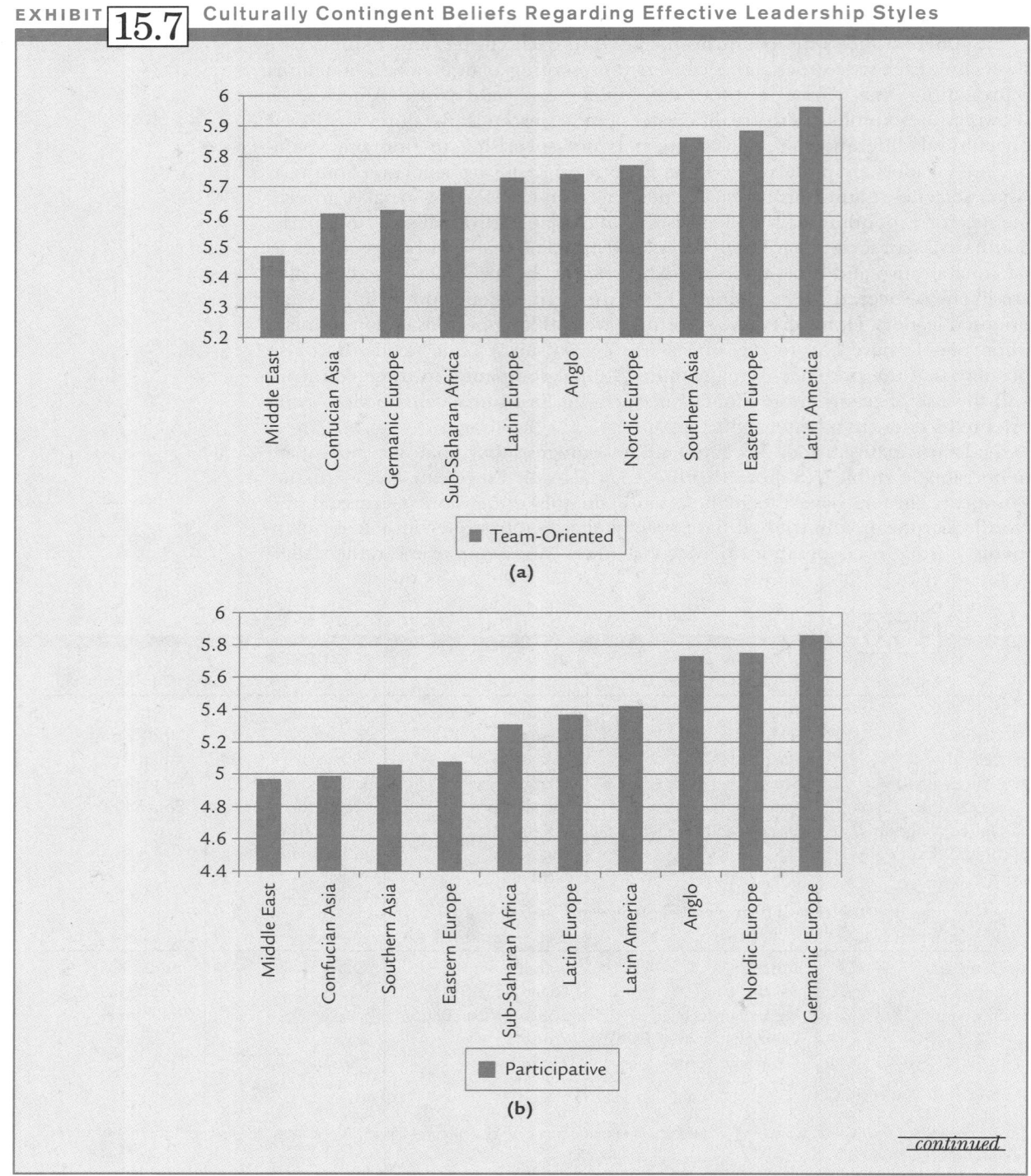

(a)

(b)

continued

EXHIBIT 15.7 Continued

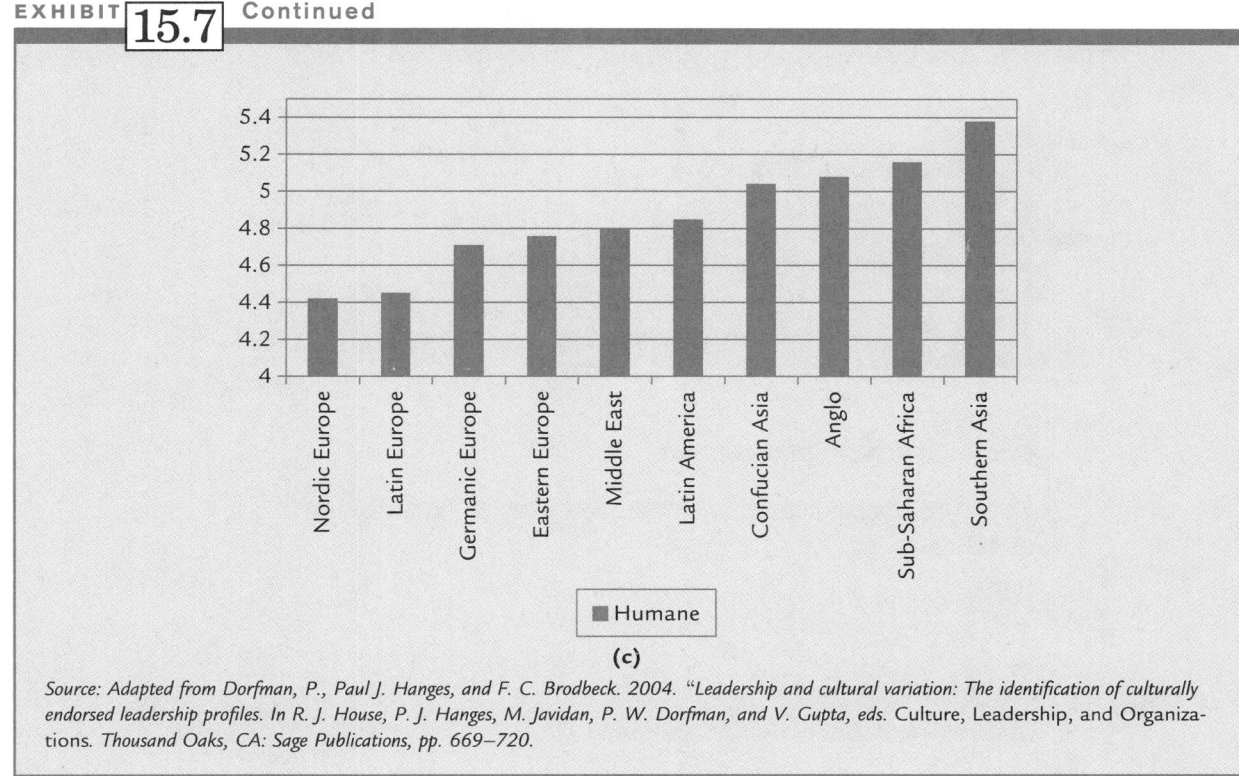

(c)

Source: Adapted from Dorfman, P., Paul J. Hanges, and F. C. Brodbeck. 2004. "Leadership and cultural variation: The identification of culturally endorsed leadership profiles. In R. J. House, P. J. Hanges, M. Javidan, P. W. Dorfman, and V. Gupta, eds. Culture, Leadership, and Organizations. Thousand Oaks, CA: Sage Publications, pp. 669–720.

freedom and having a say in decisions that affect them. Leaders who allow subordinates to have their say through participative leadership are more likely to be viewed as effective.[24] Furthermore, all these cultures have low power distance; that is, subordinates are encouraged to have a say in decision making.

The humane-oriented leader is fair, altruistic, friendly, generous, and caring.[25] All country clusters rate the humane leader highly, suggesting that this leadership orientation is almost universally seen as a very desirable trait in successful leaders. Exhibit 15.8 shows that the Southern Asian cluster scored the highest on this leadership dimension. The score can be attributed to the generally benevolent and humane orientation of most Southern Asian societies, such as India, Thailand, and Malaysia.

As for the autonomous leader, most country clusters see autonomy as an impediment to effective leadership. Results were similar for the self-protective leader. The clusters with the highest score on autonomy are the Germanic and East European clusters. Their scores, however, were slightly higher than 4, indicating that these clusters were generally indifferent as to the propensity of autonomous leadership to either contribute to or impede effective leadership. The scores for the self-protective leadership were all fairly similar and were all lower than 4, indicating that all country clusters felt that self-protective leadership hindered effective leadership. Taken together, results for autonomous and self-protective leadership are consistent with Den Hartog et al.'s findings that certain leadership characteristics, such as being a loner or egocentric, are negatively regarded universally.[26]

Thus, leadership characteristics and behaviors vary across countries because the national contexts produce differences in the repertoire of behaviors and traits

EXHIBIT 15.8   Preferred Leader Influence Tactics in Four Countries

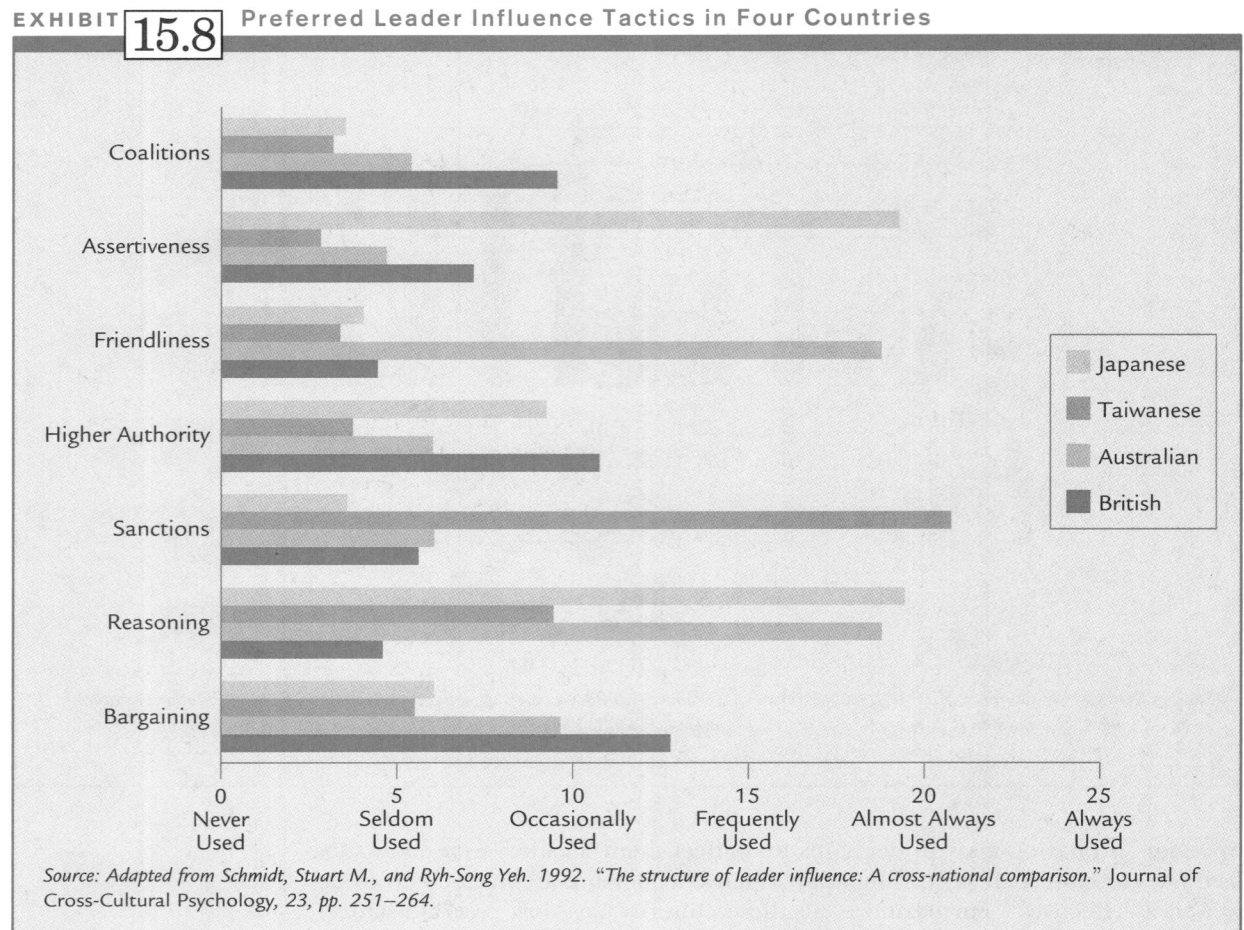

Source: Adapted from Schmidt, Stuart M., and Ryh-Song Yeh. 1992. "The structure of leader influence: A cross-national comparison." Journal of Cross-Cultural Psychology, 23, pp. 251–264.

available to managers. Both superiors and subordinates see the leader's task or person orientation based on culturally and institutionally defined sets of leader behaviors; that is, each national context has its own acceptable ways to communicate a leader's concerns for tasks or people. To lead successfully in multinational companies, managers must be particularly sensitive in using locally appropriate leadership behaviors to communicate their intended leadership styles.

The next section shows that even the basic tactics leaders use to manage subordinates vary by the national context.

National Context and Preferred Leader Influence Tactics

Beyond broad approaches to leadership behaviors, one can look at the specific tactical behaviors leaders use to influence subordinates. U.S. managers favor seven major **influence tactics**.[27] Here they are, with examples for each:

Influence tactics
Tactical behaviors leaders use to influence subordinates.

1. *Assertiveness:* Being forceful, directive, and demanding.
2. *Friendliness:* Being friendly, humble, and receptive.
3. *Reasoning:* Using logical arguments, providing reasons, and using plans.
4. *Bargaining:* Offering favors and exchanges.
5. *Sanctioning:* Using threats, rewards, and punishments.

6. *Appeals to a higher authority:* Appeals for help to higher authorities and sending problems to higher authorities.

7. *Coalitions:* Building support for ideas by networking and using friendships.

What influence tactics are used in other national contexts? One research study found that most managers, regardless of cultural background, use the same general types of influence tactics. However, different nationalities favor some over others.[28] For example, the British prefer bargaining, while the Japanese favor reasoning. Exhibit 15.8 shows the favored tactics of Taiwanese, Japanese, Australian, and British managers.

National Context and Subordinates' Expectations

Leaders cannot lead without the cooperation of subordinates. The national context also affects subordinates' expectations regarding who can be a leader, what a leader should do, and what a leader may or may not do. All levels of culture—national, business, occupational, and organizational—influence the types of leader behaviors that subordinates consider appropriate or fair. For example, at the level of organizational culture, even university students differ in the range of leader behaviors they perceive as acceptable for professors. At some universities, two 25-page papers for a semester class are a fair expectation. At other universities, students would resent this assignment and perceive it as unfair.

Just as leader's behaviors communicate their person or task orientation, subordinates accept or reject certain behaviors as legitimate prerogatives of leadership. For example, North American workers consider leadership behaviors associated with applying pressure to work, considered normal in Japan, as harsh or punitive.[29]

What makes a behavior acceptable in one country but not in another? The cultural and institutional settings provide a framework for people to interpret leader behaviors. For example, labor relations laws in some European countries mandate that managers consult with workers regarding key strategic issues, such as plant closures (Chapter 12). At the level of national culture, Hofstede suggests that the cultural value of power distance has profound effects on subordinates' expectations regarding leaders.[30]

Exhibit 15.9 shows Hofstede's ideas on how subordinates from countries with three different levels of power distance respond to leadership issues. In countries with high power-distance values, including many of the Latin and Asian countries, subordinates expect autocratic leadership. The leader often assumes the status of a father figure and acts as a caring but authoritarian master. A leader is different and is expected to show visible signs of status (e.g., a chauffeur-driven car). In low power-distance countries, such as Sweden and Norway, subordinates expect the leader to be more like them. Good leaders should involve subordinates in decision making and should forgo excessive symbols of status.

Besides power distance, other cultural values likely affect subordinates' expectations. Hofstede's work suggests that strong masculinity norms often lead to the acceptance of authoritarian leadership, although perhaps this is a paternalistic authoritarianism in the case of the Japanese. Strong uncertainty-avoidance norms may cause subordinates to expect the leader to provide more detail when giving directions. For example, workers may expect leaders to say exactly what they want, how, and when.[31]

The next Multinational Management Brief gives more examples of international differences in subordinates' preferences for leadership behaviors.

> **Subordinates' expectations**
> Expectations regarding what leaders should do and what they may or may not do.

EXHIBIT **15.9**   **Subordinates' Expectations Under Three Levels of Power Distance**

Leadership Issue	Low Power Distance (Great Britain)	Medium Power Distance (United States)	High Power Distance (Mexico)
Subordinates' dependence needs	Weak dependence on superiors	Moderate dependence on superiors	Heavy dependence on superiors
Consultation	Strongly expected as part of superior's role	Expect consultation but will accept autocratic leadership	Expect autocratic leadership
Ideal superior	Democrat	Moderate democrat	Benevolent autocratic or paternalistic father figure
Laws and rules	Apply to superiors and subordinates	Apply to all, but superiors have some privileges	Superiors above the law and take advantage of privileges
Status symbols	Viewed as not appropriate	Accepted as symbolic of authority	Very important contributions to the authority of superiors

Sources: Adapted from Hofstede, Geert. 1980. "Motivation, leadership, and organization: Do American theories apply abroad?" Organizational Dynamics, Summer, pp. 42–63; Hofstede, Geert. 1984. Culture's Consequences: International Differences in Work-Related Values. Newbury Park, CA: Sage Publications.

Multinational Management **Brief**

Subordinate Expectations and Trust in China

China's culture is characterized by a preference for familial orientation and harmony. People generally want to maintain harmonious relationships with others as a way to protect each other's face. So it is logical to expect that subordinates prefer leadership behaviors that promote harmony.

In a study of full-time Chinese employees, researchers examined task- and person-centered leaders and their subordinates' reactions. A person-centered leader (called consideration leadership style in the study) is a leader who leads through mutual trust and respect for subordinates' ideas and feelings. In contrast, a task-centered leader (or initiating structure) is focused on getting the task done. The results of the study show that leaders were more likely to display a person-centered leadership style than task-centered style. The results are not surprising, given the Chinese preference for human interactions and harmony. The study also showed that the person-centered leader was more likely to encourage Chinese employees to display organizational citizenship behaviors whereby they perform beyond what is expected. However, the results showed that not only is the task-centered leadership style important, but that it is very important if employees are expected to share knowledge. Such results are attributed to the fact that Chinese culture favors a paternalistic and authoritarian approach. Task-centered leaders can expect their subordinates to comply given their propensity to display obedience to leaders' orders. Such results show that the best Chinese leaders tend to display high levels of both person-centered and task-centered leadership.

Source: Based on Huang, Q., R. Davison, H. Liu, and J. Gu. 2008. "The impact of leadership style on knowledge-sharing intentions in China." Journal of Global Information Management, 16(4), pp. 67–91.

The classic contingency view of leadership and the national-context contingency model of leadership can guide multinational managers as to when and how to adapt leadership styles given the national context.

We now extend our discussion to consider additional contemporary views of leadership and their applications to multinational settings.

Contemporary Leadership Perspectives: Multinational Implications

This section of the chapter reviews two contemporary approaches to leadership: transformational leadership and the attribution approach. It considers how these views apply in multinational settings.

Transformational Leadership

Most experts argue that, to achieve a great organization, managers must adopt a higher form of leadership known as transformational leadership. Of importance to the multinational manager is the finding by the GLOBE researchers that transformational leadership is considered superior in almost all societies. What makes a transformational leader? What do transformational leaders do that separates them from ordinary leaders?

Studies have identified several behaviors and characteristics of transformational leaders.[32] The transformational leader:

- *Articulates a vision:* Presents in vivid and emotional terms an idealized vision of the future for the organization—what it can and should become—and makes this vision clear to followers.

- *Breaks from the status quo:* Has a strong desire to break from tradition and to do things differently, is an expert in finding ways to do things differently, challenges subordinates to find new solutions to old problems.

- *Provides goals and a plan:* Has a vision that is future oriented and provides clear steps for followers to transform the company.

- *Gives meaning or a purpose to goals:* Places the goals in emotionally laden stories or a cultural context so that subordinates see the need to follow the leader's ideals and to share a commitment to radical change, helps subordinates envision a future state of a better organization.

- *Takes risks:* Is willing to take more risks with the organization than the average leader.

- *Is motivated to lead:* Seeks leadership positions and displays strong enthusiasm for the leadership role, acts as a role model.

- *Builds a power base:* Uses personal power based on expertise, respect, and the admiration of followers.

- *Demonstrates high ethical and moral standards:* Behaves consistently and fairly with a known ethical standard.

Transformational leaders succeed because subordinates respond to them with high levels of performance, personal devotion, reverence, excitement regarding the leader's ideas, and a willingness to sacrifice for the good of the company.[33] However, true transformational leaders are rare. They seem to arise when organizations need change or face a crisis. In the next Multinational Management Brief, you can see how transformational leadership works in Malaysia.

Although transformational leaders exist in all countries, the same leadership traits and behaviors may not lead to successful transformational leadership everywhere. The charisma requires tapping into basic cultural values and evoking

Transformational leadership
Managers go beyond transactional leadership by articulating a vision, breaking from the status quo, providing goals and a plan, giving meaning or a purpose to goals, taking risks, being motivated to lead, building a power base, and demonstrating high ethical and moral standards.

Multinational Management Brief

Transformational Leadership in Malaysia

Although transformational leadership is viewed differently across societies, it is clearly valued worldwide. In a large-scale study of Malaysian CEOs, researchers provided evidence of the value of transformational leadership. The researchers examined how a transformational leader affects organizational performance as well as the ability of a company to adopt best practices of the industry. Results of the study showed not only that transformational leaders indeed influenced firm performance positively but also that it positively influenced Malaysian companies' ability to adopt best practices in the industry. A transformational leader is better able to reflect and examine what competitors are doing in order to adopt their best practices. Such results show that the transformational leader is more open to new ideas and to comparing the company's own performance with that of other companies.

Source: Based on Idris, F. and K. A. M. Ali. 2008. "The impacts of leadership style and best practices on company performances: Empirical evidence from business firms in Malaysia." Total Quality Management, 19(1–2), pp. 163–171.

national cultural myths and heroic deeds.[34] For example, Hitler built part of his charisma by tapping into the heroic myths and symbols of German culture; Gandhi capitalized on Indian culture in his struggles with the British.[35] In addition, traits associated with charisma—such as risk taking—and behaviors necessary to communicate a transformational vision may have different consequences depending on the national setting.

Den Hartog et al. provide perhaps the most definitive test of the proposition that transformational or charismatic leadership is universally endorsed as the key to effective leadership.[36] As part of the GLOBE project, they examined data from 62 different cultures and found that charismatic leadership attributes, such as encouraging, trustworthy, positive, confidence builder, and motivational were all perceived as universal attributes. Although no attempts were made to link these differences to cultural factors, the study showed that some aspects of transformational leadership may be viewed similarly in many cultures.

GLOBE project researchers also looked at whether possessing traits of a charismatic leader contributed to effective leadership.[37] The charismatic leader is decisive, performance oriented, visionary, inspiring for subordinates, and willing to sacrifice for the organization.

Next, we will examine a final perspective on leadership and its application to multinational operations.

Attributions and Leadership

Attributional approach to leadership
Emphasis on what leaders believe causes subordinates' behaviors.

The **attributional approach to leadership** emphasizes the leader's attributions regarding the causes of subordinates' behaviors. We all make attributions when we observe someone's behavior and attach a reason or motivation to it. For example, when a student walks quickly across campus, we may assume (correctly or incorrectly) that she is late for class, or we might believe that the student is hungry and going to lunch.

The most important attribution for leaders is that of responsibility for work performance. In determining how to respond to subordinates' behaviors, leaders make two key distinctions: the external attribution and the internal attribution. The *external attribution* explains a person's behavior based on factors outside the person and beyond the person's control (e.g., natural disasters, illness, faulty equipment). For example, a leader uses an external attribution when assuming an employee is late because of a severe storm. The *internal attribution* explains a person's behavior based on the characteristics of the person (e.g., personality, motivation, low ability). For example, a leader makes an internal attribution when assuming an employee was late because he is lazy.

In making such an attributional decision, the leader responds to the subordinate based on that assumption. If the subordinate's behavior is based on an internal attribution, the manager tends to correct or reward the worker. If, on

Multinational Management **Challenge**

Getting Attributions Right

Paul Jones makes some observations regarding his leadership challenges during his first year as a manager in Mexico. Jones's observations are countered by the perceptions and attributions of Sr. Gonzalez, a subordinate manager at Jones's plant.

Paul Jones:	Sr. Gonzalez:
First day: "It is well past 9:00 a.m. and the office staff just arrived. I must emphasize punctuality at the next staff meeting."	"Mr. Jones wants us to behave as if we were robots. He seems crazy about the clock. Doesn't he realize that there are legitimate reasons to be late?"
"I just toured the plant, and Gonzalez pointed out various problems. He really pressed me to meet all the supervisory staff, but there are many more pressing problems."	"Mr. Jones did not take the time or make the effort to meet the supervisors. Doesn't he realize that this neglect really hurt their feelings?"
Second month: "My managers keep asking me for advice, or, worse, asking me to solve their problems. Don't they realize that this lack of taking responsibility reflects poorly on their performance?"	"Mr. Jones does not seem to realize that many managers feel he is the boss and he must make the decisions."
"I had to correct a first-line supervisor today when he was incorrect in teaching a worker how to operate a machine. The whole plant seemed to stop and listen. These people need to get over their fear of criticism."	"Mr. Jones's actions today created an extreme embarrassment for one of my supervisors. Jones criticized him in public! Now all the supervisors are afraid to do anything for fear of a public reprimand."
"I thought things were looking up. My managers recently produced a beautiful document on how to improve procedures. Three weeks later, much to my astonishment, only one manager had made any attempt at implementation."	"Doesn't Mr. Jones realize that the managers were waiting for him to tell them when to begin?"
"I figured maybe I should try a 'U.S.-style' meeting—shirt sleeves, feet up on the desk, and open communication. But the managers just stood around looking embarrassed. I don't understand."	"Mr. Jones did not act like a plant manager at all. Can you imagine a plant manager putting his feet up on the desk? How uncivilized!"

Source: Kras, Eva S. 1995. Management in Two Cultures. *Yarmouth, ME: Intercultural Press.*

the other hand, the attribution is external, the leader modifies the work environment. Consequently, according to this view, successful leadership requires making the correct attributions regarding subordinates' behavior.[38]

In most Western nations, people tend to make internal attribution. As a result, managers more often believe that people behave in certain ways because of internal motivations, such as laziness or ambition, not because of outside factors, such as poor working conditions. This assumption is so strong in Western culture that it is called the **fundamental attribution error**.[39]

As in international negotiation, where mistakes in attribution can be a major source of misunderstanding, the challenge for the multinational leader is to understand the cultures of subordinates enough to avoid such errors. The previous Multinational Management Challenge shows how a U.S. manager working in Mexico and his Mexican subordinate imposed their own culturally biased attributions regarding the use of time, authority, and interpersonal relations. The Challenge shows what can happen when superiors and subordinates attach the wrong motivations to each other's behaviors. How would you advise these managers?

Fundamental attribution error Assumption by managers that people behave in certain ways because of internal motivations rather than outside factors.

Getting Results: Should You Do What Works at Home?

The contingency view of leadership—that leadership works differently depending on national context—suggests that managers cannot assume that the leadership styles or traits that worked successfully in their home countries will result in equally successful leadership in a foreign country.

What happens if leaders do not adapt to local conditions? The results of at least one study suggest that home-based leadership styles do not work very well in other cultural settings.[40] Based on this study, Exhibit 15.10 shows the correlation between managerial performance and leadership behaviors for two groups of U.S. managers, one working in the United States and one working as

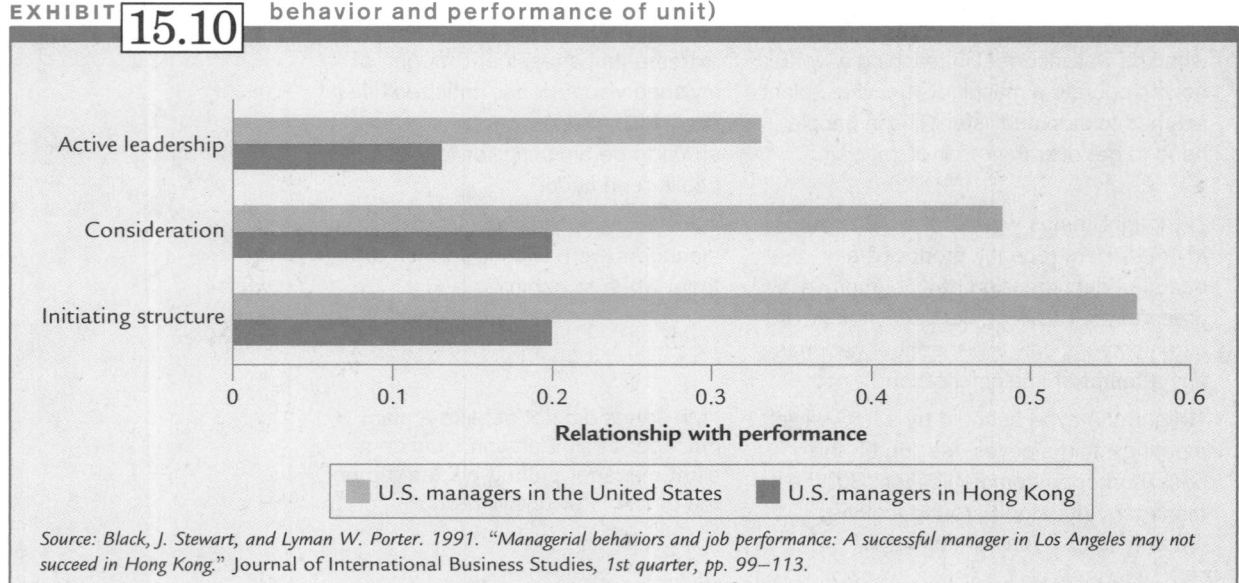

EXHIBIT 15.10

Leadership Behaviors and Job Performance of U.S. Managers in the United States and in Hong Kong (1 = perfect correlation between behavior and performance of unit)

Source: Black, J. Stewart, and Lyman W. Porter. 1991. "Managerial behaviors and job performance: A successful manager in Los Angeles may not succeed in Hong Kong." Journal of International Business Studies, 1st quarter, pp. 99–113.

expatriates in Hong Kong. A +1.0 indicates a perfect correspondence between the leadership behavior and the performance of the leader's unit; a 0 indicates no relationship; and a negative number indicates that leader's behavior reduced performance levels. As you can see from the example, typical U.S. leadership behaviors did not work as well in Hong Kong as in the United States. In particular, the highly involved hands-on leadership style that worked very well in the United States had little impact on the performance of Hong Kong workers.

A possible reason that many managers (especially from the United States) fail in international assignments may be their inability to modify their behavior and adopt leadership styles to be congruent with the cultural setting. This difficulty in adaptation is not surprising. As noted in Chapter 12, selection for an expatriate assignment usually requires prior success as a manager in the home country. Thus, before getting international assignments, most expatriate managers likely demonstrated successful leadership at home. As a result, without adequate cross-cultural training and awareness, many previously successful managers will continue to apply their home style leadership behaviors in their international assignments.

The Cultural Context and Suggested Leadership Styles

Probably because of the extreme variability among cultures and nations, there are few prescriptive theories of multicultural leadership—no simple formula identifying how to lead in every national context. However, some writings by Hofstede and Rodrigues suggest some general recommendations.[41] Using the

EXHIBIT **15.11**   National Culture and Recommended Leadership Styles

Cultural Context: Low power distance and low uncertainty avoidance
Leader Type: The democrat
Recommended Leadership Styles: Supportive, participative, and achievement
Example Country: Great Britain

Cultural Context: High power distance and low uncertainty avoidance
Leader Type: The master
Recommended Leadership Styles: Directive and supportive
Example Country: China

Cultural Context: Low power distance and high uncertainty avoidance
Leader Type: The professional
Recommended Leadership Styles: Directive, supportive, and participative
Example Country: Germany

Cultural Context: High power distance and high uncertainty avoidance
Leader Type: The boss
Recommended Leadership Style: Directive
Example Country: France

Source: Adapted from Hofstede, Geert. 1991. Cultures and Organizations: Software of the Mind. *London: McGraw-Hill; Rodrigues, Carl A. 1990. "The situation and national culture as contingencies for leadership behavior: Two conceptual models."* Advances in International Comparative Management, *5, pp. 51–68.*

dimensions of national culture considered most important by Hofstede for organizations—power distance and uncertainty avoidance—Exhibit 15.11 shows these experts' recommended leadership styles for different cultural settings.

Power distance is important for leadership because it affects both subordinates' and superiors' expectations regarding the leader's degree of directiveness or task orientation. In high power-distance countries, leaders generally behave autocratically. Subordinates also feel, "You are the boss, so tell us what to do." Hofstede suggests that managers from low power-distance countries can usually adjust to a high power-distance country without much difficulty;[42] they just develop a more authoritarian leadership style. However, he suggests that it is more difficult for managers from high power-distance countries to become less authoritarian and more participative or person-centered.

The uncertainty-avoidance norm also affects the range of acceptable leadership styles.[43] In high uncertainty-avoidance national cultures, both leaders and subordinates often feel more comfortable when the leader removes ambiguity from the work setting. In countries such as France, this may take the form of *le directeur* telling subordinates exactly what to do. In countries such as Germany, substitutes for leadership such as professional training may make the work setting predictable and allow leaders more discretion for participation.

Ultimately, multinational managers must diagnose the institutional, organizational, and cultural situations that may affect the success of their leadership style. Too many contingencies exist to predict what may work in all situations, but successful global leaders remain flexible and highly sensitive to the national context.

Summary and Conclusions

All managers who work for multinational companies should strive to become global leaders, unconstrained by national or cultural limitations and able to adjust to any national context. Toward this goal, this chapter provided background information on the nature of leadership, information crucial to understanding leadership options in a multinational setting.

First, the chapter defined leadership and introduced the global leader. Then it reviewed three classic North American views of leadership based on leadership traits, leadership behaviors, and contingency theory. Trait theories identify the personal qualities of leaders. Leadership behavior theories identify the behaviors that signify certain leadership styles; these styles are usually considered person or task centered. Contingency theories identify characteristics of the supervisor, organization, and subordinates that determine the appropriate leadership style in a given situation. The chapter also showed that the Japanese and Indians have similar views of leadership.

The national-context contingency model of leadership extended traditional contingency theories to show how culture and social institutions affect the leadership process. Culture affects the preferences that leaders have for certain styles. Culture and the nation's social institutions affect subordinates' expectations regarding the leadership behaviors considered fair or appropriate.

Using the most recent findings from the GLOBE study, you saw numerous examples of national differences in preferred leadership traits and behaviors.

The national context also affects leadership contingencies indirectly. Culture and social institutions, such as a nation's educational system or economic system, influence the characteristics of the workforce available in a country and the nature of typical companies there. In turn, the types of available workers and the typical designs of organizations and jobs limit the successful leadership options for the multinational manager. In addition to developing a national-context contingency view of leadership, the chapter reviewed the international implications of contemporary views of leadership, focusing on the transformational leader and leadership attributions.

Finally, the chapter applied elements of the national-context contingency model of leadership to suggest leadership styles for expatriate managers in selected countries. Specifically, we showed that the power-distance norm and the uncertainty-avoidance norm suggest different choices in leadership styles. Although it is impossible to identify all cultural and situational factors that affect the choice of leadership style, a careful reading of this chapter should sensitize the multinational manager to the array of complex culture issues facing today's global leader.

Discussion Questions

1. Define leadership. How might people from different national cultures define leadership? What are the implications of these definitions for multinational leaders working in the affected countries?

2. Discuss how the cultural norms of power distance and uncertainty avoidance affect the preferred leadership styles in different nations.

3. Pick a national culture with which you are familiar, and identify leadership traits and behaviors that would be detrimental to organizational effectiveness.

4. From the perspective of the subordinates, discuss why culturally inappropriate leadership behaviors might be demotivating.

5. Discuss whether transformational leadership qualities are culture free. In other words, are transformational leaders similar regardless of cultural background, or is there a different type of transformational leader for each cultural group?

6. Compare and contrast the U.S. leadership-style model with the Japanese performance-maintenance model. Use national culture dimensions to explain your findings.

Multinational Management **Skill Builder**

Leadership Challenges in Mexico

Step 1. Read the following scenario:

You have been approached by a U.S. multinational company that is considering opening a manufacturing facility in Mexico. The company will most likely employ Mexican employees, although management will come from the United States. Your consulting services are required to ensure that the U.S. management and leadership are effective in the Mexican environment. You have been asked the following questions:

- What sources of cultural and social institutional differences between the United States and Mexico are likely to pose significant challenges to U.S. managers as they lead Mexican workers?
- What specific forms may these challenges take?
- What do you propose to help your client and its managers face these problems?
- What specific forms of training or immersion programs would you recommend?

Step 2. After gathering the necessary information, prepare a presentation to answer the questions.

Endnotes

1 Dorfman, P. 2003. "International and cross-cultural leadership research." In J. Punnett, and O. Shenkar, eds. *Handbook for International Management research*, 2nd ed. Ann Arbor: University of Michigan.

2 European Foundation for Quality Management. 2009. http://www.efqm.org.

3 McCarthy, Grace. 2005. "Leadership practices in German and UK organizations." *Journal of European Industrial Training*, 29(2/3), pp. 217–261.

4 Harris, Philip R., and Robert T. Moran. 2000. *Managing Cultural Differences*. Woburn, MA: Gulf Professional Publishing; Rosen, Robert, Patricia Digh, Marshall Singer, and Carl Phillips. 2000. *Global Literacies: Lessons on Business Leadership and National Cultures*. New York: Simon & Schuster.

5 Alon, Ilan, and James M. Higgins. 2005. "Global leadership success through emotional and cultural intelligences." *Business Horizons*, 48, pp. 501–512.

6 Yukl, Gary. 1998. *Leadership in Organizations*. Upper Saddle River, NJ: Prentice Hall.

7 Likert, R. 1961. *New Patterns of Management*. New York: McGraw-Hill; Stogdill, Ralf M. and Alvin E. Coons. 1957. *Leader Behavior: Its Description and Measurement*. Columbus: Bureau of Business Research: Ohio State University.

8 Tannenbaum, R., and W. H. Schmidt. 1958. "How to choose a leadership pattern." *Harvard Business Review*, March–April, pp. 95–102.

9 Likert, R. 1967. *Human Organization: Its Management and Value*. New York: McGraw-Hill.

10 Peterson, M., Mary Yoko Brannen, and Peter B. Smith. 1994. "Japanese and U.S. leadership: Issues in current research." *Advances in International and Comparative Management*, 9, pp. 57–82.

11 Misumi, J., and M. F. Peterson. 1985. "The performance-maintenance theory of leadership: Review of a Japanese research program." *Administrative Science Quarterly*, 30, pp. 198–223.

12 Fiedler, F. E., and J. E. Garcia. 1987. *New Approaches to Effective Leadership*. Hoboken, NJ: Wiley.

13 House, R. J., and M. L. Baetz. 1979. "Leadership: Some empirical generalizations and new research directions." *Research in Organizational Behavior*, 1, pp. 341–424.

14 House, R. J., N. S. Wright, and R. N. Aditya. 1997. "Cross-cultural research on organizational leadership: A critical analysis and a proposed theory." In P. C. Earley and M. Erez, eds. *New Perspectives in International Industrial Organizational Psychology*. San Francisco: New Lexington, pp. 536–625; Rodrigues, Carl A. 1990. "The situation and national culture as contingencies for leadership behavior: Two conceptual models." *Advances in International Comparative Management*, 5, pp. 51–68.

15 Kerr, S., and J. M. Jermier. 1978. "Substitutes for leadership: Their meaning and measurement." *Organizational Behavior and Human Performance*, 22, pp. 375–404.

16 Dorfman.

17 Hofstede, Geert. 1993. "Cultural constraints in management theories." *Academy of Management Executive*, 7, pp. 81–93.

18 House, R. J., Paul J. Hanges, Mansour Javidan, Peter W. Dorfman, and Vipin Gupta. 2004. *Culture, Leadership, and Organizations*. Thousand Oaks, CA: Sage Publications; Brodbeck, Felix, and 44 associates. 2000. "Cultural variation of leadership prototypes across 22 European countries." *Journal of Occupational and Organizational Psychology*, 23, pp. 1–29; Dorfman.

19 Dorfman, P., Paul J. Hanges, and F. C. Brodbeck. 2004. "Leadership and cultural variation: The identification of culturally endorsed leadership profiles. In R. J. House, P. J. Hanges, M. Javidan, P. W. Dorfman, and V. Gupta, eds. *Culture, Leadership, and Organizations*. Thousand Oaks, CA: Sage Publications, pp. 669–720.

20 Gupta, Vipin, Paul J. Hanges, and Peter Dorfman. 2002. "Cultural clusters: Methodology and findings." *Journal of World Business* 37, pp. 11–15.

21 Jesuino, Jorge Correia. 2002. "Latin Europe cluster: From south to north." *Journal of World Business*, 37, pp. 81–89.

22 Gupta, Vipin, Gita Surie, Mansour Javidan, and Jagpdeep Chhokar. 2002. "Southern Asia cluster: Where the old meets the new?" *Journal of World Business*, 37, pp. 16–27.

23 Szabo, Erna, Felix C. Brodbeck, Deanne N. Den Hartog, Gerard Reber, Jurgen Weibler, and Rolf Wunderer. 2002. "The Germanic Europe cluster: Where employees have a voice." *Journal of World Business, 37, pp. 55–68.*

24 Ashkanasy, Neal M., Edwin Trevor-Roberts, and Louise Earnshaw. 2002. "The Anglo cluster: Legacy of the British empire." *Journal of World Business*, 37, pp. 28–39.

25 House, Hanges, Javidan, Dorfman, and Gupta.

26 Den Hartog, Deanne N., Robert J. House, Paul J. Hanges, Peter W. Dorfman, S. Antonio Ruiz-Quintanna, and 170 associates. 1999. "Culture specific and cross-culturally generalizable implicit leadership theories: Are attributes of charismatic/transformational leadership universally endorsed?" *Leadership Quarterly*, 10, pp. 219–256.

27 Kipnis, D. S., M. Schmidt, and I. Wilkinson. 1980. "Intraorganizational influence tactics: Explorations in getting one's way." *Journal of Applied Psychology*, 65, pp. 440–452.

28 Schmidt, Stuart M., and Ryh-Song Yeh. 1992. "The structure of leader influence: A cross-national comparison." *Journal of Cross-Cultural Psychology*, 23, pp. 251–264.

29 Peterson, Brannen, and Smith.

30 Hofstede, Geert. 1984. *Culture's Consequences: International Differences in Work-Related Values*. Thousand Oaks, CA: Sage.

31 Ibid.

32 Ibid; Conger, J. A., and James G. Hunt. 1999. "Overview— Charismatic and transformational leadership: Taking stock of the present and future (Part I)." *Leadership Quarterly*, 10, pp. 112–117; Conger, J. A. 1991. "Inspiring others: The language of leadership." *Academy of Management Executive*, 5, pp. 31–45.

33 Greenberg, Jerald, and Robert A. Baron. 1995. *Behavior in Organizations*. Upper Saddle River, NJ: Prentice-Hall.

34 Kets de Vries, M. F. R. 1988. "Origins of charisma: Ties that bind the leader to the led." In J. A. Conger and R. N. Kanungo, eds. *Charismatic Leadership*. San Francisco: Jossey-Bass, pp. 237–252.

35 Erez, Miriam P., and Christopher Earley. 1993. *Culture, Self Identity and Work*. Oxford: Oxford University Press.

36 Hartog et al.

37 House, Hanges, Javidan, Dorfman, and Gupta.

38 Heneman, R. L., D. B. Greenberger, and C. Anonyuo. 1989. "Attributions and exchanges: The effects of interpersonal factors on the diagnosis of employee performance." *Academy of Management Journal*, 32, pp. 466–476.

39 Mullen, B., and C. A. Riordan. 1988. "Self-serving attributions for performance in naturalistic settings: A meta-analytic review." *Journal of Applied Social Psychology*, 18, pp. 3–22.

40 Black, J. Stewart, and Lyman W. Porter. 1991. "Managerial behaviors and job performance: A successful manager in Los Angeles may not succeed in Hong Kong." *Journal of International Business Studies*, 1st quarter, pp. 99–113.

41 Hofstede, Geert. 1991. *Cultures and Organizations: Software of the Mind*. London: McGraw-Hill; Rodrigues.

42 Ibid.

43 Ibid.

Old Corporate Ways Fade as New Korean Generation Asserts Itself

Until a few years ago, there was an unwritten rule about working hours at South Korea's leading food and beverage company. "Everyone sat at their desks, fidgeting and waiting for their superiors to leave. Assistant managers waited for managers to leave. The managers waited for the bosses upstairs to leave," said Kim Jang-ok, 40, a customer service manager at Cheil Jedang Corp. So for Kim, Lee Wook-jae presents a cultural shock. Lee, a 27-year-old assistant marketing manager, doesn't wait for the bosses. He leaves when he pleases.

He also comes to work in khaki pants and an open-necked shirt, a cell telephone dangling from a cord around his neck. His black hair is dyed chestnut brown with yellow strains. "I want to be judged by what I do for the company, not by my hairstyle," Lee said. Thanks to young office workers such as Lee, a growing number of companies are abandoning South Korea's rigid corporate culture for a global one.

But staid old Korea, Inc. isn't dead. Most companies still prefer top-down management. Sons inherit businesses from fathers. Most employees address each other by their titles. Suits with ties are standard attire in most offices. The rise of Internet start-ups with their casual and egalitarian ways, the new generation of assertive youths entering the job market, and the disintegration of some of the country's top conglomerates have undermined old hierarchies. Lee, who majored in business management at Ohio State University, is among thousands of Koreans returning home every year armed with U.S. college diplomas and Western ways. "When I first dyed my hair some months ago, everyone in the office looked at me as if I did something wrong," said Lee. "After a while, they accepted it. Now they even comment on how well my latest color came out."

Women are making halting progress too in male-oriented corporate Korea. They still earn less and are promoted less, but "We no longer deliver coffee for male workers. That ended three or four years ago. We get more chances to demonstrate our abilities" said Kim Yoon-hee, 28, a colleague of Lee's at Cheil Jedang. "Still, many men look uncomfortable to talk business with women," she said. "When I sit down for contract negotiations, for example, some of the men across the table first give me a look that says, 'What is this woman doing here?'"

The old system was shaken to its roots during the Asian economic crisis of the late 1990s. People began questioning whether staffers trained to think alike were flexible enough to react to sharp global market changes. "It was not uncommon for the one-man boss to shout at a lower-ranking official briefing him, 'Who's this fool? Get out!' " said Choi Hae-pyong, describing his management experience at an electronic components arm of South Korea's largest conglomerate, Samsung. At 39, Choi is beyond dying his hair but is still adventurous enough to have quit Samsung last year with two colleagues to start their own business, making components for flat-panel computer screens. At Samsung, he said, "They put brutal pressure on employees to force good results. But under such a system, you try to keep the status quo and not make any mistakes. You don't try to be creative. Now I no longer have the safety of working in big business. But at least now I work for myself. I feel good," Choi said.

These days, more companies are urging their employees to get lean and creative. Big corporations such as Cheil Jedang, LG Electronics, and SK encourage workers to shed sober suits and stiff ties. They have also abolished many executive posts to speed up decision making. At Cheil Jedang, gone are big desks and long titles for managers. Individual merit determines wage increases and promotion. Workers who used to say "Mr. Manager Kim" now say "Mr. Kim." Employees in casual attire sit with legs crossed and talk business—in stark contrast to other big business offices where employees still work in suits and ties, and young staffers bow to the boss or stand at attention. "In the past, everybody dressed and looked more or less the same. Everybody got promoted at the same time and had the same salary increases," said Kim, the customer service manager. "In the old days, you got to the senior managers only when you were summoned," he said. "Now, we see young employees going directly to senior managers with opinions. For example, they come to me to ask for more responsible jobs, rather than the dull work of typing data into the computer."

Until recently, working for the nation's top conglomerates conferred status. Now, more college graduates prefer Internet start-ups and foreign businesses. "Loyalty to the company used to be a big motto, and your life centered on what you did at the company," said Ha Il-won, a midlevel manager at a construction arm of the SK conglomerate. "But the Asian financial crisis shattered our illusion about lifetime employment at one company. We became more individualistic." Previously, companies hired students with good school grades and required them to pass a written test. Today, many recruiters are just as likely to choose independent people who have traveled or worked abroad. "Interviewers were more interested in listening to what I had to say than asking standard questions. They asked me what I thought of antiglobalization activists," said Park Ji-sook, 24, a French major who was hired by LG Electronics while protests were going on against the World Trade Organization meeting in Seattle in late 1999. Park said she spoke well of the activists' success in attracting media attention to their demands through the well-publicized protests.

The company made her an editor of its Internet Web site.

CASE DISCUSSION QUESTIONS

1. What institutional factors are driving changes in Korean business culture?
2. How can organizations in a culture that values respect for age differences manage the changes that occur when organizational necessities require younger mangers to supervise older managers?
3. How will Korean companies manage more individualistic employees without losing the competitive advantage of a loyal workforce?

REFERENCE

1 Choe, Sang-Hun. 2001. Associated Press. http://www.asianweek .com/2001_02_02/biz4_koreanbizculture.html.

Cheung Yan: China's Paper Queen

It was August 2008, and Cheung Yan (张茵), the 51-year-old chairperson and co-founder of the Nine Dragons Paper Holdings Company ("Nine Dragons"), could look back upon a successful year. Nine Dragons had, three months earlier, acquired a controlling interest in a Vietnamese paper mill, thereby expediting the company's entry into the South-East Asian markets.[1] For Cheung, this was just another milestone in an illustrious career. In November 2006, Forbes magazine had ranked Cheung the richest woman (and the fifth-richest person) in China, with a fortune of US$ 1.35 billion.[2] By any measure, Cheung was a truly successful business leader. The firm she had founded just over a decade ago, in 1995, was by June 2007 a pulp and paper powerhouse—it had 13 giant papermaking machines, about 8,600 full-time employees, US$1.4 billion in annual revenue and US$300 million in profits.[3]

Cheung started off modestly by setting up a small scrap paper brokerage in Hong Kong in 1985. When the market did not appear large enough for someone of her ambition, she left for the United States in 1990. In the United States, with her new husband, she started a paper recycling unit called America Chung Nam. This unit collected waste paper from the United States and shipped it to China. Cheung soon realised that there was a huge opportunity for her in China—there was an ever-rising demand for export packaging there. Thus, in 1995, with a bank loan and the support of her husband and brother, Cheung established Nine Dragons in Dongguan, China. The unit started off modestly with two paper machines and made 600,000 tons of kraft linerboard per year.[4] By 2006, the company had an annual production capacity of 3.3 million tons of containerboard, with ten paper machines running and five more under construction.[5] With a huge expansion programme in place, it was expected that by 2009, Nine Dragons, in which Cheung and her family had a 72% stake, would be Asia's top producer of packaging paper, and the first in the world in terms of production capacity.

In a male-dominated industry in Asia, how had Cheung succeeded in being celebrated globally as a business leader? What were the qualities and abilities that made her such an effective strategic leader?

Havovi Joshi prepared this case under the supervision of Prof. Stephen Ko for class discussion. This case is not intended to show effective or ineffective handling of decision or business processes.

© 2008 by The Asia Case Research Centre, The University of Hong Kong. No part of this publication may be reproduced or transmitted in any form or by any means—electronic, mechanical, photocopying, recording, or otherwise (including the Internet)—without the permission of The University of Hong Kong.

Cheung Yan and the Making of Nine Dragons

Cheung Yan (also called "Zhang Yin") was one of eight children born in Lioaning province, north-east China. Her father was an army official, who was imprisoned during China's Cultural Revolution. Cheung lacked formal education and experienced early hardship, when she started work in a textile company, supporting her mother and seven siblings on a mere US$6 a month.[6] She left the textile plant in the early 1980s for a job with a small paper trading company in southern China.

In 1985, the 28-year-old Cheung relocated to Hong Kong as an accountant at a Chinese trading company, which, however, closed within a year.[7] Instead of looking for another job, Cheung, with just about US$4,000, set up a waste-paper trading business. She saw an opportunity in China's chronic paper shortages. At that time, straw was the main raw material for the manufacture of paper in China because recycled paper was unpopular due to its high moisture content. Hence, Cheung's first success was realised when she managed to procure high quality waste paper to send to China. Cheung's partner in Hong Kong, Ng Weiting, said that Cheung was successful because she was "driven and tough, and had figured out how to get the best performance out of those who worked for her."[8]

By 1990, Cheung found the Hong Kong market too small for her ambitions, and despite the fact that she spoke very little English, she left for the United States. In her view, "vision and methods matter more than language".[9] It was in the United States that Cheung really saw the huge potential of the Chinese paper making market. Along with her new husband, Liu Ming Chung,[10] she started a paper trading unit called America Chung Nam in 1990. America Chung Nam collected paper for recycling from all over the United States and shipped it to China, where it was used for manufacturing boxes for packaging. By 2004, the company, which had shipped 2.6 million tonnes of recovered paper to China, was named the top U.S. exporter to China by the *Journal of Commerce*.[11] Cheung enjoyed her stint in the United States and said that she benefited a lot from her experience there. She found that the Americans shared her long-term views about businesses and had high credibility, keeping to their promises.

As Cheung kept shipping these numerous containers of paper from the United States back to China, she realised the immense potential for manufacturing paper in China's fast-growing economy. An early effort was made to enter this business through a passive investment in a Chinese paper-making company which, however, failed. Cheung returned to China in 1995.

With the help of her husband and younger brother, Zhang Cheng Fei, Cheung availed of financing from a bank and set up Nine Dragons in Dongguan, an industrial hub located in the Pearl River Delta area near Hong Kong.

Fortunately, I had the wholehearted support from the bankers because of Nine Dragon's vision of the business and the valuable assets of the company, so I was able to get the funding. I believed that one day China would be like Europe or the USA. So that's why I started to invest in the first paper machine in Dongguan with an international approach—meaning that I imported the machines from overseas, components from the USA and Europe, and also the scale of the machines was much bigger than my peers at that time.

— *Cheung Yan, chairperson of Nine Dragons*[12]

Cheung's business model was classically simple: it followed a cycle where her companies would procure tons of waste paper from the United States and Europe (essentially developed countries where the quality of waste paper was high), and ship it to China. Freight costs of shipping to China were cheap, as container vessels transporting goods to the United States often returned empty. In China, this waste paper was recycled and used for making boxes in which Chinese-made products would be packed, and then shipped out, invariably to the same Western market from where the raw material had been sourced. When these boxes were thrown away, the cycle would begin again. As Cheung said, her inspiration came from a statement made by someone in the business, "Waste paper is like a forest: paper recycles itself, generation after generation."[13]

On 3 March 2006, Nine Dragons went public and was listed on the main board of the Hong Kong Stock Exchange. The three founders continued to be actively involved: Cheung as the chairperson; Liu, her husband, as the deputy chairperson and chief executive officer; and Zhang, her younger brother, as the deputy chief executive officer.

Nine Dragons

In China, the paper industry was strewn with manufacturers who were typically small, inefficient and environmentally unfriendly. Cheung's vision was the opposite of the market trend—she wanted Nine Dragons to be the biggest, most efficient and environmentally friendly paper company.

As of August 2008, Nine Dragons was the largest producer of containerboard products in China in terms of production capacity. It offered a large range of products in three major categories of packaging paper products—linerboard (kraftlinerboard, testlinerboard, and white top linerboard), high performance corrugating medium and coated duplex board [see Exhibit 1]. The company and its subsidiaries thus served "as a one-stop shop for a wide range of packaging paperboard products."[14] Its paper machines were located in two locations in China: Guangdong and Jiangsu. There were two more units planned at Chongging and Tianjin. The group also had operations in Sichuan to produce high value specialty paper and pulp.[15] It further produced unbleached kraft pulp through a joint venture in Inner Mongolia. In May 2008, the company acquired a 60% controlling interest in an existing paper mill in Vietnam, thereby getting a foothold into the South-East Asian markets [see Exhibit 2 for significant milestones].

The Nine Dragons group showed consistent growth in turnover and profits. For the financial year ending on 30 June 2007, revenues increased by approximately 24% over the previous year to US$1,436 million. The annual gross profit too increased by about 35% to US$369 million, while the net profit registered an increase of 47% to US$300 million [see Exhibit 3 for further financial details].

For the six months ending on 31 December 2007, the group continued to perform exceedingly well. The total revenue amounted to US$976.7 million, an increase of 44.2% over the corresponding period of the previous year. Similarly, the gross profit increased by 30.9% to approximately US$230 million over the corresponding period of the previous year, and the profit attributable to the shareholders grew 11.4% more than the same period of the previous year to US$154 million. This success was attributed to Nine Dragon's competitive advantage, that is, economies of large scale production and the lower costs associated with it.

In terms of operational efficiency, Nine Dragons continually looked at technological improvements to achieve higher product quality. To improve

EXHIBIT 1   Nine Dragon's Products

Nine Dragons' main products included linerboard (kraftlinerboard, testlinerboard, and white top linerboard), high performance corrugating medium, and coated duplex board.

Linerboard

 Kraftlinerboard was the unbleached linerboard manufactured from unbleached kraft pulp and recovered paper.

 Testerlinerboard was a more environmentally friendly, lower cost linerboard made completely from recovered paper.

 White top linerboard was a three-ply sheet, with one layer bleached, and allowed for superior printing.

High performance corrugating medium

 This product had superior strength as compared to standard corrugating medium, thereby reducing the amount of weight and material used, and the customers' shipping costs.

Coated duplex board

 This product had a glossy coated surface, and was basically used for small boxes that required high quality printing.

Source: Nine Dragons Paper (Holdings) Ltd. 2008 "Our business," http://www.ndpaper.com/eng/business/products.htm, accessed October 6, 2008.

operations and management, the company had adopted advanced management techniques and systems, such as enterprise resource planning (ERP).[16]

Vision for the Future

The plan was for Nine Dragons to be the "world's leading fully integrated paper manufacturer, from forestry to paper."[17] The company hoped to expand its

EXHIBIT **2**   Milestones in Nine Dragons' History

July 1998	The first paper machine (PM-1) achieves a successful test run, marking the entry of Nine Dragons in the Chinese paper industry.
June 2000	PM-2 commenced operations.
May 2002	PM-3 commenced operations, raising the total annual production capacity of the company to over 1 million tonnes per year. By this time, further land had been purchased in the Taicang and Dongguan areas of China, so that the production could cover a wider geographical network of the Pearl River Delta and the Yangtze River Delta.
October 2003	PM-4 commenced production, breaking the productivity records of standalone units round the world at that time.
November 2003	PM-5 commenced operation.
February 2004	Established Nine Dragons Xing An Pulp and Paper (Inner Mongolia) Co. Ltd ("ND Xing An") as an equity joint venture with China Inner Mongolia Forestry Industry Co., Ltd, which owns abundant forestry resources.
October 2004	PM-6 and PM-7 commenced production of high performance corrugating medium, which expanded the variety and market reach of the company.
April 2005	PM-8 has a successful test run.
May 2005	210MW thermal power generating units successfully commence on-grid power generation, thereby becoming the largest in the industry in terms of power generation capacity. As a result, the total thermal power generating capacity of the Dongguan production base of the company increased to 350MW, comparable to a medium scale power plant. This assured Nine Dragons a stable and sufficient electricity supply, and also eased the pressure on the local electricity supply, thereby winning government and public recognition.
December 2005	PM-9 and PM-10 begin production of corrugating medium.
March 2006	Nine Dragons is successfully listed on the main board of the Hong Kong Stock Exchange and included in the MSCI Standard Index, the MSCI Global Value and Growth Index, and the Hang Seng Index.
November 2006	Plans are announced for the third production site in Chongqing, to meet the rising containerboard demand in the region.
January 2007	PM-11 commences production, bringing the company's total annual production capacity in coated duplex board to 950,000 tonnes, the largest in China. Also, another two machines, PM-12 and PM-13, commence production of high performance corrugating medium.
August 2007	PM-14 and PM-15 commence operations, and the total annual designed capacity of the containerboard products reaches 5.35 million tpa.
September 2007	Nine Dragons finalises the location of its fourth production base in Tianjin, improving the geographical coverage in China. It is expected to commence operations in 2009.
May 2008	The company starts the development of high value specialty paper production and bamboo and wood pulp manufacturing. It also enters Vietnam by acquiring a 60% controlling interest of Cheng Yang Paper Mill Co. Ltd in Vietnam.

Source: Nine Dragons Paper (Holdings) Ltd. 2008. "About ND paper," http:/www.ndpaper.com/eng/aboutnd/major_achievements.htm, accessed October 6, 2008.

annual capacity of the overall packaging paperboard from 5.35 million tons per annum (tpa) as of June 2007 to 10.15 million tpa by 2009.

To pursue this vision, the following initiatives were planned:[18]

* To expand the containerboard production capacity, such that the company could continue to capitalise on the large scale economies of the paper

EXHIBIT 3　Nine Dragons' Income Statement from 2006 To 2008 (US$ Millions)

	30 June 2007	30 June 2006	30 June 2005	30 June 2004
Sales	1436.30	1153.72	704.51	387.41
Cost of Goods Sold	(1067.08)	(882.03)	(593.48)	(307.43)
Gross Profit	369.22	271.69	111.03	79.98
Other Gains	45.44	52.12	3.52	0.77
Selling and Marketing Expenses	(28.53)	(25.23)	(13.36)	(8.79)
Administrative Expenses	(51.29)	(34.15)	(19.71)	(9.83)
OPERATING PROFIT	334.84	264.44	81.48	62.14
Finance Costs	(9.18)	(43.04)	(26.25)	(12.42)
Profit before Tax	315.65	221.39	55.23	49.71
Income Tax Expense	(14.85)	(16.98)	(8.82)	(7.69)
NET INCOME	300.80	204.41	46.41	42.02

Source: Nine Dragons Paper (Holdings) Ltd. 2007 "Annual report." http://www.ndpaper.com, accessed September 12, 2008.

making industry to become the largest packaging paperboard manufacturer in the world.

- To widen the product range to include high performance products through which the company could get a stronghold in the high value categories market.

- To stabilise recovered paper costs (the main raw material expense of the company) by sourcing from a wider set of geographical locations across the globe, and participating in pulp production and forestry projects.

- To work towards a comprehensive and balanced geographical coverage in China, from where most of the company's business was sourced.

- To expedite the entry into the ASEAN markets, in particular, Vietnam, Laos, and Cambodia, through investment in a paper mill in Vietnam.

In April 2007, the company successfully raised about US$25 million for future core business expansion.

Cheung Yan: The Leader

Strategic Direction

Cheung clearly and simply articulated her vision as: "My desire has always been to be the leader in an industry."[19] However, for someone to have this ambitious vision and actually succeed at it would require considerable effort and determination.

My success didn't come so easily and simply. It's a lot of hard work over the past twenty years. The industry is good. That is a prerequisite definitely. And I have a passion for the business. I like the paper recycling business.

— Cheung Yan, chairperson of Nine Dragons[20]

Cheung's vision and strategy were clear—economies of scale mattered, and the bigger the better. Unlike many family-owned businesses in Asia, her company had not over-diversified. Nine Dragons continued to specialise in paper products and the paper market alone. She looked at Nine Dragons as a legacy, "a long-term business with a 100 years' foundation."[21]

As a Woman

In the male-dominated paper manufacturing industry in China, Cheung maintained that gender inequality had never been a concern for her, and claimed that men had always respected her.

> I didn't feel I was affected by any sex[ual] discrimination in the business community. Actually I felt that whether it was in China or whether it was in the USA, males and female[s] are actually now equal. And in my career development, I didn't feel that as a woman I experienced any difficulty because of that. And my belief is in any business transaction, it's not [gender] that makes the difference. It's actually [...] your intelligence [...].
>
> — Cheung Yan, chairperson of Nine Dragons[22]

In her opinion, a problem only arose when a woman lost confidence and put herself down, thinking that being a woman meant that she was inferior.

Managing the Resource Portfolio

Human Capital

Cheung believed that Nine Dragon's people were one of its critical success factors. She had defined the spirit of the company as "Spirit and Dedication, Cooperation and Aspiration, Excellent Product Quality, Enviable Market Reputation."[23]

Some of the measures followed by the company to ensure staff satisfaction and loyalty included:[24]

- A fair performance management system to realise staff potential.
- Opportunities for transfers and promotions to improve overall staff development.
- Provision of comfortable staff residences.
- A staff communication system where new recruits could meet management three times during the probation period so that assistance in settling in could be offered.
- Adoption of an opinion feedback system to strengthen communication and handle staff advice and complaints promptly.
- Strict adherence to a fair appraisal system based on performance.
- Ensuring competitive remuneration and incentive schemes adjusted annually to market levels.

Cheung claimed to be critical of "heavy-handed family-style management" and had tried to run her company professionally, with three non-family members appointed as general managers responsible for all aspects of the business.[25] However, as of June 2007, she, her husband, and her brother (the three original founders of the company) continued to have a major say in the company's affairs. Cheung was the chairperson responsible for the overall corporate development and long-term strategy, supervising the functions and performance of the Board. Her husband, Liu, was the deputy chairperson and chief executive officer responsible for the overall corporate management and planning of the company's businesses, the development of new technologies, and human resources management. He also assisted Cheung in managing government relations. Cheung's brother, Zhang, was the deputy chief executive officer and executive director, responsible for the management of the company's operations and the business of marketing, finance, procurement, and information technology (IT).

In February 2006, Cheung appointed her 25-year-old son, Lau Chun Shun, as a non-executive member of the Board of Directors. This move was criticised by analysts for nepotism, but vehemently defended by Cheung who said that her son was qualified and exposed to the paper recycling business, and Nine Dragons was, in any case, a family company.[26] She did, however, say that while he would "take priority in being considered as a successor," it would only happen when he could prove that he was capable of doing so.[27]

Government Relations

Cheung had always worked at maintaining good relations with the government and claimed that "there had never been any conflict with the government."[28] In the 1990s, the Chinese government was actively promoting foreign investment, and Nine Dragons, founded as a subsidiary of America Chung Nam to be able to benefit from preferential government policies such as tax cuts,[29] fell into that category. Moreover, as the container box manufacturing industry was still nascent then, the company had been further encouraged by the government.

In 2007, the government stipulated the Paper Industry Development Policy to ensure that there was no monopolistic behaviour and to promulgate open market competition. Cheung publicly supported this stance through the company's annual statement.

As of June 2007, Cheung had been recognised as a member of the National Committee of the Chinese People's Political Consultative Conference, vice-chairperson of the Women's Federation of Commerce of the All-China Federation of Industry and Commerce, executive vice-president of the Guangdong Overseas Chinese Enterprises Association, and an honorary citizen of the City of Dongguan.[30]

Effective Organisational Culture

Cheung had demonstrated an entrepreneurial mindset. Nine Dragons was dramatic evidence of her having pursued opportunities to become a first-mover in the industry. She had also supported innovativeness by being open to new ideas and creative processes, whether in improving technology or in going public with her family-held business. She had displayed her risk-taking abilities on several occasions, and said, "I can withstand a lot of pressure."[31] Whether in the United States, or later in China, Cheung was truly proactive, anticipating market needs. Because of her competitive aggressiveness, she had often outperformed her rivals.

Nine Dragons had been awarded the ISO Quality and Environmental Standard Certifications and the OHSAS 18001 certification[32] in recognition of its superior occupational health and safety standards. In August 2008, Cheung admitted that her company imposed fines on its workers to ensure work safety, and that these fines had amounted to approximately US$152,000 in the previous year. She was responding to a report filed by the Hong Kong-based group called Students and Scholars Against Corporate Misbehaviour ("SACOM") and two Hong Kong University Student Unions, which had described her factory as "shameful among Hong Kong funded companies" for its unsafe working conditions, poor welfare, and violation of labour laws.[33] Cheung vehemently denied the criticism and also went on to mention that the company had so far paid out about US$3,068,000 in bonuses for outstanding performances and to those who had contributed to work safety. She said that her company was capital- and technology-intensive, rather than labour-intensive.

> *The feed-in plant is what the SACOM has condemned most; however, I can assure [you] that the working conditions in the plant are at least equal to or even better than those in developed countries.*
>
> — *Cheung Yan, chairperson of Nine Dragons*[34]

The Guangdong provincial trade unions agreed with Cheung, and said that there were no major violations like those mentioned in the SACOM report, but "minor mistakes" like fines did exist, which the company had begun to amend.

Ethical Practices

In an environment where Cheung would be faced with numerous ethical conflicts, she simply claimed, "I'm an honest businesswoman."[35] In her view, anyone could see the company's results and books—after all, she said, "I run a listed company and I'm transparent. I have nothing to hide."[36]

Following Nine Dragons' listing on the Hong Kong Stock Exchange in 2006, the company's annual statement certified its adherence to the Code on Corporate Governance Practices as set out by the Hong Kong Stock Exchange.

In terms of a corporate governance structure, the company's Board of Directors served as the core, with a separate stratum of management employees looking after the day-to-day operations.[37] As of June 2007, the Board had nine directors, of which four were executive directors—Cheung; her husband, Liu; her brother, Zhang; and her husband's cousin. Cheung's son, Lau, was a non-executive Board director, and the other four non-executive Board directors were independent.

Corporate Social Responsibility

It was Cheung's belief that corporate development had to be accompanied by social responsibility. During the financial year 2007, the company made donations totalling about US$1.02 million to local charities and included subsidies to students from poor regions in China to pursue further studies in the mainland's education institutions.[38]

In terms of environmental responsibility, the company had from the very start invested substantially into facilities aimed at protecting the environment. The paper manufacturing industry was known to be a polluting one as it used substantial quantities of chemicals. Nine Dragons aimed at not just meeting the stringent industry standards set by the Chinese government, but rather becoming a role model for the industry. "No environment, no paper" was Nine Dragons' widely publicised philosophy. In December 2006, the company was awarded the "Green/Environmental Creditable Enterprise" by the Guangdong Environmental Protection Bureau in recognition of these efforts.[39]

Cheung believed that in the long run, Nine Dragons had benefited from being environmentally friendly from the very start as government policies were such that those paper makers who could not comply with these standards were being forced to leave the industry, thereby helping Nine Dragons consolidate their market position.[40] Cheung claimed that she had started appreciating the importance of environmental protection early in her life, particularly during her stints in Hong Kong and the United States.

Organisational Controls

Cheung has played a critical part in managing the balance between the strategic controls and the financial controls of the company. While ensuring that the consistently profitable Nine Dragons remains financially stable, she also made appropriate investments for future viability. For instance, recognising that the company's reliance on good quality waste paper from the United States could be a real risk in the future, she invested in a joint venture in Inner Mongolia to ensure a steady supply of kraft pulp required to manufacture containerboard.

Nine Dragons did not restrict itself to investing in just the paper machines—rather, looking towards the future, it invested in two power plants that provided it with power and steam, it acquired land use rights in case of further development and expansion, and it went ahead and constructed a shipping pier to reduce port charges and avoid potential transportation bottlenecks.

Financial Perspective

Seen from a shareholder's point of view, Nine Dragons had a strong cash flow and healthy return on equity and return on assets. Cheung and family (with about 72% shareholding in the company), were perhaps the most tangible evidence of the company's strong financial balance sheet, with a net worth of approximately US$3.4 billion in August 2007.[41]

Customer Perspective

Cheung had correctly predicted the huge demand for the paper that Nine Dragons produced. Prices remained firm, and net profit margins increased steadily from 6% in 2005 to 20% for the quarter ending in March 2007.[42] The company also used its extensive customer network to assemble a library of data which would help forecast future customer needs and demand.

Internal Business Processes

By 30 June 2007, Nine Dragons had successfully installed 13 paper-making machines, and the average utilisation rate of these machines was an impressive 94.6%.[43]

To boost morale, remuneration packages were competitive and performance-linked incentives were offered. As Cheung said, her company's lowest-paid worker earned between about US$220 and US$350 a month last year (2007), in addition to pension and other benefits, compared to the average monthly income of about US$140 for workers in the city (Dongguan).[44]

Learning and Growth

Cheung would have kept a close watch on new requirements in the market. For instance, to meet the "3R" principles of "Reduce, Reuse, Recycle," the company planned to launch lightweight, high performance corrugating medium- and light-weight linerboard products in China, in a move that would make the company a pioneer in introducing this product category into China, and help broaden the product range.[45]

To improve employee skills, Nine Dragons' staff was encouraged to pursue further studies. Staff were sent to university for advanced studies. The company also collaborated with Zhongshan University in Guangzhou to launch EMBA and MBA courses as part of their staff incentive schemes. Further, students who had dropped out of school in the poor regions of China were provided assistance to study in the South China University of Technology, and then hired after graduation.

Cheung Yan: The Successful Leader

My achievement was a natural consequence of the building of values in my enterprise. The Nine Dragons development was a step-by-step process. Today the achievements are all derived from excellent management in the company and my own long-term vision about the market. It is from the raw material market that I had a good vision of the potential of the Chinese paper market and started to build a business and become successful. In my management, I emphasized a humanized approach and also an approach that you may say is an amalgamation of the Chinese and Western management.

— *Cheung Yan, chairperson of Nine Dragons*[46]

Cheung was proud of her capacity to meet challenges. She often attributed her success to the long-term vision she had about the industry and company. Woo, an analyst at BNP Paribas, agreed, calling her a "visionary."[47] It was also believed that Cheung's "ebullient personality made her a great saleswoman and a savvy deal maker."[48]

How did Cheung, a woman from modest beginnings, succeed in being globally recognised as one of the foremost strategic business leaders of Asia? What are the special qualities and abilities she possesses that has allowed her to successfully transform her vision and dreams into reality? What must she now do to ensure that Nine Dragons continues to grow from strength to strength?

CASE DISCUSSION QUESTIONS

1. What is strategic leadership?
2. What would constitute key strategic leadership actions? What are the key elements of a "Balanced Scorecard"?
3. How has Cheung Yan seen such success as a strategic leader? What are the qualities she possesses?

CASE NOTES

1. Data sourced from Nine Dragons Paper (Holdings) Ltd. 2007. "Annual report."
2. Flannery, R. 2006. "China's richest dragon lady." November 13. http://www.forbes.com/global/2006/1113/060.html, accessed August 23, 2008.
3. Data sourced from Nine Dragons Paper.
4. Linerboard referred to the outside and inside surfaces of the corrugated panels that constituted a box. These were generally made from a mixture of kraft and recycled pulp. Kraft linerboards contained at least 80 percent virgin kraft pulp fibres.
5. Taylor, B. 2006. "Roaring dragon: China's Nine Dragon's paper emerges as a high volume recovered fiber destination." *Recycling Today*, November 1. http://www.forbes.com/global/2006/1113/060.html, accessed August 24, 2008.
6. *The Economist.* 2007. "Face value, paper queen." June 7. http://www.economist.com/people/displaystory.cfm?story_id=9298884, accessed October 6, 2008.
7. Cheng, A. 2007. "The packaging of Zhang Yin: Other people's trash has made her fortune." *Business Report*, January 21, http://www.busrep.co.za/index.php?fArticleId=3636278, accessed September 18, 2008.

8. Barboza, D. 2007. "China's queen of trash finds riches in waste paper." *International Herald Tribune*, January 15. http://www.iht.com/articles/2007/01/15/business/trash.php, accessed September 16, 2008.
9. *The Economist.*
10. Liu Ming Chung, Cheung's second husband, was a dentist by profession. He was born in Taiwan and grew up in Brazil.
11. Beck, M. 2005. "America Chung Nam: Committed to the paper loop." *Recycling International*, June. http://www.environmental-expert.com/Files%5C6496%5Carticles%5C4543%5Carticle3.pdf, accessed September 17, 2008.
12. Rao, A. 2007. "Cheung Yan interview on Talk Asia." June 3 edition. http://cnn.com/2007/WORLD/asiapcf/06/03/talkasia.cheungyan/index.html, accessed September 12, 2008.
13. Barboza, D. "China's queen of trash."
14. Nine Dragons Paper (Holdings) Ltd. 2008. "About ND paper." http://www.ndpaper.com/eng/aboutnd (accessed September 12, 2008.
15. "Pulp" is the material from which paper is made when ground and suspended in water.
16. ERP is a method used to integrate an organisation's data and processes.
17. Nine Dragons Paper (Holdings) Ltd. 2008. "Chairlady's statement in the 2007/08 interim report." http://www.ndpaper.com/eng/aboutnd/profile.htm, accessed September 12, 2008.
18. Nine Dragons Paper (Holdings) Ltd. 2008. "Annual report." http://www.ndpaper.com, accessed September 12, 2008.
19. Barboza, D. 2007. "Blazing a paper train in China: A self-made billionaire wrote her ticket on recycled cardboard." January 16. http://query.nytimes.com/gst/fullpage.html, accessed August 23, 2008.
20. Rao.
21. Ibid.

22 Ibid.

23 Nine Dragons Paper (Holdings) Ltd. "Chairlady's statement."

24 Nine Dragons Paper (Holdings) Ltd. "About ND paper."

25 Flannery, R.

26 Barboza, D. "Blazing a paper train in China."

27 Rao.

28 Ibid.

29 Siegerist, M. 2007. "China's no. 1 business woman." August 1. http://www.erim.eur.nl/portal/page/portal/ 2B188840788F43B32E0401BAC4D012257?p_ite, accessed September 29, 2008.

30 Nine Dragons Paper (Holdings) Ltd. 2008. "Annual report."

31 Cheng, A. 2007. "The packaging of Zhang Yin."

32 OHSAS 18001 certification was created by an association of specialist consultancies and certification bodies, and certified that the management system for the health and safety of the workforce complied with prescribed global best practices.

33 Lisheng, Z. 2008. "Nine Dragons paper admits firing workers." *China Daily*, August 5. http://www.chinadaily.com.cn/china/2008-05/08/content_6669958.htm, accessed 29 September 29, 2008.

34 Ibid.

35 Barboza, D. "Blazing a paper train in China."

36 Cheng, A. 2006. "Pulp making beckons China's richest woman." *International Herald Tribune*, November. http://www.iht.com/articles/ 2006/11/07/bloomberg/sxpulp.php, accessed September 16, 2008.

37 Nine Dragons Paper (Holdings) Ltd. 2008. "Annual report."

38 Ibid.

39 Ibid.

40 Government policies in China had become stricter as the new middle class was becoming more concerned about the state of the environment.

41 Flannery, R. 2007. "China's 40 richest." August 10. http://www .forbes.com/business/2007/10/08/china-40-richest-ent-cx_rf_1008chinasrich.html, accessed October 8, 2008.

42 *The Economist.*

43 Nine Dragons Paper (Holdings) Ltd. 2008. "Annual report"

44 Lisheng, Z.

45 Nine Dragons Paper (Holdings) Ltd. "Chairlady's statement."

46 Rao.

47 Barboza, D. "Blazing a paper train in China."

48 Barboza, D. "China's queen of trash."

Kimberly-Clark Andean Region: Creating a Winning Culture

The culture is innocent. It is really difficult when you are a grown-up to be a kid again.

—Sandra Benavides, Peru

The new generations have different expectations, they have been exposed to new information and trends; they are more inclined to think in terms of people than the generation we grew up in.

—Sergio Nacach, Head of Kimberly-Clark, Andean Region

Sergio not only has done a terrific job in his own region, he became the evangelist, if you will, the missionary for the remaining countries and sub-regions in Latin American Operations.

—Ramiro Garces, Vice President for Human Resources, LAO

In the summer of 2008, Ramiro Garces, vice president of human resources for the Latin American region of Kimberly-Clark, the large consumer products company, was thinking about the many management changes spreading through the company almost like a virus. Less than a decade earlier, Kimberly-Clark (K-C) had hired an Argentinean, Sergio Nacach, from Unilever. Nacach's first job had been to run Kimberly-Clark's operations in the small Central American country of El Salvador. Now, Nacach was running the Andean region for K-C and producing impressive business results. Because of his outstanding results, outgoing personality, and willingness to talk to others about what he and his colleagues were doing, his management approach was generating interest throughout the company and particularly influencing its operations in Latin America. Operations in this area already demonstrated an organizational culture and leadership approach that was largely consistent with Nacach's management style, so he did not have to struggle to implement his ideas.

Megan Anderson prepared this case under the supervision of Professor Jeffrey Pfeffer as the basis for class discussion rather than to illustrate either effective or ineffective handling of an administrative situation.

To make this different way of managing sustainable, the company needed to understand the essential elements of the Andean success. There was also the issue, articulated by another Kimberly-Clark executive not working in the Andean region, concerning the extent to which this success was largely a function of the leader's personality and leadership style, or whether the basic philosophy and management approach could be transferred to other parts of the company—or even to another company in the absence of such a leader.

Nacach also faced some challenges of his own. First of all, even within the Andean region, there was the question of what his team could do to keep the momentum and energy going—to surmount the so-called "Hawthorne effect," the idea that almost any positive change would work for a while until its effects diminished as the novelty wore off. Second, Nacach was thinking about whether this specific management style, which was very warm and emotional—Latin in its essence—really would work in other places and parts of the world characterized by more interpersonal reserve. And third, there was the question of what lessons could be drawn from the experience to help others build a winning culture.

Kimberly-Clark in Latin America and the Andean Region

In 2008, Juan Ernesto de Bedout, the group president for Kimberly-Clark's Latin American Operations (LAO) to whom Nacach reported, oversaw Central and South America and the Caribbean (except K-C Mexico, which was a separate, publicly traded company). This large presence in Latin America represented a huge change from where the company had been just a couple of decades earlier, a transformation accomplished through the efforts of de Bedout and his colleagues. When de Bedout, who holds bachelor's and master's degrees in industrial engineering from Purdue, had joined Kimberly-Clark in the early 1980s, the company was a tiny player in Latin America. Market shares for K-C's products in many countries were in the lower single digits.

Juan Ernesto de Bedout began his career for Kimberly-Clark working under Claudio Gonzalez, who was based in Mexico. Although K-C de Mexico was a thriving operation, in South and Central America, Kimberly-Clark's principal competitors, such as Johnson & Johnson and Procter & Gamble, had been operating for many years and had by far the leading market share. There were also a lot of entrepreneurial companies making similar products, often for one or just a few markets.

Kimberly-Clark had ambitions to build a much bigger organization with far greater business success, which it did over time by completing more than 30 merger and acquisition deals with different entities as well as growing organically. As de Bedout explained, "Some were buyouts, some were partnerships, some were 50/50 equity arrangements—a whole array of combinations," because Kimberly-Clark was competing for these deals with other key players. Initially, K-C offered the purchased firms and their leaders a great deal of autonomy, but then the corporation felt the necessity to bring the different pieces under more control so that marketing and manufacturing could be aligned and the company could benefit from various economies of scale in both production and distribution. "We re-engineered and reduced our footprint from roughly 50 to 25 plants, introduced an SAP financial management and control system, and initially transitioned to a matrix organizational structure organized by geography and product lines."

By 2008, the regional organizational model had evolved substantially and Kimberly-Clark had become a leading player in most Latin American markets, building its competitive advantage by being close to the market and not operating as centrally as some of the competition—an approach referred to by many senior executives as "freedom within a framework." K-C was present in all countries on the South American continent as well as throughout Central America and many Caribbean countries, and in many instances had market shares for its products exceeding 50 percent—quite an accomplishment considering the entrenched competition and the speed of its establishment in the area. In parallel, the company culture and employee engagement were rated very high even though the Latin American operations had gone through a lot of restructuring and consolidation. Ramiro Garces noted:

> Over the past years, we have built very high engagement throughout the Andean region. As a matter of fact, according to the Great Place to Work Institute, K-C Peru and K-C Ecuador were rated number one and K-C Colombia number four (2007 results) in their own countries compared to all the other companies (local and multinational) in those countries. This is no accident, as results this good have been consistent over the last years.

The Andean Region

In 2009, Kimberly-Clark´s Andean region consisted of the five countries of Peru, Ecuador, Bolivia, Venezuela, and Colombia. These five countries faced the same oil and raw material price increases as everyone else, while additionally confronting their own political and economic issues. Venezuela's economy and infrastructure faced problems, resulting from Hugo Chavez' struggles to gain power by using the country's oil wealth to exert political influence and quarrel with the United States. In Bolivia, calls for more regional autonomy within the country had been accompanied by massive demonstrations, occasional street violence, and economic conflict. Cross-border disputes and military confrontations had broken out between Colombia and its neighbors, as a leftist guerrilla movement caused tensions. Despite some natural resources, this was not a wealthy area and certainly it had neither the size nor the apparent economic vitality of, for instance, Brazil. Nonetheless, for Kimberly-Clark the Andean region was economically successful. In 2007, the Andean region accounted for a significant share of the growth in net operating income for the entire Kimberly-Clark Corporation. (Exhibit 1 shows recent financial results for the Andean region and the five countries within it.)

The Andean region's headquarters in Lima, Peru, were in an office building in a suburb. The operation in Peru had been purchased as part of the wave of acquisitions, and initially the people running the original company had stayed in charge. Although the Peruvian company was very profitable, by 2004 growth was slowing because of its already large market share. Mario Escudero, a senior manager who had been with the company since he began his career, described the culture at that time:

> It was a culture where costs were always controlled…. The solution was always to come from better products and better advertising. The sales function was considered sort of a necessary mechanism, but by no means the most glamorous…. Decisions were top-down and the senior positions had all of the power.

EXHIBIT **1**
Financial Results for the Andean Region and the Five Countries on an Index Basis (2005 = 100)

	2005	2006	2007
Andean Regional (TOTAL)			
Sales (in $ millions)	100	117	154
Operating Income (in $ millions)	100	127	225
Country A			
Sales	100	129	167
Operating Income	100	113	174
Country B			
Sales	100	106	145
Operating Income	100	192	451
Country C			
Sales	100	108	121
Operating Income	100	95	103
Country D			
Sales	100	113	138
Operating Income	100	110	146
Country E			
Sales	100	143	219
Operating Income	100	220	563

Source: Kimberly-Clark

When Nacach arrived to run Peru and Bolivia in 2004, two previous attempts to put together an integrated Andean region had encountered problems. Despite an overall similarity in outward expression, there was great diversity in management style and approach among the country managers in the region, and there was some doubt that Nacach could be successful in building a region-wide organization while creating growth and a winning culture.

Sergio Nacach

Sergio Nacach came from a lower-income middle class family in Argentina. From an early age he played competitive sports, such as volleyball and soccer, where he began to build his competitive drive. His parents were unable to pay for private schooling so he was educated in public institutions, at both the high school and university levels. He graduated with a degree in accounting and joined Unilever, a large, international consumer products company. Getting a job at Unilever was difficult for Nacach because there were scores of applicants for each opening, as it was considered a great place to begin one's career—approximately 5,000 or so applicants for 5 or 6 job openings. One of the requirements for being hired at a large multinational like Unilever at that time was having good English skills. Despite his poor English skills, Sergio was given the opportunity to join Unilever. The company was growing about 20 percent a year in Argentina where the economy was doing well. Consequently, Nacach became accustomed to being part of something that was succeeding and increasing in size.

Nacach's initial career took him through a number of different functions including purchasing and sales, as well as to different parts of Argentina. It was during his time at Unilever that he heard people complain about those in other operations—that sales could not make its numbers because of problems in manufacturing and supply, that manufacturing was having problems because purchasing had not done its job, and so forth. And he was exposed to the practice of people looking out for themselves and their own departments and pointing fingers elsewhere as the cause of problems. Nacach believed that this experience helped him understand how important it was to build a culture that was focused on doing what is best for the company as a whole.

Nacach worked at Unilever from about 1992 to 2001, when he joined Kimberly-Clark. As Garces explained, "We were looking for somebody with a lot of energy, someone who could bring new ideas…. We found Sergio, and the rest is history."

One of the attractions for Nacach in joining Kimberly-Clark was that it was somewhat decentralized and still in its entrepreneurial growth phase. After his first two-and-a-half-year assignment in El Salvador, in 2004 he moved to Peru to take over the management of Peru and Bolivia—his first two countries in the Andean sub-region of Kimberly-Clark. The other three countries were being managed by somebody else from Colombia when Nacach first joined. Soon after, however, de Bedout decided to put everything under Nacach's leadership.

Nacach had always loved people and was very much at ease with individuals from all sorts of cultures and backgrounds. His leadership style entailed reducing the barriers between himself and the other people in the company, being open, friendly, and caring. Mario Escudero recalled how Nacach began his tenure at K-C:

> He arrived in February, and in the first days of March he had a conference with the top 100 individuals in his organization. The meeting was open to leaders from human resources, supply chain, systems, marketing, and so forth. We went to a very nice but simple location, four hours outside of Lima. We went river rafting and did some other team building activities.
>
> I think what impressed people the most was Sergio's first slide in his presentation. It was about who he was. That was years ago and I still remember it. He showed us pictures of his youth, of his wife—who also worked for Kimberly-Clark—and pictures of his passion, sports. And he told us a story. He said, "My wife is pregnant so in a few months I'll have a Peruvian daughter." That won us over.

Sandra Benavides, who had been in sales with the Andean region before returning to school to get a master's degree in marketing, also commented about Nacach's way with people:

> He was not a leader that was way above you, that you could not communicate with. He was always available. He always invited you to his office. And when you got there, he would drop what he was doing to talk to you. He would never say he didn't have time to speak to you. I don't know how he did it…. There was no distance between him and the others in the company.

The Cultural Transformation

When Nacach arrived to manage Peru and Bolivia, he had a larger playing field than he had in El Salvador; bigger opportunities but also bigger challenges. He had been somewhat emboldened by his success in El Salvador to do things even more differently and to build an even greater level of success. The starting point for his leadership team was to institute management practices and a culture that would address the three biggest business challenges the region was facing.

One challenge was the sub-optimization that frequently occurred inside companies as a natural result of different units having different goals and measurements and even, in many instances, incompatible financial rewards. So one of the team´s objectives was to get sales to work effectively with marketing—in the past, marketing had done promotions and sales had not necessarily even been informed about them. Similarly, purchasing needed to work with manufacturing, and manufacturing needed to coordinate with sales so that sufficient inventory would be available but inventory levels would not be excessive. The Andean team wanted this coordination to occur on as decentralized and local a level as possible, so that the company's competitive advantage could arise from being closer and more responsive to the customers. As several Kimberly-Clark executives explained, even within these relatively small countries there were important regional differences in things ranging from language and dialect to the feast days and other holidays. To be successful, it was useful to tailor marketing campaigns and sales promotions to these local cultural variations.

Another challenge was to get people to set higher aspirations for what they could achieve, both for themselves and the company. The company had hired a greater number of younger, college- educated employees who were ready for a challenge. At the same time, many people who had worked for K-C for some time were used to operating in a more traditional structure. They did not necessarily have advanced degrees or harbor big goals for themselves in terms of advancing through the management ranks or driving an outstanding level of success.

The third challenge was to fully tap into all of the employees' ideas and abilities, to involve them more fully and completely in the company, and by so doing, to build a deeper, more emotional connection with the workforce and increase their degree of engagement. The idea was to build a company that felt and operated like a community, where people would care for and about each other, as well as the organization, and where there were bonds of friendship and respect as well as the more typical organizational titles and hierarchical levels.

Harold Mongrut, another senior manager who in 2008 moved from Peru to Colombia, commented, "Sergio is an individual who likes to start things without necessarily having them all finished on paper. He wanted us to make an attempt. We could do it and learn from the process. From the very first moment he changed many things and started doing a lot on a trial-and-error basis—do it, and then make it better."

Much, maybe even all, of what Nacach and his leadership team did to transform the Andean region was, by his own admission, reasonably simple and plain common sense, yet it seemed to work very well.

Winning Culture

Everyone in the Andean region of Kimberly-Clark agreed that in that company, the culture came first. Mongrut noted, "It is a people-oriented culture. Culture is always first in our decisions. The people from the company know that when they have a problem that has to do with people—such as payments or rewards or bonus—the company is now taking care of the people first. Culture is not just on paper, but something that we live every day." The results of the culture were evident not just in the business results but in the recognition the company had received from the Great Place to Work Institute. In Ecuador and Peru in 2007, Kimberly-Clark was ranked number one on the best places to work list, and in Colombia, it was number four.

Alberto Paredes, a supply chain manager, described the culture as being open:

It is a culture of sincerity, where anyone can say whatever crosses his or her mind. There is a culture to achieve and exceed the goals, a winning culture of people totally committed to the results. Our people always want more. Achieving the goal generates a new challenge, and that creates a virtuous circle.

(Exhibit 2 shows the values that constituted the culture of Kimberly-Clark in the Andean region.)

Two aspects of the culture seemed particularly noteworthy and unusual. The first cultural dimension was embodied in the ideas of empathy and community and had to do with how people related to and took care of each other. For instance, Sandra Benavides, who had formerly been with Andean sales before returning to school, related the following:

After two years, I had a really big family problem and everyone was so supportive. They cared about me. My numbers and business were complicated, but they let me leave when I needed to. They told me not to worry about vacation time. I was seen as a person, not a number. When I was having a bad time, they had a bad time with me, supporting me all along.

The second aspect was related, in that the company also wanted to take care of the communities in which it operated. So, an initiative called K-C 360 was launched that would soon become a strategic pillar with a much larger scope. As Harold Mongrut later noted:

All the work that has been with the community has been amazing—with our employees, their families, and all the people that live around us. In Ecuador, the company will invest money in the neighborhood so it looks better. Or in Peru, the company invested money in the hospitals so the mill workers will have better care. We are really taking steps to give back to the surrounding communities. There are 40 or 50 examples of things we are doing that make the community stronger, and we are so proud of them.

Hiring the Right People

Sergio Nacach and his team had the objective to create a winning region out of the Andean countries. In order to do that, they needed the right people. This

EXHIBIT 2   The Core Values of the Kimberly-Clark Andean Region Culture

- Culture is first.
- Always do what is best for the company.
- Freedom within a framework.
- Results oriented.
- Customer oriented.
- Personal and professional development.
- Communication and transparency.
- Empathy.
- Trust.

Source: Kimberly-Clark

entailed hiring both more skilled people and people who fit the culture. Rafael Ravettino, the initial Andean HR director, noted that the company changed its entire sales force:

> There was a time here in Latin America when sales people did not have a college degree. All their experience came from the interaction with clients or it was gained in the field. We progressively replaced our sales force, primarily with students from the top third of their class graduating from the best Peruvian universities. That was a radical change, because sales was not attractive for them. So we created a plan to show them that it was a good path towards professional development…. They became advisors for our clients, and their presence gave a big boost to our company.

Celebrations and Meetings

Starting in the first year, and beginning even as he joined the company, Nacach organized events that brought people together and celebrated the company's success. For instance, there was an annual meeting for the top leaders in the company—about 130 people—and each year's meeting had its own theme. One year, the theme was "together, we can do anything." In December, 2007, the meeting's theme was "creating our legacy." The meeting extended over four days and typically entailed traveling to a nice location and combining both fun and serious business.

In December, 2007, the group gathered at the Lima airport on Monday morning and then flew to the town of Cuzco on several different flights so that everyone would not be on the same plane. After a buffet lunch at a hotel, the group went in buses for guided tours of the town. In the evening, there was a banquet at a venue overlooking the city, complete with a speech by Nacach outlining the results of the past year—with many exclamations of "bravo!"—and recognition of various leaders and contributors with much applause and emotion and the presentation of plaques and other mementos. The next day, the group got up very early and took the train to Machu Picchu. After guided tours of the ruins and lunch, people took the train back and organized into groups for dinner on their own. On Wednesday, the group flew back to Lima in the morning and went in buses to a hotel on the outskirts of town. That afternoon, there was a personal development seminar led by a Peruvian professor. In the evening there was a group dinner. The following day, Thursday, there was an all-day session on the topics of corporate culture and leadership.

Thursday night people assembled in *Star Wars* costumes (delivered to their rooms while they were in class) for a gala dinner and celebration, complete with sound effects, a video show, music and dancing, and lots of local food and beverages. Friday morning, many people met in business groups to go over business issues and plans, and then the group dispersed as people flew back to their home countries, to where they lived in Lima, or in other parts of Peru. The meeting cost was considered an investment, and the event was extremely well organized and carried out with consummate style.

Although not as elaborate, similar meetings were held throughout the company at local levels to recognize outstanding individual and team achievements and to celebrate the company's collective success. Nacach believed these celebrations were important to show that the organization appreciated what had been accomplished, and as a way of getting people together to have fun and develop stronger social bonds and networks of relationships. The meetings also helped the various parts of the company come to know and understand each other better. They were an opportunity for personal development and also for communicating and listening.

An important change from past practice was including people from all functions at these events. As Ravettino from human resources noted, "We used to have conferences exclusively for our sales force, but in 2004 we convened all the people working with sales; people from operations, human resources, finance, supply chain, all the areas. In the past, each area presented its goal, but in this cascade [meeting], all the goals were converted into one, to create the same aim for the company."

Dreams, Not Budgets

All of these meetings and celebrations, as well as communications through newsletters and other formats, shared one element in common: although there was usually a review of financial results, the orientation was mostly toward the future, toward what could be done to exceed anything the company believed possible. The word most often used was "dreams," and there was a lot of emphasis on reaching for dreams, reaching for the stars, doing what others believed could not be done. In particular, this meant setting high goals and aspirations for what K-C in the Andean region could be and what it could accomplish.

Ramiro Garces, the head of human resources for all of Latin America, commented that throughout the region the emphasis was on, "It's not how good you are, but how good you want to be." He noted how Nacach conveyed the idea of high aspirations for success:

He has impacted the organization speaking of dreams. So the language in this culture is such that there are people willing to reach for the stars. People don't speak a whole lot about, 'We need to meet our budget numbers.' Well, everybody knows that there are budgets. But the language in this culture is, 'No, we need to reach for dreams.' And dreams exceed what the budget numbers are. During this past month [May 2008], the Andean region exceeded every number imaginable, even those which were considered unreachable. They did it, and it was amazing.

Cascades

For people to feel a part of the company and to make good decisions, they needed to have information. So the company embarked on a process of information sharing. Recognizing that this process needed to be both vigorous and ongoing, they initiated a very intentional, strategic way of cascading information down through the ranks to the lowest-level employees. Gustavo Palacio, the Andean supply chain director based in Colombia, explained the rationale for sharing information:

Managers had arrived in the past, introduced a strategy, a manner of working, and important themes, but there was no consensus among the different areas in recognizing the problem. Every time they tried to organize something, a lot of the problems were related to incorrect, unreliable information. They wanted to make changes, but the people did not think the information was credible and did not feel they could depend on it.

Alberto Paredes, another person working in the supply chain function, noted that this previous situation of inadequate information had changed. "Now, even the lowest position knows our sales projection, and we all work together to achieve it, directly or indirectly. We publish monthly reports, via e-mails or wallboards, on sales and revenues, so people develop bigger expectations."

What's Best for the Company

One way of getting people focused on what was "best for the company" was to make that phrase and what it represented part of the company culture—

repeated frequently at events and meetings and in internal communications. But it was also important to make that sentiment real through actual decisions. Ravettino noted that in the very first regional meeting held after Nacach's arrival in 2004, an important discussion and decision occurred:

> *At that time there was a corporate-wide effort to reduce head count, but if the company was projecting 15 percent growth, that goal was unrealistic. So we opened a discussion on what was best for the company. That discussion is tattooed in everyone's mind and it marked a change of mentality. We were discussing what was best for the company, not what was best for some department or person. We agreed that since we wanted to grow, the head count needed to grow as well. This is how we linked and aligned all goals in one, to avoid conflict.*

The Andean team did two other things to try and build a "best for company" decision-making process. One of these was to change the structure and create GBAs—geographic business accountability units. The GBAs were multifunctional teams responsible for the business in a defined geography. As described in a white paper written by Sergio Nacach and Mario Escudero in 2007:

> *This ... GBA is led by the sales leader in charge of the geographical area who acts as a country manager for his own geographical area.... He also has to interact with different support areas and the sectors that own the products.... The leader of this geographical team ... has the challenge to manage a multifunctional team for the GBA in order to achieve significant improvements in business aspects.... Unlike the previous structure ... in a GBA, not only sales executives ... are entitled to receive incentives, but all members receive monthly incentives associated with geographic achievement and other associated qualitative drivers.[1]*

As noted in this passage, emphasis was put on ensuring that the incentives encouraged—or at least did not discourage—coordination across functions and having people take actions consistent with what was good for the business overall. The sales leader did this by ensuring that everyone involved in a section of the business received financial rewards from its success.

Increasing Employee Engagement

Many things were done in an effort to increase employee motivation and engagement. Ravettino commented that one important change involved the way the company thought of its leaders: "We used to think that the company leaders were only the local board members, only five or six people. We decided that those five or six people did not have the power to transform the company. We established that any person in charge of even one or three people was a leader in K-C. We developed a plan to motivate those who were moving the wheels of the organization." One of Nacach's phrases, repeated often in many different settings, was to "act as a leader." By talking about many, many people as leaders, by reminding them to act as leaders, and by treating them as leaders, K-C increased the motivation of many of its people.

Another way of motivating people was to invest in their development to encourage a close identification with the company. Ravettino commented, "Four times per year we gathered these leaders to train them in personal and professional development, knowledge that they can take away and use in their daily lives. We also include some business theory or topics to broaden their business skills."

To create a greater sense of team and individual involvement, many symbolic and substantive changes were made. Alberto Paredes, the supply chain manager, commented on the importance of the change to a norm of casual dress: "Before, all administrators wore suits and ties, and even people at the production plant dressed formally. That created some personal barriers, so as part of this new culture, we eliminated that formality. We are very informal in our clothes and in the way we talk to each other." The headquarters office in Lima did not have a secured area for the senior people. People called Nacach "Sergio," and addressing people by their first names was common. All of this was intended to break down the barriers that separated people and impeded the flow of information.

In a larger sense, decentralization and delegation of decision making substantially increased. Fernando Soruco, a business area executive in Bolivia, noted that when he first came to the company as a sales manager, Bolivia was considered a subsidiary of Peru. "We followed what Peru wanted and dictated. All of the supply chain and finance managers were in Peru." Soruco noted that when Nacach came in, he gave a lot of power to the general managers. "The first change that we felt [despite] having the areas continue to report to Peru, [was that] decisions were now made at the local level."

Decentralization was considered to be a key dimension providing competitive advantage for K-C, particularly compared to the competition. The Andean region of Kimberly-Clark identified three key initiatives to take advantage of local differences within countries:

> In the first place, strategic alliances [are] with local partners that have a strong position in the area where they are originally from and that are valued by the people from the area, but they do not have strong position at the national level. These alliances are intended to transfer the regional identity from the local partners to K-C's global brands and execution. Secondly, we have the local purchase of local media, targeting inhabitants of a specific region. Lastly … active participation in regional festivities and celebrations … leveraging wherever possible the emotional aspect of local culture.[2]

These initiatives, executed through the GBA structure, allowed Kimberly-Clark to leverage global brands with local insights in each territory, thereby enabling the expansion of its market leadership.

Diffusion of the Cultural Transformation

Because of its origins and the work done so far, the Latin American region of Kimberly-Clark had a somewhat distinct flavor in terms of culture and entrepreneurial spirit. The region had a 12-person board that included three outside members—a governance arrangement that was unique in the company. Juan Ernesto de Bedout, the head of LAO, commented that setting up such a board was more demanding but provided enormous value with in-depth local insights and healthy discussions prior to key decisions.

Kimberly-Clark was connected to prestigious universities in the United States, such as Purdue and Penn State as well as universities throughout Latin America, and was committed to recruiting the best talent—not always so easy in a business whose products did not have a lot of glamour. K-C had an intern program that included PhDs and MBAs from the best schools. Even though the region's business results were excellent, de Bedout had approached the author of *Blue Ocean Strategy* to help ensure that the region would move to the next level of performance, and in meetings was always challenging his team to not rest on their laurels but to try and take their operations to an even higher level. There was definitely a spirit of continuous improvement in the management team.

The region was naturally proud of its results and was particularly pleased by the attention the Andean region was attracting from around the company. Over the years, individual teams from Poland, Spain, Russia, South Africa, the Middle East, and South Asia visited the region looking for best practices to replicate. Instead, they left with the conviction that results depended much more on a winning culture, an appropriate organizational structure, and the K-C 360 type approach rather than technological breakthroughs or other well-kept secrets. In the summer of 2008, Kimberly-Clark representatives from North Asia, South Asia, the Middle East, Africa, and Eastern Europe came to Peru to see first-hand what was going on with the culture that was producing such excellent results.

Ramiro Garces noted that the outstanding business results were the first thing to attract people's attention, and then they became interested in the culture, the decentralization, the communication strategies, and the idea of really taking care of people and the communities. But as he noted, the ideas and practices did not necessarily spread quickly:

> I have to tell you, it's not a process that took place in six months or two weeks. It's a cultural change that's been going on for the last four years. But the more the Andean region was doing these good things, the better the business results were. But you only become a believer once you start doing it. You have to put this into practice. You really have to walk your talk. You have to turn it into practice and believe in this. Otherwise, it's just another program.

What Was Next?

There was no question that Kimberly-Clark had accomplished some remarkable things in the Andean Region, in terms of business results and the way things were done around there. And there was also no question that senior leadership support was strong for Nacach and his team on their management approach.

But the history of such high-performance cultures has not been encouraging. Although such people-centered management cultures had consistently produced outstanding business results and there was an enormous amount of evidence connecting people management practices to various business outcomes, such cultures sometimes did not survive changes in leadership and their diffusion was frequently difficult. Those realities made it important not only to understand the what and the why of the successes in the five countries of the Andean region, but to think about which steps would ensure the continuation and dissemination of a set of management practices that had made such a big difference in such a short time.

CASE DISCUSSION QUESTIONS

1. Describe some of the challenges facing Kimberly-Clark in the Andean region prior to Sergio Nacach joining the company.
2. What did Nacach do to address these challenges? Be as specific as possible.
3. Describe some of the key elements of Kimberly-Clark Andean region organizational culture. Are these cultural elements consistent with the Latin American culture? Why or why not?
4. How easy will it be to transfer the organizational culture to other countries? What challenges do you

see if, for example, the organizational culture were to be implemented in the U.K.?
5. What role does organizational culture play in motivating employees of multinationals? How can such culture be established?
6. What lessons do you learn from Kimberly-Clark Andean region's efforts to build a new culture?

CASE NOTES

1 Nacach, Sergio, and Mario Escudero. 2007. "Geographic business accountability (GBA): Building competitive advantages through multifunctional teams with a market focus." unpublished, July.
2 Ibid., p. 21.

GLOSSARY

A

Achievement-motivation theory Suggestion that only some people have the need to win in competitive situations or to exceed a standard of excellence.

Achievement versus ascription How a society grants or gives status.

Anchor partners A partner that holds back the development of a successful strategic alliance because it cannot or will not provide its share of the funding.

Asia-Pacific-Economic Cooperation (APEC) A confederation of 19 nations with less specific agreements on trade facilitation in the Pacific region.

Attitudinal commitment The willingness to dedicate resources and efforts and to face risks to make the alliance work.

Attributional approach to leadership Emphasis on what leaders believe causes subordinates' behaviors.

Autocratic leadership Leaders make all major decisions themselves.

Autonomous work group Team or unit that has nearly complete responsibility for a task.

B

Backdoor recruitment Prospective employees are friends or relatives of those already employed.

Balance sheet method Attempts to equate purchasing power in the host country with purchasing power in the expatriate's home country.

Benevolent trust The confidence that the partner will behave with good will and with fair exchange.

Bonus system In Japan, employees often receive as much as 30 percent of their base salary, usually given twice a year during traditional gift-giving seasons.

Brick-and-mortar Traditional or nonvirtual business operation.

B2B Business-to-business transactions.

B2C Business-to-consumer transactions.

Buddhism Religious tradition that focuses primarily on the reality of world suffering and the ways one can be freed from suffering.

Building a relationship The first stage of the actual negotiation process, when negotiators concentrate on social and interpersonal matters.

Bureaucratic control system Focuses on managing organizational processes through budgets, statistical reports, standard operations procedures, and centralization of decision making.

Business culture The norms, values, and beliefs that pertain to all aspects of doing business in a culture.

Business-level strategies Those for a single business operation.

C

Calculative commitment Alliance partner's evaluations, expectations, and concerns regarding the potential rewards from the relationship.

Capabilities The ability to assemble and coordinate resources effectively.

Capitalist or market economy System where production is decentralized to private owners who carry out these activities to make profits.

Christianity Religion based on the life and teachings of Jesus.

Codetermination Surrender by management to workers of a share of control of the organization, traditionally reserved for management and owners.

Collectivism Set of cultural values that views people largely through the groups to which they belong.

Commitment In a strategic alliance, when partners take care of each other and put forth extra effort to make the venture work.

Comparative advantage That arising from cost, quality, or resource advantages associated with a particular nation.

Competitive advantage When a company can outmatch its rivals in attracting and maintaining its targeted customers.

Competitive negotiation Each side tries to give as little as possible and tries to win for its side.

Competitive scope How broadly a firm targets its products or service.

Competitive strategies Moves multinational firms use to defeat competitors.

Competitor analysis Profiles of your competitor's strategies and objectives.

Complementary skills One that enhances but does not necessarily duplicate an alliance partner's skills.

Concession making Process requiring each side to relax some of its demands to meet the other party's needs.

Consultative or participative leadership Leader's style falls midway between autocratic and democratic styles.

Contingency theory Assumption that different styles and leaders are appropriate for various situations.

Contract manufacturing Producing products for foreign companies following the foreign companies' specifications.

Control system Vertical organizational links, up and down the organizational hierarchy.

Convenient relativism What occurs when companies use the logic of ethical relativism to behave any way

663

they please, using the excuse of differences in cultures.

Coordination system Horizontal organizational links.

Copycat businesses Those following the me-too strategy, whereby they adopt existing strategies for providing products or services.

Corporate-level strategies How companies choose their mixture of different businesses.

Corporate social responsibility Idea that businesses have a responsibility to society beyond making profits.

Counterparry Fending off a competitor's attack in one country by attacking in another country, usually the competitor's home country.

Country clusters Groups of countries with similar cultural patterns.

Craft union Represents people from one occupational group, such as plumbers.

Credibility trust The confidence that the partner has the intent and ability to meet promised obligations and commitments.

Cross-cultural training Increases the relational abilities of future expatriates and, in some cases, of their spouses and families.

C2B Consumer-to-business transactions.

C2C Consumer-to-consumer transactions.

Cultural beliefs Our understandings about what is true.

Cultural control system Uses organizational culture to control the behaviors and attitudes of employees.

Cultural intelligence The ability to interact effectively in multiple cultures.

Cultural norms Prescribed and proscribed behaviors, telling us what we can do and what we cannot do.

Cultural paradoxes When individual situations seem to contradict cultural prescriptions.

Cultural relativism A philosophical position arguing that all cultures, no matter how different, are correct and moral for the people of those cultures.

Cultural rituals Ceremonies such as baptism, graduation, the tricks played on a new worker, or the pledge to a sorority or fraternity.

Cultural symbols These may be physical, such as national flags or holy artifacts. In the workplace, office size and location can serve as cultural symbols.

Cultural values Values that tell us such things as what is good, what is beautiful, what is holy, and what are legitimate goals in life.

Culture The pervasive and shared beliefs, norms, and values that guide the everyday life of a group.

Customer contact techniques Trade shows, catalog expositions, international advertising agencies and consulting firms, government-sponsored trade missions, and direct contact.

Decision-making control Level in the organizational hierarchy where managers have the authority to make decisions.

Defensive competitive strategies Attempts to reduce the risks of being attacked, to convince an attacking firm to seek other targets, or to blunt the impact of any attack.

Democratic leadership Leader includes subordinates in decision making.

Deontological ethical theory Focus on actions that, by themselves, have a good or bad morality regardless of their outcomes.

Developed countries Countries with mature economies, high GDPs, and high levels of trade and investment.

Developing countries Countries with economies that have grown extensively in the past two decades.

Differentiation strategy Strategy based on finding ways to provide superior value to customers.

Direct communication Communication that comes to the point and lacks ambiguity.

Direct contact Face-to-face interaction of employees.

Direct exporting Exporters take on the duties of intermediaries and make direct contact with customers in the foreign market.

Dirty tricks Negotiation tactics that pressure opponents to accept unfair or undesirable agreements or concessions.

Dispersed subunits Subsidiaries located anywhere in the world where they can most benefit the company.

Distinctive competencies Strengths that allow companies to outperform rivals.

Dominant parent Majority owner or contributor who controls or dominates the strategic and operational decision making of the alliance.

Dual system A form of vocational education in Germany that combines in-house apprenticeship training with part-time vocational school training and that leads to a skilled worker certificate.

E-commerce The selling of goods or services over the Internet.

E-commerce enablers Fulfillment specialists that provide other companies with services such as Web site translation.

E-commerce security Degree to which customers feel that their private and personal information is safeguarded by companies collecting it.

Economic analysis Of an ethical problem, focuses on what is the best decision for a company's profits.

Economic system System of beliefs (concerning work, property, and wealth), activities (extraction, production, and distribution), organizations (business firms, labor unions), and relationships (ownership, management) that provide the goods and services consumed by the members of a society.

Education Organized networks of socialization experiences that prepare individuals to act in society.

Elephant-and-ant complex Occurs in strategic alliances when two companies are greatly unequal in size.

Emerging markets Countries that are currently between developed and developing countries and are rapidly growing.

Enterprise union Represents all the people in one organization, regardless of occupation or location.

Entrepreneur Person who creates new ventures that seek profit and growth.

Entry wedge Company's competitive advantage for breaking into the established pattern of commercial activity.

Equity theory Proposal that people perceive the fairness of their rewards vis-á-vis their inputs based on how they compare themselves to others.

ERG theory Simplified hierarchy of needs: growth needs, relatedness needs, and existence needs.

Escalation of commitment Companies continue in an alliance relationship longer than necessary because of past financial and emotional investments.

Ethical analysis One that goes beyond focusing on profit goals and legal regulations.

Ethical convergence The growing pressures for multinational companies to follow the same rules in managing ethical behavior and social responsibility.

Ethical relativism Theory that each society's view of ethics must be considered legitimate and ethical.

Ethical universalism Theory that basic moral principles transcend cultural and national boundaries.

Ethnocentric IHRM All aspects of HRM for managers and technical workers tend to follow the parent organization's home country HRM practices.

Ethnocentrism When people from one culture believe that theirs are the only correct norms, values, and beliefs.

European Union (EU) Austria, Belgium, Bulgaria, Britain, Denmark, Finland, France, Germany, Greece, Ireland, Italy, Luxembourg, the Netherlands, Portugal, Romania, Spain, and Sweden, plus Norway and Switzerland in the related European Free Trade Area.

Expatriate Employee who comes from a country that is different from the one in which they working.

Expatriate glass ceiling The organizational and structural barriers preventing female managers from receiving international assignments.

Expectancy theory Assumption that motivation includes people's desire to satisfy their needs and their beliefs regarding how much their efforts at work will eventually satisfy their needs.

Export department Coordinates and controls a company's export operations.

Export management company (EMC) Intermediary specializing in particular types of products or particular countries or regions.

Export trading company (ETC) Intermediary similar to EMC, but it usually takes title to the product before exporting.

Extrinsic work values Preference for the security aspects of jobs, such as income and job security.

F

Fair exchange In a strategic alliance, when partners believe that they receive benefits from the relationship equal to their contributions.

Fiedler's theory of leadership Proposal that success of task- or person-centered leader depends on relationships between the leader and subordinates, the degree that subordinates' tasks are easily and clearly defined, and the officially granted organizational power of the leader.

Final agreement Signed contract, agreeable to all sides.

First mover advantage That of the entrepreneur who moves quickly into a new venture and establishes the business before other companies can react.

First offer First proposal by parties of what they expect from the agreement.

Flexpatriates Employees who are sent on frequent but short-term international assignments.

Focus strategy Applying a differentiation or low-cost strategy to a narrow market.

Foreign Corrupt Practices Act (FCPA) Forbids U.S. companies to make or offer illegal payments or gifts to officials of foreign governments for the sake of getting or retaining business.

Foreign direct investment (FDI) Multinational firm's ownership, in part or in whole, of an operation in another country.

Foreign subsidiaries Subunits of the multinational company located in another country.

Formal communication Communication that acknowledges rank, titles, and ceremony in prescribed social interaction.

Formal international cooperative alliance (ICA) A nonequity alliance with formal contracts specifying what each company must contribute to the relationship.

Full-time integrator Cross-unit coordination is the main job responsibility.

Functional structure Has departments or subunits based on separate business functions, such as marketing or manufacturing.

Fundamental attribution error Assumption by managers that people behave in certain ways because of internal motivations rather than outside factors.

G

General Agreement on Tariffs and Trade (GATT) Tariff negotiations among several nations that reduced the average worldwide tariff on manufactured goods.

Generic strategies Basic ways that both domestic and multinational companies keep and achieve competitive advantage.

Geographic structure Has departments or subunits based on geographical regions.

Global culture Managerial and worker values that view strategic opportunities as global and not just domestic.

Global IHRM Recruiting and selecting worldwide, and assigning the best managers to international assignments regardless of nationality.

Global integration solution Conducting business similarly throughout the world and locating company units wherever there is high quality and low cost.

Globalization The worldwide trend of cross-border economic integration that allows businesses to expand beyond their domestic boundaries.

Globalization drivers Conditions in an industry that favor transnational or international strategies over multilocal or regional strategies.

Global leader One who has the skills and abilities to interact with and manage people from diverse cultural backgrounds.

Global Leadership and Organizational Behavior Effectiveness (GLOBE) project Recent large-scale project based on Hofstede's model to determine nine cultural dimensions of 62 countries.

Global-local dilemma Choice between a local-responsiveness or global approach to a multinational's strategies.

Global mindset Mindset that requires managers to think globally, but act locally.

Global pay system Worldwide job evaluations, performance appraisal methods, and salary scales are used.

Global platform Country location where a firm can best perform some, but not necessarily all, of its value chain activities.

Global start-up/born-global firm Company that begins as a multinational company.

Global virtual team Groups of people from different parts of the world who work together by using information and communication technologies such as intranets, Web meetings, WIKIs, e-mails, and instant messaging.

Goal-directed behavior One that people use with the intention of satisfying a need.

Goal-setting theory Assumption that the mere existence of a goal is motivating.

Great person theory Leaders are born with unique characteristics that make them quite different from ordinary people.

Greenfield investments Starting foreign operations from scratch.

H

Haptics or touching Basic form of human interaction, including shaking hands, embracing, or kissing when greeting one another.

Headquarters-based compensation system Paying home country wages regardless of location.

Hierarchy of needs theory States that people have five basic types of needs: physiological, security, affiliation, esteem, and self-actualization.

High-context language One in which people state things indirectly and implicitly.

Hinduism Acceptance of the ancient traditions of India that are based on the Vedic scriptures.

Hofstede model of national culture A cultural model mainly based on differences in values and beliefs regarding work goals.

Holistic approach Each side makes very few, if any, concessions until the end of the negotiation.

Home country national Expatriate employee who comes from the parent firm's home country.

Host-based compensation system Adjusting wages to local lifestyles and costs of living.

Host country nationals Local workers who come from the host country where the unit (plant, sales unit, etc.) is located.

Humane orientation An indication of the extent to which individuals are expected to be fair, altruistic, caring, and generous.

Human resource management (HRM) Recruitment, selection, training and development, performance appraisal, compensation, and labor relations.

Hybrid structures Mixes functional, geographic, and product units.

I

Ideological union Represents all types of workers based on an ideology (e.g., communism) or religious orientation.

IHRM orientation Company's basic tactics and philosophy for coordinating IHRM activities for managerial and technical workers.

IJV and ICA performance criteria Often must include other than financial criteria, such as organizational learning.

IJV negotiation issues Points such as equity contributions, management structure, and "prenuptial" agreements regarding the dissolution of the relationship.

Independent management structure Alliance managers act like managers from a separate company.

Index of economic freedom Determines the extent of governmental intervention in a country.

Indirect exporting Intermediary or go-between firms provide the knowledge and contacts necessary to sell overseas.

Individualism Relationship between the individual and the group in society.

Induced factor conditions National resources created by a nation, such as a superior educational system.

Industrialization Cultural and economic changes that occur because of how production is organized and distributed in society.

Industrial society Characterized by the dominance of the secondary or manufacturing sectors.

Industrial union Represents all people in an industry, regardless of occupational type.

Influence tactics Tactical behaviors leaders use to influence subordinates.

Informal international cooperative alliance A nonlegally binding agreement between companies to cooperate on any value chain activity.

Inpatriate Employees from foreign countries who work in the country where the parent company is located.

Interdependent relationships Continuous sharing of information and resources by dispersed and specialized subunits.

Internal versus external control Beliefs regarding whether one controls one's own fate.

International business ethics Unique ethical problems faced by managers conducting business operations across national boundaries.

International cadre Managers who specialize in international assignments.

International cooperative alliance (ICA) An agreement for cooperation between two or more companies from different nations that does not set up a legally separate company.

International division Responsible for managing exports, international sales, and foreign subsidiaries.

International entrepreneurship The discovery, evaluation, and exploitation of market opportunities.

International franchising Comprehensive licensing agreement where the franchisor grants to the franchisee the use of a whole business operation.

International human resource management (IHRM) All the HRM functions, adapted to the international setting.

International joint venture (IJV) A separate legal entity in which two or more companies from different nations have ownership positions.

International sales intensity Amount of international sales divided by total sales of the company.

International strategic alliance Agreement between two or more firms from different countries to cooperate in any value chain activity from R&D to sales.

International strategies Selling global products and using similar marketing techniques worldwide.

Internet hosts Computer connected to the Internet with its own Internet Protocol address.

Interpreter's role To ensure the accuracy and common understanding of written and oral agreements.

Intrinsic work values Preference for openness-to-change job aspects, such as autonomy, being able to take initiative and be creative.

Islam Religion based on the submission of the will to Allah (God).

ISO 14000 The current name for the environmental protection standards of the International Organization for Standardization.

ISO 9001:2000 The current name for the technical and quality standards of the International Organization for Standardization.

J

Job characteristics model Suggests that work is more motivating when managers enrich core job characteristics, such as by increasing the number of skills a job requires.

K

Key success factors (KSFs) Important characteristics of a company or its product that lead to success in an industry.

Key success factors for expatriate assignments Relational abilities, family situation, motivation, and language skills.

Kinesics Communication through body movements.

Knowledge management Systems and mechanisms to ensure that the right form of knowledge is available to the right individual at the right time.

Leadership Ability of an individual to influence, motivate, and enable others to contribute toward the effectiveness and success of the organizations of which they are members.

Legal analysis Of an ethical problem, focuses only on meeting legal requirements of host and parent countries.

Less developed countries (LDCs) The poorest nations, often plagued with unstable political regimes, high unemployment, and low worker skills.

Levels of culture The levels of cultural influence, including national, business, and occupational and organizational culture.

Liabilities of smallness The challenges facing small businesses in getting access to necessary resources to internationalize.

Liaison roles Part of a person's job in one department to communicate with people in another department.

Licensing Contractual agreement between a domestic licenser and a foreign licensee. (Licenser usually has a valuable patent, technological know-how, a trademark, or a company name that it provides to the foreign licensee.)

Localized Web site Web site that is adapted to the local cultures.

Local-responsiveness solution Responding to differences in the markets in all the countries in which a company operates.

Local union Represents one occupational group in one company.

Location advantages Dispersing value chain activities anywhere in the world where the company can do them best or cheapest.

Long-term (Confucian) orientation An orientation toward time that values patience.

Low-context language One in which people state things directly and explicitly.

Low-cost strategy Producing products or services equal to those of competitors at a lower cost.

M

Market transitions Changes that societies go through as they move from socialism toward a market-based economy.

Masculinity Tendency of a society to emphasize traditional gender roles.

Meister In Germany, a master technician.

Metanational structure An evolution of the transnational network structure that develops extensive systems to encourage organizational learning and entrepreneurial activities.

Micromultinational Company that uses Web technology and the Internet to go global from the day it is founded.

Minireplica subsidiary Scaled-down version of the parent company, using the same technology and producing the same products as the parent company.

Mixed economy Combines aspects of capitalist and socialist economies.

Moral languages Descriptions of the basic ways that people use to think about ethical decisions and to explain their ethical choices.

Motivation A psychological process resulting in goal-directed behavior that satisfies human needs.

Motivator-hygiene theory Assumption that a job has two basic characteristics: motivators and hygiene factors.

Multidomestic strategy Emphasizing local-responsiveness issues.

Multinational company (MNC) Any company that engages in business functions beyond its domestic borders.

Multinational management The formulation of strategies and the design of management systems that successfully take advantage of international opportunities and that respond to international threats.

N

National context National culture and social institutions that influence how managers make decisions regarding the strategies of their organizations.

National-context contingency model of leadership Shows how culture and related social institutions affect leadership practices.

National culture The dominant culture within the political boundaries of the nation-state.

Natural factor conditions National resources that occur naturally, such as abundant water supply.

Need Feeling of deficit or lacking that all people experience at some time.

Need theory Of motivation, assumes that people can satisfy basic human needs in the work setting.

Negotiation steps Preparation, building the relationship, exchanging information, first offer, persuasion, concessions, agreement, and postagreement.

Nenpo system New Japanese compensation system based on yearly performance evaluations that emphasize goals, although goals are not always the same as in Western companies.

Neutral versus affective The acceptability of expressing emotions.

New ventures Entering a new market; offering a new product or service; or introducing a new method, technology, or innovative use of raw materials.

Nonverbal communication Face-to-face communication that is not oral.

North American Free Trade Agreement (NAFTA) A multilateral treaty that links the United States, Canada, and Mexico in an economic bloc that allows freer exchange of goods and services.

O

Occupational cultures Distinct cultures of occupational groups such as physicians, lawyers, accountants, and craftspeople.

Oculesics Communication through eye contact or gaze.

Offensive competitive strategies Direct attacks, end-run offensives, preemptive strategies, and acquisitions.

Olfactics Use of smells as a means of nonverbal communication.

Operant conditioning Model proposes that, if a pleasurable consequence follows a behavior, the behavior will continue, whereas if an unpleasant consequence follows a behavior, the behavior will stop.

Organizational culture The norms, values, and beliefs concerning the organization that are shared by members of the organization.

Organizational design How organizations structure subunits and use coordination and control mechanisms to achieve their strategic goals.

Output control system Assesses the performance of a unit based on results, not on the processes used to achieve the results.

Outsourcing The deliberate decision to have outsiders or strategic allies perform certain activities in the value chain.

P

Participation strategies Options multinational companies have for entering foreign markets and countries.

Particularism Dealing with other people based on personal relationships.

Passive exporting Treating and filling overseas orders like domestic orders.

Path-goal theory Four types of leadership styles that a manager might choose depending on the situation.

Performance-maintenance (PM) theory Japanese perspective on balancing task- and person-centered leader behaviors.

Performance orientation The degree to which the society encourages societal members to innovate, to improve their performance, and to strive for excellence.

Personal success characteristics Tolerance of ambiguous situations, flexibility, creativity, humor, stamina, empathy, curiosity, and knowledge of a foreign language.

Person-centered leader One who focuses on meeting employees' social and emotional needs.

Persuasion stage When each side in the negotiation attempts to get the other side to agree to its position.

Pervasive The idea that culture affects almost everything we do, everything we see, and everything we feel and believe.

Political risk The impact of political decisions or events on the business climate in a country such that a multinational's profitability and feasibility of its global operations are negatively affected.

Polycentric IHRM Firm treats each country-level organization separately for HRM purposes.

Porter's five forces model A popular technique that can help a multinational firm understand the major forces at work in the industry and its degree of attractiveness.

Postagreement Consists of an evaluation of the success of a completed negotiation.

Postindustrial society Characterized by emphasis on the service sectors.

Power distance Expectations regarding equality among people.

Preindustrial society Characterized by agricultural dominance and shaping of the economic environment.

Prescriptive ethics for multinationals Suggested guidelines for the ethical behavior of multinational companies.

Primary stakeholders People directly linked to a company's survival, including customers, suppliers, employees, and shareholders.

Problem-solving negotiation Negotiators seek mutually satisfactory ground that is beneficial to both companies.

Process theories Of motivation, arising from needs and values combined with an individual's beliefs regarding the work environment.

Product structure Has departments or subunits based on different product groups.

Profit center Unit controlled by its profit or loss performance.

Proxemics The use of space to communicate.

Punishment Consequences of a person's behavior that discourage the behavior.

Regiocentric IHRM Regionwide HRM policies are adopted.

Regional strategy Managing raw material sourcing, production, marketing, and support activities within a particular region.

Regional trade agreements Agreements among nations in a particular region to reduce tariffs and develop similar technical and economic standards.

Reinforcement Reactions to a person's behavior that encourage the person to continue the behavior.

Related diversification A mix of businesses with similar products and markets.

Religion Shared set of beliefs, activities, and institutions based on faith in supernatural forces.

Repatriation problem Difficulties that managers face in coming back to their home countries and reconnecting with their home organizations.

Resource pool All the human and physical resources available in a country.

Resources Inputs into the production or service processes.

S

Secondary stakeholders People less directly linked to a company's survival, including the media, trade associations, and special interest groups.

Secure server Internet host that allows users to send and receive encrypted data.

Sequential approach Each side reciprocates concessions made by the other side.

7d culture model Seven-dimension cultural model based on beliefs regarding how people relate to each other, how people manage time, and how people deal with nature.

Shared cultural values, norms, and beliefs The idea that people in different cultural groups have similar views of the world.

Shared management structure Occurs when both parent companies contribute approximately the same number of managers to the alliance organization.

Small business UN definition: fewer than 500 employees. Popular press definition: fewer than 100 employees. The U.S. Small Business Administration's definition varies by industry and uses both sales revenue and the number of employees.

Small business advantage Fast moving entrepreneurs can use their competitive advantage of speed. Being first to market, they can capture significant sales before large competitors react.

Small business stage model Incremental process of internationalization followed by many small businesses.

Social inequality Degree to which people have privileged access to resources and positions within societies.

Social institution A complex of positions, roles, norms, and values organizing relatively stable patterns of human resources with respect to sustaining viable societal structures within a given environment.

Socialist or command economy Production resources are owned by the state and production decisions are centrally coordinated.

Social loafing People put out less effort when they work in groups.

Sociotechnical systems (STS) approach Focuses on designing motivating jobs by blending the social system (i.e., organizational structure, culture) with technologies.

Specialized operations Subunits specializing in particular product lines, research areas, or marketing areas.

Specific versus diffuse The extent to which all aspects of an individual's life are involved in his or her work relationships.

Split-control management structure Partners usually share strategic decision making but split functional-level decision making.

Standardized Web site Web site that is similar in design and layout around the world.

Stereotyping When one assumes that all people within a culture behave, believe, feel, and act the same.

Strategic complementarity The alliance partners' strategies are complementary.

Strategy The central, comprehensive, integrated, and externally oriented set of choices of how a company will achieve its objectives.

Strategy formulation Process by which managers select the strategies to be used by their company.

Strategy implementation All the activities that managers and an organization must perform to achieve strategic objectives.

Subordinates' expectations Expectations regarding what leaders should do and what they may or may not do.

Sustainable Characteristic of strategies that are not easily defeated by competitors.

Switching costs Expenses incurred when a customer switches to a competitor's products.

SWOT The analysis of an organization's internal strengths and weaknesses and the opportunities or threats from the environment.

T

Task-centered leader One who gives subordinates specific standards, schedules, and tasks.

Task force Temporary team created to solve a particular organizational problem.

Task-related information Actual details of the proposed agreement.

Team Permanent unit of the organization designed to focus the efforts of different subunits on particular problems.

Technological leadership Being first to use or introduce a new technology.

Teleological ethical theory One that suggests that the morality of an act or practice comes from its consequences.

Third country nationals Expatriate workers who come from neither the host nor home country.

Time horizon The way cultures deal with the past, present, and future.

Training rigor Extent of effort by both trainees and trainers to prepare the expatriate.

Transformational leadership Managers go beyond transactional leadership by articulating a vision, breaking from the status quo, providing goals and a plan, giving meaning or a purpose to goals, taking risks, being motivated to lead, building a power base, and demonstrating high ethical and moral standards.

Transition economies Countries in the process of changing from government-controlled economic systems to capitalistic systems.

Transnational network structure Network of functional, product, and geographic subsidiaries dispersed

throughout the world, based on the subsidiaries' location advantages.

Transnational strategy Seeking location advantages and gaining economic efficiencies from operating worldwide.

Transnational subsidiary Has no company-wide form or function; each subsidiary does what it does best or most efficiently anywhere in the world.

TRIAD The world's dominant trading partners: the European Union, the United States, and Japan.

Turnkey operations Multinational company makes a project fully operational and trains local managers and workers before the foreign owner takes control.

U

Uncertainty avoidance How people react to what is different and dangerous.

Union membership density Proportion of workers in a country who belong to unions.

Universalism Dealing with other people based on rules.

Unrelated diversification A mix of businesses in any industry.

U.S. legal requirements for appraisals Regulating performance evaluation practices to ensure their fairness.

Utilitarianism Argument that what is good and moral comes from acts that produce the greatest good for the greatest number of people.

V

Value chain All the activities that a firm uses to design, produce, market, deliver, and support its product.

Verbal negotiation tactics Promises, threats, recommendations, warnings, rewards, punishments, normative appeals, commitments, self-disclosures, questions, commands, saying no (refusals), interruptions.

W

White-collar or professional union Represents an occupational group, similar to craft union.

Whorf hypothesis Theory that language determines the nature of culture.

Work centrality Overall value of work in a person's life.

Work obligation norms Degree to which work is seen as an obligation or duty to society.

Works council In Germany, employee group that shares plant-level responsibility with managers regarding issues such as working conditions.

World Trade Organization (WTO) A formal structure for continued negotiations to reduce trade barriers and a mechanism for settling trade disputes.

Worldwide geographic structure Has geographical units representing regions of the world.

Worldwide matrix structure Symmetrical organization, usually with equal emphasis on worldwide product groups and regional geographical divisions.

Worldwide product structure Gives product divisions responsibility to produce and sell their products or services throughout the world.